Teacher's Edition

HOLT McDOUGAL

GEOGRAPHY

Daniel D. Arreola

Marci Smith Deal

James F. Petersen

Rickie Sanders

HISTORY

HOLT McDOUGAL

HOUGHTON MIFFLIN HARCOURT

Printed in the U.S.A.

ISBN 978-0-547-49111-0

1 2 3 4 5 6 7 8 9 10 0914 19 18 17 16 15 14 13 12 11 10

4500264418 ^ B C D E F G

Contents

Inspire Students with the Story T4

Connect to 21st Century Learners T5

Experience Engaging Interactive Multimedia T6

Imagine Easy-to-Access Digital Content T7

Partnership for 21st Century Skills T8

Correlation to the National Geography Standards T10

PROGRAM HIGHLIGHTS

Inspire students with the story...

HISTORY™ video and **interactive games** transport students into what they are studying, providing them with an unforgettable virtual experience.

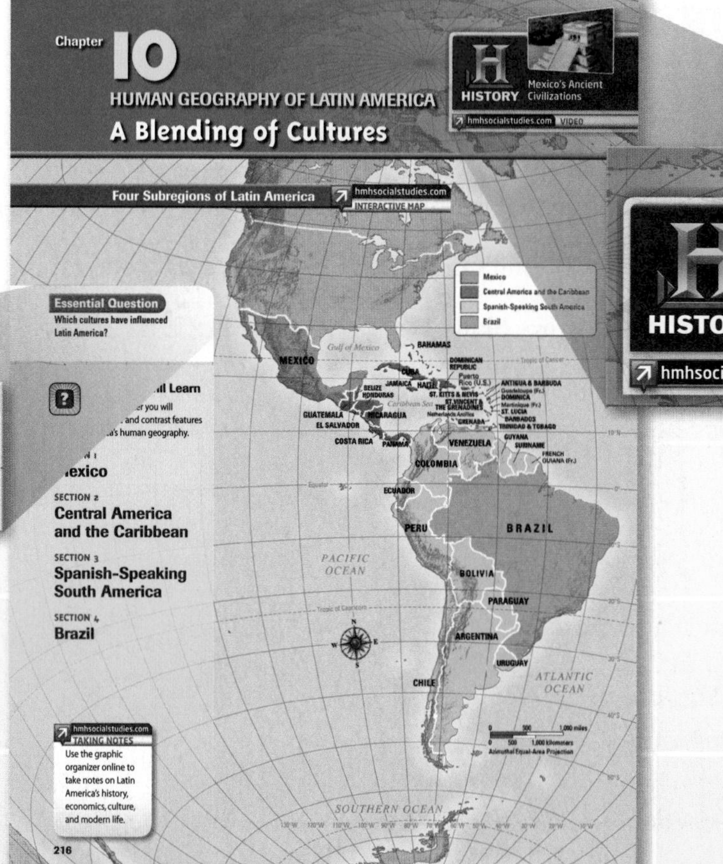

Chapter 10
HUMAN GEOGRAPHY OF LATIN AMERICA
A Blending of Cultures
Four Subregions of Latin America
HISTORY Mexico's Ancient Civilizations
hmhsocialstudies.com VIDEO
Essential Question
Which cultures have influenced Latin America?
SECTION 2
Central America and the Caribbean
SECTION 3
Spanish-Speaking South America
SECTION 4
Brazil

Essential Question

Which cultures have influenced Latin America?

The **Essential Question,** at the beginning of each chapter, engages students by connecting people, places and events and setting the main purpose for reading.

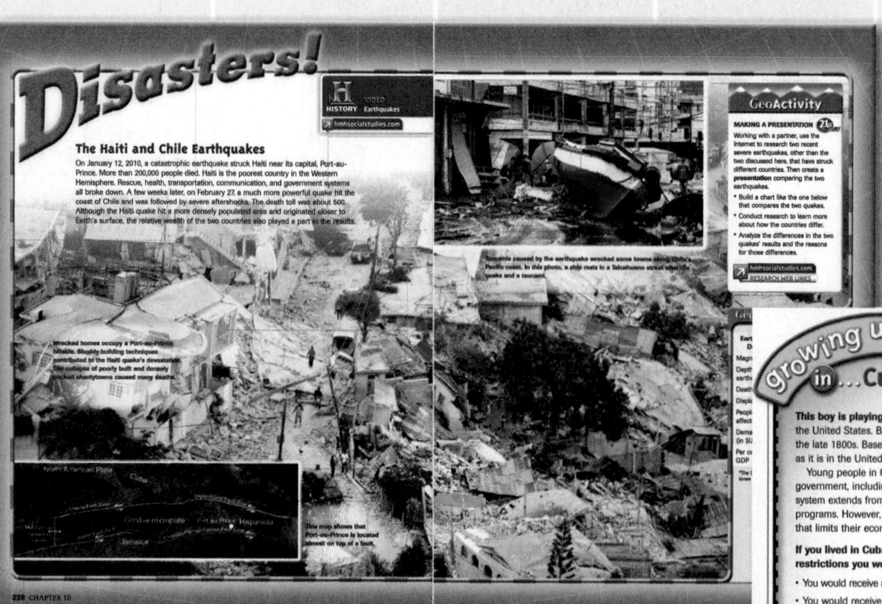

Compelling stories told with dynamic visuals bring people, places and events to life, grabbing students' interest to stimulate and encourage learning.

growing up in...Cuba

This boy is playing baseball, a sport as popular in Cuba as it is in the United States. Baseball traveled from the United States to Cuba in the late 1800s. Baseball is considered the island's national pastime, just as it is in the United States.

Young people in Cuba receive many benefits from the Communist government, including free education and health care. The education system extends from preschool programs through college to graduate programs. However, young people, like all Cubans, live in a police state that limits their economic and political freedoms.

If you lived in Cuba, here are some rights you would enjoy and restrictions you would face:

- You would receive a free education.
- You would receive free medical care.
- You would attend school from age 6 to somewhere between ages 11 and 15.
- You could attend free concerts, ballets, and plays.
- Your freedom of speech and writing would be restricted.
- Your economic opportunities would be very limited.

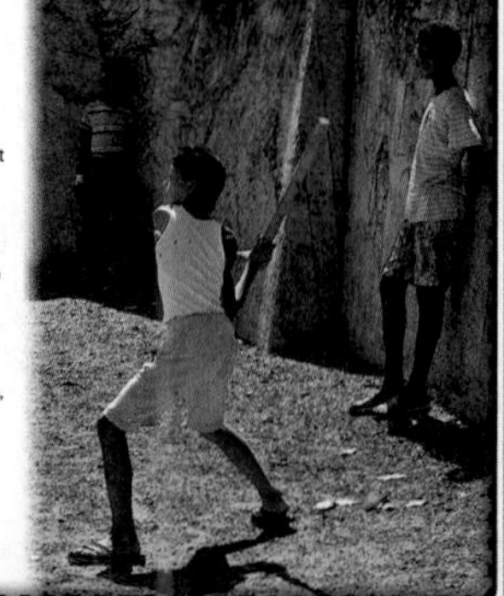

Connect to 21st century learners...

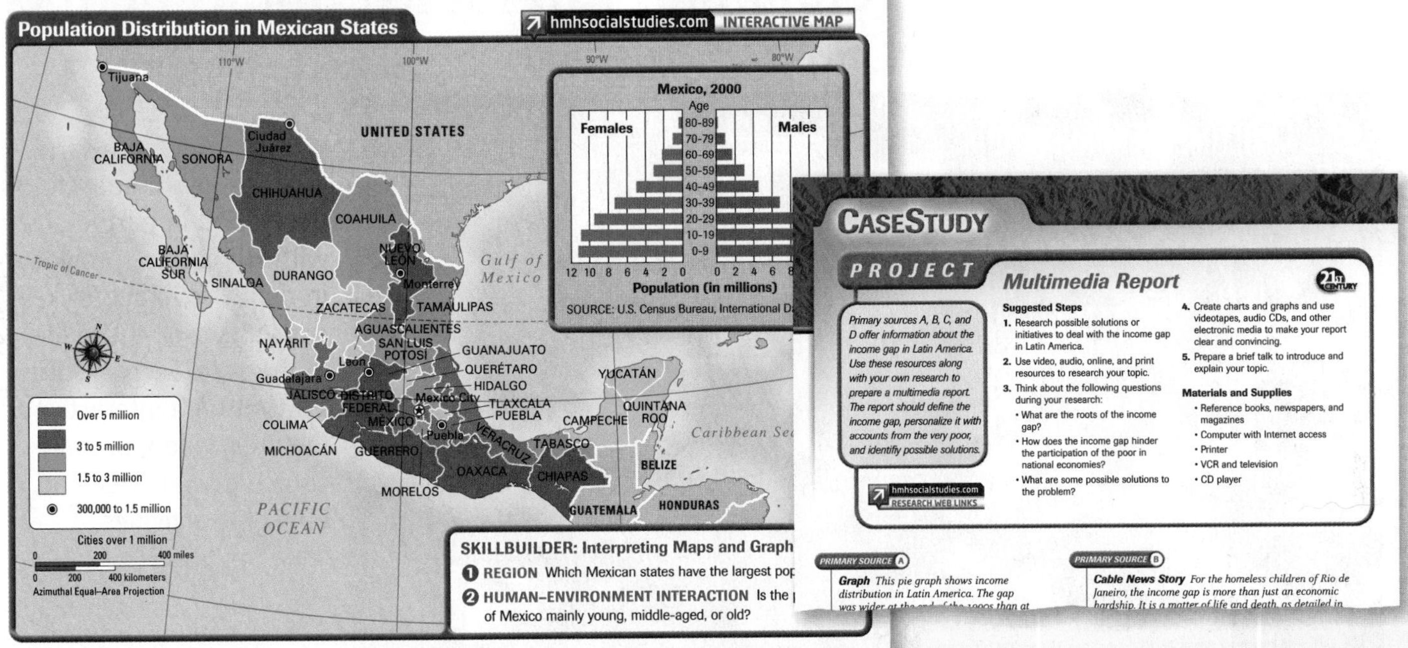

Population Distribution in Mexican States
hmhsocialstudies.com INTERACTIVE MAP
Mexico, 2000
Females
Males
Population (in millions)
SOURCE: U.S. Census Bureau, International D
UNITED STATES
Gulf of Mexico
PACIFIC OCEAN
Caribbean Sea
Over 5 million
3 to 5 million
1.5 to 3 million
300,000 to 1.5 million
Cities over 1 million
Azimuthal Equal-Area Projection
SKILLBUILDER: Interpreting Maps and Graph
REGION Which Mexican states have the largest pop
HUMAN–ENVIRONMENT INTERACTION Is the p of Mexico mainly young, middle-aged, or old?
CASESTUDY
PROJECT
Multimedia Report
Primary sources A, B, C, and D offer information about the income gap in Latin America. Use these resources along with your own research to prepare a multimedia report. The report should define the income gap, personalize it with accounts from the very poor, and identify possible solutions.
Suggested Steps
1. Research possible solutions or initiatives to deal with the income gap in Latin America.
2. Use video, audio, online, and print resources to research your topic.
3. Think about the following questions during your research:
• What are the roots of the income gap?
• How does the income gap hinder the participation of the poor in national economies?
• What are some possible solutions to the problem?
4. Create charts and graphs and use videotapes, audio CDs, and other electronic media to make your report clear and convincing.
5. Prepare a brief talk to introduce and explain your topic.
Materials and Supplies
• Reference books, newspapers, and magazines
• Computer with Internet access
• Printer
• VCR and television
• CD player
hmhsocialstudies.com RESEARCH WEB LINKS
PRIMARY SOURCE A
Graph This pie graph shows income distribution in Latin America. The gap
PRIMARY SOURCE B
Cable News Story For the homeless children of Rio de Janeiro, the income gap is more than just an economic hardship.

Holt McDougal Social Studies programs are organized to help students connect to the content and develop skills. The Student Editions are designed with:

- **Main Ideas, Big Idea, Key Terms and People,** and **Taking Notes** that prepare students to learn with focused success
- **Section sub-headings** tied to the Main Ideas that provide an outline for reading
- **Maps, visuals, charts,** and **documents** that make content accessible to all students
- **21st Century Skills** that require students to apply what they know

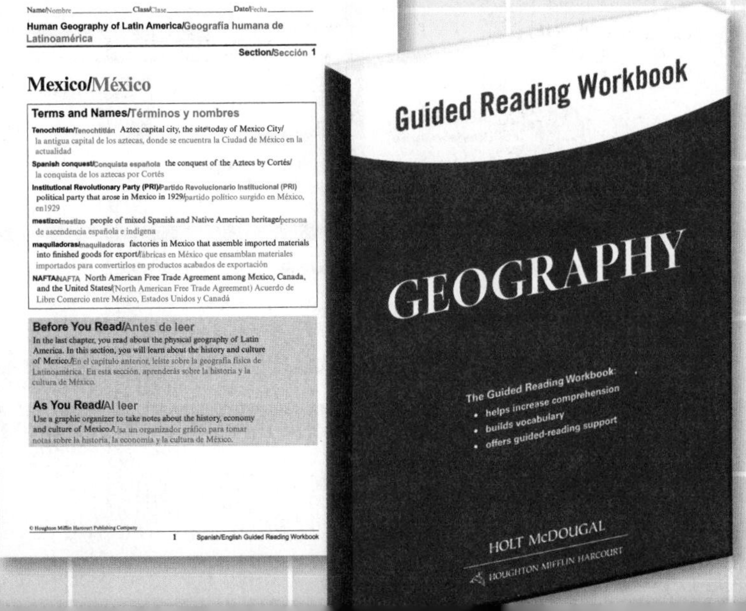

• helps increase comprehension

Guided Reading Workbooks (English and Spanish) help guide students as they read, take notes while reading adapted-level summaries, practice skills with an activity, and assess their understanding of content.

Experience

engaging interactive multimedia...

Multimedia Connections, developed in partnership with HISTORY™, provide in-depth coverage of key concepts brought to life in the **Interactive Online Edition** with interactive features, video, primary source documents, and engaging activities.

Power Presentations with Media Gallery DVD-ROM allows teachers to show, edit, and create dynamic multimedia presentations using interactive maps, informative graphics, and fine art and engages students with games and puzzles.

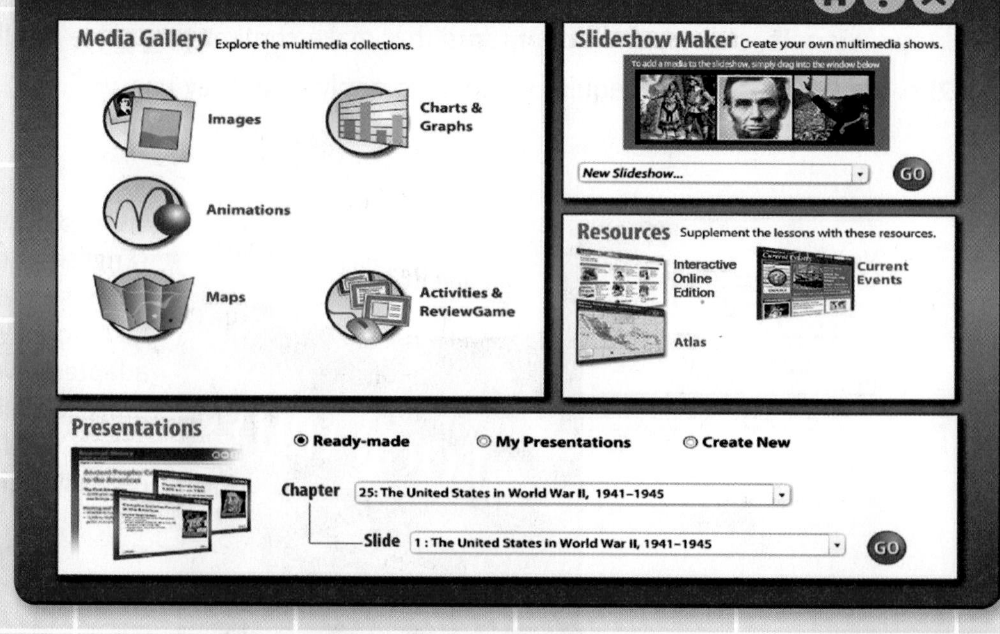

Imagine

easy-to-access, digital content...

The **Interactive Online Edition** is an interactive textbook that links the content of the Student Edition with the world of enhanced features such as activities, interactive maps, and assessments.

Premium Interactive Online Edition contains everything included in the Interactive Online Edition and:

- Additional chapter-based, interactive **Multimedia Connections** with HISTORY™ video, primary sources and maps for both the teacher and the student.
- **eReader files** of the Student Edition are also included for download to any mobile device.

The **Teacher One Stop** includes everything you need to plan, present, and assess—all on one convenient DVD. Easy to use, editable resources include:

- Reading Support
- Assessment
- Teacher Resources
- Chapter Resource Files
- Lesson Plans
- Videos
- Interactive Teacher's Edition
- Enrichment Activities
- Skill Development Activities
- Examview Assessment Suite
- MindPoint Quiz Show
- Calendar Planner
- PuzzleMaker
- State Specific Resources

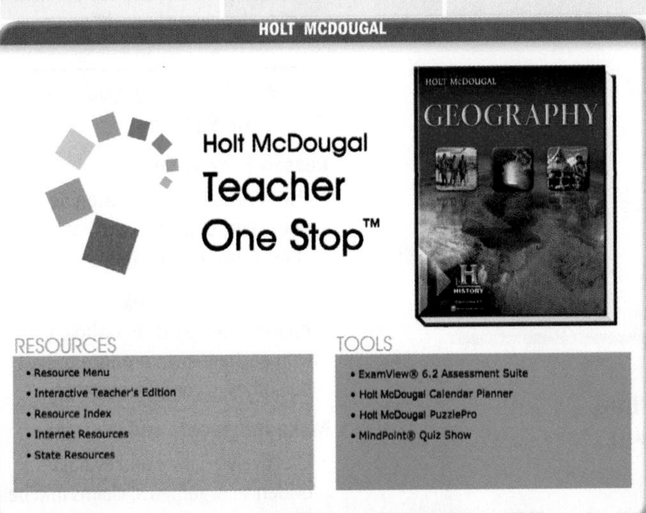

Partnership for 21st Century Skills

The Partnership for 21st Century Skills is the leading advocacy organization focused on infusing 21st century skills into education. The organization brings together the business community, education leaders, and policy makers to define a powerful vision for 21st century education to ensure every child's success as citizens and workers in the 21st century by providing tools and resources to help facilitate and drive change.

A listing of the 21st century skills (P21) outlined by the Partnership is provided here. As an Affiliate of the Partnership, Houghton Mifflin Harcourt helps support the teaching of these skills.

Throughout this book skills lessons that can be used to support the instruction of the P21 framework are indicated by this logo. 21ST CENTURY

For more information about the Partnership for 21st Century Skills, visit www.p21.org

Learning and Innovation Skills

Learning and innovation skills increasingly are being recognized as those that separate students who are prepared for a more and more complex life and work environments in the 21st century, and those who are not. A focus on creativity, critical thinking, communication and collaboration is essential to prepare students for the future.

Creativity and Innovation

Think Creatively

- Use a wide range of idea creation techniques (such as brainstorming)
- Create new and worthwhile ideas (both incremental and radical concepts)
- Elaborate, refine, analyze and evaluate their own ideas in order to improve and maximize creative efforts

Work Creatively with Others

- Develop, implement and communicate new ideas to others effectively
- Be open and responsive to new and diverse perspectives; incorporate group input and feedback into the work
- Demonstrate originality and inventiveness in work and understand the real world limits to adopting new ideas
- View failure as an opportunity to learn; understand that creativity and innovation is a long-term, cyclical process of small successes and frequent mistakes

Implement Innovations

- Act on creative ideas to make a tangible and useful contribution to the field in which the innovation will occur

Critical Thinking and Problem Solving

Reason Effectively

- Use various types of reasoning (inductive, deductive, etc.) as appropriate to the situation

Use Systems Thinking

- Analyze how parts of a whole interact with each other to produce overall outcomes in complex systems

Make Judgments and Decisions

- Effectively analyze and evaluate evidence, arguments, claims and beliefs
- Analyze and evaluate major alternative points of view
- Synthesize and make connections between information and arguments
- Interpret information and draw conclusions based on the best analysis
- Reflect critically on learning experiences and processes

Solve Problems

- Solve different kinds of non-familiar problems in both conventional and innovative ways
- Identify and ask significant questions that clarify various points of view and lead to better solutions

Communication and Collaboration

Communicate Clearly

- Articulate thoughts and ideas effectively using oral, written and nonverbal communication skills in a variety of forms and contexts
- Listen effectively to decipher meaning, including knowledge, values, attitudes and intentions
- Use communication for a range of purposes (e.g. to inform, instruct, motivate and persuade)
- Utilize multiple media and technologies, and know how to judge their effectiveness a priori as well as assess their impact
- Communicate effectively in diverse environments (including multi-lingual)

Collaborate with Others

- Demonstrate ability to work effectively and respectfully with diverse teams
- Exercise flexibility and willingness to be helpful in making necessary compromises to accomplish a common goal
- Assume shared responsibility for collaborative work, and value the individual contributions made by each team member

Information, Media and Technology Skills

People in the 21st century live in a technology and media-suffused environment, marked by various characteristics, including: 1) access to an abundance of information, 2) rapid changes in technology tools, and 3) the ability to collaborate and make individual contributions on an unprecedented scale. To be effective in the 21st century, citizens and workers must be able to exhibit a range of functional and critical thinking skills related to information, media and technology

Information Literacy

Access and Evaluate Information

- Access information efficiently (time) and effectively (sources)
- Evaluate information critically and competently

Use and Manage Information

- Use information accurately and creatively for the issue or problem at hand
- Manage the flow of information from a wide variety of sources
- Apply a fundamental understanding of the ethical/legal issues surrounding the access and use of information

Media Literacy

Analyze Media

- Understand both how and why media messages are constructed, and for what purposes
- Examine how individuals interpret messages differently, how values and points of view are included or excluded, and how media can influence beliefs and behaviors
- Apply a fundamental understanding of the ethical/legal issues surrounding the access and use of media

Create Media Products

- Understand and utilize the most appropriate media creation tools, characteristics and conventions
- Understand and effectively utilize the most appropriate expressions and interpretations in diverse, multi-cultural environments

ICT (Information, Communications and Technology) Literacy

Apply Technology Effectively

- Use technology as a tool to research, organize, evaluate and communicate information
- Use digital technologies (computers, PDAs, media players, GPS, etc.), communication/networking tools and social networks appropriately to access, manage, integrate, evaluate and create information to successfully function in a knowledge economy
- Apply a fundamental understanding of the ethical/legal issues surrounding the access and use of information technologies

Life and Career Skills

Today's life and work environments require far more than thinking skills and content knowledge. The ability to navigate the complex life and work environments in the globally competitive information age requires students to pay rigorous attention to developing adequate life and career skills.

Flexibility and Adaptability

Adapt to Change

- Adapt to varied roles, job responsibilities, schedules and contexts
- Work effectively in a climate of ambiguity and changing priorities

Be Flexible

- Incorporate feedback effectively
- Deal positively with praise, setbacks and criticism
- Understand, negotiate and balance diverse views and beliefs to reach workable solutions, particularly in multi-cultural environments

Initiative and Self-Direction

Manage Goals and Time

- Set goals with tangible and intangible success criteria
- Balance tactical (short-term) and strategic (long-term) goals
- Utilize time and manage workload efficiently

Work Independently

- Monitor, define, prioritize and complete tasks without direct oversight

Be Self-directed Learners

- Go beyond basic mastery of skills and/or curriculum to explore and expand one's own learning and opportunities to gain expertise
- Demonstrate initiative to advance skill levels towards a professional level
- Demonstrate commitment to learning as a lifelong process
- Reflect critically on past experiences in order to inform future progress

Social and Cross-Cultural Skills

Interact Effectively with Others

- Know when it is appropriate to listen and when to speak
- Conduct themselves in a respectable, professional manner

Work Effectively in Diverse Teams

- Respect cultural differences and work effectively with people from a range of social and cultural backgrounds
- Respond open-mindedly to different ideas and values
- Leverage social and cultural differences to create new ideas and increase both innovation and quality of work

Productivity and Accountability

Manage Projects

- Set and meet goals, even in the face of obstacles and competing pressures
- Prioritize, plan and manage work to achieve the intended result

Produce Results

- Demonstrate additional attributes associated with producing high quality products including the abilities to:
  - Work positively and ethically
  - Manage time and projects effectively
  - Multi-task
  - Participate actively, as well as be reliable and punctual
  - Present oneself professionally and with proper etiquette
  - Collaborate and cooperate effectively with teams
  - Respect and appreciate team diversity
  - Be accountable for results

Leadership and Responsibility

Guide and Lead Others

- Use interpersonal and problem-solving skills to influence and guide others toward a goal
- Leverage strengths of others to accomplish a common goal
- Inspire others to reach their very best via example and selflessness
- Demonstrate integrity and ethical behavior in using influence and power

Be Responsible to Others

- Act responsibly with the interests of the larger community in mind

Correlation to the National Geography Standards

World Geography correlates to the National Geography Standards through the Pupil's Edition and the Teacher's Edition. The following page references are representative of the many ways the textbook meets the National requirements.

	PUPIL'S EDITION	TEACHER'S EDITION
(1) How to use maps and other geographic representations, tools, and technologies to acquire, process, and report information from a spatial perspective		
The student knows and understands: **1.1** How to use maps and other graphic representations to depict geographic problems	5–7, 10–13, 14–19, 20–23, 71–76, 78–82, 107–115, 262–263, 266–267, 288–293, 308–309, 336–337, 338–339, 340–341, 342–343, 402–411, 484–485, 539, 542–549, 610–617, 678–687	12
1.2 How to use technologies to represent and interpret Earth's physical and human systems	4, 12–13	248, 425
1.3 How to use geographic representations and tools to analyze, explain, and solve geographic problems	5–6, 8, 10–13, 14–19, 23, 24–25, 70, 71–73, 75–77, 78–82, 96–97, 102–106, 262–267, 268–271, 288–293, 321, 336, 338, 340, 359, 394–395, 484, 540, 542, 544, 546, 548, 568, 574, 575, 585, 594, 595, 598, 610, 612, 614, 624, 626, 634, 648, 650, 653, 664, 674, 678, 680, 682, 684, 686, 720	10, 54, 55, 66, 70, 71–73, 75–77, 78–82, 96–97, 102–106, 262–267, 268–271, 288–293, 321, 336, 338, 340, 359, 394–395, 484, 540, 542, 544, 546, 548, 568, 574, 575, 585, 594, 595, 598, 610, 612, 614, 624, 626, 634, 648, 650, 653, 664, 674, 678, 680, 682, 684, 686, 720
Therefore, the student is able to: **1.A** Produce and interpret maps and other graphic representations to solve geographic problems	13, 19, 24, 25, 64, 67, 86, 97, 102–103, 120, 121, 145, 158, 190–195, 206, 215, 261–271, 281, 322, 331, 336–343, 351, 357, 373, 375, 376, 383, 402–413, 429, 442, 478–485, 540, 542, 544, 546, 548, 568, 574, 575, 585, 594, 595, 598, 610, 612, 614, 624, 626, 634, 648, 650, 653, 664, 674, 678, 680, 682, 684, 686, 720	8, 11, 12, 24, 26, 35, 52, 55, 60, 61, 62, 84, 85, 88, 119, 120, 121, 141, 145, 146, 147, 149, 150, 160, 161, 164, 176, 182, 203, 206, 216, 218, 224, 229, 234, 240, 241, 244, 275, 276, 277, 284–7, 292, 299, 304, 312, 324, 327, 328, 414, 416, 418, 419, 421, 422, 423, 425, 426, 430, 432, 436, 438, 439, 440, 443, 444, 445, 446, 449, 450, 453, 455, 456, 461, 461, 465, 469, 467, 469, 484, 540, 542, 544, 546, 548, 568, 574, 575, 585, 594, 595, 598, 610, 612, 614, 624, 626, 634, 648, 650, 653, 664, 674, 678, 680, 682, 684, 686, 720
1.B Use maps and other geographic representations to analyze world events and suggest solutions to world problems	13, 74, 78, 78, 140, 150–151, 154, 157, 172, 173, 181, 208, 245, 257, 290, 295, 312, 328–329, 392, 442, 459, 460, 470–471, 540, 542, 544, 546, 548, 568, 574, 575, 585, 594, 595, 598, 610, 612, 614, 624, 626, 634, 648, 650, 653, 664, 674, 678, 680, 682, 684, 686, 720	136, 138, 218, 236, 277, 284–7, 292, 299, 304, 312, 324, 327, 328, 414, 416, 418, 419, 421, 422, 423, 425, 426, 430, 432, 436, 438, 439, 440, 443, 444, 445, 446, 449, 450, 453, 455, 456, 461, 461, 465, 469, 467, 469, 484, 540, 542, 544, 546, 548, 568, 574, 575, 585, 594, 595, 598, 610, 612, 614, 624, 626, 634, 648, 650, 653, 664, 674, 678, 680, 682, 684, 686, 720
1.C Evaluate the applications of geographic tools and supporting technologies to serve particular purposes	13, 24, 25, 248	248
(2) How to use mental maps to organize information about people, places, and environments in a spatial context		
The student knows and understands: **2.1** How to use mental maps of physical and human features of the world to answer complex geographic questions	5, 128, 133, 177	235
2.2 How mental maps reflect the human perception of places	5, 177, 215	185c

Correlation to the National Geography Standards

	PUPIL'S EDITION	TEACHER'S EDITION
(2) How to use mental maps to organize information about people, places, and environments in a spatial context *(continued)*		
2.3 How mental maps influence spatial and environmental decision-making	5, 129, 321, 565	243, 558
Therefore, the student is able to: **2.A** Use maps drawn from memory to answer geographic questions	31, 90, 97, 122, 130, 133, 151, 171, 623	239
2.B Identify the ways in which mental maps influence human decisions about location, settlement, and public policy	128, 287, 317	215c, 547
2.C Compare the mental maps of individuals to identify common factors that affect the development of spatial understanding and preferences	205, 309	238, 565
(3) How to analyze the spatial organization of people, places, and environments on earth's surface		
The student knows and understands: **3.1** The generalizations that describe and explain spatial interaction	5–6, 60–61, 85	60
3.2 The models that describe patterns of spatial organization	7–8, 89	58, 89
3.3 The spatial behavior of people	164–165, 630–631	164–165
3.4 How to apply concepts and models of spatial organization to make decisions	66	81
Therefore, the student is able to: **3.A** Apply concepts of spatial interaction (e.g., complementarity, intervening opportunity, distance decay, connections) to account for patterns of movement in space	9, 87	82
3.B Use models of spatial organization to analyze relationships in and between places	56, 90	80, 85
3.C Explain how people perceive and use space	8, 631	67, 90
3.D Apply concepts and models of spatial organization to make decisions	57	57

GEOGRAPHY

Correlation to the National Geography Standards

	PUPIL'S EDITION	TEACHER'S EDITION
(4) The physical and human characteristics of places		
The student knows and understands: **4.1** The meaning and significance of place	7–8	5, 6, 118
4.2 The changing physical and human characteristics of places	116–122, 127–130, 201–215, 207–209, 273–277, 278–280, 350–352, 353–356, 418–423, 529–531, 542–549, 551–555, 557–559, 582–583, 584–587, 588–589, 593–595, 610–617, 619–623, 676–685, 689–692	34, 36, 38, 39, 40, 41, 44, 116–122, 127–130, 167, 180–181, 201, 274, 306, 310, 418–423, 529–531, 542–549, 551–555, 557–559, 582–583, 584–587, 588–589, 593–595, 610–617, 619–623, 676–685, 689–692
4.3 How relationships between humans and the physical environment lead to the formation of places and to a sense of personal and community identity	210–213, 320–321, 560–563, 628–631, 698–701	67, 128, 130, 137, 426
Therefore, the student is able to: **4.A** Explain place from a variety of points of view	117–119, 121, 123, 205, 210–213, 320–321, 414–423, 542, 544, 555, 565	6, 7, 33, 117, 118, 119, 121, 123, 124, 125, 134, 146, 154, 157, 161, 167, 177, 201–203, 207–209, 216, 222, 273–275, 280, 283, 288, 415–416
4.B Describe and interpret physical processes that shape places	161, 163, 205, 209, 277, 280, 287, 317, 352, 356, 414, 421–422, 424, 559, 591, 598, 599, 605, 623, 633, 692, 701	33, 39, 40, 43, 125, 126, 127, 150–151, 228–229, 278–279, 420, 421–422, 424
4.C Explain how social, cultural, as well as economic processes shape the features of places	140–142, 152, 160, 209, 212–213, 217, 527, 531, 572, 575, 577, 583, 587, 590, 657, 709, 723	71, 72, 74–76, 91–92, 94, 121, 129, 147, 148, 157, 160, 163, 180–181, 204, 217, 223–224, 238, 276, 292, 299, 417
4.D Evaluate how humans interact with physical environments to form places	130, 132, 153, 163, 213, 285, 287, 424–427, 559, 563, 595, 631, 701	210, 282, 284
(5) That people create regions to interpret earth's complexity		
The student knows and understands: **5.1** How multiple criteria can be used to define a region	7, 145–149, 166–169, 196–199, 484–485	145–146
5.2 The structure of regional systems	140–144, 145–149, 166–169, 567–572, 614–615	83, 134, 143, 166–169, 430
5.3 The ways in which physical and human regional systems are interconnected	145–149, 166–169, 560–563, 593–595	127, 150–151, 166–169, 211, 297
5.4 How to use regions to analyze geographic issues	108–115, 194–195, 355, 548–549, 628–629, 640–641, 661–663, 680–683, 710–711, 734–735	216
Therefore, the student is able to: **5.A** List and explain the changing criteria that can be used to define a region	9, 24, 134–135, 149, 169, 406–413, 544–545, 546–547, 565, 591	84, 145–148, 154, 166, 406–413, 430
5.B Describe the types and organization of regional systems	140–143, 156–157, 161–162, 218–219, 232–233, 291–292, 310–311, 314, 377–378, 384–387, 434, 503–507, 516–519, 510–513, 561	85, 86, 134, 135, 140–143, 156–157, 159, 161–162, 434
5.C Identify human and physical changes in regions and explain the factors that contribute to those changes	149, 152, 168, 194, 370–372, 595	137, 149, 150–151, 156, 221, 433, 455

Correlation to the National Geography Standards

	PUPIL'S EDITION	TEACHER'S EDITION
(5) That people create regions to interpret earth's complexity *(continued)*		
5.D Explain the different ways in which regional systems are structured	97, 152, 171, 315, 614–615	145
5.E Interpret the connections within and among the parts of a regional system	153	211
5.F Use regions to analyze geographic issues and answer geographic questions	149, 169, 356, 359, 563, 631, 633, 641, 646, 650, 663, 680–683, 736–737	119, 123, 124, 201–202, 207–208, 288
(6) How culture and experience influence people's perceptions of places and regions		
The student knows and understands: **6.1** Why places and regions serve as symbols for individuals and society	296–298, 727–29	224, 241
6.2 Why different groups of people within a society view places and regions differently	140–143, 156–157, 161–162, 180–183, 218–219, 232–233, 291–292, 310–311, 314, 377–378, 384–387, 434, 503–507, 516–519, 510–513, 571–572, 576–577, 582–583, 585–586, 588–589, 638–639, 643–644, 648–649, 654, 705–709, 714–715, 722	76, 140, 143, 163, 167, 202, 213, 217, 224, 232, 233, 235, 236–237, 249, 434
6.3 How changing perceptions of places and regions reflect cultural change	142–143, 224, 532–533, 654	142–143, 164, 180–183
Therefore, the student is able to: **6.A** Explain why places and regions are important to individual human identity and as symbols for unifying or fragmenting society	293, 308–309, 729	71, 156, 240–241
6.B Explain how individuals view places and regions on the basis of their stage of life, sex, social class, ethnicity, values, and belief systems	144, 158, 171, 183–183, 221, 224, 234, 301, 314, 383, 397, 444–445, 507, 515, 579, 572, 577, 583, 587, 605, 639	72, 76, 116, 161, 162, 163, 167, 168, 180–183, 202, 218, 219, 231, 237, 238, 249, 296, 312, 314, 434, 444–445
6.C Analyze the ways in which people's changing views of places and regions reflect cultural change	171, 184–185, 308–309, 379, 380–381, 387, 519, 646, 650, 659, 709, 715, 723	72, 164, 218, 224, 310, 312, 441
(7) The physical processes that shape the patterns of earth's surface		
The student knows and understands: **7.1** The dynamics of the four basic components of Earth's physical systems: the atmosphere, biosphere, lithosphere, and hydrosphere	27–28, 37–41, 42–45, 420–421, 597–599, 610–611, 619–623, 625–627, 689–692	27, 28, 33, 54, 420–421
7.2 The interaction of Earth's physical systems	32–36, 37–41, 54–58, 65–67, 150–151, 201–205, 207–209, 272–277, 278–280, 345–349, 415–418, 419–423, 486–490, 551–555, 622–623, 694–697	33, 37, 39, 40, 229

Correlation to the National Geography Standards

	PUPIL'S EDITION	TEACHER'S EDITION
(7) The physical processes that shape the patterns of earth's surface *(continued)*		
7.3 The spatial variation in the consequences of physical processes across Earth's surface	49-53, 59-63, 65-67, 123-126, 150-151, 415-418, 491-493, 542-543, 661-663	29, 34, 35, 38, 124, 415-418, 422
Therefore, the student is able to: **7.A** Describe how physical processes affect different regions of the United States and the world	29, 36, 46, 59, 63, 126, 161, 163, 204, 209, 277, 280, 287, 349, 418, 423, 490, 555, 564, 565, 591, 623, 692, 703	30, 31, 40, 42, 43, 55, 56-57, 59, 60, 61, 62, 66, 125-126, 228-229, 277, 415-418, 420-421
7.B Explain Earth's physical processes, patterns, and cycles using concepts of physical geography	29, 36, 41, 45, 46-47, 68, 122, 126, 349, 418, 423, 490, 555, 599, 623, 627, 678-679, 697	27, 28, 32, 33, 35, 44, 45, 48, 49-53, 56, 65, 278-280, 415-418
7.C Explain the various interactions resulting from Earth-Sun relationships	49-53	49
7.D Describe the ways in which Earth's physical processes are dynamic and interactive	41, 46-47, 59, 133, 663, 710-711	58
(8) The characteristics and spatial distribution of ecosystems on earth's surface		
The student knows and understands: **8.1** The distribution and characteristics of ecosystems	42-45, 65-67, 117-122, 201-205, 245-247, 415-418, 345-349, 487-490, 698-701	117-122, 147, 208, 415-418
8.2 The biodiversity and productivity of ecosystems	65	204, 244-246
8.3 The importance of ecosystems in people's understanding of environmental issues	58, 67, 173-174, 245-247, 323-325, 425-426, 560-563, 628-631, 734-737	205, 210, 247, 423-426
Therefore, the student is able to: **8.A** Analyze the distribution of ecosystems by interpreting relationship between soil, climate, and plant and animal life	47, 67, 122, 247, 277, 701	93, 122, 172, 174, 202, 415-418
8.B Evaluate ecosystems in terms of their biodiversity and productivity	205, 325, 418, 427, 631	205, 244-246, 418, 427
8.C Apply the concept of ecosystems to understand and solve problems regarding environmental issues	69, 247, 325, 349, 436-437, 563, 633, 640-641, 736-737	93, 175, 205, 208, 210, 246, 277, 284-285, 423-426, 436-437
(9) The characteristics, distribution, and migration of human populations on earth's surface		
The student knows and understands: **9.1** Trends in world population numbers and patterns	9, 78-82, 102, 109-115, 192-193, 196-198, 266-271, 340-343, 404-413, 480-481, 548-549, 593-595, 612-617, 668-671, 684-688	78, 80, 92, 143, 161, 212, 220, 404-413
9.2 The impact of human migration on physical and human systems	8, 82, 127-130, 137, 238, 353-354, 439-439, 448-452, 526-527, 544-545, 594-595, 705-709, 730-731	81, 127-130, 211

Correlation to the National Geography Standards

	PUPIL'S EDITION	TEACHER'S EDITION
(9) The characteristics, distribution, and migration of human populations on earth's surface *(continued)*		
Therefore, the student is able to: **9.A** Predict trends in the spatial distribution of population on Earth	79, 215	78, 220, 404–413
9.B Analyze population issues and propose policies to address such issues	79, 82, 180–183, 436–437, 595	78, 79, 128, 146, 180–183, 436
9.C Explain the economic, political, and social factors that contribute to human migration	96, 97, 161, 185, 236, 239, 243, 317, 359, 525–526, 732	80, 128, 137, 161, 176–178, 180, 181, 211, 219, 236
9.D Evaluate the impact of human migration on physical and human systems	82, 153, 185, 213, 317, 435, 519, 527, 639, 670–671, 680–681, 725	211, 301, 435–437
(10) The characteristics, distribution, and complexity of earth's cultural mosaics		
The student knows and understands: **10.1** The impact of culture on ways of life in different regions	142–143, 161–163, 180–181, 291–292, 365–366, 377–378, 440–441, 510–512, 516–517, 571–572, 638, 653–644, 648–649, 654, 708, 714–715, 722–723	75, 76, 140, 143, 163, 167, 291, 306
10.2 How cultures shape the character of a region	73–74, 135–136, 161–163, 168, 180–181, 218–220, 224–225, 232–233, 237–238, 306, 310–311, 314, 370–371, 378–379, 434–435, 445–446, 456–457, 510–512, 514–515, 576–577, 582–583, 585–586, 643–646	76, 135–136, 140, 143, 163, 167, 180–183, 218, 225, 233, 434, 439, 440, 445–447
10.3 The spatial characteristics of the processes of cultural convergence and divergence	72, 236, 300, 306–307, 310–311, 708–709	72, 236, 300, 306–307, 310–311, 708–709
Therefore, the student is able to: **10.A** Compare the role that culture plays in incidents of cooperation and conflict in the present-day world	96, 379	96
10.B Analyze how cultures influence the characteristics of regions	97, 144, 151, 158, 171, 293, 301, 387, 441, 503–504, 572, 577, 583, 587, 656–657, 709, 715, 723	72, 76, 140, 143, 163, 167, 218, 226, 232, 237–238, 291, 296–297, 314, 434, 440, 445–447
10.C Explain how cultural features often define regions	96, 221, 380–381, 383, 457	71, 72, 76, 140–143, 163, 167, 224, 240, 241
10.D Investigate how transregional alliances and multinational organizations can alter cultural solidarity	171, 182–183, 239, 243, 296–297, 315, 523	171, 182–183, 232, 310
10.E Explain the spatial processes of cultural convergence and divergence	72, 77, 182–183, 239, 659, 709	182–183

Correlation to the National Geography Standards

	PUPIL'S EDITION	TEACHER'S EDITION
(11) The patterns and networks of economic interdependence on earth's surface		
The student knows and understands: **11.1** The classification, characteristics, and spatial distribution of economic systems	91–95, 140, 159–161, 233–234, 238–239, 276–277, 292–293, 313, 372–373, 388–390, 433–434, 444–445, 461–463, 569–570, 581–582, 586–587, 644–645, 650, 652–654, 666–667, 707, 714, 721–722	91–95, 140, 159–161, 233–234, 238–239, 276–277, 292–293, 313, 433–434, 444–445, 461–463
11.2 How places of various size function as centers of economic activity	95, 167, 225–226, 433–434, 513, 518–519, 575, 637–638, 730–731	95, 167, 225–226, 433–434, 513, 518–519, 575, 637–638, 730–731
11.3 The increasing economic interdependence of the world's countries	92–93, 305, 439–449, 480–481	93, 247, 292
Therefore, the student is able to: **11.A** Classify and describe the spatial distribution of major economic systems and evaluate their relative merits in terms of productivity and the social welfare of workers	96, 145–149, 163, 185, 227, 367, 587, 646, 655, 667, 732	91, 94, 276, 433–434, 444–445, 461–463
11.B Identify and evaluate the spatial aspects of economic systems	92–93, 149, 153, 169, 331, 639, 650	91, 92, 94, 219, 233, 292, 313, 434–435
11.C Analyze the relationships between various settlement patterns, their associated economic activities, and the relative land values	227, 507, 732	225, 247
11.D Identify and analyze the historical movement patterns of people and goods and their relationships to economic activity	144, 159, 301, 367, 457, 515, 667	230, 457
11.E Analyze and evaluate international economic issues from a spatial point of view	133, 185, 252–253, 317, 331, 374, 390, 463, 473, 583, 709	93, 204, 205, 219, 234
(12) The processes, patterns, and functions of human settlement		
The student knows and understands: **12.1** The functions, sizes, and spatial arrangements of urban areas	86–90, 138, 176–178, 630–631	86–90, 176–178, 211
12.2 The differing characteristics of settlement in developing and developed countries	86–90, 138, 145–149, 176–178, 211–212, 221, 239, 301, 506, 593–595, 668–671, 712, 718–719	90, 128, 137, 145–149, 161, 176–178, 180–181, 212, 220
12.3 The processes that change the internal structure of urban areas	9, 176–178, 212–213, 221, 731	176–178, 212
12.4 The evolving forms of present-day urban areas	86, 88, 176–178, 212–213, 221	90, 176–178, 212

Correlation to the National Geography Standards

	PUPIL'S EDITION	TEACHER'S EDITION
(12) The processes, patterns, and functions of human settlement *(continued)*		
Therefore, the student is able to: **12.A** Analyze the functions of cities	90, 631	88, 90, 177
12.B Analyze the internal structure and shape of cities	96, 87, 178	87, 89, 177
12.C Classify the characteristics of settlements in developing or developed countries	96, 130, 163, 214, 215, 434–435, 633, 670–671, 715	87, 90, 128, 137, 145–149, 161, 176–178, 180–181
12.D Describe the nature, causes, and geographic impact of change in urban areas	90, 128, 132, 163, 177, 178, 221, 595, 631, 732	128, 141, 178, 218, 238, 301, 456
12.E Evaluate the physical and human impacts of emerging urban forms in the present-day world	132, 138, 178, 213, 725	178
(13) How the forces of cooperation and conflict among people influence the division and control of earth's surface		
The student knows and understands: **13.1** Why and how cooperation and conflict are involved in shaping the distribution of social, political, and economic spaces on Earth and different scales	83–86, 96, 156–157, 249–251, 298, 311–312, 319–321, 326–327, 361–363, 366–367, 376, 385–387, 431–433, 443–444, 453–454, 504–505, 517, 532–533, 568–569, 574, 600–603, 728–729	96, 156, 231–232, 249, 250, 298, 431–433, 443, 453
13.2 The impact of multiple spatial divisions on people's daily lives	21, 76, 84–86, 87–90	21, 84, 85, 89
13.3 How differing points of view and self-interests play a role in conflict over territory and resources	298, 301, 315, 320–321, 323–325, 326–327, 431–322, 368–369, 512–513, 726–729	249, 250, 298
Therefore, the student is able to: **13.A** Analyze how cooperation and conflict influence the development and control of social, political, and economic entities on Earth	251, 315, 328–328, 331, 387, 397, 473, 515, 519, 532–533, 602–603, 604, 723, 729	156, 217, 223, 232, 311, 312, 326–328, 431–433, 453
13.B Explain the changes that occur in the extent and organization of social, political, and economic entities on Earth's surface	138, 251, 321, 387, 452	138, 249
13.C Explain how external forces can conflict economically and politically with internal interests in a region	251, 387, 470–471, 729	470–471

Correlation to the National Geography Standards

	PUPIL'S EDITION	TEACHER'S EDITION
(14) How human actions modify the physical environment		
The student knows and understands: **14.1** The role of technology in the capacity of the physical environment to accommodate human modification	12–13, 248, 355–356, 369, 377, 392–393, 424–427, 494–499, 529–531, 560–563, 628–630, 698–701	138, 225–226, 248, 424–427, 463
14.2 The significance of the global impacts of human modification of the physical environment	127–130, 173–174, 210–213, 245–247, 282–285, 353–354, 424–427, 529–537, 560–563, 628–631, 668, 732	130, 210, 225–226, 245–246, 257, 282–285, 424–427
14.3 How to apply appropriate models and information to understand environmental problems	734–737	734–737
Therefore, the student is able to: **14.A** Evaluate the ways in which technology has expanded the human capability to modify the physical environment	130, 149, 153, 213, 282, 285, 287, 356, 379, 394–395, 417, 499, 523, 525, 531, 631, 659	138, 225–226, 248, 282–285, 426, 463
14.B Explain the global impacts of human changes in the physical environment	130, 175, 246–247, 256–257, 287, 325, 397, 531, 563, 640–641, 701, 736–737	130, 175, 219, 225–226, 245–246, 424–427, 437
14.C Develop possible solutions to scenarios of environmental change induced by human modification of the physical environment	150–151, 175, 257, 356, 359, 417, 429	150–151, 425, 426
(15) How physical systems affect human systems		
The student knows and understands: **15.1** How changes in the physical environment can diminish its capacity to support human activity	210–212, 282–283, 353–354, 433, 436–437, 560–563, 621	150, 205, 208, 244, 246–247, 436–437
15.2 Strategies to respond to constraints placed on human systems by the physical environment	82, 123–126, 128–129, 201, 282–283, 495–496, 561, 562–563, 580–581, 628–631, 694–697, 734–737	123–125, 151, 200, 282–283
15.3 How humans perceive and react to natural hazards	30–31, 40–41, 51–52, 150–151, 294–295, 426–437, 520–521, 597–599, 640–641, 661–663	39, 40, 51, 52, 150–151, 228–229, 436–437
Therefore, the student is able to: **15.A** Analyze examples of changes in the physical environment that have reduced the capacity of the environment to support human activity	53, 150–151, 213, 563, 633, 736–737	126, 150–151, 246–247, 436–437
15.B Apply the concept of "limits to growth" to suggest ways to adapt to or overcome the limits imposed on human systems by physical systems	133, 697	200, 205

Correlation to the National Geography Standards

	PUPIL'S EDITION	TEACHER'S EDITION
(15) How physical systems affect human systems *(continued)*		
15.C Explain the ways in which individuals and societies hold varying perceptions of natural hazards in different environments and have different ways of reacting to them	31, 151, 437, 591, 599, 605, 631, 633, 641, 663, 710–711	39, 52, 53, 151, 228–229, 437
(16) The changes that occur in the meaning, use, distribution, and importance of resources		
The student knows and understands: **16.1** How the spatial distribution of resources affects patterns of human settlement	82, 117–122, 127–130, 141, 145–146, 157, 159, 173–175, 220, 225–226, 233–234, 238, 275–277, 356, 417–418, 439–440, 448, 455–456, 468–469, 489–490, 505–506, 622–623, 652–654, 668–671, 714, 721–722, 730–732	117–122, 127–130, 141, 257, 274–275, 305, 375–377, 417–418, 439–440, 448, 455–456, 468–469, 489–490
16.2 How resource development and use change over time	141–142, 146–148, 158, 173–175, 205, 210–211, 238, 245–247, 292, 299, 364, 424–427, 490, 495–499, 644–656, 707	141, 147, 159–160, 174, 236, 424–427, 490, 495–499
16.3 The geographic results of policies and programs for resource use and management	173–175, 205, 238, 246, 276–277, 304–305, 313, 323–325, 372–373, 393, 424–426, 529–530, 650, 665–667, 699–700	147, 150, 174, 233, 246–247, 424–426
Therefore, the student is able to: **16.A** Analyze the relationships between the spatial distribution of settlement and resources	163, 214, 227, 239, 257, 277, 287, 317, 459, 470–471, 623, 659, 714	160, 204, 277, 459, 470–471
16.B Explain the relationship between resources and the exploration, colonization, and settlement of different regions of the world	122, 158, 185, 205, 239, 257, 277, 287, 459, 490, 523, 531, 655, 667, 670–671	127–128, 158, 185, 277, 459, 490
16.C Evaluate policy decisions regarding the use of resources in different regions of the world	247, 257, 285, 356, 374, 377, 427, 537, 667, 701, 732	285, 427
16.D Identify the ways in which resources can be reused and recycled	185, 325, 394–395, 397	185, 325, 394–395, 397
16.E Evaluate policies and programs related to the use of resources on different spatial scales	213, 247, 257, 331, 359, 429, 703, 723	148, 210, 246–247, 429
(17) How to apply geography to interpret the past		
The student knows and understands: **17.1** How processes of spatial change affect events and conditions	176–178, 293, 297–298, 389	176–178, 293
17.2 How changing perceptions of places and environments affect the spatial behavior of people	176–177, 181, 282–283, 448, 461, 503–504, 567–568, 712–714	129–130, 218, 230–232

Correlation to the National Geography Standards

	PUPIL'S EDITION	TEACHER'S EDITION
(17) How to apply geography to interpret the past *(continued)*		
17.3 The fundamental role that geographical context has played in affecting events in history	30–31, 40, 129–130, 230–232, 236–237, 319–321, 389, 491–493, 584–585, 648–649, 727–729	129–130, 218, 230–232
Therefore, the student is able to: **17.A** Explain how the processes of spatial change have affected history	130, 385, 321, 390, 572, 646	130, 321, 385, 390, 572, 646
17.B Assess how people's changing perceptions of geographic features have led to changes in human societies	178, 367	128, 153
17.C Analyze the ways in which physical and human features have influenced the evolution of significant historic events and movements	130, 139, 205, 379, 383, 493	130, 137, 139, 157, 161, 168, 205, 218
(18) How to apply geography to interpret the present and plan for the future		
The student knows and understands: **18.1** How different points of view influence the development of policies designed to use and manage Earth's resources	135–137, 174–175, 210–211, 354, 569–570, 600–603	135–137, 174–175, 210–211
18.2 Contemporary issues in the context of spatial and environmental perspectives	138, 174–175, 323–325, 354, 569–570	138, 174–175
18.3 How to use geographic knowledge, skills, and perspectives to analyze problems and make decisions	181–183, 252–253, 326–329, 392–395, 436–437, 467–471, 532–535	181–183, 253–255, 436–437, 467–471
Therefore, the student is able to: **18.A** Develop policies that are designed to guide the use and management of Earth's resources and that reflect multiple points of view	325, 602–603	325, 602–603
18.B Develop plans to solve local and regional problems that have spatial dimensions	247, 293, 602–603	247, 293
18.C Analyze a variety of contemporary issues in terms of Earth's physical and human systems	175, 185, 325	162, 167, 175, 462, 466, 470–471
18.D Use geography knowledge and skills to analyze problems and make decisions within a spatial context	144, 175, 293, 604	175, 253–254, 293, 426, 470–471

Senior Consultants

Daniel D. Arreola is Professor of Geography and an affiliate faculty member of the Center for Latin American Studies at Arizona State University. He has taught world regional geography for more than a decade at universities in Arizona and Texas. Dr. Arreola has published extensively on topics relating to the cultural geography of the Mexican-American borderlands. He is co-author of *The Mexican Border Cities: Landscape Anatomy and Place Personality* and author of *Tejano South Texas: A Mexican American Cultural Province.*

Marci Smith Deal is the K-12 Social Studies Curriculum Coordinator for Hurst-Euless-Bedford Independent School District in Texas. She received the 2000 Distinguished Geographer Award for the State of Texas, and was one of the honorees of the 2001 National Council for Geographic Education Distinguished Teacher Award. She has served as president for the Texas Council for Social Studies Supervisors and as vice-president for the Texas Council for Social Studies. She currently serves as a teacher consultant for National Geographic Society.

James F. Petersen is Professor of Geography at Southwest Texas State University. He served as president of the National Council for Geographic Education in 2000. As a charter member of the National Geographic Society's Alliance, Dr. Petersen has directed summer institutes and national conferences for teachers and educational organizations. He is the author of many articles on geographic education, as well as media/book reviews, textbooks, and curricular materials.

Rickie Sanders is Professor and Chair of Geography/Urban Studies at Temple University. She recently served on the team that directed the National Science Foundation/National Council for Geographic Education's "Finding A Way" project, which produced learning modules for integrating gender into geography classrooms. Dr. Sanders has received numerous awards for teaching, including the NCGE Distinguished Teaching Award and the Temple University Distinguished Teaching Award. She has numerous publications and is co-author of *Growing Up in America: An Atlas of Youth in the U.S.A.*

iii

Consultants and Reviewers

Content Consultants

C. Cindy Fan
Department of Geography
UCLA
Los Angeles, California

Howard Johnson
Department of Physical and Earth Sciences
Jacksonville State University
Jacksonville, Alabama

Cheryl Johnson-Odim
Liberal Education Division
Columbia College
Chicago, Illinois

Charles Kovacik
Department of Geography
University of South Carolina
Columbia, South Carolina

Barbara McDade
Department of Geography
University of Florida
Gainesville, Florida

Inés Miyares
Department of Geography
Hunter College
New York City, New York

Joseph Stoltman
Department of Geography
Western Michigan University
Kalamazoo, Michigan

Donald Zeigler
Department of Political Science and Geography
Old Dominion University
Norfolk, Virginia

Multicultural Advisory Board

Betty Dean
Social Studies Consultant
Pearland, Texas

C. Cindy Fan
Department of Geography
UCLA
Los Angeles, California

Cheryl Johnson-Odim
Liberal Education Division
Columbia College
Chicago, Illinois

Barbara McDade
Department of Geography
University of Florida
Gainesville, Florida

Inés Miyares
Department of Geography
Hunter College
New York City, New York

Pat Payne
Office of Multicultural Education
Indianapolis Public Schools
Indianapolis, Indiana

Betto Ramirez
Region One Education Service Center
Edinburg, Texas

Jon Reyhner
Department of Education
Northern Arizona University
Flagstaff, Arizona

Teacher Consultants

The following educators reviewed manuscript or wrote classroom activities.

Deborah Althouse
Thomas J. Anderson High School
Southgate, Michigan

Jamie Berlin
South High School
Sheboygan, Wisconsin

Heather Berry
Hazelwood East High School
St. Louis, Missouri

Jewel Berryman
Kashmere High School
Houston, Texas

Deborah Bittner
Sandra Day O'Connor High School
Helotes, Texas

Dora Bradley
Lakewood Middle School
North Little Rock, Arkansas

Denise Butler
Hillcrest High School
Dallas, Texas

Deborah Canales
Austin High School
Houston, Texas

Fred Cibik
Brown Deer High School
Brown Deer, Wisconsin

Jim Curtis
Antioch High School
Antioch, Illinois

Sam Eigel
Cody High School
Detroit, Michigan

Jan Ellersieck
Ft. Zummalt South High School
St. Peters, Missouri

iv

Thomas Figurski
Thomas J. Anderson High School
Southgate, Michigan

Karen Fletcher
Haltom High School
Haltom City, Texas

Kathy Gilbert
Mukwonago High School
Mukwonago, Wisconsin

Manuel Gomez
McAllen Memorial High School
McAllen, Texas

Richard Goodwin
Yvonne A. Ewell Township Center
Dallas, Texas

Craig Grace
Lanier High School
West Austin, Texas

David Haas
Waukegan High School
Waukegan, Illinois

Britin Hanson
Granite Hills High School
El Cajon, California

William Hoffman
Capistrano Valley High School
Mission Viejo, California

Alan Hunt
Coronado High School
El Paso, Texas

Amy Kiehl
Milwaukee Trade & Technical High School
Milwaukee, Wisconsin

Cliff Kinder
Bowie High School
Arlington, Texas

Korri Kinney
Meridian High School
Meridian, Idaho

Sherry Kusenberger
MacArthur High School
San Antonio, Texas

Rick Looze
Ft. Atkinson High School
Ft. Atkinson, Wisconsin

Jerome Love
Beaumont High School
St. Louis, Missouri

Kara Lukens
Dakota High School
Macomb, Michigan

Matt Lyons
Hastings Ninth Grade Center
Houston, Texas

Gene Mahurin
Western Hills High School
Ft. Worth, Texas

Joy McKee
Lamar High School
Arlington, Texas

Patricia Medina
Ray High School
Corpus Christi, Texas

Tim Murray
Plano Senior High School
Plano, Texas

Joseph Naumann
McCluer North High School
Florissant, Missouri

Phillip Owens
Ball High School
Galveston, Texas

Robert Parker
St. Margaret's High School
San Juan Capistrano, California

Cathy Probst
Nathan Hale High School
West Allis, Wisconsin

Dan Richardson
East Troy High School
East Troy, Illinois

Robert Schutt
Detroit High School for the Fine and Performing Arts
Detroit, Michigan

Martha B. Sharma
National Cathedral School
Washington, D.C.

Brenda Smith
Social Studies Instructional Supervisor
Colorado Springs School District #11
Colorado Springs, Colorado

Jody Smothers-Marcello
Sitka School District
Sitka, Alaska

Linda Tillis
South Oak Cliff High School
Dallas, Texas

Mark Van Hecke
Anchor Bay High School
New Baltimore, Michigan

Glenn Watt
Grayslake High School
Grayslake, Illinois

Alice White
Bryan Adams High School
Dallas, Texas

Sarah White
Dakota High School
Macomb, Michigan

Tom Wissink
Oshkosh West High School
Oshkosh, Wisconsin

Anne Woods
Orchard Farms High School
St. Charles, Missouri

Tom Wurst
Langham Creek High School
Houston, Texas

v

HISTORY™ is the leading destination for revealing, award-winning, original non-fiction series and event-driven specials that connect history with viewers in an informative, immersive and entertaining manner across multiple platforms. HISTORY is part of A&E Television Networks (AETN), a joint venture of Hearst Corporation, Disney/ABC Television Group and NBC Universal, an award-winning, international media company that also includes, among others, A&E Network™, BIO™, and History International™.

HISTORY programming greatly appeals to educators and young people who are drawn into the visual stories our documentaries tell. Our Education Department has a long-standing record in providing teachers and students with curriculum resources that bring the past to life in the classroom. Our content covers a diverse variety of subjects, including American and world history, government, economics, the natural and applied sciences, arts, literature and the humanities, health and guidance, and even pop culture.

The HISTORY website, located at **www.history.com**, is the definitive historical online source that delivers entertaining and informative content featuring broadband video, interactive timelines, maps, games, podcasts and more.

"We strive to engage, inspire and encourage the love of learning..."

Since its founding in 1995, HISTORY has demonstrated a commitment to providing the highest quality resources for educators. We develop multimedia resources for K–12 schools, two- and four-year colleges, government agencies, and other organizations by drawing on the award-winning documentary programming of A&E Television Networks. We strive to engage, inspire and encourage the love of learning by connecting with students in an informative and compelling manner. To help achieve this goal, we have formed a partnership with Houghton Mifflin Harcourt.

The Idea Book for Educators

...assroom resources that ...ng the past to life

Live webcasts

HISTORY Take a Veteran to School Day

In addition to premium video-based resources, **HISTORY** has extensive offerings for teachers, parents, and students to use in the classroom and in their in-home educational activities, including:

- ***The Idea Book for Educators*** is a biannual teacher's magazine, featuring guides and info on the latest happenings in history education to help keep teachers on the cutting edge.
- **HISTORY Classroom (www.history.com/classroom)** is an interactive website that serves as a portal for history educators nationwide. Streaming videos on topics ranging from the Roman aqueducts to the civil rights movement connect with classroom curricula.
- **HISTORY email newsletters** feature updates and supplements to our award-winning programming relevant to the classroom with links to teaching guides and video clips on a variety of topics, special offers, and more.
- **Live webcasts** are featured each year as schools tune in via streaming video.
- **HISTORY Take a Veteran to School Day** connects veterans with young people in our schools and communities nationwide.

In addition to **HOUGHTON MIFFLIN HARCOURT**, our partners include the *Library of Congress*, the *Smithsonian Institution, National History Day, The Gilder Lehrman Institute of American History,* the *Organization of American Historians*, and many more. HISTORY video is also featured in museums throughout America and in over 70 other historic sites worldwide.

Unit 1 The Basics of Geography

RAND McNALLY ATLAS A1

Chapter 1
PHYSICAL GEOGRAPHY
Looking at the Earth 4
1 The Five Themes of Geography 5
2 The Geographer's Tools 10
GEOGRAPHY SKILLS HANDBOOK 14
Chapter 1 Assessment 24

Chapter 2
PHYSICAL GEOGRAPHY
A Living Planet 26
VIDEO Viewing the Planets
1 The Earth Inside and Out 27
DISASTERS! Asteroid Hit! 30
2 Bodies of Water and Landforms 32
3 Internal Forces Shaping the Earth 37
4 External Forces Shaping the Earth 42
Chapter 2 Assessment 46

Chapter 3
PHYSICAL GEOGRAPHY
Climate and Vegetation 48
1 Seasons and Weather 49
2 Climate 54
3 World Climate Regions 59
RAND MCNALLY MAP AND GRAPH SKILLS
Interpreting Climographs 64
4 Soils and Vegetation 65
Chapter 3 Assessment 68

Chapter 4
HUMAN GEOGRAPHY
People and Places 70
1 The Elements of Culture 71
2 Population Geography 78
3 Political Geography 83
4 Urban Geography 87
5 Economic Geography 91
Chapter 4 Assessment 96

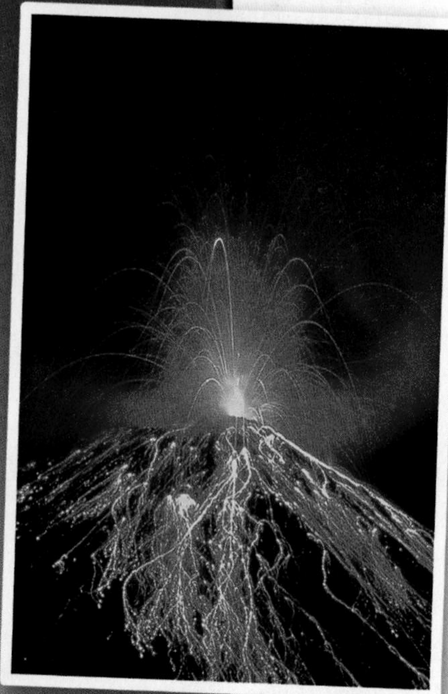

Volcano in Costa Rica (p. 2)

Nanjing Road, Shanghai, China (p. 81)

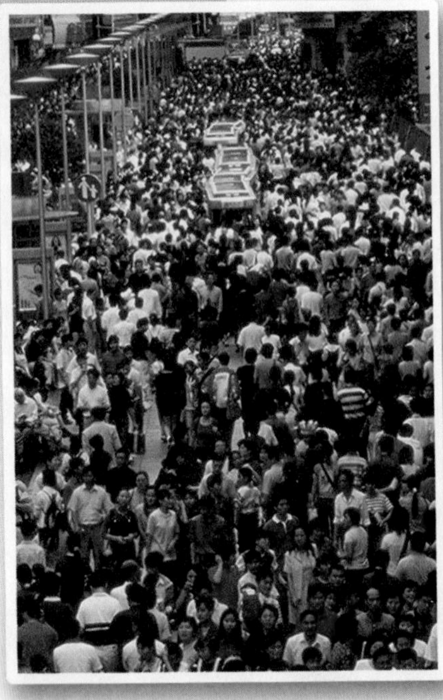

viii

The United States and Canada

Unit 2

Introduction UNIT PREVIEW: TODAY'S ISSUES 100
- The Fight Against Terrorism
- Urban Sprawl
- Diverse Societies Face Change

UNIT 2 ATLAS 102

REGIONAL DATA FILE 108

Chapter 5

PHYSICAL GEOGRAPHY OF THE UNITED STATES AND CANADA

A Land of Contrasts 116

1 Landforms and Resources 117

2 Climate and Vegetation 123

3 Human-Environment Interaction 127

RAND MCNALLY MAP AND GRAPH SKILLS Reading a Highway Map 131

Chapter 5 Assessment 132

Chapter 6

HUMAN GEOGRAPHY OF THE UNITED STATES

Shaping an Abunant Land 134

1 History and Government of the United States 135

2 Economy and Culture of the United States 140

3 Subregions of the United States 145

DISASTERS! The Dust Bowl 150

Chapter 6 Assessment 152

HISTORY MULTIMEDIA CONNECTIONS The American Revolution 153 MC1

Chapter 7

HUMAN GEOGRAPHY OF CANADA

Developing a Vast Wilderness 154

1 History and Government of Canada 155

2 Economy and Culture of Canada 159

COMPARING CULTURES Transportation 164

3 Subregions of Canada 166

Chapter 7 Assessment 170

Chapter 8

TODAY'S ISSUES

The United States and Canada 172

1 The Fight Against Terrorism 173

2 Urban Sprawl 176

RAND MCNALLY MAP AND GRAPH SKILLS Reading a Bounded-Area Map 179

UNIT CASE STUDY Diverse Societies Face Change 180

Chapter 8 Assessment 184

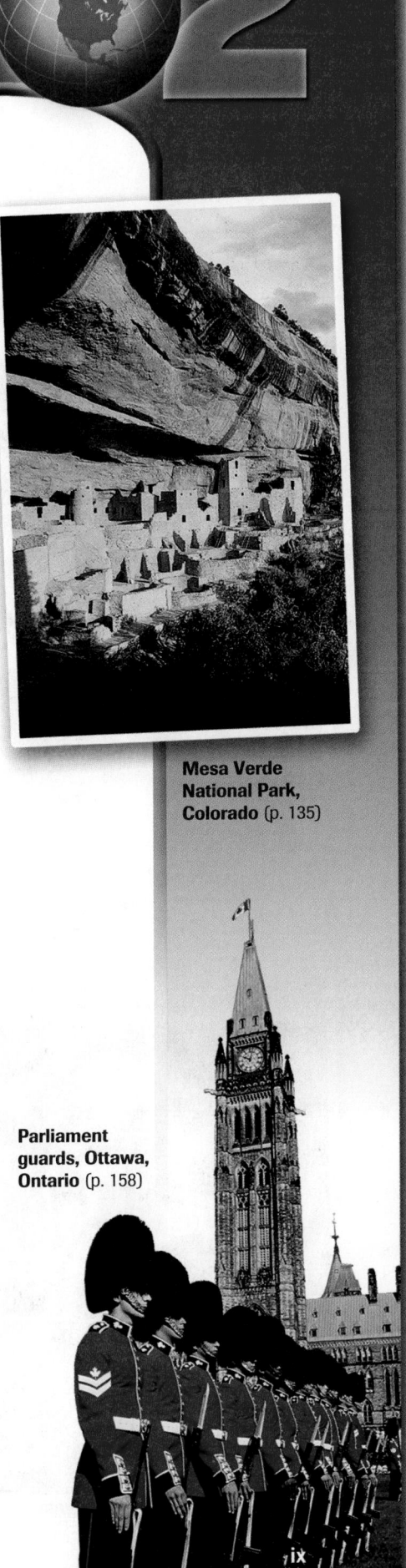

Mesa Verde National Park, Colorado (p. 135)

Parliament guards, Ottawa, Ontario (p. 158)

Unit 3 Latin America

Introduction UNIT PREVIEW: TODAY'S ISSUES 188
- Rain Forest Resources
- Giving Citizens a Voice
- The Income Gap

UNIT 3 ATLAS 190
REGIONAL DATA FILE 196

Chapter 9 PHYSICAL GEOGRAPHY OF LATIN AMERICA
From the Andes to the Amazon 200
1 Landforms and Resources 201
RAND MCNALLY MAP AND GRAPH SKILLS Interpreting a Precipitation Map 206
2 Climate and Vegetation 207
3 Human-Environment Interaction 210
Chapter 9 Assessment 214

Chapter 10 HUMAN GEOGRAPHY OF LATIN AMERICA
A Blending of Cultures 216
VIDEO Mexico's Ancient Civilizations
1 Mexico 217
2 Central America and the Caribbean 222
DISASTERS! The Haiti and Chile Earthquakes 228
3 Spanish-Speaking South America 230
4 Brazil 236
COMPARING CULTURES Festivals and Holidays 240
Chapter 10 Assessment 242
MULTIMEDIA CONNECTIONS Mexico 243 MC1

Chapter 11 TODAY'S ISSUES
Latin America 244
1 Rain Forest Resources 245
RAND MCNALLY MAP AND GRAPH SKILLS Interpreting Satellite Images 248
2 Giving Citizens a Voice 249
UNIT CASE STUDY The Income Gap 252
Chapter 11 Assessment 256

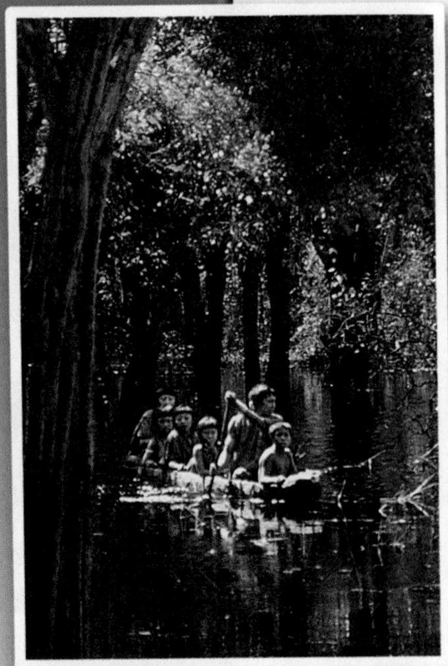

Chacobo Indians on the Amazon River, Bolivia (p. 186)

São Paulo, Brazil (p. 251)

Europe

Unit 4

Introduction UNIT PREVIEW: TODAY'S ISSUES 260
- Turmoil in the Balkans
- Cleaning Up Europe
- The European Union

UNIT 4 ATLAS 262
REGIONAL DATA FILE 268

Chapter 12 PHYSICAL GEOGRAPHY OF EUROPE
The Pensulia of Peninsulas 272
VIDEO Miraculous Canals of Venice
1 Landforms and Resources 273
2 Climate and Vegetation 278
RAND MCNALLY MAP AND GRAPH SKILLS Interpreting a Bar Graph 281
3 Human-Environment Interaction 282
Chapter 12 Assessment 286

Chapter 13 HUMAN GEOGRAPHY OF EUROPE
Diversity, Conflict, Union 288
VIDEO The Roman Republic Is Born
1 Mediterranean Europe 289
DISASTERS! Bubonic Plague 294
2 Western Europe 296
3 Northern Europe 302
COMPARING CULTURES Geographic Sports Challenges 308
4 Eastern Europe 310
Chapter 13 Assessment 316
MULTIMEDIA CONNECTIONS Ancient Greece 317 MC1

Chapter 14 TODAY'S ISSUES
Europe 318
1 Turmoil in the Balkans 319
RAND MCNALLY MAP AND GRAPH SKILLS Interpreting a Thematic Map 322
2 Cleaning Up Europe 323
UNIT CASE STUDY The European Union 326
Chapter 14 Assessment 330

The Eiffel Tower, Paris, France (p. 259)

The Wetterhorn, Switzerland (p. 310)

xi

Unit 5

Russia and the Republics

Introduction UNIT PREVIEW: TODAY'S ISSUES 334

- Regional Conflict
- The Struggle for Economic Reform
- The Soviet Union's Nuclear Legacy

UNIT 5 ATLAS 336

REGIONAL DATA FILE 342

Chapter 15 PHYSICAL GEOGRAPHY OF RUSSIA AND THE REPBULICS

A Land of Extremes 344

1 Landforms and Resources 345

2 Climate and Vegetation 350

3 Human-Environment Interaction 353

RAND MCNALLY MAP AND GRAPH SKILLS Understanding Time Zones 357

Chapter 15 Assessment 358

Chapter 16 HUMAN GEOGRAPHY OF RUSSIA AND THE REPUBLICS

A Diverse Heritage 360

1 Russia and the Western Republics 361

DISASTERS! Nuclear Explosion at Chernobyl 368

2 Transcaucasia 370

3 Central Asia 375

COMPARING CULTURES Homes and Shelters 380

Chapter 16 Assessment 382

Chapter 17 TODAY'S ISSUES

Russia and the Republics 384

1 Regional Conflict 385

2 The Struggle for Economic Reform 388

RAND MCNALLY MAP AND GRAPH SKILLS Reading Line and Pie Graphs 391

UNIT CASE STUDY The Soviet Union's Nuclear Legacy 392

Chapter 17 Assessment 396

Frozen Lake Baikal, Russia (p. 350)

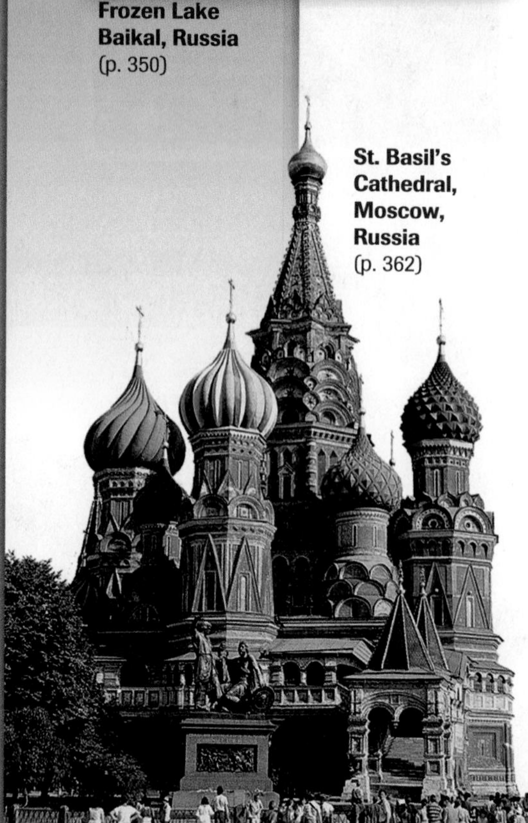

St. Basil's Cathedral, Moscow, Russia (p. 362)

xii

Africa Unit 6

Introduction UNIT PREVIEW: TODAY'S ISSUES 400
- Economic Development
- Health Care
- Effects of Colonialism

UNIT 6 ATLAS 402
REGIONAL DATA FILE 408

Chapter 18 PHYSICAL GEOGRAPHY OF AFRICA
The Plateau Continent 414
VIDEO Dams
1 Landforms and Resources 415
RAND MCNALLY MAP AND GRAPH SKILLS Reading an Economic Activity Map 419
2 Climate and Vegetation 420
3 Human-Environment Interaction 424
Chapter 18 Assessment 428

Chapter 19 HUMAN GEOGRAPHY OF AFRICA
From Human Beginnings to New Nations 430
VIDEO Gold Mines
1 East Africa 431
DISASTERS! Famine in Somalia 436
2 North Africa 438
3 West Africa 442
COMPARING CULTURES Feasts 446
4 Central Africa 448
5 Southern Africa 453
Chapter 19 Assessment 458

Chapter 20 TODAY'S ISSUES
Africa 460
1 Economic Development 461
RAND MCNALLY MAP AND GRAPH SKILLS Reading a City Map 464
2 Health Care 465
UNIT CASE STUDY Effects of Colonialism 468
Chapter 20 Assessment 472

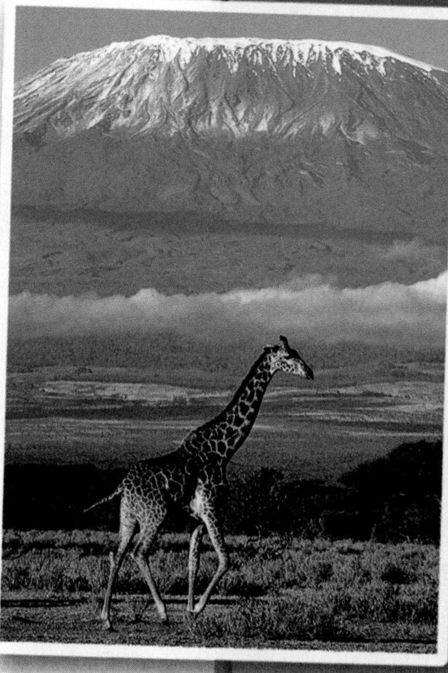

Mount Kilimanjaro, Tanzania (p. 399)

Masai Girl, Kenya (p. 434)

Sahara Desert, North Africa (p. 420)

Unit 7 Southwest Asia

Introduction UNIT PREVIEW: TODAY'S ISSUES 476
- Population Relocation
- Oil Wealth Fuels Change
- Regional Conflict Over Land

UNIT 7 ATLAS 478
REGIONAL DATA FILE 484

Chapter 21 PHYSICAL GEOGRAPHY OF SOUTHWEST ASIA
Harsh and Arid Lands 486
1 Landforms and Resources 487
2 Climate and Vegetation 491
RAND MCNALLY MAP AND GRAPH SKILLS Reading a Vegetation Map 494
3 Human-Environment Interaction 495
Chapter 21 Assessment 500

Chapter 22 HUMAN GEOGRAPHY OF SOUTHWEST ASIA
Religion, Politics, and Oil 502
VIDEO Back to Basra: After Saddam
1 The Arabian Peninsula 503
COMPARING CULTURES Religious Architecture 508
2 The Eastern Mediterranean 510
3 The Northeast 516
DISASTERS! Earthquake in Turkey 520
Chapter 22 Assessment 522

Chapter 23 TODAY'S ISSUES
Southwest Asia 524
1 Population Relocation 525
RAND MCNALLY MAP AND GRAPH SKILLS Interpreting a Population Density Map 528
2 Oil Wealth Fuels Change 529
UNIT CASE STUDY Regional Conflict Over Land 532
Chapter 23 Assessment 536

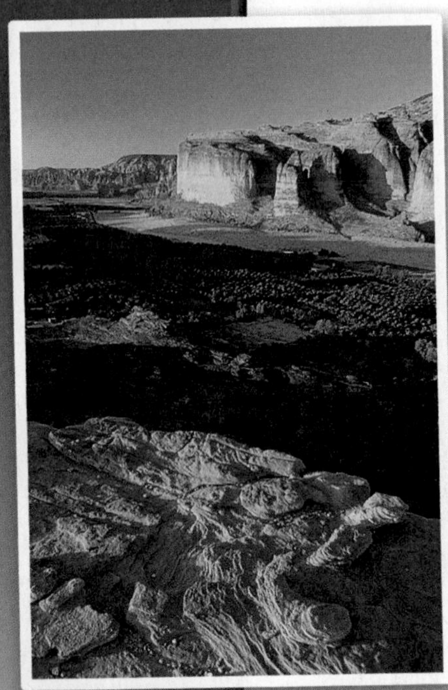

Oasis on caravan route from Yemen to Palestine (p. 475)

Kurdish family, Turkey (p. 476)

xiv

South Asia

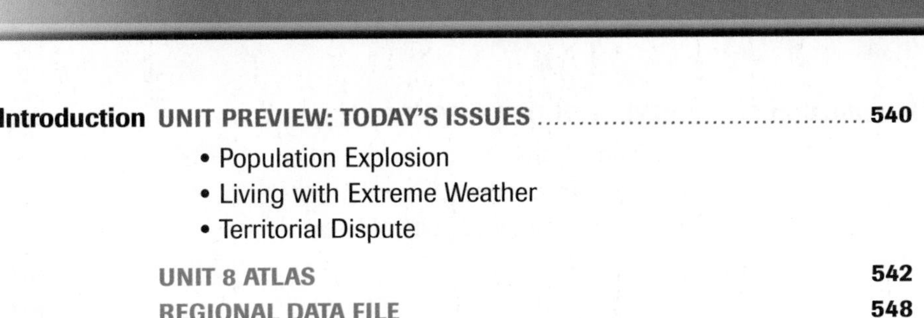

Introduction UNIT PREVIEW: TODAY'S ISSUES 540

- Population Explosion
- Living with Extreme Weather
- Territorial Dispute

UNIT 8 ATLAS 542

REGIONAL DATA FILE 548

Chapter 24 PHYSICAL GEOGRAPHY OF SOUTH ASIA

The Land Where Continents Collided 550

1 Landforms and Resources 551

2 Climate and Vegetation 556

RAND MCNALLY MAP AND GRAPH SKILLS Reading a Weather Map 559

3 Human-Environment Interaction 560

Chapter 24 Assessment 564

Chapter 25 HUMAN GEOGRAPHY OF SOUTH ASIA

A Region of Contrasts 566

VIDEO Mahatma Gandhi

1 India 567

2 Pakistan and Bangladesh 573

DISASTERS! The Cyclone of 1970 578

3 Nepal and Bhutan 580

4 Sri Lanka and the Maldives 584

COMPARING CULTURES Musical Instruments 588

Chapter 25 Assessment 590

Chapter 26 TODAY'S ISSUES

Southeast Asia 592

VIDEO Kashmir: The Legacy of Partition in India

1 Population Explosion 593

RAND MCNALLY MAP AND GRAPH SKILLS Reading a Population Pyramid 596

2 Living with Extreme Weather 597

Chapter 26 Assessment 604

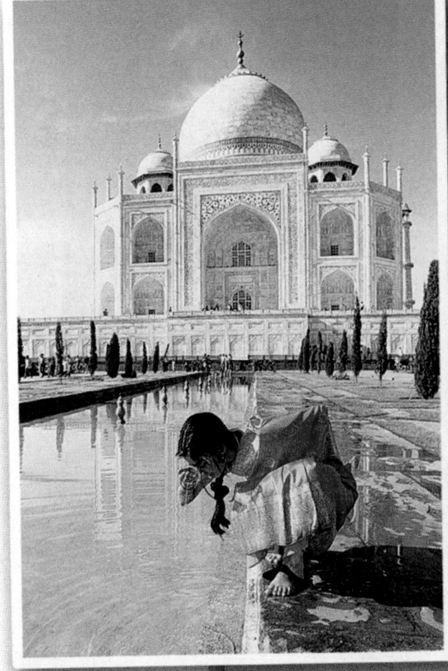

Taj Mahal, Agra, India (p. 538)

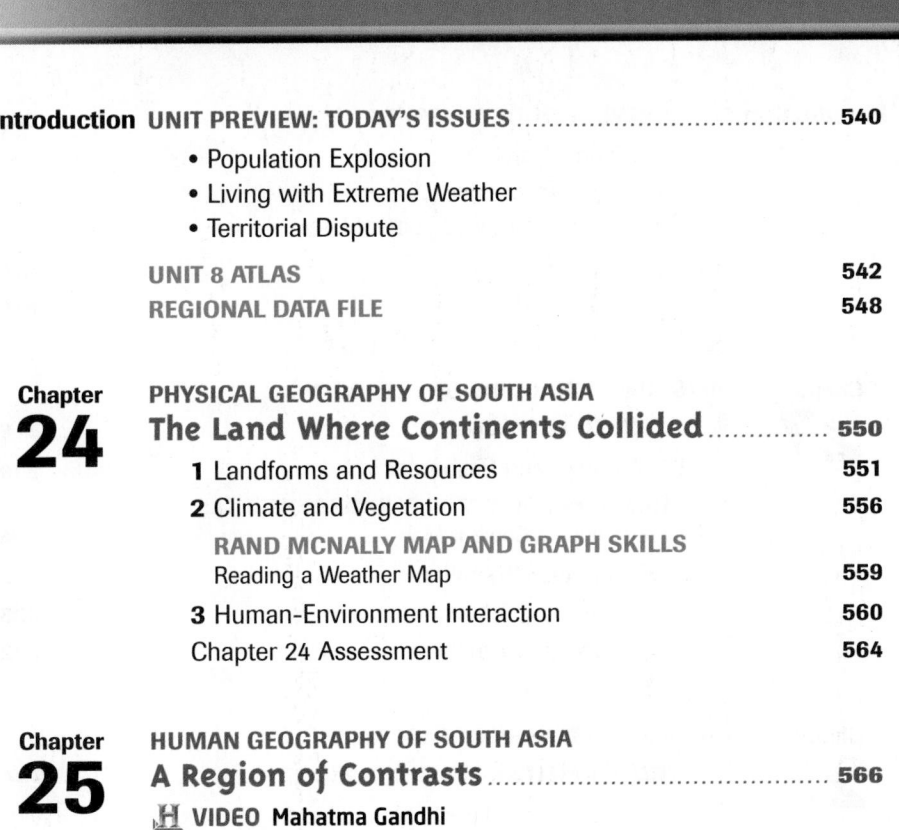

Tea Plantation, Sri Lanka (p. 586)

Unit 9

East Asia

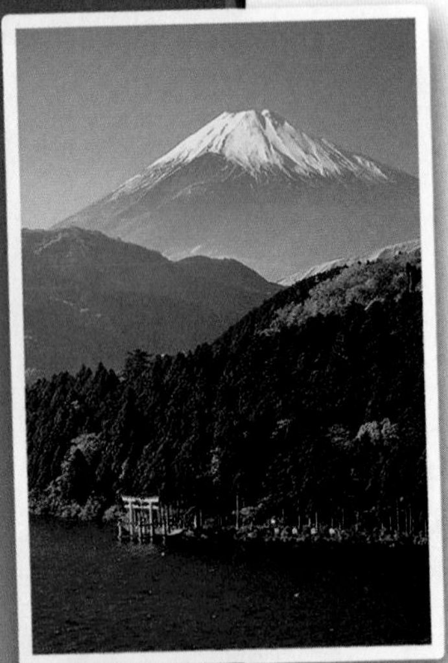
Mount Fuji, Japan (p. 607)

Potala Palace, Tibet (p. 619)

Crowded urban street, Hong Kong (p. 668)

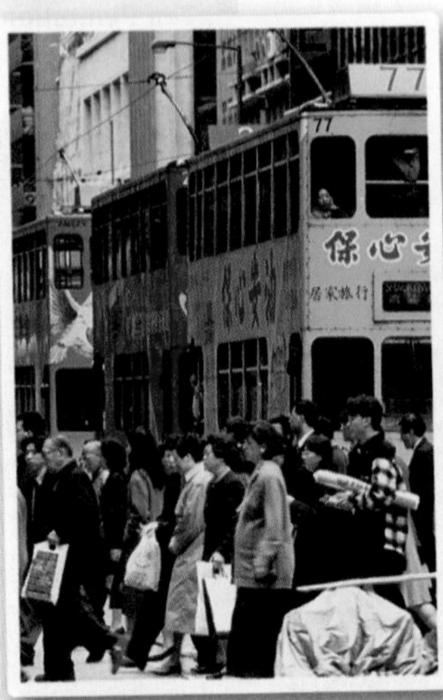

Introduction UNIT PREVIEW: TODAY'S ISSUES 608
- The Ring of Fire
- Trade and Prosperity
- Population and the Quality of Life

UNIT 9 ATLAS 610
REGIONAL DATA FILE 616

Chapter 27 PHYSICAL GEOGRAPHY OF EAST ASIA
A Rugged Terrain 618
1 Landforms and Resources 619
RAND MCNALLY MAP AND GRAPH SKILLS Interpreting a Contour Map 624
2 Climate and Vegetation 625
3 Human-Environment Interaction 628
Chapter 27 Assessment 632

Chapter 28 HUMAN GEOGRAPHY OF EAST ASIA
Shared Cultural Traditions 634
VIDEO The Great Wall of China
1 China 635
DISASTERS! Chang Jiang (Yangtze River) Flood of 1931 640
2 Mongolia and Taiwan 642
3 The Koreas: North and South 647
4 Japan 651
COMPARING CULTURES Masks 656
Chapter 28 Assessment 658
MULTIMEDIA CONNECTIONS China and the Great Wall 659 MC1

Chapter 29 TODAY'S ISSUES
East Asia 660
1 The Ring of Fire 661
RAND MCNALLY MAP AND GRAPH SKILLS Interpreting a Proportional Circle Map 664
2 Trade and Prosperity 665
UNIT CASE STUDY Population and the Quality of Life 668
Chapter 29 Assessment 672

xvi

Southeast Asia, Oceania, and Antarctica

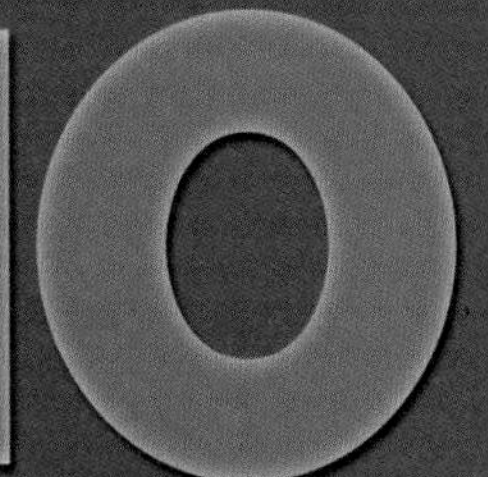

Unit 10

Introduction UNIT PREVIEW: TODAY'S ISSUES 676
- Aboriginal Land Claims
- Industrialization Sparks Change
- Global Environmental Change

UNIT 10 ATLAS 678
REGIONAL DATA FILE 684

Chapter 30 PHYSICAL GEOGRAPHY OF SOUTHEAST ASIA, OCEANIA, AND ANTARCTICA
A Region of Extremes 688
1 Landforms and Resources 689
RAND MCNALLY MAP AND GRAPH SKILLS Interpreting a Relief Map 693
2 Climate and Vegetation 694
3 Human-Environment Interaction 698
Chapter 30 Assessment 702

Chapter 31 HUMAN GEOGRAPHY OF SOUTHEAST ASIA, OCEANIA, AND ANTARCTICA
Migration and Conquest 704
VIDEO Dreamtime of the Aborigines
1 Southeast Asia 705
DISASTERS! Krakatoa 710
2 Oceania 712
COMPARING CULTURES Regional Costumes 716
3 Australia, New Zealand, and Antarctica 718
Chapter 31 Assessment 724

Chapter 32 TODAY'S ISSUES
Southeast Asia, Oceania, and Antarctica 726
1 Aboriginal Land Claims 727
2 Industrialization Sparks Change 730
RAND MCNALLY MAP AND GRAPH SKILLS Interpreting a Cartogram 733
UNIT CASE STUDY Global Environmental Change 734
Chapter 32 Assessment 738

REFERENCE

Skillbuilder Handbook R1
English Glossary........ R16
Spanish Glossary........ R26
Index........ R36
Acknowledgments........ R52

Available @ hmhsocialstudies.com
- Strategies for Studying Geography
- Strategies for Taking Standardized Tests
- Gazetteer

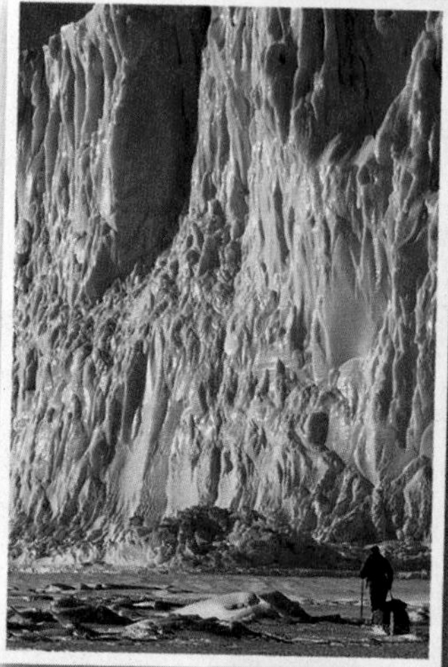

Ice Cliffs, Antarctica (p. 674)

Fishing on Cook Island (p. 714)

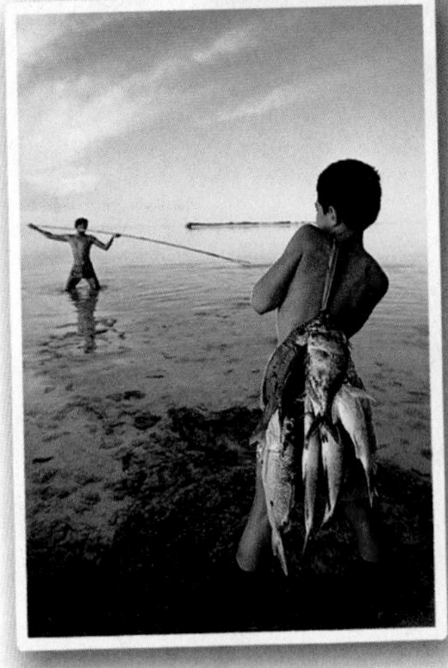

Uluru, or Ayers Rock, Australia (p. 729)

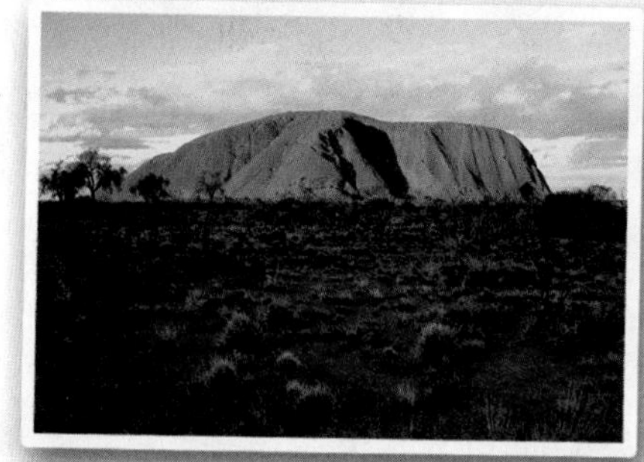

xvii

RAND McNALLY

World Atlas

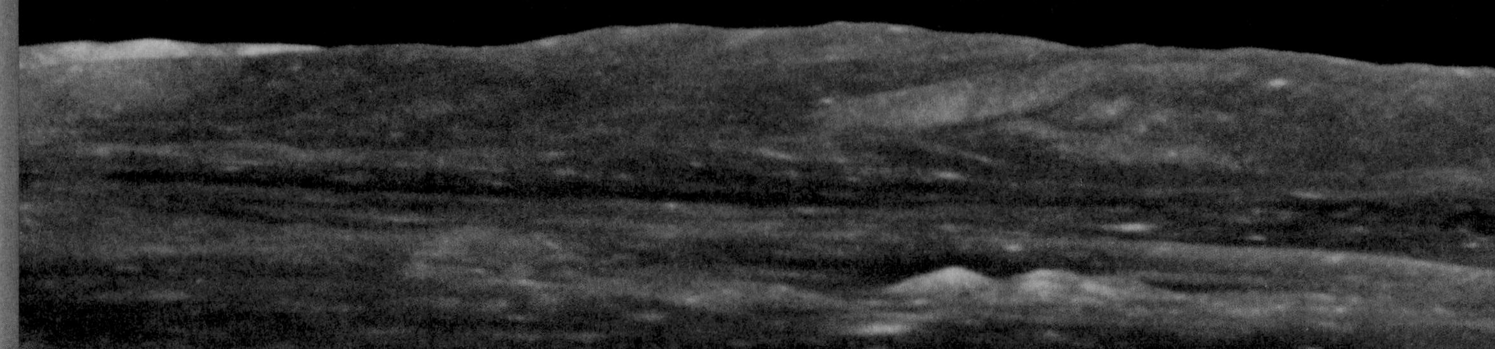

Contents

World: Physical A2
World: Political A4
World: Climate A6
World: Environments A8
World: Population A10
World: Economies A12
Plate Tectonics A14
World: Time Zones A16
United States: Physical A18
United States: Political A20
North America: Physical A22
North America: Political A23
South America: Physical A24
South America: Political A25
Europe: Physical A26
Europe: Political A28
Africa: Physical A30
Africa: Political A31
Asia: Physical A32
Asia: Political A34
Australia and Oceania A36
North and South Pole A37

Complete Legend for Physical and Political Maps

Symbols

 Lake

 Salt Lake

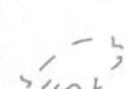 Seasonal Lake

 River

\ Waterfall

 Canal

 Mountain Peak

 Highest Mountain Peak

Cities

■ **Los Angeles** — City over 1,000,000 population

▣ **Calgary** — City of 250,000 to 1,000,000 population

• Haifa — City under 250,000 population

⊛ ***Paris*** — National Capital

★ **Vancouver** — Secondary Capital (State, Province, or Territory)

Type Styles Used to Name Features

CHINA — Country

ONTARIO — State, Province, or Territory

PUERTO RICO (U.S.) — Possession

ATLANTIC OCEAN — Ocean or Sea

A l p s — Physical Feature

Borneo — Island

Boundaries

 International Boundary

 Secondary Boundary

Land Elevation and Water Depths

Land Elevation

Meters	Feet
3,000 and over	9,840 and over
2,000 - 3,000	6,560 - 9,840
500 - 2,000	1,640 - 6,560
200 - 500	656 - 1,640
0 - 200	0 - 656

Water Depth

Meters	Feet
Less than 200	Less than 656
200 - 2,000	656 - 6,560
Over 2,000	Over 6,560

ATLAS

A1

ARCTIC OCEAN
Greenland
Jan Mayen
Arctic Circle
Iceland
Faroe Is.
British Isles
London
Baffin Island
Baffin Bay
Hudson Bay
Yukon
Mt. McKinley
20,320 Ft.
6,194m
Mackenzie
Canadian Shield
NORTH AMERICA
Rocky Mountains
Great Plains
Aleutian Islands
Vancouver
Newfoundland
St. Lawrence
Appalachian Mts.
Washington, D.C.
Cape Hatteras
Mississippi
Colorado
Los Angeles
Azores
Iberian Peninsula
Atlas Mts.
Midway Is.
Tropic of Cancer
Baja California
Gulf of Mexico
ATLANTIC
Canary Islands
Hawaiian Islands
Yucatan Peninsula
Cuba
Hispaniola
Puerto Rico
Jamaica
Caribbean Sea
Cape Verde Islands
Cape Verde
Niger
PACIFIC
Trinidad
Orinoco
OCEAN
Palmyra
Equator
Kiribati
Galapagos Islands
OCEAN
Amazon
Amazon Basin
SOUTH AMERICA
Andes
Samoa Islands
Marquesas Is.
Mato Grosso Plateau
St. Helena
Tonga Is.
Cook Islands
Tahiti
Tropic of Capricorn
Easter Island
Rio de Janeiro
Paraná
Mt. Aconcagua
22,831 Ft.
6,959m
Buenos Aires
Archipiélago Juan Fernández
Chatham Is.
Patagonia
0 1000 2000 Miles
0 1000 2000 3000 Kilometers
Copyright by Rand McNally & Co.
Robinson Projection
M-101520-1
Falkland Is.
South Georgia
Tierra del Fuego
Cape Horn
South Sandwich Is.
South Orkney Is.
South Shetland Is.
Antarctic Circle
Antarctic Peninsula
Weddell Sea
Ross Sea
Marie Byrd Land
Vinson Massif
16,066 Ft.
4,897m
N

ARCTIC OCEAN
Spitsbergen
Franz Josef Land
Novaya Zemlya
North Cape
Scandinavian Peninsula
North Sea
EUROPE
Moscow
Volga
Don
Ural Mts.
Ob'
Yenisey
Lena
Siberia
Alps
Balkan Peninsula
Black Sea
Caucasus
Mt. Elbrus 18,510 Ft. 5,642m
Caspian Sea
Aral Sea
Sardinia
Sicily
Crete
Cyprus
Mediterranean Sea
Cairo
Zagros Mts.
ASIA
Altai Mts.
Pamir
Gobi Desert
Beijing
Huang
Yangtze
Plateau of Tibet
Himalayas
Mt. Everest 29,035 Ft. 8,850m
Indus
Ganges
Sea of Okhotsk
Bering Sea
Kamchatka Peninsula
Sakhalin
Amur
Hokkaidō
Honshū
Sea of Japan (East Sea)
East China Sea
Kyūshū
Sahara Desert
Arabian Peninsula
Red Sea
AFRICA
Nile
Sahel
Mumbai (Bombay)
Arabian Sea
Deccan Plateau
Bay of Bengal
Mekong
Taiwan
Hainan Island
South China Sea
Luzon
PACIFIC
Tropic of Cancer
Mariana Islands
Wake Island
Guam
Socotra
Lakshadweep
Sri Lanka
Ethiopian Plateau
Mindanao
Palau Islands
OCEAN
Caroline Islands
Marshall Islands
Malay Peninsula
Gulf of Guinea
Congo
Congo Basin
Rift Valley
Kilimanjaro 19,340 Ft. 5,895m
Maldive Islands
Borneo
Celebes
Equator
Sumatra
Seychelles
New Guinea
Solomon Islands
Java
Timor
INDIAN
Cocos Island
Zambezi
Madagascar
Mauritius
Reunion
Kalahari Desert
Coral Sea
New Hebrides
Great Sandy Desert
New Caledonia
Fiji Is.
Tropic of Capricorn
OCEAN
AUSTRALIA
Great Dividing Range
Darling
Cape Town
Cape of Good Hope
Cape Leeuwin
Sydney
North Island
Aoraki (Mt. Cook) 12,316 Ft. 3,754m
Tasmania
South Island
Kerguelen Islands
SOUTHERN OCEAN
Antarctic Circle
Queen Maud Land
Enderby Land
Wilkes Land
Victoria Land
ANTARCTICA
Land Elevation
Meters
Feet
3,000
9,840
2,000
6,560
500
1,640
200
656
0
0
Water Depth
0
0
200
656
2,000
6,560

ATLAS

RAND McNALLY

ARCTIC OCEAN
GREENLAND (Den.)
Baffin Bay
Arctic Circle
ICELAND
FAROE IS. (Den.)
RUSSIA
ALASKA
Yukon (U.S.)
Anchorage
Aleutian Islands
CANADA
Hudson Bay
UNITED KINGDOM
IRELAND
London
Vancouver
Missouri
Newfoundland
Montréal
Ottawa
FRANCE
Chicago
New York
Washington, D.C.
UNITED STATES
Colorado
Mississippi
Azores (Port.)
PORTUGAL
Madrid
SPAIN
Los Angeles
Casablanca
MOROCCO
MIDWAY IS. (U.S.)
Houston
Tropic of Cancer
MEXICO
Gulf of Mexico
ATLANTIC
Canary Islands (Sp.)
W. SAHARA
BAHAMAS
Hawaiian Islands (U.S.)
CUBA
Mexico City
HAITI
DOM. REP.
PUERTO RICO (U.S.)
CAPE VERDE
MAURITANIA
MALI
BELIZE
JAMAICA
Caribbean Sea
SENEGAL
Niger
GUAT.
HOND.
EL. SAL.
NIC.
GAMBIA
PACIFIC
Caracas
TRINIDAD AND TOBAGO
GUINEA-BISSAU
GUINEA
BURK. FASO
COSTA RICA
VENEZUELA
GUYANA
SIERRA LEONE
COTE D'IVOIRE
GHANA
PANAMA
SURINAME
FRENCH GUIANA
LIBERIA
COLOMBIA
Equator
KIRIBATI
Galapagos Islands (Ecuador)
ECUADOR
Amazon
BRAZIL
PERU
Lima
OCEAN
OCEAN
SAMOA
AMERICAN SAMOA
COOK ISLANDS (N.Z.)
TONGA
FRENCH POLYNESIA
BOLIVIA
ST. HELENA (U.K.)
Tropic of Capricorn
PARAGUAY
Rio de Janeiro
Easter Island (Chile)
ARGENTINA
Santiago
URUGUAY
Buenos Aires
CHILE
N
0 1000 2000 Miles
0 1000 2000 3000 Kilometers

Robinson Projection
M-101519-2
FALKLAND IS. (U.K.)
South Georgia (U.K.)
South Orkney Is. (U.K.)
South Shetland Is. (U.K.)
Antarctic Circle
Weddell Sea

180° 165° 150° 135° 120° 105° 90° 75° 60° 45° 30° 15°
75° 60° 45° 30° 15° 0° 15° 30° 45° 60° 75°

National Capital
Major Cities

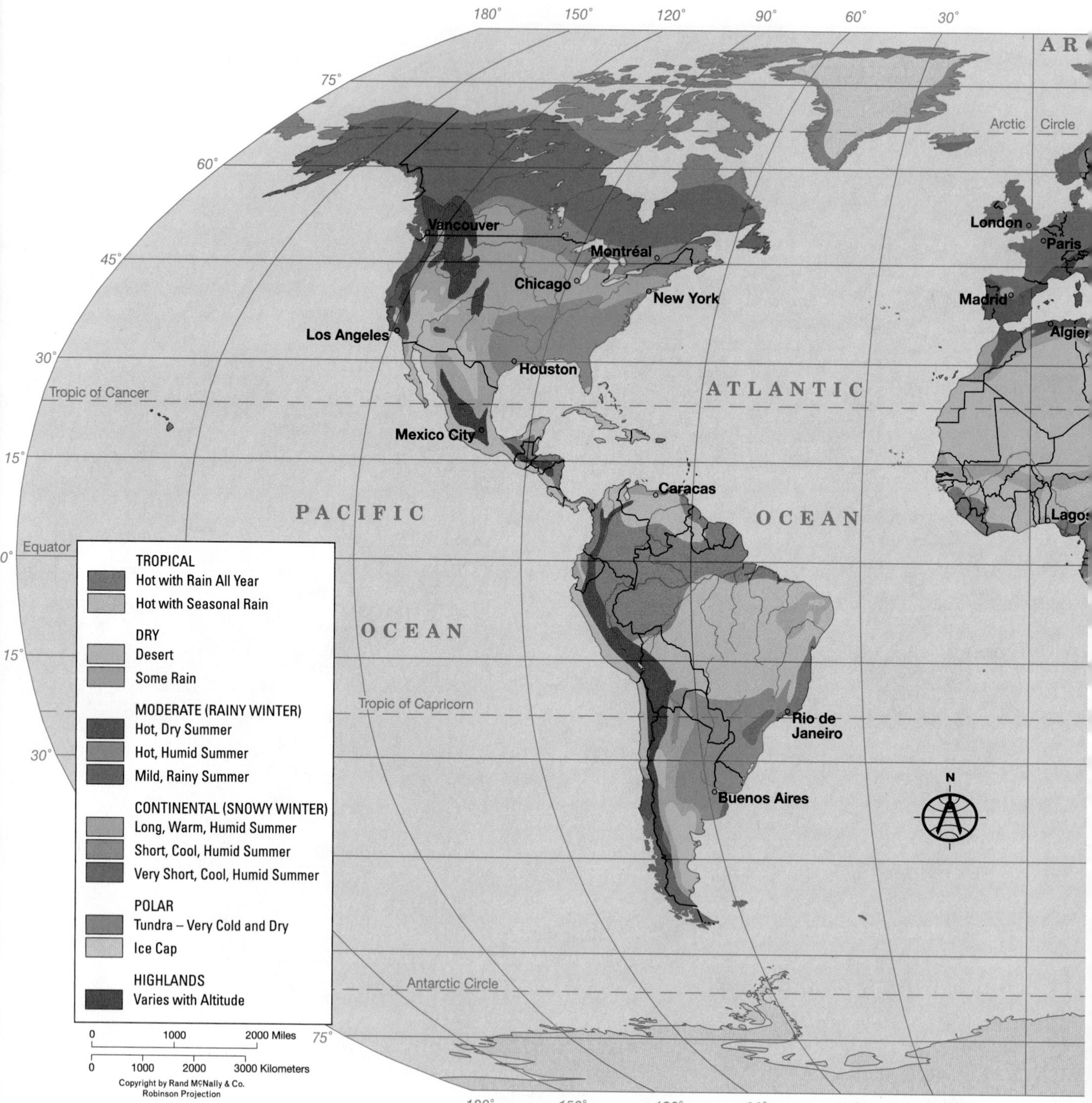

180°
150°
120°
90°
60°
30°
75°
60°
45°
30°
15°
0°
15°
30°
Arctic Circle
Tropic of Cancer
Equator
Tropic of Capricorn
Antarctic Circle
Vancouver
Montréal
Chicago
New York
Los Angeles
Houston
Mexico City
Caracas
Rio de Janeiro
Buenos Aires
London
Paris
Madrid
Lagos
PACIFIC
OCEAN
ATLANTIC
OCEAN
N
TROPICAL
Hot with Rain All Year
Hot with Seasonal Rain
DRY
Desert
Some Rain
MODERATE (RAINY WINTER)
Hot, Dry Summer
Hot, Humid Summer
Mild, Rainy Summer
CONTINENTAL (SNOWY WINTER)
Long, Warm, Humid Summer
Short, Cool, Humid Summer
Very Short, Cool, Humid Summer
POLAR
Tundra – Very Cold and Dry
Ice Cap
HIGHLANDS
Varies with Altitude
0 1000 2000 Miles
0 1000 2000 3000 Kilometers
Copyright by Rand McNally & Co.
Robinson Projection

A6

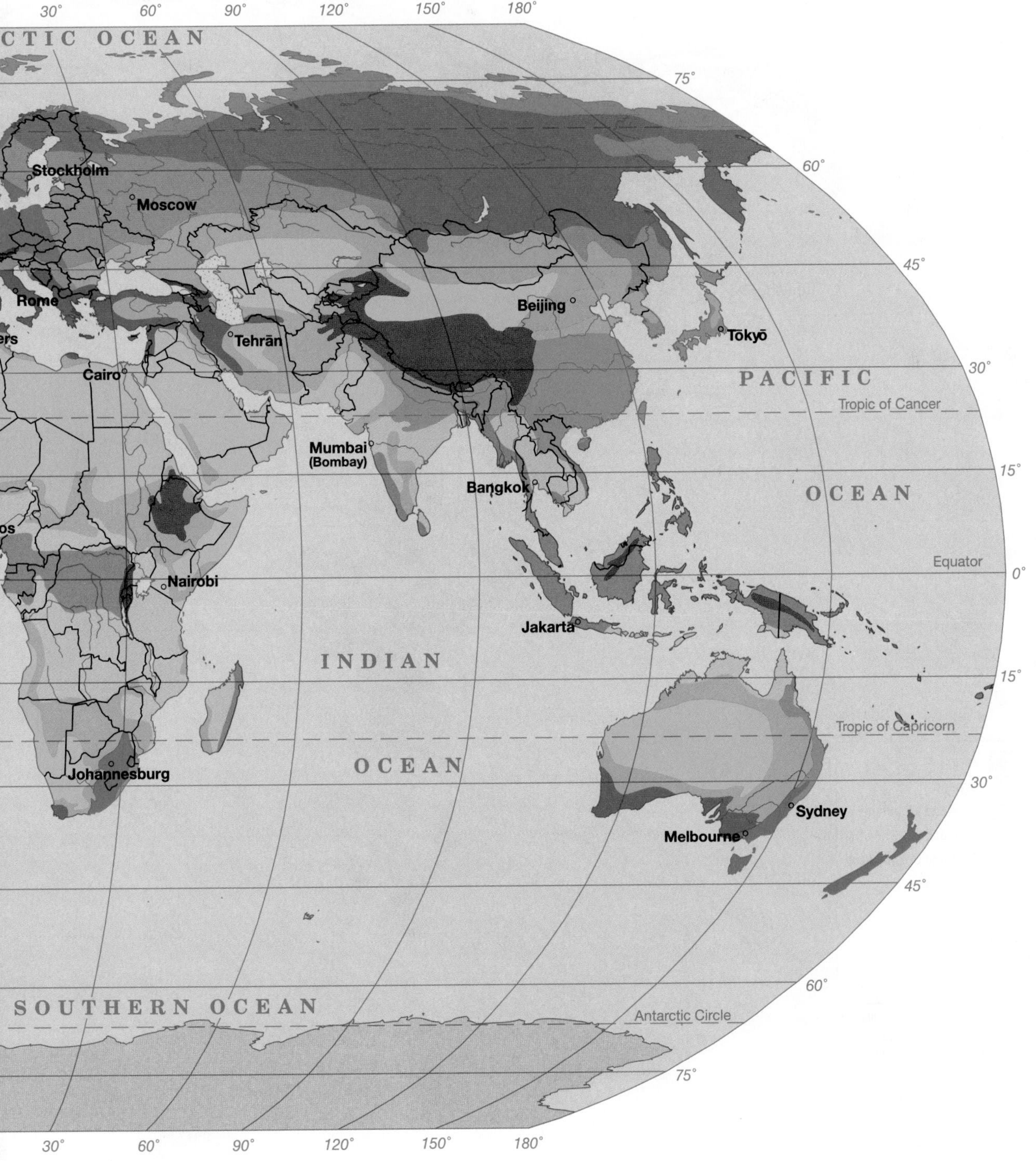

ATLAS

RAND McNALLY

A7

180° 150° 120° 90° 60° 30°

75°
60°
45°
30°
15°
0°
15°
30°
75°

ARC
Arctic Circle
Vancouver
Montréal
Chicago
New York
Los Angeles
Houston
London
Paris
Madrid
Algie
Tropic of Cancer
ATLANTIC
Mexico City
Caracas
PACIFIC
OCEAN
Lago
Equator
OCEAN
Tropic of Capricorn
Rio de Janeiro
Buenos Aires
N
Antarctic Circle

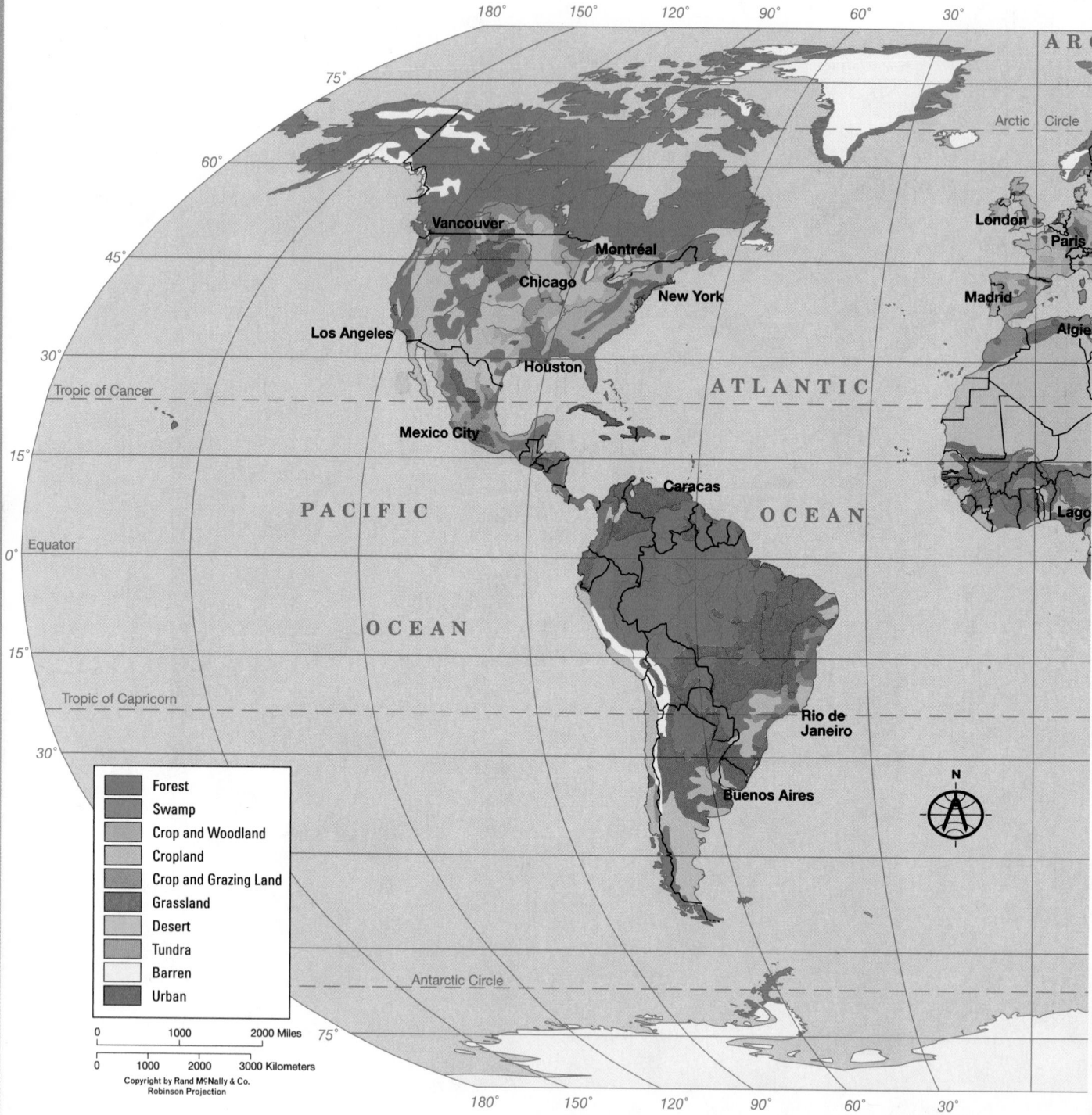

- Forest
- Swamp
- Crop and Woodland
- Cropland
- Crop and Grazing Land
- Grassland
- Desert
- Tundra
- Barren
- Urban

0 1000 2000 Miles
0 1000 2000 3000 Kilometers

Robinson Projection

180° 150° 120° 90° 60° 30°

A8

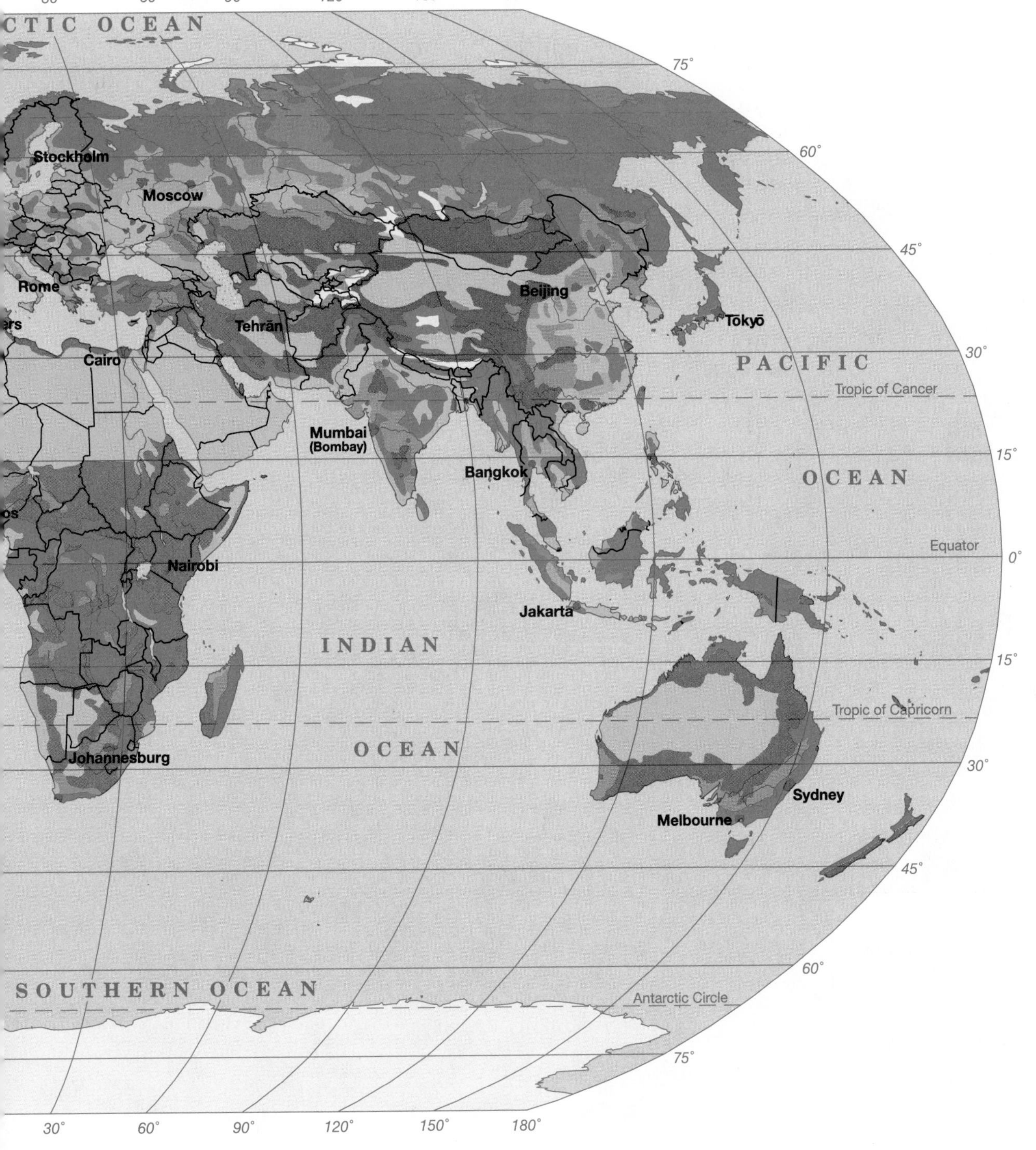
30°
60°
90°
120°
150°
180°
CTIC OCEAN
75°
Stockholm
Moscow
60°
45°
Rome
Beijing
Tehrān
Tōkyō
Cairo
30°
PACIFIC
Tropic of Cancer
Mumbai
(Bombay)
15°
Bangkok
OCEAN
Equator
0°
Nairobi
Jakarta
INDIAN
15°
Tropic of Capricorn
OCEAN
Johannesburg
30°
Sydney
Melbourne
45°
60°
SOUTHERN OCEAN
Antarctic Circle
75°
30°
60°
90°
120°
150°
180°

A9

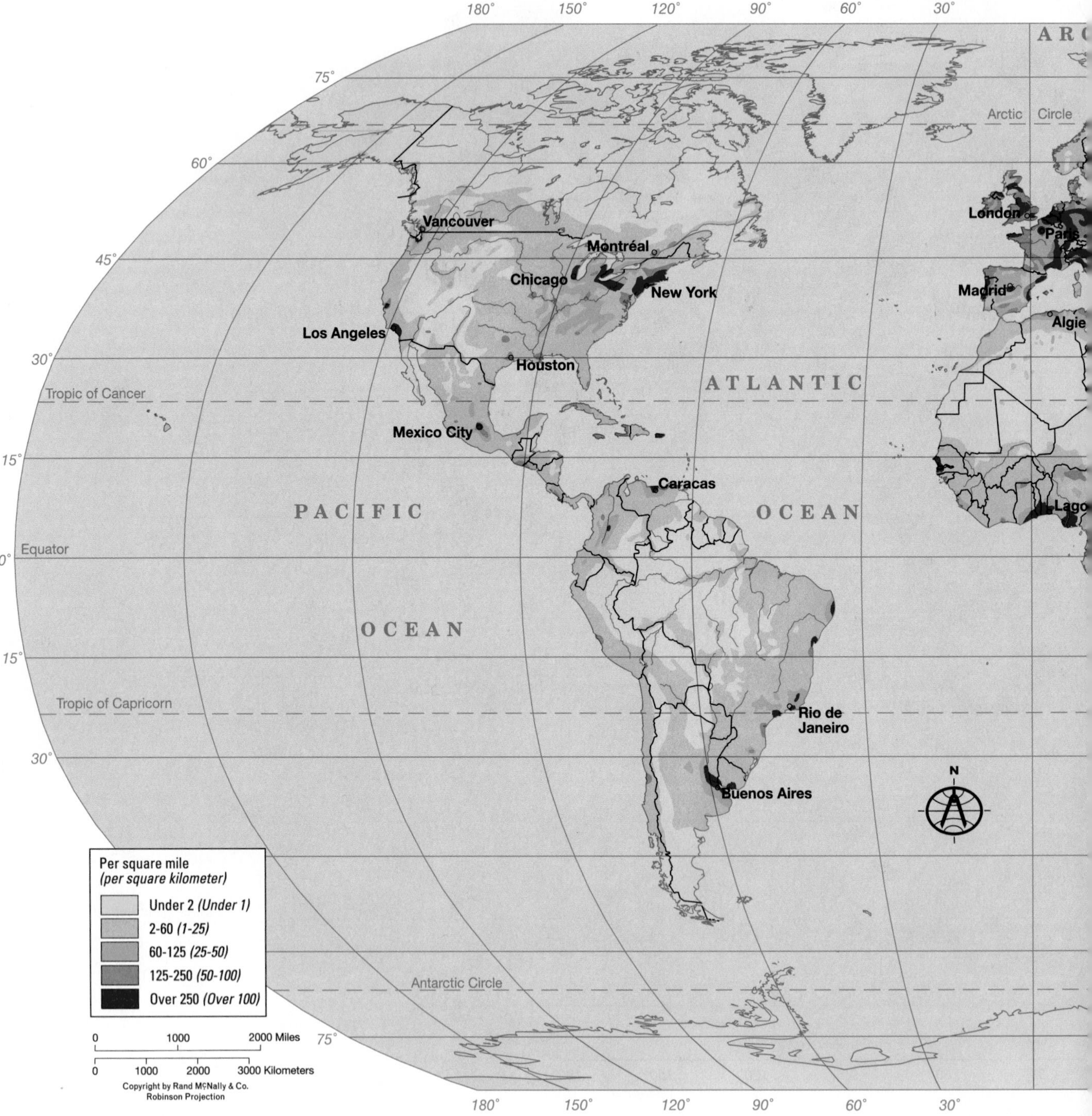
180°
150°
120°
90°
60°
30°
75°
60°
45°
30°
15°
0°
15°
30°
Arctic Circle
Tropic of Cancer
Equator
Tropic of Capricorn
Antarctic Circle
Vancouver
Montréal
Chicago
New York
Los Angeles
Houston
Mexico City
Caracas
Rio de
Janeiro
Buenos Aires
London
Paris
Madrid
PACIFIC
OCEAN
ATLANTIC
OCEAN
N
Per square mile
(per square kilometer)
Under 2 (Under 1)
2-60 (1-25)
60-125 (25-50)
125-250 (50-100)
Over 250 (Over 100)
0 1000 2000 Miles
0 1000 2000 3000 Kilometers
Copyright by Rand McNally & Co.
Robinson Projection

A10

30°
60°
90°
120°
150°
180°
TIC OCEAN
75°
60°
45°
30°
15°
0°
15°
30°
45°
60°
75°
Stockholm
Moscow
Yekaterinburg
Rome
Tehrān
Beijing
Tōkyō
Cairo
PACIFIC
Tropic of Cancer
Mumbai
(Bombay)
Bangkok
OCEAN
Equator
Nairobi
Jakarta
INDIAN
Tropic of Capricorn
OCEAN
Johannesburg
Sydney
Melbourne
SOUTHERN OCEAN
Antarctic Circle

A11

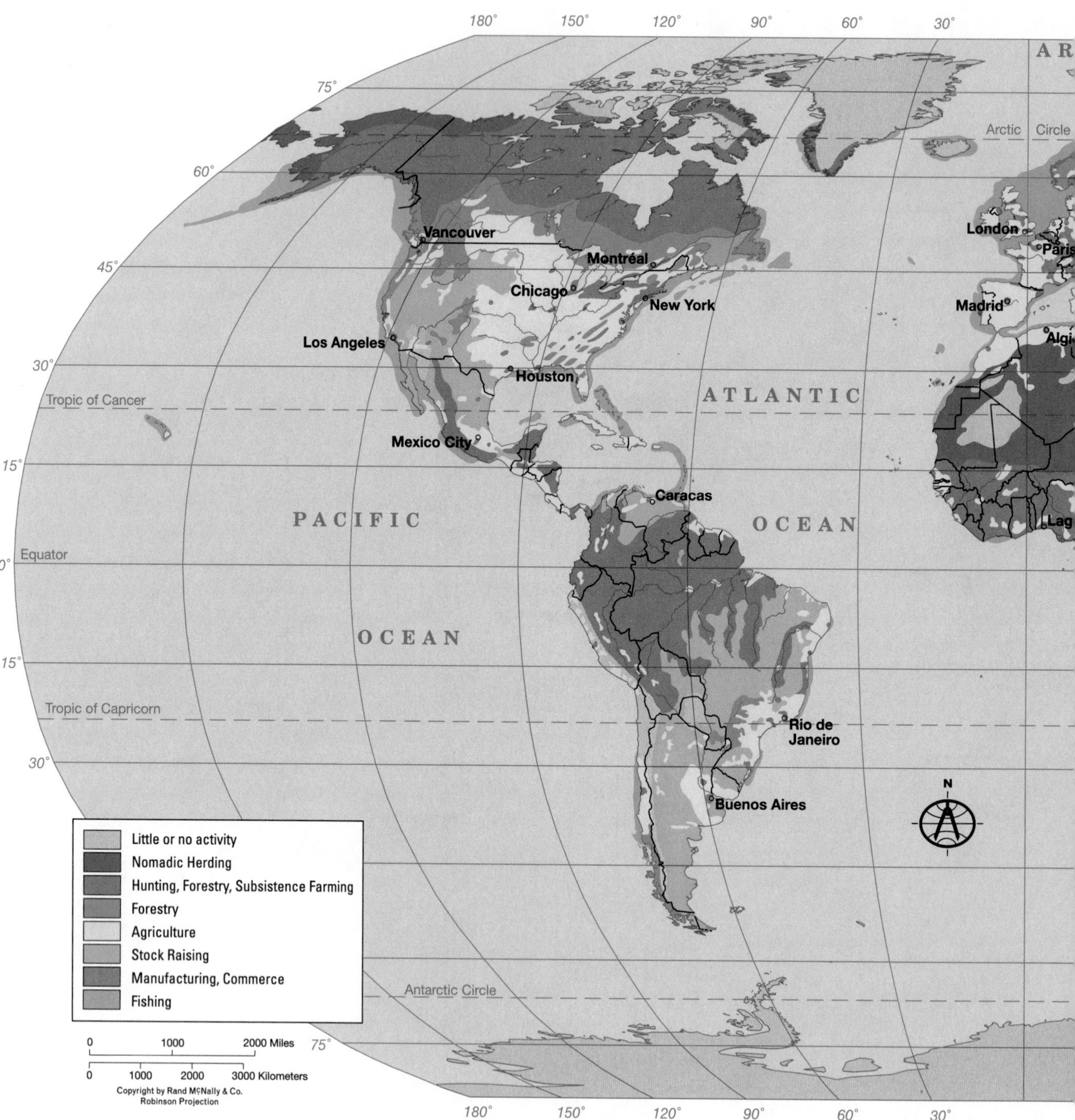
180°
150°
120°
90°
60°
30°
75°
60°
45°
30°
15°
0°
15°
30°
Arctic Circle
Tropic of Cancer
Equator
Tropic of Capricorn
Antarctic Circle
Vancouver
Montréal
Chicago
New York
Los Angeles
Houston
Mexico City
Caracas
Rio de Janeiro
Buenos Aires
London
Paris
Madrid
PACIFIC
OCEAN
ATLANTIC
OCEAN
Little or no activity
Nomadic Herding
Hunting, Forestry, Subsistence Farming
Forestry
Agriculture
Stock Raising
Manufacturing, Commerce
Fishing
0 1000 2000 Miles
0 1000 2000 3000 Kilometers
Copyright by Rand McNally & Co.
Robinson Projection
N

A12

30°
60°
90°
120°
150°
180°
CTIC OCEAN
75°
60°
45°
30°
15°
0°
15°
30°
45°
60°
75°
Stockholm
Moscow
Rome
Tehrān
Cairo
Beijing
Tōkyō
PACIFIC
Tropic of Cancer
Mumbai
(Bombay)
Bangkok
OCEAN
Equator
Nairobi
Jakarta
INDIAN
OCEAN
Tropic of Capricorn
Johannesburg
Sydney
Melbourne
SOUTHERN OCEAN
Antarctic Circle
30°
60°
90°
120°
150°
180°

A13

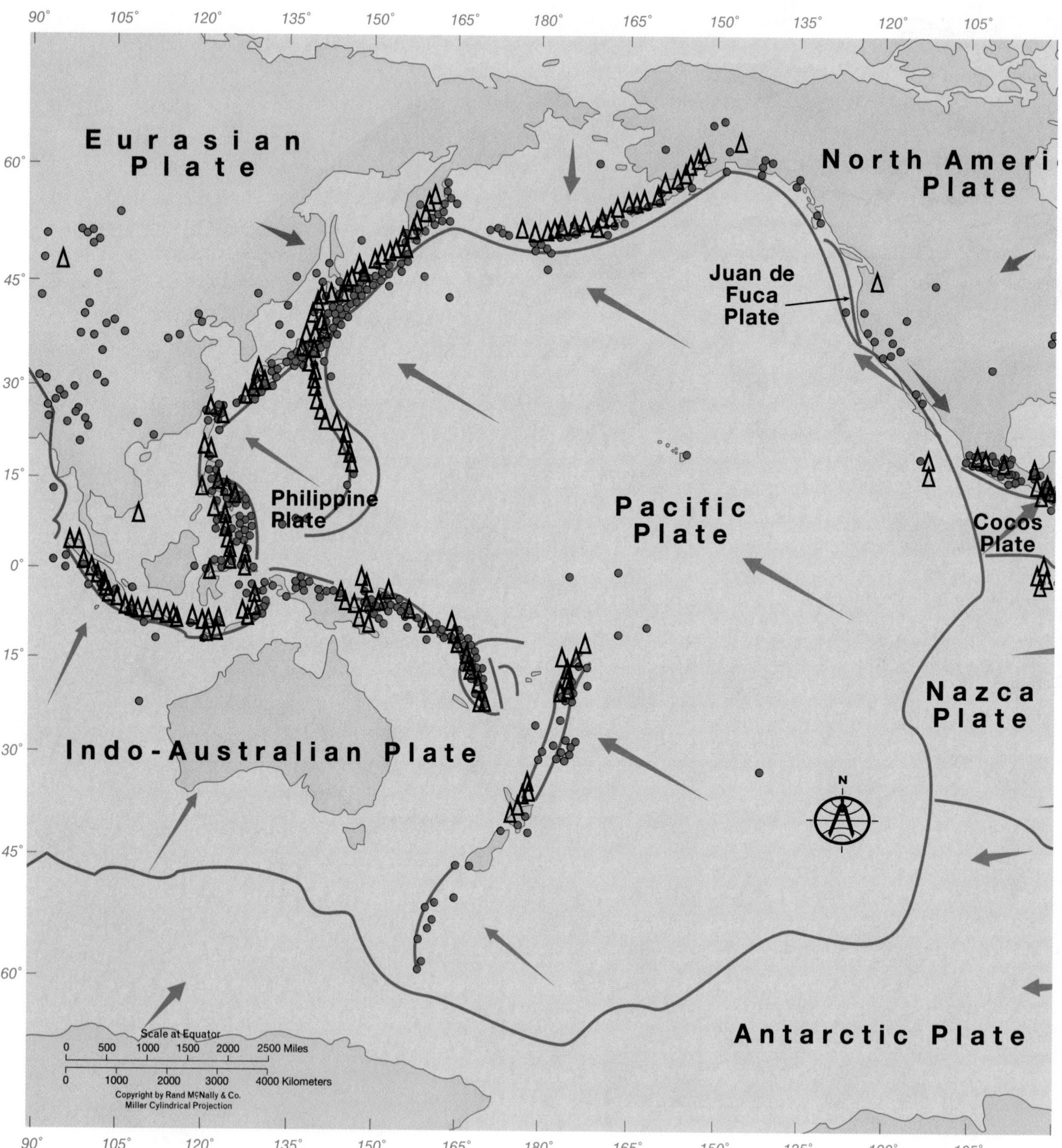
Eurasian Plate
North Ameri
Plate
Juan de Fuca Plate
Philippine Plate
Pacific Plate
Cocos Plate
Nazca Plate
Indo-Australian Plate
Antarctic Plate
N
Scale at Equator
0 500 1000 1500 2000 2500 Miles
0 1000 2000 3000 4000 Kilometers
Copyright by Rand McNally & Co.
Miller Cylindrical Projection
90° 105° 120° 135° 150° 165° 180° 165° 150° 135° 120° 105°
60° 45° 30° 15° 0° 15° 30° 45° 60°

A14

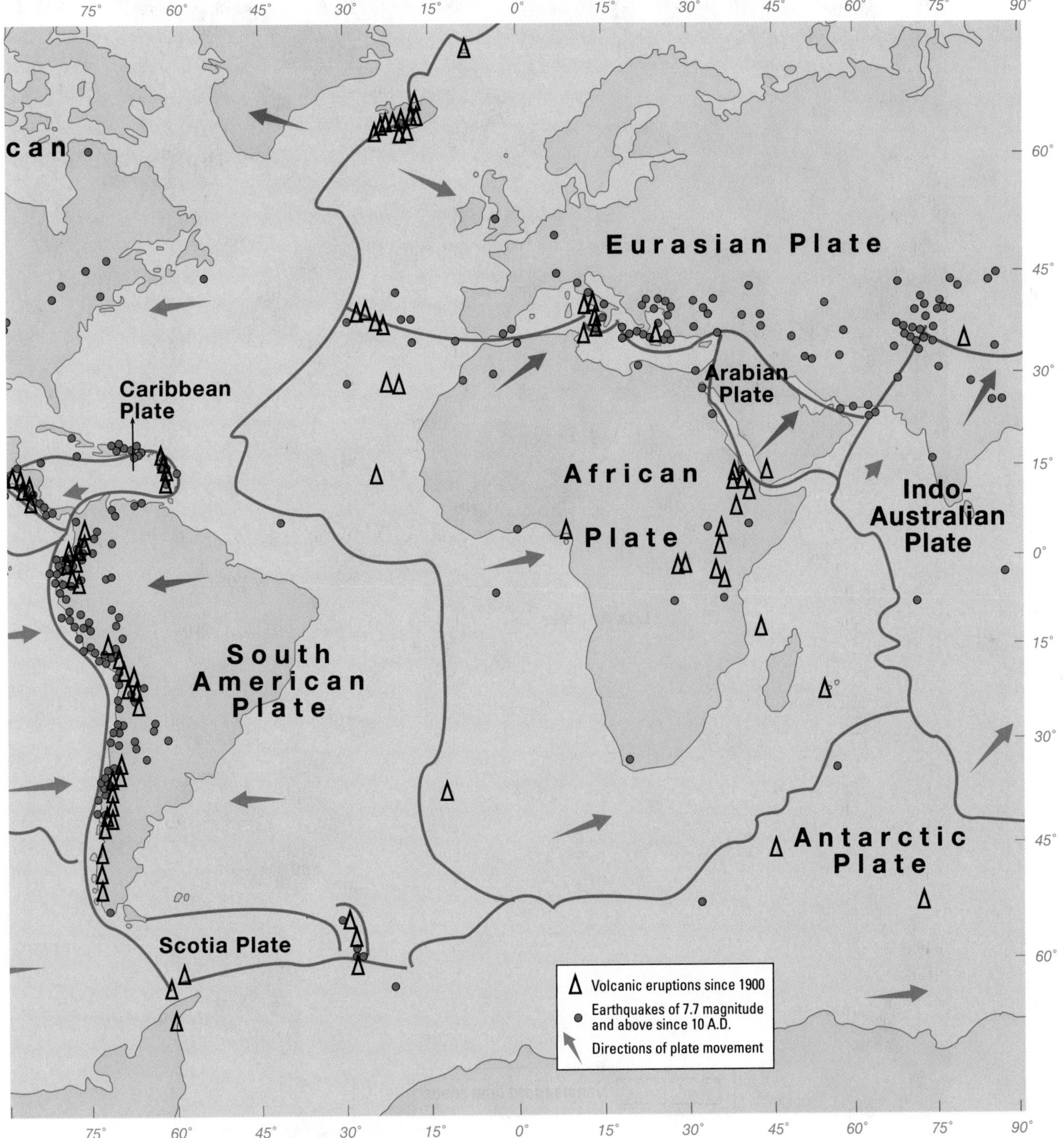

can
Eurasian Plate
Caribbean Plate
Arabian Plate
African Plate
Indo-Australian Plate
South American Plate
Antarctic Plate
Scotia Plate
Volcanic eruptions since 1900
Earthquakes of 7.7 magnitude and above since 10 A.D.
Directions of plate movement
75° 60° 45° 30° 15° 0° 15° 30° 45° 60° 75° 90°
60° 45° 30° 15° 0° 15° 30° 45° 60°

A15

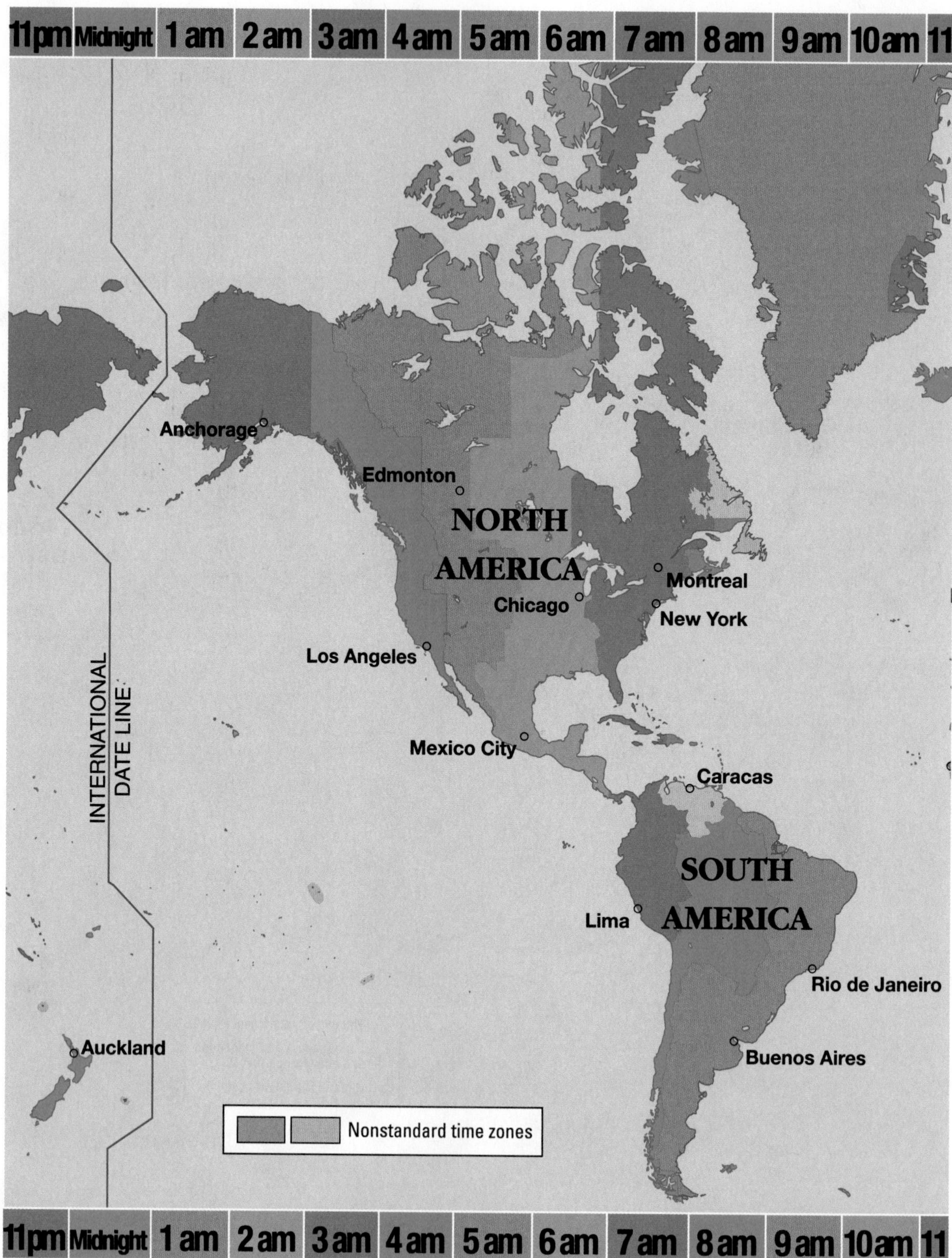
11pm
Midnight
1 am
2 am
3 am
4 am
5 am
6 am
7 am
8 am
9 am
10 am
11
INTERNATIONAL DATE LINE
Anchorage
Edmonton
NORTH AMERICA
Montreal
Chicago
New York
Los Angeles
Mexico City
Caracas
SOUTH AMERICA
Lima
Rio de Janeiro
Buenos Aires
Auckland
Nonstandard time zones

A16

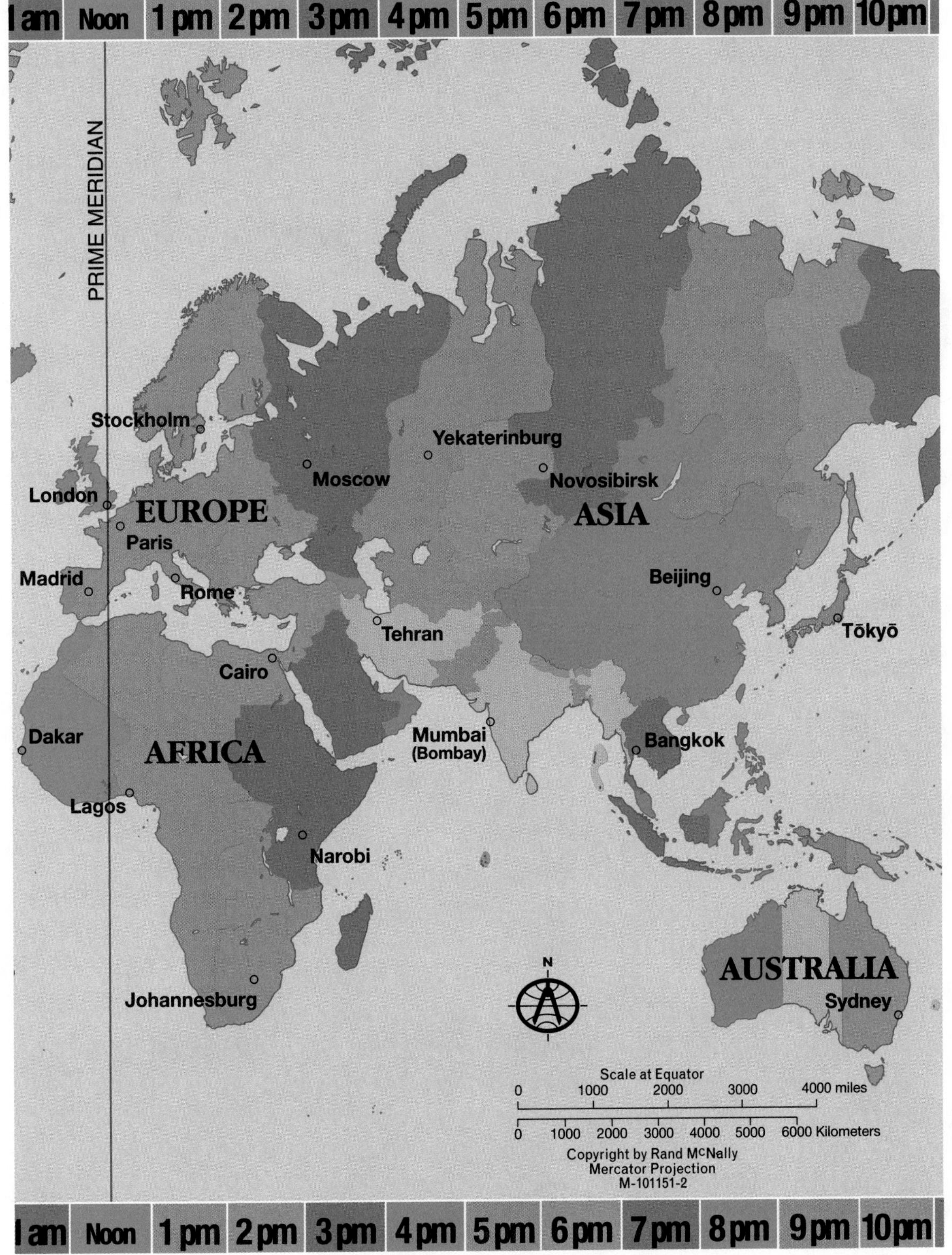

1 am
Noon
1 pm
2 pm
3 pm
4 pm
5 pm
6 pm
7 pm
8 pm
9 pm
10pm
PRIME MERIDIAN
Stockholm
London
EUROPE
Paris
Madrid
Rome
Moscow
Yekaterinburg
Novosibirsk
ASIA
Beijing
Tōkyō
Tehran
Cairo
Dakar
AFRICA
Mumbai
(Bombay)
Bangkok
Lagos
Narobi
Johannesburg
AUSTRALIA
Sydney
N
Scale at Equator
0 1000 2000 3000 4000 miles
0 1000 2000 3000 4000 5000 6000 Kilometers
Copyright by Rand McNally
Mercator Projection
M-101151-2

A17

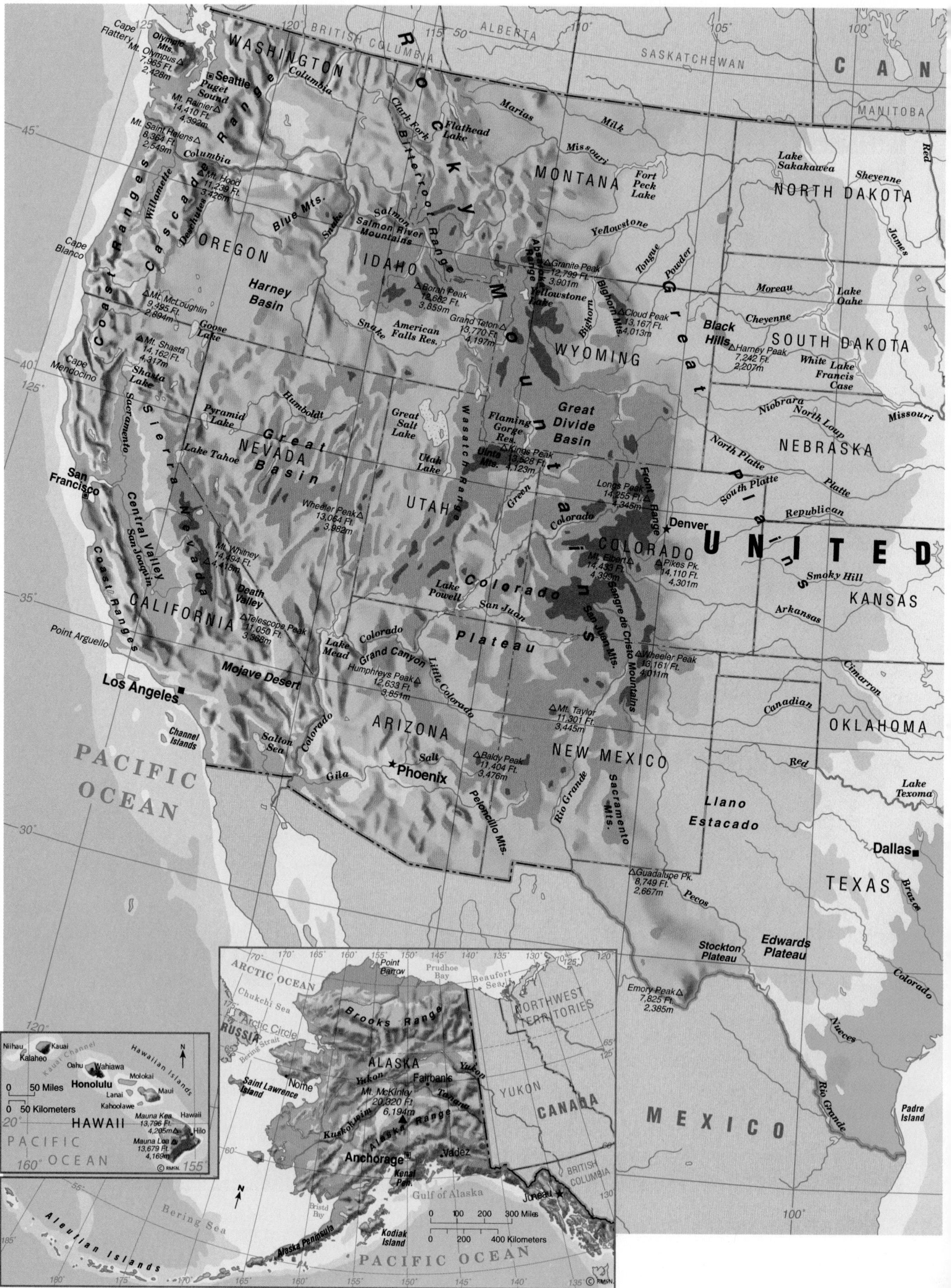
BRITISH COLUMBIA
ALBERTA
SASKATCHEWAN
MANITOBA
C A N
WASHINGTON
Cape Flattery
Olympic Mts.
Mt. Olympus 7,965 Ft. 2,428m
Seattle
Puget Sound
Mt. Rainier 14,410 Ft. 4,392m
Mt. Saint Helens 8,364 Ft. 2,549m
Columbia
Mt. Hood 11,239 Ft. 3,426m
Willamette
Deschutes
Cascade Range
Coast Ranges
Cape Blanco
OREGON
Blue Mts.
Snake
Harney Basin
Mt. McLoughlin 9,495 Ft. 2,894m
Goose Lake
Mt. Shasta 14,162 Ft. 4,317m
Shasta Lake
Cape Mendocino
Sacramento
Sierra Nevada
Pyramid Lake
Humboldt
Great Basin
NEVADA
Lake Tahoe
San Francisco
Central Valley
San Joaquin
Mt. Whitney 14,494 Ft. 4,418m
Death Valley
Telescope Peak 11,050 Ft. 3,368m
CALIFORNIA
Point Arguello
Mojave Desert
Los Angeles
Channel Islands
Salton Sea
PACIFIC OCEAN
ROCKY MOUNTAINS
Clark Fork
Flathead Lake
Bitterroot Range
Salmon
Salmon River Mountains
IDAHO
Borah Peak 12,662 Ft. 3,859m
Snake
American Falls Res.
Marias
Milk
Missouri
MONTANA
Fort Peck Lake
Yellowstone
Absaroka Range
Granite Peak 12,799 Ft. 3,901m
Yellowstone Lake
Bighorn
Bighorn Mts.
Tongue
Powder
Grand Teton 13,770 Ft. 4,197m
Cloud Peak 13,167 Ft. 4,013m
WYOMING
Great Salt Lake
Wasatch Range
Flaming Gorge Res.
Great Divide Basin
Uinta Mts.
Kings Peak 13,528 Ft. 4,123m
Utah Lake
UTAH
Green
Wheeler Peak 13,064 Ft. 3,982m
Colorado
Longs Peak 14,255 Ft. 4,345m
Front Range
Denver
COLORADO
Mt. Elbert 14,433 Ft. 4,399m
Pikes Pk. 14,110 Ft. 4,301m
Lake Powell
Colorado Plateau
San Juan
San Juan Mts.
Sangre de Cristo Mountains
Wheeler Peak 13,161 Ft. 4,011m
Lake Mead
Grand Canyon
Humphreys Peak 12,633 Ft. 3,851m
Little Colorado
ARIZONA
Salt
Gila
Phoenix
Baldy Peak 11,404 Ft. 3,476m
Peloncillo Mts.
Mt. Taylor 11,301 Ft. 3,445m
NEW MEXICO
Rio Grande
Sacramento Mts.
Guadalupe Pk. 8,749 Ft. 2,667m
Pecos
Llano Estacado
Stockton Plateau
Edwards Plateau
Emory Peak 7,825 Ft. 2,385m
Great Plains
Lake Sakakawea
Sheyenne
NORTH DAKOTA
James
Red
Moreau
Lake Oahe
Cheyenne
Black Hills
Harney Peak 7,242 Ft. 2,207m
SOUTH DAKOTA
White
Lake Francis Case
Niobrara
North Loup
Missouri
NEBRASKA
North Platte
South Platte
Platte
Republican
UNITED
Smoky Hill
KANSAS
Arkansas
Cimarron
Canadian
OKLAHOMA
Red
Lake Texoma
Dallas
TEXAS
Brazos
Colorado
Nueces
Rio Grande
Padre Island
MEXICO
ARCTIC OCEAN
Point Barrow
Prudhoe Bay
Beaufort Sea
Chukchi Sea
Arctic Circle
RUSSIA
Bering Strait
Brooks Range
NORTHWEST TERRITORIES
ALASKA
Yukon
Fairbanks
Tanana
Nome
Saint Lawrence Island
Mt. McKinley 20,320 Ft. 6,194m
Kuskokwim
Alaska Range
Anchorage
Valdez
Kenai Pen.
YUKON
CANADA
BRITISH COLUMBIA
Juneau
Gulf of Alaska
Bristol Bay
Bering Sea
Aleutian Islands
Alaska Peninsula
Kodiak Island
PACIFIC OCEAN
0 100 200 300 Miles
0 200 400 Kilometers
Niihau
Kauai
Kalaheo
Kauai Channel
Hawaiian Islands
Oahu
Wahiawa
Honolulu
Molokai
Lanai
Maui
Kahoolawe
Hawaii
Mauna Kea 13,796 Ft. 4,205m
Mauna Loa 13,679 Ft. 4,169m
Hilo
HAWAII
0 50 Miles
0 50 Kilometers
PACIFIC OCEAN
© RMN

A18

STATES
ATLANTIC OCEAN
GULF OF MEXICO
Great Lakes
Appalachian Mountains
Allegheny Plateau
Allegheny Mountains
Blue Ridge
Piedmont
Coastal Plain
Ozark Plateau
Cumberland Plateau
Land Elevation
Meters
Feet
3,000
9,840
2,000
6,560
500
1,640
200
656
0
0
Water Depth
0
0
200
656
2,000
6,560
0 100 200 300 Miles
0 100 200 300 400 Kilometers
Copyright by Rand McNally & Co.
Alber's Conic Equal Area Projection
PUERTO RICO (U.S.)
San Juan
Arecibo
Mayagüez
Ponce
Caguas
Caribbean Sea
0 25 50 Miles
0 25 50 Kilometers
Mt. Katahdin 5,268 Ft. 1,606m
Mt. Washington 6,288 Ft. 1,917m
Mt. Mitchell 6,684 Ft. 2,037m

RAND McNALLY

ATLAS

A19

WASHINGTON
OREGON
CALIFORNIA
NEVADA
IDAHO
MONTANA
WYOMING
UTAH
COLORADO
ARIZONA
NEW MEXICO
NORTH DAKOTA
SOUTH DAKOTA
NEBRASKA
KANSAS
OKLAHOMA
TEXAS
MEXICO
CANADA
BRITISH COLUMBIA
ALBERTA
SASKATCHEWAN
MANITOBA
PACIFIC OCEAN

Seattle
Olympia
Tacoma
Spokane
Portland
Salem
Boise
Helena
Sacramento
San Francisco
Oakland
San Jose
Fresno
Los Angeles
Long Beach
San Diego
Las Vegas
Carson City
Reno
Salt Lake City
Cheyenne
Denver
Colorado Springs
Santa Fe
Albuquerque
Phoenix
Tucson
El Paso
Bismarck
Pierre
Lincoln
Oklahoma City
Dallas
Fort Worth
Austin
San Antonio
Corpus Christi

HAWAII
Kauai
Oahu
Honolulu
Molokai
Maui
Hawaiian Islands
Mauna Kea 13,796 ft. 4,205 m
Mauna Loa 13,679 ft. 4,169 m
0 50 Miles
0 50 Kilometers

ALASKA
Barrow
Kotzebue
Nome
Fairbanks
Anchorage
Valdez
Seward
Kodiak
Juneau
Sitka
Dutch Harbor
Bethel
Saint Lawrence Island
Aleutian Islands
Bering Sea
Gulf of Alaska
ARCTIC OCEAN
Beaufort Sea
Chukchi Sea
Arctic Circle
Bering Strait
RUSSIA
NORTHWEST TERRITORIES
YUKON
CANADA
Whitehorse
0 100 200 300 Miles
0 200 400 Kilometers

A20

ATLAS

RAND McNALLY

A21

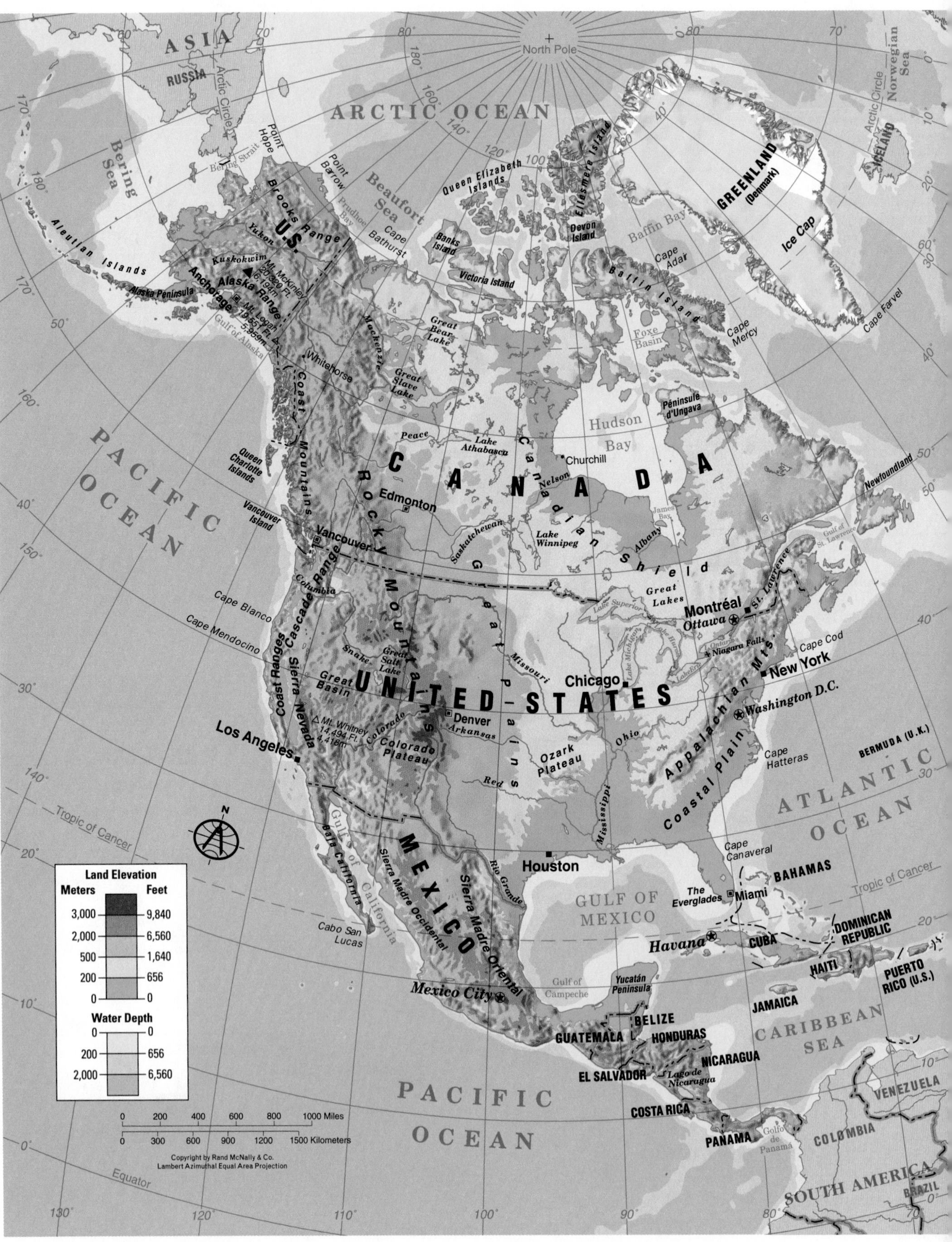
North Pole
ARCTIC OCEAN
ASIA
RUSSIA
Arctic Circle
Bering Sea
Bering Strait
Point Hope
Point Barrow
Prudhoe Bay
Beaufort Sea
Cape Bathurst
Queen Elizabeth Islands
Ellesmere Island
Devon Island
Banks Island
Victoria Island
Baffin Bay
Cape Adar
Baffin Island
Foxe Basin
Cape Mercy
GREENLAND (Denmark)
Ice Cap
Cape Farvel
ICELAND
Norwegian Sea
Aleutian Islands
Alaska Peninsula
U.S.
Brooks Range
Yukon
Kuskokwim
Mt. McKinley 20,320 Ft. 6,194m
Alaska Range
Anchorage
Mt. Logan 19,551 Ft. 5,959m
Gulf of Alaska
Whitehorse
Mackenzie
Great Bear Lake
Great Slave Lake
Coast Mountains
Queen Charlotte Islands
Vancouver Island
Vancouver
Peace
Lake Athabasca
Edmonton
Saskatchewan
Nelson
Churchill
Hudson Bay
Péninsule d'Ungava
James Bay
CANADA
Canadian Shield
Lake Winnipeg
Albany
Newfoundland
Gulf of St. Lawrence
St. Lawrence
Rocky Mountains
PACIFIC OCEAN
Columbia
Cascade Range
Cape Blanco
Cape Mendocino
Coast Ranges
Sierra Nevada
Snake
Great Salt Lake
Great Basin
Great Plains
Missouri
Lake Superior
Great Lakes
Lake Michigan
Lake Huron
Lake Ontario
Lake Erie
Niagara Falls
Montréal
Ottawa
Cape Cod
New York
Chicago
UNITED STATES
Washington D.C.
Denver
Arkansas
Mt. Whitney 14,494 Ft. 4,418m
Colorado
Colorado Plateau
Los Angeles
Ozark Plateau
Ohio
Appalachian Mts.
Coastal Plain
Cape Hatteras
BERMUDA (U.K.)
ATLANTIC OCEAN
Red
Mississippi
Tropic of Cancer
Gulf of California
Baja California
Sierra Madre Occidental
MEXICO
Sierra Madre Oriental
Rio Grande
Houston
Cape Canaveral
BAHAMAS
The Everglades
Miami
GULF OF MEXICO
Cabo San Lucas
Havana
CUBA
DOMINICAN REPUBLIC
HAITI
PUERTO RICO (U.S.)
Gulf of Campeche
Yucatán Peninsula
Mexico City
JAMAICA
BELIZE
GUATEMALA
HONDURAS
CARIBBEAN SEA
NICARAGUA
EL SALVADOR
Lago de Nicaragua
COSTA RICA
PANAMA
Golfo de Panamá
VENEZUELA
COLOMBIA
SOUTH AMERICA
BRAZIL
Equator
Land Elevation
Meters
Feet
3,000
9,840
2,000
6,560
500
1,640
200
656
0
0
Water Depth
0
0
200
656
2,000
6,560
0 200 400 600 800 1000 Miles
0 300 600 900 1200 1500 Kilometers
Copyright by Rand McNally & Co.
Lambert Azimuthal Equal Area Projection

A22

North America: Political

North Pole
ARCTIC OCEAN
ASIA
RUSSIA
Arctic Circle
Bering Sea
Bering Strait
Aleutian Islands
Beaufort Sea
Prudhoe Bay
Queen Elizabeth Islands
Ellesmere Island
Devon Island
Banks Island
Victoria Island
Baffin Bay
Baffin Island
GREENLAND (Denmark)
Godthab
ICELAND
Reykjavik
U.S.
Yukon
Fairbanks
Anchorage
Valdez
Gulf of Alaska
Whitehorse
Juneau
Mackenzie
Great Bear Lake
Great Slave Lake
Yellowknife
Peace
Hudson Bay
CANADA
Nelson
Edmonton
Calgary
Saskatoon
Saskatchewan
Lake Winnipeg
Regina
Winnipeg
Victoria
Vancouver
Seattle
Spokane
Columbia
Portland
Missouri
Thunder Bay
Lake Superior
Québec
Montréal
Ottawa
Toronto
St. Lawrence
Gulf of St. Lawrence
Newfoundland
St. John's
Saint John
Halifax
Billings
Great Salt Lake
Minneapolis
Milwaukee
Detroit
Cleveland
Boston
New York
Philadelphia
Washington D.C.
Sacramento
San Francisco
Omaha
Chicago
UNITED STATES
Denver
Colorado
Arkansas
Kansas City
Indianapolis
Cincinnati
St. Louis
Ohio
Norfolk
Las Vegas
Los Angeles
San Diego
Tijuana
Phoenix
Albuquerque
Oklahoma City
Red
Nashville
Memphis
Atlanta
Charlotte
Dallas
Mississippi
Jacksonville
Houston
New Orleans
San Antonio
Tampa
Miami
BERMUDA (U.K.)
ATLANTIC OCEAN
BAHAMAS
Nassau
Tropic of Cancer
PACIFIC OCEAN
Ciudad Juárez
Hermosillo
Gulf of California
MEXICO
Chihuahua
Rio Grande
Torreón
Culiacán
Monterrey
GULF OF MEXICO
San Luis Potosí
Guadalajara
León
Mérida
Cancún
Havana
CUBA
DOMINICAN REPUBLIC
PUERTO RICO (U.S.)
HAITI
Port-au-Prince
Santo Domingo
JAMAICA
Kingston
Mexico City
Puebla
Veracruz
Acapulco
BELIZE
Belmopan
GUATEMALA
Guatemala City
HONDURAS
Tegucigalpa
San Salvador
EL SALVADOR
NICARAGUA
Lago de Nicaragua
Managua
CARIBBEAN SEA
Caracas
VENEZUELA
COSTA RICA
San José
Panama City
PANAMA
Golfo de Panamá
COLOMBIA
Bogotá
SOUTH AMERICA
BRAZIL
Equator
National Capital
Secondary Capital (State, Province, or Territory)
City over 1,000,000 population
City of 250,000 to 1,000,000 population
City under 250,000 population
0 200 400 600 800 1000 Miles
0 300 600 900 1200 1500 Kilometers
Copyright by Rand McNally & Co.
Lambert Azimuthal Equal Area Projection

ATLAS

RAND McNALLY

A23

GULF OF MEXICO
NORTH AMERICA
CUBA
Greater Antilles
HAITI
DOMINICAN REPUBLIC
JAMAICA
PUERTO RICO (U.S.)
Lesser Antilles
BELIZE
Gulf of Honduras
MEXICO
HONDURAS
GUATEMALA
EL SALVADOR
NICARAGUA
CARIBBEAN SEA
ATLANTIC OCEAN
Cristóbal Colón Peak 18,948 Ft. 5,775m
Caracas
TRINIDAD AND TOBAGO
COSTA RICA
PANAMA
Gulf of Panama
Llanos
Orinoco
VENEZUELA
GUYANA
SURINAME
FRENCH GUIANA
Cape Orange
Magdalena
Bogotá
COLOMBIA
Galapagos Islands (Ec.)
ECUADOR
Chimborazo 20,703 Ft. 6,310m
Putumayo
Japurá
Negro
Manaus
Amazon
Ilha de Marajó
Belém
Equator
Amazon Basin
Tapajós
Tocantins
Juruá
Madeira
Selvas
BRAZIL
Andes
PERU
Ucayali
Recife
Mt. Huascarán 22,133 Ft. 6,746m
Lima
Mato Grosso Plateau
Mt. Illampu 21,066 Ft. 6,421m
Lake Titicaca
Cordillera Oriental
BOLIVIA
Brasília
São Francisco
Serra do Espinhaço
Mt. Sajama 21,463 Ft. 6,542m
Gran Chaco
PARAGUAY
Paraná
Atacama Desert
São Paulo
Rio de Janeiro
Tropic of Capricorn
Isla San Ambrosio (Chile)
Isla San Felix (Chile)
Mt. Ojos del Salado 22,615 Ft. 6,893m
ARGENTINA
PACIFIC OCEAN
Archipiélago Juan Fernández (Chile)
Santiago
Mt. Aconcagua 22,831 Ft. 6,959m
URUGUAY
Buenos Aires
Río de la Plata
Pampas
CHILE
N
Land Elevation
Meters
Feet
3,000 9,840
2,000 6,560
500 1,640
200 656
0 0
Water Depth
0 0
200 656
2,000 6,560
San Matías Gulf
Península Valdés
Chiloé
Patagonia
San Jorge Gulf
Point Medanoso
Grand Bay
West Falkland
FALKLAND ISLANDS (U.K.)
East Falkland
Strait of Magellan
Tierra del Fuego
Cape Horn
0 200 400 600 800 1000 Miles
0 300 600 900 1200 1500 Kilometers
Copyright by Rand McNally & Co.
Lambert Azimuthal Equal Area Projection
South Georgia (U.K.)
Drake Passage
South Shetland Islands (U.K.)
South Orkney Islands (U.K.)
South Sandwich Islands (U.K.)

A24

GULF OF MEXICO
Havana
CUBA
NORTH AMERICA
HAITI
DOMINICAN REPUBLIC
JAMAICA
PUERTO RICO (U.S.)
Lesser Antilles
BELIZE
MEXICO
HONDURAS
GUATEMALA
CARIBBEAN SEA
ATLANTIC OCEAN
EL SALVADOR
NICARAGUA
Barranquilla
Cartagena
Maracaibo
Caracas
TRINIDAD AND TOBAGO
Barquisimeto
Valencia
COSTA RICA
Cúcuta
Orinoco
Ciudad Guayana
PANAMA
Bucaramanga
VENEZUELA
Georgetown
Medellín
GUYANA
Paramaribo
Magdalena
Cayenne
Bogotá
SURINAME
FRENCH GUIANA
Cali
COLOMBIA
Macapá
Galapagos Islands (Ec.)
Quito
Equator
ECUADOR
Putumayo
Japurá
Negro
Amazon
Belém
Manaus
Santarém
Guayaquil
Tocantins
São Luís
Iquitos
Amazon
Fortaleza
Tapajós
Imperatriz
Juruá
Madeira
BRAZIL
Teresina
Natal
Chiclayo
Ucayali
Pôrto Velho
Trujillo
PERU
Recife
Maceió
Aracaju
Lima
Feira de Santana
Salvador
Cusco
BOLIVIA
Cuiabá
Lake Titicaca
Brasília
Arequipa
La Paz
Goiânia
Cochabamba
Montes Claros
Santa Cruz
Uberlândia
Sucre
Campo Grande
Belo Horizonte
Vitória
Paraná
Campinas
PARAGUAY
Rio de Janeiro
Antofagasta
São Paulo
Salta
Asunción
Tropic of Capricorn
Isla San Ambrosio (Chile)
San Miguel de Tucumán
Curitiba
Isla San Felix (Chile)
Caxias do Sul
Pôrto Alegre
Paraná
Córdoba
Santa Fe
Rosario
URUGUAY
Archipiélago Juan Fernández (Chile)
Valparaíso
Mendoza
Montevideo
Santiago
Buenos Aires
La Plata
PACIFIC OCEAN
Río de la Plata
N
Concepción
Mar del Plata
CHILE
Bahía Blanca
ARGENTINA
Chiloé
ATLANTIC OCEAN
Archipiélago de los Chonos
Comodoro Rivadavia
FALKLAND ISLANDS (U.K.)
West Falkland
East Falkland
Strait of Magellan
Punta Arenas
Tierra del Fuego
South Georgia (U.K.)
Drake Passage
South Sandwich Islands (U.K.)
South Shetland Islands (U.K.)
South Orkney Islands (U.K.)
National Capital
Secondary Capital (State, Province, or Territory)
City over 1,000,000 population
City of 250,000 to 1,000,000 population
City under 250,000 population
0 200 400 600 800 1000 Miles
0 300 600 900 1200 1500 Kilometers
Copyright by Rand McNally & Co.
Lambert Azimuthal Equal Area Projection

A25

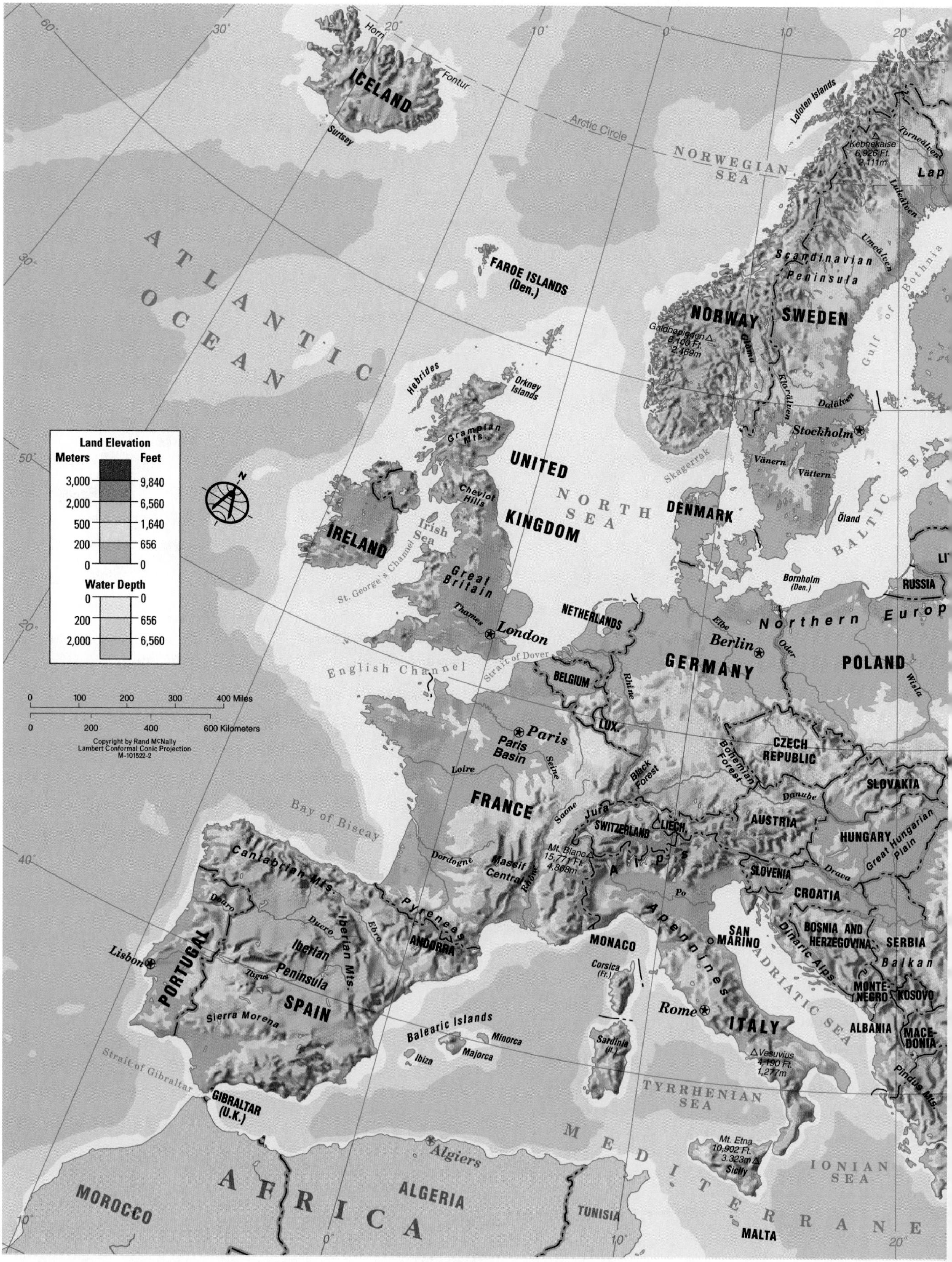

Land Elevation

Meters	Feet
3,000	9,840
2,000	6,560
500	1,640
200	656
0	0

Water Depth

Meters	Feet
0	0
200	656
2,000	6,560

0 100 200 300 400 Miles

0 200 400 600 Kilometers

Lambert Conformal Conic Projection
M-101522-2

ATLANTIC OCEAN
ICELAND
Horn
Fontur
Surtsey
Arctic Circle
NORWEGIAN SEA
Lofoten Islands
Kebnekaise 6,926 Ft. 2,111m
Torneälven
Lap
Luleälven
Umeälven
Scandinavian Peninsula
Gulf of Bothnia
FAROE ISLANDS (Den.)
NORWAY
SWEDEN
Galdhøpiggen 8,100 Ft. 2,469m
Glomma
Klarälven
Dalälven
Stockholm
Hebrides
Orkney Islands
Grampian Mts.
UNITED KINGDOM
NORTH SEA
Skagerrak
Vänern
Vättern
Öland
BALTIC SEA
Cheviot Hills
Irish Sea
IRELAND
DENMARK
Bornholm (Den.)
RUSSIA
LI
St. George's Channel
Great Britain
Thames
London
NETHERLANDS
Elbe
Berlin
Northern European
Oder
POLAND
Wisla
GERMANY
English Channel
Strait of Dover
BELGIUM
Rhine
LUX.
Paris
Paris Basin
Seine
Loire
CZECH REPUBLIC
Bohemian Forest
Black Forest
SLOVAKIA
Danube
FRANCE
Bay of Biscay
Saône
Jura
SWITZERLAND
LIECH.
AUSTRIA
HUNGARY
Great Hungarian Plain
Mt. Blanc 15,771 Ft. 4,808m
Alps
Dordogne
Massif Central
Rhône
SLOVENIA
Drava
CROATIA
Po
Cantabrian Mts.
Pyrenees
Douro
Duero
Iberian Mts.
Ebro
ANDORRA
MONACO
SAN MARINO
BOSNIA AND HERZEGOVINA
SERBIA
Dinaric Alps
Balkan
Apennines
ADRIATIC SEA
Lisbon
PORTUGAL
Iberian Peninsula
Tagus
SPAIN
Sierra Morena
Corsica (Fr.)
Rome
ITALY
MONTENEGRO
KOSOVO
ALBANIA
MACEDONIA
Balearic Islands
Minorca
Majorca
Ibiza
Sardinia (It.)
Vesuvius 4,190 Ft. 1,277m
Pindus Mts.
Strait of Gibraltar
GIBRALTAR (U.K.)
TYRRHENIAN SEA
MEDITERRANEAN
Algiers
Mt. Etna 10,902 Ft. 3,323m
Sicily
IONIAN SEA
AFRICA
MOROCCO
ALGERIA
TUNISIA
MALTA

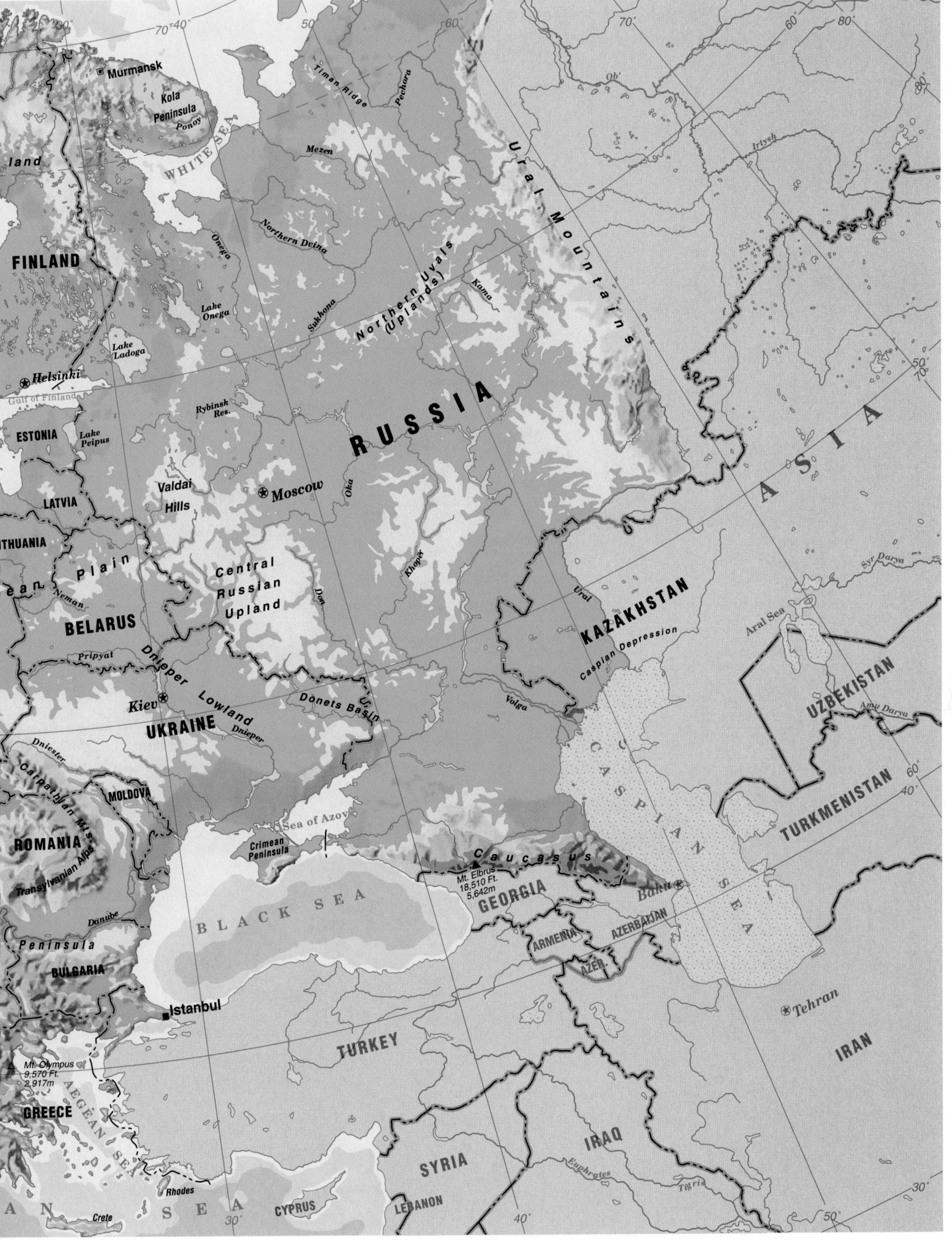

ATLAS

RAND McNALLY

A27

- ⊛ National Capital
- ★ Secondary Capital (State, Province, or Territory)
- ■ City over 1,000,000 population
- ▣ City of 250,000 to 1,000,000 population
- • City under 250,000 population

0 100 200 300 400 Miles

0 200 400 600 Kilometers

Lambert Conformal Conic Projection
M-101521-2

ATLANTIC OCEAN
ICELAND
Reykjavík
Arctic Circle
NORWEGIAN SEA
FAROE ISLANDS (Den.)
NORWAY
SWEDEN
Hammerfest
Trondheim
Bergen
Oslo
Umeå
Tampere
Gulf of Bothnia
Stockholm
Vänern
Vättern
Göteborg
Skagerrak
DENMARK
Copenhagen
BALTIC SEA
LITHUANIA
Kaliningrad
RUSSIA
Gdańsk
Szczecin
POLAND
Wisła
Warsaw
Oder
UNITED KINGDOM
SCOTLAND
Aberdeen
Glasgow
Edinburgh
NORTHERN IRELAND
Belfast
Irish Sea
IRELAND
Dublin
Cork
NORTH SEA
Liverpool
Manchester
WALES
Birmingham
ENGLAND
St. George's Channel
Cardiff
Thames
London
Plymouth
English Channel
Strait of Dover
NETHERLANDS
Amsterdam
The Hague
Hamburg
Elbe
Berlin
GERMANY
Rhine
Brussels
BELGIUM
Cologne
Bonn
LUX.
Luxembourg
Frankfurt
Dresden
Wroclaw
Prague
CZECH REPUBLIC
Kraków
Le Havre
Paris
Seine
Strasbourg
Stuttgart
Danube
Munich
SLOVAKIA
Nantes
Loire
FRANCE
Zürich
Bern
SWITZERLAND
LIECH.
Vienna
AUSTRIA
Bratislava
Budapest
HUNGARY
Bay of Biscay
Geneva
Lyon
Rhône
Bordeaux
Toulouse
SLOVENIA
Ljubljana
Zagreb
Belgrade
Milan
Turin
Venice
Po
Genoa
CROATIA
BOSNIA AND HERZEGOVINA
SERBIA
Sarajevo
Nice
MONACO
Marseille
SAN MARINO
Florence
ADRIATIC SEA
Corsica (Fr.)
ITALY
(MONT.)
Priština
KOS.
Podgorica
Skopje
ALBANIA
MACEDONIA
Tiranë
Rome
VATICAN CITY
Bari
Naples
Sardinia (It.)
Cagliari
TYRRHENIAN SEA
Palermo
Sicily
Catania
IONIAN SEA
MEDITERRANEAN SEA
Valletta
MALTA
A Coruña
Gijón
Bilbao
Porto
Valladolid
Ebro
Zaragoza
ANDORRA
PORTUGAL
Lisbon
Tagus
Madrid
Barcelona
SPAIN
Valencia
Córdoba
Palma
Seville
Málaga
Strait of Gibraltar
GIBRALTAR (U.K.)
Rabat
MOROCCO
AFRICA
Algiers
ALGERIA
Tunis
TUNISIA

A28

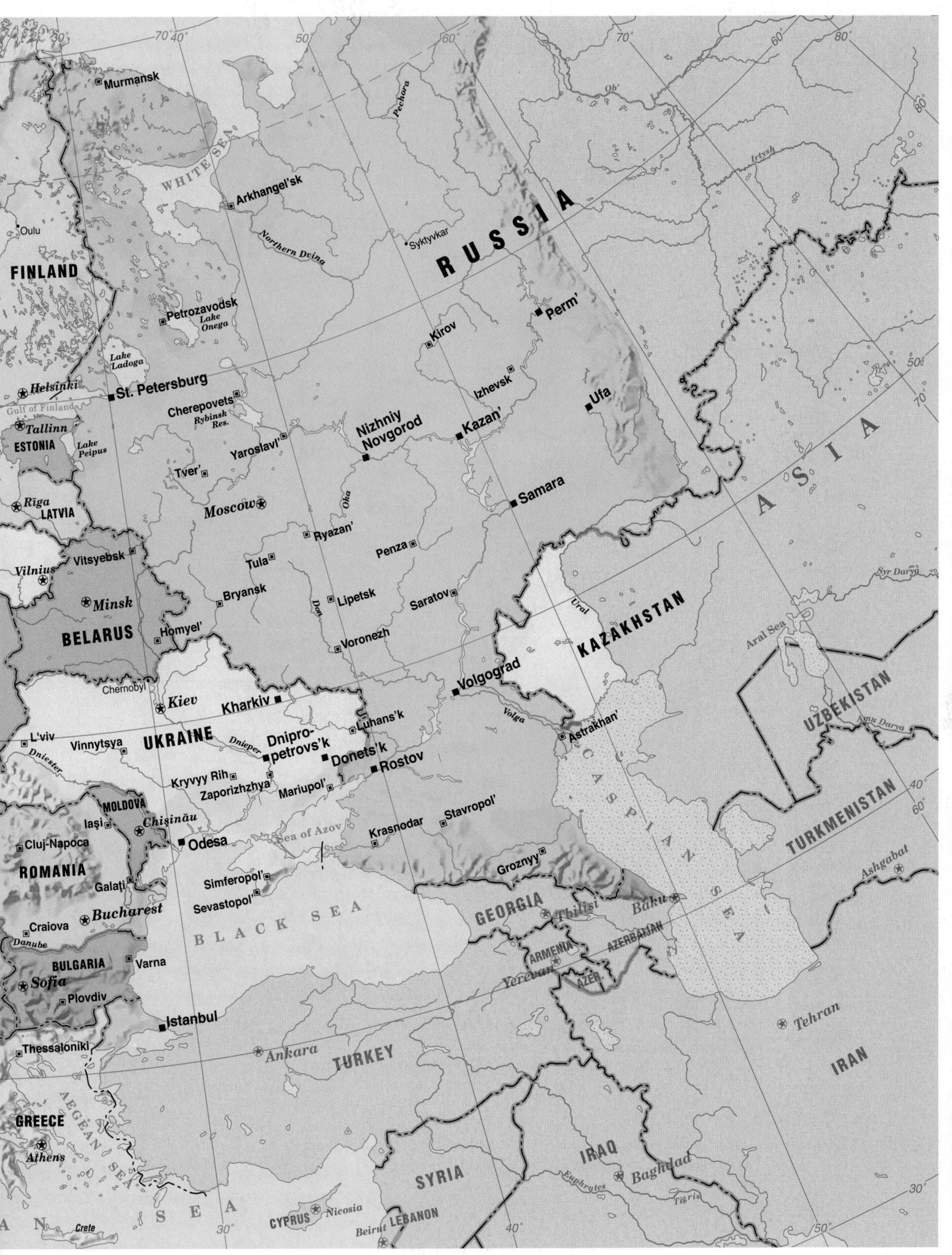
Murmansk
WHITE SEA
Arkhangel'sk
Northern Dvina
Pechora
Syktyvkar
RUSSIA
Oulu
FINLAND
Petrozavodsk
Lake Onega
Lake Ladoga
Helsinki
St. Petersburg
Gulf of Finland
Cherepovets
Rybinsk Res.
Tallinn
ESTONIA
Lake Peipus
Yaroslavl'
Tver'
Rīga
LATVIA
Moscow
Kirov
Perm'
Izhevsk
Ufa
Nizhniy Novgorod
Kazan'
Samara
Oka
Ryazan'
Penza
Tula
Vitsyebsk
Vilnius
Minsk
Bryansk
Lipetsk
Saratov
Don
BELARUS
Homyel'
Voronezh
Volgograd
Ob'
Irtysh
ASIA
Ural
KAZAKHSTAN
Syr Darya
Aral Sea
UZBEKISTAN
Amu Darya
TURKMENISTAN
Ashgabat
Chernobyl
Kiev
Kharkiv
Luhans'k
L'viv
Vinnytsya
UKRAINE
Dnieper
Dnipro-petrovs'k
Donets'k
Rostov
Dniester
Kryvyy Rih
Zaporizhzhya
Mariupol'
Volga
Astrakhan'
CASPIAN SEA
MOLDOVA
Iaşi
Chişinău
Cluj-Napoca
Odesa
Sea of Azov
Krasnodar
Stavropol'
ROMANIA
Groznyy
Galaţi
Simferopol'
Sevastopol'
Craiova
Bucharest
Danube
BLACK SEA
GEORGIA
Tbilisi
Baku
ARMENIA
AZERBAIJAN
Yerevan
AZER.
BULGARIA
Varna
Sofia
Plovdiv
Istanbul
Tehran
IRAN
Thessaloniki
Ankara
TURKEY
GREECE
Athens
AEGEAN SEA
IRAQ
Baghdad
Euphrates
Tigris
SYRIA
CYPRUS
Nicosia
Beirut
LEBANON
Crete

A29

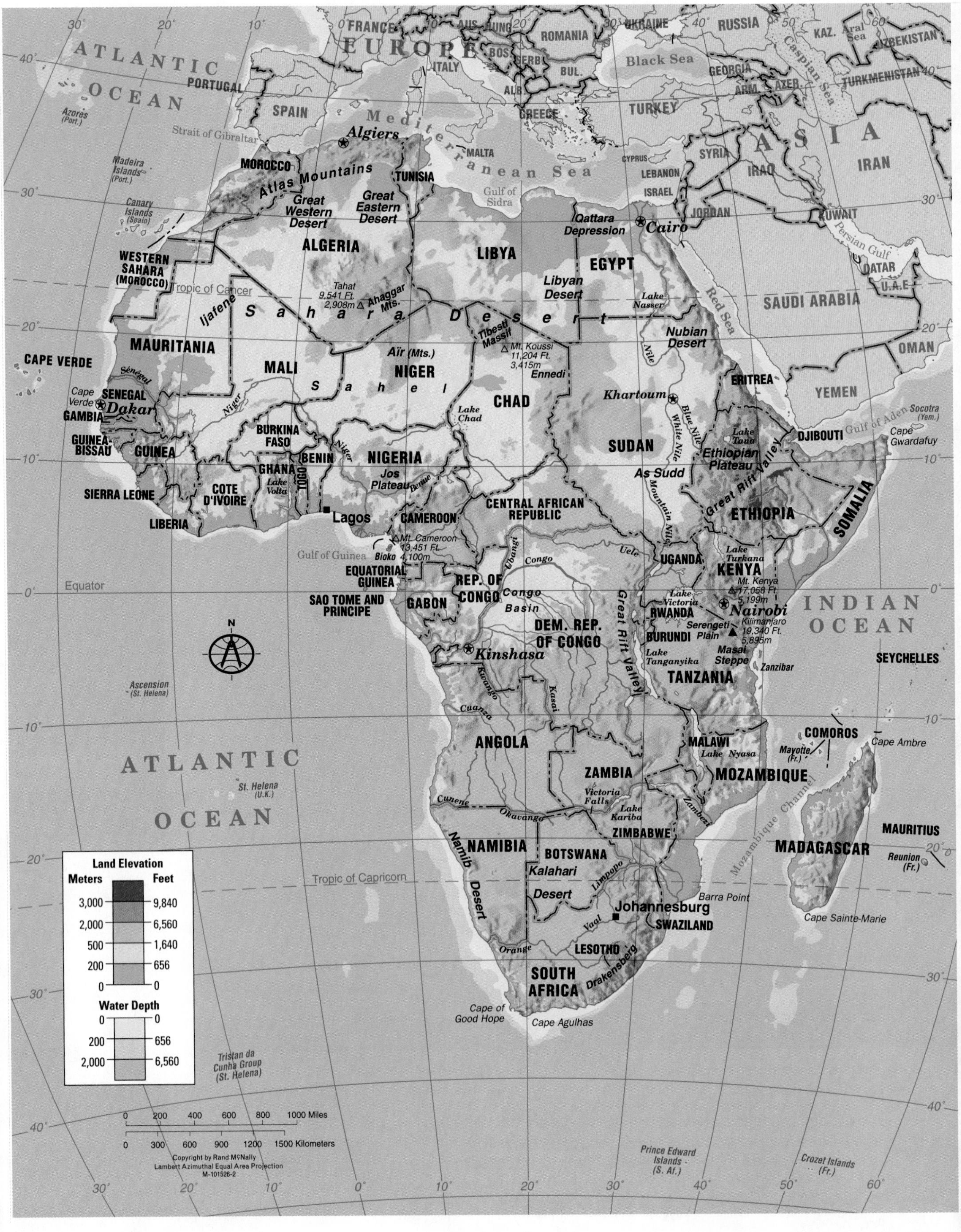

ATLANTIC OCEAN
Azores (Port.)
Madeira Islands (Port.)
Canary Islands (Spain)
PORTUGAL
SPAIN
Strait of Gibraltar
FRANCE
EUROPE
ITALY
AUS. HUNG.
BOS. SERB.
ALB.
GREECE
ROMANIA
BUL.
UKRAINE
RUSSIA
Black Sea
GEORGIA
ARM. AZER.
KAZ.
Aral Sea
UZBEKISTAN
Caspian Sea
TURKMENISTAN
TURKEY
Mediterranean Sea
MALTA
CYPRUS
SYRIA
LEBANON
ISRAEL
JORDAN
IRAQ
IRAN
ASIA
KUWAIT
Persian Gulf
QATAR
U.A.E.
SAUDI ARABIA
OMAN
YEMEN
Socotra (Yem.)
Gulf of Aden
Red Sea
Algiers
MOROCCO
TUNISIA
Atlas Mountains
Great Western Desert
Great Eastern Desert
Gulf of Sidra
Qattara Depression
Cairo
ALGERIA
LIBYA
EGYPT
WESTERN SAHARA (MOROCCO)
Tropic of Cancer
Ijafene
Tahat 9,541 Ft. 2,908m
Ahaggar Mts.
Sahara Desert
Libyan Desert
Lake Nasser
Nubian Desert
Tibesti Massif
Mt. Koussi 11,204 Ft. 3,415m
Ennedi
MAURITANIA
CAPE VERDE
MALI
Aïr (Mts.)
NIGER
CHAD
Nile
Sahel
Sénégal
Cape Verde
SENEGAL
Dakar
GAMBIA
GUINEA-BISSAU
GUINEA
Niger
BURKINA FASO
Lake Chad
Khartoum
SUDAN
ERITREA
Blue Nile
White Nile
Lake Tana
Ethiopian Plateau
DJIBOUTI
Cape Gwardafuy
SIERRA LEONE
LIBERIA
COTE D'IVOIRE
GHANA
Lake Volta
TOGO
BENIN
NIGERIA
Jos Plateau
Benue
Lagos
As Sudd
Mountain Nile
Great Rift Valley
ETHIOPIA
SOMALIA
CAMEROON
CENTRAL AFRICAN REPUBLIC
Mt. Cameroon 13,451 Ft. 4,100m
Bioko
Gulf of Guinea
Ubangi
Congo
Uele
UGANDA
Lake Turkana
KENYA
Mt. Kenya 17,058 Ft. 5,199m
EQUATORIAL GUINEA
Equator
SAO TOME AND PRINCIPE
GABON
REP. OF CONGO
Congo Basin
DEM. REP. OF CONGO
Lake Victoria
RWANDA
BURUNDI
Nairobi
Serengeti Plain
Kilimanjaro 19,340 Ft. 5,895m
Masai Steppe
Lake Tanganyika
TANZANIA
Zanzibar
INDIAN OCEAN
SEYCHELLES
Kinshasa
Ascension (St. Helena)
Kwango
Kasai
Cuanza
ANGOLA
MALAWI
Lake Nyasa
COMOROS
Mayotte (Fr.)
Cape Ambre
ZAMBIA
MOZAMBIQUE
ATLANTIC OCEAN
St. Helena (U.K.)
Cunene
Okavango
Victoria Falls
Lake Kariba
Zambezi
Mozambique Channel
ZIMBABWE
NAMIBIA
Namib Desert
BOTSWANA
Kalahari Desert
Limpopo
MADAGASCAR
MAURITIUS
Reunion (Fr.)
Tropic of Capricorn
Barra Point
Johannesburg
Vaal
SWAZILAND
Cape Sainte-Marie
Orange
LESOTHO
Drakensberg
SOUTH AFRICA
Cape of Good Hope
Cape Agulhas
Tristan da Cunha Group (St. Helena)
Prince Edward Islands (S. Af.)
Crozet Islands (Fr.)

Land Elevation

Meters	Feet
3,000	9,840
2,000	6,560
500	1,640
200	656
0	0

Water Depth

Meters	Feet
0	0
200	656
2,000	6,560

0 200 400 600 800 1000 Miles
0 300 600 900 1200 1500 Kilometers

Lambert Azimuthal Equal Area Projection
M-101526-2

A30

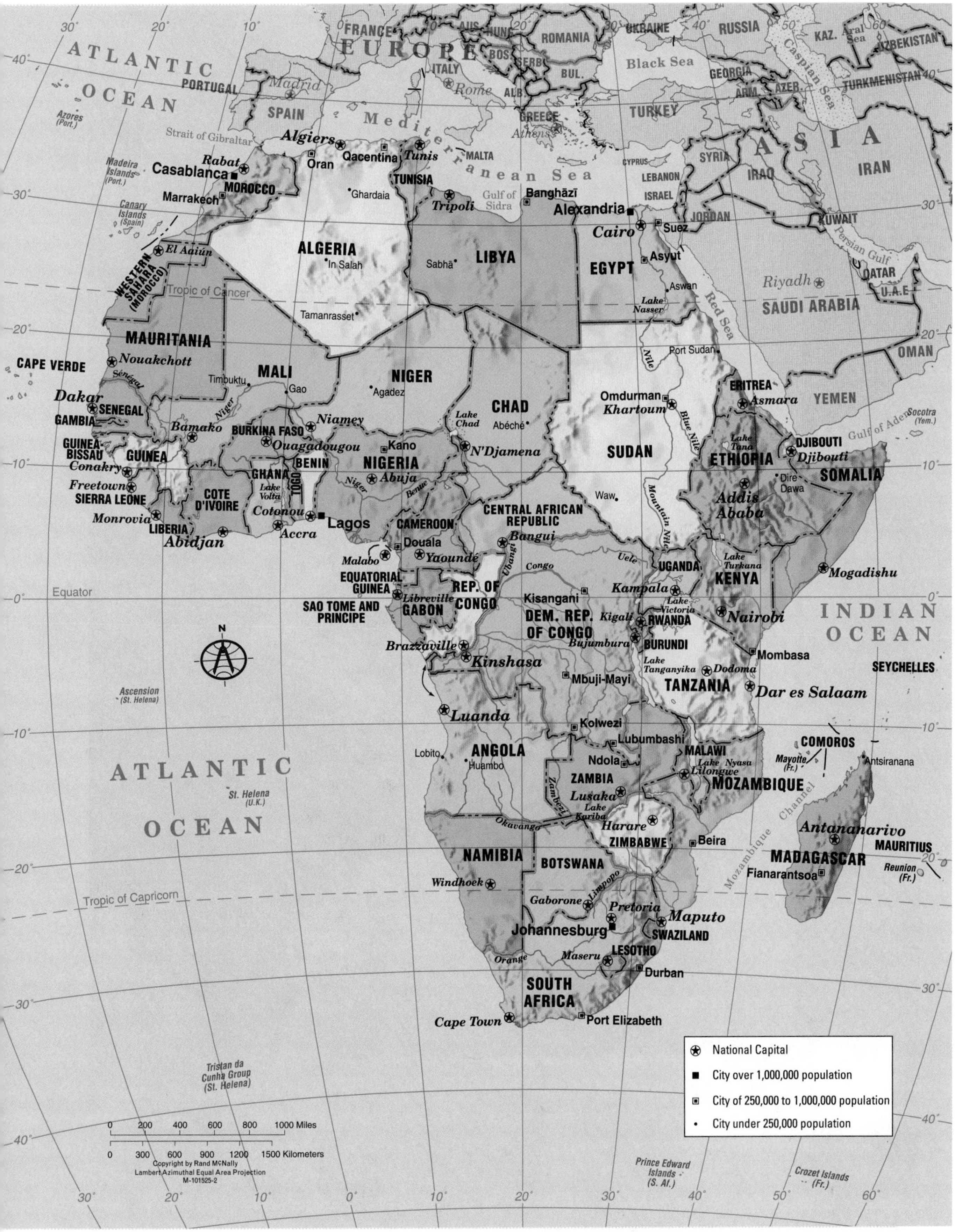

ATLANTIC OCEAN
EUROPE
ASIA
Mediterranean Sea
Black Sea
Caspian Sea
Aral Sea
Red Sea
Persian Gulf
Gulf of Aden
Gulf of Sidra
Strait of Gibraltar
Mozambique Channel
INDIAN OCEAN
Tropic of Cancer
Equator
Tropic of Capricorn

PORTUGAL
SPAIN
FRANCE
ITALY
AUS.
HUNG.
BOS.
SERB.
ALB.
GREECE
BUL.
ROMANIA
UKRAINE
RUSSIA
KAZ.
UZBEKISTAN
TURKMENISTAN
GEORGIA
ARM.
AZER.
TURKEY
CYPRUS
SYRIA
LEBANON
ISRAEL
JORDAN
IRAQ
IRAN
KUWAIT
QATAR
U.A.E.
SAUDI ARABIA
OMAN
YEMEN
MALTA

Azores (Port.)
Madeira Islands (Port.)
Canary Islands (Spain)
CAPE VERDE
MOROCCO
WESTERN SAHARA (MOROCCO)
ALGERIA
TUNISIA
LIBYA
EGYPT
MAURITANIA
MALI
NIGER
CHAD
SUDAN
ERITREA
DJIBOUTI
ETHIOPIA
SOMALIA
SENEGAL
GAMBIA
GUINEA-BISSAU
GUINEA
SIERRA LEONE
LIBERIA
COTE D'IVOIRE
BURKINA FASO
GHANA
TOGO
BENIN
NIGERIA
CAMEROON
CENTRAL AFRICAN REPUBLIC
EQUATORIAL GUINEA
SAO TOME AND PRINCIPE
GABON
REP. OF CONGO
DEM. REP. OF CONGO
UGANDA
KENYA
RWANDA
BURUNDI
TANZANIA
SEYCHELLES
ANGOLA
ZAMBIA
MALAWI
MOZAMBIQUE
COMOROS
Mayotte (Fr.)
MADAGASCAR
MAURITIUS
Reunion (Fr.)
ZIMBABWE
NAMIBIA
BOTSWANA
SWAZILAND
LESOTHO
SOUTH AFRICA
Ascension (St. Helena)
St. Helena (U.K.)
Tristan da Cunha Group (St. Helena)
Prince Edward Islands (S. Af.)
Crozet Islands (Fr.)
Socotra (Yem.)

Madrid
Rome
Athens
Algiers
Oran
Qacentina
Tunis
Rabat
Casablanca
Marrakech
Ghardaia
Tripoli
Banghāzī
Alexandria
Cairo
Suez
Asyut
Aswan
Lake Nasser
Riyadh
El Aaiún
In Salah
Sabhā
Tamanrasset
Nouakchott
Timbuktu
Gao
Agadez
Port Sudan
Omdurman
Khartoum
Asmara
Dakar
Bamako
Niamey
Lake Chad
Abéché
N'Djamena
Ouagadougou
Kano
Abuja
Conakry
Freetown
Monrovia
Abidjan
Lake Volta
Cotonou
Lagos
Accra
Lake Tana
Djibouti
Dire Dawa
Addis Ababa
Waw
Bangui
Douala
Malabo
Yaoundé
Libreville
Kisangani
Kampala
Lake Victoria
Lake Turkana
Nairobi
Mogadishu
Kigali
Bujumbura
Brazzaville
Kinshasa
Lake Tanganyika
Dodoma
Mombasa
Dar es Salaam
Mbuji-Mayi
Luanda
Kolwezi
Lubumbashi
Lobito
Huambo
Ndola
Lake Nyasa
Lilongwe
Antsiranana
Lusaka
Lake Kariba
Harare
Beira
Antananarivo
Fianarantsoa
Windhoek
Gaborone
Pretoria
Maputo
Johannesburg
Maseru
Durban
Cape Town
Port Elizabeth

Sénégal
Niger
Benue
Nile
Blue Nile
Mountain Nile
Congo
Ubangi
Uele
Zambezi
Okavango
Limpopo
Orange

⊛	National Capital
■	City over 1,000,000 population
▣	City of 250,000 to 1,000,000 population
•	City under 250,000 population

0 200 400 600 800 1000 Miles
0 300 600 900 1200 1500 Kilometers

Lambert Azimuthal Equal Area Projection
M-101525-2

A31

0 200 400 600 800 Miles

0 200 400 600 800 1000 Kilometers

Lambert Azimuthal Equal Area Projection

M-101524-2

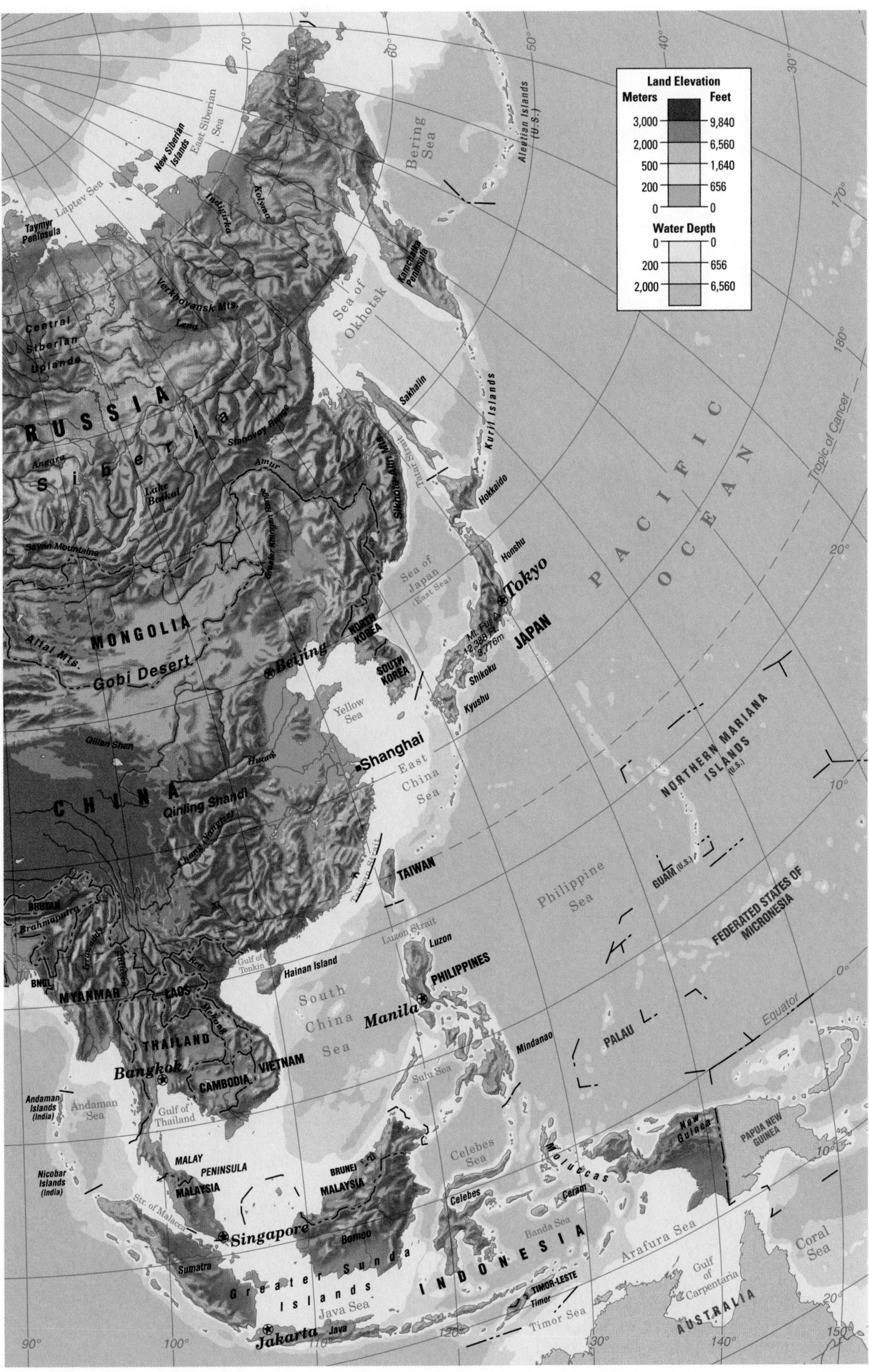
Land Elevation
Meters Feet
3,000 9,840
2,000 6,560
500 1,640
200 656
0 0
Water Depth
0 0
200 656
2,000 6,560
RUSSIA
Siberia
Central Siberian Uplands
Taymyr Peninsula
Laptev Sea
New Siberian Islands
East Siberian Sea
Bering Sea
Aleutian Islands (U.S.)
Kamchatka Peninsula
Sea of Okhotsk
Verkhoyansk Mts.
Sakhalin
Kuril Islands
Hokkaido
Honshu
Tokyo
JAPAN
Mt. Fuji 12,388 ft 3,776m
Shikoku
Kyushu
Sea of Japan (East Sea)
NORTH KOREA
SOUTH KOREA
Beijing
MONGOLIA
Gobi Desert
Altai Mts.
Lake Baikal
Sayan Mountains
Yellow Sea
Shanghai
East China Sea
CHINA
Qinling Shandi
TAIWAN
PACIFIC OCEAN
Tropic of Cancer
NORTHERN MARIANA ISLANDS (U.S.)
GUAM (U.S.)
FEDERATED STATES OF MICRONESIA
Philippine Sea
Luzon Strait
Luzon
PHILIPPINES
Manila
Hainan Island
Gulf of Tonkin
South China Sea
BHUTAN
BNGL.
MYANMAR
LAOS
THAILAND
Bangkok
CAMBODIA
VIETNAM
Andaman Islands (India)
Andaman Sea
Gulf of Thailand
Nicobar Islands (India)
MALAY PENINSULA
MALAYSIA
BRUNEI
Singapore
Str. of Malacca
Borneo
Sumatra
Greater Sunda Islands
Java Sea
Jakarta
Java
Sulu Sea
Mindanao
PALAU
Celebes Sea
Celebes
Moluccas
Ceram
Banda Sea
INDONESIA
TIMOR-LESTE
Timor
Timor Sea
New Guinea
PAPUA NEW GUINEA
Arafura Sea
Gulf of Carpentaria
AUSTRALIA
Coral Sea
Equator

ATLAS

RAND McNALLY

A33

ATLANTIC OCEAN
ARCTIC OCEAN
ICELAND
FAROE ISLANDS (Den.)
IRELAND
UNITED KINGDOM
London
Arctic Circle
Norwegian Sea
Barents Sea
SVALBARD (Nor.)
Spitsbergen
Franz Josef Land
Severnaya Zemlya
Novaya Zemlya
Kara Sea
North Sea
DENMARK
NORWAY
SWEDEN
FINLAND
PORTUGAL
SPAIN
FRANCE
Paris
GIBRALTAR (U.K.)
MOROCCO
GERMANY
POLAND
ESTONIA
LATVIA
LITH.
BELARUS
AUSTRIA
SLOVAKIA
HUNGARY
ROMANIA
MOL.
UKRAINE
Kiev
Moscow
ITALY
Adriatic Sea
BOS.
SERB.
BULGARIA
ALB.
MAC.
GREECE
Danube
Volga
ALGERIA
TUNISIA
Mediterranean Sea
Black Sea
Istanbul
Izmir
Ankara
TURKEY
GEORGIA
Tbilisi
ARM.
Yerevan
AZER.
Baku
Caspian Sea
CYPRUS
SYRIA
Damascus
Beirut
LEBANON
ISRAEL
Jerusalem
Amman
JORDAN
Cairo
Tabriz
Tehran
Euphrates
Tigris
IRAQ
Baghdad
LIBYA
EGYPT
Nile
CHAD
Kuwait
KUWAIT
SAUDI ARABIA
Riyadh
Jiddah
Red Sea
Persian Gulf
BAHRAIN
QATAR
Abu Dhabi
U.A.E.
Muscat
OMAN
Gulf of Oman
YEMEN
Sanaa
ERITREA
DJIBOUTI
ETHIOPIA
Gulf of Aden
Socotra (Yem.)
SUDAN
Blue Nile
DEM. REP. OF THE CONGO (ZAIRE)
UGANDA
KENYA
SOMALIA
RWANDA
BURUNDI
TANZANIA
ZAMBIA
MALAWI
MOZAMBIQUE
Pechora
Ob'
Yenisey
Noril'sk
RUS
Yekaterinburg
Chelyabinsk
Omsk
Novosibirsk
Barnaul
Ishim
Irtysh
Astana
Karaganda
Semipalatinsk
Öskemen
Aral Sea
KAZAKHSTAN
Lake Balkhash
Syr Darya
UZBEKISTAN
TURKMENISTAN
Tashkent
Bishkek
Almaty
Ürümqi
KYRGYZSTAN
Ashgabat
Mashhad
IRAN
Eşfahān
Dushanbe
TAJIKISTAN
Kabul
AFGHANISTAN
Islamabad
Lahore
Amritsar
PAKISTAN
Indus
Delhi
New Delhi
Brahmaputra
NEPAL
Kathmandu
Ganges
Karāchi
Hyderābād
Kānpur
Ahmadābād
INDIA
Kolkata (Calcutta)
Nāgpur
Godavari
Mumbai (Bombay)
Hyderābād
Arabian Sea
Bay of Bengal
Bangalore
Chennai (Madras)
Lakshadweep (India)
SRI LANKA
Colombo
MALDIVES
INDIAN OCEAN

0 200 400 600 800 Miles
0 200 400 600 800 1000 Kilometers

Lambert Azimuthal Equal Area Projection
M-101523-2

RAND McNALLY

A34

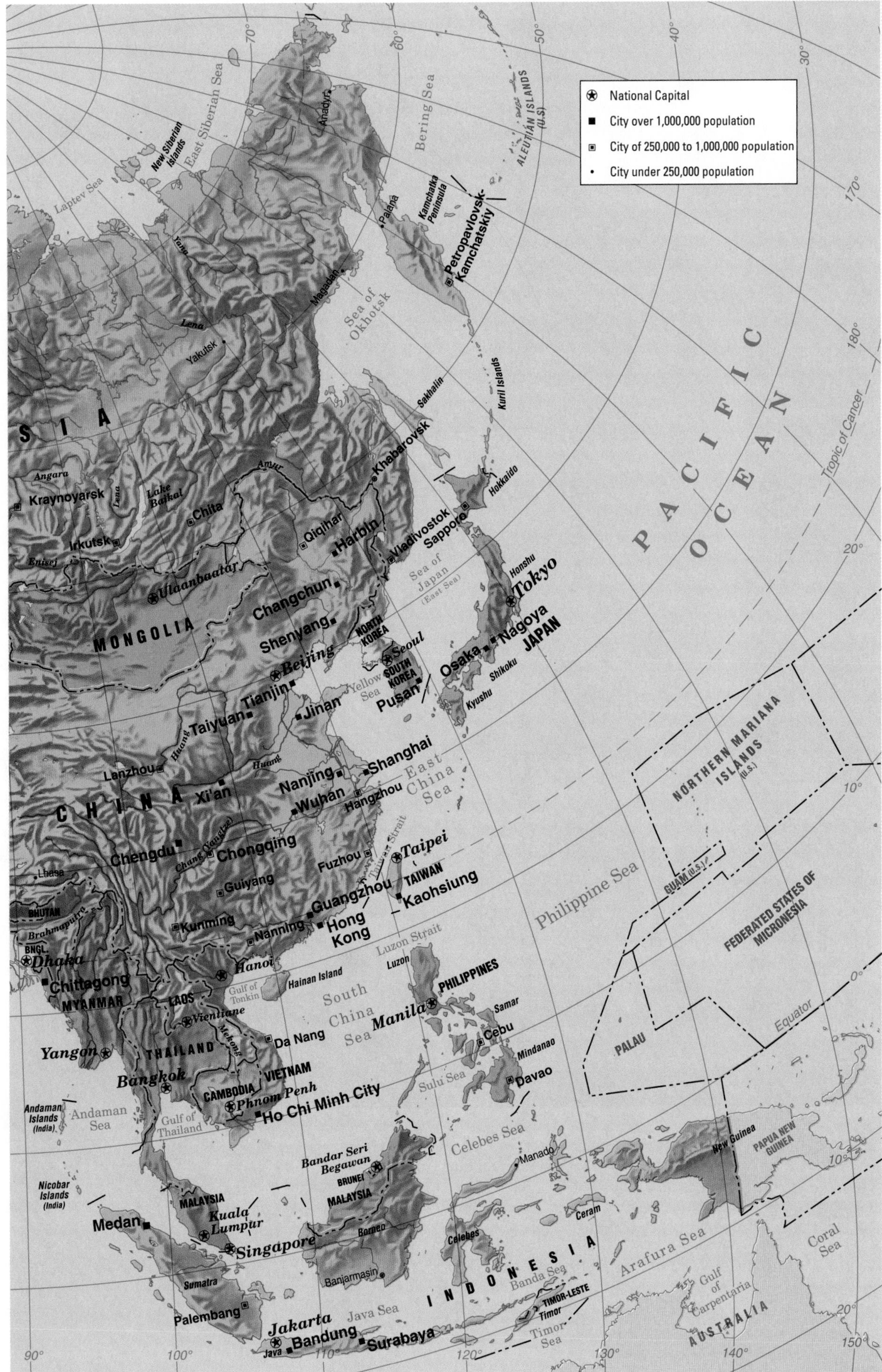

ATLAS
RAND McNALLY

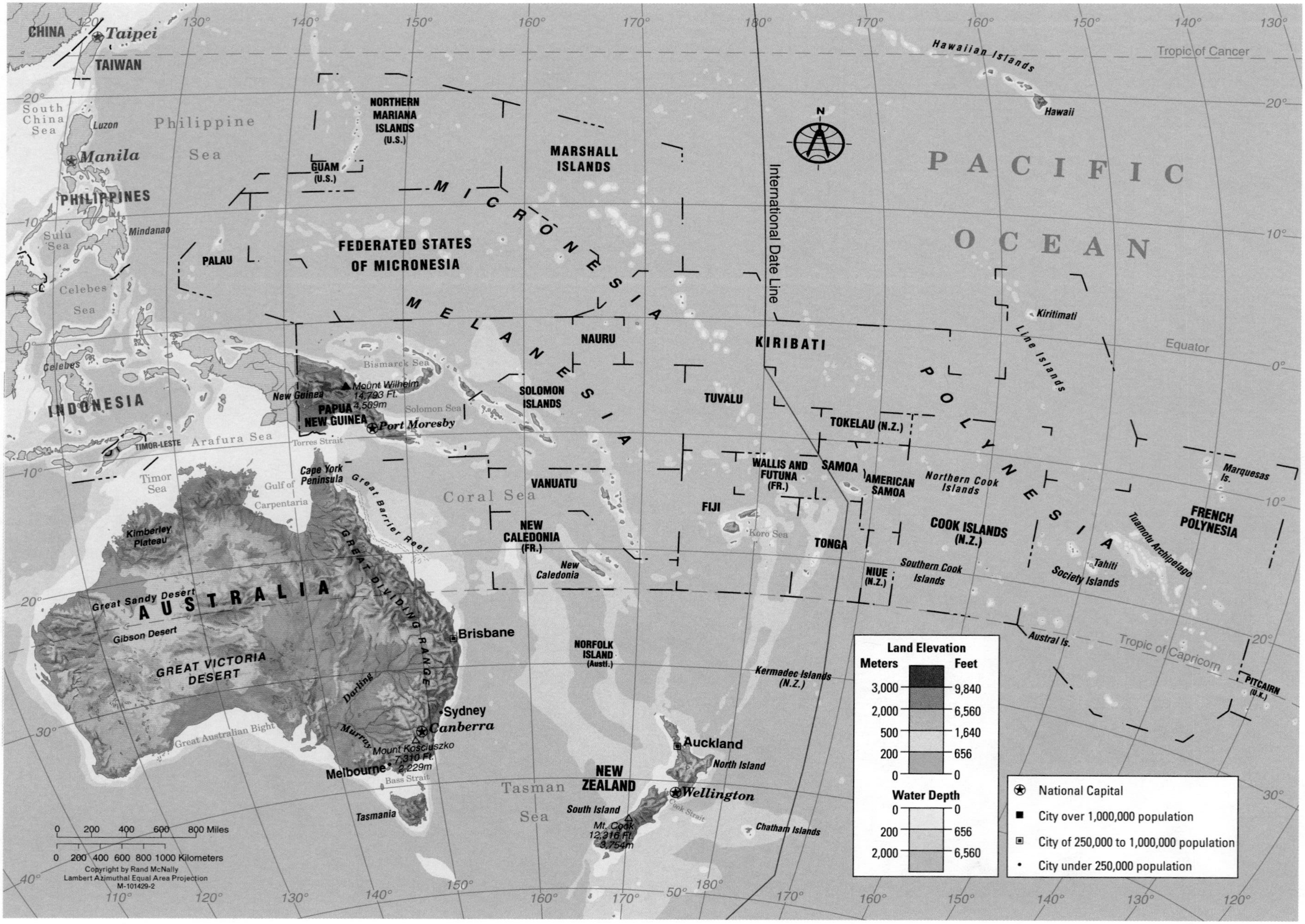

PACIFIC OCEAN

CHINA
Taipei
TAIWAN
South China Sea
Luzon
Philippine Sea
Manila
PHILIPPINES
Mindanao
Sulu Sea
Celebes Sea
Celebes
INDONESIA
TIMOR-LESTE
Timor Sea
Arafura Sea
Torres Strait
Gulf of Carpentaria
Cape York Peninsula
Great Barrier Reef
GREAT DIVIDING RANGE
Kimberley Plateau
Great Sandy Desert
AUSTRALIA
Gibson Desert
GREAT VICTORIA DESERT
Great Australian Bight
Darling
Murray
Brisbane
Sydney
Canberra
Mount Kosciuszko 7,310 Ft. 2,229m
Melbourne
Bass Strait
Tasmania
Coral Sea
Tasman Sea
NEW ZEALAND
North Island
South Island
Auckland
Wellington
Cook Strait
Mt. Cook 12,316 Ft. 3,754m
Chatham Islands
Kermadec Islands (N.Z.)
NORFOLK ISLAND (Austl.)
NEW CALEDONIA (FR.)
New Caledonia
VANUATU
SOLOMON ISLANDS
Solomon Sea
Bismarck Sea
New Guinea
Mount Wilhelm 14,793 Ft. 4,509m
PAPUA NEW GUINEA
Port Moresby
PALAU
GUAM (U.S.)
NORTHERN MARIANA ISLANDS (U.S.)
FEDERATED STATES OF MICRONESIA
MICRONESIA
MELANESIA
MARSHALL ISLANDS
NAURU
KIRIBATI
TUVALU
FIJI
Koro Sea
WALLIS AND FUTUNA (FR.)
SAMOA
AMERICAN SAMOA
TOKELAU (N.Z.)
TONGA
NIUE (N.Z.)
POLYNESIA
Northern Cook Islands
COOK ISLANDS (N.Z.)
Southern Cook Islands
Kiritimati
Line Islands
Hawaiian Islands
Hawaii
International Date Line
Tropic of Cancer
Equator
Tropic of Capricorn
Tuamotu Archipelago
Tahiti
Society Islands
Austral Is.
FRENCH POLYNESIA
Marquesas Is.
PITCAIRN (U.K.)

Land Elevation

Meters	Feet
3,000	9,840
2,000	6,560
500	1,640
200	656
0	0

Water Depth

Meters	Feet
0	0
200	656
2,000	6,560

- National Capital
- City over 1,000,000 population
- City of 250,000 to 1,000,000 population
- City under 250,000 population

0 200 400 600 800 Miles
0 200 400 600 800 1000 Kilometers

Lambert Azimuthal Equal Area Projection
M-101429-2

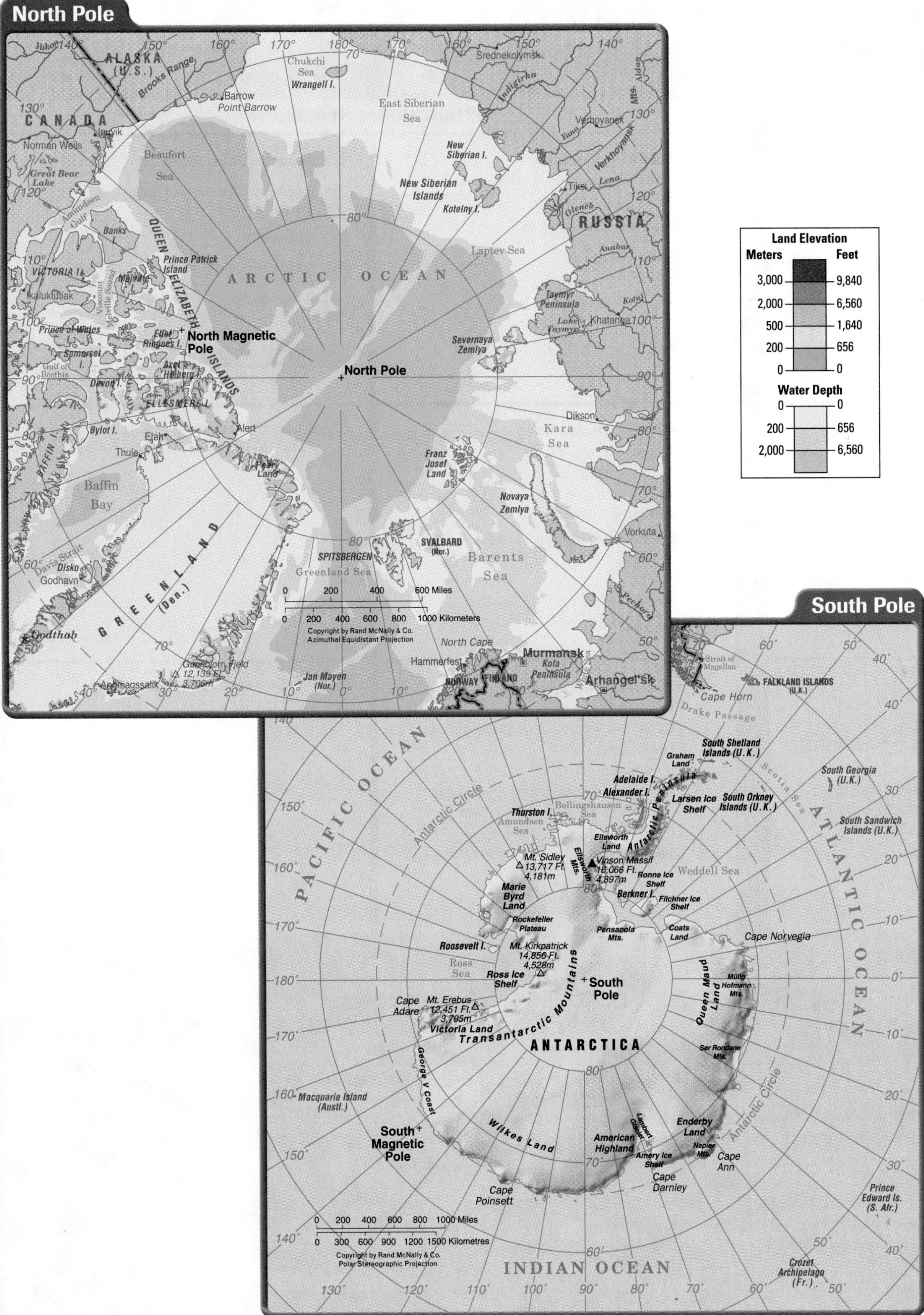
North Pole
ALASKA (U.S.)
Brooks Range
Barrow
Point Barrow
Chukchi Sea
Wrangell I.
East Siberian Sea
Srednekolymsk
Indigirka
Verkhoyansk
Verkhoyansk Mts.
Yana
Aldan
CANADA
Norman Wells
Great Bear Lake
Beaufort Sea
New Siberian I.
New Siberian Islands
Kotelny I.
Tiksi
Lena
Olenëk
RUSSIA
Amundsen Gulf
Banks I.
QUEEN ELIZABETH ISLANDS
Prince Patrick Island
VICTORIA I.
Melville
Viscount Melville Sound
ARCTIC OCEAN
Laptev Sea
Anabar
Taymyr Peninsula
Kotui
Lake Taymyr
Khatanga
Prince of Wales
Ellef Ringnes I.
North Magnetic Pole
Somerset I.
Gulf of Boothia
Devon I.
Axel Heiberg I.
North Pole
Severnaya Zemlya
ELLESMERE I.
Alert
Dikson
Kara Sea
Bylot I.
BAFFIN I.
Etah
Thule
Peary Land
Franz Josef Land
Baffin Bay
Novaya Zemlya
GREENLAND (Den.)
Vorkuta
Davis Strait
Disko
Godhavn
SPITSBERGEN
SVALBARD (Nor.)
Greenland Sea
Barents Sea
Pechora
Godthab
North Cape
Hammerfest
Murmansk
Kola Peninsula
Gunnbjorn Field 12,139 Ft. 3,700m
Jan Mayen (Nor.)
Angmagssalik
NORWAY
FINLAND
White Sea
Arhangel'sk
0 200 400 600 Miles
0 200 400 600 800 1000 Kilometers
Copyright by Rand McNally & Co.
Azimuthal Equidistant Projection
Land Elevation
Meters Feet
3,000 9,840
2,000 6,560
500 1,640
200 656
0 0
Water Depth
0 0
200 656
2,000 6,560
South Pole
Strait of Magellan
FALKLAND ISLANDS (U.K.)
Cape Horn
Drake Passage
South Shetland Islands (U.K.)
Graham Land
South Georgia (U.K.)
PACIFIC OCEAN
Adelaide I.
Alexander I.
Antarctic Peninsula
Scotia Sea
Larsen Ice Shelf
South Orkney Islands (U.K.)
Antarctic Circle
Thurston I.
Bellingshausen Sea
Amundsen Sea
South Sandwich Islands (U.K.)
ATLANTIC OCEAN
Ellsworth Land
Ellsworth Mts.
Mt. Sidley 13,717 Ft. 4,181m
Vinson Massif 16,066 Ft. 4,897m
Ronne Ice Shelf
Weddell Sea
Marie Byrd Land
Berkner I.
Filchner Ice Shelf
Rockefeller Plateau
Pensacola Mts.
Coats Land
Roosevelt I.
Mt. Kirkpatrick 14,856 Ft. 4,528m
Cape Norvegia
Ross Sea
Ross Ice Shelf
South Pole
Queen Maud Land
Mühlig-Hofmann Mts.
Cape Adare
Mt. Erebus 12,451 Ft. 3,795m
Victoria Land
Transantarctic Mountains
ANTARCTICA
Sør Rondane Mts.
George V Coast
Macquarie Island (Austl.)
Lambert Glacier
Enderby Land
South Magnetic Pole
Wilkes Land
American Highland
Napier Mts.
Amery Ice Shelf
Cape Ann
Cape Darnley
Cape Poinsett
Prince Edward Is. (S. Afr.)
0 200 400 600 800 1000 Miles
0 300 600 900 1200 1500 Kilometres
Copyright by Rand McNally & Co.
Polar Stereographic Projection
INDIAN OCEAN
Crozet Archipelago (Fr.)

ATLAS

RAND McNALLY

A37

CHAPTER 1 PLANNING GUIDE

Physical Geography: Looking at the Earth

OVERVIEW	INSTRUCTIONAL RESOURCES	
ESSENTIAL QUESTION What concepts and tools do geographers use to study the world? **Focus on the Essential Question Podcast**	**In-Depth Resources: Unit 1** • *World Geography* Atlas Activities, pp.1–4 • Building Vocabulary, p. 9 **Block Schedule Strategies** **Chapter Summaries** (English/Spanish)	**Interactive Online Edition** TOS **ExamView® Assessment Suite** (English/Spanish) TOS **CalendarPlanner** **Power Presentations with Media Gallery** **Critical Thinking Transparencies** • CT1 hmhsocialstudies.com INTERACTIVE
SECTION 1 **THE FIVE THEMES OF GEOGRAPHY** **MAIN IDEAS** • Geographers study the use of space on earth. • Geographers organize information about geography into five categories, or themes. • The five themes of geography are location, place, region, movement, and human-environment interaction.	**In-Depth Resources: Unit 1** • Guided Reading, p. 5 • Skillbuilder Practice, p. 8 • Building Vocabulary, p. 9 • Reteaching Activities, p. 10 **Guided Reading Workbook,** Section 1	**Critical Thinking Transparencies** • CT33 The Five Themes of Geography
SECTION 2 **THE GEOGRAPHER'S TOOLS** **MAIN IDEAS** • Two basic tools of geographers are maps and globes. • Most mapmaking today relies on data gathered by remote sensing, primarily by aerial photography or by satellites. • Other important tools of geographers are Geographic Information Systems (GIS) and Global Positioning Systems (GPS).	**In-Depth Resources: Unit 1** • Guided Reading, p. 6 • Guided Reading, Geography Skills Handbook, p. 7 • Building Vocabulary, p. 9 • GeoWorkshop, pp. 47–48 • Reteaching Activities, Section 2, p. 11 • Reteaching Activities, Geography Skills Handbook, p. 12 **Guided Reading Workbook,** Section 2	**Map Transparencies** • MT3 The Global Grid

ASSESSMENT

SE **Chapter Assessment,** pp. 24–25

Formal Assessment
- Chapter Tests, Forms A, B, and C, pp. 7–18

TOS **ExamView® Assessment Suite**

Strategies for Test Preparation

hmhsocialstudies.com TEST PRACTICE

SE **Section Assessment,** p. 9

Formal Assessment
- Section Quiz, p. 5

Integrated Assessment
- Rubric for a brochure, 1.13

Test Practice Transparencies TT1

SE **Section Assessment,** p. 13

Formal Assessment
- Section Quiz, p. 6

Integrated Assessment
- Rubric for a chart, 2.2
- Rubric for a database, 2.6

Test Practice Transparencies TT2

CHART KEY:

SE Student Edition	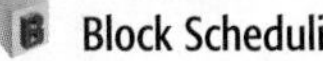 Block Scheduling	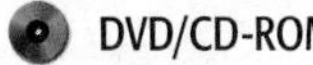 DVD/CD-ROM
TE Teacher's Edition	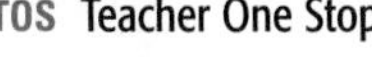 TOS Teacher One Stop	 MP3 Audio
Printable Resource	Presentation Resource	HISTORY™

Program Resources available on TOS and @ hmhsocialstudies.com

SUPPORTING RESOURCES

- Multimedia Classroom Global History Series
- Global History Teacher's Guide

Social Studies Trade Library Collection
- World Regions Trade Collection

For more information or to purchase these resources, go to 

DIFFERENTIATED INSTRUCTION

English Learners	Struggling Readers	Gifted and Talented Students
 **Spanish/English Guided Reading Workbook**  **Access for Students Acquiring English/ESL** Spanish Translations, pp. 1–4  **Chapter Summaries** (English/Spanish) TE **TE Activity** Understanding Geographic Terms, p. 6	 **Chapter Summaries** (English/Spanish) TE **TE Activity** Summarizing Main Ideas from Visuals, p. 11 Remembering the Meaning of Key Terms, p. 17	TE **TE Activity** Drawing Conclusions From Maps, p. 8

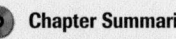

ENRICHMENT ACTIVITIES

The following activities are especially suitable for classes following block schedules.

SE **Student Edition,** pp. 2–25
- Geography Skills Handbook, pp. 14–23

hmhsocialstudies.com INTERACTIVE
- How Satellites Gather Map Data, p. 11
- Projections, p. 18

CHAPTER 1 PACING GUIDE

BLOCK SCHEDULE LESSON PLAN OPTIONS: 90-MINUTE PERIOD

DAY 1

UNIT OPENER, pp. 2–3
Class Time 90 minutes

- **Short Essay** Remind students that both geographers and historians study the world. Ask students consider how the two disciplines might be similar or different and to write a brief essay on the subject.
  Class Time 45 minutes

- **Class Discussion** Call on students to name cultures with which they are familiar. Make a list of these different groups on the board. Ask other students to suggest what characteristics makes these cultures identifiable or unique. Use students' responses to augment the list on the board. Then lead a class discussion in which students consider how some cultural characteristics might be related to the place in which specific cultures make their home.
  Class Time 45 minutes

DAY 2

SECTION 1, pp. 5–9
Class Time 90 minutes

- **Small Groups** Divide the class into five groups and assign one of the five themes of geography to each group. Have each group prepare an oral presentation in which members explain the theme and give examples of it. Allow the groups to share their presentations with the rest of the class.

DAY 3

SECTION 2, pp. 10–13
Class Time 35 minutes

- **Oral Quiz** Use the Places & Terms list on page 10 to quiz students on the section content.
  Class Time 10 minutes

- **Skillbuilder Lesson** Use the lesson about creating a sketch map on TE page 12 and the Skillbuilder Practice worksheet.
  Class Time 25 minutes

CHAPTER 1 REVIEW AND ASSESSMENT, pp. 24–25
Class Time 55 minutes

- **Review** Pair each student with a partner and have them use their GeoFocus graphic organizers to quiz each other on the chapter content.
  Class Time 15 minutes

- **Assessment** Have students complete the Chapter 1 Assessment.
  Class Time 40 minutes

TEACHER-TESTED ACTIVITY *Giving Directions*

Class Time One class period

Task Students give directions from their homes to school

Supplies
- One sheet of 8.5-by-11-inch paper per student
- Colored pens and pencils
- Straight edge

Purpose To recognize and use absolute and relative location

Activity Have students use two complete street addresses, including zip codes, as their "absolute" locations for their home and their school. Have them write the addresses on the front of their papers. Next, have students draw a map that shows a quick way to get from one address to the other. Then ask students to imagine they are giving directions to someone who has nothing to write with. Explain that they will have to give directions orally using relative location to describe the way. For example, they might suggest that a traveler "turn left where you see a red brick house with a gray roof and blue shutters." Have them write their oral directions on the back of their paper.

Joseph Naumann
Retired Geography Teacher, McCluer North High School, Florissant, Missouri

The interactive nature of the Web lets students create and manipulate maps in ways that would be difficult or impossible on paper. Students can create and customize maps of any part of the United States, from large cities to small towns; map any part of the world by inputting latitude and longitude; manipulate maps to see them in different projections; zoom in and out to see maps at different scales; and compare satellite images from different years.

Objective Students will create maps on the Internet and analyze the purposes and uses of each map.

Task Have students use Web sites to create and manipulate maps of the United States and Las Vegas, Nevada. Have them describe the maps and explain how they might be used.

Class Time 3 class periods

1. Have students read Chapter 1 and make sure they can define these terms: latitude, longitude, prime meridian, azimuthal projection, cylindrical projection, Mercator projection.

2. Have students go to the follow the links at **hmhsocialstudies.com** to the Online Map Creation site to create maps of the continental United States in Mercator, azimuthal equidistant, and equidistant cylindrical projections. To do this, they will need to type in the approximate United States boundary coordinates of 25 degrees south, 50 degrees north, 125 degrees west, and 67 degrees east. It's important that they type in coordinates west of the Prime Meridian as negative numbers. They should also be sure to select "national boundaries" and to choose the appropriate projections.

3. As they create the maps, ask students to write sentences describing what the maps look like and to explain how each projection might be useful (they should refer to pages 18–19). Ask them to write additional sentences explaining which map they think is the most useful for themselves as geography students.

4. Have students visit other Web sites at **hmhsocialstudies.com** to create maps of Las Vegas, Nevada. They will see satellite images, local street maps, and topographical maps. Ask them to write sentences describing what each map looks like and explaining some ways in which each one can be used. Under what circumstances would someone benefit from looking at one of these maps?

5. Discuss students' online map-viewing experiences as a class. In what ways can the Internet be useful in learning about maps and seeing maps of specific places? What does the Internet enable them to do that they can't do with paper maps?

Previewing the Unit

The first pages of this unit provide an introduction to physical and human geography.

Discussion Prompts

Exploring Prior Knowledge Ask students the following questions about geography to determine their prior knowledge of the discipline:

- What do geographers study? *(Some students may know that geographers study both the physical features of the earth, such as mountains and rivers, and the earth's human features, such as religion and ethnicity.)*
- How is geography different from history? *(Historians are primarily concerned with questions about time, whereas geographers are concerned with questions of space.)*

Interpreting Maps Ask students to examine the satellite image on pages 2 and 3 and answer the following questions:

- What landforms do you recognize? *(Answers will vary but may include oceans, seas, lakes, mountains, islands, and peninsulas.)*
- Do you recognize any continents? *(Answers will vary but may include North and South America, Europe, Africa, Asia, Australia, and Antarctica.)*

In-Depth Resources: Unit 1
- *World Geography* Atlas Activities, pp. 1–4

Unit 1 The Basics of Geography

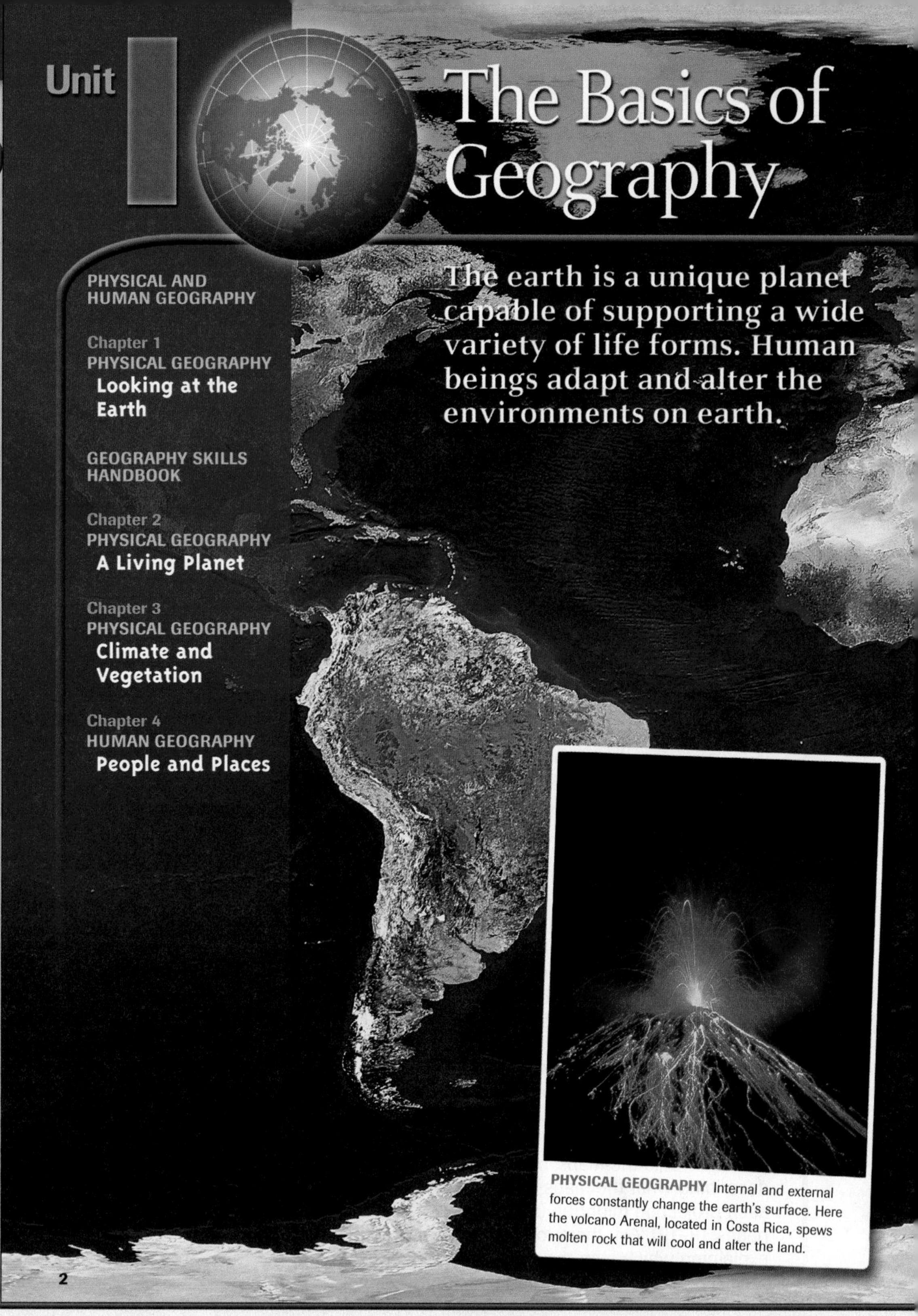

PHYSICAL AND HUMAN GEOGRAPHY

Chapter 1
PHYSICAL GEOGRAPHY
Looking at the Earth

GEOGRAPHY SKILLS HANDBOOK

Chapter 2
PHYSICAL GEOGRAPHY
A Living Planet

Chapter 3
PHYSICAL GEOGRAPHY
Climate and Vegetation

Chapter 4
HUMAN GEOGRAPHY
People and Places

The earth is a unique planet capable of supporting a wide variety of life forms. Human beings adapt and alter the environments on earth.

PHYSICAL GEOGRAPHY Internal and external forces constantly change the earth's surface. Here the volcano Arenal, located in Costa Rica, spews molten rock that will cool and alter the land.

UNIT 1 ADDITIONAL RESOURCES

BOOKS FOR THE TEACHER

De Blij, Harm J. ***The Power of Place: Geography, Destiny, and Globalization's Rough Landscape.*** Oxford University Press, 2008. How globalization may affect various levels of society.

Kunstler, James Howard. ***The Geography of Nowhere: The Rise and Decline of America's Man-Made Landscape.*** NY: Simon & Schuster, 1993. An examination of what the automobile has done to the sense of place in the United States.

Sherer, Thomas E. ***The Complete Idiot's Guide to Geography.*** NY: Simon & Schuster Macmillan, 1997. Basic maps and information about the history, culture, and customs of the world's major regions.

BOOKS FOR THE STUDENT

Goode's World Atlas. Skokie, IL: Rand McNally, 20th rev. ed., 2000. Comprehensive atlas with features on physical and human geography.

VIDEOS

Basics of Geography. United Learning, 1996. Examines landforms, water, climate, natural resources, and human-environment interaction.

INTERNET

For more about geography, visit . . .
hmhsocialstudies.com

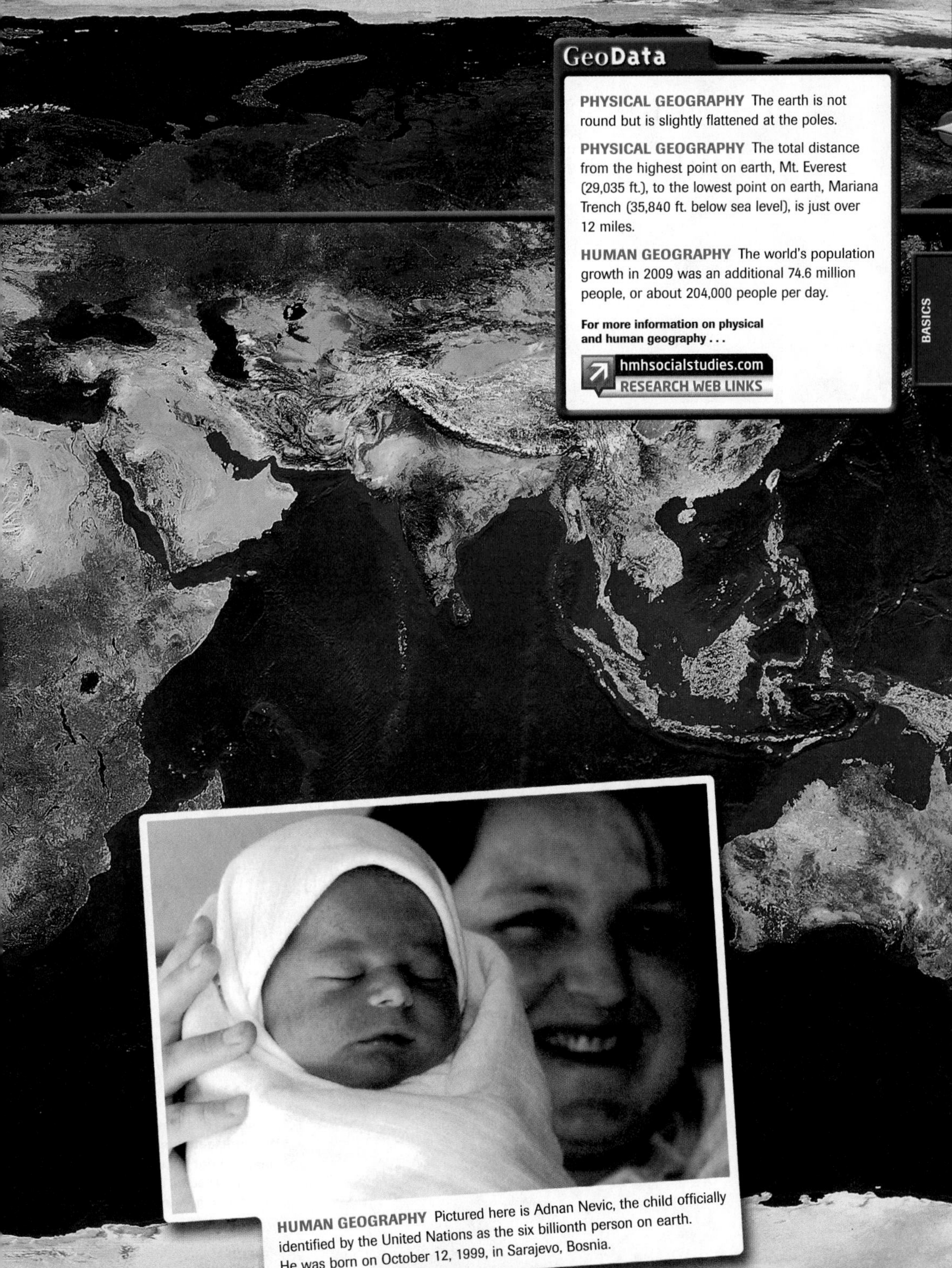

GeoData

PHYSICAL GEOGRAPHY The earth is not round but is slightly flattened at the poles.

PHYSICAL GEOGRAPHY The total distance from the highest point on earth, Mt. Everest (29,035 ft.), to the lowest point on earth, Mariana Trench (35,840 ft. below sea level), is just over 12 miles.

HUMAN GEOGRAPHY The world's population growth in 2009 was an additional 74.6 million people, or about 204,000 people per day.

For more information on physical and human geography . . .

hmhsocialstudies.com RESEARCH WEB LINKS

HUMAN GEOGRAPHY Pictured here is Adnan Nevic, the child officially identified by the United Nations as the six billionth person on earth. He was born on October 12, 1999, in Sarajevo, Bosnia.

Interpreting Photographs

Physical Geography

After a long stretch of dormancy, the volcano Arenal entered an active period in 1968, when a major eruption blew off much of the volcano's west side. The explosion devastated two villages that lay at the foot of the volcano (Pueblo Nuevo and Tabacón) and killed 78 people.

Ask students if they can think of other ways in which the earth's surface changes. *(Students may point out other natural phenomena, such as earthquakes, or they may note the changes brought about by human activities, such as dams.)*

Human Geography

Explain to students that the United States is the world's third most populous nation, after China and India. The U.S. population, approximately 307,212,000 in 2010, represented less than five percent of the world's total.

Ask students if they think that the global population is too large. Have them give reasons for their answers. *(Answers will vary.)*

ACTIVITY OPTION **STUDENTS ACQUIRING ENGLISH/ESL**

DISCUSSING HUMAN GEOGRAPHY

Objective To have students consider the cultural differences among places and regions

Class Time 20 minutes

Task Create a list characteristics that cultural geographers might use to define places and regions

Directions Tell students that people in different parts of the world have special combinations of characteristics. Then explain that cultural geographers often use these characteristics to define places and regions. Call on students to suggest characteristics—e.g., ethnicity, religion, education, cuisine, rate of television or automobile ownership, etc.—that geographers might use to differentiate among places and regions. Help students who are having difficulty with English to articulate their ideas. Write a list of students' answers on the board.

CHAPTER 1 OBJECTIVE

Explain the five themes of geography and describe basic geographic tools and technology.

Chapter 1

PHYSICAL GEOGRAPHY

Looking at the Earth

Interpreting Maps

Have students look at urban areas on the maps. Help students understand that different methods for gathering and displaying geographic information gives maps different points of emphasis.

Extension Ask students which map shows the route between Seneca Falls and Waterloo. *(the road map)* Which map shows vegetation most clearly? *(the heat sensing scan)*

Introducing the Essential Question

- Emphasize to students that geographers group many basic concepts of geography into five themes. These themes will help students understand how geographic concepts relate to each other.
- Geographers use specialized tools to help them describe our world.

hmhsocialstudies.com TAKING NOTES

Have students fill out graphic organizers in their notebooks using material from all sections in this chapter.

Critical Thinking Transparencies CT1
• GeoFocus

In-Depth Resources: Unit 1
• Building Vocabulary, p. 9

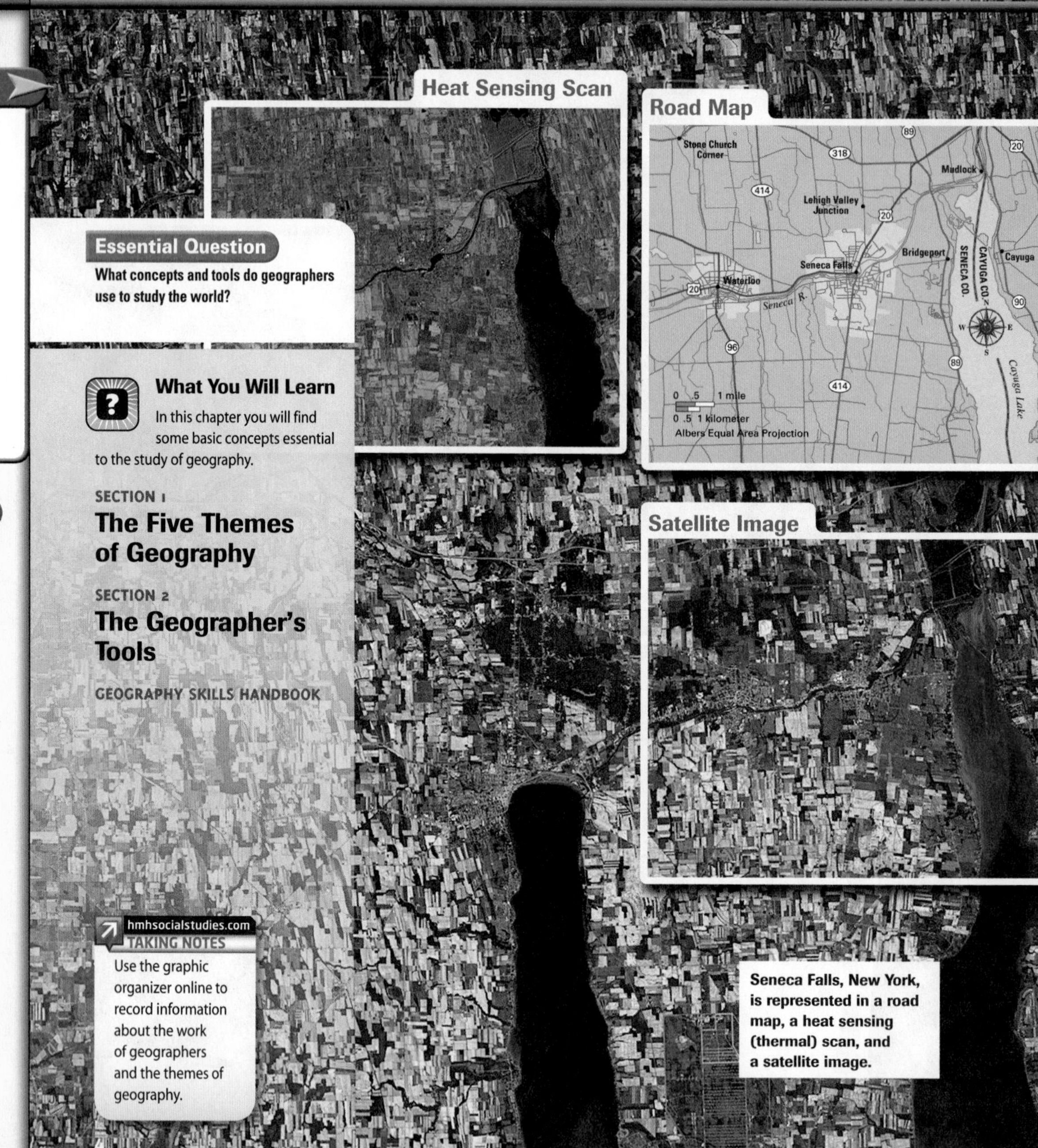

Essential Question

What concepts and tools do geographers use to study the world?

What You Will Learn

In this chapter you will find some basic concepts essential to the study of geography.

SECTION 1
The Five Themes of Geography

SECTION 2
The Geographer's Tools

GEOGRAPHY SKILLS HANDBOOK

hmhsocialstudies.com TAKING NOTES

Use the graphic organizer online to record information about the work of geographers and the themes of geography.

Seneca Falls, New York, is represented in a road map, a heat sensing (thermal) scan, and a satellite image.

CHAPTER 1 ADDITIONAL RESOURCES

BOOKS FOR THE TEACHER

Bednarz, Sarah.et al. ***Geography for Life: National Geography Standards 1994.*** Washington, D.C.: National Geographic Research and Exploration, 1994. Examination of national geography standards and description of geographic perspectives.

BOOKS FOR THE STUDENT

Sobel, Dava, and William J. H. Andrewes. ***The Illustrated Longitude.*** NY: Walker & Co., 1998. Story of the scientist who solved the problem of determining east-west location at sea.

VIDEOS

The Five Themes of Geography. Educational Video Network, 2000. Explanation of the five themes of geography.

Maps and Globes. AGC/United Learning, 2000. Four-part series on reading maps, globes, and other visual aids.

INTERNET

For more about physical geography, visit . . .

hmhsocialstudies.com

The Five Themes of Geography

Main Ideas

- Geographers view the world in terms of the use of space.
- Geographers study the world by looking at location, place, region, movement, and human-environment interaction.

Places & Terms

geography
absolute location
relative location
hemisphere
equator
prime meridian
latitude
longitude

A HUMAN PERSPECTIVE Between 1838 and 1842, Captain Charles Wilkes led an American expedition to the South Pacific and Antarctica. At one stop at a South Sea island, a friendly islander drew a map on the wooden deck planks of the ship. To Wilkes's amazement, the map accurately showed the location of the Tuamotu Archipelago—a chain of about 80 coral islands that stretches more than 1,000 miles across the South Pacific. The islander relied on personal experience sailing in the area and a mental map to accurately show the positions of the islands.

The Geographer's Perspective

Maps like the one that the islander drew are important tools in geography. The word *geography* comes from the Greek word *geographia,* which means "to describe the earth." Geographers study the world in a different way than do other social scientists. Historians look at events over time. Geographers, on the other hand, view the world by looking at the use of space on the earth and the interactions that take place there. They look for patterns and connections between people and the land that they live on. **Geography,** then, is the study of the distribution and interaction of physical and human features on the earth.

METHODS OF GEOGRAPHY Geographers use a variety of tools to study the use of space on earth. The most common one is a map. Maps are visual representations of a portion of the earth. Maps do not have to be written down to be useful. Since people began roaming the earth, they have created mental maps—maps that they carry in their minds. You use a mental map every day as you go to and from school.

The maps that you are probably most familiar with appear in printed form, such as in road atlases and books. In recent years, more maps have appeared in electronic media such as CD-ROMs and on the Internet.

Geographers also use photographs to gain visual evidence about a place. They organize information into charts, graphs, or tables to learn about geographic patterns and to understand changes over time. They may also construct scale models to make study of the real world easier. Sometimes they use graphic models to illustrate an idea.

Other basic tools used by geographers are the five themes of geography, which also describe patterns and connections in the use of space. These themes organize information about geography into five distinct categories, shown at right. These themes are important to geographic study. They help the geographer to describe the use of space.

The Five Themes

Location	Where is it?
Place	What is it like?
Region	How are places similar or different?
Movement	How do people, goods, and ideas move from one location to another?
Human-Environment Interaction	How do people relate to the physical world?

SECTION 1 OBJECTIVES

1. Explain how geographers study the world.
2. Define *location* and explain how geographers describe it.
3. Explain the themes of *place* and *region* and identify the differences among formal, functional, and perceptual regions.
4. Explain the geographic theme of *human-environment interaction.*
5. Explain the theme of *movement* and distinguish among linear, time, and psychological distances.

SKILLBUILDER: Interpreting Graphics, p. 6

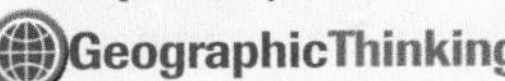

Making Comparisons, p. 6
Using the Atlas, p. 7
Seeing Patterns, pp. 8, 9
Making Generalizations, p. 9

Focus & Motivate

Ask students how the Five Themes of Geography are part of their everyday lives. *(Their school has a* location, *and* movement *is required to get there.)*

Instruct: Objective 

The Geographer's Perspective

- What tools and methods are used by geographers? *(maps, photographs, scale models, the five themes of geography)*
- Why are the five themes of geography useful? *(They organize geographic information into five distinct categories.)*

In-Depth Resources: Unit 1
- Guided Reading, p. 5
- Skillbuilder Practice, p. 8

SECTION 1 PROGRAM RESOURCES

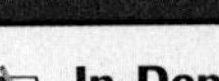
In-Depth Resources: Unit 1
- Guided Reading, p. 5
- Skillbuilder Practice, p. 8
- Building Vocabulary, p. 9
- Reteaching Activity, p. 10

Guided Reading Workbook
- Section 1

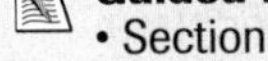
Access for Students Acquiring English/ESL
- Guided Reading, p. 1
- Skillbuillder Practice, p. 4

Formal Assessment
- Section Quiz, p. 5

Integrated Assessment
- Rubric for a brochure, 1.13

INTEGRATED TECHNOLOGY

Critical Thinking Transparency CT33
- The Five Themes of Geography

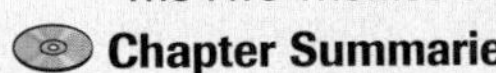
Chapter Summaries

Power Presentations

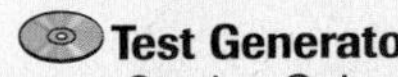
Test Generator
- Section Quiz

TEST-TAKING RESOURCES

Strategies for Test Preparation

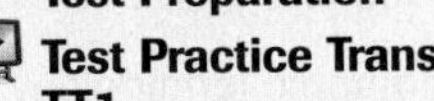
Test Practice Transparencies TT1

Online Test Practice

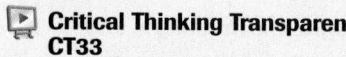

Instruct: Objective 2

Theme: Location

- What is the difference between absolute location and relative location? *(Absolute location is the exact place of a geographic feature. Relative location describes a feature's location in relation to its surroundings.)*
- How is the absolute location of a place described? *(by identifying the place's latitude and longitude)*
- How is the relative location of a place described? *(by identifying its spatial relationship to other places around it)*

Critical Thinking Transparencies CT33
- The Five Themes of Geography

Interpreting Graphics

The Geographic Grid

Point out that longitude lines begin and end at the North and South poles. The degree value of longitude lines directly opposite one another always add up to 180. Direct students' attention to the graphic showing longitude lines and ask what longitude line the Prime Meridian meets at the North and South poles. *(180°)*

SKILLBUILDER ANSWERS

1. Northern Hemisphere, Western Hemisphere **2.** 180 degrees—90° North, 90° South

The Geographic Grid

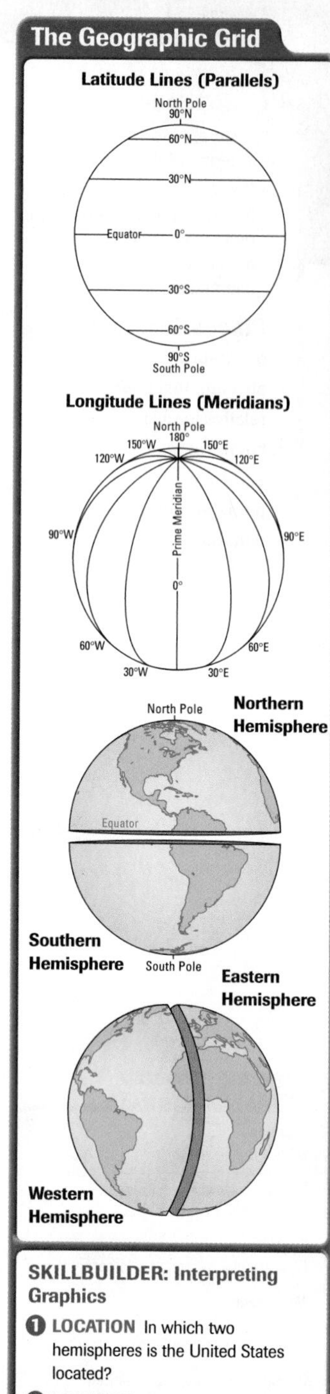

SKILLBUILDER: Interpreting Graphics

1. **LOCATION** In which two hemispheres is the United States located?
2. **LOCATION** How many degrees of latitude are there?

Theme: Location

The geographic question "Where is it?" refers to location. Geographers describe location in two ways. **Absolute location** is the exact place on earth where a geographic feature, such as a city, is found. **Relative location** describes a place in comparison to other places around it.

ABSOLUTE LOCATION To describe absolute location, geographers use a grid system of imaginary lines for precisely locating places on the earth's surface. (See the diagram at left.) Earth is divided into two equal halves. Each half of the globe is called a **hemisphere.** Because the earth is round, a hemisphere can be north and south, or east and west. The **equator** is the imaginary line that divides the north and south halves. The **prime meridian** is the imaginary line dividing the earth east and west. Sometimes this line is called the Greenwich meridian (GREHN•ich muh•RIHD•ee•uhn) line because the line runs through Greenwich, England. A

Geographic Thinking

Making Comparisons

A How is the equator different from the prime meridian?

A. Answer Equator divides the earth north and south; the prime meridian divides east and west.

LATITUDE LINES To locate places north or south, geographers use a set of imaginary lines that run parallel to the equator. These lines are called **latitude** lines. The equator is designated as the zero-degree line for latitude. Lines north of the equator are called north latitude lines, and lines south of the equator are called south latitude lines.

LONGITUDE LINES To complete the grid system, geographers use a set of imaginary lines that go around the earth over the poles. These lines, called **longitude** lines, mark positions in the east and west hemispheres. The prime meridian is the zero-degree line for longitude.

Each site on the earth can have only one absolute location. To find an absolute location using the grid system, you need to find the point where the latitude and longitude lines cross. For example, the absolute location of Melbourne, Australia, is 37° South latitude, 145° East longitude. To see how latitude and longitude lines cross and to learn more about absolute location, see page 17 in the Geography Skills Handbook.

RELATIVE LOCATION Relative location describes how a place is related to its surrounding environment. For example, you may tell a person that the library is three blocks west of the park. This helps the person find the library—if he or she knows where the park is located. Using relative location may help you become familiar with the specific characteristics of a place. Learning that Cairo, Egypt, is located near the mouth of the Nile River in Africa, for example, tells you something about Cairo, the Nile River, and even Africa itself.

DIFFERENTIATING INSTRUCTION **STUDENTS ACQUIRING ENGLISH/ESL**

UNDERSTANDING GEOGRAPHIC TERMS

Objective To familiarize students with important geographic terms

Class Time 20 minutes

Task Use geographic terminology to describe students' present location

Directions Write the boldfaced terms from this page on the board. Use a classroom map to explain each term or call on students to do so. Have students apply terms to their present location. For example, ask them to describe the absolute and relative location of their hometowns. Then ask questions like the following: Is it close to or far from the Equator? from the Prime Meridian? What city in the Southern Hemisphere is about the same distance from the Equator? What city in the Eastern Hemisphere is about the same distance from the Prime Meridian?

Place: Rio de Janeiro, Brazil
Overlooking the entrance to Guanabara Bay, Sugarloaf Mountain is a prominent landform in the skyline of Rio.
Leisure boats rest in the harbor of Botafogo Bay. There is a large commercial shipyard industry in Rio.
Headquarters of corporations and expensive housing compete for space in the scenic part of the city.

PLACE Rio de Janeiro, once the capital of Brazil, lies on the western shore of Guanabara Bay. **How would location on a bay affect the economy of a city?**

Theme: Place

The question "What is it like?" refers to place. Place includes the physical features and cultural characteristics of a location. All locations on earth have physical features that set them apart, such as climate, landforms, and vegetation. Other features are the product of humans interacting with the environment, such as by building dams, highways, or houses. Still others are the result of humans interacting with animals or with each other. In the photograph above, you can see place features of Rio de Janeiro. Since a location's culture and its use of space may change over time, the description of a place may also change.

Theme: Region

The question "How are places similar or different?" refers to region. A region is an area of the earth's surface with similar characteristics. Regions usually have more than one characteristic that unifies them. These may include physical, political, economic, or cultural characteristics. For example, the Sunbelt in the southern United States is a physical region. Geographers categorize regions in three ways: formal, functional, and perceptual regions. 

Geographic Thinking

Using the Atlas

B Refer to the U.S. map on pages A18–A19. What states might be included in the Sunbelt?

B. Answer Florida, Georgia, Mississippi, Alabama, Louisiana, Texas, New Mexico, Arizona, California

FORMAL REGIONS A formal region is defined by a limited number of related characteristics. For example, the Sahel region of Africa is a desert area characterized by specific climate, vegetation, and land use patterns. In this textbook, the regions you'll explore generally are defined by continental area and by similar cultural styles. The following are considered formal regions:

- The United States and Canada
- Latin America
- Europe
- Russia and the Republics
- Africa
- Southwest Asia
- South Asia
- East Asia
- Southeast Asia, Oceania, and Antarctica

Interpreting Photographs

Rio De Janeiro

Have students identify natural features of the city and features that are the product of human-environment interaction. *(Sugarloaf Mountain is a natural feature. Apartment buildings and docks are products of human-environment interaction.)*

CAPTION ANSWER Its location would make it ideal for shipping goods in and out of the country, shipbuilding, and leisure activities.

More About

Place

Examples of place features that are the result of humans interacting with each other include cultural life (parks and plazas), economic activities (downtown), and political behavior (courthouse, parade grounds).

Instruct: Objective 3

Theme: Place/Theme: Region

- What does the theme of *place* refer to? *(the physical and cultural features of a location)*
- What is a *region*? *(an area of the earth's surface with similar characteristics)*
- How do formal, functional, and perceptual regions differ? *(A formal region is based on related characteristics, a functional region on connections between places, and a perceptual region on people's perceptions of an area.)*

ACTIVITY OPTION | CRITICAL THINKING

MAKING COMPARISONS

Explaining the Skill Remind students that when you make comparisons, you identify similarities and differences. Point out that geographers define regions by looking at similarities and differences among places.

Applying the Skill Direct students' attention to the formal regions in the bulleted list at the bottom of page 7. Ask the following questions and write the students' answers on the board.

What characteristics do the United States and Canada have in common? *(Responses might refer to location, size, landforms, culture, history, type of government, and economy.)* How do the two countries differ? *(Responses might refer to political power, climate zones, official languages, and amount of developed land.)* Which characteristics do you think are most important in making the United States and Canada a formal region? *(Responses might include location, culture, economy, and standard of living.)*

Instruct: Objective 

Theme: Human-Environment Interaction

- What does the theme *human-environment interaction* refer to? *(the ways in which people use, change, or live with their environment)*
- What are some examples of the positive and negative effects of people altering their environments? *(positive–makes places safer or more livable; negative–pollutes, destroys natural beauty)*

FUNCTIONAL REGIONS A functional region is organized around a set of interactions and connections between places. Usually a functional region is characterized by a hub, or central place, and links to that central place. For example, a city and its suburbs may form a functional region. Highways, commuter railroads, subways, and bus lines move people from the suburbs to the city for jobs and other activities. Because the city and its suburbs are connected by a great deal of movement back and forth, they form a functional region. C

Geographic Thinking

Seeing Patterns C How might areas within a city form a functional region?

C. Answer Parts of the city are linked to and interact with each other.

PERCEPTUAL REGIONS A perceptual region is a region in which people perceive, or see, the characteristics of the region in the same way. However, the set of characteristics may not be precisely the same for all people. For example, although many people are familiar with the region called the American Midwest, they sometimes differ on how that region is defined. Some people believe the Midwest begins in Ohio. Others believe the region begins in the middle of Illinois.

Theme: Human–Environment Interaction

The question "How do people relate to the physical world?" refers to the relationship between humans and their environment. People learn to use what the environment offers them and to change that environment to meet their needs. They also learn to live with aspects of the environment that they cannot control, such as climate.

People living in similar environments do not respond to them in the same way. For example, some people view a hot, sunny climate near a body of water as ideal for recreational activities. Others may see this as an opportunity for raising citrus, olives, or grapes. Human beings work to alter their environments to make them better places or to provide needed goods. People may drain swamps or dig irrigation ditches to grow crops in a particular environment. Sometimes the alterations create new problems, such as pollution. As you study geography, you will learn about many ways humans interact with their environment.

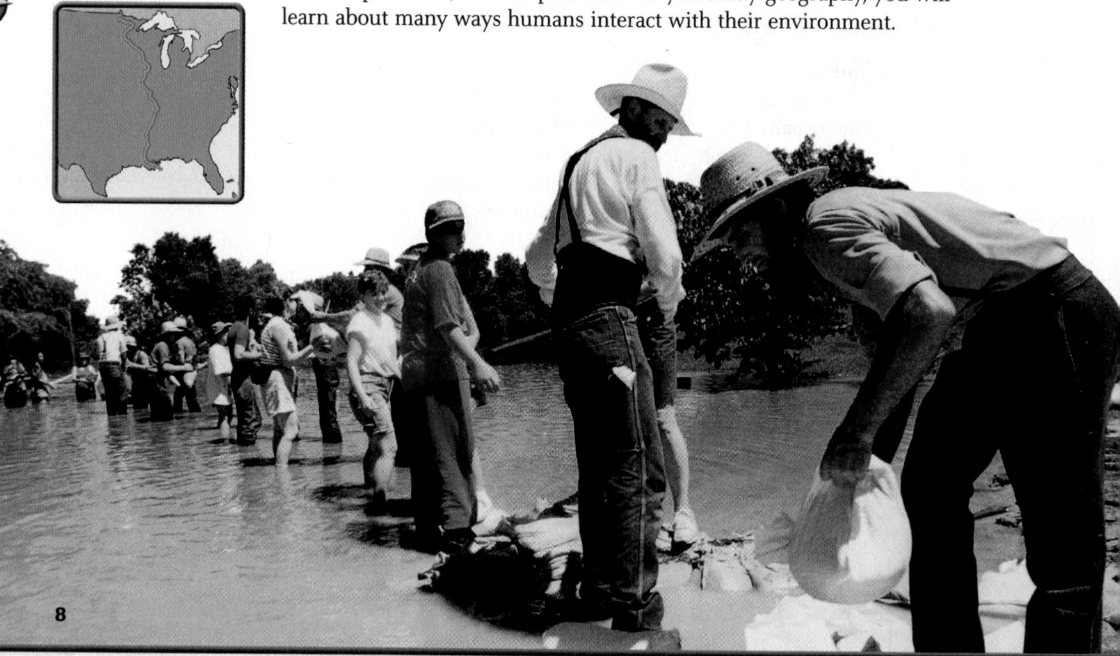

HUMAN–ENVIRONMENT INTERACTION Neighbors and friends use sandbags to hold back floodwaters during the Great Mississippi Flood of 1993. **In what ways do floods alter the landscape?**

8

Interpreting Photographs

Great Mississippi Flood

Tell students that, although the direct cause was heavy rainfall, some observers blamed human activity–such as unwise development of flood-plain areas–for the extensive damage caused by the 1993 flood. Ask students to think of other examples of human activity influencing climatic phenomena. *(Students may mention the relationship between greenhouse gasses and global warming.)*

CAPTION ANSWER Floods may move buildings, trees, or other large objects, may leave dirt and sand behind, or may change the course of a river or stream.

DIFFERENTIATING INSTRUCTION GIFTED AND TALENTED STUDENTS

DRAWING CONCLUSIONS FROM MAPS

Objective To familiarize students with specialized maps and deepen understanding of human-environment interaction

Class Time 30 minutes

Task Draw conclusions about the extent to which people have altered the environment

Directions A land use map, also called a land cover characteristics map, can provide students with the big picture of how much people have altered the environment on earth. Have students locate a land use map in a United States or world atlas. Ask students to estimate from the map what percentage of the land area of the United States and/or the world has been altered by human activities.

Theme: Movement

The question "How do people, goods, and ideas move from one location to another?" refers to movement. Geographers are interested in the ways people, goods, and ideas move from place to place. Think about the clothing you wear, the music you listen to, or the places you go for entertainment. All of these things involve movement from one place to another. Geographers analyze movement by looking at three types of distance: linear distance, time distance, and psychological distance.

LINEAR DISTANCE AND TIME DISTANCE Linear distance simply means how far across the earth a person, an idea, or a product travels. Physical geography can affect linear distance by forcing a shift in a route to avoid impassable land or water.

Time distance is the amount of time it takes for a person, an idea, or a product to travel. Modern inventions have shortened time distances. For example, in the 1800s, pioneers traveled up to six months to reach California. Today you can get there by airplane from almost any U.S. location in under six hours. With the use of the Internet, ideas can travel around the world in seconds. D

Seeing Patterns
D How do interstate highways affect linear distance and time distance?
D. Answer They move large volumes of traffic rapidly. Time distance may be reduced, or in the case of traffic jams, increased between destinations.

PSYCHOLOGICAL DISTANCE Psychological distance refers to the way people view distance. When you were younger, some locations seemed very far away. As you grew older, the distance to these locations probably seemed to shrink. Studies show that, as we become familiar with a place, we think it is closer than it actually is. Less familiar places seem to be further away. Psychological distance may influence decisions about many different human activities.

Across the world, people make important choices based on linear distance, time distance, and psychological distance. These choices make up patterns that geographers can study. In the next section, you'll read about the tools they use to study these patterns.

Section 1 Assessment

1 Places & Terms
Explain the meaning of each of the following terms.
- geography
- hemisphere
- equator
- prime meridian
- latitude
- longitude

2 Taking Notes
REGION Review the notes you took for this section.

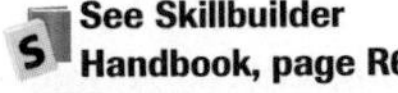

- What is a region?
- What are three types of regions?

3 Main Ideas
a. What are the five themes of geography?
b. How is place different from location?
c. Why do geographers study human-environment interaction?

4 Geographic Thinking
Making Generalizations How is the study of geography different from the study of history? **Think about:**
- use of space on earth
- relationships between people and the environment

See Skillbuilder Handbook, page R6.

EXPLORING LOCAL GEOGRAPHY Using the five themes of geography, develop a **brochure** describing your community. Use pictures or sketches, maps, and other data to complete your descriptions.

Instruct: Objective 5

Theme: Movement

- What question does the geographic theme of *movement* refer to? *(How do people, ideas, and products move from one location to another)*
- How do geographers analyze movement? *(by looking at three types of distances: linear, time, and psychological)*
- How do linear, time, and psychological distance differ? *(Linear distance refers to how far something travels, time distance refers to how long it takes to travel, and psychological distance refers to a person's perception of the distance.)*

Assess & Reteach

GeoFocus Have students complete the section on the five themes of geography in their graphic organizers.

Formal Assessment
- Section Quiz, p. 5

Reteaching Activity
Divide the class into five small groups. Assign each group one of the five themes of geography, and ask them to define the theme and brainstorm a list of five examples. Have each group share their definition and examples with the rest of the class.

In-Depth Resources: Unit 1
- Reteaching Activity, p. 10

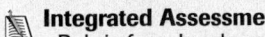

SECTION 1 ASSESSMENT ANSWERS

1. Places & Terms
geography, p. 5
hemisphere, p. 6
equator, p. 6
latitude, p. 6
longitude, p. 6
prime meridian, p. 6

2. Taking Notes
- A region is an area of the world with similar characteristics.
- formal regions, functional regions, perceptual regions

3. Main Ideas
a. location, place, region, movement, human-environment interaction
b. Location can be absolute or relative, and identifies where something is. Place describes a location's physical and cultural features.
c. to understand the relationships between human beings and the environment in which they live

4. Geographic Thinking
Geographers study the use of space on the surface of the earth. They look for patterns and connections between the people and the land. Historians look at events over time.

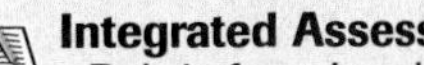

Integrated Assessment
- Rubric for a brochure, 1.13

SECTION 2 OBJECTIVES

1. Compare the advantages and disadvantages of maps and globes and identify three types of maps.
2. Describe how geographers use satellites and other tools.

GeographicThinking

Making Comparisons, p. 13
Making Generalizations, p. 13

Focus & Motivate

How might today's technology make mapmaking easier and more accurate than it was 100 years ago? *(Satellites provide more accurate information.)*

Instruct: Objective 1

Maps and Globes

- What is an advantage and a disadvantage of a globe? *(It is three-dimensional and so shows the earth as it sits in space. They are not as portable as maps.)*
- What is an advantage and a disadvantage of maps? *(They are portable; distortion occurs in flattening the earth's surface to create the map.)*
- What are three basic map types, and what do they show? *(A general reference map shows natural and man-made features. Thematic maps show specific information, such as climate zones. Nautical maps provide information needed to navigate through air or water.)*

In-Depth Resources: Unit 1
- Guided Reading, p. 6
- GeoWorkshop, p. 47

2 The Geographer's Tools

Main Ideas

- Geographers use two- and three-dimensional tools to learn about the earth.
- Geographers use computer-assisted technology to study the use of the earth's surface.

Places & Terms

globe
map
cartographer
map projection
topographic map
Landsat
Geographic Information Systems (GIS)

A HUMAN PERSPECTIVE At noon on a sunny midsummer day, sometime around 255 B.C., Eratosthenes drove a stake into the ground at the mouth of the Nile River in Alexandria, Egypt. He then noted the angle of the shadow cast by the stake. Meanwhile at Syene (modern-day Aswan, Egypt), another person drove a stake into the ground—but it cast no shadow. Using the angle of the first shadow and the distance between Syene and Alexandria, Eratosthenes calculated the circumference of the earth. By today's measurements, he was off by about 15 percent, but he was remarkably accurate considering the simple tools he used. Eratosthenes was one of the earliest geographers to use tools and critical thinking to measure and describe the earth.

Maps and Globes

A geographer's tools include maps, globes, and data that can be displayed in a variety of ways. The oldest known map is a Babylonian clay tablet created about 2,500 years ago. The tablet is about four inches high and shows the Babylonian world surrounded by water. Over the centuries, mapmaking evolved into a very complex task. However, a map's function has remained the same—to show locations of places, landforms, and bodies of water, and where they are in relation to other parts of the earth.

TWO OR THREE DIMENSIONS A **globe** is a three-dimensional representation of the earth. It provides a way to view the earth as it travels through space. But since the earth is a sphere, we can see only one half of it at any time. For certain tasks, globes are not very practical because they are not easily portable.

People often prefer to use **maps,** which are two-dimensional graphic representations of selected parts of the earth's surface. Maps are easily portable and can be drawn to any scale needed. The disadvantage of a map is that distortion occurs as the earth's surface is flattened to create the map. A **cartographer,** or mapmaker, reduces some types of distortion by using different types of map projections. A **map projection** is a way of drawing the earth's surface that reduces distortion caused by presenting a round earth on flat paper. To learn more about map projections, see the Geography Skills Handbook, pages 18–19.

This globe, created circa 1492, is turned to show Africa and Europe.

SECTION 2 PROGRAM RESOURCES

In-Depth Resources: Unit 1
- Guided Reading, Section 2, p. 6
- Guided Reading, Geography Skills Handbook, p. 7
- GeoWorkshop, pp. 47–48
- Reteaching Activities, Section 2, p. 11
- Reteaching Activities, Geography Skills Handbook, p. 12

Guided Reading Workbook
- Section 2

Access for Students Acquiring English/ESL
- Guided Reading, pp. 2–3

Formal Assessment
- Section Quiz, p. 6

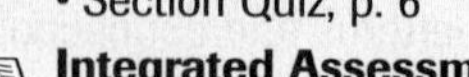

Integrated Assessment
- Rubric for a chart, 2.2
- Rubric for a database, 2.6
- Rubric for a map, 2.1

INTEGRATED TECHNOLOGY

Map Transparencies MT3
- The Global Grid

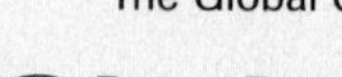

Power Presentations

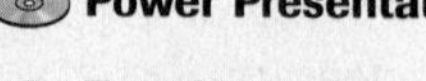

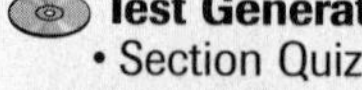

Test Generator
- Section Quiz

hmhsocialstudies.com

TEST-TAKING RESOURCES

Strategies for Test Preparation

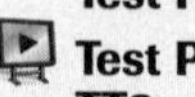

Test Practice Transparencies TT2

Online Test Practice

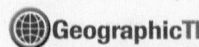

TYPES OF MAPS The three types of maps are general reference maps, thematic maps, and navigational maps. One kind of general reference map is called a **topographic map,** which is a representation of natural and man-made features on the earth. Thematic maps emphasize specific kinds of information, such as climate or population density. Sailors and pilots use the third type of map—navigation maps. You can learn more about using different maps in the Geography Skills Handbook, pages 20–23.

BACKGROUND
Navigational maps, often referred to as charts, help their users to plot a course through air or water.

The Science of Mapmaking

A cartographer decides what type of map to create by considering how the map will be used. Keeping that purpose in mind, he or she then determines how much detail to show and what size the map should be.

SURVEYING The first step in making a map is to complete a field survey. Surveyors observe, measure, and record what they see in a specific area. Today, most mapping is done by remote sensing, the gathering of geographic information from a distance by an instrument that is not physically in contact with the mapping site. These data are gathered primarily by aerial photography or by satellites.

The data gathered includes information such as elevation, differences in land cover, and variations in temperature. This information is recorded and converted to a gray image. Cartographers then use these data and computer software to construct maps. See the illustration below to learn more about satellite surveying.

BASICS

How Satellites Gather Map Data

hmhsocialstudies.com INTERACTIVE

As the satellite orbits the earth, a scanner constantly records data from the earth's surface.
Instruments measure invisible electromagnetic waves emitted by each object on earth. Because these waves are unique for every object, computers can analyze and identify them.
The data collected is converted first to code and then to pixels—electronic dots. Computer software then converts the pixels into usable images.
The first step in mapmaking is collecting data. Remote sensors gather information for constructing maps.
1
2
3
Code
97 128 151
64 97 133
46 78 102
Pixels
Image

Instruct: Objective 2

The Science of Mapmaking

- What is the first step in making a map and how is it done? *(surveying or collecting data by means of aerial photography or satellites)*
- What is GIS, and how is it used? *(a computer technology that helps mapmakers combine geographic data about a location from several sources)*
- What is GPS? *(A series of satellites that beam location information to earth.)*

Interpreting Infographics

Obtaining Map Data

Have students look at the infographic and summarize how geographic information is collected and stored. Direct their attention to the image at the bottom right. Ask what the image shows and what will be done with it. *(It shows the topography of the area scanned by the satellite. A representation of the topography will be stored in a database that cartographers can access.)*

DIFFERENTIATING INSTRUCTION LESS PROFICIENT READERS

SUMMARIZING MAIN IDEAS FROM VISUALS

Objective To help students focus on main ideas with the aid of visuals

Class Time 20 minutes

Task Create a flow chart from information presented in infographics

Directions Some students may have trouble extracting the most important information from this section. Have them focus on visuals to grasp key ideas. Explain how the two infographics on pages 11 and 12 provide key information. The first shows how geographic information gets into a database, and the second shows how geographers use the information. Have students create a simple flow chart that summarizes this process.

Satellites carry instruments that pick up and measure data.
↓
Computers analyze and convert data into images.
↓
Layers of information are stored in a computer database.
↓
Cartographers select layers of information to create maps.

SATELLITES Today, geographers rely heavily on satellites to provide geographic data. Two of the best-known satellites are Landsat and GOES. **Landsat** is actually a series of satellites that orbit more than 100 miles above Earth. Each time a satellite makes an orbit, it picks up data in an area 115 miles wide. Landsat can scan the entire Earth in 16 days.

Geostationary Operational Environmental Satellites (GOES) is a weather satellite system. The satellites fly in orbit in synch with Earth's rotation. By doing so, they always view the same area. They gather images of atmospheric conditions that are useful in forecasting the weather.

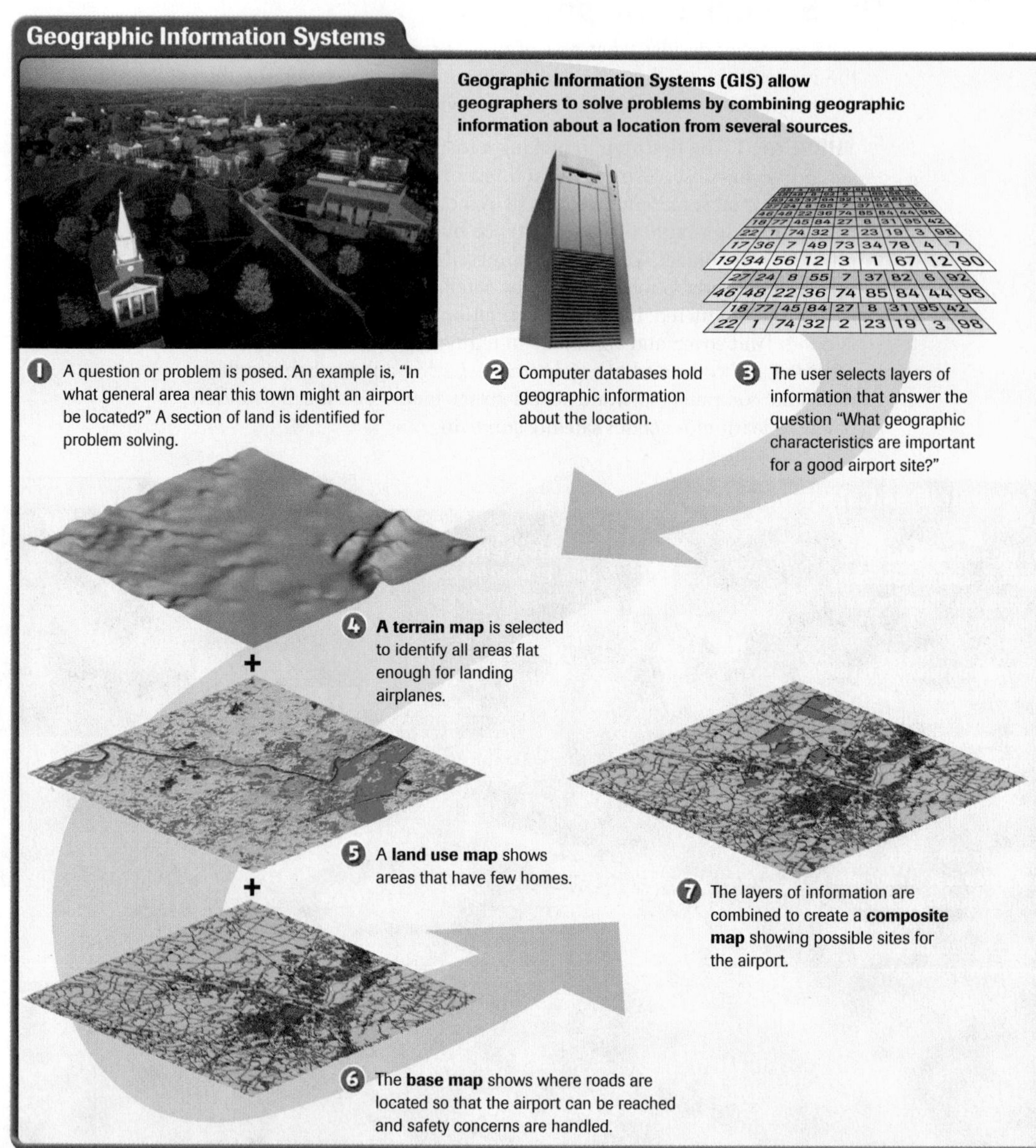

Geographic Information Systems
Geographic Information Systems (GIS) allow geographers to solve problems by combining geographic information about a location from several sources.
1 A question or problem is posed. An example is, "In what general area near this town might an airport be located?" A section of land is identified for problem solving.
2 Computer databases hold geographic information about the location.
3 The user selects layers of information that answer the question "What geographic characteristics are important for a good airport site?"
4 A terrain map is selected to identify all areas flat enough for landing airplanes.
+
5 A land use map shows areas that have few homes.
+
6 The base map shows where roads are located so that the airport can be reached and safety concerns are handled.
7 The layers of information are combined to create a composite map showing possible sites for the airport.

Interpreting Infographics

Geographic Information Systems

Note that the infographic on the previous page showed how geographic data was collected and stored. This one shows how a cartographer uses the data to make a map. Have students summarize this process, then ask what a cartographer would have to add to the composite map shown here to make it into a usable map. *(a title, labels, and a key or legend)*

More About

Geographic Information Systems

Explain to students that GIS is not a single system or a single database. The term refers to a technology that includes many computer software programs. It draws upon a number of databases, such as the National Satellite Land Remote Sensing Data Archive and the National Climatic Data Center.

ACTIVITY OPTION SKILLBUILDER LESSON

CREATING A SKETCH MAP

Explaining the Skill Tell students that they can create their own map using existing maps and other sources of information. For instance, they can use an atlas to provide general outlines of a region, and then apply data gathered from another map, a report, or a database.

Applying the Skill Direct students to sketch a copy of a physical map of their state. On a tissue overlay, have them add information from a state political map. Then have students answer the following questions:

- What do you learn about your state from the physical map? *(location of landforms and bodies of water)*
- What do you learn from the political map? *(location of counties and cities)*
- What conclusions can you draw from putting the two types of information together? *(how the locations of cities are related to landforms and bodies of water)*

For more Skillbuilder practice, see p. 5 in Section 1.

GEOGRAPHIC INFORMATION SYSTEMS The newest tool in the geographer's toolbox is **Geographic Information Systems (GIS).** GIS stores information about the world in a digital database. GIS has the ability to combine information from a variety of sources and display it in ways that allow the user to visualize the use of space in different ways.

When using the system, geographers must look at a problem and decide what types of geographic information would help them solve the problem. The information could include maps, aerial photographs, satellite images, or other data. Next, they select the appropriate layers of information. Then, GIS creates a composite map combining the information. Study the diagram on page 12 to learn more about the way GIS works.

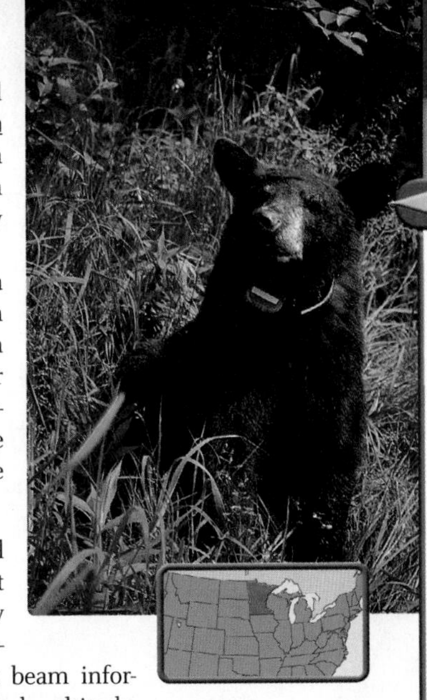

MOVEMENT Scientists use a GPS device to track this bear in Minnesota. **What other uses could be found for a GPS device?**

GLOBAL POSITIONING SYSTEM (GPS) A familiar tool of geographers is GPS or Global Positioning System. It was originally developed to help military forces know exactly where they were on the earth's surface. The system uses a series of 24 satellites called Navstars, which beam information to the earth. The exact position—latitude, longitude, altitude, and time—is displayed on a hand-held receiver. Hikers, explorers, sailors, and drivers use GPS devices to determine location. They are also used to track animals. A

Geographers use a variety of other tools including photographs, cross sections, models, cartograms, and population pyramids. These tools help geographers to visualize and display information for analysis. They are looking for patterns and connections in the data they find. You will learn how to use these tools in the Geography Skills Handbook, which follows, and in the Map and Graph Skills pages in this book.

A. Answer GPS allows the military to know their precise position. GOES alerts the military to weather problems.

Geographic Thinking

Making Comparisons
A How might the military use both GOES and GPS?

Interpreting Photographs

Tracking a Bear

Point out how the photograph shows an example of the geographic theme of movement. Make sure students understand that the device on the bear's neck transmits signals that a satellite picks up and then beams back down to earth. Ask why scientists might want to track the movement of a black bear. *(Scientists might, for example, want to determine the bear's territorial range.)*

CAPTION ANSWER Rescue crews, such as those of the U.S. Coast Guard, might use GPS devices to locate a ship lost at sea.

Assess & Reteach

GeoFocus Have students complete the section on geographer's tools in their graphic organizers.

Formal Assessment
- Section Quiz, p. 6

Reteaching Activity
Have students work with partners to create word webs that summarize this section's content on the tools of geographers.

In-Depth Resources: Unit 1
- Reteaching Activity, p. 11

Section 2 Assessment

1 Places & Terms
Explain the meaning of each of the following terms.
- globe
- map
- cartographer
- map projection
- topographic map
- GIS

2 Taking Notes
REGION Review the notes you took for this section.

Tools:

- How would a globe show a region differently than a map?
- How does GIS aid in understanding a region?

3 Main Ideas
a. What are the three basic types of maps?
b. What are some geographers' tools in addition to maps and globes?
c. How does a cartographer decide which type of map is needed?

4 Geographic Thinking
Making Generalizations How does modern technology help geographers? **Think about:**
- digital information
- satellite images

See Skillbuilder Handbook, page R6.

GeoActivity

MAKING COMPARISONS Choose a place on the earth and in an atlas, and find three maps that show the place in three different ways. Create a **chart** that lists the similarities and differences in the way the place is shown on the three maps.

SECTION 2 ASSESSMENT ANSWERS

1. Places & Terms
globe, p. 10
map, p. 10
cartographer, p. 10
map projection, p.10
topographic map, p. 11
GIS, p. 13

2. Taking Notes
- A globe shows three dimensions and does not distort landmasses. A map shows two dimensions and does distort landmasses.
- GIS brings a variety of information about an area together in one database. It can be used for planning or to study an area.

3. Main Ideas
a. general reference, thematic, and nautical maps
b. satellite data, Geographical Information System databases, and Global Positioning System data
c. A cartographer needs to consider how the map will be used.

4. Geographic Thinking
The use of satellite images, positioning systems, and a Geographic Information System provides geographers with accurate data and ways to display the information.

GeoActivity

Integrated Assessment
- Rubric for a chart, 2.2

OBJECTIVES

1. Understand the methods for determining location.
2. Learn how to interpret the different elements of a map.
3. Understand the elements and purpose of the geographic grid.
4. Examine different types of map projections.
5. Understand and interpret different types of maps.

Focus & Motivate

Ask students to name the different elements that can be found on a map and list these on the board. *(Answers will vary.)*

Instruct: Objective 

Finding Location

- How do the functions of a personal GPS device and a compass differ? *(A GPS determines absolute location, and a compass determines direction.)*
- Why do surveyors use theodolites? *(to measure angles and distances on the earth)*

 **In-Depth Resources: Unit 1**
• Guided Reading, p. 7

More About

Compasses

A compass consists of a small, lightweight magnet balanced atop a nearly frictionless pivot point. The magnet is sometimes called a needle. In response to the earth's magnetic field, the needle points toward the north. In the photograph at right, the needle is in the shape of an arrow.

GEOGRAPHY SKILLS HANDBOOK

This handbook covers the basic map skills and information that geographers rely on as they investigate the world—and the skills you will need as you study geography.

Finding Location

Mapmaking depends on surveying the earth's surface. Until recently, that activity could only happen on land or sea. Today, aerial photography and satellite imaging are the most popular ways to gather data.

A personal **GPS** device provides the absolute location to the user.

Magnetic compasses introduced by the Chinese around the 1100s helped to accurately determine direction.

Nigerian surveyors use a **theodolite,** a type of surveying instrument. It precisely measures angles and distances on the earth.

GEOGRAPHY SKILLS NOTEBOOK | **ADDITIONAL RESOURCES**

BOOKS FOR THE TEACHER

Kjellstrom, Bjorn and Carina Kjellstrom Elgin. ***Be Expert with Map and Compass: The Complete Orienteering Handbook.*** Wiley, 2009.
Basics of map and compass skills.

Ehrenberg, Ralph E. ***Mapping the World: An Illustrated History of Cartography.*** National Geographic, 2005.

BOOKS FOR THE STUDENT

Brown, Lloyd A. ***The Story of Maps.*** Boston: Little, Brown, 1949. A history of cartography from antiquity to the early 20th century, including many fascinating anecdotes from cartographers themselves.

Monmonier, Mark S. ***How to Lie with Maps.*** Chicago: Univ. of Chicago Press, 1996. A useful reference for learning how to avoid being manipulated and misled by maps.

VIDEOS

Maps: Different Types, Different Uses. Social Studies School Service. Uses animated graphics, cartoons, and live footage to explain maps and their uses.

INTERNET

For more about geography skills, visit . . .

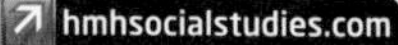 hmhsocialstudies.com

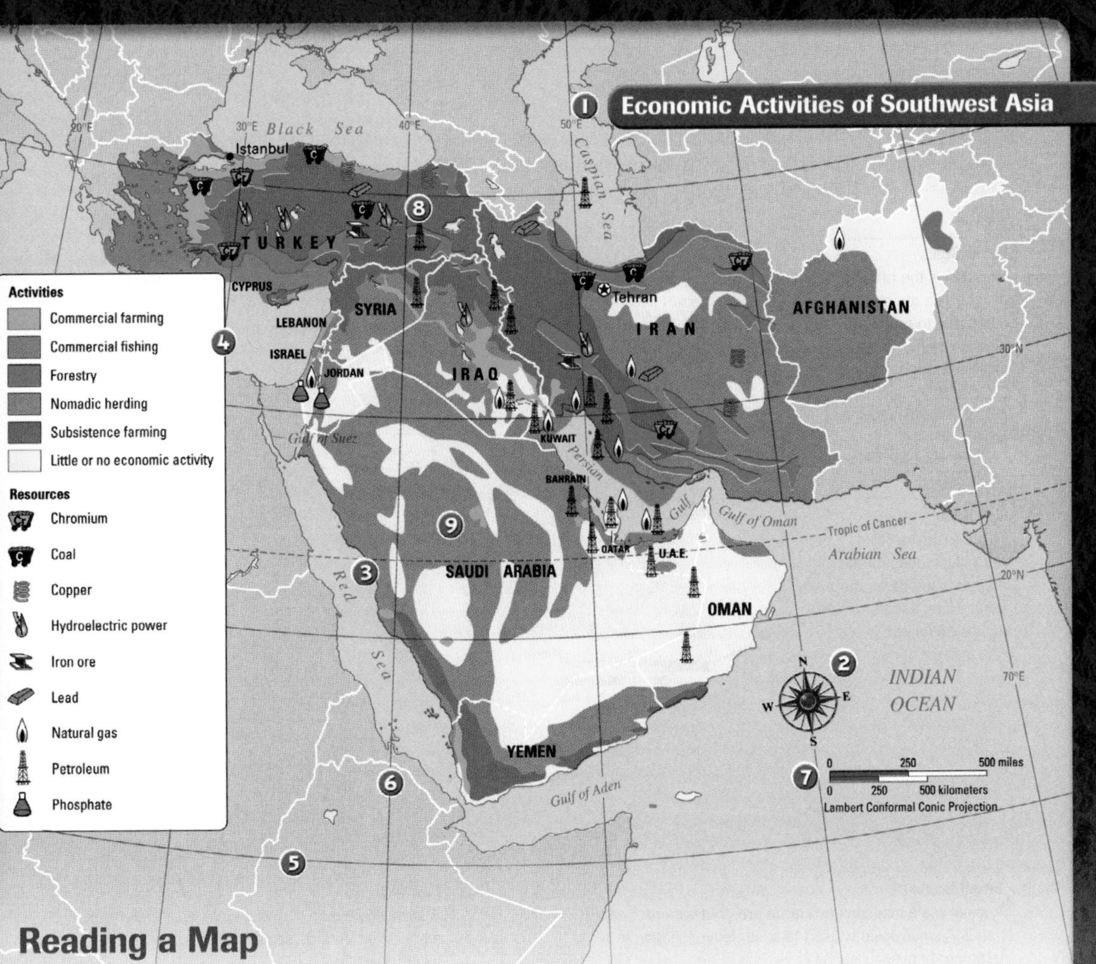

Reading a Map

Most maps have these elements, which are necessary to read and understand them.

1. **TITLE** The title explains the subject of the map and gives you an idea of what information the map conveys.
2. **COMPASS ROSE** The compass rose shows you the north (N), south (S), east (E), and west (W) directions on the map. Sometimes only north is indicated.
3. **LABELS** Labels are words or phrases that explain features on the map.
4. **LEGEND** A legend or key lists and explains the symbols and use of color on the map.
5. **LINES OF LATITUDE** These are imaginary lines that measure distance north or south of the equator.
6. **LINES OF LONGITUDE** These are imaginary lines that measure distance east or west of the prime meridian.
7. **SCALE** A scale shows the ratio between a unit of length on the map and a unit of distance on the earth.
8. **SYMBOLS** Symbols represent such items as capital cities, economic activities, or natural resources. Check the map legend for more details.
9. **COLORS** Colors represent a variety of information on a map. The map legend indicates what the colors mean.

Instruct: Objective 2

Reading a Map

- Where can you find the subject and basic information about a map? *(title)*
- What is the function of a compass rose? *(to show direction)*
- What is a legend? *(the explanatory list of symbols and colors used on a map, also called a key)*
- What map feature would you use to determine the distance between two places? *(scale)*
- What features of a map will help you find absolute locations? *(lines of latitude and longitude)*

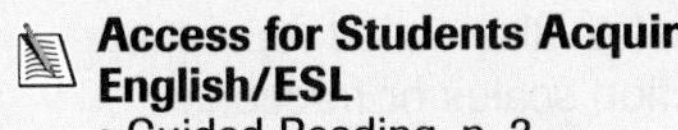

Access for Students Acquiring English/ESL
- Guided Reading, p. 3

ACTIVITY OPTION | EXPLORING LOCAL GEOGRAPHY

CREATING A NEIGHBORHOOD MAP

Objective To understand the basic features of a map

Class Time 30 minutes

Task Create a map that utilizes the basic elements of maps

Directions Have students create maps of the areas around their homes. Ask them to make imaginative use of the basic features examined above. Students might create a scale that uses the length of their footstep. Or they could use symbols to designate the location of favorite stores or homes of friends and relatives. With colors, they might show areas where they play sports or hang out. Display and discuss the maps in class.

Instruct: Objective 

Scale/Using the Geographic Grid

- What determines a map maker's choice of scale? *(the amount of detail they want to show)*
- How is a grid system useful to geographers? *(it allows geographers to establish absolute location)*
- What are the names of the latitudinal and longitudinal lines at 0°? *(the equator and prime meridian)*

Map Transparencies MT3
- The Global Grid

More About

Scale

Ratio scales, also called representative fraction scales or fractional scales, are the most accurate of all scale statements. Since they are presented numerically, they can be understood in any language.

Scale

A geographer decides what scale to use by determining how much detail to show. If many details are needed, a large scale is used. If fewer details are needed, a small scale is used.

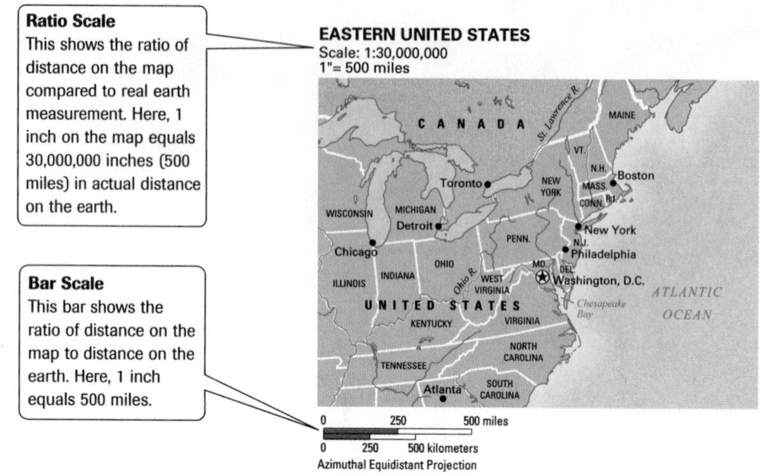

Small Scale

A small scale map shows a large area but without much detail. A small scale is used to see relative location in a region or between regions.

WASHINGTON, D.C., METRO AREA
Scale: 1:3,000,000
1"= 50 miles

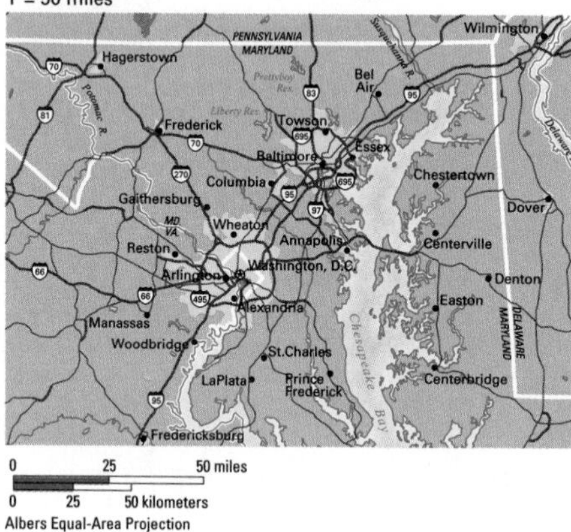

Large Scale

A large scale map shows a small area with much more detail. A large scale is used to see relative location within a region.

WASHINGTON, D.C.
Scale: 1:62,500
1"= 1 mile

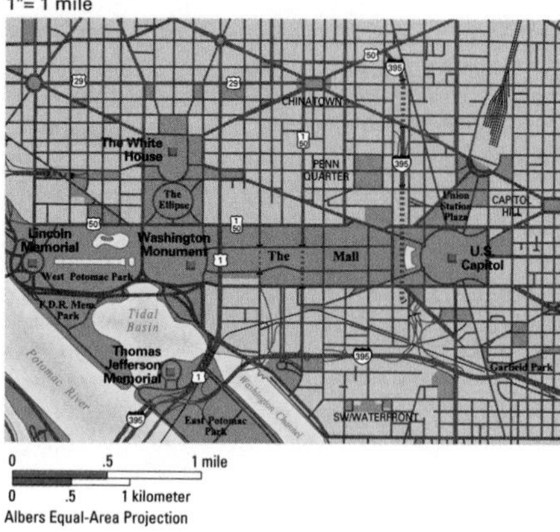

ACTIVITY OPTION — LINK TO MATHEMATICS

CREATING A SCALE

Objective To help students understand scale

Class Time 30 minutes

Task Create a map and scale for the classroom

Supplies Needed
- tape measures
- rulers
- grid paper
- pencils and erasers

Directions Divide students into groups. Have one group of students measure the dimensions of the classroom. Have another group measure the sizes of the room's larger furnishings. A third group could measure the distance of these furnishings from the walls. After students finish collecting this data, draw a map that shows the classroom and its dimensions on the chalkboard. Next, provide students with a ratio, for example, .5 inches = 1 foot, and have them redraw the map of the room on their grid paper using this ratio. Remind them to include a ratio or bar scale on their maps.

Using the Geographic Grid

As you learned in Chapter 1, geographers use a grid system to identify absolute location. The grid system uses two kinds of imaginary lines:

- latitude lines, also called parallels because they run parallel to the equator
- longitude lines, also called meridians because, like the prime meridian, they run from pole to pole

Latitude
There are 90° in North latitude and 90° in South latitude.

North Pole
90°N
Arctic Circle
60°N
30°N
Tropic of Cancer
Equator
0°
Tropic of Capricorn
30°S
60°S
Antarctic Circle
90°S
South Pole

Beginning of north polar region

Marks sun's most northerly location, on about June 21

Tropics

Marks sun's most southerly location, on about December 21

Longitude
There are 180° in West longitude and 180° in East longitude. Lines also mark the hours of the day as the earth rotates. Every 15° east or west is equal to one hour.

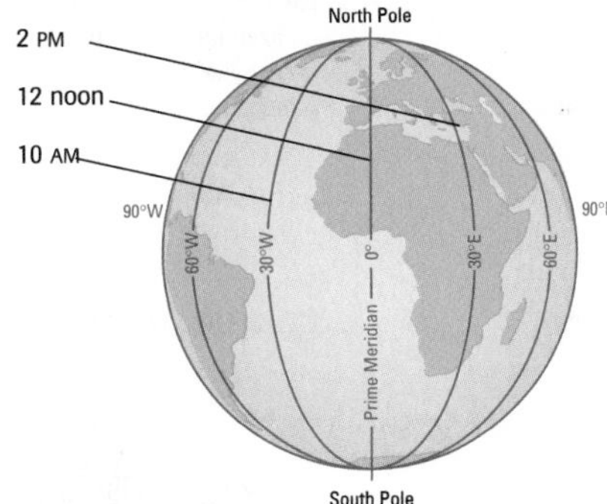

Global Grid
Absolute location can be determined by noting where latitude and longitude lines cross. For more precision, each degree is divided into 60 minutes.

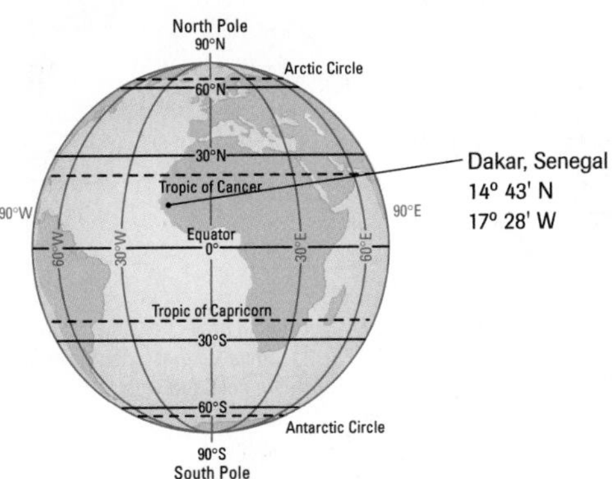

More About

The Geographic Grid

On June 21, the sun is directly over the Tropic of Cancer. On that date the sun appears in the constellation Gemini. However, earlier in history, the sun appeared in the constellation Cancer, giving the tropic its name. Similarly, on December 21, the sun is directly over the Tropic of Capricorn and appears in the constellation Sagittarius. But at one time, it appeared in the constellation Capricorn. A gradual change in the direction of the earth's axis of rotation is responsible for the change.

DIFFERENTIATING INSTRUCTION | **LESS PROFICIENT READERS**

REMEMBERING THE MEANING OF KEY TERMS

Objective To help students differentiate among key terms

Class Time 5 minutes

Task Have students use a mnemonic device to differentiate between latitude and longitude

Directions Some students may have difficulty remembering the difference between latitude and longitude. Have them use the following mnemonic device to remember the meanings of the two terms. L**a**titude goes **a**round the earth. L**o**ngitude goes **o**ver the earth.

Instruct: Objective 4

Projections

- What is a projection? *(a way of showing the curved surface of the earth on a flat map)*
- How might a projection be misleading? *(Because the earth is a sphere, projecting it onto a flat surface will cause some distortion.)*
- What are three types of projections? *(planar, or azimuthal; conical, and cylindrical)*

Interpreting Maps

Planar Projections

Have students examine the azimuthal projection on page 18. Ask them why a bar scale might be misleading if they were to measure the distance between San Francisco and Rome and try to convert the measurement using the bar scale. *(because the size and shape of the earth have been distorted by the projection)*

hmhsocialstudies.com INTERACTIVE

Projections

A projection is a way of showing the curved surface of the earth on a flat map. Because the earth is a sphere, a flat map will distort some aspect of the earth's surface. Distance, shape, direction, or area may be distorted by a projection. Be sure to check the projection of a map so you are aware of how the areas are distorted.

PLANAR PROJECTIONS

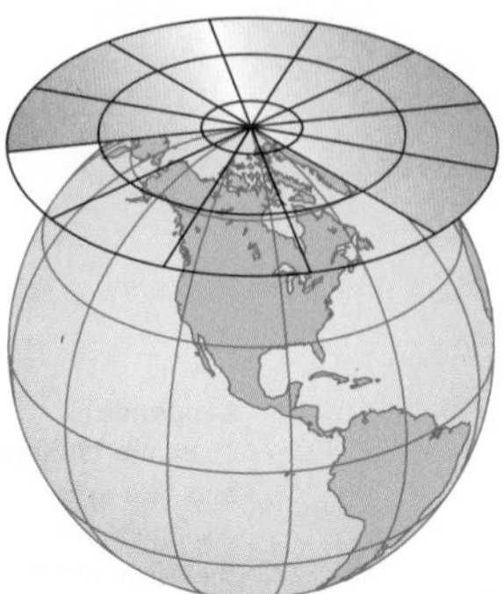

A planar projection is a projection on a flat surface. This projection is also called an azimuthal projection. It distorts size and shape. To the right is a type of planar projection.

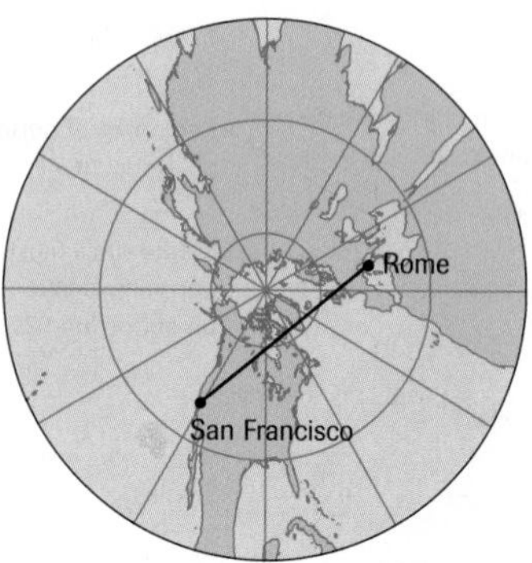

The **azimuthal** projection shows the earth so that a line from the central point to any other point on the map gives the shortest distance between the two points. Size and shape are distorted.

CONICAL PROJECTIONS

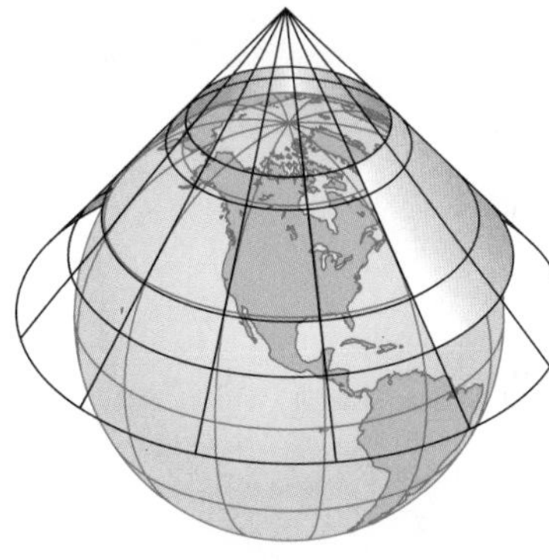

A conical projection is a projection onto a cone. This projection shows shape fairly accurately, but it distorts landmasses at the edges of the map.

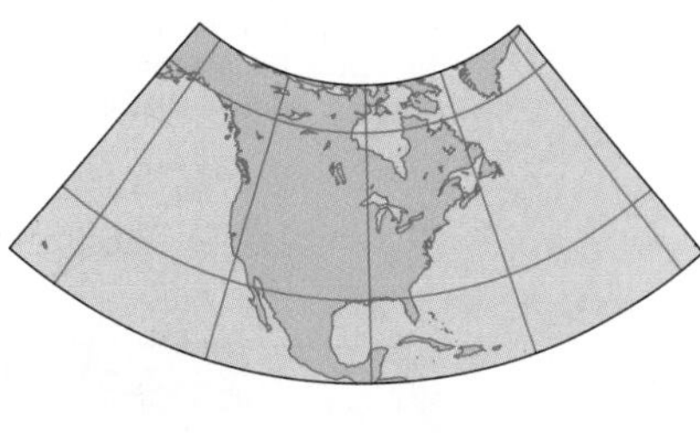

Conical projections are often used to show landmasses that extend over large areas going east and west.

ACTIVITY OPTION | **COOPERATIVE LEARNING**

COMPARING DISTANCES

Task To familiarize students with different projections and the use of map scales

Class Time 30 minutes

Objective Create a chart that compares distances measured on different types of projections

Directions Divide students into groups of four or more students. Provide each group with a list of different types of projections. Within each group, have individual students pick one projection from the list. Students will be responsible for finding a world map that uses the projection he or she chose. When students have located their maps, have them use the maps' scales to measure the distance between the location in which they live and two other locations–one in the United States and another overseas. Ask students to create charts that show the types of projections they used and the results of their measurements using those projections. Lead the class in discussing the results.

COMPROMISE PROJECTIONS

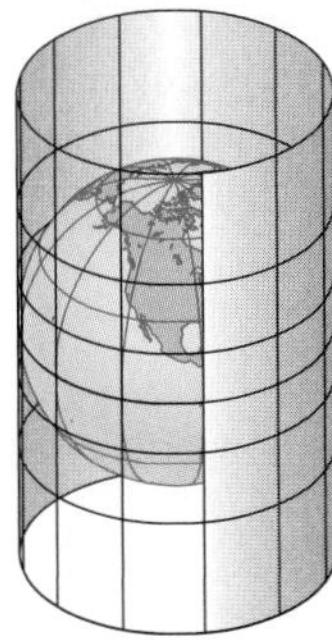

A compromise projection is a projection onto a cylinder. This projection shows the entire earth on one map. Included here are three types of compromise projections.

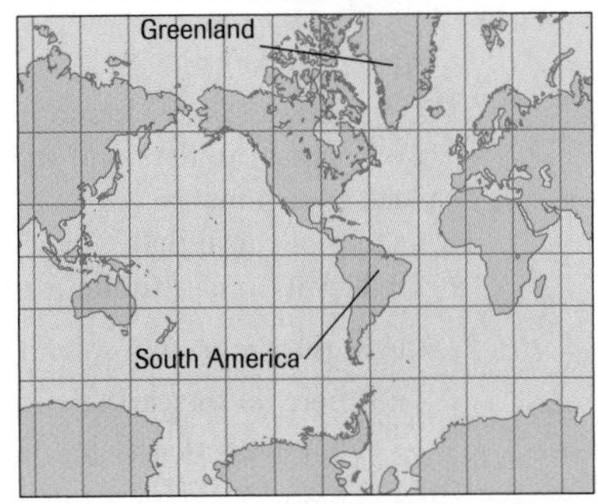

In the compromise projection called **Mercator,** the shapes of the continents are distorted at the poles and somewhat compressed near the equator. For example, the island of Greenland is actually one-eighth the size of South America.

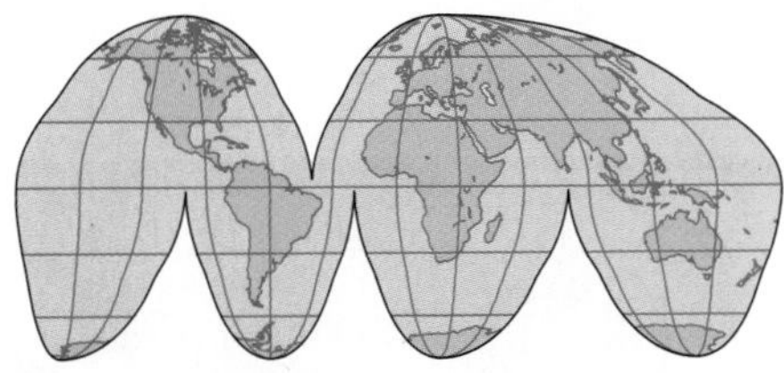

The compromise projection called **homolosine** is sometimes called an "interrupted map," because the oceans are divided. This projection shows the accurate shapes and sizes of the landmasses, but distances on the map are not correct.

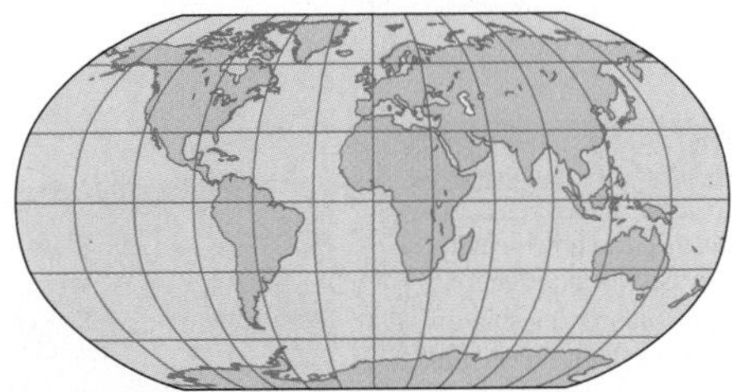

A **Robinson** projection is a type of compromise projection, commonly used in textbooks. It shows the entire earth with nearly the true sizes and shapes of the continents and oceans. However, the shapes of the landforms near the poles appear flat.

Map Practice

Use pages 14–19 to help you answer these questions. Look at the map on page 15 to answer questions 1–3.

1. How are colors used on this map?
2. Is the map a large-scale or a small-scale map? How do you know?
3. What is the approximate longitude of Buenos Aires?
4. What are the names of three lines of latitude besides the equator?
5. Which projections show shape of landmasses most accurately?

MAKING COMPARISONS Look at the maps in the atlas in this book. Create a **database** that shows the projection and scale of each map. Write a summary of your findings.

More About

Projections

Projections may seem like a dull subject, but they can create heated debates. In 1974, a German cartographer named Arno Peters introduced his "Peters' Projection." He claimed that his new world map showed more accurate proportions than maps with traditional projections–which he considered biased toward developed countries. These claims were hotly contested by cartographers. The first English version of the map was published in 1983, and it continues to cause controversy.

GEOGRAPHY SKILLS HANDBOOK ANSWERS

1. The colors show types of economic activity in Southwest Asia.
2. The map is a small-scale map because it shows a large area without much detail.
3. approximately 51° East longitude
4. Arctic Circle, Tropic of Cancer, Tropic of Capricorn
5. The conical, homolosine, and Robinson projections show the shape of landmasses most accurately.

GeoActivity

Integrated Assessment
- Rubric for a database, 2.6

Instruct: Objective 5

Using Different Types of Maps

- What is the purpose of a physical map? *(to show landforms and bodies of water)*
- How does a physical map represent relief? *(with color, shading, and contour lines)*
- What is the purpose of a political map? *(to show features of the earth's surface created by humans, such as countries, states, cities, and other political entities, such as Congressional voting districts)*

More About

Sea Level

Elevations are based on a landform's distance above or below sea level. But what if one sea is higher than another? And what if the level of the sea changes, for example, with the change of tides? For these reasons geographers measure elevation using "global mean sea level"—the height of the surface of the sea averaged over all tidal stages and over long periods of time.

Using Different Types of Maps

PHYSICAL MAPS Physical maps help you see the types of landforms and bodies of water found in a specific area. By studying the map, you can begin to understand the relative location and characteristics of a place or region.

On a physical map, color, shading, or contour lines are used to indicate elevation or altitude, also called relief.

Ask these questions about the physical features shown on a map:
- Where on the earth's surface is this area located?
- What is its relative location?
- What is the shape of the region?
- In which direction do the rivers flow? How might the direction of flow affect travel and transportation in the region?
- Are there mountains or deserts? How do they affect the people living in the area?

South Asia: Physical

On this map the green colors show land at lower elevations. As the elevation rises, the color turns to light brown, and the peaks of mountains are dark brown.

Elevation
13,100 ft. (4,000 m.)
6,600 ft. (2,000 m.)
1,600 ft. (500 m.)
650 ft. (200 m.)
0 ft. (0 m.)
Below sea level
▲ Mountain peak

0 250 500 miles
0 250 500 kilometers
Two-Point Equidistant Projection

ACTIVITY OPTION **INTERNET RESEARCH**

WRITING A RESEARCH REPORT

Objective To learn more about the use of sea level as a basis for determining elevation

Class Time 30 minutes

Task Write a report on the measurement of sea level using information gathered on the Internet

Directions Have students use the Internet to investigate sea level as a basis for determining elevation. They might examine the history of sea-level measurement, the causes of fluctuations in sea levels, how these fluctuations are measured, how global mean sea level is defined and measured, etc. Ask students to use their research to write a short report. Have students include a visual component in their reports to clarify difficult ideas and concepts.

OPTIONAL ACTIVITY If Internet access is limited, have students use the library for this activity. Ask the librarian to show students how to use the *Readers' Guide to Periodical Literature* and other indexes to find articles on sea level.

POLITICAL MAPS Political maps show features on the earth's surface that humans created. Included on a political map may be cities, states, provinces, territories, or countries.

Ask these questions about the political features shown on a map:

- Where on the earth's surface is this area located?
- What is its relative location? How might the location affect the economy or foreign policy of a place?
- What is the shape and size of the country? How might shape or size affect the people living in the country?
- Who are the neighbors in the region, country, state, or city?
- How populated does the area seem to be? How might that affect activities there?

South Asia: Political

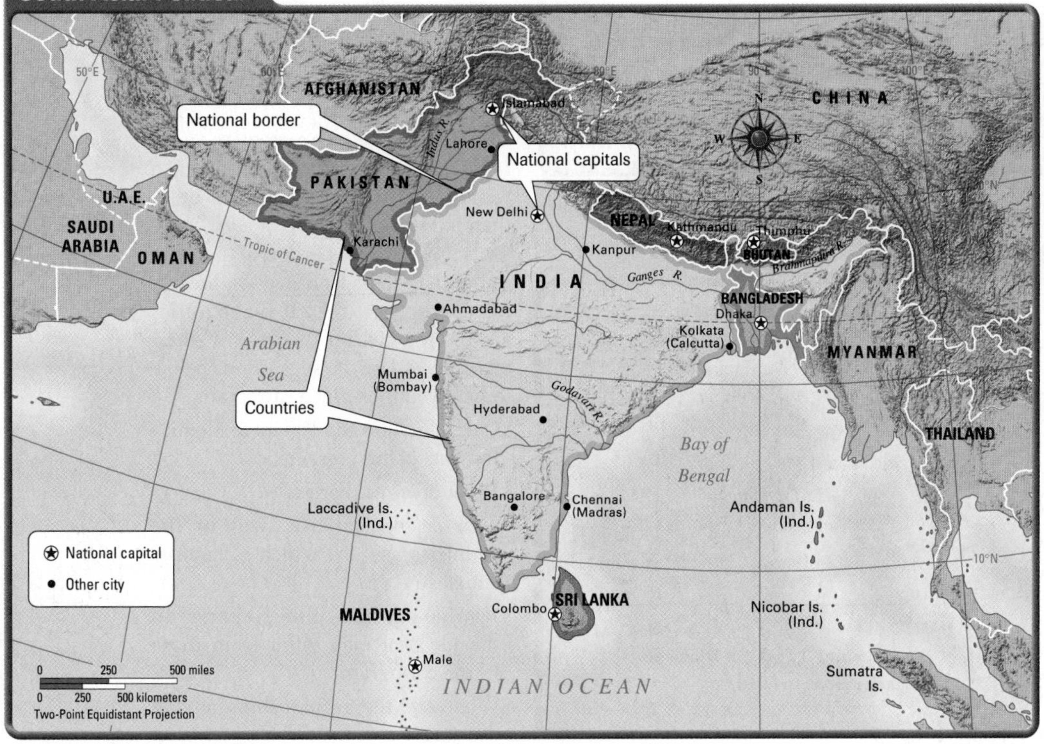

More About

Political Boundaries

The boundaries we see on political maps are not always as fixed as they seem. Boundary disputes even occur in the United States. Recently, the U.S. Supreme Court had to settle a dispute between New York and New Jersey. Leaders in each state argued that part of Ellis Island, the historic entry point for millions of immigrants to the United States, fell within their borders. In May 1998, the Supreme Court decided in favor of New Jersey.

More About

Political Boundaries

Tell students that the drawing of political boundaries becomes a heated issue every time the United States carries out its decennial census. That is because each new census influences the location and shape of congressional voting districts. Political officials, often from opposing political groups, must cooperate in adjusting old borders or drawing new ones that reflect the most recent census numbers. Recently, some of these negotiations, in North Carolina, for example, have resulted in conflicts that the U.S. Supreme Court has had to resolve.

ACTIVITY OPTION | COOPERATIVE LEARNING

RESEARCHING BOUNDARY DISPUTES

Objective To have students examine contested political boundaries

Class Time 30 minutes

Task Create a chart with maps and descriptions of border disputes

Directions Select four continents to be the objects of study. Divide students into small groups. Have them count off by fours and assign each subgroup a specific continent. Then have students use newspapers, magazines, or the Internet to find stories about disputed political borders. Ask students to select a number of articles discussing different conflicts. Then have them work together to create a chart that summarizes the conflicts. On one side of the chart they should include maps that show the contested borders. On the other side, they should write short synopses of the origins of the disputes and their current status.

Instruct: Objective 5

Thematic Maps

- What are thematic maps? *(maps that focus on specific types of information)*
- What are some examples of thematic maps? *(maps that show climate, population density, vegetation, etc.)*
- What are some of the different ways in which thematic maps are presented? *(as qualitative and flow-line maps and cartograms)*

More About

Rome's Cultural Legacy

Rome's influence traveled across the Atlantic Ocean when Spanish explorers sailed to the New World in the 15th century. The Romance language of these explorers would later spread across large areas of North and South America. In the United States today, Spanish is spoken by most of the nation's over 46 million Hispanic inhabitants.

Thematic Maps

Geographers also rely on thematic maps, which focus on specific types of information. For example, in this textbook you will see thematic maps that show climate, vegetation, natural resources, population density, and economic activities. Some thematic maps illustrate historical trends, and others may focus on the movement of people or ideas. These maps may be presented in a variety of ways.

Cultural Legacy of the Roman Empire

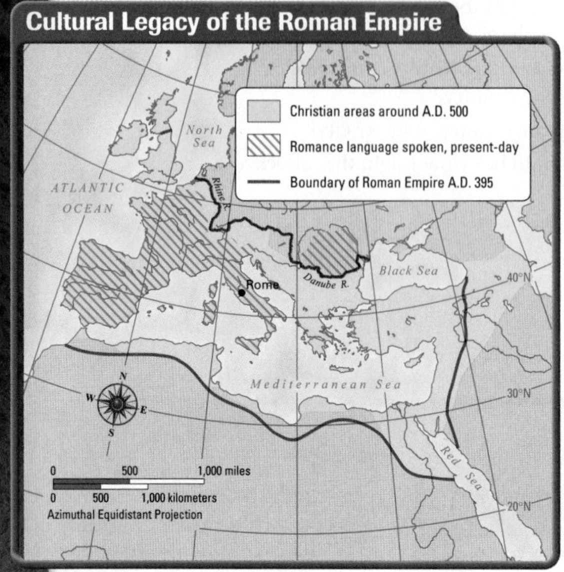

QUALITATIVE MAPS Qualitative maps use colors, symbols, dots, or lines to help you see patterns related to a specific idea. The map shown to the left shows the influence of the Roman Empire on Europe, North Africa, and Southwest Asia. Use the suggestions below to help you interpret a map.

- Check the title to identify the theme and data being presented.
- Study the legend to understand the theme and the information presented.
- Look at physical or political features of the area. How might the theme of the map affect them?
- What are the relationships among the data?

Estimated World Oil Reserves

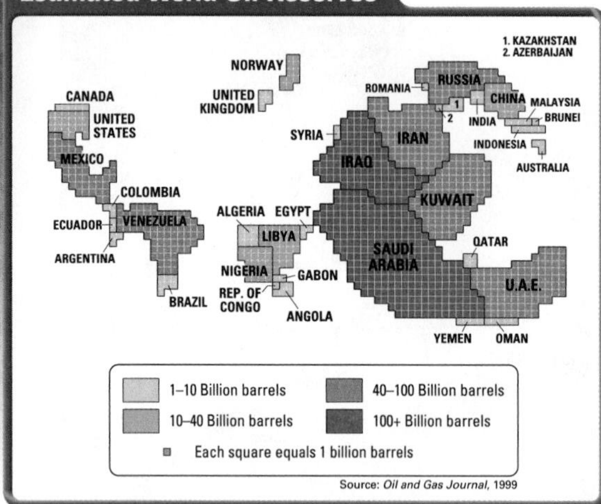

CARTOGRAMS In a cartogram, geographers present information about a country based on a set of data other than land area. The size of each country is drawn in proportion to that data rather than to its land size. On the cartogram shown to the left, the countries are represented on the basis of their oil reserves. Use the suggestions below to help you interpret a cartogram.

- Check the title and legend to identify the data being presented.
- What do sizes represent?
- Look at the relative sizes of the countries shown. Which is largest? smallest?
- How do the sizes of the countries on the physical map differ from those in the cartogram?
- What are the relationships among the data?

ACTIVITY OPTION **FIVE THEMES OF GEOGRAPHY**

PLACE

Exploring the Themes When we ask the question "What is it like?" we are often referring to place. When we describe a place, we might refer to that place's physical features, such as climate, or to its cultural characteristics, such as language or ethnicity.

Understanding the Theme Cartograms are useful for showing the characteristics of a place and how one place differs from another. In the map above, the characteristic is oil reserves. Each place (in this case, countries) is represented as larger or smaller depending on the quantity of its reserves. Ask students:

- What other political units, besides states, might be represented on a cartogram? *(states or provinces, counties, cities and towns, neighborhoods, census precincts, etc.)*
- What other features of a place might a cartographer represent on a cartogram? *(water resources, deserts, forests, religions, roads, home ownership—anything that can be measured)*

FLOW-LINE MAPS Flow-line maps illustrate movement of people, goods, ideas, animals, or even glaciers. The information is usually shown in a series of arrows. Location, direction, and scope of movement can be seen. The width of the arrow may show how extensive the flow is. Often the information is given over a period of time. The map shown to the right portrays the movement of the Bantu peoples in Africa. Use the suggestions below to help you interpret a flow-line map.

- Check the title and legend to identify the data being presented.
- Over what period of time did the movement occur?
- In what direction did the movement occur?
- How extensive was the movement?

Remember that the purpose of a map is to show a location and provide additional information. Be sure to look at the type of map, scale, and projection. Knowing how maps present the information will help you interpret the map and the ideas it presents.

Bantu Migrations

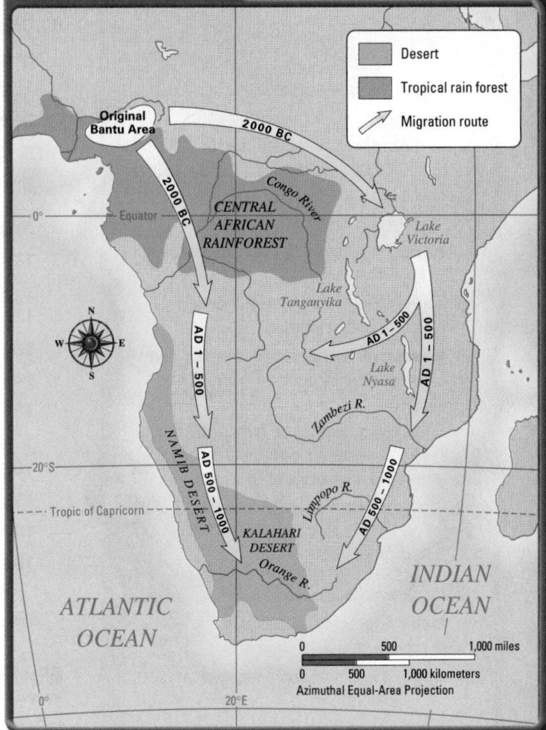

Desert
Tropical rain forest
Migration route

Original Bantu Area · 2000 BC · 2000 BC · AD 1 – 500 · AD 1 – 500 · AD 1 – 500 · AD 500 – 1000 · AD 500 – 1000

CENTRAL AFRICAN RAINFOREST · NAMIB DESERT · KALAHARI DESERT · Congo River · Zambezi R. · Limpopo R. · Orange R. · Lake Victoria · Lake Tanganyika · Lake Nyasa · Equator · Tropic of Capricorn · ATLANTIC OCEAN · INDIAN OCEAN

0 500 1,000 miles
0 500 1,000 kilometers
Azimuthal Equal-Area Projection

Map Practice

Use pages 20–23 to help you answer these questions. Use the maps on pages 20–21 to answer questions 1–3.

1. In what direction does the Ganges River flow?
2. China is the northern neighbor of which countries?
3. Which city is closer to the Thar Desert–Lahore, Pakistan or New Delhi, India?
4. Why are so few nations shown on the cartogram?
5. Which of the thematic maps would best show the location of climate zones?

EXPLORING LOCAL GEOGRAPHY Obtain a physical–political map of your state. Use the data on it to create two separate **maps.** One should show physical features only, and one should show political features only.

Interpreting Maps

Bantu Migrations

Have students examine the map on page 23. Ask them when the Bantu migrations began and when the Bantu arrived at the Orange River in southern Africa. *(The migrations began around 2000 BC. The Bantu arrived at the Orange River between AD 500 and 1000.)*

Reteaching Activity

Have students make a list of the main subheadings from the Geography Skills Handbook (Finding Location; Reading a Map; Scale, etc.). For each subheading, students should write a sentence that describes the most important thing they learned from the information under that subheading.

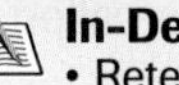
In-Depth Resources: Unit 1
- Reteaching Activity, p. 12

GEOGRAPHY SKILLS HANDBOOK ANSWERS

1. It flows east and then turns south.
2. Pakistan, India, Nepal, Bhutan, Myanmar
3. Lahore, Pakistan
4. Only the nations with oil reserves are shown. Most nations do not have oil reserves.
5. A qualitative map would be best.

GeoActivity

Integrated Assessment
- Rubric for a map, 2.1

Reviewing Places & Terms

A. 1. geography, p. 5
2. hemisphere, p. 6
3. equator, p. 6
4. prime meridian, p. 6
5. latitude, p. 6
6. longitude, p. 6
7. globe, p. 10
8. map, p. 10
9. cartographer, p.10
10. map projection, p. 10

B. Possible Responses

11. Latitude lines circle the earth.
12. The Prime Meridian marks the beginning.
13. Longitude has 180° in each hemisphere.
14. Hemispheres are divided north and south or east and west.
15. The equator separates the Northern and Southern hemispheres.
16. Longitude lines are also called meridians.
17. Cartographers work on maps and globes.
18. Map projections are needed to represent our 3-dimensional world in 2 dimensions.
19. Longitude, latitude, and possibly equator and prime meridian, are elements of the grid.
20. Geography characterizes the study of the use of land space.

Chapter 1 Assessment

VISUAL SUMMARY
LOOKING AT THE EARTH

The Five Themes of Geography

Location
- **Absolute Location** uses latitude and longitude.
- **Relative Location** uses relationships to other places.

Place This explains the characteristics of an area.

Region This looks at a larger area with similar characteristics.

Movement People, plants, animals, and ideas move through time and across space.

Human–Environment Interaction Humans interact with the environment to adjust to it or to alter it.

The Geographer's Tools

Globe A three-dimensional representation of the earth

Map A two-dimensional representation of the earth

Mapmaking
- Area is surveyed.
- High-tech tools, including satellites, are used to gather data and create maps.

Geography Skills Handbook

Map Elements Maps have elements such as a legend to aid in interpreting them.

Scale This determines how much detail is shown on a map.

Grid Gridlines help to determine absolute location.

Projection This shows the earth's surface in two dimensions but distorts either size, shape, direction, or area.

Types of Maps These include physical, political, and thematic, such as qualitative, cartographic, or flow-line.

Reviewing Places & Terms

A. Briefly explain the importance of each of the following.

1. geography
2. hemisphere
3. equator
4. prime meridian
5. latitude
6. longitude
7. globe
8. map
9. cartographer
10. map projection

B. Answer the questions about vocabulary in complete sentences.

11. Which of the above terms indicate imaginary parallel lines that circle the earth?
12. Which term marks the beginning of longitude?
13. Which of the above terms has 180° in each hemisphere?
14. How may hemispheres be divided?
15. What imaginary line separates the Northern Hemisphere from the Southern Hemisphere?
16. Which term is also known as a meridian line?
17. Would a cartographer work on a map or a globe?
18. Why are map projections needed?
19. Which of the above terms are associated with the geographic grid?
20. Which term characterizes the study of the use of land space?

Main Ideas

The Five Themes of Geography (pp. 5–9)

1. How is absolute location different from relative location?
2. What are some examples of information that would be included in a place description?
3. How is place different from region?
4. Why do geographers study movement?

The Geographer's Tools (pp. 10–13)

5. What is the purpose of a map?
6. How do satellites aid in mapmaking?
7. Why is GIS a valuable tool for examining the geography of a place?

Geography Skills Handbook (pp. 14–23)

8. How is the use of small-scale maps different from the use of large-scale maps?
9. In what ways may relief be shown on a map?
10. What are three types of thematic maps?

Main Ideas

1. Absolute location gives an exact position of a feature on the earth's surface. Relative location describes the feature's relationship to other features on the earth.
2. Physical features such as rivers or mountains, human-made features such as cities, highways, and cultural aspects may be a part of place description.
3. Place describes what a location is like. Region describes how places are similar or different.
4. Geographers study movement to understand how people, goods, and ideas move from place to place.
5. A map shows locations of places on the earth and of one place relative to another.
6. Satellites provide accurate data for a map.
7. It allows geographers to view many different aspects of a specific place.
8. Small-scale maps show large areas with less detail. Large-scale maps show smaller areas but with more detail.
9. Color, shading, or contour lines can be used to show relief.
10. Thematic maps include cartograms, and qualitative, flow-line, vegetation, climate, population density, historical, natural resources, and economic activities maps.

Critical Thinking

1. Using Your Notes

Use your completed chart to answer these questions.

5 Themes:
Tools:

a. How are relative location and place related?

b. How do thematic maps help geographers understand the five themes?

2. Geographic Themes

a. **REGION** Write a sentence describing a region that your community is a part of. Be sure to identify the region and give reasons for your answer.

b. **MOVEMENT** How are linear and time distances related to the theme of movement?

3. Identifying Themes

Into which two hemispheres would an island at 50°S, 60°W be placed? Which of the five themes are reflected in your answer?

4. Drawing Conclusions

Why was it necessary for geographers to develop a grid system?

5. Seeing Patterns

Into which formal region, functional region, and perceptual region might your community be placed?

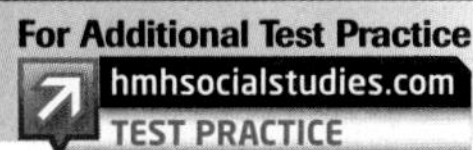

Geographic Skills: Interpreting Maps

Continents of the World

Use the map to answer the following questions.

1. **LOCATION** What is the absolute location of the continent of Australia?
2. **LOCATION** What is the relative location of South America?
3. **PLACE** What body of water is located at 45° N, 45° W?

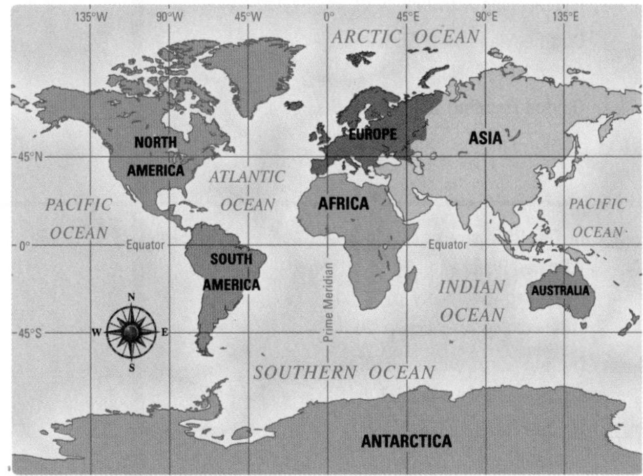

With a partner, choose and record the latitude and longitude of five locations on the map at left. Then trade your list with another set of partners. Have them search for the coordinates on your list, and do the same with their list. Then check the accuracy of the findings.

hmhsocialstudies.com

MULTIMEDIA ACTIVITY

21st CENTURY

Use the links at **hmhsocialstudies.com** to do research about GIS. Take notes on the ways GIS can be used to provide geographic information for mapmaking, site selection, and simulating environmental effects.

Creating a Multimedia Presentation Using the information you gathered about GIS, create a multimedia presentation explaining the various aspects of GIS and how it helps geographers and others solve problems.

CHAPTER 1 ASSESSMENT

Critical Thinking

1. a. Relative location may be a part of the description of the characteristics of a place.
b. A thematic map allows geographers to focus on one specific theme or idea.

2. a. Answers will vary but most likely will include a state designation. Answers should include reasons.
b. People may move across spaces that are measured in a linear way or in terms of the time it takes to cross a specific linear distance.

3. Southern Hemisphere, Western Hemisphere; location–absolute

4. Because the earth is round, it is necessary to create a method of marking a location. Without the grid system, there would be no accurate reference points.

5. Answers will vary.

GeoActivity

Integrated Assessment
- Rubric for a list, 2.2

Formal Assessment
- Chapter Test, Forms A, B, and C, pp. 7–18

Geographic Skills

1. approximately 15°-40° S, 110°-150°E

2. South America is south of North America and west of Africa.

3. the Atlantic Ocean

BASICS

MULTIMEDIA ACTIVITY

For their multimedia presentation on GIS, students should:

- Discuss the types of information that can be stored in a GIS.
- Include a section on the application of GIS information.
- Provide examples of how GIS is used.

Grading Rubric Evaluate student performances as Exceptional, Acceptable, or Poor in each of the following categories.

	Exceptional	Acceptable	Poor
Utilizes two or more media			
Clearly demonstrates an understanding of the concepts presented			
Uses a format that aids the viewer in accessing the information			
Shows technical proficiency			

CHAPTER 2 PLANNING GUIDE

Physical Geography: A Living Planet

OVERVIEW	INSTRUCTIONAL RESOURCES	
ESSENTIAL QUESTION What physical forces shape our planet? **Focus on the Essential Question Podcast**	**In-Depth Resources: Unit 1** • Building Vocabulary, p. 18 **Block Schedule Strategies** **Chapter Summaries** (English/Spanish) **Video:** Viewing the Planets hmhsocialstudies.com INTERACTIVE	**Interactive Online Edition** TOS **ExamView® Assessment Suite** (English/Spanish) TOS **CalendarPlanner** **Power Presentations with Media Gallery** **Critical Thinking Transparencies** • CT2
SECTION 1 **THE EARTH INSIDE AND OUT** **MAIN IDEAS** • The earth is the only habitable planet in the solar system. • The earth consists of a series of shells that float on one another. • The theory of continental drift explains the formation of the continents.	**In-Depth Resources: Unit 1** • Guided Reading, p. 13 • Building Vocabulary, p. 18 • Reteaching Activities, p. 19 **Outline Maps with Activities** • World: Physical, pp. 1–2 **Guided Reading Workbook,** Section 1	**Video:** Seeing Asteroids and Meteors
SECTION 2 **BODIES OF WATER AND LANDFORMS** **MAIN IDEAS** • Water covers three-fourths of the earth's surface and makes life possible. • The water on earth is continuously circulated between the atmosphere, the oceans, and the earth. • The ocean floor and the continents have similar landforms.	**In-Depth Resources: Unit 1** • Guided Reading, p. 14 • Building Vocabulary, p. 18 • Reteaching Activities, p. 20 **Outline Maps with Activities** • Ocean Currents, pp. 7–8 **Guided Reading Workbook,** Section 2	**Map Transparencies** • MT4 Oceans in Relief
SECTION 3 **INTERNAL FORCES SHAPING THE EARTH** **MAIN IDEAS** • The earth's crust consists of a number of tectonic plates. • The movement of the tectonic plates continually reshapes the surface of the earth. • Movement of the plates produces earthquakes and volcanoes.	**In-Depth Resources: Unit 1** • Guided Reading, p. 15 • Skillbuilder Practice, p. 17 • Building Vocabulary, p. 18 • Reteaching Activities, p. 21 **Guided Reading Workbook,** Section 3	**Map Transparencies** • MT5 Drifting Continents
SECTION 4 **EXTERNAL FORCES SHAPING THE EARTH** **MAIN IDEAS** • Weathering and erosion alter the surface of the earth. • Water, wind, and glaciers cause erosion that produces a variety of landforms. • Weathering and erosion help form soil.	**In-Depth Resources: Unit 1** • Guided Reading, p. 16 • Building Vocabulary, p. 18 • Reteaching Activities, p. 22 **Guided Reading Workbook,** Section 4	**Critical Thinking Transparencies** • CT34 What Causes the Earth to Change? **Map Transparencies** • MT6 Natural Hazards

ASSESSMENT

SE **Chapter Assessment,** pp. 46–47

Formal Assessment
- Chapter Tests, Forms A, B, and C, pp. 23–34

TOS **ExamView® Assessment Suite**

Strategies for Test Preparation

hmhsocialstudies.com TEST PRACTICE

SE **Section Assessment,** p. 29

Formal Assessment
- Section Quiz, p. 19

Integrated Assessment
- Rubric for a description, 4.5
- Rubric for a news article, 4.5

Test Practice Transparencies TT3

SE **Section Assessment,** p. 36

Formal Assessment
- Section Quiz, p. 20

Integrated Assessment
- Rubric for a relief map, 1.10

Test Practice Transparencies TT4

SE **Section Assessment,** p. 41

Formal Assessment
- Section Quiz, p. 21

Integrated Assessment
- Rubric for a database, 2.6

Test Practice Transparencies TT5

SE **Section Assessment,** p. 45

Formal Assessment
- Section Quiz, p. 22

Integrated Assessment
- Rubric for sketches and photographs, 1.3

Test Practice Transparencies TT6

CHART KEY:

SE Student Edition	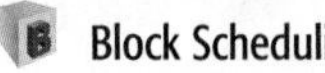 Block Scheduling	DVD/CD-ROM
TE Teacher's Edition	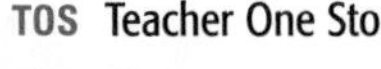 TOS Teacher One Stop	 MP3 Audio
Printable Resource	Presentation Resource	HISTORY™

Program Resources available on TOS and @ hmhsocialstudies.com

SUPPORTING RESOURCES

- Multimedia Classroom Global History Series
- Global History Teacher's Guide

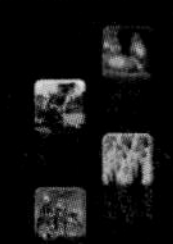

Social Studies Trade Library Collection
- World Regions Trade Collection

For more information or to purchase these resources, go to 

DIFFERENTIATED INSTRUCTION

English Learners	Struggling Readers	Gifted and Talented Students
 **Spanish/English Guided Reading Workbook**  **Access for Students Acquiring English/ESL:** Spanish Translations, pp. 5–9 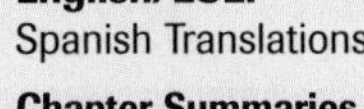 **Chapter Summaries** (English/Spanish) 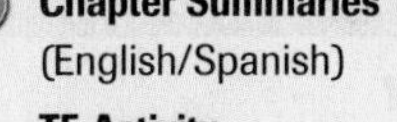 TE **TE Activity** 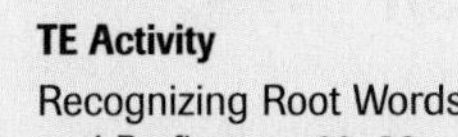 Recognizing Root Words and Prefixes, p. 28, 38	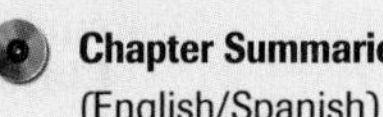 **Chapter Summaries** (English/Spanish) TE **TE Activity** Naming Different Landforms, p. 34	TE **TE Activity** Investigating the Hydrologic Cycle, p. 33

ENRICHMENT ACTIVITIES

The following activities are especially suitable for classes following block schedules.

SE **Student Edition,** p. 26–47
- Disasters! Asteroid Hit, pp. 30–31

hmhsocialstudies.com INTERACTIVE
- The Earth's Interior, p. 28
- Continental Drift Theory, p. 29
- Tectonic Plates, p. 37

BLOCK SCHEDULE LESSON PLAN OPTIONS: 90-MINUTE PERIOD

DAY 1

SECTION 1, pp. 27–29
Class Time 60 minutes

- **Diagrams** Review the section by calling on volunteers to come to the board and create labeled diagrams showing the earth's place in the solar system, the structure of the earth's interior, and the continental drift theory.

SECTION 2, pp. 32-36
Class Time 30 minutes

- **Oral Quiz** Using the Places & Terms list on page 32 and the landforms illustration on pages 34–35, provide definitions of the terms and types of landforms and ask students to identify the correct answers.

DAY 2

SECTION 3, pp. 37-41
Class Time 90 minutes

- **Demonstration** To help students visualize the four types of movement at plate boundaries, ask for two volunteers to use their bodies to demonstrate the movements. Have the two students stand close to each other, then move apart to demonstrate a divergent boundary. For a convergent boundary in which folding occurs, have the students bump into each other and fold up. For a convergent boundary in which subduction occurs, have them again bump into each other; then one should dive under while the other slides over. For a transform boundary, the students should slide past each other.
Class Time 20 minutes
- **Group Presentations** Divide students into groups and assign each group one of the following categories: earthquakes, volcanoes, tsunamis. Have each group do research on one event of their assigned category and give a class presentation on that event.
Class Time 45 minutes
- To review earthquakes, volcanoes, and the Ring of Fire, trace the Ring of Fire on a classroom world map. Ask students to name cities along the Ring of Fire that they know have been sites of earthquakes or volcanic eruptions.
Class Time 25 minutes

DAY 3

SECTION 4, pp. 42-45
Class Time 35 minutes

- **Charting** Lead the entire class in creating two charts, one on weathering and one on erosion. For the weathering chart, use the category headings "Mechanical" and "Chemical" and the topic headings "Definition," "How it happens," and "Agents that cause it." For the erosion chart, use the category headings "Water," "Wind," and "Glacier" and the topic headings "How it happens" and "What it forms."

CHAPTER 2 REVIEW AND ASSESSMENT, pp. 46-47
Class Time 55 minutes

- **Review** Have students review the chapter by using the Visual Summary on page 46. For each main idea listed in the summary, ask students to write three details that elaborate on the subject.
Class Time 20 minutes
- **Assessment** Have students complete the Chapter 2 Assessment.
Class Time 35 minutes

TEACHER-TESTED ACTIVITY *Forces Flip Chart*

Class Time One class period

Task Create a flip chart of the forces that shaped the earth

Supplies
- White paper
- Colored pens, pencils, and markers
- String
- Staplers
- Hole punches
- Glue
- Other decorative materials

Purpose Many students are not familiar with the variety of forces that shape the earth. They will gain a more thorough understanding of the different forces by creating flip charts, which they will then be able to use as a handy reference.

Activity Ask students to use pages 37–44 to compile a list of the different forces that shape the earth, such as earthquakes or erosion. Students should consider both external and internal forces. Have students use the completed lists to come up with a design for their flip charts. They might simply fold sheets of paper in half and staple them together, or the could do something more creative using other materials, as available. After they have prepared their blank flip charts, students can begin explaining and illustrating the forces they have listed. Encourage students to make their flip charts as clear as possible by explaining and illustrating just one force or movement per page.

Patricia Medina
Geography Teacher, Ray High School, Corpus Christi, Texas

The Web offers a huge variety of photographs that can help students understand the geographical concepts they are learning and see what it looks like around the country and the world. Students can generally save these photographs onto their computers and use them in their own multimedia presentations, but they should be sure to give credit to the Web sites where they found the pictures.

Objective Students will view photographs of the United States national parks to see examples of the landforms and bodies of water described in Chapter 2.

Task Have students visit Web sites with pictures of national parks in different regions of the United States. Then have them compile some of the photographs into multimedia presentations with textual descriptions of the landforms and bodies of water shown in the pictures.

Class Time 2–3 class periods

1. Have students read pages 32–36 and look at the diagram on pages 34–35. Ask them to list the geographical features that can be found near their home town.

2. Have students visit the Web sites listed at **hmhsocialstudies.com** and look at pictures for at least ten United States national parklands. They should choose sites from different parts of the country (i.e., Alaska, Hawaii, Pacific coast, Southwestern desert, Great Plains, Southeast, and Northeast). As they go through the pictures, have them look for examples of the landforms and bodies of water described on pages 32–36. Ask them to save pictures of some of the samples they find, making sure to note the URL and title of the Web site the picture came from and the photographer's name, if available.

3. Have students create multimedia presentations that showcase some of the landforms and bodies of water in the national parks. Their presentations should include pictures of at least ten landforms and bodies of water and text descriptions of each one. They should be sure to include credits for the photographs, providing the URL, Web page title, and photographer's name (if known).

CHAPTER 2 OBJECTIVE

Identify key features of the earth's physical geography and the forces shaping it.

Chapter 2

PHYSICAL GEOGRAPHY
A Living Planet

Interpreting Photographs

Ask students to examine this image of the earth taken from space.

Extension Ask students to use a globe or atlas to identify the land masses in the photograph.

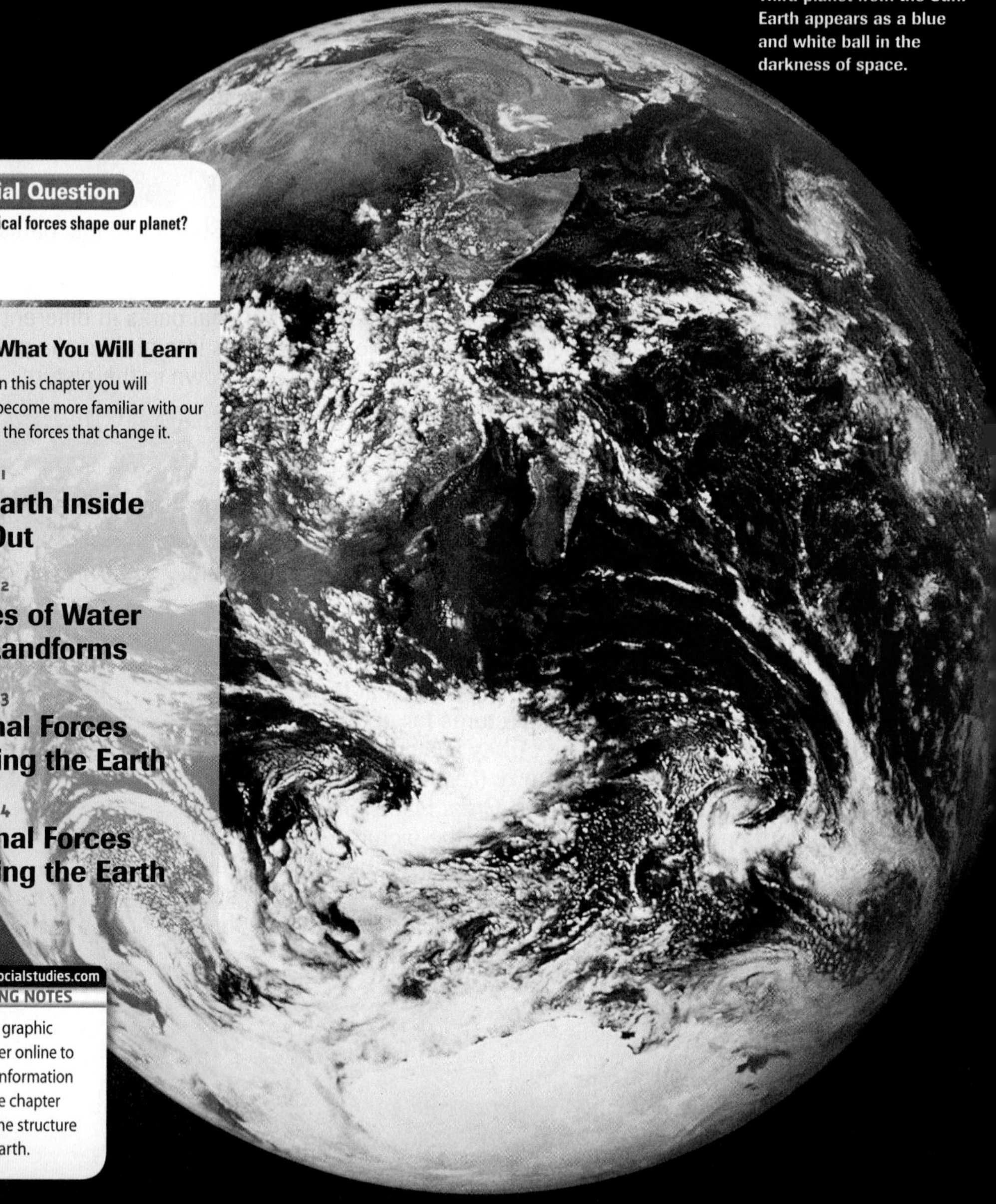

Third planet from the Sun: Earth appears as a blue and white ball in the darkness of space.

Essential Question

What physical forces shape our planet?

What You Will Learn

In this chapter you will become more familiar with our planet and the forces that change it.

SECTION 1
The Earth Inside and Out

SECTION 2
Bodies of Water and Landforms

SECTION 3
Internal Forces Shaping the Earth

SECTION 4
External Forces Shaping the Earth

hmhsocialstudies.com TAKING NOTES

Use the graphic organizer online to record information from the chapter about the structure of the earth.

Introducing the Essential Question

- Point out that our planet is constantly changing. We cannot see the forces that shape the earth's interior unless they cause earthquakes or volcanoes.
- We are more familiar with forces shaping the earth's surface, such as erosion and weathering. Sometimes these processes happen quickly, and sometimes they happen so slowly that we can only see their results.

Have students fill out graphic organizers in their notebooks using material from all sections in this chapter.

Critical Thinking Transparencies CT2
- GeoFocus

In-Depth Resources: Unit 1
- Building Vocabulary, p. 18

CHAPTER 2 ADDITIONAL RESOURCES

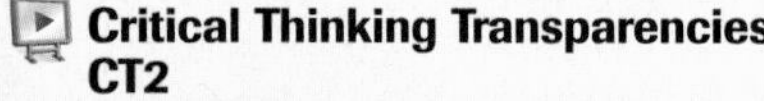

BOOKS FOR THE TEACHER

Kunzig, Robert. ***The Restless Sea.*** NY: W. W. Norton, 1999. Account of current knowledge of the world under the sea.

Mathez, Edmond A., ed. ***Earth: Inside and Out.*** NY: New Press, 2001. Examination of the structure of the earth and the processes shaping it.

BOOKS FOR THE STUDENT

Editors of Time-Life Books. ***Library of Curious and Unusual Facts: Forces of Nature.*** Alexandria, VA: Time-Life Books, 1990. Brief articles on earthquakes, meteorites, glaciers, volcanoes, tsunamis, and other natural forces.

Prager, Ellen. ***Furious Earth: The Science and Nature of Earthquakes, Volcanoes, and Tsunamis.*** NY: McGraw-Hill, 1999. Scientific explanation of tectonic forces and the earthquakes, volcanoes, and tsunamis they produce.

INTERNET

For more about physical geography, visit . . .

hmhsocialstudies.com

The Earth Inside and Out

Main Ideas

- The earth is the only habitable planet in the sun's solar system.
- The drifting of the continents shaped the world we live in today.

Places & Terms

continent	atmosphere
solar system	lithosphere
core	hydrosphere
mantle	biosphere
magma	continental drift
crust	

BASICS

A HUMAN PERSPECTIVE A quick look at a world map will convince you that the **continents,** landmasses above water on Earth, fit together like a huge jigsaw puzzle. South America and Africa are good examples. With imagination, you can see how other continents might fit together as well. The first person to suggest that the seven continents were once all one supercontinent was Englishman Francis Bacon in 1620. Bacon's idea received support in the early 1900s, when scientists found rocks in Africa that matched rocks in South America. Other evidence also supported the idea of a supercontinent millions of years ago.

The Solar System

The "home address" of the earth is the third planet in the solar system of the sun, which is a medium-sized star on the edge of the Milky Way galaxy. Its distance from the sun is 93 million miles. The **solar system** consists of the sun and eight regular planets, as well as other celestial bodies that orbit the sun. The solar system also contains comets, spheres covered with ice and dust that leave trails of vapor as they race through space. Asteroids—large chunks of rocky material—are found in space as well. As you can see in the diagram, our solar system has an asteroid belt between the orbits of Jupiter and Mars.

LOCATION This not-to-scale illustration shows the eight planets and other objects in our solar system. Pluto lost its designation as a planet in 2006. It is now considered a dwarf planet.

SECTION 1 OBJECTIVES

1. Describe the solar system and the earth's location in it.
2. Describe the earth's structure and the forces that created it.

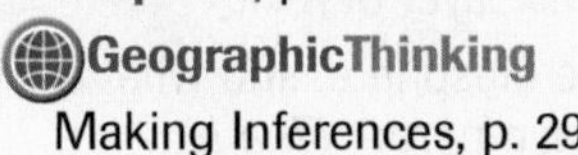

SKILLBUILDER: Interpreting Graphics, p. 28

GeographicThinking Making Inferences, p. 29

Focus & Motivate

What is unique about the earth? *(It is the only planet in our solar system that supports human life.)*

Instruct: Objective 1

The Solar System

- What does the solar system consist of? *(the sun, the eight regular planets, and other celestial bodies that orbit the sun)*
- What are comets and asteroids? *(Comets are spheres covered with ice and dust that leave trails of vapor as they race through space. Asteroids are large chunks of rocky material found in space.)*

In-Depth Resources: Unit 1
- Guided Reading, p. 13

Interpreting Graphics

The Solar System

Direct students' attention to the relative sizes of the eight regular planets and ask them to rank the planets in order of size, from smallest to largest. *(Mercury, Mars, Venus, Earth, Neptune, Uranus, Saturn, Jupiter)*

SECTION 1 PROGRAM RESOURCES

In-Depth Resources: Unit 1
- Guided Reading, p. 13
- Building Vocabulary, p. 18
- Reteaching Activity, p. 19

Guided Reading Workbook
- Section 1

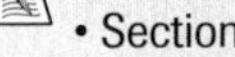
Access for Students Acquiring English/ESL
- Guided Reading, p. 5

Outline Maps with Activities
- World: Physical, pp. 1–2

Formal Assessment
- Section Quiz, p. 19

Integrated Assessment
- Rubric for a description, 4.5
- Rubric for a news article, 4.5

INTEGRATED TECHNOLOGY

Chapter Summaries

Power Presentations

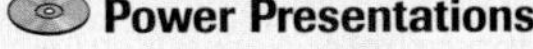
Test Generator
- Section Quiz

hmhsocialstudies.com

TEST-TAKING RESOURCES

Strategies for Test Preparation

Test Practice Transparencies TT3

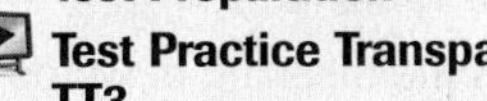
Online Test Practice

Instruct: Objective 2

The Structure of the Earth

- What are the three main layers of the earth, and what do they consist of? *(The core is made up of iron and nickel. The mantle has several layers, and can give rise to magma. The crust is a thin layer of rock.)*
- What is the biosphere, and what are its three main parts? *(The biosphere, where the earth's plants and animals live, consists of the hydrosphere, the lithosphere, and the atmosphere.)*
- What is the continental drift hypothesis? *(The earth's landmass was once a supercontinent that broke into about a dozen plates that slowly drifted apart over millions of years.)*

Outline Maps with Activities
- World: Physical, pp. 1–2

Interpreting Graphics

The Earth's Interior

Point out that this infographic provides additional details about the layers of the earth's surface and interior. Ask students what they notice about the depth of the earth's crust compared to its other layers. *(The crust is very thin compared to the mantle and core, which make up most of the earth's interior.)*

SKILLBUILDER ANSWERS

1. approximately 2,140 miles thick
2. The lithosphere is found in the crust and mantle of the earth.

The Structure of the Earth

The earth is about 24,900 miles in circumference and about 7,900 miles in diameter. Although the earth seems like a solid ball, it is really more like a series of shells that surround one another.

INSIDE THE EARTH The **core** is the center of the earth and is made up of iron and nickel. The outer core is liquid, but the inner core is solid. Surrounding the core is the **mantle,** which has several layers. The mantle contains most of the earth's mass. **Magma,** which is molten rock, can form in the mantle and rise through the **crust,** the thin layer of rock at the earth's surface. Study the diagram below to learn more about the earth's interior.

BACKGROUND Part of the upper portion of the mantle is known as the asthenosphere. It is the hot, but still mostly solid, rock below the cold, brittle rock of the lithosphere.

ON AND ABOVE THE EARTH Surrounding the earth is a layer of gases called the **atmosphere.** It contains the oxygen we breathe, protects the earth from radiation and space debris, and provides the medium for weather and climate. The solid rock portion of the earth's surface is the **lithosphere,** which includes the crust and uppermost mantle. Under the ocean, the lithosphere forms the seafloor. The huge landmasses above water are called continents. There are seven continents: North America, South America, Europe, Asia, Africa, Australia, and Antarctica. The **hydrosphere** is made up of the water elements on the earth, which include oceans, seas, rivers, lakes, and water in the atmosphere. Together, the atmosphere, the lithosphere, and the hydrosphere form the **biosphere,** the part of the earth where plants and animals live.

The Earth's Interior

hmhsocialstudies.com INTERACTIVE

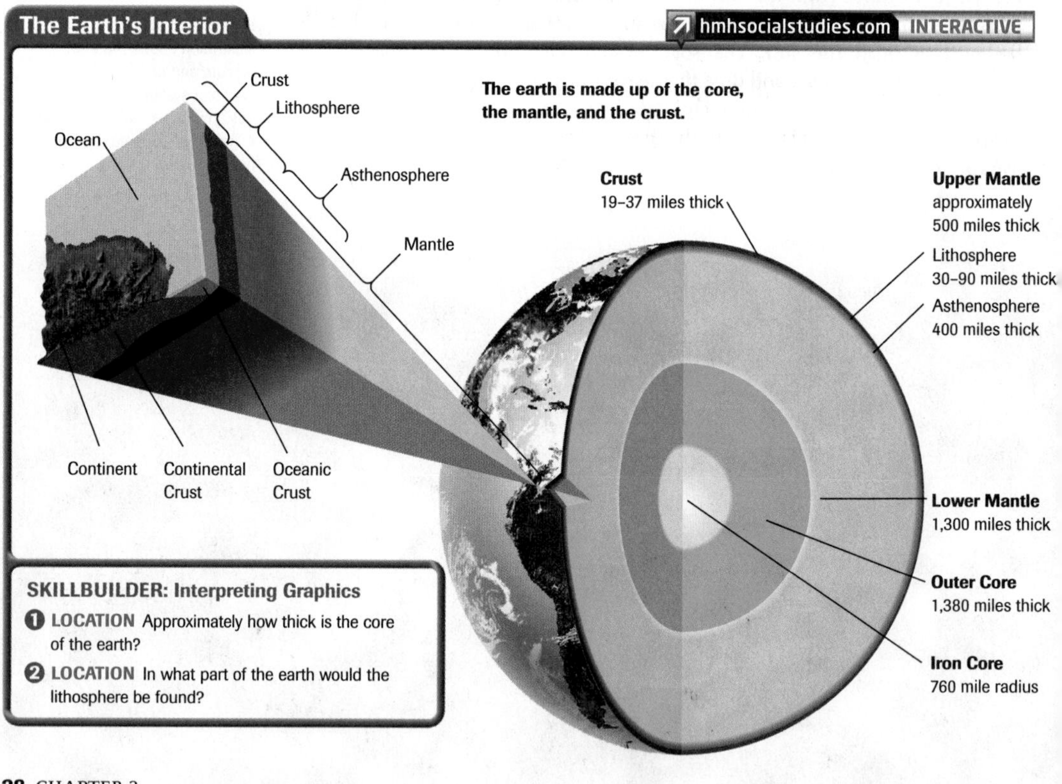

SKILLBUILDER: Interpreting Graphics

1. **LOCATION** Approximately how thick is the core of the earth?
2. **LOCATION** In what part of the earth would the lithosphere be found?

DIFFERENTIATING INSTRUCTION **STUDENTS ACQUIRING ENGLISH/ESL**

RECOGNIZING ROOT WORDS AND PREFIXES

Objective To help students understand words by identifying their roots

Class Time 15 minutes

Task Guess the meaning of words by identifying their roots

Directions Many of the terms in this section have the common root word *sphere.* Identifying the root word and the meaning of prefixes can help students learn and remember these terms. Write the words *atmosphere, lithosphere, hydrosphere,* and *biosphere* on the board. Underline the root *sphere* in each word and explain that the word can refer to anything with a ball-like shape. Explain, or have students guess the meaning of the following prefixes: *atmo* = vapor; *litho* = stone; *hydro* = water; *bio* = life. Then have them guess the words' meanings.

CONTINENTAL DRIFT In 1912, Alfred Wegener of Germany presented a new idea about continents—the **continental drift** hypothesis. It maintained that the earth was once a supercontinent that divided and slowly drifted apart over millions of years. Wegener called the supercontinent Pangaea (from a Greek word meaning "all earth"). An ocean called Panthalassa surrounded it. The supercontinent split into many plates that drifted, crashed into each other, and split apart several times before they came to their current positions. This process occurred over millions of years.

In the 1960s, scientists studying the sea floor discovered that the youngest rocks were in the middle of the ocean, at long cracks in the crust. This suggested that the new sea floor was being added, pushing the continents apart. Later in this chapter, you will learn how the rocks of Earth's surface are broken into giant plates that move and continue to shape the earth.

Continental Drift Theory

hmhsocialstudies.com INTERACTIVE

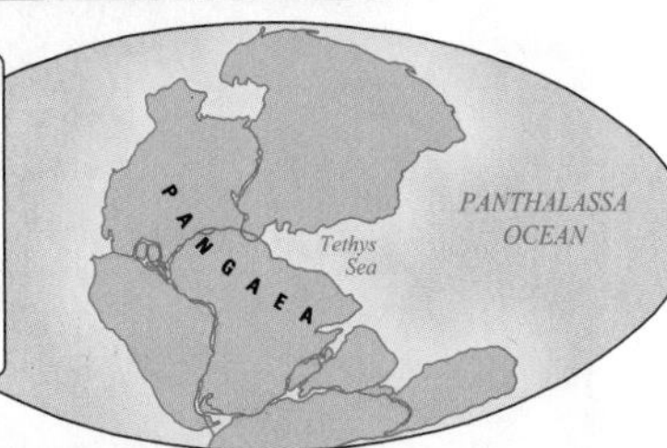

200 million years ago The supercontinent now called *Pangaea* was surrounded by an ocean, Panthalassa.

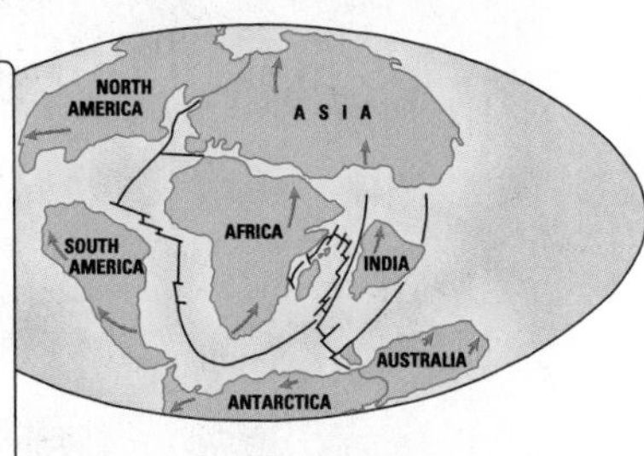

65 million years ago The supercontinent split apart and began moving in different directions. Notice that India broke away from Antarctica and Australia and drifted toward Asia.

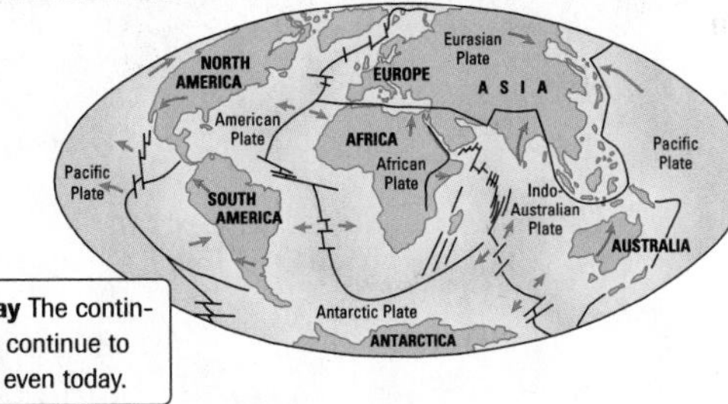

Today The continents continue to drift even today.

Interpreting Graphics

Continental Drift Hypothesis

Have students examine the three illustrations and call on volunteers to describe the general direction that each continent and India moved. *(North America and South America moved northwest; Europe, Asia, Africa, and India moved north; Australia moved northeast; and Antarctica moved southwest.)*

Assess & Reteach

GeoFocus Have students complete the section on the earth's structure in their graphic organizers.

Formal Assessment
- Section Quiz, p. 19

Reteaching Activity

Divide students into four groups and assign one of the following topics to each group: (1) the earth's location in the solar system, (2) the structure of the earth's interior, (3) the elements of the biosphere, and (4) the continental drift theory. Have each group create a diagram to explain their topic to the class.

In-Depth Resources: Unit 1
- Reteaching Activity, p. 19

SECTION 1 Assessment

1 Places & Terms

Identify and explain where on the earth these terms would be found.
- continent
- mantle
- magma
- crust
- biosphere

2 Taking Notes

PLACE Review the notes you took for this section.

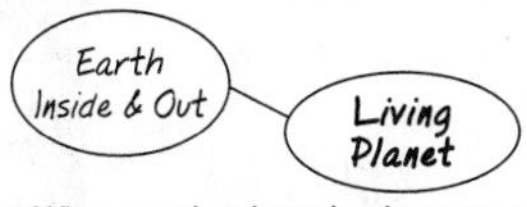

- What are the three basic parts of the earth's interior?
- What are four basic spheres found on or above the earth?

3 Main Ideas

a. What makes up the interior of the earth?

b. What makes up the biosphere?

c. How can the presence of seven continents on the earth's surface be explained?

4 Geographic Thinking

Making Inferences How do the earth's spheres influence one another? **Think about:**
- the function of the atmosphere
- the makeup of the biosphere

See Skillbuilder Handbook, page R4.

MAKING COMPARISONS Study the diagrams of continental drift on this page. Write a **description** of the location of the continents in the past in comparison with their current location.

SECTION 1 ASSESSMENT ANSWERS

1. Places & Terms

continent, p. 27
mantle, p. 28
magma, p. 28
biosphere, p. 28
crust, p. 28

2. Taking Notes
- core, mantle, crust
- atmosphere, lithosphere, hydrosphere, and biosphere

3. Main Ideas

a. The earth's interior is made up of an iron and nickel core and outer core, the mantle, and the transition zone leading to the crust.

b. The biosphere is made up of the atmosphere, lithosphere, and hydrosphere.

c. They are the result of the breakup of the supercontinent.

4. Geographic Thinking

The atmosphere and the hydrosphere make it possible for the biosphere to exist. The biosphere is where the lithosphere, atmosphere, and hydrosphere interact.

GeoActivity

Integrated Assessment
- Rubric for a description, p. 4.5

OBJECTIVES

1. Explain the series of events that caused the extinction of the dinosaurs.
2. Write and illustrate a news account of an asteroid hit.
3. Identify characteristics of asteroids.

Instruct: Objective

Asteroid Hit!

- Where and when did the asteroid that killed off the dinosaurs hit? *(near Chicxulub on the Yucatan Peninsula of Mexico, about 65 million years ago)*
- What was the immediate impact of the asteroid hit? *(It dug a huge crater, vaporized limestone and seawater, and created a fireball that caused fires thousands of miles away.)*
- How did the asteroid hit change life on earth, and how long did the effects last? *(The skies darkened for several months, acid rain poisoned lakes and rivers, and about 70 percent of all species died out. A greenhouse effect existed for perhaps a thousand years. Some plants and animals survived.)*

Interpreting Maps

Chicxulub, Mexico

Based on the site of the impact, what continents do you think the asteroid affected most? *(North and South America)*

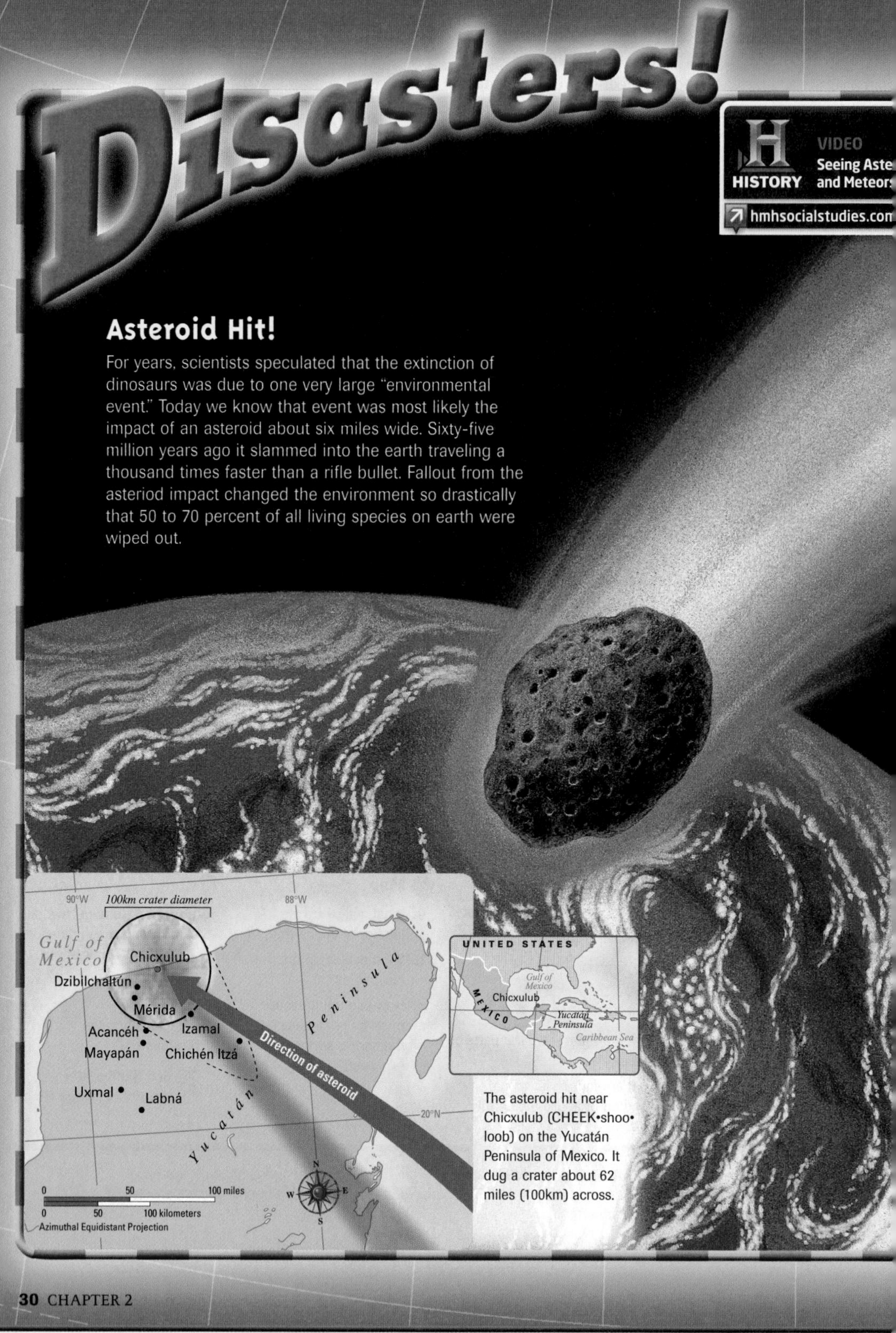

Disasters!

HISTORY VIDEO Seeing Aste
and Meteor
hmhsocialstudies.com

Asteroid Hit!

For years, scientists speculated that the extinction of dinosaurs was due to one very large "environmental event." Today we know that event was most likely the impact of an asteroid about six miles wide. Sixty-five million years ago it slammed into the earth traveling a thousand times faster than a rifle bullet. Fallout from the asteriod impact changed the environment so drastically that 50 to 70 percent of all living species on earth were wiped out.

The asteroid hit near Chicxulub (CHEEK•shoo•loob) on the Yucatán Peninsula of Mexico. It dug a crater about 62 miles (100km) across.

30 CHAPTER 2

SUPPORTING RESOURCES

BOOKS FOR THE TEACHER

Frankel, Charles. ***The End of the Dinosaurs.*** Cambridge, England: Cambridge University Press, 1999. An account of the history of the asteroid impact theory.

Lewis, John S. ***Rain of Iron and Ice.*** Reading, MA: Addison-Wesley, 1996. Scientific evidence for past and potential future asteroid hits.

BOOKS FOR THE STUDENT

Alvarez, Walter. ***T. rex and the Crater of Doom.*** Princeton, NJ: Princeton University Press, 1997. Story of the discovery of the Chicxulub crater by one of the discoverers.

Gribbon, John and Mary. ***Fire on Earth.*** NY: St. Martin's Press, 1996. Examination of how asteroid and comet collisions have affected human history.

VIDEO

Asteroids: Deadly Impact. National Geographic Television, 1997. Examination of the evidence of asteroid hits.

PERIODICALS

McKelway, Margaret. ***Identified Flying Objects.*** *National Geographic World,* July 1995, 1-6. Discussion of the dinosaur extinction theory and Chicxulub crater.

Winters, Jeffrey. ***Flying Rubble.*** *Discover,* August 1996, 26. Discussion of the composition of asteroids.

hmhsocialstudies.com INTERACTIVE

The asteroid plows into the earth at 150,000 mph, vaporizing limestone and seawater. It creates an immense fireball that causes fires thousands of miles away.

GeoActivities

CREATING A FRONT PAGE 

With a small group, use the Internet to research the Chicxulub event. Then create the front page of a **newspaper** describing the event.

- Create a map showing the impact area.
- Add an article describing the destruction caused by the asteroid.
- Write an interview with a scientist who predicts event results.

The Earth's skies are darkened for several months by 25 trillion tons of rock, dust, and smoke from the impact. Acid rain created by vaporized minerals poisons lakes and rivers. Food chains collapse, and plants and animals die.

A thick layer of carbon dioxide is trapped in the atmosphere, creating a "greenhouse effect" for perhaps a thousand years or more. Ferns, burrowing mammals, and some freshwater animals survive. Some even thrive in the new climate.

GeoData

ASTEROIDS

- Asteroids are small planetary bodies that orbit the sun.
- There are an estimated 50,000 asteroids in our solar system.
- Asteroids range in size from 20 feet to 580 miles in diameter.
- Fragments of asteroids that reach the earth are called meteorites.

TUNGUSKA EVENT

On June 30, 1908, at about 7:30 A.M., an explosion occurred over the Tunguska region of Siberia. This event might have been an asteroid hit.

- The force of the explosion was estimated at between 10 and 20 megatons of TNT.
- The fireball and explosion were seen and felt 500 miles away.
- Five hundred thousand acres of forest were flattened and burned.
- More than 600 grazing reindeer were roasted instantly.
- No crater could be found.

GeoActivities

Newspaper Page

Have each student in the group take responsibility for a particular task, including the design of the newspaper page.

Integrated Assessment
- Rubric for a news article, 4.5

More About

The Chicxulub Event

Meteorite-like objects found in present-day Belize support the theory of an asteroid impact at Chicxulub. The impact sent debris from earth soaring high above the atmosphere. When the material fell back to earth, it became superheated upon reentry, taking on the characteristic molten and hardened surface of meteorites.

ACTIVITY OPTION — COOPERATIVE LEARNING

RESEARCHING IN DIFFERENT MEDIA

Objective To explore different media in order to learn more about the Tunguska event

Class Time 30 minutes

Task Use the Internet, books, magazines, and newspapers to learn about the Tunguska event

Directions Divide students into different groups. Have each student carry out research on the Tunguska event in a different medium: Internet, magazines, newspapers, and books. After the completion of their research, have students compile their research and discuss positive and negative aspects of the different media.

SECTION 2 OBJECTIVES

1. Describe the components of the water system on earth.
2. Identify the characteristics of oceanic and continental landforms.

SKILLBUILDER: Interpreting Graphics, p. 33

GeographicThinking
Using the Atlas, p. 36
Making Comparisons, p. 36

Instruct: Objective 1

Bodies of Water

- How does the motion of the ocean help distribute heat on earth? *(Winds blow over the ocean and are either heated or cooled by the water. Winds, as they blow over the land, moderate temperatures.)*
- How does the hydrologic cycle work? *(Water from bodies of water and plants evaporates. This vapor cools, condenses, and falls to the earth as precipitation. It then flows back into bodies of water.)*

In-Depth Resources: Unit 1
- Guided Reading, p. 14

Outline Maps with Activities
- Ocean Currents, pp. 7–8

Interpreting Photographs

Iguaçu Falls

In 1984, UNESCO declared Iguaçu Falls a World Heritage Site. Ask students why UNESCO may have done so. *(because of the falls' unique beauty; to help protect and preserve the site)*

Bodies of Water and Landforms

Main Ideas
- Water covers about three-fourths of the earth's surface.
- The earth's surface displays a variety of landforms.

Places & Terms
hydrologic cycle
drainage basin
ground water
water table
landform
continental shelf
relief
topography

A HUMAN PERSPECTIVE In July 1971, astronaut James Irwin was lifted into space on the Apollo 15 mission. As he circled the earth, he was deeply moved by the beauty of our planet. Later he wrote this:

> Anyone passing through our solar system would be attracted to the blue planet. They would know that the blue color indicated water on Earth. They would know that where there is water there is probably life. They might try to meet us. We, the blue planet, stand out as a beacon to all.

The earth is unlike any other observable planet in our solar system. It is a living planet.

Bodies of Water

Without both freshwater and saltwater, life on this planet would be impossible. Water not only supports plants and animals, it helps distribute heat on the earth.

OCEANS AND SEAS The ocean is an interconnected body of salt water that covers about 71 percent of our planet. It covers a little more than 60 percent of the Northern Hemisphere and about 81 percent of the Southern Hemisphere. Even though it is one ocean, geographers divide it into four main parts: the Atlantic Ocean, the Pacific Ocean, the Indian Ocean, and the Arctic Ocean, which is sometimes considered part of the Atlantic. The largest of the oceans is the Pacific. The waters near Antarctica are sometimes called the Southern Ocean.

OCEAN MOTION The salty water of the ocean circulates through three basic motions: currents, waves, and tides. Currents act like rivers flowing through the ocean. Waves are swells or ridges produced by winds. Tides are the regular rises and falls of the ocean created by the gravitational pull of the moon or the sun. The motion of the ocean helps distribute heat on the planet. Winds blow over the ocean and are either heated or cooled by the water. When the winds eventually blow over the land, they moderate the temperature of the air over the land.

HYDROLOGIC CYCLE The **hydrologic cycle** is the continous circulation of water between the atmosphere, the oceans, and the earth. As you can see in

PLACE Iguaçu Falls at the Argentina-Brazil border has 275 separate waterfalls varying between 200 and 269 feet high. It is nearly three times wider than Niagara Falls in North America.

SECTION 2 PROGRAM RESOURCES

In-Depth Resources: Unit 1
- Guided Reading, p. 14
- Building Vocabulary, p. 18
- Reteaching Activity, p. 20

Guided Reading Workbook
- Section 2

Access for Students Acquiring English/ESL
- Guided Reading, p. 6

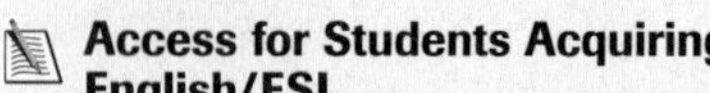

Outline Maps with Activities
- Ocean Currents, pp. 7–8

Formal Assessment
- Section Quiz, p. 20

Integrated Assessment
- Rubric for a relief map, 1.10

INTEGRATED TECHNOLOGY

Map Transparencies MT4
- Oceans in Relief

Test Generator

Power Presentations

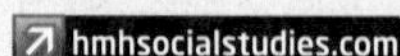

hmhsocialstudies.com

TEST-TAKING RESOURCES

Strategies for Test Preparation

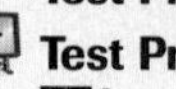

Test Practice Transparencies TT4

Online Test Practice

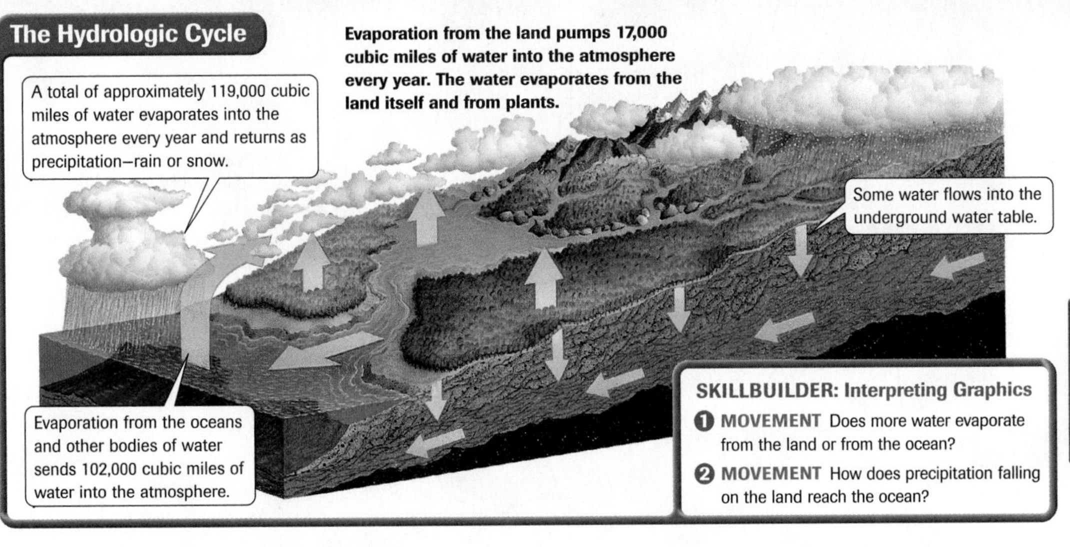

The Hydrologic Cycle
Evaporation from the land pumps 17,000 cubic miles of water into the atmosphere every year. The water evaporates from the land itself and from plants.
A total of approximately 119,000 cubic miles of water evaporates into the atmosphere every year and returns as precipitation–rain or snow.
Some water flows into the underground water table.
Evaporation from the oceans and other bodies of water sends 102,000 cubic miles of water into the atmosphere.

SKILLBUILDER: Interpreting Graphics

1. **MOVEMENT** Does more water evaporate from the land or from the ocean?
2. **MOVEMENT** How does precipitation falling on the land reach the ocean?

BASICS

the diagram above, water evaporates into the atmosphere from the surface of the oceans, other bodies of water, and from plants. The water exists in the atmosphere as vapor. Eventually, the vapor cools, condenses, and falls to earth as precipitation—rain or snow. The water soaks into the ground, evaporates to the atmosphere, or flows into rivers to be recycled.

LAKES, RIVERS, AND STREAMS Lakes hold more than 95 percent of all the earth's fresh water supply. The largest freshwater lake is Lake Baikal in Russia. Its volume of water equals 18 percent of all freshwater on earth. Freshwater lakes like the Great Lakes of North America are the result of glacial action thousands of years ago. Saltwater lakes result from changes in the earth's surface that cut off outlets to the sea. Saltwater lakes are created when creeks and rivers carry salts into a lake, and there is no outlet to carry the salt away. The Great Salt Lake in Utah is the remnant of a large freshwater lake—Lake Bonneville. Its water outflows were cut off, causing the remaining water to become more salty as the water evaporated. The largest saltwater lake is the Caspian Sea in Western Asia.

Rivers and streams flow through channels and move water to or from larger bodies of water. Rivers and streams connect into drainage systems that work like the branches of a tree, with smaller branches, called tributaries, feeding into larger and larger ones. Geographers call an area drained by a major river and its tributaries a **drainage basin.**

GROUND WATER Some water on the surface of the earth is held by the soil, and some flows into the pores of the rock below the soil. The water held in the pores of rock is called **ground water.** The level at which the rock is saturated marks the rim of the **water table.** The water table can rise or fall depending on the amount of precipitation in the region and on the amount of water pumped out of the ground.

BACKGROUND Rock layers that store water are called aquifers. The largest U.S. aquifer is the Ogallala Aquifer, which runs from South Dakota south to Texas.

Landforms

Landforms are naturally formed features on the surface of the earth. The diagram on pages 34–35 shows the different kinds of landforms.

Interpreting Infographics

The Hydrologic Cycle

Point out that the amount of water on earth is constant; the water just changes form and moves from place to place. Ask students where most precipitation falls. *(on the oceans–the oceans cover 71 percent of the planet)*

SKILLBUILDER ANSWERS

1. the ocean **2.** It runs off into rivers or goes into underground water tables that feed into streams.

Instruct: Objective 2

Landforms

- What is the topography of the ocean floor like? *(It has landforms similar to those found above water–ridges, valleys, canyons, and plains.)*
- What is the main geographic feature that distinguishes different types of landforms? *(relief, or the difference in elevation from the lowest to the highest point)*
- What are the four categories of relief? *(mountains, hills, plains, and plateaus)*

Map Transparencies MT4
- Oceans in Relief

DIFFERENTIATING INSTRUCTION GIFTED AND TALENTED STUDENTS

INVESTIGATING THE HYDROLOGIC CYCLE

Objective To familiarize students with the movement of pollution through the hydrologic cycle

Class Time 30 minutes

Task Research the Gulf of Mexico's "dead zone"

Directions The hydrologic cycle provides an excellent example of the interconnectedness of life on earth. Interested students might investigate how pesticides and fertilizers used on farms and suburban lawns enter the hydrologic cycle and cause pollution problems far from their source. Have students conduct research on the "dead zone" in the Gulf of Mexico caused by chemicals used on farms in the Mississippi River drainage basin. They might present their findings in an oral or written report, a diagram with captions, or an illustrated map.

Interpreting Graphics

Landforms at a Glance

Explain that all these landforms do not usually occur in such close proximity in the real world. Ask students to name regions of the United States or world where you would find certain types of landforms. *(volcanoes in the Pacific Northwest; prairies in the Midwest; mesas, buttes, and deserts in the Southwest; and steppes in Russia)*

Landforms at a Glance

hmhsocialstudies.com INTERACTIVE

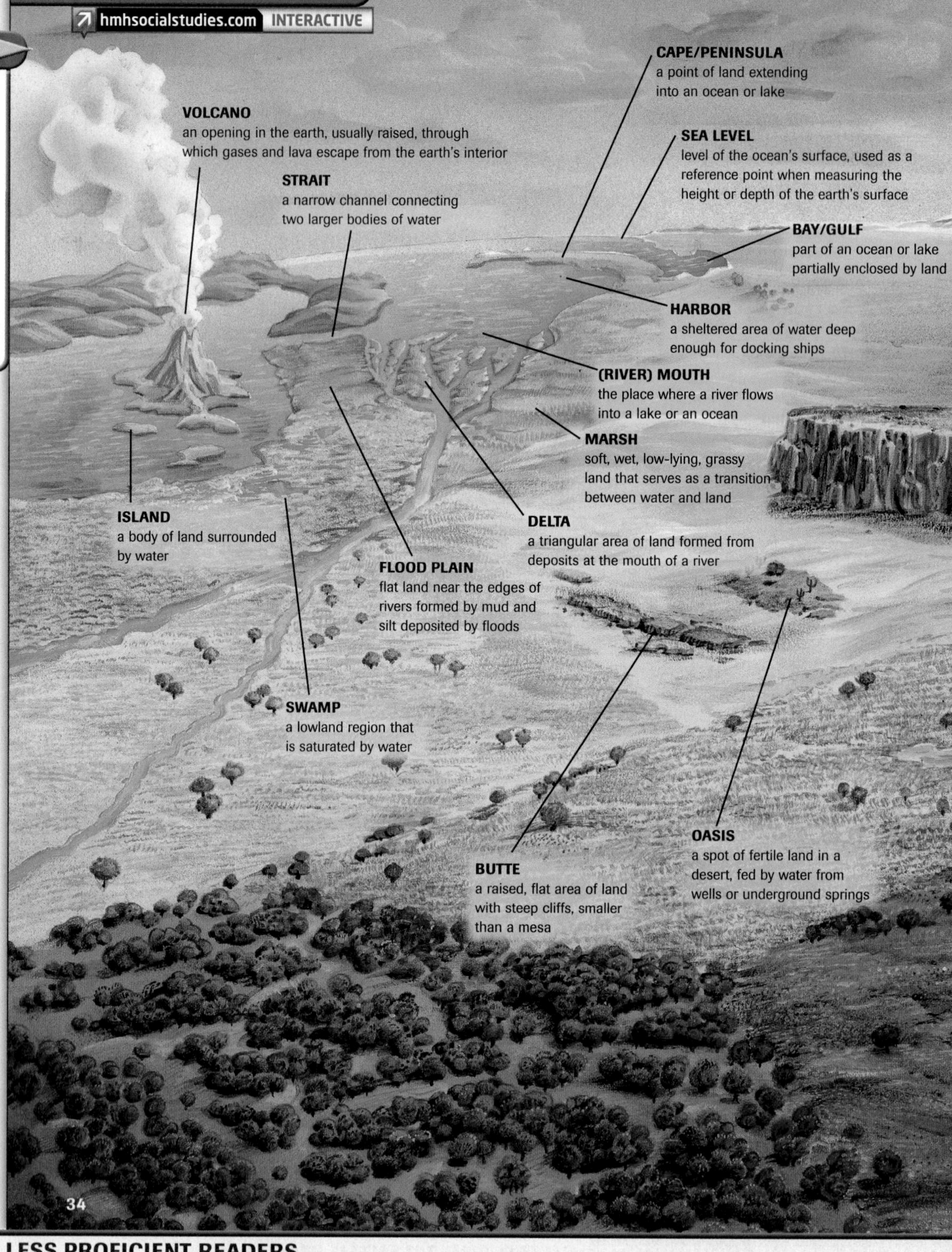

CAPE/PENINSULA
a point of land extending into an ocean or lake
VOLCANO
an opening in the earth, usually raised, through which gases and lava escape from the earth's interior
SEA LEVEL
level of the ocean's surface, used as a reference point when measuring the height or depth of the earth's surface
STRAIT
a narrow channel connecting two larger bodies of water
BAY/GULF
part of an ocean or lake partially enclosed by land
HARBOR
a sheltered area of water deep enough for docking ships
(RIVER) MOUTH
the place where a river flows into a lake or an ocean
MARSH
soft, wet, low-lying, grassy land that serves as a transition between water and land
ISLAND
a body of land surrounded by water
DELTA
a triangular area of land formed from deposits at the mouth of a river
FLOOD PLAIN
flat land near the edges of rivers formed by mud and silt deposited by floods
SWAMP
a lowland region that is saturated by water
OASIS
a spot of fertile land in a desert, fed by water from wells or underground springs
BUTTE
a raised, flat area of land with steep cliffs, smaller than a mesa
34

DIFFERENTIATING INSTRUCTION LESS PROFICIENT READERS

NAMING DIFFERENT LANDFORMS

Objective To familiarize students with the names of landforms

Class Time 15 minutes

Task Associate the names of specific landforms with maps, illustrations, and photographs of those forms

Directions In the form of maps, illustrations, and photographs, collect different examples of the various types of landforms shown on pages 34 and 35. One by one, hold up the images in front of the class. After they have identified the specific landform by referring to pages 34 and 35 in their textbooks, have students pronounce the name of the specific landform aloud.

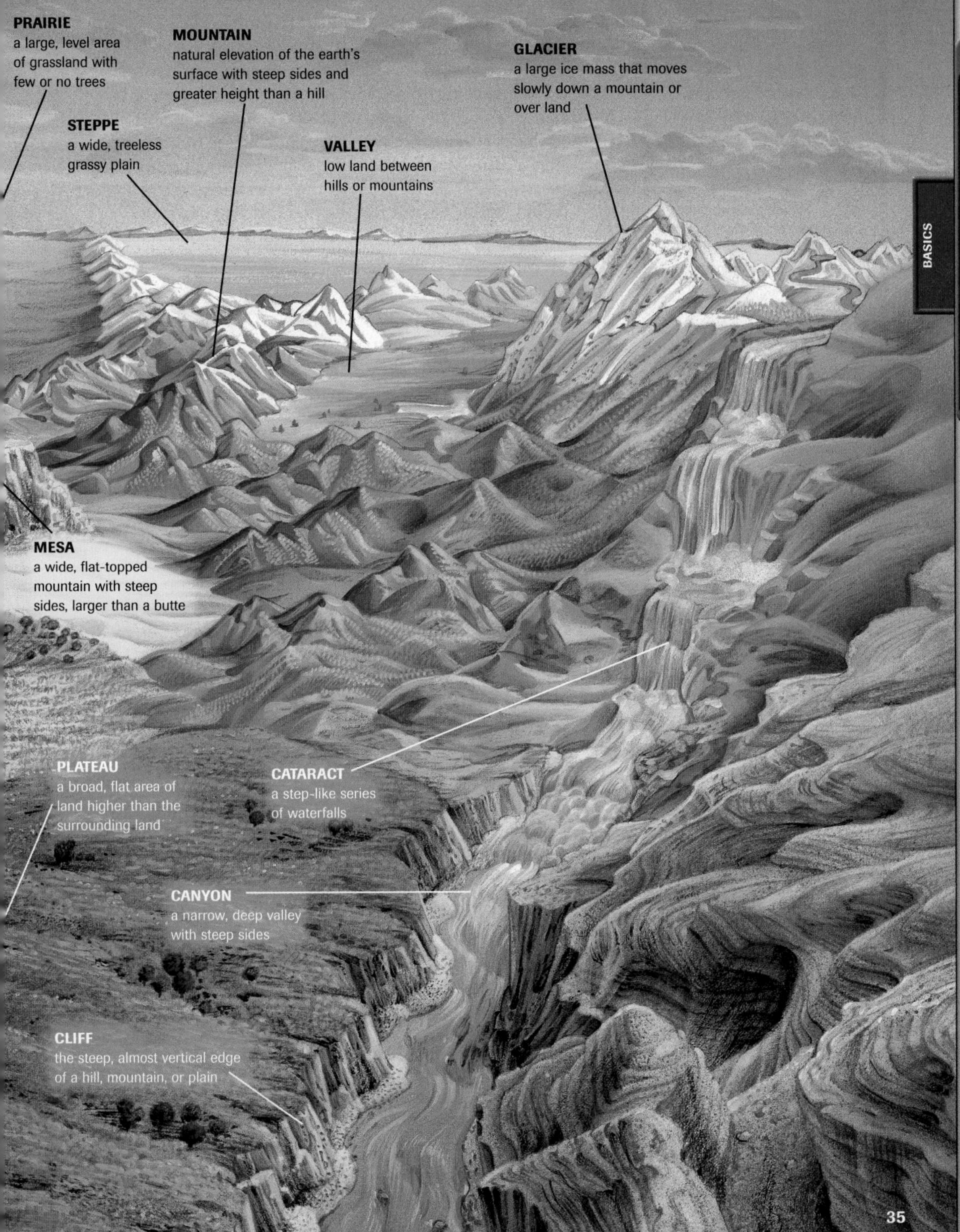
PRAIRIE
a large, level area of grassland with few or no trees
MOUNTAIN
natural elevation of the earth's surface with steep sides and greater height than a hill
GLACIER
a large ice mass that moves slowly down a mountain or over land
STEPPE
a wide, treeless grassy plain
VALLEY
low land between hills or mountains
BASICS
MESA
a wide, flat-topped mountain with steep sides, larger than a butte
PLATEAU
a broad, flat area of land higher than the surrounding land
CATARACT
a step-like series of waterfalls
CANYON
a narrow, deep valley with steep sides
CLIFF
the steep, almost vertical edge of a hill, mountain, or plain
35

More About

Landforms

Large plains with few or no trees go by different names in different parts of the world. There are the prairies of the Midwestern United States, the steppes of Russia, the veldts of South Africa, the savannas of central and eastern Africa, the *llanos* of Venezuela, the *pampas* of Argentina, and the *campos* of Brazil. Technically, prairies have tall grasses, and steppes have short grasses.

ACTIVITY OPTION EXPLORING LOCAL GEOGRAPHY

ILLUSTRATING LOCAL LANDFORMS

Objective To illustrate the topography of a local area

Class Time 20 minutes

Task Use a map and firsthand observations to create an illustration of local topography

Directions Direct students to create an illustration similar to the one on these two pages but showing the landforms of their local region. The size of the area students choose to include in their illustrations may vary. Suggest that they use a state or regional map and draw upon their own knowledge to create their illustrations. Direct students to label all the landforms in their illustrations.

Region: The Everglades

The Everglades was once a very shallow, free-flowing river that traveled 100 miles from Lake Okeechobee to the Gulf of Mexico. Although it was just a few inches deep, its width reached up to 50 miles. The Everglades National Park of today covers only one-tenth of the original wetland—the rest of the area was drained and developed. Ask students what characteristics distinguish the Everglades as a formal region. *(landform, vegetation, climate, wildlife)*

Assess & Reteach

GeoFocus Have students complete the section on bodies of water and landforms in their graphic organizers.

Formal Assessment
- Section Quiz, p. 20

Reteaching Activity
Have students work in small groups to write short-answer quizzes covering the main ideas in this section. Direct groups to exchange quizzes and write the answers.

In-Depth Resources: Unit 1
- Reteaching Activity, p. 20

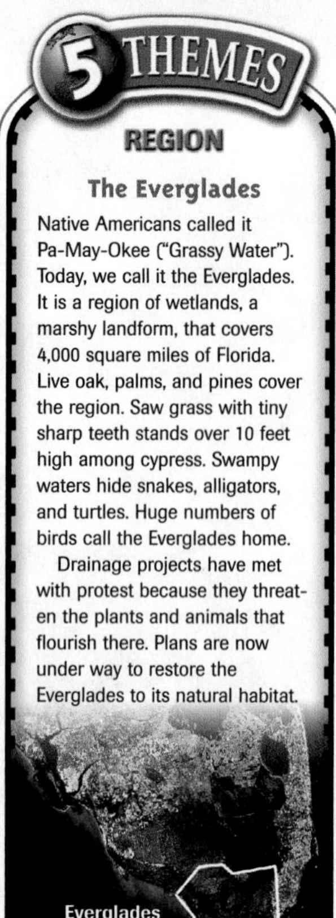

5 THEMES
REGION
The Everglades
Native Americans called it Pa-May-Okee ("Grassy Water"). Today, we call it the Everglades. It is a region of wetlands, a marshy landform, that covers 4,000 square miles of Florida. Live oak, palms, and pines cover the region. Saw grass with tiny sharp teeth stands over 10 feet high among cypress. Swampy waters hide snakes, alligators, and turtles. Huge numbers of birds call the Everglades home.
Drainage projects have met with protest because they threaten the plants and animals that flourish there. Plans are now under way to restore the Everglades to its natural habitat.
Everglades National Park

OCEANIC LANDFORMS The sea floor has landforms similar to those above water. The earth's surface from the edge of a continent to the deep part of the ocean is called the **continental shelf.** The floor of the ocean has ridges, valleys, canyons, and plains. Ridges mark places where new crust is being formed on the edges of the tectonic plates. Mountain chains similar to those on the continents themselves cover parts of the ocean floor. The longest continuous range is the Mid-Atlantic Ridge, which extends for thousands of miles north to south through the middle of the Atlantic Ocean. Islands dot the ocean surface. Islands can be formed by volcanic action, deposits of sand, or deposits of coral skeletons.

CONTINENTAL LANDFORMS To understand the types of landforms, study the illustration on pages 34–35. The major geographic feature that separates one type of landform from another is relief. **Relief** is the difference in elevation of a landform from its lowest point to its highest point. There are four categories of relief: mountains, hills, plains, and plateaus. A mountain, for instance, has great relief compared with a plain, which displays very little difference between its high and low points. A

Topography is the combination of the surface shape and composition of the landforms and their distribution in a region. A topographic map shows the landforms with their vertical dimensions and their relationship to other landforms.

In the next section, you will learn how internal forces of the earth help to build and change the landforms on the earth—and how those forces affect humans.

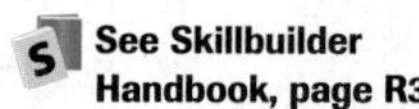

Using the Atlas
A Use the map on pages A18–A19 to determine the relief of your state.

Section 2 Assessment

1 Places & Terms
Explain the meaning of each of the following terms.
- hydrologic cycle
- ground water
- continental shelf
- relief
- topography

2 Taking Notes
MOVEMENT Review the notes you took for this section.

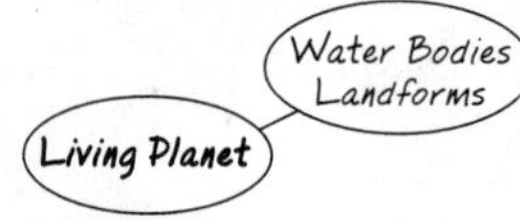

- How does the hydrologic cycle circulate water?
- How does ocean water circulate?

3 Main Ideas
a. How do the winds and the ocean distribute heat on the earth's surface?
b. How are relief and topography related?
c. How are islands formed?

4 Geographic Thinking
Making Comparisons How is the floor of the ocean similar to land above sea level? **Think about:**
- mountain chains
- other landforms

See Skillbuilder Handbook, page R3.

SEEING PATTERNS Study the Landforms at a Glance diagram on pages 34–35. Choose a part of it to reproduce in a three-dimensional **relief map.** Be sure to label the landforms clearly.

SECTION 2 ASSESSMENT ANSWERS

1. Places & Terms
hydrologic cycle, p. 32
ground water, p. 33
continental shelf, p. 36
relief, p. 36
topography, p. 36

2. Taking Notes
- Water from the surface of the earth evaporates into the atmosphere. It condenses and returns to the earth as precipitation.
- Water circulates by tides, waves, and currents.

3. Main Ideas
a. As winds blow over the ocean, they are either heated or cooled by the water. When they blow over land, they change the land temperature.
b. Relief is the difference in elevation of a landform. Topography is the relief for an entire region.
c. Islands are formed by volcanic action, deposits of sand, or by coral skeletons.

4. Geographic Thinking
There are mountain chains, valleys, canyons, and ridges both above and below the ocean.

GeoActivity

Integrated Assessment
- Rubric for a relief map, 1.10

Internal Forces Shaping the Earth

Main Ideas

- Internal forces reshape the earth's surface.
- Internal forces shaping the earth often radically alter the lives of people as well.

Places & Terms

tectonic plate	**Richter scale**
fault	**tsunami**
earthquake	**volcano**
seismograph	**lava**
epicenter	**Ring of Fire**

BASICS

SECTION 3 OBJECTIVES

1. Explain plate tectonics.
2. Identify the cause and effects of earthquakes.
3. Describe the action and location of volcanoes.

SKILLBUILDER: Interpreting Maps, p. 37

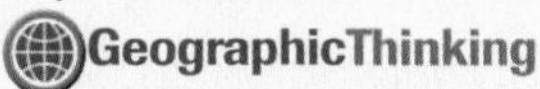

GeographicThinking

Making Comparisons, p. 38
Using the Atlas, p. 40
Seeing Patterns, p. 41
Making Generalizations, p. 41

Focus & Motivate

Ask students to discuss the consequences of the most recent major earthquake or volcanic eruption that they remember. *(Answers will vary.)*

Instruct: Objective 1 appears on p. 38

A HUMAN PERSPECTIVE Sally Ride, America's first female astronaut, wrote the following after one of her trips into space:

> I also became an instant believer in plate tectonics; India really is crashing into Asia, and Saudi Arabia and Egypt really are pulling apart, making the Red Sea even wider. Even though their respective motion is really no more than mere inches a year, the view from overhead makes the theory come alive.

From space, Ride was seeing evidence of the internal forces that have shaped the earth's surface.

Plate Tectonics

The internal forces that shape the earth's surface begin beneath the lithosphere. Rock in the asthenosphere is hot enough to flow slowly. Heated rock rises, moves up toward the lithosphere, cools, and circulates downward. Riding above this circulation system are the **tectonic plates,** enormous moving pieces of the earth's lithosphere. You can see the position of the tectonic plates in the map below.

hmhsocialstudies.com INTERACTIVE MAP

Tectonic Plates

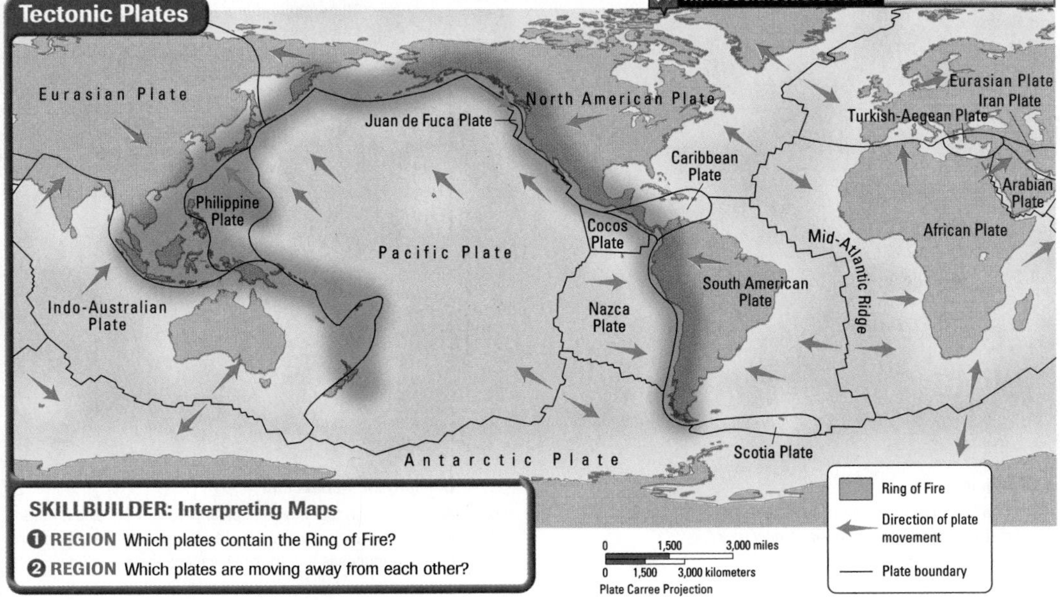

SKILLBUILDER: Interpreting Maps

1. **REGION** Which plates contain the Ring of Fire?
2. **REGION** Which plates are moving away from each other?

Interpreting Maps

The Tectonic Plates

Point out to students that the largest plates are named after the continent (or ocean) they contain. Ask students to identify these large plates. *(Eurasian, North American, South American, African, Antarctic, Indo-Australian, and Pacific)*

SKILLBUILDER ANSWERS

1. Nazca, South American, Cocos, North American, Juan de Fuca, Eurasian, Philippine, Indo-Australian, Antarctic **2.** Pacific from Nazca, Indo-Australian from Antarctic Plate, South and North American Plates from African and Eurasian Plates

SECTION 3 PROGRAM RESOURCES

In-Depth Resources: Unit 1
- Guided Reading, p. 15
- Skillbuilder Practice, p. 17
- Building Vocabulary, p. 18
- Reteaching Activity, p. 21

Guided Reading Workbook
- Section 3

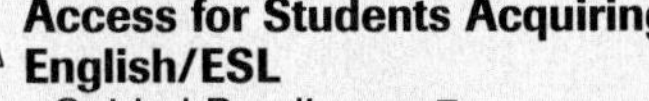

Access for Students Acquiring English/ESL
- Guided Reading, p. 7
- Skillbuillder Practice, p. 9

Formal Assessment
- Section Quiz, p. 21

Integrated Assessment
- Rubric for a database, 2.6

INTEGRATED TECHNOLOGY

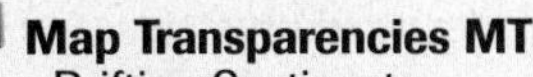

Map Transparencies MT5
- Drifting Continents

Test Generator
- Section Quiz

hmhsocialstudies.com

TEST-TAKING RESOURCES

Strategies for Test Preparation

Test Practice Transparencies TT5

Online Test Practice

Instruct: Objective 

Plate Tectonics

- What are tectonic plates, and how do they move? *(The enormous pieces of the earth's crust move by spreading; subduction; collision; and sliding past each other in a shearing motion.)*
- What is the difference between folds and faults? *(Folds occur where two plates meet and cause the layers of rock to bend. Faults occur where two plates meet and cause a fracture in the earth's crust.)*

 **In-Depth Resources: Unit 1**
- Guided Reading, p. 15

Map Transparencies MT5
- Drifting Continents

More About

The Great Rift Valley

Plates create a depression or valley where they move apart. The Great Rift Valley is a series of valleys in Africa that extend roughly 4,000 miles from Syria to Mozambique. For much of its length, the rift ranges from 25 to 60 miles wide and is flanked by steep walls that rise 2,000 to 3,000 feet.

Geographers study the movement of the plates and the changes they cause in order to understand how the earth is continually being reshaped—and how earthquakes and volcanoes occur.

PLATE MOVEMENT Tectonic plates move in one of four ways: 1) spreading, or moving apart; 2) subduction, or diving under another plate; 3) collision, or crashing into one another; 4) sliding past each other in a shearing motion. The diagrams below show details about plate movement.

When tectonic plates come into contact, changes on the earth's surface occur. Three types of boundaries mark plate movements:

- **Divergent boundary**—Plates move apart, spreading horizontally.
- **Convergent boundary**—Plates collide, causing either one plate to dive under the other or the edges of both plates to crumple.
- **Transform boundary**—Plates slide past one another. A

Geographic Thinking

Making Comparisons

A Which of the plate boundaries involves a collision of plates?

A. Answer convergent

An example of a divergent boundary is the one between Saudi Arabia and Egypt. The two plates on which those countries sit are spreading apart, making the Red Sea even wider. The Red Sea is actually a part of the Great Rift Valley in Africa. If you look at the map of Africa on page A18, you will see a string of lakes along the eastern side of Africa, including Lake Tanganyika and Lake Nyasa. These lakes, along with the Red Sea, were formed in the spreading boundary.

An example of a convergent boundary can be found in South Asia. The plate where India is located is crashing into the Asian continent and building up the Himalayas. One of the most famous examples of a transform boundary is in North America—the San Andreas Fault in

Plate Movement and Boundaries

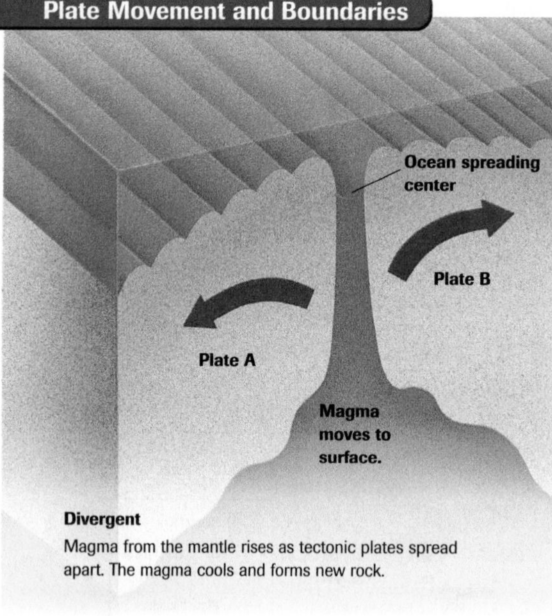

Divergent
Magma from the mantle rises as tectonic plates spread apart. The magma cools and forms new rock.

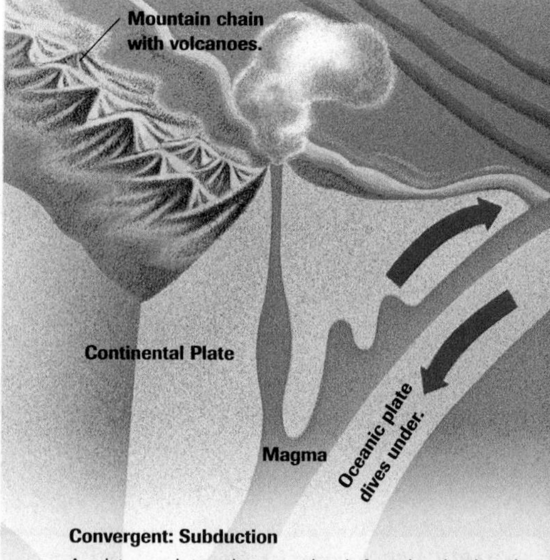

Convergent: Subduction
As plates push together, one plate is forced under the other in a process called subduction. As the bottom plate starts to melt, magma rises and forms volcanoes at the surface.

DIFFERENTIATING INSTRUCTION **STUDENTS ACQUIRING ENGLISH/ESL**

RECOGNIZING ROOT WORDS AND PREFIXES

Objective To use word roots and prefixes to understand unfamiliar terms

Class Time 20 minutes

Task Use word roots and prefixes to learn about plate boundaries

Directions Write the words *divergent, convergent,* and *transform* on the board. Then explain the following roots and prefixes in the words:

verge = to bend or incline
form = shape
di = apart
trans = across
con = together

California. Study the diagrams below to understand the movement of the plates and their effect on the surface of the earth.

FOLDS AND FAULTS When two plates meet each other, they can cause folding and cracking of the rock. The transformation of the crust by folding or cracking occurs very slowly, often only a few centimeters or inches in a year. Because the movement is slow, the rocks, which are under great pressure, become more flexible and bend or fold, creating changes in the crust. However, sometimes the rock is not flexible and will crack under the pressures exerted by the plate movement. This fracture in the earth's crust is called a **fault.** It is at the fault line that the plates move past each other.

Earthquakes

As the plates grind or slip past each other at a fault, the earth shakes or trembles. This sometimes violent movement of the earth is an **earthquake.** Thousands of earthquakes occur every year, but most are so slight that people cannot feel them. Only a special device called a **seismograph** (SYZ•muh•GRAF) can detect them. A seismograph measures the size of the waves created by an earthquake.

BACKGROUND
Seismographs measure earthquakes, but no accurate device for predicting quakes has been developed.

EARTHQUAKE LOCATIONS The location in the earth where an earthquake begins is called the focus. The point directly above the focus on the earth's surface is the **epicenter.** The map on page 37 outlines the major plate boundaries. Nearly 95 percent of all recorded earthquakes occur around those boundaries. Plate movement along the Pacific Rim

Convergent: Collision
When two continental plates collide, neither one is subducted, and the plates buckle and fold. Sometimes a double thickness of crust results in the formation of mountain ridges.

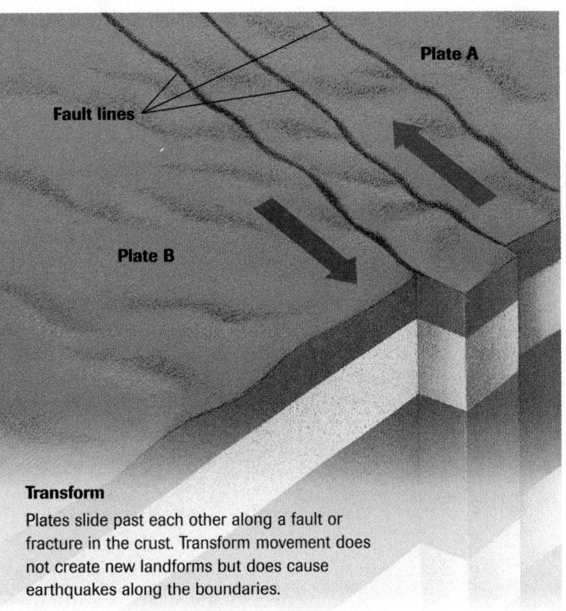

Transform
Plates slide past each other along a fault or fracture in the crust. Transform movement does not create new landforms but does cause earthquakes along the boundaries.

BASICS

More About

Faults and Earthquakes

Plate movement produces zones of faults around plate boundaries. The San Andreas Fault, for example, has a number of associated faults. While the majority of earthquakes occur in these fault zones, some occur within a plate's interior. These *intraplate earthquakes,* which mainly occur in weak areas of a plate, are usually smaller than the *interplate earthquakes,* which occur along plate boundaries.

Instruct: Objective 2

Earthquakes

- What causes earthquakes? *(the grinding and slipping of plates along a fault)*
- Where do most earthquakes occur? *(along plate boundaries)*
- What are some effects of earthquakes? *(landslides, displacement of land, fires, collapsed buildings and tsunamis)*

ACTIVITY OPTION | LINK TO PHYSICAL SCIENCE

RESEARCHING PLATE MOVEMENT

Objective To conduct research and give an oral report

Class Time 20 minutes

Task Locate information on the physical causes of plate movement and give a brief oral report

Directions Have students use Internet or library resources to research the physical causes of plate movement. Ask them to explain their findings in a brief oral report. In their reports, students should use visual aids to describe at least three types of movement.

Interpreting Photographs

Kobe Earthquake

The 1995 Kobe earthquake had a magnitude of 7.2. The quake injured about 35,000 people, destroyed or damaged about 180,000 buildings, and left 300,000 people homeless. The shaking caused around $147 billion in damage. Ask students what they think would be the most difficult aspects of living on the street. *(enduring cold air, obtaining water and food, finding restrooms)*

CAPTION ANSWER It is located near the intersection of four tectonic plates.

Instruct: Objective 3

Volcanoes

- What happens in a volcanic eruption? *(hot lava, gases, ash, dust, and rocks explode out of vents in the earth's crust, often creating a hill or mountain)*
- Where are the majority of active volcanoes located? *(in the Ring of Fire, a zone around the rim of the Pacific where eight major tectonic plates meet)* (Note: The Ring of Fire is also covered in Unit 9: East Asia.)
- Where do volcanoes that are far from the margins of tectonic plates appear? *(in "hot spots," where the crust is thin, allowing magma to melt through)*

LOCATION Victims of the 1995 earthquake in Kobe, Japan, wait out aftershocks. More than 5,000 people died in this quake. **Why does the location of Japan make it vulnerable to earthquakes?**

and from southern Asia westward to southern Europe makes this region especially vulnerable to quakes.

EARTHQUAKE DAMAGE Earthquakes result in squeezing, stretching, and shearing motions of the earth's crust that damage land and structures.

The changes are most noticeable in places where people live. Landslides, displacement of land, fires (from broken gas lines), and collapsed buildings are major outcomes of the ground motion. Aftershocks, or smaller-magnitude quakes, may occur after an initial shock and can sometimes continue for days afterward.

An earthquake is the sudden release of energy in the form of motion. C.F. Richter developed a scale to measure the amount of energy released. The **Richter Scale** uses information collected by seismographs to determine the relative strength of an earthquake. The scale has no absolute upper limit. Most people would not notice a quake that measured 2 on the scale. A 4.5 quake will probably be reported in the news. A major quake has a measurement of 7 or more. The largest quake ever measured was 9.5 in Southern Chile on May 22, 1960.

TSUNAMI Sometimes an earthquake causes a **tsunami** (tsu•NAH•mee), a giant wave in the ocean. A tsunami can travel from the epicenter of a quake at speeds of up to 450 miles per hour, producing waves of 50 to 100 feet or higher. Tsunamis may travel across wide stretches of the ocean and do damage on distant shores. For example, the 1960 quake in Chile and the nearby ocean floor created a tsunami that caused damage in Japan, almost half a world away. In December 2004, a tsunami from a quake in the Indian Ocean struck areas of Southeast Asia, South Asia, and East Africa. An estimated 225,000 people were immediately killed, and another 1.2 million were forced to leave their homes. B

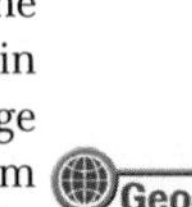

Using the Atlas
B Using the map on pages A2–3, calculate the distance the 1960 tsunami traveled.
B. Answer Chile to Japan is approximately 10,715 miles.

Volcanoes

Volcanoes are among the most spectacular of natural events. Magma, gases, and water from the lower part of the crust or the mantle collect in underground chambers. Eventually the materials pour out of a crack in the earth's surface called a **volcano.** Most volcanoes are found along the tectonic plate boundaries.

VOLCANIC ACTION When the magma flows out onto the land slowly, it may spread across an area and cool. Magma that has reached the earth's surface is called **lava.** The most dramatic volcanic action is an eruption, in which hot lava, gases, ash, dust, and rocks explode out of vents in the earth's crust. Often a hill or a mountain is created by lava. The landform may also be called a volcano.

Volcanoes do not erupt on a predictable schedule; they may be active over many years and then stop. Sometimes they remain inactive for

ACTIVITY OPTION **SKILLBUILDER LESSON**

CREATING MULTIMEDIA PRESENTATIONS

Explaining the Skill A multimedia presentation may include any combination of visual, audio, and print information. Video recordings, slide presentations, or Web pages are possible media components. Students should research their topic and then decide upon the best format for presenting their findings.

Applying the Skill Have students research the use of geothermal energy and prepare a multimedia presentation of their findings. To help students focus their research, give them these questions to answer:
- Where and how is geothermal energy used today?
- What is its potential as a significant energy source?

In-Depth Resources: Unit 1
- Skillbuilder Practice, p. 17

long periods of time—as long as hundreds of years—before becoming active again.

RING OF FIRE The **Ring of Fire,** a zone around the rim of the Pacific Ocean, is the location of the vast majority of active volcanoes. You can see the zone on the map on page 37. Eight major tectonic plates meet in this zone. Volcanic action and earthquakes occur frequently there. Other volcanoes are located far from the margins of tectonic plates. They appear over "hot spots" where magma from deep in the mantle rises and melts through the lithosphere, as in volcanoes in the Hawaiian Islands.

Hot springs and geysers are indicators of high temperatures in the earth's crust. Hot springs occur when ground water circulates near a magma chamber. The water heats up and rises to the surface. The hot springs and pools of Yellowstone Park are examples of this type of activity. A geyser is a hot spring that occasionally erupts with steam jets and boiling water. Old Faithful, a geyser in Yellowstone, erupts regularly, but most geysers are irregular in their eruptions. Countries with hot springs and geysers include the United States, Iceland, and Japan. C

Not all volcanic action is bad. Volcanic ash produces fertile soil. In some parts of the world, the hot springs, steam, and heat generated by the magma are tapped for energy. In Iceland, for example, volcanic heat and steam are used for heating and hot water in the city of Reykjavik.

Internal forces have a major role in shaping the earth. In the next section, you will learn how external forces also change the landscape.

Geographic Thinking

Seeing Patterns
C Why do the United States, Iceland, and Japan have geysers?
C. Answer They all lie on hot spots on the earth's crust.

Geography TODAY

An Island Is Born

On May 14, 2000, a team of scientists observed the birth of a new island in the South Pacific. On that day Kavachi, a volcano in the Solomon Islands, erupted for the first time since 1991. The volcano is located about 18 miles from the boundary of the Indo-Australian plate and the Pacific plate.

For at least 20 hours, the volcano erupted every 5 to 7 minutes, shooting ash and glowing lava blocks 230 feet into the air (shown below). The peak of the volcano is under water, about 2,100 feet above the sea floor. A sandy, ashen beach is forming about 6 feet below the surface of the ocean.

BASICS

Geography TODAY

An Island Is Born

About 80 percent of all volcanic activity occurs in the ocean. The lava from submarine eruptions acts differently from that of land eruptions. The lava cools rapidly in the ocean water and breaks up into sand and debris that build up a slope, or "seamount." Ask students what type of plate boundary is near Kavachi? *(a convergent boundary where subduction is occurring)*

Assess & Reteach

GeoFocus Have students complete the section on internal forces in their graphic organizers.

Formal Assessment
- Section Quiz, p. 21

Reteaching Activity
Organize the class into groups of three students. Assign each group member one of the three main headings in this section. Have each student orally summarize the main ideas under that heading for the rest of the group.

In-Depth Resources: Unit 1
- Reteaching Activity, p. 21

SECTION 3 Assessment

1 Places & Terms
Explain the meaning of each of the following terms.
- tectonic plate
- fault
- earthquake
- seismograph
- epicenter
- volcano

2 Taking Notes
MOVEMENT Review the notes you took for this section.

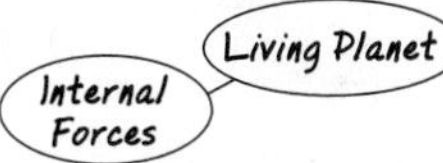

- What are four types of plate movement?
- How are folds and faults created?

3 Main Ideas
a. How does the movement of tectonic plates shape the earth's surface?
b. When does a volcano occur?
c. How do earthquakes cause damage?

4 Geographic Thinking
Making Generalizations Why do volcanoes and earthquakes occur along the Ring of Fire? **Think about:**
- tectonic plate movement
- movement of magma

SEEING PATTERNS Use the Internet to find information on the top 10 most deadly volcanoes in history. Create a **database** showing the information by continent. Summarize your findings about the location of deadly quakes in two sentences.

21st CENTURY

SECTION 3 ASSESSMENT ANSWERS

1. Places & Terms
tectonic plate, p. 37
fault, p. 39
earthquake, p. 39
seismograph, p. 39
epicenter, p. 39
volcano, p. 40

2. Taking Notes
- collision, subduction, spreading, sliding
- Flexible rock folds under pressure when two plates meet. Inflexible rock fractures, causing faults.

3. Main Ideas
a. The movement of the plates pushes up mountains, causes volcanoes to erupt, and creates faults, ridges, and sea floor spreading.
b. when hot lava, rock, gases, and ash erupt out of the ground
c. Earthquakes cause stretching, squeezing, and shearing motions of the earth's crust. This results in collapsed buildings, landslides, and displacement of land.

4. Geographic Thinking
because eight major tectonic plates meet in this zone

GeoActivity

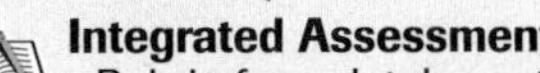
Integrated Assessment
- Rubric for a database, 2.6

SECTION 4 OBJECTIVES

1. Describe mechanical and chemical weathering.
2. Relate the processes of water, wind, and glacial erosion to the development of landforms.
3. Identify the basic components of soil.

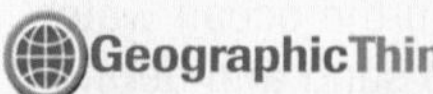

Making Comparisons, pp. 43, 44
Making Inferences, p. 45

Focus & Motivate

Ask students to describe the effects of weathering or erosion that they have seen either locally or in their travels. *(Answers will vary.)*

Instruct: Objective 1

Weathering

- How does mechanical weathering occur? *(Ice, plant growth, and human activities break rock into smaller pieces.)*
- How does chemical weathering occur? *(Elements in air or water combine with minerals in the rock to create new substances.)*
- How do the products of mechanical and chemical weathering differ? *(Mechanical weathering produces smaller particles of rock; chemical weathering produces new substances.)*

In-Depth Resources: Unit 1
- Guided Reading, p.16

Critical Thinking Transparencies CT34
- What causes the Earth to change?

CAPTION ANSWER It was carried away by wind or water.

External Forces Shaping the Earth

Main Ideas
- Wind, heat, cold, glaciers, rivers, and floods alter the surface of the earth.
- The results of weathering and erosion change the way humans interact with the environment.

Places & Terms

weathering
sediment
mechanical weathering
chemical weathering
erosion
delta
loess
glacier
glaciation
moraine
humus

A HUMAN PERSPECTIVE In Egypt, a seasonal dry wind is called khamsin ("fifty") for the number of days the season occurs. During khamsin, wind-driven sandstorms kill and injure people, close businesses and airports, and strip topsoil and seed from the ground. Sandstorms are not limited to the desert areas of Africa and Southwest Asia. For instance, a five-hour storm recently blasted Jingchang, China, causing millions of dollars of damage and killing about 300 people. Sandstorms are among the external forces that change the shape of the earth and affect the lives of the people in their paths.

Weathering

In the last section, you learned about forces within the earth that changed the land. External forces, such as weathering and erosion, also alter landscapes and in some instances create the soil that is needed for plant life. **Weathering** refers to physical and chemical processes that change the characteristics of rock on or near the earth's surface. Weathering occurs slowly over many years and even centuries. Weathering processes create smaller and smaller pieces of rock called **sediment**. Sediment is mostly identifiable as either mud, sand, or silt, which is very fine particles of rock.

MECHANICAL WEATHERING Processes that break rock into smaller pieces are referred to as **mechanical weathering**. Mechanical weathering does not change the composition of the rock—only its size. For example, when ice crystals build up in the crack of a rock, they can actually create enough pressure to fracture the rock into smaller pieces. All sorts of agents can break apart rocks. Frost and even plant roots dig into crevices in the rock, splitting it. Human activities, like road construction or drilling and blasting in mining, are also mechanical weathering forces. Eventually, the smaller broken material will be combined with organic material to become soil.

MOVEMENT A view of the Colorado River and Grand Canyon in Arizona. The canyon's depth was created by water erosion, and the width by rain and wind erosion. **What has happened to the sediment created by weathering in the canyon?**

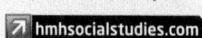

SECTION 4 PROGRAM RESOURCES

In-Depth Resources: Unit 1
- Guided Reading, p. 16
- Building Vocabulary, p. 18
- Reteaching Activity, p. 22

Guided Reading Workbook
- Section 4

Access for Students Acquiring English/ESL
- Guided Reading, p. 8

Formal Assessment
- Section Quiz, p. 22

Integrated Assessment
- Rubrics for sketches and photographs, 1.3

INTEGRATED TECHNOLOGY

Critical Thinking Transparencies CT34
- What Causes the Earth to Change?

Map Transparencies MT6
- Natural Hazards of the World

Test Generator
- Section Quiz

hmhsocialstudies.com

TEST-TAKING RESOURCES

Strategies for Test Preparation

Test Practice Transparencies TT6

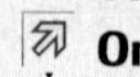

Online Test Practice

CHEMICAL WEATHERING **Chemical weathering** occurs when rock is changed into a new substance as a result of interaction between elements in the air or water and the minerals in the rock. Decomposition, or breakup, can happen in several ways. Some minerals react to oxygen in the air and begin to crumble. That is what happens when iron rusts, for example.

Other minerals break down when combined with water or carbon dioxide, which form weak acids within the rock. When sulfur and nitrogen oxides mix with water, acid rain is formed. The increase of acid rain in the 20th century is believed to be speeding up some decomposition. The location and the climate in which the rocks are located have a great deal to do with how rocks decompose. Climates that are warm and moist will produce more chemical weathering than do cool dry areas. Rocks in cold dry and hot dry areas generally experience more mechanical weathering than chemical weathering. A

Geographic Thinking

Making Comparisons
A Why would chemical weathering be rare in a desert area?
A. Answer Chemical weathering usually occurs where water is present. Desert areas have little water.

Erosion

Erosion occurs when weathered material is moved by the action of wind, water, ice, or gravity. For erosion to occur, a transporting agent, such as water, must be present. Glaciers, waves, stream flow, or blowing winds cause erosion by grinding rock into smaller pieces. Material moved from one location to another results in the lowering of some locations and increased elevation in others. For example, water might carry topsoil from a hill into a river and gradually cause the river to become more narrow. Erosion in its many forms reshapes landforms and coastal regions, as well as riverbeds and riverbanks.

WATER EROSION One form of water erosion occurs as water flows in a stream or river. The motion picks up loose material and moves it downstream. The greater the force of water, the greater the ability of the water to transport tiny rock particles, or sediment. Another form of erosion is abrasion, the grinding away of rock by transported particles. The heavier the load of sediment, the greater the abrasion on the banks and riverbed. A third eroding action of water occurs when the water dissolves chemical elements in the rock. The composition of the rock changes as a result.

Most streams erode both vertically and horizontally—that is, the valley cut by a stream gets deeper and wider, forming a V-shaped valley. As the water slows, it drops the sediment it is carrying. When a river enters the ocean, the sediment is deposited in a fan-like landform called a **delta.**

Wave action along coastlines also changes the land. Waves can reduce or increase beaches. Sediment deposited by wave action may build up sandbars or islands. Wave action is so powerful that in some locations, it erodes about three feet of beach per year. For some unfortunate people, a beach house with an ocean view

BACKGROUND
The term *delta* is used because the shape of the landform resembles the Greek letter delta (Δ).

Geography TODAY

Moving the Cape Hatteras Lighthouse

Coastal erosion led to one of the great moving projects of the 20th century. The Cape Hatteras Lighthouse (shown below), the tallest brick lighthouse in the nation, was dangerously close to disappearing into the sea. Built in 1870 on Hatteras Island off the coast of North Carolina, the lighthouse stood 1,500 feet from the sea. By 1987, it was only 160 feet away. The only way to save the historic lighthouse was to move it.

In the summer of 1999, the structure was slowly moved—10 to 355 feet per day—to a new location 1,600 feet from the sea. But erosion will also take beach from the new location, and by 2018, as much as 404 feet may be gone.

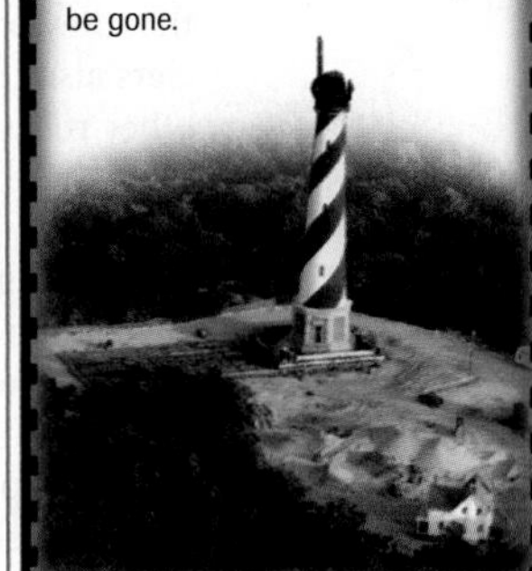

BASICS

Instruct: Objective 2

Erosion

- How does water erosion reshape stream beds and coastal regions? *(It deepens and widens streams. As streams enter the ocean, they deposit sediments forming deltas. Waves reduce beaches and build up sandbars and islands.)*
- What landforms are produced by wind erosion? *(sand dunes, sculpted rocks, and loess deposits)*
- How do glaciers change the land? *(They slice out valleys, form hills called moraines, leave ridges called eskers, and create depressions called kettles.)*

 **Map Transparencies MT6**
- Natural Hazards of the World

Geography TODAY

Moving the Cape Hatteras Lighthouse

Hatteras Island is one of the barrier islands that make up North Carolina's Outer Banks. Strong ocean currents and storms cause erosion of the island's eastern shorelines and buildup of the southern shorelines. Ask students what might happen if the erosion of Hatteras Island continues over a long period of time? *(It may be eroded away and disappear.)*

ACTIVITY OPTION **CRITICAL THINKING**

DETERMINING CAUSE AND EFFECT

Explaining the Skill Physical processes are constantly at work producing a variety of landforms. These physical processes are *causes*, and landforms are the *effects*. Geographers study these causes and effects to understand how the earth's surface came to be the way it is today and to predict what it will be like in the future.

Applying the Skill Direct students to reread the first paragraph under the heading "Water Erosion" in the middle of page 43. Then ask them to answer the following questions.

- Over a long period of time, such as millions of years, what effect would water erosion have on mountains and hills? *(It would wear them down or cut deep channels or valleys in them.)*
- If muddy streams drain into a lake that has no outlet and no other source of water, what will happen to the lake over a long period of time? *(It will fill up with sediment and became land.)*
- Why would a river bank, even a high one, be a poor choice for the site of a home? *(because the bank would be subject to erosion)*

Interpreting Photographs

Glacier in the Alaskan Range
Glaciers cover about 10 percent of the land area on earth and are found on all the continents, although most are located at the poles. The majority of the glaciers in the United States occur in Alaska. Ask students why high mountains foster the formation of glaciers. *(because temperatures are cool year round, and snowfall is high)*

CAPTION ANSWER It has moved rocks and boulders down the mountain and left them in moraines.

MOVEMENT At Chakachamna in Alaska, a glacier moves down a mountain.
What effect has the glacier had on the landform shown here?

may end up in the ocean as a result of wave action erosion.

WIND EROSION In many ways, wind erosion is similar to water erosion because the wind transports and deposits sediment in other locations. Wind speeds must reach 11 miles per hour before fine sediment can be moved. The greater the speed of the wind, the larger the particles moved. Dust storms are capable of carrying as much as 6,000 tons of sediment per cubic mile of air. As the wind slows, the sediment is dropped.

Depending on the type of wind-borne sediment, new landforms—such as sand dunes miles from seashores and rocks sculpted into fantastic forms—may be produced. Deposits of **loess** (LOH•uhs), wind-blown silt and clay sediment that produce very fertile soil, are found across the world. In northern China, for example, the deposits are several hundred feet deep. Extensive areas of loess are found in the Mississippi Valley in the United States and in the grasslands of Argentina. B

Geographic Thinking
Making Comparisons
B In what ways are water and wind erosion similar? different?
B. Answer Both transport sediment to different locations and create new landforms. Water erosion creates valleys, but wind does not.

GLACIAL EROSION A **glacier** is a large, long-lasting mass of ice that moves because of gravity. Glaciers form in mountainous areas and in regions that are routinely covered with heavy snowfall and ice. In mountain regions, glaciers move downslope as a result of gravity. Glaciers such as ice caps and ice sheets move from the highest point on land toward the lowest point.

Glaciation is the changing of landforms by slowly moving glaciers. As a glacier moves, several types of erosion occur. Rocks caught underneath the glacier are ground into finer and finer particles. Some particles are so small that they are called rock flour, which is one component of soil. Massive glaciers also cut U-shaped valleys into the land. On top of or within the ice are other rocks carried by the glacier. When the glacier melts, these rocks are left behind. Rocks left behind by a glacier may form a ridge or a hill called a **moraine.** Moraines can be found on the sides, down the center, or at the leading edge of a glacier.

Inside or under the glacier may be tunnels formed by running water. These tunnels fill up with sediment dropped by the water. When the ice melts, it leaves a long snakelike ridge called an esker. Sometimes blocks of ice are trapped in the sediment. They melt slowly and leave behind a dent or a depression in the ground. These depressions are called kettles. The kettles may be filled with water forming a small lake.

ACTIVITY OPTION **INTERNET RESEARCH**

PREPARING A NEWS REPORT

Objective To research a topic and prepare an oral news report

Class Time 30 minutes

Task Investigate how global warming has affected glaciers

Directions Tell students that from the 1600s to the late 1800s, glaciers actually advanced because world temperatures were cool enough. Direct students to **hmhsocialstudies.com**, where they can follow the links to sources of information on how world temperatures have been changing in the past century and how this change has affected glaciers. Students should present their findings in an oral news report.

OPTIONAL ACTIVITY If Internet access is limited, have students use the library for this research activity. They can start with reference books and check periodical indexes to find articles on the effect of global warming on glaciers.

Building Soil

Weathering and erosion are a part of the process of forming soil. Soil is the loose mixture of weathered rock, organic matter, air, and water that supports plant growth. Organic matter in the soil helps to support the growth of plants by providing needed plant food. Water and air share tiny pore-like spaces in the soil. When it rains, the pores are filled with water. As the water evaporates, drains away, or is used by the plants, the pores are filled with air. The texture of the soil, the amount of organic material called **humus,** and the amount of air and water in the soil all contribute to the soil's fertility—its ability to nurture plants.

SOIL FACTORS When geographers study soil, they look at five factors:

- **Parent material** The chemical composition of the original rock, or parent rock, before it decomposes affects its fertility.
- **Relief** Steeper slopes, such as mountainsides, are eroded easily and do not produce soil quickly.
- **Organisms** Organisms include plants, small animals like worms, ants, and bacteria that decompose material. They help to loosen soil and supply nutrients for plants.
- **Climate** Hot climates produce a soil different from that produced by cold climates. Wet climates and dry climates produce soils that are different from each other as well.
- **Time** The amount of time to produce soil varies, but a very rough average is about 2.5 cubic centimeters per century.

BACKGROUND
In some soils, as many as a million or more bacteria inhabit each cubic centimeter of soil.

The variety of soils—and the climates in which they are found—determine the types of vegetation that can grow in a location. Agricultural activities, such as farming, ranching, and herding, depend on this complex relationship. In the next chapter, you will learn about the climate and vegetation on the earth and how it affects human life.

BASICS

Section 4 Assessment

1 Places & Terms
Explain the meaning of each of the following terms.
- weathering
- sediment
- erosion
- delta
- glaciation
- humus

2 Taking Notes
REGION Review the notes you took for this section.

- How does weathering vary according to climate?
- What are five factors affecting soil composition?

3 Main Ideas
a. What is the difference between mechanical weathering and chemical weathering?
b. What are three types of eroding action by water?
c. What factors contribute to soil fertility?

4 Geographic Thinking
Making Inferences In what ways does erosion affect the lives of humans? **Think about:**
- water, wind, and glacial action
- results of erosion

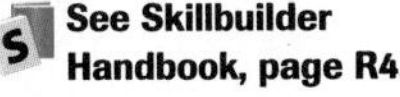
See Skillbuilder Handbook, page R4.

EXPLORING LOCAL GEOGRAPHY Choose a type of erosion that occurs in your community. Do some research to find examples of that type of erosion. Make **sketches** or take **photographs** of the effects of the erosion. Write captions for the pictures describing the type of erosion and where it was found.

Instruct: Objective 3

Building Soil

- What does soil consist of, and what factors determine its fertility? *(Soil is a loose mixture of weathered rock, organic matter, air, and water. Fertility depends on texture and the amount of humus, air, and water.)*
- What factors do geographers look at when they study soil? *(parent material, relief, organisms, climate, and time)*
- Why is the type of soil in a location important? *(It influences the types of vegetation that can grow and, thus, the location's agricultural potential.)*

Assess & Reteach

GeoFocus Have students complete the section on external forces in their graphic organizers.

Formal Assessment
- Section Quiz, p. 22

Reteaching Activity
Have students work with a partner or in a small group to create posters that illustrate the three processes described in this section: weathering, erosion, and soil-building.

In-Depth Resources: Unit 1
- Reteaching Activity, p. 22

SECTION 4 ASSESSMENT ANSWERS

1. Places & Terms
weathering, p. 42
sediment, p. 42
erosion, p. 43
delta, p. 43
glaciation, p. 44
humus, p. 45

2. Taking Notes
- Hot or dry climates produce more mechanical weathering. Warm or wet climates produce more chemical weathering.
- parent material, relief, organisms, climate, time

3. Main Ideas
a. Mechanical weathering involves the breaking down of parent material into smaller and smaller pieces. Chemical weathering decomposes the rock and may create new substances.
b. transporting rock, abrasion, and dissolution by water
c. the texture of the soil, the amount of humus, and the amount of air and water in the soil

4. Geographic Thinking
Humans may lose land for homes or fields because the surface of the earth is altered by erosion.

GeoActivity

Integrated Assessment
- Rubrics for sketches and photographs, 1.3

Reviewing Place & Terms

A. **1.** continent, p. 27
2. magma, p. 28
3. hydrologic cycle, p. 32
4. landform, p. 33
5. relief, p. 36
6. tectonic plate, p. 37
7. earthquake, p. 39
8. volcano, p. 40
9. weathering, p. 42
10. erosion, p. 43

B. Possible Responses

11. Continents are the portions of the tectonic plates that rise above the ocean.
12. Magma is found in the mantle.
13. Lava is a form of magma.
14. Mountains, hills, plains, and plateaus are all landforms.
15. It tells you the elevation of the landform from the lowest point to the highest point.
16. The hydrologic cycle constantly re-circulates the water on earth.
17. Earthquakes are caused by the movement of tectonic plates.
18. Magma is forced out of the earth. A volcano is formed by lava, which is magma that has reached the surface.
19. Weathering can be mechanical or chemical.
20. Erosion cannot occur without a transporting agent.

Chapter 2 Assessment

VISUAL SUMMARY
A LIVING PLANET

The Earth Inside and Out

- The earth's interior is made up of a series of layers that float on one another.
- The exterior of the earth is the crust.
- The presence of air and water make life on earth possible.

Bodies of Water and Landforms

- Almost three-fourths of the earth is covered with water.
- The hydrologic cycle circulates water.
- Landforms on the land and under the ocean are similar.

Internal Forces Shaping the Earth

- Huge plates on the earth's crust move because of the circulation of magma.
- Earthquakes and volcanoes are the results of plate movement.

External Forces Shaping the Earth

- Weathering and erosion cause changes in the earth's surface and build soil.
- Actions of wind, water, ice, and gravity shape the earth's surface.

Reviewing Places & Terms

A. Briefly explain the importance of each of the following.

1. continent
2. magma
3. hydrologic cycle
4. landform
5. relief
6. tectonic plate
7. earthquake
8. volcano
9. weathering
10. erosion

B. Answer the questions about vocabulary in complete sentences.

11. How are continents and tectonic plates related?
12. Where is magma found?
13. Lava is a form of which term listed above?
14. What is an example of a landform?
15. What does relief tell you about a landform?
16. What is the purpose of the hydrologic cycle?
17. What causes earthquakes?
18. How are magma and volcanoes related?
19. What are the two types of weathering?
20. What must be present for erosion to occur?

Main Ideas

The Earth Inside and Out (pp. 27–31)

1. What layers are found in the earth's interior?
2. What is the continental drift theory?

Bodies of Water and Landforms (pp. 32–36)

3. How does water reach a drainage basin?
4. What is topography?

Internal Forces Shaping the Earth (pp. 37–41)

5. What are three types of plate boundaries?
6. How are the Richter scale and a seismograph used?
7. What is the Ring of Fire?

External Forces Shaping the Earth (pp. 42–45)

8. What is the difference between weathering and erosion?
9. What are three transporting agents of erosion?
10. Why are there many different types of soil?

Main Ideas

1. The layers are the core, including the iron and nickel core and the outer core; the mantle; and the crust.
2. The theory suggests the land was one supercontinent that has broken into many plates that have drifted apart.
3. Water flows through branching tributaries and major rivers into a drainage basin.
4. Topography shows the relief of an area, the distribution of landforms, and their relationship.
5. Convergent, divergent and transform are boundary types.
6. The Richter scale uses a seismograph to determine the relative strength of an earthquake.
7. The Ring of Fire is a zone around the rim of the Pacific Ocean where there is major volcanic activity.
8. Weathering is the mechanical or chemical process of changing rocks on or near the earth's surface. Erosion occurs when wind, water, or glaciers act upon the weathered rock.
9. Wind, water, ice, and gravity are transporting agents of erosion.
10. Every location has a different combination of soil types that are influenced by five different factors: parent material, relief, organisms, climate, and time.

Critical Thinking

1. Using Your Notes

Use your completed chart to answer these questions.

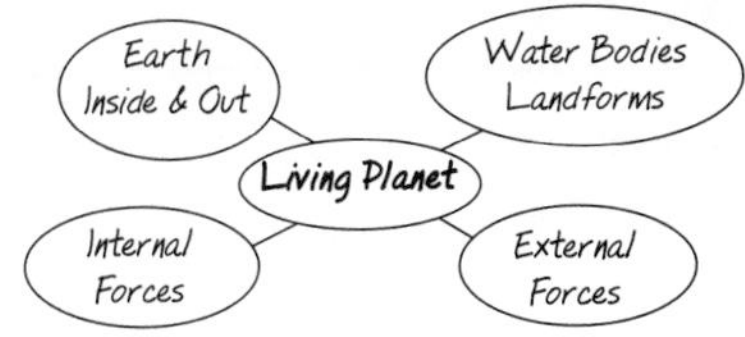

a. Why is water a critical element on the earth?

b. How do internal and external forces shape the earth?

2. Geographic Themes

a. **MOVEMENT** How does the movement of wind, water, or ice reshape the earth's surface?

b. **HUMAN–ENVIRONMENT INTERACTION** How do volcanoes and earthquakes affect human life?

3. Identifying Themes

What might be the hazards of living near the Ring of Fire? Which of the five themes apply to this situation?

4. Determining Cause and Effect

What is the relationship between tectonic plates, earthquakes, and volcanoes?

5. Making Comparisons

How is a valley created by water different from a valley created by a glacier?

For Additional Test Practice

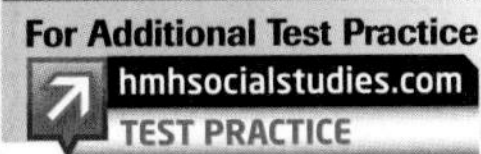

Geographic Skills: Interpreting Charts

Ten Most Deadly Earthquakes in the 20th Century

Use the information in the chart to answer the following questions.

1. **LOCATION** Which location suffered two deadly earthquakes in the 20th century?
2. **MOVEMENT** How is the magnitude of a quake related to loss of life?
3. **PLACE** What reasons might there be for so great a loss of life in Tangshan, China?

Date	Location	Deaths	Magnitude*
1976, July 27	Tangshan, China	255,000	8.0
1920, Dec. 16	Gansu, China	200,000	8.6
1927, May 22	Nan-Shan, China	200,000	8.3
1923, Sept. 1	Yokohama, Japan	143,000	8.3
1908, Dec. 28	Messina, Italy	83,000	7.5
1932, Dec. 25	Gansu, China	70,000	7.6
1970, May 31	Northern Peru	66,000	7.8
1935, May 30	Quetta, India	50,000	7.5
1990, June 20	Western Iran	40,000	7.7
1988, Dec. 7	Armenia	25,000	7.0

*Magnitude of earthquakes measured on the Richter scale developed in 1935.
SOURCES: Global Volcanism Network, Smithsonian Institution, U.S. Geological Survey, *World Almanac*

Using a base map of the world and an atlas, plot the locations of the ten most deadly earthquakes. Write a sentence describing the pattern you see in the locations.

hmhsocialstudies.com

MULTIMEDIA ACTIVITY

Use the links at **hmhsocialstudies.com** to do research about volcanic action. Focus on a variety of volcanic activities, including eruptions, geysers, hot springs, and island formation.

Creating a Multimedia Presentation Put together a presentation about volcanic activity. Include diagrams of several different types of activity and give examples of locations where the activity takes place.

BASICS

Critical Thinking

1. a. It is essential for life, and it distributes heat on the earth.
b. Internal forces build up portions of the earth, and external forces tear it down or build it up.

2. a. They act as transporting agents for erosion by moving sediment to new locations, carving out valleys, and creating new beaches and sandbars.
b. Volcanic eruptions release dangerous gases, ash, and hot lava that disrupt people's lives. Earthquakes destroy buildings and can create destructive tsunamis.

3. This zone is subject to both earthquakes and volcanic action that could be deadly; human-environment interaction.

4. The movement of tectonic plates is the cause of earthquakes and some volcanoes.

5. Running water creates v-shaped valleys, while valleys created by glaciers are u-shaped.

GeoActivity

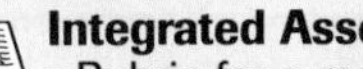

Integrated Assessment
- Rubric for a map, 2.1

Formal Assessment
- Chapter Test, Forms A, B, and C, pp. 23–34

Geographic Skills

1. Gansu, China
2. the greater the magnitude, the greater the loss of life
3. It may have a very dense or very high population. The quake may have hit at night when many people were sleeping.

MULTIMEDIA ACTIVITY

For their multimedia presentation on volcanoes, students should:

- Discuss the different varieties of volcanic activity.
- Include imaginative maps and visuals.
- Provide references to Web sites and other sources of information.

Grading Rubric Evaluate student performance as Exceptional, Acceptable, or Poor in each of the following categories.

	Exceptional	Acceptable	Poor
Utilizes two or more media			
Demonstrates understanding of concepts presented			
Shows technical proficiency			

Physical Geography: Climate and Vegetation

OVERVIEW	INSTRUCTIONAL RESOURCES	
ESSENTIAL QUESTION What factors shape climate and weather, and how is vegetation affected? **Focus on the Essential Question Podcast**	**In-Depth Resources: Unit 1** • Building Vocabulary, p. 30 **Block Schedule Strategies** **Chapter Summaries** (English/Spanish) hmhsocialstudies.com INTERACTIVE	**Interactive Online Edition** TOS **ExamView® Assessment Suite** (English/Spanish) TOS **CalendarPlanner** **Power Presentations with Media Gallery** **Critical Thinking Transparencies** • CT3
SECTION 1 **SEASONS AND WEATHER** **MAIN IDEAS** • Seasons are caused by the earth's tilt and revolution around the sun. • Daily weather is the result of many factors, including solar energy, water vapor, cloud cover, landforms and bodies of water, and air movement. • Types of extreme weather include hurricanes, tornadoes, blizzards, droughts, and floods.	**In-Depth Resources: Unit 1** • Guided Reading, p. 23 • Building Vocabulary, p. 30 • Reteaching Activities, p. 31 **Cultures Around the World** • Architecture, p. 1 **Guided Reading Workbook,** Section 1	**Cultures Transparencies** • CW1 Living in a Igloo **Video:** Tornado Alley Twister
SECTION 2 **CLIMATE** **MAIN IDEAS** • Four major factors influence the climate of a region: wind and ocean currents, latitude, altitude, and topography. • Climates change over time. • Some climate changes are natural, while others result from human activities.	**In-Depth Resources: Unit 1** • Guided Reading, p. 24 • Building Vocabulary, p. 30 • Reteaching Activities, p. 32 **Guided Reading Workbook,** Section 2	hmhsocialstudies.com INTERACTIVE • El Niño and La Niña, p. 57
SECTION 3 **WORLD CLIMATE REGIONS** **MAIN IDEAS** • Climate region definitions tell what typical weather conditions are like in a region. • Temperature and precipitation define climate regions. • A place's location on a continent, its topography, and its altitude influence its climate.	**In-Depth Resources: Unit 1** • Guided Reading, p. 25 • Skillbuilder Practice, p. 29 • Map and Graph Skills, p. 27–28 • Building Vocabulary, p. 30 • Reteaching Activities, p. 33 **Guided Reading Workbook,** Section 3	**Critical Thinking Transparencies** • CT35 Comparing Climate Regions
SECTION 4 **SOILS AND VEGETATION** **MAIN IDEAS** • Soil characteristics and climate are major influences on vegetation regions. • There are four main types of biomes: forest, grassland, desert, and tundra. • Human activities have altered the vegetation of many areas.	**In-Depth Resources: Unit 1** • Guided Reading, p. 26 • Building Vocabulary, p. 30 • Reteaching Activities, p. 34 **Guided Reading Workbook,** Section 4	**Map Transparencies** • MT7 World Soils

ASSESSMENT

SE **Chapter Assessment,** pp. 68–69

Formal Assessment
- Chapter Tests, Forms A, B, and C, pp. 39–50

TOS **ExamView® Assessment Suite**

Strategies for Test Preparation

hmhsocialstudies.com TEST PRACTICE

SE **Section Assessment,** p. 53

Formal Assessment
- Section Quiz, p. 35

Integrated Assessment
- Rubric for a chart, 2.2

Test Practice Transparencies TT7

SE **Section Assessment,** p. 58

Formal Assessment
- Section Quiz, p. 36

Integrated Assessment
- Rubric for a multimedia presentation, 5.4

Test Practice Transparencies TT8

SE **Section Assessment,** p. 63

Formal Assessment
- Section Quiz, p. 37

Integrated Assessment
- Rubric for a mobile, 1.9

Test Practice Transparencies TT9

SE **Section Assessment,** p. 67

Formal Assessment
- Section Quiz, p. 38

Integrated Assessment
- Rubric for a map, 2.1

Test Practice Transparencies TT10

CHART KEY:

SE Student Edition	Block Scheduling	DVD/CD-ROM
TE Teacher's Edition	TOS Teacher One Stop	MP3 Audio
Printable Resource	Presentation Resource	HISTORY™

Program Resources available on TOS and @ 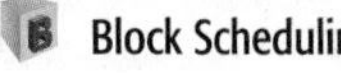

SUPPORTING RESOURCES

- **Multimedia Classroom Global History Series**
- **Global History Teacher's Guide**

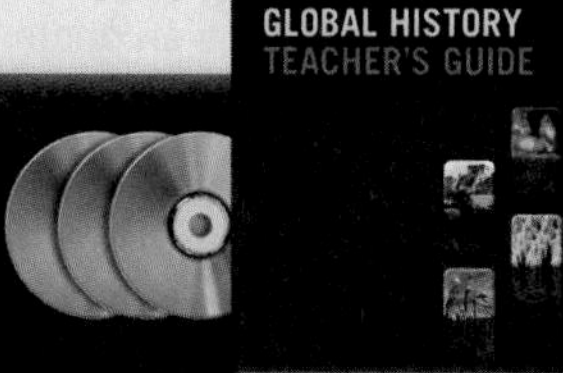

Social Studies Trade Library Collection
- World Regions Trade Collection

For more information or to purchase these resources, go to 

DIFFERENTIATED INSTRUCTION

English Learners	Struggling Readers	Gifted and Talented Students
Spanish/English Guided Reading Workbook **Access for Students Acquiring English/ESL:** Spanish Translations, pp. 10–16 **Chapter Summaries** (English/Spanish) TE **TE Activity** Identifying Climate Regions, p. 60	**Chapter Summaries** (English/Spanish) TE **TE Activity** Diagramming Information, p. 55	TE **TE Activity** Comparing Maps/Making Charts, p. 66

ENRICHMENT ACTIVITIES

The following activities are especially suitable for classes following block schedules.

SE **Student Edition,** p. 48–69
- Interpreting Climographs, p. 64

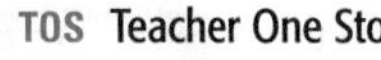
hmhsocialstudies.com INTERACTIVE
- Seasons: Northern Hemisphere, p. 49
- El Niño and La Niña, p. 57

BLOCK SCHEDULE LESSON PLAN OPTIONS: 90-MINUTE PERIOD

DAY 1

SECTION 1, pp. 49–53
Class Time 45 minutes

- **Demonstration** Using a globe and referring to the diagram on page 49 as a guide, demonstrate how the earth's tilt and revolution around the sun creates the seasons. Discuss any questions students have.
  Class Time 15 minutes

- **Flow Charts** Ask students to create flow charts that explain the three types of precipitation. Call on volunteers to share their charts with the rest of the class.
  Class Time 30 minutes

SECTION 2, pp. 54-58
Class Time 45 minutes

- **Examining Visuals** Review this section's content by discussing the maps on pages 54 and 55 and the graphics on pages 56, 57, and 58. Use the TE suggestions and Skillbuilder questions as a guide.

DAY 2

SECTION 3, pp. 59-63
Class Time 90 minutes

- **Using Maps** Display a classroom world map and ask students to open their books to the climate regions map on pages 60–61. Focus on one climate region at a time and point out on the classroom map the areas where this climate occurs. Then ask a volunteer to summarize the characteristics of this climate and note them on the board.
  Class Time 35 minutes

- **Skillbuilder Mini-Lesson** Use the mini-lesson on creating and using a database on TE page 62 and the Skillbuilder Practice worksheet.
  Class Time 55 minutes

DAY 3

SECTION 4, pp. 65-67
Class Time 20 minutes

- **Discussion** Lead a class discussion of the main ideas in this section using the Key Questions on TE pages 65 and 67 as a guide.

CHAPTER 3 REVIEW AND ASSESSMENT, pp. 68-69
Class Time 70 minutes

- **Review** Have students prepare a list of the main ideas in the chapter using the words in the Places & Terms list on the first page of each section.
  Class Time 30 minutes

- **Assessment** Have students complete the Chapter 3 Assessment.
  Class Time 40 minutes

TEACHER-TESTED ACTIVITY *Human-Environment Interaction Collage*

Class Time One class period

Task Create a collage that explores connections between a region's climate and daily life

Supplies
- Posterboard or large construction paper
- Magazines for clippings
- Access to the Internet
- Markers
- Scissors
- Glue

Purpose By examining the relationship between the climate and daily life of a region, students will gain a better understanding of the geographic theme of human-environment interaction.

Activity Separate students into groups and assign each group a region. Have each group search the Internet or look through magazines to find images with which to construct a collage. The images should illustrate the ways in which the daily life of people living in a region is related to that region's climate. Students should consider items such as dress, housing, food, and careers that are prominent within the region.

Sarah White
Geography Teacher, Dakota High School, Macomb, Michigan

TECHNOLOGY IN THE CLASSROOM

"Ask An Expert" Web sites allow students or adults to pose questions to experts on a particular subject, such as meteorology. Because many of these experts receive high volumes of questions, they do not always reply directly to the students via e-mail, but they generally post the responses on the Web site for everyone to see. They always encourage students to browse through the site to see if their question has already been answered..

Objective Students will pose questions related to Chapter 3 to experts who they find on the Internet.

Task Have students read the chapter, write questions about the topics, look for the answers on "Ask An Expert" sites, pose questions to the experts, and search the Internet to look for the same answers.

Class Time 2 class periods

1. Have students read Chapter 3. In pairs, ask them to write three questions that the chapter raises for them. The questions should help guide them toward additional information about the topics covered in the chapter but should not be questions that can be easily answered in an encyclopedia. For example, students could readily find the answer to "What is the average annual rainfall in Buffalo?" in an almanac or encyclopedia, but it might not be as easy to find out "Why does western New York have more cloudy days and higher snowfall than Chicago?"

2. Have students go to the "Ask An Expert" Web sites that they think would be appropriate for their questions., (Students will find links for such sites at **hmhsocialstudies.com**.) Ask them to check to see if any of their questions have already been answered. Have them place a checkmark next to each one they can find an answer to, and have them write the answer next to the question.

3. Have students share their unanswered questions with the class. List the questions on the board, and ask the class to vote on three questions to ask one of the experts.

4. Ask students to choose the most appropriate "Ask An Expert" sites on which to pose the questions, and have them submit the questions.

5. Have students check the sites over the next few weeks to see if their questions have been addressed. If they do not get a response, they should try another "Ask An Expert" site.

6. Have students search the Internet to see if they can find answers to their questions. They can use one of the search engines listed at **hmhsocialstudies.com**. Ask them to compare the information they find on the Internet with the answer they get from the expert. Are the answers consistent? If not, which source do they trust more, and why?

CHAPTER 3 OBJECTIVE

Explain the causes, patterns, and characteristics of the world's climate and vegetation regions.

Chapter 3

PHYSICAL GEOGRAPHY

Climate and Vegetation

Interpreting Photographs

Ask students what effects they would expect the tornado shown in this photograph to have. *(It will rip up and move or blow apart houses, trees, cars, and anything else in its path.)*

Extension Ask students to share their personal experiences of extreme weather phenomena.

Introducing the Essential Question

- Point out that weather and climate are different. Ask students to describe your region's typical weather—both short-term and long-term.
- Emphasize that weather and climate have a profound effect on a region's vegetation. Ask students to describe your region's natural vegetation.

Have students fill out graphic organizers in their notebooks using material from all sections in this chapter.

- GeoFocus

In-Depth Resources: Unit 1
- Building Vocabulary, p. 30

Essential Question

What factors shape climate and weather, and how is vegetation affected?

What You Will Learn

In this chapter you will read about the effects that climate and weather have on vegetation.

SECTION 1
Seasons and Weather

SECTION 2
Climate

SECTION 3
World Climate Regions

SECTION 4
Soils and Vegetation

Use the graphic organizer online to record information about weather, climate, and vegetation.

A tornado roars through the countryside. Tornado winds may reach speeds up to 300 miles per hour.

CHAPTER 3 ADDITIONAL RESOURCES

BOOKS FOR THE TEACHER

Lutgens, Frederick K., Edward J. Tarbuck, and Dennis Tasa. ***The Atmosphere: An Introduction to Meteorology (11th Edition).*** Prentice Hall, 2009. Basic concepts of atmospheric processes with clear examples.

McNeill, J. R. ***Something New Under the Sun: An Environmental History of the Twentieth-Century World.*** W. W. Norton and Company, 2001. How fossil fuels affect our world.

BOOKS FOR THE STUDENT

Davies, Pete. ***Inside the Hurricane.*** NY: Holt, 2000. Story of Hurricane Floyd of 1999.

VIDEOS

Nature's Fury! National Geographic Society, 1994. Study of tornadoes, hurricanes, floods, and other natural forces.

Planet Earth 3: The Climate Puzzle. Unapix, 1995. Examination of past weather patterns and predictions for the future.

INTERNET

For more about physical geography, visit . . .

hmhsocialstudies.com

Seasons and Weather

Main Ideas
- Seasons and weather occur because of the changing position of the earth in relation to the sun.
- Weather extremes are related to location on earth.

Places & Terms

solstice	hurricane
equinox	typhoon
weather	tornado
climate	blizzard
precipitation	drought
rain shadow	

BASICS

A HUMAN PERSPECTIVE The smell of thousands of decaying corpses hung in the air in what was once the thriving seaport of Galveston, Texas. The day before, winds estimated at 130 miles per hour roared through the city. A storm surge of seawater more than 15 feet high pushed a wall of debris across the island of Galveston. Through this turmoil, Isaac Cline's family huddled in their home. A trolley trestle rammed the house until at last it collapsed, and the waves poured in. Cline survived, but some of his family did not. With a death toll of up to 12,000 human lives, the hurricane that hit Galveston Island on September 8, 1900, remains the deadliest natural disaster in United States history.

Seasons

Hurricanes occur frequently in the southern and eastern United States during summer and fall. During these seasons, storm systems with strong winds form over warm ocean water.

EARTH'S TILT Seasons have an enormous impact on us, affecting the conditions in the atmosphere and on the earth that create our weather. As the earth revolves around the sun, it is tilted at a 23.5° angle in relation to the sun. Because of the earth's revolution and its tilt, different parts of the earth receive the direct rays of the sun for more hours of the day at certain times in the year. This causes the changing seasons on the earth. Notice in the diagram to the right that the northern half of the earth tilts toward the sun in summer and away from the sun in winter.

Two lines of latitude—the tropic of Cancer and the tropic of Capricorn—mark the points farthest north and south that the sun's rays shine directly overhead at noon. The day on which this occurs is called a **solstice.** In the Northern Hemisphere, the summer solstice, or the beginning of summer, is the longest day of the year. Winter solstice, the beginning of winter, is the shortest.

Another signal of seasonal change are the equinoxes. Twice a year on the **equinox,** the days and nights all over the world are equal in length. The equinoxes mark the beginning of spring and autumn.

Seasons: Northern Hemisphere

hmhsocialstudies.com INTERACTIVE

The seasons are related to the earth's tilt and revolution. Some locations receive more direct sun rays because of the earth's tilt.

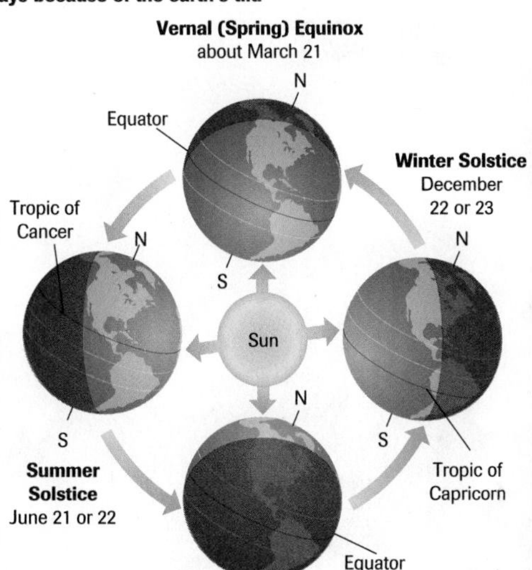

SECTION 1 OBJECTIVES

1. Explain how annual changes in the relationship between the earth and the sun cause the seasons.
2. Identify the factors that influence weather.
3. Describe the main types of extreme weather.

Geographic Thinking

Making Comparisons, pp. 50, 52
Using the Atlas, p. 51
Determining Cause and Effect, p. 53

Focus & Motivate

Ask students to explain why their region does or does not experience significant seasonal changes.

Instruct: Objective 

Seasons

- What causes the changing seasons? *(The earth's revolution and tilt cause different parts of the earth to receive the direct rays of the sun for more hours of the day at certain times of year.)*
- What is a solstice? *(the day on which the sun's rays shine directly overhead at noon at either the Tropic of Cancer or the Tropic of Capricorn)*
- What are equinoxes? *(the biannual times when the days and nights all over the world are equal in length; The equinoxes mark the beginning of spring and autumn.)*

 **In-Depth Resources: Unit 1**
- Guided Reading, p. 23

SECTION 1 PROGRAM RESOURCES

In-Depth Resources: Unit 1
- Guided Reading, p. 23
- Building Vocabulary, p. 30
- Reteaching Activity, p. 31

Guided Reading Workbook
- Section 1

Access for Students Acquiring English/ESL
- Guided Reading, p. 10

Formal Assessment
- Section Quiz, p. 35

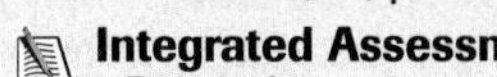

Integrated Assessment
- Rubric for a chart, 2.2

Cultures Around the World
- Architecture, p. 1

INTEGRATED TECHNOLOGY

Cultures Transparencies CW1
- Living in an Igloo

Chapter Summaries

Power Presentations

Test Generator
- Section Quiz

hmhsocialstudies.com

TEST-TAKING RESOURCES

Strategies for Test Preparation

Test Practice Transparencies TT7

Online Test Practice

Instruct: Objective 2

Weather

- What is the difference between weather and climate? *(Weather refers to conditions at one time. Climate refers to conditions over a long period.)*
- How do the three types of precipitation differ? *(Convectional precipitation occurs in hot, moist climates as a result of heated, rising air; orographic precipitation occurs where hills or mountains block moist air and force it to rise; and frontal precipitation occurs in mid-latitudes, where cold fronts push up warm fronts.)*

Cultures Around the World
• Architecture, p. 1

Weather

Weather and climate are often confused. **Weather** is the condition of the atmosphere at a particular location and time. **Climate** is the term for weather conditions at a particular location over a long period of time. Northern Russia, for example, has a cold climate. A

Geographic Thinking

Making Comparisons
A Why might geographers be more interested in the climate of a place than its weather?

A. Answer Weather is a daily event. Climate gives you information for many days or even a year.

WHAT CAUSES THE WEATHER? Daily weather is the complex result of several conditions. For example, the amount of solar energy received by a location varies according to the earth's position in relation to the sun. Large masses of air absorb and distribute this solar energy, which in turn affects the weather. Other factors include:

- **water vapor** This determines whether there will be **precipitation**—falling water droplets in the form of rain, sleet, snow, or hail.
- **cloud cover** Clouds may hold water vapor.
- **landforms and bodies of water** Water heats slowly but also loses heat slowly. Land heats rapidly but loses heat quickly as well.
- **elevation** As elevation above sea level increases, the air becomes thinner and loses its ability to hold moisture.
- **air movement** Winds move the air and the solar energy and moisture that it holds. As a result, weather can change very rapidly.

PRECIPITATION Precipitation depends on the amount of water vapor in the air and the movement of that air. As warm air rises, it cools and loses its ability to hold water vapor. The water vapor condenses, and the water droplets form into clouds. When the amount of water in a cloud is too heavy for the air to hold, rain or snow falls from the cloud. Geographers classify precipitation as convectional, orographic, or frontal, as illustrated in the diagram below.

Interpreting Diagrams

Types of Precipitation

Point out that all three types of precipitation involve moist air rising, cooling, and then dropping water. The difference is what causes the air to rise. Ask students to identify this cause for each type of precipitation. *(convectional—the sun heats the air, and warm air rises; orographic—mountains block the passage of the air and cause it to rise; frontal—cold, dense air pushes up warm, light air)*

Types of Precipitation

Convectional Typical of hot climates, convection occurs after morning sunshine heats warm moist air. Clouds form in the afternoon and rain falls.

Orographic Associated with mountain areas, orographic storms drop more rain on the windward side of a mountain and create a rain shadow on the leeward side.

Frontal Mid-latitude frontal storms feature cold dense air masses that push lighter warm air masses upwar[d], causing precipitation to form.

50

ACTIVITY OPTION **CRITICAL THINKING**

MAKING GENERALIZATIONS

Explaining the Skill In this activity, students will proceed from details they learn about weather principles to make broader assumptions about weather patterns where similar circumstances obtain.

Applying the Skill Direct students' attention to the diagram "Types of Precipitation" at the bottom of page 50 and display a physical map of the United States. Ask students to apply the information in the diagram to regions of the United States in order to answer the following questions.

- What kind of precipitation would you expect to occur in the Southeast? *(convectional)* In the Midwest? *(frontal)* In the Pacific Northwest? *(orographic)*

Convectional precipitation occurs in hot, moist climates where the sun quickly heats the air. The heated air rises, and by afternoon clouds form and rain falls. Orographic precipitation falls on the windward side of hills or mountains that block moist air and force it upward. The air cools and rain or snow falls. The land on the leeward side is called a **rain shadow** because it gets little rain from the descending dry air. Frontal movement causes most precipitation in the middle latitudes. A front is the boundary between two air masses of different temperatures or density. Rain or snow occurs when lighter, warm air is pushed upward by the colder, denser air. The rising air cools, water vapor condenses, and precipitation falls.

Weather Extremes

As air masses warm and cool and move across the earth's surface, they create weather. Sometimes the clashes between air masses cause storms, which can be severe. They disrupt the usual patterns of life and often cause major property damage and loss of human life. Hurricanes, tornadoes, blizzards, droughts, and floods are examples of extreme weather.

HURRICANES Storms that form over warm, tropical ocean waters are called **hurricanes**—also known as **typhoons** in Asia. These storms are called different names around the globe: tropical cyclones, willy-willies (Australia), *baguios* (Philippines), and *chubascos* (Mexico). Hurricanes are one way heat from the tropics is moved out of the region. Air flowing over an ocean with a water temperature of 80°F or higher picks up huge amounts of moisture and heat energy. As these water-laden winds flow into a low-pressure core, they tighten to form an "eye." The eye is usually 10 to 20 miles across and has clear, calm skies. But the winds moving around the eye may be as strong as 200 miles per hour.

The clouds and winds stretch over a vast area, sometimes as wide as 500 miles. Upper air currents blowing from the east steer the hurricanes in a westerly direction. As the hurricane hits land, it pounds the area with howling winds and very heavy rains. It may also cause a storm surge along coastal regions. This wall of seawater, pushed ashore by the winds, may rise to 16 feet or more. The low-lying coastal regions of Bangladesh in South Asia are especially vulnerable to storm surges from tropical cyclones. B

TORNADOES Unlike hurricanes, which take days to develop, tornadoes form quickly and sometimes without warning. A **tornado,** or twister, is a powerful funnel-shaped column of spiraling air.

MOVEMENT A pair of typhoons move across the Pacific Ocean. Notice the "eye" in each storm. **What is the weather inside the "eye" like?**

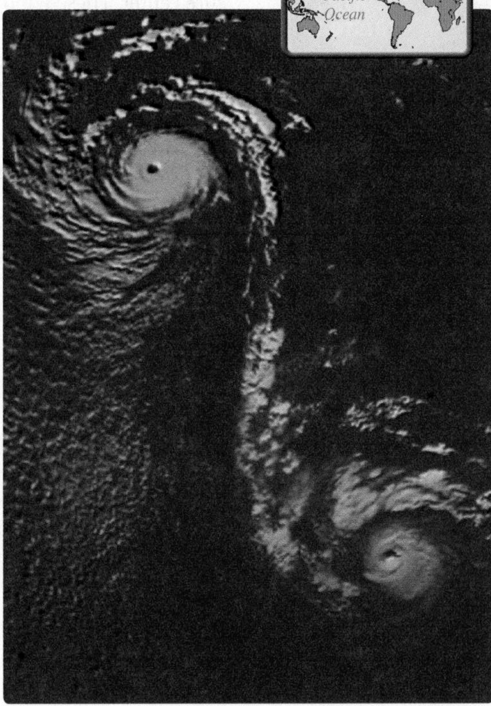

B. Answer Bangladesh is located on the Ganges River.

Geographic Thinking

Using the Atlas
B Use the map on page A34-A35. On which river delta is Bangladesh located?

BASICS

Instruct: Objective 3

Weather Extremes

- How are hurricanes, tornadoes, and blizzards similar? Different? *(Each involves strong winds. Hurricanes cover large areas and take days to form. Tornadoes develop quickly and have relatively small diameters. Blizzards are heavy snowstorms.)*
- What is a flood? *(the accumulation of melted snow and/or rain that exceeds the land's absorption capacity)*

More About

Weather Extremes

Highest temperature
136° F at El Azizia, Libya

Coldest temperature
-129° F at Vostok, Antarctica

Deadliest hurricane
Mitch 1998, Central America, over 10,800 killed

Wettest annual average
523.6 in. at Lloro, Colombia

Driest annual average
.03 in. at Arica, Chile

Biggest snowstorm
189 in., Feb. 13–19, 1959, Mt. Shasta, CA

Highest wind speed
231 mph, April 12, 1934, Mt. Washington, NH

Interpreting Photographs

Typhoons
Have students examine the typhoons in this image and ask them to describe how the wind and water appear to be moving. *(in a counter-clockwise direction)*

CAPTION ANSWER The "eye" has clear, calm skies.

ACTIVITY OPTION INTERNET RESEARCH

BLOCK SCHEDULING

REPORTING ABOUT HURRICANES

Objective To explain the formation of a hurricane

Class Time 30 minutes

Task Research how hurricanes form

Directions Assign students to small groups. Tell them to use the links at **hmhsocialstudies.com** to find out more about how hurricanes develop. Have each group explore an aspect of hurricanes: formation, onshore damage, classification and naming conventions, predication and tracking, etc.

OPTIONAL ACTIVITY If Internet access is limited, have students use reference books in the library for this activity.

5 THEMES

REGION: Tornado Alley

"Tornado Alley" is an example of a formal region, which is an area defined by a limited number of related characteristics. These characteristics include topography and weather patterns. What type of precipitation would be most common in Tornado Alley? *(frontal)*

More About

Fujita-Pearson Tornado Scale

The Fujita-Pearson tornado scale has been used since the early 1970s to rate the intensity of tornadoes. Below are some characteristics associated with the different categories.

Category	Wind Speeds (mph)	Damage
F-0	40-72	chimney damage, tree branches broken
F-1	73-112	mobile homes pushed off foundations or overturned
F-2	113-157	considerable damage, mobile homes demolished, trees uprooted
F-3	158-206	roofs and walls torn down, trains overturned, cars thrown
F-4	207-260	well-constructed walls leveled
F-5	261-318	homes lifted off foundations and carried large distances, autos thrown as far as 100 yards

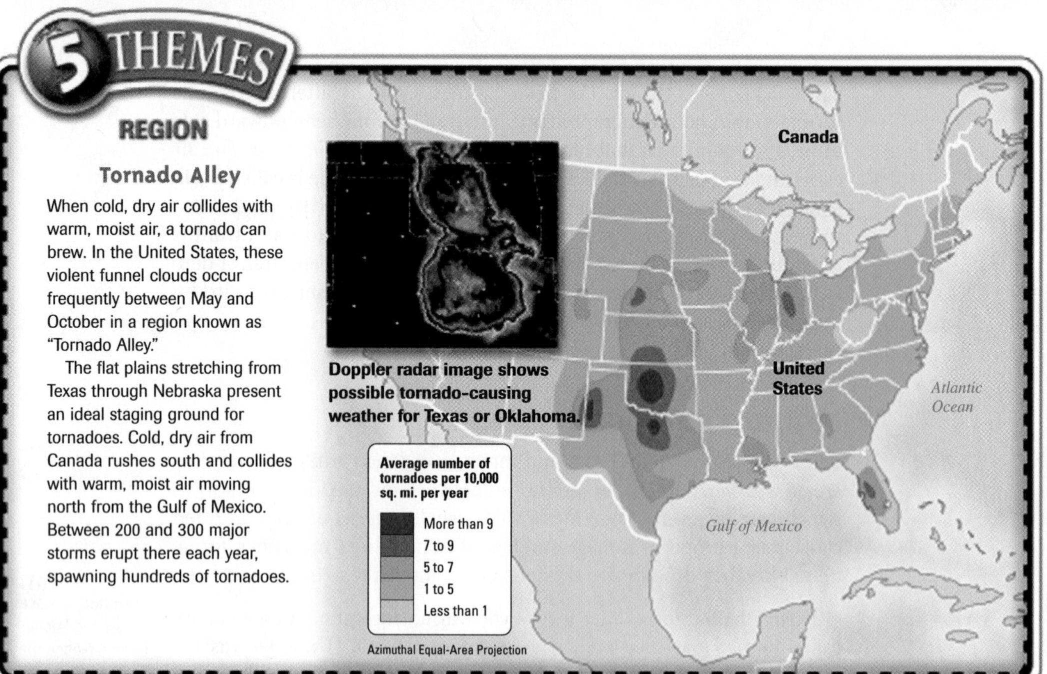
5 THEMES
REGION
Tornado Alley
When cold, dry air collides with warm, moist air, a tornado can brew. In the United States, these violent funnel clouds occur frequently between May and October in a region known as "Tornado Alley."
The flat plains stretching from Texas through Nebraska present an ideal staging ground for tornadoes. Cold, dry air from Canada rushes south and collides with warm, moist air moving north from the Gulf of Mexico. Between 200 and 300 major storms erupt there each year, spawning hundreds of tornadoes.
Doppler radar image shows possible tornado-causing weather for Texas or Oklahoma.
Canada
United States
Atlantic Ocean
Gulf of Mexico
Average number of tornadoes per 10,000 sq. mi. per year
More than 9
7 to 9
5 to 7
1 to 5
Less than 1
Azimuthal Equal-Area Projection

HISTORY
VIDEO
Tornado Alley Twister
hmhsocialstudies.com

Born from strong thunderstorms, tornadoes are capable of immense damage. In a tornado, winds swirl counter-clockwise around a low-pressure center. These winds may reach speeds of 300 miles per hour, blasting apart buildings and lifting objects as large as cars and mobile homes. Generally, tornadoes have small diameters (about 300 feet), travel about a mile, and last only a few minutes. However, the largest and most forceful can reach a mile across and stay on the ground for hours, hopscotching from one location to another. The largest outbreak of tornadoes in the United States occurred during a 16-hour period, April 3 and 4, 1974. A total of 148 tornadoes ripped through the Ohio and Tennessee valleys, killing 330 people. The largest share of tornadoes, about 3 of every 4, hit in the United States. On average, the U.S. National Weather Service counts 700 tornadoes each year. C

Geographic Thinking

Making Comparisons

C How are tornadoes different from hurricanes?

C. Answer Tornadoes form over land, are smaller in diameter, develop more quickly, have higher winds, and are shorter in duration.

BLIZZARDS A **blizzard** is a heavy snowstorm with winds of more than 35 miles per hour and reduced visibility. These weather conditions snarl traffic, endanger livestock, and trap travelers. The greatest snowfall for a 24-hour period was 76 inches (6 feet 4 inches) in Silver Lake, Colorado, in 1921. A snowstorm that lasted from February 13 to 19, 1959, dumped 189 inches (almost 16 feet) of snow on Mt. Shasta, California.

Because of their location, some areas of the country are frequently hit with snowstorms that produce huge amounts of snow. For example, the eastern and southern shores of the Great Lakes are snowbelts that experience days and days of heavy snow resulting in enormous snow depths. Around the Lake Erie and Lake Ontario areas, the annual snowfall can be as much as 450 inches (37.5 feet).

ACTIVITY OPTION **COOPERATIVE LEARNING**

DRAWING A WEATHER MAP

Objective To create a thematic map

Class Time 30 minutes

Task Make an outline map of the United States showing which areas of the country are prone to hurricanes, tornadoes, and blizzards

Directions Organize students into groups of three. While one student makes an outline map of the United States, the other two can use reference books or the Internet to find out which areas of the country are most prone to hurricanes and blizzards. By combining this information with the tornado information on page 52, students can create a composite map. Students' maps should include a key and colored or shaded areas that accurately depict the areas of the country that experience the majority of these three weather extremes.

DROUGHTS A **drought** is a long period of time without rain or with very minimal rainfall. This lack of rain results in crop failures and drastically reduced levels in water storage facilities. In the early 1930s, a drought hit the Great Plains in the United States. Dust storms damaged farms across a 150,000 square-mile region that became known as the "Dust Bowl." Suffering the effects of a harsh climate, thousands of families were forced to leave their land to find work elsewhere. (See the Dust Bowl Disaster feature on pages 150-151.) In 2000, a large portion of the southern United States was struck with a long drought. Northern Texas was particularly hard hit, with 84 straight days of no rain and extremely high temperatures.

REGION Before the drought in Texas, this boat floated on the waters of a lake now barely visible in the background.
How is life affected by drought?

BACKGROUND
A series of droughts in Texas between 1996 and 2000 caused $5.3 billion in damages.

FLOODS When water spreads over land not normally covered with water, it is called a flood. Melting snow or rainwater fills streams or rivers until they reach flood stage, the point at which the banks can no longer contain the water. The water then flows into the surrounding area, called a floodplain.

Floods take lives every year, especially in low, flat places like Bangladesh, where millions of people live on the flood plains and the delta. In 1993, flooding along the Mississippi and Missouri rivers claimed 50 lives and caused about $15 billion in damage. Nearly 150 rivers and their tributaries were involved. It was the largest flood ever to hit the United States.

In the next section, you will learn about how climate affects people's lives and how humans adapt to changes in climate.

Section 1 Assessment

1 Places & Terms
Explain the meaning of each of the following terms.
- solstice
- equinox
- weather
- climate
- precipitation

2 Taking Notes
MOVEMENT Review the notes you took for this section.

Seasons & Weather

- Which latitude lines mark the summer and winter solstices?
- How do moving air masses create weather?

3 Main Ideas
a. How do the earth's revolution and tilt affect the seasons?
b. What is the difference between weather and climate?
c. What are some examples of extreme weather?

4 Geographic Thinking
Determining Cause and Effect What must be present for any type of precipitation to occur? **Think about:**
- the cause of precipitation
- the types of precipitation

See Skillbuilder Handbook, page R9.

GeoActivity

EXPLORING LOCAL GEOGRAPHY Using your local newspaper, television, or an Internet weather forecast, make a **chart** showing predicted temperature highs and lows and precipitation for several days. Then record the actual weather on those days. Write a summary of your observations of the accuracy of the weather forecast.

Interpreting Photographs

North Texas Drought of 2000

Ask students to examine the photograph and guess what economic problems might be caused by the drought. *(loss of tourist income; depreciation of local property values; higher prices paid by consumers for water, etc.)*

CAPTION ANSWER Shortage of water supplies for humans, animals, and crops may cause death, crop failures, food shortages, or economic hardship.

Assess & Reteach

GeoFocus Have students complete the section on seasons and weather in their graphic organizers.

Formal Assessment
- Section Quiz, p. 35

Reteaching Activity
Write the three section objectives from page 49 on the board and ask students to write a summary paragraph that fulfills each objective.

In-Depth Resources: Unit 1
- Reteaching Activity, p. 31

SECTION 1 ASSESSMENT ANSWERS

1. Places & Terms
solstice, p. 49
equinox, p. 49
weather, p. 50
climate, p. 50
precipitation, p. 50

2. Taking Notes
- the Tropic of Cancer and the Tropic of Capricorn
- Air masses move heat and moisture to different parts of the globe.

3. Main Ideas
a. The earth's revolution and tilt affect the seasons by exposing different parts of the earth to direct sunlight for more or fewer hours of the day at certain times of the year.
b. Weather is the daily condition of the atmosphere. Climate is the average of a year or several years' weather.
c. hurricanes, tornadoes, blizzards, droughts, floods

4. Geographic Thinking
Precipitation occurs when warm, moist air rises and then cools and falls. Convection, mountain barriers, or fronts will cause the air to rise.

GeoActivity

Integrated Assessment
- Rubric for a chart, 2.2

Climate

SECTION 2 OBJECTIVES

1. Explain the factors that influence the climate of a region.
2. Describe the effects of El Niño, La Niña, and global warming.

SKILLBUILDER: Interpreting Maps and Graphics, pp. 54, 55, 56, 57, 58

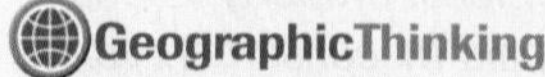

GeographicThinking

Making Comparisons, p. 55
Drawing Conclusions, p. 58

Focus & Motivate

Ask students where in the world they would most like to live based on the climate in that location. How much does climate affect the quality of life? *(Answers will vary.)*

Instruct: Objective 1 appears on p. 55.

Interpreting Maps

Global Wind Currents

Remind students that winds are identified by the direction *from* which they blow, and point out how the names of global wind currents reflect this fact. Ask students what the colors on this map represent. *(They represent the temperature of the wind currents, with orange being warm, green being cool, and blue being cold.)*

SKILLBUILDER ANSWERS

1. southeasterly **2.** The westerlies blow between 30° and 60° North latitude and 30° and 60° South latitude.

Main Ideas

- Climate reflects the seasonal patterns of weather for a location over a long period of time.
- Global climatic changes may be natural or human-made.

Places & Terms

convection
El Niño
greenhouse effect

A HUMAN PERSPECTIVE Nineteenth-century fishermen along the Peruvian coast called the event El Niño—the Spanish name for the infant Jesus—because the event occurred near Christmastime. Every two to seven years, the waters off the Peruvian coast became warmer than usual, resulting in poor fishing. Eventually, 20th-century scientists studying worldwide climate changes confirmed the truth of this folk knowledge. They discovered that El Niño brought about changes in global weather patterns that disrupted not only fishing, but also other economic activities. Droughts and floods in Asia, Africa, and North America seemed to be related to El Niño. Scientists recognized that weather and climate conditions are not isolated but are connected parts of the global climate system.

Factors Affecting Climate

Four major factors influence the climate of a region: wind and ocean currents, latitude, elevation, and topography.

WIND CURRENTS Wind and ocean currents help distribute the sun's heat from one part of the world to another through **convection,** the transfer of heat in the atmosphere by upward motion of the air. As sunlight heats the atmosphere, the air expands, creating a zone of low air pressure. Cooler dense air in a nearby high-pressure zone rushes into the low-pressure area, causing wind.

Global wind patterns are caused by the same kind of circulation on a larger scale. The hot air flows toward the poles, and the cold air moves toward the equator. The winds would blow in straight lines, but since the earth rotates they are turned at an angle. In the Northern Hemisphere, they turn to the right. In the Southern Hemisphere, they turn to the left. This bending of the winds is called the Coriolis effect.

The map to the right shows that the wind patterns are mirror images of each other in the Northern and Southern Hemispheres. Winds are identified by the direction from which they blow; a north wind blows from the north to the south.

Global Wind Currents

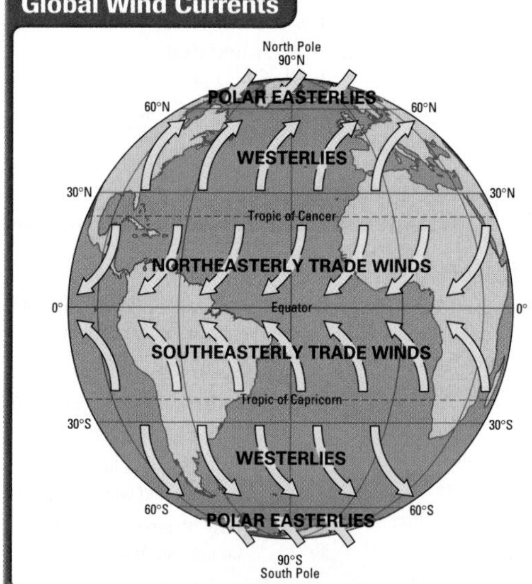

SKILLBUILDER: Interpreting Maps

1. **MOVEMENT** From which direction do the wind currents blow near the equator in the Southern Hemisphere?
2. **LOCATION** Between which latitudes do the westerlies blow?

SECTION 2 PROGRAM RESOURCES

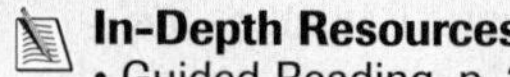

In-Depth Resources: Unit 1
- Guided Reading, p. 24
- Building Vocabulary, p. 30
- Reteaching Activity, p. 32

Guided Reading Workbook
- Section 2

Access for Students Acquiring English/ESL
- Guided Reading, p. 11

Formal Assessment
- Section Quiz, p. 36

Integrated Assessment
- Rubric for a multimedia presentation, 5.4

INTEGRATED TECHNOLOGY

Chapter Summaries

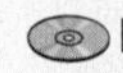

Power Presentations

Test Generator
- Section Quiz

hmhsocialstudies.com

TEST-TAKING RESOURCES

Strategies for Test Preparation

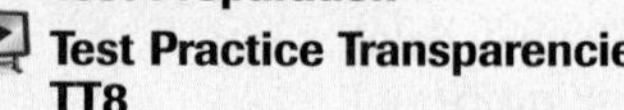

Test Practice Transparencies TT8

Online Test Practice

Global Ocean Currents

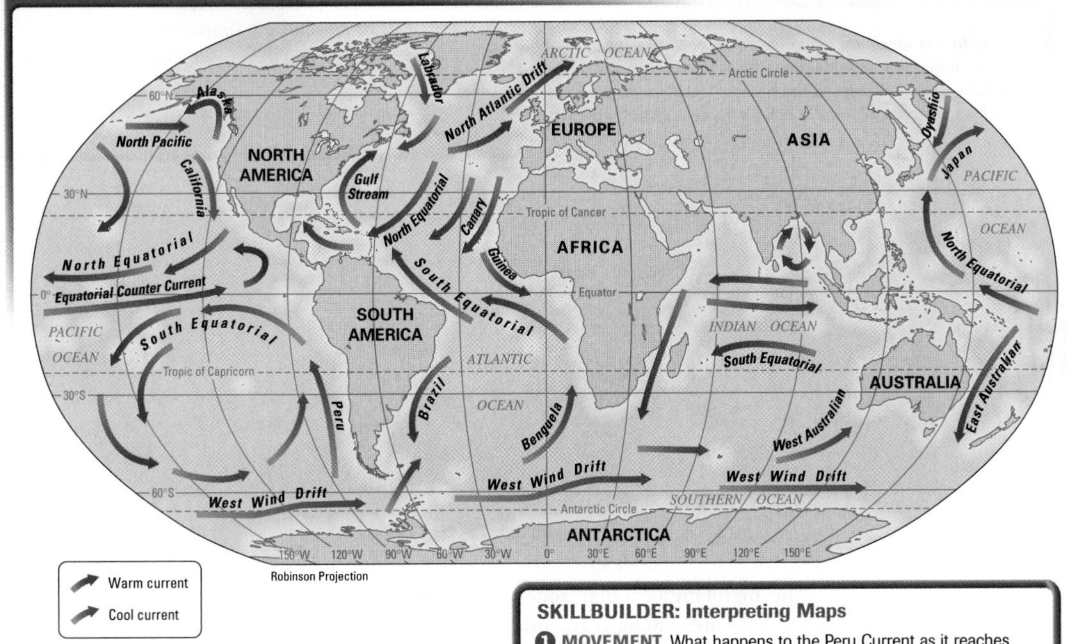

ARCTIC OCEAN
Arctic Circle
60°N
Alaska
North Pacific
California
NORTH AMERICA
Gulf Stream
Labrador
North Atlantic Drift
EUROPE
ASIA
Oyashio
Japan
PACIFIC OCEAN
30°N
Tropic of Cancer
North Equatorial
Canary
AFRICA
Guinea
North Equatorial
Equatorial Counter Current
0° Equator
South Equatorial
PACIFIC OCEAN
SOUTH AMERICA
INDIAN OCEAN
South Equatorial
ATLANTIC OCEAN
Tropic of Capricorn
30°S
Peru
Brazil
Benguela
AUSTRALIA
West Australian
East Australian
60°S
West Wind Drift
West Wind Drift
West Wind Drift
SOUTHERN OCEAN
Antarctic Circle
ANTARCTICA
150°W 120°W 90°W 60°W 30°W 0° 30°E 60°E 90°E 120°E 150°E

Warm current
Cool current

Robinson Projection

SKILLBUILDER: Interpreting Maps

1. **MOVEMENT** What happens to the Peru Current as it reaches the equator?
2. **LOCATION** Where does the West Wind Drift flow?

OCEAN CURRENTS Ocean currents are like rivers flowing in the ocean. Moving in large circular systems, warm waters flow away from the equator toward the poles, and cold water flows back toward the equator. Winds blowing over the ocean currents affect the climate of the lands that the winds cross. For example, the warmth of the Gulf Stream and the North Atlantic Drift help keep the temperature of Europe moderate. Even though much of Europe is as far north as Canada, it enjoys a much milder climate than Canada.

Ocean currents affect not only the temperature of an area, but also the amount of precipitation received. Cold ocean currents flowing along a coastal region chill the air and sometimes prevent warm air and the moisture it holds from falling to earth. The Atacama Desert in South America and the Namib Desert in Africa, for example, were formed partly because of cold ocean currents nearby. A

Geographic Thinking
Making Comparisons
A How are wind and ocean currents similar in their effect on climate?
A. Answer Both move heat from the earth's surface to other parts of the globe.

ZONES OF LATITUDE Geographers divide the earth into three general zones of latitude: low or tropical, middle or temperate, and high or polar. Tropical zones are found on either side of the equator. They extend to the tropic of Cancer in the Northern Hemisphere and the tropic of Capricorn in the Southern Hemisphere. Lands in tropical zones are hot all year long. In some areas, a shift in wind patterns causes variations in the seasons. For example, Tanzania experiences both a rainy season and a dry season as Indian Ocean winds blow in or away from the land.

BASICS

Interpreting Maps

Global Ocean Currents

Point out that ocean currents are driven by the wind, but that continents and the earth's rotation also affect their flow. Have students compare this map with the map of global wind currents on page 54. Ask how the ocean currents differ from the wind currents. *(There appears to be a greater variety of ocean currents.)*

SKILLBUILDER ANSWERS
1. It changes from a cold current to a warm one. **2.** The West Wind Drift flows off the coast of Antarctica.

Instruct: Objective 

Factors Affecting Climate

- What four factors influence the climate of a region? *(wind and ocean currents, latitude, altitude, and topography)*
- What is the general direction of wind and ocean currents? *(Warm air and water flow toward the poles, and cold air and water flow toward the Equator.)*
- How does latitude and altitude affect climate? *(The higher the latitude or altitude, the colder it gets.)*

In-Depth Resources: Unit 1
• Guided Reading, p. 24

More About

Ocean Temperature

The surface temperature of the ocean near the Equator is about 86° F (30° C). Near the poles, the surface temperature is about 28° F (-2° C).

DIFFERENTIATING INSTRUCTION LESS PROFICIENT READERS

DIAGRAMMING INFORMATION

Objective Using diagrams to help students understand concepts
Class Time 20 minutes
Task Have students answer questions based on simple diagrams
Directions Explain that the overall effect of wind and ocean currents is to moderate, or even out, climates by circulating heat and moisture. Note that temperature and precipitation are the main components of climate. Then draw a simple diagram of a land mass and an ocean current on the board. Label the ocean current "warm" and draw an arrow to represent wind blowing from the ocean onto the land. Ask students what effect the warm ocean current and wind would have on the weather on the land. *(It would warm the air and bring moisture.)* Then change the label to "cold" and ask students what effect a cold ocean current and wind would have on the weather on the land. *(It would cool the air and bring little moisture.)*

Interpreting Graphics

Climate Controls

Help students read this graph by asking them to locate 2,500 feet in elevation along the vertical axis. Then direct them to read across the horizontal axis and identify all the possible climates. Ask them to do the same thing for 15,000 feet. *(2,500 feet: tropical wet, tropical wet and dry, desert, humid subtropical, marine, humid continental, subarctic, tundra, and icecap; 15,000 feet: tundra and icecap.)*

SKILLBUILDER ANSWERS
1. between about 20° and 35° latitude and up to 7,500 feet **2.** Climates change from tropical to continental to subarctic to tundra and ice cap.

Instruct: Objective 2

Changes in Climate

- What is El Niño, and what effects does it have? *(El Niño is a warming of the waters off the west coast of South America caused by a change in the direction of the prevailing easterly wind. The change pushes warm water and heavy rains toward the Americas and brings drought to Australia and Asia.)*
- What are the effects and possible causes of global warming? *(Global warming might cause the melting of ice caps, coastal flooding, and the disappearance of islands. It may be the result of the earth's natural warming and cooling cycles, or it may be caused by human activities.)*

Climate Controls

Latitude and elevation influence climate. Notice that as you move along the latitude line, the climates at the lower altitude change. However, the greater the altitude, the fewer the climate zones no matter what latitude a location may be.

SKILLBUILDER: Interpreting Graphics
1. **LOCATION** At about what latitude and altitude would you find a desert climate?
2. **REGION** How do the climate zones change as latitude gets higher?

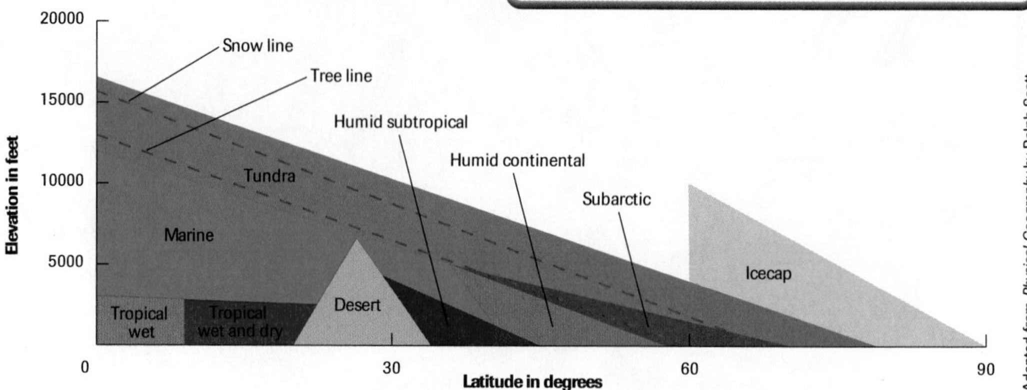

Adapted from *Physical Geography* by Ralph Scott.

The high-latitude polar zones, which encircle the North Pole and South Pole, are cold all year. Summer temperatures in the polar regions may reach a high of only 50°F.

The earth's two temperate zones lie at the middle latitudes, between the tropics and the polar regions. Within the temperate zones, climates can vary greatly, ranging from relatively hot to relatively cold. These variations occur because solar heating is greater in the summer than in the winter. So summers are much warmer.

ELEVATION Another factor in determining the climate of a region is elevation, or distance above sea level. You would think that the closer you get to the sun, the hotter it would become. But as altitude increases, the air temperature drops about 3.5°F for every 1,000 feet. Therefore, the climate gets colder as you climb a mountain or other elevated location. Climates above 12,000 feet become like those in Arctic areas—with snow and ice. For example, Mt. Kilimanjaro in east Africa is capped by snow all year long. The diagram above will help you see how latitude and elevation are related.

TOPOGRAPHY Landforms also affect the climate. This is especially true of mountain areas. Remember that moisture-laden winds cool as they move up the side of a mountain, eventually releasing rain or snow. By the time the winds reach the other side of the mountain, they are dry and become warmer as they flow down the mountain.

Changes in Climate

Climates change over time. Scientists studying ice-core samples from thousands of years ago have noted a variety of changes in temperature and precipitation. Some of the changes in climate appear to be natural while others are the result of human activities.

ACTIVITY OPTION **LINK TO MATH**

ESTIMATING TEMPERATURE AND ALTITUDE

Objective To estimate the air temperature as altitude increases

Class Time 10 minutes

Task Solve math problems that require using a rate for change in air temperature with increase in altitude

Directions Have students solve the following problems using this rate: air temperature drops 3.5°F for every 1,000-feet increase in altitude. Ask them to show how they found the answers.

1. If the temperature in a city at 3,500 feet elevation is 60°F, what is the temperature at a nearby location with an elevation of 8,500 feet? *(8,500 – 3,500 = 5,000 feet; 5 × 3.5 = 17.5°F drop in temperature; 60 – 17.5 = 42.5°F)*
2. If the temperature in a town at 5,200 feet elevation is 55°F, what is the temperate at a nearby location with an elevation of 13,200 feet? *(13,200 – 5,200 = 8,000 feet; 8 × 3.5 = 28°F drop in temperature; 55 – 28 = 27°F)*

EL NIÑO The warming of the waters off the west coast of South America—known as **El Niño**—is a natural change in the climate. About every two to seven years, prevailing easterly winds that blow over the central Pacific Ocean slow or reverse direction, changing the ocean temperature and affecting the weather worldwide. Normally, these easterlies bring seasonal rains and push warm ocean water toward Asia and Australia. In El Niño years, however, the winds push warm water and heavy rains toward the Americas. This can cause floods and mudslides there, while Australia and Asia experience drought conditions.

When the reverse occurs—that is, when the winds blow the warmer water to the lands on the western Pacific rim—the event is called La Niña. La Niña causes increases in precipitation in places such as India and increased dryness along the Pacific coasts of the Americas.

El Niño and La Niña

hmhsocialstudies.com INTERACTIVE

El Niño and La Niña act to transfer the heat on the earth's surface and in the atmosphere to other parts of the globe.

SKILLBUILDER: Interpreting Graphics

1. **MOVEMENT** In which direction do winds and water move in El Niño?
2. **LOCATION** Where does flooding occur during La Niña?

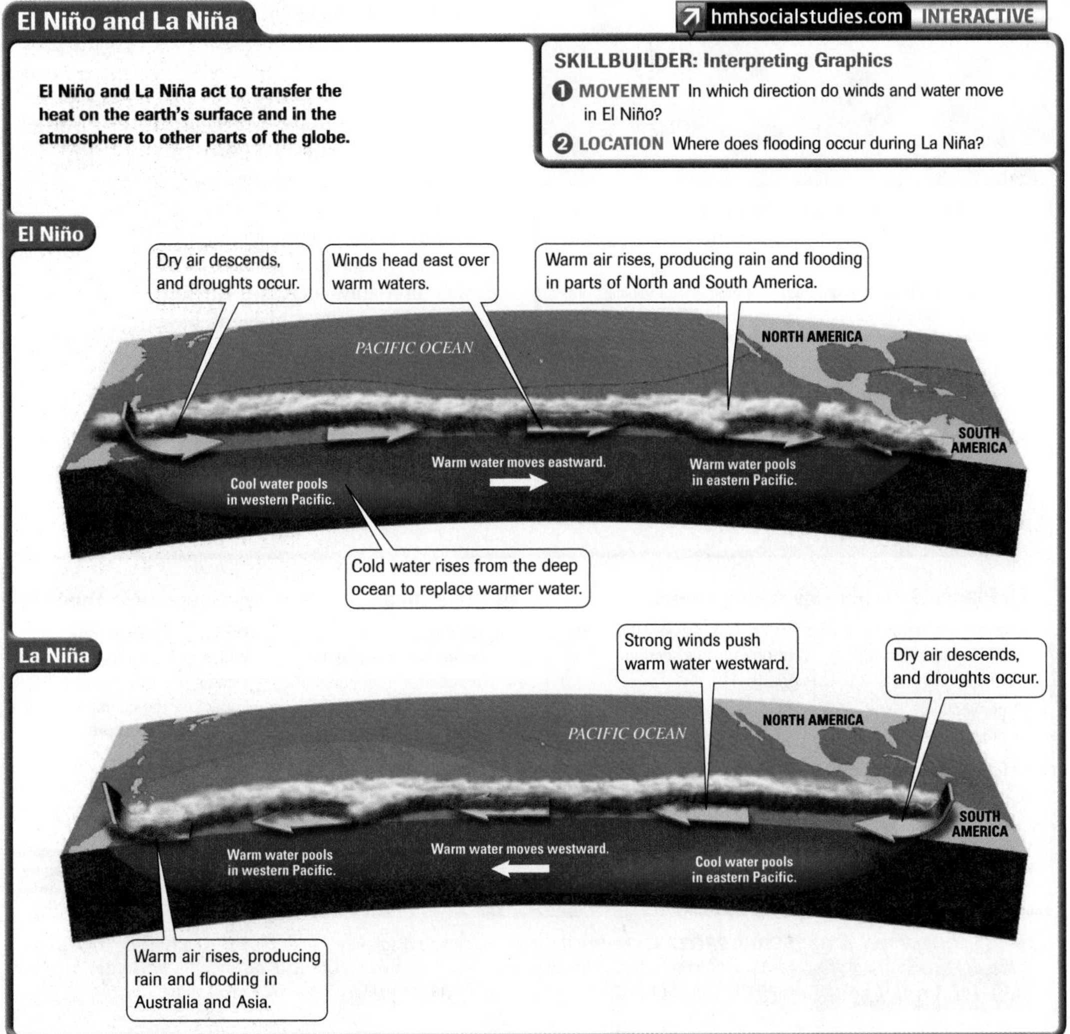
El Niño
Dry air descends, and droughts occur.
Winds head east over warm waters.
Warm air rises, producing rain and flooding in parts of North and South America.
PACIFIC OCEAN
NORTH AMERICA
SOUTH AMERICA
Warm water moves eastward.
Warm water pools in eastern Pacific.
Cool water pools in western Pacific.
Cold water rises from the deep ocean to replace warmer water.
La Niña
Strong winds push warm water westward.
Dry air descends, and droughts occur.
PACIFIC OCEAN
NORTH AMERICA
SOUTH AMERICA
Warm water pools in western Pacific.
Warm water moves westward.
Cool water pools in eastern Pacific.
Warm air rises, producing rain and flooding in Australia and Asia.

BASICS

More About

El Niño

El Niño is a Spanish term meaning "the child." The name reflects the fact that the pattern usually occurs around Christmas, and the name refers to the Christ child. *La Niña* is the feminine form of the word.

Interpreting Graphics

El Niño and La Niña

Note that these cut-away diagrams show the Pacific Ocean basin and bordering continents. Ask students why El Niño and La Niña have their strongest effects on North America, South America, Australia, and Asia. *(because these continents border the Pacific Ocean)*

SKILLBUILDER ANSWERS

1. They move from the west.
2. Australia and Asia

ACTIVITY OPTION INTERNET RESEARCH

BLOCK SCHEDULING

CREATING A CHART

Objective To conduct research and present the information in a chart

Class Time 40 minutes

Task Search the Internet for information about the effects of the most recent El Niño and report these effects by location in a chart

Directions Direct students to **hmhsocialstudies.com** and have them follow the links to find the information they need. Charts should reflect average temperatures and rainfall in years with no El Niño as well as how those numbers differ during an El Niño period.

OPTIONAL ACTIVITY If Internet access is limited, have the students use periodical indexes to locate information on the most recent El Niño.

Interpreting Graphics

Greenhouse Effect

Ask students how the layer of carbon dioxide and other gases in the atmosphere create conditions similar to those in a greenhouse. Note: If students are unfamiliar with greenhouses, point out that the same effect occurs in a car on a sunny day. *(A greenhouse's glass enclosure allows sunlight to enter and warm the air. The warm air is trapped by the glass. In the same way, the sunlight warms the air above the earth and the layer of gases prevents the heated air from escaping as readily.)*

SKILLBUILDER ANSWERS

1. factories and automobiles
2. More exhaust gases will be trapped and raise the temperature even higher.

Assess & Reteach

GeoFocus Have students complete the section on climate in their graphic organizers.

 **Formal Assessment**
- Section Quiz, p. 36

Reteaching Activity

Divide the class into two teams and direct each team to review the material under one of the two main headings in this section. Then quiz each team on that content. Keep track of the number of correct answers to see which team "wins."

 **In-Depth Resources: Unit 1**
- Reteaching Activity, p. 32

Greenhouse Effect

Some heat escapes
HEAT TRAPPING LAYER
Heat trapped
CO_2 and other gases

SKILLBUILDER: Interpreting Graphics

1. **HUMAN–ENVIRONMENT INTERACTION** Which elements in the illustration add heat to the environment?
2. **MOVEMENT** What might happen if more motor vehicles are added to the picture?

GLOBAL CLIMATE CHANGE Evidence shows that climates are changing around the world. Violent weather events, including some exceptionally harsh winters, have become more common. On average, though, air temperatures are rising. Since the late 1800s, the temperature of the earth has increased by one degree Fahrenheit. Estimates suggest that the temperature will increase from 3.2 to 7.2 degrees in the next century.

Most climate scientists argue that global warming is caused by the **greenhouse effect.** The layer of gases released by the burning of coal and oil traps some solar energy, causing higher temperatures in the same way that a greenhouse traps solar energy. However, some critics say that this warming is just part of the earth's natural cycle.

BACKGROUND The air temperature in the period between about 1500 and 1850 was so much cooler than today that it is known as a "Little Ice Age."

As more nations industrialize, the greenhouse effect and global warming will probably increase. Already, many of the world's glaciers have shrunk. There is much less ice in the Arctic Ocean than there once was. If the trend continues, ice caps will melt, flooding some coastal areas and covering low-lying islands. Many scientists also predict that weather patterns will become more erratic. For example, droughts may worsen.

Section 2 Assessment

1 Places & Terms

Explain the meaning of each of the following terms.
- convection
- El Niño
- greenhouse effect

2 Taking Notes

MOVEMENT Review the notes you took for this section.

Climate	

- What are four factors that affect climate?
- What are examples of forces that produce climate changes?

3 Main Ideas

a. What role do wind and ocean currents play in climate?
b. How do latitude and altitude affect climate?
c. How do El Niño and La Niña affect climate?

4 Geographic Thinking

Drawing Conclusions Which of the factors affecting climate has the greatest impact on the climate in your region? **Think about:**
- the four factors affecting climate
- the climate where you live

SEEING PATTERNS Review the information and diagram about El Niño and La Niña on page 57. Use the Internet to find more information on these events. Create a **multimedia presentation** explaining one of the events and how it affects the world-wide weather conditions

SECTION 2 ASSESSMENT ANSWERS

1. **Places & Terms**
   convection, p. 54
   El Niño, p. 57
   greenhouse effect, p. 58
2. **Taking Notes**
   - wind and ocean currents, latitude, altitude, and topography
   - El Niño, La Niña, and the greenhouse effect of global warming
3. **Main Ideas**
   a. They move heat and moisture from one part of the globe to another.
   b. The latitudes closer to the equator have warmer climates. An increase in elevation is equivalent to moving to higher latitudes in climate type.
   c. During El Niño, the Americas experience more rain, wave erosion, and flooding, and Asia and Australia experience more drought conditions. In La Niña periods, the reverse is true.
4. **Geographic Thinking**
   Answers will vary but most likely will include latitude or altitude.

GeoActivity

 **Integrated Assessment**
- Rubric for a multimedia presentation, 5.4

World Climate Regions

Main Ideas
- Temperature and precipitation define climate regions.
- Broad climate definitions help to identify variations in weather at a location over the course of a year.

Places & Terms
tundra
permafrost

BASICS

A HUMAN PERSPECTIVE Songs have been written celebrating April in Paris. Springtime there is mild, with temperatures in the 50°F range. But no songs have been written about April in Winnipeg, Canada. Temperatures in April there are only slightly above freezing. If you look at the two locations on a map, you will find the cities are almost the same distance north of the equator. To understand why two cities at the same latitude are so different, you need to understand climate regions. When studying climate, one of the key words is location.

PLACE This highland climate zone in Patagonia, South America, has several different climate regions, including tundra and subarctic.

Defining a Climate Region

Climate regions act like a code that tells geographers much about an area without giving many local details. To define a climate region, geographers must make generalizations about what the typical weather conditions are like over many years in a location.

The two most significant factors in defining different climates are temperature and precipitation. A place's location on a continent, its topography, and its elevation may also have an impact on the climate.

Geographers use a variety of methods to describe climate patterns. The most common method uses latitude to help define the climate. There are five general climate regions: tropical (low latitude), dry, mid-latitude, high latitude, and highland. Dry and highland climates occur at several different latitudes. Within the five regions, there are variations that geographers divide into smaller zones. You can see the varied climate regions on the map on pages 60–61.

Although the map shows a distinct line between each of the climate regions, in reality there are transition zones between the regions. As you read about climate regions, refer to the climate map. You should see the latitude-related patterns that emerge in world climate regions.

59

SECTION 3 OBJECTIVES
1. Identify the factors that define climate regions.
2. Describe the temperature and precipitation patterns of the world's major climate regions.

GeographicThinking
Making Comparisons, pp. 62, 63
Making Generalizations, p. 63

Focus & Motivate
Ask students to describe the climate in their region. *(Answers should be based on average temperatures in summer and winter, and average rainfall/precipitation.)*

Instruct: Objective 1

Defining a Climate Region

- What are two major factors that define climates? *(temperature and precipitation)*
- What other factors influence climate? *(location on a continent, topography, and altitude)*
- What are the five general climate regions? *(tropical, dry, mid-latitude, high latitude, and highland)*

In-Depth Resources: Unit 1
- Guided Reading, p. 25

Interpreting Photographs
Patagonia, South America
Ask students to examine the image and describe what kind of weather they would expect at the different elevations. *(At lower elevations, there are probably distinct seasons, with cold winters and warm summers. At higher elevations, the weather would be cooler.)*

SECTION 3 PROGRAM RESOURCES

In-Depth Resources: Unit 1
- Guided Reading, p. 25
- Skillbuilder Practice, p. 29
- Building Vocabulary. p. 30
- Reteaching Activity, p. 33
- Map and Graph Skills, pp. 27–28

Guided Reading Workbook
- Section 3

Access for Students Acquiring English/ESL
- Guided Reading, p.12
- Skillbuillder Practice, p, 14
- Map and Graph Skills, pp. 15–16

Formal Assessment
- Section Quiz, p. 37

Integrated Assessment
- Rubric for a mobile, 1.9

INTEGRATED TECHNOLOGY

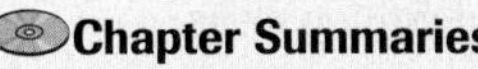
Chapter Summaries

Critical Thinking Transparencies CT35
- Comparing Climate Regions

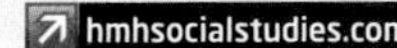

TEST-TAKING RESOURCES

Strategies for Test Preparation

Test Practice Transparencies TT9

Online Test Practice

Instruct: Objective 

Types of Climates

- How do tropical wet and tropical wet and dry climate regions differ? *(In tropical wet regions, it is always hot, and rain falls daily. Tropical wet and dry regions have rainy, warm summers and dry, cool winters.)*
- How do humid subtropical and humid continental climate regions differ? *(Humid subtropical regions have hot, humid summers and mild winters. Humid continental regions have four seasons and a great variety in temperature and precipitation.)*

Critical Thinking Transparencies CT35
- Comparing Climate Regions

Interpreting Maps

Climate Regions

Have students examine the map and make generalizations about the latitudes at which different climates are found. *(Climates with very cold temperatures–icecap, tundra, and subarctic–occur in high latitudes. Mid-latitude climates include humid continental, marine west coast, humid subtropical, Mediterranean, semiarid, and desert. Low-latitude climates include tropical wet and tropical wet and dry.)*

Types of Climates

World climates are generally divided into five large regions: tropical, dry, mid-latitude, high latitude, and highland. The regions are divided into smaller subregions that are described below.

TROPICAL WET This subregion has little variation in temperature over the year—it is always hot, with an average temperature of 80°F. The days begin sunny but by afternoon have clouded up, and rain falls almost daily. The average amount of rain in a year is more than 80 inches. Tropical wet climates are found in Central and South America as well as Africa and Southeast Asia.

Climate Regions

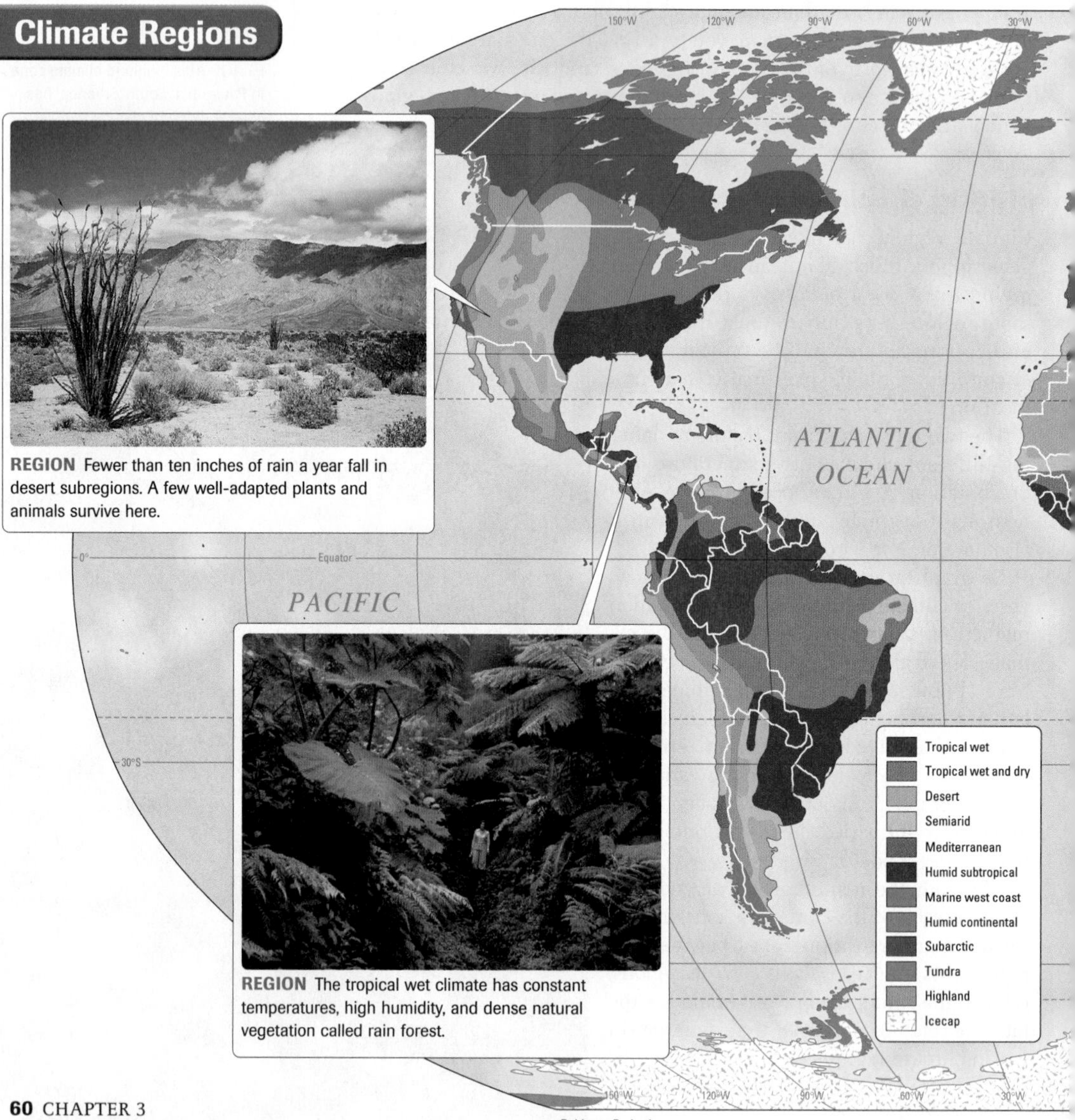

ATLANTIC OCEAN
PACIFIC
Equator
0°
30°S
150°W
120°W
90°W
60°W
30°W

Tropical wet
Tropical wet and dry
Desert
Semiarid
Mediterranean
Humid subtropical
Marine west coast
Humid continental
Subarctic
Tundra
Highland
Icecap

Robinson Projection

REGION Fewer than ten inches of rain a year fall in desert subregions. A few well-adapted plants and animals survive here.

REGION The tropical wet climate has constant temperatures, high humidity, and dense natural vegetation called rain forest.

DIFFERENTIATING INSTRUCTION — STUDENTS ACQUIRING ENGLISH/ESL

IDENTIFYING CLIMATE REGIONS

Objective To develop students' communication and writing skills

Class Time 20 minutes

Task Write captions about major world climate regions

Directions Divide students into small groups and assign each group one of the climate regions shown on pages 60 and 61. Provide each group with an image that represents the climate region that you have assigned to them. Ask students to find information about the relevant climate region in their textbooks. Then have them discuss this information and work together to write a caption for their image.

TROPICAL WET AND DRY This climate is called "tropical wet and dry" because the subregion has a rainy season in summer and a dry season in winter. Temperatures are cooler in the dry season and warmer in the wet season. Rainfall is less than in the tropical wet climate subregion and occurs mostly in the wet season. Tropical wet and dry climates are found next to tropical wet climates in Africa, South and Central America, and parts of Asia.

SEMIARID This climate subregion does receive precipitation, just not very much: about 16 inches per year. Summers are hot. Winters are mild to cold, and some semiarid locations can produce snow. The climate is found in the interior of continents, or in a zone around deserts. The region contains some of the most productive agricultural lands in the world.

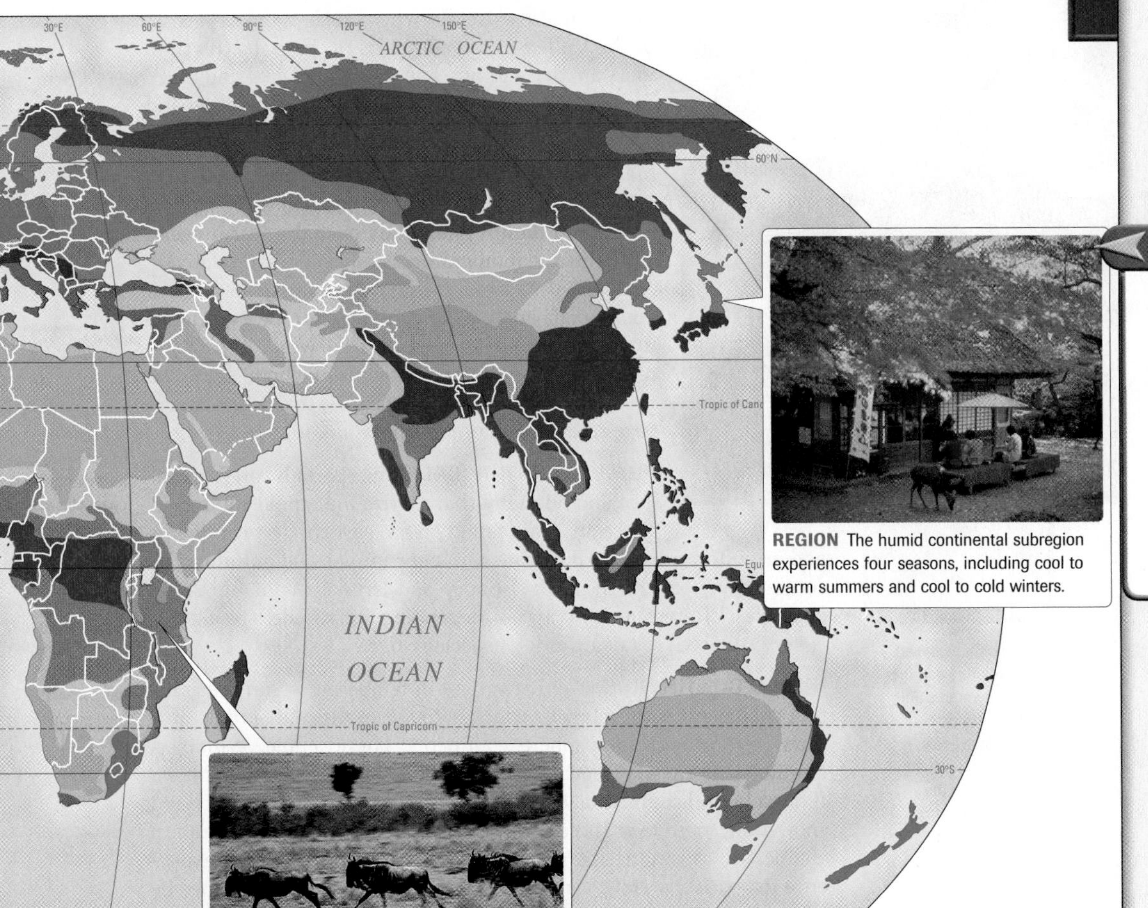

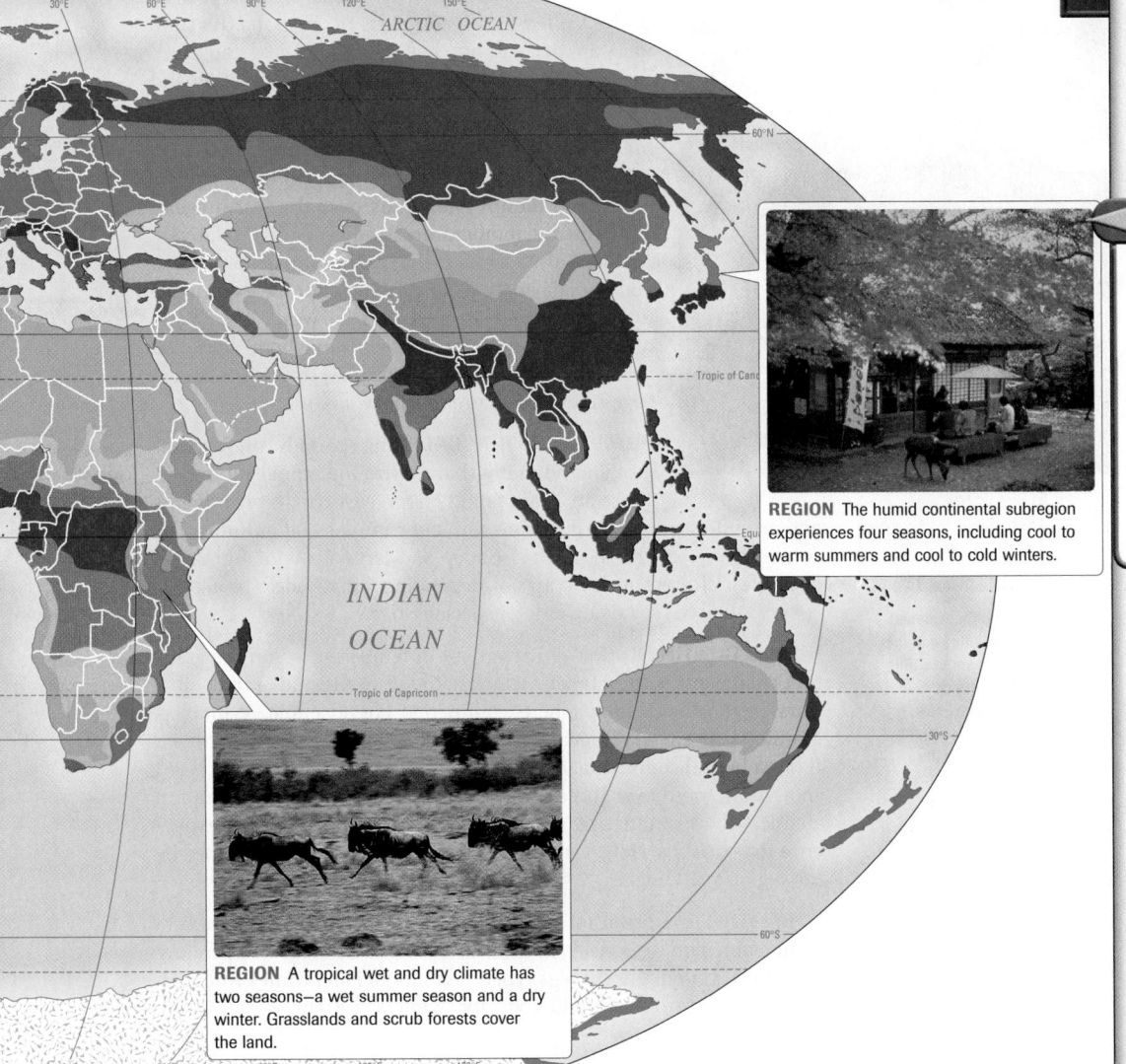

REGION The humid continental subregion experiences four seasons, including cool to warm summers and cool to cold winters.

REGION A tropical wet and dry climate has two seasons—a wet summer season and a dry winter. Grasslands and scrub forests cover the land.

More About

Tropical Wet and Dry Climate

In the tropical wet and dry climate of Southeast Asia, there is often a very marked difference between the wet and dry seasons, which are associated with seasonal winds called *monsoons.*

Interpreting Photographs

Regions

Point out that the photographs on pages 60 and 61 show vegetation associated with the various climate regions. Ask students to rank the regions based on vegetation, from sparsest to most lush. *(desert, tropical wet and dry, humid continental, tropical wet)*

ACTIVITY OPTION FIVE THEMES OF GEOGRAPHY

REGION

Exploring the Theme Remind students that a *region* is an area of the earth's surface that has certain characteristics. As the photographs on pages 60–61 show, the climate regions of the world are associated with certain types of vegetation. Geographers often look at how climate and vegetation affect land use in a region.

Understanding the Theme Have students locate the region in which they live on the map on page 60 and identify the climate of the region. Then ask the following questions.

- What are the characteristics of the region's climate?
- How does climate affect the vegetation in the region?
- How might climate affect land use in the region—in the choice of crops, for example?

More About

Deserts

The term *desert* applies not only to a climate region but also to a vegetation region. Climate is largely responsible for the formation of deserts, but human activities can contribute to the expansion of deserts. The Sahara, for example, has expanded because land bordering the desert has been overgrazed. With the plant life destroyed, the soil is easily eroded by the wind. (For a full description of this phenomenon, see pages 424–425 in Unit 6.)

DESERT Some people think a desert is nothing but sand dunes. However, deserts are categorized according to the amount of rainfall, rather than by landforms, and can be hot or cool/cold. Deserts receive less than ten inches of rain per year. Hot deserts, like the Sahara and the Arabian Desert, regularly have low humidity and high temperatures during the day. At night, temperatures drop because the dry air cannot hold heat well.

Cool/cold deserts are found in the mid-latitudes mostly in the Northern Hemisphere, often in the rain shadow of nearby mountain ranges. Summer temperatures are warm to hot, and winter temperatures range from quite cool to below freezing.

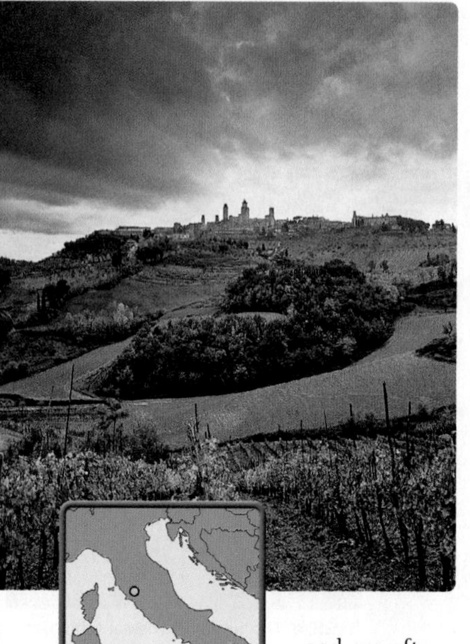

PLACE These Italian vineyards thrive in the hot dry summers and cool rainy winters of the Mediterranean climate. The climate also supports the cultivation of citrus fruit, olives, and vegetables.

MEDITERRANEAN This climate subregion is named for the land around the Mediterranean Sea where it is located. It also exists elsewhere, such as the west coast of the United States and parts of Australia. Its summers are dry and hot, and its winters cool and rainy. This climate region supports a dense population and rich agricultural activity.

MARINE WEST COAST This climate subregion, which is located close to the ocean, is frequently cloudy, foggy, and damp. The winds over the warm ocean moderate the temperatures and keep them relatively constant. Parts of the west coast of the United States and Canada and most of Western Europe experience this climate. Precipitation in marine west coast climate regions is evenly distributed throughout the year. Industrial regions with marine west coast climate may have smog (a mixture of smoke and fog). A

Geographic Thinking

Making Comparisons
A How are Mediterranean and marine west coast climates different?

A. Answer Mediterranean climate has a cool, rainy season and hot, dry summer; marine west coast has evenly distributed precipitation throughout the year.

HUMID SUBTROPICAL Long periods of summer heat and humidity characterize the humid subtropics. These areas are found on the east coast of continents and are often subject to hurricanes in late summer and autumn. The southeastern part of the United States and large areas of China are examples. Winters are mild to cool, depending on latitude. The climate is very suitable for raising crops, especially rice.

HUMID CONTINENTAL A great variety in temperature and precipitation characterizes this climate, which is found in the mid-latitude interiors of Northern Hemisphere continents. For example, Winnipeg, Manitoba, in Canada is located deep in the North American continent. It has a humid continental climate. Air masses chilled by Arctic ice and snow flow south over these areas and frequently collide with tropical air masses, causing changing weather conditions. These areas experience four seasons. However, the length of each season is determined by the region's latitude.

SUBARCTIC Evergreen forests called taiga cover the lands in the subarctic subregion, especially in Canada and Russia. Huge temperature variations occur in this subregion between summer and winter. Although the summers are short and cool, the winters are always very cold.

ACTIVITY OPTION SKILLBUILDER LESSON

CREATING AND USING A DATABASE

Explaining the Skill A database is a collection of data, or information, that is organized so that you can find information quickly and easily. The chart to the right will help you organize data on climate regions.

Applying the Skill Have students create a database of the climate regions covered on pages 60–63. Provide additional references, if needed. Students working in small groups can be responsible for particular information categories. Provide column headings as shown:

CLIMATE REGIONS

	Temperature (Range)	Precipitation (Average in Inches)	Seasons	Other Characteristics	Locations
Tropical Wet					
Tropical Wet and Dry					

In-Depth Resources: Unit 1
• Skillbuilder Practice, p. 29

Temperatures at freezing or below freezing last five to eight months of the year.

TUNDRA The flat, treeless lands forming a ring around the Arctic Ocean are called **tundra.** The climate subregion is also called tundra. It is almost exclusively located in the Northern Hemisphere. Very little precipitation falls here, usually less than 15 inches per year. The land has **permafrost**—that is, the subsoil is constantly frozen. In the summer, which lasts for only a few weeks, the temperature may reach slightly above 40°F. B

Geographic Thinking
Making Comparisons
B How are precipitation amounts in a tundra climate similar to those of a desert climate?
B. Answer Both receive 15 or less inches a year.

ICE CAP Snow, ice, and permanently freezing temperatures characterize the region, which is so cold that it rarely snows. These subregions are sometimes called polar deserts since they receive less than ten inches of precipitation a year. The coldest temperature ever recorded, 128.6°F below zero, was on the ice cap at Vostok, Antarctica.

HIGHLANDS The highlands climate varies with latitude, elevation, other topography, and continental location. In rugged mountain areas such as the Andes of South America, climates can vary based on such factors as whether a slope faces north or south and whether it is exposed to winds carrying moisture.

Understanding climate helps you understand about the general weather conditions in an area. In the next section, you will learn about the variety of soils and vegetation on the earth.

REGION Life is hard during the long, cold, and dark winter in the subarctic. The only places where the temperatures are colder are the icecaps of Greenland and the Antarctic.

Section 3 Assessment

1 Places & Terms

Identify and explain where in the region these would be found.

- tundra
- permafrost

2 Taking Notes

REGION Review the notes you took for this section.

World Climates	

- What are the five basic climate regions?
- What are the factors that determine climate?

3 Main Ideas

a. How do tropical climates differ from each other?

b. How do desert regions differ from each other?

c. How are Humid subtropical and Mediterranean climates different from each other?

4 Geographic Thinking

Making Generalizations
How are the climates of the Northern Hemisphere different from the climates of the Southern Hemisphere?
Think about:

- sizes and locations of the continents

See Skillbuilder Handbook, page R6.

MAKING COMPARISONS Study the descriptions of climates in this chapter. Then either draw pictures or find pictures that illustrate the climates. Using a hanger and string, create a **mobile** displaying world climate regions.

Interpreting Photographs

Subarctic Region

Ask students what adaptations to the cold climate they notice in this photograph. *(heavy clothing; use of sleds)*

Assess & Reteach

GeoFocus Have students complete the section on world climates in their graphic organizers.

Formal Assessment
- Section Quiz, p. 37

Reteaching Activity
Divide students into teams. Have them use the climate regions map on pages 60–61 to locate the continents, regions, or countries where each climate is found. Teams that can describe the climate region get extra "points."

In-Depth Resources: Unit 1
- Reteaching Activity, p. 33

SECTION 3 ASSESSMENT ANSWERS

1. Places & Terms
tundra, p. 63 permafrost, p. 63

2. Taking Notes
- tropical, dry, mid-latitude, high latitude and highland
- location on a continent, topography, and altitude

3. Main Ideas
a. They may be wet all the time or may have wet and dry seasons.
b. They are either semiarid or desert depending on the amount of rainfall and may be hot or cool/cold.
c. Humid subtropical is found on the east coasts of continents and has long, hot, and humid summers. Mediterranean is found on west coasts of continents and has hot dry summers.

4. Geographic Thinking
There is less land in the Southern Hemipshere, especially in the high latitudes, so there are fewer areas with high-latitude climates. There are more tropical wet areas in the Southern Hemisphere. The Northern Hemisphere has many more high-latitude and continental climates.

GeoActivity

Integrated Assessment
- Rubric for a mobile, 1.9

OBJECTIVE

Understand and interpret climographs

Instruct: Objective

Interpreting Climographs

- What is the function of a climograph? *(to show what a climate is like in a place and to facilitate comparisons of climates in different places)*
- What is shown in a climograph? *(average daily temperature and precipitation for each month of the year for a specific location)*
- Who might find a precipitation climograph useful? *(meteorologists, travelers, farmers, etc.)*

In-Depth Resources: Unit 4
- Map and Graph Skills, pp. 27–28

Access for Students Acquiring English/ESL
- Map and Graph Skills, pp. 15-16

More About

Measurement

Many scientists use the Celsius temperature scale and the metric system for climographs. To convert Celsius to Fahrenheit, multiply °C by 1.8 and add 32. To convert Fahrenheit to Celsius, subtract 32 from °F and multiply by .55. To convert inches to centimeters, multiply by 2.54. To convert centimeters to inches, multiply by .39.

RAND McNALLY **Map and Graph Skills**

Interpreting Climographs

How many seasons are in a year where you live? In some parts of the world the climate is the same all year long. Other places have only two seasons–wet and dry. Still others experience changes in temperature and precipitation almost every month. A climograph allows you to quickly determine what the climate is like in a place. If you have two climographs you may compare two different places.

THE LANGUAGE OF GRAPHS A **climograph** shows the average daily temperature and precipitation for each month of the year for a specific location. This information shows what the climate is like over a year. Use the green line on the graph to find the average temperature and the blue bars to find average rainfall.

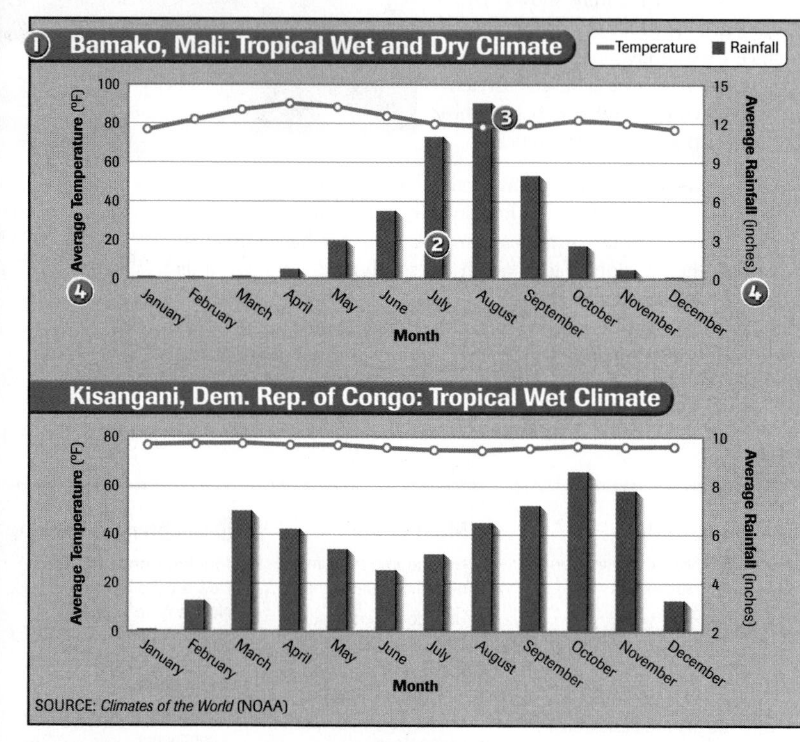

1 The title indicates the place, sometimes its absolute location, and the type of climate.

2 Each blue bar shows average rainfall for one month of the year. For example, more than 13 inches of rain falls in Bamako in August.

3 The green line shows the average temperature. For example, the July temperature in Bamako is 80°F.

4 Precipitation can be shown in inches (in.) or centimeters (cm.). Temperature can be shown in Fahrenheit (F°) or Celsius (C°) degrees.

Map and Graph Skills Assessment

1. Analyzing Data
What information is shown on each side of the vertical axis?

2. Analyzing Data
What are the rainy months in Bamako? How much rain falls in the rainiest month?

3. Drawing Conclusions
How is the tropical wet and dry climate of Bamako different from the tropical wet climate of Kisangani?

SKILLS ASSESSMENT ANSWERS

1. One side shows the average temperature, the other side shows average rainfall.

2. June, July, August, and September. August has approximately 13 inches.

3. Bamako has many months of little precipitation followed by several months of heavy precipitation. Kisangani has precipitation every month of the year.

Soils and Vegetation

Main Ideas

- Soil and climate help to determine the vegetation of a region.
- Human land use alters the vegetation in both positive and negative ways.

Places & Terms

ecosystem **biome** **deciduous** **rain forest** **coniferous** **savanna** **steppe**

BASICS

A HUMAN PERSPECTIVE In the 1870s, a settler described prairie land in Tazewell County, Illinois, as having western meadow lilies "as high as a boy's head," rippling waves of wildflowers, and grass so dense that a man on horseback 30 yards away could not be seen. At that time, the land produced crops of grains, such as corn, wheat, and oats. In most places in the world where people have settled, the land continues to be used for agricultural purposes, such as farming, herding, and timber production. Soil and vegetation have a direct impact on which of those activities the people living in a region can perform.

Soil Regions

Soil is a thin layer of weathered rock, humus, air, and water. It shapes human existence in many ways. The world's food supply depends greatly on the top six inches of soil (sometimes called topsoil). Such factors as depth, texture, and humus content of the soil determine the type of vegetation that can be supported in a region. That, in turn, helps to influence which human activities may take place there. As you study the chart below, notice the relationship of climate to the characteristics of the soil. Soil characteristics and climate are major influences in vegetation regions.

Vegetation Regions

Vegetation regions are natural environments that provide the stage for human activities such as farming, raising livestock, and producing timber. Soil, temperature, and moisture influence the type of vegetation that thrives naturally in a region. Vegetation patterns are identified on the basis of the ecosystems they support. An **ecosystem** is an interdependent community of plants and animals. The ecosystem of a region is referred to as a **biome.** Biomes are further divided into forest, grassland, desert, and tundra.

Soil Differences

Soil Characteristic	Wet Climate	Dry Climate	Warm Climate	Cold Climate
Depth	deep	shallow	deep	shallow
Texture	intermediate to fine	coarse	fine	coarse
Weathering	chemical	physical	rapid	slow
Humus Content	variable	low	low	abundant
Acidity	acidic	not acidic	less acidity	higher acidity

SOURCE: *Physical Geography,* Ralph Scott

SKILLBUILDER: Interpreting Charts

1. **PLACE** What characteristics would soil in a cold, dry climate most likely have?
2. **REGION** How does the soil in warm and wet climates differ from the soil in cold and dry climates in terms of depth and texture?

SECTION 4 OBJECTIVES

1. Explain the important characteristics of soils.
2. Identify and describe the main vegetation regions on earth.
3. Describe ways in which people have altered the environment.

SKILLBUILDER: Interpreting Charts and Maps, pp. 65, 66

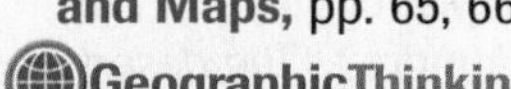

Seeing Patterns, p. 66
Making Inferences, p. 67

Focus & Motivate

Ask students why soil fertility is important? *(Soil fertility is directly related to the amount of food it can produce.)*

Instruct: Objective 

Soil Regions

- Why is the depth, texture, and humus content of soil important? *(These factors determine what vegetation can grow in a region.)*
- Besides soil, what other factor determines the vegetation in a region? *(climate)*

 **In-Depth Resources: Unit 1**
- Guided Reading, p.26

 **Map Transparencies MT7**
- World Soils

SKILLBUILDER ANSWERS

1. It would be shallow, coarse, and subject to slow, physical weathering.
2. Wet and warm climates have a deeper, finer soil.

Instruct: Objective 2 appears on p. 66.

SECTION 4 PROGRAM RESOURCES

In-Depth Resources: Unit 1
- Guided Reading, p. 26
- Building Vocabulary, p. 30
- Reteaching Activity, p. 34

Guided Reading Workbook
- Section 4

Access for Students Acquiring English/ESL
- Guided Reading, p. 13

 **Formal Assessment**
- Section Quiz, p. 38

Integrated Assessment
- Rubric for a map, 2.1

INTEGRATED TECHNOLOGY

Map Transparencies MT7
- World Soils

Chapter Summaries

Power Presentations

Test Generator
- Section Quiz

hmhsocialstudies.com

TEST-TAKING RESOURCES

Strategies for Test Preparation

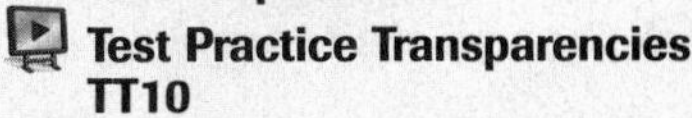

Test Practice Transparencies TT10

Online Test Practice

Instruct: Objective 2

Vegetation Regions

- What are the four main types of biomes? *(forest, grassland, desert, and tundra)*
- How are forests categorized? *(by the type of leaf they support—broadleaf or needleleaf)*
- Which types of plants thrive in the desert? In the tundra? *(The desert favors plants that can conserve water and withstand heat, such as cacti. The tundra favors plants that hug the ground, such as mosses and lichens.)*

Interpreting Maps

World Vegetation Regions

Help students see the relationship between vegetation regions and climate regions by having them compare this map with the one on pages 60–61. Ask questions such as this: In what climate or climates do tropical rain forests thrive? *(Tropical rain forests thrive in tropical wet and tropical wet and dry climates.)*

SKILLBUILDER ANSWERS

1. South America **2.** deciduous and mixed forest, coniferous forest, temperate grasslands, desert and dry shrub, and Mediterranean shrub

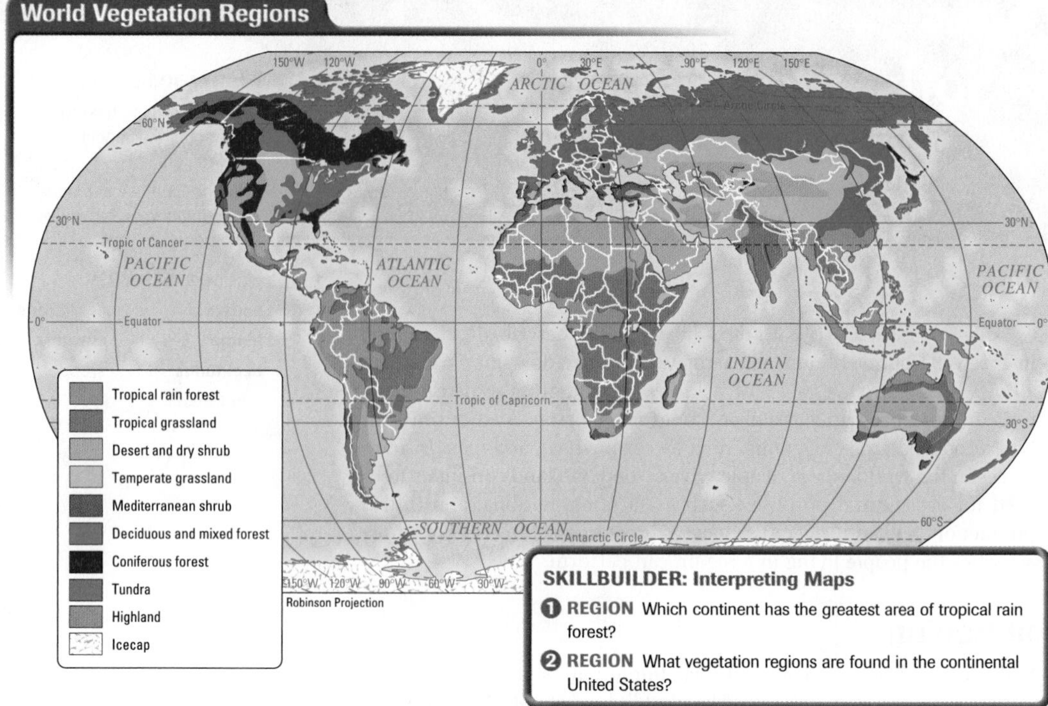

SKILLBUILDER: Interpreting Maps

1 REGION Which continent has the greatest area of tropical rain forest?

2 REGION What vegetation regions are found in the continental United States?

FORESTLANDS Forest regions are categorized by the types of trees they support—broadleaf or needleleaf. Broadleaf trees, such as maple, oak, birch, and cottonwood, are also called **deciduous** trees. The **rain forest** is located in the tropical zone and is covered with a heavy concentration of broadleaf trees. In the tropical rain forest region, some broadleaf trees stay green all year. In the deciduous region, trees shed their leaves at least once during the year. This region is located almost exclusively in the Northern Hemisphere. Sometimes deciduous trees are mixed with needleleaf trees, such as pine, fir, and cedar, to form a mixed forest region. Needleleaf trees are also called **coniferous** trees because they are cone bearing. They are found in huge stands in northern regions of North America, Asia, and Europe.

GRASSLANDS Grasslands, mostly flat regions dotted with a few trees, are called by different terms. In the tropical grassland region, the flat, grassy, mostly treeless plains are called **savanna.** In the Northern Hemisphere, the terms **steppe** or prairie are used to identify temperate grasslands. Vast areas of Eurasia are covered with steppe. In the Southern Hemisphere, the temperate grasslands may be referred to as pampas. A

DESERT AND TUNDRA The plants that live in these extreme climates are specially adapted to tolerate the dry or cold conditions. In the tundra, plants that hug the ground, such as mosses and lichen, are best adapted to survive the cold dry climate. In the desert, plants that can conserve water and withstand heat, such as cacti, sagebrush, or other shrubs, dot the landscape.

A. Answer Forests are frequently next to grasslands.

Seeing Patterns

A Study the map above. What patterns do you see in the relationship of forestlands to grasslands?

DIFFERENTIATING INSTRUCTION GIFTED AND TALENTED STUDENTS

COMPARING MAPS/MAKING CHARTS

Objective To compare climate and vegetation regions

Class Time 20 minutes

Task Create a chart comparing climate and vegetation

Directions Direct students to make a chart listing the climate regions from the map key on page 60 in a column. Then have them compare the climate map with the vegetation map on page 66 and list the type of vegetation that is associated with each climate. Ask them to draw conclusions about what other factors, besides climate, might determine the vegetation that an area will support.

Human Impact on the Environment

As you can imagine, the impact of human activities on soil and vegetation is immense. Throughout this book, you will read about the ways that human beings either have adapted to the land or have altered it to meet their needs. Human activities that affect the environment include building dams or irrigation systems, planting food crops, or slashing and burning the vegetation.

The two photographs above show you an example of a human-environment interaction. The photograph to the left shows Glen Canyon on the Colorado River before a dam was built to create a huge lake. The lake—Lake Powell—was created to provide irrigation water, hydroelectric power, and recreational facilities. The photograph on the right shows a part of Lake Powell today. It is 186 miles long, has 1,900 miles of shoreline, and in places is 500 feet deep. As you can see, this human activity has caused changes in the environment.

The next chapter will help you understand the human side of geography and its relationship to the physical world.

HUMAN–ENVIRONMENT INTERACTION Photographs of Glen Canyon show the same site before and after it was filled with the waters of Lake Powell. **How has the landscape changed as the result of the creation of the lake?**

Section 4 Assessment

1 Places & Terms

Explain the meaning of each of the following terms.

- ecosystem
- biome
- rain forest
- savanna
- steppe

2 Taking Notes

REGION Review the notes you took for this section.

Soils & Vegetation

- How are soil and vegetation linked?
- What are the four types of biomes?

3 Main Ideas

a. What soil factors influence type of vegetation in a region?

b. What is the difference between coniferous and deciduous trees?

c. What is unique about vegetation in the desert and tundra regions?

4 Geographic Thinking

Making Inferences What impact have humans had on soil and vegetation? **Think about:**

- altering the land to meet needs
- careless use of the land

EXPLORING LOCAL GEOGRAPHY Use the Internet to find out about the current vegetation of your state and what it was like before becoming populated. Draw two **maps** to show the contrast between the two time periods. Write a sentence summarizing what you learned.

Instruct: Objective 3

Human Impact on the Environment

- What are two ways in which people interact with their environment? *(by adapting to it or by altering it)*
- What are some of the ways in which people alter the environment? *(by building dams or irrigation systems, planting food crops, etc.)*

Interpreting Photographs

Glen Canyon and Lake Powell

The controversy over the creation of Lake Powell, one of the world's largest artificially created lakes, helped spawn the modern environmental movement. Ask students to infer what objections environmentalists might have had to the construction of the dam. *(The dam would alter the scenery, destroy vegetation and wildlife, and disrupt the flow of the Colorado River.)*

CAPTION ANSWER

Much of the area is covered with water.

Assess & Reteach

GeoFocus Have students complete the section on soils and vegetation in their graphic organizers.

Formal Assessment
- Section Quiz, p. 38

Reteaching Activity

Have students create illustrations of the four main biomes and write captions that summarize the section information on each biome.

In-Depth Resources: Unit 1
- Reteaching Activity, p. 34

SECTION 4 ASSESSMENT ANSWERS

1. Places & Terms

ecosystem, p. 65
biome, p. 65
rain forest, p. 66
savanna, p. 66
steppe, p. 66

2. Taking Notes

- Soil type influences the type of vegetation that can be supported.
- The four types of biomes are forest, grassland, desert, and tundra.

3. Main Ideas

a. Depth, texture, and humus content influence vegetation.
b. Coniferous trees are needleleaf and cone bearing, and deciduous trees are broadleaf.
c. Plants in these regions can tolerate dry or cold conditions.

4. Geographic Thinking

The soil and vegetation may be changed by the creation of dams, roads, and other human activities. Careless use of the land may result in damage to soil and vegetation.

GeoActivity

Integrated Assessment
- Rubric for a map, 2.1

Reviewing Places & Terms

A.
1. weather, p. 50
2. climate, p. 50
3. precipitation, p. 50
4. convection, p. 54
5. El Niño, p. 57
6. greenhouse effect, p. 58
7. ecosystem, p. 65
8. biome, p. 65
9. rain forest, p. 66
10. savanna, p. 66

B. Possible Responses

11. It is more important to consider weather when daily activities are concerned.
12. Weather is a daily activity and is part of the overall climate pattern.
13. Ecosystem, biome, rain forest, and savanna refer to vegetation.
14. Precipitation is the result of the convection movement of warm, moist air.
15. The greenhouse effect deals with increases in average global temperatures.
16. El Niños have much to do with dramatic changes in Pacific Ocean water temperatures.
17. Rain forests are found near the equator in North and South America, Africa, and Asia.
18. They are all terms for grasslands in different regions of the world.
19. The greenhouse effect could influence weather, climate, ecosystems, biomes, rain forests, and savannas.
20. A regional ecosystem is referred to as a biome.

Chapter 3 Assessment

VISUAL SUMMARY
CLIMATE AND VEGETATION

Seasons and Weather
- Seasons occur because of the earth's revolution and tilt.
- Weather is the condition of the atmosphere on a daily basis.
- Weather extremes disrupt normal patterns of living.

Climate
- Climate is the atmospheric condition over a long period of time.
- Climate is affected by wind and ocean currents, latitude, elevation, and topography.
- Global climate changes include El Niño and the greenhouse effect.

World Climate Regions
- There are five basic climate regions: tropical, dry, mid-latitude, high latitude, and highland.
- The two most significant factors in climate are temperature and precipitation.

Soils and Vegetation
- Soil characteristics include texture, depth, and humus content.
- Soil and climate are major influences on vegetation regions.
- Vegetation patterns are based on ecosystems.

Reviewing Places & Terms

A. Briefly explain the importance of each of the following.

1. weather
2. climate
3. precipitaton
4. convection
5. El Niño
6. greenhouse effect
7. ecosystem
8. biome
9. rain forest
10. savanna

B. Answer the questions about vocabulary in complete sentences.

11. In what type of situation would it be more important to know about weather instead of climate?
12. How are climate and weather related?
13. Which of the above terms deal with types of vegetation?
14. What role does convection play in precipitation?
15. Which of the above terms deals with increases in average global temperature?
16. Which of the above terms has to do with dramatic changes in Pacific Ocean water temperature?
17. What is the relative location of rain forests?
18. What does savanna have in common with steppe and prairie?
19. Which of the above terms could be affected by the greenhouse effect?
20. What is the relationship between an ecosystem and a biome?

Main Ideas

Seasons and Weather (pp. 49–53)
1. What causes the changing seasons on earth?
2. What are the major factors that cause weather?
3. What are the different types of precipitation?

Climate (pp. 54–58)

4. What are four factors that influence climate?
5. How do ocean currents affect climate?
6. What might be some causes of global warming?

World Climate Regions (pp. 59–64)

7. What general information about climate is included in a description of a climate region?
8. What are the five basic climate regions?

Soils and Vegetation (pp. 65–67)

9. How does climate affect soil?
10. How are forestlands defined?

Main Ideas

1. earth's revolution and tilt
2. solar energy, water vapor, cloud cover, landforms and bodies of water, elevation, and air movement
3. convection, orographic, and frontal
4. ocean and wind currents, latitude, elevation, and topography
5. Ocean currents move warm water from one location to another, and winds blowing over the warm waters transfer the heat to new locations.
6. Causes include a natural cycle change or the introduction of heat-trapping gases into the atmosphere by humans.
7. Temperature and precipitation averages and patterns are included in climate descriptions.
8. tropical, mid-latitude, high latitude, dry, and highland
9. Climate may affect soil depth, texture, weathering, humus, and acidity.
10. Forestlands are defined by the type of trees found there: deciduous, coniferous, or mixed.

Critical Thinking

1. Using Your Notes

Use your completed chart to answer these questions.

Seasons & Weather	
Climate	
World Climates	
Soils & Vegetation	

a. How are seasons, weather, and climate connected to each other?

b. How would knowing about the climate of a region help you determine the vegetation of the region?

2. Geographic Themes

a. **REGION** Why are there few subarctic climate zones in the Southern Hemisphere?

b. **LOCATION** How does location affect climate?

3. Identifying Themes

How might the climate of an area be affected by global warming? Which of the five themes apply to this situation?

4. Drawing Conclusions

What is incorrect about defining a desert by landforms such as sand dunes?

5. Making Inferences

Why is a hurricane such a deadly storm?

For Additional Test Practice

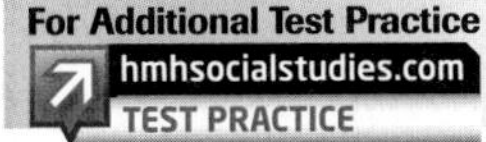

Geographic Skills: Interpreting Graphs

Temperature Variations

Use the graph to answer the following questions.

1. **MOVEMENT** Which decade (10-year span) had the highest temperatures?
2. **MOVEMENT** In approximately which year did temperatures begin to consistently rise above the average?
3. **HUMAN-ENVIRONMENT INTERACTION** What impact might the greenhouse effect have on the temperature changes?

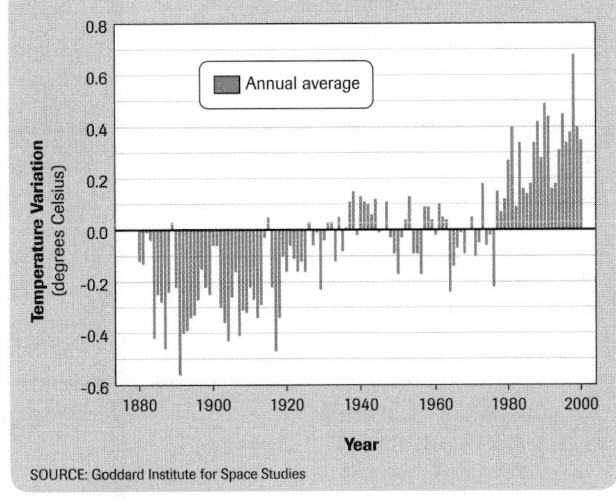

SOURCE: Goddard Institute for Space Studies

GeoActivity

Using straws, devise a three-dimensional model to show the information on the graph. Be sure to provide time frames and temperature information on your model.

hmhsocialstudies.com

MULTIMEDIA ACTIVITY

21st CENTURY

Use the links at **hmhsocialstudies.com** to do research about global warming. Choose one of the nine regions in this textbook. Focus on determining the effects of global warming on the region, especially on coastal areas.

Creating a Multimedia Presentation Combine charts, maps, or other visual images in an electronic presentation showing how the earth will be affected by global warming.

CHAPTER 3 ASSESSMENT

BASICS

Critical Thinking

1. a. Seasons and weather are aspects of climate.
b. Climate will help you to understand the type of environment in which vegetation can thrive.

2. a. The Southern Hemisphere has little land at the latitudes for subarctic climates.
b. Climate is affected by latitude, elevation, and continental location.

3. Global warming might change temperature and precipitation patterns. Human-environment interaction is involved since global warming is probably caused by human activities.

4. Desert is a designation of climate or vegetation region, not a landform.

5. Hurricanes can cause damage by high winds, rain, flooding, and storm surges over a very large area.

GeoActivity

Integrated Assessment
- Rubric for a three-dimensional model, 1.10

Formal Assessment
- Chapter Test, Forms A, B, and C, pp. 39–50

Geographic Skills

1. 1990–2000
2. 1977
3. It could be responsible for increased temperatures beginning in the 1970s.

MULTIMEDIA ACTIVITY

For their multimedia presentation on global warming, students should:
- Discuss theories about the causes of global warming.
- Focus on global warming's impact on a specific region.
- Include imaginative maps and visuals.
- Provide references to Web sites and other sources of information.

Grading Rubric Evaluate student performance as Exceptional, Acceptable, or Poor in each of the following categories.

	Exceptional	*Acceptable*	*Poor*
Utilizes two or more media			
Clearly demonstrates an understanding of the concepts presented			
Shows technical proficiency			

Human Geography: People and Places

OVERVIEW	INSTRUCTIONAL RESOURCES	
ESSENTIAL QUESTION How do geographers study people? **Focus on the Essential Question Podcast**	**In-Depth Resources: Unit 1** • Building Vocabulary, p. 41 **Block Schedule Strategies** **Chapter Summaries** (English/Spanish) hmhsocialstudies.com INTERACTIVE	**Interactive Online Edition** **ExamView® Assessment Suite** (English/Spanish) **CalendarPlanner** **Power Presentations with Media Gallery** **Critical Thinking Transparencies** • CT4
SECTION 1 **THE ELEMENTS OF CULTURE** **MAIN IDEAS** • Cultures change through innovation and the spread of ideas from one culture to another. • Language, religion, and the arts are among the most important aspects of culture.	**In-Depth Resources: Unit 1** • Guided Reading, p. 35 • Building Vocabulary, p. 41 • Reteaching Activities, p. 42 **Outline Maps with Activities** • Religions of the World, pp. 5–6 **Cultures Around the World** • Daily Life, p. 2; Fine Arts, p. 3; Music, p. 5; Arts and Crafts, p. 6	**Map Transparencies** • MT8 World Languages **Cultures Transparencies CW2–6** • Sukkoth; Cave Painting; Fulani Dancers; Panpipes; Spinning Cotton **Guided Reading Workbook,** Section 1
SECTION 2 **POPULATION GEOGRAPHY** **MAIN IDEAS** • The world's population is growing at a rapid rate because of improved living conditions. • Population density tells how heavily populated an area is.	**In-Depth Resources: Unit 1** • Guided Reading, p. 36 • Skillbuilder Practice, p. 40 • Building Vocabulary, p. 41 • Reteaching Activities, p. 43 **Guided Reading Workbook,** Section 2	**Critical Thinking Transparencies** • CT36 Population Geography Around the World **Map Transparencies** • MT9 World Population Density
SECTION 3 **POLITICAL GEOGRAPHY** **MAIN IDEAS** • The three main types of governments are democracy, monarchy, and dictatorship. • Size, shape, and location influence a nation's political geography.	**In-Depth Resources: Unit 1** • Guided Reading, p. 37 • Building Vocabulary, p. 41 • Reteaching Activities, p. 44 **Outline Maps with Activities** • World: Political, 3–4	**Guided Reading Workbook,** Section 3
SECTION 4 **URBAN GEOGRAPHY** **MAIN IDEAS** • Almost half of the world's population lives in urban areas. • Cities around the world have certain geographic characteristics and land use patterns in common.	**In-Depth Resources: Unit 1** • Guided Reading, p. 38 • Building Vocabulary, p. 41 • Reteaching Activities, p. 45 **Guided Reading Workbook,** Section 4	
SECTION 5 **ECONOMIC GEOGRAPHY** **MAIN IDEAS** • The four basic types of economic systems are traditional, command, market, and mixed. • Among the subjects studied by economic geographers are levels of economic activity and the location, quality, quantity, and type of natural resources.	**In-Depth Resources: Unit 1** • Guided Reading, p. 39 • Building Vocabulary, p. 41 • Reteaching Activities, p. 46 **Guided Reading Workbook,** Section 5	**Map Transparencies** • MT10 World Per Capita GDP

ASSESSMENT

SE **Chapter Assessment,** pp. 96–97

Formal Assessment
- Chapter Tests, Forms A, B, and C, pp. 56–67

TOS **ExamView® Assessment Suite**

Strategies for Test Preparation

hmhsocialstudies.com TEST PRACTICE

SE **Section Assessment,** p. 77

Formal Assessment
- Section Quiz, p. 51

Integrated Assessment
- Rubric for a database, 2.6

Test Practice Transparencies TT11

SE **Section Assessment,** p. 82

Formal Assessment
- Section Quiz, p. 52

Integrated Assessment
- Rubric for an explanation, 4.5

Test Practice Transparencies TT12

SE **Section Assessment,** p. 86

Formal Assessment
- Section Quiz, p. 53

Integrated Assessment
- Rubric for a database, 2.6

Test Practice Transparencies TT13

SE **Section Assessment,** p. 90

Formal Assessment
- Section Quiz, p. 54

Integrated Assessment
- Rubric for a sketch map, 2.1

Test Practice Transparencies TT14

SE **Section Assessment,** p. 95

Formal Assessment
- Section Quiz, p. 55

Integrated Assessment
- Rubric for an illustration, 1.3

Test Practice Transparencies TT15

CHART KEY:

SE Student Edition

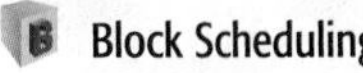

Block Scheduling

DVD/CD-ROM

TE Teacher's Edition

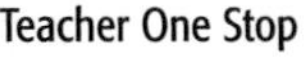

TOS Teacher One Stop

MP3 Audio

Printable Resource

Presentation Resource

HISTORY™

Program Resources available on TOS and @ hmhsocialstudies.com

SUPPORTING RESOURCES

- **Multimedia Classroom Global History Series**
- **Global History Teacher's Guide**

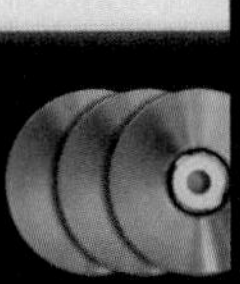

Social Studies Trade Library Collection
- World Regions Trade Collection

For more information or to purchase these resources, go to hmhsocialstudies.com

DIFFERENTIATED INSTRUCTION

English Learners	Struggling Readers	Gifted and Talented Students
 **Spanish/English Guided Reading Workbook**  **Access for Students Acquiring English/ESL:** Spanish Translations, pp. 17–21  **Chapter Summaries** (English/Spanish) 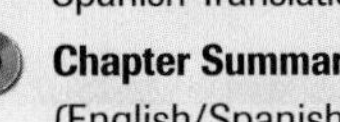 TE **TE Activity** Exploring Language Blending, p. 73 Recognizing Root Words and Prefixes, p. 75	**Chapter Summaries** (English/Spanish) TE **TE Activity** Previewing Economic Terms, p. 92	TE **TE Activity** Applying Geographic Concepts, p. 84

ENRICHMENT ACTIVITIES

The following activities are especially suitable for classes following block schedules.

SE **Student Edition,** p. 70–97 • U.S. Population Pyramids, 2000 and 2050, p. 79	hmhsocialstudies.com INTERACTIVE • World Language Families Today, p. 74

BLOCK SCHEDULE LESSON PLAN OPTIONS: 90-MINUTE PERIOD

DAY 1

SECTION 1, pp. 71–77
Class Time 55 minutes

- **Discussion** Use the Key Questions on TE pages 71, 72, 73, 75, and 77 as a guide in leading a class discussion of this section. Encourage students to offer examples and share what they know about the topics discussed.
  Class Time 35 minutes
- **Summary** Ask students to write summaries of the main ideas from their discussion of culture, language, religion, and creative expression. Call on volunteers to share their summaries.
  Class Time 20 minutes

SECTION 2, pp. 78–82
Class Time 35 minutes

- **Quiz Show** Divide students into two teams. Using the Places & Terms list on page 78 and the questions in the second and third parts of the Section 2 Assessment, quiz the teams on the key concepts in this section and keep score of correct answers. You might give extra points when students can elaborate on their answers.

DAY 2

SECTION 2, pp. 78–82
Class Time 20 minutes

- **Skillbuilder Lesson** Use the activity about seeing patterns on TE page 80 and the Skillbuilder Practice worksheet on page 40 of the *In-Depth Resources.*

SECTION 3, pp. 83–86
Class Time 40 minutes

- **Finding Examples on a Map** Display a classroom world map and call on students to point out examples of countries that are ruled by a democracy, a monarchy, and a dictatorship. Then call on volunteers to point out examples of countries in which size, shape, or location has influenced their development. Finally, ask volunteers to point out examples of natural and artificial boundaries.

SECTION 4, pp. 87–90
Class Time 30 minutes

- **Outlines** Have students create outlines of the main ideas in this section and then pair up with partners and use the outlines to quiz each other.

DAY 3

SECTION 5, pp. 91–95
Class Time 35 minutes

- **Summary Chart** Lead the class in creating a chart of economic terms that gives definitions and examples.

CHAPTER 4 REVIEW AND ASSESSMENT, pp. 96–97
Class Time 55 minutes

- **Review** Present an oral summary of the main ideas in the chapter.
  Class Time 15 minutes
- **Assessment** Have students complete the Chapter 4 Assessment.
  Class Time 40 minutes

TEACHER-TESTED ACTIVITY *How Does Your City Fit In?*

Class Time One class period

Task Analyze the local land-use patterns and their relation to the closest metropolitan region

Supplies
- Photocopies of local street map (classroom set)
- Photocopies of nearest metropolitan area (classroom set)
- Overhead transparencies of each
- Highlighters or colored pencils

Purpose By identifying the land-use patterns in their community and how they relate to the nearest large city, students will learn some of the basic components of urban geography.

Activity After students have read PE pages 87-90, have them take the map of their community and color areas that are residential, commercial, industrial, agricultural, and public or institutional. Discuss whether their community meets the definition of a suburb. Then distribute maps of the nearest metropolitan area. Have students label the central business district(s) and surrounding suburbs. After studying both maps, students can answer the following questions:

- What is the relationship of their community to the metropolitan region?
- Where are most of the jobs located and what type of jobs are they?
- What regional problems are faced by the metropolitan area?
- What are the best locations for future growth?

Bill Hoffman
Geography Teacher, Capistrano Valley, California

TECHNOLOGY IN THE CLASSROOM

Students can design their own Web sites to organize information and to share their knowledge with other kids at school and around the world. By creating a Web site, students gain experience in organizing information in a "non-linear" fashion and get a behind-the-scenes look at what goes into developing materials for the Internet. Their Web sites can be kept on the classroom computer, uploaded to the school's internal server, or uploaded to the Internet for students at other schools to view.

Objective Students will create Web sites showcasing the cultural traditions of their ancestors or older relatives.

Task Have students use the Internet and personal interviews to find out about their ancestors' or older relatives' (grandparents or great-grandparents) cultures. Have them create Web sites to illustrate the things they have learned.

Class Time 3–4 class periods

1. Have students read pages 71–77, and ask them to define the word "culture." Ask them to contribute words that describe their own culture, and list their ideas on the board.
2. Ask students to list the things they know about the culture of their ancestors and older living relatives (e.g. grandparents or great-grandparents). Their lists should mention the countries they came from, languages they spoke, religious practices, customs, and any other cultural practices students are aware of. Have them share some of the items on their lists with the class.
3. Have students use the Internet to research one of their ancestors' cultures. If their great-grandparents came from France, Mexico, and Japan, they should choose just one of those cultures. Ask them to investigate the cultural practices of people who live in that country as well as people who have immigrated from that country to the United States. Have them begin their research by using the search engines, directories, and Web sites listed at **hmhsocialstudies.com**.
4. If possible, have students continue their research by interviewing relatives who are a part of this culture or who may remember ancestors who were part of the culture.
5. Have students create Web sites showcasing the culture they have studied. The sites should include the following components: a definition of culture; the ancestors' or relatives' language, religion, migration story (how they or earlier relatives got from their home country to the United States), and cultural traditions in the "homeland" and in the United States. Have students link from a home page that introduces the culture to additional pages that provide further details, including text and pictures.
6. Have a few students create a class home page that introduces the overall project and lists links to all students' Web sites. As an option, they can place a world map on the class home page and link from places on the map to students' Web sites, corresponding to the countries their ancestors came from.

CHAPTER 4 OBJECTIVE

Explain the basic concepts of human geography, including key ideas about culture, demographics, political systems, urban growth, and economics.

Chapter 4 HUMAN GEOGRAPHY People and Places

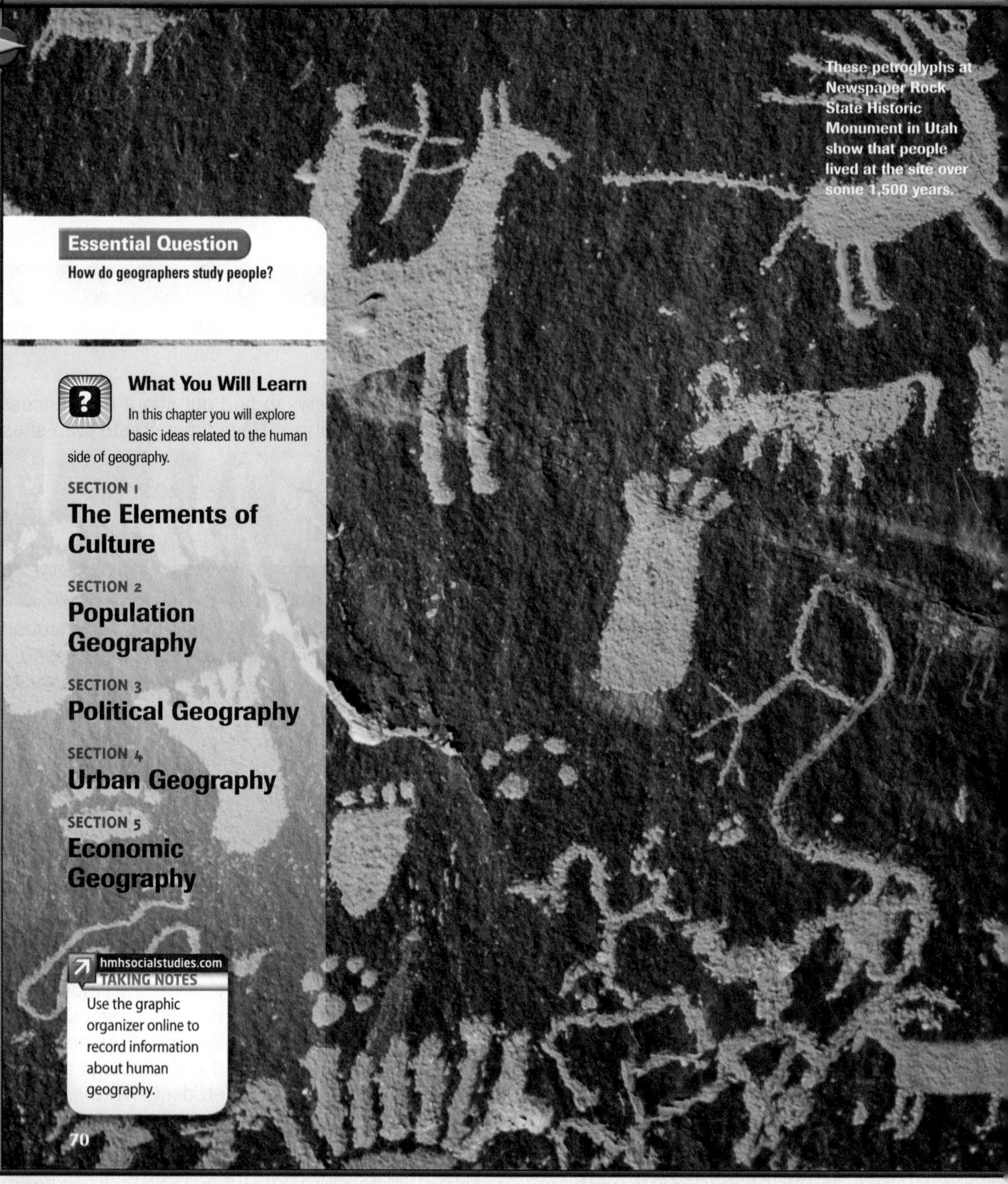

Interpreting Photographs

Point out that Newspaper Rock displays one of the largest, best-preserved collections of petroglyphs in the Southwest. The word *petroglyph* is from Greek words that mean "stone" and "to carve".

Extension Ask students to consider what the different images in the petroglyph represent. Also ask what purpose these rock carvings might have served. *(Students might answer that the images were spiritual in nature or depicted scenes of hunting and other daily life.)*

These petroglyphs at Newspaper Rock State Historic Monument in Utah show that people lived at the site over some 1,500 years.

Essential Question

How do geographers study people?

What You Will Learn

In this chapter you will explore basic ideas related to the human side of geography.

SECTION 1 **The Elements of Culture**

SECTION 2 **Population Geography**

SECTION 3 **Political Geography**

SECTION 4 **Urban Geography**

SECTION 5 **Economic Geography**

hmhsocialstudies.com TAKING NOTES

Use the graphic organizer online to record information about human geography.

70

Introducing the Essential Question

- Emphasize that the processes that happen on the earth's surface are just a part of the study of geography. The other part is human geography. Physical geography affects people in many ways, though.
- Tell students that geographers study many aspects of human life. Major divisions of human geography include cultural, population, political, urban, and economic geography.

Have students copy the graphic organizer online in their notebooks and fill it in using material from all sections in this chapter.

Critical Thinking Transparencies CT4
- GeoFocus

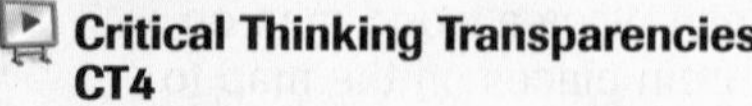

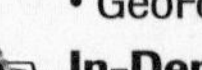

In-Depth Resources: Unit 1
- Building Vocabulary, p. 41

CHAPTER 4 ADDITIONAL RESOURCES

BOOKS FOR THE TEACHER

Tuan, Yi-Fu. ***Space and Place: The perspective of Experience.*** University of Minnesota Press, 2001. How people think and feel about space and the implications of these ideas on human geography.

BOOKS FOR THE STUDENT

Epping, Randy Charles. ***A Beginner's Guide to the World Economy.*** NY: Vintage Books, 1995. An explanation of basic economic concepts.

VIDEOS

Betrayal of Science and Reason. Stanford University Channel, 1998. Discussion of overpopulation dangers by scientists Paul and Anne Ehrlich.

Population 2000: The New Giant Cities. Gulliver Education, 1998. Examination of urban growth problems in Mexico City, Bangkok, and Cairo.

INTERNET

For more about human geography, visit . . .

hmhsocialstudies.com

The Elements of Culture

Main Ideas

- Human beings are members of social groups with shared and unique sets of behaviors and attitudes.
- Language and religion are two very important aspects of culture.

Places & Terms

culture	cultural hearth
society	acculturation
ethnic group	dialect
innovation	religion
diffusion	

BASICS

A HUMAN PERSPECTIVE In an article titled "The 100% American," anthropologist Ralph Linton described how a typical American, in eating breakfast, had borrowed from other cultures.

> He has coffee, an Abyssinian plant, with cream and sugar. Both the domestication of cows and the idea of milking them originated in the Near East, while sugar was first made in India. . . . As a side dish he may have the egg of a species of bird domesticated in Indo-China, or thin strips of the flesh of an animal domesticated in Eastern Asia.

Borrowing from other cultures is common around the world, even if we are not aware of it.

Defining Culture

What makes us similar to some people in the world but different from most others? The answer is culture. **Culture** is the total of knowledge, attitudes, and behaviors shared by and passed on by the members of a specific group. It includes all products of human work and thought. Culture acts as a blueprint for how a group of people should behave if they want to fit in with the group. It ties us to one group and separates us from other groups—and helps us to solve the problems that all humans face. Culture involves the following factors:

- food and shelter
- religion
- relationships to family and others
- language
- education
- security/protection
- political and social organization
- creative expression

A group that shares a geographic region, a sense of identity, and a culture is called a **society.** Sometimes the term **ethnic group** is used to refer to a group that shares a language, customs, and a common heritage. An ethnic group has an identity as a separate group of people within the region where they live. For example, the San peoples—known as the Bushmen of the Kalahari Desert in Africa—live in a specific territory, speak their own language, and have a social organization distinct from other groups in the region.

Society and the Individual

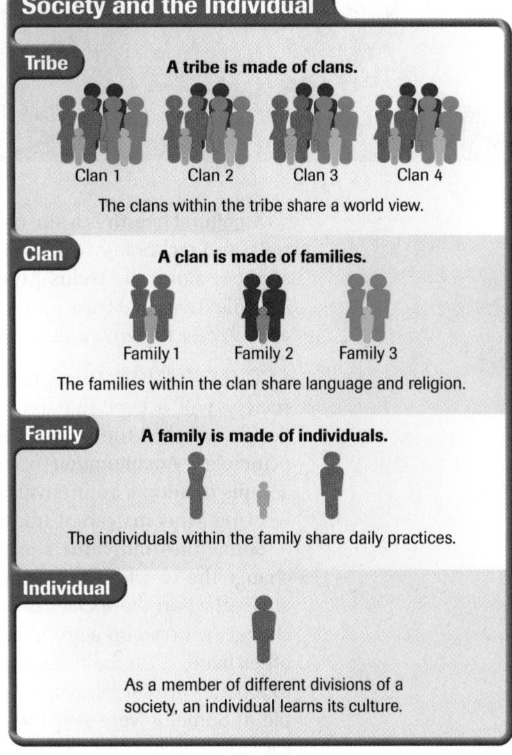

Tribe
A tribe is made of clans.
Clan 1
Clan 2
Clan 3
Clan 4
The clans within the tribe share a world view.
Clan
A clan is made of families.
Family 1
Family 2
Family 3
The families within the clan share language and religion.
Family
A family is made of individuals.
The individuals within the family share daily practices.
Individual
As a member of different divisions of a society, an individual learns its culture.

SECTION 1 OBJECTIVES

1. Define culture and explain its impact.
2. Explain how culture changes and spreads.
3. Describe how language unites and divides people and how it changes and spreads.
4. Identify and define three categories of religion.
5. Describe the world's major religions.
6. Identify modes of cultural expression

SKILLBUILDERS: Interpreting Graphics, Graphs, and Maps, pp. 74, 76

GeographicThinking
Seeing Patterns, pp. 72, 75, 77
Determining Cause and Effect, p. 77

Focus & Motivate

What elements of American culture unite us? What elements divide us? *(Answers will vary, but may include language, religion, arts, and media.)*

Instruct: Objective 1

Defining Culture

- What is culture? *(the knowledge, attitudes, and behaviors shared and passed on by members of a group)*
- How does culture affect a group of people? *(It gives them a guide for how to behave, it ties them to one group, and it separates them from other groups.)*
- What is a group that shares a culture called? *(a society)*

 **In-Depth Resources: Unit 1**
- Guided Reading, p. 35

SECTION 1 PROGRAM RESOURCES

 **In-Depth Resources: Unit 1**
- Guided Reading, p. 35
- Building Vocabulary, p. 41
- Reteaching Activity, p. 42

Guided Reading Workbook
- Section 1

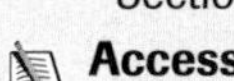 **Access for Students Acquiring English/ESL**
- Guided Reading, p. 17

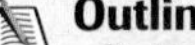 **Outline Maps with Activities**
- Religions of the World, pp. 5–6

 **Formal Assessment**
- Section Quiz, p. 51

 **Integrated Assessment**
- Rubric for a database, 2.6

Cultures Around the World
- Daily Life, p. 2
- Fine Arts, p. 3
- Dance, p. 4
- Music, p. 5
- Arts and Crafts, p. 6

INTEGRATED TECHNOLOGY

 **Cultures Transparencies CW2, 3, 4, 5, 6**
- Sukkoth
- Cave Painting
- Fulani Dancers
- Panpipes
- Spinning Cotton

 **Map Transparencies MT8**
- World Languages

hmhsocialstudies.com

TEST-TAKING RESOURCES

 **Strategies for Test Preparation**

 **Test Practice Transparencies TT31**

 **Online Test Practice**

Instruct: Objective 

Culture Change and Exchange

- In what two ways do cultures change? *(through innovation and diffusion)*
- What must happen for a cultural change to occur? *(acculturation–the acceptance of an innovation)*
- Why does cultural change take place rapidly today? *(largely because electronic technology makes it possible to speed ideas and sell goods around the world)*

 **Cultures Around the World**
- Daily Life, p. 2
- Fine Arts, p. 3
- Dance, p. 4
- Music, p. 5
- Arts and Crafts, p. 6

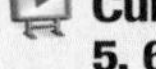 **Cultures Transparencies CW2, 3, 4, 5, 6**

Interpreting Photographs

Mongolian Yurt and Satellite Dish

Traditionally, many Mongolians were nomadic livestock herders. Their yurts, or felt tents, were collapsible, could fit on a draft animal, and could be set up in a half hour. Some Mongols still prefer to live in yurts. Ask students what this image says about cultural diffusion. *(A society may adopt some elements of another culture, but may retain key aspects of its own way of living.)*

CAPTION ANSWER The family has accepted the innovation of the satellite dish and the ideas that come through the dish to expand its world.

Culture Change and Exchange

Cultures and societies are always in the process of changing. Change comes very slowly to some societies and rapidly to others. It can come about through innovation or the spread of ideas or behaviors from one culture to another.

INNOVATION Taking existing technology and resources and creating something new to meet a need is called **innovation.** For example, to solve the need for storage of goods, some societies invented baskets woven from reeds because reeds were abundant. Other cultures developed clay pots to solve the same problem.

Innovation and invention may happen on purpose or by accident. History is filled with examples of "accidents" that changed the life of a society. For example, the first cooked meat may have happened by accident, but it led to the practice of cooking most food rather than eating it raw.

MOVEMENT A satellite dish brings the outside world to a Mongolian family living in this traditional house called a yurt. **How does this picture show acculturation?**

DIFFUSION Good ideas or inventions are hard to keep secret—they spread when people from different societies, or their ideas and inventions, come into contact with one another. This spread of ideas, inventions, or patterns of behavior is called **diffusion.** In an age of electronic technology, diffusion can happen very quickly. Television and the Internet speed ideas and facilitate the sale of goods around the globe. Almost no group of people can avoid some kind of contact with other societies. A

Geographic Thinking

Seeing Patterns

A In which locations would diffusion happen less frequently?

A. Answer in locations that are very isolated, lack transportation or communication systems

A **cultural hearth** is a site of innovation from which basic ideas, materials, and technology diffuse to many cultures. River civilizations such as those along the Indus River in South Asia, Huang He in East Asia, the Nile River in Africa, and the Tigris and Euphrates in Southwest Asia are the best known cultural hearths.

ACCULTURATION Exposure to an innovation does not guarantee that a society will accept that innovation. Individuals in the society must decide whether the innovation is useful and consistent with its basic principles. **Acculturation** occurs when a society changes because it accepts or adopts an innovation. An example of acculturation might be wearing jeans instead of traditional garments.

Sometimes individuals or a group adopt innovations that radically change the society. The resulting changes may have a positive or a negative effect on the society, depending on how the change came about. If change is forced on a group, it may have negative consequences. On the other hand, if the individuals or a group accept the change, it may lead to a better life for everyone. For example, the lives of thousands of people in Somalia were saved when they were persuaded to be vaccinated for smallpox in the 1970s.

ACTIVITY OPTION **FIVE THEMES OF GEOGRAPHY**

MOVEMENT

Exploring the Theme Cultural exchange is an example of geographic movement. Cultural exchange occurs through the movement of people, ideas, and goods. In the past, cultural exchange depended upon people traveling, but today, much cultural exchange also occurs through the media–print, radio, television, and the Internet.

Applying the Theme Direct students' attention to the photograph on page 72 and note that cultural exchanges can have both positive and negative effects. Ask students the following questions

- In what ways might exposure to television benefit this Mongolian family? *(It might be a source of news, entertainment, health information.)*
- What negative effects might exposure to television have? *(It might diminish the importance of their traditional values, and give them a distorted image of other cultures.)*
- Has television had these same effects on Americans? *(yes)*

Language

Language is one of the most important aspects of culture because it allows the people within a culture to communicate with each other. Language reflects all aspects of culture, including the physical area occupied by the society. For example, a society that lives in the subarctic or tundra region may have many different words to describe various forms of snow. However, those words would be useless for a culture in a place with no snow.

LANGUAGE AND IDENTITY Language helps establish a cultural identity. It builds a group identity and a sense of unity among those who speak the language. If a language is spoken throughout a political region, a spirit of unity and sometimes nationalism (a strong feeling of pride in one's nation) grows. Language can also divide people. If more than one language is spoken in an area, but one language seems to be favored, then conflict sometimes results. In Canada, for example, where both English and French are spoken, French Canadians pressured the government to recognize both French and English as official languages.

LANGUAGE FAMILIES Geographers estimate that between 3,000 and 6,500 languages are spoken across the world today. The languages are categorized by placing them with other similar languages in language families. (See page 74.) Today's languages evolved from earlier languages. One of the earlier languages, called Nostratic, developed in the area known today as Turkey. Nostratic is believed to be the basis of the Indo-European languages that you see on the chart on page 74. Languages as different as English, Russian, Hindi, and Greek all developed from the Indo-European family.

BACKGROUND
The language spoken by the largest number of native speakers is Mandarin Chinese, with an estimated 885 million speakers.

Versions of a language are called dialects. A **dialect** reflects changes in speech patterns related to class, region, or other cultural changes. For example, in the United States, dialects might include a Southern drawl, a Boston accent, or even street slang.

LANGUAGE DIFFUSION Like other aspects of culture, language can be diffused in many ways. It may follow trade routes or even be invented. For example, Swahili developed as a trade language between Arabic traders and Bantu-speaking tribes on Africa's east coast. Sometimes a blended language develops to aid communication among groups speaking several languages. In Louisiana, the presence of French, African, and North American peoples resulted in a blended language called Louisiana Creole.

A second way diffusion occurs is through migration. As people settle in new locations, the language they carry with them sometimes takes hold in the region. For example, colonists from Europe brought the English, Spanish, French, and Dutch languages to North and South America, Africa, Australia, and parts of Asia.

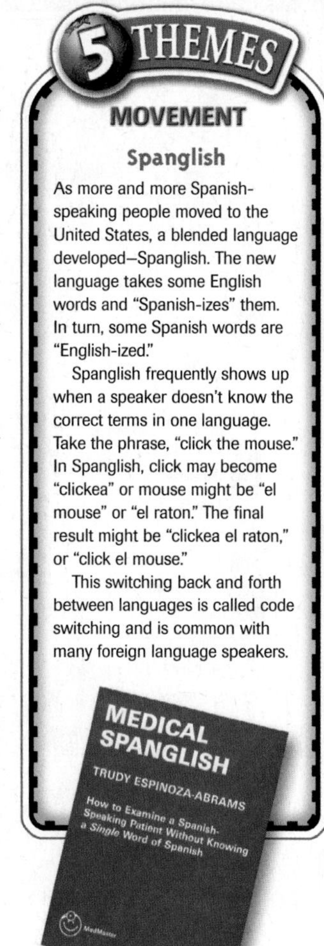

5 THEMES

MOVEMENT

Spanglish

As more and more Spanish-speaking people moved to the United States, a blended language developed—Spanglish. The new language takes some English words and "Spanish-izes" them. In turn, some Spanish words are "English-ized."

Spanglish frequently shows up when a speaker doesn't know the correct terms in one language. Take the phrase, "click the mouse." In Spanglish, click may become "clickea" or mouse might be "el mouse" or "el raton." The final result might be "clickea el raton," or "click el mouse."

This switching back and forth between languages is called code switching and is common with many foreign language speakers.

MEDICAL SPANGLISH
TRUDY ESPINOZA-ABRAMS
How to Examine a Spanish-Speaking Patient Without Knowing a Single Word of Spanish

BASICS

Instruct: Objective 3

Language

- How does language both unite and divide people? *(Language can build group identity and a feeling of pride in one's nation or group. Speakers of different languages in a region may come into conflict if one group feels the other is favored.)*
- What are some ways that language spreads? *(along trade routes, through contact between groups that blend their languages, and by migration)*

 **Map Transparency MT8**
- World Languages

5 THEMES

Movement: Spanglish

The U.S. Census Bureau estimated that in 2008 about 12.2 percent of the American populace five years old and older spoke Spanish at home. The language is most widely spoken in Florida, the Southwest, and the nation's largest cities, to which large numbers of Spanish-speakers from Mexico, Central America, the Caribbean, and other parts of the U.S. have migrated.

DIFFERENTIATING INSTRUCTION | **STUDENTS ACQUIRING ENGLISH/ESL**

EXPLORING LANGUAGE BLENDING

Objective To show how languages are blended

Class Time 15 minutes

Task Demonstrate how languages are blended with concrete examples

Directions Students may have first-hand examples of how languages are blended. Ask students to share examples of ways in which they blend English with their native language in their conversations with friends or family.

Interpreting Graphics

World Language Families

Remind students that a language family includes a number of individual languages. Note that some Native Americans in the United States speak non-Indo-European languages, but the number of speakers is too few to show on this map. Ask students what branch of the Indo-European language family English belongs to. *(Western Germanic)*

SKILLBUILDER ANSWERS

1. Indo-European **2.** Indo-European, other (Alaska)

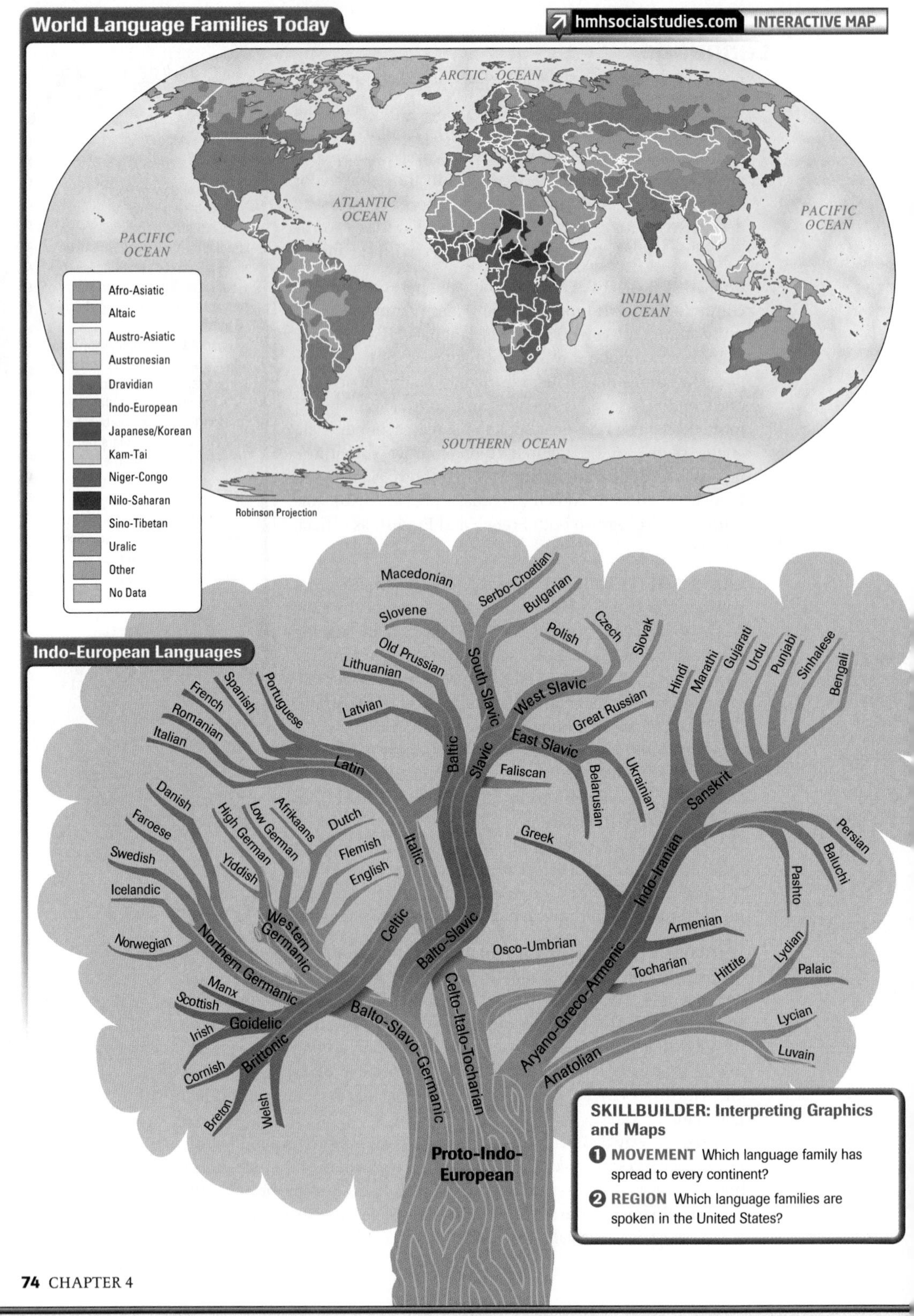

ACTIVITY OPTION CRITICAL THINKING

MAKING INFERENCES

Explaining the Skill Tell students that making inferences involves making reasonable guesses by combining what they already know with clues that are provided. For example, students can see from the map at the top of page 74 that the Indo-European language family covers more areas of the globe than any other single language family. Remind students that Europeans migrated to most parts of the world. They might therefore infer that the predominance of the Indo-European language family is due to this migration.

Applying the Skill Have students answer the following questions:

- Would a Spanish-speaker have an easier time learning French or English? Why? *(French, because it is more closely related to Spanish than to English)*
- Would you expect Greek to be more similar to Italian or to Hindi? Why? *(Hindi, because they come from the same language branch)*
- How might different languages have developed from the same family? *(by groups of people moving away, becoming separated for a long time from the original group, and being exposed to the influence of other languages)*

Religion

An aspect of culture that has a great deal of influence on people's lives is religion. **Religion** consists of a belief in a supernatural power or powers that are regarded as the creators and maintainers of the universe. Religions establish beliefs and values that define how people worship the divine being or divine forces and how they behave toward each other. Traditionally, religions have been categorized as one of three types:

- **monotheistic,** with a belief in one god
- **polytheistic,** with a belief in many gods
- **animistic** or traditional, often with a belief in divine forces in nature

SPREAD OF RELIGION Religions spread across the world through diffusion and through converts, people who give up their former beliefs for a new religion. Some religions, such as Christianity, Islam, and Buddhism, actively seek to convert people to their beliefs. Other religions, such as Judaism and Hinduism, do not. Finally, isolated pockets of religions, mostly animist, are found in Japan, Central Africa, Oceania, and among Native Americans of both North and South America. B

Geographic Thinking

Seeing Patterns
B How does location contribute to the isolation of animist practice?
B. Answer Many of the sites are difficult to reach because of their location in the middle of continents or in the oceans, and thus are isolated.

Major Religions

Several of the world's major religions began in Southwest and South Asia. Three religions from Southwest Asia—Judaism, Christianity, and Islam—are monotheistic. Of the religions that developed in South Asia, Buddhism in its original form did not involve a deity, and Hinduism features many gods.

JUDAISM Judaism developed in the dry lands near the eastern Mediterranean Sea. Its roots go back about 4,000 years, and Judaism is considered the oldest monotheistic religion. It is an ethnic religion, with a tradition of faith and culture tied tightly together. Judaism's basic laws and teachings can be found in a group of writings called the Hebrew Bible, of which the Torah is the most sacred text. The followers of Judaism, called Jews, live in many countries. Jews founded the state of Israel in 1948.

CHRISTIANITY Christianity, which is also monotheistic, is based on the teachings of Jesus, a Jew who lived in the Roman province of Judea about 2,000 years ago. Christians believe that Jesus was the Son of God. The teachings of Jesus were written down in the New Testament of the Bible. The religion was spread first by the disciples of Jesus and then by other people, such as Paul of Tarsus, whose writings had a deep impact on Christian thought. Christianity has more than 2 billion followers, more than any other faith. It has three major divisions: Roman Catholicism, Protestantism, and Eastern Orthodoxy.

ISLAM In about A.D. 610, an Arabian merchant named Muhammad reported that an angel had brought him messages from God. Muhammad began teaching these messages soon after, and they formed the basis of Islam. Followers of the faith are called Muslims. Islam is a monotheistic religion in which followers worship God, called Allah in Arabic, and observe certain rules of behavior. The holy book of the Muslims is the

BASICS

Instruct: Objective 4

Religion

- What are the three categories of religion? *(monotheistic, polytheistic, and animistic)*
- How do these categories differ? *(by the number or type of supernatural powers adherents believe in)*
- How do religions spread? *(through diffusion or conversion)*

Outline Maps with Activities
- Religions of the World, pp. 5–6

More About

Animism

Some animistic religions include a belief in one Supreme Being as well as in divine forces, or spirits, in nature.

Instruct: Objective 5

Major Religions

- What are five of the world's major religions, and where did each originate? *(Judaism, Christianity, and Islam began in Southwest Asia; Hinduism and Buddhism began in South Asia.)*
- What are three features that Judaism, Christianity, and Islam have in common? *(All three are monotheistic, have sacred texts, and began in Southwest Asia.)*

DIFFERENTIATING INSTRUCTION **STUDENTS ACQUIRING ENGLISH/ESL**

RECOGNIZING ROOT WORDS AND PREFIXES

Objective To use root words and prefixes to understand terms

Class Time 10 minutes

Task Learn terms that contain similar roots or prefixes

Directions Write the words *monotheistic, polytheistic,* and *animistic* on the board. Share with students the meanings of the following root words and prefixes.

-theism = belief in god

mono- = one

poly- = many

anima = soul

Interpreting Maps

World Religions/Worldwide Religious Membership

Ask students to describe the patterns they see in religious practice by region on the map. How do they account for the fact that traditional religion covers the largest total area but Christianity has the most members? *(Traditional religion covers the largest total area. Christianity predominates in several heavily populated regions. Islam is important in the Middle East and parts of Africa and Asia. Hinduism is important in India. Buddhism and Confucianism predominate in most of Asia. Judaism is practiced primarily in Israel and in small pockets of Europe and the United States. Traditional religions are practiced in areas where fewer people live.)*

SKILLBUILDER ANSWERS

1. Africa, South America, Australia, North America, Asia **2.** 13.2%, mostly in India

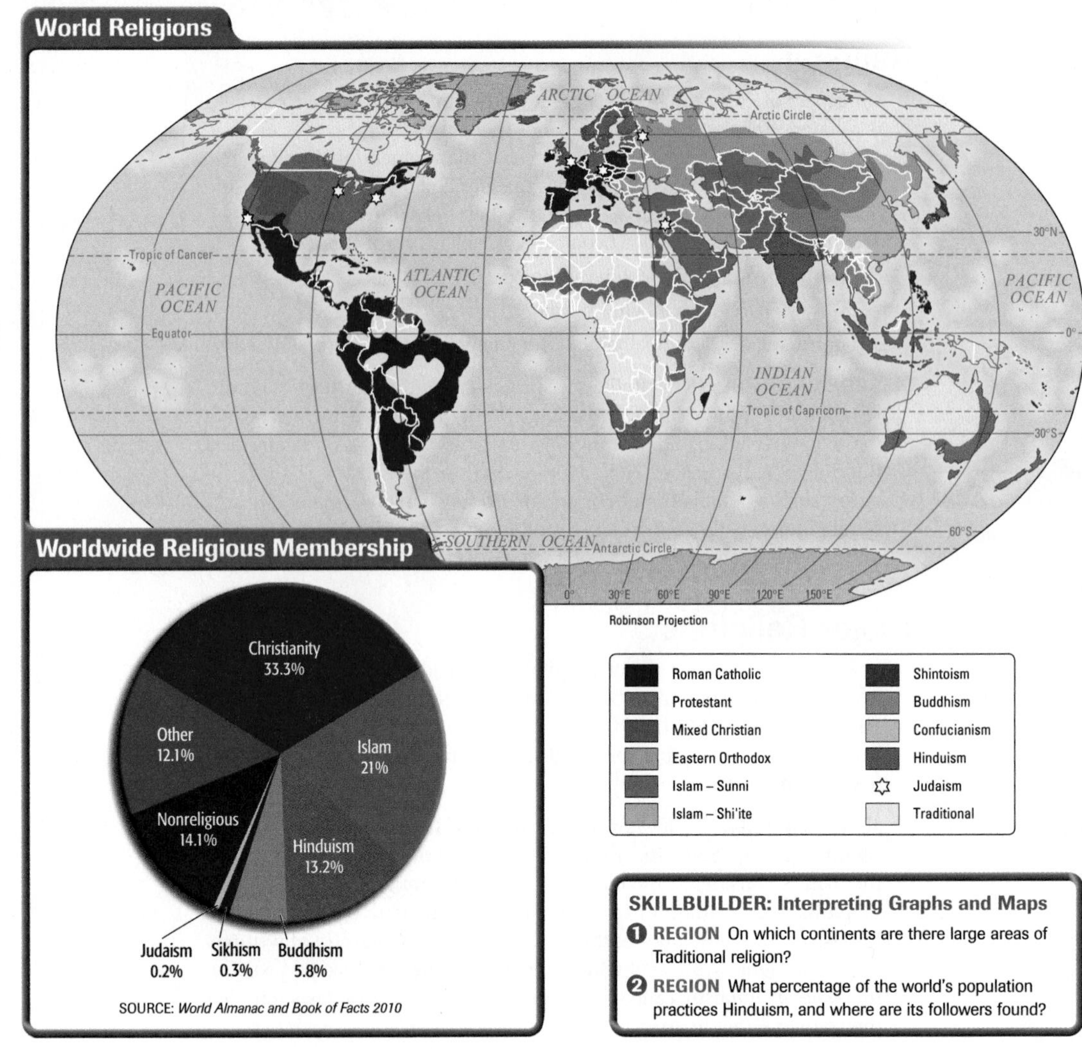

SOURCE: *World Almanac and Book of Facts 2010*

SKILLBUILDER: Interpreting Graphs and Maps

1. **REGION** On which continents are there large areas of Traditional religion?
2. **REGION** What percentage of the world's population practices Hinduism, and where are its followers found?

Qur'an. Islam spread from Arabia to the Middle East, Africa, large parts of Asia, and southeastern Europe. The two major groups within Islam are the Sunni and the Shia.

HINDUISM Of the major religions, Hinduism is the oldest, dating back about 5,000 years. It is an ethnic religion concentrated in India, but it has followers elsewhere. Hinduism is usually considered polytheistic because there are many Hindu gods. However, Hindus believe that each one represents an aspect of the supreme God, Brahman, so their religion can also be considered monotheistic. Belief in reincarnation, or rebirth, is central to Hinduism.

BUDDHISM Buddhism's origins go back to about the fifth century B.C. in northern India. Its founder, Siddhartha Gautama (also called the Buddha or Enlightened One) rejected the strict rules of Hindu society. His teachings promote a way of living in order to reach an enlightened

ACTIVITY OPTION **COOPERATIVE LEARNING** **BLOCK SCHEDULING**

INVESTIGATING WORLD RELIGIONS

Objective To compare the basic beliefs of the world's major religions

Class Time 20 minutes

Task Make lists of the most important beliefs of the world's major religions and discuss similarities and differences

Directions Divide students into groups of five and assign each group member one religion—Judaism, Christianity, Islam, Hinduism, or Buddhism—to research as homework. Instruct each student to make a list of the key beliefs of the religion. In class, have each group compare their lists and discuss the similarities and differences among the religions. Each group should prepare a brief oral summary to share with the entire class. These oral reports should clearly outline the similarities and differences among the five religions.

spiritual state called Nirvana. These beliefs spread from India to Southeast Asia, China, Japan, and Korea. Buddhism has several branches, the largest of which are Theravada, Mahayana, Tibetan Buddhism, and Zen.

OTHER ASIAN PRACTICES In parts of East Asia, three other belief systems are widely followed. They are Confucianism, Taoism, and Shinto. Sometimes these belief systems are thought of as religions and sometimes philosophies of life. All of them have specific practices and behaviors associated with them.

HUMAN–ENVIRONMENT INTERACTION This Peruvian bone flute dates back to sometime before 700 A.D. Bone flutes are among the oldest of all musical instruments.
In what way does this instrument show human-environment interaction?

Creative Cultural Expressions

C. Answer Climate may determine which natural materials are available for creating visual arts.

All cultures have ways of expressing themselves creatively. The environment and culture in which an artist lives is reflected in the artistic product. Cultures produce performing arts, visual arts, and literature.

Performing arts developed by a culture often include music, dance, theater, and film. Music is a cultural aspect found in all societies. The instruments on which the music is played and the style of music are unique to each group.

Visual arts include architecture, painting, sculpture, and textiles. The style of the visual arts will reflect materials available in the region and cultural themes. C

Geographic Thinking
Seeing Patterns C How might climate affect the visual arts of a region?

Oral and written literature, such as poems, folk tales, and stories, often illustrate aspects of the culture such as attitudes and behaviors. They can also be a reflection of the environment in which they are produced.

Throughout this book, you will find discussions of creative cultural expressions. As you study them, remind yourself that each culture is unique—as are the artistic expressions that the people from that culture produce.

Section 1 Assessment

1 Places & Terms
Explain the meaning of each of the following terms.
- culture
- society
- ethnic group
- diffusion
- acculturation
- dialect

2 Taking Notes
MOVEMENT Review the notes you took for this section.

Human Geography
Cultural

- In what ways is culture diffused?
- Which religions have spread from the place where they were founded?

3 Main Ideas
a. What factors make up culture?
b. In what ways is language spread?
c. What are some of the world's major religions?

4 Geographic Thinking
Determining Cause and Effect What role do innovation and diffusion play in changing a culture? **Think about:**
- contact with other groups
- acculturation

hmhsocialstudies.com
RESEARCH WEB LINKS

MAKING COMPARISONS Choose one of the factors of culture listed on page 71. Then select three countries. Use the Internet to find information on how each culture solves the problems associated with the factor you selected. Create a **database** showing the results of your research.

Interpreting Photographs

Peruvian Bone Flute
Bone flutes have been discovered in sites dating as far back as 10,000 years ago. Ask students what music playing might indicate about early human societies. *(From very early on, people have been concerned about more than survival and have sought ways to express and enjoy themselves.)*

CAPTION ANSWER To create the flute, an animal had to be killed and the bone carved.

Instruct: Objective 

Creative Cultural Expressions

- How do cultures express themselves creatively? *(through performing arts, visual arts and literature)*
- How do cultural expressions relate to the environment? *(materials used often reflect what is locally available; stories can reflect how people interact with the environment)*

Assess & Reteach

GeoFocus Have students complete the section on culture in their graphic organizers.

Formal Assessment
- Section Quiz, p. 51

Reteaching Activity
Using a large world map, ask students to cite examples of the cultural diffusion of language, religion, and the arts and the ways in which this diffusion occurred.

In-Depth Resources: Unit 1
- Reteaching Activity, p. 42

SECTION 1 ASSESSMENT ANSWERS

1. Places & Terms
culture, p. 71
society, p. 71
ethnic group, p. 71
acculturation, p. 72
diffusion, p. 72
dialect, p. 73

2. Taking Notes
- It diffuses when people come into contact with each other, through television, or the Internet.
- Judaism, Christianity, Islam, Hinduism, and Buddhism

3. Main Ideas
a. food and shelter, religion, relationships to family and others, language, education, security, political and social organizations
b. Language is spread by following trade or migration routes.
c. Judaism, Christianity, Islam, Hinduism, Buddhism

4. Geographic Thinking
They change cultures by bringing societies into contact with new ideas which a society or culture can either accept or reject.

GeoActivity

Integrated Assessment
- Rubric for a database, 2.6

SECTION 2 OBJECTIVES

1. Explain the factors involved in the world's population growth.
2. Describe the distribution of the world's population.
3. Describe some factors that influence population density and carrying capacity.

SKILLBUILDERS: Interpreting Graphs, Maps, and Charts, pp. 78, 79, 80, 82

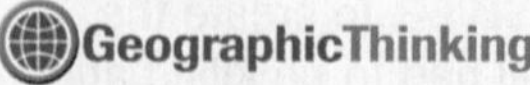

Seeing Patterns, pp. 79, 80
Making Comparisons, p. 81
Using the Atlas, p. 82
Making Inferences, p. 82

Focus & Motivate

Does the world already have too many people now, or can it support many more? *(Answers will vary.)*

Instruct: Objective 

Worldwide Population Growth

- What trend is occurring in the earth's population? *(It is increasing at a rapid rate.)*
- How is the rate of natural increase, or population growth rate, determined? *(by subtracting the mortality rate from the birthrate)*

 **In-Depth Resources: Unit 1**
- Guided Reading, p. 36

SKILLBUILDER ANSWERS

1. One billion population was not reached until the 1800s. **2.** The time to reach an additional billion in population has shortened.

2 Population Geography

Main Ideas

- People are not distributed equally on the earth's surface.
- The world's population continues to grow, but at different rates in different regions.

Places & Terms

birthrate
fertility rate
mortality rate
infant mortality rate
rate of natural increase
population pyramid
push-pull factors
population density
carrying capacity

A HUMAN PERSPECTIVE In 1999, the world's population reached 6 billion people. To get an idea of how many people that is, consider this:

If you had a *million* dollars in thousand dollar bills, the stack would be 6.3 inches high. If you had a *billion* dollars in thousand dollar bills, the stack would be 357 feet high, or about the length of a football field including the end zones. Now multiply by 6. Six billion dollars would be almost 6 football fields high.

At the world's natural growth rate in 1999, that 6 billion population figure was reached by the births of 230,000 people each day.

Worldwide Population Growth

The earth's population hit the one billion mark in the early 1800s. As the world industrialized, people grew more and better food and improved sanitation methods, and the population of the world began to soar. As more and more women reached childbearing age, the number of children added to the population also increased. As you can see in the diagram at the right, by 1930 two billion people lived on the earth. Notice that the number of years between each billion mark gets smaller.

BIRTH AND DEATH RATES A population geographer studies aspects of population such as birth and death rates, distribution, and density. To understand population growth, geographers calculate several different statistics. One is the **birthrate,** which is the number of live births per thousand population. In 2010, the highest birthrate in the world was more than 51.6 per thousand in Niger, and the lowest rate was about 7.6 per thousand in Japan. The world average birthrate is almost 20 per thousand.

Another way to study population is to look at the fertility rate. The **fertility rate** shows the average number of children a woman of childbearing years would have in her lifetime, if she had children at the current rate for her country. A fertility rate of 2.1 is necessary just to replace current population. Today, the worldwide average fertility rate is about 2.56.

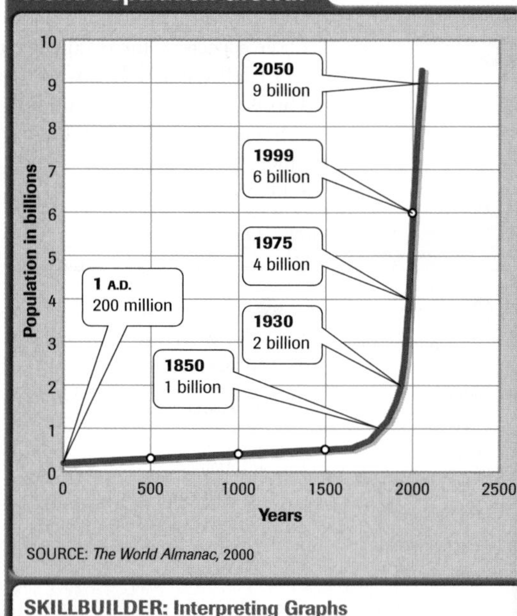

SOURCE: *The World Almanac*, 2000

SKILLBUILDER: Interpreting Graphs

1. **ANALYZING DATA** How long did it take for the population to reach one billion?
2. **MAKING GENERALIZATIONS** How have the intervals between increases changed?

SECTION 2 PROGRAM RESOURCES

 **In-Depth Resources: Unit 1**
- Guided Reading, p. 36
- Skillbuilder Practice, p. 40
- Building Vocabulary, p. 41
- Reteaching Activity, p. 43

 **Guided Reading Workbook**
- Section 2

 **Access for Students Acquiring English/ESL**
- Guided Reading, p. 18
- Skillbuillder Practice, p. 22

 **Formal Assessment**
- Section Quiz, p. 52

Integrated Assessment
- Rubric for an explanation, 4.5

INTEGRATED TECHNOLOGY

 **Critical Thinking Transparencies CT36**
- Population Geography Around the World

 **Map Transparencies MT9**
- World Population Density

  **Test Generator**
- Section Quiz

TEST-TAKING RESOURCES

 **Strategies for Test Preparation**

 **Test Practice Transparencies TT12**

 **Online Test Practice**

U.S. Population Pyramids, 2000 and 2050

A population pyramid presents a quick picture of a country's population distribution by age and sex. The effects of events in society can also be seen. Notice that in the year 2000 pyramid there is a bulge between ages 35 to 49. This reflects the "baby boom" generation born after World War II.

SKILLBUILDER: Interpreting Graphs

1. **ANALYZING DATA** How old are the people in the "baby boom" generation in the 2000 pyramid?
2. **DRAWING CONCLUSIONS** Why will the numbers for the very elderly (85+) increase so much by the year 2050?

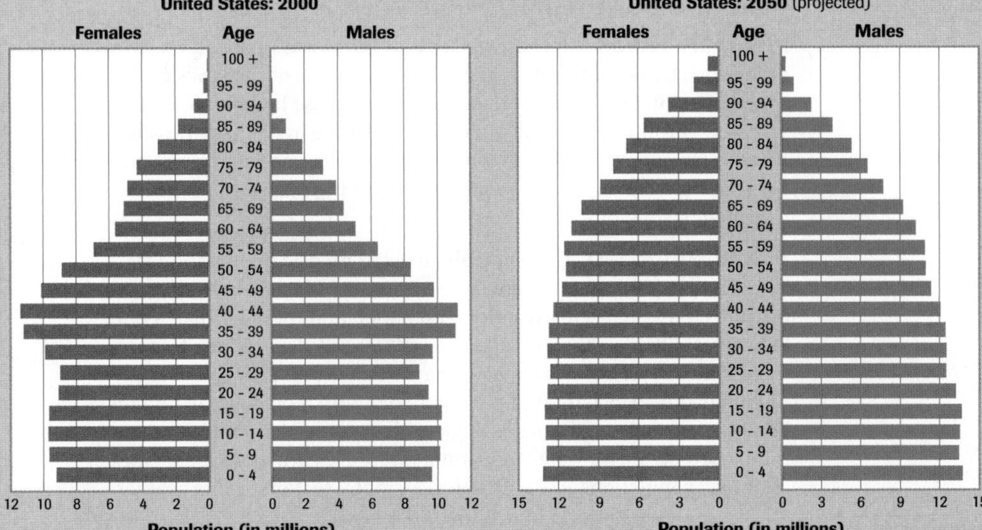

SOURCE: U.S. Census Bureau

BASICS

Interpreting Graphics

Constructing Population Pyramids to Predict Future Growth Trends

Remind students that geographers use population pyramids to predict future growth trends. For example, the population pyramids on page 79 show predicted growth trends by gender in the United States between the years 2000 and 2050. Have students research the population statistics for various ethnic groups in the United States from 1990 to 2000. Have students use that information to construct a population pyramid in order to predict future growth trends of those groups between 2000 and 2050.

SKILLBUILDER ANSWERS

1. approximately between 40 and 55

2. The numbers will increase because of the large number of "baby boomers" who will reach that age.

The **mortality rate**—also called the death rate—is the number of deaths per thousand people. In general, a society is considered healthy if it has a low mortality rate. However, some healthy nations have higher mortality rates because they have large numbers of elderly people.

For this reason, geographers also look at infant mortality rates in measuring how healthy the people of a nation are. The **infant mortality rate** shows the number of deaths among infants under age one per thousand live births. In the 1800s, the worldwide infant mortality rate was about 200 to 300 deaths per thousand live births. At the beginning of the 21st century, improved health care and nutrition led to a much lower rate worldwide. However, some parts of the world still record as many as 110 infant deaths per thousand. To find the rate at which population is growing, subtract the mortality rate from the birthrate. The difference is the **rate of natural increase,** or population growth rate. A

Geographic Thinking

Seeing Patterns

A What will the rate of natural increase be like if the birthrate is high and the mortality rate is low?

A. Answer It will increase greatly.

POPULATION PYRAMID Another way to analyze populations is to use a **population pyramid,** a graphic device that shows sex and age distribution of a population. Population pyramids help us understand population trends in countries. For example, population pyramids with wide bases have large percentages of young people, and the countries represented have rapidly growing populations.

More About

Infant Mortality Rate

For comparison purposes, the infant mortality rate of the United States is 6.2 per 1,000 live births. The rate for the United Kingdom is 4.9, and the rate for Sweden is 2.8.

ACTIVITY OPTION — INTERNET RESEARCH

CREATING AN INFOGRAPHIC

Objective To research and report on overpopulation problems

Class Time 45 minutes

Task Use the Internet to identify the potential problems that may result from a continued growth in the world population.

Directions Direct students to **hmhsocialstudies.com**. Have them follow the links to learn more about worldwide population growth and the problems that many scientists believe will result from overpopulation. Ask students to create an infographic to present their findings.

OPTIONAL ACTIVITY If Internet access is limited, have students use print resources such as reference books, almanacs, and encyclopedias.

Instruct: Objective 

Population Distribution

- Where does the majority of the world's population live? Why? *(Almost 90 per cent live in the Northern Hemisphere, and two thirds live between 20° N and 60° N. This zone has the most suitable climate and vegetation to support a large population.)*
- What portion of the world's population lives in rural areas? *(more than half)*
- Which continent has the greatest population density? *(Asia)*

Critical Thinking Transparencies CT36
- Population Geography Around the World

Interpreting Maps

World Population Density

Have students examine the map and point out that all but two of the world's twelve largest cities are in the Northern Hemisphere. Note that although Western Europe is densely populated, it has no cities with 12 million population or greater. Ask students what three regions of the world have the greatest population density. *(East Asia, South Asia, and Western Europe)*

SKILLBUILDER ANSWERS
1. Asia **2.** the Southern Hemisphere

Population Distribution

The billions of people in the world are not distributed equally across the earth. Some lands are not suitable for human habitation. In fact, almost 90 percent of the world's population lives in the Northern Hemisphere. One in four people in the world lives in East Asia, and one of every two people lives in either East Asia or South Asia. Several factors, including climate, altitude, and access to water, influence where people live.

HABITABLE LANDS Almost two-thirds of the world's population lives in the zone between 20° N and 60°N latitude. Some of the lands in this zone have suitable climate and vegetation for dense human habitation. They are warm enough and wet enough to make agriculture possible. In addition, populations are concentrated along coastal regions and river valleys. The lightly populated areas are in polar regions, heavily mountainous regions, and desert regions. B

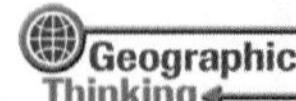

Geographic Thinking

Seeing Patterns B Why are populations concentrated along coastal regions and river valleys?

B. Answer The locations provide food and transportation.

URBAN–RURAL MIX Currently, about half the world's population lives in rural areas, but that percentage is shrinking. More people are moving into cities—particularly cities with populations of more than a million. Cities with more than 10 million people are called megacities. By 2010, there were at least 25 megacities, with a combined population of over 427 million people. The largest of these is Tokyo, with more than 35 million inhabitants. Such huge cities struggle with overcrowded conditions and immense demand for water and sanitation. You'll learn more about cities and their populations in the Urban Geography section of this chapter.

World Population Density

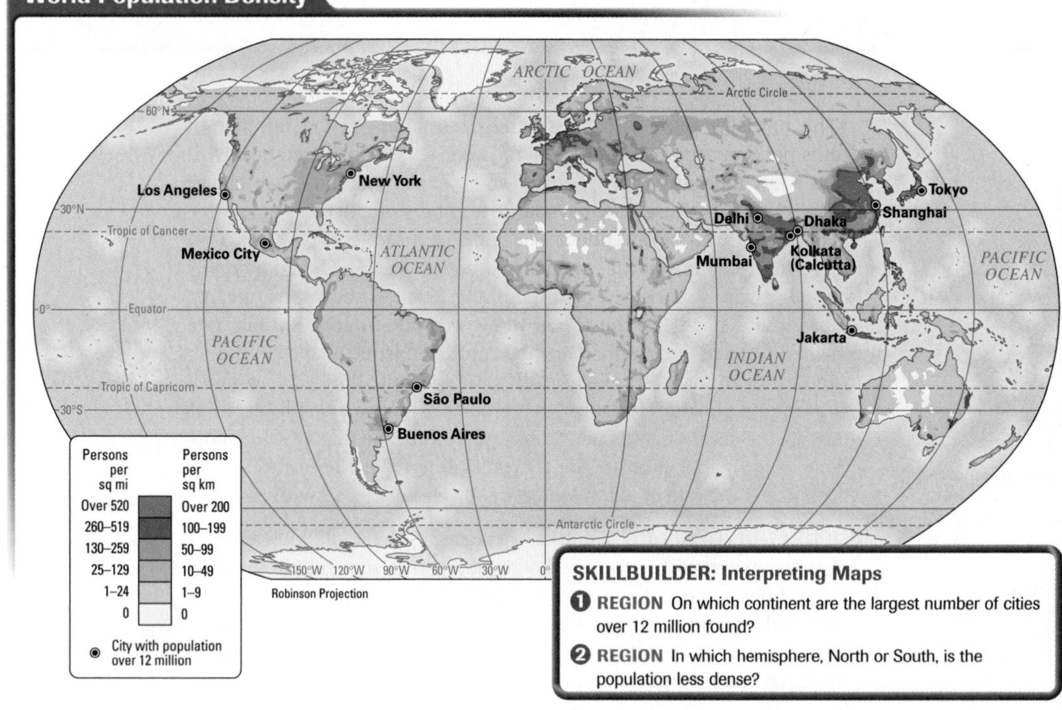

SKILLBUILDER: Interpreting Maps

1 REGION On which continent are the largest number of cities over 12 million found?

2 REGION In which hemisphere, North or South, is the population less dense?

ACTIVITY OPTION **SKILLBUILDER LESSON**

SEEING PATTERNS

Explaining the Skill A pattern is a recurring characteristic or the recurring association of two or more characteristics. One task of population geographers is to look for settlement patterns and seek explanations for those patterns.

Applying the Skill Have students use the population density map at the bottom of page 80 to answer the following questions:

- What association is there between land area, excluding areas of ice cap, and the hemisphere with the greatest population density? *(The Northern Hemisphere has the largest land area, excluding ice cap, and the greatest population density.)*
- What pattern do you see in population density of the United States? *(The eastern part of the United States is more densely populated than the western part, although both coasts are densely populated.)*

In-Depth Resources: Unit 1
- Skillbuilder Practice, p. 40

MIGRATION The large-scale migration of people from one location to another also alters the distribution of population. Reasons for migrating are sometimes referred to as **push-pull factors.**

Push factors are those that cause people to leave their homeland and migrate to another region. Environmental conditions, such as drought or other natural disasters, are examples of push factors. Other push factors are political, such as war or the persecution of certain groups of people for ethnic or religious reasons. For example, more than one million Rwandans left their country for other parts of Africa in the wake of a civil war there in 1994.

Pull factors draw or attract people to another location. Countries with good economic opportunities and high salaries are the likely destinations for migrants. Favorable climate is another pull factor. C

C. Answer Push factors are more likely to cause migration because they affect a larger number of people.

Geographic Thinking

Making Comparisons Do you think push factors or pull factors result in larger migrations?

Population Density

To understand how heavily populated an area is, geographers use a figure called **population density.** This figure is the average number of people who live in a measurable area, such as a square mile. The number is reached by dividing the number of inhabitants in an area by the total amount of land they occupy.

Because population is not distributed evenly across the land, the number may be misleading for an entire nation. Certain areas may be densely populated, while others are quite thinly populated. For example, in 2008, the estimated population density of the United States was 86.8 people per square mile. But as you can see on the population density table on the next page, Alaska—with its huge land area and small population—had a density of 1.2 people per square mile. On the other hand, New Jersey, with a small land area and large population, had a very high density at more than 1,180 people per square mile. Remember, too, that population density may change over time.

PLACE Nanjing Road in Shanghai, China, is considered one of the busiest streets in the world. **What problems do people in overcrowded cities face?**

BASICS

Interpreting Photographs

Shanghai, China

Shanghai, with a population in the metropolitan area of more than 15 million, is the largest city in China. The city has a population density of over 5,000 per square mile. Ask students what signs of cultural diffusion they see in this photograph. *(The people are wearing Western-style clothing.)*

CAPTION ANSWER Shortages of housing, water, and sanitation are problems.

Instruct: Objective 3

Population Density

- What is population density? *(the average number of people who live in a measurable area)*
- What is carrying capacity? *(the number of organisms a piece of land can support)*
- What factors influence both carrying capacity and population density? *(fertility of the land, level of technology, economic activities)*

Map Transparencies MT9
- World Population Density

ACTIVITY OPTION **LINK TO HISTORY**

BLOCK SCHEDULING

IDENTIFYING FACTORS IN U.S. IMMIGRATION

Objective To apply the concept of push-pull factors to the history of immigration to the United States

Class Time 30 minutes

Task Create a chart listing the push-pull factors that motivated immigrants to come to the United States

Directions Organize students into small groups and assign a period of U.S. history to each group. Direct them to use the Internet, history books, or encyclopedias to identify the main immigrant groups of the period and the reasons they immigrated. Students should create charts that distinguish the "push" and the "pull" factors.

Interpreting Charts

Regional Population Density

Point out that this chart lists the regions that are covered in this textbook. Students might refer back to this chart as they study each region. Students may be surprised at the high population density of Monaco. Ask students if any other statistics surprise them and why. *(Australia is less densely populated than Iceland, which most people think of as having a more forbidding climate.)*

SKILLBUILDER ANSWERS

1. Europe **2.** China has more land than Taiwan, which reduces the number of persons per square mile.

Assess & Reteach

GeoFocus Have students complete the section on population in their graphic organizers.

Formal Assessment
• Section Quiz, p. 52

Reteaching Activity
Have students create an outline of the headings in this section and write a summary of the main idea or ideas under each heading.

In-Depth Resources: Unit 1
• Reteaching Activity, p. 43

Regional Population Density

Region	Highest Density (per square mile)		Lowest Density (per square mile)	
United States and Canada	New Jersey Prince Edward I.	1,181 61.9	Alaska Nunavut	1.2 0.04
Latin America	Barbados	1,710	French Guiana	5.9
Europe	Monaco	43,784	Iceland	7.9
Russia and the Republics	Armenia	271	Kazakhstan	14.9
Africa	Mauritius	1,639	Namibia	6.6
Southwest Asia	Bahrain	2,835	Saudi Arabia	34.6
South Asia	Maldives	3,422	Bhutan	38.1
East Asia	Taiwan	1,845	Mongolia	5.1
Southeast Asia, Australia, and Oceania	Singapore	17,559	Australia	7.2

SOURCE: *The World Almanac and Book of Facts, 2010*

SKILLBUILDER: Interpreting Charts

❶ **ANALYZING DATA** Which region seems to be the most densely populated?

❷ **MAKING INFERENCES** Why might Taiwan be more densely populated than China, which is in the same region?

CARRYING CAPACITY Another aspect of population density statistics is the ability of the land to support a population. **Carrying capacity** is the number of organisms a piece of land can support. A region with fertile land may be able to support far more people than one with land of poor quality or with little land available for cultivation.

The level of technology of a group living on the land may affect carrying capacity. Improved farming techniques, such as irrigation, use of fertilizers, and mechanized farm equipment, will generally increase the carrying capacity of land.

In some locations, few if any people make their living by farming. However, other aspects of their economy allow a small area of land to support a large number of people. Notice the density of Singapore shown in the chart at left. A city state located at the tip of Malaysia, Singapore is a center of international finance and shipping. The wealth these activities bring allows people to import food. Thus, Singapore is able to support millions of people even though it has little farmable land. D

In the next section, you'll learn how the world's population forms into political units.

D. Answer Strait of Molucca and the South China Sea

Geographic Thinking

Using the Atlas
D Use the map on pages A32–A33 to find the location of Singapore. On what bodies of water is Singapore located?

Section 2 Assessment

❶ Places & Terms

Explain the meaning of each of the following terms.
- birthrate
- mortality rate
- rate of natural increase
- push-pull factors
- population density

❷ Taking Notes

PLACE Review the notes you took for this section.

- How does a population pyramid help you understand population in a place?
- What factors influence where people live?

❸ Main Ideas

a. How is the rate of natural increase determined?

b. Why must the population density figures for a country be used with caution?

c. Where does the majority of the world's population live?

❹ Geographic Thinking

Making Inferences What role has industrialization played in population growth? **Think about:**
- infant mortality rate
- improved living conditions

See Skillbuilder Handbook, page R4.

GeoActivity

SEEING PATTERNS Choose one continent to study on the satellite image on page 88. Compare the satellite image with an atlas map of the same area. Write an **explanation** of which landforms or water bodies have played a part in the distribution of population that you see in the satellite image.

SECTION 2 ASSESSMENT ANSWERS

1. Places & Terms
birthrate, p. 78
mortality rate, p. 79
rate of natural increase, p. 79
population density, p. 81
push-pull factors, p. 81

2. Taking Notes
- It shows the makeup of the population by gender and age and aids in understanding how certain events affect the population.
- climate, altitude, and access to water

3. Main Ideas

a. by subtracting the mortality rate from the birthrate

b. They may not reflect the distribution of the population or the economic activities that change the carrying capacity.

c. Two-thirds of the world's population lives in the zone between 20°N and 60°N latitude. More than half live in rural areas.

4. Geographic Thinking
With industrialization has come improved health and sanitation. The world's population has grown; more babies are born, and more people are living longer due to improved food supplies.

GeoActivity

Integrated Assessment
• Rubric for an explanation, 4.5

3 Political Geography

Main Ideas

- The world is divided into many political regions.
- Local, national, and regional governments control aspects of life within the boundaries of the unit.

Places & Terms

state	monarchy
nation	dictatorship
nation-state	communism
democracy	landlocked

BASICS

A HUMAN PERSPECTIVE Abdoulaye Sowe, a Senegalese farmer, chose a spot to build his new house near the Senegalese border guard's shack. He believed the guard shack was in Senegal. But long-time residents of the area told him that, before the shack was built, a guard used to sit near a tree that was considered the border marker. The tree was several hundred feet north of Sowe's house. Technically, Sowe now lived in the country of Gambia, not Senegal. Sowe's dilemma points out the difficulty of pinpointing borders that create political units.

Nations of the World

Governmental units of the world can be described in either political or geographic terms. Generally, we use the political term **state** to describe an independent unit that occupies a specific territory and has full control of its internal and external affairs. Often the term "country" is used to mean state.

Nation refers to a group of people with a common culture living in a territory and having a strong sense of unity. When a nation and a state occupy the same territory, that territory is called a **nation-state.** Many countries of the world are nation-states. However, it is possible for a nation not to have a territory. When that happens, the group without a territory is called a stateless nation. Examples of stateless nations include Palestinians, Kurds, and Basques.

TYPES OF GOVERNMENT All countries must choose a type of government. Generally, the type of government falls into one of these categories:

- **Democracy** Citizens hold political power, either directly or through elected representatives. Example: the United States.
- **Monarchy** A ruling family headed by a king or queen holds political power and may or may not share the power with citizen bodies. Example: the United Kingdom or Saudi Arabia.
- **Dictatorship** An individual or group holds complete political power. Example: North Korea.
- **Communism** In this government and economic system, nearly all political power and means of production are held by the government in the name of all the people.

Whatever the type of government, it must deal with issues that have to do with the territory and people of the state.

PLACE National flags fly at the United Nations headquarters in New York City.

SECTION 3 OBJECTIVES

1. Define the three categories of governments.
2. Identify the three most important geographic characteristics used to describe a country.
3. Distinguish between natural and artificial boundaries.
4. Identify the main types of regional political systems.

SKILLBUILDER: Interpreting Maps, p. 84

Geographic Thinking

Making Comparisons, p. 84
Using the Atlas, p. 85
Making Inferences, p. 86

Focus & Motivate

Why do people form political units such as countries and states? *(ease of managing an area; natural or artificial boundaries; common culture or interests)*

Instruct: Objective 

Nations of the World

- How does a state differ from a nation? *(A state is an independent political unit that occupies a specific territory and controls its internal and external affairs. A nation is a group of people with a common culture living in a territory and having a strong sense of unity. State refers to territory and government, while* nation *refers to people.)*
- What is a monarchy? *(A form of government in which a ruling family holds political power.)*

In-Depth Resources: Unit 1
- Guided Reading, p. 37

SECTION 3 PROGRAM RESOURCES

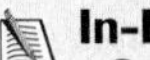

In-Depth Resources: Unit 1
- Guided Reading, p. 37
- Building Vocabulary, p. 41
- Reteaching Activity, p. 44

Guided Reading Workbook
- Section 3

Access for Students Acquiring English/ESL
- Guided Reading, p. 19

Outline Maps with Activities
- World: Political, pp. 3–4

Formal Assessment
- Section Quiz, p. 53

Integrated Assessment
- Rubric for a database, 2.6

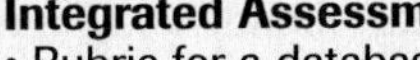

INTEGRATED TECHNOLOGY

Power Presentations

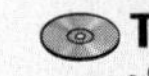

Test Generator
- Section Quiz

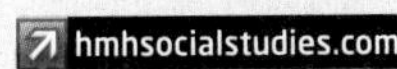

hmhsocialstudies.com

TEST-TAKING RESOURCES

Strategies for Test Preparation

Test Practice Transparencies TT13

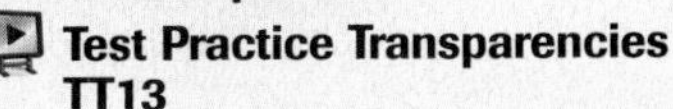

Online Test Practice

Interpreting Maps

Political Geography of the Korean Peninsula

From 1910 to the end of World War II, Japan claimed Korea as a colony. Communists took over North Korea in 1945. After Japan was defeated in World War II, the Allies divided Korea. North and South Korea formed separate governments in 1948. Ask students why Korea's size and location might make it politically vulnerable. *(It is a small country located near two strong countries, China and Japan.)*

SKILLBUILDER ANSWERS

1. It is located south and east of China, has coastlines on the Yellow Sea and the Sea of Japan (East Sea), and is across the Korea Strait from Japan.

2. The western coast is much more irregular than the eastern coast, which is smoother.

Instruct: Objective 

Geographic Characteristics of Nations

- What three geographic characteristics are important in describing a country? *(size, shape, and relative location)*
- How are size and shape important? *(A larger country may have more resources and population on which to build military or economic power. Shape influences how a country can be governed, and how goods can be transported.)*
- How is location important? *(Location can influence transportation, trade, and security.)*

Political Geography of the Korean Peninsula

1. The Yalu Jiang River is a natural boundary between North Korea and China.
2. The artificial boundary between North and South Korea was a result of an agreement ending the Korean War.
3. The Korean Peninsula is divided into two small and compact nations. Their relative location gives them access to mainland China and to Japan.

CHINA · NORTH KOREA · SOUTH KOREA · JAPAN · Shenyang · Sinuiju · Yalu Jiang · Chongjin · Kimch'aek · Hamhuag · Wonsan · Pyongyang · Korea Bay · Kaesong · Panmunjom · Seoul · Inchon · Chongju · Taejon · Taegu · Kwangju · Pusan · Yellow Sea · Sea of Japan (East Sea) · Korea Strait

0 100 200 miles; 0 100 200 kilometers; Lambert Conformal Conic Projection

SKILLBUILDER: Interpreting Maps

1. **LOCATION** What is the relative location of the Korean Peninsula?
2. **PLACE** How is the coastline on the west side of the peninsula different from the coastline on the east side?

Geographic Characteristics of Nations

Three geographic characteristics are very important in describing a country. These characteristics are: 1) size, 2) shape, and 3) relative location. The combination of these characteristics makes each nation unique. By looking at the map above, you will see how these characteristics helped shape the political geography of the Korean Peninsula.

SIZE You might assume that the physical size of a country has much to do with its wealth and power. However, this is not always true. For example, the political division of the United Kingdom known as England once controlled a significant empire of colonies around the globe. Even so, a larger nation, such as the United States, China, or Russia, has the potential to be more powerful because it has more resources and people on which to build military or economic power.

SHAPE Countries can be compact, such as Germany, or long like Chile. Some countries are fragmented, like Japan, which is made up of many islands. The shape of a country can have an impact on how easily it can be governed, how goods are moved to all areas of the country, and how it relates to neighboring countries. A

LOCATION The relative location of a country can be very important. A **landlocked** country—one surrounded by other land and with no direct outlet to the sea—must find ways to build connections to the rest of the world to get goods in and out of the country. Bolivia is an example of a landlocked country. In contrast, the location of the tiny city-state of

A. Answer It is compact but some might answer fragmented because of Alaska and Hawaii.

Geographic Thinking

Making Comparisons

A Which of the three shapes describes the United States?

DIFFERENTIATING INSTRUCTION **GIFTED AND TALENTED STUDENTS** **BLOCK SCHEDULING**

APPLYING GEOGRAPHIC CONCEPTS

Objective To apply concepts regarding a country's size, shape, and location

Class Time One class period

Task Create an annotated map of a country of their choice

Directions Instruct students to choose any country in the world and create an area map with annotations that explain how the country's size, shape, and location have affected its development. Students may choose a country they already know a great deal about, or they may choose one that requires them to do research.

Singapore in Southeast Asia gives it access to major shipping lanes between East Asia and South Asia. The resulting trade brings great wealth to the port. A nation surrounded by hostile neighbors must deal with issues of protection and security.

National Boundaries

Boundaries or borders set the limits of the territory controlled by a state. Within its borders, the state can do such things as collect taxes, set up a legal code, and declare an official language. A state may claim all of the resources found within its boundaries. Because so much is at stake, states are very protective of their borders. The two basic types of national boundaries are natural and artificial.

NATURAL BOUNDARIES A natural boundary is based on physical features of the land, such as rivers, lakes, or chains of mountains. The Rio Grande, for example, is a river that forms a natural boundary between part of Mexico and part of the United States. Natural boundaries may seem like an easy way to separate one country from another, but they do present problems. Traditionally, a river or lake boundary is fixed in the middle of the body of water. What if a river shifts its course? Which country gets additional land—or loses it? B

Geographic Thinking

Using the Atlas

B Use the map on pages A18–A19. What physical features make up the natural boundaries between the United States and Canada?

B. Answer the Great Lakes and the St. Lawrence River

ARTIFICIAL BOUNDARIES An artificial boundary is a fixed line generally following latitude or longitude lines. The 49°N latitude line that separates the United States from Canada is an example. These lines are often formally defined in boundary treaties between countries. Sometimes a conquering country imposes boundaries on lands it has taken over. The lines established may not match boundaries previously found in that location, which can lead to internal problems or even war.

Africa is a good example of how boundary lines can divide groups of people or put groups that have long been enemies together in one state. When parts of Africa were divided by European colonial powers in the 1800s, the boundary lines for Nigeria included the traditional lands of the Hausa-Fulani people, the Yoruba people, and the Ibo people. Under British control, the three groups were forced to follow British rules. When

MOVEMENT The Great Wall of China is an example of an artificial boundary. It was built to stop invading armies. **How does the wall also illustrate a type of natural boundary?**

85

BASICS

Instruct: Objective 3

National Boundaries

- Why are a state's boundaries important? *(Within its borders, a state can collect taxes, set up a legal code, declare an official language, and claim resources.)*
- What is a natural boundary based on, and what problem can it cause? *(A natural boundary is based on physical features of the land. A dispute may arise if the physical feature changes.)*
- What is an artificial boundary, and when does it cause problems? *(An artificial boundary generally follows latitude or longitude lines. Conflict may arise when an artificial boundary ignores established divisions between groups of people.)*

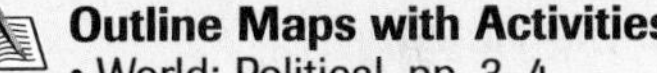

Outline Maps with Activities
- World: Political, pp. 3–4

Interpreting Photographs

Great Wall of China

Direct students to examine the photograph closely to see that the wall winds far into the distance along the mountain ridge. Ask students what other methods countries use to protect their borders. *(border patrols, forts, radar and satellite surveillance)*

CAPTION ANSWER The wall is built along the ridge of the mountains that are a natural feature of the earth.

ACTIVITY OPTION | EXPLORING LOCAL GEOGRAPHY

RESEARCHING STATE BOUNDARIES

Objective To apply concepts about boundaries to a local area

Class Time 30 minutes

Task Make a map of state boundaries and write a report on how they were determined

Directions Randomly assign a state to each student. Have them make a map of their state and label the boundaries as natural or artificial. Instruct them to do library research to find out how the boundaries were determined and include these as captions on the map.

Instruct: Objective 4

Regional Political Systems

- Why do countries form smaller political units? *(to make governing more efficient)*
- In order of increasing size, how do the following political units rank: state, city, county, country? *(city, county, state, country)*
- Which has more direct contact with the people, a city government or a state government? *(city)*

Assess & Reteach

GeoFocus Have students complete the section on political geography in their graphic organizers.

Formal Assessment
- Section Quiz, p. 53

Reteaching Activity
Organize the class into groups of four students and assign one section objective to each group member. Have each member write a short summary of that section's main idea and share the summary with the rest of the group.

In-Depth Resources: Unit 1
- Reteaching Activity, p. 44

Levels of Government

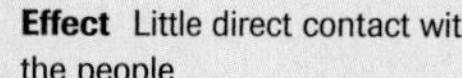

NATIONAL
Size Very large units composed of many medium and small units
Effect Little direct contact with the people
Role Deals with issues affecting the entire nation, such as security or international diplomatic relations
Example United States

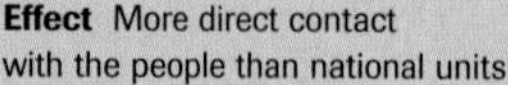

STATE/REGIONAL
Size Larger units composed of many smaller units
Effect More direct contact with the people than national units
Role Deals with issues that affect all of the smaller units, such as licensing drivers
Example States or regional groups, such as the Tennessee Valley Authority

LOCAL
Size Smaller units of government
Effect Very direct contact with the people
Role Deals with issues that are narrow in scope, such as streets and sanitation
Example A school district or town

Britain left, there was controversy over the control of the lands. One group, the Ibo, attempted to withdraw from Nigeria and form its own nation-state—Biafra. A civil war resulted, and the attempt to split away failed.

Regional Political Systems

Countries often are divided into smaller political units to make governing more efficient. The most common local units of government are cities, towns, and villages. Other types of political units might include school districts.

Smaller political units often combine to form larger regional units, such as counties, provinces, and states. Here, too, there may be districts for providing a service or product to an area that crosses several political units. For example, the Tennessee Valley Authority (TVA) regulates water usage in a seven-state region.

BACKGROUND
The TVA built dams, hydroelectric plants, and flood control projects on the Tennessee River and its tributaries.

Countries may join with each other to form international political, military, or economic units. Groups of states within a regional area may band together to promote mutual goals. An example is the European Union, which you'll learn more about in Chapter 14.

The largest political unit is the United Nations, which has nearly 200 members who work to improve political, cultural, and economic conditions across the globe. In the next section, you'll learn that almost half of the world's population lives in urban areas that include political units called cities.

Section 3 Assessment

1 Places & Terms
Explain the meaning of each of the following terms.
- state
- nation
- nation-state
- democracy
- monarchy
- dictatorship

2 Taking Notes
PLACE Review the notes you took for this section.

- What are three geographic characteristics of countries?
- What are three types of governments?

3 Main Ideas
a. How do the three basic geographic characteristics affect a nation?
b. What is the difference between natural and artificial boundaries?
c. Why do local and regional political systems exist?

4 Geographic Thinking
Making Inferences Which type of boundary would most likely cause the greatest political problems? **Think about:**
- types of natural borders
- artificial boundaries

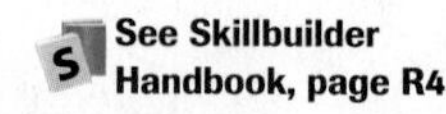

See Skillbuilder Handbook, page R4.

GeoActivity
EXPLORING LOCAL GEOGRAPHY Using a map of the United States, study the boundaries of the 50 states. Create a **database** that shows the names of states with 1) all artificial boundaries, 2) all natural boundaries, 3) mixed boundaries. Write several sentences summarizing your data.

SECTION 3 ASSESSMENT ANSWERS

1. Places & Terms
state, p. 83
nation, p. 83
nation-state, p. 83
democracy, p. 83
monarchy, p. 83
dictatorship, p. 83

2. Taking Notes
- size, shape, and relative location
- democracy, monarchy, dictatorship, and communism

3. Main Ideas
a. Size may affect the amount of political or economic power a nation has. Shape may affect how it can be governed, or how goods are moved to all areas of the country, and how it relates to neighboring countries. Location relates to issues of protection, security, and accessibility.
b. Natural boundaries use physical features to divide nations. Artificial boundaries are drawn by people to divide lands.
c. to make governments more efficient and to pursue common goals

4. Geographic Thinking
Artificial boundaries may overlap with traditional, cultural, or historic boundaries and thus cause disagreements.

GeoActivity

Integrated Assessment
- Rubric for a database, 2.6

Urban Geography

Main Ideas

- Nearly half the world's population lives in urban areas.
- Cities fulfill economic, residential, and cultural functions in different ways.

Places & Terms

urban geography
city
suburb
metropolitan area
urbanization
central business district (CBD)

BASICS

A HUMAN PERSPECTIVE Around 4500 B.C. in Sumer, an ancient country in what today is Iraq, the city of Ur was settled. Eventually it grew to be home to as many as 34,000 people. Archaeologists believe that it was one of the first cities in the world. Within the city walls, a broad avenue led up to an immense temple with a roof that loomed 80 feet above the ground. Surrounding the temple were private homes and large open markets with shops on streets resembling those in cities of Southwest Asia today. Some people lived in two-story houses with balconies and even had clay-lined drains for waste disposal. A canal ran through the city from the river to a harbor built on its northern edge. This was not an overgrown village, but a real city.

In the centuries since, cities have grown so important that geographers have developed the field of **urban geography**—the study of how people use space in cities.

Growth of Urban Areas

Today, much of the population of the world lives in cities. **Cities** are not just areas with large populations—they are also centers of business and culture. Cities are often the birthplace of innovation and change in a society. Urban lifestyles are different from those of towns, villages, or rural areas. When geographers study urban areas, they consider location, land use, and functions of the city.

URBAN AREAS An urban area develops around a main city called the central city. The built-up area around the central city may include **suburbs,** which are political units touching the borders of the central city or touching other suburbs that touch the city. These suburbs are within commuting distance of the city. Some suburbs are mostly residential, while others have a whole range of urban activities.

Smaller cities or towns with open land between them and the central city are called exurbs. The city, its suburbs, and exurbs link together economically to form a functional area called a **metropolitan area.** A megalopolis is formed when several metropolitan areas grow together. An example of a megalopolis is the corridor in the northeastern United States including Boston, New York, Philadelphia, Baltimore, and Washington, D.C.

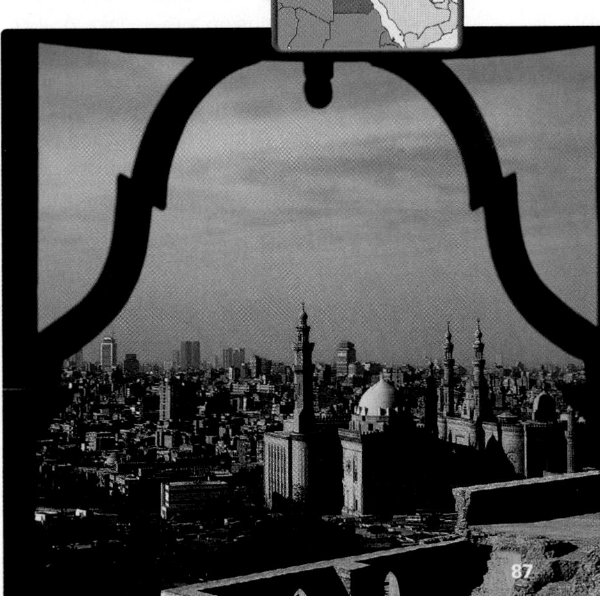

PLACE Both the old city and the new parts of Cairo, Egypt, can be seen in this view.
Why do you think the old parts of the city were not torn down and replaced with new buildings?

87

SECTION 4 OBJECTIVES

1. Explain how urban areas develop.
2. Describe common reasons for the locations of cities.
3. Identify the basic land-use patterns found in all cities.
4. Describe the functions of cities and the relationship between a city's functions and transportation.

SKILLBUILDERS: Interpreting Graphics and Maps pp. 89, 90

GeographicThinking

Using the Atlas, p. 88
Seeing Patterns, p. 89
Making Comparisons, p. 90
Making Inferences, p. 90

Focus & Motivate

Why do people live in cities? *(Students may mention economic and cultural opportunities.)*

Instruct: Objective 

Growth of Urban Areas

- What is the core of an urban area and what surrounds it? *(The core is a central city. Suburbs surround it.)*
- What does a metropolitan area consist of? *(city, suburbs, and exurbs)*
- What is meant by the term "urbanization?" *(the dramatic rise in the number of cities over the last two centuries and the changes in lifestyle that have resulted)*

In-Depth Resources: Unit 1
- Guided Reading, p. 38

CAPTION ANSWER Those parts of the city may have buildings that are important to the culture and will not be torn down even if they are old.

SECTION 4 PROGRAM RESOURCES

In-Depth Resources: Unit 1
- Guided Reading, p. 38
- Building Vocabulary, p. 41
- Reteaching Activity, p. 45

Guided Reading Workbook
- Section 4

Access for Students Acquiring English/ESL
- Guided Reading, p. 20

Formal Assessment
- Section Quiz, p. 54

Integrated Assessment
- Rubric for a sketch map, 2.1

INTEGRATED TECHNOLOGY

 **Power Presentations**

Test Generator
- Section Quiz

hmhsocialstudies.com

TEST-TAKING RESOURCES

 **Strategies for Test Preparation**

 **Test Practice Transparencies TT14**

 **Online Test Practice**

Interpreting Photographs

Satellite View of Earth at Night

Ask students to use what they have learned about the landforms and vegetation regions of the world to generalize about the types of places that lack urban areas. *(Mountainous areas, deserts, and icecaps lack urban areas.)*

CAPTION ANSWER parts of Australia, Africa, North and South America, Antarctica

Instruct: Objective 2

City Locations

- Where are many cities located? *(in places that allow good transportation, such as near a body of water, and in places with easy access to natural resources)*
- How does location affect a city's economic activities? *(The location may cause the city to specialize. For example, a location near iron ore and coal sources may result in a city becoming a steel-producing center.)*

PLACE Urban areas are clearly visible in this satellite view of earth at night. The light blue areas are "reflective" areas with either snow pack or sand.
Which regions of the earth have few urban areas?

URBANIZATION The dramatic rise in the number of cities and the changes in lifestyle that result is called **urbanization.** The trend to live in cities increased rapidly over the last two centuries. As more and more people moved into cities to find work, the cities and their surrounding areas grew. Today, some cities are enormous in physical area and have populations exceeding 10 million residents. As you can see above, cities are found on all continents except Antarctica.

City Locations

Around the world, cities have certain geographic characteristics in common. Many cities are found in places that allow good transportation, such as on a river, lake, or coast. Others are found in places with easy access to natural resources. Sacramento, California, for instance, grew rapidly after gold was discovered in 1848 in north-central California. Because of their geographic advantages, cities serve as economic bases, attracting businesses and people to work in those businesses.

Cities are often places where goods are shifted from one form of transportation to another. For example, the city of Chicago, Illinois, is a transportation hub for goods produced in the upper Great Lakes states. Goods are sent by air, truck, or train to Chicago on Lake Michigan, then to the U.S. east coast and the rest of the world. A

Cities may specialize in certain economic activities because of their location. For example, the city of Pittsburgh, Pennsylvania, which is located close to iron ore and coal sources, became a steel-producing center. The same is true for the city of Sheffield in England. Some urban areas may grow or expand because of economic activities located in the city. Brasília, the capital of Brazil, has grown to 2.6 million people since 1960 because of all the government agencies and activities there. Cultural, educational, or military activities may also attract people to a specific location.

Geographic Thinking

Using the Atlas
A Use the map of North America on page A22. What waterway leads from the Great Lakes to the Atlantic Ocean?
A. Answer the St. Lawrence Seaway

ACTIVITY OPTION FIVE THEMES OF GEOGRAPHY

HUMAN-ENVIRONMENT INTERACTION

Explaining the Theme The growth of urban areas has a tremendous impact on the environment. In an urban area, people alter the natural environment in unique ways. The operations of an urban area consume huge quantities of resources while producing waste products that can cause pollution.

Applying the Theme Direct students to use the satellite image at the top of page 88 to answer the following questions.

- About what portion of the land area on earth, excluding icecaps, has been developed into urban areas? *(about half)*
- Which two regions of the United States are the most urbanized? *(the Northeast and Great Lakes regions)*

Land Use Patterns

Urban geographers also study land use, the activities that take place in cities. Basic land use patterns found in all cities are:

- **residential,** including single-family housing and apartment buildings
- **industrial,** areas reserved for manufacturing of goods
- **commercial,** used for private business and the buying and selling of retail products

The core of a city is almost always based on commercial activity. This area of the city is called the **central business district (CBD).** Business offices and stores are found in this part of the city. In some cities, very expensive housing may also be found there. Predictably, the value of the land in the CBD is very high. In fact, the land is so expensive that skyscrapers are often built to get the most value from the land.

As you move away from the CBD, other functions become more important. For example, residential housing begins to dominate land use. Generally, the farther you get from the CBD, the lower the value of the land. Lower land values may lead to less expensive housing. Tucked into these less expensive areas are industrial activities and retail areas, such as shopping centers, markets, or bazaars. However, the patterns for urban activities vary by culture and geography. Study the models below to learn more about urban land use patterns. B

B. Answer More land is required for industrial activities, so cost of land is an important consideration in locating an industry.

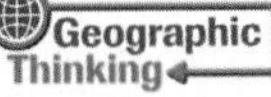

Seeing Patterns
B Why do industrial activities take place where land is less expensive?

Urban Area Models

Geographers may use a model to illustrate patterns they find in the use of space. The models below are patterns of land use in urban areas.

Concentric Zone Model

An early model showed the CBD as the "bull's-eye" of the urban area. It is surrounded by other activities.
by E. W. Burgess

Sector Model

Activities are concentrated in wedges or sectors, which may follow transportation lines or natural features such as a river.
by H. Hoyt

Multiple Nuclei Model

Districts, called nuclei, specialize in one urban activity, and are found throughout the urban area.
by C. D. Harris and E. L. Ullman

- Central business district
- Wholesale and light manufacturing
- Low-income housing
- Middle-income housing
- High-income housing
- Low-income and high-income housing
- Middle-income and high-income housing
- Heavy manufacturing
- Outlying business district
- Outer suburban housing
- Outer suburban industry
- High-income commuter zone

SKILLBUILDER: Interpreting Graphics

1. **MAKING GENERALIZATIONS** Where is low-income housing found in each of the models?
2. **MAKING COMPARISONS** What has happened to business and industry activities in the multiple nuclei model as compared to the other two models?

BASICS

Instruct: Objective 3

Land Use Patterns

- What are the three basic land use patterns found in all cities? *(residential, industrial, commercial)*
- How does land use generally change as you move away from the CBD? *(Residential housing begins to dominate.)*
- How does the value of the land generally change as you move farther from the CBD in a city? *(It decreases.)*

Interpreting Graphics

Urban Area Models

Have students examine the graphic and ask which model is most appropriate to the region in which they live. *(Answers will vary.)*

SKILLBUILDER ANSWERS

1. It is found close to wholesale and light manufacturing, and the CBD.
2. Some business and industry has developed outside the CBD and its nearby manufacturing district.

ACTIVITY OPTION | CRITICAL THINKING

MAKING INFERENCES

Explaining the Skill Making inferences involves reading between the lines to interpret the information you read. You can make inferences by studying what is stated and using your common sense and previous knowledge.

Applying the Skill Have students examine the graphic on page 89 and ask them to consider how urban area models might reflect the kind of transportation available in a city. Ask students the following questions.

- Which model might be less appropriate in a city where walking is the only form of transportation? *(the multiple nuclei model, since it would be more difficult for people to move from one nucleus to another)*
- How might a model showing suburban areas reflect the availability of automobiles? *(Suburban areas might be larger, more dispersed, and farther from the CBD when automobile transportation is available.)*

Instruct: Objective 4

The Functions of Cities

- What are some types of functions of a city? *(retail, entertainment, transportation, business, education, government, manufacturing, wholesaling, residential, recreation, religious)*
- Why is good transportation essential to a city? *(People and goods need to get from one area to another.)*

Interpreting Maps

Urban Functions: Chicago

This map shows part of Chicago's Loop, which gets its name from a rectangular loop of elevated train tracks in the area. Ask students what conclusion they might draw about Chicago's mass transit system. *(It is well developed, at least in the downtown area.)*

SKILLBUILDER ANSWERS
1. City Hall/County Building **2.** governmental, shopping, entertainment

Assess & Reteach

GeoFocus Have students complete the section on urban geography in their graphic organizers.

Formal Assessment
• Section Quiz, p. 54

Reteaching Activity
Draw a word web on the board with the word *Cities* in the center and the words *Growth, Location, Land Use,* and *Functions* in circles around the central circle. Ask students to add the main ideas under each topic heading.

In-Depth Resources: Unit 1
• Reteaching Activity, p. 45

Urban Functions: Chicago

SKILLBUILDER: Interpreting Maps
1. **LOCATION** What other government building is located near the State of Illinois Center?
2. **PLACE** What urban functions are found in the area shown?

The Functions of Cities

The city is the center of a variety of functions. The map at the left shows a portion of the CBD of Chicago, Illinois. Notice that shopping, entertainment, and government services are located there. Large office buildings occupy much of the rest of the area shown.

Many cities also have educational and cultural activities such as libraries or museums located in the CBD. The Manhattan section of New York City, for example, is home to about 70 museums. Other functions of the city—such as manufacturing, wholesaling, residential, recreation, and a variety of religious and social services—may be located in other parts of the city.

Cities need a great deal of space to accomplish these functions, which makes good transportation absolutely essential. Major cities may have several forms of mass transit, such as bus systems, subways, or commuter trains, to move thousands of people to and from the areas of the city where the various functions take place. In some areas, freeway systems link people in the suburbs to the activities in the city. Geographers often study a city's transportation system to understand how well the city is fulfilling its functions. C

In the next section, you'll learn more about economic geography that takes place across the globe.

C. Answer There may be several types of mass transit equipped to carry more passengers.

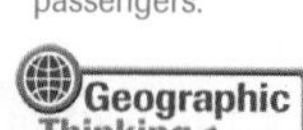

Making Comparisons
C How are city transportation systems different from those of towns or villages?

Section 4 Assessment

1 Places & Terms
Explain the meaning of each of the following terms.
- city
- suburb
- metropolitan area
- urbanization
- central business district (CBD)

2 Taking Notes
LOCATION Review the notes you took for this section.

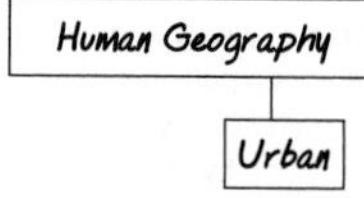

- What functions or activities are located away from the CBD?
- In what types of relative locations are many cities found?

3 Main Ideas
a. What components make up a metropolitan area?
b. What are some basic land use patterns in cities?
c. What are some functions of an urban area?

4 Geographic Thinking
Making Inferences How does land value influence the activities that take place on a piece of urban land? **Think about:**
- land use patterns
- the CBD

See Skillbuilder Handbook, page R4.

EXPLORING LOCAL GEOGRAPHY Survey the CBD of the city you live in or one close to you. Make notes of the urban functions you see there. Create a **sketch map** of your CBD. Be sure to label the areas or buildings, and the urban functions they fill.

SECTION ASSESSMENT ANSWERS

1. Places & Terms
city, p. 87
suburb, p. 87
metropolitan area, p. 87
urbanization, p. 88
central business district (CBD), p. 89

2. Taking Notes
- residential housing, industrial activities, and retail
- locations that offered good transportation or access to natural resources

3. Main Ideas
a. Metropolitan area consists of a main city, its suburbs, and exurbs.
b. residential, commercial, and industrial
c. Functions include retailing, wholesaling, government services, education, entertainment, recreation, residential, commercial, industrial, and religious and social services.

4. Geographic Thinking
The activities that generate more money are often found on very valuable land, usually in the CBD. Activities that take a lot of land, such as industrial plants, will use less valuable land.

GeoActivity

Integrated Assessment
• Rubric for a sketch map, 2.1

Economic Geography

Main Ideas
- Economic activities depend on the resources of the land and how people use them.
- The level of economic development can be measured in different ways.

Places & Terms
economy
economic system
command economy
market economy
natural resources
infrastructure
per capita income
GNP
GDP

BASICS

A HUMAN PERSPECTIVE One of the most valuable of natural resources—petroleum—wasn't always used as a source of energy. Until the world began to run on gasoline-powered machinery, oil was used for a variety of purposes. Native Americans, for instance, used "rock oil" for medicinal purposes. Egyptians used oil as a dressing for wounds. Ancient Persians wrapped oil-soaked fibers around arrows, lit them, and fired them into the city of Athens in 480 B.C.

Sometimes a resource only becomes valuable after the technology to use it is developed. In today's world, petroleum is vital to providing power for industry, commerce, and transportation. Petroleum plays a powerful role in the economies of nations that supply it and consume it.

Economic Systems

An **economy** consists of the production and exchange of goods and services among a group of people. Economies operate on a local, regional, national, or international level. Geographers study economic geography by looking at how people in a region support themselves and how economic activities are linked across regions.

TYPES OF ECONOMIC SYSTEMS The way people produce and exchange goods and services is called an **economic system.** In the world today, there are four basic types of economic systems:

- **Traditional Economy** Goods and services are traded without exchanging money. Also called "barter."
- **Command Economy** Production of goods and services is determined by a central government, which usually owns the means of production. Production does not necessarily reflect the consumer demand. Also called a planned economy.
- **Market Economy** Production of goods and services is determined by the demand from consumers. Also called a demand economy or capitalism.
- **Mixed Economy** A combination of command and market economies provides goods and services so that all people will benefit.

Economic behaviors and activities to meet human needs take place within these economic systems.

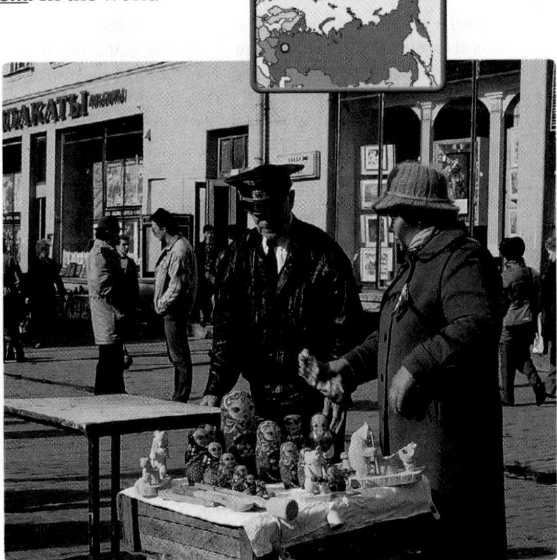

PLACE A woman sells goods on a Moscow street. Russia is changing from a command economy to a market economy.
Is the activity in this photograph an example of a command or market economy?

SECTION 5 OBJECTIVES
1. Identify the four basic types of economic systems.
2. Define the four levels of economic activity.
3. Distinguish among renewable, non-renewable, and inexhaustible resources.
4. Identify key components of economic support systems.
5. Distinguish between GNP and GDP, and between developed and developed nations.

SKILLBUILDER: Interpreting Graphics, pp. 92–93

GeographicThinking

Making Comparisons, pp. 92, 93
Using the Atlas, p. 94
Drawing Conclusions, p. 95

Instruct: Objective 

Economic Systems

- What is an economic system? *(An economic system is the way people produce and exchange goods.)*
- What are the four basic types of economic systems? *(traditional, command, market, and mixed)*
- How does a command economy differ from a market economy? *(They differ in who determines the production of goods and services. In a command economy, it is the government. In a market economy, it is consumer demand.)*

 **In-Depth Resources: Unit 1**
- Guided Reading, p. 39

CAPTION ANSWER a market economy

SECTION 5 PROGRAM RESOURCES

In-Depth Resources: Unit 1
- Guided Reading, p. 39
- Building Vocabulary, p. 41
- Reteaching Activity, p. 46

Guided Reading Workbook
- Section 5

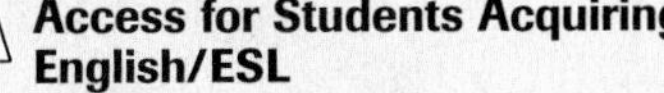
Access for Students Acquiring English/ESL
- Guided Reading, p. 21

Formal Assessment
- Section Quiz, p. 55

Integrated Assessment
- Rubric for an illustration, 1.3

INTEGRATED TECHNOLOGY

Map Transparencies MT10
- World Per Capita GDP

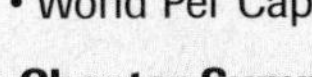
Chapter Summaries

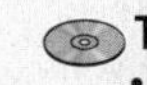
Test Generator
- Section Quiz

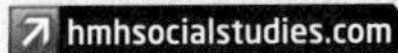
hmhsocialstudies.com

TEST-TAKING RESOURCES

Strategies for Test Preparation

Test Practice Transparencies TT15

Online Test Practice

Instruct: Objective 2

Economic Activities

- How do primary and secondary economic activities differ? *(primary activities: gather raw materials; secondary activities: add value to raw materials by changing their form)*
- What are tertiary activities? *(providing personal or professional services)*
- What are quaternary activities? *(providing information, management, and research services)*

Map Transparencies MT10
- World Per Capita GDP

Economic Activities

People may choose from a variety of methods to meet their basic needs. Some groups simply raise enough food or animals to meet their need to eat, but have little left over to sell to others. This is called subsistence agriculture. In other areas, market-oriented agriculture produces crops or animals that farmers sell to markets.

In some places, industries dominate economic activities. Small industries often involve a family of craftspersons who produce goods to be sold in a local area. Since they often take place in the home, these businesses are referred to as cottage industries. Finally, commercial industries meet the needs of people within a very large area. Economic behaviors are related to the economic activities described below.

LEVELS OF ECONOMIC ACTIVITY No matter how small or large a business is, it operates at one of four economic levels. The four levels of economic activity describe how materials are gathered and processed into goods or how services are delivered to consumers.

Primary Activities involve gathering raw materials such as timber for immediate use or to use in the making of a final product.

Secondary Activities involve adding value to materials by changing their form. Manufacturing automobiles is an example.

Tertiary Activities involve providing business or professional services. Salespeople, teachers, or doctors are examples.

Quaternary Activities provide information, management, and research services by highly-trained persons. A

The more developed an economy is, the greater the number and variety of activities you will find.

A. Answer tertiary

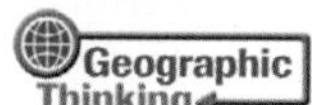

Geographic Thinking

Making Comparisons
A Into which level of activity would insurance sales fit?

Interpreting Graphics

Economics of Pencil Production
This graphic demonstrates that the production and exchange of even a very simple product like a pencil involves the use of natural resources that come from around the globe. Note that some raw materials could be obtained from several sources. Ask students what factor or factors probably determine which source is used. *(cost and delivery time, which is partly dependent on distance)*

SKILLBUILDER ANSWERS
1. copper, pumice, graphite, rubber
2. It would have easy access to the Atlantic Ocean to receive and ship goods.

Economics of Pencil Production

Making a pencil brings together economic activities and natural resources from around the world. The gathering of the raw materials (primary activity), transforming them into a pencil (secondary activity), and selling the pencil to you (tertiary activity) happen in different parts of the globe.

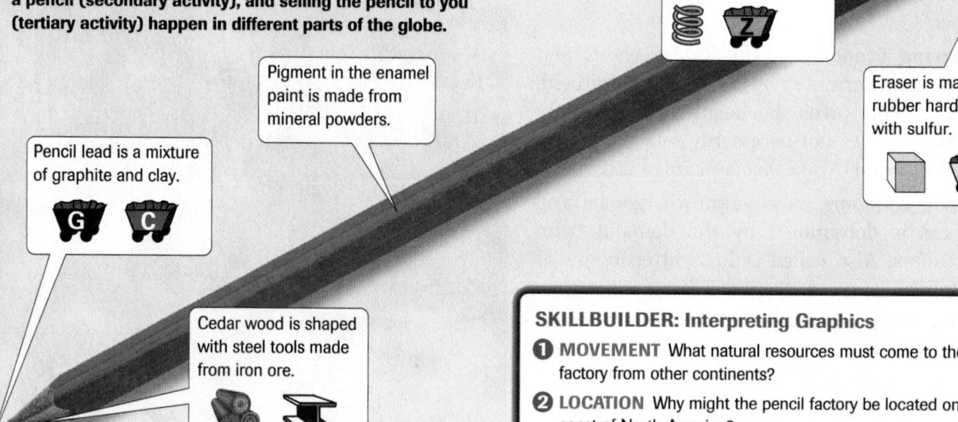

Brass eraser holder is made from copper and zinc.
Z
Pigment in the enamel paint is made from mineral powders.
Eraser is made from rubber hardened with sulfur.
S
Pencil lead is a mixture of graphite and clay.
G
C
Cedar wood is shaped with steel tools made from iron ore.

SKILLBUILDER: Interpreting Graphics
1. **MOVEMENT** What natural resources must come to the pencil factory from other continents?
2. **LOCATION** Why might the pencil factory be located on the east coast of North America?

DIFFERENTIATING INSTRUCTION **LESS PROFICIENT READERS**

PREVIEWING ECONOMIC TERMS

Objective Preview the section to understand unfamiliar terms

Class Time 20 minutes

Task Create a chart that lists and defines categories found in the section

Directions Tell students that this section explains basic terms and concepts that are used to study economic systems. In later chapters, they will apply these terms and concepts to regions they study. Direct students to scan the pages of the section and read the large headings and the boldfaced terms. Point out that the first three subsections identify categories of economic systems, of economic activity, and of natural resources. Have students create a chart that lists and defines these categories.

The Economics of Natural Resources

An important part of economic geography is understanding which resources a nation possesses. **Natural resources** are materials on or in the earth—such as trees, fish, or coal—that have economic value. Materials from the earth become resources only when the society has the technology and ability to transform those resources into goods. So, iron ore is useless until people have the technology to produce steel from it.

Natural resources are abundant but are not distributed equally around the world. As a result, when geographers study the economy of a country, they look closely at the location, quality, and quantity of its natural resources. They also divide natural resources into three basic types:

- **Renewable**—These resources can be replaced through natural processes. Examples include trees and seafood.
- **Non-renewable**—These resources cannot be replaced once they have been removed from the ground. Examples include metals, such as gold, silver, and iron, and non-metals, such as gemstones, limestone, or sulfur. Also included are fossil fuels, petroleum, natural gas, and coal. They are the basis of energy production.
- **Inexhaustible energy sources**—These resources, which are used for producing power, are the result of solar or planetary processes and are unlimited in quantity. They include sunlight, geothermal heat, winds, and tides. B

Natural resources are a major part of world trade. This is especially true of the fossil fuels, since industry relies on them for both power and raw materials in manufacturing. The value of a natural resource depends on the qualities that make it useful. For example, trees can provide lumber for building or pulp for paper. Countries trade for raw materials that they need for energy and to manufacture products.

B. Answer Fossil fuels will eventually be used up, and inexhaustible sources will not.

Geographic Thinking

Making Comparisons

B What advantage do inexhaustible energy sources have over fossil fuels?

BASICS

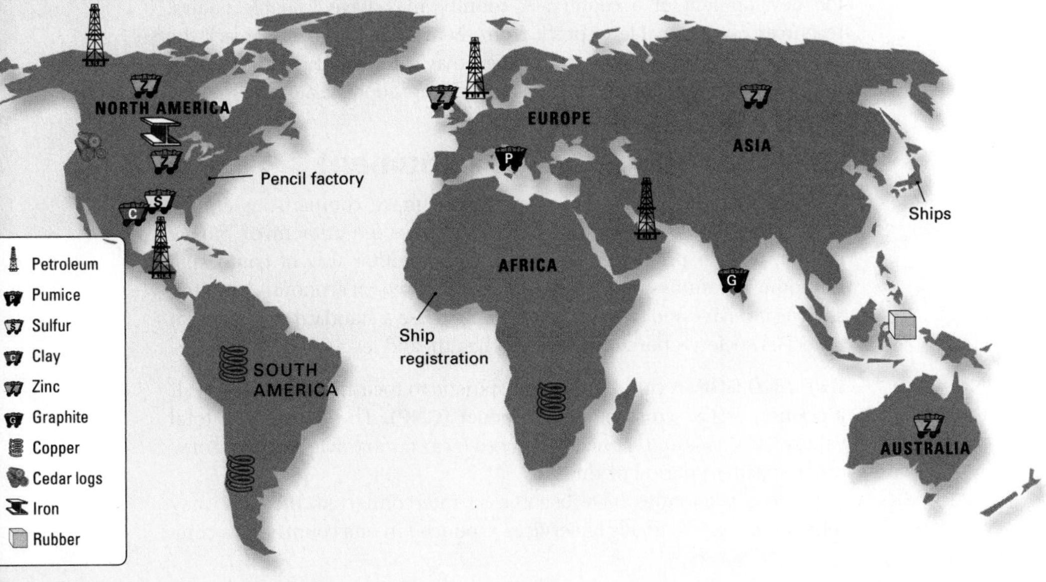

Instruct: Objective 3

The Economics of Natural Resources

- What are renewable resources? *(resources that can be replaced through natural processes, such as trees and fish)*
- What are non-renewable resources? *(resources that cannot be replaced once they have been removed from the ground, such as gold, silver, and sulfur)*
- What are inexhaustible resources? *(resources that are the result of solar or planetary processes and are unlimited in quantity, such as sunlight and wind)*

More About

Natural Resources

Some renewable resources can only be replaced through natural processes if they are used wisely. For example, a species of animal cannot be replaced if it is hunted to extinction. Some experts believe that certain non-renewable resources, on the other hand, cannot be used up because they occur in such large quantities and also can be recycled. Examples include iron and aluminum.

ACTIVITY OPTION | FIVE THEMES OF GEOGRAPHY

HUMAN-ENVIRONMENT INTERACTION

Exploring the Theme People's use of natural resources is an example of human-environment interaction. The level of technology in a society affects its use of natural resources.

Understanding the Theme Direct students to use what they have learned about the categories of natural resources on page 93 as well as their own prior knowledge to infer the answers to the following questions.

- Why would geographers be concerned about the availability of renewable resources? *(because these resources are only renewable in a given location if they are managed wisely)*
- If resources such as sunlight and wind are inexhaustible, why aren't they used more extensively for energy in place of fossil fuels? *(Some locations receive less sunlight and less wind than others. Many people have already invested in other energy producing industries.)*
- How might the high use of natural resources by some countries affect the environment of other countries? *(Rich or resource-hungry countries may import natural resources from poor or less-developed countries, and so alter the environment by such activities as cutting trees or mining.)*

Instruct: Objective 

Economic Support Systems

- What makes up a nation's infrastructure? *(basic support systems needed to keep an economy going, such as power, communications, transportation, water, sanitation, and education systems)*
- What is one of the most important aspects of infrastructure? *(transportation)*
- What do the communication system and the level of technology indicate about a country's economic development? *(how strong and highly developed the economy is)*

Instruct: Objective 

Measuring Economic Development

- What are some methods of comparing economies? *(by per capita income, by GNP, and by GDP)*
- What are the economic characteristics of developing nations? *(They have a low GDP per capita and limited development on all levels of economic activities. They lack an industrial base and struggle to provide their citizens with basic needs.)*
- What are the economic characteristics of developed nations? *(They have a high per capita income and a varied economy that features a good deal of quaternary activities.)*

Material Goods

Levels of economic development are measured in the numbers of goods and services available in a country. This graphic compares the availability of televisions and passenger cars in three countries at different stages of development.

SOURCES: Central Intelligence Agency, *The World Factbook*, 2010; *The World Almanac and Book of Facts, 2010*

DEVELOPING NATION
Ethiopia

5 televisions per 1,000 people

1 passenger car per 1,000 people

Economic Support Systems

Producing and distributing goods and services requires a series of support systems. The most important of these services is infrastructure.

INFRASTRUCTURE A nation's **infrastructure** consists of the basic support systems needed to keep an economy going, including power, communications, transportation, water, sanitation, and education systems. The more sophisticated the infrastructure, the more developed the country.

One of the most important systems in the infrastructure is transportation. Geographers look at the patterns of roads and highways, ports, and airports to get an idea of how transportation affects economic growth. For example, the country of Honduras has only one major north-south highway. The highway leads to port cities where a major export, bananas, is shipped out of the country. Areas not accessible to the major highway remain undeveloped.

Communications systems give geographers an idea of how a country is linked internally as well as with the outside world. Countries with a strong economy are linked internally and externally by high-speed Internet and satellite communications.

The level of available technology and access to it is also an indicator of the development of a country. A country may have valuable natural resources but be unable to profit from them because its people lack the skills to make use of them. Technology may be available, but a country may lack educated workers to run and maintain sophisticated equipment.

Measuring Economic Development

Geographers use a variety of standards to make comparisons among economies. One is **per capita income,** the average amount of money earned by each person in a political unit. Another way of comparing economies examines levels of development based on economic activities such as industry and commerce. Still others use a standard of living that reflects a society's purchasing power, health, and level of education.

GNP AND GDP A commonly-used statistic to measure the economy of a country is the **gross national product (GNP).** The **GNP** is the total value of all goods and services produced by a country over a year or some other specified period of time.

Because economies have become so interconnected, the GNP may reflect the value of goods or services produced in one country by a com-

ACTIVITY OPTION **COOPERATIVE LEARNING** **BLOCK SCHEDULING**

BUILDING AN ECONOMIC ENTERPRISE

Objective To examine the types of economic activities required to build selected businesses

Class Time 20 minutes

Task Develop a business plan according to economic activity categories

Directions Have students name five to ten businesses. List these on the chalkboard. Divide the class into groups of four. Then have each student count off; the "ones" will be in charge of primary activities, "twos" in charge of secondary activities, and so on. Assign a business venture from the list on the chalkboard to each group. Have each student list all the people and/or resources needed in his/her category. Have each group present its combined "operation" to the class.

94 CHAPTER 4

NATION IN TRANSITION
Turkey

328 televisions per 1,000 people

76 passenger cars per 1,000 people

DEVELOPED NATION
Japan

719 televisions per 1,000 people

449 passenger cars per 1,000 people

pany based in another country. For example, the value of sport shoes produced in Thailand by an American company is counted as U.S. production, even though the shoes were not produced in the United States. To adjust for situations like this, a second statistic is used—**GDP, or gross domestic product**—which is the total value of all goods and services produced *within* a country in a given period of time.

BACKGROUND
Developing countries that have greatly improved their GDP are called countries in transition.

DEVELOPMENT LEVELS Countries of the world have different levels of economic development. Developing nations are nations that have a low GDP and limited development on all levels of economic activities. These countries lack an industrial base and struggle to provide their residents with items to meet their basic needs.

Developed nations, on the other hand, are countries with a high per capita income and varied economy, especially with quaternary activities such as computer software development. Western European nations, Japan, Canada, and the United States have highly developed economies.

In this chapter, you've learned that human geography is a complex mix of human activities and the earth's resources. As you study the regions of the world, remember that a geographer views those regions by looking at the space and the interactions that take place there.

Section 5 Assessment

1 Places & Terms

Explain the meaning of each of the following terms.

- economy
- natural resources
- infrastructure
- per capita income
- GDP

2 Taking Notes

PLACE Review the notes you took for this section.

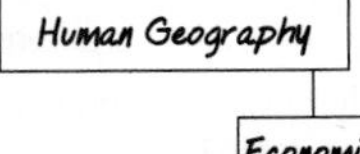

- What are the four basic economic systems?
- What are the three types of resources?

3 Main Ideas

a. What are the basic activities in each of the four economic activity levels?

b. What role do natural resources play in the economy of a country?

c. What systems are a part of a country's infrastructure?

4 Geographic Thinking

Drawing Conclusions Fossil fuels are non-renewable resources. What does this suggest about worldwide supplies of this energy?
Think about:

- industrial need for power
- alternative sources of power

MAKING COMPARISONS Study the types of economic systems on page 91. Create a series of **illustrations** showing the differences among the systems. Be sure your illustrations show the role of the consumer and the government in determining what goods or services are produced in each type of economy.

Interpreting Graphics

Material Goods

Have students examine the graphic on pages 94 and 95. Ask them which of the three nations they would prefer to live in. Then ask them to explain their choice. *(Answers will vary. Some students may prefer to live in a nation in which they could acquire a larger number of possessions, such as Japan.)*

Assess & Reteach

GeoFocus Have students complete the section on economic geography in their graphic organizers.

Formal Assessment
• Section Quiz, p. 55

Reteaching Activity
Divide the class into five groups and assign one of the five main headings in this section to each group. Have each group write a short quiz covering the content of that part of the section. Have the whole class orally answer the quizzes.

In-Depth Resources: Unit 1
• Reteaching Activity, p. 46

More About

Consumer Price Index

A Consumer Price Index (CPI) notes the current prices of a country's goods and services and compares them with a set time in the past, called the *base.* The base is given a value of 100, so a CPI of 150 would represent a 50 percent increase in prices from the starting point. The CPI is used to measure inflation, or the decrease in the buying power of a country's currency.

SECTION 5 ASSESSMENT ANSWERS

1. Places & Terms
economy, p. 91
natural resources, p. 93
infrastructure, p. 94
per capita income, p. 94
GDP, p. 95

2. Taking Notes
• traditional, command, market, and mixed
• renewable, non-renewable, and inexhaustible energy sources

3. Main Ideas
a. Primary gathers raw materials, secondary adds value to the materials by changing their form, tertiary furnishes business or professional services, and quaternary provides information management and research.
b. Natural resources may form the basis of a country's economy.
c. power, communications, transportation, water, sanitation, education

4. Geographic Thinking
Those who have fossil fuels can use them to develop their economy or sell to others who need them. Alternative sources of power will need to be used when fossil fuels run out.

GeoActivity

Integrated Assessment
• Rubric for an illustration, 1.3

Reviewing Places & Terms

A. **1.** culture, p. 71
2. diffusion, p. 72
3. rate of natural increase, p. 79
4. population density, p. 81
5. state, p. 83
6. nation, p. 83
7. urbanization, p. 88
8. economy, p. 91
9. infrastructure, p. 94
10. GDP, p. 95

B. Possible Responses

11. Urbanization is the growth in the number and size of cities.
12. Culture refers to the blueprint for the behaviors of a group.
13. Birthrate is the number of live births per thousand. Rate of natural increase takes into account the birthrate minus the mortality rate to determine the population growth.
14. Population density is found by dividing the number of people in a specific area by a specific amount of land.
15. Nation refers more to the culture of the people in a specific area. State is a political term for an independent unit that occupies a specific territory and has certain powers.
16. Diffusion refers to this spreading.
17. The economy requires the infrastructure to make it work.
18. GDP gives the total value of all goods and services produced within a country in a specific period of time.
19. Rate of natural increase and population density refer to population geography.
20. Power and transportation systems are examples of infrastructure.

Chapter 4 Assessment

VISUAL SUMMARY
PEOPLE AND PLACES

The Elements of Culture

- All human groups have a culture.
- Language and religion are a part of culture.

Population Geography

- The world's population is expanding rapidly.
- Most of the world's population lives in the Northern Hemisphere.

Political Geography

- Size, shape, and location influence political geography.
- States of the world have a variety of political systems.

Urban Geography

- Urban areas have expanded rapidly and now are home to about one half of the world's population.
- Functions of cities are similar.
- Land use patterns are unique to a place.

Economic Geography

- Resources, available technology, and economic systems shape the economy of a state.
- Economic activities are based on how goods or services are produced and traded.

Reviewing Places & Terms

A. Briefly explain the importance of each of the following.

1. culture
2. diffusion
3. rate of natural increase
4. population density
5. state
6. nation
7. urbanization
8. economy
9. infrastructure
10. GDP

B. Answer the questions about vocabulary in complete sentences.

11. What is the growth in the number of cities called?
12. Which term above refers to the blueprint for the behaviors of a group?
13. How is the birthrate different from the rate of natural increase?
14. How is population density determined?
15. How is a nation different from a state?
16. Which term refers to the spread of ideas, innovations and inventions, and patterns of behavior?
17. How are the economy and the infrastructure related to each other?
18. What does the GDP number tell you about a country's economy?
19. Which terms above are associated with population geography?
20. What are some examples of infrastructure?

Main Ideas

The Elements of Culture (pp. 71–77)

1. What is the purpose of culture?
2. Why is language so important to a culture?

Population Geography (pp. 78–82)

3. What geographic factors influence population distribution?
4. How is population density different from population distribution?

Political Geography (pp. 83–86)

5. What are the geographic characteristics of a state?
6. What is the difference between a country with a democracy and one with a dictatorship?

Urban Geography (pp. 87–90)

7. What are some characteristics of city locations?
8. What are the basic land use patterns in cities?

Economic Geography (pp. 91–95)

9. Why does a country need an infrastructure?
10. How are natural resources related to a country's economy?

Main Ideas

1. Culture provides individuals with guidelines for behavior, values and knowledge.
2. Language reflects all aspects of a culture and allows people to communicate with one another.
3. Landforms, climate, vegetation, access to water, and altitude influence where people live.
4. Density is the average number of people in a region, and distribution is where in a region people live.
5. Geographic characteristics of a state include size, shape, and location.
6. In a democracy, the citizens hold power, either directly or through elected representatives. In a dictatorship, an individual or group holds complete political power.
7. Many are found at places that allow good transportation or are near natural resources.
8. Basic land-use patterns include residential, industrial, and commercial zones.
9. A country needs infrastructure to support the economy in the production and distribution of goods and services.
10. Available natural resources may form the basis of a country's economy, either by their being processed or sold.

Critical Thinking

1. Using Your Notes

Use your completed chart to answer these questions.

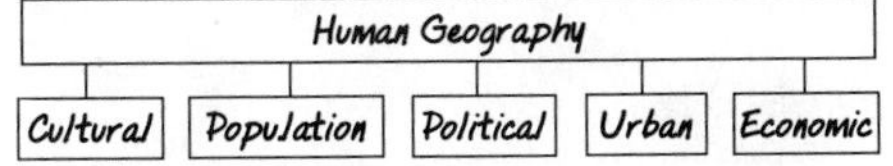

a. Which type of human geography focuses on how goods and services are produced and distributed by a country?

b. What do population geographers study?

2. Geographic Themes

a. **MOVEMENT** How might migration affect both population distribution and density?

b. **PLACE** What are some characteristics of an urban area?

3. Identifying Themes

How do landform and climate affect the distribution of population? Which of the five themes apply to this situation?

4. Making Inferences

Why might two groups of people living in the same area develop different cultures?

5. Identifying and Solving Problems

What reasons might countries have to form a regional political unit?

For Additional Test Practice

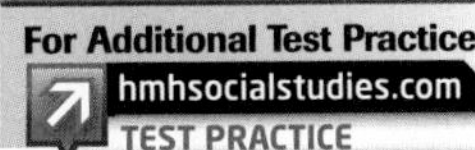

Geographic Skills: Interpreting Maps

Dominant World Cities*

Use the map to answer the following questions.

1. **REGION** Which continent has the most dominant world cities shown?
2. **REGION** Which continents do not have dominant world cities?
3. **MOVEMENT** Into which continent does the most activity appear to flow? Give a reason for your answer.

Tokyo
PACIFIC OCEAN
Los Angeles
Hong Kong
Chicago
PACIFIC OCEAN
New York
London
Frankfurt
Singapore
Mumbai
Paris
INDIAN OCEAN
São Paulo
ATLANTIC OCEAN

Dominant world city
Major world city
Major economic ties

*Based on number of international banks and transactions

Molleweide Projection

Using a blank map of the world, mark in the cities shown on this map. Then go to page 80. Add the cities with more than 12 million shown on that map. On the back of your map, write two observations about the cities on your map.

hmhsocialstudies.com

MULTIMEDIA ACTIVITY

21st CENTURY

Use the links at **hmhsocialstudies.com** to do research about population growth. Focus on the projected growth by 2050. Identify ten places where predicted growth will be the greatest and ten with little predicted growth.

Creating a Database Create a **database** showing your findings about worldwide growth. Create separate databases for the fastest growth and for the slowest growth. Be sure to label your databases.

BASICS

Critical Thinking

1. a. economic geography
b. birth and death rates, density and distribution of population

2. a. Migration may affect distribution by changing locations where people live and density by increasing or decreasing the number of people living in a specific area.
b. An urban area develops around a central city and often has a built-up area around it that includes suburbs.

3. Landforms may restrict areas for living by being too rugged or inhospitable. Severe climates restrict the number of people in an area, and a pleasant climate may attract many people; human-environment interaction

4. Even though they may be living in the same area, each group has a unique set of behaviors, attitudes, and knowledge about an area that it transmits to its members.

5. Regional political groups are often formed to deal with problems that affect all members in a special area, such as defense, environment, and trade.

GeoActivity

Integrated Assessment
- Rubric for a map, 2.1

Formal Assessement
- Chapter Tests, Forms A, B, and C, pp. 56–67

Geographic Skills

1. Europe has two.
2. Africa, Australia, Antarctica, and South America
3. Much activity goes in and out of Europe. Europe probably has a large number of international banks.

MULTIMEDIA ACTIVITY

For their database on population growth, students should:

- Focus on projected growth by 2050.
- Create separate databases for the fastest growth and for the slowest growth.
- Clearly label their databases.
- Include references to the Web sites used as sources.

Grading Rubric Evaluate student performance as Exceptional, Acceptable, or Poor in each of the following categories.

	Exceptional	Acceptable	Poor
Presents a variety of information from several sources			
Presents information accurately			
Clearly identifies sources of information			

Physical Geography of the United States and Canada

OVERVIEW	INSTRUCTIONAL RESOURCES	
CHAPTER 5 ESSENTIAL QUESTION What are the key physical features of the United States and Canada? **Focus on the Essential Question Podcast**	**In-Depth Resources: Unit 2** • Exploring Today's Issues, pp. 36–39 • Unit Atlas Activities, p. 1 • Regional Data File Activities, p. 2 • Building Vocabulary, p. 9 **Outline Maps with Activities** • The United States and Canada: Physical, pp. 9–10 • The United States and Canada: Political, pp. 11–12 **Block Schedule Strategies** **Chapter Summaries** (English/Spanish)	**Interactive Online Edition** TOS **ExamView® Assessment Suite** (English/Spanish) TOS **CalendarPlanner** **Power Presentations with Media Gallery** **Critical Thinking Transparencies** • CT5 hmhsocialstudies.com INTERACTIVE
SECTION 1 **LANDFORMS AND RESOURCES** **MAIN IDEAS** • The U.S. and Canada are countries with vast amounts of land. • The U.S. and Canada's landforms include lowlands, highlands, mountains, plateaus, basins, and islands. • Abundant natural resources have shaped lifestyles and the economy.	**In-Depth Resources: Unit 2** • Guided Reading, p. 3 • Skillbuilder Practice, p. 8 • Building Vocabulary, p. 9 • Reteaching Activity, p. 10 • GeoWorkshops, pp. 43–44 **Guided Reading Workbook,** Section 1	hmhsocialstudies.com INTERACTIVE • Natural Resources of the U.S. and Canada, p. 120 • The Mississippi River, p. 121
SECTION 2 **CLIMATE AND VEGETATION** **MAIN IDEAS** • The U.S. has more climate zones than Canada. • Canada has mostly cold climates. • The U.S. has mild, dry, and tropical climates as well as colder ones. • Natural vegetation ranges from tropical rain forests to desert shrubs to dense forests.	**In-Depth Resources: Unit 2** • Guided Reading, p. 4 • Building Vocabulary, p. 9 • Reteaching Activity, p. 11 **Guided Reading Workbook,** Section 2	**Critical Thinking Transparencies CT37** • Land and Climate of the United States and Canada
SECTION 3 **HUMAN-ENVIRONMENT INTERACTION** **MAIN IDEAS** • North American settlers first were nomadic but became more agricultural. • The building and growth of cities in Canada and the U.S. has often been based on physical factors. • Trails, waterways, railroads, and highways have been important in allowing for growth in Canada and the U.S.	**In-Depth Resources: Unit 2** • Guided Reading, p. 5 • Building Vocabulary, p. 9 • Reteaching Activity, p. 12 • Map and Graph Skills, pp. 6–7 **Guided Reading Workbook,** Section 3	**Video:** Paving America

ASSESSMENT

SE **Chapter Assessment,** pp. 132–133

Formal Assessment
- Chapter Tests, Forms A, B, and C, pp. 71–82

TOS **ExamView® Assessment Suite**

Strategies for Test Preparation

hmhsocialstudies.com TEST PRACTICE

SE **Section Assessment,** p. 122

Formal Assessment
- Section Quiz, p. 68

Integrated Assessment
- Rubric for a sketch map, 2.1

Test Practice Transparencies TT16

SE **Section Assessment,** p. 126

Formal Assessment
- Section Quiz, p. 69

Integrated Assessment
- Rubric for a data base, 2.6

Test Practice Transparencies TT17

SE **Section Assessment,** p. 130

Formal Assessment
- Section Quiz, p. 70

Integrated Assessment
- Rubric for a presentation, 3.6

Test Practice Transparencies TT18

CHART KEY:

SE Student Edition	Block Scheduling	DVD/CD-ROM
TE Teacher's Edition	TOS Teacher One Stop	MP3 Audio
Printable Resource	Presentation Resource	HISTORY™

Program Resources available on TOS and @ 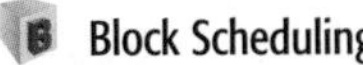 hmhsocialstudies.com

SUPPORTING RESOURCES

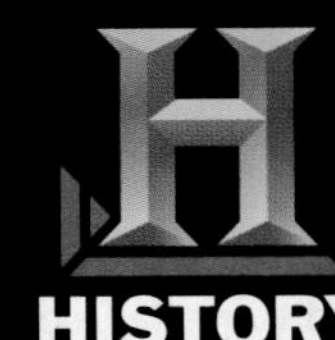

- Multimedia Classroom Global History Series
- Global History Teacher's Guide

Social Studies Trade Library Collection
- World Regions Trade Collection

For more information or to purchase these resources, go to hmhsocialstudies.com

DIFFERENTIATED INSTRUCTION

English Learners	Struggling Readers	Gifted and Talented Students
Spanish/English Guided Reading Workbook **Access for Students Acquiring English/ESL** Spanish Translations, pp. 23–28 **Chapter Summaries** (English/Spanish) TE **TE Activity** Understanding Context, p. 120	**Chapter Summaries** (English/Spanish) TE **TE Activity** Organizing Information, p. 118 Recalling Details, p. 121 Drawing Connections, p. 129	TE **TE Activity** Researching Severe Weather Events, p. 125

ENRICHMENT ACTIVITIES

The following activities are especially suitable for classes following block schedules.

SE **Student Edition,** p. 116–113
- Reading a Highway Map, p. 131

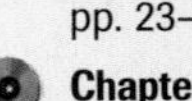 hmhsocialstudies.com INTERACTIVE
- Natural Resources of the U.S. and Canada, p. 120
- The Mississippi River, p. 121

UNIT 2 ATLAS AND CHAPTER 5 PACING GUIDE

BLOCK SCHEDULE LESSON PLAN OPTIONS: 90-MINUTE PERIOD

DAY 1

SECTION 1, pp. 98–101
Class Time 20 minutes

- **Discussion** Discuss the Unit Introduction, using the discussion prompts on TE p. 98
Class Time 10 minutes

- **Today's Issues** Introduce Today's Issues in the U.S. and Canada, using Exploring the Issues questions on PE pp. 100–101
Class Time 10 minutes

UNIT ATLAS, pp. 102–115
Class Time 30 minutes

- **Small Groups** Divide the class into four groups and have each group answer Making Comparisons questions for one section of the Unit Atlas: Physical Geography, Human Geography, Regional Patterns, and Regional Data File.

SECTION 1, pp. 116–122
Class Time 40 minutes

- **Outline Maps** In preparation for discussing Section 1, have students complete the physical map for the United States and Canada in *Outline Maps with Activities.* Students should label the countries and physical features such as mountains and rivers. They should color the map, using different colors for landforms.

DAY 2

SECTION 1, pp. 116–122
Class Time 45 minutes

- **Quiz Show** As a way to review the section, have three students volunteer to be contestants and one student be the host. Then have the rest of the class prepare questions to ask the contestants. Contestants who answer correctly can earn points. Highest points wins.
Class Time 20 minutes

- **Skillbuilder Practice** Use the Activity Option about analyzing data on TE p. 119 and the Skillbuilder Practice worksheet.
Class Time 25 minutes

SECTION 2, pp. 123–126
Class Time 45 minutes

- **Comparing the U.S. and Canada** Use a large map of the U.S. and Canada. Point to locations on the map and ask students to tell what the weather in that region is like. Then discuss with the class the similarities and differences between climates in the U.S. and Canada, including the issues of weather, landscape, vegetation.

DAY 3

SECTION 3, pp. 127–133
Class Time 35 minutes

- **Issues Chart** Lead the class in creating an issues chart which summarizes key issues and the reasons and obstacles, effects and/or outcomes associated with them. Have students make a three column chart with the headings "Issue," "Reasons/Obstacles," and "Effects/Outcomes." Within each column, the students should list information from the section like "Farming" and then "people seeking permanent settlement; needing to clear land of trees, create irrigation, plow fields" and then "altering the land/sustaining larger communities."

CHAPTER 5 REVIEW AND ASSESSMENT
pp. 132–133

- **Review** Have students prepare a summary of the chapter using the Places and Terms listed on the first page of each section.
Class Time 20 minutes

- **Assessment** Have students complete the Chapter 5 Assessment
Class Time 35 minutes

TEACHER-TESTED ACTIVITY *Appalachian Trail Map*

Class Time One class period

Task Create a map of the Appalachian Trail

Supplies
- Outline maps of the east coast of North America
- Computer access: http://www.appalachiantrail.org/hike/index.html
- Reference books
- Colored pencils and markers

Purpose To develop an understanding of the oldest mountain chain in the United States and Canada. By doing this, students will work on all five geographic themes: place, region, location, movement, and human-environment interaction. They will also practice their map skills.

Activity Have students create an accurate map of the Appalachian Trail. They should select five points of interest along the 2,160-mile-long trail. Have them include the latitude and longitude of each of those locations, and share descriptive information about them. Students' maps should reflect the different land formations and climate types the trail passes through.

Cathy Probst
Geography Teacher, Nathan Hale High School, West Allis, WI

TECHNOLOGY IN THE CLASSROOM

Electronic field trips are one of the most popular ways for students to use the Internet. Students generally visit a specified set of Web pages to see pictures and read about places, such as national parks or historic sites. This type of field trip is often an excellent substitute for an actual field trip, which may be logistically impossible.

Objective Students will take an electronic field trip to some national parks in the United States and Canada to find out what the natural landscape looks like in different parts of these countries.

Task Have students visit the Web sites to see pictures of United States and Canadian national parks. Have them create multimedia presentations that showcase four of the national parks.

Class Time 2–4 class periods

1. Ask the class if anyone has ever been on a road trip across the United States or Canada. Where did they go? What was the scenery and weather like? What did they do?
2. Have students look at the physical map of the United States and Canada on page 103 and describe some of the major landscape features they see. What are the big mountain ranges, rivers, and lakes?
3. Ask students to imagine that their class has been given some money, a bus and driver, and three months next summer to explore the continental United States and Canada. They want to focus on natural scenery, so they've chosen to visit some national parks.
4. Have students make a chart in a word processor or on paper with rows for the following fourteen national parks: **United States:** Acadia, Everglades, Great Smoky Mountains, Rocky Mountain, Yellowstone, Grand Canyon, Yosemite, Olympic; **Canada:** Gros Morne, Jasper, Nahanni, Auyuittuq, Aulavik, and Grasslands.
5. Have students, either individually or in small groups, visit the Web sites at **hmhsocialstudies.com**. They should look at the pictures of the parks and read information about the parks' plant and animal life and geology. Ask them to list in each row of their charts three distinctive features of the natural landscape they see at each park. For example, for Yellowstone, they might say "geysers," "the Grand Canyon of Yellowstone," and "bison." (If there's not enough time for students to visit every park, divide the class into groups and assign each group several parks.)
6. As they go through the field trip, have students label the national parks on blank outline maps of the United States and Canada.
7. Have each student or group choose two national parks from the United States and two from Canada. The parks should be located in different parts of the countries.
8. Ask students to create multimedia presentations to serve as "electronic brochures" for the parks they will visit over the summer. The presentations should focus on the scenery and physical geography of the parks.

Previewing the Unit

The first pages of this unit offer an overview of the United States and Canada, two of the world's largest countries, occupying four fifths of North America. The United States and Canada have a strong history of cultural diversity partnered by a rich variety of natural resources, climates, and landforms.

Discussion Prompts

Exploring Prior Knowledge Ask students the following questions about the United States and Canada to determine their prior knowledge of the region:

- What other country occupies North America? *(Mexico)*
- What are some of these countries' most famous natural landforms? *(Some answers: Niagara Falls, Rocky Mountains, Great Lakes)*

Interpreting Maps Ask students to refer to the satellite image of North America to answer the following questions:

- What states, regions, or countries do you recognize? *(Alaska, Canada, United States)*
- What differences in vegetation does the image show? *(forest or highly vegetated areas, dry/arid or mountainous regions)*

The United States and Canada

PREVIEW: TODAY'S ISSUES IN THE UNITED STATES AND CANADA

UNIT ATLAS

Chapter 5
PHYSICAL GEOGRAPHY
A Land of Contrasts

Chapter 6
HUMAN GEOGRAPHY: UNITED STATES
Shaping an Abundant Land

Chapter 7
HUMAN GEOGRAPHY: CANADA
Developing a Vast Wilderness

Chapter 8
TODAY'S ISSUES
The United States and Canada

CASE STUDY
DIVERSE SOCIETIES FACE CHANGE

The United States and Canada ar[e] two of the world's largest countr[ies] with vast lands and abundant resources. They occupy four-fift[hs] of the continent of North Americ[a]

MOVEMENT Thousands of cars enter and leave Chicago, Illinois, daily. They use the vast expressway system that links the city to its surrounding suburbs and to interstate highways.

PLACE Cowhands and tourists from around the world gather in the western Canadian city of Calgary, Alberta, each July for the Calgary Stampede—the world's largest rodeo.

98

UNIT 2 ADDITIONAL RESOURCES

BOOKS FOR THE TEACHER

Homberger, Eric. ***The Penguin Historical Atlas of North America (Penguin Historical Atlases).*** NY: Penguin USA, 1995. Informative, illustrated atlas of North American history.

BOOKS FOR THE STUDENT

Smith, Philip, ed. ***Favorite North American Indian Legends.*** Dover, 1995. Indian legends loom large in the history of North America, as this book handsomely illustrates.

VIDEOS

Travel the World By Train: North America. Pioneer Video, 1999. Train passengers get spectacular views of the United States and Canada.

INTERNET

For more on the United States and Canada, visit . . .

hmhsocialstudies.com

GeoData

LOCATION The United States and Canada extend from the Atlantic Ocean to the Pacific Ocean and from the Arctic Ocean to the Gulf of Mexico (only the United States).

REGION The two countries are often referred to as Anglo America, because both were once British colonies and also share a common language–English.

MOVEMENT Both countries were settled by immigrants from all over the world, beginning with their first settlers who migrated from Asia after the last Ice Age.

For more information on the United States and Canada . . .

hmhsocialstudies.com
RESEARCH WEB LINKS

US & CANADA

LOCATION The majestic falls of the Niagara River are shared by both the United States and Canada. The American Falls, to the left, are in New York state; Horseshoe Falls, to the right, are in Ontario, Canada.

Interpreting Photographs

Chicago Expressways

Chicago, at the southern tip of Lake Michigan, has long been a hub for transportation and the distribution of goods.

Ask students whether they have traveled on a major expressway like the one pictured and what that experience was like. *(It may have been congested with traffic and difficult to get around on, or it may have been a good way to get to and from the city.)*

Rodeos

Tell students that both the United States and Canada have cowboys because both have vast plains that support cattle ranching.

Ask students what other cultural activities the United States and Canada have in common? *(hockey, skiing, country music, etc.)*

Niagara Falls

Point out that Niagara Falls is a natural formation.

Ask students why they think so many visitors go to see Niagara Falls each year. *(The falls are unlike anything else in North America.)*

ACTIVITY OPTION INTERNET RESEARCH

PLANNING A TRIP

Objective To allow students to explore a location in the United States and Canada

Class Time 30 minutes

Task Make decisions about planning a trip

Directions Divide students into small groups and have them look for information about Niagara Falls on the Internet. Have them find information about planning a trip to Niagara Falls. Have them decide how they would get there, where they would stay, and what they would like to see in and around the area. Also have them list any special problems they may encounter (documents required to visit a foreign country, currency exchange, and so forth).

OPTIONAL ACTIVITY If Internet access is limited, bring in travel articles and travel magazines relating to Niagara Falls, including information from the Niagara Falls Tourism Board.

Previewing Today's Issues

These pages provide a preview of issues that currently affect both the United States and Canada. These topics will be fully explored in Chapter 8 (pp. 172–185). Use the discussion prompts that follow to determine students' prior knowledge and allow them to make comparisons to local events.

 **In-Depth Resources: Unit 2**
- Exploring Today's Issues, pp. 36–39

TERRORISM

The United States and Canada became allies in a war against international terrorism after the deadly terrorist attack on the United States on September 11, 2001. Many other nations joined in the fight, because terrorism threatens the safety and security of society.

Discussion Prompts

- What does the word terrorism mean to you? *(Using violence against a nation or its citizens to cause fear or intimidation for political or social ends.)*
- What antiterrorist activities are you aware of in your state? *(Answers may vary, but may include increased security at airports, government buildings, and other possible terrorist targets.)*

Today's Issues in the United States and Canada

Today, the United States and Canada face the issues previewed here. As you read Chapters 5, 6, and 7, you will learn helpful background information. You will study the issues themselves in Chapter 8.

In a small group, answer the questions below. Then have a class discussion of your answers.

Exploring the Issues

1. TERRORISM Consider news stories that you have heard about terrorist groups in other countries. Make a list of the countries and the type of terrorist activity in each.
2. URBAN SPRAWL Why is the ever-expanding spread, or sprawl, of cities and suburbs a problem? What can be done to improve the quality of life in these areas?
3. DIVERSE SOCIETIES Search the Internet for information about diversity in the United States or Canada. What strategies or actions are being taken to help these many cultures unify?

For more on these issues in the United States and Canada . . .

TERRORISM

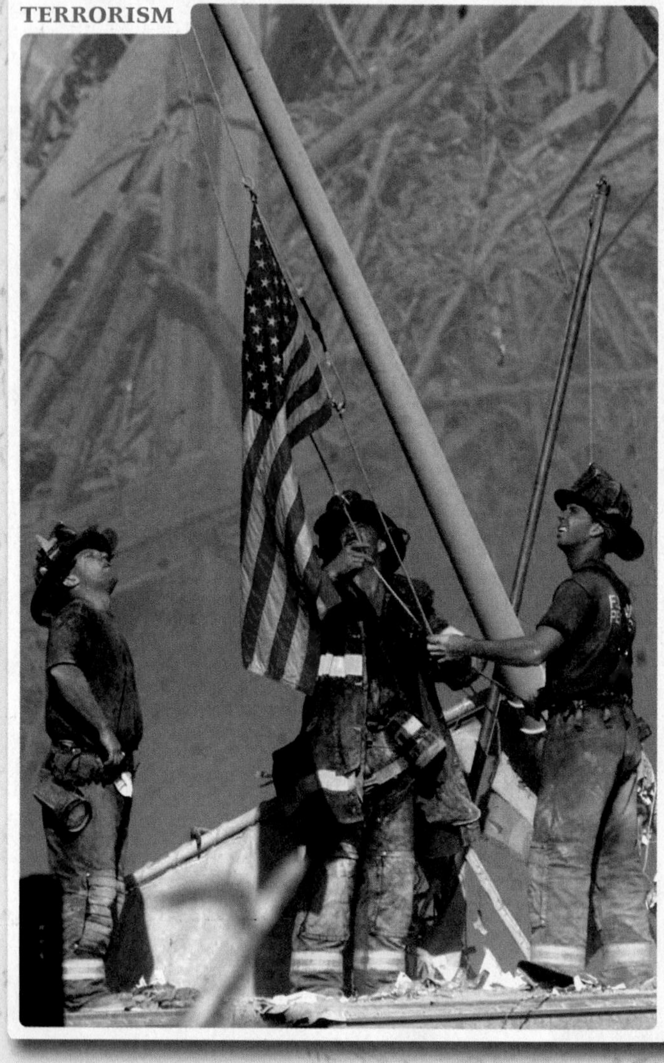

How can a country protect itself from terrorism?

A surprise attack, such as the one on the World Trade Center in New York City, is just one way terrorists attempt to intimidate governments and civilian populations to further their objectives.

EXPLORING THE ISSUES ANSWERS

1. TERRORISM Students may list Afghanistan, Israel, India, Japan, or Russia, among others, as sites of terrorist activity. They may refer to individual terrorist groups and their goals, types of weapons, and the use of tactics such as hijackings and suicide bombings.
2. URBAN SPRAWL Students may say that pollution, traffic congestion, and long commuting times are caused by urban sprawl. Suggestions for improvement will vary based on students' prior knowledge.
3. DIVERSE SOCIETIES Students may learn about Canada's issues with French-speaking citizens in Quebec or about how the latest U.S. census figures affect our society.

How can urban sprawl be controlled?

Urban communities, such as Las Vegas shown here, are trying to solve problems caused by urban areas spreading farther and farther out.

CASESTUDY

How can many cultures form a unified nation?

The diverse population of the United States is reflected in this group of California students. How to bring many cultures together as one nation is a continuing challenge for the United States, and for Canada, as well.

US & CANADA

URBAN SPRAWL

Urban sprawl has largely been caused by the use of cars, desire for less crowded living, and unrestricted and poorly planned development. Among other problems, urban sprawl causes housing costs to rise, and air and noise pollution to increase. Community activism and urban planning is helping stabilize the growth of cities.

Discussion Prompts

- What points might be made for and against rapid urban growth? *(People are happier living where they want and are willing to drive longer distances. Or, it is better for the environment to slow down urban expansion.)*
- How has urban sprawl affected you or someone you know? *(Answers will vary.)*

CASESTUDY

DIVERSE SOCIETIES

Over the years, the United States and Canada have welcomed immigrants from different areas of the world. The process of protecting and promoting diversity while remaining unified presents a challenge to both countries.

Discussion Prompts

- What is the difference between "Americanization" and multiculturalism? *(Speaking, acting, and living like other Americans; maintaining one's cultural uniqueness.)*
- Which approach do you think is healthier for a country? *(Answers will vary.)*

ACTIVITY OPTION | **COOPERATIVE LEARNING**

FINDING SOLUTIONS

Objective To perform group research and propose positive solutions to real-life problems

Class Time 30 minutes

Task Present solutions to issues

Directions Divide the class into small groups. Have each group choose one of the three issues above (terrorism, sprawl, or diversity) and use at least two sources to come up with some ideas on solving the problems related to that issue. Direct students to the Internet to do a search for articles on their particular issue. The group should prepare a report to present to the rest of the class in which they present possible solutions to issues. Assign the following tasks to one or more students in each group:

- conduct Internet research
- draft the possible solutions
- prepare the group presentation to the class

OPTIONAL ACTIVITY If Internet access is limited, have the students use the library for this research activity. Have the librarian show the students different methods for finding information on their chosen issue.

ATLAS OBJECTIVES

1. Compare data on the physical geography of Canada and the United States.
2. Examine historical and political features of both countries.
3. Identify country borders, and individual states and regions.
4. Compare economic factors between the United States and Canada.
5. Analyze population density in both countries.
6. Examine natural hazards that affect both countries.

Focus & Motivate

Ask students what they already know about the physical geography of Canada. Ask them how the maps could help them understand the geography of all of North America. *(Answers will vary. The maps help point out patterns and similarities and differences between the two countries' geography.)*

Instruct: Objective 

Comparing Data

- ***Landmass*** How does Canada compare in size to the United States? *(a little bigger)*
- ***Population*** How do the populations of Canada and the United States compare? *(The United States' population is much larger.)*
- ***Rivers*** How does the Rio Grande River compare to the Nile? *(less than half as long)*
- ***Mountains*** How does Mt. Logan in Canada compare in size to the highest mountain in the United States? *(about 800 feet shorter)*

Unit ATLAS

Patterns of Physical Geography

Use the Unit Atlas to add to your knowledge of the United States and Canada. As you look at the maps and charts, notice geographic patterns and specific details about the region.

After studying the illustrations, graphs, and physical map on these two pages, jot down answers to the following questions in your notebook.

Making Comparisons

1. Compare the world's longest river, the Nile, to the Mississippi. How much difference is there in the lengths of the two rivers?
2. Compare the landmass and population of the United States to those of Canada. What statement can be made about the two countries?
3. Compare the mountain peaks of the United States to those of Canada. What statement can be made about the height of these mountains?

Comparing Data

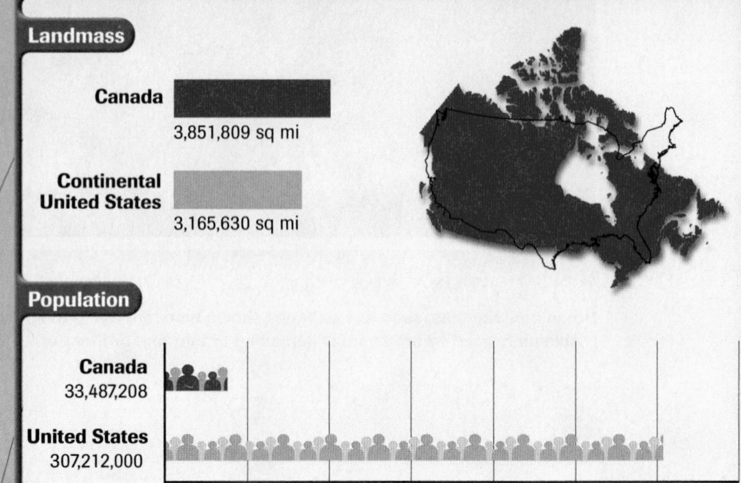

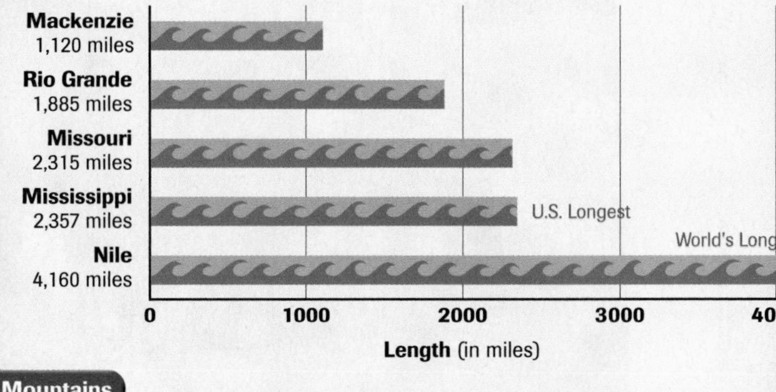

Mountains

World's Tallest **Mt. Everest**	U.S. Tallest **Mt. McKinley**	**Mt. Logan**	**Mt. St. Elias**	**Mt. Foraker**
Nepal-Tibet	United States	Canada	U.S.-Canada	United States
29,035 feet	20,320 feet	19,524 feet	18,008 feet	17,400 feet

MAKING COMPARISONS ANSWERS

1. The Mississippi River is a little more than half as long as the Nile River.
2. There are many more people per square mile in the United States, and greater landmass in Canada.
3. The United States has the tallest mountain in North America; the United States has more tall mountains than Canada.

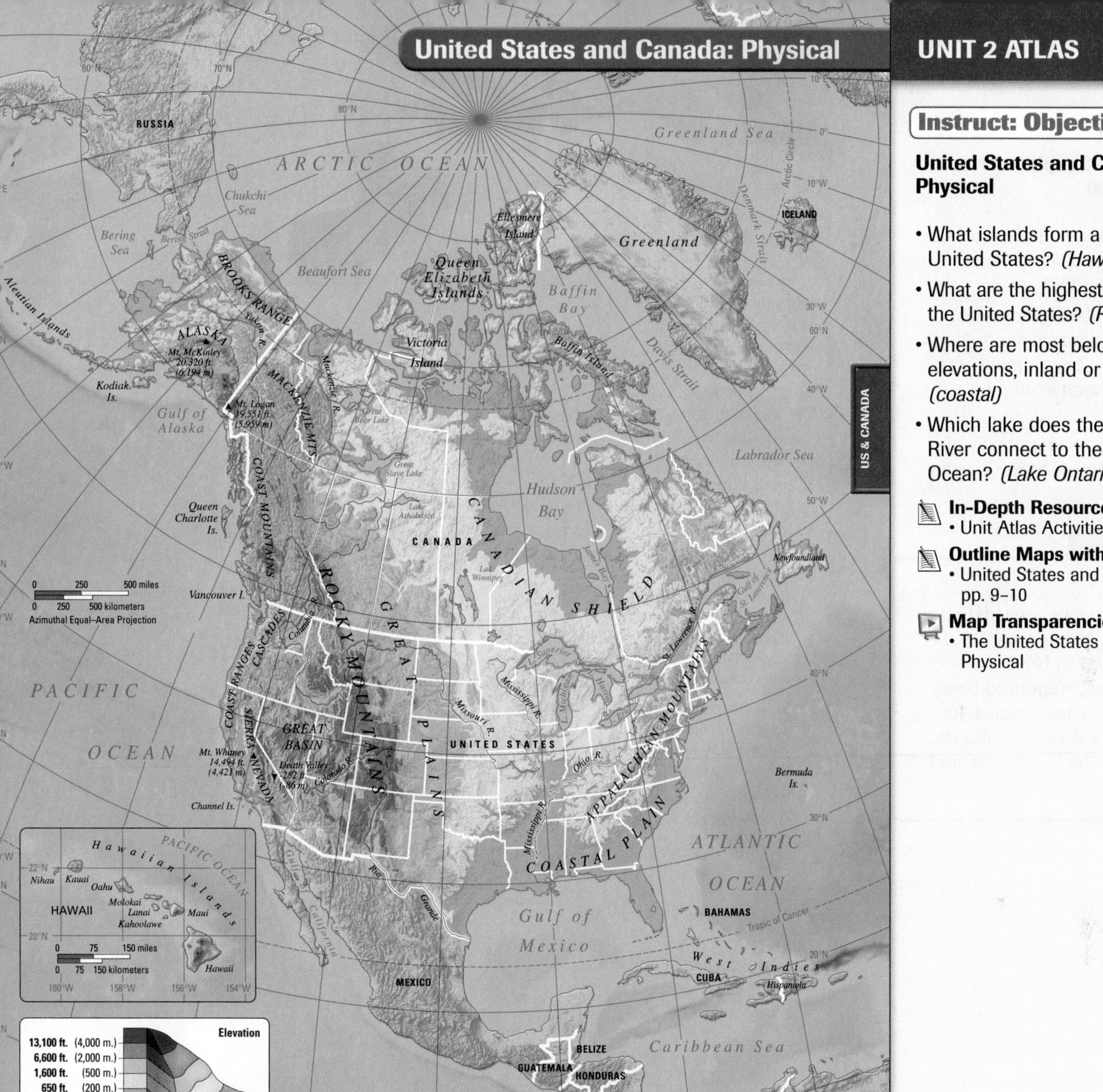

UNIT 2 ATLAS

US & CANADA

Instruct: Objective 2

United States and Canada: Physical

- What islands form a state in the United States? *(Hawaii)*
- What are the highest mountains in the United States? *(Rocky Mountains)*
- Where are most below-sea-level elevations, inland or coastal? *(coastal)*
- Which lake does the St. Lawrence River connect to the Atlantic Ocean? *(Lake Ontario)*

In-Depth Resources: Unit 2
- Unit Atlas Activities, p. 1

Outline Maps with Activities
- United States and Canada: Physical, pp. 9–10

Map Transparencies MT11
- The United States and Canada: Physical

ACTIVITY OPTION | CRITICAL THINKING

DRAWING CONCLUSIONS

Explaining the Skill By looking at a set of facts—in this case, the data presented in the chart and map—students can use their common sense and experience to form opinions, or draw conclusions. For example, information about the location of a country can tell you something about its likely climate, vegetation, and patterns of settlement.

Applying the Skill Tell students that most of the population in Canada is clustered along the border with the United States in the eastern half of the country. Ask them why this might be so. Have them consider climate, waterways, elevation, and any other factors that seem relevant. Then make up a composite list on the chalkboard based on students' suggestions. *(Answers might include milder climate; access to waterways of Great Lakes and St. Lawrence River; lower elevation means flatter country that was easier to settle and farm.)*

Instruct: Objective 3

Selected Native Peoples of North America, c. 1600

- What does the map show? *(various tribes of native peoples in North America around 1600)*
- In terms of population, how was North America then similar to North America today? *(fewer inhabitants in area of Canada than in area of United States)*
- Which native peoples probably did the most farming? *(Creek, Choctaw, Apalachee)*

More About

Native Peoples

By the time Europeans arrived, there could have been as many as 240 different tribal groups in North America. Researchers have categorized these groups by cultures and regions, for example, Northwest Coast, subarctic, western Plateau, the Southwest, and so forth.

Unit ATLAS

Patterns of Human Geography

After the coming of European settlers in the 17th century, the political map of North America changed quickly and significantly. Study the historical and political maps of the United States and Canada on these two pages. In your notebook, answer these questions.

Making Comparisons

1. What differences do you notice when you compare the map of 1600 with the map of the United States and Canada today?
2. Which names of native peoples are found as geographic names on the map on page 105?
3. Which country was more sparsely settled by native peoples in 1600?

Selected Native Peoples of North America, c. 1600

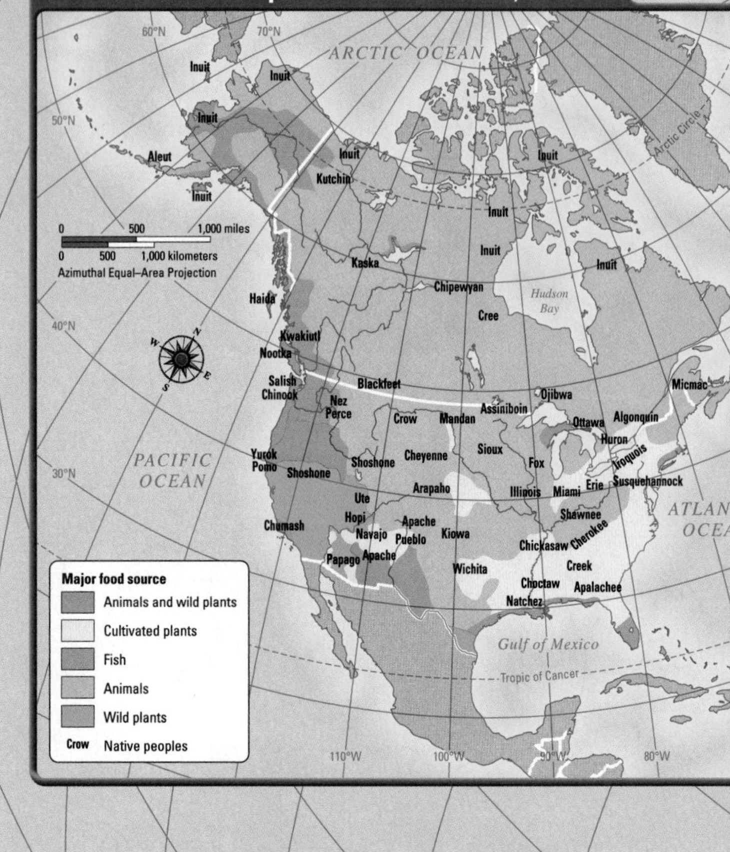

MAKING COMPARISONS ANSWERS

1. No borders or countries then; native peoples widespread across continent; game almost everywhere
2. Ottawa, Huron, Erie, Illinois
3. Canada

United States and Canada: Political

National capital
Other city
0 250 500 miles
0 250 500 kilometers
Azimuthal Equal-Area Projection

Instruct: Objective 4

United States and Canada: Political

- What is Canada's national capital? *(Ottawa)*
- What U.S. state has the longest border with Canada? *(Alaska)*
- What Canadian territory borders the Labrador Sea? *(Newfoundland)*

Outline Maps with Activities
- United States and Canada: Political, pp. 11–12

Map Transparencies MT12
- The United States and Canada: Political

More About

Shared Environment

Because of common borders, the United States and Canada have several common interests, including business practices, tourism, immigration, and trade. Common resources such as the Great Lakes have led the two countries to maintain a dialogue on air and water quality, among other environmental concerns.

ACTIVITY OPTION LINK TO LITERATURE

MAKING GEOGRAPHIC CONNECTIONS

Objective To find a piece of literature with strong geographic ties to the United States or Canada

Reading Time 2-3 hours; **Class Time** 25 minutes

Task Using literature and geography to reinforce one another

Directions Have students look for a literature selection with strong geographic ties to a specific place in North America. Suggest they look among Native American songs and stories; historical fiction; Westerns; hunting-and-fishing stories; and mid-20th-century urban tales.

Then have them develop a profile for the place in which the story takes place, including the following elements:

- climate
- topography
- settlements
- resources
- vegetation
- landforms
- population

Instruct: Objective 

Canada-U.S. Connections

- To which country do most people travel? *(about the same to each)*
- Which country has invested more in the other? *(United States has invested more in Canada.)*
- Which category of comparison is probably the most accurate? *(Tourism or trade because the information was gathered in the same year.)*

Instruct: Objective 

Economic Activities of the U.S. and Canada

- What is Canada's most widespread economic activity? *(hunting, fishing, and forestry)*
- Near what bodies of water could an American or Canadian fisherman live? *(Atlantic, Pacific, or Arctic oceans; Gulf of Mexico; Hudson Bay)*
- In what part of the United States would you find the most cattle? *(western)*

Unit ATLAS

Regional Patterns

These pages contain three thematic maps and an infographic. The infographic illustrates economic connections between the United States and Canada. The maps show economic activities, population density, and areas affected by natural hazards.

Study these two pages and then answer the questions below in your notebook.

Making Comparisons

1. Where are the areas of greatest population density found in each country? Do settlement patterns have any relationship to the threat of natural hazards?
2. Where are manufacturing and trade concentrated in the United States and Canada? Why might this be so?

Canada-U.S. Connections

CANADA

Immigration: 15,109 people (2008); 5,304 people (2002)

Trade: US $335.6 billion (2008); US $260.9 billion (2008)

Direct Investment: US $51,000 million (1998); US $103,908 million (1998)

Tourism: 15.9 million travelers (2006); 13.9 million travelers (2006)

UNITED STATES

Source: *The Europa World Year Book 2005 and 2009*

This graphic shows that the geographic nearness of the United States and Canada has resulted in economic connections.

Economic Activities of the U.S. and Canada

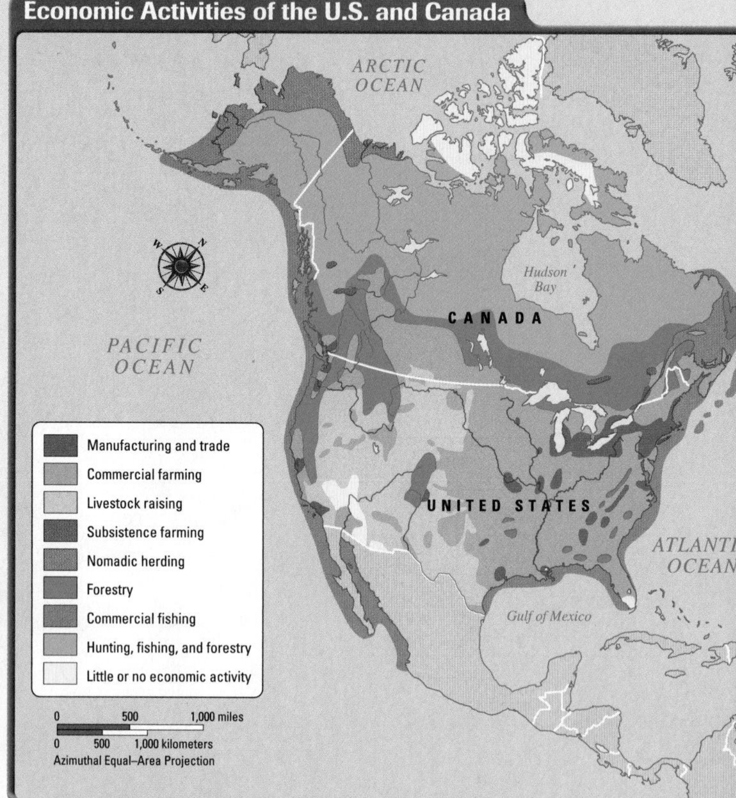

106 UNIT 2

MAKING COMPARISONS ANSWERS

1. Around bodies of water; not much, since Los Angeles is built in an area with a number of natural hazards.
2. Around major cities and important waterways; so that manufactured items can be easily transported via waterways.

Natural Hazards of the U.S. and Canada

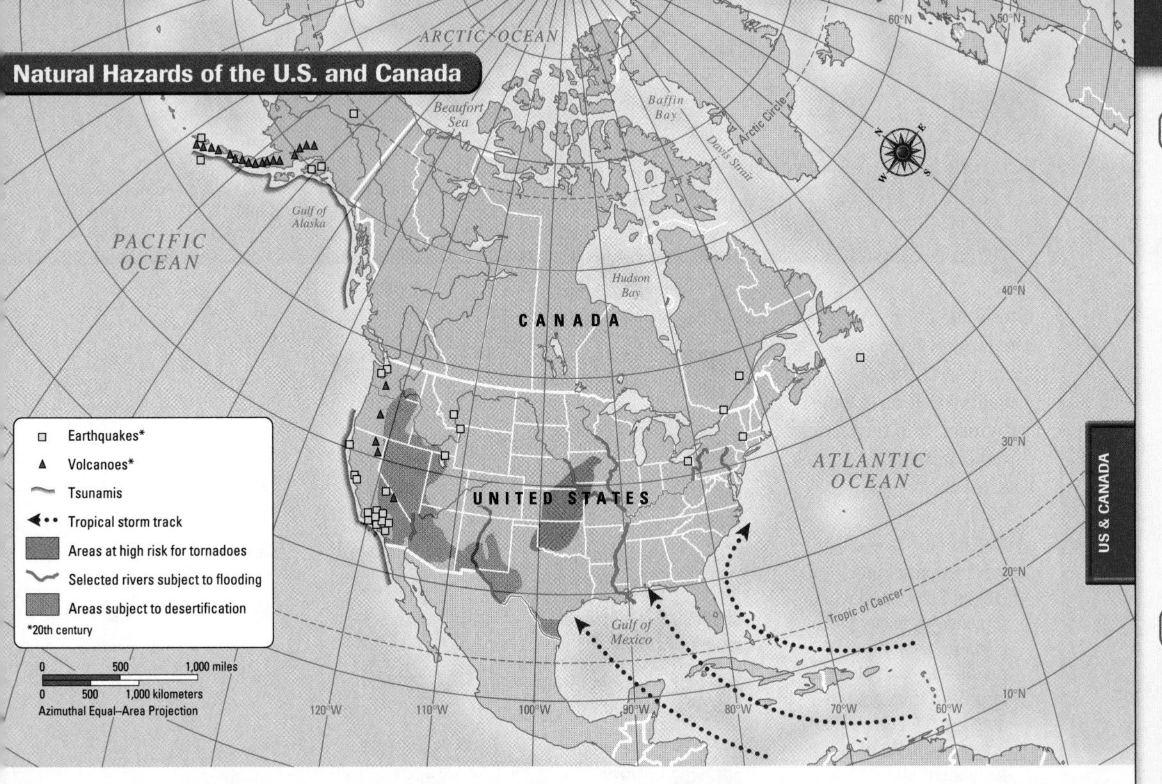

Population Density of the U.S. and Canada

107

US & CANADA

Instruct: Objective 6

Natural Hazards of the U.S. and Canada

- What natural hazards most affect Alaska? *(volcanoes and tsunamis)*
- Which part of the United States is most likely to deal with flooding? *(the South, Midwest, and West)*
- Which natural hazard most threatens the southern United States? *(tropical storms)*
- How vulnerable is Canada to natural hazards? *(It suffers few.)*

Instruct: Objective 6

Population Density of the U.S. and Canada

- In what areas is U.S. population density the highest? *(eastern United States, between Boston and Washington; around Great Lakes cities of Chicago and Detroit; southern California around Los Angeles)*
- Which color represents the most widespread population density level in the United States? *(yellow, 1–24 persons per sq mi)*
- What is the population density around Winnipeg? *(25-129 persons per sq mi/10-49 persons per sq km)*

FIVE THEMES OF GEOGRAPHY

PLACE

Exploring the Theme Many times viewing statistical information in map form can provide new insights into the data, and some reasonable conclusions can be drawn. For instance, when looking at populated areas questions naturally arise (for example, why one place is more populated than another).

Understanding the Theme Look at the map above showing population density.

- What area has the highest population density? *(Northeastern United States between Boston and Washington.)*
- What do the cities in the area with the highest population density all have in common? *(They are all close to water.)*
- Why might many people have settled there? *(Many people entered the country in this area; early cities sprung up in the area; nearness to water probably provided jobs in trade, transportation, and manufacturing.)*

DATA FILE OBJECTIVE

Examine and compare data on the United States and Canada.

Focus & Motivate

Ask students which country they think has the most states or territories. Which country do they think has the higher per capita income? *(the United States has more states than Canada has territories; the United States)*

Instruct: Objective

Regional Data File

- What political units are included in these charts? *(states, territories, provinces, the countries as a whole)*
- What U.S. political entity has the highest population density? *(District of Columbia)*
- What is the largest U.S. state in area? *(Alaska)*
- Which U.S. territory has the most inhabitants? *(Puerto Rico)*

In-Depth Resources: Unit 2
• Regional Data File Activities, p. 2

Unit ATLAS Regional Data File

Study the charts on the United States and Canada and their political subdivisions—states, provinces, and territories. In your notebook, answer these questions.

Making Comparisons

1. Which state of the United States and which province or territory of Canada have the most people? Is each also the largest in total area in its country? Locate them on the map. What is significant about their locations?
2. Which state of the United States and which province or territory of Canada have the least people? Is each also the smallest in total area in its country? Locate them on the map.

(continued on page 110)

Flag	State or Territory/ Capital	Population (2009 est.)	Population Rank (2009 est.)	Infant Mortality (per 1,000 live births) (2006)
	Alabama Montgomery	4,708,708	23	9.0
	Alaska Juneau	698,473	47	6.9
	Arizona Phoenix	6,595,778	14	6.4
	Arkansas Little Rock	2,889,450	32	8.5
	California Sacramento	36,961,664	1	5.0
	Colorado Denver	5,024,748	22	5.7
	Connecticut Hartford	3,518,288	29	6.2
	Delaware Dover	885,122	45	8.3
	District of Columbia*	599,657	50	11.3
	Florida Tallahassee	18,537,969	4	7.3
	Georgia Atlanta	9,829,211	9	8.1
	Hawaii Honolulu	1,295,178	42	5.6
	Idaho Boise	1,545,801	39	6.8
	Illinois Springfield	12,910,409	5	7.3
	Indiana Indianapolis	6,423,113	16	8.0
	Iowa Des Moines	3,007,856	30	5.1
	Kansas Topeka	2,818,747	33	7.1
	Kentucky Frankfort	4,314,113	26	7.5
	Louisiana Baton Rouge	4,492,076	25	9.9

Notes:
* The federal district of Washington, D.C., is the capital city of the United States.

For updated statistics on the United States and Canada . . .
hmhsocialstudies.com DATA UPDATE

MAKING COMPARISONS ANSWERS

1. California and Ontario. They are not the largest in land area. They are both located near significant bodies of water (Pacific Ocean, Great Lakes, Hudson Bay).
2. Wyoming and Nunavut. They are not the smallest in total land area.

Doctors (per 100,000 pop.) (2007)	Population Density (per square mile) (2008)	Urban/Rural Population (2000)	Per Capita Income[a] (US$) (2008 prelim.)	High School Graduates[b] (percent) (2008 est.)	Area Rank	Total Area[c] (square miles)
218	92.1	55/45	33,643	80.9	30	52,419
228	1.2	66/34	43,321	90.6	1	663,267
210	57.2	88/12	32,953	83.7	6	113,998
203	54.9	53/47	31,266	81.2	29	53,179
269	236.0	94/6	42,696	80.3	3	163,696
260	47.7	85/15	42,377	88.6	8	104,094
376	723.3	88/12	56,248	88.2	48	5,543
251	447.9	80/20	40,852	86.7	49	2,489
807	9,687.0	100/00	64,991	85.3	51	68
248	341.9	89/11	39,070	84.9	22	65,755
217	168.4	72/28	33,975	82.9	24	59,425
317	200.4	92/8	40,490	89.5	43	10,931
169	18.4	66/34	32,133	87.9	14	83,570
280	232.4	88/12	42,397	85.6	25	57,914
217	178.0	71/29	34,103	85.7	38	36,418
189	53.8	61/39	36,680	89.6	26	56,272
223	34.3	71/29	37,978	89.0	15	82,277
232	108.1	56/44	31,826	80.4	37	40,409
263	102.1	73/27	36,271	80.2	31	51,840

More About

Hawaii

Hawaii is often a stopping point for ships and planes crossing the Pacific Ocean since it is nearly midway between major cities in North America and Asia, such as San Francisco and Tokyo. Honolulu, the capital and most populated city, is located on the island of Oahu. In Hawaiian, *Honolulu* means "sheltered bay." Honolulu became a primary center of trade during the 1800s. During the early 1900s, Pearl Harbor near Honolulu, became a U.S. military base, and was bombed during World War II. Honolulu has since become a fast-growing city and very popular tourist spot.

ACTIVITY OPTION CRITICAL THINKING

MAKING GENERALIZATIONS

Explaining the Skill Making generalizations means making broad judgments based on information. When making generalizations, students gather information from several sources.

It is also possible to examine data presented in chart form in order to make generalizations that give insight to a larger picture. For example, comparing statistics between countries or states can lead to a better general understanding of an issue, such as health care or education.

Applying the Skill Have students compare U.S. and Canadian capitals: the District of Columbia and Ontario. Then have them compare the data for each. Have the students make two generalizations about Canada in relation to the United States. Ask the following questions:

- Which national capital city is more likely to be congested? *(the District of Columbia; population density is much higher there.)*
- Which probably has a better standard of living? *(Answers will vary. According to some measures, such as comparing infant mortality and population, Ontario comes out ahead; according to others, such as per capita income, the District of Columbia comes out ahead.)*

More About

Bismarck, North Dakota

Bismarck, North Dakota was originally founded in 1873 as the city of Edwinton. Its name was later changed to Bismarck in honor of Prussian statesman Otto von Bismarck, who was known as the “Iron Chancellor” because of his belief that the German states be welded into one empire by “blood and iron” rather by than treaties and speeches. The city of Bismarck was a railroad center for the gold mines of the Black Hills of the Dakota Territory.

Regional Data File

Making Comparisons
(continued)

3. Which six states of the United States and which three provinces or territories of Canada have the highest per capita income? Locate them on the map. What factors might account for this?

4. Which are the six most highly urbanized states of the United States? In which three provinces or territories of Canada do at least 80 percent of the people live in urban areas? Are these states and provinces or territories the same as those that have the highest per capita incomes?

(continued on page 112)

Flag	State or Territory/ Capital	Population (2009 est.)	Population Rank (2009 est.)	Infant Mortality (per 1,000 live births) (2006)
	Maine Augusta	1,318,301	41	6.3
	Maryland Annapolis	5,699,478	19	8.0
	Massachusetts Boston	6,593,587	15	4.8
	Michigan Lansing	9,969,727	8	7.4
	Minnesota St. Paul	5,266,214	21	5.2
	Mississippi Jackson	2,951,996	31	10.6
	Missouri Jefferson City	5,987,580	18	7.4
MONTANA	**Montana** Helena	974,989	44	5.8
	Nebraska Lincoln	1,796,619	38	5.6
	Nevada Carson City	2,643,085	35	6.4
	New Hampshire Concord	1,324,575	40	6.1
	New Jersey Trenton	8,707,739	11	5.5
	New Mexico Santa Fe	2,009,671	36	5.8
	New York Albany	19,541,453	3	5.6
	North Carolina Raleigh	9,380,884	10	8.1
	North Dakota Bismarck	646,844	48	5.8
	Ohio Columbus	11,542,645	7	7.8
OKLAHOMA	**Oklahoma** Oklahoma City	3,687,050	28	8.0
STATE OF OREGON 1859	**Oregon** Salem	3,825,657	27	5.5

MAKING COMPARISONS ANSWERS

3. Connecticut, (District of Columbia), Massachusetts, New Jersey, Maryland, Wyoming; Alberta, Ontario, British Columbia. Answers will vary.

4. U.S.–California, Hawaii, Massachusetts, Nevada, New Jersey, Rhode Island. Canada–Alberta, British Columbia, Ontario, Quebec. Per capita income is high in some instances but not all.

Doctors (per 100,000 pop.) (2007)	Population Density (per square mile) (2008)	Urban/Rural Population (2000)	Per Capita Income[a] (US$) (2008 prelim.)	High School Graduates[b] (percent) (2008 est.)	Area Rank	Total Area[c] (square miles)
278	42.7	40/60	35,381	89.3	39	35,385
421	580.5	86/14	48,091	87.5	42	12,407
469	833.0	91/9	50,735	88.4	44	10,555
250	177.0	75/25	35,299	87.6	11	96,716
293	65.6	71/29	42,772	91.1	12	86,939
178	62.6	49/51	29,569	78.8	32	48,430
246	86.0	69/31	35,228	85.6	21	69,704
221	6.6	54/46	34,256	90.5	4	147,042
245	23.2	70/30	37,730	89.8	16	77,354
188	23.7	92/8	40,353	83.8	7	110,561
275	147.0	59/41	42,830	90.5	46	9,350
316	1,180.7	94/6	50,919	86.9	47	8,721
244	16.4	75/25	32,091	82.0	5	121,589
396	413.6	88/12	48,076	84.1	27	54,556
254	189.7	60/40	34,439	82.9	28	53,819
244	9.3	56/44	39,321	89.0	19	70,700
267	281.1	77/23	35,511	87.0	34	44,825
173	53.1	65/35	36,899	84.9	20	69,898
274	39.5	79/21	35,956	88.1	9	98,381

More About

Measuring Per Capita Income

Many income statistics are based on household income estimates. Households are almost always based on the total population minus the "institutional population" (which includes military personnel, college students, retirees in homes, prisoners, homeless persons, and any others who do not live in households). Most income data is collected by a government through census, labor, taxation, and economic surveys.

ACTIVITY OPTION **COOPERATIVE LEARNING**

CREATING A BAR GRAPH

Objective To gather information from one type of graphic display, reconfigure it, and present it in a new format

Class Time 30 minutes

Task Make a bar graph to compare population density

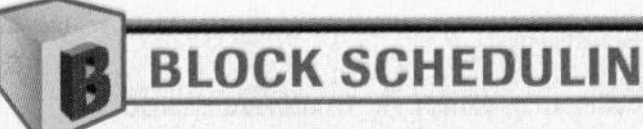

Directions Divide the class into small groups. Have students create a graph with two axes, one showing "Population Density per square mile," and the other showing "U.S. states (Maine through Oregon)." Students should decide whether to list states alphabetically, or to group states with similar rates together. Students may choose to use color to organize the data in their bar graphs. Have small groups exchange and compare their peers' graphs.

More About

Pierre, South Dakota

Pierre, South Dakota, lies on the east bank of the Missouri River. The city was named for Pierre Chouteau, an early fur trader of French descent. The first settlers arrived in 1878, and the town became the temporary state capital in 1889 and the permanent capital in 1904.

Regional Data File

Making Comparisons *(continued)*

5. Which seven states of the United States and which three provinces or territories of Canada have the highest infant mortality rate? the lowest? What relationship do these figures appear to have to the urban/rural population ratio?
6. Which U.S. territory has the largest population and largest area? Which has the smallest population and the smallest area?

(continued on page 114)

Flag	State or Territory/ Capital	Population (2009 est.)	Population Rank (2009 est.)	Infant Mortality (per 1,000 live births) (2006)
	Pennsylvania Harrisburg	12,604,767	6	7.6
	Rhode Island Providence	1,053,209	43	6.1
	South Carolina Columbia	4,561,242	24	8.4
	South Dakota Pierre	812,383	46	6.9
	Tennessee Nashville	6,296,254	17	8.7
	Texas Austin	24,782,302	2	6.2
	Utah Salt Lake City	2,784,572	34	5.1
	Vermont Montpelier	621,760	49	5.5
	Virginia Richmond	7,882,590	12	7.1
	Washington Olympia	6,664,195	13	4.7
	West Virginia Charleston	1,819,777	37	7.4
	Wisconsin Madison	5,654,774	20	6.4
	Wyoming Cheyenne	544,270	51	7.0
U.S. Territories				
	American Samoa Pago Pago	65,628 (2009 est.)	–	10.2 (2009 est.)
	Guam Agana	178,430 (2009 est.)	–	6.0 (2009 est.)
	Puerto Rico San Juan	3,966,213 (2009 est.)	–	8.3 (2009 est.)
	U.S. Virgin Islands Charlotte Amalie	109,825 (2009 est.)	–	7.6 (2009 est.)

MAKING COMPARISONS ANSWERS

5. United States: highest–Alabama, Arkansas, (District of Columbia), Louisiana, Mississippi, South Carolina, Tennessee; lowest–California, Iowa, Massachusetts, Minnesota, Utah, Washington, New Jersey, Oregon, Vermont. Canada: highest–Newfoundland, Nunavut, Yukon Territory; lowest–British Columbia, Northwest Territories, Nova Scotia. Answers will vary.
6. Puerto Rico has the largest population and area. American Samoa has the smallest population and area.

Doctors (per 100,000 pop.) (2007)	Population Density (per square mile) (2008)	Urban/Rural Population (2000)	Per Capita Income[a] (US$) (2008 prelim.)	High School Graduates[b] (percent) (2008 est.)	Area Rank	Total Area[c] (square miles)
305	278.2	77/23	40,265	86.8	33	46,055
376	1,016.4	91/9	41,008	83.0	50	1,545
230	149.0	61/39	31,884	82.1	40	32,020
219	10.6	52/48	37,375	88.9	17	77,116
264	150.7	64/36	34,330	81.8	36	42,143
214	93.1	83/17	38,575	79.2	2	268,581
208	33.3	88/12	30,291	90.3	13	84,899
374	67.4	38/62	38,880	90.4	45	9,614
274	196.7	73/27	42,876	85.7	35	42,774
270	98.6	82/18	42,356	89.3	18	71,300
232	75.5	46/54	30,831	81.5	41	24,230
259	103.9	68/32	37,314	89.0	23	65,498
184	5.5	65/35	49,719	90.9	10	97,814
1/1,253 (2003)	852 (2009 est.)	92/8 (2008)	4,357 (1999)	68.8 (2005)	–	77
1/1,022 (2007)	842 (2009 est.)	93/7 (2008)	12,722 (1999)	78.9 (2007)	–	212
1/504 (2001)	1,129 (2009 est.)	98/2 (2008)	8,185 (1999)	74.6 (2000)	–	5,324
1/680 (2005)	808 (2009 est.)	95/5 (2008)	13,139 (1999)	60.4 (2004)	–	737

113

More About

U.S. and Canadian Health Care

Canada has a diversity of joint federal-provincial and local programs to meet the health needs of its people, while the United States has a system of private insurance coverage. Although some in Canada have proposed changing their system to one like that of the United States, Canadians have resisted because statistics show their system is performing better overall

The United States spends a large portion of its Gross Domestic Product (GDP) on health care, but tens of millions of Americans remain uninsured. Many millions more are underinsured because of limits on individual health care expenditures. Canada, on the other hand, spends less of its GDP on health care, and everyone is covered.

ACTIVITY OPTION CRITICAL THINKING

ANALYZING DATA

Explaining the Skill The chart above presents many different kinds of data. Students can compare different columns of figures in the Regional Data File in order to get a deeper understanding of life in the region. For example, there is frequently a correlation between education and income. Students might examine the connection between education and income in the U.S. states listed above.

Applying the Skill Have students look at the 13 U.S. states listed above (Pennsylvania through Wyoming). Have them look at the figures for per capita income and high school graduates. Ask them if they can see any correlation between the states with the highest percentage of high-school graduates and the states with the highest per capita income. *(In some cases, the higher the percentage of high school graduates, the higher the per capita income. For example, Wyoming is number one in both categories. It has a high-school graduation rate of 90.9 percent and a per capita income of $49,719. Utah, however, is third in the percentage of high school graduates, but has the lowest per capita income.)*

Instruct: Objective

Regional Data File

- How many provinces or territories does Canada have? *(13)*
- Which Canadian province or territory is the largest? *(Nunavut)*
- Which Canadian territory or province is closest in population to the U.S. state of Connecticut? *(Alberta)*
- Which Canadian territory or province is closest in land area to the U.S. state of Alaska? *(Quebec)*

Regional Data File

Flag	State or Territory/ Capital	Population (2009 est.)	Population Rank (2009 est.)	Infant Mortality (per 1,000 live births) (2006)
	Alberta Edmonton	3,653,840	4	6.0
	British Columbia Vancouver	4,435,344	3	4.0
	Manitoba Winnipeg	1,217,163	5	7.3
	New Brunswick Fredricton	748,866	8	4.3
	Newfoundland St. John's	508,726	9	7.5
	Northwest Territories Yellowknife	42,840	11	4.1
	Nova Scotia Halifax	939,475	7	3.3
	Nunavut Iqaluit	31,762	13	15.1
	Ontario Toronto	13,014,018	1	5.2
	Prince Edward Island Charlottetown	140,638	10	5.0
	Quebec Quebec City	7,799,372	2	4.5
	Saskatchewan Regina	1,027,092	6	5.8
	Yukon Territory Whitehorse	35,550	12	8.5
	Canada Ottawa, Ontario	33,487,208 (2009 est.)	–	5.0 (2009 est.)
	United States Washington, D.C.	307,212,123 (2009 est.)	–	6.2 (2009 est.)

Making Comparisons *(continued)*

7. Which state and which province or territory is the most densely populated? Which state and which territory is the least densely populated? Are the most densely populated the smallest in area and the least populated the largest in area?

Sources:
Canadian Institute for Health Information, 2008, online
CIA World Factbook, 2010, online
Encyclopedia Britannica, online
Provincial Economic Accounts, 2007, Statistics Canada
Statistical Abstract of the United States, 2010, online
Statistics Canada, online
UNICEF 2006
U.S. Census Bureau, American FactFinder, online
The World Almanac and Book of Facts 2010

Notes:
[a] Personal income per capita in constant 2000 dollars. Because of differences in the way the two countries calculate income, Canadian and U.S. per capita income figures are not directly comparable. U.S. dollars are used for the U.S. figures, and Canadian dollars are used for the Canadian figures. The average annual exchange rate in 2001 was approximately 1.55Can$/US$.
[b] Percentage of the population, 25 years old or older, with high school diploma or higher. Figures for Puerto Rico include attainment of some upper secondary education. Figures for Canada reflect the percentage of population, aged 25 to 29 who are high school graduates.
[c] Includes land and water.

MAKING COMPARISONS ANSWERS

7. The most densely populated state is New Jersey; the least densely populated state is Alaska. The most densely populated province or territory is Prince Edward Island. The least densely populated province or territory is Nunavut.

Doctors (per 100,000 pop.) (2007)	Population Density (per square mile) (2008)	Urban/Rural Population (2000)	Per Capita Income[a] (US$) (2008 prelim.)	High School Graduates[b] (percent) (2008 est.)	Area Rank	Total Area[c] (square miles)
201	13.3	82/18	45,875	82.6	6	255,287
205	11.5	85/15	34,664	88.1	5	365,948
183	5.4	72/28	32,106	80.2	8	250,947
193	26.5	51/49	29,811	87.3	11	28,355
218	3.5	58/42	31,040	84.5	10	156,649
112	0.09	58/42	NA	69.9	3	503,951
233	44.7	56/44	30,956	86.4	12	21,425
35	0.04	43/57	NA	42.4	1	818,959
177	34.7	85/15	36,259	89.7	4	412,581
165	61.9	45/55	28,248	86.5	13	2,185
219	14.4	80/20	32,474	85.5	2	594,860
162	4.3	65/35	32,104	80.8	7	251,866
227	0.2	60/40	NA	78.7	9	186,661
195 (2008)	9.6 (2009)	80/20 (2008)	35,533 (2007)	86.7 (2006)	-	3,855,103
256 (2004)	86.8 (2009)	82/18 (2008)	46,400 (2009 est.)	85.7 (2007)	-	3,794,100

More About

Prince Edward Island

Although smallest in land area, Prince Edward Island is the most densely populated province of Canada. Inhabitants call it "The Island" or simply use its initials, "P.E.I." Charlottetown is the capital and only city on the island. Prince Edward Island is also the only Canadian province that is totally separate from the North American mainland. Positioned in the Gulf of St. Lawrence off the Atlantic coast of Canada, the island is a rich fishing area that yields lobsters, oysters, crabs, scallops, cod, flounder, hake, herring, mackerel, and tuna.

ACTIVITY OPTION CRITICAL THINKING

ANALYZING DATA

Explaining the Skill The chart above presents many different kinds of data. Students can compare different columns of figures in the Regional Data File in order to get a deeper understanding of life in the region. For example, there is frequently a correlation between the number of doctors available to serve a population and the infant mortality rate. Students might examine the connection between doctors per 100,000 people and the infant mortality rate in Canadian provinces and territories.

Applying the Skill Have students look at the 13 Canadian provinces and territories listed above. Have them look at the figures for doctors available to serve the population (measured in terms of 1 doctor per 100,000 people) and infant mortality rate (measured per 1,000 live births). Ask them if they can see any correlation between the number of doctors and the number of babies who survive. *(There seems in general to be a negative correlation—the more doctors available to serve 100,000 people, the fewer infants who die. For example, Nunavut has the fewest doctors available—only 35 per 100,000 people—and the highest number of infant deaths per 1,000 births. Nova Scotia has the highest number of doctors in proportion to population and the lowest infant mortality rate.)*

CHAPTER 5 OBJECTIVE

Identify key features of the U.S. and Canada's physical geography and human-environment interaction.

Chapter 5

PHYSICAL GEOGRAPHY OF THE UNITED STATES and CANADA
A Land of Contrasts

Interpreting Photographs

El Capitan

Ask students to examine the photograph and read the caption. Ask students during what season of the year this photograph was probably taken and what in the picture indicates that? *(It was probably taken in late winter since there is snow.)*

Introducing the Essential Question

- Tell students that the physical geography of the United States and Canada is extremely varied—from icy, tall mountains to flat, parched deserts.
- Explain that industrialization and population growth have created problems for the region's environment. Students may describe some of these problems.

Have students fill out the graphic organizers in their notebooks by using information from all the sections in this chapter.

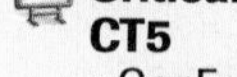

Critical Thinking Transparencies CT5
- GeoFocus

In-Depth Resources: Unit 2
- Building Vocabulary, p. 9

The 3,593-foot El Capitan is one of many cliffs that soar above the valley floor in California's Yosemite National Park.

Essential Question

What are the key physical features of the United States and Canada?

What You Will Learn

In this chapter you will explore the physical geography of the United States and Canada.

SECTION 1
Landforms and Resources

SECTION 2
Climate and Vegetation

SECTION 3
Human–Environment Interaction

hmhsocialstudies.com
TAKING NOTES

Use a graphic organizer like the one online to record information from the chapter about the physical geography of the United States and Canada.

116

CHAPTER 5 ADDITIONAL RESOURCES

BOOKS FOR THE TEACHER

McCoy, Michael. ***Cycling the Great Divide: From Canada to Mexico on America's Premier Long-Distance Mountain Bike Route.*** Seattle, WA: Mountaineers, 2000. A long-distance cycling adventure.

BOOKS FOR THE STUDENT

National Geographic Society. ***Exploring Canada's Spectacular National Parks.*** Washington, D.C.: National Geographic Society, 1998. A detailed look at Canada's national parks, including photographs.

VIDEOS

My Side of the Mountain. Paramount Studio, 1995. Tale of 13-year-old Canadian boy seeking closeness to nature.

INTERNET

For more on the physical geography of the United States and Canada, visit . . .

Landforms and Resources

Main Ideas

- The United States and Canada have vast lands and abundant resources.
- These two countries share many of the same landforms.

Places & Terms

Appalachian Mountains
Great Plains
Canadian Shield
Rocky Mountains
Continental Divide
Great Lakes
Mackenzie River

US & CANADA

CONNECT TO THE ISSUES
URBAN SPRAWL Urban development in the United States is generally determined by the location of landforms and the abundance of natural resources.

A HUMAN PERSPECTIVE The beauty and abundance of the land was a source of wonder to early explorers of North America. One who traveled the Atlantic coast referred to the "amazing extent of uncultivated land, covered with forests, and intermixed with vast lakes and marshes." A 17th-century French expedition described "a beautiful river, large, broad, and deep" (the Mississippi). Still others found "an unbounded prairie" (the Great Plains), "shining mountains" (the Rocky Mountains), and "an infinite number of fish" (along the Pacific coast). To the continent's first settlers, the land was "strong and it was beautiful all around," according to an old Native American song.

Landscape Influenced Development

The United States and Canada occupy the central and northern four-fifths of the continent of North America. Culturally, the region is known as Anglo America because both countries were colonies of Great Britain at one time and because most of the people speak English. (The southern one-fifth of the continent—Mexico—is part of Latin America.) The two countries are bound together not only by physical geography and cultural heritage, but also by strong economic and political ties.

VAST LANDS The United States and Canada extend across North America from the Atlantic Ocean on the east to the Pacific on the west, and from the Arctic Ocean on the north to the Gulf of Mexico on the south (only the United States). In total area, each ranks among the largest countries of the world. Canada ranks second, behind Russia, and the United States is third. Together, they fill one-eighth of the land surface of the earth.

ABUNDANT RESOURCES In addition to their huge landmass, the United States and Canada are rich in natural resources. They have fertile soils, ample supplies of water, vast forests, and large deposits of a variety of minerals. This geographic richness has for centuries attracted immigrants from around the world and has enabled both countries to develop into global economic powers.

LOCATION Pittsburgh, Pennsylvania, is located where the Allegheny and Monongahela rivers meet to form the Ohio River.

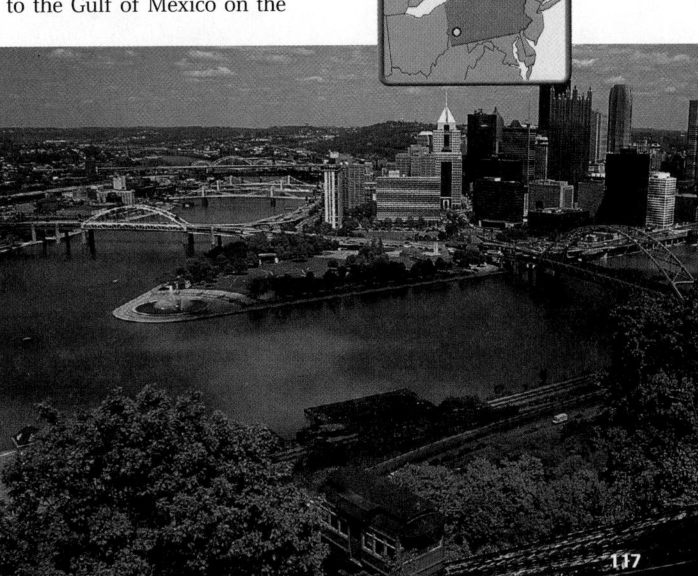

117

SECTION 1 OBJECTIVES

1. Identify the U.S. and Canada's main geographic features.
2. Examine varied landforms in relation to American and Canadian lifestyles.
3. Identify important U.S. and Canadian natural resources and how they influence life in each country.

SKILLBUILDERS: Interpreting Maps pp. 120, 121

 **GeographicThinking**

Making Comparisons, p. 119, 120
Using the Atlas, p. 121
Making Generalizations, p. 122

Focus & Motivate

How did the natural features and abundant resources help the development of the United States and Canada? *(Variety of landforms and resources drew settlers to region.)*

Instruct: Objective 1

Landscape Influenced Development

- What large bodies of water surround the United States and Canada? *(Atlantic and Pacific oceans, Gulf of Mexico, Arctic Ocean)*
- Which major landforms and/or waterways do the United States and Canada share? *(Rocky Mountains, Great Lakes, St. Lawrence River, Great Plains, Atlantic and Pacific oceans)*
- How do Canada and the United States rank in size compared with other countries? *(second and third)*

 **In-Depth Resources: Unit 2**
- Guided Reading, p. 3

SECTION 1 PROGRAM RESOURCES

 **In-Depth Resources: Unit 2**
- Guided Reading, p. 3
- Skillbuilder Practice, p. 8
- Building Vocabulary, p. 9
- Reteaching Activity, p. 10
- GeoWorkshops, pp. 43–44

 **Guided Reading Workbook**
- Section 1

 **Access for Students Acquiring English/ESL**
- Guided Reading, p. 23
- Skillbuilder Practice, p. 26

 **Formal Assessment**
- Section Quiz, p. 68

Integrated Assessment
- Rubric for a sketch map, 2.1

INTEGRATED TECHNOLOGY

Chapter Summaries

 **Power Presentations**

hmhsocialstudies.com

TEST-TAKING RESOURCES

 **Strategies for Test Preparation**

 **Test Practice Transparencies TT16**

Online Test Practice

Interpreting Maps

Landforms of North America

Have students locate the Arctic Coastal Plain and Piedmont region. Then have them identify two U.S. states or Canadian provinces located in the Great Plains. Ask them which U.S. state or Canadian province seems to have the most diverse physical landforms. *(Saskatchewan, Alberta, Wyoming, Montana, Colorado, etc.; British Columbia and Yukon Territory)*

Interpreting Photographs

East Quoddy Head in New Brunswick

This is one of the oldest lighthouses in Canada, established in 1829. It sits at the northern tip of Campobello Island just off East Quoddy Head. Ask students to describe two characteristics of the natural setting. *(rocky, small outcropping)*

Great Regina Plain in Saskatchewan

Ask students to identify within which landform(s) the Great Regina Plain is located. *(Great Plains or Interior Plains)*

Cypress Gardens in Florida

Point out that the bald cypress trees are indigenous to swampy areas in Florida. Ask students what might attract visitors to the area. *(water sports, alligator sightings, beauty of natural landscape)*

Landform Regions of the U.S. and Canada

1 East Quoddy Head in New Brunswick

2 Great Regina Plain in Saskatchewan

3 Cypress Gardens in Florida

DIFFERENTIATING INSTRUCTION — LESS PROFICIENT READERS

ORGANIZING INFORMATION

Objective To grasp the main idea by organizing textual information visually

Class Time 15-20 minutes

Task Create a chart

Directions Draw a chart on the board that students can copy in their notebooks. Have them fill in key information for each landform.

FEATURES OF CANADIAN AND U.S. LANDFORMS

Appalachian Mountains	Great Plains	Canadian Shield	Rocky Mountains
Eastern mountain chain	Mostly treeless area	Rocky, flat region	Western mountain chain
1,600 miles from Newfoundland to Alabama	4,000 feet above sea level	Lies far north in Canada	Extend 3,000 miles from Alaska to New Mexico
Include Green, Catskill, Blue Ridge, and Smoky Mountains	Run from southern Texas up through southern Canada	Covers about 1.8 million square miles	Line of highest points makes up Continental Divide
400 million years old		Encircles Hudson Bay	80 million years old

Many and Varied Landforms

All major types of landforms are found in the United States and Canada. If you look at the map on the opposite page, you will see that both countries share many of these landforms. The most prominent are eastern and western mountain chains and enormous interior plains.

THE EASTERN LOWLANDS A flat, coastal plain runs along the Atlantic Ocean and the Gulf of Mexico. One section, called the Atlantic Coastal Plain, begins as narrow lowland in the northeastern United States and widens as it extends southward into Florida. This area features many excellent harbors. A broader section of the plain—the Gulf Coastal Plain—stretches along the Gulf of Mexico from Florida into Texas. The Mississippi River empties into the Gulf from this region.

Between these plains and the nearby Appalachian (A•puh•LAY•chun) Highlands is a low plateau called the Piedmont (PEED•MAHNT). This area of rolling hills contains many fast-flowing rivers and streams.

BACKGROUND
The word *piedmont* comes from *pied,* meaning "foot," and *mont,* for "mountain." A piedmont is found at the foot of a mountain chain.

US & CANADA

THE APPALACHIAN HIGHLANDS West of the coastal plain are the Appalachian highlands. The gently sloping **Appalachian Mountains** are in this region. They are one of the two major mountain chains in the United States and Canada. Both chains run north to south. The Appalachian Mountains extend some 1,600 miles from Newfoundland in Canada to Alabama. There are several mountain ranges in the Appalachian system. Among them are the Green and the Catskill mountains in the north and the Blue Ridge and the Great Smoky mountains in the south.

Because the Appalachians are very old—more than 400 million years old—they have been eroded by the elements. Many peaks are only between 1,200 and 2,400 feet high. The Appalachian Trail, a scenic hiking path 2,160 miles long, spans almost the entire length of the chain.

THE INTERIOR LOWLANDS A huge expanse of mainly level land covers the interior of North America. It was flattened by huge glaciers thousands of years ago. The terrain includes lowlands, rolling hills, thousands of lakes and rivers, and some of the world's most fertile soils.

The interior lowlands are divided into three subregions: the Interior Plains, the Great Plains, and the Canadian Shield. The Interior Plains spread out from the Appalachians to about 300 miles west of the Mississippi River. They gradually rise from a few hundred feet above sea level to about 2,000 feet. To the west are the **Great Plains,** a largely treeless area that continues the ascent to about 4,000 feet. The **Canadian Shield** lies farther north. This rocky, mainly flat area covers nearly 2 million square miles around Hudson Bay. It averages 1,500 feet above sea level but reaches over 5,000 feet in Labrador. A

A. Answer the Canadian Shield

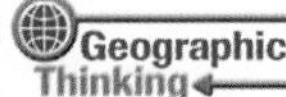

Geographic Thinking

Making Comparisons
A Which of the interior lowlands has the highest elevation?

THE WESTERN MOUNTAINS, PLATEAUS, AND BASINS West of the plains are the massive, rugged **Rocky Mountains,** the other major mountain system of the

5 THEMES

PLACE

Death Valley

Death Valley is hot–very, very hot. Temperatures can top 130°F. Few forms of life can survive its intense heat for long periods. Land features called Dead Man Pass, Funeral Mountains, and Starvation Canyon are reminders of the danger.

Death Valley (shown below) is located at the western edge of the Great Basin in California. It is the hottest point in North America. And at 282 feet below sea level, it also is the lowest point in the Western Hemisphere.

Instruct: Objective 2

Many and Varied Landforms

- Which mountain range is oldest? *(Appalachian Mountains)*
- What are two differences between the Rocky Mountains and the Appalachian Mountains? *(Rocky Mountains are younger; Appalachians are more eroded; Rockies extend over 3,000 miles)*
- What U.S. states and Canadian territories/provinces do the Great Plains encompass? *(parts of Alberta, Saskatchewan, Texas, North Dakota, South Dakota, Nebraska, and Kansas; most of Colorado, Wyoming, Montana)*

In-Depth Resources: Unit 2
- GeoWorkshops, pp. 43–44

5 THEMES

Place: Death Valley

Let students know that near the springs and marshes at Death Valley's edges, saltgrass, rushes, and pickleweed grow. Animals exist in and around the valley. Ask students why would it seem to visitors that there is no animal life, why it might be hard for animals to survive there, and what a desert might be like at night. *(The animals are not out in the daytime or are mostly nocturnal; there are few food or water sources; cold, more animal activity.)*

ACTIVITY OPTION **SKILLBUILDER LESSON**

ANALYZING DATA

Explaining the Skill Tell students that analyzing data in a map can give them a good grounding in the physical geography and natural resources of a country or continent. Explain that in the case of the United States and Canada, analyzing data can help them see areas of comparison.

Have students refer to the map on page 120 and study the various resources shown throughout Canada and the United States.

In-Depth Resources: Unit 2
- Skillbuilder Practice, p. 8

Applying the Skill Have students pair up and discuss the following questions. After 10 minutes have each pair share their answers with the class.

- Locate Prince Edward Island (refer to other country maps as necessary). How does it compare in resources to Hawaii? *(It has many more.)*
- Where does most iron ore come from? *(Great Lakes area)*
- Where are most of Alaska's resources located? *(on the coasts)*

United States and Canada. The Rockies are a series of ranges that extend about 3,000 miles from Alaska south to New Mexico. Because they are relatively young—about 80 million years old—the Rockies have not been eroded like the Appalachians. Many of their jagged, snow-covered peaks are more than 12,000 feet high. The **Continental Divide** is the line of highest points in the Rockies that marks the separation between rivers flowing eastward and westward. B

Between the Rockies and the Pacific Ocean is an area of mixed landforms. A series of ranges, including the Sierra Nevada and the Cascade Range, run parallel to the Pacific coastline from California to Alaska. North America's highest peak—Mt. McKinley (also called by its Native American name, Denali)—is in Alaska, towering 20,320 feet above sea level. Major earthquakes occur near the Pacific ranges. Between these

Geographic Thinking

Making Comparisons

B How do the Rockies differ from the Appalachians?

B. Answer The Rockies are younger and higher.

Interpreting Maps

Resources of North America

Have students examine the map. Ask what types of resources seem to appear most in the United States. *(petroleum, timber, natural gas)* Then ask which area of Canada and which area of the United States seem to have the most diverse resources. *(Ontario; Great Lakes region; northwest)*

SKILLBUILDER ANSWERS

1. Petroleum is found in the southern and western United States.

2. Hydroelectric power is more widespread in Canada than in the United States.

Natural Resources of the U.S. and Canada

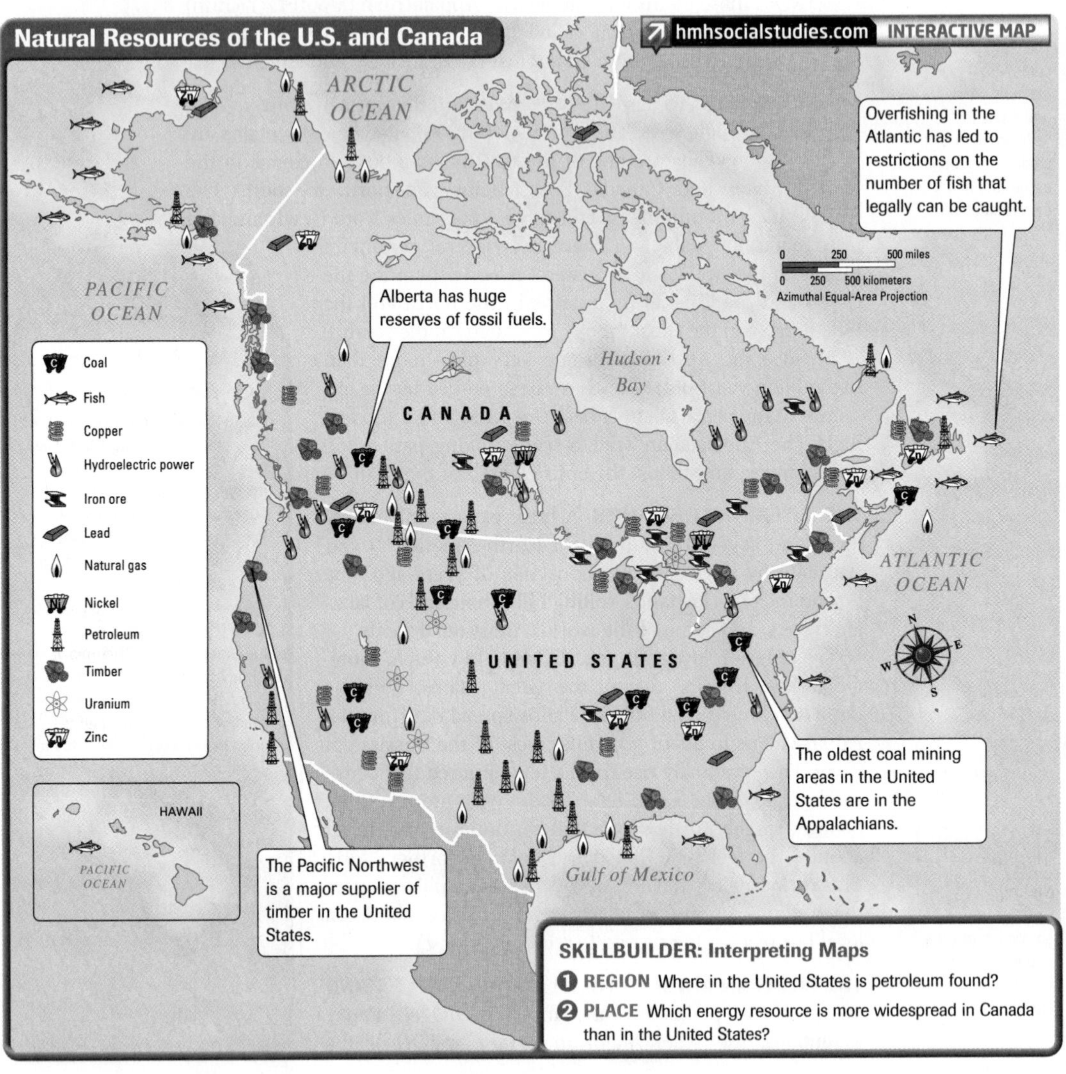

SKILLBUILDER: Interpreting Maps

1. **REGION** Where in the United States is petroleum found?
2. **PLACE** Which energy resource is more widespread in Canada than in the United States?

DIFFERENTIATING INSTRUCTION **STUDENTS ACQUIRING ENGLISH/ESL**

UNDERSTANDING CONTEXT

Objective To understand the meaning of a word by its context

Class Time 10 minutes

Task Make connections with surrounding sentences and information to help define a word

Directions Write the word *fertile* on the board. Direct students to the appearance of the word in the last paragraph (section "Land and Forests") on page 121. Have students tell you what they think the word means. Then ask them to tell you words from surrounding sentences that seem to give clues to the meaning of the word fertile. List those other words on the board. Correct or confirm the students' original definition of the word.

FERTILE
Guessed meaning: thick or a lot of it
Clue words from surrounding sentences: 1. Richest 2. Productive 3. Leading 4. Agricultural
Actual definition: "bearing or producing crops or vegetation abundantly; rich in material needed to sustain plant growth; fruitful"

ranges and the Rockies are steep cliffs, deep canyons, and lowland desert areas called basins.

THE ISLANDS Canada's northernmost lands are islands riding the icy seas near the Arctic Circle. Three of the islands—Ellesmere, Victoria, and Baffin—are huge. In North America, only Greenland is larger.

Two island chains created by volcanic activity are part of the westernmost United States. The rugged, treeless Aleutian Islands extend in an arc off the coast of Alaska. The lush, tropical Hawaiian Islands, though politically part of the United States, are not geographically part of North America. They lie in the central Pacific, about 2,400 miles to the southwest.

Resources Shape Ways of Life

The landforms of the United States and Canada hold a rich variety and abundance of natural resources. Both countries are leading agricultural and industrial nations because of this wealth of resources.

OCEANS AND WATERWAYS The United States and Canada possess ample water resources. They are bounded by three oceans—Atlantic, Pacific, and Arctic. The United States is also bounded by the Gulf of Mexico. As a result, both countries have important shipping and fishing industries.

Inland, large rivers and lakes serve as sources of transportation, hydroelectric power, irrigation, fresh water, and fisheries. Eight of the world's 15 largest lakes are found in this region. Among these are the **Great Lakes**—Huron, Ontario, Michigan, Erie, and Superior. As you will see on page 129, these lakes and the **St. Lawrence River** form one of the world's major shipping routes.

The continent's longest and busiest river system is the Mississippi-Missouri-Ohio. The Mississippi River runs almost the north-south length of the United States, from Minnesota to the Gulf of Mexico. (See map at right.) The Mississippi's main tributaries, the Ohio and Missouri rivers, are major rivers in their own right. Canada's longest river is the **Mackenzie River,** which is part of a river system that flows across the Northwest Territories to the Arctic Ocean. C

Geographic Thinking

Using the Atlas Use the map on page 103. Find the Mackenzie River. Into which body of water does it empty?

C. Answer the Arctic Ocean

LAND AND FORESTS One of the richest natural resources of the United States and Canada is the land itself. Both countries are large and contain some of the most fertile soils in the world. In fact, the land is so productive that North America is the world's leading food exporter. Much of this agricultural land is found in the plains regions and in river valleys.

hmhsocialstudies.com INTERACTIVE MAP

The Mississippi River

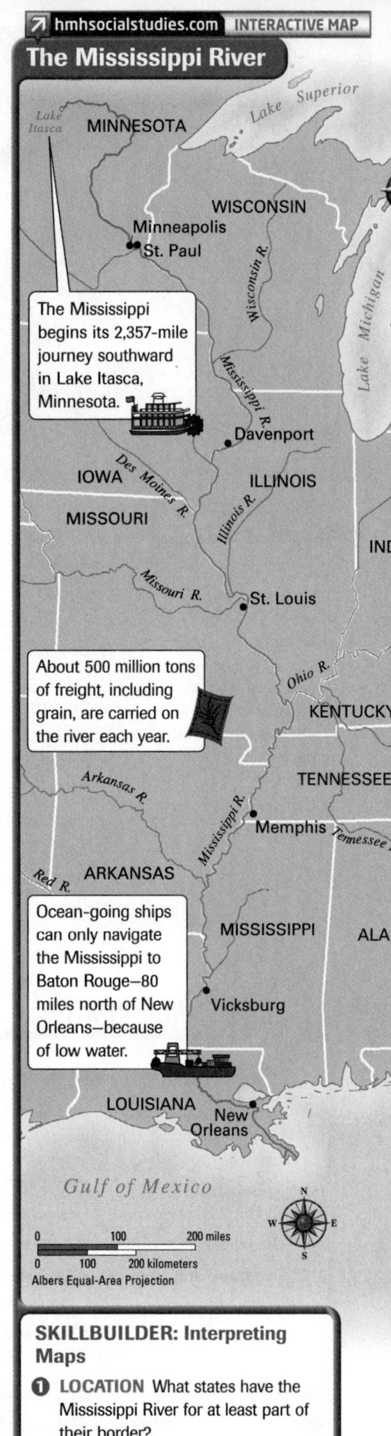

SKILLBUILDER: Interpreting Maps

1. **LOCATION** What states have the Mississippi River for at least part of their border?
2. **MOVEMENT** What rivers empty into the Mississippi?

Interpreting Maps

The Mississippi River

Have students examine the map. Ask what other two rivers besides the Mississippi are a part of North America's longest river system. *(Missouri River and Ohio River)* Then ask what resources would most likely be transported on the Mississippi. *(Grain, timber, iron)*

SKILLBUILDER ANSWERS

1. Minnesota, Wisconsin, Iowa, Illinois, Missouri, Kentucky, Tennessee, Arkansas, Mississippi, and Louisiana
2. Wisconsin, Des Moines, Illinois, Missouri, Ohio, and Arkansas rivers

Instruct: Objective 3

Resources Shape Ways of Life

- What are three common resources in the United States? *(petroleum, natural gas, coal)*
- What are three common resources in Canada? *(hydroelectric power, copper, timber)*
- Which country produces more minerals? *(neither; they are about equal)*
- Why doesn't the United States export as many minerals as Canada? *(It uses up too many to export.)*

More About

The Mississippi Delta

Located about 80 miles southeast of New Orleans, the Mississippi Delta is losing miles of land per year because of various human activities.

DIFFERENTIATING INSTRUCTION | LESS PROFICIENT READERS

RECALLING DETAILS

Some students may have trouble recalling names of the region's waterways. To help them remember key terms and important details, have them create a web or set of webs for rivers and waterways. Around each term, students can add facts about important details. You might provide a web like the one shown here as a model.

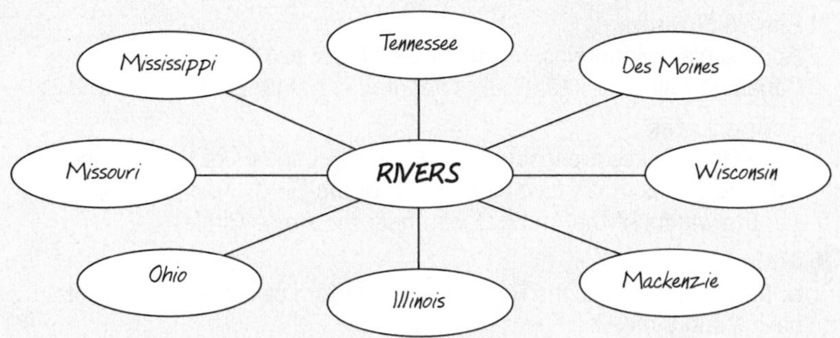

Interpreting Photographs

West Virginia Coal Mine

Tell students that coal provides one of the cheapest forms of energy. Ask students how they think a coal mine might affect the surrounding area. *(employment; economic growth or depression if closed; health risks; damage to ecosystem)*

CAPTION ANSWER the northern Great Plains

Assess & Reteach

GeoFocus Have students complete the sections on landforms and resources in their graphic organizers.

 **Formal Assessment**
- Section Quiz, p. 68

Reteaching Activity
Divide the class into small groups. Assign one section objective to each group. Have the students in each group work together to write a brief summary of that objective. Ask one member from each group to share their summaries with the class.

 **In-Depth Resources: Unit 2**
- Reteaching Activity, p. 10

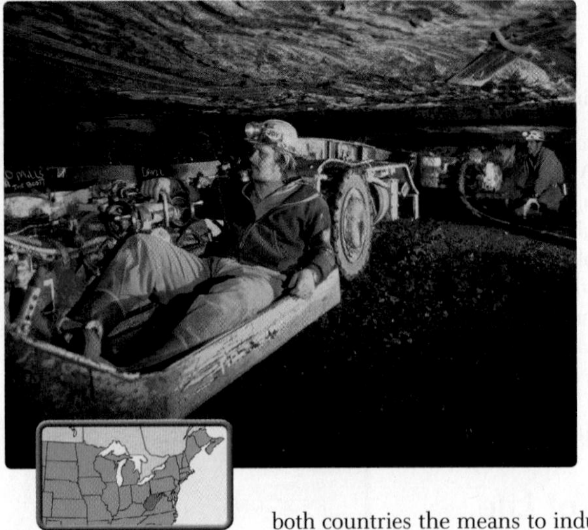

REGION This West Virginia coal mine is in one of the world's most important coal-producing regions—the Appalachian highlands. **What other region in North America is an important coal producer?**

The United States and Canada also have huge forests. About one-half of Canada is covered by woodlands, as is one-third of the United States. Canada's forests cover more land than those of the United States, but the United States has more kinds of trees because of its more varied climate. Both countries are major producers of lumber and forest products.

MINERALS AND FOSSIL FUELS As you saw on the map on page 120, the United States and Canada have large quantities and varieties of minerals and fossil fuels. These resources gave both countries the means to industrialize rapidly.

Valuable deposits of iron ore, nickel, copper, gold, and uranium are found in the Canadian Shield. Scattered among the western mountains are gold, silver, copper, and uranium. Both countries also have substantial deposits of coal, natural gas, and oil, and well-developed networks for distributing these energy-producing fossil fuels. Important coal-producing areas are the Appalachian highlands and the northern Great Plains. Significant deposits of oil and natural gas are found in the Great Plains, Alaska, and along the Gulf of Mexico. D

The United States is the world's biggest consumer of energy resources. Its need for these fuels is so great that it is a major importer. In fact, most of Canada's energy exports go to its neighbor to the south.

In the next section, you will read how some landforms of the United States and Canada have affected climate and vegetation patterns.

D. Answer Oil and natural gas are important because they are needed as fuel for industry.

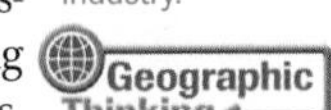

Seeing Patterns
D Why are oil and natural gas important to highly-industrialized nations?

Section 1 Assessment

1 Places & Terms
Identify and explain where in the region these would be found.
- Appalachian Mountains
- Great Plains
- Canadian Shield
- Rocky Mountains
- Great Lakes

2 Taking Notes
LOCATION Review the notes you took for this section.

Landforms	
Resources	

- What is the relative location of the Great Lakes?
- What is the relative location of most of Canada's islands?

3 Main Ideas
a. What landforms are shared by the United States and Canada?
b. Why are the Great Lakes important to both the United States and Canada?
c. Why do most of Canada's energy exports go to the United States?

4 Geographic Thinking
Making Generalizations
What makes the United States and Canada leading industrial nations? **Think about:**
- available resources
- oceans and waterways

See Skillbuilder Handbook, page R6.

GeoActivity

EXPLORING LOCAL GEOGRAPHY Using the maps on pages 103 and 118, identify the landforms located in your state. Then draw a **sketch map** of your state showing the major landforms and water bodies.

SECTION 1 ASSESSMENT ANSWERS

1. Places & Terms
Appalachian Mountains, p. 119; Great Plains, p. 119
Canadian Shield, p. 119; Rocky Mountains, p. 119; Great Lakes, p. 121

2. Taking Notes
- The Great Lakes are located between the countries of Canada and the United States in the east central part of the North American continent.
- in the waters of the Arctic Ocean near the Arctic Circle

3. Main Ideas
a. the Appalachians, the Rockies, the Interior Lowlands, intermountain basins and plateaus
b. They provide transportation, hydroelectric power, irrigation, fresh water, and fisheries for both nations.
c. The United States is the largest consumer of energy in the world. It is also close to Canada, and transportation is easier and cheaper.

4. Geographic Thinking
Both have huge reserves of important natural resources for producing products, and the ability to transport them.

GeoActivity

 **Integrated Assessment**
- Rubric for a sketch map, 2.1

Climate and Vegetation

Main Ideas

- Almost every type of climate is found in the 50 United States because they extend over such a large area north to south.
- Canada's cold climate is related to its location in the far northern latitudes.

Places & Terms

permafrost
prevailing westerlies
Everglades

CONNECT TO THE ISSUES
URBAN SPRAWL The rapid spread of urban sprawl has led to the loss of much vegetation in both the United States and Canada.

US & CANADA

A HUMAN PERSPECTIVE A little gold and bitter cold—that is what thousands of prospectors found in Alaska and the Yukon Territory during the Klondike gold rushes of the 1890s. Most of these fortune hunters were unprepared for the harsh climate and inhospitable land of the far north. Winters were long and cold, the ground frozen. Ice fogs, blizzards, and avalanches were regular occurrences. You could lose fingers and toes—even your life—in the cold. But hardy souls stuck it out. Legend has it that one miner, Bishop Stringer, kept himself alive by boiling his sealskin and walrus-sole boots and then drinking the broth.

Shared Climates and Vegetation

The United States and Canada have more in common than just frigid winter temperatures where Alaska meets northwestern Canada. Other shared climate and vegetation zones are found along their joint border at the southern end of Canada and the northern end of the United States.

If you look at the map on page 125, you will see that the United States has more climate zones than Canada. This variety, ranging from tundra to tropical, occurs because the country extends over such a large area north to south. Most of the United States is located in the mid-latitudes, where the climates are moderate. Canada is colder because so much of it lies far north in the higher latitudes.

COLDER CLIMATES The Arctic coast of Alaska and Canada have tundra climate and vegetation. Winters are long and bitterly cold, while summers are brief and chilly. Even in July, temperatures are only around 40°F. The land is a huge, treeless plain. Much of the rest of Canada and Alaska have a subarctic climate, with very cold winters and short, mild summers. A vast forest of needle-leafed evergreens covers the area. In some places, there is **permafrost,** or permanently frozen ground.

The Rocky Mountains and the Pacific ranges have highland climate and vegetation. Temperature and vegetation vary with elevation and latitude. Generally, the temperature is colder and the vegetation is more sparse in the higher, more northerly mountains. The mountains also influence the temperature and precipitation of surrounding lower areas. For example, the

MOVEMENT The snowmobile has replaced the dogsled as transportation in many parts of the Northwest Territories. Here, a mother picks up her children from school.

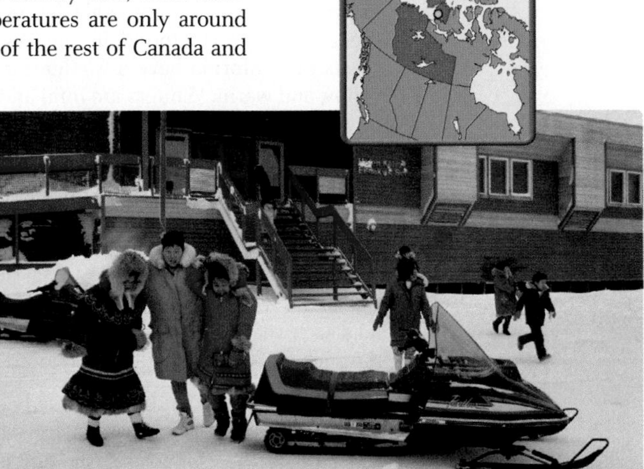

SECTION 2 OBJECTIVES

1. Examine the shared climates and vegetation of the United States and Canada.
2. Identify differences in climate and vegetation between the United States and Canada.
3. Describe the effects of extreme weather in the United States and Canada.

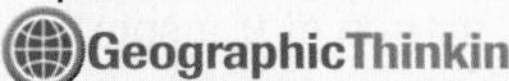

SKILLBUILDER: Interpreting Maps p. 125

GeographicThinking
Seeing Patterns, pp. 124, 126
Making Comparisons, pp. 124, 126

Focus & Motivate

In your experience, how do climates affect people's lives? *(Climates affect outdoor activities, types of jobs, transportation, and the economy of a region through such things as tourism.)*

Instruct: Objective 1

Shared Climates and Vegetation

- Why is Canada colder than the United States? *(Because it lies farther north.)*
- Which parts of Canada and the United States have the most similar climate? *(Alaska and Yukon or Northwest Territories; also area along joint U.S.-Canada border)*
- What areas in Canada and the U.S. would most likely have areas of permafrost? *(Alaska, Yukon, Northwest Territories, Nunavut)*

In-Depth Resources: Unit 2
- Guided Reading, p. 4

SECTION 2 PROGRAM RESOURCES

In-Depth Resources: Unit 2
- Guided Reading, p. 4
- Building Vocabulary, p. 9
- Reteaching Activity, p. 11

Guided Reading Workbook
- Section 2

Access for Students Acquiring English/ESL
- Guided Reading, p. 24

Formal Assessment
- Section Quiz, p. 69

Integrated Assessment
- Rubrics for a database, 2.6

INTEGRATED TECHNOLOGY

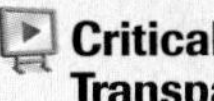

Critical Thinking Transparencies CT 37
- Land and Climate of U.S. and Canada

Power Presentations

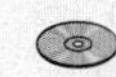

Test Generator
- Section Quiz

hmhsocialstudies.com

TEST-TAKING RESOURCES

Strategies for Test Preparation

Test Practice Transparencies TT17

Online Test Practice

More About

Transportation in Northwest Territories

The climate of the Northwest Territories is mostly subarctic, with freezing temperatures and snow for most months of the year. Transportation is more limited than in other areas, but people and goods move in and out by air service, waterways, railroads, and highways. Winter-ready vehicles such as snowmobiles have become a good source of transportation, especially in more remote areas.

Instruct: Objective 

Differences in Climate and Vegetation

- What kinds of climates do not exist in Canada? *(desert or tropical)*
- Which two states in the United States have tropical climates? *(Florida, Hawaii)*
- Where are the Everglades located? *(Florida)*
- Within which climate would you most likely find a rain forest? *(tropical)*

Critical Thinking Transparencies CT37
- Land and Climate of the United States and Canada

coastal ranges protect the coast from cold Arctic air from the interior. In the United States, the western mountains trap Pacific moisture. This makes lands west of the mountains rainy and those east very dry.

MODERATE CLIMATES The north central and northeastern United States and southern Canada near the U.S. border have a humid continental climate. Winters are cold and summers warm. Climate and soil make this one of the world's most productive agricultural areas, yielding an abundance of dairy products, grain, and livestock. In the northern part of this climate zone, summers are short. There are mixed forests of deciduous and needle-leafed evergreen trees. Most of the population of Canada is concentrated here. In the southern part of this zone, which is in the United States, summers are longer. For the most part, deciduous forests are found east of the Mississippi River and temperate grasslands are found to the west. A

The Pacific coast from northern California to southern Alaska, which includes British Columbia, has a climate described as marine west coast. This climate is affected by Pacific Ocean currents, the coastal mountains, and the **prevailing westerlies**—winds that blow from west to east in the middle of the latitudes. The summers are moderately warm. The winters are long and mild, but rainy and foggy. Vegetation is mixed, including dense forests of broad-leafed deciduous trees, needle-leafed evergreens, and giant California redwoods. The Washington coast even has a cool, wet rain forest.

Geographic Thinking

Seeing Patterns

A Why is most of Canada's population clustered in the humid continental region?

A. Answer Most of Canada's population lives in the south because the other regions are too cold.

Differences in Climate and Vegetation

The milder, dry, and tropical climates of North America are found south of 40°N latitude. Much of the United States is located in these climate zones; little of Canada is.

MILDER CLIMATES Most southern states have a humid subtropical climate. This means that summers are hot and muggy, with temperatures ranging from about 75°F to 90°F. Winters are usually mild and cool. Moist air from the Gulf of Mexico brings rain during the winter. The combination of mild temperatures and adequate rainfall provides a long growing season for a variety of crops—from citrus fruits in Florida to peanuts in Georgia. Broad-leafed evergreen trees and needle-leafed evergreen trees are found in this region. The central and southern coasts of California have a Mediterranean climate. Summers are dry, sunny, and warm. Winters are mild and somewhat rainy. Temperatures range from 50°F to 80°F year-round. A long growing season and irrigation make this a rich farming area for fruits and vegetables. B

Geographic Thinking

Making Comparisons

B Why don't central and southern California have a marine west coast climate?

B. Answer They are too far south to be significantly affected by the Pacific Ocean currents.

DRY CLIMATES The Great Plains and dry northern parts of the Great Basin have a semiarid climate. This means dry weather—only about 15 inches of rain annually—and vegetation that is mainly short grasses and shrubs. The southwestern states have a desert climate. In these states, the weather is usually hot and dry. Less than 10 inches of rain falls each year. Some cactus plants thrive, but much of the area is barren rock or sand. Large desert areas are the Mojave and the Sonoran.

TROPICAL CLIMATES In the United States, only Hawaii and southern Florida have tropical climates. The islands of Hawaii have a tropical wet climate that supports lush rain forests. Temperatures vary only

ACTIVITY OPTION **INTERNET RESEARCH**

FACT FINDING

Objective To use an Internet source to locate additional information on the United States and Canada

Class Time 30 minutes

Task Find facts on Web site

Directions Have students go to **hmhsocialstudies.com.** Ask them to click on "Research Links." Then have them select the United States and then Canada and write down two facts about each country that were not included in the textbook. Ask students to share their facts with the rest of the class.

OPTIONAL ACTIVITY If Internet access is limited, have students perform this activity with geographic reference books in the library.

Climate and Vegetation of the U.S. and Canada

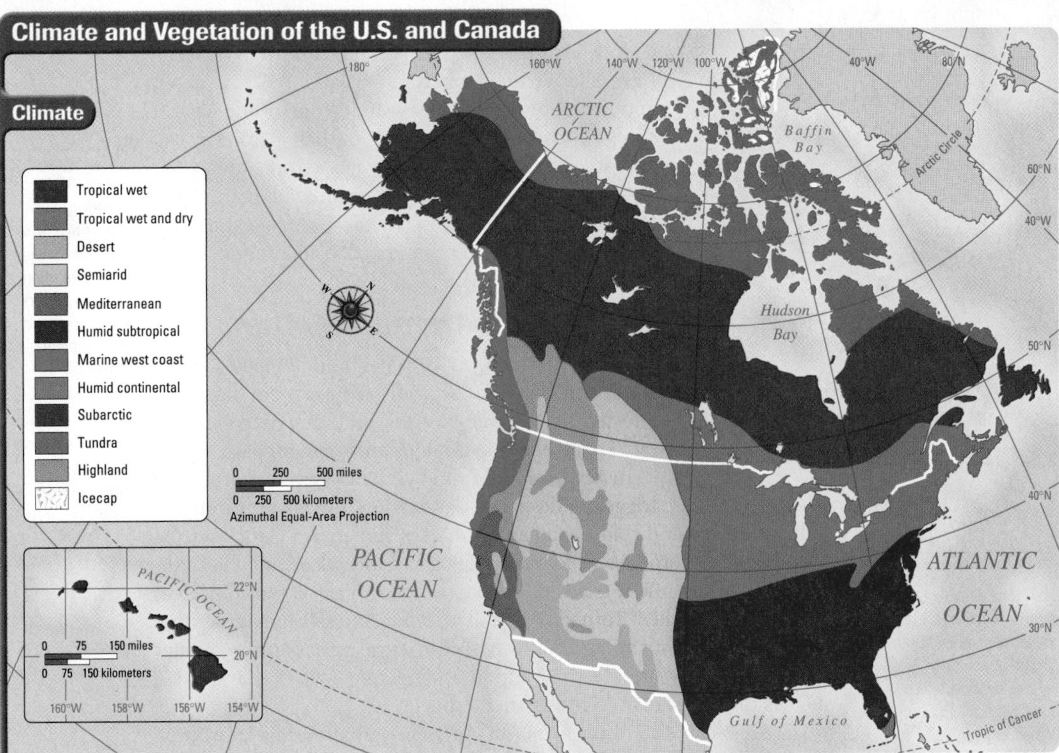

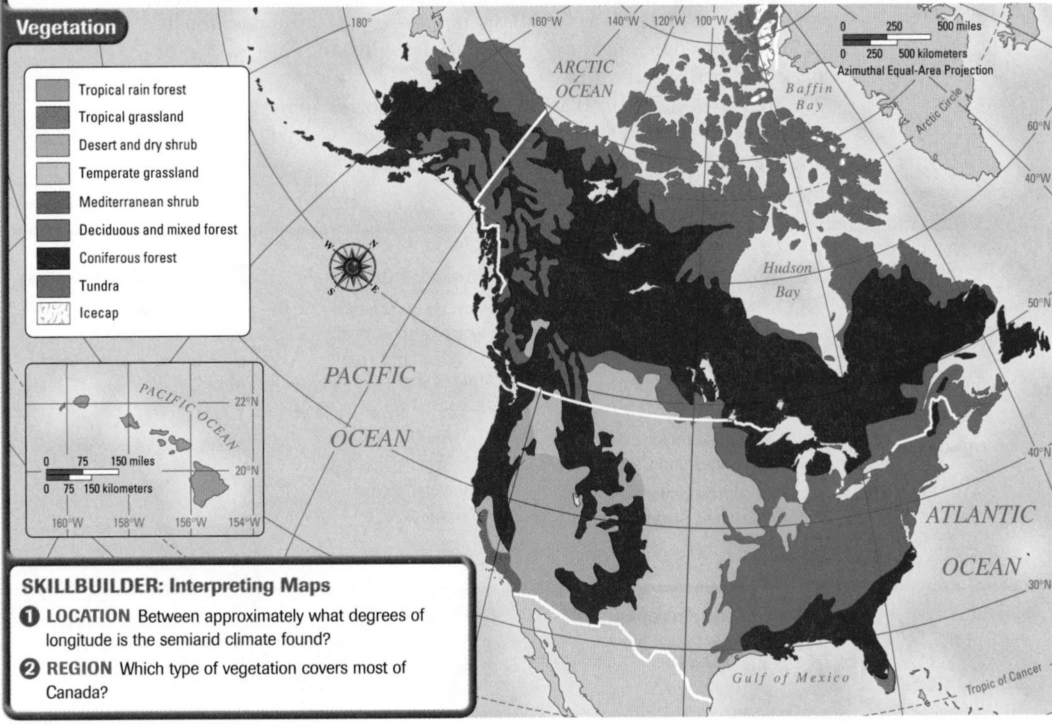

SKILLBUILDER: Interpreting Maps

1. **LOCATION** Between approximately what degrees of longitude is the semiarid climate found?
2. **REGION** Which type of vegetation covers most of Canada?

US & CANADA

Interpreting Maps

Climate and Vegetation of North America

Have students examine the map. Have them identify the most prevalent climate in the map. *(subarctic)* Have them name two states located in the semiarid climate. *(Wyoming, Colorado)* Have them list all climate types found in California. *(marine west coast, Mediterranean, semiarid, desert, and highland)*

SKILLBUILDER ANSWERS

1. between approximately 100°W and 120°W longitude **2.** coniferous forest

DIFFERENTIATING INSTRUCTION | GIFTED AND TALENTED STUDENTS

RESEARCHING SEVERE WEATHER EVENTS

Objective To develop research skills and enrich comprehension of how severe weather affects a community

Class Time One class period

Task Preparing a report about the effects of severe weather events on a community

Directions Have students do research and prepare a report on ways that a severe weather event affects a community. Have them get information on a recent severe weather event. Reports should include a description of the event (tornado, flooding, and so forth), and a brief explanation of the cause and the effects (including damage, loss of housing, disruption of daily life, lack of supplies, need for assistance, and future outlook). Encourage students to include visual aids and personal testimonials (excerpts from interviews or video footage) in their reports.

Interpreting Photographs

Snow and Ice Storms

When temperatures drop or stay just around freezing (32°F), snow can mix with rain or become sleet. This kind of ice storm, particularly with further decreases in temperature, can create dangerous conditions. Ask students what hazards are shown in the picture. *(Overhead wires and branches may be so weighed down with ice that they snap off their supports.)*

CAPTION ANSWER Hazards include slippery roads, falling trees, and downed power lines.

Instruct: Objective 3

Effects of Extreme Weather

- What kinds of extreme weather occur often in the Great Plains? *(tornadoes)*
- What areas are most at risk for flooding? *(those near major rivers)*
- What areas have suffered devastation from hurricanes? *(Gulf and Atlantic coast states)*

Assess & Reteach

GeoFocus Have students complete the section on climate and vegetation in their graphic organizer.

Formal Assessment
- Section Quiz, p. 69

Reteaching Activity

Ask students to create an outline of the information in this section. It should summarize the main points and ideas.

In-Depth Resources, Unit 2
- Reteaching Activity, p. 11

a few degrees in the 70s°F. Mount Waialeale (wy•AH•lay•AH•lay) on Kauai island receives about 460 inches of rain annually, and is one of the wettest spots on earth. Southern Florida has a tropical wet and dry climate. It is nearly always warm, but has wet and dry seasons. Vegetation is mainly tall grasses and scattered trees, like those in the **Everglades,** a huge swampland that covers some 4,000 square miles. C

Geographic Thinking

Making Comparisons
C How do climate and vegetation differ between Mediterranean and tropical climates?

C. Answer Tropical climates are warmer and wetter than the Mediterranean climate. Vegetation in tropical climates often includes lush rain forests not found in the Mediterranean climate.

Effects of Extreme Weather

Weather in the United States and Canada can be harsh and sometimes deadly. You can see the areas affected by extreme weather and climate conditions by looking at the natural hazards map on page 107.

In both cold and mild climates, severe storms can trigger widespread devastation. Warm air from the Gulf of Mexico and cold Canadian air masses sometimes clash over the plains region to produce violent thunderstorms, tornadoes, and blizzards. As you read in Unit 1, tornadoes strike so often in an area of the Great Plains that it is called "Tornado Alley." In summer and fall, hurricanes that sweep along the Atlantic and Gulf coasts can cause great damage. Winter snowstorms may bring normal life to a temporary halt in many cities, such as the one shown in the photo on this page.

REGION Deadly ice storms like this one in Watertown, New York, create chaos each winter, especially in heavily populated areas. **What are some of the hazards of this form of extreme weather?**

Disasters can also result from too much precipitation in a short time or too little over a long period. Heavy rainfall can cause flooding. Lands along major rivers, such as the Mississippi, are especially at risk. Too little rain or too much heat may bring on droughts and dust storms or spark destructive forest fires.

In this section, you read about the varied climates and vegetation of the United States and Canada. In the next section, you will learn how physical geography has shaped life in these countries.

Section 2 Assessment

1 Places & Terms

Identify and explain where in the region these would be found.
- permafrost
- prevailing westerlies
- Everglades

2 Taking Notes

REGION Review the notes you took for this section.

Climate and Vegetation	

- What climate regions do the United States and Canada share?
- What climate regions are found in the United States but not in Canada?

3 Main Ideas

a. How do the prevailing westerlies change the climate of parts of the United States and Canada?
b. In which region would you find the dry climates?
c. In which climate type would you find the Everglades?

4 Geographic Thinking

Seeing Patterns Why doesn't all of Alaska have cold, snowy winters? **Think about:**
- location
- prevailing westerlies

MAKING COMPARISONS Make a list of five Canadian cities and five U.S. cities. Then use the Internet to find out the average monthly temperature and monthly rainfall for each city. Create a **database** with the information. Then summarize your findings.

Section 2 Assessment Answers

1. Places & Terms
permafrost, p. 123; prevailing westerlies, p. 124; Everglades, p. 126

2. Taking Notes
- tundra, subarctic, humid continental, marine west coast, semiarid, highland
- tropical wet, tropical wet and dry, desert, Mediterranean, humid subtropical

3. Main Ideas
a. They bring warmer air temperatures and rain to the Pacific coast from northern California to southern Alaska.
b. the Great Plains and part of the Great Basin
c. The Everglades are found in the tropical wet and dry climate.

4. Geographic Thinking
The southern part of Alaska is located on the west coast of North America. This area is influenced by the prevailing westerlies that bring warmer air and rain to the area.

GeoActivity

Integrated Assessment
- Rubric for a database, 2.6

3 Human–Environment Interaction

Main Ideas
- Humans have dramatically changed the face of North America.
- European settlements in the United States and Canada expanded from east to west.

Places & Terms
nomad
Beringia
St. Lawrence Seaway
lock

CONNECT TO THE ISSUES
URBAN SPRAWL The spreading of cities and suburbs over wider areas—urban sprawl—is causing problems.

US & CANADA

A HUMAN PERSPECTIVE The sun-baked American Southwest was a harsh environment for its early inhabitants, the ancestors of today's Pueblo peoples. But these early settlers made good use of available resources. From the land, they took clay and stone building materials. They built multi-room, apartment-like dwellings in cliffs. This gave protection against daytime heat, nighttime cold, and human and animal enemies. From plants and animals, the early settlers got food and clothing. They survived because they adapted to their environment.

Settlement and Agriculture Alter the Land

Before humans came, North American landforms were changed only by natural forces, such as weathering and erosion. That changed when the first settlers—the ancestors of the native peoples of North America—arrived thousands of years ago.

SETTLEMENT The first inhabitants of the area of North America now known as the United States and Canada were **nomads,** people who move from place to place. Some archaeologists believe that they probably migrated from Asia over **Beringia,** a land bridge that once connected Siberia and Alaska. Alternative migration theories, such as a coastal migration, are also being investigated. These early migrants moved about the land. They hunted game, fished, and gathered edible wild plants. These first Americans made temporary settlements along coastlines and near rivers and streams. They adjusted to extremes of temperature and climate. They also adapted to the region's many natural environments, including mountains, forests, plains, and deserts.

AGRICULTURE Many early settlements became permanent after agriculture replaced hunting and gathering as the primary method of food production about 3,000 years ago. When people began to cultivate crops, they changed the landscape to meet their needs. In wooded areas, early farmers cut down trees for lumber to build houses and to burn as fuel. To plant crops, they plowed the rich soil of river valleys and flood plains using hoes of wood, stone, and bone. They dug ditches for irrigation. Vegetables they first cultivated—corn, beans, and squash—are now staples around the world.

Agriculture remains an important economic activity in the region. In fact, both countries are leading exporters of agricultural products.

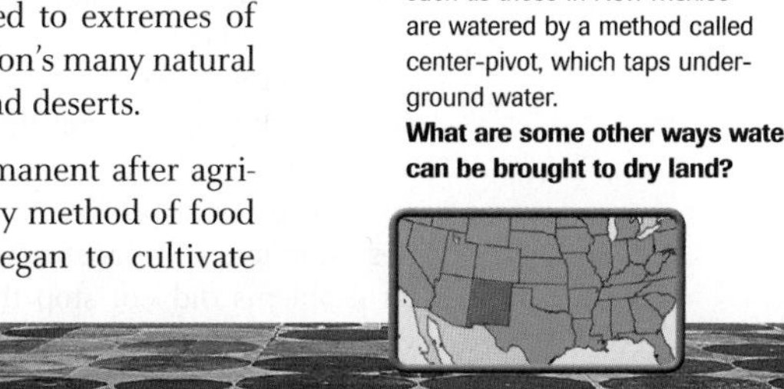

REGION Irrigation has opened land in dry areas to farming. Tracts such as these in New Mexico are watered by a method called center-pivot, which taps underground water.
What are some other ways water can be brought to dry land?

127

SECTION 3 OBJECTIVES

1. Examine how settlement and agriculture have changed the land in Canada and the U.S.
2. Describe factors that make sites suitable for building cities.
3. Identify methods of overcoming distances in the U.S. and Canada.

SKILLBUILDER: Interpreting Graphics p. 129

GeographicThinking
Making Comparisons, pp. 128, 130
Seeing Patterns, p. 129
Making Inferences, p. 130

Focus & Motivate

What reasons might people have for settling an area? *(to hunt, fish, gather edible plants, farm)*

Instruct: Objective 1 appears on p. 128.

Interpreting Photographs

Farming Tracts in New Mexico
Because of New Mexico's arid climate, people there face water-supply problems. With annual rainfall averaging 12–14 inches on the plains, farmers must rely on irrigation to ensure healthy crops. Have students speculate about the cause of undeveloped sectors in the right center of the picture. *(Irrigation pipelines are not working there; farmer is allowing those areas to lie fallow.)*

CAPTION ANSWER Other ways include building dams, using canals, pumping water from lakes and rivers, and trapping rainwater.

SECTION 3 PROGRAM RESOURCES

In-Depth Resources: Unit 2
- Guided Reading, p. 5
- Building Vocabulary, p. 9
- Reteaching Activity, p. 12
- Map and Graph Skills, pp. 6–7

Guided Reading Workbook
- Section 3

Access for Students Acquiring English/ESL
- Guided Reading, p. 25
- Map and Graph Skills, pp. 27–28

Formal Assessment
- Section Quiz, p. 70

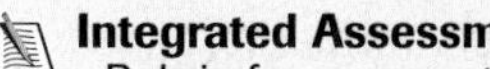
Integrated Assessment
- Rubric for a presentation, 3.6
- Rubric for a three-dimensional model, 1.10

INTEGRATED TECHNOLOGY

Power Presentations
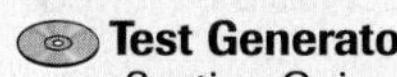
Test Generator
- Section Quiz

hmhsocialstudies.com

TEST-TAKING RESOURCES
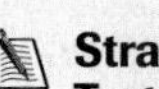
Strategies for Test Preparation

Test Practice Transparencies TT18
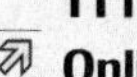
Online Test Practice

Interpreting Photographs

Los Angeles

Los Angeles has always been a city of diverse racial and ethnic groups, including whites, blacks, Latinos, Asians, and Native Americans. Although the goals of treating all residents equally and preserving their cultures are challenging, Los Angeles continues to grow and thrive.

CAPTION ANSWER Land was cleared, streets and highways were laid out, and buildings were constructed.

Instruct: Objective 

Settlement and Agriculture Alter the Land

- Where did the first inhabitants of North America come from? *(Asia)*
- Where did the first inhabitants live within North America? *(They wandered all over as nomads.)*
- What were early settlers' first food sources? *(wild game and plant foods)*

 **In-Depth Resources: Unit 2**
- Guided Reading, p. 5

Instruct: Objective 

Building Cities

- What major physical factor was most important to early settlers? *(living near water)*
- How has Montreal addressed its cold climate in urban development? *(by building underground)*
- How large an area does metropolitan Los Angeles cover? *(5,700 sq mi)*

Instruct: Objective 3 appears on p. 129

HUMAN–ENVIRONMENT INTERACTION Los Angeles sprawls out almost as far as the eye can see in this photo. **What changes were made to the environment as the city grew?**

Building Cities

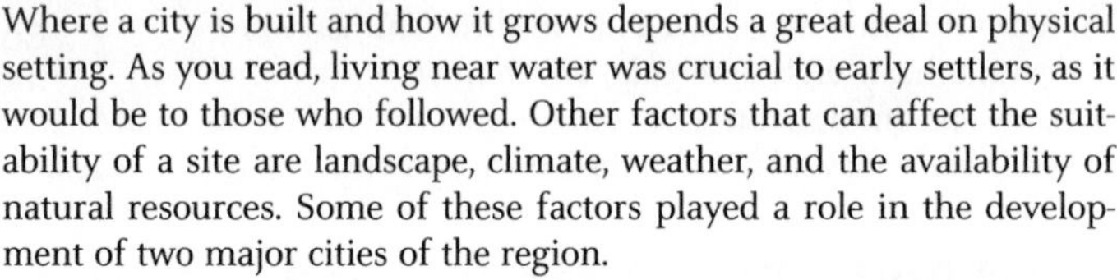

Where a city is built and how it grows depends a great deal on physical setting. As you read, living near water was crucial to early settlers, as it would be to those who followed. Other factors that can affect the suitability of a site are landscape, climate, weather, and the availability of natural resources. Some of these factors played a role in the development of two major cities of the region.

MONTREAL—ADAPTING TO THE WEATHER Montreal, Quebec, is Canada's second largest city and a major port—even though its temperature is below freezing more than 100 days each year. Montreal's location on a large island where the St. Lawrence and Ottawa rivers meet made it an appealing site to early French explorers. The French built a permanent settlement there in 1642. The community was founded at the base of Mount Royal and grew by spreading around the mountain. To make the city's severe winters more endurable, people went inside and underground. In fact, large areas of Montreal have been developed underground, including a network of shops and restaurants.

A. Answer A mild, warm climate brought many people to Los Angeles, which expanded rapidly. Montreal's cold climate forced development inside and underground.

LOS ANGELES—CREATING URBAN SPRAWL Unlike Montreal, Los Angeles, California, has a mild climate year-round. It also has a desirable location on the Pacific coast. Hundreds of thousands of people were pouring into this once small Spanish settlement by the early 1900s. As a result, the city expanded farther and farther into nearby valleys and desert-like foothills. During the 1980s, Los Angeles became the second most populous city in the United States. However, rapid population expansion brought problems. These included air pollution, inadequate water supplies, and construction on earthquake-threatened land. But such problems did not stop the city's growth. Los Angeles itself now covers about 469 square miles. Its metropolitan area spreads over 5,700 square miles. A

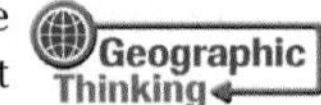

Geographic Thinking

Making Comparisons

A How has climate influenced the development of Los Angeles and Montreal?

Building cities was just one way humans interacted with their environment. Another was in the construction of transportation systems to make movement from place to place less difficult.

Overcoming Distances

The native peoples and the Europeans who followed encountered many obstacles when they moved across the land. They faced huge distances,

ACTIVITY OPTION CRITICAL THINKING

DETERMINING CAUSE AND EFFECT

Explaining the Skill Tell students that determining the cause of certain geographic events can help them understand what effects have occurred as a result.

Applying the Skill Ask students to look at a world atlas and find the Bering Strait. Then have them find information on the Bering Strait in an encyclopedia (online or in book form). On the board, create a two-column chart with the headings "Cause" and "Effects." Then ask the following questions and have students use their answers to fill in the chart.

- Where is the Bering Strait? *(Between Alaska and Russia)*
- How was it formed? *(Cause: by rising waters at the end of the last ice age)*
- How does this relate to the information you read about Beringia in this section of Chapter 5? *(Effect: separated two continents; Effect: Nomads who may have previously used the land bridge to cross between Asia and North America could no longer do so.)*

large bodies of water, formidable landforms, and harsh climates. But they spanned the continent and changed the natural environment forever.

TRAILS AND INLAND WATERWAYS Some of the early peoples who came across the land bridge from Siberia blazed trails eastward. Others followed the Pacific coast south toward warmer climates. Still others remained in the northwest, in what are now Alaska and northern Canada.

When Europeans from England and France crossed the Atlantic to North America, they set up colonies along the coast. Then, they moved inland. As they did, they carved overland trails, including the National and Wilderness roads and the Oregon and Santa Fe trails. They also used inland waterways, such as the Mississippi and Ohio rivers. To connect bodies of water, they built a network of canals. The Erie Canal across upstate New York opened in 1825 and made the first navigable water link between the Atlantic and the Great Lakes. B

North America's most important deepwater ship route—the **St. Lawrence Seaway**—was completed in the 1950s as a joint project of the United States and Canada. As you can see from the map on this page, the seaway connects the Great Lakes to the Atlantic Ocean by way of the St. Lawrence River. Ships are raised and lowered some 600 feet by a series of **locks,** sections of a waterway with closed gates where water levels are raised or lowered. The seaway enables huge, oceangoing vessels to sail into the industrial and agricultural heartland of North America.

Geographic Thinking

Seeing Patterns
B Why was it important to link waterways?
B. Answer Linking waterways allowed easy movement between different parts of the country.

The St. Lawrence Seaway

Ships using the St. Lawrence Seaway move through a series of canal locks that raise or lower the water level. This allows the vessels to navigate bodies of water that are at different levels above the sea.

Lake Superior
602 feet above sea level
Locks
Lake Huron
578 feet above sea level
Locks
Lake Erie
572 feet above sea level
Locks
Lake Ontario
246 feet above sea level
Locks
St. Lawrence River
20 feet above sea level
Sea Level

0 150 300 miles
0 150 300 kilometers
N
ONTARIO
MINN.
Duluth
L. Superior
CANADA
QUEBEC
Quebec
MAINE
Sault Ste. Marie
Sudbury
UNITED STATES
Montreal
St. Lawrence R.
WISCONSIN
Toronto
L. Huron
L. Michigan
VT.
MICH.
Ontario
N.H.
ATLANTIC OCEAN
IOWA
NEW YORK
MASS.
Chicago
Detroit
Erie
ILLINOIS
IND.
OHIO
Cleveland
PENN.
R.I.
N.J.
CONN.

SKILLBUILDER: Interpreting Graphics
1. **ANALYZING DATA** Where do ships have to make the greatest water-level adjustment?
2. **DRAWING CONCLUSIONS** Why was it important to build the St. Lawrence Seaway?

US & CANADA

Instruct: Objective 3

Overcoming Distances

- What are two obstacles early settlers faced in moving across North America? *(huge distances, large bodies of water, harsh climates, hazardous landforms)*
- Which country has the world's largest railroad system? *(U.S.)*
- Why have Canadians built their major highways east to west in the southern part of the country? *(That is where most of the population is, and highways are used to connect the main cities.)*

Interpreting Graphics

The St. Lawrence Seaway

Have students examine the graphic depicting the St. Lawrence Seaway. Have them identify the number of sets of locks, and the name of the lake not included in the seaway. *(Four locks; Lake Michigan)* Also have them identify the highest and lowest water levels of the seaway. *(602 ft.; 20 ft.)* Ask them to refer back to the map on page 120 and then determine what kinds of products might be transported on the seaway. *(coal, iron ore, timber)*

SKILLBUILDER ANSWERS

1. Ships have to make the greatest adjustment to sea level between Lake Ontario and Lake Erie–326 feet.

2. It was economically important to allow oceangoing vessels to bring trade goods into the interior of both countries.

DIFFERENTIATING INSTRUCTION | LESS PROFICIENT READERS

DRAWING CONNECTIONS

Objective To visually draw connections between textual information

Class Time 15 minutes

Task Draw a diagram that students help create

Directions Begin a diagram on the board with two ovals around the words "early settlers" and "current inhabitants," then add four ovals below that containing the words "trails," "railroads," "waterways," and "highways" (see completed example). Ask students to draw lines connecting each group to the methods of transportation it found important.

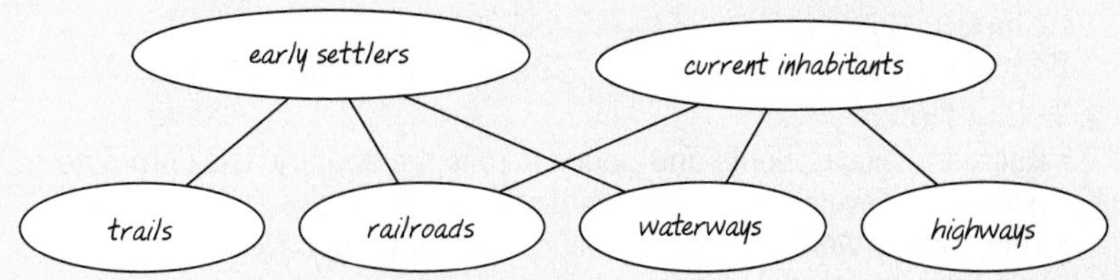

More About

Diesel Locomotives and Trucks

First perfected by Rudolf Diesel in 1897, the engine that bears his name had a dramatic impact on transportation of goods in the United States and Canada. Larger, heavier, and more fuel-efficient than steam and gas-fueled engines of equal power, diesel engines became the workhorses of the plains in the 1940s, used to haul goods across country.

More About

The St. Lawrence Seaway and the Economy

The St. Lawrence Seaway has had quite an impact on both the Canadian and U.S. economies since its completion in 1959. A major reason for its construction was to transport iron ore deposits discovered in Quebec and Newfoundland to U.S. steel mills. Today, iron ore is the second largest commodity exported from Canada to the U.S. via the St. Lawrence Seaway.

Assess & Reteach

GeoFocus Have students complete the chart they began at the start of this section.

Formal Assessment
- Section Quiz, p. 70

Reteaching Activity
Have students write a summary statement for the main idea under each of the three major headings in this section.

In-Depth Resources: Unit 2
- Reteaching Activity, p. 12

VIDEO
Paving America
hmhsocialstudies.com

TRANSCONTINENTAL RAILROADS The marriage of the steam locomotive and the railroads made crossing the continent from the Atlantic to the Pacific quicker and easier. Railroad building began in North America in the early 19th century. But many of the physical features shown on the map on page 103 presented natural barriers. To make way, railroad workers had to cut down forests, build bridges over streams, and blast tunnels through mountains.

The first transcontinental railroad was completed across the United States in 1869. A trans-Canada railroad, from Montreal to British Columbia, was completed in 1885. These railroads carried goods and passengers cross-country, promoting economic development and national unity as they went. Today, the United States has the world's largest railway system, and Canada the third largest.

NATIONAL HIGHWAY SYSTEMS Before the railroads came, there were roads that connected towns and cities and provided pathways to the interior. But it was the development of the automobile in the early 20th century that spurred roadbuilding. Today, both the United States and Canada have extensive roadway systems. The United States has about 4 million miles of roads, while Canada has about 560,000 miles.

As you read earlier, much of Canada's population is concentrated in the south. So, Canadians built their major highways east to west in the southern part of the country, connecting principal cities. The Trans-Canada Highway, Canada's primary roadway, stretches about 4,860 miles from St. John's, Newfoundland, to Victoria, British Columbia. In the United States, the interstate highway system is a network of more than 46,000 miles of highways that crisscross the country. Begun in the 1950s, it connects the United States with Canada on the north and Mexico on the south, and also runs east-west across the country. C

In this chapter, you read about the physical geography of the United States and Canada. In the next chapter, you will learn about the human geography of one of these countries—the United States.

C. Answer Both run east to west. The U.S. system also runs north and south and has many more miles of highway.

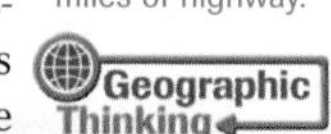

Making Comparisons
C How is the Trans-Canada Highway similar to and different from the U.S. interstate highway system?

Section 3 Assessment

1 Places & Terms
Identify and explain where in the region these would be found.
- nomad
- Beringia
- lock
- St. Lawrence Seaway

2 Taking Notes
MOVEMENT Review the notes you took for this section.

- Why are railroads important to a nation's development?
- In what ways did settlers in Canada and the United States move across the continent?

3 Main Ideas
a. What factors affect the choice of location of a city?
b. Why is the St. Lawrence Seaway important?
c. How did methods of moving people and goods across the continent change over time?

4 Geographic Thinking
Making Inferences In what ways have transportation systems crossing the continent altered the environment? **Think about:**
- construction of canals and railroads
- building cities

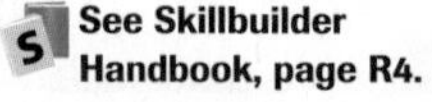
See Skillbuilder Handbook, page R4.

GeoActivity

ASKING GEOGRAPHIC QUESTIONS Obtain and study a highway map of your state. Then come up with a geographic question about the map, perhaps one considering geographic features that caused the location of a highway. Answer the question and make a **class presentation** using visuals.

SECTION 3 ASSESSMENT ANSWERS

1. Places & Terms
nomad, p. 127
Beringia, p. 127
lock, p. 129
St. Lawrence Seaway, p. 129

2. Taking Notes
- Railroads move people and goods across the country. They promote economic development and national unity.
- They moved westward using inland waterways, transcontinental railroads, and trails.

3. Main Ideas
a. The factors include: landscape, climate, weather, water, and availability of natural resources.
b. It allows oceangoing vessels to sail into the industrial and agricultural heartland of North America.
c. First, there were simple trails and waterways, and then railroads and highway systems.

4. Geographic Thinking
The building of canals and railroads first required cutting down forests, digging up the land, and building bridges and locks. Cities grew along the transportation routes. Each of these changed the natural environment.

GeoActivity

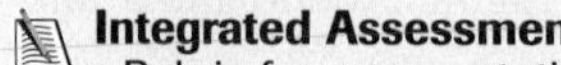

Integrated Assessment
- Rubric for a presentation, 3.6

Map and Graph Skills

Reading a Highway Map

San Antonio, Texas, is a part of a metropolitan area of more than one million people, located in south central Texas. It has been a crossroads for much of its history–for its earliest Native American settlers, the Spanish who came later, and finally, the Texans who won independence from Mexico not long after the battle of the Alamo. Looking at the map below, you can see that the city remains a meeting point, crisscrossed by interstate, U.S., state, and county highways.

THE LANGUAGE OF MAPS The primary purpose of a **highway map** is to show the location of roadways in an area and the distance between places. But highway maps usually include much other information. For example, they may identify important sites, such as airports, parks, and universities.

San Antonio and Vicinity ❶

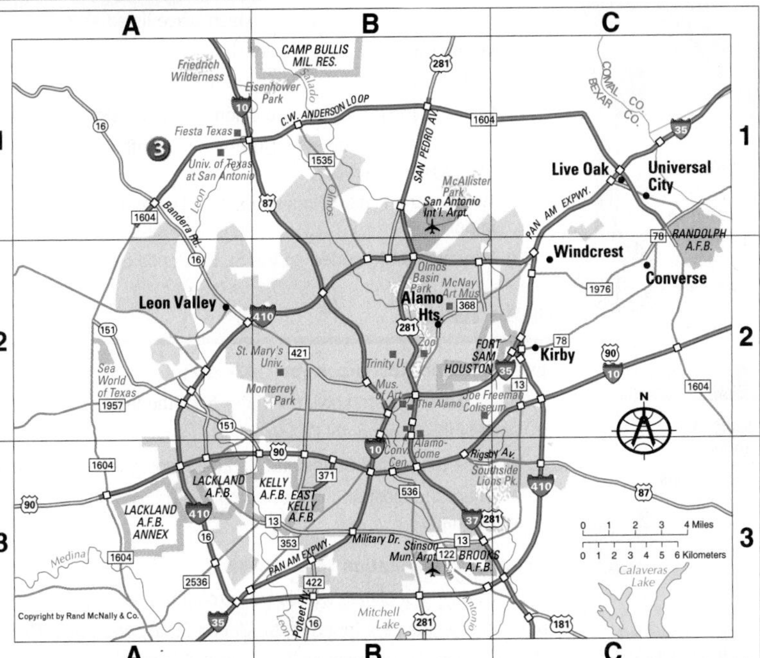

Copyright by Rand McNally & Co.

	Free Limited-Acess Highways
	Other Multilane Highways
	Principal Highways
410	Interstate Highways
281	U.S. Highways
151	State Highways
422	County Highways
	Points of Interest/ Military Installations
	Cities and Towns
❷	Airport
	City Parks
	Urbanized Area

❶ The title identifies the area covered by the map.

❷ The key shows the symbols used on the map and explains what they mean. For example, the ✈ symbol shows where airports are located.

❸ Points of interest, such as the Alamo (B-2) or Sea World (A-2), are marked by small red squares or by pink ribbons, depending on their size.

Map and Graph Skills Assessment

1. **Seeing Patterns** Which interstate highways pass through the center of San Antonio?
2. **Making Decisions** Which interstate highway and U.S. highway would you take to the Alamo when coming from the southeast?
3. **Analyzing Data** By the most direct route, how far is Live Oak from Leon Valley by highway?

OBJECTIVE

Examine key features of a highway map.

Instruct: Objective

- What is purpose of a highway map? *(to show the location of roadways, and towns and the distance between places)*
- What does the airplane symbol in the key represent? *(airports)*
- In what directions from the Alamo is Sea World of Texas located? *(west)*

In-Depth Resources: Unit 2
- Map and Graph Skills, pp. 6–7

Access for Students Acquiring English/ESL
- Map and Graph Skills, pp. 27–28

SKILLS ASSESSMENT ANSWERS

1. interstate highways 10, 35, and 37

2. U.S. Highway 181 to Interstate 37 and U.S. Highway 281

3. about 17 miles

Reviewing Places & Terms

A. 1. Appalachian Mountains, p. 119
2. Rocky Mountains, p. 119
3. Great Plains, p. 119
4. Canadian Shield, p. 119
5. Great Lakes, p. 121
6. Mackenzie River, p. 121
7. prevailing westerlies, p. 124
8. Everglades, p. 126
9. locks, p. 129
10. St. Lawrence Seaway, p. 129

B. Possible Responses

11. The Appalachian Mts., Rocky Mts., Great Plains, Canadian Shield, the Great Lakes, and the St. Lawrence Seaway are all found in U.S. and Canada.
12. The Appalachian Mountains forms a boundary.
13. The Rocky Mountains border the Great Plains.
14. Hudson Bay is found in the Canadian Shield.
15. The Great Lakes and the St. Lawrence Seaway are linked.
16. The Everglades is a huge swampland.
17. The Great Plains and the Canadian Shield are subregions of the Interior Lowlands.
18. The marine west coast is influenced by the prevailing westerlies.
19. They allow access into and out of the heart of the continent.
20. Because the St. Lawrence River is lower in elevation than the lakes, boats must be lowered into it.

Chapter 5 Assessment

VISUAL SUMMARY
PHYSICAL GEOGRAPHY OF THE UNITED STATES AND CANADA

Landforms

Major Mountain Ranges:
Rocky Mountains, Appalachian Mountains

Major Waterways:
Mississippi-Missouri-Ohio river system, Great Lakes, Mackenzie River, Columbia River, Rio Grande River, Colorado River

Interior Lowlands:
Great Plains, Canadian Shield, Interior Plains

Resources

- Both the United States and Canada have huge mineral and fossil fuel resources.
- Forest lands cover about one-third of the United States and one-half of Canada.

Climate and Vegetation

- Canada's climates and vegetation are related to its far northern location.
- The United States includes regions that are in almost every climate and vegetation zone.

Human-Environment Interaction

- Movement westward altered the land in both the United States and Canada.
- Transportation networks helped develop the land and economy of the region.

Reviewing Places & Terms

A. Briefly explain the importance of each of the following.

1. Appalachian Mountains
2. Rocky Mountains
3. Great Plains
4. Canadian Shield
5. Great Lakes
6. Mackenzie River
7. prevailing westerlies
8. Everglades
9. lock
10. St. Lawrence Seaway

B. Answer the questions about vocabulary in complete sentences.

11. Which of the places listed above are found both in the United States and Canada?
12. Which of the mountain chains form a boundary with the Canadian Shield?
13. The Great Plains are bounded on one side by which landform listed above?
14. The Hudson Bay is found in which place listed above?
15. Which two waterways are linked?
16. Which place above is a huge swampland?
17. Which of the places are subregions of the Interior Lowlands?
18. What climate region in North America is influenced by the prevailing westerlies?
19. Why are the Great Lakes and the St. Lawrence Seaway important?
20. Why are locks needed on the St. Lawrence Seaway?

Main Ideas

Landforms and Resources (pp. 117-122)

1. How do the Eastern Lowlands differ from the Interior Lowlands?
2. What is the Continental Divide?
3. Why are the United States and Canada leading food producers?
4. What are the most abundant natural resources in the United States and Canada?

Climate and Vegetation (pp. 123-126)

5. In what type of climate would you expect to find permafrost?
6. Which climates are found in the United States and not in Canada?
7. What type of vegetation covers most of Canada?

Human-Environment Interaction (pp. 127-131)

8. How did the earliest inhabitants of the United States and Canada, those who arrived before the Europeans, alter the land?
9. What problems arose in Los Angeles with rapid expansion?
10. How did the settlers of the United States and Canada overcome the distances across the continent?

Main Ideas

1. The Eastern Lowlands lie on the Atlantic and Gulf of Mexico coasts and have excellent harbors. The Interior Lowlands are huge flatlands located in the middle of the continent.
2. The Continental Divide is the line of highest points in the Rockies that marks the separation between rivers flowing eastward and westward.
3. Both nations have some of the most fertile soils in the world.
4. The United States and Canada have large supplies of timber, fossil fuels, and minerals.
5. Permafrost is found in subarctic and tundra regions.
6. Tropical wet, tropical wet and dry, desert, Mediterranean, and humid subtropical are found in the United States and not in Canada.
7. Much of Canada is covered by coniferous forest.
8. They cleared the land of trees, plowed the soil, and dug ditches for irrigation.
9. Los Angeles faced problems with air pollution, inadequate water supplies, and construction on earthquake-threatened land.
10. Settlers built trails, waterways, and railroad systems.

Critical Thinking

1. Using Your Notes

Use your completed chart to answer these questions.

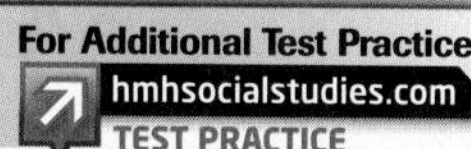

Landforms	
Resources	

a. How is the location of cities related to landforms and to climate?

b. How is Canada's economy affected by its climate and vegetation?

2. Geographic Themes

a. **MOVEMENT** Write a sentence describing the movement of people and goods across the United States and Canada over the last 200 years.

b. **PLACE** How have the Great Lakes contributed to the development of both the United States and Canada?

3. Identifying Themes

In developing their city, how did the people of Montreal solve the problems of a severe climate? Which of the five themes apply to this situation?

4. Making Inferences

What aspects of physical geography have contributed to the economic success of the United States and Canada?

5. Seeing Patterns

How did the presence of north-to-south flowing rivers in the United States affect its development?

For Additional Test Practice

hmhsocialstudies.com
TEST PRACTICE

Geographic Skills: Interpreting Maps

Physical Profile of the United States

Use the map below to answer the following questions.

1. **REGION** What might be said about the land between the Appalachians and the Mississippi?
2. **PLACE** What is the difference in altitude between the Coastal ranges and the Sierra Nevada?
3. **REGION** What happens to the land as you move west of the Mississippi?

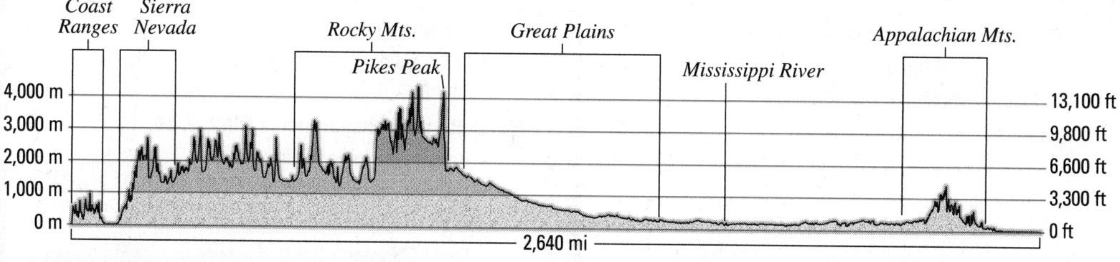

GeoActivity

Create a three-dimensional model of the cross section on this page. Use colors to indicate elevations and label the physical features you show. Create a legend for your model.

hmhsocialstudies.com

MULTIMEDIA ACTIVITY

Use the links at **hmhsocialstudies.com** to conduct research on the landforms of the United States and Canada. Focus on finding pictures of major and well-known landforms and waterways.

Creating a Multimedia Presentation From your research, select a series of pictures to include in a presentation on the theme "A Land of Contrasts." List the Web sites you used in preparing your report.

US & CANADA

Critical Thinking

1. a. Cities are less likely to be located where the climate or landforms restrict development.
b. Its cold climate limits some economic activity, but its northern location with a coniferous forest makes lumbering a large industry.

2. a. Sentences should include changes from waterways to railroad systems, and then to highway systems.
b. Located in the heartland of the continent, the Great Lakes allow both countries to move trade goods to the Atlantic.

3. The citizens of Montreal created inside and underground spaces so they would not have to go outside in the severely cold weather. Theme is human-environment interaction.

4. Abundant resources, good soil, a moderate climate, and good waterways have made possible prosperous economies in the two nations.

5. North-to-south flowing rivers allowed goods and people to be transported into and out of the interior of the country.

GeoActivity

Integrated Assessment
- Rubric for creating a three-dimensional model, 1.10

Formal Assessment
- Chapter Test, Forms A, B, and C, pp. 71–82

Geographic Skills

1. It is relatively flat.
2. approximately 6,500 feet
3. The land begins to rise and ultimately becomes the Rocky Mountains.

MULTIMEDIA ACTIVITY

For the presentation on landforms, students should:
- Present a concise well-organized presentation on landforms and waterways.
- Produce clear, imaginative visuals for the presentation.
- Include references to the Web sites used as sources.

Grading Rubric Evaluate student performance as Exceptional, Acceptable, or Poor in each of the following categories:

	Exceptional	Acceptable	Poor
Be clear, focused, and logical			
Presentation clearly states topic and purpose			
Provides necessary facts and examples			
Shows contrasts in presentation			

Human Geography of the United States

OVERVIEW	INSTRUCTIONAL RESOURCES	
ESSENTIAL QUESTION What factors shaped the development of the United States? **Focus on the Essential Question Podcast**	**In-Depth Resources: Unit 2** • Building Vocabulary, p. 17 **Block Schedule Strategies** **Chapter Summaries** (English/Spanish) **Multimedia Connections** • The American Revolution	**Interactive Online Edition** TOS **ExamView® Assessment Suite** (English/Spanish) TOS **CalendarPlanner** **Power Presentations with Media Gallery** **Critical Thinking Transparencies** • CT6 hmhsocialstudies.com INTERACTIVE
SECTION 1 **HISTORY AND GOVERNMENT OF THE UNITED STATES** **MAIN IDEAS** • Many kinds of people have settled the United States. • The industry helped cities grow rapidly. • The United States became a world power largely because of its extensive growth and abundant resources.	**In-Depth Resources: Unit 2** • Guided Reading, p. 13 • Building Vocabulary, p. 17 • Reteaching Activity, p. 18 **Guided Reading Workbook,** Section 1	**Critical Thinking Transparencies** • CT38 Subregions of the United States
SECTION 2 **ECONOMY AND CULTURE OF THE UNITED STATES** **MAIN IDEAS** • Natural resources, a stable political system, and skilled labor have helped the U.S. grow rapidly. • The U.S. has agricultural and manufacturing strength. • The U.S. has an ethnically diverse population. • The U.S. has a high quality of life overall due to economic growth.	**In-Depth Resources: Unit 2** • Guided Reading, p. 14 • Building Vocabulary, p. 17 • Reteaching Activity, p. 19 **Cultures Around the World** • Architecture, p. 7 • Fine Arts, p. 9 • Literature, p. 10 • Music, p. 11 **Guided Reading Workbook,** Section 2	**Map Transparencies** • MT13 Selected Native Peoples of North America, c. 1600 **Cultures Transparencies CW7, 9, 10, 11** • Ranch House and Bungalow • *Carmichael and O'Keeffe* • from *Walden* • Duke Ellington's Band
SECTION 3 **SUBREGIONS OF THE UNITED STATES** **MAIN IDEAS** • The U.S. has four subregions: Northeast, South, Midwest, West. • The Northeast has been a gateway for immigrants. • The Midwest is an agricultural and industrial center. • The South and the West have attracted populations with warm climates.	**In-Depth Resources: Unit 2** • Guided Reading, p. 15 • Skillbuilder Practice, p. 16 • Building Vocabulary, p. 17 • Reteaching Activity, p. 20 **Outline Maps with Activities** • United States: Physical and Political, pp. 13–14 **Guided Reading Workbook,** Section 3	**The World's Music Audio Program**

ASSESSMENT

SE **Chapter Assessment,** pp. 152–153

Formal Assessment
- Chapter Tests, Forms A, B, and C, pp. 86–97

TOS **ExamView® Assessment Suite**

Strategies for Test Preparation

hmhsocialstudies.com TEST PRACTICE

SE **Section Assessment,** p. 139

Formal Assessment
- Section Quiz, p. 83

Integrated Assessment
- Rubric for a report, 2.5

Test Practice Transparencies TT19

SE **Section Assessment,** p. 144

Formal Assessment

- Section Quiz, p. 84

Integrated Assessment
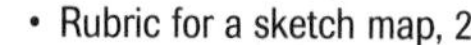
- Rubric for a sketch map, 2.1

Test Practice Transparencies TT20

SE **Section Assessment,** p. 149

Formal Assessment
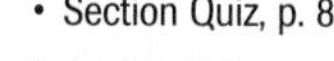
- Section Quiz, p. 85

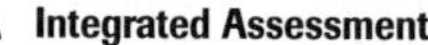
Integrated Assessment
- Rubric for a database, 2.6
- Rubric for a documentary proposal, 5.5

Test Practice Transparencies TT21

CHART KEY:

SE Student Edition	 Block Scheduling	DVD/CD-ROM
TE Teacher's Edition	TOS Teacher One Stop	 MP3 Audio
Printable Resource	Presentation Resource	HISTORY™

Program Resources available on TOS and @ hmhsocialstudies.com

SUPPORTING RESOURCES

- Multimedia Classroom Global History Series
- Global History Teacher's Guide

Social Studies Trade Library Collection
- World Regions Trade Collection

For more information or to purchase these resources, go to 

DIFFERENTIATED INSTRUCTION

English Learners	Struggling Readers	Gifted and Talented Students
 **Spanish/English Guided Reading Workbook**  **Access for Students Acquiring English/ESL** Spanish Translations, pp. 29–32 **Chapter Summaries** (English/Spanish) TE **TE Activity** Prefixes, p. 142	**Chapter Summaries** (English/Spanish) TE **TE Activity** Creating a Time Line, p. 136	TE **TE Activity** Finding a Business Site, p. 147

ENRICHMENT ACTIVITIES

The following activities are especially suitable for classes following block schedules.

SE **Student Edition,** p. 134–153 • Disasters! The Dust Bowl, pp. 150–151	hmhsocialstudies.com INTERACTIVE • Colorado River Basin, p. 149

BLOCK SCHEDULE LESSON PLAN OPTIONS: 90-MINUTE PERIOD

DAY 1

SECTION 1, pp. 135–139
Class Time 45 minutes

- **Small Group Discussion** As a way to review the section, divide the class into groups of four. Give each group an issue from the section, such as how the U.S. was founded or how the U.S. grew. Ask the groups to discuss the issue and raise all important points about that issue. Then, have each group appoint one person to speak for the group in restating the key points of their issue to the class.

SECTION 2, pp. 140–144
Class Time 45 minutes

- **Representatives** As a way to get an idea of the economic concerns related to the various subregions, divide the class into four groups, each one representing a region. Ask the students to respond to the issues you raise as though they were from that region. Possible issues to raise include: clearing more forest for agriculture, overfarming problems, restrictions on fishing, limits on the numbers of manufacturing plants in an area.

DAY 2

SECTION 3, pp. 145–151
Class Time 40 minutes

- **Regions Table** Lead the class in creating a table with four rows for the four subregions and three columns with the headings "States Included," "Nickname/Known For," and "Economic Base." Then ask them to insert the appropriate information for each subregion.
  Class Time 15 minutes
- **Skillbuilder Practice** Use the Activity Option about creating graphs and charts on TE page 146 and the Skillbuilder Practice worksheet.
  Class Time 25 minutes

SECTION 3, pp. 145–151
Class Time 50 minutes

- **Economy Map** Draw a rough outline of the U.S. on the board. Ask students to close their books and recall which areas contain which industries. Make a small map key using images of a piece of corn to represent agriculture, a steel beam to represent industrial manufacturing, and a star to represent non-manufacturing industries. Ask students to take turns going up to the board and drawing the appropriate icon in the appropriate subregion.
  Class Time 20 minutes
- **Video and/or Photograph Viewing** In preparation for the Disasters! Section, show students part of a video or some photographs related to the disaster event.
  Class Time 30 minutes

DAY 3

DISASTERS! pp. 150–151
Class Time 35 minutes

- **Discussion** Discuss the disasters section, using the discussion prompts on TE pages, 150–151.
  Class Time 15 minutes
- **News Clip** Ask the students to create a short newspaper clip about the Disaster! event as if it were from a newspaper of the time.
  Class Time 20 minutes

CHAPTER 6 REVIEW AND ASSESSMENT, pp. 152–153
Class Time 55 minutes

- **Review** Have students prepare a summary of the chapter using the words in the Places and Terms on the first page of each section.
  Class Time 20 minutes
- **Assessment** Have students complete the Chapter 6 Assessment
  Class Time 35 minutes

TEACHER-TESTED ACTIVITY — CHART AND VENN DIAGRAM

Class Time One class period

Task Create a chart with basic facts about each of the four subregions of the United States. Students will then create a Venn diagram comparing and contrasting two of the four regions.

Supplies
- notebook paper
- writing utensil
- poster-sized paper (optional)
- markers (optional)

Purpose To compare and contrast the subregions of the United States.

Activity Have students create a table showing each of the four subregions of the United States. Ask them to fill in data from the textbook under the following headings: percent of population, percent of land area, major economic activities, nickname for region, and climate. Students will then use the data to create a Venn diagram comparing and contrasting two of the four regions. (A Venn diagram is composed of two interlocking circles, with common characteristics shown in the overlapping portion of the circles.) The Venn diagram may be created on notebook paper or poster-sized paper. Data may be depicted with words, symbols, or a combination of the two.

Heather Berry
Geography Teacher, Hazelwood East, St. Louis, Missouri

A WebQuest is a structured, "inquiry-oriented" activity that asks students to solve problems by using Web resources. Students are given a task and are asked to use the Web to help them complete the task, which usually involves drawing a conclusion or solving a problem for which there is no one correct answer. WebQuests can be very simple or highly complex. Below is a simple WebQuest to complement the material in chapter 6. To learn more about WebQuests and how to design an "official" WebQuest, go to the WebQuest link at **hmhsocialstudies.com**.

Objective Students will conduct a simple WebQuest to learn more about major cities in the four subregions of the United States.

Task Have students go to the Web sites for large American cities and refer to Chapter 6 to figure out what it might be like to live in them. Ask them to list in order of preference the cities they'd most and least like to live in.

Class Time 2–3 class periods

1. Have students read pages 145–149, and discuss the similarities and differences between the four major subregions of the United States. If students have visited other subregions, have them share their experiences and observations.

2. Ask students to pretend they're considering relocating to another part of the United States. The only problem is that they don't really have an idea where they'd like to move. They will use the Internet to find out what cities in different parts of the country have to offer.

3. Have students visit the official Web sites for several United States cities, listed at **hmhsocialstudies.com**, to learn about what the cities have to offer newcomers and to help figure out where they would like to move. (If one of these cities is their home town, they can skip it and focus on the others.) Have them refer to these Web sites and the material on pages 145–149 to answer these questions for each city: What types of recreation is available in or near the city? What is the climate like? How many people live here? What types of jobs are likely to be available? What would be the best and the worst things about living in this city?

4. Have students look at their notes and at the map on page 105 and think about the characteristics of each city. Ask them to list the cities in order of preference, with the one they'd most like to live in at the top and the one they'd least like to live in at the bottom.

5. Have students summarize their decisions and explain why they ranked cities as they did.

CHAPTER 6 OBJECTIVE

Identify features of human geography in the four subregions of the United States.

Chapter 6 HUMAN GEOGRAPHY OF THE UNITED STATES

Shaping an Abundant Land

Interpreting Maps

Four Subregions of the United States

Have students name the four subregions of the United States. *(Northeast, South, Midwest, West)* Then ask students to consider what they already know about the states. Lead a discussion about other ways that U.S. subregion boundaries could be drawn. *(Example: Some students may say that Texas and Oklahoma should not be included in the South.)*

Extension Ask the students to analyze what states in a group might have in common.

Introducing the Essential Question

- Describe some of the main events in U.S. history and how they shaped the country's development.
- Point out that the differences among the subregions contribute to our country's vibrant economy and culture.

Have students fill out the diagram in their notebooks by using information from the sections in this chapter.

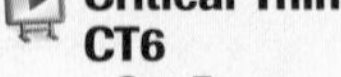
Critical Thinking Transparencies CT6
- GeoFocus

In-Depth Resources: Unit 2
- Building Vocabulary, p. 17

Four Subregions of the United States

hmhsocialstudies.com INTERACTIVE MAP

Northeast
South
Midwest
West

Essential Question

What factors shaped the development of the United States?

What You Will Learn

In this chapter you will learn about factors that shaped the human geography of the United States.

SECTION 1
History and Government of the United States

SECTION 2
Economy and Culture of the United States

SECTION 3
Subregions of the United States

hmhsocialstudies.com TAKING NOTES

Use the graphic organizer online to take notes about the history, economy, culture, and modern life of the United States and its subregions.

134

CHAPTER 6 ADDITIONAL RESOURCES

BOOKS FOR THE TEACHER

Jackson, Byron M. ***Encyclopedia of American Public Policy.*** Santa Barbara, CA: ABC-CLIO, 1999.

Bluestone, Barry, and Bennett Harrison. ***Growing Prosperity: The Battle for Growth with Equity in the Twenty-first Century.*** Boston, MA: Houghton Mifflin, 2000. A look at the U.S. economic future.

BOOKS FOR THE STUDENT

Finkelman, Paul and Peter Wallenstein. (eds.) ***The Encyclopedia of American Political History.*** Washington, D.C.: CQ Press, 2001.

VIDEOS

Lewis & Clark: The Journey of the Corps of Discovery. Florentine Films Production, 1997. Ken Burns's historical documentary of the expedition.

INTERNET

For more on the human geography of the United States, visit . . .

History and Government of the United States

Main Ideas

- The United States is a "nation of immigrants," settled by people from all over the world.
- The United States is the most diverse and highly industrialized and urbanized nation in the world.

Places & Terms

migration
Columbian Exchange
Louisiana Purchase
frontier
suburb
representative democracy

US & CANADA

CONNECT TO THE ISSUES
TERRORISM Beginning in the late 20th century, the United States has been subjected to terrorist attacks by individuals and groups opposed to its policies.

A HUMAN PERSPECTIVE Women were North America's first farmers. In all early cultures except the hunter-gatherer culture of the Southwest, women cultivated the land. They discovered which wild plants could be used as food for the family. They planted the seeds, tended the garden, harvested the crops, and prepared food for meals. Corn, beans, and squash were the first of these foods. Women also learned which leaves, bark, roots, stems, and berries could be used for medicines. Their efforts helped to ensure the survival of human settlement in North America—and the part of the land that became the United States.

Creating a Nation

The United States occupies nearly two-fifths of North America. It is the world's third largest country in both land area and population. It is rich in natural resources and is also fortunate to have a moderate climate, fertile soil, and plentiful water supplies. For thousands of years, this bounty has attracted waves of immigrants who came to find a better life. This continuing immigration is a recurring theme in the country's history; so is the constant **migration,** or movement, of peoples within the United States.

MANY PEOPLES SETTLE THE LAND As you read in Chapter 5, the first inhabitants of North America were believed to be nomads who came from Asia at least 13,000 or more years ago. These people settled the continent, spreading south along the Pacific coast and east to the Atlantic. Over the centuries, they developed separate cultures, as the map on page 104 shows. These native peoples occupied the land undisturbed until the 15th century, when Europeans began to explore what they called the "New World." The Spanish arrived first. They searched the present-day Southeast and Southwest for gold and other treasure. In 1565, they founded St. Augustine, Florida, the oldest permanent European settlement in the United States.

The French and English came later. France was interested in fisheries and the fur trade. In the early 1600s, the French settled along the northern Atlantic Coast and the St. Lawrence River in what is now Canada. The English arrived at about the same time. During the 1600s and 1700s,

HUMAN-ENVIRONMENT INTERACTION Early Native American settlers in the Southwest often built their dwellings into canyon walls. The dwellings shown are in Mesa Verde National Park in Colorado. **Why did the earliest settlers choose such locations for their dwellings?**

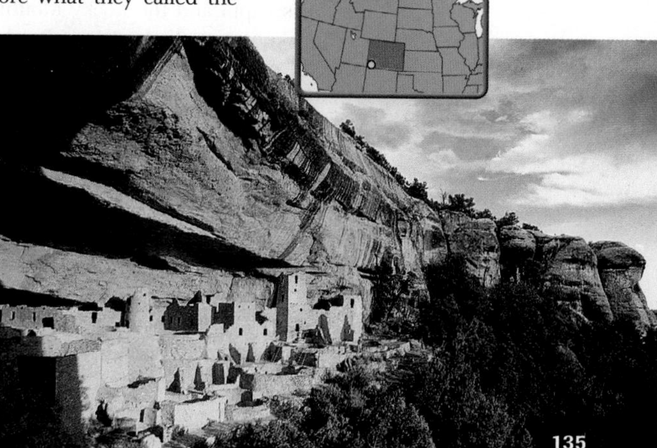

135

SECTION 1 OBJECTIVES

1. Explain how the United States was formed.
2. Describe the growth of the United States through migration and industrialization.
3. Examine United States political policy, economic growth, and social change.
4. Describe the U.S. governing system.

**GeographicThinking**

Using the Atlas, p. 137
Seeing Patterns, p. 138
Making Inferences, p. 139

Focus & Motivate

What factors might connect individual states within a subregional group in the United States? *(proximity, climate, similarity in industry or lifestyles)*

Instruct: Objective 

Creating a Nation

- What is a recurring event in the development of the United States? *(immigration; migration)*
- Who were the first Europeans to arrive in North America in the 15th century? *(Spaniards)*
- Between what two landforms did the Louisiana Purchase territory stretch? *(Mississippi River and Rocky Mountains)*

In-Depth Resources: Unit 2
- Guided Reading, p. 13

CAPTION ANSWER The canyon walls gave them protection from the weather, wild animals, and enemies, and also provided them with stone-building materials.

SECTION 1 PROGRAM RESOURCES

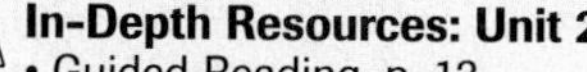
In-Depth Resources: Unit 2
- Guided Reading, p. 13
- Building Vocabulary, p. 17
- Reteaching Activity, p. 18

Guided Reading Workbook
- Section 1

Access for Students Acquiring English
- Guided Reading, p. 29

Formal Assessment
- Section Quiz, p. 83

Integrated Assessment
- Rubric for a report, 2.5

INTEGRATED TECHNOLOGY

Critical Thinking Transparencies, CT 38
- Subregions of the United States

Power Presentations

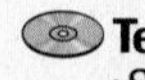
Test Generator
- Section 1 Quiz

TEST-TAKING RESOURCES

Strategies for Test Preparation

Test Practice Transparencies TT19

Online Test Practice

Interpreting Graphics

The Columbian Exchange

Ask students to identify products that Europeans brought to the Americas to cultivate for trade. *(grains, fruit, sugar cane, coffee beans, and livestock)* Ask students if they know of current "exchanges" between the continents. *(Answers will vary, but may include influenza and other viruses, Africanized honey bees, and Asian longhorn beetles.)*

More About

The Louisiana Purchase

After purchasing French territory in the West in 1803, President Thomas Jefferson made plans to carry out his dream of discovering what lay beyond the Mississippi River. After receiving government funding, he hired Meriwether Lewis and William Clark to head an expedition–the Corps of Discovery. Lewis and Clark led the expedition for more than two years, facing all of the dangers of an arduous journey into unknown territory. Through their dedication and skill, and their journals filled with detailed maps and records of climate, geography, plant and animal life, and cultural practices of Native Americans, they expanded knowledge and opened the West to further expansion.

The Columbian Exchange

MOVEMENT This infographic shows how plants, animals, and diseases were transferred between the Eastern and Western hemispheres as trade followed the voyages of Christopher Columbus to the Americas.

they settled to the south—on rivers and bays along the Atlantic coast from present-day Maine to Georgia. The English made their first permanent settlement in Jamestown, Virginia, in 1607.

European colonies often displaced Native Americans. In 1617, the Europeans brought Africans to America to work as slave laborers on cotton and tobacco plantations in the South. The coming of the Europeans also began what historians call the **Columbian Exchange.** The infographic above shows how the arrival of Europeans in the Western Hemisphere affected the lives of both Europeans and the native peoples.

Background About 600,000 Africans were brought to the United States to work as slave laborers from 1617 until the importation of slaves was banned in 1808.

ESTABLISHING AND MAINTAINING THE UNION The French and the English eventually fought in North America over trade and territory. In 1763, Great Britain gained control of all of North America east of the Mississippi River. But its control was short-lived. Britain's 13 American colonies soon began to resent the policies forced on them by a government thousands of miles away across the Atlantic. Their protests led to the American Revolution (1775–1783) and the founding of the United States of America. The new nation grew rapidly, and settlers pushed westward to the Mississippi. In 1803, the United States nearly doubled in size when the government purchased the vast plains region between the Mississippi and the Rocky Mountains from France. This territory became known as the **Louisiana Purchase.**

In the early 1800s, immigrants from Western Europe arrived in great numbers. They settled in cities in the Northeast, where industrialization was beginning. One such city was Lowell, Massachusetts, which had become a booming textile center by the 1840s. The newcomers also moved to rich farmlands in what is now the Midwest.

Meanwhile, sectionalism was growing. People were placing loyalty to their region, or section, above loyalty to the nation. The result was rising political and economic tensions between an agricultural South dependent on slave labor and the more industrialized North. These tensions led to the Civil War (1861–1865). It took four years of bloody fighting and many more years of political conflict to reunite the country.

DIFFERENTIATING INSTRUCTION LESS PROFICIENT READERS

CREATING A TIME LINE

Objective To help students grasp the chronological order of events through methods other than reading

Class Time 15 minutes

Task Create a time line on the board with students' help

Directions Draw a horizontal line on the board and cross it with six short vertical lines (for dates/events). At the left end of the time line, write "Nomads from Asia, 15,000 yrs. ago." At the right end of the time line, write "America Today." Have students give you the dates and names of four major events in the development of America to fill in the time line. *(e.g., Europeans arrive, 15th century; or American Revolution, 1775-83)*

An Industrial and Urban Society

In the second half of the 19th century, millions of Americans were on the move. They settled on newly opened lands west of the Mississippi and in the rapidly industrializing cities of the North and Midwest.

WESTWARD MOVEMENT From departure points such as Independence, Missouri, hundreds of thousands of pioneers left in covered wagons bound for the West. They blazed trails that crossed prairie, plains, desert, and mountains, moving toward the Pacific. A wagon train on the Oregon Trail might have taken up to six months to reach its destination 2,000 miles away. A

To make way for white settlers, the U.S. government removed Native Americans from their lands by treaty, or by force. In Chapter 5, you read that the first transcontinental railroad across the United States was completed in 1869. Railroads brought people to the West, and western cattle and products to markets in the East. By 1890, about 17 million people lived between the Mississippi and the Pacific. The free, open land that had been available and suitable for settlement—the **frontier**—was now fully settled.

Geographic Thinking

Using the Atlas

A Refer to the maps on pages 103 and 105. What landforms must be crossed by pioneers going from Missouri to the Pacific coast?

A. Answer the Missouri River, Great Plains, Rocky Mountains, and Coast Range

INDUSTRIALIZATION AND URBANIZATION As the West was being settled, immigrants—mainly from Western and Eastern Europe—poured into the United States. About 14 million came from 1860 to 1900.

Some joined the movement to the West. Others settled in urban areas undergoing industrialization. Cities such as New York, Boston, Pittsburgh, Cleveland, Detroit, and Chicago expanded rapidly. Both recent immigrants and large numbers of Americans from rural areas came to cities such as these to work in textile, steel, oil, food processing, and other industries. The United States was being transformed from a rural, agricultural nation to an urban, industrialized one.

World Power and Domestic Change

As the 20th century began, the United States was the dominant economic and political power in the Western Hemisphere. By the century's end, it would be the world's sole superpower.

LOOKING BEYOND ITS BORDERS The United States had tried to avoid involvement in foreign affairs during its decades of growth. Because of its ample natural and human resources, it had been almost self-sufficient from its founding. Its farms grew the food necessary for survival, and the nation's factories produced the manufactured goods it needed. It was also protected

Development of the West

1800
1803 The United States purchases French territory west of the Mississippi.
1804–1806 **Lewis and Clark** expedition explores the area of the Louisiana Purchase.
1840s **Wagon trains** begin moving pioneers to the West.
1850
1869 A symbolic **"golden spike"** is used to mark the completion of a transcontinental railroad across the United States.
1890 Land available for settlement on the western frontier has nearly disappeared.
1898 The United States continues its westward expansion, annexing Hawaii.
1900

Instruct: Objective 2

An Industrial and Urban Society

- Where did most Americans settle during the second half of the 19th century? *(industrial North and Midwest cities and west of the Mississippi)*
- What negative effects were connected with Western expansion? *(removal of Native Americans from their land)*
- What economic activities changed during the late 19th and 20th centuries? *(shift from an agricultural to an industrial nation)*

Critical Thinking Transparencies CT38
- Subregions of the United States

Interpreting Graphics

Development of the West

Have students examine the time line. Ask them to explain what the golden spike represents in the time line. *(It marks the completion of a transcontinental railroad across the U.S.)* Ask them in what year the Louisiana Purchase took place. *(1803)* Also ask what happened to western land by 1900. *(Little unclaimed land remained on the western frontier.)*

Instruct: Objective 3 appears on p. 138.

ACTIVITY OPTION | CRITICAL THINKING

DRAWING CONCLUSIONS

Explaining the Skill Tell students that an important part of understanding history is drawing conclusions based on sequences of events.

Applying the Skill Have students pair up and discuss the following questions. After 10 minutes, have each pair share their answers with the class.

- What did Lewis and Clark accomplish? *(expanded scientific and cultural knowledge of the West)*
- What impact did their accomplishments have on the United States? *(more rapid growth and settlement in the West)*
- How might railroads have expanded the development of the West? *(replaced wagon trains, facilitating the movement of goods and people)*
- How long did it take from the completion of the transcontinental railroad to the disappearance of open land on the frontier? *(21 years)*

Instruct: Objective 3

World Power and Domestic Change

- What events involved the U.S. in foreign affairs? *(world wars and global economic depression)*
- What term is used to define the United States' rank in the world community? *(superpower)*
- What were two reasons why the U.S. was largely uninvolved in foreign events during much of its history? *(physical isolation because of oceans, and self-sufficiency based on plentiful resources)*

Interpreting Time Lines

Growth of Technology

Have students examine the text box information. Ask them how the information seems to be organized or what it is intended to represent. *(major technological events in chronological order)* Ask the students to identify two categories within which technological advances have occurred. *(transportation, entertainment/information)*

Growth of Technology

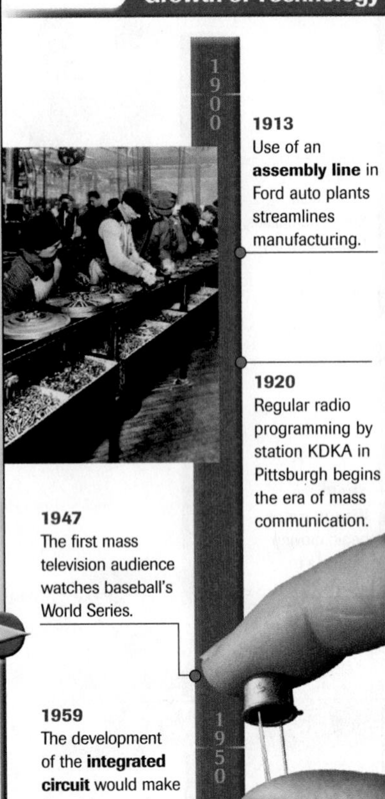

1900

1913
Use of an **assembly line** in Ford auto plants streamlines manufacturing.

1920
Regular radio programming by station KDKA in Pittsburgh begins the era of mass communication.

1947
The first mass television audience watches baseball's World Series.

1950

1959
The development of the **integrated circuit** would make the widespread use of computers possible.

1961
U.S. manned exploration of space starts as Alan B. Shepard, Jr., is launched into suborbit of the Earth.

1969
The U.S. Department of Defense develops a computer network that later leads to the Internet.

2000
Mapping **human genetic material (DNA)** is a breakthrough in biotechnology.

2000

DNA

from foreign conflicts by two vast oceans—the Atlantic and the Pacific. But a global economic depression and two world wars brought significant changes. When World War II ended in 1945, the United States was the only major nation that had escaped physical damage and had a healthy economy.

LIVING IN A GLOBAL SOCIETY Meanwhile, American political influence spread throughout the world after the Second World War. The United States became the leader of the world's non-Communist nations. Their goal was to stop the spread of communism, spearheaded by the Soviet Union (now Russia). A competition for world influence called the Cold War (roughly 1945–1991) followed. When communism in Europe collapsed in 1991, the United States emerged as the world's sole superpower. As such, it has used its diplomatic and military power to try to keep the peace and to further American interests in the international community.

A CHANGING ECONOMY The last half of the 20th century was a time of rapid social change. Large numbers of people began migrating from cities to surrounding **suburbs,** the communities outside of a city. Some Americans moved to the South and West. Also, immigrants continued to arrive by the hundreds of thousands. But now they came mainly from the countries of Latin America and Asia. B

These years saw much social unrest, especially during the 1960s and 1970s. The civil rights movement fought to gain equal rights for African Americans. The feminist movement sought equality for women. Also, many students and others protested U.S. involvement in a war between Communist and non-Communist forces in Vietnam (1955–75).

During this period, the U.S. economy boomed, despite some periods of economic downturn, or recession. The economy, too, was being transformed. Changes in technology altered the way goods were produced. The use of computers and the Internet revolutionized the workplace and the marketplace. Providing services and information surpassed industrial production in importance. This economic shift led to changes in the way people worked. Telecommuting and outsourcing became increasingly common corporate practices.

In 2008, the U.S. housing market collapsed, triggering a recession, the effects of which echoed around the globe. The U.S. financial crisis affected the economies of many nations, and more than 8 million Americans lost their jobs in fewer than 3 years. The national unemployment rate more than doubled in 10 years, rising from around 4 percent in 2000 to 10 percent by the end of 2009.

Geographic Thinking

Seeing Patterns
B What kinds of movement were taking place in the United States in the last half of the 20th century?

B. Answer People were moving from the cities to the suburbs, and from colder to warmer climates. Immigrants continued to move to the United States.

ACTIVITY OPTION **LINK TO HISTORY** **BLOCK SCHEDULING**

RESEARCH AND REPORT

Objective To help students make geographic connections between related historical events

Class Time One class period

Task Choose an event, research a related historical event, and present brief report

Directions Have students select one of the technological events briefly described in "Growth of Technology." Then have them research, either on the Internet or at the library, the geographic aspects of that and related events. For example, radio broadcasting began in Pittsburgh, but New York City became the center for national broadcasting. Have them present a brief report to the class on the reasons why.

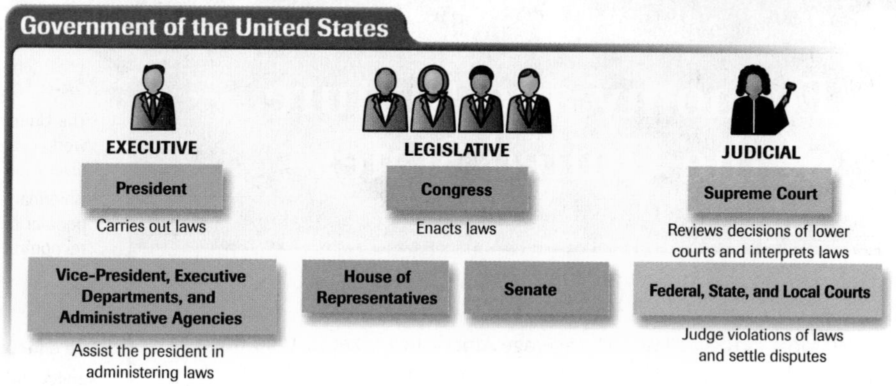

Government of the United States

EXECUTIVE	LEGISLATIVE		JUDICIAL
President	Congress		Supreme Court
Carries out laws	Enacts laws		Reviews decisions of lower courts and interprets laws
Vice-President, Executive Departments, and Administrative Agencies	House of Representatives	Senate	Federal, State, and Local Courts
Assist the president in administering laws			Judge violations of laws and settle disputes

Governing the People

One of the strengths of the United States is the political system created by the U.S. Constitution, drawn up in 1787. The United States is a **representative democracy,** where the people rule through elected representatives. It is also a federal republic, where powers are divided among the federal, or national, government and various state governments.

As you can see on the chart above, there are three separate and equal branches of the federal government. The executive branch, headed by the president, carries out the laws. The president also approves or vetoes proposed laws. The legislative branch makes the laws, and the judicial branch interprets the laws by reviewing decisions of lower courts. The 50 states also have executive, legislative, and judicial branches. They exercise powers not specifically granted to the federal government by the Constitution.

In this section, you read about the history and government of the United States. In the next, you will learn about its economy and culture.

Section 1 Assessment

1 Places & Terms

Explain the meaning of each of the following terms.

- migration
- Columbian Exchange
- Louisiana Purchase
- frontier
- suburb
- representative democracy

2 Taking Notes

MOVEMENT Review the notes you took for this section.

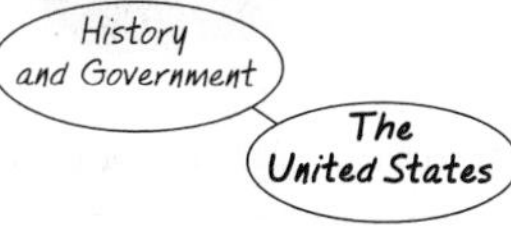

- Where did people migrate from to populate North America?
- Where did people move after the frontier was fully settled?

3 Main Ideas

a. Why did the United States attract so many immigrants?

b. How was the United States able to become a world power?

c. How are the powers of government in the United States divided?

4 Geographic Thinking

Making Inferences How did the physical geography of the United States contribute to its economic growth? **Think about:**

- land and mineral resources
- its relative global location

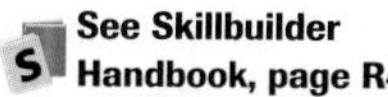
See Skillbuilder Handbook, page R4.

EXPLORING LOCAL GEOGRAPHY Make a list of physical features that would have attracted settlement to your area. Then do research or call your local historical society to find out when your community was founded and what groups settled there. Combine your findings in a **report** about your community.

US & CANADA

Interpreting Graphics

Government of the United States

Have students examine the graphic. Ask them who is the head of the executive branch of government. *(the president)* Ask them what the role of the Supreme Court is. *(to review decisions of the lower courts)* Ask them to identify who has the ability to enact bills into laws. *(both houses of Congress)*

Instruct: Objective 4

Governing the People

- When was the U.S. Constitution adopted? *(1787)*
- Define a "federal republic." *(a government that divides power among federal, state, and local governing bodies)*
- What are the three branches of government? *(executive, legislative, judicial)*

Assess & Reteach

GeoFocus Have students complete their notes on factors that have shaped the development of the United States.

Formal Assessment
- Section Quiz, p. 83

Reteaching Activity
Pass out index cards to the students and ask them to each write down one main idea from this section. Then, collect the cards and have the students help you lay out on a table or large desk the correct order of the main ideas, so that they follow the section objectives/headings.

In-Depth Resources: Unit 2
- Reteaching Activity, p. 18

SECTION 1 ASSESSMENT ANSWERS

1. Places & Terms
migration, p. 135
Columbian Exchange, p. 136
Louisiana Purchase, p. 136
frontier, p. 137
suburb, p. 138
representative democracy, p. 139

2. Taking Notes
- Asia, Africa, and Europe
- to the cities

3. Main Ideas
a. It had plentiful land for settlement, good resources, and job opportunities.
b. It was largely self-sufficient, had industrialized early, and was mainly protected from foreign conflicts.
c. divided among federal and state governments and also among executive, legislative, and judicial branches

4. Geographic Thinking
The fertile soil and mineral resources contribute to the products that form the basis of the economy. Being far away from foreign conflicts helped industry to develop and grow.

GeoActivity

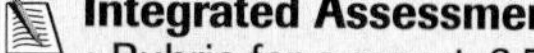
Integrated Assessment
- Rubric for a report, 2.5

SECTION 2 OBJECTIVES

1. Identify sources of economic power in the U.S.
2. Examine cultural diversity in the United States.
3. Describe American life today.

SKILLBUILDERS: Interpreting Graphs and Maps, pp. 140, 141, 142

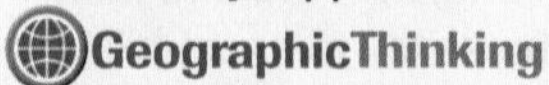

Seeing Patterns, p. 141
Making Comparisons, p. 144

Focus & Motivate

What factors make a country economically powerful? *(resources, political stability, skilled labor)*

Instruct: Objective 

The World's Greatest Economic Power

- What was the average American's job in the early days of the United States? *(farmer)*
- In what three areas is the U.S. a world leader? *(agriculture, manufacturing, global trade)*
- What percentage of the world's corn do U.S. farmers supply? *(40%)*

 **In-Depth Resources: Unit 2**
- Guided Reading, p. 14

SKILLBUILDER ANSWERS

1. agriculture in 1900, services in 1950, and services in 2000 **2.** The economy changed as more people moved to cities and industrialization expanded, and then these people required a variety of services.

Economy and Culture of the United States

Main Ideas

- The United States has the world's largest and most diversified economy.
- American products and popular culture are recognized around the world.

Places & Terms

export
free enterprise
service industry
postindustrial economy
multinational

CONNECT TO THE ISSUES
URBAN SPRAWL
Urbanization has helped economic growth, but it has also caused a variety of problems.

A HUMAN PERSPECTIVE The average American worker in 1790 was a self-employed farmer. The farmer spent each work day, sunrise to sunset, in backbreaking labor in the field. Most of the crops and livestock raised were consumed by the farm family. In the 1890s, the average American worker labored in a manufacturing or service industry, for long hours and low wages, often under unsafe conditions. Laborers in factories, for example, worked 60 hours a week for a total wage of $12; some were as young as 12 years of age.

At the start of the 21st century, the average worker was spending most of the workday in an office in front of a computer, processing information or providing services. The standard workweek was 40 hours; the government regulated workplace safety; and salaries generally covered living expenses, leisure-time activities, and perhaps, even savings.

The World's Greatest Economic Power

The United States has about 7 percent of the world's land area and about 5 percent of the world's population. But it has the world's largest economy—the most powerful, diverse, and technologically advanced in the world. The United States is a world leader in agricultural products, manufactured goods, and global trade. In fact, it accounts for more than 10 percent of the world's **exports,** which are goods sold to another country.

Three factors have contributed to the overall success of the American economy—available natural resources, a skilled labor force, and a stable political system that has allowed the economy to develop. The economy is run largely on **free enterprise.** In this economic system, private individuals own most of the resources, technology, and businesses, and can operate them for profit with little control from the government.

Major Sectors of the U.S. Economy

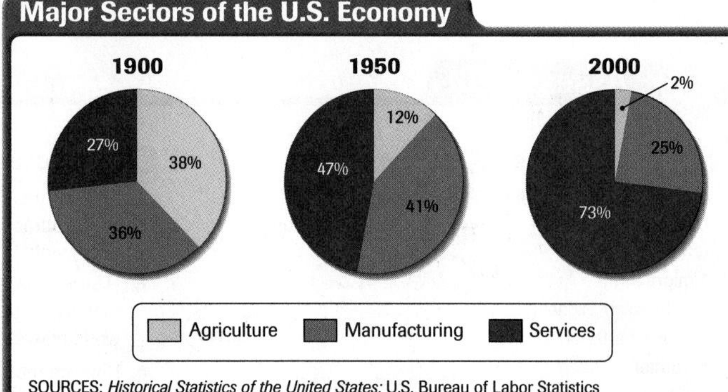

SOURCES: *Historical Statistics of the United States;* U.S. Bureau of Labor Statistics

SKILLBUILDER: Interpreting Graphs

1. **ANALYZING DATA** What were the dominant sectors of the economy in 1900, 1950, and 2000?
2. **MAKING GENERALIZATIONS** What might account for these changes in the economy?

SECTION 2 PROGRAM RESOURCES

 **In-Depth Resources: Unit 2**
- Guided Reading, p. 14
- Building Vocabulary, p. 17
- Reteaching Activity, p. 19

 **Guided Reading Workbook**
Section 2

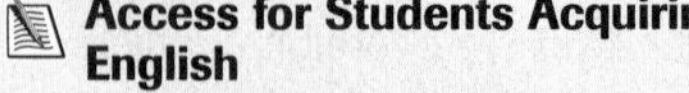

- Guided Reading, p. 30

 **Formal Assessment**
- Section Quiz, p. 84

 **Integrated Assessment**
- Rubric for a sketch map, 2.1

Cultures Around the World
- Architecture, p. 7
- Fine Arts, p. 9
- Literature, p. 10
- Music, p. 11

INTEGRATED TECHNOLOGY

 **Map Transparencies MT13**
- Selected Native Peoples of North America, c. 1600

Cultures Transparencies CW7, 9, 10, 11
- Ranch House and Bungalow
- *Carmichael and O'Keeffe*
- from *Walden*
- Duke Ellington's Band

TEST-TAKING RESOURCES

 **Strategies for Test Preparation**

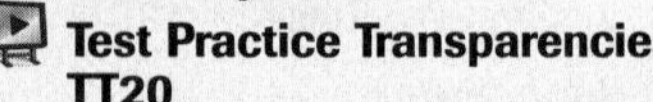

Online Test Practice

Agriculture and Industry of the United States

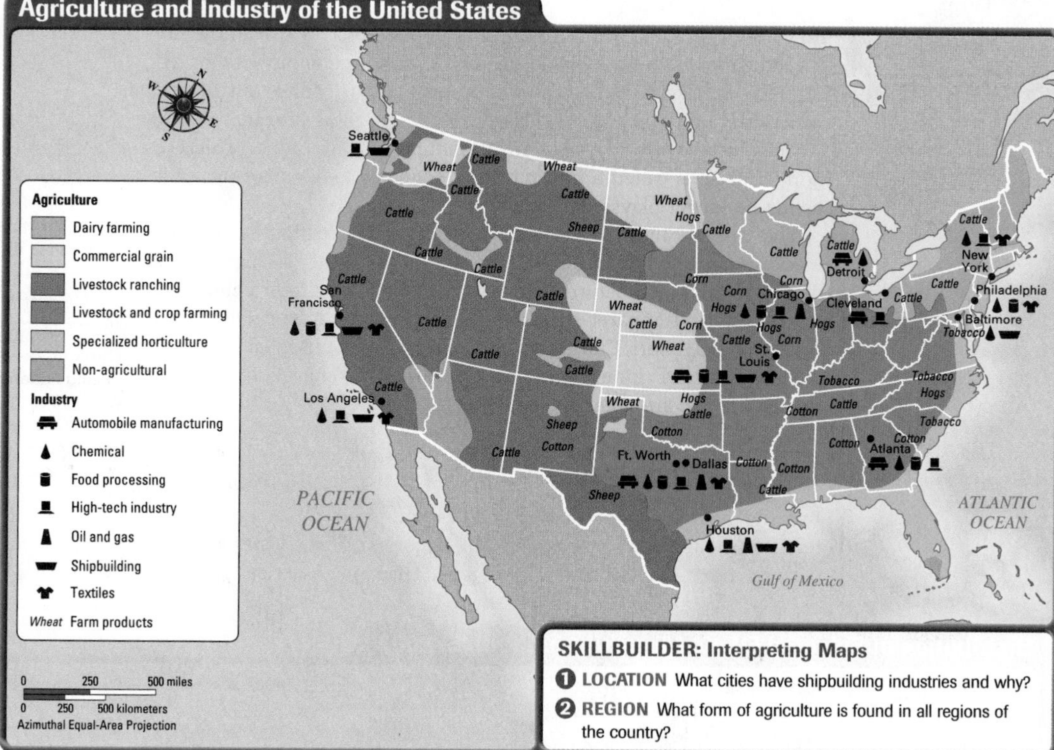

SKILLBUILDER: Interpreting Maps

❶ **LOCATION** What cities have shipbuilding industries and why?

❷ **REGION** What form of agriculture is found in all regions of the country?

AN AGRICULTURAL AND INDUSTRIAL GIANT The United States not only feeds itself but also helps to feed the world. American farms and ranches supply about 40 percent of the world's production of corn, 12 percent of its cotton, about 9 percent of its wheat, and close to 19 percent of its cattle. Fertile soil, a favorable climate, and the early mechanization of the country's farms are mainly responsible for this bounty. Different areas of the country produce different products, as you can see from the map on this page. The Midwest and South, for example, specialize in crop farming, while livestock ranching is concentrated in the West.

The industrial output of the United States is larger than that of any other country. Advances in technology, especially in electronics and computers, revolutionized industry and led to the creation of new products and methods of production. Leading industries are petroleum, steel, transportation equipment, chemicals, electronics, food processing, telecommunications, consumer goods, lumber, and mining. A

Major industrial centers have long been located along the Atlantic Coast and around the Great Lakes. In recent decades, a variety of industries have also started up in urban areas in the South and along the Pacific coast. Over time, some areas have become associated with certain products, such as Detroit (automobiles), Seattle (aircraft), and northern California, in an area called Silicon Valley (computers).

A POSTINDUSTRIAL ECONOMY The graphs on page 140 show the rich farming and manufacturing traditions of the United States. But

Geographic Thinking

Seeing Patterns
A Why might industrial centers be located near bodies of water?

A. Answer
Bodies of water can be used for transporting goods and also as sources of power.

Interpreting Maps

Agriculture and Industry of the United States

Have students identify two states that have a high-tech industry. *(Washington, California, Texas, Illinois, Missouri, Ohio, Georgia, or New York)* Ask the students to name three cities that have chemical industries. *(any of the cities named on the map except Cleveland, St. Louis, and Seattle)* Then have the students identify the northernmost area of commercial grain production. *(North Dakota, Montana, and Washington)* Ask students what type of livestock ranching is important in south/southwest Texas. *(sheep)*

SKILLBUILDER ANSWERS

1. Seattle, San Francisco, Los Angeles, Houston, St. Louis, and Baltimore have shipbuilding industries, and they are located on bodies of water. **2.** cattle raising

More About

Farming Trends

More than 800,000 American farms have vanished or been overtaken by corporate ventures since 1969. Nearly 50% of all U.S. farm production occurs on just 1% of all U.S. farms. Yet, family-run farms have recently had an opportunity to stay in business through a new trend: organic farming. Increasing consumer demand is fueling this $6 billion industry. Despite the natural difficulties and smaller crops inherent in organic farming, farmers are adopting new methods and creating a new niche in American agriculture.

ACTIVITY OPTION **INTERNET RESEARCH**

BLOCK SCHEDULING

REPORTING ON ECONOMIC TRENDS

Objective To connect geographical content to current trends

Class Time 1 hour

Task Use the Internet to research trends on growing cities and their industries

Directions Divide students into groups of 4-6. Assign one city to each group: Atlanta, Denver, Seattle, Austin. Give the same city to more than one group if necessary. Have each group work to find out current information on its city, in answer to the following questions. Is the city growing in size? What are some causes for the growth or lack thereof? What is the current major industry in that city? How does it affect the economy of that city and its residents? Have the students write a short report containing the above information and citing sources. Then have them share the reports with the class.

OPTIONAL ACTIVITY If Internet access is limited, have students use the library and assistance of a librarian to find current statistics and information through reference books, newspapers, and periodicals.

Instruct: Objective 2

A Diverse Society

- Where do the majority of Americans have their ethnic roots? *(Europe)*
- What is the second most commonly spoken language in the U.S? *(Spanish)*
- To what religious group do the majority of Americans belong? *(Christianity)*
- What are some American cultural elements that have influenced the world? *(skyscrapers, film, music)*

Map Transparencies MT13
- Selected Native Peoples of North America, c. 1600

Interpreting Maps

Distribution of Selected Ethnic Minorities in the U.S., 2000

Have students examine the map. Then ask which subregion has the highest concentration of African Americans. *(the southeast)* Ask which subregion has the highest concentration of Hispanics. *(the southwest)*

SKILLBUILDER ANSWERS

1. the West **2.** Very few remain east of the Mississippi; most are in the West.

they also indicate that the American economy today is driven by service industries. A **service industry** is any kind of economic activity that produces a service rather than a product. Nearly three out of four Americans now work in service-related jobs, such as information processing, finance, medicine, transportation, and education. This economic phase is called a **postindustrial economy,** one where manufacturing no longer plays a dominant role.

The United States is the world's major trading nation, leading the world in the value of its imports. It exports raw materials, agricultural products, and manufactured goods. Automobiles, electronic equipment, machinery, and apparel are some of its principal imports. Its North American neighbors, Canada and Mexico, are two of its most important trading partners. Many American corporations engage in business worldwide and are called **multinationals.** B

B. Answer They are exported as raw materials to other countries.

Geographic Thinking
Seeing Patterns
B Where do some of the natural resources of the United States go?

A Diverse Society

Because the United States is a nation of immigrants, it is a nation of different races and ethnic traditions. The majority of Americans, about 65 percent, trace their ancestry to Europe. Hispanic Americans, mainly

Distribution of Selected Ethnic Minorities in the U.S., 2000

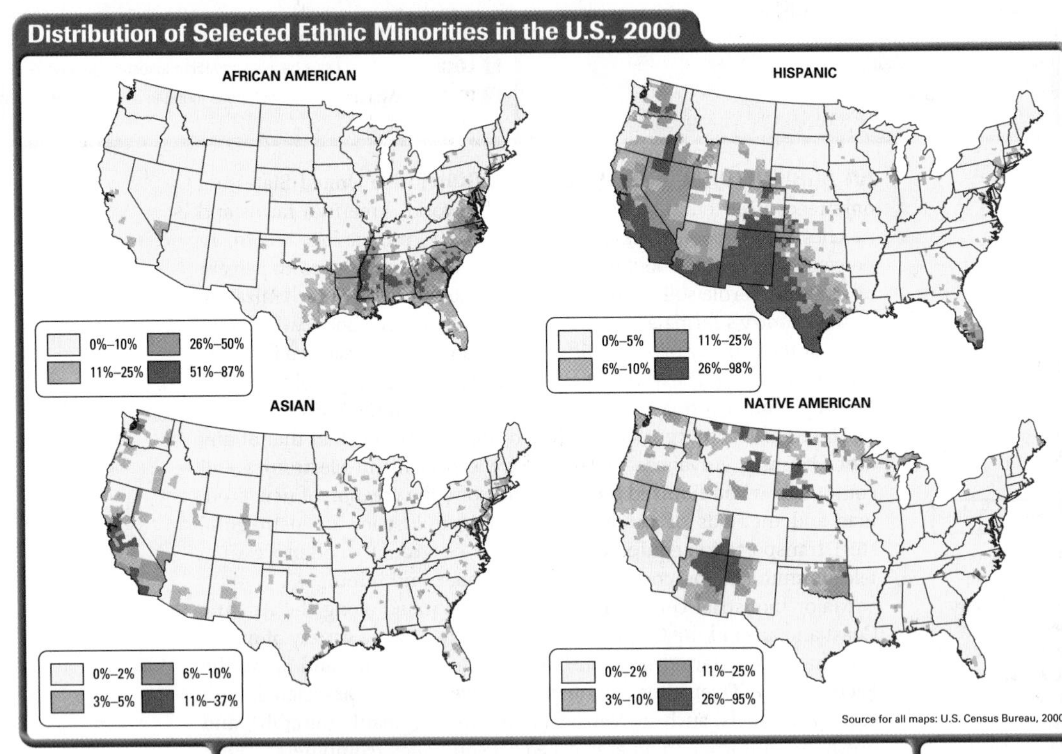

SKILLBUILDER: Interpreting Maps

1. **REGION** What subregion has significant numbers of most of the ethnic groups shown?
2. **MOVEMENT** Compare this map with the map on page 104. What has changed about the distribution of Native Americans since 1600?

DIFFERENTIATING INSTRUCTION **STUDENTS ACQUIRING ENGLISH/ESL**

PREFIXES: UN-, POST-, AND MULTI-

Objective To help ESL students understand how a prefix acts to create a new word

Class Time 10-15 minutes

Task To identify words that contain a prefix by organizing the information into a chart

Directions Have students create a three-column chart with the headings "Prefix," "Meaning," and "New Word." Remind students that a prefix is defined as letters added to the beginning of a word to form a new word, for example, *un-*, *post-*, and *multi-*. Ask them to glance through this chapter section and find three or four words that contain a prefix and put the appropriate information into the chart. A completed chart might look like this.

PREFIX	MEANING	NEW WORD
un-	not	unsafe
post-	after	postindustrial
multi-	many	multinational

from Central and South America, make up about 15 percent of the population; African Americans, about 13 percent; Asian Americans, 5 percent; and Native Americans, 1 percent. The largest ethnic groups are English, German, Irish, African, French, Italian, Scottish, Polish, and Mexican.

LANGUAGES AND RELIGION English has been the dominant language of the United States since its founding. Spanish is the second most commonly spoken language. Typically, immigrants have spoken their native language until they learned English.

BACKGROUND
English is the dominant language in countries, including Canada, the United States, and Australia, that cover one-fifth of the earth's land surface.

Religious freedom has been a cornerstone of American society. Today, more than 1,000 different religious groups practice their faiths in the United States. The majority of the American people—75 percent—are Christians. About 50 percent are Protestants and 24 percent Roman Catholics. Jews and Muslims account for about 2 percent of the religious population. About 15 percent of Americans report they do not identify with any religion.

THE ARTS AND POPULAR CULTURE The United States has a rich artistic heritage, the product of its diverse population. Its first artists were Native Americans, who made pottery, weavings, and carvings. Early European settlers brought with them the artistic traditions of their homelands. Truly American styles developed in painting, music, literature, and architecture in the 19th century. Artists depicted the country's expansive landscape and scenes of American life both on the western frontier and in the cities. One 19th-century American creation, the skyscraper, changed urban architecture all over the world.

5 THEMES
MOVEMENT
Moving the Blues
Blues music developed among African Americans in the rural South around the beginning of the 20th century. This expressive folk music, usually played on a guitar or harmonica, had its roots in Africa. The blues spread throughout the United States, as African Americans migrated to urban areas to find jobs.
The form of the blues born in the delta region of Mississippi was taken north by rural migrants to cities like Memphis, St. Louis, and Chicago (where the blues guitarist Muddy Waters settled). Blues from the Carolinas reached New York City, while the Texas blues went west to Los Angeles and Oakland.
Muddy Waters

US & CANADA

Today, motion pictures and popular music are two influential American art forms. Hollywood, California, is the center of the movie industry in the United States. American films provide entertainment for the world. Many ethnic groups contributed to the musical heritage of the United States. For example, jazz, blues, gospel, and rock 'n' roll have African-American origins. Country and bluegrass music developed among Southern whites whose ancestors came from the British Isles.

American Life Today

More than 307 million people live in the United States. The majority enjoy a high standard of living. Despite coming from many ethnic and racial groups, they generally live and work together. They are pursuing what attracted their ancestors to the New World and came to be called "the American dream," a better life for themselves and their children.

WHERE AMERICANS LIVE About 80 percent of Americans live in cities or surrounding suburbs. Americans moved first from rural areas to cities and then from cities to suburbs. The shift to the suburbs was made possible by the widespread ownership of automobiles. There is one auto

5 THEMES

Movement: Moving the Blues

Once the blues had spread across the United States, they travelled still farther. The blues style was a major inspiration to burgeoning rock 'n' rollers such as Chuck Berry and Bo Diddley, who in turn influenced English rockers Eric Clapton, Jeff Beck, and Jimmy Page.

Have students read the featurette and answer the following questions. What instruments are mostly used in blues music? What group mostly played and spread blues music? When did blues music develop? *(guitar and harmonica; African Americans; around the turn of the 20th century)*

Instruct: Objective 

American Life Today

- What has attracted most people to the United States? *(a chance for a better life)*
- Where do the majority of Americans live? *(cities and suburbs)*
- What is the gender breakdown of the workforce in America? *(about 50/50 men and women)*

Cultures Around the World
- Architecture, p. 7
- Fine Arts, p. 9
- Literature, p. 10
- Music, p. 11

 **Cultures Transparencies CW7, 9, 10, 11**
- Ranch House and Bungalow
- *Carmichael* and *O'Keeffe*
- from *Walden*
- Duke Ellington's Band

ACTIVITY OPTION | **COOPERATIVE LEARNING**

TAKING A SURVEY

Objective To conduct a survey to see which ethnic groups and languages are represented in student body

Class Time One class period

Task Conduct a survey in school

Directions Divide the class into small groups. Have each group survey a different class in school to see what nationalities and ethnic groups students (and their families) represent, as well as what languages are spoken among students and their families. Have each group present its findings to the rest of the class. Then combine the surveys to arrive at a more comprehensive picture of the school.

Interpreting Photographs

Chicago

The Chicago skyline is one of the most beautiful in the country. Set along Lake Michigan's blue waters, it contains diverse building styles that have made Chicago an architectural showplace. Chicago's buildings are as diverse as its neighborhoods and its residents.

CAPTION ANSWER boating, swimming, cycling, and jogging

Assess & Reteach

GeoFocus Have students complete their notes on the United States for the cluster diagram.

Formal Assessment
- Section Quiz, p. 84

Reteaching Activity
Have small groups of students look back at the subsection headings and quiz each other by asking a question pertaining to the main idea of each subsection. Students should alternate roles as they go through the section.

In-Depth Resources: Unit 2
- Reteaching Activity, p. 19

HUMAN–ENVIRONMENT INTERACTION Lake Michigan and its shoreline provide Chicago residents with many opportunities for recreation.
What might some of these recreational opportunities be?

for every 1.3 Americans. A highly developed transportation network that includes highways, expressways, railroads, and airlines aids mobility.

HOW AMERICANS LIVE, WORK, AND PLAY Nearly 60 percent of American adults of working age are employed. Almost half of them are women. Approximately three-fourths of all Americans in the workforce hold service industry jobs. Many are highly skilled positions, which require advanced education. Americans have always valued education, seeing it as a means to provide equality and opportunity. As a result, all children from the ages of 6 or 7 to age 16 are required to attend school. Nine out of ten students are in the public school system, where education is free through secondary school. The United States also has more than 2,600 four-year public and private colleges and universities.

Americans have a wide range of choices for leisure-time activities. As either spectators or players, they take part in sports such as baseball, basketball, football, golf, soccer, tennis, and skiing. Most major cities have professional sports teams. Americans of all ages also use their free time to engage in hobbies, visit museums and libraries, and watch television and movies. Another favorite activity is spending time on the computer, surfing the Internet or playing video games.

Unfortunately, not all Americans live well. More than one in eight lives in poverty. It is a continuing challenge for government and society to try to bring these people into the mainstream of American life. In the next section, you will learn about life in the country's subregions.

Section 2 Assessment

1 Places & Terms

Explain the meaning of each of the following terms.
- export
- free enterprise
- service industry
- postindustrial economy
- multinational

2 Taking Notes

REGION Review the notes you took for this section.

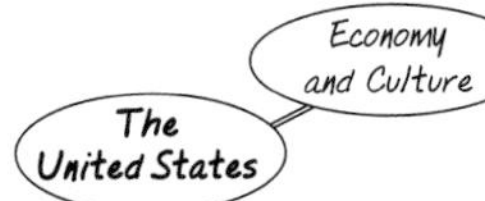

- Where are the industrial centers in the United States?
- Where do the majority of Americans live?

3 Main Ideas

a. What three factors have contributed to the success of the American economy?
b. What are the geographic origins of some American musical styles?
c. What invention made life in the suburbs possible?

4 Geographic Thinking

Making Comparisons How is the economy of the United States today different from its economy 50 years ago?
Think about:
- postindustrial economy
- multinational trade

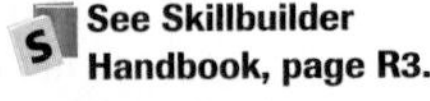
See Skillbuilder Handbook, page R3.

EXPLORING LOCAL GEOGRAPHY Study the maps on page 142. Find your state. Create a **sketch map** of your state and show the location of major ethnic groups that live in your state.

SECTION 2 ASSESSMENT ANSWERS

1. Places & Terms
export, p. 140
free enterprise, p. 140
service industry, p. 142
postindustrial economy, p. 142
multinational, p. 142

2. Taking Notes
- the Atlantic and Pacific coasts, near the Great Lakes, and in the urban areas of the South
- cities or surrounding suburbs

3. Main Ideas
a. an abundance of natural resources, skilled labor force, and stable political system
b. jazz, blues, gospel, and rock 'n' roll have origins in Africa; country and bluegrass, in the British Isles
c. the automobile

4. Geographic Thinking
The economy today is based on service industries; corporations trade worldwide.

GeoActivity

Alternative Assessment
- Rubric for a sketch map, 2.1

Subregions of the United States

Main Ideas

- The United States is divided into four major economic and cultural subregions.
- There are both similarities and differences among the subregions of the United States.

Places & Terms

New England
megalopolis
the Midwest
the South
metropolitan area
the West

CONNECT TO THE ISSUES

DIVERSE SOCIETIES While diversity can be a strength, it has also been the cause of tension and conflict among regions.

A HUMAN PERSPECTIVE America's back roads were the beat of reporter and author Charles Kuralt for more than 20 years. Beginning in the 1960s, he traveled by van through every region of the country. In his "On the Road" series for television, he reported on the uniqueness of the lives of ordinary Americans. He said that he wanted to make these trips off the beaten path because most people traveled across the country on interstate highways without seeing the "real" America. Whether he visited Minnesota's lake country or a small New England town, Kuralt spotlighted America's regional diversity. In fact, one of the key strengths of the United States is the variety of life in its subregions—the Northeast, the Midwest, the South, and the West.

The Northeast

As you can see on the map on page 134, the Northeast covers only 5 percent of the nation's land area. But about 20 percent of the population lives there. The six northern states of the subregion—Maine, Vermont, New Hampshire, Massachusetts, Rhode Island, and Connecticut—are called **New England**. The other three—Pennsylvania, New York, and New Jersey—are sometimes referred to as Middle Atlantic states. (Maryland and Delaware, which are included in the South in this book, are sometimes included in the Middle Atlantic states.)

AMERICA'S GATEWAY Because of its location along the Atlantic coast, the Northeast contains many of the areas first settled by Europeans. The region served as the "gateway" to America for millions of immigrants from all over the world. Many people still engage in fishing and farming,

LOCATION BosWash is the name given to the highly urbanized northeastern seaboard of the United States.

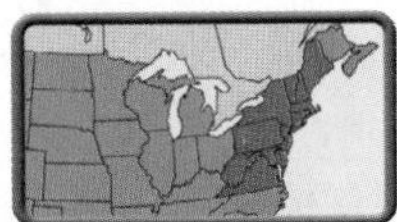

Urbanization in the Northeast

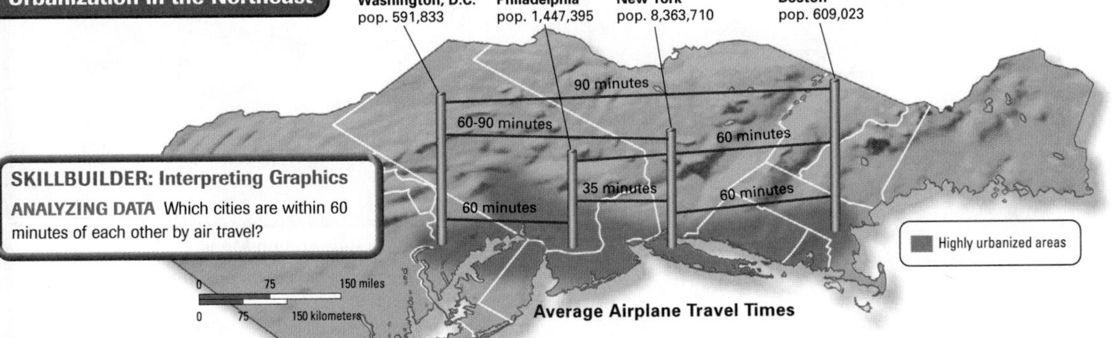

SKILLBUILDER: Interpreting Graphics

ANALYZING DATA Which cities are within 60 minutes of each other by air travel?

SECTION 3 OBJECTIVES

1. Examine the subregion known as the Northeast in the United States.
2. Examine the subregion known as the Midwest in the United States.
3. Examine the subregion known as the South in the United States.
4. Examine the subregion known as the West in the United States.

SKILLBUILDERS: Interpreting Graphics & Maps, pp. 145, 146, 149

GeographicThinking

Using the Atlas, p. 146
Making Comparisons, p. 147
Seeing Patterns, p. 149

Focus & Motivate

What accounts for the variety of ifestyles within a country's subregions? *(location, climate, types of people settling in the area, local industry)*

Instruct: Objective 1 appears on p. 146.

Interpreting Graphics

Urbanization in the Northeast

Have students examine the map. Then, ask them to identify which Northeast city listed on the map has the largest population. Ask them how long the airplane ride would be when traveling from Washington to Boston. *(New York; 90 minutes)*

SKILLBUILDER ANSWER

Washington to Philadelphia, Philadelphia to New York, New York to Boston, Philadelphia to Boston

SECTION 3 PROGRAM RESOURCES

In-Depth Resources: Unit 2
- Guided Reading, p. 15
- Skillbuilder Practice, p. 16
- Building Vocabulary, p. 17
- Reteaching Activity, p. 20

Guided Reading Workbook
Section 3

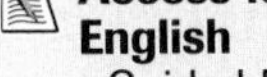
Access for Students Acquiring English
- Guided Reading, p. 31
- Skillbuilder Practice, p. 32

Formal Assessment
- Section Quiz, p. 85

Integrated Assessment
- Rubric for a database, 2.6
- Rubric for a documentary proposal, 5.5
- Rubric for a map, 2.1

Outline Maps with Activities
- United States: Physical and Political, pp. 13–14

INTEGRATED TECHNOLOGY

Power Presentations

The World's Music Audio Program

Chapter Summaries

Test Generator
- Section Quiz

hmhsocialstudies.com

TEST-TAKING RESOURCES

Strategies for Test Preparation

Test Practice Transparencies TT21

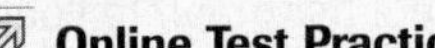
Online Test Practice

Instruct: Objective 

The Northeast

- What are two terms for state groups within the Northeast subregion? *(New England; Middle Atlantic)*
- What is one of the most significant physical factors influencing the economy in the Northeast? *(proximity to the Atlantic Ocean)*
- Why has the Northeast been referred to as the gateway to America? *(Many immigrants arrived there by boat from Europe.)*

 **In-Depth Resources: Unit 2**
- Guided Reading, p. 15

as the Northeast's early settlers did. But the region's coastal and inland waters turned it into the heart of trade, commerce, and industry for the nation. In fact, the Northeast is one of the most heavily industrialized and urbanized areas in the world. The Atlantic seaboard cities of Philadelphia, Boston, and New York City serve as international trade centers.

Coal, iron ore, and oil—found mainly in Pennsylvania—fueled the industrialization of the region. Traditional industries, such as iron and steel, petroleum, and lumber, still play a role in the region's economy. But most Northeasterners are now employed in such manufacturing and service industries as electronics, communications, chemicals, medical research, finance, and tourism. Pennsylvania, New York, and New Jersey have rich farmlands, but much of New England is too hilly or rocky to grow crops easily. A

Parts of the Middle Atlantic states are often referred to as the "rust belt" because of their declining and abandoned traditional industries. They share this term with some of the states of the Midwest. In recent times, many "rust belt" industries have moved to the warmer climates of the "sunbelt" in the South and West.

GROWTH OF THE MEGALOPOLIS The nation's first megalopolis developed in the Northeast. A **megalopolis** is a region in which several large cities and surrounding areas grow together. You can see the extent of the "BosWash" megalopolis, as it is called, in the illustration on page 145.

Geographic Thinking

Using the Atlas

A Refer to the map on page 106. What economic activities are shown for the Northeast?

A. Answer
commercial farming and fishing, forestry, and manufacturing and trade

Interpreting Maps

Population Increase By States, 1990-2000

Have students look at the map. Ask them which states in the East have shown the biggest increases in population. *(North Carolina, Georgia, and Florida)* Ask which southern state showed a population increase of less than 10 percent. *(Louisiana)*

SKILLBUILDER ANSWERS

1. Arizona, Nevada, Utah, and Colorado **2.** the Northeast, because most states in the region had a less than 10 percent increase

Population Increase by State, 1990–2000

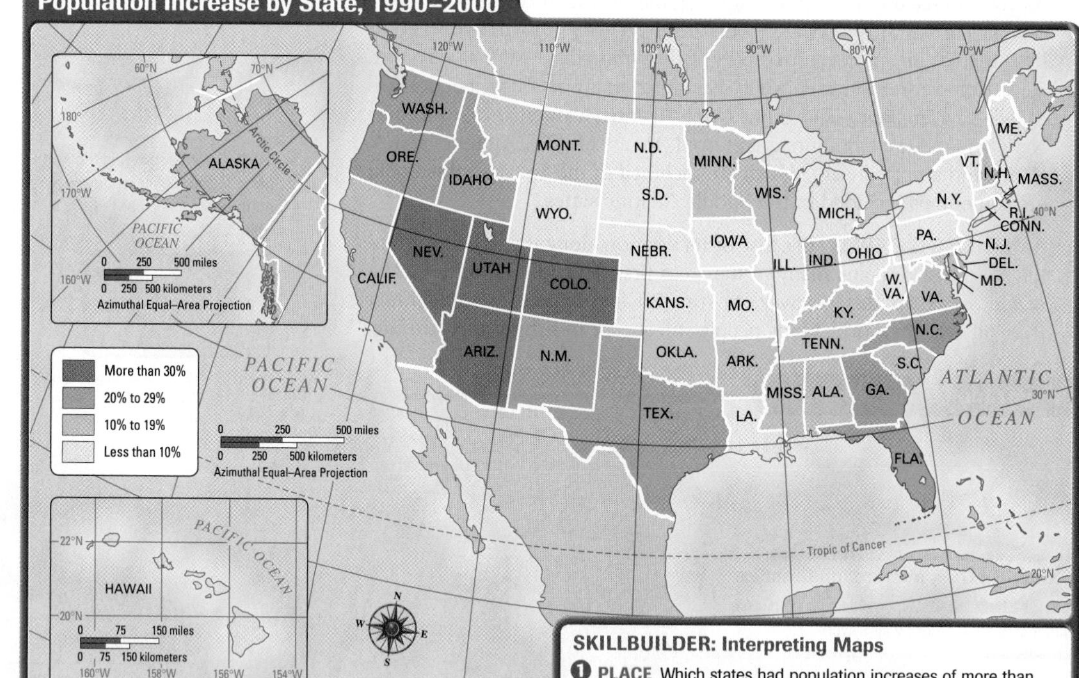

SKILLBUILDER: Interpreting Maps

❶ **PLACE** Which states had population increases of more than 30 percent?

❷ **REGION** Which region had the lowest increase in population?

ACTIVITY OPTION SKILLBUILDER LESSON

CREATING GRAPHS AND CHARTS

Objective To show differences in land and population ratios throughout the U.S. in a bar graph format

Class Time 30 minutes

Task Create a bar graph to compare population and land size in the United States' four subregions

 **In-Depth Resources: Unit 2**
- Skillbuilder Practice, p. 16

Directions Have students create a graph with two axes, one showing "Population/Land Size," the other showing "U.S. Subregions." Tell students that the graph should contain two bars, side by side, for each subregion, one for population size, one for land size. They should label the subregion underneath or above the double bars. Students should choose a color for each bar (to distinguish them) and create a graph key. Students may draw data for this chart from the Regional Data File on pages 108–113.

It stretches through 500 miles of highly urbanized areas from Boston in the north to Washington, D.C., the national capital, in the south. It contains one-sixth of the U.S. population. New York City, the country's cultural and financial center, is located here. Rapid road, rail, and air links have been vital to its economic development and expansion into the South. You will read more about urban growth in Chapter 8.

The Midwest

The subregion that contains the 12 states of the north-central United States is called the **Midwest.** Because of its central location, the Midwest is called the American heartland. It occupies about one-fifth of the nation's land and almost one-fourth of its people live there. Since the Revolutionary War, immigrants from all over the world have made it their destination. Many early settlers came from Britain, Germany, and Scandinavia. Vast, largely flat plains are a distinctive feature of the region. So are numerous waterways, including the Great Lakes and the Mississippi River and its many tributaries.

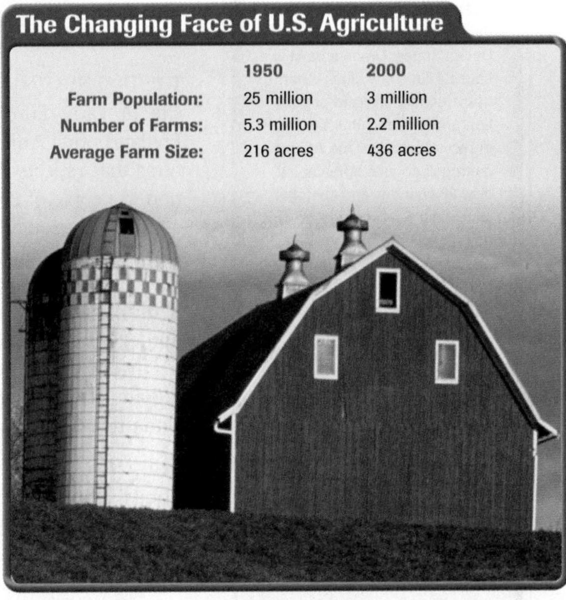

The Changing Face of U.S. Agriculture

	1950	2000
Farm Population:	25 million	3 million
Number of Farms:	5.3 million	2.2 million
Average Farm Size:	216 acres	436 acres

AGRICULTURAL AND INDUSTRIAL HEARTLAND The Midwest is the nation's "breadbasket." Fertile soil, adequate rainfall, and a favorable climate enable Midwesterners to produce more food and feed more people than farmers in any comparable area in the world. Among the main products are corn, wheat, soybeans, meat, and dairy goods. Agriculture also is the foundation for many of the region's industries, including meatpacking, food processing, farm equipment, and grain milling. Other traditional industries are steel and automaking.

Its central location and excellent waterways make the Midwest a trade, transportation, and distribution center. Chicago, Illinois, which is located near the southwestern shores of Lake Michigan, is the cultural, financial, and transportation hub of the Midwest. Most of the region's major cities developed near large bodies of water, which were essential for early transportation. Cleveland, Detroit, Chicago, and Milwaukee grew near the Great Lakes, and Cincinnati, St. Louis, Minneapolis, St. Paul, Kansas City, and Omaha developed along rivers. B

B. Answer They are near bodies of water.

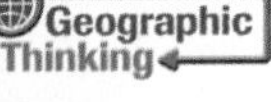

Geographic Thinking

Making Comparisons

B What do the major cities of the Midwest have in common with those of the Northeast?

CHANGING FACE OF THE MIDWEST Like other regions, the Midwest is changing. The number of farms is declining. More Midwesterners are now employed in providing services than in traditional industries. The region's metropolitan areas are expanding as urban dwellers and businesses leave the central cities for the suburbs. People and industries are also moving to the warmer South and West.

Interpreting Graphics

The Changing Face of U.S. Agriculture

Have students examine the U.S. agriculture statistics. Ask them to explain how the numbers in the two columns differ and what conclusions can be drawn from those numbers. *(Today there are fewer farms and people living on farms than in the '50s; of the farms that remain, they are larger in size than the farms of the past.)*

Instruct: Objective 2

The Midwest

- What is the Midwest most known for? *(agriculture)*
- What major industries are located in the Midwest? *(steel manufacturing and automaking)*
- What geographical factors helped make the Midwest a center for trade? *(central location and good waterways)*
- How is the Midwest changing? *(less agricultural; more service-oriented; metropolitan areas are increasing in size as suburbs grow)*

DIFFERENTIATING INSTRUCTION — GIFTED AND TALENTED STUDENTS

FINDING A BUSINESS SITE

Objective To help students use geographic information in a real-life situation

Class Time One class period

Task Produce a report that explains which of two cities would be the better location for a tire manufacturing company

Directions Tell students that they will act as the scout for a new automobile tire manufacturing company that is trying to decide on a business location. They can choose between Chicago and Detroit. Then have the students research the factors that would make each site more appealing. Have them produce a report that tells the pros and cons of each choice and argues for one site as more preferable to the other.

Instruct: Objective 3

The South

- Which southern state was England's first colony? *(Virginia)*
- What are some of the South's most important crops? *(cotton, tobacco, peanuts, rice, fruits)*
- What is a common nickname for the South? *(the "sunbelt")*
- Which southern state is sometimes grouped with the southwestern states? *(Texas)*

Connect TO THE Issues

Urban Sprawl

Have students read the information on traffic congestion in Atlanta, Georgia. Ask if anyone they know travels more than 20 miles a day by car to get to school or a job. Ask students what they think that experience is like. Ask students to share any experiences or personal knowledge of this with the class. *(parent or family member's commute might be stressful because of traffic, travel times, and so forth)*

Instruct: Objective 4 appears on p. 149.

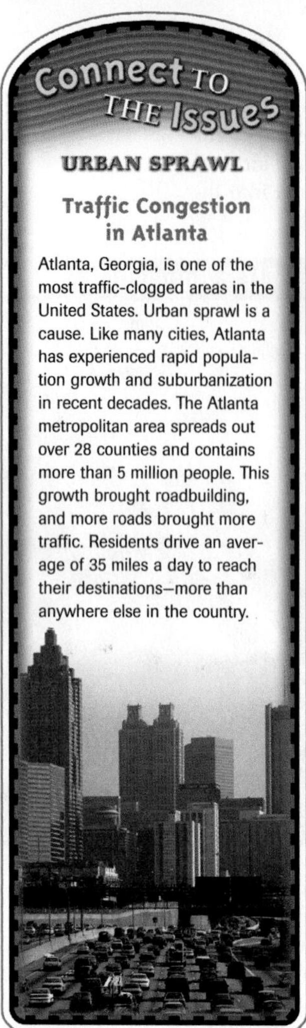

Connect TO THE Issues

URBAN SPRAWL

Traffic Congestion in Atlanta

Atlanta, Georgia, is one of the most traffic-clogged areas in the United States. Urban sprawl is a cause. Like many cities, Atlanta has experienced rapid population growth and suburbanization in recent decades. The Atlanta metropolitan area spreads out over 28 counties and contains more than 5 million people. This growth brought roadbuilding, and more roads brought more traffic. Residents drive an average of 35 miles a day to reach their destinations–more than anywhere else in the country.

The South

The South is a subregion that covers about one-fourth of the land area of the United States and contains more than one-third of its population. Among its 16 states are 11 that made up the Confederacy during the Civil War. One of these states—Texas—is sometimes included in an area of the West called the Southwest. The South's warm climate, fertile soils, and many natural resources have shaped its development.

THE OLD SOUTH Like the Northeast, the South was also the site of early European settlement. In fact, Virginia was England's first American colony. The South has a mix of cultures that reflects the diversity of its early settlers. In addition to people of British heritage, there are the descendants of Africans brought as slave laborers and Hispanics whose families first migrated from Mexico to Texas. Cajuns of French-Canadian origin and Creoles of French, Spanish, and African descent are found in Louisiana, while Florida is home to many Hispanics who came from Cuba.

Once a rural agricultural area, the South is rapidly changing and its cities growing. Along with the Southwest, it is often referred to as the "sunbelt" because of its climate.

THE NEW SOUTH Agriculture was the South's first economic activity, and cotton, tobacco, fruits, peanuts, and rice are still grown there. Also, livestock production is important in states such as Texas and Arkansas. The South's humid subtropical climate at first hindered industrialization. But the widespread use of air conditioning beginning in the 1950s and the region's vast stores of energy resources—oil, coal, natural gas, and water—gave a boost to industry.

In recent times, the South has attracted many manufacturing and service industries fleeing the harsh weather of the "rust belt." Major industries include petroleum, steel, chemicals, food processing, textiles, and electronics. The South's climate draws millions of tourists and retirees, too. Atlanta, Georgia—a financial, trade, and transportation center—is the hub of the New South. Miami, Tampa-St. Petersburg, New Orleans, Houston, Dallas-Fort Worth, and San Antonio are other rapidly growing **metropolitan areas**—large cities and nearby suburbs and towns.

The West

Look on the map on page 134, and you will see that **the West** is a far-flung subregion consisting of 13 states. It stretches from the Great Plains to the Pacific Ocean and includes Alaska to the north and Hawaii in the Pacific. The West covers about one-half of the land area of the United States but has only about one-fifth of the population. It is a region of dramatic and varied landscapes.

People settle in the West today as they did during its frontier days: wherever landforms and climate are favorable. Some areas, such as its many deserts, are sparsely settled. Nonetheless, California is the

BACKGROUND
Washington, Oregon, and Idaho are often called the Northwest. California, Arizona, New Mexico, Nevada, Colorado, Utah, and Texas are called the Southwest.

ACTIVITY OPTION **EXPLORING LOCAL GEOGRAPHY**

BLOCK SCHEDULING

DRAFTING A PROPOSAL ON EASING TRAFFIC CONGESTION

Objective To help students apply experience or local knowledge to geographical material

Class Time 30 minutes

Task Prepare a report on local traffic congestion

Directions Have students discuss traffic congestion in their area, perhaps around the school, or in a particularly busy part of town. Ask them the following questions: What causes traffic congestion around the school or in their neighborhood or town? How does it affect people? Then have them discuss solutions to the problem. Have them prepare a presentation on the problem, proposing possible solutions.

148 CHAPTER 6

BACKGROUND According to the 2000 census, the population of the West grew by 20 percent from 1990.

country's most populous state because of excellent farmland, good harbors, and a mild climate. The West is the most rapidly growing region in the United States. Los Angeles, the country's second largest city, is the West's cultural and commercial center.

DEVELOPING THE WEST The West's growth in the 20th century was helped by air conditioning and by irrigation. The map on this page, for example, shows how water from the Colorado River in Arizona has been diverted to serve many areas. Water supply aided development of inland cities such as Las Vegas, Tucson, and Phoenix.

The economic activities of the West are as varied as its climate and landscape. Among them are farming, ranching, food processing, logging, fishing, mining, oil refining, tourism, filmmaking, and the production of computers. Many cities with good harbors, including Seattle, Los Angeles, and Long Beach, make foreign trade—especially with Asia—important.

You read about the subregions of the United States in this section. In the next chapter, you will learn about the human geography of Canada.

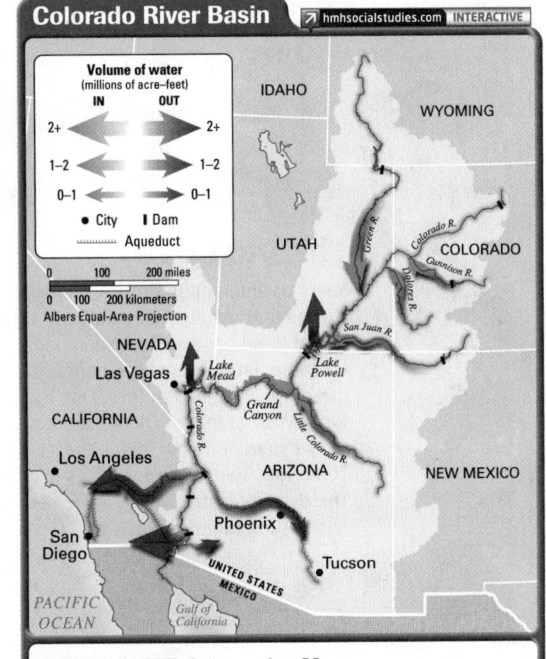

SKILLBUILDER: Interpreting Maps

1. **PLACE** What area receives the largest volume of water from the Colorado River?
2. **MOVEMENT** Which states contribute water to the Colorado River?

Instruct: Objective 

The West

- What two states are not near any other states? *(Alaska, Hawaii)*
- What is the West's current population growth? *(most rapidly growing region in country)*
- What inventions or processes helped the West grow in the 20th century? *(air conditioning, irrigation)*

US & CANADA

Interpreting Maps

Colorado River Basin

Have students examine the map. Ask them to identify three rivers that feed into the Colorado River and three states that receive water from the Colorado River. *(Gunnison, Dolores, San Juan, Green, Little Colorado Rivers; Arizona, California, Nevada, Utah)*

SKILLBUILDER ANSWERS
1. San Diego **2.** Wyoming, Colorado, New Mexico, Arizona

SECTION 3 Assessment

1 Places & Terms

Explain the meaning of each of the following terms.

- New England
- megalopolis
- the Midwest
- the South
- metropolitan area
- the West

2 Taking Notes

REGION Review the notes you took for this section.

- What are the four subregions of the United States?
- Which subregion is the largest in land area?

3 Main Ideas

a. Why is the Northeast one of the most heavily industrialized and urbanized areas?
b. How is the economy of the Midwest changing?
c. What helped the economy of the West to grow?

4 Geographic Thinking

Seeing Patterns How has air conditioning changed the economic activities of the subregions of the United States? **Think about:**

- the South and the West
- the "rust belt" and the "sunbelt"

MAKING COMPARISONS Use the Internet to find more information on the economies of the four subregions. Create a **database** comparing the top five industries in each of the four subregions.

21ST CENTURY

Assess & Reteach

GeoFocus Have students complete their notes on the United States for the cluster diagram.

 **Formal Assessment**
- Section Quiz, p. 85

Reteaching Activity
Have students look back through the section and list the main idea for each subhead in their notebooks. Then ask them to divide into pairs and compare their main ideas.

 **In-Depth Resources: Unit 2**
- Reteaching Activity, p. 20

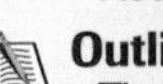 **Outline Maps with Activities**
- The United States: Physical and Political, pp. 13–14

SECTION 3 ASSESSMENT ANSWERS

1. Places & Terms
New England, p. 145
megalopolis, p. 146
the Midwest, p. 147
the South, p. 148
metropolitan area, p. 148
the West, p. 148

2. Taking Notes
- the Northeast, the Midwest, the South, and the West
- the West

3. Main Ideas
a. Its coastal and inland waters aid commerce, trade, and industry.
b. Its economy is now based on service industries rather than traditional industries.
c. air conditioning and irrigation

4. Geographic Thinking
Air conditioning made it possible to move industries to warmer climates in both the South and the West. Industries in the Midwest and Northeast "rust belt" are moving to the sunbelt of the South and West.

GeoActivity

 **Integrated Assessment**
- Rubric for a database, 2.6

OBJECTIVES

1. Identify the region affected by the Dust Bowl disaster.
2. Examine the effects of the Dust Bowl disaster on people.
3. Examine causes of severe drought and preventive measures.

Instruct: Objective

The Dust Bowl

- What happened during this disaster? *(A severe drought dried up rivers, killing crops and livestock.)*
- What important social effects were caused by the Dust Bowl disaster? *(hunger, poverty, homelessness)*
- What did many people who went to California end up doing for a living? *(working as migrant farm laborers)*
- Which two agricultural practices contributed to Dust Bowl conditions? *(overplowing and overgrazing)*

Interpreting Maps

The Dust Bowl

Ask students to examine the map. Ask them to identify the states that comprised the Dust Bowl. *(Texas, Oklahoma, New Mexico, Kansas, Nebraska, Wyoming, North and South Dakota, Montana, and Colorado)* In what region of the United States did the Dust Bowl disaster occur? *(southwestern Great Plains)* From what point south to what point north did the Dust Bowl stretch? *(from Texas to Montana/North Dakota)*

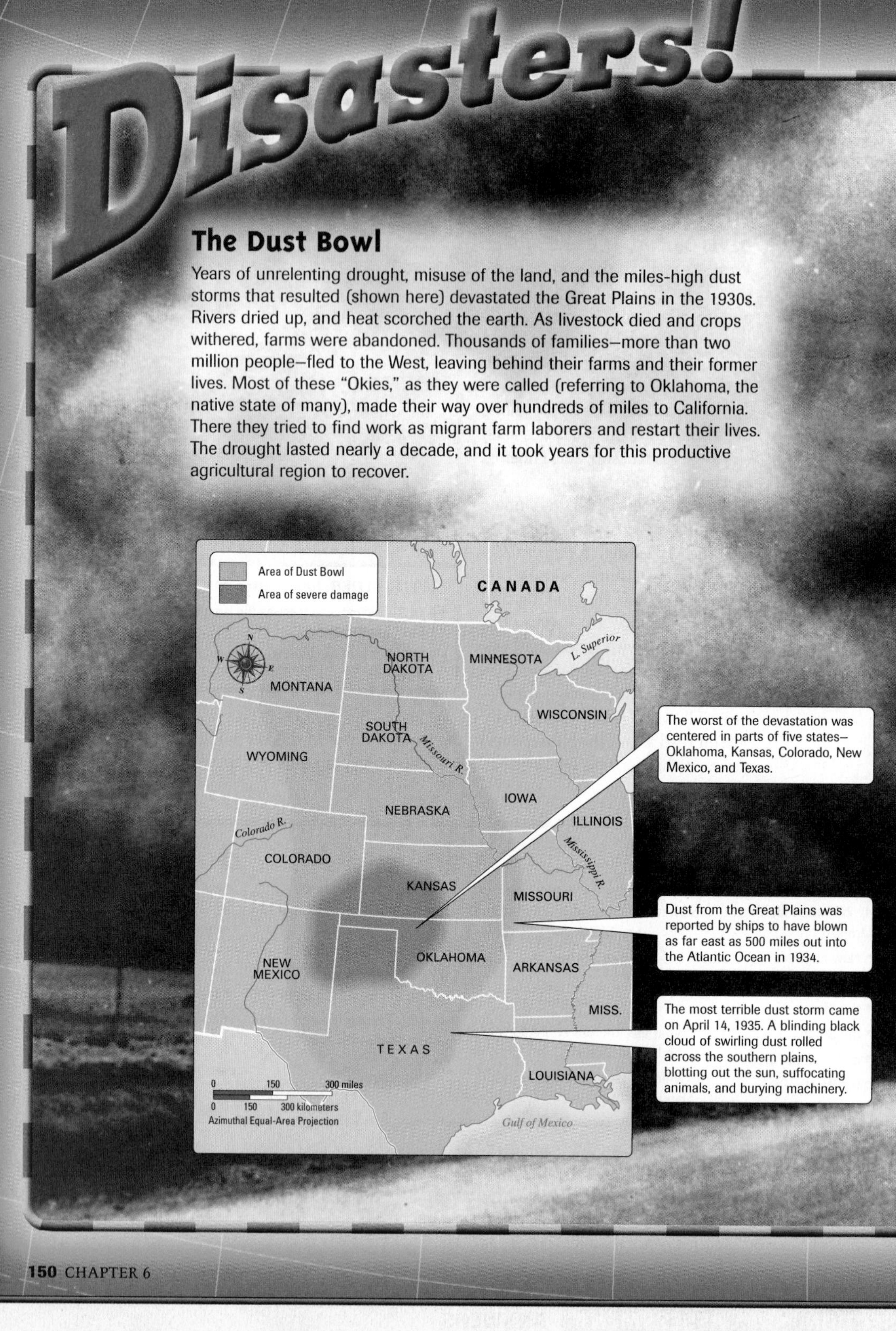
Disasters!
Area of Dust Bowl
Area of severe damage
CANADA
L. Superior
MONTANA
NORTH DAKOTA
MINNESOTA
SOUTH DAKOTA
WISCONSIN
WYOMING
Missouri R.
IOWA
NEBRASKA
ILLINOIS
Colorado R.
COLORADO
Mississippi R.
KANSAS
MISSOURI
NEW MEXICO
OKLAHOMA
ARKANSAS
MISS.
TEXAS
LOUISIANA
Gulf of Mexico
0 150 300 miles
0 150 300 kilometers
Azimuthal Equal-Area Projection
The worst of the devastation was centered in parts of five states—Oklahoma, Kansas, Colorado, New Mexico, and Texas.
Dust from the Great Plains was reported by ships to have blown as far east as 500 miles out into the Atlantic Ocean in 1934.
The most terrible dust storm came on April 14, 1935. A blinding black cloud of swirling dust rolled across the southern plains, blotting out the sun, suffocating animals, and burying machinery.

The Dust Bowl

Years of unrelenting drought, misuse of the land, and the miles-high dust storms that resulted (shown here) devastated the Great Plains in the 1930s. Rivers dried up, and heat scorched the earth. As livestock died and crops withered, farms were abandoned. Thousands of families—more than two million people—fled to the West, leaving behind their farms and their former lives. Most of these "Okies," as they were called (referring to Oklahoma, the native state of many), made their way over hundreds of miles to California. There they tried to find work as migrant farm laborers and restart their lives. The drought lasted nearly a decade, and it took years for this productive agricultural region to recover.

ADDITIONAL RESOURCES

BOOKS FOR THE TEACHER

Gregory, James Noble. ***American Exodus: The Dust Bowl Migration and Okie Culture in California.*** NY: Oxford University Press, 1989. Critical examination of the disaster.

BOOKS FOR THE STUDENT

Hesse, Karen. ***Out of the Dust.*** NY: Scholastic Press, 1997. A 15-year-old's story in first-person free verse poetry.

Ganzel, Bill. ***Dust Bowl Descent.*** Lincoln, NE: University of Nebraska Press, 1984. Photography.

VIDEO

Surviving the Dust Bowl (The American Experience Series). PBS Home Video. Boston, MA: WGBH Educational Foundation, 1998.

INTERNET

For more on the Dust Bowl (and other U.S. disasters), go to . . .

hmhsocialstudies.com

hmhsocialstudies.com INTERACTIVE

Thousands of farms like this one in Cimarron County, Oklahoma, were turned into dust-covered wastelands by the drought and dust storms of the 1930s.

Migrants from the Dust Bowl were forced to live any way they could while trying to find jobs picking vegetables or fruit. This mother and her seven children lived in a tent in a California migrant camp, eating vegetables found on the ground and birds they killed.

GeoActivity

REMEMBERING THE VICTIMS 21ST CENTURY

Use the Internet to find personal accounts of Dust Bowl families. Then create a **documentary proposal** about one of them.

- Begin with a brief overview of how the drought affected the family.
- Add a sketch map showing where they lived and copies of any photos available, with captions for each.
- Present your proposal to a panel of student producers.

hmhsocialstudies.com RESEARCH WEB LINKS

GeoData

CAUSES

- Years of poor agricultural practices, such as overplowing and overgrazing, stripped away about 96 million acres of grasslands in the southern plains.
- Seven years of drought, or dry weather, turned the soil to dust.

EFFECTS

- Hundreds of millions of tons of soil were blown away.
- Crops withered and livestock died.
- More than 2 million plains people abandoned their farms.

PREVENTIVE MEASURES

Experts in crop production and soil management proposed the use of scientific farming methods, including

- contour plowing, or plowing across a hill rather than up and down, to stop wind and water erosion
- terracing, or planting crops in stair-stepped rows, to prevent soil erosion
- planting trees to hold the soil in place and to slow the force of the wind

GeoActivities

Integrated Assessment

- Rubric for a documentary proposal, 5.5

More About

Causes of the Dust Bowl

The area that experienced the Dust Bowl disaster had been largely grassland on which ranchers raised livestock until World War I. After that, millions of acres were converted to wheat growing, which was cheaper and provided more food. Overcultivation and incorrect land use in the 1920s left the region vulnerable not only to the years of drought conditions, but to strong winds that easily carried away topsoil. The wind erosion was eventually stopped through the federally assisted planting of windbreaks, which gave the grasses a chance to re-anchor and grow. By the early 1940s, the Dust Bowl region had nearly recovered.

Interpreting Photographs

Duststorm

Churning winds of up to 90 mph blew walls of dust across the landscape. Ask students how residents might have gotten around in such an environment. *(cars would use headlights in daytime; people would wear dust masks to keep from inhaling dust)*

ACTIVITY OPTION COOPERATIVE LEARNING

ROLE PLAYING: INTERVIEW

Objective To help students grasp the effects of disaster on people by putting them in someone else's shoes

Class Time 30 minutes

Task Take turns as interviewer and interviewee

Directions Have students form pairs or break into groups of four. Have one student act as a journalist during the 1930s and ask two questions of the other student(s), who represent farmers in Oklahoma at the disaster's mid-way point. Have the other students answer the interviewer. Then rotate or switch roles. Students should each ask two questions and answer at least one, based on what they have learned in this section.

CHAPTER 6 ASSESSMENT

Reviewing Places and Terms

A. **1.** migration, p. 135
2. Columbian Exchange, p. 136
3. suburb, p. 138
4. representative democracy, p. 139
5. free enterprise, p. 140
6. service industry, p. 142
7. postindustrial economy, p. 142
8. multinational, p. 142
9. megalopolis, p. 146
10. metropolitan area, p. 148

B. Possible Responses

11. It brought people from Asia, Africa, and Europe to the United States.
12. Some examples are pumpkins, potatoes, sugar cane, and coffee.
13. Suburb, megalopolis, and metropolitan area are associated with urban geography.
14. The U.S. has a representative democracy.
15. Limited government interference and profit are advantages of free enterprise.
16. Service industries are indicators of a postindustrial economy.
17. Examples might include finance, medicine, and education.
18. The corporation will have locations in several countries.
19. The Northeast contains an example of megalopolis.
20. A suburb is a part of a metropolitan area.

Chapter 6 Assessment

VISUAL SUMMARY
HUMAN GEOGRAPHY OF THE UNITED STATES

History and Government

- The United States was populated by a diverse group of immigrants.
- The United States expanded westward and industrialized.
- The government of the United States is a representative democracy.
- At the start of the 21st century, the United States was the only remaining superpower.

Economy and Culture

- Fertile land, valuable resources, and good location help make the United States an economic leader.
- Much of the U.S. economy is based on service industries.
- Most of the U.S. population lives in urban areas.

Subregions of the United States

- The Northeast region is heavily populated and industrialized.
- The Midwest produces a variety of agricultural and manufactured goods but is shifting to some service industries.
- The South is rapidly becoming more industrialized.
- The West is a rapidly growing economic region.

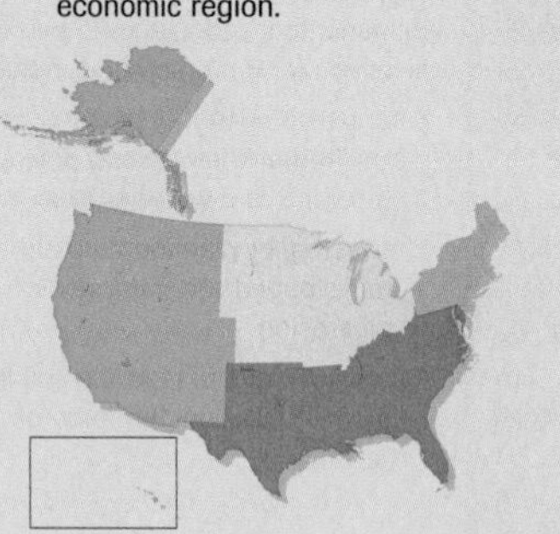

Reviewing Places & Terms

A. Briefly explain the importance of each of the following.

1. migration
2. Columbian Exchange
3. suburb
4. representative democracy
5. free enterprise
6. service industry
7. postindustrial economy
8. multinational
9. megalopolis
10. metropolitan area

B. Answer the questions about vocabulary in complete sentences.

11. What role did migration play in populating the United States?
12. What are some examples of items in the Columbian Exchange?
13. Which of the above terms are associated with urban geography?
14. What type of government does the United States have?
15. What is an advantage of free enterprise?
16. How are the service industry and postindustrial economy related?
17. What is an example of a service industry?
18. What makes a business a multinational corporation?
19. In which region is an example of a megalopolis found?
20. How are the terms suburb and metropolitan area related?

Main Ideas

History and Government of the United States (pp. 135–139)

1. Why is the United States called a "nation of immigrants?"
2. How did the Louisiana Purchase change the United States?
3. What factors led the United States to become a superpower?

Economy and Culture of the United States (pp. 140–144)

4. Why is the United States a leader in agricultural production?
5. What are some examples of the cultural diversity of the United States?
6. In what industry do most Americans work?

Subregions of the United States (pp. 145–151)

7. What changes have taken place in the industrial base of the Northeast?
8. What role did water play in the development of the Midwest?
9. What industries are found in the South today?
10. How did California become the nation's most populous state?

Main Ideas

1. It was populated by immigrants from around the world.
2. It nearly doubled the size of the country.
3. strong economy, no damage after WWII, strong political influence
4. fertile soil, favorable climate, early mechanization of farms
5. many different immigrant groups, a variety of religions, diverse arts and cultures
6. service industry
7. It has shifted from traditional industries to newer manufacturing and service industries.
8. Most of the region's major cities developed near bodies of water.
9. petroleum, steel, chemicals, food processing, textiles, high-tech, tourism
10. California's mild climate, good harbors, and natural resources

Critical Thinking

1. Using Your Notes

Use your completed chart to answer these questions.

a. What resources have been important in the development of the United States?

b. Which subregions make up the "rust belt" and which the "sunbelt"? How are they related?

2. Geographic Themes

a. **REGION** How has the economy of the South changed?

b. **MOVEMENT** How has U.S. population shifted since the country began?

3. Identifying Themes

How did air conditioning and irrigation change the population of the West? Which of the five themes apply to this situation?

4. Determining Cause and Effect

What was the effect of the United States becoming industrialized?

5. Making Generalizations

What has been the result of the United States being populated by many different groups of people?

For Additional Test Practice

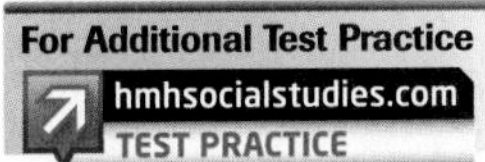

Geographic Skills: Interpreting Maps

U.S. Population and Geographic Centers

Use the map at right to answer the following questions.

1. **MOVEMENT** In which year did the population center cross the Mississippi River?
2. **MOVEMENT** How would you describe the difference between changes in the geographic center and changes in the population center?
3. **REGION** In which region was the population center from 1790 through 1850?

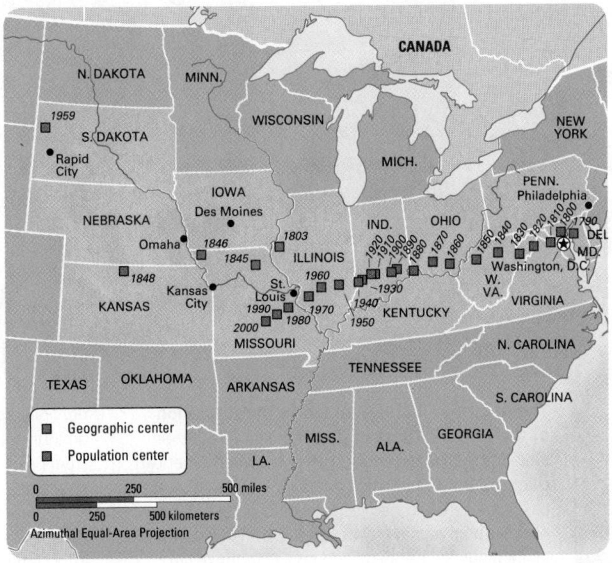

GeoActivity

Create a series of four maps showing movement of the population center of the United States in 50-year periods. Use the map on this page to help you. Start with the period from 1790 to 1840.

hmhsocialstudies.com

MULTIMEDIA ACTIVITY

Use the links at **hmhsocialstudies.com** to do research about the expansion of the United States. Look for the dates when territory was added to the United States.

Writing About Geography Write a report about your findings. Include a map showing the territory acquired to help present the information. List the Web sites that were your sources.

CHAPTER 6 ASSESSMENT

Critical Thinking

1. **a.** good soil, minerals for industries, waterways for transportation **b.** rust belt–Northeast and Midwest; Sunbelt–South and West. Industries and people are moving from rust belt to sunbelt.
2. **a.** The South has moved from primarily agricultural production to manufacturing and service industries. **b.** Population has shifted from rural to urban, and has expanded from the Northeast to the West.
3. Irrigation and air conditioning allowed the economic development of the West; region
4. The United States became a world economic leader.
5. a rich and diverse culture with contributions in many areas from a variety of groups

GeoActivity

Integrated Assessment
- Rubric for a map, 2.1

Formal Assessment
- Chapter Tests, Forms A, B, and C, pp. 86–97

Geographic Skills

1. 1980
2. The population center is moving westward every 10 years, while the geographic center has stayed the same since 1959.
3. the South

MULTIMEDIA ACTIVITY

For their research on the expansion of the United States, students should:

- Present concise, well-organized information on expansion.
- Identify dates when territories were added.
- Produce a clear, imaginative visual to complement the sentences on territorial additions.
- Include references to the websites used as sources.

Grading Rubric Evaluate student performance as Exceptional, Acceptable, or Poor in each of the following categories:

	Exceptional	Acceptable	Poor
Writing is clear, focused, and logical			
Sentences clearly state information			
Sentences provide necessary facts and examples			
Sentences use correct grammar, spelling, and punctuation			

Multimedia Classroom

The **HISTORY™ Multimedia Classroom** is a set of exciting new social studies teaching tools featuring award-winning program content. These comprehensive lesson plans, correlated to individual state and national curriculum standards, are easy to use for both teachers and students.

Each lesson contains the following:
- Short video segments that bring history topics to life
- Maps and visual materials
- Discussion and review questions
- Easily printable primary source documents
- Classroom activities and Internet-based activity links

The Multimedia Classroom has been specially designed to be versatile and easily adaptable to existing courses, lesson plans, and syllabi. Every lesson is designed to offer maximum flexibility. Teachers can select entire plans or only the elements they need, allowing them to individually tailor each lesson. Each multimedia lesson is available in CD-ROM format and is accompanied by full-length award-winning programs on DVD from HISTORY™.

For more information or to purchase go to hmhsocialstudies.com

Because some of these lessons may contain video material of a sensitive nature, we recommend that teachers and parents review these materials in their entirety before screening them to students.

MULTIMEDIA CONNECTIONS

HISTORY

THE American REVOLUTION

The American Revolution led to the formation of the United States of America in 1776. Beginning in the 1760s, tensions grew between American colonists and their British rulers when Britain started passing a series of new laws and taxes for the colonies. With no representation in the British government, however, colonists had no say in these laws, which led to growing discontent. After fighting broke out in 1775, colonial leaders met to decide what to do. They approved the Declaration of Independence, announcing that the American colonies were free from British rule. In reality, however, freedom would not come until after years of fighting.

Explore some of the people and events of the American Revolution online. You can find a wealth of information, video clips, primary sources, activities, and more at hmhsocialstudies.com.

153 MC1 MULTIMEDIA CONNECTIONS

The American Revolution

Resources 

The following resources come with printable introductions, comprehension and critical thinking questions, transcripts, and vocabulary support.

Full Length DVD

The American Revolution (30 mins)

Video Clips

- Seeds of Revolution (3:02)
- Bloodshed in Boston (2:36)
- Rebellion Arises (1:48)
- Independence! (2:36)
- A Moment of Retreat (1:28)
- The Times That Try Men's Souls (3:31)
- Victory at Saratoga (2:29)
- Final Battle (2:02)
- Victory! (1:42)

Primary Sources

- "Give Me Liberty or Give Me Death"
- The Declaration of Independence
- A Quote from *The Crisis*
- *Crossing the Delaware*
- An Account from Saratoga

"I know not what course others may take; but as for me, give me liberty or give me death!"
– Patrick Henry

"Give Me Liberty or Give Me Death"
Read an excerpt from Patrick Henry's famous speech, which urged the colonists to fight against the British.

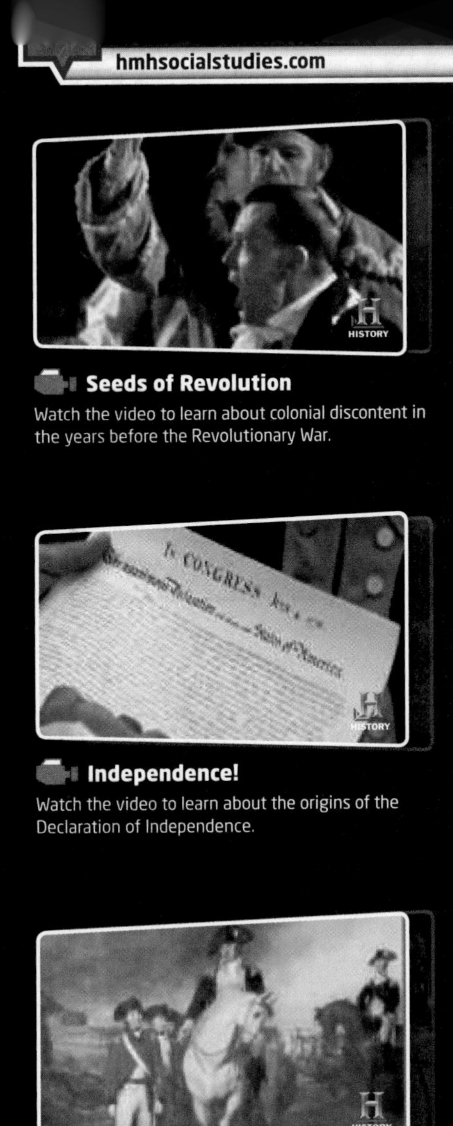

Seeds of Revolution
Watch the video to learn about colonial discontent in the years before the Revolutionary War.

Independence!
Watch the video to learn about the origins of the Declaration of Independence.

Victory!
Watch the video to learn how the American colonists won the Revolutionary War.

"Give Me Liberty or Give Me Death"

Patrick Henry was a colonial leader of Virginia and a well-known orator during the Revolutionary War. On March 23, 1775, he gave his most famous speech, titled "Give Me Liberty or Give Me Death," to the Virginia Convention at St. John's Church in Richmond, Virginia. In his speech, Henry urged Virginians to organize and prepare for war against the British. His words helped unite many American colonists.

Seeds of Revolution

In the early 1760s, most American colonists felt loyalty toward Britain's King George III and were satisfied living under British rule. But that began to change. Over the next 10 years, the colonists grew frustrated by new laws and taxes the British enacted for the colonies and by their lack of political representation in the British Parliament. The colonists' frustration turned to anger and led many to question their loyalty to a distant ruler and to think about their freedom.

Independence!

When the first battles of the Revolutionary War broke out between American colonists and British soldiers, the colonists lacked organization. But soon the colonists developed better military and political structures. In June of 1775, the Continental Congress appointed Virginian George Washington to head the army. The next year the Continental Congress approved a Declaration of Independence from Britain.

Victory!

After several years of fighting the American colonists, the British began to lack the will and resources to continue the war. In 1782, the British initiated peace talks and the next year signed the Treaty of Paris, officially ending the war. The Americans had won their independence from British rule. With this victory, Americans had much work ahead in their new nation.

Activities

- Blueprint for a Boycott
- History as It Happens
- The Midnight Ride: Fact and Fiction
- What would you Declare?
- The Landscape of War
- Proclaiming Freedom
- "Turning Points"
- Giving Up the Fight
- Moving on: The Treaty of Paris
- Extended Activities

Extended Activities

General Review Questions

General Discussion Questions

Web Links

Bibliography

CHAPTER 7 PLANNING GUIDE

Human Geography of Canada

OVERVIEW	INSTRUCTIONAL RESOURCES	
ESSENTIAL QUESTION How did Canada's large size affect its development? Focus on the Essential Question Podcast	**In-Depth Resources: Unit 2** • Building Vocabulary, p. 25 **Block Schedule Strategies** **Chapter Summaries** (English/Spanish)	**Interactive Online Edition** TOS **ExamView® Assessment Suite** (English/Spanish) TOS **CalendarPlanner** **Power Presentations with Media Gallery** **Critical Thinking Transparencies** • CT7 hmhsocialstudies.com INTERACTIVE
SECTION 1 **HISTORY AND GOVERNMENT OF CANADA** **MAIN IDEAS** • The cold climate of Canada strongly affected its development. • Rivalry was inherent between the French and English Settlers. • A transcontinental railroad was important to the expansion of Canada. • England strongly influenced Canada's political system.	**In-Depth Resources: Unit 2** • Guided Reading, p. 21 • Building Vocabulary, p. 25 • Reteaching Activity, p. 26 **Guided Reading Workbook,** Section 1	**Map Transparencies** • MT14 Canada's Territorial Growth
SECTION 2 **ECONOMY AND CULTURE OF CANADA** **MAIN IDEAS** • Canada has abundant natural resources and they are diverse. • Canada has a strong economy based soundly on exportation. • Canada's population is ethnically diverse. • Canadians enjoy many outdoor, often winter, sports and are appreciative of their native arts.	**In-Depth Resources: Unit 2** • Guided Reading, p. 22 • Skillbuilder Practice, p. 24 • Building Vocabulary, p. 25 • Reteaching Activity, p. 27 **Cultures Around the World** • Daily Life, p. 8 • Arts & Crafts, p. 12 **Guided Reading Workbook,** Section 2	**Critical Thinking Transparencies** • CT39 Governments of the United States and Canada **Cultures Transparencies** • CW8 Rock Climbing on Mt. Yamnuska • CW12 Inuit Mask **Video:** Ice Road Truckers: Tech of the Road
SECTION 3 **SUBREGIONS OF CANADA** **MAIN IDEAS** • Canada has four subregions: the Atlantic Provinces, the Core Provinces, the Prairie Provinces, and the Pacific Province and the Territories. • The Core Provinces, including Quebec and Ontario, are the most heavily populated and are centers of industry and politics.	**In-Depth Resources: Unit 2** • Guided Reading, p. 23 • Building Vocabulary, p. 25 • Reteaching Activity, p. 28 **Outline Maps with Activities** • Canada: Physical and Political, pp. 15–16 **Guided Reading Workbook,** Section 3	**The World's Music Audio Program**

ASSESSMENT

SE **Chapter Assessment,** pp. 170-171

Formal Assessment
- Chapter Tests, Forms A, B, and C, pp. 101-112

TOS **ExamView® Assessment Suite**

Strategies for Test Preparation

hmhsocialstudies.com TEST PRACTICE

SE **Section Assessment,** p. 158

Formal Assessment
- Section Quiz, p. 98

Integrated Assessment
- Rubric for a map, 2.1

Test Practice Transparencies TT22

SE **Section Assessment,** p. 163

Formal Assessment
- Section Quiz, p. 99

Integrated Assessment
- Rubric for a Venn diagram, 2.8
- Rubric for a Web page, 2.5

Test Practice Transparencies TT23

SE **Section Assessment,** p. 169

Formal Assessment
- Section Quiz, p. 100

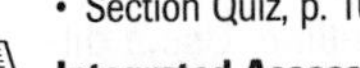
Integrated Assessment
- Rubric for a brochure, 1.13

Test Practice Transparencies TT24

CHART KEY:

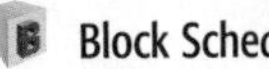

SE Student Edition	Block Scheduling	DVD/CD-ROM
TE Teacher's Edition	TOS Teacher One Stop	MP3 Audio
Printable Resource	Presentation Resource	HISTORY™

Program Resources available on TOS and @ hmhsocialstudies.com

SUPPORTING RESOURCES

- **Multimedia Classroom Global History Series**
- **Global History Teacher's Guide**

Social Studies Trade Library Collection
- Pacific Rim Trade Collection

For more information or to purchase these resources, go to hmhsocialstudies.com

DIFFERENTIATED INSTRUCTION

English Learners	Struggling Readers	Gifted and Talented Students
 **Spanish/English Guided Reading Workbook**  **Access for Students Acquiring English/ESL** Spanish Translations, pp. 33–36  **Chapter Summaries** (English/Spanish) TE **TE Activity** Suffixes, p. 156	 **Chapter Summaries** (English/Spanish) TE **TE Activity** Creating a Cultural Flow Chart, p. 160	TE **TE Activity** Following a News Trail, p. 168

ENRICHMENT ACTIVITIES

The following activities are especially suitable for classes following block schedules.

SE **Student Edition,** pp. 154–171
- Comparing Cultures: Transportation, pp. 164–165

hmhsocialstudies.com INTERACTIVE
- Comparing Cultures: Transportation, pp. 164–165

CHAPTER 7 PACING GUIDE

BLOCK SCHEDULE LESSON PLAN OPTIONS: 90-MINUTE PERIOD

DAY 1

SECTION 1, pp. 155-158
Class Time 30 minutes

- **Small Group Discussion** As a way to review the section, divide the class into groups of four. Give each group an issue from the section, such as how Canada was founded or how Canada grew or what problems were faced in the process. Ask the groups to discuss the issue and all important points about that issue. Then, have each group appoint one person to speak for the group to restate the key points of their issue to the class.

SECTION 2, pp. 159-165
Class Time 60 minutes

- **Synopsis** As a way to reconsider the information on economic sources in this section, ask students to write a brief synopsis on the key economic sources in Canada in the past, currently, and projected for the future. Then, have them divide into pairs and compare their synopses.
  Class Time 35 minutes
- **Skillbuilder Lesson** Use the lesson about Making Generalizations on TE p. 161 and the Skillbuilder Practice worksheet.
  Class Time 25 minutes

DAY 2

SECTION 2, pp. 159-165
Class Time 55 minutes

- **Growing Up Scenario** Ask the students to reread the Growing Up In . . . Canada section on page 162. Ask them to produce their own short "Growing Up In" information relating to life in the U.S.
  Class Time 25 minutes
- **Current Events Clippings** In preparation for the Comparing Cultures section, give students clippings from world news sources on modes of transportation in other parts of the world. Have them choose and read a clipping, then share their information and impressions with the class.
  Class Time 30 minutes

COMPARING CULTURES, pp. 164-165
Class Time 35 minutes

- **Discussion** Discuss the Comparing Cultures section, using the discussion prompts on TE pages 164-165.
  Class Time 15 minutes
- **Transportation Needs** Ask the students to think about what needs a country might have in terms of transportation. Ask them to mix and match what already exists in one country, with a country that doesn't have that mode of transportation. In other words, how would a bike work in Algeria, or a camel in Vietnam?
  Class Time 20 minutes

DAY 3

SECTION 3, pp. 166-171
Class Time 35 minutes

- **Regions Table** Lead the class in creating a table with four rows for the four subregions and three columns with the headings "Territories/Provinces Included," "Nickname/Known For," and "Economic Base." Then ask them to insert the appropriate information for each subregion.
  Class Time 15 minutes

CHAPTER 7 REVIEW AND ASSESSMENT, pp. 170-171
Class Time 55 minutes

- **Review** Have students prepare a summary of the chapter using the Places and Terms on the first page of each section.
  Class Time 20 minutes
- **Assessment** Have students complete the Chapter 7 Assessment.
  Class Time 35 minutes

TEACHER-TESTED ACTIVITY

The Formation of Canadian Political Boundaries

Class Time Half of class period

Task Identify the latitude and longitude lines that constitute many of Canada's political boundaries

Supplies
- Overhead projector with transparency of Canadian political map
- Atlas

Purpose To recognize how longitude and latitude lines often constitute political boundaries between and among Canadian provinces and territories.

Activity Project the Canadian map on the chalkboard and have someone quickly trace the outline. Use a different color of chalk to highlight the latitude and longitude lines that constitute boundary lines. Using the textbook or atlas, specifically identify the longitude and latitude lines. Ask the students what physical features could possibly be used to constitute boundaries not established by longitude and latitude lines.

Tim Murray
Geography Teacher, Plano Senior High School, Plano, Texas

TECHNOLOGY IN THE CLASSROOM

Keypals are pen pals who correspond via e-mail. Exchanging e-mail with keypals is one of the most popular ways for classes to use the Internet. When using keypals with your class, it's a good idea to have a goal in mind—a project to collaborate on or set of questions to ask the other class. It's also a good idea to avoid assigning individual students to their own keypals with the goal of completing a class project; if the other student does not cooperate, is out of school, etc., your student will not get the information necessary to do the project. It's better to have groups become keypals with other groups or to correspond as an entire class.

Objective Students will correspond with keypals in different parts of Canada to learn what it's like to live there.

Task Have students hypothesize what it might be like to live in each of the four subregions of Canada. Then have them find out by e-mailing questions to students in the subregions.

Class Time 2-5 class periods, over a period of weeks

1. Have students make charts with the headings of Canada's four subregions. Ask them to read pages 166-169 and take notes in the chart on the unique characteristics of each region.
2. For each region, have students write hypotheses to answer the questions "What might it be like to live in a rural part of this subregion? What about in a town or city?" They should think about what their daily life might be like, including recreation, work (themselves or their parents), the natural landscape, and the cultural groups they'd meet.
3. Locate a few Canadian classes with which to correspond, using the suggested Web sites at **hmhsocialstudies.com** or others you know about. Emphasize that this is a simple project that shouldn't take much of their (or your) time. Try to find at least one class from each of the Canadian subregions.
4. Have students label the locations of their partner schools on a large wall map of Canada, and leave the map visible in the classroom until the end of the project.
5. Divide the class into groups, and have groups write questions to ask groups of Canadian students.
6. Have groups send their questions to the Canadian students and specify a time by which they hope to hear back. As they get their responses, have them summarize the answers in a notebook or a word processed file.
7. Once students have heard back from each school, ask them to compare the responses they received to their original hypotheses. Have them write reports explaining whether their hypotheses were accurate and describing what life is like for kids their age in different parts of Canada. They should conclude by answering the question "How different is life in each of Canada's subregions from your own life?"

CHAPTER 7 OBJECTIVE

Identify features of human geography in the subregions of Canada.

Interpreting Maps

Subregions of Canada

Have students examine the map. Then ask them to name the subregions. Also have them identify the territories and provinces within each subregion. (*See map for answers.*)

Extension Ask the students to analyze the criteria for designating these subregions, including what the provinces/territories in a subregion might have in common.

Introducing the Essential Question

- Point out the area along the U.S. border where Canada's population is concentrated. Emphasize that beyond that region, there are relatively few urban areas set in the vast wilderness. Canada's prosperity has derived from both urban and rural areas, however.
- Describe the multicultural aspect of Canada's culture and the many ways of life that the country's people experience.

Have students fill out the cluster diagrams in their notebooks by using information from all the sections in this chapter.

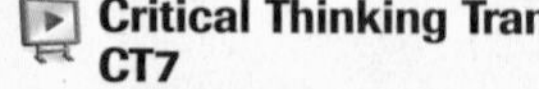

Critical Thinking Transparencies CT7
- GeoFocus

In-Depth Resources: Unit 2
- Building Vocabulary, p. 25

Chapter 7

HUMAN GEOGRAPHY OF CANADA

Developing a Vast Wilderness

Essential Question

How did Canada's large size affect its development?

What You Will Learn

In this chapter you will identify features of Canada's human geography.

SECTION 1
History and Government of Canada

SECTION 2
Economy and Culture of Canada

SECTION 3
Subregions of Canada

hmhsocialstudies.com
TAKING NOTES

Use a graphic organizer online to record information about the human geography of Canada.

Four Subregions of Canada

ARCTIC OCEAN
Beaufort Sea
Baffin Bay
Davis Strait
Labrador Sea
Hudson Bay
YUKON TERRITORY
NORTHWEST TERRITORIES
NUNAVUT
BRITISH COLUMBIA
ALBERTA
SASKATCHEWAN
MANITOBA
ONTARIO
QUEBEC
NEWFOUNDLAND
PRINCE EDWARD ISLAND
NOVA SCOTIA
NEW BRUNSWICK
Great Slave Lake
Lake Athabasca
Lake Winnipeg
James Bay
Gulf of St. Lawrence
L. Superior
L. Michigan
L. Huron
L. Erie
L. Ontario
UNITED STATES
ATLANTIC OCEAN
Gulf of Mexico
Caribbean Sea
Tropic of Cancer

Atlantic provinces
Core provinces
Prairie provinces
Pacific province and territories

0 150 300 miles
0 150 300 kilometers
Azimuthal Equal-Area Projection

154

CHAPTER 7 ADDITIONAL RESOURCES

BOOKS FOR THE TEACHER

See, Scott W. ***The History of Canada.*** Westport, CT: Greenwood Press, 2001. General history book on Canada.

Gillmor, Don and Pierre Turgeon. ***Canada: A People's History.*** Toronto, Ont: McClelland & Stewart, 2000. Companion to CBC television documentary.

BOOKS FOR THE STUDENT

Sandler, Corey. ***Econoguide 2001 Canada: Coast to Coast in Canada's Great Cities, Mountains, Parks & Attractions.*** Lincolnwood, IL: NTC/Contemporary Publishing, 2000. Interesting guidebook for Canada.

Finley, Carol. ***Art of the Far North: Inuit Sculpture, Drawing, and Printmaking.*** Minneapolis, MN: Lerner Publications, 1998.

INTERNET

For more on the human geography of Canada, visit . . .

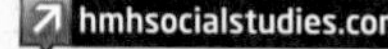

History and Government of Canada

Main Ideas
- French and British settlement greatly influenced Canada's political development.
- Canada's size and climate affected economic growth and population distribution.

Places & Terms
province
Dominion of Canada
confederation
parliamentary government
parliament
prime minister

CONNECT TO THE ISSUES
DIVERSE SOCIETIES Conflict between Canadians of French and English ancestry has been a factor throughout much of Canada's history.

A HUMAN PERSPECTIVE Around A.D. 980, a Viking named Erik the Red sailed to Greenland. Soon after, about 3,000 Vikings colonized the region. About A.D. 1000, Erik's son Leif led an expedition that landed off the Atlantic coast of North America on what is now Newfoundland. Leif called the area Vinland, after the wild grapes that grew there. The Vikings built a settlement but later abandoned it. Five centuries would pass before another European, an Italian navigator named Giovanni Caboto, would come to North America. In 1497, exploring for the English, Caboto (John Cabot in English) landed in Newfoundland and claimed the region for England. European exploration and colonization followed.

The First Settlers and Colonial Rivalry

Canada's vast size and its cold climate significantly affected its development. So did the early migrations of people across its land, the bitter territorial rivalry between the two European nations that colonized it—England and France—and their conflict with the First Nations peoples.

EARLY PEOPLES As you read in Chapter 5, one of the greatest migrations in history took place thousands of years ago, after the last Ice Age. Migrants from Asia began moving into North America across an Arctic land bridge that connected the two continents. Some early peoples remained in what are now the Canadian Arctic and Alaska. These were the ancestors of the Inuit (or Eskimos). Others, the ancestors of the North

LOCATION Quebec City, located on high ground above the St. Lawrence River, was the site of the first permanent French settlement in Canada. **Why was this a desirable location?**

CHAPTER 7 SECTION 1

SECTION 1 OBJECTIVES
1. Explain how Canada was settled.
2. Describe the unification of Canada.
3. Examine Canadian expansion and development.
4. Describe the Canadian government.

SKILLBUILDER: Interpreting Maps, p. 157

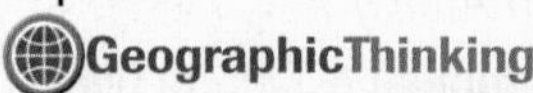
Making Comparisons, p. 157
Using the Atlas, p. 158
Drawing Conclusions, p. 158

Focus & Motivate

What factors might help unify an expansive and diverse country? *(system of government, common religions, languages)*

Instruct: Objective 1 appears on p. 156.

Interpreting Photographs

Quebec City

Tell students that the imposing building in the middle left is the Château Frontenac, a hotel.

CAPTION ANSWER The river made it readily accessible, and the high ground made it easier to defend against possible attack.

SECTION 1 PROGRAM RESOURCES

In-Depth Resources: Unit 2
- Guided Reading, p. 21
- Building Vocabulary, p. 25
- Reteaching Activity, p. 26

Guided Reading Workbook
- Section 1

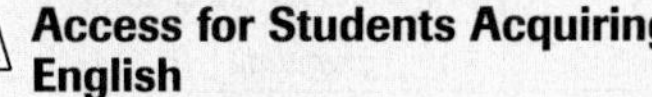
Access for Students Acquiring English
- Guided Reading, p. 33

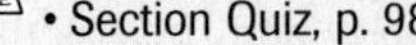
Formal Assessment
- Section Quiz, p. 98

Integrated Assessment
- Rubric for a map, 2.1

INTEGRATED TECHNOLOGY

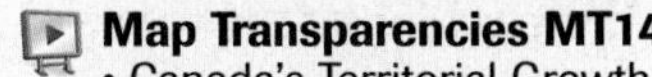
Map Transparencies MT14
- Canada's Territorial Growth

Chapter Summaries

Power Presentations

Test Generator
- Section Quiz

hmhsocialstudies.com

TEST-TAKING RESOURCES

Strategies for Test Preparation

Test Practice Transparencies TT22

Online Test Practice

Instruct: Objective 

The First Settlers and Colonial Rivalry

- Who are the Inuit? *(descendants of Asian nomads who had arrived after last Ice Age)*
- Where did the Inuit's ancestors reside in North America? *(Alaska and Canadian Arctic)*
- When did European explorers begin arriving in Canada? *(15th century)*

In-Depth Resources: Unit 2
- Guided Reading, p. 21

Instruct: Objective 

Steps Toward Unity

- What two main factors defined the differences among Canadians by the end of the 18th century? *(religion and ancestry)*
- What Canadian province or territory was once called Upper Canada? *(Ontario)*
- What Canadian province or territory was once called Lower Canada? *(Quebec)*
- Which European power won control of Canada? *(Britain)*

Interpreting Time Lines

Canadian History, 1450-1900

Have students examine the time line. Ask them to identify when the Dominion of Canada was established. Ask them what event happened in 1837. *(1867; revolts broke out)*

American Indian peoples, gradually moved south, into present-day British Columbia and beyond. When the ice melted, they moved throughout Canada. They settled where they could grow crops.

COLONIZATION BY FRANCE AND BRITAIN During the 16th and 17th centuries, French explorers claimed much of Canada. Their settlements were known as New France. The British, too, were colonizing North America along the Atlantic coast. To both countries, the coastal fisheries and the inland fur trade were important. Soon, the French and British challenged each other's territorial claims. Britain defeated France in the French and Indian War (1754–1763), forcing France to surrender its territory. But French settlers remained.

Steps Toward Unity

By the end of the 18th century, Canada had become a land of two distinct cultures—Roman Catholic French and Protestant English. Conflicts erupted between the two groups, and in 1791, the British government split Canada into two **provinces,** or political units. Upper Canada (later, Ontario), located near the Great Lakes, had an English-speaking majority, while Lower Canada (Quebec), located along the St. Lawrence River, had a French-speaking population. The land to the northwest, called Rupert's Land, was owned by a British fur-trading company.

BACKGROUND
Upper Canada was upriver—on the St. Lawrence—from Lower Canada (Quebec).

ESTABLISHING THE DOMINION OF CANADA Over the next few decades, Quebec City, Montreal, and Toronto developed as major cities in Canada. Population soared as large numbers of immigrants came from Great Britain. Railways and canals were built, and explorers moved across western lands seeking better fur-trading areas.

The conflicts between English-speaking and French-speaking settlers had not ended, however. By the late 1830s, there were serious political and ethnic disputes in both Upper and Lower Canada. The British government decided that major reform was needed. In 1867, it passed the British North America Act creating the **Dominion of Canada.** The Dominion was to be a loose **confederation,** or political union, of Ontario (Upper Canada), Quebec (Lower Canada), and two British colonies on the Atlantic coast—Nova Scotia and New Brunswick. The Dominion

Canadian History, 1450–1900

National flag of Canada, 1922–1957

1497 John Cabot claims what is now Canada for England.

1608 **Samuel de Champlain** founds the first French settlement at Quebec.

1763 Britain defeats France in the French and Indian War.

EUROPEAN SETTLEMENT 1800

1791 Britain creates Upper Canada and Lower Canada.

1800 CANADIAN UNION 1900

1837 Revolts break out in Upper and Lower Canada.

1867 Canadian provinces unite as the Dominion of Canada.

DIFFERENTIATING INSTRUCTION — STUDENTS ACQUIRING ENGLISH/ESL

SUFFIXES: -TION AND -ITY

Objective To help ESL students understand how a suffix acts to create a new word

Class Time 10-15 minutes

Task Organize words with suffixes into a chart

Directions Have students create a three-column chart with the headings "Word," "Suffix," and "Original Word." Remind students that a suffix is defined as letters added at the end of a word's base to form a new word, for example, *-tion,* and *-ity.* Ask them to glance through section titled "Steps Toward Unity," find three or four words that contain a suffix, and then put the appropriate information into a chart like the one shown here.

WORD	SUFFIX	ORIGINAL WORD
population	-tion	populate
majority	-ity	major

Territorial Growth of Canada

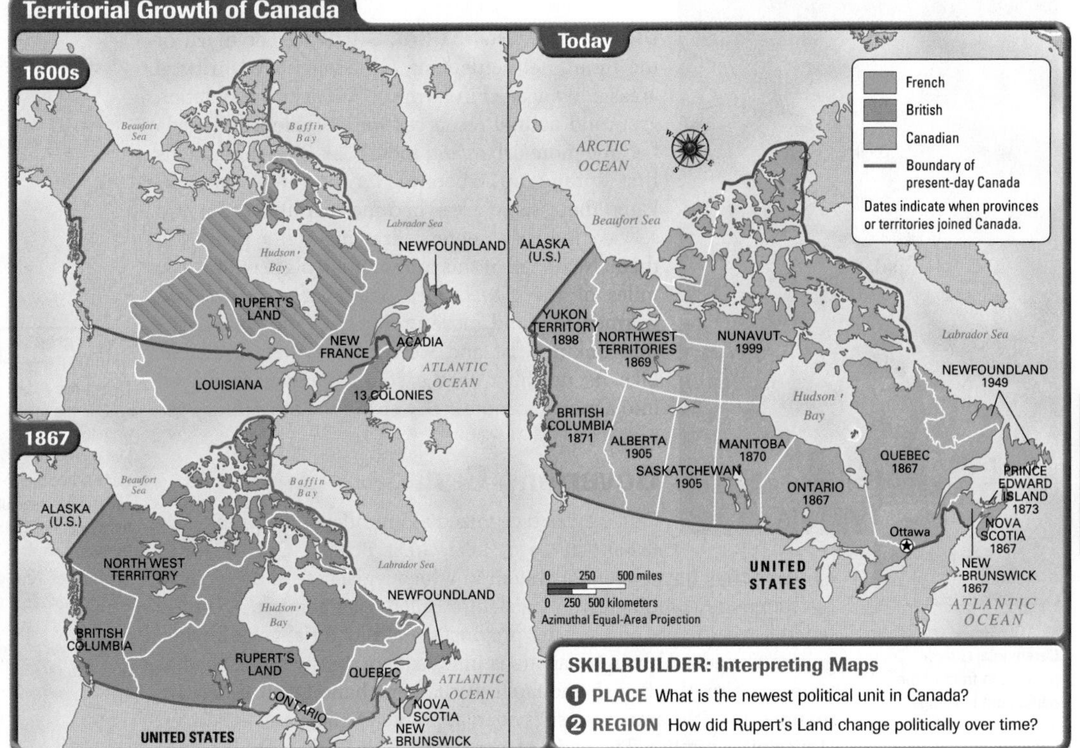

SKILLBUILDER: Interpreting Maps
1. **PLACE** What is the newest political unit in Canada?
2. **REGION** How did Rupert's Land change politically over time?

had self-government but remained part of the British Empire. Ottawa, in Ontario, became the capital.

As the map above shows, the Dominion grew rapidly. It gained control of Rupert's Land in 1869. By 1871, Canada stretched from the Atlantic to the Pacific, as Manitoba, British Columbia, and Prince Edward Island were added. Soon the Yukon Territory, Alberta, and Saskatchewan followed. Only Newfoundland remained outside the union, not joining until the mid-20th century.

Continental Expansion and Development

With so much area to settle, Canada set about making its land accessible to pioneers. Successful settlement of the west would depend on good transportation routes: roads, canals, and railroads. A

FROM THE ATLANTIC TO THE PACIFIC In 1872, the government began construction of a transcontinental railroad. In 1885, the main line of the railway, from Montreal to Vancouver, was completed. The coasts were now linked by rail. A little more than a decade later, gold was discovered in the Yukon. Fortune-hunters from around the world headed to Canada. Not long after, copper, zinc, and silver deposits also were found in Canada, prompting the building of new railroads and towns. At the same time, immigrants from other parts of Europe besides Britain were coming to Canada's vast open lands. The Dominion was taking on a new character.

Geographic Thinking

Making Comparisons
A How was Canada's westward movement similar to that of the United States?
A. Answer Both had gold rushes to the west, built railroads to span the continent, and were populated by immigrants.

US & CANADA

Interpreting Maps

Territorial Growth of Canada

Have students examine the maps. Then have them identify which country controlled more territory, France or England, in the 1600s and then in 1867. *(France in the 1600s; England in 1867)* Ask them which present-day Canadian provinces were not settled by Europeans during the 1600s. *(Yukon Territory, British Columbia, much of Northwest Territories, much of Nunavut)*

SKILLBUILDER ANSWERS
1. the territory of Nunavut **2.** It became part of the provinces of Quebec, Newfoundland, Ontario, Manitoba, Saskatchewan, and Alberta, and the Northwest Territories and Nunavut.

Instruct: Objective 

Continental Expansion and Development

- What factor was essential in the development of western Canada? *(transportation routes: roads, canals, railroads)*
- Between what two cities did the first transcontinental railroad in Canada extend? *(between Montreal and Vancouver)*
- How did Canada change after the building of railroads and discoveries of copper, zinc, and other resources? *(changed from more rural and agricultural to more industrial)*

 **Map Transparencies MT14**
- Canada's Territorial Growth

ACTIVITY OPTION CRITICAL THINKING

MAKING INFERENCES

Explaining the Skill Tell students that they should use logic and previous knowledge to make inferences about information that is not specifically stated in text. In this example, they can infer the political strategies used by Britain and France in their attempts to control Canada.

Have students refer to both the time line on page 156, the map on page 157, and the text of the "Steps Toward Unity" section. Remind students that the French supported the American colonists during the Revolutionary War.

Applying the Skill Have students pair up and answer the following questions. After 10 minutes, have each pair share their answers with the class.

- When did the British defeat the French in the French and Indian war? *(1763)*
- When did the British create Upper and Lower Canada? *(1791)*
- How might Britain's and France's roles in the American Revolutionary War have affected these events? *(The French may have hoped to secure parts of Canada by getting the American colonists as allies; the British may have created Upper and Lower Canada to secure their hold after their loss of the American colonies.)*

Interpreting Photographs 

Parliament Buildings in Ottawa

Have students examine the photograph. Ask students if they have ever seen a picture that resembles this. Ask students how Britain's influence on Canada is evident in this picture. *(similarity to British parliament and guards at Buckingham Palace)*

Instruct: Objective 4

Governing Canada

- When did Canada gain independence from Britain? *(1931)*
- How is Canada's government similar to Britain's? *(both have parliamentary government)*

Assess & Reteach

GeoFocus Have students complete their notes on the history and government of Canada for the cluster diagram.

 **Formal Assessment**
- Section Quiz, p. 98

Reteaching Activity
Organize the class into groups of six students. Assign each group a section objective (repeat as necessary). Have each group produce a few sentences or short paragraph summarizing the main information included in that objective. The groups should then share with the rest of the class.

 **In-Depth Resources: Unit 2**
- Reteaching Activity, p. 26

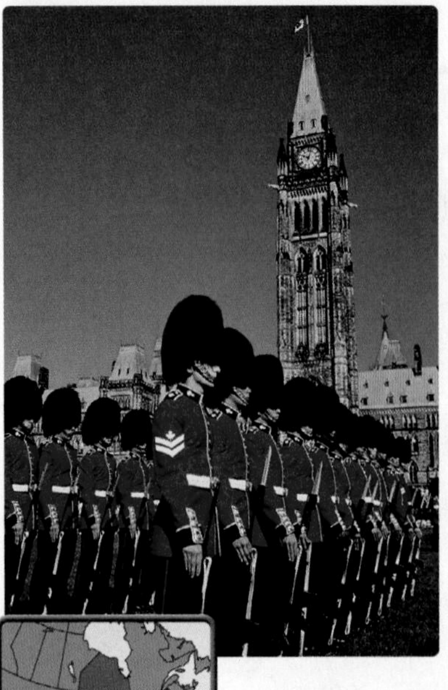

PLACE The Ceremonial Guard parades in front of the parliament buildings in Ottawa, Ontario, Canada's capital city.

URBAN AND INDUSTRIAL GROWTH For much of the time after settlement, Canadians lived in rural areas and engaged in farming. But as the population grew and natural resources were developed, Canada became more urban and industrial. Cities and towns first sprang up wherever farming was possible. Later, these same areas became manufacturing and service industry centers, drawing more people to them. Nearly all of this growth took place within 100 miles of the U.S. border. There, the climate was warmer, the land more productive, and transportation linking east and west more widely available. Like its neighbor to the south, Canada developed into a major economic power in the 20th century. B

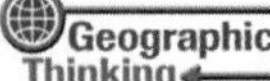

Geographic Thinking

Using the Atlas B Use the atlas on page 105. List the major Canadian cities within 200 miles of the Canadian/U.S. border.

B. Answer The list should include Montreal, Ottawa, Calgary, Vancouver, and Victoria.

Governing Canada

Canada was recognized as an independent nation by Britain in 1931. Like Great Britain, Canada has a **parliamentary government,** a system in which legislative and executive functions are combined in a legislature called a **parliament.** A central federal government and smaller provincial and territorial governments govern Canada. Although Canada is independent, its symbolic head of state remains the British monarch. Parliament handles all legislative matters. The Parliament consists of an appointed Senate and an elected House of Commons. The majority party's leader in Parliament becomes **prime minister,** or head of the government. Each of Canada's ten provinces has its own legislature and premier (prime minister). The federal government administers the territories.

In this section, you read about the history and government of Canada. In the next section, you will learn about life in Canada today.

Section 1 Assessment

1 Places & Terms

Identify and explain these terms.
- province
- Dominion of Canada
- confederation
- parliamentary government
- parliament
- prime minister

2 Taking Notes

PLACE Review the notes you took for this section.

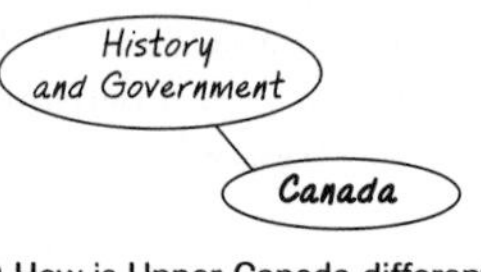

- How is Upper Canada different from Lower Canada?
- What mineral discoveries spurred development of Canada?

3 Main Ideas

a. How did the French and Indian War change Canada?

b. Where did nearly all growth in Canada's industry and urban areas take place?

c. How is Canada's federal government different from the federal government of the United States?

4 Geographic Thinking

Drawing Conclusions How did the early settlement of Canada lead to a diverse society? **Think about:**
- New France
- French and Indian War

SEEING PATTERNS Use the Internet to find the percentage of French-speaking and English-speaking citizens in each of Canada's provinces and territories. Create a **map** of Canada and write in the percentages for each province or territory.

SECTION 1 ASSESSMENT ANSWERS

1. Places & Terms

province, p. 156
Dominion of Canada, p. 156
confederation, p. 156
parliamentary government, p. 158
parliament, p. 158
prime minister, p. 158

2. Taking Notes
- Upper Canada is Protestant and English-speaking. Lower Canada is Roman Catholic and French-speaking.
- Discovery of gold, silver, copper, and zinc speeded Canada's development.

3. Main Ideas

a. After the war, the British controlled all of Canada.

b. Growth took place within 100 miles of the United States border.

c. Canada does not have a president. Instead, it has a prime minister, who also serves in the legislature. Also, its senate is appointed, not elected as is the U.S. senate.

4. Geographic Thinking

Early settlement in New France brought the French culture. Later, when Britain acquired the land, English-speakers flooded into the country. These two groups, plus the native peoples, form the basis for a diverse society.

GeoActivity

 **Integrated Assessment**
- Rubric for a map, 2.1

Economy and Culture of Canada

Main Ideas

- Canada is highly industrialized and urbanized, with one of the world's most developed economies.
- Canadians are a diverse people.

Places & Terms

First Nations
métis
reserve

CONNECT TO THE ISSUES
DIVERSE SOCIETIES
Canada is a land of immigrants with many diverse cultures.

US & CANADA

A HUMAN PERSPECTIVE The fur trade was a major economic activity in early Canada. It began in the 16th century, when Canada's Native American peoples, now known as the **First Nations,** started trading with European fishermen along the northern Atlantic coast. A brisk trade soon developed, and trappers and traders poured into Canada. They came first from France and later, from England. As the trade expanded westward, it depended heavily on daring French-Canadian boatmen called *voyageurs.* They moved animal pelts from the wilderness to trading posts, often paddling 16 hours a day. According to one trader, these hardy souls often endured "privation and hardship, not only without complaining, but even with cheerfullness."

An Increasingly Diverse Economy

Canada is one of the world's richest countries. It is highly industrialized and urbanized. As you just read, Canada's early economy was based largely on the trade of its many natural resources. Today, the manufacturing and service industries fuel the nation's economic engines.

CANADA'S PRIMARY INDUSTRIES Farming, logging, mining, and fishing are important Canadian industries. Although only about 5 percent of Canada's land is suitable for farming, Canada produces large amounts of food for domestic use and for export. Canada also is a leader in the production of newsprint—paper made from wood pulp.

Mining, too, is a major industry because of Canada's extensive mineral deposits. Uranium, zinc, gold, and silver are just a few of the minerals Canada exports to the world. Canada is also a leading exporter of oil.

Three ocean coastlines—Atlantic, Pacific, and Arctic—have given Canadians access to ample fish supplies. Traditionally, Canada has been a major exporter of fish. In recent years, however, overfishing has caused supplies to decline. As a result, some fishers have begun raising salmon and other fish on fish farms.

THE MANUFACTURING SECTOR About 13 percent of Canadians earn their living from manufacturing. Their efforts account for about one-eighth of the nation's GDP. Automobiles, steel, household appliances, electronics, and high-tech and mining equipment are just some of the products Canada manufactures.

Canadian Workers*

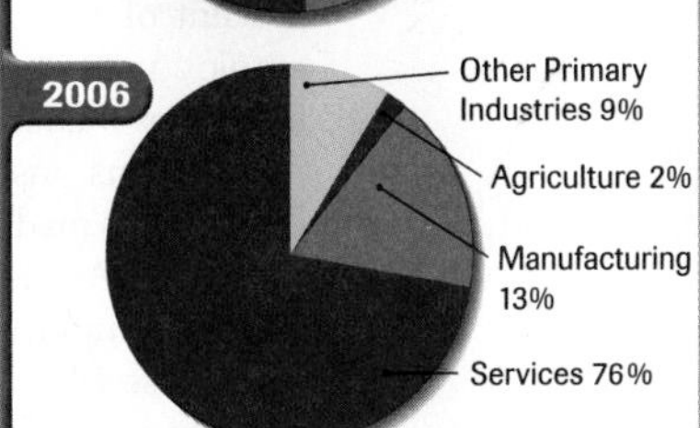

*Based on rounded employment statistics
SOURCE: *Canada Year Book 1994; Canada Year Book 1997; Statistics Canada*

SKILLBUILDER: Interpreting Graphs
1. **ANALYZING DATA** Which sector showed the greatest increase in growth from 1951 to 2006? the greatest decrease in growth?
2. **MAKING GENERALIZATIONS** What might account for these changes in the economy?

SECTION 2 OBJECTIVES

1. Identify economic power in Canada.
2. Examine cultural diversity in Canada.
3. Describe Canadian life today.

SKILLBUILDERS: Interpreting Graphs and Maps, pp. 159, 160

**GeographicThinking**
Making Comparisons, p. 160
Seeing Patterns, p. 161
Drawing Conclusions, p. 163

Focus & Motivate

What factors make an economy work? *(abundant resources, different industries, stable political system, skilled labor)*

Instruct: Objective 1

An Increasingly Diverse Economy

- What are some of Canada's industries? *(farming, logging, mining, fishing)*
- Where is most manufacturing done? *(southern Quebec and Ontario)*

 **In-Depth Resources: Unit 2**
- Guided Reading, p. 22

Interpreting Graphs

Canadian Economy

Ask students what changes in the Canadian economy have occurred since 1951. *(shift from industry to services)*

SKILLBUILDER ANSWERS
1. services increased; agriculture decreased **2.** As people moved to the cities, there were fewer farmers and a greater need for services.

SECTION 2 PROGRAM RESOURCES

 **In-Depth Resources: Unit 2**
- Guided Reading, p. 22
- Skillbuilder Practice, p. 24
- Building Vocabulary, p. 25
- Reteaching Activity, p. 27

Guided Reading Workbook
- Section 2

 **Access for Students Acquiring English**
- Guided Reading, p. 34
- Skillbuilder Practice, p. 36

Formal Assessment
- Section Quiz, p. 99

Integrated Assessment
- Rubric for a Venn diagram, 2.8
- Rubric for a Web page, 5.1

 **Cultures Around the World**
- Daily Life, p. 8
- Arts & Crafts, p. 12

INTEGRATED TECHNOLOGY

Cultures Transparencies CW8, 12
- Rock Climbing on Mt. Yamnuska
- Inuit Mask

Critical Thinking Transparencies CT39
- Governments of the U.S. and Canada

TEST-TAKING RESOURCES

 **Strategies for Test Preparation**

 **Test Practice Transparencies TT23**

Online Test Practice

Interpreting Maps

Agriculture and Industry of Canada

Have students identify two provinces that have oil and gas industries. Ask the students to name three cities that have chemical industries. Then have the students identify the largest agricultural product in Canada *(Alberta and Saskatchewan; Quebec, Montreal, Toronto, Winnipeg, or Vancouver; commercial grain)*

SKILLBUILDER ANSWERS

1. Most of Canada's industry is located in cities near the border with the United States. **2.** the colder regions of the north

More About

A Robust Economy

Although Canada has dealt with high inflation rates and economic slowdowns, it continues to thrive and be one of the largest exporters in the world. Canada is a major supplier of the world's timber, minerals, fish, and commercial grain.

Agriculture and Industry of Canada

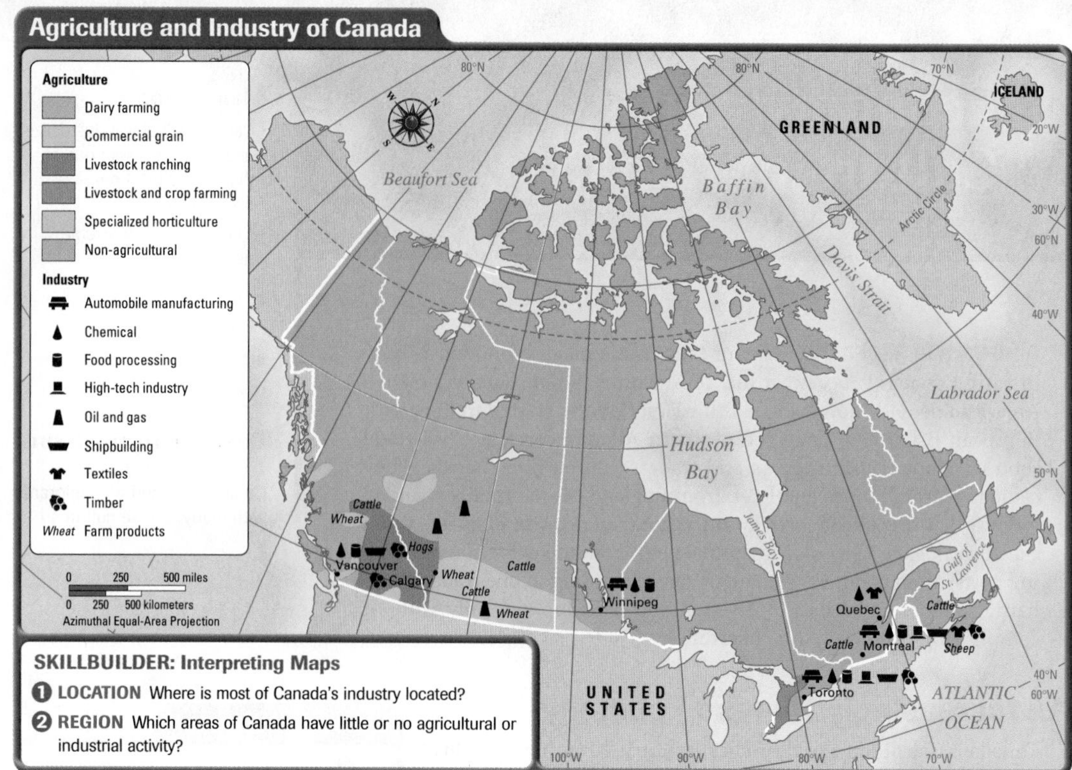

SKILLBUILDER: Interpreting Maps

❶ **LOCATION** Where is most of Canada's industry located?

❷ **REGION** Which areas of Canada have little or no agricultural or industrial activity?

Most of the manufacturing is done in the Canadian heartland, which reaches from Quebec City, Quebec, to Windsor, Ontario. **A**

SERVICE INDUSTRIES DRIVE THE ECONOMY Canada's service industries are the country's real economic powerhouse. In fact, more than 70 percent of the GDP comes from service industries. Those industries employ more Canadians than all other industries combined. Service industries include finance, utilities, trade, transportation, tourism, communications, insurance, and real estate. Canada's spectacular natural beauty has made tourism one of the fastest growing of the service industries. At the beginning of the 21st century, the Canadian tourism industry employed a higher percentage of workers—about 4 percent—than those who were engaged in agriculture.

Historically, Canada's economy has always relied on trade. The fur trade between Canada's native peoples and European fishermen was just the start of what would become a key Canadian industry. The United States is Canada's chief trading partner. This is largely because the two nations share the longest open border in the world and the same language—English. In 1994, Canada and the United States, along with Mexico, signed the North American Free Trade Agreement (NAFTA). This pact made trade between them even easier than before. At the turn of the 21st century, about 78 percent of Canada's exports went to the United States, and about 52 percent of Canada's imports came from its neighbor to the south.

Geographic Thinking

Making Comparisons

A How is the Canadian heartland similar to the northeast region of the United States?

A. Answer Both are important manufacturing regions.

DIFFERENTIATING INSTRUCTION LESS PROFICIENT READERS

CREATING A CULTURAL FLOW CHART

Objective To recall and reorganize information into a graphic organizer

Class Time 10 minutes

Task To create a flow chart based on cultural influences and ancestry in Canada

Directions Have students read the section titled "A Land of Many Cultures." Remind them to consider what they have read in other sections of this chapter as necessary. Ask them to draw a flow chart showing the settlement of Canada by different people and interactions between groups.

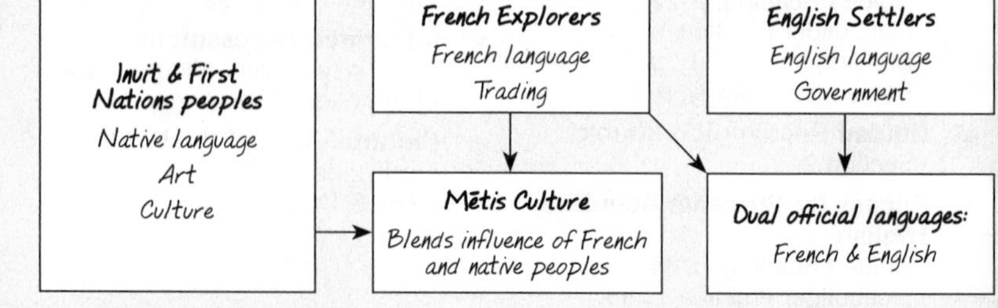

A Land of Many Cultures

From its earliest settlement, Canada has been a land of diverse cultures. The first settlers were the Inuit and the First Nations peoples who came after the last Ice Age. Many thousands of years later, the English and French arrived, bringing their languages and traditions with them. Interaction between the French and native peoples gave rise to another culture, the **métis** (may•TEES), people of mixed French and native heritage.

More recent immigrants from Europe and Asia also have made their contributions to the cultural mix. As in the United States, Canada's cultural richness has come from all corners of the world.

BACKGROUND
Official documents and information are printed both in English and in French.

LANGUAGES AND RELIGION Canada is officially a bilingual country. It has an English-speaking majority and a French-speaking minority. (Only in Quebec are French speakers in the majority.) In addition, the languages of First Nation peoples still survive, and the native languages of immigrants can be heard on many city streets.

As the English and the French settled Canada, their different cultures became a source of conflict. The English were largely Protestant, and the French were Roman Catholics. Religious and cultural conflicts between the two groups have continued over the years. Today, these two religions continue to dominate Canadian society, though Muslims, Jews, and other religious groups are represented in ever-increasing numbers. In addition, about 16 percent of Canadians report no religious affiliation.

B. Answer The harsh climate keeps the population in the south of the country. Good soil for cropland pulls people to the south as well.

Geographic Thinking
Seeing Patterns
B Which physical factors influence Canada's population distribution?

CANADA'S POPULATION Settlement patterns in Canada have always been influenced by the country's harsh environment and the accessibility of transportation routes. Canada's port cities—especially Montreal, Toronto, and Vancouver—and its rich farmlands make up the country's most densely settled areas. In fact, more than 80 percent of all Canadians live on just 10 percent of the land. This region is mostly along a 100-mile-wide strip of land just north of the U.S. border. B

US & CANADA

Instruct: Objective 2

A Land of Many Cultures

- Name two groups of people who settled Canada. *(Inuit, First Nations, French, British, Europeans)*
- What are the official languages of Canada? *(French and English)*
- What are the predominant religions of Canada? *(Protestant and Catholic)*
- What factors have most affected the settlement patterns of Canada? *(harsh climate, transportation routes)*

Interpreting Graphics

Clash of Cultures
Have students examine the "Problems/Solutions" graphic. Then ask them to summarize the main problem outlined in this chart. *(conflict between English and French cultures in Canada)* Ask them to explain how the Canadian government is trying to solve the problems. *(through promotion of cultural diversity and two official languages)*

ACTIVITY OPTION SKILLBUILDER LESSON

MAKING GENERALIZATIONS

Explaining the Skill Tell students how generalizations based on sound information can broaden their overall understanding of a country and its people.

Applying the Skill Have students take turns reading aloud from page 161 to the end of the section. Write the following questions on the board and ask students to try to formulate plausible generalizations based on the answers to the questions.

- Who were the first settlers in Canada? *(Inuit and First Nations peoples)*
- What region did they settle? *(the entire country now known as Canada)*
- Who lives in that region today? *(Inuit and First Nations peoples and Europeans)*
- Why did or didn't the original settlers probably remain in that region? *(they remained where food was still plentiful, until Europeans moved them onto reserves and took possession of the land.)*

 **In-Depth Resources: Unit 2**
- Skillbuilder Practice, p. 24

growing up in...
Canada

Have students read the description of playing hockey. Ask if they have ever played or what they think it might be like. Then ask them to compare their own lives with the lives of Canadian youth. Ask how their lives are similar or different. *(Some may not have lived in a cold climate and couldn't imagine playing ice hockey, while others may know what it's like. Students should recognize that the ages for starting schooling are similar to the U.S. and so are voting and marrying ages.)*

Instruct: Objective 

Life in Canada Today

- Who makes up the majority of Canada's work force, men or women? *(men, but not by much)*
- Within what industry sector do most Canadians work? *(service)*
- Who greatly influenced the arts in Canada? *(Inuit, First Nations people, diverse cultures)*

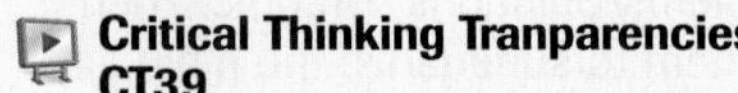

Critical Thinking Tranparencies CT39
- Governments of the United States and Canada

Cultures Around the World
- Daily Life, p. 8
- Arts & Crafts, p. 12

Cultures Transparencies CW8, 12
- Rock Climbing on Mt. Yamnuska
- Inuit Mask

growing up in... Canada

These boys are playing ice hockey on an outdoor rink in Fergus, Ontario. Hockey is Canada's national pastime. Children learn to play this Canadian-invented sport at an early age. Many boys dream of playing professional hockey in the National Hockey League. On any given day, young people and adults can be found playing or watching a game at neighborhood ice rinks.

If you lived in Canada, you would pass these milestones:
- You could attend a private preschool at age 3 or 4.
- You would begin elementary school at age 5 or 6 and would be required to attend until age 16.
- You would choose to get a job or attend a college or university after high school graduation at age 18.
- You could drive at age 16.
- You could vote at age 18.
- You could get married at age 18 without written consent.

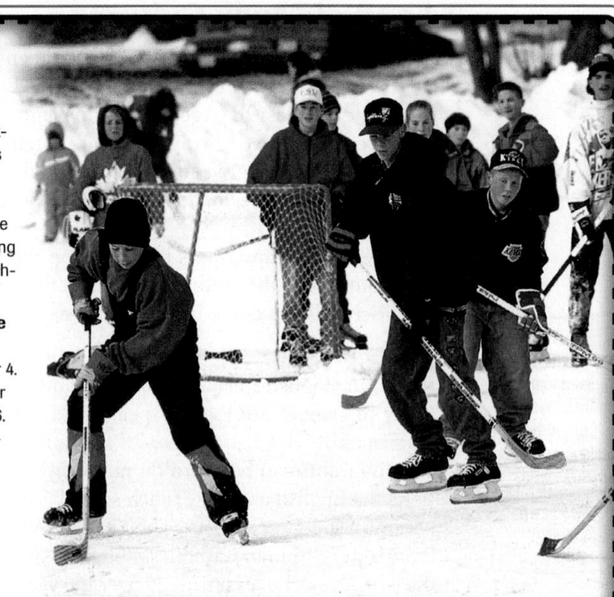

Canada's population has become increasingly urban. At the beginning of the 20th century, about one-third of the people lived in urban areas. By 2008, nearly four-fifths were city dwellers. Some Canadian population groups are clustered in certain areas. For example, about 75 percent of all French Canadians reside in Quebec. Many of Canada's native peoples are found on the country's 2,300 **reserves,** public land set aside for them by the government. The territories in the remote Arctic north are home to most of the Inuit. Large numbers of Canadians of Asian ancestry live on the West Coast. C

CONNECT TO THE ISSUES
DIVERSITY
C Which major cultural groups are found in Canada?
C. Answer French, English, native peoples, and Asians form the basis of Canada's diverse society.

Life in Canada Today

Most Canadians live active personal and professional lives and enjoy a relatively high standard of living. In 1998, Canada's labor force was nearly evenly split between men and women. Men made up about 52 percent of the work force and women, about 48 percent. As the chart on page 159 shows, Canada's service industries employ more than 75 percent of the work force. Manufacturing is a distant second, accounting for approximately 13 percent of Canadian workers. Canada's population is well educated. The oldest university, Laval, was established in Quebec during the period of French settlement. The first English-speaking universities were founded in New Brunswick and Nova Scotia in the 1780s. Today, Canada boasts a 99 percent literacy rate.

SPORTS AND RECREATION Canadians value their leisure time and use it to engage in many recreational activities. Sports such as skating, ice hockey, fishing, skiing, golf, and hunting are popular. Canadians also enjoy their professional sports teams. Canada has its own football

ACTIVITY OPTION **INTERNET RESEARCH** — **BLOCK SCHEDULING**

CULTURAL NEWS

Objective To research current news stories that reflect cultural issues raised in text

Class Time 30 minutes

Task Use the Internet to find two articles that directly relate to cultural issues discussed in the text

Directions Have students decide on a cultural issue mentioned in the section (for example, conflict between French and English). Then have them use the Internet to find two recent news stories or periodical articles that address this issue in some way. Students should summarize the main ideas of each article and share that information with the class.

OPTIONAL ACTIVITY Use the library (and librarian assistance) to find current articles relating to the issues chosen.

league and its professional ice hockey, baseball, and basketball teams compete in U.S. leagues. The Canadian love of sport goes back to its native peoples, who developed the game we know as lacrosse, and to its early European settlers, who developed ice hockey. Two annual events that are favorites nationwide are the Quebec Winter Carnival, held in Quebec City, and the Calgary Stampede, pictured on page 99.

THE ARTS Not surprisingly, Canada's long history and cultural diversity have given the nation a rich artistic heritage. The earliest Canadian literature was born in the oral traditions of the First Nations peoples. Later, the writings of settlers, missionaries, and explorers lent French and English influences to the literature.

The early visual arts included the realistic carvings of the Inuit and the elaborately decorated totem poles of the First Nations peoples of the West Coast. The artistry of the Inuit carvings has been evident since prehistoric times. Inuit carvers used ivory, whalebone, and soapstone to carve figurines of animals and people in scenes from everyday life. A uniquely Canadian style of painting developed among a group of Toronto-based artists called the Group of Seven early in the 20th century. The performing arts—music, dance, and theater—enjoyed spectacular growth during the last half of the century. The Stratford Festival in Ontario, honoring William Shakespeare, is known worldwide.

In this section, you read about life in Canada today. In the next section, you will learn more about Canada's subregions.

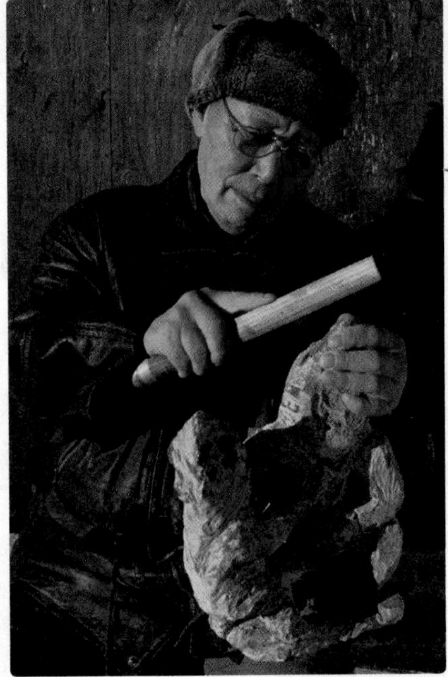

HUMAN-ENVIRONMENT INTERACTION Distinguished artist Kiawak Ashoona, an Inuit from Nunavut, works on a soapstone sculpture.

Interpreting Photographs

Inuit Art

Traditionally, most Inuit sculptures were small, stylized animals. Once made from ivory and traded with foreign explorers and settlers, Inuit art now encompasses varied styles and subject matter that reflect the Inuit communities throughout northern Canada. Stone has become the most popular material to work with, but caribou and musk-ox antlers are sometimes used as well.

Assess & Reteach

GeoFocus Have students complete their notes on Canada for the cluster diagram.

Formal Assessment
- Section Quiz, p. 99

Reteaching Activity
Have students summarize the main details of economy and culture in Canada by creating a short paragraph for each. Ask the students to pay attention to section objectives and divisions when determining the main ideas throughout the section.

In-Depth Resources: Unit 2
- Reteaching Activity, p. 27

Section 2 Assessment

1 Places & Terms

Identify and explain these terms.
- First Nations
- métis
- reserve

2 Taking Notes

REGION Review the notes you took for this section.

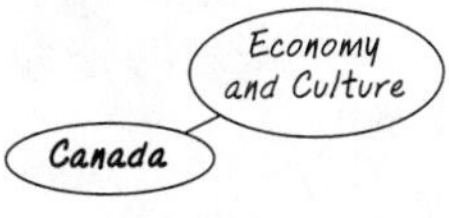

- Which industries drive Canada's economy?
- In which region is the majority of the population located?

3 Main Ideas

a. Why are Canada and the United States close trading partners?

b. How have Canada's urban areas changed?

c. What is Canada's work force like?

4 Geographic Thinking

Drawing Conclusions
How have Canada's physical resources contributed to its economic prosperity? **Think about:**
- its location
- its primary industries

See Skillbuilder Handbook, page R5.

MAKING COMPARISONS Study the information in Chapter 6, Section 2, about the U.S. economy. Create a **Venn diagram** with three circles showing the economic activities Canada and the United States have in common and those that are unique to each.

SECTION 2 ASSESSMENT ANSWERS

1. Places &Terms
First Nations, p. 159
métis, p. 161
reserve, p. 162

2. Taking Notes
- Service industries drive Canada's economy.
- the area nearest to the United States and within 100 miles of the U.S. border

3. Main Ideas
a. They share a border and the same language, and Canada has many products the United States wants.
b. They used to account for about one-third of the population but now have four-fifths of the country's population.
c. The work force is made up of about 52 percent men and 48 percent women working mostly in service industries, with only about 15 percent employed in manufacturing.

4. Geographic Thinking
Its location on three oceans gives it access to fisheries and the ability to ship goods to other locations. It has vast reserves of natural resources desired by many nations.

GeoActivity

Integrated Assessment
- Rubric for a Venn diagram, 2.8

OBJECTIVE

Identify similarities and differences in methods of transportation throughout the world.

Instruct: Objective

Transportation

- What factors affect people's choices of transportation? *(climate, roads, resources for manufacturing transportation)*
- Why are camels called "ships of the desert"? *(they carry people and cargo over long distances)*
- How would a pilot flying into Cochrane, Ontario, get to a desired location after landing? *(possibly by road, railway, or boat)*

Interpreting Photographs

Algeria, Vietnam, Canada, Peru

Have students examine the photographs. Ask them to use one word to describe the mode of transportation in each picture. *(camel, bike, boat, plane)* Then, ask them to choose one photograph and explain how transportation in that photo is similar to, or different from, what they are used to. *(Some students might get around by bikes; most have probably never seen a boat made of bark or reeds.)*

Interpreting Maps

Have students examine the world map as well as the photo captions. Ask them to name each country and continent represented in the photos here. *(Canada/North America; Algeria/Africa; Vietnam/Asia; Peru/South America)*

hmhsocialstudies.com INTERACTIVE
Comparing Cultures
Transportation
As you have read, one of the five themes of geography is movement—how people move themselves and their goods across the Earth's surface. The earliest humans moved by foot from place to place. Later, they used animals, both to ride and as pack animals. Needing to cross streams, ancient people built primitive boats from available materials, such as wood and reeds. Over the centuries, advances in technology from wheeled vehicles to the steam engine to the construction of lighter-than-air craft has enabled people in different regions to meet the challenges posed by their environments.
Canada
Algeria
Peru
In North African countries like Algeria, camels are often called "ships of the desert" because they can carry freight and people across long distances. The Arabian, or one-humped, camel shown here in the Sahara Desert can cover 40 miles a day for four days carrying 400 pounds.
Flat, smooth roadways crisscrossing Vietnam make it easy for these workers to transport hundreds of fish traps from workshops to customers on the coast by bicycle.
164 CHAPTER 7

SUPPORTING RESOURCES

BOOKS FOR THE TEACHER

Long, Stanley G. (ed.) ***Transport at the Millennium.*** Thousand Oaks, CA: Sage, 1997.

BOOKS FOR THE STUDENT

Cudahy, Brian. ***Under the Sidewalks of New York: The Story of the Greatest Subway System in the World.*** NY: Fordham Univ. Press, 1995.

INTERNET

For more on transportation, visit . . .

hmhsocialstudies.com

VIDEO
Ice Road Truckers: Tech of the Road
HISTORY
hmhsocialstudies.com

GeoActivity

RESEARCHING TRANSPORTATION
Working with a partner, use the Internet to research transportation around the world. Then prepare a report that shows the design of a **Web page** highlighting some aspect of world transportation.

- Create text to present the information you have found.
- Select suitable images.
- Locate appropriate links for visitors to your Web site.

In the northernmost reaches of Canada, roads are scarce. So, vast distances between places are more easily covered by small planes that can touch down on land or water, like this one flying into Cochrane, Ontario.

GeoData

LAND TRANSPORTATION
- In the United States, there is one car for every two persons; in Somalia, one for every 500.
- One of the world's longest single rail systems, Russia's Trans-Siberian Railway, covers a distance of 5,867 miles from Moscow to the port of Nakhodka.
- Snowmobiles have replaced dogsleds as transport in remote, cold climates of North America.
- China has more bicycles—about 540,000,000—than any other country.
- Animals, including dogs, horses, donkeys, mules, camels, and elephants, still provide transport for many people around the world.

AIR TRANSPORTATION
- In 2009, airlines flew more than 149 million passengers on 1.3 million international flights.

WATER TRANSPORTATION
- Some modern cruise ships and ocean liners are more than 900 feet long and can carry upwards of 2,000 passengers on a voyage.

This crescent-shaped boat on Lake Titicaca in Peru is made from a reedlike plant. Native peoples of the region have made these boats for centuries.

GeoActivities

Integrated Assessment
- Rubric for a Web page, 5.1

More About

Cars in the United States

Increases in auto use in the U.S. and a large group of people soon to reach driving age are making the job of auto technician ever more important. The skills required for this career have increased with the use of computerized diagnostic tools and the addition of complicated electronic components in vehicles. Technical training and certification programs have become standard in the field. Despite the tougher certification requirements, auto technician is a desirable job. In fact, more women are entering the field every day. With the likelihood of demand increasing in this field, skilled auto technicians may have big opportunities in the years ahead.

ACTIVITY OPTION | COOPERATIVE LEARNING

BLOCK SCHEDULING

ESTIMATING TRAVEL TIMES

Objective To apply geographical information to real-life situations

Class Time 15-20 minutes

Task Estimate travel times from one location to another by two different means of transportation

Directions Have students divide into pairs. Give each pair a different starting and ending point based on local trips they could take in your area. Tell each pair the total distance in miles, one way, for their route. Then have the members of each pair work together to estimate how long it would take to go from point A to point B by car (at 35 miles per hour) or by train (at 50 miles per hour). Then have them figure out the roundtrip time. Have the pairs share their results with the class.

SECTION 3 OBJECTIVES

1. Examine the subregion known as the Atlantic Provinces.
2. Examine the subregion known as the Core Provinces.
3. Examine the subregion known as the Prairie Provinces.
4. Examine the subregion known as the Pacific Province and the Territories.

SKILLBUILDER: Interpreting Graphs, p. 166.

GeographicThinking
Using the Atlas, pp. 167, 169
Seeing Patterns, p. 168
Making Inferences, p. 169

Focus & Motivate

What accounts for the variety of lifestyles within a country's subregions? *(location, climate, different people settling area, local industry)*

Instruct: Objective 1 appears on p. 167.

Interpreting Graphs

Comparing Subregions of Canada

Have students examine the graph. Then, ask them to identify which subregion has the smallest population. *(Atlantic Provinces)*

SKILLBUILDER ANSWERS

1. The most productive region is in the Core Provinces. **2.** They have more than half of Canada's land but only a small population and production compared with the Core and Prairie provinces. But they are ahead of the Atlantic Provinces in all categories.

3 Subregions of Canada

Main Ideas

- Canada is divided into four subregions–the Atlantic, Core, and Prairie Provinces, and the Pacific Province and the Territories.
- Each subregion possesses unique natural resources, landforms, economic activities, and cultural life.

Places & Terms

Atlantic Provinces
Quebec
Ontario
Prairie Provinces
British Columbia
Nunavut

CONNECT TO THE ISSUES
URBAN SPRAWL Much of Canada's population is in urban areas within 100 miles of the U.S.-Canadian border.

A HUMAN PERSPECTIVE The Grand Banks, a shallow section of the North Atlantic off the coast of Newfoundland, make up one of the earth's richest fishing grounds. In fact, it was the abundance of fish—including cod, haddock, herring, and mackerel—that first attracted Europeans to the region centuries ago. Today, thousands of hardy Canadians make their living fishing in these coastal waters. One, Alex Saunders of Labrador, remarked that "fishing is a disease. Once you start, you keep at it, do whatever's necessary. I jeopardize my home, all my possessions just to keep this boat going and keep fishing." The Grand Banks are part of the Atlantic Provinces, one of Canada's four subregions.

The Atlantic Provinces

Canada is divided into ten provinces and three territories. Each has a unique population, economy, and resources. Eastern Canada is the location of the four **Atlantic Provinces**—Prince Edward Island, New Brunswick, Nova Scotia, and Newfoundland.

HARSH LANDS AND SMALL POPULATIONS As you can see on the chart below, the Atlantic Provinces are home to just 8 percent of Canada's population. Of these people, most live in coastal cities, such as Halifax, Nova Scotia, and St. John, New Brunswick. The small population is due largely to the provinces' rugged terrain and severe weather.

Comparing the Subregions of Canada

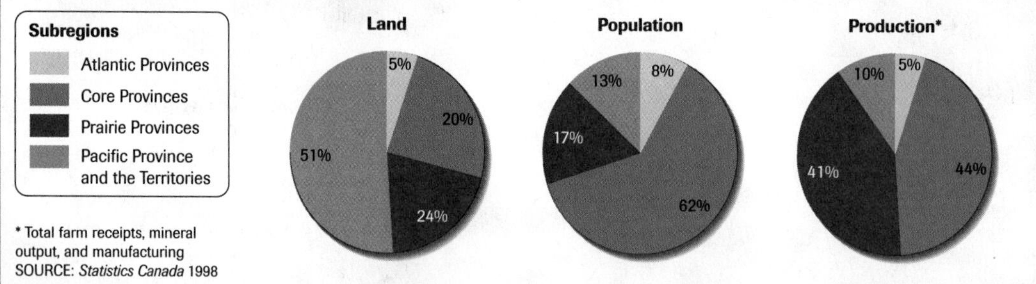

* Total farm receipts, mineral output, and manufacturing
SOURCE: *Statistics Canada* 1998

SKILLBUILDER: Interpreting Graphs
1. **ANALYZING DATA** Which subregion has the highest production?
2. **MAKING COMPARISONS** How do the Pacific Province and the Territories compare overall to the other three subregions?

SECTION 3 PROGRAM RESOURCES

In-Depth Resources: Unit 2
- Guided Reading, p. 23
- Building Vocabulary, p. 25
- Reteaching Activity, p. 28

Guided Reading Workbook
- Section 3

Access for Students Acquiring English
- Guided Reading, p. 35

Formal Assessment
- Section Quiz, p. 100

Integrated Assessment
- Rubric for a brochure, 1.13
- Rubric for a report, 2.5

Outline Maps with Activities
- Canada: Physical and Political, pp. 15–16

INTEGRATED TECHNOLOGY
- Chapter Summaries
- Power Presentations
- The World's Music Audio Program
- Test Generator
  - Section Quiz

hmhsocialstudies.com

TEST-TAKING RESOURCES
- Strategies for Test Preparation

- Test Practice Transparencies TT21
- Online Test Practice

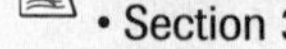

For example, about 85 percent of the land in Nova Scotia cannot be farmed because of rocky hills and poor soil. In New Brunswick, forests cover 90 percent of the land. Newfoundland—made up of the island of Newfoundland, Labrador, and nearby islands—is visited by fierce storms that roar up the Atlantic seaboard. A

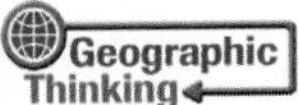

Using the Atlas
A Look at the map on page 154. Which bodies of water do the Atlantic Provinces border?
A. Answer the Atlantic Ocean, the Gulf of St. Lawrence, and the Labrador Sea

ECONOMIC ACTIVITIES Despite the sometimes harsh conditions, the people of the Atlantic Provinces have learned to use what the land and the sea offer them. For example, New Brunswick's dense forests provide the province with its largest industry—logging. This industry produces lumber, wood pulp, and paper products. The Gulf of St. Lawrence and coastal waters supply plentiful stocks of seafood for export. Also, there is mining for zinc, copper, lead, and silver.

Logging and fishing are mainstays of the economy of Nova Scotia, too. This province boasts one of the largest fish-processing plants in North America. In addition, shipbuilding and trade through the port of Halifax provide more employment and revenue. Until the 20th century, fishing was the principal industry in Newfoundland. Today, the province also has healthy mining and logging industries. Moreover, its hydroelectric-power resources are part of a system supplying power to Quebec and parts of the northeastern United States.

5 THEMES
MOVEMENT

Acadians to Cajuns

Colonists from France founded the colony of Acadia on the eastern coast of what is now Canada in 1604. Tensions flared between these settlers and later arrivals from England and Scotland, however.

In 1713, the British gained control of Acadia and renamed it Nova Scotia (New Scotland). They expelled about 4,000 descendants of the original Acadians. Many eventually settled in southern Louisiana. Today, their culture still thrives in the Mississippi Delta area, where the people are called Cajuns (an alteration of Acadian).

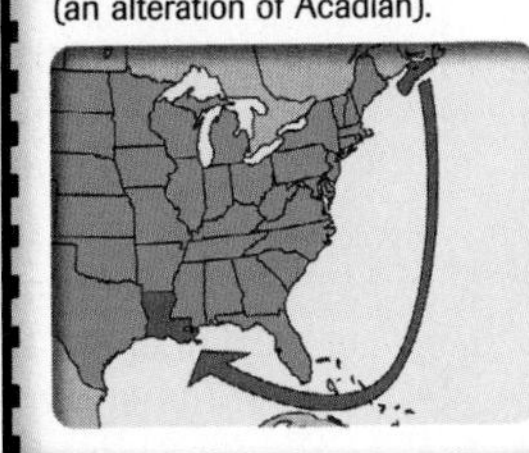

US & CANADA

The Core Provinces—Quebec and Ontario

In 1608, Samuel de Champlain, a French explorer, built a fort, the first European structure in what is now Canada, at present-day Quebec City. Four centuries later, the lands he colonized are part of the country's most dynamic region—**Quebec** and **Ontario,** Canada's Core Provinces.

THE HEARTLAND OF CANADA Quebec and Ontario are often referred to as Canada's heartland, and with good reason. Three out of five Canadians live there. Ontario is the largest province in terms of population, Quebec in land area. Most of the settlement in these inland provinces is found along the Great Lakes and the St. Lawrence River. Each province is the core of one of Canada's two major cultures. A large number of Canada's English-speaking majority live in Ontario. For most French-speaking Canadians, Quebec is home.

CANADA'S POLITICAL AND ECONOMIC CENTER Ontario and Quebec are at the center of Canada's political and economic life. Ottawa is the capital of the federal government. It is located in southeastern Ontario, right next to the border of Quebec province. Quebec has its own political importance as the heart of French Canadian life.

Ontario and Quebec also power Canada's economy. Together, they account for more than 35 percent of Canadian agricultural production, 41 percent of its mineral output, and 70 percent of its manufacturing. As

Instruct: Objective 1

The Atlantic Provinces

- Which are the Atlantic Provinces? *(Prince Edward Island, New Brunswick, Nova Scotia, and Newfoundland)*
- What factors have kept the population small in this subregion? *(poor farming lands and harsh weather)*

In-Depth Resources: Unit 2
- Guided Reading, p. 23

5 THEMES

Movement: Acadians to Cajuns

Tell students that most Cajuns speak both English and a French dialect. In recent years, they have become known for their music and cuisine. Ask students how Louisiana might be similar to and different from the Acadians' original colony in what is now Nova Scotia. *(coastal, fish as mainstay, French culture; Louisiana warmer, not an isolated peninsula)*

Instruct: Objective 2

The Core Provinces–Quebec and Ontario

- What cultures are associated with Quebec and Ontario? *(Quebec–French, Ontario–English)*
- Near what natural landforms are the larger cities in these provinces located? *(waterways: Great Lakes, St. Lawrence River)*

ACTIVITY OPTION **INTERNET RESEARCH**

SYNOPSIS OF TRENDS

Objective To connect geographical content to current trends

Class Time 1 hour

Task Use the Internet to research trends on rising cities and their industries

Directions Divide students into groups of 4-6. Assign one city to each group: Toronto, Montreal, Ottawa, Calgary. (Give more than one group the same city if necessary.) Have each group work to find current information on its city. Is the city growing in size? What are some causes for the growth or the lack thereof? What is the major industry in that city? How does it affect the economy? Have the students write a short report summarizing their findings and citing their sources. Then have them share their reports with the class.

OPTIONAL ACTIVITY If Internet access is limited, have students use the library to find current statistics and information. They may need the assistance of a librarian to locate reference books and other likely sources.

Instruct: Objective 3

The Prairie Provinces

- Which are the Prairie Provinces? *(Manitoba, Saskatchewan, Alberta)*
- For what resources are these provinces most known? *(agriculture—especially wheat—minerals, oil, coal, natural gas)*
- Which province in this subregion is home to the Métis? *(Saskatchewan)*

Interpreting Photographs

The Prairie Provinces

Have students examine the photograph. Ask them to volunteer one or two words that describe the landscape. Write the words on the board and discuss with the class the impression of the subregion this photograph creates.

Instruct: Objective 4

The Pacific Province and the Territories

- Which province and territories are included in this subregion? *(British Columbia, Yukon and Northwest Territories, Nunavut)*
- Which part of the Northwest Territories became Nunavut? *(eastern half)*
- How do the Inuit make their living in Nunavut? *(mining, logging, fishing)*

the map on page 160 shows, they supply a wide variety of products. Toronto, located on the shores of Lake Ontario, is not only the country's most populous city but also its banking and financial hub. Montreal, located on the St. Lawrence River, is Canada's second largest city. It is the center of economic and political activity in Quebec province.

The Prairie Provinces

To the west of the hustle and bustle of Ontario and Quebec lie the **Prairie Provinces**—Manitoba, Saskatchewan, and Alberta.

CANADA'S BREADBASKET Canada's Prairie Provinces are part of the Great Plains of North America. These three provinces are the center of the nation's agricultural yield. They account for 50 percent of Canada's agricultural production. The land of the Prairie Provinces, however, consists of more than just fertile soil. A significant amount of Canada's mineral output comes from this region of the country. Alberta itself has the nation's largest known deposits of coal and oil and produces 76 percent of Canada's natural gas.

A CULTURAL MIX The people of the Prairie Provinces are a diverse group. Manitoba has large numbers of Scots-Irish, Germans, Scandinavians, Ukrainians, and Poles. The town of St. Boniface boasts the largest French-Canadian population outside Quebec. The population of Saskatchewan also includes immigrants from South and East Asia and is home to the métis. Alberta is perhaps the most diverse of all. In addition to European immigrants, this province also has significant Indian, Japanese, Lebanese, and Vietnamese populations. B

B. Answer Alberta has many economic activities that would employ a variety of people, including immigrants.

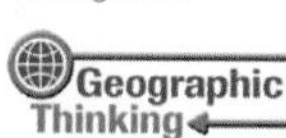

Geographic Thinking

Seeing Patterns B Why might Alberta have attracted such a diverse population?

The Pacific Province and the Territories

The province of British Columbia along with the three territories—Yukon Territory, Northwest Territories, and Nunavut—make up Canada's western and northern lands.

REGION The vast fertile plains of the Prairie Provinces, shown here in Regina, Saskatchewan, provide wheat for Canadians and the world.

DIFFERENTIATING INSTRUCTION **GIFTED AND TALENTED STUDENTS**

FOLLOWING A NEWS TRAIL

Objective Understand a current geographic situation based on events that led to it

Class Time 2 class periods

Task Create a series of articles on the events that led to the formation of Nunavut

Directions Ask students to use the library or the Internet to research the events leading to the formation of Nunavut from the area that was part of the Northwest Territories in Canada. Have students find at least 4 articles that show a progression of events. Have them print or copy the articles and create a short report that summarizes each article and then describes the events leading to the creation of the province of Nunavut. Students should be judged on the relevance of the articles they choose, the quality of their summaries, and the overall accuracy of their report.

BRITISH COLUMBIA Canada's westernmost province is **British Columbia.** Nearly all of it lies within the Rocky Mountain range. As a result, three-fourths of the province is 3,000 feet or more above sea level. More than half of the land is densely forested, and nearly one-third is frozen tundra, snowfields, and glaciers. Most of the population is found in the southwest. This is the location of British Columbia's two largest cities, Victoria and Vancouver. The economy is built on logging, mining, and hydroelectric-power production. Vancouver is Canada's largest port and has a prosperous shipping trade. C

Geographic Thinking
Using the Atlas
C Using a world map, locate Vancouver. Where might many of the goods shipped from its port be headed?
C. Answer
Vancouver is on the Pacific Ocean. Products may be headed for Asia, the United States, or Latin America.

THE TERRITORIES Canada's three territories make up 41 percent of the country's land mass. Yet, they are too sparsely populated to be provinces. The Yukon Territory, with a population around 35,000, lies north of British Columbia and is largely an unspoiled wilderness. Directly east is the Northwest Territories, an area that extends into the Arctic. It has a population of nearly 43,000 people.

Nunavut was carved out of the eastern half of the Northwest Territories in 1999. It is home to many of Canada's Inuit. (See "Geography Today" on this page.) Even though the land is rugged and climatic conditions are severe, economic activities take place in the territories. Mining, fishing, and some logging are the principal industries, and these widely scattered activities explain why the settlements are so dispersed.

In this chapter and the last, you read about the human geography of the United States and Canada. In the next chapter, you will learn about some of the issues that are facing those countries today.

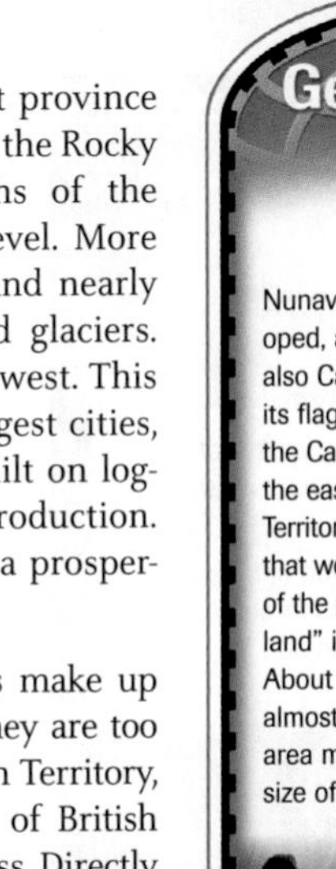
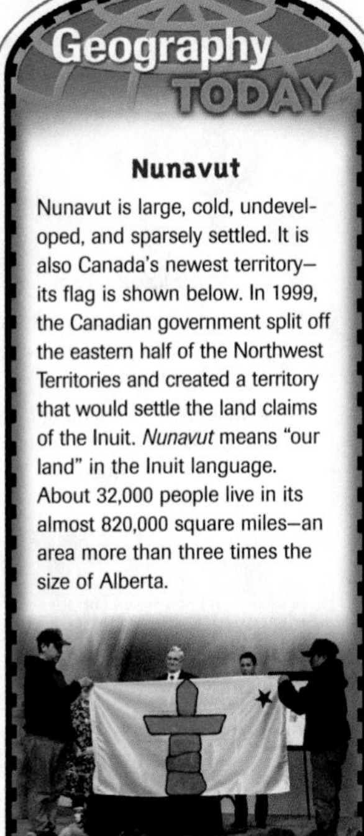

Geography TODAY

Nunavut

Nunavut is large, cold, undeveloped, and sparsely settled. It is also Canada's newest territory—its flag is shown below. In 1999, the Canadian government split off the eastern half of the Northwest Territories and created a territory that would settle the land claims of the Inuit. *Nunavut* means "our land" in the Inuit language. About 32,000 people live in its almost 820,000 square miles—an area more than three times the size of Alberta.

Section 3 Assessment

1 Places & Terms

Identify and explain where in the region these would be found.
- Atlantic Provinces
- Quebec
- Ontario
- Prairie Provinces
- British Columbia

2 Taking Notes

REGION Review the notes you took for this section.

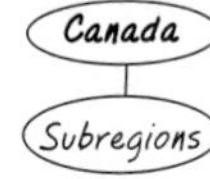

- What is the major economic activity of the Atlantic Provinces?
- Which provinces make up the Prairie Provinces?

3 Main Ideas

a. Why is the population of the Atlantic Provinces so small?
b. Why are Ontario and Quebec called the heartland of Canada?
c. What economic activities take place in British Columbia?

4 Geographic Thinking

Making Inferences Which subregions have the greatest potential for economic growth? **Think about:**
- already developed subregions
- each subregion's natural resources

See Skillbuilder Handbook, page R4.

GeoActivity

MAKING COMPARISONS Review the differences among the subregions of Canada. Create a **brochure** that illustrates the economic activities, population characteristics, and major cities of the subregions.

Geography TODAY

Nunavut

Have students read the information on the territory of Nunavut. Ask them when, why, and how Nunavut was founded. *(founded in 1999 by splitting off part of the Northwest Territories to settle an Inuit claim to the land)*

Assess & Reteach

GeoFocus Have students complete their notes on Canada for the cluster diagram.

Formal Assessment
- Section Quiz, p. 100

Reteaching Activity
Have students look back through the section and summarize, in one sen tence, the main idea for each subhead in their notebooks. Then ask them to divide into pairs and compare the main ideas they have produced.

In-Depth Resources: Unit 2
- Reteaching Activity, p. 28

Outline Maps with Activities
- Canada: Physical and Political, pp. 15–16

SECTION 3 ASSESSMENT ANSWERS

1. Places &Terms
Atlantic Provinces, p. 166
Quebec, p. 167
Ontario, p. 167
Prairie Provinces, p. 168
British Columbia, p. 169

2. Taking Notes
- Economic activity in the Atlantic Provinces includes logging, fishing, fish processing, mining, shipbuilding, trade, and production of hydroelectric power.
- The Prairie Provinces are Manitoba, Saskatchewan, and Alberta.

3. Main Ideas
a. The population is small due to the harsh climate and rugged terrain.
b. These provinces are the most heavily populated and are where Canada's major political and economic activities take place.
c. British Columbia is the site of logging, mining, and hydroelectric power production.

4. Geographic Thinking
The Prairie Provinces have large supplies of coal and natural gas that could be further developed. The Pacific Province and the Territories have a great amount of land and some minerals that could be developed.

GeoActivity
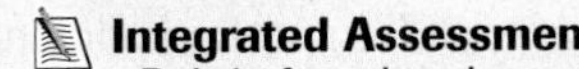
Integrated Assessment
- Rubric for a brochure, 1.13

Reviewing Places and Terms

A.
1. New France, p. 156
2. Dominion of Canada, p. 156
3. province, p. 156
4. prime minister, p. 158
5. First Nations, p. 159
6. Atlantic Provinces, p. 166
7. Quebec, p. 167
8. Ontario, p. 167
9. Prairie Provinces, p. 168
10. British Columbia, p. 169

B. Possible Responses

11. The original settlers were the First Nations peoples.
12. New France was located along the St. Lawrence River where Quebec is located today and extended into parts of present-day Manitoba, Saskatchewan, and Alberta.
13. Canada is divided into political units called provinces and territories.
14. Canada is led by a prime minister.
15. The original Dominion of Canada was made up of Quebec, Ontario, Nova Scotia, and New Brunswick.
16. Canada's core consists of Quebec and Ontario.
17. The Prairie Provinces are Canada's breadbasket.
18. Quebec has the majority of Canada's French speakers.
19. British Columbia is Canada's westernmost province.
20. The Atlantic Provinces are the smallest and least populated provinces.

Chapter 7 Assessment

VISUAL SUMMARY
HUMAN GEOGRAPHY OF CANADA

History and Government

- French and British settlement of the region had a major effect on its political development.
- The vastness of Canada and its harsh climate have affected the country's population distribution and its economic growth.

Economy and Culture

- Canada is one of the world's most industrialized and urbanized nations.
- Canada has diverse cultures.

Subregions of Canada

- The Atlantic Provinces are the smallest of the subregions.
- The Core Provinces of Canada are Quebec and Ontario.
- The Prairie Provinces are the breadbasket of Canada.
- The Pacific Province and the Territories contain huge tracts of largely undeveloped land.

Reviewing Places & Terms

A. Briefly explain the importance of each of the following.

1. New France
2. Dominion of Canada
3. province
4. prime minister
5. First Nations
6. Atlantic Provinces
7. Quebec
8. Ontario
9. Prairie Provinces
10. British Columbia

B. Answer the questions about vocabulary in complete sentences.

11. Who were the original settlers of Canada?
12. Where was New France located?
13. How is Canada divided politically?
14. What is the title of the leader of Canada?
15. Which provinces made up the original part of the Dominion of Canada?
16. Which provinces make up Canada's core?
17. Which provinces are known as Canada's "breadbasket"?
18. Which province has the majority of Canada's French speakers?
19. Which is Canada's westernmost province?
20. Which provinces are the smallest and least populated?

Main Ideas

History and Government of Canada (pp. 155–158)

1. Why were the French and the British interested in colonizing the area of North America that became the United States and Canada?
2. How did the French and Indian War change the history of Canada?
3. In what ways is the expansion and development of Canada similar to that of the United States?
4. How is Canada's government different from that of the United States?

Economy and Culture of Canada (pp. 159–165)

5. What is Canada's largest export product?
6. Which two languages and religions dominate Canadian culture?
7. Where do most Canadians live?

Subregions of Canada (pp. 166–169)

8. In which provinces would you expect to find a large fishing industry?
9. Which provinces power Canada's economy?
10. Why are the Prairie Provinces so important to the Canadian economy?

Main Ideas

1. Both were interested in the coastal fisheries and inland fur trade.
2. The British took over New France, and the country began to have two distinct cultures.
3. Both expanded westward, had immigration from a variety of countries, and had transcontinental railroads to encourage development.
4. Canada's political units are called provinces and territories. The legislature is called the Parliament, the leader is a prime minister, and the symbolic head of state is the British monarch.
5. Canada's largest trade is in forest products, including wood pulp and paper products.
6. English and French languages and Roman Catholic and Protestant religions dominate Canadian culture.
7. Most Canadians live in urban areas within 100 miles of the United States border.
8. The largest fishing industry is found in the Atlantic Provinces.
9. Quebec and Ontario power Canada's economy.
10. They produce a large percentage of all agricultural products and have huge amounts of minerals, coal, oil, and natural gas.

Critical Thinking

1. Using Your Notes

Use your completed chart to answer these questions.

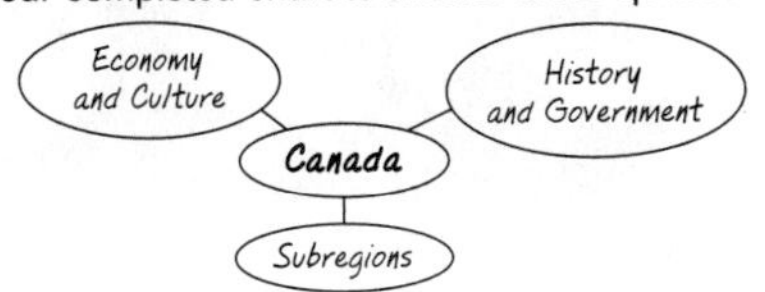

a. Which of the subregions has the least developed resources and why?

b. What types of service industry drive the Canadian economy?

2. Geographic Themes

a. **REGION** How has climate affected the distribution of population in Canada?

b. **PLACE** How are the Pacific Province and the Territories different from the rest of the subregions?

3. Identifying Themes

How did immigration shape the culture of Canada? Which of the five themes of geography applies to the development of Canadian culture?

4. Determining Cause and Effect

What impact did French and British settlement have on modern life in Canada?

5. Drawing Conclusions

Why are Quebec and Ontario considered the core of Canada?

For Additional Test Practice

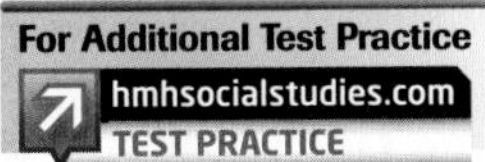

Geographic Skills: Interpreting Maps

Major Languages of Canada

Use the map to answer the questions.

1. **LOCATION** What is the relative location of the French speakers?
2. **MOVEMENT** Which native language is spoken over the widest area?
3. **REGION** What is the predominant language spoken in most areas near the U.S. border?

Choose one of the Native American languages shown on the map. Do some research to find out about the people who speak that language. Write a brief report of your findings and include a sketch map of the location of that language.

hmhsocialstudies.com

MULTIMEDIA ACTIVITY

Use the links at **hmhsocialstudies.com** to do research about the art of the Inuit people. Look for pictures of works that can be copied and background about the art itself.

Creating an Oral Presentation Put together the pictures you have copied and the information about the art for an oral presentation. Be sure to show how geography influenced the art of Canada.

US & CANADA

Critical Thinking

1. a. The Pacific Province and the Territories have the least developed resources because the land is huge and sparsely populated and the climate is harsh.

b. real estate, finance, transportation, tourism, communications, and insurance.

2. a. The harsh climate keeps most of Canada's population in the southern part of the country.

b. The land the Pacific Province and the Territories cover is much larger, is less populated than most of the rest of Canada, and is underdeveloped economically.

3. British and French settlement led to a bicultural-bilingual society. Other immigrants as well came to Canada, giving it a multicultural nature. The theme is movement.

4. Today, Canada is officially a bilingual nation. However, some French-speaking Canadians have unsuccessfully attempted to create their own country and split away from English-speaking Canada.

5. They were the first settled, and both had good natural resources and access to rivers to transport goods out of the country.

GeoActivity

 **Integrated Assessment**
- Rubric for a report, 2.5

 **Formal Assessment**
- Chapter Test, Forms A, B, and C, pp. 101–112

Geographic Skills

1. The French speakers are found in the southeast portion of Canada, bordering the United States along the St. Lawrence River.

2. Inuktitut

3. English

MULTIMEDIA ACTIVITY

For the report on Inuit art, students should:
- Present a concise well-organized oral presentation on Inuit art.
- Summarize the achievements of Inuit art.
- Produce clear, imaginative visuals for the oral presentation.
- Include references to the Web sites used as sources.

Grading Rubric Evaluate student performance as Exceptional, Acceptable, or Poor in each of the following categories:

	Exceptional	Acceptable	Poor
Writing is clear, focused, and logical			
States information topic and purpose			
Provides necessary facts and examples			
Uses correct grammar			

Today's Issues: The United States and Canada

OVERVIEW	INSTRUCTIONAL RESOURCES	
ESSENTIAL QUESTION How can the people of the United States and Canada solve the problems that face them? **Focus on the Essential Question Podcast**	**In-Depth Resources: Unit 2** • Building Vocabulary, p. 35 **Block Schedule Strategies** **Chapter Summaries** (English/Spanish)	**Interactive Online Edition** TOS **ExamView® Assessment Suite** (English/Spanish) TOS **CalendarPlanner** **Power Presentations with Media Gallery** **Critical Thinking Transparencies** • CT8 hmhsocialstudies.com INTERACTIVE
SECTION 1 **THE FIGHT AGAINST TERRORISM** **MAIN IDEAS** • Terrorism threatens the safety and security of society. • The United States launched an international war against terrorism after terrorist attacks on September 11, 2001.	**In-Depth Resources: Unit 2** • Guided Reading, p. 29 • Building Vocabulary, p. 35 • Exploring Today's Issues, pp. 36–37 • Reteaching Activity, p. 40 **Guided Reading Workbook,** Section 1	
SECTION 2 **URBAN SPRAWL** **MAIN IDEAS** • Many urban areas in North America have spread out and taken over more and more land. • Urban sprawl causes problems such as traffic congestion, air pollution, and strains on the infrastructure.	**In-Depth Resources: Unit 2** • Guided Reading, p. 30 • Map and Graph Skills, pp. 32–33 • Skillbuilder Practice, p. 34 • Building Vocabulary, p. 35 • Exploring Today's Issues, pp. 38–39 • Reteaching Activity, p. 41 **Guided Reading Workbook,** Section 2	**Map Transparencies** • MT15 National Parks of North America **Critical Thinking Transparencies** • CT40 How Urban Sprawl Affects Natural Resources
CASE STUDY **DIVERSE SOCIETIES FACE CHANGE** **MAIN IDEAS** • The United States and Canada have welcomed immigrants from around the world. • Managing diversity is a continuing challenge for both countries.	**In-Depth Resources: Unit 2** • Guided Reading, p. 31 • Building Vocabulary, p. 35 • Reteaching Activity, p. 42 **Guided Reading Workbook,** Case Study	**The World's Music Audio Program**

ASSESSMENT

SE **Chapter Assessment,** pp. 184–185

Formal Assessment
- Chapter Tests, Forms A, B, and C, pp. 116–130

TOS **ExamView® Assessment Suite**

Strategies for Test Preparation

hmhsocialstudies.com TEST PRACTICE

SE **Section Assessment,** p. 175

Formal Assessment
- Section Quiz, p. 113

Integrated Assessment
- Rubric for a report, 2.5

Test Practice Transparencies TT25

SE **Section Assessment,** p. 178

Formal Assessment
- Section Quiz, p. 114

Integrated Assessment
- Rubric for a report, 2.5

Test Practice Transparencies TT26

SE **Case Study Project,** pp. 182–183

Formal Assessment
- Case Study Quiz, p. 115

Test Practice Transparencies TT27

CHART KEY:

SE Student Edition	Block Scheduling	DVD/CD-ROM
TE Teacher's Edition	TOS Teacher One Stop	MP3 Audio
Printable Resource	Presentation Resource	HISTORY™

Program Resources available on TOS and @ 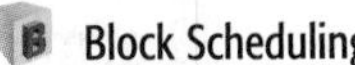

SUPPORTING RESOURCES

- **Multimedia Classroom Global History Series**
- **Global History Teacher's Guide**

Social Studies Trade Library Collection
- Latino Trade Collection

For more information or to purchase these resources, go to hmhsocialstudies.com

DIFFERENTIATED INSTRUCTION

English Learners	Struggling Readers	Gifted and Talented Students
Spanish/English Guided Reading Workbook **Access for Students Acquiring English/ESL** Spanish Translations, pp. 37–42 **Chapter Summaries** (English/Spanish) TE **TE Activity** Forms of a Word, p. 181	**Chapter Summaries** (English/Spanish) TE **TE Activity** Suffixes, p. 156	TE **TE Activity** Researching the War on Terrorism, p. 174

ENRICHMENT ACTIVITIES

The following activities are especially suitable for classes following block schedules.

SE **Student Edition,** pp. 172–185 • Reading a Bounded-Area Map, p. 179	hmhsocialstudies.com RESEARCH WEB LINKS • Case Study Project, p. 182

CHAPTER 8 PACING GUIDE

BLOCK SCHEDULE LESSON PLAN OPTIONS: 90-MINUTE PERIOD

DAY 1

SECTION 1, pp. 173–175
Class Time 90 minutes

- **Planning an Action** Divide students into small groups. Have them decide on an issue discussed in the chapter. Then ask them to organize an action in relation to that issue (such as an information campaign to make people aware of homeland security measures). Have them write up a plan and include the details of what materials they might need, how many people, how long to organize, etc.

DAY 2

SECTION 2, pp. 176–179
Class Time 90 minutes

- **Press Conference** As a way to review the section, assign each of the following issues to six pairs of students (growth of metropolitan areas, unrestricted growth, strains on the infrastructure, air pollution/water depletion, smart growth, sustainable communities). Have one student in each pair explain the issue to the class, based on the information in the section, and have the other student propose some solutions to the problem.
Class Time 45 minutes
- **Skillbuilder Lesson** Use the Activity Option about determining cause and effect on TE page 177 and the Skillbuilder Practice worksheet.
Class Time 45 minutes

DAY 3

Case Study, pp. 180–183
Class Time 35 minutes

- **Project Summary** Introduce the Case Study and discuss with the class the issues of melting pot versus mosaic. Let them share their opinions and experiences with the class.

CHAPTER 8 REVIEW AND ASSESSMENT
pp. 184–185
Class Time 55 minutes

- **Review** Have students prepare a summary of the chapter using the Places and Terms listed on the first page of each section.
Class Time 20 minutes
- **Assessment** Have students complete the Chapter 8 Assessment.
Class Time 35 minutes

TEACHER-TESTED ACTIVITY

Playing Geography Jeopardy

Class Time 1-2 class periods

Task Create a geography quiz game about the United States and Canada

Supplies
- paper, pen, pencils
- white board, markers
- score board

Purpose To enhance student knowledge of the key concepts, facts, and themes related to two of the section issues: urban sprawl and diverse societies.

Activity Form the class into two teams and select captains. Each team will use the text to develop questions or statements for game competition. Students will extract key concepts and facts related to some of the main issues of the chapter: urban sprawl and diversity. Each team will create five columns with headings that relate to the issues presented in the chapter. Create five questions per column with point values ranging from 10 to 50 per question (double bonus points may be added by the teacher). Display each group's columns on the white board. The opposing teams will attempt to answer each other's questions by rotating turns after a toss of the coin. Keep score.

Robert Schutt
Geography Teacher, Detroit High School for the Performing Arts, Detroit, Michigan

TECHNOLOGY IN THE CLASSROOM

Digital cameras are becoming increasingly popular in schools and at home. Students can take pictures of people, buildings, scenery, or other subjects and upload the pictures directly onto a computer for storage and sharing. Students will commonly incorporate these photographs into multimedia presentations or Web sites.

Objective Use digital cameras to document examples of urban sprawl in or near the community.

Task Have students learn about sprawl in Chapter 8 and on the Web. Then have them use a digital camera to take pictures of sprawl and solutions to sprawl in their town. Organize a class field trip or "walking tour," and allow students to share the camera.

Class Time 3-5 class periods

1. Have students read pages 176-178 and discuss what the book says about urban sprawl. What causes sprawl? What are the negative impacts of sprawl? What are some solutions to sprawl?
2. Ask students if they've noticed examples of sprawl in or near their town. Have them discuss the ways in which their area is experiencing sprawl-related problems, if at all.
3. Have students visit the Web sites listed at **hmhsocial studies.com** to learn more about sprawl. Ask them to take notes to answer the questions posed in step 1.
4. Ask students to plan a photojournalism project in which they document examples of sprawl and of solutions to sprawl in their community. Depending on the number of available cameras and the policy for using the cameras, you might conduct the project as a class field trip, a class "walking tour" near the school, a group project, or individual projects in which students take turns using the camera over a period of several weeks or months. If they live in an area that has not been affected by sprawl, they should focus on the features of their community that stand out as different from the examples of sprawl they've learned about.
5. Have students photograph as many examples of urban sprawl and sprawl solutions, or features that stand out as "non-sprawl," as they can. They can photograph the same types of scenes they've seen and read about in the textbook and online, and they can add new examples as they come across them.
6. Students may also interview community residents and businesspeople about their attitudes toward and experiences with sprawl. They should record the conversations either on tape or on paper.
7. Have students create multimedia presentations or a Web site showcasing what they've documented. Their presentations should contain text that describes the extent to which they think sprawl has affected their community, some quotes from the interviews (if they did any), and some possible solutions to their town's sprawl problems. If they don't think sprawl is a problem, or if they think it's a good thing, they should explain why they feel this way.

CHAPTER 8 OBJECTIVE

Learn about key issues Americans and Canadians face, and their attempts to solve problems.

Chapter 8
TODAY'S ISSUES
The United States and Canada

New York City firefighters raise the American flag amid the rubble of the World Trade Center after the terrorist attack of September 11, 2001.

Interpreting Photographs

Firefighters Raise the Flag

Ask students to examine the photograph and read the caption. Ask them to describe what action they see and what it represents to them. *(Firefighters raise the American flag at the site of the collapsed World Trade Center in New York City, September 11, 2001. Student responses will vary.)*

Essential Question

How can the people of the United States and Canada solve the problems that face them?

What You Will Learn

In this chapter you will learn about challenges facing the United States and Canada today.

SECTION 1
The Fight Against Terrorism

SECTION 2
Urban Sprawl

CASE STUDY
Diverse Societies Face Change

For more on the issues in the United States and Canada . . .

hmhsocialstudies.com CURRENT EVENTS

hmhsocialstudies.com TAKING NOTES

Use the online graphic organizer to structure your notes about some causes and effects of terrorism, urban sprawl, and diverse societies.

172

Introducing the Essential Question

- Discuss any recent events related to terrorism, urban sprawl, or societal diversity. Explore the extent of students' knowledge on these topics.
- Emphasize that these topics often generate strong sentiments and that class discussions about them should be based on verifiable facts.

Ask students to copy and fill in the graphic organizer with the causes and effects of problems facing the U.S. and Canada today.

Critical Thinking Transparencies CT8
- GeoFocus

In-Depth Resources: Unit 2
- Building Vocabulary, p. 35

CHAPTER 8 ADDITIONAL RESOURCES

BOOKS FOR THE TEACHER

Flint, Anthony. ***This Land: The Battle over Sprawl and the Future of America.*** The Johns Hopkins University Press, 2006. The dream and nightmare of our ever-expanding suburbs.

BOOKS FOR THE STUDENT

Carnes, Jim. ***Us and Them: A History of Intolerance in America.*** NY: Oxford, 1999. Individual accounts of adversity from colonial times to the present.

Duany, Andres, and Elizabeth Plater-Zybek, and Jeff Speck. ***Suburban Nation.*** NY: North Point Press, 2000. An examination of the effects of sprawl.

INTERNET

For more on issues facing the United States and Canada, visit . . .

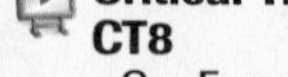

The Fight Against Terrorism

How can a country protect itself from terrorism?

Main Ideas

- Terrorism threatens the safety and security of society.
- The United States launched a war against international terrorism after being attacked on September 11, 2001.

Places & Terms

terrorism
global network
coalition
biological weapon

US & CANADA

A HUMAN PERSPECTIVE For Karl Co, a 15-year-old sophomore at Stuyvesant High School in New York City, September 11, 2001, began as "such a normal day." From his classroom, Karl had a clear view of the World Trade Center, just four blocks away. On a normal day, about 50,000 people worked in and 70,000 visited the twin towers. When the north tower burst into flames and smoke, Karl first thought, "It's a bomb. I'm going to die." Then the south tower erupted, and, shortly after, both collapsed. The students soon learned terrorists had crashed airliners into the towers, and the school was evacuated.

The September 11 Attacks

The students at Stuyvesant High had witnessed an act of **terrorism.** Terrorism is the unlawful use of, or threatened use of, force or violence against individuals or property for the purpose of intimidating or causing fear for political or social ends. Like many countries, the United States had been subjected to terrorism, both at home and abroad. But the September 11, 2001, attacks were the most destructive acts of terrorism ever committed on American soil.

On that morning, 19 Arab terrorists hijacked four airliners. They crashed two planes into the World Trade Center towers and one into the Pentagon, the U.S. military headquarters near Washington, D.C. The fourth plane crashed into a field in Pennsylvania without striking its intended target, after some passengers overwhelmed the hijackers.

THE DESTRUCTION The hijacked planes were loaded with fuel. They became destructive missiles as they crashed into their targets. Thousands of workers escaped before the damaged skyscrapers collapsed. Fire and raining debris caused nearby buildings to collapse as well. At the Pentagon, the plane tore a 75-foot hole in the building's west side.

About 3,000 people died in the attacks. The dead included 265 plane passengers and 343 New York City firefighters who had entered the towers to rescue those trapped inside. Nine buildings in the city's financial district were completely destroyed or partly collapsed, and six others suffered major damage. The disaster area covered 16 acres.

THE TERRORISTS Immediately after the attacks, investigators worked to identify both the hijackers and those who directed the attacks. The evidence pointed to a **global network,** or worldwide interconnected group, of extremist Islamic terrorists led by Osama bin Laden, a Saudi Arabian millionaire. The group, known as al-Qaeda, was formed to fight the Soviet invasion of Afghanistan in 1979. Al-Qaeda later began to oppose

BACKGROUND
Osama bin Laden offered to help the Saudi Arabian government when Iraq invaded Kuwait in 1990 and threatened Saudi Arabia. He was angered when the Saudis turned to the United States for military help instead.

SECTION 1 OBJECTIVES

1. Describe how the United States responded to the the acts of terrorism that occurred on September 11, 2001
2. Explain the difficulties the United States and its allies, such as Canada, face in fighting terrorism.

SKILLBUILDER: Interpreting Maps, p. 174

GeographicThinking

Using the Atlas, p. 174
Making Inferences, p. 175

Focus & Motivate

Ask students to recall their reactions to the events of September 11, 2001, and describe what life was like in their community in the days that followed. *(Student answers will vary.)*

Instruct: Objective 

The September 11 Attacks

- What happened in the September 11 terrorist attacks? *(Terrorists hijacked four planes. Two crashed into the World Trade Center and one into the Pentagon. Another crashed in Pennsylvania.)*
- How great was the physical destruction caused by the attacks? *(About 3,000 people died. A significant part of New York City's financial district was damaged or destroyed, and the west side of the Pentagon was left with a 75-foot hole.)*
- Who was responsible for directing the attacks? *(a global network of extremist Islamic terrorists known as al-Qaeda, led by Osama bin Laden)*

In-Depth Resources: Unit 2
- Guided Reading, p. 29
Exploring Today's Issues, pp. 36–37

SECTION 1 PROGRAM RESOURCES

In-Depth Resources: Unit 2
- Guided Reading, p. 29
- Building Vocabulary, p. 35
- Exploring Today's Issues, pp. 36–37
- Reteaching Activity, p. 40

Guided Reading Workbook
- Section 1

Access for Students Acquiring English/ESL
- Guided Reading, p. 37

Formal Assessment
- Section Quiz, p. 113

Integrated Assessment
- Rubric for a report, 2.5

INTEGRATED TECHNOLOGY

Power Presentations
Chapter Summaries
Test Generator
- Section Quiz

TEST-TAKING RESOURCES

Strategies for Test Preparation

Test Practice Transparencies TT31

Online Test Practice

Interpreting Maps

Major Terrorist Attacks Against Americans, 1979–2001

Have students examine the map. Ask them to name the continents on which terrorist attacks against Americans have taken place. *(North America, Europe, Asia, Africa)*

SKILLBUILDER ANSWER
Asia

Instruct: Objective 2

The War on Terrorism

- On the international level, how did the United States respond to the September 11 terrorist attacks? *(The United States organized a coalition to fight global terrorism. It took military action against Afghanistan and Iraq.*

More About

The Terrorists

Although all of the hijackers in the September 11 attacks were Arabs, al-Qaeda is not exclusively an Arab group. Its members come from many countries, and its network stretches across the continents of North America, South America, Europe, Africa, and Asia. It acts as an umbrella group, not only directing its own attacks, but also financing attacks by other terrorists.

Major Terrorist Attacks Against Americans, 1979-2001

SKILLBUILDER: Interpreting Maps
LOCATION What region was the site of the most attacks on Americans?

American influence in Muslim lands. It started to target Americans and U.S. allies after the Persian Gulf War in 1991. Since its founding, al-Qaeda has carried out numerous terrorist attacks. A

Geographic Thinking
Using the Atlas
A Locate Afghanistan on the political map on page A34. What is its location in relation to Saudi Arabia?
A. Answer It is about 650 miles northeast of Saudi Arabia.

The War on Terrorism

The September 11 attacks shocked and distressed not only Americans but people around the world. President George W. Bush called on other nations to join the United States in a war on terrorism.

MILITARY ACTION The United States organized a **coalition**, or an alliance, to prevent future terrorist attacks. The coalition supported military action in Afghanistan, where al Qaeda was based. The United States began bombing targets in Afghanistan in October 2001. By March 2002, Afghanistan's extremist Taliban regime had been removed from power and the al Qaeda network weakened. Yet, Taliban guerrillas continued to stage attacks throughout the country.

In March 2003, the United States launched military action against Iraq. President Bush claimed that Iraqi dictator Saddam Hussein posed a threat to national security. Hussein was overthrown, tried, and executed, but rebel attacks and religious conflicts still disrupted the country.

In 2009, President Barack Obama began to increase the number of U.S. troops in Afghanistan to secure the defeat of al Qaeda forces in the region. Corruption within the Afghan government is a lingering problem, though, and violence continues. President Obama set a goal that U.S. troops would begin leaving Afghanistan by July 2011 and that all U.S. troops be removed from Iraq by the end of 2011.

DIFFERENTIATING INSTRUCTION GIFTED AND TALENTED STUDENTS

RESEARCHING THE WAR ON TERRORISM

Objective To provide an update on the status of the war on terrorism

Class Time 15-20 minutes

Task Conduct independent research and prepare a summary update

Directions Have students work independently or in a small group to research the current status of the international war on terrorism and what has been accomplished. Direct students to prepare a summary update in a form of their own choosing, such as an oral report, poster, videotaped newscast, or written news article.

ETHNIC AND RELIGIOUS CONFLICT Terrorist attacks persist in several other countries. For example, in Mumbai, India, in November 2008, terrorist bombing and shooting attacks killed nearly 200 people. The attackers were linked to a Pakistani Muslim extremist group that reportedly aims to create an Islamic state in South Asia.

On March 29, 2010, terrorists in Russia attacked the Moscow subway system. A Chechen separatist leader later claimed responsibility for ordering the suicide bombings that killed 39 people and wounded 60 others. Russia and Chechnya, a Russian republic, have a long history of conflict.

Facing Terrorist Threats

Terrorism is a critical threat to national and global security. It is not limited to outside threats. In the past few decades both domestic and international terrorist acts have increased in violence.

TERRORIST WEAPONS AND OPERATIONS Terrorists use other weapons besides bombs and fuel-laden planes, including biological and chemical weapons. **Biological weapons** refer to bacteria and viruses that can be used to harm or kill people, animals, or plants. The United States went on an anthrax alert after traces of the anthrax bacteria were found in letters sent through the mail after the September 2001 attacks. B

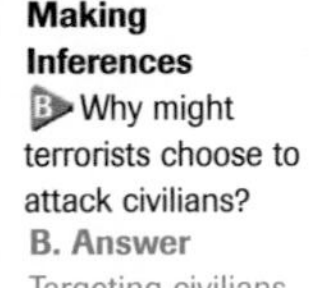

Making Inferences
B Why might terrorists choose to attack civilians?
B. Answer Targeting civilians, such as those on the Moscow subway, probably creates more fear than would an attack on the military.

RECENT THREATS On December 25, 2009, a Nigerian man was arrested for trying to blow up a plane from Amsterdam bound for Detroit, Michigan. The United States and other countries have further stepped up airport security measures in response to this failed terrorist attack.

Some domestic groups also pose threats to national security. An example is the Hutaree, a group that planned to kill law enforcement officers. Violent attacks by some U.S. militia or "patriot" groups that oppose the U.S. government increased in 2009 and 2010. These radical groups sometimes resort to violence to voice their opposition.

Section 1 Assessment

1 Places & Terms
Identify and explain the following terms.
- terrorism
- global network
- coalition
- biological weapon

2 Taking Notes
REGION Review the notes you took for this section.

	Causes	Effects
Issue 1 Terrorism		

- Why did President Obama increase the number of troops in Afghanistan?
- Why is terrorism a global problem?

3 Main Ideas
a. What happened in the terrorist attacks on the United States on September 11, 2001, and who was believed to be responsible?
b. How did the United States respond to the attacks?

4 Geographic Thinking
Drawing Conclusions What might be some difficulties facing the United States and its allies in fighting terrorism? **Think about:**
- a global network
- the variety of weapons available to terrorists

EXPLORING LOCAL GEOGRAPHY Do research to learn how the fight against terrorism is being waged in your state. Write a **press release** describing one of these antiterrorist measures.

Instruct: Objective 3

Facing Terrorist Threats

- What countries other than the United States have been the target of terrorist attacks recently? *(India, Russia)*
- What are some kinds of weapons that terrorists can use? *(bombs, planes, disease-causing bacteria and viruses, chemical weapons)*

Assess & Reteach

GeoFocus Have students complete their notes on terrorism in the graphic organizer.

Formal Assessment
- Section Quiz, p. 113

Reteaching Activity
Ask students to prepare an outline of the main ideas of the section, using the section headings in the text as the topic headings in their outlines and listing important ideas under these headings.

In-Depth Resources: Unit 2
- Reteaching Activity, p. 40

SECTION 1 ASSESSMENT ANSWERS

1. Places & Terms
terrorism, p. 173
global network, p. 173
coalition, p. 174
biological weapon, p. 175

2. Taking Notes
Causes–government corruption and continuing violence; terrorist attacks persist around the world
Effects–increased number of troops to defeat al Qaeda; increased security measures

3. Main Ideas
a. Arab terrorists in hijacked airliners attacked the World Trade Center and the Pentagon. Evidence indicated that a global terrorist network known as al-Qaeda was responsible.
b. The United States formed an international coalition to fight a war against terrorism. It also increased security at home and began to hunt for terrorists within its borders.

4. Geographic Thinking
Some extremist groups are part of a global network so it might be difficult to find out exactly who is behind the attacks or where they originated. A variety of weapons could be used in an attack, including biological or chemical weapons.

GeoActivity

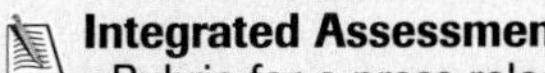
Integrated Assessment
- Rubric for a press release, 4.10

SECTION 2 OBJECTIVES

1. Examine how cities have grown without proper planning.
2. Identify the negative effects of urban sprawl.
3. Identify some possible solutions to urban sprawl.

SKILLBUILDER: Interpreting Graphs, p. 176

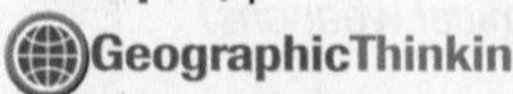

Seeing Patterns, p. 177
Making Comparisons, p. 178
Drawing Conclusions, p. 178

Focus & Motivate

How can poor urban planning affect future living conditions? *(It may affect outdoor activities, types of jobs, and transportation.)*

Instruct: Objective 1 appears on p. 177.

Interpreting Graphs

Growth of U.S. Metropolitan Areas

Have students examine the graph. Ask them what was the percentage increase between 1970 and 1980. *(10 percent)* Ask them the percentage increase between 1980 and 2000. *(3 percent)*

SKILLBUILDER ANSWERS

1. between 1970 and 1980
2. Metropolitan growth has slowed since 1980.

2 Urban Sprawl

How can urban sprawl be controlled?

Main Ideas

- Many metropolitan areas in the United States and Canada have sprawled, or spread out, farther and farther.
- Cities are focusing on smart-growth solutions to urban sprawl.

Places & Terms

urban sprawl
infrastructure
smart growth
sustainable community

A HUMAN PERSPECTIVE Richard Baron is a real estate developer who tried to address the related problems of urban sprawl and inadequate low-income housing. In 1996, he began building Murphy Park, an affordable and attractive housing complex in mid-town St. Louis, Missouri. The development has more than 400 units and contains both apartments and townhouses. It has plenty of green space, art and day-care centers, and an elementary school. More than half of Murphy Park's units are reserved for people with low income. Baron's solution—to bring the attractive features of suburban living to the city—is one of many that are being applied to the problem of urban sprawl.

Growth Without a Plan

Those Americans and Canadians who can afford it often choose to work in a city but live in its suburbs. They are usually attracted by new, upscale housing, better public services, and open space. As suburbs become more numerous, metropolitan areas become larger and more difficult to manage. (See chart to the right.)

URBAN SPRAWL Poorly planned development that spreads a city's population over a wider and wider geographical area is called **urban sprawl.** As outlying areas become more populated, the land between them and the city fills in as well.

In the United States and Canada, urban sprawl is becoming a matter of increasing concern. From 1970 to 2000, people who worked in U.S. cities moved farther and farther from urban centers. The population density of cities in the United States decreased by more than 20 percent as people in cities moved to suburbs and outlying areas. About 30,000 square miles of rural lands were gobbled up by housing developments. For example, the population of the city of Chicago decreased during this period from 3.4 million people to 2.8 million. But the Chicago metropolitan area grew from about 7.0 million persons to 7.3 million.

Canada is less populated than the United States but faces similar problems. In the 1990s, more than 75 percent of all Canadians lived in urban areas.

Growth of U.S. Metropolitan Areas

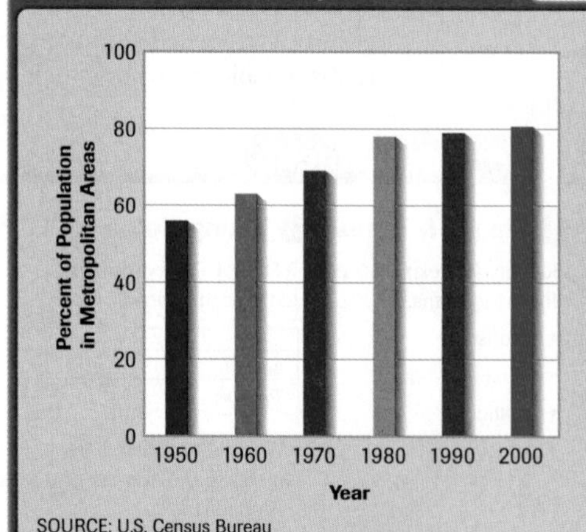

SKILLBUILDER: Interpreting Graphs

1. **ANALYZING DATA** During what time period did the largest increase in metropolitan growth occur?
2. **MAKING GENERALIZATIONS** What has happened to metropolitan growth since 1980?

SECTION 2 PROGRAM RESOURCES

In-Depth Resources: Unit 2
- Guided Reading, p. 30
- Map and Graph Skills, pp. 32–33
- Skillbuilder Practice, p. 34
- Building Vocabulary, p. 35
- Exploring Today's Issues, pp. 38–39
- Reteaching Activity, p. 41

Guided Reading Workbook
- Section 2

Access for Students Acquiring English/ESL
- Guided Reading, p. 38
- Skillbuilder Practice, p. 40
- Map and Graph Skills, pp. 41–42

Formal Assessment,
- Section Quiz, p. 114

Integrated Assessment
- Rubric for a report, 2.5

INTEGRATED TECHNOLOGY

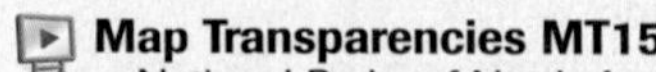
Map Transparencies MT15
- National Parks of North America

Critical Thinking Transparencies CT40
- How Urban Sprawl Affects Natural Resources

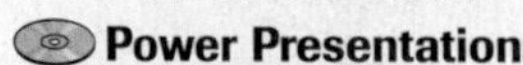
Power Presentations

TEST-TAKING RESOURCES

Strategies for Test Preparation

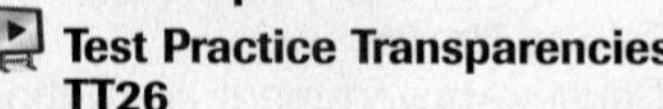
Test Practice Transparencies TT26

Online Test Practice

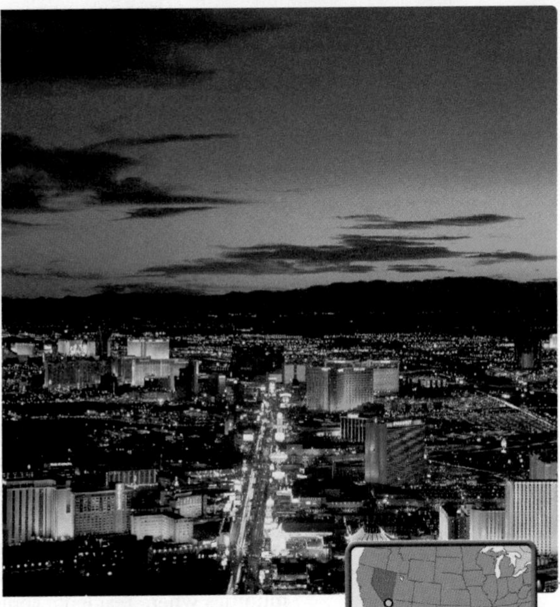

PLACE Las Vegas, Nevada, is a perfect example of urban sprawl. In the 1970s (left), it was a small city. In the 1990s (right), it became the fastest growing city in the country.
What are some of the differences between the photos of Las Vegas above?

CAUSES OF URBAN SPRAWL Sprawl occurs in metropolitan areas that allow unrestricted growth or that have no plans to contain it. Other factors include the widespread use of automobiles and the building of expressways. Autos and relatively cheap gasoline enable Americans to drive many miles to and from their jobs. Despite clogged highways and long commutes, Americans prefer their cars to mass transit. Expressways provide the means for continued reliance on the automobile.

Yet, despite sprawl, there are many reasons why Americans have moved to suburbs. Some people want open spaces or better schools and housing. Still others want to try to recapture the sense of community they experienced while growing up. They want their children to know their neighbors and have a backyard in which to play. Only recently have urban planners started to design big-city neighborhoods to give a sense of community, hoping to slow the flight to the suburbs.

A. Answer The auto has caused highway congestion, strains on the infrastructure, and air pollution.

Urban Sprawl's Negative Impact

Urban sprawl has a negative impact on the quality of life in many ways. As suburbs grow, more commuter traffic strains the infrastructure. **Infrastructure** consists of the basic facilities, services, and machinery needed for a community to function. For example, roads and bridges need maintenance. More cars on the road for more time adds to air pollution, too. Also, sources of water, such as rivers or underground aquifers (layers of water-holding rock or soil), become depleted. A

Seeing Patterns
A What problems has the automobile caused?

Urban sprawl also has other costs. The cost of providing streets, utilities, and other public facilities to suburban communities is often at least 25 per cent higher than for high-density residences in a city. Urban sprawl also separates classes of people. When those in upper-income brackets choose to live in outlying areas, lower-income residents often become isolated in inner-city areas.

Instruct: Objective 1

Growth Without a Plan

- What is urban sprawl? *(the spreading of a city's population over a wider and wider area)*
- What are two factors contributing to urban sprawl? *(unrestricted growth, unlimited use of autos, growth of expressways)*

In-Depth Resources: Unit 2
- Guided Reading, p. 30
- Exploring Today's Issues, pp. 38–39

Interpreting Photographs

Las Vegas

Have students examine the photographs. Then ask students to name two differences between Las Vegas of the 1920s (left picture) and Las Vegas today (right picture). *(Today Las Vegas is spread out, has many more buildings, and lots of lighting and roadways.)*

CAPTION ANSWER Answers will vary, but they should generally indicate that both the business and residential areas of Las Vegas have grown rapidly.

Instruct: Objective 2

Urban Sprawl's Negative Impact

- What is infrastructure? *(basic facilities, services, and installations)*
- What are two bad effects of urban sprawl? *(increased costs for housing, utilities, and other public expenses; economic class separation)*

Critical Thinking Transparencies CT40
- How Urban Sprawl Affects Natural Resources

ACTIVITY OPTION | **SKILLBUILDER LESSON**

DETERMINING CAUSE AND EFFECT

Explaining the Skill Tell students that a **cause** is an action that makes something happen. An **effect** is the event, or set of events, that result. In the exercise that follows, students are asked to examine the causes and effects of ground or water contamination.

In-Depth Resources: Unit 2
- Skillbuilder Practice, p. 34

Applying the Skill Have students use the Internet or library resources to find articles with facts about ground or water contamination. Have students ask: What is the problem? What are likely causes? How has the problem affected the environment or people's lives? What could be done to correct the problem? Then, have students write a short (1-2 paragraph) report.

Instruct: Objective 

Solutions to Sprawl

- Which Canadian and U.S. cities have adopted plans to manage growth? *(Vancouver, BC, and Portland, Oregon)*
- Name two actions that have helped limit sprawl? *(sustained communities and growth boundary lines)*

 **Map Transparencies MT15**
- National Parks of North America

Assess & Reteach

GeoFocus Have students complete the sections on causes and effects of urban sprawl in their graphic organizers.

 **Formal Assessment**
- Section Quiz, p. 114

Reteaching Activity

Ask students to summarize the main points and connected ideas of each section. Point out to students that they can use the section headings as guides.

 **In-Depth Resources: Unit 2**
- Reteaching Activity, p. 41

Solutions to Sprawl

More and more cities are developing plans for **smart growth,** which is the efficient use and conservation of land and other resources. Most often this involves encouraging development close to or inside the limits of existing cities. Good public transportation systems help to make smart growth possible by cutting down on auto traffic.

PORTLAND'S GROWTH BOUNDARY In 1979, the city of Portland, Oregon, drew a line around itself to create an urban growth boundary. Building was allowed inside the boundary. The surrounding green space was off limits to developers. This decision caused controversy but has paid off. Portland has contained urban sprawl.

VANCOUVER'S PLAN FOR SUSTAINABLE COMMUNITIES The population of metropolitan Vancouver, British Columbia, is two-and-a-half times what it was in 1961. The growth of outlying suburbs often took place at the expense of forests, farms, and flood plains. In 1995, the Greater Vancouver Regional Board adopted a plan to manage growth. It involved turning suburbs into **sustainable communities,** that is, communities where residents could live and work. The same solution was applied to Vancouver's downtown area, where about 40 percent of its residents now walk to work. This has cut down on commuting. B

Geographic Thinking
Making Comparisons
B How were the urban growth actions of Portland and Vancouver similar?
B. Answer Both cities saw urban sprawl developing and set up programs to control growth.

GRASSROOTS OPPOSITION In some metropolitan areas, citizens have banded together to offer their own solutions to urban sprawl. For example, citizens in Durham, North Carolina, opposed additional commercial development along a congested area of a nearby interstate highway. They formed CAUSE—Citizens Against Urban Sprawl Everywhere. The organization worked against sprawl through education and political activism.

In this section, you read about the challenge of urban sprawl. In the Case Study that follows, you will learn about challenges increasingly diverse societies bring to the United States and Canada.

Section 2 Assessment

1 Places & Terms
Identify and explain the following places and terms.
- urban sprawl
- infrastructure
- smart growth
- sustainable community

2 Taking Notes
HUMAN-ENVIRONMENT INTERACTION Review the notes you took for this section.

	Causes	Effects
Issue 2: Urban Sprawl		

- What are some of the causes of urban sprawl?
- What are some of the effects of urban sprawl?

3 Main Ideas
a. What happens when metropolitan areas spread farther and farther out?
b. What are some of the ways cities are dealing with urban sprawl?
c. What are some of the ways citizens are dealing with urban sprawl?

4 Geographic Thinking
Drawing Conclusions What would happen to the environment if urban sprawl were not controlled? **Think about:**
- the negative effects of urban sprawl
- the quality of life in the United States and Canada

EXPLORING LOCAL GEOGRAPHY Pair with another student and choose a metropolitan area in the United States or Canada to research. Then prepare a **report** on the condition of urban sprawl in that area and present your report to the class. Discuss the effects of urban sprawl and what steps, if any, are being taken to control the sprawl.

SECTION 2 ASSESSMENT ANSWERS

1. Places & Terms
urban sprawl, p. 176
infrastructure, p. 177
smart growth, p. 178
sustainable community, p. 178

2. Taking Notes
Causes–unrestricted growth; unlimited use of autos; growth of expressways; desire for open spaces, better schools and housing, and a sense of community
Effects–strains on infrastructure, air pollution, rising housing costs, isolation of the poor in inner cities

3. Main Ideas
a. Urban sprawl and all of its problems result from metropolitan areas spreading farther and farther out.
b. Cities are dealing with sprawl by developing plans for smart growth.
c. Citizens are banding together to offer their own solutions.

4. Geographic Thinking
Air pollution would increase, water resources could be depleted, and open land would disappear, affecting the balance of nature.

GeoActivity

 **Integrated Assessment**
- Rubric for a report, 2.5

Map and Graph Skills

Reading a Bounded-Area Map

Urban growth over time is the theme of this map of the Baltimore, Maryland, and Washington, D.C., areas. Both Baltimore and Washington grew from small cities to important metropolitan areas, spreading outward in all directions. At one time, nearly 30 miles of unsettled area separated them. Today, much of this area has been built up as the Baltimore and Washington metropolitan areas have spread.

THE LANGUAGE OF MAPS **Bounded-area maps** show the distribution of some feature of interest, such as climate, vegetation, precipitation, or, in this case, urban growth in a region. Bounded-area maps use lines, colors, and patterns to communicate information.

Urban Growth in Baltimore and Washington 1

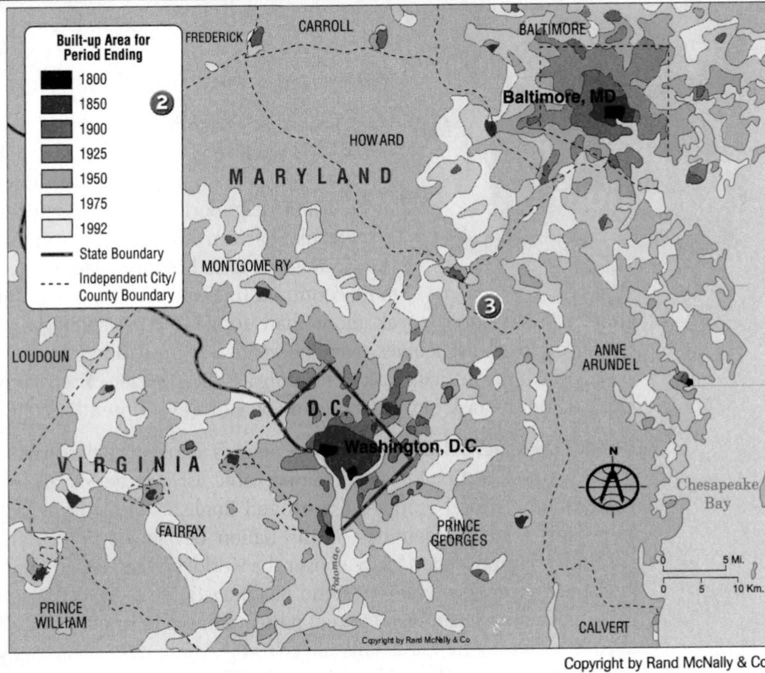

Copyright by Rand McNally & Co.

1 The title gives you the subject matter of the map.

2 The key explains the meanings of the colors and symbols.

3 This map shows the gradual spread of urban areas from two neighboring cities—Baltimore and Washington. The map covers the period of time from 1800 to 1992.

Map and Graph Skills Assessment

1. Seeing Patterns
Like most early settlements, Baltimore and Washington were founded near essential geographic features. What were they?

2. Analyzing Data
During which time period did the greatest expansion take place for the Washington metropolitan area?

3. Drawing Conclusions
At what physical location do the two metropolitan areas seem to have merged?

OBJECTIVE
Examine key features of a bounded-area map.

Instruct: Objective

Reading a Bounded-Area Map

- What is the primary purpose of a bounded-area map? *(to show the distribution of features such as climate, vegetation, precipitation, or urban growth)*
- What does the broken line in the key represent? *(boundaries of counties or independent cities)*
- What is the location of the Chesapeake Bay in relation to Baltimore and Washington? *(Baltimore is north and Washington is west of Chesapeake Bay)*

In-Depth Resources: Unit 2
- Map and Graph Skills, pp. 32–33

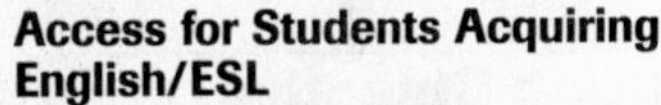

Access for Students Acquiring English/ESL
- Map and Graph Skills, pp. 41–42

SKILLS ASSESSMENT ANSWERS

1. rivers and ocean

2. between 1950–1975

3. border lines of Prince Georges, Anne Arundel, and Howard counties

CASE STUDY OBJECTIVES

1. Describe how the U.S. and Canada are like a cultural mosaic or melting pot.
2. Examine new cultural issues that the U.S. and Canada face.
3. Complete the Case Study Project by preparing a talk show discussion on whether countries can be multicultural yet unified.
4. Analyze primary sources for different views on multiculturalism in the U.S. and Canada.

SKILLBUILDER: Interpreting Graphs, p. 181

Focus & Motivate

What factors can unify or divide a multicultural country? *(language, religion, ethnicity, or race)*

Instruct: Objective 

"Mosaic" or "Melting Pot"

- Name at least two groups of immigrants who have come to the U.S. and Canada. *(Europeans, Asians, Latin Americans)*
- Why is Canada called a cultural mosaic? *(Because diverse ethnic groups have kept close ties with their ancestry and ethnicity.)*
- Why is the United States considered a melting pot? *(Because the approach to unification was to assimilate ethnic groups.)*

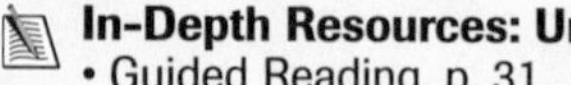
In-Depth Resources: Unit 2
• Guided Reading, p. 31

CASESTUDY

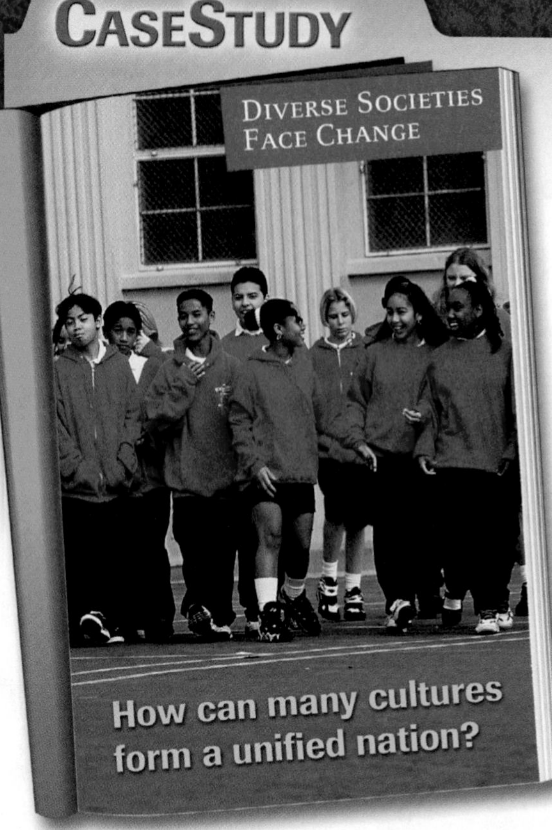

DIVERSE SOCIETIES
FACE CHANGE
How can many cultures form a unified nation?

The diverse heritage of the United States is evident in this group of students in California.

As you read earlier in this unit, the first immigrants to North America are believed to have come from Asia. They are thought to have crossed a land bridge that existed in what is now the Bering Strait thousands of years ago. Since that time, millions of people from countries all over the world have immigrated to the United States and Canada. They have come in search of a new life in a new homeland. The challenge for citizens and governments of both the United States and Canada is to make sure that these diverse peoples continue to remain unified.

"Mosaic" or "Melting Pot"

After centuries of immigration, the United States and Canada are culturally diverse. They contain large populations of the world's cultures. Ethnic neighborhoods with populations of Asians, Eastern Europeans, and Latin Americans are found in most large cities of both countries. In New York City alone, immigrant schoolchildren speak more than 100 different languages. The arrival of so many peoples over the years left the United States and Canada with the difficult task of forming a unified society. Each country approached the task of unifying its many cultures differently.

CANADA'S CULTURAL "MOSAIC" Canada's earliest settlers were its native peoples. Its first European settlers came, as you have learned, from two distinct cultural groups—French and English. All of these groups kept their separate identities as the nation developed. Also, Canada encouraged immigration from all over the world. It wanted to fill its vast lands and expand its workforce and its domestic markets. These immigrants also were encouraged to retain their cultural heritage.

As a result, many Canadians have strong ethnic ties. In fact, as you read in Chapter 7, the ethnic identity of French-speaking citizens in Quebec has been so strong that at times they have even considered separating themselves from the Canadian confederation.

The Canadian government has officially recognized the multicultural nature of Canada. In 1988, it enacted the Canadian Multiculturalism Act to protect and promote diversity. Many Canadians believe that this policy ensures equality for people of all origins and enriches their nation. But not all agree. Some Canadians feel that diversity has promoted difference at the expense of "Canadianness."

PROGRAM RESOURCES

In-Depth Resources: Unit 2
• Guided Reading, p. 31
• Building Vocabulary, p. 35
• Reteaching Activities, p. 42

Guided Reading Workbook
• Case Study

Access for Students Acquiring English
• Guided Reading, p. 39

Formal Assessment
• Case Study Quiz, p. 115

INTEGRATED TECHNOLOGY

Test Generator
• Case Study Quiz

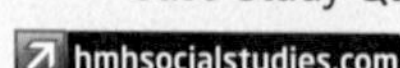
hmhsocialstudies.com

TEST-TAKING RESOURCES

Strategies for Test Preparation

Test Practice Transparencies TT27

Online Test Practice

AMERICA'S "MELTING POT" For many years, people in the United States believed that assimilation was the key. It was thought to be the best way to build one nation from many different peoples. Assimilation occurs when people from a minority culture assume the language, customs, and lifestyles of people from the dominant culture. Native Americans were an example. In the late 19th century, they were encouraged and even forced to learn English, adopt Western dress, and become Christians to assimilate into the dominant white culture.

People expected immigrants to assimilate, too. Those who did not could face prejudice because of their cultural differences. Immigrants soon learned that life would be easier if they adopted the ways of their new country—if they underwent "Americanization." Most of these immigrants had come from Europe. Many wanted to assimilate. They wanted to adopt a common language and culture—to become Americans.

New Immigrants Challenge Old Ways

The immigrants who came to the United States in the late 20th century brought different attitudes. They came mainly from Latin America and Asia. They were culturally or racially unlike earlier immigrant groups, who had come mainly from Europe. These later immigrants were less willing to give up their traditions and beliefs in order to assimilate.

DIVIDED OPINION Some Americans felt that the new immigrants did not understand what made the United States unique. According to this point of view, America's strength has come from blending its diverse cultures to create something new—an American. They also believed that encouraging different languages and customs would promote separation, not unity. In response, they wanted immigration limited and English made the official language.

SEE PRIMARY SOURCE C

Other Americans, including many educators, held different views. They thought that American society would benefit by stressing multiculturalism, as the Canadians do.

As you can see, bringing many cultures together is a continuing challenge both in the United States and in Canada. So, how can cultural diversity be preserved and national unity forged? The Case Study Project and primary sources that follow will help you explore this question.

U.S. Population by Race and Ethnicity

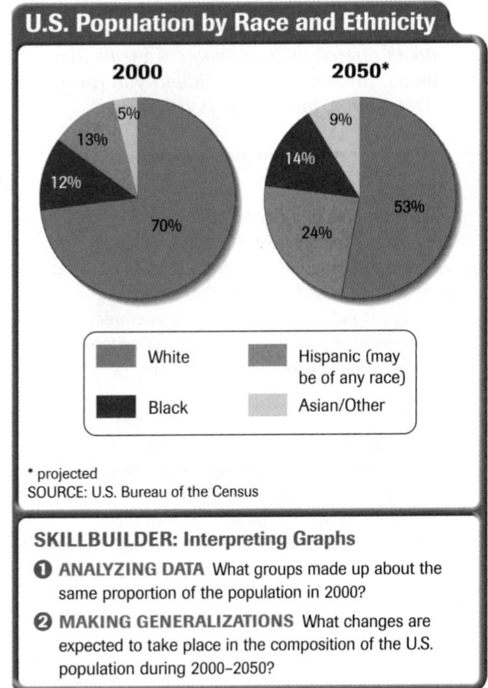

* projected
SOURCE: U.S. Bureau of the Census

SKILLBUILDER: Interpreting Graphs

1. **ANALYZING DATA** What groups made up about the same proportion of the population in 2000?
2. **MAKING GENERALIZATIONS** What changes are expected to take place in the composition of the U.S. population during 2000–2050?

US & CANADA

Instruct: Objective 2

New Immigrants Challenge Old Ways

- What is one main difference between immigrants who came to the U.S. in the early part of the 20th century and immigrants who came to the U.S. in the latter part of the 20th century? *(Those who came in late 20th century came from different areas, namely Latin America and Asia.)*
- What are the two approaches to immigration proposed as ways to unify a country? *(blending diverse cultures and remaining unified under one language or stressing multiculturalism and allowing diverse groups to maintain a strong ethnic identity)*

Interpreting Graphs

U.S. Population by Race and Ethnicity

Have students examine the graph. Ask them which race or ethnicity made up the second largest population in 2000. *(Hispanic)* Then ask which race or ethnicity is projected to make up the second largest population in 2050. *(Hispanic)*

SKILLBUILDER ANSWERS

1. Hispanics at 13 percent and African Americans at 12 percent **2.** Possible answer: The white majority of the American population will shrink, the black minority will increase only slightly, and both the Hispanic and the Asian/other ethnicities will increase markedly.

DIFFERENTIATING INSTRUCTION STUDENTS ACQUIRING ENGLISH/ESL

FORMS OF A WORD

Objective To show students how a word can change form and action in use

Class Time 10 minutes

Task Have students identify different forms of a word and use them appropriately

Directions Ask students to write the words *diverse* and *unity* in their notebooks. Tell them that diverse is an adjective and unity is a noun. Then, ask them to find different forms of those words in the text on pages 180-181. Remind them how various parts of speech are defined and used. Then, ask them to guess what part of speech each form of each word they found is, and then re-use that form in a new sentence they create. An example might be: *diversity*–a noun–"Jamie liked the diversity of languages she heard at the world religions convention."

Instruct: Objective 3

Case Study Project: Talk Show Discussion

- What is your role in the discussion? *(to present a position on the issue of unification)*
- What information should you look for in your research? *(positive and negative aspects of unifying diverse cultures)*
- What do you have to prepare for the talk show? *(an opening statement, any necessary visuals)*

Instruct: Objective 4

Using Primary Sources

- Ⓐ ***Newspaper Article*** What main point is the writer trying to make? *(that historians believe people are more interested in maintaining their ethnic identity than they used to be)*
- What is the current trend of immigration in the U.S.? *(people coming in large numbers from Latin America and Asia)*
- Ⓑ ***Social Commentary*** Why does Young say immigrants wanted to accept the melting pot idea? *(to erase historical hurts)*
- What comes before unification in the multiculturalism approach? *(pride in ethnic origins)*

CASE STUDY

PROJECT Talk Show Discussion

Primary sources A, B, C, D, and E offer differing opinions about assimilation and maintaining cultural identity. Use them along with your own research from the library or Internet to prepare for a talk show discussion on the issue of today's cultural diversity.

Suggested Steps

1. With a group totaling five students, prepare a talk show discussion on the topic, "Can Many Cultures Form a Unified Nation?" One member should act as the discussion leader. Each of the other members should select one of the following positions: for assimilation or against assimilation.
2. Think about the following questions as you prepare for your role. "Must a unified nation have a single culture?" "What are the advantages and disadvantages of assimilation, or the advantages and disadvantages of multiculturalism, in unifying a nation?"
3. Use online and print resources to research your topic.
4. Write an opening statement of your position. Prepare visuals, such as charts or graphs, if you need them to support your position.
5. Present your position as a part of the talk show. Discuss with the leader and other group members the focus question given above.

Materials and Supplies

- posterboard
- colored markers
- reference books, newspapers, and magazines
- Internet access

PRIMARY SOURCE Ⓐ

Newspaper Article *In 1998, the* Washington Post *published a series of articles titled* The Myth of the Melting Pot. *Staff writer* **William Booth** *offered the following comments about immigration and cultural identity in his piece, "One Nation, Indivisible: Is It History?"*

The immigrants of today come not from Europe but overwhelmingly from the still developing world of Asia and Latin America. They are driving a demographic shift so rapid that within the lifetimes of today's teenagers, no one ethnic group—including whites of European descent—will comprise a majority of the nation's population. . . .

[M]any historians argue that there was a greater consensus in the past on what it meant to be an American, a yearning for a common language and culture, and a desire—encouraged, if not coerced [forced] by members of the dominant white Protestant culture—to assimilate. Today, they say, there is more emphasis on preserving one's ethnic identity, of finding ways to highlight and defend one's cultural roots.

PRIMARY SOURCE Ⓑ

Social Commentary *Michelle Young is a writer and editor. Much of her work has focused on issues of multiculturalism. In the following excerpt from a 1996 article in the online publication* Career Magazine, *Young contrasts assimilation with multiculturalism.*

The melting pot concept spoke of all Americans being part of the enormous "cultural stew" we call America. . . . Many people . . . saw the United States of America as a place where historical hurts from their homelands could be erased. . . .

But America was not the nation they'd been promised, where the streets were paved with gold. Many newcomers knew that from experience because "they" were doing the paving! As a result, people began to realize that the concept of the melting pot just wasn't realistic. . . .

In contrast to the melting pot, multiculturalism encourages us to take pride in our own roots first, in our ingredients we've added to what has become America's multicultural stew. The nation's promise lies in that multicultural stew, and by appreciating our own cultures, we develop an eagerness to learn about others' origins.

ACTIVITY OPTION | INTERNET RESEARCH

ANALYZING DATA

Explaining the Skill Tell students that data comes in different forms and can be useful in helping to identify patterns, form assumptions, and make projections. Remind them that the U.S. government conducts a census every 10 years to determine the makeup of the U.S. population. The most recent census was conducted in 2010.

Applying the Skill Have students go to the Research Links in **hmhsocialstudies.com** to find information on the lastest U.S. census. Then ask them to analyze the census results to write a short report. Have students' reports tell what information the U.S. census collected; what it says about U.S. populations (assumptions); how it compares to the 2000 census results; and what the projections are for the U.S. population, based on this data.

OPTIONAL ACTIVITY For the class, bring in a hard copy of articles or published data, charts, and tables showing results of the 2010 census and final data from the 2000 census.

PRIMARY SOURCE C

Political Commentary *Patrick Buchanan is a politician who was the presidential candidate of the Reform Party in 2000. Buchanan was a strong supporter of immigration reform and assimilation, as is evident in these words posted on his Web site on August 6, 2000.*

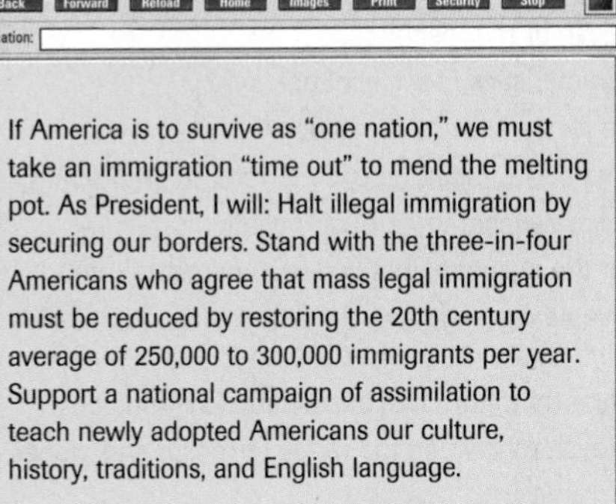
GeoNet

Back Forward Reload Home Images Print Security Stop

Location:

If America is to survive as "one nation," we must take an immigration "time out" to mend the melting pot. As President, I will: Halt illegal immigration by securing our borders. Stand with the three-in-four Americans who agree that mass legal immigration must be reduced by restoring the 20th century average of 250,000 to 300,000 immigrants per year. Support a national campaign of assimilation to teach newly adopted Americans our culture, history, traditions, and English language.

PRIMARY SOURCE D

Government Law *The Canadian Multiculturalism Act was passed by the Canadian parliament in 1988. Its purpose was to make the preservation and enhancement of multiculturalism in Canada the law of the land.*

". . . It is hereby declared to be the policy of the Government of Canada to . . . (b) recognize and promote the understanding that multiculturalism is a fundamental characteristic of the Canadian heritage and identity and that it provides an invaluable resource in the shaping of Canada's future; . . . (c) promote the full and equitable participation of individuals and communities of all origins in the continuing evolution and shaping of all aspects of Canadian society and assist them in the elimination of any barrier to that participation; . . . (f) encourage and assist the social, cultural, economic, and political institutions of Canada to be both respectful and inclusive of Canada's multicultural character; . . . (g) promote the understanding and creativity that arise from the interaction between individuals and communities of different origins."

PRIMARY SOURCE E

Government Document *The 2000 census form contained detailed racial and ethnic classifications, showing the diverse peoples that make up the population of the United States.*

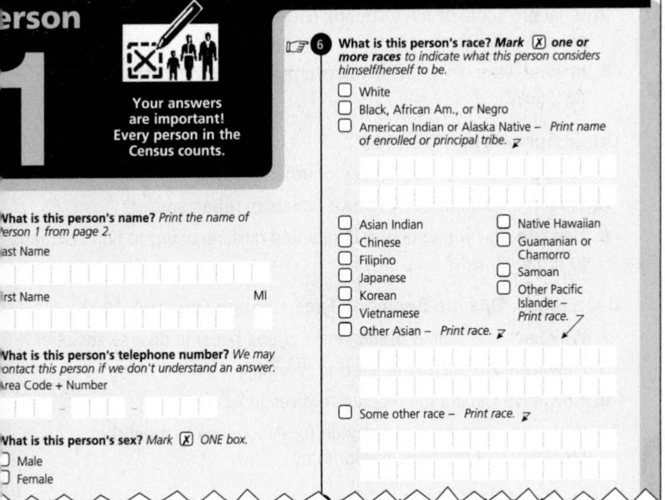
Person 1

Your answers are important! Every person in the Census counts.

What is this person's name? *Print the name of Person 1 from page 2.*

Last Name

First Name MI

What is this person's telephone number? *We may contact this person if we don't understand an answer.*

Area Code + Number

What is this person's sex? *Mark* ☒ *ONE box.*

☐ Male
☐ Female

6 What is this person's race? *Mark* ☒ *one or more races to indicate what this person considers himself/herself to be.*

☐ White
☐ Black, African Am., or Negro
☐ American Indian or Alaska Native – *Print name of enrolled or principal tribe.*
☐ Asian Indian
☐ Chinese
☐ Filipino
☐ Japanese
☐ Korean
☐ Vietnamese
☐ Other Asian – *Print race.*
☐ Native Hawaiian
☐ Guamanian or Chamorro
☐ Samoan
☐ Other Pacific Islander – *Print race.*
☐ Some other race – *Print race.*

PROJECT CheckList

Have I . . .

- ✓ fully researched my topic?
- ✓ taken into account both sides of an issue?
- ✓ created informative visuals that make my presentation clear and interesting?
- ✓ practiced the delivery of my presentation?

Instruct: Objective 5

Using Primary Sources

- Ⓒ ***Political Commentary*** What does Buchanan mean by an "immigration time-out"? *(reduce mass immigration, tighten border control)*
- Ⓓ ***Government Law*** What issues does the Canadian Multiculturalism Act address? *(support for and preservation of diverse cultural identities and increased understanding arising from that support)*
- How would the Canadian Multiculturalism Act most likely assist a Native Peoples group that claimed discrimination in the workplace? *(support their cause and help enforce equitable treatment)*
- Ⓔ ***Government Document*** How many ethnic and racial group choices does this document offer? *(15, including "Some other race")*
- What additional distinction does the document offer Native Americans? *(to include their tribal group name)*

Assess & Reteach

Have students complete the chart they began at the start of the chapter.

Formal Assessment
- Case Study Quiz, p. 115

Reteaching Activity

Have students take notes on the case study, writing down key issues and ideas about ethnic diversity in the U.S. and Canada. Then, divide the class into small groups and have each student give a brief oral "report" about the efforts of each country to unify a culturally diverse nation.

In-Depth Resources: Unit 2
- Reteaching Activity, p. 42

RUBRIC CASE STUDY PROJECT

TALK SHOW DISCUSSION

For the Case Study Project, students should:

- Research the topic and their position on the topic.
- Produce a visual or visuals that support presentation.
- Present a concise, well-organized opening statement of their position.
- Play an active role in the talk show discussion.

Grading Rubric Evaluate student performance as Exceptional, Acceptable, or Poor in each of the following categories:

	Exceptional	Acceptable	Poor
Communicates ideas and positions clearly			
Fulfills assigned role			
Cooperates with other group members			
Shares responsibility for the activity			

CHAPTER 8 ASSESSMENT

Reviewing Places & Terms

A. **1.** terrorism, p. 173
2. global network, p. 173
3. coalition, p. 174
4. biological weapon, p. 175
5. urban sprawl, p. 176
6. infrastructure, p. 177
7. smart growth, p. 178
8. sustainable community, p. 178

B. Possible Responses

9. Terrorism is meant to intimidate or cause fear for political or social ends.
10. A global network is interconnected and worldwide in scope.
11. An alliance of nations is a coalition.
12. Anthrax is a biological weapon.
13. It increases the number of cars on the roadways.
14. Basic facilities, services, and machinery are elements of infrastructure.
15. Smart growth encourages development in or near the city.
16. Suburbs and city areas were turned into sustainable communities.
17. Terrorists have formed a global network to further their objectives.
18. A biological weapon is used to harm or kill people, animals, or plants.
19. The cost of providing and maintaining streets, utilities, and other public facilities is higher in the suburbs.
20. Public transportation is a component of smart growth.

Chapter 8 Assessment

VISUAL SUMMARY
TODAY'S ISSUES IN THE UNITED STATES AND CANADA

Conflict

The Fight Against Terrorism

- Terrorists attack the United States on September 11, 2001.
- The United States increases security at home and searches for suspected terrorists within the country.
- A coalition of nations led by the United States launches a war against global terrorism.
- The war begins in Afghanistan, where those responsible for the September attacks–the al-Qaeda terrorists led by Osama bin Laden–are based.

Economics

Urban Sprawl

- Many metropolitan areas in North America have spread out farther and farther.
- This has caused problems such as traffic congestion, air pollution, strains on infrastructure, rising housing costs, and the separation of the well-off from the poor.
- Some governments and citizens are promoting "smart growth" as an answer to urban sprawl.

Government

Case Study: Diverse Societies Face Change

- Centuries of immigration from all parts of the world have given the United States and Canada diverse populations.
- The United States and Canada have approached unifying their many cultures differently.
- Bringing diverse peoples together is a continuing challenge for both countries.

Reviewing Places & Terms

A. Briefly explain the importance of each of the following.

1. terrorism	**5.** urban sprawl
2. global network	**6.** infrastructure
3. coalition	**7.** smart growth
4. biological weapon	**8.** sustainable community

B. Answer the questions about vocabulary in complete sentences.

9. What is the objective of terrorism?
10. What are the characteristics of a global network?
11. What is the name for an alliance of nations?
12. Which of the terms above might be used to refer to anthrax?
13. How does urban sprawl contribute to air pollution?
14. What are some of the elements that make up infrastructure?
15. Which term involves encouraging development close to or inside city limits?
16. What did Vancouver try to turn into sustainable communities?
17. What is the relationship between the terms terrorism and global network?
18. What is the objective of employing a biological weapon?
19. How does urban sprawl cause housing costs to rise?
20. What system is an important component of smart growth?

Main Ideas

The Fight Against Terrorism (pp. 173-175)

1. What are some of the actions governments can take when faced with terrorism?
2. What are some of the weapons used by terrorists to further their objectives?
3. In what ways have terrorist acts changed over the past few decades?

Urban Sprawl (pp. 176-179)

4. What are some of the causes of urban sprawl?
5. What are some of the negative effects of urban sprawl?
6. How are governments and concerned citizens trying to find solutions to urban sprawl?

Case Study: Diverse Societies Face Change (pp. 180-183)

7. Why have the United States and Canada become diverse societies?
8. How have Americans reacted to diversity?
9. How have Canadians reacted to diversity?
10. What are some ways suggested for Americans to meet the challenges of the new immigrants?

Main Ideas

1. Governments can increase security, attempt to find terrorists within their borders, and join in an alliance with other nations to fight terrorism.
2. Terrorists might use conventional weapons, such as bombs, but also biological or chemical weapons.
3. They have increased in violence.
4. unrestricted spread, growth of expressways, a desire for sense of community
5. more commuter traffic, air pollution, higher housing costs, low-income residents isolated in inner cities
6. developing plans for smart growth, encouraging development close by or inside city limits, good public transportation systems
7. Immigration has brought a variety of people to the two nations.
8. Many Americans have expected new immigrants to assimilate.
9. Canada established a multicultural policy.
10. Some suggest limiting immigration and making English the official language. Others think that the country's policy should recognize and respect diversity.

Critical Thinking

1. Using Your Notes

Use your completed chart to answer these questions.

	Causes	Effects
Issue 1: Terrorism		
Issue 2: Urban Sprawl		

a. How might a negative effect of urban sprawl be halted?

b. What are some of the positive effects of diverse societies?

2. Geographic Themes

a. **REGION** What are the aims of recent U.S. military action in Afghanistan?

b. **HUMAN-ENVIRONMENT INTERACTION** How has the spread of urban sprawl affected the environment?

3. Identifying Themes

If you were a government official, how would you promote smart growth? Which of the five themes are reflected in your answer? Explain.

4. Determining Cause and Effect

What actions has the United States taken to prevent terrorism?

5. Making Comparisons

How do the Canadian and American approaches to a diverse society differ?

For Additional Test Practice

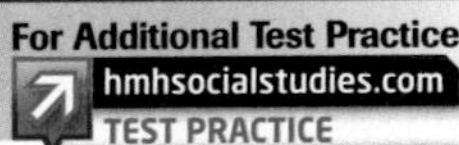

Geographic Skills: Interpreting Graphs

Region of Last Residence of Legal Immigrants to the United States, 1901–1998

Use the graph to answer the following questions.

1. **ANALYZING DATA** What was the percentage of immigrants from Europe during 1901–1910? during 1991–1998?
2. **MAKING COMPARISONS** Which two regions supplied the largest percentage of immigrants to the United States during the last century?
3. **DRAWING CONCLUSIONS** What significant change took place in the pattern of immigration during the 20th century?

Percentage (0–100)

South America
North America
Europe
Asia
Africa

1901–1910 1931–1940 1961–1970 1991–1998

NOTE: Oceania and unspecified region represent no more than 1 percent of legal immigration each decade.

SOURCE: 1998 Statistical Yearbook of the Immigration and Naturalization Service

Do research to create a chart showing the total number of immigrants from each region during the 20th century. Display the figures for each region on an outline map of the world.

hmhsocialstudies.com

MULTIMEDIA ACTIVITY

Use the links at **hmhsocialstudies.com** to research immigration to Canada. Focus on changes in the regions from which immigrants came in the 20th century.

Writing About Geography Write a report on your findings. Combine with a chart listing the regions and the percentages.

US & CANADA

Critical Thinking

1. **a.** developing plans for smart growth; turning suburbs into sustainable communities
 b. contributions to society of many cultures; benefits from interaction between individuals and communities of different origins
2. **a.** to secure the defeat of al Qaeda in the region, to protect national security, to prevent future terrorist attacks.
 b. increased pollution, depletion of local water supplies
3. developing a plan for growth, limiting growth to certain areas, making sure there is good public transportation; human-environment interaction
4. The United States formed a coalition, took steps to increase national security, and took military action in Afghanistan and Iraq.
5. Canadians have encouraged a multicultural nation to develop with recognition of many groups. Americans have supported assimilation, but there is also support for a multicultural policy.

GeoActivity

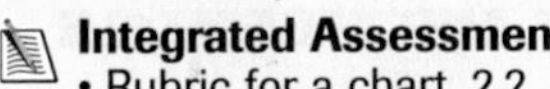

Integrated Assessment
- Rubric for a chart, 2.2

Formal Assessment
- Chapter Tests, Forms A, B, and C, pp. 116–130

Geographic Skills:

1. more than 90 percent, 1901–1910; not quite 15 percent, 1991–1998
2. Europe, other countries of North America
3. The percentage of immigrants from Europe dropped significantly, while the percentages from North America and Asia increased.

MULTIMEDIA ACTIVITY

For the report on immigration to Canada, students should:
- Present a concise, well-organized report on immigration.
- Summarize the changes in the regions from which immigrants came in the 20th century.
- Produce statistical data in the form of a chart to complement the report.
- Include references to the Web sites used as sources.

Grading Rubric Evaluate student performance as Exceptional, Acceptable, or Poor in each of the following categories:

Introductory sentence clearly states topic and purpose			
Report is clear, focused, and logical			
Provides necessary facts and examples			
Uses correct grammar, spelling, and punctuation			

Physical Geography of Latin America

OVERVIEW	INSTRUCTIONAL RESOURCES	
CHAPTER 9 ESSENTIAL QUESTION How have Latin America's varied landscapes affected the region's development? **Focus on the Essential Question Podcast**	**In-Depth Resources: Unit 3** • Unit Atlas Activities, p. 1 • Building Vocabulary, p. 9 • Exploring Today's Issues, pp. 30–33 **Outline Maps with Activities** • Latin America: Physical, pp. 17–18 • Latin America: Political, pp. 19–20 **Block Schedule Strategies** **Chapter Summaries** (English/Spanish)	**Interactive Online Edition** TOS **ExamView® Assessment Suite** (English/Spanish) TOS **CalendarPlanner** **Power Presentations with Media Gallery** **Critical Thinking Transparencies** • CT9 hmhsocialstudies.com INTERACTIVE
SECTION 1 **LANDFORMS AND RESOURCES** **MAIN IDEAS** • Latin America's landforms include highlands, lowlands, mountains, and plains. • The Andes Mountains and the Amazon River are among the most important physical features of the region. • Abundant natural resources have shaped lifestyles and the economy.	**In-Depth Resources: Unit 3** • Guided Reading, p. 3 • Map and Graph Skills, pp. 6–7 • Building Vocabulary, p. 9 • Reteaching Activity, p. 10 **Guided Reading Workbook,** Section 1	**Critical Thinking Transparencies** • CT41 Comparing Regional Geography **Map Transparencies** • MT18 Latin America: Geological Structures
SECTION 2 **CLIMATE AND VEGETATION** **MAIN IDEAS** • Latin America has a variety of climates. • The vegetation of Latin America ranges from grasslands to rain forests.	**In-Depth Resources: Unit 3** • Guided Reading, p. 4 • Building Vocabulary, p. 9 • Reteaching Activity, p. 11 • GeoWorkshop, p. 37 **Guided Reading Workbook,** Section 2	hmhsocialstudies.com INTERACTIVE • Vertical Climate Zones in Latin America, p. 208
SECTION 3 **HUMAN-ENVIRONMENT INTERACTION** **MAIN IDEAS** • Agriculture and urbanization have altered the landscape throughout Latin America. • Tourism is having a growing impact on the environment of Latin America.	**In-Depth Resources: Unit 3** • Guided Reading, p. 5 • Skillbuilder Practice, p. 8 • Building Vocabulary, p. 9 • Reteaching Activity, p. 12 **Guided Reading Workbook,** Section 3	

ASSESSMENT

SE **Chapter Assessment,** pp. 214-215

Formal Assessment
- Chapter Tests, Forms A, B, and C, pp. 134-145

TOS **ExamView® Assessment Suite**

Strategies for Test Preparation

hmhsocialstudies.com TEST PRACTICE

SE **Section Assessment,** p. 205

Formal Assessment
- Section Quiz, p. 131

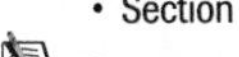
Integrated Assessment
- Rubric for a sketch map, 2.1

Test Practice Transparencies TT28

SE **Section Assessment,** p. 209

Formal Assessment
- Section Quiz, p. 132

Integrated Assessment
- Rubric for a paragraph, 4.2

Test Practice Transparencies TT29

SE **Section Assessment,** p. 213

Formal Assessment
- Section Quiz, p. 133

Integrated Assessment
- Rubric for creating a travel poster, 1.1

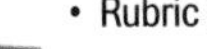
Test Practice Transparencies TT30

CHART KEY:

SE Student Edition

 Block Scheduling

 DVD/CD-ROM

TE Teacher's Edition

TOS Teacher One Stop

 MP3 Audio

 Printable Resource

 Presentation Resource

 HISTORY™

Program Resources available on TOS and @  hmhsocialstudies.com

SUPPORTING RESOURCES

- Multimedia Classroom Global History Series
- Global History Teacher's Guide

Social Studies Trade Library Collection
- Latino Trade Collection

For more information or to purchase these resources, go to  hmhsocialstudies.com

DIFFERENTIATED INSTRUCTION

English Learners	Struggling Readers	Gifted and Talented Students
 **Spanish/English Guided Reading Workbook**  **Access for Students Acquiring English/ESL** Spanish Translations, pp. 43–48  **Chapter Summaries** (English/Spanish) TE **TE Activity** Creating a Dictionary, p. 202	**Chapter Summaries** (English/Spanish) TE **TE Activity** Creating a Graphic Organizer, p. 208	TE **TE Activity** Reporting on Conservation Efforts, p. 204

ENRICHMENT ACTIVITIES

The following activities are especially suitable for classes following block schedules.

SE **Student Edition,** p. 210–215
- Interpreting a Precipitation Map, p. 206

hmhsocialstudies.com INTERACTIVE
- Resources of Latin America, p. 204
- Vertical Climate Zones in Latin America, p. 208

UNIT 3 ATLAS AND CHAPTER 9 PACING GUIDE

BLOCK SCHEDULE LESSON PLAN OPTIONS: 90-MINUTE PERIOD

DAY 1

UNIT PREVIEW, pp. 186-189
Class Time 20 minutes

- **Discussion** Discuss the Unit Introduction, using the discussion prompts on TE p. 186
  Class Time 10 minutes
- **Today's Issues** Introduce Today's Issues in Latin America, using Exploring the Issues questions on PE p. 188
  Class Time 10 minutes

UNIT ATLAS, pp. 190-199
Class Time 30 minutes

- **Small Groups** Divide the class into four groups and have each group answer Making Comparisons questions for one section of the Unit Atlas: Physical Geography, Human Geography, Regional Patterns, and Regional Data File.

SECTION 1, pp. 201-205
Class Time 40 minutes

- **Outline Maps** In preparation for discussing Section 1, have students complete the physical map for Latin America in *Outline Maps with Activities.* Students should label the countries and physical features such as mountains and rivers. They should color the map, using different colors for landforms.

DAY 2

SECTION 1, pp. 201-205
Class Time 45 minutes

- **Quiz Show** As a way to review the section, have three students volunteer to be contestants and one student be the host. Then have the rest of the class prepare questions to ask the contestants. Contestants who answer correctly can earn points. Highest points wins.
  Class Time 20 minutes

SECTION 2, pp. 207-209
Class Time 45 minutes

- **Comparing the Latin America and the United States** Use a large map of North and South America. Point to locations on the map and ask students to tell what the weather in that region is like. Then discuss with the class the similarities and differences between climates in Latin America and the United States, including the issues of weather, landscape, and vegetation.

DAY 3

SECTION 3, pp. 210-213
Class Time 35 minutes

- **Issues Chart** Lead the class in creating an issues chart that summarizes key issues and the problems and solutions associated with them. Have students make a three column chart with the headings "Issue," "Problems," and "Solutions." Within each column, the students should list information from the section. For example, under the "Issue" head, students might list the three issues of Agriculture, Urbanization, and Tourism. Then after each issue, they can list problems and solutions connected with each.
- **Skillbuilder Lesson** Use the Activity Option about identifying and solving problems on TE p. 212 and the Skillbuilder Practice worksheet.
  Class Time 25 minutes

CHAPTER 9 REVIEW AND ASSESSMENT, pp. 214-215

- **Review** Have students prepare a summary of the chapter using the Places and Terms listed on the first page of each section.
  Class Time 20 minutes
- **Assessment** Have students complete the Chapter 9 Assessment
  Class Time 35 minutes

TEACHER-TESTED ACTIVITY *Preservation Flow Chart*

Class Time One class period.

Task Create an illustrated flow chart of the struggle to preserve the rain forest. This can be done individually or in small groups of 2-3 students.

Supplies
- textbook (Chapter 9 Section 2)
- poster board or poster paper
- markers
- old magazines

Purpose The destruction of the rain forest in Brazil is multifaceted and requires a critical analysis in order to redirect human activity from further destroying this unique and vital habitat. Students will gain an appreciation for the political, economic, environmental, and social forces at work throughout this region.

Activity Have students read pages 207–208 and list those resources that can be found in the rain forest. They might supplement the text pages with research in the library or on the Internet. The list should include plants, insects, wildlife, and hardwoods. Then they should list the potential uses of these rain forest resources. Have students itemize the results of human exploitation—both the positive and negative effects. The final step is for students to create a flow chart that shows the potential dangers of the destruction of the forest and the overuse of individual resources. Allow students to draw pictures (or cut out pictures from old magazines) in a flow chart format that illustrates how the items on the students' original list are related to each other.

David Haas
Geography Teacher, Waukegan High School, Waukegan, IL

TECHNOLOGY IN THE CLASSROOM

INTERNET SIMULATION

The Internet lends itself well to simulations, in which students get to make choices and see the outcome of their decisions. Well-designed simulations allow students to use their critical thinking skills while receiving detailed and helpful feedback as to the wisdom of their decisions. There are quite a few simulations available online free of charge; some of them can be found at the Web site at **hmhsocialstudies.com.**

ACTIVITY OUTLINE

Objective Students will use an online simulation to learn about ecotourism in the Latin American rain forest.

Task Have students go through the simulation and take notes on their decisions and the outcomes. Discuss their experiences as a class, and have them write a few paragraphs explaining what they've learned.

Class Time 1–2 class periods

DIRECTIONS

1. After students have read Chapter 9, Section 3 (pages 210–213), ask them to list and discuss the ways in which the environment impacts human activity in Latin America, and vice versa.

2. Ask students to list the pros and cons of tourism, as stated in this chapter. If any of them have traveled to Latin America or the Caribbean, have them share with the class their experiences as tourists.

3. Ask students to look at the physical map of Latin America on page 190 and the vegetation map on page 207 and provide reasons why people from the United States or Canada might want to visit Latin America as tourists. What parts of the region are particularly appealing, and why?

4. Write the word "ecotourism" on the board, and ask students to provide words describing their ideas about ecotourism. Have they ever heard this term?

5. Ask students to go to the first Web site at **hmhsocialstudies.com** and go through the ecotourism simulation game, either individually or in groups. If they initially choose not to get into ecotourism, they should go back and make sure they choose the ecotourism option to see what happens. Ask them to write down their decisions and the outcomes as they go along.

6. Discuss students' experiences in the simulation. How many of them found the ecotourism project to be successful? What were the reasons for this success? How many of them had problems developing ecotourism in their village? Why did these problems occur, and what could have been done differently? Why did the village consider an ecotourism project in the first place? What were some of the major decisions that had to be made and the disagreements villagers had to discuss?

7. Have students answer the following questions:
   - What are the pros and cons of tourism in Latin American rainforest regions?
   - What are the pros and cons of ecotourism in these regions?

Previewing the Unit

The opening pages of this unit provide an overview of Latin America, a diverse region of many countries that spans a great distance on each side of the equator. Encompassing parts of North America, Central America, the Caribbean islands, and South America, Latin America is a region of diversity in its land, climates, and peoples.

Discussion Prompts

Exploring Prior Knowledge Ask students the following questions about Latin America to determine their prior knowledge of the region:

- What oceans and seas surround Latin America? *(Atlantic and Pacific oceans, Gulf of Mexico, Caribbean Sea)*
- What mountain chains are in Latin America? *(Andes, Sierra Madres)*
- What Latin American countries and cities have you heard about? *(Answers will vary.)*

Interpreting Maps Ask students to refer to the satellite image of Latin America to answer the following questions:

- What landforms do you recognize? *(Possible answers: lakes, mountains, rivers)*
- What vegetation regions do you recognize? *(forests, arid mountainous regions)*
- Do you recognize any countries? *(Answers will vary but may include Cuba, Mexico, Brazil.)*

Unit 3 Latin America

PREVIEW: TODAY'S ISSUES IN LATIN AMERICA

UNIT ATLAS

Chapter 9
PHYSICAL GEOGRAPHY
From the Andes to the Amazon

Chapter 10
HUMAN GEOGRAPHY
A Blending of Cultures

Chapter 11
TODAY'S ISSUES
Latin America

CASESTUDY
THE INCOME GAP

Latin America includes parts of North America, Central America and the Caribbean, and South America. The region covers many latitudes from north to south of the equator.

MOVEMENT Villagers from surrounding areas bring their goods to market in the Aztec city of Tenochtitlán, depicted in this mural by Diego Rivera.

HUMAN–ENVIRONMENT INTERACTION Chacobo Indians make the dugout canoes they use to explore in the Amazon River basin in northern Bolivia.

186

UNIT 3 ADDITIONAL RESOURCES

BOOKS FOR THE TEACHER

Honey, Martha. ***Ecotourism and Sustainable Development: Who Owns Paradise?*** Washington D.C.: Island Press, 2008. A balanced view of the competing demands on the environment in places visited by tourists.

BOOKS FOR THE STUDENT

Fried, Mark, trans. ***Soccer in Sun and Shadow.*** Eduardo H. Galeano. NY: Verso Books, 1999. Soccer is the most popular spectator sport in Latin America.

Menard, Valerie. ***The Latino Holiday Book: From Cinco De Mayo to Dia De Los Muertos: The Celebrations and Traditions of Hispanic-Americans.*** NY: Marlowe & Co., 2000. A good introduction to the holidays and festivals of the region.

INTERNET

For more on Latin America, visit . . .

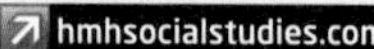

GeoData

LOCATION Latin America extends from Mexico southward across the equator to nearly reach Antarctica in the Southern Hemisphere.

REGION It is called "Latin America" because the two main languages spoken there–Spanish and Portuguese–developed from Latin.

REGION This region is bordered by two oceans (Atlantic and Pacific), the Gulf of Mexico, and the Caribbean Sea.

For more information on Latin America . . .

hmhsocialstudies.com
RESEARCH WEB LINKS

PLACE Sugarloaf Mountain is a famous landmark that looks out over Guanabara Bay in Rio de Janeiro, Brazil. The statue of Christ atop the mountain reflects the importance of the Catholic faith to millions of Latin Americans.

Interpreting Photographs

Tenochtitlàn

The Aztec capital, with 300,000 inhabitants, was one of the largest cities in the 16th-century world. Built on islands in a lake, the city streets were canals.

Ask students what they can infer from the picture about how people from surrounding villages brought their goods to market. *(The fact that the marketplace was on the water suggests that they traveled by boat.)*

Chacobo Indians

More than half of Bolivia's peoples are indigenous. Most are poor subsistence farmers with close-knit families.

Ask students what inference they can make about family life among the Chacobo Indians in Bolivia. *(Having little contact with the outside world, the Chacobo Indians live in the same way they did hundreds of years ago.)*

Rio de Janeiro

Tell students that the first schools in Brazil were founded by Portuguese Jesuits. Ask students how the Jesuits' influence might be seen in modern-day Brazil. *(The country is still mostly Catholic.)*

ACTIVITY OPTION | **COOPERATIVE LEARNING**

BLOCK SCHEDULING

CREATING A COUNTRY PROFILE

Objective To create a profile on a Latin American country

Research Time 40 minutes **Presentation Time** 20 minutes

Task Make a video (or class presentation) about a Latin American country

Directions Divide class into groups of four or five students. Assign each group a Latin American country. In this exercise, each country is vying to be the new home of the Latin American headquarters of a major news and entertainment cable channel, and has hired the student groups as public relations firms. As the first step in preparing their "campaigns," all students in each group must gather basic information about their country, including physical features, major cities, cultural attractions, and the political situation–including potential problems. Once research is completed, the students should divide the following tasks among group members:

- Videographer (or, if planning a class presentation, director and set designer)
- Scriptwriter and editor
- Presenter #1: physical features and political situation
- Presenter #2: major cities and cultural attractions

Each group should prepare an 8-minute video or live presentation that profiles its country.

Previewing Today's Issues

These pages provide a preview of issues faced by the nations of Latin America. These topics will be fully explored in Chapter 11 (pages 244–255). Use the discussion prompts that follow to determine students' prior knowledge and help them to make comparisons to local events.

In-Depth Resources: Unit 3
- Exploring Today's Issues, pp. 30–33

RESOURCES
Many Latin American countries have harvested the tropical hardwoods of the rain forests for export to the world market. Deforestation damages the global environment and destroys animal and plant life. Some plant species that might be used to make medicines to treat or cure many diseases are facing extinction.

Discussion Prompts

- What are some of the effects of deforestation? *(destruction of plants and animals; provision of timber for export; provision of land for growing crops)*
- Do you think the rest of the world has a right to interfere in how Latin America manages its rain forests? *(Answers will vary. Destruction of rain forests affects the global environment and world market.)*

Today's Issues in Latin America

Three of the most important issues that concern Latin America today are resources, democracy, and the income gap between rich and poor.

As you read Chapters 9 and 10, you will learn helpful background information. You will study the issues themselves in Chapter 11.

In a small group, answer the following questions. Then participate in a class discussion of your ideas.

Exploring the Issues

1. RESOURCES What are some resources that are becoming increasingly scarce in the world?
2. DEMOCRACY What are some threats to democracy in the world today? What conditions might be necessary for democracy to thrive?
3. INCOME GAP Why might an income gap exist in a country? How might a growing gap between rich and poor affect a country?

For more on these issues in Latin America . . .

RESOURCES

How can we preserve and develop the rain forest?

Agriculture and timber harvesting in Brazil are reducing the size of the rain forests by destroying thriving ecosystems, but are providing food and export products.

EXPLORING THE ISSUES ANSWERS

1. RESOURCES oil, trees, clean air, and water
2. DEMOCRACY political extremism, one-party rule, dictators, terrorists; to thrive, democracy requires social, economic, and political stability
3. INCOME GAP Wealth might be unevenly distributed because of historical circumstances. A growing gap between rich and poor might undermine stability.

How can Latin Americans gain a voice in government?

Demonstrators in Chile rally in support of putting former dictator General Augusto Pinochet on trial. The signs say, "Judgment for Pinochet—truth and justice for Chile."

LATIN AMERICA

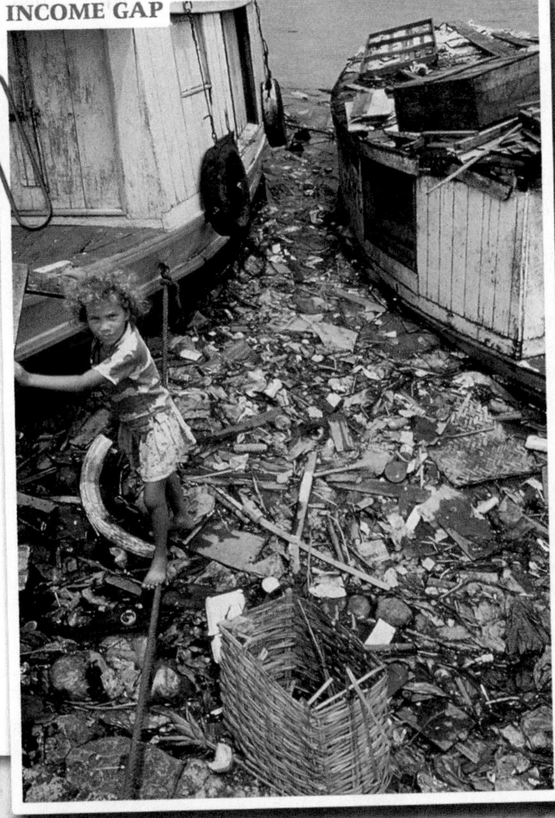

CASESTUDY

How can the economic gulf between rich and poor be bridged?

There is a growing gap between rich and poor in Latin America, with all the problems of slums, homeless children, and street crime. Here, a young girl stands above polluted water in a slum in Belém, Brazil.

189

DEMOCRACY

In order for democracy to work, people must be educated, economically secure, and able to participate in free elections. New reforms aimed at creating such an infrastructure may give democracy a chance.

Discussion Prompts

- What forces do you know about in Latin America that keep the people from gaining a voice in their government? *(Answers will vary; some students may mention military rule or one-party rule.)*
- Do you think democracy is the best form of government for Latin American countries? *(Answers will vary, but most students will probably think that democracy is better than the alternatives.)*

CASESTUDY

INCOME GAP

In Latin America there is a large gap between the rich and poor, with only a small middle class. Political stability for Latin American countries depends on narrowing this gap between the wealthy elite and the poor.

Discussion Prompts

- Why might there be a larger income gap in Latin America than in the United States? *(there is a far bigger middle class in the United States)*
- Why is economic stability necessary for political stability? *(Without economic stability and fairness, people are willing to pursue radical political solutions to improve their circumstances.)*

ACTIVITY OPTION **INTERNET RESEARCH**

WRITING A SUMMARY

Objective To develop research skills

Class Time 20 minutes

Task Write a summary of research on the rain forests and the impact of deforestation on the world's environment

Directions Direct the students to use words and phrases such as *tropical rain forests, environment,* and *deforestation* in searching the Internet. Work with students to show them how to follow links to helpful sources of information. When students have completed their research, have them write a brief summary of their findings, and offer at least one suggestion for helping the environment or the rain forests.

OPTIONAL ACTIVITY If Internet access is limited, have the students use the library for this research activity. Have the librarian show students how to use the *Reader's Guide to Periodical Literature* and other indexes to find articles on tropical rain forests and the effects of deforestation.

ATLAS OBJECTIVES

1. Compare data on the physical geography of Latin America.
2. Examine key physical features of Latin America.
3. Identify Latin American countries and borders in 1800.
4. Identify current countries and borders of Latin America.
5. Learn about Latin American religions and climates.
6. Analyze language distribution and population density in Latin America.

Focus & Motivate

Ask students what they already know about the physical geography of Latin America. Also have them list the kinds of information that maps and charts might convey about Latin America.

Instruct: Objective 

Comparing Data

- ***Landmass*** How much larger is Latin America than the United States? *(4,776,320 sq. mi.)*
- ***Population*** How many more people live in Latin America than in the United States? *(273,817,000)*
- ***Rivers*** How much greater is the Amazon's discharge rate than that of the Paraná? *(6,398,300 cubic feet per second)*
- ***Mountains*** How do the Andes Mountains compare in length to the next longest mountain chain? *(3,500 miles longer)*

Unit ATLAS

Use the Unit Atlas to add to your knowledge of Latin America, which stretches from Mexico to the tip of South America. As you look at the maps and graphs, notice geographic patterns and specific details about the region. For example, the graph gives details about two large rivers in the region.

After studying the graphs and physical map on these two pages, jot down answers to the following questions in your notebook.

Making Comparisons

1. Which river systems dominate South America?
2. How are the Andes Mountains of South America similar in location to the Rocky Mountains of the United States?
3. Compare Latin America's landmass and population to those of the United States. Based on that data, how might the overall population densities of the two compare?

Patterns of Physical Geography

Comparing Data 1

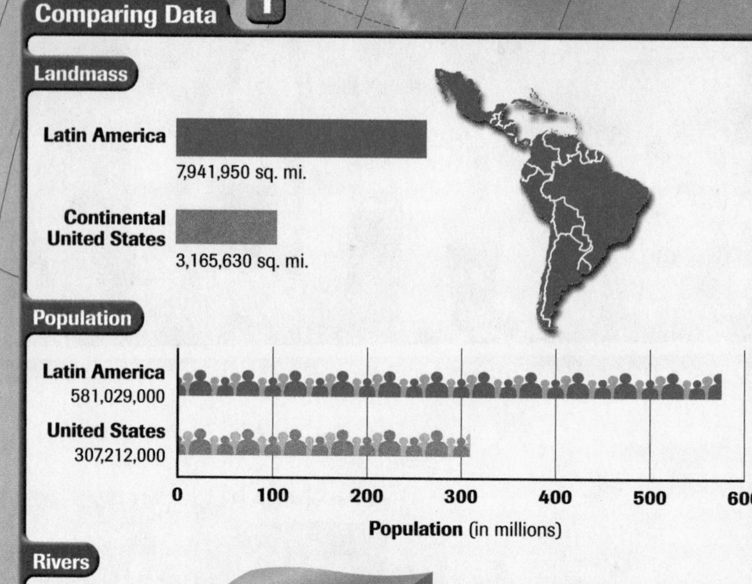

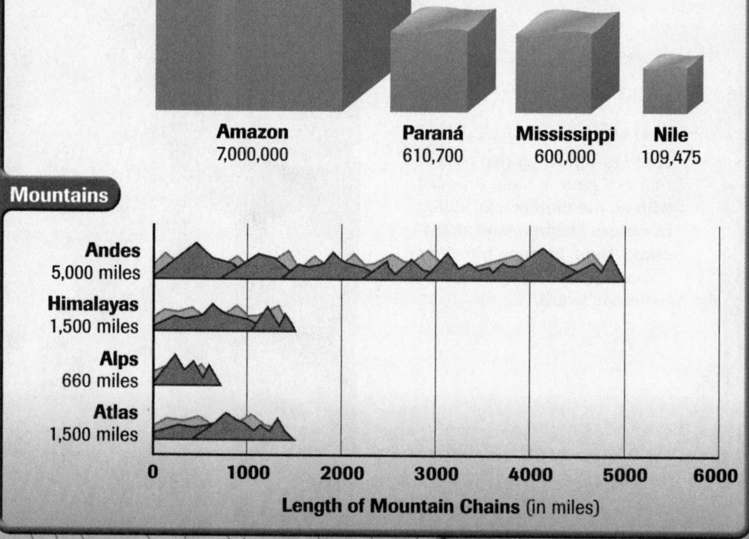

MAKING COMPARISONS ANSWERS

1. Orinoco, Amazon, and Paraná river systems
2. Both ranges are located along the western edge of the continent.
3. Both in landmass and population, Latin America is roughly twice the size of the United States, so the population densities of the two are roughly comparable.

2 Latin America: Physical

Elevation
13,100 ft. (4,000 m.)
6,600 ft. (2,000 m.)
1,600 ft. (500 m.)
650 ft. (200 m.)
0 ft. (0 m.)
Below sea level
▲ Mountain peak

0 500 1,000 miles
0 500 1,000 kilometers
Azimuthal Equal-Area Projection

191

UNIT 3 ATLAS

Instruct: Objective 2

Latin America: Physical

- What two oceans border Latin America? *(Pacific and Atlantic)*
- What are South America's highest mountains? *(Andes)*
- What mountain chain runs through Mexico? *(Sierra Madres)*
- The Amazon River empties into what ocean? *(Atlantic)*
- What body of water is south of Puerto Rico? *(Caribbean Sea)*
- Latin America is part of what two continents? *(North America and South America)*

In-Depth Resources: Unit 3
- Unit Atlas Activities, p. 1

Outline Maps with Activities
- Latin America: Physical, pp. 17–18

Map Transparencies MT16
- Latin America: Physical

LATIN AMERICA

More About

The Galápagos Islands

The Galápagos Islands lie off the coast of Ecuador. They are famous for their rare animal species. In 1835, Charles Darwin visited the islands and collected scientific data that supplied the foundation for his theory of evolution by means of natural selection. Tourism is now restricted in order to protect the rare species on the islands.

ACTIVITY OPTION | **CRITICAL THINKING**

BLOCK SCHEDULING

CREATING A DATABASE OF PHYSICAL FEATURES

Explaining the Skill A database is a collection of data, or information, that is organized so that you can find and retrieve information on a specific topic quickly and easily. Once a computerized database is set up, you can search it to find specific information without going through the entire database. The database will provide a list of all information in the database related to your topic. Learning how to use a database will help you learn how to create one.

Applying the Skill Have students work in groups of five. Using the computer or art materials, they should work together to create a grid with five categories across the top: "Mountain Ranges," "River Systems," "Highlands," "Flat Land," and "Rugged Land." Down the side, they should write the names of the Latin American countries. Assign one of the categories to each member of the group. Using the physical map as reference, students should work independently to research their category, then incorporate the information in the group's database. Have groups compare their results.

Instruct: Objective 3

Latin America, 1800

- What two present-day countries have territory that was part of the Viceroyalty of New Spain in the 1800s? *(the United States and Mexico)*
- Who ruled Guiana in 1800? *(the British, Dutch, and French)*
- Who ruled Cuba in 1800? *(the Spanish)*
- In 1800, part of what is now the United States was under what country's rule? *(Spain's)*
- What country held the most land in Latin America in 1800? *(Spain)*

More About

Viceroyalties

In an attempt to establish an effective colonial government, Spain divided its American empire into provinces. Each province was called a viceroyalty. The top official of each province was called the viceroy. He ruled in the king's name.

Unit ATLAS

Patterns of Human Geography

Study the historical and political maps of Latin America on these two pages. In your notebook, answer these questions.

Making Comparisons

1. What differences do you notice when you compare the 1800 map to the map of Latin America today?
2. What are some of the similarities between the 1800 map and the contemporary map of Latin America?
3. What former Portuguese colony in South America is the largest country in the region today?

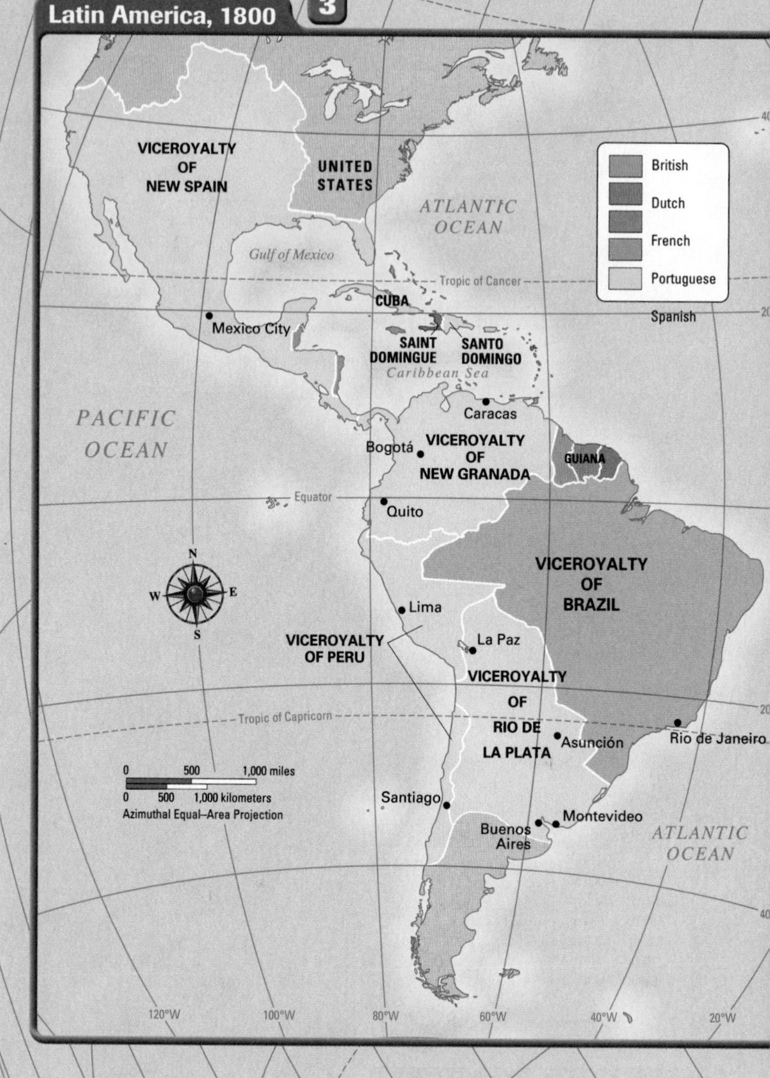

MAKING COMPARISONS ANSWERS

1. There were fewer political entities in 1800. Essentially there were five colonial subregions or provinces, not the many different countries of today.
2. The Spanish and Portuguese spheres of influence were then, and still are, the largest.
3. Brazil

4 Latin America: Political

Instruct: Objective 4

Latin America: Political

- What is the capital of Mexico? *(Mexico City)*
- What is the largest country in South America? *(Brazil)*
- What countries border Ecuador? *(Colombia and Peru)*
- What country connects Central America to South America? What is its capital? *(Panama; Panama City)*
- What do you think is the dominant language in Brazil? Why? *(Portuguese; because Brazil was settled by the Portuguese)*

Outline Maps with Activities
- Latin America: Political, pp. 19–20

Map Tranparencies MT17
- Latin America: Political

ACTIVITY OPTION CRITICAL THINKING

MAKING COMPARISONS

Explaining the Skill *Comparing* means looking at the similarities and differences between two or more things. Geographers compare landforms, resources, climate, and vegetation, as well as other elements in order to understand them better. A chart can provide a useful and concise way to display comparative information.

Applying the Skill Have each student choose a different country in Latin America and then do research to discover its constituent states or provinces. Students might find the information in an encyclopedia or on the Internet, as well as in books about individual countries. After they have completed their research, have them write a paragraph on the political structure of the country they have chosen. Then have the class as a whole make up a chart listing the results of the research. Display the chart in the classroom.

Instruct: Objective 5

Religions of Latin America

- What is the major religion of Latin America? *(Catholicism)*
- Why are most people of Latin America Catholic? *(Most of Latin America was settled by Catholic Spain and Portugal.)*

Instruct: Objective 5

Climates of Latin America

- What is the main climate of the largest country in South America? *(tropical wet and dry)*
- What is the climate of the southernmost tip of South America? *(marine west coast)*

Unit ATLAS

Regional Patterns

On these pages are several thematic maps and a pie graph. One map shows the climates of Latin America. Another depicts the urbanization of the region. A third map shows the languages of the region. Look at them and see what you can learn about Latin America. Answer these questions in your notebook.

Making Comparisons

1. What is the climate in much of the interior of South America? How does it differ from the climate along much of the coast? How might the climate have affected settlement in the interior?
2. What language do the people speak in Brazil? What language is spoken in most countries in the region?
3. Where is most of the population located in South America? Where is there less population? Why might people have settled in these areas rather than the others?

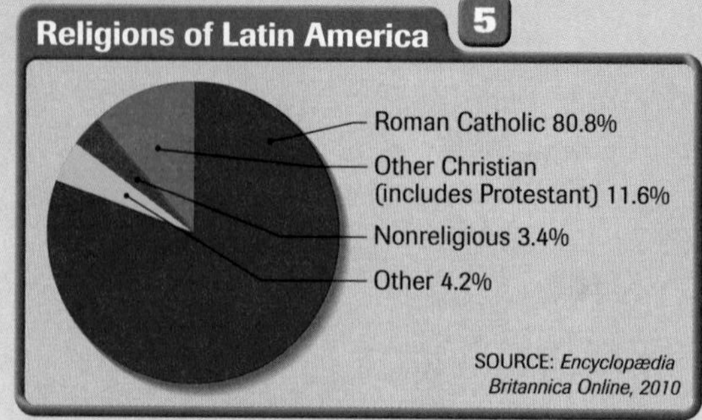

MAKING COMPARISONS ANSWERS

1. The climate is hotter and more humid in the interior, a fact that discouraged settlement.
2. Portuguese in Brazil; Spanish in most other countries
3. Most of the population is located along the eastern and southeastern coasts. The coasts were more accessible than the interior.

Languages of Latin America 6

Indo-European
Other languages
French Spoken language

0 500 1,000 miles
0 500 1,000 kilometers
Azimuthal Equal-Area Projection

Urbanization of Latin America 6

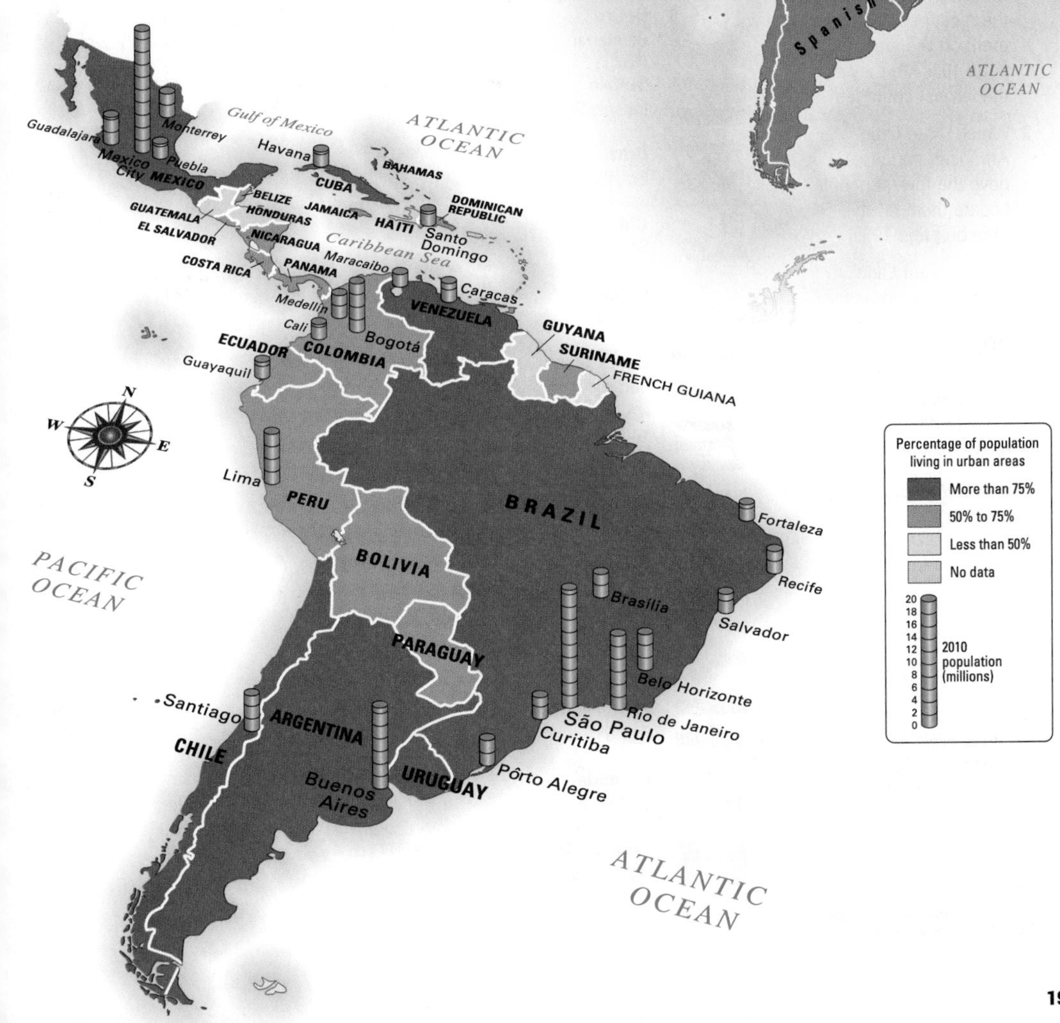

Percentage of population living in urban areas
More than 75%
50% to 75%
Less than 50%
No data
2010 population (millions)

UNIT 3 ATLAS

Instruct: Objective 6

Languages of Latin America

- What is the dominant language of Mexico? *(Spanish)*
- Why is Spanish the dominant language in most of Latin America? *(Most of Latin America was settled by Spanish-speaking peoples who then became the ruling class.)*

Instruct: Objective 

Urbanization of Latin America

- What are some of the most populated areas in Latin America? *(Mexico City, Mexico; São Paulo, Brazil; Rio de Janeiro, Brazil; Buenos Aires, Argentina; and Lima, Peru)*
- What nine countries have more than 75 percent of their population living in urban areas? *(Argentina, Bahamas, Brazil, Chile, Cuba, Mexico, Suriname, Uruguay, and Venezuela)*
- How many cities in Mexico have more than 2 million people? *(four: Guadalajara, Mexico City, Monterrey, and Puebla)*

LATIN AMERICA

ACTIVITY OPTION INTERNET RESEARCH

PRESENTING AN ORAL REPORT

Objective To explore business opportunities in Latin America

Class Time One class period

Task Research and discuss different business opportunities

Directions Have students brainstorm jobs they might be able to do in a Latin American country. Then have them use the Internet or library to find information about these jobs. Decide ahead of time what information students should be looking for, such as that about salary, availability of jobs, opportunity for advancement, ways to apply for jobs, living conditions, and so forth. Have students prepare a short oral report on their findings.

DATA FILE OBJECTIVE

Examine and compare data on Latin American countries.

Focus & Motivate

Ask students what the literacy rate and the GDP (Gross Domestic Product) are for several different countries. Ask students if there is a connection between a low literacy rate and a low GDP. Ask students why they think this might be so.

Instruct: Objective

Regional Data File

- Which four countries have the shortest life expectancy? *(Bolivia, Grenada, Guyana, and Haiti)*
- Which four countries have the lowest literacy rate? *(Belize, Guatemala, Haiti, and Nicaragua)*
- What is Guatemala's GDP? Haiti's? *($69.2 billion; $11.6 billion)*
- Use the map on page 193 to identify four countries. Then compare the literacy rate with the GDP, life expectancy, and infant-mortality rate in the four countries you have chosen. What can you infer about the correlation between literacy, GDP, and health? *(Answers will vary depending on the countries students choose. Students will probably say that a higher literacy rate is correlated with a healthier economy and greater life expectancy.)*

In-Depth Resources: Unit 3
- Regional Data File Activities, p. 2

Regional Data File

Study the charts on the countries of Latin America. In your notebook, answer these questions.

Making Comparisons

1. Which four Latin American countries have the most people? Locate them on the map on page 193. Are they also the largest countries?
2. Which three Latin American countries have the fewest people? Locate them on the map on page 193.
3. Which seven Latin American countries have the highest GDP (gross domestic product)? Which countries have the lowest? What factors might account for this?

(continued on page 198)

Country Flag	Country/ Capital	Population	Life Expectancy (years)	Birthrate (per 1,000 pop.)	Infant Mortal (per 1,000 live bi
	Antigua and Barbuda St. John's	86,000	74.8	16.6	16.3
	Argentina Buenos Aires	40,914,000	76.6	17.9	11.4
	Bahamas Nassau	308,000	69.9	16.4	14.8
	Barbados Bridgetown	285,000	73.9	12.6	12.3
	Belize Belmopan	308,000	68.2	27.3	23.1
	Bolivia La Paz, Sucre	9,775,000	66.9	25.8	44.7
	Brazil Brasília	198,739,000	72.0	18.4	22.6
	Chile Santiago	16,602,000	77.3	14.6	7.7
	Colombia Bogotá	43,677,000	74.1	18.1	17.4
	Costa Rica San José	4,254,000	77.6	17.4	8.8
	Cuba Havana	11,452,000	77.5	11.1	5.8
	Dominica Roseau	73,000	75.6	15.7	13.7
	Dominican Republic Santo Domingo	9,650,000	73.7	22.4	26.0
	Ecuador Quito	14,573,000	75.3	20.8	20.9
	El Salvador San Salvador	7,185,000	72.3	25.3	21.5
	Grenada St. George's	91,000	66.0	21.3	13.2
	Guatemala Guatemala City	13,277,000	70.3	28.0	27.8

**** Data is available for commercial vehicles only.***
***** Figure includes commercial vehicles.***

For updated statistics on Latin America . . .

MAKING COMPARISONS ANSWERS

1. Argentina, Brazil, Colombia, Mexico; in general, they are also the largest in terms of area.
2. Antigua and Barbuda, Dominica, and St. Kitts and Nevis
3. Argentina, Brazil, Chile, Colombia, Mexico, Peru, and Venezuela have the highest GDPs. Antigua and Barbuda, Belize, Dominica, Grenada, St. Kitts and Nevis, Saint Lucia, and St. Vincent and the Grenadines have the lowest GDPs. Educated work force, natural resources, manufacturing, and geographic location may all play a part.

Doctors (per 100,000 pop.) (2000–2004)	GDP[a] (billions $US)	Import/Export (billions $US)	Literacy Rate (percentage)	Televisions (per 1,000 pop.)	Passenger Cars (per 1,000 pop.)	Total Area[b] (square miles)
17	1.6	0.52/0.08	86	493	279	171
301	558	38.71/55.7	97	293	127	1,068,302
105	9.1	2.4/0.67	96	243	218	5.382
121	5.3	1.59/0.39	100	290	218	166
105	2.5	0.62/0.40	77	183	106	8,867
122	45.1	4.17/4.84	87	118	30	424,164
115	2,025	136/158.9	89	333	84	3,286,488
109	243.7	40.91/48.85	96	240	96	292,260
135	401	31.67/31.34	90	279	48	439,736
132	48.6	10.53/8.10	95	229	157	19,730
591	111.1	10.86/3.25	100	248	N/A*	42,803
50	0.7	0.29/0.09	94	232	137	291
188	80.5	12.14/5.37	87	96	75	18,815
148	108.2	14.09/13.76	91	213	28	109,483
124	42.9	7.22/4.09	80	191	21	8,124
50	1.2	0.34/0.03	96	376	174	133
90	69.2	10.91/6.77	69	61	98**	42,043

197

More About

The Bahamas

The Bahamas consist of 700 islands. Located in the western Atlantic Ocean, off the tip of the Florida coast, the Bahamas are a popular tourist destination. One of the Caribbean's major cruise-line stops, the Bahamas offer plenty of sandy beaches. Ask students why they think the Bahamas are a major tourist attraction. *(Answers may include the following reasons: nearness to the United States, climate, beaches.)*

ACTIVITY OPTION CRITICAL THINKING

ANALYZING DATA

Explaining the Skill Graphs summarize and present data in a visual format. To understand data, it is important to be able to read different types of graphs. *Circle* (or *pie*) *graphs* show the division of the whole. *Line graphs* are used for plotting over time. *Bar graphs* have vertical and horizontal axes, with labels that tell what is being measured and what units of measurement are being used. *Pictographs* use rows of icons to show comparisons.

Applying the Skill Have students choose three Latin American countries. Using the information on the maps on pages 190–195 and the information in the Regional Data File on pages 196–197, students should create three graphs that represent three types of data. Ask: Why is it important to compare data about countries? What have you learned about the countries you created graphs for? Why did you choose these types of graphs? *(Comparing data is a tool for learning about countries; answers will vary depending on the countries students choose; different graphs illustrate different types of data.)*

More About

Media

Paraguay, Venezuela, and Brazil have an abundance of telephones, television and radio stations, and newspapers. Ask students what conclusions they can draw about these countries from this information. *(The countries have a well-developed infrastructure; their populations have opportunities for widespread communications.)*

Regional Data File

Making Comparisons *(continued)*

4. Latin America has several countries with populations under 200,000. Which of these has the smallest total area?
5. Use the map on page 193 to identify one country in Central America and another in the Caribbean. For each country, calculate per capita GDP by dividing total GDP by population. Which country has the higher per capita GDP?

Country Flag	Country/ Capital	Population	Life Expectancy (years)	Birthrate (per 1,000 pop.)	Infant Mortali (per 1,000 live bir
	Guyana Georgetown	753,000	66.3	18.3	39.1
	Haiti Port-au-Prince	9,036,000	60.8	29.1	59.7
	Honduras Tegucigalpa	7,834,000	70.5	26.3	21.7
	Jamaica Kingston	2,826,000	73.5	19.7	15.2
	Mexico Mexico City	111,212,000	76.1	19.7	18.4
	Nicaragua Managua	5,891,000	71.5	23.3	25.0
	Panama Panama City	3,360,000	77.3	20.2	12.7
	Paraguay Asunción	6,996,000	75.8	28.2	24.7
	Peru Lima	29,547,000	70.7	19.4	28.6
	St. Kitts and Nevis Basseterre	40,000	73.2	17.7	13.9
	St. Lucia Castries	160,000	76.5	15.1	13.4
	St. Vincent and the Grenadines Kingstown	105,000	73.7	15.3	15.1
	Suriname Paramaribo	481,000	73.7	16.8	18.8
	Trinidad and Tobago Port of Spain	1,230000	70.9	14.4	29.9
	Uruguay Montevideo	3,494,000	76.4	13.9	11.3
	Venezuela Caracas	26,815,000	73.6	20.6	21.5
	United States Washington, D.C.	307,212,000	78.1	13.8	6.2

Sources:

Central Intelligence Agency, *The World Factbook*, 2010

The World Almanac and Book of Facts, 2010

World Health Organization (WHO), 2007

Notes:

[a] GDP (purchasing power parity) is defined as the sum value of all goods and services produced in the country, valued at prices prevailing in the United States.

[b] Includes land and water, when figures are available

MAKING COMPARISONS ANSWERS

4. Antigua and Barbuda, Dominica, Grenada, St. Kitts and Nevis, St. Lucia, and St. Vincent and the Grenadines all have populations under 200,000. Of these, St. Kitts and Nevis has the smallest area.
5. Answers will vary, depending on which countries students choose.

Doctors (per 100,000 pop.) (2000–2004)	GDP[a] (billions $US)	Import/Export (billions $US)	Literacy Rate (percentage)	Televisions (per 1,000 pop.)	Passenger Cars (per 1,000 pop.)	Total Area[b]
48	2.8	1.07/0.65	99	70	81	83,000
25	11.9	2.02/0.52	53	5	10	10,714
57	33.2	7.57/5.25	80	95	6	43,278
85	23.2	4.62/1.42	88	191	37	4,244
198	1,482	234.4/229.7	91	272	132	761,606
37	16.5	3.97/2.34	68	69	14	49,998
150	40.3	13.62/11.41	92	192	75	30,193
111	28.3	6.50/3.17	94	205	52	157,047
117	253.0	20.3/23.1	93	147	31	496,226
119	0.8	0.38/0.08	98	256	225	101
517	1.8	0.79/0.28	90	368	149	238
87	1.6	0.58/0.19	96	230	133	150
45	4.3	1.30/1.39	90	241	158	63,039
79	28.4	7.45/10.64	99	337	260	1,980
365	44.5	6.58/6.32	98	531	135	68,039
194	350.1	41.04/51.99	93	185	93	352,144
256	14,260.0	1,445/994.7	99	844	725	3,794,083

199

More About

Bolivia

High in the Andes Mountains of South America, Bolivia has the highest golf course, the highest ski resort, and the highest capital city in the world. Located between two mountain ranges, La Paz, Bolivia, is 12,000 feet above sea level.

ACTIVITY OPTION INTERNET RESEARCH

RESEARCHING DATA

Objective To gather information and present it in a graphic

Class Time 30 minutes

Task Make a bar graph to compare data on communications in different Latin American countries.

Directions Have students choose three communication categories to research. Categories may include radio stations, television stations, daily newspapers, magazines, telephones, and so forth. Then have students use the Internet, encyclopedias, or library for their research. Once students have compiled the data, they should illustrate the data in a bar graph. Collect the graphs and display them around the room.

CHAPTER 9 OBJECTIVE

Identify key features of Latin America's physical geography, climate and vegetation, and human-environment interaction.

Chapter 9 PHYSICAL GEOGRAPHY OF LATIN AMERICA

From the Andes to the Amazon

Interpreting Photographs

Angel Falls

Ask students to study the photograph and read the caption. Ask students to compare the size of the plane to the size of the waterfall. Ask students if they think people live near here. If so, what might these people be like? How has this environment affected their lives? *(Answers will vary.)*

Introducing the Essential Question

- Ask student to look through the photos in this unit and suggest objectives that describe Latin America's physical geography. Emphasize the great beauty and fragility of some of the region's landscapes.
- Challenge students to investigate the source of some foods or products that they enjoy to determine if these items' production threatens Latin American rain forests.

hmhsocialstudies.com TAKING NOTES

Have students fill out the graphic organizers in their notebooks using material from all sections in this chapter. Responses can be found in Section and Chapter Assessments (pp. 205, 209, 213, 214-215).

Critical Thinking Transparencies CT9
- GeoFocus

In-Depth Resources: Unit 3
- Building Vocabulary, p. 9

Angel Falls in eastern Venezuela is the world's tallest waterfall. Named after James Angel, an American pilot who spotted it from his airplane in 1935, it is 3,212 feet tall.

Essential Question

How have Latin America's varied landscapes affected the region's development?

What You Will Learn

In this chapter you will identify key features of Latin America's physical geography.

SECTION 1
Landforms and Resources

SECTION 2
Climate and Vegetation

SECTION 3
Human-Environment Interaction

hmhsocialstudies.com TAKING NOTES

Use the graphic organizer online to record information from the chapter about the physical geography of Latin America.

200

CHAPTER 9 ADDITIONAL RESOURCES

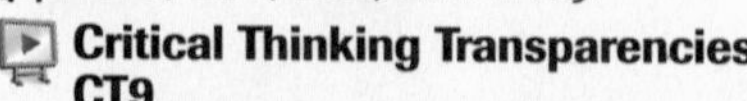

BOOKS FOR THE TEACHER

Williamson, Edwin. ***The Penguin History of Latin America.*** Penguin, 2010. Comprehensive, historical view of the region.

BOOKS FOR THE STUDENT

Schafer, Kevin (photographs) and Downs Matthews (text). ***Beneath the Canopy: Wildlife of Latin American Rain Forest.*** San Francisco: Chronicle Books, 1999. Photographs and information about the mystery and wonder of the rain forest.

VIDEOS

Ancient Voices: The Search For El Dorado. Time Life Video, 1998. An expedition into Colombia in search of the fabled kingdom of gold of the Muisca.

INTERNET

For more on the physical geography of Latin America, visit . . .

hmhsocialstudies.com

Landforms and Resources

Main Ideas

- Latin America's landforms include highlands, lowlands, mountains, and plains.
- The Andes Mountains and the Amazon River are the region's most remarkable physical features.

Places & Terms

Andes Mountains

llanos	**Orinoco River**
cerrado	**Amazon River**
pampas	**Paraná River**

CONNECT TO THE ISSUES

RESOURCES People in Latin America have often struggled over the best way to develop and use natural resources.

A HUMAN PERSPECTIVE Simón Bolívar was a general who led the South American wars of independence against Spain. In August 1819, Bolívar led approximately 2,500 soldiers on a daring march from Venezuela over the mountains into present-day Colombia. Coming from this direction, over the massive barrier of the Andes Mountains, Bolívar and his troops were able to advance unseen. Bolívar's soldiers surprised the Spanish army and won a great victory. Military leaders such as Bolívar were able to use the geography of the region to help the South American republics win their independence from Spain.

LATIN AMERICA

Mountains and Highlands

Latin America has an enormous span from north to south, as you can see from the map on page 191. It reaches from the border between the United States and Mexico down to Tierra del Fuego at the southernmost tip of South America, a distance of about 7,000 miles. It covers part of North America, all of Central and South America, and the Caribbean Islands. Its highlands, lowlands, rain forests, and plains are bounded by the Atlantic and Pacific oceans, the Gulf of Mexico, and the Caribbean Sea. The mountains of Latin America form one of the great ranges of the world.

THE ANDES MOUNTAINS The **Andes Mountains** of the South American continent are part of a chain of mountain ranges that run through the western portion of North, Central, and South America. This range is called the Rockies in the United States, the Sierra Madre in Mexico, and the Andes in South America. There are many active volcanoes throughout the region.

All along the west and south coasts of South America, the Andes Mountains are a barrier to movement into the interior. As a result, more settlement in South America has occurred along the eastern and northern coasts.

Even so, the mountain ranges of Latin America were the home of some of the most important civilizations in the hemisphere, including the Inca in Peru.

MOVEMENT Two sure-footed guanacos climb the foothills of the Andes in Patagonia, a region that includes parts of Argentina and Chile.

201

SECTION 1 OBJECTIVES

1. Identify Latin America's mountains and highlands.
2. Describe the Latin American plains, and identify the Amazon River and other rivers.
3. Identify the major islands of the Caribbean.
4. Explain the importance of the resources of Latin America.

SKILLBUILDERS: Interpreting Maps pp. 203, 204

**GeographicThinking**

Seeing Patterns p. 202
Using the Atlas p. 203
Drawing Conclusions p. 205

Focus & Motivate

How might landforms affect the way people in Latin America live? *(Mountains protect isolated communities; rivers can provide a means of transportation; plains provide soil for growing crops, grasses, and livestock.)*

Instruct: Objective 1

Mountains and Highlands

- Where are the Sierra Madre and Andes mountains located? *(Sierra Madre in Mexico; Andes in South America)*
- How has geography affected settlement in Latin America? *(Mountain ranges were a barrier to movement away from the coast, so coastal areas are more densely populated.)*
- In what mountain range did the Inca live? *(Andes)*

In-Depth Resources: Unit 3
- Guided Reading, p. 3

Map Transparencies MT18
- Latin America: Geological Structures

SECTION 1 PROGRAM RESOURCES

**In-Depth Resources: Unit 3**
- Guided Reading, p. 3
- Map and Graph Skills, pp. 6–7
- Building Vocabulary, p. 9
- Reteaching Activity, p. 10

Guided Reading Workbook
- Section 1

Access for Students Acquiring English/ESL
- Guided Reading, p. 43
- Map and Graph Skills, pp. 47–48

Formal Assessment
- Section Quiz, p. 131

Integrated Assessment
- Rubric for a sketch map, 2.1

INTEGRATED TECHNOLOGY

Critical Thinking Transparencies CT41
- Comparing Regional Geography

Map Transparencies MT18
- Latin America: Geological Structures

Chapter Summaries

Power Presentations

TEST-TAKING RESOURCES

Strategies for Taking Tests

Test Practice Transparencies TT28

Online Test Practice

Instruct: Objective 2

Plains for Grain and Livestock/ The Amazon and Other Rivers

- What are llanos? *(large, grassy, treeless plains used for grazing and farming)*
- Do you think it would be a good idea for Brazilian farmers to move to the cerrado? Why or why not? *(Yes, because these savannas have flat terrain and moderate rainfall that make them suitable for farming.)*
- What are the three major river systems in South America? *(Orinoco, Amazon, Paraná)*
- Why are the countries of Central America and the Caribbean less dependent on river systems than South America? *(because they are surrounded by water)*

5 THEMES

Human-Environment Interaction: The Gaucho

Like North American cowboys, gauchos have inspired folk music and folktales. Ask students questions to point out the parallels between gauchos and cowboys.

- What North American songs or folktales do you know about cowboys? *(Answers will vary depending on student knowledge.)*
- Why do you think gauchos and cowboys inspire music and folktales? *(Because they lead somewhat solitary lives away from others, and their work can be dangerous and demanding; their lives seem exciting or mysterious to city dwellers.)*

HIGHLANDS Other ranges in Latin America include the Guiana Highlands in the northeast section of South America. Highlands are made up of the mountainous or hilly sections of a country. The highlands of Latin America include parts of Venezuela, Guyana, Suriname, French Guiana, and Brazil. The Brazilian Highlands (see the map on page 203) are located along the east coast of Brazil.

Plains for Grain and Livestock

South America has wide plains that offer rich soil for growing crops and grasses for grazing livestock.

LLANOS OF COLOMBIA AND VENEZUELA Colombia and Venezuela contain vast plains called **llanos** (LAH•nohs), which are grassy, treeless areas used for livestock grazing and farming. They are similar to the Great Plains in the United States and the pampas of Argentina.

PLAINS OF AMAZON RIVER BASIN Brazil also contains expansive plains in the interior of the country. These are the **cerrado** (seh•RAH•doh), savannas with flat terrain and moderate rainfall that make them suitable for farming. Much of this land is undeveloped. However, the government of Brazil is encouraging settlers to move into the interior and develop the land.

PAMPAS OF ARGENTINA AND URUGUAY In parts of South America, the plains are known as **pampas** (PAHM•puhs), areas of grasslands and rich soil. Pampas are found in northern Argentina and Uruguay. The main products of the pampas are cattle and wheat grain. A culture of the gaucho has grown up in the region, centered on the horsemen of the pampas. A

5 THEMES

HUMAN-ENVIRONMENT INTERACTION

The Gaucho

Gauchos, the cowboys of Argentina and Uruguay, wear ponchos to help protect them from bad weather. They tuck the tops of their baggy trousers into riding boots. Like American cowboys and the *vaqueros* of Mexico, they wear hats with wide brims to help protect them from sun and rain on the pampas.

Their tools include the knife and the bola, a special kind of sling. It is made of stones fastened to the ends of cowhide thongs. The thrower hurls the bola at the legs of an animal, tripping it and throwing it to the ground.

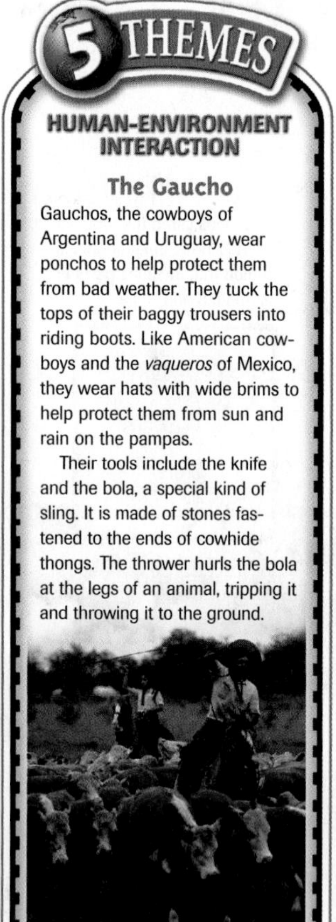

Geographic Thinking

Seeing Patterns

A How are the llanos, cerrado, and pampas of South America similar to the Great Plains of the United States?

A. Answer They are large, grassy, treeless plains ideal for cattle grazing and farming.

The Amazon and Other Rivers

The countries of Central America and the Caribbean do not have the extensive river systems that are found in South America. In North America, the Rio Grande, which forms part of the border between the United States and Mexico, is longer than any other river in Mexico, Central America, or the Caribbean. However, these areas are all bordered by water. As a result, they are less dependent on river systems for transportation than is South America.

South America has three major river systems. The Orinoco is the northernmost river system, with the Amazon also in the north, and the Paraná in the south of the continent.

ORINOCO RIVER The **Orinoco River** winds through the northern part of the continent, mainly in Venezuela. It flows more than 1,500 miles, partly along the Colombia-Venezuela border, to the Atlantic. The Orinoco River basin drains the interior lands of both Venezuela and Colombia. Some of the areas drained by the Orinoco are home to the few remaining Native American peoples, such as the Yanomamo.

DIFFERENTIATING INSTRUCTION **STUDENTS ACQUIRING ENGLISH/ESL**

CREATING A DICTIONARY

Objective To make sure students understand unfamiliar terms

Class Time 15 minutes

Task Have students use note cards to create a dictionary of words in their native language with the corresponding words in English, and the definition.

Directions Have students use the key terms, names of mountains, rivers, and other important features to create their own dictionaries. Pass out a pack of note cards to each student. Students are to write English words that are difficult for them on cards, along with the translation in their native language. Also include the definition in English.

Have students work with a partner. One partner reads the word in the native tongue, if possible, or gives the definition. The other student then provides the English term and definition. Then have students switch roles.

Background The Amazon is the second longest river in the world after the Nile.

AMAZON RIVER Farther south, the **Amazon River** flows about 4,000 miles from west to east, emptying into the Atlantic Ocean. Its branches start in the Andes Mountains of South America, close to the Pacific. Yet it flows eastward across the central lowlands toward the Atlantic. The Amazon River is fed by over 1,000 tributaries, some of which are large rivers in themselves. The Amazon carries more water to the ocean than any other river in the world. In fact, it carries more water to the ocean than the next seven largest rivers of the world combined.

PARANÁ RIVER The **Paraná River** has its origins in the highlands of southern Brazil. It travels about 3,000 miles south and west through Paraguay and Argentina, where it is fed by several rivers, and then turns eastward. The last stretch of the river, where it turns into an estuary of the Paraná and Uruguay rivers between Argentina and Uruguay, is called the Río de la Plata. An estuary is the wide lower course of a river where its current is met by the tides.

Landforms and Rivers of Latin America

Mountains
Hills and Plateaus
Plains

0 500 1,000 miles
0 500 1,000 kilometers
Azimuthal Equal-Area Projection

SKILLBUILDER: Interpreting Maps

1. **MOVEMENT** Which rivers empty into the Atlantic Ocean?
2. **REGION** What mountains run along the western edge of South America?

LATIN AMERICA

Interpreting Maps

Landforms and Rivers of Latin America

Have students locate the Orinoco, Amazon, and Paraná rivers on the map. Then have students identify the Andes Mountains. Ask students the following questions: What is the major mountain chain in Mexico? What are the major landforms of Brazil? Is the Amazon Plain located in the Caribbean, Mexico, Central America, or South America? *(Sierra Madre; hills, plateaus, river basins; South America)*

SKILLBUILDER ANSWERS

1. the Orinoco, Amazon, and Paraná
2. the Andes

Major Islands of the Caribbean

The Caribbean Islands consist of three major groups: the Bahamas, the Greater Antilles, and the Lesser Antilles. (See the map on page 191.) These islands together are sometimes called the West Indies and were the first land encountered by Christopher Columbus when he sailed to the Western Hemisphere in 1492. They served as a base of operations for the later conquest of the mainland by the Spanish.

The Bahamas are made up of hundreds of islands off the southern tip of Florida and north of Cuba. They extend southeast into the Atlantic Ocean. Nassau is the capital and largest city in the Bahamas.

B. Answer the Lesser Antilles

Geographic Thinking

Using the Atlas B Use the map on page 191. Which of the Antilles are closer to the coast of South America?

THE GREATER ANTILLES The Greater Antilles are made up of the larger islands in the Caribbean. These include Cuba, Jamaica, Hispaniola, and Puerto Rico. The island of Hispaniola is divided between the countries of Haiti and the Dominican Republic.

THE LESSER ANTILLES The Lesser Antilles are the smaller islands in the region southeast of Puerto Rico. The Lesser Antilles are divided into the Windward Islands and Leeward Islands. The Windward Islands face winds that blow across them. The Leeward Islands enjoy a more sheltered position from the prevailing northeasterly winds. B

Instruct: Objective 

Major Islands of the Caribbean

- What are the three major island groups in the Caribbean Islands? *(the Bahamas, the Greater Antilles, and the Lesser Antilles)*
- If you wanted to be protected from the wind, would you live on the Windward or Leeward Islands? Why? *(Leeward Islands, because they are protected against winds that blow across them; whereas the Windward Islands face winds that blow across them.)*

Critical Thinking Transparencies CT41
- Compairing Regional Geography

ACTIVITY OPTION | LINK TO LANGUAGE ARTS

STORYTELLING

Objective To learn about the oral tradition of storytelling

Class Time 60 minutes

Task To write and tell Latin American stories

Directions Tell students that the people of Latin America have a rich tradition of oral storytelling. For example, there are many stories about the gauchos of Argentina and Uruguay. And, although the stories of the Caribbean are different from those of the peoples of Mexico or Brazil, many have similar themes, such as reverence for nature, devotion to ancestral spirits, and origin stories. Stories teach ethics, morals, and cultural values.

Give students 30 minutes to write a story. Encourage them to use elements of Latin American geography in their stories: animals such as the jaguar or sloth, and features such as the sea, rivers, jungles, or mountains will tie the stories to Latin America. When they are done, encourage students to tell their stories rather than read them.

Instruct: Objective  4

Resources of Latin America

- What are three types of resources found in Latin America? *(mineral resources, such as gold and silver; energy resources, such as oil and natural gas; agricultural and forest resources, such as timber)*
- What country generates the most hydroelectric power and why? *(Brazil, because of its many rivers)*
- How does the global price of oil affect the economy of Mexico? *(If the price of oil declines on the global market, it can throw Mexico into recession or debt.)*

Interpreting Maps

Resources of Latin America

Have students examine the map. Discuss what types of resources are shown on the map. Point out that timber is a resource in Brazil. Ask students the following questions: From looking at the map, do you think timber is important to Brazil's economy? Why? *(Yes, because from the map it looks like timber is a major export in Brazil.)*

SKILLBUILDER ANSWERS
1. the west **2.** Mexico

Resources of Latin America

Latin America is a treasure house of natural resources. These include mineral resources, such as gold and silver, as well as energy resources, such as oil and natural gas. In addition, the region is rich in agricultural and forest resources, such as timber. These resources have drawn people to the region for centuries.

MINERAL RESOURCES Gold, silver, iron, copper, bauxite (aluminum ore), tin, lead, and nickel—all these minerals are abundant in Latin America. In addition, mines throughout the region produce precious gems, titanium, and tungsten. In fact, South America is among the world's leaders in the mining of raw materials.

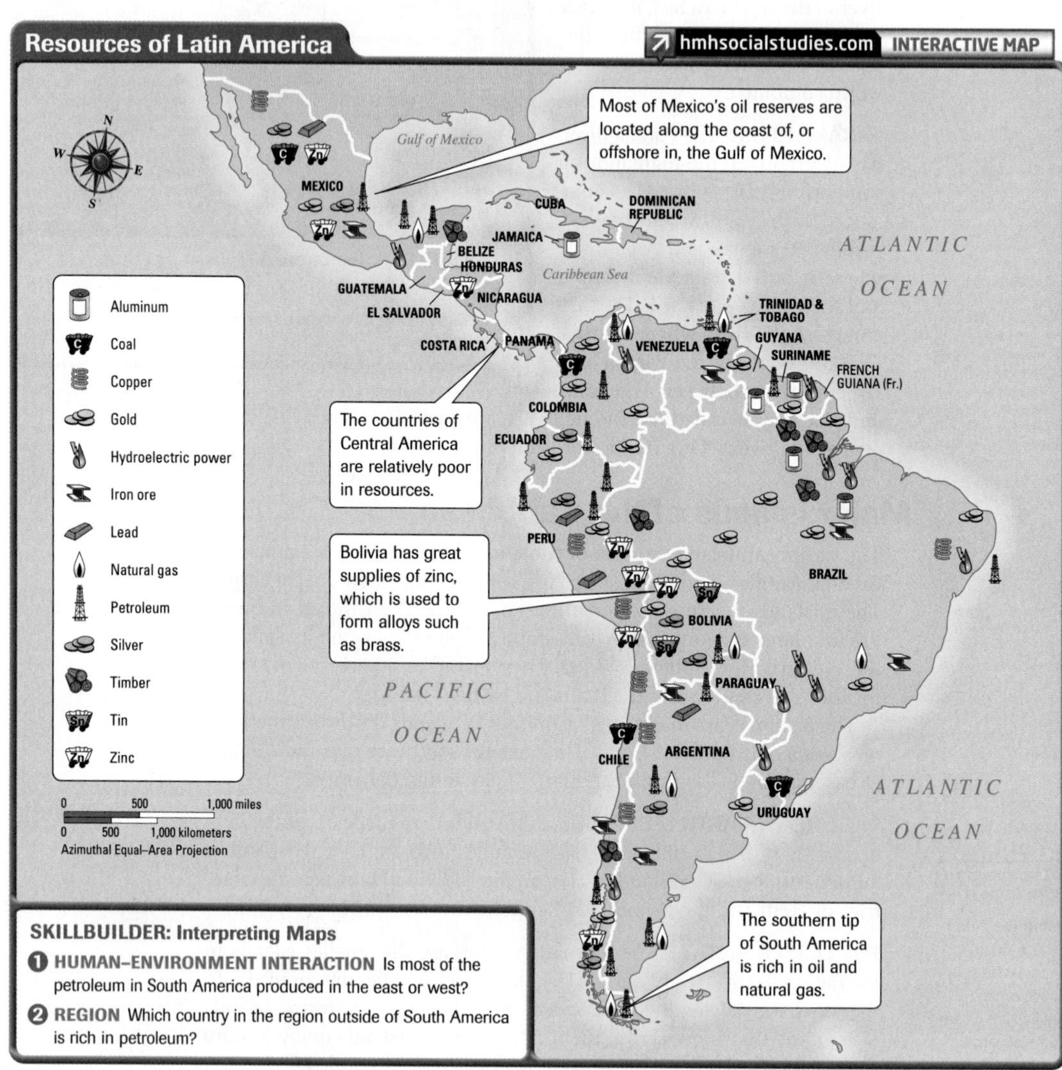

SKILLBUILDER: Interpreting Maps

1. **HUMAN-ENVIRONMENT INTERACTION** Is most of the petroleum in South America produced in the east or west?
2. **REGION** Which country in the region outside of South America is rich in petroleum?

DIFFERENTIATING INSTRUCTION **GIFTED AND TALENTED STUDENTS**

REPORTING ON CONSERVATION EFFORTS

Objective To investigate the role of ecotourism in conservation

Research Time 3 days **Class Time** 20 minutes

Task Report on Mesoamerican Ecotourism Alliance, a conservation group formed by park rangers and environmentalists in Mexico, Belize, Guatemala, and Honduras

Directions Have students research the Mesoamerican Ecotourism Alliance and give a report to the whole class. Then have the students brainstorm how they can create an ecotourism student link in your community. Ask students: How can you work with students in other schools to help the environment in our community? What type of Saturday afternoon ecotourism adventure can we create to raise money to help the environment?

Many of these minerals are mined and then exported to other parts of the world, where they are made into valuable goods. For example, Jamaica was originally a plantation economy that depended on the sale of bananas and sugar for its livelihood. Then it turned to the mining and processing of bauxite (aluminum ore) in an attempt to make the country less dependent on agriculture and tourism. Today, this resource is mainly an export that is shipped elsewhere for industrial use.

ENERGY RESOURCES Oil, coal, natural gas, uranium, and hydroelectric power are all plentiful in Latin America. Venezuela and Mexico have major oil reserves. Brazil is rich in hydroelectric power because of its many rivers (including the mighty Amazon) and waterfalls. It is also rich in oil and gas.

Trinidad has discovered vast reserves of natural gas. New factories have turned Trinidad into a major exporter of methanol and ammonia. Natural gas has also attracted developers to the island.

In Mexico and Venezuela, oil has been a very important resource. Venezuela sits on top of major oil deposits. This resource was developed into a significant oil industry. Mexico has huge oilfields centered along the Gulf coast. Because of its reserves, Mexico is able to export oil to other countries. However, changes in the global price of oil have had a great impact on the economies of these countries. C

Latin America has great variety in its climate and vegetation. You will read about each in the next section.

C. Answer They mine and otherwise develop the resources, use some, and export the rest.

CONNECT TO THE ISSUES
RESOURCES
C How do the countries of the region make use of their natural resources?

Connect to the Issues

RESOURCES

Rain Forest Medicines

Vegetation in the rain forests has yielded many products used to make modern drugs and medicines. These include quinine, which is used to treat malaria, and curare, which is used to relax muscles.

Scientists believe that many of the potential medicines and drugs of the rain forest remain undiscovered. Destroying the rain forests damages the habitats of plants or animals that might even provide a cure for cancer. In the picture below, a man is using a plant to soothe an earache.

LATIN AMERICA

Connect to the Issues

Resources: Rain Forest Medicines

Tell students that every year people destroy 33.8 million acres of tropical rain forests, which is about 64 acres every minute. Ask students:

- Do you think U.S. citizens have a responsibility to do something to help protect the rain forest? *(Accept a variety of answers; encourage students to support their arguments with reasons and evidence.)*
- What might students do to help protect the rain forests? *(Accept all answers, then narrow answers to a short list, and ask students if they would be willing to create a save-the-rain forest project.)*

Assess & Reteach

GeoFocus Have students complete the sections on landforms and resources in their graphic organizers.

Formal Assessment
Section Quiz, p. 131

Reteaching Activity
Have students organize the material in this section in a formal outline. Have them exchange their outlines with another student, and check each other's work.

In-Depth Resources: Unit 3
- Reteaching Activity, p. 10

Section 1 Assessment

1 Places & Terms

Identify and explain where in the region these would be found.

- Andes Mountains
- llanos
- cerrado
- pampas
- Orinoco River
- Amazon River
- Paraná River

2 Taking Notes

PLACE Review the notes you took for this section.

Landforms	
Resources	

- What types of landforms are found in Latin America?
- What is their relative location?

3 Main Ideas

a. How did the Andes Mountains affect settlement along the western coast of South America?

b. How are the landforms of the region both an advantage and disadvantage?

c. What effect did natural resources have on the development of the region?

4 Geographic Thinking

Drawing Conclusions How might the Amazon River have affected movement into the interior of South America?

Think about:

- the network of travel offered by a river system

S **See Skillbuilder Handbook, page R5.**

GeoActivities

SEEING PATTERNS Pair with a partner and draw a **sketch map** of Latin America's rivers and mountains. Use arrows to indicate the directions the rivers flow. Why does the Amazon flow all the way east across the continent even though its headwaters begin in the Andes Mountains along the west coast?

SECTION 1 ASSESSMENT ANSWERS

1. Places & Terms

Andes Mountains, p. 201
llanos, p. 202
cerrado, p. 202
pampas, p. 202
Orinoco River, p. 202
Amazon River, p. 203
Paraná River, p. 203

2. Taking Notes

- Andes Mountains and Amazon River are among most remarkable landforms in region; also vast plains and many island groups.
- Andes Mountains run along western coast of South America; Amazon flows from west to east in northern part of South America and flows into Atlantic; plains in Argentina and Uruguay, as well as Colombia, Venezuela, Brazil; most islands in region are in the Caribbean.

3. Main Ideas

a. They were a barrier to movement from the west coast into the interior, resulting in more settlement along the eastern and northern coasts.
b. The mountains have been a barrier to settlement; however, the rivers have been a means of transport and a source of hydroelectric power.
c. brought settlers to region; have been exported around world

4. Geographic Thinking

The river provides a way into the interior of the continent.

GeoActivity

Integrated Assessment
- Rubric for a sketch map, 2.1

OBJECTIVE

Learn how to identify precipitation patterns.

Instruct: Objective

Interpreting a Precipitation Map

- What is a precipitation map? *(identifies seasonal patterns of rainfall, snowfall, sleet in a region)*
- What is the precipitation pattern in the Amazon basin? *(heavy annual precipitation)*
- In what part of the continent is it dry most of the year? *(along west coast)*

In-Depth Resources: Unit 3
- Map and Graph Skills, pp. 6–7

Access for Students Acquiring English/ESL
- Map and Graph Skills, pp. 47–48

RAND McNALLY **Map and Graph Skills**

Interpreting a Precipitation Map

This map shows differences in annual precipitation throughout South America. Suppose you have been given a chance to live in either Manaus, Brazil, or Buenos Aires, Argentina, for a year. You don't want to live in a city where it rains a lot. Which city would you choose? To help make your decision, find the two cities on the Unit Atlas map on page 193. Then find their locations on this precipitation map.

THE LANGUAGE OF MAPS A **precipitation map** is a type of thematic map. Many precipitation maps show differences in annual precipitation within a given region.

Precipitation in South America

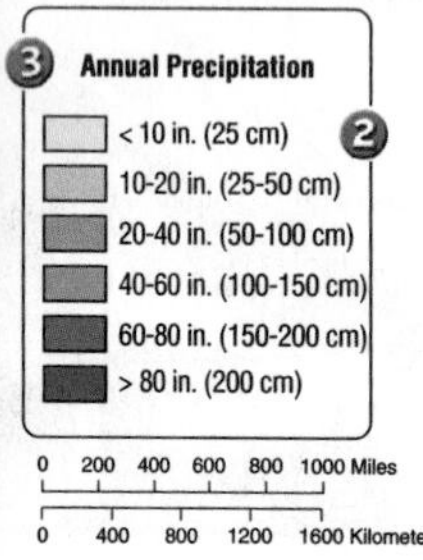

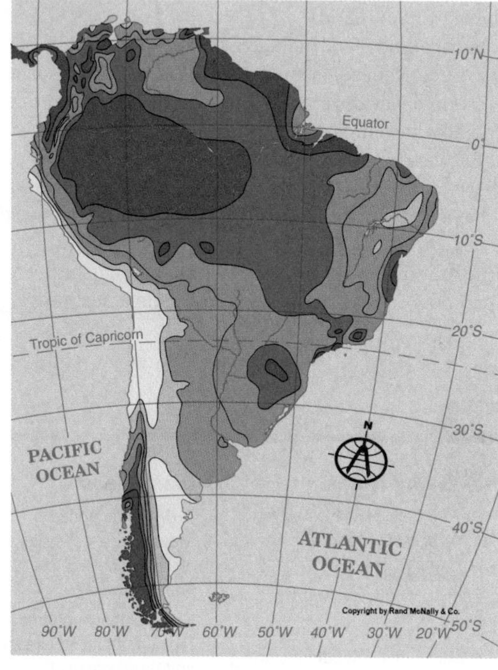

1. The title gives you the subject matter of the map.
2. The amount of annual precipitation is shown both in inches and centimeters.
3. The key shows the colors used on the map and explains their meaning. Each color shows a different range of annual precipitation.

Map and Graph Skills Assessment

1. **Making Comparisons** Where are you likely to experience more rain—in Peru or Brazil?
2. **Drawing Conclusions** Does Guyana have heavy or light annual precipitation?
3. **Making Inferences** Is there heavier annual precipitation in the northern or southern parts of the continent?

MAP SKILLS ASSESSMENT ANSWERS

1. Brazil **2.** heavy **3.** north

Climate and Vegetation

Main Ideas

- Latin America has a variety of climates, from the cold peaks of the Andes to the Amazon rain forest.
- The vegetation of Latin America ranges from grasslands to the largest rain forest in the world.

Places & Terms

rain forest

CONNECT TO THE ISSUES

RESOURCES Latin America's climate and vegetation make up a habitat that is threatened by economic development.

A HUMAN PERSPECTIVE In the 17th century, missionaries and Indians in the area of present-day Paraguay were at times attacked by jaguars, the great cats of Latin America. In 1637, packs of jaguars roamed the countryside, attacking humans. The Indians built barricades for protection from the savage cats. But the jaguars remained a source of fear. The cats were a factor that had to be taken into account in settling and protecting towns and villages. There was no question about it—jaguars and other creatures thrived in the humid climate and thick vegetation of the tropical rain forests.

A Varied Climate and Vegetation

The climate of Latin America ranges from the hot and humid Amazon River basin to the dry and desert-like conditions of northern Mexico and southern Chile. Rain forest, desert, and savanna are all found in the region.

The vegetation varies from rain forests to grasslands and desert scrub. It ranges from the thick trees of the rain forests to mosses of the tundra.

This variety of climate and vegetation is due to several factors. First, Latin America spans a great distance on each side of the equator. Second, there are big changes in elevation because of the massive mountains in the region. Third, the warm currents of the Atlantic Ocean and the cold currents of the Pacific Ocean affect the climate.

Tropical Climate Zones

The tropical climate zones of the region produce both rain forests and the tree-dotted grasslands known as savannas. Rain forests are abundant in Central America, the Caribbean, and South America. Savannas are found in South America.

TROPICAL WET **Rain forests** are dense forests made up of different species of trees. They form a unique ecosystem—a community of plants and animals living in balance. The climate in these areas is hot and rainy year round. The largest forest is the

Vegetation of Latin America

110°W 90°W 70°W 50°W
Gulf of Mexico
Caribbean Sea
PACIFIC OCEAN
ATLANTIC OCEAN
Equator
20°N 0° 20°S 40°S
0 500 1,000 miles
0 500 1,000 kilometers
Azimuthal Equal-Area Projection

- Tropical rain forest
- Tropical grassland
- Desert and dry shrub
- Temperate grassland
- Mediterranean shrub
- Deciduous and mixed forest
- Highland

SKILLBUILDER: Interpreting Maps

1. **REGION** In what part of the region is the largest rain forest?
2. **REGION** What form of vegetation covers most of the southeastern part of South America?

LATIN AMERICA

SECTION 2 OBJECTIVES

1. Describe the climate and vegetation of Latin America.
2. Identify the tropical climate zones of Latin America.
3. Identify the dry climate zones of Latin America.
4. Identify the mid-latitude climate zones of Latin America.

SKILLBUILDERS: Interpreting Maps & Graphics pp. 207, 208

GeographicThinking

Seeing Patterns, p. 209
Making Inferences, p. 209

Focus & Motivate

Ask students to use this map to compare the vegetation of their community to that of Latin America.

Instruct: Objective 

A Varied Climate and Vegetation

- What are two of Latin America's climates? *(hot and humid Amazon River basin, dry and desert-like, tropical wet, and tropical wet and dry)*
- What two types of vegetation are produced by tropical climate zones found in Central America, the Caribbean, and South America? *(rain forests and savannas)*

In-Depth Resources: Unit 3
- Guided Reading, p. 4

SKILLBUILDER ANSWERS

1. Amazon River basin in northern South America **2.** temperate grasslands and desert and dry shrub

Instruct: Objective 2 appears on p. 208.

SECTION 2 PROGRAM RESOURCES

In-Depth Resources: Unit 3
- Guided Reading, p. 4
- Building Vocabulary, p. 9
- Reteaching Activity, p. 11
- GeoWorkshop, pp. 37–38

Guided Reading Workbook
- Section 2

Access for Students Acquiring English/ESL
- Guided Reading, p. 44

Formal Assessment
- Section Quiz, p. 132

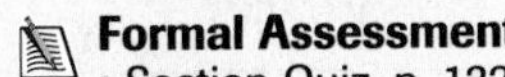

Integrated Assessment
- Rubric for a paragraph, 4.2

INTEGRATED TECHNOLOGY

Power Presentations

Test Generator
- Section Quiz

hmhsocialstudies.com

TEST-TAKING RESOURCES

Strategies for Test Preparation

Test Practice Transparencies TT29

Online Test Practice

Instruct: Objective 

Tropical Climate Zones

- What makes up an ecosystem? *(a community of plants and animals living in balance)*
- How much land is currently covered by Amazon rain forest? *(More than 2 million square miles.)*
- What countries have savannas? *(Brazil, Colombia, and Argentina)*

Instruct: Objective 

Dry Climate Zones

- What is a semiarid climate? *(dry, with some rain)*
- Which countries have regions of semiarid climate? *(Mexico, Brazil, Uruguay, Argentina)*

Interpreting Graphics

Vertical Climate Zones in Latin America

Because climatic conditions change as elevation increases, each country's topography determines which crops can be grown. Bananas and pineapples are major exports in Costa Rica. In Cuba, sugar, rice, and coffee are grown. Colombia and Jamaica are known for their coffee. Rice and sugar come from Guyana.

SKILLBUILDER ANSWERS

1. Lower elevations are more productive **2.** Most people would probably settle at low or moderate elevations.

Amazon rain forest, which covers more than two million square miles of South America. Much of this rain forest is located in Brazil.

Rain forests contain many exotic plants and creatures. Scientists have counted more than 2,500 varieties of trees in the Amazon rain forest. These include the Brazil nut tree, which grows 150 feet high. Animals include the anaconda, among the largest snakes in the world, the jaguar, and the piranha, a sharp-toothed, meat-eating fish.

BACKGROUND The anaconda lives in and near the rivers of tropical South America. It may grow as long as 25 feet.

TROPICAL WET AND DRY Wet and dry climates, found primarily in South America, support savannas, which are grasslands dotted with trees common in tropical and subtropical regions. These areas have hot climates with seasonal rain. Savannas are found in Brazil, Colombia, and Argentina.

Dry Climate Zones

Dry climate zones are found in Mexico on the North American continent and in various countries of South America. Neither Central America nor the Caribbean, though, has dry climate zones.

SEMIARID A semiarid climate is generally dry, with some rain. Vast, semiarid, grass-covered plains are often found in such climates. Desert shrubs also grow in semiarid regions. Such regions are found in Mexico, Brazil, Uruguay, and Argentina.

Vertical Climate Zones in Latin America

hmhsocialstudies.com INTERACTIVE

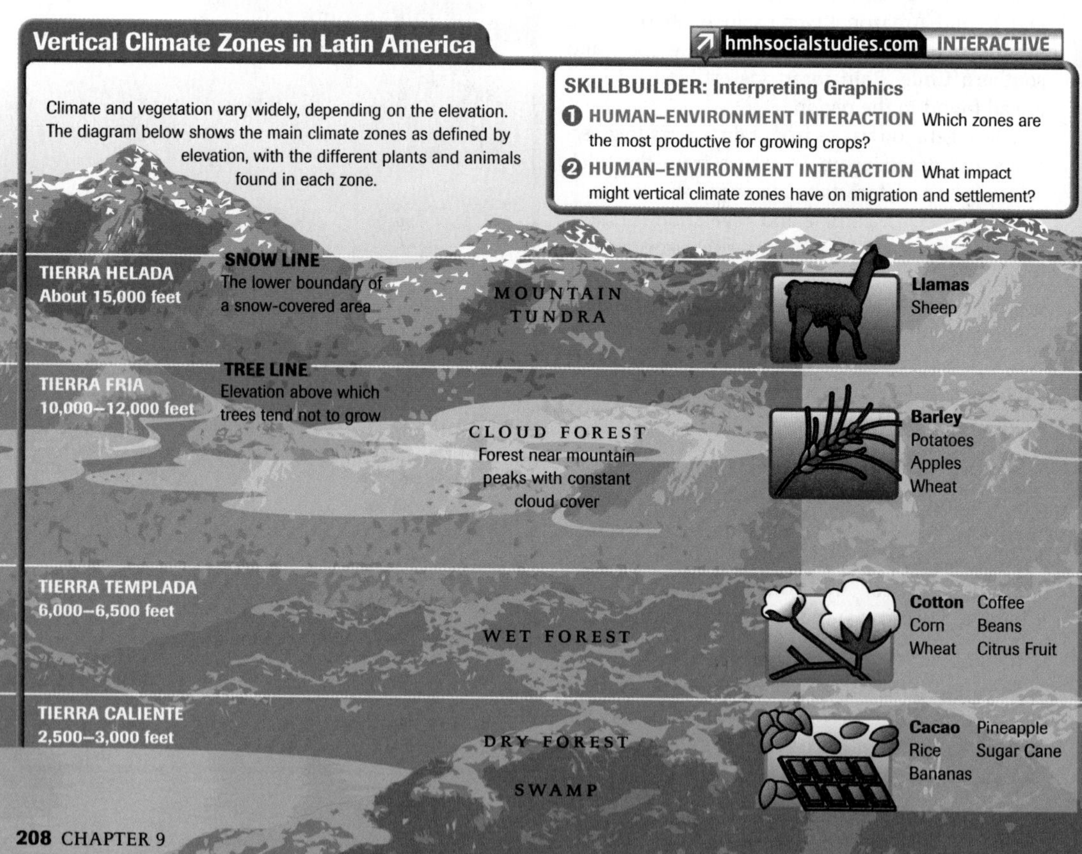

SKILLBUILDER: Interpreting Graphics

1. **HUMAN–ENVIRONMENT INTERACTION** Which zones are the most productive for growing crops?
2. **HUMAN–ENVIRONMENT INTERACTION** What impact might vertical climate zones have on migration and settlement?

DIFFERENTIATING INSTRUCTION | **LESS PROFICIENT READERS**

CREATING A GRAPHIC ORGANIZER

Objective To help students understand climate and vegetation.

Time 20 minutes

Task Create a graphic organizer

Directions Have students create a table with three rows and four columns. In the first column, have them list the following Climate Zones: Tropical, Dry, and Mid-Latitude. Above the remaining columns, have them list Climate Types, Characteristics, and Countries. Have students scan the text to find the climate types that make up the larger zone, its characteristics, and the countries where each zone is found.

CLIMATE ZONES	CLIMATE TYPES	CHARACTERISTICS	COUNTRIES
Tropical	Tropical wet Tropical wet & dry	hot, humid, rainy grasslands, rain forest, etc.	Brazil, Colombia, Argentina, etc.
Dry	Semiarid Desert		
Mid-Latitude	Humid subtropical Mediterranean Marine West Coast Highlands		

DESERT Parts of northern Mexico are classified as desert, as is much of the coast of Peru. The Atacama Desert is in northern Chile. Likewise, Argentina's southern zone, Patagonia, contains a desert. The vegetation of the region's deserts includes shrubs growing in gravel or sand.

Mid-Latitude Climate Zones

The mid-latitude, moderate climate zones in the region are located south of the equator, from approximately Rio de Janeiro in Brazil southward.

HUMID SUBTROPICAL Humid subtropical areas have rainy winters and hot, humid summers. Parts of Paraguay, Uruguay, southern Brazil, southern Bolivia, and northern Argentina (including Buenos Aires) are located in humid, subtropical climates. The vegetation is varied.

MEDITERRANEAN Mediterranean climate zones experience hot, dry summers and cool, moist winters. Part of Chile along the west coast is in this zone. The vegetation in a Mediterranean climate zone consists mainly of low shrubs and small trees.

MARINE WEST COAST Marine west coast climate zones are characterized by cool, rainy winters and mild, rainy summers. One such climate region runs along the coast of southwestern South America. Parts of southern Chile and Argentina have this climate. If you have spent time on the coast of Oregon or Washington, you have experienced a marine west coast climate. Forests are the typical vegetation.

HIGHLANDS Highland climate zones vary from moderate to cold, depending on elevation. Other factors influence highland climates, such as wind, sunlight, and landscape. Highland climates are found in the mountains of Mexico and South America. A

In the next section, you will read about how human-environment interaction affects the quality of life in Latin America.

A. Answer along the western coast of the continent, in the Andes Mountains and in Mexico

Geographic Thinking

Seeing Patterns
A Where are most of the highland climate zones located?

LATIN AMERICA

Section 2 Assessment

1 Places & Terms
Identify and explain where in the region this would be found.
- rain forest

2 Taking Notes
PLACE Review the notes you took for this section.

Climate and Vegetation

- What vegetation characterizes the Amazon River basin?
- What types of climate zones are found in Latin America?

3 Main Ideas
a. What are two reasons for the variety of climate and vegetation found in Latin America?
b. What effect might elevation have on growing crops and grazing livestock in the region?
c. What are the three main types of moderate climate zones in the region?

4 Geographic Thinking
Making Inferences How might the climate and vegetation of Latin America have affected migration, settlement, and ways of life? **Think about:**
- the impact of deserts and rain forests on settlement

ASKING GEOGRAPHIC QUESTIONS Research on the Internet the climate and vegetation in your state. Devise three geographic questions, such as "What is the dominant climate zone in my state?" Choose one of your questions and then write a **paragraph** explaining your findings. Be sure to list your sources.

21st CENTURY

Instruct: Objective 

Mid-Latitude Climate Zones

- Where are the mid-latitude climate zones in Latin America located? *(south of the Equator, from approximately Rio de Janerio in Brazil southward)*
- Where is the Latin American climate similar to that of Oregon or Washington state? *(along the southwestern coast of South America—the marine west coast)*
- What is the typical vegetation in the marine west coast, and why is this so? *(forest, because there is plenty of rain and the temperatures are mild)*

 **In-Depth Resources: Unit 3**
- GeoWorkshop, p. 37

Assess & Reteach

GeoFocus Have students complete the section on climate and vegetation in their graphic organizers.

Formal Assessment
- Section Quiz, p. 132

Reteaching Activity
Organize the class into groups of four students. Assign one of the four section objectives to each group member. Each member should write a short summary of the main idea covered under that objective. Members should then share their summaries with the rest of the group.

 **In-Depth Resources: Unit 3**
- Reteaching Activity, p. 11

SECTION 2 ASSESSMENT ANSWERS

1. Places and Terms
rain forest, p. 207

2. Taking Notes
- Rain forest
- A variety of climate zones can be found, ranging from hot and humid rain forests to desert. These include tropical wet, tropical wet and dry, semiarid, desert, humid subtropical, Mediterranean, marine west coast, and highland.

3. Main Ideas
a. The variety of climate and vegetation is due to the region's latitudinal span, elevation, and ocean currents.
b. Different crops grow better at different elevations, and different animals are better suited to different elevations.
c. humid subtropical, Mediterranean, marine west coast

4. Geographic Thinking
People tend to settle where it is easier for them to grow crops and graze their livestock. Temperate climates are easier for most settlers to adjust to.

GeoActivity

Integrated Assessment
- Rubric for a paragraph, 4.2

SECTION 3 OBJECTIVES

1. Identify how agriculture reshapes ecological the environment.
2. Describe the effects of urbanization and migration to cities.
3. Explain the positive and negative effects of tourism.

SKILLBUILDER: Interpreting Graphs p. 212

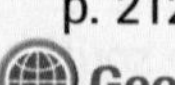 **GeographicThinking** Making Inferences, p. 213

Focus & Motivate

What is the relationship between the ecological environment and making a living? *(People grow food on the available fertile land. People who move to cities may end up in crowded, unhealthy areas.)*

Instruct: Objective 1 appears on p. 211

Interpreting Photographs

Slash-and-Burn Farming

Tell students that most farmers in the United States rotate crops each year to replenish nutrients in the soil. Ask students if there is a similar stage in the slash-and-burn process. *(After forest plants reclaim abandoned plots, the soil may eventually regain its fertility.)*

3 Human–Environment Interaction

Main Ideas

- The people of Latin America have altered the land through agriculture and urbanization.
- Tourism is having a growing impact on the environment of Latin America.

Places & Terms

slash-and-burn
terraced farming
push factors
pull factors
infrastructure

CONNECT TO THE ISSUES
INCOME GAP The income gap can be seen in the landless poor, the cities, and the tourist industry.

A HUMAN PERSPECTIVE High in the Andes Mountains, in what is present-day Peru, the ancient Inca needed fields in which to grow crops. By the 1200s, in the highlands around their capital of Cuzco and elsewhere, the Inca carved terraces out of the steep sides of the Andes Mountains. They built irrigation channels to bring water to the terraces. Because of their activity, they were able to grow crops for thousands of people on the slopes of previously barren hillsides. In this way, the Inca altered their environment to meet their needs.

Agriculture Reshapes the Environment

Native peoples were the first in the Western Hemisphere to change their environment to grow food. They burned the forest to clear land for planting and diverted streams to irrigate crops. They built raised fields in swampy areas and carved terraces out of hillsides.

SLASH-AND-BURN To clear fields, native peoples used the **slash-and-burn** technique—they cut trees, brush, and grasses and burned the debris to clear the field. This method was particularly effective in humid and tropical areas.

Today, farmers practice the same method as they move into the Amazon River basin in Brazil and clear land for farming in the rain forest. But the non-landowning poor who are clearing and then settling the

Slash-and-Burn Farming

1 Farmers cut trees, brush, and grasses to clear a field.

2 They then burn the debris and use the ashes to fertilize the soil.

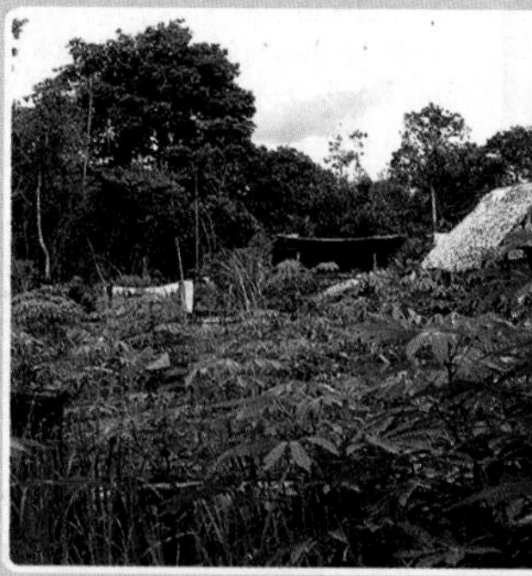

3 Farmers plant crops for a year or two, which exhausts the soil.

SECTION 3 PROGRAM RESOURCES

 **In-Depth Resources: Unit 3**
- Guided Reading, p. 5
- Skillbuilder Practice, p. 8
- Building Vocabulary, p. 9
- Reteaching Activity, p. 12

 **Guided Reading Workbook**
- Section 3

Access for Students Acquiring English
- Guided Reading, p. 45
- Skillbuilder Practice, p. 46

 **Formal Assessment**
- Section Quiz, p. 133

 **Integrated Assessment**
- Rubric for a travel poster, 1.1

INTEGRATED TECHNOLOGY

 **Power Presentations**

 **Test Generator**
- Section Quiz

hmhsocialstudies.com

TEST-TAKING RESOURCES

 **Strategies for Test Preparation**

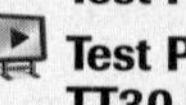 **Test Practice Transparencies TT30**

 **Online Test Practice**

Connect to the Issues
Resources
A What is the impact of slash-and-burn on the rain forest?
A. Answer The technique destroys the rain forest. This method is one of the main reasons the rain forests are shrinking.

land sometimes use destructive farming practices. After a few years, they find that the soil is exhausted—all the nutrients have been drained from the land. Then they move on and clear a new patch to farm. This is one of the reasons for the steady shrinking of the rain forests. (For more about the rain forest, see Chapter 11, Section 1, page 245.) A

TERRACED FARMING **Terraced farming** is an ancient technique for growing crops on hillsides or mountain slopes. It is an especially important technique in the mountainous areas of the region. Farmers and workers cut step-like horizontal fields into hillsides and slopes, which allow steep land to be cultivated for crops. The technique reduces soil erosion. As you read earlier, the Inca practiced terraced farming hundreds of years ago in Peru. The Aztecs of Mexico also used terraced farming.

Urbanization: The Move to the Cities

Throughout Latin America, people are moving from rural areas into the cities. They leave farms and villages in search of jobs and a better life. Cities have grown at such a rapid pace in Latin America that today the region is as urban as Europe or North America.

B. Answer Many of these factors motivate people to move to the cities in an attempt to improve their economic situation.

Connect to the Issues
Income Gap
B How might push and pull factors affect the gap between rich and poor?

FROM COUNTRY TO CITY Argentina, Uruguay, and Venezuela are the most highly urbanized countries in South America. In these countries, more than 90 percent of the people live in cities and towns. In Brazil and Chile, too, most people live in urban settings.

People move to the cities in the hope of improving their lives. Many people in rural areas struggle to make a living and feed their families by subsistence farming. With a great deal of effort, they grow barely enough food to keep themselves and their families alive.

Both push and pull factors are at work in moving peasants and farmers off the land and drawing them to the cities. **Push factors** are factors that "push" people to leave rural areas. They include poor medical care, poor education, low-paying jobs, and ownership of the land by a few rich people. **Pull factors** are factors that "pull" people toward cities. They include higher-paying jobs, better schools, and better medical care. B

Fields often remain barren or are reclaimed by brush, grass, trees, and scrub.

RAPIDLY GROWING CITIES Six cities in South America rank among the region's largest in population. These include São Paulo and Rio de Janeiro in Brazil, Buenos Aires in Argentina, Lima in Peru, Bogotá in Colombia, and Santiago in Chile. But the most populous city in all of Latin America is Mexico City. Estimates of its population vary from fewer than 9 million people for the city alone to over 21 million for the entire greater metropolitan area.

Similar problems afflict cities throughout the region. Slums spread over larger and larger urban areas. Often unemployment and crime increase. In addition to social problems, there are many environmental problems. These include high levels of air

LATIN AMERICA

Instruct: Objective 

Agriculture Reshapes the Environment

- To grow crops, native peoples in the Andes Mountains use what technique? *(terraced farming)*
- Where is the slash-and-burn technique of farming used today? *(Amazon River basin)*

 **In-Depth Resources: Unit 3**
- Guided Reading, p. 5

Instruct: Objective 2

Urbanization: The Move to the Cities

- What are the three most urbanized countries in South America? *(Argentina, Uruguay, Venezuela)*
- Why do people move to cities? *(better jobs, schools, medical care)*

More About

Urbanization

Despite the large area occupied by Brazil, more than 84 percent of Brazil's population lives in cities and towns, on a small portion of the land. The rural, less developed, and undeveloped areas are home to indigenous groups, who have had little contact with the outside world. Their distinct indentity may be undermined and lost if development continues as it has in the past.

ACTIVITY OPTION INTERNET RESEARCH

RESEARCHING FARMING IN THE RAIN FOREST

Objective To learn basic research methods

Class Time 60 minutes

Task Identify a number of sources of information about farming in the rain forest

Directions Have students use the key words "farming in rain forest" in an Internet search to research the impact of slash-and-burn and other practices on the rain forest. Ask students to find at least five facts about rain-forest farming methods. Call on different students to read their facts. Hold a class discussion on the different methods.

OPTIONAL ACTIVITY If Internet access is limited, have students use the library for this research. Have the librarian show the students how to use various indexes to find articles on the topic.

Instruct: Objective 3

Tourism: Positive and Negative Impacts

- What are two advantages of tourism? *(increased local employment and more money is introduced into local economy)*
- What are two disadvantages of tourism? *(congestion and pollution)*
- Why is there resentment between the local population and tourists in places like the Caribbean and Rio de Janeiro? *(The gap between rich tourists and less well-off residents causes resentment.)*

Interpreting Graphs

Growth of Cities, 1970–2005

Ask students to study the chart on this page. Ask students what the chart is comparing. *(the growth of cities between 1970 and 2005)* Ask them what the blue stands for, and what the green stands for. *(1970, 2005)*

SKILLBUILDER ANSWERS

1. Mexico City, Mexico City
2. São Paulo and Mexico City

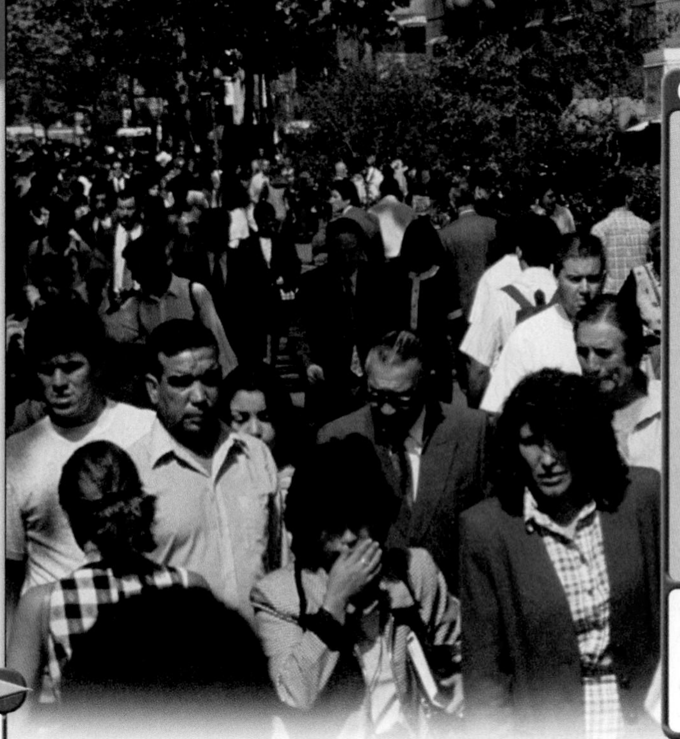

PLACE Pedestrians crowd a street in Santiago, Chile.

Growth of Metropolitian Areas, 1970–2005

People in Millions: 0, 5, 10, 15, 20

Bogotá, Buenos Aires, Lima, Mexico City, Rio de Janeiro, São Pau

1970 | 2005

SOURCE: *World Population Prospects: The 2004 Revision and World Urbanizatio Prospects: The 2005 Revision*

SKILLBUILDER: Interpreting Graphs

1. **MAKING COMPARISONS** Which city had the largest population in 1970? In 2005?
2. **MAKING COMPARISONS** Which two cities showed the biggest increase in population between 1970 and 2005?

pollution from cars and factories. Some cities have shortages of drinkable water as local supplies are used up and underwater supplies are drained.

To make matters worse, local governments cannot afford facilities to handle the population increase. This **infrastructure** includes such things as sewers, transportation, electricity, and housing.

Tourism: Positive and Negative Impacts

Tourism is a growth industry throughout Latin America. It is especially important in Mexico and the Caribbean. But despite the money it brings in to the economies of the region, tourism is a mixed blessing.

ADVANTAGES OF TOURISM Every year millions of tourists visit the resorts of Latin America, spending money and helping to create jobs. New hotels, restaurants, boutiques, and other businesses have sprung up on the islands of the Caribbean and in Mexico to serve the tourist trade. Luxurious cruise ships anchor in the ports of the region. They carry travelers who spend money on souvenirs and trips around the islands. Lavish restaurants serve expensive meals to these tourists. Staffing those ships, hotels, and restaurants are local people who profit from the visitors in their midst.

Resorts offer many activities that provide jobs for local residents. For example, local guides conduct tours of the natural wonders and beautiful scenery. Local companies may offer guided rafting trips down rivers. Sailing and snorkeling expeditions into the waters of the Caribbean and Pacific reveal exotic marine life. All of these activities bring money into the region and employ local people.

ACTIVITY OPTION | **SKILLBUILDER LESSON**

IDENTIFYING AND SOLVING PROBLEMS

Explaining the Skill Tell students that identifying and solving problems means finding and understanding the difficulties faced by a particular group of people at a certain time. In addition, it means noticing how people solved their problems.

Applying the Skill Have pairs of students discuss the following problems typical of urbanization. After 10 minutes, have each team share possible solutions to each problem with the class.

- slums *(building of low-income housing)*
- unemployment *(job training in needed skills)*
- crime *(expanding police force; reducing poverty)*
- pollution *(setting legal standards for clean air and water)*
- infrastructure *(national investment improving sewers, transportation, etc.)*

In-Depth Resources: Unit 3
- Skillbuilder Practice, p. 8

In this way, tourism can play a part in reducing the income gap between rich and poor. Jobs in hotels, restaurants, and resorts raise incomes and give the local people a stake in their society.

DISADVANTAGES OF TOURISM Despite the income and jobs that tourism brings to various places in Latin America, it causes problems as well. As resorts are built in previously unspoiled settings, congestion occurs and pollution increases.

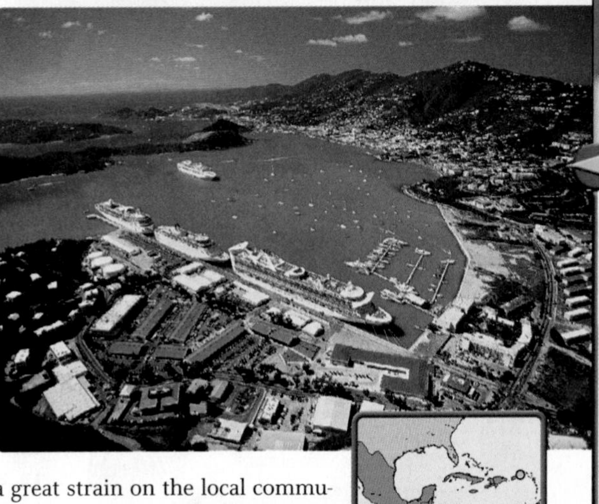

HUMAN–ENVIRONMENT INTERACTION A luxury cruise ship is docked in the beautiful harbor of Charlotte Amalie, St. Thomas in the Virgin Islands. **What might be the impact of tourists on the local economy?**

LATIN AMERICA

The tourism industry often puts a great strain on the local communities where it builds its resorts. Further, there is an obvious gap between rich tourists and less well-off local residents. This has produced resentment and hostility in places such as Jamaica in the Caribbean and Rio de Janeiro in Brazil.

More important, local governments can run up large public debts by borrowing money to build tourist facilities. Airports and harbors must be constructed. Hotels and resorts must be built. Sewage systems and shopping areas must be expanded.

Often the owners of these hotels and airlines do not live in the tourist country. Typically, they send their profits back home. Further, these absentee owners often make decisions that are not in the tourist country's best interest. The owners may be able to influence local elections and business decisions. C

In the next chapter, you will read about the human geography of Latin America, including its history, culture, economics, and daily life.

C. Answer Owners who do not live in the country can have great influence on local development, more than the local residents who live and vote there.

CONNECT TO THE ISSUES
DEMOCRACY
C How might absentee ownership of tourist facilities undermine democracy in a tourist country?

Interpreting Photographs

Harbor in Charlotte Amalie
Ask students: What can you tell about this port by studying the photograph on page 213? *(Cruise ships and yachts indicate the port is used partly for tourists and pleasure boating.)*

CAPTION ANSWER Tourists spend money that circulates in the local economy, creating jobs for local residents.

More About

Tourism in Rio de Janeiro
Tell students that Carnival, the pre-Lenten festival is held every year. Many of the local people cannot afford to take part in formal parades, with the wealthy and the tourists taking over more and more of the festival activities.

SECTION 3 Assessment

1 Places & Terms
Identify and explain the significance of each in the region.
- slash-and-burn
- terraced farming
- push factors
- pull factors
- infrastructure

2 Taking Notes
HUMAN-ENVIRONMENT INTERACTION Review the notes you took for this section.

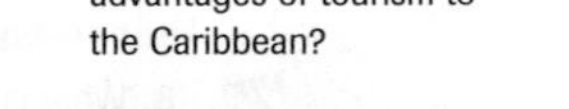

- What are the steps in slash-and-burn farming?
- What are some of the problems of cities in the region?

3 Main Ideas
a. How have humans changed the environment in Latin America to make it more suitable for agriculture?
b. What factors have drawn people from the countryside into the cities of the region?
c. What are some of the advantages of tourism to the Caribbean?

4 Geographic Thinking
Making Inferences How might the cities of Latin America deal with the increasing demands placed on them by their expanding populations? **Think about:**
- water, sewage, and electricity
- transportation and housing

See Skillbuilder Handbook, page R4.

SEEING PATTERNS Pair with a partner and create a **travel poster** about a place in the region that you would like to visit. Show various activities and sports available at the place you choose.

Assess & Reteach

Geo Focus
Have students complete their graphic organizers for this section.

Formal Assessment
- Section Quiz, p. 133

Reteaching Activity
Have students work with a partner. Using the material in this section, have each partner write five questions. Partners should then exchange papers and answer each other's questions.

In-Depth Resources: Unit 3
- Reteaching Activity, p. 12

SECTION 3 ASSESSMENT ANSWERS

1. Places & Terms
slash-and-burn, p. 210
terraced farming, p. 211
push factors, p. 211
pull factors, p. 211
infrastructure, p. 212

2. Taking Notes
- First, cut trees and brush; second, burn debris and fertilize soil with ashes; third, plant crops; fourth, once soil is exhausted, move on.
- slums, unemployment, crime, pollution, shortages of water

3. Main Ideas
a. slash-and-burn and terraced farming
b. higher-paying jobs, better schools, better medical care
c. Tourism creates jobs for local residents, which puts money in their pockets and may help to narrow the gap between rich and poor.

4. Geographic Thinking
The cities of Latin America might deal with increasing population demands by expanding their water, sewage, electrical capacities, housing, and public transportation.

GeoActivity

Integrated Assessment
- Rubric for a travel poster, 1.1

Reviewing Places & Terms

A. **1.** Andes Mountains, p. 201
2. llanos, p. 202
3. pampas, p. 202
4. Orinoco River, p. 202
5. Amazon River, p. 203
6. rain forest, p. 207
7. slash-and-burn, p. 210
8. terraced farming, p. 211
9. push factors, p. 211
10. infrastructure, p. 212

B. Possible Responses

11. The Orinoco drains Venezuela and Colombia.
12. They are located long the Pacific coast of South America.
13. Slash-and-burn involves using ashes.
14. They are plains that provide soil for growing crops and grass for grazing livestock.
15. Slums, unemployment, crime, pollution are some of the problems.
16. The Amazon drains the largest rain forest.
17. Poor medical care, poor education, low-paying jobs, few people owning most of the land are factors pulling farmers off the land.
18. The Orinoco is the northernmost of the great rivers.
19. Terraced farming is useful in the mountains.
20. Cattle and wheat grain are the main products of the pompas.

Chapter 9 Assessment

VISUAL SUMMARY
PHYSICAL GEOGRAPHY OF LATIN AMERICA

Landforms

Major Mountain Ranges: Andes, Sierra Madres

Major Rivers: Orinoco, Amazon, Paraná

Major Plains: pampas of Argentina and Uruguay, llanos of Colombia and Venezuela, cerrado of Brazil

Resources

- Latin America has important mineral and energy resources.
- Venezuela and Mexico have major oil reserves.

Climate and Vegetation

- The variety of climate and vegetation in Latin America is caused by the great distance from north to south, variations in elevation, and ocean currents.
- Latin America has many rain forests.

Human-Environment Interaction

- Two techniques that farmers have used in the region are slash-and-burn and terraced farming.
- Cities in Latin America have grown at a rapid pace, and the region is now highly urbanized.
- Tourism has both advantages and disadvantages for the region.

Reviewing Places & Terms

A. Briefly explain the importance of each of the following.

1. Andes Mountains
2. llanos
3. pampas
4. Orinoco River
5. Amazon River
6. rain forest
7. slash-and-burn
8. terraced farming
9. push factors
10. infrastructure

B. Answer the questions about vocabulary in complete sentences.

11. What two countries does the Orinoco River drain?
12. Where are the Andes Mountains located?
13. What agricultural technique involves using ashes to fertilize the soil?
14. What characteristics do the pampas and llanos have in common?
15. What are some of the problems that afflict cities throughout the region?
16. Which river drains the largest rain forest in the region?
17. What are some factors that are pushing farmers off the land and into the cities?
18. Which is the northernmost of the great rivers of South America?
19. What farming technique is especially useful in mountainous regions?
20. What are the main products of the pampas?

Main Ideas

Landforms and Resources (pp. 201–206)

1. How have the Andes Mountains affected settlement in South America?
2. What are the two main purposes for which the plains and grasslands of the region are used?
3. What are the three major island groups of the Caribbean?
4. What Caribbean island is rich in natural gas, and what impact has this had on the economy?

Climate and Vegetation (pp. 207–209)

5. In what part of the region are savannas most common?
6. How do the vertical climate zones of Latin America affect agriculture?
7. What is the dominant vegetation of the Amazon river basin?

Human-Environment Interaction (pp. 210–213)

8. What is the main disadvantage of the slash-and-burn method of growing crops?
9. What factors tend to pull people into the cities from their farms?
10. What are some of the disadvantages of tourism in the region?

Main Ideas

1. The Andes Mountains have made settlement moving east from the Pacific coast more difficult because they are a barrier to movement into the interior. As a result, more settlement has occurred along the eastern and northern coasts.
2. growing crops and grazing livestock
3. Bahamas, Greater Antilles, Lesser Antilles
4. Trinidad—factories have sprung up to manufacture methanol and ammonia; developers have been attracted to the island
5. South America
6. People grow different crops depending on the elevation at which they live.
7. rain forest
8. It quickly exhausts the soil.
9. higher-paying jobs, better schools, better medical care
10. congestion, pollution, strain on local communities, gap between rich and poor, large public debt, profits not reinvested in tourist country, influence of nonresidents on local affairs

Critical Thinking

1. Using Your Notes

Use your completed chart to answer these questions.

Landforms	
Resources	

a. Where are most of the mountains of South America located?

b. What are some examples of mineral and energy resources found in abundance in Latin America?

2. Geographic Themes

a. LOCATION Where are some of the largest plains found in Latin America?

b. REGION What are the settlement patterns of South America in terms of the interior and the coast?

3. Identifying Themes

Based on landforms and climate, which areas of Latin America would be the least agriculturally productive? Which of the five themes are reflected in your answer?

4. Drawing Conclusions

What factors must people in the region consider when they are deciding whether to move from the country to the city?

5. Making Comparisons

What are some of the advantages and disadvantages of tourism to a community?

For Additional Test Practice

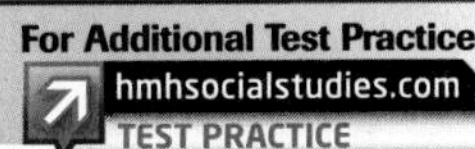

Geographic Skills: Interpreting Maps

The Tributaries of the Amazon

Use the map to answer the following questions.

1. MOVEMENT In what general direction do the Amazon and its tributaries flow?
2. PLACE Into which ocean does the Amazon empty?
3. REGION What countries are drained by the Amazon and its tributaries?

PANAMA, VENEZUELA, SURINAME, GUYANA, FRENCH GUIANA (Fr.), ATLANTIC OCEAN, COLOMBIA, ECUADOR, PERU, BRAZIL, BOLIVIA, PARAGUAY, ARGENTINA, Manaus, Belém, Brasília, Lake Titicaca, Amazon R., Negro R., Branco R., Putumayo R., Solimões R., Marañón R., Ucayali R., Purús R., Madeira R., Tapajós R., Xingu R., Tocantins R., Araguaia R., Equator 0°, 80°W, 70°W, 60°W, 50°W, 10°S, 20°S

Amazon River basin

0 250 500 miles
0 250 500 kilometers
Azimuthal Equal-Area Projection

Create your own sketch map of the physical geography of Latin America. Combine the information from this map with the information from the landforms map on page 203.

hmhsocialstudies.com

MULTIMEDIA ACTIVITY

Use the links at **hmhsocialstudies.com** to do research on the most rapidly growing cities in Latin America. Focus on the impact that rapid growth has on the residents of a city.

Writing About Geography Write a report of your findings. Include a map that shows the fastest growing cities. Combine it with a chart that lists common problems of rapid growth.

CHAPTER 9 ASSESSMENT

Critical Thinking

1. **a.** Most of mountains are along the western coast.
   b. Mineral resources include gold, silver, iron, copper, bauxite, tin, lead, and nickel. Energy resources include oil, coal, natural gas, uranium, and hydroelectric power.
2. **a.** Pampas of Argentina and Uruguay, llanos of Colombia and Venezuela, and cerrado of Brazil are among largest plains in the region.
   b. On the west coast, the Andes Mountains were a barrier that tended to limit settlement there. Along the eastern coast of South America, most of the early settlements were along the coast.
3. High-altitude zones in the mountains, semiarid, and desert zones such as the Atacama Desert in Chile would be the least agriculturally productive. Mainly region and human-environment interaction are reflected in the answer.
4. They must consider medical care, jobs, education, and opportunity.
5. Advantages: jobs for residents which help to reduce the income gap; disadvantages: pollution, congestion, and debt incurred by local governments

GeoActivity

Integrated Assessment
- Rubric for a sketch map, 2.1

Formal Assessment
- Chapter Test, Forms A, B, and C, pp. 134-145

Geographic Skills

1. The Amazon flows mainly west to east, and its tributaries flow mainly northeast and southwest.
2. the Atlantic Ocean
3. Brazil, Bolivia, Colombia, Ecuador, Peru, Venezuela (partly)

MULTIMEDIA ACTIVITY

For a report on rapidly growing cities in Latin America, students should:

- present concise, well-organized information on rapidly growing cities.
- summarize the effects that rapid growth has on a city's residents.
- produce clear, imaginative visuals (map and chart).
- include references to the Web sites used as sources.

Grading Rubric Evaluate student performance as Exceptional, Acceptable, or Poor in each of the following categories:

	Exceptional	*Acceptable*	*Poor*
Writing is clear, focused, and logical			
Sentences clearly state information			
Sentences provide necessary facts and examples			
Sentences use correct grammar, spelling, and punctuation			

CHAPTER 10 PLANNING GUIDE

Human Geography of Latin America

OVERVIEW	INSTRUCTIONAL RESOURCES	
ESSENTIAL QUESTION Which cultures have influenced Latin America? **Focus on the Essential Question Podcast**	**In-Depth Resources: Unit 3** • Building Vocabulary, p.18 **Block Schedule Strategies** **Chapter Summaries** (English/Spanish) **Multimedia Connections** • Mexico hmhsocialstudies.com INTERACTIVE	**Interactive Online Edition** TOS **ExamView® Assessment Suite** (English/Spanish) TOS **CalendarPlanner** **Power Presentations with Media Gallery** **Critical Thinking Transparencies** • CT10 **Video:** Mexico's Ancient Civilizations
SECTION 1 **MEXICO** **MAIN IDEAS** • Native and Spanish influences have shaped Mexico. • Mexico's economy may expand because of democracy and trade.	**In-Depth Resources: Unit 3** • Guided Reading, p. 13 • Skillbuilder Practice, p. 17 • Building Vocabulary, p. 18 • Reteaching Activity, p. 19 **Outline Maps with Activities** • Mexico, pp. 21–22 **Cultures around the World** • Fine Arts, p. 15	**Critical Thinking Transparencies** • CT42 Population Geography in Selected Latin American Countries **Cultures Transparencies** • CW15 Frida Kahlo **Guided Reading Workbook,** Section 1
SECTION 2 **CENTRAL AMERICA AND THE CARIBBEAN** **MAIN IDEAS** • Native peoples, Europeans, and Africans have shaped the culture of Central America and the Caribbean. • Agriculture and tourism are the basis of the economies in the region.	**In-Depth Resources: Unit 3** • Guided Reading, p. 14 • Building Vocabulary, p. 18 • Reteaching Activity, p. 20 **Outline Maps with Activities** • Central America and the Caribbean, pp. 23–24 **Cultures around the World** • Daily Life, p. 14 • Arts and Crafts, p. 17 **Guided Reading Workbook,** Section 2	**Cultures Transparencies** • CW14 Selling Food at Market • CW17 Andean Textiles **Map Transparencies** • MT19 Native Peoples of Latin America **Video:** Panama Canal: Locks **Video:** Earthquakes
SECTION 3 **SPANISH-SPEAKING SOUTH AMERICA** **MAIN IDEAS** • The culture of South America has been shaped by native peoples and settlers from Spain. • The standard of living in the region may improve through regional economic cooperation.	**In-Depth Resources: Unit 3** • Guided Reading, p. 15 • Building Vocabulary, p. 18 • Reteaching Activity, p. 21 **Outline Maps with Activities** • Spanish-Speaking South America, pp. 25–26 **Cultures around the World** • Architecture, p. 13 • Traditional Practices, p. 18	**Cultures Transparencies** • CW13 Machu Picchu • CW18 Charro **Guided Reading Workbook,** Section 3 **The World's Music Audio Program**
SECTION 4 **BRAZIL** **MAIN IDEAS** • Brazil has been shaped by native peoples, Portuguese, and Africans. • Brazil is the largest country in Latin America, both in population and territory.	**In-Depth Resources: Unit 3** • Guided Reading, p. 16 • Building Vocabulary, p. 18 • Reteaching Activity, p. 22 **Outline Maps with Activities** • Brazil, pp. 27–28 **Cultures around the World** • Dance, p. 16	**Cultures Transparencies** • CW16 Dancing the Tango **Guided Reading Workbook,** Section 4

ASSESSMENT

SE **Chapter Assessment,** pp. 242-243

Formal Assessment

- Chapter Tests, Forms A, B, and C, pp. 150-161

TOS **ExamView® Assessment Suite**

Strategies for Test Preparation

hmhsocialstudies.com TEST PRACTICE

SE **Section Assessment,** p. 221

Formal Assessment

- Section Quiz, p. 146

Integrated Assessment

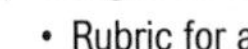

- Rubric for a chart, 2.2

Test Practice Transparencies TT31

SE **Section Assessment,** p. 227

Formal Assessment

- Section Quiz, p. 147

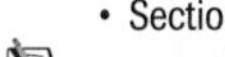

Integrated Assessment

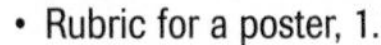

- Rubric for a poster, 1.1
- Rubric for presentation, 3.6

Test Practice Transparencies TT32

SE **Section Assessment,** p. 235

Formal Assessment

- Section Quiz, p. 148

Integrated Assessment

- Rubric for a sketch map, 2.1

Test Practice Transparencies TT33

SE **Section Assessment,** p. 239

Formal Assessment

- Section Quiz, p. 149

Integrated Assessment

- Rubric for a map, 2.1
- Rubric for a poster, 1.1

Test Practice Transparencies TT34

CHART KEY:

SE Student Edition

Block Scheduling

DVD/CD-ROM

TE Teacher's Edition

TOS Teacher One Stop

MP3 Audio

Printable Resource

Presentation Resource

HISTORY™

Program Resources available on TOS and @

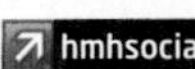

SUPPORTING RESOURCES

- **Multimedia Classroom Global History Series**
- **Global History Teacher's Guide**

Social Studies Trade Library Collection

- Latino Trade Collection

For more information or to purchase these resources, go to

DIFFERENTIATED INSTRUCTION

English Learners	Struggling Readers	Gifted and Talented Students
Spanish/English Guided Reading Workbook	**Chapter Summaries** (English/Spanish)	TE **TE Activity** Tracing Family Histories, p. 218
Access for Students Acquiring English/ESL Spanish Translations, pp. 49–53	TE **TE Activity** Creating a Graphic Organizer, p. 237	
Chapter Summaries (English/Spanish)		
TE **TE Activity** Researching Personal Histories, p. 219		

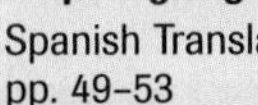

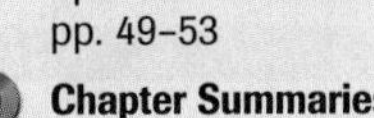

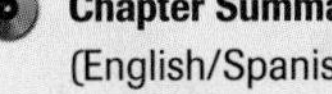

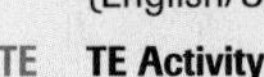

ENRICHMENT ACTIVITIES

The following activities are especially suitable for classes following block schedules.

SE **Student Edition,** pp. 216–243

- Disasters!: The Haiti and Chile Earthquakes, pp. 228–229
- Comparing Cultures: Festivals and Holidays, pp. 240–241

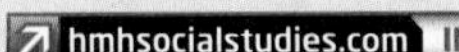

- Population Distribution in Mexican States, p. 220
- Comparing Cultures: Festivals and Holidays, pp. 240–241

CHAPTER 10 PACING GUIDE

BLOCK SCHEDULE LESSON PLAN OPTIONS: 90-MINUTE PERIOD

DAY 1

SECTION 1, pp. 217-221
Class Time 45 minutes

- **Small Group Discussion** As a way to review the section, divide the class into groups of four. Give each group an issue from the section, such as the impact of colonialism or the condition of Mexico's economy. Ask the groups to discuss the issue and raise important points about that issue. Then, have each group appoint a spokesperson to restate the key points of their issue to the class.

SECTION 2, pp. 222-229
Class Time 45 minutes

- **Economic Roundtable** To review the economic concerns of Central America and the Caribbean, divide the class into four groups, each one representing a different economic issue. Possible issues to raise include agriculture, trade, tourism, and the informal economy of the subregion.
Class Time 25 minutes

- **Skillbuilder Lesson** Use the Skillbuilder Practice worksheet for Section 1 and the Activity Option about Making Comparisons on TE page 224.
Class Time 20 minutes

DAY 2

SECTION 3, pp. 230-235
Class Time 90 minutes

- **Regions Table** Lead the class in creating a table with four rows for the headings "History," "Culture," "Economics," and "Education." Then ask students to insert the appropriate information for each topic.
Class Time 45 minutes

- **Documentary Sources** To follow up on the Disasters! feature between sections 2 and 3, show students part of a video or some photographs related to the disaster event.
Class Time 45 minutes

DAY 3

SECTION 4, pp. 236-241
Class Time 30 minutes

- **Economy Map** Draw a rough outline of Brazil on the board. Ask students to close their books and recall which areas contain which resources. Make a small map key to the side similar to that on PE p. 238. Ask students to take turns going up to the board and drawing the appropriate icon in the appropriate area.

CHAPTER 10 REVIEW AND ASSESSMENT, pp. 242-243
Class Time 60 minutes

- **Review** Have students prepare a summary of the chapter using the words in the Places and Terms on the first page of each section.
Class Time 25 minutes

- **Assessment** Have students complete the Chapter 10 Assessment
Class Time 35 minutes

TEACHER-TESTED ACTIVITY *Vocabulary Graphics*

Class Time One class period

Task Create vocabulary graphics for the vocabulary terms in Chapter 10

Supplies
- map pencils
- blank paper or pre-created sheets

Purpose To develop further understanding of vocabulary terms that are essential to grasping concepts of the chapter.

Activity For each of the vocabulary words listed under Places & Terms, have students write a definition in their own words. For words that lend themselves to illustration, have students draw a picture or make a graphic illustrating the definition. Finally, students may choose two or three terms and make an illustration showing the terms in an interrelated picture.

Joy McKee
Geography Teacher, Lamar High School, Arlington, Texas

TECHNOLOGY IN THE CLASSROOM

The Internet offers a wealth of numerical data that can be helpful for student research and to supplement topics students are learning about. Some Web sites even allow users to specify how they'd like to see the data presented. When students use this type of site, they not only practice their statistical analysis skills, but they also learn about ways that the Internet can be used to effectively organize and present numerical information. In this activity, they'll generate charts of economic and social statistics by inputting their requests into interactive forms.

Objective Students will use the interactive forms on a Web site to compare and contrast economic and social indicators for seven Latin American countries.

Task Have students compare and contrast such indicators as GDP per capita, life expectancy, and unemployment rates by using an Internet program that's specifically designed to do this type of analysis. Ask them to write an interpretation of the data.

Class Time 1 class period

1. Ask students to go to the Website at **hmhsocialstudies.com,** and explain that they're going to look at some data for Latin American countries that will tell them about the countries' economies and standards of living.
2. Have students click the boxes in the right-hand frame next to the following countries: Brazil, Chile, Peru, Dominican Republic, El Salvador, Haiti, and Mexico. Then have them click "Data Menu."
3. Ask students to select the following data fields: GDP per capita, unemployment, life expectancy (women/men), and illiteracy rate (total).
4. Discuss the meanings of these four data fields, making sure students understand what each one measures. Ask them to explain what they think each type of data reveals about a country. For example, what does it mean for one country to have a much lower life expectancy or per capita income than another country?
5. Have students click "view info." to view the data. Ask them to look carefully at the chart and compare the data for the different countries. Which country appears to be in the best shape, and which appears to have the most problems?
6. Have students return to the data field page, and discuss the meanings of some of the other indicators, such as population density, population under 15 years old, infant mortality, and spending on education. Based on what they've learned about the seven countries so far, how do they predict the countries would compare on these indicators? Have students find out by selecting these data fields and clicking "view info."
7. Have students refer to Chapter 10 to find out some of the reasons for the statistics they've seen. Ask them to write a brief description of how the countries compare to one another and explaining some of the reasons why this might be the case.

CHAPTER 10 OBJECTIVE

Identify key features of Latin America's blending of cultures.

Chapter 10

HUMAN GEOGRAPHY OF LATIN AMERICA

A Blending of Cultures

Interpreting Maps

Four Subregions of Latin America

Have students examine the map, then name the four subregions of Latin America. *(Mexico, Central America and the Caribbean, Spanish-Speaking South America, Brazil)*

Extension Have students suggest other ways the region might be divided.

Introducing the Essential Question

- Point out that the four subregions of Latin America differ in many ways but also share several cultural features.
- Describe the conflicts between the region's native cultures and the Spanish and Portuguese conquerors.
- Explain that Latin America's colonial era has affected the region's cultural and political history.

hmhsocialstudies.com TAKING NOTES

Have students copy the graphic organizer online into their notebooks and fill it in using material from all sections in this chapter.

Critical Thinking Transparencies CT10
- GeoFocus

In-Depth Resources: Unit 3
- Building Vocabulary, p. 18

Four Subregions of Latin America hmhsocialstudies.com INTERACTIVE MAP

Mexico
Central America and the Caribbean
Spanish-Speaking South America
Brazil

Essential Question

Which cultures have influenced Latin America?

What You Will Learn

In this chapter you will compare and contrast features of Latin America's human geography.

SECTION 1
Mexico

SECTION 2
Central America and the Caribbean

SECTION 3
Spanish-Speaking South America

SECTION 4
Brazil

hmhsocialstudies.com TAKING NOTES

Use the graphic organizer online to take notes on Latin America's history, economics, culture, and modern life.

216

CHAPTER 10 SUPPORTING RESOURCES

BOOKS FOR THE TEACHER

Peter H. Smith, ***Democracy in Latin America: Political Change in Comparative Perspective.*** Oxford University Press, 2005. Analysis of issues related to the move toward democracy.

McCullough, David. ***Path Between the Seas.*** NY: Simon & Schuster, 1999. A chronicle of the Panama Canal.

BOOKS FOR THE STUDENT

Santiago, Esmeralda. ***When I Was Puerto Rican.*** NY: Vintage Books, 1994. A young woman's story about growing up Puerto Rican.

Franz, Carl. ***The People's Guide to Mexico: Wherever You Go . . . There You Are!! (11th ed).*** NY: Avalon Travel Publishing, 1998. Comprehensive guide to Mexico.

VIDEOS

Touring Mexico. Questar Video, Inc., 1989. A tour of Mexico, including the history and culture.

National Geographic's Jewels of the Caribbean Sea. National Geographic video, 1994. Information on the exotic sea creatures in the Caribbean Sea.

INTERNET

For more on the human geography of Latin America, visit . . .

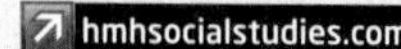

1 Mexico

Main Ideas
- Native and Spanish influences have shaped Mexico.
- Mexico's economy may expand because of democracy and trade.

Places & Terms

Spanish conquest
Tenochtitlán
Institutional Revolutionary Party (PRI)
mestizo
maquiladoras
NAFTA

CONNECT TO THE ISSUES
DEMOCRACY Economic development is helping to shape the increasingly democratic culture of Mexico.

A HUMAN PERSPECTIVE Quetzalcoatl (keht•SAHL•koh•AHT•l) was a god worshiped by the Toltec and Aztec peoples of Mexico and Central America. According to Native American legend, Quetzalcoatl traveled east across the sea. It was said that he would return some day, bringing peace. One day, messengers brought Montezuma, the Aztec emperor, news that strangers had arrived from across the sea. Montezuma thought that these strangers might be Quetzalcoatl and his servants. Instead, it was Hernando Cortés and his soldiers, who would claim the land for Spain. When the Spanish landed, the cultures of two widely separated regions came into contact, which forever changed the Aztec and Spanish worlds—and made Mexico what it is today.

Colonialism and Independence 1

The history of Mexico is the story of the conflict between native peoples and settlers from Spain and the Spanish conquest of the region. The result was a blending of Indian and Spanish cultures that has greatly affected Mexico's development.

NATIVE AMERICANS AND THE SPANISH CONQUEST The territory of present-day Mexico was originally occupied by many different native peoples. These people included the residents of Teotihuacán, an early city-state, the Toltecs, the Maya (in the Yucatán Peninsula), and the Aztecs, as well as a number of other smaller groups or tribes.

The rich fabric of native life in Mexico was torn apart by the **Spanish conquest**. In 1519, Hernando Cortés landed on the coast of Mexico. Cortés and his men marched into the interior of the country until they reached the Aztec city of **Tenochtitlán** (teh•NOH•tee•TLAHN), the site today of Mexico City. By 1521, Cortés and his soldiers had conquered the Aztecs.

COLONY AND COUNTRY For centuries afterward, Mexico was a part of the Spanish empire. Mexico's abundant resources, such as gold and silver, made it a great prize. In 1821, Mexico achieved independence from Spain under Agustín de Iturbide, who proclaimed himself emperor in 1822. Then,

PLACE Independence Monument stands at a busy intersection of the Paseo de la Reforma in Mexico City.

217

SECTION 1 OBJECTIVES

1. Explain colonialism and independence in Mexico.
2. Understand the blending of the native and Spanish influences in Mexico.
3. Understand the economics of cities and factories in Mexico.
4. Explore Mexican life today.

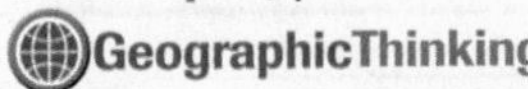

SKILLBUILDER: Interpreting Maps and Graphs, p. 220

GeographicThinking
Seeing Patterns, p. 219
Making Generalizations, p. 221

Focus & Motivate

Ask students what they know about colonialism and independence in the United States. What similarities might there be between the U.S. struggle for independence and that of Mexico? *(fought against European control)*

Instruct: Objective 1

Colonialism and Independence

- The conflict between which groups has affected Mexico's development? *(native people, settlers from Spain)*
- How was life changed by the Spanish conquest? *(The rich fabric of native life was torn apart.)*
- How might Mexico be different if the Spanish had never conquered it? *(might have been exclusively Native American culture)*

In-Depth Resources: Unit 3
- Guided Reading, p. 13
- Skillbuilder Practice, p. 17

SECTION 1 PROGRAM RESOURCES

In-Depth Resources: Unit 3
- Guided Reading, p. 13
- Skillbuilder Practice, p. 17
- Building Vocabulary, p. 18
- Reteaching Activity, p. 19

Guided Reading Workbook
- Section 1

Access for Students Acquiring English
- Guided Reading, p. 49
- Skillbuilder Practice, p. 53

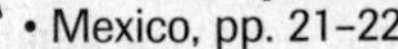

Outline Maps with Activities
- Mexico, pp. 21–22

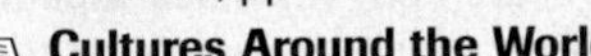

Cultures Around the World
- Fine Arts, p. 15

Formal Assessment
- Section Quiz, p. 146

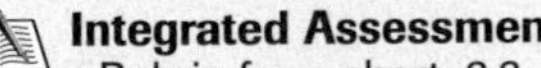

Integrated Assessment
- Rubric for a chart, 2.2

INTEGRATED TECHNOLOGY

Critical Thinking Transparencies CT42
- Population Geography in Selected Latin American Countries

Cultures Transparencies, CW15
- Frida Kahlo

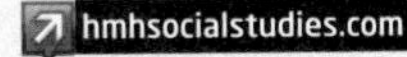

hmhsocialstudies.com

TEST-TAKING RESOURCES

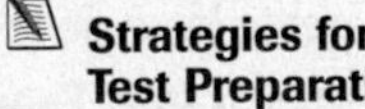

Strategies for Test Preparation

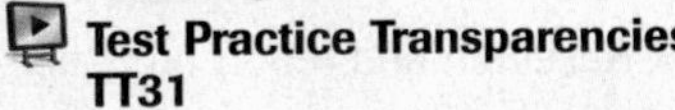

Test Practice Transparencies TT31

Online Test Practice

Interpreting Timelines

Mexican History

Have students study the timeline of Mexican history on this page. Have them compare the following dates in U.S. history to those in Mexican history: 1776 (Declaration of Independence); 1860–1865 (American Civil War); 1914–1918 (World War I).

Instruct: Objective 2

A Meeting of Cultures

- Mexico is built on top of the ruins of what culture? *(Aztec)*
- Why are José Orozco and Diego Rivera important to Mexico's culture? *(They painted the history of Mexico in murals.)*
- How is the influence of Mexico's ancient cultures still visible? *(name "Mexico" comes from an Aztec word; there is a large mestizo population; art is a blend of European and Native American influences; architecture.)*

Cultures Around the World
• Fine Arts, p. 15

Cultures Transparencies CW15
• Frida Kahlo

Mexican History

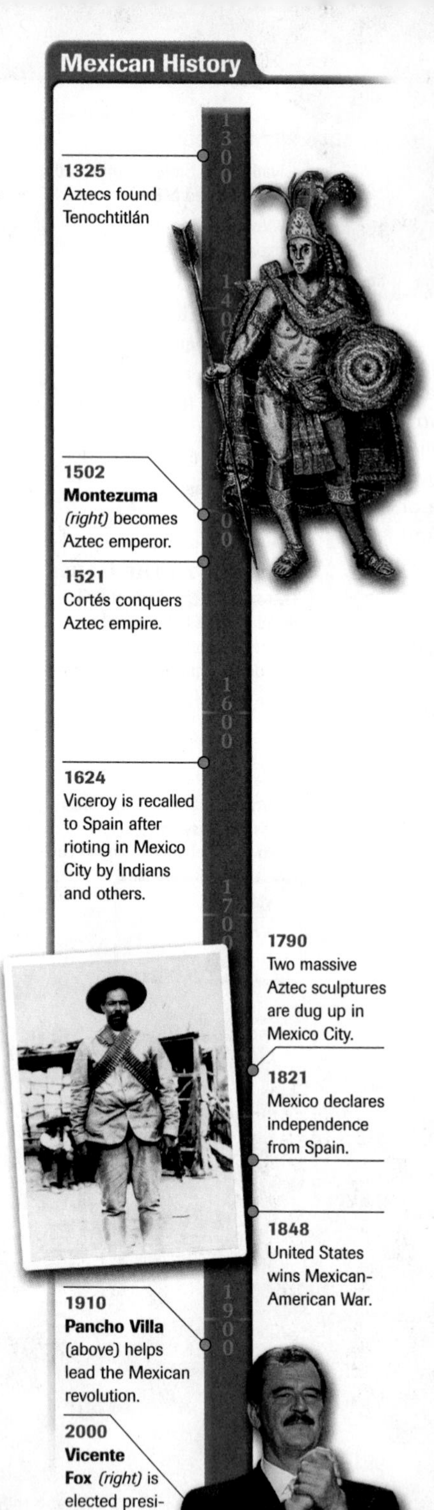

1325
Aztecs found Tenochtitlán

1502
Montezuma *(right)* becomes Aztec emperor.

1521
Cortés conquers Aztec empire.

1624
Viceroy is recalled to Spain after rioting in Mexico City by Indians and others.

1790
Two massive Aztec sculptures are dug up in Mexico City.

1821
Mexico declares independence from Spain.

1848
United States wins Mexican-American War.

1910
Pancho Villa (above) helps lead the Mexican revolution.

2000
Vicente Fox *(right)* is elected president of Mexico.

beginning in the mid-19th century, Benito Juárez led a reform movement and became president of Mexico. He worked for separation of church and state, better educational opportunities, and a more even distribution of the land.

Under Spanish rule, and even after independence, land had been unequally distributed. A few rich landowners owned haciendas (estates or ranches) that covered most of Mexico's farmland. Landless peasants worked on these haciendas. Juárez tried to remedy this problem by giving some land to the peasants.

Juárez was eventually succeeded by Porfirio Díaz, a dishonest politician who ruled Mexico for more than 30 years. His harsh and corrupt rule brought about a revolution and civil war, led by Francisco Madero, Pancho Villa, and Emiliano Zapata. A new constitution was adopted in 1917. It redistributed nearly half of Mexico's farmland to peasants.

ONE-PARTY RULE In 1929, a new political party arose in Mexico. This was the **Institutional Revolutionary Party (PRI).** It helped to maintain political stability for much of the 20th century. It continued the policy of redistributing land to the peasants. However, it held onto power by fraud and corruption.

In 1997, two parties opposed to the PRI won a large number of seats in the congress. Then, in 2000, National Action Party (PAN) candidate Vicente Fox was elected president. For the first time in 71 years, the PRI did not control Mexico's government. But the 2006 election of Fox's successor, Felipe Calderón, was marred by charges of fraud. Calderón's opponents tried to keep him from taking office. A

CONNECT TO THE ISSUES
DEMOCRACY

How did the PRI both help and hinder democracy?
A. Answer
The PRI helped to introduce democracy, stability, and land reform in Mexico. However, it also tolerated fraud and corruption.

A Meeting of Cultures 2

The culture of Mexico is a blend of Spanish influences with original native cultures. Mexico's native population has helped to shape the country's self-image.

THE AZTECS AND THE SPANISH Before the arrival of the Spanish, Mexico was a place of many advanced native cultures. For example, the Aztec empire arose in the Valley of Mexico, a mountain basin about 7,500 feet above sea level. According to legend, the Aztec people arrived there around A.D. 1200 from the deserts of northern Mexico. Then they built their capital of Tenochtitlán, a city of beautiful temples, palaces, gardens, and lakes. Canals linked parts of the city. People grew food on islands in Lake Texcoco surrounding the city. Tenochtitlán was where the Aztecs practiced human sacrifice in their temples.

218

DIFFERENTIATING INSTRUCTION | GIFTED AND TALENTED STUDENTS

TRACING FAMILY HISTORIES

Objective Help students learn about their personal heritage

Research Time 1 week; **Class Time** 30 minutes

Task Research and report on genealogy search

Directions Have students use the key words "genealogy" in an Internet search to find out about their ancestors. The key phrase will link students up with a number of genealogy search engines and databases. Some search engines have separate indexes for different countries of origin. Have students supplement their Internet research with personal interviews with members of older generations in their families.

Have students try to research at least three generations back. Have them give a short speech on one aspect about their heritage that enriches their lives.

When Cortés and the Spanish conquered the Aztec empire, they destroyed most of the capital and built Mexico City on top of the ruins of Tenochtitlán. Today, though, ancient Aztec ruins and relics keep turning up as modern projects in Mexico City are built. Like the ruins, the past is still very much present in Mexico. B

Geographic Thinking

Seeing Patterns B What does Mexico City's site on top of the Aztec city suggest about the location?
B. Answer It suggests that the site was a good one, with a surrounding lake and adequate amounts of nearby farmland.

The Spanish brought their language and Catholic religion, both of which dominate modern Mexico. In spite of Spanish cultural diffusion, though, Mexico's Indian heritage remains very strong. In fact, the name of the country comes from *Mexica,* an older name for the Aztecs. Mexico has a large **mestizo** population—people of mixed Spanish and Native American heritage.

HUMAN–ENVIRONMENT INTERACTION This painting by Juan O'Gorman (1905-1982) portrays Father Miguel Hidalgo, a Mexican priest and a leader of the revolt against Spanish rule in 1810. **What does the painting suggest about Hidalgo's support among the people?**

LATIN AMERICA

MEXICAN PAINTERS Mexico has a long heritage of architecture and art. In the 20th century, Mexico's tradition of painting took the form of public art. Many important painters portrayed the history of Mexico on the walls of its public buildings. Among the important Mexican mural painters of the 20th century were José Orozco, Diego Rivera, David Siqueiros, and Juan O'Gorman. (See the Diego Rivera mural showing the city of Tenochtitlán on page 186.) Frida Kahlo was an important Mexican painter known for her self-portraits. Most of the important Mexican painters blended European and Native American influences.

AN ARCHITECTURAL HERITAGE The Native Americans constructed beautiful temples and public buildings, often in the shape of pyramids. At Teotihuacán, for example, the people built a city of pyramids, many of which were topped with temples. The Aztec city of Tenochtitlán was filled with temples and palaces before it was demolished by the Spanish. The Spanish buildings included beautiful missions that were scattered throughout the territory they conquered. Later the Spanish built huge cathedrals, such as the Metropolitan Cathedral in Mexico City. This cathedral is located on the main square, or zocalo, of the city.

Economics: Cities and Factories 3

Mexico continues to struggle with two main economic challenges. First, it is attempting to close a long-standing gap between rich and poor people. Second, it is attempting to develop a modern industrial economy. Mexico had traditionally been an agricultural society, but it started to industrialize in the middle of the 20th century.

Interpreting Paintings

Juan O'Gorman Mural

Shown here is a detail of a mural whose title is *Retablo de la Independencía (Altar of Independence)*, painted in Chapultepec Castle in Mexico City. Have students speculate about why a priest might lead a revolution against Spanish rule in Mexico. *(Father Hidalgo might have objected to the oppression of the poor peasants because of his religious beliefs.)* Obtain pictures of some other murals by other artists, and hold a class discussion about how Mexican murals help to keep cultural history alive.

Instruct: Objective 3

Economics: Cities and Factories

- Why are Mexicans moving to cities? *(job opportunities)*
- What is the most important part of Mexico's economy today? *(manufacturing)*
- What was NAFTA designed to do? *(break down many economic barriers among the three countries, create jobs, and bring greater prosperity)*

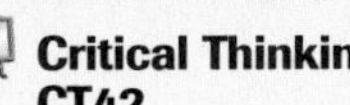

Critical Thinking Transparencies CT42
- Population Geography in Selected Latin American Countries

DIFFERENTIATING INSTRUCTION | STUDENTS ACQUIRING ENGLISH/ESL

RESEARCHING PERSONAL HISTORIES

Objective Help students expand their knowledge of their family history

Class Time 30 minutes

Task Research personal family history

Directions Have students interview a family member about their family's heritage, and then have students write a short essay about their heritage. Or, students can write about a friend's family.

Essays should include information on the family's history and cultural traditions. Have students speak a sentence or two in their native language, and then read the whole essay to the class in English.

Have them include a photograph or drawing of a family memento or artifact that expresses their family's heritage.

Interpreting Maps

Population Distribution in Mexican States

Population maps can help governments plan for the future. For example, if we see that the population is getting older, we would need to plan for more geriatric care facilities and hospitals. Ask students: what would we need to think about if the population were getting younger? (*education, jobs, health care for newborns and children, and so forth*)

SKILLBUILDER ANSWERS

1. Jalisco, Veracruz, Distrito Federal, Puebla **2.** The population of Mexico is very young.

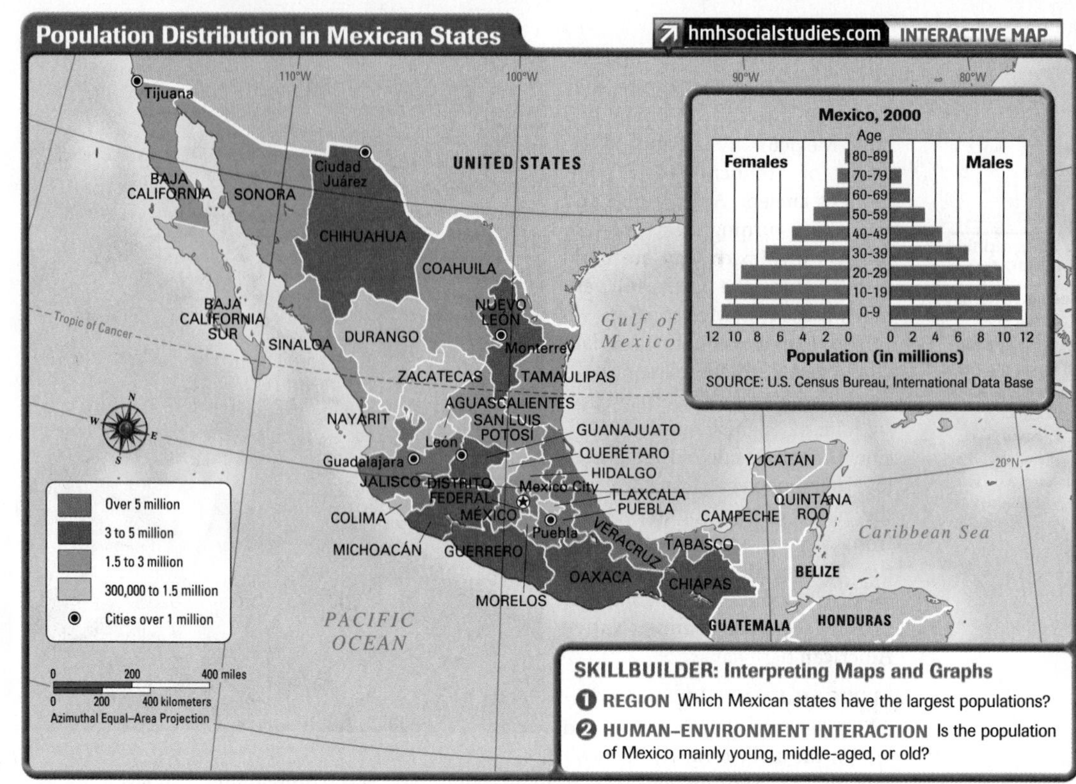

SKILLBUILDER: Interpreting Maps and Graphs

❶ **REGION** Which Mexican states have the largest populations?

❷ **HUMAN–ENVIRONMENT INTERACTION** Is the population of Mexico mainly young, middle-aged, or old?

POPULATION AND THE CITIES Mexicans are moving to cities because they see economic opportunities there. Jobs in cities provide a way to narrow the gap between rich and poor because such jobs pay more than those in rural areas. Mexico's population of about 52 million in 1970 almost doubled by the year 2000. Its population is largely very young.

OIL AND MANUFACTURING Mexico's economy includes a large industry based on its oil reserves in and along the coast of the Gulf of Mexico. Mexico has emphasized its oil industry as an important part of developing an industrial economy. The profits from oil have helped to finance development, especially in manufacturing industries.

Manufacturing is the most important part of Mexico's recent economic development. Many of the new factories are located in the north of the country, along the border with the United States. **Maquiladoras** are factories in Mexico that assemble imported materials into finished products that are then exported, mostly to the United States. These products include electronic equipment, clothing, and furniture.

Mexico is a member, along with the United States and Canada, of **NAFTA** (North American Free Trade Agreement). This agreement has broken down many economic barriers among the three countries. NAFTA was designed to create jobs and bring prosperity to millions of people, but the treaty has received mixed reviews. Critics say it has contributed to environmental damage and cost many Mexican farmers their livelihoods, among other charges.

ACTIVITY OPTION EXPLORING LOCAL GEOGRAPHY

COMMUNITY PLANNING

Objective To see the connection between the current population and future needs of the community

Class Time 30 minutes

Task Create a plan for future needs of the community

Directions Obtain information from the local chamber of commerce or city government, or use information from the U.S. census on the population statistics for the community. Have students speculate what the local government needs to plan for in the coming years based on population information. Have students write a short report on their speculations.

Their report should include specific recommendations for dealing with either a growing population (likely in urban locations) or a shrinking population (possibly in rural communities). For example, if the population is growing, then there may be a need for more school construction, but if the population is shrinking, then there may be a need for school consolidation.

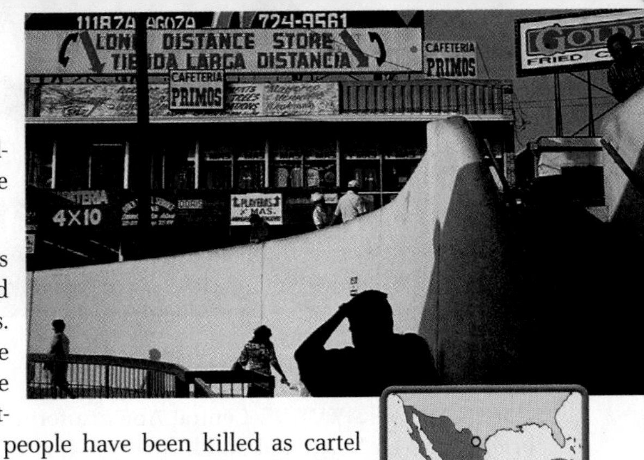

4 Facing Challenges

The people of Mexico face big challenges. Safety, jobs, and education are foremost among their concerns.

SAFETY Every year, illegal drugs worth billions of dollars are shipped through Mexico to the United States. Brutal gangs compete to control the trade. In 1989, fighting between the gangs, also known as cartels, escalated. Since then, countless innocent people have been killed as cartel violence erupted in public places. The increased violence has also damaged Mexico's tourist industry and driven down foreign investment in Mexican businesses. In 2006 President Calderón declared war on the drug traffickers, but success has been limited.

MOVEMENT Pedestrians use a walkway in crossing from Nuevo Laredo, Mexico, into Laredo, Texas. Shop signs are in English and Spanish.

EMIGRATION Many Mexicans leave their country and travel to the United States in search of work. Although many of these immigrants enter the United States with proper documentation, many others do so illegally, but take the risk to look for jobs. The money that the immigrants send back to their families in Mexico can be essential to local economies. However, as the recession that took hold in 2008 limited employment opportunities in the United States, many Mexican immigrants lost their jobs or had less money to send home.

C. Answer
Improved education may help people get jobs and earn more money.

CONNECT TO THE ISSUES
INCOME GAP
C How might the income gap be narrowed in Mexico?

WORK AND SCHOOL Mexico suffers from high unemployment. Without education and training, young workers cannot find good jobs. In recent years, school-attendance rates of eligible students have improved. Today, about 85 percent of school-age children attend school. Education will become even more important as Mexico becomes more industrialized. C

SECTION 1 Assessment

1 Places & Terms
Identify and explain the following terms.
- Spanish conquest
- Tenochtitlán
- Institutional Revolutionary Party (PRI)
- mestizo
- maquiladoras
- NAFTA

2 Taking Notes
REGION Review the notes you took for this section.

- Which two main cultures blended to form modern Mexico?
- Where do most of Mexico's people live today?

3 Main Ideas
a. How might democratic reforms and improved trade agreements contribute to a stronger economy in Mexico?
b. What effect might Mexico's young population have on its development?
c. In what ways have Native American and Spanish influences shaped Mexico?

4 Geographic Thinking
How might a shortage of jobs in Mexico affect the movement of its people?
Think about:
- why one might travel to the United States in search of work
- what factors in Mexico might lead people to move

MAKING COMPARISONS Pair with a partner and make a chart of the ten most heavily populated states of Mexico arranged in order from most to least heavily populated. Then compare your chart with a map, and mark those states that are closest to the U.S. border.

Instruct: Objective 4

Facing Challenges

- What are three challenges Mexico faces? *(safety, emigration, work and school)*
- Why do Mexicans emigrate to the United States? *(to find work)*
- Why is education important to Mexico? *(Young workers need education to get good jobs in an industrialized society.)*

Assess & Reteach

GeoFocus Have students complete their notes on Mexico for the cluster diagram.

Formal Assessment
- Section Quiz, p. 146

Reteaching Activity
Have students write an outline of this section. Have a peer evaluate the outline.

In-Depth Resources: Unit 3
- Reteaching Activity, p. 19

Outline Maps with Activities
- Mexico, pp. 21–22

SECTION 1 ASSESSMENT ANSWERS

1. Places & Terms
Spanish conquest, p. 217
Tenochtitlán, p. 217
Institutional Revolutionary Party, p. 218
mestizo, p. 219
maquiladoras, p. 220
NAFTA, p. 220

2. Taking Notes
- Spanish and native cultures
- Most of the people live in the cities.

3. Main Ideas
a. Both should contribute to the growth of a free-market economy that should lead to greater prosperity for all.
b. Mexico's expanding young population will present a challenge to its educational system. If young people can be trained and educated with job skills for the global economy, then Mexico's young population might contribute to its prosperity.
c. Mexican art, architecture, food, language, religion, and politics all show the interaction of Spanish and native influences.

4. Geographic Thinking
A shortage of jobs in Mexico might drive its people to emigrate.

GeoActivity

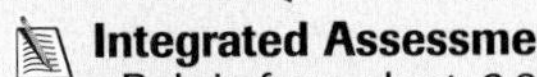
Integrated Assessment
- Rubric for a chart, 2.2

SECTION 2 OBJECTIVES

1. Describe the history of Central America.
2. Describe the history of the Caribbean.
3. Identify the cultural blends in the region.
4. Identify economic conditions in the region.
5. Explore the modern life in the region.

SKILLBUILDERS: Interpreting Maps & Charts, pp. 222, 224

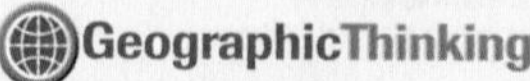

Using the Atlas, p. 223
Making Comparisons, p. 224
Drawing Conclusions, p. 227

Focus & Motivate

Discuss with students what the economy of your community is based on. Then ask students, based on their prior knowledge, what they think the economy of Central America and the Caribbean might be based on. *(bananas, coffee, tourism)*

Instruct: Objective 1 appears on p. 223

Interpreting Maps

Native Peoples, 1492

Point out that the wooden snake that accompanies the map was carved by a Taino artist. The Taino people lived on what are now Cuba, Jamaica, Hispaniola, and Puerto Rico.

SKILLBUILDER ANSWERS

1. Carib **2.** Atlantic Ocean, Gulf of Mexico, Pacific Ocean, and Caribbean Sea

2 Central America and the Caribbean

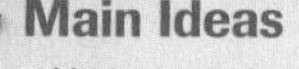

Main Ideas

- Native peoples, Europeans, and Africans have shaped the culture of this region.
- The economies of the region are based primarily on agriculture and tourism.

Places & Terms

cultural hearth
United Provinces of Central America
Panama Canal
calypso
reggae
informal economy

CONNECT TO THE ISSUES
INCOME GAP The people of Central America and the Caribbean face an uneven distribution of income as one of the effects of colonialism.

A HUMAN PERSPECTIVE Central America forms an isthmus, a land bridge between North and South America. It also divides two oceans. This geographic fact has made the region attractive to the United States and other major world powers and has helped to keep the area fragmented and politically unstable. For example, in the early 20th century, the United States wanted to build a canal across Panama that would connect the Atlantic and Pacific oceans. In 1903, Panama was still a province of Colombia, which did not like the idea. The United States encouraged a revolution in Panama, and when it won its independence, Panama granted the United States a ten-mile-wide zone in which to build a canal. Central America had become a crossroads of world trade.

Native and Colonial Central America 1

Central America is a cultural hearth as well as a crossroads. A **cultural hearth** is a place from which important ideas spread. Usually, it is the heartland or place of origin of a major culture. The Mayan people built a great civilization in the area that spread throughout the region. The homeland of the Maya stretched from southern Mexico into northern Central America. During the 800s, the Maya began to abandon many of their cities. Why they did so remains a mystery to be solved by archaeologists.

Wooden snake carved by a Taino artist

Native Peoples, 1492

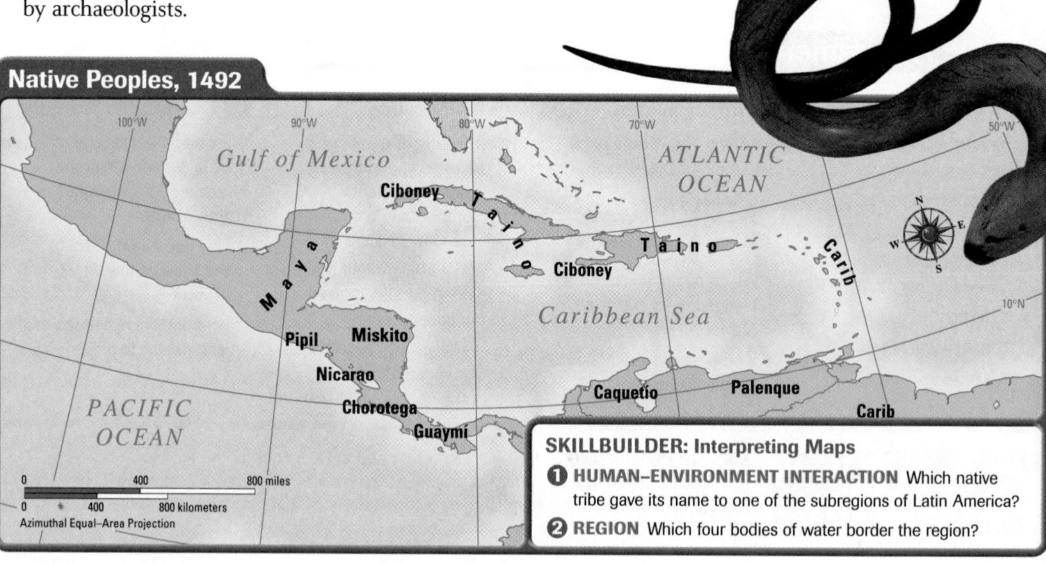

SKILLBUILDER: Interpreting Maps

1. **HUMAN-ENVIRONMENT INTERACTION** Which native tribe gave its name to one of the subregions of Latin America?
2. **REGION** Which four bodies of water border the region?

SECTION 2 PROGRAM RESOURCES

In-Depth Resources: Unit 3
- Guided Reading, p. 14
- Building Vocabulary, p. 18
- Reteaching Activity, p. 20

Guided Reading Workbook
- Section 2

Access for Students Acquiring English
- Guided Reading, p. 50

Outline Maps with Activities
- Central America and the Caribbean, pp. 23–24

Formal Assessment
- Section Quiz, p. 147

Integrated Assessment
- Rubric for a poster, 1.1
- Rubric for a presentation, 3.6

Cultures Around the World
- Daily Life, p. 14
- Arts & Crafts, p. 17

INTEGRATED TECHNOLOGY

Cultures Transparencies CW14, 17
- Selling Food at Market
- Andean Textiles

Map Transparency MT19
- Native Peoples of Latin America

Power Presentations

Test Generator
- Section Quiz

TEST-TAKING RESOURCES

Strategies for Test Preparation
Test Practice Transparencies TT00
Online Test Practice

MAYAN INFLUENCE The Maya built many cities with temples and palaces in present-day Belize, Guatemala, El Salvador, and Honduras. Each city was an independent state ruled by a god-king and served as a center for religious ceremony and trade. One of their most spectacular cities was Tikal, located in the dense, steamy jungle of northern Guatemala, considered the center of Mayan civilization. The pyramids at Tikal were among the tallest structures in the Americas until the 20th century. The influence of the Maya spread over a region from Mexico to El Salvador. The Mayan culture was carried to other regions through military alliances and trade.

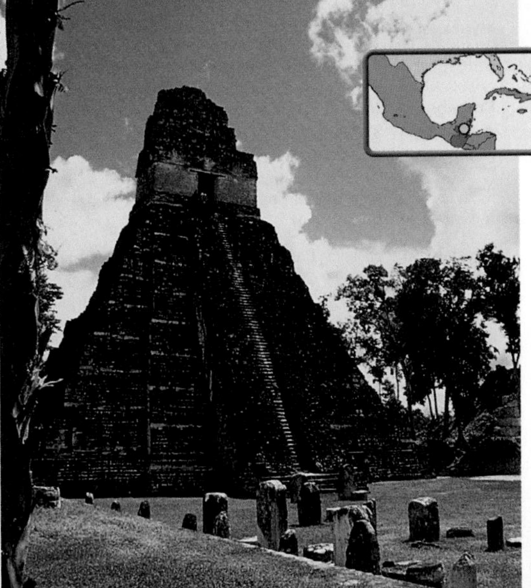

HUMAN–ENVIRONMENT INTERACTION This pyramid at Tikal towers over the great plaza of the ancient city. A temple sits on top of the pyramid. **What might this and similar buildings at Tikal suggest about Mayan civilization?**

THE SPANISH IN CENTRAL AMERICA The Spanish conquest of the Aztecs in Mexico opened the door to Spanish control of Central America. Spain ruled Central America until the 19th century. Mexico declared its independence from Spain in 1821. Up to that point, Central America had been governed from Mexico. In 1823, however, the whole region declared its independence from Mexico and took the name of the **United Provinces of Central America.**

By the late 1830s, the United Provinces had split into separate nations. These became El Salvador, Nicaragua, Costa Rica, Guatemala, and Honduras. Later, Panama broke off from Colombia and became an independent country in Central America. Belize, a former British colony, broke away from British Honduras.

LATIN AMERICA

A. Answer Because the Caribbean was made up of separate islands, each could be separately colonized by European powers.

Geographic Thinking

Using the Atlas A Use the maps on pages 216 and 222. Why might the Caribbean have been settled by more European powers than was Central America?

Native and Colonial Caribbean 2

Although Central America was ruled by Spain, the Caribbean was settled and claimed by many European powers. In addition, Africans who were brought to the Caribbean as slaves played an important role in the settling of the Caribbean. A

CARIBBEAN INFLUENCES When Christopher Columbus reached the Caribbean islands in 1492, he thought he had reached the East Indies in Asia. Therefore, he called the natives "Indians." The inhabitants of these islands called themselves the Taino (TY•noh). The Spanish settled some of the islands and established sugar plantations, which were well suited to the climate and soil of the islands. They attempted to use the Taino as forced labor, but many of the natives died from disease and mistreatment.

To replace the Taino, European slave traders brought Africans to the Caribbean by force and put them to work on plantations. As a result, Africans have had a lasting influence on Caribbean life and culture.

Instruct: Objective 1

Native and Colonial Central America

- Why is ancient Central America considered a cultural hearth? *(The Mayan people built a great civilization in this crossroad region.)*
- What brought about the United Provinces of Central America? *(When Mexico declared its independence from Spain, the region declared its independence from Mexico.)*

In-Depth Resources: Unit 3
- Guided Reading, p. 14

Map Transparency MT19
- Native Peoples of Latin America

Interpreting Photographs

Pyramids at Tikal

Two massive pyramids sit at the center of a royal-religious complex. Surrounding the two main pyramids are 350 temples and palaces scattered over 6.5 square miles.

CAPTION ANSWER Mayan civilization was very advanced.

Instruct: Objective 2

Native and Colonial Caribbean

- Where did the African influence in the Caribbean come from? *(Africans were brought by force by slave traders to replace Taino natives.)*
- Who were the European powers in the Caribbean, and how did most of them earn their wealth? *(Spanish, French, British, Dutch, and Danish; made their wealth in sugar trade)*

ACTIVITY OPTION | INTERNET RESEARCH

PREPARING A NEWS BRIEF

Objective To summarize information

Class Time 45 minutes

Task To write a short news story about the discovery of Tikal

Directions Tikal began as a small farming village around 600 B.C. It grew slowly until, by about A.D. 700 it was one of the largest Mayan cities, with a population of nearly 60,000 people. Thousands more lived in the surrounding area.

Students can access links through **hmhsocialstudies.com** to research Tikal. Have them find what they consider the most important three to five facts. Students should write a news brief that describes the discovery of the ancient site. Call on several students to read their news briefs. These may also be recorded if video equipment is available.

Interpreting Charts

Caribbean Colonies

Have students study the chart on this page. Point out the titles across the top: the country, colony, and the cultural influences. Explain to students that to better understand the current culture of a country, it is useful to understand its history.

SKILLBUILDER ANSWERS
1. Great Britain **2.** Spain and France

Instruct: Objective 3

Cultural Blends

- What are the two major cultural blends of Central America? *(Native Americans and Spanish settlers)*
- What are the cultural blends of the Caribbean Islands? *(Native American, European, African and mixed)*
- Why is there such a cultural blend in the Caribbean Islands? *(The original inhabitants were displaced by different European powers who then introduced the slave trade.)*

Cultures Around the World
- Daily Life, p. 14
- Arts & Crafts, p. 17

Cultures Transparencies CW14, 17
- Selling Food at Market
- Andean Textiles

Caribbean Colonies

Country	Colony	Major Cultural Influences
Spain	Cuba, Dominican Republic, Puerto Rico	Spanish language Catholic religion
France	Haiti, Guadeloupe, Martinique	French language Catholic religion
Great Britian	Jamaica, Barbados, St. Lucia, St. Vincent, Grenada, Trinidad and Tobago, British Virgin Islands	English language Protestant and Catholic religions
Netherlands	Netherlands Antilles	Dutch language Protestant religion
Denmark	Danish West Indies [1]	Danish language [2] Protestant religion

[1] Became U.S. Virgin Islands in 1917. [2] English is now the official language.

SKILLBUILDER: Interpreting Charts

1. **REGION** Which European country had the most colonies in the Caribbean?
2. **PLACE** In the colonies of which European countries was the Catholic religion dominant?

A COLONIAL MOSAIC By the 19th century, the Spanish, French, British, Dutch, and Danish all claimed islands in the Caribbean. Most of the European powers were there to profit from the sugar trade. This trade depended on the forced labor of workers brought in chains from Africa.

CARIBBEAN INDEPENDENCE The first independence movement in Latin America began as a slave revolt in the Caribbean on the island of Haiti. In the 18th century, Haiti was a French colony with an important sugar industry. Africans brought to the island by force worked on the sugar plantations and other plantations. In the 1790s, Toussaint L'Ouverture (too•SAN•loo•vehr•TOOR) led a slave rebellion in Haiti and took over the government of the island. By 1804, Haiti had achieved independence from France. Cuba achieved independence from Spain in 1898 as a result of the Spanish-American War. After an occupation by United States forces, the island became self-governing in 1902. Jamaica and Trinidad and Tobago did not achieve full independence from Great Britain until 1962.

Cultural Blends 

Central America and the Caribbean are close to each other geographically, and their cultures show a blending of influences. This mixture affects everything from religion to language.

CULTURE OF CENTRAL AMERICA As you've read, the culture of Central America blends two major elements: Native American influences with those of Spanish settlers. The Spanish were the dominant group of European settlers in Central America—their language remains dominant in the area today. Catholicism is the major religion, although Protestant missionaries are active in the region.

The Spanish took land away from the natives of the region. The conquerors cut down forests, opened up land for grazing livestock, and introduced new crops, such as wheat. They created large farms and ranches, built towns, and moved the native peoples off the land and into the towns. All this altered the way of life in the region.

CULTURE OF THE CARIBBEAN A greater variety of influences was at work in the Caribbean. The Spanish, French, British, Danish, and Dutch existed side by side with the African and Native American. Residents of the islands are of European, African, or mixed ancestry. B

African influences were especially important. Most of the people are descendants of the African slaves brought to the islands to work on the

B. Answer The culture of the Caribbean is more diverse because of all the different European countries that established colonies there and the large number of Africans.

Making Comparisons
B How does the culture of the Caribbean differ from the culture of Central America?

ACTIVITY OPTION | **SKILLBUILDER LESSON** | **BLOCK SCHEDULING**

MAKING COMPARISIONS

Explaining the Skill Making comparisons involves finding both similarities and differences between two or more things. Countries, events, ideas, beliefs, and institutions can be compared in order to understand them thoroughly. Tell students that making comparisons between regions and subregions can help them put geographic information in perspective.

For additional Skillbuilder Practice, see p. 217 in Section 1.

Applying the Skill Ask students to compare the cultures of Central America and the Caribbean. On the board, create a Venn diagram. Then ask the following question and use students' answers to fill the diagram.

- What languages are spoken in each subregion? *(mainly Spanish in Central America; Spanish, French, English, Dutch, Danish in Caribbean)*
- What colonial powers ruled each subregion? *(Spanish in Central America; Spanish, French, English, Dutch in Caribbean)*
- Which subregion had the strongest African influence? *(African influence strongest in Caribbean because of slaves on sugar plantations)*

growing up in...Cuba

This boy is playing baseball, a sport as popular in Cuba as it is in the United States. Baseball traveled from the United States to Cuba in the late 1800s. Baseball is considered the island's national pastime, just as it is in the United States.

Young people in Cuba receive many benefits from the Communist government, including free education and health care. The education system extends from preschool programs through college to graduate programs. However, young people, like all Cubans, live in a police state that limits their economic and political freedoms.

If you lived in Cuba, here are some rights you would enjoy and restrictions you would face:

- You would receive a free education.
- You would receive free medical care.
- You would attend school from age 6 to somewhere between ages 11 and 15.
- You could attend free concerts, ballets, and plays.
- Your freedom of speech and writing would be restricted.
- Your economic opportunities would be very limited.

sugar plantations. They left a lasting mark on all aspects of culture in the islands, including village life, markets, and choice of crops.

The religions of the Caribbean include Catholic and Protestant, as well as Santeria, which combines certain African practices and rituals with Catholic elements. Voodoo is practiced on the island of Haiti. The religious and political Rastafari movement originated in Jamaica.

Spanish is spoken on the most populous islands in the Caribbean: Cuba, with a population of about 11 million, and the Dominican Republic, with a population of about 9.7 million. There are also many French speakers (Haiti alone has a population of more than 6 million). English dominates in Jamaica, with a population of almost 3 million. There is a smattering of Dutch and Danish also spoken in the region.

Economics: Jobs and People 

In general, most of the people in the countries of the region are poor. This is, in part, a legacy of colonialism. The early success of the sugar crop benefited colonial planters, not the native or African laborers. Also, the region faced competition in the sugar market, and eventually the sugar trade declined. Further, the fact that natural resources were exported and not used locally left the region economically weakened.

FARMING AND TRADE Sugar cane plantations in the Caribbean provide the region's largest export crop. Other important export crops are bananas, citrus fruits, coffee, and spices. All these crops are well adapted to the climate and soil of the region. Many people work on the plantations that grow crops for export. But the pay is poor, and as a result, average per-capita income in the Caribbean is very low.

growing up in...

Cuba

Cuba is a multiracial society with a population of mainly Spanish and African origins. The black population is descended from enslaved Africans imported to Cuba and its neighbors, particularly Jamaica.

Ask students if they are surprised that baseball is popular in Cuba. Ask what other sports might also be popular in Cuba. *(soccer is also popular)*

Instruct: Objective 

Economics: Jobs and People

- What are three reasons for poverty in the region? *(colonialism, decline in sugar market, and depleted natural resources)*
- Why is the Panama Canal important? *(major trade route connecting the Caribbean Sea and Pacific Ocean)*
- How are economics in Central America and the Caribbean related to population patterns? *(In Central America people live in rural areas and work as farmers; in the Caribbean most people live in urban areas and work in tourism.)*

ACTIVITY OPTION | LINK TO LANGUAGE ARTS

CREATING A TRAVEL JOURNAL

Objective To learn more about the subregion

Class Time 15 minutes

Task To write an entry in a travel journal about a country in Central America or the Caribbean

Supplies Needed

- journal
- pen or pencil
- travel magazines

Directions Have students obtain travel magazines and travel brochures about different countries in Central America or the Caribbean. Then have students write a short journal entry imagining they are traveling through one of the countries. If desired, students can write on additional countries while covering this unit.

5 THEMES

Movement: The Panama Canal

Although the United States built and ran the canal for most of its history, the U.S. government agreed to a series of treaties that turned control of the canal over to Panama. Ask students why the canal is important to trade. *(The canal provides a shortcut for cargo ships, cutting a 15,000 mile voyage in half.)*

Instruct: Objective 5

Popular Culture, Tourism, and Jobs

- What countries have influenced and shaped music in Central America and the Caribbean? *(Africa, Spain, and the United States)*
- What is an informal economy? *(jobs outside official channels, without benefits or protection for workers)*
- Why might reggae be popular in the Caribbean? *(Reggae addresses social and religious issues.)*

MOVEMENT

The Panama Canal

Panama is a unique crossroads, linking North America and South America and the Caribbean Sea and the Pacific Ocean.

Before the Panama Canal was built, sea travel from the east coast to the west coast of North America meant a journey of about 15,000 miles. The canal cut the coast-to-coast journey more than in half. Now, ships move through a series of locks shown on the map at right.

Sailing through the Panama Canal from the Caribbean to the Pacific Ocean, you actually sail from northwest to southeast, not from east to west.

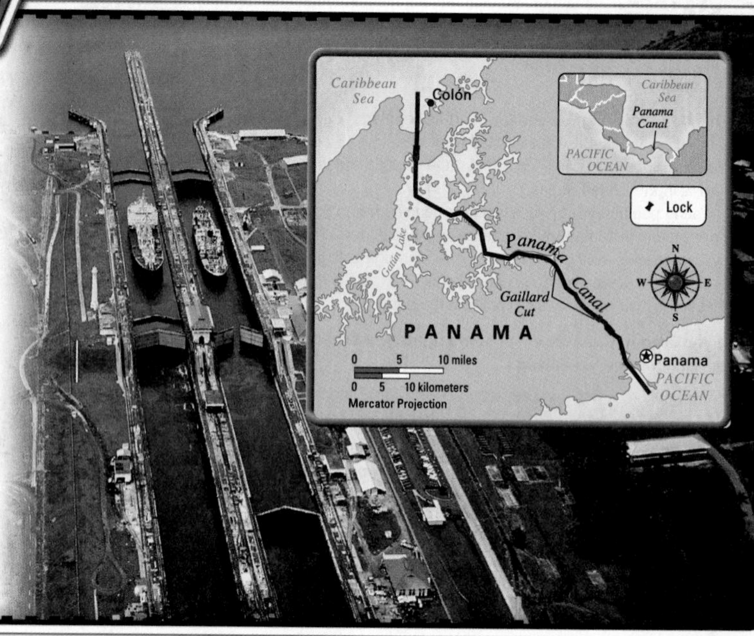

HISTORY

VIDEO
Panama Canal: Locks
hmhsocialstudies.com

In Central America, too, the main source of income is the commercial farming practiced on large plantations. These farms produce 10 percent of the world's coffee and 10 percent of the world's bananas. Central America's mines and forests also provide resources for export.

Trade is important because of the **Panama Canal**, which cuts through the land bridge and connects the Atlantic and Pacific oceans. Ships from both hemispheres use the canal, making Panama a crossroads of world trade. The canal made possible the exchange of both goods and ideas.

CONNECT TO THE ISSUES
RESOURCES
 What resources are exported from Central America and the Caribbean?
C. Answer sugar, bananas, citrus, spices, and coffee

WHERE PEOPLE LIVE AND WHY Population patterns in Central America and the Caribbean are directly related to their economies. Both Central America and the Caribbean have populations of between 35 million and 42 million people. In Central America, most people make their living on farms and, as a result, live in rural areas.

Many of the islands in the Caribbean are densely populated. More than 11 million people live on Cuba, the largest of the islands. Most people live in urban areas, where they hope to find jobs in tourism. The cities attract people who are seeking a better way of life. Unfortunately, many end up living in slums. The region is working to find a way to channel more of the profits from tourism and farming to benefit local communities.

Popular Culture, Tourism, and Jobs 5

Education and jobs are a major concern to the people of Central America and the Caribbean. Music, heavily influenced and shaped by the African heritage in the region, is an important part of the popular culture of Central America and the Caribbean.

ACTIVITY OPTION **COOPERATIVE LEARNING**

CREATING A TRAVEL POSTER

Objective To create a travel poster

Class Time 30 minutes

Task Have students work in small groups to create a travel poster

Supplies Needed

- poster board
- glue
- old magazines

Directions Have students work together to extract information from this chapter about one of the countries or subregions. Have groups brainstorm what they want to show on their poster. When completed, display the posters around the room. Within each group, assign the following tasks to individual students:

- acquire art supplies
- find pictures
- conduct research
- design and draw the poster

HUMAN-ENVIRONMENT INTERACTION Many of Bob Marley's songs reflect his faith and political beliefs. **How might popular culture express important ideas and political beliefs?**

MUSIC OF THE CARIBBEAN Both reggae and calypso music started in the Caribbean. **Calypso** music began in Trinidad. Calypso combines musical elements from Africa, Spain, and the Caribbean. Calypso songs are accompanied by steel drums and guitars, and they have improvised lyrics.

Reggae developed in Jamaica in the 1960s. Many reggae songs deal with social problems and religion. African music, Caribbean music, and American music all fed into the roots of reggae. Bob Marley of Jamaica was a pioneer of reggae. The music of the Caribbean is one of the elements that lures tourists to the region, creating jobs for local residents.

BACKGROUND
Bob Marley's son, David "Ziggy" Marley, is carrying on his father's musical legacy.

TOURISM AND THE INFORMAL ECONOMY Rapid population growth in the Caribbean is contributing to high unemployment, especially among the young. Many people flee rural areas and move to the cities in search of jobs. Too often, however, they lack job skills. There are schools to help prepare students for jobs in agriculture and tourism.

Tourism is, in fact, an increasingly important industry. Local residents of the islands are able to find jobs working in the hotels, resorts, and restaurants there. In addition, people can make a living working as guides and assistants on fishing excursions, sailing trips, snorkeling adventures, hiking expeditions, and other activities for tourists.

People also find jobs in the **informal economy,** which takes place outside official channels, without benefits or protection for workers. These include jobs such as street vending, shining shoes, and a variety of other activities and services that provide people with a small income.

In Section 3, you will read about Spanish-speaking South America.

LATIN AMERICA

Section 2 Assessment

1 Places & Terms
Identify and explain the following places and terms.
- cultural hearth
- United Provinces of Central America
- Panama Canal
- calypso
- reggae
- informal economy

2 Taking Notes
REGION Review the notes you took for this section.

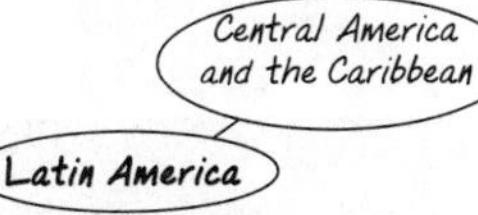

- What European countries had colonies in the Caribbean?
- Which European country settled most of Central America?

3 Main Ideas
a. What are the major groups that blended to form the culture of this region?
b. What are some major sources of income in the economies of Central America and the Caribbean?
c. What forms of music have evolved in the region?

4 Geographic Thinking
Drawing Conclusions How did the establishment of sugar plantations by Europeans affect the settlement of the Caribbean? **Think about:**
- the people brought in to work on the plantations

MAKING COMPARISONS Pair with a partner and make a **poster** about the Panama Canal. Do research on the Internet and illustrate your poster with maps and diagrams of the locks in the canal. Provide statistical data about the canal that compares it with other canals, such as the Suez Canal.

Interpreting Photographs

Bob Marley
Have students bring to class photos of their favorite recording artists. Have students give a little information about each artist.

CAPTION ANSWER The words and music of a popular song can communicate ideas about social justice and equality—for example, Bruce Springsteen's *American Skin* or Lauryn Hill's *The Miseducation of Lauryn Hill.*

More About

The Informal Economy
Like the informal economy, a cottage industry is another way in which individuals are able to survive and feed themselves outside the structure of larger businesses or industries.
A cottage industry is a small-scale business carried on at home by family members using their own equipment.

Assess & Reteach

GeoFocus Have students complete their notes on Central America and the Caribbean for the cluster diagram.

 **Formal Assessment**
- Section Quiz, p. 147

Reteaching Activity
Have students write a summary of this section. Call on several students to read their summaries to the rest of the class.

 **In-Depth Resources: Unit 3**
- Reteaching Activity, p. 20

 **Outline Maps with Activities**
- Central America and the Caribbean, pp. 23–24

SECTION 2 ASSESSMENT ANSWERS

1. Places & Terms
cultural hearth, p. 222; United Provinces of Central America, p. 223; Panama Canal, p. 226; calypso, p. 227; informal economy, p. 227; reggae, p. 227

2. Taking Notes
- Spain, France, Great Britain, Netherlands, Denmark
- Spain

3. Main Ideas
a. The culture of Central America blended Native American influences with those of the Spanish settlers. The Caribbean blended Spanish, French, British, Danish, and Dutch influences with African and Native American elements.
b. commercial farming, tourism, and trade
c. calypso and reggae

4. Geographic Thinking
The sugar plantations of the Caribbean attracted European settlers who, in using the native peoples (the Taino) as forced labor, exposed them to disease and mistreatment that resulted in many deaths. Africans were brought by force to work on the plantations.

GeoActivity

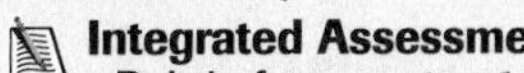 **Integrated Assessment**
- Rubric for a poster, 1.1

OBJECTIVES

1. Identify the source of the Haiti earthquake.
2. Evaluate the impact of the Haiti and Chile earthquakes.
3. Analyze the reasons for the different outcomes of the quakes.

Instruct: Objective

The Haiti and Chile Earthquakes

- What role did the location of the fault play in the destruction of Port-au-Prince? *(contributed greatly to the destruction, because the fault practically underlies the city)*
- How might a country's economic situation affect the death toll caused by an earthquake? *(In a richer country, rescue systems and hospitals are probably more advanced, expensive building codes can be followed, transportation and communication systems can better get help to where it is needed, and so on.)*

Interpreting Maps

Fault Lines in the Caribbean

Ask students to examine the map. Ask them to identify other islands that are threatened by the instability of the Gonâve microplate. *(Cuba and Jamaica)* Which two major tectonic plates meet in the region? *(North American and Caribbean plates)*

Disasters!

HISTORY VIDEO Earthquakes

hmhsocialstudies.com

The Haiti and Chile Earthquakes

On January 12, 2010, a catastrophic earthquake struck Haiti near its capital, Port-au-Prince. More than 200,000 people died. Haiti is the poorest country in the Western Hemisphere. Rescue, health, transportation, communication, and government systems all broke down. A few weeks later, on February 27, a much more powerful quake hit the coast of Chile and was followed by severe aftershocks. The death toll was about 500. Although the Haiti quake hit a more densely populated area and originated closer to Earth's surface, the relative wealth of the two countries also played a part in the results.

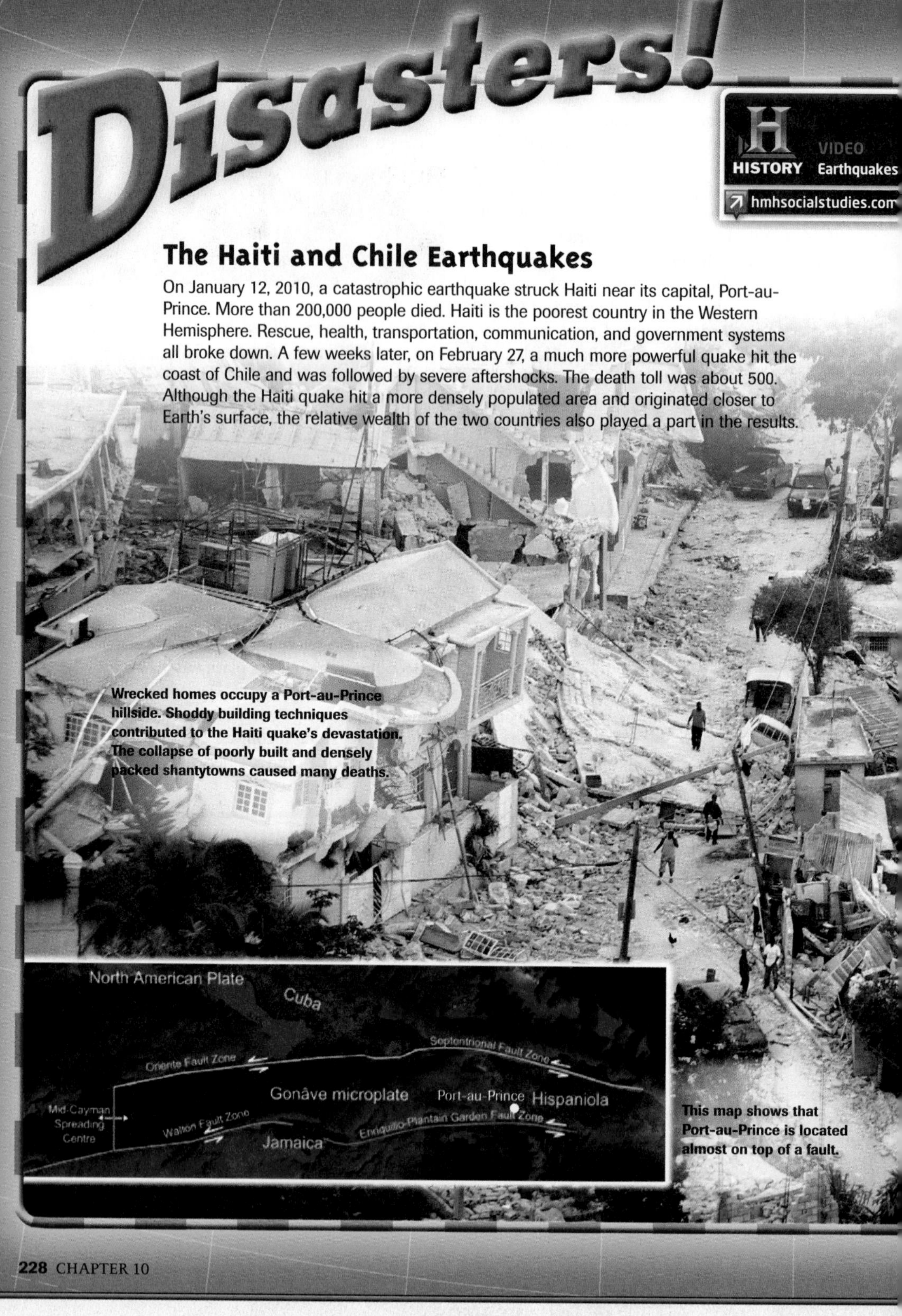

Wrecked homes occupy a Port-au-Prince hillside. Shoddy building techniques contributed to the Haiti quake's devastation. The collapse of poorly built and densely packed shantytowns caused many deaths.

This map shows that Port-au-Prince is located almost on top of a fault.

SUPPORTING RESOURCES

BOOKS FOR THE TEACHER

U.S. Government, ***Haiti Earthquake Tragedy 2010—A Chronicle of the Devastation and American Relief Efforts, Destruction of Port au Prince, Operation Unified Response.*** 2010. Collection of U.S. government documents about the earthquake.

De Boer, Jelle Zeilinga and Donald Theodore Sanders, ***Earthquakes in Human History: The Far-Reaching Effects of Seismic Disruptions.*** Princeton University Press, 2007. The repercussions of earthquakes on all aspects of human experience.

BOOKS FOR THE STUDENT

Susan Hough, ***Earthshaking Science: What We Know (and Don't Know) about Earthquakes.*** Princeton University Press, 2004.

INTERNET

For more on the earthquakes in Haiti and Chile, visit . . .

hmhsocialstudies.com

Tsunamis caused by the earthquake wrecked some towns along Chile's Pacific coast. In this photo, a ship rests in a Talcahuano street after the quake and a tsunami.

GeoActivity

MAKING A PRESENTATION 21st CENTURY

Working with a partner, use the Internet to research two recent severe earthquakes, other than the two discussed here, that have struck different countries. Then create a **presentation** comparing the two earthquakes.

- Build a chart like the one below that compares the two quakes.
- Conduct research to learn more about how the countries differ.
- Analyze the differences in the two quakes' results and the reasons for those differences.

GeoData

Earthquake Details	Haiti	Chile
Magnitude	7.0	8.8*
Depth of earthquake	8.1 miles	21.7 miles
Deaths	230,000	500
Displaced	1.3 million	800,000
People affected	3 million	2 million
Damage (in $US)	at least 8 billion	30 billion
Per capita GDP	$1,300	$14,700

*The Chile earthquake was some 500 times more powerful than the Haiti quake.

GeoActivities

Integrated Assessment
- Rubric for a presentation, 3.6

Interpreting Photographs

Tsunamis on the Chilean Coast

The photo shows the town of Talcahuano, Chile, after a tsunami had struck. Ask students to identify the main threat posed by a tsunami. *(loose debris from wrecked buildings and boats being pushed farther inland by the powerful waves)*

More About

Aftershocks

Smaller quakes, called aftershocks, often follow a major earthquake. Within a week of the February 27 quake, Chile had experienced more than 130 aftershocks, 13 of which were above magnitude 6.0.

ACTIVITY OPTION COOPERATIVE LEARNING

BLOCK SCHEDULING

ROLE PLAYING: INTERVIEW

Objective To help students grasp the human consequences of disaster by putting students in someone else's shoes

Class Time 30 minutes

Task Take turns as interviewer and interviewee

Directions Have students form pairs or break into groups of four. Have one student act as a journalist in the aftermath of the earthquakes of 2010 and ask two questions of the other student(s), who represent residents of Haiti or Chile during the worst of the events. Have the other students answer the interviewer. Then have students rotate or switch roles. Students should each ask two questions and answer at least one, based on what they have learned in this section. Questions might include the following: Did you lose family members or friends in the disaster? What damage did your home sustain? Did you have to find shelter in a tent or elsewhere? What assistance have you received from relief agencies? How do you think your community will cope or rebuild?

SECTION 3 OBJECTIVES

1. Describe the Spanish conquest and independence movements in South America.
2. Identify the cultural mosaic of South America.
3. Explain economic resources and trade.
4. Describe future prospects in South America.

SKILLBUILDER: Interpreting Maps, p. 234

GeographicThinking

Seeing Patterns, p. 231
Drawing Conclusions, p. 235

Focus & Motivate

Ask students what they think might have happened to the native people of South America when the Spanish conquerors came. Ask students if they think it would be possible today for one country to conquer another. *(Answers will vary.)*

Instruct: Objective 

Conquest and the End of Spanish Rule

- What ancient civilization was located in the Andes Mountains of Peru? *(Inca)*
- What is one lasting legacy of the Inca? *(Quechua language)*
- How did colonialism affect the development of government in South America? *(Colonialism created strong militaries and weak governments undermined by social divisions.)*

 **In-Depth Resources: Unit 3**
- Guided Reading, p. 15

3 Spanish-Speaking South America

Main Ideas

- Native peoples and settlers from Spain have shaped the culture of South America.
- Regional economic cooperation will help raise people's standards of living.

Places & Terms

Inca **Mercosur**
Quechua

CONNECT TO THE ISSUES
INCOME GAP The countries of South America are trying to find ways to narrow the gap between rich and poor.

A HUMAN PERSPECTIVE In the early 1500s, the Inca empire was at the height of its glory. Then Spanish soldiers under the command of Francisco Pizarro invaded the South American empire. The Spanish attacked the Inca army, killed many of its warriors, and took the emperor prisoner. The Spaniards held him for ransom. Although the Inca filled a room with silver and gold to win his release, the Spanish executed the emperor. This broke the spirit of the Inca nation, already weakened by civil war, and the Spanish conquered the rest of the empire. As in Mexico, Central America, and the Caribbean, the Spanish conquest would have a deep effect on the history and culture of South America.

Conquest and the End of Spanish Rule 

South America is divided into two main regions, based in part on whether the people speak Spanish or Portuguese. In this section, you will learn about Spanish-speaking South America. This region is composed of Argentina, Bolivia, Chile, Colombia, Ecuador, Guyana, Paraguay, Peru, Uruguay, and Venezuela. Suriname is a Dutch-speaking country. French Guiana is a part of France.

THE INCA This civilization was created by the **Inca**—descendants of people who may have crossed a land bridge from Siberia to Alaska and eventually found their way to South America. When they reached the west coast of South America, they encountered the Andes Mountains, which rise to heights of more than 20,000 feet in some places. In spite of the

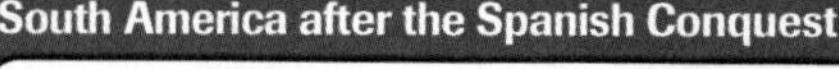

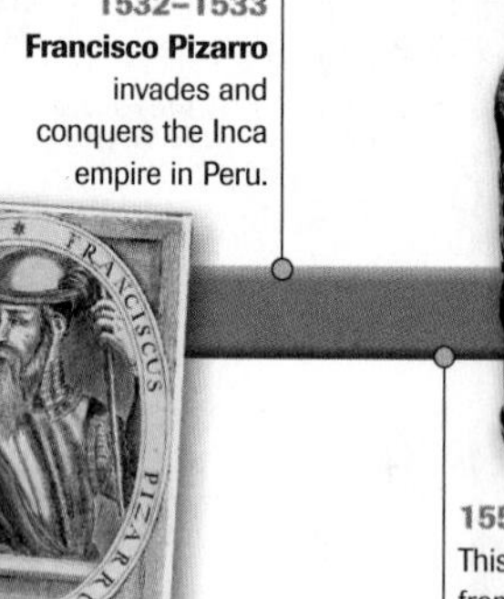

1532–1533 **Francisco Pizarro** invades and conquers the Inca empire in Peru.

1550 This **ceremonial goblet** from Cuzco shows a jaguar, sacred to the Inca.

1608 Jesuit state of Paraguay is established.

1647 Santiago, Chile, is destroyed by an earthquake.

1739 Spanish establish viceroyalty of New Granada, encompassing all territory between Orinoco and Amazon rivers.

230

SECTION 3 PROGRAM RESOURCES

 **In-Depth Resources: Unit 3**
- Guided Reading, p. 15
- Building Vocabulary, p. 18
- Reteaching Activity, p. 21

 **Guided Reading Workbook**
- Section 3

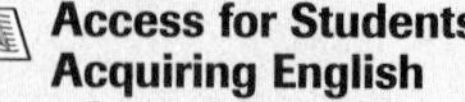 **Access for Students Acquiring English**
- Guided Reading, p. 51

 **Outline Maps with Activities**
- Spanish-Speaking South America, pp. 25–26

 **Formal Assessment**
- Section Quiz, p. 148

 **Integrated Assessment**
- Rubric for a sketch map, 2.1

 **Cultures Around the World**
- Architecture, p. 13
- Traditional Practices, p. 18

INTEGRATED TECHNOLOGY

Cultures Transparencies CW13, 18
- Machu Picchu
- Charro

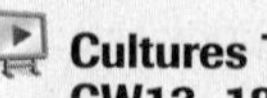

TEST-TAKING RESOURCES

 **Strategies for Test Preparation**

 **Test Practice Transparencies TT33**

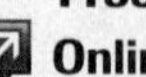 **Online Test Practice**

A. Answer A road system would have made communication faster and more efficient. It would have made the movement of troops easier.

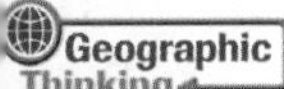
Geographic Thinking

Seeing Patterns
A How might a road system have helped to hold the Inca empire together?

harsh terrain, the Inca were able to build an advanced civilization.

They built their empire on the foundation of earlier cultures. From their capital at Cuzco in Peru, the Inca extended their power. They brought other tribes under their control and built a great empire.

By 1500, the Inca empire extended 2,500 miles along the west coast of South America. It ran from present-day Ecuador in the north to Argentina in the south. A road system that was about 20,000 miles long crossed mountains and deserts to link the empire. A

THE SPANISH CONQUEST As you read earlier, Pizarro and his soldiers invaded and conquered the Inca empire. The Spanish were primarily interested in claiming the gold and silver of the Inca.

The Spanish settlers forced the natives to work in mines and on farms and ranches. The Spanish landlords received the rights to the labor of the natives from officials in Spain, who passed laws to protect the Indians. But in spite of the laws, many of the settlers abused the natives or worked them to death.

The Spanish conquest had a devastating effect on the native population. Many Indians died while working in the silver mines at Potosí, Bolivia. These mines provided vast wealth for Spain. Natives were also forced to move to new villages so they could be controlled more easily. B

CONNECT TO THE ISSUES
DEMOCRACY
B What effect might the disruption of Inca life have had on the development of democracy in the region?

B. Answer It probably made it more difficult for democracy to develop, since it undermined a sense of community.

The Spanish forced their own language and religion on the conquered peoples. The **Quechua** (KEHCH•wuh) language of the Inca was overshadowed by Spanish as the settlers became the dominant culture. Likewise, the Inca religion of the native peoples was replaced by the Catholic religion of the conquerors as the official religion. Spanish rule in the region continued for almost 300 years. But one lasting legacy of the Inca is that millions of native peoples still speak Quechua.

INDEPENDENCE MOVEMENTS Inspired by the American Revolution (1776) and the French Revolution (1789), the countries of South America sought their independence from Spain in the first half of the 19th century. Two great leaders of independence movements in the region in the first half of the 19th century were Simón Bolívar and José

LATIN AMERICA

More About

Simón Bolívar

Simón Bolívar became disillusioned with Latin America's political chaos after independence. Before his death in 1830, he complained bitterly that those who worked for South American independence had plowed the sea.

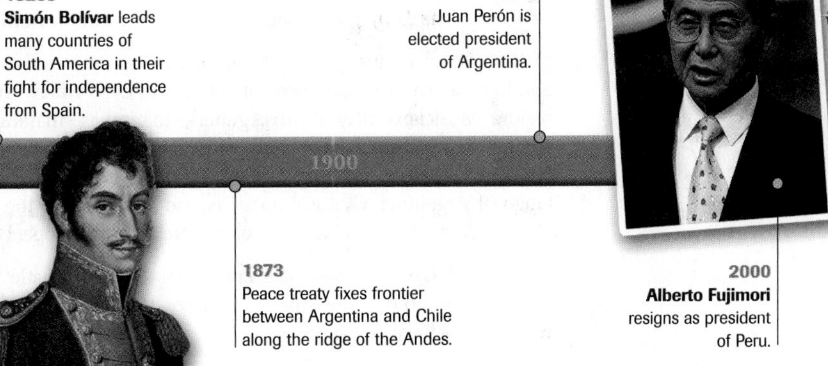

1777
Spain and Portugal resolve disputes about colonies in South America.
1820s
Simón Bolívar leads many countries of South America in their fight for independence from Spain.
1946
Juan Perón is elected president of Argentina.
1800
1900
1780
Peruvian Indians rebel against Spain.
1873
Peace treaty fixes frontier between Argentina and Chile along the ridge of the Andes.
2000
Alberto Fujimori resigns as president of Peru.

Interpreting Time Lines

South America after the Spanish Conquest

Ask students to look at the time line on this page, then ask them which came first, the earthquake in Chile or the peace treaty between Chile and Argentina. *(earthquake)* Point out to students that a timeline helps them see the events of history in the order in which they occurred.

ACTIVITY OPTION FIVE THEMES OF GEOGRAPHY

REGION

Exploring the Theme Cultural ties are maintained or destroyed based on a group's ability to control its region. When the Spanish invaded South America and conquered the Inca, the culture of the Inca people was undermined.

Understanding the Theme Discuss with students that language and religion are primary to a culture. By undermining native languages, the cultural identity is threatened. By weakening native religions, the backbone of the culture is destroyed.

- Why might conquering nations attempt to destroy the language and religion of the people they conquer? *(Destroying native language and religion makes it easier for the conqueror's language, religion, and so forth to find a place among the conquered.)*
- What other sources of information might we have about the Inca if their language and religion were undermined? *(artifacts, architecture, art works)*

Connect TO THE Issues

Democracy: Coup in Chile

In 1993, voters elected Eduardo Frei president of Chile. Pinochet was the commander-in-chief of the army until 1998, when he was arrested in Britain. He was taken back to Chile to stand trial for crimes against humanity. He died in 2006. Since the fall of the Pinochet government, tourism has increased in Chile. Ask students why tourism might improve with the election of a democratic government. *(tourists more willing to spend money to support a country with a democratically elected government)*

Instruct: Objective 

A Cultural Mosaic

- What is a cultural mosaic? *(societies with different cultures living near each other, but keeping their separate identities)*
- What sorts of music are popular in South America? *(popular, folk, street, classical)*
- Why are the literature, music, and arts and crafts of South America important? *(They express the different peoples and cultures that make up South America.)*

 **Cultures Around the World**
- Architecture, p. 13
- Traditional Practices, p. 18

Cultures Transparencies CW13, 18
- Machu Picchu
- Charro

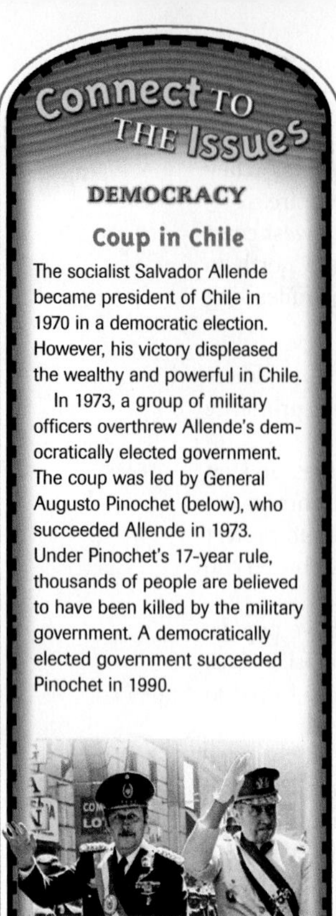

de San Martín. Bolívar helped to liberate the countries of Colombia, Venezuela, Ecuador, and Bolivia. José de San Martín helped to free the countries of Argentina, Chile, and Peru from Spanish rule.

Connect TO THE Issues
DEMOCRACY
Coup in Chile
The socialist Salvador Allende became president of Chile in 1970 in a democratic election. However, his victory displeased the wealthy and powerful in Chile.
In 1973, a group of military officers overthrew Allende's democratically elected government. The coup was led by General Augusto Pinochet (below), who succeeded Allende in 1973. Under Pinochet's 17-year rule, thousands of people are believed to have been killed by the military government. A democratically elected government succeeded Pinochet in 1990.

Argentina and Chile were the first to achieve independence because they were the farthest from Lima, the center of Spanish control. However, once independence was achieved, geography contributed to the failure of various countries to unify or work together for common goals. The continent has tended to be populated around its edges, with mountains and rain forests limiting interaction. This has contributed to underdevelopment and political instability. C

CONNECT TO THE ISSUES
DEMOCRACY
C How might better interaction and communication affect the development of democracy?

C. Answer They are likely to improve the prospects of democracy, which depends upon the free exchange of ideas and movement of people.

GOVERNMENT BY THE FEW Oligarchy (government by the few) and military rule have characterized the governments of many of the countries of South America since they won their independence from Spain. In fact, before his death in 1830, Simón Bolívar had become discouraged about the future of democracy in Latin America.

Throughout South America, authoritarian rule—which stresses obedience to authority over individual freedom—delayed the development of democracy. Although many South American nations gained freedom in the 1800s, hundreds of years of colonialism had their effects. Strong militaries, underdeveloped economies, and social class divisions still exist in the region today.

A Cultural Mosaic 2

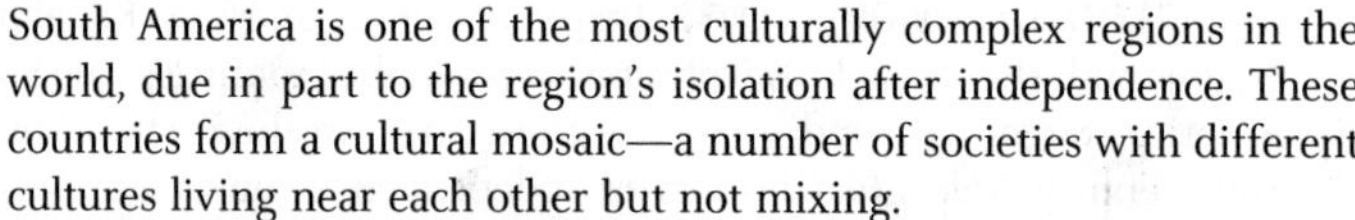

South America is one of the most culturally complex regions in the world, due in part to the region's isolation after independence. These countries form a cultural mosaic—a number of societies with different cultures living near each other but not mixing.

LITERATURE Spanish-speaking South America has a strong literary heritage. Particularly in the last quarter of the 20th century, South American writers claimed the world's attention with their extraordinary novels. Perhaps the most famous of these writers is Gabriel García Márquez of Colombia, who won the Nobel Prize for literature in 1982. Among his best-known novels are *One Hundred Years of Solitude* (1967) and *The General in His Labyrinth* (1989), a novel about Simón Bolívar.

MUSIC Popular music and folk music are important artistic traditions in South America. You can hear street music everywhere throughout the region. Musicians play drums, guitars, marimbas, maracas, and flutes, among other instruments. This music combines Indian, African, and European elements to make a thick cultural brew, as can be heard in the tango of Argentina. Classical music is also important in the region. Many cities in South America have symphony orchestras and opera companies.

ARTS AND CRAFTS Beautiful craftwork and handmade items can be found throughout Latin America. Pottery, textiles, glasswork, and metalwork all manage to combine beauty and usefulness. Many handmade

ACTIVITY OPTION **LINK TO HUMANITIES**

EXPLORING CULTURES

Objective To have a multisensory South American cultural experience

Class Time 60 minutes

Task To create mini-booths of South American food, music, and art

Supplies Needed
- food
- art, music, literature from South America
- art materials

Directions Have students work in small groups to make food, and find examples of art, literature, and music from a South American country that they choose. Have each group use art materials to create a booth. In one booth, students can read literature, in another play CDs, in another serve food, and in another display art pieces.

Arts and Crafts in South America

A Peruvian in Ollantaytambo carries craft items for sale. Her wares include hand-woven hats, scarves, and gloves.

Handmade furniture is still found throughout the region. This carpenter shows a chair that he has made in his workshop in Sicuani, Peru.

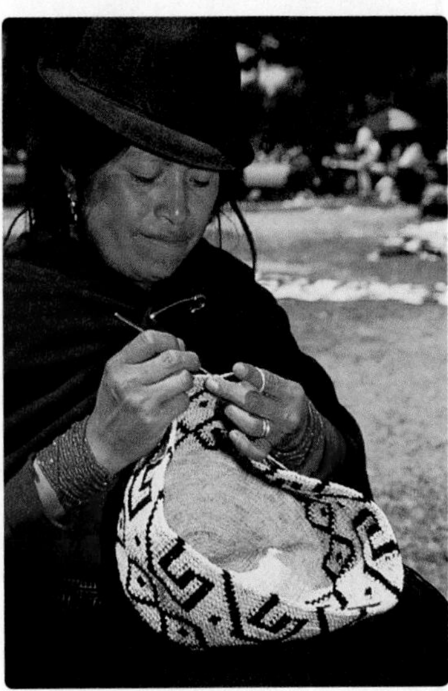

A Cotopaxi native woman weaves a basket at an open market in Alameda Park in Quito, Ecuador.

items are decorated with folk art or Indian religious symbols. Beautiful examples of handmade items can be found in tools and other household items throughout the region. Indian weavers, for example, make ponchos from the wool of the animals of the region, such as llamas and alpacas.

Economics: Resources and Trade 

Most economies in South American countries are based upon agriculture and the mining and extraction of resources such as oil and minerals. However, the income gap between rich and poor reflects the region's poverty and failure to develop economically after independence. Economic development of the entire region holds out the hope of improving the lives of millions of people.

ECONOMIES OF THE REGION One of the advantages in the region is that it produces a wide variety of products. This is because of its unique combination of resources, landforms, climate, and vegetation. In the north, Guyana, Suriname, and French Guiana grow crops for export on large farms. Colombia and Venezuela both have huge oil reserves that are probably their greatest economic asset.

In the west, Peru has an important fishing industry. Ecuador exports huge quantities of shrimp. Bolivia has deposits of tin, zinc, and copper.

In the south, Argentina produces great quantities of grain and livestock on its vast pampas. Uruguay is a prosperous agricultural country that has major farming and grazing areas in its portion of the pampas. Paraguay exports products such as soybeans, cotton, and animal hides.

Interpreting Photographs

Arts and Crafts in South America

These three photographs show various craftspeople displaying their wares. Ask students if there is any craft (such as pottery, carpentry, or weaving) that they practice or would like to practice.

Instruct: Objective 

Economics: Resources and Trade

- What makes the region able to produce a wide variety of products? *(a unique combination of resources, landforms, climate, and vegetation)*
- What country is South America's greatest economic success story? *(Chile)*

ACTIVITY OPTION COOPERATIVE LEARNING

RESOURCES CHART

Objective To make a chart that shows the resources of South America

Class Time 45 minutes

Task Work in small groups to create resources charts of several different countries in South America

Directions Assign a different country in South America to each group. Have groups use the material in this section, and any additional research, to create a chart that shows the resources of their assigned country. Within each group, assign the following tasks to individual students:
- research and make a list of resources
- research what part of the country the resources come from
- design chart
- make chart

Interpreting Maps

The Mercosur Trade Group

Point out the map and chart to students. Remind students that the goals of a free-trade zone are to help make the economies of the member nations more stable and to increase trade.

SKILLBUILDER ANSWERS

1. eight **2.** All border the Atlantic except Paraguay

Instruct: Objective 4

Education and the Future

- Is the literacy rate in South America higher or lower than in other parts of Latin America? *(higher)*
- What indications are there that the literacy rate is high in South America? *(South America supports colleges, universities, and technical schools, and there are many daily newspapers and books published)*
- Why is a high literacy rate important to a country? *(A high literacy rate means more people are educated and can get better jobs.)*

The Mercosur Trade Group
Caribbean Sea
VENEZUELA
GUYANA
SURINAME
FRENCH GUIANA
COLOMBIA
ECUADOR
PERU
BRAZIL
PACIFIC OCEAN
ATLANTIC OCEAN
BOLIVIA
PARAGUAY
ARGENTINA
URUGUAY
CHILE
N
S
E
W
Member
Associate member
Non-member
0 500 1,000 miles
0 500 1,000 kilometers
Azimuthal Equal-Area Projection
Geographic Cooperation: A Common Market
• Mercosur is an economic common market that began operating in the southern cone of South America in 1995.
• Goals of a free-trade zone among member nations:
1. to make member economies more stable;
2. to increase trade within region and thereby decrease dependency on unstable global markets;
3. to channel some of the profits of improving economies to those people and groups that most need help.
• The name Mercosur is formed from the Spanish phrase Mercado Común del Sur, which means Southern Common Market.
• There are more than 265 million consumers in this market.
• The combined Gross Domestic Product of the member nations is more than 1.3 trillion dollars a year.

SKILLBUILDER: Interpreting Maps

1 **REGION** How many countries in South America are not full members of Mercosur?

2 **LOCATION** What characteristics do the members of Mercosur share in terms of location?

CHILE'S SUCCESS STORY Chile is South America's greatest economic success story. It has been able to participate in the global economy by trading the products of its mines and fields with nations as far away as Japan. The export of fruit and vegetables to North American markets is an important part of Chile's economy because its harvest comes during the Northern Hemisphere's winter. Chile also has huge deposits of copper, which remains its largest export. However, Chile has recently begun to focus on its own hemisphere. It has been a leader in working for economic cooperation in the region, where it is an associate member of Mercosur. (See the chart and map above.) Associate members are countries with free-trade agreements with Mercosur.

Education and the Future 

The people of Spanish-speaking South America face a number of challenges. Education is a critical issue as young people move to the cities in search of jobs.

LITERACY IN SOUTH AMERICA The countries of Spanish-speaking South America have higher literacy rates than do the countries of Central America and the Caribbean, or Mexico and Brazil. In several countries, including Chile and Uruguay, literacy rates are higher than 90 percent. Moreover, the literacy rates for women are about the same as for men in those three countries; in fact, in Uruguay, the rate is slightly

ACTIVITY OPTION | CRITICAL THINKING

MAKING INFERENCES

Explaining the Skill Explain to students that inferences are ideas and meanings not stated in the material. Making inferences means reading between the lines to extend the information provided. Inferences are based on careful reading of what is stated in the material as well as one's own common sense and previous knowledge.

Applying the Skill Have students read the information on "Education and the Future" in this section. Then have students write answers to the following questions:

- In general, how would you describe the school systems in South America? *(They are good.)*
- From what you know about Central America and the Caribbean, why might South America have a higher literacy rate? *(Answers will vary. All should be supported by information from the text.)*
- Why is a high literacy rate desirable for a country? *(An educated public is economically more successful and this creates political stability.)*

higher for women. Most of the countries of South America support colleges, universities, and technical schools that train students for careers. As measured by the number of students in school and copies of daily newspapers and books published per capita, most of the countries of the region show high rates of education and literacy.

THE CASE OF CHILE Chile's literacy rate for the total adult population is around 96 percent. For young people between the ages of 15 and 24, it is even higher—close to 99 percent. Chilean readers can choose among numerous national and regional newspapers, many of them available online.

Education is very important in Chile. When they are between the ages of 6 and 13, all children must attend school, and public education is free. But after primary school, enrollment drops to less than 60 percent. Higher education has suffered because of political unrest. The universities had been independent and of high quality. Then a military coup led by General Augusto Pinochet overthrew Salvador Allende's government in 1973. Afterwards, the military introduced reforms that undermined higher education. Nonetheless, since Pinochet's departure from power in 1990, universities have regained some of their independence and standards. Today, there are many business schools in Chile that have contributed to the country's economic success.

Chile suffered a setback, however, when a magnitude 8.8 earthquake struck the country on February 27, 2010. Severe aftershocks followed. Rebuilding may take several years.

REGION The writer Isabel Allende, niece of Salvador Allende, is an important novelist in Latin America. Her most famous book may be *The House of the Spirits* (1982).

Interpreting Photographs

Isabel Allende

Ask students why writers are so important to a culture. Write several key words on the board from students' answers. Guide students to understand that writers tell about the culture and the people. Have one student begin a story about your class. Ask several students to tell a story about your class or community.

Assess & Reteach

GeoFocus Have students complete their notes on South America for the cluster diagram.

Formal Assessment
- Section Quiz, p. 148

Reteaching Activity
Restate the goals for this section. Have students write one or two sentences that describe the important ideas for each of the goals.

In-Depth Resources: Unit 3
- Reteaching Activity, p. 21

Outline Maps with Activities
- Spanish-Speaking South America, pp. 25–26

Section 3 Assessment

1 Places & Terms
Identify and explain the importance of each of the following.
- Inca
- Quechua
- Mercosur

2 Taking Notes
PLACE Review the notes you took for this section.

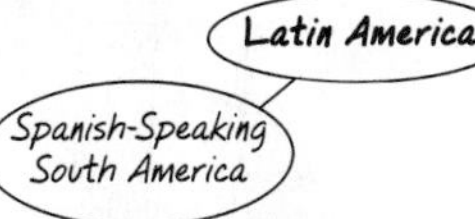

- Which countries besides Spain sent settlers to South America?
- Which countries in South America have the highest literacy rates?

3 Main Ideas
a. What have been some obstacles to democratic government in South America?
b. What was the extent of the Inca empire in South America?
c. What are some of the arts and crafts of the region?

4 Geographic Thinking
Drawing Conclusions Why might the southern cone of South America have decided to form a trade group?
Think about:
- the geography of the region
- the region's economies

See Skillbuilder Handbook, page R5.

SEEING PATTERNS Pair with a partner and draw a **sketch map** of South America. Fill in the map with the names of the various countries and the dominant language spoken in each.

SECTION 3 ASSESSMENT ANSWERS

1. Places & Terms
Inca, p. 230
Quechua, p. 231
Mercosur, p. 234

2. Taking Notes
- Portugal, France, and the Netherlands sent settlers.
- Argentina, Chile, and Uruguay

3. Main Ideas
a. oligarchy, military rule, authoritarian rule, underdeveloped economies, and class divisions
b. 2,500 miles along the west coast of South America
c. pottery, textiles, glasswork, and metalwork

4. Geographic Thinking
The countries of the region saw an opportunity to improve their standard of living by acting together to create a free-trade zone. Trade within the region should increase economic prosperity and this, in turn, will create profits that can be channeled to those who need help.

GeoActivity

Integrated Assessment
- Rubric for a sketch map, 2.1

SECTION 4 OBJECTIVES

1. Explain the two major divisions of South America.
2. Describe the national culture of Brazil.
3. Explain the economic strength of Brazil.
4. Describe Brazilian life today.

SKILLBUILDER: Interpreting Maps, p. 238

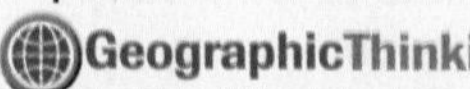

Making Comparisons, p. 237
Drawing Conclusions, p. 239

Focus & Motivate

Ask students how Brazil might be similar to the cultures of other Latin American countries, and how it might be different. *(Answers will vary.)*

Instruct: Objective 

History: A Divided Continent

- What resource was Portugal's source of wealth in Brazil? *(sugar)*
- Why did the patterns of settlement occur along the coast? *(The interior was difficult to settle because it was heavily forested.)*

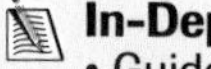

In-Depth Resources: Unit 3
- Guided Reading, p. 16

Interpreting Maps

Treaty of Tordesillas

Remind students that the Treaty of Tordesillas divided South America between Portugal and Spain. Ask students what group was not included in this treaty. (*native peoples*)

4 Brazil

Main Ideas

- Native peoples, Portuguese, and Africans have shaped Brazil.
- Brazil has the largest territory and the largest population of any country in Latin America.

Places & Terms

Treaty of Tordesillas
Carnival
samba
capoeira

CONNECT TO THE ISSUES
RESOURCES Brazil is a giant country rich in natural resources that must be developed and used wisely.

A HUMAN PERSPECTIVE In 1807, Napoleon's armies invaded Portugal. As the French army approached the capital of Lisbon, the Portuguese royal family boarded ships to escape capture. They sailed to Brazil, Portugal's largest colony, taking their court and royal treasury with them. For the next 14 years, Brazil was the heart of the Portuguese empire. During that time Brazilians developed a sense of their own independence. As you will read, a member of the Portuguese royal family was to play a decisive role in gaining Brazil's freedom from Portugal.

History: A Divided Continent 

Geography played an important role in the colonization of South America by Spain and Portugal. The two European powers reached an agreement to divide South America. In the resulting **Treaty of Tordesillas** (1494), Portugal gained control over the land that became present-day Brazil. In this section, you will look at Portuguese-speaking Brazil, the largest country in South America.

NATIVE PEOPLES AND PORTUGUESE CONQUEST

The territory of Brazil was originally home to native peoples divided into hundreds of tribes and language groups. Various estimates place the number of native peoples between one million and five million when the first colonists arrived in the early 1500s.

The first Portuguese colonists hoped to find gold or silver but were disappointed when they could find neither. Then they cleared out huge areas of forest where they created sugar plantations. Brazil soon became a source of wealth for Portugal because the demand for sugar was so great.

The patterns of settlement were along the coast, where cities such as Rio de Janeiro were established, rather than in the interior where rain forests made farming difficult. Eventually, the colonists cleared more land in the west for sugar plantations. In the process, the Portuguese conquered the native tribes and put them to work on the plantations. When natives died from diseases brought by the colonists, the Portuguese brought African slaves to Brazil by force to replace them. Today millions of Brazilians are of mixed European, African, and native ancestry.

Treaty of Tordesillas

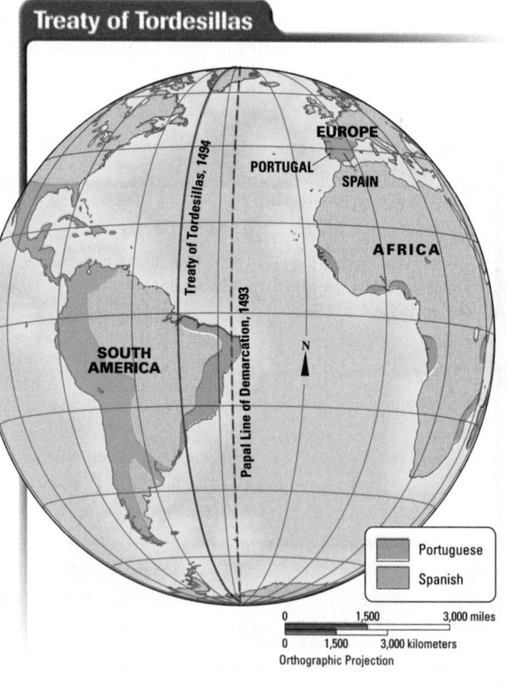

SECTION 4 PROGRAM RESOURCES

In-Depth Resources: Unit 3
- Guided Reading, p. 16
- Building Vocabulary, p. 18
- Reteaching Activity, p. 22

Guided Reading Workbook
- Section 4

Access for Students Acquiring English
- Guided Reading, p. 52

Outline Maps with Activities
- Brazil, pp. 27–28

Formal Assessment
- Section Quiz, p. 149

Integrated Assessment
- Rubric for a map, 2.1
- Rubric for a poster, 1.1

Cultures Around the World
- Dance, p. 16

INTEGRATED TECHNOLOGY

Cultures Transparencies CW16
- Dancing the Tango

Power Presentations

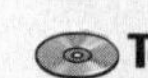

Test Generator
- Section Quiz

hmhsocialstudies.com

TEST-TAKING RESOURCES

Strategies for Test Preparation

Test Practice Transparencies TT34

Online Test Practice

INDEPENDENCE FOR BRAZIL Brazil remained a Portuguese colony from 1500 to 1822. After Napoleon's defeat in 1815, many people in Brazil demanded independence from Portugal. However, the Portuguese government wanted Brazil to remain a colony. But the Brazilians kept pushing for independence. Finally, thousands of them signed petitions asking Dom Pedro, the son of Portugal's king, to rule Brazil as an independent country. He agreed, and in September of 1822, he declared Brazil's independence from Portugal.

A National Culture 2

The culture of Brazil includes Portuguese influences, Native American elements, and African influences. But unlike other South American countries, Brazil has had more success in blending its ethnic groups.

THE PEOPLE OF BRAZIL When the first Europeans arrived in 1500, millions of native people lived in what is now Brazil. Thousands of them died from diseases brought by Europeans. Today, more than 500,000 native people live in Brazil, most in the Amazon rain forest.

Brazil has become home to many immigrants from other nations. Large numbers of people from Portugal, Germany, Italy, and Spain have settled there, as have immigrants from Lebanon and Syria. Brazil also has the largest Japanese population outside Japan. A

Geographic Thinking

Making Comparisons
A How does the population of Brazil resemble that of the United States?
A. Answer Like the United States, Brazil has welcomed immigrants from many different nations.

LANGUAGE AND RELIGION The Portuguese brought their language and their Catholic religion with them to Brazil. Today, Brazil has the largest Catholic population in the world. In addition, Protestants make up more than 15 percent of the population. Many other Brazilians, mainly those of African or mixed ancestry, practice religions that combine African beliefs with Catholicism.

ARCHITECTURE OF BRASÍLIA The architect Oscar Niemeyer designed the buildings for the new capital of Brasília, which was built in the interior of Brazil beginning in 1957. Part of the reason for locating the capital 600 miles inland was to draw people into the interior. The move of the government to the new capital city in 1960 signaled the opening of the country's west.

HUMAN-ENVIRONMENT INTERACTION Oscar Niemeyer designed these government offices for Brasília. The Senate meets in the domed building, and the Chamber of Deputies meets in the bowl-like building.

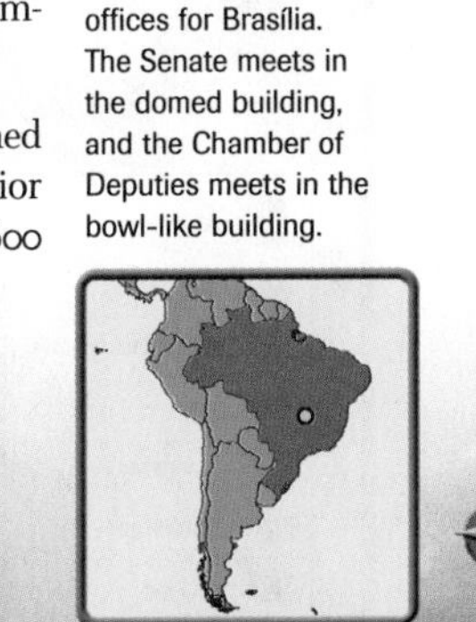

LATIN AMERICA

237

Instruct: Objective 2

A National Culture

- What three influences have shaped the culture of Brazil? *(Portuguese, Native American, African)*
- What are the primary language and religion of Brazil? *(Portuguese, Catholic)*

Interpreting Photographs

Brasília

Have students study the photograph on this page, then ask for their responses to the architecture. Ask them if they would like to work in the domed building. Why or why not? Ask them if they would like to work in the bowl. Why or why not? Ask students if they believe the environment where they spend time is important. Why or why not?

DIFFERENTIATING INSTRUCTION LESS PROFICIENT READERS

CREATING A GRAPHIC ORGANIZER

Objective To provide a framework for recalling key terms and details

Class Time 20 minutes

Task Make a web diagram of key details

Directions Have students create a web or set of webs for history, culture, economics, and daily life. Around each main head, students can add facts and important details. You might provide a web like the one shown here as a model.

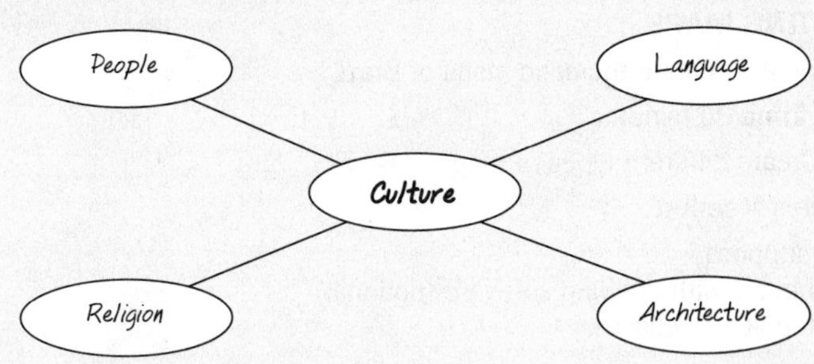

Instruct: Objective 3

An Economic Giant Awakens

- What has made Brazil an industrial power? *(natural resources, rivers, reserves of oil and natural gas, vast area, people)*
- What is an important part of the economy in the western interior? *(agriculture, because grasslands provide rich farmland)*

Interpreting Maps

Natural Resources of Brazil

Ask students what resources are found near Salvador. *(gold, petroleum, hydroelectric power)*

SKILLBUILDER ANSWERS

1. in the north **2.** in the interior

An Economic Giant Awakens 

Brazil is a growing economic power. Much of this power is based on its vast area, its abundance of natural resources, and its people. Its economy is the tenth largest in the world. Its diverse population of almost 200 million people contributes to its economic strength.

AN INDUSTRIAL POWER Natural resources have helped make Brazil an industrial power. It has deposits of iron and bauxite, as well as other minerals used in manufacturing. In addition, tin and manganese reserves are abundant. It also has supplies of gold, silver, titanium, chromite, tungsten, and quartz.

More than a thousand rivers, including the Amazon, flow through Brazil. Power plants located along these rivers produce electricity. In addition, Brazil's large reserves of oil and natural gas contribute to its industrial might.

Brazil is one of the most industrialized of South American countries, with one of the largest steel plants in the region. It is a leading maker of automobiles. More than 90 percent of new cars use ethanol, a fuel that comes from sugar cane and is less expensive than imported oil. B

CONNECT TO THE ISSUES
RESOURCES
B How do Brazil's natural resources contribute to its industrial success?
B. Answer Rather than having to import resources that are converted into goods, Brazil has a rich supply of resources within the country to use in manufacturing.

MIGRATION TO THE CITIES Despite its economic successes, Brazil remains a country with a vast gap between the rich and the poor. Increasing urbanization is one result of attempts by many Brazilians to improve their lives by seeking jobs in the cities.

The movement of people in Brazil from country to city reflects changes in agriculture that pushed people off the land. It also reflects the growth in manufacturing that pulled people to the cities. In 1960, about 22 percent of the population lived in the cities. By 2008, more than 86 percent of the people lived in cities.

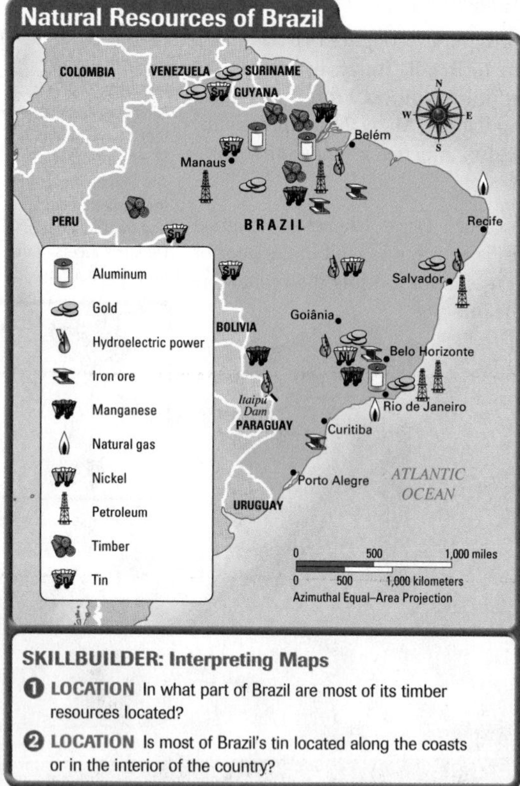

SKILLBUILDER: Interpreting Maps

1. **LOCATION** In what part of Brazil are most of its timber resources located?
2. **LOCATION** Is most of Brazil's tin located along the coasts or in the interior of the country?

MIGRATION TO THE INTERIOR There has also been a move into the interior. About 80 percent of the people live within 200 miles of the sea. But the government is encouraging settlement of the interior to develop its many resources. Commercial agriculture is an important part of the economy in the western interior. That is because of the *cerrado*—the fertile grasslands, similar to the Great Plains in the United States, that provide rich farmland. Many Brazilians are willing to move to the interior to improve their economic situation.

ACTIVITY OPTION **COOPERATIVE LEARNING**

CREATING MAPS

Objective To create thematic maps of Brazil

Class Time 30 minutes

Task Create different types of maps of Brazil

Supplies Needed

- art supplies
- computer with drawing software (optional)
- textbook and atlases

Directions Divide the class into groups. Assign one of the following maps to each group: climate, natural resources and land uses, political, physical, population. Using computer graphics or art materials, have groups create their assigned maps. Encourage students to be creative in the materials they use to create their maps. When completed, display the maps around the room. Within each group, assign the following tasks to individual students:

- researcher
- map designer
- map creator
- editor

GeoFocus Have students complete their notes on Brazil for the cluster diagram.

Brazilian Life Today 4

Brazil is a country of great variety in its city life, music, and holidays.

FROM CARNIVAL TO MARTIAL ARTS The most colorful feast day in Brazil is **Carnival.** In Rio de Janeiro, people in costumes ride on floats through the streets. Carnival takes place to the music of the **samba,** a Brazilian dance with African influences.

Capoeira is a martial art and dance that developed in Brazil from African origins. Angolans who were taken to Brazil by the Portuguese brought this martial art and dance with them.

PLACE Young men practice the martial art of capoeira.

CITY LIFE IN RIO DE JANEIRO Brasília is the political capital of Brazil, and São Paulo is its economic heart and largest city, but Rio de Janeiro is the cultural center. The residents of Rio are among the country's leaders in important cultural activities and institutions.

Rio has one of the most spectacular natural settings in the world. Sugarloaf Mountain, Guanabara Bay, and Copacabana Beach are just a few of the breathtaking sights.

There is a darker side to life in Rio, and that is caused by the widening gap between rich and poor. Desperately poor slums, called *favelas,* dot the hillsides. Crime waves and drug abuse are two results of the poverty. Recently, however, government officials have launched programs to bring in electrical power, paved streets, and sewers. C

In the next chapter, you will read about three important issues that affect Latin America—resources, democracy, and the income gap.

C. Answer
Severe poverty and a growing income gap can undermine a democracy and make it less stable.

CONNECT TO THE ISSUES
INCOME GAP
C What might be the impact of poverty and the income gap on democratic government?

LATIN AMERICA

SECTION 4 Assessment

1 Places & Terms
Identify and explain the importance of each of the following.
- Treaty of Tordesillas
- Carnival
- samba
- capoeira

2 Taking Notes
PLACE Review the notes you took for this section.

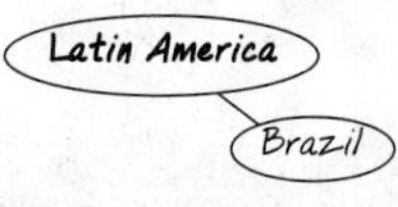

- Which European country sent the most settlers to Brazil?
- Who lived in Brazil before the European settlers arrived?

3 Main Ideas
a. What crop did settlers first grow in Brazil and what effect did it have on the makeup of the population?
b. How do Brazil's rivers contribute to its wealth?
c. What are some aspects of Brazilian culture that show an African influence?

4 Geographic Thinking
Drawing Conclusions What is the relationship between coast and interior in the settling of Brazil? **Think about:**
- the patterns of settlement along the coast
- the resources of the interior

EXPLORING LOCAL GEOGRAPHY Rio de Janeiro is almost two different cities–one rich and one poor. Pair with a partner and draw a **map** that divides your city, town, or neighborhood in two. Decide which parts are better off than others. What resources and features distinguish one part from another?

Instruct: Objective 4

Brazilian Life Today

- Which city is the cultural center of Brazil? *(Rio de Janeiro)*
- Why are drug abuse and crime so high in Rio de Janeiro? *(high poverty level and large income gap)*
- How does poverty contribute to drug abuse and high crime rates? *(When people feel desperate, they often turn to drugs and crime.)*

Cultures Around the World
- Dance, p. 16

Cultures Transparencies CW16
- Dancing the Tango

Assess & Reteach

Formal Assessment
- Section Quiz, p. 149

Reteaching Activity
Ask students what they found most interesting about Brazil. After a brief class discussion, have students write a couple of paragraphs on what they found interesting, and why. Read a few of the paragraphs aloud in class.

In-Depth Resources: Unit 3
- Reteaching Activity, p. 22

Outline Maps with Activities
- Brazil, pp. 27–28

SECTION 4 ASSESSMENT ANSWERS

1. Places & Terms
Treaty of Tordesillas, p. 236
Carnival, p. 239
samba, p. 239
capoeira, p. 239

2. Taking Notes
- Portugal
- native peoples of many tribes and language groups

3. Main Ideas
a. The settlers cleared huge areas of the forest for sugar plantations. Many natives died on the plantations and were replaced by enslaved Africans brought by force to Brazil.
b. Brazil's many rivers produce hydroelectric power.
c. Capoeira and the samba both have African elements.

4. Geographic Thinking
People from Europe first settled along the coast. Later, they moved into the interior to develop its resources.

GeoActivity

Integrated Assessment
- Rubric for a map, 2.1

OBJECTIVES

- Identify similarities and differences in festivals and holidays around the world.

Instruct: Objective

Festivals and Holidays

- What is the main purpose of festivals and holidays? *(celebration)*
- What special kind of significance do holidays often have? *(religious)*
- Which of the holidays shown does not have its origin in religion? *(Chinese New Year)*

Interpreting Maps

Have students examine the world map as well as the photo captions. Ask them to name each country and continent represented in the photos here. *(Brazil in South America; Italy in Europe; India in Asia; Hong Kong in Asia)*

hmhsocialstudies.com INTERACTIVE

Comparing Cultures

Festivals and Holidays

Different cultures around the world have their own festivals and holidays—occasions for celebration. Often these special days have a religious significance. Carnival, for example, is a period of merrymaking that is celebrated in many Christian countries just before Lent, a season of fasting and penitence. On these two pages, you will learn about this and other festivals around the world. Three of the festivals—those in Brazil, Venice, and India—have their roots in religion. One of the holidays—that in Hong Kong—celebrates the beginning of a new year.

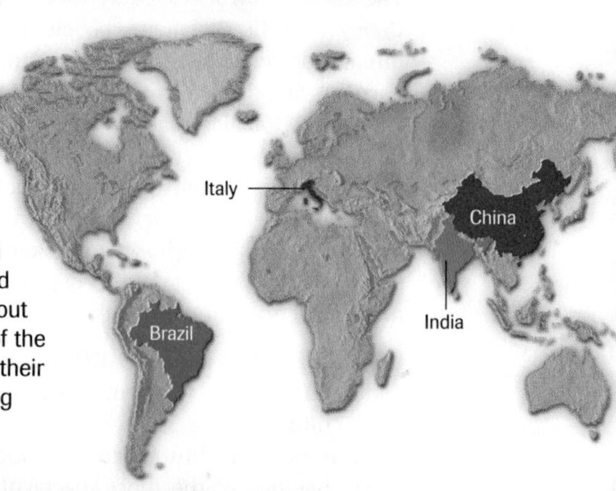

Samba dancers in Rio de Janeiro, Brazil, celebrate Carnival by dancing in the streets. Carnival is the period of merrymaking just before Lent.

In Venice, Italy, masks are used to celebrate Carnival, a revel that features elaborate costumes.

SUPPORTING RESOURCES

BOOKS FOR THE TEACHER

Starza, O. M. ***The Jagannatha Temple at Puri: Its Architecture, Art and Cult*** (Studies in South Asian Culture, Vol. 15). Boston: Brill Academic Publishers, 1993. Created in the 12th century, the temple of Jagannatha (Juggernaut) at Puri is one of India's great centers of pilgrimage.

Vianna, Hermano, and John C. Chasteen, ed. ***The Mystery of Samba: Popular Music and National Identity in Brazil.*** Chapel Hill: Univ of North Carolina Pr, 1999. A readable study of the popular music of Brazil, translated from the Portuguese.

BOOKS FOR THE STUDENT

McGowan, Chris, and Ricardo Pessanha. ***The Brazilian Sound: Samba, Bossa Nova, and the Popular Music of Brazil.*** Philadelphia: Temple Univ Pr, 1998. A survey of Brazilian popular music.

INTERNET

For more on festivals and holidays around the world, visit . . .

hmhsocialstudies.com

The Juggernaut in Puri, India, is a wooden image of the Hindu god Krishna mounted on a cart. The term comes from a Sanskrit word that means "lord of the world." The cart moves on 16 wheels through crowds of Hindu pilgrims on various festival days.t

In Hong Kong, a dragon is paraded by a boy to celebrate the New Year. In Chinese culture, the New Year is an important holiday.

GeoActivity

CREATING A POSTER

Working with a partner, use the Internet to research one of the festivals or holidays listed below. Then create a **poster** about the holiday.

- Use visuals and captions to describe the festival or holiday you have chosen.
- Research a different festival and make a second poster to compare festivals from different countries.

hmhsocialstudies.com RESEARCH WEB LINKS

GeoData

FESTIVALS AND HOLIDAYS AROUND THE WORLD

RELIGIOUS

Christianity
Christmas
Easter

Judaism
Rosh Hashanah
Passover

Islam
Feast of Sacrifice
Festival of Breaking Fast
Ashura

Hinduism
Holi
Diwali

OTHER
Independence Day
New Year's Day
Cinco de Mayo
Bastille Day
May Day
Kwanzaa
Thanksgiving

GeoActivities

GeoActivities

Integrated Assessment
- Rubric for a poster, 1.1

Interpreting Photographs

Rio, Venice, Puri, Hong Kong

Have students examine the photographs. Ask them to describe each picture. Then ask them to choose one photograph and explain how it is similar to or different from a holiday they celebrate.

More About

The Juggernaut

Sometimes during the procession of the Juggernaut through the streets, people are accidently crushed under the wheels of the cart. The crowds of pilgrims are sometimes so thick that careless worshippers have been known to fall under one of the 16 wheels of the cart.

ACTIVITY OPTION | INTERNET RESEARCH

PLANNING A VACATION

Objective To develop basic research and planning skills

Class Time 30 minutes

Task Use the Internet and other means of research to create a travel presentation

Directions Have students use the Internet to learn about vacations in one of the places shown on these two pages. Have students create a brochure that promotes tourist vacations in one of these places using computer-generated graphics, art materials, photographs, or slides.

Reviewing Places & Terms

A. 1. Tenochtitlán, p. 217
2. PRI, p. 218
3. NAFTA, p. 220
4. cultural hearth, p. 222
5. United Provinces of Central America, p. 223
6. Panama Canal, p. 226
7. Inca, p. 230
8. Mercosur, p. 234
9. Treaty of Tordesillas, p. 236
10. Carnival, p. 239

B. Possible Responses

11. Lake Texcoco surrounded Tenochtitlán.
12. Vicente Fox's election signaled the end of one-party rule.
13. The canal cuts the distance and travel time for ships.
14. Spain and Portugal signed the Treaty of Tordesillas.
15. Chile and Bolivia are associate members.
16. Rio de Janeiro celebrates Carnival in a colorful way.
17. The United States and Canada are also members of NAFTA.
18. These areas were homelands to the Maya and the Inca.
19. El Salvador, Nicaragua, Costa Rica, Guatemala, and Honduras made up the United Provinces of Central America.
20. The Inca spoke Quechua.

Chapter 10 Assessment

VISUAL SUMMARY
HUMAN GEOGRAPHY OF LATIN AMERICA

Subregions of Latin America

Mexico
- Native peoples and Spanish settlers have shaped the history and culture of Mexico.
- Economic expansion and an increasingly democratic government have developed together.

Central America and the Caribbean
- Native peoples, settlers from many European countries, and Africans have shaped Central America and the Caribbean.
- The economies of the region rely primarily on agriculture and tourism.

Spanish-Speaking South America
- The countries of South America are developing strategies to improve their economies.
- Among these strategies are wide-ranging trade agreements, including Mercosur.

Brazil
- Brazil is the giant of Latin America.
- Settled originally by the Portuguese, Brazil has welcomed immigrants from all over the world.
- Its economy is among the ten largest in the world.

Reviewing Places & Terms

A. Briefly explain the importance of each of the following.

1. Tenochtitlán
2. Institutional Revolutionary Party (PRI)
3. NAFTA
4. cultural hearth
5. United Provinces of Central America
6. Panama Canal
7. Inca
8. Mercosur
9. Treaty of Tordesillas
10. Carnival

B. Answer the questions about vocabulary in complete sentences.

11. What body of water surrounded Tenochtitlán?
12. Whose election signaled the end of one-party rule in Mexico?
13. Why is the Panama Canal important to world trade?
14. Which two European powers signed the Treaty of Tordesillas?
15. Which countries are associate members of Mercosur?
16. In what city of Brazil is Carnival celebrated in a particularly colorful way?
17. Which countries besides Mexico are members of NAFTA?
18. Why are Central America and the Andes Mountains around Cuzco cultural hearths?
19. Which countries made up the United Provinces of Central America?
20. What language did the Inca speak?

Main Ideas

Mexico (pp. 217–221)

1. What was the Spanish attitude toward Aztec culture?
2. What are the maquiladoras?

Central America and the Caribbean (pp. 222–229)

3. In terms of who settled there, how is the Caribbean different from Mexico and Central America?
4. Which two parts of the economy provide most of the income in Central America and the Caribbean?
5. What are some of the most important export crops in the region?

Spanish-Speaking South America (pp. 230–235)

6. Which countries are full members of Mercosur?
7. Which countries have literacy rates higher than 90 percent?
8. What happened to the Inca language after the Spanish conquest?

Brazil (pp. 236–241)

9. What is the ethnic makeup of Brazil?
10. What are some of the darker aspects of life in Brazil today?

Main Ideas

1. The Spanish did not respect Aztec culture, and destroyed much of it.
2. They are factories in Mexico, often located along the U.S. border, that assemble imported materials into manufactured goods for export.
3. The Caribbean had settlers from many countries in Europe, while Mexico and Central America had settlers mostly from Spain.
4. agriculture and tourism
5. bananas, coffee, sugar cane, citrus, and spices
6. Argentina, Brazil, Paraguay, and Uruguay
7. See unit Regional Data File.
8. Quechua is still spoken by millions of people in the Andes.
9. Brazil has taken in immigrants from around the world, including people from Portugal, Germany, Italy, Spain, Lebanon, Syria, Japan, and Africa.
10. poverty, slums, crime, drugs

Critical Thinking

1. Using Your Notes

Use your completed chart to answer these questions.

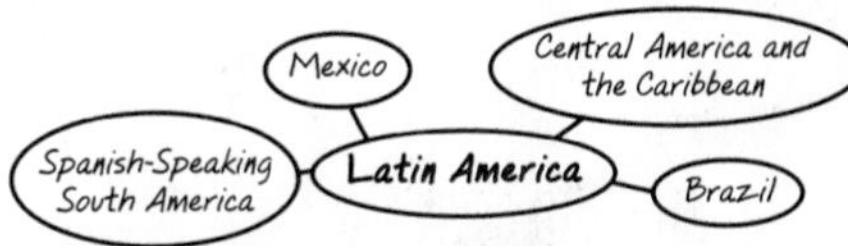

a. Which two European countries colonized the most territory in Latin America?

b. What are some of the ways in which Latin America is developing economically in recent years?

2. Geographic Themes

a. **HUMAN–ENVIRONMENT INTERACTION** How has the Amazon River been used and developed?

b. **MOVEMENT** What has restricted the movement of people from the coast of South America into the interior?

3. Identifying Themes

Interaction between European powers and native peoples occurred throughout the region. What are some of the consequences of this interaction? Which of the five themes are reflected in your answer?

4. Identifying and Solving Problems

What are some of the ways that individual citizens of Latin America are working to improve their economic situation?

5. Making Comparisons

How are Spanish-speaking and Portuguese-speaking South America alike and different?

For Additional Test Practice

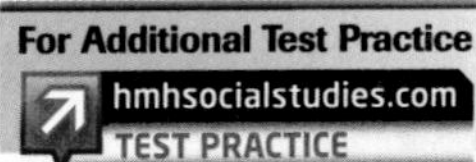

Geographic Skills: Interpreting Maps

City of Tenochtitlán

Use the map to answer the questions.

1. **PLACE** This is a Spanish map of the Aztec city of Tenochtitlán. Why did the city require roadway connections to the mainland?
2. **MOVEMENT** Why might this site have been a good location for a city?
3. **HUMAN–ENVIRONMENT INTERACTION** What purpose might the canals within the city have served?

Create a map of a fortress city of your design. Your map should make use of the natural advantages afforded by the site you have chosen.

hmhsocialstudies.com

MULTIMEDIA ACTIVITY

Use the links at **hmhsocialstudies.com** to do research on economic growth in Latin America. Focus on the impact of free-market reforms on the income gap.

Creating Graphs and Charts Present a report of your findings. Include a chart that shows which countries have introduced free-market reforms and what impact these reforms have had on closing the income gap.

Critical Thinking

1. a. Spain and Portugal
b. maquiladoras in Mexico, the exploitation of resources in Brazil, tourism in the Caribbean, and the industrialization of subregions

2. a. Power plants located along the river produce electricity.
b. mountains and the rain forest

3. The destruction of the cultures of the native peoples, with the language and religion of the European countries becoming dominant in the region. Region is the theme that best applies.

4. moving to the cities in search of better jobs, getting training and education, looking for work in tourism and other growth industries, participating in the informal economy, and taking jobs in factories

5. Both were settled by people who came from a dominant country in Europe. Both have become more diverse over the years. However, Spanish-speaking South America is divided into a number of countries, while Portuguese-speaking South America is composed only of Brazil.

GeoActivity

Integrated Assessment
- Rubric for a map, 2.1

Formal Assessment
- Chapter Test, Forms A, B, and C, pp. 150-161

Geographic Skills

1. because surrounded by a lake

2. because the island location provided some security and protection

3. They connected the city, providing avenues of transportation for people and goods, for example, in getting products to market.

For their report on economic growth in Latin America, students should:

MULTIMEDIA ACTIVITY

- present concise, well-organized information on economic growth;
- summarize the impact of free-market reforms;
- produce a clear, imaginative visual to complement the report on economic growth;
- include references to the Web sites used as sources.

Grading Rubric Evaluate student performance as Exceptional, Acceptable, or Poor in each of the following categories:

	Exceptional	Acceptable	Poor
Writing is clear, focused, and logical			
States information clearly			
Provides necessary facts and examples			
Uses correct grammar, spelling, and punctuation			

Multimedia Classroom

The **HISTORY™ Multimedia Classroom** is a set of exciting new social studies teaching tools featuring award-winning program content. These comprehensive lesson plans, correlated to individual state and national curriculum standards, are easy to use for both teachers and students.

Each lesson contains the following:

- Short video segments that bring history topics to life
- Maps and visual materials
- Discussion and review questions
- Easily printable primary source documents
- Classroom activities and Internet-based activity links

The Multimedia Classroom has been specially designed to be versatile and easily adaptable to existing courses, lesson plans, and syllabi. Every lesson is designed to offer maximum flexibility. Teachers can select entire plans or only the elements they need, allowing them to individually tailor each lesson. Each multimedia lesson is available in CD-ROM format and is accompanied by full-length award-winning programs on DVD from HISTORY™.

For more information or to purchase go to hmhsocialstudies.com

Because some of these lessons may contain video material of a sensitive nature, we recommend that teachers and parents review these materials in their entirety before screening them to students.

HISTORY

MULTIMEDIA CONNECTIONS

Mexico

Teotihuacán, established around 200 B.C., was the first great civilization of ancient Mexico. At its height around the middle of the first millennium A.D., the "City of the Gods" was one of the largest cities in the world. It covered 12 square miles and was home to some 200,000 people. The Pyramid of the Sun, above, was the largest building in Teotihuacán.

For centuries after the fall of Teotihuacán, present-day Mexico was home to a number of great empires, including the highly sophisticated Aztec civilization. The arrival of the Spanish in the early 1500s forever changed life for Mexico's ancient peoples, and Mexican culture today is dominated by a blend of indigenous and Spanish cultures.

Explore the history of Mexico from ancient to modern times online. You can find a wealth of information, video clips, primary sources, activities, and more at hmhsocialstudies.com.

Mexico: Courage and Conquest

Resources 

The following resources come with printable introductions, comprehension and critical thinking questions, transcripts, and vocabulary support.

Full Length DVD

Mexico: Courage and Conquest (3 hrs 20 mins)

Video Clips

- Mexico's Ancient Civilizations (3:44)
- The Arrival of the Spanish (3:15)
- Catholicism and the Crown (3:39)
- Miguel Hidalgo's Call to Arms (3:13)
- Independence for Texas (4:36)
- The Mexican-American War (3:42)
- Transforming the Nation (4:44)
- The Peasant Revolution (5:08)
- Power Plays and Politics (3:31)
- Mexico in the Modern Era (2:09)

Maps

- Site Plan of Tenochtitlán
- Mexico, 1824-1867

Activities

- The Columbian Exchange
- The Struggle for Equality
- Mexico's Reform Movements
- A Hundred Years of Change
- Women and the Revolution
- Comparing Constitutions

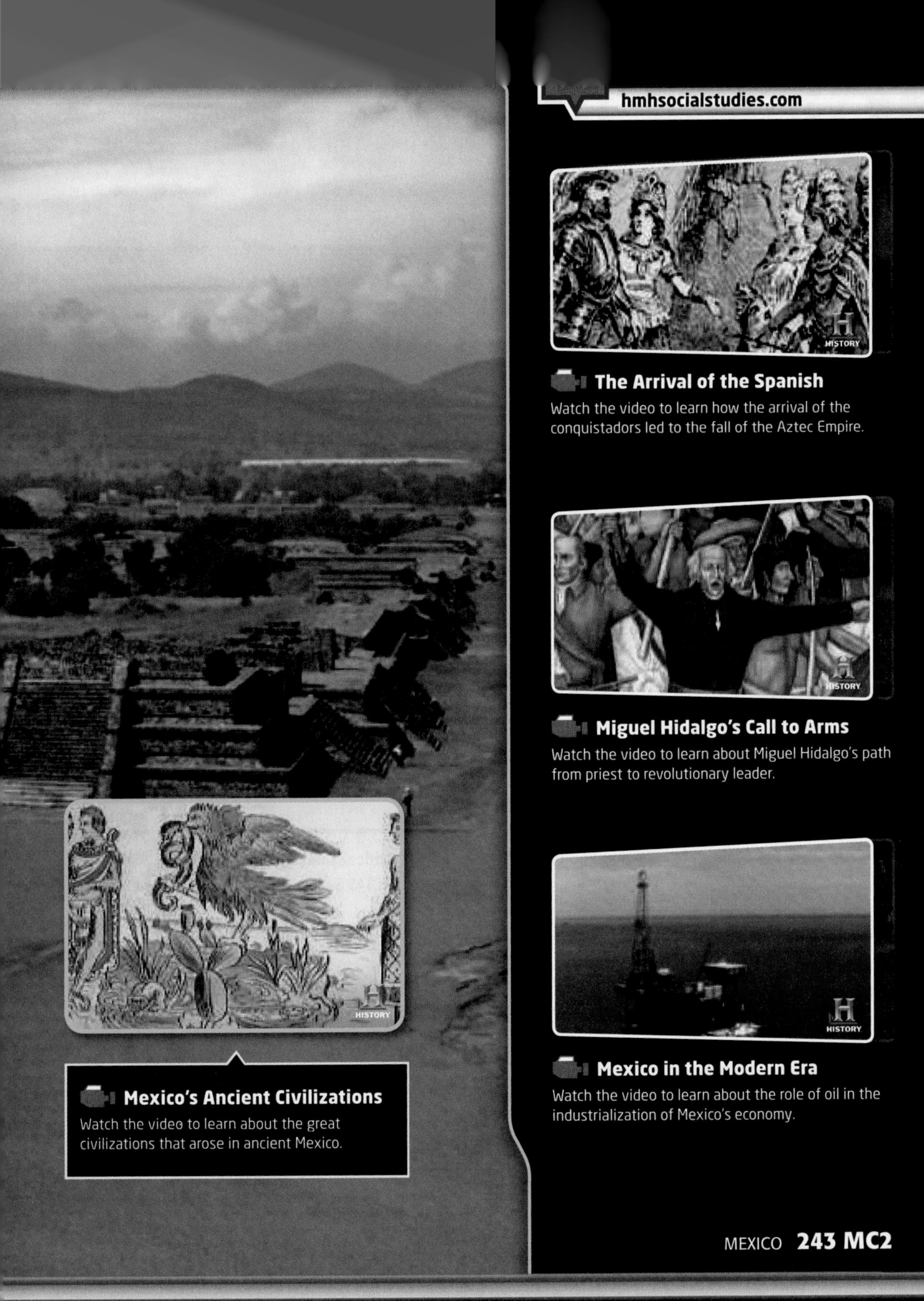

hmhsocialstudies.com
The Arrival of the Spanish
Watch the video to learn how the arrival of the conquistadors led to the fall of the Aztec Empire.
Miguel Hidalgo's Call to Arms
Watch the video to learn about Miguel Hidalgo's path from priest to revolutionary leader.
Mexico in the Modern Era
Watch the video to learn about the role of oil in the industrialization of Mexico's economy.
Mexico's Ancient Civilizations
Watch the video to learn about the great civilizations that arose in ancient Mexico.
MEXICO 243 MC2

Primary Sources

- Pyramid of the Sun
- The Fall of Tenochtitlán
- On Female Education
- Concerning the Caste System
- Observations on Texas, 1827
- Treaty of Guadalupe Hidalgo, 1848
- The Plan of San Luis Potosí
- Photograph of Zapata
- Response to U.S. Intervention, 1915
- Disembarkation at Veracruz

? General Review Questions

? General Discussion Questions

Web Links

Bibliography

Mexico's Ancient Civilizations

The first people to live in what is now Mexico were migratory hunters that eventually settled and established civilizations in the region. Powerful groups came to dominate the area, including the Maya and the Toltecs. The latest arrivals to the region, the Aztecs, would build the greatest empire of ancient Mexico.

The Arrival of the Spanish

Aztec mythology told of the eventual return of the god Quetzalcoatl. When Spanish explorer Hernán Cortés arrived in Mexico in 1519, many believed the prophecy had been fulfilled. Moctezuma II, the Aztec king, first welcomed the newcomers, believing they might be descendants of Quetzalcoatl. Soon after, though, the Aztecs realized the Spanish were in fact a powerful enemy. The conquistadors and their Indian allies overpowered the Aztecs, and Tenochtitlán, the ancient Aztec capital, was destroyed in 1521.

Miguel Hidalgo's Call to Arms

During the Spanish Inquisition, a Catholic priest named Miguel Hidalgo was banished to the city of Dolores for his controversial beliefs that were in opposition to Church doctrine. In Dolores, Hidalgo dedicated himself to helping improve life for Indians and mestizos. On September 16, 1810, he called for revolution against Spanish rule in his "Grito de Dolores." His actions helped spark the independence movement and later earned him the name "Father of the Mexican Revolution."

Mexico in the Modern Era

In the late 1930s, Mexico's Institutional Revolutionary Party, or PRI, nationalized the oil industry. The country prospered from its vast oil deposits. PRI's leaders had promised economic reform and a more equal distribution of wealth. Yet the disparity between Mexico's socioeconomic classes remained virtually unchanged.

CHAPTER 11 PLANNING GUIDE

Today's Issues: Latin America

OVERVIEW	INSTRUCTIONAL RESOURCES	
ESSENTIAL QUESTION How can citizen participation help solve Latin America's challenges? **Focus on the Essential Question Podcast**	**In-Depth Resources: Unit 3** • Building Vocabulary, p. 29 **Block Schedule Strategies** **Chapter Summaries** (English/Spanish)	**Interactive Online Edition** TOS **ExamView® Assessment Suite** (English/Spanish) TOS **CalendarPlanner** **Power Presentations with Media Gallery** **Critical Thinking Transparencies** • CT11 hmhsocialstudies.com INTERACTIVE
SECTION 1 **RAIN FOREST RESOURCES** **MAIN IDEAS** • Rain forest resources are subjected to competing demands from different groups. • The quality of life on earth is threatened as rain forests are destroyed.	**In-Depth Resources: Unit 3** • Guided Reading, p. 23 • Map and Graph Skills, pp. 26–27 • Skillbuilder Practice, p. 28 • Building Vocabulary, p. 29 • Exploring Today's Issues, pp. 30–31 • Reteaching Activity, p. 34 **Guided Reading Workbook,** Section 1	**Map Transparencies** • MT20 Natural Resources and Rain Forests of Latin America
SECTION 2 **GIVING CITIZENS A VOICE** **MAIN IDEAS** • Democracy is beginning to overcome obstacles in Latin America. • Political, economic, and social reform all play a part in the success of democracy in Latin America.	**In-Depth Resources: Unit 3** • Guided Reading, p. 24 • Building Vocabulary, p. 29 • Exploring Today's Issues, pp. 32–33 • Reteaching Activity, p. 35 **Guided Reading Workbook,** Section 2	**Critical Thinking Transparencies** • CT43 Evolution of Democracy in Latin America
CASE STUDY: **THE INCOME GAP** **MAIN IDEAS** • The income gap in Latin America reflects the legacy of colonialism. • In many parts of Latin America, there is a wide (and widening) income gap between rich and poor.	**In-Depth Resources: Unit 3** • Guided Reading, p. 25 • Building Vocabulary, p. 29 • Reteaching Activity, p. 36 **Guided Reading Workbook,** Case Study	

ASSESSMENT

SE **Chapter Assessment,** pp. 256-257

Formal Assessment
- Chapter Tests, Forms A, B, and C, pp. 165-179

TOS **ExamView® Assessment Suite**

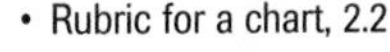

Strategies for Test Preparation

hmhsocialstudies.com TEST PRACTICE

SE **Section Assessment,** p. 247

Formal Assessment
- Section Quiz, p. 162

Integrated Assessment
- Rubric for a chart, 2.2

Test Practice Transparencies TT35

SE **Section Assessment,** p. 251

Formal Assessment
- Section Quiz, p. 163

Integrated Assessment
- Rubric for a report, 2.5

Test Practice Transparencies TT36

SE **Case Study Project,** p. 254–255

Formal Assessment
- Case Study Quiz, p. 164

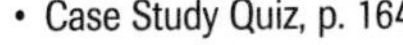

Test Practice Transparencies TT37

CHART KEY:

SE Student Edition	Block Scheduling	DVD/CD-ROM
TE Teacher's Edition	TOS Teacher One Stop	MP3 Audio
Printable Resource	Presentation Resource	HISTORY™

Program Resources available on TOS and @ hmhsocialstudies.com

SUPPORTING RESOURCES

- **Multimedia Classroom Global History Series**
- **Global History Teacher's Guide**

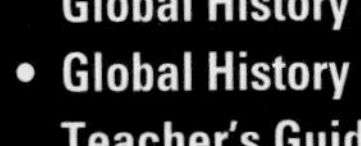

Social Studies Trade Library Collection
- Latino Trade Collection

For more information or to purchase these resources, go to hmhsocialstudies.com

DIFFERENTIATED INSTRUCTION

English Learners	Struggling Readers	Gifted and Talented Students
Spanish/English Guided Reading Workbook **Access for Students Acquiring English/ESL** Spanish Translations, pp. 56–59 **Chapter Summaries** (English/Spanish)	**Chapter Summaries** (English/Spanish)	TE **TE Activity** Researching a Food Web, p. 246

ENRICHMENT ACTIVITIES

The following activities are especially suitable for classes following block schedules.

SE **Student Edition,** pp. 244–257
- Interpreting Satellite Images, p. 248

hmhsocialstudies.com RESEARCH WEB LINKS
- Case Study Project, p. 254

CHAPTER 11 PACING GUIDE

BLOCK SCHEDULE LESSON PLAN OPTIONS: 90-MINUTE PERIOD

DAY 1

SECTION 1, pp. 245-248
Class Time 90 minutes

- **Planning an Action** Divide students into small groups. Have them decide on an issue discussed in the chapter. Then ask them to organize an action in relation to that issue (such as a information campaign to make people aware of competing demands on the rain forest or a peaceful protest to raise awareness of the income gap). Have them write up a plan and include the details of what materials they might need, how many people, how long to organize, etc

DAY 2

SECTION 2, pp. 249-251
Class Time 90 minutes

- **Press Conference** As a way to review the section, assign each of the following issues to pairs of students (competing demands on the rain forest, the links between economic prosperity and political democracy, the income gap). Have one student in each pair explain the issue to the class, based on the information in the section, and have the other student propose some solutions to the problem.
Class Time 30 minutes
- **Skillbuilder Practice** Use the Activity Option about drawing conclusions on TE p. 254 and the Skillbuilder Practice worksheet.
Class Time 25 minutes

DAY 3

SECTION 3, pp. 252-255
Class Time 35 minutes

- **Project Summary** Introduce the Case Study and discuss with the class the issues of the income gap. Let students share their opinions and experiences with the class.

CHAPTER 11 REVIEW AND ASSESSMENT
pp. 256-257
Class Time 55 minutes

- **Review** Have students prepare a summary of the chapter using the words in the Places and Terms on the first page of each section.
Class Time 20 minutes
- **Assessment** Have students complete the Chapter 11 Assessment.
Class Time 35 minutes

TEACHER-TESTED ACTIVITY *Making a Magazine Cover*

Class Time 1-2 class periods.

Task Create a magazine cover entitled "Reformer of the Year"

Supplies
- encyclopedias and other hard copy resources
- Internet
- unlined 8 1/2-by-11-inch paper
- colored pencils or markers

Purpose The students will be able to research people (not necessarily elected politicians) who have started or led reform movements in politics, economics, or land ownership for any time since 1800.

Activity Allow some time to identify a reformer in Latin America in the last century or two. Have students draw a magazine cover with the picture of the reformer. There should also be a headline, as well as objects or events that sum up his or her achievements. On the back of the cover, the students should identify who the reformer was, what he/she did, when he/she made the contribution(s), and a summary of whether the reform was a success or failure and why.

Tom Wurst
Geography Teacher, Langham Creek High School, Houston, Texas

TECHNOLOGY IN THE CLASSROOM

Flow charts and similar graphic organizers can be very helpful in illustrating cause and effect relationships between topics students are studying. If students create flow charts on the computer, rather than on paper-based charts, they will be able to more easily manipulate, add, and change information. Flow charts and other graphic organizers can be created in special software programs designed for that purpose or in word processors or multimedia presentation programs.

Objective Create a flow chart to illustrate concepts presented in Chapter 11

Task Have students create a flow chart on the computer to show the relationship between deforestation, urbanization, and the income gap.

Class Time 1 class period

1. Have students read Chapter 11, and hold a class discussion on the relationship between deforestation, urbanization, and the income gap. How does urbanization contribute to the income gap? (See pages 252-255.) How does the income gap contribute to deforestation? (See "Geographic Thinking," page 247.) How might deforestation contribute to urbanization? (See page 211.) Ask students to take notes on the discussion.
2. Have students, either individually, in pairs, or in small groups, create flow charts on the computer to show the relationship between deforestation, urbanization, and the income gap. They should use either a word processor (with a drawing tool), a presentation program, or a graphic organizer program. Have them begin by inserting three large circles and entering one of these terms—"deforestation," "urbanization," "income gap"—into each circle.
3. Have students draw arrows from one circle to another to indicate cause and effect relationships.
4. Have students insert text boxes with details on the relationship between the topics in the three circles. For example, they might have a text box that explains why the income gap can lead to increased deforestation. Have them insert their text boxes along the cause/effect arrows. They might need to move their circles and arrows to create space for the text boxes.
5. Students can obtain additional information to enter into their flow charts at the Web site at **hmhsocialstudies.com.**

CHAPTER 11 OBJECTIVE

Learn that Latin Americans face serious issues, and are actively seeking solutions to their problems.

Chapter 11

TODAY'S ISSUES

Latin America

Interpreting Photographs

Timber Harvesting

Have students examine the photograph, especially the contrast between foreground and background. Ask what the picture tells them about the relationship of people to rain forest in this area. *(Certain trees may represent a valuable resource; others may be cleared out for farmland.)*

Essential Question

How can citizen participation help solve Latin America's challenges?

What You Will Learn

In this chapter you will read about important issues facing Latin Americans.

SECTION 1
Rain Forest Resources

SECTION 2
Giving Citizens a Voice

CASE STUDY
The Income Gap

For more on these issues in Latin America . . .

hmhsocialstudies.com CURRENT EVENTS

hmhsocialstudies.com TAKING NOTES

Use the graphic organizer online to take notes on causes and effects of some aspect of each issue.

Timber harvesting (as shown here in Bahia, Brazil) and agriculture have had a devastating effect on the Latin American rain forest.

244

Introducing the Essential Question

- Explore what students already know about destruction or preservation of rain forests around the world. Discuss any recent news stories related to the topic.
- Introduce the history of political repression in Latin America with a review of essential freedoms that citizens of the United States enjoy. Point out that those freedoms have sometimes been denied to certain segments of U.S society, such as women and members of minority groups.

Ask students to copy and fill in the graphic organizer with some causes and effects of problems facing Latin America.

Critical Thinking Transparencies CT11
- GeoFocus

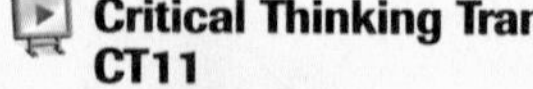

In-Depth Resources: Unit 3
- Building Vocabulary, p. 29

CHAPTER 11 ADDITIONAL RESOURCES

BOOKS FOR THE TEACHER

Zerner, Charles, ed. ***People, Plants, and Justice; The Politics of Nature Conservation.*** NY: Columbia University Press, 2000. Examines the social and environmental consequences of market-linked nature conservation schemes.

BOOKS FOR THE STUDENT

Hecht, Susanna, and Alexander Cockburn. ***The Fate of the Forest.*** NY: Verso, 1989. Discusses the developers, destroyers, and defenders of the Amazon rain forest. Topics include deforestation, forest conservation, and rain forest ecology.

VIDEOS

Decade of Destruction, Bullfrog Films. (Classroom version.) A view of the complex factors that lead to destruction of the Amazonian rain forests.

INTERNET

For more on the issues facing Latin America, visit . . .

hmhsocialstudies.com

Rain Forest Resources

How can we preserve and develop the rain forest?

Main Ideas

- Special-interest groups make competing demands on the resources of the rain forest.
- As the rain forests are destroyed, the quality of life on Earth is threatened.

Places & Terms

biodiversity
deforestation
global warming
debt-for-nature swap

A HUMAN PERSPECTIVE In 1997, biologist Marc van Roosmalen made an incredible discovery. An Amazonian Indian had brought the biologist a tiny monkey huddled inside a tin can. Van Roosmalen realized that the monkey was a kind of pygmy marmoset never before seen by scientists. Over the next three years, Van Roosmalen and his colleagues located the native region of this creature and along the way observed plants and animals unknown to science. These scientists had confirmed the richness of plant and animal life in the Amazon rain forest of Brazil. But for other people, the forest (once cleared) holds the promise of something more—land for farming and timber for sale.

Rain Forest Land Uses

The rain forest is an important global resource. Its vegetation helps to clean the earth's atmosphere, regulate the climate, and shelter several million species of plants, insects, and other wildlife. Scientists have just begun to investigate and understand the rain forest's **biodiversity**—its wide range of plant and animal species. And yet, this variety of life is being destroyed at a rapid rate. At the end of the 20th century, nearly 50 million acres of rain forest worldwide were being destroyed every year.

CLEARING THE RAIN FORESTS The world's demand for timber is great. The Amazon rain forest contains tropical hardwoods, such as mahogany and cedar, that are harvested for export by the timber industry.

Native peoples, living in poverty, travel into the rain forest in search of land on which they can grow crops. They clear the forest,

Major Rain Forests of Latin America

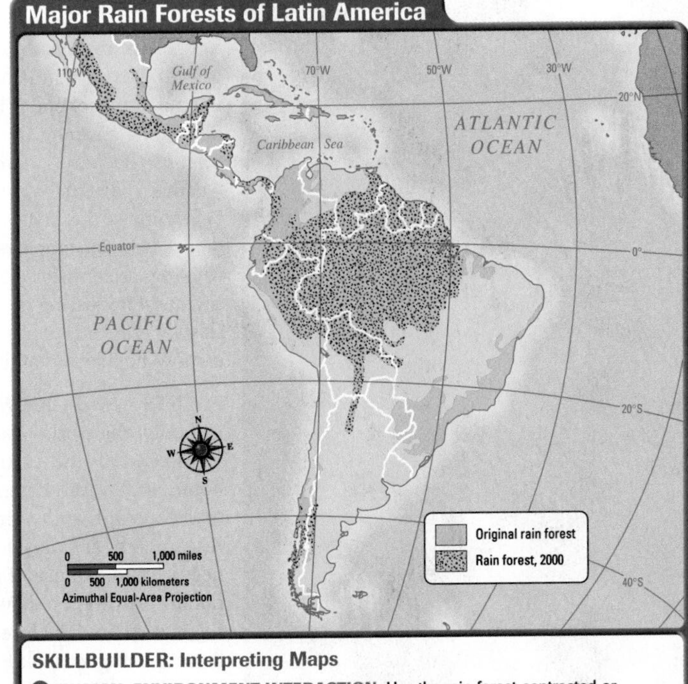

SKILLBUILDER: Interpreting Maps

1. **HUMAN-ENVIRONMENT INTERACTION** Has the rain forest contracted or expanded in recent years? Why might this be so?
2. **REGION** Around what latitude is most of the rain forest clustered? Why might this be?

LATIN AMERICA

SECTION 1 OBJECTIVES

1. Describe uses of the rain forest.
2. Explain the social costs of destruction of the rain forest.
3. Discuss how destruction of the rain forest can be prevented.

SKILLBUILDER: Interpreting Maps, p. 245

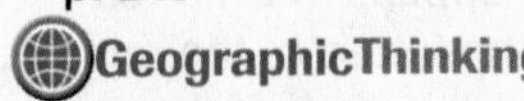
GeographicThinking

Using the Atlas, p. 246
Seeing Patterns, p. 247
Making Inferences, p. 247

Focus & Motivate

Open a discussion about what students already know about the rain forest and its destruction. Ask students what right they think outsiders have to tell a country how to manage its land. Under what circumstances might outsiders have or not have this right?

Instruct: Objective 1 appears on p. 246

Video Resource Book
- Costa Rica, pp. 11–20

SKILLBUILDER ANSWERS

1. The rain forest has contracted due to harvesting of timber and clearing of land for farming and livestock grazing.
2. around the Equator at 0° latitude; ideal climate—hot and humid—for growth of rain forests

SECTION 1 PROGRAM RESOURCES

In-Depth Resources: Unit 3
- Guided Reading, p. 23
- Map and Graph Skills, pp. 26–27
- Skillbuilder Practice, p. 28
- Building Vocabulary, p. 29
- Exploring Today's Issues, pp. 30–31
- Reteaching Activity, p. 34

Guided Reading Workbook
- Section 1

Access for Students Acquiring English
- Guided Reading, p. 54
- Skillbuilder Practice, p. 57
- Map and Graph Skills, pp. 58-59

Formal Assessment
- Section Quiz, p. 162

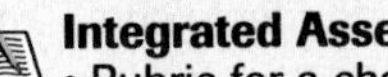
Integrated Assessment
- Rubric for a chart, 2.2

INTEGRATED TECHNOLOGY

Map Transparencies MT20
- Natural Resources and Rain Forests of Latin America

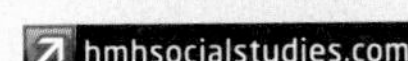
hmhsocialstudies.com

TEST-TAKING RESOURCES

Strategies for Test Preparation

Test Practice Transparencies TT35

Online Test Practice

Instruct: Objective 

Rain Forest Land Uses

- How is the rain forest an important global resource? *(Its vegetation helps to clean the earth's atmosphere, regulate the climate, and shelter plants, insects, and wildlife.)*
- Why is what happens in Brazil so important to the future of the rain forests? *(More than half of the Amazon rain forest is located in Brazil, and Brazil's population is growing rapidly, which means expansion into the rain forest.)*

 **In-Depth Resources: Unit 3**
- Guided Reading, p. 23
- Skillbuilder Practice, p. 28

 **Map Transparencies MT20**
- Natural Resources and Rain Forests of Latin America

Instruct: Objective 

The Price of Destruction

- What is deforestation? *(cutting down and clearing away trees)*
- What is global warming? *(increasing average temperature of atmosphere and shifting world weather patterns)*

Interpreting Photographs

Tracking Birds

The quetzal chooses to live in the canopies of trees on mountain ranges at an altitude between 4,000 and 10,000 feet.

CAPTION ANSWER Scientists might wish to identify birds' habitats and migratory patterns.

not realizing that the soil is not very fertile. Also, cutting down the trees exposes the land to erosion. After a few years, this new farmland becomes less productive, resulting in the need for more timber clearing.

Livestock, too, have been introduced into the rain forest. Ranchers need land on which to graze their cattle, and by clearing the forests for pasture, they can produce a steady supply of beef for the export market.

POPULATION PRESSURES More than half of the Amazon rain forest is located in Brazil. That country's growing population is contributing to the rain forest's decline. The estimated population of Brazil in 2000 was about 173 million people. With an annual growth rate between half a percent and 1 percent, Brazil's population is expected to reach 200 million by 2020. With that many people to shelter, some developers want to build homes on land now covered by the rain forest. A

Geographic Thinking

Using the Atlas

A Use the map on page 191. In what other countries besides Brazil is the Amazon rain forest located?

A. Answer Colombia, Ecuador, Bolivia, Peru, and Venezuela

HUMAN–ENVIRONMENT INTERACTION A naturalist and a biologist attach a radio transmitter to a bird to track its movements in the rain forest. **Why might scientists wish to track birds?**

The Price of Destruction

There is a cost to pay for **deforestation**—cutting down and clearing away of trees—in the rain forest. The short-term benefits are offset by the high price Latin America and the world are paying in damage to the environment.

ENVIRONMENTAL CONCERNS Rain forests help to regulate the earth's climate. They do this by absorbing carbon dioxide and producing oxygen. As the forests disappear, however, much less carbon dioxide is absorbed. The carbon dioxide that is not absorbed builds up in the atmosphere. This buildup prevents heat from escaping into space. The temperature of the atmosphere begins to rise, and weather patterns start to change. By the beginning of the 21st century, evidence of this **global warming** appeared around the world, causing scientific concern. A common method for clearing the rain forest, known as slash-and-burn (see pages 210–211), produces carbon dioxide and other harmful gases.

BACKGROUND These gases are referred to as greenhouse gases because they help keep heat in the atmosphere.

PLANTS AND ANIMALS IN DANGER Although the world's rain forests cover about 6 percent of the earth's surface, they are home to an estimated 50 percent of the world's plant and animal species. Medical researchers are developing the processes needed to make use of the many plants that rain-forest dwellers have harvested for thousands of years. The forest dwellers have used these plants to make medicines that heal wounds and cure disease. What is lost as the rain forests disappear is more than biodiversity and a stable environment. The rain forests also hold secrets of nature that might improve and extend the quality of people's lives.

DIFFERENTIATING INSTRUCTION **GIFTED AND TALENTED STUDENTS**

RESEARCHING A FOOD WEB

Objective To understand the interdependencies of rain forest plants, insects and animals

Research Time One week

Task Students report on wildlife food sources

Directions Have students use the Internet and library to research the animals and plants that live in the rain forest. Have each student research the diet of one large carnivore, such as the jaguar or boa constrictor. Then have them work backwards, noting the diets of each item in the food web. Have students determine the status of each population (stable or shrinking, widely available or scarce) and note what the weakest link in the food web currently is. Students should prepare a written report with diagrams to show their findings.

Moving Toward Solutions

Saving the rain forests of Latin America is an issue that affects people around the world. Creative solutions will be required to make sure that the forests are not sacrificed to economic development.

A JUGGLING ACT A central problem facing many Latin American countries is how to balance competing interests. Some countries in the region are attempting to restrict economic development until they can find the right balance between economic growth and the preservation of the rain forests.

For example, grassroots organizations are closely observing development projects in the rain forests. Their mission is to educate people about the value of the rain forests and, when necessary, to organize protests against plans that would damage the environment.

FIGHTING ECONOMICS WITH ECONOMICS Some people think that since economic gain is at the heart of rain forest destruction, the affected governments should be paid to preserve the forests. One such plan is known as a **debt-for-nature swap.** B

Many Latin American nations are burdened by tremendous debt. They've borrowed money to improve living conditions, and now they are struggling to pay it back. In a debt–for–nature swap, an environmental organization agrees to pay off a certain amount of government debt. In return, the government agrees to protect a certain portion of the rain forest. Governments get debt relief; environmentalists get rain forest preservation. This approach was successful in Bolivia. There, an international environmental group paid off some government debt in exchange for the protection of an area of forest and grassland.

The movement to preserve the rain forests has many supporters in the region, as well as around the world. The battle to preserve the rain forests may be one in which everybody wins.

Geographic Thinking

Seeing Patterns
B How might the income gap affect the use of the rain forest?
B. Answer There might be pressure on governments to develop the resources of the rain forest in order to help narrow the income gap.

Section 1 Assessment

1 Places & Terms

Identify and explain the following places and terms.

- biodiversity
- deforestation
- global warming
- debt-for-nature swap

2 Taking Notes

HUMAN–ENVIRONMENT INTERACTION Review the notes you took for this section.

	Causes	Effects
Issue 1: Resources		

- Why are the rain forests being destroyed?
- What effect might the destruction of the rain forest have on climate?

3 Main Ideas

a. What are some of the important resources of the rain forest?

b. What are some of the costs of the destruction of the rain forest?

c. What are some factors that might slow destruction of the rain forest?

4 Geographic Thinking

Making Inferences What might happen to the rain forest in the future? **Think about:**

- economic pressures to destroy the rain forest
- reasons to preserve the rain forest

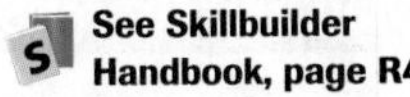
See Skillbuilder Handbook, page R4.

MAKING COMPARISONS Pair with a partner and make a **chart** of the largest rain forests in the world. Then make a copy of a map of the world and color in on the map the rain forests on your chart.

LATIN AMERICA

Instruct: Objective 3

Moving Toward Solutions

- What juggling act do Latin American countries face? *(balancing economic growth with preservation of rain forest)*
- What is a debt-for-nature-swap? *(government debts paid in exchange for preserving forests)*
- How might the international community help Latin American governments preserve the rain forests? *(might help governments with economic development)*

More About

Protecting the Environment

Environmentalists have also been working to protect the marine environment in Latin America. Land-based pollution, such as agrochemical runoff and sewage, threatens marine life. In 1999, the Land-Based Sources of Marine Pollution protocol was adopted and signed—though not yet ratified—by Costa Rica, France, Netherlands, and the United States.

Assess & Reteach

GeoFocus Have students complete the sections on causes and effects of rain forest depletion in their graphic organizers.

Formal Assessment
- Section Quiz, p. 162

Reteaching Activity

Have students write an essay or short story about the photograph on p. 246.

In-Depth Resources: Unit 3
- Exploring Today's Issues, pp. 30–31
- Reteaching Activity, p. 34

SECTION 1 ASSESSMENT ANSWERS

1. Places & Terms

biodiversity, p. 245
deforestation, p. 246
global warming, p. 246
debt-for-nature swap, p. 247

2. Taking Notes

- because of demands for timber, farm land, and grazing land
- Destruction of the rain forest might cause a change in global weather patterns that will lead to warmer climates.

3. Main Ideas

a. timber; the role the forest plays in regulating climate; the rare plants and animals

b. global warming, destruction of species, loss of medicines

c. concerns about environment, efforts of international environmental groups, debt-for-nature swaps, potential medicinal properties of rain forest species

4. Geographic Thinking

Mounting concerns about its negative impact may slow, or possibly even stop, destruction of the rain forest. Eventually, careful management and harvesting of the rain forest could reverse its steady decline.

GeoActivity

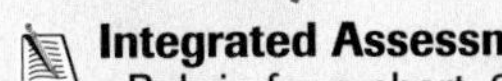
Integrated Assessment
- Rubric for a chart, 2.2

OBJECTIVE

Learn how to interpret satellite images.

Instruct: Objective

Interpreting Satellite Images

- What is a satellite image? *(visible-light, radar, or infrared picture of the earth's surfaces taken from space)*
- Which satellite image would you look at to get an idea of the vegetation in an area? *(Landsat)*

In-Depth Resources: Unit 3
- Map and Graph Skills, pp. 26–27

More About

Satellite Imagery

Another kind of satellite imagery is provided by radar. Radar images use microwave radiation reflected off the earth's surface to detect flooded areas. Smooth surfaces such as rivers, lakes, and flooded areas appear dark; rain forest appears medium bright.

More About

Mapping the Rain Forest

Geographic Information Systems (GIS) store information in a digital database. GIS allows geographers to solve problems by combining geographic information about a location from several sources. The information includes maps, aerial photographs, satellite images, and other data. GIS creates a composite map combining the information.

Extension Have students use GIS to answer a geographic question or solve a geographic problem in their area. For example, students might use GIS to find possible sites for a park or a dam.

RAND McNALLY **Map and Graph Skills**

Interpreting Satellite Images

Satellites are orbiting "eyes in the skies." They can give us detailed views of landforms, vegetation, and bodies of water. The satellite image below shows part of the rain forest in the state of Rondônia in Brazil.

THE LANGUAGE OF MAPS A **satellite image** is a visible-light, radar, or infrared picture of land or water taken from space. Depending on the equipment used, satellite images can show land features such as those shown below—ground vegetation and a lake as well as a river that shows some flooding (in the loop below the center of the image). **Landsat satellites** are orbiting satellites that measure reflected light to show features on the earth's surface, including vegetation. A landsat satellite image shows changes in vegetation over time by using a series of images.

A Satellite View of the Rain Forest

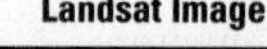

Landsat Image

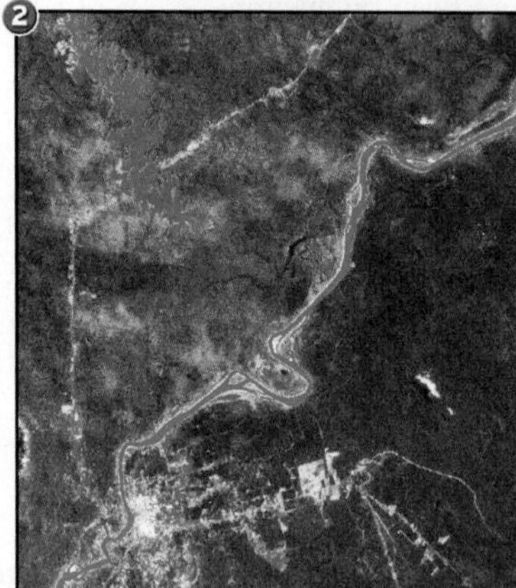

Sketch Map

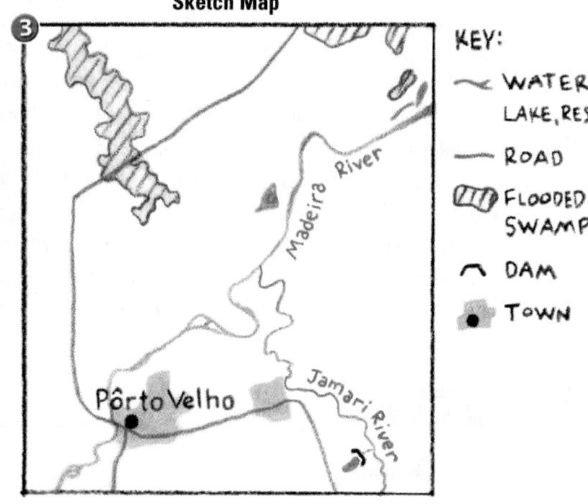

1 Satellite images are useful in constructing maps, updating maps, and making them more explicit.

2 In Landsat images, shallow water appears light blue. Thick vegetation appears red. Sparse vegetation appears white.

3 A researcher made a sketch of the Landsat image, adding names of towns and rivers.

Map and Graph Skills Assessment

1. Making Inferences
The town of Pôrto Velho is near the intersection of what two means of transportation?

2. Making Decisions
In what direction would you travel in going from Pôrto Velho to the Jamari River?

3. Drawing Conclusions
What sort of vegetation predominates in the Landsat image? How can you tell?

SKILLS ASSESSMENT ANSWERS

1. road and river

2. east

3. Thick vegetation appears red.

Giving Citizens a Voice

How can Latin Americans gain a voice in government?

Main Ideas

- Despite obstacles, democracy is beginning to succeed in Latin America.
- The success of Latin American democracies depends on political, economic, and social reforms.

Places & Terms

oligarchy **caudillo**
junta **land reform**

A HUMAN PERSPECTIVE From the late 1970s through the early 1980s, the Argentine military waged a campaign of terror against those who supported political reform. As many as 30,000 people mysteriously disappeared. People accused of being terrorists and revolutionaries were kidnapped and questioned. Some were tortured, and then killed or "disappeared"—their bodies were never found. In an effort to learn the truth about their loved ones, a group of women, calling themselves the Mothers of Plaza de Mayo, staged weekly protests in the plaza in Buenos Aires. Their protests were part of the larger attempt by citizens of the region to gain a voice in how their governments were being run.

LATIN AMERICA

A Struggle to Be Heard

Latin Americans today seek more democratic governments. Democracy depends on free and fair elections, citizen participation, majority rule with minority rights, and guaranteed freedoms. However, Latin America has shown little support for democratic rule until recently.

THE LEGACY OF COLONIALISM After the Spanish conquest of the region in the 16th century, Native Americans in Central and South America were ruled by governors who took their orders from the king and queen of Spain. Even when Latin American countries won their independence during the 1800s, they continued to be governed mainly by small groups of Spanish colonists.

This government by the few, known as **oligarchy** (AHL•ih•GAHR•kee), was not democratic. The government censored the press, limited free speech, and punished dissent. It also discriminated against all who were not part of the Spanish ruling class. Elections were held, but there was never any doubt who was in charge. If the government was unable to control the people, the military would step in, seize power, and form a new, harsher government known as a **junta** (HOON•tah), which was run by the generals.

THE RULE OF THE *CAUDILLO* Throughout the 20th century, many Latin American countries were ruled by a **caudillo** (kow•DEE•yoh), a military dictator or political boss, such as Juan Perón in Argentina. The caudillo's

"My goodness, if I'd known how badly you wanted democracy I'd have given it to you ages ago."

SECTION 2 OBJECTIVES

1. Describe the struggle for democratic government in Latin America.
2. Identify some conditions for establishing stable democracies.

GeographicThinking

Seeing Patterns, p. 250
Drawing Conclusions, p. 251

Focus & Motivate

Open a discussion on why Latin Americans might want democracy. What are the advantages of democratic government? What are the disadvantages? *(advantages–freedom of speech, freedom to choose elected representatives, equality, opportunity; disadvantages–sometimes harder to get things done because different voices must be listened to)*

Instruct: Objective 1

A Struggle to Be Heard

- What is a junta? *(military government run by generals)*
- What is a caudillo? *(military dictator or political boss)*
- How did colonialism contribute to oligarchy in Latin America? *(people were used to rule by a few Spanish colonists)*

In-Depth Resources: Unit 3
- Guided Reading, p. 24

Critical Thinking Transparencies CT43
- Evolution of Democracy in Latin America

SECTION 2 PROGRAM RESOURCES

In-Depth Resources: Unit 3
- Guided Reading, p. 24
- Building Vocabulary, p. 29
- Exploring Today's Issues, pp. 32–33
- Reteaching Activity, p. 35

Guided Reading Workbook
- Section 2

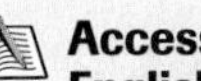
Access for Students Acquiring English
- Guided Reading, p. 55

Formal Assessment
- Section Quiz, p. 163

Integrated Assessment
- Rubric for a report, 2.5

INTEGRATED TECHNOLOGY

Critical Thinking Transparencies CT43
- Evolution of Democracy in Latin America

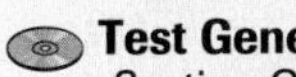
Chapter Summaries

Test Generator
- Section Quiz

hmhsocialstudies.com

TEST-TAKING RESOURCES

Strategies for Test Preparation

Test Practice Transparencies TT36

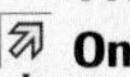
Online Test Practice

Instruct: Objective 2

Establishing Stable Democracies

- What is one goal of political reform? *(to establish constitutional, democratic government)*
- What is land reform? *(the breaking up of large land holdings and giving land to peasant farmers)*
- Why is land reform important in helping to establish democracies? *(Land reform distributes wealth more evenly, which contributes to political and economic stability.)*

In-Depth Resources: Unit 3
- Exploring Today's Issues, pp. 32–33

Interpreting Graphs

Elections

Although the response in some Latin American countries to whether democracy is the best form of government might appear to be lukewarm according to a regional polling organization, Latinobarometro, democracy did better than any other form of government in the poll. Point out to students that the photograph suggests a positive involvement by people in the democratic process.

support came from the military and the wealthy. Surprisingly, the caudillo was sometimes elected directly by the people.

For example, from the 1920s until the end of the 20th century, Mexico was governed by caudillos who were members of the *Partido Revolucionario Institucional* (PRI), or the Institutional Revolutionary Party. For 71 years the PRI dominated Mexican politics.

Opposition parties were legal, but the PRI used fraud and corruption to win elections. Opposition parties made big gains in the 1997 congressional elections. In 2000, Vicente Fox became the first non-PRI president since the adoption of Mexico's constitution in 1917. Finally, it seemed Mexico was ready to fully accept democracy.

BACKGROUND
Caudillo is a Spanish word that means "leader" or "chief."

Establishing Stable Democracies

Creating democracies in Latin America requires political, economic, and land reforms.

THE GOALS OF REFORM One goal of political reform is to establish constitutional government. A freely elected government that respects the law is the basis of democracy. Participation of citizens in political affairs is also critical. This requires that people be well educated and provided with economic security.

Political and economic stability are two sides of the same coin. A lack of prosperity is usually accompanied by social and political unrest. A

Geographic Thinking
Seeing Patterns
A What effect might the income gap have on political stability in a democracy?
A. Answer An income gap is likely to undermine political stability by stirring up social and political unrest.

Argentina in the 1980s was one example of how economic problems damaged a developing democracy. In 1983, Raúl Alfonsín was elected president of Argentina in that nation's first free election in many years. He was faced with a ruined economy after years of military rule.

Argentina suffered from inflation—a rise in the prices of goods and services. To fight inflation, the newly-elected president froze all wages and prices. He issued a new currency to replace the peso. (Later, the peso was brought back.) At first these measures seemed successful, but by 1989, inflation was severe again. In 1989, Argentina elected a new president, Carlos Menem. He introduced a number of capitalist reforms. These included reducing government spending and selling off state-controlled industries and utilities.

Another goal of reform is to recognize and increase the role of women in politics. Throughout the region, women are running for office and taking an active role in government. For example, Marta Suplicy was elected mayor of São Paulo, Brazil, in 2000.

LAND REFORM Latin American countries had been ruled by a wealthy elite. Economic power, as well as land, was in the hands of the few. To spread the wealth more fairly, some governments set up a program of **land reform,** the process of breaking up large landholdings and giving portions of the land to land-poor peasant farmers.

Attitudes on Democracy

Latinobarometro, a Chilean organization, conducts polls asking Latin Americans from a number of countries what they think about different political issues. Recently, the organization asked residents of various countries the following question:

Is democracy the best system of government?

Brazil	50% agree
Central America	49%
Ecuador	41%
Mexico	45%
Paraguay	44%
Peru	21%
Uruguay	86%

SOURCE: *Latinobarometro,* 1998

ACTIVITY OPTION **COOPERATIVE LEARNING**

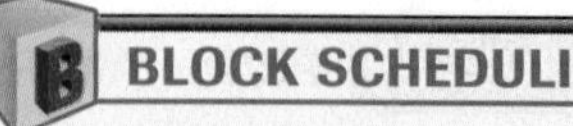

WRITING A DIALOGUE

Objective To deepen the understanding of the struggle for democracy
Class Time 60 minutes
Task Create a dialogue

Directions Have students work in small groups. Within each group, assign each student a role, such as president, general, wealthy land owner, Native American, and farmer. The students should write a dialogue in which they discuss, in their assigned roles, their thoughts about democracy, the future of their country, and their place in a democratic society. Have some groups present their dialogues to class.

In Mexico, for example, the process of land reform began with Benito Juarez. He was a Zapotec Indian from a small farm who was elected Mexico's president in 1858. One of his main reform goals was to redistribute the land so that rich landowners could not keep other Mexicans in a cycle of poverty. After the Mexican Revolution in the early part of the 20th century, there was another attempt at land reform. This gave people a better chance at economic equality.

All of these reforms have been aimed at creating stability. With a sound foundation, democracy has a better chance of taking root.

REGION Marta Suplicy holds a press conference after being elected mayor of São Paulo, Brazil, in 2000. **What does her election suggest about the role of women in politics in Brazil?**

Interpreting Photographs

Mayor of São Paulo

Ask students why the participation of women in politics is a healthy sign. *(It suggests that democracy is working because all citizens have a voice in government.)*

CAPTION ANSWER Her election suggests that women are assuming increasingly important political roles in the region.

Assess & Reteach

GeoFocus Have students complete the sections in their graphic organizers on causes and effects of the struggle for democracy.

Formal Assessment
- Section Quiz, p. 163

Reteaching Activity

Have students write an outline of the section. Suggest they use the headings as the main topics, and add three to five points under each heading.

In-Depth Resources: Unit 3
- Reteaching Activity, p. 35

Section 2 Assessment

1 Places & Terms

Identify and explain the following places and terms.

- oligarchy
- junta
- caudillo
- land reform

2 Taking Notes

HUMAN-ENVIRONMENT INTERACTION Review your notes.

	Causes	Effects
Issue 2: Democracy		

- What problems has democracy faced in Latin America?
- What are some of the effects of political reform in the region?

3 Main Ideas

a. How did colonialism affect the development of democracy?

b. What are some of the goals of political reform in the region?

c. Why was land reform necessary, and what was its purpose?

4 Geographic Thinking

Drawing Conclusions What are the prospects of democracy in the region?

Think about:
- political reforms
- economic reforms

SEEING PATTERNS Pair with a partner and choose a country in Latin America to research on the Internet. Then prepare a **report** on the condition of democracy in that country and present your report to the class. Discuss what kind of government the country has, the number and names of political parties, and the nature of its legislative and executive functions.

SECTION 2 ASSESSMENT ANSWERS

1. Places & Terms

oligarchy, p. 249
junta, p. 249
caudillo, p. 249
land reform, p. 250

2. Taking Notes
- colonialism, government by the few, government by the military, and government by dictators and bosses
- political stability and economic prosperity

3. Main Ideas

a. Colonialism created oligarchies, juntas, and caudillos.

b. constitutional government, free elections, rule of law, citizen participation in political affairs, economic and political stability

c. Land and wealth tended to be in the hands of the few. Land reform spreads the wealth more evenly among more people.

4. Geographic Thinking

The prospects of democracy in the region are good as long as economic progress is made. However, a severe economic downturn might undermine whatever progress has been made.

GeoActivity

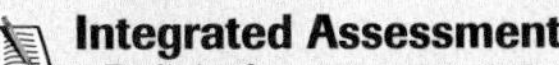

Integrated Assessment
- Rubric for a report, 2.5

CASE STUDY OBJECTIVES

1. Explain the problem of the income gap in Latin America.
2. Describe possible solutions to the income gap.
3. Complete the Case Study Project by preparing a multimedia report on the income gap in Latin America.
4. Analyze primary sources for different views on the income gap in Latin America.

Focus & Motivate

Ask students what the presence of banks and other financial institutions tells them about Bogotá. *(that there is a high level of economic activity in Bogatá; that financial institutions assist the movement of money and goods)*

Instruct: Objective 

The Nature of the Problem

- What are three different aspects of the income gap? *(moral issue, economic dilemma, political problem)*
- Why do the doors to economic equality appear shut to the poor? *(little education; few marketable skills)*
- Why should the wealthy classes help the poor? *(poverty breeds desperation, which leads to social unrest)*

 **In-Depth Resources: Unit 3**
- Guided Reading, p. 25

CASESTUDY
THE INCOME GAP
How can the economic gulf between rich and poor be bridged?

Bogotá, Colombia's glittering financial district

Along the oceanfront in Rio de Janeiro, Brazil, gleaming office buildings and hotels share the boulevards with trendy restaurants and exclusive shops.

Behind all this glitter and glamour, however, is another world, hidden from sight—the *favelas*, or slums, of Rio. Here, the poor live among swamps and garbage dumps, and on barren hillsides.

These contrasting conditions are evidence of what economists call an income gap. This is the difference between the quality of life enjoyed by the rich and the poor. In many Latin American countries, the gap is widening. Some solutions have been proposed for this problem.

The Nature of the Problem

As you've learned in this unit, the income gap in Latin America has many causes, some of which reflect the impact of colonialism in the region. There are three angles to exploring the income gap: it is a moral issue, an economic dilemma, and a political problem.

A MORAL ISSUE Some people argue that Latin America's income gap raises important ethical questions. How can any caring society, they ask, justify vast wealth in the hands of a few while most people live in poverty from which they will likely never escape? Some leaders within the Roman Catholic Church and other faiths have argued that narrowing the gap between rich and poor in Latin America is more than just an economic necessity; it is a matter of social justice.

AN ECONOMIC DILEMMA Most Latin American countries now have free-market economies with a minimum of government rules. A free-market economy offers many people the freedom and rewards they need to create wealth. However, in Latin America the poor often lack the basic skills that would make taking part in the economy possible.

Often, the poor have little education. Many cannot read. Most cannot find jobs. Those who find work may end up sweeping streets or shining shoes. Conditions in the slums breed disease and encourage crime. In fact, the life spans of slum dwellers are shorter than those of the middle and upper classes. To the poor of Latin America, the doors to economic equality appear shut.

A POLITICAL PROBLEM Poverty can make people desperate. Those who think they have nothing to lose are sometimes willing to take great risks.

CASE STUDY PROGRAM RESOURCES

 **In-Depth Resources: Unit 3**
- Guided Reading, p. 25
- Building Vocabulary, p. 29
- Reteaching Activity, p. 36

 **Guided Reading Workbook**
- Case Study

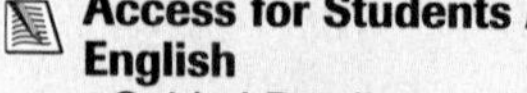 **Access for Students Acquiring English**
- Guided Reading, p. 56

 **Formal Assessment**
- Case Study Quiz, p. 164

INTEGRATED TECHNOLOGY

 **Power Presentations**

 **Test Generator**
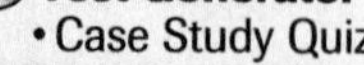
- Case Study Quiz

hmhsocialstudies.com

TEST-TAKING RESOURCES

 **Strategies for Test Preparation**

 **Test Practice Transparencies TT37**

 **Online Test Practice**

SEE PRIMARY SOURCE C

Throughout history, battles have been waged and governments have been overthrown by citizens protesting what they regard as an unjust society in which a few have too much while the many have too little.

Argentina, Bolivia, Brazil, Colombia, El Salvador, and Guatemala have all seen bloody rebellions put down by harsh military measures. In the process, human rights and human dignity have been violated. The story is usually the same. The rebels seek economic justice, and the military protects the wealthy. Clearly, attitudes will have to change before the poor in Latin America will be able to participate fully in their nations' economies. Some attitudes are already changing as, for example, more money is going to education.

Possible Solutions

The income gap in Latin America varies from one country to another. For example, according to a 2006 report issued by the United Nations' Development Program, 46 percent of all Ecuadorans and 64 percent of Colombians live below the national poverty level. In contrast, the percentage of people living in poverty is 17 percent in Chile and 6 percent in Uruguay.

SEE PRIMARY SOURCE A

EDUCATION, POLITICS, AND ECONOMICS Many of the countries of the region have put in place free-market economies that they hope will eventually help to narrow the gap by providing economic opportunity and stability for all citizens.

Along with market economies, democracy is now seen by many countries as an essential part of the equation needed to achieve widespread prosperity. Democracy provides an outlet for protest and opposition so that policies can be adjusted to reflect the will of the majority of the people.

Finally, education is an important part of the mix. A literate, well-educated population will be needed to fill the jobs that will become available in an increasingly complex economy. A case study project on the income gap follows on the next two pages.

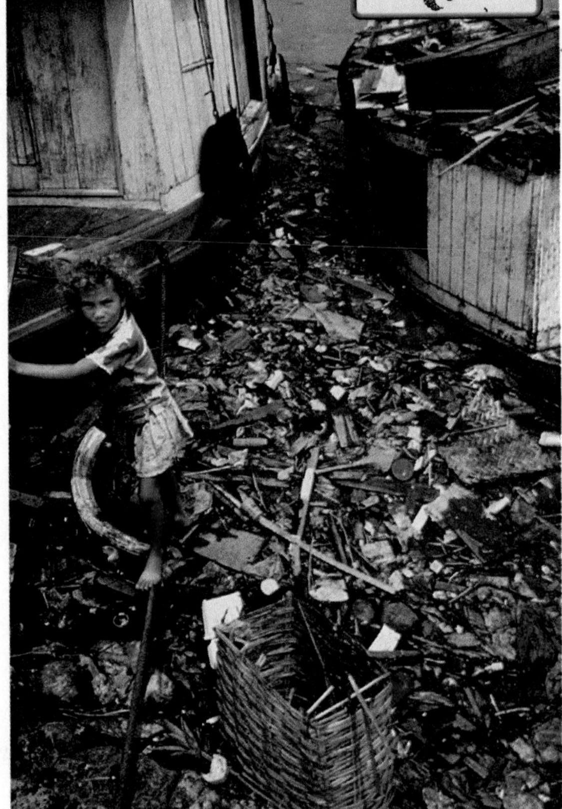

REGION A girl plays amid garbage and polluted water in Belém, Brazil. **What do the photographs on these pages suggest about the distribution of money in the region?**

Instruct: Objective 2

Possible Solutions

- What do countries hope to accomplish with free-market economies? *(to narrow income gap by providing economic opportunity and stability)*
- Why is democracy important for narrowing the income gap? *(Democracy provides citizens with a voice so policies can be adjusted to reflect the will of the people.)*
- What role does education play in narrowing the income gap? *(to give people job skills)*

Interpreting Photographs

Belém, Brazil

Ask students to study the photograph on this page. Discuss with them what they see in the photograph.

CAPTION ANSWER The photograph suggests that the income gap is wide and that there is money in the region but that it is unevenly distributed.

ACTIVITY OPTION | CRITICAL THINKING

IDENTIFYING AND SOLVING PROBLEMS

Explaining the Skill Identifying problems means finding and understanding the difficulties faced by people in certain situations. Solving problems means understanding how people develop remedies for those problems.

For this exercise, have students review information they have studied about revolutions and revolutionary leaders in Latin America. After the class discussion, have students write an editorial either for or against a revolutionary movement.

Applying the Skill Following the class discussion, students are to imagine that they are newspaper editors in a Latin American country where rebel forces are fighting against the government. Each student should write an editorial stating the nature of the conflict, summarizing key events of the rebellion and proposing solutions to the problems that lie behind the conflict. Each "editor" should take a stand supporting either the rebels or the government, and provide reasons for his or her position.

Instruct: Objective 3

Case Study Project: Multimedia Report

- What is your research goal for the project? *(to learn about the income gap and possible solutions)*
- What questions should you consider in the process? *(the roots of the income gap; effect on the poor; possible solutions)*
- What should you produce for the project? *(multimedia report including charts, graphs, video, CDs, and other electronic media)*

Instruct: Objective 

Using Primary Sources

- Ⓐ ***Graph*** What percentage of the population in Latin America owns only 8 percent of the income? *(the poorest 40 percent)*
- What percentage of the income does the wealthiest 20 percent control? *(62 percent)*
- Ⓑ ***Cable News Story*** Why are the street children afraid to sleep at night? *(the possibility of being murdered by death squads)*
- How many homeless children are murdered each year? *(Some estimates say about 500 per year)*

CASESTUDY

PROJECT  Multimedia Report

21st CENTURY

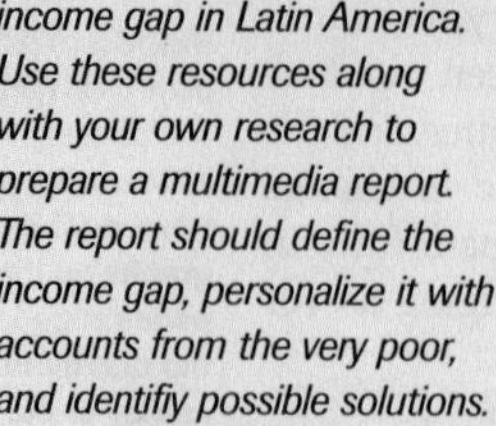

Primary sources A, B, C, and D offer information about the income gap in Latin America. Use these resources along with your own research to prepare a multimedia report. The report should define the income gap, personalize it with accounts from the very poor, and identify possible solutions.

hmhsocialstudies.com
RESEARCH WEB LINKS

Suggested Steps

1. Research possible solutions or initiatives to deal with the income gap in Latin America.
2. Use video, audio, online, and print resources to research your topic.
3. Think about the following questions during your research:
   - What are the roots of the income gap?
   - How does the income gap hinder the participation of the poor in national economies?
   - What are some possible solutions to the problem?
4. Create charts and graphs and use videotapes, audio CDs, and other electronic media to make your report clear and convincing.
5. Prepare a brief talk to introduce and explain your topic.

Materials and Supplies

- Reference books, newspapers, and magazines
- Computer with Internet access
- Printer
- VCR and television
- CD player

PRIMARY SOURCE A

Graph *This pie graph shows income distribution in Latin America. The gap was wider at the end of the 1990s than at the end of the 1970s.*

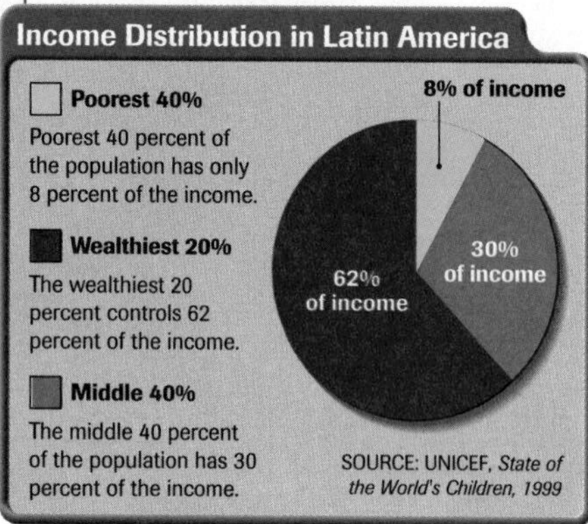

Income Distribution in Latin America
Poorest 40%
Poorest 40 percent of the population has only 8 percent of the income.
Wealthiest 20%
The wealthiest 20 percent controls 62 percent of the income.
Middle 40%
The middle 40 percent of the population has 30 percent of the income.
8% of income
30% of income
62% of income
SOURCE: UNICEF, State of the World's Children, 1999

PRIMARY SOURCE B

Cable News Story *For the homeless children of Rio de Janeiro, the income gap is more than just an economic hardship. It is a matter of life and death, as detailed in this report filed by CNN correspondent Marina Marabella.*

April 29, 1996—Four men, including three police officers, went on trial in Rio Monday for the 1993 slaying of eight street children. The murder, the worst massacre of children on record in Brazil, took place outside Candelaria Cathedral in the city center. . . .

Of all the dangers faced by Rio's homeless children, the one they fear the most is being murdered by death squads while they sleep. "When we can, we sleep during the day," said Ricardo, 13. "It's too risky at night." . .

Yvonne Bezerra de Mello has spent years helping Brazil's estimated 2,000 to 3,000 street children. "Until now, no policemen were ever convicted for killing street kids. This is a very good step for Brazilian justice," she said.

She and other human rights activists say the death squads that murder Brazil's homeless children are hired by shopkeepers and others to get rid of those suspected of stealing. . . .

[O]fficial police estimates say about 500 of Rio's homeless children are murdered each year.

ACTIVITY OPTION **SKILLBUILDER LESSON**

DRAWING CONCLUSIONS

Explaining the Skill Tell students that drawing conclusions means analyzing what they have read and forming an opinion about its meaning. To draw conclusions, they look closely at facts, combine them with inferences they make, and then use their common sense and experience to decide what the facts mean.

For addtional Skillbuilder Practice, see p. 246 in Section 1.

Applying the Skill Have students look at the information in primary sources **A** and **B** above. Then have them consider the following questions.

- Why do shopkeepers and others hire death squads to murder Brazil's homeless children? *(to get rid of those suspected of stealing)*
- How are poverty and the income gap at the root of this situation? *(economic motives are given—shopkeepers accuse children of stealing)*
- How might a narrowing of the income gap help solve this problem? *(If there were less poverty, children might not have to live in the streets and steal; business owners might feel less threatened by the street crime they attribute to homeless children)*

PRIMARY SOURCE C

Newspaper Report *On September 5, 2000, Steven Gutkin filed this story from Caracas, Venezuela, to* The Times of India Online. *It shows clearly that the consequences of the income gap can be found throughout Latin America.*

Caracas–The Sambil shopping mall in eastern Caracas is Latin America's largest. It boasts 450 stores, two movie theatres, an amusement park, a 30,000-gallon aquarium–and a McDonald's where Big Macs cost a half day's pay for the average Venezuelan worker.

A slum just a few miles to the west has open sewers running alongside tin shacks perched on unstable hillsides, flies buzzing in uncollected garbage and idle young men nursing bullet wounds. Blanca Vera, 65, lifts her baby granddaughter's blouse to reveal blotches on her tiny stomach. "This is from the pollution," she says.

[I]nequality of wealth and opportunity is a huge obstacle to development in Latin America. The existence of so many have-nots threatens to undermine the success of the region's two great experiments of recent years: democracy and free markets.

In Chile, the highest-paid 6 percent of workers get 30 percent of salaries, while 75 percent of workers get just 4 percent, according to the United Nations' Economic Commission for Latin America and the Caribbean.

Some blame the growing inequality on globalization. . . . Yet most economists say the real culprit is not globalization but misguided state policies that deprive the poor of a decent education, fail to collect taxes, and encourage corruption.

There's another factor that's harder to define but likely is just as real: a culture of elitism that regards poor people as unworthy. "You can't operate in a globalized economy with a narrow, tiny elite sector that has absolutely no connection or appreciation of the vast majority of people in society," says Michael Shifter, a Latin America specialist at the Washington-based Inter-American Dialogue.

PRIMARY SOURCE D

Magazine Article *There are some initiatives to deal with the consequences of poverty. A reporter for the British magazine,* The Economist, *wrote about a program in Pôrto Alegre, Brazil, to help street children.*

"Is it true that in your country parents can be jailed for beating their children?" 16-year-old Jose asks your correspondent. Clearly there is no need to ask what made him run away from home, to become, briefly, one of Brazil's "street children." Luckily for him, the city on whose streets he ended up sleeping is Pôrto Alegre. Its municipal council this year, for the second year running, won an award given by the Abrinq Foundation, a Brazilian children's rights charity, to the local authority with the best social services for children. After only a short while on the streets, Jose now sleeps in a council-run dormitory and spends most of his days in the city's "Open School," which allows current and former street children to come and go as they please, aiming gradually to draw them back to something like a normal life and perhaps to an education. . . .

Pôrto Alegre is one of a handful of cities . . . that are trying. The services they offer are modest: a shelter where the children can sleep, eat, and wash; a day center staffed with a few teachers, drug counsellors, and so on; and some staff to patrol the streets at night looking for children in need.

PROJECT CheckList

Have I . . .

- ✓ fully researched my topic?
- ✓ searched for a mix of media sources from which to build my report?
- ✓ created informative visuals that make my report clear and convincing?
- ✓ practiced the delivery of my presentation?
- ✓ made sure that I am familiar with the video and audio equipment I plan to use?

Instruct: Objective 4

Using Primary Sources

- Ⓒ ***Newspaper Report*** What two great experiments in the region does the writer say the income gap may undermine? *(democracy and free markets)*
- What does the writer say are some of the possible causes of the income gap? *(globalization, poor education for many, tax failure, corruption, elitism)*
- Ⓓ ***Magazine Article*** What initiative does this article describe? *(a program to help street children)*
- What are some of the services that can help street children? *(shelter, beds, food, soap and water, day center, teachers, drug counselors)*

Assess & Reteach

GeoFocus Have students complete the cause-and-effect charts they began at the start of this chapter.

Formal Assessment
- Case Study Quiz, p. 164

Reteaching Activity
Have students write a short paragraph describing the effects of the income gap and summarizing possible solutions.

In-Depth Resources: Unit 3
- Reteaching Activity, p. 36

RUBRIC CASE STUDY PROJECT

MULTIMEDIA REPORT

For the Case Study Project, students should:
- Research solutions or initiatives to deal with the income gap.
- Use a variety of resources in their research.
- Prepare a brief speech to introduce topic.
- Present a report containing a variety of data.

Grading Rubric Evaluate student performance as Exceptional, Acceptable, or Poor in each of the following categories:

	Exceptional	Acceptable	Poor
Communicates ideas and positions clearly			
Provides necessary facts and examples			
Makes use of a variety of research sources			
Makes use of electronic media			

CHAPTER 11 ASSESSMENT

Reviewing Places & Terms

A.
1. biodiversity, p. 245
2. deforestation, p. 246
3. global warming, p. 246
4. debt-for-nature swap, p. 247
5. oligarchy, p. 249
6. junta, p. 249
7. caudillo, p. 249
8. land reform, p. 250

B. Possible Responses

9. The plant and animal life of the rain forest might lead to new medicines or other discoveries that will improve lives.
10. Tropical hardwoods such as mahogany and cedar are being harvested.
11. Carbon dioxide is harming the atmosphere.
12. Such swaps reduce government debt.
13. It represents the rule of the wealthy few rather than all of the people.
14. The military seizes power in an attempt to control the people.
15. The caudillo gains support from the military, the wealthy, and sometimes the people.
16. Land-poor peasant farmers benefit from land reform.
17. Biodiversity is decreasing, although the rate of decrease may be slowing.
18. The government agrees to protect part of its rain forest.
19. Large landowners and the wealthy tend to lose land in a program of land reform but they gain in social stability.
20. Oligarchy, junta, and cuadillo, represent the negative impact of colonialism.

Chapter 11 Assessment

VISUAL SUMMARY
TODAY'S ISSUES IN LATIN AMERICA

Environment

Rain Forest Resources
- There are a number of competing demands on the resources of the rain forest.
- Farmers, ranchers, environmentalists, the timber industry, and pharmaceutical companies all have their own interests in the rain forests of the region.
- Intelligent management and development of the rain forests depend on careful balancing of these competing interests.

Government

Giving Citizens a Voice
- After a long struggle to overcome the legacy of colonialism, most countries in Latin America are struggling toward more democratic forms of government.
- Political stability and economic progress often go hand in hand.

Economics

Case Study: The Income Gap
- The gap between rich and poor in Latin America presents a challenging problem.
- It is likely that a widening income gap will undermine political stability in the region.
- For this reason, government, businesses, and education must all work together to try to narrow the gap.

Reviewing Places & Terms

A. Briefly explain the importance of each of the following.

1. biodiversity
2. deforestation
3. global warming
4. debt-for-nature swap
5. oligarchy
6. junta
7. caudillo
8. land reform

B. Answer the questions about vocabulary in complete sentences.

9. Why is the biodiversity of the rain forest important?
10. What are some examples of the kinds of trees being harvested in the rain forest?
11. What is one byproduct of slash-and-burn clearing of the rain forest that is harming the atmosphere?
12. Why is it in the interest of governments to participate in debt-for-nature swaps?
13. Why is an oligarchy undemocratic?
14. Why is a junta undemocratic?
15. From where does the caudillo gain support?
16. Who benefits from land reform?
17. Is the biodiversity of the region increasing or decreasing?
18. In a debt-for-nature swap, what does the government agree to do?
19. Who loses in a program of land reform?
20. Which of the eight terms listed above represent the negative impact of colonialism on the politics of the region?

Main Ideas

Rain Forest Resources (pp. 245–248)

1. Why is the rain forest an important global resource?
2. What are some of the reasons the rain forest is being cleared?
3. What is one mission of the grassroots organizations in the rain forest?

Giving Citizens a Voice (pp. 249–251)

4. Who are some democratically elected leaders in the region?
5. What are some of the elements upon which democracy depends?
6. What sorts of reforms are essential to stable democracy in the region?

Case Study: The Income Gap (pp. 252–255)

7. Which groups have argued that the income gap presents a moral issue?
8. What is the basic economic dilemma confronted by poor people in Latin America?
9. Why is the income gap a political issue?
10. Do all countries of Latin America have a similar income gap? Explain.

Main Ideas

1. It helps to clean the atmosphere, regulate climate, and shelter many species.
2. to harvest timber, clear farm land, clear grazing land for livestock, provide room for population growth
3. to observe development projects, educate people, and mount protests
4. Vicente Fox in Mexico, Marta Suplicy in Brazil
5. free and fair elections, citizen participation, majority rule, minority rights, constitutional freedoms, equal rights, educated population
6. Political reform, economic reform, and land reform are essential to stable democracies.
7. religious groups such as the Catholic Church and other religious faiths in the region
8. The poor often lack the education and job skills they need to participate in the economy.
9. because the gap between rich and poor is likely to undermine political stability
10. No. The income gap varies widely from country to country, with some, such as Brazil, having a fairly wide gap while others, such as Ecuador, Paraguay, and Uruguay, having a fairly narrow gap.

Critical Thinking

1. Using Your Notes

Use your completed chart to answer these questions.

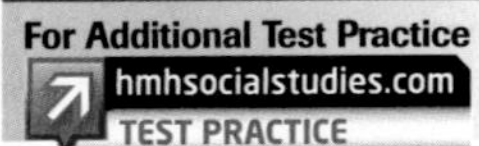

	Causes	Effects
Issue 1: Resources		
Issue 2: Democracy		

a. How might the income gap undermine democracy?

b. What effect might the exploitation of rain forest resources have upon the income gap in the region?

2. Geographic Themes

a. **MOVEMENT** What effect has the movement of people had on the rain forest?

b. **REGION** What are some of the major historical facts that have hindered the development of democracy in Latin America?

3. Identifying Themes

How might the use and development of the region's resources be connected to the gap between rich and poor? Which of the five themes apply to this situation?

4. Making Decisions

If you were a government official in the region, how might you try to balance competing demands on rain forest resources?

5. Drawing Conclusions

How might democratic government in the region promote economic prosperity?

For Additional Test Practice
hmhsocialstudies.com
TEST PRACTICE

Geographic Skills: Interpreting Graphs

Poverty in Latin America

Use the graph to answer the following questions.

1. **REGION** In which three countries of Latin America is the percentage of people living in poverty the lowest?
2. **REGION** In which three countries is the poverty rate highest?
3. **PLACE** Brazil is the largest country in the region, in terms of both area and population. What is its poverty rate?

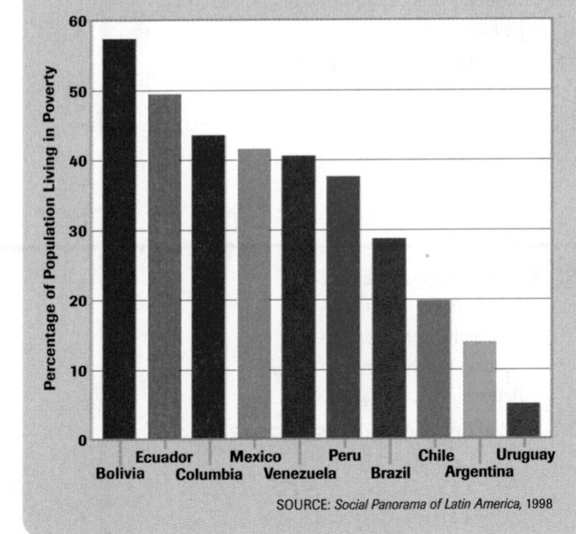

SOURCE: *Social Panorama of Latin America, 1998*

Create a poster showing the effects of poverty and the income gap in one or more countries in the region. Include a map, as well as photographs and diagrams.

hmhsocialstudies.com
MULTIMEDIA ACTIVITY

Use the links at **hmhsocialstudies.com** to research on the Amazon rain forest. Focus on solutions and strategies to slow the dwindling of the rain forest.

Creating Multimedia Presentations Combine charts, maps, or other visual images in an electronic presentation showing strategies for preserving the rain forest.

21st CENTURY

LATIN AMERICA

Critical Thinking

1. a. It undermines political and economic stability.
b. The use of resources might enable poor people to gain economic footholds through small farms or ranches. On the other hand, the exploitation of resources might generate profits that end up with foreign companies.

2. a. People are moving into the rain forest, where they are farming land and grazing livestock.
b. the legacy of colonialism (oligarchy, income gap) and the rule of the caudillos

3. There are pressures to develop and exploit the resources of the region in order to promote economic prosperity. The themes of region, movement, and human-environment interaction apply.

4. A government official might allow development of rain forest resources while imposing stricter rules and regulations on such use.

5. Democratic government promotes political, social, and economic stability, which are important to achieving prosperity.

GeoActivity

Integrated Assessment
• Rubric for a poster, 1.1

Formal Assessment
• Chapter Test, Forms A, B, and C, p. 165-179

Geographic Skills

1. Chile, Argentina, Uruguay
2. Bolivia, Ecuador, Colombia
3. about 28 percent

MULTIMEDIA ACTIVITY

For the presentation on the rain forest, students should:

- Offer a concise, well-organized presentation on preserving the rain forest.
- Include clear, imaginative visuals.
- Cite references to the Web sites used as sources.

Grading Rubric Evaluate student performance as Exceptional, Acceptable, or Poor in each of the following categories:

	Exceptional	Acceptable	Poor
Writing is clear, focused, and logical			
Clearly states topic and purpose			
Provides necessary facts and examples			
Shows contrasts			

UNIT 4 ATLAS AND CHAPTER 12 PLANNING GUIDE
Physical Geography of Europe

OVERVIEW	INSTRUCTIONAL RESOURCES	
CHAPTER 12 ESSENTIAL QUESTION What effect does Europe's physical geography have on its people? **Focus on the Essential Question Podcast**	**In-Depth Resources: Unit 4** • Exploring Today's Issues, pp. 30–33 • Unit Atlas Activities, p. 1 • Regional Data File Activities, p. 2 • Building Vocabulary, p. 9 **Outline Maps with Activities** • Europe: Physical, pp. 29–30 • Europe: Political, pp. 31–32 **Block Schedule Strategies** **Chapter Summaries** (English/Spanish)	**Interactive Online Edition** TOS **ExamView® Assessment Suite** (English/Spanish) TOS **CalendarPlanner** **Power Presentations with Media Gallery** **Critical Thinking Transparencies** • CT12 **Video:** Miraculous Canals of Venice hmhsocialstudies.com INTERACTIVE
SECTION 1 **LANDFORMS AND RESOURCES** **MAIN IDEAS** • Europe is composed of many peninsulas and islands. • Europe's landforms also include large plains and mountain ranges. • Abundant natural resources have shaped lifestyles and the economy.	**In-Depth Resources: Unit 4** • Guided Reading, p. 3 • Building Vocabulary, p. 9 • Reteaching Activities, p. 10 **Guided Reading Workbook,** Section 1	hmhsocialstudies.com INTERACTIVE • Natural Resources of Europe, p. 276
SECTION 2 **CLIMATE AND VEGETATION** **MAIN IDEAS** • Warm ocean currents moderate Western Europe's climate. • Northern and Eastern Europe have much colder climates. • Naturally occurring vegetation ranges from desert scrub to deciduous and coniferous forest.	**In-Depth Resources: Unit 4** • Guided Reading, p. 4 • Map and Graph Skills, pp. 6–7 • Building Vocabulary, p. 9 • Reteaching Activities, p. 11 **Guided Reading Workbook,** Section 2	**Critical Thinking Transparencies** • CT44 Comparing Regional Climates
SECTION 3 **HUMAN–ENVIRONMENT INTERACTION** **MAIN IDEAS** • In the Netherlands, people reclaimed the land to suit their needs. • In Venice, people adapted to the watery environment. • Most of Europe has been deforested.	**In-Depth Resources: Unit 4** • Guided Reading, p. 5 • Skillbuilder Practice, p. 8 • Building Vocabulary, p. 9 • Reteaching Activities, p. 12 **Guided Reading Workbook,** Section 3	**Map Transparencies** • MT23 Environmental Challenges of Europe

ASSESSMENT

SE **Chapter Assessment,** pp. 286–287

Formal Assessment
- Chapter Tests, Forms A, B, and C, pp. 183–194

TOS **ExamView® Assessment Suite**

Strategies for Test Preparation

hmhsocialstudies.com TEST PRACTICE

SE **Section Assessment,** p. 277

Formal Assessment
- Section Quiz, p. 180

Integrated Assessment
- Rubric for a Venn diagram, 2.8

Test Practice Transparencies TT38

SE **Section Assessment,** p. 281

Formal Assessment
- Section Quiz, p. 181

Integrated Assessment
- Rubric for a chart, 2.2

Test Practice Transparencies TT39

SE **Section Assessment,** p. 285

Formal Assessment
- Section Quiz, p. 182

Integrated Assessment
- Rubric for a cause-and-effect chart, 2.2

Test Practice Transparencies TT40

CHART KEY:

SE Student Edition	 Block Scheduling	DVD/CD-ROM
TE Teacher's Edition	TOS Teacher One Stop	 MP3 Audio
Printable Resource	Presentation Resource	 HISTORY™

Program Resources available on TOS and @ hmhsocialstudies.com

SUPPORTING RESOURCES

- Multimedia Classroom Global History Series
- Global History Teacher's Guide

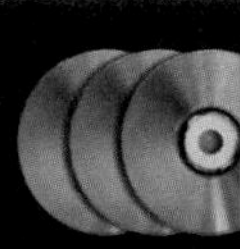

Social Studies Trade Library Collection

- World Regions Trade Collection

For more information or to purchase these resources, go to hmhsocialstudies.com

DIFFERENTIATED INSTRUCTION

English Learners	Struggling Readers	Gifted and Talented Students
Spanish/English Guided Reading Workbook **Access for Students Acquiring English/ESL:** Spanish Translations, pp. 60–63 **Chapter Summaries** (English and Spanish) TE **TE Activity** Understanding Economic Terms, p. 276	**Chapter Summaries** (English and Spanish) TE **TE Activity** Recalling Details, p. 274	TE **TE Activity** Preparing an Environmental Progress Report, p. 284

ENRICHMENT ACTIVITIES

The following activities are especially suitable for classes following block schedules.

SE **Student Edition,** pp. 272–285
- Interpreting a Bar Graph, p. 281

- Natural Resources of Europe, p. 276
- Making a Polder, p. 282

BLOCK SCHEDULE LESSON PLAN OPTIONS: 90-MINUTE PERIOD

DAY 1

UNIT PREVIEW, pp. 258–261
Class Time 20 minutes

- **Discussion** Discuss the Unit Introduction using the discussion prompts on TE pp. 258–259.
  Class Time 10 minutes
- **Today's Issues** Introduce Today's Issues in Europe using Exploring the Issues questions on PE pp. 260–261.
  Class Time 10 minutes

UNIT ATLAS, pp. 262–271
Class Time 30 minutes

- **Small Groups** Divide the class into four groups and have each group answer Making Comparisons questions for one section of the Unit Atlas: Physical Geography, Human Geography, Regional Patterns, and Regional Data File.

SECTION 1, pp. 273–277
Class Time 40 minutes

- **Outline Maps** In preparation for discussing Section 1, have students complete the physical map for Europe in *Outline Map Activities.* Students should label the countries and physical features such as mountains and rivers. They should color the map, using different colors for different landforms.

DAY 2

SECTION 1, pp. 273–277
Class Time 45 minutes

- **Press Conference** As an interesting way to review the section, have a group of four students field questions about the landforms and resources of Europe. The rest of the class should prepare questions to ask the group of four either as homework or in class.
  Class Time 20 minutes
- **Skillbuilder Lesson** Use the Activity Option about drawing conclusions on TE p. 275 and the Skillbuilder Practice worksheet.
  Class Time 25 minutes

SECTION 2, pp. 278–281
Class Time 45 minutes

- **Comparing Europe and the United States** Make two transparencies—one a weather map of Europe and one a weather map of the United States. Have students compare the two maps by pointing out similarities and differences between the weather in Europe and that in the United States. After the discussion, have students draw a Venn diagram in which they list similarities and differences between European weather and U.S. weather.

DAY 3

SECTION 3, pp. 282–285
Class Time 35 minutes

- **Summary Chart** Lead the entire class in creating a three-column summary chart about the examples of human-environment interaction in this section. The headings for the three columns should be "Dutch polders," "Venetian canals," and "European deforestation." Within each column, the students should list important information from the text.

CHAPTER 12 REVIEW AND ASSESSMENT, pp. 286–287
Class Time 55 minutes

- **Review** Have students prepare a summary of the chapter using the Places & Terms listed on the first page of each section.
  Class Time 20 minutes
- **Assessment** Have students complete the Chapter 12 Assessment.
  Class Time 35 minutes

TEACHER-TESTED ACTIVITY *Eastern European Jigsaw*

Class Time One class period

Task Create a two-dimensional jigsaw puzzle map of Eastern Europe

Supplies
- Overhead projector with blank transparency film and marking pens
- Construction paper, assorted colors
- Poster board

Purpose To recognize the shapes of Eastern European countries. Many students do not recognize the shapes of countries, and this is particularly true in areas that have experienced significant boundary changes, as has been the case in Eastern Europe.

Activity Have students trace a political outline map of Eastern Europe from the Unit Atlas (p. 265) to a sheet of blank transparency film. Project this tracing onto construction paper, using different colors for adjacent countries. Have students retrace, then cut out, the country shapes. Have them label the back of each jigsaw piece with the name of the country. Use the pieces to create a political map of Eastern Europe on the poster board. The completed jigsaw puzzle can be used by students to drill themselves in sight/shape recognition of Eastern European countries.

Richard Goodwin
Geography Teacher, Dallas Independent School District

With the advent of the World Wide Web and multimedia presentation programs, which both employ hyperlinks to go from page to page, it has become increasingly common to organize and present information in a non-linear manner. Students can create this type of presentation using a multimedia software program. They will design a primary page that links directly to several other pages with details about different aspects of the topic introduced on the first page.

Objective Students will create a hyperlinked multimedia presentation that illustrates aspects of European physical geography and the relationship between physical geography and life in Europe. This project will give them practice not only in designing a multimedia presentation but also in organizing information in a non-linear manner.

Task Have students read Chapter 12 and look for some of the most interesting and unique features of European physical geography. Then have them design multimedia presentations with hyperlinks from a map on the first page that provide text and pictures to describe these features.

Class Time 2–3 class periods

1. Have students read Chapter 12. As they read, ask them to list the following geographical features, specifying the names of individual examples: peninsulas and islands, mountain ranges, lakes, seas and oceans, rivers, far northern regions, canals.

2. After they have read the chapter and made their lists, discuss these questions as a class:
   - How do mountain ranges, oceans, seas, lakes, and rivers affect the daily lives of European people?
   - What is life like in the far north of Europe?
   - Why were canals built in two European cities, and how do people use these canals?

3. Discuss with the class how they might illustrate their knowledge of European physical geography by creating multimedia presentations. Ask them to imagine that their first page contains a map, from which they link to other pages providing more information about the places on the map (provide an example, if possible). Discuss the ways in which this presentation would differ from a slide show that moves one-by-one through a series of slides, or from a written report.

4. Divide the class into small groups of two to four and ask groups to use a multimedia presentation program to create pages that contain a large map of Europe. They can find the map online at **hmhsocialstudies.com,** or they can scan in their own map.

5. Have groups select one specific example from the chapter for each geographical feature listed in step 1 (for example, the Scandinavian Peninsula, or the Venetian canals).

6. Ask students to insert text over the map indicating the name of each geographical feature and to create hyperlinks from each feature to additional pages or slides.

7. Have students place text and images on the slides to describe how each geographical feature is unique, and to explain how it affects human life in that part of Europe.

Previewing the Unit

The first pages of this unit provide an overview of Europe. The diversity of its peoples and cultures has produced great material and cultural riches, but has also led to conflict.

Discussion Prompts

Exploring Prior Knowledge Ask students the following questions about Europe to determine their prior knowledge of the region:

- What mountain chains are found in Europe? *(the Alps, Pyrenees, Apennines, Carpathian, and Baltic Mountains)*
- What other continents are nearby? *(Africa and Asia)*

Interpreting Maps Ask students to refer to the satellite image of Europe to answer the following questions:

- What landforms do you recognize? *(islands, peninsulas, mountains, lakes)*
- Do you recognize any countries? *(Answers will vary, but may include Italy, Spain, and England.)*

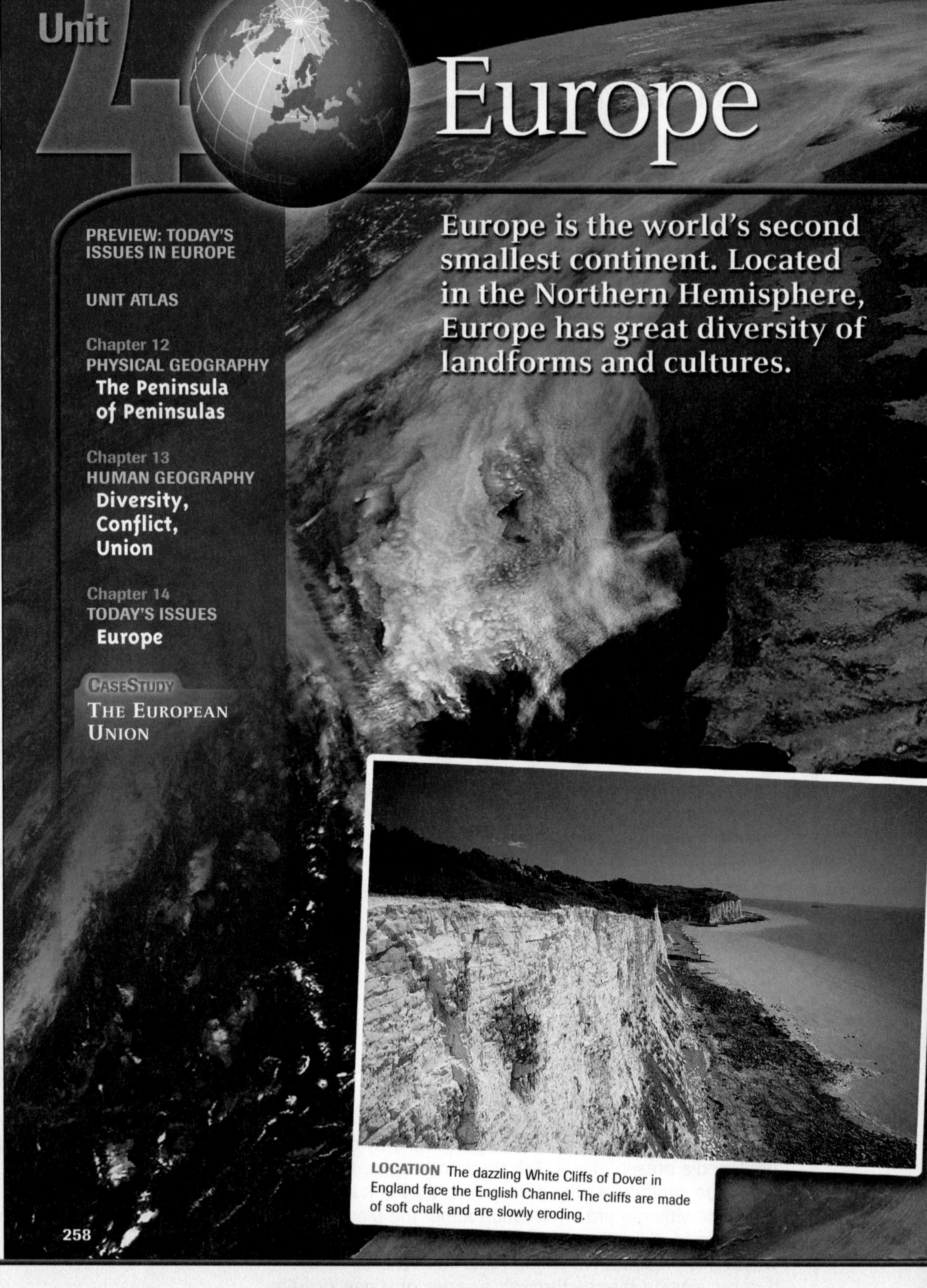

Unit 4 Europe

PREVIEW: TODAY'S ISSUES IN EUROPE

UNIT ATLAS

Chapter 12
PHYSICAL GEOGRAPHY
The Peninsula of Peninsulas

Chapter 13
HUMAN GEOGRAPHY
Diversity, Conflict, Union

Chapter 14
TODAY'S ISSUES
Europe

CASESTUDY
THE EUROPEAN UNION

Europe is the world's second smallest continent. Located in the Northern Hemisphere, Europe has great diversity of landforms and cultures.

LOCATION The dazzling White Cliffs of Dover in England face the English Channel. The cliffs are made of soft chalk and are slowly eroding.

UNIT 4 ADDITIONAL RESOURCES

BOOKS FOR THE TEACHER

Ostergren, Robert C. and Jon G. Rice, ***The Europeans: A Geography of People, Culture, and Environment.*** The Guilford Press, 2004. Thematic introduction to key geographical issues.

Barnes, Ian. ***The History Atlas of Europe.*** NY: Macmillan, 1998. Informative, illustrated atlas of European history.

BOOKS FOR THE STUDENT

Cussans, Thomas, et al. ***The Times Atlas of European History.*** NY: Harper Collins, 1994. Excellent maps showing historic periods in Europe.

VIDEOS

In the Shadow of Vesuvius. Vestron Video, 1989. Physical and cultural geography at Pompeii, by National Geographic.

INTERNET

For more on the geography of Europe, visit . . .

hmhsocialstudies.com

GeoData

REGION Many people view the Ural Mountains as the eastern border of Europe, but for historic and cultural reasons, Russia and other former republics of the Soviet Union are in Unit 5.

PLACE Europe's coastline is longer than that of Africa, the world's second largest continent.

HUMAN-ENVIRONMENT INTERACTION Historically, Europeans used the oceans and seas to make voyages for exploration and trade. Their culture spread around the world.

For more information on Europe . . .

hmhsocialstudies.com
RESEARCH WEB LINKS

PLACE The Eiffel Tower stands 984 feet above the Paris skyline. It was completed in 1889 for an International Exposition celebrating the French Revolution.

MOVEMENT Europeans are wildly enthusiastic about soccer. Teams and fans travel to matches held all over the world. The teams in this game represent two European powerhouses, Germany and Italy.

259

Interpreting Photographs

White Cliffs of Dover

The ancient Greeks and Romans referred to the island as Albion, which translates roughly as "white land."

Ask students what they can infer about the Greeks and Romans from their use of this name. *(They must have traveled to the island by boat and seen the white cliffs.)*

The Eiffel Tower

Point out that the Eiffel Tower was the tallest structure in the world when it was built, but that it was not meant to be permanent.

Ask students why they think the Eiffel Tower wasn't torn down, and what gives the tower its appeal. *(Many people liked the extraordinary structure, and it became identified with Paris.)*

Soccer Game

Tell students that people usually support a team for geographic reasons.

Ask students if they support any sports teams. If they do, ask them what they would do if they had to move to the school or town of their favorite team's rival. *(They would remain loyal to their favorite team, or they would want to fit in with their new community, and so would support their former rival.)*

ACTIVITY OPTION | COOPERATIVE LEARNING

CREATING A MONTAGE

Objective To allow students to explore aspects of Europe

Class Time 30 minutes

Task Create a poster of features of Europe

Supplies Needed

- old magazines and newspapers
- poster board
- glue
- markers

Directions Divide students into small groups and have them look for photographs on the Internet or in magazines and newspapers that fall into the same categories as the photographs above. Each poster should display European landforms, human-made landmarks, and athletic activities. Each image should have a caption that includes the location.

Today's Issues in Europe

Previewing Today's Issues

These pages provide a preview of issues faced by the nations of Europe. These topics will be fully explored in Chapter 14 (pages 318–329). Use the discussion prompts that follow to determine students' prior knowledge and allow them to make comparisons to local events.

In-Depth Resources: Unit 4
• Exploring Today's Issues, pp. 30–33

CONFLICT

In the former Yugoslavia, ethnic tensions between Serbs, Croats, and Bosnians erupted into war during the 1990s. Today, tensions still simmer in the Balkans and other parts of Europe.

Discussion Prompts

- Do you know of other conflicts in Europe? *(Answers will vary but may include conflicts in Northern Ireland and the Basque separatist movement.)*
- Do you know of cultural or religious conflicts in the United States? *(Answers will vary.)*

Today, Europe faces the issues previewed here. As you read Chapters 12 and 13, you will learn helpful background information. You will study the issues themselves in Chapter 14.

In a small group, answer the questions below. Then participate in a class discussion of your answers.

Exploring the Issues

1. CONFLICT Search a print or online newspaper for articles about ethnic or religious conflicts in Europe today. What do these conflicts have in common? How are they different?
2. POLLUTION Make a list of possible pollution problems faced by Europe and those faced by the United States. How are these problems similar? Different?
3. UNIFICATION To help you understand the issues involved in unifying Europe, compare Europe to the United States. Imagine what might occur if each U.S. state were its own country. List five problems that might result.

For more on these issues in Europe . . .

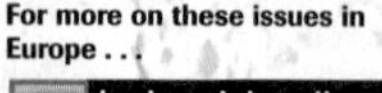

CONFLICT

How can people resolve their differences?

In central Bosnia, a child stands near the ruins of a Muslim mosque. Bosnian Croats destroyed the mosque during an "ethnic cleansing" campaign to drive out Muslims during the 1992-1995 Bosnian war.

EXPLORING THE ISSUES ANSWERS

1. CONFLICT Students may learn that many of the conflicts in Europe have common causes: religious and linguistic differences. However, the Northern Ireland conflict is between Christians, while the Balkans conflict involves Christians and Muslims.
2. POLLUTION Students may say that Europe and the United States have similar problems: air pollution, water pollution, toxic waste, and oil spills. The differences cited will vary, depending on each student's level of prior knowledge.
3. UNIFICATION Problems could include the need for passports for interstate travel, taxes on goods shipped across state lines, different currencies, different postage, no central authority to resolve conflicting laws, difficulty in extraditing criminals, and some states' refusal to recognize other states' marriages and contracts.

POLLUTION

How can Europeans clean up their environment?

On February 13, 2000, cyanide-polluted water from a Romanian mine reached Hungary. The cyanide killed thousands of fish, some of which are shown here washed up on the banks of the Tisza River.

CASESTUDY

What will become of the European Union?

Since 1950, European nations have been working together to develop an economic alliance that is now known as the European Union (EU). However, disagreements remain over many issues.

UNIFICATION
WHAT DOES HE SAY?..
I DON'T KNOW, I DON'T SPEAK TURKISH
ADMISSIONS
EU
DELIGNE

EUROPE

POLLUTION

Pollution is most severe in the former communist nations of Eastern Europe. To compete with Western economies, countries like Romania, Hungary, Poland, and Czechoslovakia promoted rapid industrialization. Despite recent clean-up efforts, contamination continues to haunt the region.

Discussion Prompts

- What are the competing interests surrounding industrial pollution? *(Pollution controls may curtail number of jobs or affect the cost of finished products, but the health of citizens may be worth that cost.)*
- How has pollution affected your community or state? *(Answers will vary.)*

CASESTUDY

UNIFICATION

To give students an opportunity to gain a deeper understanding of the issues surrounding the European Union, direct them to the Case Study, which begins on page 326 and concludes with a Case Study Project on page 328.

Discussion Prompts

- What have you heard or read about the European Union in news sources? *(Answers will vary.)*
- How are U.S. citizens affected by decisions made by the European Union? *(Answers may include changes in the price of imported goods; changes to U.S. foreign policy.)*

ACTIVITY OPTION | INTERNET RESEARCH

WRITING A NEWS SYNOPSIS

Objective To develop basic research skills on the Internet

Class Time 20 minutes

Task Identify two sources of information for one of the three issues introduced about Europe, and write a brief description or synopsis of the source

Directions Direct students to the Web site for *World Geography* at **hmhsocialstudies.com.** Click on the Current Events button and follow the links to sources of information on these or other European issues.

OPTIONAL ACTIVITY If Internet access is limited, have the students use the library for this research activity. Have the librarian show the students how to use the *Readers' Guide to Periodical Literature* and other indexes to find articles on the issues in Europe.

ATLAS OBJECTIVES

1. Compare data on the physical geography of Europe.
2. Examine key physical features of Europe.
3. Identify European countries and borders in 1914.
4. Identify current political features of Europe.
5. Learn about European religions and climates.
6. Analyze language distribution and population density in Europe.

Focus & Motivate

Ask students what they already know about the physical geography of Europe. Have them list the kinds of information that maps and charts might convey about Europe. *(Answers will vary but may include physical, political, and language information.)*

Instruct: Objective 1

Comparing Data

- **Landmass** How does Europe compare in size to the United States? *(about half the size)*
- **Population** How do the populations of Europe and the United States compare? *(Europe's population is more than 200 million greater.)*
- **Rivers** How does the Rhine River compare in length to the Mississippi? *(about half as long as the Mississippi)*
- **Mountains** How does Mont Blanc compare in size to the highest mountain in the world? *(a little more than half as high)*

Unit ATLAS

Patterns of Physical Geography

Use the Unit Atlas to add to your knowledge of Europe. As you look at the maps and charts, notice geographic patterns and specific details about the region. For example, the chart gives details about the rivers and mountains of Europe.

After studying the graphs and physical map on these two pages, jot down answers to the questions below in your notebook.

Making Comparisons

1. Compare Europe's size and population to that of the United States. Based on that data, how might the population densities of the two compare?
2. Compare Europe's longest river, the Danube, to the Mississippi. How much difference is there in the lengths?
3. Which countries have many mountains? How might those mountains affect human life there?

Comparing Data

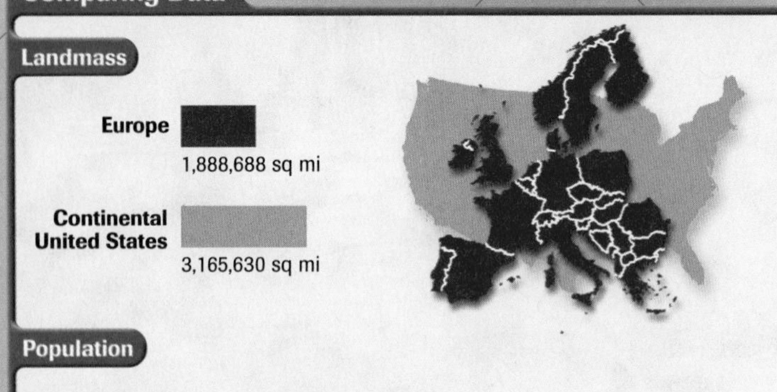

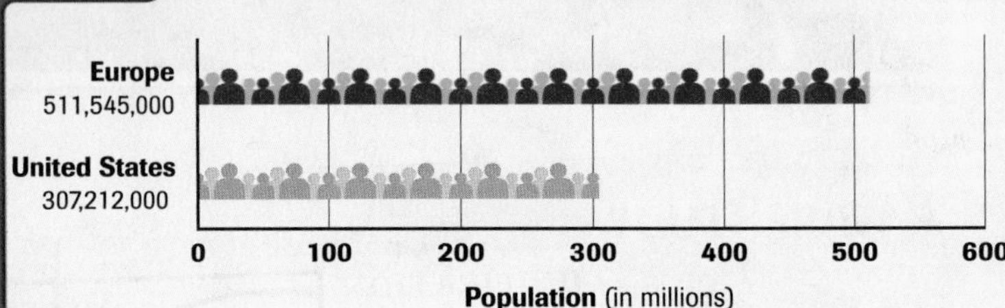

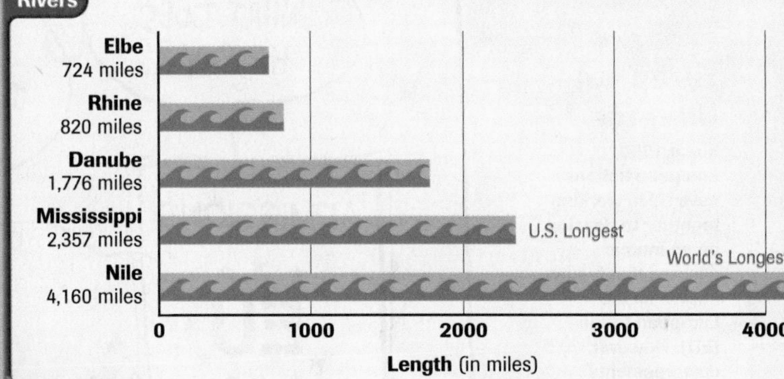

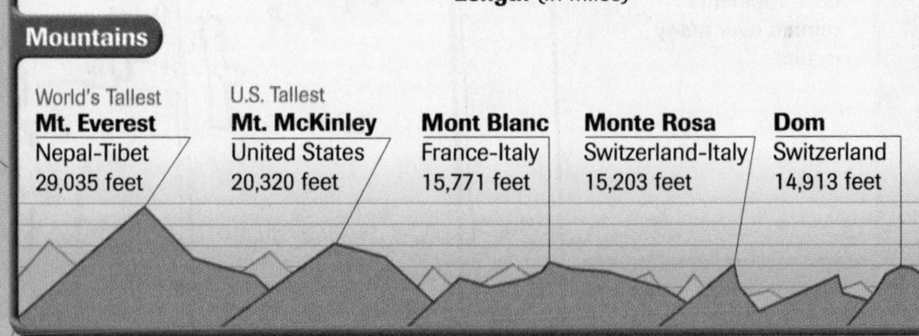

MAKING COMPARISONS ANSWERS

1. Europe is about 59 percent the size of the United States but has roughly 1.6 times as many people. Its population density is probably about three times that of the United States.
2. The Mississippi is 581 miles longer than the Danube.
3. The mountainous countries include Norway, Switzerland, Italy, Austria, Slovakia, Romania, Slovenia, Bosnia-Herzegovina, Yugoslavia, Albania, Macedonia, Bulgaria, and Greece. Transportation and farming may be difficult. The climate is probably colder than in nearby countries without mountains. Their economies may benefit from tourism.

Instruct: Objective 2

Europe: Physical

- What are Europe's highest mountains? *(the Alps)*
- What are the Apennines? *(mountains in Italy)*
- What seas border Denmark? *(North, Baltic)*

In-Depth Resources, Unit 4
- Unit Atlas Activities, p. 1

Outline Maps with Activities
- Europe: Physical, pp. 29–30

Map Transparencies MT21
- Europe: Physical

More About

Fjords

Carved out by glaciers during the Ice Ages, fjords are a characteristic landform of Norway (visible in this map along its western coast.) Fjords also exist in other parts of the world, including New Zealand, Chile, Alaska, and British Columbia. They can extend far inland and reach depths of more than 4,000 feet. Villages are typically found at the head of fjords, where an entering stream may create a delta that lends itself to small-scale farming and settlement.

ACTIVITY OPTION CRITICAL THINKING

BLOCK SCHEDULING

MAKING COMPARISONS

Explaining the Skill Students will demonstrate their ability to recognize similar features in a physical map by using the key and the display itself.

Applying the Skill Have students create a table with two columns and six rows. Label the columns "Elevation" and "Countries." Under "Elevation," label the rows with the six elevation categories from the map legend in ascending order. Have students use the map to rank the following nations according to overall elevation: Denmark, France, Netherlands, Spain, Switzerland. *(lowest: Netherlands, Denmark, France, Spain; highest: Switzerland)* Have students compare their tables when they are finished.

Instruct: Objective 3

Europe, 1914

- What does this map show? *(the nations of Europe in 1914, before World War I)*
- Why do you think 1914 was chosen for the date of this map? *(because political boundaries in Europe changed a great deal after that)*
- How was Great Britain different in 1914 than it is today? Austria? *(Great Britain included Ireland; Austria was Austria-Hungary and much larger.)*

More About

Austria-Hungary

Austria-Hungary was one of the main European empires of the late 1800s. Ruled by the Hapsburg dynasty, it contained various peoples and cultures within its borders but had no strong sense of national identity. After World War I, the empire split into the independent states of Austria, Hungary, Czechoslovakia, and Yugoslavia.

Unit ATLAS

Patterns of Human Geography

After World War I (1914–1918), the political map of Europe changed radically. Empires disappeared, and new countries were born. Study the political maps of Europe in 1914 and Europe today to see what changes took place in the 20th and 21st centuries. Then answer these questions in your notebook.

Making Comparisons

1. Which nations appear on the map of Europe today but don't appear on the 1914 map?
2. Which nations existed in 1914 but no longer exist today?
3. Which nations are larger now than they were in 1914?
4. Which nations are smaller than they were in 1914?

Europe, 1914

This map shows the nations of Europe in 1914, before the outbreak of World War I.

Madeira Is. (Port.)

Canary Is. (Sp.)

MAKING COMPARISONS ANSWERS

1. Poland, Ireland, Austria, Hungary, Czech Republic, Slovakia, Slovenia, Croatia, Bosnia and Herzegovina, Macedonia, Kosovo, Liechtenstein
2. Austria-Hungary
3. Italy, Romania
4. Germany, United Kingdom

Europe: Political

hmhsocialstudies.com
INTERACTIVE MAP

National capital
Other city

Azimuthal Equidistant Projection

265

Instruct: Objective 4

Europe: Political

- What four countries on the eastern side of the Baltic Sea were once part of Russia? *(Finland, Estonia, Latvia, Lithuania)*
- What European countries border the Black Sea? *(Romania, Bulgaria)*
- What countries were formed from the old state of Austria-Hungary? *(Austria, Hungary, Czech Republic, Slovakia, Slovenia, Croatia, Bosnia and Herzegovina, Romania, Serbia, Montenegro, Macedonia)*

 **Outline Maps with Activities**
- Europe: Political, pp. 31–32

 **Map Transparencies MT22**
- Europe: Political

EUROPE

More About

The End of the Soviet Union

The collapse of the Soviet bloc brought about the formation of new countries. Two nations emerged from the former Czechoslovakia: the Czech Republic and Slovakia. Several new states have also separated from Yugoslavia: Slovenia, Croatia, Macedonia, Bosnia and Herzegovina, Serbia, Kosovo, and Montenegro. In addition, the fall of Communist governments in Bulgaria, Romania, Poland, and East Germany (now reunited with West Germany) has led to unprecedented economic and political changes in those countries.

ACTIVITY OPTION | LINK TO MATH

CALCULATING TRAVEL TIMES

Objective To use a map scale and make calculations that give a sense of distances and spatial relationships in Europe

Class Time 15–25 minutes

Task Figure distances and travel times between European cities

Supplies Needed
- Paper, pencil, ruler
- Calculators (optional)

Directions In Europe, trains generally provide fast, efficient, and comfortable service. Have students use the map scale on the political map above to calculate the distance in kilometers of each stage in this train itinerary: Lisbon–Madrid–Barcelona–Paris–Brussels–Berlin–Warsaw. Then, assuming an average speed of 90 km/hour, have them calculate the time it would take to travel between each city. Offer extra credit for converting calculations from kilometers to miles. *(Lisbon to Madrid, 5.5 hours; Madrid to Barcelona, 5.5 hours; Barcelona to Paris, approx. 9 hours; Paris to Brussels, 2.7 hours; Brussels to Berlin, 6.9 hours ; Berlin to Warsaw, about 5.5 hours.)*

Instruct: Objective 5

Major Religions of Europe

- Which religion in Europe has the most followers? *(Roman Catholic)*
- What do you think the category "Other" includes? *(religions like Buddhism, Hinduism, and others)*
- How do the figures for Muslims and Jews compare? *(There are 2% more Muslims than Jews.)*

Instruct: Objective 5

Climates of Europe

- What type of climate is common in much of northwestern Europe? *(moderate, mild rainy winter)*
- What is the typical climate of southern Europe? *(moderate, hot dry summer)*
- Where is the semiarid climate found? *(Spain, Portugal)*

Unit ATLAS

Regional Patterns

These two pages contain a pie graph and three thematic maps. The pie graph shows the religions of Europe. The maps show other important features of Europe: its generally mild climate, its diversity of languages, and its high population density. After studying these two pages, answer the questions below in your notebook.

Making Comparisons

1. Where are the coldest climates to be found in Europe? Is the population density high or low in those areas? Give possible reasons for that pattern.
2. What do you notice about the number of languages in Europe? Do they belong to one language group or several? Explain whether the pattern of languages would be more likely to increase or decrease conflict in the region.

Major Religions of Europe*

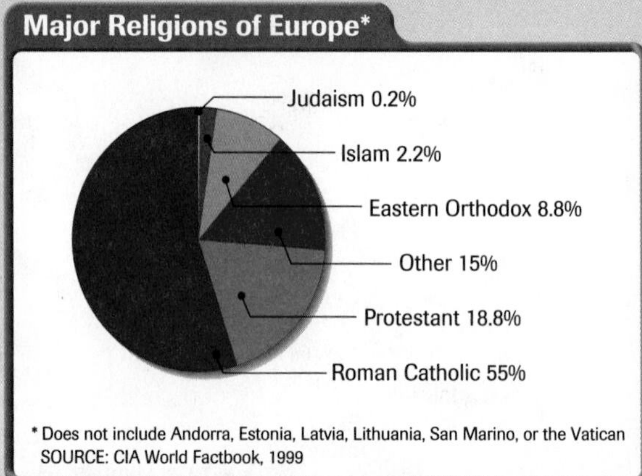

* Does not include Andorra, Estonia, Latvia, Lithuania, San Marino, or the Vatican
SOURCE: CIA World Factbook, 1999

Climates of Europe

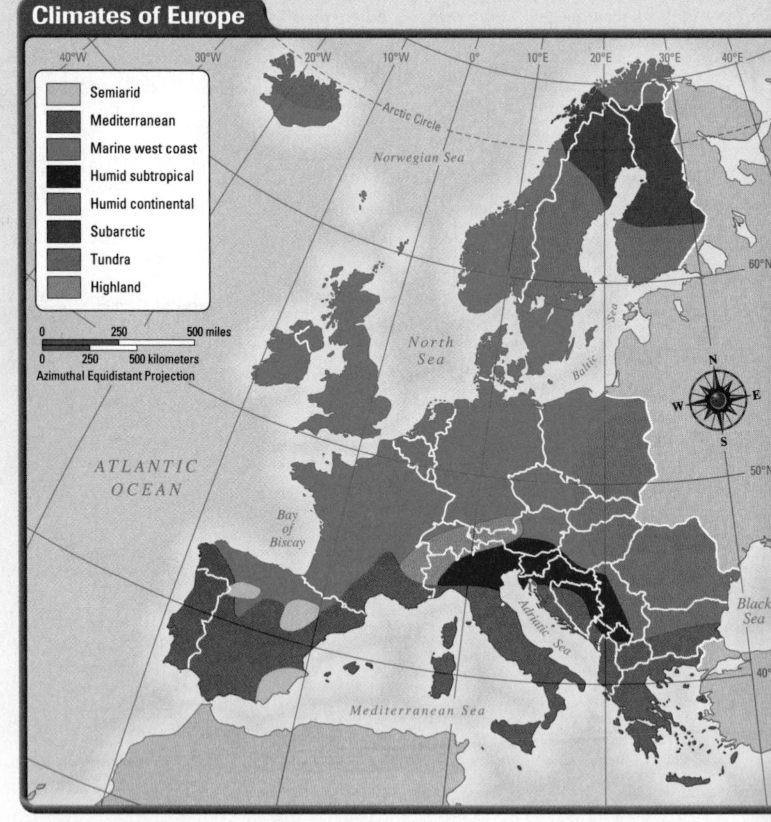

MAKING COMPARISONS ANSWERS

1. They are in the far northern parts of Norway, Sweden, and Finland, plus Iceland. Population density is very low there, probably because the weather is so harsh.
2. There are many languages and language groups. This would probably increase conflict because it would make it harder for people to understand one another.

Instruct: Objective 6

Languages of Europe

- What languages are included in the Romance group? *(Portuguese, Spanish, French, Provençal, Italian, Romanian)*
- Where are Germanic languages spoken? *(in north-central Europe, Scandinavia, and the British Isles)*
- What do Finnish, Sami, and Hungarian have in common? *(They are part of the Finno-Ugric group.)*

Instruct: Objective 

Population Density of Europe

- What color is used to show lowest population density? *(yellow)*
- What island has very low population density? *(Iceland)*
- In what part of Europe is the population density highest? *(north-central Europe)*

Languages of Europe

Population Density of Europe

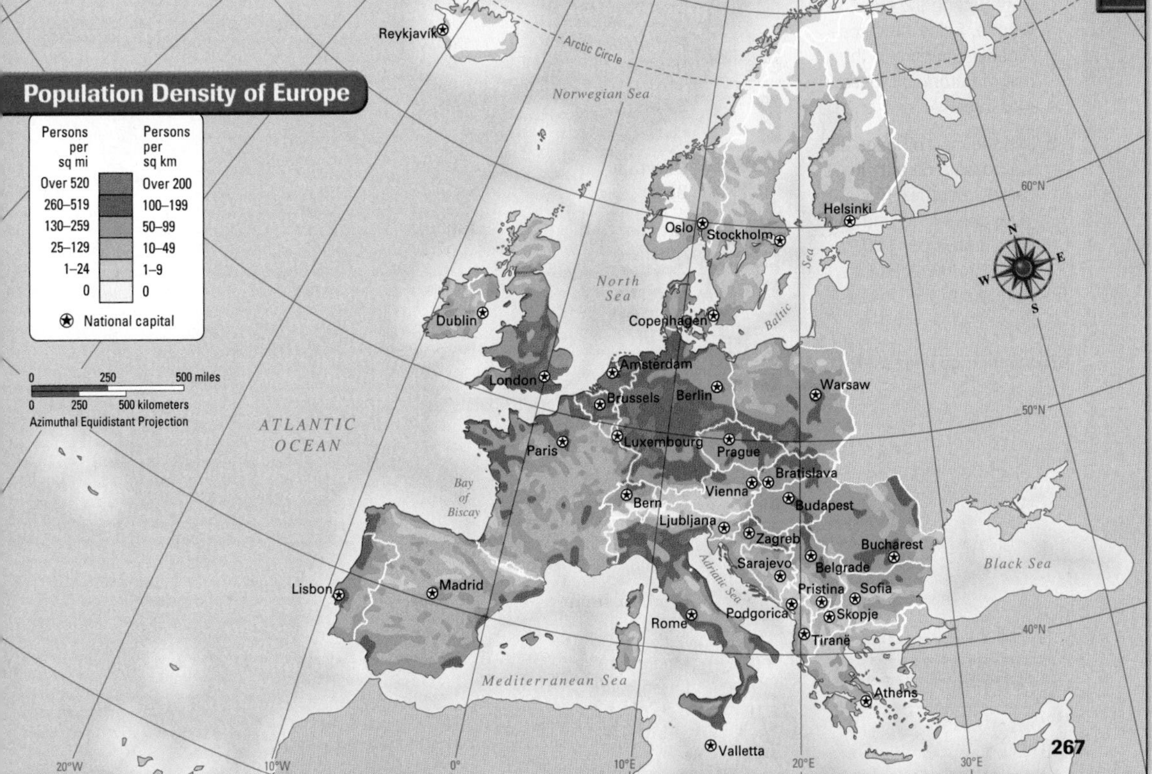

267

DIFFERENTIATING INSTRUCTION GIFTED AND TALENTED STUDENTS

CREATING POPULATION DENSITY TABLES

Objective To gather information from one type of graphic display, reconfigure it, and present it in a new format

Class Time 20 minutes

Task Make a table showing population density of cities

Directions Have students create a table like the one shown. Ask them to use the population density map to determine density for all the cities shown and list the cities in the proper rows according to their population density. Have students compare their tables when they're finished.

DENSITY (persons / sq mi)	CITIES
Over 520	London, Amsterdam, Madrid, Brussels, Luxembourg, Paris
260-519	Rome, Berlin, Warsaw, Prague, Vienna, Bratislava, Bucharest, Budapest, Bern, Belgrade
130-259	Oslo, Stockholm, Helsinki, Copenhagen, Zagreb
25-129	Dublin, Sofia, Skopje, Ljubliana, Tirana, Athens
1-24	Sarajevo, Reykjavik
0	—

OBJECTIVE

Examine and compare data on European countries.

Focus & Motivate

Ask students what they think is the total number of European nations. *(38)*

Instruct: Objective

Regional Data File

- What is the largest country in Europe in terms of area? the most populous? *(France; Germany)*
- Which European country has the most televisions per 1,000 people? How does the United States compare? *(San Marino; the U.S. has fewer)*
- Which country has the most doctors per 100,000 people? How does the United States compare? *(Monaco; the U.S. has less than half that)*

In-Depth Resources: Unit 4
- Regional Data File Activities, p. 2

Unit ATLAS

Regional Data File

Study the charts on the countries of Europe. In your notebook, answer these questions.

Making Comparisons

1. Make a list of the top five European countries in GDP. Where are each of these countries located, relative to the rest of Europe? What pattern do you notice?
2. In 2000, Albania had an infant mortality rate of 41.3, and its life expectancy, number of doctors, and literacy rate were among the worst in Europe. Today, how does Albania compare to the rest of Europe on these measures?
3. Use the map on page 265 to choose a country in Eastern Europe. How many televisions and cars does it have per 1,000 people? How does that compare to the United States?

(continued on page 270)

Country Flag	Country/ Capital	Population	Life Expectancy (years)	Birthrate (per 1,000 pop.)	Infant Mo (per 1,000 live
	Albania Tiranë	3,639,000	77.9	16.3	18.6
	Andorra Andorra la Vella	84,000	82.5	10.4	3.8
	Austria Vienna	8,210,000	79.5	8.7	4.4
	Belgium Brussels	10,414,000	79.2	10.2	4.4
	Bosnia & Herzegovina Sarajevo	4,613,000	78.5	8.8	9.1
	Bulgaria Sofia	7,205,000	73.1	9.5	17.9
	Croatia Zagreb	4,489,000	75.3	9.6	6.4
	Czech Republic Prague	10,212,000	76.8	8.8	3.8
	Denmark Copenhagen	5,501,000	78.3	10.5	4.3
	Finland Helsinki	5,250,000	78.9	10.4	3.5
	France Paris	64,058,000	80.9	12.6	3.3
	Germany Berlin	82,330,000	79.3	8.2	4
	Greece Athens	10,737,000	79.7	9.5	5.2
	Hungary Budapest	9,906,000	73.4	9.5	7.9
	Iceland Reykjavík	307,000	80.7	13.4	3.2
	Ireland Dublin	4,203,000	78.2	14.2	5
	Italy Rome	58,126,000	80.2	8.2	5.5
	Kosovo Pristina	1,805,000	69.5	19	46.4
	Liechtenstein Vaduz	35,000	80.1	9.8	4.3
	Luxembourg Luxembourg	490,000	79.3	11.7	4.6

For updated statistics on Europe . . .

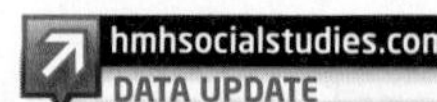

MAKING COMPARISONS ANSWERS

1. Germany, France, United Kingdom, Italy, Spain. They form a bloc in the western half of Europe. They are among the largest European countries in terms of population.
2. Albania has cut its infant mortality rate in half, and its literacy rate is comparable to that of the rest of Europe (and much higher than that of the United States), but it still has a low number of doctors. Its life expectancy rate is about average.
3. Answers will vary depending on country chosen.

Doctors (per 100,000 pop.) (2000–2004)	GDP[a] (billions $US)	Import/Export (billions $US)	Literacy Rate (percentage)	Televisions (per 1,000 pop.)	Passenger Cars (per 1,000 pop.)	Total Area[b] (square miles)
131	22.6	3.6/1.2	99	146	48	11,100
370	4.2	1.8/.09	100	440	590	181
338	323.1	136/129	98	526	512	32,382
449	381.4	315/296.1	99	532	471	11,787
134	29.3	9.95/4.36	97	112	N/A	19,741
356	90.4	23.27/16.23	98	429	470	42,823
244	79.2	22.1/10.57	98	286	312	21,831
351	256.7	99.97/106.4	99	487	388	30,450
293	197.7	84.07/91.9	99	776	358	16,639
316	181.4	54.1/57.88	100	643	457	130,559
337	2,113.0	532.2/456.8	99	620	464	248,429
337	2,812.0	931.3/1,187	99	581	551	137,847
438	339.2	61.47/18.64	96	480	400	50,942
333	186.3	74.56/78.61	99	447	293	35,919
362	12.2	2.83/4.22	99	505	609	39,769
279	177	64.9/107.3	99	406	404	27,135
420	1,756	358.7/369	98	492	597	116,306
N/A	5.3	2.6/0.53	92	N/A	N/A	4,203
N/A	4.16	2.6/2.47	100	469	N/A	62
266	38.1	18.69/14.05	100	599	620	998

More About

Health Indicators

Have students note the various ways the data is measured. For example, doctors are measured per 100,000 residents. Ask students whether this statistic shows an actual number or a rate? *(It shows a rate.)* How would they determine the actual number of doctors in Monaco? *(Divide the total population figures by 100,000, then multiply that number by the doctors/thousand figure.)*

ACTIVITY OPTION | CRITICAL THINKING

ANALYZING DATA

Explaining the Skill In many cases it is necessary to perform additional tasks with the raw data presented in a chart in order to get a deeper understanding of a real-life situation. For instance, economists use import/export figures to determine a country's trade balance. When exports exceed imports, a country has a trade surplus. When imports exceed exports, a country has a trade deficit. Economists also compare exports to total GDP to figure out the relative importance of foreign trade in a country's economy.

Applying the Skill Have students choose five countries and calculate whether each has a trade surplus or a deficit by subtracting the import figure from the export figure (a positive number is a surplus; a negative number is a deficit). They can then calculate the degree to which each economy is export-based by dividing exports by total GDP (producing a percentage figure). Ask: Which do you think is preferable: a trade surplus or a trade deficit? Why?

More About

Europe's Smallest Nations

Andorra, Liechtenstein, Luxembourg, Malta, Monaco, and San Marino are remnants of old principalities or kingdoms that now survive on tourism or other specialized economic activities. In fact, these tiny countries can show surprising economic features.

Luxembourg, for example, is one-fortieth the size of Iceland but has an economy more than twice as large.

Unit ATLAS Regional Data File

Making Comparisons *(continued)*

4. Europe has several countries with populations under 100,000 people. Which of these has the smallest total area?

5. Use the map on page 265 to identify the two countries on the Scandinavian Peninsula. For each of those countries, calculate per capita GDP by dividing total GDP by population. Which country has the higher per capita GDP?

Country Flag	Country/ Capital	Population	Life Expectancy (years)	Birthrate (per 1,000 pop.)	Infant M (per 1,000 li
	Macedonia Skopje	2,067,000	74.7	11.9	9
	Malta Valletta	405,000	79.4	10.4	3.
	Monaco Monaco	33,000	80.1	9.1	5.
	Montenegro Cetinje and Podgorica	672,000	77.2	11.1	10.
	Netherlands Amsterdam	16,716,000	79.4	10.4	4.
	Norway Oslo	4,661,000	79.9	11	3.
	Poland Warsaw	38,483,000	75.6	10	6.8
	Portugal Lisbon	10,708,000	78.2	10.3	4.8
	Romania Bucharest	22,215,000	72.5	10.5	22.9
	San Marino San Marino	30,000	80.8	9.7	5.5
	Serbia Belgrade	7,379,000	73.9	9.2	6.8
	Slovakia Bratislava	4,463,000	75.4	10.6	6.8
	Slovenia Ljubljana	2,006,000	76.9	9	4.3
	Spain Madrid	40,525,000	80	9.7	4.2
	Sweden Stockholm	9,060,000	80.8	10.1	2.8
	Switzerland Bern	7,604,000	80.9	9.6	4.2
	United Kingdom London	61,113,000	79	10.7	4.9
	Vatican City Vatican City	1,000	N/A	N/A	N/A
	United States Washington, D.C.	307,212,000	78.1	13.8	6.2

Sources:
Central Intelligence Agency, *The World Factbook*, 2010
The World Almanac and Book of Facts, 2010
World Health Organization (WHO), 2007

Notes:
[a] GDP (purchasing power parity) is defined as the sum value of all goods and services produced in the country valued at prices prevailing in the United States.
[b] Includes land and water, when figures are available

MAKING COMPARISONS ANSWERS

4. Vatican City

5. Norway's per capita GDP in U.S. dollars is $59,322; Sweden's is $36,777.

Doctors (per 100,000 pop.) (2000–2004)	GDP[a] (billions $US)	Import/Export (billions $US)	Literacy Rate (percentage)	Televisions (per 1,000 pop.)	Passenger Cars (per 1,000 pop.)	Total Area[b] (square miles)
219	18.8	4.94/3.03	96	273	122	9,781
318	9.7	3.94/2.46	93	549	582	122
581	0.98	0.92/0.72	99	758	N/A	1
N/A	6.64	0.60/0.17	N/A	N/A	199	5,415
315	652.3	358.9/397.6	99	540	418	16,033
313	276.5	64.5/122	100	653	436	125,021
247	686.2	141.7/134.7	99	387	311	120,728
342	232.2	58.79/41.43	93	567	560	35,672
190	256.3	49.2/38.1	97	312	153	91,699
N/A	1.7	3.74/4.63	96	875	N/A	24
N/A	77.0	18.35/8.82	96	277	199	29,913
318	115.3	46.47/45.05	99	418	291	18,859
225	56.5	22.9/24.3	99	362	484	7,827
330	1,368.0	293.2/215.7	98	555	501	194,897
328	333.2	121.1/132.8	99	551	464	173,732
361	316.1	177.2/190.1	99	457	513	15,942
230	2,165.0	473.6/351.3	99	661	463	94,526
N/A	N/A	N/A	100	N/A	N/A	0.2
256	14,260.0	1,445/994.7	99	844	725	3,794,083

More About

Vatican City

Vatican City, the headquarters of the Roman Catholic Church, is an independent state in the heart of Rome. It has its own telephone system, post office, and radio station, as well as its own army and banking system. The pope is the ultimate authority, with absolute power over all Vatican affairs.

ACTIVITY OPTION COOPERATIVE LEARNING

CREATING A BAR GRAPH

Objective To gather information from one type of graphic display, reconfigure it, and present it in a new format

Class Time 30 minutes

Task Make a bar graph to compare infant mortality rates

Directions Divide the class into small groups. Have students create a bar graph with two axes, one showing "Infant Mortality per 1,000 live births" the other showing "European Countries (M-Z)". Direct students to evaluate the data before plotting it. They should make a judgment as to whether it is preferable to list countries alphabetically or to group nations with similar rates together. Students may elect to use color to organize the information in their bar graphs. Have small groups exchange and compare their peers' graphs.

CHAPTER 12 OBJECTIVE

Identify key features of Europe's physical geography, climate and vegetation, and human-environment interaction.

Chapter 

12 PHYSICAL GEOGRAPHY OF EUROPE
The Peninsula of Peninsulas

Miraculous Canals of Venice

hmhsocialstudies.com VIDEO

Interpreting Photographs

Sognafjord

Direct the students' attention to the houses set on steep slopes above the water, and to the gray, chilly weather conditions.

Extension Have students write a brief journal entry describing a day in the life of a resident of Sognafjord.

Introducing the Essential Question

- Tell students that, for most Europeans, the sea is just a few hours away. For millions of Europeans, the sea is practically at their doorstep. Describe some ways this proximity to the sea might have affected Europe's history.
- Emphasize that Europe has a temperate climate, thanks to the sea's warming effect. Other problems plague the region, however, including centuries of environmental damage.

Have students fill out graphic organizers in their notebooks using material from all sections in this chapter.

 **Critical Thinking Transparencies CT12**
- GeoFocus

In-Depth Resources: Unit 4
- Building Vocabulary, p. 9

Sognafjord, north of the city of Bergen, Norway, has only about five and a half hours of light per day in mid-December.

Essential Question

What effect does Europe's physical geography have on its people?

What You Will Learn

In this chapter you will read about key features of Europe's physical geography.

SECTION 1
Landforms and Resources

SECTION 2
Climate and Vegetation

SECTION 3
Human–Environment Interaction

hmhsocialstudies.com TAKING NOTES

Use the graphic organizer online to record information from the chapter about the physical geography of Europe.

272

CHAPTER 12 ADDITIONAL RESOURCES

BOOKS FOR THE TEACHER

Blanning, T. C. W. (ed.). ***The Oxford Illustrated History of Modern Europe.*** Oxford University Press, 2001. Continuity and change in Europe since 1789.

BOOKS FOR THE STUDENT

Lambert, David. ***The Mediterranean Sea.*** Austin: Raintree/Steck-Vaughn, 1997. The physical geography of the Mediterranean region.

Rebuffat, Gaston. ***Starlight and Storm.*** NY: Modern Library, 1999. Adventure in the Alps.

VIDEOS

Alpine Adventure. Readers Digest Home Entertainment, 1994. Tour of the Alps.

Iceland River Challenge. Vestron Video, 1985. National Geographic rafting expedition in Iceland.

INTERNET

For more on the physical geography of Europe, visit . . .

hmhsocialstudies.com

Landforms and Resources

Main Ideas

- Europe is composed of many peninsulas and islands.
- Europe's landforms also include large plains and mountain ranges.

Places & Terms

fjord · ***Massif Central***
uplands · **peat**
Meseta

CONNECT TO THE ISSUES
UNIFICATION Resources helped Western Europe develop industry before other regions. The European Union began in Western Europe.

SECTION 1 OBJECTIVES

1. Identify the main peninsulas and islands.
2. Explain how mountains and uplands affect European life.
3. Describe major rivers and their uses.
4. Explain the importance of plains in Europe.
5. Identify key natural resources and describe connections between resources and daily life in Europe.

SKILLBUILDERS: Interpreting Maps, pp. 273, 275, 276

GeographicThinking
Seeing Patterns, pp. 274, 275
Drawing Conclusions, p. 277

Focus & Motivate

How might landforms and resources have helped make Europe rich and powerful? *(Seafaring and trade were common; resources supported industry.)*

Instruct: Objective 1 appears on p. 274.

A HUMAN PERSPECTIVE Elephants in Europe? In 218 B.C., Hannibal, a general from Carthage in North Africa, attacked the Roman Empire, which was at war with Carthage. He moved 38 war elephants and an estimated 60,000 troops across the Mediterranean Sea to Spain. To reach Italy, his armies had to cross the Pyrenees Mountains, the Rhone River, and the Alps. Hannibal used rafts to float the elephants across the Rhone. In the Alps, steep paths and slick ice caused men and animals to fall to their deaths. Despite this, Hannibal arrived in Italy with 26,000 men and a few elephants, and he defeated Rome in many battles. His crossing of the Alps was a triumph over geographic barriers.

Peninsulas and Islands

On a map you will see that Europe is a large peninsula stretching to the west of Asia. Europe itself has many smaller peninsulas, so it is sometimes called a "peninsula of peninsulas." Because of these peninsulas, most locations in Europe are no more than 300 miles from an ocean or sea. As you can imagine, the European way of life involves using these bodies of water for both business and pleasure.

NORTHERN PENINSULAS In northern Europe is the Scandinavian Peninsula. Occupied by the nations of Norway and Sweden, it is bounded by the Norwegian Sea, the North Sea, and the Baltic Sea. More than almost any other place in Europe, this peninsula shows the results of the movement of glaciers during the Ice Age. The glaciers scoured away the rich topsoil and left only thin, rocky soil that is hard to farm.

In Norway, glaciers also carved out **fjords** (fyawrdz), which are steep U-shaped valleys that connect to the sea and that filled with seawater after the glaciers melted. Fjords provide excellent harbors for fishing boats. The fjords are often separated by narrow peninsulas.

The Jutland Peninsula is directly across the North Sea from Scandinavia. Jutland forms the largest part of Denmark and a small part of Germany. This peninsula is an extension of a broad

Major European Peninsulas

SKILLBUILDER: Interpreting Maps
1. **LOCATION** Where are Europe's major peninsulas located in relation to each other?
2. **REGION** Why might each peninsula be considered a region?

SKILLBUILDER ANSWERS

1. The Scandinavian Peninsula is the northernmost of them; the Jutland Peninsula is directly south of Scandinavia; farther south lie the Iberian, Italian, and Balkan peninsulas; the Iberian is the westernmost of those three, while the Balkan Peninsula is the easternmost.
2. Answers will vary but might mention that each peninsula is a clearly defined landform, and several of them are separated from the rest of Europe by mountains.

SECTION 1 PROGRAM RESOURCES

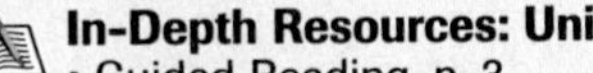
In-Depth Resources: Unit 4
- Guided Reading, p. 3
- Building Vocabulary, p. 9
- Reteaching Activity, p. 10

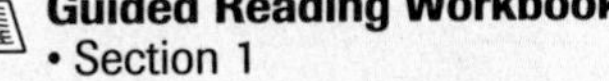
Guided Reading Workbook
- Section 1

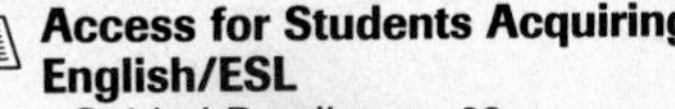
Access for Students Acquiring English/ESL
- Guided Reading, p. 60

Formal Assessment
- Section Quiz, p. 180

Integrated Assessment
- Rubric for a Venn diagram, 2.8

INTEGRATED TECHNOLOGY

Chapter Summaries
Power Presentions
Test Generator
- Section Quiz

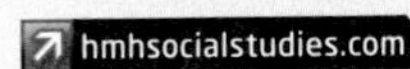

TEST-TAKING RESOURCES

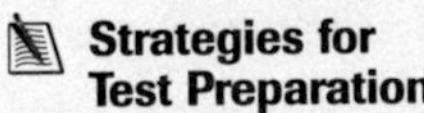
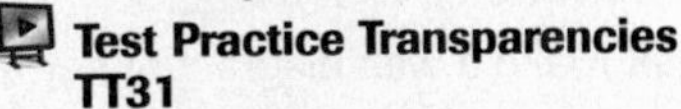
Strategies for Test Preparation
Test Practice Transparencies TT31
Online Test Practice

Instruct: Objective 

Peninsulas and Islands

- Why can Europe be called "a peninsula of peninsulas"? *(It is a large peninsula made up of smaller ones.)*
- What European islands are located in the North Atlantic? In the Mediterranean Sea? *(Great Britain, Ireland, Iceland, Greenland; Corsica, Sardinia, Sicily, Crete)*

 **In-Depth Resources: Unit 4**
- Guided Reading, p. 3

Instruct: Objective 

Mountains and Uplands

- What are the large upland areas of Spain and France? *(the Meseta and the Massif Central)*
- How do mountains and uplands affect life in Europe? *(They make the movement of people, goods, and ideas more difficult. They also affect the weather.)*

Interpreting Photographs

Swiss Alps

Point out the contrast between the rugged mountains and the green valley. Then have students list some of the attractions that might draw visitors to the Alps, as well as some of the drawbacks to this environment. *(Hiking, skiing, and the beauty of the alpine scenery would be attractions. Isolation and harsh winter weather might be drawbacks.)*

CAPTION ANSWER They might shelter the valley from winds, making the climate milder; they might make transportation difficult and isolate the valley.

plain that reaches across northern Europe. Its gently rolling hills and swampy low-lying areas are very different from the rocky land of the Scandinavian Peninsula.

SOUTHERN PENINSULAS The southern part of Europe contains three major peninsulas:

- The Iberian Peninsula is home to Spain and Portugal. The Pyrenees Mountains block off this peninsula from the rest of Europe.
- The Italian Peninsula is home to Italy. It is shaped like a boot, extends into the Mediterranean Sea, and has 4,700 miles of coastline.
- The Balkan Peninsula is bordered by the Adriatic, Mediterranean, and Aegean Seas. It is mountainous, so transportation is difficult.

ISLANDS Another striking feature of Europe is its islands. The larger islands are Great Britain, Ireland, Iceland, and Greenland, all located in the North Atlantic. Although far from mainland Europe, Iceland and Greenland were settled by Scandinavians and have maintained cultural ties with the mainland. Over the centuries, many different groups have occupied the smaller Mediterranean Sea islands of Corsica, Sardinia, Sicily, and Crete. All of Europe's islands have depended upon trade. A

A. Answer Islands provide relatively quick access to seas and oceans, so transporting goods by ship is a natural occupation for islanders.

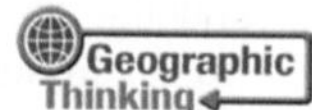

Seeing Patterns A What geographic advantages do islands have that help to promote trade?

Mountains and Uplands

The mountains and uplands of Europe may be viewed as walls because they separate groups of people. They make it difficult for people, goods, and ideas to move easily from one place to another. These landforms also affect climate. For example, the chilly north winds rarely blow over the Alps into Italy, which has a mild climate as a result.

MOUNTAIN CHAINS The most famous mountain chain in Europe is the Alps. On a map you can see that the Alps arc across France, Italy, Germany, Switzerland, Austria, and the northern Balkan Peninsula. They cut Italy off from the rest of Europe. Similarly, the Pyrenees restrict movement from France to Spain and Portugal. Both ranges provide opportunities for skiing, hiking, and other outdoor activities.

Running like a spine down Italy, the Apennine Mountains divide the Italian Peninsula between east and west. The Balkan Mountains block

HUMAN-ENVIRONMENT INTERACTION The Wetterhorn in the Swiss Alps stands 12,142 feet above the city in the valley below. **How do the mountains affect the lives of the people in the valley?**

274

DIFFERENTIATING INSTRUCTION **LESS PROFICIENT READERS**

RECALLING DETAILS

Objective To provide a framework for recalling key terms and details

Class Time 20 minutes

Task Make a web diagram of key terms

Directions Have students create a web or set of webs for peninsulas, islands, and mountains and uplands. Around each key term, students can add facts about location and other important details. You might provide a web such as the one shown here as a model.

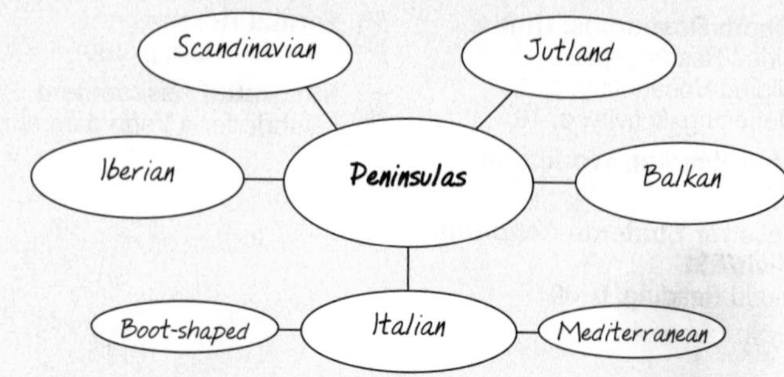

off the Balkan Peninsula from the rest of Europe. Historically, they also have isolated the peninsula's various ethnic groups from each other.

UPLANDS Mountains and uplands differ from each other in their elevation. **Uplands** are hills or very low mountains that may also contain mesas and high plateaus. Some uplands of Europe are eroded remains of ancient mountain ranges. Examples of uplands include the Kjølen (CHUR•luhn) Mountains of Scandinavia, the Scottish highlands, the low mountain areas of Brittany in France, and the central plateau of Spain called the ***Meseta*** (meh•SEH•tah). Other uplands border mountainous areas, such as the Central Uplands of Germany, which are at the base of the Alps. About one-sixth of French lands are located in the uplands called the ***Massif Central*** (ma•SEEF sahn•TRAHL).

BACKGROUND
Brittany is a region located on a peninsula in northwest France.

Rivers: Europe's Links

Traversing Europe is a network of rivers that bring people and goods together. These rivers are used to transport goods between coastal harbors and the inland region, aiding economic growth. Historically, the rivers also have aided the movement of ideas.

Two major castle-lined rivers—the Danube and the Rhine—have served as watery highways for centuries. The Rhine flows 820 miles from the interior of Europe north to the North Sea. The Danube cuts through the heart of Europe from west to east. Touching 9 countries over its 1,771-mile length, the Danube River links Europeans to the Black Sea.

Many other European rivers flow from the interior to the sea and are large enough for ships to traverse. Through history, these rivers helped connect Europeans to the rest of the world, encouraging both trade and travel. Europeans have explored and migrated to many other world regions. B

Rivers of Europe

SKILLBUILDER: Interpreting Maps
1. **MOVEMENT** Which rivers empty into the North Sea? Into the Mediterranean Sea?
2. **PLACE** What port is at the mouth of the Rhine?

B. Answer
Because they flow toward seas, the rivers help Europeans to travel to other regions.

Geographic Thinking
Seeing Patterns
B How does the direction in which European rivers flow aid in linking Europeans to the world?

Fertile Plains: Europe's Bounty

One of the most fertile agricultural regions of the world is the Northern European Plain (see the map on page 263), stretching in a huge curve across parts of France, Belgium, the Netherlands, Denmark, Germany, and Poland. Relatively flat, this plain is very desirable agricultural land that has produced vast quantities of food over the centuries. However, the plain's flatness has also allowed armies and groups of invaders to use it as an open route into Europe. Smaller fertile plains used for farming also exist in Sweden, Hungary, and Lombardy in northern Italy.

Instruct: Objective 

Rivers: Europe's Links

- Where does the Danube flow? *(through the heart of Europe, from west to east, and into the Black Sea)*
- How are rivers used in Europe? *(to transport goods and people and forge links between regions and with the world)*

Interpreting Maps

Rivers of Europe

Have students make a list of rivers shown on the map and describe their courses. *(Loire: north through France to the Bay of Biscay; Seine: north through Paris to the coast; Rhone: south through Lyon to the Mediterranean; Elbe: north through Germany to the North Sea; Oder and Vistula: north through Poland to the Baltic)*

SKILLBUILDER ANSWERS

1. The Elbe and the Rhine empty into the North Sea; the Ebro, the Rhone, and the Tiber flow into the Mediterranean. **2.** Rotterdam

Instruct: Objective 

Fertile Plains: Europe's Bounty

- What is the most important plain in Europe? *(the Northern European Plain)*
- Why is it important? *(It produces lots of food, but is also an avenue for invasion.)*
- Where are some other plains in Europe? *(Sweden, Hungary, Lombardy)*

ACTIVITY OPTION | **SKILLBUILDER LESSON**

DRAWING CONCLUSIONS

Explaining the Skill Point out that students can sometimes make connections and draw conclusions based on related features of physical geography. For example, if you know that snowfall produces water and that it snows a lot in the Alps, you can conclude that the Alps are a well-watered region.

Have students refer to the map above and note the location of major rivers in northern Europe. Also have them recall the location of the Northern European plain.

Applying the Skill Have pairs of students discuss the following questions. After 10 minutes, have each team share their answers with the class.

- How do rivers benefit agriculture? *(They water fields and deposit fertile soil.)*
- What conclusion can you draw about the relationship between rivers and the Northern European Plain? *(Rivers are a key reason for the productivity of this plain.)*

For addtional Skillbuilder practice, see p. 282 in Section 3.

Interpreting Maps

Europe's Natural Resources
Have students examine the map. Then ask what resources each pair of the following countries has in common: United Kingdom and Belgium; Spain and Finland; Sweden and Bulgaria; Switzerland and Italy. *(UK and Belgium: coal; Spain and Finland: zinc, copper, fish; Sweden and Bulgaria: copper, iron, lead; Switzerland and Italy, both resource poor)*

SKILLBUILDER ANSWERS
1. Petroleum is plentiful in the North Sea; there are some deposits in Eastern Europe. **2.** Portugal, Switzerland, Italy, Ireland, Greece

Instruct: Objective 

Resources Shape Europe's Economy/Resources Shape Life

- What resources does Europe have in abundance? *(coal and iron ore)*
- Why are those resources important? *(They are essential for making steel.)*
- Why do the Irish burn peat? *(Because Ireland lacks other kinds of energy resources, and peat can be burned as fuel.)*

Natural Resources of Europe

hmhsocialstudies.com INTERACTIVE MAP

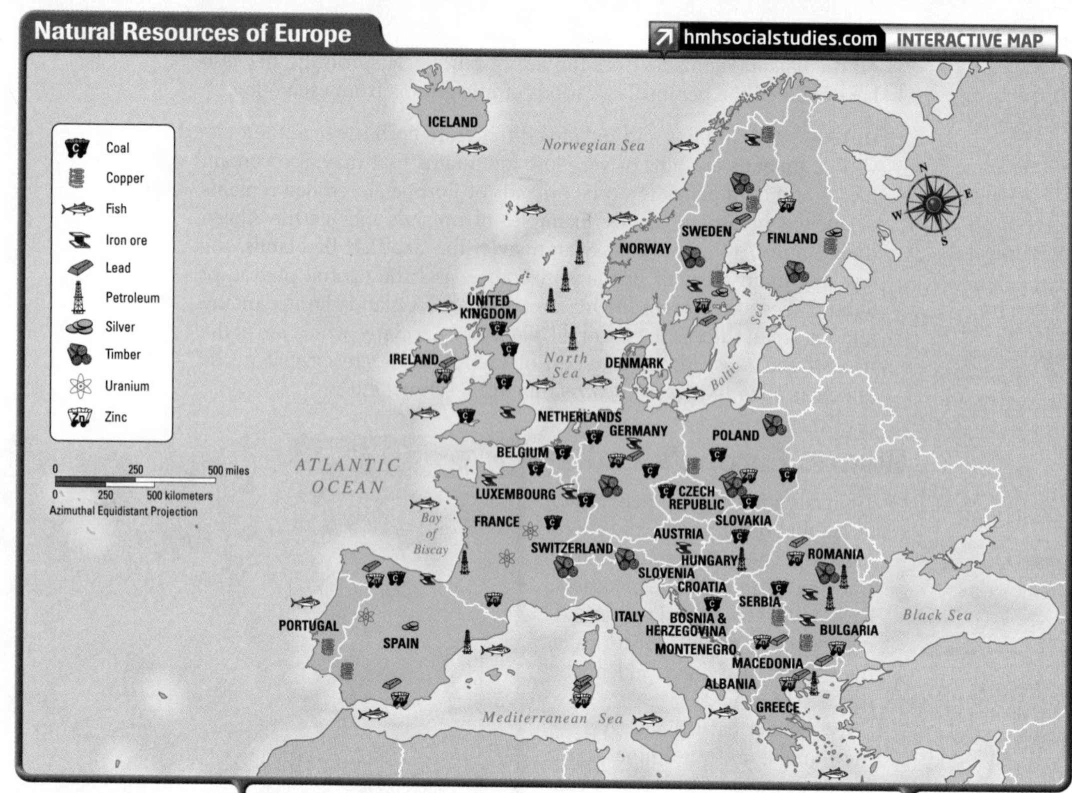

SKILLBUILDER: Interpreting Maps
1 **LOCATION** Where are major petroleum deposits found in Europe?
2 **REGION** Which countries in Europe have relatively few natural resources?

Resources Shape Europe's Economy

Europe has abundant supplies of two natural resources—coal and iron ore—needed for an industrialized economy. The map above shows a band of coal deposits stretching from the United Kingdom across to Belgium and the Netherlands and from there to France, Germany, and Poland. Near many of these coal deposits are iron ore deposits. Having both of these resources makes it possible to produce steel. The Ruhr (roor) Valley in Germany, the Alsace-Lorraine region of France, and parts of the United Kingdom are heavily industrialized because these minerals are found there and good transportation exists. But as a result, these regions have suffered from industrial pollution. (See Chapter 14 for more on pollution.) C

CONNECT TO THE ISSUES
POLLUTION
C What types of pollution might industry create?
C. Answer water pollution and air pollution

ENERGY Oil and natural gas were found beneath the North Sea floor in 1959. Energy companies began to tap gas fields between the United Kingdom and the Netherlands. In 1971, new technologies made it possible to construct offshore oil rigs in the North Sea despite its deep, stormy waters. Norway, the Netherlands, the United Kingdom, and Denmark now pump oil from rigs as far as 400 miles out in the ocean. The North Sea oil fields are major sources of petroleum for the world.

DIFFERENTIATING INSTRUCTION | STUDENTS ACQUIRING ENGLISH/ESL

UNDERSTANDING ECONOMIC TERMS

Objective To categorize terms of similar economic activities
Class Time 10 minutes
Task Create a category chart
Directions Write the words "industrial" and "agricultural" on the board and have students explain their meaning. Point out that the terms refer to two broad types of economic activity.

Have students look at the map "Natural Resources of Europe" on this page and identify resources linked to industrial and agricultural activity. Then have them think of other natural resources that are identified with industry and agriculture. List those resources on a chart such as the one shown here.

INDUSTRIAL	AGRICULTURAL
coal	timber
iron	soil
oil	water
copper	air

AGRICULTURAL LAND About 33 percent of Europe's land is suitable for agriculture. The world average is 11 percent, so Europe is especially well off. The land produces a variety of crops: grains, grapes, olives, and even cork. Timber is cut from vast forests on the Scandinavian Peninsula and in the Alps.

BACKGROUND
Cork is the outer bark of the cork oak tree.

Resources Shape Life

As is true of every region, the resources available in Europe help shape the lives of its people. Resources directly affect the foods people eat, the jobs they hold, the houses in which they live, and even their culture. For example, traditional European folk tales often take place in deep, dark forests that were a major part of the European landscape centuries ago.

The distribution of resources also creates regional differences within Europe. For instance, because Ireland lacks energy sources, the Irish cut peat from large beds and burn it as fuel. **Peat** is partially decayed plant matter found in bogs. In contrast, coal is plentiful in other parts of Europe and has been mined for centuries. For example, generations of Polish miners have worked the mines that modern-day Poles work.

Just as landforms and resources influence the lives of people, so does climate. In Section 2, you will learn that the climates of Europe are mild near the Atlantic Ocean and grow harsher inland. You will also learn about the climates of the Mediterranean and the Arctic regions.

PLACE Harvesting peat is common in Ireland because other fuel sources are scarce. **Why is it cut in blocks?**

Interpreting Photographs

Cutting Peat

Have students note the slabs of peat cut from the peat bog. Ask them if they believe peat is a renewable resource. *(Peat is a non-renewable resource.)* Ask students how life would change if peat were no longer available as a fuel source. *(People who had relied on peat would have to turn to other sources of fuel.)*

CAPTION ANSWER The size and shape of peat is similar to logs, so it will fit in fireplaces and stoves. It has to dry before it can be burned.

Assess & Reteach

GeoFocus Have students complete the sections on landforms and resources in their graphic organizers.

Formal Assessment
• Section Quiz, p. 180

Reteaching Activity
Organize the class into groups of six students. Assign one section objective to each group member. Each member should write a short summary of that section's main idea. Members should then share their summaries with the rest of the group.

In-Depth Resources: Unit 4
• Reteaching Activity, p. 10

SECTION 1 Assessment

1 Places & Terms

Identify and explain where in the region these would be found.

- fjord
- uplands
- *Meseta*
- *Massif Central*
- peat

2 Taking Notes

PLACE Review the notes you took for this section.

Landforms	
Resources	

- What types of landforms are found in Europe?
- What resources help with farming?

3 Main Ideas

a. Why is Europe called a "peninsula of peninsulas"?

b. How are the landforms of Europe both an advantage and a disadvantage to life in Europe?

c. How did natural resources help Europe to become industrialized?

4 Geographic Thinking

Drawing Conclusions What role did the waterways of Europe play in the development of its economy? **Think about:**

- the nearness to seas and oceans
- the network of rivers

EXPLORING LOCAL GEOGRAPHY Do research to learn the top three natural resources in your state. Then study the map on page 276 to determine which European country has the most resources in common with your state. Create a **Venn Diagram** showing the resources your state has in common with that country and the resources that are different.

SECTION 1 ASSESSMENT ANSWERS

1. Places & Terms
fjord, p. 273
uplands, p. 275
Meseta, p. 275
Massif Central, p. 275
peat, p. 277

2. Taking Notes
- peninsulas, islands, mountains, uplands, plains
- fertile soil helps with farming.

3. Main Ideas
a. Europe is a large peninsula extending west of Asia, and it has many smaller peninsulas of its own.
b. The mountains provide opportunities for sports but make travel difficult; the plains are good for farming but provide an open invasion route.
c. Europe had abundant supplies of coal and iron ore, which are needed for industrial growth.

4. Geographic Thinking
Rivers helped move people, goods, and ideas within Europe and also flowed to the sea; the closeness of the sea helped Europeans trade with the rest of the world.

GeoActivity

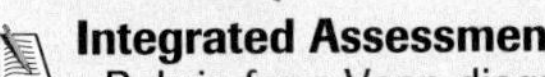

Integrated Assessment
• Rubric for a Venn diagram, 2.8

SECTION 2 OBJECTIVES

1. Explain how winds warm much of Europe.
2. Describe the climate of inland Europe.
3. Identify climatic characteristics in the Mediterranean.
4. Describe the climatic effect on vegetation in the Land of the Midnight Sun.

SKILLBUILDER: Interpreting Graphs, p. 278

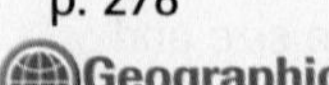**GeographicThinking**
Making Comparisons, p. 279
Using the Atlas, p. 279
Making Decisions, p. 280

Focus & Motivate

What kinds of climatic and natural landforms act as tourist attractions? *(snow-packed mountains, hot springs, sunny beaches, and other unique natural phenomena)*

Instruct: Objective 1 appears on p. 279.

SKILLBUILDER ANSWERS
Paris is farther north but has a milder climate. It is milder because it does not become as hot in summer or as cold in winter.

2 Climate and Vegetation

Main Ideas
- Much of Europe has a relatively mild climate because of ocean currents and warm winds.
- Eastern Europe has a harsher climate because it is farther from the Atlantic Ocean.

Places & Terms
North Atlantic Drift
sirocco
mistral

CONNECT TO THE ISSUES
POLLUTION Industrial air pollution leads to acid rain, which kills trees and other vegetation.

A HUMAN PERSPECTIVE Because of Greece's mild climate, the ancient Greeks spent much time outdoors. Greek men liked to talk with their friends in the marketplace. They also enjoyed sports. Large crowds gathered for athletic contests that were held during religious festivals. The most important of these was a footrace held every four years in the town of Olympia, a contest called the Olympic Games. In time, these games came to include other sports such as wrestling. In this form, they were the model for our modern Olympics. If ancient Greece had had a cold climate, we might not have Olympic Games today.

Westerly Winds Warm Europe

A marine west coast climate exists in much of Europe—from northern Spain across most of France and Germany to western Poland. It also exists in the British Isles and some coastal areas of Scandinavia. With warm summers and cool winters, the region enjoys a milder climate than do most regions at such a northern latitude.

The nearby ocean and the dominant winds create this mild climate. The **North Atlantic Drift,** a current of warm water from the tropics, flows near Europe's west coast. The prevailing westerlies, which blow west to east, pick up warmth from this current and carry it over Europe. No large mountain ranges block the winds, so they are felt far inland. They also carry moisture, giving the region adequate rainfall.

Climographs: Fargo and Paris

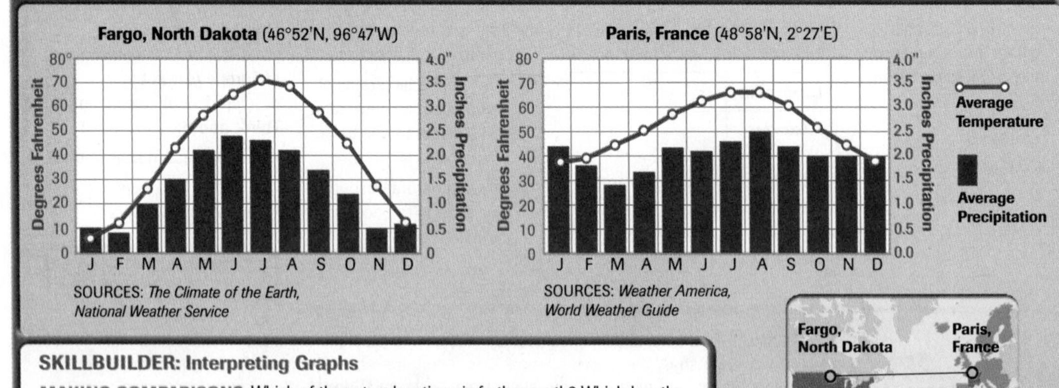

SKILLBUILDER: Interpreting Graphs
MAKING COMPARISONS Which of these two locations is farther north? Which has the milder climate? Explain how you determined which was milder.

SECTION 2 PROGRAM RESOURCES

 **In-Depth Resources: Unit 4**
- Guided Reading, p. 4
- Map and Graph Skills, pp. 6–7
- Building Vocabulary, p. 9
- Reteaching Activity, p. 11

 **Guided Reading Workbook**
- Section 2

Access for Students Acquiring English/ESL
- Guided Reading, p. 61
- Map and Graph Skills, pp. 64–65

 **Formal Assessment**
- Section Quiz, p. 181

 **Integrated Assessment**
- Rubric for a chart, 2.2

INTEGRATED TECHNOLOGY

 **Critical Thinking Transparencies CT44**
- Comparing Regional Climates

 **Power Presentations**

 **Test Generator**
- Section Quiz

TEST-TAKING RESOURCES

 **Strategies for Test Preparation**

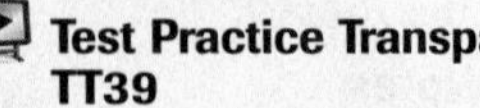
Test Practice Transparencies TT39
Online Test Practice

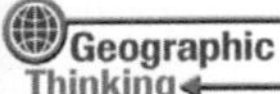

Geographic Thinking

Making Comparisons

A Would you expect the high Alps to be more or less densely populated than the surrounding region? Why?

A. Answer They would be less densely populated because of the harsher climate.

The Alps create a band of harsher conditions next to this climate zone. Because of their high elevation, the Alps have a much colder climate. Above 5,000 feet, snow can reach a depth of 33 feet in winter. A

FORESTS TO FARMS Originally, mixed forests covered much of the marine west coast climate region. Over the centuries, people cleared away most of the forest so they could settle and farm the land. Today, farmers in the region grow grains, sugar beets, livestock feed, and root crops such as potatoes.

Harsher Conditions Inland

People who live far from the Atlantic Ocean do not benefit from the moderating influence of the westerlies. As a result, much of Sweden and Finland and the eastern parts of Poland, Slovakia, and Hungary have a humid continental climate, as does all of Romania. These places have cold, snowy winters and either warm or hot summers (depending upon their latitude). In general, the region receives adequate rainfall, which helps agriculture.

Like most of Europe, the region has suffered much deforestation, but the forests that do survive tend to be coniferous. The region also has broad fertile plains that were originally covered with grasses. Today, farmers grow grains such as wheat, rye, and barley on these plains. Other major crops include potatoes and sugar beets.

The Sunny Mediterranean

A mild climate lures people to live and vacation in the region bordering the Mediterranean Sea. This Mediterranean climate extends from southern Spain and France through Italy to Greece and other parts of the Balkan Peninsula. Summers are hot and dry with clear, sunny skies, while winters are moderate and wet. One reason for the climate is that mountain ranges block cold north winds from reaching the Iberian, Italian, and Balkan peninsulas.

SPECIAL WINDS An exception to this pattern is the Mediterranean coast of France, which is not protected by high mountains. In winter, this coast receives the **mistral** (MIHS•truhl), a cold, dry wind from the north. B

Most Mediterranean countries experience a wind called the sirocco. The **sirocco** (suh•RAHK•oh) is a hot, steady south wind that blows from North Africa across the Mediterranean Sea into southern Europe. Some siroccos pick up moisture from the sea and produce rain; others carry dust from the desert.

Geographic Thinking

Using the Atlas

B Locate southern France on the map on page 263. What type of landform borders the Mediterranean Sea there?

B. Answer a plain

REGION In some Mediterranean fields, such as this one in southern France, olive trees and grape vines are grown side by side. **Why might farmers choose to plant a field with two crops instead of one?**

EUROPE

Instruct: Objective 1

Westerly Winds Warm Europe

- What is the North Atlantic Drift? *(a current of warm water flowing near Europe's west coast)*
- How does the North Atlantic Drift affect temperature and rainfall? *(It warms westerly winds that elevate temperature and carry moisture.)*

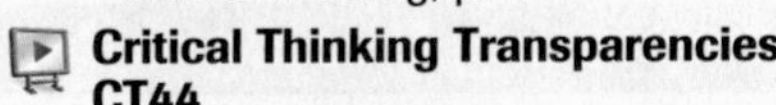

In-Depth Resources: Unit 4
- Guided Reading, p. 4

Critical Thinking Transparencies CT44
- Comparing Regional Climates

Instruct: Objective 2

Harsher Conditions Inland

- What extremes of climate are common in northeastern and east central Europe? *(Summers are warm or hot, and winters snowy and cold.)*
- What moderating climatic influence is lacking? *(warm westerly winds produced by the North Atlantic Drift)*

Instruct: Objective 3

The Sunny Mediterranean

- What parts of Europe benefit from the Mediterranean climate? *(southern Spain and France, Italy, Greece, parts of the Balkans)*
- How are the mistral and the sirocco similar? How are they different? *(Both are strong Mediterranean winds; the mistral is cold, dry, and comes from the north in winter; the sirocco is a hot south wind.)*

CAPTION ANSWER They might plant two crops as insurance, in case one fails.

ACTIVITY OPTION **INTERNET RESEARCH**

BLOCK SCHEDULING

WRITING A TRAVEL ARTICLE

Objective To obtain more information on weather, climate, and optimal seasons for travel

Class Time One class period

Task Write main copy points of an article for a travel magazine

Directions Have students search the Internet for information appropriate to a travel article about the Mediterranean. (Updated links are available through **hmhsocialstudies.com.**) Tell them to include information on weather, climate, and what they might see during a particular season of the year.

OPTIONAL ACTIVITY If Internet access is limited, students may use encyclopedias, travel guides, and books on the region.

Instruct: Objective 4

Land of the Midnight Sun

- Why do trees not grow in upper Scandinavia? *(The subsoil is always frozen.)*
- What vegetation grows in the land of the Midnight Sun? *(lichens, mosses)*
- How does the climate affect agriculture in Scandinavia? *(The cold limits agriculture to southern Scandinavia.)*

Interpreting Photographs

Jukkasjärvi's ice hotel can accommodate about 100 guests. Temperatures in the hotel hover between 19°F and 23°F. The hotel staff provides guests with cold-weather suits and sleeping bags. Also, beds are covered with reindeer skins to keep guests warm at night.

CAPTION ANSWER Cold winter temperatures keep the hotel from melting.

Assess & Reteach

GeoFocus Have students complete the section on climate and vegetation in their graphic organizers.

Formal Assessment
- Section Quiz, p. 181

Reteaching Activity

Have students read over their notes on climate and vegetation. Ask for two examples of how climate directly affects vegetation. *(extreme cold in northern Scandinavia freezes subsoil so that no trees can grow; warm winds help crops in England and France)*

In-Depth Resources: Unit 4
- Reteaching Activity, p. 11

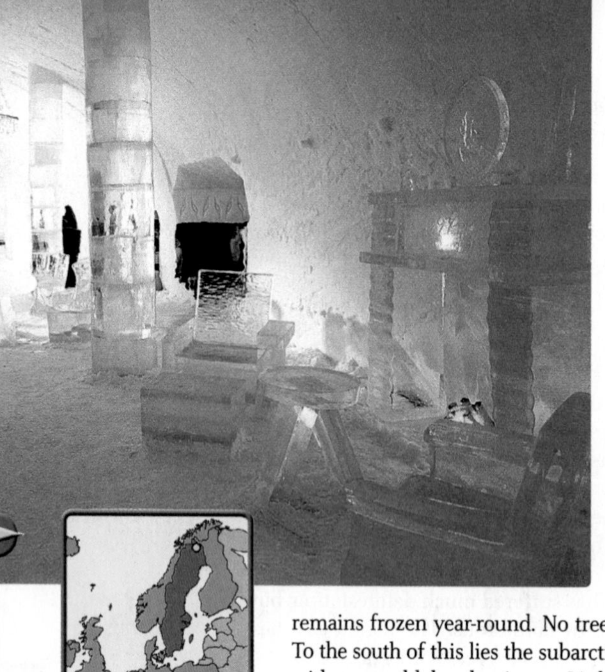

PLACE In the village of Jukkasjärvi, Sweden, the Ice Hotel is built every winter out of 10,000 tons of ice and 30,000 tons of snow. **How does climate make this possible?**

THE CLIMATE ATTRACTS TOURISTS The Mediterranean region has primarily evergreen shrubs and short trees that grow in climates with hot, dry summers. The region's major crops are citrus fruits, olives, grapes, and wheat. The sunny Mediterranean beaches also attract thousands of people, making tourism a major industry in the region.

Land of the Midnight Sun

In far northern Scandinavia, along the Arctic Circle, lies a band of tundra climate. As explained in Chapter 3, the land in such a climate is often in a state of permafrost, in which the subsoil remains frozen year-round. No trees grow there—only mosses and lichens. To the south of this lies the subarctic climate, which is cool most of the time with very cold, harsh winters. Little grows there but stunted trees. Because of the climate, agriculture is limited to southern Scandinavia.

BACKGROUND
A lichen is an organism made of a fungus and an alga growing together.

This far northern region witnesses sharp variations in the amount of sunlight received throughout the year. Winter nights are extremely long, as are summer days. North of the Arctic Circle, there are winter days when the sun never rises and summer days when the sun never sets. The region is often called the Land of the Midnight Sun.

In the next section, you will read about ways in which Europeans have altered their environment—both positively and negatively.

Section 2 Assessment

1 Places & Terms

Identify these terms and explain how they affect climate.
- North Atlantic Drift
- mistral
- sirocco

2 Taking Notes

REGION Review the notes you took for this section.

Climate and Vegetation	

- Which regions of Europe have the harshest, coldest climates?
- Which climate zones produce the richest variety of vegetation?

3 Main Ideas

a. How do the North Atlantic Drift and the prevailing westerlies affect Europe's climate?
b. How are a mistral and a sirocco different?
c. Why is northern Scandinavia sometimes called the Land of the Midnight Sun?

4 Geographic Thinking

Making Decisions If you wanted to attract tourists to far northern Scandinavia, how would you advertise the region? **Think about:**
- recreational activities suitable for such a climate

MAKING COMPARISONS Choose a place in Europe, and then find a place in North America at about the same latitude. Do Internet research to learn about the climate and vegetation of the two places. Create a **chart** comparing the two.

SECTION 2 ASSESSMENT ANSWERS

1. Places & Terms
North Atlantic Drift, p. 278
mistral, p. 279
sirocco, p. 279

2. Taking Notes
- the Alps and far northern Scandinavia
- the marine west coast and humid continental climates

3. Main Ideas

a. The North Atlantic Drift is a warm ocean current, and the prevailing westerlies carry its warmth over northwestern Europe, making the climate milder there.

b. A mistral is a cold, dry north wind; a sirocco is a hot, steady south wind that blows from North Africa across the Mediterranean Sea into southern Europe.

c. North of the Arctic Circle, there are summer days when the sun never sets.

4. Geographic Thinking

Answers will vary, but students might emphasize winter sports or talk about the beauty of the Midnight Sun in summer.

GeoActivity

Integrated Assessment
- Rubric for a chart, 2.2

Map and Graph Skills

Interpreting a Bar Graph

How much rain and snow does your area receive in a year? Average yearly precipitation varies widely throughout the United States, with extremes ranging from a low of less than 2 inches a year in Death Valley, California, to as much as 151.25 inches a year in Yakutat, Alaska. The figures for average yearly precipitation don't reveal how much rain or snow falls in a given month, but they can provide a general indication of a place's suitability for agriculture or other activities.

THE LANGUAGE OF GRAPHS A **bar graph** is a visual way of showing quantities. On a bar graph, it is easy to see how different examples in a category compare; the longer the bar, the greater the quantity. Depending on the subject, the quantities are expressed using measurements such as inches, dollars, or tons. The categories vary from graph to graph. Time periods and places are common categories. Below, a bar graph shows annual precipitation for several European cities.

Average Annual Precipitation in Europe

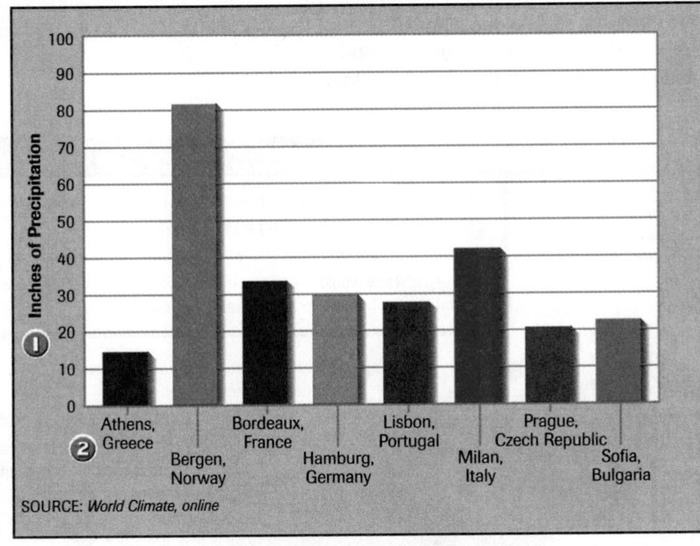

1 The vertical axis tells you that on this graph, the precipitation is expressed in inches.

2 The horizontal axis tells you that the category is selected cities of Europe.

2 A quick glance at this bar graph tells you which cities have high and low amounts of precipitation. By examining the bars more carefully and measuring their heights against the horizontal lines, you can estimate actual amounts of precipitation.

Map and Graph Skills Assessment

1. Analyzing Data
Which cities on this graph have the lowest and highest amounts of annual precipitation?

2. Drawing Conclusions
To which city would you move if your doctor advised you to live in a dry climate?

3. Analyzing Data
What is the average annual precipitation for these eight cities?

OBJECTIVE

Understand and interpret bar graphs.

Instruct: Objective

Interpreting a Bar Graph

- How many inches of precipitation would you expect if you spent a year in Hamburg, Germany? *(about 30)*
- If you moved from Sofia to Bordeaux, how much more annual precipitation would you expect? *(about 10 inches)*
- Who might find a precipitation bar graph useful? *(meteorologists, travelers, people who live near rivers, etc.)*

 **In-Depth Resources: Unit 4**
- Map and Graph Skills, pp. 6–7

 **Access for Students Acquiring English/ESL**
- Map and Graph Skills, pp. 64–65

More About

Bergen, Norway

The west-coast city of Bergen is Norway's second largest city, after Oslo. Bergen is sometimes called the "gateway to the fjords" because many travelers use the city as a starting point for visits to major fjords, such as the Sognafjord and Hardangerfjord. Moist air carried by the Gulf Stream brings frequent precipitation to Bergen. Each year, the city experiences as many as 274 wet days—days with over .01 inches of rain or melted snow.

SKILLS ASSESSMENT ANSWERS

1. Athens with about 15 inches of precipitation and Bergen with about 82 inches

2. Athens, which receives less than 20 inches of precipitation per year

3. about 33 inches (answers may vary slightly)

SECTION 3 OBJECTIVES

1. Describe land reclamation in the Netherlands.
2. Examine the unique environment of Venice.
3. Identify reasons for deforestation in Europe.

SKILLBUILDER: Interpreting Graphics & Maps, pp. 282, 284

GeographicThinking Making Comparisons, p. 283, 285

Focus & Motivate

In what ways do people interact with their environment? *(by adapting to it or by changing it to suit their needs)*

Instruct: Objective 

Polders: Land from the Sea

- What is a polder? *(land in the Netherlands that is drained and dried)*
- What is remarkable about the Zuider Zee? *(The Dutch built a dike across its entrance and gradually it became a freshwater lake.)*

 **In-Depth Resources: Unit 4**
- Guided Reading, p. 5
- Skillbuillder Practice, p. 8

SKILLBUILDER ANSWERS

1. Rain has to wash salt out of the soil. Alfalfa replenishes nutrients.
2. no need to wash salt from soil before farming

3 Human–Environment Interaction

Main Ideas

- The Dutch and the Venetians altered lands to fit their needs by constructing polders and canals.
- Uncontrolled logging and acid rain destroy forests.

Places & Terms

dike	terpen
polder	Zuider Zee
seaworks	Ijsselmeer

CONNECT TO THE ISSUES
POLLUTION Water pollution is creating conditions that kill the fish in Venice's lagoon.

A HUMAN PERSPECTIVE "1800 DIE IN WIND-WHIPPED FLOOD WATERS!" February 1, 1953, witnessed a disaster in the Netherlands. Winds estimated at 110 to 115 miles per hour piled up gigantic waves that ripped through **dikes**—earthen banks—holding back the North Sea. When the storm was over, 4.5 percent of the Netherlands was flooded, and thousands of buildings were destroyed. The Netherlands is prone to floods because much of its land is below sea level.

Polders: Land from the Sea

An old saying declares, "God created the world, but the Dutch created Holland." (Holland is another name for the Netherlands.) Because the Dutch needed more land for their growing population, they reclaimed land from the sea. At least 40 percent of the Netherlands was once under the sea. Land that is reclaimed by diking and draining is called a **polder.**

Making a Polder

hmhsocialstudies.com INTERACTIVE

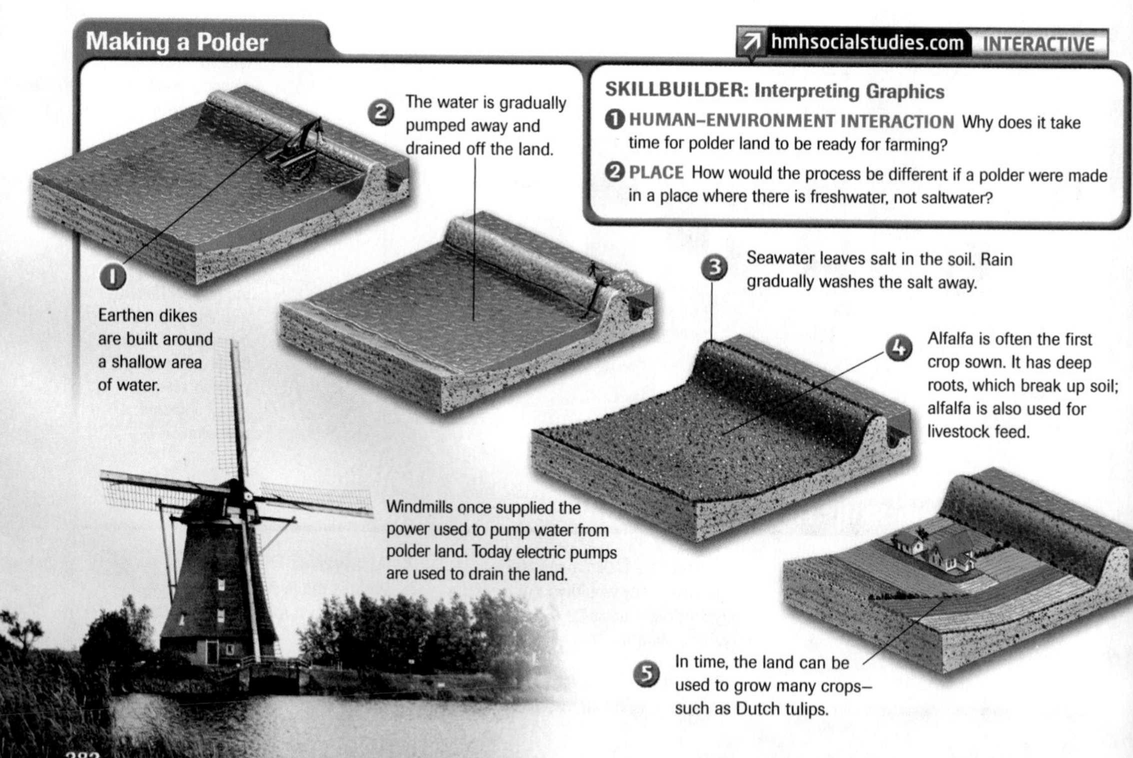

1 Earthen dikes are built around a shallow area of water.
2 The water is gradually pumped away and drained off the land.
3 Seawater leaves salt in the soil. Rain gradually washes the salt away.
4 Alfalfa is often the first crop sown. It has deep roots, which break up soil; alfalfa is also used for livestock feed.
5 In time, the land can be used to grow many crops—such as Dutch tulips.
Windmills once supplied the power used to pump water from polder land. Today electric pumps are used to drain the land.

SKILLBUILDER: Interpreting Graphics

1. **HUMAN-ENVIRONMENT INTERACTION** Why does it take time for polder land to be ready for farming?
2. **PLACE** How would the process be different if a polder were made in a place where there is freshwater, not saltwater?

282

SECTION 3 PROGRAM RESOURCES

 **In-Depth Resources: Unit 4**
- Guided Reading, p. 5
- Skillbuillder Practice, p. 8
- Building Vocabulary, p. 9
- Reteaching Activity, p. 12

Guided Reading Workbook
- Section 3

Access for Students Acquiring English/ESL
- Guided Reading, p. 62
- Skillbuillder Practice, p. 63

Formal Assessment
- Section Quiz, p. 182

Integrated Assessment
- Rubric for a cause-and-effect chart, 2.2
- Rubric for a sketch map, 2.1

INTEGRATED TECHNOLOGY

Map Transparencies MT23
- Environmental Challenges of Europe

 **Power Presentations**

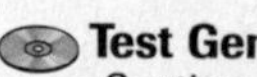 **Test Generator**
- Section Quiz

hmhsocialstudies.com

TEST-TAKING RESOURCES

 **Strategies for Test Preparation**

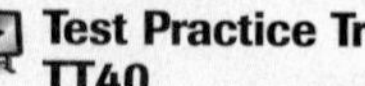 **Test Practice Transparencies TT40**

 **Online Test Practice**

SEAWORKS The Dutch erected **seaworks,** structures that are used to control the sea's destructive impact on human life. Those seaworks include dikes and high earthen platforms called **terpen.** The dikes hold back the sea, while the terpen provide places to go for safety during floods and high tides.

Over the centuries, the Dutch found ways to reinforce the dikes and to control water in the low-lying areas the dikes protected. In the 1400s, the Dutch began using their windmills to power pumps that drained the land. When the French conqueror Napoleon viewed a site with 860 windmills pumping an area dry, he reportedly said, "Without equal." Today the pumps use electric motors instead of windmills. A

Geographic Thinking

Making Comparisons

A What are possible disadvantages of windmills and of electric pumps?

A. Answer Windmills wouldn't work on still days; electric pumps wouldn't work during power outages.

TRANSFORMING THE SEA Another remarkable Dutch alteration of their environment was the transformation of the **Zuider Zee** (ZEYE•duhr ZAY). It was an arm of the North Sea and is now a freshwater lake. The idea was originally proposed in 1667. But it was not until the late 1800s and early 1900s that the Dutch perfected a plan to build dikes all the way across the entrance to the Zuider Zee. Since no saltwater flowed into that body of water, it eventually became a freshwater lake. It is now called **Ijsselmeer** (EYE•suhl•MAIR). The land around the lake was drained, creating several polders that added hundreds of square miles of land to the Netherlands.

Waterways for Commerce: Venice's Canals

BACKGROUND
A land link to Venice was built in 1846. A railway bridge connected Venice to the mainland.

Like the Netherlands, Venice, Italy, is a place where humans created a unique environment. About 120 islands and part of the mainland make up the city of Venice. Two of the largest islands are San Marco and Rialto. A broad waterway called the Grand Canal flows between them.

Moving people or goods in Venice depends upon using the more than 150 canals that snake around and through the islands. Consequently, to get from one place to another in Venice, you generally have two choices: take a boat or walk. Almost anything that is moved on wheels elsewhere is moved by water in Venice.

AN ISLAND CITY GROWS Venice began when people escaping invaders took shelter on inhospitable islands in a lagoon. They remained there and established a settlement that eventually became Venice. The city is located at the north end of the Adriatic Sea, a good site for a port. As a result, trade helped Venice grow.

BUILDING ON THE ISLANDS Building Venice required construction techniques that took into account the swampy land on the islands. Builders sunk wooden pilings into the ground to help support the structures above. So many pilings were required that oak forests in the northern Italian countryside and in Slovenia were leveled to supply the wood. The weight of the buildings is so great that it has compressed the underlying ground. This is one of the reasons that Venice is gradually sinking. Other reasons include rising sea levels and the removal of too much groundwater by pumping.

PROBLEMS TODAY Severe water pollution threatens historic Venice. Industrial waste, sewage, and saltwater are combining to eat away the

EUROPE

More About

Windmills

The first windmills date back to 7th-century Persia, where they were used to grind grain. Between the 12th and 19th centuries, they were common in Europe. The classic Dutch windmill consists of a wooden tower with a rotating top or cap, which allows the sails or blades to face the wind. Although electric pumps have replaced most Dutch windmills, modern windmills are now used to generate electricity in many parts of the world.

Instruct: Objective 2

Waterways for Commerce: Venice's Canals

- Why is water transport so important in Venice? *(because the city is made up of islands and canals)*
- Why did Venice grow? *(It is on the Adriatic Sea, a good location for a port and for trade.)*
- What problems face Venice today? *(sinking, pollution, flooding, algae)*

ACTIVITY OPTION | CRITICAL THINKING

MAKING COMPARISONS

Explaining the Skill Tell students that looking at similarities and differences between regions or countries can help them put geographic information in perspective.

Applying the Skill Ask students to compare the physical geography of Venice and the Netherlands. On the board, create a flow chart. Then ask the following questions and have students use their answers to fill in the chart.

What key geographic factors do the Netherlands and Venice have in common? *(Both have a problem with swampy land and flooding.)* How have they dealt with the problem? *(The Netherlands built polders and drained the land. Venice built canals and sunk pilings into the ground.)* What were the results? *(The Netherlands has succeeded in reclaiming land. Venice is sinking and in continual danger of flooding.)*

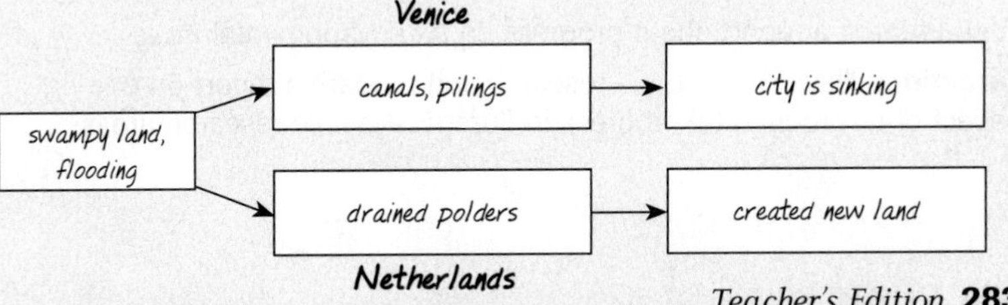

Interpreting Maps

Canals of Venice

Have students examine the map and locate Venice on the inset map of Italy. Have them identify the three canals named on the map. Ask why early settlers might have chosen Venice as a place to settle. *(The canals are Grand, St. Mark's, and Giudecca. Settlers might have chosen this site because it would be easily defensible and provide sailors and traders with easy access to the sea.)*

SKILLBUILDER ANSWERS

1. People and goods can move by both land and water.

2. The islands have become completely urbanized.

Instruct: Objective 

A Centuries-Old Problem: Deforestation

- What actions have led to deforestation in Europe? *(clearing of forests for fuel and building; industrial pollution)*
- How is acid rain produced? *(sulfur emissions from factories combine with water vapor)*
- How much of Europe's forest land has been affected by acid rain? *(one-fourth)*

Map Transparencies MT23
- Environmental Challenges of Europe.

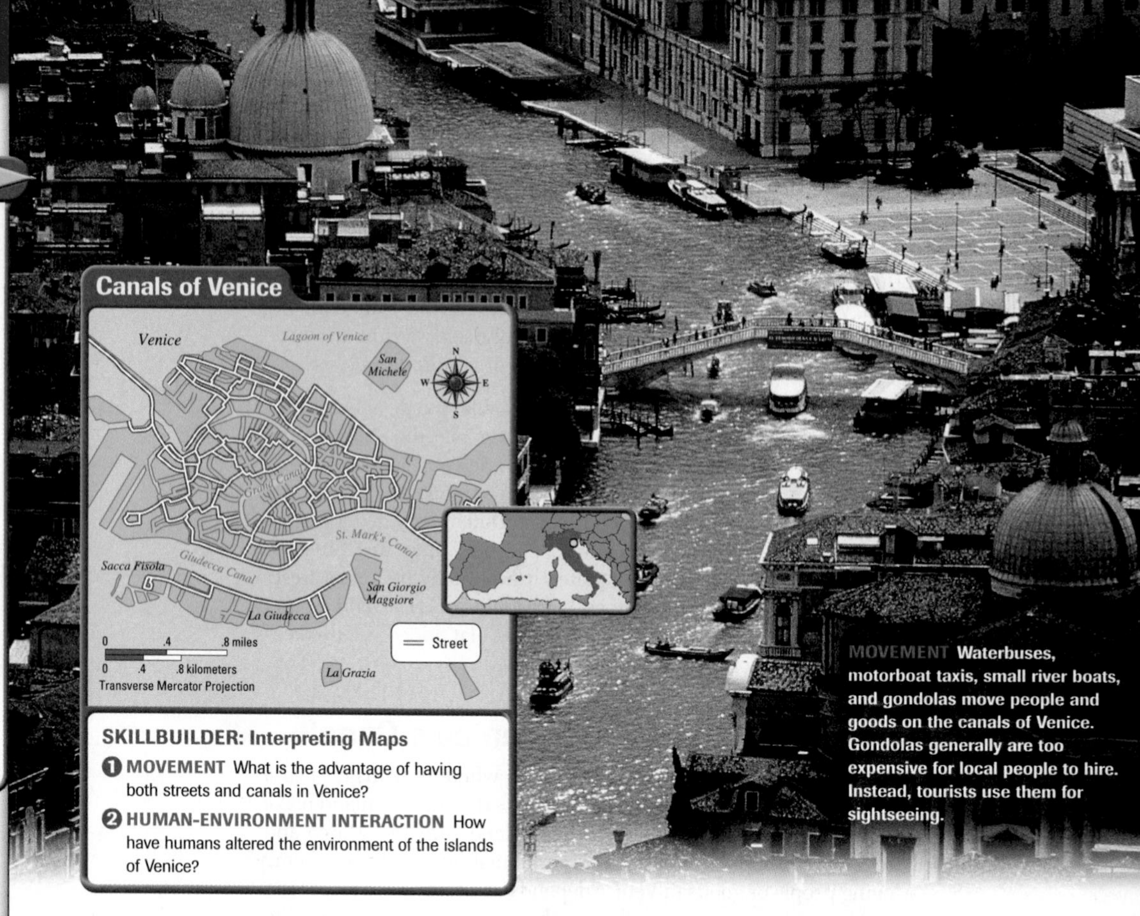

SKILLBUILDER: Interpreting Maps

1. **MOVEMENT** What is the advantage of having both streets and canals in Venice?
2. **HUMAN-ENVIRONMENT INTERACTION** How have humans altered the environment of the islands of Venice?

MOVEMENT Waterbuses, motorboat taxis, small river boats, and gondolas move people and goods on the canals of Venice. Gondolas generally are too expensive for local people to hire. Instead, tourists use them for sightseeing.

foundations of buildings and damage the buildings themselves. Erosion has allowed increased amounts of seawater into the lagoon. Because of this, floods also endanger the city. In November 1966, six feet of floodwater engulfed the city and ruined many of its buildings and the artwork that they housed. Agricultural runoff flowing into Venice's harbor creates conditions that promote algae growth, sometimes called "killer algae." These algae grow rapidly and, after they die, decay. The decaying process uses up oxygen in the water, so that fish also die. Dead fish attract insects and create a stench, especially in warm weather.

A Centuries-Old Problem: Deforestation

Throughout history, humans have damaged and destroyed Europe's forests. The term deforestation means the clearing of forests from an area. Often when we think of deforestation, we think of losing the great rain forests of the world, such as those in South America, which you learned about in Unit 3. But people have also been clearing the forests of Europe since ancient times. Forests provided wood to burn for fuel and to use as building material for ships and houses. When Europeans began to develop industry in the 1700s and 1800s, they needed even

DIFFERENTIATING INSTRUCTION | **GIFTED AND TALENTED STUDENTS**

PREPARING AN ENVIRONMENTAL PROGRESS REPORT

Objective To develop research skills and deepen understanding of human-environment interaction

Class Time One class period for presentations

Task Prepare a report about progress on an environmental issue

Directions Have students do research and prepare a report on one aspect of environmental progress in Europe. Possible research areas include recycling, anti-pollution efforts, species preservation, forest conservation, and urban development. Reports should identify an environmental problem, explain efforts to solve it, and describe the results. Reports should emphasize progress in a given area. Encourage students to include charts, graphs, illustrations, and other visual aids in their reports if possible.

HUMAN–ENVIRONMENT INTERACTION A forest in Bohemia in the Czech Republic is dying from the effects of acid rain.
Why would restoring the forest be a slow process?

more wood to make charcoal for blast furnaces. Eventually, they used coal as a fuel in place of wood, but not before huge areas of Europe had lost their native forests.

ACID RAIN STRIPS FORESTS In the 1960s, people noticed that many trees of the Black Forest in Germany were discolored, losing needles and leaves, and dying. In time, scientists identified one cause of the tree deaths as acid rain. Europe's factories produce high amounts of sulfur dioxide and nitrogen oxide emissions. These combine with water vapor and oxygen to form acid rain or snow. Winds carry the emissions to other parts of Europe, affecting an estimated one-fourth of all European forests. This problem has hit Scandinavia particularly hard, since the prevailing winds blow in that direction. As mentioned earlier, the Black Forest in Germany also has suffered extreme damage. To save the remaining forests, nations must work together to reduce air pollution. You can read more about this in Chapter 14. B

As you will read in Chapter 13, the ways people live upon the land and interact with each other make up the human geography of Europe.

B. Answer Such a union might foster cooperation among member nations in the clean-up effort.

CONNECT TO THE ISSUES
UNIFICATION
B How might a union of nations affect the clean-up effort?

SECTION 3 Assessment

1 Places & Terms

Identify and explain where in the region these would be found.

- dike
- polder
- seaworks
- terpen
- Zuider Zee
- Ijsselmeer

2 Taking Notes

HUMAN-ENVIRONMENT INTERACTION Review your notes for this section.

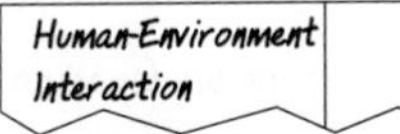

- What are examples of human adaptation to the environment?
- What are examples of an environment changed by humans?

3 Main Ideas

a. How have the people of the Netherlands been able to create more land for their country?
b. How has pollution affected the city of Venice?
c. How has industrialization hurt the forests of Europe?

4 Geographic Thinking

Making Comparisons What is similar about the ways that the people of the Netherlands and the people of Venice interact with their environments? **Think about:**

- seaworks in the Netherlands
- canals in Venice

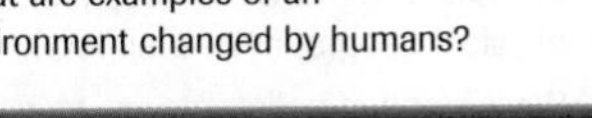
See Skillbuilder Handbook, page R3.

SEEING PATTERNS Pollution has affected both Venice and the forests of Scandinavia. Create two **cause-and-effect charts** outlining the causes and effects of pollution in each place. Then write a sentence or two summarizing the similarities.

Interpreting Photographs

Acid Rain

Ask students to look closely at the photograph. Ask: How does this photo convey the devastation caused by acid rain? Is it more or less effective than a text description? Explain. *(The stripped trees and dark, stormy sky create an impression of complete destruction. It is more effective than words because the image is so direct and powerful.)*

CAPTION ANSWER because trees grow slowly, and because acid rain might still cause damage

EUROPE

Assess & Reteach

GeoFocus Have students complete the section on human-environment interaction in their graphic organizers.

Formal Assessment
- Section Quiz, p. 182

Reteaching Activity
Have students summarize the main details of human-environment interaction discussed in this section by creating a two-column chart. The left column should list the topics: polders, Venice, deforestation. The right column should list main points about each.

In-Depth Resources: Unit 4
- Reteaching Activity, p. 12

SECTION 3 ASSESSMENT ANSWERS

1. Places & Terms
dike, p. 282
polder, p. 282
seaworks, p. 283
terpen, p. 283
Zuider Zee, p. 283
Ijsselmeer, p. 283

2. Taking Notes
- Traveling by boat in Venice is an adaptation to the environment.
- Building polders and deforestation have changed the environment.

3. Main Ideas
a. They built dikes, drained the land of seawater, and gradually turned it into productive farmland.
b. Water pollution is destroying the foundations of Venice's buildings.
c. Factories emit chemicals into the air, which combine with water vapor and oxygen to create acid rain, which has damaged and killed many trees.

4. Geographic Thinking
Both have learned to live in places strongly affected by the sea; both must contend with flooding.

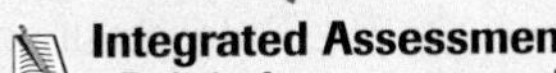

Integrated Assessment
- Rubric for a cause-and-effect chart, 2.2

CHAPTER 12 ASSESSMENT

Reviewing Places & Terms

A. 1. fjord, p. 273
2. uplands, p. 275
3. Meseta, p. 275
4. Massif Central, p. 275
5. peat, p. 277
6. mistral, p. 279
7. polder, p. 282
8. seaworks, p. 283
9. terpen, p. 283
10. Zuider Zee, p. 283

B. Possible Responses

11. Fjords are steep, U-shaped valleys that connect to the sea and are filled with seawater. They are found in Norway.
12. Mesetas and the Massif Central are uplands.
13. It is called the Massif Central.
14. It is an ocean current whose warmth is carried by the westerlies and makes the climate of much of Europe milder.
15. The mistral blows along the Mediterranean coast of France.
16. Peat is burned for fuel.
17. A terpen is a type of seaworks.
18. The Dutch built dikes across the entrance to the Zuider Zee, which eventually became a freshwater lake called Ijsselmeer.
19. Polders are land that is reclaimed from the sea by diking and draining; they are found in the Netherlands.
20. Polders, seaworks, and terpens are all associated with human-environment interaction.

Chapter 12 Assessment

VISUAL SUMMARY
PHYSICAL GEOGRAPHY OF EUROPE

Landforms

Major Peninsulas: Scandinavian, Jutland, Iberian, Italian, Balkan

Major Mountain Ranges: Alps, Pyrenees, Carpathians, Apennines, Balkans

Major Rivers: Danube, Rhine, Seine, Loire, Elbe, Oder

Resources

- Oil from North Sea oil rigs is an important energy source for Europe.
- Coal and iron ore are found in abundance, making heavy industry possible.

Climate and Vegetation

- The North Atlantic Drift and the prevailing westerlies moderate much of Europe's climate.
- Lands bordering the Mediterranean Sea have a climate that encourages large-scale commercial agriculture.

Human-Environment Interaction

- Polders are an example of how Europeans have altered their environment.
- The canals of Venice demonstrate how Europeans have adapted to their environment.
- Deforestation of the land is a long-standing environmental problem in Europe.

Reviewing Places & Terms

A. Briefly explain the importance of each of the following.

1. fjord
2. uplands
3. *Meseta*
4. *Massif Central*
5. peat
6. mistral
7. polder
8. seaworks
9. terpen
10. Zuider Zee

B. Answer the questions about vocabulary in complete sentences.

11. What are fjords and where are they found?
12. Which of the above terms are examples of uplands?
13. What is France's highland area called?
14. How does the North Atlantic Drift influence climate?
15. In what part of Europe would you find the mistral?
16. How is peat used?
17. Which of the above terms is a type of seaworks?
18. How did the Zuider Zee become Ijsselmeer?
19. What are polders and where are they found?
20. Which of the above terms are associated with human-environment interaction?

Main Ideas

Landforms and Resources (pp. 273-277)

1. How do the mountain ranges of Europe impact the lives of the people who live near them?
2. Why are the rivers of Europe an important aspect of its geography?
3. Where are the most important oil fields of Europe located, and which countries pump oil from them?

Climate and Vegetation (pp. 278-281)

4. How do the prevailing westerlies affect the climate of Europe? Explain which part of Europe is most affected.
5. In which climate area of Europe would you find citrus fruits growing? Explain why.
6. What types of vegetation are found on the Scandinavian Peninsula?

Human-Environment Interaction (pp. 282-285)

7. Why did the Dutch build seaworks?
8. In what ways have the people of the Netherlands changed the physical geography of their land?
9. What kinds of pollutants are found in the Venice canals?
10. Why were forests chopped down in Europe?

Main Ideas

1. They create a colder, harsher climate, make travel more difficult, and provide recreational opportunities.
2. They encouraged travel and trade, and made the movement of people, goods, and ideas easier.
3. They are in the North Sea; Norway, Denmark, the United Kingdom, and the Netherlands pump oil from them.
4. They make the climate of northwestern Europe milder by bringing warmth from the North Atlantic Drift over the land.
5. Citrus fruits grow in the Mediterranean because it is a warm climate.
6. Mosses, lichens, and stunted trees are found on the Scandinavian Peninsula.
7. The Dutch built seaworks to reduce the destructive impact of the sea on their lives.
8. The people of the Netherlands reclaimed land from the sea, and they also turned an arm of the sea into a freshwater lake.
9. Industrial waste and sewage are found in Venice's canals.
10. Forests were chopped down in Europe to construct ships and buildings, and to burn as fuel.

Critical Thinking

1. Using Your Notes
Use your completed chart to answer these questions.

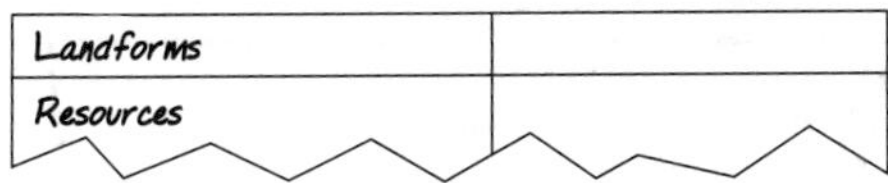

a. Which of the human-environment interactions try to make the best use of landforms?
b. Which interactions focus on problems with resources?

2. Geographic Themes
a. **PLACE** In what ways has the physical geography of the Balkan Peninsula affected the people who live there?
b. **LOCATION** How would you describe Europe's location relative to bodies of water and to other regions?

3. Identifying Themes
Considering the climate and landforms, evaluate which areas of Europe would be the most agriculturally productive. Which of the five themes apply to this situation?

4. Identifying and Solving Problems
What factors must the people of Venice consider when dealing with the water pollution in their city?

5. Making Comparisons
How are the Scandinavian Peninsula and the Italian Peninsula alike and how are they different? Discuss landforms, resources, and climates.

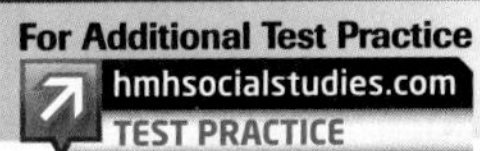

Geographic Skills: Interpreting Maps

Mountain Ranges of Europe
Use the map to answer the following questions.
1. **MOVEMENT** Which mountains hinder travel between Spain and France?
2. **REGION** Which mountain ranges are in Eastern Europe?
3. **LOCATION** What is the relative location of the Alps?

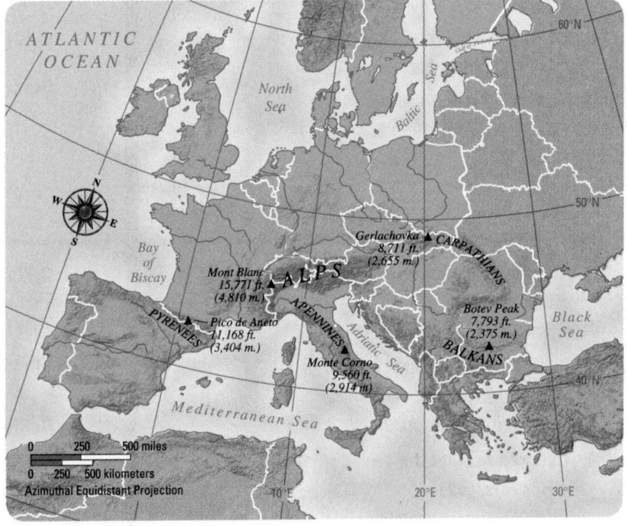

Create your own sketch map of the physical geography of Europe. Combine the information from this map with the information from the rivers map on page 275 and the peninsulas map on page 273.

hmhsocialstudies.com
MULTIMEDIA ACTIVITY

Use the links at **hmhsocialstudies.com** to do research about acid rain in Europe. Focus on one aspect of acid rain, such as how the European Union is fighting acid rain or how European students learn about acid rain.

Writing About Geography Write a report of your findings. Include a map or a chart that visually presents information on acid rain. List the Web sites that you used in preparing your report.

CHAPTER 12 ASSESSMENT

Critical Thinking

1. a. the construction of polders and the use of pilings to support buildings in Venice
b. deforestation and the construction of polders (to provide more land)
2. a. Mountains made travel difficult and isolated different ethnic groups from each other and isolated the region from the rest of Europe.
b. Europe is west of Asia, north of the Mediterranean Sea and Africa, east of the Atlantic Ocean, and south of the Arctic Ocean.
3. The British Isles, the Northern European Plain, and the Lombardy Plain of Italy are the most agriculturally productive; region.
4. How to preserve their historic buildings without creating such stringent anti-pollution measures that industry, and thus the economy, suffers.
5. Both are long and narrow and surrounded by water, and both have some mountainous areas; as for differences, the Italian Peninsula has a mild climate, while much of the Scandinavian Peninsula has a harsh climate; Scandinavia has many more natural resources.

GeoActivity

Integrated Assessment
- Rubric for a sketch map, 2.1

Formal Assessment
- Chapter Test, Forms A, B, and C, pp. 183–194

Geographic Skills

1. the Pyrenees
2. the Balkans and Carpathians
3. They are in the southern part of Europe, north of the Mediterranean and Adriatic seas.

MULTIMEDIA ACTIVITY

For the report on acid rain, students should:
- Present a concise, well-organized report on acid rain in Europe.
- Summarize efforts to control the problem.
- Produce a clear, imaginative visual to complement the report.
- Include references to the Web sites used as sources.

Grading Rubric Evaluate student performance as Exceptional, Acceptable, or Poor in each of the following categories:

	Exceptional	Acceptable	Poor
Writing is clear, focused, and logical			
Clearly states the topic and purpose in the introductory sentence			
Provides necessary facts and examples			
Uses correct grammar, spelling, and punctuation			

Human Geography of Europe

OVERVIEW	INSTRUCTIONAL RESOURCES	
ESSENTIAL QUESTION How have cultural differences caused conflict among Europeans? **Focus on the Essential Question Podcast**	**In-Depth Resources: Unit 4** • Building Vocabulary, p.18 **Block Schedule Strategies** **Chapter Summaries** (English/Spanish) **Multimedia Connections** • Ancient Greece hmhsocialstudies.com INTERACTIVE	**Interactive Online Edition** TOS **ExamView® Assessment Suite** (English/Spanish) TOS **CalendarPlanner** **Power Presentations with Media Gallery** **Critical Thinking Transparencies** • CT13 **Video:** The Roman Republic Is Born
SECTION 1 **MEDITERRANEAN EUROPE** **MAIN IDEAS** • Ancient Greek and Roman civilizations shaped Mediterranean culture. • The Roman Empire influenced the development of language and spread Christianity. • The region's economy is becoming less dependent on agriculture and more dependent on industry.	**In-Depth Resources: Unit 4** • Guided Reading, p. 13 • Building Vocabulary, p. 18 • Reteaching Activities, p. 19 **Outline Maps with Activities** • Mediterranean Europe, pp. 33–34 **Cultures Around the World** • Architecture, p. 19	**Map Transparencies** • MT24 The Roman Empire **Cultures Transparencies** • CW19 The Parthenon **Video:** The Black Death **Guided Reading Workbook,** Section 1
SECTION 2 **WESTERN EUROPE** **MAIN IDEAS** • Language and religion are important cultural differences. • Nationalism led to the rise of modern nation-states. • Western Europe has a strong and diversified economy and an impressive artistic legacy.	**In-Depth Resources: Unit 4** • Guided Reading, p. 14 • Building Vocabulary, p. 18 • Reteaching Activities, p. 20 **Outline Maps with Activities** • Western Europe, pp. 35–36 **Cultures Around the World** • Fine Arts, p. 21	**Critical Thinking Transparencies** • CT45 Cities of the United States, Canada and Europe **Cultures Transparencies** • CW21 Pierre Auguste Renoir **Guided Reading Workbook,** Section 2
SECTION 3 **NORTHERN EUROPE** **MAIN IDEAS** • Migrating peoples settled Northern Europe. • Great Britain helped to develop representative government and, through its empire, to spread the English language throughout the world. • Northern Europeans generally enjoy a high standard of living and have experienced limited cultural diversity.	**In-Depth Resources: Unit 4** • Guided Reading, p. 15 • Building Vocabulary, p. 18 • Reteaching Activities, p. 21 **Outline Maps with Activities** • Northern Europe, pp. 37–38 **Cultures Around the World** • Daily Life, p. 20 • Music, p. 22 **Guided Reading Workbook,** Section 3	**Cultures Transparencies CW20, 22** • Cross-Country Skiing • Playing Bagpipes
SECTION 4 **EASTERN EUROPE** **MAIN IDEAS** • Eastern Europe is a cultural crossroads. • Communist policies in Eastern Europe slowed economic development. • Ethnic and religious diversity has defined regional culture but also has created intense conflict.	**In-Depth Resources: Unit 4** • Guided Reading, p. 16 • Skillbuilder Practice, p. 17 • Building Vocabulary, p. 18 • Reteaching Activities, p. 22 **Outline Maps with Activities** • Eastern Europe, pp. 39–40	**Cultures Transparencies CW23, 24** • Folk Dancing • Bohemian Crystal **Cultures Around the World** • Dance, p. 23 • Arts and Crafts, p. 24 **Guided Reading Workbook,** Section 4

ASSESSMENT

SE **Chapter Assessment,** pp. 316–317

Formal Assessment
- Chapter Tests, Forms A, B, and C, pp. 199–210

TOS **ExamView® Assessment Suite**

Strategies for Test Preparation

SE **Section Assessment,** p. 293

Formal Assessment
- Section Quiz, p. 195

Integrated Assessment
- Rubric for quiz-show questions and answers, 3.7
- Rubric for a presentation, 3.6

Test Practice Transparencies TT41

SE **Section Assessment,** p. 301

Formal Assessment
- Section Quiz, p. 196

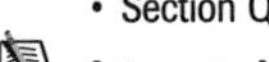
Integrated Assessment
- Rubric for a Venn diagram, 2.8

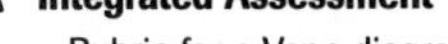

Test Practice Transparencies TT42

SE **Section Assessment,** p. 307

Formal Assessment
- Section Quiz, p. 197

Integrated Assessment

- Rubric for a chart, 2.2

Test Practice Transparencies TT43

SE **Section Assessment,** p. 315

Formal Assessment
- Section Quiz, p. 198

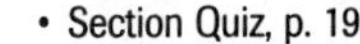

Integrated Assessment
- Rubric for a time line, 2.4

Test Practice Transparencies TT44

CHART KEY:

SE Student Edition

TE Teacher's Edition

Printable Resource

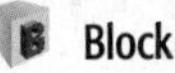
Block Scheduling

TOS Teacher One Stop

Presentation Resource

DVD/CD-ROM

MP3 Audio

HISTORY™

Program Resources available on TOS and @ 

SUPPORTING RESOURCES

- Multimedia Classroom Global History Series
- Global History Teacher's Guide

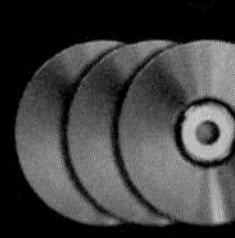

Social Studies Trade Library Collection
- Ancient World History Trade Collection

For more information or to purchase these resources, go to 

DIFFERENTIATED INSTRUCTION

English Learners

Spanish/English Guided Reading Workbook

Access for Students Acquiring English/ESL
Spanish Translations, pp. 66–70

Chapter Summaries (English/Spanish)

TE **TE Activity**
Using Proper Nouns, p. 298

Struggling Readers

Chapter Summaries (English/Spanish)

TE **TE Activity**
Previewing Key Facts, p. 304

Gifted and Talented Students

TE **TE Activity**
Preparing a Research Report, p. 305
Exploring the New Germany, p. 312

ENRICHMENT ACTIVITIES

The following activities are especially suitable for classes following block schedules.

SE **Student Edition,** p. 288–317
- Disasters! Bubonic Plague, pp. 294–295
- Comparing Cultures: Geographic Sports Challenges, pp. 308–309

hmhsocialstudies.com INTERACTIVE
- Major Industries of France and Germany, p. 299
- Comparing Cultures: Geographic Sports Challenges, pp. 308–309

BLOCK SCHEDULE LESSON PLAN OPTIONS: 90-MINUTE PERIOD

DAY 1

SECTION 1, pp. 289-295
Class Time 45 minutes

- **Defining Periods** Divide the class into four groups. Assign each group one of the following historical periods: classical, Middle Ages, Renaissance, modern. Ask students in each group to define their period in terms of major influences, trends, and events and to explain what role location and movement may have played in each. Have a spokesperson for each group present its findings to the class.

SECTION 2, pp. 296-301
Class Time 45 minutes

- **Documentary** Develop an outline for "Cultures Collide," a documentary showing how differences in French and German culture influenced Western European culture and history. Suggest that students consider questions of language, religion, nationalism, conflict, and conflict resolution. Have students begin by brainstorming. Write their ideas of what should be included on the chalkboard. Lead students in refining and organizing the outline, then have them work in pairs to provide additional details.

DAY 2

SECTION 3, pp. 302-309
Class Time 90 minutes

- **Exploring Movement** Review section by discussing the role of movement in the human geography of Northern Europe. Ask students how each of the following involved movement: Vikings, the British Empire, the Industrial Revolution, the Irish potato famine, advances in representative government. You may wish to point out that movement also applies to ideas. Challenge students to offer additional examples.
Class Time 45 minutes

- **Comparing Great Britain and the Nordic Countries** As a preliminary activity, have students look at an unlabeled transparency of Northern Europe. Fill in the names of the countries as students identify them. Then ask students to identify relevant information for each group of countries using the following categories: economy; culture and customs; languages; religion; government; leisure. Begin with Great Britain and write students' findings on the chalkboard. Proceed in a similar manner for the Nordic countries. Then have students write one or two paragraphs discussing similarities and differences between the two. Encourage students to share points from their writing with the rest of the class.
Class Time 45 minutes

DAY 3

SECTION 4, pp. 310-315
Class Time 30 minutes

- **Exploring Diversity and Conflict** Divide the class into small groups and have them determine how language, religion, topography, and communism contributed to cultural diversity and political conflict in Eastern Europe. Then have students present and compare their findings.

CHAPTER 13 REVIEW AND ASSESSMENT, pp. 316-317
Class Time 60 minutes

- **Review** Have students compare the cluster diagrams they made for each of Europe's subregions. Lead them in a discussion of the similarities and differences among the regions.
Class Time 25 minutes

- **Assessment** Have students complete the Chapter 13 Assessment.
Class Time 35 minutes

TEACHER-TESTED ACTIVITY

ABC Book of Europe

Class Time 3–4 class periods

Task Create an ABC Book of the human geography of Europe

Supplies
- Colored pencils/markers
- Stencils
- Typing paper
- Rulers
- Use of a computer lab, if available

Purpose To review the key terms in the human geography of Europe

Activity Divide students into groups of four. Within each group, assign a student to Mediterranean, Western, Northern, or Eastern Europe. Each group member should then review the corresponding section of Chapter 13 and make an alphabetical listing of key events, religions, languages, and ethnic groups for that subregion. After completing their lists, students should combine the information from the four subregions.

Group members should next divide up the alphabet equally, with each member being responsible for six letters. Have them choose one term per letter to explain and illustrate. (Some alphabet letters may be omitted.) After completing their explanations and illustrations, two group members should work together to create a Title Page, and two should work together to create a Table of Contents indicating the alphabet letter, the event, and the subregion.

Jan Ellersieck
Geography Teacher, Ft. Zumalt South High School, St. Peters, Missouri

Graphic organizers can be extremely helpful when students are gathering information from a variety of sources, comparing and contrasting subject matter, or trying to understand how certain topics are structured. If students create graphic organizers on the computer, they will be able to more easily manipulate, add, and change information than on paper-based graphic organizers. Graphic organizers can be created in special software programs designed for that purpose, or in the form of simple charts or tables in a word processor or spreadsheet program.

Objective Students will create a simple graphic organizer on the computer to compare and contrast two subregions of Europe. They will not only learn more about the subregions, but they will also learn how to organize information in a useful way on the computer.

Task Have students input information on the history, cultures, and economies of two European subregions into a simple graphic organizer that they create on the computer. Then have them write paragraphs explaining what their graphic organizer shows.

Class Time 1 period

1. Ask each student to choose two of the subregions of Europe discussed in Chapter 13 to compare and contrast.

2. Have students use the computer to make graphic organizers that will enable them to compare and contrast the two subregions. The type of organizer they create will depend on the computer program they are using, but two simple and effective examples would be charts with columns and rows, or "idea webs" with circles or ovals extending out of a main topic circle (the main topic would be "Subregions of Europe").

3. Have students go through the sections of Chapter 13 that discuss their subregions and ask them to enter information into the graphic organizer illustrating facts about the subregions' history, modern-day cultures, and economy. The facts they enter should address the following questions: What are the origins of the current form of government in this subregion's countries? What are some cultural customs in this subregion? What are some characteristics of the modern economy in this subregion? Students should be sure to list at least two details for each of these three sections (history, culture, and economy) for each subregion.

4. Have students conduct Internet research to find additional information to add to their graphic organizers. As they add new information, they can increase the size of the rows or columns (if they made a chart) or add and move the circles (if they made an "idea web"). Go to **hmhsocialstudies.com** for useful research links to other Web sites.

5. Have students use word processors to write a two to three-paragraph report answering the question "How do these two subregions differ? How are they alike?" They should refer to their graphic organizers for specific examples to include in their report.

CHAPTER 13 OBJECTIVE

Identify features of human geography in the four subregions of Europe.

Chapter 13

HUMAN GEOGRAPHY OF EUROPE
Diversity, Conflict, Union

hmhsocialstudies.com VIDEO

Interpreting Maps

Four Subregions of Europe
Have students examine the map and then analyze the characteristics of these subregional groupings, including what the countries in each group might have in common.

Extension Have students suggest other ways the region might be divided.

Introducing the Essential Question

- Show students that the four subregions of Europe have widely varied physical environments. These environments have helped to shape the subregions' cultures, which are also highly diverse. These differences have often led to conflict, both within and between subregions.
- European immigrants have brought countless culture traits with them to the United States, which has deep historical connections with all four European subregions.

Have students complete cluster diagrams in their notebooks using material from all sections in this chapter.

 **Critical Thinking Transparencies CT13**
- GeoFocus

 **In-Depth Resources: Unit 4**
- Building Vocabulary, p. 18

Four Subregions of Europe

Essential Question

How have cultural differences caused conflict among Europeans?

What You Will Learn

In this chapter you will compare and contrast features of Europe's human geography.

SECTION 1
Mediterranean Europe

SECTION 2
Western Europe

SECTION 3
Northern Europe

SECTION 4
Eastern Europe

hmhsocialstudies.com TAKING NOTES

Use the graphic organizer online to take notes about the history, economics, culture, and modern life of each subregion of Europe.

Mediterranean
Western
Northern
Eastern

0 250 500 miles
0 250 500 kilometers
Azimuthal Equidistant Projection

288 CHAPTER 13

CHAPTER 13 ADDITIONAL RESOURCES

BOOKS FOR THE TEACHER

McEvedy, Colin. ***The New Penguin Atlas of Recent History: Europe Since 1815.*** Penguin, 2003. Updated maps along with information on the events that have shaped modern Europe.

BOOKS FOR THE STUDENT

Bourbon, Fabio. ***Spain.*** NY: Smithmark, 1992. Good general guide to Spanish history and geography.

Leapman, Michael. ***Portrait of Britain.*** NY: DK Publishing, 1999. Lavishly illustrated history and travel guide to Britain.

VIDEOS

The Three Musketeers. Dir. Richard Lester. 1974. USA Home Video. Classic Alexandre Dumas story about French royal guards, set in 17th-century France.

INTERNET

For more on the human geography of Europe, visit . . .

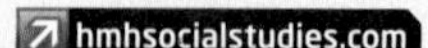

Mediterranean Europe

Main Ideas

- The ancient Greek and Roman civilizations and the Renaissance all began in Mediterranean Europe.
- In the 20th century, the region has seen economic growth and political turmoil.

Places & Terms

city-state **Renaissance**
republic **aqueduct**
Crusades

CONNECT TO THE ISSUES
UNIFICATION Membership in the European Union has helped the economies of the Mediterranean nations.

A HUMAN PERSPECTIVE Have you ever heard the saying, "All roads lead to Rome"? The Mediterranean region was home to the two great civilizations of ancient Europe—ancient Greece and ancient Rome. The city of Rome was founded in about 753 B.C., and Rome conquered a huge empire by about A.D. 100. To aid communication and make it possible for the army to march quickly to distant locations, Rome built a large network of well-paved roads. In ancient Europe, most roads did indeed lead to Rome, enabling that city to control a vast region.

A History of Ancient Glory

Two geographic advantages helped the Mediterranean to become the region where European civilization was born. First, the mild climate made survival there easier than in other areas. So societies had time to develop complex institutions such as government. Second, the nearby Mediterranean Sea encouraged overseas trade. When different societies trade with each other, they also exchange ideas. The spread of ideas often leads to advances in knowledge.

GREECE: BIRTHPLACE OF DEMOCRACY Beginning about 2000 B.C., people from the north moved onto the Balkan Peninsula. They built villages there. The region is mountainous, so those villages were isolated from each other and developed into separate city-states. A **city-state** is a political unit made up of a city and its surrounding lands.

Ancient Greece left a lasting legacy to modern civilization. The city-state of Athens developed the first democracy, a government in which the people rule. In Athens, all free adult males were citizens who had the right to serve in the law-making assembly. Athenian democracy helped inspire the U.S. system of government. And Greek science, philosophy, drama, and art helped shape modern culture.

In the 400s B.C., conflict weakened Greece. Several city-states fought a costly series of wars with Persia, an empire in southwest Asia. Then Athens fought a ruinous

PLACE In Athens, ancient ruins such as the Parthenon, shown here, stand near modern buildings.

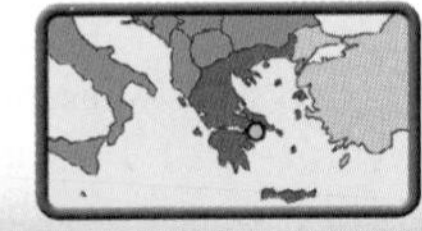

EUROPE

289

SECTION 1 OBJECTIVES

1. Identify the two great civilizations of ancient Europe.
2. Identify major historic events leading to modern times.
3. Analyze how history shaped culture and language.
4. Understand how the region's economy has changed.
5. Identify problems created by urban growth.

SKILLBUILDER: Interpreting Maps and Graphs, pp. 290, 292

GeographicThinking

Making Comparisons, p. 291
Using the Atlas, p. 293
Identifying and Solving Problems, p. 293

Focus & Motivate

Ask students why Mediterranean countries have preserved their ancient architecture. *(It is part of their cultural heritage; it attracts tourists.)*

Instruct: Objective 1 appears on p. 290.

Interpreting Photographs

Athens

Have students identify the Parthenon. Explain that it is a Greek temple built in 447–438 B.C. Ask students why they think it was built high on a high hill. *(Temples were often built in high places to be closer to the gods.)*

SECTION 1 PROGRAM RESOURCES

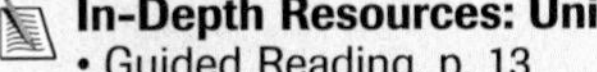

In-Depth Resources: Unit 4
- Guided Reading, p. 13
- Building Vocabulary, p. 18
- Reteaching Activity, p. 19

Guided Reading Workbook
- Section 1

Access for Students Acquiring English/ESL
- Guided Reading, p. 66

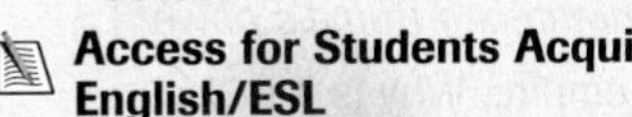

Formal Assessment
- Section Quiz, p. 195

Outline Maps with Activities
- Mediterranean Europe, pp. 33–34

Integrated Assessment
- Rubric for quiz-show questions and answers, 3.7
- Rubric for a presentation, 3.6

Cultures Around the World
- Architecture, p. 19

INTEGRATED TECHNOLOGY

Cultures Transparency CW19
- Parthenon

Map Transparencies MT24
- The Roman Empire

The World's Music Audio Program

hmhsocialstudies.com

TEST-TAKING RESOURCES

Strategies for Test Preparation

Test Practice Transparencies TT41

Online Test Practice

Instruct: Objective 1

A History of Ancient Glory

- What geographic factors fostered early European civilization? *(mild climate; the Mediterranean Sea, which encouraged trade)*
- What were the forms of government in ancient Greece and Rome? *(Greece was a democratic city-state. Rome was a republic and then an empire.)*
- How has ancient Greece shaped modern culture and democracy? *(Greek science, philosophy, and the arts influenced modern cultural development. Athenian democracy inspired democracy in the U.S.)*

In-Depth Resources: Unit 4
- Guided Reading, p. 13

Cultures Transparency CW19
- Parthenon

Map Transparencies MT24
- The Roman Empire

SKILLBUILDER ANSWERS
1. the Rhine and the Danube
2. Christianity

Instruct: Objective 

Moving Toward Modern Times

- What were the Crusades? *(a series of wars aimed at taking the Holy Land back from the Muslims)*
- Why was the Renaissance important culturally? *(It renewed interest in the arts and learning.)*

Cultural Legacy of the Roman Empire

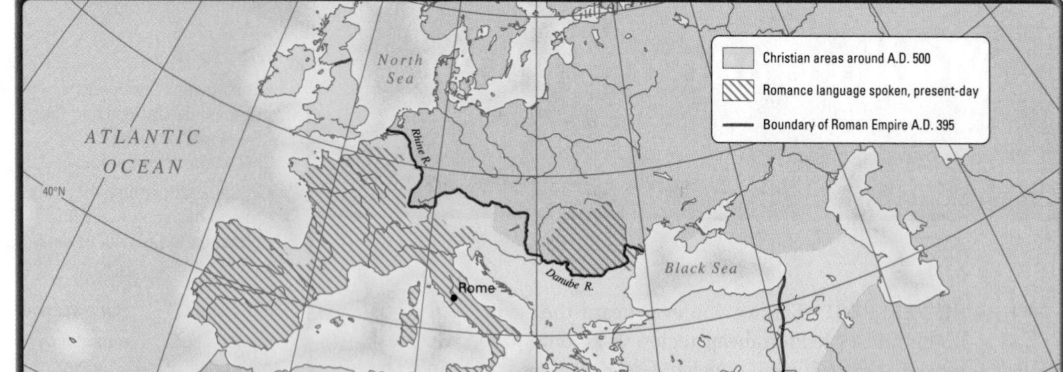

SKILLBUILDER: Interpreting Maps

1. **REGION** Which waterways formed part of the northern boundary of the Roman Empire?
2. **MOVEMENT** Which Roman cultural influence was more widespread, Christianity or Romance languages?

war with Sparta, a rival Greek city-state. Finally, in 338 B.C., Macedonia (a kingdom to the north) conquered Greece. Beginning in 336 B.C., the Macedonian general Alexander the Great conquered Persia and part of India. His empire spread Greek culture but broke apart after his death.

THE ROMAN EMPIRE As Greece lost power, a state to the west was rising. That state, Rome, ruled most of the Italian Peninsula by 275 B.C. At the time, Rome was a **republic,** a government in which citizens elect representatives to rule in their name.

BACKGROUND
The Roman republic was a model for modern governments such as those of France and the United States.

The Roman Empire grew by conquering territory overseas, including the Iberian and Balkan peninsulas. At home in Italy, unrest over inequalities led to decades of turmoil that caused Romans to seek strong leaders. Rome began to be ruled by an emperor, ending the republic.

One of Rome's overseas territories was Palestine, the place where Jesus was born. Christianity spread from there across the empire, and by the late 300s, Christianity was Rome's official religion.

By A.D. 395, the empire was too big for a single government, so it split into a western and an eastern half. The Western Roman Empire grew weak, in part because of German invaders from the north, and fell in A.D. 476. The Eastern Roman Empire lasted nearly 1,000 years longer.

Moving Toward Modern Times

After 476, the three Mediterranean peninsulas had very different histories. The Balkan Peninsula stayed part of the Eastern Roman Empire

ACTIVITY OPTION **CRITICAL THINKING**

DRAWING CONCLUSIONS

Explaining the Skill Drawing conclusions means analyzing what you have read and then deciding what the meaning of the information is. To draw conclusions, look at the facts and then use your own common sense and experience to decide what the facts mean.

Applying the Skill Have students look at the map on page 290. Tell them to use it to draw conclusions that will help them answer the following questions.

- Why did the Romans refer to the Mediterranean Sea as "our sea"? *(It was completely encompassed by the Roman Empire.)*
- The Punic Wars between Carthage (a great sea power located in what is now Tunisia) and Rome (a great land power) began in 264 B.C. and ended with the destruction of Carthage in 146 B.C. Why was Rome so intent on destroying Carthage? *(Carthaginian control of the Mediterranean Sea would have severely threatened Rome's power.)*
- Note the location of Rome relative to its empire. Why is it in the approximate center rather than on the edge? *(As the Romans conquered surrounding territory they were able to extend their empire farther from its capital.)*

(also called the Byzantine Empire) for nearly 1,000 years. Beginning in the 1300s, Italy saw the birth of the Renaissance, and in the 1400s, Portugal and Spain launched the Age of Exploration.

ITALIAN CITY-STATES The invaders who overran the Italian Peninsula had no tradition of strong central government. Italy eventually became divided into many small states and remained so for centuries.

In 1096, European Christians launched the **Crusades,** a series of wars to take the Holy Land from the Muslims. Italians earned large profits by supplying the ships that carried Crusaders to the Middle East. Italian cities such as Florence and Venice became rich from banking and foreign trade. This wealth helped them grow into powerful city-states.

BACKGROUND The Renaissance shaped modern life by stressing classical culture, material comfort, and the value of individuals.

The Renaissance, which began in the Italian city-states, was a time of renewed interest in learning and the arts that lasted from the 14th through 16th centuries. It was inspired by classical art and writings. Renaissance ideas spread north to the rest of Europe.

But the wealth of Italy did not protect it from disease. In 1347, the bubonic plague reached Italy from Asia and in time killed millions of Europeans. (See pages 294–295.)

SPAIN'S EMPIRE In the 700s, Muslims from North Africa conquered the Iberian Peninsula. Muslims controlled parts of the Iberian Peninsula for more than 700 years. Spain's Catholic rulers, Ferdinand and Isabella, retook Spain from the Muslims in 1492.

Also in 1492, Queen Isabella paid for Christopher Columbus's first voyage. Portugal had already sent out many voyages of exploration. Both Spain and Portugal established colonies in the Americas and elsewhere. Their empires spread Catholicism and the Spanish and Portuguese languages throughout the world.

REGION Italian Renaissance paintings often show the Virgin Mary and baby Jesus. Muslim art, like the Spanish wall design below (*bottom*), often uses calligraphy to praise God.

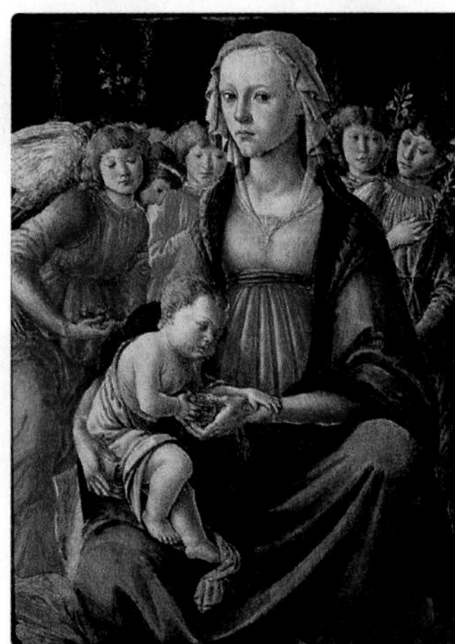

The Virgin and Child Surrounded by Five Angels, Sandro Botticelli

A Rich Cultural Legacy

Mediterranean Europe's history shaped its culture by determining where languages are spoken and where religions are practiced today. And the people of the region take pride in the artistic legacy of the past.

ROME'S CULTURAL LEGACY Unlike many areas of Europe that Rome conquered, Greece retained its own language. Greek was, in fact, the official language of the Byzantine Empire. In contrast, Portuguese, Spanish, and Italian are Romance languages that evolved from Latin, the language of Rome.

The two halves of the Roman Empire also developed different forms of Christianity. The majority religion in Greece today is Eastern Orthodox Christianity. Roman Catholicism is strong in Italy, Spain, and Portugal. A

A. Answer Both spread religion and language.

Geographic Thinking

Making Comparisons

A What is similar about the cultural legacies left by the Roman and Spanish empires?

CENTURIES OF ART This region shows many signs of its past civilizations. Greece and Italy have ancient ruins, such as the Parthenon, that reveal what classical

Alhambra Palace, Granada, Spain

Instruct: Objective 3

A Rich Cultural Legacy

- What effect did Roman conquest have on language? *(Romance languages evolved from Latin.)*
- How did the division of the Roman Empire affect religion? *(Two forms of Christianity developed: Eastern Orthodox Christianity and Roman Catholicism.)*
- What aspects of ancient Greece and Rome are still culturally significant? *(art, architecture, government, and science)*

More About

Florence

The Italian city of Florence is nestled in the beautiful landscape of Italy's Tuscany region. The city of Florence grew wealthy through banking and trade. The wealth of noble families, such as the Medicis, allowed them to patronize artists such as Michelangelo and Donatello. Today, the beautiful Tuscan landscape and the magnificent art and architecture of Florence continue to attract visitors from all over the world.

ACTIVITY OPTION **LINK TO HUMANITIES**

BLOCK SCHEDULING

EXPLORING CLASSICAL ARCHITECTURE

Objective To explore a specific example of how ancient Greek culture has remained an important cultural influence

Class Time One class period

Task Create a chart comparing the Parthenon to the Lincoln Memorial

Directions Divide the class into small groups. Have each group use an encyclopedia or other sources to find pictures and information about the Parthenon and the Lincoln Memorial. Tell them to include location, year(s) built, and at least one physical similarity and difference on their charts.

Have groups compare their findings. Then ask them to determine the number of years that passed between the building of the two and the distance between them.

	PARTHENON	LINCOLN MEMORIAL
Location		
Date(s) Built		
Similarities		
Differences		

Instruct: Objective 

Economic Change

- How has the economy changed since World War II? *(Manufacturing and service industries are increasing.)*
- What are some of the region's economic problems? *(The entire region lacks adequate energy resources; Italy's southern region remains largely undeveloped.)*
- How has membership in the EU spurred economic growth for some Mediterranean countries? *(by promoting trade and increasing financial aid opportunities)*

Interpreting Graphs

Economic Activity

Ask students what changes might have resulted in such significant decreases in agricultural activity between 1952 and 1995. *(Students might suggest that less demand for agricultural goods in 1995 resulted in the decrease, or they might guess that these countries chose to import agricultural goods rather than produce the goods themselves.)*

SKILLBUILDER ANSWERS

1. Trade and "other" increased; agriculture and industry decreased.
2. It might have increased because government and service industries have been growing.

Instruct: Objective 5 appears on p. 293.

architecture was like. Spain has Roman **aqueducts,** structures that carried water for long distances, and Muslim mosques, places of worship.

The region also has a long artistic legacy, which includes classical statues, Renaissance painting and sculpture, and modern art produced by such artists as Pablo Picasso of Spain. The pictures on page 291 contrast Renaissance Italian art with Muslim Spanish art.

Economic Change

Because of the Mediterranean region's sunny climate and historic sites, tourism has long been a large part of its economy. In other ways, the economy has been changing rapidly since World War II.

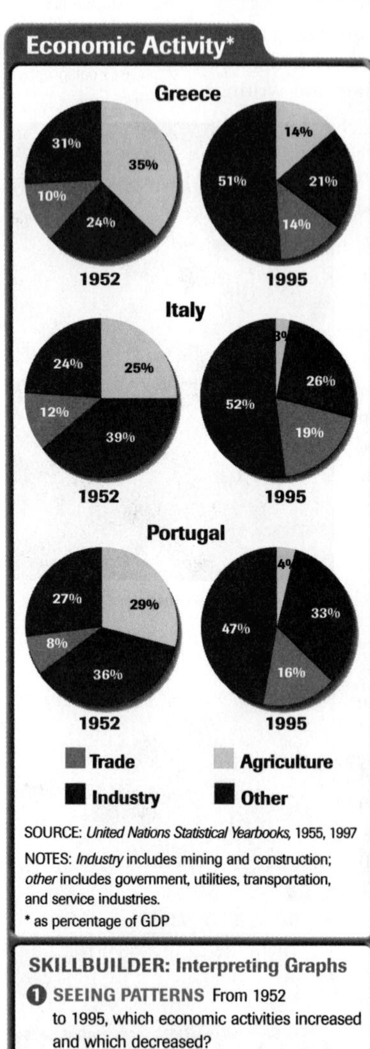

SOURCE: *United Nations Statistical Yearbooks*, 1955, 1997

NOTES: *Industry* includes mining and construction; *other* includes government, utilities, transportation, and service industries.

* as percentage of GDP

SKILLBUILDER: Interpreting Graphs

1. **SEEING PATTERNS** From 1952 to 1995, which economic activities increased and which decreased?
2. **MAKING INFERENCES** Why do you think the category "other" changed so significantly? Give possible reasons.

AGRICULTURE TO INDUSTRY In general, the Mediterranean nations are less industrial than those of Northern and Western Europe. For centuries, the region's economy was based on fishing and agriculture. Fishing remains important, and olives, grapes, citrus, and wheat are still major agricultural crops.

But in the late 20th century, the region's economy grew and changed. Today, manufacturing is increasing. The making of textiles is Portugal's biggest industry. Spain is a leading maker of automobiles, and Italy is a major producer of clothing and shoes. Service industries, such as banking, also make up a much larger part of the economy than before.

In the 1980s, Greece, Portugal, and Spain joined the European Union (EU). This aided growth by promoting trade with other EU nations and by making financial aid from the EU available.

BACKGROUND The EU is an economic and political alliance of 27 nations. Italy was one of the founding members.

ECONOMIC PROBLEMS The region still faces economic challenges. For example, Italy's northern region is much more developed than its southern half. The reasons for this include the following:

- The north is closer to other industrial countries of Europe, such as Germany and France.
- The south has poorer transportation systems.
- The government tried to promote growth in the south but made bad choices. It started industries that did not benefit the local people.

Another problem is that the entire Mediterranean region is poor in energy resources and relies heavily on imported petroleum. This makes the region vulnerable because trade problems or wars could halt oil supplies and prevent industries from functioning.

Modern Mediterranean Life

Mediterranean Europe saw political turmoil in the 20th century. Two dictators, Benito Mussolini in Italy

ACTIVITY OPTION **INTERNET RESEARCH**

UPDATING INFORMATION

Objective To gather current economic information

Class Time One class period

Task Update information shown for 1995 on the "Economic Activity" graph

Directions Have students choose one of the countries indicated on the graph and search the Internet to update the information shown. Remind students that all statistics for a particular country should be from the same year. Research links are available at **hmhsocialstudies.com.**

OPTIONAL ACTIVITY If access to the Internet is limited, students may use almanacs, magazines, and newspapers to conduct their research.

and Francisco Franco in Spain, ruled for long periods. After Franco died in 1975, Spain set up a constitutional government. After World War II, Italy became a republic but has had dozens of governments since then. Greece has also experienced political instability.

THE BASQUES Spain has had an ongoing conflict with a minority group. The Basque people live in the western foothills of the Pyrenees. Their language is the only pre-Roman language still spoken in southwestern Europe. In the late 1970s, Spain granted the Basque region self-rule. But some Basques want complete independence and have used violence to fight for it. The conflict remains unresolved. B

Geographic Thinking

Using the Atlas

B Locate the Basque language on the map on page 267. What other country besides Spain has Basque speakers?
B. Answer France

PLACE Pamplona, Spain, holds a festival in which young men run through the streets before a herd of stampeding bulls. **What might this activity show about Spanish culture?**

CITY GROWTH The transition from agriculture to manufacturing and service industries has encouraged people to move from the country to the city. Urban growth has created housing shortages, pollution, and traffic jams. The people of Mediterranean Europe want to preserve their historic cities, so they are trying to solve these problems. For example, Athens is expanding its subway system to reduce traffic and pollution. A portion of this project was completed in time for the 2004 Olympics, but work will continue until 2013.

Despite their problems, Mediterranean cities give intriguing insight into the past. In Rome and Athens, classical ruins stand near modern buildings. Florence has glorious works of Renaissance art. Granada, Spain, has Catholic cathedrals and a Muslim palace. In Section 2, you will read about Western Europe, a region that also has a rich history.

EUROPE

Section 1 Assessment

1 Places & Terms

Identify these terms and explain their importance in the region's history or culture.
- city-state
- republic
- Crusades
- Renaissance
- aqueduct

2 Taking Notes

REGION Review the notes you took for this section.

- What are the two ancient civilizations of this region?
- What type of movement is the result of recent economic change?

3 Main Ideas

a. How was the Renaissance an example of the movement of ideas?
b. What is Rome's cultural legacy in Mediterranean Europe today?
c. How has Mediterranean Europe's economy changed since World War II?

4 Geographic Thinking

Identifying and Solving Problems What might help preserve the historic cities of Mediterranean Europe?
Think about:
- how to provide housing and reduce both pollution and traffic

ASKING GEOGRAPHIC QUESTIONS Review the paragraph about the Crusades on page 291. Write three to five geographic questions about the Crusades, such as "Why did many Crusaders purchase supplies for their ships in Italy?" Do research to answer as many of your questions as possible. Then create a set of **quiz show questions and answers.** 21st Century

Instruct: Objective 5

Modern Mediterranean Life

- What is a major indicator of political instability in Italy? *(Italy has had many governments since World War II.)*
- Why have the Basques been a source of turmoil in Spain? *(Some want complete independence and have used violence to gain this end.)*

More About

The Basques

The Basques are among the most ancient of Europe's ethnic groups. Basques live in a section of the Pyrenees Mountains along the Bay of Biscay, straddling the Spanish-French border. Although the Basques were granted limited independence by Spain in 1978, the ETA—a terrorist organization demanding a Basque homeland—continues to be active.

CAPTION ANSWER Spaniards value courage.

Assess & Reteach

GeoFocus Have students complete the sections on Mediterranean Europe in their cluster diagrams.

Formal Assessment
- Section Quiz, p. 195

Reteaching Activity

Organize the class into groups of six students. Assign one section objective to each group member. Each member should write, and then share with their groups, a short summary of that section's main idea.

In-Depth Resources: Unit 4
- Reteaching Activity, p. 19

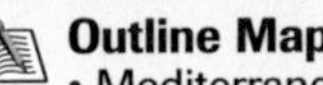

Outline Maps with Activities
- Mediterranean Europe, pp. 33–34

Section 1 Assessment Answers

1. Places & Terms
city-state, p. 289
republic, p. 290
Crusades, p. 291
Renaissance, p. 291
aqueduct, p. 292

2. Taking Notes
- the two ancient civilizations were Greece and Rome
- Economic change has caused movement from the country to the city.

3. Main Ideas
a. The ideas of the Renaissance began in the city-states of Italy and over time spread to Northern Europe.
b. Latin evolved into Italian, Spanish, and Portuguese; Roman Catholicism and Eastern Orthodox Christianity developed during the Roman Empire.
c. Traditional farming and fishing are less important; service industries have grown.

4. Geographic Thinking
Answers will vary, but students might suggest building housing on the outskirts of cities; increasing public transportation to reduce pollution; levying high taxes on fuel to discourage the use of cars.

GeoActivity

Integrated Assessment
- Rubric for quiz-show questions and answers, 3.7

OBJECTIVE

Describe how the bubonic plague arrived and spread throughout much of Europe.

Instruct: Objective

Bubonic Plague

- What brought the plague to Europe? *(trading ships)*
- How is bubonic plague caused and spread? *(by flea bites; infected humans spread the disease by coughing, sneezing, and spitting)*
- How severe was the devastation caused by the plague? *(25 million Europeans died)*

Interpreting Maps

Spread of the Bubonic Plague

Look at the areas on the map that were affected by the plague in 1347 and those affected in 1350 and 1351. What do the areas within each of the two groups have in common? *(Earliest affected areas were on the Mediterranean; areas affected in 1350–1351 generally were much farther north; none were on the Mediterranean.)*

Disasters!

HISTORY VIDEO The Black De

hmhsocialstudies.com

Bubonic Plague

By the 1300s, Italian merchants were growing rich from the trade in luxury goods from Asia. Then in October 1347, trading ships sailed into the port of Messina, Sicily, carrying a terrifying cargo—the disease we now call bubonic plague. Over the next four years, the plague spread along trade routes throughout Europe. An estimated 25 million Europeans died, about one-fourth to one-third of the population. In terms of its death toll, the plague (also called the Black Death) was the worst disaster Europe ever suffered.

Spread of the Bubonic Plague

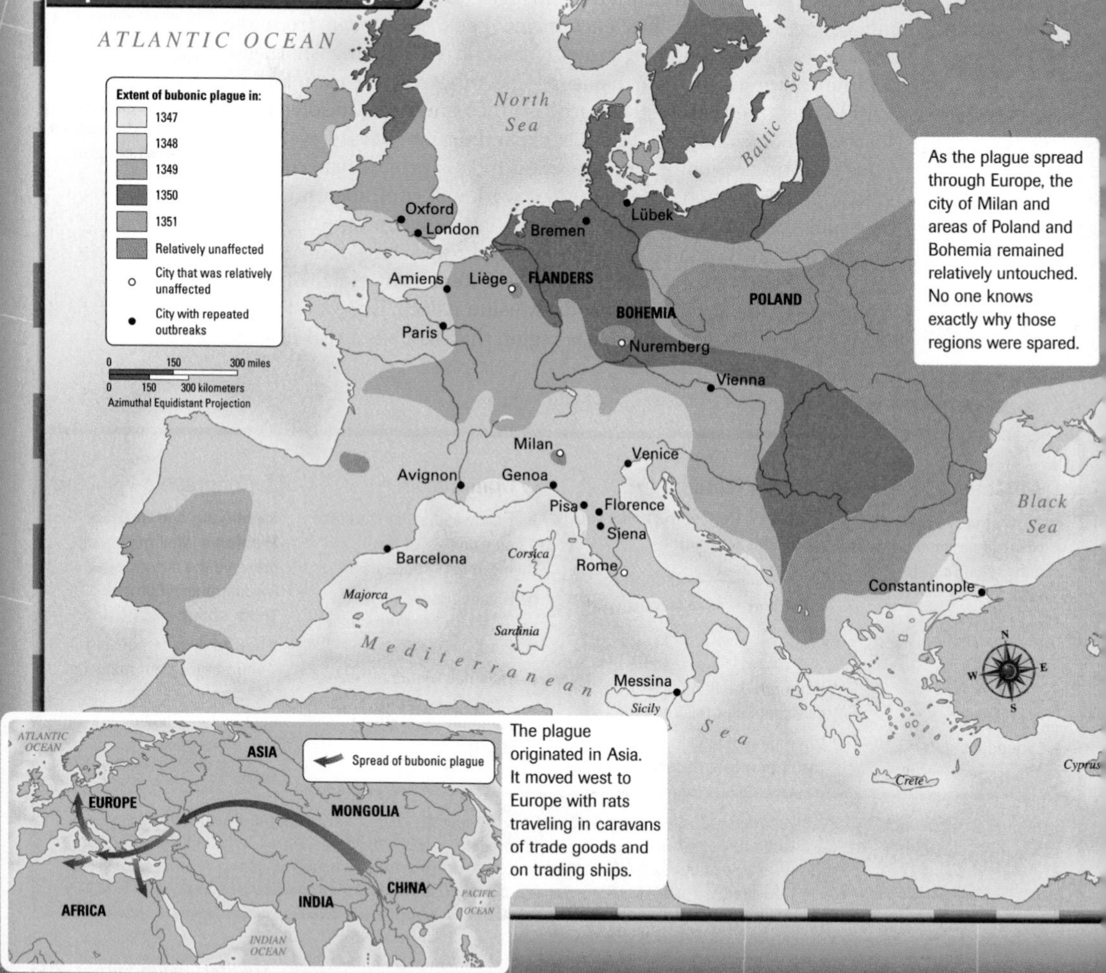

As the plague spread through Europe, the city of Milan and areas of Poland and Bohemia remained relatively untouched. No one knows exactly why those regions were spared.

The plague originated in Asia. It moved west to Europe with rats traveling in caravans of trade goods and on trading ships.

SUPPORTING RESOURCES

BOOKS FOR THE TEACHER

Cowie, Leonard W. ***Plague and Fire, London 1665–66.*** NY: Putnam, 1970. Contains original accounts of the 1665 plague outbreak in London, and the Great Fire in 1666.

BOOKS FOR THE STUDENT

Biel, Timothy Levi. ***The Black Death.*** San Diego: Lucent Books, 1989. Detailed information about the Middle Ages contributes to the reader's understanding of the plague's impact on life in Europe.

PERIODICALS

R. Skelton. **"The Great Plague,"** *National Geographic World,* vol. 283 (Mr 1999), pp. 16–20.

VIDEOS

The Black Death. Chip Clements, producer. Ancient Mysteries Series, 1997. VHS video. A documentary about the plague in 14th-century Europe.

INTERNET

For more on the Bubonic Plague, go to . . .

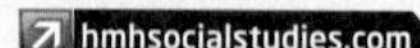
hmhsocialstudies.com

hmhsocialstudies.com INTERACTIVE

Transmission of the Plague

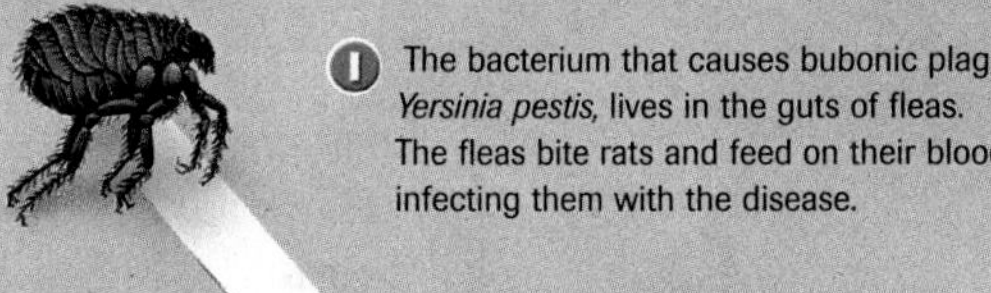

1 The bacterium that causes bubonic plague, *Yersinia pestis,* lives in the guts of fleas. The fleas bite rats and feed on their blood, infecting them with the disease.

2 Sometimes, an infected rat comes into contact with humans. Because the rat is dying, the fleas jump onto the humans to feed off them.

3 People catch bubonic plague from flea bites. In some, the plague enters their lungs, becoming pneumonic plague. These victims cough, sneeze, and spit up infected blood and saliva—spreading the disease more quickly.

GeoActivity

UNDERSTANDING EPIDEMICS

Working with a partner, use the Internet to research an epidemic on the time line below and create a **presentation** about it.

- Create a diagram showing the symptoms of the disease and the methods of treating it.
- Add a map of the region affected by this epidemic.
- Last, write a report explaining how the epidemic affected society.

GeoData

PREVENTIVE MEASURES

In the 1300s, most doctors recommended these methods of purifying the air to prevent plague:

- Burn richly scented incense.
- Fill the house with flowers.
- Sprinkle the floors with vinegar.
- Have doctors wear a bird mask with perfume in the beak.

OTHER DISASTROUS EPIDEMICS

1507–1518
Smallpox killed one-third to one-half of the people of Cuba, Haiti, and Puerto Rico.

1918–1919
About 30 million people died from an influenza outbreak that spread around the world.

2000
A UN report said that AIDS had killed 19 million people worldwide. Seven African countries had 20 percent of their population infected.

GeoActivities

Understanding Epidemics

Integrated Assessment
- Rubric for a presentation, 3.6

More About

Bubonic Plague

The bubonic plague is sometimes called the Black Death. The name comes from one of the disease's symptoms. After the onset of the disease, egg-sized swellings form at the site of an infected flea bite. These swellings are usually located in the armpits, groin, or neck. Next, blood vessels around the infected areas begin to break, causing purplish blotches under the skin that turn black as the blood dries. These black blotches give the disease its name.

ACTIVITY OPTION COOPERATIVE LEARNING

INVESTIGATING THE BUBONIC PLAGUE

Objective To inform students about the status of the bubonic plague today

Class Time 30 minutes

Task Gather information on current status of the bubonic plague

Directions Divide students into groups and have them research different aspects of the bubonic plague's current status. For example, one group might concentrate on recently reported cases of the plague. Another group might look into the types of treatment now available for victims of the disease.

SECTION 2 OBJECTIVES

1. Identify cultural divisions in Western Europe.
2. Explain the development of nation-states.
3. Analyze Western European economies.
4. Examine artistic achievements in Western Europe.
5. Describe features of modern life.

SKILLBUILDER: Interpreting Maps, p. 299

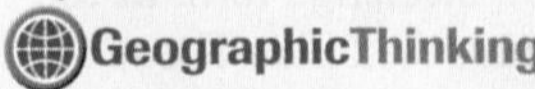

GeographicThinking

Seeing Patterns, p. 298
Making Comparisons, p. 299
Using the Atlas, p. 301
Making Generalizations, p. 301

Focus & Motivate

Ask students what factors might link the countries of Western Europe and make them a key subregion of Europe. *(shared history and religion; shared economic systems)*

Instruct: Objective 1

A History of Cultural Divisions

- Why are France and Germany the dominant countries of Western Europe? *(They are the largest countries and have good access to resources, ports, and trade routes.)*
- How did language differences develop in Western Europe? *(Because Rome conquered France but not Germany, French reflects Latin influences, while lands to the east speak Germanic languages.)*

In-Depth Resources: Unit 4
- Guided Reading, p. 14

2 Western Europe

Main Ideas

- France and the Germanic countries developed very different cultures.
- These cultural differences led to conflicts that shaped the history of Western Europe.

Places & Terms

Benelux	**nationalism**
Reformation	**Holocaust**
feudalism	**Berlin Wall**

CONNECT TO THE ISSUES
UNIFICATION France and Germany have resolved their past conflicts and now cooperate in the European Union.

A HUMAN PERSPECTIVE Today, the French call Émile Durkheim the father of French sociology (the study of society). But he wasn't always honored. During World War I, some French patriots considered him a disloyal foreigner. Why? Perhaps it was because he had a German last name and came from Lorraine, a region that had switched between French and German rule many times. France and Germany have long had a deep rivalry, based in part on cultural differences.

A History of Cultural Divisions

France and Germany are the dominant countries in Western Europe. They are the two largest countries, and their access to resources, ports, and trade routes helped them to build productive economies.

French culture is strong in France and Monaco; German culture is strong in Germany, Austria, and Liechtenstein. Switzerland and the **Benelux** countries of Belgium, the Netherlands, and Luxembourg have their own cultures—but also have been influenced by Germany and France. Western Europe's cultural divisions have historic roots.

ROME TO CHARLEMAGNE One cultural division, language, dates from ancient times. By 50 B.C., the Roman Empire had conquered the Celtic tribes in what is now France. French is one of the Romance languages that evolved from Latin (Rome's language). But Rome never fully conquered the Germanic tribes that migrated into the lands east of France. Germanic languages are still spoken there. (See the chart on page 297.)

Western European History

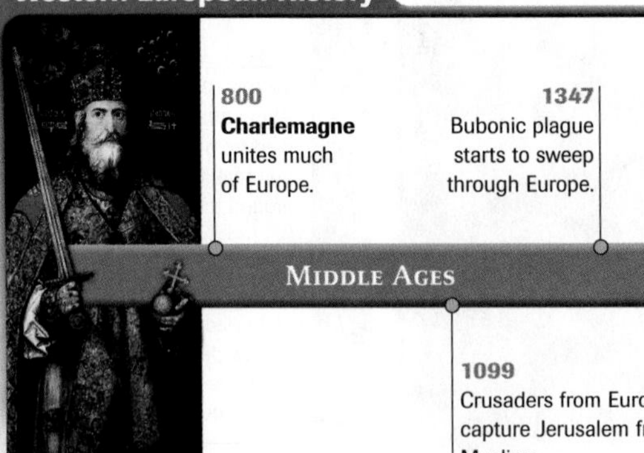

MIDDLE AGES

800 **Charlemagne** unites much of Europe.

1099 Crusaders from Europe capture Jerusalem from Muslims.

1347 Bubonic plague starts to sweep through Europe.

RENAISSANCE AND REFORMATION

1455 First printing of Gutenberg Bible

1516 **Leonardo da Vinci** moves to France, bringing Renaissance ideas.

1517 **Martin Luther** criticizes the Catholic Church. The Reformation begins.

SECTION 2 PROGRAM RESOURCES

In-Depth Resources: Unit 4
- Guided Reading, p. 14
- Building Vocabulary, p. 18
- Reteaching Activity, p. 20

Guided Reading Workbook
- Section 2

Access for Students Acquiring English/ESL
- Guided Reading, p. 67

Outline Maps with Activities
- Western Europe, pp. 35–36

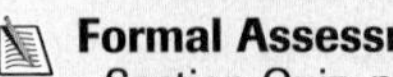

Formal Assessment
- Section Quiz, p. 196

Integrated Assessment
- Rubric for a Venn diagram, 2.8

Cultures Around the World
- Fine Arts, p. 21

INTEGRATED TECHNOLOGY

Critical Thinking Transparencies CT45
- Cities of the United States, Canada, and Europe

Cultures Transparencies CW21
- Pierre Auguste Renoir

The World's Music Audio Program

hmhsocialstudies.com

TEST-TAKING RESOURCES

Strategies for Test Preparation

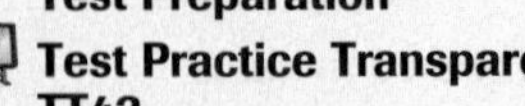

Test Practice Transparencies TT42

Online Test Practice

In the late 700s, a Germanic king, Charlemagne, conquered most of the region. However, his empire began to fall apart soon after his death. Western Europe remained a region of small, competing kingdoms.

THE REFORMATION A religious movement created new differences. During the Renaissance (see Section 1), scholars questioned authority. Some people even began to question the Catholic Church. In 1517, Martin Luther published 95 statements that criticized church practices that he believed were wrong. That began the **Reformation**, a period when many Christians broke away from the Catholic Church and started Protestant churches. Mutual hostility led Catholics and Protestants to fight religious wars that tore Europe apart.

Today, France is mostly Catholic. The Netherlands, Switzerland, and Germany contain both Protestants and Catholics. In Germany, Protestants live mainly in the north and Catholics in the south of the country. A

CONNECT TO THE ISSUES
CONFLICT
A Why might conflict result if neighboring countries adopt different religions?
A. Answer They might see each other as enemies to their own faith and go to war.

5 THEMES
REGION
Diversity of Languages

Nation	Languages Spoken
Austria	German
Belgium	Flemish, French, German
Germany	German
France	French
Liechtenstein	German, Alemannic dialect
Luxembourg	Luxembourgian, German, French
Monaco	French, English, Italian, Monegasque dialect
Netherlands	Dutch
Switzerland	German, French, Italian, Romansch

SOURCE: *The National Geographic Desk Reference, World Book*

The Rise of Nation-States

The period between the fall of Rome and the Renaissance is called the Middle Ages. During this time, Europeans gradually developed the nation-state, an independent nation of people with a common culture.

NATIONALISM During the centuries after Rome fell, **feudalism** gradually developed in Europe. This was a political system in which powerful lords owned most of the land. They gave some land to nobles in exchange for military service by those nobles. Over time, strong kings gained power over feudal lords, and nationalism evolved. **Nationalism** is the belief that people should be loyal to their nation, the people with whom they share land, culture, and history.

Nationalism often causes groups to want their own countries, so it contributed to the rise of modern nation-states. France was one of the

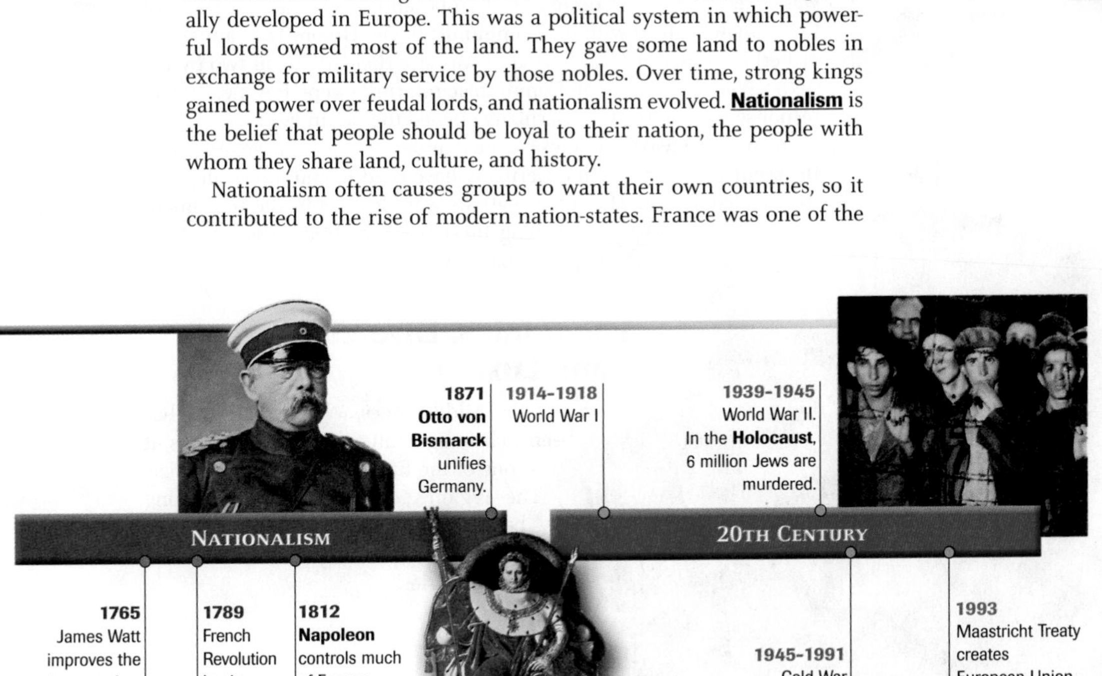
NATIONALISM
1765 James Watt improves the steam engine.
1789 French Revolution begins.
1812 Napoleon controls much of Europe.
1871 Otto von Bismarck unifies Germany.
20TH CENTURY
1914–1918 World War I
1939–1945 World War II. In the Holocaust, 6 million Jews are murdered.
1945–1991 Cold War
1993 Maastricht Treaty creates European Union.

EUROPE

5 THEMES

Region: Diversity of Languages

Have students read the chart and identify the main languages spoken in each country. Point out that Flemish is a variant of Dutch; Alemannic is an ancient Germanic dialect; Luxembourgian is a mixture of German and French. Ask students why Flemish would be spoken in northern Belgium, and why German and French would blend in Luxembourg. *(northern Belgium borders the Netherlands; Luxembourg lies between France and Germany)*

Instruct: Objective 2

The Rise of Nation-States

- What is a nation-state? *(an independent nation of people with a common culture)*
- How did nation-states emerge from feudal societies? *(Strong kings gained power over feudal lords and formed countries.)*
- How was Germany divided and then re-united? *(It split after World War II into Communist and non-Communist nations, then came together again in 1990 after reforms swept Europe.)*

ACTIVITY OPTION **LINK TO HISTORY**

MAKING A TIME LINE

Objective To summarize key historical information

Class Time 30 minutes

Task Make a time line showing key events in the history of a country

Supplies Needed

- Chart paper or large sheets of drawing paper
- Encyclopedias or books on European history

Directions Have students choose a Western European country and conduct research on key events in that country's history. Students should select events they feel are most significant and construct a time line based on those events. Remind them to follow the example of the time line on this page, illustrating it if they wish. Display time lines in class and ask students to compare and contrast them.

Instruct: Objective 3

Economics: Diversity and Luxury

- Why is Western Europe's economy so strong? *(It has both agriculture and industry.)*
- What economic challenge does Germany face? *(fostering growth in the East, which has a lower standard of living and older factories)*

More About

The Geography of the Holocaust

The Holocaust was mainly carried out at concentration camps in German-occupied territory. Some were forced-labor camps, located in areas where natural resources or factories could be harnessed for production. Other camps were primarily death camps for the murder of Jews, Roma (Gypsies), and other groups targeted by the Nazis. These camps were located in Poland, the Baltic states, and the Soviet Union. Prisoners were shipped in by train.

Interpreting Photographs

Castle Reichenstein

For feudal kings and nobles, castles served as homes and, during times of war, as fortresses and bases of military operations.

CAPTION ANSWER Having the hill at the back of the castle prevented having to defend that side, and it was easier to shoot down on attackers climbing a slope.

first nation-states. By the late 1600s, French kings held absolute power, which they often used to benefit themselves, not their people. In 1789, the people began a rebellion—the French Revolution. They deposed the king and formed a republic. But in a few years, an army officer named Napoleon Bonaparte seized power. In 1804, he made himself emperor. Napoleon tried to conquer all of Europe but was defeated.

The nation-states of Europe became strong rivals. From the 1600s to 1945, wars repeatedly broke out between France and Austria or between France and the German states (later Germany). Germany did not unify as a nation until 1871. It was one of many European countries affected by a new wave of nationalism in the 1800s.

Western Europe also experienced industrial growth in the 1800s. Industrialism caused European nations to set up colonies in other lands in order to gain raw materials and markets. Many European nations saw each other as rivals in the race to gain colonies. You will learn more about the effects of colonialism as you read this book. B

B. Answer It would want colonies to provide raw materials; it would sell finished goods to those colonies.

Geographic Thinking

Seeing Patterns B Why might industrialism cause a country to want colonies?

MODERN CONFLICTS The nationalistic rivalry and competition for colonies among European nations helped cause World War I. The Allied Powers (including France) fought the Central Powers (Germany, Austria-Hungary, and their allies). The Allied Powers won and imposed harsh terms on Germany. German resentment over those terms helped cause World War II, in which Germany, led by Adolf Hitler and the Nazis, tried to conquer Europe. The Nazis also carried out the **Holocaust**, a program of mass murder of two-thirds of European Jews and the murder of other minorities. In 1945, the Allies defeated Germany.

BACKGROUND The Nazis were a political party that created a government that controlled all aspects of German life. They held many racist beliefs.

After the war, Germany was split into two nations. West Germany was allied with non-Communist Europe and the United States. East Germany was allied with the Communist Soviet Union. The capital city of Berlin, located in East Germany, was also divided, cut in two by the **Berlin Wall**. In 1989, anti-Communist reforms swept Europe, and in response to protests, East Germany opened the Berlin Wall.

In 1990, the two Germanys reunited under a democratic government. In recent years, France and Germany have tried to end the rivalry that so often led to war. These two nations were leaders in the movement toward establishing the European Union. (See the Case Study on pages 326–329.)

REGION Picturesque old castles, such as the Castle Reichenstein in Germany, were built for defense purposes. Now they are tourist attractions.
Why do you think this castle was built on a hillside?

Economics: Diversity and Luxury

Since the Middle Ages, Western Europe has been rich in agriculture, and in the 1800s, it was one of the first regions to industrialize. The region's economy remains strong because it includes agriculture and manufacturing, plus high-tech and service industries.

298

DIFFERENTIATING INSTRUCTION STUDENTS ACQUIRING ENGLISH/ESL

USING PROPER NOUNS

Objective To help ESL students expand their knowledge of proper nouns

Class Time 30 minutes

Task Create a chart of proper nouns and adjectives

Directions Help ESL students expand their knowledge of proper nouns by creating a chart of European nations and nationalities. Pair proficient English speakers with students acquiring English and have each pair create a two-column chart with the headings "Country" and "Nationality."

COUNTRY	NATIONALITY
Austria	Austrian
Belgium	Belgian
France	French
Germany	German
Italy	Italian
Poland	Polish
Spain	Spanish
Switzerland	Swiss

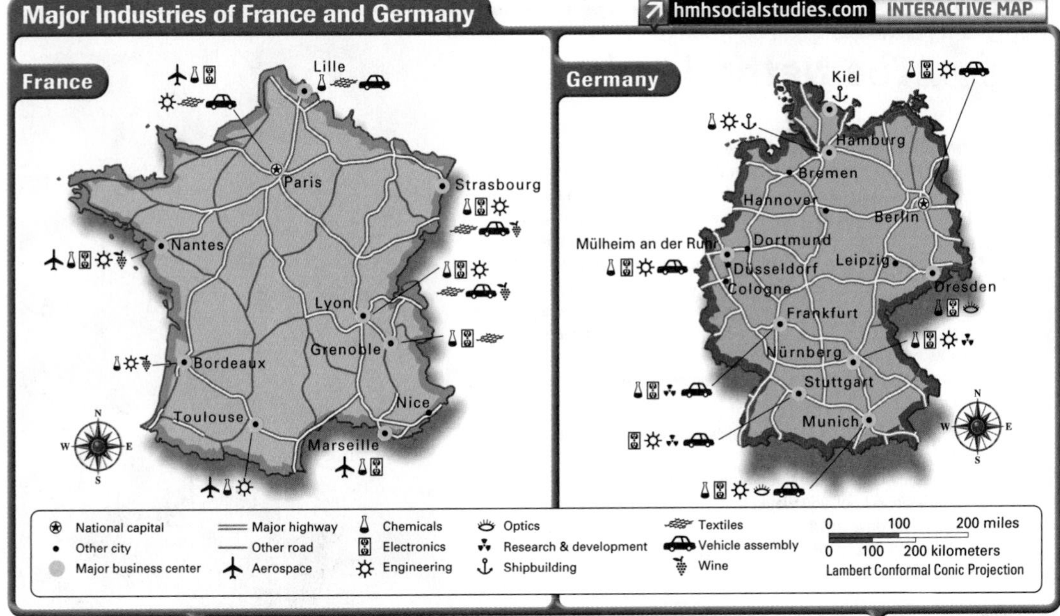

SKILLBUILDER: Interpreting Maps

1. **LOCATION** What is the relative location of business centers? Give possible reasons.
2. **MOVEMENT** Use the Unit Atlas to find the border between France and Germany. Which French and German cities might make good international trading partners?

AGRICULTURE TO HIGH-TECH Dairy farming and livestock provide most of the agricultural income in Belgium, France, the Netherlands, and Switzerland. These countries produce and export dairy products. In addition, France is the largest producer of agricultural products in Western Europe. Its major crops include wheat, grapes, and vegetables.

Western Europe was a leader in developing industry because it was rich in coal and iron ore. Today, the region has three of Europe's top manufacturing nations: France, Germany, and the Netherlands. The maps above show the major industries of France and Germany.

High-tech and service industries are also very important. Electronics is a major product of the Netherlands. Germany also produces electronics, as well as scientific instruments. France has one of the world's fastest passenger trains, the TGV (*train à grande vitesse*, or high-speed train), and a space program. France also relies heavily on nuclear energy. Nuclear plants produce 80 percent of its electricity. C

Switzerland specializes in the service industry of banking. One reason for this is that Switzerland refuses to fight in wars, so people believe that money is safer there.

TOURISM AND LUXURY Because of its varied scenery, mild climate, and historic sites, Western Europe is popular with tourists. Tourism is a major part of the French, Swiss, and Austrian economies.

Western Europe exports luxury goods to the world. For example, some German cars and Swiss watches are considered status symbols.

Geographic Thinking

Making Comparisons

C Which high-tech industry do Germany and the Netherlands have in common?

C. Answer electronics

EUROPE

Interpreting Maps

Major Businesses of France and Germany

Have students examine the maps and map key. Ask them to make a list of businesses that France and Germany have in common, and ones they don't have in common. Also ask where optical goods and textiles are made. *(Both have chemicals, electronics, engineering, and vehicle assembly. France has textiles and wine, while Germany has optics, research and development, and ship building. Optics are found in Dresden and Munich; textiles in Strasbourg, Lyon, Grenoble, Paris, and Lille.)*

SKILLBUILDER ANSWERS

1. They are close to ports and borders; that makes international trade easier. **2.** Frankfurt and Strasbourg; Stuttgart and Strasbourg

ACTIVITY OPTION **LINK TO ECONOMICS**

BLOCK SCHEDULING

EVALUATING EUROPEAN IMPORTS

Objective To assess the impact of European imports on American life

Class Time 20 minutes

Task Make lists of Western European products found in the United States

Directions Ask each student to make a list of European imports, both by category and name, if possible. Then work with students to make a composite list of imports on the board. Have students analyze the list.

Ask: How important do you think these goods are to Americans and to the American economy? How would American life be different if these goods were not available? How do you think this list would compare with a list of American exports to Western Europe? What general conclusions can you draw from this exercise?

growing up in...

The Netherlands

Have students read the description of mud walking and share their opinions about it. Ask if they have ever done anything similar, and what it was like. Then ask them to compare their own lives with the milestones listed for Dutch youth. Ask how their lives are similar and different. *(Some students may wonder why people would want to walk in the mud, while others may say that it sounds like fun.)*

Instruct: Objective 4

Great Music and Art

- Which Western European countries were home to famous composers? *(Germany and Austria)*
- Who were some great European composers? *(Bach, Beethoven, Mozart)*
- Which countries or regions are famed for their painting? *(France, Netherlands, Flanders)*

Cultures Around the World
- Fine Arts, p. 21

Cultures Transparencies CW21
- Pierre Auguste Renoir

growing up in...The Netherlands

These girls are doing *wadlopen,* or mud walking. As many as 25,000 people a year take part in this popular Dutch pastime. When the tide goes out on the Waddenzee (part of the North Sea), it leaves mud flats. Mud walking can be extremely strenuous exercise; at times, the mud can reach up to a person's thighs! The activity can also be risky. If the mud walkers don't leave the flats before the tide returns, they are in danger of being drowned.

Another popular activity for young people in the Netherlands is ice skating. The Netherlands has an extensive network of canals that link its major rivers. During the Middle Ages, the Dutch began to skate on these frozen canals in the winter. The sport of speed skating originated in the Netherlands.

If you grew up in the Netherlands, you would pass these milestones:
- You would go to school from age 5 to age 18.
- In primary school, you would learn to swim, usually by age 9.
- You could drive at 18.
- You could vote at 18.
- You could marry at 18.

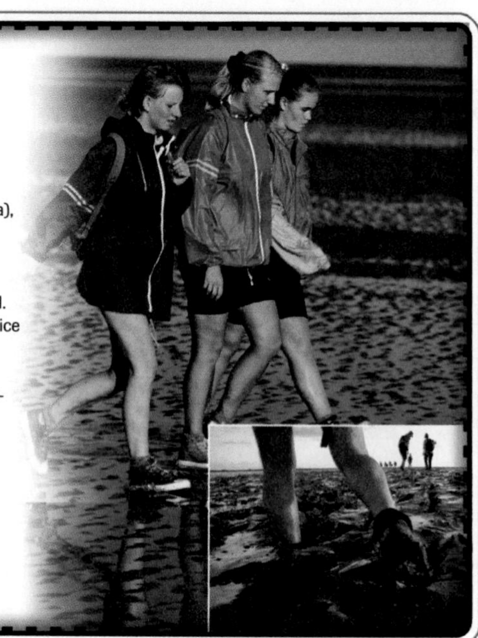

France is famous for its high-fashion clothing and gourmet foods. The Netherlands exports high-quality flower bulbs, such as colorful tulips.

ECONOMIC PROBLEMS One nation in the region, Germany, has had economic struggles. When Germany reunified, it faced difficulties because the West had a much higher standard of living. East Germany's factories were outdated, and many shut down. Germany has been working to foster growth in the former East Germany—for example, by spending billions of dollars on infrastructure. Yet, in 2005, the number of jobless workers remained twice as high in the East as in the West.

Great Music and Art

Each Western European country has a distinct identity, shaped in part by language and religion. Even with these differences, one thing is true of the region as a whole—it has a strong artistic legacy.

MUSIC Germany and Austria are famous for music. Johann Sebastian Bach, who wrote music for church services, was German. So was Ludwig van Beethoven, who composed symphonies and other works. He wrote music even after going deaf. Austrian composers include Wolfgang Amadeus Mozart, who was a child genius.

PAINTING France and the Netherlands have had many important painters. Jan Van Eyck was a painter from Flanders (a region now divided among France, the Netherlands, and Belgium) who perfected techniques for using oil paints. Jan Vermeer and Rembrandt were Dutch artists who painted with great realism. Major French painters include the impressionist Claude Monet and postimpressionists Paul Cézanne and Paul Gauguin, who paved the way for modern art.

BACKGROUND Many landscape paintings of the Netherlands show its flat, low terrain. The sea is also a frequent subject.

ACTIVITY OPTION **SKILLBUILDER LESSON**

CREATING MULTIMEDIA PRESENTATIONS

Explaining the Skill Tell students that multimedia productions combine various media–including text, images, and sound–in a slide-show or documentary-style format. Using presentation software, students can copy images and sound on a computer and combine these elements with their own text to produce effective presentations on a topic.

Applying the Skill Have pairs of students work together to prepare a 10-minute multimedia presentation on an aspect of Western European music or art. Students should choose a specific topic, such as a particular composer, artist, or style. Tell students to research their topic in print resources and on the Web. They should gather information for the text portion of their presentation and copy images and sound onto the computer. They can then use the presentation software to arrange the components, and write text to accompany the visuals and sound. Have them give their presentations in class.

For additional Skillbuilder practice, see p. 310, Section 4.

Modern Life

Because of their strong economies, Western Europeans enjoy a high standard of living and generally can afford to buy material goods such as cars and computers. Most Western Europeans live in cities.

CITY LIFE In general, Western European cities are interesting and pleasant places to live. Most have good public transportation systems. They offer many cultural attractions: movies, concerts, art galleries, and museums. Crime rates are lower than in the United States.

As a rule, Europeans live in smaller homes than Americans do. Because of this, they often socialize in public places. Friends might meet in cafes, sitting at outdoor tables if the weather is nice. Also, most cities have many lovely parks that their citizens regularly enjoy. D

One difference between Western Europe and the United States is that Europeans receive more paid vacation time. For example, Germans have about 30 vacation days a year. Vacationing Europeans often leave the city to engage in outdoor activities like biking, hiking, or skiing.

RECENT CONFLICTS In recent decades, immigration has been a source of conflict here. In the 1980s, increasing numbers of "guest workers" from Yugoslavia and Turkey came to West Germany for jobs. When the German economy declined, some angry Germans committed discrimination and even violence against immigrants. In response, millions of other Germans protested racism.

Austria has also faced tensions. Political leader Joerg Haider made controversial remarks that defended former Nazis and that immigrants found insulting. Many feared a rebirth of racist politics, so in 2000 Haider had to resign as party head—yet he remained a force in Austrian public life.

In Section 3, you will read about Northern Europe, a region that includes the Nordic countries, the United Kingdom, and Ireland.

Geographic Thinking

Using the Atlas

D Refer to the climate map on page 266. What role does climate play in Western Europeans' enjoyment of the outdoors?

D. Answer Western Europe has a generally mild climate, which allows people to spend more time outdoors.

SECTION 2 Assessment

1 Places & Terms

Identify these terms and explain their importance in the region's history or culture.

- Benelux
- Reformation
- feudalism
- nationalism
- Holocaust
- Berlin Wall

2 Taking Notes

REGION Review the notes you took for this section.

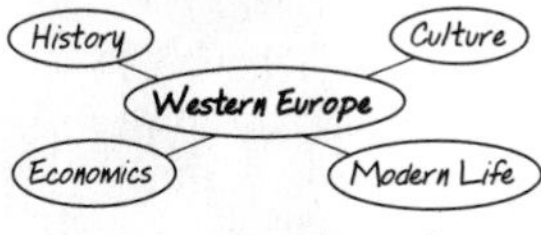

- What are major aspects of Western Europe's artistic legacy?
- What are some characteristics of modern life in Western Europe?

3 Main Ideas

a. How do language and religion reflect the cultural division in Western Europe?

b. Which Western European leaders tried to unify Europe through conquest?

c. In what way does Western Europe have a diverse economy?

4 Geographic Thinking

Making Generalizations
How does the economic strength of a nation affect its willingness to welcome immigrants? **Think about:**

- whether immigrants are more welcome when jobs are scarce or plentiful
- the experience of Germany since the 1980s

MAKING COMPARISONS Study the two maps on page 299. Create a **Venn Diagram** showing the businesses that France and Germany have in common and those that each have separately.

Instruct: Objective 5

Modern Life

- What is the standard of living in Western Europe? *(generally high)*
- What are the cities like? *(They are pleasant, interesting places, with good transportation and cultural attractions.)*
- How has immigration produced conflict in Western Europe? *(Immigrants have been subject to racism and violence.)*

Critical Thinking Transparency CT45
- Cities of the United States, Canada, and Europe

Assess & Reteach

GeoFocus Have students complete their notes on Western Europe in their cluster diagrams.

Formal Assessment
- Section Quiz, p. 196

Reteaching Activity
Have pairs of students review the section by looking back at the subsection headings. One student should turn the first heading into a question and the other should answer it. Students can alternate roles as they move through the section.

In-Depth Resources: Unit 4
- Reteaching Activity, p. 20

Outline Maps with Activities
- Western Europe, pp. 35–36

SECTION 2 ASSESSMENT ANSWERS

1. Places & Terms

Benelux, p. 296
Reformation, p. 297
feudalism, p. 297
nationalism, p. 297
Holocaust, p. 298
Berlin Wall, p. 298

2. Taking Notes

- Music and painting are major aspects of Western Europe's artistic legacy
- urban living, socializing outdoors, and conflict between some groups

3. Main Ideas

a. French is a Romance language, while German is a Germanic language; France is mainly Roman Catholic, while Germany is split between Catholics and Protestants.

b. Charlemagne, Napoleon, and Hitler all tried to conquer Europe.

c. While Western Europe still maintains some agriculture, it is also strong in manufacturing, service, and high-tech industries.

4. Geographic Thinking

Answers will vary, but most students will say that immigrants are more welcome when a nation's economy is strong and there are more jobs than workers.

GeoActivity

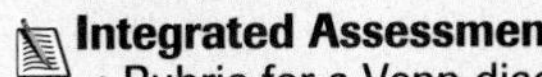
Integrated Assessment
- Rubric for a Venn diagram, 2.8

leading to the modern age.
3. Identify the major trends in Northern Europe's economy.
4. Examine modern Northern European culture.
5. Learn about life in Northern Europe.

SKILLBUILDER: Interpreting Maps, p. 304

GeographicThinking
Seeing Patterns, pp. 303, 305
Using the Atlas, p. 306
Determining Cause and Effect, p. 307

Focus & Motivate

Ask students which Northern European countries are closely tied geographically and historically. *(Nordic countries and countries of the British Isles)*

Instruct: Objective 1

A History of Seafaring Conquerors

- What are some of the groups that invaded Northern Europe? *(Celts, Romans, Germanic tribes, Vikings)*
- What cultural impact did the British Empire have in many parts of the world? *(It resulted in the spreading of the English language and culture.)*

developing representative government and industry.

Places & Terms
Nordic countries
Silicon Glen
parliament
euro

CONNECT TO THE ISSUES
UNIFICATION Some nations in Northern Europe have held back from full participation in the European Union.

A HUMAN PERSPECTIVE In World War II, Germany perfected a new military tactic, the blitzkrieg. Using a massive force of dive-bombers, tanks, and artillery, the German army rapidly surprised, attacked, and defeated a foe before it could mount a defense. Germany used blitzkriegs to invade Poland, Belgium, the Netherlands, and France. But Germany couldn't launch a swift land attack against the United Kingdom on the island of Great Britain. Germany tried to destroy Britain by first bombing it from the air, but such a campaign took time, so Britain was able to fight back. In time, Britain and its allies won the war. Throughout its history, Britain's status as an island has been a geographic advantage.

A History of Seafaring Conquerors

Today, Northern Europe consists of the United Kingdom, Ireland, and the Nordic countries. The **Nordic countries** are Denmark, Finland, Iceland, Norway, and Sweden. The history of this region has been a history of using the sea and of conquest.

EARLY CONQUERORS In ancient times, waves of migrating people settled Northern Europe. Each new group tended to push the previous residents out of its way. As a result, the earlier groups ended up living at the tips or along the coasts of Northern Europe's peninsulas and islands. For example, the Sami, descendants of one of the earliest migrating groups, now live in far northern Scandinavia and Finland.

Ancient Britain was invaded by many peoples, including the Celts. Rome conquered southern Britain by about A.D. 80. In the 400s, Germanic tribes invaded, driving out the Romans and pushing the Celts north and west.

Beginning about 795, a group of seafaring warriors from Denmark, Norway, and Sweden terrorized Europe. These Norsemen, or Vikings, sailed in long ships to coastal towns and conducted hit-and-run raids. They conquered parts of Britain and sailed to Iceland, Greenland, and even North America. They also had a settlement in Normandy (a part of France named for the Norsemen) and moved into Russia.

In 1066, William the Conqueror of Normandy conquered England (the largest kingdom in Britain) and began to rule it. The Normans spoke French, and over time the English language acquired many words of French origin.

MOVEMENT This helmet is from Sutton Hoo, an Anglo-Saxon burial site in England. The Anglo-Saxons began invading England in the 400s.

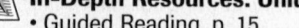

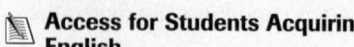

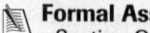

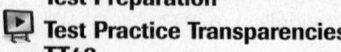

SECTION 3 PROGRAM RESOURCES

In-Depth Resources: Unit 4
- Guided Reading, p. 15
- Building Vocabulary, p. 18
- Reteaching Activity, p. 21

Guided Reading Workbook
- Section 3

Access for Students Acquiring English
- Guided Reading, p. 68

Outline Maps with Activities
- Northern Europe, pp. 37–38

Formal Assessment
- Section Quiz, p. 197

Integrated Assessment
- Rubric for a chart, 2.2

Cultures Around the World
- Daily Life, p. 20
- Music, p. 22

INTEGRATED TECHNOLOGY

Cultures Transparencies CW20, 22
- Cross-Country Skiing
- Playing Bagpipes

The World's Music Audio Program

TEST-TAKING RESOURCES

Strategies for Test Preparation

Test Practice Transparencies TT43

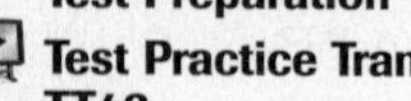

Online Test Practice

DREAMS OF EMPIRE Denmark, Sweden, and Norway each became a kingdom during the 900s. Sweden was a strong power in the 1600s, but no Nordic country ever became a major empire.

In contrast, Great Britain built an empire that strongly affected the rest of the world. First, the English set out to control the British Isles. Over time, England won control of its neighbors, Wales, Ireland, and Scotland. In 1801, the nation became known as the United Kingdom of Great Britain and Ireland.

Britain drew on its geographic advantages to grow in strength. As you read earlier, Britain's status as an island helped protect it. After 1066, no outside power ever successfully invaded Britain. In addition, the British people had much experience as sailors. This helped them to build a strong navy and to develop overseas trade.

Drawing on its economic and naval strength, Great Britain built a global empire. By the 1800s, it had colonies in the Americas, Asia, Africa, and Oceania. A popular saying declared, "The sun never sets on the British Empire." One consequence of the empire is that the English language and British culture spread worldwide. A

A. Answer A navy can be used both for transport and for battles.

Geographic Thinking

Seeing Patterns
A Why would a strong navy be helpful in building an empire?

Moving into the Modern Age

Great Britain played a role in shaping our modern world in two ways. It helped to develop representative government. Also, the industrial revolution started in Britain and spread to other countries.

REPRESENTATIVE GOVERNMENT Britain's government is a monarchy that also has a parliament. A **parliament** is a representative lawmaking body whose members are elected or appointed. (In some cases, they inherit the position.) Over the centuries, English rulers lost power to the English Parliament, so a more representative government evolved. For example, in 1215 nobles forced the king to sign the Magna Carta. That

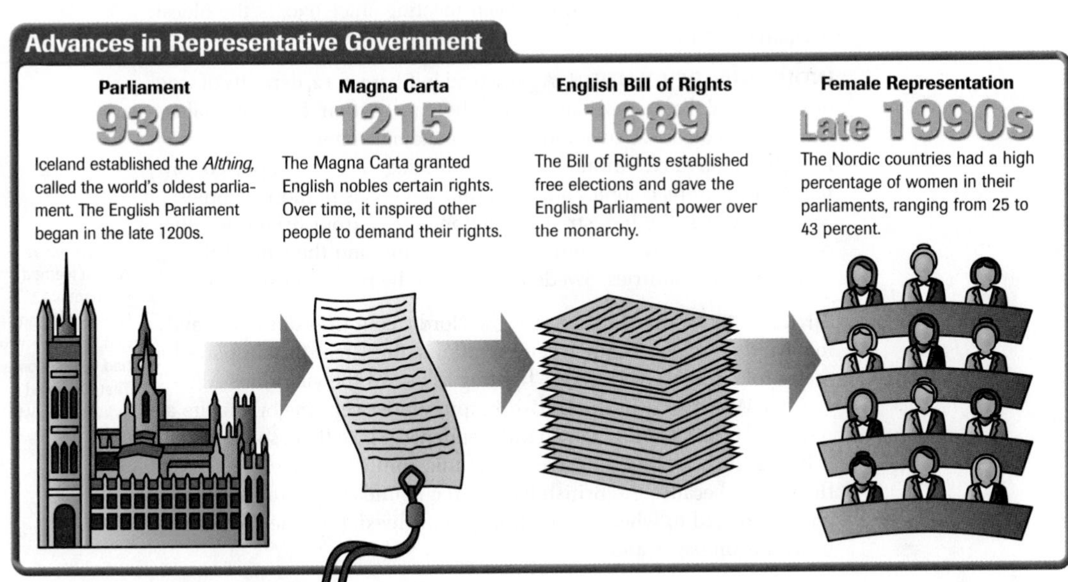

Advances in Representative Government
Parliament
930
Iceland established the *Althing,* called the world's oldest parliament. The English Parliament began in the late 1200s.
Magna Carta
1215
The Magna Carta granted English nobles certain rights. Over time, it inspired other people to demand their rights.
English Bill of Rights
1689
The Bill of Rights established free elections and gave the English Parliament power over the monarchy.
Female Representation
Late 1990s
The Nordic countries had a high percentage of women in their parliaments, ranging from 25 to 43 percent.

Instruct: Objective 2

Moving into the Modern Age

- How have Northern European countries advanced representative government? *(England's Magna Carta inspired ideas such as trial by jury and no taxation without representation; Iceland's parliament, dating from 930, demonstrates the viability of this type of government.)*
- How did the Industrial Revolution motivate Britain to build an empire? *(Britain's colonies were a source of raw materials and also markets for finished products.)*
- How did the English cause long-standing and continuing unrest in Ireland? *(by seizing Catholic lands and giving them to Scottish and English Protestants, leaving the Catholic minority in the North, in particular, in poverty)*

In-Depth Resources: Unit 4
- Guided Reading, p. 15

More About

Magna Carta

The Magna Carta, or "Great Charter," was drawn up by English noblemen and members of the clergy in an effort to curb the excessive greed and tyranny of King John of England. Abandoned by most of his supporters, John had no choice but to affix his seal to the document. The charter, which has 63 sections, sets forth the liberties to which English people are entitled. It has been a source of inspiration for constitutions in many other countries.

ACTIVITY OPTION | **CRITICAL THINKING**

MAKING COMPARISONS

Explaining the Skill Making comparisons means looking at the similarities and differences between two or more things. By comparing Northern European advances in representative government to representative government in the United States, students will come to appreciate the influence of Northern Europe.

Applying the Skill Direct students' attention to the chart on page 303. Ask the following question for each of the first three items: What governing body (or document) in the United States is similar? *(Parliament: Congress; Magna Carta: Declaration of Independence; English Bill of Rights: U.S. Bill of Rights)* Lead students to conclude that Northern Europe had a significant influence on the development of representative government in the United States.

Interpreting Maps

British Empire, 1900

Tell students that the British Empire began in 1497, when John Cabot sailed to North America and claimed it for England. The first permanent English settlement in North America was established in 1607 in Jamestown, Virginia. In the 18th century, prior to the American Revolution, land in North America accounted for nine-tenths of the British Empire. Ask students approximately how much of North America belonged to the British Empire in 1900. *(less than half)* Have students determine approximately what percentage of countries in the empire had at least one ocean border. *(almost all)* Ask what this suggests about how the empire developed. *(It was claimed or conquered by English seafarers.)*

SKILLBUILDER ANSWERS

1. British colonies were spread around the globe, so it was always daytime somewhere in the Empire.
2. The government wanted to control shipping and travel lanes among its colonies as well as between its colonies and Britain itself.

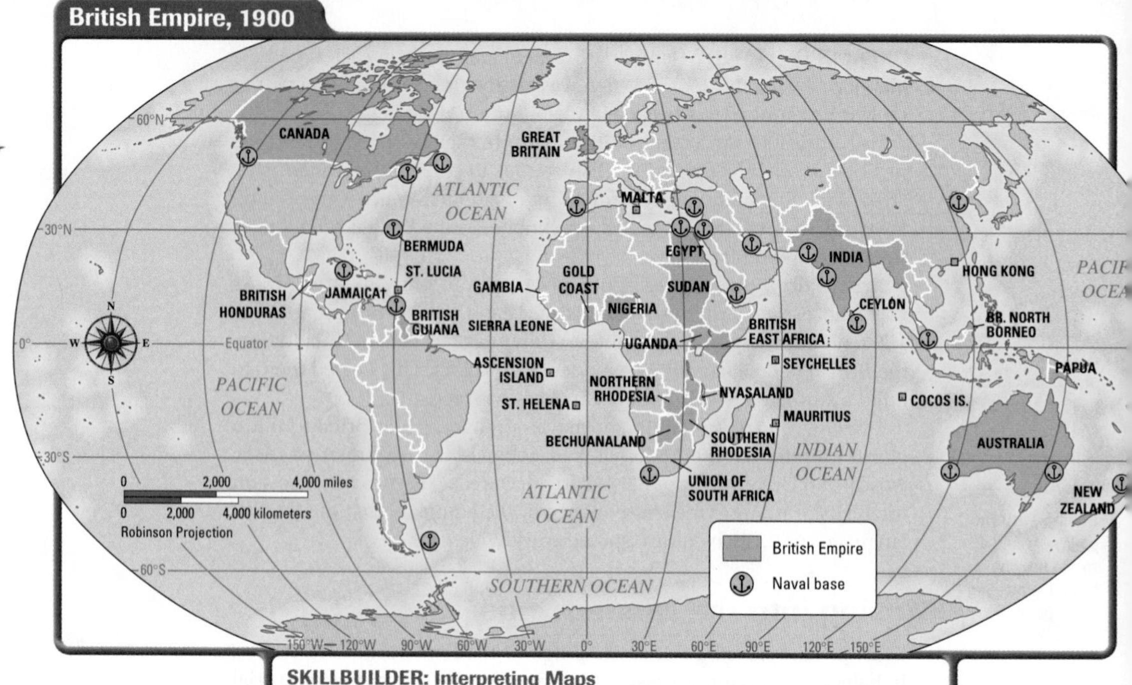

SKILLBUILDER: Interpreting Maps

❶ **REGION** Why were people able to say, "The sun never sets on the British Empire"?
❷ **LOCATION** Why do you think Britain built naval bases where it did?

document inspired such political ideas as trial by jury and no taxation without representation. Those ideas later spread to the United States, Canada, and various British colonies.

The Nordic countries also developed representative government. Iceland's parliament, which has been meeting since 930, is the oldest parliament in the world.

INDUSTRIAL REVOLUTION As you read in Chapter 12, deposits of iron ore and coal helped Britain to be the first nation to industrialize. Industry used coal as fuel and iron to make machinery. The growth of industry motivated Britain's empire building. Britain imported raw materials from its colonies and sold finished goods to those colonies.

In the 1800s, the industrial revolution spread from Britain to other countries, especially Belgium, France, Germany, and the United States. Of the Nordic countries, Sweden developed the most industry.

BACKGROUND
As you learned in Chapter 12, France, Belgium, and Germany also had coal deposits. That promoted industrial growth.

SINCE 1900 In the 20th century, the Nordic countries did not heavily involve themselves in other nations' affairs. But Great Britain played a major role in both world wars, fighting as one of the victorious Allies.

After World War II, the British Empire underwent major change as nearly all of its colonies gained independence. Since then, some former colonies, such as Nigeria, have had ethnic conflicts. Many of the conflicts arose because the British had set the boundaries of their colonies without regard to where rival ethnic groups lived. (See the Case Study in Unit 6, on pages 468–471.)

DIFFERENTIATING INSTRUCTION LESS PROFICIENT READERS

PREVIEWING KEY FACTS

Objective To preview the most important elements in the text

Class Time 20 minutes

Task List key facts in notebooks

Directions Previewing important points helps less proficient readers become more focused as they read. To help students better understand the development of the British Empire, write on the chalkboard the items that follow and have students read each aloud. Then tell students to copy the items in their notebooks and, as they read the section, to write down the importance of each to the development of the British Empire.

- Wales, Ireland, Scotland *(first countries controlled by England)*
- Britain is an island *(easier to defend)*
- strong navy *(enabled Britain to acquire colonies through conquest)*
- demand for raw materials and markets *(led to empire building)*
- the Americas, Asia, Africa, Oceania *(British colonies in each)*

THE IRISH QUESTION The British still face a problem that has roots in the past. Protestant English rulers strengthened their hold on Catholic Ireland by seizing Irish land and giving it to Scottish and English Protestants. That left many Irish in poverty. In the 1840s, potato crops failed and caused famine. Over a million Irish fled to other lands.

Many Irish called for independence, and in 1921, Britain divided Ireland into two states. The Republic of Ireland gained independence in 1921. Northern Ireland, which had a Protestant majority, remained part of the United Kingdom. Since then, religious conflict and anti-British violence have plagued Northern Ireland. B

Geographic Thinking

Seeing Patterns

B How have politics, economics, and religion all contributed to the conflict in Northern Ireland?

B. Answer British rule of Ireland, British control of Irish land, and distrust between Catholics and Protestants have all helped fuel the conflict.

Economics: Diversity and Change

Today, Northern Europe has a highly developed and varied economy. Manufacturing and traditional economic activities such as fishing and forestry remain important. As is true in all developed countries, the service and information economies are growing.

INDUSTRY AND RESOURCES Sweden and the United Kingdom have many types of manufacturing in common. For example, both nations have strong motor vehicle and aerospace industries. Both also produce paper products, food products, and pharmaceuticals.

Northern Europe's economy benefits from its many natural resources. Sweden exports timber. Iceland relies heavily on its fishing industry, and Norway earns a large portion of its income from North Sea oil.

HIGH-TECH Technology is swiftly changing the economy of Northern Europe. For example, the production of computer software and hardware has been a major part of Ireland's economy since the 1970s. In the 1990s, the section of Scotland between Glasgow and Edinburgh became known as **Silicon Glen**, because it had so many high-tech companies, which use silicon computer chips. However, from 2000 to 2006, many of those companies moved their plants to Eastern Europe to lower costs. Scotland's economy now depends on service industries.

BACKGROUND
The word *glen* is from the Scottish term for valley.

UNION OR INDEPENDENCE? Most nations of this region joined the European Union (EU), but Norway has chosen not to do so. Even in nations belonging to the European Union, people have mixed feelings about the EU policy that they should adopt a common currency called the **euro.** In September 2000, Denmark voted against adopting the euro. Economics professor Jesper Jespersen agreed with that decision. He said, "I believe Denmark should retain its own currency . . . [because] our economy is in many ways independent of the eurozone [the region using the euro]." (See the Case Study on pages 326–329 for more about the EU.)

Connect to the Issues

UNIFICATION

Norway Rejects the EU

In 1994, Norwegians voted 52 percent to 48 percent against joining the European Union. Norway did not become a separate nation until 1905, so many Norwegians feared losing their independence and national identity.

Another reason for the vote against joining is that the economy was booming. This prosperity was due to Norway's status as the world's second-largest exporter of crude oil. Some Norwegians feared that Norway would lose control over its valuable oil resources if it joined the EU.

Instruct: Objective 3

Economics: Diversity and Change

- What role do natural resources play in Europe's economy? *(Sweden exports timber; fishing is a major industry in Iceland; oil is a major source of income in Norway)*
- Where is Silicon Glen and why is it important economically? *(Scotland; its many high-tech companies produce personal computers and computer notebooks)*
- Name a Northern European country that has chosen not to join the European Union. *(Norway)*

Connect TO THE Issues

Unification:
Norway Rejects the EU

Norway and Iceland are the only two Nordic countries that were not members of the European Union as of the year 2007. Switzerland and several of the Balkan countries are not members either. Pros and cons of EU membership are explored further in the Unit's Case Study. Ask students:

- Do you think that Norwegians made the right choice when they voted not to join the EU? Explain. *(Some may say that potential loss of independence and control of resources were too much to risk; others may think that the EU will become one of the dominant economic forces in the world, in which case Norway may lose out.)*

DIFFERENTIATING INSTRUCTION **GIFTED AND TALENTED STUDENTS**

PREPARING A RESEARCH REPORT

Objective To study Britain's role in India

Class Time 30 minutes

Task Write a report on British rule in India

Directions Have students work in small groups to research and prepare a report on British rule in India. Their reports should explain how Britain became established in India, the impact of British rule in India, and events leading to independence. Ask students to draw conclusions as to whether Britain's impact was positive or negative and to give reasons for their opinions.

Instruct: Objective 

Cultural Similarities and Modern Art

- How did the Reformation affect religion in Northern Europe? *(Protestantism became firmly established.)*
- In what ways have Great Britain and Ireland influenced world literature? *(Shakespeare's plays are still performed; Wordsworth popularized everyday speech in poetry; James Joyce explored new techniques for expressing human thought.)*

 **Cultures Around the World**
- Daily Life, p. 20
- Music, p. 22

Cultures Transparencies CW20, 22
- Cross-Country Skiing
- Playing Bagpipes

More About

Ibsen

Henrik Ibsen was born in 1828 in Norway. Although he began to write while still in his teens, his first successful play, *Brand,* was not performed until 1885. Ibsen's plays, which are largely realistic and strongly plotted, often deal with social issues. In *A Doll's House,* for example, a woman decides to leave the comfort of her home and marriage for a life of her own. Other plays by Ibsen include *Hedda Gabler* and *Peer Gynt.*

CAPTION ANSWER Jobs and cultural attractions might be some of the reasons that people move to London.

Instruct: Objective 5 appears on p. 307.

Cultural Similarities and Modern Art

Throughout most of history, Northern Europe has not been culturally diverse. Even today, the Nordic nations have populations that consist mostly of one ethnic group. In recent years, however, the United Kingdom, particularly its capital London, has grown more diverse. That is partially due to immigration from former colonies, such as India. By the year 2005, more than 1.8 million of London's 7.2 million residents belonged to an ethnic minority.

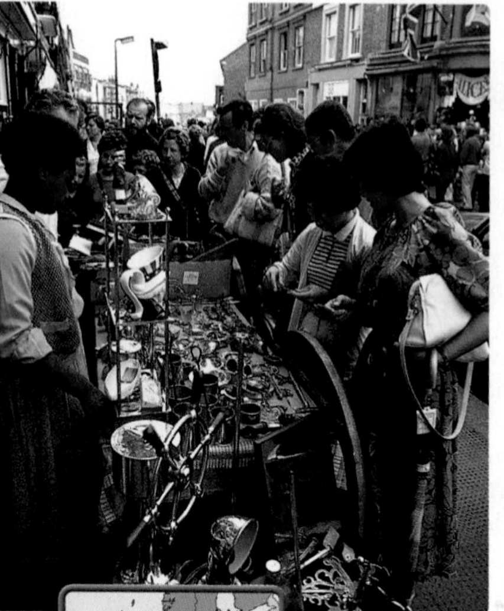

MOVEMENT Portobello Road in London has antique shops and stalls. As shown here, immigration has given London a diverse population. **What might draw people to a city like London?**

SIMILAR LANGUAGES AND RELIGIONS The language map on page 267 shows the effect of historic migrations into this region. Most people of Northern Europe speak a Germanic language. When Germanic tribes migrated to the Scandinavian Peninsula and the British Isles, they pushed the previous inhabitants north and west. Today, the Sami language is spoken in the far north. Celtic languages such as Welsh, Irish Gaelic, and Scottish Gaelic survive on the northern and western edges of the British Isles.

C. Answer Swedish, Norwegian, Danish, Icelandic, Faeroese, and English

Geographic Thinking

Using the Atlas Refer to the language map on page 267. Which Germanic languages are spoken in Northern Europe?

The Reformation, which began in nearby Germany in the 1500s, swept through Northern Europe. Several different Protestant churches took root there. Most of the region is still Protestant. Only Ireland kept Catholicism as its main faith.

MODERN CULTURE AND LITERATURE The Nordic countries have influenced many modern cultures. The Norwegian playwright Henrik Ibsen is sometimes called the father of modern drama. Ingmar Bergman, a Swedish director, influenced movies with his intensely personal films. Both men raised psychological issues in their work that remain important in modern life.

Great Britain and Ireland have had their strongest artistic influence on world literature. Many people consider William Shakespeare the greatest playwright of all time. Nearly 400 years after his death, his works are still performed on stage and also adapted for movies. The English poet William Wordsworth popularized the use of everyday speech in poetry. English novelists of the 1800s, such as Charlotte Brontë, influenced later novels. The Irish novelist James Joyce shaped modern fiction by exploring techniques to portray human thought.

Life in Northern Europe

In Northern Europe, most people live in cities and have a high standard of living. One aspect that distinguishes Northern Europe from most other regions is that its women have made great strides toward political equality. In the late 1990s, women made up 25 percent of the parliament in Iceland, 36 percent in Norway, 37 percent in Finland and Denmark, and 43 percent in Sweden.

SOCIAL WELFARE Overall, the governments of Northern Europe take great responsibility for the welfare of their people. This is especially true

ACTIVITY OPTION **LINK TO LITERATURE** **BLOCK SCHEDULING**

PRESENTING WORKS FROM NORTHERN EUROPE

Objective To introduce students to works by well-known Northern European authors

Class Time 90 minutes

Task Choose and present a reading or dramatization from a work by a Northern European writer

Directions Ask students to name the writers mentioned in "Cultural Similarities and Modern Art," along with their respective genres as you list them on the chalkboard. Ask for additional names of Northern European writers with whom students may be familiar. Divide the class into small groups and have them choose an author. Each group should then select a poem or a passage to present to the class. Students should be prepared to explain the importance of the work selected and give the context of the selected passage. Tell groups to divide their selection so that each may read a portion and to practice reading their selections out loud before reading them to the class.

of the Nordic countries, which provide many welfare services for their citizens. For example, Finland, Norway, and Sweden give families a yearly allowance to help raise their children. The Nordic governments help fund national health insurance programs. Britain also has a national health insurance program. To pay for the programs, the people in those countries have very high taxes.

DISTINCTIVE CUSTOMS Some social customs of Northern Europe have gained worldwide fame. For example, the British are known for afternoon tea, a small meal of sandwiches, breads, cakes, and tea. Swedes developed the smorgasbord. It is a large assortment of hot and cold dishes served buffet style. Finns are famous for their sauna, in which people sit in a hot room to work up a sweat that cleans the skin's pores. Afterward, they plunge into a cold bath or icy lake.

BACKGROUND
Because of Sweden's closeness to the sea, smorgasbords feature a variety of seafood such as salmon and herring.

LEISURE Even though the Nordic countries have some of the coldest climates in Europe, outdoor sports remain popular there. Some of the sports in the winter Olympics developed in Norway and the other Nordic countries. They include cross-country skiing and ski jumping.

Many British enjoy horseback riding, horse jumping, and fox hunting. These traditionally were pastimes for the wealthy upper classes on their large country estates. In addition, the British developed two sports that are unique. Rugby is a form of football, and cricket is played with a ball, a bat, and wickets. Spread by British colonialism, cricket is played around the world.

In Section 4, you will read about Eastern Europe, a region that continues to be torn apart by ethnic conflicts.

MOVEMENT

Tea Time

Nothing seems more English than tea, but it is really an import from Asia. Dutch traders introduced tea to Europe, and it was sold for the first time in England in 1657. Tea soon became Britain's national beverage.

Perhaps one reason for its popularity is that clean water was scarce; boiling water for tea purified it. Tea also had caffeine, giving tea drinkers energy during the long stretch between the midday meal and supper. The custom of taking food with afternoon tea began in the 1800s.

Section 3 Assessment

1 Places & Terms

Identify these terms and explain their importance in the region's history, culture, or economy.
- Nordic countries
- parliament
- Silicon Glen
- euro

2 Taking Notes

REGION Review the notes you took for this section.

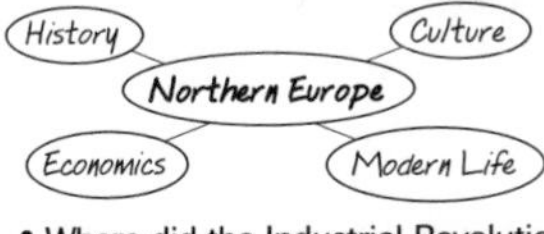

- Where did the Industrial Revolution begin and to where did it spread?
- What are some characteristics of governments in Northern Europe?

3 Main Ideas

a. How did conquest influence the languages spoken in Northern Europe?
b. How did the Industrial Revolution spur the growth of Britain's empire?
c. How did the Reformation affect Northern Europe?

4 Geographic Thinking

Determining Cause and Effect Why is there conflict in Northern Ireland? **Think about:**
- the history of Britain's relationship with Ireland
- religious differences
- arguments for and against a union of the Republic of Ireland and Northern Ireland

GeoActivity

SEEING PATTERNS Compare the map on page 304 with the world map on pages A4 and A5 to learn the present names of former British colonies. Then do research to learn which former colonies still use English as an official language. Present this information on a **chart.**

Instruct: Objective 

Life in Northern Europe

- What gains have women in Nordic countries made toward political equality in the 1990s? *(They made up 25 percent or greater of the parliaments of Iceland, Norway, Finland, Denmark, and Sweden.)*
- What welfare services do the countries of Northern Europe fund? *(subsidized child care, national health care, and national health insurance)*

5 THEMES

Movement: Tea Time

Tell students that tea cultivation is an example of diffusion. First used in China thousands of years ago, tea was transported to Japan around A.D. 800. After tea was introduced to Europeans, growers shipped seeds and plants to several Asian colonies. Today tea is grown for worldwide export and local consumption in Asia, Africa, South America, and Australia.

Assess & Reteach

GeoFocus Have students complete the section on Northern Europe in their cluster diagrams.

 **Formal Assessment**
- Section Quiz, p. 197

Reteaching Activity
Have students prepare an outline of the section. Then have them take turns challenging each other to explain the importance of a main point.

 **In-Depth Resources: Unit 4**
- Reteaching Activity, p. 21

 **Outline Maps with Activities**
- Northern Europe, pp. 37–38

SECTION 3 ASSESSMENT ANSWERS

1. Places & Terms
Nordic countries, p. 302
parliament, p. 303
Silicon Glen, p. 305
euro, p. 305

2. Taking Notes
- It began in Britain and spread to Belgium, France, Germany, and the United States.
- They are representative, have many women participating, and take great responsibility for the social welfare of their citizens.

3. Main Ideas
a. The conquering Germanic tribes pushed out the speakers of other languages; the conquering Normans spoke French, and many French words became part of the English language.
b. Britain wanted colonial markets and raw materials.
c. With the exception of Ireland, all of the countries are mostly Protestant.

4. Geographic Thinking
Students may say that the Irish hate British rule because it caused past suffering and Catholics dislike Protestants because they took Catholics' land. Catholics may want the two countries united, while the Protestants of Northern Ireland would not want to become a minority.

GeoActivity

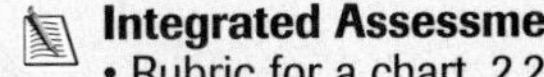 **Integrated Assessment**
- Rubric for a chart, 2.2

OBJECTIVE

Identify and explore geographically inspired sports.

Instruct: Objective

Geographic Sports Challenges

- What sports grew out of the need to overcome challenging land forms and climate? *(mountain climbing and skiing)*
- What is one theory that explains the origin of surfing? *(Polynesian sailors may have surfed to reach land from outlying canoes.)*
- How does the Iditarod reflect the culture and climate of Alaska? *(The Inuits first used dog sledding as a means of transportation. The Iditarod commemorates a 1925 emergency mission by dog sled.)*

Cultures Transparencies CW20
- Cross-Country Skiing

Interpreting Photographs

Geographic Sports Challenges

What do the sports in each of the photographs have in common? *(They require an individual to challenge himself or herself against an element of the natural environment.)*

hmhsocialstudies.com INTERACTIVE

Comparing Cultures

Geographic Sports Challenges

Over time, humans have found ways to enjoy even the most forbidding climates and terrains. Some popular sports evolved from activities that people used to overcome geographic challenges, such as mountains or snowy climates. Other sports were created to take advantage of special geographic features, such as recurring winds or waves. On these two pages, you will learn about geographically inspired sports from around the world.

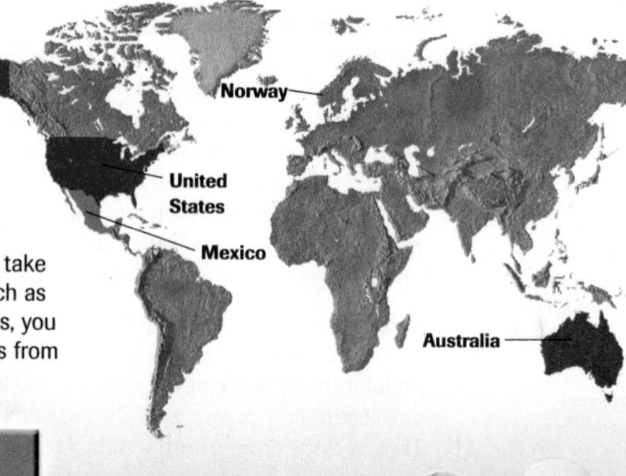

Surfing, shown here off the coast of Australia, dates back to prehistoric times. It may have originated when Polynesian sailors of the Pacific Islands needed to reach land from large canoes floating offshore.

Skiing originated as a means of travel in northern Europe, and ski jumping probably evolved in hilly Norway. In 1924, ski jumping became an Olympic sport. Competitors are judged not only on how far they jump but also on the technique they use.

SUPPORTING RESOURCES

BOOKS FOR THE TEACHER

Weihenmayer, Erik. ***Touch the Top of the World.*** NY: Dutton, 2001. Blind as the result of a degenerative eye disorder, the author describes his struggle to succeed as a world-class mountain climber.

BOOKS FOR THE STUDENT

Paulsen, Gary. ***Woodsong.*** NY: Bradbury Press, 1990. A memoir of the author's first run in the Iditarod.

Knox-Johnston, Robin. ***A World of My Own.*** NY: W. W. Norton, 1994 (reprint edition). Recounts the author's adventure as the first person to sail around the world alone.

VIDEOS

Hang Gliding Extreme. Dir. Paul Hamilton. Flying Yosemite, Telluride, and other spectacular U.S. sites.

Doc Ball—Surfing's Legendary Lensman. Dir. Carl Ackerman. 2000 Telly Award Winner focuses on surfer photographer Doc Ball.

INTERNET

For more on geographic sport challenges, visit . . .

hmhsocialstudies.com

Acapulco, Mexico, is famous for its cliff diving. This dangerous sport often involves diving from heights nearly three times higher than those used in Olympic platform diving. Cliff divers have been killed by hitting their heads on rocks.

The Iditarod Sled Dog Race is held in Alaska. Susan Butcher, shown here, was the first person to have won it three years in a row. The Inuit people first used sled dogs to travel across snow-covered terrain; racing evolved later.

GeoActivity

EXPLORING MOUNTAIN CLIMBING 

Working with a small group, use the Internet to research mountain climbing, another geographic sports challenge. Then create a **presentation** about the sport.

- Draw a world map, label popular mountains to climb, and give their altitudes.
- Make a chart listing the dangers of mountain climbing.

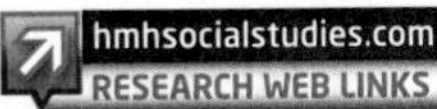
hmhsocialstudies.com
RESEARCH WEB LINKS

GeoData

Skiing
- Skis that are more than 4,000 years old have been found in Scandinavian bogs.
- Skiing was once a military skill. Norwegian troops skied in the Battle of Oslo in 1200.

Surfing
- The explorer James Cook first reported seeing surfing in 1778.
- European missionaries banned surfing in 1821. It was revived in 1920 by a Hawaiian, Duke Kahanamoku.

Cliff Diving
- Women did not compete at Acapulco until 1996.
- Divers enter the water at speeds of up to 65 mph.

Sled Dog Racing
- The Iditarod honors a 1925 emergency mission to deliver medicine to Nome, Alaska.
- During the 1985 race, a moose charged across Susan Butcher's path. The collision that resulted killed 2 dogs and wounded 13 other dogs.

GeoActivity

Exploring Mountain Climbing

 **Integrated Assessment**
- Rubric for a chart, 2.2

More About

Cliff Diving in Acapulco

In the early 1930s, young men living around Acapulco, a city on Mexico's Pacific coast, began to meet at *la quebrada*—a Spanish word for ravine. They challenged each other to dive from the ravine's cliffs—from heights of up to 130 feet—into a small canal at the bottom. Soon locals and tourists were coming to watch these spectacular leaps. Thus began the tradition of cliff diving at *La Quebrada* in Acapulco.

ACTIVITY OPTION | EXPLORING LOCAL GEOGRAPHY

APPRECIATING JUMPING DISTANCE RECORDS

Objective To gain an understanding of record-breaking distances for different sports

Class Time 30 minutes

Task To compare world-record distances to local surroundings

Directions Have groups of students carry out further research on record-breaking distances in sports, such as ski jumping, high diving, the long jump, etc. Have them record these distances and then make comparisons with local surroundings. For example, provide students with tape measures or yardsticks to measure out the distances in the hallway or elsewhere on school property. Or, have students compare the world records to the heights of local buildings or other landmarks.

SECTION 4 OBJECTIVES

1. Define Eastern Europe as a cultural crossroads.
2. Analyze Eastern European turmoil in the 20th century.
3. Explain how the economy of Eastern Europe has developed.
4. Explain how ethnic and religious diversity has defined Eastern European culture.
5. Identify the challenges involved in moving toward economic growth and political freedom.

SKILLBUILDERS: Interpreting Maps and Graphs, pp. 312, 313

GeographicThinking
Seeing Patterns, p. 314
Making Inferences, p. 315

Focus & Motivate

Ask students how cultural diversity can enrich a society. What problems might it cause? *(People from different cultures can learn from each other; cultural differences may cause conflict.)*

Instruct: Objective 

History of a Cultural Crossroads

- What is a cultural crossroads? *(a place where many cultures cross paths)*
- Why have many empires tried to control Eastern Europe? *(because it is an important crossroads)*
- What defines Eastern Europe as a cultural crossroads? *(its location between Asia and the rest of Europe; migration of many different peoples to the region)*

 **In-Depth Resources: Unit 4**
- Guided Reading, p. 16
- Skillbuilder Practice, p. 17

4 Eastern Europe

Main Ideas
- Eastern Europe has great cultural diversity because many ethnic groups have settled there.
- Many empires have controlled parts of the region, leaving it with little experience of self-rule.

Places & Terms
cultural crossroads
balkanization
satellite nation
market economy
folk art
anti-Semitism

CONNECT TO THE ISSUES
CONFLICT Nationalism and ethnic differences have fueled conflicts that have torn apart the Balkans in recent times.

A HUMAN PERSPECTIVE Eastern Europe has many plains that allow invaders to move from east to west and vice versa. In World War II, Germany invaded the Communist Soviet Union, killing millions. After the war, the Soviet Union decided to protect itself from invasion by setting up a political barrier. So it established Communist governments in the nations of Eastern Europe, which lay between the Soviet Union and its enemies to the west. Soviet dictator Joseph Stalin wanted Eastern Europe to "have governments whose relations to the Soviet Union are loyal." For decades, the Soviet Union crushed political reform and free trade in Eastern Europe. The region is still recovering.

History of a Cultural Crossroads

Eastern Europe's location between Asia and the rest of Europe shaped its history. Many groups migrated into the region, creating great diversity. Strong empires ruled parts of Eastern Europe, delaying the rise of independent nation-states there. Today the region includes Albania, Bosnia and Herzegovina, Bulgaria, Croatia, the Czech Republic, Hungary, Kosovo, Macedonia, Montenegro, Poland, Romania, Slovakia, Slovenia, and Serbia.

CULTURES MEET Eastern Europe is a **cultural crossroads**, or a place where various cultures cross paths. Since ancient times, people moving between Europe and Asia—traders, nomads, migrants, and armies—have passed through this region. Because the region is an important crossroads, many world powers have tried to control it.

Eastern European History, 1389–2000

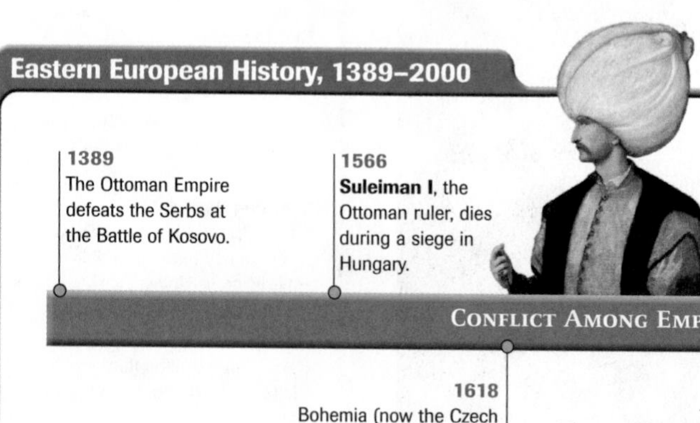

1389 The Ottoman Empire defeats the Serbs at the Battle of Kosovo.

1566 **Suleiman I**, the Ottoman ruler, dies during a siege in Hungary.

1618 Bohemia (now the Czech Republic) revolts against its Austrian ruler, starting the Thirty Years' War.

1686 The Austrians drive the Ottomans out of Hungary.

1795 The Russian ruler **Catherine the Great** divides Poland among Russia, Prussia, and Austria.

1867 Hungary demands equal status with Austria. The empire becomes Austria-Hungary.

CONFLICT AMONG EMPIRES

SECTION 4 PROGRAM RESOURCES

 **In-Depth Resources: Unit 4**
- Guided Reading, p. 16
- Skillbuilder Practice, p. 17
- Building Vocabulary, p.18
- Reteaching Activity, p. 22

Guided Reading Workbook
- Section 4

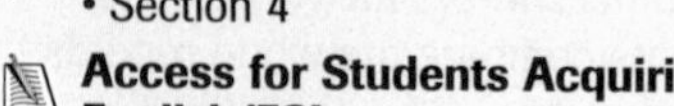 **Access for Students Acquiring English/ESL**
- Guided Reading, p. 69
- Skillbuillder Practice, p. 70

Outline Maps with Activities
- Eastern Europe, pp. 39–40

Formal Assessment
- Section Quiz, p. 198

Integrated Assessment
- Rubric for a time line, 2.4

Cultures Around the World
- Dance, p. 23
- Arts and Crafts, p. 24

INTEGRATED TECHNOLOGY

 **Cultures Transparencies CW23, 24**
- Folk Dancing
- Bohemian Crystal

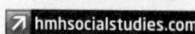

The World's Music Audio Program

hmhsocialstudies.com

TEST-TAKING RESOURCES

 **Strategies for Test Preparation**

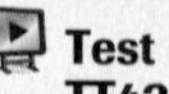 **Test Practice Transparencies TT42**

 **Online Test Practice**

EMPIRES AND KINGDOMS By about A.D. 100, ancient Rome held the Balkan Peninsula, Bulgaria, Romania, and parts of Hungary. After the Roman Empire was split, the Byzantine Empire held onto those lands for centuries. In the 1300s and 1400s, the Ottoman Empire of Turkey (see Unit 7) gradually took over the southern part of Eastern Europe.

BACKGROUND
Romania means "land of the Romans."

Various Slavic groups moved into Eastern Europe from the 400s through the 600s. Several kingdoms, such as Poland in the north and Serbia on the Balkan Peninsula, formed. In the late 800s, a non-Slavic group called the Magyars swept into what is now Hungary and in time established a kingdom. The Ottomans later conquered it.

Beginning in the 1400s, the nation of Austria became a great power. Austria drove the Ottomans out of Hungary and took control of that state. In the late 1700s, Austria, Prussia (a German state), and Russia divided up Poland among themselves. Poland ceased to exist.

Turmoil in the 20th Century

Responding to centuries of foreign rule, most ethnic groups in Eastern Europe fiercely guarded their identities. Many wanted their own nation-states, even though few had a history of self-rule. These characteristics sparked many conflicts in Eastern Europe during the 20th century. A

CONNECT TO THE ISSUES
CONFLICT
A What might happen if two different ethnic groups wanted to establish a nation on the same land?
A. Answer They might go to war to see who could win control of that land.

WAR AFTER WAR By 1908, the Balkan nations of Bulgaria, Greece, Montenegro, Romania, and Serbia had broken free from the Ottoman Empire. In 1912, Greece, Bulgaria, and Serbia went to war against the Ottomans, who lost most of their remaining European territory. In 1913, the Balkan countries fought over who should own that territory. Their actions led to a new word, **balkanization.** The term refers to the process of a region breaking up into small, mutually hostile units.

The Slavic nation of Serbia also wanted to free the Slavs in Austria-Hungary. In 1914, a Serb assassinated an Austrian noble, sparking World War I. Austria-Hungary and Serbia each pulled their allies into the conflict until most of Europe was involved. After the war, Austria and Hungary split apart. Albania, Bulgaria, Czechoslovakia, Poland, and Yugoslavia gained independence. The Ottoman Empire ended and was replaced by the nation of Turkey.

EUROPE

TWO WORLD WARS

1914 A Serb kills Austrian **Archduke Francis Ferdinand.** World War I erupts.

1918 The Kingdom of Serbs, Croats, and Slovenes (later Yugoslavia) is created.

1939 Germany overruns Poland. World War II starts.

1939–1945 Nazis carry out the Holocaust.

COMMUNISM AND DEMOCRACY

1945 **Josip Broz Tito** becomes dictator of Yugoslavia.

1946–1948 Communist governments are set up in Eastern Europe.

1989 Czechoslovakia, Hungary, Romania, and Poland end Communist rule.

2000 Yugoslavia elects a reform leader, Vojislav Kostunica, as president.

311

Instruct: Objective 2

Turmoil in the 20th Century

- What does the term *balkanization* describe? *(the breaking up of a region into mutually hostile areas)*
- How has ethnicity led to turmoil in Eastern Europe? *(People wanted to preserve their ethnicity. Many groups wanted their own nation-states.)*
- How did the Soviet Union's withdrawal from Eastern Europe create instability? *(Groups in many areas returned to ethnic loyalties.)*

Interpreting Time Lines

Eastern European History, 1389–2000

Remind students that time lines present historic events in chronological order. Ask: What period does this time line cover? *(1389–2000)* What do the illustrations have in common? *(They show people who were important to history.)* What patterns do you see in the events presented? *(conquest and revolt)*

ACTIVITY OPTION | **LINK TO HISTORY**

BLOCK SCHEDULING

MAKING A TIME LINE

Objective To learn more about the history of a particular country

Class Time 90 minutes

Task Create time lines for individual countries of Eastern Europe

Supplies
- plain shelf paper
- felt-tip pens
- photocopier

Directions Have students work in pairs to create a time line for an Eastern European country of their choice. Tell them to read about the country in encyclopedias or history books. They should select important historic events and be prepared to explain reasons for their choices. If they wish they may illustrate their work. Display the time lines in the classroom.

In 1939, Germany seized Poland, starting World War II. Near the end of that war, the Soviet Union advanced through Eastern Europe as part of an Allied strategy to crush Germany from two sides. The Soviet Union later refused to withdraw from Eastern Europe until it had set up Communist governments there. Eastern Europe became a region of **satellite nations**—nations dominated by another country.

RECENT CHANGES The Soviet Union controlled Eastern Europe for four decades. But by the late 1980s, the Soviet Union had severe economic problems, and a new leader, Mikhail Gorbachev, was making reforms. As one reform, he gave Eastern Europe more freedom.

The impact was dramatic. Eastern Europeans demanded political and economic reforms. In 1989, Czechoslovakia, Hungary, Poland, and Romania ended Communist control of their governments and held free elections. In 1990, Bulgaria and Yugoslavia followed suit.

Instability followed. The old governments had taught people to be loyal only to the Communist Party. After those governments fell, people

MOVEMENT In 1989, the desire for democracy swept Eastern Europe. Country after country saw demonstrations like this one in Budapest, Hungary.

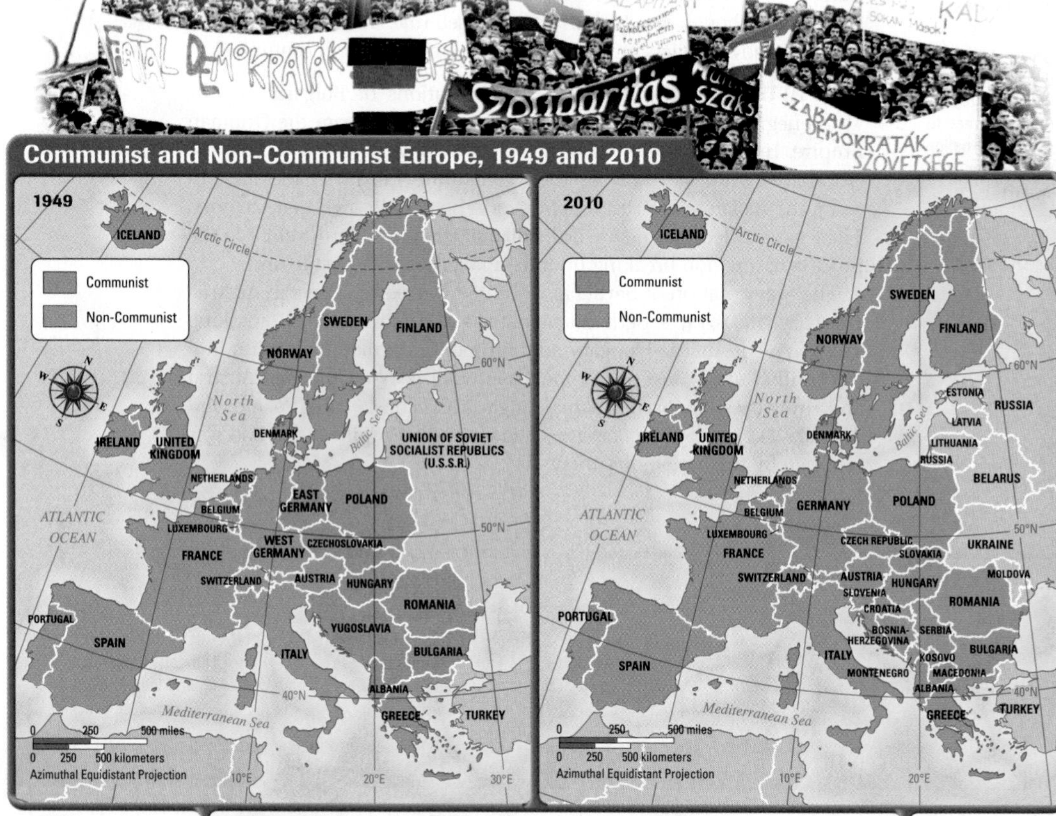

SKILLBUILDER: Interpreting Maps

1. **LOCATION** In 1949, near what country were the Communist nations of Europe located?
2. **REGION** How would you describe the political change that happened in the region?

Interpreting Maps

Communist and Non-Communist Europe, 1949 and 2000

Have students compare the communist countries that appear in orange on the 1949 map with the same land area on the 2000 map. Have them identify new countries on the 2000 map and determine from which 1949 countries they were created. *(Czech Republic, Slovakia: formerly Czechoslovakia; Slovenia, Croatia, Bosnia and Herzegovina, Macedonia: formerly Yugoslavia)* Ask which country underwent unification. *(East Germany with West Germany)* Ask which countries' boundaries remain unchanged. *(Romania, Bulgaria, Poland, Greece)* Ask which country has become smaller. *(Yugoslavia)*

SKILLBUILDER ANSWERS

1. the Soviet Union **2.** All the communist governments were overthrown.

DIFFERENTIATING INSTRUCTION — GIFTED AND TALENTED STUDENTS

EXPLORING THE NEW GERMANY

Objective To explore ethnic identity and political divisiveness

Class Time 50 minutes

Task Research and write a report on the division of Germany

Directions Draw students' attention to Germany as it appears on the 1949 and 2010 maps and ask how the country changed. *(East and West Germany were reunified.)* Then have students research and write a report on the reunification of Germany. Tell them to include the following: when and why Germany was divided; the effect of the division on the East German economy and people; how reunification came about. Then ask students to compare division and reunification in Germany with strong ethnicity in the Balkans. *(Germans were once divided but desired to be a single nation; Balkan ethnic groups want their own nation states; both are motivated by ethnicity and nationalism.)*

returned to ethnic loyalties. That was especially true in Yugoslavia, a nation consisting of six republics. In the early 1990s, four of the six Yugoslav republics voted to become separate states. Serbia objected, leading to civil war. (See Chapter 14 for details.) In contrast, Czechoslovakia peacefully split into the Czech Republic and Slovakia.

Developing the Economy

Because of its fertile plains, Eastern Europe has traditionally been a farming region. After 1948, the Soviet Union promoted industry there.

INDUSTRY Under communism, the government owned all factories and told them what to produce. This system was inefficient because industries had little motive to please customers or to cut costs. Often, there were shortages of goods. Eastern European nations traded with the Soviet Union and each other, so they didn't keep up with the technology of other nations. As a result, they had difficulty selling goods to nations outside Eastern Europe. And their outdated factories created heavy pollution.

After 1989, most of Eastern Europe began to move toward a **market economy**, in which industries make the goods consumers want to buy. Many factories in Eastern Europe became privately owned instead of state owned. The changes caused problems, such as inflation, the closing of factories, and unemployment. Since then, however, many factories have cut their costs and improved production. As a result, the Czech Republic, Hungary, and Poland have all grown economically. B

Per Capita GDP in Eastern Europe

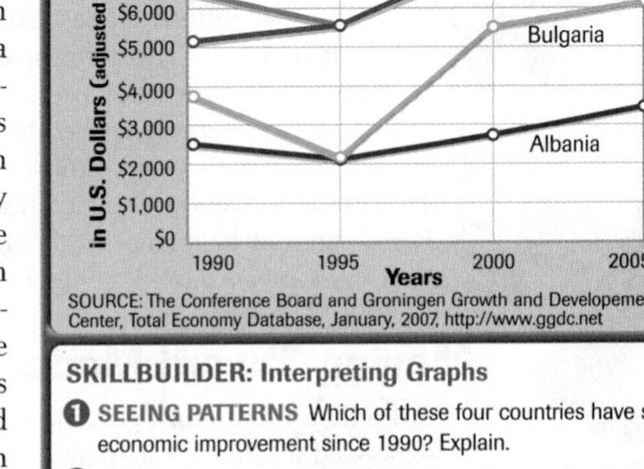

SOURCE: The Conference Board and Groningen Growth and Developement Center, Total Economy Database, January, 2007, http://www.ggdc.net

SKILLBUILDER: Interpreting Graphs

1. **SEEING PATTERNS** Which of these four countries have seen economic improvement since 1990? Explain.
2. **DRAWING CONCLUSIONS** In terms of per capita GDP, which country has the best standard of living? Explain.

CONNECT TO THE ISSUES
UNIFICATION
B Do you think the nations of Eastern Europe wanted to join the European Union? Why or why not?
B. Answer Yes, they might join to gain increased trade opportunities and financial aid as the Mediterranean countries have.

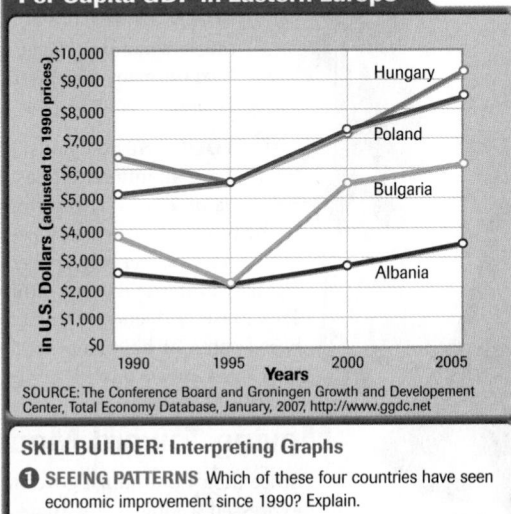

LINGERING PROBLEMS Some Eastern European nations have had trouble making economic progress—for many different reasons.

- Albania's economic growth is slowed by old equipment, a lack of raw materials, and a shortage of educated workers.
- Few of Romania's citizens have money to invest in business. In addition, the Romanian government still owns some industries. Foreigners don't want to invest their money in those industries.
- The civil wars of the 1990s damaged Yugoslavia and its former republics of Bosnia and Herzegovina and Croatia. Equipment and buildings were destroyed; workers were killed or left the country.

In general, it will take years for Eastern Europe to overcome the damage caused, in part, by decades of Communist control.

Instruct: Objective 3

Developing the Economy

- Why did Eastern European countries move from farming to industry? *(The Soviet Union promoted industry.)*
- How did communist governments restrict economic development? *(Factories were state owned and told what they could produce.)*
- How has moving toward a market economy been of benefit in Eastern Europe? *(Factories can make products that are in demand.)*

Interpreting Graphs

Per capita GDP in Eastern Europe

In the United States, the per capita GDP rose by more than $7,000 during the same six-year period of 1990–2005. Ask: Which country on the chart had the greatest increase? *(Poland)* How much did it rise? *(Close to $3000.)* How does that compare with the increase in the United States? *(less than ½)* In 2005 the U.S. per capita GDP was about $30,500. Have students compare this with the information on the chart and ask for their conclusions. *(The U.S. standard of living is much higher than that of Eastern European countries. The per capita GDP in the United States is more than 3 times greater than that of Hungary, which had the highest GDP in the region.)*

SKILLBUILDER ANSWERS

1. Hungary and Poland; their per capita GDP has consistently risen since 1990. **2.** Hungary has the highest per capita GDP and therefore a better standard of living.

ACTIVITY OPTION | CRITICAL THINKING

MAKING INFERENCES

Explaining the Skill Tell students that making inferences involves reading between the lines to interpret the information they read. Students can make inferences by studying what is stated and using their common sense and previous knowledge.

Applying the Skill Have the students review the benefits and problems connected to the development of a market economy in Eastern Europe. (benefits: factories are free to produce goods that are in demand; problems: inflation, the closing of businesses, unemployment)

Ask students:

- Of the countries on the graph, which benefited most from conversion to a market economy? Explain your answer. *(Hungary and Poland, because they have shown an improvement in GDP)*
- Which countries have suffered from problems caused by the conversion? Explain. *(Bulgaria and Albania; their GDP dropped)*
- What specific problems has Albania had to address? *(old equipment, a lack of raw materials, and few educated workers)*

Instruct: Objective 

A Patchwork Culture

- What effect does the variety of Eastern European languages have on the region? *(It makes unification difficult.)*
- How does religion contribute to the region's cultural diversity? *(A variety of religions adds to cultural diversity.)*
- What influences shape the folk art of Eastern Europe? *(religious beliefs, customs, Byzantine art)*

 **Cultures Around the World**
- Dance, p. 23
- Arts and Crafts, p. 24

 **Cultures Transparencies CW23, 24**
- Folk Dancing
- Bohemian Crystal

More About

Romanian Folk Art

Folk art in Romania takes many forms, including embroidery, intricate wood carving, pottery, and ceramic stoves, which may still be found in rural cottages. The type of folk art and the decorative elements used often reflect a particular geographic area. Woodcarving is especially evident in heavily forested areas, such as those in the Carpathian Mountains. Transylvania is known for religious icons painted on glass.

Instruct: Objective 5 appears on p. 315.

A Patchwork Culture

Because Eastern Europe contains a variety of ethnic groups, the region as a whole is a patchwork of different languages and religions.

CULTURAL DIVERSITY The map on page 267 shows the languages of Eastern Europe. The number of languages makes it difficult to unify the region. In some places, the national language is most closely related to a language spoken in a different region. For example, Hungarian is related to Finnish, and Romanian is related to Italian, French, and Spanish. Neither are related to the Slavic languages of the countries around them. This pattern was created by long-ago migrations.

Similarly, many different religions can be found in Eastern Europe. The Roman Empire introduced Catholicism, and after Rome fell, the Byzantine Empire spread Eastern Orthodox Christianity. Some countries also have a Protestant minority. And under the Ottoman Empire, some Eastern Europeans converted to Islam.

The region also has a small Jewish minority. Jews once made up a much higher percentage of Eastern Europeans, but in the Holocaust, Nazi Germany killed 6 million Jews. About half of them were from Poland. After World War II, many surviving Jews migrated to Israel.

FOLK ART Religious belief, rural customs, and Byzantine art have all influenced Eastern European folk art. In general, **folk art** is produced by rural people with traditional lifestyles instead of by professional artists. Eastern European folk artists create items such as pottery, woodcarving, and embroidered traditional costumes. C

Many Eastern European ethnic groups also have their own folk music. This music influenced the region's classical musicians. Frédéric Chopin based some of his piano music on Polish dances. Anton Dvořák wove Czech folk music into his compositions.

These figures are folk art depictions of traditional costumes from the mountains of southern Poland.

Geographic Thinking

Seeing Patterns
C Why do you think folk art has remained important in Eastern Europe?
C. Answer because traditional agricultural activities remained important in the Eastern European economy

Moving Toward Modern Life

Since their Communist governments fell, many Eastern Europeans have expressed a longing for more economic growth and political freedom. These goals provide the region with some major challenges.

LESS URBAN DEVELOPMENT Eastern Europe has several large cities, such as Prague in the Czech Republic. More than 1,000 years old, Prague is one of Europe's most interesting cities, with quaint buildings, a rich history of music and culture, and thriving industries.

In general, though, Eastern Europe is much less urban than the rest of Europe. For example, the percentage of city dwellers is only 40 percent in Bosnia and Herzegovina and only 37 percent in Albania.

As Eastern Europe develops more industry, its cities will grow. That will have both positive and negative effects. Cities are often places of culture, learning, and modern technology. But urban growth creates problems such as pollution, traffic jams, and housing shortages.

CONFLICT As you read earlier, many Eastern Europeans have fierce loyalties to their own ethnic groups. One result of that has been conflict. For example, many Serbs hate Croats (KROH•ATS) because they believe the Croats betrayed them in World War II by working with the Nazis.

ACTIVITY OPTION **LINK TO WORLD LANGUAGES**

CHARTING REGIONAL LANGUAGE DIFFERENCES

Objective To reinforce the significance of language diversity

Class Time 30 minutes

Task Create a chart of Eastern European languages

Directions Have pairs of students create a chart of Eastern European languages arranged by language group. Tell them to copy the chart and fill it in using the map on page 267. Have them use their charts to answer the following questions:

- Ask how many languages they were able to identify. *(10)*
- Ask whether additional languages are spoken in Eastern Europe. *(yes, as indicated by the dotted areas on the map)*
- Ask whether the multiplicity of languages may have been a factor in balkanization. *(Yes. People who speak the same language often want their own nation-state, and distrust others who do not speak their language.)*

EASTERN EUROPEAN LANGUAGES

Major Indo-European	Other Indo-European	Uralic

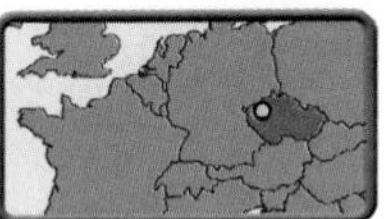

PLACE Crossing the Vltava River in Prague is the famous 650-year-old Charles Bridge. The bridge is now reserved for pedestrians. **Why do you think cars are banned from this bridge?**

Eastern European minority groups have often faced discrimination. Throughout history, Jews have suffered from **anti-Semitism**, which is discrimination against Jewish people. Another minority that experiences prejudice is the Romany, or Gypsy, people who are scattered across Eastern Europe. Traditionally, the Romany have moved from place to place. Because of this, other groups often look down on them.

DEMOCRACY To obtain true democracy, Eastern Europeans need to overcome old hatreds and work together. They also need to accept democratic ideals such as the rule of law—which means that government officials must obey the law. The dictators that ruled Eastern Europe in the past did not do so. But in recent years, Eastern Europeans have often held their leaders accountable. For example, in 2000, the Yugoslav people forced a dictator to accept election results that turned him out of office. You will read about this event in Chapter 14, along with other major issues of European life today.

EUROPE

Section 4 Assessment

1 Places & Terms

Identify these terms and explain their importance in the region.

- cultural crossroads
- balkanization
- satellite nation
- market economy
- folk art
- anti-Semitism

2 Taking Notes

REGION Review the notes you took for this section.

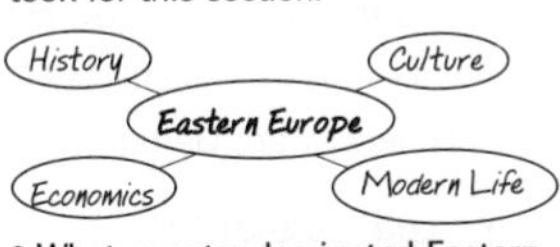

- What country dominated Eastern Europe after World War II?
- What problems did the move toward a market economy cause?

3 Main Ideas

a. Why is Eastern Europe considered a cultural crossroads?

b. What role did the Soviet Union play in the rise and fall of communism in Eastern Europe?

c. What are some important ways that Eastern Europe is different from Western Europe?

4 Geographic Thinking

Making Inferences The Balkan region has been called the "powder keg of Europe." Why do you think it earned that name? **Think about:**

- the wars in 1912 and 1913
- World War I

See Skillbuilder Handbook, page R4.

EXPLORING LOCAL GEOGRAPHY Like Eastern Europe, most places in the United States have been controlled by various cultural groups or nations over time. Research the history of your area and create a **time line,** like the one on pages 310-311, listing changes in control.

Instruct: Objective 5

Moving Toward Modern Life

- How might the growth of industry create urban problems? *(It will cause cities to grow, potentially causing increased pollution, housing shortages, and traffic jams.)*
- What minority groups have suffered discrimination? *(Jews, the Romany)*
- In what ways might extreme ethnic loyalty inhibit the development of democracy? *(Democracy calls for cooperation. Groups who hate each other cannot work together effectively.)*

CAPTION ANSWER to prevent damage to the ancient structure

Assess & Reteach

GeoFocus Have students complete the section on Eastern Europe in their cluster diagrams.

Formal Assessment
- Section Quiz, p. 198

Reteaching Activity
Have the students work in pairs and assign each a main heading of Section 4. Tell students to create questions regarding the main points of the material under their assigned heading. Have them take turns asking each other their questions and providing answers. Then have students ask their questions of the class as a whole.

In-Depth Resources: Unit 4
- Reteaching Activity, p. 22

Outline Maps with Activities
- Eastern Europe, pp. 39–40

SECTION 4 ASSESSMENT ANSWERS

1. Places & Terms

cultural crossroads, p. 310
balkanization, p. 311
satellite nation, p. 312
market economy, p. 313
folk art, p. 314
anti-Semitism, p. 315

2. Taking Notes

- The Soviet Union dominated the region.
- inflation, the closing of factories, and unemployment

3. Main Ideas

a. It is located between Asia and the rest of Europe, so many groups have migrated through or settled in the region; as a result, many different cultures have influenced the region.

b. After World War II, the Soviet Union sponsored Communist governments there. In the late 1980s, Soviet reforms allowed Eastern Europe more freedom, resulting in the overthrow of Communist governments.

c. Differences in Eastern Europe include less industry, less urbanization, and a history of Communist rule.

4. Geographic Thinking

The countries of the region have frequently turned against each other; in addition, the event that sparked World War I took place there.

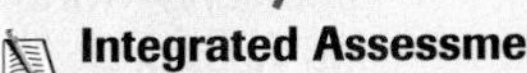

GeoActivity

Integrated Assessment
- Rubric for a time line, 2.4

Reviewing Places & Terms

A. **1.** city-state, p. 289
2. republic, p. 290
3. Benelux, p. 296
4. nationalism, p. 297
5. Berlin Wall, p. 298
6. Nordic countries, p. 302
7. euro, p. 305
8. cultural crossroads, p. 310
9. balkanization, p. 311
10. satellite nation, p. 312

B. Possible Responses

11. Benelux and the Nordic countries are regions.
12. A supporter of nationalism would probably want a distinct national currency and therefore would oppose the euro.
13. Berlin Wall and balkanization are terms that are related to conflict.
14. Eastern European countries were satellite nations of the Soviet Union.
15. Many cultures pass through a cultural crossroads and interact with one another there; without movement, the cultural crossroads would not exist.
16. Greece was organized into city-states, and Rome was a republic.
17. Benelux is in Western Europe.
18. It comes from the Balkan Peninsula (the Balkan region).
19. The United States is a republic, and many Americans feel strong nationalism.
20. The Scandinavian and Jutland peninsulas are located in Nordic countries.

Chapter 13 Assessment

VISUAL SUMMARY
HUMAN GEOGRAPHY OF EUROPE

Subregions of Europe

Mediterranean Europe

- The influence of ancient Greece, ancient Rome, and Renaissance Italy on art, philosophy, religion, and language shaped modern life.
- In the late 1900s, Mediterranean Europe began to have more manufacturing and service industries.

Western Europe

- Germany and France developed very different cultures, and throughout history, conflicts between them involved much of Europe.
- Western Europe has a highly developed economy. It is a leader in the economic and political alliance known as the European Union.

Northern Europe

- This region was a leader in the Industrial Revolution and the rise of representative government.
- The region has a history of seafaring conquerors. Great Britain established an empire that spread British culture and the English language worldwide.

Eastern Europe

- Because it is a cultural crossroads, Eastern Europe has a diverse culture with many ethnic groups.
- Domination by outside powers, most recently the Soviet Union, has characterized the region's history.

Reviewing Places & Terms

A. Briefly explain the importance of each of the following.

1. city-state
2. republic
3. Benelux
4. nationalism
5. Berlin Wall
6. Nordic countries
7. euro
8. cultural crossroads
9. balkanization
10. satellite nation

B. Answer the questions about vocabulary in complete sentences.

11. Which of the terms above are the names of regions?
12. Would a supporter of nationalism want to adopt the euro? Explain.
13. Which of the terms above have to do with conflict?
14. In which part of Europe did the countries become satellite nations of the Soviet Union?
15. How does the geographic theme of movement relate to a cultural crossroads?
16. Which ancient civilization was organized into city-states and which was a republic?
17. In what part of Europe is Benelux found?
18. What is the origin of the term *balkanization*?
19. Which of the terms above can also be applied to the United States? Explain.
20. Which two major peninsulas are found in the Nordic countries?

Main Ideas

Mediterranean Europe (pp. 289–295)

1. What legacy did ancient Athens leave for modern governments?
2. What effect did the empires of Spain and Portugal have on the rest of the world?
3. Why does Spain have a conflict with the Basque people?

Western Europe (pp. 296–301)

4. How did the Reformation create new cultural divisions?
5. How did nationalism lead to conflicts?
6. For what artistic legacy are Germany and Austria famous?

Northern Europe (pp. 302–309)

7. Who were the Vikings, and what did they do?
8. What geographic advantages helped Great Britain build its empire?

Eastern Europe (pp. 310–315)

9. Why did independent nation-states develop later in Eastern Europe than in Western Europe?
10. What problems existed in the Eastern European economy under Communist rule?

Main Ideas

1. It was the first democracy.
2. They spread Roman Catholicism and the Spanish and Portuguese languages.
3. Because of linguistic and cultural differences, some Basques want complete freedom from Spain and have used violence to achieve it.
4. It led to the rise of Protestantism, and Protestants and Catholics have fought each other in many wars.
5. First, it helped inspire the French Revolution, and second, it led to rivalry among nations, often ending in wars.
6. They are famous for music; composers include Bach, Beethoven, and Mozart.
7. They were seafaring warriors from Denmark, Norway, and Sweden. They terrorized Europe and moved to Iceland, Greenland, North America, Normandy, and Russia.
8. Its iron ore and coal helped it industrialize; being an island helped protect it from invasion and also encouraged the development of a navy; its industrial and naval strength enabled it to build its empire.
9. Eastern Europe had little history of self-rule.
10. Government control of industrial planning led to inefficiency and reduced the motive to please customers; the factories were outdated and created heavy pollution.

Critical Thinking

1. Using Your Notes

Use your completed chart to answer these questions.

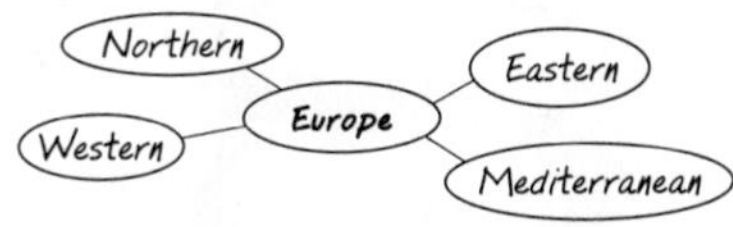

a. What similarities exist between the ways the Roman Empire and the British Empire influenced other regions of the world?

b. In what ways are Eastern Europe and Northern Europe different?

2. Geographic Themes

a. LOCATION Do you think the location of France and Germany relative to the rest of Europe is a geographic advantage or disadvantage? Explain.

b. MOVEMENT What geographic reason might account for the fact that Spain and Great Britain colonized much of the Americas?

3. Identifying Themes

Explain which countries were the first to develop industry and which developed industry later. If you identify those countries on a map, what spatial patterns do you see? Which geographic themes relate to your answer?

4. Seeing Patterns

How did ancient migrations affect the pattern of where certain languages are spoken in Europe today? Give examples.

5. Making Inferences

Millions of Europeans have migrated to other parts of the world. What are some geographic factors that you think might have encouraged this?

For Additional Test Practice

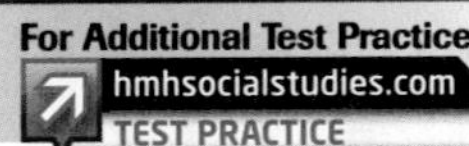

Geographic Skills: Interpreting Maps

A Divided Germany

Use the map to answer the following questions.

1. PLACE How did the size of West Germany compare with that of East Germany?
2. LOCATION In which of the two countries was the city of Berlin located?
3. LOCATION Which of the two Germanys was closer to the Soviet Union?

West Germany was divided into several zones after World War II. Use a history book or historical atlas to learn which three countries controlled those zones. Create a historical map showing the zones.

hmhsocialstudies.com

MULTIMEDIA ACTIVITY

Use the links at **hmhsocialstudies.com** to do research about the population of a single society in Europe. Look for such information as age distribution, religions, ethnic or minority groups, and literacy rates.

Constructing a Population Pyramid Use the information you have gathered to construct a population pyramid describing the population characteristics of the European society you have chosen.

CHAPTER 13 ASSESSMENT

Critical Thinking

1. a. Both controlled other regions and spread their language and culture.
b. Northern Europe remained independent, while Eastern Europe was dominated by foreign powers; Northern Europe is ethnically homogenous, while Eastern Europe is diverse.

2. a. It is an advantage; its central location promotes trade and political or military influence.
b. They are located near the Atlantic Ocean and could sail directly west to the Americas.

3. Great Britain, Belgium, France, Germany, and Sweden were the first. Eastern and Mediterranean Europe developed industry later. Relevant themes are place, location, and region; in addition, movement (of ideas) is implied by the answer.

4. The migration of Germanic peoples caused Germanic languages to be dominant in much of Western Europe (except France), the Nordic countries, and Great Britain. The migration of Slavic people had a similar effect on Eastern Europe.

5. Widespread access to the sea encouraged ocean voyages; limited land encouraged emigration; ethnic and religious conflicts may have prompted some migrations.

GeoActivity

Integrated Assessment
- Rubric for a sketch map, 2.1

Formal Assessment
- Chapter Test, Forms A, B, and C, pp. 199–210

Geographic Skills

1. West Germany was approximately twice the size of East Germany.
2. East Germany
3. East Germany

MULTIMEDIA ACTIVITY

For their report on the population in a European society, students should:

- Provide information on different characteristics of the population.
- Produce a clear population pyramid.
- Include references to the Web sites used as sources.

Grading Rubric Evaluate student performance as Exceptional, Acceptable, or Poor in each of the following categories:

	Exceptional	Acceptable	Poor
Graphic is clear and accurate			
Title and headings clearly state the topic and categories			
Clearly lists sources			

Multimedia Classroom

The **HISTORY™ Multimedia Classroom** is a set of exciting new social studies teaching tools featuring award-winning program content. These comprehensive lesson plans, correlated to individual state and national curriculum standards, are easy to use for both teachers and students.

Each lesson contains the following:

- Short video segments that bring history topics to life
- Maps and visual materials
- Discussion and review questions
- Easily printable primary source documents
- Classroom activities and Internet-based activity links

The Multimedia Classroom has been specially designed to be versatile and easily adaptable to existing courses, lesson plans, and syllabi. Every lesson is designed to offer maximum flexibility. Teachers can select entire plans or only the elements they need, allowing them to individually tailor each lesson. Each multimedia lesson is available in CD-ROM format and is accompanied by full-length award-winning programs on DVD from HISTORY™.

For more information or to purchase go to  hmhsocialstudies.com

Because some of these lessons may contain video material of a sensitive nature, we recommend that teachers and parents review these materials in their entirety before screening them to students.

HISTORY

MULTIMEDIA CONNECTIONS

ANCIENT GREECE

The Acropolis of Athens symbolizes the city and represents the architectural and artistic legacy of ancient Greece. *Acropolis* means "highest city" in Greek, and there are many such sites in Greece. Historically, an acropolis provided shelter and defense against a city's enemies. The Acropolis of Athens—the best known of them all—contained temples, monuments, and artwork dedicated to the Greek gods. Archaeological evidence indicates that the Acropolis was an important place to inhabitants from much earlier eras. However, the structures that we see today on the site were largely conceived by the statesman Pericles during the Golden Age of Athens in the 5th century B.C.

Explore the Acropolis of ancient Greece and learn about the legacy of Greek civilization. You can find a wealth of information, video clips, primary sources, activities, and more at hmhsocialstudies.com.

317 MC1 MULTIMEDIA CONNECTIONS

Ancient Greece

Resources hmhsocialstudies.com

The following resources come with printable introductions, comprehension and critical thinking questions, transcripts, and vocabulary support.

Full Length DVD

Ancient Greece (45 minutes)

Video Clips

- Athens' Spiritual Citadel (1:43)
- Athena as Divine Guardian (1:47)
- At War with the Persians (1:56)
- Pericles and the Golden Age (3:37)
- The Panathenaia Festival (3:52)
- Origins of Western Culture (4:29)
- Dionysus and Greek Theater (1:57)
- The Death of a Philosopher (1:13)
- Bringing Down the Parthenon (4:10)
- Elgin's Contested Collection (1:43)
- Mysteries and Discoveries (5:11)

Primary Sources

- *Oedipus Rex*
- *The Republic*
- *The Histories*
- The Porch of the Caryatids
- A Panathenaic Amphora
- Greek Fables
- A Greek Funeral Stele

The Parthenon

Watch the video to see what the Parthenon, one of the most important temples on the Acropolis, might have looked like after it was completed.

The Persian Wars

Watch the video to find out how Athens emerged as the principal Greek city-state at the conclusion of the Persian Wars.

The Goddess Athena

Watch the video to learn how, according to Greek mythology, Athena became the protector of Athens.

Legacy of Greece

Watch the video to analyze *The School of Athens*, a painting by the Italian Renaissance artist Raphael, which pays tribute to the legacy of ancient Greece in philosophy and science.

Maps

- Greco-Persian Wars
- The Athenian Acropolis

Activities

- Women of Ancient Greece
- Greek Games and Festivals
- Quotable Greek Philosophers
- Taking to the Greek Stage
- A New Trial for Socrates
- To Return or Not to Return?
- Things to See in Athens

General Review Questions

General Discussion Questions

Web Links

Bibliography

Lesson Preview

The Parthenon

No other building on the Acropolis was as magnificent as the Parthenon. Begun by Pericles in 447 B.C., the Parthenon took about 15 years to build. When finished, the marble temple was more than 225 feet long and 100 feet wide. However, the Parthenon was impressive for the elegant proportion of its columns, not for its size. Visitors did not enter the temple; they could only view it from outside. As they walked around the Parthenon, visitors admired the colorful sculptures that rose in the frieze above its columns until they finally glimpsed the huge gold and ivory statue of Athena standing within.

The Persian Wars

From about 490 to 479 B.C., the Greek city-states fought the vast and powerful Persian Empire. Surprisingly, Greece defeated the Persians at their first major battle at Marathon, a town that lay not far from Athens. According to legend, an Athenian messenger ran from Marathon to Athens after the battle to announce the Greeks' victory. He completed the 26-mile run but died from exhaustion after he delivered the message. This legend inspired the modern marathon race.

The Goddess Athena

According to Greek mythology, Athena, the goddess of wisdom, and Poseidon, the god of the sea, competed for a city in Greece by presenting it with valuable gifts. Poseidon gave the city a spring, but the people had little use for its salty water. Athena planted an olive tree, which would provide the city with food, oil, and wood. The goddess won and named her city Athens.

Legacy of Greece

Raphael's *The School of Athens* depicts the great philosophers of ancient Greece. Its central figures are Plato on the left—portrayed as Leonardo da Vinci—and his student, Aristotle, on the right. Raphael portrayed himself in a less significant area of the painting, peering out from among a group of scholars.

CHAPTER 14 PLANNING GUIDE

Today's Issues: Europe

OVERVIEW	INSTRUCTIONAL RESOURCES	
ESSENTIAL QUESTION How can international cooperation ease the tensions of Europe's past and present? **Focus on the Essential Question Podcast**	**In-Depth Resources: Unit 4** • Building Vocabulary, p.29 **Block Schedule Strategies** **Chapter Summaries** (English/Spanish)	**Interactive Online Edition** TOS **ExamView® Assessment Suite** (English/Spanish) TOS **CalendarPlanner** **Power Presentations with Media Gallery** **Critical Thinking Transparencies** • CT14 hmhsocialstudies.com INTERACTIVE
SECTION 1 **TURMOIL IN THE BALKANS** **MAIN IDEAS** • A series of foreign conquests increased diversity and contributed to ethnic tension in the Balkans. • World War II intensified turmoil in Yugoslavia as various ethnic groups aligned themselves with the Nazis or the Allies. • Disagreement among ethnic groups over whether Bosnia and Herzegovina should become independent led to war in 1992.	**In-Depth Resources: Unit 4** • Guided Reading, p. 23 • Building Vocabulary, p. 29 • Exploring Today's Issues, pp. 30–31 • Reteaching Activities, p. 34 • Map and Graph Skills, pp. 26–27 **Guided Reading Workbook,** Section 1	**Critical Thinking Transparencies** • CT46 Political Unrest in the Balkans
SECTION 2 **CLEANING UP EUROPE** **MAIN IDEAS** • European countries are working together to clean up water pollution. • European countries are attempting to reduce air pollution both individually and, as members of the European Union, collectively.	**In-Depth Resources: Unit 4** • Guided Reading, p. 24 • Skillbuilder Practice, p. 28 • Building Vocabulary, p. 29 • Exploring Today's Issues, pp. 32–33 • GeoWorkshop, pp. 37–38 • Reteaching Activities, p. 35 **Guided Reading Workbook,** Section 2	
CASE STUDY: **THE EUROPEAN UNION** **MAIN IDEAS** • France and West Germany initiated the process of unification as a way to prevent war. • The European Union faces complex economic and political issues as it attempts to build a consolidated Europe.	**In-Depth Resources: Unit 4** • Guided Reading, p. 25 • Building Vocabulary, p. 29 • Reteaching Activities, p. 36 **Guided Reading Workbook,** , Case Study	**Map Transparencies** • MT25, The European Union, 2000

ASSESSMENT

SE **Chapter Assessment,** pp. 330–331

Formal Assessment
- Chapter Tests, Forms A, B, and C, pp. 214–225

TOS **ExamView® Assessment Suite**

Strategies for Test Preparation

hmhsocialstudies.com TEST PRACTICE

SE **Section Assessment,** p. 321

Formal Assessment
- Section Quiz, p. 211

Integrated Assessment
- Rubric for a map, 2.1

Test Practice Transparencies TT45

SE **Section Assessment,** p. 325

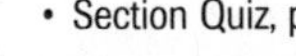

Formal Assessment
- Section Quiz, p. 212

Integrated Assessment
- Rubric for a news article, 4.5

Test Practice Transparencies TT46

SE **Case Study Project,** pp. 328–329

Formal Assessment
- Case Study Quiz, p. 213

Test Practice Transparencies TT47

CHART KEY:

SE Student Edition	 Block Scheduling	 DVD/CD-ROM
TE Teacher's Edition	 TOS Teacher One Stop	 MP3 Audio
Printable Resource	 Presentation Resource	HISTORY™

Program Resources available on TOS and @ hmhsocialstudies.com

SUPPORTING RESOURCES

- Multimedia Classroom Global History Series
- Global History Teacher's Guide

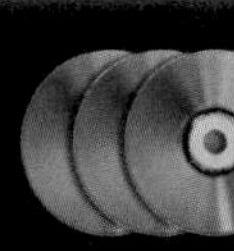

Social Studies Trade Library Collection
- Modern World History Trade Collection

For more information or to purchase these resources, go to hmhsocialstudies.com

DIFFERENTIATED INSTRUCTION

English Learners	Struggling Readers	Gifted and Talented Students
 **Spanish/English Guided Reading Workbook**  **Access for Students Acquiring English/ESL** Spanish Translations, pp. 71–76  **Chapter Summaries** (English/Spanish) TE **TE Activity** Understanding Environmental Terms, p. 324	**Chapter Summaries** (English/Spanish) TE **TE Activity** Creating an Issues Chart, p. 327	TE **In-Depth Resources: Unit 4** GeoWorkshop, p. 374

ENRICHMENT ACTIVITIES

The following activities are especially suitable for classes following block schedules.

SE **Student Edition,** p. 318–331 • Interpreting a Thematic Map, p. 322	hmhsocialstudies.com INTERACTIVE • The European Union, 2007, p. 327

BLOCK SCHEDULE LESSON PLAN OPTIONS: 90-MINUTE PERIOD

DAY 1

SECTION 1, pp. 319-322
Class Time 90 minutes

- **In-Depth Report** Have students write a brief essay discussing the connection between geography, history, and current issues. Tell students to use information in the section as the basis for their writing. Collect the essays and read from them as a basis for discussion.
  Class Time 45 minutes
- **Service Project** Have students research relief efforts conducted by the International Federation of Red Cross and Red Crescent in Kosovo and other parts of the former Yugoslavia. Divide students into small groups. Have each group draft a plan as to how their class or school could contribute to the relief efforts. Each plan should include a target population, a goal, and timetables.
  Class Time 45 minutes

DAY 2

SECTION 2, pp. 323-325
Class Time 90 minutes

- **Comparing Air and Water Pollution** Have students review their notes on the causes and effects of pollution. Then have them compare the causes and effects of water pollution with those of air pollution. Ask what generalizations they can make regarding common causes, effects, and solutions.
  Class Time 20 minutes
- **Summary Chart** Lead students in creating a summary chart of action taken to control pollution in Europe. Supply two column heads: "European Union" and "Individual Countries." Challenge students to suggest measures in addition to those covered in the section. Discuss which methods students think are most effective and why.
  Class Time 25 minutes
- **Video** Conduct the Before Viewing activities included in the Video Resource Book (p. 24). Ask students to prepare a list of questions that they would like the video to answer. Present *Greece: Urbanization and the Environment* (23 minutes), and afterward have students ask and answer their prepared questions. Follow up with the questions and activities in the Video Resource Book (pp. 26–30) to review themes presented in the film.
  Class Time 45 minutes

DAY 3

CASE STUDY 3, pp. 326-329
Class Time 35 minutes

- **Project Summary** Have students summarize their presentations on EU expansion on large sheets of newsprint, using bullet points for each main item. Display these summaries with the visuals students made for the project. Compare the points of view of the various countries. Then have students identify reasons for and against membership as you list them on the chalkboard.

CHAPTER 14 REVIEW AND ASSESSMENT, pp. 330-331
Class Time 55 minutes

- **Review** Have students review the chapter by relating the Places & Terms on the first page of each section to the causes-and-effects chart they have made of the chapter.
  Class Time 20 minutes
- **Assessment** Have students complete the Chapter 14 Assessment.
  Class Time 35 minutes

TEACHER-TESTED ACTIVITY *Comparing Pollution Problems*

Class Time 2–3 class periods

Task Have students review daily newspapers for articles on air or water pollution in the United States or other countries

Supplies
- Daily local newspaper
- Library
- Copies of class set of selected news articles

Purpose To have students become aware of the global and local nature of air and water pollution and what is or is not being done to remedy the problems.

Activity Have students read Section 2 and help them collect news articles on pollution. The class may be divided into small groups and assigned specific types of pollution, such as air, water, or noise pollution. Have each group create a written summary report on the articles they have selected. The activity can be conducted over several class periods and then compiled into a final report comparing Europe's pollution problems to those of the United States or other nations. Use the reports as a basis for class discussion.

Craig T. Grace
Geography Teacher, Lanier High School, West Austin, Texas

TECHNOLOGY IN THE CLASSROOM

A WebQuest is a structured, inquiry-oriented activity that asks students to solve problems by using Web resources. Students are given a task and are asked to use the Web to help them complete the task, which usually involves drawing a conclusion or solving a problem for which there is no single correct answer. WebQuests can be very simple or highly complex. Below is a simple WebQuest to complement the material in Chapter 14. To learn more about WebQuests and how to design an "official" WebQuest, go to the WebQuest link at **hmhsocialstudies.com.**

Objective Students will use the Web to prepare presentations to the EU, pretending that they are representing specific EU and non-EU countries. (This activity would work well as a precursor to the panel discussion on page 328.)

Task Students prepare a chart outlining a European nation's status in and attitude toward the EU as they relate to that nation's current environmental and social issues.

Class Time 90 minutes

1. Have students join with partners and ask each pair to choose one European country. Try to get a good mix of countries throughout the classroom.
2. Ask students to pretend that they are going to represent their selected country at a European Union meeting. They will attend the meeting whether or not their country is an EU member.
3. Inform students that their goal at the EU meeting will be to explain to other country representatives their country's position on the EU (whether or not it wants to participate and why, or how it likes being a part of the EU if it already is) and what their country might do to be a better member of the European community (e.g., cleaning up the environment or reducing social problems).
4. Have students make charts with the headings "EU Status," "Environment," and "Social Situation."
5. Have students use the Web sites at **hmhsocialstudies.com** to find information about their country to add to their charts. They should look for information explaining: their country's status with and attitude toward the EU; current environmental problems within their country; current social problems, such as tensions with immigrant or minority groups.
6. Have students look carefully at the charts they have created and discuss with their partners the things they might say in a five-minute presentation to the EU. Remind them of their goal, as described in step 3.
7. **Optional Activity** Ask students to create multimedia slide shows that they would present at the EU meeting. Their slide shows should include specific information about the three categories they investigated.

CHAPTER 14 OBJECTIVE

Learn that Europeans face serious issues and are actively seeking solutions to their problems.

Chapter **14**

TODAY'S ISSUES
Europe

Interpreting Photographs

War in the Balkans

A young girl stands in front of the bombed ruins of a mosque's minaret in central Bosnia. A minaret is a tall, slender tower attached to a mosque.

Extension Ask students to investigate the architecture of mosques to find out the function of the minaret.

Introducing the Essential Question

- Describe the Balkans' early history to students, emphasizing that since antiquity many cultures and faiths have occupied the region.Conflict among these groups still shadows the Balkans.
- Remind students that Europe began to industrialize in the 18th century. Centuries of industrialization have burdened Europe with serious pollution problems. One of the European Union's goals is cleaning up the pollution.

Ask students to fill in the graphic organizer with the causes and effects of the issues facing Europe today.

Critical Thinking Transparencies CT14
- GeoFocus

In-Depth Resources: Unit 4
- Building Vocabulary, p. 29

Essential Question

How can international cooperation ease the tensions of Europe's past and present?

Throughout the 1990s, ethnic conflict tore apart the Balkan region.

What You Will Learn

In this chapter you will read about serious issues facing Europe today and how Europeans are working to resolve them.

SECTION 1
Turmoil in the Balkans

SECTION 2
Cleaning Up Europe

CASE STUDY
The European Union

For more on these issues in Europe

hmhsocialstudies.com
CURRENT EVENTS

hmhsocialstudies.com
TAKING NOTES

Use the graphic organizer online to take notes on the causes and effects of the issues.

318

CHAPTER 14 ADDITIONAL RESOURCES

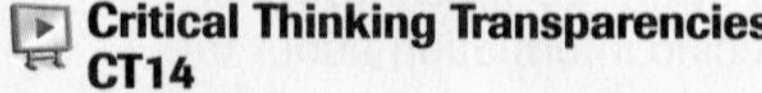

BOOKS FOR THE TEACHER

Wallace, Helen, Mark A. Pollack, Alsdair Young. ***Policy-Making in the European Union.*** Oxford University Press, 2010. How the EU develops policies and the global reach of those policies.

Rubin, Barnett R., ed. ***Toward Comprehensive Peace in Southeast Europe.*** The Twentieth Century Fund, 1997.

BOOKS FOR THE STUDENT

Filipovic, Zlata. Transl. by Christina Pribichevich-Zoric. ***Zlata's Diary: A Child's Life in Sarajevo.*** London: Viking Penguin, 1995. One teen's account of the Yugoslav conflict.

PERIODICALS

"Eastern Europe's Environment: Clean Up Or Clear Out." *Economist,* December 11, 1999.

Purvis, Andrew, Dejan Anastasijevic, and Michael Fitzgerald, **"Deadly Discharge."** *Time South Pacific,* February 28, 2000.

INTERNET

For more on today's issues in Europe, visit . . .

hmhsocialstudies.com

Turmoil in the Balkans

How can people resolve their differences?

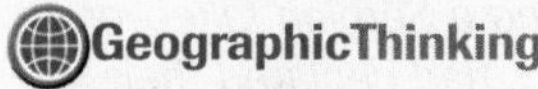

Main Ideas

- Yugoslavia was a nation of many ethnic groups distributed among six republics.
- When Serbia tried to dominate Yugoslavia, other republics broke away. This sparked conflict.

Places & Terms

Slobodan Milošević
South Slavs
ethnic cleansing
KLA
Vojislav Kostunica

A HUMAN PERSPECTIVE The Serbian leader **Slobodan Milošević** (SLOH•buh•DAHN muh•LOH•suh•VIHCH) tried to increase Serbia's power over the rest of Yugoslavia. As a result, in 1991 and 1992, four republics left Yugoslavia. Serbia went to war against them but lost. In 1999, an international court accused Milošević (who was the Yugoslav president by then) and Serbian troops of war crimes in those conflicts. Many nations ended trade with Yugoslavia in protest, and the country grew poorer.

In 2000, Yugoslavia voted Milošević out of office. When he refused to accept the election results, thousands of people protested until he admitted defeat. In doing so, the Yugoslav people showed that they wanted peace and a normal relationship with the world. This may have been a turning point in the long history of conflict in the Balkans.

EUROPE

Roots of the Balkan Conflict

One conflict in the Balkans is that different groups want control of the same land. The causes of this conflict go back centuries. In the 500s, Slavic people migrated from Poland and Russia and settled in the Balkan Peninsula. They were called the **South Slavs**. Each group of South Slavs (the Croats, the Slovenes, and the Serbs) formed its own kingdom.

FOREIGN RULERS In the 1300s, the Muslim Ottoman Empire tried to conquer the Balkan Peninsula. In 1389, the Ottomans defeated the Serbian Empire at the Battle of Kosovo Polje. The Ottomans also ruled Bosnia and Herzegovina. Elsewhere in the Balkans, Austria ruled Slovenia, and Hungary ruled Croatia. Over time, foreign rule created differences among the South Slavs. For instance, under Muslim rule, the Serbs clung to Christianity, while many Bosnians converted to Islam.

Both Serbs and Albanians had lived in Kosovo, a part of the Serbian Empire. When the Muslims seized power, many Serbs fled Kosovo, so the region became more Albanian in culture.

YUGOSLAVIA IS FORMED In 1878, Serbia broke free of the Ottoman Empire. Many Serbs wanted all the South Slavs to be free of foreign rule and to unite in one nation. That desire helped to spark World War I.

In 1918, the Kingdom of the Serbs, Croats, and Slovenes was formed. In 1929, the king renamed it Yugoslavia (which means "Land of the South Slavs") to help end ethnic divisions.

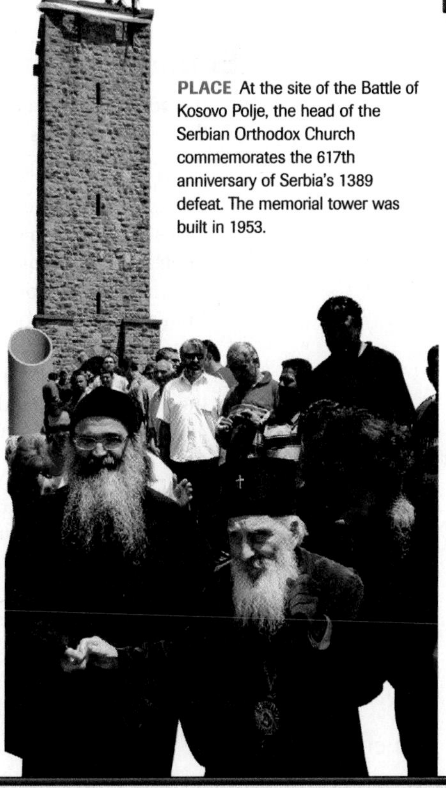

PLACE At the site of the Battle of Kosovo Polje, the head of the Serbian Orthodox Church commemorates the 617th anniversary of Serbia's 1389 defeat. The memorial tower was built in 1953.

SECTION 1 OBJECTIVES

1. Analyze the roots of the Balkan conflict.
2. Identify immediate causes of fighting in the Balkans near the end of the 20th century.

GeographicThinking
Seeing Patterns, p. 320
Making Comparisons, p. 321
Drawing Conclusions, p. 321

Focus & Motivate

Ask students what impressions they have formed of the Balkans from articles and news reports. *(Possible answers may refer to armed conflict between Bosnians and Serbs, ethnic cleansing, the UN peacekeeping mission, and the ousting of Milošević.)*

Instruct: Objective 1

Roots of the Balkan Conflict

- What effect did a series of foreign rulers have on the Balkans? *(It created different loyalties and increased the diversity of religion.)*
- How did events in World War II contribute to ethnic tension in Yugoslavia? *(Croats cooperated with the Nazis in the massacre of Jews and Serbs; other Yugoslavs fought against the Nazis.)*
- How was Yugoslavia reorganized in 1946? *(into six republics: Bosnia and Herzegovina, Croatia, Macedonia, Montenegro, Serbia, Slovenia)*

In-Depth Resources: Unit 4
- Guided Reading, p. 23
- Exploring Today's Issues, pp. 30–31

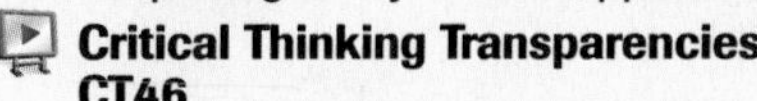

Critical Thinking Transparencies CT46
- Political Unrest in the Balkans

SECTION 1 PROGRAM RESOURCES

In-Depth Resources: Unit 4
- Guided Reading, p. 23
- Building Vocabulary, p. 29
- Exploring Today's Issues, pp. 30–31
- Reteaching Activity, p. 34
- Map and Graph Skills, pp. 26–27

Guided Reading Workbook
- Section 1

Access for Students Acquiring English/ESL
- Guided Reading, p. 71
- Map and Graph Skills, pp. 75–76

Formal Assessment
- Section Quiz, p. 211

Integrated Assessment
- Rubric for a map, 2.1

INTEGRATED TECHNOLOGY

Critical Thinking Transparencies CT46
- Political Unrest in the Balkans

Power Presentations

Test Generator
- Section Quiz

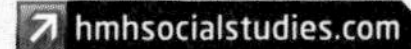

hmhsocialstudies.com

TEST-TAKING RESOURCES

Strategies for Test Preparation

Test Practice Transparencies TT45

Online Test Practice

Instruct: Objective 2

Ethnic Tension Boils Over

- What led the Yugoslavian army to invade Slovenia and Croatia in 1991? *(Fearing a Serbian takeover, both republics had declared their independence.)*
- Why did war break out in Croatia? *(There was longstanding hatred between Croats and Croatia's large minority of Serbs.)*
- What acts of military aggression did Serbs commit in Bosnia and Herzegovina and Kosovo? *(invaded Bosnia and Herzegovina to block its move for independence; tried to control Kosovo and to wipe out Albanian culture there)*

Conflict in the Balkans, 1990–Present

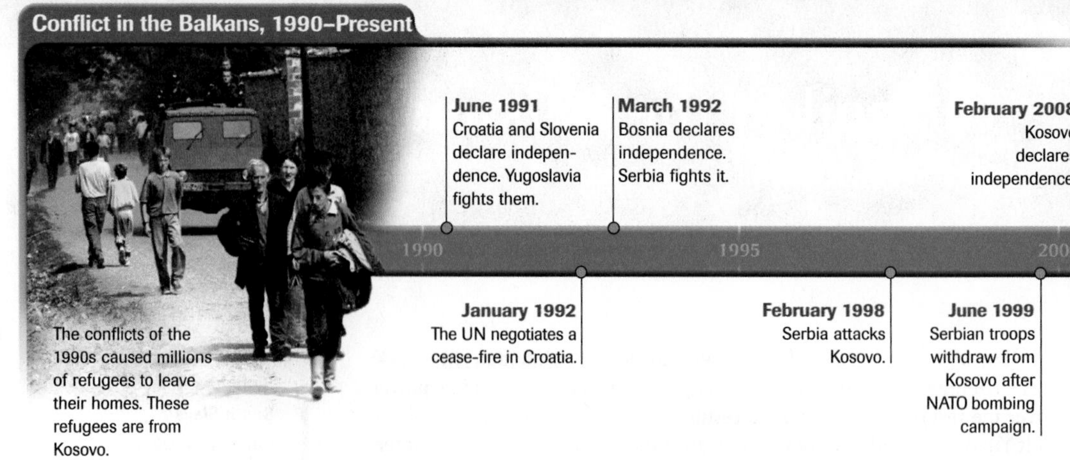
June 1991
Croatia and Slovenia declare independence. Yugoslavia fights them.
March 1992
Bosnia declares independence. Serbia fights it.
February 2008
Kosovo declares independence.
1990
1995
2000
January 1992
The UN negotiates a cease-fire in Croatia.
February 1998
Serbia attacks Kosovo.
June 1999
Serbian troops withdraw from Kosovo after NATO bombing campaign.

The conflicts of the 1990s caused millions of refugees to leave their homes. These refugees are from Kosovo.

COMMUNIST RULE During World War II, Germany and Italy invaded Yugoslavia. The Croats cooperated with the Nazis, and the Croat leader ordered the massacre of Jews and Serbs. Many other Yugoslavs joined the Chetniks or the Partisans, two rival groups fighting the Nazis.

One Partisan leader was Josip Broz Tito, head of the Communist Party. After the war, Tito became the dictator of Yugoslavia. He encouraged the Serbs, Croats, and other groups to think of themselves as Yugoslavs.

In 1946, a new constitution organized Yugoslavia into a nation of six republics: Bosnia and Herzegovina, Croatia, Macedonia, Montenegro, Serbia, and Slovenia. Serbia had two self-governing provinces, Kosovo and Vojvodina. The map on page 322 shows that Croatia and Bosnia were ethnically mixed and contained many Serbs. A

A. Answer It might increase conflict among the groups and therefore decrease stability.

Geographic Thinking

Seeing Patterns A How might having a mixed population affect the stability of Croatia and Bosnia?

Ethnic Tension Boils Over

In 1980, Tito died, and the presidency began to rotate among leaders from the many republics and provinces. No single person ran the country.

FEAR OF SERBIA Slobodan Milošević began to propose the creation of a Greater Serbia. Serbia would expand its borders to include other territories with Serbian populations. This plan alarmed Croats and Bosnians. Then in 1991, Serbia blocked a Croat from becoming president.

In response, Slovenia and Croatia declared their independence. In June 1991, the Serbian-led Yugoslav army invaded both republics. The Slovenes quickly achieved freedom. But Croatia had a large Serbian minority, and past Serb-Croat hatreds exploded in all-out war. The fighting claimed thousands of lives before the United Nations arranged a cease-fire in January 1992. Slovenia and Croatia remained free.

WAR IN BOSNIA In March 1992, Bosnia and Herzegovina declared independence. Bosnia's Muslims and Croats backed the move, but its Serbs (and Serbia) launched a war to stop it. The Serbs used murder and violence to get rid of Bosnia's Muslims and Croats. The policy of trying to eliminate an ethnic group through violence is called **ethnic cleansing**. More than 200,000 people died, while over 2 million people fled their homes.

In 1995, the United States sponsored peace negotiations, and in December, a peace treaty was signed. Bosnia remained independent.

BACKGROUND By 1992, only Serbia and Montenegro remained part of Yugoslavia.

ACTIVITY OPTION | INTERNET RESEARCH

WRITING A NEWS SYNOPSIS

Objective To update information regarding ethnic conflict or its resolution in the Balkans

Class Time One class period

Task Research and present a one-minute news brief on the state of ethnic conflict or resolution in the Balkans

Directions Have students use the links at **hmhsocialstudies.com** and other Internet Web sites to find information on the current status of ethnic conflict or resolution in the Balkans. Tell them to use the information to prepare a one-minute news synopsis on the situation. Then have students present their findings in class.

OPTIONAL ACTIVITY If Internet access is limited, students may search for information in current newspapers and periodicals.

WAR IN KOSOVO Serbia saw Kosovo as a sacred part of its heritage and regained control of the province in 1912. But by the 1990s, Kosovo was inhabited mostly by Muslim Albanians, who spoke a non-Slavic language.

Serbia, led by Milošević, tried to assert control over Kosovo and to wipe out its Albanian culture. In response, Kosovo demanded independence. In the 1990s, a group called the Kosovo Liberation Army (**KLA**) began to carry out attacks against Serbian officials. The Serbian government responded by bombing villages and began a campaign of ethnic cleansing against Albanians. B

Geographic Thinking
Making Comparisons
B How were Serbia's actions in Kosovo similar to its actions in Bosnia and Herzegovina?
B. Answer In both conflicts, Serbia carried out a campaign of ethnic cleansing against Muslims.

In March 1999, NATO started bombing Serbia to force it to stop the violence. In June, Serbian troops withdrew from Kosovo. International officials then found evidence that the Serbs had tortured and massacred Kosovars. Milošević died in prison in 2006, after being arrested and put on trial for war crimes.

AN UNCERTAIN FUTURE In 2000, the Yugoslav people elected a reform leader named **Vojislav Kostunica** (VAW•yee•SLAHV kahsh•TOO•neet•sah) as president.

Despite this hopeful event, the country faced problems. The decade of wars had created widespread poverty and millions of refugees. Also, many Kosovars and Montenegrins wanted independence from Serbia.

In 2003, a country called Serbia and Montenegro was formed, but it was short-lived. In 2006, Montenegro gained independence. In 2007, the UN proposed a plan for Kosovo to stay within Serbia but gain self-rule. Kosovo declared its independence in 2008, but Serbia has refused to recognize it as a country.

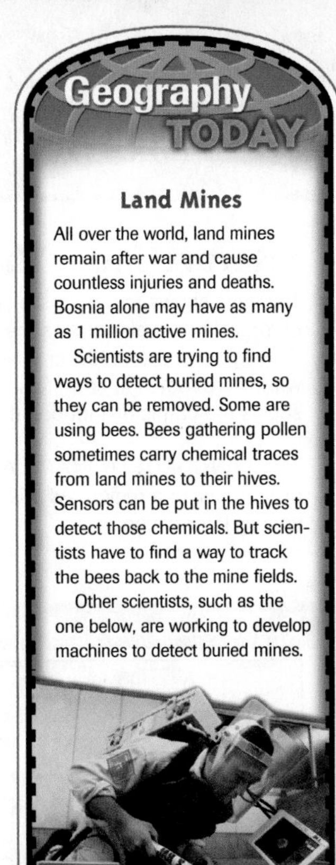

Land Mines

All over the world, land mines remain after war and cause countless injuries and deaths. Bosnia alone may have as many as 1 million active mines.

Scientists are trying to find ways to detect buried mines, so they can be removed. Some are using bees. Bees gathering pollen sometimes carry chemical traces from land mines to their hives. Sensors can be put in the hives to detect those chemicals. But scientists have to find a way to track the bees back to the mine fields.

Other scientists, such as the one below, are working to develop machines to detect buried mines.

Geography TODAY

Land Mines

First used extensively during World War II, land mines continue to injure or kill someone somewhere in the world approximately every twenty minutes. In some Third World countries, doctors who perform resulting amputations must do so without anesthesia for patients. Millions of land mines remain buried, with armies burying additional land mines every year.

- How do land mines continue to foster hostility after an armed conflict has ended? *(land mines continue to kill and maim civilians)*
- How is life in the United States different from that in countries where land mines are buried? *(people have no fear of injury from land mines; removal is not an issue, nor is rehabilitation from land mine injuries)*

EUROPE

Section 1 Assessment

1 Places & Terms

Identify these terms and explain their relationship to the issue.

- Slobodan Milošević
- South Slavs
- ethnic cleansing
- KLA
- Vojislav Kostunica

2 Taking Notes

PLACE Review the notes you took for this section.

	Causes	Effects
Issue 1: Conflict		

- Where was the historic battle in which the Ottomans defeated the Serbs?
- Which two republics suffered brutal wars after independence?

3 Main Ideas

a. How did Tito try to overcome the differences among ethnic groups in Yugoslavia?

b. What was the plan to create Greater Serbia?

c. How did the rest of the world get involved in the Balkan conflicts?

4 Geographic Thinking

Drawing Conclusions
Was Milošević's effort to make Serbia stronger successful? Give examples.
Think about:
- the reaction of other Yugoslav republics to Serbia's actions
- the reaction of the international community

MAKING COMPARISONS Working from a history book, historical atlas, or other resource, make a sequence of **maps** showing changes in the political boundaries of the Balkans over the last 100 years. Possible dates for maps include 1912, 1919, 1946, 1995, 2003, and 2008.

Assess & Reteach

GeoFocus Have students complete the section on the Balkans in their cause-and-effect charts.

Formal Assessment
- Section Quiz, p. 211

Reteaching Activity
Have students work in pairs. Tell them to take turns reading either a cause or an effect from their charts. The student not reading should identify the item as either a cause or an effect and tell what effect it had or what caused it.

In-Depth Resources: Unit 4
- Reteaching Activity, p. 34

SECTION 1 ASSESSMENT ANSWERS

1. Places & Terms
Slobodan Milošević, p. 319
South Slavs, p. 319
ethnic cleansing, p. 320
KLA, p. 321
Vojislav Kostunica, p. 321

2. Taking Notes
- Kosovo
- Croatia and Bosnia and Herzegovina

3. Main Ideas
a. He urged people to think of themselves as Yugoslavs instead of as Serbs, Croats, Slovenes, etc.
b. The plan was for Serbia to take back lands that had been given to other republics but which had Serbian populations.
c. The UN negotiated peace in Croatia and Bosnia, and NATO bombed Serbia to stop its violence in Kosovo.

4. Geographic Thinking
No, ultimately he weakened Serbia. Most of the other Yugoslav republics declared independence rather than remain in federation with Serbia, the international community condemned Serbian violence, and warfare damaged Serbia's economy.

GeoActivity

Integrated Assessment
- Rubric for a map, 2.1

OBJECTIVE

Understand and interpret thematic maps.

Instruct: Objective

Interpreting a Thematic Map

- What are the two main ethnic groups in Croatia? *(Croat and Serb)*
- Which republic has the largest Muslim areas? *(Bosnia and Herzegovina)*
- Where are ethnic Albanians concentrated? *(Kosovo and Macedonia)*

In-Depth Resources: Unit 4
- Map and Graph Skills, pp. 26–27

Access for Students Acquiring English/ESL
- Map and Graph Skills, pp. 75–76

More About

Ethnic Albanians in Macedonia

In February 2001, ethnic Albanians in Macedonia began to fight against government forces. The rebel groups said that their aim was to secure equal constitutional rights for Macedonia's Albanians. But Macedonian officials feared that the real aim of the rebels was to create a new ethnic Albanian state that would include Kosovo, areas of southern Serbia, and areas of western and northern Macedonia.

RAND MCNALLY **Map and Graph Skills**

Interpreting a Thematic Map

This map shows the republics and provinces that made up the former country of Yugoslavia. It also shows the major ethnic and religious groups throughout the region. In the 1990s, civil wars raged throughout this part of Europe. These wars were rooted in centuries-old ethnic and religious conflicts. This map shows the ethnic distribution that contributed to those conflicts.

THE LANGUAGE OF MAPS A **thematic map** illustrates a specific feature, or features, of a region. As this map shows, thematic maps may use color to convey information.

Ethnic Groups in the Former Yugoslavia

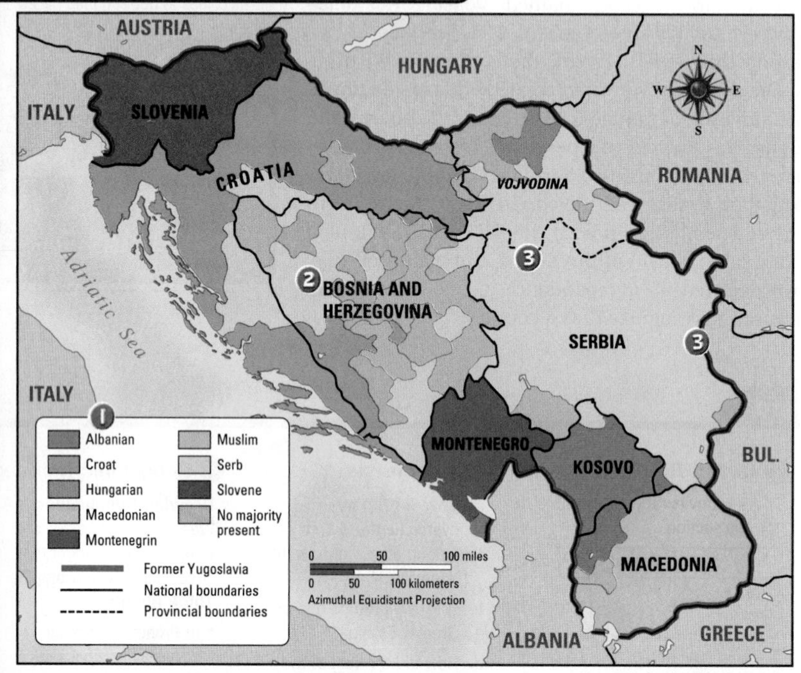

1. The key illustrates the colors used and what they represent. It also shows symbols for boundaries.

2. The different colored areas on the map indicate the majority ethnic group in each area. The colors do not imply that no one from a different group lives in the area.

3. This map shows three types of political boundaries: the boundary of the former Yugoslavia, boundaries of the republics that were part of it, and boundaries of provinces that belonged to the republic of Serbia.

Map and Graph Skills Assessment

1. Analyzing Data
Which republics had Serbs as part of their populations?

2. Drawing Conclusions
What republic had the most diverse population?

3. Making Inferences
How did the ethnic composition of the most diverse republic relate to its relative location?

SKILLS ASSESSMENT ANSWERS

1. Croatia, Bosnia and Herzegovina, Serbia

2. Bosnia and Herzegovina

3. Several of its ethnic groups are the same as the majority population of neighboring republics: its location created its diversity.

322 CHAPTER 14

Cleaning Up Europe

How can Europeans clean up their environment?

Main Ideas
- Pollution has many complex causes and results. It often spreads across borders, contaminating a region.
- The nations of Europe are cooperating to try to clean up their environment.

Places & Terms
cyanide
European Environmental Agency
particulates
smog
ozone

A HUMAN PERSPECTIVE In January 2000, a gold mine in Romania released cyanide into local streams. The **cyanide,** a deadly poison, flowed into the Tisza River in Hungary. Before the accident, the river held some of Europe's rarest fish. The poison killed an estimated 80 percent of the fish in the Tisza. Balazs Meszaros, whose family has commercially fished the Tisza for generations, said, "Now I don't know how I am going to live." Even worse than the loss of jobs was the threat to health. Experts feared that the poison would seep into wells and contaminate crops and livestock. The damage will take years to undo.

Pollution is a complex example of human-environment interaction. People damage the environment, which in turn affects human lives. For instance, pollution is thought to cause 1 out of every 17 deaths in Hungary. Because cleaning up pollution is time-consuming, difficult, and costly, it remains a serious issue in Europe—and around the world.

Saving Europe's Water

As the story of the Tisza demonstrates, pollution rarely remains at its point of origin but often spreads to neighboring regions. As a result, water pollution is a problem that concerns almost all of Europe.

CAUSES OF WATER POLLUTION Mines and factories create much of Europe's water pollution. Industries often discharge chemicals into streams and rivers. Factories sometimes bury solid waste. Poisons from this waste seep into ground water and contaminate wells and rivers. And, as you read in Chapter 12, the burning of coal and other fuels causes acid rain. Acid rain changes the chemistry of lakes and rivers, often killing fish.

The link between industry and pollution creates a dilemma. Most countries want to develop industry, and some accept environmental damage as the price they must pay for progress. Other nations force industry to use pollution controls, but these are usually expensive.

EUROPE

HUMAN-ENVIRONMENT INTERACTION A cyanide spill poisoned Eastern Europe's streams and rivers. These dead fish are from the Tisza River in Hungary.

SECTION 2 OBJECTIVES

1. Identify causes of water pollution in Europe and some solutions.
2. Understand the causes of air pollution, the problems it creates, and some solutions.

Geographic Thinking
Seeing Patterns, p. 325

Assess & Reteach

How do humans negatively affect their environment and why should we be concerned? *(Sewage and industrial waste cause air and water pollution; they contaminate the air, water, and food we need to live.)*

Instruct: Objective 

Saving Europe's Water

- How does industry create water pollution? *(by discharging chemicals into rivers and streams, by burying solid waste that leaches into ground water, and by burning coal that creates acid rain)*
- What are some other common sources of water pollution? *(sewage, chemical fertilizers, oil spills)*
- What measures has Europe taken to solve water pollution? *(created a commission to protect the Rhine River; passed laws; set up the European Environmental Agency)*

In-Depth Resources: Unit 4
- Guided Reading, p. 24
- Skillbuilder Practice, p. 28
- Exploring Today's Issues, pp. 32–33
- GeoWorkshops, pp. 37–38

SECTION 2 PROGRAM RESOURCES

In-Depth Resources: Unit 4
- Guided Reading, p. 24
- Skillbuilder Practice, p. 28
- Building Vocabulary, p. 29
- Exploring Today's Issues, pp. 32–33
- Reteaching Activity, p. 35
- GeoWorkshops, pp. 37–38

Guided Reading Workbook
- Section 2

Access for Students Acquiring English/ESL
- Guided Reading, p. 72
- Skillbuilldler Practice, p. 74

Formal Assessment
- Section Quiz, p. 212

Integrated Assessment
- Rubric for a news article, 4.5

Video Resource Book
- Greece, pp. 21–30

INTEGRATED TECHNOLOGY

Chapter Summaries

Test Generator
•Section Quiz

hmhsocialstudies.com

TEST-TAKING RESOURCES

Strategies for Test Preparation

Test Practice Transparencies TT46

Online Test Practice

Instruct: Objective 2

Improving Europe's Air Quality

- What causes air pollution? *(burning of fossil fuels and garbage, and forest fires; chemicals released into the air)*
- Why is it important to clean up the air? *(Air pollution causes asthma, bronchitis, emphysema, and possibly lung cancer; it creates acid rain, which destroys forests and damages buildings.)*
- What is the European Union doing to limit air pollution? *(requiring thermal insulation in new buildings to reduce the burning of fossil fuels; calling for vans and cars to reduce fuel emissions)*

Interpreting Photographs

Coke Plant

Explain to students that coke is used in the production of steel. Then ask why owners of this plant might have chosen to build near a railroad line. *(because the railroad provides a relatively cheap and efficient way to transport coal to the plant)*

CAPTION ANSWER the railroad

Industry is not the only source of water pollution. Other sources include the following:

- **Sewage** Ideally, cities should have treatment plants that remove harmful substances from sewage before it is released into bodies of water. But in Poland, for example, from 1988 to 1990, 44 percent of the cities had no sewage treatment plants. The water in most of Poland's rivers is unsafe to drink. It has also contaminated the soil so that some crops are toxic.
- **Chemical fertilizers** Rain washes fertilizers from fields into bodies of water, where they cause algae and plants to grow faster than fish can eat them. The plants and algae die and decay, a process that uses up oxygen. The lack of oxygen kills fish—which then decay, using more oxygen. In time, these bodies of water can no longer support life.
- **Oil spills** For example, in December 1999, a tanker sank off the west coast of France and spilled 10,000 tons of oil that spread along 250 miles of coastline. The oil killed tens of thousands of shorebirds.

CLEANING UP THE WATER Because water pollution spreads so easily, nations must cooperate to solve the problem. For example, pollution levels in the Rhine River rose sharply in the mid-1900s. To correct this, representatives from France, Germany, Luxembourg, the Netherlands, and Switzerland formed the International Commission for the Protection of the Rhine. Since it began meeting in 1950, the commission has recommended programs such as the treatment of sewage before it enters the Rhine. As a result, pollution of the Rhine has decreased.

In addition, the European Union has passed environmental laws that its member nations must obey. The EU also set up the **European Environmental Agency,** which provides the EU with reliable information about the environment.

HUMAN–ENVIRONMENT INTERACTION This mill in Nowa Huta, Poland, is making coke—a byproduct of coal. The smokestacks cause heavy air pollution.
What else besides the smokestacks might be causing air pollution?

Improving Europe's Air Quality

Although they are often considered separately, the different types of pollution are connected. For example, water pollution can be caused by air pollution—because rain washes chemicals out of dirty air and into bodies of water.

CAUSES OF AIR POLLUTION Air pollution is made up of harmful gases and **particulates,** very small particles of liquid or solid matter. Many human activities create air pollution by expelling these gases and particulates into the atmosphere.

- **Using fossil fuels** The burning of petroleum, gas, and coal causes much air pollution. It contributes

DIFFERENTIATING INSTRUCTION **STUDENTS ACQUIRING ENGLISH/ESL**

UNDERSTANDING ENVIRONMENTAL TERMS

Non-native speakers may be unfamiliar with terms relating to pollution. Associating such terms to the element they pollute should help them increase their vocabulary.

Directions Have students make a chart listing types of pollution. Write *air pollution* and *water pollution* on the chalkboard for students to copy as the chart's column headings. Also write the following terms on the chalkboard: *cyanide, particulates, smog,* and *ozone.* Have students reread the section to find the terms listed and then to write them in the correct column. They should find the definition of each term in a dictionary and write it on their charts.

AIR POLLUTION	WATER POLLUTION
cyanide: poisonous chemical compounds	ozone
sewage	smog
chemicals	particles
etc.	etc.

BACKGROUND
The word *smog* was formed by combining the words *smoke* and *fog*.

to the formation of **smog**—a brown haze that occurs when the gases released by burning fossil fuels react with sunlight to create hundreds of harmful chemicals. One such chemical is **ozone**, a form of oxygen that causes health problems.

- **Fires** Forest fires caused by careless human behavior and the burning of garbage release smoke and particulates into the atmosphere.
- **Chemical use** Dry cleaning, refrigeration, air conditioning, and the spraying of pesticides are among the human activities that release harmful chemicals into the air.
- **Industry** Factories discharge chemicals such as sulfur into the air. The factories of former Communist countries have been especially heavy polluters. Because of this, air pollution levels are much higher in the former East Germany than in the United States. A

Geographic Thinking
Seeing Patterns
A You learned in Chapter 13 that Eastern Europe used old technology. How might this relate to pollution?
A. Answer Older technology would not have the most recent advances in protecting or restoring the environment.

RESULTING PROBLEMS Breathing polluted air can contribute to respiratory diseases such as asthma, bronchitis, and emphysema. Air pollution is also suspected to be one of the causes of lung cancer. In addition, air pollution harms livestock and stunts plant growth. It also causes acid rain, which kills forests and damages buildings, such as the famous Parthenon in Athens, Greece.

CLEANING UP THE AIR Individual European countries are passing laws to make their air safer to breathe. France, for example, now requires improved thermal insulation of new buildings. This reduces the need to burn fossil fuels for heat. Other European governments are also passing laws to protect the air.

Nations are also cooperating to clean the air. For example, in 1998, the members of the European Union agreed that, starting in 2000, they would require reduced emissions from cars and vans. As that example indicates, a leader in the effort to restore Europe's environment will be the European Union—which is discussed in the following Case Study.

EUROPE

Section 2 Assessment

1 Places & Terms
Identify these terms and explain their relationship to the issue.
- cyanide
- European Environmental Agency
- particulates
- smog
- ozone

2 Taking Notes
HUMAN-ENVIRONMENT INTERACTION Review the notes you took for this section.

	Causes	Effects
Issue 2: Pollution		

- What river has an international group been trying to save?
- What diseases are linked to air pollution?

3 Main Ideas
a. What dilemma is faced by countries that are developing industry?
b. What is a harmful result of burning fossil fuels?
c. Why is the European Union a leader in the fight against pollution?

4 Geographic Thinking
Seeing Patterns How are the different types of pollution interrelated?
Think about:
- how air pollution, water pollution, and buried waste cause other types of pollution

See Skillbuilder Handbook, page R8.

EXPLORING LOCAL GEOGRAPHY Find out how your community deals with pollution. Learn about laws passed by your local government, environmental safeguards used by industry, or water treatment facilities. Then write a **news article** on the subject.

Assess & Reteach

GeoFocus Have students complete the section on cleaning up Europe in their cause-and-effect charts.

Formal Assessment
- Section Quiz, p. 212

Reteaching Activity
Ask students to review their completed notes for the chapter and decide whether each effect is desirable or undesirable, giving reasons for their answers. Challenge them to offer solutions for the negative effects.

In-Depth Resources: Unit 4
- Reteaching Activity, p. 35

SECTION 2 ASSESSMENT ANSWERS

1. Places & Terms
cyanide, p. 323
European Environmental Agency, p. 324
particulates, p. 324
smog, p. 325
ozone, p. 325

2. Taking Notes
- the Rhine
- asthma, bronchitis, emphysema, lung cancer

3. Main Ideas
a. accepting environmental damage as the price of industrial growth or insisting on pollution controls, which are expensive and may slow growth
b. air pollution due to the formation of smog and ozone
c. Because pollution crosses national boundaries, international cooperation is needed to solve the problem, and the EU is an international alliance.

4. Geographic Thinking
Air pollution can pollute water when rain washes chemicals from the air; water pollution can contaminate soil when poisoned water is used in farming; poisons from buried waste can seep into water supplies.

GeoActivity

Integrated Assessment
- Rubric for a news article, 4.5

CASE STUDY OBJECTIVES

1. Describe the first steps toward European unification.
2. Examine issues facing the European Union.
3. Complete the Case Study Project by taking part in a panel discussion on the challenges of future EU expansion.
4. Analyze primary sources for different information and opinions about expansion.

SKILLBUILDER: Interpreting Maps, p. 327

Focus & Motivate

Ask students why it might be difficult to unite Europe. What factors of culture, politics, economics, and physical geography might stand in the way? *(Differing languages, currencies, and economic policies are obstacles. Different resources may mean different priorities.)*

Instruct: Objective 

Steps Toward Unity

- Which countries first began the process of European unification? *(France, West Germany, Italy, and the Benelux countries)*
- Why did they arrange joint control over coal and steel resources? *(Joint dependence on industrial resources would make it hard to go to war against each other.)*
- What document created the European Union? *(the Maastricht Treaty of 1993)*

 **In-Depth Resources: Unit 4**
- Guided Reading, p. 25

CASE STUDY

UNIFICATION: THE EUROPEAN UNION

What will become of the European Union?

EU headquarters in Brussels, Belgium

Europe's long history of conflict reached a crisis in World War II (1939-1945). In the wake of that destructive war, two goals emerged: to rebuild the nations' shattered economies and to prevent new conflict. Some people believed the best way to achieve both goals was to unify Europe. As you read the Case Study, consider the pros and cons of that idea.

Steps Toward Unity

The first step toward unification was an industrial alliance. In 1951, France, West Germany, Italy, and the Benelux countries signed a treaty that gave control of their coal and steel resources to the European Coal and Steel Community (ECSC). Because the nations would depend on each other for industrial resources, their economies would suffer if they fought again. No country could prepare for war secretly because each knew what the others were manufacturing. Further, the ECSC would set a tone of cooperation that would help Europe rebuild its economy.

The next step came in 1957 with the formation of the European Economic Community (EEC), also called the Common Market. This alliance removed trade barriers, set common economic goals, and allowed people to live and work in any member country. Between 1958 and 1968, trade among the EEC nations quadrupled.

In 1967, the EEC merged with the ECSC and another European alliance to become the European Community (EC). In 1973, the EC began to admit other European nations. In 1993, the Maastricht Treaty took effect, and the European Union (EU) replaced the EC. By 2007, the EU included 27 member nations. (See the map on page 327.)

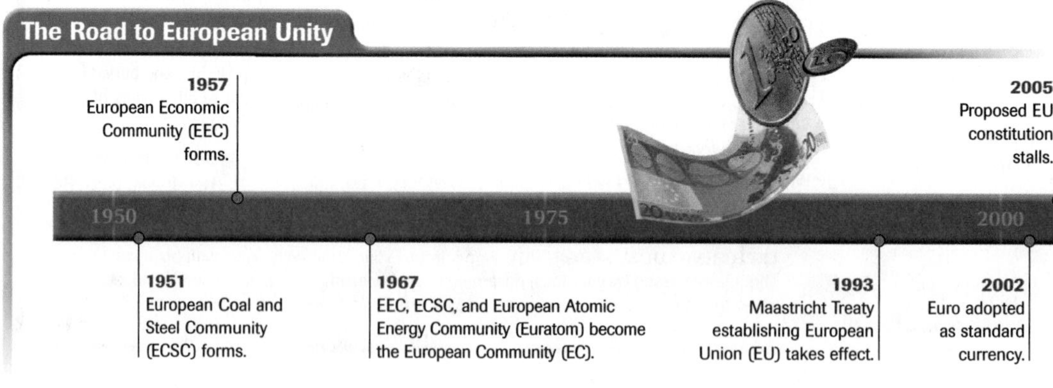
The Road to European Unity
1957
European Economic Community (EEC) forms.
2005
Proposed EU constitution stalls.
1950
1975
2000
1951
European Coal and Steel Community (ECSC) forms.
1967
EEC, ECSC, and European Atomic Energy Community (Euratom) become the European Community (EC).
1993
Maastricht Treaty establishing European Union (EU) takes effect.
2002
Euro adopted as standard currency.

CASE STUDY PROGRAM RESOURCES

 **In-Depth Resources: Unit 4**
- Guided Reading, p. 25
- Building Vocabulary, p. 29
- Reteaching Activity, p. 36

 **Guided Reading Workbook**
- Case Study

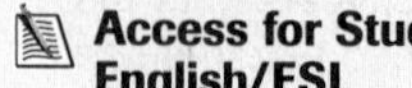 **Access for Students Acquiring English/ESL**
- Guided Reading, p. 73

Formal Assessment
- Section Quiz, p. 213

INTEGRATED TECHNOLOGY

 **Map Transparencies MT25**
- The European Union, 2000

 **Power Presentations**

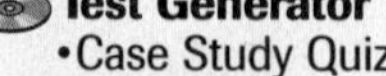 **Test Generator**
- Case Study Quiz

 hmhsocialstudies.com

TEST-TAKING RESOURCES

 **Strategies for Test Preparation**

 **Test Practice Transparencies TT47**

 **Online Test Practice**

Issues Facing the EU Today

In a little more than 50 years, the EU has increased from 6 nations to 27. In time it might expand to 30 countries that presently have almost 560 million people. Such rapid growth creates many challenges.

GROWING PAINS Many of the Eastern European nations that joined the EU in 2004 and 2007 had a Communist past. Generally, they are less prosperous than Western Europe and have little experience with democracy. Such differences may create friction among EU members.

SEE PRIMARY SOURCE D

Some Europeans fear rising tensions if Turkey joins the EU. Turkey is a Muslim nation, while the countries of Europe are predominantly Christian. Turkey also has a record of human rights abuses and of conflict with Greece. Turkey's membership process is moving slowly.

ECONOMICS AND POLITICS The Maastricht Treaty set the goal of replacing national currencies with a single currency. Having a common currency improves business efficiency and increases trade. In 2002, 12 countries began to use the new euro (symbol €) for all transactions. To adopt the euro, member states had to meet certain economic standards.

SEE PRIMARY SOURCE B

Even so, some Europeans had reservations about the euro. They feared losing control of economic factors, such as the ability of each country to set its own interest rates. Denmark and the United Kingdom chose not to adopt the euro.

As the EU grew, people realized that its original structures were inadequate to unite more than 20 nations. In 2002, work began on a new constitution. The changes created fears that the EU would become a "supernation" and replace individual nations. In 2005, the Netherlands and France rejected the constitution. All members had to accept the constitution for it to go into effect, so the process halted. EU leaders wrote the Lisbon Treaty to replace the failed constitution. The Lisbon Treaty contained many changes proposed for the constitution.

The European Union, 2007

hmhsocialstudies.com INTERACTIVE MAP

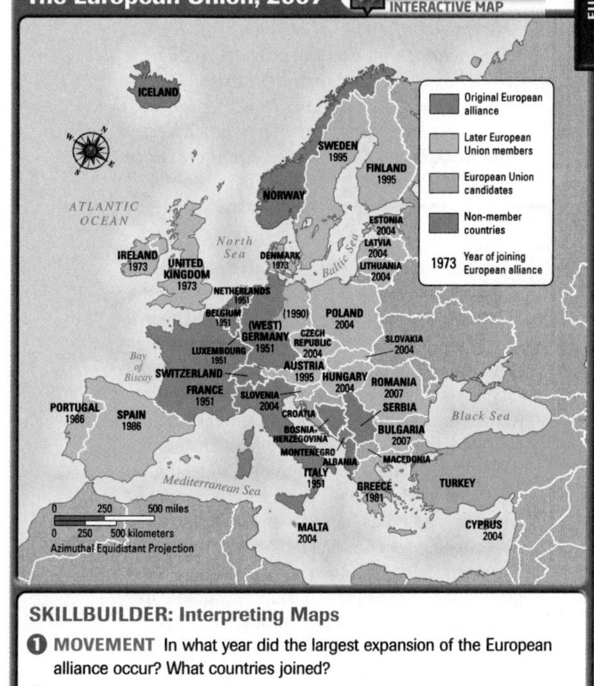

SKILLBUILDER: Interpreting Maps

1. **MOVEMENT** In what year did the largest expansion of the European alliance occur? What countries joined?
2. **REGION** Which region of Europe has the most non-member countries? Why?

Instruct: Objective 2

The European Union Today

- How are recent Eastern European members different from other EU members? *(less prosperity and experience with democracy)*
- Why do people think that tensions might increase if Turkey joins the EU? *(Turkey is culturally different, and it has a history of human rights abuses and conflicts with Greece.)*
- Why are some countries reluctant to adopt the euro? *(They fear losing control of their economies.)*
- Why do people fear a strong EU? *(They do not want a "supernation" to replace individual countries.)*

EUROPE

Interpreting Maps

The European Union, 2007

Have students examine the map. Then ask them to provide the following information: date and membership of the original European alliance; the most recent members who joined in 2007. *(The original 1951 alliance included France, Italy, Luxembourg, Belgium, the Netherlands, and Germany. The most recent members are Bulgaria and Romania.)*

SKILLBUILDER ANSWERS

1. 2004; Cyprus, the Czech Republic, Estonia, Hungary, Latvia, Lithuania, Malta, Poland, Slovakia, and Slovenia.
2. Nearly all of Turkey lies in Asia, so it has not been part of Europe historically or culturally.

DIFFERENTIATING INSTRUCTION | LESS PROFICIENT READERS

CREATING AN ISSUES CHART

Objective To help less proficient readers better understand the issues related to the expansion of the European Union

Class Time 20 minutes

Task Create a chart summarizing the key issues and concerns

Directions Have students copy the chart shown here and fill in the left column with the issues. Then have them fill in the right column of the chart by describing in their own words the concerns related to each issue in the left column. Have students share their answers with a classmate.

ISSUE	CONCERNS
Eastern European members	less prosperity, less experience with democracy
Accepting Turkey into EU	cultural differences, history of human rights issues and conflicts with Greece
Adoption of euro	less financial control
Ratification of constitution	fears that a "supernation" will replace existing nations

Instruct: Objective 3

Case Study Project: Panel Discussion

- What is your research goal? *(to learn how EU expansion might affect a country of a certain type)*
- What questions should you consider in the process? *(how expansion would affect the economy; how adopting the euro affects new EU members; political and cultural effects that might arise)*
- What should you produce for the project? *(a 1–2 minute summary of my position and a visual aid)*

Instruct: Objective 4

Using Primary Sources

- Ⓐ***News Article*** How has EU expansion affected the UK work-force? *(More than 640,000 Eastern Europeans have entered the work-force of the United Kingdom.)*
- Ⓑ***Radio Interview*** Does Marketa Sichtarova want the Czech Republic to adopt the euro quickly? Explain. *(No, hasty adoption might hurt the economy; ECB policies don't fit new members' economic needs.)*

More About

Challenges Facing the EU

When the United States went to war against Iraq in 2003, EU members responded individually rather than as an alliance. The UK joined the fight; France and Germany opposed the war. Expanding the EU to include more nations with varied backgrounds may increase the chance of such conflicts.

CASESTUDY

PROJECT Panel Discussion

Primary sources A to E on these two pages present information and opinions on expansion of the EU. Use these sources and your own research to prepare for a panel discussion on EU expansion. You might use the Internet and the library for research.

Suggested Steps

1. Form a group of three students. Each student will represent one type of country: an original EU member, a recent EU member, and an EU candidate.
2. Research how future expansion might affect your type of country. Consider the following questions during your research:
   - How do people in your type of country feel about EU membership?
   - How might future expansion affect the economies of your type of country?
   - What potential problems face nations who want to adopt the euro?
   - What political or cultural issues might arise because of EU expansion?
3. Create a visual to be shown during the panel discussion.
4. Hold a discussion before the class. Each member should give a short 1-2 minute summary of his or her position; then the panel should discuss their differences.

Materials and Supplies

- Writing paper
- Posterboard
- Encyclopedias and reference books
- Computer
- Internet access
- Felt-tip markers

PRIMARY SOURCE A

News Article *One of the goals of the European Union was for citizens to be able to travel freely among member states. This article, published by BBC News on May 22, 2007, explains how that policy has affected the workforce of the United Kingdom since the EU expanded.*

Almost 8,000 Romanian and Bulgarian workers registered to work in the UK in the three months after their countries joined the European Union in January. The Home Office [a British government department] added that a further 49,000 workers from eight other Eastern European countries, which are already in the EU, applied to work in the UK. More than 640,000 workers from Eastern Europe have sought work in the UK since the EU expanded in May 2004. The [British] government has restricted rights for Bulgarian and Romanian workers. Romania and Bulgaria joined the European Union in January 2007—but the government decided not to allow its workers free access to the British labour market.

PRIMARY SOURCE B

Radio Interview *In an interview given in 2003, just before the Czech Republic joined the EU, Czech economist Marketa Sichtarova discussed the economic effects of the euro on countries just joining the eurozone (the region using the euro).*

The eurozone comprises very different countries. There are countries such as Ireland, which suffers from high inflation. It is relatively easy to fight inflation by higher interest rates. But there are also countries like Germany which . . . suffer from high unemployment. It is also relatively easy to fight unemployment by cutting interest rates. Now, what should the European Central Bank [ECB] do? Hike the rates to help Ireland or cut the rates to help Germany? Countries within the eurozone are very different but they seem almost the same when compared to the new candidate countries, such as the Czech Republic . . . Adopting euro is a very good idea; however, adopting euro too early would mean high inflation, economic slowdown, and high unemployment.

ACTIVITY OPTION SKILLBUILDER LESSON

DISTINGUISHING FACT FROM OPINION

Explaining the Skill Tell students that it is important to distinguish fact from opinion when they read. Remind them that facts are objective statements or pieces of information that are verifiable, while opinions are expressions of personal views that cannot be verified as true or false. Point out that facts are often used to support opinions and that primary sources often contain both facts and opinions.

Applying the Skill Have students look for facts and opinions in primary sources **A** and **B** above. Then ask whether the following ideas from these sources are more likely to be facts or opinions, and why.

- Almost 8,000 Romanian and Bulgarian workers registered to work in the UK in the three months after their countries joined the European Union in January. *(fact: verifiable by government records)*
- The policies of the ECB will be . . . deadly for the Czech economy. *(opinion: a prediction that is not verifiable because it refers to the future)*
- Adopting the euro is a very good idea. *(opinion: states one economist's view, which is not verifiable*

PRIMARY SOURCE C

Survery Data *Eurobarometer is a company that surveys public opinion for the EU. In 2007, it asked people in all the current EU nations whether they supported further expansion.*

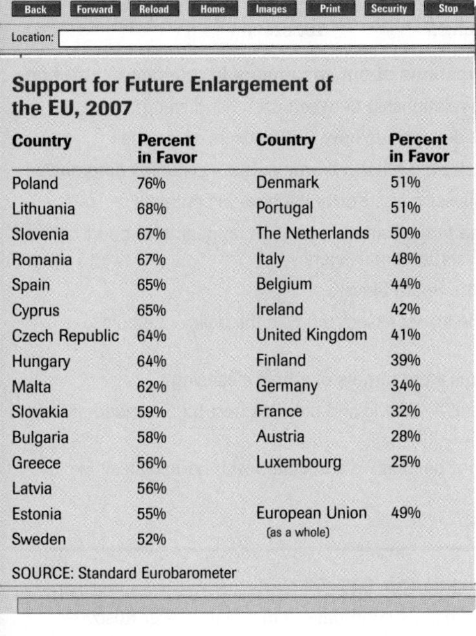

GeoNet

Back Forward Reload Home Images Print Security Stop

Location:

Support for Future Enlargement of the EU, 2007

Country	Percent in Favor	Country	Percent in Favor
Poland	76%	Denmark	51%
Lithuania	68%	Portugal	51%
Slovenia	67%	The Netherlands	50%
Romania	67%	Italy	48%
Spain	65%	Belgium	44%
Cyprus	65%	Ireland	42%
Czech Republic	64%	United Kingdom	41%
Hungary	64%	Finland	39%
Malta	62%	Germany	34%
Slovakia	59%	France	32%
Bulgaria	58%	Austria	28%
Greece	56%	Luxembourg	25%
Latvia	56%		
Estonia	55%	European Union (as a whole)	49%
Sweden	52%		

SOURCE: Standard Eurobarometer

PRIMARY SOURCE D

Background Paper *EurActiv.com is a web site offering independent journalism about the European Union. One of their services is to give background for major issues, such as Turkey's desire to become a member state.*

A number of stumbling blocks remain on the road to Turkey's EU accession. . . . Ever since the foundation of modern day Turkey in 1923, this country with a predominantly Muslim population has been a secular democracy closely aligned with the West. . . . Throughout Europe, the arguments that surround Turkey's projected accession revolve around a series of issues ranging from demographic through geographic to political. One commonly raised point is that, if and when it were to join the EU, Turkey would become the EU's most populated member state. . . . Another argument is rooted in the age-old debate on whether it is possible to establish geographic borders for Europe, and whether Turkey "fits" within these borders. . . . Perhaps the most sensitive of all arguments center on the cultural and religious differences. . . . The EU member states' concerns over Turkey's human rights record as well as global and regional security-related issues have also been key factors behind Turkey's prolonged application process.

PRIMARY SOURCE E

Political Cartoon *In December 2006, the French cartoonist Frederick Deligne offered this view of Turkey's request for EU membership.*

WHAT DOES HE SAY?..
I DON'T KNOW, I DON'T SPEAK TURKISH
ADMISSIONS
EU
DELIGNE

PROJECT CheckList

Have I . . .

- ✓ researched perspectives of countries of my type
- ✓ answered all relevant questions
- ✓ prepared a 1-2 minute summary of my position and answers to opposing views
- ✓ created a visual for the discussion?

Instruct: Objective 4

Using Primary Sources

- Ⓒ ***Background Pape*** Why is Turkey's population a stumbling block to its membership in the EU? *(It would immediately become the most populated nation in the EU.)*
- What might cause EU members to worry that Turkey is not democratic enough? *(its human rights record)*
- Ⓓ ***Data*** Do the original members of the EU favor or oppose expansion of the EU? *(mostly oppose)*
- How do Romania and Bulgaria, the two newest EU members, feel about expansion? *(mostly favor it)*
- Ⓔ ***Political Cartoon*** Does the cartoon offer a hopeful or pessimistic view of Turkey's chance at EU membership? Explain. *(pessimistic because the man's hand has been slammed in the door)*
- Which possible source of conflict is emphasized by the line *I don't speak Turkish?* *(cultural differences)*

Assess & Reteach

GeoFocus Have students complete the cause-and-effect chart they began at the start of this chapter.

Formal Assessment
- Case Study Quiz, p. 213

Reteaching Activity
Have students write a short paragraph describing historical efforts to unite Europe and summarizing key issues surrounding European integration.

In-Depth Resources: Unit 4
- Reteaching Activity, p. 36

RUBRIC CASE STUDY PROJECT

PANEL DISCUSSION

For the Case Study Project, students should:

- Based on research, summarize the position of a country in a certain category on the subject of EU expansion.
- Produce a clear, imaginative visual that complements their presentation.
- Present a concise, well-organized summary of their position.
- Play an active role in the panel discussion.

Grading Rubric Evaluate student performance as Exceptional, Acceptable or Poor in each of the following categories:

	Exceptional	Acceptable	Poor
Communicates ideas and positions clearly			
Fulfills assigned role			
Cooperates with other group members			
Shares responsibility for the activity			

CHAPTER 14 ASSESSMENT

Reviewing Places & Terms

A. Answers

1. Slobodan Milošević, p. 319
2. South Slavs, p. 319
3. ethnic cleansing, p. 320
4. KLA, p. 321
5. Vojislav Kostunica, p. 321
6. cyanide, p. 323
7. European Environmental Agency, p. 324
8. particulates, p. 324
9. smog, p. 325
10. ozone, p. 325

B. Possible Responses

11. Ozone is a gas found in smog.
12. It poisoned many fish, wiped out livelihoods, and endangered health.
13. Milošević led Serbia into war and international conflict; Kostunica was a reform leader elected to replace Milošević.
14. Both were president of Yugoslavia.
15. The report might include cyanide, particulates, smog, and ozone.
16. They were Slavic people who migrated from Poland and Russia and settled in the Balkan Peninsula.
17. Slobodan Milošević is associated with that policy.
18. Muslims and Croats were targeted in Bosnia, and Albanians were targeted in Kosovo.
19. They are enemies because Milošević was the leader when Serbia tried to wipe out Albanian culture in Kosovo, and the KLA was the group that attacked Serbian officials in an attempt to liberate Kosovo.
20. Air pollution is associated with particulates, which are very small particles of airborne liquid or solid matter.

Chapter 14 Assessment

VISUAL SUMMARY
TODAY'S ISSUES IN EUROPE

Conflict

Turmoil in the Balkans

- Yugoslavia was a nation of many ethnic groups distributed among six republics.
- Serbia tried to dominate Yugoslavia, causing several republics to declare independence. Brutal wars followed. The UN and the United States negotiated peace.
- Seeking to re-establish control over Kosovo, Serbia tried to drive Albanians from Kosovo. NATO intervened to stop the violence.

Environment

Cleaning Up Europe

- Industry, sewage, agriculture, and other activities have caused water and air pollution in Europe.
- Pollution has caused disease, damaged buildings, and harmed livestock.
- Both national and international efforts are being made to clean up Europe.

Economics

The European Union

- After the destruction of World War II, France, Germany, Italy, and the Benelux countries joined in an economic alliance to foster cooperation.
- In time, this alliance began to admit other nations and to pursue more general goals.
- The alliance became the European Union (EU) in 1993. The EU faced the issues of adopting a common currency, settling political and economic differences, and expanding EU membership.

Reviewing Places & Terms

A. Briefly explain the importance of each of the following.

1. Slobodan Milošević
2. South Slavs
3. ethnic cleansing
4. KLA
5. Vojislav Kostunica
6. cyanide
7. European Environmental Agency
8. particulates
9. smog
10. ozone

B. Answer the questions about vocabulary in complete sentences.

11. What is the relationship between ozone and smog?
12. What effect did cyanide have on the rivers of Europe?
13. How are Slobodan Milošević and Vojislav Kostunica different?
14. What do Milošević and Kostunica have in common?
15. Which of the terms listed above might appear in a report by the European Environmental Agency?
16. Who were the South Slavs?
17. Who was the leader associated with the policy of ethnic cleansing?
18. Which groups were targets of ethnic cleansing?
19. Can Slobodan Milošević and the KLA best be described as allies or enemies? Explain.
20. Which type of pollution is associated with particulates? Explain.

Main Ideas

Turmoil in the Balkans (pp. 319–322)

1. How did historic events contribute to the conflict over Kosovo?
2. How did the diversity of Bosnia and Herzegovina's population contribute to the conflict there?
3. What did international officials discover after Serbian forces withdrew from Kosovo?
4. What are possible sources of future conflict in the Balkans?

Cleaning Up Europe (pp. 323–325)

5. What are the effects of acid rain?
6. Which region became heavily polluted under Communist rule?
7. Why is pollution such a difficult issue to resolve?

The European Union (pp. 326–329)

8. What organizations were forerunners of the European Union?
9. Why did European leaders believe that an economic alliance would help prevent war?
10. What are some possible problems associated with admitting formerly Communist countries to the EU?

Main Ideas

1. The Serbs lost their independence at Kosovo Polje in 1389 and wanted to regain the province; over time, however, the population of Kosovo became mostly Albanian.
2. Croats and Muslims favored independence; Serbs did not; this led to fighting among them.
3. The Serbs had carried out torture and massacres.
4. anger over past wrongs, ethnic loyalty, poverty, and the desire of Montenegro and Kosovo for independence
5. It harms river and lake environments, damages buildings, and kills trees.
6. Eastern Europe
7. It crosses national boundaries, and is difficult and costly to clean up.
8. European Coal and Steel Community (ECSC), the European Economic Community (EEC)—also called the Common Market—and the European Community (EC)
9. The members would depend on each other for resources, so their economies would suffer if they fought each other.
10. There might be tension because they have less developed economies and little experience of democratic rule.

Critical Thinking

1. Using Your Notes

Use your completed chart to answer these questions.

	Causes	Effects
Issue 1: Conflict		
Issue 2: Pollution		

a. Which of these issues has caused physical damage to Europe? Explain.

b. Do you think the issues are linked? Explain.

2. Geographic Themes

a. REGION In what way is the European Union creating a new region?

b. MOVEMENT What natural processes spread pollution from its point of origin?

3. Identifying Themes

Reread the story about the Tisza River on page 323. How do the five themes of geography relate to that story?

4. Making Inferences

What factors do you think led the Yugoslav people to vote Slobodan Milošević out of office?

5. Drawing Conclusions

How important is international cooperation in solving Europe's problems? Explain using specific examples.

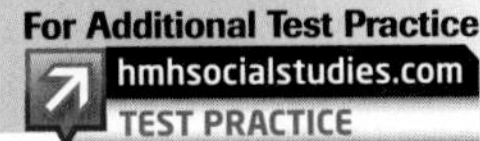

Geographic Skills: Interpreting Graphs

EU Trade, 2003
(as percentage of total trade)

Use the graph to answer the following questions.

1. PLACE Which country does the highest percentage of its trade within the EU?
2. PLACE Which two countries do the lowest percentage of trade within the EU?
3. MOVEMENT Judging by the countries shown here, is there more trade within the EU or between the EU and non-member countries? Explain.

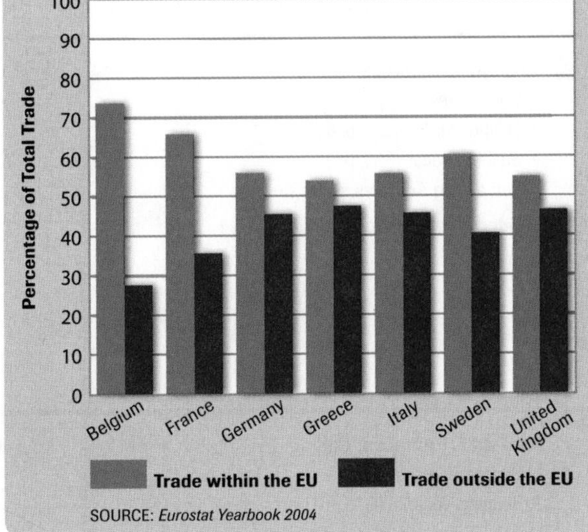

SOURCE: *Eurostat Yearbook 2004*

Research trade statistics for Austria, Denmark, Finland, Ireland, Luxembourg, Netherlands, Portugal, and Spain. Create an expanded graph by adding data for these EU countries to those already shown.

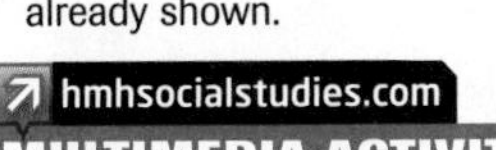

MULTIMEDIA ACTIVITY 21st CENTURY

Use the links at **hmhsocialstudies.com** to do research about pollution in Europe. Learn about the "Green" political parties and their views on what should be done.

Writing About Geography Write a summary of your findings. Include a chart listing the programs proposed by the "Green" political parties. List the Web sites that were your sources.

EUROPE

Critical Thinking

1. a. Both pollution and conflict have damaged buildings, the land itself, and caused injuries and deaths.
   b. Both conflict and pollution might lead to further support for the EU.
2. a. by using a common currency, promoting trade and free travel among members, and abiding by the same laws
   b. winds, precipitation, the motion of rivers and oceans, and water seeping through soil
3. industrial pollution shows human-environment interaction; Romanian gold mine and Tisza River are locations; characteristics of the Tisza before and after the spill describe place; river spreading cyanide is movement; affected area is a region
4. They may have been tired of war; they may have felt isolated by international disapproval.
5. It is essential. This is demonstrated by the pressure brought on Serbia by the UN and NATO, and by the international efforts to clean up pollution that crosses national boundaries.

GeoActivity

Integrated Assessment
- Rubric for a graph, 2.3

Formal Assessment
- Chapter Test, Forms A, B, and C, pp. 214–225

Geographic Skills

1. Belgium
2. Greece and the United Kingdom
3. within the European Union because each does over 50% of its trade with EU countries

MULTIMEDIA ACTIVITY

For the report on pollution in Europe, students should:

- Present a concise, well-organized report that emphasizes the impact of pollution on politics in Europe.
- Summarize efforts of political parties (such as the "Greens") to control pollution.
- Produce a clear, imaginative visual to complement the report.
- Include references to the Web sites used as sources.

Grading Rubric Evaluate student performance as Exceptional, Acceptable, or Poor in each of the following categories:

	Exceptional	Acceptable	Poor
Writing is clear, focused, and logical			
Introductory sentence clearly states the topic and purpose			
Provides necessary facts and examples			
Uses correct grammar, spelling, and punctuation			

Physical Geography of Russia and the Republics

OVERVIEW	INSTRUCTIONAL RESOURCES	
CHAPTER 15 ESSENTIAL QUESTION How do the extremes of the region's physical geography affect the people of Russia and the Republics? **Focus on the Essential Question Podcast**	**In-Depth Resources: Unit 5** • Unit Atlas Activities, p. 1 • Building Vocabulary, p. 9 • Exploring Today's Issues, pp. 28–31 **Outline Maps with Activities** • Russia and the Republics: Physical, pp. 41–42 • Russia and the Republics: Political, pp. 43–44 **Block Schedule Strategies** **Chapter Summaries** (English/Spanish)	**Interactive Online Edition** TOS **ExamView® Assessment Suite** (English/Spanish) TOS **CalendarPlanner** **Power Presentations with Media Gallery** **Critical Thinking Transparencies** • CT15 hmhsocialstudies.com INTERACTIVE
SECTION 1 **LANDFORMS AND RESOURCES** **MAIN IDEAS** • Flat plains stretch across the western and central areas of the region. • The southern and eastern areas of the region are more mountainous. • Russia and the Republics are rich in resources, but many resources are in isolated regions with brutal climates.	**In-Depth Resources: Unit 5** • Guided Reading, p. 3 • Skillbuilder Practice, p. 8 • Building Vocabulary, p. 9 • Reteaching Activities, p. 10 **Guided Reading Workbook,** Section 1	**Critical Thinking Transparencies** • CT47 Lakes and Rivers in Russia and the Republics
SECTION 2 **CLIMATE AND VEGETATION** **MAIN IDEAS** • Humid continental and subarctic climates dominate much of the region. • A major influence on the region's climates is its distance from the moderating influence of the sea. • From north to south, the region's vegetation zones are tundra, forest, steppe, and desert.	**In-Depth Resources: Unit 5** • Guided Reading, p. 4 • Building Vocabulary, p. 9 • Reteaching Activities, p. 11 **Guided Reading Workbook,** Section 2	**Map Transparencies** • MT28 Russia and the Republics: Climate Zones
SECTION 3 **HUMAN-ENVIRONMENT INTERACTION** **MAIN IDEAS** • Irrigation policies in Central Asia have caused a dramatic shrinkage of the Aral Sea. • The region's harsh climate has been both an obstacle and an advantage for its inhabitants. • The Trans-Siberian Railroad opened up the resources of Siberia to development.	**In-Depth Resources: Unit 5** • Guided Reading, p. 5 • Building Vocabulary, p. 9 • Reteaching Activities, p. 12 • GeoWorkshop, pp. 35–36 • Map and Graph Skills, pp. 6–7 **Guided Reading Workbook,** Section 3	

ASSESSMENT

SE **Chapter Assessment,** pp. 358-359

Formal Assessment
- Chapter Tests, Forms A, B, and C, pp. 229-240

TOS **ExamView® Assessment Suite**

Strategies for Test Preparation

hmhsocialstudies.com TEST PRACTICE

SE **Section Assessment,** p. 349

Formal Assessment
- Section Quiz, p. 226

Integrated Assessment
- Rubric for a poster, 1.1

Test Practice Transparencies TT48

SE **Section Assessment,** p. 352

Formal Assessment
- Section Quiz, p. 227

Integrated Assessment
- Rubric for a graph, 2.3

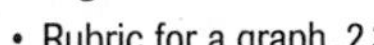
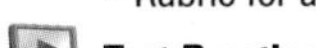
Test Practice Transparencies TT49

SE **Section Assessment,** p. 356

Formal Assessment
- Section Quiz, p. 228

Integrated Assessment
- Rubric for a Venn diagram, 2.8

Test Practice Transparencies TT50

CHART KEY:

SE Student Edition	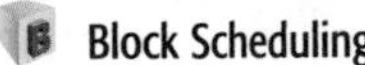 Block Scheduling	DVD/CD-ROM
TE Teacher's Edition	TOS Teacher One Stop	 MP3 Audio
Printable Resource	Presentation Resource	 HISTORY™

Program Resources available on TOS and @ hmhsocialstudies.com

SUPPORTING RESOURCES

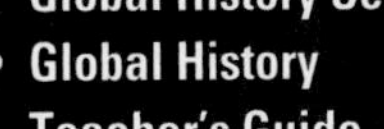

- Multimedia Classroom Global History Series
- Global History Teacher's Guide

Social Studies Trade Library Collection

- World Regions Trade Collection

For more information or to purchase these resources, go to  hmhsocialstudies.com

DIFFERENTIATED INSTRUCTION

English Learners	Struggling Readers	Gifted and Talented Students
 **Spanish/English Guided Reading Workbook** **Access for Students Acquiring English/ESL** Spanish Translations, pp. 77–82 **Chapter Summaries** (English/Spanish) TE **TE Activity** Locating and Describing Landforms, p. 346	 **Chapter Summaries** (English/Spanish) TE **TE Activity** Locating and Describing Landforms, p. 346	 TE **TE Activity** Making Predictions, p. 355

ENRICHMENT ACTIVITIES

The following activities are especially suitable for classes following block schedules.

SE **Student Edition,** p. 344–359 • Understanding Time Zones, p. 357	hmhsocialstudies.com INTERACTIVE • Rail Routes Across Russia, p. 355

UNIT 5 ATLAS AND CHAPTER 15 PACING GUIDE

BLOCK SCHEDULE LESSON PLAN OPTIONS: 90-MINUTE PERIOD

DAY 1

UNIT PREVIEW, pp. 332-335
Class Time 45 minutes

- **Discussion** Discuss the Unit Introduction, using the discussion prompts on TE pages 332–333.
  Class Time 20 minutes

- **Today's Issues** Introduce Today's Issues in Russia and the Republics using the Exploring the Issues questions on PE page 334.
  Class Time 25 minutes

UNIT ATLAS, pp. 336-343
Class Time 45 minutes

- **Small Groups** Divide the class into four groups and have each group prepare a summary of the patterns they see in one section of the Unit Atlas: Physical Geography, Human Geography, Regional Patterns, and Regional Data File. Have each group share their summary with the entire class.

DAY 2

SECTION 1, pp. 345-349
Class Time 40 minutes

- **Oral Quiz** Orally quiz the class on the section's content, using the prompts on TE pages 345–348.

SECTION 2, pp. 351-352
Class Time 50 minutes

- **Skillbuilder Lesson** Use the lesson on creating a sketch map on TE page 351, in which students depict the major influences on the climates of the region.
  Class Time 25 minutes

- **Comparing Russia and Canada** Using the vegetation map of Russia and the Republics on PE page 351 and the vegetation map of Canada on PE page 125, have students compare the vegetation regions of Russia and Canada.
  Class Time 25 minutes

DAY 3

SECTION 3, pp. 353-357
Class Time 35 minutes

- **Oral Summary** Call on student volunteers to orally summarize the main ideas in the three main subsections of this section.

CHAPTER 15 REVIEW AND ASSESSMENT, pp. 358–359
Class Time 50 minutes

- **Review** Have students work in pairs and use their GeoFocus graphic organizers to review the chapter's main ideas.
  Class Time 15 minutes

- **Assessment** Have students complete the Chapter 15 Assessment.
  Class Time 35 minutes

TEACHER-TESTED ACTIVITY *Creating a Mnemonic Aid*

Class Time One-half class period

Task Create a mnemonic to aid in learning the names of Russia and the Republics.

Supplies
- Notebook paper
- Pen/Pencil°

Purpose Students often have difficulty remembering the names of Russia and the Central Asian Republics. A memory helper may be needed.

Activity Most of us are familiar with the elementary mnemonic that helped us remember the names of the Great Lakes—H.O.M.E.S (Huron, Ontario, Michigan, Erie, and Superior). Have students invent a creative mnemonic that can help them and classmates remember the names of Russia and the Republics. Allow students to offer their suggestions to the class for possible adoption by others to help them remember the names.

Dan Richardson
Geography Teacher, East Troy High School, East Troy, Illinois

TECHNOLOGY IN THE CLASSROOM

The Internet is an excellent way to access and compare photographs and other images. The United States Geological Survey's Earthshots site provides satellite images of different parts of the Earth. The images, which were taken over periods of three or four decades, allow students to see changes to the environment over time and are thus excellent tools in the geography classroom.

Objective Students will view online satellite images of the Aral Sea, analyze what they see, and draw maps showing changes to the sea.

Task Have students look at satellite images of the Aral Sea and discuss what the images reveal. Have them outline the sea's shore in 1964, the present time, and fifty years from now and write one or two paragraphs explaining the reasons for the changes they observe.

Class Time 2 class periods

1. Have students read pages 353–354, about the Aral Sea. Discuss the problems the sea is facing and the reasons for these problems.
2. Have students go to the Earthshots page (link from **hmhsocialstudies.com**). If you have a little extra time, have students go to the first link ("First time readers: start at Garden City, Kansas"). This section will introduce them to the satellite images and explain how to "read" the images they will see. If you do not have time for this introduction, provide the class with a brief overview of what satellite images are and what the colors mean (see the Garden City article).
3. Ask students to select the Aral Sea article. Have them read the article and view the satellite images from each year.
4. Ask students to explain in writing or a class discussion what the satellite images show. In particular, they should describe the evidence they see that indicates that the Aral Sea is shrinking.
5. Give each student a blank outline map from the link at **hmhsocialstudies.com**. Ask them to compare this map to the satellite images. Which year's satellite image does the sea on the outline map most resemble?
6. Have students use red pencils or markers to outline the sea on the map as it appeared in 1964. Then have them use green pencils to outline how the sea might appear fifty years from now, based on what they have learned about what's happening to it and the changes they noticed on the satellite images. Alternately, have them draw the outlines of the sea for 1964, the present time, and fifty years from now on separate pieces of paper.
7. Have students word process paragraphs describing the changes to the Aral Sea, the reasons for these changes, and predictions for the sea's future. They should be sure to discuss the ways in which the region's climate and physical geography exacerbate problems caused by the diversion of the rivers.

Previewing the Unit

These opening pages provide an overview of Russia and the Republics, a region distinguished by its huge area, extremes in climates, and turbulent political history. The breakup of the Soviet Union in 1991 resulted in the creation of 15 independent republics and unleashed conflict among the region's many ethnic groups.

Discussion Prompts

Exploring Prior Knowledge Ask students the following questions about Russia and the Republics to determine their prior knowledge of the region:

- On what two continents is Russia located? *(Europe and Asia)*
- What are Russian winters like? *(long and cold)*

Interpreting Maps Ask students to refer to the satellite image of this region to answer the following questions:

- What pole is this region near? *(the North Pole)*
- What oceans border Russia? *(Arctic and Pacific)*
- What landforms do you recognize? *(mountains and plains)*

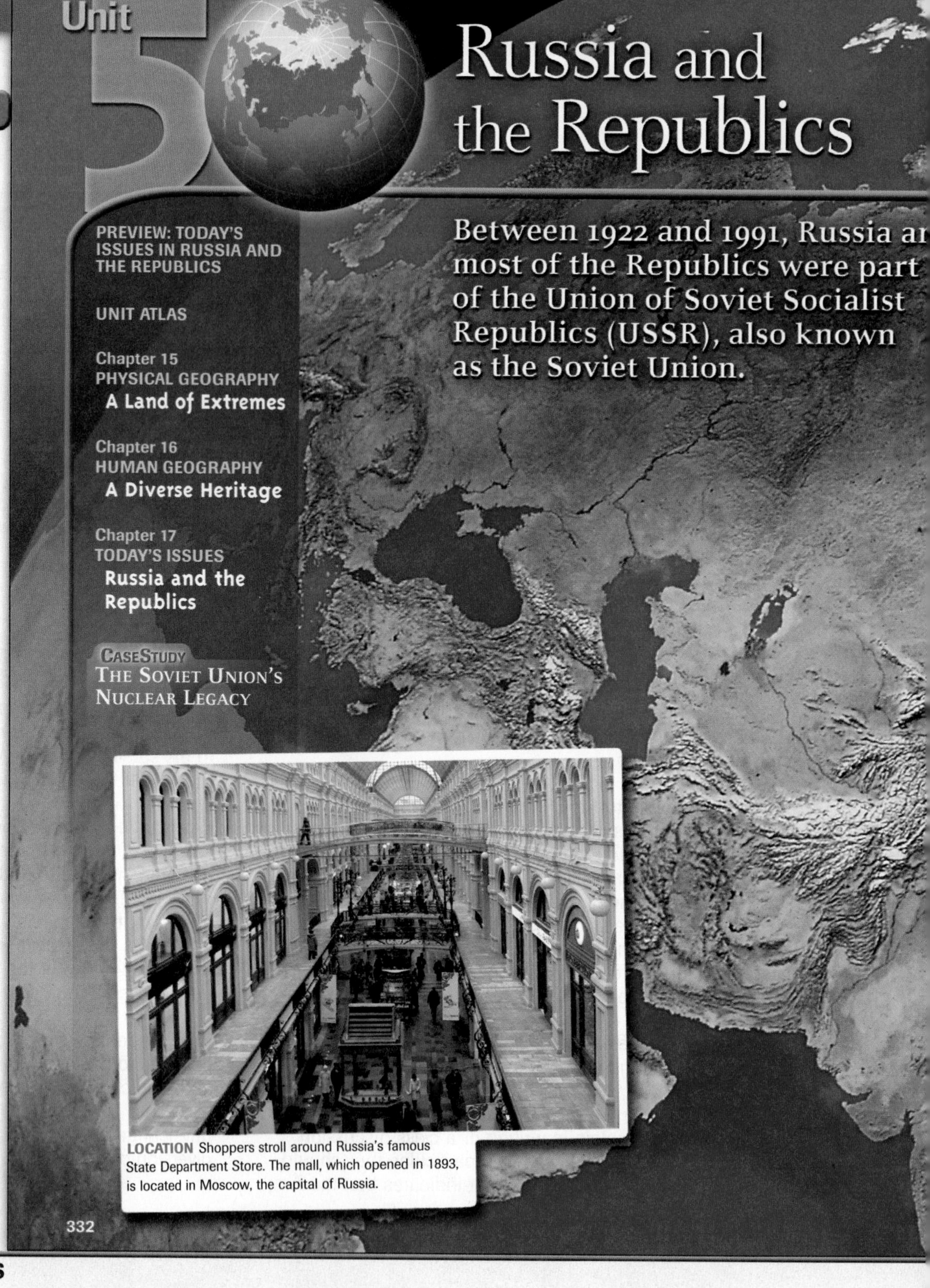

Unit 5

Russia and the Republics

Between 1922 and 1991, Russia and most of the Republics were part of the Union of Soviet Socialist Republics (USSR), also known as the Soviet Union.

PREVIEW: TODAY'S ISSUES IN RUSSIA AND THE REPUBLICS

UNIT ATLAS

Chapter 15
PHYSICAL GEOGRAPHY
A Land of Extremes

Chapter 16
HUMAN GEOGRAPHY
A Diverse Heritage

Chapter 17
TODAY'S ISSUES
Russia and the Republics

CASESTUDY
THE SOVIET UNION'S NUCLEAR LEGACY

LOCATION Shoppers stroll around Russia's famous State Department Store. The mall, which opened in 1893, is located in Moscow, the capital of Russia.

332

UNIT 5 ADDITIONAL RESOURCES

BOOKS FOR THE TEACHER

Longworth, Philip. ***Russia: The Once and Future Empire from Pre-History to Putin.*** St. Martin's Press, 2006.

Gorbachev, Mikhail. ***On My Country and the World.*** NY: Columbia University Press, 2000. A discussion of Russia's past, present, and future by the last leader of the Soviet Union.

BOOKS FOR THE STUDENT

Insight Guide: Russia, Belarus & Ukraine. Maspeth, NY: Langenscheidt, 2000. Travel guide with information on history, culture, and contemporary life.

Taplin, Mark. ***Open Lands.*** South Royalton, VT: Steerforth Press, 1997. Travelogue of journey through the region.

VIDEOS

Russia: Then and Now Series—The Rise and Fall of the Soviet Union. Educational Videos, 1994. History of Russia from the Bolshevik Revolution to the collapse of the Soviet Union.

Trans-Siberia. Publishers Choice Video, 1995. A view of the vast expanse of Russia.

INTERNET

For more on the geography of Russia and the Republics, visit . . .

hmhsocialstudies.com

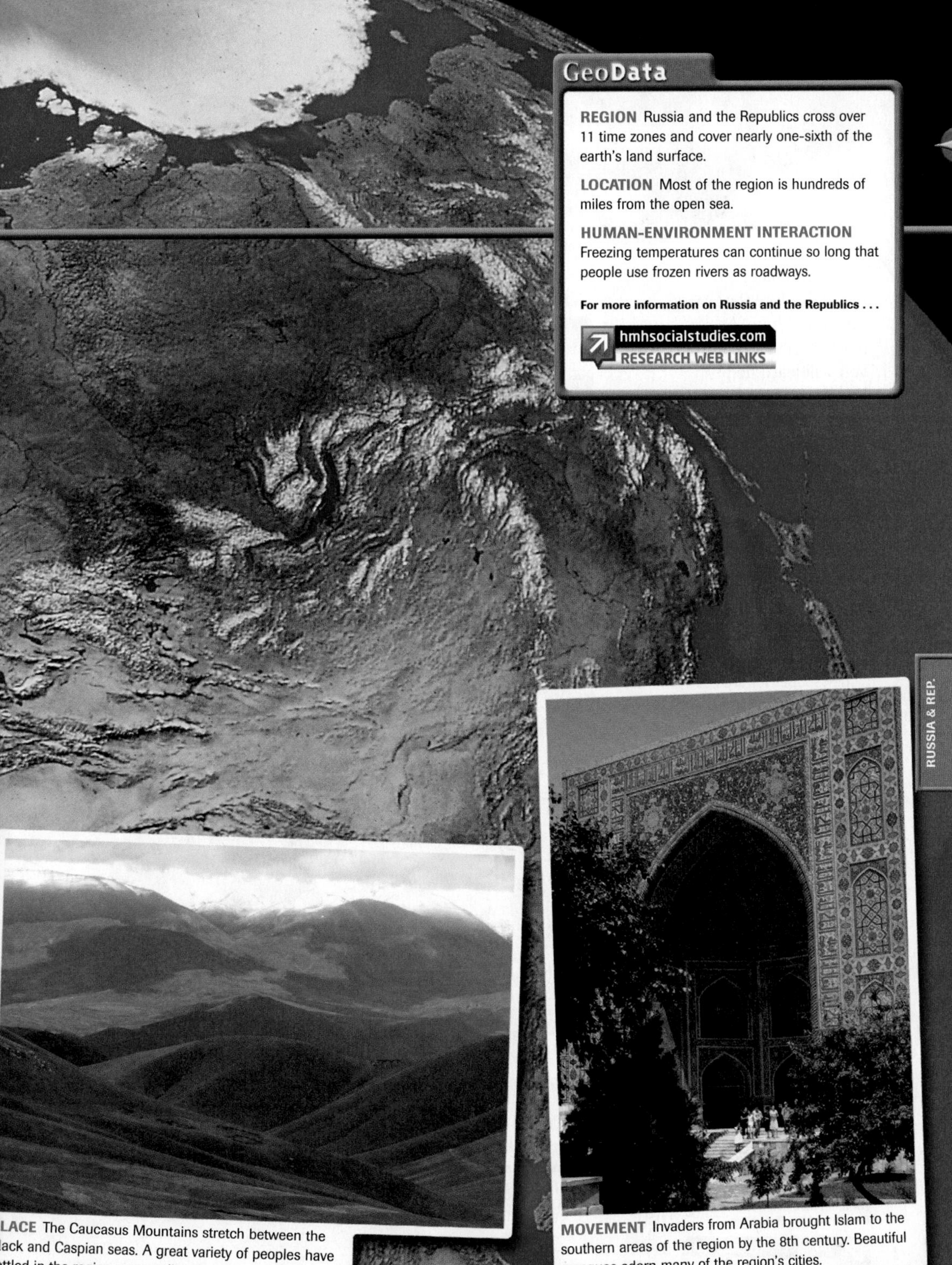

GeoData

REGION Russia and the Republics cross over 11 time zones and cover nearly one-sixth of the earth's land surface.

LOCATION Most of the region is hundreds of miles from the open sea.

HUMAN-ENVIRONMENT INTERACTION Freezing temperatures can continue so long that people use frozen rivers as roadways.

For more information on Russia and the Republics . . .

hmhsocialstudies.com
RESEARCH WEB LINKS

LACE The Caucasus Mountains stretch between the ack and Caspian seas. A great variety of peoples have ttled in the region surrounding the mountains.

MOVEMENT Invaders from Arabia brought Islam to the southern areas of the region by the 8th century. Beautiful mosques adorn many of the region's cities.

Interpreting Photographs

Moscow's State Department Store

This ornate building dates back to the reign of the czars in Russia. During the rule of Soviet communists, few goods could be found in the mall. Today, it features cafes and shops that sell mostly Western luxury goods.

Ask students how the State Department Store, also known as GUM, compares with American shopping malls. *(It is much older and more ornate. Store names and advertising are not conspicuous.)*

Caucasus Mountains

The republics of Georgia, Azerbaijan, Armenia, and parts of Russia are located in the Caucasus Mountains region.

Have students locate the Caucasus Mountains between the two large seas on the left of the satellite map. Then ask students what pattern of settlement the photograph shows. *(small farms or villages in the mountain valleys)*

Mosque in Samarqand

Samarqand, located in the republic of Uzbekistan, is one of the oldest cities in Central Asia. It dates back to the 300s B.C. and has been invaded and ruled by many groups of people during its long history.

Ask students to identify the distinctive features in this example of Islamic architecture. *(simple, graceful lines; elaborate exterior decoration with mosaics and gold; dome, arched doorways, and towers)*

ACTIVITY OPTION | COOPERATIVE LEARNING

CREATING A TRAVEL BROCHURE

Objective To identify distinctive physical and cultural characteristics of Russia and the Republics

Class Time 60 minutes

Task Create a travel brochure showing some of the highlights of the region

Directions Divide students into small groups. Direct individual members of each group to choose one of the countries in this region, identify a tourist attraction, and provide a photograph and description of the attraction. Group members should then compile their information to create a travel brochure for the region. The completed brochures should be visually appealing and clear and easy to read.

Previewing Today's Issues

These pages provide a preview of three key issues that Russia and the Republics face today: conflict between regional minorities, change from a command economy to a market economy, and the nuclear legacy of the Soviet Union. These topics will be more fully explored in Chapter 17.

 **In-Depth Resources, Unit 5**
- Exploring the Issues, pp. 28–31

CONFLICT
After the fall of the Soviet Union in 1991, several groups took advantage of the weakened central authority to seek independence. In the Russian republic of Chechnya, rebels began to fight for independence from Russia. Russia has invaded Chechnya twice to stop the rebellion.

Discussion Prompt

- What emotion do you see in the face of the Chechen woman in this photograph? *(Responses will vary. Students may say that the woman appears grim or determined to carry on in the midst of violence and destruction.)*

Today's Issues in Russia and the Republics

Today, Russia and the Republics face the issues previewed here. As you read Chapters 15 and 16, you will learn helpful background information. You will study the issues themselves in Chapter 17.

In a small group, answer the questions below. Then participate in a class discussion of your answers.

Exploring the Issues

1. CONFLICT Search a newspaper for articles about conflicts in Russia and the Republics today. What do these conflicts have in common? How are they different?
2. ECONOMIC CHANGE Think about the different economic systems you learned about in Chapter 4. How might changing from a command economy to a market economy be difficult?
3. NUCLEAR LEGACY What impact could Soviet nuclear programs have on the region's economy?

For more on these issues in Russia and the Republics . . .

CONFLICT

How do new nations establish law and order?

After the collapse of the Soviet Union in 1991, groups in different parts of the region took up arms to fight for independence. This photo shows a woman and child from a region of Russia called Chechnya. Russia invaded Chechnya twice in the 1990s to end an independence movement in the region.

334 UNIT 5

EXPLORING THE ISSUES ANSWERS

1. CONFLICT Students might discuss the legacy of the Soviet Union or the role of regional ethnic and religious differences.
2. ECONOMIC CHANGE Students might point out the difficulty of shifting decisions about production and distribution from the central government to consumers.
3. NUCLEAR LEGACY Students might note that Soviet nuclear programs caused serious environmental and health problems and that economic resources must now be allocated to deal with these problems.

ECONOMIC CHANGE

How does a nation change its economic system?

For more than 70 years, the Soviet government made all the important economic decisions in the region. This cartoon illustrates a major economic challenge faced by the region's new leaders: to move their nations from a command economy to a market economy while maintaining economic stability.

CASESTUDY

NUCLEAR LEGACY

How have Soviet decisions affected new leaders?

In 1965, Soviet officials exploded a nuclear bomb to create this lake in Kazakhstan. The blast exposed nearby residents to harmful radiation. The region's new leaders inherited many problems caused by Soviet nuclear programs.

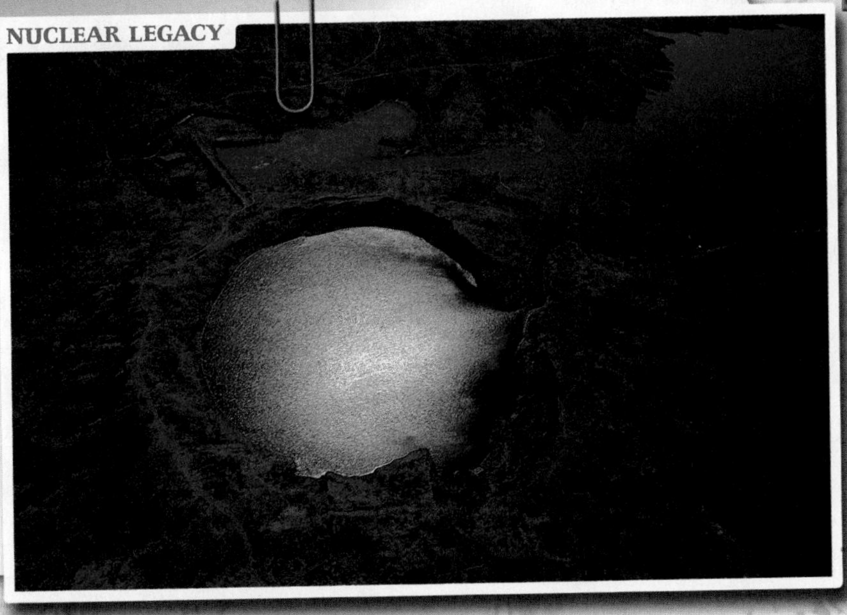

ECONOMIC CHANGE

When Russia changed from a command to a market economy, the necessary institutions were not in place. When price controls were lifted, prices rose, and the people's standard of living fell. More than a third of Russians lived in poverty during the 1990s.

Discussion Prompts

- What do you think are some benefits and drawbacks of a command economy? *(It might allow for greater focus of wealth and resources; it denies individuals the freedom to make their own economic decisions.)*
- What are some benefits and drawbacks of a market economy? *(It gives individuals the freedom to make their own economic decisions; wealth and resources might be allocated to enterprises not helpful to society as a whole.)*

CASESTUDY

NUCLEAR LEGACY

The Soviet Union has had many serious problems with nuclear energy and weapons, the most publicized of which was the explosion of a nuclear power plant at Chernobyl in 1986. It was the worst nuclear accident in history.

Discussion Prompts

- What do you know about the problems of nuclear waste disposal and contamination in the United States? *(Answers will vary.)*
- What level of environmental problems do you think Americans are willing to tolerate? *(Answers will vary.)*

ACTIVITY OPTION **INTERNET RESEARCH**

DISCUSSING RUSSIA'S NUCLEAR LEGACY

Objective To use the Internet to locate information about Russia's nuclear problems for a class discussion

Class Time 40 minutes

Task Locate information about the various aspects of Russia's nuclear problems and discuss the information found

Directions Direct students to **hmhsocialstudies.com** and have them follow the links to sources of information on various nuclear problems in Russia.

OPTIONAL ACTIVITY If Internet access is limited, have the students use such library resources as *Infotrac* or the *Readers' Guide to Periodical Literature* to find articles on this subject.

UNIT 5 ATLAS

ATLAS OBJECTIVES

1. Identify key physical features of Russia and the Republics.
2. Compare data on the region's physical geography with that on the United States.
3. Contrast the political boundaries of the former Soviet Union with those of Russia and the Republics.
4. Investigate the religious and ethnic groups of the region.
5. Identify relationships between climate and population density in Russia and the Republics.

Focus & Motivate

Ask students to give a general description of the physical geography of Russia and the Republics based on what they already know. *(Answers will vary.)*

Instruct: Objective 

Russia and the Republics: Physical

- What landform is predominant in western Russia? *(plains)*
- What two landforms are predominant in eastern Russia? *(plateaus and mountains)*
- Other than Russia, what is the region's largest republic? *(Kazakhstan)*
- What three large seas lie on Russia's western borders? *(Baltic Sea, Black Sea, Caspian Sea)*

 **In-Depth Resources, Unit 5**
- Unit Atlas Activities, p. 1

 **Outline Maps with Activities**
- Russia and the Republics: Physical, pp. 41–42

 **Map Transparencies MT26**
- Russia and the Republics: Physical

Unit ATLAS

Patterns of Physical Geography

Russia and the Republics span two continents. The part of the region that lies to the west of the Ural Mountains is part of Europe. The part of the region that lies to the east of the Urals is part of Asia.

Use the Unit Atlas to add to your knowledge of Russia and the Republics. As you study the maps and charts, notice geographic patterns and specific details about the region.

Jot down answers to the following questions in your notebook.

Making Comparisons

1. What ocean lies to the north of Russia and the Republics? How might this ocean affect the region's climate?
2. How much deeper is Lake Baikal than the deepest lake in the United States?
3. Based on these maps and charts, which region do you think has the higher population density: Russia and the Republics or the United States? Why?

Comparing Data

Lakes

	World's Deepest **Lake Baikal**	U.S. Deepest **Crater Lake**	**Caspian Sea**	**Lake Issyk-Kul**
Location	Asia (Russia)	North America	Europe-Asia	Asia (Kyrgyzstan)
Depth	5,715 feet	1,932 feet	3,363 feet	2,303 feet

Depth (feet): 0, 1,000, 2,000, 3,000, 4,000, 5,000, 6,000

MAKING COMPARISONS ANSWERS

1. The Arctic Ocean lies to the region's north. Since there are no mountains to block the Arctic air from moving into the region, the temperature of the ocean air will affect neighboring areas.
2. 3,783 feet
3. the United States, because it has far less land for about the same number of people

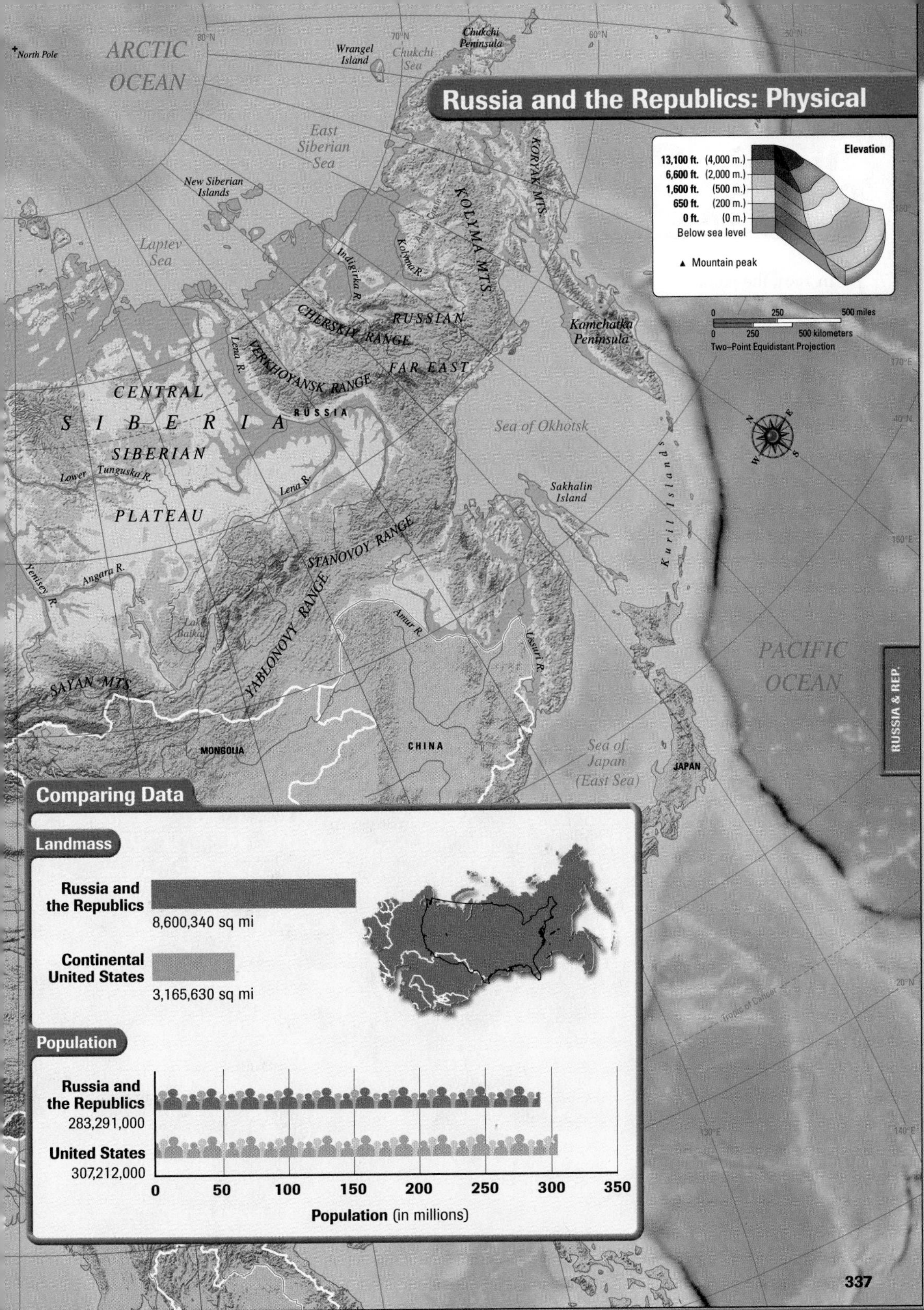

Russia and the Republics: Physical

Elevation: 13,100 ft. (4,000 m.); 6,600 ft. (2,000 m.); 1,600 ft. (500 m.); 650 ft. (200 m.); 0 ft. (0 m.); Below sea level

▲ Mountain peak

Two-Point Equidistant Projection

Comparing Data

Landmass

Russia and the Republics	8,600,340 sq mi
Continental United States	3,165,630 sq mi

Population

Russia and the Republics	283,291,000
United States	307,212,000

Population (in millions): 0, 50, 100, 150, 200, 250, 300, 350

Instruct: Objective 2

Comparing Data

- **Lakes** How does the deepest lake in the United States compare with the three deepest bodies of water in Russia and the Republics? *(It is shallower than all three.)*
- **Landmass** How many times larger is the land area of Russia and the Republics than that of the United States? *(It is over two times the size of the United States.)*
- **Population** How does the population of Russia and the Republics compare with that of the United States? *(The U.S. population is slightly larger.)*

ACTIVITY OPTION FIVE THEMES OF GEOGRAPHY

LOCATION

Exploring the Theme Students will notice from the physical map that the region's republics fall into three groups based on location. One group lies in western Russia, one in the Caucasus Mountain region, and one in south central Asia.

Understanding the Theme Ask students to make a chart that groups the republics by location. Then have them answer the following questions.

- Based on neighboring countries, what cultural influences would you expect in the western part of the region? *(Eastern European and Scandinavian)*
- Based on neighboring countries, what cultural influences would you expect on the republics in the Caucasus Mountain region? *(Russian and Southwest Asian)*
- Based on neighboring countries, what cultural influences would you expect on the republics in south central Asia? *(Asian)*

Instruct: Objective 3

Russia and the Republics: Political

- About what proportion of Soviet land area became part of independent countries with the breakup of the USSR? *(about one-fourth)*
- Into how many independent republics did the former Soviet Union break up? *(15)*
- How do the other republics differ from Russia? *(They are much smaller. They are located inland and in the west and central part of the region.)*

Outline Maps with Activities
- Russia and the Republics: Political, pp. 43–44

Map Transparencies MT27
- Russia and the Republics: Political

Unit ATLAS

Patterns of Human Geography

In 1991, the political geography of Russia and the Republics changed dramatically. For decades, the region's 15 republics had been part of the Soviet Union. Each of the republics became independent after 1991, when the Soviet Union collapsed.

Study the map of the former Soviet Union and the map of Russia and the Republics today. Then answer these questions in your notebook.

Making Comparisons

1. Where are most of the region's smaller republics located?
2. What was the largest republic in the Soviet Union? What is the largest republic in the region today?
3. To which of the Soviet Socialist Republics did Kaliningrad belong?

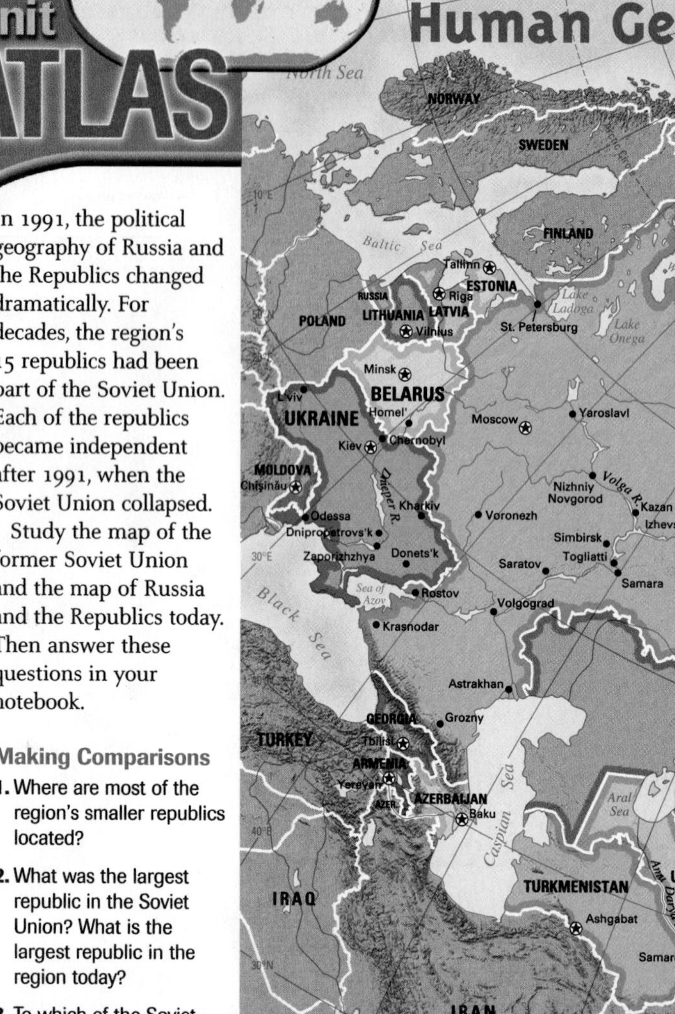

MAKING COMPARISONS ANSWERS

1. in the west and southwest
2. The R.S.F.S.R. was the largest republic during the Soviet Era. Russia is the largest republic in the region today.
3. to the R.S.F.S.R.

Russia and the Republics: Political

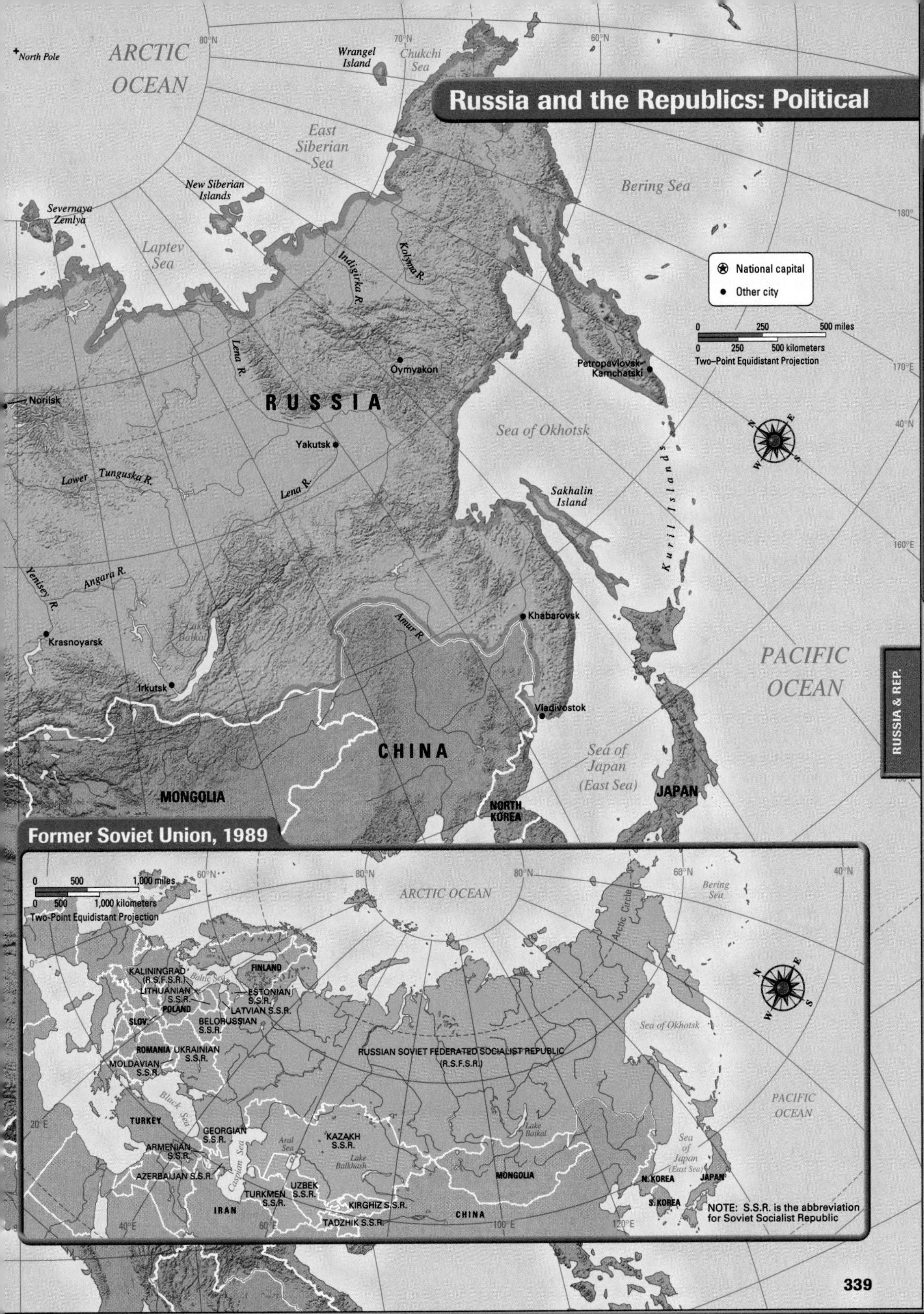

Former Soviet Union, 1989

NOTE: S.S.R. is the abbreviation for Soviet Socialist Republic

More About

The Republics

Although the region's 15 republics are now separate, independent nations, many of them belong to a voluntary association called the Commonwealth of Independent States. This association was intended to take over some of the governing functions of the former Soviet Union, such as coordinating policies in such areas as defense and foreign relations. However, the Commonwealth republics have had difficulty agreeing on policies. Lithuania, Latvia, and Estonia do not belong to the Commonwealth.

ACTIVITY OPTION | COOPERATIVE LEARNING

MAKING CHARTS

Objective To locate information about the governments and economies of the republics and summarize the information in a chart

Class Time 20 minutes

Task Use reference books or online reference sources to find basic information about the governments and economies of the 15 republics and present the information in a chart

Directions Divide students into small groups and assign several countries to each group. Each group member will be responsible for finding information about one country. Direct each group to create a chart to share with the rest of the class. Each group's chart should identify the type of government and economy of each country and summarize important characteristics.

Instruct: Objective 

Religions of Russia and the Republics /Climates of Russia and the Republics

- Into what religious category do the majority of the people in Russia and the Republics fit? *(other and nonreligious)*
- Which two religions claim about equal numbers of the people? *(Islam and Christian)*
- In what three climate zones of the region do few or no people live? *(tundra, subarctic, and desert)*
- Where do the few people who live within these climate zones tend to settle? *(along rivers and the coast)*

Unit ATLAS

Regional Patterns

These two pages contain a pie graph and three thematic maps. The pie graph shows the religions of Russia and the Republics. The maps show other important features of the region: its different climates, numerous ethnic groups, and population density. After studying these two pages, answer the questions below in your notebook.

Making Comparisons

1. Where is the population of Russia and the Republics most dense? Which climate do those areas have? How might climate affect population density?
2. How would you describe the ethnic and religious populations of Russia and the Republics? Which is the most widespread ethnic group in the region?

Religions of Russia and the Republics

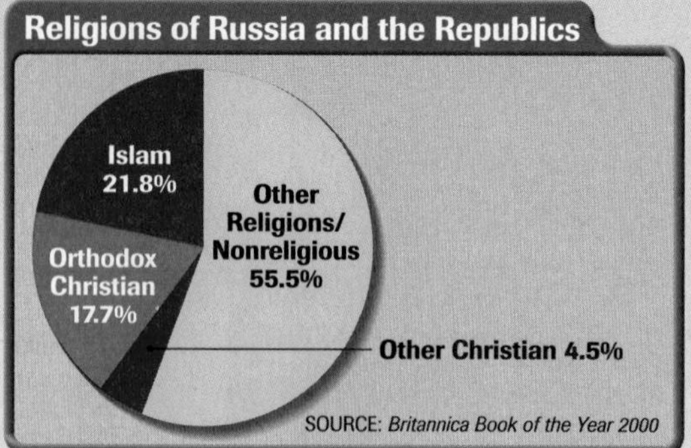

SOURCE: *Britannica Book of the Year 2000*

Climates of Russia and the Republics

MAKING COMPARISONS ANSWERS

1. The population is densest in the central-western area of the region, which has a humid continental climate. People probably chose to live in this area because the climate is more moderate than in other areas of the region.
2. The religiously affiliated part of the population is divided mainly between Orthodox Christianity and Islam. The ethnic profile of the region is more complex, but Russians form the majority of the population.

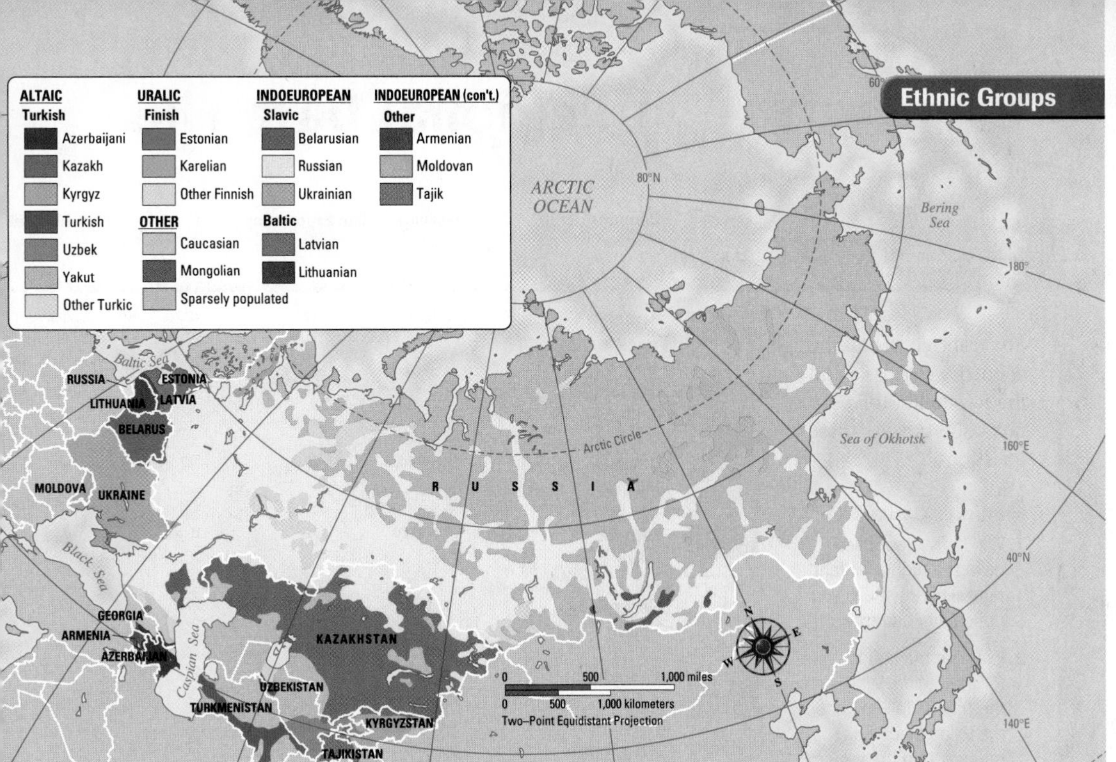

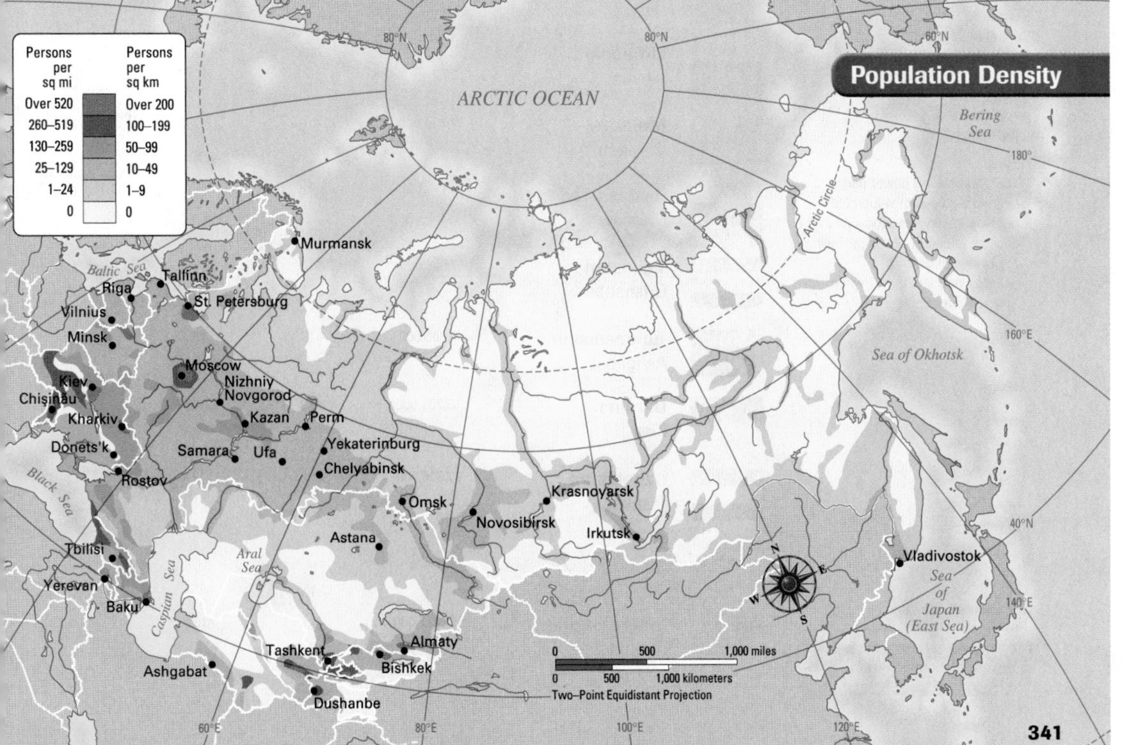

341

UNIT 5 ATLAS

Instruct: Objective 5

Ethnic Groups/Population Density

- What pattern do you see in the ethnic groups of the republics? *(Each republic has its own dominant ethnic group.)*
- Which republic has the largest number of ethnic groups? *(Russia)*
- What are the three most densely populated cities in the region? *(Moscow, St. Petersburg, and Kiev)*
- Is the population concentrated in the European or Asian part of the region? *(European)*

ACTIVITY OPTION | CRITICAL THINKING

MAKING INFERENCES

Explaining the Skill Remind students that an inference is a reasonable guess based on prior knowledge and clues that are provided. Readers might make many kinds of inferences based on the information provided in the maps on these pages.

Applying the Skill Direct students to use the climate and population density maps on pages 340 and 341 to answer the following questions.

- If you traveled across eastern Russia, what kind of settlement patterns and landscape would you expect to see? *(vast areas of wilderness with a few small settlements along rivers)*
- If you traveled through western Russia and the republics, what kind of settlement patterns would you expect to see? *(large cities and metropolitan areas with agricultural land in-between)*
- What would you expect life to be like in eastern Russia? *(harsh, isolated, lacking in material comforts and luxuries)*

DATA FILE OBJECTIVE

Use statistics to draw conclusions about standards of living in Russia and the Republics.

Focus & Motivate

Ask students to read across the headings at the top of the chart and explain what these categories of information can reveal about standards of living in a region or country. *(They give a sense of the socio-economic status of each country.)*

Instruct: Objective

Regional Date File

- How do the GDPs of Russia and the Republics compare to GDP of the United States? *(They are drastically lower.)*
- How do the numbers of televisions and passenger cars compare with those in the United States? *(They are all much lower except for televisions in Latvia.)*
- From these statistics, what conclusions can you draw about the standards of living in the republics? *(The standards of living are lower than that in the United States.)*
- What inconsistency do you see between the infant mortality rate and the number of doctors in the republics? *(The republics have many doctors–a higher proportion than the United States does–and yet the infant mortality rates are very high.)*

In-Depth Resources: Unit 5
• Regional Data File Activities, p. 2

Unit ATLAS

Regional Data File

Study the charts on the countries of Russia and the Republics. In your notebook, answer these questions.

Making Comparisons

1. Which five republics have the highest infant mortality rates? Do you notice any pattern?
2. Examine the literacy rates for the region. What do the figures tell you about the value placed on education in the region?

Country Flag	Country/ Capital	Population	Life Expectancy (years)	Birthrate (per 1,000 pop.)	Infant Mortality (per 1,000 live births)
	Armenia Yerevan	2,967,000	72.7	12.7	20.2
	Azerbaijan Baku	8,239,000	66.7	17.6	54.6
	Belarus Minsk	9,649,000	70.6	9.7	6.4
	Estonia Tallinn	1,299,000	72.8	10.4	7.3
	Georgia T'bilisi	4,616,000	76.7	10.7	16.2
	Kazakhstan Astana	15,399,000	67.9	16.6	25.7
	Kyrgyzstan Bishkek	5,432,000	69.4	23.4	31.3
	Latvia Riga	2,232,000	72.2	9.8	8.8
	Lithuania Vilnius	3,555,000	74.9	9.1	6.5
	Moldova Chişinău	4,321,000	70.8	11.1	13.1
	Russian Federation Moscow	140,041,000	66.0	11.1	10.6
	Tajikistan Dushanbe	7,349,000	65.3	26.9	41.0
	Turkmenistan Ashgabat	4,885,000	67.9	19.7	45.4
	Ukraine Kiev	45,701,000	68.3	9.6	9.0
	Uzbekistan Tashkent	27,606,000	71.9	17.6	23.4
	United States Washington, D.C.	307,212,000	78.1	13.8	6.2

Sources:
Central Intelligence Agency, *The World Factbook*, 2010
The World Almanac and Book of Facts, 2010
World Health Organization (WHO), 2007

Notes:
[a] GDP (purchasing power parity) is defined as the sum value of all goods and services produced in the country valued at prices prevailing in the United States.
[b] Includes land and water, when figures are available

For updated statistics on Russia and the Republics . . .

MAKING COMPARISONS ANSWERS

1. Azerbaijan, Kyrgyzstan, Tajikistan, Turkmenistan, and Kazakhstan have the highest infant mortality rates. These republics are all concentrated in the southwestern area of the region near the Caspian Sea.
2. High literacy rates suggest that education is taken very seriously in the region.

Doctors (per 100,000 pop.) (2000–2004)	GDP[a] (billions $US)	Import/Export (billions $US)	Literacy Rate (percentage)	Televisions (per 1,000 pop.)	Passenger Cars (per 1,000 pop.)	Total Area[b] (square miles)
359	16.2	2.55/0.72	99	241	N/A	11,506
355	85.1	5.45/13.16	99	257	58	33,436
455	111.9	22.4/18.04	99	331	187	80,155
448	24.5	9.32/9.23	99	567	380	17,462
409	20.8	4.48/1.77	100	516	55	26,911
354	175.1	25.15/41.64	99	240	91	1,049,155
251	11.7	2.38/1.33	99	49	37	76,641
301	32.4	8.85/6.72	99	757	332	24,938
397	53.4	15.63/14.68	99	422	422	25,174
264	10.2	3.14/1.24	99	297	68	13,067
425	2,117	196.8/295.6	99	421	182	6,592,772
203	13.8	2.91/1	99	328	16	55,251
418	33.6	4.44/8.29	99	198	N/A	188,456
295	294.3	45.58/41.49	99	433	120	233,090
274	77.6	6.51/9.47	99	280	N/A	172,742
256	14,260.0	1,445/994.7	99	844	725	3,794,083

More About

Infant Mortality Rates

Infant mortality rate is one of the statistics that indicate the general level of health of the people in a region or country. The infant mortality rates in many of the republics remain quite high, but they have dropped drastically in recent years; the republics have begun to develop as independent nations after cutting free from the U.S.S.R. and then the C.I.S. in the 1990s.

ACTIVITY OPTION INTERNET RESEARCH

RESEARCHING AND PRESENTING AN ORAL REPORT

Objective To identify the reasons behind specific statistics

Class Time 60 minutes

Task Locate information explaining why Russia and the Republics have such high infant mortality rates and present the findings in an oral report

Directions Direct students to use the key words *infant mortality rates* and *russia and the republics* to locate online sources of information explaining the reasons for the high infant mortality rates in this region. Have students present and discuss their findings.

OPTIONAL ACTIVITY If Internet access is limited, direct students to use such library resources as *Infotrac* or *Readers' Guide to Periodical Literature* to locate articles on this subject.

CHAPTER 15 OBJECTIVE

Identify key features of the landforms, resources, climate, vegetation, and human-environment interaction in Russia and the Republics.

Chapter 15 PHYSICAL GEOGRAPHY OF RUSSIA AND THE REPUBLICS
A Land of Extremes

Russia's Lake Baikal is the world's deepest lake and holds over 20 percent of the earth's fresh water. Russians treasure Lake Baikal as much as Americans treasure the Grand Canyon.

Essential Question

How do the extremes of the region's physical geography affect the people of Russia and the Republics?

What You Will Learn

In this chapter you will compare and contrast the physical characteristics of Russia and the Republics.

SECTION 1
Landforms and Resources

SECTION 2
Climate and Vegetation

SECTION 3
Human–Environment Interaction

hmhsocialstudies.com
TAKING NOTES

Use the graphic organizer online to record information from the chapter about the physical geography of Russia and the Republics.

344

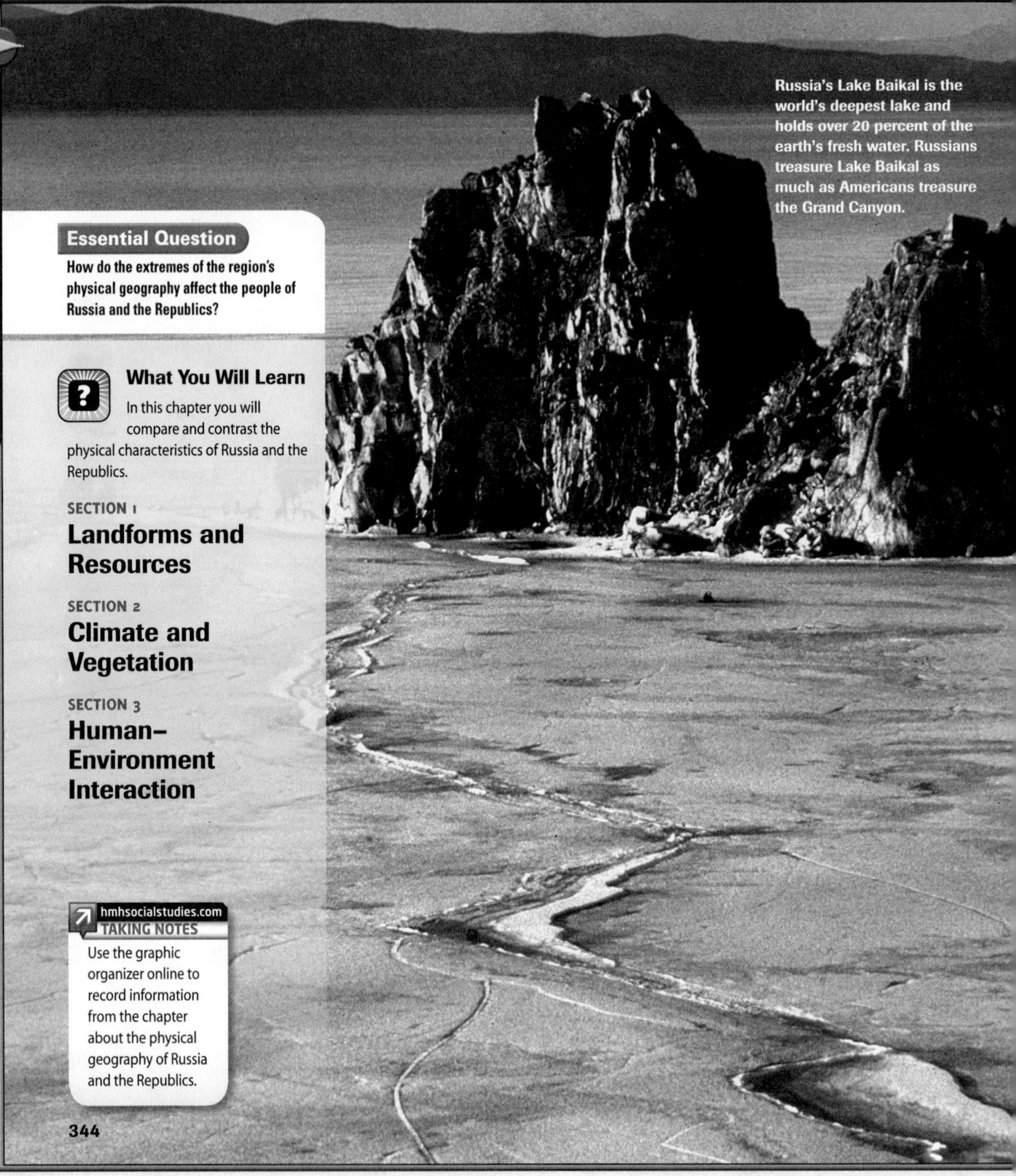

Interpreting Photographs

Lake Baikal

Share with students that certain areas of Lake Baikal have extraordinarily clean water. Relate how a visitor to the lake described its waters as "a transparent turquoise in which a silver coin could be spotted 120 feet below the surface."

Extension Have students write a brief journal entry that describes why Lake Baikal is such an important resource.

Introducing the Essential Question

- Emphasize the huge differences that one can find in this region's physical geography—from frozen Siberian plains to baking deserts raked by dust-laden winds.
- Discuss any topics related to nuclear weapons or nuclear waste that may be current. Point out that nuclear weapons still trouble the region although the Cold War has ended.

hmhsocialstudies.com
TAKING NOTES

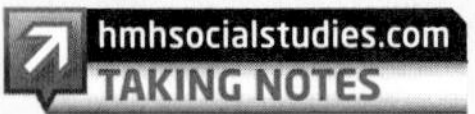

Have students fill out graphic organizers in their notebook using material from all sections of this chapter.

Critical Thinking Transparencies CT15
- GeoFocus

In-Depth Resources: Unit 5
- Building Vocabulary, p. 9

CHAPTER 15 ADDITIONAL RESOURCES

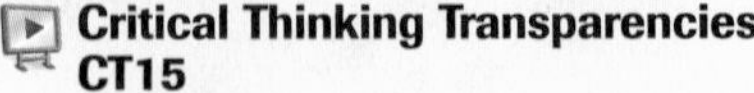

BOOKS FOR THE TEACHER

Tayler, Jeffrey. ***Siberian Dawn.*** St. Paul, MN: Ruminator Books, 2000. Travelogue of journey across Russia.

BOOKS FOR THE STUDENT

Nebesky, Richard, et. al., ***Lonely Planet Russia, Ukraine & Belarus.*** Oakland, CA: Lonely Planet, 2000. Travel guide with information on the landscape of the region.

VIDEOS

Napoleon Invades Russia. Ambrose, 1997. An examination of Napoleon's defeat by the Russian winter.

Russia: Video Visits. IVN, 1995. Tour of Russia.

INTERNET

For more about Russia and the Republics, visit . . .

hmhsocialstudies.com

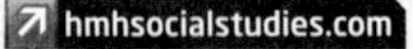

Landforms and Resources

Main Ideas

- Flat plains stretch across the western and central areas of the region. In the south and east, the terrain is more mountainous.
- Many resources in Russia and the Republics are in hard-to-reach regions with brutal climates.

Places & Terms

chernozem
Ural Mountains
Eurasia
Transcaucasia
Central Asia
Siberia

CONNECT TO THE ISSUES
ECONOMIC CHANGE Leaders must strike a balance between environmental protection and economic growth.

A HUMAN PERSPECTIVE Russia and the Republics occupy a tremendous expanse of territory—approximately three times the land area of the United States. The region sprawls across the continents of both Europe and Asia and crosses 11 time zones. When laborers in the western city of Kaliningrad are leaving their jobs after a day's work, herders on the region's Pacific coast are just beginning to awaken their animals for the next day's grazing.

Northern Landforms

The geography of Russia and the Republics is the geography of nearly one-sixth of the earth's land surface—over eight and a half million square miles. In spite of this huge size, the region's landforms follow a simple overall pattern. You can divide the northern two-thirds of the region into four different areas. Moving from west to east, they are the Northern European Plain, the West Siberian Plain, the Central Siberian Plateau, and the Russian Far East. (See the physical map on pages 336–337 of the Unit Atlas.)

THE NORTHERN EUROPEAN PLAIN The Northern European Plain is an extensive lowland area. It stretches for over 1,000 miles from the western border of Russia and the Republics to the Ural Mountains.

One of the world's most fertile soils—**chernozem,** or black earth—is abundant on this plain. It sometimes occurs in layers three feet deep or more. Because of the high quality of its soil, many of the region's agricultural areas are located on this plain.

More than 75 percent of the region's 283 million people live on this plain. Three of the region's largest cities are located there: Moscow, Russia's capital; St. Petersburg; and Kiev, the capital of Ukraine.

PLACE Ukraine, which lies on the Northern European Plain, has been called the region's breadbasket because of the enormous grain crops produced on its farms.

RUSSIA & REP.

SECTION 1 OBJECTIVES

1. Describe the terrain of the northern two thirds of the region.
2. Describe the terrain of the southern third of the region.
3. Identify two main drainage basins and three main lakes of the region.
4. Identify resources and explain why they are difficult to develop.

SKILLBUILDERS: Interpreting Maps & Graphs, pp. 347, 348

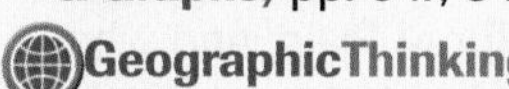

Using the Atlas, p. 347
Seeing Patterns, p. 348
Making Generalizations, p. 349

Focus & Motivate

Would you expect that Russia and the Republics are rich or poor in natural resources? Why? *(rich, because the region covers such a huge area)*

Instruct: Objective 1

Northern Landforms

- In general, how does the landscape of the northern two thirds of the region change from west to east? *(It rises in elevation, changing from plains to plateaus to mountains.)*
- Which area has the richest agricultural land, the most people, and the largest cities? *(the Northern European Plain)*

In-Depth Resources: Unit 5
- Guided Reading, p. 3

SECTION 1 PROGRAM RESOURCES

In-Depth Resources: Unit 5
- Guided Reading, p. 3
- Skillbuilder Practice, p. 8
- Building Vocabulary, p. 9
- Reteaching Activity, p. 10

Guided Reading Workbook
- Section 1

Access for Students Acquiring English/ESL
- Guided Reading, p. 77
- Skillbuillder Practice, p. 80

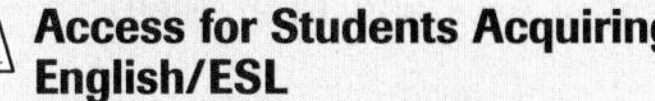

Formal Assessment
- Section Quiz, p. 226

Integrated Assessment
- Rubric for a poster, 1.1

INTEGRATED TECHNOLOGY

Critical Thinking Transparencies CT47
- Lakes and Rivers in Russia and the Republics

Chapter Summaries

TEST-TAKING RESOURCES

Strategies for Test Preparation

Test Practice Transparencies TT4

Online Test Practice

Instruct: Objective 2

Southern Landforms

- What physical features characterize the southern third of Russia and the Republics? *(towering mountains, barren uplands, and semiarid grasslands)*
- What border do the Caucasus Mountains form? *(the border between Russia and Transcaucasia)*
- Where is the Turan Plain, and what is it like? *(It is located between the Caspian Sea and the mountains and uplands of Central Asia. It is very dry and has two large deserts.)*

WEST SIBERIAN PLAIN The **Ural Mountains** separate the Northern European and West Siberian plains. Some geographers recognize the Urals as a dividing line between Europe and Asia. Others consider Europe and Asia to be a single continent, which they call **Eurasia.**

The West Siberian Plain lies between the Urals and the Yenisey River and between the shores of the Arctic Ocean and the foothills of the Altay Mountains. Because the plain tilts northward, its rivers flow toward the Arctic Ocean.

CENTRAL SIBERIAN PLATEAU AND RUSSIAN FAR EAST Although extensive plains lie east of the Yenisey River, uplands and mountains are the dominant landforms. High plateaus—with average heights of 1,000 to 2,000 feet—make up the Central Siberian Plateau, which lies between the Yenisey and Lena rivers.

East of the Lena River lies the Russian Far East and its complex system of volcanic ranges. The Kamchatka Peninsula alone contains 120 volcanoes, 20 of which are still active. The Sakhalin and Kuril islands lie south of the peninsula. Russia seized the islands from Japan after World War II. Japan still claims ownership of the Kuril Islands.

BACKGROUND Russia and Japan never signed a formal peace treaty after World War II ended in 1945. Technically, they are still at war.

Southern Landforms

The southern areas of Russia and the Republics feature towering mountains, barren uplands, and semiarid grasslands.

THE CAUCASUS AND OTHER MOUNTAINS The Caucasus Mountains stretch across the land that separates the Black and Caspian seas. The mountains form the border between Russia and **Transcaucasia**—a region that consists of the republics of Armenia, Azerbaijan, and Georgia. Farther east, along the southern border of Russia and the Republics, rises a colossal wall of mountains, including the Tian Shan, shown below.

Some of these mountains are located along the southeastern border of **Central Asia**—a region that includes the republics of Kazakhstan,

LOCATION The Tian Shan, which is Chinese for "Heavenly Mountains," stretch for nearly 1,500 miles, mainly between China and Kyrgyzstan. **Why might a river be flowing at the base of these mountains?**

Interpreting Photographs

Tian Shan

Direct students' attention to the river banks in the photograph, and ask what might account for their sheer sides. *(The river has, over time, carved out these bluffs.)*

CAPTION ANSWER It was probably formed by the runoff of melting precipitation from the mountain.

DIFFERENTIATING INSTRUCTION **STUDENTS ACQUIRING ENGLISH/ESL**

LOCATING AND DESCRIBING LANDFORMS

Objective To provide a method of organizing and visualizing information about landforms

Class Time 20 minutes

Task Label landforms on an outline map and list key facts about them

Directions As they read the text, have students label important landforms and regions of Russia and the Republics on an outline map and list one or two key facts under each label. Students should include these labels: Northern European Plain, West Siberian Plain, Central Siberian Plateau, Russian Far East, Ural Mountains, Yenisey River, Lena River, Caucasus Mountains, Transcaucasia, Tian Shan, Central Asia, and Turan Plain.

Transcaucasia and Central Asia

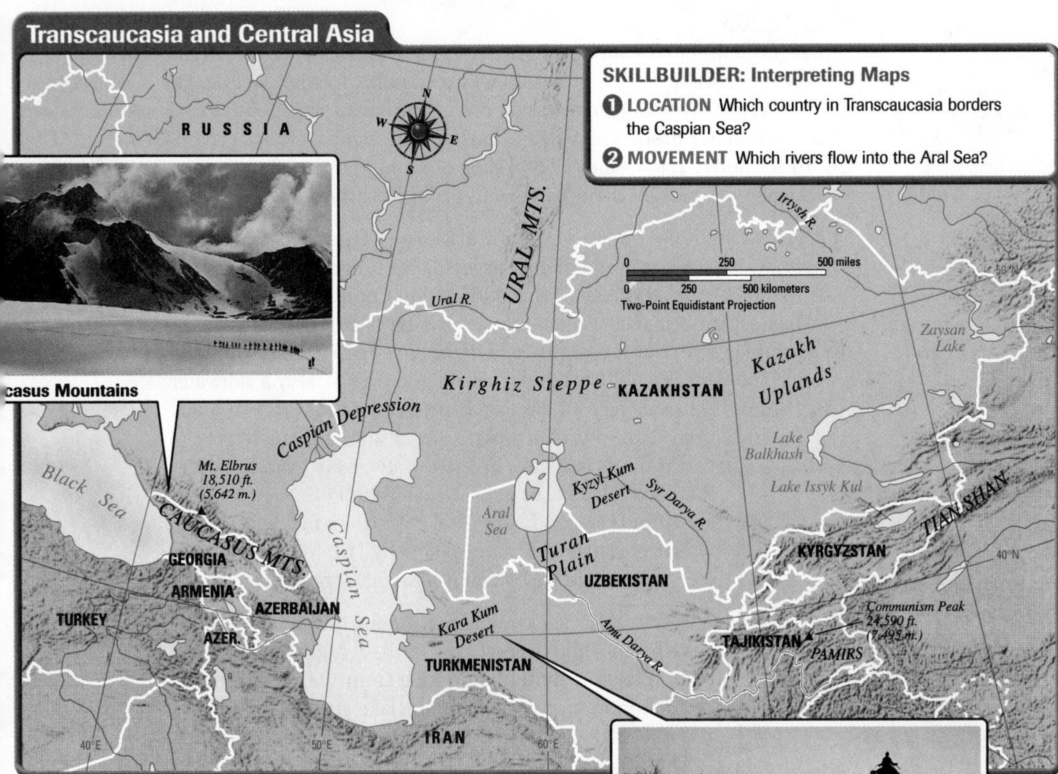

casus Mountains

Kara Kum Desert

SKILLBUILDER: Interpreting Maps

1. **LOCATION** Which country in Transcaucasia borders the Caspian Sea?
2. **MOVEMENT** Which rivers flow into the Aral Sea?

Kyrgyzstan, Tajikistan, Turkmenistan, and Uzbekistan. These ranges are so high that they prevent moist air from entering the region from the south, contributing to the arid climate of Central Asia. (A)

Geographic Thinking

Using the Atlas

(A) Examine the climate map on page 340. What is the relationship between landforms and climate zones in Central Asia?

A. Answer The high mountains in the southeastern part of the region contribute to the semiarid and desert climate.

THE TURAN PLAIN An extensive lowland called the Turan Plain lies between the Caspian Sea and the mountains and uplands of Central Asia. Although two major rivers, the Syr Darya and Amu Darya, cross the plain, much of the lowland is very dry. Two large deserts stretch across the plain—the Kara Kum and the Kyzyl Kum.

Rivers and Lakes

Some of the world's longest rivers flow through the vast plains of Russia and the Republics. The region also boasts some of the largest and deepest lakes in the world.

DRAINAGE BASINS AND RIVERS The region's rivers flow through a number of large drainage basins. You may recall from Chapter 2 that a drainage basin is an area drained by a major river and its tributaries. The main drainage basins in Russia and the Republics are the Arctic Ocean, Caspian Sea, Pacific Ocean, Baltic Sea, Black Sea, and Aral Sea basins.

The Arctic basin is the region's largest. The basin's three powerful rivers—the Ob, the Yenisey, and the Lena—drain an area of more than

Interpreting Maps

Have students compare the map of Transcaucasia and Central Asia with the climate map on page 340. Ask them to identify the climate zones in which the two photographs were taken. *(highland and desert)*

SKILLBUILDER ANSWERS

1. Azerbaijan **2.** Amu Darya and Syr Darya

Instruct: Objective 3

Rivers and Lakes

- What is the region's largest drainage basin, and what three rivers drain into it? *(Arctic Ocean basin; Ob, Yenisey, and Lena rivers)*
- What are the two largest lakes in the region? *(Caspian and Aral seas)*
- Why is Lake Baikal unique? *(It is the world's deepest lake and holds 20 percent of the world's fresh water.)*

Critical Thinking Transparencies CT47

- Lakes and Rivers in Russia and the Republics

ACTIVITY OPTION | INTERNET RESEARCH

CREATING A TRAVEL BROCHURE

Objective To visualize the terrain of Central Asia

Class Time 30 minutes

Task Search the Internet for photographs and create a travel brochure

Directions Direct students to **hmhsocialstudies.com** and have them follow the links to find photographs of the landscape of Central Asia. Have them work in small groups to compile the photographs and write captions for a travel brochure.

BLOCK SCHEDULING

OPTIONAL ACTIVITY If Internet access is limited, have students use such library resources as *Infotrac, The Readers' Guide to Periodical Literature*, or travel books to find photographs of this region.

Instruct: Objective 4

Regional Resources

- What are some of the resources that have been developed in Russia and the Republics? *(coal, iron ore, oil, natural gas, and timber)*
- Why might extracting and transporting the region's resources be difficult? *(because many resources are located in climatically severe areas of Siberia)*
- What other challenges face regional leaders? *(balancing economic growth with respect for the environment)*

Interpreting Graphs

Fossil Fuels

Ask students what these two circle graphs indicate about Russia's energy supplies. *(Russia has abundant energy supplies.)*

SKILLBUILDER ANSWERS

1. Russia **2.** about 48,185,604,264 cubic meters

Interpreting Photographs

Oil Field Workers

Ask students what they can infer about the climate in which these laborers are working. Have them explain the basis for their inference. *(Because the men are wearing heavy coats and gloves, students can infer that very cold temperatures are a feature of the climate.)*

three million square miles. These rivers deliver water to the Arctic Ocean at a combined rate of nearly 1,750,000 cubic feet per second. B

The Volga River, the longest river on the European continent, drains the Caspian Sea basin. The Volga begins near Moscow and flows southward for about 2,300 miles until it arrives at the Caspian. This important waterway carries about 60 percent of Russia's river traffic.

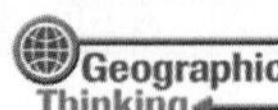

Geographic Thinking

Seeing Patterns B Examine the map on pages 336–337. Why might many of the region's rivers flow toward the north?

B. Answer because many of the rivers begin in the mountainous areas in the southern part of the region

LAKES In addition to some of the world's longest rivers, Russia and the Republics also boast some of the largest lakes on our planet. Two of them, the Caspian and Aral seas, are located in Central Asia.

The Caspian Sea, which is actually a saltwater lake, stretches for nearly 750 miles from north to south, making it the largest inland sea in the world. The Aral Sea, which lies east of the Caspian, is also a saltwater lake. Since the 1960s, the Aral has lost about 87 percent of its water volume. This enormous loss is the result of extensive irrigation projects that have diverted water away from the rivers that feed the lake. In 2005, Kazakhstan built a dam to separate the smaller North Aral Sea from the South Aral, which is saltier and more polluted. The North Aral now receives enough water that it has largely recovered.

Fossil Fuels

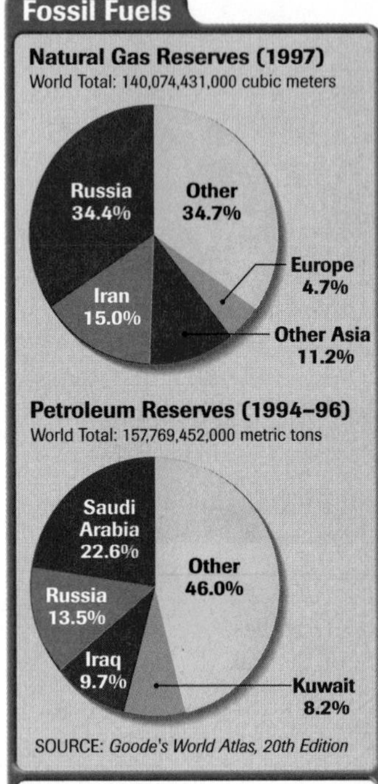

SKILLBUILDER: Interpreting Graphs

1. **ANALYZING DATA** What country had the largest reserves of natural gas in 1997?
2. **ANALYZING DATA** About how many cubic meters of natural gas did Russia have in 1997?

LAKE BAIKAL The crown jewel among the region's lakes is Lake Baikal—the deepest lake in the world. At its deepest point, Baikal is more than a mile from the surface to the bottom. From north to south, the lake stretches for nearly 400 miles. It holds 20 percent of the world's fresh water.

Though it has some pollution, most of Lake Baikal is remarkably clean. Thousands of species of plants and animals live in the lake. Twelve hundred species, including the world's only freshwater seal, are unique to Lake Baikal.

Regional Resources

Russia and the Republics have a great wealth of natural resources, but regional leaders have struggled to manage them. One challenge has been how to transport resources from harsh, distant regions. Another has been how to use the resources without damaging the environment.

LOCATION Workers adjust machinery at the Samotlor oil field in Russia.

ACTIVITY OPTION **FIVE THEMES OF GEOGRAPHY**

HUMAN-ENVIRONMENT INTERACTION

Exploring the Theme In order to survive, human beings must use the natural resources on earth, but in a *sustainable* way. Because political leaders in the past did not heed basic principles of conservation, Russia and the Republics have some of the most severe environmental problems of any region on earth.

Understanding the Theme Direct students' attention to the paragraph on page 348 that discusses the shrinkage of the Aral Sea. Then ask students the following questions:

- Why might people in the Aral Sea area be reluctant to cut back on irrigation projects? *(Without irrigation, crops cannot grow, and income would be lost.)*
- What steps might be taken to prevent further shrinkage of the Aral Sea? *(switch to crops that require less water, ration the water used for irrigation, and promote other economic activities in the region)*

ABUNDANT RESOURCES Russia and the Republics boast huge reserves of coal, deposits of iron ore, and other metals. The region is also a leading producer of oil and natural gas. Petroleum deposits around the Caspian Sea are among the world's largest.

Russia's vast forests hold one-fifth of the world's timber resources. And the region's powerful rivers make it one of the world's largest producers of hydroelectric power.

RESOURCE MANAGEMENT Harsh climates, rugged terrain, and vast distances make it difficult for Russia and the Republics to remove resources from the ground and transport them to markets. Many of these resources are located in the frigid arctic and subarctic region of **Siberia**—the part of Russia that lies on the continent of Asia. Businesses find it difficult to attract workers to this severe region. C

Geographic Thinking

Seeing Patterns Why might workers be unwilling to take jobs in Siberia?

C. Answer They are probably reluctant to move to a region with such a harsh climate.

When businesses have been able to exploit regional resources successfully, they have often done so at great cost to the environment. Mining operations have caused significant damage, as has the production of oil and gas. Russia's hydroelectric plants have also caused substantial damage. Dams and the plants' discharge of unusually hot water—known as thermal pollution—have caused significant damage to surrounding plant and animal habitats.

Dramatic political and economic change in recent years will continue to make resource management difficult. Leaders will have to balance the need for economic growth with their responsibility to protect the environment.

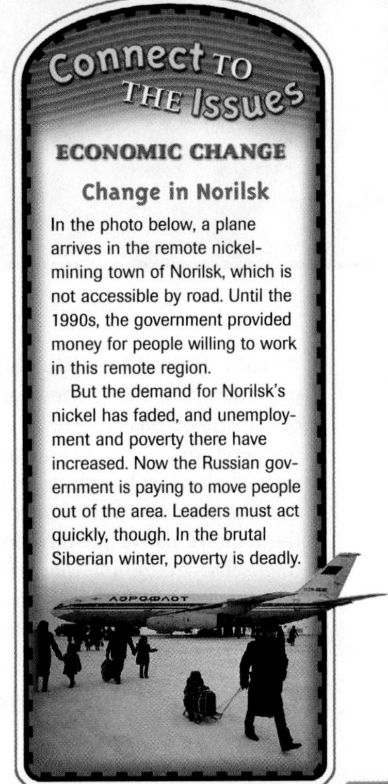

ECONOMIC CHANGE

Change in Norilsk

In the photo below, a plane arrives in the remote nickel-mining town of Norilsk, which is not accessible by road. Until the 1990s, the government provided money for people willing to work in this remote region.

But the demand for Norilsk's nickel has faded, and unemployment and poverty there have increased. Now the Russian government is paying to move people out of the area. Leaders must act quickly, though. In the brutal Siberian winter, poverty is deadly.

RUSSIA & REP.

Connect TO THE Issues

Economic Change: Change in Norilsk

When Norilsk Nickel was established under the Soviet's command economy, the government provided housing, health care, day care, and other social services to workers. In a market economy, paying for such benefits make a company less profitable. Trimming the labor force is one way to reduce costs. Ask students to name other factors that would make it expensive to produce and market Norilsk's nickel. *(the difficulty of extracting the nickel from the frozen ground, heating costs, the cost of transporting the nickel from a region that is inaccessible by road)*

Assess & Reteach

GeoFocus Have students complete the section on landforms and resources in their graphic organizers.

Formal Assessment
- Section Quiz, p. 226

Reteaching Activity
Have students work in small groups and use the notes they took in their GeoFocus graphic organizers to quiz each other on the section's content.

In-Depth Resources: Unit 5
- Reteaching Activity, p. 10

Section 1 Assessment

1 Places & Terms
Explain the importance of each of the following terms and places.
- chernozem
- Ural Mountains
- Eurasia
- Transcaucasia
- Central Asia
- Siberia

2 Taking Notes
REGION Review the notes you took for this section.

Landforms	
Resources	

- What is the name of the region's westernmost lowland?
- What mountain range separates Russia from Transcaucasia?

3 Main Ideas
a. Why might a large part of the region's population live on the Northern European Plain?
b. What factor contributes to the dry conditions on the Turan Plain?
c. Why is the Volga one of the region's most important rivers?

4 Geographic Thinking
Making Generalizations
Why has resource management been a problem for leaders in Russia and the Republics? **Think about:**
- where resources are located
- how resources are extracted or used

EXPLORING LOCAL GEOGRAPHY Do more research on Lake Baikal and on the deepest lake in the state in which you live. Make a **poster** that visually compares the size and depth of the two lakes. Provide other information on your poster, including the volume of water in each of the lakes.

SECTION 1 ASSESSMENT ANSWERS

1. Places & Terms
chernozem, p. 345
Ural Mountains, p. 346
Eurasia, p. 346
Transcaucasia, p. 346
Central Asia, p. 346
Siberia, p. 349

2. Taking Notes
- Northern European Plain
- Caucasus Mountains

3. Main Ideas
a. because most of the major agricultural regions are located there
b. The mountains along the southeastern border of the region prevent moist air from entering the region from the south.
c. because it carries a great deal of the region's river traffic

4. Geographic Thinking
Answers will vary, but students might mention how difficult it is to access resources in remote and harsh regions of Siberia. They should also mention that the extraction of resources has often taken place with too little regard to the effects on the environment.

GeoActivity

Integrated Assessment
- Rubric for a poster, 1.1

SECTION 2 OBJECTIVES

1. Identify the main climates of Russia and the Republics and the influences on the region's weather.
2. Describe four major vegetation regions of Russia and the Republics.

SKILLBUILDER: Interpreting Maps, p. 351

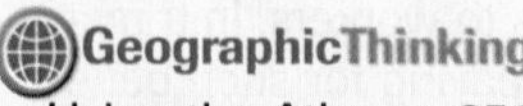

Using the Atlas, p. 351
Determining Cause and Effect, p. 352

Focus & Motivate

What North American country has climates and vegetation regions similar to those in Russia and the Republics? Why are they similar? *(Canada, because much of Canada lies in the same latitudes)*

Instruct: Objective 

A Climate of Extremes

- What are the two main climates of the region? *(humid continental and subarctic)*
- What are three influences on these two climates? *(high latitude, the wall of mountains in the southeast, and continentality)*
- What effects does continentality have on the region's climates? *(It causes low precipitation and extreme temperatures.)*

 **In-Depth Resources: Unit 5**
- Guided Reading, p. 4

 **Map Transparencies MT28**
- Russia and the Republics: Climates Zones

2 Climate and Vegetation

Main Ideas
- Much of Russia and the Republics lies in subarctic and tundra climate zones.
- In the region's southern areas, semiarid and desert climates feature warmer winters and hot summers.

Places & Terms
continentality
taiga

CONNECT TO THE ISSUES
CONFLICT Ethnic conflict has disrupted the flow of tourist dollars into some areas of the region.

A HUMAN PERSPECTIVE Large areas of Russia and the Republics are extremely cold during much of the year. For example, the Siberian town of Oymyakon has reportedly had temperatures as low as −95°F. At such temperatures, the cold can crack steel and cause tires to explode. When you exhale, your breath freezes into crystals that fall to the ground and make a noise that Siberians call "the whispering of the stars." Some of the region's native peoples believe that, in the coldest weather, words themselves freeze, and that, when warmer weather arrives and thaws the crystals, the words come to life and begin to speak. "Suddenly the air fills with out-of-date gossip, unheard jokes, and cries of forgotten pain."

A Climate of Extremes

As you can see on the climate map on page 340, Russia and the Republics have some very cold climates. But the region also features warmer climates, such as the subtropical areas of Transcaucasia, and the semiarid and desert zones of Central Asia.

MAJOR CLIMATE REGIONS Humid continental and subarctic climates dominate much of Russia and the Republics. These climates reflect the influence of the region's high latitude and the impact of the wall of mountains in the southeast. The region's enormous size also has a major effect on its climates. Much of the region is hundreds of miles from the moderating influence of the sea. The effect of this distance on climate is called **continentality.**

Distance from the sea affects the amount of precipitation the region gets, as well as its temperatures. Most of the region's moisture comes from the Atlantic Ocean. But the air coming from the ocean loses its moisture as it travels farther and farther inland. Distance from the seas also results in extreme temperatures. In Siberia, average monthly temperatures rarely exceed 50°F and sometimes drop below -90°F.

The long stretches of cold weather in the region have a unique impact on daily life. Siberians, for example, use frozen rivers and lakes as roads for part of the year. Temperatures are so consistently low that the region is covered by a layer of permanently frozen subsoil called permafrost. This layer can reach depths of 1,500 feet.

MOVEMENT The crew driving this truck is using the frozen surface of Lake Baikal to transport cargo.

SECTION 2 PROGRAM RESOURCES

 **In-Depth Resources: Unit 5**
- Guided Reading, p. 4
- Building Vocabulary, p. 9
- Reteaching Activity, p. 11

 **Guided Reading Workbook**
- Section 2

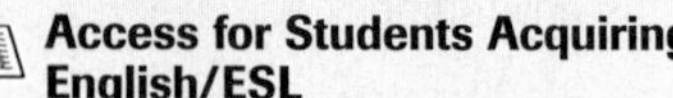 **Access for Students Acquiring English/ESL**
- Guided Reading, p. 78

 **Formal Assessment**
- Section Quiz, p. 227

Integrated Assessment
- Rubric for a graph, 2.3

INTEGRATED TECHNOLOGY

 **Map Transparencies MT28**
- Russia and the Republics: Climates Zones

 **Power Presentations**

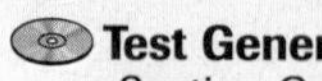 **Test Generator**
- Section Quiz

hmhsocialstudies.com

TEST-TAKING RESOURCES

 **Strategies for Test Preparation**

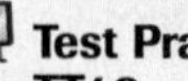 **Test Practice Transparencies TT49**

 **Online Test Practice**

While humid continental and subarctic climates dominate the northern and eastern areas of the region, Russia and the Republics also have warmer climates. A wall of mountains in the southeastern areas of the region blocks moist air traveling northward from the Indian and Pacific oceans. The mountains contribute to the semiarid and desert climates of Central Asia.

In Transcaucasia, moist air from the Mediterranean Sea contributes to a subtropical climate zone. The region's health resorts were a favorite destination of tourists until ethnic conflict made traveling there dangerous. A

Geographic Thinking

Using the Atlas
A Examine the map on page 340. In which climate region do you think the layer of permafrost will be deepest?
A. Answer in the tundra

Vegetation Regions

Russia and the Republics have four major vegetation regions. These regions run east to west in wide strips. Moving from north to south, they are the tundra, forest, temperate grassland, and desert.

TUNDRA The tundra region of Russia and the Republics falls mostly in the Arctic climate zone. Only specific types of vegetation—such as mosses, lichens, small herbs, and low shrubs—are able to survive in the tundra's polar conditions.

FOREST South of the tundra lies the largest forest on earth—the **taiga.** The taiga contains primarily coniferous trees. Many fur-bearing animals,

Vegetation Regions of Russia and the Republics

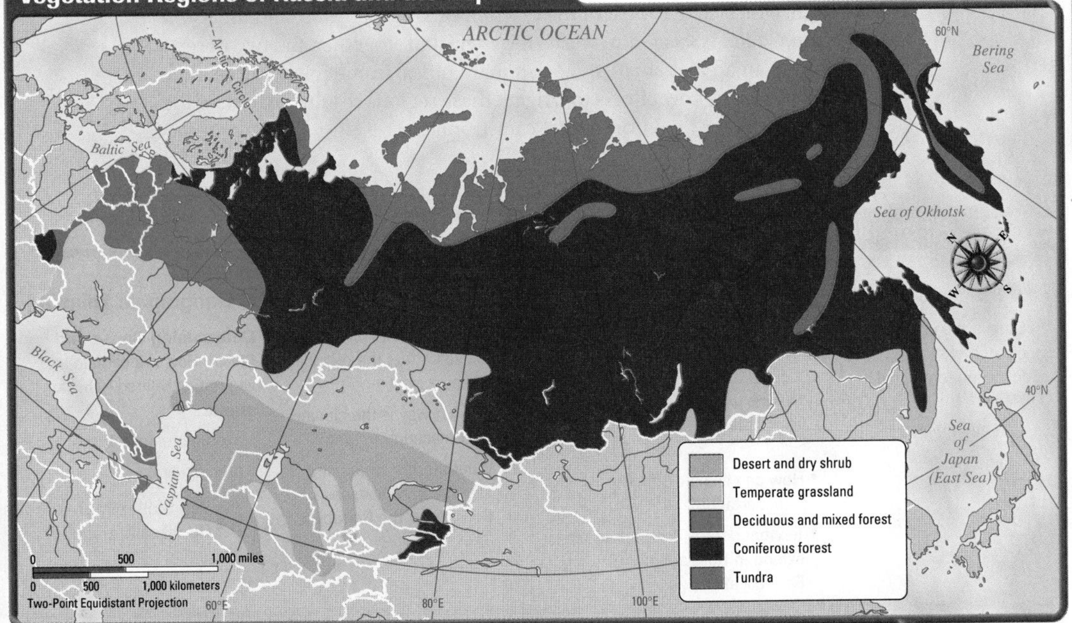

ARCTIC OCEAN
Arctic Circle
Bering Sea
Baltic Sea
Sea of Okhotsk
Black Sea
Caspian Sea
Sea of Japan (East Sea)
60°N
40°N
60°E
80°E
100°E
Desert and dry shrub
Temperate grassland
Deciduous and mixed forest
Coniferous forest
Tundra
0 500 1,000 miles
0 500 1,000 kilometers
Two-Point Equidistant Projection

SKILLBUILDER: Interpreting Maps

1. **REGION** What kind of vegetation is most common to the east of the Caspian Sea?
2. **LOCATION** At what latitudes does the tundra give way to coniferous forests?

RUSSIA & REP.

Instruct: Objective 2

Vegetation Regions

- From north to south, what are the four main vegetation regions of Russia and the Republics? *(tundra, forest, steppe, and desert)*
- What is the name of the largest forest on earth? *(the taiga)*
- What kind of vegetation does the steppe have? *(grass)*

Interpreting Maps

Vegetation Regions of Russia and the Republics

Ask students to compare this vegetation map with the climate map on page 340. *(The tundra climate and vegetation zones are nearly the same. The subarctic climate zone consists primarily of coniferous forest. The humid continental climate zone consists of deciduous and mixed forest, coniferous forest, and temperate grassland. The semiarid climate zone corresponds with temperate grassland. The desert climate zone corresponds with the desert and dry shrub vegetation zone.)*

SKILLBUILDER ANSWERS
1. desert and dry shrub **2.** generally between 70°N and the Arctic Circle

ACTIVITY OPTION **SKILLBUILDER LESSON**

CREATING A SKETCH MAP

Explaining the Skill Tell students that a sketch map is a rough outline map that does not include a lot of detail. A sketch map can be made to highlight the location of specific features or to show important influences on a region. In this activity, students will create a sketch map to show the major influences on the climates of Russia and the Republics.

Applying the Skill Have students draw a simple outline map of Europe and Asia and mark the boundaries of Russia and the Republics. Direct students to reread the text on climate on pages 350–351 and indicate on their map, using arrows and labels, the major influences on the region's climates.

For additional Skillbuilder Practice, see p. 345 in Section 1.

Interpreting Photographs

Siberian Reindeer Herders
About 15 different groups of reindeer-herding people live in Siberia, following a way of life that is centuries old. These people depend on reindeer much as the Native Americans of the North American plains depended on the buffalo. The reindeer provide food, clothing, and bedding. Ask students what might be appealing about this way of life. *(living close to nature, being self-sufficient and independent, having an active life, working at a variety of tasks to meet everyday needs)*

CAPTION ANSWER The deep snow and the fog caused by the breath of the reindeer are signs that it is extremely cold.

Assess & Reteach

GeoFocus Have students complete the section on climate and vegetation in their graphic organizers.

Formal Assessment
• Section Quiz, p. 227

Reteaching Activity
Have students form groups and create their own study guides for this section by outlining the main ideas.

In-Depth Resources: Unit 5
• Reteaching Activity, p. 11

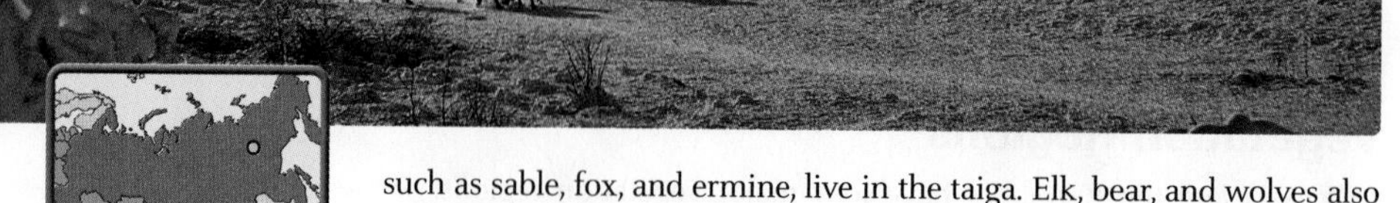

REGION Siberian herders lead reindeer through the taiga. The breathing of the reindeer is the cause of much of the fog floating above the herd. **What does this image suggest about the region's climate?**

such as sable, fox, and ermine, live in the taiga. Elk, bear, and wolves also make their homes in the forest.

South of the taiga, deciduous trees begin to mix with coniferous species. In lower latitudes, the deciduous trees become dominant.

STEPPE The steppe is the name of the temperate grassland that extends from southern Ukraine through northern Kazakhstan to the Altay Mountains. The highly fertile chernozem soil is found in the steppe and helps to make the grassland a major source of grain for Russia and the Republics.

DESERT Deserts and semiarid lands occupy the wide plains in the west and central areas of Central Asia. The two main deserts are the Kara Kum, which covers most of the republic of Turkmenistan, and the Kyzyl Kum, which is located in western Uzbekistan. Together, the two deserts occupy an area of about 230,000 square miles. In the following section, you will learn how efforts to irrigate these regions resulted in one of the world's greatest environmental catastrophes.

Section 2 Assessment

1 Places & Terms
Explain the importance of each of the following terms and places.
- continentality
- taiga

2 Taking Notes
REGION Review the notes you took for this section.

- How can climate affect transportation?
- To what depths can permafrost extend in Russia and the Republics?

3 Main Ideas
a. How does distance from the sea affect the region's climate?
b. In what way is the climate of Transcaucasia unique?
c. What are the major vegetation regions in Russia and the Republics?

4 Geographic Thinking
Determining Cause and Effect How are climate and vegetation related? **Think about:**
- average temperatures
- precipitation

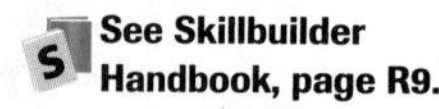
See Skillbuilder Handbook, page R9.

GeoActivity
SEEING PATTERNS Choose a city in Russia and the Republics. Collect data on the average monthly temperatures and precipitation in the city. Then create a **climograph** that illustrates the results of your research.

SECTION 2 ASSESSMENT ANSWERS

1. **Places & Terms**
continentality, p. 350 taiga, p. 351
2. **Taking Notes**
• Residents of Siberia, for example, use frozen rivers and lakes as roads for part of the year.
• as much as 1,500 feet
3. **Main Ideas**
a. It limits the amount of precipitation and results in extreme temperatures.
b. It has subtropical and highland climate zones.
c. tundra, forest, temperate grassland or steppe, and desert
4. **Geographic Thinking**
Answers will vary but should show a strong relationship between climate and vegetation.

GeoActivity

Integrated Assessment
• Rubric for a graph, 2.3

Human-Environment Interaction

Main Ideas

- The region's harsh climate has been both an obstacle and an advantage to its inhabitants.
- Attempts to overcome the region's geographic limits have sometimes had negative consequences.

Places & Terms

runoff

Trans-Siberian Railroad

CONNECT TO THE ISSUES
ECONOMIC CHANGE New regional leaders must solve economic problems caused by the former Soviet Union.

A HUMAN PERSPECTIVE Since the 1960s, irrigation policies in Central Asia have had a dramatic impact on the Aral Sea. A recent visitor to an old Aral fishing village described the change: "I stood on what had once been a seaside bluff . . . but I could see no water. The sea was twenty-five miles away." The dried-up seabed had become a graveyard for abandoned ships. The powerful winds were covering local populations with polluted dust picked up from the seabed. Thousands of people have left the region, and those who remain risk illness, or even death. In this section, you will read more about the complex relationship between the environment and the people of Russia and the Republics.

The Shrinking Aral Sea

Between 1960 and the present, the Aral Sea lost about 80 percent of its water. Central Asian leaders now face one of the earth's greatest environmental tragedies.

A DISAPPEARING LAKE The Aral Sea receives most of its water from two rivers, the Amu Darya and the Syr Darya. Before the 1960s, these rivers delivered nearly 13 cubic miles of water to the Aral Sea every year. But in the 1950s, officials began to take large amounts of water from the rivers to irrigate Central Asia's cotton fields. Large-scale irrigation projects, such as the 850-mile-long Kara Kum canal, took so much water from the rivers that the flow of water into the Aral slowed to a trickle. The sea began to evaporate.

EFFECTS OF AGRICULTURE Agricultural practices in Central Asia caused other problems for the Aral Sea. Cotton growers used pesticides and fertilizers. These chemicals were being picked up by **runoff**—rainfall not absorbed by the soil that runs into streams and rivers. The runoff carried the chemicals into the rivers that feed the Aral, with devastating effects. Of the 24 native species of fish once found in the sea, none is left today.

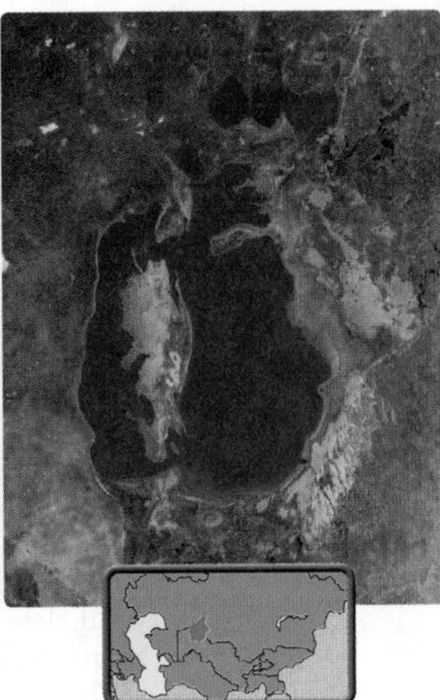

HUMAN-ENVIRONMENT INTERACTION These two images, taken in 1976 and 1997, show what happened after agricultural officials began diverting water from the rivers that feed the Aral Sea.

RUSSIA & REP.

SECTION 3 OBJECTIVES

1. Identify the causes and effects of the shrinkage of the Aral Sea.
2. Describe how Russia's harsh winter has been both an obstacle and an advantage to the country.
3. Explain the significance of the Trans-Siberian Railroad.

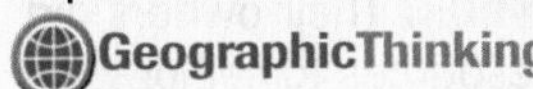

SKILLBUILDER: Interpreting Maps, p. 355

GeographicThinking
Using the Atlas, p. 354
Seeing Patterns, p. 355
Making Decisions, p. 356

Focus & Motivate

What would you do if environmental pollution seriously damaged your health or threatened to shorten your life span? *(file a lawsuit, protest, join an environmental group, move)*

Instruct: Objective 1

The Shrinking Aral Sea

- Why has the Aral Sea lost about 80 percent of its water since 1960? *(because officials have diverted water from the two major rivers that feed the Aral Sea)*
- What other environmental problems affect the area? *(pollution from pesticides and fertilizers have killed native fish species and damaged the residents' health)*
- What would have to be done to keep the lake at its present levels? *(significantly limit the amount of land in the region given to agricultural use)*

In-Depth Resources: Unit 5
- Guided Reading, p. 5

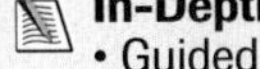

SECTION 3 PROGRAM RESOURCES

In-Depth Resources: Unit 5
- Guided Reading, p. 5
- Map and Graph Skills, pp. 6–7
- Building Vocabulary, p. 9
- Reteaching Activity, p. 12
- GeoWorkshop, pp. 35–36

Guided Reading Workbook
- Section 3

Access for Students Acquiring English/ESL
- Guided Reading, p. 79
- Map and Graph Skills, pp. 81–82

Formal Assessment
- Section Quiz, p. 228

Integrated Assessment
- Rubric for a Venn diagram, 2.8

INTEGRATED TECHNOLOGY

Power Presentations

Test Generator
- Section Quiz

hmhsocialstudies.com

TEST-TAKING RESOURCES

Strategies for Test Preparation

Test Practice Transparencies TT50

Online Test Practice

Interpreting Photographs

Exposed Floor of the Aral Sea

Ask students what kind of vegetation region the area shown in the photograph most resembles and what that might indicate about the climate in the Aral Sea region. *(The area resembles a desert. The climate probably became drier.)*

CAPTION ANSWER Their owners did not have the resources to sell or move them elsewhere.

Instruct: Objective 2

The Russian Winter

- What problems do Siberia's residents face in the winter and in the summer? *(Temperatures drop so much during winter that basic human activities become painful. In the summer, insects become a serious problem.)*
- How does Siberia's climate affect construction? *(Heated buildings thaw the permafrost, which can cause buildings to sink, tilt, and fall over.)*
- How did Russia's harsh winter help the country in the early 1800s? *(It helped to turn back Napoleon's invading armies.)*

PLACE Camels walk by the rusting hulks of abandoned ships on what was once the floor of the Aral Sea. **Why might the ships have been abandoned?**

Soon the damage spread beyond the lake. The retreating waters of the Aral exposed fertilizers and pesticides, as well as salt. Windstorms began to pick up these substances and dump them on nearby populations.

This pollution has caused a sharp increase in diseases. The incidence of throat cancer and respiratory diseases has risen dramatically. Dysentery, typhoid, and hepatitis have also become more common. Child mortality rates in Central Asia are among the highest in the world.

BACKGROUND Scientists have reportedly found salt from the Aral Sea as far away as the coast of the Arctic Ocean.

SAVING THE ARAL Scientists estimate that even to keep the lake at its present levels, you would have to remove 9 of the 18 million acres that are now used for farming. This would create terrible hardship for the farmers who depend on those fields for their livelihood. But many argue that only such drastic measures can save the Aral.

The Russian Winter

The frigid landscapes of Siberia lie far from Central Asia. But the rugged inhabitants of Siberia are also familiar with hardship.

COPING IN SIBERIA More than 32 million people make their homes in Siberia. The climate presents unique challenges to its inhabitants, especially during winter. A

Scientists have recorded the most variable temperatures on earth in Siberia. In the city of Verkhoyansk, temperatures have ranged from –90°F in the winter to 94°F in the summer—a span of 184 degrees. But most of the time it is cold. Temperatures drop so low that basic human activities become painful. A worker in the Siberian mining center at Norilsk explained how he and fellow workers turned up their collars and turned down the ear flaps of their fur caps so that only their eyes were visible. "Even then," he reported, "your eyes would be so cold that you'd close one until the one you were looking with froze, and then swap over."

The change of seasons brings little relief. Warmer weather melts ice and snow and leaves pools of water that become breeding grounds for mosquitoes and black flies. The problem becomes severe in the spring.

Geographic Thinking

Using the Atlas

A Examine the maps on pages 340–341. What relationship do you see between population density and climate?

A. Answer Most of the region's population is concentrated in the humid continental climate zone.

ACTIVITY OPTION **CRITICAL THINKING**

DETERMINING CAUSE AND EFFECT

Explaining the Skill A cause is an action that makes something happen. An effect is the event that is the result of the cause. Often, one cause can have multiple effects or can set off a series of effects.

Applying the Skill Have students reread the section on "The Shrinking Aral Sea" on pages 353–354 and ask them to create a cause-and-effect diagram similar to the one shown here, which lists a series of effects that resulted from diverting water for irrigation.

CAUSE

Water for irrigation is diverted from rivers that feed Aral Sea.

⇓

EFFECTS

The diversion decreases the amount of water flowing into the Aral.

⇓

The retreating waters expose salt and fertilizers and pesticides on the Aral's sea bed.

⇓

Windstorms pick up the exposed substances and drop them on people.

⇓

Diseases and mortality rates increase.

Swamps form when northward flowing rivers, swollen by spring rains, run into still-frozen water further north. Soon, enormous black clouds of insects are attacking Siberia's residents.

The climate also affects construction in Siberia. Permafrost makes the ground in Siberia iron-hard. However, a heated building will thaw the permafrost. As the ground thaws, buildings sink, tilt, and eventually topple over. To prevent such problems, builders raise their structures a few feet off the ground on concrete pillars.

WAR AND "GENERAL WINTER" Russia's harsh climate has caused difficulties for its inhabitants, but it has also, at times, come to their aid.

In the early 1800s, the armies of the French leader Napoleon Bonaparte were taking control of Europe. In the spring of 1812, Napoleon decided to extend his control over Russia. He gathered his army together in Poland and from there began the march on Moscow.

But as his troops advanced, so did the seasons. When Napoleon arrived in Moscow in September, the Russian winter was not far behind. Moreover, the citizens of Moscow had set fire to their city before fleeing, so there was no shelter for Napoleon's troops.

Napoleon had no choice but to retreat during the bitter Russian winter. He left Moscow with 100,000 troops. But by the time his army arrived back in Poland, the cruel Russian winter had helped to kill more than 90,000 of his soldiers. Some historians believe that Russia's "General Winter" succeeded in defeating Napoleon where the armies of Europe had failed. B

B. Answer the kind of terrain that would have to be crossed and the location of agricultural regions that might serve as sources of food

Geographic Thinking

Seeing Patterns

B Besides climate, what other geographic factors might an army invading Russia have to consider?

Crossing the "Wild East"

At the end of the 19th century, Siberia was similar to the "Wild West" of the United States. Travel through the region was dangerous and slow. For these reasons, Russia's emperor ordered work to start on a **Trans-Siberian Railroad** that would eventually link Moscow to the Pacific port of Vladivostok.

Instruct: Objective 3

Crossing the "Wild East"

- What made the building of the Trans-Siberian Railroad an enormous undertaking? *(The rails had to be laid across thousands of miles of a bitter cold, undeveloped region.)*
- Why did Russian officials want to build the Trans-Siberian Railroad? *(to speed up travel and populate the region so that its resources could be developed)*
- How did the railroad affect the development of the region? *(Millions of settlers came, and resources such as coal and iron ore were extracted.)*

RUSSIA & REP.

Rail Routes Across Russia

hmhsocialstudies.com INTERACTIVE MAP

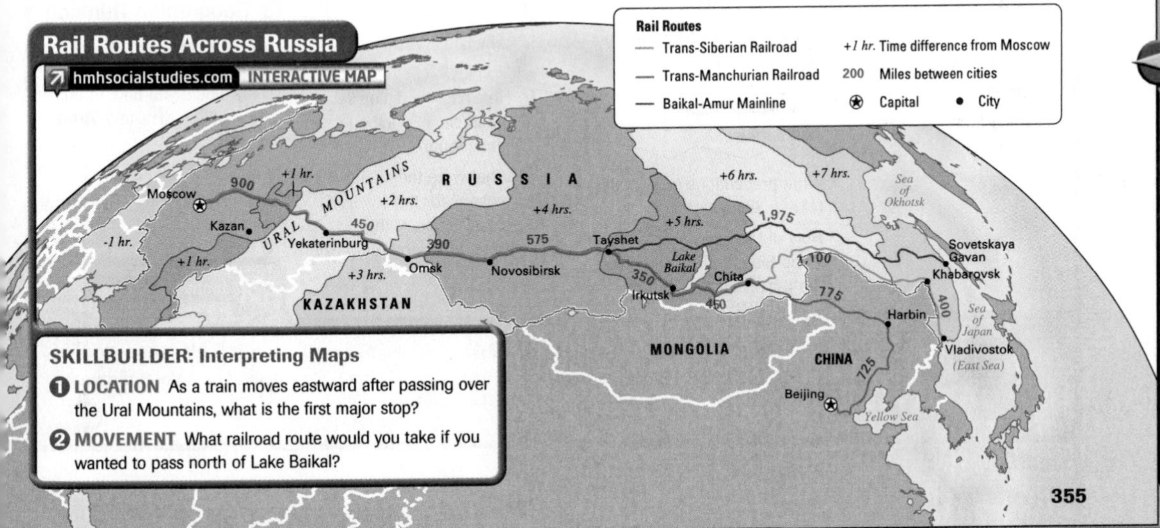

SKILLBUILDER: Interpreting Maps

1. **LOCATION** As a train moves eastward after passing over the Ural Mountains, what is the first major stop?
2. **MOVEMENT** What railroad route would you take if you wanted to pass north of Lake Baikal?

Interpreting Maps

Rails Across Russia

Ask students what part of Siberia the railroad crosses and why this route may have been chosen. *(It crosses the southern part of Siberia. The southern part is probably warmer than the northern part and thus easier to cross.)*

SKILLBUILDER ANSWERS

1. Yekaterinburg **2.** the Baikal-Amur Mainline

DIFFERENTIATING INSTRUCTION GIFTED AND TALENTED STUDENTS

MAKING PREDICTIONS

Objective To use prior knowledge to make predictions

Class Time 15 minutes

Task Predict some of the difficulties workers had in building the Trans-Siberian Railroad

Directions Ask students to use what they have learned about the physical geography of Siberia to make a list of some of the difficulties workers probably experienced in building the railroad. Then have students do library or Internet research to check their predictions and to add to their lists.

Interpreting Photographs

Trans-Siberian Railroad

The present-day Trans-Siberian Express makes the trip from Moscow to Vladivostok in seven days. Ask students what they can tell from the photograph about the land that the railroad crosses. *(It crosses vast stretches of wilderness, where there are forested mountains and open plains and where the climate is cold and snowy.)*

CAPTION ANSWER They transport goods between distant regions more quickly.

Assess & Reteach

GeoFocus Have students complete the section on human-environment interaction in their graphic organizers.

Formal Assessment
- Section Quiz, p. 228

Reteaching Activity

Have students work in small groups to write quizzes on the section's main ideas. Then direct groups to exchange and answer the quizzes.

In-Depth Resources: Unit 5
- Reteaching Activity, p. 12

MOVEMENT A train from Ukraine travels on Trans-Siberian tracks on its journey toward Vladivostok. **What impact do railroads have on commerce?**

AN ENORMOUS PROJECT The project was a massive undertaking. The distance to be covered was more than 5,700 miles, and the tracks had to cross seven time zones. Between 1891 and 1903, approximately 70,000 workers moved 77 million cubic feet of earth, cleared more than 100,000 acres of forest, and built bridges over several major rivers.

RESOURCE WEALTH IN SIBERIA Russian officials did not undertake this massive project simply to speed up travel. They also wanted to populate Siberia in order to profit from its many resources.

Ten years after the completion of the line in 1904, nearly five million settlers, mainly peasant farmers, had taken the railway from European Russia to settle in Siberia.

As migrants streamed into Siberia, resources, such as coal and iron ore, poured out. Siberia, one author wrote, began to yield riches that "she has under guard of eternal snow and ice, so long held in trust for future centuries." In the years that followed, the railroad would aid the political and economic development of Russia and the Republics, which you will read about in the next chapter.

Section 3 Assessment

1 Places & Terms

Explain the importance of the following terms.
- runoff
- Trans-Siberian Railroad

2 Taking Notes

REGION Review the notes you took for this section.

- What precautions must builders take in Siberia? Why?
- How did the construction of the Trans-Siberian Railroad affect the region's landscape?

3 Main Ideas

a. Why is the Aral Sea shrinking?

b. How has the region's harsh climate helped its inhabitants?

c. What were the main reasons for the construction of the Trans-Siberian Railroad?

4 Geographic Thinking

Making Decisions If you were a regional leader, what steps would you take to end the Aral Sea disaster? **Think about:**
- how your solutions will affect people in the region

hmhsocialstudies.com RESEARCH WEB LINKS

GeoActivity

MAKING COMPARISONS Do more research on the Trans-Siberian Railroad. Then do research on the construction of the transcontinental railroad in the United States. Use a **Venn diagram** to compare and contrast the two projects.

SECTION 3 ASSESSMENT ANSWERS

1. Places & Terms

runoff, p. 353 — Trans-Siberian Railroad, p. 355

2. Taking Notes
- They build on concrete pillars so that the heat from the buildings does not thaw the permafrost, causing the buildings to topple over.
- Workers moved 77 million cubic feet of earth and cleared more than 100,000 acres of forest.

3. Main Ideas

a. Large-scale irrigation projects have diverted water away from its main tributaries, the Amu Darya and Syr Darya.

b. The region's harsh winter has helped to defeat invading armies.

c. Russia's leaders wanted to speed up travel times, populate Siberia, and exploit its wealth of resources.

4. Geographic Thinking

Answer will vary, but students should take into consideration the fact that thousands of people depend on the irrigated lands for their livelihood.

GeoActivity

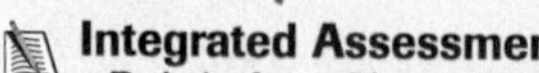

Integrated Assessment
- Rubric for a Venn diagram, 2.8

Map and Graph Skills

Understanding Time Zones

In 1884, international officials agreed to divide the map of the earth's surface into 24 time zones, one for each hour of the day. Because the earth rotates 360° each day, each zone was to represent 15° longitude (360° ÷ 24 hours = 15°). Officials used the prime meridian (0°) as the starting point for the time zones. They named this base time Greenwich Mean Time (GMT). The International Date Line was set at 180° longitude. To the east of this line, the calendar date is one day earlier than to the west.

THE LANGUAGE OF MAPS A **time zone map** shows the time zones that are in use around the world today. Officials have adjusted the boundaries of many time zones to keep political units, such as countries, within a single time zone.

Non-standard time zones

Time varies from the standard time zone by less than an hour.

Time Zones of the World

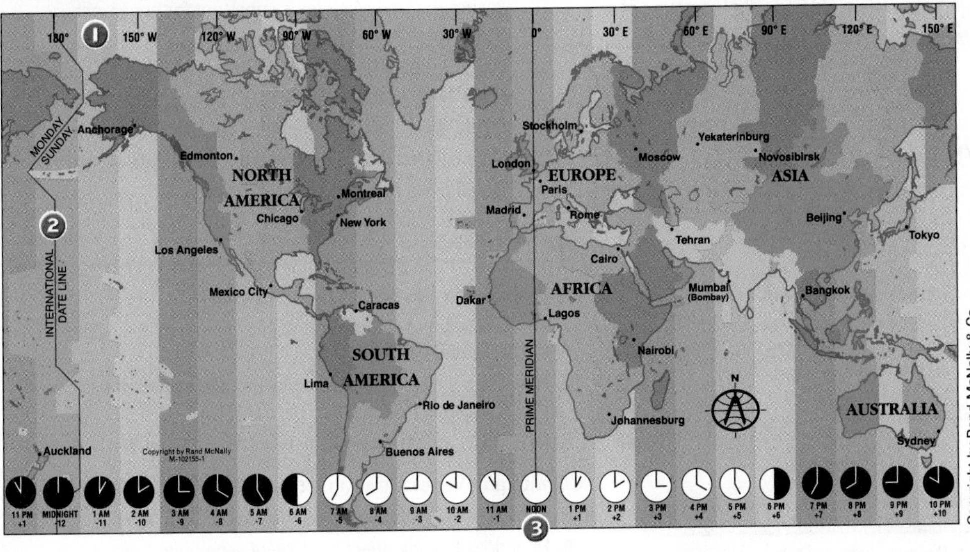

1. Each band of color represents one time zone.

2. Officials set the International Date Line at 180°, but the line moves east or west of it in places to avoid dividing countries.

3. Positive and negative numbers show the difference between local time and Greenwich Mean Time.

Map and Graph Skills Assessment

1. Drawing Conclusions
How many time zones are there in the continental United States?

2. Making Comparisons
What is the current time in the time zone in which you live? What is the current time in Greenwich, England?

3. Drawing Conclusions
If it is 6:00 Sunday morning in New York, what are the day and time in Auckland, New Zealand?

OBJECTIVE
Understand and interpret time zones.

Instruct: Objective

Understanding Time Zones

- What information do you gain from the map legend? *(It indicates that the tan areas have non-standard time zones. It also indicates that the numbers in each zone refer to the hours to be added or subtracted from Greenwich time.)*
- If it is 1:00 P.M. in Moscow, what time is it in Novosibirsk? *(4 P.M.)*
- What is the significance of the international date line? *(It marks where a new calendar day begins.)*

In-Depth Resources, Unit 5
- Map and Graph Skills, pp. 6–7
- GeoWorkshop, pp. 35–36

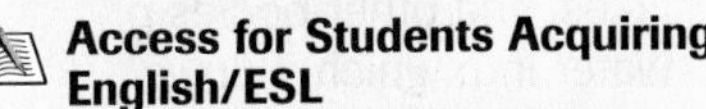

Access for Students Acquiring English/ESL
- Map and Graph Skills, pp. 81–82

More About

Time Zones

In the United States, the lower 48 states are divided into four major time zones: Eastern, Central, Mountain, and Pacific. Alaska and Hawaii are in different time zones to the west.

SKILLS ASSESSMENT ANSWERS

1. 4

2. Answers will vary.

3. Monday night at 11:00

Reviewing Places & Terms

A. **1.** chernozem, p. 345
2. Ural Mountains, p. 346
3. Eurasia, p. 346
4. Transcaucasia, p. 346
5. Central Asia, p. 346
6. Siberia, p. 349
7. continentality, p. 350
8. taiga, p. 351
9. runoff, p. 353
10. Trans-Siberian Railroad, p. 355

B. Possible Responses
11. The railroad crosses Siberia.
12. Transcaucasia is south of the Caucasus Mountains.
13. Chernozem is a fertile soil found on the Northern European Plain.
14. If runoff holds dangerous substances, it will affect the rivers, lakes, and other bodies of water into which it flows.
15. Kazakhstan, Kyrgyzstan, Tajikistan, Turkmenistan, and Uzbekistan are located there.
16. Many geographers consider this range to be a major boundary line between Europe and Asia.
17. It is often called Siberia.
18. This region is called the taiga.
19. Because of the region's distance from surrounding seas, it receives limited precipitation.
20. Eurasia includes Europe and Asia.

Chapter 15 Assessment

VISUAL SUMMARY
PHYSICAL GEOGRAPHY OF RUSSIA AND THE REPUBLICS

Landforms

Major Geographical Areas: Northern European Plain, West Siberian Plain, Central Siberian Plateau, Russian Far East, Turan Plain

Important Mountain Ranges: Urals, Caucasus, Tian Shan

Important Rivers and Lakes: Caspian and Aral seas, Lake Baikal, Volga, Ob, Yenisey, and Lena rivers

Resources

- Regional resources include huge coal reserves and deposits of iron ore and other metals.
- The Caspian Sea region has enormous reserves of oil and gas.

Climate and Vegetation

- Continentality and a wall of high southeastern mountains have a major impact on the climate of Russia and the Republics.

Human-Environment Interaction

- The shrinking of the Aral Sea is an example of the dramatic impact that agricultural policies can have on the environment.
- The hardships faced by Napoleon's army show how Russia's environment influenced human events.
- The construction of the Trans-Siberian Railway changed the population distribution and economic geography of the region.

Reviewing Places & Terms

A. Briefly explain the importance of each of the following.

1. chernozem
2. Ural Mountains
3. Eurasia
4. Transcaucasia
5. Central Asia
6. Siberia
7. continentality
8. taiga
9. runoff
10. Trans-Siberian Railroad

B. Answer the questions about vocabulary in complete sentences.

11. What is the name of the region crossed by the Trans-Siberian Railroad?
12. Which region is located south of the Caucasus Mountains?
13. What is chernozem and where is it found?
14. How can runoff affect the environment?
15. What are the five republics located in Central Asia?
16. Why are the Ural Mountains important for geographers?
17. What is the name of the non-European part of Russia?
18. Which vegetation region allows Russia to boast one-fifth of the world's timber resources?
19. Why do Russia and the Republics receive limited precipitation?
20. Which landmass is named after the continents of Asia and Europe?

Main Ideas

Landforms and Resources (pp. 345–349)

1. What facts could you provide to give an idea of the enormous size of Russia and the Republics?
2. How does the tilt of the West Siberian Plain affect the region's physical geography?
3. How is the region's use of its resources affected by climate?

Climate and Vegetation (pp. 350–352)

4. What are major influences on the region's climate?
5. How does latitude affect the type of vegetation found in Russia's forests?
6. Where is the steppe located in Russia and the Republics?

Human-Environment Interaction (pp. 353–357)

7. What effect have irrigation projects had on the Aral Sea?
8. How has the shrinking of the Aral Sea affected public health in the surrounding region?
9. What factors contribute to the formation of swamps in Siberia, and how do the swamps affect people living in the region?
10. How long did it take to complete the main line of the Trans-Siberian Railway?

Main Ideas

1. The region covers approximately three times the land area occupied by the United States and sprawls across the continents of both Europe and Asia.
2. The region's rivers flow northward, taking much needed water from the arid lands of the south.
3. Many of the region's resources are located in frigid arctic and subarctic regions of Siberia and are virtually inaccessible.
4. high latitude, mountain barriers, and distance from the sea
5. In lower latitudes, coniferous trees begin to give way to deciduous trees.
6. It extends from southern Ukraine through Kazakhstan to the Altay Mountains.
7. They reduced the flow of water into the sea, which then began to shrink.
8. The shrinking exposed the polluted seabed of the Aral. Windstorms spread the pollution over nearby populations, causing increases in many diseases.
9. Northward flowing rivers, swollen by spring rains, run into still-frozen water further north. The resulting swamps become breeding grounds for insects.
10. The railway was built between 1891 and 1903.

Critical Thinking

1. Using Your Notes

Use your completed chart to answer these questions.

Landforms	
Resources	

a. Which region contains a large number of volcanoes?

b. Who was "General Winter"?

2. Geographic Themes

a. **HUMAN-ENVIRONMENT INTERACTION** How has Siberia's climate affected transportation in the region?

b. **MOVEMENT** What impact did the Trans-Siberian Railway have on Russia's population?

3. Identifying Themes

What factor might explain why Russia and the Republics receive relatively little precipitation and frequently experience extreme temperatures? Which of the five themes applies to this situation?

4. Determining Cause and Effect

What is a major factor contributing to the large subtropical climate zone in Transcaucasia?

5. Drawing Conclusions

Given what you have read about the dependency of Central Asian farmers on the water from the Amu Darya and Syr Darya rivers, how likely do you think it is that the Aral Sea will eventually recover?

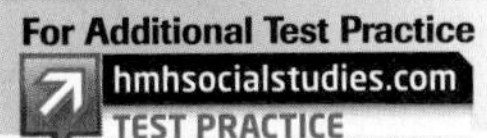

Geographic Skills: Interpreting Maps

Mineral Resources and Pollution

Use the map to answer the following questions.

1. **REGION** This map shows how close mining sites are to polluted areas. Why might the two be related?
2. **MOVEMENT** How might locating a mining site near a river affect the spread of pollution?
3. **PLACE** Why might the areas around Moscow and St. Petersburg be polluted even though there seem to be few mining sites nearby?

GeoActivity

Do more research on mining pollution's impact on public health in one area of the region. Use presentation software to share your results.

hmhsocialstudies.com

MULTIMEDIA ACTIVITY

Use the links at **hmhsocialstudies.com** to conduct research on Siberia. Focus on how people cope with the region's low temperatures. For example, investigate the kinds of clothing people wear or how they move about in the winter.

Writing About Geography Write a report of your findings. Include photos or illustrations that visually present information about life in the region. List the Web sites that you used in preparing your report.

CHAPTER 15 ASSESSMENT

Critical Thinking

1. a. the Russian Far East
b. "General Winter" describes the impact of the Russian winter on invading troops, including Napoleon's.

2. a. When Siberia's rivers and lakes freeze during the winter, people often use them for roads.
b. It increased the population of Siberia dramatically. Within ten years after the railway's completion, nearly five million people had taken the railway from European Russia to settle in Siberia.

3. continentality, or the effect of distance from the moderating influence of surrounding seas; location

4. the moist air flowing into the region from the Mediterranean Sea

5. Opinions will vary, but some students may argue that a solution is unlikely because the removal of millions of acres of farmland from irrigation to save the sea would be too high a cost for the region's farmers.

GeoActivity

Integrated Assessment
- Rubric for a presentation, 5.4

Formal Assessment
- Chapter Tests, Forms A, B, and C, pp. 229–240

Geographic Skills

1. because mine operators have not taken adequate measures to reduce the impact of their mines on the surrounding environment
2. If pollution from the mine is discharged into the river, the river will carry the pollution downstream.
3. Students might point out that, as large urban areas, the two cities generate considerable pollution.

INTERNET ACTIVITY

For their report on coping in Siberia, students should:

- Present a concise, well-organized report.
- Summarize different ways in which inhabitants face the region's challenges.
- Produce a clear, imaginative visual to complement the report.
- Include references to the web sites used as sources.

Grading Rubric Evaluate student performance as Exceptional, Acceptable, or Poor in each of the following categories:

	Exceptional	*Acceptable*	*Poor*
Writing is clear, focused, and logical			
Introductory sentence clearly states the topic and purpose			
Provides necessary facts and examples			
Uses correct grammar, spelling, and punctuation			

Human Geography of Russia and the Republics

OVERVIEW	INSTRUCTIONAL RESOURCES	
ESSENTIAL QUESTION How did the expansion of Russia affect the region's people? **Focus on the Essential Question Podcast**	**In-Depth Resources: Unit 5** • Building Vocabulary, p. 17 **Block Schedule Strategies** **Chapter Summaries** (English/Spanish)	**Interactive Online Edition** TOS **ExamView® Assessment Suite** (English/Spanish) TOS **CalendarPlanner** **Power Presentations with Media Gallery** **Critical Thinking Transparencies** • CT16 hmhsocialstudies.com INTERACTIVE
SECTION 1 **RUSSIA AND THE WESTERN REPUBLICS** **MAIN IDEAS** • From modest beginnings, Russia expanded to become the largest country in the world. • In the 1900s, Soviet leaders adopted a command economy to move their society toward communism. • Russian traditions have remained strong through periods of economic and political change.	**In-Depth Resources: Unit 5** • Guided Reading, p. 13 • Building Vocabulary, p. 17 • Reteaching Activities, p. 18 **Outline Maps with Activities** • Russia and the Western Republics, pp. 45–46 **Cultures Around the World** • Architecture, p. 25 • Daily Life, p. 26 • Fine Arts, p. 27 • Music, p. 29 **Guided Reading Workbook,** Section 1	**Map Transparencies** • MT29 Russian and Soviet Expansion: 1462–2000 **Cultures Transparencies** • CW25 St. Basil's Cathedral • CW26 Caviar • CW27 Chagall • CW29 Stravinsky **Video:** The Romanovs **Video:** Chernobyl: Nuclear Meltdown
SECTION 2 **TRANSCAUCASIA** **MAIN IDEAS** • Transcaucasia has been a gateway between Europe and Asia. • The region has a long history of outside control. • The Caspian Sea's oil and gas reserves have given the region great economic potential.	**In-Depth Resources: Unit 5** • Guided Reading, p. 14 • Skillbuilder Practice, p. 16 • Building Vocabulary, p. 17 • Reteaching Activities, p. 19 **Outline Maps with Activities** • Transcaucasia: Physical and Political, pp. 47–48 **Cultures Around the World** • Dance, p. 28 • Arts and Crafts, p. 30 **Guided Reading Workbook,** Section 2	**Cultures Transparencies** • CW28 Georgian Folk Dance • CW30 Traditional Rugs
SECTION 3 **CENTRAL ASIA** **MAIN IDEAS** • A trade route called the Silk Road made Central Asia a historical crossroads. • Soviet officials drew borders in Central Asia that have contributed to the region's instability. • Central Asians have preserved some nomadic traditions despite decades of colonization.	**In-Depth Resources: Unit 5** • Guided Reading, p. 15 • Building Vocabulary, p. 17 • Reteaching Activities, p. 20 **Outline Maps with Activities** • Central Asia, pp. 49–50 **Guided Reading Workbook,** Section 3	**Critical Thinking Transparencies** • CT48, Great Games in Central Asia

ASSESSMENT

SE **Chapter Assessment,** pp. 382–383

Formal Assessment
- Chapter Tests, Forms A, B, and C, pp. 244–255

TOS **ExamView® Assessment Suite**

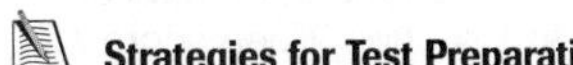

Strategies for Test Preparation

SE **Section Assessment,** p. 367

Formal Assessment

- Section Quiz, p. 241

Integrated Assessment
- Rubric for an oral report, 3.6
- Rubric for a multimedia presentation, 5.4

Test Practice Transparencies TT51

SE **Section Assessment,** p. 374

Formal Assessment
- Section Quiz, p. 242

Integrated Assessment

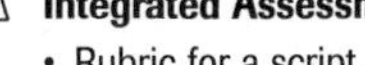

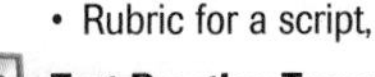

- Rubric for a script, 5.5

Test Practice Transparencies TT52

SE **Section Assessment,** p. 379

Formal Assessment

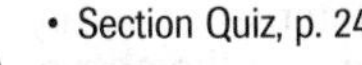

- Section Quiz, p. 243

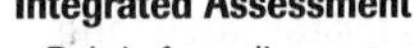

Integrated Assessment
- Rubric for a diary entry, 4.3
- Rubric for an exhibit, 1.5

Test Practice Transparencies TT53

CHART KEY:

SE Student Edition

Block Scheduling

DVD/CD-ROM

TE Teacher's Edition

TOS Teacher One Stop

MP3 Audio

Printable Resource

Presentation Resource

HISTORY™

Program Resources available on TOS and @ hmhsocialstudies.com

SUPPORTING RESOURCES

- **Multimedia Classroom Global History Series**
- **Global History Teacher's Guide**

Social Studies Trade Library Collection

- World Regions Trade Collection

For more information or to purchase these resources, go to

DIFFERENTIATED INSTRUCTION

English Learners	Struggling Readers	Gifted and Talented Students
Spanish/English Guided Reading Workbook **Access for Students Acquiring English/ESL** Spanish Translations, pp. 83–86 **Chapter Summaries** (English/Spanish) TE **TE Activity** Charting Key Words and Ideas, p. 371	**Chapter Summaries** (English/Spanish) TE **TE Activity** Previewing the Section, p. 376	TE **TE Activity** Researching Russian History, p. 362

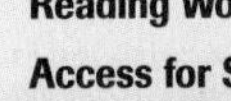

ENRICHMENT ACTIVITIES

The following activities are especially suitable for classes following block schedules.

SE **Student Edition,** p. 360–383
- Disasters! Nuclear Explosion at Chernobyl, pp. 368–369
- Comparing Cultures: Homes and Shelters, pp. 380–381

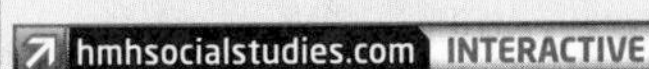

- History of Russia, 1555–2000, pp. 362–363
- Silk Production, p. 376
- Comparing Cultures: Homes and Shelters, pp. 380–381

CHAPTER 16 PACING GUIDE

BLOCK SCHEDULE LESSON PLAN OPTIONS: 90-MINUTE PERIOD

DAY 1

SECTION 1, pp. 361–369
Class Time 90 minutes

- **Discussion** Lead a class discussion of this section using the TE questions and prompts as a guide. Share with students the "More About" information on TE pages 364 and 367.
  Class Time 40 minutes
- **Freewriting** Ask students to review the photographs, map, and timeline in this section and freewrite about their dominant impressions of this region. Call on volunteers to share what they have written.
  Class Time 50 minutes

DAY 2

SECTION 2, pp. 370–374
Class Time 90 minutes

- **Examining Visuals** Use the maps on PE pages 370 and 373 and the photographs on PE pages 371, 372, and 374 to review this section's content.
  Class Time 45 minutes
- **Skillbuilder Lesson** Use the lesson on making inferences on TE page 372 and the Skillbuilder Practice worksheet.
  Class Time 45 minutes

DAY 3

SECTION 3, pp. 375–381
Class Time 40 minutes

- **Quiz Show** Divide students into two teams and use the "Instruct" questions on TE pages 376, 377, and 378 and the Section Assessment questions to quiz the teams on the main ideas in this section. Keep score of correct answers.

CHAPTER 16 REVIEW AND ASSESSMENT, pp. 382–383
Class Time 50 minutes

- **Review** Pair each student with a partner and have them use their GeoFocus graphic organizers to quiz each other on the chapter content.
  Class Time 15 minutes
- **Assessment** Have students complete the Chapter 16 Assessment.
  Class Time 35 minutes

TEACHER-TESTED ACTIVITY *Writing a Position Paper*

Class Time Two class periods

Task Write a one-page position paper on the economic future of Russia and the Republics

Supplies
- Textbook
- Notebook paper
- Pen/pencil
- Computer lab or library for research

Purpose To have students make inferences about the future of Russia and the Republics based on the information drawn from Chapter 16, as well as supplemental research.

Activity Write the following statement on the board: "As Russia and the Republics continue to develop their natural resources, the region's people will become more prosperous." Have students evaluate this statement using relevant sections in the textbook. Students might carry out further research using the Internet or library resources. After completing their research, students should decide whether or not they agree with the above statement and then write a one-page position paper defending their position. Day one is for research, and day two is for writing their paper.

Jamie Berlin
Geography Teacher, South High School, Sheboygan, Wisconsin

TECHNOLOGY IN THE CLASSROOM

Knowing how to conduct an effective Internet search is a powerful skill for students to acquire. There are a variety of search engines, and the same search techniques can be used on many of them. This activity has students use the Alta Vista search engine–not because it is necessarily the best one, but because its help screen contains good examples of simple search strategies that can be used at a variety of search engines. Please refer to the "Choose the Best Search Engine for Your Information Needs" link at **hmhsocialstudies.com** for information on how to determine the most effective search engine.

Objective Students will use a popular search engine to refine a search on the Silk Road.

Task Have students review some basic search techniques and use the Alta Vista search engine to look for Web sites about the Silk Road. After refining their searches, have them illustrate maps with the information they have found.

Class Time Two class periods

1. Ask students to describe their experiences searching the Internet. Why might it be helpful to know how to conduct a good search?

2. As a class, go over the "Examples" at the Alta Vista Search Cheat Sheet (link from **hmhsocialstudies.com**). Be sure to introduce students to the method of using quotes and the + and - signs in a search. Inform them that these search tools will work with Alta Vista, as well as many other search engines (but not all of them).

3. Ask students to assume they are going to search the Web for information about the Silk Road, including its history and the route in modern times. What keywords might they try typing into Alta Vista? Would they use quotes or the + or - signs? List their ideas on the board. Some ideas might include "Silk Road" and + "Silk Road" +Tashkent.

4. Have students try their keyword combinations in Alta Vista (link from **hmhsocialstudies.com**). When they get to the results pages, have them count the "hits" they get and record the number. Then have them look at the first page of results. By looking at the titles and descriptions of the sites, can they determine whether these sites might have relevant information? How many sites on the first page look promising?

5. If they have found a number of sites that do not seem to be about the Silk Road (e.g. sites for tour companies), ask them to brainstorm what they can do to narrow the results, and have them experiment with these ideas (hint: -movie; -hotels).

6. Have students continue to refine their searches until they find at least four Web sites discussing the history of the Silk Road and/or the Silk Road today. Give each student a blank outline map of Asia, and have them draw the Silk Road on their maps. Ask them to illustrate their maps with at least ten things they have learned about the Silk Road and this region. They may include pictures and text captions. On a separate page, they should list the URLs and titles of the Web sites they have used.

CHAPTER 16 OBJECTIVE

Identify features of human geography in the three subregions of Russia and the Republics.

Chapter **16**

HUMAN GEOGRAPHY OF RUSSIA AND THE REPUBLICS

A Diverse Heritage

Interpreting Maps

Three Subregions of Russia and the Republics

Have students examine the map and ask them to compare the sizes of the three subregions shown.

Extension Have students suggest other ways the region might be divided.

Introducing the Essential Question

- Emphasize that the region's huge size has posed both advantages and disadvantages for its people and their governments. Ask students to suggest what those might be.
- Explain that the region includes many different ethnic groups with very different ways of life. Point out that the physical geography of Russia and the Republics has helped create these differences.

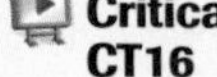

hmhsocialstudies.com TAKING NOTES

Have students complete the cluster diagrams in their notebooks, using material from all sections of this chapter.

Critical Thinking Transparencies CT16
- GeoFocus

In-Depth Resources: Unit 5
- Building Vocabulary, p. 17

Three Subregions of Russia and the Republics

ARCTIC OCEAN
North Sea
Barents Sea
Kara Sea
Laptev Sea
East Siberian Sea
Sea of Okhotsk
Black Sea
Caspian Sea
RUSSIA
ESTONIA
LATVIA
LITHUANIA
BELARUS
MOLDOVA
UKRAINE
GEORGIA
ARMENIA
AZERBAIJAN
KAZAKHSTAN
UZBEKISTAN
TURKMENISTAN
KYRGYZSTAN
TAJIKISTAN
Arctic Circle
Tropic of Cancer
Tropic of Capricorn
INDIAN OCEAN

Russia and the Western Republics
Transcaucasia
Central Asia

0 500 1,000 miles
0 500 1,000 kilometers
Two-Point Equidistant Projection

Essential Question

How did the expansion of Russia affect the region's people?

What You Will Learn

In this chapter you will learn about the history, culture, and economy of Russia and the Republics.

SECTION 1
Russia and the Western Republics

SECTION 2
Transcaucasia

SECTION 3
Central Asia

hmhsocialstudies.com TAKING NOTES

Use the graphic organizer online to take notes about the history, economics, culture, and modern life of each subregion of Russia and the Republics.

360

CHAPTER 16 ADDITIONAL RESOURCES

BOOKS FOR THE TEACHER

Hiro, Dilip. ***Inside Central Asia: A Political and Cultural History of Uzbekistan, Turkmenistan, Kazakhstan, Kyrgyzstan, Tajikistan, Turkey, and Iran.*** Overlook, 2009. A comprehensive view of a volatile region, with an emphasis on post-Soviet history.

BOOKS FOR THE STUDENT

Karny, Yo'av. ***Highlanders.*** NY: Farrar, 2001. An examination of the ethnic cultures of the Caucasus.

Curtis, Glenn E., ed. ***Armenia, Azerbaijan, and Georgia: Country Studies.*** Washington, D.C.: Library of Congress, 1995. Handbook on Transcaucasia.

VIDEOS

Living in Russia Today. Idea Bank, 1998. A portrait of life in modern Russia.

The Face of Russia. WETA, 1998. A three-part cultural history of Russia.

INTERNET

For more on the human geography of Russia and the Republics, visit . . .

hmhsocialstudies.com

Russia and the Western Republics

Main Ideas

- From modest beginnings, Russia expanded to become the largest country in the world.
- The rise and fall of the Soviet Union affected the world's political geography.

Places & Terms

Baltic Republics
czar
Russian Revolution
USSR
Cold War
command economy
collective farm

CONNECT TO THE ISSUES

ECONOMIC CHANGE The region is struggling to move from a command economy to a market economy.

A HUMAN PERSPECTIVE Early in the 1500s, the Russian leader Ivan the Great put an end to two centuries of foreign rule in his homeland. Russia then entered a period of explosive growth. From its center in Moscow, Russia expanded at a rate of about 55 square miles a day for the next four centuries. During the expansion, Russians made so much progress toward the east that they swallowed up a future U.S. state, Alaska. Russia had taken control of the territory by the late 18th century but did not sell it to the United States until 1867.

A History of Expansion

Russia's growth had lasting effects on nearby lands and peoples. You can see these effects even today in the republics to its west: Belarus, Moldova, Ukraine, and the **Baltic Republics** of Estonia, Latvia, and Lithuania. But Russian expansion not only affected its neighbors. It also had an impact on the entire world's political geography.

BIRTH OF AN EMPIRE The Russian state began in the region between the Baltic and Black seas. In the ninth century, Vikings from Scandinavia came to the region to take advantage of the river trade between the two seas. They established a settlement near what is now Kiev, a city near the Dnieper River. In time, the Vikings adopted the customs of the local Slavic population. Soon the settlement began to expand.

Expansion was halted in the 13th century with the arrival of invaders from Mongolia, called Tatars. The ferocity of those Mongol warriors is legendary. It is said that "like molten lava, they destroyed everything in their path." The Tatars sacked Kiev between 1237 and 1240.

The Mongols controlled the region until the 1500s, when Ivan the Great, the powerful prince of Moscow, put an end to their rule. Russia continued once again to expand to the east. By the end of the 17th century, it had built an empire that extended to the Pacific Ocean. As the leaders of Russia added more territory to their empire, they also added more people. Many of these people belonged to different ethnic groups, spoke different languages, and practiced different religions.

MOVEMENT This 1862 painting imagines a dramatic scene when Ivan the Great cast the Tatar king (or khan) out of Russia.

SECTION 1 OBJECTIVES

1. Summarize the history of Russia.
2. Explain how the former Soviet command economy worked.
3. Describe the cultural background and achievements of Russia and the Western Republics.
4. Describe ways in which Russian life has changed and remained the same.

SKILLBUILDER: Interpreting Maps, p. 362

GeographicThinking

Using the Atlas, p. 363
Seeing Patterns, pp. 365, 367
Making Inferences, p. 367

Focus & Motivate

What are some achievements of Russian culture? *(Students might mention great Russian dancers or writers.)*

Instruct: Objective 1 appears on p. 362.

More About

The Baltic Republics

Estonia, Latvia, and Lithuania, perhaps more so than other republics in the region, strongly identify with the West. Each has sought to cultivate closer relationships with Europe, for example, by reforming their economic and legal systems to bring them in line with European models. The republics tried to strengthen their Western identity by joining the European Union in 2004.

SECTION 1 PROGRAM RESOURCES

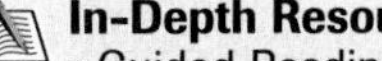

In-Depth Resources: Unit 5
- Guided Reading, p. 13
- Building Vocabulary, p. 17
- Reteaching Activity, p. 18

Guided Reading Workbook
- Section 1

Access for Students Acquiring English/ESL
- Guided Reading, p. 83

Outline Maps with Activities
- Russia and the Western Republics, pp. 45–46

Formal Assessment
- Section Quiz, p. 241

Integrated Assessment
- Rubric for an oral report, 3.6

Cultures Around the World
- Architecture, p. 25
- Daily Life, p. 26
- Fine Arts, p. 27
- Music, p. 29

INTEGRATED TECHNOLOGY

Map Transparencies MT29
- Russian and Soviet Expansion: 1462–2000

Cultures Transparencies CW25, 26, 27, 29
- St. Basil's Cathedral
- Caviar
- Chagall
- Stravinsky

hmhsocialstudies.com

TEST-TAKING RESOURCES

Strategies for Test Preparation

Test Practice Transparencies TT51

Online Test Practice

Interpreting Maps

Russian and Soviet Expansion

Have students examine the map and ask them to identify the period of greatest expansion of Russian territory. *(1599 to 1689)*

SKILLBUILDER ANSWERS

1. between 1463 and 1598

2. between 1599 and 1689

Instruct: Objective 

A History of Expansion

- How did the Russian empire develop? *(In the 800s Vikings settled in the region between the Baltic and Black seas and mixed with the local Slavs. After a period of foreign rule that ended in the 1500s, Russia began to expand, reaching the Pacific by the 1700s.)*
- What was a major goal of Czar Peter the Great? *(to modernize Russia and establish more contact with the West)*
- What were the political and economic results of the Russian Revolution of 1917? *(the overthrow of the Russian Empire and the czars, and establishment of a command economy)*

 **In-Depth Resources: Unit 5**
• Guided Reading, p. 13

 **Map Transparencies MT29**
• Russian and Soviet Expansion: 1462–2000

Russian and Soviet Expansion

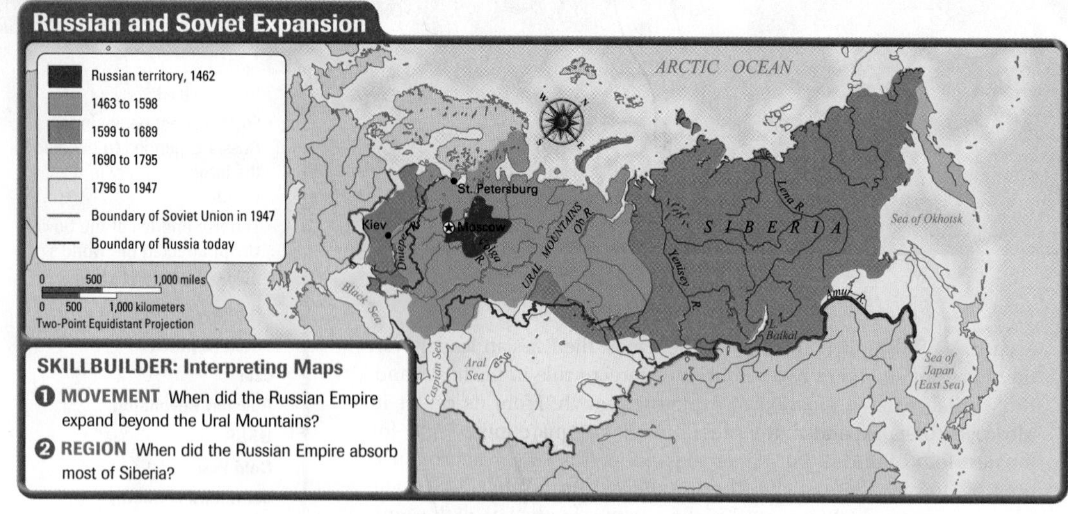

SKILLBUILDER: Interpreting Maps

1. **MOVEMENT** When did the Russian Empire expand beyond the Ural Mountains?
2. **REGION** When did the Russian Empire absorb most of Siberia?

RUSSIA LAGS BEHIND WESTERN EUROPE Russia's territorial growth was rapid, but its progress in other ways was less impressive. Russian science and technology lagged behind that of its European rivals. Peter the Great, who was **czar**—or emperor—of Russia from 1682 to 1725, tried to change this. For example, he moved Russia's capital from Moscow to a city on the Baltic Sea. The new capital, named St. Petersburg, provided direct access by sea to Western Europe. Russians called St. Petersburg their "window to the West."

BACKGROUND The word *czar* comes from the Latin for *Caesar,* the title of address for Roman emperors.

Peter the Great made impressive strides toward modernizing Russia, but the empire continued to trail behind the West. While the Industrial Revolution swept over many Western European countries in the first half of the 1800s, Russia did not even begin to industrialize until the end of the century. When industry did come to Russia, it resulted in harsh working conditions, low wages, and other hardships. These problems contributed to the people's anger at the czars who ruled Russia.

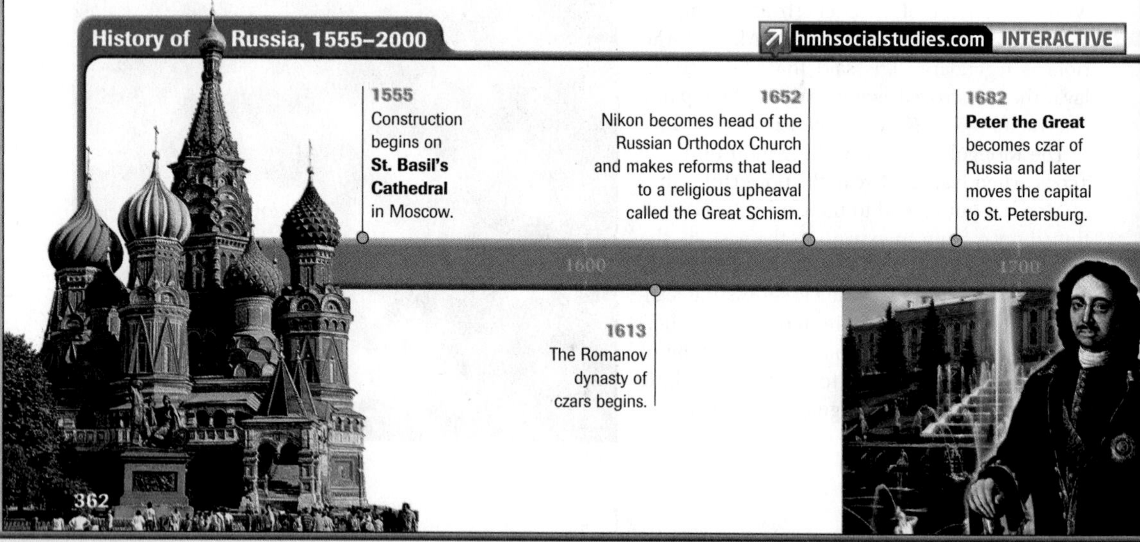

History of Russia, 1555–2000
hmhsocialstudies.com INTERACTIVE
1555
Construction begins on St. Basil's Cathedral in Moscow.
1652
Nikon becomes head of the Russian Orthodox Church and makes reforms that lead to a religious upheaval called the Great Schism.
1682
Peter the Great becomes czar of Russia and later moves the capital to St. Petersburg.
1600
1700
1613
The Romanov dynasty of czars begins.
362

DIFFERENTIATING INSTRUCTION GIFTED AND TALENTED STUDENTS

RESEARCHING RUSSIAN HISTORY

Objective To learn more about Russian history

Class Time 15 minutes

Task Conduct independent research and prepare an oral report

Directions Have students work independently or in a small group to research the conditions in Russia that contributed to the Russian Revolution of 1917. Direct students to prepare an oral report for the class and allow time for the class to ask questions.

THE RISE AND FALL OF THE SOVIET UNION During World War I (1914–1918), the Russian people's anger exploded into revolt. In 1917, the **Russian Revolution** occurred, ending the rule of the czars. The Russian Communist Party, led by V. I. Lenin, took control of the government. The Party also took charge of the region's economy and gave Communist leaders control over all important economic decisions.

BACKGROUND *Soviet* comes from the Russian word for a governmental council, or assembly.

By 1922, the Communist Party had organized the different peoples absorbed during the centuries of Russia's imperial expansion. This new nation was called the Union of Soviet Socialist Republics (**USSR**), or the Soviet Union for short. The leaders of the Soviet Union ruled the nation from its new capital in Moscow.

By the time World War II broke out in 1939, Joseph Stalin had taken over the leadership of the USSR. In 1941, he led the Soviet Union in the fight against Nazi Germany. However, as the war dragged on, relations between the Soviet Union and its allies—including the United States—began to worsen.

A. Answer because the nations of Eastern Europe were so close to the Soviet Union and its center of power–Moscow

Using the Atlas A Examine the map on page 339. Why do you think the Soviet Union had so much power over Eastern Europe?

After the war, Stalin installed pro-Soviet governments in the Eastern European countries that his armies had liberated from Germany. U.S. leaders feared that a new stage of Russian expansion was beginning and that Stalin would spread communism all over the globe. By the late 1940s, tensions between the United States and the Soviet Union led to conflict. Diplomats called this conflict the **Cold War** because it never grew into open warfare between the two nations. A

The rivalry between the two superpowers continued into the mid-1980s. At that time, Soviet leader Mikhail Gorbachev started to give more economic and political freedom to the Soviet people. This began a process that led to the collapse of the Communist government and the Soviet Union in 1991—and the end of the Cold War.

After the fall of the Soviet Union, the region was divided into 15 independent republics. Of these, Russia, formally known as the Russian Federation, is the largest and most powerful. Today, Russia has a popularly elected president. Its legislature, the Federal Assembly, is divided into two chambers—the Federation Council and the State Duma.

VIDEO
The Romanovs
hmhsocialstudies.com

More About

Russian Revolutions

Explain to students that two revolutions took place in 1917. The first, known as the February Revolution, resulted in the overthrow of the imperial government. This paved the way for the Bolsheviks, who took power during the second, October Revolution, that took place just eight months later.

RUSSIA & REP.

1812 The French general, **Napoleon** (below), retreats during winter after a failed attack on Russia.

1861 Czar Alexander II issues an order freeing all Russian serfs, that is, peasants held in servitude.

1991 The Soviet Union falls, and Russia becomes independent.

2000 The Russians elect **Vladimir Putin** president.

1800 1900

1917 The Russian Revolution occurs. **Lenin** (above left), then **Stalin** (above right), take power.

1922 Russia becomes part of the Soviet Union.

363

Interpreting Timelines

History of Russia, 1500–2000

Tell students that this timeline shows some key events in the past 500 years of Russian history. St. Basil's Cathedral, for example, is significant because it is a famous example of Russian Byzantine architecture and was built by Russia's first czar, Ivan IV. Ask students what date marks the end of czarist rule in Russia. *(1917, the date of the Russian Revolution)*

ACTIVITY OPTION LINK TO HISTORY

WRITING A REPORT

Objective To learn more about Russian leaders of the 1900s

Class Time 20 minutes

Task Research the rule of a Russian leader of the 1900s and write a brief report

Directions Have students choose one of the Russian leaders mentioned on page 363–V. I. Lenin, Joseph Stalin, Mikhail Gorbachev, or Vladimir Putin–and research their rule of Russia or the Soviet Union. Ask them to write a one-page report summarizing what they learn. Then allow time for a class discussion in which students share what they learned about Russian life.

Instruct: Objective 2

Building a Command Economy

- What is the economic goal of communism? *(to have citizens own property together and everyone share the wealth)*
- How did Soviet leaders institute a command economy? *(They took over property, businesses, and industries and made all economic decisions. They moved people onto collective farms.)*
- What was the result of these actions? *(Industrial and agricultural production increased, but millions starved or were killed.)*

More About

The Soviet Command Economy

The Soviet leaders intended for the economy to be self-sufficient, meaning that the country would produce all the necessary goods itself and not depend on foreign trade. But communist leaders promoted defense and heavy industries over the production of consumer goods and crops, causing shortages in such basic needs as food, clothing, and housing.

REGION The Soviet government's control over the economy was often inefficient. Citizens had to wait in line for hours, even to buy basic consumer goods, such as a handbag.

Building a Command Economy

The Communists who overthrew czarist Russia in 1917 had strong ideas about the future. When they put their ideas into practice, they drastically transformed the economic geography of the region.

AN ECONOMIC DREAM The Communists had been inspired by the work of Karl Marx, a German philosopher who had examined the history of economic systems. Marx believed that the capitalist system was doomed because it concentrated wealth in the hands of a few and left everyone else in poverty. He predicted that a Communist system would replace capitalism. In a Communist society, he argued, citizens would own property together, and everyone would share the wealth.

A HARSH REALITY To move their society toward communism, Soviet leaders adopted a **command economy**—one in which the central government makes all important economic decisions. The government took control of the major sources of the state's wealth, including land, mines, factories, banks, and transportation systems. Government planners decided what products factories would manufacture, what crops farms would grow, and even what prices merchants would charge for their goods.

Rapid industrialization became a major goal of Soviet planning. Even farming became an industry under Stalin. The Soviet government created enormous **collective farms** on which large teams of laborers were gathered to work together. People were moved to the farms by the thousands. By 1939, nearly nine out of ten farms were collectives. The Soviets had firmly established their power over the countryside.

Although industrial and agricultural production increased, the region's people had to make great sacrifices for this rapid transformation. Millions of citizens starved to death in famines caused, in part, by the creation of collective farms. Those who survived soon realized that only a small number of individuals had benefited from the economic changes.

Many people tried to do something about this betrayal, but at great risk. Under Stalin's rule, the police swiftly punished any form of protest. Some historians estimate that Stalin was responsible for the deaths of more than 14 million people.

Since the fall of the Soviet Union in 1991, leaders in Russia and the Republics have tried to reduce the state's monopoly on economic power and return some control to private individuals and businesses. You will learn more about these changes in Chapter 17. B

B. Answer because, after decades of centralized decisionmaking, it will take time for citizens to learn how to function in a new economy

CONNECT TO THE ISSUES
ECONOMIC CHANGE
B Considering how long the Soviet command economy lasted, why might the change to a market economy be hard for the region's citizens?

ACTIVITY OPTION | **CRITICAL THINKING**

MAKING COMPARISONS

Explaining the Skill Remind students that when you compare things, you look for similarities, and when you contrast things, you look for differences. In this activity, students will compare and contrast the Soviet command economy with the U.S. market economy.

Applying the Skill Have students refer to the text on page 364 and use as their own knowledge of the U.S. market economy to answer the following questions:

- How did the ownership and control of industries in the Soviet command economy differ from that in the U.S. market economy? *(In the Soviet command economy, the government owned and controlled industries. In the American market economy, some industries are owned and controlled by individuals while others are owned by groups of stockholders and controlled by corporate boards.)*
- How does the American government's role in the nation's economy compare with that of the former Soviet Union's? *(Like the Soviet government, the American government passes laws and regulations that industries and businesses must follow; but these laws and regulations do not cover all business decisions.)*

A Rich Culture

Russia and the Western Republics faced hard times under the czars and the communists. But these leaders could not destroy the cultural and spiritual traditions of the region's people.

ETHNICITY AND RELIGION The region has a rich variety of ethnic groups because of the many peoples absorbed during the centuries of Russian expansion. Russia has the greatest ethnic diversity of the region's republics. Russians make up the largest ethnic group there, with about 80 percent of the total. But nearly 70 other peoples live in Russia, including Finnish, Turkic, and Mongolian peoples. (See the map on page 341 of the Unit Atlas.)

Russia and the Western Republics are home to a great number of religions. Most Russians follow Orthodox Christianity, a religion Russia adopted in the 10th century. But the region is home to many other religions, including Buddhism and Islam. Judaism is also an important religion in the region. However, persecution has led large numbers of Jews to emigrate, especially to Israel and the United States. C

ARTISTIC GENIUS Religion and art are closely related in Russia and the Western Republics. The art and architecture of Orthodox Christian churches, for example, are among the region's earliest artistic achievements. Even today, citizens adore the beautiful onion-shaped domes and the icons—images of sacred Christians—that ornament the churches.

Regional culture went through great change after Peter the Great began to promote communication with Western Europe. As Russian artists combined artistic ideas from the West with their own experiences, a truly golden age of culture began.

C. Answer The extraordinary variety of peoples and religions in the region were absorbed during the centuries of expansion.

Geographic Thinking

Seeing Patterns
C How did the expansion of the Russian Empire affect the ethnic and religious makeup of the region?

HUMAN-ENVIRONMENT INTERACTION The two churches in this photo are on Kizhi Island, in Karelia, Russia. The churches' onion domes help to prevent the accumulation of snow during the winter.
How can architecture reflect the influence of geography?

Instruct: Objective 3

A Rich Culture

- What is the ethnic and religious makeup of Russia and the Western Republics? *(Orthodox Christianity is the dominant religion, but Buddhism, Islam, and Judaism are also practiced.)*
- What are notable aspects of Russian culture? *(Orthodox Christian churches with onion domes, such Russian writers as Pushkin and Dostoyevsky, such musicians as Tchaikovsky and Stravinsky, and such ballet dancers as Baryshnikov)*
- How did the Communist Party stifle artistic expression in the visual arts? *(by requiring artists to follow the style of socialist realism, which promoted Soviet ideals)*

Interpreting Photographs

Russian Churches

The art and architecture of the Eastern Orthodox Christian religion is also known as *Byzantine.* The name comes from the Byzantine Empire, which flourished from the 300s to the 1400s. In Russia, paired churches were built for winter and summer use. The smaller winter churches needed less heat for the smaller number of people who came in the winter.

CAPTION ANSWER Here, the church domes reflect the need to guard against potential damage from harsh Russian winters.

365

ACTIVITY OPTION **INTERNET RESEARCH**

MAKING A POSTER

Objective To learn more about Russian culture

Class Time 40 minutes

Task Research one aspect of Russian culture and depict it in a poster

Directions Direct students to research Russian art, architecture, writing, music, dance, or theater by using key words to find information on the Internet. Have students create posters that depict cultural achievements from the past or present. Display students' posters in the classroom.

BLOCK SCHEDULING

OPTIONAL ACTIVITY If Internet access is limited, direct students to use the library catalog and periodical indexes to find books and magazines with pictures and information on Russian culture.

Instruct: Objective 

Tradition and Change in Russian Life

- How has life changed in the region's cities since the end of the Soviet Union? *(People are exposed to more outside influences, including books, magazines, newspapers, movies, music, clothing, and foods from around the world.)*
- How has life stayed the same? *(People still eat such traditional foods as rye bread and kasha. They still enjoy visiting* dachas *and* banyas.*)*
- Why is the preservation of customs and traditions important in Russia? *(It helps make the transition from the isolated Soviet past to the more open society of the present less difficult.)*

Interpreting Photographs

Soviet Posters

Have students examine the smaller poster and ask if anyone knows how the image might be related to the flag of the former Soviet Union. *(The imagery echoes the hammer and sickle of the Soviet flag.)*

 **Cultures Around the World**
- Architecture, p. 25
- Daily Life, p. 26
- Fine Arts, p. 27
- Music, p. 29

 **Cultures Transparencies CW25, 26, 27, 29**
- St. Basil's Cathedral
- Caviar
- Chagall
- Stravinsky

Soviet Poster Art

REGION The Communist Party recruited artists to help promote Soviet industry. The poster above, from 1947, and the one below, from 1931, promise punishment for laziness and rewards for hard work.

In the 18th and 19th centuries, audiences around the world marveled at the work of writers such as Aleksandr Pushkin and Feodor Dostoyevsky. Their dramatic scenes and colorful psychological studies give an important portrait of Czarist Russia.

Great composers such as Peter Tchaikovsky and Igor Stravinsky also earned worldwide attention, as did the Russian ballet. Russian ballet companies, such as the Kirov and Bolshoi, are famous for producing magnificent dancers and creative choreographers, such as Mikhail Baryshnikov.

Art underwent another major change after the Communist Party began to outlaw artists who did not work in the official style. This style, called socialist realism, promoted Soviet ideals by optimistically showing citizens working to create a socialist society. In spite of the censorship, many artists took great risks to continue producing original work. Since the collapse of the Soviet Union, artistic expression has begun to gain strength.

Tradition and Change in Russian Life

Since the collapse of the Soviet Union, the region is more open to the influence of other countries—especially those in the West. At the same time, the region's people continue to honor their traditions and work hard to preserve them.

A MORE OPEN SOCIETY The region's people—especially in larger cities—have begun to enjoy more social and cultural opportunities. Large cities, such as Moscow and St. Petersburg, now resemble major cities in the West. City dwellers can read books, magazines, and newspapers from all over the world. They are able to keep up with new movies, music, and clothing trends. They can also experience a wide variety of foods and cuisines.

Although the variety of social and cultural opportunities has increased, native traditions have survived. For example, in spite of the many cuisines now available in Russian cities, many Russians still favor their traditional foods. Many of the foods, such as rye bread,

ACTIVITY OPTION | EXPLORING LOCAL GEOGRAPHY

EXAMINING GEOGRAPHIC INFLUENCES ON ART

Objective To study geographic influences on artistic production

Class Time 30 minutes

Task Students will prepare a brief essay or oral report that examines the relationship between art and geography

Directions Assist students in choosing a locally produced work of art. Allow them to choose among a variety of media, such as painting, sculpture, theater, music, or writing. Then have students consider how the work of art they chose reflects features of local physical and human geography. Ask them to write a brief essay or prepare a short oral report that describes these relationships. After the completion of the activity, lead the classroom in discussing how advances in communication and transportation might affect the relation between art and geography.

366 CHAPTER 16

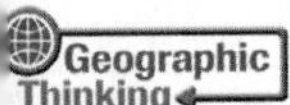

Seeing Patterns
D How do Russian foods reflect regional geography?

D. Answer Many of Russia's most popular foods are made using the grains produced on the region's farms.

reflect the large crops of grain produced on the region's steppes. Kasha is another popular food made from grain. It is cooked and eaten with butter. Even Russia's national drink, vodka, is made from rye or wheat grains. D

DACHAS* AND *BANYAS Only a quarter of Russia's population lives in rural areas. Even so, many Russians cherish the nation's countryside. Nearly 30 percent of the population own homes in the country, where they spend weekends and vacations. These homes, called *dachas,* are usually small, plain houses and often have gardens in which to grow vegetables.

One of the customs that Russians enjoy both in the countryside and the cities is visiting a *banya.* A *banya* is a bathhouse in which Russians perform a cleaning ritual that combines a dry sauna, steam bath, and often a plunge into ice-cold water.

Russians begin the ritual by warming up in a sauna heated to around 200°F. They then move into a steam room, where they use birch twigs to ease the muscles and perfume the body. After spending time in the steam room, many bathers plunge into an icy-cold pool—which might be a hole cut in the ice of a river or a lake. The ice bath is followed by hot tea, and the process is repeated. A visit to the *banya* can sometimes last for two to three hours.

The preservation of such customs and traditions by the Russian people has played an important role since the fall of the Soviet Union. It has helped to make the change from the isolated Soviet past to the more open society of the present less difficult.

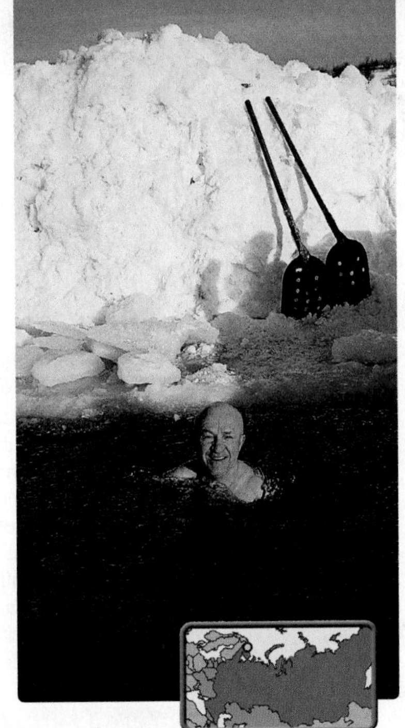

PLACE A man enjoys an ice-cold dip during his trip to the *banya.*

RUSSIA & REP.

More About

The Russian *Banya*

All Russian towns have a public *banya*, and larger towns have more than one. At the *banya*, Russians generally meet a circle of friends who go there on the same day each week. Russians welcome foreign visitors at their *banyas.*

Assess & Reteach

GeoFocus Have students complete their notes on Russia and the Western Republics in their graphic organizers.

Formal Assessment
- Section Quiz, p. 241

Reteaching Activity
Have pairs of students review the section by looking back at the boldfaced headings and vocabulary words. One student should ask a question about a heading or vocabulary word and the other should answer it. Students can alternate roles as they work through the section.

In-Depth Resources: Unit 5
- Reteaching Activity, p. 18

Outline Maps with Activities
- Russia and the Western Republics, pp. 45–46

Section 1 Assessment

1 Places & Terms

Explain the importance of each of the following terms and places.

- Baltic Republics
- czar
- Russian Revolution
- USSR
- Cold War
- command economy
- collective farm

2 Taking Notes

REGION Review the notes you took for this section.

Russia and the Western Republics → Russia and the Republics

- How did the Russian Empire lag behind its European rivals?
- How did the Communist Party control artistic expression?

3 Main Ideas

a. What was the extent of the Russian Empire's expansion between the 9th century and the end of the 17th century?

b. What were the origins of the Soviet Union?

c. How did the Soviet Union come to an end?

4 Geographic Thinking

Making Inferences How did the economic policies of the Soviet Union affect its human geography? **Think about:**

- industrialization
- collective farms

See Skillbuilder Handbook, page R4.

EXPLORING LOCAL GEOGRAPHY You read in this section how Russia's traditional food is related to its geography. Do research on the traditional foods where you live, and try to determine how they might be related to the physical or human geography of your region. Explain the connections that you find in an **oral report.**

SECTION 1 ASSESSMENT ANSWERS

1. Places & Terms

Baltic Republics, p. 361
czar, p. 362
Russian Revolution, p. 363
USSR, p. 363
Cold War, p. 363
command economy, p. 364
collective farm, p. 364

2. Taking Notes

- Russian scientific and technological progress was much slower
- by requiring artists to work in the official style, called socialist realism

3. Main Ideas

a. from a small settlement at Kiev in the ninth century, to the Pacific Ocean by the end of the 17th century

b. Communist revolutionaries overthrew the Russian government in 1917 and formed the Union of the Soviet Socialist Republics in 1922.

c. In the mid-1980s, Soviet leader Mikhail Gorbachev began to give more economic and political power to the Soviet people. This started a process that eventually led to the collapse of the Soviet Union in 1991.

4. Geographic Thinking

The Soviet Union's rapid industrialization, and creation of collective farms caused severe famines in which millions starved to death.

Integrated Assessment
- Rubric for an oral report, 3.6

OBJECTIVES

1. Explain what happened at Chernobyl in 1986.
2. Describe the causes and consequences of the disaster at Chernobyl.
3. Research the Chernobyl disaster and prepare a multimedia presentation.

Instruct: Objective

Nuclear Explosion at Chernobyl

- When and why did the nuclear explosion at Chernobyl occur? *(It occurred in April 1986. A poorly planned safety experiment and a faulty reactor design caused the explosion.)*
- What were some of the consequences of the explosion? *(Radioactive dust was spread for thousands of miles and contaminated roughly 100,000 square miles of land in Ukraine, Russia, and Belarus; 31 people died immediately.)*

Interpreting Maps

Spread of Radiation from Chernobyl

Have students examine the map on page 370. Then ask them to consult other maps and make a list the areas of North America that were affected by the spread of the radioactive cloud from Chernobyl. *(Greenland, Baffin Island, Davis and Hudson straits.)*

Disasters!

HISTORY VIDEO Chernobyl: Nuclear Meltdown

hmhsocialstudies.com

Nuclear Explosion at Chernobyl

On April 28, 1986, engineer Cliff Robinson arrived at Sweden's Forsmark nuclear power plant. He was startled when a radiation detector went off as he entered his office. When he checked the radiation levels on his clothing, he could not believe his eyes. "My first thought," said Robinson, "was that a war had broken out and that somebody had blown up a nuclear bomb." What Forsmark had detected was a radioactive cloud from the city of Chernobyl—site of a Soviet nuclear power plant nearly 800 miles away.

One of Chernobyl's nuclear reactors had exploded, spewing radioactive dust across the region. It took two days for Soviet officials to admit that the explosion had occurred. The blast killed 31 people. No one is certain what toll accident-related diseases will take on the region's population in the future.

Workers test radiation levels from a helicopter. After the explosion, hundreds of thousands of workers helped in cleanup operations. Many were exposed to radiation and required emergency medical treatment.

The Spread of Radiation from Chernobyl

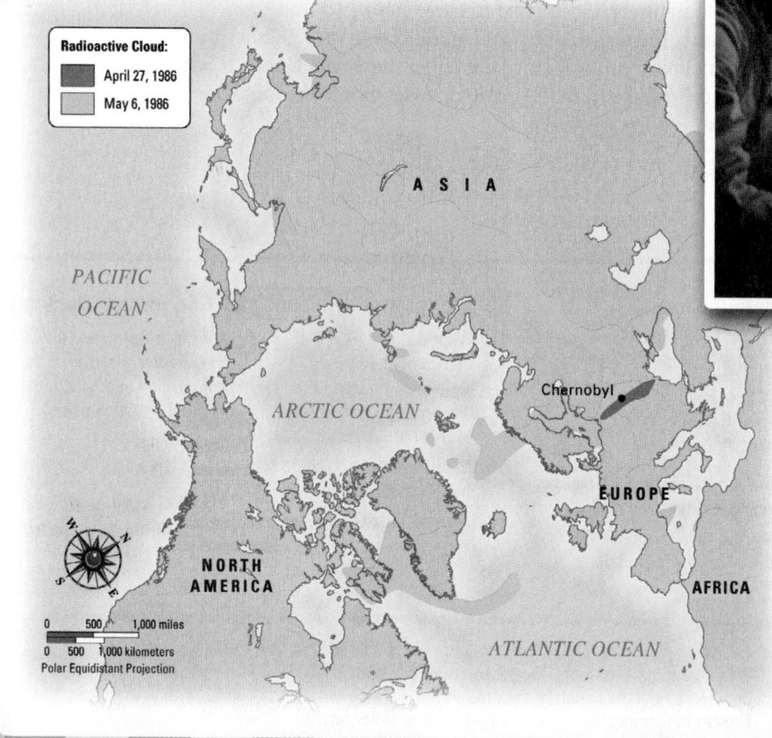

The radioactive cloud from Chernobyl eventually spread over the entire Northern Hemisphere.

SUPPORTING RESOURCES

BOOKS FOR THE TEACHER

Medvedev, Zhores A., ***The Legacy of Chernobyl.*** NY: W.W. Norton & Co., 1990. Account of the disaster by a former Soviet scientist.

Read, Piers Paul. ***Ablaze.*** NY: Random House, 1993. Story of the disaster and its aftermath.

BOOKS FOR THE STUDENT

Helgerson, Joel. ***Nuclear Accidents.*** NY: Franklin Watts, 1988. A study of Chernobyl and earlier nuclear accidents.

Gale, Robert Peter, and Thomas Hauser. ***Final Warning.*** NY: Warner Books, 1988. Story of American medical aid to Chernobyl victims.

PERIODICALS

"Radiation Damages Chernobyl Children." *Science News.* 27 April 1996. Examination of genetic mutations in children exposed to radioactive fallout from Chernobyl.

Wasserman, Harvey. **"In the Dead Zone."** *The Nation.* 29 April 1996. Discussion of effects of the Chernobyl disaster and problems with nuclear reactors around the world.

VIDEOS

Best of Nightline: Chernobyl Nuclear Disaster *(1986).* MPI Home Video, 1990. News account of the disaster.

Chernobyl Plant—Aftermath *(1987).* MPI Home Video, 2001. *Nightline* followup on the disaster.

Serious health problems, such as thyroid cancer, have increased dramatically among children since the accident at Chernobyl.

A close-up of the damage at Chernobyl's Unit 4 reactor (left). The color image below shows the concrete and steel "sarcophagus," or enclosure, later built around the contaminated reactor.

GeoActivity

PLANNING A PRESENTATION

With a partner, use the Internet to research Chernobyl today. Plan a **multimedia presentation** about the disaster's legacy.

- Design charts, graphs, and maps that show the disaster's impact on public health and the environment.
- Include personal stories from individuals whose lives have been affected by the explosion.

GeoData

DAMAGE REPORT

- The Chernobyl plant is located about 80 miles north of Kiev, Ukraine's capital.
- The plant once employed nearly 9,200 people.
- On April 26, 1986, a poorly planned safety experiment led to the explosion at Chernobyl, which was made worse by a faulty reactor design.
- The reactor explosion was the world's worst civilian nuclear accident.
- The explosion contaminated around 100,000 square miles of land in Ukraine, Russia, and Belarus.
- Officials evacuated and resettled approximately 250,000 people from different towns around Chernobyl.
- Chernobyl continued to produce electricity until December 15, 2000, when officials finally shut down its last operating reactor.
- Costs related to the disaster have been estimated at over $300 billion.

GeoActivity

Planning a Presentation

Integrated Assessment
- Rubric for a multimedia presentation, 5.4

More About

Chernobyl

It is not certain how much radiation clean-up and recovery workers were exposed to at Chernobyl. But some scientists have estimated that levels may have reached 165 millisieverts. Doses above 10 millisieverts pose significant threats to the human body.

ACTIVITY OPTION | COOPERATIVE LEARNING

LEARNING ABOUT CHERNOBYL'S "LIQUIDATORS"

Objective To learn more about the long-term affects of radiation exposure

Class Time 30 minutes

Task Write a status report on the fate of Chernobyl's "liquidators"

Directions Divide students into groups of three. Ask each group to use the Internet or other resources to do research on Chernobyl's "liquidators"–the name given to the emergency clean-up and recovery crews deployed at Chernobyl in the months after the accident. Ask students to focus on health problems that the liquidators and their children may have experienced since the accident. Have them use the results of their research to write a short report on the current status of the liquidators.

In putting together their status reports, one group member should be responsible for writing. Another member should compile charts and graphs. The third member will look for maps, photographs, and illustrations that complement the report.

SECTION 2 OBJECTIVES

1. Identify some effects of the use of Transcaucasia as a migration route.
2. Summarize some of the historic influences on Transcaucasia.
3. Describe the economy of Transcaucasia.
4. Identify characteristics of the people of the region.

SKILLBUILDERS: Interpreting Maps, pp. 370, 373

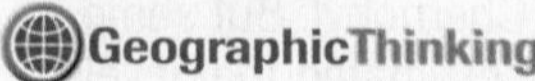

Seeing Patterns, p. 373
Determining Cause and Effect, p. 374

Focus & Motivate

Point out Transcaucasia on a world map and ask students what they notice about the size and location of the region's three republics. *(The republics are relatively small and are between the Black and Caspian seas.)*

Instruct: Objective 

A Gateway of Migration

- How has its role as a gateway between Europe and Asia affected Transcaucasia? *(It brought different people and languages to the region.)*
- How have the region's different ethnic groups related since the fall of the Soviet Union? *(Relationships are tense, and the region has experienced several ethnic conflicts since the fall of the USSR.)*

 **In-Depth Resource: Unit 5**
- Guided Reading, p. 14

SKILLBUILDER ANSWERS
1. Turkic **2.** Armenian

Transcaucasia

Main Ideas
- Transcaucasia has been a gateway between Europe and Asia.
- The Caspian Sea's oil and gas reserves have given the region great economic potential.

Places & Terms
Red Army
supra

CONNECT TO THE ISSUES
CONFLICT Ethnic tensions in Transcaucasia erupted in conflict after the fall of the Soviet Union.

A HUMAN PERSPECTIVE Throughout history, human beings have migrated through Transcaucasia, which today consists of the republics of Armenia, Azerbaijan, and Georgia. Recent discoveries have shown just how early such migrations began. In the summer of 1999, a team of scientists discovered two 1.7-million-year-old human skulls in the Transcaucasian republic of Georgia. They were the oldest human fossils found outside Africa. Reports suggest that the skulls could belong to the first people to have migrated from Africa.

A Gateway of Migration

People have long used Transcaucasia as a migration route, especially as a gateway between Europe and Asia. Trade routes near the Black Sea led to the thriving commercial regions of Mediterranean Europe. And trade routes leading to the Far East began on the shores of the Caspian Sea.

A VARIETY OF CULTURES Because of the presence of so many trade routes, Transcaucasia has been affected by many different peoples and cultures. Today, more than 50 different peoples live in the region.

Migrants brought a great variety of languages to the region. Arab geographers called the region *Jabal Al-Alsun,* or the "Mountain of Language." The Indo-European, Caucasian, and Altaic language families are the region's most common.

MIGRATION BRINGS RELIGIONS The people of Transcaucasia follow a number of different religions. However, most of the region's people belong to either the Christian or the Islamic faith.

Languages Around the Caucasus

SKILLBUILDER: Interpreting Maps
1. **REGION** Which is the most common language group in Azerbaijan?
2. **PLACE** Which language is spoken in the Nagorno-Karabakh region of Azerbaijan?

SECTION 2 PROGRAM RESOURCES

 **In-Depth Resources: Unit 5**
- Guided Reading, p. 14
- Skillbuilder Practice, p. 16
- Building Vocabulary, p. 17
- Reteaching Activity, p. 19

 **Guided Reading Workbook**
- Section 2

Access for Students Acquiring English/ESL
- Guided Reading, p. 84
- Skillbuilder Practice, p. 86

Outline Maps with Activities
- Transcaucasia: Physical and Political, pp. 47–48

 **Formal Assessment**
- Section Quiz, p. 242

Integrated Assessment
- Rubric for a script, 5.5

Cultures Around the World
- Dance, p. 28
- Arts and Crafts, p. 30

INTEGRATED TECHNOLOGY

 **Cultures Transparencies CW28, 30**
- Georgian Folk Dance
- Traditional Rugs

 **The World's Music Audio Program**

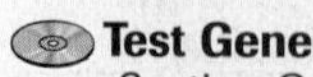 **Test Generator**
- Section Quiz

hmhsocialstudies.com

TEST-TAKING RESOURCES

 **Strategies for Test Preparation**

 **Test Practice Transparencies TT52**

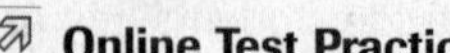 **Online Test Practice**

These faiths arrived in the region at an early date, because Transcaucasia is close to the areas in Southwest Asia where the two religions began. Armenia and Georgia, for example, are among the oldest Christian states in the world. Armenia's King Tiridates III converted to Christianity in A.D. 300. A year later, he made his state the first in the world to adopt Christianity.

Not long after the 7th-century beginnings of Islam in Southwest Asia, Muslim invaders stormed into the southern Caucasus and converted many Transcaucasians to Islam. Today, the great majority of Azerbaijan's people are Muslim.

PLACE The beautiful Karmravor Church is located in the Armenian village of Ashtarak. It dates from the 7th century. **How long after Armenia adopted Christianity was the church built?**

CONFLICT The region's diverse population has not always lived together in harmony. Tensions seldom erupted into open hostility under the rigid rule of the Soviets. However, after the collapse of the USSR in 1991, tensions among different groups have resulted in violence. Civil war broke out in Georgia, and Armenia fought a bitter war with Azerbaijan over a disputed territory called Nagorno-Karabakh. A

A. Answers because of the rigid control of central authorities

CONNECT TO THE ISSUES
CONFLICT
A Why did ethnic tensions seldom erupt into violence during the Soviet era?

The story of conflict is not new to Transcaucasia. Its history of conflict, as you will read below, can be explained, in part, by its location.

A History of Outside Control

Over the centuries, Transcaucasia has been a place where the borders of rival empires have come together. Imperial armies have repeatedly invaded the region to protect and extend those borders.

CZARIST AND SOVIET RULE In the 18th century, the troops of the Russian Empire joined the list of invaders. Russia's southward expansion had begun as early as the 1500s, but it was only in the 1700s that the czar's army began making progress south of the Caucasus Mountains.

The inhabitants of the region resisted the Russians, but the czar's troops prevailed. By 1723, Peter the Great's generals had taken control of Baku, the capital of Azerbaijan. In 1801, Russia annexed Georgia. In 1828, Russian armies took control of a large stretch of Armenian territory, including the plain of Yerevan. By the late 1870s, the czar's troops had added Transcaucasia to the Russian Empire.

After the Russian Revolution in 1917, the Transcaucasian republics enjoyed a brief period of independence. By the early 1920s, however, the **Red Army**—the name of the Soviet military—had taken control of the region.

Interpreting Photographs

Karmravor Church

This domed Armenian church reflects a regional modification of Byzantine design. The Karmravor Church is built in the shape of a cross with a dome over the central area. Ask students what adjectives they would use to describe the style of this church. *(simple, graceful, classic)*

CAPTION ANSWER more than 300 years

More About

The Name *Transcaucasia*

The regional name *Transcaucasia* combines the prefix *trans-* ("across") and a variant of *Caucasus*, in reference to the mountain chain. The name thus means "across the Caucasus Mountains." The word *Caucasian*, in reference to the white race, originated with an 18th Century German anthropologist who claimed that the white race originated in the Caucasus area. His theories were later discredited.

Instruct: Objective 2

A History of Outside Control

- For how many centuries did Russia or the Soviet Union control either part or all of Transcaucasia? *(for almost three centuries)*
- How have they fared since achieving their independence from the Soviet Union? *(They are struggling to rebuild their economies.)*

DIFFERENTIATING INSTRUCTION | STUDENTS ACQUIRING ENGLISH/ESL

CHARTING KEY WORDS AND IDEAS

Objective To help ESL students link key words and concepts

Class Time 20 minutes

Task Create a chart of the region's republics and main ideas about them

Directions Help ESL students create a chart like the one shown here, which categories and summarizes key concepts about the region.

TRANSCAUCASIA	
Republics	Armenia, Georgia, Azerbaijan
Language families	Indo-European, Caucasian, Altaic
Religions	Christianity, Islam
Agriculture	Tea, fruits, wine from grapes
Industries.	Oil, iron, steel, chemicals, consumer goods

Instruct: Objective 3

Economic Potential

- What are some of Transcaucasia's main agricultural products? *(tea and fruits)*
- What is the region's most important industry? *(oil)*
- Which Transcaucasian country stands to gain more revenue if the Caspian Sea is considered a sea rather than a lake? Why? *(Azerbaijan, because it would have the legal rights to the large oil reserves off its coast.)*

5 THEMES

Place: Trouble in Georgia

The situation in Georgia is so unstable that foreigners are advised to avoid traveling outside the capital of Tbilisi. Besides the area of Abkhazia, the area of South Ossetia also has attempted to secede from the country. Ask students why government officials might resist the breakup of the country. *(It would make the country smaller and diminish its economic resources.)*

In the decades following the Soviet takeover, the people of Transcaucasia experienced the same painful economic and political changes as the rest of the Soviet Union. Many people lost their lives in famines triggered by the shift to collective farming or were killed because of their political beliefs. The republics of Transcaucasia regained their political independence in 1991 after the fall of the Soviet Union. Since then, the region's leaders have struggled to rebuild their nations' economies.

Background
Stalin was especially harsh on Transcaucasia, even though he was from the Georgian town of Gori.

Economic Potential

Today, economic activity in the Transcaucasian republics ranges from the tourism and wine industries of subtropical Georgia to large-scale oil production in Azerbaijan.

AGRICULTURE AND INDUSTRY Although much of Transcaucasia's terrain is mountainous, each of the republics has a significant agricultural output. Transcaucasians have taken advantage of the region's climate and the potential of the limited amount of land fit for farming.

The humid subtropical lowlands and foothills of the region are ideal for valuable crops such as tea and fruits. Grapes are one of the most important fruit crops. Georgians use the grapes cultivated along their Black Sea coast to produce their famous wines. Georgia's mild climate also once fueled a profitable tourist industry.

There was little industry in Transcaucasia before the Soviet Union took control of the region. Soviet planners transformed Transcaucasia from a largely agricultural area into an industrial and urban region.

PLACE

Trouble in Georgia

In the late 1980s, more than 3.6 million tourists visited Georgia each year. But tourism slowed to a trickle after ethnic conflict broke out in the region in the early 1990s.

One conflict took place in Abkhazia—a resort area that stretches for more than 100 miles along Georgia's Black Sea coast. Ethnic Abkhazians sought independence and rebelled against Georgia, which sent troops to prevent the uprising. The conflict remained unresolved at the beginning of 2001.

In this photo, from 1993, soldiers help a boy flee from street fighting in Sokhumi, the capital of Abkhazia.

ACTIVITY OPTION | SKILLBUILDER LESSON

MAKING INFERENCES

Explaining the Skill Point out that students of geography must often make inferences, or "read between the lines," to understand the relationships between countries. For example, after reading that the Soviet Union ruled the people of Transcaucasia with a heavy hand, students might reasonably infer that the people of the region have negative feelings toward Russians.

Applying the Skill Have students reread the text under the heading "A History of Outside Control" on pages 371–372, and have them refer to the map on page 360. Then ask them to answer the following questions:

- Why would the three countries of Transcaucasia be easy for a country like Russia to take over? *(They are very small, Russia is very large, and the different ethnic groups have not united and formed a national identity.)*
- How might these countries react if Russia once again became a strong, powerful country? *(They might fear takeover and seek a protective alliance with another strong country.)*

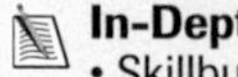
In-Depth Resources: Unit 5
- Skillbuilder Practice, p. 16

A number of industrial centers built by the Soviets continue to produce iron, steel, chemicals, and consumer goods for the region's economy. But today, the oil industry is most important. The oil industry has an impact not only on oil-rich republics, such as Azerbaijan. It also affects Armenia and Georgia because oil producers want to build pipelines across their territory to bring the oil to market.

LAND OF FLAMES The significance of oil in the region has a long history. In fact, the name Azerbaijan means "land of flames." The republic's founders chose the name because of the fires that erupted seemingly by magic from both the rocks and the waters of the Caspian Sea. The fires were the result of underground oil and gas deposits.

DIVIDING THE CASPIAN SEA Since the breakup of the Soviet Union, Azerbaijan and the other four countries bordering the Caspian Sea have argued about whether the Caspian is an inland sea or a lake. The resolution of this argument will decide how resources are divided among the five countries.

If the Caspian is a sea, then each country has legal rights to the resources on its own part of the sea bed. If it is a lake, the law says that most of the resource wealth must be shared equally among each of the countries. Azerbaijan, with large reserves off its coast, says the Caspian is an inland sea. Russia, with few offshore reserves, insists that the Caspian is a lake. B

The oil industry has given the region's people hope for a better life. But oil revenue has benefited few Transcaucasians. Many continue to live in poverty.

B. Answer Such definitions can determine the legal rights of the people who live nearby.

Seeing Patterns

B How can the geographic definition of a body of water affect economic relationships?

Dividing the Caspian

As Lake

KAZAKHSTAN
RUSSIA
Caspian Sea
Joint area
UZBEKISTAN
GEORGIA
AZERBAIJAN
Baku
TURKMENISTAN
AZER.
ARMENIA
IRAN

As Inland Sea

KAZAKHSTAN
RUSSIA
Caspian Sea
UZBEKISTAN
GEORGIA
AZERBAIJAN
Baku
TURKMENISTAN
AZER.
ARMENIA
IRAN

SKILLBUILDER: Interpreting Maps

REGION Which are the five countries that border the Caspian Sea?

RUSSIA & REP.

Modern Life in Transcaucasia

Although times are tough for many, the region has much to offer, including a well-educated population and a reputation for hospitality.

AN EDUCATED PEOPLE The educational programs of the Soviet Union had a largely positive impact on its people. At the time of the Russian Revolution, only a small percentage of Transcaucasia's population was literate. Communist leaders decided to train a new generation of skilled workers who would be prepared to undertake the tasks of industrial development and modernization. They succeeded, as literacy rates in Transcaucasia rose to nearly 99 percent, among the highest in the world. Today, high quality educational systems remain a priority for Transcaucasians.

HOSPITALITY In their quest for a modern system of education, Transcaucasians have not forgotten the value of their traditions. Among the most important are the region's mealtime celebrations.

Interpreting Maps

Dividing the Caspian

The proven oil reserves around the Caspian Sea are between 17 and 33 billion barrels. The entire region has not been fully explored, however, and potential reserves may be much higher. Ask students how development of the oil resources of the Caspian Sea might affect the environment. *(It might result in water pollution and a reduction in plant and animal life.)*

SKILLBUILDER ANSWERS

Azerbaijan, Russia, Kazakhstan, Turkmenistan, and Iran

Instruct: Objective 

Modern Life in Transcaucasia

- What are two characteristics of Transcaucasians? *(Many Transcaucasians are well-educated and hospitable.)*
- What is the literacy rate in the region? *(almost 99%)*
- How do Georgians celebrate a *supra*? *(with lots of food and drink and many toasts)*

Cultures Around the World
- Dance, p. 28
- Arts and Crafts, p. 30

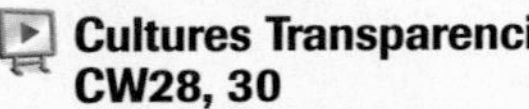

Cultures Transparencies CW28, 30
- Georgian Folk Dance
- Traditional Rugs

ACTIVITY OPTION | CRITICAL THINKING

MAKING DECISIONS

Explaining the Skill The debate over oil rights in the Caspian Sea demonstrates how a decision about a geographic terms can have political and economic consequences. The distinction between some geographic terms is not precise, as students will learn about the definitions of *lake* and *sea*.

Applying the Skill Remind students that the Caspian Sea is the largest inland body of water in the world. Then share with students the following definitions of *sea* and *lake* from *The American Heritage Dictionary:*

lake 1. a. large inland body of fresh water or salt water

sea 2. b. a relatively large body of salt water completely or partially enclosed by land **c.** a relatively large landlocked body of fresh water

Ask students to give their opinions on whether the Caspian Sea is a lake or an inland sea and explain the basis of their opinions. Then have the class vote on the issue.

Interpreting Photographs

Georgian *Supra*

Ask students to identify some of the foods shown in the photographs and to generalize about what they have in common. *(The foods include corn, tomatoes, grapes, pears, and bread. Most of the food is fresh produce.)*

CAPTION ANSWER Georgia's subtropical climate zone is suited for the cultivation of the grapes and other fresh fruits and vegetables on the table.

Assess & Reteach

GeoFocus Have students complete the section on Transcaucasia in their graphic organizers.

Formal Assessment
• Section Quiz, p. 242

Reteaching Activity
Have students use their GeoFocus graphic organizer notes to write a summary report on Transcaucasia.

In-Depth Resources: Unit 5
• Reteaching Activity, p. 19

Outline Maps with Activities
• Transcaucasia, pp. 47–48

PLACE At a dinner party held in the Georgian town of Kutol, a woman raises her glass to deliver a toast. **How do the foods you see in the image reflect what you have read about Georgia's climate?**

The Georgian ***supra***, or dinner party, is one of the best examples of such gatherings. The word *supra* means tablecloth but also refers to any occasion at which people gather to eat and drink.

A *supra* involves breathtaking quantities of food and drink. Meals begin at a table spread with a great number of cold dishes. Two or three hot courses and fruit and desserts follow those. Georgians add locally grown foods, such as grated walnuts, garlic, and an array of herbs and spices to their recipes. And they are able to serve meals with remarkable freshness, thanks to the region's mild climate.

In addition to food and drink, a *supra* is accompanied by a great number of toasts, short speeches given before taking a drink. Georgians take the toasts very seriously because they show a respect for tradition, eloquence, and the value of bringing people together—a goal of great importance for the future of the region.

Section 2 Assessment

1 Places & Terms
Explain the importance of each of the following terms.
• Red Army
• *supra*

2 Taking Notes
REGION Review the notes you took for this section.

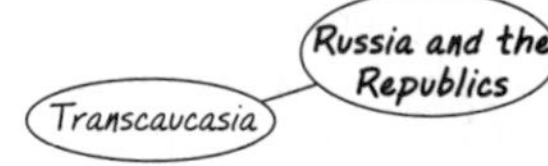

• How do Transcaucasia's republics differ in terms of religion?
• What sorts of activities take place during a Georgian *supra*?

3 Main Ideas
a. How would you describe the ethnic and linguistic makeup of Transcaucasia?
b. What roles did Russia and the Soviet Union play in Transcaucasia?
c. How has the oil industry affected the people of Transcaucasia?

4 Geographic Thinking
Determining Cause and Effect How did the economic goals of the Soviet Union affect educational values in Transcaucasia? **Think about:**
• Transcaucasia's economy before the 1920s
• the impact of economic changes on the region's workers

MAKING COMPARISONS Carry out more research on the religions of Transcaucasia. Then write a **script** for a five minute documentary that compares the architectural styles used in two different houses of worship.

SECTION 2 ASSESSMENT ANSWERS

1. Places & Terms
Red Army, p. 371 supra, p. 374

2. Taking Notes
• Armenia and Georgia are among the oldest Christian states in the world, while the majority of people in Azerbaijan are Muslims
• Great quantities of food and drink are served and are accompanied by many short speeches, called toasts.

3. Main Ideas
a. Many different languages are spoken in this region, which is home to more than 50 different peoples.
b. The Russian Empire took control of Transcaucasia by the late 1870s. The Soviet Union ruled Transcaucasia from the early 1920s until 1991.
c. Oil reserves have attracted foreign oil firms and given some hope of prosperity. But oil wealth has not reached the majority of Transcaucasians, many of whom live in poverty.

4. Geographic Thinking
Soviet planners stressed formal education in order to transform Transcaucasia into an industrial and urban region.

GeoActivity

Integrated Assessment
• Rubric for script, 5.5

Central Asia

Main Ideas

- Soviet officials drew borders in Central Asia that are making it difficult for the region's new leaders to establish stability.
- Central Asians have preserved many cultural traditions despite decades of colonization.

Places & Terms

Silk Road	**nomad**
Great Game	**yurt**

CONNECT TO THE ISSUES
NUCLEAR LEGACY Soviet nuclear testing will have a long-term impact on the region.

A HUMAN PERSPECTIVE Central Asia has inspired the dreams of many adventurers—and presented them with many dangers. In the 19th century, agents of the mighty British Empire found that even they were not safe there. In 1842, two British officers were captured in the Central Asian city of Bukhoro. For months, the city's ruler kept the men in an underground bug-pit that swarmed with ticks, rats, and scaly vermin. In June of that year, he forced the two officers to dig their own graves and then beheaded them. In spite of the dangers, people have journeyed across Central Asia throughout history.

A Historical Crossroads

Today, Central Asia consists of five independent republics: Kazakhstan, Kyrgyzstan, Tajikistan, Turkmenistan, and Uzbekistan. Travelers first began to make their way across the region in large numbers around 100 B.C. Many of them joined caravans making the 4,000-mile journey between China and the Mediterranean Sea.

THE SILK ROAD Traders called this route the **Silk Road,** after the costly silk they bought in China. In addition to silk, traders carried many other goods on their horses and camels. These included gold, silver, ivory, jade, wine, spices, amber, linen, porcelain, grapes, perfumes—even

The Silk Road

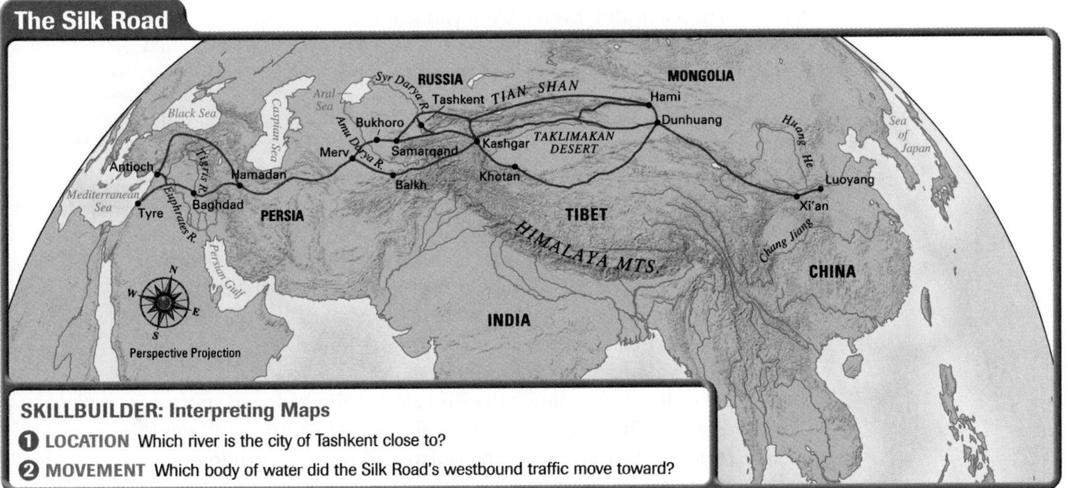

SKILLBUILDER: Interpreting Maps
1. **LOCATION** Which river is the city of Tashkent close to?
2. **MOVEMENT** Which body of water did the Silk Road's westbound traffic move toward?

RUSSIA & REP.

SECTION 3 OBJECTIVES

1. Explain the historical importance of Central Asia.
2. Describe the environmental problems and promise of the region.
3. Explain how Soviet policies contributed to the region's instability and identify some unifying forces.
4. Describe the traditional lifestyle of nomads in Central Asia.

SKILLBUILDERS: Interpreting Maps, Graphics, and Graphs, pp. 375, 376, 377

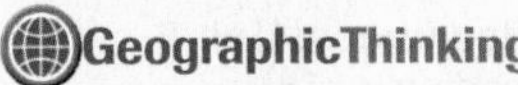

GeographicThinking
Seeing Patterns, p. 377
Using the Atlas, p. 378
Drawing Conclusions, p. 379

Focus & Motivate

Ask students to share what they know about Central Asia. If students know little, make the point that this region is one that few people know much about.

Instruct: Objective 1 appears on p. 376

Interpreting Maps

The Silk Road

Ask students to speculate about why there are so many alternative routes between Dunhuang and Merv. *(Students might suggest that the difficulty of the region's terrain prompted travelers to search for the easiest routes.)*

SKILLBUILDER ANSWERS
1. the Syr Darya
2. the Mediterranean Sea

SECTION 3 PROGRAM RESOURCES

In-Depth Resources: Unit 5
- Guided Reading, p. 15
- Building Vocabulary, p. 17
- Reteaching Activity, p. 20

Guided Reading Workbook
- Section 3

Access for Students Acquiring English/ESL
- Guided Reading, p. 85

Outline Maps with Activities
- Central Asia, pp. 49–50

Formal Assessment
- Section Quiz, p. 243

Integrated Assessment
- Rubric for a diary entry, 4.3
- Rubric for an exhibit, 1.5

INTEGRATED TECHNOLOGY

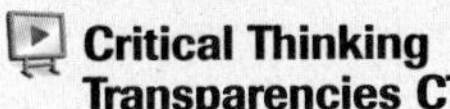

Critical Thinking Transparencies CT48
- Great Games in Central Asia

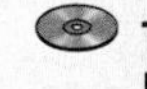

The World's Music Audio Program

hmhsocialstudies.com

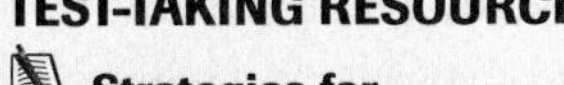

TEST-TAKING RESOURCES

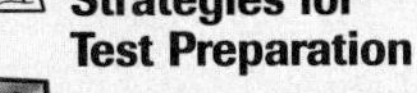

Strategies for Test Preparation

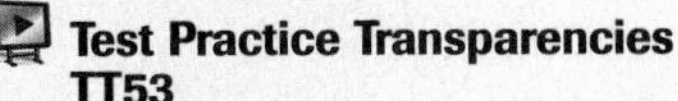

Test Practice Transparencies TT53

Online Test Practice

Instruct: Objective 

A Historical Crossroads

- What was the Silk Road? *(a trade route between China and the Mediterranean Sea, used between 100 B.C. and the 1300s)*
- How did the Silk Road affect Central Asia? *(Besides being a route for transporting goods, it also spread ideas, technology, and religion.)*
- What two countries struggled for control of Central Asia in the 1800s? *(Russia and Great Britain)*

In-Depth Resources: Unit 5
- Guided Reading, p. 15

Critical Thinking Transparencies CT48
- Great Games in Central Asia

Interpreting Graphics

Silk Production

Have students examine the infographic on page 376. Make sure they understand that silk clothing is made of fibers produced by insects. Ask students to name other sources of clothing fibers. *(cotton and rayon from plants; wool and leather from animals; nylon and polyester from petrochemicals, etc.)*

Silk Production

hmhsocialstudies.com INTERACTIVE

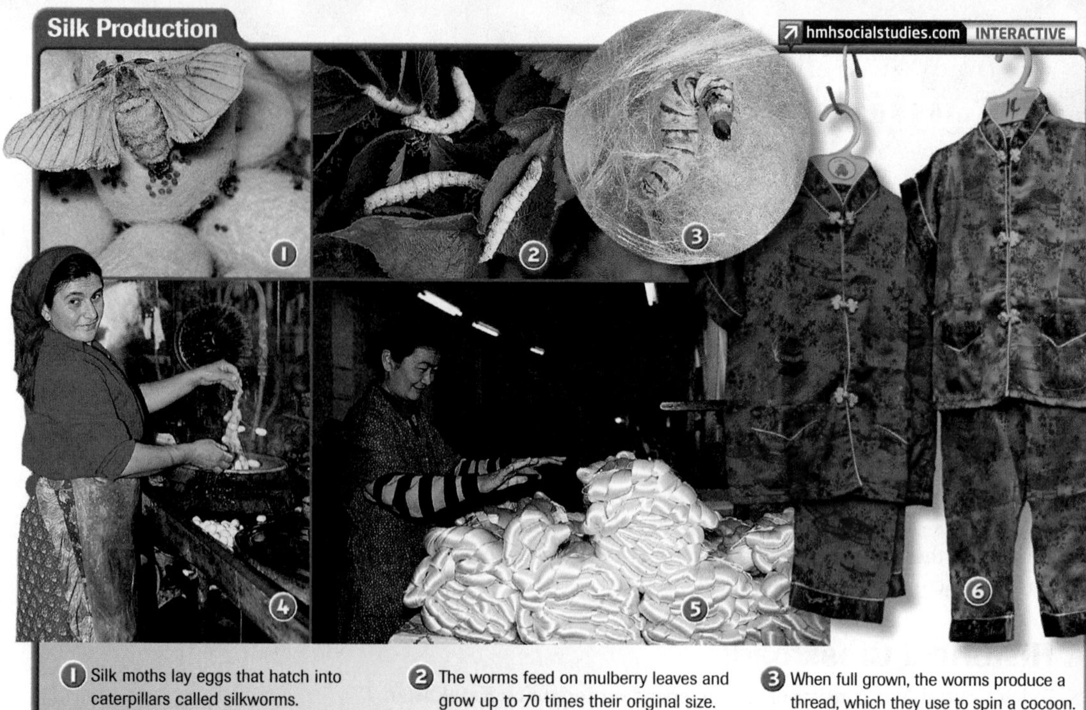

1. Silk moths lay eggs that hatch into caterpillars called silkworms.
2. The worms feed on mulberry leaves and grow up to 70 times their original size.
3. When full grown, the worms produce a thread, which they use to spin a cocoon.
4. This Kyrgyz woman is dipping cocoons in hot water to loosen the threads that she will then wind onto a reel.
5. A single cocoon yields about 3,000–5,000 feet of thread. It takes about 3,000 cocoons to make just one pound of raw silk.
6. Silk garments are popular items at a market.

ostriches and acrobats. The Silk Road also became a route for spreading ideas, technology, and religion.

Traffic on the Silk Road slowed in the 14th century, giving way to less expensive sea routes. Even so, you can still experience the legacy of the Silk Road in the magnificent cities—such as Samarqand and Bukhoro—built to take advantage of the trade.

Background Bukhoro and Samarqand marked halfway points where travelers could meet and take advantage of the cities' markets and services.

THE GREAT GAME Interest in Central Asia exploded again in the 19th century when Great Britain and the Russian Empire began to struggle for control of the region. Russian troops were moving southward, and British leaders wanted to stop the advance before the troops could threaten Britain's possessions in India.

Both sides recruited daring young officers who made journeys through the region in disguise. These officers worked to create maps of Central Asia and to win local leaders to their side. Arthur Connoly—one of the British officers executed in Bukhoro—called this struggle between the two empires the **Great Game.**

By the end of the 19th century, the Russian Empire had won control of Central Asia. In the 1920s, the Soviet Union took control and governed the region until 1991. Since the collapse of the Soviet Union, the Central Asian republics have been independent.

DIFFERENTIATING INSTRUCTION LESS PROFICIENT READERS

PREVIEWING THE SECTION

Objective To help students build a mental framework for the material they will read

Class Time 10 minutes

Task Use the headings and visuals to preview the section

Directions Demonstrate for students how they can build a mental outline of the information to be covered in this section by reading the headings and examining the visuals first. As you preview the section, make an outline of the headings on the board.

An Uncertain Economic Future

In Chapter 15, you read about the problems caused by Soviet irrigation programs in Central Asia. Other Soviet programs have also caused problems in the region.

NUCLEAR TESTING Until the late 1980s, the Soviet nuclear industry was the economic mainstay of Semey (renamed Semipalatinsk), a city in northeastern Kazakhstan. Between 1949 and 1989, scientists exploded 470 nuclear devices in "the Polygon," a vast nuclear test site southwest of Semey.

The nuclear tests were so close to Semey that citizens could see the mushroom clouds of the above-ground explosions. Later, underground explosions cracked walls in towns 50 miles away. The testing caused widespread health problems. Winds spread nuclear fallout over a 180,000-square-mile area, exposing over a million people to dangerous levels of radiation. Exposure caused dramatic increases in the rates of leukemia, thyroid cancer, birth defects, and mental illness. Although testing at the site ended in 1989, the harmful effects of radiation will continue for years to come. A

Geographic Thinking

Seeing Patterns

A What are the harmful effects of nuclear testing?

A. Answer Fallout from nuclear testing causes serious environmental damage and public health problems.

PETROLEUM AND PROSPERITY More hopeful is the potential for oil to bring wealth to Central Asia. Regional leaders see great promise in the oil and gas reserves of the Caspian Sea. In addition, engineers have recently discovered oil fields in Kazakhstan and Turkmenistan. These discoveries have triggered what many are calling the new "Great Game," as nations all over the world begin to compete for profits from the region's resources.

For Central Asia's resources to benefit its people, however, leaders must first establish stable political and legal institutions. The cultural geography of Central Asia, though, will make this goal especially difficult to achieve.

Cultures Divided and Conquered

Central Asia has a large number of ethnic groups, as the chart to the right shows. Before the Russian Revolution, each group lived in a particular region where it could follow its own way of life.

SOVIETS FORM NATIONS When the Soviets took control of Central Asia, they used the differences among the ethnic groups to establish their own authority in the region.

Soviet planners carved the region into five new nations that corresponded to the largest ethnic groups—Kazakh, Kyrgyz, Tajik, Turkmen, and Uzbek. However, when they drew the borders of these nations, they deliberately left large numbers of one ethnic group as minorities in the neighboring republics of other ethnic groups.

That explains why Uzbeks form about 24 percent of the population of Tajikistan and why two of the major

Ethnic Groups

Central Asia

Group	Percent
Uzbek	41
Kazakh	15
Russian	12
Tajik	12
Turkmen	7
Kyrgyz	6
Karakalpak	1
Tatar	1
Ukrainian	1
German	1
Other	4

SOURCE: *CIA World Factbook*

SKILLBUILDER: Interpreting Charts

REGION What is the second largest ethnic group in Central Asia?

Instruct: Objective 2

An Uncertain Economic Future

- What environmental problem has caused widespread health problems in Central Asia? *(radioactive fallout caused by Soviet nuclear testing)*
- What are some of these health problems? *(dramatic increases in the rates of leukemia, thyroid cancer, birth defects, and mental illness)*
- What resource may help bolster the region's economies? *(oil)*

Instruct: Objective 3

Cultures Divided and Conquered

- How did the Soviets contribute to the instability of the nations of Central Asia? *(They drew regional borders that exploited ethnic tensions.)*
- What is the largest ethnic group in the region? *(Uzbek)*
- What are two forces that unify the people of the region? *(the religion of Islam and Turkic languages)*

SKILLBUILDER ANSWER

Kazakhs

ACTIVITY OPTION **CRITICAL THINKING**

SEEING PATTERNS

Explaining the Skill Seeing patterns means making note of similar events, activities, or characteristics among various groups or at different places. Seeing patterns of ethnic conflict may help students appreciate the importance of respecting different cultures and finding ways to work and live together.

Applying the Skill After students read the section "Cultures Divided and Conquered" on pages 377–378, ask students the following questions:

- What kinds of problems might arise when one ethnic group forms the majority and another the minority of the population in a country? *(The majority group may control most of the country's wealth and hold most of the power and discriminate against the minority.)*
- What differences between ethnic groups might become sources of conflict? *(religion, language, customs, traditions)*
- In what other parts of the world have ethnic differences caused conflict ? *(on almost every continent)*

growing up in...

Kyrgyzstan

Kyrgyz children typically live in extended families, and social life centers on the family. Ask students to compare the way they celebrate birthdays with the way this family is celebrating. Then ask how much the lack of televisions and telephones would affect their way of life. *(Students probably celebrate their birthdays with a much simpler meal. They might feel cut off from the world if they did not have televisions and telephones.)*

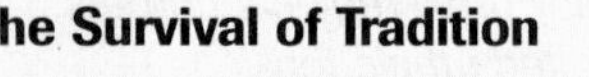

Instruct: Objective 4

The Survival of Tradition

- Why do the nomads of Central Asia have few possessions? *(because they are always on the move and must carry what they own)*
- What is a yurt made of, and what is it like inside? *(It is made of felt stretched over a wooden frame. Hanging inside the yurt are reed mats and woven bags. Handwoven carpets are used for sleeping and for covering the floor and wall.)*
- How are the Kyrgyz people preserving the nomadic tradition? *(by organizing a network of shepherd families willing to take in tourists)*

growing up in... Kyrgyzstan

Like children in the other former Soviet republics, the young people of Kyrgyzstan face a future filled with challenges. But most of the country's young people are prepared to meet those challenges. Children in Kyrgyzstan go to school from the ages of 6 to 15, and the nation's literacy rate stands at more than 97 percent.

The children in this photo are celebrating a birthday with their family. They are in a yurt set up for the occasion. Among the dishes on the table are *manti* (sheep dumplings), *irkat* (a salad made of noodles and grated carrots), and *kymys* (a drink made from fermented horse milk).

If you lived in Kyrgyzstan, here is what you might experience:

- Since 75 percent of Kyrgyz practice Islam, you might be Muslim.
- You might become a farmer, since nearly half of Kyrgyzstan's people earn their living that way.
- You might find it hard to keep in touch with friends since just 8 out of 100 people own phones.
- Watching TV would also be difficult. Only 2 out of 10 people own a TV.
- You would earn the right to vote and become eligible for military service at the age of 18.

cities inside Uzbekistan, Samarqand and Bukhoro, are populated by ethnic Tajiks. Ethnic Uzbeks also make up 9 percent of Turkmenistan's and nearly 14 percent of Kyrgyzstan's populations. Soviet leaders tried to prevent opposition to their rule by using the tensions that existed among these different groups. B

LANGUAGE AND RELIGION Although the peoples of Central Asia are divided by a number of ethnic and political loyalties, there are unifying forces in the region as well. Islam, which was brought by Muslim warriors from Southwest Asia in the 8th and 9th centuries, is one of the strongest. Also, most Central Asians speak languages related to Turkish. Many people also speak Russian, once the region's official language.

Geographic Thinking

Using the Atlas

B Look at the maps on pages 338–339 and 341. Compare the political and ethnic borders in Central Asia. In which regions do you see a potential for conflict?

B. Answer Students should note that conflict could occur where political and ethnic borders do not coincide with each other.

The Survival of Tradition

Central Asia endured decades of upheaval under Russian and Soviet rule. Even so, many of the region's traditions have survived.

NOMADIC HERITAGE The expansive grasslands of Central Asia are ideal for nomadic peoples. **Nomads** are people who have no permanent home. As seasons change, they move from place to place with their animals in search of food, water, and grazing land.

During the years of Soviet control, the number of nomads in Central Asia decreased dramatically as officials forced people onto collective farms. Even so, you can still find nomads in the region. In central Kyrgyzstan, for example, herders set up their tents near Lake Song-Köl during the summer months. They bring their animals there to graze on the lush pastures of the valley.

ACTIVITY OPTION **FIVE THEMES OF GEOGRAPHY**

HUMAN-ENVIRONMENT INTERACTION

Exploring the Theme Remind students that geographers look at the way people respond to their environment to meet their needs and wants. People living in similar environments may respond in different ways. Some responses have far less impact on an environment than others.

Understanding the Theme Have students use what they learn from the section entitled "The Survival of Tradition" on pages 378–379 to answer the following questions.

- How does the lifestyle of Central Asian nomads change the environment? *(It changes the environment very little. Their livestock eat the grasses of the grasslands, but unless they overgraze, these grasses grow back. The nomads probably also hunt game, but unless they overhunt, the game reproduces.)*
- Which do you think would change the environment of the Central Asian grasslands more—a nomadic way of life or large-scale, permanent farms? *(Large-scale, permanent farms would completely alter the environment.)*

Because they are always on the move and must carry what they own, nomads have few possessions. They usually carry what is most useful. Even so, many of the possessions of Central Asia's nomads are both useful and beautiful.

YURTS Among the most valuable of the nomads' possessions are their tents—called **yurts.** Yurts are light and portable. They usually consist of several layers of felt stretched around a wooden frame, often made of willow. The outermost layer of felt is coated with the waterproof fat of sheep.

As the photo on page 378 shows, the inside of a yurt can be stunningly beautiful. To block the wind, nomads hang reed mats, intricately woven with the grasses of the steppe. For storage, they suspend woven bags on their tent walls. The inlaid wooden saddles of their horses and their carved daggers also ornament the yurt.

Perhaps the most beautiful and useful of all the yurt's furnishings are the handwoven carpets. Their elaborate designs, colored with natural plant and beetle dyes, have made the carpets famous. Nomads use them for sleeping, or as floor coverings, wall linings, and insulation.

PRESERVING TRADITIONS The nomadic lifestyle of the peoples of Central Asia is not nearly as widespread as it once was. But many people are working hard to preserve the tradition. One group has organized a network of shepherds' families in Kyrgyzstan who are willing to take in guests. In this way, tourists can experience the daily life of the shepherds, who, in turn, receive a source of income for their families. Central Asians will benefit greatly from such imaginative and productive uses of their traditions.

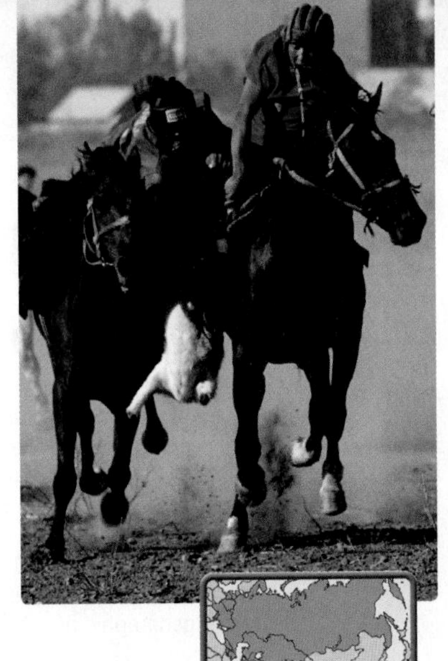

PLACE
Kyrgyz men play a form of polo that uses a goat carcass instead of a ball.

RUSSIA & REP.

Assess & Reteach

GeoFocus Have students complete the section on Central Asia for the graphic organizers.

Formal Assessment
- Section Quiz, p. 243

Reteaching Activity
Have students work in pairs to outline the main ideas of this section.

In-Depth Resources: Unit 5
- Reteaching Activity, p. 20

Outline Maps with Activities
- Central Asia, pp. 49–50

Section 3 Assessment

1 Places & Terms
Explain the importance of each of the following terms.
- Silk Road
- Great Game
- nomad
- yurt

2 Taking Notes
REGION Review the notes you took for this section.

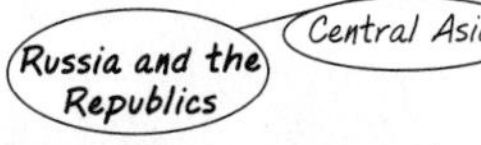

- What were some of the objects traded or transported over the Silk Road?
- Why have some people suggested that a new Great Game is beginning in Central Asia?

3 Main Ideas
a. What was the cause of the Great Game?
b. What impact has Soviet nuclear testing had in Central Asia?
c. What are two important unifying forces in Central Asia?

4 Geographic Thinking
Drawing Conclusions How did the Soviet Union use the human geography of Central Asia to establish control of the region? **Think about:**
- ethnic groups in the region
- how Soviet planners drew borders

SEEING PATTERNS Carry out more research on the lives of nomads in Central Asia. Focus on the period before the Soviet Union took control of the region. Then make up a **diary entry** that describes the daily activity of a typical nomadic family.

SECTION 3 ASSESSMENT ANSWERS

1. Places & Terms
Silk Road, p. 375
Great Game, p. 376
nomad, p. 378
yurt, p. 379

2. Taking Notes
- Traders exchanged goods such as silk, metals, and spices, but the road was also a conduit for the exchange of ideas, technology, and religion.
- because of the international competition for the region's petroleum resources

3. Main Ideas
a. Russia's expansion into Central Asia worried British leaders, who believed that the expansion was a threat to their possessions in India.
b. The radiation released by nuclear testing has poisoned the surrounding land and caused severe public health problems.
c. Many Central Asians are Muslim and speak languages related to Turkish.

4. Geographic Thinking
Soviet planners drew borders that increased ethnic tensions in the region. They hoped that turning people in the region against each other would help to prevent opposition to Soviet rule.

GeoActivity

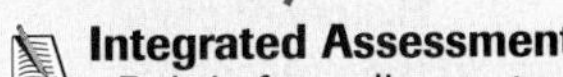

Integrated Assessment
- Rubric for a diary entry, 4.3

OBJECTIVE

Identify ways in which homes and shelters in different regions reflect local geography.

Instruct: Objective

Homes and Shelters

- How do yurts fit the nomadic lifestyle of Mongolian herders? *(They are portable.)*
- How do igloos reflect the environment of Arctic peoples? *(They are made of blocks of snow, which is plentiful in the Arctic region.)*
- Why do the Korowai of Irian Jaya live in tree houses? *(for protection from rival tribes, insects, and snakes)*
- Why do the people in Guadix live in caves? *(for protection against the region's extreme temperatures)*

More About

Igloos

The Inuit people of Canada and Greenland use igloos mainly in the winter as hunting-ground shelters. During the summer, they use sealskin or cloth tents.

hmhsocialstudies.com INTERACTIVE

Comparing Cultures

Homes and Shelters

The geography of the region in which people live influences the nature of their homes and shelters. People who live in forested areas, for example, might build log cabins. People living in grasslands, on the other hand, may use thatch–plant stalks and leaves–to build their homes. On these two pages, you will learn how homes in different parts of the world reflect local geographic possibilities and limitations.

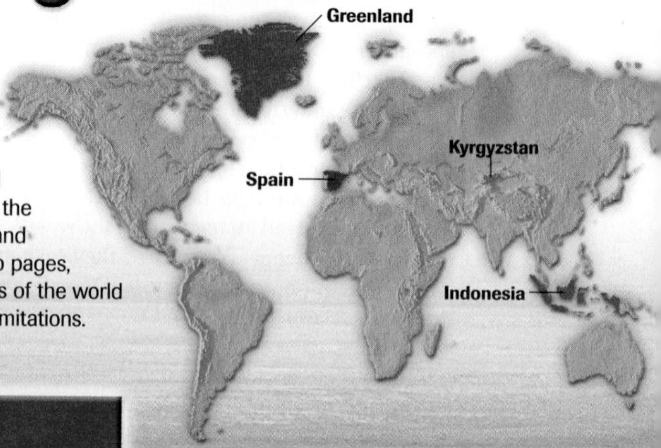

Greenland
Spain
Kyrgyzstan
Indonesia

Arctic peoples in Canada and Greenland take advantage of their environment by using blocks of snow to build dome-shaped winter shelters called igloos. They sometimes add windows made with sheets of ice or seal intestines.

The portable yurts of Kyrgyz herders are suited to their nomadic lifestyle.

380 CHAPTER 16

COMPARING CULTURES ADDITIONAL RESOURCES

BOOKS FOR THE TEACHER

Horning, Jonathan. ***Simple Shelters: Tents, Tipis, Yurts, Domes and Other Ancient Homes.*** Walker & Company, 2009. How stick-frame structures like those common in Central Asia fulfill physical and cultural needs of nomadic peoples.

BOOKS FOR THE STUDENT

Nelson, Peter. ***Treehouses: The Art and Craft of Living Out on a Limb.*** Boston: Houghton Mifflin, 1994. A treatment of treehouse living in the past and present.

Kempe, D. K. C. ***Living Underground: A History of Cave and Cliff Dwelling.*** London: Herbert, 1988. History of cave dwellers up to the present day.

PERIODICALS

Stiny, Andrew. **"Yurts of the San Juans."** *Backpacker,* Feb 1994. Description of a yurt camp in Colorado.

Steinmetz, George. **"Irian Jaya's People of the Trees."** *National Geographic,* Feb. 1996. Information on the tree-dwelling people of Indonesia.

INTERNET

For more about homes in different regions, visit . . .

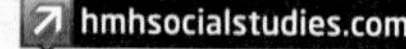

The Korowai of Irian Jaya, Indonesia, live in tree houses that protect them from rival tribes, as well as the insects, scorpions, and snakes of the rain forest.

GeoActivity

CREATING AN EXHIBIT 
Working with a partner, use the Internet to do research on homes in a region other than those shown on these two pages. Create an **exhibit** that shows the relationship between the region and its homes.

- Construct a model of the homes you are researching.
- Add a world map to the exhibit that shows where the homes are located.

People in the Spanish town of Guadix have turned underground caves into homes to protect against the region's extreme temperatures.

GeoData

Igloos
- The blocks of snow in an igloo are about 2 feet high, 4 feet long, and 8 inches thick.
- An experienced builder can finish an igloo in one to two hours.

Caves
- About 50 percent of Guadix's inhabitants live underground.
- Some of Guadix's caves are quite luxurious, with marble floors, modern kitchens, fax machines, and Internet connections.

Tree Houses
- The Korowai people build tree houses as high as 150 feet above ground.
- Korowai tree houses have separate areas for men and women, each with its own entrance.

Yurts
- A nomadic family can set up their yurt in approximately a half-hour.
- Felt—the material used to cover yurts—is a fabric of compressed animal fibers, such as wool or fur.

GeoActivity

Creating an Exhibit

Integrated Assessment
- Rubric for an exhibit, 1.5

More About

Cave Dwellers

People who live in caves are sometimes called *troglodytes*—from a Greek word meaning "those who enter holes."

ACTIVITY OPTION | COOPERATIVE LEARNING

PREPARING TO BUILD A HOME

Objective To investigate the relationship between homes and geography

Class Time 30 minutes

Task Create a list of factors that a home-builder in a specific place would need to consider

Directions Divide students into pairs and assign a place to each pair. (Each place should have relatively distinct physical or human geography.) Explain to each pair that a long-lost relative has left them property and that they should make plans to build a home on their new property. Ask students to investigate the geography of the place where their inherited property is located and make a list of the factors that they will need to consider when they are building their house. One student should focus on physical geography, and the other student should focus on human geography.

Reviewing Places & Terms

A. 1. Baltic Republics, p. 361
2. czar, p. 362
3. Russian Revolution, p. 363
4. USSR, p. 363
5. Cold War, p. 363
6. command economy, p. 364
7. collective farm, p. 364
8 Red Army, p. 371
9. Silk Road, p. 375
10. yurt, p. 379

B. Possible Responses

11. The emperors were known as czars.
12. Estonia, Latvia, and Lithuania are the former Soviet republics located on the Baltic Sea.
13. The Russian Revolution ended the rule of the czars.
14. The Soviet Union is also known as the Union of Soviet Socialist Republics (USSR).
15. The conflict is known as the Cold War.
16. In a command economy, the central government makes all major economic decisions.
17. By creating collective farms, the Soviet Union transformed agriculture into an industry.
18. The Soviet military was called the Red Army.
19. Cities such as Samarqand grew up along the Silk Road.
20. Central Asia's felt-covered dwellings are called yurts.

Chapter 16 Assessment

VISUAL SUMMARY
HUMAN GEOGRAPHY OF RUSSIA AND THE REPUBLICS

Subregions of Russia and the Republics

Russia and the Western Republics
- The explosive growth of the Russian Empire and the following decades of Soviet rule have had a lasting impact on both the physical and human geography of the region.
- The dramatic economic changes that accompanied the rise and fall of the Soviet Union affected both Russia and the Republics and the world.

Transcaucasia
- Migrating peoples have created a mosaic of languages and ethnicities in Transcaucasia.
- Today, leaders in Transcaucasia are struggling to maintain harmony among the region's different cultural groups and bring stability to the region's three newly-independent republics.

Central Asia
- Central Asia's fractured cultural geography still reflects the political goals of the old Soviet government.
- Powerful unifying forces, such as Islam, may help the region's new republics as they continue to rebuild their social and economic systems.

Reviewing Places & Terms

A. Briefly explain the importance of each of the following.

1. Baltic Republics
2. czar
3. Russian Revolution
4. USSR
5. Cold War
6. command economy
7. collective farm
8. Red Army
9. Silk Road
10. yurt

B. Answer the questions about vocabulary in complete sentences.

11. What were the emperors of the Russian Empire called?
12. What are the names of the three former Soviet republics located on the Baltic Sea?
13. What event ended the Russian Empire and the rule of the czars?
14. What is another name for the Soviet Union?
15. What was the name of the 20th-century conflict between the United States and the Soviet Union?
16. In what type of system are all major economic decisions made by the central government?
17. How did the Soviet Union turn agriculture into an industry?
18. What was the name of the Soviet military?
19. What caravan route contributed to the growth of magnificent trading cities such as Samarqand?
20. What is the name for the felt-covered dwellings of Central Asia's nomads?

Main Ideas

Russia and the Western Republics (pp. 361–369)

1. What former Soviet republics are located west of Russia?
2. What event delayed the growth of Russia before the 16th century?
3. What were the origins of the Cold War?
4. What is the largest religious group in Russia and the Western Republics?

Transcaucasia (pp. 370–374)

5. Of what republics does Transcaucasia consist?
6. Transcaucasia's location between which two seas made it an ideal migration route?
7. What factors may have contributed to instability in Transcaucasia?

Central Asia (pp. 375–381)

8. Of what republics does Central Asia consist?
9. Why did the Silk Road cross over Central Asia?
10. How did Islam become a major religion in Central Asia?

Main Ideas

1. Belarus, Estonia, Latvia, Lithuania, Moldova, and Ukraine
2. Expansion was halted by the 13th-century invasion of the Tartars. They controlled the region until the 1500s.
3. Stalin's installation of pro-Soviet governments in Eastern Europe after World War II caused U.S. leaders to fear the expansion of Communism. The resulting tensions between the two superpowers gave rise to the Cold War.
4. Orthodox Christians
5. Armenia, Azerbaijan, and Georgia
6. Black and Caspian seas
7. Historically, Transcaucasia has been located at the meeting point of rival empires that have sought to defend and extend their borders. The cultural complexity of the region has also presented challenges to regional stability.
8. Kazakhstan, Kyrgyzstan, Tajikistan, Turkmenistan, and Uzbekistan
9. because the region was located between two of the major endpoints of the route: China and the Mediterranean Sea
10. It was brought to the region by Muslim warriors from Southwest Asia in the eighth and ninth centuries.

Critical Thinking

1. Using Your Notes
Use your completed chart to answer these questions.

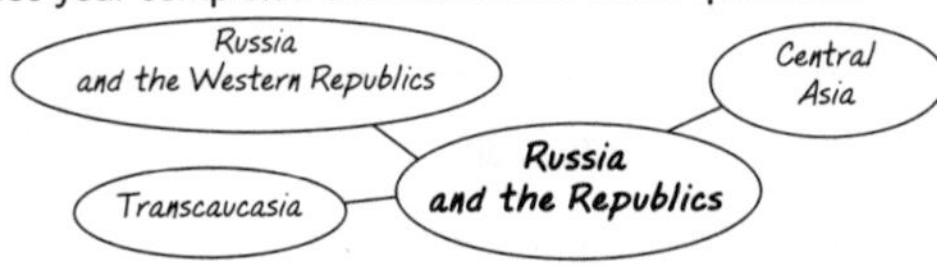

a. What percentage of the Russian population lives in rural areas?
b. What are the main religions in Transcaucasia?

2. Geographic Themes
a. PLACE Why did Azerbaijan's founders call it the "land of flames"?
b. LOCATION Where was the Soviet nuclear test site called "the Polygon" located?

3. Identifying Themes
Which country in Russia and the Western Republics has the greatest ethnic diversity, and what is its largest ethnic group? Which of the five themes applies to this situation?

4. Making Comparisons
How did the rise of the Soviet Union affect Transcaucasia and Central Asia?

5. Making Generalizations
How can the type of government that a country has affect the kind of work the country's artists create?

For Additional Test Practice
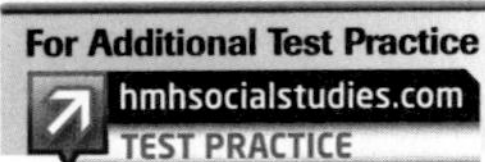

Geographic Skills: Interpreting Maps

Central Moscow
Use the map to answer the following questions.
1. LOCATION On what river does Russia's capital lie?
2. MOVEMENT Which of the ring roads would you take to visit Gorky Park?
3. MOVEMENT In which direction would you walk to get from Lenin's tomb to the State Department Store?

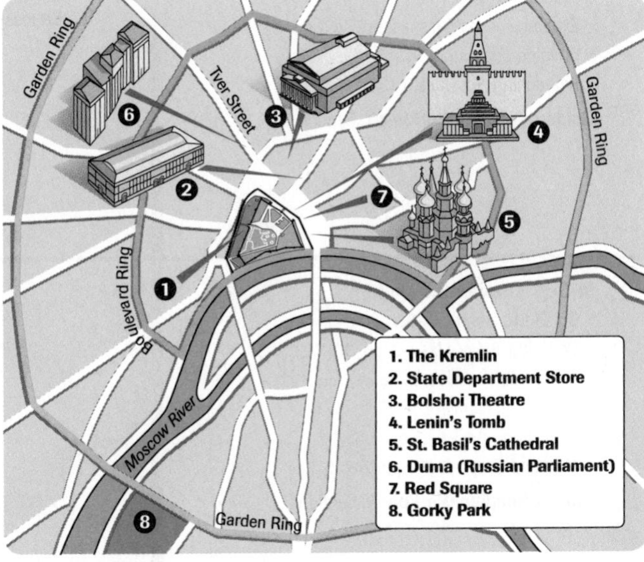

Choose one of the buildings shown on this map, and carry out further research on that building. Create a poster that includes a sketch of the site's floor plan and a paragraph about the history of the building.

hmhsocialstudies.com
MULTIMEDIA ACTIVITY

Use the links at **hmhsocialstudies.com** to do research on two of the former Soviet republics to the west of Russia. Focus on the characteristics of the republics' geography and people.

Creating Charts and Graphs Use your research to create charts and graphs that compare the two republics that you have chosen. List the Web sites that you used in preparing your report.

CHAPTER 16 ASSESSMENT

Critical Thinking

1. a. about 25 percent
   b. Christianity and Islam
2. a. because of the fires that erupted from its underground gas and oil deposits
   b. in northeastern Kazakhstan
3. Russia; Russian; region
4. The Soviet Union took control over both regions and dramatically altered their governments and economies to serve its own ends.
5. Some governments determine or restrict the types of work that artists produce.

GeoActivity

Integrated Assessment
- Rubric for a poster, 1.1

Formal Assessment
- Chapter Tests, Forms A, B, and C, pp. 244–255

RUSSIA & REP.

Geographic Skills

1. Moscow River
2. Garden Ring
3. north

MULTIMEDIA ACTIVITY

For their charts and graphs on Western Republics, students should:
- Focus on data and information that is suitable for charts and graphs.
- Produce a clear, imaginative visual to complement the report.
- Make sure that their data is concise and well-organized.
- Include references to the Web sites used as sources.

Grading Rubric Evaluate student performance as Exceptional, Acceptable, or Poor in each of the following categories:

	Exceptional	Acceptable	Poor
Topics and purposes of charts and graphs are clearly stated			
Charts and graphs compare both physical and human geography			
Data and information are easy to read and interpret			
Uses correct grammar, spelling, and punctuation.			

CHAPTER 17 PLANNING GUIDE

Today's Issues: Russia and the Republics

OVERVIEW	INSTRUCTIONAL RESOURCES	
ESSENTIAL QUESTION How has the fall of the Soviet Union affected the region? **Focus on the Essential Question Podcast**	**In-Depth Resources: Unit 5** • Building Vocabulary, p. 27 **Block Schedule Strategies** **Chapter Summaries** (English/Spanish)	**Interactive Online Edition** TOS **ExamView® Assessment Suite** (English/Spanish) TOS **CalendarPlanner** **Power Presentations with Media Gallery** **Critical Thinking Transparencies** • CT17 hmhsocialstudies.com INTERACTIVE
SECTION 1 **REGIONAL CONFLICT** **MAIN IDEAS** • Regional tensions, once under Soviet control, have flared up since the collapse of the Soviet Union in 1991. • Progress in peace talks, declining public support, and the human and economic costs of war may help end some of the conflicts.	**In-Depth Resources: Unit 5** • Guided Reading, p. 21 • Exploring Today's Issues, pp. 28–29 • Building Vocabulary, p. 27 • Reteaching Activities, p. 32 **Guided Reading Workbook,** Section 1	hmhsocialstudies.com INTERACTIVE • The Caucasus, p. 385
SECTION 2 **THE STRUGGLE FOR ECONOMIC REFORM** **MAIN IDEAS** • Russia has sold many government-owned businesses in an effort to move from a command to a market economy. • Russia's economic changes have not yet benefited most Russians. • The enormous size of Russia and widespread criminal activity have hindered economic reform.	**In-Depth Resources: Unit 5** • Guided Reading, p. 22 • Exploring Today's Issues, pp. 30–31 • Skillbuilder Practice, p. 26 • Building Vocabulary, p. 27 • Reteaching Activities, p. 33 • Map and Graph Skills, pp. 24–25 **Guided Reading Workbook,** Section 2	
CASE STUDY **THE SOVIET UNION'S NUCLEAR LEGACY** **MAIN IDEAS** • The region's new leaders must face the nuclear legacy of the Soviet Union. • This legacy includes nuclear power plants of questionable safety, as well as an arsenal of nuclear weapons, whose security is of great concern to world leaders.	**In-Depth Resources: Unit 5** • Guided Reading, p. 23 • Building Vocabulary, p. 27 • Reteaching Activities, p. 34 **Guided Reading Workbook,** Case Study	**Critical Thinking Transparencies** • CT49, Major Producers of Nuclear Power, 1999 **Map Transparencies** • MT30, Disaster at Chernobyl

ASSESSMENT

SE **Chapter Assessment,** pp. 396–397

Formal Assessment
- Chapter Tests, Forms A, B, and C, pp. 259–273

TOS **ExamView® Assessment Suite**

Strategies for Test Preparation

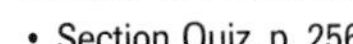

hmhsocialstudies.com TEST PRACTICE

SE **Section Assessment,** p. 387

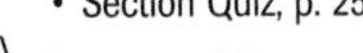

Formal Assessment
- Section Quiz, p. 256

Integrated Assessment
- Rubric for flash cards, 1.7

Test Practice Transparencies TT54

SE **Section Assessment,** p. 390

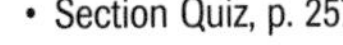

Formal Assessment
- Section Quiz, p. 257

Integrated Assessment
- Rubric for guidelines, 4.11

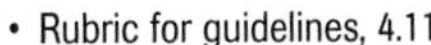

Test Practice Transparencies TT55

SE **Case Study Project,** p. 394–395

Formal Assessment
- Case Study Quiz, p. 258

Test Practice Transparencies TT56

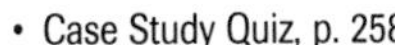

CHART KEY:

SE Student Edition	Block Scheduling	DVD/CD-ROM
TE Teacher's Edition	TOS Teacher One Stop	MP3 Audio
Printable Resource	Presentation Resource	HISTORY™

Program Resources available on TOS and @ hmhsocialstudies.com

SUPPORTING RESOURCES

- **Multimedia Classroom Global History Series**
- **Global History Teacher's Guide**

Social Studies Trade Library Collection
- Modern World History Trade Collection

For more information or to purchase these resources, go to hmhsocialstudies.com

DIFFERENTIATED INSTRUCTION

English Learners	Struggling Readers	Gifted and Talented Students
Spanish/English Guided Reading Workbook **Access for Students Acquiring English/ESL** Spanish Translations, pp. 87–92 **Chapter Summaries** (English/Spanish) TE **TE Activity** Recognizing Words with Multiple Meanings, p. 386	**Chapter Summaries** (English/Spanish) TE **TE Activity** Rereading for Main Ideas, p. 394	TE **TE Activity** Internet Research, p. 393

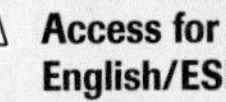

ENRICHMENT ACTIVITIES

The following activities are especially suitable for classes following block schedules.

SE **Student Edition,** pp. 384–397
- Reading Line and Pie Graphs, p. 391

hmhsocialstudies.com INTERACTIVE
- The Caucasus, p. 385

BLOCK SCHEDULE LESSON PLAN OPTIONS: 90-MINUTE PERIOD

DAY 1

SECTION 1, pp. 385–387
Class Time 90 minutes

- **Debates** Divide students into four groups and have each group research one of the conflicts discussed in this section: the Chechen-Russian conflict, the South Ossetian-Georgian conflict, the Abkhazian-Georgian conflict, or the Armenian-Azerbaijan conflict. Have each group prepare and stage a debate in which they present opposing viewpoints in each conflict.

DAY 2

SECTION 2, pp. 388–391
Class Time 90 minutes

- **Charting** Review the section content by leading the class in creating a problems-solutions chart that lists the economic problems Russia is struggling with and the solutions that leaders have tried.
Class Time 45 minutes
- **Skillbuilder Lesson** Use the lesson on making decisions on TE page 389 and the Skillbuilder Practice worksheet.
Class Time 45 minutes

DAY 3

CHAPTER 17 REVIEW AND ASSESSMENT, pp. 396–397
Class Time 90 minutes

- **Review** Have students review the chapter by using the Main Ideas at the beginning of Section 1 on PE page 385 and of Section 2 on PE page 388. For each main idea, have students write three to four details that elaborate on the subject.
Class Time 40 minutes
- **Assessment** Have students complete the Chapter 16 Assessment.
Class Time 50 minutes

TEACHER-TESTED ACTIVITY

Population Densities of the Former Soviet Republics

Class Time One class period

Task Calculate the population density of each former Soviet republic using the information given in the Regional Data File

Supplies Needed:
- Pencil
- Calculator
- Ruler
- Spreadsheet program (optional)

Purpose To create new information using the textbook's Regional Data File as a resource

Activity Have students create a table or spreadsheet with 4 columns and 17 rows. Headings in the first row should read from left to right: Nation; Population; Area (sq. miles); Population Density. Write or key in the republic names in the Nations column. For the Population Density column, divide the population of each nation by its area, or key in a formula. Use a fill command to complete the table.

Martin A. Van Hecke
Geography Teacher, Anchor Bay High School, New Baltimore, Michigan

TECHNOLOGY IN THE CLASSROOM

The Web is well-suited to helping students learn about current and recent events. Updates to current stories can be posted within minutes after they occur, and recent news stories can be told using text, audio, video, and still pictures.

One good way to keep students "on-task" and to ensure that they use appropriate Web sites for their current issues research is to have them look through a limited set of pre-selected sites. The teacher should choose sites sponsored by organizations that are generally considered reliable, such as major news sources, television networks, or nonprofit organizations. If the teacher presents students with a list of appropriate sites, they can save a good deal of classroom time, and students will be less likely to end up at sites that are irrelevant or inappropriate.

Objective Students will look through a pre-selected set of Web sites to gather information about the situation in Chechnya. One of the sites contains a photojournalism slideshow with audio.

Task Have students pretend to be journalists who have interviewed Russian soldiers and Chechen civilians in Chechnya. Have them gather information for their interviews on the Web and write a summary of the interview.

Class Time 2 class periods

1. Have students read pages 385–387 and discuss the "Main Ideas" questions on page 387. Ask them to explain in a class discussion why the Caucasus region is so troubled.
2. Ask students to imagine that they are journalists who have sneaked into Chechnya to find out what's going on there. Their goal is to interview one Russian soldier and one Chechen civilian.
3. Have students go to the Web sites listed at **hmhsocial studies.com** to find out about the situation in Chechnya. Then have them transcribe their interviews, with questions and answers. Each interview should pose at least six questions that require the interviewee to explain what has happened in his or her life since the Russians invaded Chechnya. Some good questions might be: Why did the Russians invade Chechnya? What is your daily life like? What do you think will happen here in the future? The Russian and the Chechen should have different perspectives on these questions.

CHAPTER 17 OBJECTIVE

Describe the major challenges that Russia and the Republics face today.

Chapter 17 TODAY'S ISSUES Russia and the Republics

Interpreting Photographs

Explain to students that the photograph on page 384 shows a woman and child returning to Grozny, the capital of Chechnya, during a lull in the fighting in 1996.

Extension Ask students to examine the photograph and discuss the impact the war might have had on the city and its inhabitants.

Introducing the Essential Question

- Describe how political repression can cover up conflicts between groups that have been forced to coexist in a huge, powerful country. This was the situation in the Soviet Union.
- Discuss how difficult it might be for Americans to change their entire economic system—including all their assumptions and expectations about making and spending money. For many people in Russia and the Republics, this is the situation they faced after the dissolution of the Soviet Union.

Have students fill out graphic organizers in their notebooks using material from all sections in this chapter.

Critical Thinking Transparencies CT17
- GeoFocus

In-Depth Resources: Unit 5
- Building Vocabulary, p. 27

Essential Question
How has the fall of the Soviet Union affected the region?

What You Will Learn
In this chapter you will analyze major challenges that face Russia and the Republics.

SECTION 1
Regional Conflict

SECTION 2
The Struggle for Economic Reform

CASE STUDY
The Soviet Union's Nuclear Legacy

For more on these issues in Russia and the Republics . . .

hmhsocialstudies.com CURRENT EVENTS

hmhsocialstudies.com TAKING NOTES
Use the graphic organizer online to take notes on causes and effects of some aspect of each issue.

This woman and child are from the Russian Republic of Chechnya. Russia invaded Chechnya twice in the 1990s to prevent the republic from becoming independent.

384

CHAPTER 17 ADDITIONAL RESOURCES

BOOKS FOR THE TEACHER

Zürcher, Christoph. ***The Post-Soviet Wars: Rebellion, Ethnic Conflict, and Nationhood in the Caucasus.*** NYU Press, 2009. Emphasis is on Chechnya, Armenia, Azerbaijan, Georgia, and Dagestan.

BOOKS FOR THE STUDENT

Goldman, Marshall. ***Lost Opportunity.*** New York: W.W. Norton, 1994. Analysis of the failure of economic reforms in Russia.

VIDEOS

Living in Russia Today. BFA/Phoenix, 1998. Russians discuss their government and their future.

INTERNET

For more about issues facing Russia and the Republics, visit . . .

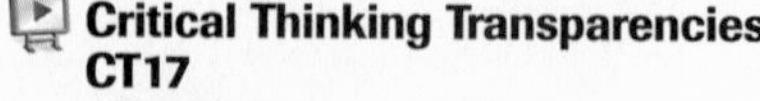

Regional Conflict

How do new nations establish law and order?

Main Ideas

- Regional tensions, once under Soviet control, have flared up in Russia and the Republics.
- Some of the most violent conflicts have occurred in the Caucasus region.

Places & Terms

Caucasus
Chechnya
Nagorno-Karabakh

A HUMAN PERSPECTIVE The powerful central government of the Soviet Union once maintained tight control over Russia and the Republics. But when the Soviet Union collapsed in 1991, central authority weakened. Crime, conflict, and other signs of instability increased. As one former Soviet citizen put it, "We're floating in a zone of half-lawlessness, half-law. . . . We destroyed the old system but replaced it with nothing. There is a vacuum."

A number of ethnic and religious groups have taken advantage of this vacuum to seek control over their own affairs. In several regions, their demands have resulted in conflict. Leaders in these regions have tried to gain control over the conflicts and bring them to an end. The test for many leaders has been how to preserve law and order without returning to the undemocratic rule of the Soviet era.

A Troubled Caucasus

Among the different subregions of the former Soviet Union, the Caucasus has experienced some of the most violent conflicts. The **Caucasus,** or Caucasia, is a region that straddles the Caucasus Mountains, which stretch between the Black and Caspian seas. To the north of the mountains lie republics that are part of Russia—including Chechnya, Dagestan, Ingushetia, and North Ossetia. To the south are the republics of Transcaucasia, which were once part of the Soviet Union but are now independent countries: Armenia, Azerbaijan, and Georgia.

The Caucasus is a land of great complexity. Inhabitants of the region, which is about the size of the state of California, speak dozens of distinct languages and belong to approximately 50 different ethnic groups.

The Caucasus — hmhsocialstudies.com INTERACTIVE MAP

SKILLBUILDER: Interpreting Maps

1. **LOCATION** On what seacoast is Abkhazia situated?
2. **LOCATION** In what countries do North and South Ossetia lie?

RUSSIA & REP.

CHAPTER 17 SECTION 1

SECTION 1 OBJECTIVES

1. Explain the reasons for the conflicts in the Caucasus since the collapse of the Soviet Union in 1991.
2. Identify factors that may help resolve the conflicts in the Caucasus.

SKILLBUILDER: Interpreting Maps, p. 385

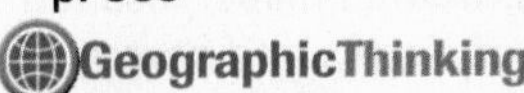

Seeing Patterns, p. 386
Making Comparisons, p. 387

Focus & Motivate

Ask students to recall what they have learned so far about reasons for conflict in the region around the Caucasus. *(There is tension between the many ethnic groups in the region.)*

Instruct: Objective 1 appears on p. 386

Interpreting Maps

Direct students' attention to the small size of the internal Russian republics of Chechnya, Dagestan, Ingushetia, and North Ossetia and the Georgian regions of South Ossetia and Abkhazia. Ask what these small regions would be similar to in the United States. *(states)*

SKILLBUILDER ANSWERS

1. the Black Sea **2.** North Ossetia lies in Russia, and South Ossetia lies in Georgia.

SECTION 1 PROGRAM RESOURCES

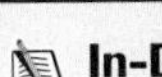 **In-Depth Resources: Unit 5**
- Guided Reading, p. 21
- Exploring Today's Issues, pp. 28–29
- Building Vocabulary, p. 27
- Reteaching Activity, p. 32

 **Guided Reading Workbook**
- Section 1

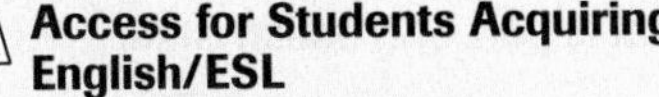
Access for Students Acquiring English/ESL
- Guided Reading, p. 87

Formal Assessment
- Section Quiz, p. 256

Integrated Assessment
- Rubric for flash cards, 1.7

INTEGRATED TECHNOLOGY

 **Chapter Summaries**

 **Power Presentations**

TEST-TAKING RESOURCES

 **Strategies for Test Preparation**

 **Test Practice Transparencies TT54**

Online Test Practice

Instruct: Objective 

A Troubled Caucasus

- What is the reason for the war between Russia and Chechnya? *(Many Chechens want independence from Russia.)*
- What two areas of Georgia have fought for independence, and what were the results? *(South Ossetia and Abkhazia; both conflicts resulted in thousands of deaths and severe refugee problems)*
- Over what region have Armenia and Azerbaijan fought, and what was the result? *(They fought for control of Nagorno-Karabakh. Armenia is now in control of the territory.)*

 **In-Depth Resources: Unit 5**
- Guided Reading, p. 21
- Exploring Today's Issues, pp. 28-29

Interpreting Photographs

Bomb Attack in Argun, Chechnya

Point out that Russia's republics in Caucasia are close to the Caspian Sea. Ask students to consider why internal republics in this area might be important to Russia. *(because they are close to the region's sizeable oil resources)*

CAPTION ANSWER Answers will vary, but students may point out the familiarity of Chechen rebels with their own territory.

As the Soviet Union began to break up in the late 1980s, several of these ethnic groups began to take up arms to win their own independent territories. In the following decade, hundreds of thousands of people died in the conflicts that resulted.

CHECHNYA Among the republics that remained part of Russia after the collapse of the Soviet Union, **Chechnya** has experienced the worst violence. In response to Chechnya's demand for independence, Russia invaded Chechnya twice in the 1990s, causing over 100,000 casualties.

Russia first invaded Chechnya in 1994. By the spring of 1995, Russian troops were in control of more than two-thirds of the republic's territory, and they had captured the capital, Grozny, and other major towns. But Chechen rebels continued to fight from hideouts in the surrounding mountains. Unable to defeat the rebels, Russia reluctantly entered into a peace agreement with Chechnya, ending the first phase of the war in August 1996.

Russia invaded Chechnya again in October 1999 after a series of bombings blamed on Chechen terrorists. In the following years, the conflict seemed to have calmed, but in March 2010 bombs went off in the Moscow subway, killing or injuring dozens. Widows of Chechen rebels were named as the bombers.

PLACE This was the main street in Grozny, the Chechen capital (February 2000). **Why might the Russian army have trouble defeating the Chechen rebels?**

BACKGROUND Chechens are the largest ethnic group in Chechnya and are predominantly Muslim.

GEORGIA The Republic of Georgia has also experienced instability. From 1989 to 1992, the Ossetian people living in the region of South Ossetia fought against Georgian troops to unite South Ossetia with North Ossetia, in Russia. A 1992 truce calmed the region, but the peace did not last. In August 2008, Georgia tried to regain control of South Ossetia by launching a military attack. Russia promptly sent troops into South Ossetia and bombed targets elsewhere in Georgia. After several days of heavy fighting, the Georgian troops were defeated. The opposing countries signed a ceasefire, but Russia maintained a military presence in the area.

Abkhazia, a once-popular resort area on the Black Sea, is another troubled region. Abkhazians declared independence in 1992 and forced up to 250,000 ethnic Georgians living there to leave. Many died while fleeing across snow-covered mountains. In 2008, fighting in South Ossetia spread to Abkhazia, and all Georgian troops were pushed out. The situation remains unsettled and tense. A

A. Answer Both conflicts involved minority ethnic groups seeking independence from Georgia, and both resulted in thousands of deaths and severe refugee problems.

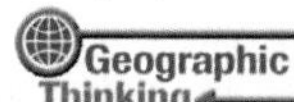

Geographic Thinking

Seeing Patterns
A How are the two conflicts in Georgia that you read about similar?

ARMENIA AND AZERBAIJAN Conflict has also plagued the region south of Georgia, where Armenia and Azerbaijan fought over a mountainous area of Azerbaijan called **Nagorno-Karabakh.** Leaders in Azerbaijan say that the region's history proves that Nagorno-Karabakh belongs to them. Armenia claims Nagorno-Karabakh because over three-quarters of its population is ethnic Armenian.

DIFFERENTIATING INSTRUCTION — STUDENTS ACQUIRING ENGLISH/ESL

RECOGNIZING WORDS WITH MULTIPLE MEANINGS

Objective To help ESL students understand a key word with multiple meanings

Class Time 5 minutes

Task Explain two of the meanings of the word *republic* as it is used in this section

Directions ESL students may be confused by the two ways in which the word *republic* is used in this section. It refers not only to such independent nations as Armenia and Georgia but also to such local political units as Chechnya, which form part of an independent nation. Write the following two definitions of *republic* on the board. Explain that the second definition refers to a local political unit similar to the states of the United States.

republic a nation-state in which the power resides in citizens who vote for representatives

republic a political and territorial unit that is part of a nation-state

The dispute began long ago and was raging in the early 1920s, when the Soviet army took control of the region. Soviet authorities kept the dispute under control until the late 1980s, when Armenians and Azerbaijanis began to fight for control over the region.

The fighting continued on and off for nearly six years. Eventually Armenia won control of the territory. A cease-fire was declared in 1994, but by then, tens of thousands of people had died. Nearly a million had become refugees.

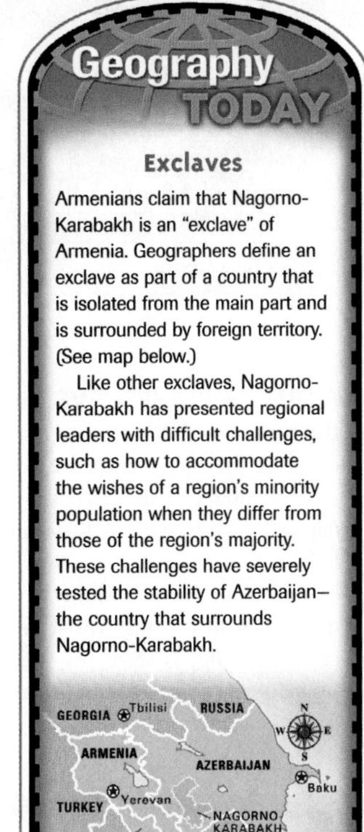

Exclaves

Armenians claim that Nagorno-Karabakh is an "exclave" of Armenia. Geographers define an exclave as part of a country that is isolated from the main part and is surrounded by foreign territory. (See map below.)

Like other exclaves, Nagorno-Karabakh has presented regional leaders with difficult challenges, such as how to accommodate the wishes of a region's minority population when they differ from those of the region's majority. These challenges have severely tested the stability of Azerbaijan—the country that surrounds Nagorno-Karabakh.

Hope on the Horizon?

In spite of all this conflict in the region, many believe that there is some hope for the future. In April 2001, U.S. Secretary of State Colin Powell hosted a round of direct talks between the presidents of Armenia and Azerbaijan. The talks, which were held in Florida, were aimed at reaching a lasting peace settlement between the two nations. However, as of 2007, the dispute had not been resolved.

Fighting has continued in Chechnya, and the human costs of the war have continued to mount. In February 2001, Russian officials reported that more than 15,000 soldiers (2,700 Russians and 13,000 Chechen guerrillas) had died since the second war began. Since then, the Russian army has had sporadic success shutting down the rebels. Before a full peace can be achieved, agreement must be reached on the fates of some 25,000 to 180,000 refugees who have been forced from their homes in the disputed areas. In the next section, you will read more about the economic challenges faced by Russian leaders since the fall of the Soviet Union.

Section 1 Assessment

1 Places & Terms

Explain the importance of each of the following places.

- Caucasus
- Chechnya
- Nagorno-Karabakh

2 Taking Notes

REGION Review the notes you took for this section.

	Causes	Effects
Issue 1: Conflict		

- Why might Abkhazia's tourist industry have declined in the 1990s?

3 Main Ideas

a. Why did ethnic tensions in Russia and the Republics seldom result in armed conflict before the 1990s?

b. Why did Russian troops invade Chechnya in 1994 and 1999?

c. What led to the conflict between Armenia and Azerbaijan?

4 Geographic Thinking

Making Comparisons Why might ethnic differences cause problems in one region or society but not in another? **Think about:**

- the type of government in the region

ASKING GEOGRAPHIC QUESTIONS Search for articles on a conflict in Caucasia. Create **flash cards** that raise geographic questions about the conflict, such as "How did geography help keep Russian troops from defeating Chechen rebels?" The back of the card might read "Rebels hid in the region's mountainous terrain." Consider features of both physical and human geography. 21st CENTURY

RUSSIA & REP.

Geography TODAY

Exclaves

Ask students to imagine that a neighboring U.S. state became an exclave of another country. Ask what problems might develop from such a situation. *(People would have to travel through a foreign country to get from one state to another. The resources of that state would be lost to the country.)*

Instruct: Objective 2

Hope on the Horizon?

- What steps have been taken to resolve the conflict between Armenia and Azerbaijan? *(Their leaders have been making progress in peace talks.)*
- What issue must be resolved before a full peace can be achieved in Chechnya? *(The refugee problem must be resolved.)*

Assess & Reteach

GeoFocus Have students complete their notes on the issue of conflict in their cause-and-effect charts.

Formal Assessment
- Section Quiz, p. 256

Reteaching Activity

Have students work in groups to write quizzes on the main ideas of the section, using the notes in their GeoFocus charts. Then direct the groups to exchange quizzes and answer them.

In-Depth Resources: Unit 5
- Reteaching Activity, p. 32

SECTION 1 ASSESSMENT ANSWERS

1. Places & Terms

Caucasus, p. 385
Chechnya, p. 386
Nagorno-Karabakh, p. 386

2. Taking Notes

- Instability and conflict in the region made it unattractive to visitors.

3. Main Ideas

a. Tight control by the central government kept ethnic tensions from erupting into open warfare before the fall of the Soviet Union in 1991.
b. They wanted to end Chechnya's fight for independence from Russia.
c. a dispute over Nagorno-Karabakh, a territory in Azerbaijan with a majority Armenian population

4. Geographic Thinking

Ethnic conflict may be discouraged in regions with a powerful central government that can control its population with force.

GeoActivity

Integrated Assessment
- Rubric for flash cards, 1.7

SECTION 2 OBJECTIVES

1. Describe how Russia is changing its economic system.
2. Identify obstacles to reforming Russia's economy.

SKILLBUILDER: Interpreting Maps, p. 389

GeographicThinking
Seeing Patterns, p. 389
Drawing Conclusions, p. 390

Focus & Motivate

How would Americans be affected if the prices of goods in their country increased 250 percent but their earnings stayed the same? *(Their standard of living would decline. Most people would not be able to afford any luxuries, and many would have difficulty meeting their basic needs for food, shelter, and clothing.)*

Instruct: Objective 

Steps Toward Capitalism

- What steps did Russia take in the 1990s to move toward a capitalist economic system? *(removed price controls, privatized government-owned businesses)*
- What percentage of Russians lived below the poverty line at the end of the 1990s? *(40%)*

 **In-Depth Resources: Unit 5**
- Guided Reading, p. 22
- Exploring Today's Issues, pp. 30–31

CAPTION ANSWER because few privately owned businesses, such as fast-food chains, were allowed under the Soviet Union's communist economy

The Struggle for Economic Reform

How does a nation change its economic system?

Main Ideas
- Russia has struggled to move from a command economy to a market economy.
- Russia's enormous size and widespread criminal activity have made economic reform difficult.

Places & Terms
privatization
distance decay

A HUMAN PERSPECTIVE Russians have faced many hardships since the breakup of the Soviet Union. But few have been as difficult to overcome as the collapse of the Soviet command economy. After the Soviet Union collapsed in 1991, the region's people began to participate in a capitalist system. One Russian bitterly summed up the sudden transition in this way: "You developed your capitalist markets in the West over hundreds of years, and our government wants our people to go to sleep one night in a Communist world and wake up the next morning in a capitalist one." One of the toughest problems facing Russia's leaders is how to carry out economic reforms without causing too much turmoil for the nation's citizens.

Steps Toward Capitalism

After the Soviet collapse, Russia tried to move quickly toward a capitalist system. This meant ending the tight control that the central government held over economic activity.

PRIVATIZATION In January 1992, Russia removed the price controls that had been set by the Soviet government on goods sold within the country. The effect was dramatic. Almost immediately, the prices of many goods increased by 250 percent.

In the same year, Russia began to sell government-owned businesses to individuals and private companies. This process was called **privatization.** But few Russians had enough money to buy large businesses. So, leaders offered vouchers to the public. The vouchers were like loans that could be used to purchase businesses. The purchasers promised to repay the government with future profits.

But the policy had mixed success. Many of the new businesses were not profitable, and their owners were unable to repay their vouchers. The failures contributed to an economic crash in Russia in 1998. In spite of this shaky start, though, over 60 percent of the country's workforce worked in the private sector by the end of the 20th century.

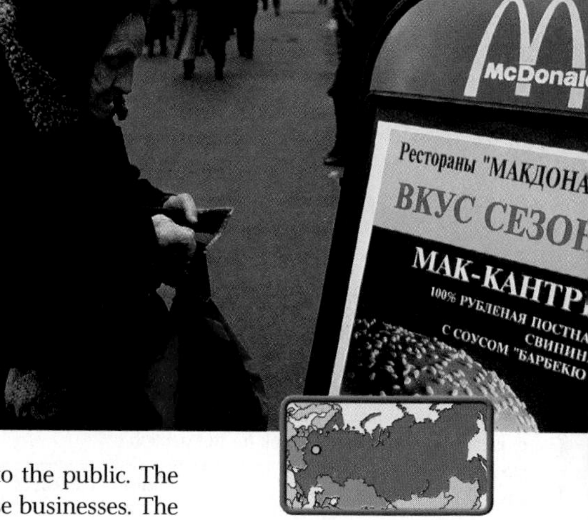

PLACE The many Western fast-food chains popping up in Moscow are symbols of economic change.
Why might fast-food chains have been rare in Russia before 1991?

THE HIGH COST OF ECONOMIC CHANGE Since the 1998 crash, Russia's economy has moved slowly toward recovery. But the movement toward a market economy has yet to benefit most Russians. By the end of the 1990s, nearly 40 percent of the Russian population lived

SECTION 2 PROGRAM RESOURCES

 **In-Depth Resources: Unit 5**
- Guided Reading, p. 22
- Exploring Today's Issues, pp. 30–31
- Skillbuilder Practice, p. 26
- Building Vocabulary, p. 27
- Reteaching Activity, p. 33
- Map and Graph Skills, pp. 24–25

 **Guided Reading Workbook**
- Section 2

Access for Students Acquiring English/ESL
- Guided Reading, p. 88
- Skillbuilder Practice, p. 90
- Map and Graph Skills, pp. 91–92

 **Formal Assessment**
- Section Quiz, p. 257

 **Integrated Assessment**
- Rubric for guidelines, 4.11

INTEGRATED TECHNOLOGY

 **Power Presentations**

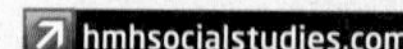

TEST-TAKING RESOURCES

 **Strategies for Test Preparation**

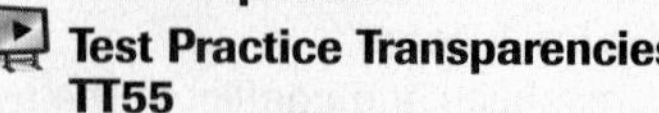 **Test Practice Transparencies TT55**

 **Online Test Practice**

far below the poverty line. Some people even wondered whether things had been better under the Soviet Union.

Obstacles to Economic Reform

Russians have made slow, if painful, strides toward capitalism. Even so, many obstacles remain. Russia's enormous size and the rise of organized crime are among the most important.

DISTANCE DECAY A major obstacle facing economic reformers is **distance decay.** This means that long distances between places make communication and transportation difficult. Russia is an enormous nation, stretching across 11 time zones. Spread over this vast area are 89 different regional governments. The interaction and cooperation of these regional leaders with Moscow is crucial if the government's economic reforms are to be successful. But because the central government in Moscow has been weak, officials far from the capital sometimes refuse to carry out the government's reform programs.

In the spring of 2000, Russian President Vladimir Putin created seven large federal districts to gain more control over regional leaders. Each has its own governor-general. Putin hoped that the heads of the new federal districts would force regional officials to carry out the economic reforms that Moscow wanted. A

A. Answer Citizens may feel that the new districts will return too much power to the central government.

Seeing Patterns
A Some Russians have objected to the creation of new federal districts. Why might there be disagreement over the districts?

SKILLBUILDER: Interpreting Maps
1. **PLACE** What is the capital of the Northwest Federal District?
2. **LOCATION** Approximately how many miles separate Moscow and Khabarovsk?

Instruct: Objective 2

Obstacles to Economic Reform

- Why has Russia's size made it difficult to implement economic reforms? *(Emboldened by their distance from Moscow, some regional leaders have chosen to ignore government reforms.)*
- What step did Russian President Vladimir Putin take to gain more control over regional leaders? *(He created large federal districts with governors-general responsible to Moscow.)*
- How has the growth of organized crime slowed economic reform in Russia? *(by making illegal activity more lucrative than honest business and reducing government tax revenues)*

RUSSIA & REP.

Interpreting Maps

Federal District of Russia

Ask students what pattern they see in the size of the federal districts in Russia moving from west to east. Have students explain a possible reason for this pattern. *(The districts increase in size from west to east. This pattern reflects the fact that the western part of Russia is more densely populated than the eastern part.)*

SKILLBUILDER ANSWERS
1. St. Petersburg **2.** about 4,000 miles

ACTIVITY OPTION **SKILLBUILDER**

MAKING DECISIONS

Explaining the Skill Point out that every decision has consequences, some of which are positive and some negative. In this activity, students will chart the pros and cons of two courses of action and decide which one they favor.

Applying the Skill Tell students that Russian leaders had a choice to make in moving from a command to a market economy. They could make the change gradually over a number of years, or as rapidly as within a year. Ask students to work in small groups to make a chart like the one shown, listing the pros and cons of the two choices.

CHOICES	PROS	CONS
Rapid change to market economy	Faster influx of much-needed hard currency	
Gradual change to market economy	more time to establish new economic and legal institutions	

In-Depth Resources: Unit 5
• Skillbuilder Practice, p. 26

Interpreting Photographs

Russian Crime

Point out to students that photos of Russian police operations often hide the faces of officers. Ask students why this might be so. *(Showing the faces of officers might allow organized criminals to identify the officers and put them in danger.)*

CAPTION ANSWER It makes it even more difficult for Russian officials to carry our economic reforms.

Assess & Reteach

GeoFocus Have students complete the section on economic issues in their cause-and-effect charts.

Formal Assessment
- Section Quiz, p. 257

Reteaching Activity
Have students use their GeoFocus notes to write a summary of the economic problems that Russia faces.

In-Depth Resources: Unit 5
- Reteaching Activity, p. 33

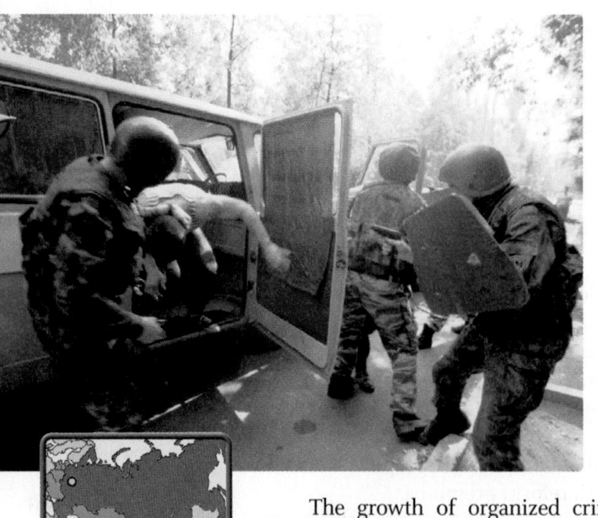

PLACE Officers from a special police force in Moscow arrest a suspected mafia car thief in August 1997. **Why might organized crime present a special problem for the Russian government?**

ORGANIZED CRIME As the government tries to improve the economy, it must also face a powerful enemy—organized crime. The "Russian mafia," as criminal organizations in the republic are sometimes labeled, grew rapidly during the 1990s.

By the end of the decade, the mafia had created its own economy. In 1998, the government estimated that organized criminals controlled 40 percent of private companies and 60 percent of state-owned enterprises. Russian criminal activity also expanded outside of Russia. The mafia even tried to sell a Russian submarine to drug barons in Colombia.

The growth of organized crime has slowed economic reform by rewarding illegal activity over honest business. And because illegal activities often go undetected, the government cannot collect taxes on them. Russian officials have taken initiatives to combat organized crime, including the addition of more officers to a special tax police.

FUTURE PROSPECTS In 2001, Russia's prime minister reported increases in revenues. However, the global economic crisis of 2008 struck Russia hard, and unemployment increased dramatically. By 2010, the situation had improved somewhat.

Russia's political future is also cause for concern. President Putin had tightened control of Russians' freedoms. In 2008 Dmitry Medvedev was elected president of Russia, but Putin was named prime minister. As a result, many people—Russians and Westerners—worried that Putin's repressive policies would continue.

Section 2 Assessment

1 Places & Terms
Explain the importance of each of the following terms.
- privatization
- distance decay

2 Taking Notes
REGION Review the notes you took for this section.

	Causes	Effects
Issue 2: Economy		

- Why did the Russian government issue vouchers in 1992?
- What impact might organized crime have on government revenue?

3 Main Ideas
a. What is one of the toughest issues facing Russia's economic reformers?
b. How has Russia moved toward a capitalist system?
c. What are some of the obstacles to economic reform?

4 Geographic Thinking
Drawing Conclusions Why did President Putin establish seven new federal districts in Russia? **Think about:**
- the number of its regional governments
- Russia's size

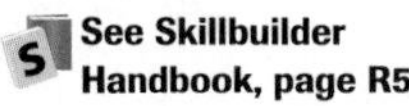
See Skillbuilder Handbook, page R5.

SEEING PATTERNS Do research on a U.S. company doing business in Russia. Create a set of **guidelines** that the company might follow in conducting business in Russia.

SECTION 2 ASSESSMENT ANSWERS

1. **Places & Terms**
privatization, p. 388 distance decay, p. 389
2. **Taking Notes**
- to help Russian citizens purchase government-owned businesses during the privatization process
- The government receives no tax revenues from criminal activities because they are illegal and usually go undetected.
3. **Main Ideas**
a. how to carry out economic reforms without causing too much turmoil for Russia's citizens
b. by loosening its tight control over the economy; by ending price controls and initiating privatization programs.
c. distance decay and organized crime
4. **Geographic Thinking**
Putin may have believed that he would be better able to maintain control over Russia with seven district governors overseeing the 89 regional governments, some of which are thousands of miles from Moscow.

GeoActivity

Integrated Assessment
- Rubric for guidelines, 4.11

Map and Graph Skills

Reading Line and Pie Graphs

Russia's economy has changed dramatically since the fall of the Soviet Union. To keep track of these changes and plan for the future, economists gather statistics. Presenting statistical data visually in graph form makes the data easier to read.

THE LANGUAGE OF GRAPHS **Line graphs** show the relation between two variables. The line graph below shows changes in Russia's unemployment rate. The vertical axis lists rates of unemployment. The horizontal axis shows the passage of time.

Pie graphs use percentages to show the relationship of parts to a whole. The pie represents the whole, and each slice of the pie represents a part. The pie graph below shows the distribution of income in Russia.

Economic Conditions in Russia

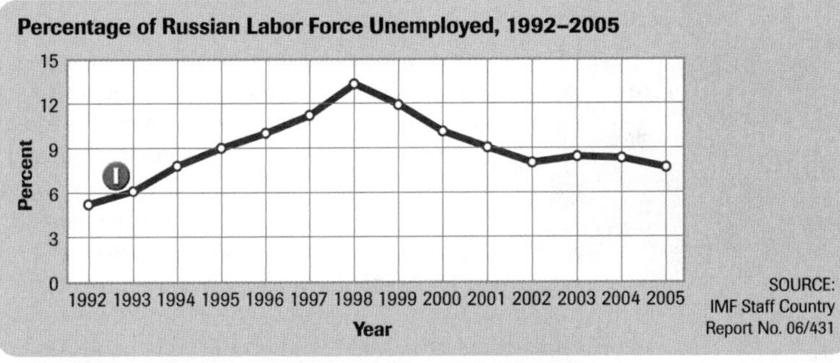

1 After the Soviet Union and its command economy collapsed in 1991, Russia became a separate republic. As it struggled to reform its economy, the rate of unemployment began to rise.

2 In 2009, only 18.5 percent of Russia's population earned more than $9600 per year.

3 The color key shows the income ranges that correspond to the different slices of the pie graph.

Map and Graph Skills Assessment

1. Seeing Patterns
What was the trend in Russia's unemployment rate after 1992? When did it begin to change?

2. Analyzing Data
What was Russia's unemployment rate in 1995?

3. Analyzing Data
About how much did the largest percentage of Russians earn in 2009?

OBJECTIVE

Understand and interpret line and pie graphs.

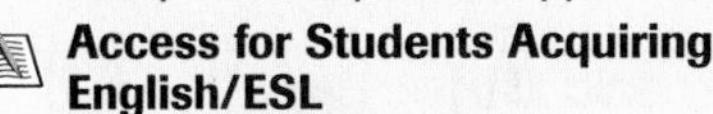

Reading Line and Pie Graphs

- Why might the presentation of statistical data in graph form be useful? *(It makes data easy to read and interpret.)*
- What is the purpose of line graphs? *(to show the relation between two variables)*
- How do pie graphs represent data? *(The pie represents the whole, and each wedge represents a part of the whole.)*

In-Depth Resources: Unit 5
- Map and Graph Skills, pp. 24–25

Access for Students Acquiring English/ESL
- Map and Graph Skills, pp. 91–92

More About

Poverty in Russia

In 1999, Russian officials estimated that a Russian citizen needed to earn at least $330 per year in order to be able to afford an adequate amount of food. Ask students if they think that figure has gone up or down since 1999. *(Answers will vary. Students might suggest that crime has driven up prices, so the figure would be higher today.)*

SKILLS ASSESSMENT ANSWERS

1. rising; 1998

2. 9 percent

3. $5761-$9600

CASE STUDY OBJECTIVES

1. Describe the concerns of world leaders about the fate of Soviet nuclear weapons.
2. Understand the consequences of the Soviet nuclear legacy.
3. Prepare a damage assessment on the region's nuclear situation.
4. Analyze primary sources on the Soviet's nuclear legacy.

SKILLBUILDER: Interpreting Maps, p. 392

Focus & Motivate

What problems with Soviet nuclear power have you learned about so far? *(the Chernobyl explosion and nuclear testing in Central Asia)*

Instruct: Objective 1

An Unwelcome Legacy

- What were the concerns of world leaders about nuclear weapons when the Soviet Union broke apart? *(location and control of weapons; fate of the nuclear scientists)*
- What fears did world leaders have about the region's nuclear reactors? *(They feared another disaster like Chernobyl, because many of the region's reactors were dangerous.)*

In-Depth Resources: Unit 5
- Guided Reading, p. 23

Critical Thinking Transparencies CT49
- Major Producers of Nuclear Power, 1999

Map Transparencies MT30
- Disaster at Chernobyl

SKILLBUILDER ANSWER
1. 2 **2.** because of the four reactors in nearby St. Petersburg

CASESTUDY

THE SOVIET UNION'S NUCLEAR LEGACY
How have Soviet decisions affected new leaders?

In 1988, Russia destroyed its SS-12 missles, in accordance with the terms of a 1987 treaty between the U.S. and the USSR.

As you have read, the breakup of the Soviet Union sparked regional conflicts and economic hardship. Equally serious were the problems caused by the Soviet Union's nuclear programs. These included nuclear warheads atop ballistic missiles, poorly constructed and maintained nuclear power stations, and decaying nuclear waste dumps. All threatened the region's people and environment.

An Unwelcome Legacy

When the USSR fell apart in the early 1990s, leaders around the world had serious concerns about the fate of the region's nuclear weapons. The Soviet Union, which had once controlled those weapons, was now separated into 15 independent republics. World leaders wanted to know who was in control of the weapons, where they were located, and how well they were protected. They also wondered what would become of the nuclear scientists who had worked on the weapons systems.

The weapons industry was just part of the problem. As the 1986 disaster at Chernobyl had so clearly shown, many of the region's nuclear reactors were badly built and poorly managed. Many reactors of the same design as the one that exploded at Chernobyl still exist. Observers fear another disaster may occur in the region.

Selected Nuclear Reactors in Former Soviet Republics

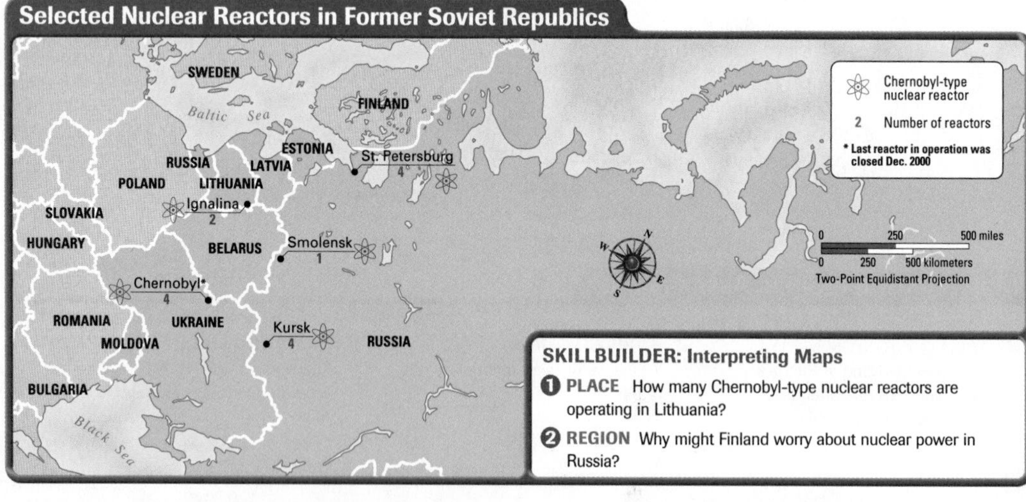

SKILLBUILDER: Interpreting Maps
1. **PLACE** How many Chernobyl-type nuclear reactors are operating in Lithuania?
2. **REGION** Why might Finland worry about nuclear power in Russia?

CASE STUDY PROGRAM RESOURCES

In-Depth Resources: Unit 5
- Guided Reading, p. 23
- Building Vocabulary, p. 27
- Reteaching Activity, p. 34

Guided Reading Workbook
- Case Study

Access for Students Acquiring English/ESL
- Guided Reading, p. 89

Formal Assessment
- Case Study Quiz, p. 258

INTEGRATED TECHNOLOGY

Critical Thinking Transparencies CT49
- Major Producers of Nuclear Power, 1999

Map Transparencies MT30
- Disaster at Chernobyl

hmhsocialstudies.com

TEST-TAKING RESOURCES

Strategies for Test Preparation

Test Practice Transparencies TT56

Online Test Practice

392 CHAPTER 17

The Consequences of Collapse

The nuclear legacy of the USSR has had serious political, economic, and environmental consequences.

POLITICAL TENSIONS When the communist government could no longer keep the USSR together, the security of the region's nuclear materials became uncertain. This has caused political tension between the region's leaders and other nations, especially the United States.

In January 2000, a task force of former U.S. officials issued a report that suggested just how important the issue is. The report said that the possibility of Russian nuclear materials being stolen or misused is "the most urgent unmet national security threat" facing the United States. The task force recommended a $30 billion program to help ensure the safety of Russia's nuclear weapons.

SEE PRIMARY SOURCE C

ECONOMIC HEALTH The Soviet Union's nuclear legacy also affects the economic health of Russia and the former Soviet Republics. For example, many regional leaders have been reluctant to shut down aging Soviet reactors because of the expense of building new plants that run on other kinds of fuel, such as natural gas.

Some republics have taken questionable steps to revive their economies. For instance, Russian lawmakers recently approved plans to make their country the world's nuclear dump. In January 2001, the Duma, or legislature, gave preliminary approval to a plan to import, store, and treat nuclear waste from other countries. Officials hope the project will earn Russia as much as $21 billion over the next ten years.

ENVIRONMENTAL PROSPECTS Plans for the disposal of other nations' nuclear waste angered Russian environmentalists. But other developments have given some hope that the region's environmental prospects might improve. In December 2000, the government of Ukraine finally shut down the last active reactor at Chernobyl. Officials there pledged to spend millions of dollars on a new protective dome for the site.

Help has also come from overseas. In October 2000, a U.S.-funded treatment plant opened near the White Sea. The 17-million-dollar facility will treat radioactive waste from Russia's fleet of nuclear submarines—waste that used to be dumped in the sea.

SEE PRIMARY SOURCE E

You will learn more about these developments as you examine the primary sources and complete the Case Study Project on the following pages.

PLACE A Ukrainian official examines a nuclear missile just before it is to be dismantled as part of a U.S.-sponsored program.
Why would the United States sponsor this program in Ukraine?

Instruct: Objective 2

The Consequences of Collapse

- Why has the questionable security of the region's nuclear materials caused political tension between the United States and the region's leaders? *(U.S. leaders fear the possibility of the nuclear materials being stolen or misused)*
- What are some of the economic issues surrounding the Soviet nuclear legacy? *(Regional leaders are reluctant to shut down aging Soviet reactors because of the cost of alternative energy sources.)*
- What corrective steps have been taken to address one area of nuclear contamination? *(Ukraine shut down the last active reactor at Chernobyl and plans to build a new protective dome.)*

Interpreting Photographs

Ukrainian Nuclear Missiles

After the breakup of the Soviet Union, four nations, rather than one, had control of nuclear weapons: Russia, Ukraine, Belarus, and Kazakhstan. Before surrendering their nuclear missiles, Ukrainian officials wanted guarantees that their independence would be secure. Ask students why the Ukraine might be concerned about its security. *(It is a small nation that was under Russia's control for a long time.)*

CAPTION ANSWER Students might note that the U.S. should be concerned about the location of nuclear weapons in a region still struggling to achieve stability.

ACTIVITY OPTION | INTERNET RESEARCH

BLOCK SCHEDULING

RESEARCHING NUCLEAR WASTE

Objective To find out why the disposal of nuclear waste is such a difficult problem

Class Time 30 minutes

Task Use the Internet to investigate the problem of nuclear waste disposal and give an oral report

Directions Have students use the key words *nuclear waste disposal* to find web sites explaining why the disposal of nuclear wastes is such a difficult problem. Ask students to share what they find in a brief oral report. Updated links on this topic are also available through **hmhsocialstudies.com.**

OPTIONAL ACTIVITY If Internet access is limited, direct students to use such library resources as science reference books and periodicals to research the topic.

Instruct: Objective 3

Case Study Project: Damage Assessment Report

- What basic information should a damage assessment report contain? *(causes, effects, and steps being taken to solve problems)*
- What kinds of information are used to enliven a damage assessment report? *(interesting statistics, compelling stories, and first-person accounts)*
- What do you need to add visual interest to the assessment? *(maps, charts, graphs, and photos)*

Instruct: Objective 4

Using Primary Sources

- Ⓐ **Photograph** What does the photograph convey about Russia's use of nuclear weapons in the past? *(It shows that Russia was capable of using these weapons irresponsibly—to create a reservoir, for example.)*
- Ⓑ **Photograph** What does this recent photograph reveal about Russia's nuclear program? *(Russia is still a nuclear power.)*
- Ⓒ **Editorial Commentary** What is the viewpoint of the author of this editorial? *(The United States should spend money to eliminate the risks from Russia's nuclear weapons before they are sold to potential aggressors.)*
- Do you agree with this viewpoint? *(Some students may agree that the money would be well spent. Others may think that other countries should share the costs.)*

CASESTUDY

PROJECT

Damage Assessment Report

Primary sources A to E on these two pages offer different views of the Soviet Union's nuclear legacy. Use these resources and your own research to prepare a damage assessment report of the region's nuclear situation today.

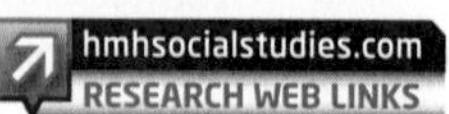

Suggested Steps

1. Choose a nuclear threat to investigate and examine its political, economic, and environmental consequences.
2. Use online and print resources to research your topic.
3. Be sure your damage assessment includes both causes and effects. Also, explain the steps being taken by regional officials to address the problems.
4. Search for interesting statistics, compelling stories, and first-person accounts to enliven your assessment.
5. Provide maps, charts, graphs, and photos to add visual interest to the assessment.
6. Prepare a brief oral introduction that introduces and explains your topic.

Materials and Supplies

- posterboard
- colored markers
- computer with Internet access
- reference books, newspapers, and magazines
- printer

PRIMARY SOURCE Ⓐ

Photograph *In 1965, Soviet officials used a nuclear bomb to create this reservoir in Semey, Kazakhstan.*

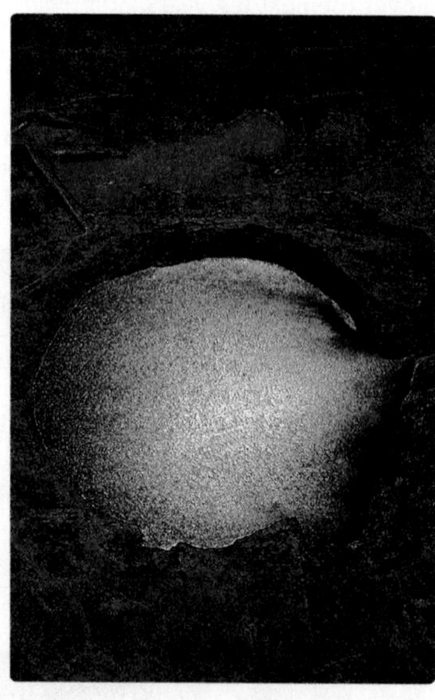

PRIMARY SOURCE Ⓑ

Photograph *Scientists and technicians pass through a checkpoint at Moscow's Kurchatov Institute, Russia's leading nuclear research center.*

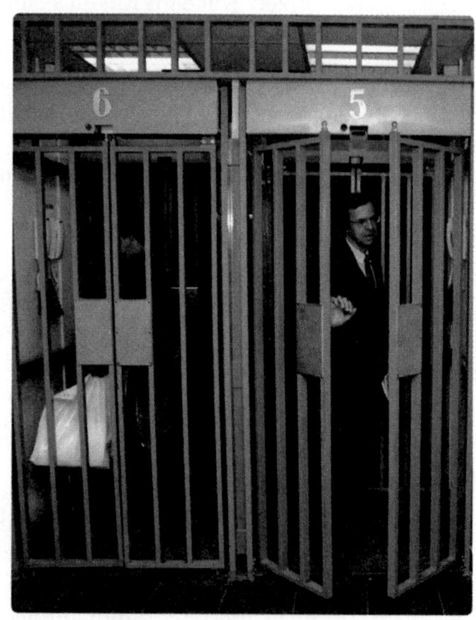

DIFFERENTIATING INSTRUCTION **LESS PROFICIENT READERS**

REREADING FOR MAIN IDEAS

Objective To encourage less proficient readers to read informative articles twice

Class Time 20 minutes

Task Read an editorial once to learn the subject and then reread it to identify main ideas

Directions Tell students that a good strategy for reading informative articles is to read or skim them first to gain an idea of the subject, and then to reread them to identify the main ideas. To have students practice this strategy, ask them to read the editorial commentary at the top of page 395 once and then tell what the subject of the editorial is. *(the danger posed by Russia's inadequately secured nuclear weapons)* Then ask them to reread this article and identify the main ideas. *(The United States no longer has to fear a nuclear attack from Russia. But Russia's nuclear bombs and other weapons are inadequately guarded by poorly paid workers, who could sell out to enemies. Enemies could also recruit unemployed nuclear scientists. The United States should spend money to eliminate this risk.)*

PRIMARY SOURCE C

Editorial Commentary *On January 21, 1999, the* New York Times *offered its comments on Russia's nuclear legacy.*

There is no longer any threat of Russia's deliberately attacking the United States. But Moscow's still-formidable stocks of nuclear bombs, nuclear ingredients, and biological and chemical warfare agents pose a different kind of danger. Much of this material is inadequately secured, and the workers guarding it are paid poorly or not at all. That creates an unacceptably high risk that some material could be sold to potential aggressors like Iraq, Libya, North Korea, or Serbia. Many Russian weapons scientists are also unemployed or unpaid and vulnerable to foreign recruitment.

During the Cold War, the United States spent trillions of dollars to deter Russia from using its nuclear, biological, and chemical weapons. It would not take much more than $10 billion to eliminate most of the risks from those weapons today.

PRIMARY SOURCE E

News Report *In his dispatch of September 30, 1997,* London Daily Telegraph *reporter Christopher Lockwood relates yet another terrible tale from Russia's nuclear legacy of an environmental disaster waiting to happen.*

Nothing on the outside indicates what lies within the retired Russian supply ship *Lepse* except the presence of a Kalashnikov-armed guard and the fact that the vessel is moored at the farthest possible point of the Atomplot shipyard in Murmansk.

In fact, *Lepse* may well be the most terrifying vessel on Earth, loaded with a deadly cargo of warped nuclear-reactor parts and spent fuel rods that would be sufficient to poison the world's population. . . .

For the past six years, Norway and Finland have been negotiating with Russia in an attempt to clear up the mess left by Russia's Northern Fleet, which had its headquarters in Severomorsk, near Murmansk. About 200 disused nuclear reactors and tens of thousands of fuel rods are haphazardly stored at its bases around Murmansk, in the Kola Peninsula.

"If there is a catastrophe in the Kola Peninsula, it can affect the whole of Europe's climate, perhaps for hundreds of years," said Norwegian Defense Minister Joergen Kosmo.

PRIMARY SOURCE D

News Report *On December 15, 2000, 14 years and 7 months after the reactor explosion at Chernobyl, Ukraine's president ordered the plant closed. The excerpt below, written by* New York Times *reporter Michael Wines, outlines the economic impact that the shutdown will have.*

The closing of Unit 3 [the plant's last working reactor] will cut off 5 percent of the electricity supply in a nation already deeply in [debt] to Russia for natural gas and dogged by shortages in its shoddily run power grid.

The closing will also gradually eliminate jobs of thousands of Ukrainians whose work depends, directly or indirectly, on Chernobyl's continued operation as a power plant. Beyond the layoffs at the plant itself, thousands of Ukrainians provide goods or services to Chernobyl workers.

Ukraine also faces immense costs in the future—$750 million to cover the disaster site with a new [protective dome], hundreds of additional millions of dollars to remove 180 tons of lethal melted fuel and steel from the damaged core of Unit 4 and to store it safely, millions to build a new heating system and other necessities for the crews that will permanently care for the idle reactor site and millions for solid and liquid waste-processing plants to handle the fuel from the closing of Unit 3.

PROJECT CheckList

Have I . . .

- ✓ fully researched my topic?
- ✓ balanced my report by discussing both sides of the issue?
- ✓ created informative visuals that make my report clear and interesting?
- ✓ practiced explaining my report?
- ✓ anticipated questions others might ask and prepared answers?

Instruct: Objective

Using Primary Sources

- Ⓓ **News Report** What are some of the economic costs associated with the closing of the nuclear power plant at Chernobyl? *(Thousands of workers will lose their jobs, and thousands of others will lose business.)*
- Do you think the costs are worth the benefits? Why or why not? *(Most students will probably think the costs are necessary because the risk to people's health is so great.)*
- Ⓔ **News Report** What nuclear hazard does this news article describe? *(poorly stored nuclear wastes from Russia's Northern Fleet in the Kola Peninsula)*
- What countries are especially concerned about this situation? Why? *(Norway and Finland, because they are located near the site)*
- What other countries should be concerned? Why? *(All countries of the world, because there are enough nuclear wastes to poison the entire world's population)*

Assess & Reteach

GeoFocus Have students complete the cause-and-effect chart they started at the beginning of the chapter.

Formal Assessment
- Case Study Quiz, p. 258

Reteaching Activity

Lead the class in summarizing this case study by making a list on the board of problems that the region faces as a result of the Soviet Union's nuclear programs.

In-Depth Resources: Unit 5
- Reteaching Activity, p. 34

RUBRIC CASE STUDY PROJECT

DAMAGE ASSESSMENT REPORT

The report should:

- clearly explain the causes and effects of the problem
- describe steps that are or can be taken to solve the problem
- include interesting statistics, a story, or a first-person account to engage the reader
- contain informative, visually appealing graphics

Grading Rubric Evaluate student performance as Exceptional, Acceptable, or Poor in each of the following categories:

	Exceptional	Acceptable	Poor
Focus and purpose of the report are clearly stated			
Includes personal accounts to engage the reader			
Contains an attractive visual complement			
Uses correct grammar, spelling, and punctuation			

Reviewing Places & Terms

A. **1.** Caucasus, p. 385
2. Chechnya, p. 386
3. Nagorno-Karabakh, p. 386
4. privatization, p. 388
5. distance decay, p. 389

B. Possible Responses
6. Chechnya is in Russia.
7. Nagorno-Karabakh is claimed by Armenia and Azerbaijan.
8. Privatization is one step a nation could take to move from a command economy to a market economy.
9. Caucasia is also known as the Caucasus.
10. Distance decay describes this decreasing interaction.

Chapter 17 Assessment

VISUAL SUMMARY

TODAY'S ISSUES IN RUSSIA AND THE REPUBLICS

Conflict

Regional Conflict

- Since the fall of the Soviet Union in 1991, a number of ethnic and religious groups have sought more control over their own affairs. Their demands have frequently led to conflict.
- Regional leaders who are trying to end these conflicts face a dilemma. How can they maintain order without resorting to the undemocratic rule of the past?

Economics

The Struggle for Economic Reform

- Another dilemma facing leaders in Russia and the former Soviet republics is how to move away from the old Soviet command economy toward a market economy.
- Leaders are struggling to make reforms without causing too much turmoil for citizens.

Government

The Soviet Union's Nuclear Legacy

- The impact of Soviet nuclear programs did not end with the fall of the Soviet Union in 1991. Russia and the Republics inherited the former state's nuclear weapons, power plants, and waste.
- This legacy has had serious political, economic, and environmental consequences.

Reviewing Places & Terms

A. Briefly explain the importance of each of the following.

1. Caucasus
2. Chechnya
3. Nagorno-Karabakh
4. privatization
5. distance decay

B. Answer the questions about vocabulary in complete sentences.

6. In which nation is Chechnya located?
7. Which region is the subject of a dispute between Armenia and Azerbaijan?
8. How might a nation move from a command economy to a market economy?
9. What is another name for Caucasia?
10. What is the name for the decreasing interaction between places as the distance between them increases?

Main Ideas

Regional Conflict (pp. 385–387)

1. What is the connection between the fall of the Soviet Union and the outbreak of ethnic conflicts in Russia and the Republics?
2. Why might ethnic tensions in the Caucasus be stronger than in other regions?
3. In the Russian part of Caucasia, where has the most serious conflict taken place?

The Struggle for Economic Reform (pp. 388–391)

4. What has been one of the major goals of Russian economic reformers?
5. How have reformers moved Russia toward a market economy?
6. What are some of the problems faced by economic reformers?

Case Study: The Soviet Union's Nuclear Legacy (pp. 392–395)

7. Why were world leaders concerned about the security of nuclear weapons in Russia and the Republics after 1991?
8. What other aspect of the Soviet nuclear legacy concerned observers?
9. How has the United States assisted Russia in dealing with the nuclear legacy of the Soviet Union?
10. How are the nuclear policies of Russia related to its economic problems?

Main Ideas

1. Ethnic groups have taken advantage of weakening central authority to seek more autonomy in the region.
2. because there are about 50 different ethnic groups in a region the size of California
3. the Republic of Chechnya
4. to move Russia from a command economy to a market economy
5. by ending the tight control of economic activity held by the central government
6. making reforms without causing too much turmoil for the country's citizens, distance decay, organized crime
7. because the nation that had once controlled those weapons had separated into 15 independent republics, leaving the security of the weapons in question
8. The safety of the region's nuclear reactors was also a concern, especially in light of the 1986 disaster at Chernobyl.
9. by funding a nuclear waste treatment plant near the White Sea, for example
10. Regional leaders have been reluctant to shut down aging reactors, for example, because they consider the alternative forms of energy generation to be too expensive.

Critical Thinking

1. Using Your Notes

Use your completed chart to answer these questions.

	Causes	*Effects*
Issue 1: Conflict		
Issue 2: Economy		

a. What caused several ethnic groups in the Caucasus to believe they might successfully demand independence in the 1990s?

b. What is the intended effect of Russia's new federal districts?

2. Geographic Themes

REGION Why did the division of the USSR into 15 independent republics concern observers of the region's nuclear programs?

3. Identifying Themes

Why did the United States fund a nuclear waste treatment plant near the White Sea? Which of the five themes applies to this situation?

4. Making Inferences

Why might Russian economic reformers worry about causing too much hardship for citizens?

5. Drawing Conclusions

Why do you think Russian legislators want to import, store, and treat nuclear waste from other countries in spite of the environmental risks involved?

For Additional Test Practice

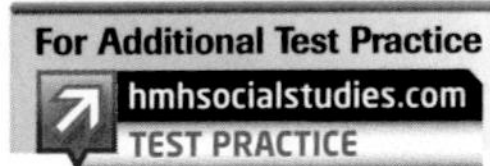

Geographic Skills: Interpreting Graphs

Global Male Life Expectancy

Use the graph to answer the following questions.

1. PLACE How does male life expectancy in Russia differ from world trends?
2. PLACE What was the life expectancy of Russian men in 1990? In 2000?
3. PLACE What might account for the dip in life expectancy for Russian men?

Create another line graph that shows how the population of Russia changed during the same period of time.

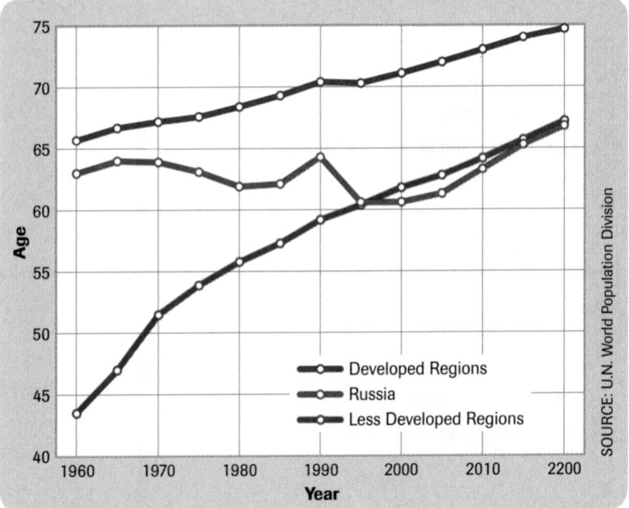

hmhsocialstudies.com

MULTIMEDIA ACTIVITY

Use the links at **hmhsocialstudies.com** to do research on current economic conditions in Russia. Compare the statistics you find on the Russian economy, such as inflation and poverty rates, with statistics on the U.S. economy.

Creating a Multimedia Presentation Create a multimedia presentation of your findings. Include maps and graphs that visually present the information that you discovered.

21st CENTURY

CHAPTER 17 ASSESSMENT

Critical Thinking

1. a. the breakup of the Soviet Union and the weakening of central authority
b. to increase central authority and secure the cooperation of regional governments

2. It was uncertain what effect the breakup would have on the control and security of the region's nuclear weapons.

3. to assist Russia in treating radioactive waste from its fleet of nuclear submarines—waste formerly dumped into the sea; human-environment interaction

4. Answers will vary, but students might suggest that if reformers create too much financial hardship, the Russian people might revolt against the government.

5. Their goal is to earn money, which will help Russia in its struggle for economic stability.

RUSSIA & REP.

GeoActivity

Integrated Assessment
- Rubric for a line graph, 2.3

Formal Assessment
- Chapter Tests, Forms A, B, and C, pp. 259–273

Geographic Skills

1. There is a large dip in life expectancy beginning around the 1990s.

2. about 64; about 61

3. the fall of the Soviet Union in 1991 and the resulting economic hardship

MULTIMEDIA ACTIVITY

For their multimedia presentation on the Russian economy, students should:

- Present a concise, well-organized presentation.
- Make sure that comparisons covers comparable data and time periods.
- Include imaginative visual complements in the presentation.
- Include references to the Web sites used as sources.

Grading Rubric Evaluate student performance as Exceptional, Acceptable, or Poor in each of the following categories:

	Exceptional	*Acceptable*	*Poor*
Focus and purpose of comparisons are clearly stated			
Includes comparative charts, graphs, and maps			
Data and information are easy to read and interpret			
Uses correct grammar, spelling, and punctuation			

Physical Geography of Africa

OVERVIEW	INSTRUCTIONAL RESOURCES	
CHAPTER 18 ESSENTIAL QUESTION How has the physical geography of Africa affected the lives of the continent's people? **Focus on the Essential Question Podcast**	**In-Depth Resources: Unit 6** • Unit Atlas Activities, p. 1 • Building Vocabulary, p. 9 • Exploring Today's Issues, pp. 32–35 **Outline Maps with Activities** • Africa: Physical, pp. 51–52 • Africa: Political, pp. 53–54 **Block Schedule Strategies** **Chapter Summaries** (English/Spanish)	**Interactive Online Edition** TOS **ExamView® Assessment Suite** (English/Spanish) TOS **CalendarPlanner** **Power Presentations with Media Gallery** **Critical Thinking Transparencies** • CT18 **Video:** Dams hmhsocialstudies.com INTERACTIVE
SECTION 1 **LANDFORMS AND RESOURCES** **MAIN IDEAS** • Much of Africa consists of a huge plateau. • Distinctive African landforms include rift valleys and the Great Escarpment. • Africa has abundant natural resources, such as minerals and oil.	**In-Depth Resources: Unit 6** • Guided Reading, p. 3 • Building Vocabulary, p. 9 • Reteaching Activities, p. 10 • Map and Graph Skill, pp. 6–7 **Guided Reading Workbook,** Section 1	**Critical Thinking Transparencies** • CT50 Gold Production in Selected Countries, 1989–1999
SECTION 2 **CLIMATE AND VEGETATION** **MAIN IDEAS** • Africa is home to the Sahara, the largest desert in the world. • Nearly 90 percent of Africa lies within the tropics. • Along the equator is rain forest. To the north and south of the rain forest lie grasslands.	**In-Depth Resources: Unit 6** • Guided Reading, p. 4 • Building Vocabulary, p. 9 • Reteaching Activities, p. 11 **Guided Reading Workbook,** Section 2	
SECTION 3 **HUMAN-ENVIRONMENT INTERACTION** **MAIN IDEAS** • The desert is spreading into the Sahel, a band of grassland that lies along the edge of the Sahara. • The oil industry has damaged the environment in Nigeria. • The Aswan High Dam has helped to control flooding of the Nile but has created some problems.	**In-Depth Resources: Unit 6** • Guided Reading, p. 5 • Skillbuilder Practice, p. 8 • Building Vocabulary, p. 9 • Reteaching Activities, p. 12 **Guided Reading Workbook,** Section 3	

ASSESSMENT

SE **Chapter Assessment,** pp. 428–429

Formal Assessment
- Chapter Tests, Forms A, B, and C, pp. 277–288

TOS **ExamView® Assessment Suite**

Strategies for Test Preparation

hmhsocialstudies.com TEST PRACTICE

SE **Section Assessment,** p. 418

 **Formal Assessment**
- Section Quiz, p. 274

 **Integrated Assessment**
- Rubric for a Venn diagram, 2.8 

 **Test Practice Transparencies** TT57

SE **Section Assessment,** p. 423

 **Formal Assessment**
- Section Quiz, p. 275

 **Integrated Assessment**
- Rubric for a chart, 2.2 

 **Test Practice Transparencies** TT58

SE **Section Assessment,** p. 427

 **Formal Assessment**
- Section Quiz, p. 276

 **Integrated Assessment**
- Rubric for a cause-and-effect chart, 2.2 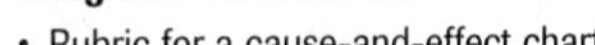

 **Test Practice Transparencies** TT59

CHART KEY:

SE Student Edition	 Block Scheduling	 DVD/CD-ROM
TE Teacher's Edition	 TOS Teacher One Stop	 MP3 Audio
 Printable Resource	 Presentation Resource	 HISTORY™

Program Resources available on TOS and @  hmhsocialstudies.com

SUPPORTING RESOURCES

- **Multimedia Classroom Global History Series**
- **Global History Teacher's Guide**

Social Studies Trade Library Collection
- World Regions Trade Collection

For more information or to purchase these resources, go to  hmhsocialstudies.com

DIFFERENTIATED INSTRUCTION

English Learners	Struggling Readers	Gifted and Talented Students
 **Spanish/English Guided Reading Workbook**  **Access for Students Acquiring English/ESL** Spanish Translations, pp. 93–98  **Chapter Summaries** (English/Spanish) TE **TE Activity** Understanding Geographic Terms, p. 416	**Chapter Summaries** (English/Spanish) TE **TE Activity** Understanding Important Facts, p. 417	TE **TE Activity** Writing a Position Paper, p. 426

ENRICHMENT ACTIVITIES

The following activities are especially suitable for classes following block schedules.

SE **Student Edition,** pp. 414–429 • Reading an Economic Activity Map, p. 419	hmhsocialstudies.com INTERACTIVE • Basins of Africa, p. 415

UNIT 6 ATLAS AND CHAPTER 18 PACING GUIDE

BLOCK SCHEDULE LESSON PLAN OPTIONS: 90-MINUTE PERIOD

DAY 1

UNIT PREVIEW, pp. 398–401
Class Time 20 minutes

- **Discussion** Discuss the Unit introduction, using the discussion prompts on TE pages 398–399.
Class Time 10 minutes

- **Today's Issues** Introduce Today's Issues in Africa using the Exploring the Issues questions on PE page 400.
Class Time 10 minutes

UNIT ATLAS, pp. 402–413
Class Time 40 minutes

- **Discussion** Select one student for each section of the Unit Atlas: Physical Geography, Human Geography, Regional Patterns, and Regional Data File. Have the students use the questions in the book to lead the class in Making Comparisons question-and-answer sessions for their assigned sections.

SECTION 1, pp. 415–419
Class Time 30 minutes

- **Outline Maps** In preparation for discussing Section 1, have students complete the physical map for Africa on pages 51–52 in *Outline Maps with Activities.* Students should label the countries and physical features such as mountains, rivers, and lakes.

DAY 2

SECTION 1, pp. 415–419
Class Time 25 minutes

- **Tour Itinerary** Have groups of students prepare an itinerary for a tour of the most important landforms and resources in Africa. The groups should share their itineraries with the class. Have the class discuss differences in the proposed tours.

SECTION 2, pp. 420–423
Class Time 40 minutes

- **Small Groups** Divide the class into groups to discuss Africa's climate and vegetation in comparison to the United States.
Class Time 15 minutes

- **Panel Discussion** Have one student from each of the groups form a panel to discuss slash-and-burn farming in terms of the need to preserve rain forests. After 15 minutes, allow the entire class to ask questions or volunteer opinions.
Class Time 25 minutes

SECTION 3, pp. 424–427
Class Time 25 minutes

- **Skillbuilder Lesson** Use the lesson about determining cause and effect on TE page 425 and the Skillbuilder Practice worksheet.
Class Time 25 minutes

DAY 3

SECTION 3, pp. 424–427
Class Time 35 minutes

- **Summary Lists** Divide the class into four groups. Two groups should discuss environmental damage in Nigeria and two should discuss the Aswan High Dam. Each group should create a list of the most important causes and effects associated with its topic. At the end of 25 minutes, have the four groups share their results with the class. Compile a summary list of all causes and effects on the board.

CHAPTER 18 REVIEW AND ASSESSMENT, pp. 428–429
Class Time 55 minutes

- **Review** Pair students. Have each pair in turn select a question from Reviewing Places & Terms or Main Ideas and ask another pair to respond.
Class Time 20 minutes

- **Assessment** Have students complete the Chapter 18 Assessment.
Class Time 35 minutes

TEACHER-TESTED ACTIVITY

Traversing Major Geographic Features of Africa

Class Time One class period

Task Use geographic skills to compare two dominant geographic features of Africa

Supplies
- Additional maps and atlases

Purpose To examine and compare the Sahara Desert and the Nile River

Activity Have groups of 3–4 students plan a trip up the Nile River or across the Sahara Desert. Help students plan their trips by suggesting things they might consider, such as distance, physical features, types of climate and vegetation, and language. Encourage students to be realistic in considering routes, methods of transportation, length of time needed for trips, difficulties that might be encountered, and the supplies they will need. As students craft their itineraries, periodically introduce "unexpected difficulties" for the groups to overcome —e.g., flooding, loss of supplies, severe sandstorms, etc. At the end of the project, groups should report to the whole class and explain their plans and contingency actions. Afterwards, lead a class discussion about the differences between the two trips.

Alice White
Geography Teacher, Bryan Adams High School, Dallas, Texas

TECHNOLOGY IN THE CLASSROOM

Computer drawing programs allow students to create original drawings and designs right on the computer. While using the mouse to draw can take some getting used to, the advantages of drawing on the computer are that it is easy to erase or change parts of the picture, the images can be saved digitally, and even students who do not think they are good at art can take advantage of stamps and other special effects offered by most drawing programs.

Objective Students will use a computer drawing program to illustrate the causes and consequences of desertification in Africa.

Task Have students research the causes and consequences of desertification in the Sahel and use the computer to draw pictures of what they have learned.

Class Time 1–2 class periods

1. Have students read pages 424–425 and look at the images of desertification. Discuss the reasons why desertification is occurring and the possible consequences of desertification.

2. Have a student point out the Sahel region on a world wall map so that everyone can locate this region of African desertification.

3. Ask students to picture what it might look like in an area that is suffering from desertification. What images come to their minds?

4. Have students read more about desertification and look at the pictures at the United Nations Secretariat of the Convention to Combat Desertification Web site listed at **hmhsocialstudies.com**. They should take notes to help answer the questions "What are some causes and consequences of desertification, and what might it look like in a region that is facing desertification?" Ask them to focus their research on desertification in the Sahel region of Africa.

5. Have students use a computer drawing program to create posters depicting causes and/or consequences of desertification in Africa. They can first look at the example at the United Nations Convention to Combat Desertification Information for Public and Media page, available at **hmhsocialstudies.com**. (They should scroll down, select "Posters," and view the poster of the man with the skulls). Their posters should employ images and colors to illustrate the idea of desertification, rather than being text-based.

6. Have students print the posters on a color printer and share them with the class. Alternately, have them display the posters from a central computer with projection device as they explain to classmates how the posters illustrate the causes or consequences of desertification.

Previewing the Unit

The first pages of this unit provide an overview of Africa, the world's second-largest continent. It contains 53 countries and many more ethnic groups. Africa's rich resources led to centuries of colonial exploitation and a legacy of problems that still plague the continent today.

Discussion Prompts

Exploring Prior Knowledge Ask students the following questions about Africa to determine their prior knowledge of the continent.

- Where is Africa situated in relation to the United States? *(east and south across the Atlantic Ocean)*
- What major desert is found in Africa? *(Sahara)*

Interpreting Maps Ask students to refer to the satellite image of Africa to answer the following questions:

- Does the image provide an indication of the continent's size? *(It appears vast compared to Europe.)*
- What does the image indicate about Africa's nearness to other continents? *(Most of Africa is distant from other continents.)*

Unit 6

Africa

PREVIEW: TODAY'S ISSUES IN AFRICA

UNIT ATLAS

Chapter 18 PHYSICAL GEOGRAPHY **The Plateau Continent**

Chapter 19 HUMAN GEOGRAPHY **From Human Beginnings to New Nations**

Chapter 20 TODAY'S ISSUES **Africa**

CASE STUDY EFFECTS OF COLONIALISM

Africa is the world's second largest continent. Its unique location—almost centered over the equator—affects its vegetation, climate, and population patterns.

LOCATION A man prays in front of the pyramids at Giza in Egypt.

MOVEMENT People travel to a market outside of Mali's Great Mosque in Djenné. The mosque is one of the world's largest mud-brick buildings.

UNIT 6 ADDITIONAL RESOURCES

BOOKS FOR THE TEACHER

Dowden, Richard. ***Africa: Altered States, Ordinary Miracles.*** PublicAffairs, 2010. A sweeping portrait of sub-Saharan Africa.

BOOKS FOR THE STUDENT

Haley, Alex. ***Roots.*** NY: Doubleday, 1976. Fictionalized history based on the author's search for his African ancestors.

Murray, Jocelyn, ed. ***Cultural Atlas of Africa.*** Rev. ed. NY: Checkmark, 1998. Valuable resource for history, ethnography, and geography of Africa.

VIDEOS

Wonders of the African World with Henry Louis Gates, Jr. PBS Home Video, 1999. The acclaimed historian leads viewers on a six-hour journey through Africa's past and present.

INTERNET

For more on Africa, visit . . .

hmhsocialstudies.com

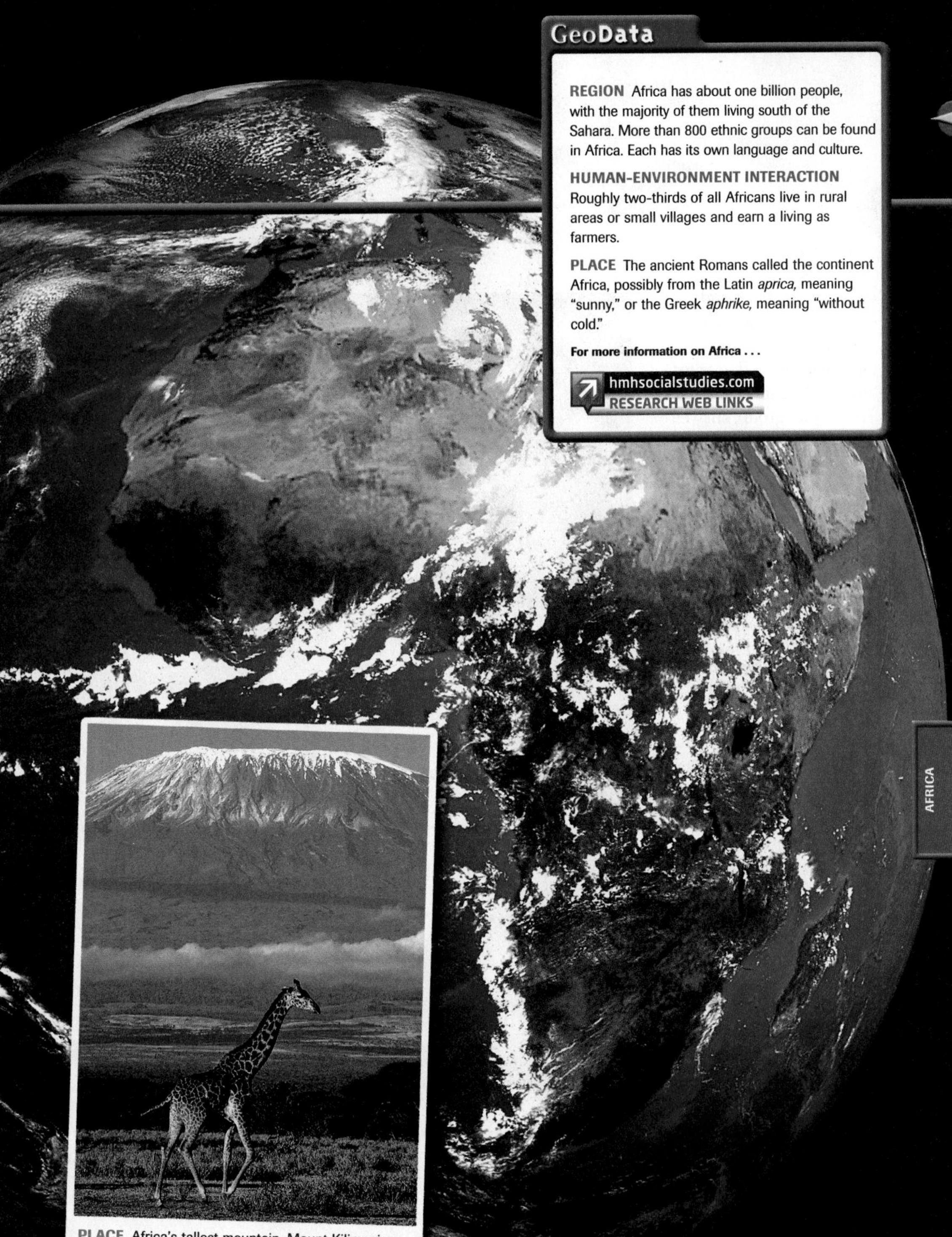

GeoData

REGION Africa has about one billion people, with the majority of them living south of the Sahara. More than 800 ethnic groups can be found in Africa. Each has its own language and culture.

HUMAN-ENVIRONMENT INTERACTION Roughly two-thirds of all Africans live in rural areas or small villages and earn a living as farmers.

PLACE The ancient Romans called the continent Africa, possibly from the Latin *aprica,* meaning "sunny," or the Greek *aphrike,* meaning "without cold."

For more information on Africa . . .

hmhsocialstudies.com
RESEARCH WEB LINKS

PLACE Africa's tallest mountain, Mount Kilimanjaro, towers above northeastern Tanzania as a giraffe roams the grassy plain below.

399

Interpreting Photographs

Pyramids at Giza, Egypt

The great pyramids were built in the 26th century B.C. They stand less than ten miles west of Giza, a suburb of the modern city of Cairo. Ask students what they can infer about the duration of civilization in the area. *(People have lived there since ancient times.)*

Market and Great Mosque in Djenné, Mali

Founded in the 13th century, Djenné became an early center for the gold trade and for Muslim learning. Ask students what the photograph shows about the way that Djenné's inhabitants adapted to their environment. *(They built with mud rather than wood or stone, which were scarce.)*

Mount Kilimanjaro in Tanzania

Kilimanjaro is a large mountain mass that extends about 50 miles and contains three extinct volcanoes. The youngest and highest volcanic cone, Kibo, rises to 19,340 feet. Tell students that Kilimanjaro is located about 200 miles from the equator. Ask students to account for the presence of snow at that location. *(Kilimanjaro's high elevation creates a colder climate.)*

ACTIVITY OPTION | COOPERATIVE LEARNING

MAKING A TOURIST BROCHURE

Objective To allow students to learn more about regions of Africa

Class Time 30 minutes

Task Prepare a brochure to attract tourists

Directions Divide students into small groups and assign each group a subregion of Africa. Have them find information and photographs on the Internet or in printed sources. Have each student take on one (or more) of these tasks:

- researcher
- designer
- writer
- cartographer
- illustrator
- typist

Place finished brochures on display for comments.

Previewing Today's Issues

These pages provide a preview of issues faced by the nations of Africa today. These issues will be fully explored in Chapter 20 (pages 460-473). Use the discussion prompts that follow to determine students' prior knowledge and allow them to make comparisons to local issues.

In-Depth Resources: Unit 6
- Exploring Today's Issues, pp. 32–35

ECONOMIC DEVELOPMENT
As a result of past exploitation, many African countries today rely mainly on the export of raw materials. They lack infrastructures and diversified economies.

Discussion Prompts

- Why were European colonizers interested in Africa? *(Students may say slaves, diamonds, gold.)*
- What raw materials does the United States import from Africa? *(Students may say oil, or agricultural products like coffee.)*

Today's Issues in Africa

Africa faces the issues previewed here. As you read Chapters 18 and 19, you will learn background information. You will study the issues themselves in Chapter 20. In a small group, answer the questions below. Then have a class discussion of your answers.

Exploring the Issues

1. ECONOMIC DEVELOPMENT Make a list of some of the pros and cons of economic development. How would economic development benefit people living in Africa?
2. HEALTH CARE Search the Internet for information about how African nations are trying to slow the spread of various diseases. What strategies and actions are being employed by these countries?
3. EFFECTS OF COLONIALISM Find one news story about political or ethnic violence. How might colonialism be a cause or have contributed to the problem?

For more on these issues in Africa . . .
hmhsocialstudies.com
CURRENT EVENTS

ECONOMIC DEVELOPMENT

How can African nations develop their economies?

African nations rely too much on the exportation of natural resources. These miners in Johannesburg, South Africa, mine gold, one of the country's main exports.

EXPLORING THE ISSUES ANSWERS

1. ECONOMIC DEVELOPMENT Students may say that economic development can create a higher standard of living but can also undermine traditional cultures and damage the environment. Students' ideas for limiting negative effects will vary, based on their level of prior knowledge.
2. HEALTH CARE Most students will find that many African countries are using comprehensive education programs to help teach their citizens about AIDS.
3. EFFECTS OF COLONIALISM Answers will vary depending on the news story chosen, but may include such causes as longstanding enmity between ethnic groups or abuses by corrupt leaders.

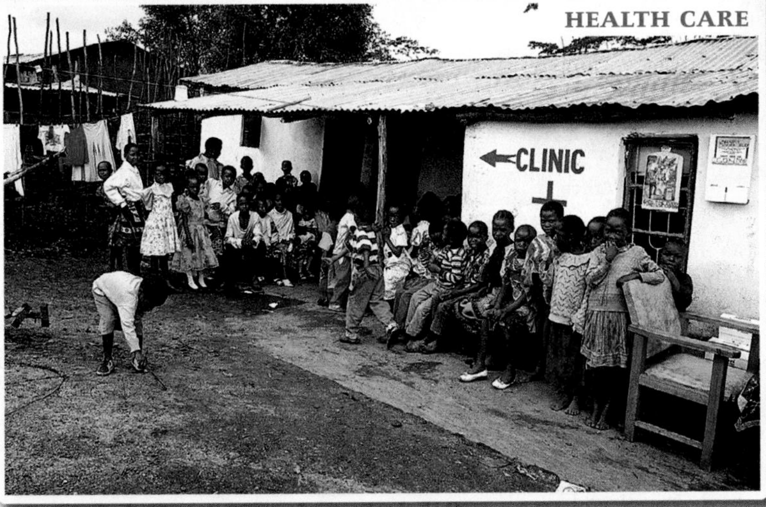

How can African countries eliminate the diseases that threaten their people and cultures?

A health clinic in Nairobi, Kenya, attempts to slow the spread of AIDS through various education programs.

CASESTUDY

How can African nations bring peace and stability to their people?

Many African countries are still suffering from the effects of colonialism. Africa's problems after colonialism are shown in this cartoon about the Democratic Republic of the Congo (formerly known as Zaire). This cartoon shows that there are no easy solutions.

AFRICA

HEALTH CARE

The spread of AIDS created a crisis in many African countries. Life expectancies declined sharply, and industries lost workers. Millions of people have died. In recent years, the situation has improved somewhat.

Discussion Prompts

- How might the high death rate affect economic growth? *(Economic growth will halt and maybe even decline as nations lose their workers.)*
- What is being done to prevent AIDS in the United States? *(education, AIDS research)*

CASESTUDY

EFFECTS OF COLONIALISM

Most African countries face political challenges that affect economic growth. To help students understand this issue, direct them to the Case Study that begins on page 468 and concludes with a Case Study Project on pages 470-471.

Discussion Prompts

- What current problems in Africa have you heard about on the news? *(Answers will vary but may include post-apartheid issues, civil or ethnic wars.)*
- What similar issues has the United States faced? *(Answers may include racism, the Civil War, or anti-immigrant feelings.)*

ACTIVITY OPTION | **INTERNET RESEARCH**

DISTINGUISHING FACT FROM OPINION

Objective To evaluate research materials

Class Time 30 minutes

Task Locate three sources for one of the issues introduced about Africa. Then write a brief description identifying whether each source is primarily a statement of fact or an expression of opinion

Directions Direct students to the Web site for World Geography at **hmhsocialstudies.com.** Click on the current events button and follow the links to sources of information on these or other issues in Africa.

OPTIONAL ACTIVITY If Internet access is limited or unavailable, have the students use classroom resources or the library for this activity.

ATLAS OBJECTIVES

1. Compare data on the physical geography of Africa.
2. Examine key physical features of Africa.
3. Identify African borders and colonial territories in 1913.
4. Identify current African political borders.
5. Learn about the religions and population density of Africa.
6. Analyze language distribution in Africa.

Focus & Motivate

Ask students what they have heard about travel in Africa. *(safaris and tours by small planes, camels, or boats on the Nile)* Ask what they would expect to find on a map featuring African landforms. *(Answers will vary but may include deserts, rivers, grasslands, and mountains.)*

Instruct: Objective 

Comparing Data

- **Landmass** About what proportion of the landmass of Africa is taken up by the Sahara? *(about a third)*
- **Population** How do Africa and the United States compare in population? *(Africa has almost 700 million more people.)*
- **Rivers** How do the three longest rivers of Africa compare in length to the Mississippi? *(They are all longer.)*
- **Deserts** How does the Sahara compare in size to the Mojave? *(more than 233 times larger)*

Unit ATLAS

Patterns of Physical Geography

Use the Unit Atlas to add to your knowledge of Africa. As you look at the maps and charts, notice geographic patterns and specific details about the region. After studying the graphs and physical map on these two pages, jot down in your notebook the answers to the questions below.

Making Comparisons

1. Compare Africa's size and population to that of the United States. How much larger in terms of population and size is Africa compared to the United States?
2. Compare Africa's longest river, the Nile, to the Mississippi. How much difference is there in the lengths?
3. How much bigger is the Sahara than the largest desert in the United States? What is the difference in size between the Sahara and the continental United States?

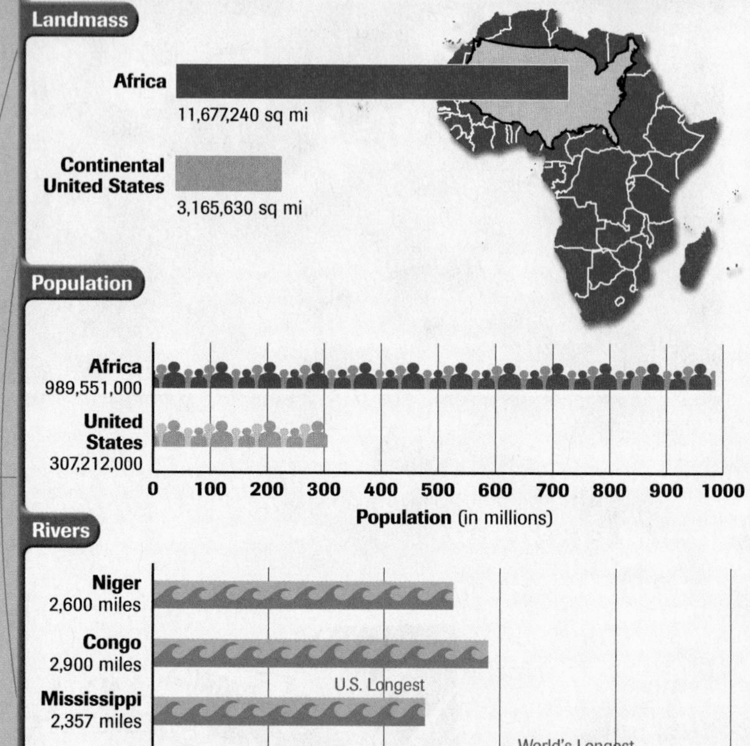

MAKING COMPARISONS ANSWERS

1. Africa is about 3.69 times as large as the United States, and Africa has about 3.2 times more people.
2. The Nile is 1,803 miles longer.
3. 3,485,000 sq. miles; 334,370 sq. miles

Africa: Physical

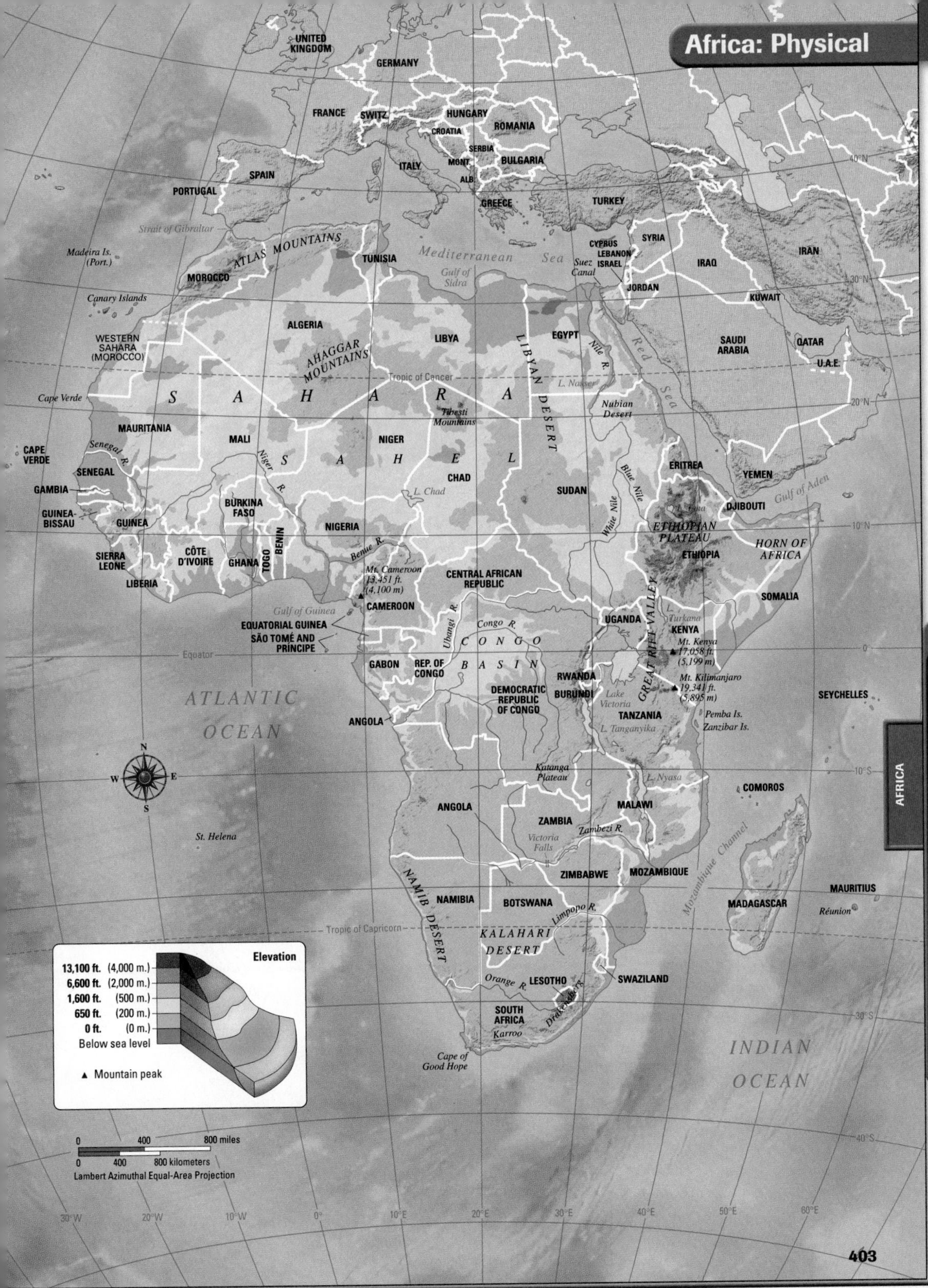

Elevation

13,100 ft. (4,000 m.)
6,600 ft. (2,000 m.)
1,600 ft. (500 m.)
650 ft. (200 m.)
0 ft. (0 m.)
Below sea level

▲ Mountain peak

0 400 800 miles
0 400 800 kilometers
Lambert Azimuthal Equal-Area Projection

403

UNIT 6 ATLAS

Instruct: Objective 2

Africa: Physical

- Where are the Atlas Mountains? *(North Africa near the Mediterranean coast)*
- Where are the lowest elevations in Africa? *(along the coasts)*
- What countries border Lake Victoria? *(Uganda, Kenya, Tanzania)*
- Which country contains the greatest area of high plateau elevations? *(Ethiopia)*

In-Depth Resources: Unit 6
- Unit Atlas Activities, p. 1

Outline Maps with Activities
- Africa: Physical, pp. 51–52

Map Transparencies MT31
- Africa: Physical

More About

The Nile River

Although the Nile River has been famous since ancient times, its source remained a mystery for centuries. The Nile is formed by the joining of three main streams: the Atbara and the Blue Nile (which both flow out of the Ethiopian Plateau) and the White Nile. It wasn't until 1862 that explorers found the place where the White Nile exits Lake Victoria—and even that wasn't the final answer. The Nile's remotest source is the Ruvironza River of Burundi, which flows into the Kagera River, which in turn feeds Lake Victoria.

ACTIVITY OPTION FIVE THEMES OF GEOGRAPHY

BLOCK SCHEDULING

LOCATION

Exploring the Theme Remind students that *location* answers the question of "where." There are two types of location. *Absolute location* uses longitude and latitude to identify precisely where something is. *Relative location* tells where something is in relation to something else.

Understanding the Theme Ask students to use the physical map of Africa on page 403 to answer the following questions about relative location.

- What continents are close to Africa? *(Asia, Europe)*
- What oceans surround Africa? *(Atlantic, Indian)*
- Where is Africa in relation to the Mediterranean Sea? *(Africa is directly south of the Mediterranean.)*

Instruct: Objective 3

Colonialism in Africa, 1913

- Which European nation colonized a part of Africa less than 50 miles away from its southernmost point? *(Spain)*
- Which European nation colonized only one large area? *(Belgium in the Belgian Congo)*
- Are more political boundaries evident on the map of Africa in 1913 or on the map of Africa today? *(Africa today)*

More About

Madagascar

Madagascar is the world's fourth largest island. Although it lies only a few hundred miles from Southern Africa, it is culturally very different. Madagascar was settled about 2,000 years ago by people from Indonesia. During the colonial period, Madagascar was a French colony. It gained independence in 1960. The official languages are Malagasy—an Austronesian language related to many languages of Southeast Asia and the Pacific Islands—and French.

Unit ATLAS

Patterns of Human Geography

In the years preceding World War I (1914–1918), the political map of Africa changed dramatically. European colonial powers had replaced traditional African states and empires. Study the political maps of Africa in 1913 and Africa today to see how the continent changed by the end of the 20th century. Then answer these questions in your notebook.

Making Comparisons

1. What independent nations appear on the map of Africa in 1913 and also appear on the map of Africa today?
2. Which two European powers controlled the most land in Africa in 1913? Which country controlled the least amount?
3. Which countries in Africa today formed French West Africa in 1913?
4. Which three African countries emerged from colonialism with the most territory?

Colonialism in Africa, 1913

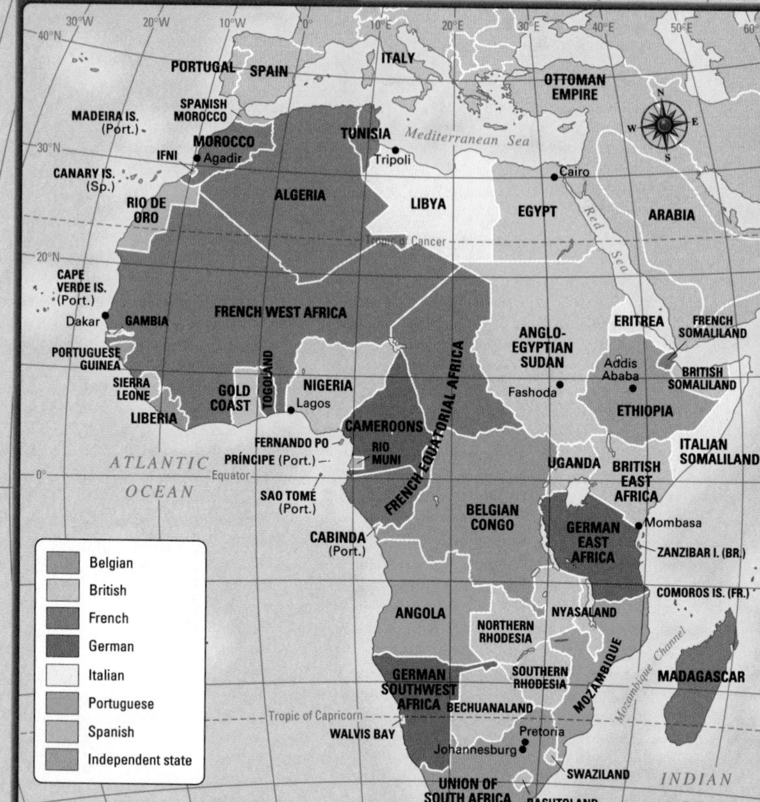

MAKING COMPARISONS ANSWERS

1. Liberia, Ethiopia, South Africa. (South Africa became a self-governing dominion under the British crown in 1910. The British and Afrikaners ruled the Union of South Africa together from 1910 to 1961, when South Africa became a republic.)
2. France, Britain; Spain.
3. Niger, Mali, Mauritania, Benin, Burkina Faso, Côte d'Ivoire, Guinea, Senegal
4. Algeria, Sudan, Democratic Republic of the Congo.

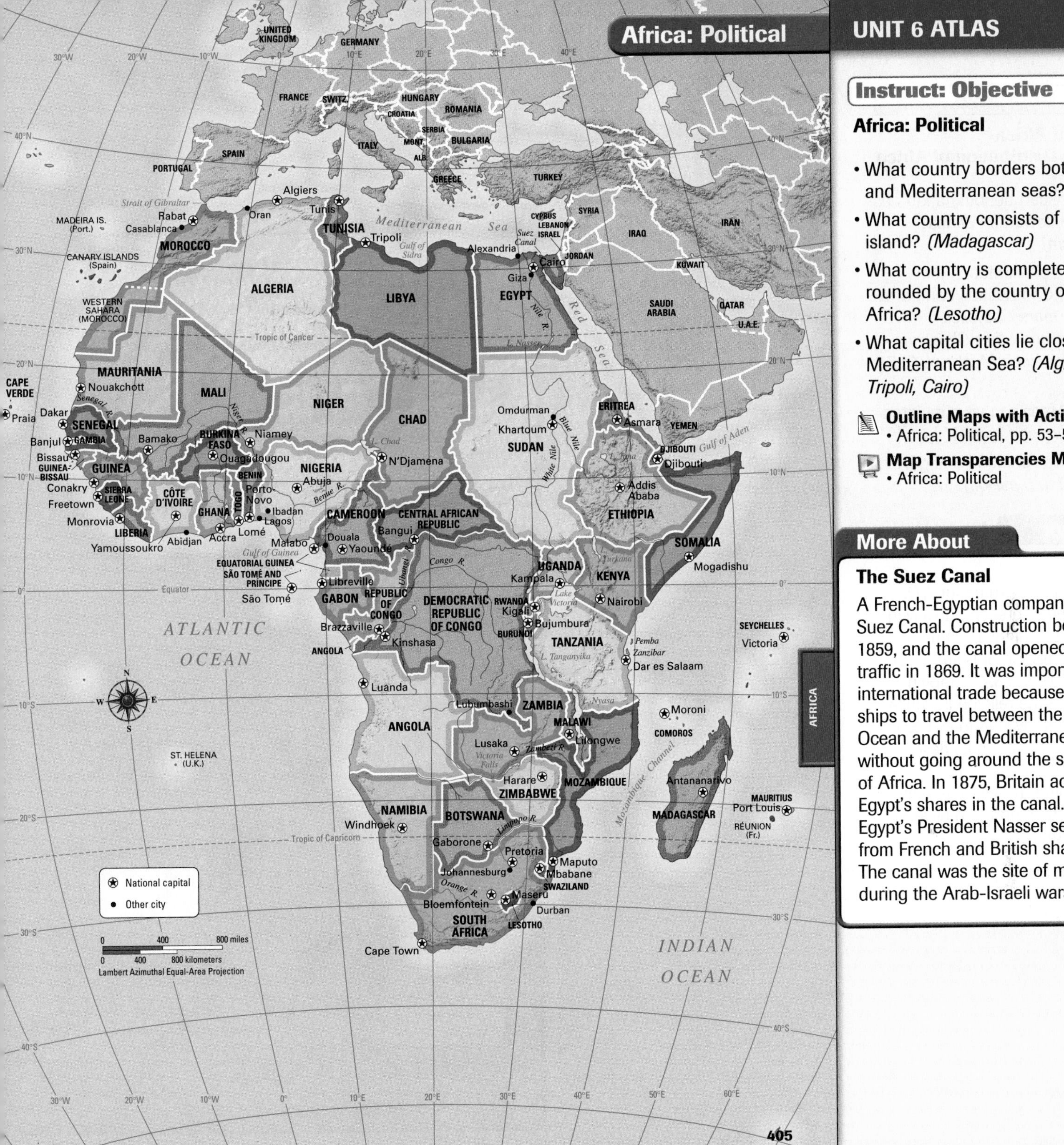

Instruct: Objective 4

Africa: Political

- What country borders both the Red and Mediterranean seas? *(Egypt)*
- What country consists of a large island? *(Madagascar)*
- What country is completely surrounded by the country of South Africa? *(Lesotho)*
- What capital cities lie close to the Mediterranean Sea? *(Algiers, Tunis, Tripoli, Cairo)*

Outline Maps with Activities
- Africa: Political, pp. 53–54

Map Transparencies MT32
- Africa: Political

AFRICA

More About

The Suez Canal

A French-Egyptian company built the Suez Canal. Construction began in 1859, and the canal opened to sea traffic in 1869. It was important to international trade because it allowed ships to travel between the Indian Ocean and the Mediterranean Sea without going around the southern tip of Africa. In 1875, Britain acquired Egypt's shares in the canal. In 1956, Egypt's President Nasser seized control from French and British shareholders. The canal was the site of much conflict during the Arab-Israeli wars.

ACTIVITY OPTION LINK TO HISTORY

WRITING AN OBITUARY

Objective To write about the life of Cecil Rhodes, emphasizing his part in the British colonization of Africa

Class Time 40 minutes

Task Research the life of Cecil Rhodes and write an obituary

Directions Have students locate Northern and Southern Rhodesia on the map of colonies in 1913. Ask them to identify which European power held those colonies. *(Great Britain)* Explain that those two colonies were named for Cecil John Rhodes, a British man who dreamed of building a railway from the Cape (in South Africa) to Cairo. Direct students to write an obituary for Rhodes that emphasizes the role he played in the colonization of Africa.

Instruct: Objective 5

Religions of Africa/ Population Distribution of Africa

- Which Christian denomination has the most followers in Africa? *(Catholicism)*
- How do the percentages for Muslims and Christians compare? *(There are more Catholics, Protestants, and other Christians–45.8 percent–than Muslims–40.5 percent.)*
- What are Africa's most populated cities? *(Cairo and Lagos)*
- What is the population category for Algiers? *(2 to 6 million)*

More About

Islam in Africa

Muhammad was born about A.D. 570. He began to preach publicly in 613, and his teachings became the basis for the religion of Islam. After Muhammad died in 632, Arabian traders spread the religion in Africa as they traveled by ship to its coasts and by caravan through its deserts. West Africa became a center of Muslim learning. Today Islam has many followers in northern Nigeria and in East Africa.

Unit ATLAS

Regional Patterns

These two pages contain a graph and two thematic maps. The graph shows the religions of Africa. The maps show other important features of Africa: its diversity of languages and its population distribution. After studying these two pages, jot down in your notebook the answers to the questions below.

Making Comparisons

1. Where are most of the people in Africa living? In what areas of Africa are the fewest people living?
2. What geographic factors may account for these population patterns?
3. What do you notice about the number of languages in Africa? Do they belong to one language group or several?

Religions of Africa

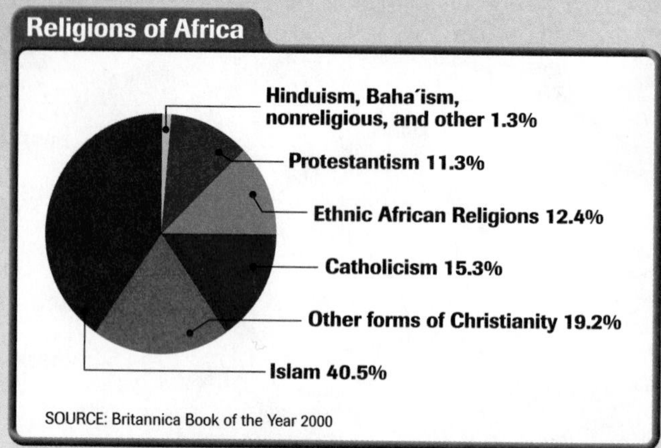

SOURCE: Britannica Book of the Year 2000

Population Distribution of Africa

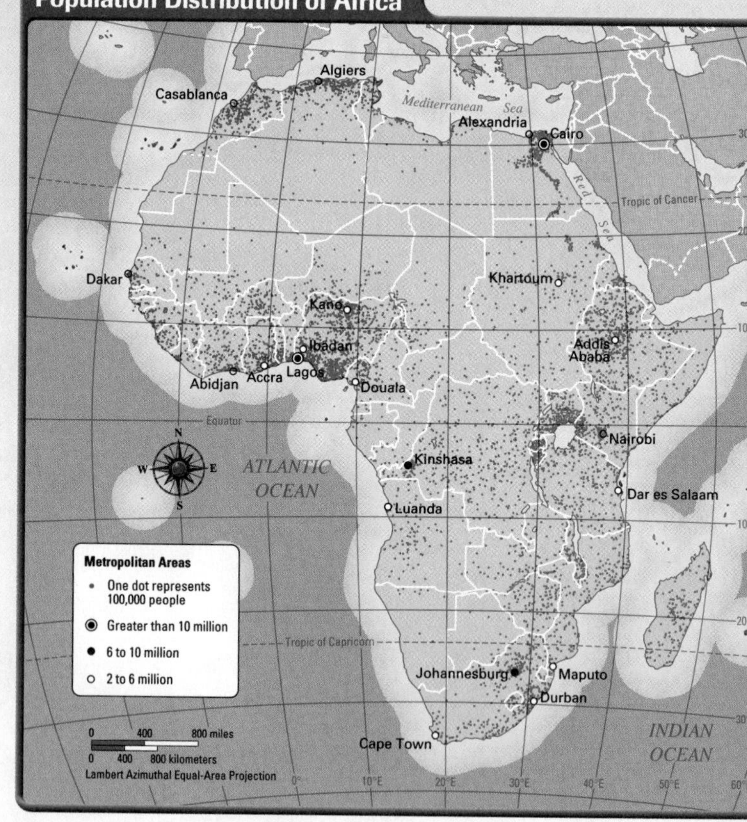

MAKING COMPARISONS ANSWERS

1. densest in northern coast of Morocco and Algeria, Nile River region, West African coast around Nigeria, around Lake Victoria, southeastern coast of South Africa; lowest in the Sahara and Kalahari Deserts
2. The highest density populations exist near a water source such as a lake, river, sea, or ocean. The lowest density populations occur in deserts, which do not have an abundance of natural resources to support life.
3. There are many languages that belong to many language groups.

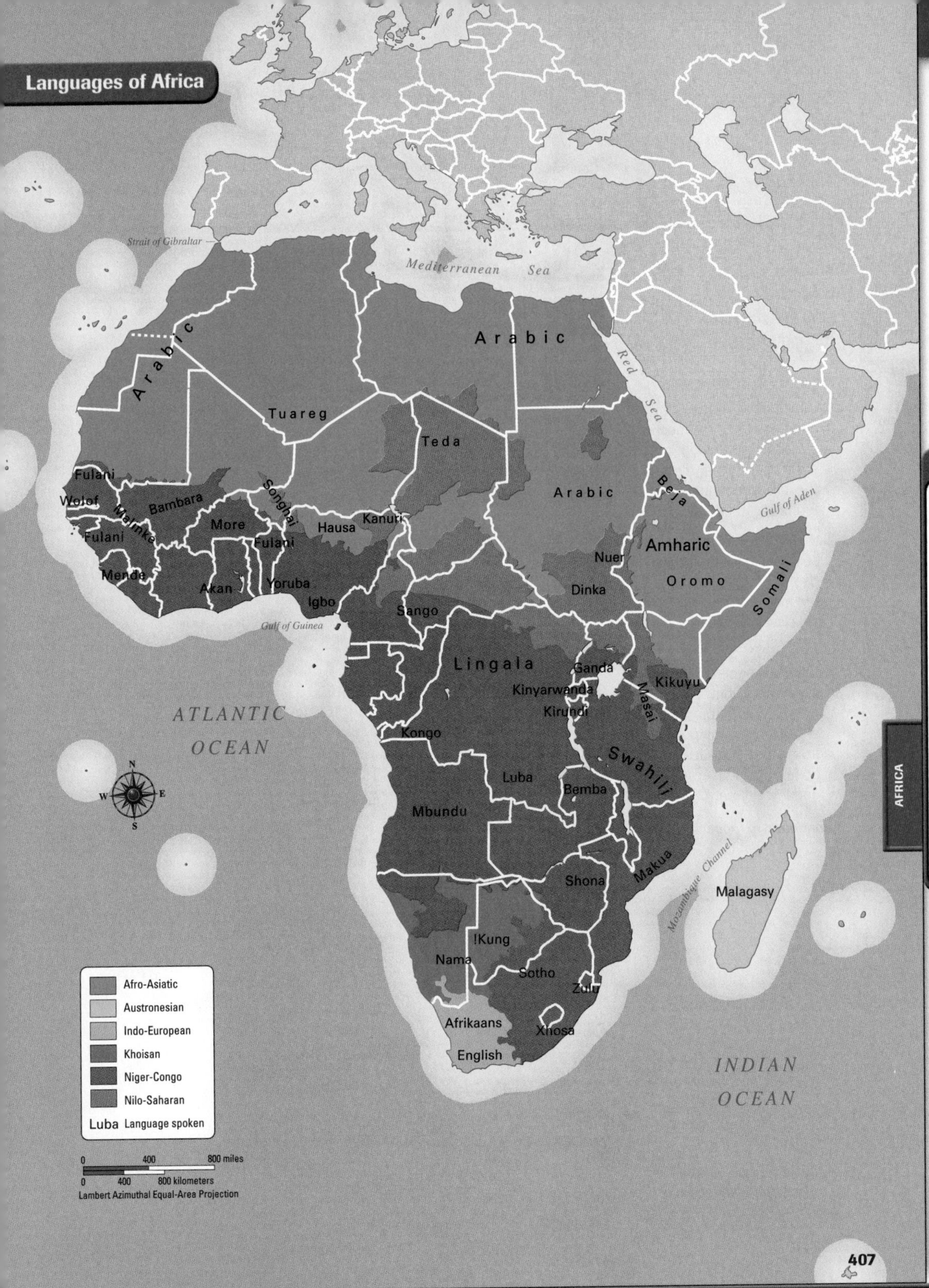

Languages of Africa

Arabic, Tuareg, Teda, Fulani, Wolof, Malinke, Bambara, More, Songhai, Hausa, Kanuri, Fulani, Mende, Akan, Yoruba, Igbo, Sango, Arabic, Beja, Amharic, Nuer, Dinka, Oromo, Somali, Lingala, Ganda, Kikuyu, Kinyarwanda, Kirundi, Masai, Kongo, Swahili, Luba, Bemba, Mbundu, Makua, Shona, Malagasy, !Kung, Nama, Sotho, Zulu, Afrikaans, Xhosa, English

Strait of Gibraltar, Mediterranean Sea, Red Sea, Gulf of Aden, Gulf of Guinea, ATLANTIC OCEAN, INDIAN OCEAN, Mozambique Channel

- Afro-Asiatic
- Austronesian
- Indo-European
- Khoisan
- Niger-Congo
- Nilo-Saharan
- Luba Language spoken

0 400 800 miles
0 400 800 kilometers
Lambert Azimuthal Equal-Area Projection

Instruct: Objective 6

Languages of Africa

- What languages are spoken at the southern tip of Africa? *(English, Afrikaans, Xhosa)*
- What language group does Masai belong to? *(Nilo-Saharan)* Tuareg? *(Afro-Asiatic)*
- What are the most widespread language groups in Africa? *(Afro-Asiatic, Niger-Congo)*

More About

Swahili

Swahili, one of the Bantu languages that belong to the Niger-Congo group, shows how the movement of people can affect culture and language. Swahili uses Bantu grammar but contains many words of Arabic origin. The language evolved as Arabian traders had contact with Bantu-speaking peoples of Africa's east coast. Trading caravans then spread the language inland. Today Swahili is the official language of Tanzania. Swahili is taught throughout the world and in U.S. African Studies programs.

AFRICA

DIFFERENTIATING INSTRUCTION GIFTED AND TALENTED STUDENTS

LEARNING SWAHILI

Objective To learn basic traveler's vocabulary in Swahili

Class Time 30 minutes

Task Make flashcards of Swahili words and phrases

Directions Have students use the Internet or print sources to learn basic Swahili words and phrases that would be useful for travelers. They should make at least a dozen flash cards like the one shown by writing the Swahili word or phrase on the front and the English translation on the back.

DATA FILE OBJECTIVE

Examine and compare data on African countries.

Focus & Motivate

Ask students to identify the three African countries with the largest total areas. *(Sudan, Algeria, Democratic Republic of the Congo)* Which three countries have the highest value of exports? *(South Africa, Algeria, Nigeria)*

Instruct: Objective

Regional Data File

- Which country has the lowest life expectancy? How does the United States compare? *(Angola; U.S. life expectancy is more than twice as long.)*
- Which country has the lowest literacy rate? Which has the highest? *(Burkina-Faso; Seychelles)*
- Which country has the highest infant mortality rate? How many doctors does it have per 100,000 persons? *(Angola; eight)*

In-Depth Resources: Unit 6
- Regional Data File Activities, p. 2

Regional Data File

Study the charts on the countries of Africa. In your notebook, answer these questions.

Making Comparisons

1. Which three African countries have the most people? Locate them on the map. Are they also the largest countries in terms of total area?
2. Which two African countries have the fewest people? Locate them on the map. Are they the smallest countries in terms of total area?
3. Look at Angola's life expectancy, infant mortality, and number of doctors. Judging from these statistics, does Angola have good health care?

(continued on page 410)

Country Flag	Country/ Capital	Population	Life Expectancy (years)	Birthrate (per 1,000 pop.)	Infant Mortali (per 1,000 live birt
	Algeria Algiers	34,178,000	74.0	16.9	27.7
	Angola Luanda	12,799,000	38.2	43.7	180.2
	Benin Porto-Novo	8,792,000	59.0	39.2	64.6
	Botswana Gaborone	1,991,000	61.9	22.9	12.6
	Burkina Faso Ouagadougou	15,746,000	52.9	44.3	84.5
	Burundi Bujumbura	9,511,000	57.8	41.8	64.9
	Cameroon Yaoundé	18,879,000	53.7	34.1	63.3
	Cape Verde Praia	429,000	71.6	23.5	41.4
	Central African Republic, Bangui	4,511,000	44.4	32.8	80.6
	Chad N'Djamena	10,329,000	47.7	40.9	98.7
	Comoros Moroni	752,000	63.5	35.2	66.6
	Congo, Democratic Republic of, Kinshasa	68,693,000	54.4	42.6	81.2
	Congo, Republic of, Brazzaville	4,013,000	54.2	41.4	79.8
	Côte d'Ivoire Yamoussoukro	20,617,000	55.5	32.1	68.1
	Djibouti Djibouti	725,000	60.3	26.3	58.3
	Egypt Cairo	78,867,000	72.1	25.4	27.3
	Equatorial Guinea Malabo	633,000	61.6	36.5	81.6
	Eritrea Asmara	5,647,000	61.9	34.2	43.3

For updated statistics on Africa . . .

MAKING COMPARISONS ANSWERS

1. Nigeria, Egypt, Ethiopia. They rank in the upper third in area.
2. São Tomé & Príncipe, Seychelles. They are the smallest and are all islands.
3. Based on those statistics, Angola does not have good health care.

Doctors (per 100,000 pop.)	GDP[a] (billions $US)	Import/Export (billions $US)	Literacy Rate (percentage)	Televisions (per 1,000 pop.)	Passenger Cars (per 1,000 pop.)	Total Area[b] (square miles)
113	244.3	39.51/52.03	70	107	56	919,595
8	113.9	12.81/40.02	67	15	9	481,354
4	13.4	1.54/1.02	35	44	15	43,483
40	24.1	3.67/2.96	81	21	42	231,804
5	19.1	1.08/0.65	22	11	2	105,869
3	3.27	0.32/0.08	59	15	1	10,745
19	42.6	3.74/3.41	68	34	9	183,568
49	1.7	0.77/0.10	77	5	31	1,557
8	3.3	0.24/0.15	49	6	0	240,535
4	15.9	2.12/3.16	26	1	N/A	495,755
15	0.5	0.14/0.32	57	4	N/A	838
11	21.6	5.2/6.1	67	2	3	905,568
20	16.7	2.72/7.54	84	13	7	132,047
12	35.6	6.50/8.99	49	65	6	124,503
18	2.04	1.56/0.34	68	48	N/A	8,880
54	470.4	43.98/22.91	87	170	27	386,662
30	22.9	2.85/8.27		116	N/A	10,831
5	4.10	0.59/0.01	59	16	N/A	46,842

More About

The African Union

The African Union (AU) began life in 1964 as the Organization of African Unity (OAU). The main objectives of the OAU were to promote solidarity among African States in their attempts to overcome the effects of colonialism. From 1999 through 2002, the OAU was disbanded and replaced by the AU in order to promote "accelerated socio-economic integration of the continent, which will lead to greater unity and solidarity between African countries and peoples." Every one of the 53 nations of Africa is a member.

ACTIVITY OPTION — CRITICAL THINKING

MAKING INFERENCES

Explaining the Skill Remind students that making inferences involves using their own knowledge to go beyond what is stated directly by the text. For example, they might infer from a high literacy rate that a country has a good system of schools that most of its citizens attend.

Applying the Skill Ask students these questions to help them make inferences from the data file.

- Which African nations have life expectancies of 50 years or less? *(Angola, Central African Republic, Chad, Guinea-Bissau, Lesotho, Liberia, Malawi, Mozambique, Nigeria, Somalia, South Africa, Swaziland, Zambia, Zimbabwe)*
- What might you infer about these countries? *(that they have high poverty rates, persistent health problems, violent conflicts, or a combination of these conditions)*

More About

Libya

In recent years Libya has abandoned its international isolation and dramatically improved its relations with the West. Under the leadership of Colonel Gaddafi, Libya once supported a range of militant organizations. Libya's suspected involvement in terrorist attacks in Europe during the 1980s, including the 1988 bombing of a plane above Lockerbie, Scotland, led to UN sanctions against this North African nation. However, in 2003, Libya took responsibility for the Lockerbie bombing and soon after renounced weapons of mass destruction. Since then, relations between Libya and the West have steadily improved.

Regional Data File

Making Comparisons

(continued)

4. Use the map on page 405 to choose a country in East Africa. How many televisions and cars does it have per 1,000 people? How does that compare to the United States?

5. Make a list of the top three African countries in GDP. Where are these countries located? Do you notice any pattern?

6. Use the map on page 405 to identify two countries in Southern Africa. For each of those countries, calculate per capita GDP by dividing total GDP by population. Which country has the higher per capita GDP?

(continued on page 412)

Country Flag	Country/ Capital	Population	Life Expectancy (years)	Birthrate (per 1,000 pop.)	Infant Mortali (per 1,000 live birt
	Ethiopia Addis Ababa	85,237,000	55.4	43.7	80.8
	Gabon Libreville	1,515,000	53.1	35.6	51.9
	Gambia, The Banjul	1,778,000	53.8	37.8	68.8
	Ghana Accra	23,888,000	60.1	28.7	51.2
	Guinea Conakry	10,058,000	57.1	37.5	65.2
	Guinea-Bissau Bissau	1,534,000	47.9	35.9	99.8
	Kenya Nairobi	39,003,000	57.9	36.6	54.7
	Lesotho Maseru	2,131,000	40.4	24.1	77.4
	Liberia Monrovia	3,442,000	41.8	42.3	138.2
	Libya Tripoli	6,324,000	77.3	25.1	21.7
	Madagascar Antananarivo	20,654,000	62.9	38.1	54.2
	Malawi Lilongwe	15,029,000	50.0	41.7	86.0
	Mali Bamako	13,443,000	51.8	46.4	115.9
	Mauritania Nouakchott	3,129,000	60.4	34.1	63.4
	Mauritius Port Louis	1,284,000	74.0	14.4	12.2
	Morocco Rabat	31,285,000	75.5	19.7	29.8
	Mozambique Maputo	21,669,000	41.2	38.0	105.8
	Namibia Windhoek	2,109,000	51.2	22.5	45.5

MAKING COMPARISONS ANSWERS

4. Answers will vary based on the country chosen.

5. Egypt in North Africa, Nigeria in West Africa, and South Africa in Southern Africa; all three are located on seacoasts.

6. Answers will vary based on the countries chosen.

Doctors (per 100,000 pop.)	GDP[a] (billions $US)	Import/Export (billions $US)	Literacy Rate (percentage)	Televisions (per 1,000 pop.)	Passenger Cars (per 1,000 pop.)	Total Area[b] (square miles)
3	75.9	7.32/1.61	43	5	1	435,186
29	20.8	2.30/5.87	63	251	N/A	103,347
11	2.t4	0.24/0.08	40	3	4	4,363
15	36.6	9.81/5.74	58	115	4	92,456
11	10.6	1.12/0.97	30	47	N/A	94,926
12	0.94	0.20/0.13	42	N/A	N/A	13,946
14	63.52	9.03/4.48	85	22	8	224,962
55	3.31	1.83/0.87	85	16	N/A	11,720
N/A	1.63	7.14/1.20	58	26	5	43,000
56	92.3	26.82/33.97	83	139	87	679,362
29	20.5	1.84/1.04	69	23	N/A	226,657
2	12.8	1.63/0.95	63	3	0	45,745
8	15.4	2.36/0.29	46	13	5	478,767
11	6.49	1.48/1.40	51	95	4	397,955
106	15.9	3.55/2.06	84	248	97	788
51	146.7	31.83/15.61	52	165	42	172,414
3	20.2	3.10/1.95	48	5	5	309,496
30	13.5	4.39/3.48	85	38	N/A	318,696

More About

Mauritius

The island nation of Mauritius shows how political stability can foster economic growth. It gained independence in 1968 and became a stable democracy. This attracted foreign investment. Mauritius now has one of Africa's highest per capita incomes. It has a diversified and growing economy with increased life expectancy and improved infrastructure. It has two television stations, radio stations, a good telephone system, and nearly 200,000 Internet users.

Using Maps to Predict Future Growth Trends

Refer students to the maps in the Unit 6 Atlas and the Regional Data File. Have them use these resources to predict growth trends of African societies.

ACTIVITY OPTION EXPLORING LOCAL GEOGRAPHY

CREATING A DATA FILE

Objective To compare data about an African country to data about a U.S. state

Class Time 30 minutes

Task Create a data file

Directions Refer students to the U.S. data file on pages 108-113 to learn the total area of their state. Tell them to choose an African country of a similar size. Then have them create a chart comparing the two, using the categories of total area, population, infant mortality, and number of doctors. If they wish, they may research other categories to add to the chart.

More About

Medicine in Africa

The number of doctors per 100,000 population is only one aspect of health care in Africa. In many African nations, 80 to 90 percent of the people use traditional medicine. Recent studies of traditional medicine have shown that certain plants help counteract parasites, and certain herbs are useful for treating malaria. In Uganda, Zambia, and Mozambique, both traditional and modern health practitioners work together to combat the AIDS epidemic. These programs may prove more effective than modern medicine alone.

Regional Data File

Making Comparisons *(continued)*

7. Choose three countries and examine their GDP and life expectancy figures. What might be the relationship between a country's GDP and its life expectancy?

Country Flag	Country/ Capital	Population	Life Expectancy (years)	Birthrate (per 1,000 pop.)	Infant M (per 1,000 li
	Niger Niamey	15,306,000	52.6	51.6	116.
	Nigeria Abuja	149,229,000	46.9	36.7	94.4
	Rwanda Kigali	10,746,000	56.8	38.1	67.2
	Sao Tome and Principe São Tomé	213,000	68.3	38.5	37.1
	Senegal Dakar	13,712,000	59	36.8	58.9
	Seychelles Victoria	87,000	73	15.9	12.3
	Sierra Leone Freetown	5,132,000	55.2	39.1	81.9
	Somalia Mogadishu	9,832,000	49.6	43.7	109.2
	South Africa Cape Town/Johannesburg	49,052,000	48.9	19.9	44.4
	Sudan Khartoum	41,088,000	51.4	33.7	82.4
	Swaziland Mbabane	1,337,000	47.9	28.1	69.7
	Tanzania Dodoma	41,049,000	52	34.3	69.3
	Togo Lomé	6,032,000	59.7	36.5	56.8
	Tunisia Tunis	10,486,000	75.8	15.4	22.6
	Uganda Kampala	32,370,000	52.7	47.8	64.8
	Zambia Lusaka	11,863,000	38.6	40.2	101.2
	Zimbabwe Harare	11,393,000	45.8	31.5	32.3
	United States Washington, D.C.	307,212,000	78.1	13.8	6.2

Sources:

Central Intelligence Agency, *The World Factbook*, 2010

The World Almanac and Book of Facts, 2010

World Health Organization (WHO), 2007

Notes:

[a] GDP (purchasing power parity) is defined as the sum value of all goods and services produced in the country valued at prices prevailing in the United States.

[b] Includes land and water, when figures are available

MAKING COMPARISONS ANSWERS

7. Answers will vary depending on the countries chosen. In many cases, higher GDP is associated with longer life expectancy, but the correlation is not automatic.

Doctors (per 100,000 pop.)	GDP[a] (billions $US)	Import/Export (billions $US)	Literacy Rate (percentage)	Televisions (per 1,000 pop.)	Passenger Cars (per 1,000 pop.)	Total Area[b] (square miles)
2	10.8	0.80/0.43	29	15	1	484,191
28	353.2	42.1/45.43	68	69	0	356,669
5	10.4	0.79/0.21	70	101	1	10,169
49	0.29	0.91/0.01	85	229	N/A	386
6	23.2	3.86/1.65	39	41	11	75,749
151	1.7	0.66/0.37	92	214	71	176
3	4.5	0.56/0.22	35	13	2	27,699
N/A	5.7	0.80/0.30	38	14	N/A	246,201
77	488.6	70.24/67.93	86	138	N/A	471,011
22	92.8	6.82/8.46	61	173	1	967,499
16	5.9	1.64/1.57	82	112	41	6,704
2	57.5	5.55/2.74	69	21	1	364,900
4	5.29	1.40/0.73	61	22	9	21,925
134	83.2	19.04/14.43	74	190	53	63,170
8	42.2	4.11/3.15	67	28	2	91,136
12	18.6	4.13/4.39	81	145	0	290,586
16	0.3	2.03/1.09	91	35	52	150,804
256	14,260.0	1,445/994.7	99	844	725	3,794,083

More About

Dr. Wangari Maathai

Dr. Maathai is internationally known for her environmental activism. She was born in 1940 in Kenya and received her doctorate from the University of Nairobi. Dr. Maathai celebrated Earth Day in 1977 by founding the Green Belt Movement to reverse the effects of deforestation. She helped local women by hiring them to plant trees. Since then, millions of trees have been planted. In 2004, Dr. Maathai won the Nobel Peace Prize for her contributions to sustainable development, democracy, and peace.

ACTIVITY OPTION | COOPERATIVE LEARNING

HOLDING A PANEL DISCUSSION

Objective To draw conclusions about regional patterns based on economic information

Class Time One class period

Task Hold a panel discussion on the economies of African subregions

Directions Each student in class should choose (or be assigned) a different African nation. Organize students into five groups, based on the subregions shown on page 430. Each student should use the Internet or print resources to learn about his or her country's exports and should use the data file to calculate that country's per capita GDP. The groups should then discuss each member's research and use the combined data to draw conclusions about economic patterns in the subregion. They can use these questions as a guide:

- Do the countries of this subregion tend to rely on the export of one main product or many products?
- Do all the countries of this subregion rely on the same exports?
- Do any countries of the subregion have a higher per capita GDP than others? If so, is there a difference in their export patterns?

CHAPTER 18 OBJECTIVE

Identify key features of Africa's physical geography, climate and vegetation, and human-environment interaction.

Chapter 18

PHYSICAL GEOGRAPHY OF AFRICA
The Plateau Continent

Interpreting Photographs

Victoria Falls

Direct the students' attention to the high falls and deep chasm. Tell them that the falls plunge 355 feet. David Livingstone named them after Great Britain's Queen Victoria when he first saw the falls in 1855. The Kalolo-Lozi people call the falls *Mosi-oa-Tunya*, or "The Smoke That Thunders." Ask what the effect of these physical features might be on human life in the area. *(They prevent the smooth transport of goods and people.)*

Introducing the Essential Question

- Lead students to recall the images of African landscapes that they have seen on TV or in movies. Point out that those landscapes range from the hottest, largest desert in the world to practically impenetrable jungles.
- Encourage students to imagine themselves in those varied environments and to consider how their surroundings would affect their daily lives.

hmhsocialstudies.com TAKING NOTES

Have students fill out the graphic organizer in their notebooks using material from all sections of this chapter. Explain that the information will help them understand human interaction with the environment.

Critical Thinking Transparencies CT18
- GeoFocus

The Zambezi River plunges over Victoria Falls on the border between Zambia and Zimbabwe.

Essential Question

How has the physical geography of Africa affected the lives of the continent's people?

What You Will Learn

In this chapter you will read about how Africa's landforms, climate, and resources affect life there.

SECTION 1
Landforms and Resources

SECTION 2
Climate and Vegetation

SECTION 3
Human–Environment Interaction

hmhsocialstudies.com TAKING NOTES

Use the online graphic organizer to record information about the physical geography of Africa.

414

CHAPTER 18 ADDITIONAL RESOURCES

BOOKS FOR THE TEACHER

Moorehead, Alan. ***The White Nile.*** NY: Harper, 1960. Nile River exploration in the 1800s.

Montgomery, Sy. ***Walking With the Great Apes: Jane Goodall, Dian Fossey, Birute Galdikas.*** Boston: Houghton, 1991. Three women who studied African primates.

BOOKS FOR THE STUDENT

Ridgeway, Rick. ***The Shadow of Kilimanjaro.*** NY: Holt, 1998. An explorer walks across Kenya from Kilimanjaro to the Indian Ocean and considers the land from a conservationist point of view.

PERIODICALS

Victor, David G., and Jesse H. Ausubel. **"Restoring the Forests."** *Foreign Affairs.* Nov./Dec. 2000: 127-45.

Strait, G. Carroll. **"Facing Desertification."** *World & I.* Oct. 2000: 140-48.

INTERNET

For more on the physical geography of Africa, visit . . .

hmhsocialstudies.com

Landforms and Resources

Main Ideas

- A large plateau covers most of Africa.
- Africa's natural resources made it appealing to European colonizers.

Places & Terms

basin
Nile River
rift valley
Mount Kilimanjaro
escarpment

CONNECT TO THE ISSUES
COLONIALISM Africa's valuable resources still attract the world's industrialized countries.

A HUMAN PERSPECTIVE Angola's rebel leader Jonas Savimbi kept his forces fighting by bargaining with arms dealers and haggling with international diamond traders. Diamonds—one of the world's most precious and valuable gems—have enriched some of Africa's countries, including Botswana and South Africa. However, in other diamond-rich countries such as Angola, people use diamonds to fund costly and bloody civil wars. Rebel groups in Angola and the Angolan government sold diamonds on the world market and then used the money from the sale to buy weapons. The sale of diamonds funded a war that killed more than 500,000 Angolans and left more than 4 million homeless. A country's or continent's resources are used for a variety of purposes.

A Vast Plateau

Africa's shape and landforms are the result of its location in the southern part of the ancient supercontinent of *Pangaea,* which you read about in Chapter 2. About 200 million years ago, *Pangaea* began to break up. Over thousands of years, North and South America, Antarctica, Australia, and India drifted into their current positions. Present-day Africa, however, moved very little.

AFRICA'S PLATEAU A huge plateau covers most of Africa. It rises inland from narrow lowlands along the coast. Except for the coasts of Mozambique and Somalia, much of the continent lies at least 1,000 feet above sea level. This plateau is Africa's most prominent physical feature. As a result, geographers sometimes refer to Africa—the world's second largest continent—as the "plateau continent."

BASINS AND RIVERS Throughout this plateau lie several huge **basins,** or depressions, which you'll notice on the map on the right. Each basin spans more than 625 miles across and is as much as 5,000 feet deep. Water collects in the Chad Basin, and rivers flow through the Sudan, Congo, and Djouf basins.

Basins of Africa hmhsocialstudies.com INTERACTIVE

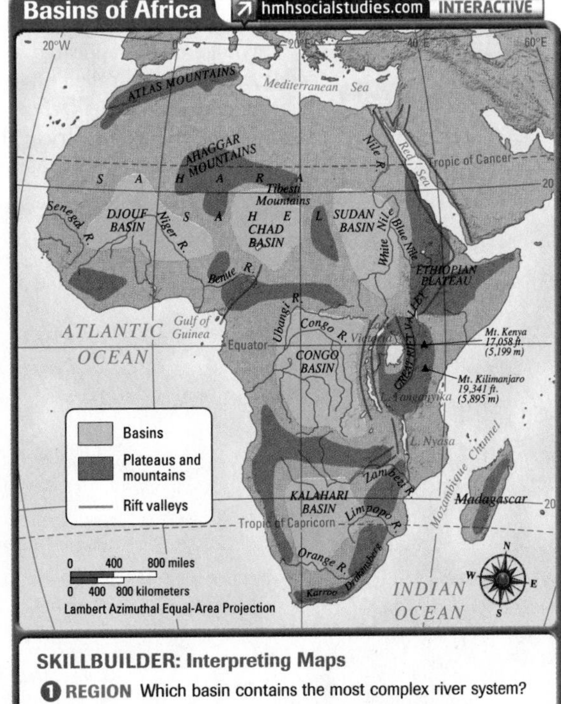

SKILLBUILDER: Interpreting Maps
1. **REGION** Which basin contains the most complex river system?
2. **LOCATION** Which basin lies completely south of the equator?

SECTION 1 OBJECTIVES

1. Identify the main features of Africa's vast plateau.
2. Describe the distinctive African landforms of rift valleys, lakes, mountains, and escarpments.
3. Explain how the continent's wealth of mineral resources affects Africans.
4. Identify Africa's major commodities.

SKILLBUILDER: Interpreting Maps, p. 415

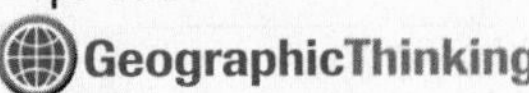
GeographicThinking
Using the Atlas, p. 416
Making Comparisons, p. 417
Seeing Patterns, p. 418

Focus & Motivate

Ask students what resources they think Africa has and why those resources are valuable. *(oil, gold, diamonds, coffee; they are used by industries and consumers worldwide.)*

Instruct: Objective 

A Vast Plateau

- What is Africa's most prominent physical feature? *(a plateau)*
- Why are Africa's rivers difficult to navigate? *(They meander and contain waterfalls, rapids, and gorges.)*
- How might this affect the economy? *(It is hard to transport goods.)*

In-Depth Resources: Unit 6
- Guided Reading, p. 3

SKILLBUILDER ANSWERS
1. Congo Basin **2.** Kalahari Basin

SECTION 1 PROGRAM RESOURCES

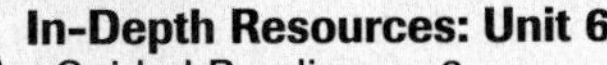
In-Depth Resources: Unit 6
- Guided Reading, p. 3
- Building Vocabulary, p. 9
- Reteaching Activity, p. 10
- Map and Graph Skills, pp. 6–7

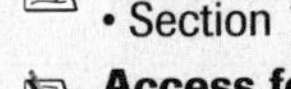
Guided Reading Workbook
- Section 1

Access for Students Acquiring English/ESL
- Guided Reading, p. 93
- Map and Graph Skills, pp. 97–98

Formal Assessment
- Section Quiz, p. 274

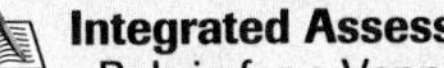
Integrated Assessment
- Rubric for a Venn diagram, 2.8

INTEGRATED TECHNOLOGY

Critical Thinking Transparencies CT50
- Gold Production in Selected Countries, 1989–1999

Power Presentations

Test Generator
- Section 1 Quiz

hmhsocialstudies.com

TEST-TAKING RESOURCES

Strategies for Test Preparation

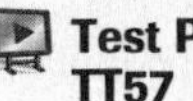
Test Practice Transparencies TT57

Online Test Practice

More About

The Congo River

The Congo River flows in a sweeping curve through the Congo Basin and drains most of Central Africa. Despite its waterfalls and rapids, much of the lower Congo River is navigable and is a major artery. It was named for the historic kingdom of Kongo, which was located near its mouth.

Instruct: Objective 2

Distinctive African Landforms

- Where are the most distinctive landforms found, and what are they? *(East Africa; rift valleys)*
- What is the Great Escarpment? *(a steep slope marking the edge of the continent's plateau in Southern Africa)*

Interpreting Photographs

Tanzania's Great Rift Valley

Point out the absence of roads and the steep slope that the people must climb. Rift valleys in this region of Africa average 30 to 40 miles wide. Ask students how rift valleys might affect transportation networks. *(Roads and railways would be difficult to build because they would require bridges or massive embankments.)*

CAPTION ANSWER Over millions of years, the earth's continental plates pulled apart, forming huge cracks that became the rift valleys.

The world's longest river, the **Nile River,** flows more than 4,000 miles through Uganda and Sudan and into Egypt. Its waters have provided irrigation for the region for thousands of years. More than 95 percent of Egyptians depend on the Nile for their water. In fact, the average population density along the Nile is more than 3,320 people per square mile. Compare that to the average population density of 216 people per square mile in all of Egypt.

Africa's rivers contain many waterfalls, rapids, and gorges. These features make the rivers less useful for transportation than shorter rivers on other continents. The 2,900-mile-long Congo River forms the continent's largest network of waterways. But a series of 32 cataracts, or waterfalls, makes large portions of that river impassable.

Furthermore, meandering courses also make Africa's rivers difficult to use for transportation. For example, the Niger River begins in West Africa and flows north toward the Sahara, where it forms an interior delta and turns to the southeast. It then cuts through Nigeria and forms another huge delta as it empties into the Gulf of Guinea. A

Geographic Thinking

Using the Atlas A Use the physical map on page 403 to find out what other rivers in Africa follow winding courses.

A. Answer Congo, Zambezi, Nile

Distinctive African Landforms

Africa does not have a long chain of mountains, such as the Rocky Mountains in North America or the Himalayas in Asia. However, Africa's valleys and lakes add to the continent's varied landscape.

RIFT VALLEYS AND LAKES The continent's most distinctive landforms are in East Africa. As the continental plates pulled apart over millions of years, huge cracks appeared in the earth. The land then sank to form long, thin valleys—called **rift valleys.** The rift valleys, which you can see on the map on page 415, show that the eastern part of Africa is pulling away from the rest of Africa. These rift valleys stretch over 4,000 miles from Jordan in Southwest Asia to Mozambique in Southern Africa.

PLACE Masai tribespeople climb the walls of the Great Rift Valley in Tanzania. **How were the rift valleys formed?**

416

DIFFERENTIATING INSTRUCTION **STUDENTS ACQUIRING ENGLISH/ESL**

UNDERSTANDING GEOGRAPHIC TERMS

Objective To create a resource that will help students acquire vocabulary

Class Time 20 minutes

Task Create a personal dictionary of geographic terms

Directions Have students work in pairs to make a personal dictionary of unfamiliar geographic terms. They should list the landforms and proper names of landforms in this section and describe them. You might provide a list like the one shown to model the activity.

DICTIONARY OF GEOGRAPHIC TERMS
basin: huge depressions, or sunken areas, in plateaus
Nile River: world's longest river; flows through Uganda, Sudan, and Egypt
rift valleys: long valleys formed by cracks between continental plates

A cluster of lakes formed at the bottoms of some of these rift valleys. These African lakes are unusually long and deep. Lake Tanganyika, the longest freshwater lake in the world, stretches about 420 miles and reaches a depth of more than 4,700 feet.

However, Africa's largest lake, Lake Victoria, sits in a shallow basin between two rift valleys. It is the world's second largest freshwater lake but is only 270 feet deep. B

Geographic Thinking
Making Comparisons
B How is Lake Victoria different from Lake Tanganyika?
B. Answer Lake Victoria is shallow and wide, while Lake Tanganyika is deep and long.

MOUNTAINS Africa contains mainly volcanic mountains. Mount Kenya and **Mount Kilimanjaro,** Africa's highest mountain, are both volcanoes. Volcanic activity also produced the Ethiopian Highlands, the Tibesti Mountains in the Sahara, and Mount Cameroon in West Africa. In addition, volcanic rock covers the Great Escarpment in Southern Africa. An **escarpment** is a steep slope with a nearly flat plateau on top. The Great Escarpment marks the edge of the continent's plateau in Southern Africa.

Connect to the Issues
ECONOMIC DEVELOPMENT
Oil Pipeline

The people of Chad and Cameroon gaze out at the construction of a new 665-mile oil pipeline with a sense of hope and worry. With new income from the oil, Chad plans to improve education, social services, and its infrastructure.

However, leaders are concerned because past African oil exploration has caused corruption, civil wars, poverty, and serious environmental damage.

Furthermore, people in Cameroon worry because the pipeline travels through otherwise untouched tropical rain forest. This pipeline represents a test for new African development policies.

Africa's Wealth of Resources

The story of Africa's natural resources is at once a story of plenty and one of scarcity. Africa has a huge amount of the world's minerals. But many African countries lack the industrial base and money to develop them.

A WEALTH OF MINERALS Africa's minerals make it one of the world's richest continents in terms of resources. African nations contain large amounts of gold, platinum, chromium, cobalt, copper, phosphates, diamonds, and many other minerals. For example, South Africa is the world's largest producer of chromium. Chromium is an element used in manufacturing stainless steel.

South Africa also produces nearly 80 percent of the world's platinum and has 30 percent of the world's gold reserves. Another important resource, cobalt, is used in high-grade steel for aircraft and industrial engines. African nations produce about 50 percent of the world's cobalt, mostly from the Democratic Republic of the Congo. Ores and minerals account for more than half of the total value of Africa's exports.

Africa's great mineral wealth, however, has not meant economic prosperity for most of its population. In the 19th and 20th centuries, European colonial rulers developed Africa's natural resources for export to Europe to manufacture goods there. As a result, many African nations have been slow to develop the infrastructure and industries that could turn these resources into valuable products. C

C. Answer European colonial powers removed resources from the continent to help run their own industrial economies.

CONNECT TO THE ISSUES
ECONOMIC DEVELOPMENT
C Why hasn't Africa's mineral wealth translated into wealth for most of its citizens?

OIL RESOURCES Nigeria, Libya, Algeria, and Angola are Africa's leading petroleum producers. Other countries, such as Gabon, have huge untapped oil reserves. Nigeria, Libya, Algeria, and Angola combine to produce about one-tenth of the world's oil.

Angola illustrates why valuable resources don't always benefit most Africans. Recently discovered offshore oil deposits will likely enable

Connect TO THE Issues

Oil Pipeline

Three African nations—Algeria, Libya, and Nigeria—belong to OPEC (Organization of Petroleum Exporting Countries). OPEC seeks to increase its members' economic strength by coordinating their petroleum policies. Ask students how oil drilling might create positive and negative effects for Chad. *(Positive—might provide funds for education, social services, infrastructure; negative—might lead to corruption, conflict, and environmental damage.)*

More About

Impact of Oil Money

Oil money doesn't always create conflict and unequal distribution of income. Alaska's oil industry has provided citizens with jobs and income. Further, each Alaskan receives an annual dividend (more than $1,900 in 2000) from royalties paid to their state for oil operations.

Instruct: Objective 

Africa's Wealth of Resources

- What important minerals are found in Africa? *(gold, platinum, chromium, cobalt, copper, phosphates, diamonds)*
- Why does oil-rich Angola have a poor public infrastructure? *(Oil money was spent on a civil war.)*

Critical Thinking Transparencies CT50
- Gold Production in Selected Countries, 1989–1999

DIFFERENTIATING INSTRUCTION **LESS PROFICIENT READERS**

UNDERSTANDING IMPORTANT FACTS

Objective To help students understand the importance of key facts

Class Time 30 minutes

Task Make a chart of resources and their uses

Directions Create a two-column chart on the chalkboard. Prompt students to name Africa's mineral resources and diverse commodities and list them in the left column. Then have students draw on the text and their own prior knowledge to list the way resources are used.

RESOURCES	USES
gold	money, jewelry, decoration
plantinum	jewelry, electrical wire, surgical instruments
chromium	manufacture of stainless steel and some paints
copper	coins, pipes, electrical wire

Instruct: Objective 4

Diversity of Resources

- What are two profitable commodities besides oil? *(coffee, lumber)*
- What problem does logging cause? *(depletes forests)*
- How do most Africans earn their living? *(by farming)*

Interpreting Photographs

Processing Coffee

Coffee seeds must be extracted from berries. A pulping machine contains a rotating disk and sharp plate that remove skin and pulp from ripened coffee berries. The remaining pulp is removed by fermenting wetted seeds in holding tanks. Then the seeds are dried. Ask students to describe how mechanized the work in the photo appears. *(Not very mechanized; no conveyor belts are used; workers carry drums of berries.)*

Assess & Reteach

GeoFocus Have students complete the sections on landforms and resources in their graphic organizers.

Formal Assessment
- Section Quiz, p. 274

Reteaching Activity
Have students work in pairs to list the physical features and resources of Africa. Then have them take turns quizzing each other.

In-Depth Resources: Unit 6
- Reteaching Activity, p. 10

Angola to surpass Nigeria as Africa's most oil-rich country. American oil companies pay Angola a fee for drilling rights and the oil. However, the Angolan government spent much of the money on fighting a civil war. This war, which raged from 1975 to 2002, may have claimed half a million lives. With loans from abroad, Angola has started to rebuild its schools, hospitals, and other public infrastructure. D

Seeing Patterns D How does Angola make money from its resources?

D. Answer It charges a fee to foreign governments for the right to remove the resources.

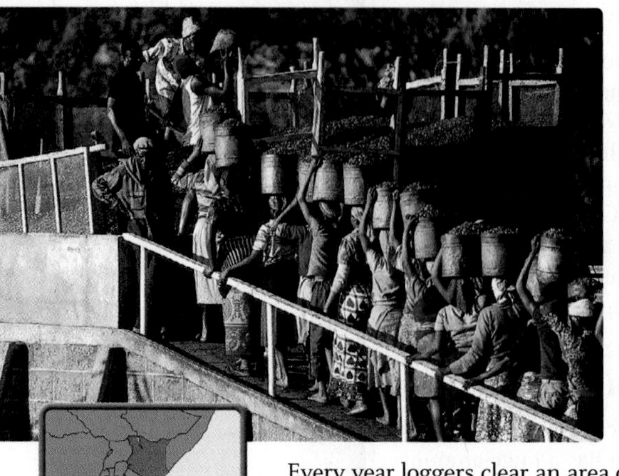

MOVEMENT Kenyan workers carry coffee berries to a pulping machine.

Diversity of Resources

From rain forests to roaring rivers, Africa possesses an incredible diversity of resources.

MAJOR COMMODITIES After oil, coffee is the most profitable commodity in Africa. Even though few Africans drink coffee, the continent grows 10 percent of the world's supply.

Lumber is another important commodity. Ethiopia leads African nations in lumber exports and ranks eighth worldwide in that area. However, logging is depleting Africa's forests. Every year loggers clear an area of land in Africa about twice the size of New Jersey. Other major commodities include sugar, palm oil, and cocoa. Côte d'Ivoire is the world's largest exporter of cocoa beans, the main ingredient in chocolate.

Agriculture is the single most important economic activity in Africa. About two-thirds of Africans earn their living from farming. In addition, farm products typically account for a third of the continent's exports. Farmers benefit from Africa's climate, which you will read about in the next section.

Section 1 Assessment

1 Places & Terms
Identify and explain where in the region these would be found.
- basin
- Nile River
- rift valley
- Mount Kilimanjaro
- escarpment

2 Taking Notes
PLACE Review the notes you took for this section.

Landforms	
Resources	

- What types of landforms are found in Africa?
- What kinds of resources does Africa possess?

3 Main Ideas
a. Why is Africa called the "plateau continent"?
b. What are some of Africa's distinctive landforms?
c. Why do you think Africa's abundance of natural resources has not translated into economic wealth for most of its population?

4 Geographic Thinking
Seeing Patterns How has Africa's physical geography affected its ability to use its resources for economic development? **Think about:**
- its use of rivers for transportation

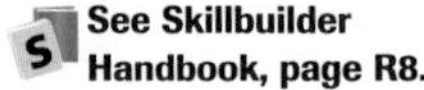
See Skillbuilder Handbook, page R8.

EXPLORING LOCAL GEOGRAPHY Examine a physical map of your state or region. Then study the map on page 403 to determine which African country has the most similar physical geography to your region or state. Create a **Venn diagram** identifying which physical features your state or region has in common with that country and the features that are different.

SECTION 1 ASSESSMENT ANSWERS

1. Places & Terms
basin, p. 415
Nile River, p. 416
rift valley, p. 416
Mount Kilimanjaro, p. 417
escarpment, p. 417

2. Taking Notes
- Africa contains rivers, great lakes, some large mountains but no long mountain chains, and the rift valleys.
- Africa possesses a wide array of resources including oil, gold, platinum, copper, and many others.

3. Main Ideas
a. Much of Africa lies at least 1,000 feet above sea level.
b. rift valleys; long, deep lakes; and volcanic mountains
c. European colonialism, difficult terrain, and unnavigable rivers have prevented Africans from taking advantage of abundant resources.

4. Geographic Thinking
Africa's rivers, though long, did not provide an efficient transportation network because of their many waterfalls and rapids.

GeoActivity

Integrated Assessment
- Rubric for a Venn diagram, 2.8

Map and Graph Skills

Reading an Economic Activity Map

Subsistence farming and nomadic herding are the primary economic activities in large sections of Africa. Even though African nations have a wealth of natural resources, mining and drilling for these resources are not evenly distributed throughout the continent. The thematic map below shows a wide variety of economic activities in Africa.

THE LANGUAGE OF MAPS An **economic activity map** is a thematic map that shows the location of economic activities over a large area such as a continent.

Economic Activities in Africa

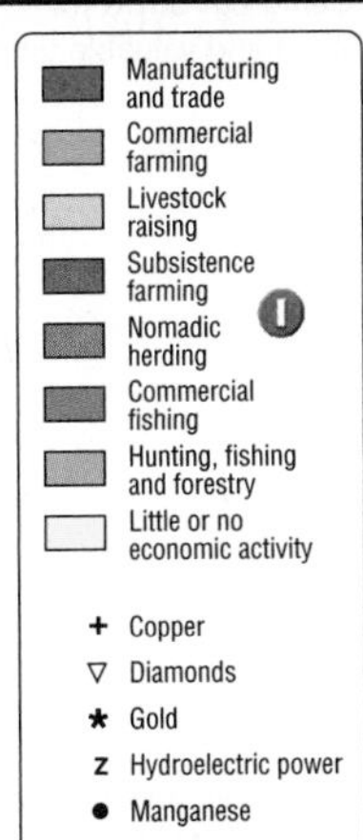

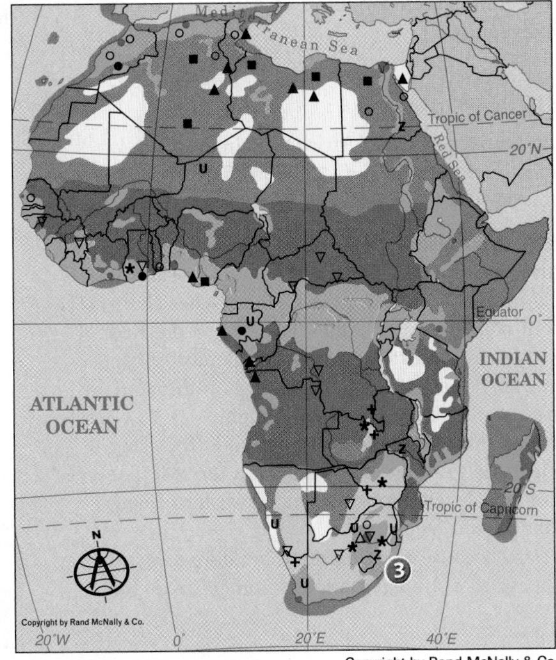

Copyright by Rand McNally & Co.

1 Each color represents the economic activity in which the majority of people are engaged.

2 The black symbols represent major drilling and mining for natural resources.

3 The symbols and colors show the combination of economic activities and natural resources in a particular location. For example, this map shows that Southern Africa contains livestock raising, mining, commercial fishing, and commercial farming.

Map and Graph Skills Assessment

1. Making Generalizations
In what region of Africa does most of the livestock raising take place?

2. Making Inferences
Why do you think so many manufacturing and trade centers are located near rivers or on the coasts?

3. Drawing Conclusions
What is the most common type of farming done in Africa?

OBJECTIVE

Understand and interpret economic activity maps.

Instruct: Objective

Reading an Economic Activity Map

- What is an economic activity map? *(a thematic map that shows the location of a region's economic activities)*
- What do the colors on an economic activities map represent? *(the economic activity in which the majority of people are engaged)*
- What are the primary economic activities in most of Africa? *(subsistence farming and nomadic herding)*

In-Depth Resources: Unit 6
- Map and Graph Skills, pp. 6–7

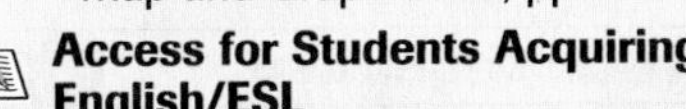
Access for Students Acquiring English/ESL
- Map and Graph Skills, pp. 97–98

Interpreting Maps

Manufacturing and Trade in Africa

Ask students to look at the map on page 419 and find the areas with significant manufacturing and trading activity. Have students compare the location of these areas with the same locations on the political map on page 405 of the Unit Atlas. Ask students if they notice any patterns. *(Most of the trading and manufacturing centers are near national capitals or large cities.)*

MAP SKILLS ASSESSMENT ANSWERS

1. southern Africa

2. Rivers and coasts provide convenient access transportation for manufactured goods.

3. subsistence farming

SECTION 2 OBJECTIVES

1. Explain the distribution of warm climates in Africa.
2. Describe Africa's rainfall patterns.
3. Examine Africa's tropical grasslands.
4. Describe rain-forest biodiversity and practices that endanger it.

SKILLBUILDER: Interpreting Maps, p. 421

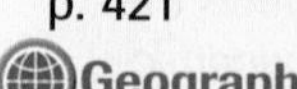

GeographicThinking

Using the Atlas, p. 421
Seeing Patterns, p. 422
Making Comparisons, p. 423

Focus & Motivate

Ask students how climate in Africa might affect agriculture. *(Desert conditions make farming difficult, while tropical conditions foster it.)*

Instruct: Objective 

A Warm Continent

- What deserts are located in Africa? *(Sahara, Kalahari, Namib)*
- Why is so much of Africa tropical? *(Nearly 90 percent lies between the tropics of Cancer and Capricorn.)*

In-Depth Resources: Unit 6
- Guided Reading, p. 4

CAPTION ANSWER It might destroy valuable farmland and grazing lands.

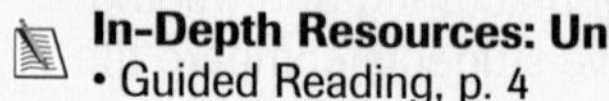

Climate and Vegetation

Main Ideas
- Africa contains dry and hot deserts, warm tropics, and permanently snow-capped mountains.
- Africa's vegetation includes thick rain forests, tall grasslands, and desert areas.

Places & Terms

Sahara **Serengeti Plain**
aquifer **canopy**
oasis

CONNECT TO THE ISSUES
ECONOMIC DEVELOPMENT Africa's tropical rain forests are being cut down for farmland and valuable timber.

A HUMAN PERSPECTIVE In 1352, 48-year-old Ibn Battuta, a great traveler from Morocco, set out for the empire of Mali in West Africa. His most challenging obstacle was the Sahara, a desert nearly the same size as the continental United States. Battuta and his caravan set out in February. They traveled only in early morning and early evening to avoid the midday heat. Even so, they battled brutally high temperatures and the constant threat of thirst. Reaching Mali around April, Batutta had covered more than 1,000 miles, all on foot. The Sahara today remains just as hazardous—fewer than 2 million of Africa's approximately one billion people live in it.

A Warm Continent

You can see from the map on page 421 that Africa lies almost entirely between the tropic of Cancer and the tropic of Capricorn. This location gives most of Africa warm, tropical temperatures.

THE DESERTS Two deserts, the Kalahari and Namib, can be found in Southern Africa. In North Africa lies the **Sahara,** the largest desert in the world. (Sahara actually means "desert" in Arabic.) It stretches about 3,000 miles across the continent, from the Atlantic Ocean to the Red Sea, and also runs 1,200 miles from north to south. Temperatures can rise above 130° in the summer, hot enough to cook an egg on the sand. But in winter, temperatures can fall below freezing at night.

Only about 20 percent of the Sahara consists of sand. Towering mountains, rock formations, and gravelly plains make up the rest. For instance, the Tibesti Mountains, located mostly in northwestern Chad, rise to heights of more than 11,000 feet.

Travel in the Sahara is risky because of the extreme conditions. Many travelers rely on the camel as desert transportation. A camel can go for

PLACE Rolling sand dunes are only a small part of the Sahara's varied landscape.
How might an expanding desert affect the lives of the people living near it?

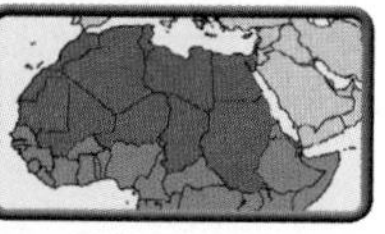

420

SECTION 2 PROGRAM RESOURCES

In-Depth Resources: Unit 6
- Guided Reading, p. 4
- Building Vocabulary, p. 9
- Reteaching Activity, p. 11

Guided Reading Workbook
- Section 2

Access for Students Acquiring English/ESL
- Guided Reading, p. 94

Formal Assessment
- Section Quiz, p. 275

Integrated Assessment
- Rubric for a chart, 2.2

INTEGRATED TECHNOLOGY

Power Presentations

Test Generator
- Section 2 Quiz

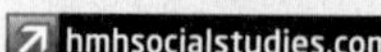
hmhsocialstudies.com

TEST-TAKING RESOURCES

Strategies for Test Preparation

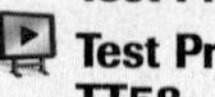
Test Practice Transparencies TT58

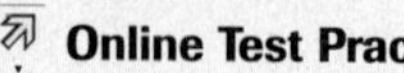
Online Test Practice

up to 17 days without water. In addition, its eyelashes protect the eyes from blowing sand, and the nostrils can be squeezed shut.

Ironically, as much as 6,000 feet under this hottest and driest of places lie huge stores of underground water called **aquifers**. In some places, this water has come to the surface. Such a place is called an **oasis.** It supports vegetation and wildlife and is a critical resource for people living in the desert.

THE TROPICS Africa has a large tropical area—the largest of any continent. In fact, nearly 90 percent of the continent lies within the tropics of Cancer and Capricorn, as you can see on the map to the right. Temperatures run high most of the year. A town in eastern Ethiopia holds the world record for the highest average annual temperature—93.9°F (34.4°C). In that same town the average daily high temperature was 106°F (41.1°C).

In humid regions of the tropics, variance in temperature between winter and summer are slight. Differences in night and day temperatures tend to be greater than differences between seasons. An African saying describes nighttime as the "winter" of the tropics. A

Climates of Africa

Tropical wet
Tropical wet and dry
Desert
Semiarid
Mediterranean
Humid subtropical
Marine west coast
Highland

0 400 800 miles
0 400 800 kilometers
Lambert Azimuthal Equal-Area Projection

SKILLBUILDER: Interpreting Maps

1 **REGION** What climate zones are found only in Southern Africa?

2 **PLACE** What is Africa's most dominant climate zone?

Using the Atlas

A Which climate regions of Africa do the tropics of Cancer and Capricorn pass through?

A. Answer Cancer passes through desert, and Capricorn passes mostly through desert and semiarid.

Sunshine and Rainfall

Rainfall in Africa is often a matter of extremes. Some parts get too much rain, while other parts receive too little. The amount of rainfall can vary greatly from year to year as well as season to season. These variations have had a tremendous impact on East Africa, which endured several droughts in the 1980s and 1990s, and again in 2005–2006.

RAINFALL PATTERNS The rain forest in Central Africa receives the most precipitation, as rain falls throughout the year. Most of the rest of Africa, however, has one or two rainy seasons. Africa's tropical savanna stretches through the middle of the continent. It covers nearly half the total surface area of Africa. Rainy seasons in this area can last up to six months. The closer an area is to the equator, the longer the rainy season. The closer an area is to the desert, the longer the dry season.

Africa's west coast also receives a great deal of rain. The region around Monrovia, Liberia, experiences an average annual rainfall of more than 120 inches. In contrast, many parts of Africa barely get 20 inches of rain over the course of a year. In the Sahara and other deserts, rain may not

AFRICA

Interpreting Maps

Climates of Africa

Have students examine the map. Ask them how many different climates are shown. Ask what the map shows that might account for the diversity of climates. Ask what influences on climate the map omits. *(There are eight climates; the continent extends through many degrees of latitude; the map omits elevation and prevailing winds.)*

SKILLBUILDER ANSWERS

1. humid subtropical and marine west coast **2.** desert

More About

Camels

Camels are protected from blowing sand by double rows of eyelashes and haired ear openings. In addition, their wide-spreading soft feet keep them from sinking into the sand. Camels can carry a rider at eight to ten miles per hour for 18 hours.

Instruct: Objective 2

Sunshine and Rainfall

- What region receives the most rain? *(Central Africa)*
- How long can dry spells last in desert regions? *(five or six years)*
- What relationship do rainfall patterns in Africa have to the equator? *(Rainfall is heaviest near the equator.)*

ACTIVITY OPTION | CRITICAL THINKING

MAKING GENERALIZATIONS

Explaining the Skill Tell students that a generalization is a broad statement summarizing several different pieces of information. It is important when making generalizations not to leap to false conclusions based on a single piece of information. Using several different types of sources–such as maps, graphs, photographs, and written material–helps one to make accurate generalizations.

Applying the Skill Point out to students that pages 420-421 have three different sources of information about the Sahara: text, a photograph, and a map. Have students study all three. Then ask if this generalization is true: "The Sahara is covered with sand dunes." *(No.)* What is the basis for their answer? *(The text says dunes cover only 20 percent of the Sahara.)* Ask students to form their own generalizations about the desert. *(The Sahara is vast and arid but contains oases where vegetation grows; the Sahara is consistently dry but has a variety of landforms.)*

Instruct: Objective 3

A Grassy Continent

- What vegetation covers most of Africa? *(tropical grassland)*
- Why is the Serengeti still covered with wild grass? *(The climate is too dry, and the soil is too hard for crops.)*
- Which animals thrive there? *(wildebeests, gazelles, zebras)*

Instruct: Objective 

Africa's Extremes

- What vegetation is typical of Central Africa? *(tropical rain forest)*
- How much diversity can be found in a square acre of rain forest? *(almost 100 types of trees and hundreds of bird species)*
- What danger exists from the slash-and-burn farming method? *(rain forests may gradually disappear)*

Interpreting Photographs

Serengeti National Park

Tell students that the park has become a refuge not only for the wildebeests in the photograph, but also for elephants. Increasing human populations and farming operations are displacing elephants that live outside the park.

CAPTION ANSWER It protects wildlife from hunters and allows animals to live in their natural habitat.

fall for years. Children living in those areas may not see rain until they are five or six years old!

AFRICA'S MODERATE AREAS A Mediterranean climate exists on the northern and southern tips of the continent. Clear, blue skies in these places are normal. Rain falls usually only in the winter—December and January in North Africa and June and July in Southern Africa. Summer temperatures in Johannesburg, South Africa, average around 68°F.

A Grassy Continent

Africa's vegetation—like its climate—is almost mirrored north and south of the equator. Africa's vegetation consists of grasslands, rain forests, and a wide variety of other plant life.

TROPICAL GRASSLAND Tropical grassland covers most of the continent. One example of this grassland is the **Serengeti Plain** in northern Tanzania. Its dry climate and hard soil prevent the growth of trees and many crops, but these conditions are perfect for growing grass. Serengeti National Park, located within the Serengeti Plain, contains some of the best grasslands in the world. Some of these grasses can grow taller than the average person. The abundance of grass makes Serengeti National Park an ideal place for grazing animals. Huge herds of wildebeests, gazelles, and zebras roam there. It is the place where the largest numbers of land mammals still make annual migrations.

BACKGROUND *Serengeti* means "endless plains" in the Masai language.

PLACE These wildebeests live in Serengeti National Park, which was founded in 1951. **How might the park help conservation efforts in Africa?**

Africa's Extremes

An enormous tropical rain forest stretches across Central Africa.

RAIN FOREST The major rain forests of Africa sit on the equator in the area of the Congo Basin. One square acre of rain forest can contain almost 100 different kinds of trees. It may also be home to hundreds of species of birds. The massive number of plants, leaves, and trees block out much of the sunlight that would otherwise hit the floor of the rain forest. Beneath this umbrella of vegetation, the air is hot and filled with moisture. As a result, plants and other vegetation quickly decompose, or decay. For example, a fallen leaf in Europe decomposes in about a year. A leaf on the jungle floor in Africa decomposes in about six weeks. B

Most animals in a rain forest live in the canopy. The **canopy** refers to the uppermost layer of branches, about

B. Answer The large number of plants and trees block out sunlight and trap moisture underneath.

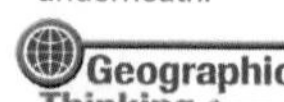

Seeing Patterns B How do rain forests maintain such a high level of moisture?

ACTIVITY OPTION **INTERNET RESEARCH**

WRITING A NEWS REPORT

Objective To develop research skills

Class Time 30 minutes

Task Write a news report using two sources

Directions Direct students to the Web site for *World Geography* at **hmhsocialstudies.com.** Click on the Current Events button and follow the links to sources of information on current issues in Africa. They should find two sources of information about current environmental issues in Nigeria or Egypt and use those sources to write a brief news report.

OPTIONAL ACTIVITY If Internet access is limited or unavailable, have students use library reference sources to find sources.

BLOCK SCHEDULING

150 feet above the ground. Birds, monkeys, and flying foxes move from tree to tree and enjoy the bounty of the rain forest. A large number of snakes live in these rain forests, too. The Gaboon viper, the largest African viper, can weigh as much as 18 pounds and have fangs more than two inches long. Another snake, the black-necked cobra, can shoot its venom more than eight feet through the air.

However, farmers using slash-and-burn agricultural methods are endangering the existence of the rain forest. As you read in Chapter 9, slash-and-burn farming is a method in which people clear fields by cutting and burning trees and other vegetation, the ashes of which fertilize the soil. After farmers have exhausted the soil, they burn another patch of forest. Slash-and-burn farming is responsible for the nearly complete destruction of Madagascar's rain forest. Experts estimate that over half of Africa's original rain forest has been destroyed.

BACKGROUND The National Cancer Institute estimates that 70 percent of the plants found useful for cancer treatment are found only in rain forests.

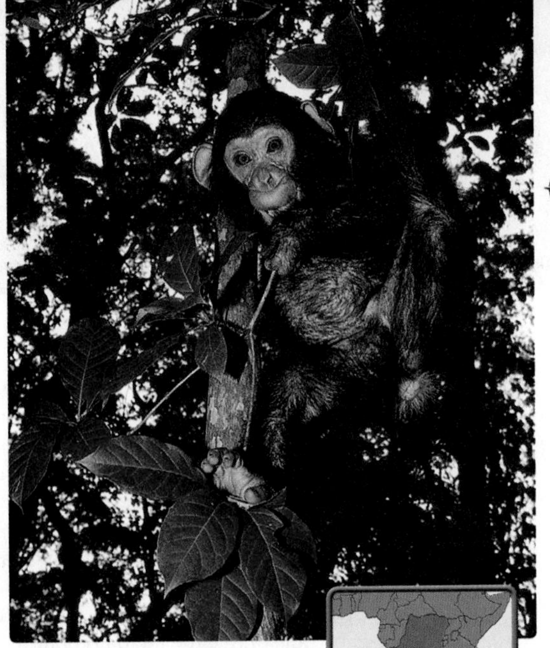

MOVEMENT Animals, such as this chimpanzee, move about the Ituri rain forest in the Democratic Republic of the Congo.

VARIETIES OF PLANTLIFE All of Africa's regions contain a variety of vegetation. North Africa contains sizable oak and pine forests in the upper reaches of the Atlas Mountains. The mangrove tree of West Africa sprouts up along river banks in swamps and river deltas. Mangrove tree roots are breeding grounds for fish. They also help to build up dry land by holding silt. In the next section, you will read about different ways that people in Africa have interacted with their environment.

AFRICA

Section 2 Assessment

1 Places & Terms

Explain the meaning of each of the following terms.

- Sahara
- aquifer
- oasis
- Serengeti Plain
- canopy

2 Taking Notes

PLACE Review the notes you took for this section.

- What are the different climates found in Africa?
- How does climate affect the vegetation of Africa?

3 Main Ideas

a. What is the largest climatic feature in Africa?

b. Why does most of Africa have high temperatures?

c. What are the different kinds of vegetation growing in Africa?

4 Geographic Thinking

Making Comparisons What are the similarities between the climates of Africa north and south of the equator?

Think about:

- the Sahara
- where the equator cuts across Africa

hmhsocialstudies.com RESEARCH WEB LINKS

MAKING COMPARISONS Choose a place in Africa and a place in the United States at about the same latitude. Use encyclopedias or the Internet to compare the climate and vegetation of the two places. Create a **chart** comparing the two locations.

21st CENTURY

Interpreting Photographs

Chimpanzee in Ituri Rain Forest

Have students examine the photograph. Ask them what might happen to the chimpanzee and its habitat if present trends continue. *(They might disappear due to human encroachment and farming.)*

More About

Climate and Burning

Many scientists warn that carbon dioxide produced by the burning of rain forests will form a layer that traps heat in Earth's atmosphere. Slash-and-burn farming may contribute to a global warming trend and accelerate the alteration of Earth's climates.

Assess & Reteach

GeoFocus Have students complete the sections on climate and vegetation in their graphic organizers.

Formal Assessment
- Section Quiz, p. 275

Reteaching Activity
Have students write a paragraph about Africa's climate and vegetation. Ask several students to read their paragraphs aloud, and have the class suggest additional points that could be included.

In-Depth Resources: Unit 6
- Reteaching Activity, p. 11

SECTION 2 ASSESSMENT ANSWERS

1. Places & Terms
Sahara, p. 420
aquifer, p. 421
oasis, p. 421
Serengeti Plain, p. 422
canopy, p. 423

2. Taking Notes
- tropical wet, tropical wet and dry, desert, semiarid, Mediterranean, humid subtropical, marine west coast, highland
- The Serengeti receives enough rain to nourish grasses, but little rain falls in North Africa and Southern Africa. On the northern and southern tips of the continent, plant life flourishes in a Mediterranean climate.

3. Main Ideas
a. the Sahara
b. because Africa straddles the equator and nearly 90 percent of it lies within the Tropics
c. Africa has a variety of forests, lush grasslands, and large rain forests.

4. Geographic Thinking
The northern and southern tips both have Mediterranean climate. Northern and southern Africa each has a desert and a tropical area.

GeoActivity

Integrated Assessment
- Rubric for a chart, 2.2

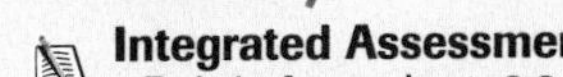

SECTION 3 OBJECTIVES

1. Describe the process of desertification.
2. Explain the harm caused by oil operations in Nigeria.
3. Examine the good and bad effects of the Aswan High Dam.

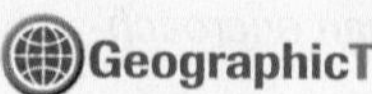

GeographicThinking

Using the Atlas, p. 425
Seeing Patterns, pp. 426, 427
Drawing Conclusions, p. 427

Focus & Motivate

Ask students what harm might be done when humans harvest or extract natural resources. *(alteration or destruction of landforms; threats to wildlife; pollution)*

Instruct: Objective 

Desertification of the Sahel

- What process threatens the Sahel? *(desertification)*
- What happens when livestock overgraze vegetation and farmers clear land to plant crops? *(Soil is exposed, and erosion may occur.)*
- What can be done to slow the process of desertification? *(increase tree planting, use land more efficiently)*

In-Depth Resources: Unit 6
- Guided Reading, p. 5

3 Human–Environment Interaction

Main Ideas

- The Sahara's expansion is causing problems for Africa's farmers.
- The Nigerian oil industry has caused serious environmental damage in the Niger delta.

Places & Terms

Niger delta
Sahel
desertification
Aswan High Dam
silt

CONNECT TO THE ISSUES
COLONIALISM European colonialism has caused political, economic, and environmental problems in Africa today.

A HUMAN PERSPECTIVE Akierou Awe lives in a mud-brick house in Nigeria's **Niger delta,** a region that contains most of Nigeria's oil. On the morning of July 10, 2000, Awe's four sons had been collecting fuel from a leaking pipeline to help scrape out a living in this poverty-stricken region. They hoped to resell the fuel for more than the going rate of 21 cents a quart. Suddenly, an explosion shook the area, and a fire spread along a mile-long stretch of the pipeline. The blast killed more than 300 people, including three of Awe's sons. This accident is one of many in the recent past that have claimed the lives of hundreds of Nigerians. Nigeria has become one of the top oil producers in the world, but at the cost of thousands of lives and major environmental ruin in the region.

Desertification of the Sahel

Sahel means "shore of the desert" in Arabic. You can see from the physical map on page 403 that the Sahel is a narrow band of dry grassland that runs east to west along the southern edge of the Sahara. People use the Sahel for farming and herding. Since the 1960s, the desert has spread into the Sahel. This shift of the desert is called desertification. **Desertification** is an expansion of dry conditions into moist areas that are next to deserts. Normally, it results from nature's long-term cycle, but as you can see in the illustration below, human activity is speeding up the process.

HUMAN CAUSES OF DESERTIFICATION Geographers and other scientists have identified several human activities that increase the pace of desertification. For example, allowing overgrazing of vegetation by

The Process of Desertification

1. The Sahel receives little rainfall. The vegetation lives in a fragile state, having barely enough water and food to survive.
2. Farming, overgrazing by livestock, and burning wood for fuel all contribute to desertification.

424

SECTION 3 PROGRAM RESOURCES

In-Depth Resources: Unit 6
- Guided Reading, p. 5
- Building Vocabulary, p. 9
- Skillbuilder Practice, p. 8
- Reteaching Activity, p. 12

Guided Reading Workbook
- Section 3

Access for Students Acquiring English/ESL
- Guided Reading, p. 95
- Skillbuilder Practice, p. 96

Formal Assessment
- Section Quiz, p. 276

Integrated Assessment
- Rubric for a cause-and-effect chart, 2.2
- Rubric for a map, 2.1

INTEGRATED TECHNOLOGY

Power Presentations

Test Generator
- Section 3 Quiz

TEST-TAKING RESOURCES

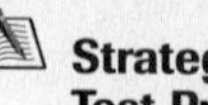
Strategies for Test Preparation

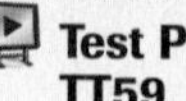
Test Practice Transparencies TT59

Online Test Practice

livestock exposes the soil. Animals also trample the soil, making it more vulnerable to erosion.

Farming also increases the pace of desertification. When farmers clear the land to plant crops, they expose the soil to wind, which can cause erosion. In addition, when farmers drill for water to irrigate crops, they put further stress on the Sahel. Widespread drilling and more irrigation increase salt levels in the soil, which prevent the growth of vegetation.

Increasing population levels are an indirect cause of desertification. More people require more food. As a result, farmers continue to clear more land for crops, burn more wood for fuel, and overfarm the land they already have.

RESULTS OF DESERTIFICATION Desertification has affected many parts of Africa. For example, large forests once existed around Khartoum, Sudan. In addition, desertification is slowly destroying a tropical rain forest around Lake Chad in the southern edge of the Sahel. Slowing desertification is difficult. Some African countries have increased tree planting and promoted more efficient use of forests and farmland in hopes of slowing the process. A

Geographic Thinking

Using the Atlas
A Refer to the physical map on page 403. What countries are probably most affected by desertification of the Sahel?
A. Answer Sudan, Chad, Niger, Mali, Mauritania

Harming the Environment in Nigeria

Another environmental issue concerns the discovery of oil in Nigeria in 1956. Rich oil deposits in the Niger delta made Nigeria one of Africa's wealthiest countries. However, in drilling for oil, the Nigerian government and foreign oil companies have often damaged the land and harmed the people living in the Niger delta.

A MAJOR OIL PRODUCER Nigeria is the sixth leading oil exporter in the world. Two million barrels are extracted each day, much of it shipped to the United States. Oil accounts for 80 to 90 percent of Nigeria's income.

During the 1970s, high oil prices made Nigeria one of the wealthiest nations in Africa. As a result, the government borrowed heavily against the future sale of its oil. However, oil prices eventually fell, and the Nigerian government owed millions of dollars to other nations, including the United States. Mismanagement, poor planning, corruption, and a decline in oil prices left Nigeria poorer than before the oil boom.

Instruct: Objective 2

Harming the Environment in Nigeria

- What made Nigeria one of Africa's wealthiest countries? *(discovery of oil there in 1956, high oil prices in the 1970s)*
- How did the Nigerian government later impoverish the nation? *(borrowing, mismanagement, poor planning, corruption)*
- How did foreign oil companies harm Nigeria? *(non-existent or slow clean-up operations of oil spills, often resulting in fires that caused acid rain, soot, and respiratory diseases)*

3 During desertification, dry grasses die and are replaced by tougher plants like shrubs. These plants do not cover the soil as well as grass.
4 With less vegetation covering the soil, any rain that falls evaporates quickly. Over the years, the wind then blows the dry soil into a desert-like state.

AFRICA

Interpreting Infographics

The Process of Desertification

Have students examine the infographic. Explain that desertification takes place gradually; the four stages pictured here show "snapshots in time" of a place undergoing that process. Direct students' attention to the background. Ask how it relates to the four overlaid cross-sections of land. *(The background depicts the desertification process in another way; it shows the gradual nature of the process.)* Ask why Sahel vegetation is fragile. *(Little rain falls.)*

ACTIVITY OPTION **SKILLBUILDER LESSON**

DETERMINING CAUSE AND EFFECT

Explaining the Skill Remind students that a cause is an event that makes something happen; in geography, both physical processes and human actions can be causes. An effect is the result of a cause. Tell students that geographers must be careful to look for all the causes of a particular situation, or they might recommend the wrong course of action.

Refer students to the text and infographic on pages 424-425 on the topic of desertification.

Applying the Skill Ask pairs of students to answer the following questions. After 10 minutes, have them share their answers with the class.

- Which causes of desertification are physical processes, and which are human actions? *(physical: a climate with little rain; human: clearing land for farming, overgrazing livestock)*
- Which actions are recommended to slow the process of desertification? *(better land use and irrigation methods; planting trees)*
- Do the actions address physical or human causes? *(human)*

In-Depth Resources: Unit 6
- Skillbuilder Practice, p. 8

More About

Conditions in Nigeria

The current state of the Nigerian infrastructure hinders economic development. Periodic blackouts force poor households to discard much-needed perishable food. The telephone system is inadequate, clean water is scarce, and roads are poor. And ironically, gasoline supplies remain low in the country that is the sixth biggest exporter of crude oil.

Instruct: Objective 3

Controlling the Nile

- How did construction of the dam affect the surrounding area? *(relocation of many people and Abu Simbel; loss of ancient treasures)*
- What have been negative effects of the dam? *(decreased soil fertility, increased salt in soil, increased rates of disease)*

Interpreting Photographs

Aswan High Dam

Tell students that Lake Nasser extends south from the dam for 200 miles in Egypt and 100 miles in Sudan. Ask students how the photograph enhances the map. *(It aids visualizing the dam and comprehending its vast size.)*

CAPTION ANSWER more farmable land, efficient control of the water supply, hydroelectric power, commercial fishing

DESTROYING THE LAND AND PEOPLE The damage caused by oil companies and the Nigerian government has been severe. More than 4,000 oil spills have occurred in the Niger delta over the past four decades. Cleanup operations have been slow and sometimes non-existent. Fires often resulted, causing acid rain and massive deposits of soot, and people in the region contracted respiratory diseases. In addition, between 1998 and 2000, oil pipeline explosions killed more than 2,000 people. Many of these explosions were not accidents but were caused intentionally. Bandits, in cooperation with corrupt government officials and the military, drain fuel from the pipelines and then resell it. Once the bandits finish draining oil, local villagers arrive. They use small cans to collect any spilled oil and then sell it. B

Aswan High Dam

HUMAN–ENVIRONMENT INTERACTION The Aswan High Dam has helped Egypt control the flooding of the Nile River.
What are some of the benefits of the Aswan High Dam?

Geographic Thinking

Seeing Patterns
B Why did bandits and corrupt government officials drain fuel from the pipelines?

B. Answer It was a way for them to make money. They would steal the oil and then resell it.

A NEW START In 1999, Nigeria adopted a new constitution, and in May, Olusegun Obasanjo became Nigeria's new president. Although a former Nigerian military leader himself, he distanced himself from the armed forces. He started many economic reforms and fired corrupt government officials.

In April 2007, Nigeria elected a new president, Umara Musa. When Musa took office it was the first time a Nigerian civilian-run government changed hands. Now he faces the task of finding ways for Nigeria to benefit from oil.

Controlling the Nile

Egypt faces environmental challenges caused by another resource—water. Throughout history, the Egyptians have tried to control the floodwaters of the Nile River. Ancient Egyptians built canals and small dams. In spite of these efforts, though, the people still experienced cycles of floods and droughts. To solve these problems, Egyptians completed the first Aswan Dam on the Nile in 1902, which quickly became outmoded.

THE ASWAN HIGH DAM Four miles upriver from the first Aswan Dam, the Egyptians cut a huge channel through the land beside the Nile River. The builders used the rocks from the channel as a base for their new creation—the **Aswan High Dam**—which was completed in 1970. Lake Nasser, which Egypt shares with Sudan, is the artificial lake created behind the dam. It stretches for nearly 300 miles.

DIFFERENTIATING INSTRUCTION **GIFTED AND TALENTED STUDENTS**

WRITING A POSITION PAPER

Objective To develop research skills and write a persuasive statement using facts as evidence

Class Time One class period

Task Write a position paper either supporting or opposing construction of the Three Gorges Dam in China

Directions Point out that the same geographic issue often arises in more than one place. For example, China is constructing the Three Gorges Dam for many of the same reasons that led to the construction of the Aswan High Dam. Yet protestors have raised concerns about environmental and humanitarian losses. Have students do independent research on the construction and anticipated effects of Three Gorges Dam. Students may use the Internet and other printed sources of information. (There is a discussion of this topic on pages 628–630 in Unit 9.) Then each student should write a position paper that tries to persuade Chinese officials either to halt or continue the project.

The dam gives farmers a regular supply of water. It holds the Nile's floodwaters, releasing them as needed so that farmers can use the water effectively for irrigation. As a result of the dam, farmers can now have two or three harvests per year rather than one. Irrigation canals even keep some fields in continuous production through the use of artificial fertilizers. The dam has increased Egypt's farmable land by 50 percent. The dam has also helped Egypt avoid droughts and floods.

BACKGROUND
The channel next to the Aswan High Dam produces about 40 percent of Egypt's electricity, and Lake Nasser supports commercial fishing.

PROBLEMS WITH THE DAM Though the dam has provided Egypt with many benefits, it has also created some problems. During the dam's construction, many people had to be relocated, including thousands of Nubians, whose way of life was permanently changed. In addition, one of ancient Egypt's treasures, the temples at Abu Simbel, had to be moved. Other smaller ancient treasures could not be saved and now lie at the bottom of Lake Nasser.

The dam also decreased the fertility of the soil around the Nile. First, the river no longer deposits its rich **silt**, or sediment, on the farmland. Farmers must now rely on expensive artificial fertilizers to enrich the soil. Second, this year-round irrigation has resulted in a rising water table in Egypt. As a result, salts from deep in the earth have decreased the fertility of the soil. Before the dam was built, floodwaters flushed out the salt. Now expensive field drains have to be installed. C

Geographic Thinking
Seeing Patterns
C How do farmers fertilize their land now that the dam traps all the silt?
C. Answer
Farmers must buy expensive artificial fertilizers.

Rates of malaria and other diseases have increased due to greater numbers of mosquitos, which thrive in the still waters of Lake Nasser and the irrigation canals. Furthermore, because Lake Nasser holds the floodwaters, Egyptians lose millions of gallons of fresh water every year to evaporation. Measuring the success of the Aswan High Dam is difficult. For all the ways it has helped Egyptians, it has also created new problems.

More About
The Temples of Abu Simbel
Built by the pharaoh Ramses II, the two temples at Abu Simbel were carved out of a sandstone cliff. Realizing that the lake created by the Aswan High Dam would cover the temples, the Egyptian government and UNESCO launched a campaign to save them. Workers, engineers, and scientists dug away the top of the cliff, disassembled the temples, and rebuilt them on higher ground. Included in the salvaged treasures were four magnificent 66-foot statues of Ramses II.

Assess & Reteach
GeoFocus Have students complete the human-environment interaction section of their graphic organizers.

Formal Assessment
• Section Quiz, p. 276

Reteaching Activity
Divide students into small groups and have them briefly discuss the environmental issues raised in this section. Ask a student from each group to summarize the discussion and share that summary with the class.

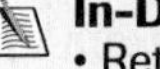
In-Depth Resources: Unit 6
• Reteaching Activity, p. 12

AFRICA

Section 3 Assessment

1 Places & Terms
Explain the meaning or identify the location of each of the following terms.
- Niger delta
- Sahel
- desertification
- Aswan High Dam
- silt

2 Taking Notes
HUMAN-ENVIRONMENT INTERACTION Review the notes you took for this section.

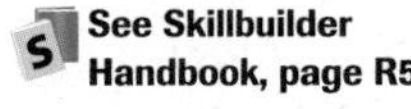

- Which activities illustrate human control of the environment?
- Which examples illustrate an environment changed by humans?

3 Main Ideas
a. What are some of the causes of desertification?
b. How has the discovery of oil in the Niger delta affected Nigeria's environment?
c. What were some of the reasons that the Egyptian government built the Aswan High Dam?

4 Geographic Thinking
Drawing Conclusions Do you think that the benefits of the Aswan High Dam have outweighed its problems?
Think about:
- the dam's effect on Egypt's food supply and farmers

See Skillbuilder Handbook, page R5.

ASKING GEOGRAPHIC QUESTIONS Study the map of the Aswan High Dam on page 426. Write three geographic questions about the map, such as one concerning the location of the dam. Write a **report** answering one of your three questions. Then present your findings to the class.

SECTION 3 ASSESSMENT ANSWERS

1. Places & Terms
Niger delta, p. 424
Sahel, p. 424
desertification, p. 424
Aswan High Dam, p. 426
silt, p. 427

2. Taking Notes
- The Aswan High Dam controls flooding of the Nile River.
- Humans have increased the rate of desertification; the oil industry has damaged the environment in the Niger River delta.

3. Main Ideas
a. overgrazing, trampling of the soil by livestock, irrigation, overfarming
b. Oil spills and large fires resulted in acid rain and massive soot deposits.
c. The Egyptian government needed to increase the food supply and control the Nile's sometimes dangerous flooding.

4. Geographic Thinking
Some might say that the benefits of more food, hydroelectric power, and flood control outweigh the problems. Others might say that the relocation of the Nubians, the expense of artificial fertilizers and field drains, and the increased incidence of diseases outweigh the benefits.

GeoActivity

Integrated Assessment
• Rubric for a cause-and-effect chart, 2.2

Reviewing Places & Terms

A. 1. Nile River, p. 416
2. rift valley, p. 416
3. escarpment, p. 417
4. Sahara, p. 420
5. oasis, p. 421
6. Serengeti Plain, p. 422
7. Sahel, p. 424
8. desertification, p. 424
9. Aswan High Dam, p. 426
10. silt, p. 427

B. Possible Responses

11. Silt enhances the fertility of the soil.
12. The Nile is the world's longest river.
13. This movement creates rift valleys.
14. The Sahara is the world's largest desert.
15. Desertification occurs in grassy areas overtaken by desert sands.
16. The Serengeti Plain is home to the world's largest herds of migrating mammals.
17. Oases support vegetation and are critical resources for people living in the desert.
18. The Sahel is a delicately balanced region of wild grasses adjacent to the Sahara.
19. An escarpment, the Great Escarpment, marks the edge of the continent's plateau.
20. Aswan High Dam is an example of human-environment interaction.

Chapter 18 Assessment

VISUAL SUMMARY
PHYSICAL GEOGRAPHY OF AFRICA

Landforms and Resources

- A large plateau covers most of Africa.
- Long, thin valleys, called rift valleys, stretch along East Africa.
- Africa contains many valuable resources including oil, diamonds, and gold.

Climate and Vegetation

- The Sahara, the largest desert in the world, stretches across northern Africa.
- Nearly 90 percent of Africa lies within the Tropics.
- A large, grassy area called the Serengeti Plain provides an ideal natural habitat for Africa's wild animals.

Human-Environment Interaction

- Desertification results from nature's cycle, farming, overgrazing, and clearing too much land for crops.
- People and the environment in Nigeria have suffered as a result of the country's poor management and corruption of the oil industry.
- The Aswan High Dam helped to increase Egypt's food supply but has also caused environmental problems.

Reviewing Places & Terms

A. Briefly explain the importance of each of the following.

1. Nile River
2. rift valley
3. escarpment
4. Sahara
5. oasis
6. Serengeti Plain
7. Sahel
8. desertification
9. Aswan High Dam
10. silt

B. Answer the questions about vocabulary in complete sentences.

11. What is sediment that is deposited on farmland by rivers and also acts as a fertilizer?
12. What is the longest river in the world?
13. What does the pulling apart of continental plates create?
14. What is the largest desert in the world?
15. What is the process in which dry conditions spread into areas that are moist?
16. Where do Africa's large mammal migrations take place?
17. What supports vegetation and is a critical resource for people living in the desert?
18. What is a narrow region of grassland on the southern edge of the Sahara?
19. What marks the edge of Africa's plateau in Southern Africa?
20. Which of the terms above is an example of how humans have adapted to the environment?

Main Ideas

Landforms and Resources (pp. 415–419)

1. In what ways does the Nile River support life?
2. What are some of the abundant resources in Africa?
3. Why does oil in Angola not always benefit Angolans?

Climate and Vegetation (pp. 420–423)

4. What is the physical geography of the Sahara?
5. What is the general pattern of rainfall in Africa?
6. How does the Serengeti Plain help support much of Africa's wildlife?
7. What are some of the benefits of rain forests?

Human-Environment Interaction (pp. 424–427)

8. How might desertification affect people's lives in the Sahel?
9. What are some problems created by the Nigerian oil industry?
10. What are some of the problems created by the Aswan High Dam?

Main Ideas

1. The Nile River irrigates farmland and provides a means of transportation.
2. oil, gold, diamonds, and chromium
3. The Angolan government charges a fee for oil drilling rights but uses little of the money for education, public health, or economic infrastructure.
4. Only a small portion is sandy. The rest contains rocky, gravelly areas and some 11,000-foot-tall mountains.
5. The closer a place is to the equator, the more rain the place receives.
6. The grasslands of the Serengeti provide wildlife with an abundant food supply.
7. Rain forests can provide medicines, and they provide much of the world's plant and animal diversity.
8. People there are losing farmland for crops and grassland for their animals.
9. Careless extraction of oil has led to massive fires, acid rain, oil spills, soot deposits, and health problems.
10. Farmers now have to use expensive artificial fertilizers and field drains, people had to be relocated, and the still waters behind the dam have increased rates of mosquito-borne diseases.

Critical Thinking

1. Using Your Notes
Use your completed chart to answer these questions.

Landforms	
Resources	

a. Why has Africa not been able to take advantage of its abundant resources?

b. What are some of the problems facing Africa's rain forests?

2. Geographic Themes

a. **REGION** What are some of the aspects of Africa's physical geography that make interior transportation difficult?

b. **LOCATION** In what way does Africa's location impact its climate?

3. Identifying Themes
How does desertification alter Africa's surrounding environment? Which of the five themes of geography apply to this situation?

4. Making Generalizations
How has the Aswan High Dam affected the lives of Egyptians?

5. Seeing Patterns
Has the Nigerian oil industry and the Aswan High Dam had positive or negative effects on the surrounding environment? Explain.

For Additional Test Practice

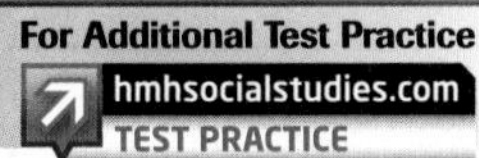

Geographic Skills: Interpreting Maps

Profile of Africa
Use the profile to answer the following questions.

1. **PLACE** What is the tallest landform on the map?
2. **MOVEMENT** How many feet would a person have to climb to reach the peak of the Ahaggar Mountains from the lowest point at this latitude?
3. **REGION** How does this profile illustrate Africa's nickname as the plateau continent?

Sketch your own profile of Africa. Use this profile as a model for your own map. Examine the physical map on page 403 and choose a latitude from which to draw your profile.

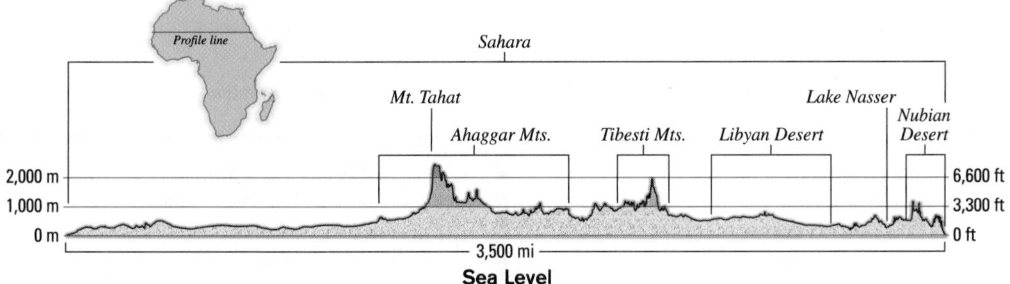

hmhsocialstudies.com
MULTIMEDIA ACTIVITY

Use the links at **hmhsocialstudies.com** to do research about desertification. Focus on determining the long-term effects of desertification in the Sahel.

Creating a Multimedia Presentation Combine charts, maps, or other visual images in an electronic presentation showing how the Sahel will be affected by desertification.

AFRICA

Critical Thinking

1. **a.** As a result of colonialism, the economies of many African nations are based on exporting resources instead of processing them.
   b. slash and burn farming; logging
2. **a.** Africa's rivers contain many rapids and waterfalls, which make travel on them difficult.
   b. Located inside the tropics, Africa has high temperatures.
3. The desert overtakes forests, grassland, and farmland; movement and human-environment interaction
4. It has improved the lives of most Egyptians by providing a steady water supply for farming. It is also a source of electricity for Egypt. Negative results include the relocation of the Nubian people, the need for expensive fertilizers and field drains, and increased rates of mosquito-borne diseases.
5. The Nigerian oil industry has had many negative effects, including acid rain, and oil spills. The Aswan High Dam has improved the environment by more efficiently irrigating the land, but hurt the environment by preventing silt from reaching that farmland.

GeoActivity

Integrated Assessment
- Rubric for a map, 2.1

Formal Assessment
- Chapter Test, Forms A, B, and C, pp. 277–288

Geographic Skills

1. Mt. Tahat
2. about 7,000 feet
3. Much of the profile is fairly flat and lies between 1,000-2,000 feet.

MULTIMEDIA ACTIVITY

For the multimedia presentation on desertification, students should:

- Explain the anticipated long-term effects of desertification, focusing especially on the Sahel.
- Use maps, charts, graphs, photographs, and other visuals to convey information.
- Organize the presentation in a logical order.
- Include references to Web sites and other materials used as sources.

Grading Rubric Evaluate student performance as Exceptional, Acceptable, or Poor in each of the following categories.

	Exceptional	*Acceptable*	*Poor*
Uses appropriate visuals, such as maps, graphs, and charts			
Has sufficient explanation to help audience interpret the visuals			
Is organized logically			
Credits sources			

Human Geography of Africa

OVERVIEW	INSTRUCTIONAL RESOURCES	
ESSENTIAL QUESTION What role has foreign intervention played in Africa's past and present? **Focus on the Essential Question Podcast**	**In-Depth Resources: Unit 6** • Building Vocabulary, p. 19 **Block Schedule Strategies** **Chapter Summaries** (English/Spanish) **Video:** Gold Mines hmhsocialstudies.com INTERACTIVE	**Interactive Online Edition** TOS **ExamView® Assessment Suite** (English/Spanish) TOS **CalendarPlanner** **Power Presentations with Media Gallery** **Critical Thinking Transparencies** • CT19
SECTION 1 **EAST AFRICA** **MAIN IDEAS** • East Africa has a history of trade and disruptive European colonialism. • Farming and some tourism shape East African economies.	**In-Depth Resources: Unit 6** • Guided Reading, p. 13 • Building Vocabulary, p. 19 • Reteaching Activities, p. 20 **Outline Maps with Activities** • East Africa, pp. 55–56 **Cultures Around the World** • Arts and Crafts, p. 36	**Map Transparencies** • MT33 The Origin of Early Humans **Cultures Transparencies** • CW36 Making Jewelry **Guided Reading Workbook,** Section 1 **The World's Music Audio Program**
SECTION 2 **NORTH AFRICA** **MAIN IDEAS** • Ancient Egyptian civilization and Muslim invasion are features of North African history. • Some North African countries have oil economies.	**In-Depth Resources: Unit 6** • Guided Reading, p. 14 • Building Vocabulary, p. 19 • Reteaching Activities, p. 21 • GeoWorkshop, pp. 39–40 **Outline Maps with Activities** • North Africa, pp. 57–58	**Map Transparencies** • MT34 Expansion of Islam, 750–1500 **Cultures Transparencies** • CW32 Playing Mancala **Cultures Around the World** • Daily Life, p. 32 **Guided Reading Workbook,** Section 2
SECTION 3 **WEST AFRICA** **MAIN IDEAS** • West Africa has a history of trading empires and stateless societies. • West Africa has a rich cultural tradition, including crafts and music.	**In-Depth Resources: Unit 6** • Guided Reading, p. 15 • Skillbuilder Practice, p. 18 • Building Vocabulary, p. 19 • Reteaching Activities, p. 22 **Outline Maps with Activities** • West Africa, pp. 59–60 **Cultures Around the World** • Architecture, p. 31; Fine Arts, p. 33 • Traditional Practices, p. 34; Music, p. 35	**Critical Thinking Transparencies** • CT51 Ancient Empires of Africa **Cultures Transparencies** • CW31 Dogon Village • CW33 Senufo Mask • CW34 Benin Bronze • CW35 Kora **Video:** Origins of Thanksgiving Holiday **Guided Reading Workbook,** Section 3
SECTION 4 **CENTRAL AFRICA** **MAIN IDEAS** • Bantu migrations and European colonialism are features of Central African history. • Central Africa struggles with the effects of colonialism.	**In-Depth Resources: Unit 6** • Guided Reading, p. 16 • Building Vocabulary, p. 19 • Reteaching Activities, p. 23 **Outline Maps with Activities** • Central Africa, pp. 61–62	**Guided Reading Workbook,** Section 4
SECTION 5 **SOUTHERN AFRICA** **MAIN IDEAS** • The gold trade was important to Southern Africa's ancient states. • Today, Southern Africa is trying to grow economically.	**In-Depth Resources: Unit 6** • Guided Reading, p. 17 • Building Vocabulary, p. 19 • Reteaching Activities, p. 24 **Outline Maps with Activities** • Southern Africa, pp. 63–64	**Guided Reading Workbook,** Section 5 **The World's Music Audio Program**

ASSESSMENT

SE **Chapter Assessment,** pp. 458–459

Formal Assessment
- Chapter Tests, Forms A, B, and C, pp. 294–305

TOS **ExamView® Assessment Suite**

Strategies for Test Preparation

hmhsocialstudies.com TEST PRACTICE

SE **Section Assessment,** p. 435

Formal Assessment
- Section Quiz, p. 289

Integrated Assessment
- Rubric for a time line, 2.4

Test Practice Transparencies TT60

SE **Section Assessment,** p. 441

Formal Assessment
- Section Quiz, p. 290

Integrated Assessment
- Rubric for an illustration, 1.3

Test Practice Transparencies TT61

SE **Section Assessment,** p. 445

Formal Assessment
- Section Quiz, p. 291

Integrated Assessment
- Rubric for a chart, 2.2

Test Practice Transparencies TT62

SE **Section Assessment,** p. 452

Formal Assessment
- Section Quiz, p. 292

Integrated Assessment
- Rubric for a sketch map, 2.1

Test Practice Transparencies TT63

SE **Section Assessment,** p. 457

Formal Assessment
- Section Quiz, p. 293

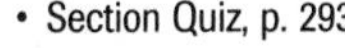

Integrated Assessment
- Rubric for a map, 2.1

Test Practice Transparencies TT64

CHART KEY:

SE Student Edition	 Block Scheduling	 DVD/CD-ROM
TE Teacher's Edition	TOS Teacher One Stop	MP3 Audio
 Printable Resource	 Presentation Resource	 HISTORY™

Program Resources available on TOS and @ hmhsocialstudies.com

SUPPORTING RESOURCES

- **Multimedia Classroom Global History Series**
- **Global History Teacher's Guide**

Social Studies Trade Library Collection
- World Regions Trade Collection

For more information or to purchase these resources, go to 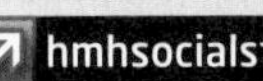

DIFFERENTIATED INSTRUCTION

English Learners

Spanish/English Guided Reading Workbook

Access for Students Acquiring English/ESL
Spanish Translations, pp. 99–104

Chapter Summaries
(English/Spanish)

TE **TE Activity**
Learning Unfamiliar Words, p. 439

Struggling Readers

Chapter Summaries
(English/Spanish)

TE **TE Activity**
Identifying Details Related to a Theme, p. 433

Gifted and Talented Students

TE **TE Activity**
Holding a Panel Discussion, p. 454

ENRICHMENT ACTIVITIES

The following activities are especially suitable for classes following block schedules.

SE **Student Edition,** pp. 430–459
- Disasters! Famine in Somalia, pp. 436–437
- Comparing Cultures: Feasts, pp. 446–447

hmhsocialstudies.com INTERACTIVE
- Expansion of Islam, 750–1500, p. 439
- Empires of West Africa, 1050–1500, p. 442
- Infrastructure of Central Africa, p. 450

BLOCK SCHEDULE LESSON PLAN OPTIONS: 90-MINUTE PERIOD

DAY 1

SECTION 1, pp. 431–435
Class Time 35 minutes

- **Discussion** Lead the class in a discussion that compares the early history of East Africa ("Continental Crossroads," PE pages 431–432) with its later history ("Colonization Disrupts Africa," pp. 432–433).
  Class Time 15 minutes
- **Writing** Have students write scripts for a newscast from East Africa. Suggest that they focus on either economic or health-care issues.
  Class Time 20 minutes

DISASTERS! pp. 436–437
Class Time 15 minutes

- **Discussion** Use the questions on TE page 436 to lead the class in a discussion of the issues concerning famine in Somalia.
  Class Time 15 minutes

SECTION 2, pp. 438–441
Class Time 40 minutes

- **Student Reports** Divide the class into four groups based on the four headings in Section 2. Have each group prepare a report on the assigned content, with each member exploring a main idea. After each group presents its report, allow five minutes for questions from the class.
  Class Time 40 minutes

DAY 2

SECTION 3, pp. 442–445
Class Time 30 minutes

- **Summary Chart** Lead the entire class in creating a three-column summary chart about the rich heritage of West Africa, drawing information from the text. The headings for the three columns should be "Government," "Economics," and "Culture."

COMPARING CULTURES, pp. 446–447
Class Time 20 minutes

- **Discussion** Ask students what they notice about the photographs. Use the questions on TE page 446 to lead the class in a discussion about the settings of the feasts and the types of food eaten.
  Class Time 20 minutes

SECTION 4, pp. 448–452
Class Time 40 minutes

- **Panel of Experts** Have five students form a panel to discuss colonialism and its effects in Central Africa. Allow them to field questions from the class for ten minutes. Follow with another five-student panel to discuss hopeful signs in post-colonial Central Africa.
  Class Time 20 minutes
- **Political Cartoons** Have pairs of students work together to create rough sketches of political cartoons about colonialism in Africa.
  Class Time 20 minutes

DAY 3

SECTION 5, pp. 453–457
Class Time 30 minutes

- **Discussion** Introduce Section 5 with the map "Ethnic Groups of Southern Africa" on PE page 454. Focus on the Skillbuilder questions.
  Class Time 10 minutes
- **Jigsaw Groups** Divide the class into four groups based on the four headings in Section 5. Tell the groups that they have 10 minutes to create lists of the most important information in their part of Section 5. Each group member must copy the list. Then re-divide the class into groups of four students, consisting of one person from each of the original groups. Each student should teach the other members of the new group about his or her assigned content.
  Class Time 20 minutes

CHAPTER 19 REVIEW AND ASSESSMENT, pp. 458–459
Class Time 60 minutes

- **Review** Have pairs of students review the chapter by taking turns asking each other the Main Ideas questions in the Section Assessments.
  Class Time 25 minutes
- **Assessment** Have students complete the Chapter 19 Assessment.
  Class Time 35 minutes

TEACHER-TESTED ACTIVITY *Scavenger Hunt*

Class Time One class period

Task To allow students to learn independently and cooperatively about Africa

Supplies
- Textbook
- Tape
- Construction paper (cut into small squares)
- Question sheets

Purpose To seek out the different terms associated with the history and cultures of Africa

Activity Have students read Section 3 out loud and Section 4 silently; allow 15 minutes for completion of the reading. Each student will have a paper that has nine questions covering the two sections. Not every sheet is the same. Students may not write down the answers on anything; instead, they will leave their seats, without their book, and begin to search for the answers, which have been hidden around the room. Once the student feels that he or she has found a correct answer, he or she will tape the answer to his or her sheet. As students finish, they will approach the teacher to see if their answers are correct. The first five students to successfully complete the hunt receive prizes.

Karen Fletcher
Geography Teacher, Haltom High School, Haltom City, Texas

TECHNOLOGY IN THE CLASSROOM

Electronic field trips are one of the most popular ways for students to use the Internet. Students generally visit a specified set of Web pages to see pictures and read about places, such as national parks or historic sites. This type of field trip is often an excellent substitute for an actual field trip, which may be logistically impossible.

Objective Students will take an electronic field trip to look for examples of traditional arts from the different regions of the African continent. They will create multimedia presentations showing what they have found.

Task Have students pretend that they are taking a trip to Africa to learn more about traditional arts. Have them use Chapter 19 and the Web to gather examples from different regions of Africa, and have them showcase their findings in multimedia presentations.

Class Time 3 class periods

1. Have students pretend they have a year to travel around Africa and visit each of the regions covered in Chapter 19. Their goal will be to learn as much as possible about traditional African arts and to compare the artistic traditions of the different regions.
2. Divide the class into small groups or pairs, and have groups choose examples of African arts, including music and dance, from Chapter 19 and the Web sites listed at **hmhsocialstudies.com**. They should try to find at least two examples from each region of Africa. They can take notes and save images from the Internet into a folder on the computer or a disk. They can also save audio files or bookmark the links to these files to include in their presentations. Ask them to make sure they record the source of each file they save, citing the title and URL of the Web site it came from and the artist's name, if known.
3. Have students create multimedia presentations that showcase what they have learned.

CHAPTER 19 OBJECTIVE

Identify features of human geography in the five subregions of Africa.

Chapter 19 HUMAN GEOGRAPHY OF AFRICA

From Human Beginnings to New Nations

hmhsocialstudies.com VIDEO

Five subregions of Africa

Have students study the map. Remind them that Africa consists of 53 nations. Ask them to comment on the countries in terms of size. *(They vary widely.)*

Introducing the Essential Question

- Ask students to recall what they have learned about Africa's physical geography. Point out that the continent's climate and vegetation posed challenges to early explorers, but the lure of Africa's resources was more powerful than the difficulties.
- Emphasize that foreign intervention has not only marked Africa's past, but also continues to shadow its present and future.

GeoFocus

Have students complete a cluster diagram in their notebooks using material from all sections of this chapter. Tell students that this will help them identify similarities and differences among subregions.

 **Critical Thinking Transparencies CT19**
- GeoFocus

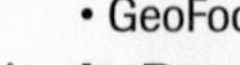 **In-Depth Resources: Unit 6**
- Building Vocabulary, p. 19

Five Subregions of Africa

MOROCCO
WESTERN SAHARA (MOROCCO)
ALGERIA
TUNISIA
LIBYA
EGYPT
MAURITANIA
MALI
NIGER
CHAD
SUDAN
ERITREA
DJIBOUTI
SENEGAL
GAMBIA
GUINEA
GUINEA-BISSAU
SIERRA LEONE
LIBERIA
CÔTE D'IVOIRE
BURKINA FASO
GHANA
TOGO
BENIN
NIGERIA
CAMEROON
CENTRAL AFRICAN REPUBLIC
ETHIOPIA
SOMALIA
EQUATORIAL GUINEA
SÃO TOMÉ AND PRÍNCIPE
GABON
REP. OF CONGO
DEMOCRATIC REPUBLIC OF CONGO
UGANDA
KENYA
RWANDA
BURUNDI
TANZANIA
ANGOLA
ZAMBIA
MALAWI
MOZAMBIQUE
COMOROS
ZIMBABWE
NAMIBIA
BOTSWANA
MADAGASCAR
SWAZILAND
SOUTH AFRICA
LESOTHO
Mediterranean Sea
Red Sea
Gulf of Aden
Gulf of Guinea
Lake Victoria
L. Tanganyika
L. Nyasa
Mozambique Channel
ATLANTIC OCEAN
INDIAN OCEAN
Tropic of Cancer
Equator
Tropic of Capricorn
East Africa
North Africa
West Africa
Central Africa
Southern Afric
0 400 800 miles
0 400 800 kilometers
Lambert Azimuthal Equal-Area Projection

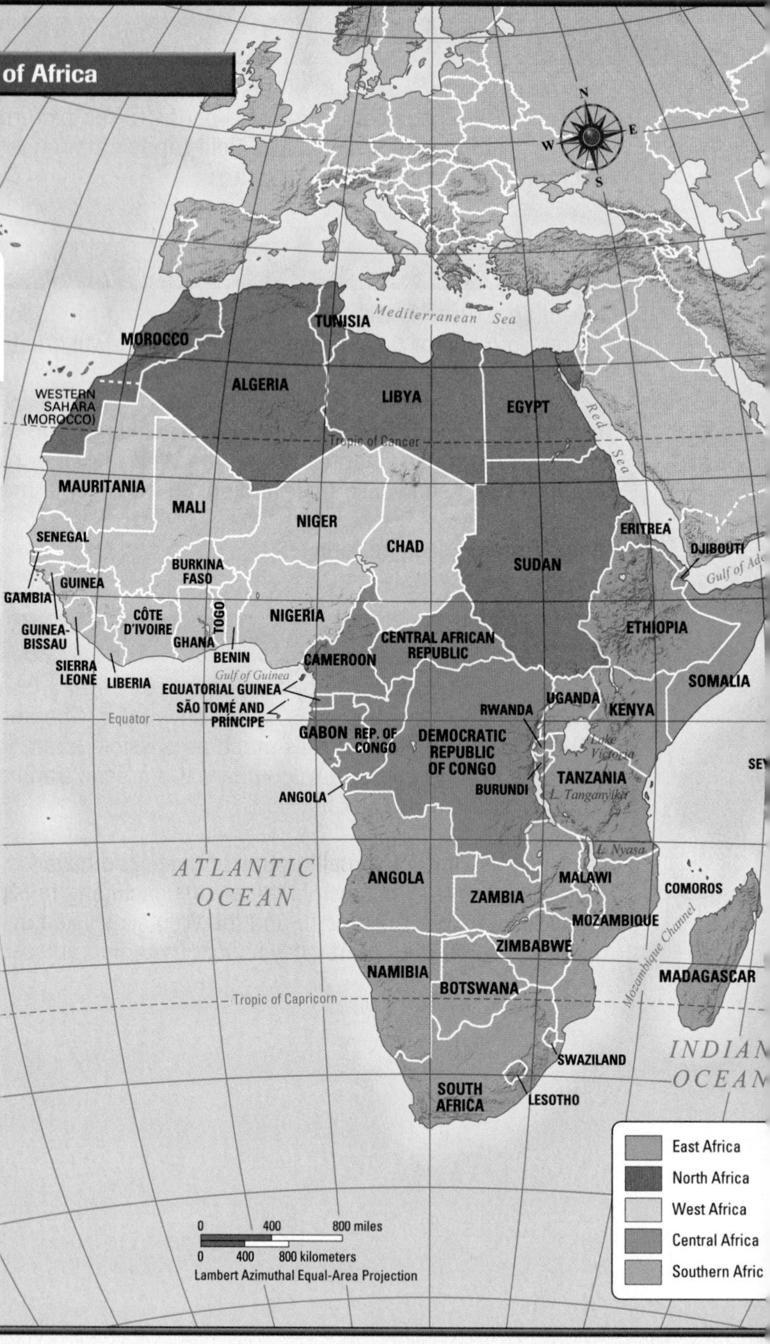

Essential Question

What role has foreign intervention played in Africa's past and present?

What You Will Learn

In this chapter you will examine the connections between Africa's past and present.

SECTION 1
East Africa

SECTION 2
North Africa

SECTION 3
West Africa

SECTION 4
Central Africa

SECTION 5
Southern Africa

hmhsocialstudies.com TAKING NOTES

Use the graphic organizer online to take notes about the history, economics, culture, and modern life of each subregion of Africa.

430

CHAPTER 19 ADDITIONAL RESOURCES

BOOKS FOR THE TEACHER

Meredith, Martin. ***The Fate of Africa: A History of Fifty Years of Independence.*** PublicAffairs, 2006. Readable account of the major upheavals in modern Africa.

Pakenham, Thomas. ***The Scramble for Africa, 1876-1912.*** NY: Random, 1991. European countries gain control of Africa.

BOOKS FOR THE STUDENT

No More Strangers Now: Young Voices from a New South Africa. McKee, Tim (ed.) NY: DK, 1998. Teens discuss *apartheid.*

Rasmussen, R. Kent. ***Modern African Political Leaders.*** NY: Facts on File, 1998. Profiles eight leaders of African nations.

VIDEOS

Wilds of Madagascar. Prod. National Geographic Society, 1988. Documentary of British expedition addressing problem of conservation.

INTERNET

For more on the human geography of Africa, visit . . .

hmhsocialstudies.com

East Africa

Main Ideas

- East Africa is known as the "cradle of humanity."
- East Africa's location has made it a trading center.

Places & Terms

Olduvai Gorge
Aksum
Berlin Conference
cash crop
Masai
pandemic

CONNECT TO THE ISSUES
ECONOMIC DEVELOPMENT East Africa's political conflicts have limited its economic development.

A HUMAN PERSPECTIVE East Africa is called the "cradle of humanity" because of the large number of prehistoric human remains found in the region. In 1931, Louis Leakey, an English archaeologist, began doing research in **Olduvai Gorge,** located in northern Tanzania. Olduvai Gorge has contained the most continuous known record of humanity. The gorge has yielded fossils from 65 individual hominids, or humans that walk upright. In 1959, Leakey and his wife, Mary Leakey, discovered a fossil there of a species called *Homo habilis,* the first human creatures to make stone tools. They lived about two million years ago. Throughout history, East Africa has been a crossroads of humanity because of its geographic position near seas and oceans.

Continental Crossroads

Bounded on the east by the Red Sea and Indian Ocean, East Africa includes Burundi, Djibouti, Eritrea, Ethiopia, Kenya, Rwanda, Seychelles, Somalia, Tanzania, and Uganda. Scientists believe that the world's first humans lived there.

A TRADING COAST East Africa was also a place where early civilizations developed. An important civilization was **Aksum,** which emerged in present-day Ethiopia in the A.D. 100s. Its location on the Red Sea and the Indian Ocean made it an important trading center and contributed to its expansion and power. People from Aksum regularly traded with the people of Egypt and the eastern Roman Empire.

During the sixth century, however, Aksum lost many trading partners, and several geographic factors weakened the empire. Traders on routes between the eastern Mediterranean region and Asia began passing through the Persian Gulf rather than

East African Trade, A.D. 1000

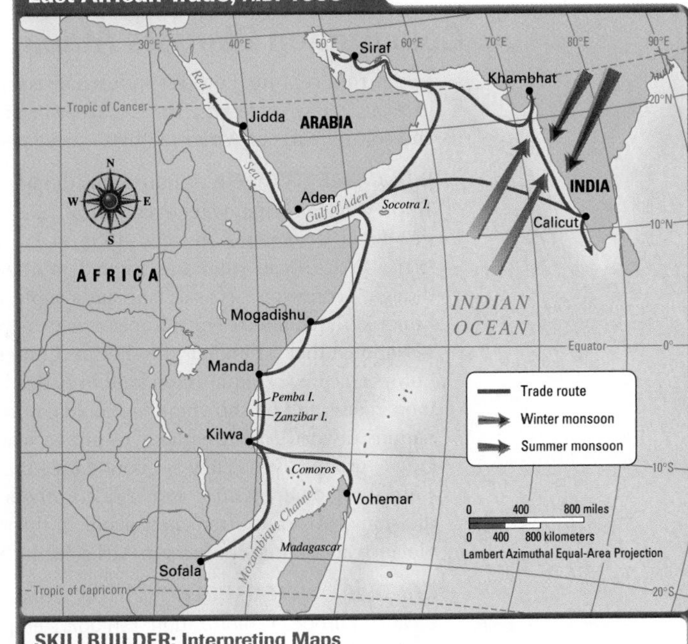

SKILLBUILDER: Interpreting Maps
1. **MOVEMENT** How far would a trader have to travel to go from Calicut to Sofala?
2. **HUMAN–ENVIRONMENT INTERACTION** Which monsoon would a trader rely on to sail from Africa to India?

SECTION 1 OBJECTIVES

1. Examine East Africa's history as a continental crossroads.
2. Describe the disruptive effect of colonization on East Africa.
3. Analyze East Africa's economies of farming and tourism.
4. Describe the cultures of East Africa's major ethnic groups.
5. Examine the state of health care in East Africa.

SKILLBUILDER: Interpreting Maps, p. 431

GeographicThinking
Seeing Patterns, pp. 432, 433, 435
Making Generalizations, p. 435

Focus & Motivate

Ask students how proximity to the Red Sea, Southwest Asia, and the Indian Ocean affected East Africa. *(It promoted trade, bringing people, goods, and ideas to the region.)*

Instruct: Objective 

Continental Crossroads

- What contributed to the rise of early civilizations in East Africa? *(location on seas and trade)*
- What effect did international trade have on East Africa? *(It became a cultural crossroads.)*

In-Depth Resources: Unit 6
- Guided Reading, p. 13

Map Transparencies MT33
- The Origin of Early Humans

SKILLBUILDER ANSWERS
1. about 3,500 miles
2. summer monsoon

SECTION 1 PROGRAM RESOURCES

In-Depth Resources: Unit 6
- Guided Reading, p. 13
- Building Vocabulary, p. 19
- Reteaching Activity, p. 20

Guided Reading Workbook
- Section 1

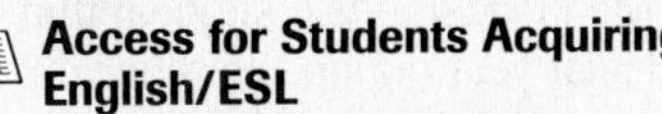
Access for Students Acquiring English/ESL
- Guided Reading, p. 99

Outline Maps with Activities
- East Africa, pp. 55–56

Formal Assessment
- Section Quiz, p. 289

Integrated Assessment
- Rubric for a time line, 2.4
- Rubric for a news report, 3.6

Cultures Around the World
- Arts and Crafts, p. 36

INTEGRATED TECHNOLOGY

Chapter Summaries

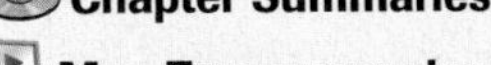
Map Transparencies MT33
- Origin of Early Humans

Cultures Transparencies CW36
- Making Jewelry

hmhsocialstudies.com

TEST-TAKING RESOURCES

Strategies for Test Preparation

Test Practice Transparencies TT60

Online Test Practice

Interpreting Time Lines

East Africa, 0-1500, and East Africa, 1750-2000

Have students examine the time lines. Explain that the two time lines use different scales. The time line on page 432 covers 1,500 years, while the time line on page 433 covers only 250 years. Ask students what the dates on the time line indicate. *(milestones in East African history)* Ask why 1497 is important. *(Europeans visit East Africa.)* Ask students what the two men pictured at the right have in common. *(They were both African leaders.)*

Instruct: Objective 2

Colonization Disrupts Africa

- What happened at the Berlin Conference of 1884-1885? *(European nations divided Africa in order to obtain its resources.)*
- What African countries managed to remain free of European control? *(Liberia and Ethiopia)*
- How did colonialism cause conflicts in East Africa after independence? *(Europeans set boundaries that combined peoples that were enemies.)*

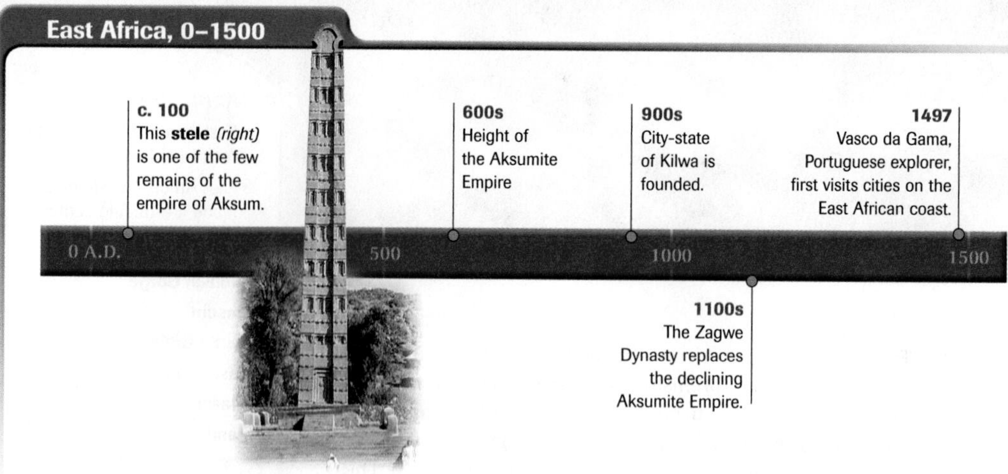
East Africa, 0–1500
c. 100 This **stele** *(right)* is one of the few remains of the empire of Aksum.
600s Height of the Aksumite Empire
900s City-state of Kilwa is founded.
1497 Vasco da Gama, Portuguese explorer, first visits cities on the East African coast.
0 A.D.
500
1000
1500
1100s The Zagwe Dynasty replaces the declining Aksumite Empire.

the Red Sea. In addition, the cutting down of forests and overuse of the soil led to a population decline, which reduced the empire's power.

Around the seventh century, Arab, Persian, and Indian traders once again made East Africa an international trading center. By 1300, many trading cities dotted the eastern coast of Africa. The trading city of Kilwa emerged as one of the most important cities of the time. Kilwa flourished on the southern coast of what is now Tanzania. All this movement of goods, ideas, and people made East Africa a cultural crossroads.

Colonization Disrupts Africa

In the 19th century, Europe's industrialized nations became interested in Africa's raw materials. Those European nations wanted to colonize and control parts of Africa to obtain those resources.

SCRAMBLE FOR AFRICA Europeans did not want to fight over Africa. To prevent European wars over Africa, 14 European nations convened the **Berlin Conference** in 1884–1885 to lay down rules for dividing Africa. No African ruler was invited to attend this conference, even though it concerned Africa's land and people. By 1914, only Liberia and Ethiopia remained free of European control. A

Nations that attended the Berlin Conference decided that any European country could claim land in Africa by telling other nations of their claims and by showing they could control the area. The European nations divided Africa without regard to where African ethnic or linguistic groups lived. They set boundaries that combined peoples who were traditional enemies and divided others who were not. Europe's division of Africa is often cited as one of the root causes of the political violence and ethnic conflicts in Africa in the 20th century.

ETHIOPIA AVOIDS COLONIZATION Ethiopia is one country that escaped European colonization. Ethiopia's emperor, Menelik II, skillfully protected his country from the Italian invasion with weapons from France and Russia. In addition, the Ethiopian army had a greater knowledge of the area's geography than did the Italians. As a result, Ethiopia defeated Italy in 1896.

Geographic Thinking

Seeing Patterns
A Which group of nations participated in the Berlin Conference? Which group did not?

A. Answer Fourteen European nations participated—no African countries were invited.

BACKGROUND
The Ethiopian victory was the first time native Africans successfully defended themselves against a colonial power.

ACTIVITY OPTION **LINK TO HISTORY**

BLOCK SCHEDULING

REPORTING ON THE MAU MAU REBELLION

Objective To learn about the origins and goals of the Mau Mau rebels

Class Time 50 minutes

Task Prepare a news report on the Mau Mau Rebellion

Directions Working in small groups, students should research the Mau Mau and prepare a news report on the group's origins, goals, and actions. Remind students that comprehensive news reports should include maps showing the location of rebel bases or the regions affected by the uprising and interviews with British and Mau Mau leaders. Also suggest that they focus on the news events for a particular year during the rebellion (1952-1960).

East Africa, 1750–Present

1855	Kassa Hailu consolidates his rule over present-day Ethiopia.
1873	East Africa's busiest slave market, Zanzibar, closes.
1896	Ethiopian forces under **Menelik II** *(far left)* defeat Italians.
1952	The Mau Mau rebellion against the British begins in Kenya.
1978	**Jomo Kenyatta** *(below)*, Kenya's first prime minister and an important African leader, dies.
1994	Hundreds of thousands die in battles between the Hutu and the Tutsi ethnic groups in Rwanda.
2003	Darfur refugee crisis begins in Sudan.
2005	Somali piracy in Indian Ocean becomes critical.

1750 1875 2000

CONFLICT IN EAST AFRICA By the 1970s, most of East Africa had regained its independence from Europe. However, internal disputes and civil wars became a serious problem. For example, in Rwanda, tensions left over from the colonial era combined with ethnic animosity to set off a massacre in 1994.

One cause of those problems was that European colonial powers had not prepared East African nations for independence. Furthermore, the ethnic boundaries created by the Europeans forced cultural divisions that had not existed before colonialism. Those cultural divisions often caused internal conflicts among native groups. Colonialism also greatly affected the economy of East Africa, which today centers around tourism and farming.

Farming and Tourism Economies

Agriculture forms the economic foundation of East Africa. In addition, East Africa's world-famous wildlife parks generate millions of dollars of revenue.

FARMING IN EAST AFRICA East Africa is about 60 percent rural. Since European colonization in the 19th century, countries have relied more on **cash crops** such as coffee, tea, and sugar, which are grown for direct sale. They bring in much-needed revenue but reduce the amount of farmland that otherwise could be devoted to growing food for use in the region. Relying on cash crops for revenue can be risky because the price of crops varies according to the world market. B

East Africa's agricultural balance is changing, however, because people are leaving farms for greater economic opportunities in cities. For example, Addis Ababa, the capital of Ethiopia, has grown by more

B. Answer Cash crops bring in revenue for a country but take up farmland needed to grow food for people living in the country.

Geographic Thinking

Seeing Patterns

B How does growing cash crops both help a country's economy and hurt the people living in the country?

5 THEMES

REGION

Ethiopia-Eritrea War

In 1993, Eritrea gained its independence from Ethiopia after a violent and bloody war. But in 1998, the two countries became embroiled in a border conflict over the town of Badme.

In 1999, the fighting became full-scale conventional warfare. More than 100,000 people were killed on both sides. In 2000 the two countries signed a peace agreement, but 5 years later they still had not settled their differences. An international commission in 2005 found Eritrea guilty of illegally causing an unjustified war. Ethiopia and Eritrea remain bitter enemies.

AFRICA

More About

Menelik II

Menelik II was born in 1844 and died in 1913. As a ruler and later emperor, he is noted for uniting a number of semi-independent Ethiopian states into a nation. He founded the capital city of Addis Ababa.

5 THEMES

Region: Ethiopia-Eritrea War

Ethiopia survived as an independent country in spite of being occupied by Italy from 1936 to 1941. Eritrea has a history of domination by other countries, including Italy and Great Britain in the 20th century. Eritrea's agricultural economy was virtually destroyed by the war with Ethiopia.

- What did the international commission conclude in 2005? *(It found Eritrea guilty of causing an unjustified war.*

Instruct: Objective 3

Farming and Tourism Economies

- Why is it risky for East Africa to rely on cash crops? *(Crop prices vary on the world market.)*
- Why is East Africa's agricultural base changing? *(People are seeking economic opportunities in cities.)*
- What threatens East Africa's wildlife parks? *(More land is needed to grow food for the increasing population.)*

DIFFERENTIATING INSTRUCTION **LESS PROFICIENT READERS**

IDENTIFYING DETAILS RELATED TO A THEME

Objective To trace a theme throughout text

Class Time 20 minutes

Task List events that relate to the theme of movement

Directions Tell students that tracing a theme such as movement may help them better understand what they read. Remind them that movement involves travel and the exchange of goods and ideas. Ask students to reread the text under the headings "Continental Crossroads" and "Colonization Disrupts Africa" and identify events related to movement. Have each student make a list of class responses like the one shown here.

MOVEMENT
trade across Red Sea and Indian Ocean
Arabians, Persians, and Indians trade with East Coast cities
Europeans colonize Africa
Italy invades Ethiopia
Africans force Europeans from Africa

growing up in...
Kenya

Age-based groupings are observed throughout a Masai's life. Stages for males occur approximately every 15 years. Junior warriors protect the herds during their teens and must live apart from the main Masai group. At about age 30, the men become senior warriors who may marry and have children. At later stages they become junior and senior elders.

- What similarities do you see between Masai customs and those of the United States? *(child care done mostly by girls, ear piercing)*

Instruct: Objective 

Maintaining Traditional Cultures

- What two major ethnic groups inhabit East Africa? *(Masai and Kikuyu)*
- Why did the Mau Mau rebellion occur? *(The Kikuyu organized a Mau Mau society to overthrow British rule.)*
- How do the Masai and Kikuyu compare in the kinds of work they do? *(Most Masai are herders and farmers; Kikuyu are traditionally herders but today work in a variety of jobs.)*

 **Cultures Around the World**
• Arts and Crafts, p. 36

 **Cultures Transparencies CW36**
• Making Jewelry

growing up in...Kenya

The Masai are members of an ethnic group that live in Kenya. All Masai children address adults as either "mother" or "father."

A typical Masai girl *(pictured at the right)* takes on responsibilities that include:
- household chores
- child care
- the processing and distribution of milk

Each boy is assigned to a group called an age-set. Boys at the bottom of the age-set do the following:
- herd young animals
- learn to protect the herd from predatory animals

Between the ages of 14 and 18, boys receive a new name in a ceremony marking their transition from youth to manhood.

Around eight years of age, boys and girls have the upper part of their ears pierced. Two years later, the lower lobes are pierced. Wooden plugs are inserted into the holes to increase their size. Masai consider large ear lobes to be beautiful.

than one million people since 1991. However, such rapid population growth can put a strain on a city's resources and a country's agricultural production.

TOURISM CREATES WEALTH AND PROBLEMS One of the main economic activities in East Africa is tourism. The region's vast wildlife parks in Kenya, Uganda, and Tanzania are world famous. In 1938, Europeans created the game reserves because they were killing animals for sport at a high rate. Most African peoples did not need the parks because they hunted only for survival. However, the wild animal parks, which are no longer used for hunting, have now become important sources of income for Africans, generating millions of dollars each year from tourists.

BACKGROUND
Serengeti National Park in Tanzania covers nearly 6,000 square miles and contains 35 species of plains animals and 350 species of birds.

Competing demands for the parkland exist, though. For example, Kenya's increasing population requires more food. As a result, some groups want to eliminate or reduce the size of the wildlife reserves to create more farmland. Some desperate farmers have even begun to plow the land around the parks.

Maintaining Traditional Cultures

East Africa's position as a major trading region has given it a diverse culture. It is a melting pot of more than 160 different ethnic groups.

CULTURES OF EAST AFRICA Two major ethnic groups in East Africa are the **Masai** and the Kikuyu. The Masai, whom you read about above, are an East African ethnic group that lives on the grasslands of the rift valleys in Kenya and Tanzania. Most of the Masai herd livestock and farm the land.

Typical Masai dress includes clothes made from calfskin or buffalo hide. Women wear long skirt-like robes, while men wear a shorter

ACTIVITY OPTION **COOPERATIVE LEARNING** — **BLOCK SCHEDULING**

DEBATING THE ISSUES

Objective To help students understand the pros and cons of conservation

Class Time One class period

Task Debate the question of conserving wildlife areas

Directions Divide students into groups of three. Each group member should research the issue of conserving wildlife areas in relation to human needs. One student should favor conservation, one should oppose it, and one should act as the moderator. Hold the debates before the class.

434 CHAPTER 19

version of the robe. They often grease their clothes with cow fat to protect themselves from the sun and rain. The Masai are also known for making intricate beadwork and jewelry.

The Kikuyu are the largest ethnic group in Kenya, numbering around 6.6 million. Their homeland is centered around Mount Kenya. Like the Masai, the Kikuyu traditionally were herders. However, today the Kikuyu live throughout the country and work in a variety of jobs. During British colonial rule, the Kikuyu organized a society called the Mau Mau, which fought against the British. The British killed around 11,000 Africans—mostly Kikuyu—during the Mau Mau rebellion between 1952 and 1960. C

Geographic Thinking

Seeing Patterns

C How have the lives of the Kikuyu changed during the last century?

C. Answer The Kikuyu were traditionally farmers and herders, but now they work in a variety of jobs.

Health Care in Modern Africa

The people of East Africa face many health care problems. The most critical is acquired immune deficiency syndrome (AIDS), which spread throughout Africa in the 1980s and 1990s.

HEALTH CARE IN AFRICA AIDS has become a pandemic and is having a devastating effect on the continent. A **pandemic** is an uncontrollable outbreak of a disease affecting a large population over a wide geographic area.

AIDS is caused by the human immunodeficiency virus (HIV). People infected with HIV do not necessarily have AIDS and can carry HIV for years without knowing it. As a result, AIDS statistics can be misleading. The number of people who have AIDS lags behind the number of those infected with HIV. Though AIDS education is increasing, some governments hide the scope of the disease. Many doctors in Africa say that more AIDS cases exist than are reported.

Some medical geographers predict that the populations of Africa's worst affected countries could decline by 10 to 20 percent.

You will read more about AIDS and other major health issues in Chapter 20. In the next section , you will learn about North Africa.

Section 1 Assessment

1 Places & Terms

Identify these terms and explain their importance in the region's history or culture.

- Olduvai Gorge
- Aksum
- Berlin Conference
- cash crop
- Masai
- pandemic

2 Taking Notes

PLACE Review the notes you took for this section.

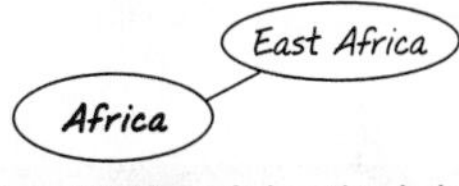

- How did Aksum's location help the empire grow?
- What are some of the problems created by tourism?

3 Main Ideas

a. Why did East Africa become an international trading center early in its history?

b. How did the Berlin Conference change Africa?

c. How is AIDS affecting the population of Africa?

4 Geographic Thinking

Making Generalizations In what way has colonialism affected East Africa? **Think about:**

- the Berlin Conference
- problems in the 20th century

See Skillbuilder Handbook, page R6.

SEEING PATTERNS Do research to learn about two ethnic groups other than the Masai and the Kikuyu in East Africa. Create a **time line** tracing the origins of those ethnic groups to the present day. Examine the groups' history, movement patterns, and evolution of their lifestyles.

AFRICA

Instruct: Objective 5

Health Care in Modern Africa

- What is East Africa's most critical health-care problem? *(AIDS)*
- What is the difference between HIV and AIDS? *(AIDS is the disease; the human immunodeficiency virus, or HIV, is its cause)*
- How does the difference affect AIDS statistics? *(Statistics may mislead because they reflect people with AIDS now, not those who are already infected with HIV.)*

Assess & Reteach

GeoFocus Have students complete their notes on East Africa for their cluster diagrams.

Formal Assessment
- Section Quiz, p. 289

Reteaching Activity
Have students review what they have learned about East Africa by listing the main points for each heading in the section. Have a brief follow-up class discussion.

In-Depth Resources: Unit 6
- Reteaching Activity, p. 20

Outline Maps with Activities
- East Africa, pp. 55–56

SECTION 1 ASSESSMENT ANSWERS

1. Places & Terms
Olduvai Gorge, p. 431
Aksum, p. 431
Berlin Conference, p. 432
cash crop, p. 433
Masai, p. 434
pandemic, p. 435

2. Taking Notes
- Aksum's location gave it ready access to Asia and Europe.
- competing demands on land set aside in wildlife parks; growing population needs more farmland

3. Main Ideas
a. East Africa's position on the Red Sea and the Indian Ocean made it a convenient location for trade with Asia and Europe.
b. It divided Africa without considering the wishes of native Africans or traditional tribal boundaries. The Berlin Conference is often cited as a root cause of Africa's 20th-century violence.
c. AIDS is killing many people in Africa.

4. Geographic Thinking
Colonialism is responsible for much of the political violence and lack of economic growth in East Africa. The Berlin Conference gave control of Africa to many European powers, which divided Africa without regard to traditional ethnic boundaries and exploited it economically.

GeoActivity

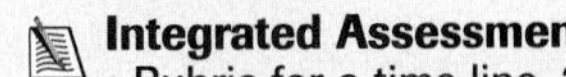
Integrated Assessment
- Rubric for a time line, 2.4

OBJECTIVE

Understand the causes of famine and explore the responses by local and international communities.

Instruct: Objective

Famine in Somalia

- What was the principal natural cause of famine? *(drought)*
- What human factors complicated the famine in Somalia? *(Somali criminals disrupted relief shipments; civil war)*
- How did Somalia's history cause the famine? *(The influence of foreign colonizers brought about changes such as the increased reliance on cash crops and livestock.)*

Interpreting Maps

Famine in the Horn of Africa

Ask students to examine the map. Tell them that northeastern Somalia has thin, infertile desert soils. In addition, that region receives an average of less than four inches of rainfall a year. Ask students to use this information to determine which Somali clan lives in the worst area for agriculture. *(the Daarood)* Ask students to use the map to estimate what percentage of Somalia is arable land. *(25 percent or less)* What percentage of Somalia is prone to drought? *(80 percent or more)*

Disasters!

Famine in Somalia

Famine—an extreme and long-term shortage of food—causes widespread hunger and sometimes death to millions of people. Natural causes, such as weather, plant diseases, and massive insect infestations, can cause famine. Drought is the most common natural cause. In addition, human beings can cause famine. Wars and political violence often destroy crops and prevent the adequate distribution of food. The worst famines usually involve a combination of both human and natural causes. The Horn of Africa, which includes Ethiopia and Somalia, has been the site of recent famines in the 1980s and 1990s.

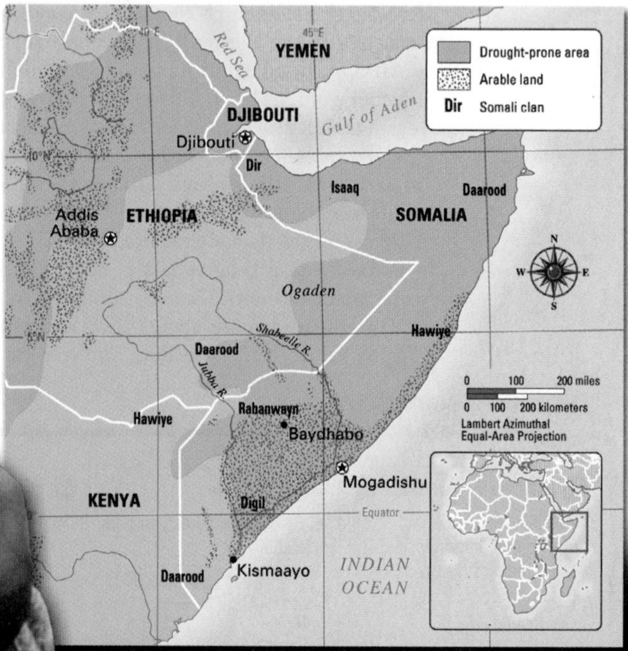

SUPPORTING RESOURCES

BOOKS FOR THE TEACHER

Bowden, Mark. ***Black Hawk Down: A Story of Modern War.*** NY: Atlantic, 1999. U.S. Special Forces team lands in Mogadishu in 1993.

Peterson, Scott. ***Me Against My Brother: At War in Somalia, Sudan, and Rwanda.*** NY: Routledge, 2000. Covers U.S. mission in Somalia.

BOOKS FOR THE STUDENT

Ocko, Stephanie. ***Water: Almost Enough for Everyone.*** NY: Atheneum, 1995. A study of world climate patterns and water shortages.

PERIODICALS

McGirk, Tim, et al. **"Hell Freezes Over."** *Time.* 5 Mar. 2001: 46-49. Discusses drought and starvation in Afghanistan.

Robinson, Simon. **"Birth of a Nation."** *Time.* 8 Jan. 2001: 44-45. Recounts Somalia's efforts to rebuild.

INTERNET

For more information on famines, visit . . .

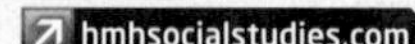

Natural Causes
A lack of rain in successive seasons resulted in drought. Drought prevented the growth of enough food to feed the country's population.

Human Causes
Somali gunmen often looted relief shipments and then extracted payment for protecting relief workers. Other political causes, such as disagreements between warring factions, also prevented the delivery of food supplies.

Results

Thirsty Somalis plead for water delivered by the International Red Cross in Baidoa, Somalia, in 1992. Aid agencies estimated that famine killed between 25 and 50 people a day in this town in 1992.

GeoActivity

UNDERSTANDING FAMINE

Working with a partner, use the Internet to research different international aid organizations. Then write a **news report** about those organizations.

- Create a visual aid comparing the various groups.
- Include information about how the groups are funded.

hmhsocialstudies.com
RESEARCH WEB LINKS

GeoData

FAMINE IN SOMALIA
In the early 1990s, more than 300,000 Somalis died of famine, and another 30,000 died in a related civil war.

- Principal causes included drought, desertification, and civil war.
- Underlying causes, such as increased growth of cash crops and reliance on livestock, stemmed from a history of foreign intervention dating back to Italian and British colonization in the 19th century.

OTHER FAMINES

1876–1878 India
Drought caused famine that killed about five million people.

1932–1934 Soviet Union
Between six and eight million peasants died because of actions by the government.

1958–1960 China
Around 20 million people died during government reforms.

GeoActivities

Understanding Famine

Integrated Assessment
- Rubric for news report, 3.6

More About

Drought and Famine

In 2000, drought conditions were severe in the countries of India, Afghanistan, and Pakistan. Hundreds of thousands of animals, including camels, died of thirst. In India, millions of people lacked water, and officials called for international aid to prevent high death tolls. In Pakistan, people fled hard-hit areas. The World Food Program, which fed several million people in Afghanistan, tried to persuade villagers not to flee their homes but to dig deeper wells and clean up irrigation channels.

ACTIVITY OPTION | COOPERATIVE LEARNING

BLOCK SCHEDULING

PREPARING FOR A PANEL DISCUSSION

Objective To allow students to explore the issues of famine
Class Time One class period
Task Prepare for and hold a panel discussion

Directions Working in small groups, students should use the Internet or print sources to find two or three articles about drought and famine. Tell groups to assign a role—such as researcher, scribe, or presenter—to each member. Have each group discuss its articles and write a summary. The presenters from each group should then use the summaries to hold a panel discussion.

SECTION 2 OBJECTIVES

1. Examine roots of civilization in North Africa.
2. Analyze the impact of oil on the economies of North Africa.
3. Describe the culture of North Africa.
4. Examine changing roles for women in North Africa.

SKILLBUILDER: Interpreting Maps, p. 439

GeographicThinking

Using the Atlas, p. 439
Making Comparisons, p. 440
Drawing Conclusions, p. 441

Focus & Motivate

What landforms or resources do you think help to make civilization possible? *(waterways and potable water sources, fertile land for agriculture)*

Instruct: Objective 

Roots of Civilization in North Africa

- What form of government did ancient Egypt have? *(monarchy led by god-kings called pharaohs)*
- What practices did the ancient world acquire from Egypt? *(use of geometry to set boundaries; medical treatments)*
- How did Muslims gain control of North Africa? *(military conquest)*

In-Depth Resources: Unit 6
• Guided Reading, p. 14

CAPTION ANSWER The Nile provided rich soil and water, enabling civilization to grow in Egypt.

2 North Africa

Main Ideas

- The Nile River valley and ancient Egypt, one of the world's great civilizations, formed a cultural hearth.
- North Africa shares the Arabic language and the Islamic religion and culture with Southwest Asia.

Places & Terms

Carthage
Islam
rai

CONNECT TO THE ISSUES
ECONOMIC DEVELOPMENT The discovery of oil in North Africa has helped the region's economy to grow.

A HUMAN PERSPECTIVE According to legend, around 814 B.C. a Phoenician queen founded **Carthage,** one of the great cities of ancient Africa. She located it on a peninsula on the Gulf of Tunis. The location was ideal. The Lake of Tunis protected the rear of the peninsula from invasion. In addition, because Carthage was on the coast of the Mediterranean Sea, it had access to trading routes. Consequently, it became a trading and commercial force in the ancient world for hundreds of years. Carthage's history shows that a city's or a civilization's geographic position always plays an important part in its ability to thrive and grow.

Roots of Civilization in North Africa

North Africa includes Algeria, Egypt, Libya, Morocco, Sudan, and Tunisia. Egypt and the Nile River valley formed a cultural hearth, a place where ideas and innovations come together to change a region. Those ideas and innovations reached other regions through cultural diffusion.

EGYPT BLOSSOMS ALONG THE NILE The Nile River made possible the existence of the great civilization of ancient Egypt. The river flooded at roughly the same time every year, providing the people with water and rich soil for their crops. The ancient Greek historian Herodotus remarked in the fifth century B.C. that Egypt was the "gift of the Nile."

Egyptians had been living in farming villages around the Nile River since 3300 B.C. Each village followed its own customs and rituals. Around 3100 B.C., a strong king united all of Egypt and established the first Egyptian dynasty. The history of ancient Egypt would span 2,600 years and around 30 dynasties. Monarchs called pharaohs ruled over Egypt. They were worshipped as gods. The Egyptians built huge, elaborate temples to worship their many gods and pyramids to house some of their rulers' remains.

Movement influenced ancient Egypt and the Nile valley. Egyptian ideas about farming, the building of their cities, and their system of

HUMAN-ENVIRONMENT INTERACTION An irrigation ditch from the Nile River nourishes the fields outside Al Fayyam, Egypt. **Why has Egypt been called the "gift of the Nile"?**

SECTION 2 PROGRAM RESOURCES

In-Depth Resources: Unit 6
• Guided Reading, p. 14
• Building Vocabulary, p. 19
• Reteaching Activity, p. 21
• GeoWorkshop, pp. 39–40

Guided Reading Workbook
• Section 2

Access for Students Acquiring English/ESL
• Guided Reading, p. 100

Outline Maps with Activities
• North Africa, pp. 57–58

Formal Assessment
• Section Quiz, p. 290

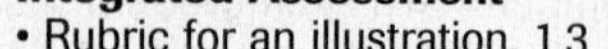
Integrated Assessment
• Rubric for an illustration, 1.3

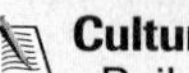
Cultures Around the World
• Daily Life, p. 32

INTEGRATED TECHNOLOGY

Map Transparencies MT34
• Expansion of Islam, 750–1500

Test Generator
• Section Quiz

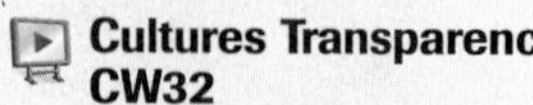
Cultures Transparencies CW32
• Playing Mancala

TEST-TAKING RESOURCES

Strategies for Test Preparation

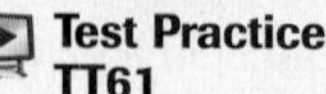
Test Practice Transparencies TT61

Online Test Practice

writing may have come from the Mesopotamians, who lived in what is now Southwest Asia. Egyptians pioneered the use of geometry in farming to set boundaries after the Nile's annual flood. Furthermore, Egyptian medicine was famous throughout the ancient world. Egyptians could make splints for broken bones and effectively treat wounds and fevers. Trade and travel on the Nile River, the Mediterranean and Red seas, and overland trade routes helped spread those practices.

ISLAM IN NORTH AFRICA North Africa lies close to Southwest Asia and across the Mediterranean Sea from Europe. As a result, it has been invaded and occupied by many people and empires from outside Africa. Greeks and Romans from Europe and Phoenicians and Ottoman Turks from Southwest Asia all invaded North Africa.

Islam, however, remains the major cultural and religious influence in North Africa. Islam, a monotheistic religion, is based on the teachings of Muhammad, whom you will read about in Chapter 22. Muslim invaders from Southwest Asia brought their language, culture, and religion to North Africa. Beginning in A.D. 632, the successors of Muhammad began to spread Islam through conquest and through trade. Around 634, Muslim armies swept into lower Egypt, which was then part of the Byzantine Empire. By 750, Muslims controlled most of North Africa. Muslims bound their territory together with a network of sea-linked trading zones. They used the Mediterranean Sea and the Indian Ocean to connect North Africa and Europe with Southwest Asia. A

Expansion of Islam, 750–1500

hmhsocialstudies.com INTERACTIVE

Extent of Islam 750
Extent of Islam 900
Extent of Islam 1100
Extent of Islam 1500

Lambert Azimuthal Equal-Area Projection

SKILLBUILDER: Interpreting Maps

1. **PLACE** On which continent did Islam begin?
2. **MOVEMENT** Between which years did Islam achieve its greatest growth in Africa?

Geographic Thinking

Using the Atlas

A Using the map on this page and the unit atlas on page 405, identify the first Islamic countries in Africa.

A. Answer parts of what are now Morocco, Algeria, Tunisia, Libya, and Egypt

Economics of Oil

North Africa began with an economy based on agriculture. Over the course of its history, it evolved into an economy based on the growth of cash crops and mining. Today, the economy revolves around the discovery of oil in the region.

BLACK GOLD Oil has transformed the economies of some North African countries, including Algeria, Libya, and Tunisia. In Algeria, oil has surpassed farm products as the major export and source of revenue. Furthermore, oil makes up about 99 percent of Libya's exports. Libya and Algeria supply the European Union with much of its oil and gas.

Interpreting Maps

Expansion of Islam, 750-1500

Tell students that Muhammad began the religion of Islam in the city of Mecca and several years later emigrated to Medina. Have students locate these two cities on the map. Then ask them to use the map to determine why Cairo and Alexandria were part of the first wave of Islamic expansion. *(The overland route from Arabia to Africa runs north of the Red Sea and then west. That route ran past Cairo and Alexandria.)*

Map Transparencies MT34
- Expansion of Islam, 750–1500

SKILLBUILDER ANSWERS

1. Asia **2.** between 900 and 1100

Instruct: Objective 2

Economics of Oil

- How has North Africa's economic base evolved? *(from agriculture to cash crops and mining and finally oil)*
- What North African countries have economies transformed by oil? *(Libya, Algeria, Tunisia)*
- Why has the oil industry failed to benefit local workers? *(Local workers' lack of training and education forces oil companies to hire foreign workers.)*

AFRICA

DIFFERENTIATING INSTRUCTION | STUDENTS ACQUIRING ENGLISH/ESL

LEARNING UNFAMILIAR WORDS

Objective To help ESL students expand their vocabulary

Class Time 30 minutes

Task Create cluster diagrams of related words

Directions Pair ESL students with English-proficient students to create cluster diagrams of related words. Suggest that they use the terms *Egypt* or *Islam* at the center of their clusters. Encourage them to discuss the meaning of unfamiliar terms as they work. Have students display their diagrams. A model cluster diagram is shown at right.

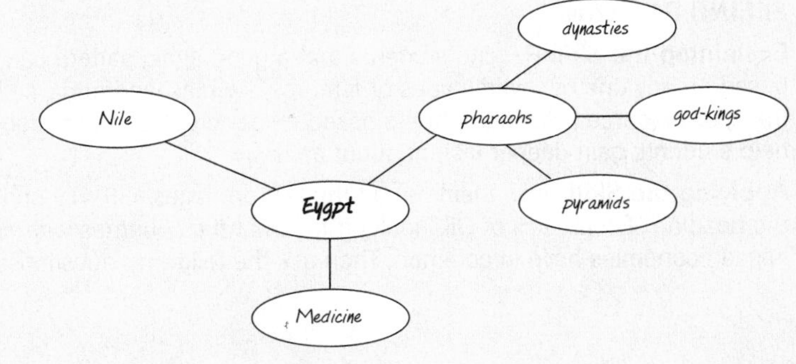

Instruct: Objective 

A Culture of Markets and Music

- What major influences combine in North African culture? *(Arabic, traditional African ethnic groups)*
- How are prices set for products sold at *souks*? *(bartering and haggling between buyer and seller)*
- How has *rai* music changed since its beginnings? *(from carefree music for urban youths into a form of protest)*

 **Cultures Around the World**
- Daily Life, p. 32

Cultures Transparencies CW32
- Mancala

The World's Music Audio Program

Although oil has helped the economies of those countries, it has also caused some problems. For example, Libya's labor force cannot meet the demands of the oil industry because of a lack of training and education. Oil companies therefore are forced to give many high-paying jobs to foreign workers. Despite the oil industry, overall unemployment is still a problem. As a result, large numbers of North Africans have migrated to Europe in search of jobs.

A Culture of Markets and Music

North African culture is a combination of Arabic influences and traditional African ethnic groups.

NORTH AFRICAN *SOUKS* *Souks,* or marketplaces, are common features of life in North Africa. A country *souk* opens early in the morning. Tents are erected, and storytellers, musicians, and fortunetellers entertain the crowds. A typical city *souk* is located in the *medina,* or old section, of a North African town or city. A *medina* has narrow, winding streets. Some of the best *souks* in North Africa can be found in Marrakesh, Morocco. The markets are known for high-pressure sales, and shoppers must be prepared to bargain fiercely for the lowest price. B

Geographic Thinking

Making Comparisons

B How are country and city *souks* alike? Different?

B. Answer Country and city *souks* are alike in that people travel from many places to come to the market, and all sorts of bartering takes place for a range of products. Country *souks* open early in the morning, and merchants set up tents. A city *souk* usually takes place in the old section of a city.

In both the city and the country, people fill the *souks* throughout the day. All kinds of bartering and haggling take place for a range of products, including brightly colored clothes, spices, and a variety of foods. The aroma of lamb, spices, and animals fills the air. It is also a place where one can eat traditional foods such as couscous, a kind of steamed grain.

PROTEST MUSIC Algeria is home to ***rai,*** a kind of music developed in the 1920s by poor urban children. *Rai* was at first carefree and centered around topics for youths. The music is fast paced and contains elements of popular Western music.

Before Algerian independence in 1962, however, performers began using *rai* to communicate Algerian resentment toward their French

MOVEMENT Moroccans flood this typical market in Marrakesh.
What role do markets play in the movements of goods and people?

Interpreting Photographs

Market in Marrakesh, Morocco

Ask students to examine the photograph. Ask them what *souks* have in common with U.S. shopping malls. *(Like* souks, *malls are gathering places that may provide forms of entertainment or exhibits, as well as goods for sale.)* What are differences between the two? *(Malls are usually filled with chain stores;* souks *feature small shops run by individuals.)*

CAPTION ANSWER People travel to a central location to buy goods, which have often been transported there from another place.

ACTIVITY OPTION | **CRITICAL THINKING**

SEEING PATTERNS

Explaining the Skill Remind students that a geographic pattern can be based on any one of several types of features, such as landforms, cultural traits, or resources. Seeing patterns based on geographic information can help students gain deeper insight about an issue.

Applying the Skill Have them reread the text on pages 439-440 under the heading "Economics of Oil," looking for what the countries with oil-based economies have in common. Then ask the following questions:

- How has the discovery of oil affected several North African economies? *(Oil is a major export and source of revenue.)*
- Why does the oil industry hire foreign workers? *(Local workers lack skills and education.)*
- How can North African countries improve their local economies? *(establish a better educational system)*

colonizers. After independence, the Algerian government tried to ban *rai*. In the 1990s, Islamic fundamentalists have criticized *rai* for its Western-style qualities. *Rai* is now used as a form of rebellion against Islamic fundamentalists, especially by women.

Changing Roles of Women

Modern life in North Africa is in a constant state of change. The role of women, especially, has shifted during the past several years.

PLACE Teenagers socialize in front of stylish shops in Casablanca, Morocco.

WOMEN AND THE FAMILY North African households tend to be centered around males. Men go out to work in offices or on farms. Few women hold jobs after they marry. Men and women also generally eat and pray separately.

Women's roles, however, are changing, especially in Tunisia, where having more than one wife at a time has been abolished. It has also increased the penalty for spousal abuse. Moreover, either spouse can now seek a divorce. In addition, Tunisia no longer permits preteen girls in arranged marriages and requires equal pay for equal jobs.

Women in North Africa have also made gains outside the home, particularly in cities. Growing numbers of them, for instance, have professional jobs. Women hold 20 percent of Tunisia's parliamentary seats and manage a growing number of the businesses in Tunis, the capital of Tunisia.

In the next section, you will read about how trade formed the foundation of ancient civilizations in West Africa.

AFRICA

Section 2 Assessment

1 Places & Terms

Identify these terms and explain their importance in the region's history or culture.

- Carthage
- Islam
- *rai*

2 Taking Notes

PLACE Review the notes you took for this section.

- What is the single biggest cultural influence in North Africa?
- Which commodity supports some of North Africa's economies?

3 Main Ideas

a. How did the Nile help support the growth of ancient Egypt?

b. Where did Islam spread after its beginnings in Southwest Asia?

c. In which ways have women's roles changed in North Africa?

4 Geographic Thinking

Drawing Conclusions

How has Islam influenced life in North Africa? **Think about:**

- its impact on women
- the religion that people practice

SEEING PATTERNS Use the Internet or encyclopedias to learn about all the economic and recreational activities supported by the Nile River. Then create an **illustration** of the Nile River with those activities taking place.

21st CENTURY

Instruct: Objective 4

Changing Roles of Women

- What was the traditional role for North African women? *(stay at home, eat and pray apart from men)*
- How has marriage law changed in Tunisia? *(Polygamy has been abolished, pre-teen girls cannot marry, spousal abuse is punished more severely, and either spouse can seek divorce.)*
- What gains have Tunisian women made outside the home? *(They hold professional jobs, sit in Parliament, and run businesses)*

In-Depth Resources: Unit 6
- GeoWorkshop, pp. 39–40

Assess & Reteach

GeoFocus Have students complete their notes on North Africa for their cluster diagrams.

Formal Assessment
- Section Quiz, p. 290

Reteaching Activity
Have students discuss the section in terms of culture. Ask them to contribute information about cultural influences in ancient North Africa and modern North Africa.

In-Depth Resources: Unit 6
- Reteaching Activity, p. 21

Outline Maps with Activities
- North Africa, pp. 57–58

SECTION 2 ASSESSMENT ANSWERS

1. Places & Terms
Carthage, p. 438 rai, p. 440
Islam, p. 439

2. Taking Notes
- Islam is the single biggest cultural influence in North Africa. Muslim armies conquered most of North Africa by A.D. 750, and the region has remained Muslim.
- Oil supports some of North Africa's economies.

3. Main Ideas
a. The Nile flooded at roughly the same time every year, which made it a reliable source of irrigation for Egyptian farmers.
b. Islam spread from Southwest Asia to parts of Africa, Europe, and other parts of Asia.
c. In Tunisia, at least, women are working outside the home more often and are holding professional jobs. In addition, they have equal marriage rights with men, and polygamy has been abolished.

4. Geographic Thinking
Islam has influenced many facets of life in North Africa. Men and women follow prescribed, separate patterns of behavior.

GeoActivity

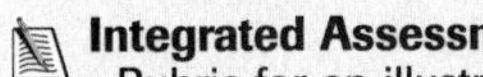

Integrated Assessment
- Rubric for an illustration, 1.3

SECTION 3 OBJECTIVES

1. Examine the history of West Africa, including trade and government.
2. Analyze West African economies.
3. Describe cultural symbols of West Africa and West African music.

SKILLBUILDERS: Interpreting Maps and Graphs, pp. 442, 443

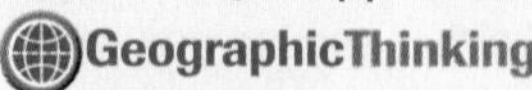

Seeing Patterns, pp. 443, 444
Making Comparisons, p. 445

Focus & Motivate

Ask students what geographic feature lies between the Mediterranean and West Africa. *(the Sahara)* What means of transport made trade across the Sahara possible? *(camels)*

Instruct: Objective 

A History of Rich Trading Empires

- How did location help the three West African empires? *(They were on trade routes across the Sahara.)*
- What helped Ghana thrive besides its gold-salt trade? *(It taxed traders passing through its territory.)*

In-Depth Resources: Unit 6
• Guided Reading, p. 15

Critical Thinking Transparencies CT51
• Ancient Empires

SKILLBUILDER ANSWERS
1. about 1,900 to 2,000 miles, depending on which route was taken
2. Songhai

West Africa

Main Ideas
- Wealth from the gold and salt trades supported a series of West African empires.
- West Africa has a rich cultural tradition that has influenced many parts of the world.

Places & Terms
Gorée Island
stateless society
Ashanti

CONNECT TO THE ISSUES
COLONIALISM European nations took raw materials from West Africa. Today many West African countries rely on exports to support their economies.

A HUMAN PERSPECTIVE A visit to **Gorée Island,** off the coast of Senegal, can be a moving experience. This island served as one of the busiest points for exporting slaves during the slave trade. From the mid-1500s to the mid-1800s, Europeans transported about 20 million Africans through Gorée Island. The island has a slave house, a dark, damp building that housed captive Africans. Europeans packed these captives onto slave ships bound for plantations in the Americas. Approximately 20 percent of all Africans died on the transatlantic voyage—and the rest never saw their West African homes or families again. Slavery had a profound effect on West Africa that is still being felt there today.

A History of Rich Trading Empires

West Africa includes Benin, Burkina Faso, Cape Verde, Chad, Côte d'Ivoire, Gambia, Ghana, Guinea, Guinea-Bissau, Liberia, Mali, Mauritania, Niger, Nigeria, Senegal, Sierra Leone, and Togo. West Africa is a cultural hearth, and its ideas and practices spread to North America and Europe.

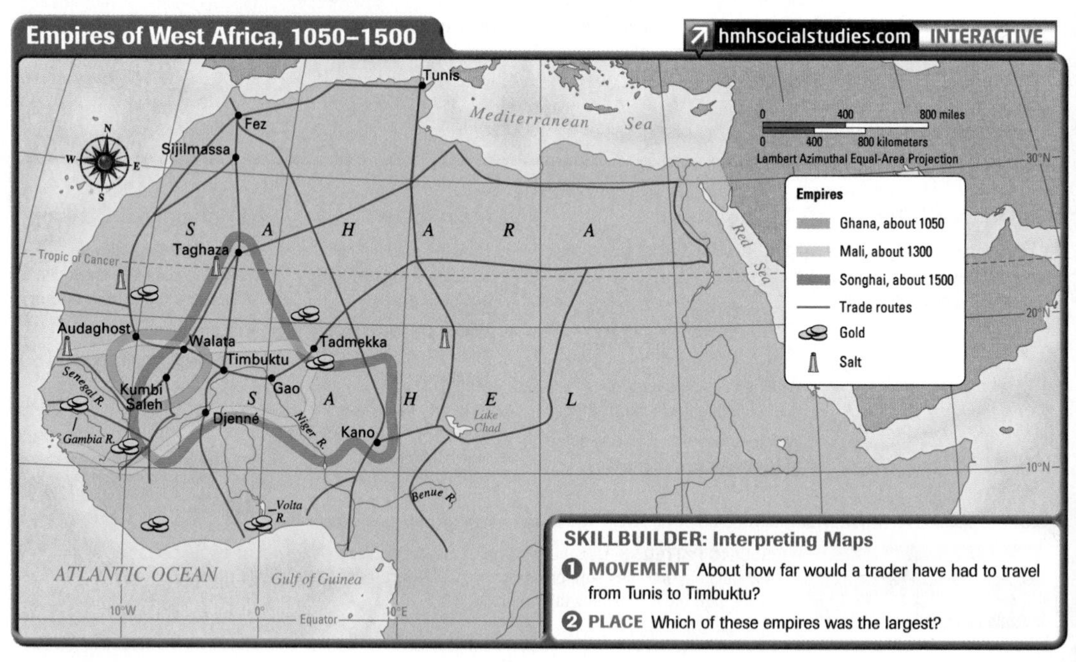

SKILLBUILDER: Interpreting Maps
❶ **MOVEMENT** About how far would a trader have had to travel from Tunis to Timbuktu?
❷ **PLACE** Which of these empires was the largest?

SECTION 3 PROGRAM RESOURCES

In-Depth Resources: Unit 6
• Guided Reading, p. 15
• Skillbuilder Practice, p. 18
• Building Vocabulary, p. 19
• Reteaching Activity, p. 22

Guided Reading Workbook
• Section 3

Access for Students Acquiring English/ESL
• Guided Reading, p. 101
• Skillbuilder Practice, p. 104

Outline Maps with Activities
• West Africa, pp. 59–60

Formal Assessment
• Section Quiz, p. 291

Integrated Assessment
• Rubric for a chart, 2.2

Cultures Around the World
• Architecture, p. 31
• Fine Arts, p. 33
• Traditional Practices, p. 34
• Music, p. 35

INTEGRATED TECHNOLOGY

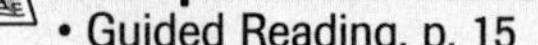

Critical Thinking Tranparencies CT51
• Ancient Empires of Africa

Cultures Transparencies CW31, 33, 34, 35
• Dogon Village
• Benin Bronze
• Senufo Mask
• Kora

TEST-TAKING RESOURCES

Strategies for Test Preparation

Test Practice Transparencies TT62

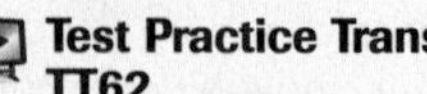

Online Test Practice

THREE TRADING EMPIRES The empires of Ghana, Mali, and Songhai thrived in West Africa because of their location on trade routes across the Sahara. Gold and salt were the main products traded. By A.D. 200, trade across the Sahara had existed for many years.

Many of the trade routes crossed an area farmed by the Sonike people. They called their leader *ghana,* or war chief. Traders began to refer to this area as Ghana, which grew rich from taxing the traders who passed through its territory. Traders exchanged mostly gold and salt. Ghana became an empire around A.D. 800 but began to decline in power by the end of the 11th century. A

Geographic Thinking

Seeing Patterns

A Why did three empires prosper and grow in this area of West Africa?

A. Answer
Because of gold and salt deposits, the empires became destinations for traders crossing the Sahara.

By 1235, the kingdom of Mali emerged. Mali's first great leader, Sundiata, conquered Ghana. He promoted agriculture and reestablished the gold and salt trade. Some experts estimate that until 1350, about two-thirds of the world's gold came from West Africa. Around 1400, Mali declined because of a lack of leadership and the discovery of new gold fields farther east.

Around 1400, the empire of Songhai replaced Mali. Sunni Ali ruled for 28 years, beginning in 1464. In 1591, a Moroccan army invaded Songhai and defeated it, destroying the empire.

STATELESS SOCIETIES West Africa is filled with many different cultures and peoples. Before colonialism, some of these people lived in what are called stateless societies.

A **stateless society** is one in which people rely on family lineages to govern themselves, rather than an elected government or a monarch. A lineage is a family or group that has descended from a common ancestor. Members of a stateless society work through their differences to cooperate and share power.

One example of a stateless society is the Igbo of southeast Nigeria. Relying on family lineages worked well for the Igbo and other African societies. However, many stateless societies faced challenges from 18th- and 19th-century European colonizers, who expected one ruler to govern the society.

BACKGROUND
One stateless society, the Nuer of southern Sudan, organized thousands of people without an official ruler.

West Africa Struggles Economically

Trade is as important to West Africa today as it was in the past. The economic well-being of West Africa is based on the sale of its products to industrialized countries in Europe, North America, and Asia. The economies of West Africa range in strength from the relatively solid economy of Ghana to the weak economy of Sierra Leone.

GNP Per Capita, 1987–1997

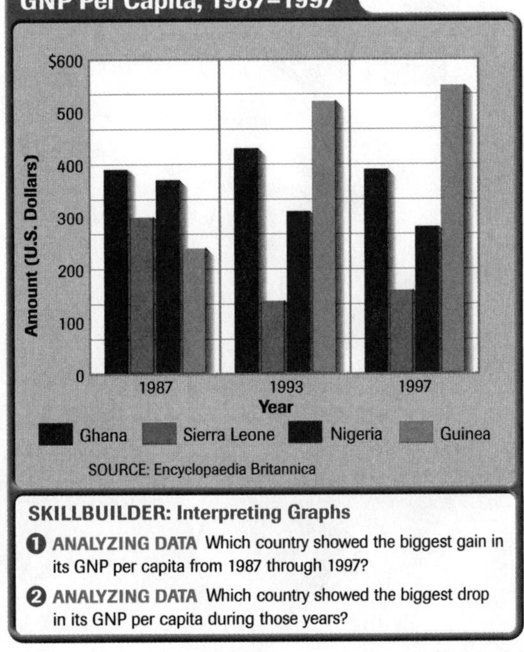

SKILLBUILDER: Interpreting Graphs

1. **ANALYZING DATA** Which country showed the biggest gain in its GNP per capita from 1987 through 1997?
2. **ANALYZING DATA** Which country showed the biggest drop in its GNP per capita during those years?

AFRICA

More About

The Igbo

The Igbo of southeastern Nigeria remain divided into subgroups that govern themselves by village councils. These councils include heads of lineages, elders, and men who enjoy economic success within the group. This complex social structure allows most individuals some decision-making power, making Igbo villages fairly democratic.

Instruct: Objective 2

West Africa Struggles Economically

- What is the basis of West Africa's economic well-being? *(trade)*
- What has helped Ghana achieve healthy economic growth in recent years? *(political stability)*

SKILLBUILDER ANSWERS
1. Guinea **2.** Sierra Leone

ACTIVITY OPTION **SKILLBUILDER LESSON**

CREATING GRAPHS AND CHARTS

Explaining the Skill Tell students that different types of graphs can help them to analyze data in different ways. For example, the bar graph on page 443 makes it easy to compare the GNP per capita for different countries. However, it is not the most useful graph for seeing a single country's changes over time. To study that pattern, line graphs are helpful. Tell students that they can reconfigure the existing bar graph as a line graph.

In-Depth Resources: Unit 6
- Skillbuilder Practice, p. 18

Applying the Skill On the chalkboard, copy the *x* and *y* axes from the graph on page 443. Select four students, one for each country, and give each a different color of chalk. Have each student determine his or her country's GNP per capita for the three years, place appropriate dots on the new graph, and connect the dots with a continuous line.

- Which country shows a steadily rising line? *(Guinea)*
- Which country shows a steadily falling line? *(Nigeria)*
- Which country's GNP per capita remained fairly stable? *(Ghana)*

Instruct: Objective 3

Cultural Symbols of West Africa/Music in Daily Life

- For what colorful cloth are the Ashanti well known? (asasia, *called* kente *cloth by Westerners)*
- What influences are found in West African popular music? *(traditional African melodies and American jazz, blues, reggae)*

Cultures Around the World
- Architecture, p. 31
- Fine Arts, p. 33
- Traditional Practices, p. 34
- Music, p. 35

Cultures Transparencies CW31, 33, 34, 35
- Dogon Village
- Benin Bronze
- Senufo Mask
- Kora

The World's Music Audio Program

Interpreting Photographs

Ashanti Weaver

Have students examine the photograph and insert. In West Africa, weaving on this type of strip loom is traditionally a man's activity. Ask students how that compares to what they know of weaving in other countries. *(It is often a woman's job.)* Ask students to name the ways that they have seen *kente* cloth used. *(hats, ties, stoles, and other accessories)*

CAPTION ANSWER agility, good eyesight, coordination

GHANA'S STABILITY Ghana's economy relies primarily on the export of gold, diamonds, magnesium, and bauxite to the industrialized world. Ghana's per capita output is about twice that of the poorest African countries. Oil production is expected to increase also. In addition, Ghana has committed to upgrading its agricultural sector.

Ghana's transition from colonialism to democracy has had setbacks, including military rule and civil war. However, every four years since 1992, Ghana has held free and fair elections. As a result of this new political stability, the economy is growing at a healthy rate. But other West African countries have not been as fortunate. B

Geographic Thinking

Seeing Patterns

B How is the economy of Ghana similar to those of the ancient West African kingdoms?

B. Answer It relies on natural resources as the basis for its wealth.

PROBLEMS IN SIERRA LEONE Some of the worst economic conditions in West Africa exist in Sierra Leone, which once produced some of the world's highest-quality diamonds. However, years of political instability and civil wars have left the economy in shambles. In addition, a relatively uneducated population—with a 35 percent literacy rate—leaves a shortage of skilled workers. Finally, the road and transportation system contains few highways and only about 560 miles of paved roads. In contrast, Benin, another West African country close to Sierra Leone in size, has almost twice that amount of paved roadways.

HUMAN-ENVIRONMENT INTERACTION A Ghanaian weaver makes *kente* cloth. **What are some skills that a weaver might need?**

Cultural Symbols of West Africa

West African cultures, such as the Ashanti and Benin, have produced elaborate craftwork and colorful textiles.

ASHANTI CRAFTS The **Ashanti,** who live in what is now Ghana, are known for their work in weaving colorful *asasia*—what Westerners usually call *kente* cloth. The designs of *kente* cloth contain colorful woven geometric figures with specific meanings. Only royalty were allowed to wear *kente* cloth.

Other crafts include making masks and carving wooden stools. An Ashanti stool symbolizes the unity between ancestral spirits and the living members of a family. Fathers often give their sons a stool as their first gift. In the case of kings, the stool represents the unity of the state with its people.

BENIN ART The kingdom of Benin, which has no direct connection with the current

444

ACTIVITY OPTION **FIVE THEMES OF GEOGRAPHY**

MOVEMENT

Exploring the Theme Remind students that geographers frequently examine the transport of goods as part of the theme of movement. Explain that it is also possible to study the negative side of this theme; in some cases, it is most helpful to analyze why goods do not move easily.

Understanding the Theme Ask students to reread the paragraph under the heading "Problems in Sierra Leone." Direct them to look specifically for information related to movement. Then ask the following questions:

- How many miles of roads are there in Sierra Leone? *(only about 560)*
- How does this affect the ability to transport goods? *(It is difficult to transport goods if no roads exist.)*
- How does the road system affect the economy of Sierra Leone? Explain. *(It has a negative effect because trade depends on the transport of goods.)*

country of Benin, arose in what is now Nigeria in the 1200s. Benin artists made beautiful objects of metal and terra cotta. However, their most important works were fashioned from brass and are called Benin "bronzes." They include statues, masks, and jewelry. A common subject of Benin "bronzes" was that of the queen mother.

Music in Daily Life

Music is a large part of life in West Africa. West African music has become an important influence on world music.

WEST AFRICAN MUSIC West African popular music involves a blend of traditional African music with American forms of jazz, blues, and reggae—which also had their origins in West Africa because of the slave trade and the contact between the two regions. Over the years, West African musicians used French and English lyrics to attract an international audience. West African music is played on a wide variety of drums and other instruments such as the kora, a cross between a harp and a lute. The kora originated in what is now Guinea-Bissau.

King Sunny Adé, also known as the "minister of enjoyment," is a popular musician from Nigeria. King Sunny and his band, the African Beats, play an informal type of music characterized by tight vocals, complex guitar work, traditional talking drums, percussion instruments, and the pedal steel guitar and accordion.

In Section 4, you can read more about culture and life in Central Africa.

MOVEMENT King Sunny Adé's music blends sounds from North America and West Africa.
How do you think music moved from West Africa to North America?

Assessment

1 Places & Terms

Identify these terms and explain their importance in the region's history or culture.

- Gorée Island
- stateless society
- Ashanti

2 Taking Notes

HUMAN-ENVIRONMENT INTERACTION Review the notes you took for this section.

- How did natural resources affect the ancient empires in West Africa?
- How do stateless societies differ from those with a centralized government?

3 Main Ideas

a. What three empires flourished because of trade in West Africa?

b. What are some of the roadblocks to economic development in West Africa?

c. What is the significance of the stool in Ashanti society?

4 Geographic Thinking

Making Comparisons How do the economics of Sierra Leone and Ghana differ?
Think about:
- Ghana's political stability
- the state of infrastructure in Sierra Leone

MAKING COMPARISONS Review the information about the West African economies on pages 443–444. Using the Internet or encyclopedias, find the per capita income of four other West African countries during the last ten years. Then create a **chart** comparing their growth or decline during that time.

Interpreting Photographs

Musician King Sunny Adé

Point out to students that King Sunny Adé plays a guitar, rather than an African instrument such as the kora, mentioned in the text. Ask students why they think he chooses the guitar over something more traditionally African. *(perhaps for the same reason that many West African musicians sing in English or French—to gain an international audience)*

CAPTION ANSWER Enslaved Africans brought many aspects of West African culture to the Americas.

Assess & Reteach

GeoFocus Have students complete their notes on West Africa for their cluster diagrams.

Formal Assessment
- Section Quiz, p. 291

Reteaching Activity

Have students review the main ideas for this section by creating two lists. One list should have the heading "Ongoing Problems" and the other "Contributions to World Culture."

In-Depth Resources: Unit 6
- Reteaching Activity, p. 22

Outlines Maps with Activities
- West Africa, pp. 59–60

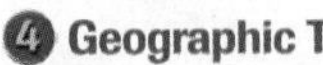

SECTION 3 ASSESSMENT ANSWERS

1. Places & Terms
Gorée Island, p. 442
stateless society, p. 443
Ashanti, p. 444

2. Taking Notes
- Gold provided the ancient empires of West Africa with a valuable commodity to enrich their societies.
- People use family lineages to govern themselves in a stateless society, rather than one central government.

3. Main Ideas
a. Ghana, Mali, and Songhai were supported by the gold-salt trade.
b. They include reliance on export of raw materials, political instability, an uneducated population, and poor roads and transportation systems.
c. The stool symbolizes the unity between the ancestral spirits and the living members of Ashanti families.

4. Geographic Thinking
Ghana's economy has benefited from nearly ten years of political stability. Sierra Leone is still suffering from civil war, which is destroying its infrastructure and is preventing economic growth.

GeoActivity

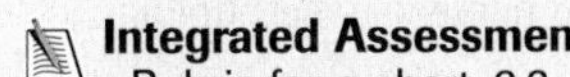
Integrated Assessment
- Rubric for a chart, 2.2

OBJECTIVE

Understand that people all over the world celebrate harvest feasts.

Instruct: Objective

Feasts

- What are the names of the harvest festivals of India, China, and Ghana? *(Sankranti, the moon festival, Homowo harvest feast)*
- Why do the Chinese celebrate their festival with moon-shaped pastries? *(because they time planting and harvesting by the moon)*
- What crops are central to the Homowo harvest festival? *(corn, okra)*

Interpreting Photographs

- What color seems to have significance in the Chinese moon festival? *(red, the color of the candles, paper lanterns, and moon pastries)*
- Why do you suppose banana leaf plates are traditional for Sankranti? *(perhaps as a symbol of harvest)*
- Judging from the photographs, what do all these feasts seem to have in common? *(They are celebrated in groups, probably of family members.)*

hmhsocialstudies.com INTERACTIVE

Comparing Cultures

VIDEO
Origins o
Thanksg
Holiday

hmhsocialstudies.

Feasts

All over the world, people celebrate certain events by holding a ritual feast. The autumn harvest, when the season's crops are gathered, is an important time in most cultures. As a result, many people have a special meal to celebrate the earth's bounty. Most harvest feasts are accompanied by a legend or story that tells of the feast's origins. For example, most Americans trace Thanksgiving, their harvest feast, to 1621, when Pilgrims invited Native Americans to join them in a three-day celebration marking the harvest.

United States
China
Ghana
India

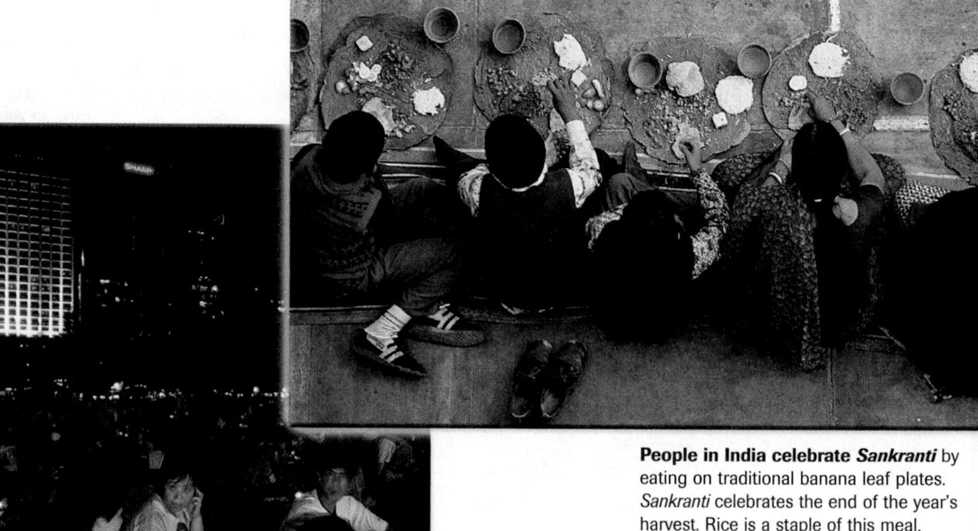

People in India celebrate *Sankranti* by eating on traditional banana leaf plates. *Sankranti* celebrates the end of the year's harvest. Rice is a staple of this meal.

Chinese celebrate the moon festival in Hong Kong. Throughout history, the Chinese have planted and harvested according to the moon. The Chinese eat moon-shaped pastries filled with red bean and lotus seed paste.

446

SUPPORTING RESOURCES

BOOKS FOR THE TEACHER

Thompson, Sue Ellen. ***Holiday Symbols, 2nd Edition.*** Detroit: Omnigraphics, 2000. A reference work on more than 900 holiday symbols from the United States and around the world.

BOOKS FOR THE STUDENT

Webb, Lois Sinaiko. ***Holidays of the World Cookbook for Students.*** Phoenix: Oryx, 1995. A collection of recipes and world customs.

Copage, Eric V. ***A Kwanzaa Fable.*** NY: Morrow, 1995. After his father's death, a 13-year-old boy experiences the harvest-based holiday.

PERIODICALS

Schorow, Stephanie. **"Many Cultures Reap Harvest Celebrations."** *Boston Herald.* 23 Nov. 2000: 63. Includes festivals in South Africa and Sri Lanka.

INTERNET

For more on feasts, visit . . .

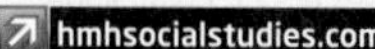

Americans gather for their Thanksgiving feast. Roast turkey, potatoes, and pumpkin pie are traditional dishes for this meal.

A Ga chief in Ghana shares ceremonial food and drink during the Homowo harvest feast. The meal includes palm oil fish stew consisting of steamed corn dough, bream (fish), and okra.

GeoActivity

EXPLORING TRADITIONAL FEASTS

Working with a small group, use the Internet to research another feast from another culture. Then create a **presentation** about this feast.

- Write a short paragraph about the origin of the feast.
- Gather pictures of the traditional foods eaten at the feast.
- Identify other rituals besides eating that are part of this celebration.

GeoData

Homowo harvest feast

- According to traditional beliefs, any Ga person failing to celebrate Homowo will incur the wrath of deceased ancestors and die.
- Some Homowo events include opening the fishing season and house purification.

Thanksgiving

- Abraham Lincoln officially proclaimed Thanksgiving a national holiday in 1863. Canada first adopted Thanksgiving as a national holiday in 1879.

Sankranti

- A general housecleaning and the burning of unwanted possessions symbolizes the destruction of evil. Children also fill the sky wih kites in a kite-flying spectacle.

Moon Festival

- During the Tang Dynasty (A.D. 618–906), the moon festival was made an official holiday.
- During the Yuan Dynasty (1279–1368), Mongolians had taken over China. So the Chinese hid messages inside moon cakes to communicate with each other about their plans for rebellion.

GeoActivities

Exploring Traditional Feasts

Integrated Assessment
- Rubric for a presentation, 3.6

More About

Harvest Feasts

Tell students that harvest feasts are particularly significant in agricultural societies. A bountiful harvest ensures that there will be enough food to survive the winter or the next planting cycle. Today, the United States is mainly an urban, postindustrial society, yet it still honors its agricultural past. Not only does it hold an annual harvest feast, but many people use cornstalks, multi-colored corn, pumpkins, and gourds as autumn decorations.

ACTIVITY OPTION EXPLORING LOCAL GEOGRAPHY

BLOCK SCHEDULING

LEARNING ABOUT THANKSGIVING FOODS

Objective To learn about the geographic origins of foods

Class Time 30 minutes

Task Create an annotated Thanksgiving menu

Directions Working in pairs, students should plan a traditional Thanksgiving menu, based on what their families serve or on the photograph above. Then they can use encyclopedias or the Internet to learn which of those foods are native to the Americas and which came from overseas. Finally, they should create an annotated menu, giving the origins of the agricultural products and animals that are featured in each dish.

The groups can be evaluated using the rubric shown.

	Exceptional	Acceptable	Poor
The menu is for a complete dinner			
The menu contains traditional foods			
The geographic origin of each food is listed			

SECTION 4 OBJECTIVES

1. Identify key events in the history of Central Africa.
2. Describe how colonialism led to economic problems in Central Africa.
3. Identify changing themes in Central African art.
4. Examine educational programs in Central Africa.

SKILLBUILDERS: Interpreting Maps, pp. 448, 450

GeographicThinking
Seeing Patterns, pp. 449, 452

Focus & Motivate

Have students consider what they read about other subregions. Ask what similarities they might expect to find in Central Africa. *(effects of colonialism, economic and political struggles)*

Instruct: Objective 1 appears on p. 449

SKILLBUILDER ANSWERS

1. about 3,000 years
2. rain forest, desert, rivers, lakes

Central Africa

Main Ideas

- The Bantu migrations helped to populate the African continent.
- European nations divided Africa without regard to ethnic groups or language.

Places & Terms

Bantu migrations
King Leopold II
Mobutu Sese Seko
Fang sculpture

CONNECT TO THE ISSUES

COLONIALISM European colonial policies so divided Africans that the region suffers from ethnic conflict today.

A HUMAN PERSPECTIVE A Congo riverboat ride from Kinshasa to Kisangani in the Democratic Republic of the Congo is a journey all visitors should take. The riverboat is essentially a floating village. Each barge shakes with music and dancing. In addition, the Congolese fill the riverboat with market stalls stocked with all types of food. The smell of smoked fish and a variety of live animals, including monkeys, tortoises, and crocodiles, fills the air. Farmers slaughter pigs and goats on board, and merchants bargain with each other for a range of products. The journey can present a valuable snapshot of life in Central Africa.

Bantu Migrations and Colonial Exploitation

Central Africa includes Cameroon, Central African Republic, Democratic Republic of the Congo, Republic of the Congo, Equatorial Guinea, Gabon, and São Tomé and Princípe. Europeans first began their African colonization in Central Africa.

BANTU MIGRATIONS The Bantu are a group of peoples and cultures who speak one of the Bantu languages. Beginning around 2000 B.C. in what is now southeastern Nigeria, the Bantu people moved southward throughout Africa. On the way they spread their languages and their cultures. This mass migration is called the **Bantu migrations.**

The Bantu may have begun this journey because of a land shortage. The Bantu migrations are a key event in Africa's history. They produced a great diversity of cultures but also helped link various areas of the continent. Today, around 120 million Africans speak one of the hundreds of Bantu languages.

Bantu Migrations, 2000 B.C.–A.D. 1000

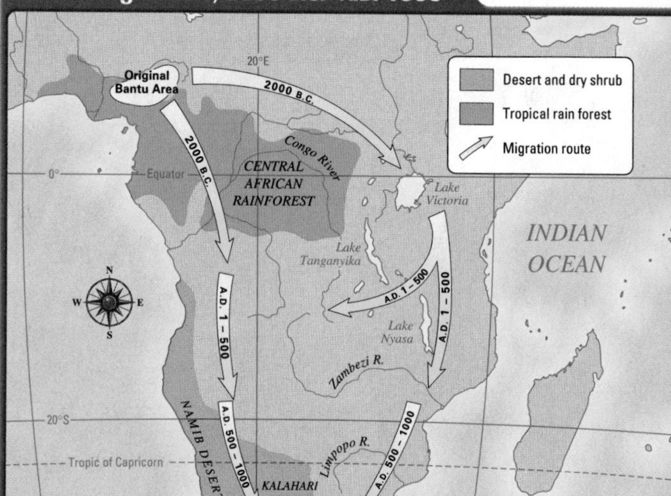

SKILLBUILDER: Interpreting Maps
1. **MOVEMENT** About how many years did it take the Bantu to reach Southern Africa?
2. **HUMAN–ENVIRONMENT INTERACTION** What physical obstacles did the Bantu have to overcome on their journey south?

SECTION 4 PROGRAM RESOURCES

In-Depth Resources: Unit 6
- Guided Reading, p. 16
- Building Vocabulary, p. 19
- Reteaching Activity, p. 23

Guided Reading Workbook
- Section 4

Access for Students Acquiring English/ESL
- Guided Reading, p. 102

Outline Maps with Activities
- Central Africa, pp. 61–62

Formal Assessment
- Section Quiz, p. 292

Integrated Assessment
- Rubric for a sketch map, 2.1

INTEGRATED TECHNOLOGY

Power Presentations

Test Generator
- Section Quiz

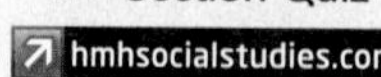

TEST-TAKING RESOURCES

Strategies for Test Preparation

Test Practice Transparencies TT52

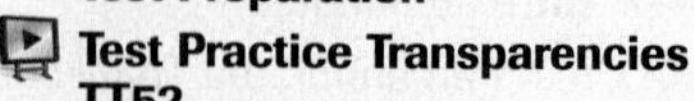
Online Test Practice

Geographic Thinking

Seeing Patterns

A How did European traders obtain slaves from Africa's interior?

A. Answer African merchants who wanted European goods brought potential slaves to the Europeans on the coast to trade.

THE SLAVE TRADE Europeans wanted slaves for their plantations in the Americas. In the 15th century, the Portuguese established the island of São Tomé, off the coast of what is now Gabon, as the initial base for trade in African captives. European traders traveled to Africa and waited on the coast. African merchants then brought potential slaves to them. The merchants traded for guns and other goods. A

Many African rulers took part in the slave trade. They already had been selling slaves to other African rulers and Arabs. So, they saw no difference in selling them to Europeans. Some Africans, however, objected. One African ruler protested to the king of Portugal. Nevertheless, by the end of the slave trade in 1870, Europeans had transported millions of slaves to the Americas and Europe.

IN THE RUBBER COILS.

MOVEMENT King Leopold II of Belgium (shown as a serpent) takes control of Central Africa. **What does the cartoon suggest about the king's view of Africa's resources?**

START OF COLONIALISM In the mid-1800s, Central Africa consisted of hundreds of different ethnic groups, which followed traditional religions and spoke hundreds of different languages. Politically, they ranged from large empires to small villages. Europeans had been in Africa since the mid-15th century but had stayed mainly on the coast. The rugged interior geography of Africa prevented further movement.

But that changed when **King Leopold II** of Belgium developed an interest in the Congo after it had been explored in the 1870s. He wanted to open the African interior to European trade along the Congo River. By 1884, Leopold controlled this area and paved the way for the Berlin Conference, which you read about in Section 1. The Berlin Conference established this area as the Congo Free State. Leopold used forced labor to gather rubber, palm oil, ivory, and other resources. B

CONNECT TO THE ISSUES
COLONIALISM

B Why did Africa become such a prized place for European powers?

B. Answer Africa became valuable to European leaders when they realized that it possessed a great deal of natural resources.

EFFECTS OF COLONIALISM During the 19th and 20th centuries, primarily the Belgians and French colonized Central Africa. Most Central African countries gained their independence in the 1960s, but the borders imposed on the Africans during colonialism posed problems. Those borders disrupted long-standing systems of government in Africa, did not consider ethnic regions, and grouped traditional enemies together.

Before colonization, a village, a tribal chief, or a group of elders would consult with various leaders within a village to make decisions that affected only that village. This type of organization is a stateless society, which you read about on page 443 in Section 3. During colonization, Europeans installed more centralized governments that destroyed the organizing principle of stateless societies. After colonization ended, new African governments in the 1960s were then forced to govern a diverse population. Inexperienced leaders were often corrupt and abused their power.

AFRICA

Instruct: Objective 1

Bantu Migrations and Colonial Exploitation

- Why are the Bantu migrations a key event? *(They produced a diversity of cultures but also linked various areas of Africa.)*
- How did the Portuguese open the African slave trade to Europeans? *(by establishing an island trading base)*
- What role did King Leopold of Belgium play in the early colonial period? *(He paved the way for European colonialism by gaining control of the region around the Congo River.)*

In-Depth Resources: Unit 6
- Guided Reading, p. 16

Interpreting Cartoons

In the Rubber Coils

Have students study the cartoon. Tell them that Leopold ruled the Congo as his own personal colony, exploiting it to make himself rich. Rubber workers who didn't meet their quotas often had their hands cut off or saw their families taken hostage. In 1904, word of the "rubber terror" began to reach Europe; by 1908, protests forced Leopold to cede control of the Congo to the Belgian parliament. Ask students when they think this cartoon was published. *(probably between 1904 and 1908)*

CAPTION ANSWER The cartoon suggests that the king felt no guilt over taking Africa's resources.

ACTIVITY OPTION | CRITICAL THINKING

DETERMINING CAUSE AND EFFECT

Explaining the Skill Tell students that causes can have many effects. Some effects will be immediate, while others may be long-term. In the case of the Congo, King Leopold's agents used brutal force to make Africans work for them. Ask students to consider what the immediate and long-term effects of such violence might be.

Applying the Skill Have pairs of students discuss Leopold's motives and the immediate and long-term effects of his rule in the Congo. Have them answer the following questions and then take part in a class discussion.

- What caused King Leopold II to take over the Congo? *(desire for trade, resources, wealth)*
- What was the immediate effect of the violence against the people of the Congo? *(They were terrorized into submission and forced to work.)*
- What might be the long-term effects of the violence? *(hatred or distrust toward Europeans; a legacy of autocratic, abusive government)*

Interpreting Maps

Infrastructure of Central Africa

Have students examine the map. Remind them that infrastructure refers to the structures that a nation needs to function. Ask them which of the features listed in the legend fall under the category of infrastructure. *(roads, railroads, airports, ports)* Which fall under the category of natural features? *(rivers, waterfalls, rapids)* Ask them what topic both the infrastructure and natural features relate to. *(transportation)*

SKILLBUILDER ANSWERS

1. Colonial powers wanted to remove resources from the interior and get them to the coast for transport to Europe. **2.** Boat, truck, train

Instruct: Objective 

The Economic Legacy of Colonialism

- What types of infrastructure did European colonizers develop in Central Africa? *(only whatever helped them remove resources)*
- Why did economic problems caused by colonization continue in the independent Democratic Republic of the Congo? *(Mobutu Sese Seko was a corrupt leader.)*
- What will help the Democratic Republic of the Congo benefit from its rich resources? *(political stability and improved infrastructure)*

Infrastructure of Central Africa

hmhsocialstudies.com INTERACTIVE

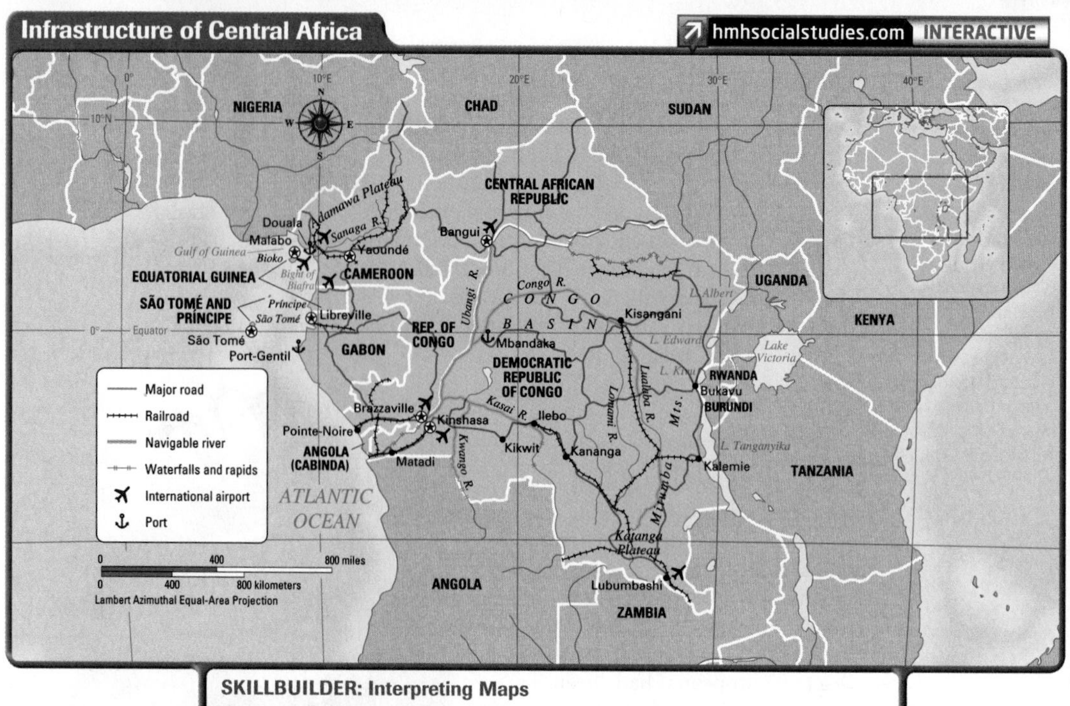

SKILLBUILDER: Interpreting Maps

1 MOVEMENT Why do you think most of the transport routes begin in the middle of the continent and end on the coast?

2 MOVEMENT What different modes of transport would you use to take goods from Kisangani in the Democratic Republic of the Congo to the coast?

The Economic Legacy of Colonialism

The economic geography of Central Africa is similar to that of the other regions of Africa. Many of the countries suffer from a lack of infrastructure and rely too much on the export of raw materials.

ECONOMIC EFFECTS Central Africa's economy is still recovering from the effects of colonialism: the loss of resources, the disruption of its political systems, and the cultural and ethnic oppression of its people. European colonizers invested little in Central Africa. The only economic infrastructure they developed was to aid the removal of raw materials. They left little money to develop roads, railroads, airports, or a productive education system for the people of those countries. C

CONNECT TO THE ISSUES
ECONOMIC DEVELOPMENT
C Why are many African countries still having difficulty developing their economies?
C. Answer European colonial powers left a state of political chaos with little money to invest in education, businesses, and economic infrastructure.

CONGO'S ECONOMIC CHAOS A good example of economic problems caused by colonization can be seen in the Democratic Republic of the Congo. The country possesses huge amounts of natural resources such as gold, copper, and diamonds. However, European colonization and a personal desire for power and riches by postcolonial leaders left the country in a state of disarray.

In the Democratic Republic of the Congo, for example, **Mobutu Sese Seko,** the country's leader from 1967 until 1997, brought the country's businesses under national control. He then began to take kickbacks in order to profit from this reorganization. The country's economy, educational system, and social structure began a rapid decline thereafter.

ACTIVITY OPTION EXPLORING LOCAL GEOGRAPHY

MAPPING LOCAL INFRASTRUCTURE

Objective To provide a basis for comparison with Africa's infrastructure

Class Time 40 minutes

Task Create a map of local transportation networks

Directions Provide students with maps of your local community (often available in telephone books or as insets on state road maps). Have students create maps showing local highways, railroads, navigable rivers and canals, and airports. Then they should compare their maps to the one on page 450 and compare their local infrastructure to that of Central Africa.

Mobutu used the army to maintain his own power. His regime finally gave way in 1997 to that of Laurent Kabila. But Kabila's leadership only led to more violence in Central Africa. Angola, Namibia, Zimbabwe, Chad, Rwanda, and Uganda all became involved in the fighting. In 2001, Kabila was assassinated, and his son Joseph succeeded him. In 2006 Joseph Kabila was democratically elected in what was considered a very fair process. Kabila's governement has given many people in the Democratic Republic of the Congo hope, but the country is still struggling to establish a stable political system.

The Influence of Central African Art

Central African art shares common ideas and themes with art in other parts of Africa, including expressions of traditional African cultures and the struggle against colonialism.

CENTRAL AFRICAN ART During the 20th century, some Central African art reflected attitudes toward colonialism. After gaining independence in the 1960s, however, many countries wanted to establish their own identities. As a result, these countries banned Western influences in their art. For example, in the 1970s, Mobutu Sese Seko launched a program to promote African—in particular, Congolese—culture above that of the West. Artists who participated tried to recover the personality of African art by using materials they considered African in origin. D

Today, artists from a new generation who did not experience colonialism are coming of age. They are focusing on issues of political instability, urban life, social justice, and crime.

FANG SCULPTURE Prior to the 20th century, few people in Europe knew much about African art. However, in 1907 the famous Spanish artist Pablo Picasso saw a display of African **Fang sculpture** in Paris, and it captivated him. After that, Picasso began using African themes in his work.

The Fang, who live in Gabon, southern Cameroon, and Equatorial Guinea, are famous for their carvings. They carve wooden masks, which are painted white with facial features outlined in black. They also carve boxes that contain the skulls and bones of deceased ancestors. These boxes are decorated with figures to protect their contents.

Compare this traditional Fang mask and Picasso's *Bust of a Man,* painted in 1907.

CONNECT TO THE ISSUES
COLONIALISM
D How might Mobutu's arts program have been a reaction against colonialism?

D. Answer The Congolese had been under foreign control for so long, he may have felt the need to help the people assert their national identity.

Improving Education

In recovering from the effects of colonialism, Central African countries are placing their hopes on education. Improved education should produce more skilled workers and citizens who are better able to participate in democratic governments.

Instruct: Objective 3

The Influence of Central African Art

- What theme dominated Central African art for most of the 20th century? *(attitudes toward colonialism)*
- How has Central African art changed since independence? *(Younger artists who did not experience colonialism are now exploring the issues of political instability, urban life, social justice, and crime.)*
- How did Picasso spread the influence of Central African art? *(He used African themes after he saw Fang sculpture.)*

Interpreting Art

Features to compare include: shape of the head; hairstyle; eyes; eyebrows; lips; nose; textures; colors; overall expression.

Instruct: Objective 4 appears on p. 452

ACTIVITY OPTION **INTERNET ACTIVITY**

CREATING ILLUSTRATED REPORTS ON ART

Objective To identify African artists and themes in art

Class Time 50 minutes

Task Prepare illustrated reports about African art or artists

Directions Direct students to the Web site for *World Geography* at **hmhsocialstudies.com** to research African art and artists. Tell students to focus on the political, social, and economic issues expressed in current African art. Have them write brief reports, accompanied by illustrations.

BLOCK SCHEDULING

OPTIONAL ACTIVITY If Internet access is limited or unavailable, have students use the library to find art books or magazine articles on African art or African artists.

Connect TO THE Issues

Health Care: Ebola Virus

Ebola spreads easily in health-care settings where precautions, such as the wearing of masks and gloves, are not used. Many African hospitals are underequipped, so they have difficulty containing Ebola outbreaks. Ask how local governments can help prevent the spread of Ebola. *(equip health-care facilities better; improve sanitation)*

Instruct: Objective 

Improving Education

- What problems does Central Africa have in education? *(few teachers and secondary schools, high dropout rate)*
- How do language barriers hinder education? *(Schools often teach in a language not used at home.)*

Assess & Reteach

GeoFocus Have students complete their notes on Central Africa for their cluster diagrams.

 **Formal Assessment**
- Section Quiz, p. 292

Reteaching Activity

Have the class review the section by identifying major events in Central African history, current problems, and cultural expressions of independence. Write the answers on the chalkboard.

 **In-Depth Resources: Unit 6**
- Reteaching Activity, p. 23

 **Outline Maps with Activities**
- Central Africa: Physical and Political, pp. 61–62

Connect TO THE Issues

HEALTH CARE

Ebola Virus

The Ebola virus, named after the Ebola River, first emerged in 1976 in the northern Democratic Republic of the Congo.

People affected by the virus develop fever, severe headaches, and loss of appetite. Blood clots form on internal organs, such as the liver and brain. This causes uncontrolled bleeding from parts of the body, such as the eyes or ears. Death usually occurs within 2 to 21 days, and no known cure exists.

One outbreak occurred in October 2000 in Uganda. Those cases appeared in a refugee camp. Unsanitary conditions are one cause of disease associated with the Ebola virus.

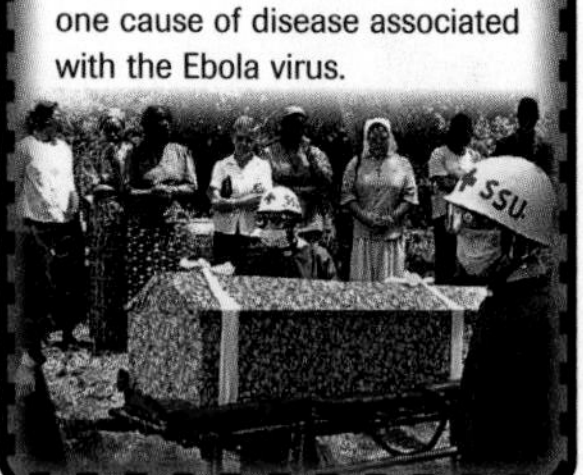

EDUCATION FACES BARRIERS Adequate schooling for many of Africa's young people is in short supply. In 2001, experts estimated that less than half of sub-Saharan Africa's 16- to 20-year-olds attended school. Education problems in Central Africa include a shortage of trained teachers, a high dropout rate, and a shortage of secondary schools.

Central Africa's more than 700 languages also pose barriers. The language used in school is often different from the one used at home. For example, in Gabon—a former colony of France—French is the only language of instruction, though most people speak one of the Bantu languages outside the classroom.

BACKGROUND People from other countries make up the entire staff at the one technical school and the three secondary schools in São Tomé and Princípe.

LEARNING IN CENTRAL AFRICA Students' education varies in Central Africa. In Cameroon, most children leave school at around the age of 12. In the Central African Republic, children between the ages of 6 and 14 are required to go to school.

Many Central African countries are improving their educational systems, however. In 1991, Cameroon created two new universities. In addition, Libreville University in Gabon, founded in the 1970s, now has more than 4,000 students.

The Republic of the Congo offers vocational, agricultural, and teacher training courses. In addition, many countries are starting programs to educate young people about health care issues such as the spread of disease. Those countries hope that better education will slow the spread of AIDS, the Ebola virus, cholera, and other diseases.

You will read in Section 5 about how ancient trade networks and gold formed the economic foundation of Southern Africa.

SECTION 4 Assessment

1 Places & Terms

Identify these terms and explain their importance in the region's history or culture.
- Bantu migrations
- King Leopold II
- Mobutu Sese Seko
- Fang sculpture

2 Taking Notes

MOVEMENT Review the notes you took for this section.

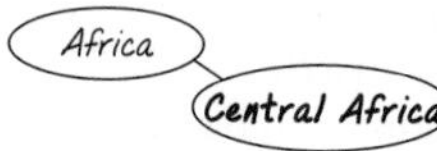

- How did the Bantu migrations affect Africa's population?
- Who were the first Europeans to establish the African slave trade?

3 Main Ideas

a. How did colonialism in Central Africa begin?

b. What are the subjects of the works of today's artists in Central Africa?

c. What problems does education face in Central Africa?

4 Geographic Thinking

Seeing Patterns How did colonialism affect most African countries? **Think about:**
- their natural resources
- 20th century conflicts

See Skillbuilder Handbook, page R8.

EXPLORING LOCAL GEOGRAPHY Review the information about the Central African infrastructure on page 450. Create a **sketch map** showing all the major roads, highways, and railroads in your own neighborhood.

SECTION 4 ASSESSMENT ANSWERS

1. Places & Terms

Bantu migrations, p. 448
King Leopold II, p. 449
Mobutu Sese Seko, p. 450
Fang sculpture, p. 451

2. Taking Notes
- The Bantu migrations resulted in many Africans speaking one of the Bantu languages.
- The Portuguese began the slave trade.

3. Main Ideas

a. Europeans first established coastal trading stations, then moved into Central Africa to exploit its natural resources.

b. Today's artists are focusing on issues of political instability, urban life, social justice, and crime.

c. It suffers from a shortage of trained teachers, a high dropout rate, and a shortage of secondary schools.

4. Geographic Thinking

Colonial powers disrupted long-standing systems of government and pitted groups of Africans against each other. This led to abusive governments after the countries gained independence.

GeoActivity

 **Integrated Assessment**
- Rubric for a sketch map, 2.1

Southern Africa

Main Ideas

- Great Zimbabwe and the Mutapa Empire thrived on the gold trade.
- The wealth of Southern Africa is tied to the land, and conflicts over land and resources often result.

Places & Terms

Great Zimbabwe
Mutapa Empire
apartheid
Nelson Mandela

CONNECT TO THE ISSUES
HEALTH CARE AIDS threatens Southern Africa's youth and could significantly reduce the region's population.

A HUMAN PERSPECTIVE In April 2000 in Zimbabwe, armed men attacked the farmhouse of a white farmer whose family has lived in Zimbabwe for generations. A political crisis that goes back to Britain's colonial rule caught white farmers in a violent crossfire. British colonial rule ended in 1980, but more than 4,000 white farmers in Zimbabwe still own one-third of the best land in a country of about 10 million blacks. The British and the white farmers have made attempts to equalize land ownership, but Zimbabwe's leaders have not taken advantage of these opportunities. Instead, they have targeted individual white farmers who own that land. This conflict illustrates a critical issue in all of Southern Africa—that blacks far outnumber whites but still own little of the land.

Gold Trade Builds Empires

Southern Africa includes Angola, Botswana, Comoros, Lesotho, Madagascar, Malawi, Mauritius, Mozambique, Namibia, South Africa, Swaziland, Zambia, and Zimbabwe. The history of Southern Africa involves a blending of colonialism with African cultures and the development of gold-trading empires.

GOLD TRADE SPAWNS GREAT ZIMBABWE The majority of the people in Southern Africa are Bantu-speaking peoples, including the Shona people. Around 1000, the Shona established a city called **Great Zimbabwe** in what is now the country of Zimbabwe.

From the 1200s to the 1400s, Great Zimbabwe became the capital of a thriving gold-trading area. But for unknown reasons, around 1450 the Shona abandoned Great Zimbabwe. One theory is that cattle grazing had exhausted the nearby grasslands, and overfarming had ruined the soil.

MUTAPA EMPIRE According to local legend, a man named Mutota left Great Zimbabwe around 1440 and settled in a fertile valley to the north. He founded a new state to replace Great Zimbabwe. By the time Mutota died, the **Mutapa Empire** extended throughout all of present-day Zimbabwe except the eastern part.

PLACE Pictured below are the walls of Great Zimbabwe. **What do the materials used to build the walls reveal about the local physical geography?**

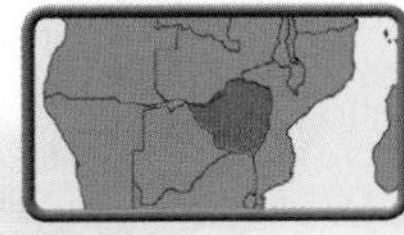

SECTION 5 OBJECTIVES

1. Identify events and issues in Southern African history.
2. Examine Southern African economic development.
3. Describe Southern African celebrations and daily life.

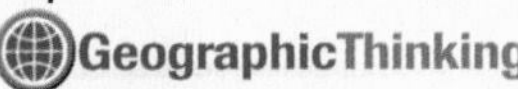

SKILLBUILDER: Interpreting Maps, p. 454

GeographicThinking

Seeing Patterns, pp. 454, 457
Making Comparisons, p. 455
Identifying and Solving Problems, p. 457

Focus & Motivate

Ask students what news stories they have seen recently about Southern Africa. *(Answers may include stories on land policy in Zimbabwe or AIDS.)*

Instruct: Objective 

Gold Trade Builds Empires

- What economic activity caused Southern Africa to thrive centuries ago? *(gold trade)*
- How did the British gain control in South Africa? *(They fought and defeated the Zulu and the Dutch farmers, or Boers.)*
- Why did foreign nations object to South Africa's policy of apartheid? *(It harshly discriminated by segregating blacks and depriving them of land.)*

 **In-Depth Resources: Unit 6**
- Guided Reading, p. 17

CAPTION ANSWER There was a large supply of stones in the area.

SECTION 5 PROGRAM RESOURCES

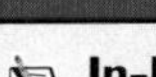 **In-Depth Resources: Unit 6**
- Guided Reading, p. 17
- Building Vocabulary, p. 19
- Reteaching Activity, p. 24

Guided Reading Workbook
- Section 5

 **Access for Students Acquiring English/ESL**
- Guided Reading, p. 103

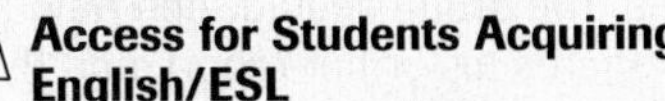

 **Outline Maps with Activities**
- Southern Africa, pp. 63–64

 **Formal Assessment**
- Section Quiz, p. 293

 **Integrated Assessment**
- Rubric for a map, 2.1

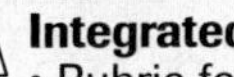

INTEGRATED TECHNOLOGY

 **Power Presentations**

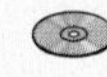 **Test Generator**
- Section Quiz

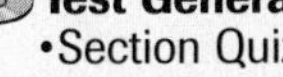

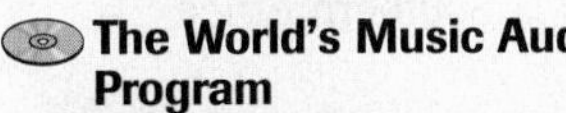 **The World's Music Audio Program**

hmhsocialstudies.com

TEST-TAKING RESOURCES

 **Strategies for Test Preparation**

 **Test Practice Transparencies TT64**

 **Online Test Practice**

The Mutapa Empire thrived on the gold trade. In the 1500s, however, the Portuguese arrived and began interfering with the politics there. Soon, the Mutapa Empire began to decline. This event showed the increasing role Europeans would play in Southern Africa.

ETHNIC CLASH FOR SOUTHERN AFRICA As Europeans migrated to Southern Africa in the 1700s and 1800s, their presence led to conflicts with Africans. As the map below shows, many different ethnic groups were already living in Southern Africa. They competed with each other and with the Europeans for control of the land. In the early 19th century, the Zulu controlled a large area in Southern Africa. However, the British defeated the Zulu and by the late 19th century had taken over their land. A

In the 1890s, the British battled the Dutch farmers, or Boers, in the Boer War for control of the region. The Boers had arrived in Southern Africa in the mid-1600s. The British won the war and formed the Union of South Africa in 1902. South Africa is currently a country in the region of Southern Africa.

A. Answer Africans and Europeans competed for control of the land.

Geographic Thinking

Seeing Patterns
A What led to the conflicts between Europeans and groups of people already living in Southern Africa?

THE POLICY OF APARTHEID IN SOUTH AFRICA In 1948, the white minority government of South Africa instituted a policy of **apartheid,** or complete separation of the races. It banned social contact between blacks and whites and established segregated schools, hospitals, and neighborhoods. Although blacks made up 75 percent of the population, they received only a small percentage of the land. The government kept the best land for whites.

In 1912, blacks had founded the African National Congress (ANC) to fight for their rights. In 1949, **Nelson Mandela** emerged as one of the

BACKGROUND
Segregation is the separation of people on the basis of race or ethnicity.

Ethnic Groups of Southern Africa

SKILLBUILDER: Interpreting Maps

1. **REGION** Which country in Southern Africa contains the most ethnic groups?
2. **PLACE** What might the concentration of ethnic groups in the eastern portion of the map indicate about the number of conflicts in that area?

More About

The Boers

Having first settled near the Cape of Good Hope in the mid-17th century, the Boers were primarily Dutch or Huguenot (French Protestant). Their descendents, called Afrikaaners, strongly supported the policy of apartheid.

More About

The Policy of Apartheid

White supremacy and racial segregation existed in South Africa before 1948. Official policy implemented after that time not only separated whites from nonwhites but nonwhites from each other. Nonwhites included Asians (mostly Indians) and people known in South Africa as Coloured (mixed black, white, and Malayan). African groups, including the Zulu, the Xhosa, and the Ndebele, were also separated from each other.

Interpreting Maps

Ethnic Groups of Southern Africa

Have students locate the Swazi, Zulu, and Xhosa groups on the map. These three ethnic groups speak languages that are part of the Nguni branch of Bantu languages, the only Bantu languages that have a clicking sound as part of their phonetic system.

SKILLBUILDER ANSWERS
1. Mozambique **2.** More ethnic groups usually lead to more conflict.

DIFFERENTIATING INSTRUCTION GIFTED AND TALENTED STUDENTS

HOLDING A PANEL DISCUSSION

Objective To develop research skills and gain greater understanding of current events in Southern Africa

Class Time One class period

Task Hold a panel discussion on current issues in Southern Africa

Directions Working in small groups, each student should select a different nation in Southern Africa and prepare a report on current events there. They should focus on issues such as politics, health care, education, or economic development. They may use the Internet or print sources such as newspapers and news magazines. The group should then hold a panel discussion in which each member shares his or her report, and the group as a whole reaches conclusions about trends in the region.

leaders of the ANC, and he led a long struggle to end apartheid that resulted in his being imprisoned. By the 1980s, nations around the world—including the United States—pressured South Africa to end apartheid. In 1989, F. W. de Klerk became the president, and he wanted to change South Africa.

As a result, South Africa experienced a peaceful revolution, and the government ended its apartheid laws. An election that involved members of all races in South Africa took place in 1994. Mandela, having been released from prison, won the election and became president. In 1996, the government passed a new, democratic constitution that guarantees the rights of all citizens.

Southern Africa Grows Economically

The economies of Southern African countries are some of the most advanced in Africa. However, many countries are struggling to raise the standard of living for blacks, who get the worst jobs, own the least productive land, and attend the worst schools.

SOUTH AFRICA The policy of apartheid has hurt the economy of South Africa. Because of apartheid, foreign nations imposed economic sanctions that prevented their countries from conducting business with or investing in South Africa. In addition, the policy led to poor education of blacks, creating an uneducated mass of young people. As a result, two economies exist in South Africa.

One segment of South Africa has an upper-middle-income economy like that of the United States. South Africa possesses great cities with huge industrial complexes, such as Johannesburg and Cape Town. It also has modern, mechanized farms and large ranches. In contrast, though, South Africa also has poverty-stricken rural areas. Black townships and shantytowns also fill portions of the cities. Furthermore, the government currently faces problems arising from unequal land distribution and a severe housing shortage. B

B. Answer South Africa possesses great cities with industrial complexes and modern farms and ranches. There are also shantytowns, poverty-stricken areas, and a severe housing shortage.

Geographic Thinking
Making Comparisons
B What are the two segments of South Africa's economy?

SUCCESS AT A COST Botswana illustrates a problem that exists in many African countries today. It made a great deal of money from valuable resources but has serious agricultural problems and an unequal distribution of wealth. Botswana gained its independence from Britain in 1966 and subsequently experienced long-term economic growth. In 1966, its per capita income stood at $69. In 1997, that figure had risen to $3,900 per capita.

Southern Africa, 1800–2000

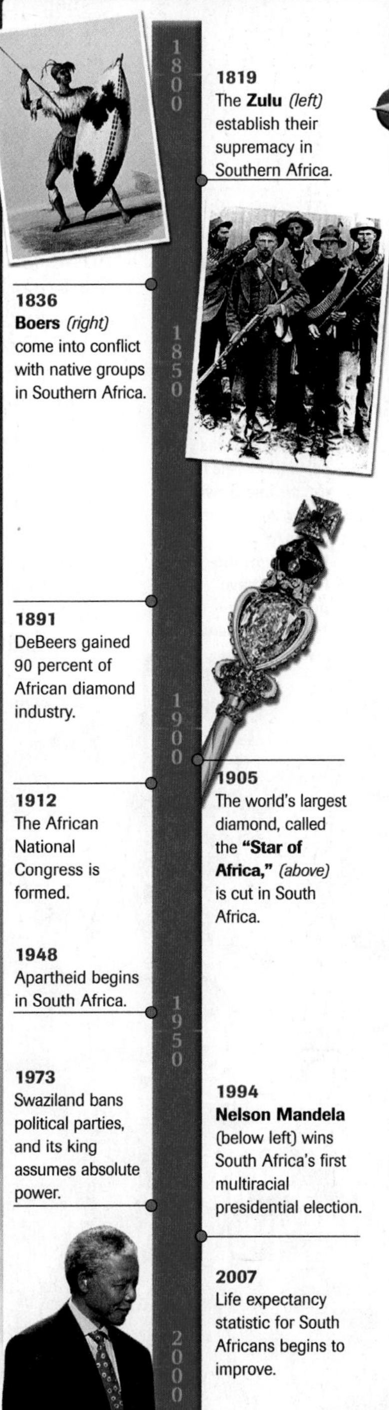

1800
1819
The **Zulu** *(left)* establish their supremacy in Southern Africa.
1836
Boers *(right)* come into conflict with native groups in Southern Africa.
1850
1891
DeBeers gained 90 percent of African diamond industry.
1900
1905
The world's largest diamond, called the **"Star of Africa,"** *(above)* is cut in South Africa.
1912
The African National Congress is formed.
1948
Apartheid begins in South Africa.
1950
1973
Swaziland bans political parties, and its king assumes absolute power.
1994
Nelson Mandela (below left) wins South Africa's first multiracial presidential election.
2007
Life expectancy statistic for South Africans begins to improve.
2000

Interpreting Time Lines

Southern Africa, 1800-Present

Have students examine the time line and photographs. Ask them to identify 20th-century milestones for Southern Africa's blacks *(1912, formation of ANC; 1994, South Africa's first multi-racial election)* Ask them to explain the significance of the 1994 election. *(It was the first multiracial election in South Africa, and it paved the way for a new democracy and the creation of a new constitution guaranteeing equal rights.)*

Instruct: Objective 2

Southern Africa Grows Economically

- How did apartheid hurt South Africa's economy? *(Foreign nations imposed economic sanctions; blacks remained largely uneducated.)*
- What "two economies" exist in South Africa today? *(one upper-middle-income and modern; one poverty-stricken rural or urban shantytown)*
- How has Botswana's diamond wealth created agricultural problems? *(It created an income gap, which allows rich people to buy productive land from poor farmers, who then must move to less productive land.)*

ACTIVITY OPTION **INTERNET ACTIVITY**

BLOCK SCHEDULING

REPORTING THE NEWS

Objective To develop Internet research skills

Class Time 40 minutes

Task Write a news story about post-apartheid conditions in South Africa

Directions Direct students to the Web site for *World Geography* at **hmhsocialstudies.com.** Click on the Current Events button and follow the links to sources of information on the issues. Remind students that a good news story should answer the questions *who, what, where, when, why,* and *how.*

OPTIONAL ACTIVITY If Internet access is limited or unavailable, direct students to library resources, particularly newspapers and periodicals, for this activity.

Instruct: Objective 3

Celebrations of Southern Africa/ Living in Southern Africa

- How does modern Johannesburg reflect the problems created by apartheid? *(It is divided into spacious suburbs of mostly whites and poor townships inhabited by blacks)*
- What jobs do most blacks perform in Southern Africa? *(mainly menial and unskilled jobs, or traditional jobs such as farming)*

More About

Combating AIDS in Botswana

At Debswana, the largest diamond-mining company in Botswana, close to one-third of all workers are infected with HIV. Debswana announced in 2001 that it would pay up to 90 percent of the costs of HIV medication for employees and their spouses. Since 2004, Debswana requires all its contractors to have an AIDS prevention program.

Interpreting Photographs

Ndebele Houses

Tell students that, in addition to painting their homes in this distinctive manner, Ndebele women also create elaborate beadwork. There are many groups of Ndebele, however, and only the Ndzundza (about 20,000 people) still practice these traditional arts. Ask students what words or phrases they might use to describe the painted houses. *(colorful, geometric designs)*

CAPTION ANSWER for decoration or as a symbol of cultural pride

Botswana's wealth is based on minerals. People discovered diamonds there shortly after the country's independence from Britain. By 1995, Botswana had become a major diamond producer. It is now the world's leader in diamond production. Diamonds account for about half of government revenue. A problem, however, is the uneven distribution of the profits—an issue in many African countries. C

CONNECT TO THE ISSUES
ECONOMIC DEVELOPMENT
C How has Botswana increased its wealth?
C. Answer exporting diamonds

The vast majority of the people work as farmers and never benefit from the diamond revenue. A minority of the population grows wealthy from diamond money. One problem developing from this unequal distribution is that wealthy people are purchasing large tracts of land for cattle ranching from poor farm owners. As a result, poor farmers often move to less productive land. Meat production then increases, but overall food production actually decreases. The country winds up producing only 50 percent of the food needed to feed its population. The rest must be imported or come from international aid.

AIDS AFFECTS SOUTHERN AFRICA By 2006, the most severe AIDS-affected countries were in Southern Africa. In Zimbabwe and Botswana, for example, about 25 percent of all adults were infected with HIV, the virus that causes AIDS. In Botswana, the life expectancy was 60 years old in 1994; it had declined to 39 years of age in 1999, but has risen to above 61 again since then. The disease also has far-ranging implications for any country's economic well-being. In Botswana, many highly trained diamond sorters have died from the disease.

REGION Colorfully painted Ndebele houses, like the one shown below, are common in South Africa.
Why might the Ndebele have painted their houses in this way?

Celebrations of Southern Africa

Southern Africa is a rich mosaic of cultures and traditions. More than any other region, it is a mix of African and European cultures.

A VARIETY OF DANCES Celebrations and festivals are a large part of life in Southern Africa. The Chewa people perform a dance called the *gule wa mkulu,* which reflects their traditional religious beliefs. Dancers dress in ragged costumes of cloth and animal skins. They wear masks and sometimes walk on stilts.

The Tumbuka people in northern Malawi perform the *vimbuza,* a dance performed by healers who wish to cure people of sickness. Other dances include the *benji* dance of the Yao people in southern Malawi. This dance, performed by Yao warriors, pokes fun at what these warriors saw as the desire of the European militaries to march and have parades.

ACTIVITY OPTION **CRITICAL THINKING**

MAKING COMPARISONS

Explaining the Skill Tell students that comparisons between countries can help them gain a better perspective on the issues. Refer students to pages 455 and 456, which contain information about the societies and economies of South Africa and Botswana.

Applying the Skill After students have had the opportunity to review the text, ask the following questions:

- What resources provided an economic basis for South Africa and Botswana? *(mineral resources of diamonds and gold)*
- How do the two countries compare today in terms of social divisions and distribution of wealth? *(both have a wealthy minority and large populations of poor workers)*
- What might help both countries achieve greater economic growth? *(social equality with more even distribution of wealth)*

In Madagascar, during the *hira gasy* festival, costumed groups of 25 or more people play music, perform dances, and act out stories. The themes are upbeat and praise the virtues of honesty and respect for elders.

Living in Southern Africa

Johannesburg, South Africa, is one of Southern Africa's largest cities and offers its residents a variety of opportunities and experiences.

JOHANNESBURG About 100 years ago, Johannesburg began as a small mining town and grew because of nearby gold reserves. Today, greater Johannesburg is a city of more than six million people with many different ethnicities and lifestyles. The center of Johannesburg looks like most modern big cities, with a cluster of skyscrapers dotting the skyline. However, as a result of apartheid, greater Johannesburg developed into two different cities. To the north lie the spacious suburbs that were once exclusively white. To the south are poor black townships. D

Geographic Thinking
Seeing Patterns
D What resource fueled the growth of both Johannesburg and Great Zimbabwe?
D. Answer
Both cities were founded and grew because of the mining of nearby gold deposits.

MODERN AND TRADITIONAL LIFESTYLES Some Southern Africans live a modern lifestyle as doctors, lawyers, and businesspeople. These people live in tree-lined suburbs that look no different from those found in the United States. Many blacks, on the other hand, because of apartheid's legacy, still work in menial and unskilled jobs. They still live in the former black-only homelands and shantytowns.

Some ethnic groups of Southern Africa follow more traditional patterns as farmers, traders, or herders. For example, the Zulu either work in menial jobs, such as mining, or cling to their traditional roles as farmers and metalworkers. The Zulu have a long tradition of making hoes, spears, axes, and other tools and weapons.

In the next chapter you will read more about major issues facing Africa today, including economic development, health care, and the effects of colonialism.

Section 5 Assessment

1 Places & Terms

Identify these terms and explain their importance in the region's history or culture.

- Great Zimbabwe
- Mutapa Empire
- apartheid
- Nelson Mandela

2 Taking Notes

PLACE Review the notes you took for this section.

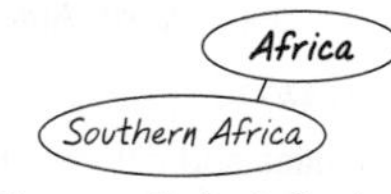

- What was the basis for the growth of Great Zimbabwe?
- How would you describe the occupations of the people who live in Southern Africa?

3 Main Ideas

a. Who ended the system of apartheid in South Africa?

b. How has AIDS affected Botswana's economy?

c. What are some of the major traditional cultural activities in Southern Africa?

4 Geographic Thinking

Identifying and Solving Problems How did apartheid affect the economy of South Africa? **Think about:**

- how blacks were treated
- international economic sanctions

MAKING COMPARISONS Review the information about Botswana's economy on pages 455–456. Using the Internet or encyclopedias, find out where the major natural resources are located in each country of the region. Then create a **resources map** of Southern Africa.

More About

The Zulu in Modern Times

The Zulu are the largest black ethnic group of South Africa. In 1975, the Zulu chief Mangosuthu Gatsha Buthelezi founded the Inkatha Freedom Party, with the goal of fighting apartheid. Inkatha advocated more evolutionary change than did the African National Congress (ANC). In the late 1980s and the 1990s, Inkatha was the ANC's main rival for black political allegiance, but it never expanded much beyond its Zulu base.

Assess & Reteach

GeoFocus Have students complete their notes on Southern Africa for their cluster diagrams.

Formal Assessment
- Section Quiz, p. 293

Reteaching Activity
Have students write a paragraph summarizing the content of the section.

In-Depth Resources: Unit 6
- Reteaching Activity, p. 24

Outline Maps with Activities
- Southern Africa, pp. 63–64

AFRICA

SECTION 5 ASSESSMENT ANSWERS

1. Places & Terms
Great Zimbabwe, p. 453
Mutapa Empire, p. 453
apartheid, p. 454
Nelson Mandela, p. 454

2. Taking Notes
- The Shona people established Great Zimbabwe because it was situated on the trade routes of a gold-trading area.
- Some people are doctors, lawyers, and businesspeople, but others perform menial and unskilled jobs. Still others are traditional farmers, herders, traders, miners, and metalworkers.

3. Main Ideas
a. Nelson Mandela and F.W. de Klerk
b. Botswana is losing many highly trained diamond sorters to AIDS.
c. Some include *gule wa mkulu*, which reflects traditional religious beliefs; *vimbuza*, a healing dance; and *Hira Gasy*, a major costumed festival.

4. Geographic Thinking
Apartheid hurt the economy because of international economic sanctions, which forbid other countries from conducting business in South Africa. Apartheid also led to poor education of blacks, which left a large underclass of unskilled workers.

GeoActivity

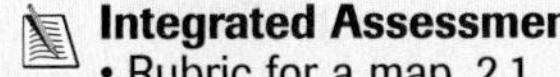
Integrated Assessment
- Rubric for a map, 2.1

Reviewing Places & Terms

A. **1.** Berlin Conference, p. 432
2. pandemic, p. 435
3. Islam, p. 439
4. stateless society, p. 443
5. Ashanti, p. 444
6. Bantu migrations, p. 448
7. Fang sculpture, p. 451
8. Great Zimbabwe, p. 453
9. apartheid, p. 454
10. Nelson Mandela, p. 454

B. Possible Responses

11. The policy of apartheid was used to separate the races.
12. Picasso was influenced by Fang sculpture.
13. The Berlin Conference divided African lands among European powers.
14. Carved wooden stools serve as thrones to the Ashanti kings.
15. A stateless society relies on lineage and family relationships to govern.
16. Nelson Mandela was leader of the ANC and, eventually, president of South Africa.
17. Islam has the largest cultural and religious influence in North Africa.
18. Great Zimbabwe thrived on gold trade.
19. A pandemic describes a widespread disease.
20. Bantu migrations helped to bring this sense of unity of language.

Chapter 19 Assessment

VISUAL SUMMARY
HUMAN GEOGRAPHY OF AFRICA

Subregions of Africa

East Africa
- East Africa's location on the Red Sea and Indian Ocean has made it a major trading center throughout history.
- AIDS has become a major health problem in East Africa.

North Africa
- The Nile River supported the growth of ancient Egypt.
- Islam is the major cultural and religious influence in North Africa.

West Africa
- Gold and salt provided the basis for three great empires in West Africa.
- Many of West Africa's economies rely too much on exporting raw materials.

Central Africa
- The Bantu migrations helped to populate the African continent.
- Colonialism caused long-term damage to the economies and cultures of African nations.

Southern Africa
- Gold provided the basis for great empires in Southern Africa.
- Apartheid hurt the economy of South Africa because of international economic sanctions and inadequate education of blacks.

Reviewing Places & Terms

A. Briefly explain the importance of each of the following.

1. Berlin Conference
2. pandemic
3. Islam
4. stateless society
5. Ashanti
6. Bantu migrations
7. Fang sculpture
8. Great Zimbabwe
9. apartheid
10. Nelson Mandela

B. Answer the questions about vocabulary in complete sentences.

11. Which term is used to describe the policy used to separate blacks and whites in South Africa?
12. What type of art influenced some of Pablo Picasso's work?
13. What meeting by European nations set the rules and conditions for the takeover of Africa?
14. Which African people place a high value on wooden stools?
15. What is the system called that uses family lineages to govern people?
16. Who led the ANC in the second half of the 20th century and helped to end apartheid in South Africa?
17. What is the largest cultural and religious influence in North Africa?
18. Which empire thrived on the gold trade in Southern Africa?
19. What term describes a disease outbreak affecting a large population in a wide geographic area?
20. What movement of people helped to bring a sense of unity of language to much of Africa?

Main Ideas

East Africa (pp. 431–437)

1. How did East Africa's location help it to become a major international trading center?
2. What impact did the Berlin Conference have on Africa?

North Africa (pp. 438–441)

3. How did Islam become the biggest influence in North Africa?
4. How have women's roles in North Africa changed over the years?

West Africa (pp. 442–447)

5. What are the similarities and differences among the three West African kingdoms of Ghana, Mali, and Songhai?
6. What are some of the problems faced by West African economies?

Central Africa (pp. 448–452)

7. Why were the Bantu migrations important in African history?
8. What are some of the problems facing education in Central Africa?

Southern Africa (pp. 453–457)

9. How have natural resources affected the economy of Southern Africa?
10. How was apartheid brought to an end?

Main Ideas

1. Its location on the Red Sea and the Indian Ocean gave it easy access to trade routes to Asia.
2. It legitimized the European takeover of Africa.
3. The Muslims invaded North Africa and established their influence by A.D. 750.
4. They have gotten more professional and career opportunities outside the home and have made social progress.
5. All three thrived on the gold-and-salt trade, but Songhai was larger than either Mali or Ghana.
6. They have poor transportation infrastructure, rely too much on exporting raw materials, and experience political instability.
7. They helped to unify Africa; many people in Africa speak a Bantu language.
8. a shortage of teachers, a high dropout rate, and few secondary schools.
9. Diamonds, platinum, and other resources have helped enrich many countries in Southern Africa.
10. Nelson Mandela and F.W. de Klerk cooperated to end the policy.

Critical Thinking

1. Using Your Notes

Use your completed chart to answer these questions.

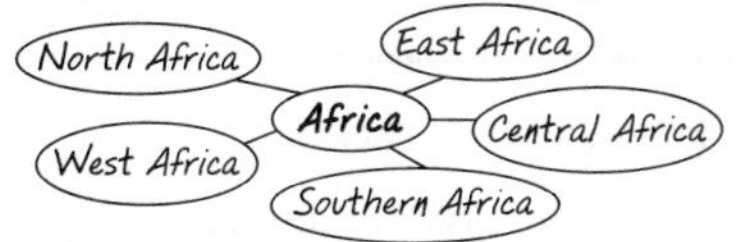

a. How were the precolonial kingdoms of West Africa similar to or different from the precolonial kingdoms of Southern Africa?

b. How did colonialism change Africa and its people?

2. Geographic Themes

a. MOVEMENT How did the movement of Islam from Southwest Asia to North Africa affect the African continent?

b. HUMAN-ENVIRONMENT INTERACTION What role did natural resources play in the colonization of Africa?

3. Identifying Themes

How did natural resources affect the formation of ancient African kingdoms and empires? Which of the five themes apply to this situation?

4. Making Comparisons

How did stateless societies in Africa differ from centralized governments?

5. Determining Cause and Effect

What prompted the Berlin Conference, and what effects did it have on Africa's culture and economy?

For Additional Test Practice

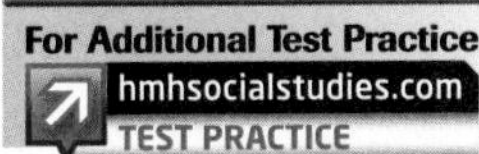

Geographic Skills: Interpreting Graphs

Languages of Nigeria

Use the graph below to answer the following questions.

1. ANALYZING DATA What percentage of Nigerians speak English?
2. MAKING GENERALIZATIONS Which language group is the most commonly spoken?
3. MAKING INFERENCES How might the number of languages in Nigeria affect a newly formed democratic government?

GeoActivity

Choose another country in Africa. Then using the library, encyclopedias, or other reference books, create your own language pie chart.

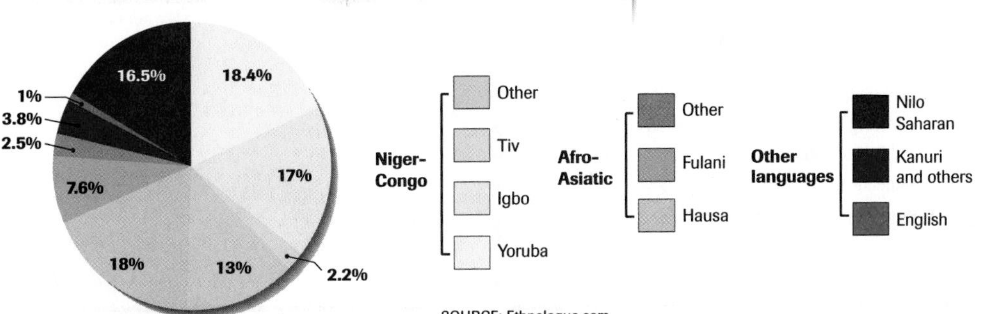

SOURCE: Ethnologue.com

hmhsocialstudies.com

MULTIMEDIA ACTIVITY

Use the links at **hmhsocialstudies.com** to do research on the people of one African country. Look for such information as age range, religions, ethnic groups, literacy rates, and per capita income.

Constructing a Population Pyramid Using the information you have gathered, construct a population pyramid describing the population characteristics of the society you have chosen.

AFRICA

Critical Thinking

1. a. In both regions, empires benefited from the gold trade and a location on trade routes. Only the West African empires traded for salt.
b. It disrupted cultural and political boundaries and is blamed for causing much of the 20th-century violence. Also, African economies were geared to supplying—not processing—raw materials.

2. a. Islam and Arabic spread from North Africa to other regions.
b. They motivated Europeans to colonize Africa.

3. Trade in gold aided the growth of ancient African empires located on trade routes. location, movement, and human-environment interaction

4. In a stateless society, people knew or were related to their leaders, and felt that their interests were being taken into account. In a centralized government, leaders make decisions for society, often without considering everyone's viewpoint.

5. European powers convened the Berlin Conference to divide Africa in order to exploit the continent economically.

GeoActivity

Integrated Assessment
- Rubric for pie chart, 2.3

Formal Assessment
- Chapter Test, Forms A, B, and C, pp. 294–305

Geographic Skills

1. one percent
2. Niger-Congo
3. It might be hard to communicate with such a diverse population.

MULTIMEDIA ACTIVITY

For the report on an African society, students should:

- Describe several aspects of the country's human geography.
- Include references to Web sites used as sources.
- Produce a clear population pyramid.

Grading Rubric Evaluate student performance as Exceptional, Acceptable, or Poor in each of the following categories.

	Exceptional	*Acceptable*	*Poor*
Graphic is clear and accurate			
Titles and headings clearly state the topic and categories			
Clearly lists sources			

Today's Issues: Africa

OVERVIEW	INSTRUCTIONAL RESOURCES	
ESSENTIAL QUESTION How are Africans trying to solve the challenges that their countries face? **Focus on the Essential Question Podcast**	**In-Depth Resources: Unit 6** • Building Vocabulary, p. 31 **Block Schedule Strategies** **Chapter Summaries** (English/Spanish)	**Interactive Online Edition** TOS **ExamView® Assessment Suite** (English/Spanish) TOS **CalendarPlanner** **Power Presentations with Media Gallery** **Critical Thinking Transparencies** • CT20 hmhsocialstudies.com INTERACTIVE
SECTION 1 **ECONOMIC DEVELOPMENT** **MAIN IDEAS** • Most African economies are in decline. • African nations struggle to eliminate debt and build cooperation. • Economic diversification and education are keys to progress.	**In-Depth Resources: Unit 6** • Guided Reading, p. 25 • Exploring Today's Issues, pp. 32–33 • Building Vocabulary, p. 31 • Reteaching Activities, p. 36 • Map and Graph Skills, pp. 28–29 **Guided Reading Workbook,** Section 1	**Critical Thinking Transparencies** • CT52 Estimated Illiteracy Rates in Selected African Countries, 2001
SECTION 2 **HEALTH CARE** **MAIN IDEAS** • Serious diseases threaten Africa. • The AIDS epidemic harms Africa's economies. • African countries pursue strategies to combat AIDS.	**In-Depth Resources: Unit 6** • Guided Reading, p. 26 • Skillbuilder Practice, p. 30 • Exploring Today's Issues, pp. 34–35 • Building Vocabulary, p. 31 • Reteaching Activities, p. 37 **Guided Reading Workbook,** Section 2	
CASE STUDY **EFFECTS OF COLONIALISM** **MAIN IDEAS** • European colonialism damaged Africa. • Post-colonial Africa struggles for political stability. • The case study project focuses on Africa's current status.	**In-Depth Resources: Unit 6** • Guided Reading, p. 27 • Building Vocabulary, p. 31 • Reteaching Activities, p. 38 **Guided Reading Workbook,** Case Study	**Map Transparencies MT35** • Challenges of Postcolonial Africa

ASSESSMENT

SE **Chapter Assessment,** pp. 472-473

Formal Assessment
- Chapter Tests, Forms A, B, and C, pp. 309-323

TOS **ExamView® Assessment Suite**

Strategies for Test Preparation

hmhsocialstudies.com TEST PRACTICE

SE **Section Assessment,** p. 463

Formal Assessment
- Section Quiz, p. 306

 **Integrated Assessment**
- Rubric for a news article, 4.5

 **Test Practice Transparencies** TT65

SE **Section Assessment,** p. 467

 **Formal Assessment**
- Section Quiz, p. 307

 **Integrated Assessment**
- Rubric for a chart, 2.2

 **Test Practice Transparencies** TT66

SE **Case Study Project,** p. 470-471

 **Formal Assessment**
- Section Quiz, p. 308

 **Test Practice Transparencies** TT67

CHART KEY:

SE Student Edition	 Block Scheduling	 DVD/CD-ROM
TE Teacher's Edition	TOS Teacher One Stop	 MP3 Audio
Printable Resource	 Presentation Resource	HISTORY™

Program Resources available on TOS and @  hmhsocialstudies.com

SUPPORTING RESOURCES

- **Multimedia Classroom Global History Series**
- **Global History Teacher's Guide**

Social Studies Trade Library Collection
- Modern World History Trade Collection

For more information or to purchase these resources, go to 

DIFFERENTIATED INSTRUCTION

English Learners	Struggling Readers	Gifted and Talented Students
 **Spanish/English Guided Reading Workbook**  **Access for Students Acquiring English/ESL** Spanish Translations, pp. 105–110  **Chapter Summaries** (English/Spanish) TE **TE Activity** Analyzing Primary Sources, p. 470	TE **TE Activity** Connecting Problems and Solutions, p. 462	TE **TE Activity** Making Comparisons, p. 469

ENRICHMENT ACTIVITIES

The following activities are especially suitable for classes following block schedules.

SE **Student Edition,** pp. 460–473 • Reading a City Map, p. 464	hmhsocialstudies.com RESEARCH WEB LINKS • Case Study Project, p. 470

BLOCK SCHEDULE LESSON PLAN OPTIONS: 90-MINUTE PERIOD

DAY 1

SECTION 1, pp. 461-464
Class Time 55 minutes

- **Small Groups** Divide the class into small groups that team less proficient readers and ESL students with proficient readers. Have the groups read and discuss Section 1. Suggest that they use the Geographic Thinking questions in the inner margins as discussion prompts.
  Class Time 25 minutes
- **Cause-and-Effect Chart** On the board, copy the Issue 1 section of the GeoFocus chart on page 460. Have volunteers list causes and effects on the chart. Students should copy the completed chart in their notebooks.
  Class Time 15 minutes
- **Map Discussion** Ask the class to study the city map on page 464 and answer the questions. Then have students locate the university, transportation networks, and stock exchange. Ask them to explain how these relate to economic development.
  Class Time 15 minutes

SECTION 2, pp. 465-467
Class Time 35 minutes

- **Independent Study** Have students use the Internet and print sources to research the diseases listed in the chart on page 465. They should look for causes, prevention, and socio-economic effects. Have students write a summary of their findings.

DAY 2

SECTION 2, pp. 465-467
Class Time 20 minutes

- **Discussion** Have students share their findings of the day before. Then direct their attention to the map on page 466. Have the class discuss the social and economic impacts on nations that have 20 percent or more of their population living with HIV or AIDS.

CASE STUDY, pp. 468–471
Class Time 70 minutes

- **Discussion** Use the questions on TE pages 470–471 to lead a class discussion of the five primary sources.
  Class Time 25 minutes
- **Creating a News Report** Divide students into six groups. Have each group select a different African country to report on. Suggest that the group assign specific roles—such as researcher, writer, editor, broadcaster, and camera operator—to each member. Have the groups use the Internet and print resources to research their country. Then they should write and practice their broadcasts. If possible, they should tape their broadcasts as homework.
  Class Time 45 minutes

DAY 3

CASE STUDY, pp. 468-471
Class Time 30 minutes

- **News Reports** Have the teams give their reports or play recordings of them.

CHAPTER 20 REVIEW AND ASSESSMENT, pp. 472-473
Class Time 60 minutes

- **Review** Have pairs of students work together to write summary outlines for each of the three issues: economic development, health care, and the effects of colonialism.
  Class Time 25 minutes
- **Assessment** Have students complete the Chapter 20 Assessment.
  Class Time 35 minutes

TEACHER-TESTED ACTIVITY

Mapping Ethnic Boundaries

Class Time One class period

Task Sketch the colonial political and ethnic boundaries of an African country

Supplies
- Overhead transparency of the map on page 469
- Construction paper in various colors
- Pens

Purpose To show students the incredible difference between the boundaries of the various ethnic groups in Africa and the political boundaries established by European colonizers

Activity Project the map from page 469 on the overhead screen. Discuss the colonization of Africa and the boundaries drawn in Africa by European colonizers. Students may form cooperative groups of 2–4 members. Designate one country per group. Using the overhead screen, students should trace an outline of their assigned country. Groups should then draw and color the various ethnic group boundaries within their country. Tape country maps on a classroom wall and allow a representative from each group to discuss how many ethnic groups are in their country. End with class discussion on the effects of colonialism.

Korri Kinney
Geography Teacher, Meridian High School, Meridian, Idaho

TECHNOLOGY IN THE CLASSROOM

The Internet offers a wealth of numerical data that can be helpful for student research and to supplement topics students are learning about. Some Web sites even allow users to specify how they'd like to see the data presented. Spreadsheet programs are also useful in helping students to compare data. In this activity, students will generate online charts of economic and social statistics for African countries, input the data into a spreadsheet, and compare the statistics.

Objective Students will use the interactive forms on a Web site to generate data about African countries. They will input the data into a spreadsheet and write reports comparing the data.

Task Have students use a Web site to compare and contrast such indicators as GDP per capita, life expectancy, and unemployment rates for several African countries. Ask them to input their findings into a spreadsheet, conduct additional Internet research on one of the countries, and write reports about what they have learned.

Class Time 2-3 class periods

1. Ask students to go to **hmhsocialstudies.com** and find the Web sites listed for this activity. In the first site, click the boxes in the right-hand frame next to the following countries: Botswana, Chad, Democratic Republic of the Congo, Nigeria, Somalia, and Uganda. Then have them click "Data Menu."
2. Ask students to select the following data fields: GDP per capita, unemployment, population under 15, and infant mortality.
3. Discuss the meanings of these four data fields, making sure students understand what each one measures. Ask them to explain what they think each type of data reveals about a country. For example, what does it mean for one country to have a much higher population under 15 years, or greater GDP per capita than another country?
4. Have students click "view info." to view the data. Then have them input the data into a spreadsheet program.
5. Have students repeat steps 2-4 for the same countries but using these data fields: life expectancy, illiteracy rate (total), telephones, refugees. Have them input this data into the same spreadsheet.
6. Have students repeat steps 1-4 for the United States.
7. Have students go to the U.S. Department of State Background Notes site, listed at **hmhsocialstudies.com**, to find out more about the history, government and political conditions, and economies one of the African countries they've looked at. Have them take notes on the factors that might contribute to that country's current economic and social situation.
8. Have students refer to their spreadsheets, their notes, and Chapter 20 to write reports that answer the following questions: What historical, political, and economic factors have contributed to the current situation in Africa? Why might African countries differ from each other in economic and social factors? How do African countries compare to the United States in economic and social factors, and what are some of the reasons for these differences? What are some possible solutions to the economic and social problems facing Africa?

CHAPTER 20 OBJECTIVE

Learn that Africans face serious issues and a health-care crisis, and are seeking solutions.

Chapter 20 TODAY'S ISSUES Africa

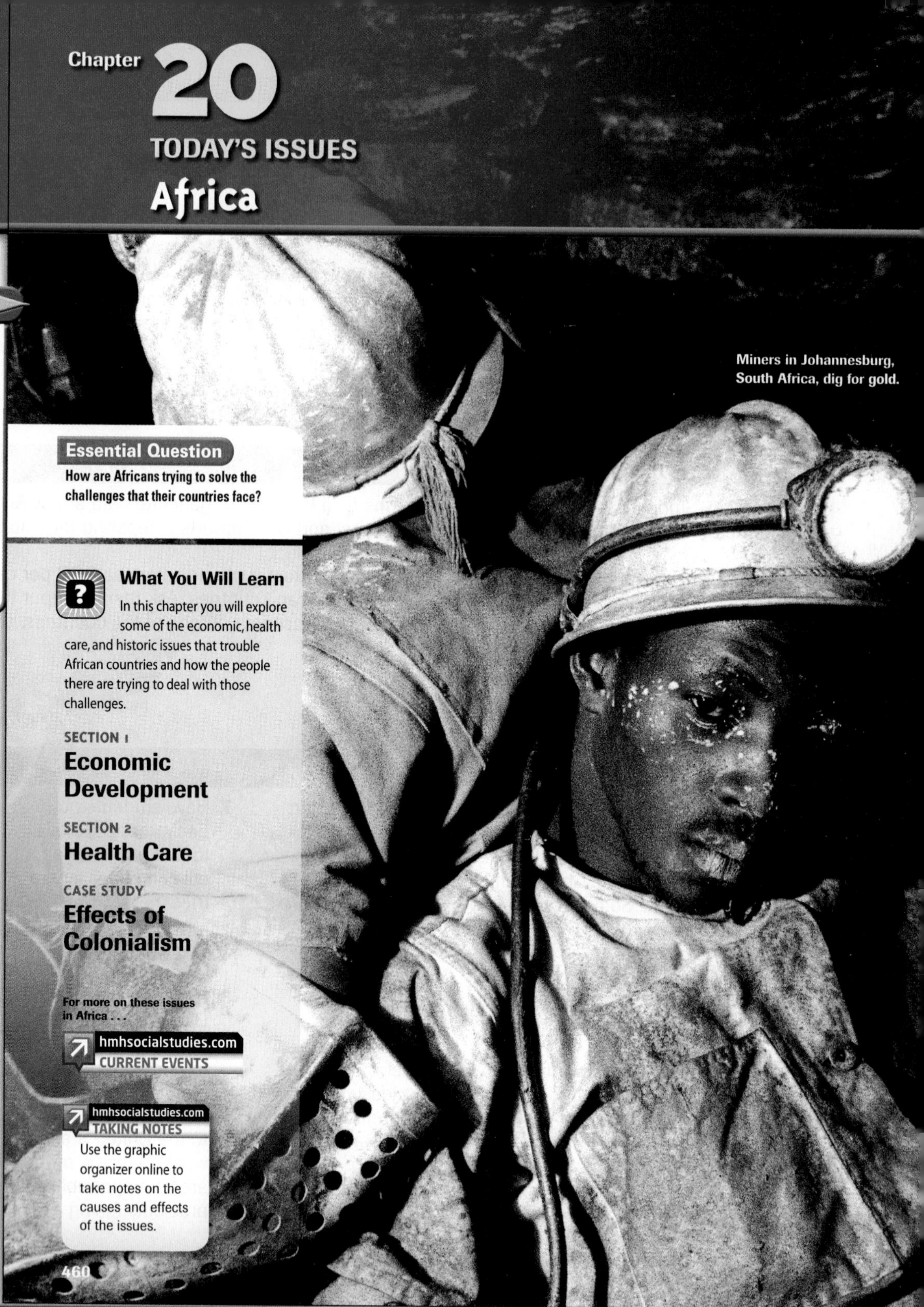

Interpreting Photographs

South African Miners

Have students examine the photograph. Direct their attention to the crowded situation for the workers and to the expression on the man facing the camera. Ask what they can infer from this image. *(Gold mining is hard labor; blacks typically perform difficult and dangerous jobs in South Africa.)*

Introducing the Essential Question

- Lead a discussion about students' learning to help themselves when they face problems. Point out that Africans are trying to figure out how to solve their problems without relying on outside aid.
- Compare health care issues in the United States with health care challenges in Africa.

Ask students to fill in the graphic organizer to help them understand the causes and effects of issues facing African nations today.

 **Critical Thinking Transparencies CT20**
- GeoFocus

 **In-Depth Resources: Unit 6**
- Building Vocabulary, p. 31

Miners in Johannesburg, South Africa, dig for gold.

Essential Question

How are Africans trying to solve the challenges that their countries face?

What You Will Learn

In this chapter you will explore some of the economic, health care, and historic issues that trouble African countries and how the people there are trying to deal with those challenges.

SECTION 1
Economic Development

SECTION 2
Health Care

CASE STUDY
Effects of Colonialism

For more on these issues in Africa . . .

hmhsocialstudies.com CURRENT EVENTS

hmhsocialstudies.com TAKING NOTES

Use the graphic organizer online to take notes on the causes and effects of the issues.

460

CHAPTER 20 ADDITIONAL RESOURCES

BOOKS FOR THE TEACHER

Moyo, Dambisa. ***Dead Aid: Why Aid Is Not Working and How There Is a Better Way for Africa.*** Douglas & Mcintyre Ltd., 2010. An argument that the West's well-intentioned aid is often worse than no aid at all.

Ayittey, George B.N. ***Africa in Chaos.*** NY: St. Martin's, 1999. Analysis of post-colonial failures in Africa.

BOOKS FOR THE STUDENT

Hochschild, Adam. ***King Leopold's Ghost.*** Boston: Houghton, 1999. Leopold's cruel reign in the Congo.

Gourevitch, Philip. ***We Wish to Inform You That Tomorrow We Will Be Killed with Our Families.*** NY: Farrar, 1998. Account of the 1994 Hutu-Tutsi conflict.

PERIODICALS

"The Cruelest Curse." *Economist.* 24 Feb. 2001: 8-11. Study of AIDS in South Africa.

McGeary, Johanna. **"Death Stalks a Continent."** *Time.* 12 Feb. 2001: 36-44. Analytical report on AIDS in Africa including victims' personal stories.

INTERNET

For additional information on issues in Africa, visit . . .

hmhsocialstudies.com

Economic Development

How can African nations develop their economies?

Main Ideas
- Africa's history of colonization has had long-term effects on its economy.
- Barriers to African economic development include illiteracy, foreign debt, and a lack of manufacturing industries.

Places & Terms
"one-commodity" country
commodity
diversify

A HUMAN PERSPECTIVE Mauwa Funidi wonders about the future of her country, the Democratic Republic of the Congo, as she looks around the rundown university library where she works. She has not been paid her salary of 12 dollars per month in many months. Classes at the university have been suspended because of a lack of funds. Funidi survives by selling bags of charcoal on the streets of Kisangani. Funidi, like many Africans, is trying to scrape out a living on a continent where people's standard of living declined for the first 30 years of independence and made little improvement after that. Many African countries have vowed to change their fortunes with better government, better relations with neighbors, more investment in education, and a diverse economy.

Africa's Economy Today

Most African nations have little manufacturing of their own. Their economies are based on providing raw materials—oil, minerals, or agricultural products—to the world's industrialized countries.

A HISTORY OF PROBLEMS As you learned in the previous chapter, European colonizers exploited Africa's resources and people during the past few centuries. Millions of Africans were sold into slavery, and countless others have died in Africa from harsh working conditions while obtaining raw materials for foreign interests. In addition, the land has been mined and drilled with little regard for the environment. This history of exploitation has limited Africa's economic growth and fostered political instability. Without political stability, consistent economic growth is difficult.

AFRICA'S ECONOMY Today, most African countries are worse off economically than they were in the 1960s, when many of them gained independence. More than half of the African countries are in the World Bank's lowest income category of less than $975 Gross National Income per person. In 2007, Africa accounted for only 2.5 percent of total world GNP and 1.5 percent of total dollar value of world exports—both

HUMAN-ENVIRONMENT INTERACTION Much of Africa's infrastructure is undeveloped. With few paved roads, trucks get bogged down on muddy roads, such as this one in the Democratic Republic of the Congo.

AFRICA

461

SECTION 1 OBJECTIVES
1. Analyze the current status of Africa's economy.
2. Identify ways to develop the economies of African nations.
3. Explain the role education plays in developing Africa's economies.

SKILLBUILDER: Interpreting Maps, p. 462

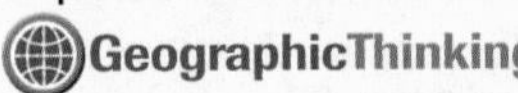
GeographicThinking
Seeing Patterns, pp. 462, 463
Making Generalizations, p. 463

Focus & Motivate

Ask students to name things that have helped promote industry and trade in other parts of the world. *(technology, investment, infrastructure, education)*

Instruct: Objective 1 appears on p. 462

Interpreting Photographs

Truck on Muddy Congolese Road
Have students examine the photograph. Direct their attention to the width of the road and the deep ditch it is in. Ask them to discuss the difference between dirt roads and paved roads. *(Paved roads are more easily traveled in bad weather. Dirt roads can become muddy, rutted, and sometimes impassable.)*

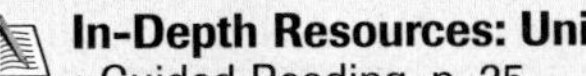
SECTION 1 PROGRAM RESOURCES

In-Depth Resources: Unit 6
- Guided Reading, p. 25
- Building Vocabulary, p. 31
- Exploring Today's Issues, pp. 32–33
- Reteaching Activity, p. 36
- Map and Graph Skills, pp. 28–29

Guided Reading Workbook
- Section 1

Access for Students Acquiring English/ESL
- Guided Reading, p. 105
- Map and Graph Skills, pp. 109–110

Formal Assessment
- Section Quiz, p. 306

Integrated Assessment
- Rubric for a news article, 4.5

INTEGRATED TECHNOLOGY

Critical Thinking Transparencies CT52
- Estimated Illiteracy Rates in Selected African Countries, 2001

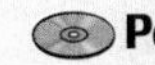
Power Presentations

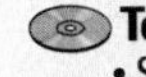
Test Generator
- Section 1 Quiz

hmhsocialstudies.com

TEST-TAKING RESOURCES

Strategies for Test Preparation

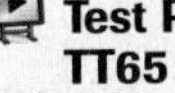
Test Practice Transparencies TT65

Online Test Practice

Instruct: Objective 

Africa's Economy Today

- What is a major historic cause of Africa's economic problems? *(European colonialism)*
- How might African nations achieve economic growth? *(fostering political stability, building infrastructure, developing high technology)*

 **In-Depth Resources: Unit 6**
- Guided Reading, p. 25
- Exploring Today's Issues, pp. 32–33

Instruct: Objective 

On the Road to Development

- What are Western leaders doing to help African economies? *(urging their countries to forgive Africa's debts)*
- What are African nations doing to help their economies? *(organizing for regional cooperation)*
- Why do economists urge African nations to diversify? *(exporting one commodity creates economic instability because prices vary constantly on the world market)*

Interpreting Maps

One-Commodity Countries

Have students examine the map. Ask them whether most exports are mineral resources or agricultural products. *(minerals)* Ask them to name a disadvantage of relying solely on the export of minerals. *(In contrast to agricultural products, minerals are non-renewable resources.)*

SKILLBUILDER ANSWERS
1. petroleum **2.** West Africa

small numbers compared to Africa's population and natural resources. The whole of Africa's economy is about as large as that of Argentina's.

Furthermore, the economic infrastructure needed for substantial growth is not in place. Roads, airports, railroads, and ports are not adequate to help African nations further their economic growth. A

In addition, most Africans don't have access to computers or other aspects of high technology. High technology has fueled economic growth in other parts of the world such as North America, Europe, and Asia.

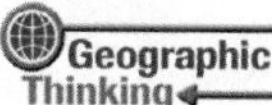

Geographic Thinking

Seeing Patterns A Why do you think good roads are important to the functioning of an economy?

A. Answer Good roads help to ensure the efficient movement of goods, services, and people from one place to another.

On the Road to Development

Despite this legacy of exploitation, African nations are struggling to build economies based on the careful use of natural and human resources.

REDUCING DEBT AND INCREASING COOPERATION When the colonial nations pulled out of Africa, they often left the newly independent nations without money for transportation, education, and businesses. To build their economies, African countries borrowed heavily. By 1997, total public debt of sub-Saharan African governments—about 227 billion dollars—was strangling them. As a result, many Western leaders have urged their countries to forgive Africa's debts so that it has more money to build its economies.

BACKGROUND
In 1998, over 57 percent of Africa's total GNP went to repaying its debts.

Another way that Africa seeks to improve its economy is through regional cooperation. The Economic Community of West African States (ECOWAS) and the Southern African Development Community (SADC) are both striving to promote trade. For example, ECOWAS is working toward removing duties and creating a common currency. Efforts of SADC include working to improve the transportation and communication infrastructures.

"One-Commodity" Countries

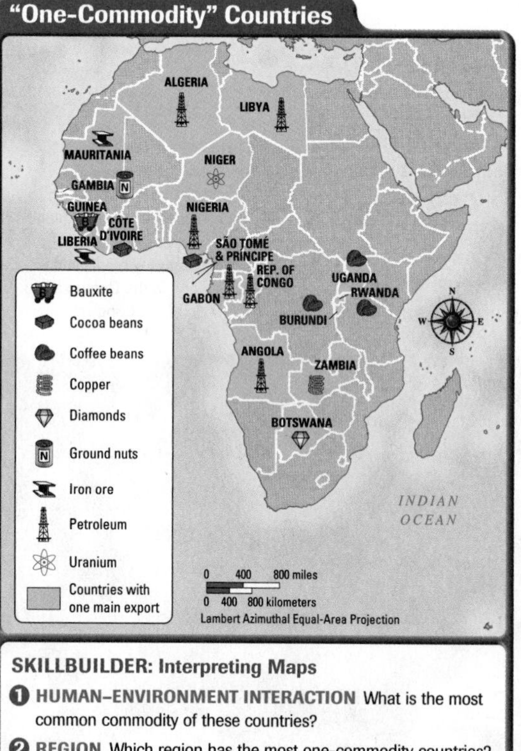

SKILLBUILDER: Interpreting Maps
1. **HUMAN-ENVIRONMENT INTERACTION** What is the most common commodity of these countries?
2. **REGION** Which region has the most one-commodity countries?

BUILDING INDUSTRIES The economy of many African nations is based on the export of raw materials. Furthermore, several of Africa's countries rely on just one or two principal commodities for much of their earnings. These are called **"one-commodity" countries.** A **commodity** is an agricultural or mining product that can be sold. The value of a commodity varies from day to day based on worldwide supply and demand. That makes the economies of the producing nations—especially "one-commodity" countries—unstable. Economists believe African nations must **diversify**, or create variety in, their economies and promote manufacturing to achieve economic growth and stability.

DIFFERENTIATING INSTRUCTION **LESS PROFICIENT READERS**

CONNECTING PROBLEMS AND SOLUTIONS

Objective To help less proficient readers better understand the relationship between problems and solutions discussed in the text

Class Time 20 minutes

Task Create a chart listing problems and solutions

Directions Have pairs of students reread the text under "On the Road to Development." Tell them to list the problems faced by African nations and the solutions to those problems on a chart like the one shown.

PROBLEMS	SOLUTIONS
colonial powers left no money	regional cooperation to promote trade
African nations deeply in debt	Western nations forgive Africa's debt
little infrastructure	regional cooperation to improve infrastructure
one-commodity countries	vary products and promote manufacturing

BACKGROUND
The Highland's Water Project of Lesotho will eventually allow the country to generate its own electricity, instead of having to buy it from South Africa.

Some African nations are making strides toward that goal. In East Africa, Djibouti is using its location on the Gulf of Aden to establish a major international shipping center.

Educating Workers

A key to developing Africa's economies is improving its education system to provide people with a high level of skills. African nations must also find ways to prevent their educated citizens from leaving the continent.

IMPROVING EDUCATION A large barrier to economic growth in Africa is an unschooled population. In 2008, Africa south of the Sahara had a primary school enrollment rate of only 76 percent, the lowest of any world region. In some countries, such as Angola and Somalia, civil wars have all but destroyed the school systems. B

Some African countries, however, are making progress. For example, in Algeria, 96 percent of the country's children complete their primary education. Mauritius has also made huge gains. As of 2008, over 84 percent of Mauritians age 15 and older were literate.

REVERSING THE BRAIN DRAIN Another priority is slowing the departure of African professionals to Western countries. In 1983, the International Organization for Migration began a campaign to encourage these professionals to return home.

As Africa moves into the 21st century, efforts to improve education, invest in industry, and create stable governments provide hope for the future.

Seeing Patterns
B Why do you think education is important to Africa's economy?
B. Answer
Educated citizens and highly skilled workers can infuse the economy with new ideas, more efficiency, and higher productivity levels.

Geography TODAY

Hi-Tech Tracking

As the scorching sun of the Kalahari Desert beats down on Attorney Hlongwane, he puts information into a palm-sized computer. Hlongwane tracks animals in the same desert as his Makuleke ancestors did. But now he uses high technology to follow animals such as hippos and crocodiles.

Some of the data will help protect certain species from drought. Tracking with hand-held computers both protects Africa's resources and shows how well-educated people can solve problems.

Geography TODAY

Hi-Tech Tracking

In 1998, Louis Liebenberg received an International Award for Enterprise for developing this technology. The trackers can easily use display screens and icon pictures to record and transmit precise information. How might this technology help promote tourism? *(by helping track and save animals that might attract visitors to the area)*

Instruct: Objective 3

Educating Workers

- How can education help Africa's economies grow? *(by providing skilled workers)*
- What countries have achieved great progress in educating their citizens? *(Algeria, Mauritius)*

Critical Thinking Transparencies CT52
- Estimated Illiteracy Rates in Selected African Countries, 2001

AFRICA

SECTION 1 Assessment

1 Places & Terms

Explain the meaning of each of the following terms.
- "one-commodity" country
- commodity
- diversify

2 Taking Notes

PLACE Review the notes you took for this section.

	Causes	Effects
Issue 1		

- What are some of the causes of economic problems of African countries?
- What impact is Africa's debt having on its ability to build its economy?

3 Main Ideas

a. What has happened to people's incomes over the last half-century?
b. What is one problem for "one-commodity" countries?
c. Why is improving education important to Africa's economy?

4 Geographic Thinking

Making Generalizations What actions should African nations take to form a solid economic foundation? **Think about:**
- economic cooperation
- education

See Skillbuilder Handbook, page R6.

EXPLORING LOCAL GEOGRAPHY Find out how your city or state promotes economic development. Learn about laws passed to promote growth or tax breaks given to certain industries. Then write a **news article** on the topic.

Assess & Reteach

GeoFocus Have students complete the section on economic development in their cause-and-effect charts.

Formal Assessment
- Section Quiz, p. 306

Reteaching Activity
Have students review this section by writing a paragraph about the ways education and improved infrastructures can benefit African economies.

In-Depth Resources: Unit 6
- Reteaching Activity, p. 36

SECTION 1 ASSESSMENT ANSWERS

1. Places & Terms
"one-commodity" country, p. 462
commodity, p. 462
diversify, p. 462

2. Taking Notes
- Africa's history of exploitation, from slavery to colonialism, has caused many of Africa's current problems.
- African nations are hampered by debt; they are spending money to pay back debt rather than on growing their economies.

3. Main Ideas
a. African incomes have decreased over the past half-century.
b. A commodity's price varies according to the world market. If the price drops, then that country's economy will suffer, and it will have no income from other commodities to offset the loss.
c. Improved education creates a pool of more highly skilled workers.

4. Geographic Thinking
Economic cooperation will help many African countries because it allows them to pool resources. Education will produce a higher-skilled citizenry, which will help economic production.

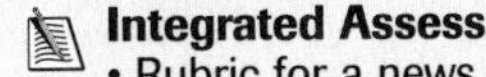

Integrated Assessment
- Rubric for a news article, 4.5

CHAPTER 20 MAP SKILLS

OBJECTIVE
Learn how to read a city map.

Instruct: Objective

Reading a City Map

- How might a city map differ from a road map? *(It is usually at a larger scale to show details that a visitor to the city might find useful.)*
- What kinds of details might be useful for a tourist? *(train stations, tourist information centers, street names, museums, etc.)*
- What is a grid system, and how does it work? *(Letters at a map's top and bottom and numbers on a map's sides are used to identify grid sections that readers can use to find sites listed in the map's index.)*

In-Depth Resources: Unit 6
- Map and Graph Skills, pp. 28–29

Access for Students Acquiring English/ESL
- Map and Graph Skills, pp. 109–110

Interpreting Maps

Johannesburg, South Africa

Have students look at the map on page 464, and ask them to identify the principal buildings in grids C-1 *(General Hospital)* and C-3 *(Supreme Court)*. Also, tell students to imagine they are standing at the corner of Simmonds and Market streets. Ask them how miles they would to travel if they wanted to visit Johannesburg's Art Gallery. *(about four miles)*

RAND MCNALLY **Map and Graph Skills**

Reading a City Map

Johannesburg, South Africa, is one of the youngest major cities in the world. It grew rapidly following the discovery of gold in 1886. Today, it is South Africa's largest city and the country's financial and industrial center. Looking at the city map below, you can see that the streets of the city center are laid out in a grid. A grid is something resembling a framework of crisscrossing parallel bars.

THE LANGUAGE OF MAPS A **city map** is essentially another kind of road map. However, it is usually set at a larger scale than a state road map in order to show greater detail to guide both visitors and residents. Many city maps show the names of streets, major tourist attractions, bus and train stations, and other useful buildings.

Johannesburg, South Africa

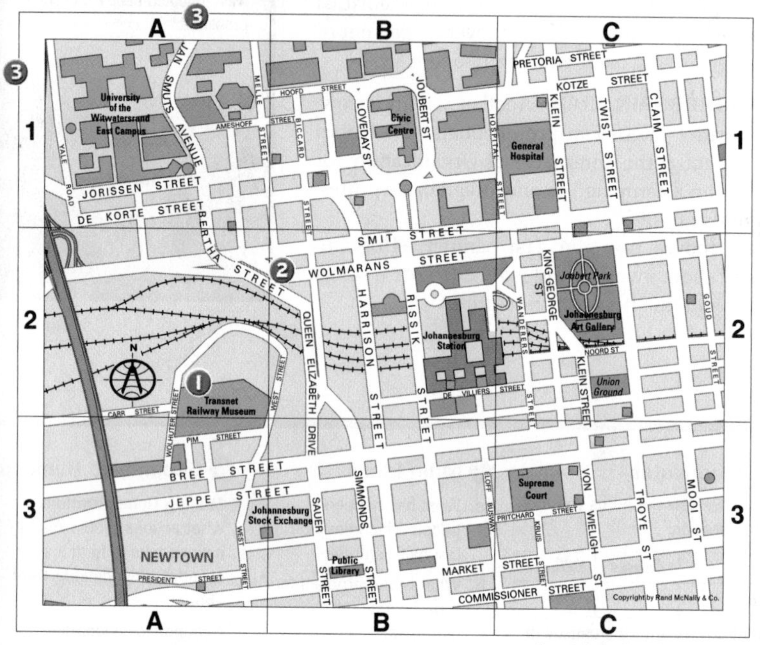

Copyright by Rand McNally & Co.

Johannesburg•

	Parks
	Principal buildings
	Rail/Bus stations
	Major highways
	Streets and roads
	Railways

0 0.1 0.2 Mi.
0 0.1 0.2 0.3 Km.

1. Points of interest are shown to help tourists plan their visit.
2. Labeling major streets is necessary to guide people around the city.
3. Letters at the top and bottom and numbers on the sides identify the grid sections created by the black lines. The grid sections help readers find places on the map. Most city maps have an index listing places on the map and the grid sections where they appear.

Map and Graph Skills Assessment

1. Making Generalizations
If you took the train into Johannesburg, how would you get to the railway museum by foot and about how long would it take?

2. Drawing Conclusions
Where is the most likely place for a picnic in this part of the city? What are the place's index coordinates?

3. Making Inferences
If you spent a weekend in Johannesburg, what are at least five activities available to you in the city?

SKILLS ASSESSMENT ANSWERS

1. De Villiers Street toward Rissik
left on Rissik Street
right on Bree Street
right on West Street
left on Pim Street
Approximately one mile would take about 20 minutes walking.

2. Joubert Park; 2-C

3. Answers will vary but may include the Johannesburg Art Gallery, the Transnet Railway Museum, the civic center, Joubert Park, the university campus, the supreme court, and the stock exchange.

Health Care

How can African countries eliminate the diseases that threaten their people and cultures?

Main Ideas

- Epidemic diseases are killing Africa's people in huge numbers.
- African nations and countries around the world are using a variety of methods, including education, to eradicate disease.

Places & Terms

AIDS
cholera
malaria
tuberculosis
UNAIDS

A HUMAN PERSPECTIVE On June 1, 2001, Nkosi Johnson died from the human immunodeficiency virus (HIV)—the virus that causes **acquired immune deficiency syndrome (AIDS).** At the time, he was the longest living South African child born with HIV. In February, he celebrated his 12th birthday—but weighed just 27 pounds. Living with a foster mother, the child had become a symbol of hope in a nation suffering from AIDS. He frankly discussed the problems of the disease and received cheers at the 13th International AIDS conference in Durban, South Africa, in July 2000. His plight was typical of many on the continent, as African nations struggle to deal with this and other diseases.

Disease and Despair

Controlling AIDS and other diseases is essential if Africans are to improve their quality of life and live a normal lifespan.

SERIOUS DISEASES African nations are threatened by a variety of diseases. Inadequate sanitation and lack of a clean water supply can lead to **cholera,** an infection that is often fatal if not treated. In 2000–2001, widespread flooding caused some cases of cholera in Mozambique, but international relief efforts prevented a widespread outbreak.

Diseases in Africa, 1900 and 2010

Leading Diseases 1900

Malaria
First reference in Greece around 400 B.C.

Sleeping Sickness
First described around A.D. 1300 in present-day Mali.

Smallpox
First evidence c. 1156 B.C. in Egypt. Eradicated A.D. 1977.

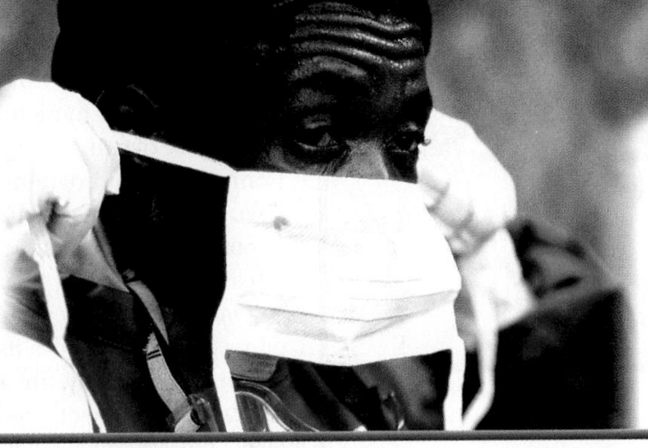

Leading Diseases 2010

Malaria
Almost 90 percent of world's estimated 863,000 malaria deaths occur in Africa.

Sleeping Sickness
Number of cases has dropped, but disease still affects almost 10,000.

AIDS
Origins of HIV traced to Central Africa in 1959.

SKILLBUILDER: Interpreting Charts

1. **MAKING COMPARISONS** What was a leading disease in Africa in 1900 but not in 2010?
2. **DRAWING CONCLUSIONS** What disease occurs in Africa in 2010 but not in 1900?

SECTION 2 OBJECTIVES

1. Identify major diseases in Africa and their impact on the population.
2. Describe strategies to fight the spread of disease in Africa.

SKILLBUILDERS: Interpreting Charts and Maps, pp. 465, 466

GeographicThinking
Using the Atlas, p. 466
Making Comparisons, p. 467
Identifying and Solving Problems, p. 467

Focus & Motivate

Ask students to think of news reports they've seen about Africa. What diseases cause problems there? *(AIDS, malaria, cholera, sleeping sickness)*

Instruct: Objective 1 appears on p. 466

Interpreting Charts

Diseases in Africa, 1900 and 2010

Have students examine the chart. Tell them that sleeping sickness produces fever, inflammation of the lymph nodes, and extreme tiredness. Sleeping sickness frequently ends in death. It is caused by a parasite that is introduced into the human blood stream when a person is bitten by an infected tsetse fly. Similarly, mosquitoes spread the parasite responsible for malaria.

SKILLBUILDER ANSWERS
1. smallpox **2.** AIDS

SECTION 2 PROGRAM RESOURCES

In-Depth Resources: Unit 6
- Guided Reading, p. 26
- Skillbuilder Practice, p. 30
- Building Vocabulary, p. 31
- Exploring Today's Issues, pp. 34–35
- Reteaching Activity, p. 37

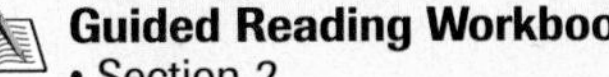
Guided Reading Workbook
- Section 2

Access for Students Acquiring English/ESL
- Guided Reading, p. 106
- Skillbuilder Practice, p. 108

Formal Assessment
- Section Quiz, p. 307

Integrated Assessment
- Rubric for a chart, 2.2

INTEGRATED TECHNOLOGY

Power Presentations

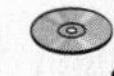
Test Generator
- Section 2 Quiz

hmhsocialstudies.com

TEST-TAKING RESOURCES

Strategies for Test Preparation

Test Practice Transparencies TT66

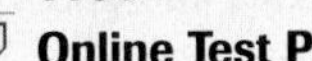
Online Test Practice

Instruct: Objective 1

Disease and Despair/ AIDS Stalks the Continent

- What diseases threaten Africans? *(cholera, malaria, tuberculosis, AIDS)*
- What causes cholera? *(inadequate sanitation and lack of a clean water supply)*
- How has AIDS affected Africa's human populations and economies? *(life expectancies have dropped; earnings and GDP have fallen)*

In-Depth Resources: Unit 6
- Guided Reading, p. 26
- Exploring Today's Issues, p. 34–35

Instruct: Objective 2

Nations Respond

- What methods have Africans used to fight various diseases? *(spraying to kill insects, immunization, improved public-health facilities)*
- Why is Brazil working with South Africa on AIDS prevention? *(Brazil's public-health policies are considered a model for developing countries.)*
- What common strategy has helped Uganda and Senegal control the spread of HIV? *(education programs)*

Interpreting Maps

AIDS in Africa, 2000

Have students examine the map. Have them identify the countries worst hit by AIDS. *(Botswana, Lesotho, Swaziland, Zimbabwe)*

SKILLBUILDER ANSWERS

1. Southern Africa **2.** North Africa

Mosquitos carrying **malaria**—an infectious disease marked by chills and fevers that is often fatal—are common in African countries. The disease has become resistant to standard drugs because of overuse of those drugs in treating the disease during the past several decades. AIDS and HIV, however, create the most severe problems. About 67 percent of the world's adult AIDS cases are in sub-Saharan Africa. More than 90 percent of all new cases of children with AIDS are in sub-Saharan African nations. AIDS is often accompanied by **tuberculosis**, a respiratory infection spread between humans.

AIDS Stalks the Continent

In 2008, AIDS took the lives of around two million people worldwide. Of these, 1.4 million lived in sub-Saharan Africa. In Swaziland, three of every four deaths were attributed to AIDS. The AIDS epidemic in Swaziland has caused life expectancy there to drop from 58 to 37 years. In 2008, 22.4 million people in sub-Saharan Africa were living with either HIV or AIDS.

BACKGROUND According to the U.S. Agency for International Development, by 2010, nearly 30 million children had lost at least one parent to AIDS.

A HIGH PRICE TO PAY Widespread disease has economic consequences. People who are sick work less or not at all, earn less, and thus are pushed further into poverty. Economists predicted that by 2010, the GDP of South Africa would be 17 percent lower than it would have been if not for AIDS. Furthermore, AIDS patients' medical care is also expensive. **UNAIDS**, the UN program that studies the world's AIDS epidemic, estimates that $4.63 billion will be needed to fight AIDS in Africa.

AIDS in Africa, 2000

Adults living with HIV/AIDS, 2000
- Greater than 20%
- 11% – 20%
- 6% – 10%
- 1% – 5%
- Less than 1%
- Data not available

Source: UNAIDS Report on the Global HIV/AIDS Epidemic, June, 2000.

SKILLBUILDER: Interpreting Maps
1. **REGION** Which subregion has the highest infection rate?
2. **REGION** Which subregion has the lowest infection rate?

Nations Respond

Response to these epidemics comes both from African nations and from countries around the world.

A VARIETY OF ANSWERS To fight malaria and other insect-borne diseases, African nations have used spraying programs since the 1930s to reduce the number of insects. In 2000, the Global Fund for Children's Vaccines pledged more than $250 million for use over the next five years for immunization programs in Africa, Asia, Latin America, and Europe.

Some African countries are fighting disease by improving their health care systems. Gabon, for example, has used oil revenues to improve its health care system substantially. In addition, the African Development Fund approved a loan of nearly 12.3 million dollars to enable Mozambique to upgrade its public health facilities. A

A. Answer Libya, Algeria, Angola, Republic of the Congo, and Nigeria

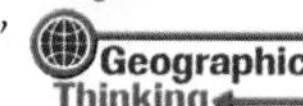

Geographic Thinking

Using the Atlas

A Using the atlas and the map on the left, which other countries could rely on revenues from oil to improve their health care systems?

ACTIVITY OPTION **SKILLBUILDER LESSON**

IDENTIFYING AND SOLVING PROBLEMS

Explaining the Skill Tell students that they can gain a better perspective on issues by thinking in terms of identifying and solving problems.

Applying the Skill Allow students five minutes to discuss the information about AIDS on pages 466 and 467. Then ask the following questions:

In-Depth Resources: Unit 6
- Skillbuilder Practice, p. 30

- How has AIDS affected the people of Sub-Saharan Africa? *(Millions have died, life expectancies have dropped.)*
- Why does AIDS create economic problems? *(Sick people work and earn less; people and nations become poorer.)*
- What measures can help control AIDS? *(improved health care, education programs)*

STRATEGIES AGAINST AIDS Fighting and preventing AIDS is being done on many levels. In December 2000, South Africa and Brazil reached an agreement to work together on AIDS prevention and care. Brazil's public health policies to combat AIDS and other diseases are considered a model for developing countries.

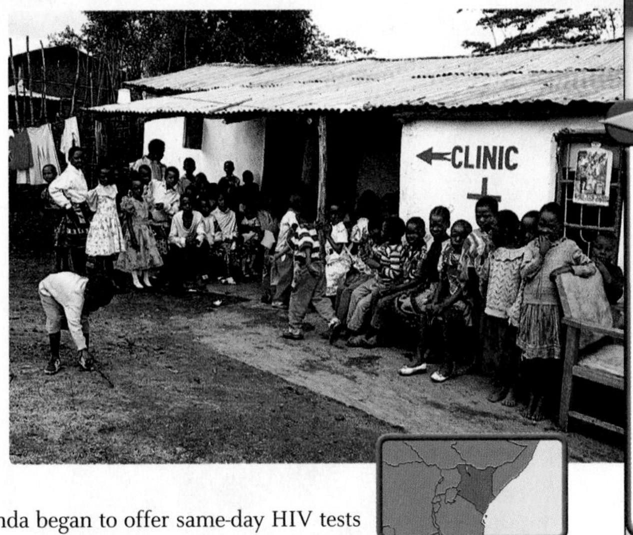

PLACE Kenyans gather outside a health clinic near Nairobi to learn about the dangers of AIDS.

B. Answer Senegal used education at the outset to keep infection rates low; Uganda used education as well as treatment programs.

Geographic Thinking

Making Comparisons
B What are the differences in the ways that Uganda and Senegal have tried to slow the spread of AIDS?

SUCCESS STORIES In the 1900s, two countries, Uganda and Senegal, had success in reducing the spread of HIV. Uganda's government has spearheaded efforts to combat AIDS. For example, in 1997, Uganda began to offer same-day HIV tests and education programs. Infection rates among 15 to 24 year olds dropped by 50 percent. On the other hand, Senegal has controlled the spread of the disease from the outset through an intensive education program. Infection rates have remained around two percent. B

UNAIDS says that the number of people newly infected with HIV in 2008 in sub-Saharan Africa dropped to 1.9 million, down from 2.3 million in 2001. However, UNAIDS cautions that the drop in HIV infection rates could mean that almost as many people are dying of AIDS as are being infected with HIV. Nevertheless, with many African nations taking action, they can build an effective health care system and make progress against the epidemics that threaten their peoples and cultures.

Interpreting Photographs

Kenyans Seek Information about AIDS

Have students examine the photograph. Ask them what age group is most represented. *(children, young people)* Ask them how might education programs help slow the spread of AIDS. *(Lack of education and communication keeps people uninformed about the dangers of the disease and how it spreads.)*

Assess & Reteach

GeoFocus Have students complete the section on health care in their cause-and-effect charts.

Formal Assessment
• Section Quiz, p. 307

Reteaching Activity
Have students prepare a chart listing diseases that threaten Africa in one column and solutions in another.

In-Depth Resources: Unit 6
• Reteaching Activity, p. 37

AFRICA

Section 2 Assessment

1 Places & Terms
Explain the meaning of each of the following terms.
- AIDS
- cholera
- malaria
- tuberculosis
- UNAIDS

2 Taking Notes
PLACE Review the notes you took for this section.

	Causes	Effects
Issue 2		

- What are some of the serious diseases affecting African countries?
- How has AIDS affected Swaziland?

3 Main Ideas
a. What are some of the causes of cholera and malaria?
b. How is AIDS affecting the population of Africa's countries?
c. Why might the drop in HIV infection rates not indicate progress in slowing AIDS?

4 Geographic Thinking
Identifying and Solving Problems How have African nations slowed the spread of the continent's diseases?
Think about:
- the different programs
- international cooperation

MAKING COMPARISONS Using encyclopedias or the Internet, find out what the leading diseases are in the United States and identify their primary causes. Compare your findings to the leading diseases in Africa in a **chart** on the topic.

21st CENTURY

SECTION 2 ASSESSMENT ANSWERS

1. Places & Terms
AIDS, p. 465
cholera, p. 465
malaria, p. 466
tuberculosis, p. 466
UNAIDS, p. 466

2. Taking Notes
- cholera, malaria, tuberculosis, sleeping sickness, AIDS
- AIDS has reduced life expectancy by 19 years and causes 3 out of 4 deaths in the country.

3. Main Ideas
a. Lack of adequate sanitation and clean water spreads cholera, and malaria is a mosquito-borne disease.
b. AIDS is reducing Africa's population; 2.4 million people died of AIDS in 2000 in sub-Saharan Africa.
c. because almost as many people may be dying of AIDS as are being infected with HIV

4. Geographic Thinking
African nations have adopted many ways to control the spread of diseases, including spraying programs for insects, vaccinations, domestic health-care improvement, and education and treatment programs.

GeoActivity

Integrated Assessment
• Rubric for a chart, 2.2

CASE STUDY OBJECTIVES

1. Describe the effects of European colonialism on Africa.
2. Examine the challenges of independence in postcolonial Africa.
3. Complete the Case Study Project by preparing a news report on postcolonial Africa from one country's point of view.
4. Analyze primary sources for different views on postcolonial Africa.

SKILLBUILDER: Interpreting Maps, p. 469

Focus & Motivate

Ask students what factors might create political instability in postcolonial Africa. Have them consider history, economics, and ethnicity. *(Centuries of European rule left African countries unprepared for democracy, with little economic infrastructure and borders that combined warring ethnic groups.)*

Instruct: Objective 

Colonizing Africa

- Why did Portuguese ships first come to Africa? *(They were looking for trade routes to Asia.)*
- Why were Europeans interested in Africa? *(They wanted raw materials for their own industrial economies and to establish markets where they could sell goods.)*
- What aspects of Africa were damaged by colonialism? *(ethnic boundaries, environment, economy)*

 **In-Depth Resources: Unit 6**
• Guided Reading, p. 27

Map Transparencies MT35
• Challenges of Postcolonial Africa

CASE STUDY

EFFECTS OF COLONIALISM

How can African nations bring peace and stability to their people?

Young people celebrate Namibia's independence from South Africa in 1990.

Africa, at the beginning of the 19th century, was home to great empires and rich cultures such as the Zulu, the Ashanti, and the Hausa. At the end of the 19th century, Africa was a place of European colonial power and oppression. European governments and financial agents based in such places as French West Africa, Belgian Congo, and British East Africa controlled much of the continent. Africa has not been the same since. Much of the poverty and violence of the 20th century is the direct result of colonialism. As you read the Case Study, consider how Africa might overcome the legacy of European colonialism.

Colonizing Africa

During the 15th century, Portuguese ships, looking for trade routes to Asia, landed in Africa. Soon other European countries established coastal trading stations there.

EUROPEANS IN AFRICA By the mid-1800s, Europeans knew of Africa's rich natural resources. They wanted these raw materials to fuel their own industrial economies and to establish markets to sell and trade their goods. In 1884–1885, the Berlin Conference, which you read about in Chapter 19, set down rules for dividing up Africa. European colonial control of Africa began to end in the early 20th century, but most African countries gained their independence in the 1960s. The Europeans did long-term damage to Africa, affecting its cultural and ethnic boundaries, and ruining its economy.

Challenges of Independence

When the European colonial powers were forced to leave Africa, the newly independent African countries did not have stable governments in place. For the next 40 years, many of the newly established African nations and their peoples suffered through dictatorships and civil wars. Many of these conflicts had lasting consequences for the continent's economy and the people's well-being.

COLONIAL TRANSITION European governments did not understand the incredible ethnic diversity in Africa. Certain African ethnic groups are living together today only because European colonizers established national borders that grouped them together. Examine the map on page 469 and you will see the ethnic and cultural complexity in

CASE STUDY PROGRAM RESOURCES

 **In-Depth Resources: Unit 6**
• Guided Reading, p. 27
• Building Vocabulary, p. 31
• Reteaching Activity, p. 38

 **Guided Reading Workbook**
• Case Study

 **Access for Students Acquiring English/ESL**
• Guided Reading, p. 107

 **Formal Assessment**
• Case Study Quiz, p. 308

INTEGRATED TECHNOLOGY

 **Map Transparencies MT35**
• Challenges of Postcolonial Africa

 **Test Generator**
• Case Study Quiz

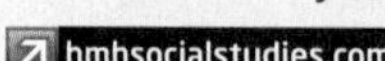

hmhsocialstudies.com

TEST-TAKING RESOURCES

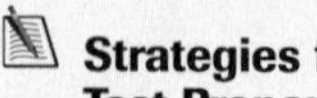 **Strategies for Test Preparation**

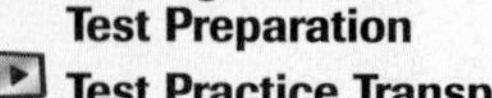 **Test Practice Transparencies TT67**

 **Online Test Practice**

SEE PRIMARY SOURCE B

Africa. Each area marked by a red line is an ethnic group. Many of these groups now reside together in the present-day countries created by Europeans. Many groups living in the same country are historical enemies. For example, German and Belgian colonial governments aggravated historically tense relations between the Hutu and Tutsi ethnic groups in present-day Rwanda and Burundi. In the early 1990s, the ethnic violence between these two groups resulted in a war that led to the deaths of hundreds of thousands of people.

Because of the way these colonial borders were drawn, many African governments had difficulty getting different ethnic groups to cooperate in building stable democracies. Dictators, such as Mobutu Sese Seko of what is now the Democratic Republic of the Congo, became common. In addition, many Africans had no experience living in democratic governments.

Traditional Ethnic Boundaries of Africa

N W E S

Ethnic group

0 400 800 miles
0 400 800 kilometers
Lambert Azimuthal Equal-Area Projection

SKILLBUILDER: Interpreting Maps

1. **PLACE** Which modern-day country probably contains the most traditional ethnic groups?
2. **REGION** Which subregion of Africa was probably the least affected by the postcolonial reconstruction of Africa's boundaries?

CAUSE FOR HOPE Establishing a democratic tradition is a primary goal for many African nations. Only through political stability can a nation bring peace and prosperity to its people. In the past decade, some African nations have been making progress. In 1994, the white minority government in South Africa finally yielded power to the black majority, ending decades of government-sanctioned racial discrimination and social injustice.

SEE PRIMARY SOURCE D

Furthermore, in 2001, Ghana swore in a new president in a peaceful transfer of power, unlike the coups and assassinations that had occurred during previous changes of government. These events are promising in a continent that is hoping for radical progress in the 21st century. Complete the Case Study Project on the following two pages to learn more about how Africa is dealing with the effects of colonialism.

MOVEMENT Voters line up during elections in South Africa.
How will elections help improve the lives of people in Africa?

Interpreting Maps

Traditional Ethnic Boundaries of Africa

Ask students to examine the different boundaries, and ask them what they can infer from these lines about the European division of Africa. *(It bore no relation to ethnic boundaries; the ethnic boundaries have survived the colonial divisions.)*

SKILLBUILDER ANSWERS
1. Nigeria **2.** North Africa

Instruct: Objective 2

Challenges of Independence

- How do Africa's diverse ethnic groups contribute to political instability? *(They often do not cooperate to build stable democracies.)*
- What countries are making progress to establish democracies in spite of the legacy of colonial rule? *(South Africa, Ghana)*

Map Transparencies MT35
- Challenges of Postcolonial Africa

Interpreting Photographs

Voting Line During South African Elections

Have students examine the photograph, and ask them what the long lines may indicate. *(The voters are very determined to participate fully in the democratic process.)*

CAPTION ANSWER Free and fair elections will give people a stake in their country and help reduce political violence.

ACTIVITY OPTION | CRITICAL THINKING

MAKING COMPARISONS

Explaining the Skill Tell students that comparing similar events in different countries can help them gain a better understanding of the issues. Provide students an opportunity to discuss the issues presented on pages 468 and 469.

Applying the Skill Ask students the following questions:

- What history is common to almost all African countries? *(European colonialism)*
- What postcolonial experiences do most African governments have in common? *(difficulty in getting diverse ethnic groups to help build stable democracies)*
- What can other African nations learn from South Africa and Ghana? *(the importance of majority rule and peaceful transfers of power)*

Instruct: Objective 

Case Study Project: News Report

- What is your research goal for the project? *(to assess the current status of your country)*
- What factors should you consider in your research? *(precolonial, colonial, and postcolonial history highlighting the country's people, resources, and colonizers)*
- What should you produce for the project? *(a taped news report on the current status of your country)*

Instruct: Objective 

Using Primary Sources

- (A) **Eyewitness Account** What does the account reveal about the Belgian opinion of Africans in 1899? *(They see Africans as unworthy of humane treatment.)*
- What is missing from the vice consul's account? *(a moral stance, shock at the inhumane approach)*
- (B) **Statement of Principle** What is the writer's approach to past European injustices? *(forget them so that Africa can look to the future)*
- What does the writer recommend to solve African problems? *(African unity)*

CASE STUDY

PROJECT

News Report 

Primary sources A, B, C, D, and E on these two pages are about colonial and postcolonial Africa. Use these resources along with your own research to prepare a news report on postcolonial Africa.

Suggested Steps

1. Select one African country to study.
2. Use online and print resources to research your country's precolonial, colonial, and postcolonial history.
3. Highlight its people, resources, colonizers, and postcolonial activity.
4. Prepare a news report on the current status of your country, covering such topics as conflicts, the health and welfare of its people, the economy, and prospects for the future.
5. Practice your news report in front of a small audience. Ask them for ways to improve it.
6. Use a tape recorder or video recorder to tape your broadcast.

Materials and Supplies

- computer with Internet access
- reference books, newspapers, magazines, and encyclopedias
- tape recorder or video recorder

PRIMARY SOURCE (A)

Eyewitness Account *In his desire for more and more rubber from the Congo, Belgian King Leopold II adopted terrorism as his preferred method of persuasion. In 1899, the British vice consul offered this eyewitness account.*

An example of what is done was told me up the Ubangi [River]. This officer's method was to arrive in canoes at a village, the inhabitants of which invariably bolted on their arrival; the soldiers were then landed, and commenced looting, taking all the chickens, grain, etc. out of the houses; after this, they attacked the natives until able to seize their women; these women were kept as hostages until the chief of the district brought in the required number of kilograms of rubber. The rubber having been brought, the women were sold back to their owners for a couple of goats apiece, and so he continued from village to village until the requisite amount of rubber had been collected.

PRIMARY SOURCE (B)

Statement of Principle *Kwame Nkrumah was the leader of postcolonial Ghana until he was overthrown in 1966. In his book,* I Speak of Freedom, *published in 1961, he wrote about his hopes for postcolonial Africa.*

For centuries, Europeans dominated the African continent. The white man [claimed] the right to rule and to be obeyed by the non-white; his mission, he claimed, was to "civilize" Africa. Under this cloak, the Europeans robbed the continent of vast riches and inflicted unimaginable suffering on the African people.

All this makes a sad story, but now we must be prepared to bury the past with its unpleasant memories and look to the future. All we ask of the former colonial powers is their goodwill and cooperation to remedy past mistakes and injustices and to grant independence to the colonies in Africa.

It is clear that we must find an African solution to our problems, and that this can only be found in African unity. Divided we are weak; united, Africa could become one of the greatest forces for good in the world.

DIFFERENTIATING INSTRUCTION — STUDENTS ACQUIRING ENGLISH/ESL

ANALYZING PRIMARY SOURCES

Objective To analyze primary sources for tone

Class Time 25 minutes

Task Identify a writer's tone by looking at word choice

Directions Students whose first language is not English may be misled by the tone of articles. Pair these students with native speakers and assign each pair a different written primary source from pages 470-471. Explain that identifying tone can help them understand how writers try to influence the reader emotionally. Suggest that each pair read its piece and think of words—such as "angry" or "optimistic"—to describe the writer's attitude. They should list words or phrases that convey that attitude.

PRIMARY SOURCE C—an angry tone
"How ironic, tragic even"
"African leaders, out of desperation"
"must now turn to the former slave-masters and colonizers for a 'bail-out'"

PRIMARY SOURCE C

News Analysis *Ron Daniels, writing in the magazine* Black World Today, *offered this analysis of the Trade and Development Act of 2000. This law recognizes the need to promote economic growth and reduce poverty in Africa, but the law only helps a small number of countries.*

How ironic, tragic even, that as we prepare to enter a new century and millennium, Africa, the motherland, is so afflicted by poverty, underdevelopment, hunger, disease, corruption, and debt that African leaders, out of desperation . . . , are in effect begging to be recolonized. How ironic that the continent whose historical underdevelopment under slavery and colonialism, whose vast human and material resources contributed mightily to the enrichment and development of Europe and America must now turn to the former slave-masters and colonizers for a "bail-out."

PRIMARY SOURCE D

Editorial Commentary *On January 8, 2001, the* New York Times *editorial page included this essay on the changes that have taken place in Ghana. The editorial was titled "An African Success Story."*

In its first two decades of independence, the West African nation of Ghana was an archetypal political disaster, brought low by successive coups and dictatorships, corruption and near total economic collapse. Today, Ghana is a welcome African example of legitimate democracy and successful economic reform. In an unusually peaceful transfer of power, a civilian government that grew out of a military regime has accepted an election defeat and surrendered power to the opposition.

John Kufuor, an Oxford-trained lawyer and businessman, and the leader of Ghana's opposition New Patriotic Party, was sworn in as president yesterday. He defeated John Atta Mills, the incumbent vice president, in an election widely viewed as free and fair. President Jerry Rawlings, the charismatic former flight lieutenant who has dominated Ghana for nearly 20 years, stepped down after reaching a constitutional two-term limit as elected president.

PRIMARY SOURCE E

Political Cartoon *Cartoonist Alan King drew this cartoon in 1996. The cartoon appeared in the* Ottawa Citizen *in Ottawa, Canada. King shows the unending cycle of indecisive attitudes on the part of the international community. The Democratic Republic of the Congo, which was formerly known as Zaire, suffers from these indecisive attitudes.*

PROJECT CheckList

Have I . . .

 fully researched the country I chose to investigate?

 included information about the current status of the country?

✓ taped my broadcast in the form of an actual news report?

Instruct: Objective 4

Using Primary Sources

- Ⓒ **News Analysis** What does the writer identify as the way African leaders want to solve problems? *(recolonization)*
- Does the writer approve of this? Explain. *(No, he calls it ironic and tragic.)*
- Ⓓ **Editorial Commentary** How does the editorial describe Ghana's past? *("a disaster . . . of political coups and dictatorships, corruption, near total economic collapse")*
- Why does the commentator write favorably of Ghana? *(A peaceful transfer of power occurred that favors democratic government.)*
- Ⓔ **Political Cartoon** Who do the people in the cartoon represent? *(the international community)*

Assess & Reteach

GeoFocus Have students complete the section on colonialism in their cause-and-effect charts.

Formal Assessment
- Case Study Quiz, p. 308

Reteaching Activity
Have students discuss and compare historical and recent perspectives on the African situation and list common themes.

In-Depth Resources: Unit 6
- Reteaching Activity, p 38

RUBRIC CASE STUDY PROJECT

NEWS REPORT

For the Case Study Project, students should:

- Summarize a country's current status in terms of conflicts, health and welfare, and the economy.
- Report opinions on the country's future prospects.
- Present this information in the format of a news broadcast.
- Tape the broadcast on either audiotape or videotape.

Grading Rubric Evaluate student performance as Exceptional, Acceptable, or Poor in each of the following categories:

	Exceptional	Acceptable	Poor
Presents comprehensive information			
Shows evidence of research			
Organizes the presentation logically			
Speaks clearly			

CHAPTER 20 ASSESSMENT

Reviewing Places & Terms

A. **1.** "one-commodity" country, p. 462
2. commodity, p. 462
3. diversify, p. 462
4. AIDS, p. 465
5. cholera, p. 465
6. malaria, p. 466
7. tuberculosis, p. 466
8. UNAIDS, p. 466

B. Possible Responses
9. It is known as a "one-commodity" country.
10. The disease is called malaria.
11. The respiratory disease that often accompanies AIDS is called tuberculosis.
12. Countries diversify to create growth.
13. Poor sanitation and polluted water supply can help spread cholera.
14. This product is called a commodity.
15. UNAIDS tracks the world's AIDS problem.

Chapter 20 Assessment

VISUAL SUMMARY
TODAY'S ISSUES IN AFRICA

Economics

Economic Development
- Africa's economy suffered because many European nations exploited Africa for its resources.
- African nations are concentrating on economic cooperation and economic diversification to build their economies.
- Many African nations are improving their educational systems to produce skilled workers.

Environment

Health Care
- Diseases are killing millions in Africa. They include cholera, malaria, tuberculosis, and AIDS.
- AIDS is threatening the continent's population and reducing life expectancies in many countries.
- Many African nations are improving efforts to educate citizens about AIDS.

Government

Effects of Colonialism
- European nations began colonizing Africa once exploration revealed a vast amount of valuable natural resources.
- Colonialism caused much political and ethnic violence because it disrupted many long-standing political and ethnic boundaries.

Reviewing Places & Terms

A. Briefly explain the importance of each of the following.

1. "one-commodity" country
2. commodity
3. diversify
4. AIDS
5. cholera
6. malaria
7. tuberculosis
8. UNAIDS

B. Answer the questions about vocabulary in complete sentences.

9. What is a nation called when it relies on one product for its economic well-being?
10. What is the name of the disease that is carried by a mosquito and was also a leading disease in both 1900 and 2000?
11. What is the name of the respiratory disease that often accompanies AIDS?
12. What is the process whereby countries employ many different ways to help their economies grow?
13. What disease is spread by poor sanitation and a polluted water supply?
14. What is a product called that is bought and sold and has value in a worldwide market?
15. Which organization tracks the world's AIDS problem?

Main Ideas

Economic Development (pp. 461–464)

1. How has Africa's economic status changed during the past 40 years?
2. What is one of the main problems preventing Africa from spending money on economic development?
3. What is a danger with a country's having only one valuable product that it relies on for its economic well-being?

Health Care (pp. 465–467)

4. How are African nations fighting some of the diseases afflicting their continent?
5. What are some of the economic implications of disease in Africa?
6. What do Uganda's and Senegal's AIDS programs have in common?
7. Why might the drop in HIV infection rates be misleading?

Effects of Colonialism (pp. 468–471)

8. What are some of the empires and peoples that controlled areas of Africa at the beginning of the 19th century?
9. What was one of the main reasons that European countries wanted to control Africa?
10. Why did colonization cause so much political and ethnic violence in the 20th century?

Main Ideas

1. Many African countries are worse off economically than they were 40 years ago. Incomes in Africa have decreased, while they have grown in most of the rest of the world.
2. international debt, which is about 227 billion dollars
3. They have little flexibility or few alternatives if that product loses value on the world market.
4. spraying programs, education programs, international cooperation, and improved domestic health care
5. AIDS and other diseases are killing off some of Africa's workers, thereby making economic growth difficult.
6. education programs about AIDS
7. It could mean that almost as many people are dying of AIDS as are being infected by HIV.
8. Zulu, Ashanti, Hausa
9. Africa's wealth of natural resources would benefit Europe's industries.
10. Europeans did not understand the ethnic diversity in Africa, so when they established colonies, they grouped together enemies and split apart allies. This caused long-term disruption on the continent when colonies later became nations.

Critical Thinking

1. Using Your Notes

Use your completed chart to answer these questions.

	Causes	Effects
Issue 1: Economic Development		
Issue 2: Health Care		

a. What is the primary foundation for most African nations' economies?

b. How might disease and economic development be related?

2. Geographic Themes

a. **MOVEMENT** How are diseases such as malaria and cholera spread?

b. **REGION** In what way is the modern map of Africa not a true reflection of the continent's people?

3. Identifying Themes

How would you relate one of the five themes of geography to the primary way in which African nations support their economies?

4. Making Inferences

How do you think Africa's economic health affects the spread of diseases such as cholera and AIDS?

5. Drawing Conclusions

How important do you think regional cooperation is in building Africa's economy? Why?

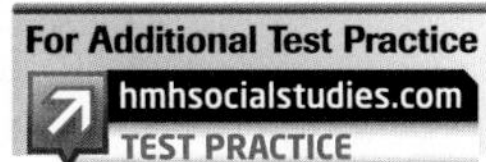

Geographic Skills: Interpreting Maps

Dates of African Independence

Use the map at right to answer the following questions.

1. **PLACE** Which two countries remained free of European control?
2. **PLACE** Which country most recently gained its independence?
3. **REGION** Which decade saw the most countries gain independence?

Morocco 1956; Tunisia 1956; Algeria 1962; Libya 1951; Egypt 1922; Western Sahara* 1976; Cape Verde 1975; Mauritania 1960; Mali 1960; Niger 1960; Chad 1960; Sudan 1956; Eritrea 1993; Djibouti 1977; Ethiopia; Senegal 1960; Gambia 1965; Guinea-Bissau 1974; Guinea 1958; Burkina Faso 1960; Benin 1960; Togo 1960; Nigeria 1960; Sierra Leone 1961; Liberia; Côte d'Ivoire 1960; Ghana 1957; Equatorial Guinea 1968; Cameroon 1960; Central African Republic 1960; Somalia 1960; São Tomé & Príncipe 1975; Gabon 1960; Rep. of Congo 1960; Dem. Rep. Congo 1960; Uganda 1962; Kenya 1963; Rwanda 1962; Burundi 1962; Tanzania 1961; Seychelles 1976; Comoros 1975; Angola 1975; Zambia 1964; Malawi 1964; Mozambique 1975; Zimbabwe 1980; Namibia 1990; Botswana 1966; Madagascar 1960; Mauritius 1968; South Africa 1910; Swaziland 1968; Lesotho 1966

Independent countries

Countries that gained independence:
- before 1954
- 1955–1964
- after 1964

1960 Date of independence

*Now part of Morocco

GeoActivity

Choose one country in West Africa that was once controlled by France. Then using the library, encyclopedias, or other reference books, research how France's influence is still felt today in that country's economy, government, schools, and language.

hmhsocialstudies.com

MULTIMEDIA ACTIVITY

Use the links at **hmhsocialstudies.com** to do research on the postcolonial economy of one African country. Look for attempts to diversify the economy, education programs, growth in per capita income, and amount of manufacturing.

Writing About Geography Write a report of your findings. Include charts, pie graphs, and other visuals to help present the information. List the Web sites that you used as sources.

21st Century

AFRICA

CHAPTER 20 ASSESSMENT

Critical Thinking

1. a. the exportation of raw materials to industrialized countries
b. Disease is killing many African workers, thereby reducing economic growth.

2. a. Mosquitoes and unsanitary conditions spread germs, which move through the air and water.
b. The modern map of Africa was essentially set up by European colonial powers and does not respect the cultural or ethnic diversity of the continent. The map is a set of arbitrary boundaries. It would look different if the continent had never been colonized.

3. African nations are essentially supported by the harvesting, mining and exportation of natural resources, which relates to the themes of movement and human-environment interaction.

4. Africa's poor economic health means that there is little money to build proper health and sanitation facilities.

5. Regional cooperation is extremely important. Countries with small economies need to pool their resources to build better roads, better schools, and adequate health facilities.

GeoActivity

Integrated Assessment
- Rubric for research, 2.5

Formal Assessment
- Chapter Test, Forms A, B, and C, pp. 309–323

Geographic Skills

1. Ethiopia; Liberia
2. Eritrea
3. the 1960s

MULTIMEDIA ACTIVITY

For the report on a post-independence economy, students should:
- Organize the report logically, with introductory and summary paragraphs.
- Cover diversification, education, growth, and manufacturing.
- Use charts, graphs, photographs, and other visuals to support the major points.
- Include references to Web sites used as sources.

Grading Rubric Evaluate student performance as Exceptional, Acceptable, or Poor in each of the following categories.

	Exceptional	Acceptable	Poor
Has separate paragraphs for the introduction, each topic, and conclusion			
Supports main points with visuals			
Uses correct grammar, spelling, and punctuation			
Lists sources			

Physical Geography of Southwest Asia

OVERVIEW	INSTRUCTIONAL RESOURCES	
CHAPTER 21 ESSENTIAL QUESTION How do the physical features and resources of Southwest Asia affect its people and their influence?  **Focus on the Essential Question Podcast**	 **In-Depth Resources: Unit 7** • Unit Atlas Activities, p. 1 • Building Vocabulary, p. 9 • Exploring Today's Issues, pp. 28–31  **Outline Maps with Activities** • Southwest Asia: Physical, pp. 65–66 • Southwest Asia: Political, pp. 67–68  **Block Schedule Strategies**  **Chapter Summaries** (English/Spanish)	 **Interactive Online Edition** TOS **ExamView® Assessment Suite** (English/Spanish) TOS **CalendarPlanner**  **Power Presentations with Media Gallery**  **Critical Thinking Transparencies** • CT21  hmhsocialstudies.com INTERACTIVE
SECTION 1 **LANDFORMS AND RESOURCES** **MAIN IDEAS** • Southwest Asia forms a land bridge connecting Asia, Africa, and Europe. • Southwest Asian landforms had a major impact on movement in the region. • The most valuable resources in Southwest Asia are oil and water.	 **In-Depth Resources: Unit 7** • Guided Reading, p. 3 • Building Vocabulary, p. 9 • Reteaching Activities, p. 10  **Guided Reading Workbook,** Section 1	
SECTION 2 **CLIMATE AND VEGETATION** **MAIN IDEAS** • Most of Southwest Asia has a very arid climate. • Vast deserts are spread across the region, including the famous Rub al-Khali, also known as the Empty Quarter. • Irrigation is critical to growing crops in this very dry region.	**In-Depth Resources: Unit 7** • Guided Reading, p. 4 • Skillbuilder Practice, p. 8 • Building Vocabulary, p. 9 • Map and Graph Skills, pp. 6–7 • Reteaching Activities, p. 11  **Guided Reading Workbook,** Section 2	 **Critical Thinking Transparencies** • CT53 Deserts in Southwest Asia
SECTION 3 **HUMAN-ENVIRONMENT INTERACTION** **MAIN IDEAS** • Water is critical to regional physical survival and economic development. • The discovery of oil increased the global economic importance of Southwest Asia. • Spills are always a possibility when oil is transported from one location to another.	 **In-Depth Resources: Unit 7** • Guided Reading, p. 5 • Building Vocabulary, p. 9 • Reteaching Activities, p. 12 • Geoworkshops, pp. 35–36  **Guided Reading Workbook,** Section 3	 **Map Transparencies** • MT38 Oil Pipelines in Southwest Asia

ASSESSMENT

SE **Chapter Assessment,** pp. 500–501

Formal Assessment
- Chapter Tests, Forms A, B, and C, pp. 327–338

TOS **ExamView® Assessment Suite**

 **Strategies for Test Preparation**

SE **Section Assessment,** p. 490

 **Formal Assessment**
- Section Quiz, p. 324

Integrated Assessment
- Rubric for a map, 2.1

 **Test Practice Transparencies** TT68

SE **Section Assessment,** p. 493

 **Formal Assessment**
- Section Quiz, p. 325

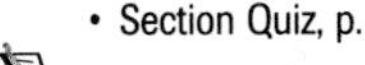 **Integrated Assessment**

- Rubric for a database, 2.6

 **Test Practice Transparencies** TT69

SE **Section Assessment,** p. 499

 **Formal Assessment**
- Section Quiz, p. 326

 **Integrated Assessment**

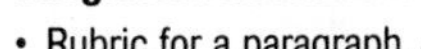
- Rubric for a paragraph, 4.2

 **Test Practice Transparencies** TT70

CHART KEY:

SE Student Edition	 Block Scheduling	 DVD/CD-ROM
TE Teacher's Edition	 TOS Teacher One Stop	 MP3 Audio
Printable Resource	 Presentation Resource	HISTORY™

Program Resources available on TOS and @ hmhsocialstudies.com

SUPPORTING RESOURCES

- Multimedia Classroom Global History Series
- Global History Teacher's Guide

Social Studies Trade Library Collection
- World Regions Trade Collection

For more information or to purchase these resources, go to 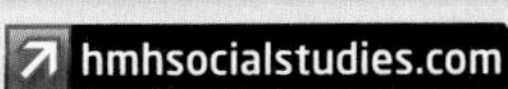

DIFFERENTIATED INSTRUCTION

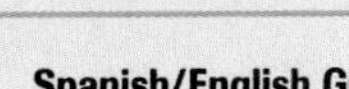

English Learners	Struggling Readers	Gifted and Talented Students
 **Spanish/English Guided Reading Workbook**  **Access for Students Acquiring English/ESL** Spanish Translations, pp. 111–116  **Chapter Summaries** (English/Spanish) TE **TE Activity** Pronouncing Difficult Words, p. 488	**Chapter Summaries** (English/Spanish) TE **TE Activity** Creating Outlines, p. 497 Writing a Short News Feature, p. 481	TE **TE Activity** Learning About Oil Processing, p. 498

ENRICHMENT ACTIVITIES

The following activities are especially suitable for classes following block schedules.

SE **Student Edition,** pp. 486–501
- Reading a Vegetation Map, p. 494

hmhsocialstudies.com INTERACTIVE
- Processing Petroleum, p. 498

BLOCK SCHEDULE LESSON PLAN OPTIONS: 90-MINUTE PERIOD

DAY 1

UNIT PREVIEW, pp. 474–477
Class Time 20 minutes

- **Discussion** Discuss the Unit Introduction using the discussion prompts on TE pages 474–475.
  Class Time 10 minutes

UNIT ATLAS, pp. 478–485
Class Time 30 minutes

- **Small Groups** Divide the class into four small groups and have each group answer Making Comparisons questions for one section of the Unit Atlas: Physical Geography, Human Geography, Regional Patterns, and Regional Data File.

SECTION 1, pp. 487–490
Class Time 40 minutes

- **Outline Maps** In preparation for discussing Section 1, have students complete the physical map for Southwest Asia in *Outline Maps with Activities.* Ask students to label countries and physical features, and have them color the maps, using different colors for different landforms.

DAY 2

SECTION 1, pp. 487–490
Class Time 45 minutes

- **Game Show** As an interesting way to review the section, have groups of students work together to create a game show whose questions are drawn from the content of Section 1. Allow students to use a popular television game show as a model.

SECTION 2, pp. 491–494
Class Time 45 minutes

- **Comparing Southwest Asia and the United States** Have students use the Internet or a national newspaper to compare current temperatures in U.S. cities and cities in Southwest Asia. Ask students to create climographs for two cities in the U.S. and two cities in Southwest Asia.

DAY 3

SECTION 3, pp. 495–499
Class Time 40 minutes

- **Brainstorming** Lead the entire class in a brainstorming review of Section 3. Write the two main subsection headings ("Providing Precious Water" and "Oil From the Sand") on the board. Then call on individual students to recall as many ideas as possible from each subsection. Write the answers on the board. When the lists are complete, work with students to rank the ideas in order of importance.

CHAPTER 21 REVIEW AND ASSESSMENT, pp. 500-501
Class Time 50 minutes

- **Review** Have students prepare a summary of the chapter, using the Places & Terms listed on the first page of each section.
  Class Time 20 minutes
- **Assessment** Have students complete the Chapter 21 Assessment.
  Class Time 30 minutes

TEACHER-TESTED ACTIVITY: *Crossword Puzzle for Southwest Asia*

Class Time One class period

Task Create a crossword puzzle using key terms in Chapter 21

Supplies
- Sheets of graph paper with large, quarter-inch, squares
- Pencils and erasers
- Notebook paper
- Textbook

Purpose Designing a crossword puzzle that utilizes the new terms in Chapter 21 may be an effective and enjoyable way for students to familiarize themselves with the chapter's vocabulary.

Activity Divide students into small groups and ask each group to create a list of at least 20 terms from Chapter 21. Have students work together to design a crossword puzzle that uses these words for answers. Explain to students that words can be placed on the graph paper horizontally or vertically but not diagonally. After students have placed as many words as possible in their puzzle, have them write clues for each word. Remind them to number the clues and answers with corresponding numbers.

Help students with difficult design issues. For example, students may not know how to handle two-word vocabulary items, such as *Jordan River.* You might suggest crafting clues such as "The _______ River is a dividing line between Israel and Jordan." After they have completed their puzzles, have students exchange and try to solve each other puzzles.

Jim Curtis
Geography Teacher, Antioch High School, Antioch, Illinois

TECHNOLOGY IN THE CLASSROOM

Spreadsheet programs can be invaluable for analyzing and comparing data. Most spreadsheet programs allow the user to input numbers into rows and columns and to then create charts and graphs based on those numbers. These charts and graphs present the data in a visual manner and make it much easier to compare the numbers.

Objective Students will create spreadsheet charts to compare water availability with population statistics.

Task Have students hypothesize which Southwest Asian countries are facing the greatest water-related problems and use a spreadsheet program to create charts comparing the statistics.

Class Time 2 class periods

1. After students read Chapter 21, have them discuss the reasons why water is such an important resource in Southwest Asia. Then ask them to explain the relationship between population and water availability. What might happen to water availability in a country with a high population growth rate? What might eventually happen to the population growth rate in a country that is experiencing severe water shortages?
2. Ask students to hypothesize which Southwest Asian countries might face the greatest water scarcity problems in the future. Have them list the top four countries with a brief explanation as to why they have chosen these four.
3. Have students enter the names of the sixteen Southwest Asian countries in the left-hand column of a spreadsheet. They should leave two blank rows at the top for a title and a header.
4. In the header row, have students label three columns with these headings: "total annual renewable fresh water," "population," and "population growth rate."
5. Have students go to the Web site at **hmhsocialstudies.com** to see a list of water availability and population statistics for countries around the world. Have them look up the "Total annual renewable fresh water available by country" figures for each Southwest Asian country and enter these numbers into the appropriate cells in the spreadsheet.
6. Have students look at the Regional Data File on pages 484–485 and record in the spreadsheet the population and birthrate for each country.
7. Ask students to use the spreadsheet program's charting or graphing feature to create bar or column charts that compare countries based on each of the three measurements.
8. Ask students to look carefully at their three charts and to explain which countries appear to be at the greatest risk for severe water shortages. Have them use a word processor to write essays that describe what the charts reveal and compare that information to their original hypotheses. They should conclude by providing some solutions that these countries might try, based on what they have read in the chapter.

Previewing the Unit

The first pages of this unit provide an overview of Southwest Asia. This region is birthplace to several of the world's major religions. It is a region blanketed by vast deserts and blessed with a tremendous wealth of resources.

Discussion Prompts

Exploring Prior Knowledge Ask students the following questions about Southwest Asia to determine their prior knowledge of the region:

- What religions are practiced in Southwest Asian countries? *(Judaism, Christianity, and Islam)*
- What bodies of water are in Southwest Asia? *(Red Sea, Persian Gulf, Mediterranean Sea, Dead Sea, etc.)*

Interpreting Maps Ask students to refer to the satellite image of Southwest Asia to answer the following questions:

- What continents do you recognize, from left to right? *(Africa, Europe, and Asia)*
- Do you recognize any countries? *(Answers will vary.)*

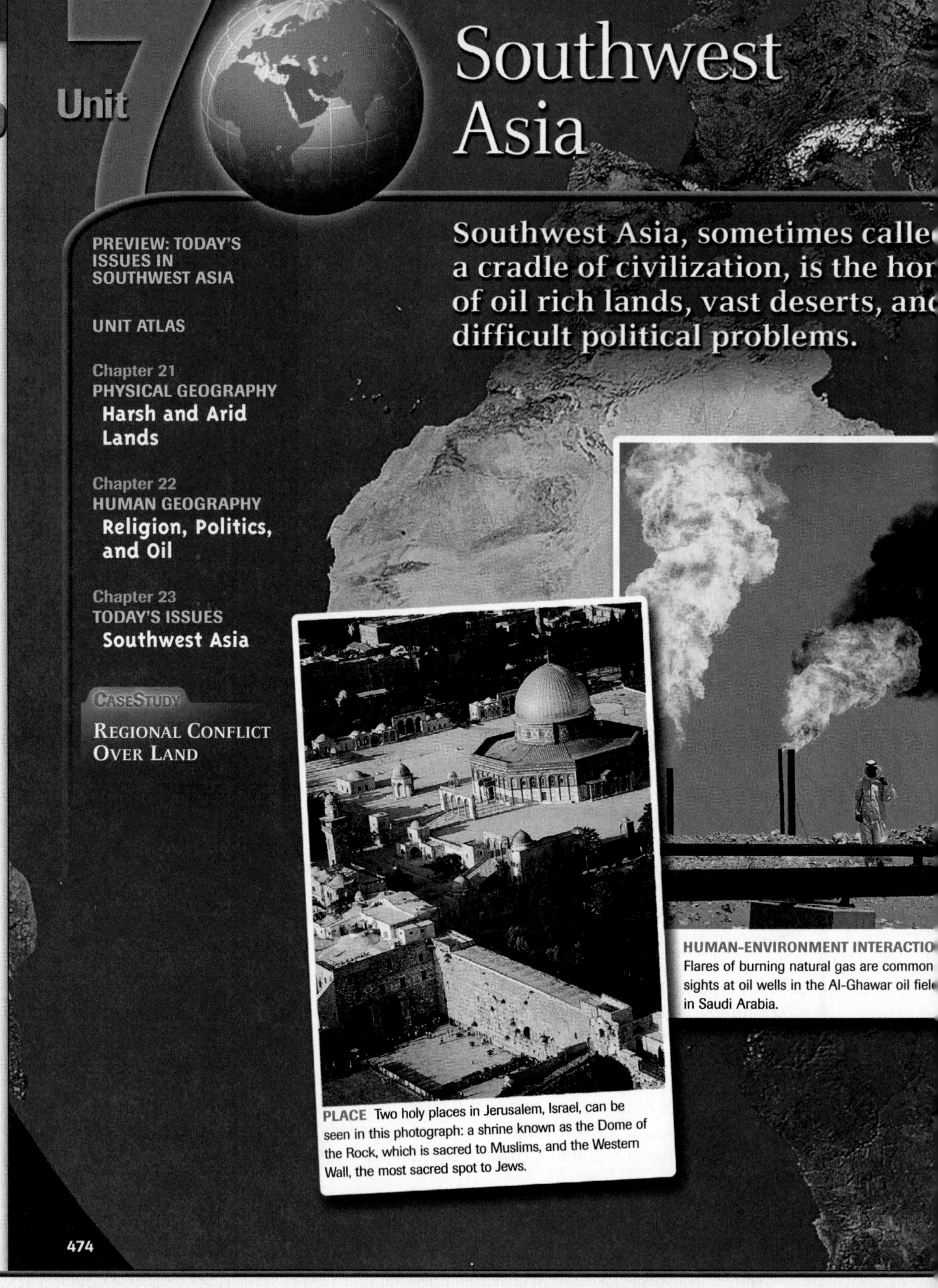

Unit 7
Southwest Asia
Southwest Asia, sometimes calle
a cradle of civilization, is the hor
of oil rich lands, vast deserts, anc
difficult political problems.
PREVIEW: TODAY'S ISSUES IN SOUTHWEST ASIA
UNIT ATLAS
Chapter 21
PHYSICAL GEOGRAPHY
Harsh and Arid Lands
Chapter 22
HUMAN GEOGRAPHY
Religion, Politics, and Oil
Chapter 23
TODAY'S ISSUES
Southwest Asia
CASESTUDY
REGIONAL CONFLICT OVER LAND
474

PLACE Two holy places in Jerusalem, Israel, can be seen in this photograph: a shrine known as the Dome of the Rock, which is sacred to Muslims, and the Western Wall, the most sacred spot to Jews.

HUMAN-ENVIRONMENT INTERACTIO Flares of burning natural gas are common sights at oil wells in the Al-Ghawar oil fiel in Saudi Arabia.

UNIT 7 ADDITIONAL RESOURCES

BOOKS FOR THE STUDENT

National Geographic Atlas of the Middle East. National Geographic, 2008. Photos, flags, graphs, and commentary, along with updated maps of countries and some cities.

BOOKS FOR THE STUDENT

Bienkowski, Piotr, ed. and Alan Millard, ed. ***Dictionary of the Ancient Near East.*** Philadelphia: Univ. of Penn. Press, 2000. A useful reference covering Mesopotamia, Iran, Anatolia, the Caucasus, Levant, and Arabia.

Haviv, Itai. ***Trekking and Canyoning in the Jordanian Dead Sea Rift.*** Desert Breeze Press, 2000. Maps, descriptions, and lore of some of the region's hidden treasures.

INTERNET

For more on the geography of Southwest Asia, visit . . .

hmhsocialstudies.com

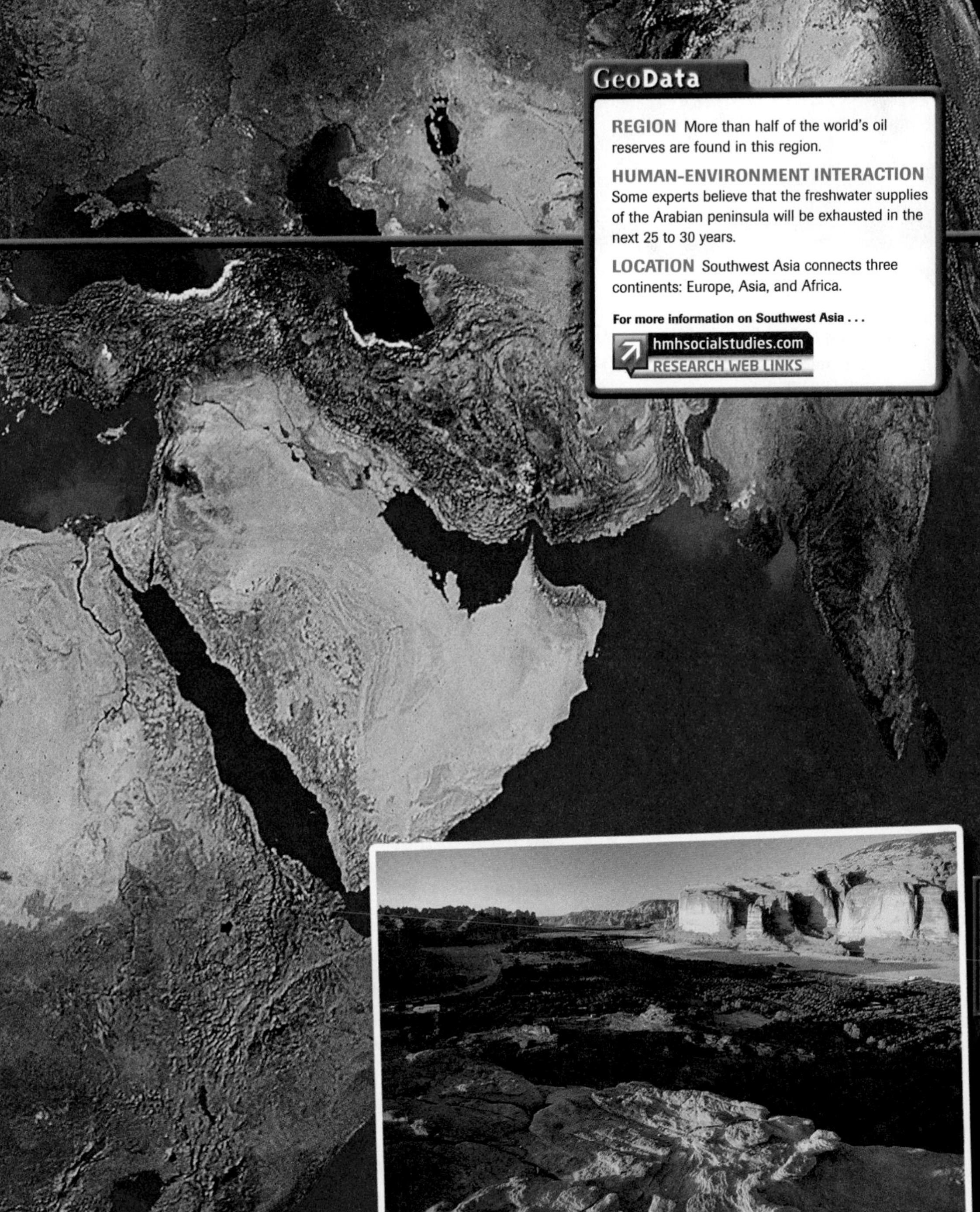

GeoData

REGION More than half of the world's oil reserves are found in this region.

HUMAN-ENVIRONMENT INTERACTION Some experts believe that the freshwater supplies of the Arabian peninsula will be exhausted in the next 25 to 30 years.

LOCATION Southwest Asia connects three continents: Europe, Asia, and Africa.

For more information on Southwest Asia . . .

hmhsocialstudies.com RESEARCH WEB LINKS

MOVEMENT Crossing the desert areas of Southwest Asia by land would be almost impossible without oases to provide water and a resting place. This oasis was on the caravan route from Yemen to Palestine.

Interpreting Photographs

Dome of the Rock and the Western Wall

Ask students what they can infer from the picture and caption about people from this region. *(Sacred places are important; both Jews and Muslims live in the region.)*

Saudi Arabian Oil Field

Ask students what this picture might have to do with their own lives. *(The fuel used in their families' automobiles may come from Saudi Arabia.)*

Oasis

Tell students that some oases are large enough for crops and that some are large enough to support cities. Ask students if they know where Palestine is. *(It is a historical region in Southwest Asia roughly coextensive with modern Israel and the West Bank.)*

ACTIVITY OPTION | COOPERATIVE LEARNING

CREATING A TRAVEL POSTER

Objective To allow students to explore aspects of Southwest Asia

Class Time 30 minutes

Task Create a travel poster about Southwest Asia

Directions Have students gather in small groups. Assign each group a country in Southwest Asia and have students search the Internet and magazines for pictures that represent their country. Groups are to assign each member a task, such as gathering supplies, designing the poster, searching for photos, or writing captions for the pictures.

Previewing Today's Issues

These pages provide a preview of issues faced by the nations of Southwest Asia. These topics will be fully explored in Chapter 23 (pages 524–537). Use the discussion prompts that follow to determine students' prior knowledge and encourage them to make comparisons to local issues.

In-Depth Resources: Unit 7
- Exploring Today's Issues, pp. 28–31

POPULATION RELOCATION
Ethnic conflict in Southwest Asia has caused the displacement of many of the region's people, including Kurds, Jews, and Palestinians.

Discussion Prompts

- Ask students to identify the main events that cause populations to relocate. *(Answers may include war, natural disaster, economic distress, environmental degradation, political or religious persecution.)*
- Do you think the United States should be involved in conflicts in this region? Why or why not? *(Answers will vary, but students should consider the issue from a number of different perspectives.)*

Unit PREVIEW 7

Today's Issues in Southwest Asia

Today, Southwest Asia faces the issues previewed here. As you read Chapters 21 and 22, you will learn helpful background information. You will study the issues themselves in Chapter 23.

In a small group, answer the questions below. Then participate in a class discussion of your answers.

Exploring the Issues

1. POPULATION RELOCATION Think about why a group of people may leave a place they call home. What problems might relocation cause for the group? Then make a list of the reasons people relocate and the problems that are caused by moving.
2. ECONOMIC DEVELOPMENT Make a list of major rivers found in the region and a list of major rivers found in the United States. How do the lists compare? What does this suggest about scarce resources in the region?
3. REGIONAL CONFLICT Study the cartoon on page 477. Who are the figures in the cartoon?

For more on these issues in Southwest Asia . . .

POPULATION RELOCATION

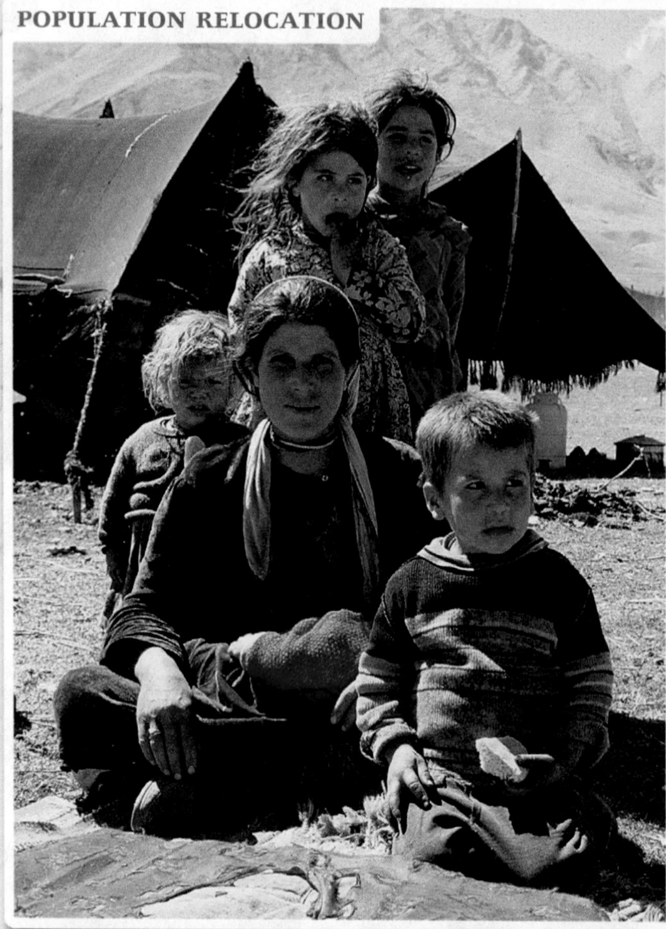

What kind of population movement is taking place in Southwest Asia?

This nomadic Kurdish family rests in the hills of eastern Turkey. The Kurds claim a homeland that crosses the boundaries of five countries: Turkey, Iraq, Iran, Syria, and Armenia.

EXPLORING THE ISSUES ANSWERS

1. POPULATION RELOCATION Students might say that people are driven from their homelands by such forces as political persecution or ecological dangers. Or they may suggest that people move for the greater economic or political opportunities abroad. Unfamiliar languages and discrimination might be among the problems faced after relocation.
2. ECONOMIC DEVELOPMENT Students should note that water resources are relatively limited in Southwest Asia.
3. REGIONAL CONFLICT The figures represent people in the Arab and Israeli communities who claim the city of Jerusalem.

ECONOMIC DEVELOPMENT

How can oil wealth help develop the region's economies?

Pollution from burning oil field wastes is one of the costs that oil-rich nations must deal with. Yet wealth from oil fields, like this one in southern Iraq, may be used to develop economic activities that do not depend on oil.

CASESTUDY

Who should control Jerusalem?

In this cartoon, the dove symbolizes peace between Arabs and Israelis in Southwest Asia. Jerusalem plays a vital role in the peace process.

REGIONAL CONFLICT

SW ASIA

ECONOMIC DEVELOPMENT

Saudi Arabia is the world's largest producer of oil. Oil revenues make up 90 to 95 percent of the export earnings and around 35 to 40 percent of the country's GDP (gross domestic product). In 2007, Saudi Arabia supplied the United States with about 1.4 million barrels of crude oil per day.

Discussion Prompts

- Do you think the United States should protect Saudi Arabia in time of war to protect U.S. oil interests? *(Answers will vary.)*
- If more resources were devoted to alternative energy sources, such as wind or solar power, what might happen to Saudi Arabia's economy? *(It would probably decline.)*

CASESTUDY

REGIONAL CONFLICT

Many different religious groups consider Jerusalem a holy city. For Jews, it is the site of King Solomon's Temple and the capital of their homeland. For Christians, Jerusalem is a sacred place where Jesus preached and was crucified. Jerusalem is where Muslims believe their prophet Muhammad rose to heaven.

Discussion Prompts

- What do you see as the major conflicts in Jerusalem? *(Answers will vary, but the complexity of the conflict should be emphasized.)*
- What initiatives would you make to bring peace to the region? *(Answers will vary.)*

ACTIVITY OPTION EXPLORING LOCAL GEOGRAPHY

EXAMINING THE LOCAL ECONOMY

Objective To familiarize students with their local economy

Class Time 30 minutes

Task Create a chart or graph that shows key elements of the local economy

Directions Divide students into research teams and have them use the Internet or library resources to carry out research on their state or local economy. Using their research, each team should create a chart or graph that shows major economic sectors of their state or locality. For example, students may wish to find data for the "gross state product." They could use this data to create a pie graph that shows how much different economic sectors—such as mining, agriculture, manufacturing, etc.—contribute to the state's economy. After students have completed their charts and graphs, lead a discussion about the diversity, or lack of diversity, in the local economy. Compare these results with those of Saudi Arabia or another nation in Southwest Asia.

ATLAS OBJECTIVES

1. Compare data on the physical geography of Southwest Asia.
2. Examine key physical features of Southwest Asia.
3. Identify Southwest Asian countries and borders in 1948 and 1967.
4. Identify current political features of Southwest Asia.
5. Learn about ethnic groups and ethnic regions in Southwest Asia.
6. Analyze religious groups and economic activity in Southwest Asia.

Focus & Motivate

Ask students what they already know about the physical features of Southwest Asia. Ask students if they have heard or read about this region. *(Some students may mention stories from the Bible or the Koran.)*

Instruct: Objective 

Comparing Data

- ***Landmass*** How much smaller is Southwest Asia than the United States? *(about 50,000 square miles)*
- ***Population*** How do the populations of Southwest Asia and the United States compare? *(They are nearly the same; there are about 2,251,000 fewer people in Southwest Asia.)*
- ***Deserts*** How much larger than the An-Nafud is the Rub al-Khali? *(The Rub al-Khali is 10 times larger.)*

 **In-Depth Resources: Unit 7**
- Unit Atlas Activities: p. 1

 **Outline Maps with Activities**
- Southwest Asia: Physical, pp. 65–66

 **Map Transparencies MT36**
- Southwest Asia: Physical

Unit ATLAS

Patterns of Physical Geography

Use the Unit Atlas to add to your knowledge of Southwest Asia. As you look at the maps and charts, notice geographic patterns and specific details about the region. For example, the chart gives details about the mountains and deserts of Southwest Asia.

After studying the graphics and physical map on these two pages, jot down answers to the following questions in your notebook.

Making Comparisons

1. Which of Southwest Asia's deserts is slightly larger than the Mojave Desert of the United States?
2. How do the tallest mountains of Southwest Asia compare to the tallest U.S. mountain?
3. Which mountain chains cut off Turkey and Iran from the rest of the region? How might isolation affect the way a country develops economically?

Comparing Data

Landmass

Southwest Asia 2,673,262 sq mi

Continental United States 3,165,630 sq mi

Population

Southwest Asia 304,961,000

United States 307,212,000

0 50 100 150 200 250 300 350

Population (in millions)

Deserts

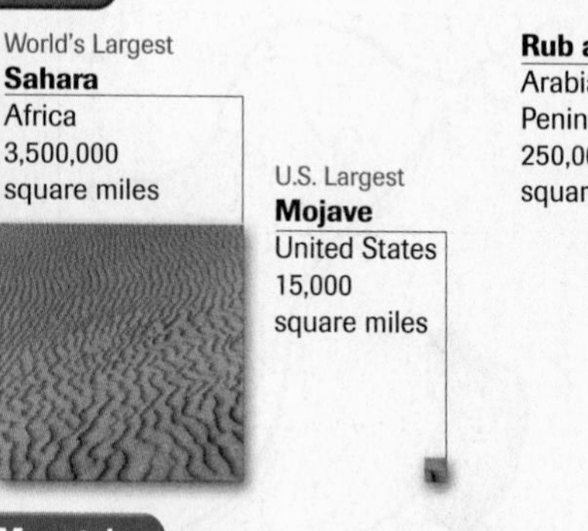

World's Largest **Sahara** Africa 3,500,000 square miles

U.S. Largest **Mojave** United States 15,000 square miles

Rub al-Khali Arabian Peninsula 250,000 square miles

An-Nafud Arabian Peninsula 25,000 square miles

Negev Israel 4,700 square miles

Mountains

World's Tallest **Mt. Everest** Nepal-Tibet 29,035 feet

U.S. Tallest **Mt. McKinley** United States 20,320 feet

Damavand Iran 18,606 feet

Mt. Ararat Turkey 16,945 feet

Mt. Hermon Lebanon-Syria 9,232 feet

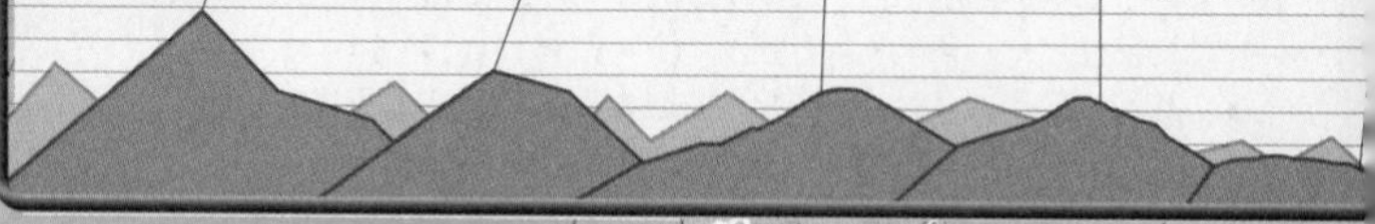

MAKING COMPARISONS ANSWERS

1. An-Nafud
2. They are not as tall.
3. Taurus and Zagros; it may make trade and communication more difficult.

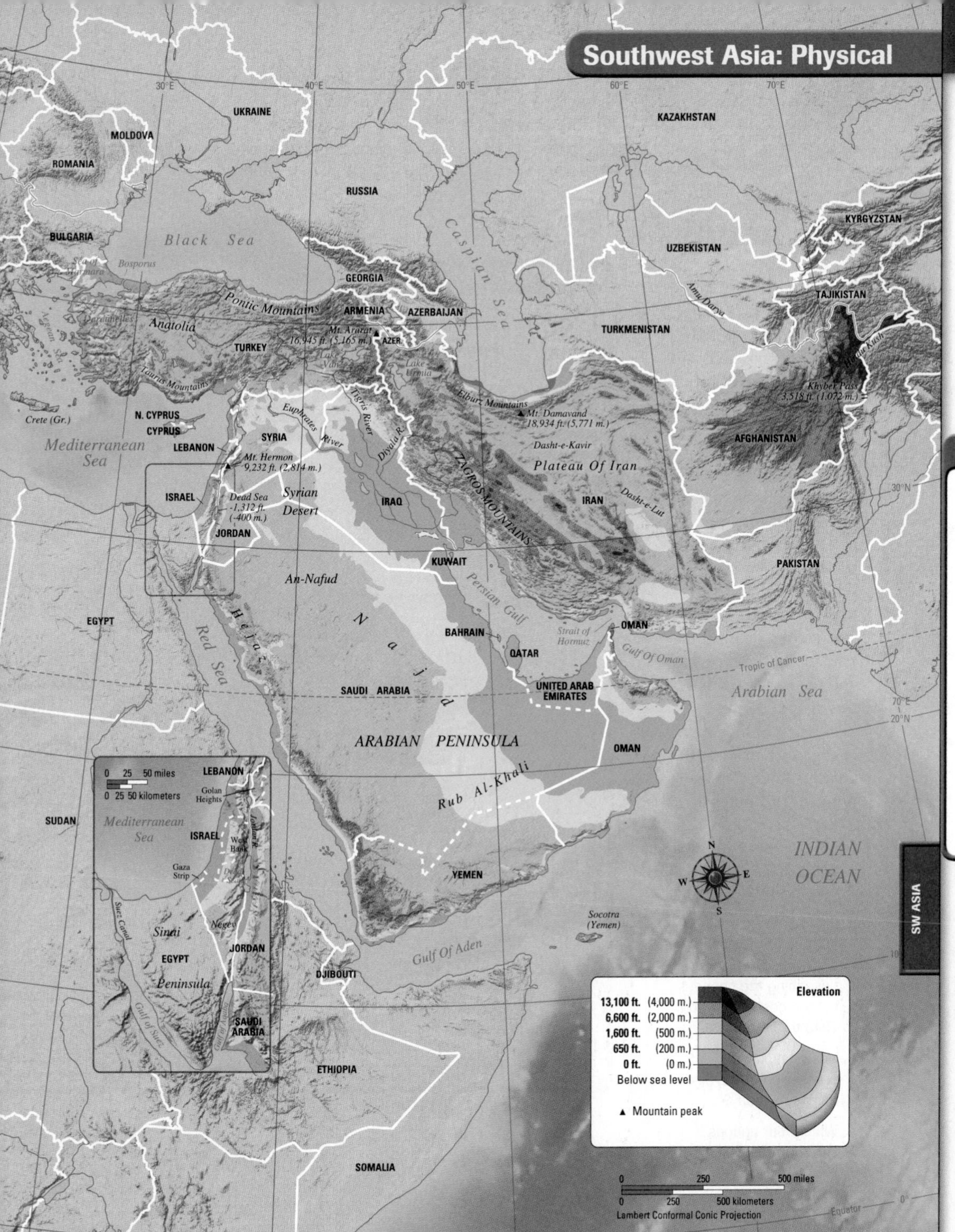

Instruct: Objective 2

Southwest Asia: Physical

- What sea is north of Turkey? *(Black Sea)*
- What gulfs separate Saudi Arabia and Iran? *(Persian Gulf and Gulf of Oman)*
- What sea lies between Jordan and Israel? *(Dead Sea)*

More About

The "Middle East"

Students may have heard the term "Middle East" used to describe much of Southwest Asia. Tell students that "Middle East" shows a Western point of view. Explain that Americans and Europeans started using the term to distinguish the region from the "Near East," which included parts of Eastern Europe, North Africa, and the "Far East," which included China, Japan, and Indochina. Point out that all these regions are "east" only in that they are regions in the Eastern Hemisphere.

ACTIVITY OPTION | COOPERATIVE LEARNING

CONSTRUCTING A CHART

Objective To examine the physical map of Southwest Asia

Task Create a chart that lists major physical features of Southwest Asia

Class Time 20 minutes

Directions Divide students into groups of four. Within each group, assign one of the following categories to each student: 1) mountains and plateaus; 2) bodies of water; 3) deserts; and 4) rivers. Have students examine the map and make a list of the physical features for which they are responsible. Then have them work together to create a chart with four columns, one for each of the categories. Ask them to list features under the appropriate columns and to illustrate their charts with a small selection of images of the region's physical features.

Instruct: Objective 3

Territorial Changes between 1947 and 1967

- When was a Jewish state proposed by the United Nations? *(1947)*
- Where is the Gaza Strip located? *(On the Mediterranean Coast just northeast of the Sinai Peninsula)*
- What is the origin of the name "West Bank"? *(The West Bank is located on the west bank of the Jordan River.)*

More About

A Jewish State

In 1917, senior officials in the British government issued the Balfour Declaration, which supported a proposal for the founding of a Jewish state in the ancient Jewish homeland, in the land of Israel.

Unit ATLAS

Patterns of Human Geography

Following World War II (1939–1945) and the Holocaust, the United Nations proposed a plan to partition the Palestine Mandate into two nations, one Jewish and the other Arab. After Arabs rejected the plan, Jews created the State of Israel. Since that time, most Arab countries and groups have refused to recognize Israel's right to exist.

Study the political map of Southwest Asia and the Israel maps at the right to see how possession of the lands changed. Then write the answers to these questions in your notebook.

Making Comparisons

1. Which areas did Israel gain in 1967?
2. Study both maps of Israel and the political map and write a sentence describing the changes in land possession from 1948 to the present.
3. What nation is in possession of the Sinai Peninsula today?
4. Which four nations surround the Golan Heights? Who controls the area?

Israel, 1948 and 1967

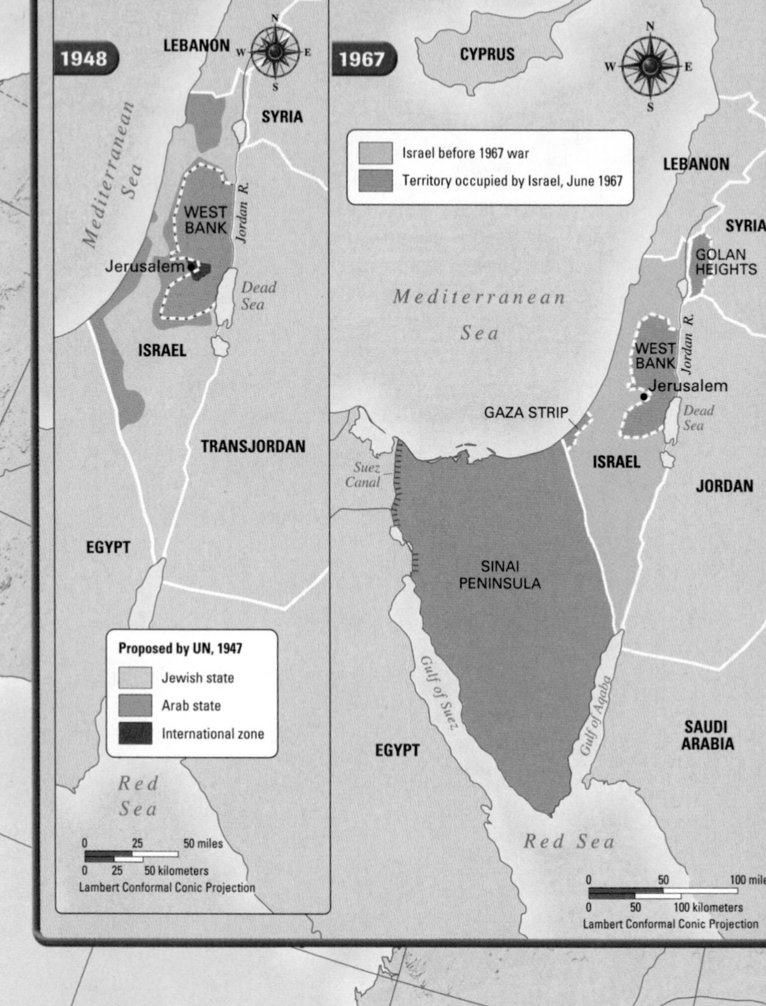

MAKING COMPARISONS ANSWERS

1. West Bank, Golan Heights, Gaza Strip, Sinai Peninsula
2. It was very small in 1948, grew larger by 1967. At present, it is smaller than it was in 1967, but larger than 1948.
3. Egypt
4. Israel, Lebanon, Syria, and Jordan; Israel

Southwest Asia: Political

Instruct: Objective 4

Southwest Asia: Political

- What is the largest country in Southwest Asia? *(Saudi Arabia)*
- Why is control of the Suez Canal important to Egypt? *(Those in control of the canal control lucrative shipping lanes in and out of the Mediterranean Sea.)*
- How do you think Israel has survived among powerful Arab states that are hostile to it? *(Answers will vary, but some students might be aware of Israel's diverse economy, strong military, and support from the United States.)*

Outline Maps with Activities
- Southwest Asia: Political, pp. 67–68

Map Transparencies MT37
- Southwest Asia: Political

DIFFERENTIATING INSTRUCTION LESS PROFICIENT READERS

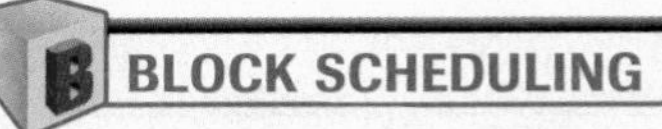

BLOCK SCHEDULING

WRITING A SHORT NEWS FEATURE

Objective To consider the impact of political conflict on individuals

Task Write a news feature

Class Time 60 minutes

Directions Divide students into research teams, being careful to pair less proficient readers with more advanced readers. Have teams use the Internet or the library to carry out research on the daily lives of Jews and Palestinians in Southwest Asia. Encourage teams to cooperate in helping members who might have difficulties with reading. Each team should prepare a short news feature that describes how the conflict surrounding Israel impacts the daily lives of a Palestinian and a Jew. Call on several students to read their features to the class.

Instruct: Objective 5

Ethnic Groups of Southwest Asia/ Ethnic Regions of Southwest Asia

- What is the major ethnic group of Southwest Asia? *(Arab)*
- What ethnic group dominates Saudi Arabia? *(Semitic)*
- Why do you think there is often conflict among different ethnic groups? *(Answers will vary.)*

Unit ATLAS

Regional Patterns

These two pages contain a graph and three thematic maps. The graph and two of the maps show the ethnic and religious diversity of Southwest Asia. The third map shows you how people in the region earn a living. After studying these two pages, answer the questions below in your notebook.

Making Comparisons

1. What percentage of the population is Kurdish and where are Kurds found in the region?
2. What area has holy places for three major religions? Why might the location of these places be a problem?
3. What energy sources are found in the region?
4. What is the main economic activity in the region? What does that suggest about the land and the population on it?

Ethnic Groups of Southwest Asia*

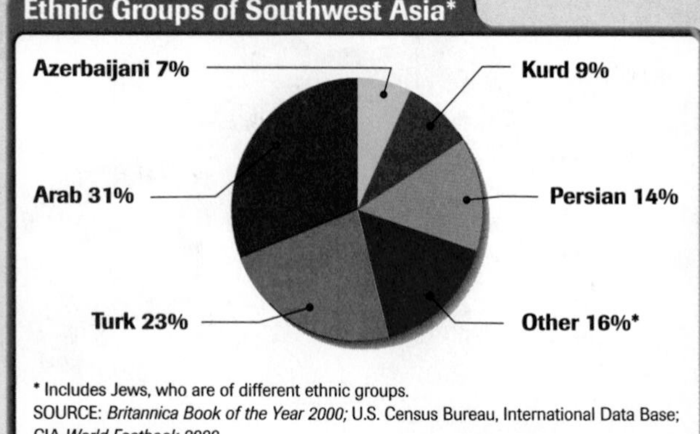

* Includes Jews, who are of different ethnic groups.
SOURCE: *Britannica Book of the Year 2000;* U.S. Census Bureau, International Data Base; CIA *World Factbook 2000*

Ethnic Regions of Southwest Asia

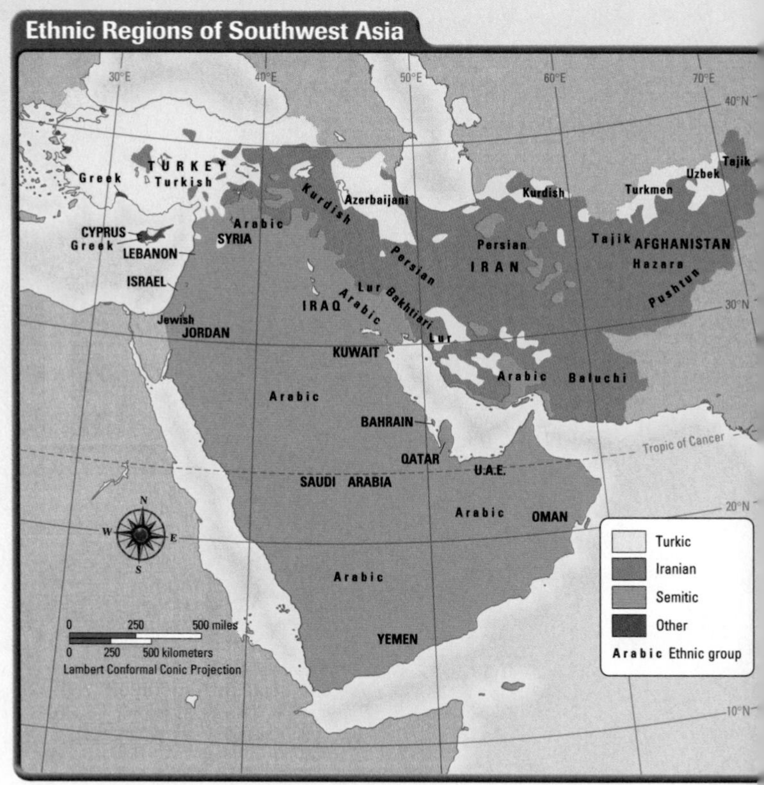

MAKING COMPARISONS ANSWERS

1. 9 percent; Turkey, Iraq, Iran
2. West Bank, Israel. The holy places might be controlled by a group that does not allow access.
3. petroleum, natural gas, coal, and hydroelectric power
4. nomadic herding; a lot of open areas with little population

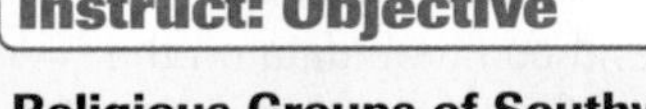

Instruct: Objective 6

Religious Groups of Southwest Asia/Economic Activities of Southwest Asia

- What is the most widespread religious group in Southwest Asia? *(Sunni Muslim)*
- What is the dominant religion of Iran? *(Shi'ite Muslim)*
- What is a major reason for U.S. interest in Saudi Arabia and the Persian Gulf? *(oil)*

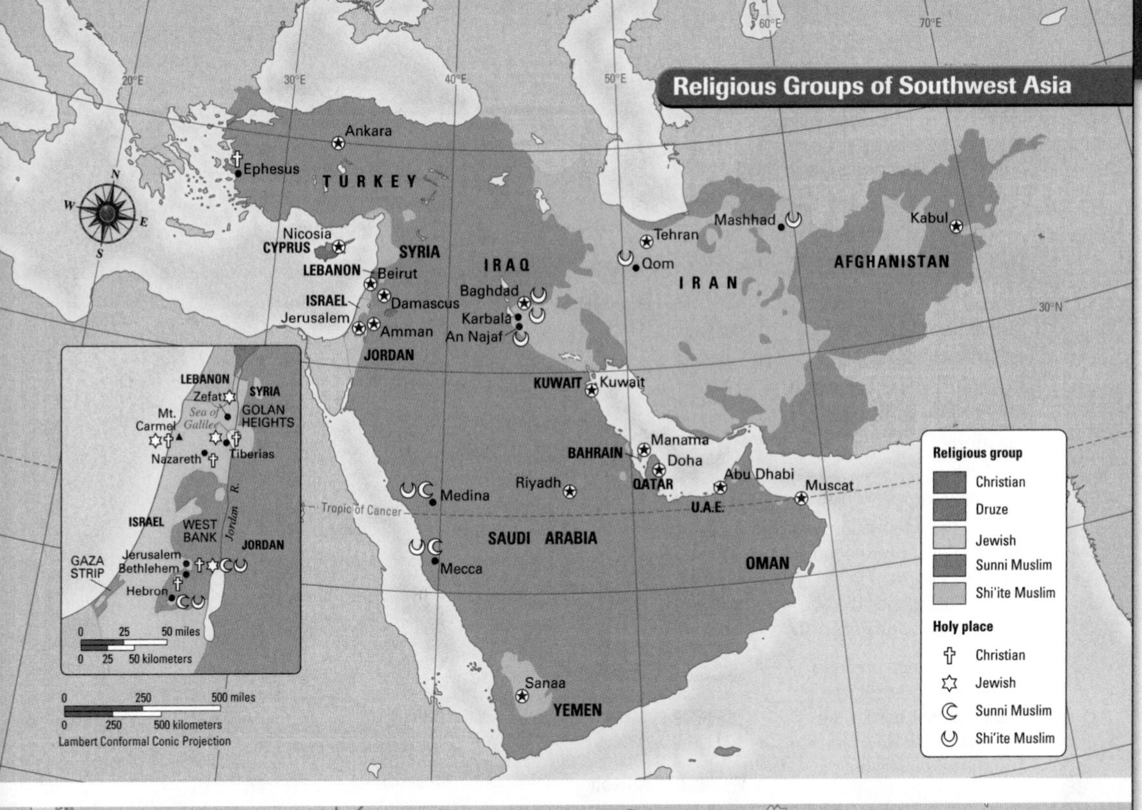

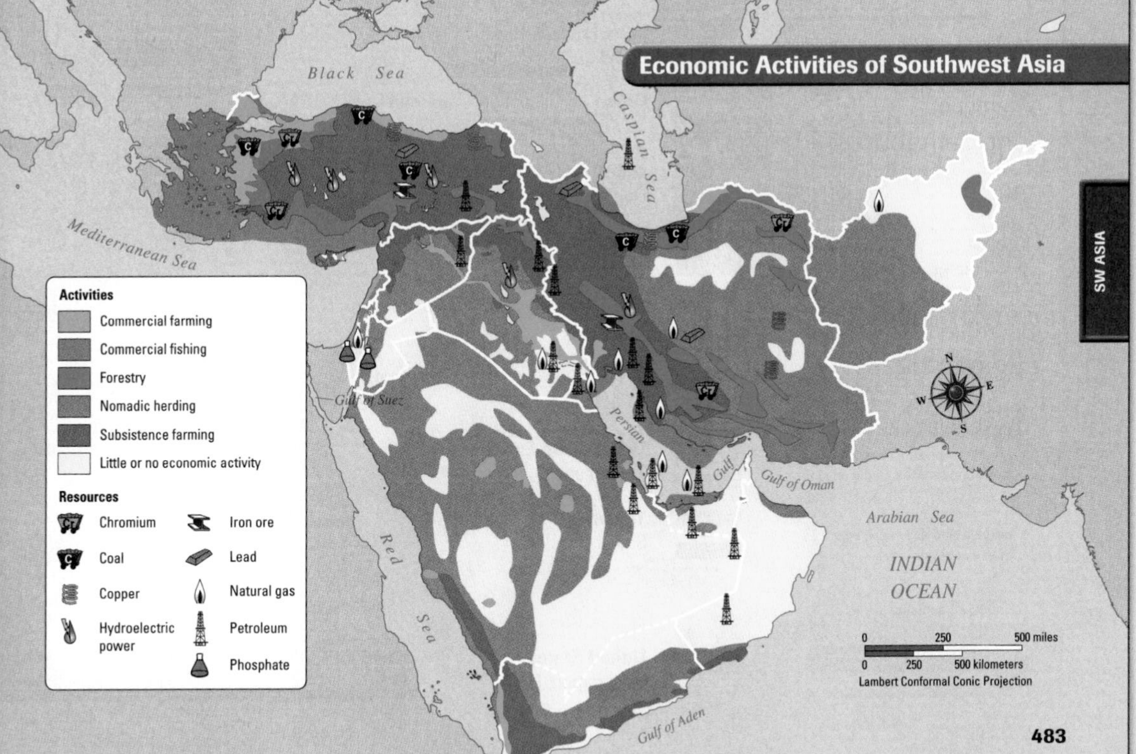

ACTIVITY OPTION | INTERNET RESEARCH

BLOCK SCHEDULING

PRESENTING AN ORAL REPORT

Objective To explore possibilities of working in Southwest Asia

Task Research job opportunities

Class Time 45 minutes

Directions Have students brainstorm to think about jobs they might be able to do in a Southwest Asian country. Using the Internet or library to research information about available jobs, have students look for information about salary, availability of the jobs, opportunity for advancement, and ways to apply for the jobs. Have students prepare a short oral report on their findings.

DATA FILE OBJECTIVE

Examine and compare data on the countries of Southwest Asia.

Focus & Motivate

Ask students which countries in Southwest Asia have the most televisions and cars per 1,000 population. *(televisions: Oman; cars: Lebanon)*

Instruct: Objective

Regional Data File

- Which four Southwest Asian countries have the highest literacy rate? *(Cyprus, Israel, Jordan, Kuwait)*
- Which Southwest Asian country has a life expectancy the same or greater than that of the United States? *(Jordan)*

In-Depth Resources: Unit 7
- Regional Data File Activities, p. 2

Regional Data File

Study the information on the countries of Southwest Asia. In your notebook, answer these questions.

Making Comparisons

1. Study the information to determine which nations are the poorest. On which categories did you base your judgment?
2. Using the map on page 479, make a list of the nations that border the Persian Gulf. How many of those nations have more exports than imports?

Country Flag	Country/ Capital	Population	Life Expectancy (years)	Birthrate (per 1,000 pop.)	Infant Mortality (per 1,000 live births)
	Afghanistan Kabul	28,396,000	44.4	38.4	153.1
	Bahrain Manama	729,000	75.2	17.0	15.1
	Cyprus Nicosia	1,085,000	77.5	11.3	9.7
	Iran Tehran	66,429,000	71.1	17.2	35.8
	Iraq Baghdad	28,946,000	69.9	30.1	44.7
	Israel Jerusalem	7,234,000	80.7	19.8	4.2
	Jordan Amman	6,269,000	79.9	27.4	17.4
	Kuwait Kuwait	2,693,000	77.7	21.8	9.0
	Lebanon Beirut	4,017,000	73.7	17.1	21.8
	Oman Muscat	3,418,000	74.1	34.8	16.9
	Qatar Doha	833,000	75.4	15.6	12.7
	Saudi Arabia Riyadh	28,687,000	76.3	28.6	11.6
	Syria Damascus	21,763,000	74.2	25	16.7
	Turkey Ankara	76,806,000	71.9	18.7	25.8
	United Arab Emirates Abu Dhabi	4,798,000	76.1	16.0	12.7
	Yemen Sanaa	22,858,000	63	35.3	58.4
	United States Washington, D.C.	307,212,000	78.1	13.8	6.2

Sources:

Central Intelligence Agency, *The World Factbook*, 2010

The World Almanac and Book of Facts, 2010

World Health Organization (WHO), 2007

Notes:

[a] GDP (purchasing power parity) is defined as the sum value of all goods and services produced in the country valued at prices prevailing in the United States.

[b] Includes land and water, when figures are available

For updated statistics on Southwest Asia . . .

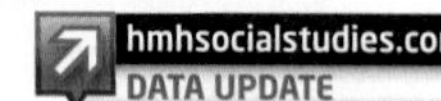

MAKING COMPARISONS ANSWERS

1. Answers may vary: Students may say that Afghanistan, Iraq, Jordan, and Syria are among the poorest countries because relatively few of the people can afford to buy consumer goods such as televisions and cars.
2. 7 of 8; Iraq does not.

Doctors (per 100,000 pop.)	GDP[a] (billions $US)	Import/Export (billions $US)	Literacy Rate (percentage)	Televisions (per 1,000 pop.)	Passenger Cars (per 1,000 pop.)	Total Area[b] (square miles)
19	23.4	5.3/0.55	28	14	1	250,001
109	28	10.27/12.5	87	446	257	257
234	22.9	6.68/1.14	98	154	327	3,571
87	876	57.16/70.16	77	154	23	636,296
66	112	55.4/38	74	82	29	168,754
382	206.9	47.4/44.35	97	328	235	8,019
203	33.1	12.31/6.99	90	83	63	35,637
153	148.7	20.8/49.77	93	480	341	6,880
325	47.8	16.25/3.5	87	355	349	4,015
132	69.4	18.41/29.34	81	575	95	82,031
222	101.2	20.87/37.43	89	866	321	4,416
137	581.3	86.61/180.5	79	263	N/A	830,000
140	102.5	13.1/10.13	80	68	15	71,498
135	859.8	140.8/102.2	87	328	76	301,384
202	200.4	141/174	78	309	67	32,278
33	58.2	7.12/5.56	50	286	15	203,850
256	14,260.0	1,445/994.7	99	844	725	3,794,083

485

More About

Cyprus

The island of Cyprus has been inhabit ed since approximately 8000 B.C., and since that time has been the site of successive waves of invasion by the Phoenicians, Egyptians, Greeks, Romans, Ottoman Turks and many others. The most recent occupation was by Great Britain from 1878 until 1960, when Cyprus became an independent republic. Tensions between the Greek-Cypriot majority and the Turkish-Cypriot minority soon escalated into a full-blown conflict, and in 1974 Turkish troops invaded the island. Since 1975 Cyprus has been unofficially partitioned into two states. In 1983 The Turkish-Cypriot state declared its independence—but only Turkey officially recognizes the Turkish Republic of Northern Cyprus.

ACTIVITY OPTION | CRITICAL THINKING

ANALYZING DATA

Explaining the Skill Data can be used to understand the needs and future needs of a country. For example, by looking at population patterns, we can determine the age of the population. Countries with a younger population may need more schools. Countries with an aging population may need more health care facilities.

Applying the Skill Have students choose a Southwest Asian country. Using the information in the Regional Data File on pages 484 and 485 and the charts and maps on pages 478 to 483, have students determine the possible future needs for their chosen country. Have students write a needs list for that country. Students should then write a paper explaining the reasons they chose the needs on their list.

CHAPTER 21 OBJECTIVE

Identify key aspects of Southwest Asia's physical geography, climate and vegetation, and human-environment interaction.

Chapter 21

PHYSICAL GEOGRAPHY OF SOUTHWEST ASIA
Harsh and Arid Lands

Interpreting Photographs

Arabia's An-Nafud Desert

Have students examine the photograph and read the caption. To give students a sense of how high 600 feet is, tell them that it is equal to two football fields.

Extension Ask students if they know of any plants or animals that live in deserts.

Introducing the Essential Question

- Discuss recent water shortage issues in your community, state, or region. Point out that even in drought years the United States has much greater water resources than much of Southwest Asia.
- Challenge students to imagine what their daily lives would be like if we could not import oil. This scenario emphasizes the significance of oil in Southwest Asia.

Have students fill out the graphic organizers in their notebooks using material from all sections in this chapter.

Critical Thinking Transparencies CT21
- GeoFocus

In-Depth Resources: Unit 7
- Building Vocabulary, p. 9

Essential Question

How do the physical features and resources of Southwest Asia affect its people and their influence?

What You Will Learn

In this chapter you will explore the harsh landscapes of Southwest Asia and investigate how the land and its resources affect life in the region.

SECTION 1
Landforms and Resources

SECTION 2
Climate and Vegetation

SECTION 3
Human–Environment Interaction

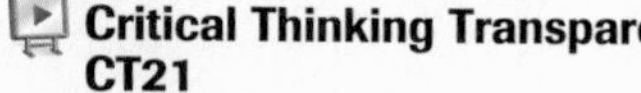

hmhsocialstudies.com TAKING NOTES

Use the graphic organizer online it to record information from the chapter about the physical geography of Southwest Asia.

Wind-shaped sand dunes in Arabia's An-Nafud Desert sometimes reach a height of 600 feet.

486

CHAPTER 21 ADDITIONAL RESOURCES

BOOKS FOR THE TEACHER

Kaplan, Robert D. ***Eastward to Tartary.*** NY: Random House, 2000. Account of Kaplan's travels in Southwest Asia.

Wallach, Janet. ***Desert Queen.*** NY: Doubleday, 1996. A biography of British diplomat Gertrude Bell, who helped to draw Southwest Asia's problematic borders.

BOOKS FOR THE STUDENT

Horwitz, Tony. ***Baghdad Without a Map.*** NY: E.P. Dutton, 1991. A reporter for the *Wall Street Journal* chronicles his travels throughout Southwest Asia.

VIDEOS

Lawrence of Arabia. Columbia Tristar Home Video, 1962. Story of a World War I British officer set in the Arabian Desert.

The Middle East in Transition. Southern California Center for International Studies, 1994. Discussions by U.S. presidents and other officials of U.S. government policies toward Southwest Asia.

INTERNET

For more on the physical geography of Southwest Asia, visit . . .

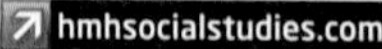

Landforms and Resources

Main Ideas
- The Southwest Asian landforms have had a major impact on movement in the region.
- The most valuable resources in Southwest Asia are oil and water.

Places & Terms
Golan Heights
wadi
Tigris River
Euphrates River
Jordan River
Dead Sea

CONNECT TO THE ISSUES
RESOURCES Enormous oil reserves have brought changes to the economic and political standing of this region.

A HUMAN PERSPECTIVE Artillery shells and sniper fire rained down on the lands below a small plateau in southwestern Syria. Airplanes bombed the military positions on the plateau itself. Families in nearby villages huddled in their homes, hoping for the shelling to stop. Israeli Army engineers struggled to build a road to enable tanks to reach the top. Thousands died in the 1967 war when Syria and Israel fought for control of the **Golan Heights,** also called Al Jawlan, a hilly plateau overlooking the Jordan River and the Sea of Galilee. This landform's strategic location has made it the site of conflict in Southwest Asia for decades. It is one of many landforms that divide the region.

Landforms Divide the Region

People sometimes picture Southwest Asia as a region of rippling sand dunes and parched land occasionally interrupted with an oasis. But the lands of Southwest Asia actually range from green coastal plains to snow-peaked mountains. Southwest Asia forms a land bridge connecting Asia, Africa, and Europe. As you can see on the map on page 37, the region is situated at the edge of a huge tectonic plate. Parts of the Arabian Peninsula are pulling away from Africa, and parts of the Anatolian Peninsula are sliding past parts of Asia. Still other plates are pushing up mountains in other areas of the Asian continent.

PENINSULAS AND WATERWAYS The most distinctive landform in Southwest Asia is the Arabian Peninsula, which is separated from the continent of Africa by the Red Sea on the southwest and from the rest of Asia by the Persian Gulf on the east. The Red Sea covers a rift valley created by the movement of the Arabian plate. The Zagros, Elburz, and Taurus mountains at the north side of the plate cut off part of the region from the south. Another important landform in the region is the Anatolian Peninsula, which is occupied by the country of Turkey. It marks the beginning of the Asian continent. (See the map on page 479.)

Both peninsulas border on strategic waterways. On the southwest side of the Arabian Peninsula are the Red Sea and a strategic opening to the Mediterranean Sea—the Suez Canal. Goods from Asia flow through this canal to ports in Europe and North Africa.

PLACE The Golan Heights are a strategic location near the source of water in the region. **How will control of this area affect those who live on lands below the top of the plateau?**

SW ASIA

487

CHAPTER 21 SECTION 1

SECTION 1 OBJECTIVES
1. Describe important landforms of Southwest Asia.
2. Describe the region's key resources.

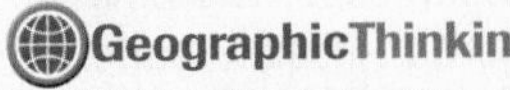

SKILLBUILDER: Interpreting Maps, pp. 488

 **GeographicThinking**
Making Comparisons, p. 488, 490
Drawing Conclusions, 490

Focus & Motivate

How might landforms divide the people of Southwest Asia? *(Deserts, mountains, and bodies of water are all potential barriers.)*

Instruct: Objective 1

Landforms Divide the Region

- What are two of the major peninsulas in Southwest Asia? *(Arabian and Anatolian)*
- What river serves as a boundary between Israel and Jordan? *(Jordan River)*

In-Depth Resources: Unit 7
- Guided Reading, p. 3

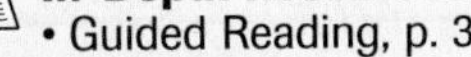

Interpreting Photographs

Golan Heights
Have students examine the photograph and ask them to consider why high ground might be militarily useful. *(A surprise attack against a force occupying high ground would be difficult, since they have a commanding view of the surrounding area.)*

CAPTION ANSWER It allows control of the water supplies and the people below.

SECTION 1 PROGRAM RESOURCES

 **In-Depth Resources: Unit 7**
- Guided Reading, p. 3
- Building Vocabulary, p. 9
- Reteaching Activity, p.10

Guided Reading Workbook
- Section 1

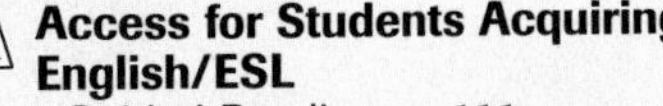
Access for Students Acquiring English/ESL
- Guided Reading, p. 111

 **Formal Assessment**
- Section Quiz, p. 324

Integrated Assessment
- Rubric for a map, 2.1

INTEGRATED TECHNOLOGY
 Chapter Summaries
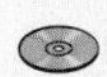 Power Presentations
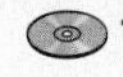 Test Generator

TEST-TAKING RESOURCES
 Strategies for Test Preparation
 Test Practice Transparencies TT68
Online Test Practice

More About

The Bosporus and the Dardanelles Straits

Turkey recently issued new rules governing the passage of ships through these straits, which link the Black and Mediterranean seas. The new rules have angered Russian leaders, who suspect that Turkey is trying to control the passage of oil tankers and influence decisions over the routes of oil pipelines needed to transport oil from newly discovered reserves in the Caspian Sea.

Interpreting Maps

Tigris-Euphrates River Valley Today

Have students examine the map and ask them what capital city is situated near the Tigris and Euphrates rivers. *(Baghdad, Iraq)*

SKILLBUILDER ANSWERS

1. Anatolian Plateau **2.** Zagros Mountains, Anatolian Plateau

The Anatolian Peninsula is located between the Black Sea and the Mediterranean Sea. Two narrow waterways, the Bosporus Strait and the Dardenelles Strait, are situated at the west end of the peninsula. Both straits have always been highly desirable locations for controlling trade and transportation to Russia and the interior of Asia.

Farther south is a narrow passageway leading from the Arabian Sea to the Persian Gulf called the Straits of Hormuz. These straits are the only waterway to the huge oilfields of Kuwait, Saudi Arabia, and Iraq. Because access to oil is essential to the world-wide economy, this waterway is very important.

BACKGROUND The Persian Gulf is also called the Arabian Gulf.

PLAINS AND HIGHLANDS Much of the Arabian Peninsula is covered by plains. Because of the dry, sandy, and windy conditions, few activities using the land take place here. Most of the land is barren with some low hills, ridges, and **wadis,** which are riverbeds that remain dry except during the rainy seasons. On the southwestern corner of the peninsula, a range of mountains—the Hejaz Mountains—pokes out of the land. People living on the Arabian Peninsula have adapted to the harsh conditions by living nomadic lives in search of water.

The heart of Iran is a plateau surrounded by mountains. Isolated and very high, the land is a stony, salty, and sandy desert. The foothills surrounding the plateau are able to produce some crops. Much of the Anatolian Peninsula is also a plateau. Some areas are productive for agriculture, while other areas support flocks of grazing animals such as sheep and goats. The Northern Plain of Afghanistan, a well-watered agricultural area, is surrounded by high mountains that isolate it from other parts of the region. A

Geographic Thinking

Making Comparisons

A How are the plateaus of Iran and Anatolia different?

A. Answer Some areas of Anatolia are productive for agriculture and herding; much of Iran's plateau is not.

Tigris-Euphrates River Valley Today

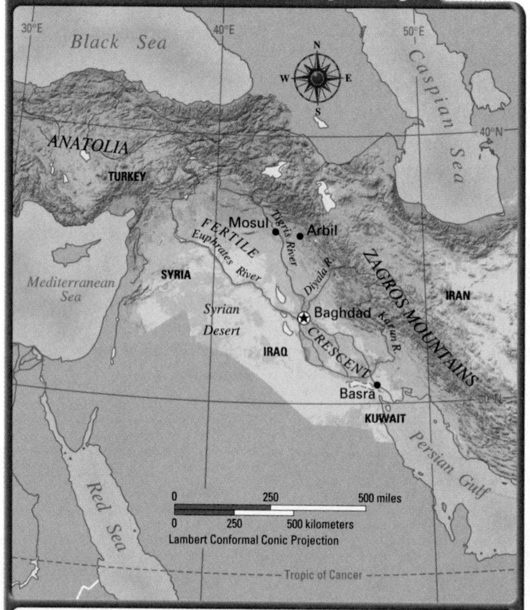

SKILLBUILDER: Interpreting Maps

1. **PLACE** The sources of two rivers are located on which landform?
2. **PLACE** Which landforms isolate the Fertile Crescent from other parts of the region?

MOUNTAINS Rugged mountains divide the land and countries. As you study the map on page 479, you will see that the Hindu Kush Mountains of Afghanistan are linked with other ranges of mountains that frame southern Asia. Afghanistan is landlocked and mountainous, so contact with the outside world is difficult.

The Zagros Mountains on the western side of Iran help isolate that country from the rest of Southwest Asia. The Elburz Mountains south of the Caspian Sea cut off easy access to that body of water by Iran. Finally, the Taurus Mountains separate Turkey from the rest of Southwest Asia. In spite of these physical barriers, people, goods, and ideas move through the entire region. One of the ways they move is by water.

DIFFERENTIATING INSTRUCTION STUDENTS ACQUIRING ENGLISH/ESL

PRONOUNCING DIFFICULT WORDS

Objective To learn the correct pronunciation of new words

Class Time 20 minutes

Task To work with a student mentor to learn to sound out new words from the text

Directions Have ESL students make a list of words from this section that they find difficult to pronounce. Ask them to work together with a student mentor who can help them to properly pronounce each word. Suggest that they write out phonetic spellings next to each word on their lists.

5 THEMES

PLACE

The Dead Sea

The Dead Sea is a landlocked salt lake, so salty that almost nothing can live in the water. It has been described as the world's largest spa. (A spa is a place with healing waters.) For thousands of years, people have come to the edges of the landlocked sea to bathe in its mineral waters and soak in its black mineral mud.

Imagine floating in water so salty that you cannot sink. Salt concentration in the Dead Sea water is 31.5 percent, nine times higher than in the world's oceans. The evaporation rate of the water is about 55 inches per year, keeping the water very salty despite the flow of fresh water from the Jordan River.

WATER BODIES Southwest Asia is almost completely surrounded by bodies of water. They provide vital avenues for trade and access to other parts of the region and to the rest of the world. However, because much of the region is arid, there are few rivers that flow the entire year. As you can see on the map on page 488, two of the most important rivers—the **Tigris** and the **Euphrates**—supported several ancient river valley civilizations in an area called the Fertile Crescent. They included Sumerians, Assyrians, Babylonians, and Chaldeans.

Today, the Tigris and Euphrates flow through parts of Turkey, Syria, and Iraq. The valleys are fertile, well watered, and good for agriculture. The two rivers flow almost parallel to each other for hundreds of miles before joining at a place called Shatt al Arab. They spread out into slow moving water and swamps, finally emptying into the Persian Gulf. B

CONNECT TO THE ISSUES

B RESOURCES Why is control of water resources important in this region?

B. Answer Such control allows agriculture to take place.

Tumbling down from the mountains of Lebanon near Mt. Hermon, the **Jordan River** provides one of the most precious resources in the entire region—water. Farther south, the river serves as a natural boundary between Israel and Jordan. The Jordan River flows into the salty waters of the **Dead Sea,** a landlocked salt lake. The Dead Sea is so salty that only bacteria can live in the waters. Thousands of years ago the earth was heaved up on the south end of present-day Israel. The outlet to the sea was blocked, creating the salt lake. The Dead Sea is 1,349 feet below sea level—the lowest place on the exposed crust of the earth. (See The Dead Sea, above.)

SW ASIA

Resources for a Modern World

It is almost impossible to think about resources in Southwest Asia without including oil. It is the region's most abundant resource. Major oil

5 THEMES

Place: The Dead Sea

The diversion of water from the Jordan River, the Dead Sea's main tributary, has caused the sea to shrink in recent years. A mark made by British explorers in 1917 to identify the sea's edge now lies nearly 50 feet up a cliff, and a road now runs between the cliff and the sea's new shoreline. Ask students if they know how the Dead Sea got its name. *(They may guess that the high salt content makes the sea's waters nearly uninhabitable for plant and animal life.)*

Instruct: Objective 2

Resources for a Modern World

- Why do so many countries, including the United States, depend on Southwest Asia? *(for its oil reserves)*
- What is another vital resource in much of Southwest Asia? *(water)*
- How might the area around the Dead Sea contribute to the region's economy? *(Salts, such as sodium chloride, could be extracted for use in manufacturing and chemical processes.)*

ACTIVITY OPTION **INTERNET RESEARCH**

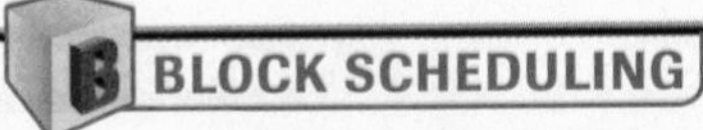

BLOCK SCHEDULING

CREATING A POSTER

Objective To learn more about the physical and human geography around the Dead Sea

Class Time 30 minutes

Task Make a poster about the Dead Sea Scrolls

Directions Divide students into small groups and ask them to use the Internet to carry out research on the Dead Sea Scrolls. Encourage students to investigate the climatic conditions that allowed the scrolls to survive for so long. Have students use their research to create a poster that illustrates the importance of the discovery. Students may wish to include pictures of the scrolls, maps, timelines, translations from the scrolls, etc.

Interpreting Photographs

Oil Workers

Have students examine the photograph and ask them what the worker in the photo is doing. *(He appears to be turning a valve that controls the flow of petroleum in the pipe.)*

CAPTION ANSWER Roads will be built to import equipment, supplies, and workers, possibly housing will be built for workers.

Assess & Reteach

GeoFocus Have students complete the sections on landforms and resources in their graphic organizers.

Formal Assessment
- Section Quiz, p. 324

Reteaching Activity

Have students write a sentence for each vocabulary word in the section. Sentences should reflect an understanding of the word.

In-Depth Resources: Unit 7
- Reteaching Activity, p. 10

HUMAN–ENVIRONMENT INTERACTION Men work at an oil drilling compound in the Rub al-Khali desert.
How will oil drilling change this area?

fields are located in the Arabian Peninsula, Iran, and Iraq, with natural gas fields close by. Since these fossil fuels run cars and trucks, factories, and power plants all over the world, they provide the major portion of income for nations with petroleum reserves.

AN OIL-RICH REGION Today, about one-half of the world's oil reserves are found in Southwest Asia, along the coast of the Persian Gulf, and at offshore drilling sites in the Gulf itself. The presence of these large reserves has made the region important because so many countries, including the United States, depend on its oil.

OTHER RESOURCES The most valuable resource in parts of Southwest Asia is water. In mountainous lands such as Turkey, Iran, Lebanon, and Afghanistan, water is plentiful compared to the rest of the region. It can be harnessed for hydroelectric power. However, elsewhere, water is a scarce resource that must constantly be guarded and carefully used. Efforts to conserve water have been a part of the culture of the people living in the region for thousands of years. C

Southwest Asia has deposits of other resources such as coal, metallic minerals such as copper, and non-metallic minerals such as potash and phosphates. However, the deposits are scattered and not very large. Iran and Turkey have good-sized deposits of coal. Around the Dead Sea are significant reserves of salts such as calcium chloride. However, these salt deposits, which are used in manufacturing and chemical processes, have not been heavily developed.

The harsh land and the desert climate that you will learn about in the next section make life in this region a challenge.

Geographic Thinking
Making Comparisons
C Why might hydroelectric power be better to use than oil?
C. Answer It can be renewed, but once oil is used, it is gone forever.

Section 1 Assessment

1 Places & Terms

Identify and explain where in the region these would be found.
- Golan Heights
- wadi
- Tigris River
- Euphrates River
- Jordan River
- Dead Sea

2 Taking Notes

LOCATION Review the notes you took for this section.

Landforms	
Resources	

- Which waterways are considered important for trade?
- In which area of the region are the greatest deposits of oil found?

3 Main Ideas

a. In what ways do landforms divide the region?

b. Why are the Red Sea and Suez Canal of strategic value in the region?

c. How did the presence of oil in the region change the region's importance in the global economy?

4 Geographic Thinking

Drawing Conclusions Which resource do you believe is more important in Southwest Asia—water or oil?
Think about:
- the scarcity of water
- the economic value of oil

See Skillbuilder Handbook, page R5.

GeoActivity

MAKING COMPARISONS Study the map on page 483, focusing on energy sources in the region. Create a **map** that shows the location of these energy sources. Label each country that has such sources.

SECTION 1 ASSESSMENT ANSWERS

1. Places & Terms
Golan Heights, p. 487
wadi, p. 488
Tigris River, p. 489
Euphrates River, p. 489
Jordan River, p. 489
Dead Sea, p. 489

2. Taking Notes
- Red Sea and Suez Canal, Bosporus Strait, Dardanelles Strait, Strait of Hormuz
- Arabian Peninsula and the Persian Gulf area

3. Main Ideas
a. It is difficult to cross desert areas—isolating them from other areas. There are few waterways to connect the area.
b. They allow easy sea trade between ports in southern and eastern Asia and those in Europe and North Africa.
c. Oil is so scarce that almost all nations need to import it, making the region very strategic and valuable.

4. Geographic Thinking
Water and oil are irreplaceable but water is necessary for life. However, money from oil sales could be used to find water, to buy water from elsewhere, or to develop ways to treat salt water.

GeoActivity

Integrated Assessment
- Rubric for a map, 2.1

Climate and Vegetation

Main Ideas
- Most of Southwest Asia has a very arid climate.
- Irrigation is critical to growing crops in this very dry region.

Places & Terms
Rub al-Khali
oasis
salt flat

CONNECT TO THE ISSUES
POPULATION RELOCATION The climate of Southwest Asia limits interaction between countries in the region.

A HUMAN PERSPECTIVE In the spring of 1999, three Canadian explorers retraced the steps of Sir Wilfred Thesiger's 1946 epic journey across the Rub al-Khali on the Arabian Peninsula. It is one of the most extreme deserts in the world. Like Sir Wilfred, they crossed using camels, not four-wheel drive vehicles. But unlike Sir Wilfred, the Canadians were equipped with late 20th-century explorers' tools—personal location beacons, a satellite phone for communications, and laptop computers for recording details of the journey. Crossing this great arid expanse was physically challenging and took 40 days to complete. But for many of the region's inhabitants, survival in the lands of this region is a challenge every day.

Variety in Arid Lands

Southwest Asia is extremely arid. Most areas receive less than 18 inches of precipitation a year. A huge portion of its land area is covered with rough, dry terrain that varies from huge tracts of sand dunes to great salt flats. Study the Map Skills on page 494 to learn more about desert vegetation. Because the region is so dry, its rivers do not flow year round. The vegetation and animals living in the desert can survive on little water and in extreme temperatures. In many areas of Southwest Asia, irrigation has transformed the deserts into productive farmland.

In other parts of the region, a Mediterranean climate prevails, making the land green and lush for at least part of each year. The land in Southwest Asia is broken up by ranges of mountains and plateaus. As a result, highland climates are found in many parts of the region.

MOVEMENT A Bedouin caravan crosses a dry, rocky desert in Judea, a part of Israel.
How do conditions in the desert restrict movement?

Deserts Limit Movement

Spread across the region, the deserts effectively reduce travel and limit almost all human-environment interaction. The surfaces of the desert may be covered with sand, salt, or rocks.

SANDY DESERTS The most famous desert in the region is the **Rub al-Khali,** also known as the Empty Quarter. A local name for the desert is the "place where no one comes out." It is a vast desert

SW ASIA

SECTION 2 OBJECTIVES
1. Describe the variety in arid lands.
2. Describe how deserts limit movement.
3. Identify semiarid lands.
4. Describe well-watered coast lands.

SKILLBUILDER: Interpreting Maps, p. 492

 **GeographicThinking**
Seeing Patterns, p. 492
Making Comparisons, p. 493

Focus & Motivate
Ask students what climate patterns predominate in Southwest Asia. *(desert climate)*

Instruct: Objective 1
Variety in Arid Lands

- How much precipitation do most areas of Southwest Asia receive annually? *(less than 18 inches)*
- What characterizes much of the region's terrain? *(rough, dry tracts that vary from high sand dunes to expansive salt flats)*

 **In-Depth Resources: Unit 7**
- Guided Reading, p. 4

Interpreting Photographs
Bedouin Caravan
Tell students that Bedouins are nomadic Arab tribes who live in the deserts of Southwest Asia.

CAPTION ANSWER The brutal heat and dry conditions restrict human movement.

Instruct: Objective 2 appears on p. 492.

SECTION 2 PROGRAM RESOURCES

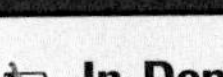 **In-Depth Resources: Unit 7**
- Guided Reading, p. 4
- Skillbuilder Practice, p. 8
- Building Vocabulary, p. 9
- Reteaching Activity, p. 11
- Map and Graph Skills, pp. 6–7

Guided Reading Workbook
- Section 2

Access for Students Acquiring English/ESL
- Guided Reading, p. 112
- Skillbuilder Practice, 114
- Map and Graph Skills, pp. 115–116

 **Formal Assessment**
- Section Quiz, p. 325

 **Integrated Assessment**
- Rubric for a database, 2.6

INTEGRATED TECHNOLOGY

Critical Thinking Transparencies CT53
- Deserts in Southwest Asia

 **Power Presentations**

hmhsocialstudies.com

TEST-TAKING RESOURCES
 **Strategies for Test Preparation**
 **Test Practice Transparencies TT69**

Online Test Practice

Instruct: Objective 2

Deserts Limit Movement

- What are two types of deserts found in Southwest Asia? *(sand and salt deserts)*
- What are four of Southwest Asia's most important sand deserts? *(Rub al-Khali, An-Nafud, Syrian, and Negev deserts)*
- How are salt flats formed? *(Dry winds increase evaporation in an area. The evaporated moisture is not replenished because high mountains block moist air from entering the area. Chemical salts remain, creating the salt flat.)*

Critical Thinking Transparencies CT53
• Deserts in Southwest Asia

Interpreting Maps

Climates of Southwest Asia

Have students examine the climate map and ask them where they might expect to find most of the region's population. *(Students might guess that population density is greatest in areas with Mediterranean climates.)*

SKILLBUILDER ANSWERS 1. desert **2.** It is higher and winds have lost their moisture by the time they reach the interior.

Climates of Southwest Asia

SKILLBUILDER: Interpreting Maps
1. **REGION** What is the dominant climate of the region?
2. **LOCATION** Why might the interior of the Anatolian Plateau be semiarid?

approximately the size of Texas—on the Arabian Peninsula. It is one of the largest sandy deserts in the world, covering about 250,000 square miles with sand ridges and dunes that reach as high as 800 feet. During the summer, the temperature on the surface of the sand often exceeds 150°F. As many as 10 years may pass without rainfall.

Next to the Rub al-Khali is the An-Nafud Desert. An occasional oasis interrupts its reddish dunes. An **oasis** is an area in the desert where vegetation is found because water is available, usually from underground springs. Severe sandstorms and brutal heat make this desert a barrier to travel across the Arabian Peninsula.

Extending north from the An-Nafud is the Syrian Desert. It separates the coastal regions of Lebanon, Israel, and Syria from the Tigris and Euphrates valleys. (See the map on page 479.) Finally, the desert area in southern Israel is the Negev Desert. Unlike some deserts, this one produces crops through extensive irrigation, developed by Jewish farmers. A

SALT DESERTS As you learned in Chapter 3, lands in the rain shadow of a mountain range are usually arid or semiarid. Lands in Iran are good examples of this effect. In Iran, the high mountains block rain, and dry winds increase evaporation. So when winds evaporate the moisture in the soil, chemical salts remain, creating a **salt flat.** In Iran there are two salt flat deserts—the Dasht-e Kavir in central Iran and the Dasht-e Lut in eastern Iran. The lands here are salt-crusted, surrounded by quicksand-like salt marshes, and extremely hot. These rugged lands are almost uninhabited and are barriers to easy movement across Iran.

Geographic Thinking

Seeing Patterns
A How is it possible for crops to be produced in desert areas?
A. Answer It is possible only when water is available through irrigation.

ACTIVITY OPTION | SKILLBUILDER LESSON

CREATING AND USING A DATABASE

Explaining the Skill A database is a collection of data, or information, that is organized so that you can find and retrieve specific information easily. Once a computerized database is set up, you can search it to find specific information without going through the entire database.

Applying the Skill Have students construct a database on some aspect of climate or vegetation in Southwest Asia. For example, students might create a database of weather extremes in the region (see the chart). Assist students in identifying the types of information that should be included in their database. Have students use the Internet or library resources to develop and fill in the database.

WEATHER EXTREMES IN SOUTHWEST ASIA				
Year	Place	Date	Highest Temperature	Lowest Temperature
2000				
2001				

In-Depth Resources: Unit 7
• Skillbuilder Practice, p. 8

Semiarid Lands

On the fringes of the deserts are regions with a semiarid climate. These semiarid areas have warm to hot summers with enough rainfall to support grass and some low-growing shrubs. Both cotton and wheat can be grown in this climate. The lands offer good pasture for animals. In Turkey, large herds of mohair goats graze on these lands. Their hair, and fabrics made from it, are among Turkey's exports.

PLACE Workers pick cotton in a field in Turkey.
Which of Turkey's climates would be good for cotton production?

B. Answer
Both have Mediterranean climates, and those areas are heavily populated.

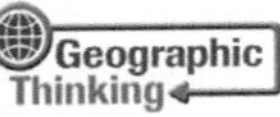

Making Comparisons
B How are Turkey and southern California similar?

Well-Watered Coast Lands

Although much of Southwest Asia is arid or semiarid, it does have some areas with adequate rainfall. Along the Mediterranean coast and across most of Turkey, hot summers and rainy winters like those in southern California create a good climate for growing citrus fruits, olives, and vegetables. Because of mild winter temperatures in winter and heavy irrigation in the dry summer, farmers can grow crops year round. The Mediterranean climate is a comfortable one in which to live, so these areas are heavily populated. B

For thousands of years, the valleys of the Tigris and Euphrates have been the site of intensive farming. Both Turkey and Iraq have constructed dams on the rivers to provide irrigation water all year long.

Climate, vegetation, and landforms have had a major impact on human-environment interaction in Southwest Asia. In the next section, you will see how oil and water have shaped life in this region.

Section 2 Assessment

1 Places & Terms
Identify and explain where in the region these would be found.
- Rub al-Khali
- oasis
- salt flat

2 Taking Notes
PLACE Review the notes you took for this section.

Climate and Vegetation	

- What are the two types of deserts in this region?
- Why are the coast lands heavily populated?

3 Main Ideas
a. How do deserts affect movement in the region?
b. In what ways are the semiarid lands different from the desert?
c. What agricultural products are raised in the coastal areas?

4 Geographic Thinking
Making Comparisons How do the two types of deserts in the region differ from each other? **Think about:**
- characteristics of deserts
- location of deserts

hmhsocialstudies.com
RESEARCH WEB LINKS

MAKING COMPARISONS Do some research on the deserts identified in this section. Create a **database** showing information about those deserts. Consider including such information as type, location, and size.

SW ASIA

Instruct: Objective 3

Semiarid Lands

- What kind of vegetation might one find in the semiarid regions of Southwest Asia? *(grasses, some low-growing shrubs, as well as cotton and wheat)*
- What kind of animals might be found grazing on land in the semi-arid zones of Turkey? *(mohair goats)*

Instruct: Objective 4

Well-Watered Coast Lands

- What U.S. state has a climate similar to Turkey's? *(California)*
- What sorts of crops are suited to a Mediterranean climate? *(citrus fruits, olives, and vegetables)*
- What countries have taken advantage of the agricultural benefits of the Tigris and Euphrates rivers? *(Turkey and Iraq)*

CAPTION ANSWER semiarid

Assess & Reteach

GeoFocus Have students complete the sections on climate and vegetation in their graphic organizers.

Formal Assessment
- Section Quiz, p. 325

Reteaching Activity
Have each student write an outline of the section. Then pair students. Have them exchange outlines and correct their partners' work.

In-Depth Resources: Unit 7
- Reteaching Activity, p. 11

SECTION 2 ASSESSMENT ANSWERS

1. Places & Terms
Rub al-Khali, p. 491
oasis, p. 492
salt flat, p. 492

2. Taking Notes
- sandy and salt
- They are well watered and have a comfortable climate.

3. Main Ideas
a. Most movement is around them, not through them.
b. Semiarid lands have enough rainfall to support vegetation.
c. citrus fruits, olives, vegetables

4. Geographic Thinking
Some are sandy; some are salt flats; some are located in high, windy areas or in rain shadows.

GeoActivity
Integrated Assessment
- Rubric for a database, 2.6

OBJECTIVE

Understand and interpret vegetation maps.

Instruct: Objective

Reading a Vegetation Map

- What is represented on a vegetation map? *(the location of particular types of plants in a region)*
- What kinds of plants are shown or not shown on a vegetation map. *(A region's natural vegetation is shown, but plants introduced as agricultural crops are generally not shown.)*
- How would you characterize the boundaries between different vegetation regions. *(They gradually blend into each other.)*

In-Depth Resources: Unit 7
- Map and Graph Skills, pp. 6–7

Access for Students Acquiring English/ESL
- Map and Graph Skills, pp. 115–116

More About

Vegetation in Southwest Asia

One of the most revered plants in Southwest Asia is the majestic Cedar of Lebanon *(Cedrus Libani)*. The Cedars of Lebanon are tall coniferous trees with massive trunks and irregular heads of spreading branches. The beautiful red wood produced from the tree is incredibly fragrant and is prized for its resistance to decay and insects. The tree has been a national emblem of Lebanon for hundreds of years and is pictured on the country's flag. (See page 484.)

RAND McNALLY **Map and Graph Skills**

Reading a Vegetation Map

Southwest Asia is a region with large areas of vegetation specially adapted for dry conditions. The natural vegetation of a region depends on many factors, including soil type, location, elevation, and climate type.

THE LANGUAGE OF MAPS A **vegetation map** shows the location of major types of plants in a region. It includes the natural vegetation found in the area and usually does not include plants introduced as agricultural crops. The map uses colors to indicate the vegetation types. Unlike the map boundaries, the boundaries on earth for the areas are not rigid but gradually blend into each other.

Vegetation of Southwest Asia

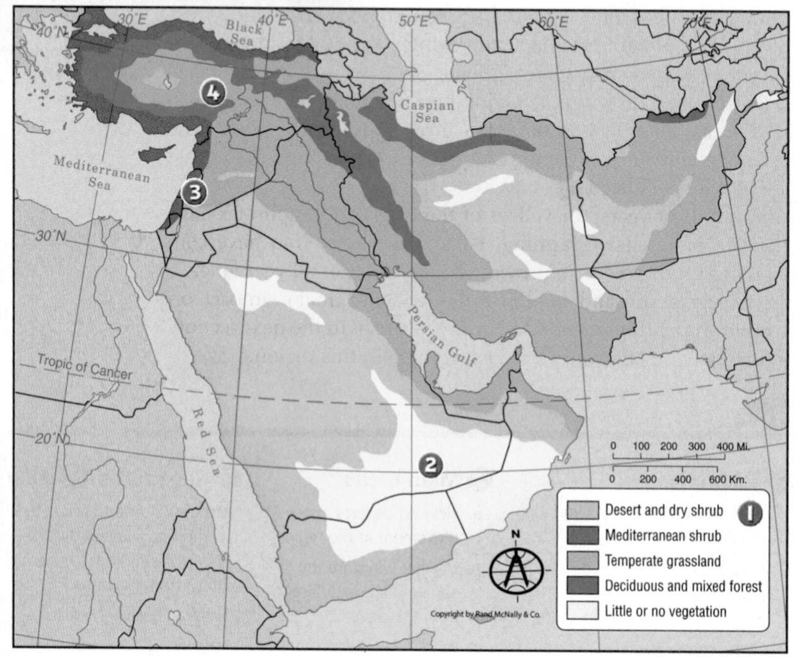

Copyright by Rand McNally & Co.

1. The key illustrates the types of vegetation found in the region. Each color on the map represents the major vegetation in that area.
2. This area has little or no vegetation, and probably is a desert.
3. Areas along the coasts of large bodies of water often have different vegetation from the kinds found inland.
4. Look for patterns that might give you clues about landforms in the region. Here, the mixed forest may indicate a mountainous area.

Map and Graph Skills Assessment

1. **Making Generalizations** What type of vegetation is found in the lands bordering the Persian Gulf?
2. **Making Comparisons** Along which bodies of water is the vegetation region different from regions farther inland?
3. **Drawing Conclusions** In general, how would you describe the vegetation of this region?

SKILLS ASSESSMENT ANSWERS

1. temperate grassland
2. Mediterranean Sea, Black Sea, Persian Gulf
3. some grasslands and temperate forests, but mostly desert shrub

Human–Environment Interaction

Main Ideas
- Water is critical to regional physical survival and economic development.
- Discovery of oil increased the global economic importance of Southwest Asia.

Places & Terms
drip irrigation **crude oil**
desalinization **refinery**
fossil water

CONNECT TO THE ISSUES
RESOURCES Southwest Asian nations face the challenge of how to use the income from oil resources to develop their economies.

A HUMAN PERSPECTIVE Icebergs for fresh water? In 1977, a Saudi prince, Muhammad ibn Faisal, formed a company to investigate the possibility of towing icebergs from Antarctica to the port of Jidda on the Red Sea. The icebergs would then be melted to release huge quantities of fresh water. It cost one million dollars to find out that no ship was powerful enough to tow an enormous iceberg, and there was no way to keep the iceberg from breaking up on the way. In 1981, the iceberg project was suspended. This story illustrates just how precious fresh water is in Southwest Asia. For centuries, people living in the region have struggled to find fresh water for themselves and for crops.

Providing Precious Water

Even though oil brings a great deal of money into Southwest Asia, the most critical resource in this dry region is water. Fresh water supplies are available only in small amounts and not consistently. Ancient civilizations constantly faced the problem of finding and storing water in order to survive and prosper. Today, the same challenge exists for modern nations. To find reliable water supplies, nations today use both ancient and modern practices. The pictures on page 496 include examples of both ancient and modern techniques for providing water.

DAMS AND IRRIGATION SYSTEMS Ancient practices can provide water for small fields but are not efficient for large-scale farming. To meet the needs of large farms and growing populations, countries must construct dams and irrigation systems. Turkey is building 22 dams and 19 power plants on the upper Euphrates and Tigris rivers. The project will provide water and hydroelectricity for parts of the country. As of 2005, 8 power plants were completed. They produced 18.7 kilowatt-hours of electricity that year, nearly half of Turkey's output. But the project is controversial—Syria and Iraq, which lie downstream from the dams, fear they will receive much less water for irrigation or hydroelectricity.

The National Water Carrier project in Israel carries water from the northern part of the country to sites in the nation's center and south. The water comes primarily from Lake Kinneret (Sea of Galilee), but also from mountain areas, including the Golan Heights, and the Jordan River. Some of the water is used for agricultural projects in the Negev, and some for

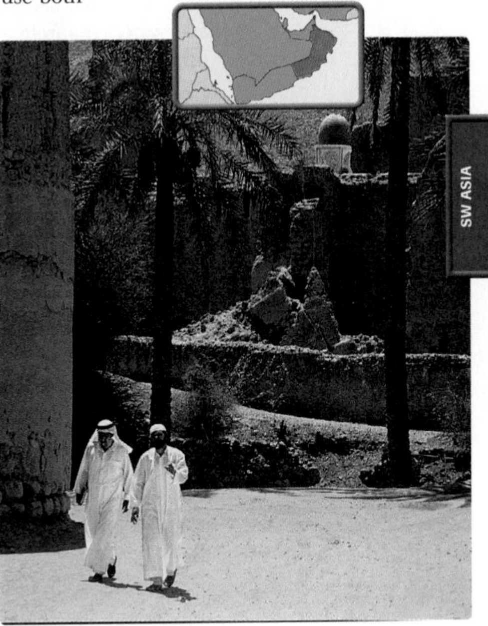

PLACE Date palms thrive in this oasis in the arid country of Oman.
Where does the water for an oasis come from?

SW ASIA

SECTION 3 OBJECTIVES
1. Examine the procurement and distribution of water resources in Southwest Asia.
2. Describe the formation, production, and movement of oil in the region.

SKILLBUILDER: Interpreting Maps, p. 498

GeographicThinking
Making Comparisons, p. 496
Seeing Patterns, p. 497
Using the Atlas, p. 499
Making Inferences, p. 499

Focus & Motivate

Ask students if they are familiar with any controversies surrounding the use of oil and water resources in the United States. *(2010 oil disaster in the Gulf of Mexico, proposals for drilling in the Arctic National Wildlife Refuge; water shortages in the Southwest)*

Instruct: Objective 1

Providing Precious Water

- What is the most critical resource in Southwest Asia? *(water)*
- Why might the distribution and use of water in Southwest Asia cause political disputes? *(because water resources, such as rivers, often flow through several countries)*
- What are some modern methods for water development and use? *(development: desalinization and waste-water treatment; use: drip irrigation)*

In-Depth Resources: Unit 7
- Guided Reading, p. 5
- GeoWorkshop, pp. 35–36

CAPTION ANSWER underground springs

SECTION 3 PROGRAM RESOURCES

In-Depth Resources: Unit 7
- Guided Reading, p. 5
- Building Vocabulary, p. 9
- Reteaching Activity, p. 12
- GeoWorkshop, pp. 35–36

Guided Reading Workbook
- Section 3

Access for Students Acquiring English/ESL
- Guided Reading, p, 113

Formal Assessment
- Section Quiz, p. 326

Integrated Assessment
- Rubric for a paragraph, 4.2

INTEGRATED TECHNOLOGY
Map Transparencies MT38
- Oil Pipelines in Southwest Asia

hmhsocialstudies.com

TEST-TAKING RESOURCES
Strategies for Test Preparation
Test Practice Transparencies TT70
Online Test Practice

Interpreting Photographs

Water Systems

Have students examine the picture of the noria. Ask students if they know how the function of this waterwheel might differ from the function of a waterwheel at a gristmill or a sawmill. *(The purpose of the noria is to raise water from a stream. Waterwheels at mills are used to power machinery.)*

More About

Qanats

Underground *qanat* tunnels are built by specialists called *muqanni* (*qanat* diggers). The gently sloping tunnels use gravity to transport water from its source, usually at the base of mountains. *Qanat* tunnels can measure up to 20 or 30 miles long.

Water Systems

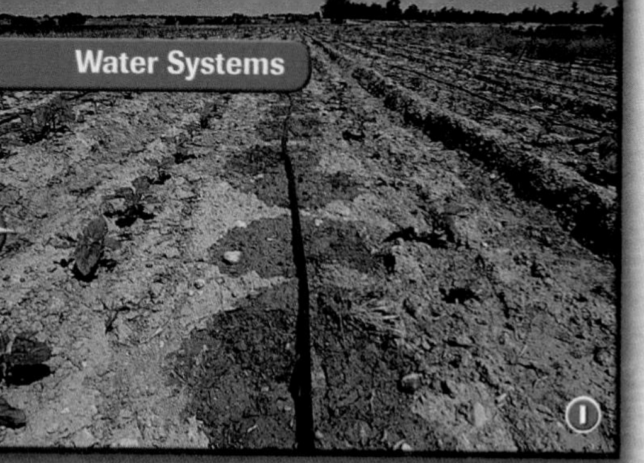

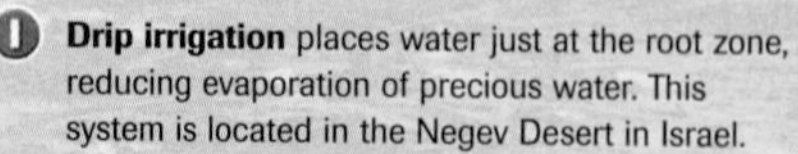

1 **Drip irrigation** places water just at the root zone, reducing evaporation of precious water. This system is located in the Negev Desert in Israel.

2 A bag of water is collected by using this pump. It is a part of a **qanat**—a system of underground brick-lined tunnels and wells that collect runoff water from the mountains.

3 This **irrigation canal** in Oman has delivered water for over a thousand years. The canals are carefully maintained to provide water for agriculture.

4 A **noria**—or waterwheel run by the flow of water or by animal power—is used to lift water from the river to the fields. These two are located in Syria on the Orontes River.

drinking water. Because the water sources flow through several countries and water resources are limited, the National Water Carrier project has been a source of tension between Israel, Jordan, and Syria. A

MODERN WATER TECHNOLOGY Several countries in the region use **drip irrigation.** Developed by Israelis, this system uses small pipes that slowly drip water just above ground to conserve water used for crops. Other nations are developing ways to use ocean water. **Desalinization,** the removal of salt from ocean water, is done at technically sophisticated water treatment plants. However, the desalinated water may be too salty to use for irrigation so it is used in sewage systems. Desalinization plants are very expensive and cannot provide adequate quantities of water to meet all the needs of people in Southwest Asia. Another alternative source of water, especially for agriculture, is the treatment of wastewater. Wastewater treatment plants constructed in the region fail to generate enough water to meet all the needs.

Water pumped from underground aquifers is called **fossil water,** because it has been in the aquifer for very long periods of time. Fossil water has very little chance of being replaced because this region has too little rainfall to recharge the aquifers. It is estimated that at the current rate water is being pumped, only about 25 to 30 years of water usage remain. Finding ways to conserve or even reuse water must be a top priority for the nations of this region.

Geographic Thinking

Making Comparisons
A How are the water projects of Turkey and Israel different?
A. Answer Turkey's includes hydroelectric power, and Israel's does not.

ACTIVITY OPTION CRITICAL THINKING

CREATING MULTIMEDIA PRESENTATIONS

Explaining the Skill Movies, CD-ROMs, television, and computer software are different kinds of media. To create a multimedia presentation, you need to collect material from different media and organize it into one presentation.

Applying the Skill Have students carry out research on different methods, such as *qanats,* that people have developed to bring water to their homes and fields. Students should consider modern systems as well as older methods of moving water.

- What role does gravity play in the process? *(Hydraulic engineers must work with or against this force to move water.)*
- What means have been used to move water from one location to another? *(pumps, norias, Archimedean screws, etc.)*
- Why might the types of materials used to convey water, such as brick tunnels or metal pipes, be important? *(Materials that do not pollute the water may be preferable if the water is to be consumed.)*

Oil From the Sand

The oil fields discovered in the sands of Southwest Asia have been a bonanza for the region. These fields contain about one-half of all of the petroleum reserves in the world. Petroleum is the source of gasoline for automobiles, heating oil, and the basis of many chemicals used to make everything from fertilizers to plastics. Thus, petroleum products are an important part of the world economy. Having huge oil resources makes Southwest Asia a very important region economically.

FORMING PETROLEUM Oil and natural gas deposits were formed millions of years ago when an ancient sea covered the area of Southwest Asia. Microscopic plants and animals lived and died in the waters. Their remains sank and became mingled with the sand and mud on the bottom of the sea. Over time, pressure and heat transformed the material into hydrocarbons, which form the chemical basis of oil and natural gas.

Oil and natural gas do not exist in large pools beneath the ground, but are trapped inside rocks. You could hold a rock containing oil in your hand and not be able to see the oil because it is trapped in the microscopic pores of the rock. The more porous the rock, the more oil can be stored. A barrier of nonporous rock above the petroleum deposit prevents the gas or oil from moving out of the rock and to the surface.

Engineers use sophisticated equipment to extract, or remove, the oil. It also takes technical skill and special equipment to find deposits of oil. For this reason, oil was not discovered in some parts of the region until the 1920s and 1930s.

Geography TODAY

Ruins vs. Water

In 2000, archaeologists in southeastern Turkey unearthed parts of the ancient city of Zeugma, revealing magnificent Roman mosaics—only to realize that a man-made lake would soon submerge the new find.

Located about half a mile away from an historic treasure, Birecik Dam is part of a chain of dams located on the Euphrates River. It was built to provide water for irrigation and hydroelectric power for the region.

Archaeologists had only a few months to save outstanding examples of Roman art, such as the mosaic you see below. The rising waters covered the art before all of it could be rescued.

EARLY EXPLORATION Industrialization and the increasing popularity of automobiles made petroleum a highly desired resource. Beginning in the late 1800s, oil companies searched all over the world for oil resources. The first Southwest Asia oil discovery was in 1908 in Persia, now known as Iran. In 1938, oil companies found more oil fields in the Arabian Peninsula and Persian Gulf. Then, World War II interrupted further exploring. In 1948, oil companies discovered portions of what would become one of the world's largest oil fields at *al-Ghawar,* just on the eastern edge of the Rub al-Khali. This field contains more than one-quarter of all Saudi Arabia's reserves of oil. B

B. Answer Earlier discoveries showed oil was present in the region. Searches continued to see if more was present.

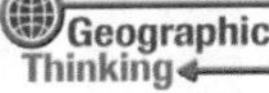

Geographic Thinking

Seeing Patterns

B Why did oil companies continue to search for oil deposits in Southwest Asia?

TRANSPORTING OIL Petroleum that has not been processed is called **crude oil.** Crude oil pumped from the ground must be moved to a **refinery.** The job of a refinery is to convert the crude oil into useful products. Pipelines transport the crude oil either to refineries or to ports where the oil is picked up by tankers and moved to other places for processing. Study the diagram on page 498 to learn how oil is processed and moved.

SW ASIA

Instruct: Objective 2

Oil from the Sand

- When and why did the demand for petroleum explode? *(By the late 1800s, industrializing countries were using a large volume of petroleum for fuel. Demand increased with the rising popularity of cars.)*
- What is the difference between crude oil and refined oil? *(Petroleum that comes directly from the ground is called crude oil. Crude oil must be refined to produce useful fuels, such as gasoline.)*
- Why might transporting oil be risky? *(because of the potential for a spill and serious damage to the environment)*

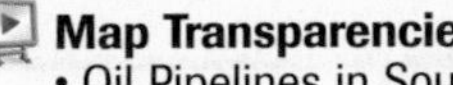

Map Transparencies MT38
- Oil Pipelines in Southwest Asia

Geography TODAY

Ruins vs. Water

Zeugma is just one of many cultural treasures endangered by increasing urbanization and population pressures in Turkey. To call attention to these threatened sites, a group of archeologists joined forces in 1993 to found the TAY (Archeological Settlements of Turkey) Project . Since then, they have worked to create an online database of archeological sites. The project Web site features an interactive collection of site inventories and photographs.

DIFFERENTIATING INSTRUCTION **LESS PROFICIENT READERS**

CREATING OUTLINES

Objective To help students focus on main ideas

Class Time 15 minutes

Task Create an outline from a written text

Directions Have students read "Oil From the Sand" on pages 497–499. To help them understand the major points, ask them to create an outline of the section. Introduce a hierarchy of numbers and letters they can use to create their outline. Then have them list the main head, sub-heads, and two or three of the main points from each sub-head. Encourage students to use their own words to rephrase main ideas.

For example:

I. Oil From the Sand
  A. Forming Petroleum
    1. Petroleum deposits were formed millions of years ago.
    2. Oil and natural gas are trapped in the microscopic pores of rocks.
    3. Engineers use complex equipment to remove oil from the ground.

More About

Processing Petroleum

Crude oil is composed of many different types of hydrocarbons. Different types of hydrocarbons are useful in different ways. Some hydrocarbons, for example, are useful for making kerosene. Others are suitable for gasoline. A major function of refineries is to separate different hydrocarbons. Because different hydrocarbons have different boiling points, one way that a refinery separates hydrocarbons is by heating crude oil. Once the boiling point of a specific hydrocarbon is reached, it vaporizes. After this separated vapor condenses, it is ready for further processing.

Interpreting Maps

Oil Pipelines in Southwest Asia

Have students examine the map. Ask them which passageway lies between the Persian Gulf and the Gulf of Oman and why the passageway is important. *(The Strait of Hormuz is important because oil tankers from various ports on the Persian Gulf must pass through it.)*

SKILLBUILDER ANSWERS

1. around the Persian Gulf
2. northwest to Mediterranean Sea

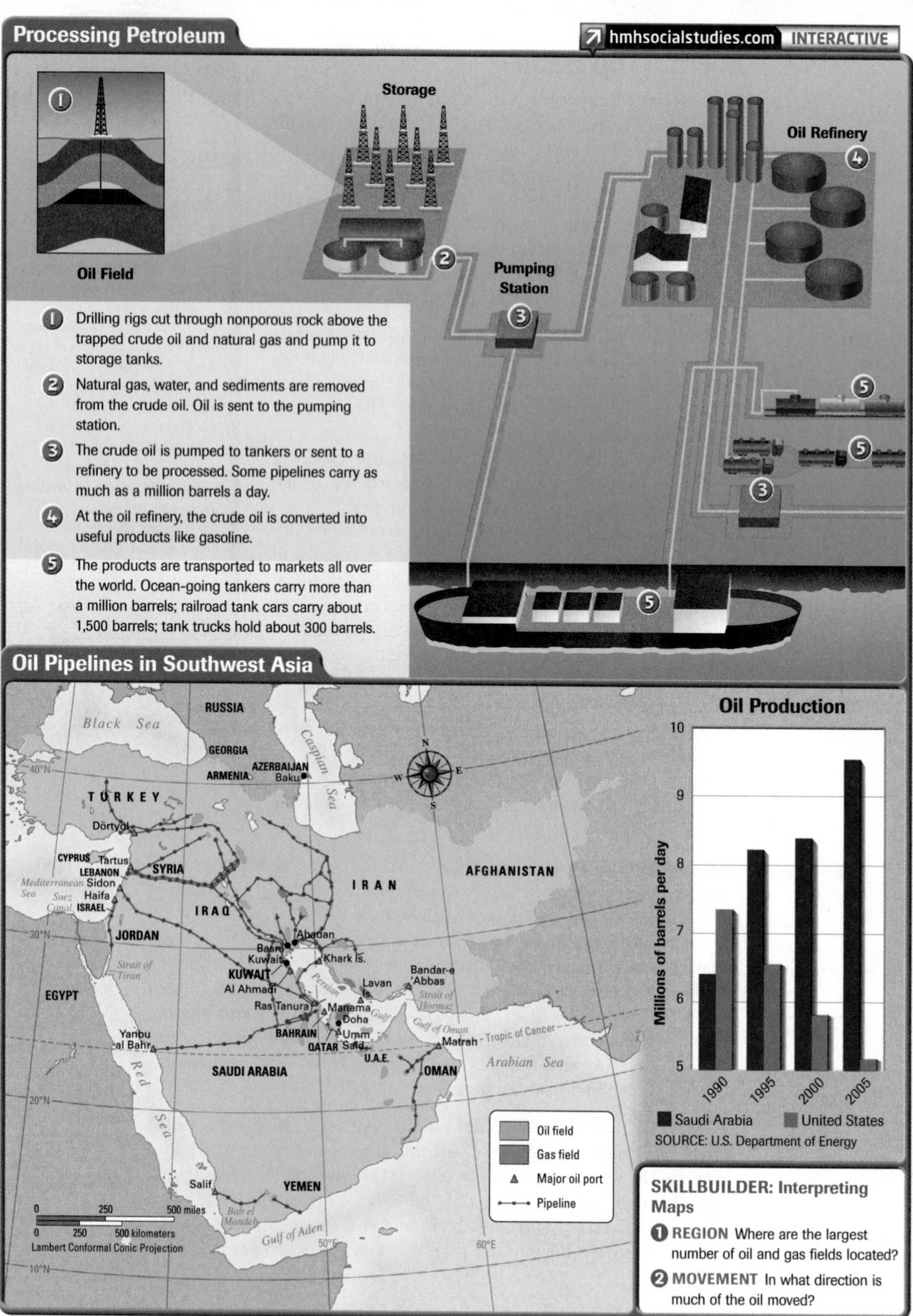
Processing Petroleum
hmhsocialstudies.com INTERACTIVE
Oil Field
Storage
Pumping Station
Oil Refinery
1 Drilling rigs cut through nonporous rock above the trapped crude oil and natural gas and pump it to storage tanks.
2 Natural gas, water, and sediments are removed from the crude oil. Oil is sent to the pumping station.
3 The crude oil is pumped to tankers or sent to a refinery to be processed. Some pipelines carry as much as a million barrels a day.
4 At the oil refinery, the crude oil is converted into useful products like gasoline.
5 The products are transported to markets all over the world. Ocean-going tankers carry more than a million barrels; railroad tank cars carry about 1,500 barrels; tank trucks hold about 300 barrels.
Oil Pipelines in Southwest Asia
RUSSIA
Black Sea
GEORGIA
ARMENIA
AZERBAIJAN
Baku
Caspian Sea
TURKEY
Dörtyol
CYPRUS
Tartus
LEBANON
Sidon
SYRIA
Mediterranean Sea
Suez Canal
Haifa
ISRAEL
JORDAN
IRAQ
IRAN
AFGHANISTAN
Abadan
Basra
Kuwait
Kharg Is.
KUWAIT
Al Ahmadi
Lavan Is.
Bandar-e 'Abbas
Strait of Hormuz
Strait of Tiran
EGYPT
Ras Tanura
Manama
Doha
Persian Gulf
BAHRAIN
Umm Said
QATAR
U.A.E.
Gulf of Oman
Matrah
Tropic of Cancer
Arabian Sea
OMAN
Yanbu al Bahr
Red Sea
SAUDI ARABIA
Salif
YEMEN
Bab el Mandeb
Gulf of Aden
40°N
30°N
20°N
10°N
50°E
60°E
0 250 500 miles
0 250 500 kilometers
Lambert Conformal Conic Projection
Oil field
Gas field
Major oil port
Pipeline
Oil Production
Millions of barrels per day
10
9
8
7
6
5
1990
1995
2000
2005
Saudi Arabia
United States
SOURCE: U.S. Department of Energy
SKILLBUILDER: Interpreting Maps
1 REGION Where are the largest number of oil and gas fields located?
2 MOVEMENT In what direction is much of the oil moved?

498 CHAPTER 21

DIFFERENTIATING INSTRUCTION GIFTED AND TALENTED STUDENTS

LEARNING ABOUT OIL PROCESSING

Objective To learn more about oil processing

Class Time 30 minutes

Task Create a chart that explains and illustrates the refining process

Directions Divide students into groups that will carry out in-depth research on the processing of crude oil. Have each team use the Internet or library resources to investigate how crude oil is transformed into usable form, employing such methods as fractional distillation or chemical processing. Each team will be responsible for creating a chart that explains and illustrates the process.

Placement of pipelines depends on the location of existing ports or access to worldwide markets. Study the map on page 498. Notice that in this region, the pipelines move the crude oil to ports on the Persian Gulf, the Red Sea, and the Mediterranean Sea. From these locations, oil tankers carry the petroleum to markets in the rest of the world. C

In some places, refineries process the crude oil near ports. Tanks to hold the oil products are located at port facilities. Many Southwest Asian nations have updated and outfitted their ports to service the very large ocean-going tankers.

Geographic Thinking

Using the Atlas

C Use the maps on pages 481 and 498. What countries would likely receive oil shipments from ports located on the Mediterranean Sea?

C. Answer any nation in Europe, possibly on to North American sites, and some North African sites

RISKS OF TRANSPORTING OIL Moving oil from one location to another always involves the risk of oil spills. The largest oil spill ever recorded occurred in January 1991, during the Persian Gulf War. A series of tankers and oil storage terminals in Kuwait and on islands off its coast were blown up by Iraqi forces. An estimated 240 to 460 million gallons of crude oil were spilled into the water and on land.

Buried pipelines in Southwest Asia help reduce the danger of above-ground accidents. However, oil spills on land do happen. Because oil is such a valuable commodity, the pipelines are carefully monitored for any drop in pressure that might signal a leak in the line. Any leaks are quickly repaired.

On the other hand, ocean-going tankers transporting oil are at a much higher risk for causing pollution. Many tankers operate in shallow and narrow waterways such as the Red Sea, the Suez Canal, the Persian Gulf, and the Straits of Hormuz. Here, there is danger of oil spills due to collisions or running aground. Most modern tankers have double hulls so that minor accidents will not result in oil spills. In addition, oil-producing nations in Southwest Asia have taken legal steps to protect their environments.

In the next chapter, you will learn more about the people and cultures of the subregions of Southwest Asia.

More About

Oil Spills

A major oil spill occurred in March 1989, when a 986-foot tanker, the *Exxon Valdez*, ran aground on Bligh Reef in Alaska. The accident caused the release of nearly 11 million gallons of oil—an amount equal to the volume of about 13 to 15 Olympic-sized swimming pools.

An even worse disaster began on April 20, 2010, when a BP (formerly British Petroleum) drilling rig in the Gulf of Mexico exploded, causing the well to gush crude oil into the water. Plant and animal life, tourism, and fishing industries were all devastated.

Section 3 Assessment

1 Places & Terms

Identify and explain where in the region these would be found.

- drip irrigation
- desalinization
- fossil water
- crude oil
- refinery

2 Taking Notes

HUMAN-ENVIRONMENT INTERACTION Review the notes you took for this section.

- What are some ways water is supplied in this region?
- In what ways is oil moved from the source to the market place?

3 Main Ideas

a. Why must both ancient and modern water supply methods be used in the region?

b. Why might water projects in Southwest Asia cause controversy?

c. What are some of the risks in transporting oil?

4 Geographic Thinking

Making Inferences What impact has technology had on the supply of oil and water in the region? **Think about:**

- finding large reserves of oil or water
- environmental hazards

hmhsocialstudies.com RESEARCH WEB LINKS

ASKING GEOGRAPHIC QUESTIONS Study the map of oil pipelines on page 498. Devise three geographic questions about the map, such as "What problems might there be in choosing locations for these pipelines?" Choose one of your questions and write several **paragraphs** answering the question. Present your findings to the class. Be sure to identify your data sources. 21st CENTURY

SW ASIA

Assess & Reteach

GeoFocus Have students complete the section on human-environment interaction in their graphic organizers.

Formal Assessment
- Section Quiz, p. 326

Reteaching Activity

Have students write a paragraph that summarizes each of the two main sub-sections of the section about human-environment interaction in Southwest Asia.

In-Depth Resources: Unit 7
- Reteaching Activity, p. 12

SECTION 3 ASSESSMENT ANSWERS

1. Place & Terms

drip irrigation, p. 496
desalinization, p. 496
fossil water, p. 496
crude oil, p. 497
refinery, p. 497

2. Taking Notes

- qanats, noria, drip irrigation, desalinization of sea water, processing wastewater
- pipeline to rail cars, ocean-going tankers, tank trucks

3. Main Ideas

a. Water supplies are short, and the area is in need of any technology it can get, old or new.

b. Supplies may be taken by nations upstream, depriving people downstream of needed water.

c. Pipelines may leak or break. Tankers may run aground or be in collisions.

4. Geographic Thinking

It has brought great wealth to the region, but also environmental hazards and danger of pollution.

GeoActivity

Integrated Assessment
- Rubric for a paragraph, 4.2

CHAPTER 21 ASSESSMENT

Reviewing Places & Terms

A.
1. Golan Heights, p. 487
2. wadi, p. 488
3. Tigris River, p. 489
4. Euphrates River, p. 489
5. oasis, p. 492
6. salt flat, p. 492
7. drip irrigation, p. 496
8. desalinization, p. 496
9. crude oil, p. 497
10. refinery, p. 497

B. Possible Responses

11. You would most likely find a wadi on the Arabian Peninsula.
12. The Golan Heights is a plateau.
13. Several ancient civilizations were located in the Tigris and Euphrates river valleys.
14. Drip irrigation and desalinization refer to water usage.
15. Refineries process crude oil into usable products.
16. Many refineries are built near oil fields and ports.
17. Drip irrigation reduces the evaporation of scarce water.
18. Iran has salt flat deserts.
19. Underground springs are often the source of water for an oasis.
20. It is expensive and too salty for crop use.

Chapter 21 Assessment

VISUAL SUMMARY

PHYSICAL GEOGRAPHY OF SOUTHWEST ASIA

Landforms

Peninsulas: Anatolian, Arabian

Mountain Ranges: Hindu Kush, Elburz, Zagros, Taurus

Major Waterways: Tigris, Euphrates, Jordan, Red Sea-Suez Canal, Bosporus Strait, Straits of Hormuz

Resources

- Water is a scarce resource.
- Oil is an abundant resource that shapes the region's economy.

Climate and Vegetation

Deserts:
- Rub al-Khali, An-Nafud, Syrian, and Negev are mostly sandy.
- Dasht-e Kavir and Dasht-e Lut are salt flat deserts.

Human-Environment Interaction

- Water is provided through both old and new technologies.
- Oil is pumped from the ground, processed, and transported out of Southwest Asia.

Reviewing Places & Terms

A. Briefly explain the importance of each of the following.

1. Golan Heights
2. wadi
3. Tigris River
4. Euphrates River
5. oasis
6. salt flat
7. drip irrigation
8. desalinization
9. crude oil
10. refinery

B. Answer the questions about vocabulary in complete sentences.

11. Where would you most likely find a wadi?
12. The Golan Heights are an example of which type of landform?
13. Where were several ancient river valley civilizations located?
14. Which terms above deal with water usage?
15. Why are refineries needed?
16. Where might you find a refinery?
17. Why is drip irrigation used?
18. Where would you find a salt flat desert in Southwest Asia?
19. What is the source of water for an oasis?
20. What are drawbacks to using water from a desalinization plant?

Main Ideas

Landforms and Resources (pp. 487–490)

1. How do the landforms of the region restrict movement?
2. What are the most valuable resources in the region and why are they valuable?
3. How large are the oil reserves in the region?

Climate and Vegetation (pp. 491–494)

4. What types of deserts are found in the region?
5. Why is extensive irrigation needed in the region?
6. Where in the region are well-watered lands found?

Human-Environment Interaction (pp. 495–499)

7. What are some examples of the ways in which water is provided in the region?
8. In what ways do major water projects cause political problems?
9. Where are the major oil fields in the region located?
10. What are some dangers in transporting oil?

Main Ideas

1. Mountains are difficult to cross, there are few rivers to use for transportation, and deserts are too hot and arid for humans.
2. water because it is scarce and necessary for life; oil because it is strategic fuel
3. about one-half of the world's supplies
4. sandy and salt flat deserts
5. Most of the area is either desert or semiarid.
6. in river valleys and on the coastlands
7. ancient and modern methods such as drip irrigation and desalinization
8. Some nations will lose out on water taken upstream and not shared downstream.
9. Saudi Arabia and the Persian Gulf
10. pipelines may leak, tankers may collide or break up

CHAPTER 21 ASSESSMENT

Critical Thinking

1. Using Your Notes
Use your completed chart to answer these questions.

Landforms	
Resources	

a. How are landforms and desert climate connected?
b. How is oil production related to the economy of the region?

2. Geographic Themes
a. **LOCATION** Why is the relative location of Southwest Asia important to world trade of oil?
b. **PLACE** Why is the Persian Gulf considered a strategic location?

3. Identifying Themes
Why are the Tigris and Euphrates rivers so important to Southwest Asia? Which of the five themes applies to this situation?

4. Making Generalizations
In what ways do oil and water shape the lives of the people of Southwest Asia?

5. Making Inferences
How does climate affect the distribution of population in the region?

For Additional Test Practice
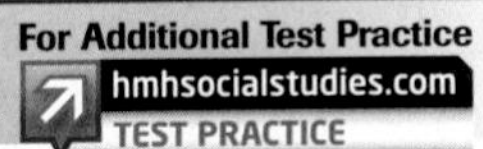

Geographic Skills: Interpreting a Cartogram

Estimated Worldwide Oil Reserves
Use the cartogram at the right to answer the following questions. (See page 22 or page 733 for more on cartograms.)

1. **PLACE** Which nations have the greatest oil reserves?
2. **PLACE** What is the approximate amount of reserves for the United States?
3. **REGION** How does this cartogram help to explain the importance of the region?

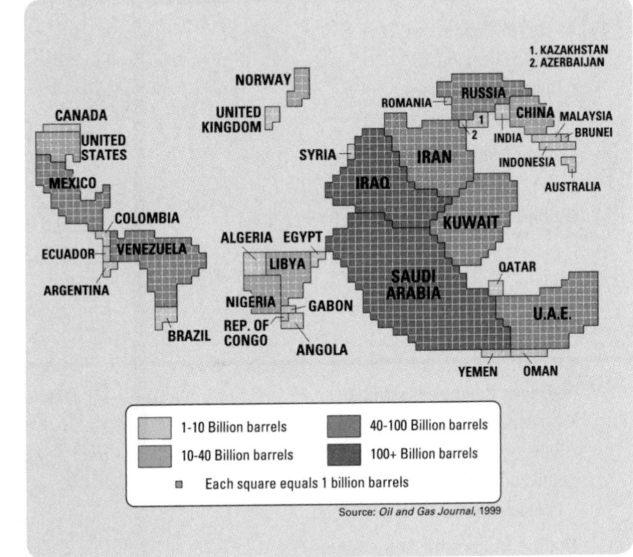

Create a three-dimensional model to show the information on the cartogram. Be sure to label each of the countries and give an approximate total amount of oil reserves.

hmhsocialstudies.com
MULTIMEDIA ACTIVITY

Use the links at **hmhsocialstudies.com** to do research about oil production. Find out what products are made from crude oil.

Creating Graphs and Charts Create an illustrated chart showing the types of products that are produced from petroleum. List the Web sites that you used in preparing your report.

21st CENTURY

SW ASIA

Critical Thinking

1. **a.** both restrict movement; some landforms cause desert areas to form
 b. It is the basis of the regional economy.
2. **a.** It is easily accessible for trade in Asia, Africa, Europe, and the Americas.
 b. It is near major oil fields in the Persian Gulf area and the Arabian Peninsula.
3. They provide water and transportation for the region; place
4. Water is scarce and is needed for human and agricultural purposes. Oil provides the base for the economy.
5. Dense populations will be found in areas with adequate water supplies.

GeoActivity

Integrated Assessment
• Rubric for a three-dimensional model, 1.10

Formal Assessment
• Chapter Test, Forms A, B, and C, pp. 327–338

Geographic Skills

1. Saudi Arabia, Iraq
2. 21 billion barrels
3. The supplies of oil in the region surpass the supplies in any other part of the world.

MULTIMEDIA ACTIVITY

For their illustrated charts on petroleum products, students should:
• Write an introductory overview.
• Use different mediums to illustrate products.
• Include references to the Web sites used as sources.

Grading Rubric Evaluate student performance as Exceptional, Acceptable, or Poor in each of the following categories:

	Exceptional	Acceptable	Poor
Graphic is clear and accurate			
Titles and headings clearly state the topic and categories			
Clearly lists sources			

Human Geography of Southwest Asia

OVERVIEW	INSTRUCTIONAL RESOURCES	
ESSENTIAL QUESTION How have religion and oil affected political issues in Southwest Asia? **Focus on the Essential Question Podcast**	**In-Depth Resources: Unit 7** • Building Vocabulary, p. 17 **Block Schedule Strategies** **Chapter Summaries** (English/Spanish)	**Interactive Online Edition** TOS **ExamView® Assessment Suite** (English/Spanish) TOS **CalendarPlanner** **Power Presentations with Media Gallery** **Critical Thinking Transparencies** • CT22 **Video:** Back to Basra: After Saddam hmhsocialstudies.com INTERACTIVE
SECTION 1 **THE ARABIAN PENINSULA** **MAIN IDEAS** • The Arabian Penisula is heavily influenced by Islam. • Saudi Arabia takes its name from the Saud family, which established control over much of peninsula by the end of the 1920s. • Oil production dominates the region's economy.	**In-Depth Resources: Unit 7** • Guided Reading, p. 13 • Building Vocabulary, p. 17 • Reteaching Activities, p. 18 **Outline Maps with Activities** • The Arabian Peninsula, pp. 69–70 **Guided Reading Workbook,** Section 1	
SECTION 2 **THE EASTERN MEDITERRANEAN** **MAIN IDEAS** • The holy places of three religions are found in this subregion. • After World War I, Britain and France took control over most of the region. • There is a great deal of political tension among the nations in this subregion.	**In-Depth Resources: Unit 7** • Guided Reading, p. 14 • Skillbuilder Practice, p. 16 • Building Vocabulary, p. 17 • Reteaching Activities, p. 19 **Outline Maps with Activities** • The Eastern Mediterranean, pp. 71–72 **Cultures Around the World** • Daily Life, p. 38 • Arts and Crafts, p. 40 • Dance, p. 41 **Guided Reading Workbook,** Section 2	**Map Transparencies** • MT39 Creation of Israel **Cultures Transparencies CW38, 40, 41** • Living on a Kibbutz • Turkish Ceramic Tiles • Whirling Dervishes **The World's Music Audio Program**
SECTION 3 **THE NORTHEAST** **MAIN IDEAS** • The vast majority of people in the Northeast are Muslim, but most are not part of the Arab culture. • The nations in the Northeast range from developed to very poorly developed. • Political problems in many of the nations in the Northeast have hampered economic progress.	**In-Depth Resources: Unit 7** • Guided Reading, p. 15 • Building Vocabulary, p. 17 • Reteaching Activities, p. 20 **Outline Maps with Activities** • The Northeast, pp. 73–74 **Cultures Around the World** • Architecture, p. 37 • Fine Arts, p. 39 • Traditional Practices, p. 42 **Guided Reading Workbook,** Section 3	**Critical Thinking Transparencies** • CT54 Selected Cities of Southwest Asia **Cultures Transparencies CW37, 39, 42** • Petra • Islamic Calligraphy • Praying at the Western Wall **The World's Music Audio Program**

ASSESSMENT

SE **Chapter Assessment,** pp. 522–523

Formal Assessment
- Chapter Tests, Forms A, B, and C, pp. 342–353

TOS **ExamView® Assessment Suite**

Strategies for Test Preparation

hmhsocialstudies.com TEST PRACTICE

SE **Section Assessment,** p. 507

Formal Assessment
- Section Quiz, p. 339

Integrated Assessment
- Rubric for line graph, 2.3

Test Practice Transparencies TT71

SE **Section Assessment,** p. 515

Formal Assessment
- Section Quiz, p. 340

Integrated Assessment
- Rubric for a sketch map, 2.1

Test Practice Transparencies TT72

SE **Section Assessment,** p. 519

Formal Assessment
- Section Quiz, p. 341

Integrated Assessment
- Rubric for a database, 2.6
- Rubric for a demonstration, 1.10

Test Practice Transparencies TT73

CHART KEY:

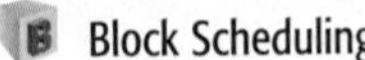

SE Student Edition	Block Scheduling	DVD/CD-ROM
TE Teacher's Edition	TOS Teacher One Stop	MP3 Audio
Printable Resource	Presentation Resource	HISTORY™

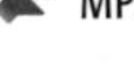

Program Resources available on TOS and @ hmhsocialstudies.com

SUPPORTING RESOURCES

- **Multimedia Classroom Global History Series**
- **Global History Teacher's Guide**

Social Studies Trade Library Collection
- World Regions Trade Collection

For more information or to purchase these resources, go to

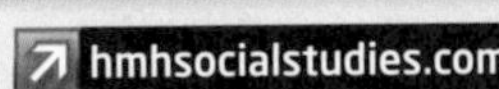

DIFFERENTIATED INSTRUCTION

English Learners	Struggling Readers	Gifted and Talented Students
 **Spanish/English Guided Reading Workbook** **Access for Students Acquiring English/ESL** Spanish Translations, pp. 117–120  **Chapter Summaries** (English/Spanish) TE **TE Activity** Using Dictionaries and Thesauri, p. 505	 **Chapter Summaries** (English/Spanish) TE **TE Activity** Seeing Main Ideas, p. 513	TE **TE Activity** Creating an Art History Booklet, p. 504

ENRICHMENT ACTIVITIES

The following activities are especially suitable for classes following block schedules.

SE **Student Edition,** pp. 502–523 • Disasters! Earthquake in Turkey, pp. 520–521	hmhsocialstudies.com INTERACTIVE • Comparing Cultures: Religious Architecture, pp. 508–509

BLOCK SCHEDULE LESSON PLAN OPTIONS: 90-MINUTE PERIOD

DAY 1

SECTION 1, pp. 503–509
Class Time 90 minutes

- **Short Essay** Have students write a short essay that compares different calendrical systems. They should focus on the Jewish and Muslim calendars and the calendar that is commonly used in the United States. Have them use the Internet or print resources in the library to research the subject. Encourage students to include drawings and illustrations in their essays.
  Class Time 45 minutes
- **Documentary** Have students develop an outline for "Ramadan," a documentary exploring Islam's holy month. Ask students to discuss the religious significance of Ramadan and to consider the different traditions associated with the holy month, such as fasting.
  Class Time 45 minutes

DAY 2

SECTION 2, pp. 510–515
Class Time 90 minutes

- **Multimedia Presentation** Divide students into small groups. Have each group use library or Internet resources to do research on the Ottoman Empire. Ask students to use their research to create a multimedia presentation that will provide a basic overview of the Ottoman Empire for people who are unfamiliar with it. Encourage students to include a brief written or audio outline of the empire's history; discussions of major leaders and events; visual examples of important architectural and artistic achievements; descriptions of interesting features of Ottoman life; and a consideration of the legacy of the Ottoman Empire in Southwest Asia today.

DAY 3

SECTION 3, pp. 516–521

CHAPTER 22 REVIEW AND ASSESSMENT, pp. 522-523
Class Time 90 minutes

- **Review** Have students compare the cluster diagrams they made for each subregion of Southwest Asia. Lead them in discussing the similarities and differences among the subregions.
  Class Time 35 minutes
- **Assessment** Have students complete the Chapter 22 Assessment.
  Class Time 55 minutes

TEACHER-TESTED ACTIVITY *Reinforcing the Five Themes*

Class Time One class period

Task Use classroom work stations to apply the five themes to Southwest Asia

Supplies
- Notebook and pencil
- Textbook atlas
- Pictures of Southwest Asia
- Five classroom stations

Purpose To review knowledge of material in the chapter and apply the five geographic themes to Southwest Asia

Activity This can be done either as an individual or a small group activity. Students or groups will move from station to station within an allotted amount of time. **Station One:** Students will give the *absolute location* of 3–5 capital cities and the *relative location* of 3–5 historical places. **Station Two:** Students will view a set of pictures and then write complete sentences describing those *places.* **Station Three:** Students will view pictures of oil fields in Iraq, Iran, Kuwait, or another OPEC nation and explain how the images represent *human-environment interaction.* **Station Four:** Students will view pictures of port cities in Southwest Asia, and explain the importance of *movement* of various goods from Southwest Asia to the United States. **Station Five:** Students will view pictures of Southwest Asian art and architecture, and explain what makes it unique to the *region.*

Anne Woods
Geography Teacher, Orchard Farms High School, St. Charles, Missouri

TECHNOLOGY IN THE CLASSROOM

Students can design their own Web sites to organize information and to share their knowledge with other kids at school and around the world. By creating a Web site, students gain experience in organizing information in a "non-linear" fashion and get a "behind-the-scenes" look at what goes into developing materials for the Internet. Their Web sites can be kept on the classroom computer, uploaded to the school's internal server, or uploaded to the Internet for students at other schools to view.

Objective Students will create Web sites to inform other students about oil and its role in Southwest Asia.

Task Have students conduct Internet research to complete a graphic organizer about different aspects of oil and its importance in Southwest Asia. Then have them create Web sites that reflect what they have learned and that link to pages with additional information.

Class Time 2–4 class periods

1. After students have read Chapter 22, discuss the importance of oil to the economies of Southwest Asian countries. Why does oil "dominate" the economy, as stated on page 505?

2. Draw an idea web on the board, formatted as one main circle with four spoke circles coming out of it. The main circle should contain the word "oil," and the spokes should contain the subtopics "production process," "economy," "environment," and "politics." Have students contribute words and ideas to add to details circles for each of these four subtopics. Their ideas should come from both Chapters 21 and 22.

3. Tell students that they will be designing Web sites to inform other students about the topics they have placed in their idea web. Discuss the reasons why this Web site might be valuable. One reason should be that these topics are frequently highlighted in the news but that there are not many good sources of basic background information about them.

4. Divide the class into groups of four, and have each group focus on one of these aspects of oil: its location and the extraction process; its importance in the Southwest Asian economy; environmental issues related to its production, transport, and use; political issues related to its production and trade.

5. Ask each group to use the links at **hmhsocialstudies.com** and any other resources they can find to add details to their portion of the idea web.

6. Have groups design Web pages that provide background information and details about their assigned subtopic. For example, the group concentrating on politics might make a home page that summarizes recent and historical events, such as current news stories, the 1970s oil embargo, or the Persian Gulf War. The sites should provide some background text, pictures or other graphics, and links to additional Web sites. Make sure students cite the sources for the images they use in the Web site (see link at **hmhsocialstudies.com** for citation format).

7. Have several students design a home page for the entire site that links to groups' home pages. Upload the site onto the server, and register it with your favorite search engines.

CHAPTER 22 OBJECTIVE

Identify key features of human geography in Southwest Asia.

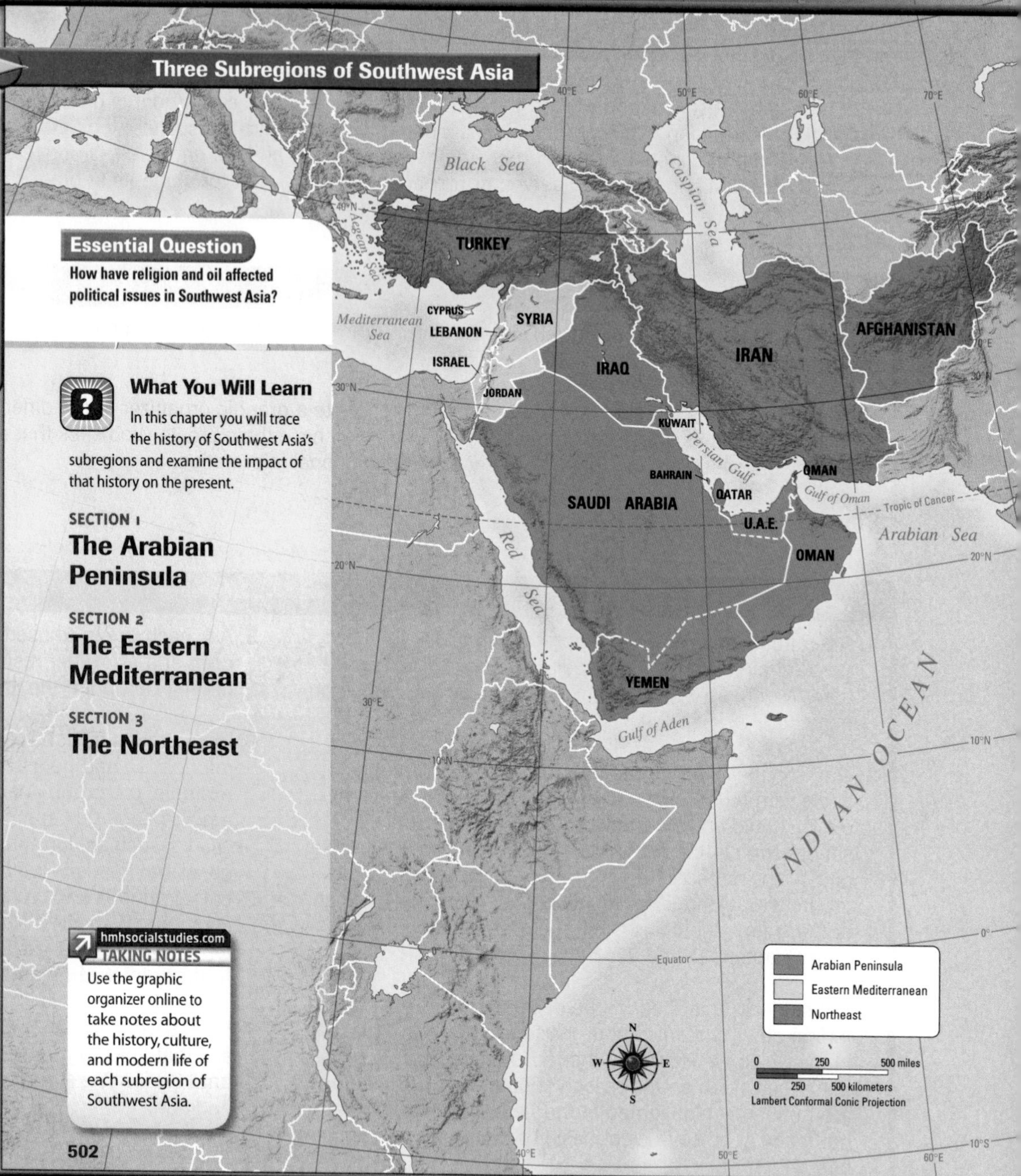

Chapter **22** HUMAN GEOGRAPHY OF SOUTHWEST ASIA

Religion, Politics, and Oil

HISTORY

Back to Basra: After Saddam

hmhsocialstudies.com VIDEO

Interpreting Maps

Three Subregions of Southwest Asia

Have students examine the map of Southwest Asia. Remind students of the region's location at the confluence of three different continents.

Extension Ask students what criteria might have been used to determine the borders of the three subregions.

Introducing the Essential Question

- Challenge students to recall what they have learned in other classes about the history of Southwest Asia. Emphasize the impact made on history by the three monotheistic religions that began in the region.
- Ask students to recall news stories they have read or heard lately that relate to Southwest Asia. Discuss those stories to determine the role of religion or oil on political events.

hmhsocialstudies.com TAKING NOTES

Have students fill out the cluster diagrams in their notebooks using material from all sections in this chapter.

Critical Thinking Transparencies CT22
- GeoFocus

In-Depth Resources: Unit 7
- Building Vocabulary, p. 17

Three Subregions of Southwest Asia
Black Sea
Caspian Sea
Aegean Sea
Mediterranean Sea
TURKEY
CYPRUS
SYRIA
LEBANON
ISRAEL
JORDAN
IRAQ
IRAN
AFGHANISTAN
KUWAIT
Persian Gulf
BAHRAIN
QATAR
SAUDI ARABIA
U.A.E.
OMAN
Gulf of Oman
Tropic of Cancer
Arabian Sea
Red Sea
YEMEN
Gulf of Aden
INDIAN OCEAN
Equator
40°E
50°E
60°E
70°E
40°N
30°N
20°N
10°N
0°
10°S
30°E
Arabian Peninsula
Eastern Mediterranean
Northeast
0 250 500 miles
0 250 500 kilometers
Lambert Conformal Conic Projection
N
S
E
W

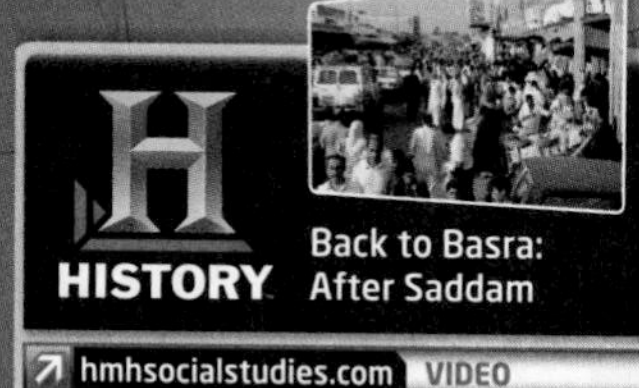

Essential Question

How have religion and oil affected political issues in Southwest Asia?

What You Will Learn

In this chapter you will trace the history of Southwest Asia's subregions and examine the impact of that history on the present.

SECTION 1
The Arabian Peninsula

SECTION 2
The Eastern Mediterranean

SECTION 3
The Northeast

hmhsocialstudies.com TAKING NOTES

Use the graphic organizer online to take notes about the history, culture, and modern life of each subregion of Southwest Asia.

502

CHAPTER 22 ADDITIONAL RESOURCES

BOOKS FOR THE TEACHER

Wright, Robin. ***Dreams and Shadows: The Future of the Middle East.*** Penguin, 2009. A guardedly optimistic view of the Middle East from a veteran observer.

Sasson, Jack, Karen Rubinson, and John Baines, eds. ***Civilizations of the Ancient Near East.*** Peabody, MA: Hendrickson, 2001. A four-volume study of the region.

BOOKS FOR THE STUDENT

Sasson, Jean P. ***Princess: A True Story of Life Behind the Veil in Saudi Arabia.*** Van Nuys, CA: Windsor-Brooke Books, 2001. Account of the position of women in Saudi society.

Settle, Mary Lee. ***Blood Tie.*** South Carolina: University of South Carolina Press, 1995. A novel that touches on the recent social changes in Turkey.

VIDEOS

The Message: The Story of Islam. Dir. by Moustapha Akkad, 1977. Epic tale of the beginning of Islam.

INTERNET

For more on the human geography of Southwest Asia, visit . . .

hmhsocialstudies.com

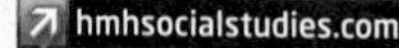

The Arabian Peninsula

Main Ideas

- The Arabian Peninsula is heavily influenced by the religious principles of Islam.
- Oil production dominates the economy of the region.

Places & Terms

Mecca	**mosque**
Islam	**theocratic**
Muhammad	**OPEC**

CONNECT TO THE ISSUES
RELIGIOUS CONFLICT Muslim claims to land in the region laid the foundation for future conflict.

A HUMAN PERSPECTIVE Two million people pour into the Saudi Arabian city of Mecca for a few weeks each year. They come from all over the world. In the past, the trip to Mecca involved a difficult journey across oceans and over miles of desert. Today, pilgrims arrive on airplanes. These people are fulfilling the Islamic religious duty of hajj, which is a pilgrimage to the holiest city of Islam—**Mecca**. For five or more days, all are dressed in simple white garments and all perform special activities, rituals, and ceremonies. It is a powerful example of spiritual devotion by the followers of one of the three major religions that claim a home in Southwest Asia.

Islam Changes Desert Culture

The modern nations in this subregion are Bahrain, Kuwait, Oman, Saudi Arabia, Qatar, United Arab Emirates, and Yemen. They are located at the intersection of three continents: Africa, Asia, and Europe. Because of this location, there were many opportunities for trade, and exchange of culture and religion.

TOWN AND DESERT In the past, some towns in the subregion served as trade centers for caravans moving across the deserts. Other cities were ports where goods were exchanged from the Silk Roads in East Asia, Indian Ocean trade from South Asia, and Mediterranean Sea trade from Europe. Still other towns were near oases and fertile lands along major rivers.

Nomadic desert dwellers called Bedouins moved across the peninsula from oasis to oasis. They adapted to the harsh conditions of the desert and built a culture based on strong family ties. They often fought against other families and clans for pasturelands for their livestock. Their fighting skills would eventually help to spread a new religion that developed in the region—Islam.

Islam is a monotheistic religion based on the teachings of its founder, **Muhammad**. Muhammad lived part of his life in the city of Mecca.

PLACE Thousands of Muslim pilgrims gather at the site of the Ka'aba in Mecca. The Ka'aba is the black box at the right in the picture.

SECTION 1 OBJECTIVES

1. Discuss the influence of Islam in Southwest Asia.
2. Describe the history of theocracy and colonialism in the region.
3. Explain the importance of oil for the regional economy.
4. Describe modern Arabic life.

GeographicThinking

Using the Atlas, p. 505
Making Comparisons, p. 506
Drawing Conclusions, p. 507

Focus & Motivate

Have students discuss what they already know about Islam. Prompt them with questions, such as "Who was the founder of Islam?" *(Muhammad)*

Instruct: Objective 1

Islam Changes Desert Culture

- What is Islam? *(a monotheistic religion based on the teachings of its founder, Muhammad)*
- How did Islam help to unite the region culturally? *(by requiring specific duties–the Five Pillars–of its adherents)*

In-Depth Resources: Unit 7
- Guided Reading, p. 13

Interpreting Photographs

The Ka'aba in Mecca

Have students examine the photograph and ask how it might reflect the region's climate. *(The Ka'aba's location out of doors suggests that pilgrims expect hospitable temperatures and little precipitation.)*

SECTION 1 PROGRAM RESOURCES

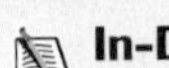

In-Depth Resources: Unit 7
- Guided Reading, p. 13
- Building Vocabulary, p. 17
- Reteaching Activity, p. 18

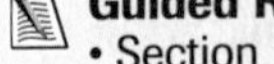

Guided Reading Workbook
- Section 1

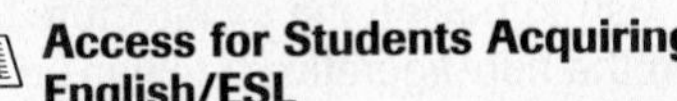

Access for Students Acquiring English/ESL
- Guided Reading, p. 117

Outline Maps with Activities
- The Arabian Peninsula, pp. 69–70

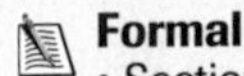

Formal Assessment
- Section Quiz, p. 339

Integrated Assessment
- Rubric for a line graph, 2.3

INTEGRATED TECHNOLOGY

Chapter Summaries

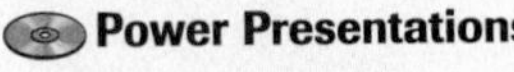

Power Presentations

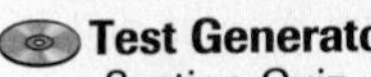

Test Generator
- Section Quiz

hmhsocialstudies.com

TEST-TAKING RESOURCES

Strategies for Test Preparation

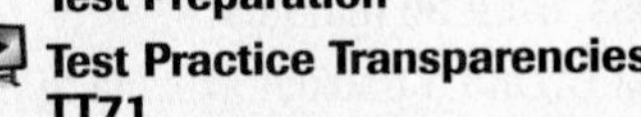

Test Practice Transparencies TT71

Online Test Practice

Instruct: Objective 2

Governments Change Hands

- What type of governments predominated in lands controlled by Muslims? *(theocratic)*
- How did World War I affect the region? *(It resulted in the breakup of the Muslim-held Ottoman Empire and British and French control of the region.)*
- Who rules Saudi Arabia? *(the Saud family)*

Interpreting Time Lines

Arabian Peninsula History

Have students study the time line and read "Governments Change Hands." Ask how much time passed between the peak and the breakup of the Ottoman Empire. *(around 350 years)*

ISLAM BRINGS A NEW CULTURE The new religion united the people of the Arabian Peninsula in a way that had not been done previously. Islam requires certain religious duties of all who follow its teachings. The basic duties are called the Five Pillars. By performing these religious duties, all converts to Islam, called Muslims, practiced a similar culture. The Five Pillars are:

- **Faith** All believers must testify to the following statement of faith: "There is no God but Allah, and Muhammad is the Messenger of Allah."
- **Prayer** Five times a day, Muslims face toward the holy city of Mecca to pray. They may do this at a place of worship called a **mosque** or wherever they find themselves at the prayer times.
- **Charity** Muslims believe they have a responsibility to support the less fortunate by giving money for that purpose.
- **Fasting** During the Islamic holy month of Ramadan, Muslims do not eat or drink anything between sunrise and sunset. This action reminds Muslims that there are things in life more important than eating. It is also a sign of self-control and humility.
- **Pilgrimage** All able Muslims are expected to make a pilgrimage (hajj) to Mecca at least once during their lifetime.

BACKGROUND
Ramadan is the ninth month of the 12-month lunar year calendar used by Muslims. It does not match the calendar used by most Americans.

THE SPREAD OF ISLAM As more and more people on the Arabian Peninsula began to convert to Islam, they spread its teachings. Armies of Bedouin fighters moved across the desert, conquered lands, and put Muslim leaders in control. Arabic language and Islamic teachings and culture spread across Southwest Asia. Muslim armies spread across three continents—Asia, Africa, and Europe. By the Middle Ages, a large area of the world was controlled by Muslim empires.

Governments Change Hands

The governments of lands controlled by Muslims were **theocratic.** This means religious leaders control the government. Rulers relied on religious law and consulted with religious scholars on running the country.

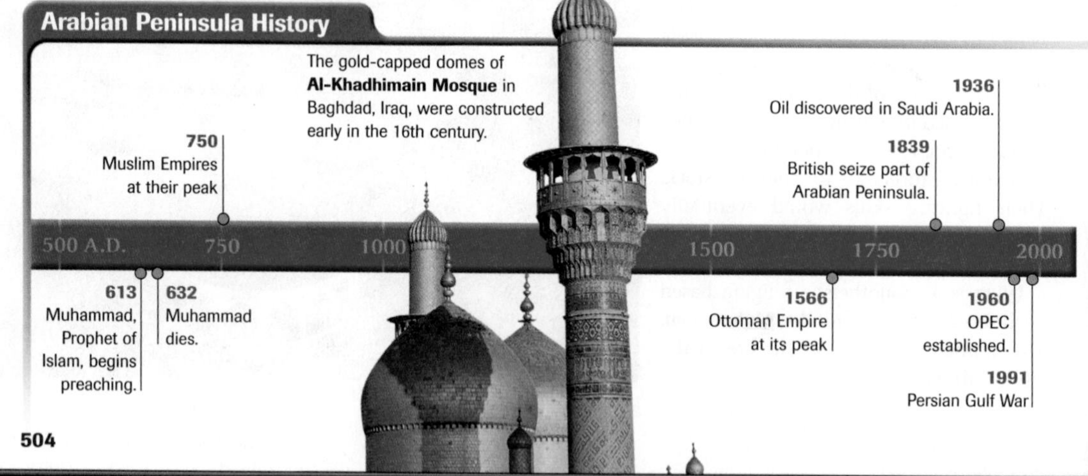
Arabian Peninsula History
The gold-capped domes of **Al-Khadhimain Mosque** in Baghdad, Iraq, were constructed early in the 16th century.
500 A.D.
750
1000
1500
1750
2000
613 Muhammad, Prophet of Islam, begins preaching.
632 Muhammad dies.
750 Muslim Empires at their peak
1566 Ottoman Empire at its peak
1839 British seize part of Arabian Peninsula.
1936 Oil discovered in Saudi Arabia.
1960 OPEC established.
1991 Persian Gulf War

DIFFERENTIATING INSTRUCTION **GIFTED AND TALENTED STUDENTS**

CREATING AN ART HISTORY BOOKLET

Objective To learn about Islamic art and architecture

Class Time 30 minutes

Task Create a booklet explaining and illustrating important themes and traditions in Islamic art and architecture

Directions Introduce students to the rich artistic legacy of Southwest Asia. Then have students use the Internet or library resources to carry out research on Islamic art. Ask them to use their research to put together a short booklet that explains and illustrates some aspect of Islamic art or architecture. For example, students may wish to outline the architecture of mosques, or they may choose to focus on the non-figurative traditions of Islamic art.

In all the modern nations of this subregion, the legal system is wholly or largely based on Islamic law (Shari'ah).

COLONIAL POWERS TAKE CONTROL Toward the end of the 1600s, the leaders of Muslim nations were weak. At the same time, countries like Britain and France were growing in power and establishing empires throughout the world. Much of Southwest Asia fell under the control of those two nations, especially after World War I and the breakup of the Muslim-held Ottoman Empire. The region was valuable to colonial powers for two reasons: because of the Suez Canal, a vital link between colonial holdings in the rest of Asia and European ports, and because oil was discovered there after 1932.

However, only a part of the region was colonized. On the Arabian Peninsula, a new power was rising. It was Abdul al-Aziz Ibn Saud. A daring leader, Abdul al-Aziz consolidated power over large areas of the Arabian Peninsula in the name of the Saud family. By the end of the 1920s, only small countries on the Persian Gulf and parts of Yemen remained free of his control. The whole area became known as Saudi Arabia in 1932. Descendants of Abdul al-Aziz still rule Saudi Arabia today. A

Geographic Thinking

Using the Atlas
A Using the map on page 479, make a list of the countries that were not under the control of Abdul al-Aziz.
A. Answer
Kuwait, Qatar, Bahrain, UAE, and Oman

Oil Dominates the Economy

The principal resource in the economy of the Arabian Peninsula is oil. The region grew in global importance as oil became more important to the economies of all nations. Arabian Peninsula nations make almost all of their export money and a large share of GDP from oil, so oil prices are very important to them. Large increases in oil prices allow the oil-producing nations to funnel money into development of other parts of their economies, especially water development projects.

In 1960, a group of oil-producing nations, including Saudi Arabia and Kuwait, established an organization to coordinate policies on selling petroleum products. The group is the Organization of Petroleum Exporting Countries, also known as **OPEC**. The purpose of OPEC is to help members control worldwide oil prices by adjusting oil prices and production quotas. OPEC is a powerful force in international trade. Other Southwest Asian members include Qatar, the United Arab Emirates, Iran, and Iraq.

BACKGROUND
Other members of OPEC include Algeria, Gabon, Indonesia, Libya, Nigeria, and Venezuela.

Connect TO THE Issues

RESOURCES

Oil and the Economy

Many of the oil-producing countries are heavily dependent on oil as a major source of business. Kuwait, which is almost floating on oil because its resources are so great, generates about one-half of its GDP from petroleum. Notice in the chart below that the nations in this subregion are dependent on oil for at least 30 percent of their GDP.

Because oil is a non-renewable resource, it will eventually run out. These nations must work to find other sources of income to replace oil revenues when they are depleted.

Oil Income Percentage of GDP*

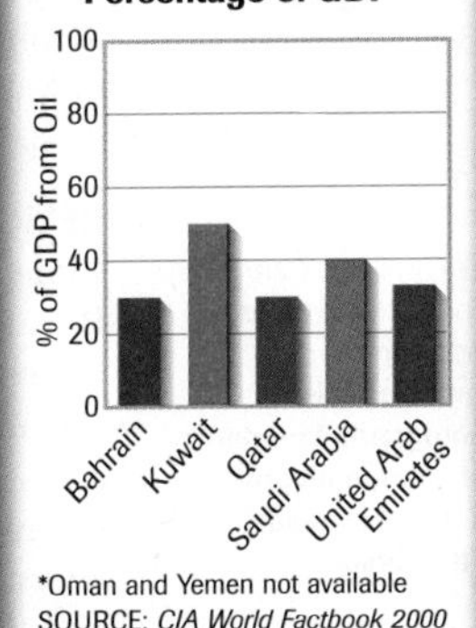

*Oman and Yemen not available
SOURCE: *CIA World Factbook 2000*

Modern Arabic Life

Changes in the nations of the Arabian Peninsula during the 20th century were dramatic. The region is developing quickly with an emphasis on modernizing. Use of Western technology and machines undermined traditional ways of life. Camels, which used to be the mainstay of life in

SW ASIA

Instruct: Objective 3

Oil Dominates the Economy

- Why might leaders on the Arabian Peninsula be concerned about changes in the price of oil? *(because their economies are heavily dependent on revenues from the sale of oil)*
- When and why was OPEC created? *(1960; to help member nations control world wide oil prices)*

Connect TO THE Issues

Resources: Oil and the Economy

Because its oil and gas reserves are limited, Bahrain has developed one of the Arabian Peninsula's more diversified economies. Bahrain's government has used oil revenues to build advanced transportation and communication systems. It has also developed non-oil sector enterprises such as ship repair and aluminum refining. Tourism is also a significant source of income. Why might such diversification be important even in countries with large reserves of oil? *(because of the fluctuation in oil demand and the development of alternative sources of energy)*

Instruct: Objective 4 appears on p. 506.

DIFFERENTIATING INSTRUCTION **STUDENTS ACQUIRING ENGLISH/ESL**

USING DICTIONARIES AND THESAURI

Objective To build student vocabularies and reading skills

Class Time 30 minutes

Task Use a dictionary and a thesaurus to understand and rephrase text

Directions Divide students into teams of three and supply each team with a dictionary and a thesaurus. Try to pair more advanced readers with students acquiring English. Have students read *Oil Dominates the Economy*. Then have them rewrite this subsection using different words and phrasing. Have them use the dictionary to clarify difficult words and the thesaurus to find alternative words that they can use to rewrite the passage.

Instruct: Objective 

Modern Arabic Life

- How do changing modes of transportation reflect the rapid modernization taking place on the Arabian Peninsula? *(Cars, trucks, and motorcycles are replacing the once ubiquitous camel.)*
- How has the demography of Southwest Asia changed since the 1960s? *(The urban population of the region went from 25 percent to around 60 percent.)*
- What spiritual tradition do Muslims observe during the month of Ramadan? *(fasting between dawn and sunset)*

the Arabian Peninsula, are no longer used as extensively as they once were. Pick-up trucks, automobiles, and motorcycles have replaced them.

Gone, too, are some of the traditional marketplaces called bazaars or souks (sooks). These open-air markets brought together buyers and sellers with a great variety of merchandise, food, and entertainment. The market was a place to meet neighbors or friends, or to conduct business. Today, Western-style supermarkets or malls may be the shopping location of choice instead of the traditional bazaar.

THE CHANGE TO URBAN LIFE Cities were always a part of life in Southwest Asia. However, because of changes in the economy, the entire area is much more urbanized. Millions of people abandoned their lives as villagers, farmers, and nomads and moved into cities. In 1960, the region was about 25 percent urbanized. By the 1990s, this number had risen to about 58 percent. According to estimates, 70 percent of the population will live in cities by 2015. Saudi Arabia has an urban population of 81 percent. Over 4 million people jam the capital, Riyadh. B

As the economy switched to providing petroleum and petroleum products, the types of jobs available in cities changed as well. Workers who could read and write and had technical skills were in great demand. Arabic nations on the peninsula scrambled to upgrade educational systems to meet the needs of the technological age. When those needs could not be fully met, foreign workers were brought in to work at jobs the native population could not fill. As a result, a large number of foreign workers now live in peninsula countries. In some cases, such as Qatar, only one in five workers is a native of the land.

Geographic Thinking

Making Comparisons

B How does the percentage of people living in cities of the Arabian Peninsula compare to that of the United States?

B. Answer Southwest Asian figures are smaller. The U.S. rate is about 80 percent.

RELIGIOUS DUTIES SHAPE LIVES Despite its rapid modernization, some aspects of Muslim culture have remained the same for centuries. If you traveled to Southwest Asia, one of the first things you would likely notice is that women cover their heads, hair, and sometimes faces with a scarf or veil. This is in keeping with the belief that covering those parts of the body is pleasing to God. Women's roles have gradually expanded during the 20th century. More Arabic women are becoming educated and are able to pursue careers in other nations. Because

PLACE Camels are transported to pasture land by truck. **How does this photograph illustrate the change oil production has made in the region?**

Interpreting Photographs

Arabian Camels

Tell students that Arabian camels are able to go without water for days without becoming sick. Also explain that the camels can regain lost weight in minutes by drinking as much as 25 gallons of water. Ask why such an animal might be suited to Southwest Asia *(because of the limited supply of water)*

CAPTION ANSWER Before oil production, the camel would not have been moved by truck.

ACTIVITY OPTION **CRITICAL THINKING**

MAKING DECISIONS

Explaining the Skill Making decisions involves choosing between two or more options, or courses of action. In most cases, decisions have consequences, or results. Sometimes decisions may lead to new problems. By examining the decisions made by others, students may be better able to consider the import and possible consequences of their own decisions.

Applying the Skill Have students read the passages on modern Arabic life. Ask them to consider how the rapid changes and modernization on the Arabian Peninsula might compel the region's Muslims to make difficult decisions about the observance of traditional religious practices.

- How might a shift to a Western work environment create conflict? *(Non-Muslim managers may not be familiar with the five daily prayer times required of the faithful.)*
- As Muslim women enter the workplace, will they decide to retain their traditional Muslim dress? *(Answers will vary.)*
- If the individual becomes more important in society, how might this impact Islam's requirement of charity? *(People may decide that they are only responsible for themselves and not others.)*

Connect to the Issues

Resources Why might it be important for women to become more educated?

C. Answer They can contribute to the development of the economy.

family is viewed as very important, many women stay at home to manage household affairs. C

As you read earlier in this section, all Muslims are expected to perform certain activities. One of the duties, prayer, is performed at prescribed times—dawn, noon, mid-afternoon, sunset, and before bed. Faithful Muslims stop the activities they are engaged in to carry out this responsibility. In some countries, traffic stops during prayer time. If a person is not near a place of worship, he or she may unroll a small prayer rug on which to kneel to pray. On Fridays, the day for congregational prayer, Muslims assemble for prayers at a mosque.

Fasting in the month of Ramadan is another duty that shapes the lives of Muslims. During this month, adult Muslims do not eat or drink from before dawn until sunset. Fasting is a way of reminding Muslims of the spiritual part of their lives. After sunset, Muslims may eat a light meal of lentil or bean soup, a few dates, yogurt, and milky tea. A festival, 'Id al-Fitr, marks the end of Ramadan. New clothes, gifts, and elaborate dinners, along with acts of charity, are part of the celebration.

Since the Muslim culture is found throughout Southwest Asia, many of the same activities of modern life on the Arabian peninsula take place in other areas of Southwest Asia as well. However, as you will learn in the next section, other groups with different religions and lifestyles also live in the region.

PLACE The female doctor above shows a blend of traditional and modern lifestyles. **How does this photograph illustrate changes in the roles of women in the region?**

Interpreting Photographs

Doctor on a Motorcycle

Have students look at the photograph and answer the question. After they answer the question, ask them how the photograph illustrates the persistence of traditional expectations of women. *(She is wearing a veil.)*

CAPTION ANSWER She is riding a motorcycle and is working outside the home.

Assess & Reteach

GeoFocus Have students complete the sections on the Arabian Peninsula for their cluster diagrams.

Formal Assessment
- Section Quiz, p. 339

Reteaching Activity

Have students use the material in this section as a basis for creating a list of questions they have about Islam.

In-Depth Resources: Unit 7
- Reteaching Activity, 18

Outline Maps with Activities
- The Arabian Peninsula, 69–70

SW ASIA

Section 1 Assessment

1 Places & Terms

Explain the meaning of each of the following terms.
- Mecca
- Islam
- Muhammad
- mosque
- theocratic
- OPEC

2 Taking Notes

REGION Review the notes you took for this section.

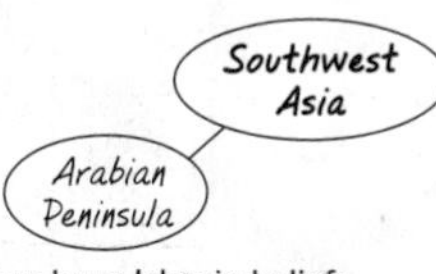

- How have Islamic beliefs affected this region?
- Why did this region grow in economic importance?

3 Main Ideas

a. What are the Five Pillars of Islam?

b. Why was the region of Southwest Asia important to colonial powers?

c. What is the purpose of OPEC?

4 Geographic Thinking

Drawing Conclusions How has the presence of large deposits of oil changed the lives of the people of the Arabian peninsula? **Think about:**
- where people live
- the types of jobs available

MAKING COMPARISONS Use the Internet to find more information on the increase in oil production over the last 25 years for the nations shown in the graph on page 505. Create a **line graph** showing the increases in oil production for the five nations.

SECTION 1 ASSESSMENT ANSWERS

1. Places & Terms

Mecca, p. 503	mosque, p. 504
Islam, p. 503	theocratic, p. 504
Muhammad, p. 503	OPEC, p. 505

2. Taking Notes
- They helped build empires and shape the lives of the people today.
- Huge reserves of oil necessary for industry are located here.

3. Main Ideas

a. They are the religious duties all Muslims practice: faith, prayer, charity, fasting, and pilgrimage.

b. It had oil and access to the Suez Canal.

c. It helps members control oil prices by adjusting oil prices and production quotas.

4. Geographic Thinking

People live in urban areas and work in technical jobs, not as farmers or herders.

GeoActivity

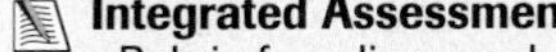
Integrated Assessment
- Rubric for a line graph, 2.3

OBJECTIVE

Examine the religious architecture of different cultures.

Instruct: Objective

Religious Architecture

- Why might houses of worship located in different regions look so radically different. *(Answers will vary, but students may mention different religious or cultural traditions; the availability of materials; climatic restrictions; the vision of individual architects, etc.)*
- What is another name for a Buddhist temple that has multiple tiers? *(pagoda)*
- What is the name of a tower at a mosque from which believers are called to prayer? *(minaret)*

More About

Mosque Architecture

Another major feature of mosques is the *mihrab.* The *mihrab* is a niche, or recess in a wall, that indicates the direction of Mecca. Students may recall that Muslims face Mecca when they pray.

hmhsocialstudies.com INTERACTIVE

Comparing Cultures

Religious Architecture

Throughout the world and across time, people have created spaces in their communities for the worship of God. Sometimes the space is reserved for only a special few, such as priests. Other times the space is designed to bring many worshippers together to create a sense of community. Religious requirements, available building materials, and artistic expression come together in the "houses of god."

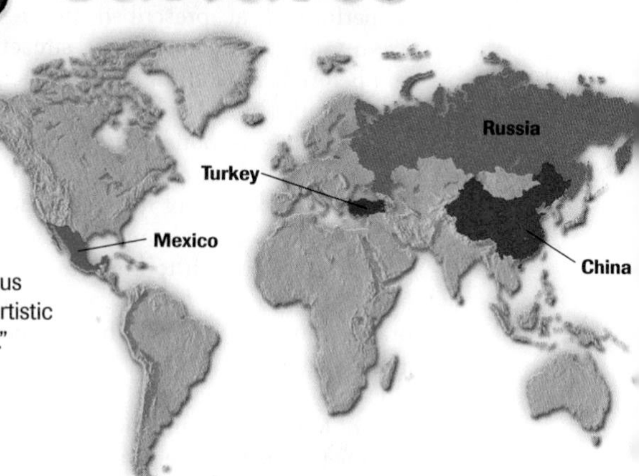

A Buddhist temple, such as this one located in Chufu, China, is called a pagoda if it has multiple tiers. The temple itself is usually a wooden hall with several tiled roofs that curve up on the edges.

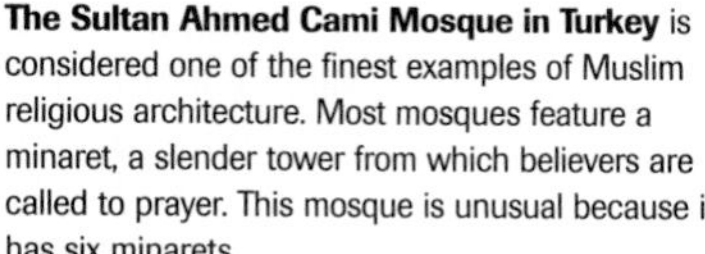

The Sultan Ahmed Cami Mosque in Turkey is considered one of the finest examples of Muslim religious architecture. Most mosques feature a minaret, a slender tower from which believers are called to prayer. This mosque is unusual because it has six minarets.

ADDITIONAL RESOURCES

BOOKS FOR THE TEACHER

Fisher, Robert. ***Buddhist Art and Architecture.*** NY: Thames and Hudson, 1993. Overview of Buddhist art and architecture in many different countries.

Grabar, Oleg. ***The Dome of the Rock.*** NY: Rizzoli, 1996. Exploration of the cultural and religious significance of Jerusalem's Dome of the Rock.

BOOKS FOR THE STUDENT

Chiat, Marilyn J. ***America's Religious Architecture: Sacred Places for Every Community.*** NY: J. Wiley & Sons, 1997. A photographic history of places of worship in the United States, including churches, synagogues, mosques, and meeting halls.

Macaulay, David. ***Cathedral: The Story of its Construction.*** Boston, MA: Houghton Mifflin, 1973. Macaulay lucidly illustrates and explains how Gothic cathedrals were built.

INTERNET

To learn more about religious architecture, visit . . .

hmhsocialstudies.com

St. Basil's Cathedral in Moscow, Russia, is really eight smaller churches around a main one. The basic plan of the church forms a cross. The exterior was originally white. The colorful domes are covered with roof tiles that were added in the 17th century.

The Pyramid of the Sun in Mexico predates the region's Aztec temples. There was once an altar at the pyramid's top, but archaeologists have not determined to which god or gods this monument was dedicated.

GeoActivity

CREATING A MODEL

Choose one of the major religions of the world. With a small group, use the Internet to research more about the religious architecture of that religion.

- Create a model of a worship space showing the unique aspects of that religion's architecture.
- Create a brochure explaining your model.

GeoData

PLACES OF WORSHIP

THE MOSQUE

- Muslims are instructed to face toward Mecca when they pray. Inside the mosque, a special recess in the wall—*mihrab*—marks the direction of Mecca.
- The Sultan Ahmed Cami Mosque is also called the Blue Mosque because of the bluish haze given to the interior by 21,043 blue-glazed tiles on the walls.

THE PYRAMID

- Standing 216 feet high and 720 by 760 feet at the base, the Pyramid of the Sun is one of the largest structures of its type in the Western Hemisphere.

ST. BASIL'S CATHEDRAL

- St. Basil's was built by Ivan IV, also called Ivan the Terrible, as an offering to God for military victories over Tatar armies.
- Legend has it that the architect of St. Basil's was blinded so that he could never create anything similar to St. Basil's.

GeoActivities

Creating a Model

Integrated Assessment
- Rubric for a model, 1.10

More About

Russian Orthodox Churches

Call students' attention to the crosses on St. Basil's, each of which has three bars. Explain that the top bar, according to the Orthodox Christian tradition, stands for the sign that was placed above Christ's head at the crucifixion and that the bottom two bars indicate where his arms and feet were placed.

ACTIVITY OPTION — EXPLORING LOCAL GEOGRAPHY

BLOCK SCHEDULING

EXAMINING ARCHITECTURAL SYMBOLISM

Objective To explore the symbolism of religious architecture

Class Time 20 minutes

Task Create a chart or write a report

Directions Have students choose a house of worship in the region in which they live. Ask them to do research on the importance or symbolism of the different features of the building. Then have students create a chart or write a report that describes these features. For example, if students choose a Jewish synagogue or temple, one element they may wish to discuss is the Ark in which the sacred religious texts are kept. Encourage students to include helpful illustrations or photographs in their reports and charts.

SECTION 2 OBJECTIVES

1. Discuss the holy places of different religious groups in the Eastern Mediterranean.
2. Outline the history of political unrest in the region.
3. Discuss the region's economy.
4. Learn about modern life.

SKILLBUILDER: Interpreting Maps, p. 512

 **GeographicThinking**

Using the Atlas, p. 512
Making Comparisons, p. 514
Seeing Patterns, p. 515
Determining Cause and Effect, p. 515

Focus & Motivate

Ask students if they know of conflict between different religious groups in the United States. *(Students may remark that such conflicts are relatively rare and that freedom of religion is protected by the First Amendment to the Constitution.)*

Instruct: Objective 

Religious Holy Places

- Which three monotheistic religions were founded in Southwest Asia? *(Judaism, Christianity, and Islam)*
- Why is Jerusalem important to all three groups? *(because it is a vital part of each of their religious histories and belief systems)*
- What site in Jerusalem has prompted clashes between Jews and Muslims *(the Temple Mount)*

 **In-Depth Resources: Unit 7**
- Guided Reading, p. 14

The Eastern Mediterranean

Main Ideas
- The holy places of three religions are found in this subregion.
- There is a great deal of political tension among nations in this subregion.

Places & Terms

Western Wall
Dome of the Rock
Zionism
Palestine Liberation Organization (PLO)

CONNECT TO THE ISSUES
REGIONAL CONFLICT Arab refusal to accept the creation of the State of Israel led to conflict in the region.

A HUMAN PERSPECTIVE On September 28, 2000, riots began in Jerusalem after a visit by an Israeli political leader to the Temple Mount, Judaism's holiest site. Muslims also have holy places located there. Palestinian leaders called for riots. Hundreds of people died in the violence that followed.

To understand why a simple visit to a holy place would cause such problems, it is necessary to understand the history of the region. There is enormous disagreement over control of Jerusalem and of the lands Arabs call the Occupied Territories. (See the map on page 480.) In fact, the relations between Arabs and Israelis affect the entire region of the Eastern Mediterranean.

Religious Holy Places

Three major monotheistic religions—Judaism, Christianity, and Islam—were founded in Southwest Asia. All three claim Jerusalem as a holy city. The City of Jerusalem, which covers 42 square miles, has Jewish, Christian, Armenian Christian, and Muslim sections. Followers of all three religions come to the Old City to visit locations with strong spiritual meaning.

JEWISH SACRED SITES For Jews, Jerusalem, the capital of Israel, is the center of their modern and ancient homeland. Located in the old part of the city, the Temple Mount once housed the Temples. There, King Solomon built the First Temple, which was destroyed by the Babylonians in 586 B.C. The Second Temple was constructed after the Jews returned to their homeland in 538 B.C. Modern Jews come to pray at the holiest site in Jerusalem, a portion of the Second Temple known as the **Western Wall**. It is the only remaining piece of the Second Temple, which was destroyed in A.D. 70 by the Romans.

CHRISTIAN SACRED SITES For Christians, Jerusalem is the sacred location of the final suffering and crucifixion of Jesus. Towns and villages important in the life of Jesus are found near Jerusalem. Every year, Christians visit places like the Mount of Olives and the Church of the Holy Sepulchre by the thousands. When Jerusalem was under Muslim control, Christians launched the Crusades to regain the lands and place them under the control of Christians. Eventually, the lands returned to the control

PLACE Christian pilgrims walk on the road to the Mount of Olives on a holy day—Palm Sunday.

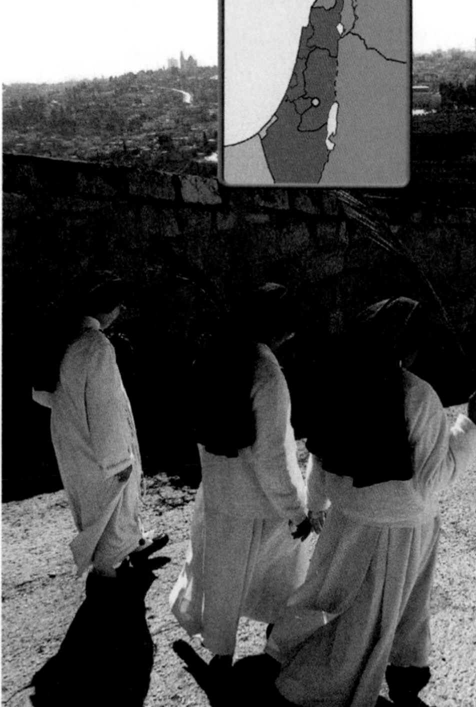

SECTION 2 PROGRAM RESOURCES

 **In-Depth Resources: Unit 7**
- Guided Reading, p. 14
- Skillbuilder Practice, p. 16
- Building Vocabulary, p. 17
- Reteaching Activity, p. 19

Guided Reading Workbook
- Section 2

Access for Students Acquiring English/ESL
- Guided Reading, p. 118
- Skillbuilder Practice, p. 120

Outline Maps with Activities
- The Eastern Mediterranean, pp. 71–72

Formal Assessment
- Section Quiz, p. 340

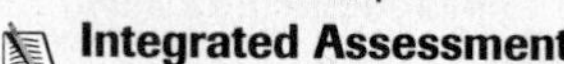 **Integrated Assessment**
- Rubric for a sketch map, 2.1

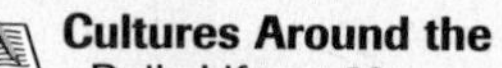 **Cultures Around the World**
- Daily Life, p. 38
- Arts and Crafts, p. 40
- Dance, p. 41

INTEGRATED TECHNOLOGY

 **Map Transparencies MT39**
- Creation of Israel

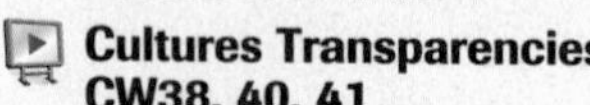 **Cultures Transparencies CW38, 40, 41**
- Living on a Kibbutz
- Turkish Ceramic Tiles
- Whirling Dervishes

hmhsocialstudies.com

TEST-TAKING RESOURCES

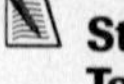 **Strategies for Test Preparation**

 **Test Practice Transparencies TT72**

 **Online Test Practice**

of Muslims and remained that way until World War I.

ISLAMIC SACRED SITES After Mecca and Medina, Jerusalem is considered the third most holy city to Muslims. A shrine there, called **Dome of the Rock,** houses the spot where Muslims believe their prophet Muhammad rose into heaven. The Dome of the Rock and a nearby mosque, Al-Aqsa, are located on the Temple Mount, the site of the Jewish Temples. Because these most holy sites are so close together, they have been the site of clashes between Jews and Muslims. A

CONNECT TO THE ISSUES
REGIONAL CONFLICT
A What problems might emerge when three different religious groups claim the same area as a holy place?
A. Answer France and Britain were each given control of parts of the Middle East by the League of Nations, to rule until independence.

PLACE Muslim visitors gather at the Dome of the Rock, a holy site in the city of Jerusalem. **How did control of Jerusalem change over many centuries?**

A History of Unrest

The nations of the Eastern Mediterranean have been plagued with a history of political tension and unrest. The Ottoman Empire, a Muslim government based in Turkey, ruled the Eastern Mediterranean lands from 1520 to 1922. But the Ottoman Empire grew weaker and less able to solve problems with groups seeking independence. By the beginning of the 20th century, its collapse was not far away. The Ottoman Empire sided with Germany during World War I. At the end of the war, the Ottoman Empire fell apart. Britain and France received Ottoman lands in the Eastern Mediterranean as part of the war settlement.

THE LEGACY OF COLONIALISM After World War I, Britain and France divided the Ottoman lands in the Eastern Mediterranean region. France took the northern portion, including the present-day countries of Lebanon and Syria. Britain controlled the southern section, which included the present-day nations of Jordan and Israel. Britain and France were supposed to rule these lands until they were ready for independence. During the time of their control, the French frequently played different religious groups against each other. Those tensions remain in the region today. The Syrians hated the French and in the 1920s and 1930s rebelled against them. Lebanon became independent in 1943, and Syria gained independence in 1946.

BACKGROUND
The League of Nations gave the Ottoman lands to France and Britain.

BRITISH PALESTINE MANDATE The land controlled by Britain was known as the Palestine Mandate. In the 19th century, a movement called **Zionism** began. Its goal was to reestablish a Jewish state in the Jewish homeland. Jewish settlers started buying land and settling there, joining the resident Jewish community. By 1914, about 12 percent of the region's population was Jewish. After World War I, the British took command of the area and continued to allow Jewish and Arab immigration. Early on, Arabs and Jews in the region cooperated. But as more and more Jews poured into Palestine to escape persecution in Germany, the Arabs resisted the establishment of a Jewish state. In 1939, to reduce tensions the British halted Jewish immigration to Palestine.

SW ASIA

Interpreting Photographs

Dome of the Rock

Have students examine the photograph of the Dome of the Rock. Explain that abstract forms, such as arabesque, are far more common than naturalistic forms in Islamic art. Ask students if they recognize the characters on the upper band of the façade. *(Some students may recognize the Arabic calligraphy.)*

CAPTION ANSWER Jerusalem was first Jewish, the later controlled by the Roman Empire, then in the hands of the Muslims, then the Christians, back to the Muslims, then to the British, and finally to Israel.

Instruct: Objective 2

A History of Unrest

- For how long did the Muslim government of the Ottoman Empire rule the Eastern Mediterranean? *(from 1520 to 1922)*
- What nations divided the region after World War I, and what areas did each control? *(France took the northern portion, including present-day Lebanon and Syria, and Britain took the southern section, including present-day Jordan and Israel.)*
- Which European countries were most deeply involved in the history of the Eastern Mediterranean in the 1900s? *(Great Britain and France)*

Map Transparencies MT39
- Creation of Israel

ACTIVITY OPTION | **SKILLBUILDER LESSON**

CREATING GRAPHS AND CHARTS

Explaining the Skill Graphs use pictures and symbols to show information. Bar, line, and pie graphs are common types of graphs. Charts present information in visual forms that organize information in a way that makes it easy to read and understand. Tables and diagrams are examples of commonly used charts.

Applying the Skill Have students carry out further research on population and ethnic groups in the Eastern Mediterranean, particularly on the 19th and 20th century growth of the Jewish and Arab populations in the area of the Palestine Mandate. After they have completed their research, ask students to select a graph style to summarize and display their findings. To get students started ask the following questions:

- What type of graph might be best suited to showing change over time? *(Line graphs are commonly used to represent change over time.)*
- What type of graph gives the quickest read on population segments? *(A pie graph shows relative percentages at a glance.)*

In-Depth Resources: Unit 7
- Skillbuilder Practice, p. 16

Interpreting Maps

Creation of Israel

Explain to students that one of the most momentous events in the history of Judaism is the Exodus—the liberation of Israelites from slavery in Egypt in the 13th century B.C., under the leadership of Moses. Have students look at the map on page 512 and ask where Egypt is located relative to Israel. *(to the southwest)*

SKILLBUILDER ANSWERS
1. Jordan River, Dead Sea **2.** Israel, Syria, Iraq, and Saudi Arabia

More About

Exodus

The Israelites' liberation from Egyptian slavery is commemorated every year with the holiday of Passover, which takes place during the Hebrew month of Nisan (concurrent with March or April). Jews celebrate Passover with a special meal called a Seder. During the Seder, the story of the Exodus is retold, and foods with symbolic significance are eaten to celebrate and renew Judaism's dedication to freedom.

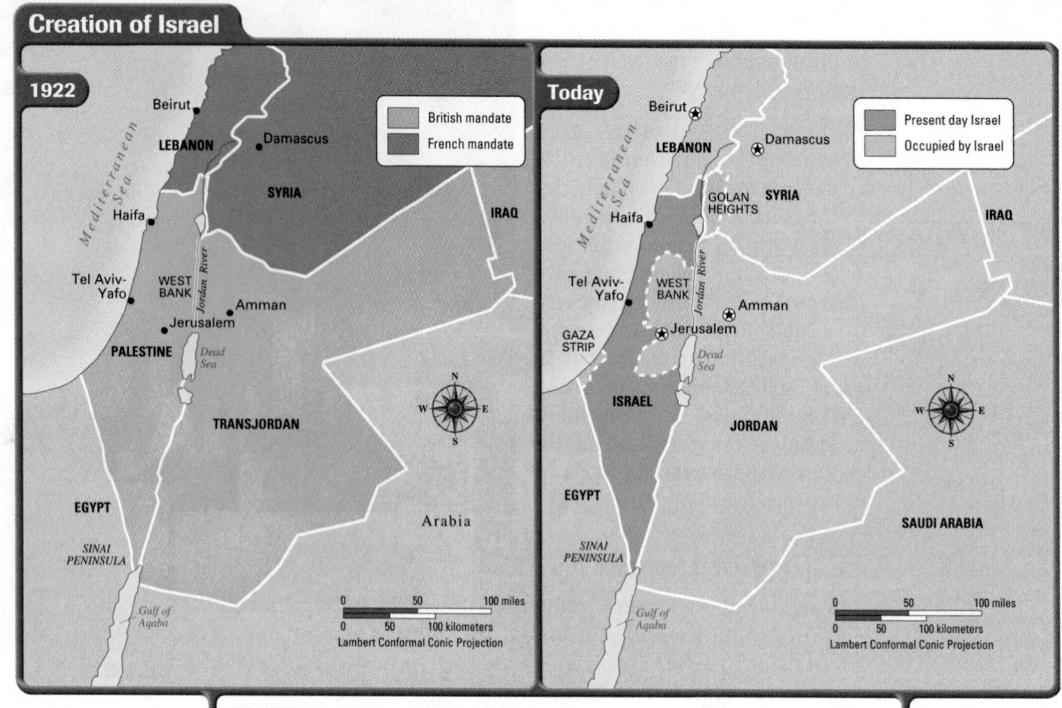

SKILLBUILDER: Interpreting Maps
❶ **PLACE** Which bodies of water form a natural boundary between Jordan and Israel?
❷ **PLACE** Today, what four countries border Jordan?

As you study the map on this page, you will see that the area controlled by the British was divided into two sections—Transjordan and Palestine. The land was divided to give one of Britain's Arab allies a kingdom. An Arab government jointly ruled Transjordan with the British. Britain controlled the Palestine Mandate, along with local governments that included both Jews and Arabs.

CREATING THE STATE OF ISRAEL At the end of World War II, thousands of Jewish survivors of the Holocaust wanted to settle in the Palestine Mandate, the historic Jewish homeland. World opinion supported the establishment of a Jewish nation-state. Britain eventually referred the question of a Jewish homeland to the United Nations. In 1947, the United Nations developed a plan to divide Palestine into two states—one for Arabs and one for Jews.

Arabs in the region did not agree with the division. However, the nation of Israel was established on May 14, 1948. Immediately, the surrounding Arab nations of Egypt, Syria, Lebanon, Jordan, Iraq, Saudi Arabia, and Yemen invaded Israel to destroy the newly established state. Israeli troops fought back and won. By the 1950s, Israel was a firmly established nation. The 1948 war was the beginning of hostilities that continue to this day. B

B. Answer Israel held more land and occupied certain Arab territories.

Using the Atlas
B Use the Atlas on page 480. How was the land Israel occupied in 1967 different from the land it held in 1948?

ACTIVITY OPTION **INTERNET RESEARCH**

BLOCK SCHEDULING

UNDERSTANDING THE JEWISH SEDER

Objective To learn about the traditions and symbolism in a Jewish Seder

Class Time 30 minutes

Task Use research to compose an oral report about Jewish Seders

Directions Ask students to use the Internet to carry out research on the Jewish Seder, the religious meal served during the festival of Passover. Have them use their research to create a short oral report. Remind students to consider important elements of the Seder, including the Haggadah, a special book with commentaries on the story of Exodus, and the symbolic foods served at the meal. Also encourage students to add visual aids to their reports.

OPTIONAL ACTIVITY If Internet access is limited or unavailable, have students use printed sources in the library.

During the 1948 war many Palestinian Arabs fled their homes or were forced out and now live in UN-sponsored refugee camps. A comparable number of Jewish refugees fled from Arab countries, and most became Israeli citizens. In 1964, the **Palestine Liberation Organization (PLO)** was formed to regain the land of Israel for Palestinian Arabs. Over the years, the PLO has pursued political and violent means of pursuit of its goals. The Palestinian National Authority has administered the West Bank since 1994. Since 2007, an organization called Hamas, which means "Islamic Resistance Movement," has controlled Gaza.

CKGROUND
fugee is a
on who leaves
e or country
nd safety in
her location.

Modernizing Economies

The nations in the Eastern Mediterranean subregion are relatively young. Most became independent shortly after World War II. Cyprus received its independence from Britain in 1960. These nations face many economic problems. Political divisions, refugees, lack of water, and a weak infrastructure make it difficult to develop healthy economies.

REFUGEES AND CIVIL WARS The 1948 Arab-Israeli war produced a large number of refugees, Arab and Jewish. Today, Palestinian refugees are scattered across many of the countries in the region. Some still live in UN-sponsored camps. Jewish refugees and their descendants make up about half of Israel's population. PLO attacks against Jordanian and Lebanese forces resulted in political instability and led Jordan to expel the PLO in 1970. Cross-border attacks against Israelis by the PLO and Hezbollah have led to Israeli counterattacks.

Civil wars in Lebanon and Cyprus have also caused huge economic problems. Since the 1970s, the northern part of Cyprus has been controlled by Turkish Cypriots, who have declared independence. Lebanon was hard hit by a civil war that lasted from 1975 to 1976. The conflict widened to include other nations. Some Israeli troops remained in Lebanon until 2000, and Syrian troops remained until 2004.

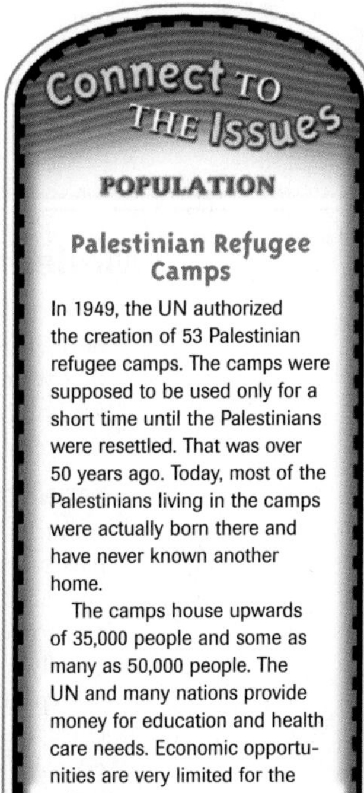

Palestinian Refugee Camps

In 1949, the UN authorized the creation of 53 Palestinian refugee camps. The camps were supposed to be used only for a short time until the Palestinians were resettled. That was over 50 years ago. Today, most of the Palestinians living in the camps were actually born there and have never known another home.

The camps house upwards of 35,000 people and some as many as 50,000 people. The UN and many nations provide money for education and health care needs. Economic opportunities are very limited for the refugees.

MODERN INFRASTRUCTURE Israel has advanced modern infrastructure and irrigation systems. Other nations of the Eastern Mediterranean subregion have great potential for development. They have a good climate for producing citrus crops and many places for tourists to visit. They are well located for connections to international markets in Europe, Asia, and Africa.

What many of them lack, however, is an infrastructure that would support a growing economy. Roads in war-torn areas, for example, must be rebuilt. Especially needed are irrigation systems to make the area bloom. Better communication systems and power sources are needed for developing high tech industries in the region. Israel has been able to build sophisticated industries such as computer software development.

Instruct: Objective 3

Modernizing Economics

- What change in the Eastern Mediterranean's population geography has put a strain on regional economies? *(the large number of Palestinian refugees)*
- What are other obstacles to regional economic development? *(conflict and poor infrastructures)*
- Why might the economic potential of the subregion's nations be promising? *(because of their potential for developing agriculture, tourism, and trade)*

DIFFERENTIATING INSTRUCTION **LESS PROFICIENT READERS**

SEEING MAIN IDEAS

Objective To have students focus on main ideas

Class Time 20 minutes

Tasks Read the text and focus on the main ideas

Directions As students read the section on the Eastern Mediterranean, ask them to write two sentences for each of the major subsections (Religious Holy Places; A History of Unrest; Modernizing Economies; Modern Life). The two sentences for each subsection should reiterate what, for them, are the two most important ideas. After students have written their summaries, divide them into pairs. Ask them to exchange and read each other's summaries and then discuss whether or not they agree that the summaries have captured the most important ideas.

growing up in...

Israel

Political tensions in Israel have made it difficult for young people of different religious and cultural backgrounds to come together. Israeli pianist and conductor Daniel Barenboim has tried to build bridges between divided groups by organizing workshops for young musicians. The workshops bring together young musicians from Israel and the surrounding region for music lessons, rehearsals, and concerts. Barenboim believes that music can foster greater understanding among different cultures. Ask students how music can do this. *(Answers will vary.)*

Instruct: Objective 4

Modern Life

- What kind of food items might you find at an Eastern Mediterranean meal? *(hummus, baba ganouzh, tabbouleh, chicken or lamb, kolaicha, etc.)*
- What cultural group forms the majority of people in the Eastern Mediterranean? *(Muslim Arabs)*
- What are some of the larger religious groups in Lebanon? *(Shi'ite Muslims, Druze, and Maronite and Eastern Orthodox Christians)*

Cultures Around the World
- Daily Life, p. 38
- Arts and Crafts, p. 40
- Dance, p. 41

Cultures Transparencies CW38, 40, 41
- Living on a Kibbutz
- Turkish Ceramic Tiles
- Whirling Dervishes

growing up in...Israel

This young woman is a member of the Israel Defense Forces. Unmarried Jewish young women are required to serve for two years. They serve in various parts of the armed forces, in jobs such as tank instructors, helicopter pilots, military police, rescue workers, and office workers. They are not required to serve in active combat units. Service in the armed forces helps build unity and identity for Israelis.

If you lived in Israel, you would pass these milestones:

- You would go to school from age 5 to age 15. Most study to age 18 or later.
- At age 14, you would choose between going to a technical school or a more academic school.
- You could begin working at age 15.
- You could drive at age 17.
- You could get married at age 17.
- You would enter the armed forces at age 18: men for 3 years, women for 2 years.

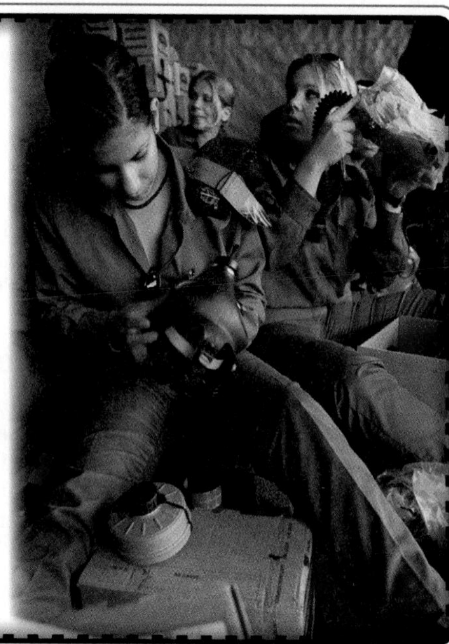

Modern Life

Modern life in the Eastern Mediterranean is a curious blend of old and new. Strong cultural traditions exist but they are combined with changes that were brought about by modern innovations. Cell phones, computers, and Internet access are increasingly common. One aspect of life here that remains quite traditional, however, is the dining experience.

EATING OUT, EATING IN Eating in restaurants in Eastern Mediterranean countries is not as common as in the United States. Some Arab restaurants have separate sections for men and women. Arab cafes serving coffee and tea are generally for men only. Most meals are eaten in the home. Families and sometimes friends gather to have meals. The last meal of the day is usually served between 8 and 11 P.M.

Typically, a meal begins with small portions of hummus, ground chickpeas mixed with lemon juice and parsley, and baba ganouzh, an eggplant dip served with pita, a flat bread with a pocket. A salad called tabbouleh, made of bulgur (cracked wheat), parsley, onions, mint, tomatoes, and lemon juice, is common. Chicken or lamb is more likely to be served as a main course than beef. Many meals are finished with fresh fruit or sweets such as kolaicha, a sweet cake made of barley flour, sugar, oil, and cardamom seed. Thick coffee or tea is also served. The host of a dinner may not eat with the guests so that he can attend to all their needs during the meal. C

A VARIETY OF CUTURES Muslim Arabs make up the majority of people who live in the countries of the Eastern Mediterranean. However, in several nations, especially Lebanon and Israel, there is a variety of cultures.

C. Answer In the U.S., many families eat out regularly. Men and women are not separated in restaurants.

Geographic Thinking
Making Comparisons
C In what ways is the dining experience in this region different from that of the United States?

ACTIVITY OPTION **COOPERATIVE LEARNING** | **BLOCK SCHEDULING**

EXPLORING EASTERN MEDITERRANEAN CUISINE

Objective To learn more about regional foods

Class Time 30 minutes

Task Create an in-depth recipe booklet

Directions Divide students into small groups. Assign each a dish from the region. Teachers could assign foods described on page 514, such as hummus or baba ganouzh, or they might assign other dishes not mentioned in the text, such as falafel. Have students use the Internet or library resources to locate a recipe for their assigned dish. Once a group has located its recipe, students in the group should divide the ingredients among themselves and carry out further research on those ingredients. Have students use their research to put together a booklet that features the written recipe, pictures of the dish, and pictures and interesting information about the recipes' different ingredients.

Since the seventh century, Lebanon has been a refuge for both Muslims and Christians. Many of the Muslims there are Shi'ites, as compared to the Sunni majorities in many of the other nations in this region. A small group of Druze also live in Lebanon. This tightly knit group is very secretive about its religious practices. The members live in the mountainous areas of Lebanon and also in Israel and Syria. Christians of the Maronite tradition (Roman Catholics following Eastern Orthodox practices) and the Eastern Orthodox tradition make up a large minority in Lebanon. Together, these groups present a wide variety of cultures and religious practices. The variety makes it difficult to build unity in the country.

PLACE A woman walks along the beachfront of Beirut, Lebanon. **How does Lebanon's relative location make it a refuge for Muslims and Christians?**

D. Answer
Because space is so limited, it may cause friction between groups, or it may force them to get along so that there is peace.

Israel is a land with a tremendous variety of immigrants. The majority of immigrants are Jewish, and they arrive from all over the globe. They come from the United States, Eastern Europe, the Mediterranean region, Russia, and Ethiopia. The focus of Jewish culture helps to draw most of this diverse group together.

In addition, Israel is home to about 1 million Arabs of several different groups. Bedouins live in the Negev Desert. Druze, Sunni Muslims, and Circassians, who come from the Caucasus Mountains area, also live in Israel with a small number of Christians and people following the Baha'i faith. The combination of all these groups brings a variety of languages and lifestyles to Israel. D

Geographic Thinking
Seeing Patterns
D How might the small size of Israel and Lebanon affect the way groups of people living there relate to each other?

In the next section, you will learn about countries in this region with ethnic backgrounds that are Turkish or Persian.

SECTION 2 Assessment

1 Places & Terms

Explain the meaning of each of the following terms.

- Western Wall
- Dome of the Rock
- Zionism
- Palestine Liberation Organization

2 Taking Notes

PLACE Review the notes you took for this section.

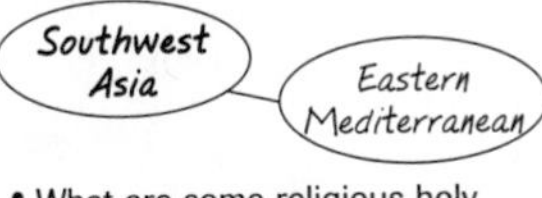

- What are some religious holy places found in this subregion?
- What factors have made it difficult to develop this subregion economically?

3 Main Ideas

a. How did mandate rule affect the region?

b. What impact have refugees and civil wars had on modernizing the economies of this subregion?

c. In addition to Muslims, what other groups live in the Eastern Mediterranean nations?

4 Geographic Thinking

Determining Cause and Effect How did Arab rejection of the nation of Israel increase tension in the region? **Think about:**

- religious prejudices
- division of land

See Skillbuilder Handbook, page R9.

MAKING COMPARISONS Review the maps on page 480 and page 512. Create a series of four **sketch maps** that show how the Eastern Mediterranean subregion changed from 1948 to the present. Write a caption on each map describing the change from the previous map.

SW ASIA

Interpreting Photographs

Beirut, Lebanon

Tell students that in Lebanon one can snow ski in the morning and then take a swim in the Mediterranean Sea later in the afternoon. This is possible because the Lebanon Mountains rise up above a very narrow coast. Even the highest ski resorts are just a short drive from the coast. Ask students why tourists may be reluctant to take advantage of such wonders. *(because of the religious and ethnic conflict in the region)*

CAPTION ANSWER It is located near countries with large populations of Muslims, some of whom do not get along. Christians have resided in Lebanon for centuries.

Assess & Reteach

GeoFocus Have students complete the section on the Eastern Mediterranean in their graphic organizers.

Formal Assessment
- Section Quiz, p. 340

Reteaching Activity
Ask students to find current newspaper articles about Israel, the West Bank, the Gaza Strip, Jordan, Lebanon, or Syria and bring them to class. Have students read and discuss several articles to learn about the Eastern Mediterranean region. Then have students make a bulletin board of the articles.

In-Depth Resources: Unit 7
- Reteaching Activity, p. 19

Outline Maps with Activities
- The Eastern Mediterranean, pp. 71–72

SECTION 2 ASSESSMENT ANSWERS

1. Places & Terms
Western Wall, p. 510; Dome of the Rock, p. 511; Zionism, p. 511; Palestine Liberation Organization, p. 513

2. Taking Notes
- the city of Jerusalem, the Western Wall, and the Dome of the Rock
- political divisions, refugees, lack of water, and weak infrastructure

3. Main Ideas
a. The land was divided between France and Britain. France encouraged internal religious tensions in its part to keep control of the area. The British divided their lands to reward an ally in World War I, creating Transjordan.
b. civil wars destroyed infrastructures; refugees need expensive services and often are unemployed
c. Jews, Christians, Druze, Maronite Christians, Greek Orthodox, and Baha'i

4. Geographic Thinking
Jews, Christians, and Muslims regard places in Jerusalem as holy and want access to them. Arab rejection of Israel, war, and terrorism against Israelis have further divided Arabs and Jews.

Integrated Assessment
- Rubric for a sketch map, 2.1

SECTION 3 OBJECTIVES

1. Describe the blend of cultures in Southwest Asia.
2. Examine land disputes.
3. Explain plans for economic reform.
4. Describe traditional and modern life in the subregion.

SKILLBUILDER: Interpreting Maps, p. 516

GeographicThinking
Seeing Patterns p. 518
Making Inferences, p. 519

Focus & Motivate

List the countries of the Northeast on the board and ask students what they know about them. Write students' responses on the board. *(Responses will vary, but teachers might prompt students by mentioning current events related to the different countries.)*

Interpreting Maps

Northeast Ethnic Areas

Afghanistan's population is 84 percent Sunni Muslim and 15 percent Shi'ite Muslim. In Iraq, about 60–65 percent of the population is Shi'ite and 32–37 percent Sunni. In Iran, the figures are 89 percent Shi'ite and 10 percent Sunni. Over 99 percent of Turkey's population is Muslim—almost all of them Sunni. What is the difference between Kurds and Shi'ites? *(Kurds are a cultural group; Shi'ites are a religious group.)*

SKILLBUILDER ANSWERS 1. Turkey **2.** 600 miles long and between 200 and 300 miles wide

Instruct: Objective 1 appears on p. 517.

3 The Northeast

Main Ideas

- The nations in this subregion are Muslim but most are not part of the Arab culture.
- The nations in the Northeast range from developed to very poorly developed.

Places & Terms

Kurds
Mesopotamia
Sunni
Shi'ite
Taliban

CONNECT TO THE ISSUES
POPULATION RELOCATION The Kurds' movement across this subregion has caused conflict.

A HUMAN PERSPECTIVE On March 16, 1988, Iraqi Air Force planes released poisonous gases over the Kurdish town of Halabja, Iraq. An estimated 5,000 **Kurds,** an ethnic group in Southwestern Asia, died from the chemical weapons attack. The Kurdish people have occupied the lands they call Kurdistan for thousands of years. In the modern world, most of those lands are located in Turkey, Iraq, and Iran. For most of the 20th century, these three nations disagreed with the Kurds over control of these lands. In fact, clashes over land have been the focus of much unrest in the northeastern part of Southwest Asia.

A Blend of Cultures

The nations in this subregion include Turkey, Iran, Iraq, and Afghanistan. They are mostly Muslim in religion, but only Iraq is Arabic in cultural life. All these nations were influenced by early civilizations and empires in the region.

EARLY CIVILIZATIONS Part of the cultural hearth known as the Fertile Crescent is located here. Some of the earliest civilizations in the world developed in Iraq along the Tigris and Euphrates rivers. Sumer, Babylonia, Assyria, and Chaldea all built empires in **Mesopotamia,** the "land between the rivers."

The Hittites, whose empire stretched across what is Turkey today, brought innovations such as the use of iron weapons. Persia, which developed in the region occupied by Iran today, introduced innovations in government organization.

ETHNIC AND RELIGIOUS VARIETY Living in this subregion are members of many ethnic groups, including Turks, Kurds, and Persians. The map on page 482 shows where these groups live. They speak languages such as Turkish and Farsi, which are different from the Arabic that is spoken in the rest of the region.

Though most of the different ethnic groups follow Islam, tensions exist. After the death of Muhammad, Muslims divided into two main branches—the **Sunni** and the **Shi'ite.** About four out of five Muslims are Sunni. Most Iranians are Shi'ite.

Northeast Ethnic Areas

Kurdish area
Shi'ite area of Iraq
Black Sea
RUSSIA
GEORGIA
ARMENIA
AZERBAIJAN
Caspian Sea
TURKEY
AZER.
SYRIA
IRAQ
IRAN
SAUDI ARABIA
KUWAIT
Persian Gulf
0 150 300 miles
0 150 300 kilometers
Lambert Conformal Conic Projection

SKILLBUILDER: Interpreting Maps
1. **REGION** Which country has the largest area inhabited by Kurds?
2. **REGION** What is the approximate size of the area inhabited by the Kurds?

SECTION 3 PROGRAM RESOURCES

In-Depth Resources: Unit 7
- Guided Reading, p. 15
- Building Vocabulary, p. 17
- Reteaching Activity, p. 20

Guided Reading Workbook
- Section 3

Access for Students Acquiring English/ESL
- Guided Reading, p. 119

Outline Maps with Activities
- The Northeast, pp. 73–74

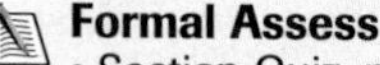
Formal Assessment
- Section Quiz, p. 341

Integrated Assessment
- Rubric for a database, 2.6

Cultures Around the World
- Architecture, p. 37
- Fine Arts, p. 39
- Traditional Practices, p. 42

INTEGRATED TECHNOLOGY

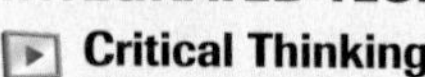
Critical Thinking Transparencies CT54
- Selected Cities of Southwest Asia

Cultures Transparencies CW37, 39, 42
- Petra
- Islamic Calligraphy
- Praying at The Western Wall

TEST-TAKING RESOURCES

Strategies for Test Preparation

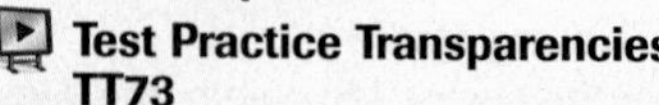
Test Practice Transparencies TT73

Online Test Practice

516 CHAPTER 22

Clashes Over Land

Clashes over land in this region increased after World War I. Some were disagreements over homelands claimed by ethnic groups whose demands for land were ignored. Other disputes were over control of valuable oil fields.

HOMELANDS AND REFUGEES The Kurds have been called a stateless nation. At the end of World War I, they were promised a homeland but never received it. Clashes between the Kurds and the governments of Turkey, Iran, and Iraq have prevented the Kurds from becoming a nation-state.

Because of its location, Iran has become home to refugees fleeing oppressive governments in both Afghanistan and Iraq. In fact, Iran has the largest refugee population of any nation in the world. Iraqi Shi'ites persecuted by their government have sought refuge with fellow Shi'ites in Iran. Decades of war drove many Afghan refugees to Iran, although some began to return in 2002. A

A. Answer Groups may cross from one country to another or one region to another to claim land or to find safety.

CONNECT TO THE ISSUES
POPULATION RELOCATION
A How might land claims and refugee status affect movement across the region?

CONTROL OF OIL FIELDS Access to the oil-rich regions on the Persian Gulf is strategically important for all nations that import oil. Between 1980 and 1990, Iran and Iraq fought a war over control of oil fields. Then, in 1990–1991, Iraq invaded Kuwait, starting the Persian Gulf War. The United States and 32 other nations fought to drive the Iraqis out of Kuwait and keep oil fields open.

Clashes Over Leadership

The war on terrorism declared by President George W. Bush led to clashes over leadership in the Northeast subregion. Within a month of the attacks against the United States on September 11, 2001, the United States and the coalition forces fought in Afghanistan, where the terrorists responsible for the attacks were being harbored. In 2003, fear for national security prompted the United States to declare war on Iraq and its leader, Saddam Hussein.

OVERTHROW OF THE TALIBAN A fundamentalist Muslim political group called the **Taliban** was protecting Osama bin Laden and his al-Qaeda terrorist network in Afghanistan. On October 7, 2001, U.S.-led coalition forces launched Operation Enduring Freedom to seize the terrorists' financial assets and destroy their infrastructure. By March 2002, the Taliban had been removed from power. A transitional government, headed by Hamid Karzai, replaced the repressive regime. However, some Taliban and al-Qaeda leaders, including Osama bin Laden, managed to escape the coalition forces.

PLACE In Afghanistan, coalition forces prepare explosives to blow up caves that shelter Taliban forces.
What difficulties did the coalition forces face fighting in the mountainous terrain of Afghanistan?

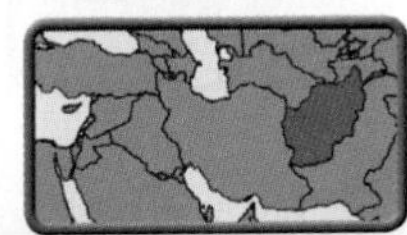

Instruct: Objective 1

A Blend of Cultures

- What is Mesopotamia? *(an ancient region between the Tigris and Euphrates rivers that was home to numerous early civilizations)*
- What are the two main branches of Islam? *(Sunni and Shi'ite)*

In-Depth Resources: Unit 7
- Guided Reading, p. 15

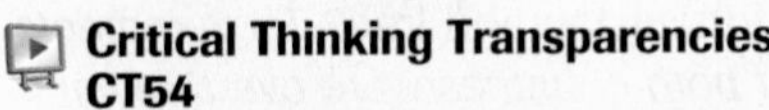

Critical Thinking Transparencies CT54
- Selected Cities of Southwest Asia

Instruct: Objective 2

Clashes Over Land

- Why are the Kurds considered a stateless nation? *(They are a nation of people without a land to legally occupy.)*
- Why does Iran have such a large refugee population? *(Refugees from Iraq and Afghanistan have fled to Iran in large numbers.)*
- How have oil resources fueled clashes over land? *(Powerful nations want control over these resources and are willing to fight for them.)*

Interpreting Photographs

International Coalition

About 70 countries joined the United States to combat terrorism in Afghanistan. Ask students why it was important for the United States to have international support for the war on terrorism. *(to supply military, humanitarian, financial support, intelligence)*

CAPTION ANSWER Rugged, unknown territory where the enemy could hide.

Instruct: Objective 3 appears on p. 518.

ACTIVITY OPTION **LINK TO RELIGION**

MAKING A CHART

Objective To understand some of the differences between different branches of Islam

Class Time 20 minutes

Task Make a chart that shows different branches of Islam

Directions Have students use the Internet or library resources to do research on Islam. Ask them to focus on identifying different branches or sects of Islam. Students should use their research to create a chart that shows the different groups they have identified. They should also write a brief explanation of what makes each group unique. Students may wish to use a chart like the one shown at right.

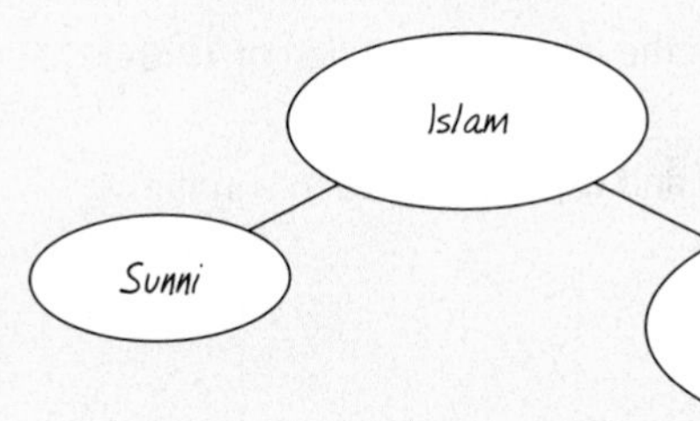
Islam
Sunni
Shi'ite: After the death of the Prophet Muhammad's son-in law, Ali...

Instruct: Objective 

Clashes Over Leadership

- Why did the United States take military action against Afghanistan and Iraq? *(to combat terrorism and protect national security)*
- What is the Taliban? *(a fundamentalist Muslim political group)*
- What happened to the leaders of Afghanistan and Iraq? *(governments of both countries were overthrown but Osama bin Laden avoided capture)*

Instruct: Objective 

Reforming Economies

- Which nations in the Northeast are making progress in modernizing their economies? *(Turkey and Iran)*
- What is a major obstacle to economic reform in most of the region's nations? *(political problems and devastating wars)*

Interpreting Photographs

Iranian Revolution Monument

Tell students that the monument was built in 1971 to celebrate the 2500th anniversary of the Persian Empire. After the 1978–1979 Revolution, it was renamed the Azadi, or Freedom, Monument. Ask students to guess how tall the monument is. *(Students may guess from the size of the people in the photograph that the monument is about 150 feet high.)*

CAPTION ANSWER To remind or inspire people to support their country.

OVERTHROW OF SADDAM HUSSEIN After the Persian Gulf War ended in 1991, the United Nations ordered Saddam Hussein to destroy his biological and chemical weapons. President George W. Bush, however, believed that the Iraqi dictator was continuing to develop weapons of mass destruction (WMD). As a result, American and British forces launched Operation Iraqi Freedom in March 2003. Saddam was removed from power (he was later executed), but no WMD were found. Then the long process of working toward democracy in Iraq began. A new constitution was adopted, and in 2005, Jalal Talabani, a Kurd, was elected president.

Reforming Economies

The nations in this subregion face a variety of economic challenges. All of them have limited agricultural land. Production must become more efficient in order to produce surplus crops to sell elsewhere. Most of these nations have oil or natural gas resources that can generate revenue. This money is needed to update and expand transportation systems, communication systems, power generation plants, and water and sanitation systems.

MAKING PROGRESS Turkey is making progress in modernizing its economy. Turkey is developing its water resources and hydroelectric plants to supply energy and to boost production of cotton and other agricultural products. It is the only nation in this subregion that produces significant amounts of steel. Turkey straddles two continents—Europe and Asia—which makes it ideally located for trade. B

In Iran, government attitudes toward fostering economic growth have swung back and forth. Starting in 1997, a reformist government supported growth. Since 2005, anti-reformists have ruled, and Iran's economy has remained flat.

Geographic Thinking

Seeing Patterns B Why might Turkey's location increase its desire to develop international trade?

B. Answer It is ideally located in both Europe and Asia and could benefit from trade with either continent.

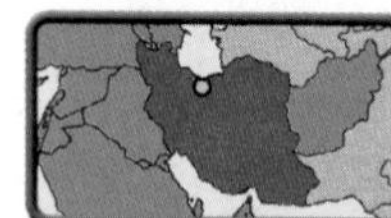

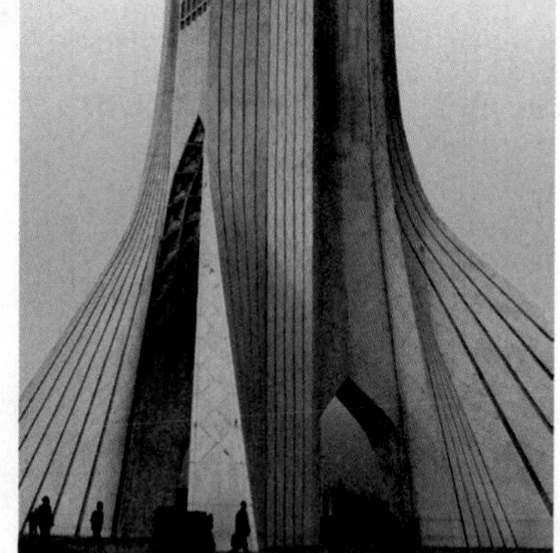

PLACE This monument located in Tehran is dedicated to the Iranian Revolution. **Why might the government have built such a monument?**

PROGRESS INTERRUPTED For many years, war and political problems in Iraq and Afghanistan prevented these countries from improving their economies. In Iraq, rebellion against U.S. forces and religious conflicts have caused major violence. For instance, during 2006, more than 34,000 Iraqi civilians were killed. Oil drilling and shipping has often been disrupted. As a result, the Iraqi people have lacked food, medical supplies, electricity, and even gasoline.

Afghanistan is one of the poorest nations in the world. Most of its people are engaged in agriculture and animal herding, but its most profitable crop is opium. Afghanistan has great mineral

ACTIVITY OPTION **LINK TO HISTORY**

CREATING A TIME LINE

Objective To familiarize students with the Iranian Revolution of 1978–1979

Class Time 40 minutes

Task Create a time line that identifies and explains key events in the Iranian Revolution

Directions Have students use the Internet or library to learn about the Iranian Revolution. Have them take note of important dates and events as they carry out their research. Ask students to use this information to create a time line that shows important key dates and events leading up to, during, and after the Revolution. Encourage students to make their time lines large enough to include explanatory notes for important entries and, when possible, to add visuals to their time lines.

518 CHAPTER 22

resources, but civil war and turmoil during the U.S.-led war against the Taliban in 2001 and 2002 interrupted any attempts at progress in the area. After the Taliban regime was removed from power, the Afghan economy was still threatened by government corruption and the resurgence of the Taliban.

PLACE An Iranian woman works on a wool rug. The high quality hand-woven rugs are a valuable trade item.
How does the photograph demonstrate a traditional lifestyle?

Modern and Traditional Life

Internal struggles in this subregion have lasted long after the initial wars have ended. In each country, a division exists between those who want to adopt a modern lifestyle and those who want to preserve more traditional ways.

Nowhere was this division more apparent than in Afghanistan. There, the Taliban imposed strict rules on people's behavior. After the Taliban regime was toppled in 2002, newly installed president Hamid Karzai began restoring civil liberties and improving education. The Taliban has strengthened since then, however, and has killed hundreds of Afghan civilians. Taliban violence often targets women and girls seeking an education.

In Turkey, Iran, and Iraq, groups similar to the Taliban exist but have not been able to gain control of the governments there. These fundamentalist Muslim groups have very different ideas from each other about the way people should behave. It has led to conflicts within the societies that have sometimes flared into serious political problems.

In the next chapter, you will study more about issues that affect the countries of Southwest Asia.

Section 3 Assessment

1 Places & Terms
Explain the meaning of each of the following terms.
- Kurds
- Mesopotamia
- Sunni
- Shi'ite
- Taliban

2 Taking Notes
REGION Review the notes you took for this section.

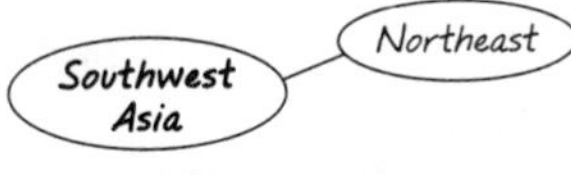

- What role has oil played in clashes over land in this subregion?
- Why are there so many refugees in this subregion?

3 Main Ideas
a. How are the people who live in the Northeast different from those who live in other parts of Southwest Asia?
b. What do the nations in this subregion need to do to develop their economies?
c. Why did the United States overthrow some of the leaders in the subregion?

4 Geographic Thinking
Making Inferences What impact do political problems have on economic progress? **Think about:**
- the economies of Turkey and Iran
- the economies of Iraq and Afghanistan

SEEING PATTERNS Review the information on ethnic and religious variety, and national economies of the countries in this section. Also visit the Internet for more information on the topics. Then create a **database** showing your information.

SW ASIA

Interpreting Photographs

Rug Weaving

Have students examine the photograph and ask what other economic activity is necessary to support weavers. *(sheep-raising would be required to supply the wool)*

CAPTION ANSWER The rug is being produced by hand and not a machine.

Instruct: Objective 

Modern and Traditional Life

- What is an important cultural division in societies in the Northeast? *(between those who want to adopt modern lifestyles and those who want to preserve traditional ways)*
- Why have conflicts arisen between fundamentalist Muslim groups and the governments of Turkey, Iran, and Iraq? *(They have very different ideas about how people should behave.)*

Cultures Transparencies CW37, 39, 42
- Petra
- Islamic Calligraphy
- Praying at the Western Wall

Assess & Reteach

GeoFocus Have students complete the sections on the Northeast in their cluster diagrams.

Formal Assessment
- Section Quiz, p. 341

Reteaching Activity
Have students work with a partner to review the section's main subjects.

In-Depth Resources: Unit 7
- Reteaching Activity, p. 20

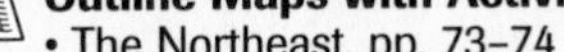

Outline Maps with Activities
- The Northeast, pp. 73–74

SECTION 3 ASSESSMENT ANSWERS

1. Places & Terms
Kurds, p. 516
Mesopotamia, p. 516
Sunni, p. 516
Shi'ite, p. 516
Taliban, p. 517

2. Taking Notes
- Attempts to control valuable oil fields have led to war in the subregion.
- Some refugees are fleeing oppressive governments. Others are trying to claim homelands promised but never received.

3. Main Ideas
a. They are different ethnically and speak languages other than Arabic.
b. They need to modernize their infrastructure including transportation, communication systems, power, water, and sanitation.
c. to fight international terrorism.

4. Geographic Thinking
Countries that have political problems are not able to focus on developing the nation economically. Infrastructure may be damaged by war.

GeoActivity

Integrated Assessment
- Rubric for a database, 2.6

OBJECTIVES

1. Understand the magnitude of the destruction caused by the 1999 earthquake in Turkey.
2. Research the causes and effects of earthquakes and create a demonstration.
3. Examine Richter and Mercalli Intensity scales.

Instruct: Objective

Earthquake in Turkey

- What caused the 1999 earthquake in Turkey? *(The Anatolian Plate was squeezed between the Arabian and Eurasian plates and thrust westward.)*
- Where was the epicenter of the quake? *(near Izmit)*
- How many people lost their lives as a result of the earthquake? *(about 17,000 people)*

Interpreting Maps

North Anatolian Fault

Have students examine the maps on pages 520 and 528. Ask why earthquakes in Turkey might be especially deadly. *(because the North Anatolian Fault runs through a region with a relatively high population density)*

Disasters!

Earthquake in Turkey

As the Arabian Plate pushes northward, it squeezes the Anatolian Plate into the Eurasian Plate. Caught like a slippery seed squeezed between two fingers, the Anatolian Plate slips westward. This movement causes the earth to quake. At 3 A.M. on August 17, 1999, residents of Gölcük, a city near Izmit, Turkey, were thrown from their beds by 45 seconds of earth-shaking terror. When it was over, the quake—which measured 7.4 on the Richter Scale—had taken the lives of 17,000 people and caused billions of dollars of damage.

Izmit, Turkey, was at the epicenter of the quake. It is located on one of the world's most active fault lines—the North Anatolian Fault. Since 1939, 11 major quakes have hit along the Anatolian Fault Line.

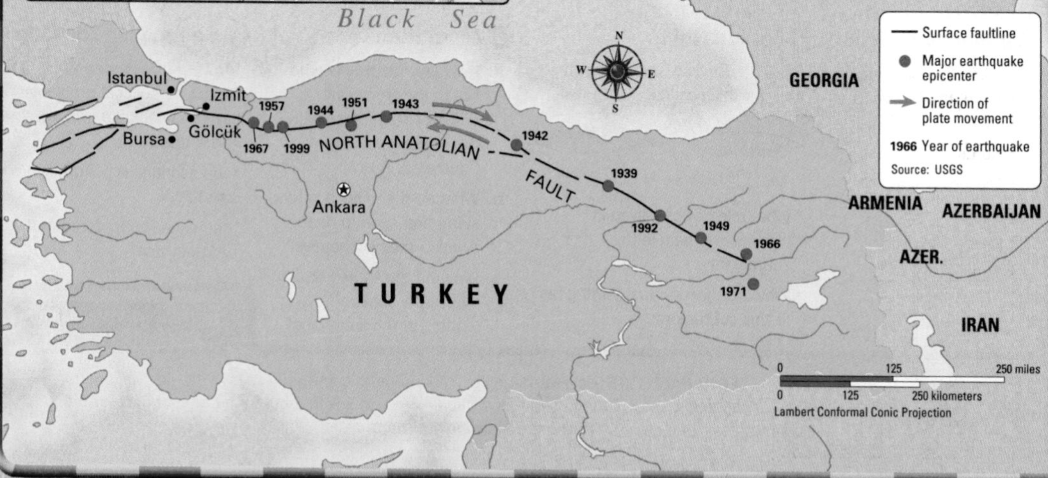

Surface faultline
Major earthquake epicenter
Direction of plate movement
1966 Year of earthquake
Source: USGS

ADDITIONAL RESOURCES

BOOKS FOR TEACHERS

Tang, Alex K. ed. ***Izmit (Kocaeli), Turkey, Earthquake of August 17, 1999.*** Reston, VA: American Society of Civil Engineers, 2000. Engineers investigate the performance of critical facilities, such as water and electric utilities, after the earthquake.

Davis, Mike. ***Ecology of Fear.*** NY: Metropolitan Books, 1998. A fascinating study of the relationship between an urban environment and its natural ecosystems and the influence of politics on public safety.

BOOKS FOR STUDENTS

Kurzman, Dan. ***Disaster! The Great San Francisco Earthquake and Fire of 1906.*** NY: William Morrow, 2001. The story of the famous earthquake that virtually leveled San Francisco in April 1906.

VIDEOS

Earthquakes. Dir. Laurence Jankowski. Ft. Collins, CO: Scott Resources, 1985.

History of 20th-Century Disasters. Prod. Helen Hill. Princeton, NJ: Films for the Humanities & Sciences, 1996.

INTERNET

For more about earthquakes, visit . . .

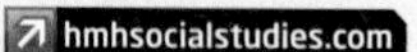

The quake destroyed 85,000 buildings. Many of the buildings were poorly constructed with inferior building materials. Floors of buildings "pancaked" and crushed the residents.

About 40,000 families were made homeless by the quake. Survivors were housed in 168 tent cities. Unfortunately, few were winterized, and thousands of people shivered through Turkey's winter.

hmhsocialstudies.com INTERACTIVE

GeoActivity

MAKING A DEMONSTRATION 21ST CENTURY

Working with a small group, use the Internet to research the causes and effects of earthquakes. Then create a **demonstration** about earthquakes.

- Build a model or create a diagram showing how an earthquake occurs.
- Create a chart showing the type of damage caused by earthquakes.
- Add a world map showing the major fault lines.

hmhsocialstudies.com RESEARCH WEB LINKS

GeoData

THE MERCALLI INTENSITY SCALE

- The Mercalli Intensity Scale measures an earthquake's effect on people and buildings.
- Mercalli ranges from I to XII. Here are some examples.

I. No damage
VI. Pictures fall off the wall
VII. Slight damage to structures
X. Most masonry structures destroyed; landslides; ground cracked
XII. Total damage

RICHTER SCALE

- The Richter Scale measures the magnitude of energy released during an earthquake.
- Here are some examples of Richter Scale measurements:

2 Just felt
4.5 Damage newsworthy
7 A major quake
8 Great damage
8.9 Largest quake ever recorded

GeoActivities

Making a Demonstration

Integrated Assessment

- Rubric for a demonstration, 1.10

More About

U.S. Earthquakes

One of the worst earthquakes in U.S. history struck California on April 18, 1906, running along the northernmost 430 kilometers of the San Andreas Fault. The epicenter of the quake was near San Francisco, which experienced violent shocks and strong shaking that lasted around 45 to 60 seconds. The quake was felt in southern Oregon, to the south of Los Angeles, and in central Nevada. It has been estimated that more than 3,000 deaths were caused directly by the earthquake or the resulting fires.

ACTIVITY OPTION FIVE THEMES OF GEOGRAPHY

LOCATION AND HUMAN-ENVIRONMENT INTERACTION

Exploring the Themes Location answers the question "Where is it?" Geographers answer this question in both absolute and relative terms. When geographers study human-environment interaction, they look at the ways in which people learn to use what the environment offers them, how they change the environment to suit their needs, and how they learn to live with aspects of the environment that lie outside their control, such as earthquakes.

Understanding the Themes Remind students that earthquakes usually occur at specific locations—where tectonic plates grind or slip past each other at a fault. Nearly 95 percent of all recorded earthquakes occur around major plate boundaries. Ask students to do research on the Internet or in the library and answer the following questions.

- What do agencies responsible for public safety recommend doing to protect yourself in the event of an earthquake? *(Answers will vary, but students should discuss both indoor and outdoor measures.)*
- What can engineers do to reduce the potential damage of earthquakes to buildings? *(Answers will vary, but students might mention technology that makes use of rubber bearings "tuned" to combat the low frequency vibrations of earthquakes.)*

Reviewing Places & Terms

A.
1. Mecca, p. 503
2. Islam, p. 503
3. OPEC, p. 505
4. Western Wall, p. 510
5. Dome of the Rock, p. 511
6. Zionism, p. 511
7. Palestine Liberation Organization, p. 513
8. Sunni, p. 516
9. Shi'ite, p. 516
10. Taliban, p. 517

B. Possible Responses

11. Because Muhammad lived part of his life in Mecca, it is considered a holy city.
12. Sunni and Shi'ite are branches of Islam.
13. Sunni Islam has the largest number of followers.
14. Both sites are located in Jerusalem.
15. The Dome of the Rock is associated with Islam.
16. It is the only remaining part of the Jewish temple destroyed by the Romans.
17. OPEC is concerned with international oil trade.
18. The PLO want to gain lands in Israel for Palestinian Arabs.
19. The goal of Zionism was to re-establish a Jewish state in the Jewish homeland.
20. Afghanistan

Chapter 22 Assessment

VISUAL SUMMARY
HUMAN GEOGRAPHY OF SOUTHWEST ASIA

Subregions of Southwest Asia

The Arabian Peninsula
- The teachings of Islam shape the lives of the people of the region.
- Oil forms the basis of the economy of the region.
- The subregion has experienced rapid modernization.

The Eastern Mediterranean
- The region has holy places of three religions: Judaism, Christianity, and Islam.
- The Jewish nation-state of Israel was created in 1948.
- Political unrest in the region has disrupted life and created problems with refugees and the economy.

The Northeast
- The region has a variety of ethnic groups, most of whom practice Islam.
- The region has economies that range from developed to one of the poorest nations in the world—Afghanistan.
- There are divisions among the people of this region over modern and traditional lifestyles.

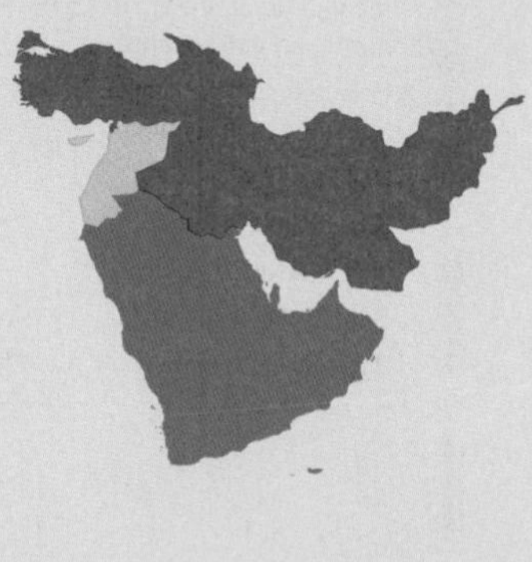

Reviewing Places & Terms

A. Briefly explain the importance of each of the following.

1. Mecca
2. Islam
3. OPEC
4. Western Wall
5. Dome of the Rock
6. Zionism
7. Palestine Liberation Organization
8. Sunni
9. Shi'ite
10. Taliban

B. Answer the questions about vocabulary in complete sentences.

11. Why is Mecca an important site to Muslims?
12. How are Islam, Sunni, and Shi'ite related to each other?
13. Which branch of Islam has the largest number of followers?
14. Where are the Western Wall and the Dome of the Rock located?
15. With which religion is the Dome of the Rock associated?
16. Why is the Western Wall important to Jews?
17. Which of the terms above is associated with international oil trade?
18. What is the goal of the Palestine Liberation Organization?
19. How was Zionism connected to the formation of the State of Israel?
20. In which country were members of the Taliban harboring terrorists?

Main Ideas

The Arabian Peninsula (pp. 503–509)

1. How did the teachings of Islam unite the people of the Arabian Peninsula?
2. Why is oil so important to the economies of the Arabian Peninsula?
3. How has modern Arabic life changed in the past 50 years?

The Eastern Mediterranean (pp. 510–515)

4. For which religions is Jerusalem a holy city?
5. Why was the State of Israel created?
6. What factors have made it difficult to build healthy economies in the Eastern Mediterranean countries?
7. How are populations of Lebanon and Israel different from other countries in the region?

The Northeast (pp. 516-521)

8. How are language, ethnic groups, and religion in the Northeast region different from other parts of Southwest Asia?
9. What steps need to be taken to improve the economies of the Northeast region?
10. Why are there internal struggles in some of the nations of the Northeast region?

Main Ideas

1. It brought a set of religious duties that were required of all followers.
2. The nations make almost all of their export money from the sale of oil, and much of their GDP is from oil.
3. Life is much more urbanized.
4. Judaism, Christianity, Islam
5. as the re-established Jewish homeland for refuge from persecution
6. Factors include political divisions, refugees, lack of water, and a weak infrastructure.
7. Both have a variety of ethnic groups and religious sects.
8. Most areas are Kurdish, Turkic, or Persian, not Arabic in culture, and the people who live there do not speak Arabic but Turkish and Farsi. This subregion has many more Shi'ites than the other parts of the region.
9. They need a modern infrastructure, including transportation systems, communication systems, power generation, and water and sanitation systems.
10. Some groups wish to pursue a traditional lifestyle, while others want to adopt a more modern lifestyle.

Critical Thinking

1. Using Your Notes

Use your completed chart to answer these questions.

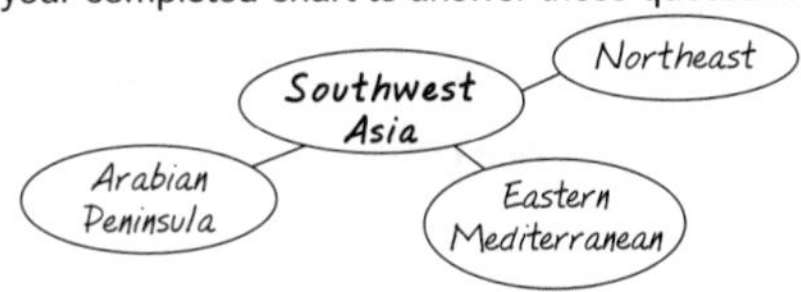

a. How is Israel different from the other nations in the region?

b. How must infrastructure be changed in the region?

2. Geographic Themes

a. **HUMAN-ENVIRONMENT INTERACTION** What impact does the presence of oil in the region have on the economies of the countries in Southwest Asia?

b. **LOCATION** How would Israel's relative location be described?

3. Identifying Themes

Which nations are dealing with large numbers of refugees or immigrants? Which of the five themes applies to this situation?

4. Making Inferences

How has the presence of many different ethnic groups in this region caused political unrest?

5. Making Generalizations

In what ways has oil production changed life in Southwest Asia?

For Additional Test Practice

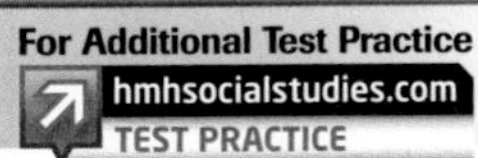

Geographic Skills: Interpreting Maps

Ottoman Empire, 1683

Use the map at the right to answer the following questions.

1. **LOCATION** What is the relative location of the Ottoman Empire?
2. **PLACE** On which continents was the Ottoman Empire located?
3. **PLACE** Which large bodies of water are within the Ottoman Empire?

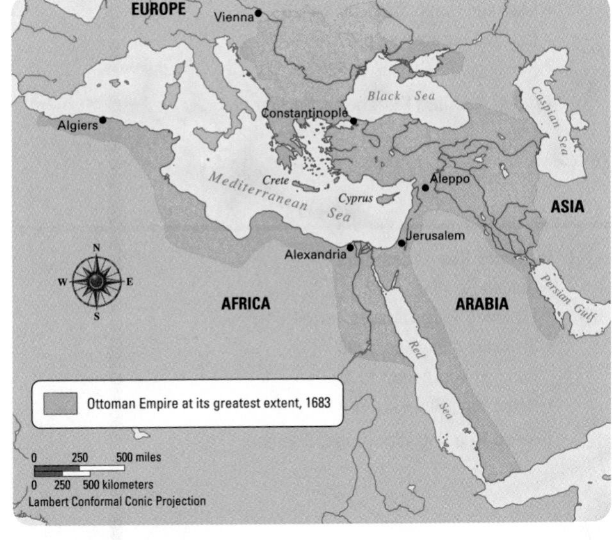

On a current map showing the same area as in the map at the right, outline the Ottoman Empire. Make a list of the modern countries that were once a part of the Ottoman Empire.

hmhsocialstudies.com

MULTIMEDIA ACTIVITY

Use the links at **hmhsocialstudies.com** to do research about OPEC. Make a list of the current members of the organization. Focus on the impact on the price of oil as a result of actions taken by the group.

Analyzing Data Study the data you collected on oil prices and the actions of OPEC. Create charts or graphs to illustrate the information. Then write a generalization about the information you found.

CHAPTER 22 ASSESSMENT

Critical Thinking

1. a. Israel is a Jewish nation.
b. It must be modernized and expanded.

2. a. It generates revenue that can be used to diversify and expand economies.
b. It is in the Eastern Mediterranean, between Lebanon, Syria, and Jordan.

3. Israel, Lebanon, Jordan, and Iran; movement

4. many of the region's different ethnic groups have competing land claims

5. The region is wealthier, more urbanized, and has a large number of guest workers.

GeoActivity

Integrated Assessment
- Rubric for a map, 2.1

Formal Assessment
- Chapter Test, Forms A, B, and C, pp. 342–353

Geographic Skills

1. It surrounds large parts of the Red and Mediterranean seas and extends north into Europe.

2. Europe, Asia, Africa

3. Mediterranean, Black, and Red seas

SW ASIA

MULTIMEDIA ACTIVITY

For their charts and graphs on OPEC data, students should:

- Be sure to list all member countries.
- Create visuals that show fluctuations in oil prices that result from OPEC actions.
- Include references to the Web sites used as sources.

Grading Rubric Evaluate student performance as Exceptional, Acceptable or Poor in each of the following categories.

	Exceptional	Acceptable	Poor
Presents information accurately			
Presents information in a style that will aid the viewer in understanding the information			
Uses bar, line, or pie graphs			
Is presented neatly			

CHAPTER 23 PLANNING GUIDE

Today's Issues: Southwest Asia

OVERVIEW	INSTRUCTIONAL RESOURCES	
ESSENTIAL QUESTION What can the people of Southwest Asia do to solve long-standing problems? **Focus on the Essential Question Podcast**	**In-Depth Resources: Unit 7** • Building Vocabulary, p. 27 **Block Schedule Strategies** **Chapter Summaries** (English/Spanish)	**Interactive Online Edition** TOS **ExamView® Assessment Suite** (English/Spanish) TOS **CalendarPlanner** **Power Presentations with Media Gallery** **Critical Thinking Transparencies** • CT23 hmhsocialstudies.com INTERACTIVE
SECTION 1 **POPULATION RELOCATION** **MAIN IDEAS** • Economic opportunities in Southwest Asia attract foreign guest workers. • Political factors have shifted the region's population. • Refugee problems have resulted in complex and often violent conflicts.	**In-Depth Resources: Unit 7** • Guided Reading, p. 21 • Exploring Today's Issues, pp. 28–29 • Map and Graph Skills, pp. 24–25 • Building Vocabulary, p. 27 • Reteaching Activities, p. 32 **Guided Reading Workbook,** Section 1	**Critical Thinking Transparencies** • CT55 Refugees of Southwest Asia, 1999
SECTION 2 **OIL WEALTH FUELS CHANGE** **MAIN IDEAS** • Oil wealth has both political and economic consequences in Southwest Asia. • The region's nations are trying to diversify their economies by improving infrastructure and resource use. • Some nations are developing human resources through education.	**In-Depth Resources: Unit 7** • Guided Reading, p. 22 • Exploring Today's Issues, pp. 30–31 • Skillbuilder Practice, p. 26 • Building Vocabulary, p. 27 • Reteaching Activities, p. 33 **Guided Reading Workbook,** Section 2	
CASE STUDY **REGIONAL CONFLICT OVER LAND** **MAIN IDEAS** • The conflict between Israelis and Arabs over land and statehood in Southwest Asia disrupts life in the region. • A serious point of contention is the status of the city of Jerusalem. • The international community has tried to craft proposals for the solution of this difficult issue.	**In-Depth Resources: Unit 7** • Guided Reading, p. 23 • Building Vocabulary, p. 27 • Reteaching Activities, p. 34 **Guided Reading Workbook,** Case Study	**Map Transparencies** • MT40 Southwest Asia: Religious Groups

ASSESSMENT

SE **Chapter Assessment,** pp. 536–537

Formal Assessment
- Chapter Tests, Forms A, B, and C, pp. 357–371

TOS **ExamView® Assessment Suite**

Strategies for Test Preparation

hmhsocialstudies.com TEST PRACTICE

SE **Section Assessment,** p. 527

Formal Assessment
- Section Quiz, p. 354

Integrated Assessment
- Rubric for a Venn diagram, 2.8

Test Practice Transparencies TT74

SE **Section Assessment,** p. 531

Formal Assessment
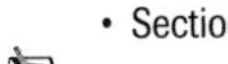
- Section Quiz, p. 355

Integrated Assessment
- Rubric for a map, 2.1

Test Practice Transparencies TT75

SE **Case Study Project,** pp. 534-535

Formal Assessment
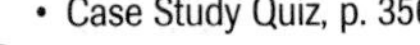
- Case Study Quiz, p. 356

Test Practice Transparencies TT76

CHART KEY:

SE Student Edition	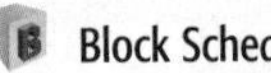 Block Scheduling	 DVD/CD-ROM
TE Teacher's Edition	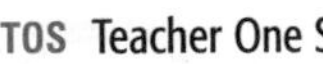 TOS Teacher One Stop	MP3 Audio
Printable Resource	 Presentation Resource	 HISTORY™

Program Resources available on TOS and @ hmhsocialstudies.com

SUPPORTING RESOURCES

- **Multimedia Classroom Global History Series**
- **Global History Teacher's Guide**

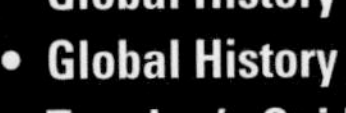

Social Studies Trade Library Collection
- Modern World History Trade Collection

For more information or to purchase these resources, go to  hmhsocialstudies.com

DIFFERENTIATED INSTRUCTION

English Learners	Struggling Readers	Gifted and Talented Students
 **Spanish/English Guided Reading Workbook** **Access for Students Acquiring English/ESL** Spanish Translations, pp. 121–126 **Chapter Summaries** (English/Spanish)	 **Chapter Summaries** (English/Spanish)	TE **TE Activity** Creating a Travel Itinerary, p. 526

ENRICHMENT ACTIVITIES

The following activities are especially suitable for classes following block schedules.

SE **Student Edition,** pp. 524–537 • Interpreting a Population Density Map, p. 528	hmhsocialstudies.com INTERACTIVE • Jerusalem: The Old City, p. 533

BLOCK SCHEDULE LESSON PLAN OPTIONS: 90-MINUTE PERIOD

DAY 1

SECTION 1, pp. 524–528
Class Time 90 minutes

- **In-Depth Report** Have students write essays that discuss the connection between geography, history, and today's issues in Southwest Asia. Ask students to use information from Section 1 as the basis for their essay. Collect the essays and select a few to read to the class to engage students in a classroom discussion.
Class Time 45 minutes

- **Oral Reports** Divide students into groups and assign each group a nation in Europe with a sizeable Kurdish community (e.g., Germany, France, Netherlands, Switzerland, Belgium, etc.). Students should use the Internet or library resources to do research on their assigned community. Have students use their research to create short oral reports that describe each community. After they have delivered their reports, lead students in a classroom discussion comparing the different communities.
Class Time 45 minutes

DAY 2

SECTION 2, pp. 529–531
Class Time 90 minutes

- **Group Debates** Divide students into groups of four or more and have them create a list of the costs and benefits associated with the use of oil. Within each group, half of the members should argue on behalf of oil's benefits, and the other half should focus on the costs.
Class Time 45 minutes

- **Classroom Discussion** Lead a classroom discussion in which students consider different ways in which they or their families could change their behavior in order to reduce the nation's demand for oil. Write students' responses on the board. Conclude the discussion by asking students which of the suggestions they think would be most effective.
Class Time 45 minutes

DAY 3

SECTION 3, pp. 532–535
Class Time 35 minutes

- **Project Summary** Have each student write an analysis of the Case Study Peace Conference. Students should provide a brief explanation of the peace proposal that was discussed. They should also explain the positions of various groups toward the proposal as well as their own opinions.

CHAPTER 23 REVIEW AND ASSESSMENT, pp. 536–537
Class Time 55 minutes

- **Review** Have students review the chapter by relating the Places & Terms on the first page of each section to the causes and effects chart they have completed for the chapter.
Class Time 20 minutes

- **Assessment** Have students complete the Chapter 23 Assessment.
Class Time 35 minutes

TEACHER-TESTED ACTIVITY *Allocating Oil Revenues*

Class Time One class period

Task Create a pie chart showing students' ideas of how a Southwest Asian government should spend money

Supplies Needed:
- Markers or colored pencils
- Notebook paper
- A circular shape to trace for the pie chart

Purpose To explore the problems faced in Southwest Asia by allocating money generated by oil production

Activity After reading the chapter, have the students create a list of problems faced by people in Southwest Asia. Working in groups of three, students will create a pie chart showing how they would allocate oil revenues to address those problems. Have them decide what percentage of the money should be put toward a problem, and why. Reasons for the expenditures should be written next to each section of pie. Next, divide the class up into groups representing the four most mentioned problems and debate which should receive the most money and why. Students can then reflect on their debate or pie charts by finishing the following sentences: The most important problem was . . . . The idea most people disagreed about was . . . . The argument that most changed my mind was . . . .

Matt Lyons
Geography Teacher, Hastings Ninth Grade Center, Houston, Texas

TECHNOLOGY IN THE CLASSROOM

The Internet can be an ideal place for students to learn about complicated issues, such as political controversies, because they can find background information as well as editorials or other expressions of opinion. One challenge is to keep students focused and to make sure they can tell the difference between factual statements and opinion pages. A good way to do this is to specify the sites they will look at and require them to answer specific questions about the things they read.

Objective Students will use the Internet to find out about the background of the Israeli-Palestinian conflict, the different points of view, and recent events related to this issue.

Task Have students use specified Web sites to take notes on the Israeli-Palestinian issue. Have them locate and summarize recent news articles about the situation. Conclude by having them summarize the point of view in two opinion pieces in the Jerusalem *Post.*

Class Time 2–3 class periods

1. Have students read pages 532–535 and ask them to summarize the reasons for the conflict over Jerusalem.
2. Ask students if they have heard anything about the Middle East peace process and the current struggles between Palestinians and Israelis. Discuss what they have heard on the news.
3. Have students use the material in the chapter and on the first three Web sites at **hmhsocialstudies.com** to list the main issues at stake in the Middle East struggle. Then have them list Palestinian and Israeli views on these issues.
4. Have students use the Web sites they have already been to, plus the online news sources at **hmhsocialstudies.com**, to locate two or three recent news stories on the Middle East struggle. Have them read the articles and, for each one, answer these six journalistic questions: who, what, where, when, how, and why?
5. Ask students to discuss the articles with the class. What are the main issues being argued right now? What has happened in the past week or month?
6. Have students go to the Jerusalem *Post* online (available by linking from **hmhsocialstudies.com**) and link to "Opinion" at the top of the screen. Ask them to find two editorials or op-ed articles related to the Israeli-Palestinian situation. If they cannot find any, they can change the date in their browser's location window to read yesterday or the day before. Have them summarize the editorials and articles in brief paragraphs, explaining the point of view the author has taken on the issue.
7. Hold a closing discussion on the reasons why it can be informative to find news articles and editorials online. What are the benefits of using the Internet for this purpose? *(it's current and easy to search)* What are some benefits of being able to locate and read editorials?

CHAPTER 23 OBJECTIVE

Examine serious issues faced by the people of Southwest Asia.

Chapter 23 TODAY'S ISSUES Southwest Asia

A Kurdish family rests at its camp in eastern Turkey. Many Kurds are nomadic and move across lands in several countries.

Interpreting Photographs

Kurdish Family

Ask students to study the photograph and read the caption. Have them discuss what daily life as a nomad might be like.

Introducing the Essential Question

- Lead a discussion about national identity and what it means to be a country. Emphasize the significance of land to that identity. This chapter deals in part with people who feel they are a country but have no land to call their own.
- Remind students what they have learned about the roles of religion and oil in the region's history. Specific situations related to both are examined more closely in this chapter.

hmhsocialstudies.com TAKING NOTES

Have students fill out the cause-and-effect charts in their notebooks using material from all sections in this chapter.

Critical Thinking Transparencies CT23
- GeoFocus

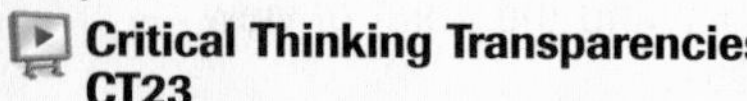

In-Depth Resources: Unit 7
- Building Vocabulary, p. 27

Essential Question

What can the people of Southwest Asia do to solve long-standing problems?

What You Will Learn

In this chapter you will trace sources of some conflicts in Southwest Asia and investigate possible solutions to those conflicts.

SECTION 1
Population Relocation

SECTION 2
Oil Wealth Fuels Change

CASE STUDY
Regional Conflict Over Land

For more on these issues in Southwest Asia . . .

hmhsocialstudies.com CURRENT EVENTS

hmhsocialstudies.com TAKING NOTES

Use the graphic organizer online to record information about solving economic and political problems in Southwest Asia.

524

CHAPTER 23 ADDITIONAL RESOURCES

BOOKS FOR THE TEACHER

Akram Khater, Fouad. ***Sources in the History of the Modern Middle East***. Wadsworth Publishing, 2010. A primary source reader provides first-hand accounts of significant events.

Brentjes, Burchard. ***The Armenians, Assyrians & Kurds: Three Nations, One Fate?*** Campbell, CA: Rishi Publications, 1997. A history of the persecution endured by Assyrians, Armenians, and Kurds.

VIDEOS

Search for Peace in the Middle East. A&E Network, 1998. A documentary of the Middle East featuring newsman Mike Wallace.

The Gates of Jerusalem: A History of the Holy City. Quasar, 1996. A tour of the city with insights into its past, present, and future.

BOOKS FOR THE STUDENT

Clot, André. ***Suleiman the Magnificent: The Man, His Life, His Epoch.*** London, Saqui Books, 1999. Biography of the 16th-century sultan who reigned during the peak of Ottoman power.

INTERNET

For more on today's issues in Southwest Asia, visit . . .

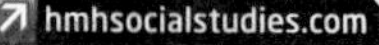
hmhsocialstudies.com

Population Relocation

What kind of population movement is taking place in Southwest Asia?

Main Ideas
- Economic growth brings foreign workers to the region.
- Political factors have shifted the region's population.

Places & Terms
guest workers
stateless nation
Palestinians
West Bank
Gaza Strip

A HUMAN PERSPECTIVE In the 1980s, Kurds living in Turkey were attacked by the Turkish military. The parents of 10-year-old Garbi Yildirim feared for their son's safety. Reluctantly they sent him from Turkey to live with relatives in Germany. When Garbi reached his 18th birthday, he was notified by the German government that he would have to return to Turkey. Upon his return, he knew that he would have to serve in the Turkish military. This meant he would have to use weapons against his own people—the Kurds. He refused to return to Turkey and was placed in a deportation prison to await the recommendation of a German court on the case. Garbi's case is an example of the problems some ethnic groups face in Southwest Asia.

New Industry Requires More Workers

Life in Southwest Asia in 1900 seemed only slightly different from life there in 1100. Some people lived in villages or cities while others moved livestock from one source of water to another.

Then, in the early years of the 20th century, everything changed. Geologists discovered huge deposits of petroleum and natural gas under the sands and seas of Southwest Asia. Western oil companies quickly leased land in the region and supplied the technology and the workers to pump the fuel from the ground.

Many countries in Southwest Asia grew enormously wealthy from oil profits. The oil boom set off decades of rapid urbanization. Extensive road construction made cities and towns more accessible. Many thousands of people migrated to the cities in search of jobs and a chance to share in the region's newfound riches. So many jobs were available that some were left unfilled.

FOREIGN WORKERS To fill the job openings, companies recruited people, mostly from South and East Asia. These **"guest workers"** are largely unskilled laborers. They fill jobs that the region's native peoples find culturally or economically unacceptable. In parts of the Arabian Peninsula, the immigrant workers actually outnumber the native workers. For example, in 2005, about 90 percent of the United Arab Emirates (UAE) work force was made up of foreigners.

PLACE Great wealth makes this United Arab Emirates golf club possible. In the middle of the desert, it features green fairways, a pool, and a freshwater lake. Guest workers fill jobs at sites like this.

SECTION 1 OBJECTIVES

1. Discuss reasons for the region's large number of guest workers and the impact they have on the region.
2. Examine the situation of political refugees in Southwest Asia.

SKILLBUILDER: Interpreting Graphs, p. 526

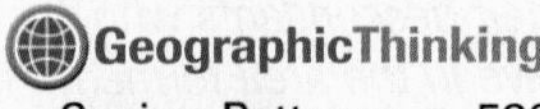

Seeing Patterns, p. 526
Making Comparisons, p. 527
Identifying and Solving Problems, p. 527

Focus & Motivate

Ask students why people from one country would go work in another country. *(because economic opportunities in their own country may not be so great)*

Instruct: Objective 

New Industry Requires More Workers

- Why did so many foreign workers come to Southwest Asia? *(to work in the oil industry)*
- What kind of positions do guest workers in Southwest Asia fill? *(mostly jobs that the region's native peoples find culturally or economically unacceptable)*
- What kinds of problems might the use of guest workers cause? *(cultural misunderstandings, segregation and discrimination, lack of job security, competition with local workforces, weakening national identity)*

In-Depth Resources: Unit 7
- Guided Reading, p. 21
- Exploring Today's Issues, pp. 28–29

SECTION 1 PROGRAM RESOURCES

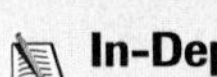

In-Depth Resources: Unit 7
- Guided Reading, p. 21
- Building Vocabulary, p. 27
- Map and Graph Skills, pp. 24–25
- Exploring Today's Issues, pp. 28–29
- Reteaching Activity, p. 32

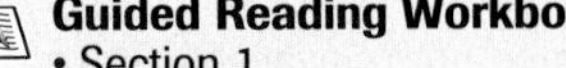

Guided Reading Workbook
- Section 1

Access for Students Acquiring English/ESL
- Guided Reading, p. 121
- Map and Graph Skills, pp. 125–126

Formal Assessment
- Section Quiz, p. 354

Integrated Assessment
- Rubric for a Venn diagram, 2.8

INTEGRATED TECHNOLOGY

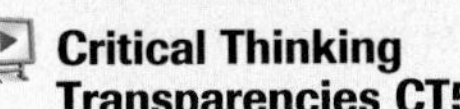

Critical Thinking Transparencies CT55
- Refugees of Southwest Asia, 1999

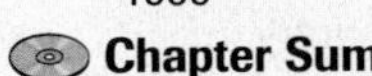

Chapter Summaries

Power Presentations

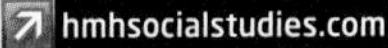

hmhsocialstudies.com

TEST-TAKING RESOURCES

Strategies for Test Preparation

Test Practice Transparencies TT74

Online Test Practice

Instruct: Objective 2

Political Refugees Face Challenges

- What group in Southwest Asia is a stateless nation? *(Kurds)*
- What lands did Allies intend for the Kurds after World War I? *(parts of Turkey, Iraq, and Syria)*
- Who are the Palestinians? *(the Arabs and their descendants who lived or still live in the area formerly called Palestine and now called Israel)*

Critical Thinking Transparencies CT55
- Refugees of Southwest Asia, 1999

Interpreting Graphs

Foreign Workers

Tell students that guest workers are used by countries all over the world. In the early 1960s, Germany experienced an economic boom that resulted in a shortage of workers. To solve the problem, Turks were invited as *Gastarbeiter*, or guest workers. Turks now make up about two-and-a-half percent of the German population. Ask students how these Southwest Asian countries compare to Germany in terms of their populations of foreign workers. *(Germany has a much smaller portion of foreign workers than any of these 5 countries.)*

SKILLBUILDER ANSWERS **1.** United Arab Emirates **2.** Foreign workers are a significant part of the labor force in all these countries.

Foreign Workers

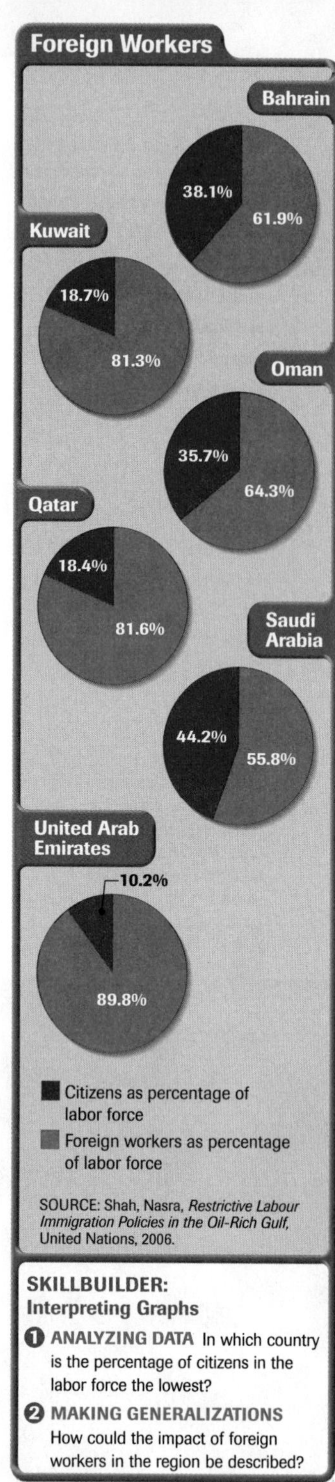

SOURCE: Shah, Nasra, *Restrictive Labour Immigration Policies in the Oil-Rich Gulf*, United Nations, 2006.

SKILLBUILDER: Interpreting Graphs

1. **ANALYZING DATA** In which country is the percentage of citizens in the labor force the lowest?
2. **MAKING GENERALIZATIONS** How could the impact of foreign workers in the region be described?

PROBLEMS OF GUEST WORKERS The presence of so many guest workers has led to problems. Cultural differences often exist between the guest workers and their employers. Misunderstandings over certain customs can result in severe penalties. For example, a Filipino man was given six months in jail and expelled from the UAE for brushing past a woman on a bus. Arabs viewed his behavior as insulting to the woman.

Sometimes the workers must live in special districts apart from the Arab population. Some workers have been abandoned. Others receive no wages for months at a time. Many immigrants find themselves unemployed and without money to get back home.

The large number of guest workers is a concern to the governments of Southwest Asia. Some government officials worry that depending on these workers will prevent their nation's own workers from developing their skills. Others worry about the intolerance and even violence that these workers face. And, finally, some fear the immigrants could weaken their country's sense of national identity. Solving the cultural and economic issues over guest workers will be a challenge to the governments of the region. A

Geographic Thinking

Seeing Patterns
A How did changes in the economy of the region change the make-up of the population?
A. Answer Foreign workers from Asia and Africa came to the region to fill jobs.

Political Refugees Face Challenges

Rapidly changing economic conditions have caused population shifts in Southwest Asia. Political conflict in the region has also caused relocation.

STATELESS NATION One of the longest conflicts has been over the ethnic group known as the Kurds. After World War I, the Allies recommended creating a national state for the group. Instead, the land intended for the Kurds became part of Turkey, Iraq, and Syria. The Kurds became a **stateless nation**—a nation of people without a land to legally occupy. Turkey, Iraq, Iran, and Syria tried to absorb the Kurds into their populations but were not successful. The Kurds resisted control in each of the countries. Governments forcibly moved thousands of Kurds in an attempt to control them.

In Iraq, this forced migration ruined Kurdish homes, settlements, and farms. As you read in Chapter 22, the Iraqi government used deadly chemical weapons on settlements of Kurds to kill them or force them to leave the area. In the year 2000, as many as 70,000 Kurds had been displaced from areas they called home. Many of the Kurds have been forced to live in crowded relocation camps.

DIFFERENTIATING INSTRUCTION

BLOCK SCHEDULING

CREATING A TRAVEL ITINERARY

Objective To give students a more in-depth perspective on a country of Southwest Asia

Class Time 30 minutes

Task Create a travel itinerary for a week-long trip to a country in Southwest Asia

Directions Have students use the Internet to plan a weeklong trip to a country in Southwest Asia. Encourage students to think of their trip not only as vacation, but also as a journey on which they can gain first-hand experience of some of the issues discussed in this section. For example, if students choose Iraq, in addition to visiting Baghdad, they may also wish to visit the thriving Kurdish city of Sulaymaniyah in northern Iraq.

After students have completed their research, have them create a day-by-day itinerary that lists the places they will visit, the sites and people they hope to see, their means of transportation, and other details they think are important.

OPTIONAL ACTIVITY If Internet access is limited or unavailable, have students use printed sources in the library. Country guides published by travel publishers of travel guides would be an especially helpful resource.

PALESTINIAN REFUGEES Another group, some of whom have been displaced in the region, are the **Palestinians.** They are the Arabs and their descendants who lived or still live in the area formerly called the Palestine Mandate. Today, much of that land is part of Israel. The Palestinians are a group of people, like the Kurds, who consider themselves a stateless nation.

As you read in Chapter 22, following World War II, the UN promised states in the Palestine Mandate to both Arabs and Jews. (See map on page 480.) Arabs rejected the UN plan because they claimed as their homeland all of the land that was granted to the Jews.

PLACE Palestinian and Israeli teens discuss concerns they share about their future in the region. **How could discussion affect these students' future?**

B. Answer Jewish refugees settled in Israel. Palestinian refugees were moved into camps.

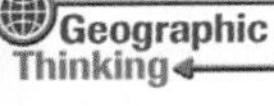

Making Comparisons

B How did the treatment of Palestinian refugees and Jewish refugees from Arab countries differ?

In 1948 when Israel was founded, and during the 1948–1949 war, between 520,000 and 1,000,000 Arabs fled Israel. An equal number of Jews fled their homes in Arab lands. Most moved to Israel and became citizens. Fifty-two refugee camps for Arab Palestinians were established in Lebanon, Jordan, Syria, the West Bank, and the Gaza Strip. The **West Bank** is a strip of land on the west side of the Jordan River. Jordan annexed the land in 1948, but Israel captured it in 1967. The **Gaza Strip** is a 139-square-mile plot of land along the Mediterranean Sea. It was annexed by Egypt in 1948, then captured by Israel in 1967. Israel withdrew completely in 2005. B

Although many refugees live in the areas the UN proposed for an Arab state, they have not been allowed to return to Israel. The number of Palestinians living in the camps or in other parts of Southwest Asia has swelled to over 4.3 million. Thousands have lived and died in refugee camps without ever establishing an Arab state. Their rejection of Israel is at the heart of many conflicts in the region.

Section 1 Assessment

1 Places & Terms

Identify and explain where in the region these would be found.

- guest workers
- stateless nation
- Palestinians
- West Bank
- Gaza Strip

2 Taking Notes

MOVEMENT Review the notes you took for this section.

	Causes	Effects
Issue 1: Population Relocation		

- What are the causes of population movement in the region?
- What is a "stateless nation"?

3 Main Ideas

a. Why is there a need for guest workers in this region?

b. What makes the Kurds a stateless nation?

c. In which areas are Palestinian refugee camps found?

4 Geographic Thinking

Identifying and Solving Problems What problems are created by the presence of guest workers in the region, and how might the problems be solved? **Think about:**

- cultural differences
- national identity

See Skillbuilder Handbook, page R10.

GeoActivity

MAKING COMPARISONS Do some additional research to find out more about the land claims of the Kurds and the Palestinians. Then create a **Venn diagram** showing the ways in which the Kurds' and the Palestinians' land claims are similar to and different from each other.

SW ASIA

Interpreting Photographs

Palestinian and Israeli Teens

After students examine the photograph and read the caption, ask why it might be difficult to bring Israeli and Palestinian teens together. *(The conflict between Israelis and Palestinians has hurt so many people in both communities, it might be difficult for people to overcome their anger in order to establish dialogues.)*

CAPTION ANSWER Discussion could help ease tensions that could otherwise threaten their future.

More About

Daily Life for Palestinians

Because of fears of more suicide bombers and other attackers killing Israeli citizens, the Israeli government has set up security checkpoints between Israeli cities and Palestinian areas. Tens of thousands of Palestinians must pass through such checkpoints in order to get to work in Israel—an often frustrating and humiliating experience.

Assess & Reteach

GeoFocus Have students complete the section on population relocation in their cause-and-effect charts.

Formal Assessment
- Section Quiz, p. 354

Reteaching Activity

Have students write an outline of this section, and then have students exchange their outline with another student who will check their work.

In-Depth Resources: Unit 7
- Reteaching Activity, p. 32

SECTION 1 ASSESSMENT ANSWERS

1. Places & Terms

guest workers, p. 525
stateless nation, p. 526
Palestinians, p. 527
West Bank, p. 527
Gaza Strip, p. 527

2. Taking Notes

- economic and political factors
- Kurds are a nation of people without a land to occupy legally.

3. Main Ideas

a. They fill jobs that the region's native peoples find culturally or economically unacceptable.

b. They claim land for a national state but do not legally occupy it.

c. Lebanon, Syria, Jordan, West Bank, Gaza Strip

4. Geographic Thinking

Problems include misunderstandings over cultural customs, mistreatment and violence toward guest workers, and fears about loss of national identity. Answers may vary on solutions.

GeoActivity

Integrated Assessment
- Rubric for a Venn diagram, 2.8

OBJECTIVE

Understand and interpret population density maps.

Instruct: Objective

Interpreting a Population Density Map

- What can you learn from a population density map? *(the distribution and density of a population in a region)*
- How is population density meas ured? *(by dividing the total population in an area by the unit of land area, such as a square mile or kilometer)*
- How are the results of this equation stated? *(as numbers of persons per square mile or kilometer)*

In-Depth Resources, Unit 7
- Map and Graph Skills, pp. 24–25

Access for Students Acquiring English/ESL
- Map and Graph Skills, pp. 125–126

Interpreting Maps

Population Density of Southwest Asia

In 1963, the American composers Duke Ellington and Billy Strayhorn toured Southwest Asia on behalf of the U.S. State Department. During the trip, they visited the city of Esfahan. Strayhorn chose the name of the city for one of his most beautiful songs–"Isfahan". Ask students to use other maps in the Unit to find out why Esfahan is so heavily populated. *(It is located at the foot of the Zagros Mountains–probably in a well-watered valley suitable for agriculture and industry.)*

RAND McNALLY **Map and Graph Skills**

Interpreting a Population Density Map

How crowded is the area in which you live? Are there cities near you that have very large populations? Population density maps help geographers learn the distribution as well as the density of the population. Notice how the map below shows that Southwest Asia has areas of very dense population and other areas where almost no one lives.

THE LANGUAGE OF MAPS A **population density map** shows where people live and how crowded the conditions are. Population density is measured by dividing the total population in an area by the total number of square miles or square kilometers. The results are stated as numbers of persons per square mile or square kilometer. The density is indicated by colors. Population maps also use symbols to show cities with large populations.

Population Density of Southwest Asia

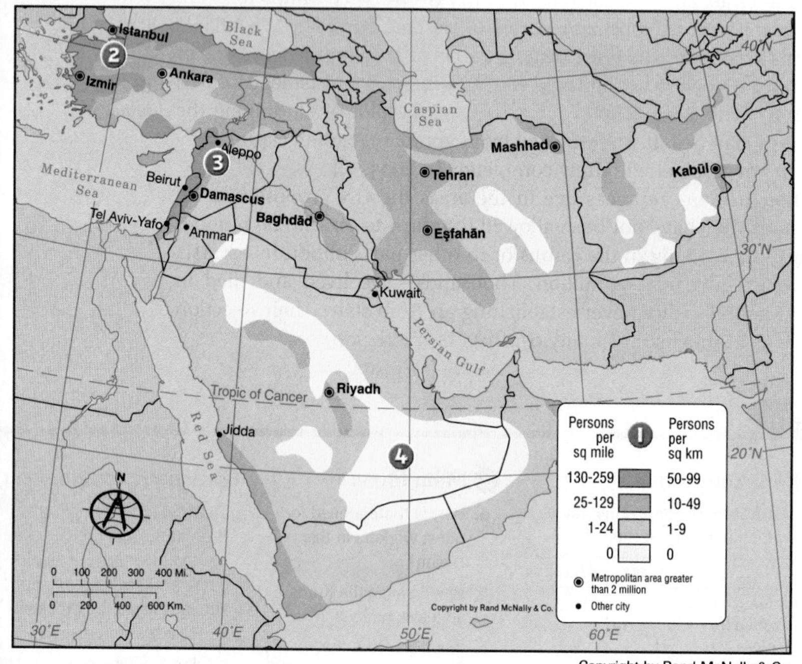

1. The key uses colors to show ranges of population density and symbols to show cities of different sizes.
2. Notice that densities are greater near large cities.
3. Population density patterns show heavier populations in some areas near water.
4. Uninhabited areas usually are regions with inhospitable climates or landforms.

Map and Graph Skills Assessment

1. **Drawing Conclusions** In which parts of the region are the largest number of cities found?
2. **Making Comparisons** Which of the two cities, Aleppo or Beirut, is more densely populated?
3. **Making Generalizations** Use the atlas map on page 481. Which country has the largest areas of uninhabited land?

SKILLS ASSESSMENT ANSWERS

1. In the northwest part of the region especially along Eastern Mediterranean coast lands.
2. Beirut
3. Saudi Arabia

Oil Wealth Fuels Change

How can oil wealth help develop the region's economies?

Main Ideas
- Oil wealth brings political and economic changes to the region.
- To achieve a diversified economy, countries need to improve infrastructure and resource use.

Places & Terms
strategic commodity
human resources

A HUMAN PERSPECTIVE On October 2, 1995, Queen Noor of the Kingdom of Jordan gave a speech on the role of women in Southwest Asian economies. In her speech, she identified an important change in the economies of Southwest Asia:

> The changing environment in our region holds the promise of new opportunity for businessmen and women. Middle Eastern women are overcoming discriminatory socio-cultural constraints [limitations] that once denied them equal access to services and hindered [slowed] their participation in the economy.

Queen Noor described one of the ways in which countries in the region are using the skills of their people to change the economy. Today, money earned from the region's most important export—oil—is helping to build a more diverse economy.

Meeting the Global Demand

At the start of the 21st century, oil fueled the world's industries and transportation—and its economies. This "black gold" was so vital that oil became a **strategic commodity,** a resource so important that nations will go to war to ensure its steady supply.

Southwest Asia contains much of the oil supply. As you learned in Chapter 21, about 64 percent of the world's proven oil deposits and 34 percent of its reserves of natural gas are found in this region. By the year 2020, exports from Southwest Asia will probably provide about 44.5 million barrels of oil per day, or about 50 percent of world demand.

These oil reserves haven't always been of great benefit. One problem is that the world's oil prices rise and fall unpredictably. As a result, Southwest Asian countries cannot always plan how much revenue oil will bring in. Unpredictable oil prices have also made it difficult for the region's nations to have steady economic growth. For instance, when oil prices were low in 1996 and 1997, Southwest Asia's economies grew slowly. Because of that experience, the nations of that region realized that they could not continue to base their economies only on oil.

World Oil Demand

Millions of barrels per day (0–120): 1995, 2000, 2010*, 2020*

SOURCES: Congressional Research Service and the International Energy Agency

*projected

SKILLBUILDER: Interpreting Graphs
1. **MAKING GENERALIZATIONS** By about how much will oil demand increase by the year 2020?
2. **ANALYZING DATA** During which decade is demand projected to increase most sharply?

SW ASIA

SECTION 2 OBJECTIVES
1. Explain the global importance of oil.
2. Discuss the importance of using oil revenues to diversify regional economies.

SKILLBUILDER: Interpreting Graphs, p. 529

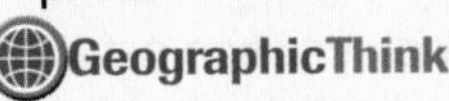

Seeing Patterns, p. 530
Making Comparisons, p. 531
Determining Cause and Effect, p. 531

Focus & Motivate

Ask students to name direct or indirect ways in which oil is important in their lives. *(for transportation, for heating oil, as the basis for plastics)*

Instruct: Objective 

Meeting the Global Demand

- What is a strategic commodity? *(a resource so important that nations will go to war to ensure its steady supply)*
- What portion of the world's proven oil deposits are located in Southwest Asia? *(about 64 percent)*
- Why is it difficult for Southwest Asian countries to plan how much revenue oil will bring in? *(The world's oil prices rise and fall unpredictably.)*

In-Depth Resources: Unit 7
- Guided Reading, p. 22
- Exploring Today's Issues, pp. 30–31

SKILLBUILDER ANSWERS
1. It will increase by around 55 million barrels between 1995 and 2020.
2. 2010 to 2020

SECTION 2 PROGRAM RESOURCES

In-Depth Resources: Unit 7
- Guided Reading, p. 22
- Skillbuilder Practice, p. 26
- Building Vocabulary, p. 27
- Exploring Today's Issues, pp. 30–31
- Reteaching Activity, p. 33

Guided Reading Workbook
- Section 2

Access for Students Acquiring English/ESL
- Guided Reading, p. 122
- Skillbuilder Practice, p. 124

Formal Assessment
- Section Quiz, p. 355

Integrated Assessment
- Rubric for a map, 2.1

INTEGRATED TECHNOLOGY

 **Chapter Summaries**

 **Test Generator**
- Section Quiz

hmhsocialstudies.com

TEST-TAKING RESOURCES

 **Strategies for Test Preparation**

 **Test Practice Transparencies TT75**

Online Test Practice

Instruct: Objective 2

Using Oil Wealth to Diversify

- What are three ways in which Southwest Asian nations can use oil revenues to promote economic growth? *(modernize infrastructures, develop other resources, and improve educational systems)*
- What non-oil resources can nations in the region develop? *(water and mineral resources)*
- Why might it be difficult for women to receive an education in some parts of the region? *(because many societies in Southwest Asia have strict rules governing the behavior for women)*

Interpreting Photographs

Desert Irrigation

Have students examine the photographs and the caption. Ask them to consider what political advantage might accrue to a nation that develops its own agricultural resources. *(Such a nation would be less vulnerable to the demands of other nations that once supplied it with such a vital resource.)*

Using Oil Wealth to Diversify

To promote more economic growth, the oil-rich nations of Southwest Asia face three challenges in the way that they use oil profits. First, each has to modernize its infrastructure. Second, each has to develop its agricultural, mineral, and water resources. Finally, the people of each nation have to gain access to higher education and job training.

MODERNIZING THE INFRASTRUCTURE The region has improved its infrastructure. Saudi Arabia, for example, has built new roads in rural areas, irrigation networks, and facilities to store agricultural products. It has also built desalinization plants that remove the salt from seawater and provide water for cities and industrial use.

BACKGROUND Water produced by desalinization is not always pure enough for drinking purposes but can be used in sanitation.

Other nations have constructed airports, shopping malls, and port facilities. These efforts are not always well coordinated, though. Some years ago, the UAE built four international airports to serve an area about the size of the state of Maine. Needless to say, these airports are greatly underused.

Toward the end of the 20th century, nations in the region began putting together information technology systems to serve businesses. Dubai launched a plan in 2000 called Internet City. The plan made it possible for its government to conduct business on-line.

HUMAN–ENVIRONMENT INTERACTION Using overhead sprinkler systems to bring water to desert areas will make them green. Compare the watered fields to the rest of the Negev Desert shown in the lower picture.

DEVELOPING RESOURCES To create a diversified economy, nations of the area have to develop resources besides oil. One of the greatest needs is to develop agriculture. The region's arid conditions mean that the area is not able to produce great quantities of food. To trap much-needed water for agricultural production, governments have built dams. They have also dug deep wells to tap the water trapped in huge underground reservoirs.

Saudi Arabia can boast several economic success stories. By 1985, improvements in agriculture allowed the Saudis to completely meet the nation's demand for dairy products, red meat, poultry, and eggs. The biggest Saudi success story, however, was wheat production. The Saudis were determined to reduce their dependence on imported wheat. They improved water supplies so that grain production could be expanded. By 1992, they were producing more than four million tons of grain per year. This was enough to actually meet their needs and to have wheat to export. This diversification of the Saudi economy would not have happened without significant investment in infrastructure. That investment, in turn, was made possible by oil profits. A

A. Answer Agriculture could not expand without additional water sources.

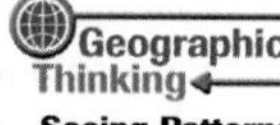

Geographic Thinking

Seeing Patterns A How are the expansion of water production and increased agricultural output connected?

ACTIVITY OPTION **SKILLBUILDER LESSON**

ANALYZING DATA

Explaining the Skill Analyzing data means examining and drawing conclusions about information—usually in the form of statistics. For example, students could look at the statistics used to produce the graph on page 529 and determine that the rate of world oil demand is increasing.

Applying the Skill Have students go to **hmhsocialstudies.com** and follow the links to the U.S. Department of Energy's (DOE) Web site. Have students use the site to locate statistical information that you assign or that is of interest to them. For example, students might use the DOE's Country Analysis Briefs to learn about average gasoline prices in different regions of the United States. Once they have located and analyzed the data, have students write a paragraph that summarizes the information. Then ask students the following questions:

- What was the intent or purpose of the researchers who compiled and published the data? *(Answers will vary.)*
- What conclusions can be drawn based on the selected data? *(Answers will vary.)*

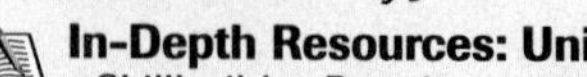

In-Depth Resources: Unit 7
- Skillbuilder Practice, p. 26

Other nations are making efforts to develop other mineral resources. Oman revived its copper industry and chromium mines. Chromium is used in steel production for jet aircraft. Expanding these industries allowed the Omani economy to reduce its dependence on oil profits. B

Geographic Thinking
Making Comparisons
B How is the diversification of Oman's economy different from that of Saudi Arabia?
B. Answer Saudi Arabia developed its agricultural base and Oman developed its industrial base.

HUMAN RESOURCES People are a valuable resource in any nation. Southwest Asian nations are developing their **human resources**—the skills and talents of their people. Many of those nations also realize that they must invest in all their people, including women. Providing education and technology training is critical. Nations are expanding the opportunities for their citizens to gain an education. For example, Kuwait has established free education for all children through the university level. For students who wish to study outside the country, the government pays the fees and provides money to cover living expenses.

Many societies in Southwest Asia have strict rules concerning women's roles in society. Often it is difficult for women to get an education and find employment. However, the shortage of workers in the region has opened economic opportunities for women. Important economic and political changes are taking place in Southwest Asia. As the nations work to develop their physical and human resources, opportunities for all who live there will expand. A successful economy is built on the efforts of all its people working together toward the goal of diversification.

PLACE Muslim girls in Tehran, Iran, discuss a lesson.
Why is it important for all citizens to be educated?

Interpreting Photographs

Muslim Girls

Have students examine the photograph and the caption. Ask whether they think that an education in Iran is similar to an education in the United States. *(Students may guess that religious instruction plays a greater role in Iran than in the United States.)*

CAPTION ANSWER A country needs educated citizens to build a solid economy.

Assess & Reteach

GeoFocus In their cause-and-effect charts, have students complete the section on how oil wealth fuels change.

Formal Assessment
- Section Quiz, p. 355

Reteaching Activity
Ask students to make a list of five important words from this section. Then have them write five sentence that correctly use each word.

In-Depth Resources: Unit 7
- Reteaching Activity, p. 33

Section 2 Assessment

SW ASIA

1 Places & Terms
Identify and explain the meaning of these terms.
- strategic commodity
- human resources

2 Taking Notes
REGION Review the notes you took for this section.

	Causes	Effects
Issue 2: Economic Development		

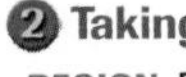

- Why are this region's resources so valuable?
- What changes need to be made to the region's infrastructure?

3 Main Ideas
a. What effect have unpredictable oil prices had on the economy of the region?
b. What steps have nations in the region taken to diversify their economic base?
c. Why must the human resources of the region be developed?

4 Geographic Thinking
Determining Cause and Effect How has oil wealth changed the economy of the region? **Think about:**
- the cost of modernizing the infrastructure
- the need for a diverse economy

See Skillbuilder Handbook, page R9.

MAKING COMPARISONS Do some research to find information about the projected freshwater supplies for the nations in the region. Create a set of symbols to represent the projected water supply figures. Then draw a **map** of the region, and place the appropriate water supply symbol on each nation.

SECTION 2 ASSESSMENT ANSWERS

1. Places & Terms
strategic commodity, p. 529 human resources, p. 531

2. Taking Notes
- They are necessary for transportation and industry everywhere in the world.
- The infrastructure needs modernizing. Key resources need to be developed.

3. Main Ideas
a. The unpredictable prices have made it difficult to have a steadily growing economy.
b. Some nations have improved agricultural production and water projects, developed other minerals, and modernized the infrastructure.
c. Human resources must be developed to keep up with technological developments and to fill jobs in the economy.

4. Geographic Thinking
Oil wealth provides the funds for updating of the infrastructure and for development of a diversified economy.

GeoActivity

Integrated Assessment
- Rubric for a map, 2.1

CASE STUDY OBJECTIVES

1. Explain the issues surrounding the control of Jerusalem.
2. Look at some of the proposed solutions to the conflict.
3. Organize a peace conference.
4. Discuss different perspectives on the control of the city.

Focus & Motivate

Ask students to discuss what they know about Jerusalem. *(Answers will vary.)*

Instruct: Objective 1

Control of Jerusalem

- What proposal did the UN make after World War II regarding Jerusalem? *(that it should become an international city under the control of an international body)*
- What actually happened to the city? *(In 1948 Jordan took control of East Jerusalem and the Old City and drove out Jews; in 1967 Israel won control of the city.)*
- How does the Israeli government handle the holy sites in Jerusalem? *(Israel allows each religion to control its own holy sites.)*

In-Depth Resources: Unit 7
- Guided Reading, p. 23

Map Transparencies MT40
- Southwest Asia: Religious Groups

Interpreting Time Lines

Arab-Israeli Conflict

Have students examine the time line and ask if they know which U.S. president oversaw the 1978 Camp David Accords. *(Jimmy Carter)*

CASESTUDY

REGIONAL CONFLICT OVER LAND

Who should control Jerusalem?

Jerusalem checkpoints deepen Palestinian resentment.

Conflict between Jews and Arabs over land and statehood in Southwest Asia disrupts life in the region. One aspect of this conflict centers around Jerusalem. The city is sacred to Jews, Christians, and Muslims. Control of Jerusalem is a deeply emotional issue that affects the region's politics and population.

Control of Jerusalem

After World War II, the UN recommended that the city of Jerusalem become an international city. It would be under the control of an international body rather than an Arab or a Jewish government. At the end of the Arab-Israeli war in 1948, Jerusalem was divided between Arabs and Israelis. Jordan took the Old City and East Jerusalem, driving out many Jews. The Israelis took control of West Jerusalem. During the Six-Day War of 1967, the Israelis captured the rest of Jerusalem, uniting the city.

Jordan had not allowed Jews to go to the Western Wall and had discriminated against Christians. When the Israelis captured the city, Jews, Christians, and Muslims were given control of their holy sites.

After Israelis gained control of the entire city of Jerusalem, the city expanded. Palestinian Arabs opposed this growth. Most Palestinians in Jerusalem and elsewhere have maintained they should have the "right of return" to Israel. Most Israelis believe that Palestinians should be able to return to the West Bank and Gaza Strip, which include most of the land the UN partition plan intended for an Arab state.

Arab-Israeli Conflict (time line 1940–2010)

- **1948** The State of Israel is created. Arabs attack immediately. Jordan takes West Bank and East Jerusalem. Egypt takes Gaza Strip.
- **1967** Israel takes control of all of Jerusalem, West Bank, and Gaza Strip at the end of the Six-Day War.
- **1978** Camp David Accords set up 1979 peace treaty between Egypt and Israel.
- **1993** Oslo Accords allow Palestinians self-rule in West Bank and Gaza. PLO renounces terrorism and violence. Israel and PLO recognize each other.
- **1994** Jordan and Israel sign a peace treaty.
- **2003** A "road map" for peace calls for establishing a Palestinian state and security guarantees for Israel.
- **2005** Israel withdraws from the Gaza Strip.

CASE STUDY PROGRAM RESOURCES

In-Depth Resources: Unit 7
- Guided Reading, p. 23
- Building Vocabulary, p. 27
- Reteaching Activity, p. 34

Guided Reading Workbook
- Case Study

Access for Students Acquiring English/ESL
- Guided Reading, p. 123

Formal Assessment
- Case Study Quiz, p. 356

INTEGRATED TECHNOLOGY

Map Transparencies MT40
- Southwest Asia: Religious Groups

hmhsocialstudies.com

TEST-TAKING RESOURCES

Strategies for Test Preparation

Test Practice Transparencies TT42

Online Test Practice

Jerusalem: The Old City

hmhsocialstudies.com INTERACTIVE

West Bank
Israel
West Bank
OLD CITY
Israel
West Jerusalem
East Jerusalem
N W E S
Muslim Quarter
DOME OF THE ROCK (Muslim)
Christian Quarter
Jewish Quarter
Western Wall (Jewish)
DAVID'S TOWER
Armenian Quarter
Temple Mount or Haram ash-Sharif
Al-Aqsa Mosque (Muslim)

Proposed Solutions to the Conflict

SEE PRIMARY SOURCE D

The emotional and political issue of who should control Jerusalem makes it a very difficult diplomatic problem to solve. Israel made Jerusalem its capital in 1950. The Palestinians claim Jerusalem as the capital of their nation, and neither is willing to give it up to the other group. The following solutions have been proposed for control of Jerusalem:

- Palestinians retain control of certain parts of East Jerusalem while Israel annexes several Jewish settlements near Jerusalem in exchange for other land.
- Israel retains control of Jerusalem and continues to give each religious group control over its holy sites in the Old City. This is basically how the city is controlled today under Israeli jurisdiction.
- An international agency has control of all holy sites.

On the following pages, you will find primary sources that present different views on the control of the city of Jerusalem. Use them to help you form an opinion about the best way to solve the problem.

Instruct: Objective 

Proposed Solutions to the Conflict

- Why is the control of Jerusalem such a difficult diplomatic problem to solve? *(because it is both an emotional and political issue)*
- What two groups of people want control of Jerusalem? *(Israelis and Palestinians)*

More About

Jerusalem's History

The three monotheistic religions have important sacred places in Jerusalem very close to each other. Three thousand years ago, King David made Jerusalem the capital of Israel. His son Solomon built the First Temple in Jerusalem, center of Jewish worship. This Temple was destroyed, then later rebuilt. Today all that remains of the Second Temple complex is the Western Wall, Judaism's holiest site. Two thousand years ago, Jesus taught in Jerusalem. Christians built the Church of the Holy Sepulchre where they believe Jesus was buried. In 691, Muslims completed the Dome of the Rock on the Temple Mount, where Muslims believe Muhammad ascended to heaven.

SW ASIA

DIFFERENTIATING INSTRUCTION **GIFTED AND TALENTED STUDENTS**

BLOCK SCHEDULING

PARTICIPATING IN A DEBATE

Objective To help students understand the complexity of the Arab-Israeli conflict

Class Time 45 minutes

Task Debate important issues in the Arab-Israeli conflict

Directions Divide students into competing teams that will take different sides on one or more issues of importance in the Israeli-Arab conflict. Possible issues of debate might include Arab refusal to recognize the creation of the State of Israel, Palestinian claims to property lost in the 1948 war, Palestinian terrorist attacks against Israeli civilians, or the construction of new Jewish settlements in territories claimed by Palestinians.

Each team should prepare for the debate with a period of intensive research. They should concentrate on finding information and arguments that support their position. Teachers should structure the debate so as to give each team several chances to present arguments for their position and to respond to the arguments of their opponents.

Instruct: Objective 3

Case Study Project: A Peace Conference

- What is your research goal for the project? *(to prepare a peace conference that presents both Israeli and Arab solutions for control of Jerusalem)*
- What questions should you consider in the process? *(what are the attitudes of the different parties to a proposed solution)*
- What materials should you prepare to make the discussion as clear as possible? *(visuals, maps, charts, graphs, etc.)*

CASE STUDY

PROJECT

A Peace Conference

Primary sources A, B, C, D, and E on these two pages offer differing views about control of Jerusalem. Use these resources along with your own research to prepare a peace conference that presents both Israeli and Arab solutions for control of Jerusalem.

Suggested Steps

1. Choose one of the proposed solutions to the control of Jerusalem to investigate.
2. Use online and print resources to research the positions of Israelis, Palestinians, and Americans.
3. Create visuals—maps, charts, graphs—to make the conference discussion clearer.
4. Select two or three representatives from each group to take part in the conference. The rest of the class should act as journalists, take notes on the presentation, and be prepared to ask questions of the representatives.

Materials and Supplies

- Posterboard
- Markers
- Reference books, newspapers, and magazines
- Video monitor with VCR or DVD capability
- Computer with Internet access/printer

PRIMARY SOURCE A

United Nations Resolution *UN Resolution 181, adopted on November 29, 1947, declared that Jerusalem would become an international city with both Jewish and Muslim inhabitants.*

Part III City of Jerusalem

A. The City of Jerusalem shall be established as a *corpus separatum* [separate body] under a special international regime and shall be administered by the United Nations. The Trusteeship Council shall be designated to discharge the responsibilities of the Administering Authority on behalf of the United Nations.

* * *

C. 1(a) To protect and to preserve the unique spiritual and religious interests located in the city of the three great monotheistic faiths throughout the world, Christian, Jewish, and Moslem; to this end to ensure that order and peace, and especially religious peace, reign in Jerusalem.

(b) To foster co-operation among all the inhabitants of the city in their own interests as well as in order to encourage and support the peaceful development of the mutual relations between the two Palestinian peoples throughout the Holy Land.

PRIMARY SOURCE B

Official Statement *This statement was made December 31, 2000, by the Palestinian cabinet. It reflects opposition to President Clinton's plan for resolving the issue of "right of return" and control of the holy sites in Jerusalem.*

The Palestinian leadership confirms its commitment to the full right of refugees to return to their lands and homes in accordance with Resolution 194, the cabinet said, referring to the United Nations resolution adopted in December 1948.

Our people will never, under any circumstances, concede one inch from our Jerusalem and our Islamic and Christian holy sites.

ACTIVITY OPTION **CRITICAL THINKING**

DISTINGUISHING FACT FROM OPINION

Explaining the Skill Facts are events, dates, statistics, or statements that can be proved to be true. Opinions are the judgments, beliefs, and feelings of a writer or speaker. By identifying facts and opinions, you will be able to think critically when a person is trying to influence your own opinion.

Applying the Skill Provide students with an objective and demonstrably factual article about an important event or issue in the conflict between Israelis and Arabs over land and statehood in Southwest Asia. Also provide students with an article that is clearly biased toward one side or the other and contains misleading or false information about the same event or issue. Have students read and compare the articles and then initiate a discussion about the two perspectives. Ask students the following questions:

- What are the backgrounds and interests of the authors and publishers of the two articles? *(Answers will vary.)*
- How might the deliberate publishing of misleading information, or propaganda, give an advantage in the conflict? *(Students might say that a good propagandist can manipulate public opinion.)*

PRIMARY SOURCE C

Government Position *Abba Eban, Israeli foreign minister from 1966 to 1974, explained the significance of Israel's unification of Jerusalem in the Six-Day War in his speech for the General Assembly of the United Nations, June 19, 1967. Eban expressed his joy at the reunification of Jerusalem and the opening of access to all faiths, which had not been the case under Jordanian rule.*

Jerusalem, now united after her tragic division, is no longer an arena for gun emplacements and barbed wire. . . For 20 years there has not been free access by men of all faiths to the shrines which they hold in unique reverence. This access now exists. Israel is resolved to give effective expression, in cooperation with the world's great religions, to the immunity and sanctity of all the Holy places. . . Israel waged her defensive struggle in pursuit of two objectives—security and peace.

PRIMARY SOURCE D

Editorial Commentary *Kenneth L. Woodward, religion editor for* Newsweek *magazine, expresses an opinion about why any solution for the Jerusalem question is one that is important not just to Jews and Arabs but to millions of others.*

Thus, for billions of believers who may never see it, Jerusalem remains a city central to their sacred geography. This is why the future of the city is not just another Middle Eastern conflict between Arabs and Jews. . . . Both Israel and the Palestinians have real roots in the Holy Land, and both want to claim Jerusalem as their capital. The United Nations, supported by the Vatican, would have the city internationalized under its jurisdiction. The issue, however, is not merely one of geopolitics. There will be no enduring solution to the question of Jerusalem that does not respect the attachments to the city formed by each faith. Whoever controls Jerusalem will always be constrained by the meaning the city has acquired over three millenniums of wars, conquest and prophetic utterance.

PRIMARY SOURCE E

Political Cartoon *Mark Fiore drew this cartoon about the situation in Jerusalem. What message is the cartoonist sending about prospects for peace between Israelis and Palestinians?*

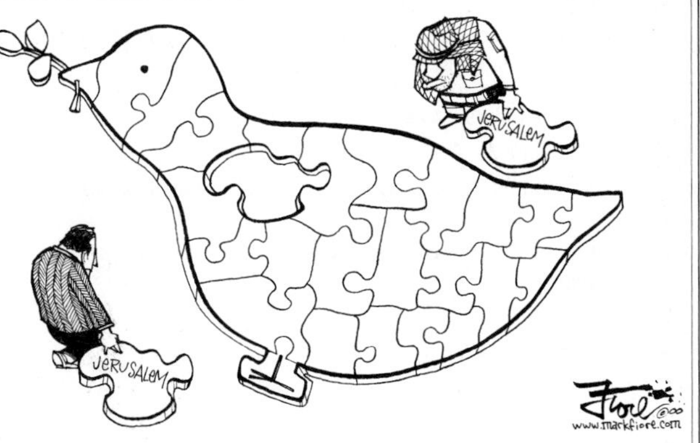

PROJECT CheckList

Have I . . .

- ✓ looked at all sides of the issue?
- ✓ identified the key players and their points of view?
- ✓ created informative visuals that make my presentation clear and interesting?
- ✓ practiced the delivery of my presentation?

Instruct: Objective  4

Using Primary Sources

- Ⓐ ***United Nations Resolution*** What does the UN resolution call for? *(establishing Jerusalem as an independent city to be administered by the UN)*
- Ⓑ ***Official Statement*** What international resolution does the Palestinian cabinet mention in support of the Palestinian "right of return"? *(UN Resolution 194)*
- Ⓒ ***Government Position*** How do you think Eban might view the current quandary over Jerusalem? Why? *(Students may say that he would be dismayed and disappointed by the lingering conflict because he had been so positive in 1967.)*
- Ⓓ ***Editorial Commentary*** What does Woodward mean by a "sacred geography"? *(Students may compare this concept to the notion of "perceptual regions," which they read about in Unit 1.)*
- Ⓔ ***Political Cartoon*** What does the dove in the cartoon represent? *(peace)*

Assess & Reteach

GeoFocus Have students complete the cause-and-effect chart they started at the beginning of the chapter.

 **Formal Assessment**
- Case Study Quiz, p. 356

Reteaching Activity
Have students review the section and discuss the pros and cons of United Nations Resolution 181.

 **In-Depth Resources: Unit 7**
- Reteaching Activity, p. 34

RUBRIC CASE STUDY PROJECT

BLOCK SCHEDULING

A PEACE CONFERENCE

For the Case Study Project, students should:

- Consider the positions of both Israelis and Palestinians toward the proposal.
- Produce visuals—such as maps, charts, and graphs—that will help clarify the arguments made on behalf of or against the proposal.
- Prepare incisive questions to ask the representatives participating in the conference.

Grading Rubric Evaluate student performance as Exceptional, Acceptable, or Poor in each of the following categories:

	Exceptional	Acceptable	Poor
Communicates ideas and positions clearly			
Fulfills assigned role			
Cooperates with other group members			
Shares responsibility for the activity			

Reviewing Places & Terms

A. **1.** guest workers, p. 525
2. stateless nation, p. 526
3. Palestinians, p. 527
4. West Bank, p. 527
5. Gaza Strip, p. 527
6. strategic commodity, p. 529
7. human resources, p. 531

B. Possible Responses
8. There are not enough native people to fill jobs in the countries.
9. West Bank and Gaza Strip
10. West Bank
11. The Kurds claim land as a homeland, but do not control it.
12. Palestinians
13. It is vital for transportation and major industries.
14. It is vital to life, and places without it are unoccupied.
15. all able bodied workers regardless of sex

Chapter 23 Assessment

VISUAL SUMMARY
TODAY'S ISSUES IN SOUTHWEST ASIA

Population

Population Relocation
- Urban areas in the region have grown significantly since the 1960s.
- Thousands of foreign workers fill jobs in the region.
- Kurds claim homelands in four countries: Turkey, Iraq, Iran, and Syria.
- Arab Palestinians claim lands in Israel.

Economics

Oil Wealth Fuels Change
- Huge oil resources shape the region's economy.
- The infrastructure needs to be updated.
- The region's economy must be diversified.
- Human resources need to be developed.

Conflict

Regional Conflict Over Land
- Jerusalem is holy to three major religions: Judaism, Christianity, and Islam.
- Israel controls Jerusalem.
- Control of holy sites in Jerusalem is one aspect of the conflict.
- Arab Palestinians claim the "right of return" to Jerusalem, after leaving it as the result of wars.

Reviewing Places & Terms

A. Briefly explain the importance of each of the following.
1. guest workers
2. stateless nation
3. Palestinians
4. West Bank
5. Gaza Strip
6. strategic commodity
7. human resources

B. Answer the questions about vocabulary in complete sentences.
8. Why is it necessary to have guest workers in Southwest Asia?
9. Which terms above refer to land areas?
10. Which of the above borders the location of Jerusalem?
11. Why might the Kurds be considered a stateless nation?
12. Which group claims the right of return to Israel?
13. Why is oil considered a strategic commodity?
14. In what way could water be considered a strategic commodity?
15. What groups make up human resources?

Main Ideas

Population Relocation (pp. 525-528)
1. What concerns have been raised about foreign workers in the region?
2. Why don't the Kurds have a homeland?
3. Which lands are claimed by Arab Palestinians?
4. Where do a large majority of Palestinians live?

Oil Wealth Fuels Change (pp. 529-531)
5. Why must nations stop depending solely on oil wealth?
6. Which areas of the region's economy need to be developed and diversified?
7. Why is providing education and technology training an important aspect of developing human resources?

Religious Conflict Over Land (pp. 532-535)
8. How did the Israelis gain control of Jerusalem?
9. What attachments do Jews, Christians, and Muslims have to Jerusalem?
10. What are some proposed solutions to the issue of control of Jerusalem?

Main Ideas

1. Concerns include too much dependence on foreign workers, fears about intolerance and violence, and a weakened national identity.
2. Lands promised to them after World War I were never given to them.
3. Israel, the West Bank, and the Gaza Strip
4. in the West Bank and the Gaza Strip
5. Prices and demand for oil change and income cannot be assured.
6. the infrastructure, additional resources especially water, and human resources
7. A successful economy depends on using the skills of the entire working population.
8. They retained part of it in the 1948 Arab-Israeli war and captured the rest in the war of 1967.
9. Major holy sites of all three religions are in Jerusalem.
10. Palestinian control of parts of East Jerusalem and Israeli annexation of Jewish neighborhoods near Jerusalem; internationalizing control of the holy sites; retaining its current status with each religious group controlling its holy sites

Critical Thinking

1. Using Your Notes

Use your completed chart to answer these questions.

	Causes	Effects
Issue 1: Population Relocation		
Issue 2: Economic Development		

a. How did the Kurds become a stateless nation?

b. What effect has an expanding economy had on population relocation in the region?

2. Geographic Themes

a. **MOVEMENT** How are rapid urbanization and guest workers related?

b. **REGION** Why is this region considered to be a strategic location?

3. Identifying Themes

Why do deserts make movement difficult? Which of the five themes applies to this situation?

4. Making Inferences

Why must some oil wealth be used to develop water resources in the region?

5. Making Decisions

Which of the proposed solutions for the control of Jerusalem do you favor and why?

For Additional Test Practice

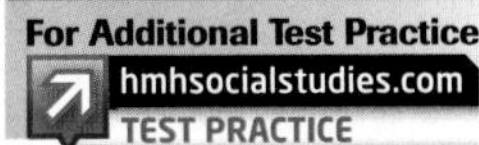

Geographic Skills: Interpreting Graphs

Availability of Water Resources*

Use the graph at the right to answer the following questions.

1. **MAKING COMPARISONS** Which country is projected to have the greatest available water supplies by 2050? Which country will have the least?
2. **MAKING INFERENCES** What are some reasons why the availability of water resources will decrease?

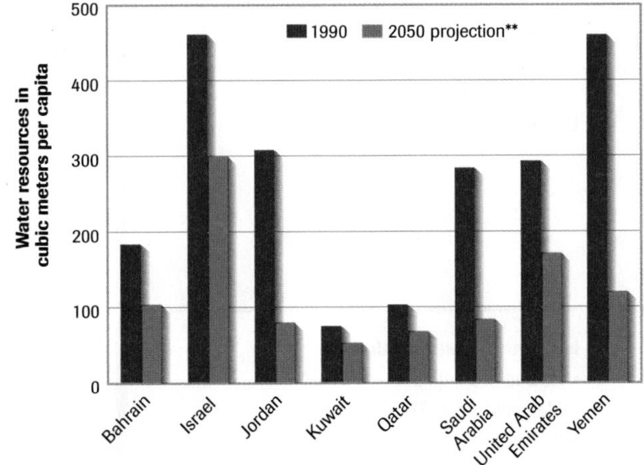

* Freshwater resources of below 1,000 cubic meters per year per capita will likely cause chronic water shortages.

**Estimates are based on a high projection of population increase.

SOURCE: Adapted from Robert Engelman and Pamela LeRoy, *Sustaining Water: An Update*, Population Action International, Washington D.C. 1995

Use the Regional Data File to create a chart showing the population of the nations listed in the Water Stress Index. Create a second bar graph showing water stress by placing the countries in order by population.

hmhsocialstudies.com

MULTIMEDIA ACTIVITY

21st CENTURY

Use the links at **hmhsocialstudies.com** to do research on water scarcity in the region and proposed solutions to the problem. Focus on finding a solution that would be environmentally friendly.

Identifying and Solving Problems Using the information you gathered, propose a solution to the need for fresh water in Southwest Asia. Support your proposal with charts or graphs illustrating both the need for water and the sources of fresh water.

CHAPTER 23 ASSESSMENT

Critical Thinking

1. a. They failed to gain a state in lands promised to the Kurds at the end of World War I.
b. It increased the demand for workers, resulting in an increase of foreign workers.

2. a. As urbanization has increased in Southwest Asia, guest workers are needed.
b. It has about two-thirds of all the oil resources in the world, making it an important region for all industrialized nations.

3. Lack of water makes travel across deserts hazardous; movement

4. If scarce water supplies are not improved, it will be difficult for the economy to expand and diversify.

5. Answers will vary but should include reasons for the decision.

GeoActivity

Integrated Assessment
- Rubric for a chart, 2.2

Formal Assessment
- Chapter Test, Forms A, B, and C, pp. 357–371

Geographic Skills

1. Israel, Kuwait

2. increased population, greater use in industry and agriculture

MULTIMEDIA ACTIVITY

For their projects addressing the need to develop regional water resources, students should:

- Provide charts and graphs illustrating the need for water.
- Identify potential sources of fresh water.
- Consider projects that will develop such resources without harming the environment.

Grading Rubric Evaluate student performance as Exceptional, Acceptable, or Poor in each of the following categories:

	Exceptional	Acceptable	Poor
Presents information clearly and accurately			
Presents information in a manner that will aid the viewer in understanding the information			
Uses bar, line, or pie graph styles			
Presents information neatly			

Physical Geography of South Asia

OVERVIEW	INSTRUCTIONAL RESOURCES	
CHAPTER 24 ESSENTIAL QUESTION How do the region's mountains and rivers affect life in South Asia? **Focus on the Essential Question Podcast**	**In-Depth Resources: Unit 8** • Unit Atlas Activities, p. 1 • Building Vocabulary, p. 9 • Exploring Today's Issues, pp. 30–33 **Outline Maps with Activities** • South Asia: Physical, pp. 75–76 • South Asia: Political, pp. 77–78 **Block Schedule Strategies** **Chapter Summaries** (English/Spanish)	**Interactive Online Edition** TOS **ExamView® Assessment Suite** (English/Spanish) TOS **CalendarPlanner** **Power Presentations with Media Gallery** **Critical Thinking Transparencies** • CT24 hmhsocialstudies.com INTERACTIVE
SECTION 1 **LANDFORMS AND RESOURCES** **MAIN IDEAS** • South Asia is a subcontinent defined by high mountains and extensive coasts. • Great river systems flow through much of South Asia. • The Maldives and Sri Lanka are island countries that belong to South Asia.	**In-Depth Resources: Unit 8** • Guided Reading, p. 3 • Building Vocabulary, p. 9 • Reteaching Activity, p. 10 **Guided Reading Workbook,** Section 1	**Map Transparencies** • MT43 South Asia: Natural Resources **Critical Thinking Transparencies** • CT56 Major Rivers of South Asia
SECTION 2 **CLIMATE AND VEGETATION** **MAIN IDEAS** • South Asia has half of the world's twelve climate zones. • Monsoons and cyclones are common types of extreme weather. • Vegetation reflects the various climate zones and ranges from desert shrub to the lush greenery of the rain forests.	**In-Depth Resources: Unit 8** • Guided Reading, p. 4 • Map and Graph Skills, pp. 6–7 • Building Vocabulary, p. 9 • Reteaching Activity, p. 11 **Guided Reading Workbook,** Section 2	
SECTION 3 **HUMAN–ENVIRONMENT INTERACTION** **MAIN IDEAS** • Hindus believe that the Ganges River is sacred. • Pollution in the Ganges poses an extreme health hazard. • Bangladesh depended on manual labor to dam the Feni River as a means of flood control.	**In-Depth Resources: Unit 8** • Guided Reading, p. 5 • Skillbuilder Practice, p. 8 • Building Vocabulary, p. 9 • Reteaching Activity, p. 12 **Guided Reading Workbook,** Section 3	

ASSESSMENT

SE **Chapter Assessment,** pp. 564–565

Formal Assessment
- Chapter Tests, Forms A, B, and C, pp. 375–386

TOS **ExamView® Assessment Suite**

Strategies for Test Preparation

hmhsocialstudies.com TEST PRACTICE

SE **Section Assessment,** p. 555

Formal Assessment
- Section Quiz, p. 372

Integrated Assessment
- Rubric for a news article, 4.5

Test Practice Transparencies TT77

SE **Section Assessment,** p. 558

Formal Assessment
- Section Quiz, p. 373

Integrated Assessment
- Rubric for a sketch map, 2.1

Test Practice Transparencies TT78

SE **Section Assessment,** p. 563

Formal Assessment
- Section Quiz, p. 374

Integrated Assessment
- Rubric for a written report, 2.5

Test Practice Transparencies TT79

CHART KEY:

SE Student Edition	Block Scheduling	DVD/CD-ROM
TE Teacher's Edition	TOS Teacher One Stop	MP3 Audio
Printable Resource	Presentation Resource	HISTORY™

Program Resources available on TOS and @ 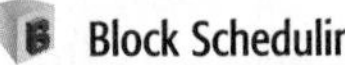

SUPPORTING RESOURCES

- Multimedia Classroom Global History Series
- Global History Teacher's Guide

Social Studies Trade Library Collection

- World Regions Trade Collection

For more information or to purchase these resources, go to 

DIFFERENTIATED INSTRUCTION

English Learners	Struggling Readers	Gifted and Talented Students
Spanish/English Guided Reading Workbook **Access for Students Acquiring English/ESL** Spanish Translations, pp. 127–132  **Chapter Summaries** (English/Spanish) TE **TE Activity** Expanding Vocabulary, p. 553	 **Chapter Summaries** (English/Spanish) TE **TE Activity** Identifying Proper Nouns, p. 561	TE **TE Activity** Writing a Report about Mineral Resources, p. 554

ENRICHMENT ACTIVITIES

The following activities are especially suitable for classes following block schedules.

SE **Student Edition,** pp. 550–563
- Reading a Weather Map, p. 559

 hmhsocialstudies.com INTERACTIVE
- Formation of the Himalayas, p. 551
- Natural Resources of South Asia, p. 554

BLOCK SCHEDULE LESSON PLAN OPTIONS: 90-MINUTE PERIOD

DAY 1

UNIT PREVIEW, pp. 538–541
Class Time 20 minutes

- **Discussion** Use the discussion prompts on TE pages 538–539 to discuss the Unit Introduction.
  Class Time 10 minutes
- **Doday's Issues** Introduce Today's Issues in South Asia, using Exploring the Issues questions on PE page 540.
  Class Time 10 minutes

UNIT ATLAS, pp. 542–549
Class Time 30 minutes

- **Working in Pairs** Have students work in pairs to answer the Making Comparisons questions for one section of the Unit Atlas: Physical Geography, Human Geography, Regional Patterns, and Regional Data File.

SECTION 1, pp.551–555
Class Time 40 minutes

- **Outline Maps** Make two transparencies—one showing the outline of South Asia and the other showing the outline of the United States. Have students identify and compare the natural boundaries of each. Discuss the impact of natural boundaries on a region's history and development.

DAY 2

SECTION 1, pp. 551–555
Class Time 45 minutes

- **Places & Terms** Have students define each place and term listed on page 551 and determine which countries each applies to, using the map on page 543. Tell them to fill in the first two sections of the chapter's GeoFocus chart in their notebooks, using the places and terms where appropriate.

SECTION 2, pp. 556–559
Class Time 45 minutes

- **Annotated Maps.** This activity expands on the Skillbuilder Maps that appear on PE page 557. Organize the class into small groups and assign a country to each. Have them prepare an outline map of their country on which they indicate applicable climate zones. Tell them to list the major characteristics of each type of climate and the type of vegetation associated with each. Display the maps in the classroom and have the class compare them.

DAY 3

SECTION 3, pp. 560–563
Class Time 40 minutes

- **Class Discussion**
  Lead a class discussion on human interaction with rivers in South Asia, focusing on the Ganges in India and the Feni in Bangladesh. Ask questions such as:
- How do Hindus in India regard the Ganges?
- How do they interact with the river?
- What problems are created as a result?
- What are possible solutions?
  Then have students define the problem posed by the Feni and explain how the people of Bangladesh interacted to solve it. Discuss the difference in cultural attitudes suggested by the two situations.

CHAPTER 24 REVIEW AND ASSESSMENT, pp. 564–565
Class Time 50 minutes

- **Review** Have students prepare a summary of the chapter by outlining the main ideas in each section.
  Class Time 25 minutes
- **Assessment** Have students complete the Chapter 24 Assessment.
  Class Time 35 minutes

TEACHER-TESTED ACTIVITY *Managing Inadequate Resources*

Class Time One class period

Task Experience the inequity of resources worldwide as compared to population.

Supplies
- Different objects to represent various resources such as candy, tacks, or paper clips.
- Current resource information for China, India, the United States, France, and Uganda.

Purpose Many students do not grasp the crippling effect the lack of resources can have on a country. This activity will provide a hands-on look at these effects. The activity provides a basis for discussions about how populations may affect countries and/or regions.

Activity Divide class into groups according to the population of countries in the region. (For example, China and India would have the most students.) Assign different objects to represent health care, clean water, life expectancy, infant mortality rate, agricultural production and literacy rates. According to current information, groups should receive an appropriate number of items representing each resource. Students should discuss how the resources available in their country might affect individuals: socially, politically, and economically.

For an even more effective approach, students should divide their resources among group members. They may do this evenly or one person may receive a disproportionate amount of food, health care or clean water. Once the resources have been divided, have the students write about what life would be like for them if they lived in this country.

Jerome Love
Geography Teacher, Beaumont High School, St. Louis, MO

TECHNOLOGY IN THE CLASSROOM

Spreadsheet programs can be invaluable in analyzing and comparing data. Most spreadsheet programs allow the user to input numbers into rows and columns and to then create charts and graphs based on those numbers. These charts and graphs present the data in a visual manner, and make it much easier to compare the numbers.

Objective Students will use a spreadsheet program to graph precipitation statistics for several South Asian cities. They will analyze the data to make predictions and inferences about monsoon-related rainfall.

Task Have students input precipitation data for seven South Asian countries into a spreadsheet. Then have them create column, bar, or line graphs to show the average precipitation throughout the year for each city, and ask them to compare the cities to see how each is affected by the monsoons.

Class Time Two class periods (may be one period if students do the activity in groups)

1. Discuss the causes and effects of the monsoons, as described on pages 556-558.
2. Ask students to look at one of the maps of South Asia in the chapter and predict which of these cities–Islamabad, Colombo, Chittagong, Thimphu, Kathmandu, New Delhi, or Gan (Maldives)–will be the hardest-hit by the monsoons. They should base their predictions on what they've read in the chapter and discussed as a class.
3. Ask students to create a spreadsheet with the left column listing the months of the year and the top row listing the above South Asian cities.
4. Have students go to the Web site at **hmhsocialstudies.com** and look up each of the cities on their list. For each one, they should record the average precipitation for each month in the appropriate cells of the spreadsheet.
5. Have students use the spreadsheet program's charting or graphing feature to create column, bar, or line graphs of each city's average precipitation. The charts should show the months along the horizontal line (x-axis) and the amount of precipitation up the vertical line (y-axis).
6. If you're short on time or computers, or to simplify the activity, have students create their spreadsheets in groups. Ask each group to create only one chart. Then have them print out the charts and display them so that everyone can compare the figures.
7. Ask students to compare the charts and to answer these questions based on what they've graphed: Which cities are most affected by the monsoons? Which cities seem to be affected by precipitation patterns other than the monsoons? In or near which cities would you expect to have the most frequent flooding? When do you think that flooding would occur?
8. Discuss students' answers as a class. Then discuss the ways that the spreadsheet and graph helped them analyze the data. Would this assignment have been easier or more difficult if they'd just done it "by hand?"

Previewing the Unit

The first pages of this unit provide an overview of South Asia. The region comprises three of the world's most populous countries, as well as some of the smallest and most remote. Religion has played an important role in shaping the region's cultures and continues to have a strong impact.

Discussion Prompts

Exploring Prior Knowledge Ask students the following questions about South Asia to determine their prior knowledge of the region:

- What is the largest country in South Asia? *(India)*
- What famous mountain range is located in the northern part of South Asia? *(the Himalayas)*

Interpreting Maps Have students look at the satellite image of South Asia to answer the following questions:

- What landforms do you recognize? *(mountains, islands, rivers)*
- What island country do you recognize? *(Sri Lanka)*
- What other countries do you recognize? *(Answers will vary but will probably include India.)*

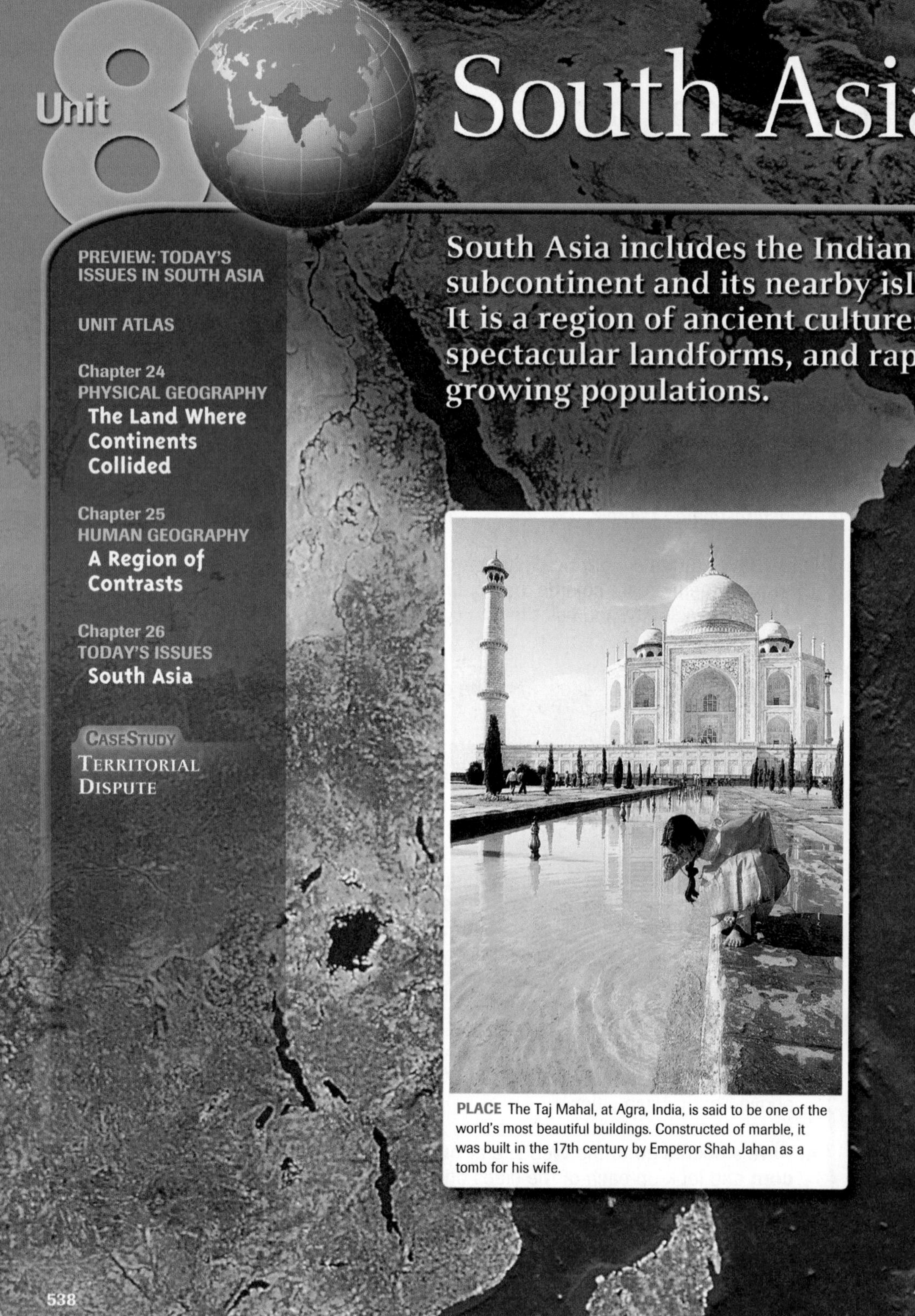

Unit 8
South Asia
South Asia includes the Indian subcontinent and its nearby isla
It is a region of ancient cultures, spectacular landforms, and rapid growing populations.
PREVIEW: TODAY'S ISSUES IN SOUTH ASIA
UNIT ATLAS
Chapter 24
PHYSICAL GEOGRAPHY
The Land Where Continents Collided
Chapter 25
HUMAN GEOGRAPHY
A Region of Contrasts
Chapter 26
TODAY'S ISSUES
South Asia
CASESTUDY
TERRITORIAL DISPUTE
538

PLACE The Taj Mahal, at Agra, India, is said to be one of the world's most beautiful buildings. Constructed of marble, it was built in the 17th century by Emperor Shah Jahan as a tomb for his wife.

UNIT 8 ADDITIONAL RESOURCES

BOOKS FOR THE TEACHER

Coll, Steve. ***On the Grand Trunk Road: A Journey into South Asia.*** Penguin, 2009. Observations by the South Asia bureau chief for *The Washington Post.*

Ludden, David. ***India and South Asia: A Short History.*** Oneworld Publications, 2002. Includes histories of all the region's countries.

BOOKS FOR THE STUDENT

Dehejia, Vidya, ed. ***India Through the Lens: Photography 1840-1911.*** NY: Prestel, 2001. Beautiful photographs of the people and landscapes of colonial India.

SOFTWARE

Microsoft Encarta World Atlas 2000. Enables user to isolate states, countries, and regions. Features multimedia treatment of faraway places.

INTERNET

For more information about South Asia, visit . . .

hmhsocialstudies.com

GeoData

LOCATION South Asia is mainly a triangular peninsula that juts out from the Asian mainland into the Indian Ocean.

REGION The seven countries of South Asia have great cultural and religious diversity.

HUMAN-ENVIRONMENT INTERACTION Life in South Asia is greatly influenced by its varied landforms and its extreme weather, especially the seasonal monsoons.

For more information on South Asia . . .

hmhsocialstudies.com RESEARCH WEB LINKS

REGION The world's highest mountains, the majestic snow-capped Himalayas, form the northern border of the Indian subcontinent. Mt. Everest, to the right, is the world's tallest peak at 29,035 feet.

LOCATION Elephants wearing richly decorated cloth coverings are central figures in the 14-night Esala Perahera festival in Kandy, Sri Lanka. It is one of many religious festivals held in South Asia.

Interpreting Photographs

The Taj Mahal

Covered in carved white marble, the ornamentation of the Taj Mahal includes verses from the Qur'an, the sacred text of Islam.

Ask students what this might suggest about the connection between religion and culture in South Asia. *(Religon has influenced culture.)*

The Himalayas

Nepal and Bhutan are both located in the Himalayas.

Ask students how they think the mountains might affect life in these countries. *(possible answers: people are isolated; limited land for farming; cold climate)*

Sri Lankan Religious Festival

Perahera is a Buddhist festival.

Ask students what elements in the photograph are probably traditional? *(the elephant and its richly ornamented covering; the shelter over the animal)*

ACTIVITY OPTION COOPERATIVE LEARNING

CREATING A TRAVEL BROCHURE

Objective To allow students to explore aspects of South Asia

Class Time 30 minutes

Task Create a travel brochure of South Asia

Supplies Needed

- Sheets of 11-by-17-inch paper
- Old magazines and newspapers
- Glue or paste
- Markers

Directions Organize students into small groups and have them look for photographs of South Asia on the Internet or in magazines. The photographs should fall into the categories of place, region, or location. Tell students to try and present the region as a whole, rather than one or two areas or countries. Tell them to write captions indicating location and why what is shown would be of interest to a visitor from another country.

Assign the following roles to one or more students in each group:

- text researcher and writer
- photo researcher
- designer

Previewing Today's Issues

These pages provide a preview of issues faced by the nations of South Asia. The issues will be fully explored in Chapter 26 (pages 600–603). Use the discussion prompts that follow to determine students' prior knowledge and allow them to make comparisons to local events.

 **In-Depth Resources: Unit 8**
- Exploring Today's Issues, pp. 30–33

POPULATION
India's population of more than a billion people continues to grow rapidly. Indian officials are seeking ways to stem the rate of growth in order to provide their people with a decent standard of living.

Discussion Prompts

- What areas of the United States have experienced rapid population growth? *(Students may name the Sun Belt, California, or cities such as Seattle and Las Vegas.)*
- Can you give an example of how population growth has affected an area of the United States? *(Answers may vary but might include lack of sufficient water and electricity in California.)*

Today's Issues in South Asia

Today, South Asia faces the issues previewed here. As you read Chapters 24 and 25, you will learn helpful background information. You will study the issues themselves in Chapter 26.

In a small group, answer the questions below. Then have a class discussion of your answers.

Exploring the Issues

1. POPULATION What might be some of the effects of rapid population growth on both humans and the environment?
2. EXTREME WEATHER Consider news stories that you have heard or read about that refer to extreme weather in various parts of South Asia. Make a list of the types of extreme weather that affect South Asians.
3. TERRITORIAL DISPUTE Search the Internet for the latest information about the dispute over Kashmir. What position does each side hold?

For more on these issues in South Asia . . .

POPULATION EXPLOSION

How can South Asia's population growth be managed?
Many problems come with rapid population growth, including crowded cities. Kolkata, pictured here, had a population of more than 4 million in the 1990s, and a population density of more than 61,900 persons per square mile.

EXPLORING THE ISSUES ANSWERS

1. POPULATION Students may mention poverty, lack of adequate living space, shortage of food and water, increased traffic and pollution.
2. EXTREME WEATHER Students may list monsoons, cyclones, and flooding.
3. TERRITORIAL DISPUTES Students may mention anti-India militant attacks and demonstrations that took place in 2008. In 2009, the U.S. State Department announced that the United States would not appoint an envoy to mediate the conflict. Pakistan and India continue to disagree on the topic of Kashmir.

EXTREME WEATHER

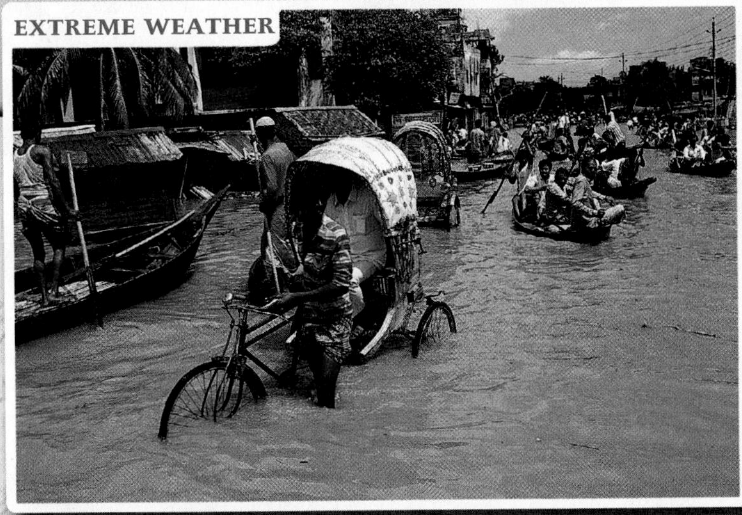

How do people cope with extreme weather?

People find a way to continue with their lives despite the severe flooding that plagues South Asia during the summer monsoons. Residents of Dhaka, Bangladesh, shown here, navigate flooded streets as best they can.

CASESTUDY

How can India and Pakistan resolve their dispute over Kashmir?

India and Pakistan have spent millions of dollars to develop nuclear weapons in their continuing dispute over Kashmir. This has left less money to spend on improving the lives of their citizens.

TERRITORIAL DISPUTE

EXTREME WEATHER

South Asia's weather includes seasonal monsoons and devasting cyclones, or hurricanes. Bangladesh's low elevation makes it particularly vulnerable to flooding.

Discussion Prompts

- Have you ever experienced extreme weather? *(Answers may vary, but may include floods, hurricanes, tornadoes, drought, and heavy snowfalls.)*
- How does extreme weather affect areas of the United States? *(Answers may include flooding in the Midwest that damages homes and businesses; hurricanes on the eastern and Gulf coasts that destroy property and even lives.)*

CASESTUDY

TERRITORIAL DISPUTE

To help students gain a deeper understanding of the issues involved in the Kashmir conflict, direct them to the Case Study, which begins on page 600 and which concludes with a Case Study Project on page 602.

Discussion Prompts

- What are some reasons for territorial disputes? *(Possible answers: Ethnic groups claim the same land; rich natural resources; strategic location.)*
- Why might the United States be concerned over India and Pakistan's dispute over Kashmir? *(It could lead to nuclear war.)*

ACTIVITY OPTION **INTERNET RESEARCH**

COMPILING NEWS SOURCES

Objective To identify relevant sources of information

Class Time 20 minutes

Task Search the Internet for two sites of information for each of the three issues introduced about South Asia. Have students begin an electronic or a hard-copy file of possible sources for further research.

Directions Direct students to the Web site for *World Geography* at **hmhsocialstudies.com.** Click on the Current Events button and follow to sources of information on these issues.

OPTIONAL ACTIVITY If Internet access is limited, have the students use the library. Tell students to use the *Readers' Guide to Periodical Literature* and other indexes to find and list sources of information on the three issues in South Asia.

ATLAS OBJECTIVES

1. Compare data on the physical geography of South Asia.
2. Examine key physical features of South Asia.
3. Identify features of South Asia's first great civilization.
4. Identify political features of South Asia.
5. Examine geographical distribution of religions practiced in South Asia.
6. Analyze population density and economic activity in South Asia.

Focus & Motivate

Ask students to name some countries in South Asia. Ask what else they know about the region's physical geography. Ask what other kinds of information they might expect to find on maps and charts of South Asia. *(Answers will vary but may include information relevant to religion, language, and ethnicity.)*

Instruct: Objective 

Comparing Data

- ***Landmass*** How does the size of South Asia compare to that of the United States? *(roughly half the size)*
- ***Population*** Is the population of South Asia greater or less than that of the United States? By approximately how much? *(greater by more than five times as much)*
- ***Rivers*** Which rivers in South Asia are the longest? *(Indus and Brahmaputra)*
- ***Mountains*** Which of the world's mountains is the tallest? *(Mount Everest)*

Unit ATLAS

Patterns of Physical Geography

Use the Unit Atlas to add to your knowledge of South Asia. As you look at the maps and charts, notice geographic patterns and specific details about the region. For example, the chart to the right gives details about the rivers and mountains of South Asia.

After studying the illustrations, graphs, and physical map on these two pages, jot down in your notebook the answers to the following questions.

Making Comparisons

1. How much longer is the Nile than each of the three major rivers of South Asia?
2. Compare the size and population of South Asia to that of the United States. Which is larger in terms of size? Which is larger in terms of population?
3. How do the tallest mountains of South Asia compare to the tallest U.S. mountain?

Comparing Data

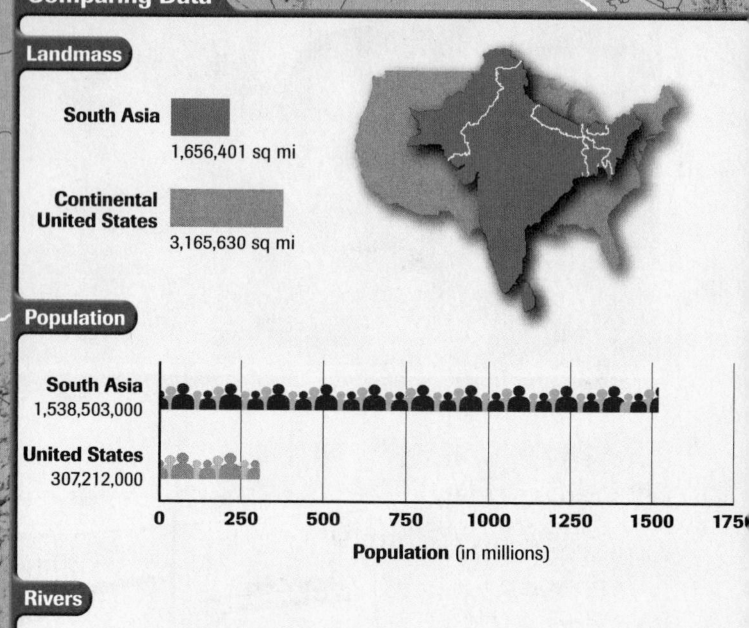

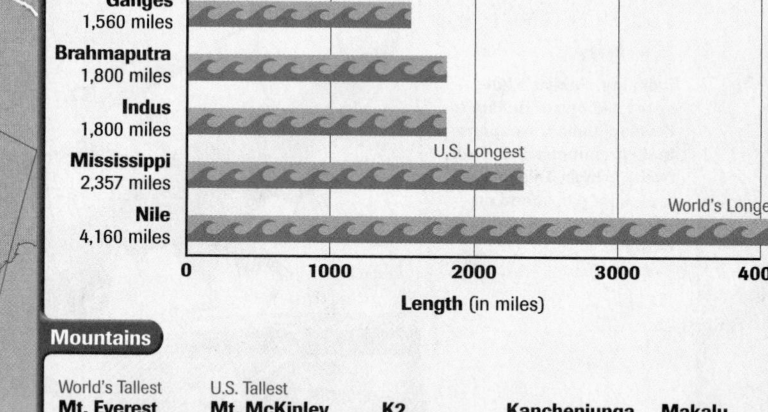

Mountains

World's Tallest **Mt. Everest** Nepal-China 29,035 feet	U.S. Tallest **Mt. McKinley** United States 20,320 feet	**K2** Pakistan 28,250 feet	**Kanchenjunga** India-Nepal 28,208 feet	**Makalu** Nepal-China 27, 824 feet

542 UNIT 8

MAKING COMPARISONS ANSWERS

1. The Nile is about 2,600 miles longer than the Ganges and about 2,300 miles longer than the Brahmaputra and the Indus.
2. The continental United States is about twice as large as South Asia, but has only about one-fifth of the population.
3. The tallest mountains of South Asia are about 7,500 to 8,700 feet taller than Mt. McKinley.

South Asia: Physical

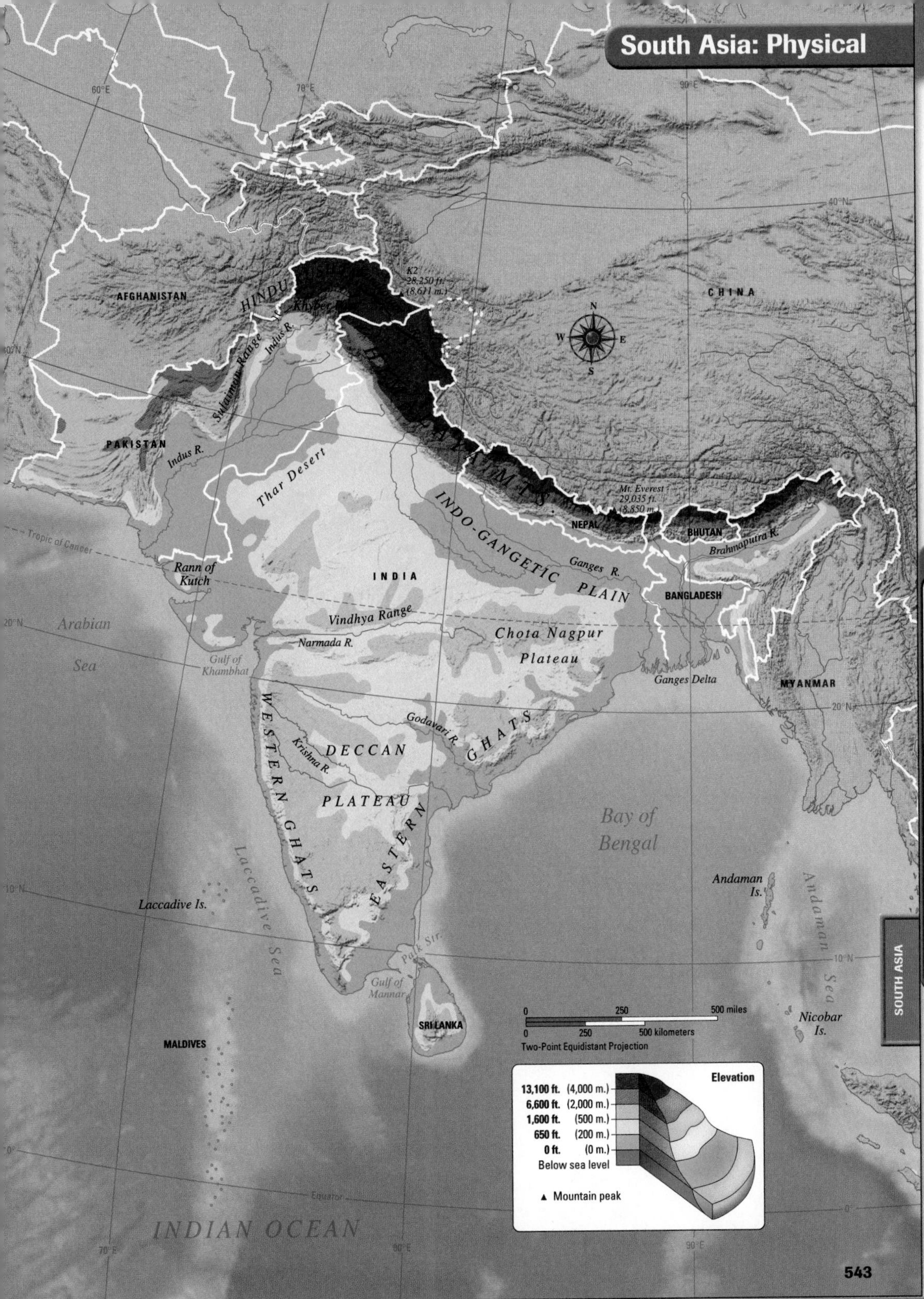

AFGHANISTAN
HINDU KUSH
K2 28,250 ft. (8,611 m.)
Khyber Pass
Indus R.
Sulaiman Range
HIMALAYA MTS.
CHINA
PAKISTAN
Indus R.
Thar Desert
INDO-GANGETIC PLAIN
Mt. Everest 29,035 ft. (8,850 m.)
NEPAL
BHUTAN
Brahmaputra R.
Ganges R.
Tropic of Cancer
Rann of Kutch
INDIA
BANGLADESH
Arabian Sea
Vindhya Range
Narmada R.
Chota Nagpur Plateau
Gulf of Khambhat
Ganges Delta
MYANMAR
WESTERN GHATS
Godavari R.
EASTERN GHATS
DECCAN PLATEAU
Krishna R.
Bay of Bengal
Laccadive Sea
Andaman Is.
Andaman Sea
Laccadive Is.
Palk Str.
Gulf of Mannar
SRI LANKA
Nicobar Is.
MALDIVES
0 250 500 miles
0 250 500 kilometers
Two-Point Equidistant Projection

Elevation
13,100 ft. (4,000 m.)
6,600 ft. (2,000 m.)
1,600 ft. (500 m.)
650 ft. (200 m.)
0 ft. (0 m.)
Below sea level
▲ Mountain peak

INDIAN OCEAN
Equator

543

SOUTH ASIA

UNIT 8 ATLAS

Instruct: Objective 2

South Asia: Physical

- What are South Asia's highest mountains? *(Himalaya Mountains)*
- What large island lies off the coast of India? *(Sri Lanka)*
- Which two major rivers empty into the Ganges Delta? *(Ganges, Brahmaputra)*

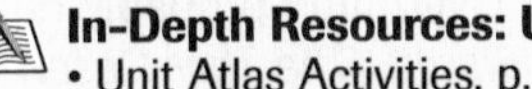

In-Depth Resources: Unit 8
- Unit Atlas Activities, p. 1

Outline Maps with Activities
- South Asia: Physical, pp. 75–76

Map Transparencies MT41
- South Asia: Physical

More About

The Vindhya Range

The tectonic collision that created the Himalayas also pushed up the mountain ranges of Central India. A Hindu myth explains why the Vindhya Range is so much lower than the Himalayas. According to this story, gods living in the Himalayas were upset because Vindhya was so tall that he blocked the sun. To remedy the situation, they sent a wise man to Vindhya. When Vindhya bowed low to his visitor out of respect, the sage ordered him to stay that way until he returned—which he never did.

ACTIVITY OPTION | CRITICAL THINKING

SEEING PATTERNS

Explaining the Skill Identifying patterns may be of use in understanding the nature of a subject. For example, observing brown bats over a period of time may lead us to note the following patterns in their behavior: they come out at night, eat insects, and fly. These patterns add to our knowledge of the animal.

Applying the Skill Tell students that observing patterns of elevation will add to their understanding of South Asia's overall topography. Have students look at the physical map on page 543. Then ask the following questions.

- What is the general pattern of elevation from south to north? *(There is a gradual increase from the lowest elevation at the southern tip to the Himalayas—India's highest elevation—in the north.)*
- What is the general pattern from east to west and from west to east? *(Elevation is lowest at the two coasts and gradually increases as one proceeds inland.)*
- How does the elevation pattern of Sri Lanka compare with that of continental South Asia? *(It is very similar, except that the island has no high mountains.)*

Instruct: Objective 3

Indus Valley Civilization

- What appear to be the natural boundaries of the Indus Valley civilization? *(mountain ranges; desert; Arabian Sea to the south)*
- To what physical feature does the civilization appear to conform? *(the Indus River)*
- Why did the civilization probably not expand eastward? *(The Thar Desert would have been inhospitable.)*

More About

Indus Valley Civilization

The ancient Indus Valley civilization comprised at least 70 population sites, spread out over 500,000 square miles. The economy was based on crops and livestock, with cotton forming the basis of a textile industry. Archaeological excavations have revealed sculptures of stone, cast-bronze, and terra-cotta that show a high degree of artistry. The reason for the civilization's decline remains unknown.

Unit ATLAS

Patterns of Human Geography

The first great civilization of South Asia developed along the banks of the Indus River more than 4,000 years ago. Study the historical map of the Indus Valley civilization and the political map of South Asia on these two pages. In your notebook, jot down the answers to these questions.

Making Comparisons

1. In which countries of modern South Asia was the Indus Valley civilization located? Which of these countries is the larger country?
2. What might have been some of the reasons for a civilization developing at that location?
3. What modern city or cities are closest to the locations of ancient Mohenjo-Daro, Harappa, Kalibangan, and Lothal? (In some cases, more than one city will be an acceptable answer.)

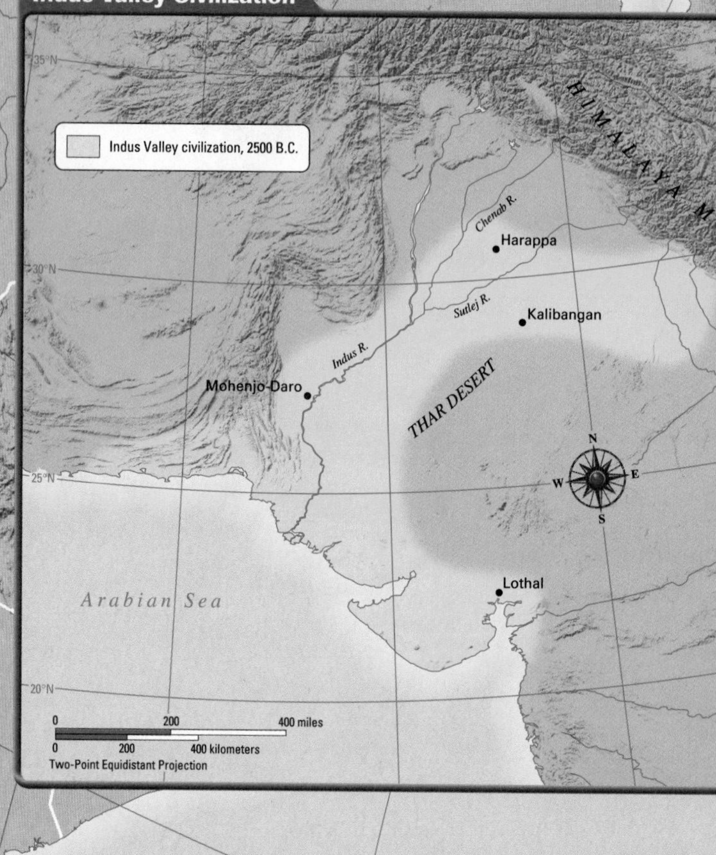

MAKING COMPARISONS ANSWERS

1. Pakistan and India; India is larger.
2. Most early civilizations, including that of the Indus Valley, developed near rivers because they provided water, fertile soil, and a means of transportation.
3. Mohenjo-Daro–Hyderabad; Harappa–Lahore and Faisalabad; Kalibangan–Jaipur, Delhi, and New Delhi; Lothal–Ahmadabad and Surat

South Asia: Political

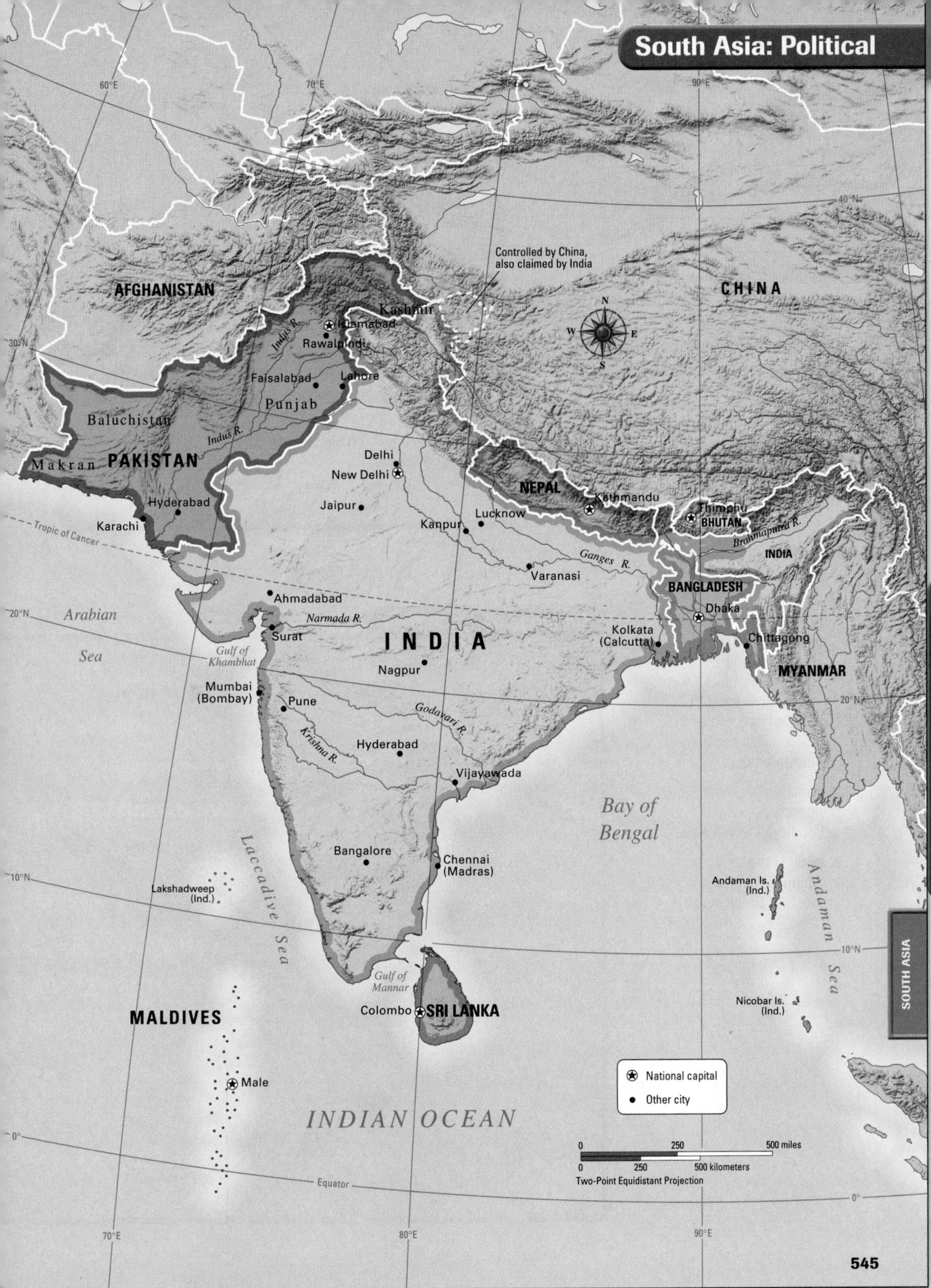

AFGHANISTAN
PAKISTAN
INDIA
CHINA
NEPAL
BHUTAN
BANGLADESH
MYANMAR
SRI LANKA
MALDIVES
Controlled by China, also claimed by India
Kashmir
Islamabad
Rawalpindi
Faisalabad
Lahore
Punjab
Baluchistan
Makran
Indus R.
Hyderabad
Karachi
Delhi
New Delhi
Jaipur
Lucknow
Kanpur
Kathmandu
Thimphu
Brahmaputra R.
Ganges R.
Varanasi
Dhaka
Chittagong
Kolkata (Calcutta)
Ahmadabad
Narmada R.
Surat
Gulf of Khambhat
Nagpur
Mumbai (Bombay)
Pune
Godavari R.
Krishna R.
Hyderabad
Vijayawada
Bangalore
Chennai (Madras)
Lakshadweep (Ind.)
Colombo
Gulf of Mannar
Male
Andaman Is. (Ind.)
Nicobar Is. (Ind.)
Arabian Sea
Laccadive Sea
Bay of Bengal
Andaman Sea
INDIAN OCEAN
Tropic of Cancer
Equator
National capital
Other city
0 250 500 miles
0 250 500 kilometers
Two-Point Equidistant Projection

UNIT 8 ATLAS

Instruct: Objective 

South Asia: Political

- Which country physically dominates South Asia *(India)*
- Which countries do not have a common border with India? *(Maldives and Sri Lanka)*
- Which countries bordering India are likely to be remote? Explain. *(Nepal and Bhutan because they are so mountainous; possibly Maldives and Sri Lanka because they are islands.)*

 **Outline Maps with Activities**
- South Asia: Political, pp. 77–78

 **Map Transparencies MT42**
- South Asia: Political

More About

Bhutan: The Forbidden Kingdom

Until the last half of the twentieth century, Bhutan was a feudal kingdom forbidden to outsiders. This policy of isolationism was reinforced by its relative inaccessibility, for its borders are alternately composed of jungle or mountains. Until 1963, Western visitors to Bhutan numbered fewer than a hundred.

ACTIVITY OPTION | LINK TO HISTORY

CREATING A TIME LINE

Objective To provide historical information about the names of the countries listed

Class Time 20 minutes

Task Create a time line

Directions Have students work in small groups. Tell them to look in books or on the Internet to find out the following information about Pakistan, Bangladesh, and Sri Lanka: **1.** When during the last hundred years did each country adopt its current name? **2.** What was the old name? **3.** What does the new name mean? Tell students to make a timeline showing the dates and brief explanations for the changes. Students might use a different color for each country.

(In 1947, Britain granted India independence. Then India was divided into the two countries of India and Pakistan. Pakistan was made up of two different areas separated by over 1,000 miles called East Pakistan and West Pakistan. The name Pakistan means "land of the pure." Bangladesh was East Pakistan from 1947 to 1971. It gained independence in 1971 and took the name of Bangladesh, which means "Bengal nation." Sri Lanka was formerly known as Ceylon. Ceylon became independent in 1948. In 1972, the country changed its name to Sri Lanka, which means "resplendent land.")

Instruct: Objective 5

South Asia: Religions by Country

- In which country does the population practice only one religion? *(Maldives)* What is the religion? *(Islam)*
- In which country are the most religions practiced? *(India)*
- Which religion is practiced by the majority of the population in the most countries? *(Islam)*

Instruct: Objective 5

Religions of South Asia

- In which country are minority religions the most scattered? *(India)*
- Do borders in South Asia tend to indicate a difference in religion? *(sometimes but not always)*
- What might the "traditional" category of religion stand for? *(Students may say that traditional religions are tied to a country's ancient beliefs, myths, and folklore.)*

Unit ATLAS

Regional Patterns

These two pages contain a graph and three thematic maps. The graph shows the religions of South Asia. The maps show other important information about religion, population density, and economics. Study these two pages and then jot down in your notebook the answers to the questions below.

Making Comparisons

1. What percentage of the population of Sri Lanka is Hindu, and where are most of the Hindus located? Why might Hindus have settled in Sri Lanka rather than in other areas?
2. Which is the most densely populated country of South Asia?
3. What is the main economic activity in much of South Asia?

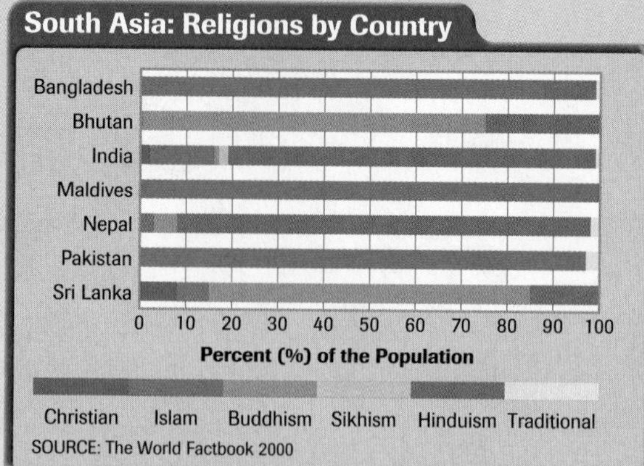

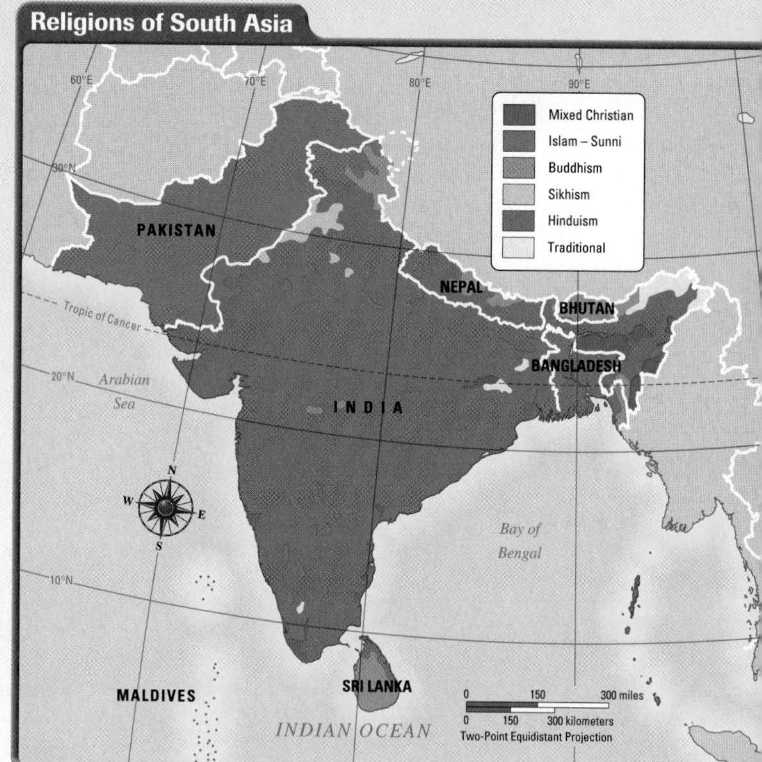

MAKING COMPARISONS ANSWERS

1. about 15 percent; along the northern and eastern coasts; these coastal areas are easily accessible to India, from where the Hindus came
2. Bangladesh
3. farming

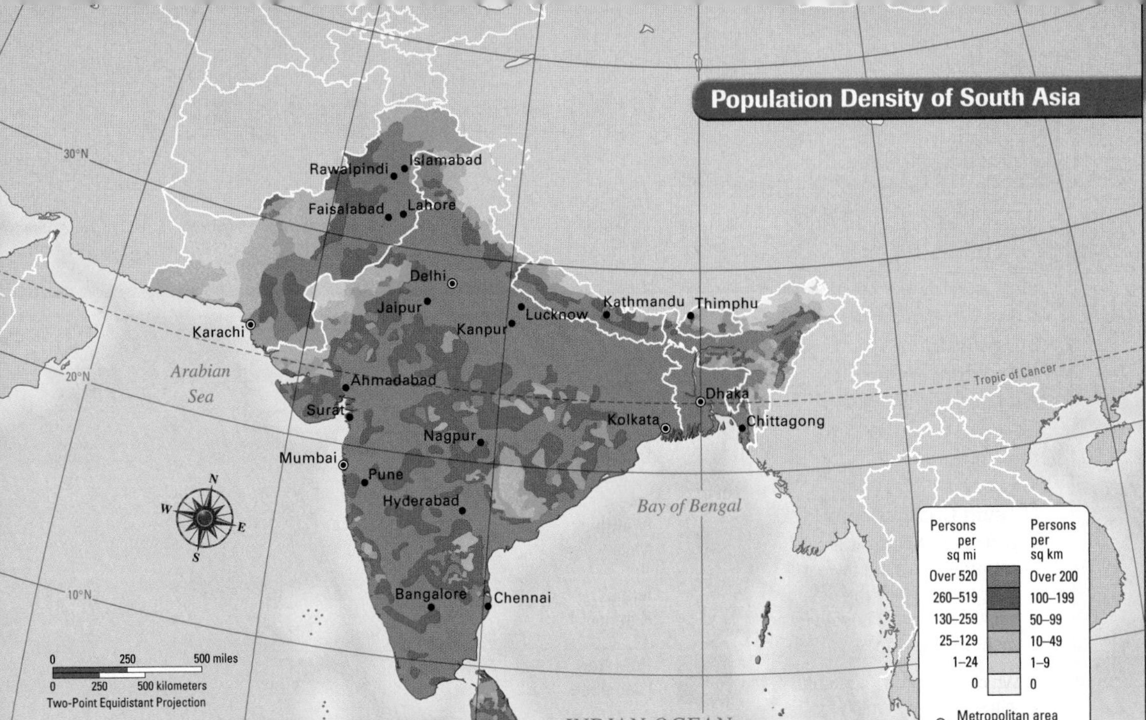

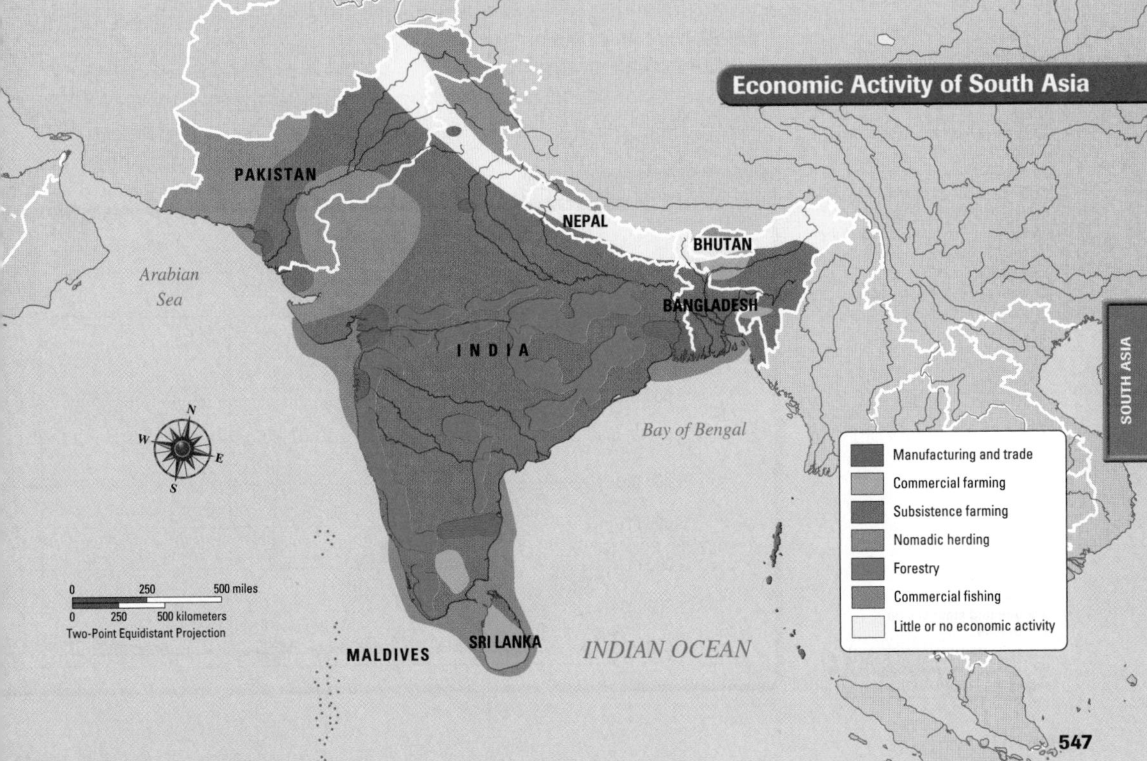

Instruct: Objective 6

Population Density of South Asia

- Which five South Asian cities have the largest populations? *(Dhaka, Delhi, Karachi, Kolkata, and Mumbai)*
- Of the most densely populated areas in South Asia, which is the largest? *(the eastern half of northern India and Bangladesh)* Why might this be so? *(Major river systems are located there.)*

Instruct: Objective 6

Economic Activity of South Asia

- Which areas have the least amount of economic activity? *(Nepal and Bhutan)*
- Ask students to give examples of how location and economic activities are related in South Asia. *(Answers may include fishing off the coasts of India, Pakistan, and Bangladesh; commercial farming where the river systems provide water; manufacturing on the coasts, where materials may be imported and exported easily.)*
- What is the relationship between the high density urban areas of India and manufacturing? *(Manufacturing attracts workers; industry is likely to locate in high density areas where there are plenty of potential workers.)*

ACTIVITY OPTION | EXPLORING LOCAL GEOGRAPHY

REGIONAL ECONOMIC ACTIVITY

Objective To gather and present regional economic data

Class Time 30 minutes

Task Creating a map of regional economic activity

Supplies Needed

- Oversized sheet of paper
- Markers

Directions Tell students to use the library or the Internet to find out what economic activities are important to their region or state. Have them write their findings on a sketch of the region or state that you or a volunteer has made. Then discuss connections between the activities noted and the locations where they take place.

DATA FILE OBJECTIVE

Examine and compare data on South Asian countries.

Focus & Motivate

Ask students whether they know which country in South Asia has more than one billion people. *(India)* Ask them to imagine what it would be like to live in a country with that many people. *(Answers will vary.)*

Instruct: Objective

Regional Data File

- Which country is made up of a series of islands? *(Maldives)*
- Which country has the lowest infant mortality rate? *(Sri Lanka)* Which has the highest? *(Pakistan)*
- Ask how students would expect the rate of infant mortality to affect life expectancy. *(A high infant mortality rate would lower life expectancy.)*

In-Depth Resources: Unit 8
- Regional Data File Activities, p. 2

Regional Data File

Study the information on the countries of South Asia. In your notebook, jot down the answers to these questions.

Making Comparisons

1. Which two South Asian countries have the fewest people? Are they the smallest in area? Locate them on the map.
2. Which nation do you think is the poorest? Which factors did you consider in making your choice?

Country Flag	Country/ Capital	Population	Life Expectancy (years)	Birthrate (per 1,000 pop.)	Infant Mortality (per 1,000 live births)
	Bangladesh Dhaka	156,051,000	60.3	24.7	59.0
	Bhutan Thimphu	691,000	66.1	20.1	49.4
	India New Delhi	1,156,898,000	66.1	21.7	50.8
	Maldives Male	396,000	73.9	14.6	29.5
	Nepal Kathmandu	28,563,000	65.5	23.2	47.5
	Pakistan Islamabad	174,579,000	65.3	25.9	67.4
	Sri Lanka Colombo	21,325,000	75.1	16.3	18.6
	United States Washington, D.C.	307,212,000	78.1	13.8	6.2

Sources:
Central Intelligence Agency, *The World Factbook*, 2010
The World Almanac and Book of Facts, 2010
World Health Organization (WHO), 2007

Notes:
[a] GDP (purchasing power parity) is defined as the sum value of all goods and services produced in the country valued at prices prevailing in the United States.
[b] Includes land and water, when figures are available

Profile of South Asia

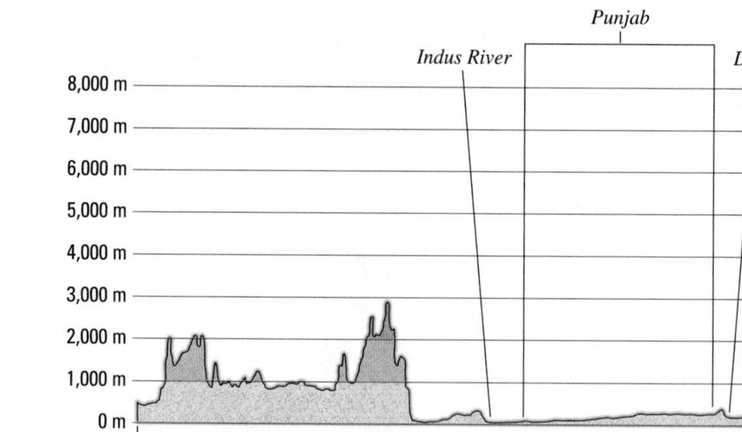

For updated statistics on South Asia . . .

548 UNIT 8

MAKING COMPARISONS ANSWERS

1. Bhutan and the Maldives; they also are the smallest countries in area.
2. Answers will vary, depending on which measures the students use to evaluate the countries' poverty. (In 2009, Nepal had the lowest GDP per capita--about $1,200.)

Doctors (per 100,000 pop.) (2000–2004)	GDP[a] (billions $US)	Import/Export (billions $US)	Literacy Rate (percentage)	Televisions (per 1,000 pop.)	Passenger Cars (per 1,000 pop.)	Total Area[b] (square miles)
26	242.2	20.22/15.91	48	7	0	55,599
5	4.34	0.53/0.51	47	6	N/A	18,147
60	3,561	253.9/165	61	75	7	1,269,346
92	1.7	0.78/0.09	96	38	11	116
21	33.3	3.63/0.91	49	6	2	56,827
74	448.1	28.31/17.87	50	105	9	310,403
55	96.5	9.6/7	91	102	24	25,332
256	14,260.0	1,445/994.7	99	844	725	3,794,083

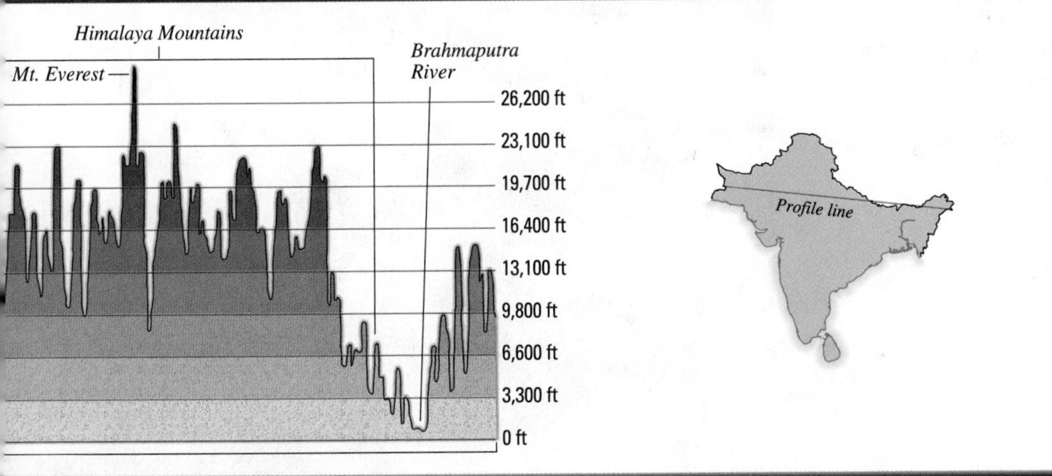

549

More About

Indicators of Wealth

Point out that not all cultures place a high value on material possessions such as televisions and cars. For example, in Bhutan there were no automobiles before 1961 because there were no roads. Bhutan's ruler cautioned that technology would be of little benefit if it were allowed to destroy the values and way of life of the Bhutanese.

ACTIVITY OPTION CRITICAL THINKING

ANALYZING DATA

Explaining the Skill Tell students that data can be used to make statistical projections. For example, if there are 100,000 people in a city and the birthrate is 20 infants per 1,000 people, then 2,000 infants will be born in that year. However, when we factor in an infant mortality rate of 7 per 1,000 live births, newborn infants will represent an increase in population of only 1986.

Applying the Skill Tell students to look at the columns in the Regional Data File labeled Population, Birthrate, and Infant Mortality. Then ask the following questions about Sri Lanka.

- How would you project how many babies will be born in Sri Lanka in 2012? *(divide total population by 1,000 and multiply by 16.3)*
- How would you project how many of those infants will die? *(divide number of projected births by 1,000 and multiply by 18.6)*
- What would be the final step in projecting population increase using these three types of data? *(subtract number of babies dying before age one from projected number born)*
- What other factors might affect population figures? *(life expectancy, war, disasters, epidemics, emigration, refugees coming into a country)*

CHAPTER 24 OBJECTIVE

Identify key features of South Asia's physical geography, climate and vegetation, and human-environment interaction.

Chapter **24**

PHYSICAL GEOGRAPHY OF SOUTH ASIA

The Land Where Continents Collided

Interpreting Photographs

Peaks and Valleys in Pakistan

Ask students how the mountains and valleys of Pakistan might have affected movement within the country. *(Movement was probably difficult because of the rugged terrain.)*

Introducing the Essential Question

- Review the theory of plate tectonics with students. Point out that the Indo-Australian Plate under India is still moving at a measurable rate. In 10 million years it will have pushed more than 900 miles into Asia.
- Discuss the hazards of living in a region dominated by monsoons, where deadly droughts can alternate with equally dangerous floods. Compare your region's climate dangers with those faced by people in Bangladesh, for example, where in 1998 floodwaters covered two-thirds of the country.

hmhsocialstudies.com
TAKING NOTES

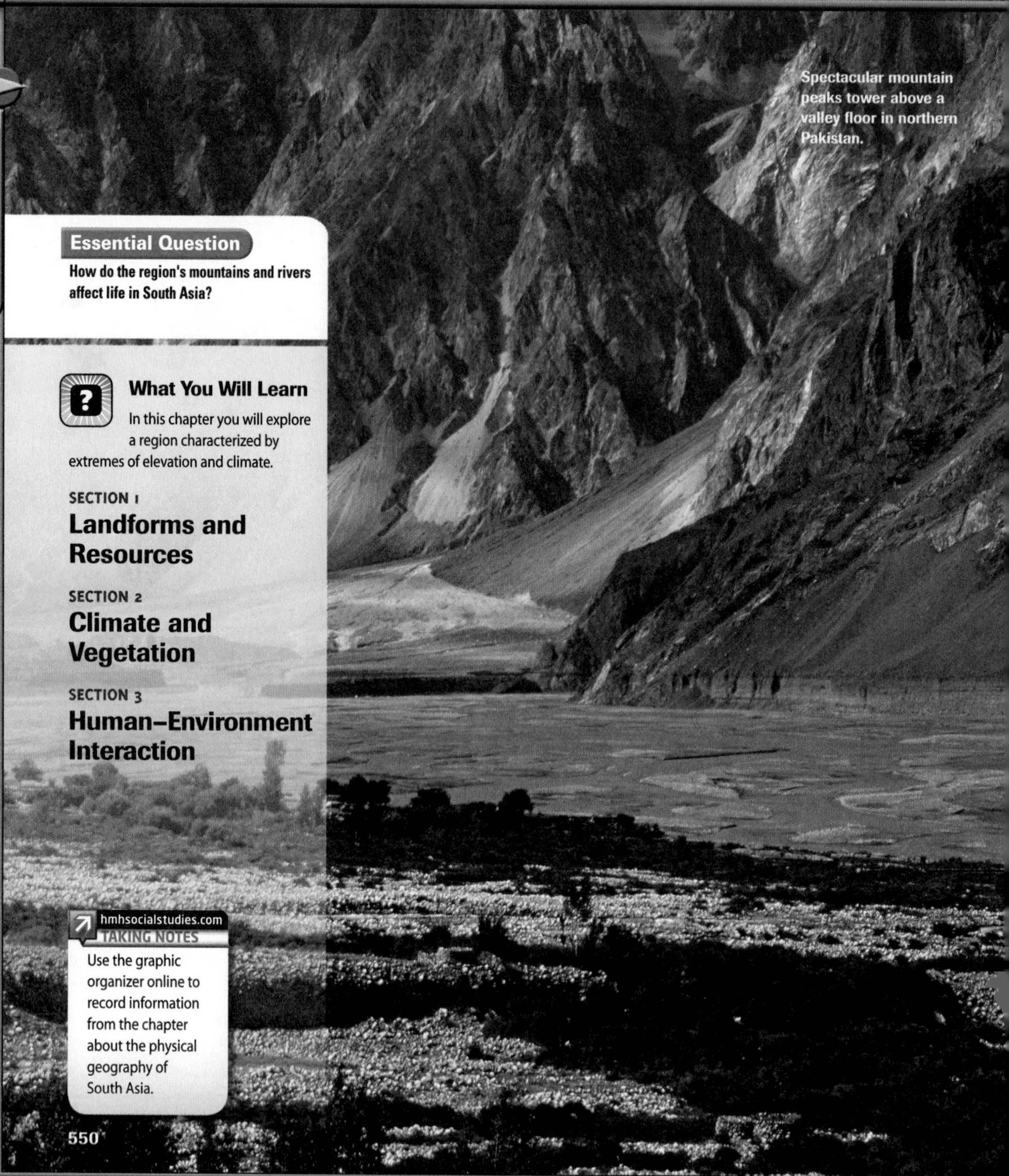

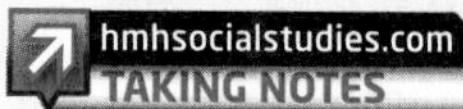

Have students fill out the graphic organizer as they take notes from each section of the chapter.

Critical Thinking Transparencies CT24
- GeoFocus

In-Depth Resources: Unit 8
- Building Vocabulary, p. 9

Spectacular mountain peaks tower above a valley floor in northern Pakistan.

Essential Question

How do the region's mountains and rivers affect life in South Asia?

What You Will Learn

In this chapter you will explore a region characterized by extremes of elevation and climate.

SECTION 1
Landforms and Resources

SECTION 2
Climate and Vegetation

SECTION 3
Human-Environment Interaction

hmhsocialstudies.com
TAKING NOTES

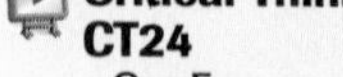

Use the graphic organizer online to record information from the chapter about the physical geography of South Asia.

550

CHAPTER 24 ADDITIONAL RESOURCES

BOOKS FOR THE TEACHER

Haberman, David L. ***River of Love in an Age of Pollution: The Yamuna River of Northern India.*** University of California Press, 2006. Interplay of religion and industrialization and how they affect a river held as sacred.

BOOKS FOR THE STUDENT

Hooper, Neil. ***Maldive Islands.*** Broomall, PA: Chelsea House, 1989. Part of the series *Let's Visit Places & Peoples of the World.*

VIDEOS

Himalayan River Run. National Geographic, 1987. Navigating white water on Nepal's Dudh Kosi River.

INTERNET

For more on the physical geography of South Asia, visit . . .

hmhsocialstudies.com

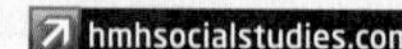

Landforms and Resources

Main Ideas

- South Asia is a subcontinent of peninsulas bordered by mountains and oceans.
- A wide variety of natural resources helps sustain life in the region.

Places & Terms

Himalaya Mountains
subcontinent
alluvial plain
archipelago
atoll

CONNECT TO THE ISSUES
TERRITORIAL DISPUTE
Kashmir is an area in the western Himalayas on the border of India and Pakistan. It has been a source of dispute between the two countries.

A HUMAN PERSPECTIVE Thousands of years ago, the Hindus of what is now north India imagined a gigantic mountain reaching more than 80,000 miles into the sky. They believed that this enormous peak, called Mt. Meru, was the center of the physical and spiritual world. In their writings, they described "rivers of sweet water" flowing down the sides of the mountain. While Mt. Meru exists only in myth, it did have a real-life inspiration—Mt. Everest, the world's tallest mountain peak at 29,035 feet above sea level. Mt. Everest and the other towering peaks of the **Himalaya Mountains** have been a lure to mountain climbers around the world. Many climbers had died on Everest's icy slopes before Sir Edmund Hillary and Tenzing Norgay, his Sherpa guide, became the first people to reach its summit in 1953.

Mountains and Plateaus

The Himalayas are part of South Asia, a region that includes seven countries—India, Pakistan, Bangladesh, Bhutan, Nepal, Sri Lanka, and the Maldives. South Asia is sometimes called a **subcontinent,** a large landmass that is smaller than a continent. In fact, it is often referred to as the Indian subcontinent because India dominates the region. Although South Asia is about half the size of the continental United States, it has more than one billion inhabitants—one-fifth of the world's population.

Formation of the Himalayas

hmhsocialstudies.com INTERACTIVE

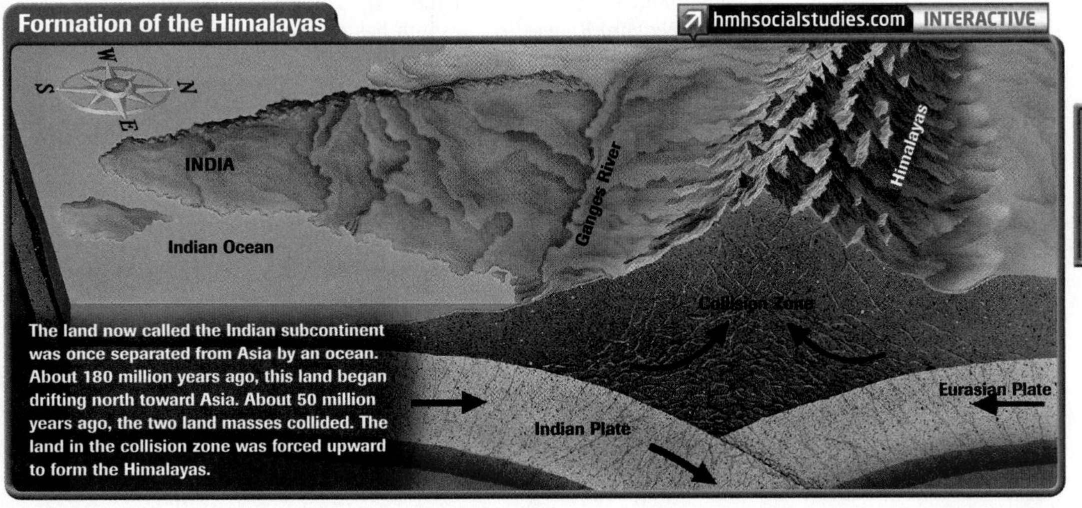

The land now called the Indian subcontinent was once separated from Asia by an ocean. About 180 million years ago, this land began drifting north toward Asia. About 50 million years ago, the two land masses collided. The land in the collision zone was forced upward to form the Himalayas.

SOUTH ASIA

SECTION 1 OBJECTIVES

1. Describe the subcontinent of South Asia.
2. Identify major rivers and their importance to South Asian life.
3. Identify and compare the two island countries that make up part of South Asia.
4. Learn about the variety of natural resources in South Asia.

SKILLBUILDER: Interpreting Maps, p. 554

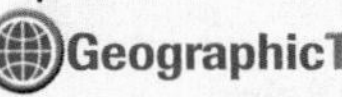

Seeing Patterns, pp. 552, 555
Using the Atlas, p. 553

Focus & Motivate

Ask what natural resources are important to the people of South Asia and why. *(Answers may include rivers for irrigation and drinking; rich soil for growing cotton and rice; Himalayas as a natural barrier to China)*

Instruct: Objective 1 appears on p. 552.

Interpreting Graphics

Formation of the Himalayas
Scientists predict that as the two tectonic plates that formed the Himalayas continue to push against each other, India will eventually become one huge mountain range. Ask students which tectonic plates collided to form the Himalayas. *(Indian and Eurasian plates)*

SECTION 1 PROGRAM RESOURCES

In-Depth Resources: Unit 8
- Guided Reading, p. 3
- Building Vocabulary, p. 9
- Reteaching Activity, p. 10

Guided Reading Workbook
- Section 1

Access for Students Acquiring English/ESL
- Guided Reading, p. 127

Formal Assessment
- Section Quiz, p. 372

Integrated Assessment
- Rubric for a news article, 4.5

INTEGRATED TECHNOLOGY

Critical Thinking Transparencies CT56
- Major Rivers of South Asia

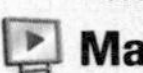
Map Transparencies MT43
- South Asia: Natural Resources

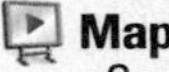

Power Presentations

Chapter Summaries

TEST-TAKING RESOURCES

Strategies for Test Preparation

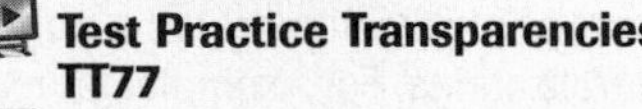
Test Practice Transparencies TT77

Online Test Practice

Instruct: Objective 

Mountains and Plateaus

- Why is South Asia sometimes called a subcontinent? *(its landmass is similar to a continent but smaller)*
- What caused the formation of mountain ranges in the northern part of the region? *(a collision of tectonic plates)*

 **In-Depth Resources: Unit 8**
- Guided Reading, p. 3

Instruct: Objective 

Rivers, Deltas, and Plains

- What are the three great rivers of South Asia? *(Ganges, Indus, Brahmaputra)*
- Where is the Indo-Gangetic Plain? *(It extends from Pakistan across northern India and Bangladesh.)* Why is it important in terms of population? *(It is the most heavily populated part of South Asia, containing about three-fifths of India's population.)*

Critical Thinking Transparencies CT56
- Major Rivers of South Asia

Connect TO THE Issues

Extreme Weather: The Ganges Delta

In the United States, spring rains often cause rivers to overflow, which may result in property damage and even loss of life. In 1927 the flooded Mississippi River covered almost 30,000 square miles. Have students compare causes of river floods in the U.S. and South Asia. *(Melting snows are a cause common to both, but the U.S. does not have monsoons.)*

As you saw on the map on page 543, natural barriers help to separate the South Asian subcontinent from the rest of Asia. The Himalayas and other mountain ranges form the northern border, while water surrounds the rest of the region. The South Asian peninsula, which extends south into the Indian Ocean, is bordered by the Arabian Sea to the west and the Bay of Bengal to the east.

NORTHERN MOUNTAINS Millions of years ago, the land that is now South Asia was actually part of East Africa. About 50 million years ago, it split off and drifted northward. As the illustration on page 551 shows, it collided with Central Asia. The gradual collision of these two large tectonic plates forced the land upward into enormous mountain ranges. These mountains, which are still rising, now form the northern edge of the South Asian subcontinent.

The magnificent Himalayas are a system of parallel mountain ranges. They contain the world's highest mountains, with nearly two dozen peaks rising to 24,000 feet or above. The Himalayas stretch for 1,500 miles and form a giant barrier between the Indian subcontinent and China. Mt. Everest, the world's tallest peak, sits at the heart of the Himalayas. Nestled high up within these mountains are the remote, landlocked kingdoms of Nepal and Bhutan. A

Geographic Thinking

Seeing Patterns

A What role have the Himalayas played in the development of Nepal and Bhutan?

A. Answer Nepal and Bhutan have mainly developed in isolation because of their mountain location.

Connect TO THE Issues

EXTREME WEATHER

THE GANGES DELTA

Water, water, and more water! Three major rivers meet in Bangladesh to form the Ganges Delta at the Bay of Bengal, shown in the satellite photo below. They are the Brahmaputra, the Ganges, and the Meghna.

These rivers bring rich alluvial soil to the delta, a region covering 65,500 square miles. But above all, these rivers bring water. Every summer, melting snow and monsoon-driven rains force the rivers to burst their banks. In fact, so much water comes that central Bangladesh is turned into an inland sea before the land dries.

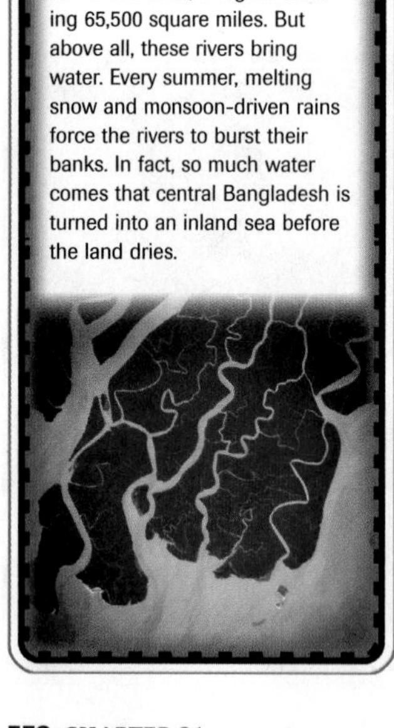

The Hindu Kush are mountains that lie at the west end of the Himalayas. They form a rugged barrier separating Pakistan from Afghanistan to the north. For centuries, the Hindu Kush stood in the way of Central Asian tribes trying to invade India. Bloody battles have been fought over control of major land routes through these mountains, including the Khyber Pass. The mighty Karakoram Mountains rise in the northeastern portion of the chain. They are the home of the world's second highest peak, K2.

SOUTHERN PLATEAUS The collision of tectonic plates that pushed up the Himalayas also created several smaller mountain ranges in central India, including the Vindhya (VIHN•dyuh) Range. To the south lies the Deccan Plateau. This large tableland tilts east, toward the Bay of Bengal, and covers much of southern India. Two mountain ranges, the Western Ghats and the Eastern Ghats, flank the plateau, separating it from the coast. These mountains also block most moist winds and keep rain from reaching the interior. As a result, the Deccan is a largely arid region.

Rivers, Deltas, and Plains

The Northern Indian Plain, or Indo-Gangetic Plain, lies between the Deccan Plateau and the northern mountain ranges. This large lowland region stretches across northern India and into Bangladesh. It is formed by three great river systems: the Indus, the Ganges, and the Brahmaputra.

BACKGROUND

The name *Himalayas* is Sanskrit for "abode of snow."

GREAT RIVERS The three great rivers of South Asia have their origins among the snowcapped peaks of the high

ACTIVITY OPTION **SKILLBUILDER LESSON**

MAKING GENERALIZATIONS

Explaining the Skill Making generalizations means to make broad judgments based on information from several sources. By examining the impact of physical geography on a region's people, it is possible to make generalizations. For example, an examination of population patterns along the world's great rivers leads to the generalization that people tend to settle in flood plains.

Additional Skillbuilder practice can be found on page 560.

Applying the Skill Have pairs of students answer the following questions. After 10 minutes, have them share their answers with the class.

- How have the northern mountain ranges been of benefit to South Asia? *(The Hindu Kush Mountains protected India from invasion by tribes from Central Asia.)*
- Why have Bhutan and Nepal developed in relative isolation? *(They are located in a remote part of the Himalayas.)*
- What generalization can you make about the effect of the northern mountain ranges on the history and lifestyle of people in South Asia? *(Mountains have both protected and isolated them.)*

Himalayas. The Indus flows west and then south through Pakistan to the Arabian Sea. The Ganges drops down from the central Himalayas and flows eastward across northern India. The Brahmaputra winds its way east, then west and south through Bangladesh. The Ganges and Brahmaputra eventually meet to form one huge river delta before entering the Bay of Bengal.

FERTILE PLAINS These rivers play a key role in supporting life in South Asia. Their waters provide crucial irrigation for agricultural lands. They also carry rich soil, called alluvial soil, on their journey down from the mountains. When the rivers overflow their banks, they deposit this soil on **alluvial plains,** lands that are rich farmlands. As a result, the Indo-Gangetic Plain is one of the most fertile farming regions in the world.

The Indo-Gangetic Plain is also the most heavily populated part of South Asia. In fact, the area contains about three-fifths of India's population. Many of the subcontinent's largest cities, including New Delhi and Kolkata in India, and Dakha in Bangladesh, are located there. Population densities at the eastern end of the plain, particularly in the Ganges-Brahmaputra delta, are especially high, as you can see on the map on page 547. To the west, in the area between the Indus and Ganges rivers, the plain becomes drier and requires more irrigation. To the south lies one of the world's most arid regions—the Thar, or Great Indian Desert. B

Geographic Thinking

Using the Atlas
B Use the map on page 543. Locate the Thar Desert. What two countries share its land?
B. Answer India and Pakistan.

Offshore Islands

Two island groups are also countries of South Asia—Sri Lanka and the Maldives. Sri Lanka is located in the Indian Ocean just off India's southeastern tip. The Maldives island group is situated farther off the Indian coast to the southwest.

SRI LANKA: THE SUBCONTINENT'S "TEAR DROP" Sri Lanka (sree LAHNG•kuh) is a large, tear-shaped island country. It is a lush tropical land of great natural beauty. Dominating the center of the island is a range of high, rugged mountains that reach more than 8,000 feet in elevation. Many small rivers cascade from these mountains to the lowlands below. The northern side of the island consists of low hills and gently rolling farmland. Circling the island is a coastal plain that includes long, palm-fringed beaches.

THE MALDIVES ARCHIPELAGO The Maldives comprise an **archipelago,** or island group, of more than 1,200 small islands. These islands stretch north to south for almost 500 miles off the Indian coast near the equator. The islands (shown at right) are the low-lying tops of submerged volcanoes, surrounded by coral reefs and shallow lagoons. This type of island is called an **atoll.** The total land area of the Maldives is 115 square miles (roughly twice the size of Washington, D.C.). Only about 200 of the islands are inhabited.

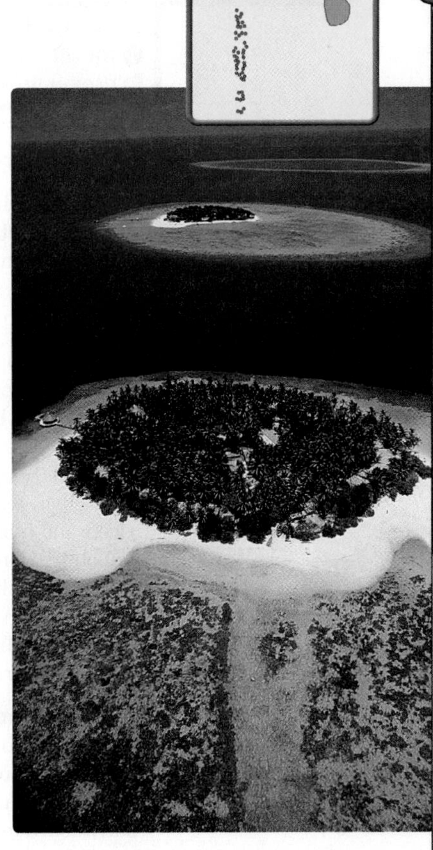

PLACE Not one of the more than 1,200 small coral islands that make up the Maldives rises more than six feet above the Indian Ocean.
How might global warming affect these islands?

Instruct: Objective 3

Offshore Islands

- What are the two island countries that are part of South Asia? *(the Maldives and Sri Lanka)*
- Which country is composed of many small islands? *(the Maldives)* What type of islands are they? *(atolls)*
- What is the main geological difference between the Maldives and Sri Lanka? *(Sri Lanka is a single large island. The Maldives island group is made up of hundreds of islands that are the tops of submerged volcanoes.)*

Interpreting Photographs

Atolls of the Maldives

Remind students that fewer than 20 percent of the Maldives are inhabited. Have students look closely at the larger island in the photograph for evidence of habitation. *(The gray and brown patches appear to be buildings. There is a structure built at the end of a pier in the left portion of the photo.)* Ask what might explain the circles of lighter blue water surrounding the islands. *(coral reefs)*

CAPTION ANSWER Melting of the polar ice caps could cause the islands to be submerged as water levels rise in the world's oceans.

DIFFERENTIATING INSTRUCTION **STUDENTS ACQUIRING ENGLISH/ESL**

EXPANDING VOCABULARY

Objective To categorize terms relating to landforms

Class Time 10 minutes

Task Create a word web relating to landforms

Directions Have students copy the web shown here in their notebook. Tell them to fill in the empty balloons with the new vocabulary words as they read through the section. Suggest that they add balloons for additional words that they want to remember as well. Upon completion of the section, pair students with native speakers and have them practice using the terms in sentences.

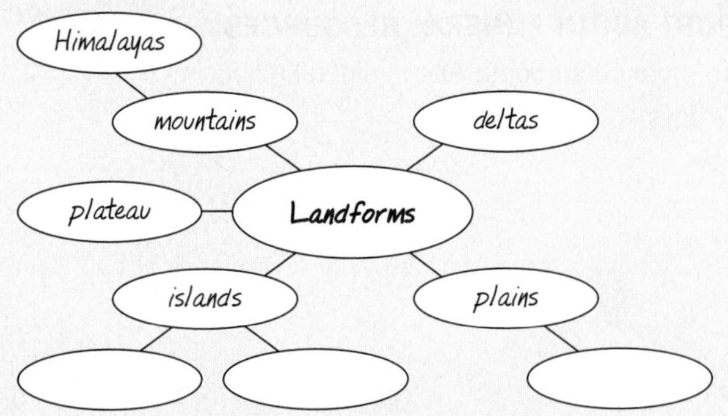

Interpreting Maps

Natural Resources of South Asia

Have students determine the location of each mineral on the chart. Then ask which resources are common to Pakistan, India, and Bangladesh. *(natural gas)*

SKILLBUILDER ANSWERS 1. Most are found along the western coast of the Indian subcontinent. **2.** Perhaps Nepal's isolated, mountainous terrain has not allowed exploration for minerals.

Instruct: Objective 4

Natural Resources

- What are South Asia's main water resources and how are they beneficial? *(River systems provide water for irrigation. Rivers and coastal waters are sources of fishing, and provide transportation and power.)*
- What mineral resources have led to the development of industries in India? *(iron ore: the steel industry; mica: the computer industry)*
- Why is deforestation a problem? *(It causes erosion, flooding, landslides, and loss of fields.)*

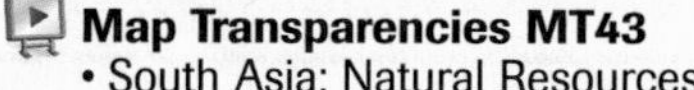

Map Transparencies MT43
- South Asia: Natural Resources

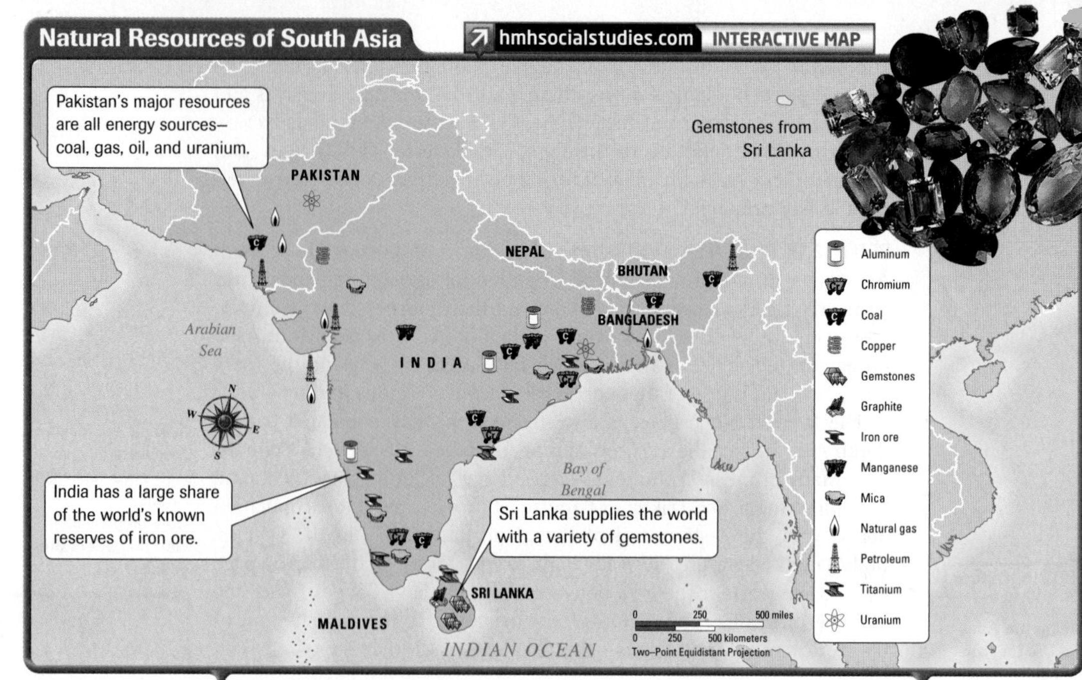

SKILLBUILDER: Interpreting Maps

1. **LOCATION** How would you describe the distribution of petroleum resources in South Asia?
2. **REGION** Why might terrain be a reason no major mineral resources are shown in Nepal?

Natural Resources

The natural beauty of the southern islands is just one of the many physical assets of South Asia. In fact, the subcontinent boasts a wide variety of natural resources that support human life. At the same time, South Asia's rapidly growing population puts great pressure on its land and resources.

WATER AND SOIL South Asia relies heavily on its soil and water resources to provide food through farming and fishing. The great river systems that bring alluvial soil down from the mountains help enrich the land. They also bring the water necessary for crops to grow. Both small- and large-scale irrigation projects divert the water to the farmlands that need it. Many types of fish are also found in South Asian rivers and coastal waters, including mackerel, sardines, carp, and catfish.

South Asian waters also provide a means of transportation and power. Boats travel the rivers and coastlines, carrying goods and people from town to town. Governments also are working to harness hydroelectric energy from the waters. For example, India and Pakistan have a number of hydroelectric and irrigation projects underway.

FORESTS Timber and other forest products are another important resource in South Asia. Rain forests in India produce hardwoods like sal and teak, along with bamboo and the fragrant sandalwood. Highland forests in Bhutan and Nepal have thick stands of pine, fir, and other softwood trees. Deforestation is a severe problem, however. It causes

BACKGROUND Only one-tenth of India's original forest cover remains uncut.

DIFFERENTIATING INSTRUCTION **GIFTED AND TALENTED STUDENTS**

BLOCK SCHEDULING

WRITING A REPORT ABOUT MINERAL RESOURCES

Objective To learn more about South Asia's mineral resources

Research Time 2 days

Task Write a report

Directions Have students choose a mineral resource from the map on page 554 and do research to learn about its importance to the South Asian country or countries in which it is found. Tell them to write a brief report, including information on how the mineral is extracted, its uses, whether it is used internally or exported, its economic significance, and any environmental impact its extraction may have.

soil erosion, flooding, landslides, and loss of wildlife habitats. Overcutting has devastated formerly dense forests in India, Bangladesh, and Sri Lanka.

MINERALS Much of South Asia's energy is still generated from mineral resources. For example, India ranks fourth in the world in coal production and has enough petroleum to supply about half its oil needs. India, Pakistan, and Bangladesh also have important natural gas resources. Uranium deposits in India provide fuel for nuclear energy.

South Asia also has large iron-ore deposits, particularly in India's Deccan Plateau. India is one of the world's leading exporters of iron ore, which is also used in that country's large steel industry. Other South Asian minerals include manganese, gypsum, chromium, bauxite, and copper.

India supplies most of the world's mica, a key component in electrical equipment. This is one of the reasons that India has a growing computer industry. Mica is also found in Nepal. India and Sri Lanka both have substantial gemstone deposits. India is traditionally known for its diamonds, while Sri Lanka produces dozens of types of precious and semi-precious stones. The island is most famous for its beautiful sapphires and rubies.

In this section, you read about the landforms and resources of South Asia. In the next section, you will learn about climate and vegetation.

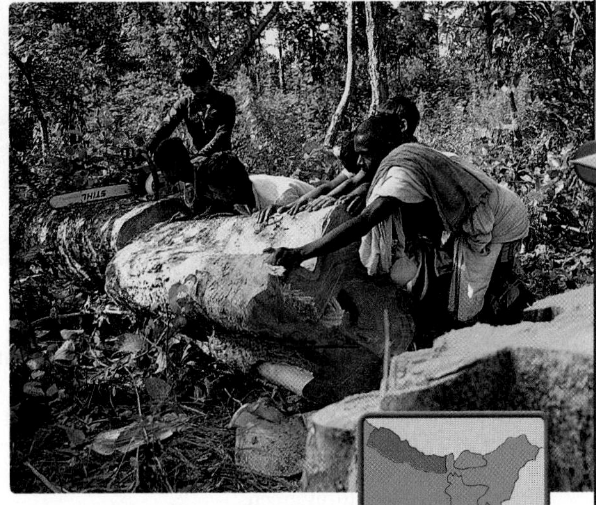

HUMAN-ENVIRONMENT INTERACTION These Nepalese are harvesting timber from depleted forests in southern Nepal. **What are some ways deforestation might affect the lives of South Asians?**

Interpreting Photographs

Harvesting Wood

Deforestation is also a problem in Nepal, where wood is needed for fuel and building material. As more trees are cut, ground water run-off causes erosion, which depletes the soil.

CAPTION ANSWER They would face a scarcity of timber for fuel and construction, and also soil erosion and the loss of habitats for wildlife.

Assess & Reteach

GeoFocus Have students complete the sections on landforms and resources in their GeoFocus graphic organizers.

Formal Asessment
- Section Quiz, p. 372

Reteaching Activity
Have students work in pairs. Tell them to take turns asking and answering a question about each subhead under the four main headings of the section.

In-Depth Resources: Unit 8
- Reteaching Activity, p. 10

Section 1 Assessment

1 Places & Terms
Identify and explain where in the region these would be found.
- Himalaya Mountains
- subcontinent
- alluvial plain
- archipelago
- atoll

2 Taking Notes
PLACE Review the notes you took for this section.

Landforms	
Resources	

- What mountain ranges separate the subcontinent from the rest of Asia?
- Why might South Asia have a large steel industry?

3 Main Ideas
a. When and how was South Asia formed?
b. What are South Asia's three largest rivers, and what is their source?
c. How do the island countries that lie off the subcontinent's coast differ from one another?

4 Geographic Thinking
Seeing Patterns How do the Himalayas contribute to South Asia's resource wealth?
Think about:
- river systems
- agriculture

See Skillbuilder Handbook, page R8.

SOUTH ASIA

MAKING COMPARISONS Do research on one of the mountain climbing expeditions to the peak of Mt. Everest. Write a **news article** about the expedition and present it to the class. Use standard sentence structure, spelling, grammar, and punctuation.

SECTION 1 ASSESSMENT ANSWERS

1. Places & Places
Himalaya Mountains, p. 551
subcontinent, p. 551
alluvial plain, p. 553
archipelago, p. 553
atoll, p. 554

2. Taking Notes
- Hindu Kush, Karakoram, and Himalayan mountains
- because of its large deposits of iron ore, used for producing steel

3. Main Ideas
a. About 50 million years ago, a large section of land broke away from East Africa, drifted northward, and collided with Central Asia.
b. The Himalayas are the source of the Indus, Ganges, and Brahmaputra rivers.
c. Sri Lanka is a tear-shaped island to the subcontinent's southeast; the Maldives, to the southwest, is an archipelago.

4. Geographic Thinking
The region's great river systems begin in the mountains. The water and alluvial soil that the rivers bring from the mountains are crucial to the region's agricultural production.

GeoActivity

Integrated Assessment
- Rubric for a news article, 4.5

SECTION 2 OBJECTIVES

1. Examine climate zones and weather patterns.
2. Identify the main types of vegetation.

SKILLBUILDER: Interpreting Maps, p. 557

Seeing Patterns, p. 557
Using the Atlas, p. 558
Making Inferences, p. 558

Focus & Motivate

Ask students what type of climate and vegetation they would expect South Asia to have. *(Answers will vary but will probably include tropical or hot climate.)*

Instruct: Objective 1 appears on p. 557

Interpreting Photographs

People of the Thar Desert

Have students comment on the way the people are dressed. Why might they choose this type of garment? *(for protection from the sun and wind)*

CAPTION ANSWER The Thar Desert's climate is probably very hot and dry, and little vegetation grows in the sandy soil.

Climate and Vegetation

Main Ideas

- Climate conditions in South Asia range from frigid cold in the high mountains to intense heat in the deserts.
- Seasonal winds affect both the climate and vegetation of South Asia.

Places & Terms

monsoon

cyclone

CONNECT TO THE ISSUES

EXTREME WEATHER Seasonal droughts and flooding take a heavy toll in lives and property in South Asia each year.

A HUMAN PERSPECTIVE Every April and May, much of South Asia bakes in the heat. People endure temperatures that regularly top 100°F. Dust fills the air, and streams dry up. People walk for miles looking for water. Then—when it seems that no one can survive another day—the clouds roll in. The skies open up, and the rains come. People celebrate when the land turns green.

But their celebration is short-lived, as the downpour continues. Soon, the ground can hold no more water. Rivers overflow their banks. Families are forced from their homes as towns and cities are flooded. Thousands may die before the waters eventually recede, and the land dries out. South Asians see this cycle repeat itself each year.

Climate—Wet and Dry, Hot and Cold

Half of the climate zones that exist on Earth can be found in South Asia. This means that South Asians must adapt to widely varying conditions.

CLIMATE ZONES South Asia has six main climate zones, as you can see on the map on page 557. The highland zone has the coldest climate. This is the area of the Himalayas and other northern mountains, where snow exists year-round. The lower elevations, which include the lush foothills and valleys of Nepal, Bhutan, and northern India, are much warmer. They are in the humid subtropical zone that stretches across South Asia. The Indo-Gangetic Plain also occupies much of this region.

The semiarid zone—a region of high temperatures and light rainfall—is found at the western end of the Plain and in parts of the Deccan Plateau. The desert zone covers much of the lower Indus Valley, in the borderlands of western India and southern Pakistan. The driest part of

MOVEMENT Camels, who can go days without water, are used to move goods and people across the sands of the Thar Desert, which straddles northwest India and southeast Pakistan.
What does this photo show about the climate and vegetation of the Thar Desert?

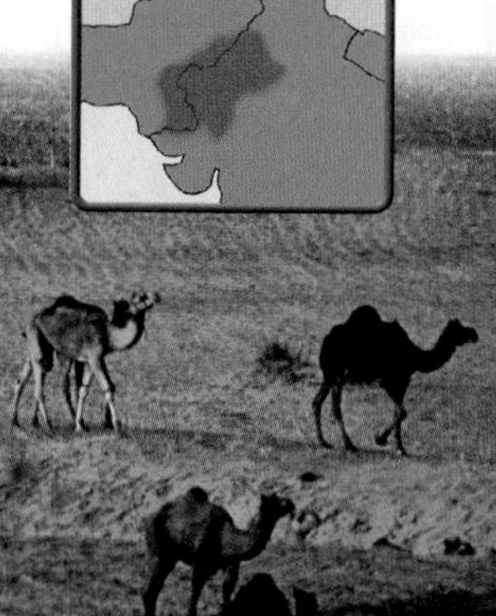

SECTION 2 PROGRAM RESOURCES

In-Depth Resources: Unit 8
- Guided Reading, p. 4
- Building Vocabulary, p. 9
- Reteaching Activity, p. 11
- Map and Graph Skills, pp. 6–7

Guided Reading Workbook
- Section 2

Access for Students Acquiring English/ESL
- Guided Reading, p. 128
- Map and Graph Skills, pp. 131–132

Formal Assessment
- Section Quiz, p. 373

Integrated Assessment
- Rubric for a sketch map, 2.1

INTEGRATED TECHNOLOGY

Power Presentations

Test Generator
- Section Quiz

TEST-TAKING RESOURCES

Strategies for Test Preparation

Test Practice Transparencies TT78

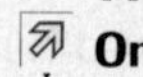

Online Test Practice

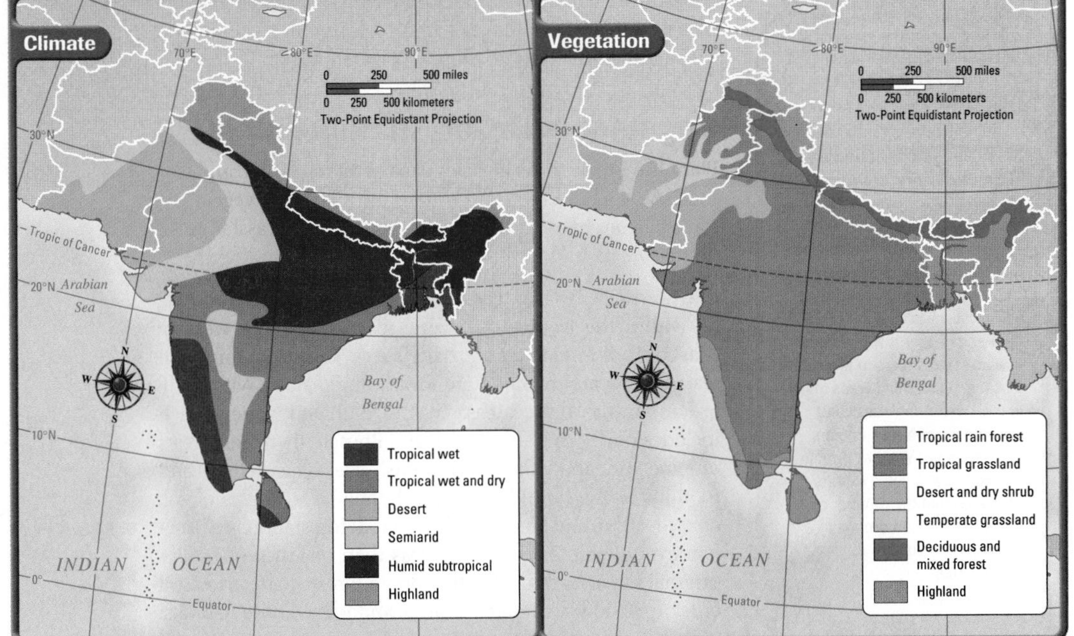

SKILLBUILDER: Interpreting Maps

❶ **LOCATION** Which countries have only one type of vegetation?

❷ **REGION** Which areas of South Asia receive the most rainfall?

this area, the Thar Desert, gets very little rain—averaging 10 inches a year. The tropical wet zone is found along the western and eastern coasts of India and in Bangladesh. Temperatures are high, and rainfall is heavy. In fact, Cherrapunji in northeastern India holds the world's record for rainfall in a month—366 inches. Southern Sri Lanka also has a tropical wet climate, while the north is tropical wet and dry.

MONSOONS AND CYCLONES Although climate varies in South Asia, the region as a whole is greatly affected by **monsoons,** or seasonal winds. Each year, from October through February, dry winds blow across South Asia from the northeast. From June through September, the winds blow in from the southwest, bringing moist ocean air. Heavy rains fall, especially in the southwestern and Ganges Delta portions of South Asia. The illustration on page 598 shows how the monsoons blow across the region.

This rainfall is crucial to life on the subcontinent. Yet, the monsoons can cause severe hardship for millions, especially those living in the lowlands of India and Bangladesh. The monsoons also are highly unpredictable. Some areas may get too little rain, while others get too much. The monsoons are a sometimes beneficial, sometimes difficult feature of life in South Asia. A

The most extreme weather pattern of South Asia is the **cyclone,** a violent storm with fierce winds and heavy rain. Cyclones are most destructive in Bangladesh, a low-lying coastal region where high waves can swamp large parts of the country. A severe cyclone can cause

A. Answer The monsoons bring needed water for life in the region, but too little or too much can cause hardships or even death for South Asians.

Geographic Thinking

Seeing Patterns

A How are the monsoons both beneficial and destructive to South Asia?

Interpreting Maps

Climate and Vegetation of South Asia

Tell students to look for connections or patterns between the climate and vegetation maps. For example, What climates are likely to produce tropical rain forests? *(tropical wet and humid subtropical)*

SKILLBUILDER ANSWERS

1. Bhutan has only deciduous and mixed forest vegetation, and Bangladesh and Sri Lanka have only tropical rain forest vegetation. **2.** the tropical wet areas along the southwestern coasts of India and Sri Lanka and much of southern Bangladesh

Instruct: Objective 1

Climate—Wet and Dry, Hot and Cold

- How many climate zones does South Asia have? *(six)*
- What are monsoons? *(seasonal winds)*
- How do monsoons affect climate during the course of a year? *(They blow dry weather from the northeast during October through February; from June through September they bring moisture from the southwest, causing heavy rains.)*
- What is South Asia's most extreme type of weather? *(cyclone)* Which country is most affected by it? *(Bangladesh)*

In-Depth Resources: Unit 8
- Guided Reading, p. 4

ACTIVITY OPTION | CRITICAL THINKING

DETERMINING CAUSE AND EFFECT

Explaining the Skill A cause is an action that makes something happen. An effect is the result of the cause. A single event may have several causes. It is also possible for one cause to result in several effects. An examination of the causes of weather patterns in South Asia and their effect on the people who live there is key to an understanding of the region.

Applying the Skill Tell students that weather patterns are important factors in understanding life in South Asia. Then ask the following questions.

- What causes heavy seasonal rains in southern and eastern South Asia? *(monsoons)*
- What is the predictable effect of a severe cyclone? *(high waves)*
- What damage is often caused in Bangladesh by the high waves of a cyclone? *(flooding, destruction, death)*

Instruct: Objective 2

Vegetation: Desert to Rain Forest

- In which countries are forests found? *(India, Bangladesh, Nepal, Bhutan, Sri Lanka, Pakistan)*
- What kinds of trees grow in the various climate zones? *(tropical wet: teak, ebony, bamboo, and mangroves in the deltas; highlands: evergreens; subtropical: sal, oak, chestnut, palm)*

Human-Environment Interaction: Saving the Tigers

Like the Bengal tiger, huge numbers of American bison were hunted nearly to extinction.

What human activities have affected the tiger? *(killing them in great numbers; destroying habitat; recent attempts to save them)* Why is it important to save these animals? *(Answers may include importance to cultural and natural heritage.)*

Assess & Reteach

GeoFocus Have students finish entering information for this section on their GeoFocus graphic organizers.

Formal Assessment
- Section Quiz, p. 373

Reteaching Activity
Have students create an outline of the information in Section 2. Tell them to use the main headings and subheadings to form the outline's structure.

In-Depth Resources: Unit 8
- Reteaching Activity, p. 11

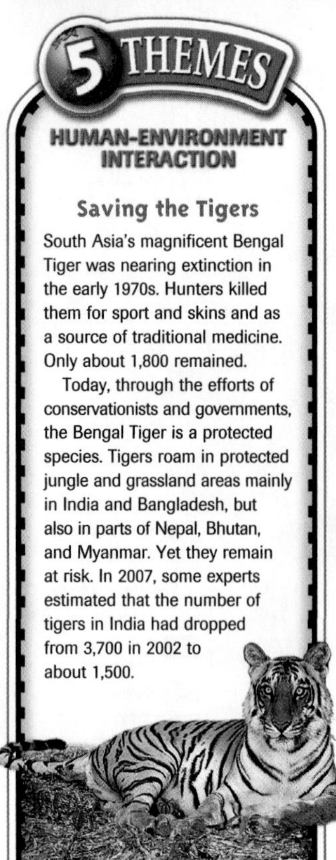

5 THEMES
HUMAN-ENVIRONMENT INTERACTION

Saving the Tigers

South Asia's magnificent Bengal Tiger was nearing extinction in the early 1970s. Hunters killed them for sport and skins and as a source of traditional medicine. Only about 1,800 remained.

Today, through the efforts of conservationists and governments, the Bengal Tiger is a protected species. Tigers roam in protected jungle and grassland areas mainly in India and Bangladesh, but also in parts of Nepal, Bhutan, and Myanmar. Yet they remain at risk. In 2007, some experts estimated that the number of tigers in India had dropped from 3,700 in 2002 to about 1,500.

widespread damage and kill thousands of people. In the Disasters! feature on pages 578–579, you will read about a cyclone that killed more than 300,000 in 1970.

Vegetation: Desert to Rain Forest

Plant life in South Asia varies according to climate and altitude. As you can see on the map on page 557, vegetation ranges from desert shrub and temperate grasslands to dense forests in the wettest areas.

VEGETATION ZONES The most forested parts of South Asia lie within the tropical wet zone, particularly the western coast of India and southern Bangladesh. Lush rain forests of teak, ebony, and bamboo are found there, along with mangroves in the delta areas. In the highland zone, which includes northern India, Nepal, and Bhutan, there are forests of pine, fir, and other evergreens. The river valleys and foothills of the humid subtropical zone have forests of sal, oak, chestnut, and various palms. But deforestation is a problem everywhere. For example, less than one-fifth of India's original forests remain. Cutting down forests has caused soil erosion, flooding, climate changes, and lost wildlife habitats.

In the semiarid areas of South Asia, such as the Deccan Plateau and the Pakistan-India border, there is less vegetation. The main plant life is desert shrubs and grasses. The driest areas, like the Thar Desert, have little plant life, and as a result, few people live there. The tropical wet and dry climate of northern Sri Lanka produces both grasses and trees. How South Asians interact with their environment will be discussed in the next section. B

B. Answer mostly between 1 to 24 persons per square mile

Using the Atlas
B Use the atlas on pages 543 and 547. What is the average population density in the Thar Desert?

Section 2 Assessment

1 Places & Terms
Explain the importance of each of the following places and terms.
- monsoon
- cyclone

2 Taking Notes
PLACE Review the notes you took for this section.

- How many different climate zones does South Asia have?
- What percentage of India's original forest remains today?

3 Main Ideas
a. In what part of South Asia is there a desert climate?
b. What are monsoons, and when do they affect South Asia?
c. Where are South Asia's tropical rain forests located?

4 Geographic Thinking
Making Inferences What might be some of the long-term effects of deforestation on life in South Asia?
Think about:
- soil erosion and flooding
- climate changes
- lost wildlife habitats

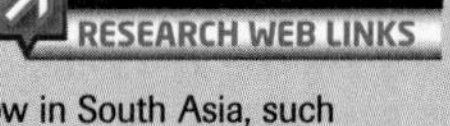

GeoActivity

SEEING PATTERNS Do more research on the different trees that grow in South Asia, such as teak, ebony, and bamboo. Create a **sketch map** of the region that shows where these various trees grow.

SECTION 2 ASSESSMENT ANSWERS

1. Places & Terms
monsoon, p. 557 cyclone, p. 557

2. Taking Notes
- six
- less than one-fifth

3. Main Ideas
a. in the northwest
b. Monsoons are seasonal winds. Dry monsoons blow in from the northeast from October through February. Southwesterly monsoons that come from June through September bring moist ocean air that results in heavy rains.
c. in Bangladesh and along the western coasts of India and Sri Lanka

4. Geographic Thinking
Answers will vary, but should include reference to the effect on agriculture caused by soil erosion and climate changes and the displacement of people from lands that become flooded.

GeoActivity

Integrated Assessment
- Rubric for a sketch map, 2.1

Map and Graph Skills

Reading a Weather Map

Suppose you have decided to take a trip to South Asia and want to know what the weather in the area you are going to visit will be like. To see what the weather is predicted to be for the next several days, you would look at a weather map. Most daily newspapers and news broadcasts show weather maps for a region or a country every day.

THE LANGUAGE OF MAPS A **weather map** shows weather conditions and patterns for a specific area at a point in time. Weather maps show temperatures, precipitation, weather fronts (rapid changes in weather), and air pressure. The weather map below shows weather conditions in South Asia on a typical February day during the winter monsoon season.

Weather Map of South Asia

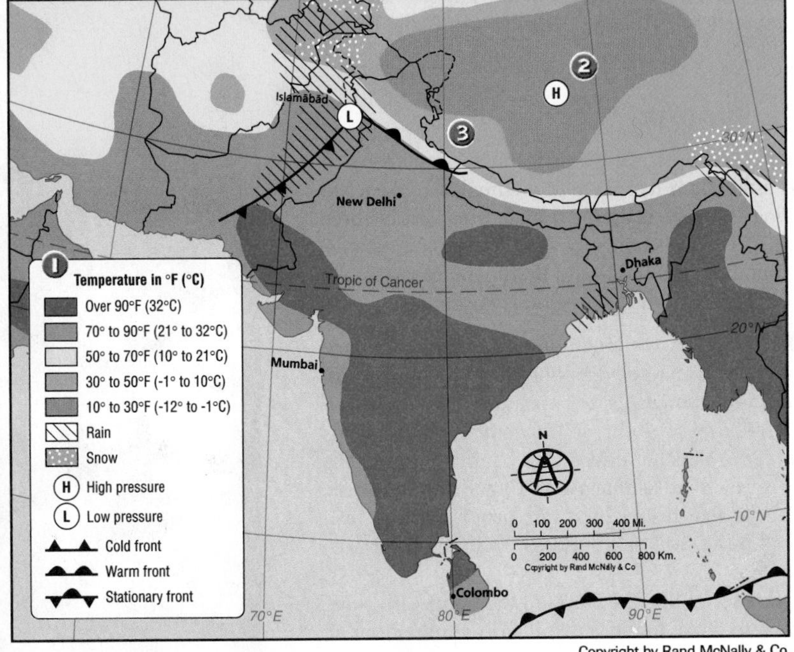

1. The key shows colors and patterns that are used to indicate temperatures and precipitation. The temperatures are shown in both Fahrenheit and Celsius.

2. Letter symbols on the map represent high and low pressure systems. Air pressure is the force of the air pressing down on the earth's surface.

3. These symbols show weather fronts. In addition to showing whether a warm front or a cold front is approaching an area, the symbols show in which direction the front is moving.

Map and Graph Skills Assessment

1. **Drawing Conclusions** Which South Asian cities are having temperatures over 70°F?

2. **Making Comparisons** Which area of South Asia would have the most pleasant weather conditions for a visitor at the time?

3. **Making Inferences** Judging from the map, will the weather in northwestern India stay the same or change?

OBJECTIVE

Learn to interpret a weather map

Instruct: Objective

Reading a Weather Map

- Which city is likely to experience rain in the next few days? *(New Delhi)* Why do you think so? *(A cold front bringing rain is moving towards New Delhi.)*
- What is the general temperature pattern from north to south? *(temperatures increase as one travels south)*
- Which country does not reflect this pattern? *(Sri Lanka)*

In-Depth Resources: Unit 8
- Map and Graph Skills, pp. 6–7

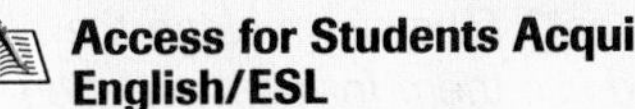

Access for Students Acquiring English/ESL
- Map and Graph Skills, pp. 131–132

SKILLS ASSESSMENT ANSWERS

1. Mumbai, New Delhi, Dhaka, Colombo
2. Answers may vary but could point to area at the north of region where temperatures range from 50 to 90 degrees with no precipitation shown.
3. It will change because a cold front is moving into India from Pakistan.

SECTION 3 OBJECTIVES

1. Learn about the relationship between Hindus and the Ganges.
2. Examine the interaction between the people of Bangladesh and the Feni River.

SKILLBUILDER: Interpreting Maps, p. 561

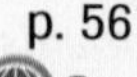

GeographicThinking

Using the Atlas, p. 562
Making Inferences, p. 563

Focus & Motivate

Have students think about what they have learned already about South Asia. What are some examples of how people there interact with their environment? *(They farm along the rivers and use them for transportation and hydroelectric power. They have deforested large areas, and extracted mineral resources.)*

Instruct: Objective 1

Living Along the Ganges

- What do Hindus believe about the Ganges? *(It is sacred.)*
- How do Hindus interact with the Ganges? *(They bathe in it, drink the water, scatter the ashes of the dead on it, and worship along it.)*
- In what ways is the Ganges a health hazard? *(Its extreme pollution causes illnesses, many of which are life-threatening.)*

In-Depth Resources: Unit 8
- Guided Reading, p. 5
- Skillbuilder Practice, p. 8

3 Human–Environment Interaction

Main Ideas
- Rivers play a central role in the lives of South Asians.
- Water pollution and flooding pose great challenges to South Asian countries.

Places & Terms

Hinduism	**storm surge**
Ganges River	**estuary**

CONNECT TO THE ISSUES
POPULATION The large population of South Asia is in danger of using up the region's water resources.

A HUMAN PERSPECTIVE **Hinduism** is the religion of most Indians. During one Hindu religious festival, millions of Indians gather near the city of Allahabad, where the Ganges and Yamuna rivers meet. A temporary tent city goes up, complete with markets, temples, and teahouses. People visit the market stalls and pray at the temples. They also watch plays based on Hindu myths and legends.

Mainly, though, the Hindus wait for the appointed moment when they will wade into the Ganges and wash their sins away in its holy waters. To Hindus, the **Ganges River** is not only an important water resource, but it is also a sacred river. It is the earthly home of the Hindu goddess Ganga.

Living Along the Ganges

The Ganges is the most well-known of all the South Asian rivers. It flows more than 1,500 miles from its source in a Himalayan glacier to the Bay of Bengal. Along the way, it drains a huge area nearly three times the size of France. This area is home to about 350 million people. Although it is shorter than both the Indus and Brahmaputra rivers, the impact of the Ganges on human life in the region is enormous.

A SACRED RIVER The Ganges is extremely important for the livelihood of Indians. It provides water for drinking, farming, and transportation. Just as important, though, is the spiritual significance of the river. The Ganges is known in India as *Gangamai,* which means "Mother Ganges." In Bangladesh, where the Ganges joins the Brahmaputra, the river is called the Padma. According to Hindu beliefs, the Ganges is a sacred river that brings life to its people. As you read above, the Hindus worship the river as a goddess, and they believe its waters have healing powers.

Many temples and sacred sites line the banks of the Ganges. In some places, wide stone steps lead down to the water. Pilgrims come from all parts of the world to drink and bathe in its waters. They also come to scatter the ashes of deceased family members on the river.

At Varanasi (shown at right), one of the most sacred sites on the Ganges, thousands of people gather every day. As the sun rises, Hindu pilgrims enter the water for purification and prayer. They float baskets of flowers and burning candles on the water, as bells ring and trumpeters blow on conch shells. It is a daily celebration of their faith in the Ganges and its sacred waters.

SECTION 3 PROGRAM RESOURCES

In-Depth Resources: Unit 8
- Guided Reading, p. 5
- Skillbuilder Practice, p. 8
- Building Vocabulary, p. 9
- Reteaching Activity, p. 12

Guided Reading Workbook
- Section 3

Access for Students Acquiring English/ESL
- Guided Reading, p. 129
- Skillbuilder Practice, p. 130

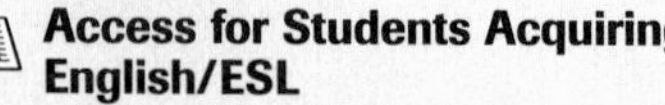

Formal Assessment
- Section Quiz, p. 374

Integrated Assessment
- Rubric for a written report, 2.5
- Rubric for a presentation, 5.4

INTEGRATED TECHNOLOGY

Power Presentations

Test Generator
- Section Quiz

TEST-TAKING RESOURCES

Strategies for Test Preparation

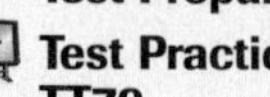

Test Practice Transparencies TT79

Online Test Practice

A POLLUTED RIVER Unfortunately for the people of India, the Ganges is in trouble. After centuries of intense human use, it has become one of the most polluted rivers in the world. Millions of gallons of raw sewage and industrial waste flow into the river every day. The bodies of dead animals float on the water. Even human corpses are thrown into the river. As a result, the water is poisoned with toxic chemicals and deadly bacteria. Thousands of people who bathe in the river or drink the water become ill with stomach or intestinal diseases. Some develop life-threatening illnesses, such as hepatitis, typhoid, or cholera.

Since 1986, the Indian government has tried to restore the health of the river. Plans have called for a network of sewage treatment plants to clean up the water and for tougher regulations on industrial polluters. So far, however, progress has been slow. Few of the proposed treatment plants are in operation, and factories and cities are still dumping waste into the river.

Pollution in the Ganges remains an enormous problem. It will take a great deal of time, effort, and money to clean up the river. It will also require a change in the way people view the river. According to many Hindu believers, the Ganges is too holy to be harmed by pollution. If there is a problem with the water, they believe that "Mother Ganges" will fix it.

The Ganges River

Length	1,560 miles
Source	Gangotri glacier, western Himalayas, 10,302 feet above sea level
Mouth	Bay of Bengal
Delta Area	65,500 square miles in India and Bangladesh
Name, in Hindi	Gangamai, or Ganga

SKILLBUILDER: Interpreting Maps

REGION Which countries are part of the Ganges river basin?

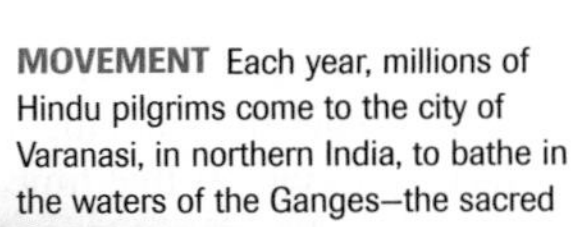

MOVEMENT Each year, millions of Hindu pilgrims come to the city of Varanasi, in northern India, to bathe in the waters of the Ganges—the sacred river of their religion.

SOUTH ASIA

561

Interpreting Maps

The Ganges River

Have students read the chart and then locate the source and the mouth of the Ganges. Ask them to identify the general direction in which the river flows. *(northwest to southeast)*

SKILLBUILDER ANSWER India, Bangladesh, Nepal, Bhutan

DIFFERENTIATING INSTRUCTION LESS PROFICIENT READERS

IDENTIFYING PROPER NOUNS

Objective Identify and briefly define proper nouns

Class Time 20 minutes

Task Create a list of proper nouns that appear in the section

Directions Review with students the definition of a proper noun (the name of a particular person, place, or thing) and remind them that proper nouns begin with a capital letter. Tell students that they will be reading about the interaction of South Asians with important rivers. Have students identify the proper noun that names a river in each main heading and write the full name of each in their notebooks. *(Ganges River, Feni River)* Tell students to add to the list of proper nouns as they read the section and to supply one- or two-word definitions as they do so. *(Example: Hinduism-religion)*

Interpreting Photographs

Building the Feni River Dam

Ask students how the photograph depicts interaction between humans and their environment. *(The people building the dam are attempting to change their environment by controlling the river's flood waters.)*

CAPTION ANSWER Unskilled labor is cheap, and Bangladesh is a relatively poor country with a large population but few financial and technological resources.

Instruct: Objective 2

Controlling the Feni River

- How did the Feni River cause hardship for the people of Bangladesh? *(Flooding–often intensified by storm surges–caused great destruction.)*
- What solution did the Bangladeshis decide on? *(building a dam)*
- What was the main means of implementation? *(manual labor)*
- What crucial test did the dam pass? *(It held against a storm surge.)*

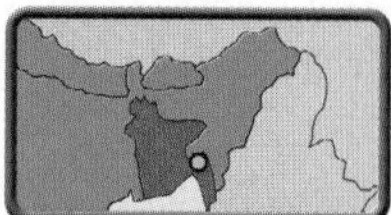

HUMAN-ENVIRONMENT INTERACTION Bangladeshi workers carry hundred-pound bags of clay across the Feni River bottom at low tide. The bags were used in the construction of the dam pictured on the next page. **What might be a reason for using people rather than trucks for this job?**

Controlling the Feni River

Just as the Ganges is the lifeblood of India, the rivers of Bangladesh are crucial to that country's survival. Many rivers emerge from the Chittagong Hills in the southeast. One of these rivers is the Feni, which flows into the Bay of Bengal just east of the huge delta that makes up most of the southern part of the country. The Feni begins as a small hill stream, but it becomes a wide, slow-moving river by the time it enters the bay. A

Geographic Thinking

Using the Atlas

A Use the map on page 543. Find the highest elevated area in Bangladesh–the Chittagong Hills. What is their elevation?

A. Answer at least 1,600 feet above sea level

A RIVER OVERFLOWS The Feni flows through a low-lying coastal plain that borders the Bay of Bengal before it reaches the sea. This flat, marshy area is subject to flooding during the wet season. At that time, monsoon rains swell the river and may cause it to overflow its banks. Also a problem are the cyclones that sweep across the Bay of Bengal. They bring high waters—called **storm surges**—that swamp low-lying areas. You saw a photo of this area on page 552.

Over the years, storm surges at the mouth of the Feni River have caused tremendous hardship. Sea water surges up the river and onto the coastal flatlands. Villages and fields are flooded, causing great destruction. On smaller streams, villagers sometimes build earthen dikes to block the water and protect their farmlands. But such structures are not effective against the flooding of large rivers.

In the 1980s, engineers in Bangladesh proposed building an earthen dam for the Feni. Closing the Feni to build the dam would be very difficult, though. The mouth of the river is nearly a mile wide, posing major problems for dam construction. The cost of building such a dam would also be enormous. A poor country like Bangladesh has limited financial and technological resources.

USING PEOPLE POWER Bangladesh did have one key asset for such a project—abundant human resources. With its large population, the country had plenty of unskilled workers available for construction work. To help plan the job, Bangladesh hired engineers from the Netherlands. As you read in Unit 4, the Dutch have had great experience in flood control.

ACTIVITY OPTION **INTERNET RESEARCH**

BLOCK SCHEDULING

WRITING A NEWS UPDATE

Objective To obtain updated information on flood control in Bangladesh

Class Time 45 minutes

Task Write a report summarizing flooding and flood control in Bangladesh since 1985

Directions Have students search the Internet for updated information on flooding and flood control in Bangladesh since 1985. Tell them to use the information to write a brief report summarizing the information. Direct students to **hmhsocialstudies.com** for updated links.

OPTIONAL ACTIVITY If access to the Internet is limited, have students use an index such as *The Readers' Guide to Periodical Literature* to find magazine and newspaper articles on the subject.

From the beginning in 1984, the project emphasized the use of cheap materials and low-tech procedures. The first step was to lay down heavy mats made of bamboo, and reeds weighted with boulders. This was done to prevent erosion of the river bottom. Workers piled more boulders on top and then covered them with clay-filled bags. After six months' work, they had built a partial closure across the mouth of the Feni River.

At that point, gaps in the wall still allowed water to flow in and out. Engineers had chosen February 28, 1985—the day of lowest tides—as the day to close the river. When the tide went out, 15,000 workers rushed to fill in the gaps with clay bags. In a seven-hour period, they laid down 600,000 bags. When the tide came back, the dam was closed.

B. Answer Dams like the one on the Feni can control the overflow of water caused by storms, saving lives and property.

COMPLETING THE DAM After that, dump trucks and earthmovers added more clay to raise the dam to a height of 30 feet. Then, workers placed concrete and brick over the sides of the dam and built a road on top. Bangladesh now had the largest **estuary** (an arm of the sea at the lower end of a river) dam in South Asia. But a crucial question remained—would the dam hold against a major storm?

The test came three months later, when a cyclone roared into the Bay of Bengal. A storm surge hit the dam, but the dam held. The lands and villages behind the dam were spared the worst effects of the storm. The success of the Feni River closure offers hope for similar solutions in other low-lying areas of Bangladesh and South Asia. B

Connect to the Issues
EXTREME WEATHER
B Why might dams such as the one on the Feni River help to prevent the effects of extreme weather?

In this chapter, you read about the physical geography of South Asia. In the next chapter, you will learn about the human geography of the region—its history, government, economy, and culture.

Section 3 Assessment

1 Places & Terms
Identify and explain the significance of each in the region.
- Hinduism
- Ganges River
- storm surge
- estuary

2 Taking Notes
PLACE Review the notes you took for this section.

- What do the people of India call the Ganges River?
- Why do pilgrims visit the Ganges?

3 Main Ideas
a. What is the spiritual significance of the Ganges for India's Hindus?
b. Why are rituals performed in the Ganges dangerous?
c. How have Bangladesh is sought to prevent storm surges from flooding coastal lowlands?

4 Geographic Thinking
Making Inferences Why might pilgrims continue to bathe in and drink water from the Ganges River even though it is polluted? **Think about:**
- how much pilgrims know about the river
- the religious importance of the river

SOUTH ASIA

GeoActivity

EXPLORING LOCAL GEOGRAPHY Learn more about common religious beliefs where you live. Are there places in your community that believers hold to be sacred? Create a **report** that describes your findings.

Assess & Reteach

GeoFocus Have students complete the GeoFocus chart they began at the start of this chapter.

Formal Assessment
- Section Quiz, p. 374

Reteaching Activity
Have students take turns defining the places and terms on page 560. After each word has been defined, have volunteers tell how the term relates to interaction between humans and the environment in South Asia.

In-Depth Resources: Unit 8
- Reteaching Activity, p. 12

Section 3 Assessment Answers

1. Places & Terms
Hinduism, p. 560
Ganges River, p. 560
storm surge, p. 562
estuary, p. 563

2. Taking Notes
- Gangamai, or "Mother Ganges," or Ganga
- to drink and bathe in its sacred waters and to scatter the ashes of deceased family members in the river

3. Main Ideas
a. They worship the river as a goddess and believe that it can heal.
b. The river is polluted with sewage and industrial waste and, therefore, can cause illness.
c. by building a dam across the Feni River, for example

4. Geographic Thinking
Some people may be unaware of the severity of the pollution. For others, the importance of religious observance may outweigh concerns for personal safety. Also, many believe that "Mother Ganges" will fix the pollution problem.

GeoActivity

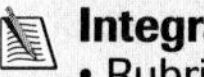
Integrated Assessment
- Rubric for a written report, 2.5

CHAPTER 24 ASSESSMENT

Reviewing Places & Terms

A.
1. Himalaya Mountains, p. 551
2. subcontinent, p. 551
3. archipelago, p. 553
4. atoll, p. 553
5. monsoon, p. 557
6. cyclone, p. 557
7. Hinduism, p. 560
8. Ganges River, p. 560
9. storm surge, p. 562
10. estuary, p. 563

B. Possible Responses

11. The Maldives form an archipelago.
12. Hinduism is the religion of most of India's people.
13. The world's tallest peak is in the Himalaya Mountains.
14. The Ganges River is supposedly home to the goddess.
15. Cyclones form the most extreme weather pattern.
16. Subcontinent is another name for South Asia's landmass.
17. An estuary is the broad seaward end of a river mouth.
18. Storm surges are caused by cyclones in the Bay of Bengal.
19. Monsoons play a large role in South Asia.
20. An atoll is the top of a submerged volcano surrounded by coral reefs.

Chapter 24 Assessment

VISUAL SUMMARY
PHYSICAL GEOGRAPHY OF SOUTH ASIA

Landforms

Mountains and Plateaus: Himalayas, Hindu Kush, Karakoram Mountains, Eastern and Western Ghats, and Vindhya Range; Deccan and Karnataka plateaus

Rivers, Deserts, and Plains: Indus, Ganges, and Brahmaputra rivers; Thar Desert; Indo-Gangetic Plain

Islands: Sri Lanka, Maldives Archipelago

Resources

- South Asia counts heavily on its soil and water resources for farming, fishing, transportation, and power.
- Coal, petroleum, uranium, and natural gas are plentiful in South Asia. The region also boasts large deposits of iron ore and other minerals, as well as substantial but dwindling timber resources.

Climate and Vegetation

- South Asia's climate ranges from frigid cold in the mountainous north to intense heat in the desert regions to the south.
- Seasonal winds, called monsoons, have an enormous impact on the region's vegetation.

Human-Environment Interaction

- The people of South Asia have strong economic and spiritual ties to their great rivers, especially the Ganges.
- Even so, the region's unpredictable storms and severe problems with water pollution have complicated these ties.

Reviewing Places & Terms

A. Briefly explain the importance of each of the following.

1. Himalaya Mountains
2. subcontinent
3. archipelago
4. atoll
5. monsoon
6. cyclone
7. Hinduism
8. Ganges River
9. storm surge
10. estuary

B. Answer the questions about vocabulary in complete sentences.

11. What geographic term above can be used to describe the Maldives?
12. What is the religion of most of India's people?
13. Where is the world's tallest mountain peak?
14. Which river is home to the Hindu goddess Gangamai?
15. What is the most extreme weather pattern in South Asia?
16. What is another name for South Asia's landmass?
17. What is the name of the broad seaward end of a river mouth?
18. What is caused by the cyclones that sweep across the Bay of Bengal?
19. What seasonal winds play a large role in South Asia?
20. What island type is the top of a submerged volcano surrounded by coral reefs?

Main Ideas

Landforms and Resources (pp. 551–555)

1. Which mountain ranges resulted from the collision of what is now the Indian subcontinent with Asia?
2. What two tectonic plates were involved in this collision?
3. In which directions do the three major rivers originating in the Himalayas flow?
4. Why is India's supply of mica important?

Climate and Vegetation (pp. 556–559)

5. When are South Asia's monsoon seasons?
6. What are the advantages and disadvantages of the southwest monsoons?
7. Why are the people in Bangladesh vulnerable to cyclones?

Human-Environment Interaction (pp. 560–563)

8. Why is the Ganges River so polluted?
9. Why do Hindu pilgrims bring the ashes of deceased family members to the river?
10. How long did it take the Bangladeshi people to build a dam across the Feni River?

Main Ideas

1. Himalaya Mountains
2. The northward moving Indian plate struck the Eurasian plate.
3. The Indus flows west then south through Pakistan; the Ganges flows eastward across northern India; and the Brahmaputra winds its way east, then west and south through Bangladesh.
4. because this mineral is a key component in electrical equipment
5. From October through February, dry monsoons blow from the northeast. From June through September, moisture-laden monsoons arrive from the southwest.
6. They bring much needed rainfall, but sometimes in such quantities that severe hardship results, especially for people in flood-prone lowlands.
7. because most of the country is located in a low-lying coastal region
8. because of inadequate sewage systems and the under-regulated disposal of industrial waste and human and animal remains
9. because the river is sacred to Hindus
10. about a year, during 1984–1985

Critical Thinking

1. Using Your Notes
Use your completed chart to answer these questions.

Landforms	
Resources	

a. Where is the Deccan Plateau?
b. What is the most heavily populated plain in South Asia?

2. Geographic Themes
a. LOCATION Which bay is located south of Bangladesh?
b. PLACE Which island's center is dominated by a range of high rugged mountains?

3. Identifying Themes
How can you explain the enormous wall of mountain ranges that separate South Asia from the rest of Asia? Which of the five themes applies to this situation?

4. Making Inferences
Why might the Khyber Pass be considered of crucial military importance?

5. Making Generalizations
How does weather cause suffering in South Asia?

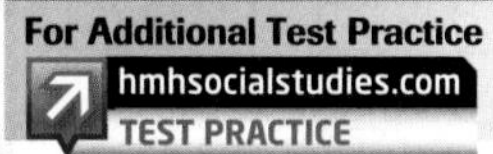

Geographic Skills: Interpreting Maps

Precipitation in South Asia
Use the maps at right to answer the following questions.
1. REGION In which season does South Asia get most of its precipitation?
2. REGION How much precipitation does central India receive during the winter?
3. PLACE How much rainfall does Bangladesh receive in the summer?

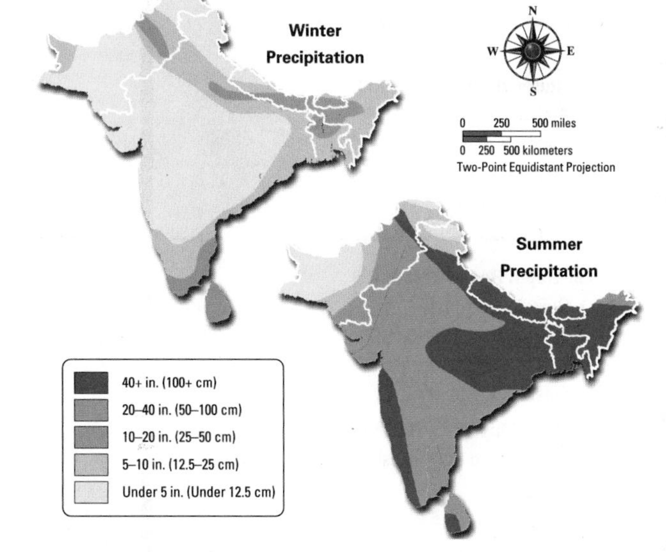

GeoActivity

Do more research on precipitation in South Asia. Focus on the drought that struck the region in 2000—what some observers have called the worst drought in 100 years. Use presentation software to share your results.

hmhsocialstudies.com
MULTIMEDIA ACTIVITY

Use the links at **hmhsocialstudies.com** to do research on the different kinds of wildlife that are found in South Asia. Try to identify specific areas in the region where these different animals live.

Creating a Sketch Map Use your research to create a sketch map that shows the locations of different animal habitats. Add pictures and captions to your map. Use the captions to explain why the locations are suited to specific animals.

SOUTH ASIA

Critical Thinking

1. a. It covers much of southern India.
b. Indo-Gangetic Plain
2. a. Bay of Bengal
b. Sri Lanka
3. the collision of two tectonic plates 50 million years ago; movement
4. because it is one of the few land routes between Central and South Asia
5. Lack of rainfall and hot temperatures bring drought to some South Asian regions, while too much rain and heavy winds cause floods, destruction of property, and loss of life in other regions.

GeoActivity

Integrated Assessment
• Rubric for a presentation, 5.4

Formal Assessment
• Chapter Test, Forms A, B, and C, pp. 375–386

Geographic Skills

1. summer
2. under 5 inches
3. more than 40 inches

MULTIMEDIA ACTIVITY

For the sketch map on the wildlife of South Asia, students should:
• Present a clear, well-organized overview of the location of different animal habitats.
• Explain why certain locations are suited to specific animals.
• Produce a clear, imaginative visual combining a sketch map with pictures.
• Include references to the Web sites used as sources.

Grading Rubric Evaluate student performance as Exceptional, Acceptable, or Poor in each of the following categories:

	Exceptional	Acceptable	Poor
Sketch map is clear, focused, and logical			
Provides necessary facts and examples			
Uses pictures and captions to illustrate and explain map			
Captions use correct grammar, spelling, and punctuation			

CHAPTER 25 PLANNING GUIDE

Human Geography of South Asia

OVERVIEW	INSTRUCTIONAL RESOURCES	
ESSENTIAL QUESTION How have various cultures affected South Asia's past and present? **Focus on the Essential Question Podcast**	**In-Depth Resources: Unit 8** • Building Vocabulary, p. 18 **Block Schedule Strategies** **Chapter Summaries** (English/Spanish) **Video:** Mahatma Gandhi hmhsocialstudies.com INTERACTIVE	**Interactive Online Edition** TOS **ExamView® Assessment Suite** (English/Spanish) TOS **CalendarPlanner** **Power Presentations with Media Gallery** **Critical Thinking Transparencies** • CT25
SECTION 1 **INDIA** **MAIN IDEAS** • India gained independence from Britain through nonviolent resistance. • Agriculture is India's main economic activity, although industry is also important. • Hinduism is the main religion in a land of rich cultural diversity.	**In-Depth Resources: Unit 8** • Guided Reading, p. 13 • Building Vocabulary, p. 18 • Reteaching Activity, p. 19 **Outline Maps with Activities** • India, pp. 79–80 **Cultures Around the World** • Architecture, p. 43 • Daily Life, p. 44 • Arts and Crafts, p. 46 • Literature, p. 48	**Map Transparencies** • MT44 Ancient Empires of South Asia **Critical Thinking Transparencies** • CT57 The Lives of Gandhi and Nehru **Cultures Transparencies CW43, 44, 46, 48** • Swayambhunath • Wearing Saris • Brass Work • from the *Ramayana* **Guided Reading Workbook,** Section 1
SECTION 2 **PAKISTAN AND BANGLADESH** **MAIN IDEAS** • Pakistan and Bangladesh are new countries that were once part of India. • Both Pakistan and Bangladesh are largely dependent on agriculture. • Islam is the main religion in both countries and strongly influences culture.	**In-Depth Resources: Unit 8** • Guided Reading, p. 14 • Skillbuilder Practice, p. 17 • Building Vocabulary, p. 18 • Reteaching Activity, p. 20 **Outline Maps with Activities** • Pakistan and Bangladesh, pp. 81–82 **Cultures** • Music, p. 47	**Cultures Transparencies** • CW47 Playing the Drums **Guided Reading Workbook,** Section 2
SECTION 3 **NEPAL AND BHUTAN** **MAIN IDEAS** • Nepal and Bhutan are remote mountain kingdoms. • Tourism represents a means of economic growth in both countries. • Most Nepalese are Hindus, while Buddhism is the official religion of Bhutan.	**In-Depth Resources: Unit 8** • Guided Reading, p. 15 • Building Vocabulary, p. 18 • Reteaching Activity, p. 21 **Outline Maps with Activities** • Nepal and Bhutan, pp. 83–84 **Cultures Around the World** • Traditional Practices, p. 45	**Cultures Transparencies** • CW45 Celebrating Tshechu **Guided Reading Workbook,** Section 3 **The World's Music Audio Program**
SECTION 4 **SRI LANKA AND THE MALDIVES** **MAIN IDEAS** • Tensions between Sri Lanka's two main ethnic groups, the Sinhalese and the Tamils, has led to civil war. • Sri Lanka and the Maldives are ethnically diverse, with religion playing a major role in both cultures. • Global warming threatens the Maldives with obliteration through flooding.	**In-Depth Resources: Unit 8** • Guided Reading, p. 16 • Building Vocabulary, p. 18 • Reteaching Activity, p. 22 **Outline Maps with Activities** • Indian Ocean, pp. 85–86 **Guided Reading Workbook,** Section 4	

ASSESSMENT

SE Chapter Assessment, pp. 590–591

Formal Assessment
- Chapter Tests, Forms A, B, and C, pp. 391–402

TOS ExamView® Assessment Suite

Strategies for Test Preparation

SE Section Assessment, p. 572

Formal Assessment
- Section Quiz, p. 387

Integrated Assessment
- Rubric for a political cartoon, 1.2

Test Practice Transparencies TT80

SE Section Assessment, p. 577

Formal Assessment

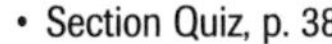

- Section Quiz, p. 388

Integrated Assessment

- Rubric for a chart, 2.2
- Rubric for a press release, 4.10

Test Practice Transparencies TT81

Formal Assessment

- Section Quiz, p. 389

Integrated Assessment

- Rubric for a letter, 4.3

Test Practice Transparencies TT82

SE Section Assessment, p. 587
- Section Quiz, p. 390

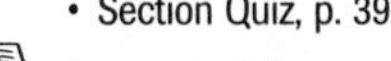

Integrated Assessment

- Rubric for a travel poster, 1.1
- Rubric for a multimedia presentation, 5.4

Test Practice Transparencies TT83

CHART KEY:

SE Student Edition

Block Scheduling

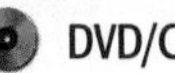

DVD/CD-ROM

TE Teacher's Edition

TOS Teacher One Stop

MP3 Audio

Printable Resource

Presentation Resource

HISTORY™

Program Resources available on TOS and @ hmhsocialstudies.com

SUPPORTING RESOURCES

- Multimedia Classroom Global History Series
- Global History Teacher's Guide

Social Studies Trade Library Collection
- Modern World History Trade Collectiion

For more information or to purchase these resources, go to hmhsocialstudies.com

DIFFERENTIATED INSTRUCTION

English Learners

Spanish/English Guided Reading Workbook

Access for Students Acquiring English/ESL
Spanish Translations, pp. 133–137

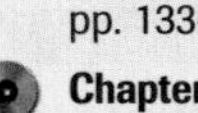

Chapter Summaries
(English/Spanish)

TE **TE Activity**
Increasing Vocabulary, p. 575

Struggling Readers

Chapter Summaries
(English/Spanish)

TE **TE Activity**
Previewing Economic Terms, p. 581

Gifted and Talented Students

TE **TE Activity**
Writing on Women Prime Ministers, p. 574
Summarizing a Book, p. 582

ENRICHMENT ACTIVITIES

The following activities are especially suitable for classes following block schedules.

SE **Student Edition,** pp. 566–587
- Disasters! The Cyclone of 1970, pp. 578–579
- Comparing Cultures: Musical Instruments, pp. 588–589

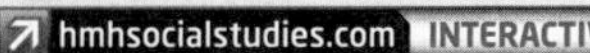

- Ancient Empires of India, p. 567
- Comparing Cultures: Musical Instruments, pp. 588–589

BLOCK SCHEDULE LESSON PLAN OPTIONS: 90-MINUTE PERIOD

DAY 1

SECTION 1, pp. 567–572
Class Time 90 minutes

- **Documentary** Have students create an outline for a documentary emphasizing India's diversity and complexity. Organize students into small groups, assigning a chapter section to each. Have groups share and compare their work.
  Class Time 45 minutes
- **Skillbuilder Lesson** Use the Activity Option about making comparisons on TE page 568 and the Skillbuilder Practice worksheet.
  Class Time 45 minutes

DAY 2

SECTION 2, pp. 573–579
Class Time 45 minutes

- **Comparing Pakistan and Bangladesh** Have students define each place and term and tell what relationship it has to Pakistan, Bangladesh, or both. Ask students to decide whether the term represents a difference or a similarity between the two countries. (Some terms may be interpreted as either.) Then tell students to find other differences and similarities within the section. Have them keep track of these items in their notebooks.

SECTION 3, pp. 580–583
Class Time 45 minutes

- **Venn Diagram** Tell students that a Venn diagram is a useful way to keep track of similarities and differences. Draw a Venn diagram on the chalkboard. Ask students what Nepal and Bhutan have in common in terms of geographic features, government, economies, religion, and cultural life. Note them in the overlapping section. Tell students to copy the diagram and to label the remaining two sections Nepal (left side) and Bhutan (right side). Have students complete the diagram by noting specific details that may differ between countries. Then complete the diagram on the board with the class.

DAY 3

SECTION 4, pp. 584–589
Class Time 35 minutes

- **Essay** Have students write a brief essay on the Maldives and Sri Lanka, in which they include information on the past, present, and future of the islands.

CHAPTER 25 REVIEW AND ASSESSMENT, pp. 590–591
Class Time 55 minutes

- **Review** Review the chapter by having students identify the countries in each subregion of South Asia. Have them determine why each country or pair of countries would qualify as a subregion. (Tell them to begin by thinking about climate, landforms, and location.)
  Class Time 20 minutes
- **Assessment** Have students complete the Chapter 25 Assessment.
  Class Time 35 minutes

TEACHER-TESTED ACTIVITY

Reactions to Natural Disasters

Class Time 2 to 3 class periods

Task Create a news documentary on an historic natural disaster and the government's, citizens', and international community's response

Supplies
- Research time in the media center or Internet laboratory

Purpose To recognize the parallels between the effects of monsoons in South Asia with natural disasters in other regions of the world. This research activity will allow students to discover how different people reacted to the disaster. They will also examine the area today and uncover what precautions, if any, the government and/or people have made against further disasters.

Activity Students should select a natural disaster in a region other than South Asia to research. Students should examine how local and international governments reacted, and decide if their actions were appropriate. The students should compare and contrast the governments' reactions with those of individuals. Again, they should determine if these actions were appropriate. Finally, they should examine the region today and discover what measures governments and individuals have taken to combat future disasters. They should comment about whether or not they feel these actions will be successful. Once the research phase is completed students should compile their findings into a television news program documenting the disaster.

Jewel Berryman
Geography Teacher, Kashmere High School, Houston, Texas

TECHNOLOGY IN THE CLASSROOM

One of the advantages of teaching with the Internet is that it offers an incredible variety of photographs and other images to help supplement textbook material. These images are sometimes presented as "slide shows" in which the user clicks through a series of images, usually with brief captions under each one.

Objective Students will view a slide show of the Indus Valley region to learn more about the early Indus Valley civilization and to see what it looks like in this part of South Asia.

Task Have students view an Internet slide show of the Indus Valley civilization, including pictures of the landscape, excavation sites, and artifacts that have been excavated. Ask them to share their findings with the class.

Class Time 2-3 class periods (including presentations)

1. Have students read about the Indus Valley civilization on pages 567 and 573.
2. Ask students to locate the Indus River on the map on page 545. What countries does it run through?
3. Divide the class into six groups. Ask each group to go through fifteen of the slides in the Indus Valley slide show available through **hmhsocialstudies.com**.
4. Ask students to take notes that answer these questions for each slide: What is pictured in the slide? If shown, what does the landscape look like? What does the slide and caption reveal about life in the ancient Indus Valley civilization? What does the slide and caption reveal about the modern-day Indus Valley?
5. Have each group choose two slides to share with the rest of the class. They should briefly describe each slide and explain what the slide reveals about ancient and modern life in the Indus Valley. If you have a computer projection device in the classroom, groups can save the slides on the computer and show them to the class.
6. Discuss as a class how the slide show helped "bring to life" what they read in the textbook about the Indus Valley civilization and this part of South Asia. What additional information did they gain from viewing the slides? What do the slides show about the landscape and natural environment? What do the slides show about ancient and modern cultures?

CHAPTER 25 OBJECTIVE

Identify features of human geography in the seven countries of South Asia.

Chapter 25
HUMAN GEOGRAPHY OF SOUTH ASIA
A Region of Contrasts

hmhsocialstudies.com VIDEO

Interpreting Maps

Four Subregions of South Asia

Have students look at the map and identify the countries that make up the four subregions of South Asia. Ask them to analyze what the countries in each group have in common.

Introducing the Essential Question

- Introduce the topics of religious and ethnic conflict in South Asia. Point out that these conflicts developed out of the waves of invasion that the region has experienced—invasions that began centuries ago.
- Ask students how South Asia has been portrayed in the media. Emphasize that the region is one of dramatic contrasts—from sumptuous palaces to high-tech companies, villages frozen in time to cities humming with activity.

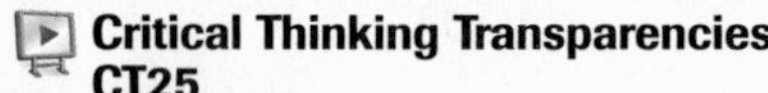

Have students complete cluster diagrams in their notebooks using material from all sections in this chapter.

Critical Thinking Transparencies CT25
- GeoFocus

In-Depth Resources: Unit 8
- Building Vocabulary, p. 18

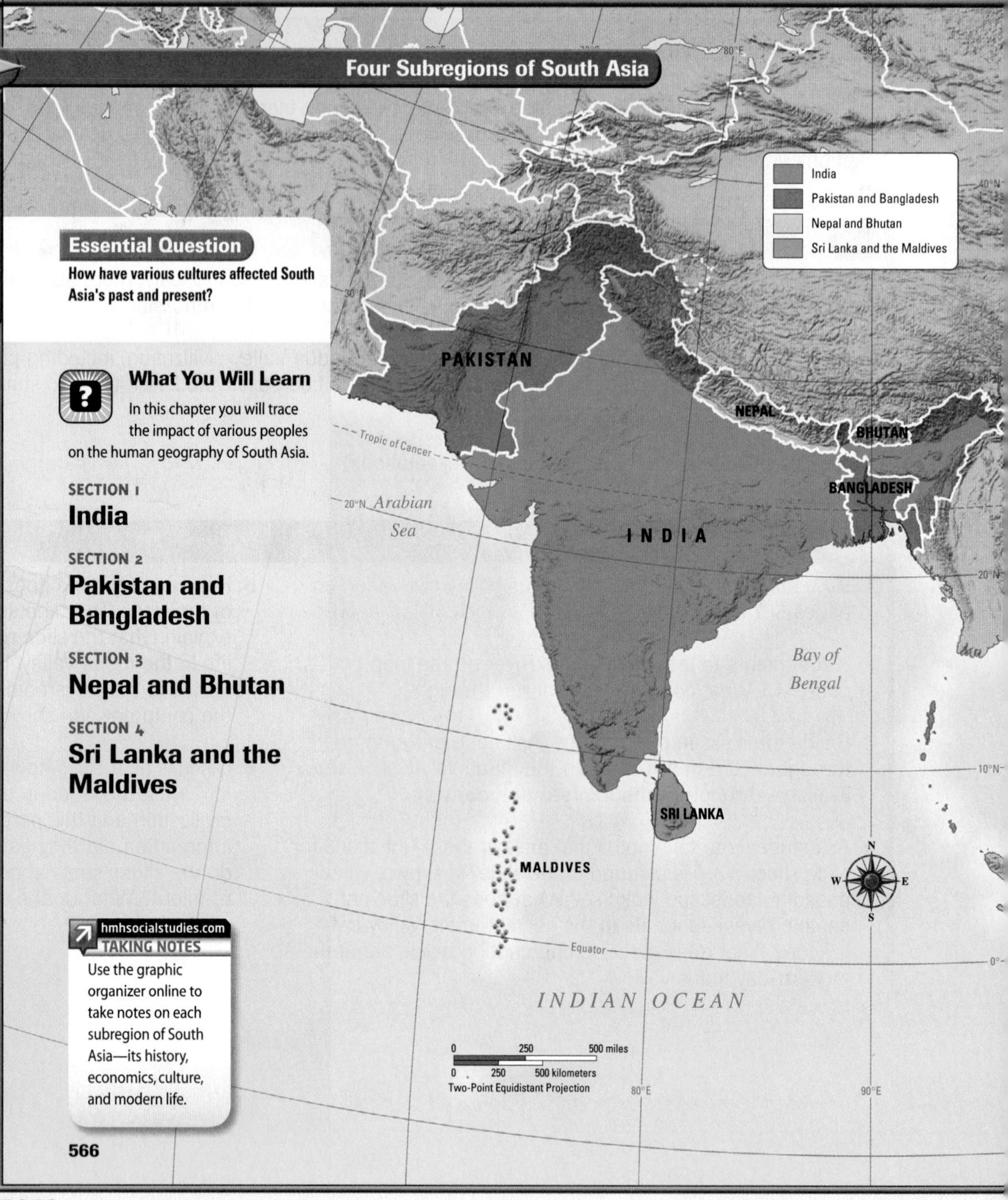

Four Subregions of South Asia

India
Pakistan and Bangladesh
Nepal and Bhutan
Sri Lanka and the Maldives

PAKISTAN
NEPAL
BHUTAN
BANGLADESH
INDIA
SRI LANKA
MALDIVES
Arabian Sea
Bay of Bengal
INDIAN OCEAN
Tropic of Cancer
Equator
Two-Point Equidistant Projection

Essential Question

How have various cultures affected South Asia's past and present?

What You Will Learn

In this chapter you will trace the impact of various peoples on the human geography of South Asia.

SECTION 1
India

SECTION 2
Pakistan and Bangladesh

SECTION 3
Nepal and Bhutan

SECTION 4
Sri Lanka and the Maldives

hmhsocialstudies.com TAKING NOTES

Use the graphic organizer online to take notes on each subregion of South Asia—its history, economics, culture, and modern life.

566

CHAPTER 25 ADDITIONAL RESOURCES

BOOKS FOR THE TEACHER

Bryant, Edwin F. and Laurie L. Patton, eds. ***The Indo-Aryan Controversy: Evidence and Inference in Indian History.*** Routledge, 2005. Survey of the arguments about the origins of Indian culture.

BOOKS FOR THE STUDENT

Whyte, Mariam. ***Bangladesh.*** Tarrytown, NY: Marshall Cavendish, 1999. A brief history of the country that was known as East Pakistan before it became independent.

Wanasundera, Nanda P. ***Sri Lanka.*** North Bellmore, NY: Marshall Cavendish, 1991. Tells the story of how the former colony of Ceylon became a nation.

VIDEOS

Bhutan: The Last Shangri-La. PBS Home Video. (The Living Edens series.) 1997. This haven for wild creatures reflects the Bhutanese respect for all living things.

Gandhi. Richard Attenborough, dir. Columbia Tristar Home Video, 1982. Biography of Mohandas Ghandi, and his role in Indian independence.

INTERNET

For more on the human geography of South Asia, visit . . .

hmhsocialstudies.com

1 India

Main Ideas

- India is the largest country in South Asia and has the most developed economy.
- Indian culture is deeply influenced by religion.

Places & Terms

Mughal Empire
raj
nonviolent resistance
land reform
Green Revolution
caste system

CONNECT TO THE ISSUES
POPULATION India's huge and diverse population presents many social, economic, and political challenges.

A HUMAN PERSPECTIVE At midnight on August 14, 1997, India celebrated the 50th anniversary of its independence from Great Britain. Thousands of people flooded the streets of the capital, New Delhi, and waved the orange, white, and green flag of India. Fifty years before, Prime Minister Jawaharlal Nehru had spoken to the nation. "A moment comes," he said, "when we step out from the old to the new, . . . and when the soul of a nation, long suppressed, finds utterance [expression]." Since then, India has emerged as a modern and powerful country. But it has also preserved its links to the past.

Invasions, Empires, and Independence

India is an ancient land. Its culture and history date back more than 4,000 years. For centuries, foreign invaders came to conquer India but were absorbed into Indian life. As a result, Indian culture is a blend of many different customs and traditions.

EARLY HISTORY Indian civilization began in the Indus Valley (now in Pakistan) around 2500 B.C. A thousand years later, invaders crossed the mountains of the Hindu Kush and spread across northern India. They were Aryans, a light-skinned people from the plains north of Iran. Aryan culture played a key role in the development of Indian civilization.

The Aryans established small kingdoms on the Ganges Plain. They pushed darker-skinned, native Indians, called Dravidians, toward the south. Later, Persian and Greek invaders occupied the Indus Valley. But they did not conquer the Aryan kingdoms of the Ganges.

Two great Indian empires eventually emerged on the lower Ganges. Beginning in 321 B.C., the Mauryan Empire united most of India. The great Mauryan leader Asoka helped spread Buddhism throughout Asia. Several centuries later, the Gupta Empire came to power. It ruled over northern India during an age of peace and prosperity.

New waves of invaders from Central Asia and, later, Southwest Asia began entering India in the A.D. fifth century. Muslims conquered the Indus

Ancient Empires of India

hmhsocialstudies.com INTERACTIVE MAP

SKILLBUILDER: Interpreting Maps
1. **LOCATION** What is the farthest north-south and east-west extent of the Gupta Empire?
2. **MOVEMENT** Which empire moved farthest south?

SECTION 1 OBJECTIVES

1. Learn about foreign rule and independence in India.
2. Define the nature of India's government and identify some of its challenges.
3. Understand the basics of India's economy.
4. Learn about life in modern India.
5. Explore Indian culture with respect to diversity and religion.

SKILLBUILDERS: Interpreting Maps, pp. 567, 569

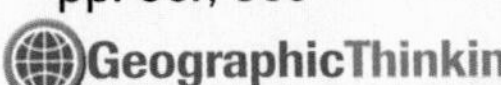

Using the Atlas, p. 568
Seeing Patterns, p. 569
Making Comparisons, p. 570
Making Inferences, p. 572

Focus & Motivate

Have students name important political figures in India. Then ask them to name familiar aspects of Indian culture. *(Answers will vary but may include Gandhi and the Nehrus; Hinduism, elephants, tigers, saris, spicy food)*

Instruct: Objective 1 appears on p. 568

SOUTH ASIA

Interpreting Maps

Ancient Empires of India

Have students look at the map and determine what physical features limited the expansion of the Mughal Empire. *(Himalayas; Indian Ocean)*

SKILLBUILDER ANSWERS 1. from about 33°N to 18°N latitude and from about 89°E to 67°E longitude **2.** the Mughal empire

SECTION 1 PROGRAM RESOURCES

In-Depth Resources: Unit 8
- Guided Reading, p. 13
- Building Vocabulary, p. 18
- Reteaching Activity, p. 19

Guided Reading Workbook
- Section 1

Access for Students Acquiring English/ESL
- Guided Reading, p. 133

Outline Maps with Activities
- India, pp. 79–80

Formal Assessment
- Section Quiz, p. 387

Integrated Assessment
- Rubric for a political cartoon, 1.2

Cultures Around the World
- Architecture, p. 43
- Daily Life, p. 44
- Arts & Crafts, p. 46
- Literature, p. 48

INTEGRATED TECHNOLOGY

Cultures Transparencies CW43, 44, 46, 48

Critical Thinking Transparencies CT57
- The Lives of Gandhi and Nehru

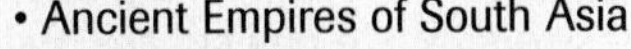

Map Transparencies MT44
- Ancient Empires of South Asia

The World's Music Audio Program

hmhsocialstudies.com

TEST-TAKING RESOURCES

Strategies for Test Preparation

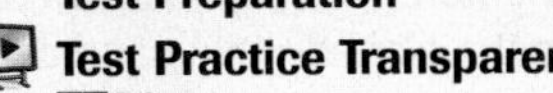

Test Practice Transparencies TT80

Online Test Practice

Interpreting Time Lines

Indian History, 1850–Present

Remind students that the history of India spans more than four thousand years. Ask what century is represented by most of the time line. *(the 20th century)* How long did Britain rule India? *(90 years)*

Instruct: Objective 

Invasions, Empires, and Independence

- How did the Mughal Empire change Indian culture? *(introduced Islam)*
- What tactic did Ghandi and his followers use? *(nonviolent resistance)*

 **In-Depth Resources: Unit 8**
- Guided Reading, p. 13

Outline Maps with Activities
- India, pp. 79–80

Map Transparencies MT44
- Ancient Empires of South Asia

Instruct: Objective 

Governing the World's Largest Democracy

- Who was India's first prime minister? *(Nehru)*
- Why are Muslim-Hindu relations of concern to the Indian government? *(The Muslim minority is huge.)*
- How have Sikhs and Tamils expressed dissatisfaction with the government? *(By assassinating two prime ministers: the Sikhs killed Indira Gandhi; the Tamils killed Rajiv Gandhi.)*

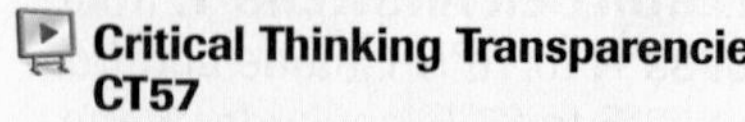

Critical Thinking Transparencies CT57
- The Lives of Gandhi and Nehru

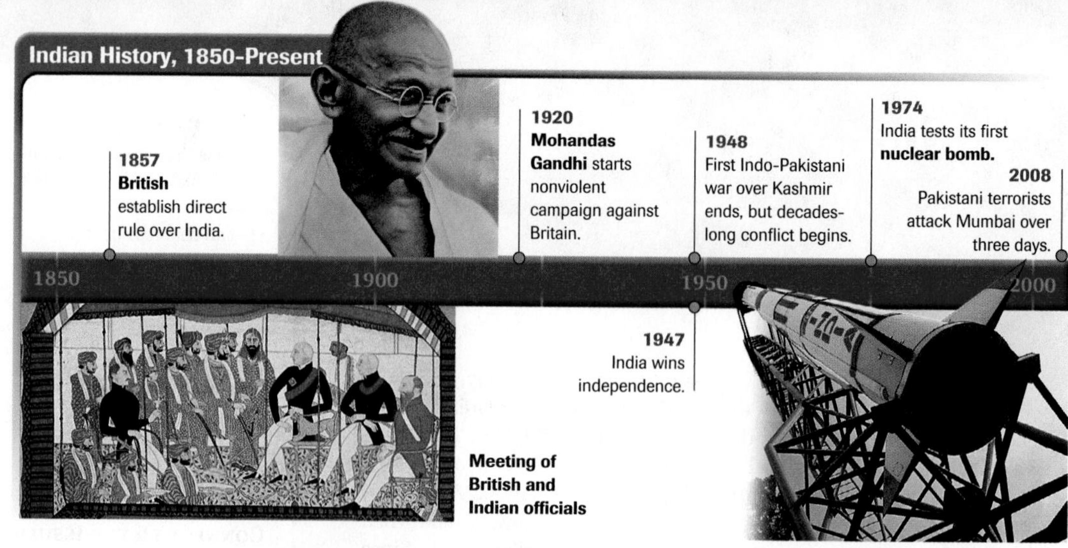

Indian History, 1850-Present
1857 British establish direct rule over India.
1920 Mohandas Gandhi starts nonviolent campaign against Britain.
1948 First Indo-Pakistani war over Kashmir ends, but decades-long conflict begins.
1974 India tests its first nuclear bomb.
2008 Pakistani terrorists attack Mumbai over three days.
1850
1900
1950
2000
1947 India wins independence.

Meeting of British and Indian officials

Valley and then occupied the Ganges Plain. By the early 1500s, they had established the **Mughal Empire** throughout much of India. Muslim rule brought new customs that sometimes conflicted with those of the native Hindus.

EUROPEANS ARRIVE Also in the 1500s, European traders came to India, looking for spices, cloth, and other goods not available in Europe. They soon established trade relations with India's rulers. French, Dutch, and Portuguese traders set up trading colonies in India—but it was the British who finally won out.

Through its trading arm, the British East India Company, Britain gained control over India's trade with Europe in 1757. In 1857, the British government put down a revolt and established direct rule over India. The period of direct British control, called the **raj,** lasted for nearly 90 years.

British rule brought some benefits to India, but most Indians did not like colonialism. The great Indian leader Mohandas Gandhi began an opposition movement based on **nonviolent resistance**—a protest movement that does not use violence to achieve its goals. Eventually, Britain gave in and granted India its freedom. At midnight on August 14, 1947, India became independent.

Independence also brought the division of India. The Muslims of West and East Pakistan (now Pakistan and Bangladesh, respectively) chose to separate from India, which was strongly Hindu, and form a separate country. This division caused violence to break out between Hindus and Muslims. Mass migrations across the new borders caused great hardship and suffering. A

A. Answer Bangladesh

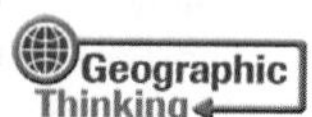

Using the Atlas

A Use the atlas on page 545. Locate India, West Pakistan (now Pakistan), and East Pakistan (now Bangladesh). Which country does not share a border with China?

Governing the World's Largest Democracy

India's first prime minister, Jawaharlal Nehru, was an associate of Gandhi. Under Nehru's leadership, India adopted a constitution and became a democratic republic in 1950. With a population of more than one billion, India is presently the world's largest democracy.

ACTIVITY OPTION | **SKILLBUILDER LESSON**

MAKING COMPARISONS

Explaining the Skill Making comparisons means looking at the similarities and differences between two or more things. Making comparisons between the United States and another country or region can provide points of reference for information about the country being studied.

Applying the Skill Have students compare the transition of the United States and India from British rule to independence. As students respond to the questions that follow, write their answers on the chalkboard under columns headed *United States* and *India.* Discuss the differences and similarity.

- When did the American colonies and India became independent from Britain? *(1776 and 1947)*
- What means did each use to obtain independence? *(America fought a war; India employed nonviolent resistance)*
- What form of government did each country choose? *(democratic republic)*

For additional Skillbuilder practice, see page 576.

Indian democracy reflects elements of both the American and the British systems. Like the United States, India is a federation of states held together by a strong central government. However, like Britain, it is a parliamentary democracy. The leader of the majority party in parliament becomes prime minister and head of the government.

Many different ethnic, cultural, and religious factors influence Indian politics. One major factor is relations between Hindus and Muslims. India is strongly Hindu, but its Muslim minority numbers around 150 million people. So, Indian leaders must take Muslim interests into account. Two other minorities, Sikhs and Tamils, also play a key role in Indian politics. In 1984, Sikhs who were angered by Indian policies assassinated Prime Minister Indira Gandhi, the daughter of Nehru. Seven years later, Tamil extremists assassinated Indira Gandhi's son, Prime Minister Rajiv Gandhi. Despite such violence, India manages to resolve most of its political conflicts peacefully. In a challenging postcolonial world, Indian democracy has survived.

BACKGROUND
Mohandas Gandhi, the founder of modern India, was also assassinated. A Hindu extremist who opposed Gandhi's attempts to resolve the Hindu-Muslim conflict killed him.

Economic Challenges

Another challenge for India is to promote economic growth and raise standards of living. The government has adopted a variety of policies to achieve these goals. But progress has been slow. India has one of the world's largest economies, but per capita income remains low. About half of India's people live in poverty.

DEPENDENCE ON FARMING About two-thirds of India's people rely on farming for their livelihood. The majority of farms, however, are very small, and crop yields are low. Most farm families struggle to survive on what they can grow for themselves.

One solution being considered for this problem is **land reform**—a more balanced distribution of land among farmers than now exists. In the late 1990s, 5 percent of India's farm families owned nearly 25 percent of India's farmland. Because the large landowners have great political influence, land-reform proposals have never made much progress. B

One change has made a major difference, though. After a series of famines in the 1960s, agricultural scientists introduced new

B. Answer
More land might allow farm families to grow more crops and might also give them more political power.

Geographic Thinking
Seeing Patterns
B What changes might come about through land reform?

Agriculture and Industry of India

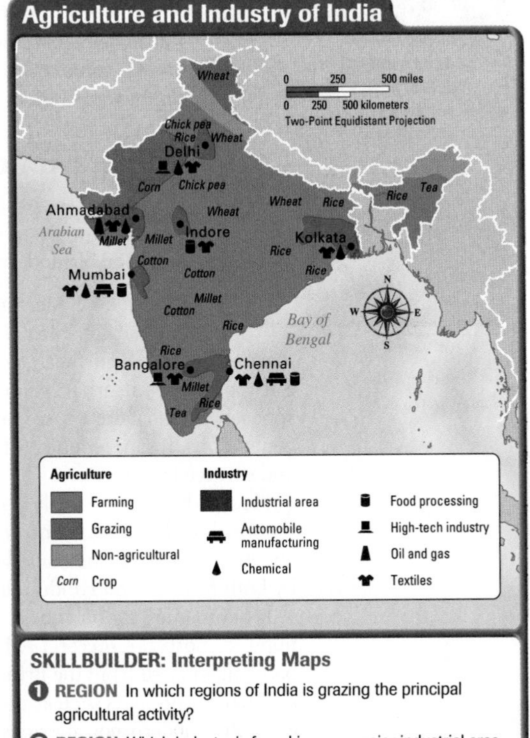

SKILLBUILDER: Interpreting Maps

1. **REGION** In which regions of India is grazing the principal agricultural activity?
2. **REGION** Which industry is found in every major industrial area of India?

SOUTH ASIA

Instruct: Objective 3

Economic Challenges

- Why has land reform been so difficult to enact? *(Powerful families control close to 25 percent of the farmland.)*
- What program has improved agricultural yield? *(the Green Revolution)* How has it done so? *(by developing higher-yielding grain varieties and using new farming techniques)*
- What industrial centers are the most progressive? *(Mumbai and Bangalore)*

Interpreting Maps

Agriculture and Industry of India

Have students locate the industrial areas on the map. How are they alike? *(They each have at least one city)* Why? *(Industry requires many workers.)* Ask students what they notice about the location of cities in industrial areas. *(Most are on the coasts.)* Why might this be an advantage? *(access to shipping both for importing raw materials and exporting finished goods)*

SKILLBUILDER ANSWERS 1. north and northwestern India
2. textiles

ACTIVITY OPTION **INTERNET RESEARCH**

BLOCK SCHEDULING

PROVIDING AN ECONOMIC UPDATE

Objective To obtain current information on India's rice production

Class Time 30 minutes

Task Write a brief report on the economic significance of India's rice crop

Directions Have students search the Internet to find information on the importance of rice to India's economy. Their report should include as much of the following data as possible: how much rice is raised, consumed domestically, and exported. Students also should compare production with previous years and with that of other rice-producing countries. They may wish to include a graph.

OPTIONAL ACTIVITY If Internet access is limited, students may consult reference books and indexes such as *Facts on File* for articles about the subject.

Geography TODAY

The Green Revolution

Although India has succeeded in raising enough food to feed its people, problems of distribution and potential threats to the environment remain. Besides introducing high-yielding hybrid seeds and improved irrigation methods, India's Green Revolution has relied heavily on fertilizers and pesticides. How might such innovations prove harmful? *(Pesticide residues may impair the health of humans; insects often develop immunities to pesticides, which leads farmers to use increasingly toxic chemicals.)*

Instruct: Objective 4

Life in Modern India

- What is the center of daily life? *(marriage and family)*
- How are traditional marriages different from most marriages in the United States? *(They are arranged by the families.)*
- What popular leisure activities are similar to those in the United States? *(sports, music, films)*
- Why has India's government placed a high priority on education? *(Raising low literacy rates is essential if Indians are to find work in factories and offices.)*

Geography TODAY

The Green Revolution

India could not feed its vast population in the 1950s. It needed foreign aid. Today, with a population of more than one billion, India is self-sufficient. The turnaround resulted from what was called the Green Revolution.

Starting in the 1950s, scientists set out to change the way Indians farmed. They proposed expanded use of machinery and increased irrigation, as well as trying chemical fertilizers and new types of high-yield crops. Today, India even grows a surplus of such crops as wheat and rice.

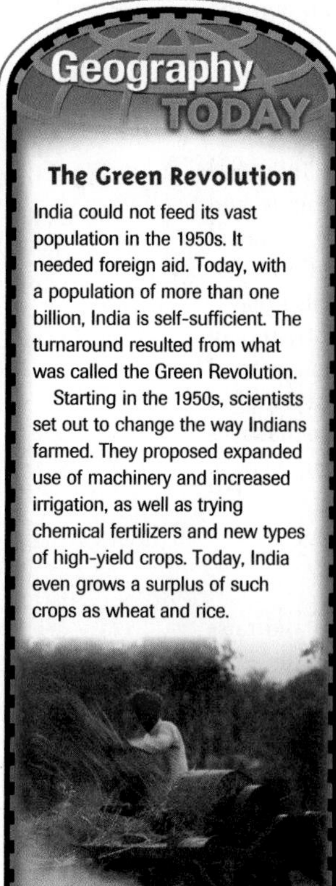

farming techniques and higher-yielding grain varieties to improve production. This program, later called the **Green Revolution,** increased crop yields. The increases were especially dramatic for wheat, but rice production also expanded. Still, many peasant farmers lack the land and money to take advantage of these technological improvements.

GROWING INDUSTRY Although agriculture is the main economic activity in India, industry is also an important element. Cotton textiles have long been a major product of India. Beginning in the late 1940s, however, other industries began to develop. As the map on page 569 shows, India is now a major producer of iron and steel, chemicals, machinery, and food products. The main industrial regions are centered around Kolkata (Calcutta) in the east, Mumbai (Bombay) and Ahmadabad in the west, Chennai (Madras) in the south, and Delhi in the north. C

Geographic Thinking

Making Comparisons C How has economic development changed India?

C. Answer India is becoming more industrial, and its industries have expanded from textiles to include metals, chemicals, machinery, and food processing.

The western industrial zone has led the way in the modernization of Indian industry. Today, Mumbai is India's most prosperous city and leading commercial center. Its industries include metals, chemicals, and electronics. Other areas are now following Mumbai's lead. The southern city of Bangalore has become India's high-tech center. It is home to hundreds of computer software companies that are taking advantage of India's low wages and highly skilled workers. To some observers, Bangalore represents the future of the modern Indian economy.

Life in Modern India

While India's economy is modernizing, many Indians still live and work in traditional ways. This blend of old and new is typical of modern life in India.

DAILY LIFE Marriage and family remain at the center of Indian life. Most Indians follow the custom of arranged marriages—in which marriage partners are chosen by their families. But more affluent urban young people increasingly choose their own spouses. Indian families are large. Often many relatives from several generations live under one roof. Marriages are usually male-dominated, and divorce is rare.

Most Indians eat a largely vegetarian diet based on rice, legumes, and flatbreads called *chapati* or roti. Some Indians eat meat, fish, and chicken, often in spicy dishes called curry. But meat consumption is limited by both Muslim and Hindu religious practices.

Indians enjoy sports, music, and movies. Some of the country's most popular sports are soccer, field hockey, and cricket—a sport similar to baseball adopted from the British. Classical Indian music, featuring traditional instruments such as the sitar and the tabla, still has a large audience. But modern pop music is finding favor with India's youth. They also flock to movie theaters, where foreign films compete with local productions. The Indian film industry is based in Mumbai.

ACTIVITY OPTION **CRITICAL THINKING**

CREATING MULTIMEDIA PRESENTATIONS

Explaining the Skill Review with students the components of a multimedia presentation: text, images, and sound. Have them use presentation software to combine these elements to produce a multimedia presentation.

Applying the Skill Have students work in pairs or small groups to create a multimedia presentation on one of the following elements of Indian culture: music, art, literature, or dance. Have them choose one aspect, such as writings from a particular region or the works of a specific artist. Tell them to begin by researching their topic and then writing the script.

growing up in... India

These young women from the state of Rajasthan dress in traditional clothing to attend a fair. Festivals of all kinds are part of life for people of all ages in India. The traditional clothing worn by females in India includes embroidered skirts, head shawls, and lots of jewelry. In many places, however, Western-style clothing has replaced the traditional, especially for young people. Even though changes are taking place, females in India are treated differently from males both inside and outside the home. Females, for example, have more family responsibilities and less access to higher education and professional jobs.

If you lived in India, you would pass these milestones:

- You would receive some schooling, as Indian law provides free education from age 6 through age 14. In some areas, though, you could be working even before the age of 10.
- In school, you would study history, geography, science, math, and moral education.
- You might be married at age 16 if you were a female living in a rural area and at age 17 if you were a female in an urban area.
- You could enter the military at age 17 if you were a male.
- You could vote at age 18.

EDUCATION Most Indians still work on farms or in small craft industries. As the economy changes, though, more people are finding work in factories and offices. Education is a key factor in this change. In towns and cities, most middle-class children attend school. Literacy—the ability to read and write—has risen steadily since the 1950s. In city slums and rural areas, however, school attendance is irregular and literacy rates are low. The government has placed a high priority on improving public education to better prepare its citizens for the future.

Indian Culture

The culture of India is a rich blend of the different linguistic, ethnic, and religious groups.

MANY LANGUAGES The Indian constitution recognizes 18 major language groups, but more than 1,000 languages and dialects are spoken in India. Hindi is the official language. English, too, is widely spoken as a common language, especially by those working in government and business. Southern India is a distinct subregion, dating back to the Aryan conquest of northern India. The language and ethnicity of this region is Dravidian rather than Indo-European. Southern India has four major languages: Telugu, Tamil, Kannada, and Malayalam.

HINDUISM India is a land of great variety, but the dominant force in the lives of most Indians is Hinduism. Hinduism is a complex religion with roots in Aryan culture. Hindus, who make up around 80 percent of the population, believe in many gods. They also believe in reincarnation—the rebirth of souls after death. The moral consequences of a person's actions, known as karma, help determine how a person is reincarnated.

BACKGROUND
Hinduism is not based on the teachings of one person or deity like many other religions. It has been shaped by many ethnic, religious, and cultural groups.

SOUTH ASIA

growing up in...
India

As in India, Bangladesh also provides free schooling at the primary level, although attendance is low. Attendance at the high-school level is even lower, with fewer than five million students attending secondary schools. Boys are more likely to go to school than girls, who more often remain at home to help with household chores.

Why is illiteracy so high in Bangladesh? *(A high percentage of young people, especially girls, receive little if any schooling.)*

Instruct: Objective 5

Indian Culture

- How do the languages of India reflect ethnic diversity? *(India has more than a thousand spoken languages and dialects, which stem from its rich ethnic diversity; Southern India's languages are Dravidian, as are its people.)*
- What do the Hindus believe about karma and reincarnation? *(that karma, or the moral consequences of one's actions, determines how a person is reborn)*

Cultures Around the World
- Architecture, p. 43
- Daily Life, p. 44
- Arts and Crafts, p. 46
- Literature, p. 48

Cultures Transparencies CW43, 44, 46, 48
- Swayambhunath
- Wearing Saris
- Brass Work
- from the *Ramayana*

ACTIVITY OPTION FIVE THEMES OF GEOGRAPHY

MOVEMENT

Exploring the Theme Movement is an important element in the study of human geography. Migrations of people from one region to another have created ethnic diversity as well as ethnic tensions.

Understanding the Theme Tell students that the movement of various groups into and within India has had a major impact on the languages spoken there. Then ask the following questions.

- What movement of peoples led to the establishment of Hindi in northern India? *(the Aryan conquest)*
- How does movement explain why people in southern India speak languages that are not Indo-European? *(When Arayans conquered northern India they pushed the Dravidians south. The Dravidians speak languages that are not Indo-European.)*
- How does movement explain the fact that English is a common language in India? *(The British were a major presence in India for nearly 200 years.)*

Interpreting Photographs

Shiva

Shiva is India's oldest god and represents many things. He is worshiped as both creator and destroyer, as Lord of Beasts and God of Fertility. He is often portrayed as a great yogi. In addition to portraying Shiva as destroyer, what aspects of Shiva does this painting suggest? *(His position is one of a yogi; the animals suggest that he is Lord of Beasts.)*

Assess & Reteach

GeoFocus Have students complete their GeoFocus notes on India in their cluster diagrams.

Formal Assessment
- Section Quiz, p. 387

Reteaching Activity
Have students work in small groups. Assign each group a section objective and tell them to find and list information in that section that supports the objective. Give groups time to share and compare their work with the rest of the class.

In-Depth Resources: Unit 8
- Reteaching Activity, p. 19

Outline Maps with Activities
- India, pp. 79–80

REGION Shiva is one of the major gods of Hinduism. As in this 18th-century painting, Shiva is often represented in the character of a many-headed, many-armed destroyer or restorer.

The **caste system** was the Aryan system of social classes. Today, it remains one of the cornerstones of Hinduism. Four basic castes made up the original system: the Brahmans (priests and scholars), the Kshatriyas (rulers and warriors), the Vaisyas (farmers and merchants), and the Sudras (artisans and laborers).

Over time, these castes were further divided into smaller groupings. Outside the system altogether were the dalits, or untouchables, who had the lowest status in Indian society. (This class was officially eliminated in the Indian constitution.)

According to Hindu belief, each person is born into a caste and has a certain moral duty, known as dharma, that is specific to that caste. A person can move into a different caste only through reincarnation. While the system brought social order, it also caused discrimination and limited people's ability to improve their lot in life.

OTHER RELIGIONS Other faiths also play a key role in Indian life. These include Jainism, Christianity, Sikhism, and Buddhism—which originated in northern India. Islam also exerts a strong cultural influence in certain parts of the country. But millions of Muslims left the country after India won independence in 1947. They chose to move to the new Muslim states founded in the northwestern and northeastern parts of the subcontinent. You will read about those states—now called Pakistan and Bangladesh—in the next section.

Section 1 Assessment

1 Places & Terms
Identify these terms and explain their importance in the region.
- Mughal Empire
- raj
- nonviolent resistance
- land reform
- Green Revolution
- caste system

2 Taking Notes
PLACE Review the notes you took for this section.

- Before Europeans arrived, which groups of people contributed to India's history?
- What are some of the major influences on Indian politics today?

3 Main Ideas
a. What happened after the Europeans arrived in India?
b. What is the traditional Indian custom regarding marriage?
c. What are the central beliefs of the Hindu religion?

4 Geographic Thinking
Making Inferences What might be some of the problems caused by the Hindu caste system? **Think about:**
- being born into a caste
- being able to move into a different caste only through reincarnation

SEEING PATTERNS Review the information about the arrival of Europeans in India on page 568. Then use the Internet or encyclopedias to learn more about British policies and actions during their rule. Create a **political cartoon** that illustrates British policies, actions, or attitudes during that time.

SECTION 1 ASSESSMENT ANSWERS

1. Places & Terms
Mughal Empire, p. 568; raj, p. 568; nonviolent resistance, p. 568; land reform, p. 569; Green Revolution, p. 570; caste system, p. 572

2. Taking Notes
- Aryans, Persians, Greeks, then Muslims
- Because of the large Muslim minority, Indian leaders must take Muslim interests into account. The Sikhs and the Tamils also play a role.

3. Main Ideas
a. Several European countries set up trading colonies, but the British won out and eventually ruled over India for nearly 200 years.
b. Many Indians follow the traditional custom of arranged marriages, although wealthy urban people now often choose their own spouses.
c. Hindus believe in many gods and also in reincarnation, the rebirth of the soul after death. One's actions help determine how one is reincarnated. Hinduism is rooted in the caste system. One is born into a particular caste and only through reincarnation can one move to another caste.

4. Geographic Thinking
discrimination and the inability to improve one's lot in life

GeoActivity

Integrated Assessment
- Rubric for a political cartoon, 1.2

2 Pakistan and Bangladesh

Main Ideas
- Pakistan and Bangladesh are Muslim countries formed as a result of the partition of British India.
- Both Pakistan and Bangladesh have large populations and face great economic challenges.

Places & Terms
Indus Valley civilization
partition
Kashmir
microcredit
entrepreneur
Ramadan

CONNECT TO THE ISSUES
EXTREME WEATHER
Bangladesh is severely affected by seasonal monsoons and cyclones.

A HUMAN PERSPECTIVE Some workers in the port of Chittagong, Bangladesh, have an unusual job. They are ship breakers. When ocean-going ships reach the end of their useful life, they take their last voyage to Chittagong. There, ship breakers wait on the beach with sledgehammers, crowbars, torches, and wrenches. They attack each ship, tearing it apart piece by piece. Within weeks, they can dismantle a ship. Then, they sell its scrap metal for recycling purposes. The job doesn't pay very well, but it is necessary work for the shipping industry, the workers, and the Bangladeshi economy.

New Countries, Ancient Lands

Like India, Pakistan and Bangladesh are young countries with an ancient history and with rapidly growing populations. They, too, are striving to make their way in the modern world.

EARLY HISTORY The largest of the world's first civilizations arose in what is now Pakistan. The **Indus Valley civilization** began around 2500 B.C. It featured well-planned cities like Harappa and Mohenjo-Daro, which had brick buildings (shown below) and sophisticated sanitation systems. The map on page 544 depicts the extent of the civilization at the height of its power. It fell around 1500 B.C., and the Aryans invaded soon after. Later on, the Mauryan, Gupta, and Mughal empires ruled the territory that included modern Pakistan and Bangladesh. The British were the next to take control of the region.

PLACE The ruins of Mohenjo-Daro, one of the great cities of the ancient Indus Valley civilization, lie on the Indus River in south-central Pakistan.

573

SECTION 2 OBJECTIVES

1. Examine the modern political history of Pakistan and Bangladesh.
2. Analyze the economies of the two countries.
3. Identify religious orientation and ethnicity of the Pakistani and Bangladeshi peoples.
4. Learn about modern family life and culture.

SKILLBUILDERS: Interpreting Maps and Graphs, pp. 574, 575

GeographicThinking
Making Comparisons, pp. 575, 577
Seeing Patterns, p. 577

Focus & Motivate

Ask students to look at the map on page 545. Ask what country separates Pakistan from Bangladesh. *(India)* How were these three countries once related? *(They were a single country–India.)*

Instruct: Objective 1

New Countries, Ancient Lands

- What was the largest early civilization? *(Indus Valley civilization)*
- What country was created as a result of partitioning? *(West and East Pakistan)*
- What was the outcome of Pakistan's 1971 civil war? *(East Pakistan became Bangladesh, an independent country.)*

In-Depth Resources: Unit 8
- Guided Reading, p. 14

Outline Maps with Activities
- Pakistan and Bangladesh, pp. 81–82

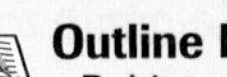

SECTION 2 PROGRAM RESOURCES

In-Depth Resources: Unit 8
- Guided Reading, p. 14
- Skillbuilder Practice, p. 17
- Building Vocabulary, p. 18
- Reteaching Activity, p. 20

Guided Reading workbook
- Section 2

Access for Students Acquiring English/ESL
- Guided Reading, p. 134
- Skillbuilder Practice, p. 137

Formal Assessment
- Section Quiz, p. 388

Outline Maps with Activities
- Pakistan and Bangladesh, pp. 81–82

Integrated Assessment
- Rubric for a chart, 2.2
- Rubric for a press release, 4.10

INTEGRATED TECHNOLOGY

Power Presentations

Chapter Summaries

Test Generator
- Section Quiz

TEST-TAKING RESOURCES

Strategies for Test Preparation

Test Practice Transparencies TT81

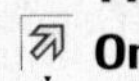

Online Test Practice

Interpreting Maps

The Indian Subcontinent

Have students determine the approximate distance between West and East Pakistan. *(more than a thousand miles)* How might this have contributed to the independence movement in East Pakistan? *(The distance would have intensified cultural differences; people living in East Pakistan may have felt that they already were living in a separate country.)*

SKILLBUILDER ANSWERS 1. Part of Kashmir had been included in the territory of India, while another part was disputed by India and Pakistan. **2.** West Pakistan had become Pakistan; East Pakistan had become Bangladesh; and Ceylon had become Sri Lanka.

Instruct: Objective 

Struggling Economies

- What is the basis for the economies of Pakistan and Bangladesh? *(agriculture)*
- What crops are produced for domestic consumption and for export? *(Pakistan grows cotton and rice for export, and wheat for domestic consumption. Bangladesh produces rice for domestic consumption and jute for export.)*
- How has microcredit spurred the growth of small businesses? *(Small businesses may apply as a group for a loan.)*

The Indian Subcontinent

1947: KASHMIR, WEST PAKISTAN, INDIA, EAST PAKISTAN, CEYLON; N, S, E, W; Disputed by India and Pakistan; 0 250 500 miles; 0 250 500 kilometers; Two-Point Equidistant Projection

1972: KASHMIR, PAKISTAN, CHINA, NEPAL, BHUTAN, INDIA, BANGLADESH, SRI LANKA; N, S, E, W; Disputed by India and Pakistan; Disputed by India and China; Cease-fire line; 0 250 500 miles; 0 250 500 kilometers; Two-Point Equidistant Projection

SKILLBUILDER: Interpreting Maps

1. **PLACE** What had happened to the territory of Kashmir by 1972?
2. **REGION** What other changes had taken place in South Asia from 1947 to 1972?

PARTITION AND WAR The end of British rule in 1947 brought the **partition,** or division, of British India. Two new countries were created—India (predominantly Hindu) and mainly Muslim Pakistan (separated into West Pakistan and East Pakistan). Partition led to much violence between Muslims and Hindus. About one million people died in the conflict. Another 10 million fled across national borders. Muslims in India moved to Pakistan, while Hindus in Pakistan crossed into India.

West Pakistan and East Pakistan shared a religious bond, but ethnic differences and their 1,100-mile separation eventually drove them apart. The people of East Pakistan began to call for their own state. But the government in West Pakistan opposed such a move. Civil war broke out in 1971. That year, with help from India, East Pakistan won its independence as Bangladesh.

BACKGROUND Bangladesh means "land of the Bangla (or Bengal)-speaking people."

MILITARY RULE Both Pakistan and Bangladesh have had political struggles since independence. Short periods of elected government have alternated with long periods of military rule. Political corruption has plagued both countries. Pakistan also has fought several destructive wars with India over the territory of **Kashmir.** These wars are discussed in the Case Study in Chapter 26. Both Bangladesh and Pakistan have had women prime ministers, a rarity in the Muslim world.

Struggling Economies

Pakistan and Bangladesh have large, rapidly growing populations. In fact, Bangladesh is the eighth most populous country in the world. Both

DIFFERENTIATING INSTRUCTION **GIFTED AND TALENTED STUDENTS**

WRITING ON WOMEN PRIME MINISTERS

Objective To expand students' knowledge of the achievements of South Asian women

Class Time 45 minutes

Task Write a report on Indira Gandhi, Benazir Bhutto, or Sheikh Hasina Wazed

Directions Tell students to write about prime ministers Indira Gandhi, Benazir Bhutto, or Sheikh Hasina Wazed. The report should include the background of the subject and explain how she became prime minister in a country where women are often poorly educated and underprivileged. Students should also discuss what problems the subject faced as prime minister and whether the country benefited from her leadership. Tell students to include a visual summarizing the main points for class discussion.

have economies that depend primarily on agriculture. As in India, per capita incomes are low, and much of the population lives in poverty. Bangladesh is one of the poorest countries in the world.

SUBSISTENCE FARMING Most farmers in Pakistan and Bangladesh work small plots of land and struggle to grow enough crops to feed their families. The government has tried to help modernize farming methods, but many farmers continue to follow less productive traditional ways. Climate also hinders crop yields. Large areas of Pakistan are arid, while Bangladesh is severely affected by seasonal monsoons and cyclones.

The most productive farming areas of Pakistan are the irrigated portions of the Indus Valley. Here, farmers grow enough cotton and rice to allow for export. The farmers also produce substantial amounts of wheat for domestic consumption. The moist delta lands of Bangladesh are ideal for the cultivation of rice, the country's principal food crop. The main export crop is jute (a plant used in the production of rope, carpets, and industrial-quality sacks). Fishing, mainly for freshwater fish, is also vital to the economy of Bangladesh.

SMALL INDUSTRY Neither Pakistan nor Bangladesh is highly industrialized. Most factories are relatively small and lack the capital, resources, and markets required for expansion. Even so, both countries are trying to increase their industrial base. They have growing textile industries that provide an important source of revenue and employment. Both countries export cotton garments, and Pakistan also exports wool carpets and leather goods. A

A. Answer Both are populous countries with struggling economies that depend on agriculture. They are trying to increase their industrial base.

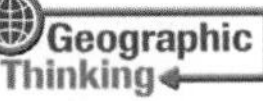

Making Comparisons
A How do the economies of Pakistan and Bangladesh compare with each other?

An important economic development has been the introduction of **microcredit.** This policy makes small loans available to poor **entrepreneurs,** people who start and build a business. Businesses that are too small to get loans from banks can often join forces to apply for these microloans. They then accept joint responsibility for repaying the loan. This program, begun in Bangladesh, has helped small businesses grow in South Asia and has raised living standards for many producers, especially women.

More About
Jute

Jute is a mainstay of the economy in Bangladesh. This plant, which grows to a height of about four feet, provides one of the world's most useful fibers. Jute is most commonly made into burlap bags for shipping produce. Its other uses include clothing, twine, and rugs. Bangladesh has grown jute for many centuries and produces more jute than any other country.

Economic Activity in Pakistan and Bangladesh

Textiles in Pakistan

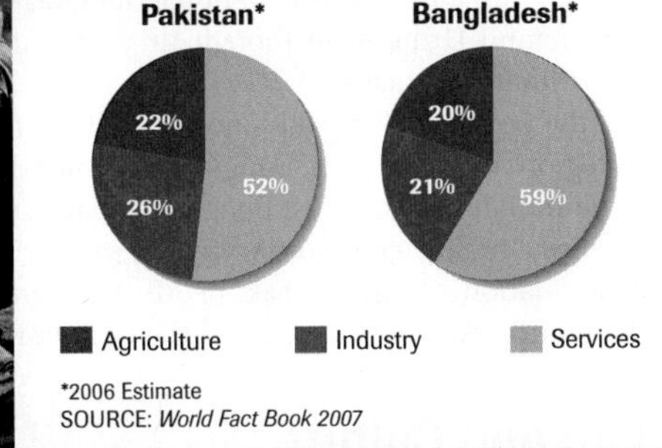

*2006 Estimate
SOURCE: *World Fact Book 2007*

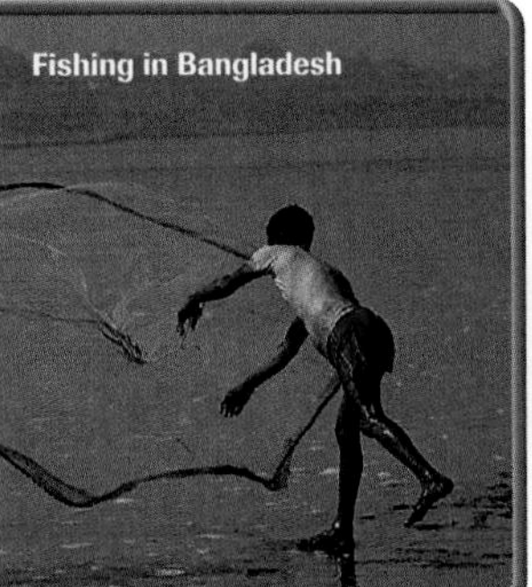
Fishing in Bangladesh

SKILLBUILDER: Interpreting Graphs

1. **MAKING COMPARISONS** Which of the two countries is more industrialized?
2. **ANALYZING DATA** In both Pakistan and Bangladesh, which economic sector employs the most people?

SOUTH ASIA

Interpreting Graphs
Economic Activity in Pakistan and Bangladesh

A cottage industry is a small-scale industry carried on at home by family members using their own equipment. In Bangladesh, the most important cottage industry centers on textiles. Direct students to the picture at the left of the graph. Where are these textiles being displayed? *(at an outdoor market)* How might microcredit assist people involved in both activities pictured? *(A microcredit loan might lead to expanded textile production and eventual export. Fishers might use capital to purchase a small boat and increase yield.)*

SKILLBUILDER ANSWERS

1. Pakistan is somewhat more industrialized than Bangladesh. **2.** The two countries employ more people in the services sector of the economy than any other.

DIFFERENTIATING INSTRUCTION **STUDENTS ACQUIRING ENGLISH/ESL**

INCREASING VOCABULARY

Objective To expand knowledge of farming and business terms

Class Time 20 minutes

Task Create a chart of terms relating to farming and business

Directions Use the chalkboard to present the chart. Ask students to name some additional terms used in business and farming. Write them on the chart. Have them identify and add appropriate vocabulary words *(microcredit, entrepreneurs)*. Tell them to copy the chart into their notebooks and to add new words as they think of them.

FARMING	BUSINESS
crops	profit
irrigation	investment

Instruct: Objective 

One Religion, Many Peoples

- What religion do most Pakistanis and Bangladeshis practice? *(Islam)*
- What is Ramadan? *(a month-long period of fasting observed by Muslims)*
- Why did Pakistan's government choose Urdu as the national language? *(to avoid favoring any ethnic group with regional origins in the country; Mujahirs migrated to Pakistan during partition)*

Interpreting Photographs

A Muslim Prayer Service

Have students look at the photograph. What might they conclude about how Muslims honor Allah (God) while praying? *(They remove their shoes, kneel, and bow their heads. All face in the same direction.)*

Instruct: Objective 

Modern Life and Culture

- Why is Rabindranath Tagore a cultural icon or hero in Bangladesh? *(Poetry is very popular and Tagore was a renowned poet who won the 1913 Nobel Prize for Literature.)*
- What forms of artistic expression are popular? Why do you think so? *(classical and folk music; qawwali; in Bangladesh, folk dances that tell stories.)*

 **In-Depth Resources: Unit 8**
- Skillbuilder Practice, p. 17

One Religion, Many Peoples

Most of the people of Pakistan and Bangladesh are Muslims. In both countries, Islam is an important unifying force. At the same time, ethnic differences promote cultural diversity, particularly in Pakistan.

ISLAMIC CULTURE Islam has long played an important role in Pakistan and Bangladesh. Both lands were key parts of the Muslim Mughal Empire that ruled the Indian subcontinent for centuries, and their cultures bear the stamp of Islam. The faithful observe Islamic customs. These include daily prayer and participation in **Ramadan,** a month-long period of fasting from sunrise to sunset. Mosques in both countries are often large and impressive structures.

The two countries differ somewhat in their Islamic practices, however. In general, Pakistan is stricter in imposing Islamic law on its citizens. For example, many Pakistanis follow the custom of *purdah,* the seclusion of women. This custom prevents women from having contact with men who are not relatives. When women appear in public, they must wear veils. In Bangladesh, purdah is much less common and religious practices are less strict.

REGION Most Pakistanis are Sunni Muslims. Here, men attend a Muslim prayer service in a mosque in Karachi.

ETHNIC DIVERSITY Pakistan is also more ethnically diverse than Bangladesh. Pakistan has five main ethnic groups—Punjabis, Sindhis, Pathans, Muhajirs, and Balochs. Each group has its own language. The Punjabis make up almost half of the population. Each group has its own regional origins within the country except for the Muhajirs, who migrated from India as a result of the partition in 1947. To avoid favoring one region or group over another, the government chose Urdu—the language of the Muhajirs—as the national language. Today, most Pakistanis understand Urdu, even though they may use another language as their primary language.

In contrast, the people of Bangladesh are mainly Bengalis. Bengal is the historic region that includes Bangladesh (once known as East Bengal) and the Indian state of West Bengal. Bengalis speak a language based on Sanskrit, the ancient Indo-Aryan language. Bangladesh also has a small population of Urdu-speaking Muslims and various non-Muslim tribal groups. About 16 percent of the population are Hindus.

BACKGROUND
Punjabi is the principal spoken language of Pakistan because the majority of Pakistanis are Punjabis. Arabic is a secondary language for Muslim Pakistanis.

Modern Life and Culture

As in India, life in Pakistan and Bangladesh revolves around the family. Arranged marriages are common, and families tend to be large. Most people live in small villages, in simple homes made of such materials as sun-baked mud, bamboo, or wood. The large cities are busy places,

ACTIVITY OPTION **CRITICAL THINKING**

MAKING COMPARISONS

Explaining the Skill Making comparisons is an effective technique for helping students form an overall picture of two different things.

Applying the Skill Tell students that comparing Pakistan and Bangladesh in terms of religion, language, and ethnicity will help them better understand each country's culture. Then ask the following questions.

- How do Islamic practices differ between the two countries? *(Pakistan is stricter about imposing Islamic law. Pakistani women must wear a veil in public; many do not have contact with men other than relatives.)*
- Which country has the greatest diversity of language and ethnicity? *(Pakistan)*
- Why is Pakistan more ethnically diverse? *(Most people in Bangladesh trace their roots to a single region, Bengal. Ethnic groups in Pakistan originated in five separate regions; an additional group, the Mujahirs, migrated there.)*

crowded with traffic and pedestrians. People in both countries enjoy sports such as soccer and cricket, and also enjoy going to see movies.

A LOVE OF POETRY Poetry is a special interest in both Pakistan and Bangladesh, where the tradition of oral literature is strong. Many Pakistanis memorize long poems and can recite them by heart. Poets are popular figures, and poetry readings—called *mushairas*—can draw thousands of people, much like a rock concert does in some countries.

The greatest literary figure in Bangladesh is the poet Rabindranath Tagore, who won the Nobel Prize for Literature in 1913. Although Tagore was born in Calcutta (now Kolkata), India, he wrote about the Ganges and his Bengal homeland. Bangladesh adopted his song, "My Golden Bengal," as its national anthem.

MUSIC AND DANCE Music and dance are also important forms of expression in Bangladesh and Pakistan. Both countries share music traditions similar to those of India. Folk music of various types is popular in cities and in rural areas. *Qawwali*—a form of devotional singing performed by Muslims known as Sufis—is famous not only in South Asia but also in parts of Europe and the United States. Bangladesh also has a long tradition of folk dances, in which elaborately costumed dancers act out Bengali myths, legends, and stories. B

You have been reading about Pakistan and Bangladesh, India's western and eastern neighbors. Next, you will learn about India's northern neighbors, Nepal and Bhutan.

B. Answer Music and dance are important as cultural expressions and as ways of showing religious devotion.

Seeing Patterns
B What roles do music and dance play in the lives of the people of Pakistan and Bangladesh?

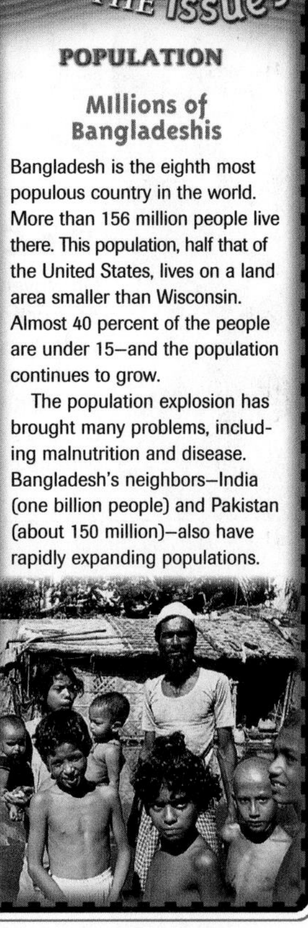

POPULATION

Millions of Bangladeshis

Bangladesh is the eighth most populous country in the world. More than 156 million people live there. This population, half that of the United States, lives on a land area smaller than Wisconsin. Almost 40 percent of the people are under 15—and the population continues to grow.

The population explosion has brought many problems, including malnutrition and disease. Bangladesh's neighbors—India (one billion people) and Pakistan (about 150 million)—also have rapidly expanding populations.

Section 2 Assessment

1 Places & Terms
Identify each of the following places and terms.
- Indus Valley civilization
- partition
- Kashmir
- microcredit
- entrepreneur
- Ramadan

2 Taking Notes
PLACE Review the notes you took for this section.

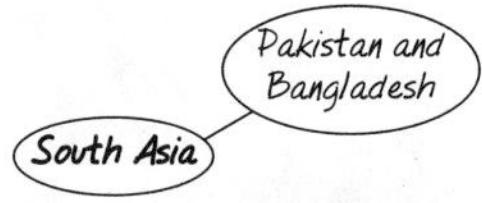

- How were the countries of Pakistan and Bangladesh formed?
- What role does farming play in the economies of Pakistan and Bangladesh?

3 Main Ideas
a. What have been some of the problems for Pakistan and Bangladesh since they were formed?
b. What role does Islam play in Pakistan and Bangladesh?
c. How would you describe Pakistan's ethnic makeup?

4 Geographic Thinking
Making Comparisons How do Pakistan and Bangladesh differ in their Islamic practices? **Think about:**
- the treatment of women
- how much of Pakistan follows strict Islamic law

MAKING COMPARISONS Review the information about Islam on page 576. Then use the Internet or an encyclopedia to compare Islam in Pakistan or Bangladesh with a Muslim country in either Africa or Southwest Asia. Create a **chart** comparing the two countries using such topics as treatment of women, eating practices, and how strictly a country enforces Islamic law.

SOUTH ASIA

Connect TO THE Issues

Population: Millions of Bangledeshis

In the year 2009 the population density of Bangladesh was estimated at more than 2,800 people per square mile. This is much higher than most other countries.

When considering population, why is density a key factor? *(When people are crowded together they put a greater demand on physical resources, municipal services, and basic necessities.)*

Assess & Reteach

GeoFocus Have students complete their GeoFocus notes for this subregion of South Asia.

Formal Assessment
- Section Quiz, p. 388

Reteaching Activity
Divide students into four groups and assign each a main heading of the section. Tell them to review the material under the heading and to list the main points in two columns labeled "Pakistan" and "Bangladesh." Then have them create a Venn diagram that shows what is unique about each country, and what they have in common. Transfer completed diagram to chart paper or poster board.

In-Depth Resources: Unit 8
- Reteaching Activity, p. 20

Outline Maps with Activities
- Pakistan and Bangladesh, pp. 81–82

SECTION 2 ASSESSMENT ANSWERS

1. Places & Terms
Indus Valley civilization, p. 573
partition, p. 574
Kashmir, p. 574
entrepreneur, p. 575
microcredit, p. 575
Ramadan, p. 576

2. Taking Notes
- Partition of India in 1947 created the divided country of West Pakistan and East Pakistan; East Pakistan became Bangladesh in 1971.
- Farming is very important, but difficult conditions and inefficient farming methods cause problems.

3. Main Ideas
a. establishing democracy; making farming more productive; increasing industrialization
b. Islam is a huge influence in both countries. In general, though, Islamic law has been more strictly imposed in Pakistan.
c. Pakistan is a diverse country, with five main ethnic groups. The Punjabis are the largest group.

4. Geographic Thinking
Pakistan is stricter in imposing Islamic law. Pakistan follows purdah, the seclusion of women. In Bangladesh, purdah is less common, and religious practices are more relaxed.

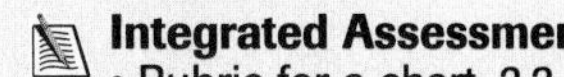

Integrated Assessment
- Rubric for a chart, 2.2

OBJECTIVES

1. Learn about the cyclone of 1970.
2. Explain the dynamics of tropical storms.

Instruct: Objective

The Cyclone of 1970

- What types of devastation resulted from the 1970 cyclone? *(loss of life, homelessness, crop destruction, fishing boat wreckage)*
- What has been done to reduce storm damage? *(construction of concrete structures on stilts; reinforcement of school buildings)*
- Why do more violent storms occur in Bangladesh than in other South Asian countries? *(Bangladesh has a low-lying coastal plain.)*

Interpreting Maps

Bangladesh

Ask which main rivers flow through Bangladesh to empty into the Bay of Bengal. *(Ganges, Meghna, Brahmaputra)* What does this suggest about the likelihood of flooding? *(Rivers generally flow from higher to low-lying areas, so the coastline is likely to be subject to flooding.)*

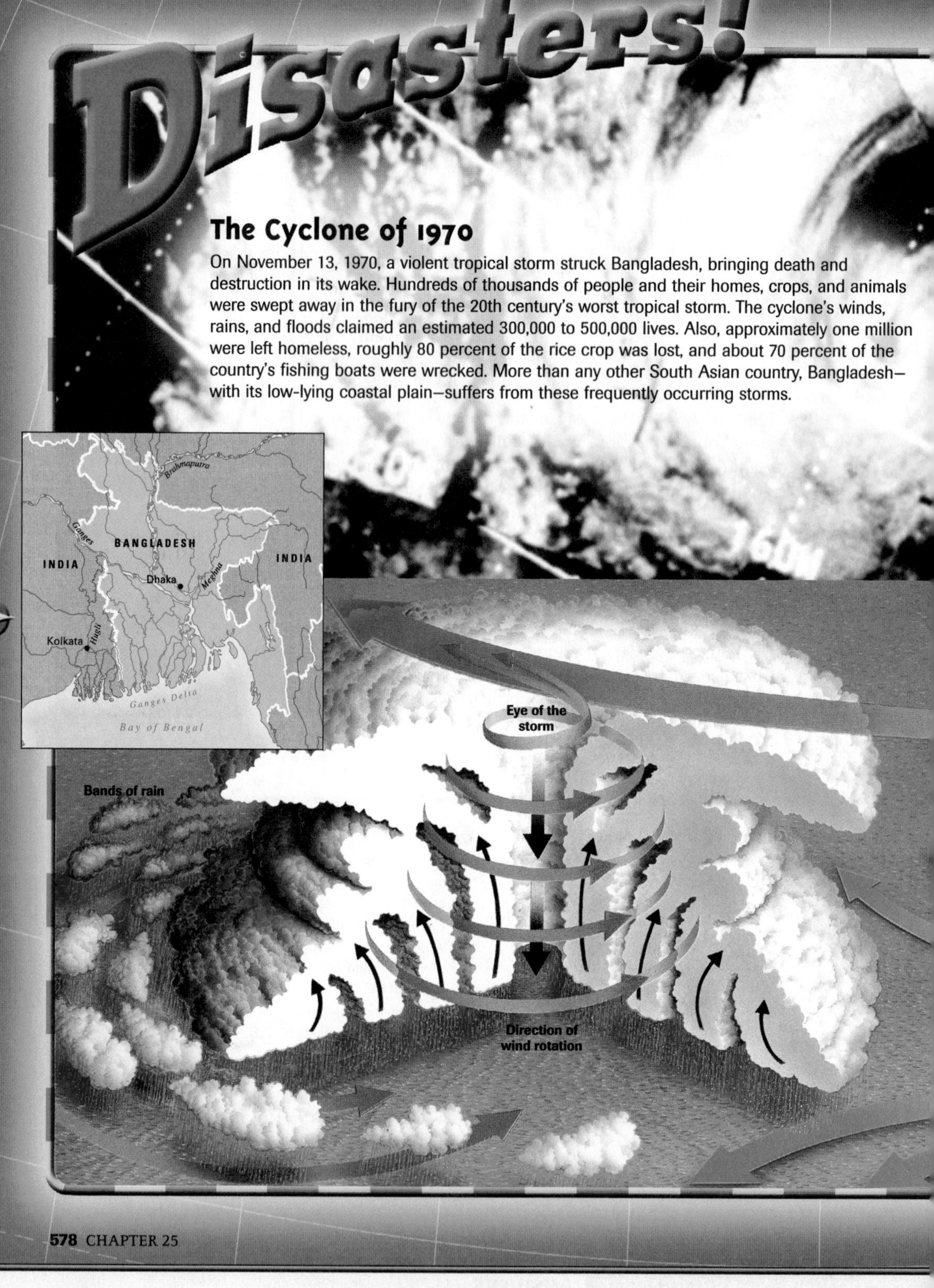

Disasters!

The Cyclone of 1970

On November 13, 1970, a violent tropical storm struck Bangladesh, bringing death and destruction in its wake. Hundreds of thousands of people and their homes, crops, and animals were swept away in the fury of the 20th century's worst tropical storm. The cyclone's winds, rains, and floods claimed an estimated 300,000 to 500,000 lives. Also, approximately one million were left homeless, roughly 80 percent of the rice crop was lost, and about 70 percent of the country's fishing boats were wrecked. More than any other South Asian country, Bangladesh—with its low-lying coastal plain—suffers from these frequently occurring storms.

578 CHAPTER 25

SUPPORTING RESOURCES

BOOKS FOR THE TEACHER

Van Schendel, Willem. ***A History of Bangladesh.*** Cambridge University Press, 2009. Chronology of a little-known country, starting with the geological history of the delta.

Ryan, Paul Ryder. ***Bangladesh 2000: On the Brink of Civil War.*** Cummington, MA: Munewata Press, 2000. Focuses on the current situation in Bangladesh.

BOOKS FOR THE STUDENT

Brace, Steve. ***Bangladesh.*** Austin, TX: Raintree Steck-Vaughn, 1995. Part of the Economically Developing Countries series.

Monan, Jim. ***Bangladesh: The Strength to Succeed.*** Herndon, VA: Stylus Publishing, 1995. Part of the Oxfam Country Profiles series.

INTERNET

For more information on cyclones and other storms, visit . . .

hmhsocialstudies.com

hmhsocialstudies.com INTERACTIVE

The damage inflicted on this village in Bangladesh in 1991 is typical of the destructive force of a cyclone's winds and the torrential rains and floods that are a part of this weather system.

Concrete shelters constructed on stilts, as shown here, and reinforced school buildings are refuges from high floodwaters and winds that can knock down all but the strongest buildings.

GeoActivity

ANNOUNCING THE DAMAGE 21ST CENTURY

Use the Internet to research the cyclone of November 1970. Read accounts of its destructive force. Gather data on the storm itself and the damage that it caused. Then prepare a **press release** about the storm.

- Begin with an overview of the storm.
- Provide a map and statistics.
- Present your press release to a group of student reporters.

hmhsocialstudies.com RESEARCH WEB LINKS

GeoData

TROPICAL STORMS

Violent tropical storms are called cyclones in the Indian Ocean, typhoons in the northwestern Pacific Ocean, and hurricanes in the Atlantic Ocean. These storms:

- develop over tropical waters in the late summer and fall when ocean temperatures are warmest
- usually begin as a cluster of thunderstorms that start to spiral and then form a single violent storm
- may be as wide as 675 miles
- have winds that range from 75 to 150 miles per hour
- generally last a week but some may take two or three weeks to die out
- produce heavy flooding that is the cause of most of the destruction and deaths
- inflict most of their damage along coastlines

OTHER BANGLADESHI STORMS

- May 28–29, 1963–22,000 deaths
- May 11–12, 1965–17,000 deaths
- June 1–12, 1965–30,000 deaths
- April 30, 1991–139,000 deaths

GeoActivities

Integrated Assessment

- Rubric for a press release, 4.10

More About

Cyclones

The Earth's rotation causes the winds of a cyclone to spiral. In the Northern Hemisphere they generally blow in a counterclockwise direction. In the Southern Hemisphere they blow clockwise.

Which way are the cyclones striking Bangladesh most likely to blow? *(counterclockwise)*

ACTIVITY OPTION | COOPERATIVE LEARNING

WRITING A NEWS SYNOPSIS

Objective To learn about the 2003 cold snap in Bangladesh

Class Time 30 minutes

Task Prepare a news synopsis

Directions Tell students that although moonsoons may cause flooding and bring cyclones, Bangladesh has been subject to other types of destructive weather as well. Have students use the Internet or do library research to learn about the 2003 cold snap in Bangladesh. Tell them to write a news synopsis in which they provide specifics of temperature and duration, area affected, and impact of the cold. Organize the students into groups of four. Have one student do research in the library. Have another do research on the Internet. Have a third student organize the information under the categories mentioned above. Have the fourth student write the synopsis.

SECTION 3 OBJECTIVES

1. Define Nepal and Bhutan as mountain kingdoms.
2. Compare aspects of the economies of Nepal and Bhutan.
3. Learn about culture and religion.

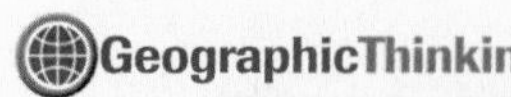

GeographicThinking

Making Comparisons, p. 581
Seeing Patterns, p. 583
Drawing Conclusions, p. 583

Focus & Motivate

Ask what associations students make with Nepal and Bhutan. *(Most will probably name the Himalayas.)* Ask students what they know about how people in these regions live. *(Answers will vary but probably will be limited, which is the point to make: until very recently, few Westerners had visited these remote countries.)*

Instruct: Objective 

Mountain Kingdoms

- What major geographic feature do Nepal and Bhutan have in common? *(high mountains)*
- What factors contribute to the remoteness of Nepal and Bhutan? *(mountainous topography; they are landlocked)*
- What type of government do the two countries have? *(constitutional monarchies)*

 **In-Depth Resources: Unit 8**
- Guided Reading, p. 15

CAPTION ANSWER

Possibly because the Buddhist religion forms a rich part of the history and culture of Bhutan.

3 Nepal and Bhutan

Main Ideas

- Nepal and Bhutan are landlocked Himalayan kingdoms.
- Rugged terrain and an isolated location have had a great impact on life in Nepal and Bhutan.

Places & Terms

constitutional monarchy
Sherpa
Siddhartha Gautama
mandala

CONNECT TO THE ISSUES

ECONOMIC DEVELOPMENT Decades of isolation and difficult topography have limited economic growth in Nepal and Bhutan.

A HUMAN PERSPECTIVE In the novel *Lost Horizon,* James Hilton described an imaginary mountain valley called Shangri-La, hidden high in the Himalayas. He wrote, "The floor of the valley, hazily distant, welcomed the eye with greenness; sheltered from winds . . . completely isolated by the lofty and sheerly unscalable ranges on the further side." Shangri-La was an earthly paradise: a land of peace, harmony, and beauty, where hunger, disease, and war did not exist. Hilton located this mythical land somewhere in Tibet, but it could just as easily have been in Nepal or Bhutan. Although neither of these countries is a paradise, both are remote lands of great beauty and peace.

Mountain Kingdoms

Nepal and Bhutan share a number of important characteristics. Both are located in the Himalayas, a factor that has had a great impact on their history and economic development. Both also are kingdoms with strong religious traditions.

GEOGRAPHIC ISOLATION The main geographic feature of Nepal and Bhutan is their mountainous landscape. Each country consists of a central upland of ridges and valleys leading up to the high mountains, with a small lowland area along the Indian border. The towering, snow-capped Himalayas run along the northern border with China. They are craggy and forbidding and have steep mountain passes and year-round ice fields. The world's tallest mountain peak, Mt. Everest, is located there.

The rugged landscape of Nepal and Bhutan has isolated the two countries throughout their histories. Their mountainous terrain and landlocked location—neither country has access to the sea—made them hard to reach and difficult to conquer and settle. China controlled Bhutan briefly in the 18th century. In the 19th century, Great Britain had influence over both countries because of its control of neighboring India. But Nepal and Bhutan generally remained independent and isolated. In fact, until the past few decades, foreigners rarely entered either country.

EVOLVING MONARCHIES For much of their history, Nepal and Bhutan were split into small religious kingdoms or ruling states. Hindu kings ruled in Nepal, while Buddhist priests controlled Bhutan. In time, unified kingdoms emerged in both countries, led by hereditary monarchs who passed the throne on to their heirs.

Today, the governments of both Nepal and Bhutan are **constitutional monarchies**—kingdoms in which the ruler's powers are limited by a

REGION Richly decorated cloths that display Buddhist religious symbols, such as the cloth shown below, have covered the thrones of Bhutanese rulers. **Why might there be religious symbols on a throne cloth used by secular rulers?**

SECTION 3 PROGRAM RESOURCES

 **In-Depth Resources: Unit 8**
- Guided Reading, p. 15
- Building Vocabulary, p. 18
- Reteaching Activity, p. 21

 **Guided Reading Workbook**
- Section 3

Access for Students Acquiring English/ESL
- Guided Reading, p. 135

 **Outline Maps with Activities**
- Nepal and Bhutan, pp. 83–84

 **Formal Assessment**
- Section Quiz, p. 389

 **Integrated Assessment**
- Rubric for a letter, 4.3

 **Cultures Around the World**
- Traditional Practices, p. 45

INTEGRATED TECHNOLOGY

 **Cultures Transparencies CW45**
- Celebrating Tshechu

 **The World's Music Audio Program**

 **Power Presentations**

 **Chapter Summaries**

hmhsocialstudies.com

TEST-TAKING RESOURCES

 **Strategies for Test Preparation**

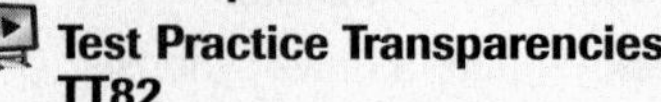 **Test Practice Transparencies TT82**

Online Test Practice

PLACE A blend of the old and the new is evident in the architecture of this square in Kathmandu, Nepal's capital city. **Why might this rich cultural tradition make Kathmandu attractive to tourists?**

constitution. Bhutan held its first democratic elections in 2008. Nepal's government is in transition to a federal democratic republic. Both governments face difficult political challenges, including the need to balance the interests of their two powerful neighbors, China and India. Both countries also face difficult economic challenges.

Developing Economies

Decades of isolation and difficult topography have limited economic development in Nepal and Bhutan. Now each country is trying to find effective ways to promote economic growth.

LIMITED RESOURCES Nepal and Bhutan are poor countries with economies based mainly on agriculture. Because of the mountainous terrain, neither country has much land suitable for cultivation. Most farm plots are small, soils are poor, and erosion is a problem. Farmers create terraces on the mountainsides to increase the amount of farmland and limit soil loss, a process you read about in Chapter 9. Common farm products include rice, corn, potatoes, and wheat. Common livestock are cattle, sheep, and yaks—longhaired animals related to the ox. In Bhutan, the government has promoted the growing of fruit for export and has tried to improve farming practices.

The timber industry is very important to both countries, although deforestation is a problem. The forests of Nepal are being cut down at a rate of more than 1 percent a year. But some timberlands remain. Around 70 percent of Bhutan is still forested. A growing manufacturing sector of the economy includes wood products, food processing, and cement production. Most trade for both countries is with India. A

A. Answer Both countries raise crops and livestock, have timber industries, and are increasing their manufacturing sectors.

Geographic Thinking

Making Comparisons

A What activities are important to the economies of Nepal and Bhutan?

INCREASING TOURISM One of the fastest growing industries in Nepal is tourism. Tourists come from around the world to visit the valley of Kathmandu, the capital, and to climb the Himalayas. Hotels and restaurants, transportation, and other services have grown to meet the needs of the tourist industry. But tourism is a mixed blessing. It has

SOUTH ASIA

Interpreting Photographs

Kathmandu

Many temples in Kathmandu and throughout Nepal are built in the pagoda style, which Nepalese architects created.

What two types of architecture does the photograph show? *(Buildings typical of both the East and West.)*

CAPTION ANSWER Tourists might find the city's architecture both historically interesting and exotic.

Instruct: Objective 2

Developing Economies

- What is the economic base in Nepal and Bhutan? *(agriculture)*
- How has tourism affected Nepal? *(It has generated income but damaged the environment.)*
- Why does Bhutan regulate tourism? *(The government is concerned about its impact on the lives of its people.)*

DIFFERENTIATING INSTRUCTION | **LESS PROFICIENT READERS**

PREVIEWING ECONOMIC TERMS

Objective To recognize terms relating to the economics of farming and tourism

Class Time 10 minutes

Task Create a list of terms

Directions Review with students how the majority of people make their living in the countries studied in the first two sections. *(agricultural)* Have students name some terms associated with farming economies and list them on the chalkboard under the heading "Farming." Tell students to copy the list and to add additional terms as they study Nepal and Bhutan. Repeat the procedure for terms related to the tourism industry.

Interpreting Graphics

Mountains of Bhutan and Nepal

Visitors to the Himalayas go there for a variety of reasons, the most notable of which is to climb the world's tallest mountains. Others, however, go to study Old World animals such as the bharal (a blue sheep) or to photograph the area and its people. Travelers also are motivated by spiritual needs or by a desire to experience a different way of life.

CAPTION ANSWER Sherpas are used to living and working at the high altitudes of the Himalayas.

Instruct: Objective 3

Rich Cultural Traditions

- What is the religion of most Nepalese? *(Hinduism)*
- What is the official religion of Bhutan? *(Buddhism)*
- What historic event connects Nepal with Buddhism? *(Siddhartha Gautama, the Buddha, was born there.)*
- What traditions are reflected in the festivals of Bhutan and Nepal? *(religious stories are told through dance; musicians play traditional songs; Bhutanese hold archery contests)*

Cultures Around the World
• Traditional Practices, p. 45

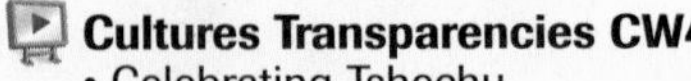
Cultures Transparencies CW45
• Celebrating Tshechu

Mountains of Bhutan and Nepal

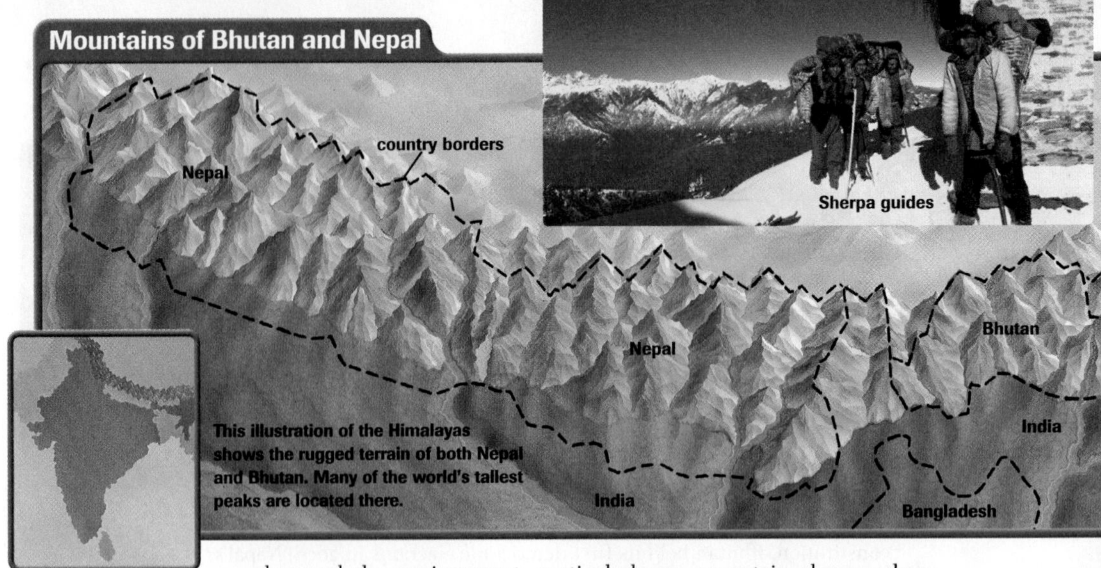

This illustration of the Himalayas shows the rugged terrain of both Nepal and Bhutan. Many of the world's tallest peaks are located there.

HUMAN-ENVIRONMENT INTERACTION The Sherpa are known for their mountaineering skills and their ability to carry heavy loads at high altitudes.
Why might mountain climbers seek out the Sherpas as guides and porters?

damaged the environment, particularly on mountain slopes, where increased trash and pollution have been most noticeable.

Bhutan, which offers many of the same natural attractions as Nepal, has taken a different approach to tourism. Concerned about the impact of tourists on national life, Bhutan regulates the tourist industry. It allows only limited numbers of visitors and keeps some areas of the country off-limits. Even so, tourism is providing increasing revenues to Bhutan and offers significant economic potential for the future.

Rich Cultural Traditions

Visitors to Nepal and Bhutan come not only for the spectacular mountain scenery but also for a glimpse of the rich cultural traditions of the Himalayan people.

A MIX OF PEOPLES Various ethnic groups inhabit the Himalayan region. In Nepal, the majority of the people are Indo-Nepalese Hindus whose ancestors came from India many centuries ago. These groups speak Nepali, a variation of Sanskrit, an ancient Indo-Aryan language. Nepal also has a number of groups of Tibetan ancestry. Among them are the **Sherpas.** These people from the high Himalayas are the traditional mountain guides of the Everest region.

The main ethnic group in Bhutan is the Bhote, who also trace their origins to Tibet. Most Bhotes live in two-story houses made of wood and stone. The families live on the second floor, while the first floor is reserved for livestock. Bhutan also has a sizable Nepalese minority in the southern lowlands. The Nepalese have preserved their language and customs, even though the government of Bhutan has tried to assimilate them into national life.

BACKGROUND Another Nepalese people, the Gurkhas from the valleys west of Kathmandu, are known as fierce fighters. They have been recruited since the mid-19th century to serve in the British and Indian armies.

RELIGIOUS CUSTOMS Religion is a powerful force in both Nepal and Bhutan. Although the great majority of Nepalese are Hindus, Buddhism also has deep roots in Nepal. The founder of Buddhism, **Siddhartha Gautama,** known as the Buddha, was born on the borders of present-day

DIFFERENTIATING INSTRUCTION: GIFTED AND TALENTED STUDENTS

SUMMARIZING A BOOK

Objective To learn more about Siddhartha Gautama, known as the Buddha

Research/Reading 3 days **Class Time** 20 minutes

Task Write and present a book report

Directions Much has been written about Siddhartha. Suggest that interested students read a book, or part of one, about him and summarize the contents for the class. Tell students to include the title, author, year written, and what the book is based on. Most accounts will be fictionalized but based on facts. Suggested reading: *Siddhartha* by Herman Hesse.

Nepal and India in the sixth century B.C. Buddhist teachings initially took hold in Nepal but were later replaced by Hinduism when Hindu rulers came to power. Today, Hindu practices still show traces of Buddhist influence.

Buddhism is the official religion of Bhutan. The Bhutanese people practice a Tibetan style of Buddhism, which includes the use of **mandalas**—geometric designs that are symbols of the universe and aid in meditation. Early communities in Bhutan were organized around large fortress-monasteries, which are still found in many parts of the country. Also scattered around the countryside are small shrines that were built to house sacred relics and are excellent examples of Buddhist architecture.

REGION Masked dancers perform a traditional ceremony during a religious festival in Bhutan.

B. Answer Rugged terrain would make charges by cavalry or field troops difficult.

Seeing Patterns B Why might archery have been a particularly useful military option in Bhutan?

THE ARTS AND RECREATION Folk art and festivals are an important feature of Himalayan culture. Artisans make beautiful metal bells, swords, and jewelry, and carve intricate wooden sculptures. They also weave colorful textiles from silk, cotton, and wool. During festivals in Nepal and Bhutan, musicians play traditional songs on flutes, drums, and long brass horns. At the same time, people in elaborate costumes perform dances based on religious stories. Bhutan is also famous for its archery competitions. This tradition goes back to ancient times, when Bhutanese warriors were known as the finest archers in the Himalayas. B

In this section, you read about life in South Asia's mountainous north. Next, you will learn about life in the southern islands.

Interpreting Photographs

Bhutanese Dancers

Buddhist monks learn and perform dance-dramas as a means of teaching about their faith. One such dance, the sacred drum dance, portrays good triumphing over evil and is believed to benefit the community in which it is performed.

Assess & Reteach

GeoFocus Have students complete their GeoFocus notes on Nepal and Bhutan.

Formal Assessment
- Section Quiz, p. 389

Reteaching Activity
Organize the class into thirds and assign each a subject area covered in this section: "Mountain Kingdoms," "Developing Economies," "Cultural Life." Have students within each group work independently to determine similarities and differences between Nepal and Bhutan. Then have students volunteer information to create a Venn diagram similar to the one made for Section 2 (TE p. 577). Transfer diagram to chart paper or poster board.

In-Depth Resources: Unit 8
- Reteaching Activity, p. 21

Outline Maps with Activities
- Nepal and Bhutan, pp. 83–84

Section 3 Assessment

1 Places & Terms
Identify these terms and explain their importance in the region.
- constitutional monarchy
- Sherpa
- Siddhartha Gautama
- mandala

2 Taking Notes
REGION Review the notes you took for this section.

- What effect does the mountainous terrain have on the economies of Nepal and Bhutan?
- What religions are practiced in Nepal and Bhutan?

3 Main Ideas
a. What kind of government do Nepal and Bhutan have today?
b. How is tourism affecting the economies of these two countries?
c. What are some of the important features of Himalayan culture?

4 Geographic Thinking
Drawing Conclusions How has the physical geography of Nepal and Bhutan affected their development? **Think about:**
- the mountainous landscape
- their landlocked location

See Skillbuilder Handbook, page R5.

EXPLORING LOCAL GEOGRAPHY Review the information about arts and recreation on this page. Then do research about a festival, athletic competition, or craft that is unique to your city, state, or region. Write a **letter** to a friend in another city, state, or country describing the event or product.

SOUTH ASIA

SECTION 3 ASSESSMENT ANSWERS

1. Places & Terms
constitutional monarchy, p. 580; Siddhartha Gautama, p. 582; sherpa, p. 582; mandala, p. 583

2. Taking Notes
- Because of the mountainous terrain, neither country has much land for farming; many farmers create terraces on the sides of mountains to create more farmland and limit soil loss.
- Nepal is mainly Hindu, but the founder of Buddhism was born there; the people of Bhutan practice Buddhism.

3. Main Ideas
a. In Bhutan, the king is the supreme ruler, while in Nepal the king shares power with an elected parliament.
b. Tourism in Nepal is helping its economy, but has caused pollution. Bhutan severely restricts tourism to protect the country.
c. folk art and festivals

4. Geographic Thinking
The mountainous terrain and landlocked locations have isolated these two countries and made them difficult to settle. However, those features have also protected the countries from invaders and allowed them to develop independently.

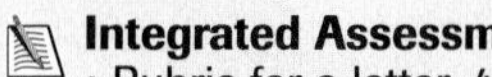

Integrated Assessment
- Rubric for a letter, 4.3

SECTION 4 OBJECTIVES

1. Identify early settlers of Sri Lanka and the Maldives.
2. Summarize religious, ethnic, and cultural life there.
3. Explore their economic strengths and challenges.

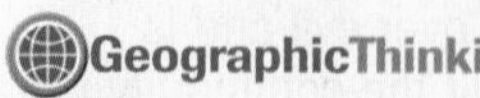

Using the Atlas, p. 585
Making Comparisons, p. 586
Seeing Patterns, p. 587

Focus & Motivate

Ask students what advantages and disadvantages there might be to living on an island. *(disadvantages: isolation, lack of farmland; advantages: unique cultures, access to beaches and fishing)*

Instruct: Objective 1

History of the Islands

- Which two ethnic groups settled in ancient Sri Lanka? *(Sinhalese and Tamils)*
- How has this been the cause of violence in the twentieth century? *(tensions led to civil war in the 1980s and continue to erupt in violence)*
- Who settled the Maldives? *(Buddhists and Hindus from Sri Lanka and India)*
- What religion had the Maldives adopted by the twelfth century? *(Islam)*

In-Depth Resources: Unit 8
- Guided Reading, p. 16

CAPTION ANSWER Tigers are native to Asia and they are noted for their ferocity.

4 Sri Lanka and the Maldives

Main Ideas
- Sri Lanka and the Maldives are island countries with strong connections to the South Asian subcontinent.
- Sri Lanka and the Maldives face difficult challenges that affect their political and economic development.

Places & Terms
Sinhalese
Tamils
sultan

CONNECT TO THE ISSUES
TERRITORIAL DISPUTE Tamil rebels in Sri Lanka are fighting to establish an independent state.

A HUMAN PERSPECTIVE For centuries, Sri Lanka and the Maldives have been ports of call for ships from around the world. The Greeks, Romans, Persians, Chinese, and Arabs all knew about these islands. Arab traders referred to Sri Lanka as Serendib, and they called the Maldives the "Money Isles" for their abundance of cowrie shells—seashells first used in ancient times as currency. Later, European traders came for spices, ivory, pearls, and other goods. Throughout history, visitors have been drawn to these islands in the Indian Ocean. The explorer Marco Polo referred to the Maldives as "one of the wonders of the world."

History of the Islands

Because the islands are close to India, Sri Lanka and the Maldives have strong ties to the Indian subcontinent. Even so, each country has its own distinct history.

SETTLEMENT OF SRI LANKA In the sixth century B.C., people from the northern plains of India crossed the narrow strait separating the subcontinent from Sri Lanka. They came to be known as the **Sinhalese**. They absorbed the island's native inhabitants and created an advanced civilization on Sri Lanka. They adopted Buddhism and built sophisticated irrigation systems that allowed farming on land that was dry. In the fourth century A.D., another group of Indians began to arrive. These were the **Tamils**—Dravidian Hindus from southern India. The Tamils brought a different culture and language to Sri Lanka. They settled the northern end of the island, while the Sinhalese moved farther south.

Europeans began to colonize Sri Lanka in the 16th century. First came the Portuguese, followed by the Dutch. The British took control of the island—which they called Ceylon—in 1796 and ruled until its independence in 1948. In 1972, Ceylon changed its name to Sri Lanka and became a republic.

After independence, tensions grew between the Sinhalese and Tamil populations. The minority Tamils (about 18 percent of the population) claimed discrimination at the hands of the Sinhalese majority (about 74 percent). They began to call for an independent state to be called *Tamil Eelam* (Precious Land of the Tamils). In the 1980s, civil war broke out between the government and the rebels, who were called the Tamil Tigers. Violence had claimed at least 70,000 lives before the Tamil Tigers were finally defeated by Sri Lankan government troops in 2009.

PLACE The Tamil Tigers are anti-government rebels in Sri Lanka. This is their emblem. **Why might a tiger have been chosen for this militant group's name?**

A MUSLIM STATE IN THE MALDIVES The Maldives were settled by Buddhists and Hindus from Sri Lanka and India some time around

SECTION 4 PROGRAM RESOURCES

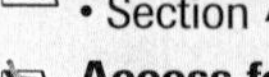

In-Depth Resources: Unit 8
- Guided Reading, p. 16
- Building Vocabulary, p. 18
- Reteaching Activity, p. 22

Guided Reading Workbook
- Section 4

Access for Students Acquiring English/ESL
- Guided Reading, p. 136

Outline Maps with Activities
- Indian Ocean, pp. 85–86

Formal Assessment
- Section Quiz, p. 390

Integrated Assessment
- Rubric for a travel poster, 1.1
- Rubric for a multimedia presentation, 5.4

Cultures around the World
- Music, p. 47

INTEGRATED TECHNOLOGY

Culture Transparencies, CW47
- Playing Drums

Power Presentation

Test Generator
- Section Quiz

hmhsocialstudies.com

TEST-TAKING RESOURCES

Strategies for Test Preparation

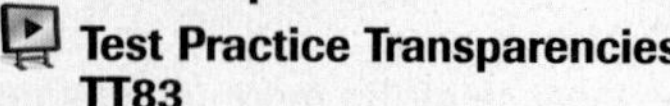

Test Practice Transparencies TT83

Online Test Practice

the sixth century B.C. Later, Arab traders made frequent visits. By the 12th century, the population had converted to Islam. Six dynasties of Muslim rulers, or **sultans,** governed the Maldives after that, despite periods of foreign intervention. In 1968, the Maldives declared itself a republic, headed by an elected president. With its 1,200 islands comprising a land area of just 115 square miles and its population of only about 396,000 people, the Maldives is one of the world's smallest independent countries.

Life in the Islands

As in the rest of South Asia, religion and ethnicity are key factors in the social and cultural life of Sri Lanka and the Maldives.

A. Answer It was a trade stop on the way from North Africa to the Far East.

Geographic Thinking

Using the Atlas
A Using the atlas on page 543, locate Sri Lanka and the continents of Africa and Asia. Why might this island have been visited by Arab traders during its history?

ETHNIC MOSAIC OF THE ISLANDS Sri Lanka is a diverse mix of ethnic and religious groups. Sinhalese Buddhists make up about 69 percent of the population, while Tamil Hindus make up about 18 percent. Almost 8 percent of the people are Muslims, who are descended from the early Arab traders. There is also a small community of Christians of mixed European descent, known as Burghers. A

Most Sinhalese live in the southern, western, and central parts of the country. The Tamils are concentrated in the northern Jaffna Peninsula, where much of the fighting has taken place. Another group of Tamils lives in the central highlands. These people are the descendants of Indian migrants who came to work on British plantations in the 19th century. Muslims live mainly in the eastern lowlands. The capital city, Colombo, is a busy urban center. But most Sri Lankans continue to live in smaller towns and villages scattered across the country.

The population of the Maldives is also multi-ethnic. Most of the people are descended from the early Sinhalese and Dravidian inhabitants, who mixed with Arab, Southeast Asian, and Chinese traders over the centuries. The official language is Divehi, a language unique to the Maldives. Arabic, Hindi, and English are also commonly spoken.

CULTURAL LIFE IN SRI LANKA Religion plays a key role in the culture of Sri Lanka. Buddhist and Hindu temples, Muslim mosques, and Christian churches dot the landscape.

PLACE Large statues of Buddha, such as the 46-foot Sleeping Buddha of Polonnaruwa, shown here, are found all over Sri Lanka. **What might be a reason for the number of these statues?**

SOUTH ASIA

585

Instruct: Objective 2

Life in the Islands

- Why are these countries' populations described as "ethnic mosaics"? *(Both countries have multi-ethnic populations.)*
- What role does religion play in island life? *(Both Hinduism and Buddhism influence Sri Lankan art and literature; Islam is the Maldivian state religion, and has a strong cultural influence.)*
- What is *bodu beru*? *(a traditional Maldivian form of music and dance based on drumming)*

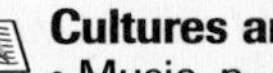

Cultures around the World
• Music, p. 47

Culture Transparencies, CW47
• Playing Drums

Interpreting Photographs

Polonnaruwa, Sri Lanka

Polonnaruwa was the capital of a Sinhalese kingdom during the twelfth century. Several Buddhist shrines were built there at that time.

CAPTION ANSWER Shrines dedicated to the Buddha serve as places of worship for Sri Lankans and visitors.

ACTIVITY OPTION | LINK TO ART

CREATING A POSTER

Objective To find examples of Sri Lankan art and crafts
Class Time 30 minutes
Task Create a poster

Directions Have students work in pairs or small groups. Tell them to search the Internet, magazines, and books for Sri Lankan masks, costumes, and traditional crafts such as lacquer work and wood carving. Students should then print out or photocopy the examples to use in making a poster on Sri Lankan art and crafts. Tell them to color any black and white copies of color images and to add captions for each image.

Instruct: Objective 3

Economic Activity in the Islands

- On what does the economy of Sri Lanka depend? *(rice farming; crops–including tea, rubber, and coconuts–raised on plantations for export; gem mining)*
- What caused the tourist industry in Sri Lanka to collapse? *(civil war)*
- How does the economy of the Maldives differ from those of other South Asian countries? *(lack of land limits farming; most food must be imported)*
- What economic challenges does each country face? *(Sri Lanka: civil unrest, decline of plantation agriculture, deforestation; the Maldives: threat of flooding caused by global warming)*

Interpreting Graphs

World Tea Production

Have students look at the graph on the production of tea around the world. Ask them which two countries account for about half of the world's tea production. *(India and China)* Sri Lanka accounts for about 9 percent of the world's tea. Ask which African country accounts for the same percentage. *(Kenya)*

Art and literature are strongly influenced by those religious traditions. Folk dancing is a notable cultural tradition. The most famous style is *Kandyan* dancing, the national dance. The dances tell the stories of local kings and heroes and are performed at Buddhist festivals. During the yearly *Perahera* festival, dancers dressed in glittering silver headpieces and jewelry leap and spin in complex, acrobatic movements.

CULTURAL LIFE IN THE MALDIVES Muslim customs have a strong influence on the culture of the Maldives. Islam is the state religion, and no other religions are allowed. One of the highlights of Maldivian culture is *bodu beru* ("big drum") music and dance based on drumming. In a *bodu beru* performance, dancers sway to the drumbeat with increasing intensity. This musical tradition has strong African influences.

B. Answer Some of the economic challenges might be to modernize agriculture, expand industrialization, keep population growth in check, find ways to protect against the ravages of natural disasters, and attract foreign aid and tourism.

Economic Activity in the Islands

Like small countries everywhere, the Maldives and Sri Lanka face tough economic challenges. Yet, each country has made good use of its resources to promote economic growth. Today, Sri Lanka has the highest per capita income in South Asia, and the Maldives is not far behind. B

Geographic Thinking

Making Comparisons

B What might be some of the economic challenges facing small developing countries such as Sri Lanka and the Maldives?

ECONOMIC STRENGTHS Like most of South Asia's economies, the economy of Sri Lanka is based on agriculture—mainly rice farming. But unlike most other countries of the region, Sri Lanka has large areas devoted to plantation agriculture. These large farms produce crops such as tea, rubber, and coconuts for export. While this type of agriculture is

REGION Workers pick tea leaves on a plantation in Sri Lanka.

World Tea Production

SOURCE: *Goode's World Atlas, 2000*

ACTIVITY OPTION **EXPLORING LOCAL GEOGRAPHY**

CREATING A CROP REPORT

Objective To learn more about an agricultural product that is important to your region or state

Class Time 30 minutes

Task Create a report on a regional crop

Directions Have students work individually or in small groups to research and write an article about a regional agricultural product. Tell them to include how the product is raised and harvested, and whether it is consumed locally or widely distributed. Students should also include uses, if appropriate, as well as the product's signficance to the local economy.

declining, Sri Lanka is still one of the world's leading tea-producing countries. Although manufacturing is increasing, other sectors of the Sri Lankan economy are less important. Overcutting has damaged the timber industry, and the fishing and mining industries are relatively small. One exception is gem mining. Sri Lanka is famous for its gemstones—including sapphires, rubies, and topaz.

BACKGROUND
One of the world's most famous gems–a star sapphire called the "Star of India"–is actually from Sri Lanka.

The economy of the Maldives is different from the economies of the rest of South Asia. Farming is limited by a lack of land, and most food has to be imported. Fishing—for tuna, marlin, and sharks—was long the main economic activity. It still provides one-fourth of the jobs and a large share of the country's export earnings. But it has been replaced in importance by tourism. The islands' beautiful beaches, coral reefs, and impressive marine life draw visitors from around the world.

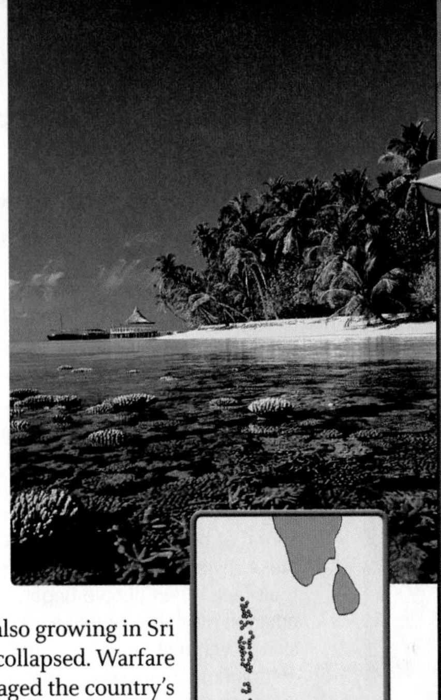

TOUGH CHALLENGES Until the 1980s, tourism was also growing in Sri Lanka. Then civil war began, and the tourist industry collapsed. Warfare has also disrupted other economic activities and damaged the country's infrastructure—its roads, bridges, power systems, and other services. Until peace returns to Sri Lanka, the economy is likely to struggle. While the Maldives is at peace, it faces a challenge of a different kind: global warming. The islands lie very low in the water, and any rise in sea level—caused by melting of the polar icecaps—could flood them completely. Scientists say this could happen by the end of the 21st century.

In this chapter, you read about modern life in South Asia. In the next chapter, you will read about issues facing South Asians.

LOCATION Tourist resorts in the Maldives are built only on previously uninhabited islands.
What might be a reason for locating the resorts on such islands?

Interpreting Photographs

Beaches of the Maldives

In an effort to preserve the lifestyle and culture of the people who inhabit Male, the nation's capital, the government does not allow tourists to stay there. Tourist resorts are located on uninhabited islands.

Which other country in South Asia is also restricting tourism? *(Bhutan)*

CAPTION ANSWER The tourist resorts might be located on these islands because they would have room for development that is not available on the inhabited islands.

Section 4 Assessment

1 Places & Terms

Identify these terms and explain their importance in the region.
- Sinhalese
- Tamils
- sultan

2 Taking Notes

MOVEMENT Review the notes you took for this section.

- How were the islands of the Maldives settled?
- Where do the different ethnic groups in Sri Lanka live?

3 Main Ideas

a. What happened between the Sinhalese and the Tamils after Sri Lanka gained independence?
b. What are some of the aspects of cultural life in the Maldives?
c. What are some of the economic strengths of Sri Lanka and the Maldives?

4 Geographic Thinking

Seeing Patterns How do the Maldives's 1,200 islands affect its economy? **Think about:**
- fishing for food or sport
- the number of beaches

See Skillbuilder Handbook, page R8.

SOUTH ASIA

SEEING PATTERNS Review the information about tourism in the Maldives on this page. Do research on different activities for tourists and different places to visit in the country. Then create a **travel poster** advertising the Maldives as an ideal tourist destination.

Assess & Reteach

GeoFocus Have students complete their GeoFocus notes for Section 4.

Formal Assessment
- Section Quiz, p. 390

Reteaching Activity
Proceed as you have done for Sections 2 and 3, with each student comparing the Maldives and Sri Lanka in the following areas: "History," "Modern Life," and "Economic Activity." Then have the class provide information for a third Venn diagram drawn on chart paper or poster board. Display the three diagrams in the classroom, where they may be used for additional review and discussion.

In-Depth Resources: Unit 8
- Reteaching Activity, p. 22

Outline Maps with Activities
- Indian Ocean, pp. 85–86

SECTION 4 ASSESSMENT ANSWERS

1. Places & Terms
Sinhalese, p. 584
Tamils, p. 584
sultan, p. 585

2. Taking Notes
- Buddhists and Hindus from Sri Lanka and India settled the Maldives, and some Arab traders also settled there.
- Sinhalese: in southern, western, and central Sri Lanka; the Tamils: the north and the central highlands; Muslims: in the east

3. Main Ideas
a. The Tamils claimed discrimination and began to call for an independent state. Civil war broke out.
b. Islam shapes cultural life. A cultural highlight is the *bodu beru*, a popular tradition of music and dance.
c. Sri Lanka: rubber, coconuts, tea, sapphires, rubies, and topaz; the Maldives: fishing and tourism

4. Geographic Thinking
Fishing accounts for one-fourth of the jobs and much of its export earnings. Tourists come from all over the world to enjoy the beaches.

GeoActivity

Integrated Assessment
- Rubric for a travel poster, 1.1

OBJECTIVE

Broaden knowledge of musical instruments associated with particular cultures.

Instruct: Objective

Musical Instruments

- What are the four basic types of instruments? *(wind, percussion, string, and keyboard)*
- What do scholars believe about the origin of music? *(that all cultures have had music, possibly from earliest times)*
- Why do you think the musician playing the didgeridoo is dressed the way he is? *(He is probably performing in a ritual ceremony.)*

 **Cultures Around the World**
• Music, p. 47

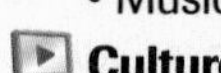 **Cultures Transparencies, CW47**
• Playing Drums

Interpreting Photographs

Bagpipes

The bagpipe is one of the oldest wind instruments with a reed, and was played by musicians in ancient Greece, Rome, and Persia. Most often associated with Scotland, where it was adopted by Highlanders in the 18th century, many countries, including France, Ireland, Italy, Romania, Spain, and Egypt, have versions of the bagpipe.

hmhsocialstudies.com INTERACTIVE

Comparing Cultures

Musical Instruments

No one is certain when or where people began to make music or what the first musical instrument was. Scholars believe, though, that music has been part of all cultures, possibly even from the earliest times. The first musical instrument may have been the human voice mimicking the sound of birds. People also used their own bodies to make rhythms, by clapping their hands or stomping their feet. When people began to make instruments, they adapted available materials, such as wood and animal skins. Eventually, musicians developed four basic types of instruments: percussion, wind, string, and keyboard. Today, there are thousands of different musical instruments. Some are closely associated with certain countries or regions.

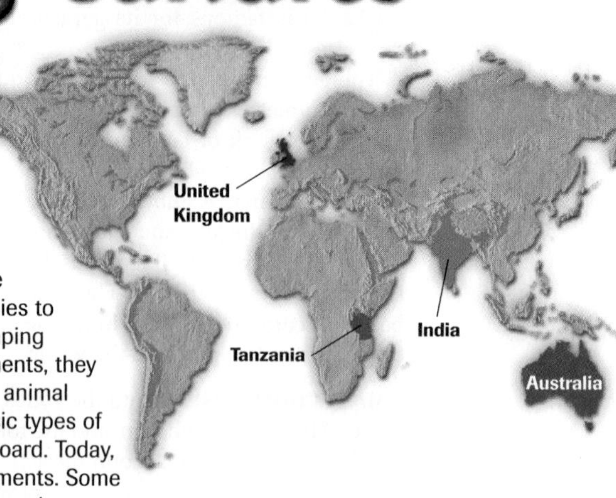

The bagpipe is a wind instrument that is associated with Scotland, although it is played in other countries. It consists of an animal skin or rubberized cloth bag fitted with one or more pipes that produce a continuous flow of sound when blown.

The drum is a percussion instrument from Africa that probably was made first from wood or stone. It is played by striking with hands or other objects. These drums are made of skins stretched over frames.

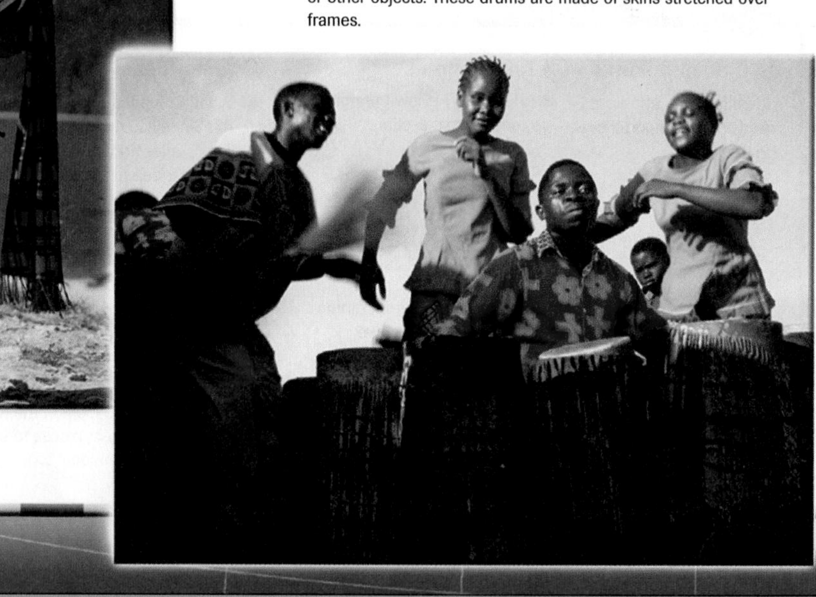

SUPPORTING RESOURCES

BOOKS FOR THE TEACHER

Titon, Jeff Todd, Linda Fujie, and David Locke (eds.) Munich, Germany: Schirmer, 2000. ***Worlds of Music: An Introduction to the Music of the World's Peoples.*** Thoughtful survey of world cultures and music.

BOOKS FOR THE STUDENT

Broughton, Simon (ed.). ***World Music, the Rough Guide: Africa, Europe and the Middle East.*** NY: Rough Guides, 2000. Easy-to-understand introduction to popular, folk, and classical music traditions of three regions.

Broughton, Simon, and Mark Ellingham (eds.). ***The Rough Guide to World Music: Latin and North America, Caribbean, India, Asia and Pacific.*** NY: Rough Guides, 2000. Guide to pop and traditional music; includes recommendations for CDs and cassettes.

INTERNET

For more on music and musical instruments, visit . . .

hmhsocialstudies.com

The didgeridoo is a wind instrument played by aboriginal people in Australia. Made of bamboo or a hollow sapling, it can be as long as five feet. It is generally painted and used in ritual ceremonies.

sitar is a stringed instrument ı India. It has a wooden body is used mainly to play classical ic. Anoushka Shankar, shown with her sitar, is the daughter med sitarist Ravi Shankar, who ght the instrument to the world's ntion with his playing in the 1960s.

GeoActivity

FORMING A BAND 
With a small group, research other musical instruments. Plan a band that includes at least one of each of the four types of instruments. Then create **a multimedia presentation.**

- Provide visuals of each instrument.
- Write a description of each instrument's sound.
- Make an audiotape that has the sound of each instrument and play it in class.

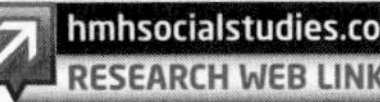
hmhsocialstudies.com
RESEARCH WEB LINKS

GeoData

OTHER INSTRUMENTS

ASIA

- Empty conch shells with broken tips give off a loud sound when blown and have been used in ceremonies for centuries in many regions, including the islands of Polynesia.

EUROPE

- The organ is the oldest keyboard instrument and was found in ancient Greece more than 2,000 years ago. It gave birth to other keyboard instruments such as the harpsichord, clavichord, and piano.

THE AMERICAS

- Native American cultures have strongly emphasized the voice in making music.

AFRICA

- Wall paintings in 4,000-year-old tombs in Egypt show musicians playing lutes.
- Some African cultures still use a stone gong—a hanging stone that gives off a sound when struck.

GeoActivities

Integrated Assessment
- Rubric for a multimedia presentation, 5.4

More About

Percussion Instruments

There are different categories of percussion instruments: drums produce sound when struck; rattles produce sound by vibrating. Percussion instruments have been used since ancient times and may be found in cultures throughout the world. Many percussion instruments, such as the timpani, or kettledrums, originated in Asia. Drums have been used to send messages and are still used in various rituals.

ACTIVITY OPTION | COOPERATIVE LEARNING

WRITING A PRESS RELEASE

Objective To research forms of traditional American music

Class Time 30 minutes

Task Create an illustrated press release announcing a forthcoming music festival

Directions Organize the class into small groups and have each choose one of the following topics: Appalachian folk music, jazz, or Native American music. (Each topic should be covered by at least one group.) Tell each group to write a press release announcing a festival featuring one of the three types of music.

Students should include information about how their topic reflects our cultural heritage and instruments traditionally associated with the music, as well as date, time, and place. Tell them to include drawings and photographs showing musical instruments associated with the type of music presented.

Assign the following roles to one or more students in each group:

- text researcher and writer
- photo researcher
- designer

Reviewing Places & Terms

A. **1.** Mughal Empire, p. 568
2. nonviolent resistance, p. 568
3. caste system, p. 572
4. partition, p. 574
5. Kashmir, p. 574
6. microcredit, p. 575
7. Sherpa, p. 582
8. mandala, p. 583
9. Sinhalese, p. 584
10. Tamils, p. 584

B. Possible Responses

11. Gandhi used nonviolent resistance to protest.
12. India and Pakistan have fought over Kashmir.
13. South Asians seek financial aid known as microcredit.
14. It was formed by partition.
15. They established the Mughal Empire.
16. The Tamils arrived in Sri Lanka from India.
17. The Sinhalese created an advanced civilization in Sri Lanka.
18. The sherpas guide mountain climbers in the Everest region.
19. Mandalas are designs that function as symbols.
20. The caste system is a strict system of social classes.

Chapter 25 Assessment

VISUAL SUMMARY
HUMAN GEOGRAPHY OF SOUTH ASIA

Subregions of South Asia

India
- India is the largest country in South Asia and dominates the region.
- India is the world's largest democracy; Hinduism is its principal religion.

Pakistan and Bangladesh
- Pakistan and Bangladesh were both eventually formed after the partition of India.
- Farming is the main source of people's livelihoods.
- Islam is the primary cultural force in those countries.

Nepal and Bhutan
- Nepal and Bhutan developed in relative isolation because of the Himalaya Mountains.
- Nepal has a religious mix of both Hindus and Buddhists, while Bhutan is a predominantly Buddhist country.

Sri Lanka and the Maldives
- Sri Lanka contains a variety of ethnic and religious groups, including Sinhalese Buddhists, Tamil Hindus, and Muslims.
- Sri Lanka's economy is based on farming and gem mining, while the Maldives relies on fishing and tourism.

Reviewing Places & Terms

A. Briefly explain the importance of each of the following.

1. Mughal Empire
2. nonviolent resistance
3. caste system
4. partition
5. Kashmir
6. microcredit
7. Sherpa
8. mandala
9. Sinhalese
10. Tamils

B. Answer the questions about vocabulary in complete sentences.

11. How did the great Indian leader Mohandas Gandhi protest British control of India?
12. Over which territory have India and Pakistan fought several wars?
13. What financial aid do poor South Asian entrepreneurs seek?
14. How was the country of West and East Pakistan formed after Indian independence?
15. What did the Muslims establish in India during the 16th century?
16. What people arrived in Sri Lanka from southern India and occupied the northern portion of the island?
17. Who created an advanced civilization in Sri Lanka and built sophisticated irrigation systems?
18. Who guides mountain climbers in the Everest region?
19. What are geometric designs that are symbols of the universe and aid in meditation?
20. What is a Hindu system of social classes?

Main Ideas

India (pp. 567–572)

1. How did Britain gain control of India?
2. What are the major economic activities in India?
3. What are the major languages of India?

Pakistan and Bangladesh (pp. 573–579)

4. What are some of the characteristics of the Indus Valley civilization?
5. What manufactured products are produced in Pakistan and Bangladesh?
6. What type of literature is important in Pakistan and Bangladesh?

Nepal and Bhutan (pp. 580–583)

7. What are some of the groups of people that live in Nepal?
8. What are some important religious customs in Bhutan?

Sri Lanka and the Maldives (pp. 584–589)

9. What are the two major ethnic groups in Sri Lanka and where did they come from?
10. What are some of the challenges facing the economies of Sri Lanka and the Maldives?

Main Ideas

1. European countries set up trading posts in India. Eventually, Britain established direct rule over the country.
2. Two-thirds of India's people rely on farming. There are also manufacturing and high-tech industries.
3. There are 18 major languages in India and hundreds of lesser ones. Hindi is the official language, although English is widely spoken.
4. It was a highly developed urban civilization, with well-planned cities and advanced sanitation systems.
5. Both countries export cotton clothes, while Pakistan also exports wool carpets and leather products.
6. Poets are popular figures, and poetry readings draw thousands.
7. The majority of people in Nepal are Indo-Nepalese Hindus. Also, there are a large number of people of Tibetan ancestry.
8. People in Bhutan practice a Tibetan-style Buddhism. The country has many small Buddhist shrines that house sacred relics.
9. The Sinhalese (Indo-Aryans) came from northern India, and the Tamils (Dravidian Hindus) arrived from southern India.
10. Civil war has disrupted tourism in Sri Lanka, damaged other economic activities, and destroyed some of the country's infrastructure. Global warming threatens the existence of the Maldives.

Critical Thinking

1. Using Your Notes
Use your completed chart to answer these questions.

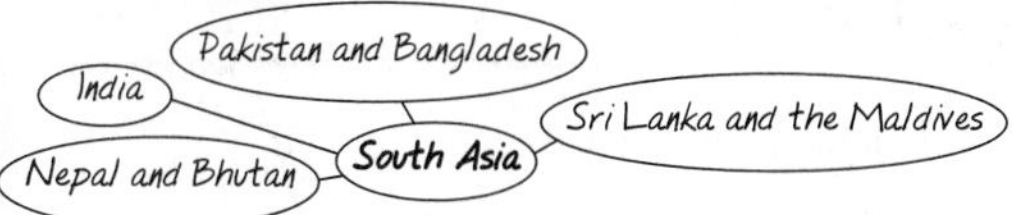

a. What role does agriculture play in the economies of the South Asian countries?
b. What are the major religions practiced in the region?

2. Geographic Themes
a. **HUMAN-ENVIRONMENT INTERACTION** How did the mountainous terrain and the landlocked location of Nepal and Bhutan affect their development?
b. **LOCATION** How do the landforms and location of the Maldives ensure that its economy is different from other South Asian countries?

3. Identifying Themes
What groups of people first populated the Indian subcontinent and eventually helped to populate all of South Asia? Which of the five themes apply to this situation?

4. Making Comparisons
How do Pakistan and Bangladesh differ in their practice of Islam?

5. Determining Cause and Effect
What are some of the reasons for the ongoing violence between the Tamils and the Sinhalese in Sri Lanka?

For Additional Test Practice

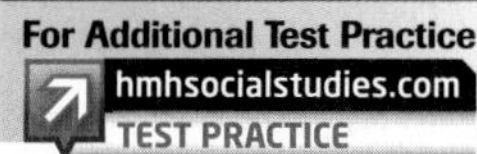

Geographic Skills: Interpreting Maps

Languages of South Asia

Use the map at right to answer the following questions.

1. **LOCATION** How many major languages are spoken in South Asia?
2. **REGION** Which language group is the most commonly spoken?
3. **MOVEMENT** How might the number of languages in South Asia affect its developing economies?

Choose a country in South Asia in which more than one language is spoken, and prepare a chart showing the number of people speaking each language. Use library references or the Internet for your research.

hmhsocialstudies.com
MULTIMEDIA ACTIVITY

Use the links at **hmhsocialstudies.com** to do research on the people of one South Asian country. Look for such information as life expectancy, religions, ethnic groups, literacy rates, and per capita income.

Writing About Geography Write a report about your findings. Use standard grammar, spelling, sentence structure, and punctuation in your report. List the Web sites that you used as sources.

CHAPTER 25 ASSESSMENT

Critical Thinking

1. a. Agriculture is the primary economic activity in every South Asian country but the Maldives.
b. India and Nepal are mostly Hindu. Pakistan, Bangladesh, and the Maldives are mostly Muslim. Bhutan and Sri Lanka are mainly Buddhist.
2. a. They were difficult to settle, but they developed independently, and were less susceptible to invasion.
b. Because the Maldives is a group of islands, it has developed a thriving fishing and tourist economy.
3. Around 1500 B.C., Aryans spread across northern India and pushed native Indians farther south. Persian and Greek invaders also occupied the Indus Valley, and around A.D. 1500 Muslims arrived; movement
4. Pakistan is stricter in enforcing Islamic law.
5. Long-standing ethnic differences are the major cause of the violence.

GeoActivity

Integrated Assessment
- Rubric for making a chart, 2.2

Formal Assessment
- Chapter Test, Forms A, B, and C, pp. 391–402

Geographic Skills

1. 24
2. Indo-European
3. The many different languages of the region could create economic problems. People may have difficulty communicating, and this could impede the flow of goods and services.

MULTIMEDIA ACTIVITY

For the report on the people of one South Asian country, students should:
- Present a concise, well-organized report on the people of one country.
- Summarize data and information.
- Produce clear, imaginative visuals to complement the report.
- Include references to the Web sites used as sources.

Grading Rubric Evaluate students performances as Exceptional, Acceptable, or Poor in each of the following categories.

	Exceptional	*Acceptable*	*Poor*
Writing is clear, focused, and logical			
Introductory sentence clearly states the topic and purpose			
Report provides necessary facts and examples			
Report uses correct grammar, spelling, and punctuation			

CHAPTER 26 PLANNING GUIDE

Today's Issues: South Asia

OVERVIEW	INSTRUCTIONAL RESOURCES	
ESSENTIAL QUESTION How can the people and governments of South Asia work together to solve the region's challenges? **Focus on the Essential Question Podcast**	**In-Depth Resources: Unit 8** • Building Vocabulary, p. 29 **Block Schedule Strategies** **Chapter Summaries** (English/Spanish)	**Interactive Online Edition** TOS **ExamView® Assessment Suite** (English/Spanish) TOS **CalendarPlanner** **Power Presentations with Media Gallery** **Critical Thinking Transparencies** • CT26 **Video:** Kashmir: The Legacy of Partition in India hmhsocialstudies.com INTERACTIVE
SECTION 1 **POPULATION EXPLOSION** **MAIN IDEAS** • At its present rate of increase, India's population is projected to reach 1.5 billion people in another 40 years. • Indians are slow to embrace the idea of having smaller families. • Education is key to slowing the growth rate of India's population.	**In-Depth Resources: Unit 8** • Guided Reading, p. 23 • Map and Graph Skills, pp. 26–27 • Building Vocabulary, p. 29 • Exploring Today's Issues, pp. 30–31 • Reteaching Activity, p. 34 **Guided Reading Workbook,** Section 1	**Critical Thinking Transparencies** • CT58 Literacy Rates and Life Expectancy
SECTION 2 **LIVING WITH EXTREME WEATHER** **MAIN IDEAS** • Summer and winter monsoons are seasonal wind systems that blow across South Asia. • Summer monsoons bring much of the rain on which agriculture in South Asia is dependent. • Extreme weather associated with monsoons may cause crop failure, homelessness, and death.	**In-Depth Resources: Unit 8** • Guided Reading, p. 24 • Skillbuilder Practice, p. 28 • Building Vocabulary, p. 29 • Exploring Today's Issues, pp. 32–33 • Reteaching Activity, p. 35 • GeoWorkshop, pp. 37–38 **Guided Reading Workbook,** Section 2	**Map Transparencies** • MT45 Summer and Winter Monsoons
CASE STUDY **TERRITORIAL DISPUTE** **MAIN IDEAS** • Since 1947, India and Pakistan have been involved in a dispute over the territory of Kashmir. • India and Pakistan both have nuclear weapons, which raises the possibility of a nuclear war over Kashmir. • Huge sums of money spent by both countries on arms could have been used instead for education and to address other social problems.	**In-Depth Resources: Unit 8** • Guided Reading, p. 25 • Building Vocabulary, p. 29 • Reteaching Activity, p. 36 **Guided Reading Workbook,** Case Study	hmhsocialstudies.com INTERACTIVE • Kashmir, p. 601

ASSESSMENT

SE **Chapter Assessment,** pp. 604–605

Formal Assessment
- Chapter Tests, Forms A, B, and C, pp. 406–420

TOS **ExamView® Assessment Suite**

Strategies for Test Preparation

SE **Section Assessment,** p. 595

Formal Assessment
- Section Quiz, p. 403

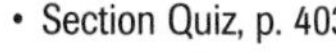

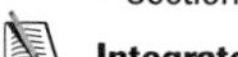

Integrated Assessment
- Rubric for a line graph, 2.3

Test Practice Transparencies TT84

SE **Section Assessment,** p. 599

Formal Assessment
- Section Quiz, p. 404

Integrated Assessment
- Rubric for a newspaper article, 4.5

Test Practice Transparencies TT85

SE **Case Study Project,** pp. 602–603

Formal Assessment
- Case Study Quiz, p. 405

Test Practice Transparencies TT86

CHART KEY:

SE Student Edition	Block Scheduling	DVD/CD-ROM
TE Teacher's Edition	TOS Teacher One Stop	MP3 Audio
Printable Resource	Presentation Resource	HISTORY™

Program Resources available on TOS and @ hmhsocialstudies.com

SUPPORTING RESOURCES

- Multimedia Classroom Global History Series
- Global History Teacher's Guide

Social Studies Trade Library Collection
- Modern World History Trade Collection

For more information or to purchase these resources, go to

DIFFERENTIATED INSTRUCTION

English Learners	Struggling Readers	Gifted and Talented Students
 **Spanish/English Guided Reading Workbook**  **Access for Students Acquiring English/ESL** Spanish Translations, pp. 138–143  **Chapter Summaries** (English/Spanish)	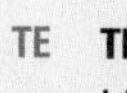 **Chapter Summaries** (English/Spanish) TE **TE Activity** Identifying Primary Sources, p. 601	 **In-Depth Resources: Unit 8** GeoWorkshop, p. 37

ENRICHMENT ACTIVITIES

The following activities are especially suitable for classes following block schedules.

SE **Student Edition,** pp. 592–605 • Reading a Population Pyramid, p. 596	hmhsocialstudies.com INTERACTIVE • Farming Calendar in India, p. 597 • Summer and Winter Monsoons, p. 598 • Kashmir, p. 601

BLOCK SCHEDULE LESSON PLAN OPTIONS: 90-MINUTE PERIOD

DAY 1

SECTION 1, pp. 593–596
Class Time 60 minutes

- **Panel Discussion** Have students prepare questions that a moderator of a panel discussion might ask regarding population growth in South Asia. Tell them to cover four general categories: extent of the problem, effects, projections for the future, and possible solutions. Have a panel of four students respond as the remaining students take turns asking questions.
  Class Time 45 minutes

- **Population Pyramid** Have students use the population pyramid on page 596 to answer the questions at the bottom of the page.
  Class Time 15 minutes

SECTION 2, 597–599
Class Time 30 minutes

- **Cause and Effect Chart** Tell students to fill in information on extreme weather on the GeoFocus chart that appears at the beginning of the chapter.

DAY 2

CASE STUDY, pp. 600–603
Class Time 20 minutes

- **Case Study Project** Have students begin gathering information for the Case Study project. They may complete the project as homework.

CHAPTER 26 REVIEW AND ASSESSMENT, pp. 604–605
Class Time 70 minutes

- **Review** Have students prepare a summary of the chapter using the Places & Terms listed on the first page of each section.
  Class Time 35 minutes

- **Assessment** Have students complete the Chapter 26 Assessment
  Class Time 35 minutes

TEACHER-TESTED ACTIVITY

Role Play a Summit Meeting on Kashmir

Class Time 1–2 class periods

Task Using Case Study text and primary source excerpts provided students will role-play and debate the Kashmir conflict.

Supplies
- Case Study primary sources
- If desired, further research materials about the Kashmir dispute.

Purpose To understand the complexity surrounding the Kashmir conflict. Many students find it difficult to appreciate all facets of such struggles throughout the world.

Activity Divide students into groups representing the Indian government, the Pakistani government, the Kashmir government, the President of the United States, the U.S. Secretary of State, and the United Nations. Using provided readings, students should prepare for a summit meeting with the purpose of finding a peaceful solution to the conflict. The United Nations and United States will mediate. Set up the meeting so that each group has an opportunity to present its concerns. Allow time for open discussion. Remember the point of the activity is for students to understand the complexity; after all, governments have been debating this question for over fifty years.

Kara Lukens
Geography Teacher, Dakota High School, Macomb, Michigan

TECHNOLOGY IN THE CLASSROOM

One significant advantage of using the Internet to obtain news is that many online news sources update their information hourly or even more often. The news is therefore likely to be more current than radio or TV news, not to mention the daily newspapers. Students can search online news sources to get updates on current events topics they've been discussing or to learn more about recent events related to a region or topic they're studying.

Objective Students will search an online news source to find out about recent events in Kashmir and recent updates on tensions between India and Pakistan.

Task Have students type keywords into an online news source's search engine to locate three recent articles on the Kashmir situation or on tensions between India and Pakistan. They'll conclude by writing paragraphs summarizing the situation.

Class Time 1-2 class periods

1. Have students read about the conflict over Kashmir and tensions between India and Pakistan on pages 600-603.

2. Ask students to make charts with the headings "India" and "Pakistan." Have them list each country's argument as to why it wants to control Kashmir.

3. Have students go to one or more of the online news sources listed at **hmhsocialstudies.com** and search for articles on the Kashmir situation and on relations between India and Pakistan. They should try searching with the keywords "Kashmir" and "India and Pakistan."

4. Have students read the three most recent articles they've found and summarize them by answering these questions: What is the title of the article? Who wrote the article? When was the article written? What is the article's main idea? What does the article say about India? What does the article say about Pakistan?

5 Hold a class discussion in which students describe the most recent news from this region.

6. Have students use a word processor to write a few paragraphs describing the situation in Kashmir, explaining the relationship between Kashmir, India, and Pakistan, and summarizing recent developments in this area.

CHAPTER 26 OBJECTIVE

Learn that South Asians face serious issues, and are actively seeking solutions to their problems.

Chapter 26 TODAY'S ISSUES South Asia

HISTORY
Kashmir: The Legacy of Partition in India
hmhsocialstudies.com VIDEO

Have students look at the photograph of a street in Kolkata. Then ask how they would describe the scene. *(crowded; busy)* What might it be like to live there? *(Answers will vary but may include constant noise, inadequate living space.)*

Introducing the Essential Question

- Remind students that a billion is a thousand millions. Challenge students to suggest ways to visualize one billion—of objects, dollars, or people. Then explain that India alone has more than a billion people. Pakistan and Bangladesh also have very large populations and extreme population density in some areas.
- Review what students learned earlier about monsoons. Students will learn more about the havoc that monsoons can unleash on South Asia in this chapter.

As students note cause and effect they will develop a better understanding of the magnitude or complexity of the issue. Use the Critical Thinking Transparency to examine the issue further.

Critical Thinking Transparencies CT26
- GeoFocus

In-Depth Resources: Unit 8
- Building Vocabulary, p. 29

Essential Question

How can the people and governments of South Asia work together to solve the region's challenges?

What You Will Learn

In this chapter you will examine the stresses that rapid population growth and weather extremes put on the people of South Asia.

SECTION 1
Population Explosion

SECTION 2
Living with Extreme Weather

CASE STUDY
Territorial Dispute

For more on these issues in South Asia . . .

hmhsocialstudies.com CURRENT EVENTS

hmhsocialstudies.com TAKING NOTES

Use the graphic organizer online to take notes on each issue and to analyze the causes and effects of some aspect of each issue.

Kolkata is one of India's most densely populated cities.

592

BOOKS FOR THE TEACHER

Marston, Daniel P. and Chandar S. Sundaram (eds.). ***A Military History of India and South Asia: From the East India Company to the Nuclear Era.*** Indiana University Press, 2008. Includes coverage of the conflict in Kashmir.

BOOKS FOR THE STUDENT

Norton, James, K., ed. ***India and South Asia: Global Studies.*** Blacklick, OH: Dushkin/McGraw-Hill, 1995. Articles on democracy, the caste system, cleaning up the Ganges River, the ecology of the Himalayas, and more.

INTERNET

For more on issues facing South Asia, visit . . .

hmhsocialstudies.com

Population Explosion

How can South Asia's population growth be managed?

Main Ideas

- Explosive population growth in South Asia has contributed to social and economic ills in the region.
- Education is key to controlling population growth and improving the quality of life in South Asia.

Places & Terms

basic necessities

illiteracy

A HUMAN PERSPECTIVE On May 11, 2000, at 5:05 A.M., a baby girl was born in a New Delhi hospital. Her parents named her Astha, which means "faith" in the Hindi language. Ordinarily, Astha's birth would not have made news. After all, an estimated 70,000 babies are born in India every day—25,637,000 each year. Astha, however, was special. With this child's birth, the population of India officially hit 1 billion. It was the second country to reach a billion in population; China was the first.

Growing Pains

India's milestone was a mixed blessing. Its population at the beginning of the 21st century is growing so quickly that many of its citizens lack life's **basic necessities**—food, clothing, and shelter. The question for India, and for South Asia as a whole, is how to manage population growth so that economic development can continue.

POPULATION GROWS When India gained its independence from Britain in 1947, the population stood at 300 million. By 2000, the population had more than tripled. India's population is so large that even an annual growth rate of less than 2 percent is producing a population explosion. Unless that growth slows down, in 2045, India will be home to more than 1.5 billion people—all living in a land about one-third the size of the United States. India will be the most populous country in the world, surpassing China.

India is not alone in its skyrocketing population. In fact, of the 10 most populous countries in the world in 2010, three were located in South Asia: India, Pakistan, and Bangladesh. South Asia is home to 27 percent of the world's population. But these people live on less than 3 percent of the world's land area.

INADEQUATE RESOURCES As South Asia's population has increased, regional governments have found it more and more difficult to meet the needs of their people. Widespread poverty and **illiteracy**, the inability to read or

REGION The homeless poor are a common sight in many of India's large cities, such as Mumbai, pictured below. **What might be some ways in which the homeless can be helped?**

SOUTH ASIA

SECTION 1 OBJECTIVES

1. Identify the reasons for and problems created by India's population explosion.
2. Analyze why population growth in India is difficult to manage.

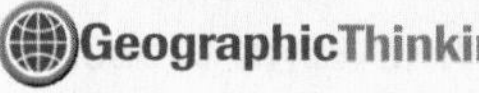

SKILLBUILDER: Interpreting Maps and Graphs, p. 594

GeographicThinking

Seeing Patterns, p. 594

Making Inferences, p. 595

Focus & Motivate

Ask students what problems would result from a population explosion. *(Answers may include homelessness, unemployment, and poor sanitation.)*

Instruct: Objective 1

Growing Pains

- Why would a population increase of only 2 percent lead to a population explosion in India? *(India already has a billion people. In 40 years a 2 percent increase would result in an additional half billion people.)*
- What percentage of the world's population lives in South Asia? *(22 percent)*

In-Depth Resources: Unit 8
- Guided Reading, p. 23
- Exploring Today's Issues, pp. 30–31

CAPTION ANSWER Governments might provide food, shelter, clothing, and even jobs.

SECTION 1 PROGRAM RESOURCES

In-Depth Resources: Unit 8
- Guided Reading, p. 23
- Map and Graph Skills, pp. 26–27
- Building Vocabulary, p. 29
- Exploring Today's Issues, pp. 30–31
- Reteaching Activity, p. 34

Guided Reading Workbook
- Section 1

Access for Students Acquiring English/ESL
- Guided Reading, p. 138
- Map and Graph Skills, pp. 142–143

Formal Assessment
- Section Quiz, p. 403

Integrated Assessment
- Rubric for a line graph, 2.3

INTEGRATED TECHNOLOGY

Critical Thinking Transparencies CT58
- Literacy Rates and Life Expectancy

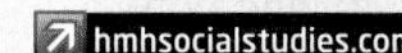

TEST-TAKING RESOURCES

Strategies for Test Preparation

Test Practice Transparencies TT84

Online Test Practice

Interpreting Maps

Population Density in Indian States

Have students look at the population density map. How much of India falls into the most densely populated category? *(at least half)*

SKILLBUILDER ANSWERS 1. about 2045 **2.** the United States

Instruct: Objective 

Managing Population Growth

- Why are large families still considered desirable despite concerns about population? *(Children supplement income and support parents in their old age.)*
- Why is education fundamental to the slowing of population growth? *(Health education can reduce the need for large families by reducing the infant mortality rate. Educated parents will be less reliant on their children to supplement family income.)*
- What difficulties are South Asian governments encountering in providing adequate education? *(inadequate funds; the inability to keep up with the needs of an exploding population)*

Critical Thinking Transparencies CT58
- Literacy Rates and Life Expectancy

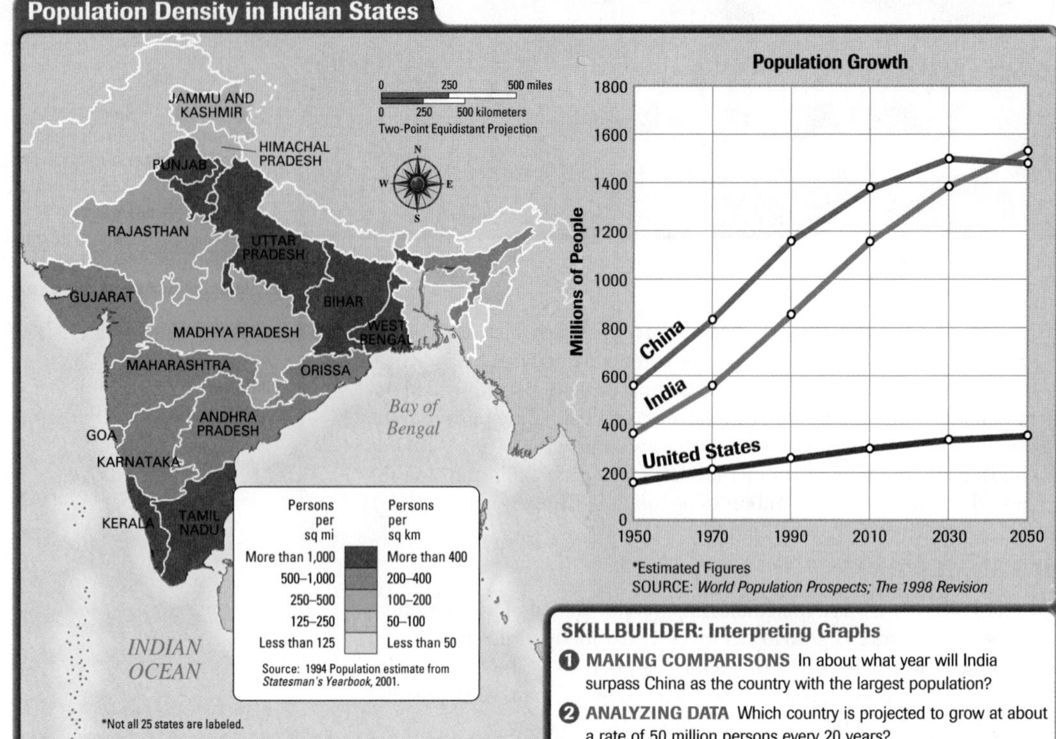

write, have left millions without hope that their lives would improve. Poor sanitation and the lack of health education have led to outbreaks of disease, which have overwhelmed the region's limited health care systems.

Officials estimate that in order to keep pace with population growth, India will have to do the following *every year*: build 127,000 new village schools, hire nearly 400,000 new teachers, construct 2.5 million new homes, create 4 million new jobs, and produce an additional 6 million tons of food.

Managing Population Growth

South Asia has struggled for decades to find solutions to its population explosion. But efforts have met with only limited success.

SMALLER FAMILIES Today, India spends much of its nearly $1 billion annual health-care budget encouraging Indians to have smaller families. "Let's have small families for a stronger India" is one of the slogans of the campaign. For many reasons, however, these programs have had only limited success. Indian women usually marry before age 18 and start having babies early. Also, for the very poor, children are a source of income. They can beg for money in the streets as early as their third birthday and can work the fields not too many years later. A

For many Indians, children represent security in old age. The more children a family has, the more likely someone will be around to take care of the parents when they are elderly. Also, the infant mortality rate

A. Answer Fewer people would mean less drain on India's natural and financial resources and would promote economic growth.

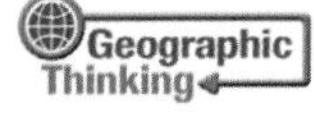

Seeing Patterns
A How might smaller families affect India's economic development?

ACTIVITY OPTION **INTERNET RESEARCH**

 **BLOCK SCHEDULING**

MAKING A CHART

Objective To compare the three most populous countries in terms of population, size, and density

Class Time 20 minutes

Task Create a chart showing the population, size (land area), and population density of India, China, and the United States

Directions Tell students to use the Internet to research population data for India, China, and the United States. Have them create a chart comparing the statistics for each country. Tell them to fill in four columns labeled from left to right as follows: Country, Population, Size, Density. Direct students **hmhsocialstudies.com** to for updated links.

OPTIONAL ACTIVITY If Internet access is limited, have the students use the library to find the information in reference books, government and United Nations publications, or in current magazine or newspaper articles.

is very high in South Asia—around 51 per 1,000 live births in India, 59 per 1,000 in Bangladesh, and 67 per 1,000 in Pakistan, compared to 6 per 1,000 in the United States. As a result, parents try to have many children to ensure that at least some will reach adulthood.

EDUCATION IS A KEY Many factors that affect population growth can be changed through education. However, South Asia's governments have a difficult task ahead of them because education funds are limited. For example, India spends about $300 per pupil annually on primary and secondary education. (Only a small fraction of this sum is spent on girls.) By contrast, annual per pupil spending on education in the United States is $6,582 for primary students and $8,157 for secondary students. That is more than 20 times as much.

Education is essential to break the cycle of poverty. It also helps to improve the status of females by giving them job opportunities outside the home. Better health education also can reduce the need for large families by ensuring that more babies reach adulthood. The future development of South Asia depends on the success of such efforts to control population growth.

The Indian government recently took a big step to improve education. In 2009, the government made education a fundamental right by approving "The Right of Children to Free and Compulsory Education Act."

BACKGROUND
Statistics for 2007 showed that about 91 percent of Indian boys aged 6 to 12 are in school, compared to about 88 percent of girls.

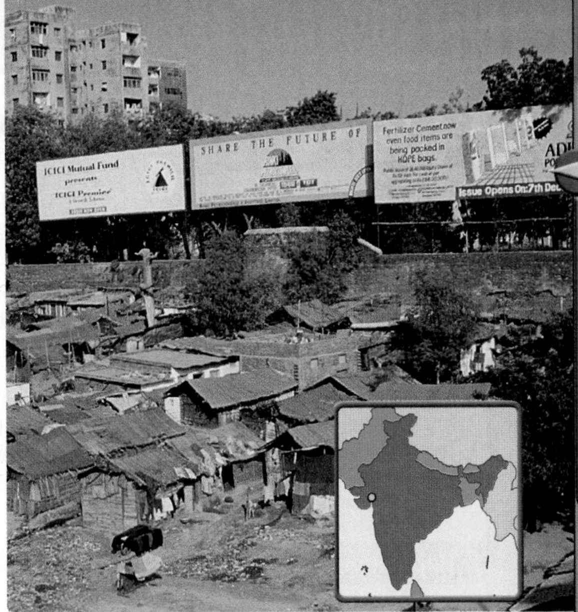

HUMAN-ENVIRONMENT INTERACTION The rural poor build settlements on unused land in many cities, such as these in Ahmadabad, India.
Why might the rural poor be attracted to urban areas?

Interpreting Photographs

Shanty Settlement
Ask students what contrast they see in the way people live in Ahmadabad? *(Some live in apartment buildings while others live in makeshift shacks.)*

CAPTION ANSWER Urban areas can provide more job opportunities than can rural areas.

Assess & Reteach

GeoFocus Have students complete Issue 1 of the GeoFocus chart they began at the start of this section.

Formal Assessment
• Section Quiz, p. 403

Reteaching Activity
Have students work together in pairs. Tell them to use their notes to write three questions regarding the causes and effects of the population explosion in South Asia. Then have them take turns using the questions to quiz each other on the section.

In-Depth Resources: Unit 8
• Reteaching Activity, p. 34

SECTION 1 Assessment

1 Places & Terms
Explain the importance of each of the following terms and places.
- basic necessities
- illiteracy

2 Taking Notes
PLACE Review the notes you took for this section.

	Causes	Effects
Issue 1: Population		

- How much did India's population grow in the second half of the 20th century?
- If this growth rate continues, what will India's population be in 2045?

3 Main Ideas
a. Why is the size of India's population a problem?
b. How has the government of India addressed population issues?
c. Why have government programs had mixed success?

4 Geographic Thinking
Making Inferences How does the population density in India compare to that in the United States? **Think about:**
- population size
- territorial size

hmhsocialstudies.com
RESEARCH WEB LINKS

GeoActivity

MAKING COMPARISONS Carry out further research focused on comparing 20th-century population growth in a city in India and one in the United States. Use the data that you gather to create a **line graph** that compares population growth in these two cities.

SOUTH ASIA

SECTION 1 ASSESSMENT ANSWERS

1. Places & Terms
basic necessities, p. 593 illiteracy, p. 593

2. Taking Notes
• It more than tripled.
• 1.5 billion

3. Main Ideas
a. Because the population has grown so quickly, it is difficult to find the resources to meet people's basic needs.
b. by promoting smaller families and funding education
c. Many parents continue to have large numbers of children because of India's high infant mortality rates, for the added incomes and to insure that they have caregivers when they are elderly.

4. Geographic Thinking
India's population is more than three times that of the United States. Moreover, India has only about one-third the territory of the United States. Compared to the United States, India's population density is extremely high.

GeoActivity

Integrated Assessment
• Rubric for a line graph, 2.3

OBJECTIVE

Interpret a population pyramid.

Instruct: Objective

Reading a Population Pyramid

- Each bar on the graph represents an age span of how many years? *(five)*
- What kinds of data does the graph enable you to compare? *(number of males and females within a specific age group; number of males or females in different age groups)*
- Where does the largest drop in population occur in the upper portion of the graph? *(between ages 70–74 and 75–79)*

In-Depth Resources: Unit 8
- Map and Graph Skills, pp. 26–27

Access for Students Acquiring English/ESL
- Map and Graph Skills, pp. 142–143

RAND McNALLY **Map and Graph Skills**

Reading a Population Pyramid

Every nation has a certain distribution of population by age group. India, for instance, has a young population; the majority of people are under the age of 30. To show how the population of a country is distributed by age, a population pyramid is a very useful tool.

THE LANGUAGE OF GRAPHS A **population pyramid** is a type of bar graph. It shows the number or percentage of people that fall into specific age groups. It may also compare the distribution of age groups by sex, ethnic group, or some other category. The population pyramid below shows the distribution of age groups by sex in India.

Population of India, 2010

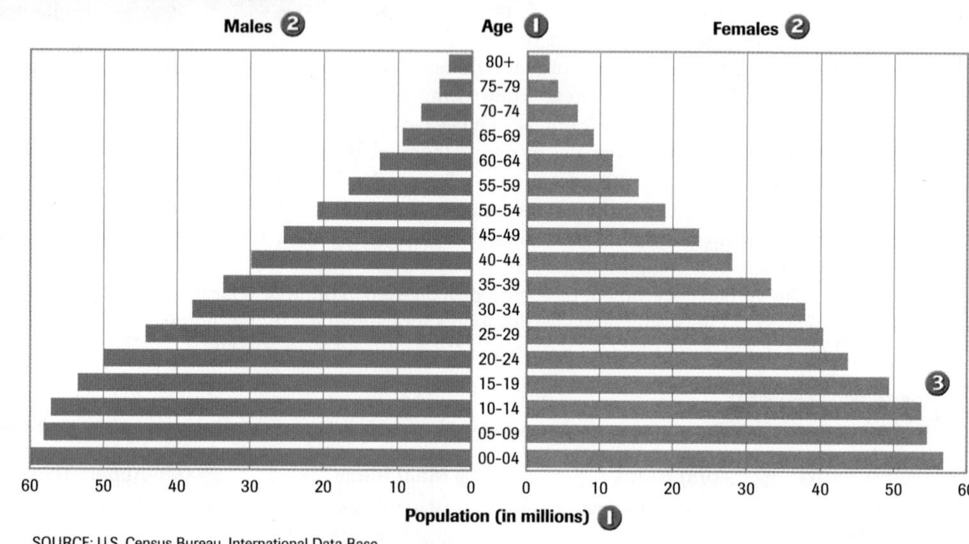

SOURCE: U.S. Census Bureau, International Data Base

1 The horizontal axis shows population in millions. The vertical axis lists age groups.

2 The left side of the pyramid shows the population distribution of males in India. The right side shows females.

3 Notice that there is a steady drop in population as Indians reach their late teens. This indicates that the life expectancy of Indians is relatively short.

Map and Graph Skills Assessment

1. **Analyzing Data** Find the bar on the pyramid that would be your age and sex. How many millions of persons fall into that group in India?
2. **Making Comparisons** What age group is the largest? What is the largest age group by sex?
3. **Making Inferences** What might be said about the male/female composition of the population of India?

SKILLS ASSESSMENT ANSWERS

1. Answers will vary with the age and sex of the student.
2. The largest groups are 0-4 and 5-9, which are almost equal; they have a total of about 240 million. The largest age group by sex is males from 0-4, with about 64 million.
3. Answers may vary but should indicate that, in general, there are more males than females in the younger age ranges.

2 Living with Extreme Weather

How do people cope with extreme weather?

Main Ideas

- South Asia experiences a yearly cycle of floods, often followed by drought.
- The extreme weather in South Asia leads to serious physical, economic, and political consequences.

Places & Terms

summer monsoon

winter monsoon

A HUMAN PERSPECTIVE In May 1996, a fierce tornado tore through northern Bangladesh, leaving more than 700 people dead and 30,000 injured. Winds reached speeds of 125 mph. Within 30 minutes, nearly 80 villages had been destroyed. In the town of Rampur, Reazuddin Ahmed and his family sought shelter behind a concrete wall. All the while, houses were tossed into the air around them. Babul Ahmed, Reazuddin's 10-year-old son, described his family's terror: "It was dust and wind everywhere. We prayed to God: 'Save us.'" The tornado that terrorized the family was not unusual. It was just one of many types of extreme weather that plague South Asia and make life both difficult and dangerous.

The Monsoon Seasons

South Asia is home to an annual cycle of powerful, destructive weather, including the monsoon. The monsoon is a wind system, not a rainstorm. There are two monsoon seasons—the moist summer monsoon and the dry, cool winter monsoon. (The illustrations on the next page show the monsoon pattern in winter and summer.)

The **summer monsoon** is a wind system that blows from the southwest across the Indian Ocean toward South Asia from June through September. These winds stir up powerful storms that release vast amounts of rain and cause severe flooding.

The **winter monsoon** is a wind system that blows from the northeast across the Himalayas toward the sea from October through February. Unlike the summer monsoon, the winter winds carry little moisture. A drought can result if the summer monsoon has failed to bring normal levels of moisture. From March through May, there are no strong prevailing wind patterns.

Impact of the Monsoons

The monsoon winds shape the rhythms of life for South Asia's people and also affect relations between its countries.

PHYSICAL IMPACT The rains that accompany the summer monsoons are critical to the agriculture of

Farming Calendar in India

hmhsocialstudies.com INTERACTIVE

SOURCE: India-Country Studies

SKILLBUILDER: Interpreting Graphics

1. **ANALYZING DATA** During what season is there no agricultural activity?
2. **MAKING INFERENCES** Which season is the most productive?

SOUTH ASIA

SECTION 2 OBJECTIVES

1. Define summer and winter monsoons.
2. Learn how the monsoons affect South Asians.

SKILLBUILDERS: Interpreting Maps and Graphics, pp. 597, 598

GeographicThinking

Using the Atlas, p. 598
Seeing Patterns, p. 599
Identifying and Solving Problems, p. 599

Focus & Motivate

Ask students how people in their communities cope with extreme weather. *(seek shelter, lay in provisions)*

Instruct: Objective 1

The Monsoon Seasons

- What are the monsoons? *(wind systems that blow across South Asia)*
- During what months does each monsoon run? *(summer monsoon: from June–September; winter monsoon: October–February)*

In-Depth Resources: Unit 8
- Guided Reading, p. 24
- Exploring Today's Issues, pp. 32–33

SKILLBUILDER ANSWERS 1. hot season and one month of wet season **2.** the cool season because planting and harvesting take place during these months

Instruct: Objective 2 appears on p. 598

SECTION 2 PROGRAM RESOURCES

In-Depth Resources: Unit 8
- Guided Reading, p. 24
- Skillbuilder Practice, p. 28
- Building Vocabulary, p. 29
- Exploring Today's Issues, pp. 32–33
- Reteaching Activity, p. 35
- GeoWorkshop, pp. 37–38

Guided Reading Workbook
- Section 2

Access for Students Acquiring English/ESL
- Guided Reading, p. 139
- Skillbuilder Practice, p. 141

Formal Assessment
- Section Quiz, p. 404

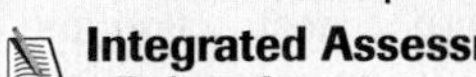

Integrated Assessment
- Rubric for a newspaper article, 4.5

INTEGRATED TECHNOLOGY

Map Transparencies MT45
- Summer and Winter Monsoons

Chapter Summaries

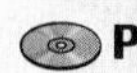

Power Presentations

TEST-TAKING RESOURCES

Strategies for Test Preparation

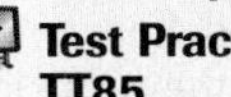

Test Practice Transparencies TT85

Online Test Practice

Interpreting Maps

Summer and Winter Monsoons

Have students note the direction of the winds of the summer and winter monsoons. Then have them look at the physical map of South Asia on page 543. Ask where the summer monsoons pick up water. *(from the ocean)* Ask why the winter monsoon blows dry and cool. *(It comes from the north and crosses the Himalayas.)*

 **Map Transparencies MT45**
• Summer and Winter Monsoons

SKILLBUILDER ANSWERS

1. The winds blow from the southwest across the Indian Ocean toward South Asia. **2.** The winds blow from the northeast across the Himalayas toward the sea.

Instruct: Objective 

Impact of the Monsoons

- What seasonal disasters do monsoons sometimes cause? *(flooding, cyclones, and drought)*
- How do the monsoons affect the economy? *(Monsoon rains are essential to agriculture, the main economic activity; extreme weather caused by monsoons destroys crops, causing loss of income.)*
- How is the Farakka dam an example of how water may affect politics? *(India built the dam to bring water to Kolkata. The dam severely reduced the amount of water available in Bangladesh and caused a lengthy political dispute.)*

 **In-Depth Resources: Unit 8**
• GeoWorkshops, pp. 37–38

Summer and Winter Monsoons

hmhsocialstudies.com INTERACTIVE

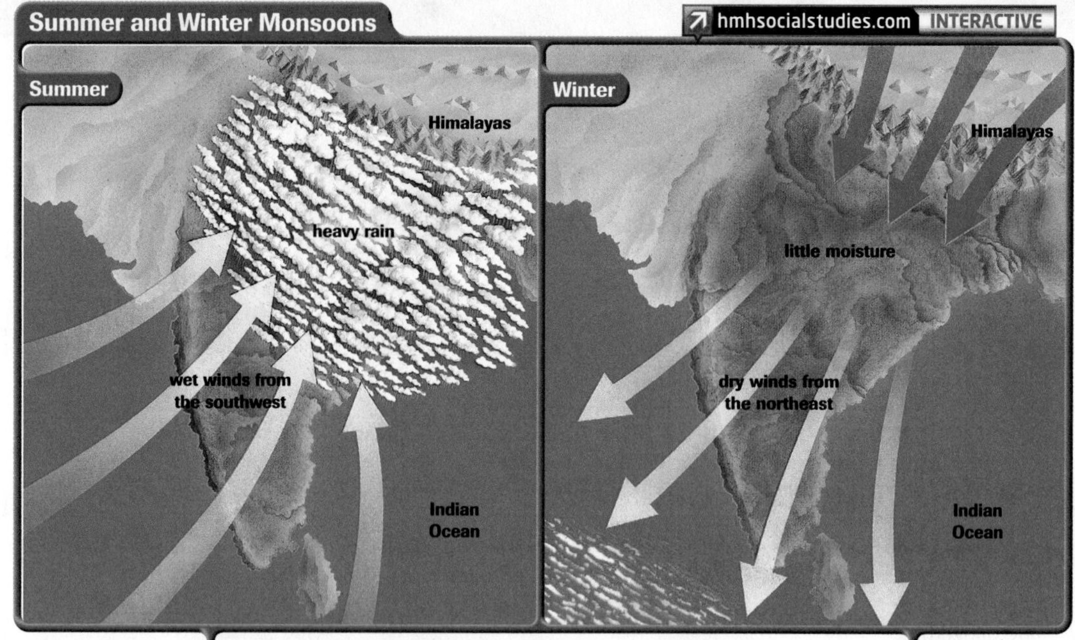

SKILLBUILDER: Interpreting Maps

1. **MOVEMENT** What direction do the summer monsoon winds follow?
2. **MOVEMENT** What direction do the winter monsoon winds follow?

South Asia, as the farming calendar on page 597 shows. They help nourish the rain forests, irrigate crops, and produce the floodwaters that deposit layers of rich sediment to replenish the soil. However, heavy flooding can also damage crops.

At the same time, the summer monsoon can cause tremendous devastation. Cyclones are common and deadly companions to the summer monsoon. (These storms are called hurricanes in North America.) Cyclones destroy farmland, wipe out villages, and cause massive flooding. Their fury is legendary. As you read in the Disasters! feature on pages 578–579, the 1970 cyclone that struck the southern coast of Bangladesh killed more than 300,000 people. It left hundreds of thousands homeless and destitute. In fact, because of the monsoons, Bangladesh was the site of some of the worst natural disasters of the 20th century.

The droughts that come with the dry winter monsoon bring their own problems. Lush landscapes can become arid wastelands almost overnight. These droughts—along with storms and floods—cause havoc for the people and economies of South Asia. A

Geographic Thinking

Using the Atlas

A Use the maps on page 545 and this page. What country of South Asia seems least affected by the summer and winter monsoons?

A. Answer
Pakistan

ECONOMIC IMPACT The climate of South Asia makes agriculture difficult. Crops often disappear under summer floodwaters or wither in drought-parched soil. With so many mouths to feed, the countries of South Asia must buy what they cannot grow, and the threat of famine is ever present. But the people suffer from more than just crop failures. They may also lose their homes and families to weather-related catastrophes. Most people are too poor to rebuild their homes and lives, and

ACTIVITY OPTION SKILLBUILDER LESSON

SEEING PATTERNS

Explaining the Skill Seeing patterns can be a useful tool for assessing problems. For example, if a single traffic accident occurs at an intersection within a ten-year-period, it is considered to be an isolated incident. But if ten accidents occur at the same intersection within a year, one may reasonably conclude that the intersection poses a safety hazard to which a solution must be found.

 **In-Depth Resources: Unit 8**
• Skillbuilder Practice, p. 28

Applying the Skill Have students look for patterns relating to weather and its impact. Then ask the following questions.

- What weather pattern occurs in South Asia? *(torrential rains followed by dry, cool winds and a hot season)*
- What pattern of destruction and human suffering does extreme weather cause? *(high winds and excessive rain cause crop ruination, loss of homes and other structures, injury, and death)*
- To which aspect of the pattern have solutions been applied? *(the result)* Why? *(the weather cannot be controlled)* Give examples of solutions applied. *(building houses on stilts, using stronger building materials, building cyclone shelters)*

governments often lack the necessary resources to provide significant help. However, the people of South Asia have taken some steps to prevent or lessen damage. These include building houses on stilts, erecting concrete cyclone shelters, and building dams to control floodwaters.

The region also receives international aid. Other governments and international agencies have lent billions of dollars to South Asian nations. But often this aid does not go far because of the frequency of disasters. Also, the aid burdens these countries with heavy debts. B

Geographic Thinking

Seeing Patterns
B How might the governments of South Asia use foreign aid?
B. Answer The aid could be used to rebuild destroyed areas after disaster strikes and to help in the construction of dams and cyclone shelters.

POLITICAL TENSIONS Conditions caused by the weather patterns in South Asia have also caused political disputes. For instance, to bring water to the city of Kolkata, India constructed the Farakka dam across the Ganges at a point just before it enters Bangladesh. (See map on page 545.) Because India and Bangladesh share the Ganges, the dam left little water for drinking and irrigation in southern Bangladesh. Many Bangladeshi farmers lost farmland, and some illegally fled to India.

The two countries finally settled the dispute in 1997, when they signed a treaty giving each country specific water rights to the Ganges. Still, the dispute provided a graphic example of the role weather plays in both the politics and economics of South Asia. In the Case Study that follows, you will read about another political conflict—a territorial dispute between India and Pakistan.

REGION Dams on the Ganges divert water to irrigate Indian farms. But the dams decrease water downstream in Bangladesh.
Why might such a result cause conflict between India and Bangladesh?

Interpreting Photographs

The Ganges and Bangladesh
Have students look at the map on page 543 to determine the approximate distance between the dam and the area of Bangladesh shown. *(about 800 miles)* Ask what they conclude from this. *(Dams may affect areas hundreds of miles downriver from where they are built.)*

CAPTION ANSWER One country might feel that it has just as much does the other country.

Assess & Reteach

GeoFocus Have students complete their notes for this section of the GeoFocus cause-and-effect chart.

Formal Assessment
• Section Quiz, p. 404

Reteaching Activity
Have students write a short paragraph summarizing the main idea presented under the heading "The Monsoon Seasons" and for each subhead under the heading "Impact of the Monsoons." Then review the main ideas as a class.

In-Depth Resources: Unit 8
• Reteaching Activity, p. 35

Section 2 Assessment

1 Places & Terms
Explain the importance of each of the following terms and places.
• summer monsoon
• winter monsoon

2 Taking Notes

PLACE Review the notes you took for this section.

	Causes	Effects
Issue 2: Extreme Weather		

• What are cyclones called in the United States?
• What kind of devastation can cyclones cause?

3 Main Ideas
a. Why do some people mistake monsoons, which are actually wind systems, for rainstorms?
b. What problems are associated with the winter monsoon?
c. What are some of the economic effects of monsoons?

4 Geographic Thinking
Identifying and Solving Problems How have attempts to address the challenges of South Asian weather patterns sometimes resulted in political disputes? How might disputes be avoided in the future?
Think about:
• the importance of water to the region
• who owns rivers

ASKING GEOGRAPHIC QUESTIONS Do research on the issue of water distribution in one South Asian country. Then, come up with a geographic question about the issue, perhaps one considering how geography can be used to improve the situation. Answer the question and write a **newspaper article** about the issue.

SOUTH ASIA

SECTION 2 ASSESSMENT ANSWERS

1. Places & Terms
summer monsoon, p. 597 winter monsoon, p. 597

2. Taking Notes
• hurricanes
• they can destroy farmland, wipe out villages, and cause massive flooding.

3. Main Ideas
a. because the summer monsoons carry moist, Indian Ocean air and stir up powerful storms that release vast amounts of rain
b. The winter monsoons can mean long periods of drought.
c. Monsoons can disrupt agricultural production and cause famine.

4. Geographic Thinking
When India dammed the Ganges river to bring water to the city of Kolkata, it prevented much-needed water from arriving at communities downstream in Bangladesh. Planning water policy at the regional instead of the national level may help to avoid problems in the future.

Integrated Assessment
• Rubric for a newspaper article, 4.5

CASE STUDY OBJECTIVES

1. Describe the controversy over Kashmir.
2. Examine the threat of nuclear war.
3. Complete the Case Study Project by writing a newspaper story explaining how people have suffered from the Kashmir conflict.
4. Analyze primary sources for personal reflections about the conflict from Indians, Pakistanis, and Kashmiris.

SKILLBUILDER: Interpreting Maps, p. 601

Focus & Motivate

Ask students why it might be difficult for two countries to resolve a 50-year-old conflict regarding Kashmir, a region that they have already partitioned in effect. *(The longer conflicts go on the less likely that one of the parties will back down; countries are generally unwilling to give up territory over which they have control.)*

Instruct: Objective 1 appears on p. 601

Interpreting Time Lines

Kashmir Conflict

Although he hoped that Kashmir might become independent, Maharaja Hari Singh ultimately ceded Kashmir to India. Direct students' attention to the time line. Ask:

- What historic event led to the beginning of the Kashmir conflict? *(India's and Pakistan's independence)*
- How long has Kashmir been a disputed region? *(more than 50 years)*

CASE STUDY

TERRITORIAL DISPUTE

How can India and Pakistan resolve their dispute over Kashmir?

Snowcapped mountains tower over a village in the valley of the Suru River in the disputed territory of Kashmir.

Kashmir is a territory of towering mountains, dense forests, and fertile river valleys. It is strategically located at the foot of the Himalayas and is surrounded by India, Pakistan, and China. Since 1947, India and Pakistan have fought to control this territory of 12 million people. The territorial dispute has caused three Indo-Pakistani wars and, in just the last decade alone, cost up to 75,000 lives. It poses a threat to the political stability of South Asia and the economic well-being of the countries involved. And, because both India and Pakistan have nuclear weapons, the Kashmir conflict has the potential to lead to nuclear war.

A Controversy Over Territory

In 1947, the British government formally ended its colonial rule over the Indian subcontinent after 90 years. It partitioned, or divided, the subcontinent into two independent countries. India had a predominantly Hindu population. Pakistan was mostly Muslim. Britain gave each Indian state the choice of joining either country or remaining independent. Muslim states joined with Pakistan, while Hindu states remained part of India. Kashmir, however, had a unique problem.

POLITICS AND RELIGION Kashmir was mainly Muslim, but its leader, the Maharajah of Kashmir, was a Hindu. Faced with a difficult decision, the maharajah tried to keep Kashmir independent. But the plan failed. The maharajah then ceded Kashmir to India in 1947, but Pakistani soldiers invaded Kashmir. After a year's fighting, India still controlled much of the territory. Since then, India and Pakistan have fought two

KASHMIR CONFLICT (1940 – 2000)

- **1947** India and Pakistan gain independence.
- **1948** Year-long **Indo-Pakistani war** over Kashmir ends.
- **1965** Second Indo-Pakistani war is fought.
- **1971** India and Pakistan fight again over Kashmir.
- **1972** Cease-fire agreement signed by India and Pakistan.
- **1974** India explodes its first nuclear device.
- **1998** **Pakistan** begins nuclear testing.
- **1999** Indian and Pakistani military clash at cease-fire line.

CASE STUDY PROGRAM RESOURCES

In-Depth Resources: Unit 8
- Guided Reading, p. 25
- Building Vocabulary, p. 29
- Reteaching Activity, p. 36

Guided Reading Workbook
- Case Study

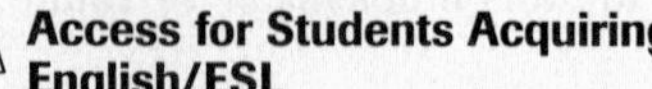

Access for Students Acquiring English/ESL
- Guided Reading, p. 140

Formal Assessment
- Case Study Quiz, p. 405

Integrated Assessment
- Rubric for a table, 2.3

INTEGRATED TECHNOLOGY

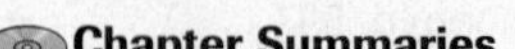
Chapter Summaries

Power Presentations

hmhsocialstudies.com

TEST-TAKING RESOURCES

Strategies for Test Preparation

Test Practice Transparencies TT86

Online Test Practice

more wars, in 1965 and in 1971. Although a cease-fire was signed in 1972, the situation remains unresolved. As you can see on the map below, India and Pakistan each control part of the disputed territory. Even China controls a portion, having seized a remote northern mountain area in 1962.

A QUESTION OF ECONOMICS There's more to this conflict than just politics and religion. The Indus River flows through Kashmir, and many of its tributaries originate in the territory. The Indus is a critical source of drinking and irrigation water for all of Pakistan. As a result, the Pakistanis are unwilling to let India control such a vital resource. Kashmir has become a strategic prize that neither country is willing to give up.

A Nuclear Nightmare

SEE PRIMARY SOURCE B

In 1998, India and Pakistan each tested nuclear weapons. The rest of the world was horrified by the thought that the 50-year-old dispute over Kashmir might finally end with vast areas of South Asia destroyed by nuclear bombs. After the tests, both nations vowed to seek a political solution to the conflict. But the possibility of a nuclear war has made the dispute even more dangerous. Despite frequent cease-fires, the border clashes have continued. Also, Pakistan is supporting Muslims in Kashmir who have been fighting Indian rule since the late 1980s.

SEE PRIMARY SOURCE A

A QUESTION OF PRIORITIES Both India and Pakistan have large populations and widespread poverty. The money that they have spent on troops, arms, and nuclear programs might have been used to educate millions of children and to address many social problems.

SEE PRIMARY SOURCE E

Resolving the status of Kashmir would offer the people of India, Pakistan, and Kashmir the peace they need to begin improving the quality of their lives. It would also reduce political tensions in the region. The Case Study Project and primary sources that follow will help you to explore the Kashmir question.

Kashmir hmhsocialstudies.com INTERACTIVE MAP

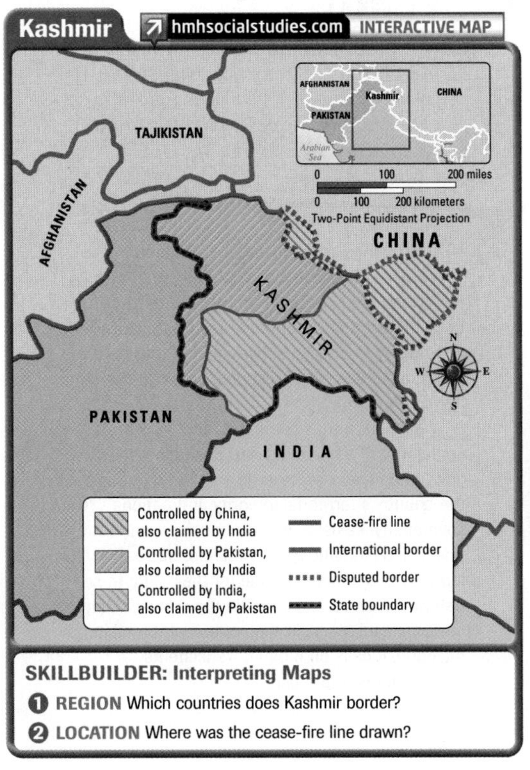

SKILLBUILDER: Interpreting Maps

1. **REGION** Which countries does Kashmir border?
2. **LOCATION** Where was the cease-fire line drawn?

Instruct: Objective 1

A Controversy Over Territory

- How has China become involved in the Kashmir controversy? *(It seized a remote northern area in 1962.)*
- What part has religion played in the controversy over Kashmir? *(Kashmir's Hindu leader ceded Kashmir to India in 1947. Then Pakistan invaded because most people living in Kashmir were Muslim.)*
- How has the Indus River contributed to the dispute? *(It flows through Kashmir and is a major source of drinking and irrigation water for Pakistan, which therefore wishes to control it.)*

In-Depth Resources: Unit 8
- Guided Reading, p. 25

Instruct: Objective 2

A Nuclear Nightmare

- Why is the testing of nuclear weapons by India and Pakistan of concern to other nations? *(A nuclear war between the countries would probably destroy a large area of South Asia.)*
- What does the Kashmir dispute suggest about the priorities of India and Pakistan? *(obtaining control of Kashmir is more important than solving domestic problems such as poverty and illiteracy.)*

SKILLBUILDER ANSWERS 1. India, Pakistan, China, and Afghanistan **2.** approximately across the middle of the disputed territory

DIFFERENTIATING INSTRUCTION **LESS PROFICIENT READERS**

IDENTIFYING PRIMARY SOURCES

Objective To preview the types of primary sources that students may encounter

Class Time 20 minutes

Task Prepare a chart of primary sources

Directions Review the difference between primary and secondary sources. Then have students make a list of primary, or firsthand, sources in their notebooks. Tell students to share items from their lists as you compile their ideas on the board. If students have failed to list one or more of the primary sources appearing on pages 602 and 603, ask them if a government document is a primary source or a secondary source. This will enable students to add the items to their lists. Label the first column Primary Sources and add a second column labeled Example. Tell students to copy the chart in their notebooks and to add to it as they encounter new types of primary sources.

Instruct: Objective 3

Case Study Project: A Newspaper Feature

- What is your research goal? *(To find personal reflections of people affected by the Kashmir conflict)*
- Where will you search for personal stories? *(In magazine and newspaper articles; on the Internet)*
- What will you produce for the project? *(a newspaper feature story)*

Instruct: Objective 4

Using Primary Sources

- Ⓐ ***Government Document*** How does the document describe Pakistan's official position regarding Kashmir? *(Pakistan will continue to support Kashmir's right to self-determination.)*
- What does it ask of India? *(that India honor its commitments as set forth in UN resolutions)*
- Ⓑ ***Government Policy Declaration*** What does the declaration seek to deny? *(that Kashmir is a nuclear flashpoint)*
- What position of India's does the declaration defend? *(maintaining a nuclear deterrent)*
- What do the words "those who refuse to make any such commitment" refer to? *(Pakistan's silence regarding the use of first-strike nuclear weapons)*

CASE STUDY

PROJECT

A Newspaper Feature

Primary sources A, B, C, D, and E offer different views of the dispute over Kashmir. Use these resources along with your own research to write a newspaper feature on how the people of Kashmir, India, and Pakistan have suffered in this conflict. Include their own words.

hmhsocialstudies.com RESEARCH WEB LINKS

Suggested Steps

1. Divide into small groups representing ordinary Kashmiris (such as women, farmers, and rebel soldiers), as well as Indian and Pakistani officials or soldiers. Then begin gathering personal accounts about the conflict from newspapers, magazines, and Internet sites.
2. Search for visuals—illustrations, maps, photographs, political cartoons, charts, and graphs—that help illustrate the points you are making.
3. When everyone in the class has collected enough material, work together to plan the feature story.
4. When you have finished planning, prepare the feature.
5. Share your project with other groups at your school or in your community.

Materials and Supplies

- Reference books, newspapers, and magazines
- Computer with Internet access and printer

PRIMARY SOURCE A

Government Document *The Ministry of* ***Foreign Affairs of Pakistan*** *published this policy statement on Kashmir in 1999, after a visit to the United States by the* ***Pakistani prime minister, Nawaz Sharif.***

In order to find an early and just solution to the 50-year old . . . Kashmir dispute, Pakistan has welcomed offers of good offices and third-party mediation. It has encouraged the international community to play an active role and facilitate the peaceful settlement of disputes between Pakistan and India.

While Pakistan is committed to a peaceful settlement of the Jammu and Kashmir dispute, adequate measures have been taken to safeguard the country's territorial integrity and national sovereignty. Pakistan will continue to extend full political, diplomatic and moral support to the legitimate Kashmiri struggle for their right to self-determination as enshrined in the relevant United Nations resolutions. In the context of the bilateral dialogue, it calls on India to translate its commitments into reality.

PRIMARY SOURCE B

Government Policy Declaration *At a state dinner in India for President Bill Clinton in March 2000,* ***Indian President Kocheril Raman Narayanan*** *warned that India would fight to protect its interests in Kashmir.*

It has been suggested that the Indian subcontinent is the most dangerous place in the world today, and Kashmir is a nuclear flashpoint. These alarmist descriptions will only encourage those who want to break the peace and indulge in terrorism and violence. The danger is not from us who have declared solemnly that we will not be the first to use nuclear weapons, but rather it is from those who refuse to make any such commitment.

We are publicly committed to the abolition of nuclear weapons together with other nuclear powers who possess them in awesome stockpiles capable of destroying the world many times over. India does not threaten any other country and will not engage in an arms race, but India will maintain a minimum credible nuclear deterrent—no more, no less—for her own security.

ACTIVITY OPTION **CRITICAL THINKING**

SEEING PATTERNS

Explaining the Skill Tell students that seeing patterns can be helpful in analyzing a problem and may even lead to solutions.

Applying the Skill Have students look for similar patterns in primary sources A and B and in sources C and D. Then ask the following questions.

- What patterns do you see in sources A and B? *(Both countries are defensive about their positions and both suggest directly or indirectly that the fault lies with the other.)*
- What pattern appears in sources C and D? *(Both recount the hardships borne by the Kashmiri people as a result of the conflict.)*
- How might one pattern affect the other? *(The failure of India and Pakistan to resolve their differences will continue to take its toll on the people of Kashmir.)*
- What conclusion or solution might this suggest? *(India and Pakistan should consider the welfare of the Kashmiri people as their first priority.)*

PRIMARY SOURCE C

Political Speech *Mehbooba Mufti is a leader of the Jammu and Kashmir People's Democratic Party, a political party in Kashmir. In 1999, she spoke about the conflict and her hope that the dispute will be peacefully resolved.*

Everything has changed, mostly for the worse. Take just the physical destruction of whatever we had, the schools, the colleges, the roads, the bridges, the buildings, everything we had for the last 50 years, that has been more or less destroyed. We used to have a very good education system, with very good teachers, but now that has gone. . . .

I think Kashmir finally has to become a bridge between India and Pakistan. Finally. Maybe not today, maybe not tomorrow, but after some years, it is finally going to become a bridge. Have an open relationship. It's a dream!

PRIMARY SOURCE D

Personal Story *Kashmiri native Mohammed Aziz lives in Kargil, a city on the border between the Pakistani- and Indian-controlled regions of Kashmir. In 1999, he described how the conflict had affected his hometown.*

We never know when the shell will come. . . . For the last three years, no one sleeps well there. Whoever flees leaves everything there. He takes nothing with him. The cattle are left on their own. Nobody cares for them, so we don't know what happens to them. . . .

Before, tourism was OK. Before the shelling there used to be 25 hotels, but now I don't think any hotel is open. We can't calculate the damage. . . .

The children's education is stopped, and whoever is ill dies because there is no medication nor anyone to care for them. Whoever resides in Kargil, does so at his own risk.

PRIMARY SOURCE E

Political Cartoon *This 1998 political cartoon shows how the development of nuclear weapons by India and Pakistan has caused economic suffering among the people of both countries.*

PROJECT CheckList

Have I . . .

- ✓ fully researched my topic?
- ✓ located primary source quotations to tell my story?
- ✓ taken into account both sides of the issue?
- ✓ arranged the quotations so that they tell a coherent, interesting story?
- ✓ created informative visuals that make my story clear and interesting?

Instruct: Objective 4

Using Primary Sources

- Ⓒ ***Political Speech*** How has the conflict affected the residents of Kashmir? *(Most physical structures have been damaged or destroyed. Without schools the educational system is no longer in place.)*
- What is the speaker's hope for Kashmir? *(that it will become independent, a "bridge" between India and Pakistan)*
- Ⓓ ***Personal Story*** Where does Mohammed Aziz live? *(in Kargil, a city on the border where conflict occurs)*
- How has the conflict affected the people in Kargil? *(They fear for their lives. Tourism has collapsed and there is no schooling or medicine.)*
- Ⓔ ***Political Cartoon*** Why is the man with the gun in the cartoon? *(He is the starter and is meant to suggest that Pakistan and India are in a nuclear arms race.)*

Assess & Reteach

GeoFocus Have students complete the GeoFocus cause-and-effect chart they began at the beginning of this chapter.

Formal Assessment
- Case Study Quiz, p. 405

Reteaching Activity
Have students write a two-minute news summary of the issues involved in the Kashmir conflict.

In-Depth Resources: Unit 8
- Reteaching Activity, p. 36

RUBRIC CASE STUDY PROJECT

BLOCK SCHEDULING

NEWSPAPER FEATURE

For the Case Study Project, students should:

- Summarize the nature of the conflict over Kashmir.
- Produce clear, imaginative visuals that complement their presentation.
- Present a well-organized feature story.
- Present a variety of points of view and personal stories.

Grading Rubric Evaluate student performances as Exceptional, Acceptable, or Poor in each of the following categories:

	Exceptional	Acceptable	Poor
Writing is clear, focused, and logical			
Provides necessary facts and examples			
Feature presents different views of conflict			
Visuals are informative and interesting			

Reviewing Places & Terms

A. **1.** basic necessities, p. 593
2. illiteracy, p. 593
3. summer monsoon, p. 597
4. winter monsoon, p. 597

B. Possible Responses

5. Summer monsoons stir up powerful storms that release vast amounts of rain and cause severe flooding.
6. The summer monsoons blow from the southwest across the Indian Ocean toward South Asia from June through September.
7. Food, shelter, and clothing are examples of basic necessities.
8. The winter monsoons blow from the northeast across the Himalayas from October through January.
9. Illiteracy is the inability to read or write.
10. The Indian government found it difficult to provide basic necessities for its people.

Chapter 26 Assessment

VISUAL SUMMARY
TODAY'S ISSUES IN SOUTH ASIA

Economics

Population Explosion
- Though only about one-third the size of the United States, India has over three times as many people.
- India's government has taken steps to control population growth but has had only mixed success.
- Many parents continue to have large numbers of children because of India's high infant mortality rates, the extra income brought in by children, and the need for caregivers as parents age.

Environment

Living with Extreme Weather
- The physical damage caused by extreme weather patterns in South Asia, such as cyclones, can be devastating to the region's people.
- The impact of extreme weather is not limited to physical damage. These forces can also disrupt the economy and cause serious political tensions.

Government

Case Study: Territorial Dispute
- Kashmir is a strategically located territory, surrounded by Pakistan, India, and China.
- India and Pakistan have fought three wars over this territory since 1947.
- Money spent by India and Pakistan for armaments, including nuclear weapons, has not been available to help improve the lives of the people of these countries.

Reviewing Places & Terms

A. Briefly explain the importance of each of the following.

1. basic necessities
2. illiteracy
3. summer monsoon
4. winter monsoon

B. Answer the questions about vocabulary in complete sentences.

5. Which winds stir up powerful storms in South Asia that release vast amounts of rain and cause severe flooding?
6. Which winds blow from the southwest across the Indian Ocean toward South Asia from June through September?
7. Food, shelter, and clothing are all examples of what?
8. Which winds blow from the northeast across the Himalayas from October through February?
9. What is the term for the inability to read or write?
10. What was the Indian government finding difficult to provide for its people?

Main Ideas

Population Growth (pp. 593–596)

1. Currently, about how many babies are born in India every day? Annually?
2. Why might the lack of basic necessities in a region concern demographers—people who study population?
3. Why might a high rate of infant mortality affect the size of families?
4. What percentage of the world's population is found in South Asia?
5. How would education play an important role in slowing population growth?

Living with Extreme Weather (pp. 597–599)

6. What are South Asia's two monsoon seasons? How do they differ?
7. When do these wind seasons occur?
8. What are some of the precautions that people in South Asia have taken to lessen the damage caused by cyclones?
9. What type of international aid have the countries of South Asia received?
10. What political tensions have resulted from the effects of extreme weather?

Case Study: Territorial Dispute over Kashmir (pp. 600–603)

11. Where is Kashmir located?
12. What countries have fought three wars over control of Kashmir?
13. When and why did the dispute over Kashmir begin?
14. Why are world leaders particularly concerned about the dispute?
15. What might happen if the dispute were resolved?

Main Ideas

1. 42,000; 15,330,000
2. Without basic necessities, population growth can cause severe economic and social problems.
3. Parents may have more children because some of their children will not survive.
4. 22 percent
5. Education would improve the standard of living, give females opportunities for jobs, and help to reduce infant mortality.
6. The summer monsoon is moist, and the winter monsoon is dry and cool.
7. summer monsoon: June–September, winter monsoon: October–February.
8. building houses on stilts, erecting concrete shelters, and building dams
9. billions of dollars in loans from other countries and international agencies
10. India and Bangladesh quarrelled over water rights to the Ganges.
11. at the foot of the Himalayas, surrounded by India, Pakistan, China, Afghanistan
12. India and Pakistan
13. In 1947, Kashmir's Hindu leader ceded this mostly Muslim territory to India, which is mainly Hindu.
14. India and Pakistan possess nuclear weapons
15. Resolving the dispute would free up money that could be used to help people improve their lives.

Critical Thinking

1. Using Your Notes
Use your completed chart to answer these questions.

	Causes	Effects
Issue 1: Population		
Issue 2: Extreme Weather		

a. Why might parents in India want a large family?
b. Why is Kashmir economically important to Pakistan?

2. Geographic Thinking
a. **REGION** How is the religious make-up of Kashmir related to conflict over the territory?
b. **MOVEMENT** Why might people in India and the other heavily populated countries in South Asia move to other parts of the world?

3. Identifying Themes
Why is Bangladesh especially vulnerable to the cyclones that occasionally devastate the region? Which of the five themes applies to this situation?

4. Making Comparisons
Why might India and Bangladesh fear the weather that can arrive during the summer?

5. Determining Cause and Effect
How might the dispute over Kashmir affect the social and educational programs in the region?

For Additional Test Practice
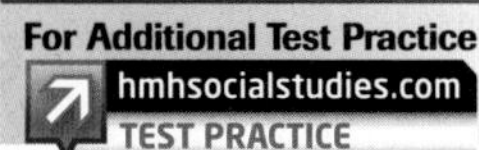

Geographic Skills: Interpreting Graphs

Ethnic Indian Population Outside of India

Use the graph at right to answer the following questions.

1. **PLACE** On what continent outside of South Asia do most Indians live?
2. **PLACE** About how many Indians live in South America?
3. **LOCATION** Why do you think most ethnic Indians living outside of India live in South Asian countries?

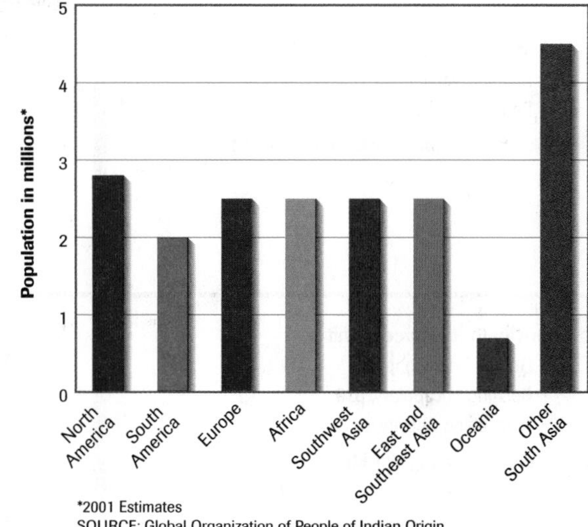

*2001 Estimates
SOURCE: Global Organization of People of Indian Origin

Carry out research on people from India who live in the United States. Create a table of the five cities with the largest populations of people from India.

hmhsocialstudies.com
MULTIMEDIA ACTIVITY

Use the links at **hmhsocialstudies.com** to continue research on population growth in India. Focus on how the limited availability of basic necessities has affected the daily life of the country's people.

Creating a Multimedia Presentation Use your research to create an electronic presentation. Combine charts, maps, images, objects, and written accounts to provide your audience with a picture of daily life in India.

SOUTH ASIA

Critical Thinking

1. a. for the extra income generated by children or to have someone to take care of them when they get old
b. The Indus river, which flows through the territory, is a critical source of drinking water and irrigation for Pakistan
2. a. In 1947, Kashmir's leader ceded his territory to India, which is mostly Hindu. Even so, many people in this Muslim majority region have fought to make the territory part of Pakistan, which is mainly Muslim.
b. because they might be able to make a better living somewhere else
3. because of its location on a low-lying coastal plain; location is the main theme
4. Summer monsoons bring heavy rains and storms that sweep across India and Bangladesh.
5. The money that India and Pakistan spend on troops and weapons cannot be spent on education or other social programs.

GeoActivity

Integrated Assessment
• Rubric for a table, 2.3

Formal Assessment
• Chapter Test, Forms A, B, and C, pp. 406–420

Geographic Skills

1. North America
2. 2 million
3. because these countries are closest to India; also, the culture would be similar

MULTIMEDIA ACTIVITY

For the multimedia presentation, students should:
- Produce a concise, well-organized report on population growth in India.
- Present clear, imaginative visuals of daily life and basic necessities.
- Include references to the Web sites used as sources.
- Use a variety of charts, maps, images, and so forth to describe daily life.

Grading Rubric Evaluate student performance as Exceptional, Acceptable, or Poor in each of the following categories:

	Exceptional	Acceptable	Poor
Presentation is clear, focused, and logical			
Provides facts and examples			
Makes use of a variety of visuals, including maps, charts, and images			
Uses a variety of sources			

UNIT 9 ATLAS AND CHAPTER 27 PLANNING GUIDE

Physical Geography of East Asia

OVERVIEW	INSTRUCTIONAL RESOURCES	
CHAPTER 27 ESSENTIAL QUESTION How have the extremes of East Asia's physical geography affected its people? **Focus on the Essential Question Podcast**	**In-Depth Resources: Unit 9** • Unit Atlas Activities, p. 1 • Building Vocabulary, p. 9 • Exploring Today's Issues, pp. 30–33 **Outline Maps with Activities** • East Asia: Physical, pp. 87–88 • East Asia: Political, pp. 89–90 **Block Schedule Strategies** **Chapter Summaries** (English/Spanish)	**Interactive Online Edition** TOS **ExamView® Assessment Suite** (English/Spanish) TOS **CalendarPlanner** **Power Presentations with Media Gallery** **Critical Thinking Transparencies** • CT27 hmhsocialstudies.com INTERACTIVE
SECTION 1 **LANDFORMS AND RESOURCES** **MAIN IDEAS** • East Asia includes diverse countries and climates and significantly rugged terrain. • East Asia's landforms include mountains, plateaus, peninsulas, and islands. • Uneven distribution of natural resources has shaped lifestyles and the economy.	**In-Depth Resources: Unit 9** • Guided Reading, p. 3 • Map and Graph Skills, pp. 6–7 • Building Vocabulary, p. 9 • Reteaching Activity, p. 10 **Guided Reading Workbook,** Section 1	hmhsocialstudies.com INTERACTIVE • Resources of East Asia, p. 622
SECTION 2 **CLIMATE AND VEGETATION** **MAIN IDEAS** • China and Mongolia have many high latitude climate zones. • North and South Korea and Japan have more moderate mid-latitude climates. • Mongolia is semiarid and desert. • Islands such as Hainan and Taiwan are more tropical.	**In-Depth Resources: Unit 9** • Guided Reading, p. 4 • Building Vocabulary, p. 9 • Reteaching Activity, p. 11 **Guided Reading Workbook,** Section 2	**Map Transparencies** • MT48 Climate, and Agricultural Products of East Asia
SECTION 3 **HUMAN-ENVIRONMENT INTERACTION** **MAIN IDEAS** • China has been faced with the serious issue of flooding during its long history. • The building of the Three Gorges Dam is an attempt to address the serious flooding problems on the Chang Jiang River. • Lack of space and large populations have caused the Japanese to come up with clever solutions.	**In-Depth Resources: Unit 9** • Guided Reading, p. 5 • Skillbuilder Practice, p. 8 • Building Vocabulary, p. 9 • Reteaching Activity, p. 12 **Guided Reading Workbook,** Section 3	**Critical Thinking Transparencies** • CT59 Contrasting China and Japan

ASSESSMENT

SE **Chapter Assessment,** pp. 632–633

Formal Assessment
- Chapter Tests, Forms A, B, and C, pp. 424–435

TOS **ExamView® Assessment Suite**

Strategies for Test Preparation

hmhsocialstudies.com TEST PRACTICE

SE **Section Assessment,** p. 623

Formal Assessment
- Section Quiz, p. 421

Integrated Assessment
- Rubric for a map, 2.1

Test Practice Transparencies TT87

SE **Section Assessment,** p. 627

Formal Assessment
- Section Quiz, p. 422

Integrated Assessment
- Rubric for a poster, 1.1

Test Practice Transparencies TT88

SE **Section Assessment,** p. 631

Formal Assessment
- Section Quiz, p. 423

Integrated Assessment
- Rubric for a chart/graph, 2.2

Test Practice Transparencies TT89

CHART KEY:

SE Student Edition	Block Scheduling	DVD/CD-ROM
TE Teacher's Edition	TOS Teacher One Stop	MP3 Audio
Printable Resource	Presentation Resource	HISTORY™

Program Resources available on TOS and @ 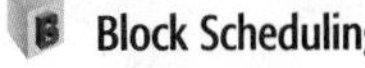

SUPPORTING RESOURCES

- Multimedia Classroom Global History Series
- Global History Teacher's Guide

Social Studies Trade Library Collection
- World Regions Trade Collection

For more information or to purchase these resources, go to hmhsocialstudies.com

DIFFERENTIATED INSTRUCTION

English Learners	Struggling Readers	Gifted and Talented Students
Spanish/English Guided Reading Workbook **Access for Students Acquiring English/ESL** Spanish Translations, pp. 144–149  **Chapter Summaries** (English/Spanish) TE **TE Activity** Spelling Similar Words, p. 626	**Chapter Summaries** (English/Spanish) TE **TE Activity** Organizing Information, p. 620 Noting Details, p. 622	**In-Depth Resources: Unit 9** TE **TE Activity** Exploring Language Origins, p. 615

ENRICHMENT ACTIVITIES

The following activities are especially suitable for classes following block schedules.

SE **Student Edition,** pp. 618–631
- Interpreting a Contour Map, p. 624

 hmhsocialstudies.com INTERACTIVE
- Resources of East Asia, p. 622
- Building the Three Gorges Dam, pp. 628–629

UNIT 9 ATLAS AND CHAPTER 27 PACING GUIDE

BLOCK SCHEDULE LESSON PLAN OPTIONS: 90-MINUTE PERIOD

DAY 1

UNIT PREVIEW, pp. 606-609
Class Time 20 minutes

- **Discussion** Discuss the Unit Introduction, using the discussion prompts on TE pages 606–609.
  Class Time 10 minutes
- **Today's Issues** Introduce Today's Issues in East Asia, using Exploring the Issues questions on PE p. 608.
  Class Time 10 minutes

UNIT ATLAS, pp. 610-617
Class Time 30 minutes

- **Small Groups** Divide the class into four groups and have each group answer Making Comparisons questions for one section of the Unit Atlas: Physical Geography, Human Geography, Regional Patterns, and Regional Data File.

SECTION 1, pp. 618-623
Class Time 40 minutes

- **Map Summary** Have students examine the maps on pages 620 and 622, focusing on Japan. Then have students looks at the map in the Map and Graph Skills activity, page 624. Students should write a brief paragraph or bulleted list of information on Hokkaido. The list should include natural resources, surrounding bodies of water, important cities, highest and lowest elevation points, and its proximity to other countries in East Asia.

DAY 2

SECTION 1, pp. 618-623
Class Time 45 minutes

- **Panel Discussion** As a way to review the section, have four students volunteer to be panelists, each representing information from the four subsections of Section 1, and a fifth student to be the facilitator. Then have the rest of the class prepare questions to ask the panelists. The facilitator should gather the questions, direct them to the panelists, and keep time limits on answers.
  Class Time 20 minutes
- **Map and Graph Skills** Complete the map skills activity with students.
  Class Time 25 minutes

SECTION 2, pp. 625-627
Class Time 45 minutes

- **Comparing the United States and East Asia** Have students review the map on page 626. Then make a two-column list on the board (one listing U.S. states in the map, another listing East Asian cities. Work with students to draw lines connecting the appropriate U.S. state to its comparable (in climate) East Asian city. Follow up with a brief discussion on the climates. Questions asked might include: What is the weather like there? What kinds of vegetation would grow there? How might the elevations be similar?

DAY 3

SECTION 3, pp. 628-631
Class Time 45 minutes

- **Pro-Con Chart** Lead the class in creating a two-column Pro-Con chart that summarizes the pros and cons of building the Three Gorges Dam in China.
  Class Time 25 minutes
- **Skillbuilder Lesson** Use the Activity Option about Making Decisions on TE p. 629 and the Skillbuilder Practice worksheet.
  Class Time 20 minutes

CHAPTER 27 REVIEW AND ASSESSMENT, pp. 632-633
Class Time 45 minutes

- **Review** Have students summarize the chapter in three paragraphs, each focusing on a main idea for the section.
  Class Time 20 minutes
- **Assessment** Have students complete the Chapter 27 Assessment.
  Class Time 25 minutes

TEACHER-TESTED ACTIVITY *Mysteries in Geography*

Class Time One class period

Task Create sets of clues for a mystery in East Asian geography

Supplies
- Overhead projector
- Marking pens
- Blank overhead transparencies

Purpose To have student apply knowledge of geographic features in East Asia in writing clue sets.

Activity Divide students into four groups. Have each group choose a geographic attribute of East Asia (for example, mountains, river systems, deserts, plateaus, or plains). The groups should keep the selection a secret from the other groups. Each group will create three sets of clues consisting of three clues each for a physical geography feature in East Asia. Students should make as many sets as time allows. After the groups are finished they should quiz the other students and see who can guess the physical feature in the shortest time.

Brenda G. Smith
Instructional Supervisor, Social Studies, Colorado Springs District 11, Colorado Springs, CO

TECHNOLOGY IN THE CLASSROOM

The Web lends itself well to student research because of the availability of Web sites with valuable, up-to-date information that include text and pictures. However, the Web also contains many sites that are not up-to-date or that have irrelevant, erroneous, or inappropriate information.

One good way to keep students "on-task" and to ensure that they use appropriate Web sites is to have them look through a limited set of pre-selected sites. The teacher should choose sites sponsored by organizations that are generally considered reliable, such as major news sources, television networks, nonprofit organizations, or museums. If the teacher presents students with a list of appropriate sites, they can save a good deal of classroom time, and students will be less likely to end up at sites that are irrelevant or inappropriate.

Objective Students will look through a pre-selected set of Web sites to gather information about the Yangtze River and the Three Gorges Dam.

Task Have students visit the Web sites to find out what it's like today and what it will be like for city dwellers, farmers, and wildlife after the dam is completed.

Class Time 2–3 class periods

1. Have students read about the Yangtze River and the Three Gorges Dam on pages 628-630. Have students make sure they can locate the Yangtze River on a map of China (page 620).
2. Ask them to list the pros and cons of building the dam, according to what they've read.
3. Discuss with the class how students think the Yangtze River Valley and its people will be affected by the dam, based on what they've read so far.
4. Divide the class into small groups, and ask groups to imagine that they're journalists who have been sent to the Yangtze River to report on what life is like there today and how people and the environment will be affected when the dam is completed.
5. Ask each group of "journalists" to visit the Web sites at **hmhsocialstudies.com** to find out what life is like today for city dwellers (e.g. shopkeepers and businesspeople), farmers, and animals living in and near the river. Then have them find out how these three groups will be affected by the dam.
6. Have groups create multimedia presentations containing "before the dam" and "after the dam" sections, showing how each group lives now and how it will fare after the dam is completed.

Previewing the Unit

The introduction to this unit provides an overview of East Asia, which includes mainland China, Japan, North Korea, South Korea, Mongolia, and Taiwan. East Asia represents diverse cultures and peoples, and has a rich tradition and history, as well as political conflicts and concerns about population.

Discussion Prompts

Exploring Prior Knowledge Ask students the following questions about East Asia to determine their prior knowledge of the region:

- What countries are considered part of East Asia? *(China, Mongolia, Taiwan, North Korea, South Korea, Japan)*
- Where is Japan located? *(islands off east coast of Asia)*

Interpreting Maps Ask students to refer to the satellite image of East Asia to answer the following questions:

- Do you recognize specific countries? *(Answers will vary, but may include China, Japan, North and South Korea, Taiwan)*
- What landforms can you identify? *(islands, lakes, mountains, oceans, seas, peninsulas)*
- Can you tell which types of vegetation or kinds of climate East Asia includes? *(Answers will vary, but may include desert, forest, and grasslands.)*

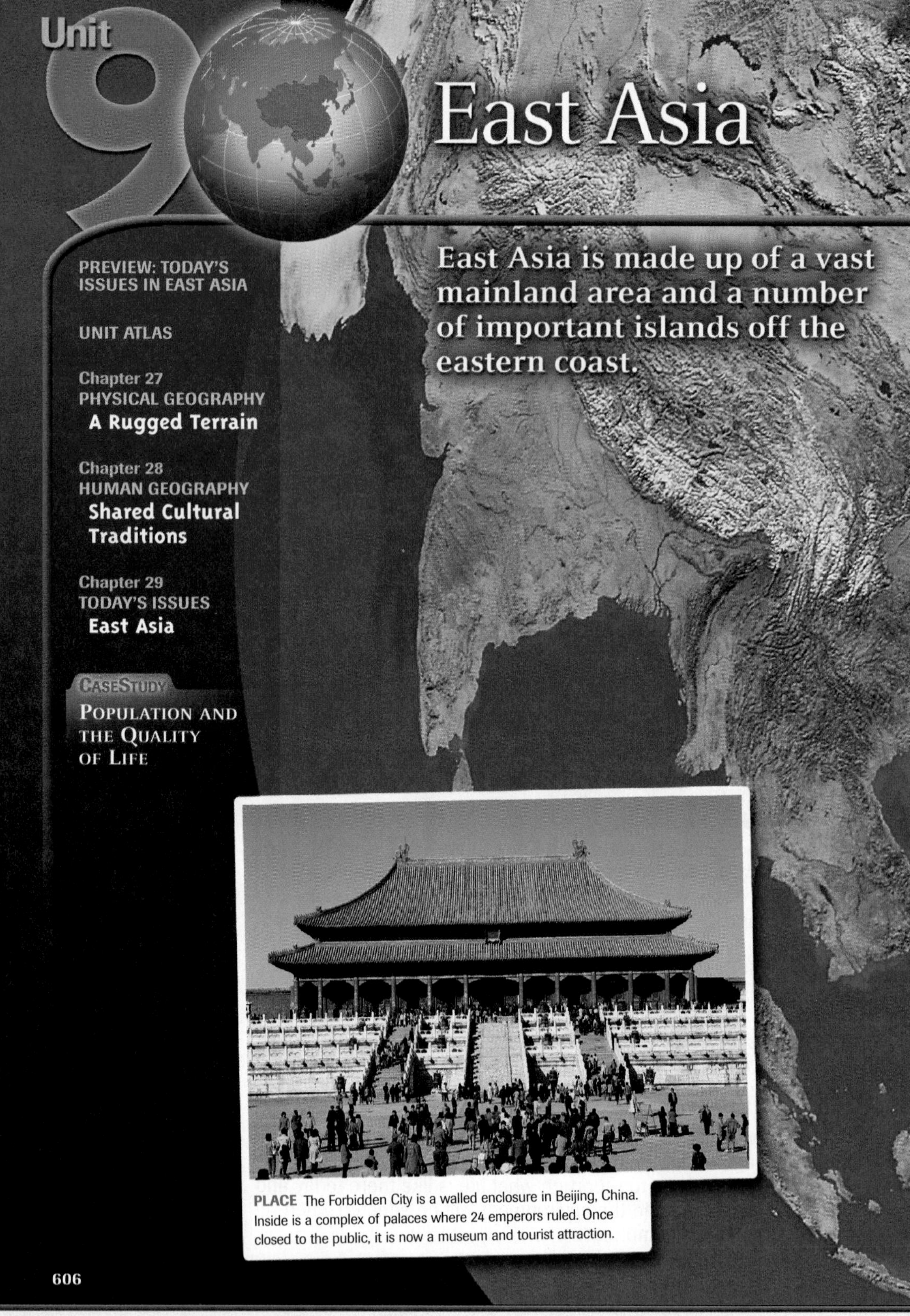

Unit 9 East Asia

East Asia is made up of a vast mainland area and a number of important islands off the eastern coast.

PREVIEW: TODAY'S ISSUES IN EAST ASIA

UNIT ATLAS

Chapter 27
PHYSICAL GEOGRAPHY
A Rugged Terrain

Chapter 28
HUMAN GEOGRAPHY
Shared Cultural Traditions

Chapter 29
TODAY'S ISSUES
East Asia

CASESTUDY
POPULATION AND THE QUALITY OF LIFE

PLACE The Forbidden City is a walled enclosure in Beijing, China. Inside is a complex of palaces where 24 emperors ruled. Once closed to the public, it is now a museum and tourist attraction.

UNIT 9 ADDITIONAL RESOURCES

BOOKS FOR THE TEACHER

Ebrey, Patricia Buckley, Anne Walthall, and James Palais. ***East Asia: A Cultural, Social, and Political History.*** Wadsworth Publishing, 2008. A wide-ranging survey with special attention to gender issues, material culture, and Korea's increasingly prominent role in global politics.

Sullivan, Lawrence R. and Nancy R. Hearst. ***Historical Dictionary of the People's Republic of China: 1949-1997.*** Lanham, MD: Scarecrow Press, 1997. Informative history of modern China.

BOOKS FOR THE STUDENT

Rubinfien, Leo. ***A Map of the East.*** Boston, MA: David R. Godine, 1992. A pictorial, nonfiction approach.

Penkala, Maria. ***A Correlated History of the Far East: China, Korea, Japan.*** Rutland, VT: Tuttle, 1969. Includes over 30 maps.

VIDEOS

Exotic Far East. International Video Network, 1991. Description and travel video which includes Japan and Korea.

INTERNET

For more on East Asia, visit . . .

hmhsocialstudies.com

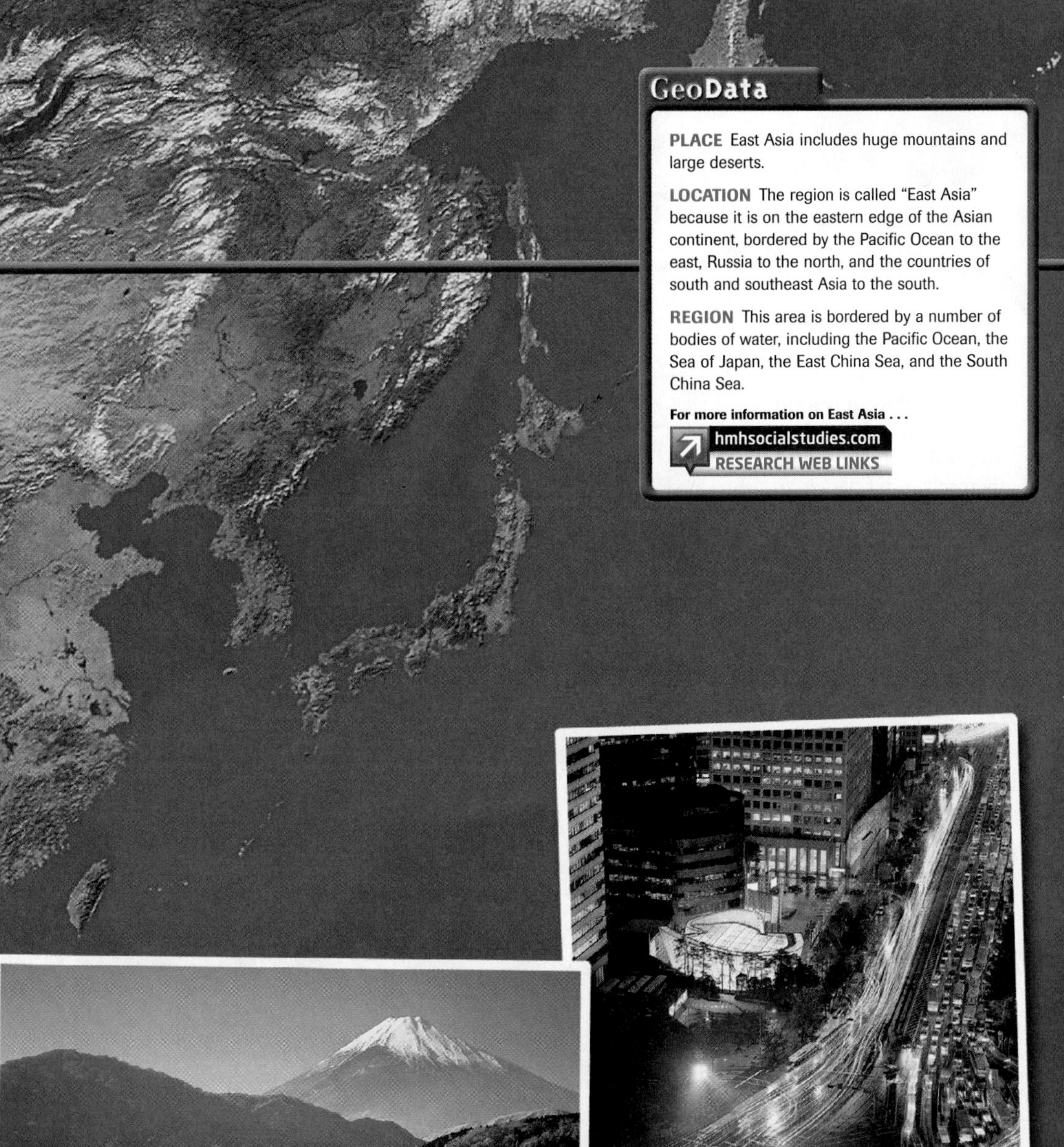

GeoData

PLACE East Asia includes huge mountains and large deserts.

LOCATION The region is called "East Asia" because it is on the eastern edge of the Asian continent, bordered by the Pacific Ocean to the east, Russia to the north, and the countries of south and southeast Asia to the south.

REGION This area is bordered by a number of bodies of water, including the Pacific Ocean, the Sea of Japan, the East China Sea, and the South China Sea.

For more information on East Asia . . .

hmhsocialstudies.com
RESEARCH WEB LINKS

LOCATION Mount Fuji, the highest peak in Japan at 12,388 feet, is a volcano that last erupted in 1707. It is considered a sacred mountain.

HUMAN–ENVIRONMENT INTERACTION This 600-year-old structure was a gate in the wall that once surrounded Seoul, South Korea. It is now in the center of the city's traffic.

EAST ASIA

607

Interpreting Photographs

The Forbidden City

The Forbidden City was so named because only the emperor had complete access to its grounds. Even family members and members of the government were given only limited access.

Ask students what this suggests about China during the Ming Dynasty in the 1400s. *(The emperor had great power and lived well.)*

Mount Fuji

Fuji means "everlasting life," and the mountain has become a sacred symbol of Japan. Each summer, many Japanese climb to the shrine located on its peak.

Ask students why they think the Japanese climb this mountain that though famous, is still an active volcano. *(They admire the mountain's heights and respect the mountain as a symbol of the country and of everlasting life.)*

Seoul, Korea

Since the 1950s, Seoul's population has been rapidly increasing. The city has one of the highest population densities in the world.

Ask students if they have ever visited such a big city. If they have, what was it like? If they haven't, would they like to, and why? *(Answers will vary based on experiences and personal opinions.)*

ACTIVITY OPTION | COOPERATIVE LEARNING

PUTTING TOGETHER A TOUR PACKAGE

Objective To help students explore East Asia and make choices that might help others

Class Time 30 minutes

Task Put together a "tour package" of suggested sites to visit in East Asia

Directions Divide students into small groups and have them look through guide books and magazines. They may also view tourism or travel sites about East Asia on the Internet. Ask each group to pick one country. Then within each group, have one student create a list of 5-10 specific sites that a visitor should try to see while in that country. Have another student in the group make a blank brochure to be filled in with information about a tour to these sites. Have a third student assemble pictures to illustrate the brochure. Have a fourth student write one paragraph of copy for each site. Then have the different groups display their brochures in the classroom.

Previewing Today's Issues

These pages provide a preview of issues that currently affect countries in East Asia. These topics will be fully explored in Chapter 29 (pp. 660-674). Use the discussion prompts that follow to determine students' prior knowledge and allow them to make comparisons to local events.

 **In-Depth Resources: Unit 9**
- Exploring Today's Issues, pp. 30–33

PHYSICAL FORCES

In the late 1960s and 1970s, geophysicists felt that their improved understanding of plate tectonics would lead quickly to improved earthquake prediction. Unfortunately that has not happened, and scientists and policy makers have shifted their focus toward safer building construction and disaster management.

Discussion Prompts

- Do you know of other countries besides Japan that have recently experienced one or more earthquakes? *(Answers will vary, but may include the United States, Haiti, Chile, Turkey, Honduras.)*
- Do you know what measures your own country has taken in terms of dealing with earthquakes? *(Answers will vary.)*

Today's Issues in East Asia

Today, East Asia faces the issues previewed here. As you read Chapters 27 and 28, you will learn helpful background information. You will study the issues themselves in Chapter 29.

In a small group, answer the questions below. Then participate in a class discussion of your answers.

Exploring the Issues

1. PHYSICAL FORCES What might be some of the effects of earthquakes and volcanoes on daily life in the region? How might the effects be similar or different in an urban and a rural area?
2. TRADE What are some items you or your family have bought that were made in East Asia?
3. POPULATION Parts of East Asia are very crowded. What might be some of the advantages and challenges of living around so many people?

For more on these issues in East Asia . . .

PHYSICAL FORCES

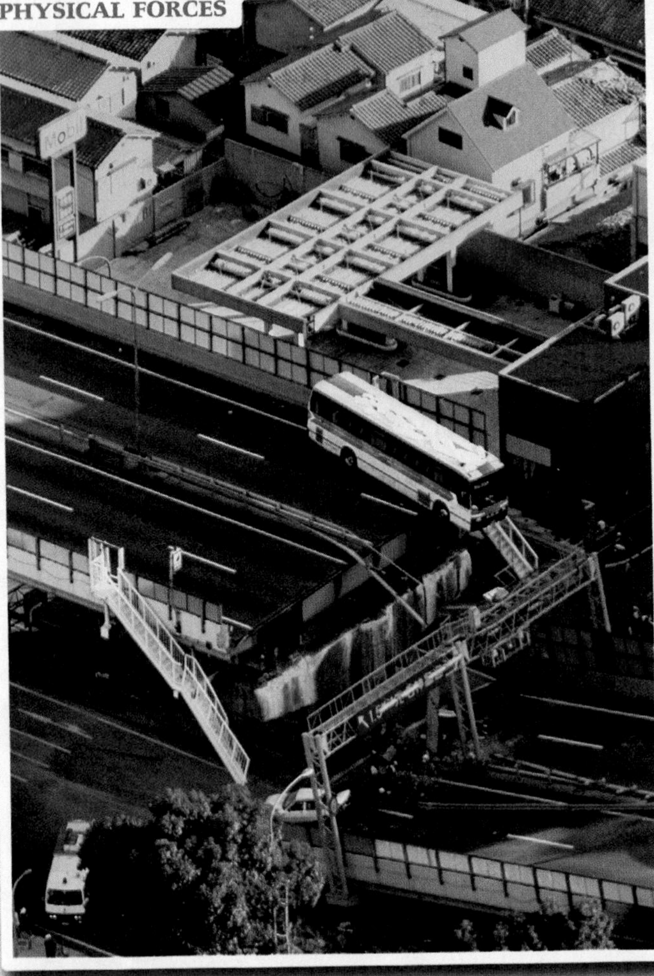

How might people in East Asia prepare for earthquakes and volcanoes?

A bus teeters on the edge of a highway torn apart by an earthquake in Kobe, Japan, in 1995.

EXPLORING THE ISSUES ANSWERS

1. PHYSICAL FORCES Students may say that earthquakes and volcanoes destroy buildings and roadways in cities, and crops and villages in the country.
2. TRADE Students may say they and their families have bought televisions, clothing, cars, computers or electronic games that were made in East Asia.
3. POPULATION Advantages could include greater community support, access to cultural events, more activities, and better job opportunities. Disadvantages could include overcrowding, higher cost of living, pollution, exposure to crime, and stress.

TRADE

What are some benefits of global trade?

Hong Kong is a thriving center of trade and economic activity. Once a colony of Britain, it is now a part of China. Its wealth and trading expertise are helping China compete with leading industrial nations.

CASESTUDY

What pressures does population put on the environment?

Subway attendants in Tokyo push people into crowded subway trains. Japan has a large number of people living on a small amount of land.

POPULATION

EAST ASIA

609

UNIT 9

TRADE

Although trade with East Asian countries such as China and Japan has been restricted at different times in history due to embargoes, trade throughout East Asia, and especially China, has grown enormously in the last 20 years.

Discussion Prompts

- How might East Asia's trade growth have occurred? *(growth of world market, fewer trade restrictions, no wars interrupting trade, desire for the resources or labor of other nations)*
- How does Chinese trade growth affect your life? *(Students may notice many products they buy are made in China or may know of companies that manufacture goods in China.)*

CASESTUDY

POPULATION

To give students the chance to gain a richer understanding of the issues related to overpopulation in East Asia, direct them to the Case Study, which begins on page 668 and concludes with a Case Study Project on page 670.

Discussion Prompts

- What have you heard or read about overpopulation in East Asia? *(Answers will vary.)*
- How is heavy population density handled in large United States cities? *(In many American cities, population density is relieved by sprawl, or movement of people to suburbs.)*

ACTIVITY OPTION **INTERNET RESEARCH**

BLOCK SCHEDULING

WRITING A NEWS SUMMARY

Objective To develop research skills and become more familiar with current events in East Asia

Class Time 20 minutes

Task Discover three news items or articles from three different sources on one of the specified topics—earthquakes, trade, or overpopulation—then write a summary of the article.

Directions Direct students to the Web to conduct a search for current articles or news items on overpopulation, trade, or earthquakes in East Asia.

OPTIONAL ACTIVITY If Internet access is limited, have the students use the library for their research. Have the librarian show the students different methods for finding current information on the issues in newspapers and magazines.

ATLAS OBJECTIVES

1. Compare data on the physical geography of East Asia.
2. Examine key physical features of East Asia.
3. Identify dynasties and periods of expansion in China.
4. Identify current political features of East Asia.
5. Learn about East Asian religions and vegetation.
6. Analyze language distribution and population density in East Asia.

Focus & Motivate

Ask students what they already know about the physical geography of East Asia. *(Answers will vary.)* Ask them how the maps could help them understand the geography of East Asia. *(The maps help show patterns, similarities, and differences in countries' geography.)*

Instruct: Objective 

Comparing Data

- ***Landmass*** How does East Asia compare in size to the United States? *(larger)*
- ***Population*** How do the populations of East Asia and the United States compare? *(East Asia's population is more than one billion people larger.)*
- ***Rivers*** How does the Chang Jiang compare in length to the Mississippi River? *(It is about 1,500 miles longer.)*
- ***Mountains*** How does Mt. Fuji compare in size to the highest mountain in the United States? *(Mt. McKinley is about 8,000 feet taller.)*

Unit ATLAS

Patterns of Physical Geography

Use the Unit Atlas to add to your knowledge of East Asia. As you look at the maps and charts, notice geographic patterns and specific details about the region. For example, the charts on pages 610–611 give details about the rivers and mountains of East Asia.

After studying the pictures, graphs, and physical map on these two pages, jot down in your notebook the answers to the following questions.

Making Comparisons

1. What three main river systems run from west to east in China?
2. Which of the bodies of water surrounding Japan is the largest?
3. Compare East Asia's size and population to those of the United States. Based on that data, how might the population densities of the two compare?

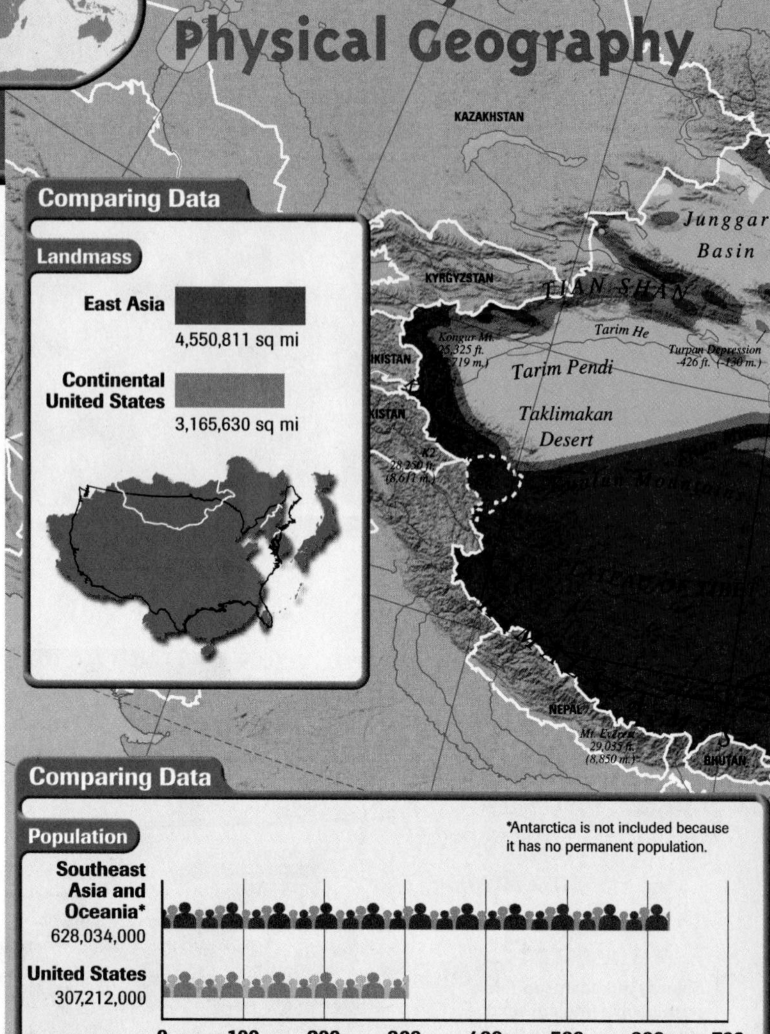

MAKING COMPARISONS ANSWERS

1. Huang He, Chang Jiang, Xi Jiang
2. Pacific Ocean
3. The population density of East Asia is much higher than that of the United States.

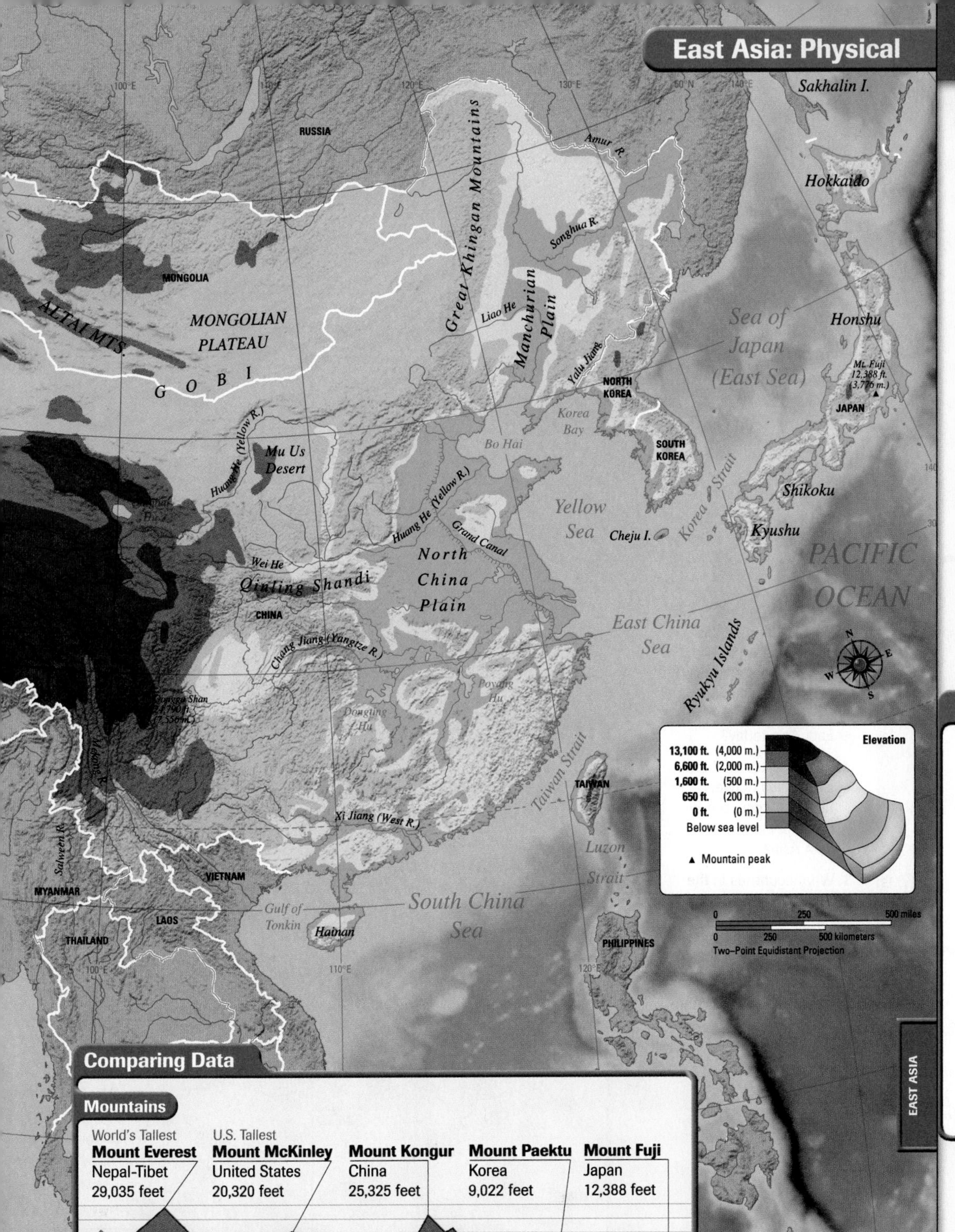

Comparing Data

Mountains

World's Tallest	U.S. Tallest			
Mount Everest	**Mount McKinley**	**Mount Kongur**	**Mount Paektu**	**Mount Fuji**
Nepal-Tibet	United States	China	Korea	Japan
29,035 feet	20,320 feet	25,325 feet	9,022 feet	12,388 feet

611

UNIT 9 ATLAS

Instruct: Objective 2

East Asia: Physical

- What countries are made up of islands in East Asia? *(Japan, Taiwan)*
- What is the highest mountain in Asia? *(Mount Everest)*
- On what type of landmass are North and South Korea located? *(peninsula)*
- What body of water do North and South Korea share with China? *(Yellow Sea)*
- Where are the Altai Mountains? *(Mongolia)*

In-Depth Resources: Unit 9
- Unit Atlas Activities, p. 1

Outline Map with Activities
- East Asia: Physical, pp. 87–88

Map Transparencies MT46
- East Asia: Physical

More About

Mount Everest

Mount Everest has been revered and seen as a challenge by many adventurers. Local Tibetans named Mount Everest *Chomolungma*, which means "Goddess Mother of the World" or "Goddess of the Valley."

Mount Everest was not recognized as the highest point in the world until 1852, when a British governmental survey determined its height. Peak XV, as it was then called, was renamed in 1865 for Sir George Everest, British surveyor general of India during the 1830s.

ACTIVITY OPTION CRITICAL THINKING

DRAWING CONCLUSIONS

Explaining the Skill Drawing conclusions means that students must analyze what they have read and form an opinion about its meaning. To draw conclusions they must look at the facts and then use common sense and experience to decide what the facts mean. Students will demonstrate their ability to draw conclusions from information presented in a physical map by using the key and visual display.

Applying the Skill Have students look closely at the physical map of East Asia. Ask them to look at the elevation key and describe one pattern they see reflected in the physical map. Then ask them to draw some conclusion about that pattern. For example, there is a pattern of the elevations moving upward from coast to inland on the East Asian islands. *(One conclusion might be that volcanoes formed the islands.)*

Instruct: Objective 3

Expansion of the Chinese Empire

- What does this map show? *(the borders of the country during various dynasties and how they compare to current Chinese borders)*
- China had many dynasties, why were these four most likely chosen for this map? *(They were dynasties that did a lot in terms of expanding China's borders.)*
- How does China differ from the time of the Qing Dynasty? *(It is smaller in size now.)*

More About

The Great Wall of China

The Great Wall was made up of different walled fortifications that served as military outposts for a variety of Chinese kingdoms. The wall was expanded by linking together these different sections. Later rulers added on to the wall. The wall was unattended, repaired, and rebuilt throughout the centuries as invasions and military strategy required. Much of what is left today was constructed during the Ming Dynasty (1368-1644).

Unit ATLAS

Patterns of Human Geography

Over the course of centuries, the political map of East Asia has changed. The Chinese empire expanded over thousands of years, absorbing much of the region. Study the historical and political maps of East Asia on these two pages. In your notebook, answer these questions.

Making Comparisons

1. What differences do you notice when you compare the historical map of the Chinese empire to the map of East Asia today?
2. What are some of the similarities between the historical map and the contemporary map of East Asia?
3. What countries in the region used to be a part of the Chinese empire but are now independent? Which country in the region was never a part of the empire?

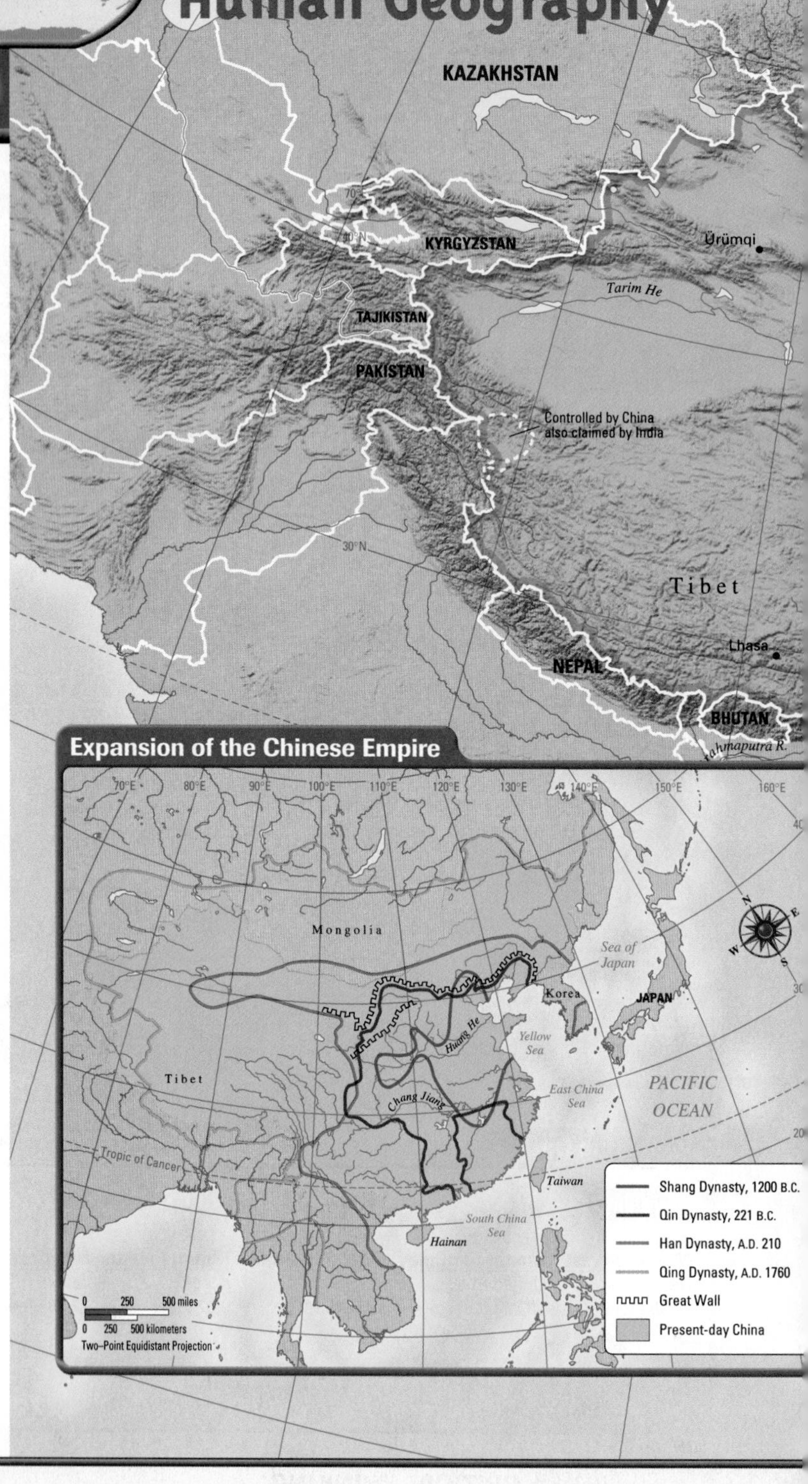

MAKING COMPARISONS ANSWERS

1. Parts of the Chinese empire have become independent countries.
2. China is still very large and encompasses Manchuria and Tibet.
3. North and South Korea, Mongolia. Japan was never part of China.

East Asia: Political

Instruct: Objective 4

East Asia: Political

- What other countries did parts of the Chinese empire once include? *(Russia, Mongolia, Korea, Vietnam, Laos, Thailand, Nepal, etc.)*
- What other country's border is closest to the Great Wall of China? *(Mongolia)*

 **Outline Maps with Activities**
- East Asia: Political, pp. 89–90

 **Map Transparencies MT47**
- East Asia: Political

More About

Hong Kong

Hong Kong became an important center of trade largely because of its natural harbor. In the 19th century, British merchants developed Hong Kong as a commercial port. After World War II, it remained under British jurisdiction. During that time, Hong Kong grew as a financial and trade center. It was known for producing inexpensive products. Britain returned control of Hong Kong to China in 1997 when its 99-year lease on the territory expired. Despite overcrowding, political unrest, fluctuations in trade, and lack of natural resources, Hong Kong has become a leading player for China's strongly emerging trade markets.

EAST ASIA

613

ACTIVITY OPTION | **LINK TO ART**

FINDING SCROLL PAINTINGS

Objective To find art history information and illustrations on either Chinese or Japanese scroll painting

Class Time 45 minutes

Task Use library resources to find information about scroll paintings

Directions Have students select either China or Japan to focus on. Have students use the library to find two sources of information on scroll painting within their chosen country. Sources should include at least two visual examples of scroll painting. Have students note the preferred media, style, and subject matter, and share examples with the class. Students should then exchange their findings in a group discussion.

Instruct: Objective 5

Religions of East Asia

- In terms of religion, into which group do the majority of people in East Asia fall? *(nonreligious)*
- Which category probably includes Confucianism? *(Other)*

Instruct: Objective 

Vegetation of East Asia

- What type of vegetation is most common in East Asia? *(temperate grassland)*
- What is the typical vegetation around the Yellow Sea? *(Deciduous and mixed forest)*
- Which country has the most diverse vegetation? *(China)*

Unit ATLAS

Regional Patterns

These two pages contain a graph and three thematic maps. The graph shows the religions of East Asia. The maps show other important features of East Asia: its vegetation, languages, and population density. After studying these two pages, answer the questions below in your notebook.

Making Comparisons

1. Where is most of the population located in China? Why might people have settled in these areas rather than in other areas?
2. Which is the smallest country in East Asia?
3. What is the vegetation in much of southern China, Taiwan, southern Korea, and southern Japan? How does it differ from the vegetation in Mongolia?

Religions of East Asia

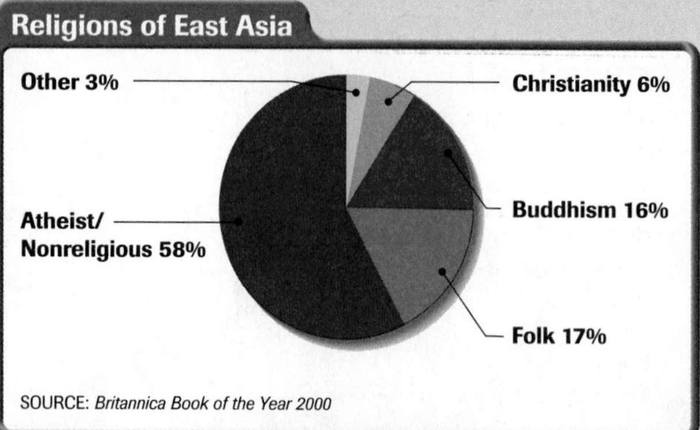

Vegetation of East Asia

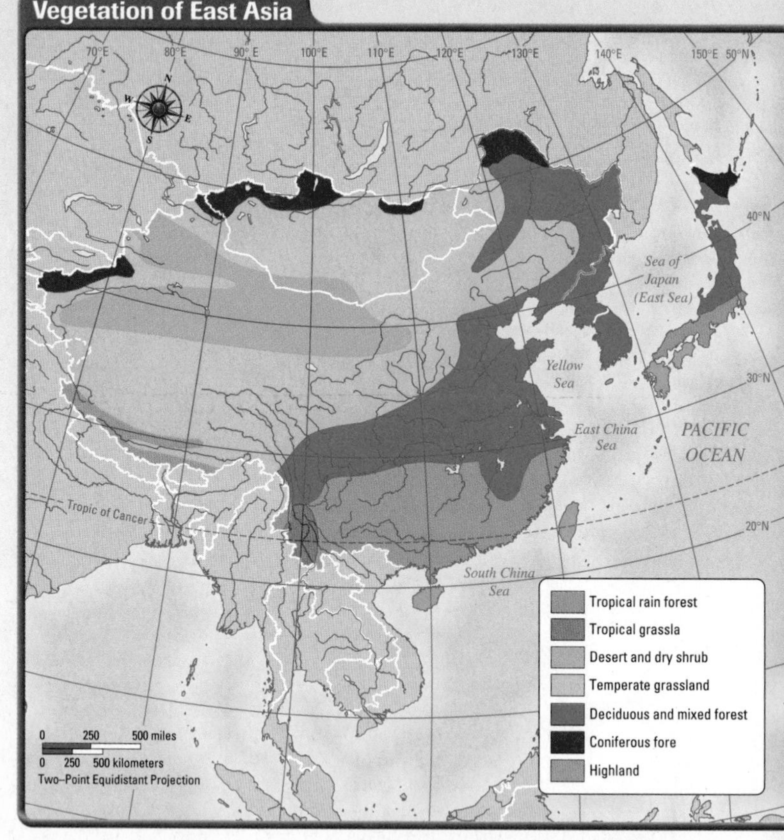

MAKING COMPARISONS ANSWERS

1. In the eastern part of China; because of water resources, farmland, and more temperate climate.
2. Taiwan
3. Tropical rain forest. Mongolia is filled with temperate grasslands.

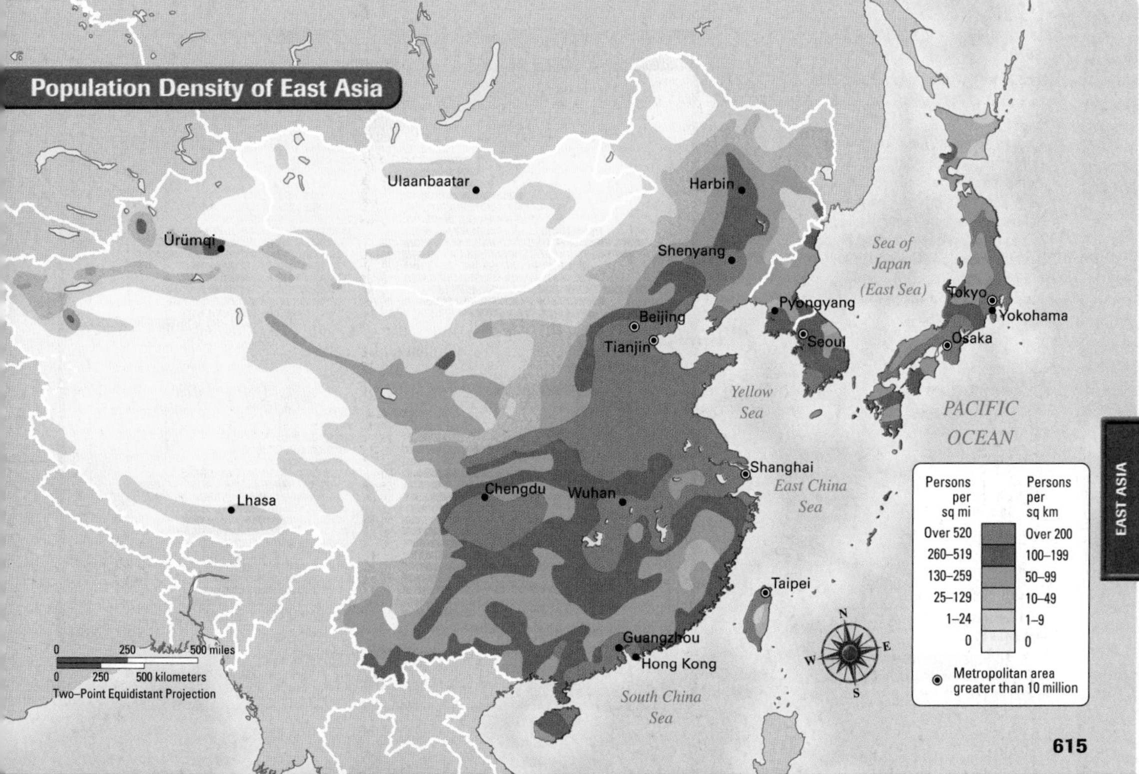

615

EAST ASIA

UNIT 9 ATLAS

Instruct: Objective 6

Languages of East Asia

- Which country has the most diverse languages? *(China)*
- Where is Min Chinese spoken? *(Taiwan and in one eastern section of China)*
- What do North and South Korea, Japan, and Mongolia have in common? *(They speak one primary language.)*

Instruct: Objective 6

Population Density of East Asia

- Which color represents the most common population density level in South Korea? *(dark orange, representing 260–519 persons per sq. mile)*
- Which country contains the lowest overall population density? *(Mongolia)*
- Identify three cities in very high population density areas. *(Beijing, Osaka, Tokyo, Taipei, Shanghai, among others)*

DIFFERENTIATING INSTRUCTION — GIFTED AND TALENTED STUDENTS

EXPLORING LANGUAGE ORIGINS

Objective To research and write about the origins of a particular language

Class Time One class period

Task Research the origin of a particular East Asian language and write a brief report

Directions Assign a particular East Asian language (such as Mandarin, Tibetan, Mongolian, Japanese, or Korean) to each student. Have the students use library and Internet sources to find at least two sources of specific information on the origins of that language. Then have them write a brief report that includes a bibliography of references.

DATA FILE OBJECTIVE

Examine and compare data on East Asian countries.

Focus & Motivate

Ask students which country they think has the smallest land area. Which country has the lowest literacy rate? *(Taiwan; China)*

Instruct: Objective

Regional Data File

- What is the smallest country in terms of population? The largest in terms of population? *(Mongolia; China)*
- Which East Asian country has the most televisions per person? How does the United States compare? *(Japan; the United States has more.)*
- Which country in East Asia has the most doctors per person? *(North Korea)*

In-Depth Resources: Unit 9
- Regional Data File Activities, p. 2

Regional Data File

Study the charts on the countries of East Asia. In your notebook, answer these questions.

Making Comparisons

1. Which countries have the most people? Are they also the largest countries in area?
2. Where in the region are the highest elevations located? What might this suggest about settlement patterns in the region?

Country Flag	Country/ Capital	Population	Life Expectancy (years)	Birthrate (per 1,000 pop.)	Infant Mortali (per 1,000 live birt
	China* Beijing	1,333,613,000	73.5	14	20.3
	Japan Tokyo	127,079,000	82.1	7.6	2.8
	Mongolia Ulaanbaatar	3,041,000	67.7	21.1	39.9
	North Korea Pyongyang	22,665,000	63.8	14.8	51.3
	South Korea Seoul	48,509,000	78.7	8.9	4.3
	Taiwan Taipei	22,974,000	77.9	9.0	5.4
	United States Washington, D.C.	307,212,000	78.1	13.8	6.2

Sources:

Central Intelligence Agency, *The World Factbook, 2010*

The World Almanac and Book of Facts, 2010

World Health Organization (WHO), 2007

Notes:

* Figures do not include Hong Kong or Macao, both Special Administrative Regions.

[a] GDP (purchasing power parity) is defined as the sum value of all goods and services produced in the country valued at prices prevailing in the United States.

[b] Includes land and water, when figures are available.

China Population Pyramids, 2000 and 2050

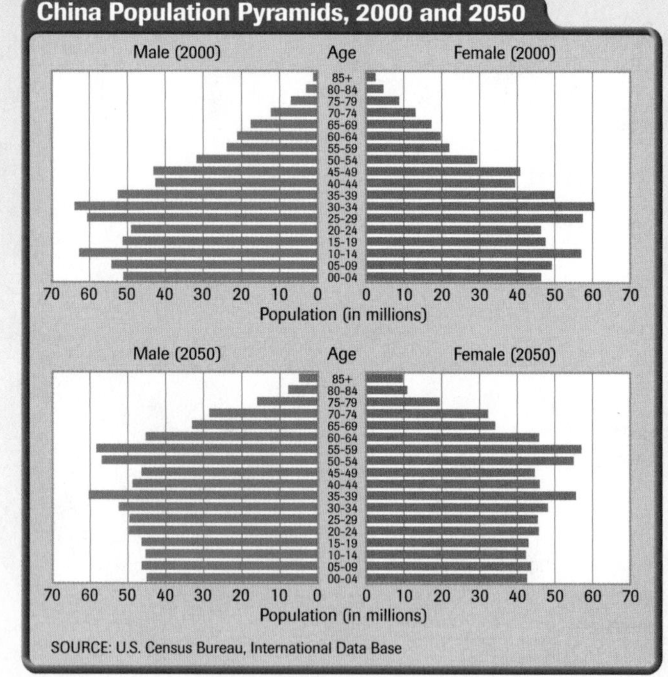

SOURCE: U.S. Census Bureau, International Data Base

For updated statistics on East Asia . . .

MAKING COMPARISONS ANSWERS

1. China and Japan. China is the largest, but Japan is smaller than China or Mongolia.
2. The highest elevations are in the western part of the region; there is less settlement in the west and more in the east.

Doctors (per 100,000 pop.) (2000-2004)	GDP[a] (billions $US)	Import/Export (billions $US)	Literacy Rate (percentage)	Televisions (per 1,000 pop.)	Passenger Cars (per 1,000 pop.)	Total Area[b]
106	8,791	921.5/1,194	91	291	16	3,705,407
198	4,141	490.6/516.3	99	719	449	145,883
263	9.5	2.13/1.90	98	58	N/A	603,909
329	40	3.57/2.06	99	55	N/A	46,541
157	1,343	313.4/355.1	98	364	219	38,023
N/A	708.4	174.7/203.7	96	327	N/A	13,892
256	14,260.0	1,445/994.7	99	844	725	3,794,083

Profile of East Asia

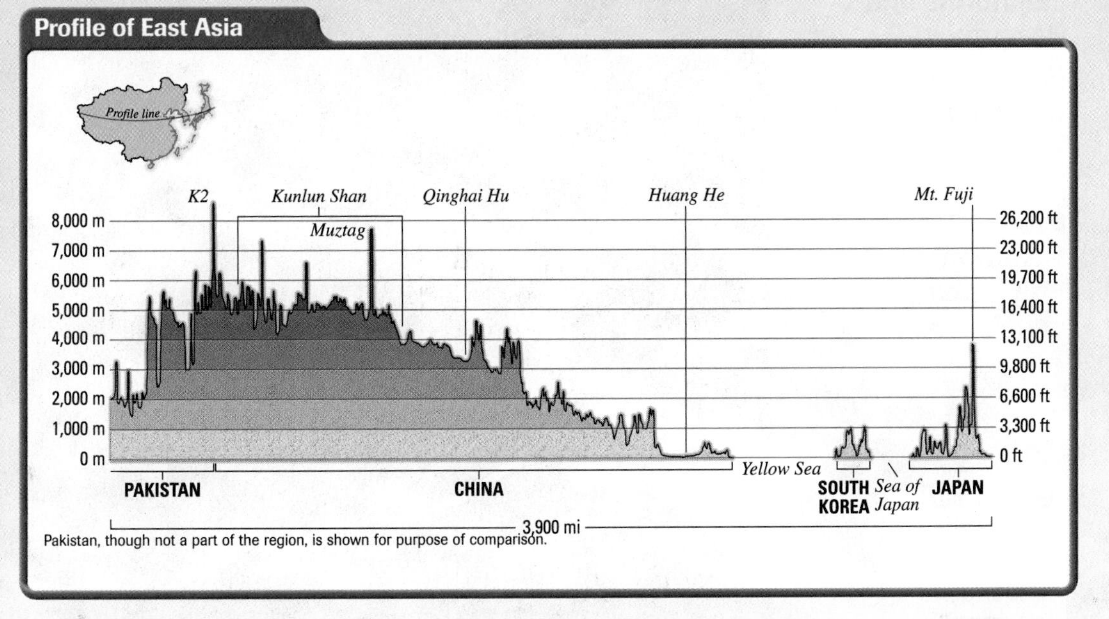

Pakistan, though not a part of the region, is shown for purpose of comparison.

More About

The Population of China

Have students examine the pyramid charts for China's population for 2010 and estimated population for 2050. Tell students how China's population has grown significantly throughout its history, even doubling at times. But population growth really accelerated during the 20th century. The Chinese government began a series of family-planning strategies in the 1950s. Those, in addition to famine and epidemics, slowed the Chinese population growth overall. China's current population growth rate is fairly low for a country of its size, but the enormous population still produces a large annual net population growth.

Using Maps to Predict Future Growth Trends

Refer students to the maps in the Unit 9 Atlas and the Regional Data File. Have them use these resources to predict growth trends of East Asian societies.

ACTIVITY OPTION CRITICAL THINKING

MAKING COMPARISONS

Explaining the Skill *Comparing* means looking at the similarities and differences between two or more things. *Contrasting* means examining only the differences between them. It is often helpful to get a fuller picture of a country and what life might be like there through comparison of data with one's own country. If, for instance, one compares population with land size, one can see how density could be the same or different in one country versus another.

Applying the Skill Have students choose one country to compare with the United States. Ask them to focus on four categories of information (such as number of televisions, passenger cars, population, and land area). Then have them write brief statements about how the two countries are similar or different in these categories and what they may say about that country's lifestyle as compared to that of the United States. Since they know what life is generally like in the United States, they can make comparisons and begin to gain a fuller idea of life in another country.

CHAPTER 27 OBJECTIVE

Identify key features of East Asia's physical geography, climate, vegetation, and human-environment interaction.

Chapter **27**

PHYSICAL GEOGRAPHY OF EAST ASIA
A Rugged Terrain

The Great Wall is a line of fortifications across northern China. The first walls were constructed mainly of tamped earth. Construction of the brick and stone wall we see today began in the 1400s. Its effectiveness against invaders was limited.

Essential Question

How have the extremes of East Asia's physical geography affected its people?

What You Will Learn

In this chapter you will learn about the landforms, climate, and resources of East Asia.

SECTION 1
Landforms and Resources

SECTION 2
Climate and Vegetation

SECTION 3
Human–Environment Interaction

hmhsocialstudies.com
TAKING NOTES

Use the graphic organizer online to record information about the physical geography of East Asia.

Interpreting Photographs

The Great Wall of China

Have students examine the photograph and read the caption. Ask students what characteristics may have made the wall effective or ineffective as a means of protection. *(Effective: view across distance, easier movement over rugged terrain; Ineffective: difficulty in guarding its vast expanse, maintaining and repairing structures)*

Introducing the Essential Question

- Discuss this question with students: Do Americans tend to think of East Asians in stereotypical ways? Emphasize that the extremes of the region's physical geography have led to the development of countless different ways of life. As a result, millions of East Asians defy any assumptions we may make about them.
- Emphasize that people have lived in China for thousands of years. Over the millennia, people have changed their environment in many ways.

Have students fill out the graphic organizers in their notebooks by using information from all the sections in this chapter.

Critical Thinking Transparencies CT27
- GeoFocus

In-Depth Resources: Unit 9
- Building Vocabulary, p. 9

CHAPTER 27 ADDITIONAL RESOURCES

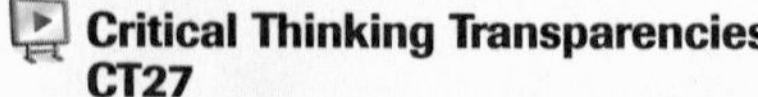

BOOKS FOR THE TEACHER

National Geographic Atlas of China. National Geographic, 2009. More than 300 maps and photos enhance this look at the latest information from the Asian giant.

Booth, Alan. ***The Road to Sata: A 2000-Mile Walk Through Japan.*** Tokyo: Kodansha, 1997. A vivid account of the author's trek from north to south.

BOOKS FOR THE STUDENT

Harrer, Heinrich. ***Seven Years in Tibet.*** NY: Jeremy P. Tarcher/Putnam, 1997. Adventures of an Austrian who visited the Tibetan holy city of Lhasa.

VIDEOS

Above All Else: The Everest Dream. Miramar/Unapix, 1999. Documentary follows Alan Hobson and Jamie Clarke on their third attempt to conquer Mt. Everest.

Touring Korea. Questar Video, 1988. Produced by Encounter Video Inc. Captures the history and legends, as well as the factories and cities, of South Korea.

SOFTWARE

China! The Grand Tour. CD-ROM. Hopkins, MN: Hopkins Technology, 1995.

INTERNET

For more on the physical geography of East Asia, visit . . .

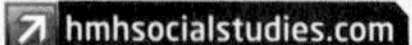

Landforms and Resources

Main Ideas

- East Asia has a huge mainland area that includes rugged terrain.
- East Asia has a number of important islands off its eastern coast.

Places & Terms

Kunlun Mountains
Qinling Shandi Mountains
Huang He
Chang Jiang
Xi Jiang

CONNECT TO THE ISSUES
PHYSICAL FORCES East Asia's rough terrain and unevenly distributed resources have influenced settlement and ways of life in the region.

A HUMAN PERSPECTIVE Time and again in its early history, China was attacked by invaders from the steppes of Central Asia. The Chinese built and extended the Great Wall over many centuries in an attempt to keep out such invaders from Mongolia. From the Yellow Sea to the Gobi Desert, the wall twisted for thousands of miles across China. The wall was built by hundreds of thousands of peasant workers. Many died from the backbreaking labor or the severe weather. The Great Wall remains one of the largest building feats in history—partly because it had to cross mile after mile of China's difficult terrain.

Landforms: Mountains and Plateaus

East Asia stretches from the western provinces of China to the eastern coast of Japan. Mongolia, Taiwan, North Korea, and South Korea are the other countries in the region. East Asia includes high mountains, vast deserts, cold climates, and Pacific waters. The mostly rugged terrain was formed by the collision of tectonic plates. One result of these natural barriers was to limit people's movement and increase their isolation.

MOUNTAIN RANGES OF THE REGION High mountains in the region limited contact between people living in China and in other parts of Asia. The world's highest mountains are located on the western edge of East Asia in southwestern and northwestern China and western Mongolia. The **Kunlun Mountains,** which are located in the west of China, are the source of two of China's great rivers, the Huang He (Yellow) and the Chang Jiang (Yangtze). In southeastern and east central China, the **Qinling Shandi Mountains** divide the northern part of China from the south.

PLATEAUS AND PLAINS The landscape of East Asia is among the roughest in the world. The mountain areas in the western part of the region restricted movement and were underpopulated. Although few flat surfaces exist, the region has some low basins and barren deserts. These include the Plateau of Tibet (also known as the Xizang Plateau), the Tarim Pendi Basin in western China, and the Taklimakan Desert in western China. All these areas are sparsely populated.

PLACE The Potala Palace in Lhasa, Tibet, has many floors and more than 1,000 rooms. It was once the residence of the Dalai Lama and other monks and is now a major pilgrimage site.

SECTION 1 OBJECTIVES

1. Examine how mountains and plateaus affected China's development.
2. Identify important peninsulas and islands in East Asia.
3. Describe major rivers and their uses.
4. Identify key natural resources and describe how they influence daily life in East Asia.

SKILLBUILDER: Interpreting Maps
pp. 620, 622

GeographicThinking
Seeing Patterns, p. 622
Drawing Conclusions, p. 623

Focus & Motivate

How might the distribution of natural resources across East Asia have helped some countries and harmed others? *(China has been able to sustain a large population and produce many goods and export resources; Japan, South Korea, and Taiwan have limited natural resources and often have to purchase resources from elsewhere.)*

Interpreting Photographs

The Potala Palace

Potala means "Pure Land" or "High Heavenly Realm" and probably refers to Mount Potala in India since the Tibetan Buddhists believe the Dalai Lama is connected to an important holy person who once lived there.

Instruct: Objective 1 appears on p. 620.

SECTION 1 PROGRAM RESOURCES

In-Depth Resources: Unit 9
- Guided Reading, p. 3
- Map and Graph Skills, pp. 6–7
- Building Vocabulary, p. 9
- Reteaching Activity, p. 10

Guided Reading Workbook
- Section 1

Access for Students Acquiring English/ESL
- Guided Reading, p. 144
- Map and Graph Skills, pp. 148–149

Formal Assessment
- Section Quiz, p. 421

Integrated Assessment
- Rubric for a map, 2.1

INTEGRATED TECHNOLOGY

Chapter Summaries

Power Presentations

Test Generator
- Section Quiz

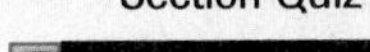

TEST-TAKING RESOURCES

Strategies for Test Preparation

Test Practice Transparencies TT87

Online Test Practice

Instruct: Objective 

Landforms: Mountains and Plateaus

- What are three natural barriers that have limited people's movements in East Asia? *(deserts, high mountains, rugged terrain, large bodies of water)*
- What is the source of China's Huang He and Chang Jiang rivers? *(Kunlun Mountains)*
- Which vast desert stretches across parts of China and Mongolia? *(Gobi)*

In-Depth Resources: Unit 9
- Guided Reading, p. 3

Interpreting Maps

Rivers and Mountains of East Asia

Have students make a list of major rivers and mountain ranges in China. *(Kunlun Mountains, Qinling Shandi; Huang He, Chang Jiang, Xi Jiang)*

SKILLBUILDER ANSWERS
1. Plateau of Tibet **2.** Xi Jiang

Instruct: Objective 

Peninsulas and Islands

- Which peninsula contains two independent countries? *(The Korean Peninsula)*
- How are Japan and Taiwan similar? *(Both are located on islands off the coast of Asia.)*
- What Chinese island is near Vietnam? *(Hainan)*

Rivers and Mountains of East Asia

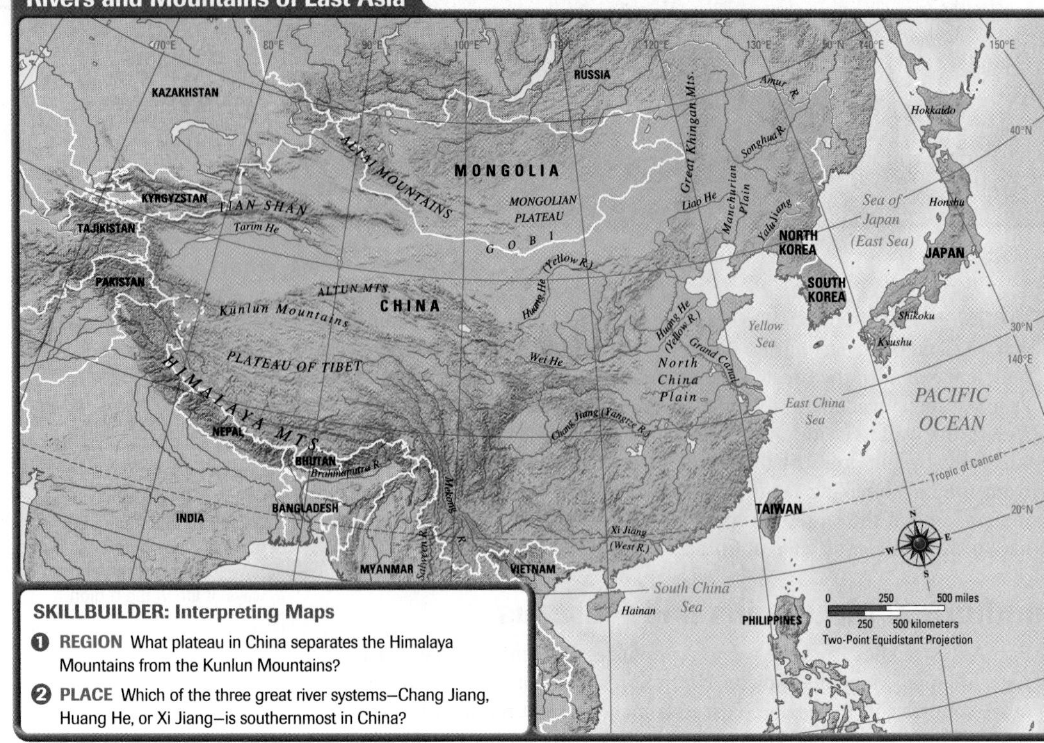

SKILLBUILDER: Interpreting Maps
1. **REGION** What plateau in China separates the Himalaya Mountains from the Kunlun Mountains?
2. **PLACE** Which of the three great river systems—Chang Jiang, Huang He, or Xi Jiang—is southernmost in China?

One of the largest deserts in the world—the Gobi—stretches from northwest China into Mongolia. It covers more than 500,000 square miles, which is larger than Texas and California combined. The Mongolian Plateau reaches into northeastern China. Northern China encompasses the Manchurian Plain and the North China Plain.

Peninsulas and Islands

East Asia includes a number of important peninsulas. Most of these form a part of China, although one peninsula contains independent nations. In addition, a number of islands off the coast of China include possessions of China as well as independent nations.

THE COAST OF CHINA The eastern coast of China features several peninsulas. These include the Shandong Peninsula, the Leizhou Peninsula, and the Macao Peninsula. Macao was owned by Portugal until 1999, when it returned to Chinese control. Because of its peninsulas, China has a long coastline that has allowed several major port cities, such as Shanghai, to develop. Bordering China on the east is the Korean Peninsula, which contains the two independent nations of North Korea and South Korea.

THE ISLANDS OF EAST ASIA An important feature of East Asia is the continental shelf—the submerged border of the continent—that extends east from China. A number of islands stand above this

DIFFERENTIATING INSTRUCTION **LESS PROFICIENT READERS**

ORGANIZING INFORMATION

Objective To remember details by organizing textual information visually

Class Time 15-20 minutes

Task Create a chart

Directions Draw a chart on the board or have students draw the chart in their notebooks. Have them fill in key information for each landform.

LANDFORMS OF EAST ASIA

Mountain Ranges	Plateaus	Peninsulas	Islands
Kunlun (China)	Plateau of Tibet (China)	Korean Penninsula (North and South Korea)	Hokkaido, Honshu, Shikoku, Kyushu (Japan)
Quinlang Shandi (China)	Tarim Pendi Basin (China)	Shandong (China)	Taiwan
Altai Mountains (Mongolia)	Taklimakan Desert (China)	Macao (China)	Hainan (China)
Himalaya Mountains (China)	Mongolian Plateau (Mongolia)	Leizhou (China)	

continental shelf. The isolation of the islands has permitted them to develop in greater security and peace than parts of the mainland. Further, many of these islands have developed trading economies.

The islands off China include Hainan and part of Hong Kong. Long one of the major harbors in the world, Hong Kong (while originally a part of China) used to be a British colony. In 1997, Hong Kong once again came under the authority of mainland China.

The smaller nations of East Asia are located on islands and peninsulas. For example, Japan is an island nation with enormous economic power. Taiwan is a separate island that at one time belonged to mainland China—and is still claimed by China.

BACKGROUND Japan is made up of four main islands and numerous smaller islands.

River Systems

China has three great rivers, which have been critical to the development of China's civilization. The rivers have helped to feed hundreds of millions of people because of the fields and crops they irrigate.

THE HUANG HE The **Huang He** (or Yellow River) of northern China starts in the Kunlun Mountains in the west. It winds east for about 3,000 miles before emptying into the Yellow Sea. Both the sea and the river get their names from the yellow silt, or particles of soil, that the river carries to its delta. Another name for the river is "China's Sorrow" because of the terrible floods that it has caused.

THE CHANG JIANG The **Chang Jiang** (or Yangtze River) is the longest river in all of Asia. The name Chang Jiang means "long river." It flows about 3,900 miles from Xizang (Tibet) to the East China Sea. The river has been a major trade route since ancient times. Even today, the Chang Jiang carries most of the goods shipped on China's waterways. But this river, too, floods frequently, causing a great deal of damage to nearby villages, as well as to the surrounding countryside. A

A. Answer Rivers provided a way into the interior of a country long before roads and other means of transportation existed.

CONNECT TO THE ISSUES A How might rivers facilitate trade?

THE XI JIANG The **Xi Jiang** (or West River) runs its course in the south of China. It flows eastward through southeast China and joins up with

MOVEMENT Workers pull a boat ashore along the Huang He (Yellow River). **What are some of the uses that people might make of a river?**

EAST ASIA

621

Instruct: Objective 3

River Systems

- Where does the Huang He begin and where does it end? *(Kunlun Mountains; Yellow Sea)*
- How long is the Chang Jiang? *(about 3,900 miles)*
- Which is the southernmost of the three great river systems of China? *(Xi Jiang)*

Interpreting Photographs

The Huang He

Tell students that although the Huang He carries a large volume of water toward the sea each year, much of that water never reaches the sea because it is diverted into irrigation routes or it evaporates. The Huang He carries a great deal of silt downstream. In fact, it is considered the world's muddiest river. Have students list some problems that could occur along such a river. *(Flooding, pollution, erosion of land)*

CAPTION ANSWER transportation, irrigation, water source, hydroelectric power

ACTIVITY OPTION | EXPLORING LOCAL GEOGRAPHY

LIVING ALONG A RIVER

Objective To activate student understanding through prior or experiential knowledge and research

Class Time Two class periods (one for research, one for sharing of reports)

Task Write a brief report on a local river's impact on a community

Directions Have students choose a local river or a river they are familiar with in the United States. Ask them to do some research on how that river affects the community (e.g., the flooding of the Mississippi) and then write a brief report. Have students share their reports with the class.

Interpreting Maps

Resources of East Asia

Have students examine the map. Ask what types of resources seem to appear most in China. *(petroleum, hydroelectric power, fishing, coal)* Then ask which area of East Asia seems to have the fewest resources. *(southwestern China)*

SKILLBUILDER ANSWERS

1. hydroelectric power and iron ore
2. northeastern China

Instruct: Objective 

Resources of East Asia

- According to the map, which countries have fewer than three natural resources? *(South Korea, Taiwan)*
- Which countries would need to import coal? *(North and South Korea, Taiwan)*
- Which country most likely exports the most minerals? *(China)*

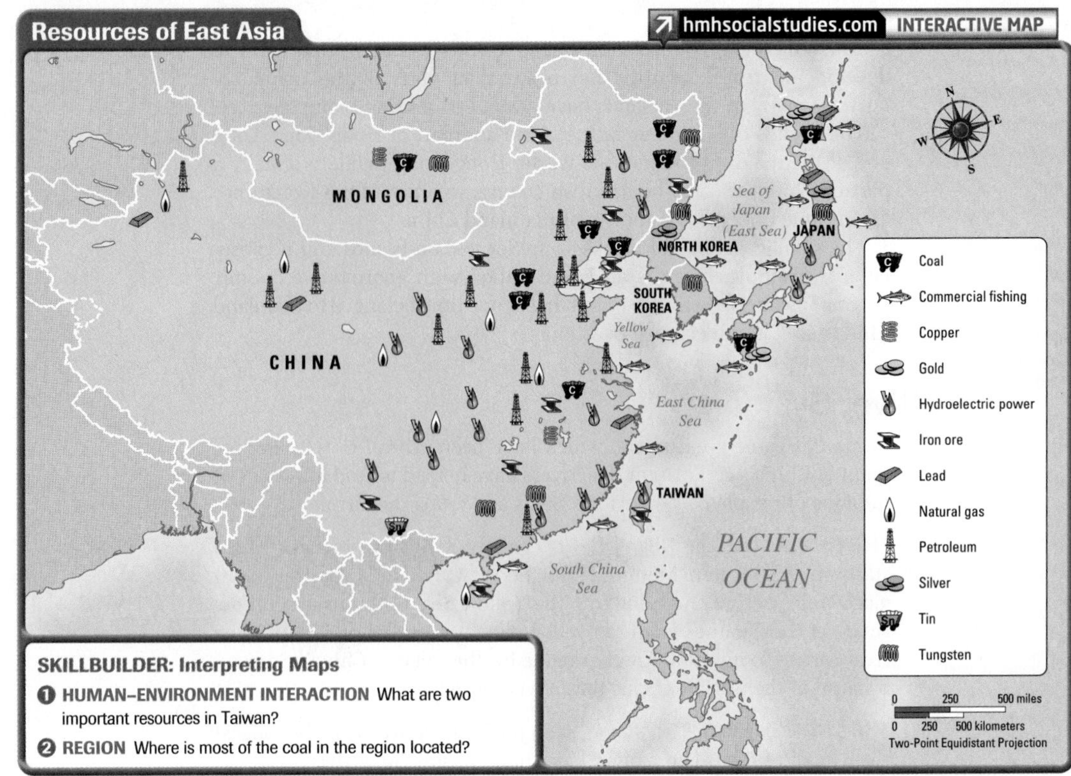

SKILLBUILDER: Interpreting Maps

1. **HUMAN–ENVIRONMENT INTERACTION** What are two important resources in Taiwan?
2. **REGION** Where is most of the coal in the region located?

the Pearl River (Zhu Jiang) to flow into the South China Sea. The Xi Jiang joins with three other rivers to form an estuary (where the river's current meets the ocean's tides) between Hong Kong and Macao. Important mineral resources are located in this river's valley.

OTHER RIVERS OF THE REGION The Yalu Jiang is another important river of the region. The Yalu, which is about 500 miles long, forms the border between North Korea and China. It is important historically because in 1950, Chinese troops entered the Korean War by crossing the river and attacking United Nations forces.

B. Answer Japan, South Korea, and Taiwan have limited natural resources.

Resources of East Asia

Natural and mineral resources are unevenly distributed throughout East Asia. China, for example, is rich in natural resources. Mongolia and North Korea also have substantial mineral resources. However, Japan, South Korea, and Taiwan have limited natural resources. Even so, these latter three nations have grown into major economic powers. B

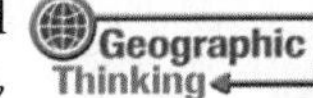
Geographic Thinking

Seeing Patterns B What are the three nations of the region that have grown into major economic powers, and what do they have in common?

LAND AND FORESTS The number of mountains in East Asia means that the amount of land available for agriculture is limited. For this reason, China's population is concentrated in the east, where river basins are located. The land in these valleys is highly productive, allowing the Chinese to grow rice and many other crops. In contrast, the mountainous western regions of China are more sparsely populated.

DIFFERENTIATING INSTRUCTION | LESS PROFICIENT READERS

NOTING DETAILS

Objective To provide support for noting and remembering important details

Class Time 20 minutes

Task Answer questions working with another person

Directions Have students form pairs and work together to answer the following questions. After 10 minutes have each pair share answers with the class.

- Which country contains gold as a natural resource? *(Japan)*
- Which countries contain silver? *(North Korea, Japan)*
- Where does most iron ore come from? *(China)*
- Which part of China has tin as a natural resource? *(in the south)*

Forests are also abundant in the region. China, Japan, Taiwan, and both North Korea and South Korea all have forest resources. Japan has been able to keep most of its forests in reserve by buying timber and other forest products from other regions of the world.

MINERAL AND ENERGY RESOURCES China has large energy reserves of petroleum, coal, and natural gas, and Korea has coal reserves. Japan also has deposits of coal. China's resources have enabled it to be self-sufficient for much of its history. In contrast, Japan's shortage of resources has forced it to trade for what it needs.

China's mineral resources include iron ore, tungsten, manganese, molybdenum, magnesite, lead, zinc, and copper. North and South Korea possess important tungsten, gold, and silver reserves. Japan has reserves of lead, silver, and coal.

C. Answer They provide power, irrigation, and a means of transportation.

WATER RESOURCES China's long river systems are important to the country's economy. They provide crop irrigation, hydroelectric power, and transportation. To control flooding on the Chang Jiang and produce more electricity, China constructed the Three Gorges Dam. (See pages 628–630.) The Huang He and Xi Jiang also provide hydroelectric power and a means of transportation. C

Seeing Patterns C In what ways might river systems be important to an economy?

People in East Asia look to the sea for food. In fact, Japan has developed one of the largest fishing industries in the world. Japanese factory ships process huge amounts of seafood for human consumption throughout the world, as well as in Japan.

You will read about East Asia's climate zones in the next section. You will also read about its vegetation.

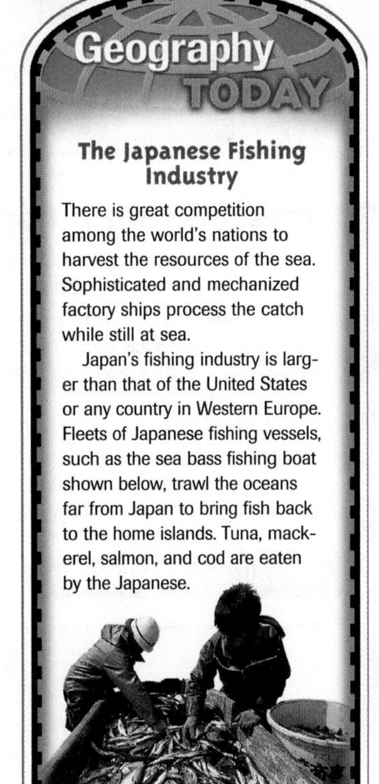

The Japanese Fishing Industry

There is great competition among the world's nations to harvest the resources of the sea. Sophisticated and mechanized factory ships process the catch while still at sea.

Japan's fishing industry is larger than that of the United States or any country in Western Europe. Fleets of Japanese fishing vessels, such as the sea bass fishing boat shown below, trawl the oceans far from Japan to bring fish back to the home islands. Tuna, mackerel, salmon, and cod are eaten by the Japanese.

Section 1 Assessment

1 Places & Terms

Identify each of the following places and terms.

- Kunlun Mountains
- Qinling Shandi Mountains
- Huang He
- Chang Jiang
- Xi Jiang

2 Taking Notes

PLACE Review the notes you took for this section.

Landforms	
Resources	

- What types of landforms are found in East Asia?
- What are their relative locations?

3 Main Ideas

a. How might the river basins of China have affected settlement patterns?

b. How are the landforms of East Asia an advantage to life in the region?

c. What effect might natural resources have had on the development of East Asia?

4 Geographic Thinking

Drawing Conclusions How might China's three large river systems have affected the development of agriculture and trade in the area? **Think about:**

- the obstacles that mountains and deserts present to agriculture
- the network of travel and communication offered by a river system

EAST ASIA

GeoActivity

SEEING PATTERNS Pair with a partner and draw a **map** of East Asia's rivers and mountains. Use arrows to indicate the directions the rivers flow. Why do the three main rivers of China flow all the way east across the continent even though their headwaters begin in the mountains of the west?

Geography TODAY

The Japanese Fishing Industry

In addition to the fish mentioned in the text, clams, eels, oysters, pollock, sardines, scallops, and squid are all harvested in abundance by the Japanese fishing industry. This is because fish are a chief source of protein in the Japanese diet.

Some of this product of Japan's fishing industry is used in sushi. This is a common seafood-and-rice dish served throughout Japan that is becoming popular worldwide. It often contains cooked rice flavored with vinegar and may be pressed, rolled, or hand formed. It can include sheets of seaweed and various kinds of raw fish and vegetables.

Assess & Reteach

GeoFocus Have students complete the sections on landforms and resources in their GeoFocus graphic organizers.

Formal Assessment
- Section Quiz, p. 421

Reteaching Activity
Divide the class into small groups. Distribute index cards that contain a word or phrase from each subhead (for example, "River Systems") to each group. Have the students in each group write a brief summary or explanation of how that word or phrase applies to the section. Members from each group should then share their summaries with the class.

In-Depth Resources: Unit 9
- Reteaching Activity, p. 10

SECTION 1 ASSESSMENT ANSWERS

1. Places & Terms
Kunlun Mountains, p. 619; Qinling Shandi Mountains, p. 619; Huang He, p. 621; Chang Jiang, p. 621; Xi Jiang, p. 621

2. Taking Notes
- mountains, plateaus, plains, deserts
- The Pacific Ocean forms its eastern border; the mountains of western and southern China separate it from the countries of South Asia, and the countries of Southeast Asia. Deserts separate the region from Russia to the north.

3. Main Ideas
a. People settled along the rivers because the rivers supplied water to irrigate crops.
b. The mountains and surrounding seas provided China with some isolation from invasions. The islands of the region also provided security and peace. The river systems provided rich farmland.
c. Most of the population of China is concentrated in the east because of the river basins that provide rich farmland. Rivers systems provide transportation and electric power.

4. Geographic Thinking
The Chang Jiang has been a major trade route since ancient times. All three rivers have irrigated vast areas of rich farmland.

GeoActivity

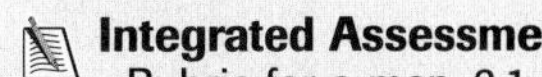

Integrated Assessment
- Rubric for a map, 2.1

OBJECTIVE

Learn how to use a contour map.

Instruct: Objective

Interpreting a Contour Map

- What unit of measure is used in the map to determine elevations? *(meters)*
- Based on the map key, approximately how many miles is Mt. Asahi from Sapporo? *(75-80 miles)*
- At about what elevation is the city of Sapporo? *(200 meters)*

 **In-Depth Resources: Unit 9**
- Map and Graph Skills, pp. 6–7

 **Access for Students Aquiring English/ESL**
- Map and Graph Skills, pp. 148–149

RAND McNALLY **Map and Graph Skills**

Interpreting a Contour Map

Suppose that you are vacationing on the Japanese island of Hokkaido. As part of your trip, you will be climbing Mount Asahi, the highest point on the island. The members of your group decide to study a contour map to understand the challenge that faces you. You can use a contour map to get a better idea of elevation and the steepness of the mountain.

THE LANGUAGE OF MAPS A **contour map** shows elevations and surface configuration by means of contour lines. Contour lines are lines on a map that show points of equal elevation. These lines are also called isolines. Numbers on the contour lines show the elevation in meters.

Elevation on Hokkaido

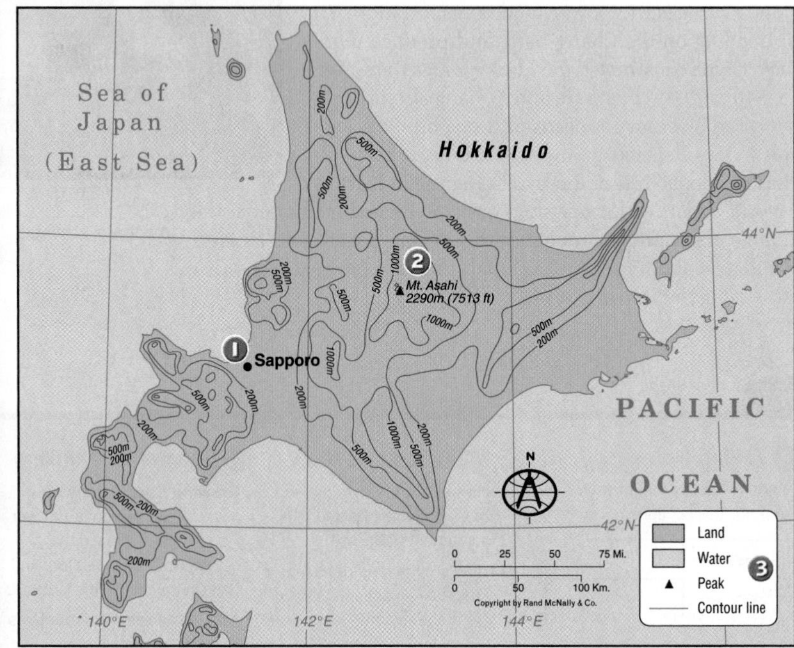

1 Sapporo, the largest city on the island, is situated at a low elevation.

2 Mount Asahi is the highest point on the island.

3 The key shows that Mount Asahi is a peak. The key shows that the red lines are contour lines. If you were to follow one contour line around its entire perimeter, you would remain at the same elevation throughout your walk.

Map and Graph Skills Assessment

1. Seeing Patterns
How high, in meters, is Mount Asahi? What is the elevation of the last contour line on the map before the peak?

2. Making Decisions
From what direction of the compass would you approach Mount Asahi if you wanted to make the steepest climb?

3. Drawing Conclusions
Where on the island do the isolines converge most densely to show a very dramatic increase in elevation?

MAP SKILLS ASSESSMENT ANSWERS

1. 2290; 1000 meters

2. west

3. in a peninsula on the east of the island at around 44 degrees latitude

Climate and Vegetation

Main Ideas
- East Asia has a dry highland climate in the west.
- The region has a humid climate in the east.

Places & Terms
typhoon
Taklimakan Desert
Gobi Desert

CONNECT TO THE ISSUES
POPULATION To feed its population, East Asian countries have had to farm in highly productive ways.

A HUMAN PERSPECTIVE Kublai Khan was the ruler of the Mongol Empire (which included China) in the 13th century. In 1281, the Great Khan sent a huge fleet against Japan. A **typhoon**—a tropical storm that occurs in the western Pacific—swept across the Sea of Japan and sank the Mongol ships or dashed them against the rocky Japanese shore. The typhoon had changed the course of history. Typhoons occur in parts of East Asia, but in other ways the weather is similar to that of the United States. Both are at the same latitude, and both have similar climate zones.

High Latitude Climate Zones

The climates in the highest latitudes present a serious challenge to all but the most hardy nomads and herders. These zones generally have severely cold climates. In addition, they tend to be very dry.

SUBARCTIC Subarctic climate zones occur in a small sliver along Mongolia's and China's northern borders with Russia. The summers in these areas range from cool to cold. The winters are brutally cold, testing the survival skills of the inhabitants. The climate is generally dry.

The typical vegetation of this region is the northern evergreen forest. Varieties of mosses and lichens also grow on rocks and tree trunks throughout subarctic zones.

HIGHLAND Highland climates are found mostly in western China. The temperature in highland zones varies with latitude and elevation. In general, the farther north the latitude and the higher the elevation, the colder the climate. The severe climate and topography of the western highlands are two of the reasons that the area is sparsely populated.

The vegetation in the highlands also varies with elevation. Forests and alpine tundra are the typical vegetation. Vast tundras reach as far as the eye can see. Tundras have no trees, and the soil a few feet below the surface is permanently frozen. In this environment, only mosses, lichens, and shrubs can grow. Because of the cold and the difficulty of growing crops, few people scratch out a living here.

HUMAN-ENVIRONMENT INTERACTION A 78-year-old woman tends sheep from the back of a camel in a semiarid zone typical of Mongolia. **What does the occupation of sheepherding and livestock grazing suggest about the vegetation in Mongolia?**

625

SECTION 2 OBJECTIVES
1. Describe the high latitude climate zones of East Asia.
2. Identify the mid-latitude zones of the region.
3. Describe the dry zones of East Asia.
4. Identify the tropical zones of the region.

SKILLBUILDER: Interpreting Maps p. 626

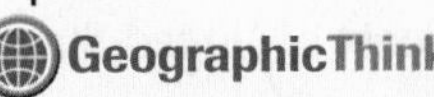

Making Comparisons, p. 627
Making Inferences, p. 627

Focus & Motivate

Ask students how climate and vegetation might affect people's lives. *(It may affect settlement, movement, and the economy, in terms of available natural resources or tourism.)*

Instruct: Objective 

High Latitude Climate Zones

- What two words best describe the climates in the higher latitudes of East Asia? *(Answers will vary, but should include "dry" and "cold.")*
- Where are the subarctic regions in East Asia? *(along Mongolia's and China's northern borders with Russia)*
- What types of vegetation grow on tundras? *(lichen, shrubs, mosses)*

 **In-Depth Resources: Unit 9**
- Guided Reading, p. 4

CAPTION ANSWER There is a lot of grassland for grazing animals.

SECTION 2 PROGRAM RESOURCES

 **In-Depth Resources: Unit 9**
- Guided Reading, p. 4
- Bulding Vocabulary, p. 9
- Reteaching Activity, p. 11

 **Guided Reading Workbook**
- Section 2

 **Access for Students Acquiring English/ESL**
- Guided Reading, p. 145

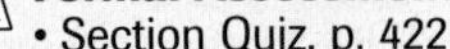 **Formal Assessment**
- Section Quiz, p. 422

 **Integrated Assessment**
- Rubric for a poster, 1.1

INTEGRATED TECHNOLOGY

 **Map Transparencies MT48**
- Climate and Agricultural Products of East Asia

  **Power Presentations**

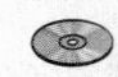 **Test Generator**
- Section Quiz

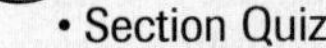  hmhsocialstudies.com

TEST-TAKING RESOURCES

 **Strategies for Test Preparation**

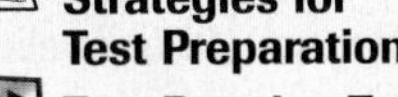 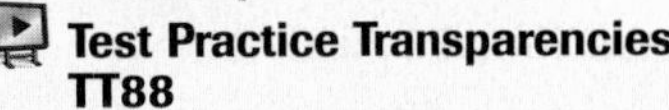 **Test Practice Transparencies TT88**

 **Online Test Practice**

Interpreting Maps

Climate Comparison, East Asia and North America

Have students examine the map for places of comparision other than the mainland U.S. states. *(The Canadian province of Alberta and the commonwealth of Puerto Rico are also used to indicate similar climates.)*

SKILLBUILDER ANSWERS

1. southeastern coast of United States
2. Taiwan

Instruct: Objective 

Mid-latitude Zones

- What types of vegetation are found in humid continental zones? *(forests, grasslands)*
- What factors make the mid-latitude zones more favorable to agriculture? *(sufficient rainfall, moderate climates)*

 **Map Transparencies MT48**
- Climate and Agricultural Products of East Asia

Instruct: Objective 

Dry Zones

- Where are most deserts found in East Asia? *(west central area of mainland)*
- What makes up most of the vegetation in semiarid zones? *(short grasses)*

Climate Comparison, East Asia and North America

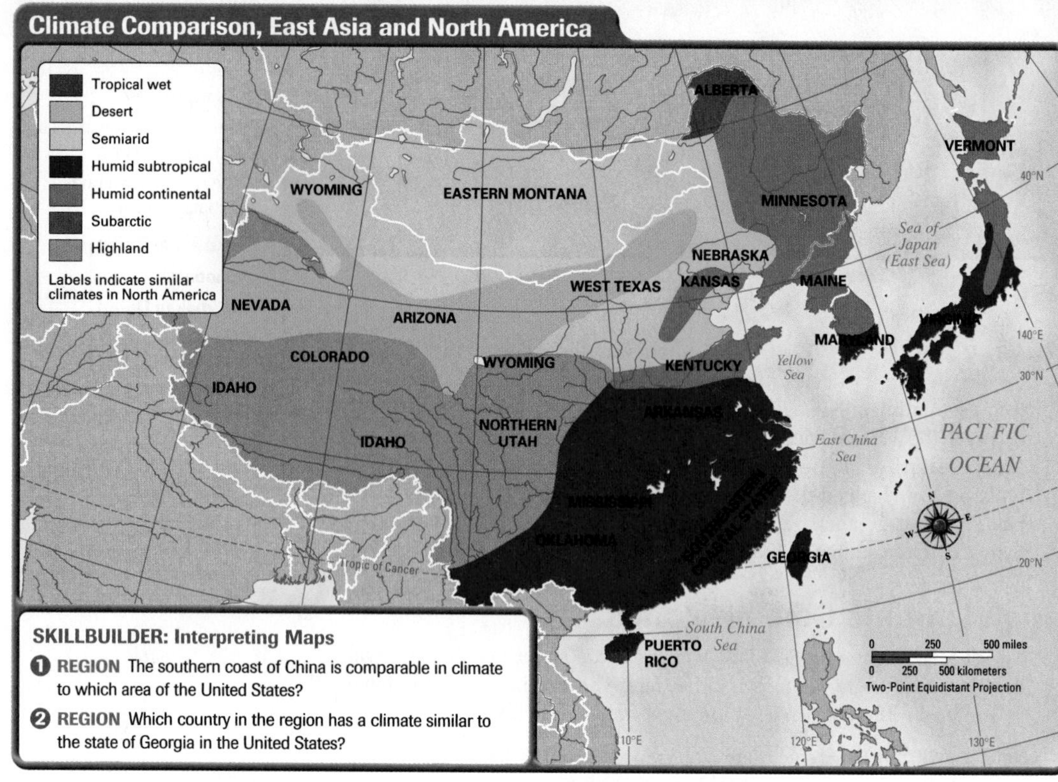

SKILLBUILDER: Interpreting Maps

1. **REGION** The southern coast of China is comparable in climate to which area of the United States?
2. **REGION** Which country in the region has a climate similar to the state of Georgia in the United States?

Mid-Latitude Zones

Mid-latitude zones are much more comfortable to live in because of their moderate climates. The land is productive, and the rainfall is sufficient for agriculture. An important resource of these zones is their forests.

HUMID CONTINENTAL Northeastern China, North Korea, northern South Korea, and northern Japan all have humid continental climates. The forests of the region are mainly coniferous in the humid continental zone. Temperate grasslands ideal for grazing are also found in these areas. However, over the years agriculture has transformed the landscape and replaced many of the forests.

HUMID SUBTROPICAL Southeastern China, southern South Korea, southern Japan, and northern Taiwan are in a humid subtropical zone. The forests in such zones are both deciduous and coniferous. The broad-leafed, deciduous trees are usually found in the north. The coniferous forests are especially typical of areas with sandy soils in the south. However, loggers and farmers have greatly reduced the forests in the southeast. A

A. Answer Climate and vegetation are best for growing crops.

CONNECT TO THE ISSUES
POPULATION
A Why might most of East Asia's population be centered in the mid-latitude zones?

Dry Zones

Dry zones of the region include both steppes and deserts. There is relatively little vegetation. These zones are not well suited to agriculture

DIFFERENTIATING INSTRUCTION | **STUDENTS ACQUIRING ENGLISH/ESL**

SPELLING SIMILAR WORDS

Objective To help ESL students differentiate between words that sound or look similar but are either spelled, pronounced, or defined differently

Class Time 20 minutes

Task Recall differences in similar words

Directions Write four pairs of similar words on the chalkboard. Define the words for the students. Ask them to make a numbered list up to 8. Erase the words from the board, and then read aloud each word, and use it in a sentence. Ask the students to write out the correct word next to each number. The following are words from the chapter that may be included in the exercise:

- steppes/steps
- feet/feat
- desert/dessert
- severe/sever
- two/too

and so have not been much settled by people. Instead, nomads have used the semiarid areas to graze livestock.

SEMIARID Parts of the Mongolian Plateau make up the semiarid zones of the region. The vegetation of semiarid zones consists mainly of short grasses, which provide food for grazing animals and livestock.

DESERT Most of the deserts in the region are found in the west central area of the mainland. The **Taklimakan Desert** is located in western China between the Tian Shan and Kunlun Mountains. The **Gobi Desert** is located in northern China and southeast Mongolia. The Gobi is a prime area for finding dinosaur fossils, since thousands of these animals roamed through the region millions of years ago. B

Geographic Thinking

Making Comparisons
B Why might the dry zones of the region be less densely populated?

B. Answer Dry zones are not well suited to agriculture.

Tropical Zones

The tropical zones of East Asia contain mainly wet climates. The most common vegetation is the rain forest.

TROPICAL WET The tropical climate zone in East Asia is fairly small. It includes a small strip of land along China's southeastern coast, the island of Hainan, and the southern tip of Taiwan. These areas have high temperatures, heavy rainfall, and high humidity every month of the year. The tropical rain forest in these places is made up of tall dense forests of broadleaf trees.

In the next section, you will read how human-environment interactions affect the quality of life in rural China and urban Japan.

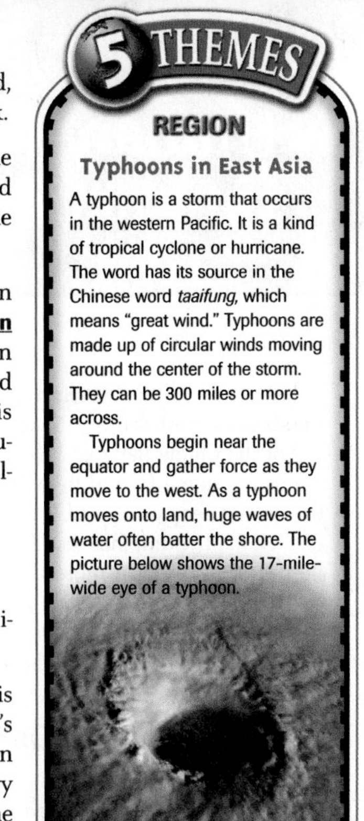

REGION

Typhoons in East Asia

A typhoon is a storm that occurs in the western Pacific. It is a kind of tropical cyclone or hurricane. The word has its source in the Chinese word *taaifung*, which means "great wind." Typhoons are made up of circular winds moving around the center of the storm. They can be 300 miles or more across.

Typhoons begin near the equator and gather force as they move to the west. As a typhoon moves onto land, huge waves of water often batter the shore. The picture below shows the 17-mile-wide eye of a typhoon.

Section 2 Assessment

1 Places & Terms

Identify each of the following places and terms.
- typhoon
- Taklimakan Desert
- Gobi Desert

2 Taking Notes

PLACE Review the notes you took for this section.

Climate	
Vegetation	

- What types of climate are found in East Asia?
- What vegetation characterizes the western reaches of China?

3 Main Ideas

a. In what ways are the climates of the United States and China similar?
b. What effect might severe weather (such as typhoons) have on crops?
c. What has been the human impact on mid-latitude climate zones in the region?

4 Geographic Thinking

Making Inferences How might the climate and vegetation of East Asia have affected patterns of settlement in the region? **Think about:**
- the impact of deserts, steppes, and tundra on patterns of settlement

See Skillbuilder Handbook, page R4.

EXPLORING LOCAL GEOGRAPHY East Asia has many kinds of climate. Pair with a partner and make a **poster** that shows the climate of East Asia in which you would most want to live. Include photographs, postcards, maps, and charts. Is there any location in the United States that is similar to your preferred climate?

EAST ASIA

Instruct: Objective 4

Tropical Zones

- Which island has a tropical climate? *(Hainan, China)*
- What are three features of a tropical climate? *(rain forest, heavy rainfall, high temperatures)*

5 THEMES

Region: Typhoons in East Asia
Have students read the information in the text box and answer the following questions.
- What does *typhoon* mean in Chinese? *(great wind)*
- What other type of storm is a typhoon most like? *(hurricane)* What do you call the center of a typhoon? *(eye)*

Assess & Reteach

GeoFocus Have students fill in the climate and vegetation section of their graphic organizers.

Formal Assessment
- Section Quiz, p. 422

Reteaching Activity
Have students summarize the main idea of each part of the chapter section in one or two sentences. Then have them share their sentences with the class.

In-Depth Resources: Unit 9
- Reteaching Activity, p. 11

SECTION 2 ASSESSMENT ANSWERS

1. Places & Terms
typhoon, p. 625
Taklimakan Desert, p. 627
Gobi Desert, p. 627

2. Taking Notes
- semiarid, desert, highland, humid continental, humid subtropical, tropical wet, subarctic
- The vegetation in western China is mostly forest and tundra. There are also extensive deserts in western China.

3. Main Ideas
a. Both are at the same latitude and both have similar climate zones.
b. Severe weather might destroy crops and make growing crops more difficult.
c. Agriculture has transformed the landscape and replaced many of the forests.

4. Geographic Thinking
The more temperate climate of the east, along with more arable land, drew most settlers to the eastern areas of the region. The land is productive, in part, because of the rainfall.

GeoActivity

Integrated Assessment
- Rubric for a poster, 1.1

SECTION 3 OBJECTIVES

1. Describe China's Three Gorges Dam project.
2. Identify methods of dealing with overcrowding in Japan.

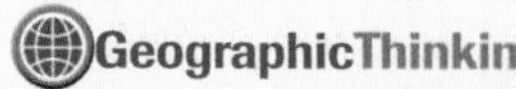

Seeing Patterns, pp. 629, 630
Using the Atlas, p. 630
Determining Cause and Effect, p. 631

Focus & Motivate

How might people address environmental obstacles? *(changing their way of living or creating something to change the environment)*

Instruct: Objective 1 appears on p. 629

Interpreting Photographs

Building the Three Gorges Dam

Direct students to the photo on the left. Ask them what will happen to the town when the water finally reaches the level of the suspension bridge. *(It will be submerged.)* Then direct students to the photo on the right, which was taken in May, 2006. How will this landscape change when the project is complete? *(A vast lake will have grown wider behind the dam.)* Ask students to provide examples of how this project relates to the Five Themes of Geography: Location, Place, Region, Movement, and Human-Environment Interaction.

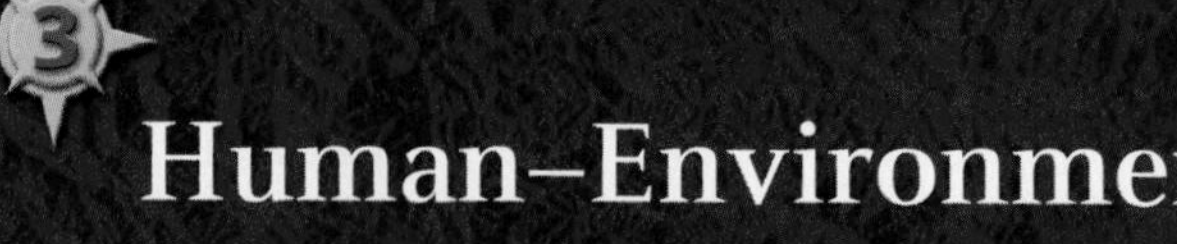

Human–Environment Interaction

Main Ideas

- The Chinese constructed the Three Gorges Dam to control flooding.
- The Japanese have developed creative ways to use their limited amounts of land.

Places & Terms

Three Gorges Dam
PCBs
landfill

CONNECT TO THE ISSUES

PHYSICAL FORCES One reason why the Three Gorges Dam was built is to control flooding of the Chang Jiang.

A HUMAN PERSPECTIVE Hundreds of thousands of Chinese died in floods in the 20th century. Most of these deaths were caused by the flooding of the Chang Jiang and the Huang He rivers. These vast river floodplains are home to, and help feed, hundreds of millions of people, and this makes people vulnerable to the rivers' wrath. In addition to the many deaths, the flooding has also forced millions of people to abandon their homes. You will read more about one such flood in Chapter 28 (pages 640–641). In the early 1990s, the Chinese began building an enormous dam on the Chang Jiang to help control flooding. This is one example of how East Asians have shaped their environment.

The Three Gorges Dam

The **Three Gorges Dam** was built on the Chang Jiang in China. The dam is helping to control flooding along the great river, the third longest in the world after the Nile and the Amazon. But the dam is also generating power and is expected to allow ships to sail farther into China.

Building the Three Gorges Dam

hmhsocialstudies.com INTERACTIVE

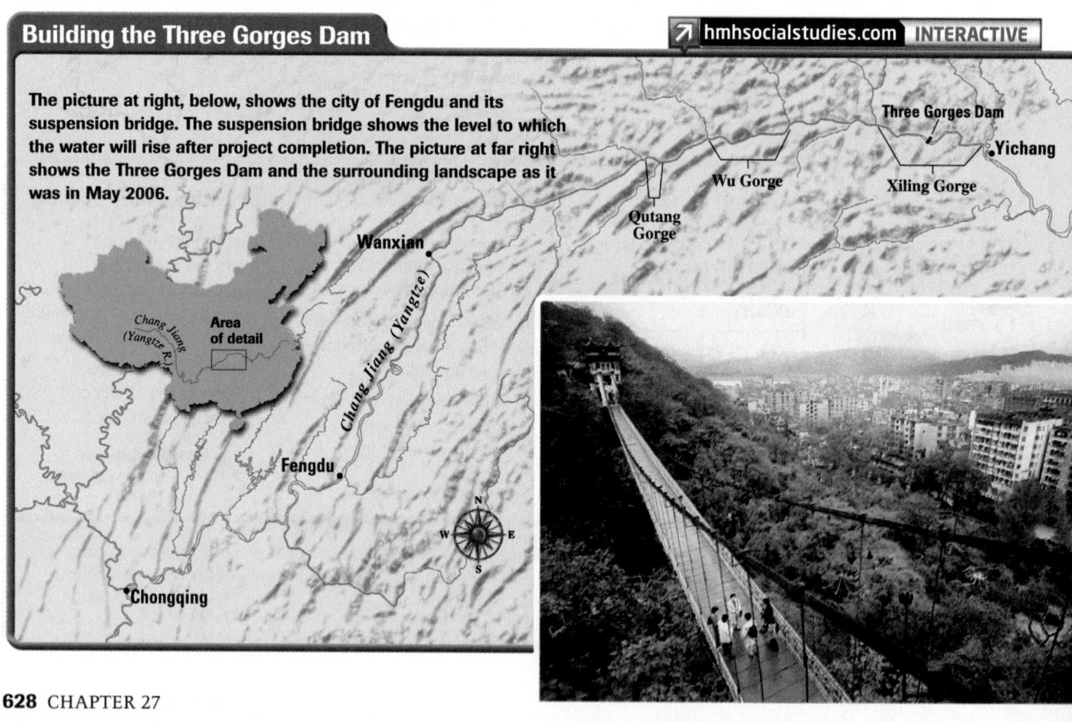

The picture at right, below, shows the city of Fengdu and its suspension bridge. The suspension bridge shows the level to which the water will rise after project completion. The picture at far right shows the Three Gorges Dam and the surrounding landscape as it was in May 2006.

SECTION 3 PROGRAM RESOURCES

In-Depth Resources: Unit 9
- Guided Reading, p. 5
- Skillbuilder Practice, p. 8
- Building Vocabulary, p. 9
- Reteaching Activity, p. 12

Guided Reading Workbook
- Section 3

Access for Students Acquiring English/ESL
- Guided Reading, p. 146
- Skillbuilder Practice, p. 147

Formal Assessment
- Section Quiz, p. 423

Integrated Assessment
- Rubric for a chart, 2.2

INTEGRATED TECHNOLOGY

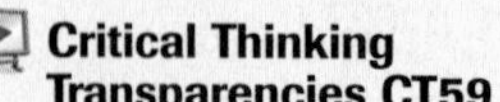

Critical Thinking Transparencies CT59
- Contrasting China and Japan

Power Presentations

Test Generator
- Section Quiz

hmhsocialstudies.com

TEST-TAKING RESOURCES

Strategies for Test Preparation

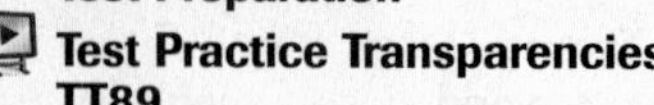

Test Practice Transparencies TT89

Online Test Practice

AN ENGINEERING FEAT The Three Gorges Dam is China's largest construction project and is the world's biggest dam. The dam towers more than 600 feet high and spans a valley more than one mile wide. This dam will create a reservoir around 400 miles long. More than 1,000 towns and villages have disappeared under the waters since the reservoir began filling.

POSITIVE EFFECTS The building of the Three Gorges Dam is a complicated issue because it has had both positive and negative effects. Experts disagreed about whether the dam should be built. But the Chinese government, which began construction of the dam in 1994, argued that the dam will have three positive effects.

First, the dam will help control the frequent flooding of the Chang Jiang, which causes great damage and loss of life. This is critical because the Chang Jiang irrigates about half of China's crops. Also, the river drains about one-fifth of China's total land area.

Second, the dam will generate huge amounts of electrical power. Giant turbines will produce electricity that will be hooked up to electrical grids in central and eastern China. This will improve the reliability of electricity throughout China. By some estimates, the dam's turbines will produce about 2 percent of China's electrical power. (See the bar chart below for a comparison of the projected generating capacity of the Three Gorges Dam with other large dams.)

Finally, the dam will make it easier for ships to reach China's interior. A series of locks along the river raise ocean-going ships up from the river to the reservoir. The Chang Jiang carries more than half of the goods moving on China's interior waterways. The dam and the locks will increase shipping capacity and decrease shipping costs. A

A. Answer control flooding; generate electrical power; improve shipping

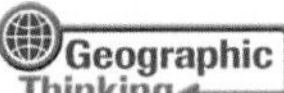

Seeing Patterns
A What are three benefits of building the dam?

Instruct: Objective 1

The Three Gorges Dam

- Where was the Three Gorges Dam built? *(on the Chang Jiang River)*
- What was the main reason for building the dam? *(to prevent flooding)*
- Why have experts disagreed about whether the dam should have been built? *(because the dam is having positive and negative effects)*

In-Depth Resources: Unit 9
- Guided Reading, p. 5

Facts and Figures

- Length of river: 3,915 miles
- Length of reservoir: 410 miles
- Height of dam: 607 feet
- Width of dam: 1.4 miles
- Number of turbines: 26, generating 18,200 megawatts of electricity
- Lives lost to flooding: about one million deaths in 20th century
- Location of dam: about 1,500 miles from the ocean
- Many hundreds of miles from headwaters in western mountains of China

Electric Generating Capacity of World's Largest Dams

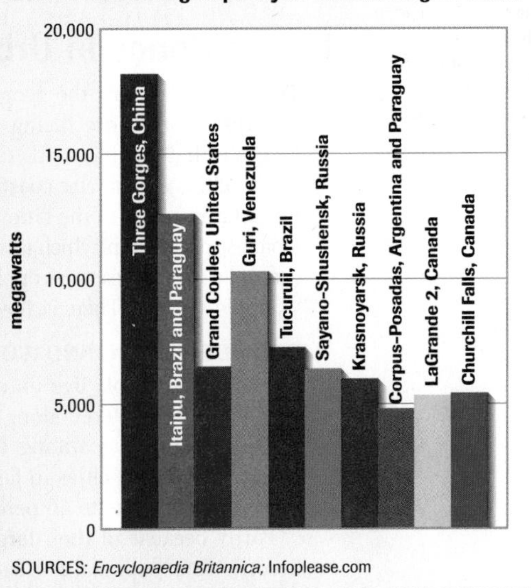

SOURCES: *Encyclopaedia Britannica;* Infoplease.com

EAST ASIA

Interpreting Graphs

Electrical Generating Capacity of World's Largest Dams

Direct students to the list of facts and figures and the bar chart. Ask them which two dams generate about the same amount of electricity. *(Grand Coulee, United States, and Sayano-Shushensh, Russia; also LaGrande 2 and Churchill Falls, Canada)* Ask students which countries have more than one of the world's largest dams. *(Brazil, Paraguay, Russia, Canada)*

ACTIVITY OPTION **SKILLBUILDER LESSON**

MAKING DECISIONS

Explaining the Skill Making decisions involves choosing between two or more options or courses of action. In most cases, decisions have consequences, or results. Tell students that by examining both sides of a complicated geography issue, they may be able to make a decision and understand its consequences.

In-Depth Resources: Unit 9
- Skillbuilder Practice, p. 8

Applying the Skill Ask students to look at the graphics on the building of the Three Gorges Dam and to review the information in the section.

- What are the most important benefits of the Three Gorges Dam? *(flood control, hydroelectric power, better transportation for ships, creating a water reservoir)*
- What are the most important negative effects of building the dam? *(loss of people's homes and historical sites, loss of animal habitats)*
- If you were a member of the Chinese government, would you have voted for or against the dam project? *(Answers will vary.)*

Interpreting Photographs

Endangered Animals

Direct students' attention to the three photographs. Ask students to describe two or three ways that animals can become endangered. *(elimination of natural habitat, lack of food and water to survive and reproduce, overhunting, disease or illness)* Ask students what other animals might be affected by the building of the Three Gorges Dam. *(fish, other birds, insects, other mammals that live nearby or use the river for food/water source)*

CAPTION ANSWER It will eliminate their natural habitat and change environmental factors like temperature and precipitation.

Instruct: Objective 2

Use of Space in Urban Japan

- Why does Japan have so little livable land space? *(because it is very mountainous)*
- What negative impact has population density had on Japan? *(noise and air pollution, small living spaces, high population densities)*
- What are a few ways Japan has overcome the obstacle of limited space? *(use of landfill, adjusting to smaller environments, adapting spaces through simple and movable furnishings)*

Critical Thinking Transparencies CT59
- Contrasting China and Japan

HUMAN–ENVIRONMENT INTERACTION The river dolphin, the white crane, and the alligator are just three of the species endangered by the construction of the Three Gorges Dam. **Why might the dam be a threat to various species?**

NEGATIVE EFFECTS Most observers agree that the Three Gorges Dam will also have negative effects. The central issue is whether the negative impact on the environment will be greater than the positive benefits.

First, the human costs of the dam are enormous. As of 2010, between one million and two million people have been forced to relocate for the dam's construction. Some estimate that millions more may eventually have to leave their homes once the dam's long-term effects become clear. Also, hundreds of archaeological, historical, and scenic sites are being submerged.

Second, construction of the dam cost more money than originally anticipated. The Chinese government first estimated the cost at approximately $11 billion. However, construction costs totaled an estimated $26 billion.

Third, environmental concerns about the dam trouble many observers. The giant reservoir created by the dam has put hundreds of square miles of land under water. This reduces the habitat of many animals. It is feared that abandoned factories submerged under the reservoir are leaking contaminating chemicals into the water. The huge reservoir has affected the climate and temperature of the region as well as the plant and animal life. Such species as the alligator, leopard, sturgeon, white crane, and river dolphin may not survive.

The main part of the Three Gorges Dam was completed in 2006. However, the Chinese government has not been careful in protecting the environment from the consequences of building the dam. Many people question whether the benefits of the Three Gorges Dam will outweigh its human and environmental costs. B

B. Answer These include displaced people, high cost, and environmental destruction.

Seeing Patterns

B What might be some negative effects of the dam?

Use of Space in Urban Japan

Throughout history, the geographic challenges facing Japan have been different from those facing China. One of the most important challenges is that Japan is made up of a series of mountainous islands. Most of the cities are on the coasts of these islands. But because of nearby mountains, many of the cities cannot expand to absorb any more of the Japanese population, which is more than 127 million people. Tokyo is a good example. The largest metropolitan area in the world, it holds more than 35 million people. There is, however, no more land for the city to grow.

CROWDED LIVING AND WORKING SPACES More than 60 percent of the Japanese people live on only about three percent of the land. The population is clustered along the narrow flat coastal plains. C

These plains are among the most densely populated areas in the world. The largest cities in Japan are Tokyo, Yokohama, Osaka, Nagoya, and Sapporo. Close to 66 percent of the people in Japan live in cities.

Partly because of their large populations, some Japanese cities have become very polluted. For example, in the 1950s and 1960s, a number

C. Answer Most of the interior portions of the Japanese islands are mountainous.

Using the Atlas

C Use the map on page 615. Why might the Japanese people live on such a small percentage of coastal land?

ACTIVITY OPTION **INTERNET RESEARCH**

DEVELOPING RESEARCH SKILLS

Objective To develop research skills about current environmental events

Class Time 20 minutes

Task Find two Web sites that present information on currently endangered species in East Asia

Directions Have pairs or small groups of students use the Internet to find appropriate sites with information on endangered species. Have them take a few notes about one or two animals and then share the information with the class.

B BLOCK SCHEDULING

OPTIONAL ACTIVITY If Internet access is limited, have the students use the periodicals section of the library to find current information on endangered animals in East Asia. Ask the librarian for assistance.

of Japanese cities experienced poisoning from mercury and **PCBs**—industrial pollutants that build up in tissue and can cause disease and birth defects. PCBs were banned in 1977. Water pollution laws were revised several times from 1989 to 2000. Soil pollution controls took effect in 2003. However, cars and factories still cause massive air pollution.

HUMAN-ENVIRONMENT INTERACTION Capsule hotels in Japan provide tiny rooms for overnight guests.

ADAPTING TO LIMITED SPACE

The Japanese have shown great ingenuity in adapting to limited space. Because of the cost of land, houses are small by U.S. standards. The rooms are separated by sliding screens and are sparsely furnished. People sleep on thin mattresses called futons that can be rolled up and stored during the day.

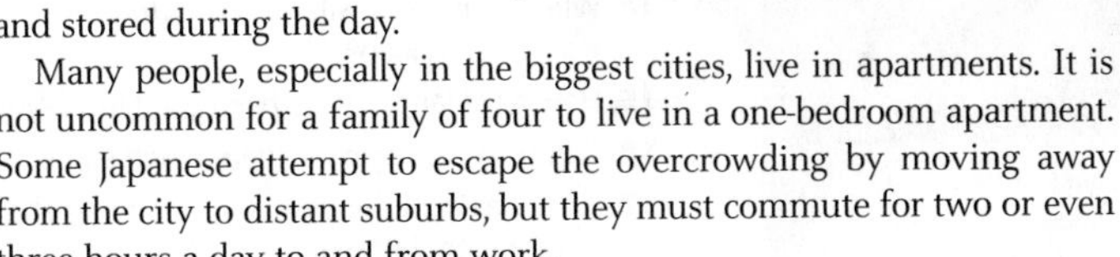

Many people, especially in the biggest cities, live in apartments. It is not uncommon for a family of four to live in a one-bedroom apartment. Some Japanese attempt to escape the overcrowding by moving away from the city to distant suburbs, but they must commute for two or even three hours a day to and from work.

One solution to the shortage of space is landfill. **Landfill** is a method of solid waste disposal in which refuse is buried between layers of dirt to fill in low-lying ground. The Japanese have used landfill to reclaim land for most of the major cities on the coast. Tokyo, for example, has built factories and refineries on landfill sites. Landfill sites have also enlarged some of Japan's ports.

You will explore more about how East Asians live in the next chapter, on human geography.

Interpreting Photographs

Capsule Hotel

Direct students to the details of the photograph. Ask them to make a list of five features/items they know would be in the average hotel room that are also included in this capsule. *(Answers might include television, bed, phone, light, climate control, curtains or door for privacy)*

Assess & Reteach

GeoFocus Have students complete their graphic organizers by filling in the section on human-environment interaction.

Formal Assessment
- Section Quiz, p. 423

Reteaching Activity

Ask students to create an outline of the information in this section. The outline should list main points and connected ideas. Have students use the section objectives and headings as guides.

In-Depth Resources: Unit 9
- Reteaching Activity, p. 12

Section 3 Assessment

1 Places & Terms

Identify and explain the significance of each in the region.
- Three Gorges Dam
- PCBs
- landfill

2 Taking Notes

HUMAN–ENVIRONMENT INTERACTION Review the notes you took for this section.

Human-Environment Interaction	

- Which of the examples in this chapter illustrate human adaptation to the environment?
- Which examples illustrate an environment changed by humans?

3 Main Ideas

a. What might be a positive effect of the Three Gorges Dam?

b. What might be a negative effect of the Three Gorges Dam?

c. Why are most of Japan's large cities located along its coast?

4 Geographic Thinking

Determining Cause and Effect What were some of the reasons that led to the building of the Three Gorges Dam? **Think about:**
- the effects of living near an unpredictable river

hmhsocialstudies.com
RESEARCH WEB LINKS

EAST ASIA

ASKING GEOGRAPHIC QUESTIONS Pair with a partner and research a dam in the United States to compare with the Three Gorges Dam. Devise three geographic questions about the dams, such as "How much concrete was used in the construction of the dams?" Then make a **chart** or **graph** in which you provide data to answer the questions. Be sure to identify your sources.

SECTION 3 ASSESSMENT ANSWERS

1. Places & Terms

Three Gorges Dam, p. 628
PCBs, p. 631
landfill, p. 631

2. Taking Notes
- The Japanese have adapted to the space limitations resulting from having a large number of people living in a relatively small area of land.
- The Three Gorges Dam will change the environment to eliminate flooding.

3. Main Ideas

a. eliminate flooding, generate electricity, improve shipping

b. people displaced, very expensive, damage environment

c. center of Japan is mountainous, with flat plains along the coast

4. Geographic Thinking

Flooding was the primary problem. It devastated villages, destroyed crops and farmland, and took many lives.

GeoActivity

Integrated Assessment
- Rubric for chart, 2.2

Reviewing Places & Terms

A. 1. Kunlun Mountains, p. 619
2. Huang He, p. 621
3. Chang Jiang, p. 621
4. Xi Jiang, p. 621
5. typhoon, p. 625
6. Taklimakan Desert, p. 627
7. Gobi Desert, p. 627
8. Three Gorges Dam, p. 628
9. PCBs, p. 631
10. landfill, p. 631

B. Possilble Responses

11. The Three Gorges Dam is on the Chang Jiang.
12. A typhoon is a kind of cyclone or hurricane.
13. The Kunlun Mountains is the source.
14. The Xi Jiang joins other rivers to form an estuary.
15. Tokyo has built factories and refineries on landfill sites and enlarged its ports.
16. The Gobi Desert contains fossils.
17. PCBs have contributed to poisoning and pollution.
18. The Taklimakan Desert is located in western China.
19. The Huang He has that name.
20. The Three Gorges Dam is supposed to contain flooding.

Chapter 27 Assessment

VISUAL SUMMARY
PHYSICAL GEOGRAPHY OF EAST ASIA

Landforms

Major Mountain Ranges: Himalayas, Kunlun, Altun, Altay, Qinling Shandi

Major Rivers: Huang He, Chang Jiang, Xi Jiang

Major Deserts: Taklimakan, Gobi

Major Plateaus and Plains: Plateau of Tibet, Tarim Pendi Basin, Mongolian Plateau, Manchurian Plain, North China Plain

Resources

- China, Mongolia, and North Korea have significant natural resources.
- Japan, South Korea, and Taiwan have limited natural resources.

Climate and Vegetation

- East Asia has a dry continental climate in the west and a humid climate in the east.
- Its mid-latitude zones, both humid continental and humid subtropical, are the most densely populated areas.

Human-Environment Interaction

- The Three Gorges Dam was built along the Chang Jiang to control flooding.
- Urban Japan is very crowded, and people must adapt to space limitations.

Reviewing Places & Terms

A. Briefly explain the importance of each of the following.

1. Kunlun Mountains	**6.** Taklimakan Desert
2. Huang He	**7.** Gobi Desert
3. Chang Jiang	**8.** Three Gorges Dam
4. Xi Jiang	**9.** PCBs
5. typhoon	**10.** landfill

B. Answer the questions about vocabulary in complete sentences.

11. On which river will the Three Gorges Dam attempt to control flooding?
12. What is another name for a tropical cyclone or hurricane?
13. What is the source of two of China's great rivers?
14. Which river joins with others to form an estuary between Hong Kong and Macao?
15. How have landfill sites been used in Tokyo?
16. Where in the region is there a rich supply of dinosaur fossils?
17. What has contributed to the poisoning and pollution of the environment in Japanese cities?
18. Which desert is located in western China near the Kunlun Mountains?
19. Which river is known as "China's Sorrow"?
20. What project is supposed to contain flooding?

Main Ideas

Landforms and Resources (pp. 619-624)

1. Why are the Kunlun Mountains especially important to China?
2. What is the approximate size of the Gobi Desert?
3. What are some of the important islands off the coast of China?
4. Why are China's three river systems so important to the country?

Climate and Vegetation (pp. 625-627)

5. In which latitude and climate zones is most of China's productive agricultural land located?
6. What landforms make up the dry zones of the region?
7. What two factors affect vegetation and temperature in the highland climate?

Human-Environment Interaction (pp. 628-631)

8. What are some benefits of the Three Gorges Dam?
9. What are some drawbacks of the dam?
10. What are some of the ways in which the Japanese have adapted to living in a crowded space?

Main Ideas

1. source of two of China's rivers
2. The Gobi is more than 500,000 square miles.
3. Hainan, Hong Kong, and Taiwan
4. The rivers irrigate crops and help to feed the people.
5. The mid-latitude zones, both humid continental and humid subtropical, are the sites of China's most productive crop fields.
6. The dry zones are made up of deserts and plains including the Mongolian plateau and the Taklimakan and Gobi deserts.
7. latitude and elevation
8. control flooding, generate electricity, and make shipping easier
9. displace people, cost more money than was estimated, and damage the environment
10. ingenious use of space in houses and apartments; long commutes to suburbs; landfill; artificial islands

Critical Thinking

1. Using Your Notes

Use your completed chart to answer these questions.

Landforms	
Resources	

a. Where are the highest mountains in China located?

b. What are some energy resources found in abundance in China and Korea?

2. Geographic Themes

a. **LOCATION** Where is the largest desert found in East Asia?

b. **REGION** Write a sentence or two describing the settlement patterns of East Asia in terms of its mountains and coasts.

3. Identifying Themes

Based on landforms and climate, which areas of East Asia would be the least agriculturally productive? Which of the five themes are reflected in your answer?

4. Making Decisions

What factors must people in China consider when they are trying to decide what to do about flooding along one of their great rivers?

5. Drawing Conclusions

How does a typhoon create so much damage?

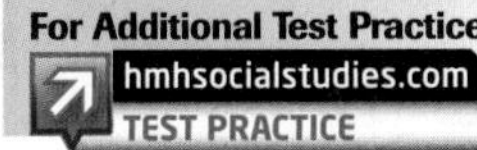

Geographic Skills: Interpreting Maps

Precipitation in East Asia

Use the map at right to answer the following questions.

1. **REGION** Which parts of the region have the least precipitation?
2. **REGION** Which parts of the region have the most precipitation?
3. **MOVEMENT** How might precipitation patterns have affected settlement in the region?

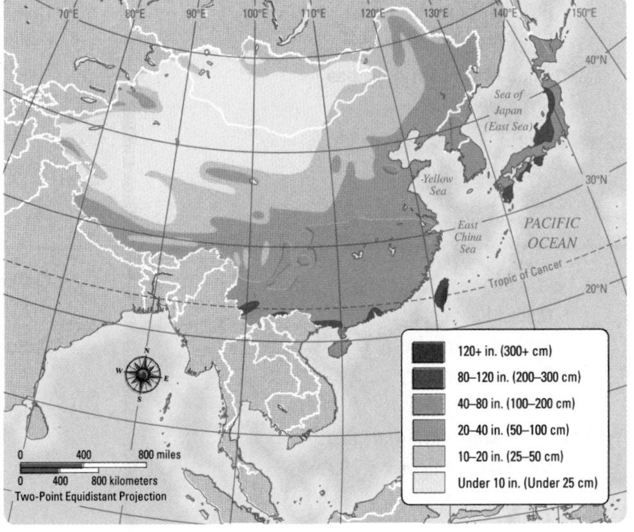

Create a way to display the map information in graph form. Be sure to list the six countries of the region by name in your graph.

hmhsocialstudies.com

MULTIMEDIA ACTIVITY

Use the links at **hmhsocialstudies.com** to do research on the most productive agricultural regions of East Asia. You might focus on the impact that precipitation has had on settlement patterns and crop growth.

Creating Multimedia Presentations Combine charts, maps, or other visual images in an electronic presentation that shows the most productive farming areas and the most common crops in the region.

Critical Thinking

1. a. the western edge of East Asia in southwestern and northwestern China and western Mongolia
b. China has oil, coal, and natural gas, and Korea has coal.

2. a. the Gobi in northern China and southeast Mongolia
b. Most of the people in East Asia live along the eastern coast of the continent where there is good farmland fed by the three great rivers of China. On the islands, such as Japan, people also tend to live along the coast and not in the mountainous interior.

3. the western areas of mountains and deserts; region, human-environment interaction

4. how many people will be displaced by the flooding and by the building of the dam; how much money the dam will cost compared to how much the repeated flooding will cost; the effect on the environment and the possible loss of species

5. because of its strong circular winds and huge waves of water

GeoActivity

Integrated Assessment
- Rubric for a graph, 2.3

Formal Assessment
- Chapter Test, Forms A, B, and C, pp. 424-435

EAST ASIA

Geographic Skills

1. the west and northwest, in China and Mongolia

2. southeast China, Taiwan, and Japan

3. People settled in areas that had more precipitation because these were more agriculturally productive.

MULTIMEDIA ACTIVITY

For a multimedia presentation on productive farming areas and common crops, students should do the following:

- Present a concise, well-organized presentation on farming areas and crops.
- Summarize the impact of precipitation on settlement and crop growth.
- Produce clear, imaginative visuals for the presentation.
- Include references to the Web sites used as sources.

Grading Rubric Evaluate student performance as Exceptional, Acceptable, or Poor in each of the following categories:

	Exceptional	*Acceptable*	*Poor*
Writing is clear, focused, and logical			
Presentation clearly states topic and purpose			
Provides necessary facts and examples			
Shows productive areas and common crops			

CHAPTER 28 PLANNING GUIDE

Human Geography of East Asia

OVERVIEW	INSTRUCTIONAL RESOURCES	
ESSENTIAL QUESTION How has China influenced the cultures of East Asia? **Focus on the Essential Question Podcast**	**In-Depth Resources: Unit 9** • Building Vocabulary, p. 18 **Block Schedule Strategies** **Chapter Summaries** (English/Spanish) **Multimedia Connections** • China and the Great Wall **Video:** The Great Wall of China hmhsocialstudies.com INTERACTIVE	**Interactive Online Edition** TOS **ExamView® Assessment Suite** (English/Spanish) TOS **CalendarPlanner** **Power Presentations with Media Gallery** **Critical Thinking Transparencies** • CT28
SECTION 1 **CHINA** **MAIN IDEAS** • China is an ancient civilization that has dominated East Asia. • China has undergone conflicts, invasion, and revolutionary changes. • China has a strong economy and rich culture. • China is the most populous country in the world.	**In-Depth Resources: Unit 9** • Guided Reading, p. 13 • Building Vocabulary, p. 18 • Reteaching Activity, p. 19 **Outline Maps with Activities** • China, pp. 91–92 **Cultures Around the World** • Architecture, p. 49 • Fine Arts, p. 51	**Critical Thinking Transparencies** • CT60 Population for China and Japan, 2025 **Cultures Transparencies CW49, 51** • Great Wall • Landscape Painting **Map Transparencies** • MT49 The Silk Road **Video:** China: Boxer Uprising **Guided Reading Workbook,** Section 1
SECTION 2 **MONGOLIA AND TAIWAN** **MAIN IDEAS** • Mongolia developed as an independent, strong empire, while Taiwan grew from Chinese settlement. • Mongolia and Taiwan have different economies, the former agricultural and the latter trade-based. • Mongolian lifestyles have changed little over the years, while Taiwan is more influenced by the West.	**In-Depth Resources: Unit 9** • Guided Reading, p. 14 • Skillbuilder Practice, p. 17 • Building Vocabulary, p. 18 • Reteaching Activity, p. 20 **Outline Maps with Activities** • Mongolia and Taiwan, pp. 93–94	**Cultures Transparencies** • CW53 Celebrating Naadam **Cultures Around the World** • Traditional Practices, p. 53 **Guided Reading Workbook,** Section 2
SECTION 3 **THE KOREAS: NORTH AND SOUTH** **MAIN IDEAS** • The Korean peninsula is divided into two separate countries, one capitalist, one Communist. • The Korean ancestry and cultural influences are largely Manchurian and northern Chinese. • The two Koreas are making attempts at unification.	**In-Depth Resources: Unit 9** • Guided Reading, p. 15 • Building Vocabulary, p. 18 • Reteaching Activity, p. 21 **Outline Maps with Activities** • The Koreas: North and South, pp. 95–96 **Guided Reading Workbook,** Section 3	hmhsocialstudies.com INTERACTIVE • The Korean War, 1950-1953, p. 648
SECTION 4 **JAPAN** **MAIN IDEAS** • Ancient Japan was isolated and had periods of strong military leadership. • Japan had been the strongest economic power in East Asia. • The Japanese must deal with issues relating to lack of land and natural resources, overcrowding, pollution, and a slowed economy.	**In-Depth Resources: Unit 9** • Guided Reading, p. 16 • Building Vocabulary, p. 18 • Reteaching Activity, p. 22 **Outline Maps with Activities** • Japan, pp. 97–98 **Cultures Around the World** • Daily Life, p. 50 • Literature, p. 52 • Arts and Crafts, p. 54	**Cultures Transparencies CW50, 52, 54** • Practicing Martial Arts • Haiku • Practicing Origami **Guided Reading Workbook,** Section 4

ASSESSMENT

SE **Chapter Assessment,** pp. 658–659

Formal Assessment
- Chapter Tests, Forms A, B, and C, pp. 440–451

TOS **ExamView® Assessment Suite**

Strategies for Test Preparation

SE **Section Assessment,** p. 639

Formal Assessment
- Section Quiz, p. 436

Integrated Assessment
- Rubric for an oral report, 3.6
- Rubric for presentation, 3.6

Test Practice Transparencies TT90

SE **Section Assessment,** p. 646

Formal Assessment
- Section Quiz, p. 437

Integrated Assessment
- Rubric for a poster, 1.1

Test Practice Transparencies TT91

SE **Section Assessment,** p. 650

Formal Assessment
- Section Quiz, p. 438

Integrated Assessment
- Rubric for a Venn diagram, 2.8

Test Practice Transparencies TT92

SE **Section Assessment,** p. 655

Formal Assessment
- Section Quiz, p. 439

Integrated Assessment
- Rubric for an oral report, 3.6
- Rubric for a graph, 2.3

Test Practice Transparencies TT93

CHART KEY:

SE Student Edition	Block Scheduling	DVD/CD-ROM
TE Teacher's Edition	TOS Teacher One Stop	MP3 Audio
Printable Resource	Presentation Resource	HISTORY™

Program Resources available on TOS and @ 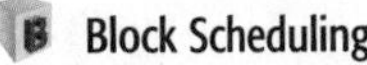

SUPPORTING RESOURCES

- Multimedia Classroom Global History Series
- Global History Teacher's Guide

Social Studies Trade Library Collection
- Pacific Rim Trade Collection

For more information or to purchase these resources, go to 

DIFFERENTIATED INSTRUCTION

English Learners	Struggling Readers	Gifted and Talented Students
Spanish/English Guided Reading Workbook **Access for Students Acquiring English/ESL** Spanish Translations, pp. 150–154 **Chapter Summaries** (English/Spanish) TE **TE Activity** Charting Proper Nouns, p. 638	**Chapter Summaries** (English/Spanish) TE **TE Activity** Creating a Comparison Chart, p. 649	TE **TE Activity** Making a Business Plan, p. 644

ENRICHMENT ACTIVITIES

The following activities are especially suitable for classes following block schedules.

SE **Student Edition,** pp. 634–659
- Disasters! Chang Jiang (Yangtze River) Flood of 1931, pp. 640–641

- The Korean War, 1950–1953, p. 648
- Comparing Cultures: Masks, pp. 656–657

BLOCK SCHEDULE LESSON PLAN OPTIONS: 90-MINUTE PERIOD

DAY 1

SECTION 1, pp. 635-639
Class Time 45 minutes

- **Time Line** Have students create their own time lines of events based on the textual information in the section. This should differ from the time line on pages 636-637, and include information from each of the subsections in this section of the chapter. Then have students explain to the class why they chose certain events to include in their time lines.
  Class Time 25 minutes
- **Face the Facts** To help students understand the importance of facts, have them make a bulleted list of 10-15 facts from the section (for example, most of China's workers, about 60%, work on farms). Then have students share their lists with the class.
  Class Time 20 minutes

DISASTERS! pp. 640-641
Class Time 45 minutes

- **Discussion** Discuss the Disasters! feature, using the questions on the TE pages 640-641.
  Class Time 20 minutes
- **News Brief** Ask the students to use the information in the Disasters! feature to create short (30-second) fictional news briefs to be read aloud, as if they were newscasters, to the class.
  Class Time 25 minutes

DAY 2

SECTION 2, pp. 642-646
Class Time 45 minutes

- **Trivial Pursuit** Use index cards to write questions (for example, Who was Genghis Khan? When did Marco Polo visit China? What is an "economic tiger"?) on one side, and the answers on the other side. Have students divide into two teams and play "Trivial Pursuit," based on these cards.
  Class Time 25 minutes
- **Skillbuilder Lesson** Use the Activity Option about making comparisons on TE page 643 and the Skillbuilder Practice worksheet.
  Class Time 20 minutes

SECTION 3, pp. 647-650
Class Time 45 minutes

- **Summary Chart** Lead the class in creating a two-column chart about facts and historical events for North Korea and South Korea, with the countries' names as the column headings.
  Class Time 25 minutes
- **Role Play** As a way to consider the issue of reunification of North and South Korea, have two students act as representatives for each country. As if in a press conference, have them answer questions about reunification, considering the information they learned about each country. The rest of the class poses the questions.
  Class Time 20 minutes

DAY 3

SECTION 4, pp. 651-657
Class Time 45 minutes

- **Synopsis** Have students write a one- to two-paragraph synopsis on Japan's economy. Their synopses should include information on the strengths or weaknesses of the economy in the past and present, what the economy is based on, and how it affects Japanese citizens.
  Class Time 20 minutes
- **Video and/or Photograph Viewing** As a means of relating to information in the Comparing Cultures feature on masks, show students part of a video or some photographs about mask-making in one or more parts of the world.
  Class Time 25 minutes

CHAPTER 28 REVIEW AND ASSESSMENT, pp. 658-659
Class Time 45 minutes

- **Review** Have students prepare a summary of the chapter using the words in the Places and Terms on the first page of each section.
  Class Time 20 minutes
- **Assessment** Have students complete the Chapter 28 Assessment.
  Class Time 25 minutes

TEACHER-TESTED ACTIVITY *Journals in Geography*

Class Time One period

Task Create journal entries

Supplies
- pen and paper
- computer

Purpose To have students process knowledge of the human geography of one or more countries of the region

Activity Have students write journal entries as either a missionary or salesperson traveling through East Asia. The journal should include evidence of knowledge of the history, culture, economics, and daily life of the country visited. For example, students might describe food eaten, sights visited, people encountered, and so forth to give their journals some lively details.

Robert Parker
Geography Teacher, St. Margaret, San Juan Capistrano, CA

TECHNOLOGY IN THE CLASSROOM

Although we frequently think of computers and the Internet as visual media, they can also be very useful in storing and transmitting sounds. Students may already be accustomed to listening to music on the computer, but they may not have used computers to listen to other people speak or to record their own voices. The recent versions of most Internet browsers support audio, and most computers allow the user to record sounds, provided they have a microphone. The sound files students will download for activity are in au format. Recent versions of their Internet browser should allow them to play the files automatically, but double-check before having students do the activity. When they create their presentations, they should insert the files as hyperlinks rather than as separate sound files (see the directions below).

Objective Students will listen to audio files of East Asian foreign languages and create multimedia presentations containing some of these files and new ones they record.

Task Have students listen to some basic words in Mandarin, Japanese, Korean, and Taiwanese and design presentations that allow the user to listen to these files.

Class Time One period

1. Have students look at the map of East Asian languages on page 615. How many languages can they count?

2. Have students go to the link at **hmhsocialstudies.com** and listen to the words "hello," "good-bye," "yes," and "no" in Mandarin, Japanese, Korean, and Taiwanese ("Min Chinese" on the map) (these are all considered "basic words"). As they listen, ask them to write down the pronunciations in each language.

3. Ask students whether these words sound similar in the different languages. Do any two of these languages resemble each other, or are they all very different?

4. Have students look at the language map on page 615 and at the Rivers and Mountains map on page 620. Ask them to explain how the physical geography of East Asia might contribute to the existence of so many different languages.

5. Divide the class into small groups of three or four students, and have them create multimedia presentations that begin with a home page showing a map of East Asia. The maps should show the locations of the four languages they've heard. They should create links from each language on the map to new pages that let users see three to five words from each language, with English translations. The link should also let the user hear the words pronounced.

   To insert the spoken words, students should go to each word on the Web site and copy its hyperlink location. They should then return to their presentation program, select the "insert hyperlink" option, and paste the hyperlink they've just copied. When the user clicks on that hyperlink, he or she will be directed to the recording of that word. The user will need to be online in order to hear the words.

6. If you have recording equipment, allow groups to record themselves saying some of the words. How close can they get to the pronunciation on the Web sound files? Have them save their own voices and add them to the presentation, making sure to label the links as their own pronunciation rather than that of native speakers.

7. Have groups try out each other's presentations to see how they work.

CHAPTER 28 OBJECTIVE

Identify key features of shared cultural traditions in East Asia.

Chapter **28**

HUMAN GEOGRAPHY OF EAST ASIA

Shared Cultural Traditions

hmhsocialstudies.com VIDEO

Interpreting Maps

Four Subregions of East Asia

Have students identify the four subregions of East Asia and the countries within each subregion. *(China, Mongolia and Taiwan, North Korea and South Korea, Japan.)*

Extension Ask students to analyze what the countries in a subregion might have in common.

Introducing the Essential Question

- Archaeologists have found Chinese writing that is about 4,500 years old. Point out to students that this is one indicator of the long history of Chinese culture. Over the centuries, that culture has often dominated other peoples in East Asia.
- Emphasize that, in spite of Chinese domination, the other cultures—Japanese, Korean, Mongolian, and Taiwanese—have maintained their own distinct characteristics.

hmhsocialstudies.com TAKING NOTES

Have students fill out the cluster diagrams by using information from all the sections in this chapter.

Critical Thinking Transparencies CT28
- GeoFocus

In-Depth Resources: Unit 9
- Building Vocabulary, p. 18

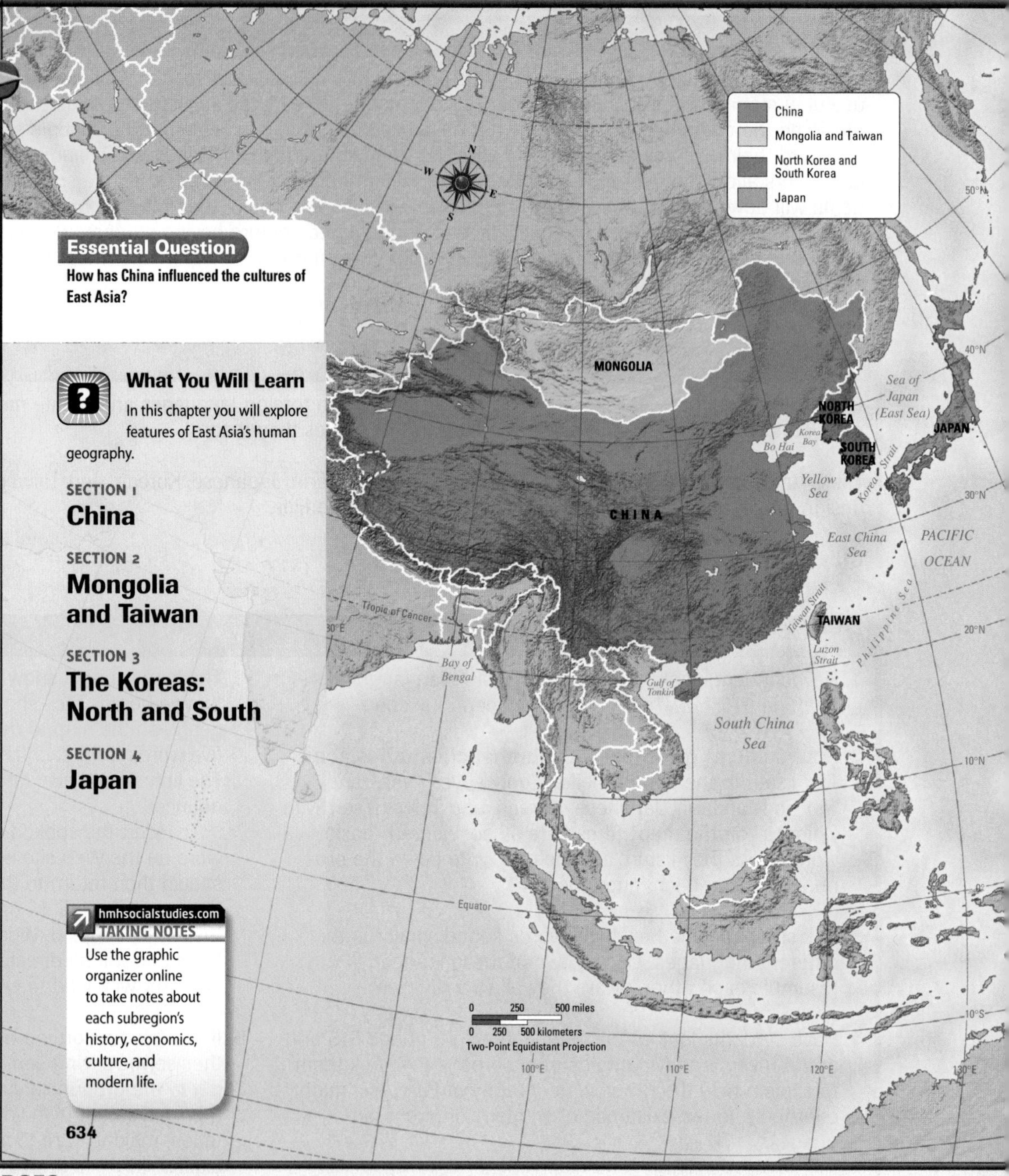

Essential Question

How has China influenced the cultures of East Asia?

What You Will Learn

In this chapter you will explore features of East Asia's human geography.

SECTION 1
China

SECTION 2
Mongolia and Taiwan

SECTION 3
The Koreas: North and South

SECTION 4
Japan

hmhsocialstudies.com TAKING NOTES

Use the graphic organizer online to take notes about each subregion's history, economics, culture, and modern life.

China
Mongolia and Taiwan
North Korea and South Korea
Japan

MONGOLIA
CHINA
NORTH KOREA
SOUTH KOREA
JAPAN
TAIWAN
Sea of Japan (East Sea)
Korea Bay
Bo Hai
Yellow Sea
Korea Strait
East China Sea
PACIFIC OCEAN
Taiwan Strait
Philippine Sea
Luzon Strait
South China Sea
Gulf of Tonkin
Bay of Bengal
Tropic of Cancer
Equator
0 250 500 miles
0 250 500 kilometers
Two-Point Equidistant Projection

634

CHAPTER 28 ADDITIONAL RESOURCES

BOOKS FOR THE TEACHER

Catchpole, Brian. ***The Korean War.*** NY: Carroll & Graf, 2000. A one-volume overview of the war.

Editors of Time-Life Books. ***The Mongol Conquests: Time Frame AD 1200–1300*** Alexandria, VA: Time-Life Books, 1989. Overview of military campaigns and court politics.

BOOKS FOR THE STUDENT

Severin, Timothy. ***In Search of Genghis Khan.*** NY: Atheneum, 1992. History, with photos.

Moore, Janet Gaylord. ***The Eastern Gate: An Invitation to the Arts of Japan and China.*** Cleveland, OH: Collins, 1979. Introduction to sculpture, painting, and architecture.

VIDEOS

The King of Masks Pien Lien. Samuel Goldwyn Films. Culver City, CA: Columbia TriStar Home Video, 2000. Subtitled film of an artist seeking an apprentice to carry on his work.

INTERNET

For more on the human geography of East Asia, visit . . .

hmhsocialstudies.com

China

Main Ideas

- China is the world's most populous country.
- China has been the dominant culture of East Asia since ancient times.

Places & Terms

dynasty
spheres of influence
Boxer Rebellion
Mao Zedong
Confucianism
Taoism
Buddhism

CONNECT TO THE ISSUES
POPULATION China's huge population puts a great strain on the environment.

A HUMAN PERSPECTIVE In ancient times, China had been open to attack from nomadic horsemen who roamed the plains of northern China and Mongolia. Around 220 B.C., the emperor Shi Huangdi decided to build a protective wall by closing the gaps between smaller walls built by earlier rulers. Hundreds of thousands of peasants were used as forced labor to build the wall. From the Yellow Sea in the east to the Gobi Desert in the west, the wall twisted and turned for thousands of miles, partially protecting China from the barbarian warriors beyond its borders. Later rulers would rework Shi Huangdi's construction to build what we know today as the Great Wall of China.

China's Early History

China is the world's oldest continuous civilization. The beginnings of that civilization extend back into the mists of prehistory. Because of China's geography—the long distances that separated it from Europe and other continents—it followed its own direction.

EARLY CIVILIZATION AND THE DYNASTIES China has been a settled society for more than 4,000 years. In its earliest days, China was made up of a number of Stone Age cultures. Then it was ruled by dynasties. A **dynasty** is a series of rulers from the same family. The first Chinese dynasty was the Shang. This dynasty arose during the 1700s B.C. It ruled a central area in China for about 600 years until it was overthrown by the Zhou Dynasty, which ruled part of northern China.

The next important dynasty, the Qin (chihn), gave its name to China. In 221 B.C., the Qin Dynasty united a number of smaller states under a strong central government and established an empire. The first Qin emperor was Shi Huangdi. The Chinese empire, ruled by different dynasties, lasted for more than 2,000 years.

Another important Chinese dynasty was that of the Han. These rulers pushed the empire into central Asia, home to many nomadic tribes. Many other dynasties followed over the centuries.

In 1644, the Manchu people of Manchuria invaded China and established the Qing (chihng) Dynasty. In 1911, the Manchus were overthrown by revolutionaries, and this ended the dynasties and the Chinese empire.

PLACE Thousands of life-sized terra cotta (clay) soldiers have been unearthed by archaeologists near the tomb of the emperor Shi Huangdi near Xian, China.

SECTION 1 OBJECTIVES

1. Explain China's early history and isolation.
2. Describe the growth of China through European contact and political change.
3. Examine China's economy.
4. Describe China's cultural heritage.
5. Analyze China's ability to address current obstacles.

Geographic Thinking
Seeing Patterns, p. 639
Making Generalizations, p. 639

Focus & Motivate

What factors combine to make a culture grow and last? *(location, climate, lack of outside interference, inventions that sustain/improve life, similar goals, ideologies, and lifestyles)*

Instruct: Objective 

China's Early History

- Why did Shi Huangdi build a wall in northern China? *(to protect China from invasion by nomadic peoples)*
- How was China governed in its early history? *(by dynastic rule)*
- What are some achievements China made in its early history? *(expansion of territory, organized government)*

 **In-Depth Resources: Unit 9**
• Guided Reading, p. 13

 **Cultures Around the World**
• Architecture, p. 49

Cultures Transparencies CW49
• Great Wall

SECTION 1 PROGRAM RESOURCES

In-Depth Resources: Unit 9
• Guided Reading, p. 13
• Building Vocabulary, p. 18
• Reteaching Activity, p. 19

Guided Reading Workbook
• Section 1

Access for Students Acquiring English
• Guided Reading, p. 150

Outline Maps with Activities
• China, pp. 91–92

Cultures Around the World
• Architecture, p. 49
• Fine Arts, p. 51

Formal Assessment
• Section Quiz, p. 436

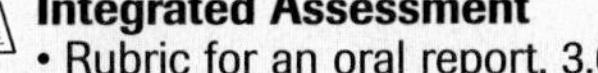
Integrated Assessment
• Rubric for an oral report, 3.6
• Rubric for a presentation, 3.6

INTEGRATED TECHNOLOGY

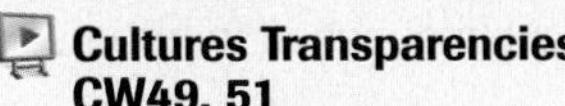
Cultures Transparencies CW49, 51
• Great Wall
• Landscape Painting

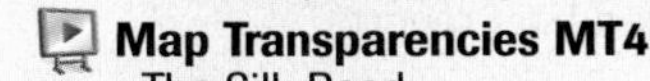
Map Transparencies MT49
• The Silk Road

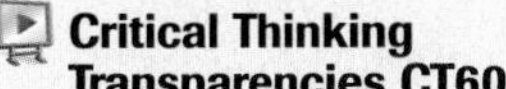
Critical Thinking Transparencies CT60
• Population Projections for China and Japan, 2025

hmhsocialstudies.com

TEST-TAKING RESOURCES

Strategies for Test Preparation

Test Practice Transparencies TT90

Online Test Practice

Instruct: Objective 2

China Opens Up to the World

- When did Europeans begin exploration of China? *(13th century)*
- How was Europe able to gain access to Chinese markets in the 19th century? *(China had a weak military and ineffective government.)*
- Which political group has held considerable power in China for the last 50 years? *(Communist Party)*

Map Transparencies MT49
- The Silk Road

Interpreting Time Lines

Chinese History, 600 B.C.–2000

Have students examine the time line. Ask them what the vase signifies. *(It represents the porcelain created during the Ming Dynasty.)* Ask them what year Marco Polo left Venice to travel to China. *(1271)* Ask what happened to northern Korea in 1627. *(It fell under China's control.)*

China Opens Up to the World

HISTORY VIDEO China: Boxer Uprising hmhsocialstudies.com

Even though China remained isolated from other regions for centuries, that started to change in the 13th century. At that time, European travelers began to visit China. Marco Polo, for example, traveled from Venice, Italy, to China in the 13th century and wrote a book about his adventures, *The Travels of Marco Polo.*

China and Europe had few contacts until the 19th century, when European powers sought access to Chinese markets. At that point, China had a weak military and an ineffective government. Europeans took advantage of China and forced it to sign a series of treaties that granted special privileges to the Europeans. Consequently, China was carved up into **spheres of influence** controlled by Britain, France, Germany, Russia, and Japan. This outside control angered China, which burst forth in the **Boxer Rebellion** of 1900. Chinese militants attacked and killed Europeans and Chinese Christians in China. A multinational force of about 20,000 soldiers finally defeated the Boxers.

BACKGROUND The Boxers were a secret society whose Chinese name meant "fists of righteous unity."

REVOLUTION AND CHANGE After the Boxer Rebellion, the Qing Dynasty, founded by the Manchus, attempted to reform the Chinese government, but it was too late. Many individuals and groups wanted to form a republic, which would give the people a voice in their government. In 1912, Sun Yat-sen and others founded the *Kuomintang,* or Nationalist Party. However, the republic, led by Sun Yat-sen, was undermined by civil war throughout China.

When Sun Yat-sen died in 1925, a general named Chiang Kai-shek took over the Nationalist Party. Chiang's troops fought against the warlords of China and united most of the country in the 1920s. However, throughout the 1920s and 1930s, the Chinese Communist Party became an increasingly powerful force in China.

The Nationalists and the Communists fought for control of China. In 1949, the Communists, under the leadership of **Mao Zedong,** finally defeated the Nationalists. Mao and the Communists ruled mainland China (now called The People's Republic of China) from Beijing. Chiang Kai-shek and the Nationalists fled to the island of Taiwan.

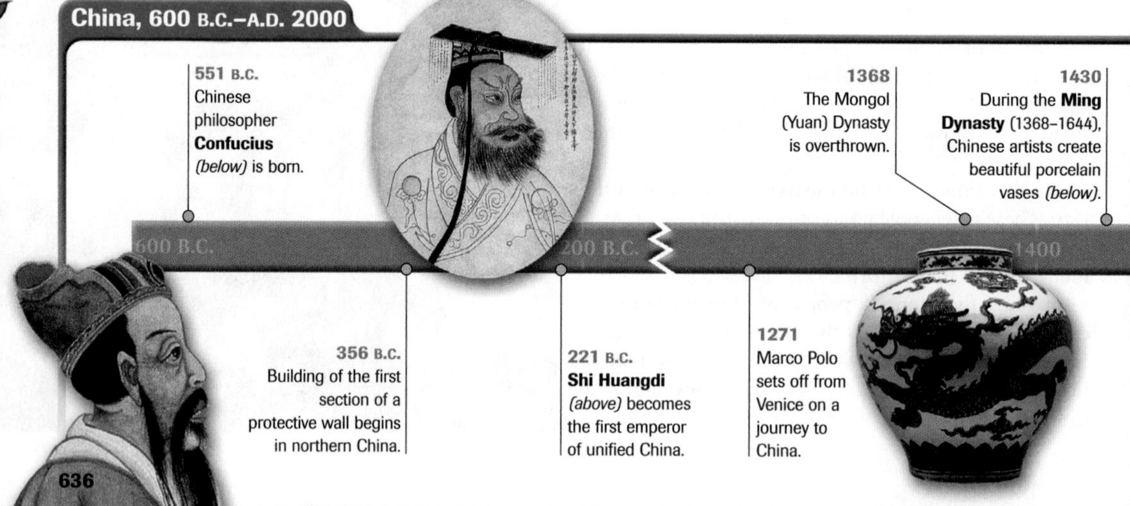

China, 600 B.C.–A.D. 2000
551 B.C. Chinese philosopher Confucius (below) is born.
1368 The Mongol (Yuan) Dynasty is overthrown.
1430 During the Ming Dynasty (1368–1644), Chinese artists create beautiful porcelain vases (below).
600 B.C.
200 B.C.
1400
356 B.C. Building of the first section of a protective wall begins in northern China.
221 B.C. Shi Huangdi (above) becomes the first emperor of unified China.
1271 Marco Polo sets off from Venice on a journey to China.
636

ACTIVITY OPTION **LINK TO HISTORY**

RESEARCHING HISTORICAL FIGURES

Objective To help students connect geographical information to historical figures

Class Time One class period

Task Research a historical figure and present a brief report

Directions Have students select one of the following historical figures: Emperor Shi Huangdi, Emperor Shunzhi, or Mao Zedong. Have them research, either on the Internet or at the library, how the chosen historical figure affected some aspect of China, such as territory, economics, politics, arts, or daily life. Then have students present a brief report to the class.

After Mao died in 1976, Deng Xiaoping, a moderate, became China's most powerful leader through the 1980s. In 2003, Hu Jintao became president and Wen Jiabao became premier. The two took responsibility for overseeing economic reforms to improve the standard of living.

Rural and Industrial Economies

When the Communist Party came to power in China in 1949, its leaders promised to modernize China by encouraging the growth of industry. From the 1950s through the 1970s, the central government tried to do this by planning all economic activities. That approach led to more failures than successes. Since the 1980s, though, China has allowed the marketplace and the consumer to play a role in the economy. As a result, China now has one of the fastest growing economies in the world.

THE RURAL ECONOMY In spite of this economic growth, China remains a largely rural society, self-sufficient in agriculture. Its great river valleys provide rich soil for crops such as rice to feed the vast population. Most of China's workers—about 60 percent—work on farms.

Farming is possible only on about 13 percent of China's land because so much of western China is made up of mountains and deserts. Even so, China manages to grow enough food to feed its people. Much of the population is concentrated in the areas where food can be grown.

The eastern river basins of China produce crops such as rice, maize, wheat, and sweet potatoes. This productivity is aided by the long growing season in southern China. Farmers there can grow two or more crops on the same land during each year. A

A. Answer The rich farming land is in the east, while mountains and deserts make up the west.

CONNECT TO THE ISSUES
POPULATION
A Why is so much of China's population in the east and so little in the west?

THE INDUSTRIAL ECONOMY The industrial heartland of China is in the northeast. Here are abundant resources important to manufacturing, such as coal, iron ore, and oil. (See map, page 622.) In addition, the northeast has better transportation systems than the rest of the country.

Shanghai leads China as a center of manufacturing and is one of the great industrial centers in the world. Other Chinese cities with many factories and industries include Beijing and Tianjin. Southeastern China

1557 Portuguese found colony of Macao on peninsula in China.

1627 Manchu armies overrun northern Korea.

1661 **Shunzhi** *(left),* Qing emperor who came to the throne as a child, dies of smallpox.

1720 China takes control of Tibet.

1839 War breaks out between Britain and China.

1949 **Mao Zedong** (left) and the Communists gain power in China.

1989 Chinese troops fire on student demonstrators in Tiananmen Square in Beijing.

1600 1800 2000

EAST ASIA

Instruct: Objective 3

Rural and Industrial Economies

- What did the Communist party want for China's economy? *(modernization, growth of industry)*
- At what point did China's economy begin to grow more rapidly? *(1980s)*
- Where does most agriculture occur in China? *(eastern river basins)*
- Where does China get the resources that fuel the industrial economy? *(in the northeast of the country)*
- What item is especially popular as an export to the United States? *(textiles)*

More About

Ming Porcelain

Thin white porcelain became popular during the Ming Dynasty. Much Ming-era porcelain was decorated with a blue underglaze. The pigment used for this decoration was called Mohammedan blue because it was imported from the Kashan district of Persia. Since it was difficult to obtain the pigment, production of the blue-glazed porcelain was occasionally interrupted. The imported pigment was used on Ming porcelain until the end of the 16th century, when ways of refining native cobalt were developed.

ACTIVITY OPTION INTERNET RESEARCH

B BLOCK SCHEDULING

LEARNING ABOUT TIANANMEN SQUARE

Objective To see how historical events affect current events

Class Time 30 minutes

Task Use the Internet to research past and current events

Directions Have students use the Internet to research events relating to Tiananmen Square. Then have them find recent news stories and articles relating to this event. Ask them to write a short summary of events (past and current) and then to explain how they think this historical event affects the Chinese people today. *(Their answers may include information about how people refer to the place and the events there, the site today, commemorative events held in the square, and so forth.)*

OPTIONAL ACTIVITY If Internet access is limited or unavailable, have students use the library for this research. Ask librarians for assistance in locating materials.

Instruct: Objective 4

A Rich and Complex Culture

- Which countries were influenced by Chinese culture? *(Japan, Korea)*
- Name two important Chinese inventions. *(paper, printing, gunpowder, compass, silk cloth)*
- What are the predominant religions or ethical traditions in China? *(Confucianism, Taoism, Buddhism)*

Critical Thinking Transparencies CT60
- Population Projections for China and Japan, 2025

Cultures Around the World
- Fine Arts, p. 51

Cultures Transparencies CW51
- Landscape Painting

Interpreting Photographs

Chinese Artifacts

Have students examine the artifacts. Ask them what the items displayed here represent. *(important inventions and articles in Chinese cultural history)*

More About

Jade

Jade is actually a name for either of two minerals that are often emerald or apple green in color. They are typically highly polished and carved into jewelry and other objects. Jadeite is the more desirable mineral and has a glassy luster, while nephrite often has an oily appearance. Either form of jade may be white or have red, gray, or green color due to the presence of iron, chromium, or manganese in the stone.

has industrial centers in Guangzhou, Hangzhou, Suzhou, Wuhan, and Wuxi.

China has developed heavy industries, such as steel and machinery. It also produces consumer goods. For example, the country has a huge textile (cloth) industry that produces goods for the home market and export. Many textiles are exported to the United States. B

Connect to the Issues
Trade
B Why might trade between the United States and China be important to both countries?
B. Answer
The U.S. is a rich market for Chinese goods, and China is a huge market for U.S. goods.

A Rich and Complex Culture

As the world's oldest continuous civilization, China has one of the world's richest cultures. The country has highly developed art, architecture, literature, painting, sculpture, pottery, printing, music, and theater. In all these areas, the Chinese have made influential contributions to the cultures of Korea, Japan, and other countries in the region.

FROM POTTERY TO PAINTING Some of the earliest Chinese works of art have been found in burial sites. Pottery, bronze vessels, and jade disks have been discovered in the excavation of old tombs. In addition, paintings have been found on tiles decorating the walls of tombs. Chinese artists created beautiful works using different materials, such as clay, bronze, jade, ivory, and lacquer.

Background
Other important Chinese art forms include calligraphy and brush painting.

Chinese Artifacts

An ancient Chinese coin *(above left)* is from about 450 B.C. The jade pendant *(above right)* is from about 250 B.C.

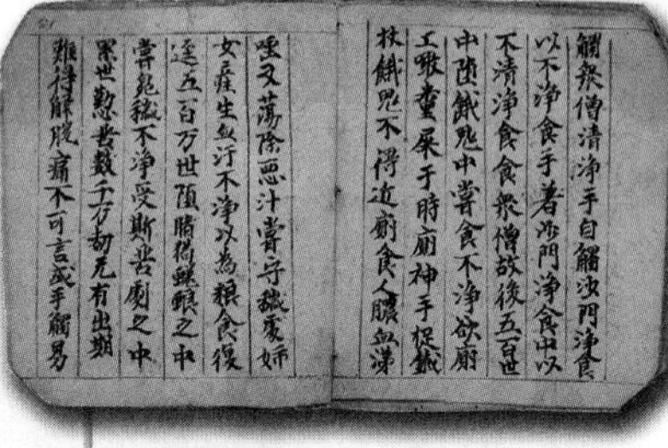

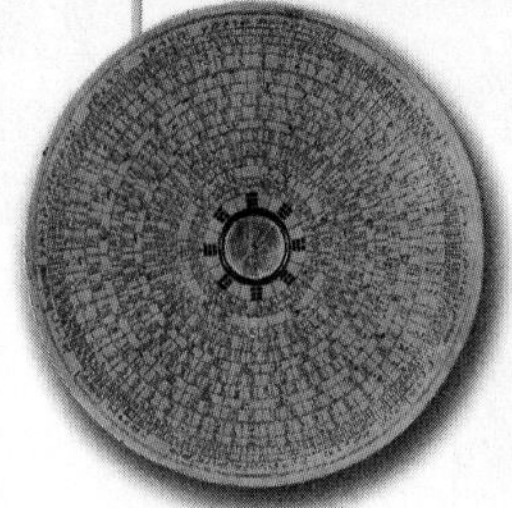

This printed book *(above)* from about A.D. 1000 contains a Buddhist prayer. This navigational compass *(left)* dates from the 18th century.

CHINESE INVENTIONS The Chinese introduced many inventions to the world, such as paper, printing, and gunpowder. Other Chinese inventions include the compass, porcelain, and silk cloth.

RELIGIOUS AND ETHICAL TRADITIONS China has three major religions or ethical traditions. The beliefs of most people include elements of all three. Those traditions have influenced beliefs throughout the region.

Confucius was a Chinese philosopher who lived from 551 to 479 B.C. He believed in respect for the past and for one's ancestors. He thought that in an orderly society, children should obey their parents and parents should obey the government and emperor. He stressed the importance of education in a well-run society. His thinking about the importance of order, education, and hierarchy in a well-ordered society is called **Confucianism.**

Taoism gets its name from a book called the *Tao-te Ching,* based on the teaching of Lao-tzu, who lived in the sixth century B.C. He believed in the importance of preserving and restoring harmony in the individual and in the universe. He also thought the government should leave the people alone and do as little as possible. Another of his major beliefs was that the individual should seek harmony with nature.

Buddhism came to China from India and grew into an important religion in China by the 300s A.D. Confucianism and Taoism influenced Buddhism as it developed in China. Among ideas important in Buddhism are rebirth and the end of the rebirth cycle.

DIFFERENTIATING INSTRUCTION **STUDENTS ACQUIRING ENGLISH/ESL**

CHARTING PROPER NOUNS

Objective To help ESL students expand their knowledge of varying forms of proper nouns

Class Time 20 minutes

Task Create a chart of varying forms of proper nouns

Directions On the board, create a three-column chart with the headings "Person/Source," "Religion/Ethical Tradition," and "Believer." Fill in one item in each row of the chart below to get students started. Then have students complete the chart. *(Blanks should be filled with Confucius/Confucianist, Taoism/Taoist, Buddha/Buddhism)*

PROPER NOUNS		
PERSON/SOURCE	RELIGION/ ETHICAL TRADITION	BELIEVER
	Confucianism	
Lao Tzu Tao Te Ching		
		Buddhist

The Most Populous Country

One out of every five people in the world lives in China. This makes it the most populous country in the world.

POPULATION PATTERNS China's estimated population in 2010 was about 1.34 billion. Somewhere between 40 and 50 Chinese cities have populations of more than one million people. Many of China's 22 provinces and five autonomous regions have more people than entire countries. In 2010, Henan province was estimated to have a population of more than 98 million people—more than the population of Germany. C

Seventy percent of the people live in 14 provinces located in the east. (See map, page 615.) About 6 percent of the people live in the west on 55 percent of the land.

Geographic Thinking

Seeing Patterns
C What does the immense size of China suggest about its future?
C. Answer
It faces enormous problems but will be a major force in the world.

HEALTH CARE One of the great achievements of China since 1950 has been to provide health care for its enormous and far-flung population. The country has pursued a dual strategy in developing its health-care system.

On the one hand, people make use of traditional Chinese medicines, including herbal remedies. Acupuncture is another important part of Chinese medicine.

On the other hand, China's doctors also use Western medicine to treat disease. Western drugs and surgery have their place in the treatment of illness. Most Chinese cities have hospitals, and the villages have clinics staffed by trained medical workers called "barefoot doctors."

In the next section, you will read about two of China's neighbors, Mongolia and Taiwan. China has greatly influenced both places.

POPULATION

One-Child Policy

Because of its rapidly growing population, China adopted a policy of one child per family in 1979. The country also outlawed early marriage. A man must be 22 and a woman 20 before they can marry. Those policies have reduced China's birthrate dramatically.

However, the government policy of one child per family has run into opposition. Rural families, in particular, feel the need for more than one child to help work on their farms. In 2002, the government reaffirmed the one-child policy but promised extra help to rural families.

Section 1 Assessment

1 Places & Terms

Identify each of the following places and terms.
- dynasty
- spheres of influence
- Boxer Rebellion
- Mao Zedong
- Confucianism
- Taoism
- Buddhism

2 Taking Notes

REGION Use your notes to answer the questions below.

- What are aspects of China's cultural legacy?
- What are some Chinese dynasties?

3 Main Ideas

a. Why is China's rural economy still so important?
b. What are some of China's most important religious ideas?
c. Why is population such an important issue in China?

4 Geographic Thinking

Making Generalizations How has China's rugged terrain affected its relations with other countries and civilizations? **Think about:**
- the mountains and deserts to the west
- the ocean to the east

See Skillbuilder Handbook, page R6.

GeoActivity

SEEING PATTERNS Pair with a partner and investigate an invention of the Chinese, such as printing or the compass. Then present your findings to the class in a brief **oral report** accompanied by an illustration of the invention.

EAST ASIA

Instruct: Objective 

The Most Populous Country

- What is China's most recent population estimate? *(1.33 billion people)*
- In what part of China do most inhabitants live? *(in the East)*
- Besides Western practices, what methods do Chinese doctors use to treat illnesses? *(acupuncture, herbal remedies, traditional Chinese medicine)*

Connect TO THE Issues

Population: One-Child Policy

Ask students to describe two aspects of China's population control policy. *(one-child limit, restrictions on marrying age)* Why would some families oppose a one-child limit? *(to have help on their farms, to have more than one gender, to have a large family, religious reasons, etc.)*

Assess & Reteach

GeoFocus Have students use their notes to complete the cluster diagram on China.

Formal Assessment
- Section Quiz, p. 436

Reteaching Activity
Assign each student a key term from the list on page 635 or a subsection headline (in green type), and have them create a flashcard defining the term or summarizing the section. Have students break into small groups to quiz each other with their flash cards.

In-Depth Resources: Unit 9
- Reteaching Activity, p. 19

Outline Maps with Activities
- China, pp. 91–92

Section 1 Assessment Answers

1. Places & Terms
dynasty, p. 635; spheres of influence, p. 636; Boxer Rebellion, p. 636; Mao Zedong, p. 636; Confucianism, p. 638; Taoism, p. 638; Buddhism, p. 638

2. Taking Notes
- China's cultural legacy can be seen in the art, architecture, literature, painting, sculpture, pottery, printing, music, and theater of the region.
- Important Chinese dynasties include Shang, Zhou, Qin, Han, Qing.

3. Main Ideas
a. China remains a largely rural society and its rural economy helps to feed its huge population.
b. Confucianism, Taoism, and Buddhism are all important in China.
c. China has the largest population in the world, over one billion people, and most of the people live on a small portion of the land.

4. Geographic Thinking
Most of the terrain has provided protection and security from the outside world. The exception is in the north, where nomadic tribes have been able to invade China. However, its mountainous terrain allowed it to develop in relative isolation.

GeoActivity

Integrated Assessment
- Rubric for an oral report, 3.6

OBJECTIVE

1. Identify the region affected by the Chang Jiang (Yangtze River) flood.
2. Examine the effects of the 1931 flood on people.
3. Examine other similar disasters.

Instruct: Objective

Chang Jiang (Yangtze River) Flood of 1931

- In what region of China did the 1931 flood occur? *(east/southeast)*
- What caused the Chang Jiang flooding in 1931? *(heavy monsoon rains)*
- Name three cities that were affected by the 1931 flood? *(Nanjing, Wuchang, Hanyang, and Hankou)*

Interpreting Maps

China

Ask students to examine the map. Ask them what significance the Three Gorges Dam has for the cities affected by the 1931 flood. *(The dam is very close to those cities and is intended to prevent such a flood in the future.)*

Disasters!

Chang Jiang (Yangtze River) Flood of 1931

Throughout Chinese history, the flooding of the Chang Jiang has cost millions of lives. On average, the Chang Jiang has caused a major flood about every 50 years, although in the past century or so the floods have been more frequent. The floods of 1931 and 1954 were particularly devastating. The 1931 flood resulted from monsoon rains. In May and June of that year, six enormous waves poured down the river, demolishing dams and dikes. More than 35,000 square miles of land were flooded and many thousands of people died. Floods along the Chang Jiang continue to the present day. Bad floods occurred in both 1996 and 1998.

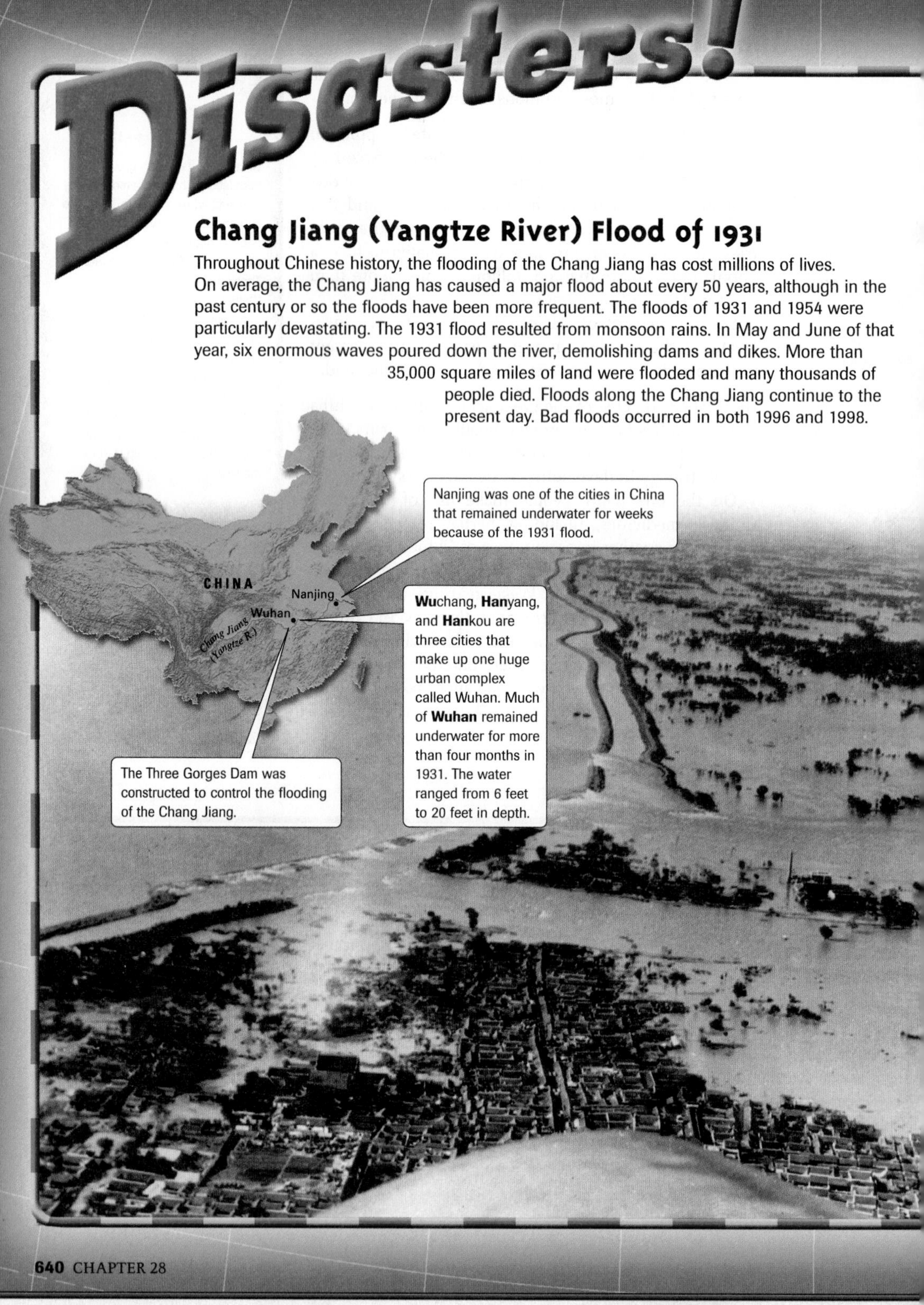

CHINA
Nanjing
Wuhan
Chang Jiang (Yangtze R.)
Nanjing was one of the cities in China that remained underwater for weeks because of the 1931 flood.
Wuchang, **Han**yang, and **Han**kou are three cities that make up one huge urban complex called Wuhan. Much of **Wuhan** remained underwater for more than four months in 1931. The water ranged from 6 feet to 20 feet in depth.
The Three Gorges Dam was constructed to control the flooding of the Chang Jiang.

SUPPORTING RESOURCES

BOOKS FOR THE TEACHER

Gifford, Rob. ***China Road: A Journey into the Future of a Rising Power.*** Random House, 2008. National Public Radio China correspondent on his 3,000-mile journey along China's "Mother Road."

BOOKS FOR THE STUDENT

Newson, Lesley. ***Devastation! The World's Worst Natural Disasters.*** NY: DK Publications, 1998. Covers more than 550 disaster sites with photos and information.

Wade, Nicolas (ed.). ***The Science Times Book of Natural Disasters.*** NY: Lyons Press, 2000. Good reference book.

VIDEO

Great Wall Across the Yangtze River. PBS Video. Boston, MA. A documentary focusing on Three Gorges Dam.

INTERNET

For more on flooding on the rivers of China, visit . . .

hmhsocialstudies.com

hmhsocialstudies.com INTERACTIVE

In the city of Hankou during the flood, wealthy people traveled in boats while poor tradespeople waded up to their necks through the water.

This panoramic aerial view of one of the Chinese cities flooded in 1931 was taken by Charles Lindbergh. He was the American aviator who had made the first solo flight across the Atlantic Ocean in 1927.

Along the Chang Jiang, human labor is still essential for flood control. These laborers work with shovels and other tools to fortify the banks of the river with dirt to prevent flooding.

GeoActivity

UNDERSTANDING FLOODS 21st CENTURY

Working with a partner, use the Internet to research one of the floods listed below. Then create a **presentation** about it.

- Create a diagram showing the extent of the flood, the damage caused by it, and the number of lives lost.
- Add a map of the affected region.
- Write a paragraph explaining how the flood affected the people and life of the region.

hmhsocialstudies.com RESEARCH WEB LINKS

GeoData

OTHER DEADLY RIVER FLOODS

1850

1887
Huang He in northeastern China; possibly more than 1,000,000 people killed

1889
Johnstown, Pennsylvania, on May 31; about 2,200 deaths (more than any other river flood in U.S. history)

1911
Chang Jiang in China; 100,000 killed

1937
Mississippi and Ohio rivers; about 250 killed

1988
Three major rivers in Bangladesh; about 1,600 deaths

1993
Mississippi River; millions of acres flooded; about 50 dead

1998
Chang Jiang in China during July and August; about 4,000 dead

2000

GeoActivities

Integrated Assessment
- Rubric for a presentation, 3.6

Interpreting Photographs

Flood of 1931

Ask students to imagine themselves in the situations depicted in the photographs. Then ask them the following questions. What happened to the people who lived in the area during the flood? *(lost homes, possessions, farms, crops, and perhaps even family members and neighbors)* How did people get around during the flood? *(by wading or by boats)*

More About

The Johnstown Flood

The Johnstown flood of 1889 was caused by a dam giving way. The dam of the South Fork Reservoir, about 12 miles east of the city, burst during heavy rains. In addition to all the lives lost, the resulting flood destroyed millions of dollars worth of property.

ACTIVITY OPTION | LINK TO CREATIVE WRITING

WRITING A DIARY ENTRY

Objective To help students gain a personal understanding of the effects of a disaster on people

Class Time 30 minutes

Task Write a fictional diary entry in the voice of a victim of a disaster

Directions Have students write a one-page diary entry from the perspective of a victim of the 1931 Yangtze River flood. Ask them to describe the scene and its effects on either their lives or people they know. Have them use the information on these two pages, plus any additional research relating to this flood to help them create a fictional account.

SECTION 2 OBJECTIVES

1. Examine Mongolia's and Taiwan's early history and links to China.
2. Describe the cultures of Mongolia and Taiwan.
3. Examine Mongolia and Taiwan's economies.
4. Describe daily life and Western influences in Mongolia and Taiwan.

SKILLBUILDER: Interpreting Maps, p. 643

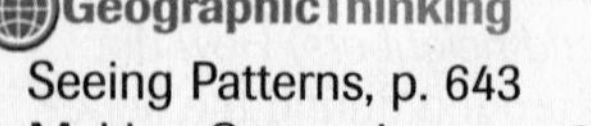

Seeing Patterns, p. 643
Making Comparisons, p. 645
Drawing Conclusions, p. 646

Focus & Motivate

What factors contribute to the formation of an empire? *(natural resources, strong military, leadership, common goals)*

Instruct: Objective 1 appears on p. 643.

Interpreting Graphics

A Mongol Army on the Move

Ask students where Genghis Khan might have ridden in the Mongol army. *(in the yurt or possibly on his own horse)* Ask students to name at least two weapons of a Mongol warrior. *(lance, dagger, bow and arrows)*

2 Mongolia and Taiwan

Main Ideas

- Taiwan and Mongolia have developed in the shadow of their giant neighbor—China.
- The countries of the region include both capitalist and socialist economies.

Places & Terms

economic tiger

Pacific Rim

CONNECT TO THE ISSUES

TRADE Trade has helped Taiwan achieve prosperity, while Mongolia has not been as economically successful.

A HUMAN PERSPECTIVE The Mongols of the Asian steppe lived their lives on horseback. In 1206, a great leader named Temujin (later called Genghis Khan) united the Mongol clans and led them in conquering much of Asia. He is reported to have said, "Man's greatest good fortune is to chase and defeat his enemy, seize his total possessions, leave his married women weeping and wailing, and ride his horse." The Mongols eventually created the largest unified land empire in history, extending from the Pacific coast of China westward into Europe.

A History of Nomads and Traders

The histories of Mongolia and Taiwan have been closely connected to that of China.

THE MONGOLIAN EMPIRE The Mongols were nomadic herders for thousands of years. Mongol history was changed forever by Genghis Khan, a title that means "supreme conqueror." Genghis Khan died in 1227, having conquered all of Central Asia and begun the conquest of

A Mongol Army on the Move

A Mongol army was like a moving city. The cavalry of 10,000 was accompanied by an even greater number of family members and by tens of thousands of horses and livestock.

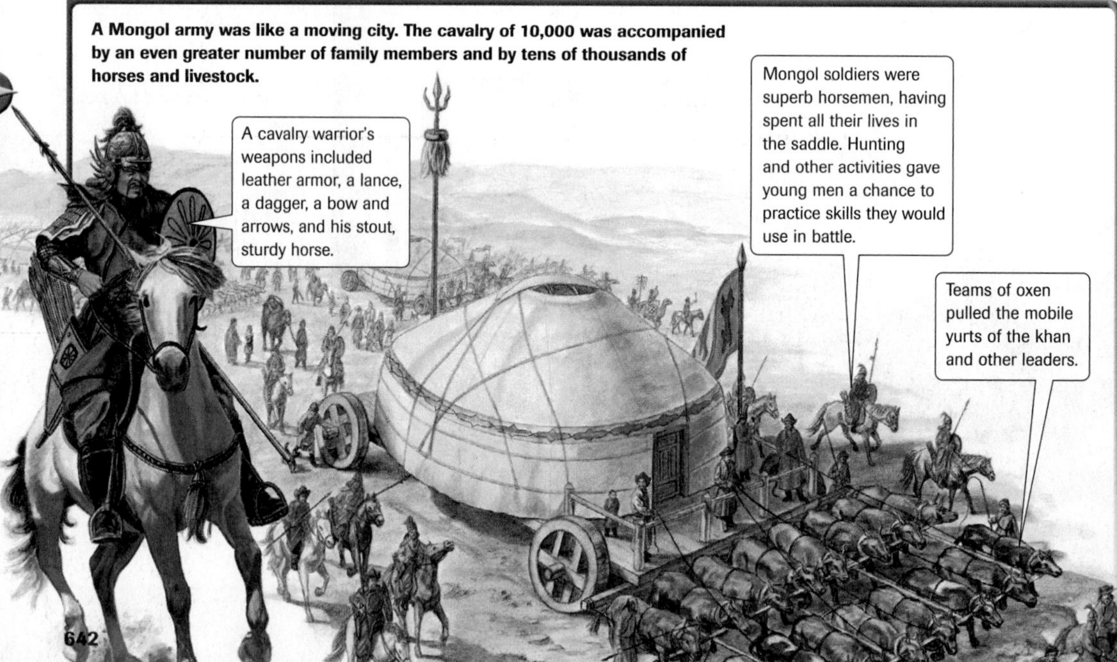

A cavalry warrior's weapons included leather armor, a lance, a dagger, a bow and arrows, and his stout, sturdy horse.
Mongol soldiers were superb horsemen, having spent all their lives in the saddle. Hunting and other activities gave young men a chance to practice skills they would use in battle.
Teams of oxen pulled the mobile yurts of the khan and other leaders.

642

SECTION 2 PROGRAM RESOURCES

In-Depth Resources: Unit 9
- Guided Reading, p. 14
- Skillbuilder Practice, p. 17
- Building Vocabulary, p. 18
- Reteaching Activity, p. 20

Guided Reading Workbook
- Section 2

Access for Students Acquiring English
- Guided Reading, p. 151
- Skillbuilder Practice, p. 154

Outline Maps with Activities
- Mongolia and Taiwan, pp. 93–94

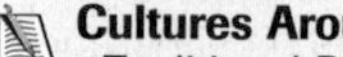

Cultures Around the World
- Traditional Practices, p. 53

Formal Assessment
- Section Quiz, p. 437

Integrated Assessment
- Rubric for a poster, 1.1

INTEGRATED TECHNOLOGY

Cultures Transparencies CW53
- Celebrating Naadam

Power Presentations

hmhsocialstudies.com

TEST-TAKING RESOURCES

Strategies for Test Preparation

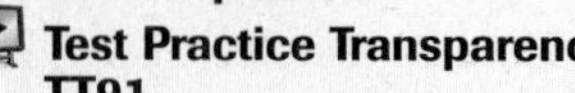
Test Practice Transparencies TT91

Online Test Practice

China. He was succeeded by his son Ogadai, who continued his policies of conquest and expansion. Mongol armies commanded by other sons and grandsons of Genghis Khan moved east, west, and south out of Mongolia.

The Mongol empire broke up in the 1300s. Eventually the Chinese gained control of Mongolia in the 17th century. The Chinese ruled Mongolia for hundreds of years. Only in 1911 were the Mongolians finally able to push the Chinese out and achieve their independence.

Under the influence of its powerful neighbor Russia, Mongolia became the Mongolian People's Republic in 1924. For about 72 years, the Communists ruled Mongolia. However, after the fall of the Soviet Union in 1989, the Communist Party in Mongolia lost its power. The country began moving toward political democracy and a free-enterprise economy. A

The Mongol Empire, 1294

SKILLBUILDER: Interpreting Maps
1 **REGION** Which khanate controlled Mongolia and China?
2 **MOVEMENT** What object may have restricted movement between the Gobi desert and the heartland of China?

Geographic Thinking

Seeing Patterns
A What are some of the countries that have controlled or been controlled by Mongolia over the centuries?

A. Answer
Mongolia has controlled parts of China, as well as other countries in the area (such as Russia); Mongolia has been controlled by China and Russia.

TAIWAN'S LINK TO CHINA The island of Taiwan experienced many prehistoric migrations from southern China and southeast Asia. Malay and Polynesian peoples also settled there. Over the centuries, other settlers and groups of people from China settled on the island. In the sixth century, for example, some Han Chinese arrived. Later, when famine struck Fujian province in the 17th century, a large number of Chinese migrated from the mainland. That contributed to the large Chinese settlements on the island. The Manchu Dynasty conquered Taiwan in 1683. (See Unit Atlas, page 613.)

The Japanese seized Taiwan (then called Formosa) after winning a war with China in 1895. Japan kept the island until its defeat in World War II. Then Chinese Nationalists took control of the island as part of their fight with the Communists for control of mainland China. When the Nationalists lost to the Communists in 1949, they moved their government to Taiwan. There they established the Republic of China. However, the People's Republic of China has never recognized Taiwan as a separate country and considers it a province.

Cultures of Mongolia and Taiwan

China is a cultural hearth that has influenced its neighbors. It has been the source for many of the important ideas and inventions that have shaped Mongolia and Taiwan and the rest of the region.

MONGOLIA Mongolia has both ruled and been ruled by China. Kublai Khan was the Mongol emperor of China when Marco Polo visited in the 13th century. In the mid-14th century, the Chinese rose up against their

Instruct: Objective 

A History of Nomads and Traders

- What animal was especially important to the Mongols? *(horse)*
- What did Genghis Khan's name mean? *(supreme conqueror)*
- Who controlled Mongolia in the 18th and 19th centuries? *(China)*
- Which country has had the most influence and control in Taiwan? *(China)*

 **In-Depth Resources: Unit 9**
- Guided Reading, p. 14

Interpreting Maps

The Mongol Empire, 1294

Have students identify the Khanate that would include most of Tibet. *(Chagatal Khanate)* Ask the students how the Mongol Empire compared to China's boundaries today. *(It was much larger, expanding farther north, east, and west of China's current borders)*

SKILLBUILDER ANSWERS
1. Khanate of the Great Khan
2. The Great Wall

Instruct: Objective 

Cultures of Mongolia and Taiwan

- What native Mongol traditions are still in practice in Mongolia? *(herding livestock, Three Games of Men festival)*
- What are some examples of Chinese culture in Taiwan? *(Buddhism, common language is Mandarin)*

 **Cultures Around the World**
- Traditional Practices, p. 53

Cultures Transparencies CW53
- Celebrating Naadam

SKILLBUILDER LESSON **MAKING COMPARISONS**

COMPARING TWO COUNTRIES

Explaining the Skill Making comparisons involves finding both similarities and differences between two or more things. Tell students that making comparisons among events, ideas, beliefs, and institutions can help them better understand those countries.

Applying the Skill Have students make a three-column chart as shown at right with the headings "Taiwan," "Issue," and "Mongolia," and the issues listed in the central column. Then ask students to complete the chart, based on information in this section of the chapter.

In-Depth Resources: Unit 9
- Skillbuilder Practice, p. 17

TAIWAN	ISSUE	MONGOLIA
Independent, but China claims as territory	Chinese control	Independent; was under Chinese rule from 17th-20th centuries
Taiwan restricted to island	History of expansion, growth	Mongolia developed an empire
Heavily influenced by China; share language and culture	Culture	Moderate Chinese influence, most in distant past
Highly successful manufacturing and trading economy	Economy	Based on livestock

Instruct: Objective 3

Two Very Different Economies

- How is Mongolia's current economy different from its historical practices? *(Mongolia is now a market economy and is exporting natural resources)*
- What is an economic tiger? *(a country whose economy grows rapidly due to cheap labor, technology, and exports)*
- Why might foreign companies want to work with Taiwanese companies? *(cheap labor for production of goods)*
- What industry is most successful in Taiwan? *(technology)*

Interpreting Photographs

Mongolian Goatherds

Goats provide the soft cashmere wool that is in increasing demand worldwide. Ask students if they can think of an American practice with live stock that is similar to painting the horns of goats. *(tagging or branding cattle, etc.)*

CAPTION ANSWER to be able to tell, especially at a distance, which goats belong to your herd

Mongol rulers and drove them out of China. In the 17th century, the Chinese under the Manchus conquered Mongolia, which they ruled for hundreds of years. This interaction produced a profound cultural influence as the Mongols adopted many aspects of Chinese culture.

The most important festival in Mongolia is the annual Naadam festival of the Three Games of Men. The festival, which dates back 2,300 years, begins each year on July 11. The three games are wrestling, archery, and horse racing. The competitors are highly skilled, and winners receive titles proclaiming their abilities. All of these contests have their roots in the ancient way of life of the Mongolian people.

TAIWAN Unlike Mongolia, Taiwan has a population that is almost exclusively Chinese. Thus, the culture of the island is Chinese. The capital city of Taipei includes Buddhist temples as well as museums of Chinese art. The island has many universities and about 30 daily newspapers. The population is well-educated, and most of the people speak the official language of Northern Chinese (also called Mandarin).

BACKGROUND The population of Taiwan is one of the best educated in Asia, second only to that of Japan.

The people of Taiwan combine a number of religious and ethical beliefs. More than 90 percent practice a blend of Buddhism, Confucianism, and Taoism. A small number are Christian and an even smaller percentage practice other religions.

Two Very Different Economies

The economies of Mongolia and Taiwan have roots in the past. Raising livestock, a part of the nomadic life, is at the core of the Mongolian economy. Because Taiwan is an island, trade is key to its economy.

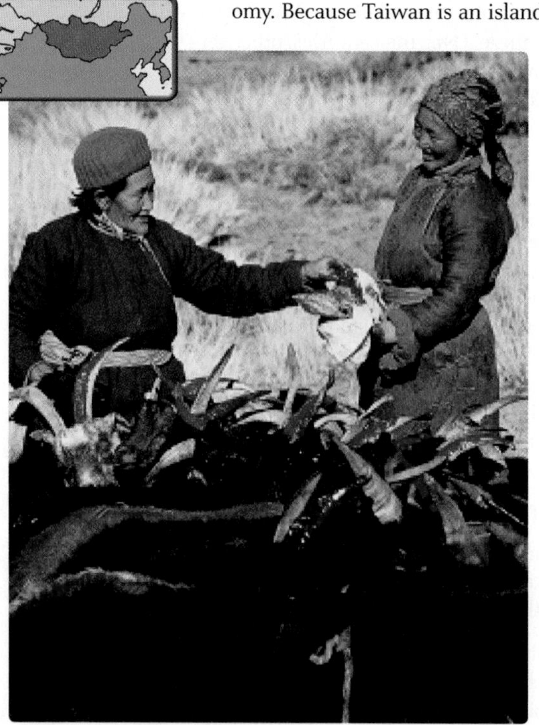

HUMAN-ENVIRONMENT INTERACTION A Mongolian mother and daughter use red paint to mark the horns of their goats. **What purpose might marking goats serve?**

ECONOMIC PROSPECTS FOR MONGOLIA A large part of the population of Mongolia still engages in herding and managing livestock. For centuries, the economy was based on the nomadic herding of sheep, goats, camels, horses, and cattle. More goats are being raised to meet the demands of the cashmere industry, which uses soft wool from goats of the region. Of the millions of animals kept in herds in the country, nearly a third are sheep. Animals and animal products are used for domestic consumption as well as for export.

Although livestock remains the basis of the economy, Mongolia is now committed to the development of other industries. Under the Communist government, the state owned and operated most of the factories in the country. The Soviets guided Mongolia's economy for about 70 years. When the Soviet Union fell

DIFFERENTIATING INSTRUCTION **GIFTED AND TALENTED STUDENTS**

MAKING A BUSINESS PLAN

Objective To help students use geographical information in a real-life situation

Class Time One class period

Task Produce a report showing whether it is better to import parts or whole items from Taiwan for (assembly and) sale in the United States

Directions Tell students that they will need to determine whether or not Taiwan would be a good place to manufacture either parts or entire cell phones for an American company. Have students find resource information, either on the Internet or through a library, on the production of cell phones in Taiwan.

Have students ask the following questions: Are many cell phones manufactured in Taiwan? If so, are any American companies manufacturing their cell phones there? If so, are those companies leaders in the market in terms of cell phones? Have students write a brief report and suggest whether or not it would benefit an American cell phone company to produce all or part of their phones in Taiwan.

apart, Mongolia was one of the first Communist countries to attempt to shift to a market economy. The transition has been difficult as the country has turned increasingly from a Soviet-style managed economy to a free-market economy.

Mongolia has large deposits of fuels such as coal and petroleum. It also has rich deposits of metals such as copper, gold, and iron. Those resources are used in both manufacturing and construction, industries which are of growing importance to the economy.

TAIWAN'S ECONOMIC SUCCESS Taiwan has one of the world's most successful economies. It has succeeded despite the fact that it has few natural resources. However, it has a highly trained and motivated work force.

Taiwan's prosperity is based on its strong manufacturing industries and its trade with other nations. Among the most successful products of its factories are radios, televisions, calculators, and computers. Taiwanese companies sell their products around the world.

Taiwan is considered one of the economic tigers of Asia, along with Singapore and South Korea. An **economic tiger** is a nation that has rapid economic growth due to cheap labor, high technology, and aggressive exports. It is one of the very prosperous economies of the western Pacific. These economies are highly industrialized and trade with nations around the world. They are part of the **Pacific Rim**—the countries surrounding the Pacific Ocean. The Pacific Rim is an economic and social region. It includes the countries of East Asia, Southeast Asia, Australia, New Zealand, Chile, and the west coast of the United States. B

Geographic Thinking

Making Comparisons

B What are some differences between the economies of Mongolia and Taiwan?

B. Answer Although Mongolia is changing, its economy is still based on herding and livestock, while the economy of Taiwan is based on manufacturing and trade.

Connect TO THE Issues

TRADE

Trade and Taiwan

Taiwan has a trading economy, and its success as a trader has made it one of the economic tigers of the region.

The electronics industry is at the core of Taiwan's prosperity. Its capitalist economy has developed a number of profitable computer companies that export personal computers all over the globe.

In addition to its electronic products, Taiwan exports many other products. These include machinery, steel, textiles, plastics, and chemicals.

Daily Life in Mongolia and Taiwan

The daily life of people in Mongolia and Taiwan shows traditional influences as well as modern influences. This blending of old and new can be seen in both work and play.

HERDING IN MONGOLIA As you learned earlier in this section, the people of Mongolia were nomads who guided their animals from grassland to grassland. The land through which they traveled has an unpredictable, hostile environment. The climate is extreme. Long, cold winters lasting six months alternate with short, hot summers of only two months. Severe winter weather makes it difficult for livestock to survive. Bad weather can kill animals from intense cold and starvation.

Nomads live in tents called yurts that are made of felt covered with leather. This is the traditional form of shelter in Mongolia. Yurts can even be found in the capital of Ulaanbaatar.

Today, many of the people of Mongolia still spend their days raising sheep, cattle, and goats. Some still follow the nomadic way of life, but most people care for livestock on farms and ranches. Often these farms have small villages in the center, with shops, offices, and houses.

Connect TO THE Issues

Trade: Trade and Taiwan

Have students read the information in the text box and ask them to make a list of some electronics that might be produced in an economy such as Taiwan's. *(televisions, stereos, MP3 players, video and DVD recording and playing equipment)* Besides exporting completed products, how could Taiwan's trade affect the American economy? *(by providing parts for American companies' electronics or by manufacturing full products for American companies)*

Instruct: Objective 

Daily Life in Mongolia and Taiwan

- What traditional influences can be seen in daily life in Mongolia? *(Herding as an economic practice, the use of yurts, nomadic life)*
- Do most Americans live in rural areas like people in Mongolia or urban areas like the people in Taiwan? *(urban)*
- When did Little League become popular in Taiwan? *(after World War II)*

ACTIVITY OPTION **FIVE THEMES OF GEOGRAPHY: MOVEMENT**

 **BLOCK SCHEDULING**

ASSESSING WESTERN INFLUENCE

Objective To examine the effect of Western influence on life in East Asia

Class Time 30 minutes

Task Make a list of American products students think are popular in East Asia, and then briefly research for confirmation

Directions Have students work in small groups to make a list of five American products and/or events (including sports, entertainment, etc.) they think would be popular in East Asia. Then, have students research briefly on the Internet or at a library, especially through travel resources (including photos), for confirmation on their choices. *(Answers will vary, but may include denim jeans, pop music, fast-food restaurants, soft drinks, and baseball.)*

Extension Have the class discuss the pros and cons of these Western influences in East Asia.

Interpreting Photographs

Baseball in Taiwan

Ask students what other ways Americans and East Asians might be able to participate together in baseball. *(through the Olympics; East Asian players on professional American teams and vice versa; exhibition games; viewing games on television from other parts of the world)*

Assess & Reteach

GeoFocus Have students complete their notes on Mongolia and Taiwan as subregions of East Asia.

Formal Assessment
- Section Quiz, p. 437

Reteaching Activity
Divide students into pairs, then have them alternate assigning subsection headings and turning those headings into questions for the other student. Students should alternate subsections and questioning each other as they go through the entire section.

In-Depth Resources: Unit 9
- Reteaching Activity, p. 20

Outline Maps with Activities
- Mongolia and Taiwan, pp. 93–94

MOVEMENT Taiwan's team celebrates winning the Little League World Series in Williamsport, Pennsylvania, in 1996.

WESTERN INFLUENCES IN TAIWAN Although Mongolia remains relatively isolated from the West, Taiwan has opened itself to many Western influences.

For example, baseball has become popular in Taiwan and in other parts of Asia, particularly Japan. As a part of this general interest in the sport, Little League baseball has also become popular in parts of Asia.

Little League became popular after World War II. In 1974, the United States banned teams from foreign countries from the Little League World Series. In part, that was a response to the success of Taiwan's teams which, throughout the 1970s, dominated the World Series. However, they were restored to competition in 1976. By 2007, there were leagues in the United States and more than 70 other countries.

In the next section, you will read about two countries that share one peninsula: North Korea and South Korea.

Section 2 Assessment

1 Places & Terms

Identify each of the following places and terms.
- economic tiger
- Pacific Rim

2 Taking Notes

REGION Use your notes to answer the questions below.

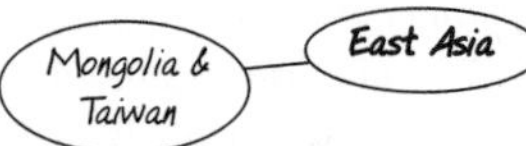

- How are the economies of Mongolia and Taiwan different from one another?
- What effect did Genghis Khan have on the history of the region?

3 Main Ideas

a. In which ways has China influenced its neighbors?

b. What are some of the characteristics of an economic tiger?

c. In what ways does the modern life of Mongolia and Taiwan show a blending of ancient and modern traditions?

4 Geographic Thinking

Drawing Conclusions How might the locations of Mongolia and Taiwan have made them open to the influence of China? **Think about:**
- the relative locations of Taiwan and Mongolia

SEEING PATTERNS Pair with a partner and do Internet research on Little League baseball in Taiwan or some other country in East Asia. Create a **poster** showing various teams in the region. You might include photographs and charts in your poster, listing the names of teams, their win-loss records, and any other information your research turns up.

SECTION 2 ASSESSMENT ANSWERS

1. Places & Terms
economic tiger, p. 645   Pacific Rim, p. 645

2. Taking Notes
- The economy of Mongolia is based on herding and managing livestock; the economy of Taiwan is based on trade and manufacturing.
- Genghis Khan intertwined the history of Mongolia and China.

3. Main Ideas

a. China ruled Mongolia for centuries. Taiwan has been settled mainly by people from China, beginning mostly in the 17th century.

b. An economic tiger is a highly industrialized nation with strong economic growth based on cheap labor and high technology.

c. The people of Mongolia still do much herding of livestock; however, today most of the livestock is kept on farms and ranches. Most of Taiwan's culture, history, and language has come from China, but it has been very much influenced by the West.

4. Geographic Thinking
Mongolia shares a border with China, and throughout history, there has been movement of people and cultural traditions between them. Taiwan has had waves of settlers from China, beginning in the 17th century.

GeoActivity

Integrated Assessment
- Rubric for a poster, 1.1

The Koreas: North and South

Main Ideas

- The Korean peninsula is divided into two separate countries.
- North Korea is a Communist country, and South Korea is a republic.

Places & Terms

Three Kingdoms
Seoul
Pyongyang

CONNECT TO THE ISSUES
TRADE South Korea is one of the economic tigers of the region, and much of its prosperity depends upon industry and trade.

A HUMAN PERSPECTIVE Korea is surrounded by water on three sides and by mountains on its northern border. In the 17th and 18th centuries, Korea chose self-protected isolation and became known as "the hermit kingdom." This isolation has continued in North Korea, which has little contact with other nations even today. However, that may be changing.

A Divided Peninsula

Korea is a peninsula. To the east lies the Sea of Japan (East Sea). To the west lies the Yellow Sea. To the south lies the Korea Strait. To the north lie China and Russian Siberia. Korea's location has shaped its history.

ANCIENT KOREA AND FOREIGN INFLUENCES The ancestors of today's Koreans probably migrated into the peninsula from Manchuria and North China many thousands of years ago. Over the course of the centuries, different clans or groups controlled different parts of the country. About 2000 B.C., the first state, called Choson, arose in Korea.

Around 100 B.C., China conquered the northern half of the peninsula. This began the history of invasions by China and Japan. Because of its location, Korea has been a buffer between the two countries.

After being partially conquered by China, the Koreans gradually won back their territory. By the late 300s, the **Three Kingdoms** had formed in the peninsula. These were Koguryo in the northeast, Paekche in the southwest, and Silla in the southeast. In the 660s, Silla conquered the other two kingdoms and controlled the peninsula for hundreds of years.

PLACE Ky'ongbok Palace is located in Seoul, South Korea. **What does the setting of the palace amidst the bustle of Seoul suggest about the culture?**

SECTION 3 OBJECTIVES

1. Examine the history of North Korea and South Korea.
2. Identify other influences on Korean culture.
3. Describe the effect of war and conflict on Korean life.
4. Describe the economic and human resources of North and South Korea.

SKILLBUILDER: Interpreting Maps, p. 648

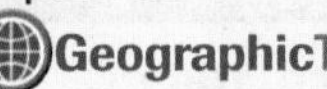
GeographicThinking

Seeing Patterns, p. 649
Drawing Conclusions, p. 650

Focus & Motivate

What geographic factors can affect development of an area? *(location, climate, natural barriers like water and mountains)*

Instruct: Objective 1 appears on p. 648.

Interpreting Photographs

Ky'ongbok Palace

Have students examine the photograph. Ask them to describe details that offer clues to South Korea's landscape, climate, and culture. *(mountains, fall colors mean seasonal change, Chinese-influenced architecture)*

CAPTION ANSWER appreciation for nature, for peace and quiet

SECTION 3 PROGRAM RESOURCES

In-Depth Resources: Unit 9
- Guided Reading, p. 15
- Building Vocabulary, p. 18
- Reteaching Activity, p. 21

Guided Reading Workbook
- Section 3

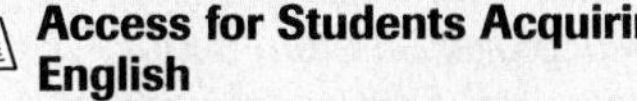
Access for Students Acquiring English
- Guided Reading, p. 152

Outline Maps with Activities
- The Koreas: North and South, pp. 95–96

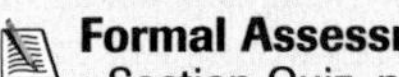
Formal Assessment
- Section Quiz, p. 438

Integrated Assessment
- Rubric for a Venn diagram, 2.8

INTEGRATED TECHNOLOGY

Power Presentions

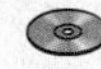
Test Generator
- Section Quiz

hmhsocialstudies.com

TEST-TAKING RESOURCES

Strategies for Test Preparation

Test Practice Transparencies TT92

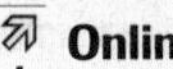
Online Test Practice

Instruct: Objective 1

A Divided Peninsula

- What bodies of water surround Korea? *(Sea of Japan [East Sea], Yellow Sea, Korea Strait)*
- What natural features influenced the settlement of Korea? *(isolation of peninsula, mountainous areas)*

In-Depth Resources: Unit 9
- Guided Reading, p. 15

Interpreting Maps

The Korean War, 1950-1953

Have students examine the maps and map key. Ask them who had control over most of Korea in the first phase of the Korean War. *(Communist forces)* Ask them who had control of most of Korea at the end of the war. *(It was nearly equally divided.)*

SKILLBUILDER ANSWERS

1. Communist forces **2.** Border changed little although South Korea gained territory.

Instruct: Objective 

Influences on Korean Culture

- What Chinese religions or philosophies greatly influenced Korea? *(Confucianism and Buddhism)*
- Which country in the Korean peninsula has been influenced the most by Communism since World War II? *(North Korea)*

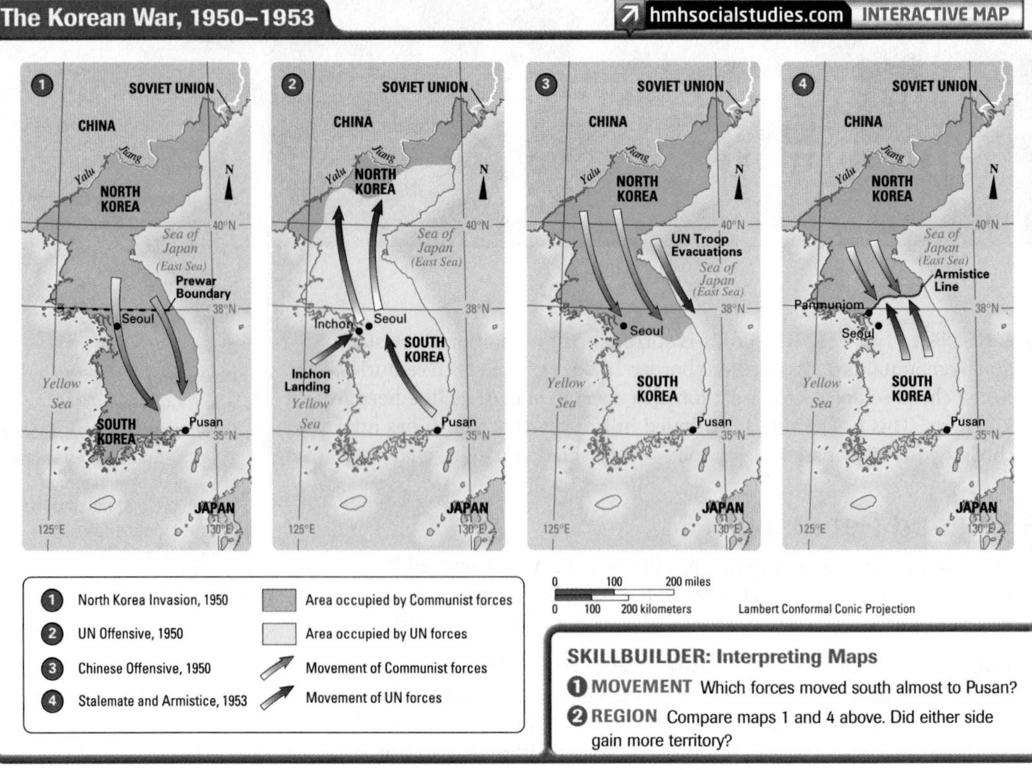

In 1392, a general named Yi S'ong-gye became ruler of Korea. He founded a dynasty that lasted for hundreds of years. But the dynasty ended in 1910, when Japan took control of the entire peninsula. The Japanese ruled Korea until they were defeated in World War II in 1945.

TWO KOREAS: NORTH AND SOUTH After Japan's defeat in the war, the northern part of Korea was controlled by the Soviet Union, and the southern half was supported by the United States. In 1950, Korean troops from the North invaded South Korea, starting the Korean War. The war ended in 1953 with a treaty that divided the peninsula between the Communist state of North Korea and the democratic country of South Korea. The two nations remained hostile toward each other, but since 2000, they have taken some small steps towards reunification.

Influences on Korean Culture

The shadow cast by China has fallen across the Korean peninsula. Korean culture, including language, art, and religion, shows this influence.

THE CHINESE INFLUENCE In philosophy and religion, Korea has adapted many ideas from China. Confucianism (see Section 1) is a system of teachings based on the beliefs of the Chinese scholar Confucius. His ideas stressing social order have influenced many Koreans. Buddhism, which came to Korea by way of China, has also influenced many Koreans. In turn, Korea has influenced its neighbors. For example, Buddhism spread from Korea to Japan.

ACTIVITY OPTION | CRITICAL THINKING

DETERMINING CAUSE AND EFFECT

Explaining the Skill Explain to students that a *cause* is an action that makes something happen. An *effect* is the event that is a result of the cause. A single event may have several causes. It is also possible for one cause to result in several effects. Geographers identify cause-and-effect relationships to help them understand changes in geographic relationships.

Applying the Skill Distribute two index cards to each student (or to groups of students). Assign causes and effects from this section to various students or groups. Have them write the assigned cause or effect on one index card. Then, have them determine the converse (either cause or effect) and write that on the second index card. Collect all of the cause cards, then all of the effect cards and lay them out in separate areas. Have students work in pairs or small groups. Have them choose one cause card (other than one they created) and then find the appropriate matching effect card. *(Some cause/effect pairs: World War II/Japan no longer controls Korea; Soviet and U.S. influence over different parts of Korea/Korean War; 1953 Treaty ending Korean War/Division of North and South Korea)*

OTHER CULTURAL INFLUENCES Since World War II, two major influences have had a profound effect on Korea. First, Communism has molded the culture of North Korea. Non-Communist South Korea, on the other hand, has been greatly influenced by Western culture.

In North Korea, the government only allows art that glorifies Communism or the folk tradition. In South Korea, artists have more freedom of expression. They work with themes drawn from their own history and culture, as well as themes drawn from Western art.

Moving Toward Unity

The most important recent development in North Korea and South Korea is the movement toward unification. However, the communist North and democratic South must overcome years of mutual hostility.

AN ARMED SOCIETY After World War II, both North Korea and South Korea built up huge armies. The armed forces of South Korea number more than 600,000 soldiers and sailors. The armed forces of North Korea are even larger, numbering well over one million. In addition, North Korea probably has chemical weapons has tested nuclear weapons.

Both countries have existed with the threat of war for many years. Only recently has there been an attempt to defuse the situation. War has been a real possibility along the border between the countries, which is guarded by nearly 2 million troops on both sides. A

A SINGLE FLAG There are signs of hope, however. In June 2000, the leaders of both Koreas held a summit meeting at which they declared their intention to reunite the two countries. Shortly after, the defense

A. Answer different political and economic systems as well as different allies

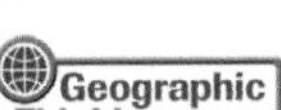

Geographic Thinking

Seeing Patterns

A What have been the main differences dividing North Korea and South Korea?

growing up in... South Korea

Young people, like most other South Koreans, follow at least some of the teachings of Confucius. For example, education is highly valued. The state requires by law that students obtain a primary education, and this schooling is free. The majority of children attend secondary schools. More than one million students attend college-level schools in South Korea.

However, in addition to traditional ideas and ways of life, there is a strong western influence in South Korea. This can be seen in the Western clothes worn by these students as they enjoy an outing in the Nampodong shopping district in Pusan, South Korea.

If you lived in South Korea, you would pass these milestones:

- You would be required by law to attend school through 6th grade.
- You would next attend middle school—grades 7 through 9.
- You would then probably attend high school—grades 10 through 12.
- You would be able to vote at age 20.
- The average age for a first marriage is 29 for men and 26 for women.
- The average age of women at the birth of their first child is 27.

EAST ASIA

Instruct: Objective 3

Moving Toward Unity

- What action have both Korean countries taken since World War II? *(building of armies)*
- What significant event occurred in June 2000? *(Both Koreas held a summit meeting to discuss unification.)*

growing up in...

South Korea

Have students read the description of education in South Korea. Ask students how the South Korean approach to education is similar to or different from the American approach. *(The United States also values education and offers free schooling.)* Also, ask students to compare their own lives with the milestones listed for South Korea's youth. How are their lives similar or different? *(Answers will vary.)*

DIFFERENTIATING INSTRUCTION LESS PROFICIENT READERS

CREATING A COMPARISON CHART

Objective To gather textual information and place it in a visual format

Class Time 30 minutes

Task Create chart to compare geographic features of North and South Korea

Directions Create a four-column, three-row chart (such as the one at right) on the board. Write in the column and row headings, and have students give you the appropriate information to fill in.

COUNTRY	ECONOMY	POLITICAL SYSTEM	LARGEST CITIES
North Korea	Based on raw material/natural resources	Communist	Pyongyang
South Korea	Based on industry and trade	Democratic	Seoul

Instruct: Objective 3

Economic and Human Resources

- What type of economy did both North and South Korea have prior to the Korean War? *(agricultural)*
- How are North and South Korea's economies different today? *(North Korea has abundant natural resources and raw materials, while South Korea has aggressive trade, high technology, and ship- and auto-building industries)*
- Which Korean country has a larger population? *(South Korea)*

Assess & Reteach

GeoFocus Have students complete their graphic organizers and note-taking for the subregion of North Korea and South Korea.

Formal Assessment
- Section Quiz, p. 438

Reteaching Activity
Have students look back through the section and summarize the main ideas of each subsection in their notebooks. Ask them to try to match the main ideas they produce with the objectives for this chapter section listed on page 647 of the Teacher's Edition.

In-Depth Resources: Unit 9
- Reteaching Activity, p. 21

Outline Maps with Activities
- The Koreas: North and South, pp. 95–96

chiefs of the two Koreas met and agreed to reduce tensions along their border. They agreed to discuss clearing land mines so they could rebuild a rail link between the two countries. Perhaps most importantly, families in North Korea and South Korea were allowed to visit each other.

At the summer Olympics held in Sydney, Australia, in 2000, there was another sign of a thaw. The two Koreas marched into the Olympic Stadium under a new flag designed for a single, unified Korea.

There are also setbacks to reunification. One occurred in 2010, when a South Korean ship exploded and sank. Many South Koreans suspected that North Korea had torpedoed the ship.

Economic and Human Resources

Before the Korean War, the economies of North Korea and South Korea were agricultural. After the war, industry gained in importance in both countries.

ECONOMIC PATTERNS If North Korea and South Korea reunite, they will form an economic powerhouse. North Korea will be able to provide natural resources and raw materials for South Korea's industries.

South Korea, like Taiwan, is one of the economic tigers of Asia. It is a highly successful and competitive economy. It has the world's largest shipbuilding industry, as well as large automobile, steel, and chemical industries. South Korea is today one of the world's top trading nations.

POPULATION PATTERNS Most of the people in Korea live on plains along the coast or in river valleys among the mountains of the peninsula. South Korea has 45 percent of the Korean peninsula's land area but about 66 percent of its people. **Seoul** is by far the largest city in South Korea, with a population of more than 10 million. The largest city in North Korea is **Pyongyang,** with more than 2.5 million people.

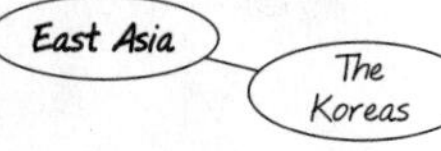

1 Places & Terms
Identify and explain the significance of each of the following in the region.
- Three Kingdoms
- Seoul
- Pyongyang

2 Taking Notes
REGION Use your notes to answer the questions below.

- In which ways has China influenced the culture of Korea?
- Which countries in the region have invaded Korea?

3 Main Ideas
a. What impact has the border between North Korea and South Korea had upon life in both countries?
b. How is the economy of South Korea different from that of North Korea?
c. Which two major influences have shaped North Korea and South Korea since World War II?

4 Geographic Thinking
Drawing Conclusions How has Korea's physical location affected its history? **Think about:**
- the definition of a peninsula
- the location of Korea's neighbors

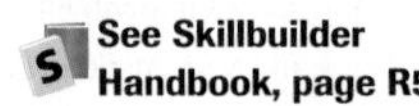

See Skillbuilder Handbook, page R5.

GeoActivity

SEEING PATTERNS Both Taiwan and South Korea are considered economic tigers of East Asia. What are some characteristics that they share? Make a **Venn diagram** showing the similarities and differences between the two.

SECTION 3 ASSESSMENT ANSWERS

1. Places & Terms
Three Kingdoms, p. 647; Seoul, p. 650; Pyongyang, p. 650

2. Taking Notes
- The language shows Chinese influence; Confucianism and Buddhism both came to Korea by way of China.
- Japan and China have both invaded Korea.

3. Main Ideas
a. The border between North Korea and South Korea has been the site of tension and danger. Both countries have had huge armies stationed along the border.
b. South Korea's economy is highly industrialized; North Korea has natural resources and raw materials, but its economy is not as developed as South Korea's.
c. Since World War II, Communism had shaped the culture of North Korea, and Western democracy has shaped South Korea.

4. Geographic Thinking
Korea has been at some times in its history fairly isolated, but at other times, it has interacted with China and Japan, as well as other countries.

GeoActivity

Integrated Assessment
- Rubric for a Venn diagram, 2.8

Japan

Main Ideas

- Japan has an ancient culture and traditions.
- Japan is the economic giant of East Asia.

Places & Terms

samurai

shogun

CONNECT TO THE ISSUES

PHYSICAL FORCES Japan is vulnerable to devastating earthquakes and huge ocean waves because of its location.

A HUMAN PERSPECTIVE The Japanese flag shows a red sun against a white background. The red sun symbolizes Amaterasu, the sun goddess. According to myth, the Japanese emperor and his family are descended from the goddess. The Japanese call their country *Nippon,* which means "source of the sun." The name *Japan* may have come from a Chinese phrase meaning "origin of the sun," or it may have come from *Chipangu,* a name for the country recorded by Marco Polo.

Samurai and Shogun

Japan lies east of China—toward the rising sun. In their earliest history, the Japanese were close enough to China to feel its civilizing effects, but they were far enough away to be protected from invasion.

ANCIENT JAPAN The original inhabitants of Japan may have come to the islands from the mainland of Asia and from the South Pacific. There is some evidence to suggest that the ancestors of today's Japanese came eastward through Siberia and Korea and entered Japan. By about 1,500 years ago, most of Japan was actively growing food, such as rice. Weapons and tools made of bronze and iron were introduced, along with textiles.

Until the A.D. 300s, Japan was not a unified country. It was made up of hundreds of clans ruling separate territories. Then, by the fifth century, the Yamato clan had become the ruling clan. It claimed descent from the sun goddess, and by the seventh century, its leaders called themselves emperors of Japan.

In 794, the rulers moved the capital to the city of Heian (modern Kyoto). The era from 794 to 1185 is called the Heian period. During this time, Japan's central government was strong, but eventually the great landowners and clan chiefs began to act as independent rulers.

Professional soldiers called **samurai** served the interests of the landowners and clan chiefs. The samurai (the word means "one who guards") served as a bodyguard of warriors loyal to the leader of a clan.

THE SHOGUNS In 1192, after a struggle between two powerful clans, the Japanese emperor created the position of shogun. The **shogun** was the general of the emperor's army with the powers of a military dictator.

PLACE This 1597 woodblock print shows a samurai field marshall. **What were important skills and gear for a samurai?**

EAST ASIA

SECTION 4 OBJECTIVES

1. Examine Japan's history.
2. Describe Japan's economic development.
3. Identify aspects of Japanese culture.
4. Examine current aspects of life in Japan.

SKILLBUILDER: Interpreting Maps, p. 653

GeographicThinking

Seeing Patterns, p. 652

Making Inferences, p. 655

Focus & Motivate

What aspects of being an island nation are helpful or harmful to Japan's development? *(Helpful: protected by water barriers, isolation can create strong independent culture; Harmful: lack of resources, lack of land to absorb expanding populations)*

Instruct: Objective 1 appears on p. 652.

Interpreting Graphics

Samurai: field marshall

Have students examine the print. Then, ask them to describe the nature of this historical figure. Ask them what details of the illustration support their description. *(Tough, strong, mean; sword and spear, armor, helmet, frowning face, glaring eyes)*

CAPTION ANSWER courage, fierceness, determination

SECTION 4 PROGRAM RESOURCES

In-Depth Resources: Unit 9
- Guided Reading, p. 16
- Building Vocabulary, p. 18
- Reteaching Activity, p. 22

Guided Reading Workbook
- Section 4

Access for Students Acquiring English
- Guided Reading, p. 153

Outline Maps with Activities
- Japan, pp. 97–98

Cultures Around the World
- Daily Life, p. 50
- Literature, p. 52
- Arts and Crafts, p. 54

Formal Assessment
- Section Quiz, p. 439

Integrated Assessment
- Rubric for an oral report, 3.6
- Rubric for a mask, 1.10
- Rubric for a graph, 2.3

INTEGRATED TECHNOLOGY

Cultures Transparencies CW50, 52, 54
- Practicing Martial Arts
- Haiku
- Practicing Origami

The World's Music Audio Program

Test Generator
- Section Quiz

hmhsocialstudies.com

TEST-TAKING RESOURCES

Strategies for Test Preparation

Test Practice Transparencies TT93

Online Test Practice

Instruct: Objective 

Samurai and Shogun

- From where did the original inhabitants of Japan most likely come? *(Mainland Asia, South Pacific)*
- From whom did the Yamato clan claim descent? *(the sun goddess)*
- For whom did the samurai work? *(landowners and clan chiefs)*

 **In-Depth Resources: Unit 9**
- Guided Reading, p. 16

Instruct: Objective 

An Economic Powerhouse

- Where do most Japanese people live within Japan? *(in cities)*
- Which island of Japan is considered the main island? *(Honshu)*
- How is Japan able to manufacture many items for trade without natural resources? *(It imports the natural resources it needs.)*
- How has Japan's economy recently changed? *(It has slowed down since the 1990s.)*

Interpreting Time Lines

Japanese History, 1500-2000

Have students examine the time line. Ask them what U.S. military figure was characterized in a Japanese woodcut. *(Commodore Perry)* Ask them to name the three shoguns represented in this time line *(Tokugawa Ieyasu, Tsunayoshi, Yoshimune)*

All officials, judges, and armies were under his authority. The shoguns appointed governors, called *daimyo,* to each province. They were responsible for maintaining order.

Rule by the shoguns lasted for about 700 years. During those years, the Japanese fought off Mongol invasions and saw the arrival of Portuguese traders, who brought Christianity and firearms to Japan in the 1500s. In 1853, Commodore Matthew Perry's arrival to Japan from the United States ended Japan's isolation. In 1868, the last shogun resigned, and the emperor became head of the government.

EMERGING WORLD POWER During the late 19th century, Japan's government began bringing Japan into the modern age. By the early 20th century, Japan had become a major power.

During the early years of the 20th century, Japan expanded its empire. (See map on next page.) Its interests and those of the United States came into conflict in the Pacific region. On December 7, 1941, the Japanese launched a surprise attack on the U.S. naval base at Pearl Harbor in Hawaii. The attack brought the United States into World War II, which ended with Japan's defeat and surrender in 1945. A

After World War II, the United States headed the occupation of Japan and introduced political and economic reforms. Eventually Japan became a democracy—a constitutional monarchy with an emperor and an elected parliament.

Geographic Thinking

Seeing Patterns
A How might Japan's 20th century empire have reflected its history?

A. Answer Japan's martial history of samurai and shoguns was continued in the 20th century in military conquest.

An Economic Powerhouse

After its defeat in World War II, Japan transformed itself into one of the world's most powerful economies. It experienced an economic boom, even though it has few natural resources. Japan is second only to the United States in the size of its economy.

PEOPLE AND PRODUCTS The population of Japan is more than 127 million. About 79 percent of Japan's people live in cities. Sixty percent of the people live on 2.7 percent of the land. Japan has few minorities, and those few often experience discrimination.

Japanese History, 1500–2000

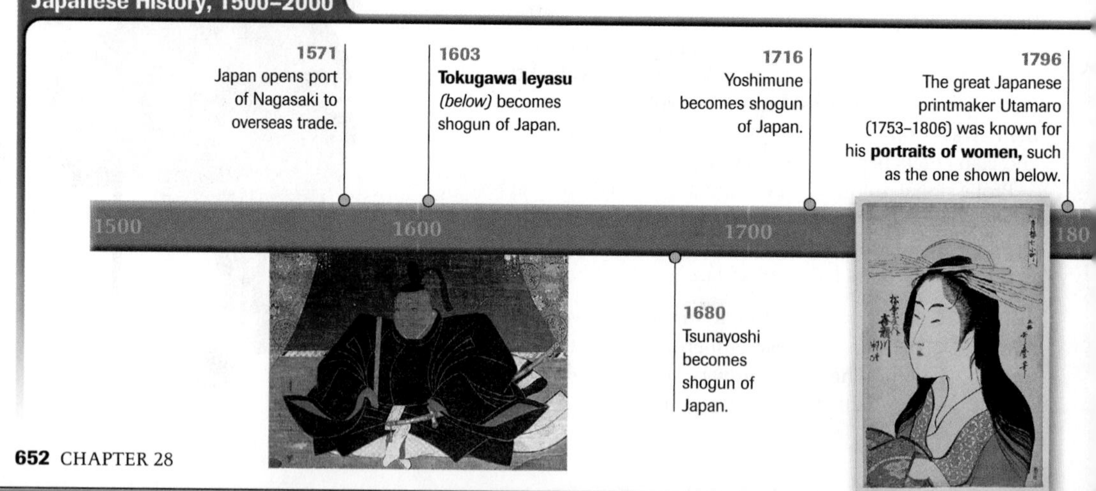
1571
Japan opens port of Nagasaki to overseas trade.
1603
Tokugawa Ieyasu *(below)* becomes shogun of Japan.
1716
Yoshimune becomes shogun of Japan.
1796
The great Japanese printmaker Utamaro (1753–1806) was known for his **portraits of women,** such as the one shown below.
1500
1600
1700
180
1680
Tsunayoshi becomes shogun of Japan.

ACTIVITY OPTION | LINK TO ART

JAPAN REFLECTED IN PRINTS

Objective To show students how art can reflect the geographical features of a country

Class Time 30 minutes

Task To have students find reproductions of Japanese woodcuts that show some of the geography of Japan

Directions Have students use the library to find books with reproductions of Japanese prints that show Japanese landscapes. Ask each student to share one reproduction with the class and describe what it tells about Japan. (You can guide students to information by looking up the following topics or artists: ukiyo-e, woodblock or printing, woodcuts, Hokusai, Hiroshige.)

Japanese Empire, 1942

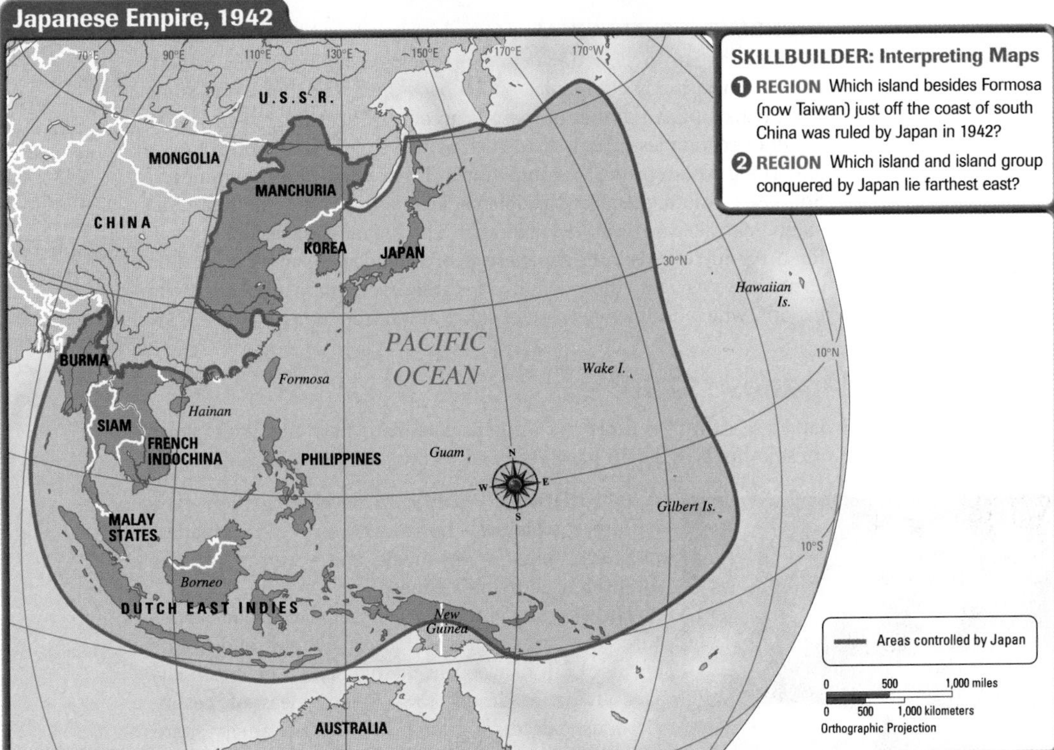

SKILLBUILDER: Interpreting Maps

1. **REGION** Which island besides Formosa (now Taiwan) just off the coast of south China was ruled by Japan in 1942?
2. **REGION** Which island and island group conquered by Japan lie farthest east?

Interpreting Maps

Japanese Empire, 1942

Have students examine the map. Ask them how many countries or parts of countries Japan controlled in 1942. Then ask them what geographical features, if any, those countries seem to have in common. *(Seven or more; many are islands or island nations and colonies)*

SKILLBUILDER ANSWERS:
1. Hainan **2.** Wake and Gilbert Islands.

Most of Japan's population and most of its industry and manufacturing are located in a corridor hundreds of miles long along the east coast of the main island of Honshu, with Tokyo as its anchor. The people who live in this corridor form the work force that produces goods sold around the world.

Manufacturing and trade are at the heart of Japan's economy. Japan imports most of the natural resources for its industrial needs. Among the resources it imports are coal and petroleum. Then it uses those resources and others to manufacture products for export to the global market. Among the most important of those products are cars, trucks, and electronic equipment such as televisions and computers.

A strong alliance between business and government has been one of the reasons for Japan's economic success during the second half of the 20th century. After the war, the United States gave economic assistance to Japan. Financial support from the government helped Japanese businesses develop products to market abroad.

1945
The **mushroom cloud** *(below)* is from an atomic bomb dropped on Nagasaki on August 9, 1945.

1853
A Japanese woodcut shows **Commodore Perry** *(above)* upon his arrival in Japan.

ACTIVITY OPTION **CRITICAL THINKING**

DRAWING CONCLUSIONS

Explaining the Skill Drawing conclusions means analyzing what you have read and forming an opinion about its meaning. To draw conclusions, people look at the facts and then use their common sense and experience to decide what the facts mean. Tell students that an important part of understanding the "big picture" of geography is drawing conclusions from individual features or events.

Applying the Skill Have students pair up and discuss the following questions. What aspects of Japanese culture have been influenced by other countries? Which countries? What aspects of Japanese culture are unique to Japan? Why do you think that is so? After 10 minutes have each pair share their answers with the class. *(Answers will vary but should include language, religion, art, music, government; China, United States, Europe; Kabuki and Noh theater, strong emphasis on harmony with nature in architecture; sumo wrestling)*

Instruct: Objective 3

Japanese Culture

- Which city is an excellent example of traditional Japanese culture? *(Kyoto)*
- What do the Japanese believe is important in designing buildings? *(They should harmonize with nature.)*

Cultures Around the World
- Literature, p. 52
- Arts and Crafts, p. 54

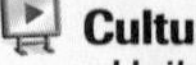

Cultures Transparencies CW52, 54
- Haiku
- Practicing Origami

Instruct: Objective  **4**

Life in Today's Japan

- How does the Japanese school system compare with American education? *(It is more structured and requires more years to complete.)*
- What are private college preparatory schools called in Japan? *(juku)*
- What two problems are the Japanese attempting to address for the future? *(pollution and overcrowding)*

Cultures Around the World
- Daily Life, p. 50

Cultures Transparencies CW50
- Practicing Martial Arts

CAPTION ANSWER It values craftsmanship and tradition.

ECONOMIC SLOWDOWN After four decades of rapid growth, Japan's economy began to slow down in the 1990s. As the economic growth rate declined, many companies scaled back their operations, and some went bankrupt. A number of reasons accounted for this slowdown.

Other economies in East Asia, such as those of Taiwan, South Korea, and Hong Kong, provided competition. Then, when the economies of Southeast Asia encountered problems, Japanese investments there lost value. Many banks proved vulnerable. The Japanese stock market suffered big losses. Also, the Japanese people tended to save rather than spend. As a result, the economy became even more dependent on exports, which declined because of competition from other countries. B

B. Answer Downturns in the economy of one can affect others in region.

CONNECT TO THE ISSUES
TRADE
B How are the economies of the region connected?

Japanese Culture

Japanese culture reflects the influences of both East and West. From these influences, Japan has developed its own unique culture.

PLACE Toyozo Arakawa, one of Japan's leading potters, was named a "Living National Treasure" in 1955.
What does the naming of a person as a national treasure say about a culture?

A TRADITIONAL PEOPLE In developing their early culture, the Japanese borrowed from China. Japanese language, religion, art, music, and government were all influenced by the Chinese.

The city of Kyoto is a monument to Japanese culture. The city contains Buddhist temples and Shinto shrines built of wood in the old style. The entire city is a living testament to Japanese ideas of beauty. Gardens, palaces, and temples all reflect a very spare, elegant, and refined style. In Kyoto and throughout Japan, great emphasis is placed on achieving harmony between a building and its natural surroundings.

Traditional drama is still performed in Japan. Noh plays developed during the 14th century. They deal with subjects drawn from history and legend and are performed by actors wearing masks. In the 17th century, Kabuki plays developed. They have colorful scenery, an exaggerated acting style, and vivid costumes.

Japanese painting was influenced by Chinese techniques and themes. Many early Japanese paintings show Buddhist themes that often came to Japan by way of China. Some examples of Japanese artistic works include long picture scrolls, ink paintings, and wood-block prints.

BACKGROUND
A tradition of print-making native to Japan is called *ukiyo-e,* which means "pictures of the floating world," the Japanese term for scenes from everyday life.

WESTERN INFLUENCES Since the day in 1853 when Commodore Perry sailed his fleet into Tokyo Bay, Japan has been open to Western influences. Those influences are visible in modern-day Japan.

Sports like baseball, golf, sumo wrestling, soccer, and tennis are popular in Japan. The clothes worn by most people are Western in style, although traditional clothing is worn on special occasions.

Western music is also popular in Japan. Rock music is popular among younger Japanese. They listen to Western groups and form rock bands of their own. Many cities in Japan have symphony orchestras that play Western classical music. Jazz is also popular.

Japan has been successful at balancing its traditional styles in art, theater, music, and architecture with influences from the West.

ACTIVITY OPTION **EXPLORING LOCAL GEOGRAPHY**

SOLVING A REAL PROBLEM

Objective To help students apply local experience or knowledge to geographical material

Class Time 30 minutes

Task Have a group discussion on overcrowding in cities

Directions Have students break into small groups and discuss the issue of overcrowding in cities. Ask them: What causes overcrowding in cities? How does it affect people? Then, have them discuss ideas for solving the problem or avoiding the problem in the future. They must suggest at least two reasonable ideas.

654 CHAPTER 28

Life in Today's Japan

The people of Japan are educated and disciplined. This work force has enabled Japan to achieve prosperity.

EDUCATION Japan's educational system is highly structured. Students often attend school six days a week. They have a shorter summer vacation than American students—just six weeks in late July and August. Students attend six years of elementary school and three years of junior high school. Education is free during those years. Then they spend three years in high school. At the same time, many students attend classes at private schools called *juku* to help get them into good colleges.

Competition among students is high to gain admission to the best universities. Japan has more than 1,000 universities and technical colleges. Universities that rank at the top of the educational system include the University of Tokyo, Kyoto University, Keio University, and Waseda University.

CHANGES IN SOCIETY The Japanese are making some changes in the way their society is run. People are now increasingly demanding an end to pollution and overcrowding. Furthermore, workers at all skill levels are asking for shorter workdays and more vacation time.

In the next chapter, you will read about three important issues in East Asia. These include trade, the pressures of a large population, and the dangers posed by volcanoes around the Pacific Ocean.

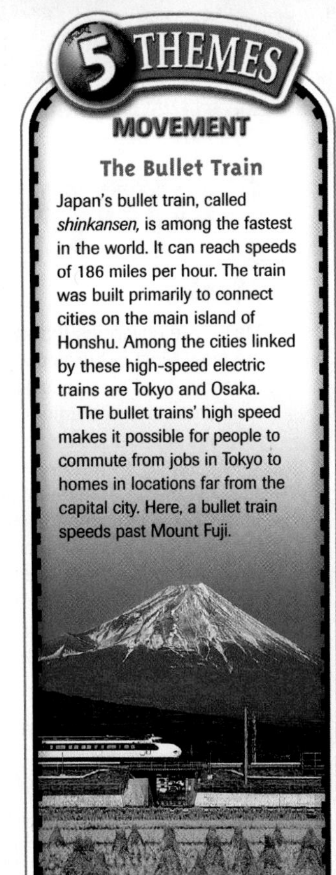

The Bullet Train

Japan's bullet train, called *shinkansen*, is among the fastest in the world. It can reach speeds of 186 miles per hour. The train was built primarily to connect cities on the main island of Honshu. Among the cities linked by these high-speed electric trains are Tokyo and Osaka.

The bullet trains' high speed makes it possible for people to commute from jobs in Tokyo to homes in locations far from the capital city. Here, a bullet train speeds past Mount Fuji.

Section 4 Assessment

1 Places & Terms

Identify and explain the significance of each of the following in the region.

- samurai
- shogun

2 Taking Notes

REGION Use your notes to answer the questions below.

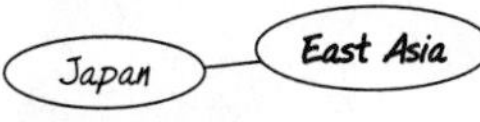

- What happened to Japan in World War II?
- What is the importance of education in Japan today?

3 Main Ideas

a. What is the basis of Japan's economic prosperity?

b. What are some examples of traditional Japanese culture?

c. How did the Western world influence Japan beginning in the 19th century?

4 Geographic Thinking

Making Inferences How might Japan's isolation and its uniform population have both helped and hindered it in its attempts to achieve prosperity? **Think about:**

- the advantages of uniformity
- the importance of creativity

SEEING PATTERNS Japan has some very distinctive cultural forms, such as Kabuki theater and sumo wrestling. Present a brief **report** to the class on some aspect of Japanese culture, illustrated by visuals that you have found in your research.

EAST ASIA

Instruct: Objective 4 appears on p. 654.

5 THEMES

Movement: The Bullet Train

Have students read the information in the text box. Tell students that additional expenditures on bullet trains and new routes have been criticized in recent years as much too expensive for the already overburdened Japanese economy. Ask students what they think about the idea of such trains? Would bullet trains work in our country? *(Answers will vary, although some students may note that the distances to be covered are much greater in this country.)*

Assess & Reteach

GeoFocus Have students complete their graphic organizers and notetaking for the subregion of Japan.

Formal Assessment
- Section Quiz, p. 439

Reteaching Activity

Have students review the section and summarize the main idea of each part of this chapter section in their notebooks. Then ask them to divide into pairs and compare the main ideas they have produced. Ask them to evaluate how their main ideas match the objectives for the section.

In-Depth Resources: Unit 9
- Reteaching Activity, p. 22

Outline Maps with Activities
- Japan, pp. 97–98

SECTION 4 ASSESSMENT ANSWERS

1. Places & Terms

samurai, p. 651 shogun, p. 651

2. Taking Notes

- Japan was defeated by the United States and its allies and then occupied at the end of the war.
- Education is highly valued in Japan, and competition to get into the best colleges is fierce.

3. Main Ideas

a. Manufacturing and trade are at the heart of Japan's economy.

b. Buddhist temples and Shinto shrines, Kabuki and Noh drama, and scroll paintings are all examples of traditional Japanese culture.

c. Japan's isolation ended with the arrival of Commodore Perry in 1853. Then it became a major military and industrial power.

4. Geographic Thinking

The uniformity of its population and its isolation as an island permitted it to develop without much outside interference. Its people generally shared the same values and beliefs, making it easy to focus on common goals. However, this uniformity might have made people less receptive to creative differences and independent thinking.

GeoActivity

Integrated Assessment
- Rubric for an oral report, 3.6

OBJECTIVES

Compare the art of mask-making in different cultures of the world.

Instruct: Objective

Masks

- What are some uses for masks? *(ceremonial, theatrical, burial, festival)*
- When are masks used in the United States? *(Mardi Gras in New Orleans, Native American ceremonies)*
- How long have masks been in existence? *(at least 30,000 years)*

Interpreting Maps

Have students examine the world map as well as the photo captions. Ask them to name each continent and country represented on the map. *(North America–United States; Africa–Angola; Asia–Indonesia and Japan)*

hmhsocialstudies.com INTERACTIVE

Comparing Cultures

Masks

Masks are coverings that disguise the face. Most cultures use masks for a variety of purposes. Followers sometimes wear ceremonial masks during religious celebrations. Actors wear theatrical masks during performances such as those in the classical drama of ancient Greece, China, and Japan. Mourners sometimes placed burial masks over the faces of the dead before they were buried. In ancient Egypt, they placed the mask directly on the mummy or else on the mummy case. Participants sometimes wear festival masks during celebrations such as Mardi Gras in New Orleans or Carnival in Rio de Janeiro.

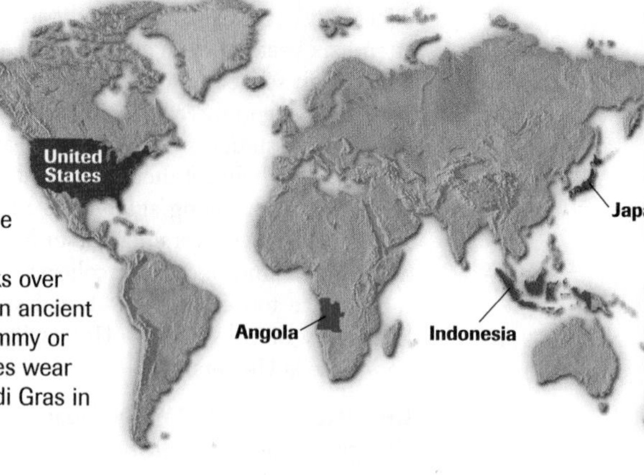

This mask from Angola represents a female ancestor with an elaborate headdress. A member of the Chokwe culture in Africa created this mask out of wood and fibers in the 20th century.

A masked dancer in Bali, Indonesia, performs a ritual dance. Balinese dancers move to the music of gongs and flutes. In their dances, each movement and gesture helps to tell the story.

656 CHAPTER 28

SUPPORTING RESOURCES

BOOKS FOR THE TEACHER

Nunley, John W., and Cara McCarty. ***Masks: Faces of Culture.*** NY: Abrams, 1999.

Emigh, John. ***Masked Performance: The Play of Self and Other in Ritual and Theatre.*** Philadelphia, PA: Univ. of Pennsylvania Press, 1996.

BOOKS FOR THE STUDENT

MacNair, Peter, et al. ***Down from the Shimmering Sky: Masks of the Northwest Coast.*** Seattle, WA: Univ. of Washington Press, 1998.

Finley, Carol. ***The Art of African Masks: Exploring Cultural Traditions.*** Minneapolis, MN: Lerner Publications, 1999.

VIDEO

National Geographic: ***Bali: Masterpiece of the Gods.*** Questar Inc., 1991.

Joseph Campbell's The Power of Myth. Vol. 6: The Masks of Eternity. Mystic Fire, 1991.

INTERNET

For more on masks, visit . . .

hmhsocialstudies.com

Native American ceremonial masks were used to calm angry spirits. This mask is a product of the Iroquois culture of the northeast woodlands and was used in healing ceremonies.

Japanese masks and costumes are worn by a performer in a Noh drama, the classical drama of Japan. Masked performers create music and dance in a highly stylized manner.

GeoActivity

MAKING MASKS 

Use the Internet to research how to make different kinds of masks. Choose materials that are easy to obtain. Then make a **mask** that you will show to the class.

- Use a technique about which you have found information.
- Write a description of the procedure you followed to make the mask.
- Display your mask in an area set aside in the classroom.

hmhsocialstudies.com RESEARCH WEB LINKS

GeoData

ODD FACTS ABOUT MASKS

- In Europe, masks have been discovered that date back as early as 30,000 years ago to Paleolithic times.
- The solid gold death mask of the pharaoh Tutankhamen, which covered the head of his mummy, weighs 22.5 pounds.
- Masks were worn by the performers of tragedies and comedies in ancient Greece.
- The Senesi people of New Guinea use masks that include skirts that cover much of the body.
- The Aleuts of Alaska cover the faces of their dead with wooden masks.
- Death masks made of plaster are sometimes put on the face of the dead to preserve their features for posterity. Death masks exist for Napoleon Bonaparte and Ludwig van Beethoven.
- The mask worn by actor Clayton Moore in the television show *The Lone Ranger* was sold at auction for $33,000.

GeoActivities

Integrated Assessment
- Rubric for a mask, 1.10

Interpreting Photographs

Looking through the Mask

Have students look at the photograph of the Angolan mask. Ask students to describe the expression on the face of the mask. What details in the mask support your description? *(Answers will vary, but may include the following: The face looks sad or even scared because of the squinting eyes and clenched teeth.)*

Have students look at the Native American mask and read the caption. Ask students what features of this mask might help "calm angry spirits"? *(silly smile, gentle eyes, nonthreatening, even comic expression)*

Have students look at the Japanese and Indonesian masks and read the captions. Ask students to list similarities between the masks. *(both used in performance, both masks of human faces, both white with painted black and red details)*

ACTIVITY OPTION | COOPERATIVE LEARNING

RESEARCHING AND SHARING

Objective To help students see similarities and differences between cultural uses and production of masks

Class Time 30 minutes

Task Research one culture's masks and share information through interviews

Directions Divide the class into small groups. Assign each group a cultural group or region (Native American, especially Pacific Northwest, Japanese, African, or Indonesian), and have students research mask-making and use in their assigned culture. Students should find information specifically on materials used and the uses of the masks. Give each student a specific role. Roles might include the following:

- research the materials used
- research the context for the use of masks
- research the role and status of the mask maker in assigned culture

Then have the groups exchange information.

Reviewing Places & Terms

A. **1.** dynasty, p. 635
2. Boxer Rebellion, p. 636
3. Mao Zedong, p. 636
4. Confucianism, p. 638
5. Pacific Rim, p. 645
6. Three Kingdoms, p. 647
7. Seoul, p. 650
8. Pyongyang, p. 650
9. samurai, p. 651
10. shogun, p. 651

B. Possible Responses

11. The Pacific Rim is the region extending from New Zealand in the western Pacific to Chile in the eastern Pacific.
12. Samurai means "one who guards."
13. Pyongyang is the largest city in North Korea.
14. Seoul has a population of about 10 million.
15. The Boxer Rebellion was ended by a multinational force of about 20,000.
16. A shogun was a leader who had the powers of a military dictator.
17. Confucianism emphasizes respect for the past and for ancestors.
18. Mao Zedong ruled China from 1949 to 1976.
19. The Shang and the Han were Chinese dynasties.
20. Koguryo, Paekche, and Silla were the Three Kingdoms of Korea.

Chapter 28 Assessment

VISUAL SUMMARY
HUMAN GEOGRAPHY OF EAST ASIA

Subregions of East Asia

China
- China has more people than any other country in the world.
- It is about the same size as the United States in area.
- It has been the dominant culture in the region since ancient times.

Mongolia and Taiwan
- The histories of Mongolia and Taiwan have been closely linked with that of China.
- They have pursued separate paths of development—Mongolia has had a managed economy, while Taiwan has a capitalist economy based on manufacturing and trade.

The Koreas: North and South
- The Korean peninsula is divided into two separate countries: Communist North Korea and capitalist South Korea.
- Recently, the two countries have begun discussing the possibility of becoming one country.

Japan
- Japan is a great industrial power.
- It has managed to achieve economic prosperity despite its small land area and limited resources.

Reviewing Places & Terms

A. Briefly explain the importance of each of the following.

1. dynasty
2. Boxer Rebellion
3. Mao Zedong
4. Confucianism
5. Pacific Rim
6. Three Kingdoms
7. Seoul
8. Pyongyang
9. samurai
10. shogun

B. Answer the questions about vocabulary in complete sentences.

11. Which area extends from New Zealand in the western Pacific to Chile in the eastern Pacific?
12. What term means "one who guards"?
13. What is the largest city in North Korea?
14. Which city in the Koreas has about 10 million residents?
15. What event did it take a multinational force of 20,000 soldiers to end?
16. Which term describes a leader with the powers of a military dictator?
17. In which system of thought was there respect for the past and one's ancestors?
18. Who ruled the People's Republic of China from 1949 to 1976?
19. The Shang and the Han are examples of what?
20. Koguryo, Paekche, and Silla made up what?

Main Ideas

China (pp. 635-641)

1. In what ways has China influenced other cultures in the region?
2. How is China able to feed its enormous population?
3. What are some of the basic beliefs of Confucianism?

Mongolia and Taiwan (pp. 642-646)

4. What kind of economy does Mongolia have, and what activity is at its core?
5. What kind of economy does Taiwan have?

The Koreas: North and South (pp. 647-650)

6. Why did North Korea become a communist state and South Korea a democracy?
7. Why is South Korea considered an economic tiger?

Japan (pp. 651-657)

8. Why did Japan emerge onto the world scene in the 19th century?
9. Why is the city of Kyoto in Japan important?
10. Where does Japan get its resources, and how does it use them in its industries?

Main Ideas

1. language, inventions, religious traditions, and fine arts
2. Vast river basins in the east have rich soil.
3. respect for the past, the value of an orderly society, and the importance of education
4. Mongolia has had a state-run economy, although it is attempting to shift to a market economy; herding and managing livestock
5. Taiwan has a manufacturing economy and trades with the rest of the world.
6. Japan controlled Korea through World War II. With Japan's defeat, the northern part of Korea came under the control of the Soviet Union and the southern part came under the influence of the United States.
7. because it is highly prosperous, with successful shipbuilding, automobile, steel, and chemical industries
8. mainly because of the visit by the American fleet commanded by Commodore Perry
9. Kyoto's Buddhist temples, Shinto shrines, gardens, and palaces are a monument to traditional Japanese culture.
10. Japan imports resources then uses them to make products that are sold around the world.

Critical Thinking

1. Using Your Notes

Use your completed chart to answer these questions.

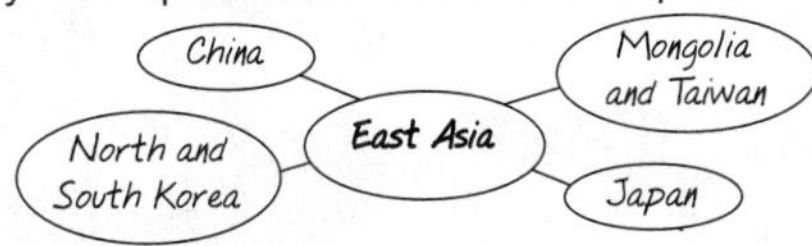

a. What are some of the ways in which China has influenced the culture of East Asia?

b. What seems to be the general direction of economic development in the region?

2. Geographic Themes

a. **HUMAN-ENVIRONMENT INTERACTION** How have the river basins of eastern China supported a high population density?

b. **REGION** What are some of the natural barriers that have provided isolation or security to the different countries of the region?

3. Identifying Themes

Interaction between cultures occurred throughout the region. What are some of the consequences of this interaction? Which of the five themes are reflected in your answer?

4. Making Inferences

What might be the effect of innovations of modern life, such as computers and the Internet, on the development of democracy and free-market economies in the region?

5. Making Comparisons

How would you compare the economic prosperity and success of managed and capitalist economies in the region?

For Additional Test Practice

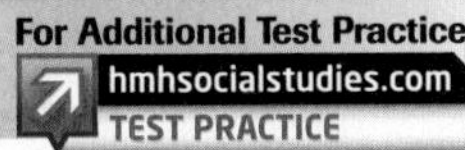

Geographic Skills: Interpreting Graphs

Stock Market in South Korea

Use the graph at right to answer the following questions.

1. **ANALYZING DATA** When did the stock market in South Korea reach its lowest level?
2. **MAKING COMPARISONS** What was its highest level before its plunge?
3. **DRAWING CONCLUSIONS** What level did it reach by the year 2000? What does this suggest about the economy of South Korea?

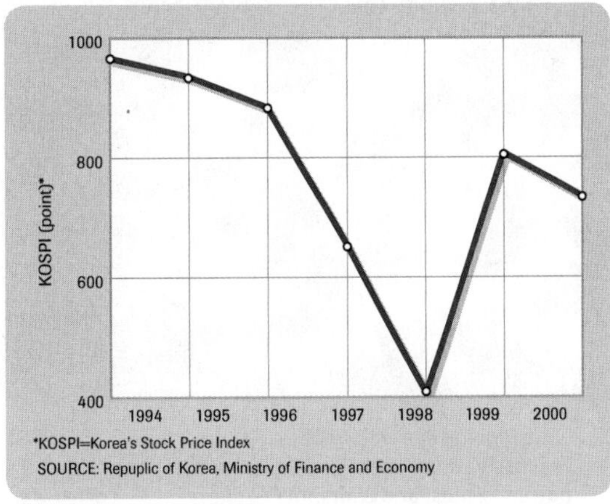

*KOSPI=Korea's Stock Price Index

SOURCE: Repuplic of Korea, Ministry of Finance and Economy

The stock market in South Korea has seen dramatic ups and downs corresponding to the economic crises in the region in recent years.

Research stock market activity in one or more of the other countries in the region. Show your findings in a graph tracking stock market activity for the late 1990s.

hmhsocialstudies.com

MULTIMEDIA ACTIVITY

Use the links at **hmhsocialstudies.com** to do research on the Mongol conquests. Focus on the reasons for the success of their conquests and whether the results of their conquests were mainly negative or positive.

Analyzing Data Present the results of your research in a chart that shows the positive and negative effects of the Mongol conquests.

EAST ASIA

Critical Thinking

1. a. Chinese language, inventions, religious and ethical ideas, artistic traditions, and ruling dynasties
b. Japan, Taiwan, and South Korea have capitalist economies. China and Mongolia are moving toward free-market economies. North Korea has a managed economy.

2. a. The river basins provide rich farm land to support the population.
b. China has been protected by the mountains and deserts of the west and northwest. Japan and Taiwan are islands. Korea is a peninsula.

3. China influenced the cultures of the region. But there was mutual interaction. Mongolia, for example, ruled China under Genghis Khan and Kublai Khan. Japan's prosperity served as a model for other economies in the region. Themes include region and human-environment interaction.

4. Computers and the Internet encourage the spread of information that governments cannot control. This encourages democracy and free-market economies.

5. The free-market, capitalist economies have been much more successful than the state-controlled economies.

GeoActivity

Integrated Assessment
- Rubric for a graph, 2.3

Formal Assessment
- Chapter Test, Forms A, B, and C, pp. 440-451

Geographic Skills

1. 1998
2. About 960 in 1994
3. About 730; it has recovered from the 1998 low, although it was still not as high as it was in 1994.

MULTIMEDIA ACTIVITY

For a chart on the Mongol conquests, students should:

- Present a concise, well-organized presentation on the positive and negative effects of the conquests.
- Summarize the impact of the conquests.
- Produce clear, imaginative visuals for the presentation.
- Include references to the Web sites used as sources.

Grading Rubric Evaluate student performance as Exceptional, Acceptable, or Poor in each of the following categories:

	Exceptional	Acceptable	Poor
Presentation is clear, focused, and logical			
Chart clearly states topic and purpose			
Provides neccessary facts and examples			
Shows positive and negative effects			

Multimedia Classroom

The **HISTORY™ Multimedia Classroom** is a set of exciting new social studies teaching tools featuring award-winning program content. These comprehensive lesson plans, correlated to individual state and national curriculum standards, are easy to use for both teachers and students.

Each lesson contains the following:

- Short video segments that bring history topics to life
- Maps and visual materials
- Discussion and review questions
- Easily printable primary source documents
- Classroom activities and Internet-based activity links

The Multimedia Classroom has been specially designed to be versatile and easily adaptable to existing courses, lesson plans, and syllabi. Every lesson is designed to offer maximum flexibility. Teachers can select entire plans or only the elements they need, allowing them to individually tailor each lesson. Each multimedia lesson is available in CD-ROM format and is accompanied by full-length award-winning programs on DVD from HISTORY™.

For more information or to purchase go to hmhsocialstudies.com

Because some of these lessons may contain video material of a sensitive nature, we recommend that teachers and parents review these materials in their entirety before screening them to students.

MULTIMEDIA CONNECTIONS

HISTORY

China and the Great Wall

Today, the Great Wall of China is an impressive symbol of the Asian giant's power, genius, and endurance. It wasn't always so. For much of its history, the Chinese people saw the Great Wall as a symbol of cruelty and oppression. This is just one way in which the wall differs from what we think we know. In contrast to popular notions, the wall that draws tourists to Beijing by the millions was not built 2,000 years ago. Nor is the Great Wall a single wall. Instead, it was patched together from walls built over many centuries. And for all its grandeur, the wall failed to keep China safe from invasion.

Explore facts and fictions about the Great Wall online. You can find more information, video clips, primary sources, activities, and more at hmhsocialstudies.com.

China and the Great Wall

Resources 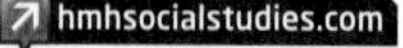

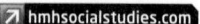

The following resources come with printable introductions, comprehension and critical thinking questions, transcripts, and vocabulary support.

Full Length DVD

Modern Marvels: Great Wall of China (50 mins)

Video Clips

- The Great Wall of China (2:30)
- Great Wall Facts and Fictions (3:24)
- A Land of Walls Within Walls (2:51)
- New Philosophies Emerge (1:33)
- The First Emperor of China (3:18)
- Constructing the Great Wall (3:52)
- The Human Costs of Building (3:19)
- China's Shortest Dynasty (3:59)
- A Mongol Empire in China (4:26)
- Ming Dynasty Wall Building (2:30)
- Guarding Against Invaders (3:18)
- Twentieth-Century China (4:06)

Primary Sources

- *The Analects* of Confucius
- A Legalist's View of Learning
- Memorial Stone Inscription
- Terra-cotta Tomb Soldiers
- Memoirs of an Italian Traveler
- The Gazetteer of Nanjing
- Hall of Supreme Harmony
- A Protest of the Opium Trade

CLICK THROUGH INTER/ACTIVITIES
hmhsocialstudies.com

The Great Wall of China
Watch the video to learn the history and significance of the magnificent, mysterious walls that snake across northern China.

A Land of Walls Within Walls
Watch the video to learn how the Great Wall fits within the ancient Chinese tradition of wall-building.

The Human Costs of Building
Watch the video to learn about the miseries that awaited the men who built the wall.

Twentieth-Century China
Watch the video to examine the role that the wall has played in modern Chinese history.

Maps
- The Qin Empire
- The Han Empire

Activities
- Replicas of the Great Wall
- A Philosophical Debate
- Leaders Envision the Wall
- Silk Road Exchange
- Asia's Unparalleled Empire
- On the Road with Marco Polo
- Understanding Modern China

General Review Questions

General Discussion Questions

Web Links

Bibliography

Lesson Preview

The Great Wall of China
The Great Wall of China winds up to 4,000 miles across the Chinese landscape, from where the mountains meet the Yellow Sea to the eastern edge of the Gobi Desert. Yet the full history of this remarkable structure was long unknown in the West. Nor has the wall always been popular with the Chinese people, who at times have chipped away big chunks of it. Yet the wall endures and continues to capture our imaginations.

A Land of Walls Within Walls
Qin Shi Huangdi, China's first emperor, is credited with building the first version of the wall. But the idea of constructing an immense barrier across China's northern frontier developed from an ancient tradition. For centuries, the Chinese had built walls—around houses, temples, and huge tracts of land. In fact, during the Warring States period, warlords built some 2,800 miles of walls in frantic efforts to keep their enemies at bay.

The Human Costs of Building
Cold, heat, thirst, starvation, beatings by overseers—all were among the hardships that workers faced when they were sent north to build the wall. The laborers' sacrifices are highlighted in the story of the faithful Lady Meng, who traveled to the wall to find her husband, only to find him dead. Legend tells us that the corpses of men who died working on the wall were simply thrown in with the dirt and rocks that filled its center.

Twentieth-Century China
During the 20th century, the Great Wall's fortunes rose and fell just as the wall itself climbs up and down mountains. Early in the century, Western tourists were entranced with the wall's grandeur. The Chinese, however, were indifferent. During the Communist Revolution, the Great Wall was briefly a symbol of the people's struggle. Later, it became an emblem of imperial oppression. As China opened to the West, the Great Wall again became a positive image—both for Western visitors and the Chinese.

CHAPTER 29 PLANNING GUIDE

Today's Issues: East Asia

OVERVIEW	INSTRUCTIONAL RESOURCES	
ESSENTIAL QUESTION How have rapid changes affected the people of East Asia? **Focus on the Essential Question Podcast**	**In-Depth Resources: Unit 9** • Building Vocabulary, p. 29 **Block Schedule Strategies** **Chapter Summaries** (English/Spanish)	**Interactive Online Edition** TOS **ExamView® Assessment Suite** (English/Spanish) TOS **CalendarPlanner** **Power Presentations with Media Gallery** **Critical Thinking Transparencies** • CT29 hmhsocialstudies.com INTERACTIVE
SECTION 1 **THE RING OF FIRE** **MAIN IDEAS** • Japan and Taiwan are part of a geologically active area called the Ring of Fire. • Japan has faced disastrous earthquakes, volcanoes, and tsunamis. • Japan has focused on disaster preparedness as a way to cope with the danger.	**In-Depth Resources: Unit 9** • Guided Reading, p. 23 • Map and Graph Skills, pp. 26–27 • Building Vocabulary, p. 29 • Exploring Today's Issues, pp. 30–31 • Reteaching Activity, p. 34 • GeoWorkshop, pp. 37–38 **Guided Reading Workbook,** Section 1	**Map Transparencies** • MT50 The Ring of Fire
SECTION 2 **TRADE AND PROSPERITY** **MAIN IDEAS** • Once isolated East Asian countries have grown into economic powerhouses. • The 1990s decline of Asian economies had global impact.	**In-Depth Resources: Unit 9** • Guided Reading, p. 24 • Skillbuilder Practice, p. 28 • Building Vocabulary, p. 29 • Exploring Today's Issues, pp. 32–33 • Reteaching Activity, p. 35 **Guided Reading Workbook,** Section 2	**Critical Thinking Transparencies** • CT61 Exports from Jakota Triangle Countries
CASE STUDY **POPULATION AND THE QUALITY OF LIFE** **MAIN IDEAS** • Population growth and lack of resources and/or land space have plagued East Asian countries since the middle of the 20th century. • The quality of life in various countries has been affected by this tremendous growth.	**In-Depth Resources: Unit 9** • Guided Reading, p. 25 • Building Vocabulary, p. 29 • Reteaching Activity, p. 36 **Guided Reading Workbook,** Case Study	

ASSESSMENT

SE **Chapter Assessment,** pp. 672–673

Formal Assessment
- Chapter Tests, Forms A, B, and C, pp. 455–466

TOS **ExamView® Assessment Suite**

Strategies for Test Preparation

hmhsocialstudies.com TEST PRACTICE

SE **Section Assessment,** p. 663

Formal Assessment
- Section Quiz, p. 452

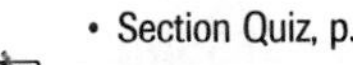

Integrated Assessment
- Rubric for a brochure, 1.13

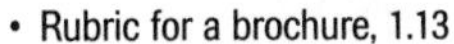

Test Practice Transparencies TT94

SE **Section Assessment,** p. 667

Formal Assessment
- Section Quiz, p. 453

Integrated Assessment
- Rubric for a class report, 2.5

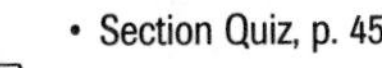

Test Practice Transparencies TT95

SE **Case Study Project,** pp. 670–671

Formal Assessment
- Case Study Quiz, p. 454

Integrated Assessment
- Rubric for a bar graph, 2.3

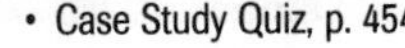

Test Practice Transparencies TT96

CHART KEY:

SE Student Edition	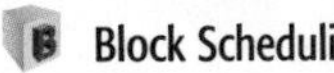 Block Scheduling	 DVD/CD-ROM
TE Teacher's Edition	TOS Teacher One Stop	 MP3 Audio
 Printable Resource	 Presentation Resource	 HISTORY™

Program Resources available on TOS and @ hmhsocialstudies.com

SUPPORTING RESOURCES

- Multimedia Classroom Global History Series
- Global History Teacher's Guide

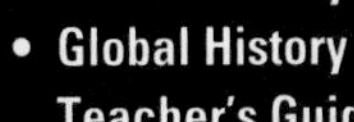

Social Studies Trade Library Collection
- Pacific Rim Trade Collection

For more information or to purchase these resources, go to hmhsocialstudies.com

DIFFERENTIATED INSTRUCTION

English Learners	Struggling Readers	Gifted and Talented Students
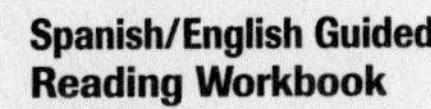 **Spanish/English Guided Reading Workbook**  **Access for Students Acquiring English/ESL** Spanish Translations, pp. 155–160  **Chapter Summaries** (English/Spanish)	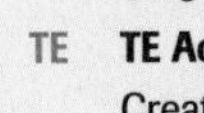 **Chapter Summaries** (English/Spanish) TE **TE Activity** Creating an Earthquake Preparation Diagram, p. 662	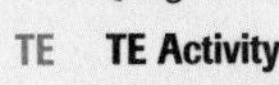 **In-Depth Resources: Unit 9** GeoWorkshop, p. 37 TE **TE Activity** Preparing a Progress Report, p. 669

ENRICHMENT ACTIVITIES

The following activities are especially suitable for classes following block schedules.

SE **Student Edition,** pp. 660–673
- Interpreting a Proportional Circle Map, p. 664

hmhsocialstudies.com RESEARCH WEB LINKS
- Case Study Project, p. 670

CHAPTER 29 PACING GUIDE

BLOCK SCHEDULE LESSON PLAN OPTIONS: 90-MINUTE PERIOD

DAY 1

SECTION 1, pp. 660-663
Class Time 65 minutes

- **Small Group Discussion** As a way to review the section, divide the class into groups of four. Give each group a question to consider. Create the questions based on information in the section (for example, How does living in the Ring of Fire affect people's lives? How can disasters such as earthquakes be prepared for?). Ask the groups to propose answers to the question and then apply that topic to their own knowledge and experience in discussing that topic in a more general way (e.g., earthquakes, disaster preparedness), or in relation to something else (e.g., flood plains, hurricane zones).
Class Time 30 minutes

MAP AND GRAPH SKILLS, p. 664

- **Map and Graph Skills** Complete the map skills activity on PE page 664, and the Map and Graph Skills worksheet.
Class Time 35 minutes

DAY 2

SECTION 2, pp. 665-667
Class Time 60 minutes

- **Clippings** As a way to extend information beyond the chapter section, give students a number of current periodicals and newspapers with world news coverage. Have them try to find articles that somehow relate to general or specific issues covered in the section (e.g., trade, economy, technology or auto industries in Asia, recession, child labor, population growth, environmental concerns). Have them clip out an article and then let everyone read their clipping to the class.
Class Time 60 minutes

- **Skillbuilder Lesson** Use the activity option about distinguishing facts from opinions on TE page 670 and the Skillbuilder Practice worksheet.
Class Time 30 minutes

DAY 3

CASE STUDY, pp. 668-671
Class Time 35 minutes

- **Class Debate** Introduce the Case Study by reviewing the information that is given on the issue of overpopulation in China. Then divide the class into two teams. Have one team argue in favor of a one-child policy and the other team argue against it. Have one or more representatives from the teams stand up and make points to support their position or to counter the other team's argument.

CHAPTER 29 REVIEW AND ASSESSMENT, pp. 672-673
Class Time 55 minutes

- **Review** Have students prepare a summary of the chapter using the words in the Places and Terms list on the first page of each section.
Class Time 20 minutes

- **Assessment** Have students complete the Chapter 29 Assessment.
Class Time 35 minutes

TEACHER-TESTED ACTIVITY: *Environmental Debate*

Class Time 2-3 class periods

Task To debate the pros and cons of environmental, economic, and population issues facing East Asia

Supplies
- newspapers
- library
- Internet access

Purpose To have students research possible solutions to various economic, political, and population pressures on the environment in East Asia

Activity Divide students into the number of groups that you would like to investigate the different aspects of population pressures on the region's environment, as seen, for example, in the effects of pollution on land, air, and water. Have each group divide into two smaller groups, one pro and one con, regarding possible solutions or strategies, such as the Three Gorges Dam, land reclamation projects, family planning, and so forth. After the students research and debate, have the entire group come to consensus on option(s) that could be implemented.

Craig T. Grace
Geography Teacher, Lanier High School, West Austin, TX

TECHNOLOGY IN THE CLASSROOM

Because it's so easy to publish on the Internet, any individual or organization can use the Internet to publicize its viewpoints. While this fact may cause people to question the validity of Web-based sources, the Web can be put to good use in the classroom if students are given guidance and are encouraged to think carefully about the sources of information they come across. Students can use the Internet to learn about different opinions on an issue, to help formulate their own opinions, and to gain experience in "reading between the lines" of media messages.

Objective Students will read and discuss opposing viewpoints on the Web that are related to economic issues discussed in chapter 29.

Task Have students go to four Web sites to see what two companies and two nonprofit organizations say about factory labor in China. Then hold a class debate or discussion on the issues.

Class Time 1-2 class periods

1. Have students read pages 665-667. Ask them to summarize the reasons why the "Asian economic miracle" occurred and why it collapsed. Then ask if they've heard about sweatshops, and discuss what they know about the sweatshop issue.
2. Inform students that there are different viewpoints on the issue of overseas labor and sweatshops. Companies that employ cheap labor overseas, as in East Asia, claim that they're providing needed jobs and helping to raise the standard of living in those countries. Labor organizations and other nonprofit groups argue that many overseas factory workers are paid too little to meet the cost of living in their countries and are often mistreated.
3. Ask students where they might go for information on these different viewpoints. How can they find out what each side is saying? Discuss the benefits and difficulties of using the Internet to learn about opposing points of view. Students probably know that, since anyone can publish anything on the Internet, many opinions and viewpoints can be found. While it's easy to access information and to learn about different points of view, it's also important to figure out who is saying what and why they are making these statements.
4. Have students go to the Web sites listed at **hmhsocialstudies.com** to read opposing viewpoints on the issue of factory labor employed by American companies in China. Ask them to take notes on the different arguments they read, including specific examples when possible.
5. Ask students to go to the home page for each Web site to learn more about the organization that sponsors the site, and ask them to write sentences answering the questions "Who sponsors this Web site? What are this organization's goals? Why do you think this organization has published its point of view on the Web?"
6. Have students hold a class debate or discussion on the arguments that have been presented on the Web sites. They should also discuss the motivations of the sponsoring organizations and the reasons why the organizations have published their opinions on the Web.

CHAPTER 29 OBJECTIVE

To learn about current issues East Asians face, and the attempts to solve these problems

Chapter 29 TODAY'S ISSUES East Asia

Interpreting Photographs

Kobe, Japan Earthquake

Ask students to examine the photograph and read the caption. What aspects of a city could be affected by such a disaster? *(roads, buildings, power supplies, overtaxing of hospitals, police, and rescue workers)*

Introducing the Essential Question

- Ask students if they knew that an active volcano is visible from an urban agglomeration of some 35 million people—the Greater Tokyo area. Although Mount Fuji has not erupted since the early 18th century, it is considered an active volcano. However, the chance of its erupting is low. In contrast, earthquakes pose considerable risk to Japan.
- Explain that the West began industrializing in the 1700s, while the countries of East Asia did not begin to industrialize until the mid- to late-1800s or even the 1900s. Emphasize that this relatively rapid industrialization has had both positive and negative effects.

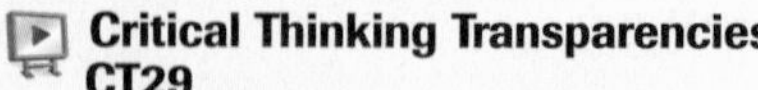

hmhsocialstudies.com TAKING NOTES

Ask students to fill in the graphic organizer with the causes and effects of problems facing East Asia.

Critical Thinking Transparencies CT29
- GeoFocus

In-Depth Resources: Unit 9
- Building Vocabulary, p. 29

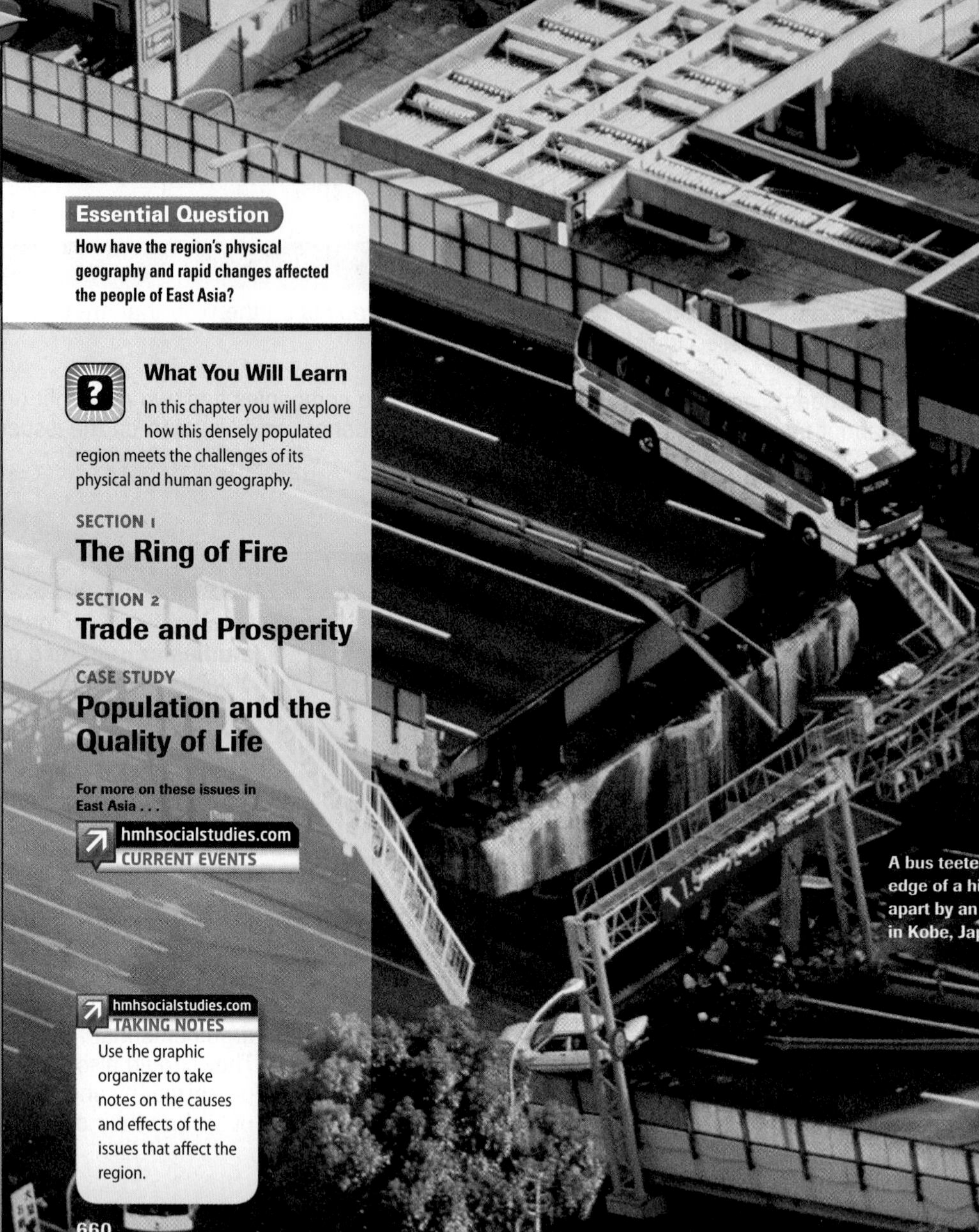

Essential Question

How have the region's physical geography and rapid changes affected the people of East Asia?

What You Will Learn

In this chapter you will explore how this densely populated region meets the challenges of its physical and human geography.

SECTION 1
The Ring of Fire

SECTION 2
Trade and Prosperity

CASE STUDY
Population and the Quality of Life

For more on these issues in East Asia . . .

hmhsocialstudies.com CURRENT EVENTS

hmhsocialstudies.com TAKING NOTES

Use the graphic organizer to take notes on the causes and effects of the issues that affect the region.

A bus teeters on the edge of a highway torn apart by an earthquake in Kobe, Japan, in 1995.

660

CHAPTER 29 ADDITIONAL RESOURCES

BOOKS FOR THE TEACHER

Beeson, Mark. ***Regionalism and Globalization in East Asia: Politics, Security, and Economic Development.*** Palgrave Macmillan, 2007. East Asia's rapid development, within the historical context.

Houston, James D. ***In the Ring of Fire: A Pacific Basin Journey.*** San Francisco: Mercury House, 1997. A traveler's journey around the Ring of Fire.

BOOKS FOR THE STUDENT

Kielburger, Craig, and Kevin Major. ***Free the Children: A Young Man Fights Against Child Labor.*** NY: HarperCollins, 1998. A personal encounter with a global problem.

VIDEO

Great Quakes. The Learning Channel's three-video set covering earliest records of quakes to recent disasters. Blends science and history.

INTERNET

For more on issues facing East Asia, visit . . .

hmhsocialstudies.com

The Ring of Fire

How might people in East Asia prepare for earthquakes and volcanoes?

Main Ideas

- The islands of Japan form part of a geologically active area called the Ring of Fire.
- Because of its location, Japan has faced disastrous earthquakes, volcanic eruptions, and tsunamis.

Places & Terms

Ring of Fire
Great Kanto earthquake
tsunami

A HUMAN PERSPECTIVE On January 17, 1995, at 5:46 A.M., a severe earthquake rocked Kobe, Japan's sixth largest city. When the dust settled and the last of the fires burned out, about 6,000 people lay dead, and more than 40,000 suffered injuries. The government quickly began rebuilding the port city, but psychologists warned that reviving the spirit of Kobe's people would take time. Many lost family members. Entire neighborhoods vanished. A year after the quake, nearly 50,000 people were still living in temporary shelters, and anger grew against the government. Clearly, much more than glass, steel, bricks, and mortar would be needed to bring Kobe fully back to life.

Physical Forces in the Ring of Fire

Like Kobe, many Japanese cities are threatened by earthquakes. This is because Japan is part of the **Ring of Fire**—a chain of volcanoes that line the Pacific Rim. (See the map on the next page.)

SHIFTING PLATES As you learned in Unit 1, the outer crust of the earth is made up of a number of shifting tectonic plates that continually bump and slide into each other. When a dense oceanic plate meets a less dense continental plate, the oceanic plate slides under the continental plate in a process called subduction. The area where the oceanic crust is subducted is called a trench.

In East Asia, the Pacific oceanic plate encounters the Eurasian continental plate. When the oceanic plate moves under the continental plate, it crumples the continental crust, building mountains and volcanoes such as those that form the Ring of Fire.

At the same time, tremendous stress builds up along the edges of the plates. The stress keeps building until eventually the plates move suddenly and violently. The result is an earthquake.

HUMAN-ENVIRONMENT INTERACTION An elderly woman is carried from a collapsing building during the earthquake in Kobe, Japan, in 1995.
What damage is apparent in the photograph?

EAST ASIA

SECTION 1 OBJECTIVES

1. Identify the physical forces in the Ring of Fire.
2. Describe the geology of Japan.
3. Examine issues relating to disaster preparedness.

SKILLBUILDER: Interpreting Maps, p. 662

GeographicThinking
Making Comparisons, p. 662
Making Inferences, p. 663

Focus & Motivate

Ask students how a country in an area more prone to natural disasters can prepare for them? *(building codes, training of rescue personnel, disaster drills)*

Instruct: Objective 1 appears on p. 662.

Interpreting Photographs

Kobe, Japan

Have students examine the photograph. Ask students what hazards rescue workers might face in such a disaster. *(fire, collapsing buildings, inability to move rubble without equipment, severe stress, and so forth)*

CAPTION ANSWER Fire, collapsed buildings, cracks in roads, falling power lines.

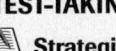

SECTION 1 PROGRAM RESOURCES

In-Depth Resources: Unit 9
- Guided Reading, p. 23
- Map and Graph Skills, pp. 26–27
- Building Vocabulary, p. 29
- Exploring Today's Issues, pp. 30–31
- Reteaching Activity, p. 34
- GeoWorkshop, pp. 37–38

Guided Reading Workbook
- Section 1

Access for Students Acquiring English
- Guided Reading, p. 155
- Map and Graph Skills, pp. 159–160

Formal Assessment
- Section Quiz, p. 452

Integrated Assessment
- Rubric for a brochure, 1.13

INTEGRATED TECHNOLOGY

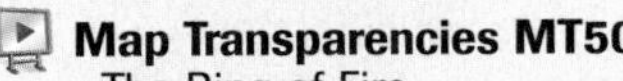
- The Ring of Fire

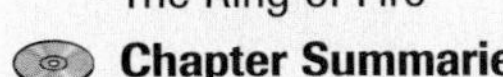

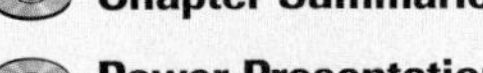

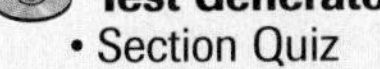
- Section Quiz

TEST-TAKING RESOURCES

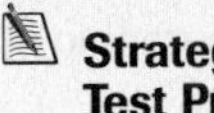
Strategies for Test Preparation

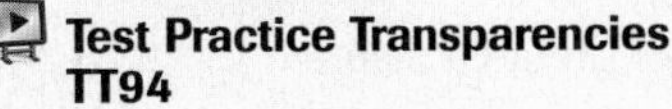

Online Test Practice

Instruct: Objective 

Physical Forces in the Ring of Fire

- What is the process of subduction? *(an oceanic plate sliding under a continental plate)*
- Why is East Asia part of the Ring of Fire? *(because of the volcanoes that encircle much of the Pacific Ocean)*
- What causes an earthquake? *(violent shifting of the earth's tectonic plates)*

 **In-Depth Resources: Unit 9**
- Guided Reading, p. 23
- Exploring Today's Issues, pp. 30–31

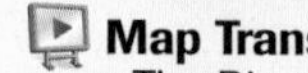 **Map Transparencies MT50**
- The Ring of Fire

Instruct: Objective 

The Geology of Japan

- What famous site in Japan is a volcano? *(Mt. Fuji)*
- How many earthquakes occur in an average year in Japan? *(1,000)*
- Where did the massive Kanto earthquake occur? *(Tokyo, Japan)*
- What causes tsunamis? *(underwater earthquakes, underwater volcanic eruptions, coastal landslides)*

Interpreting Maps

The Ring of Fire

Have students examine the map. Ask students how many other continents are adjacent to the Ring of Fire. *(three)*

SKILLBUILDER ANSWERS
1. Japan **2.** Pacific Ocean

The Geology of Japan

The Japanese islands exist because of subduction. The islands were formed by volcanoes created as the Pacific plate slid under the Eurasian plate. But the same forces that build islands can also destroy them.

VOLCANOES Living along the Ring of Fire means living with volcanic activity. From the time historical records were first kept, at least 60 volcanoes have been active on the islands of Japan. In fact, the best-known landform in Japan, Mt. Fuji, is a volcano.

EARTHQUAKES AND TSUNAMIS Earthquakes like the one that destroyed Kobe are common in Japan. An average of 1,000 quakes occur there each year. Most are too mild to affect people's lives. Some, however, cause many deaths and massive destruction. In 1923, the **Great Kanto earthquake** and the fires it caused killed an estimated 140,000 people and left the city of Tokyo in ruins. The quake partially or completely destroyed nearly 700,000 homes. A

Another geological threat to Japan comes from the sea. When an earthquake occurs under the ocean floor, part of the floor moves. If the quake is strong enough, this shift may produce a **tsunami,** a huge wave of great destructive power. Underwater volcanic eruptions and coastal landslides can also cause tsunamis. Some waves have reached heights of over 100 feet.

A. Answer About 6,000 people died in the Kobe quake, while about 140,000 died in the Great Kanto earthquake.

Geographic Thinking
Making Comparisons
A How many lives were lost in the Great Kanto earthquake compared to the Kobe earthquake?

The Ring of Fire

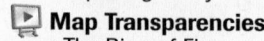

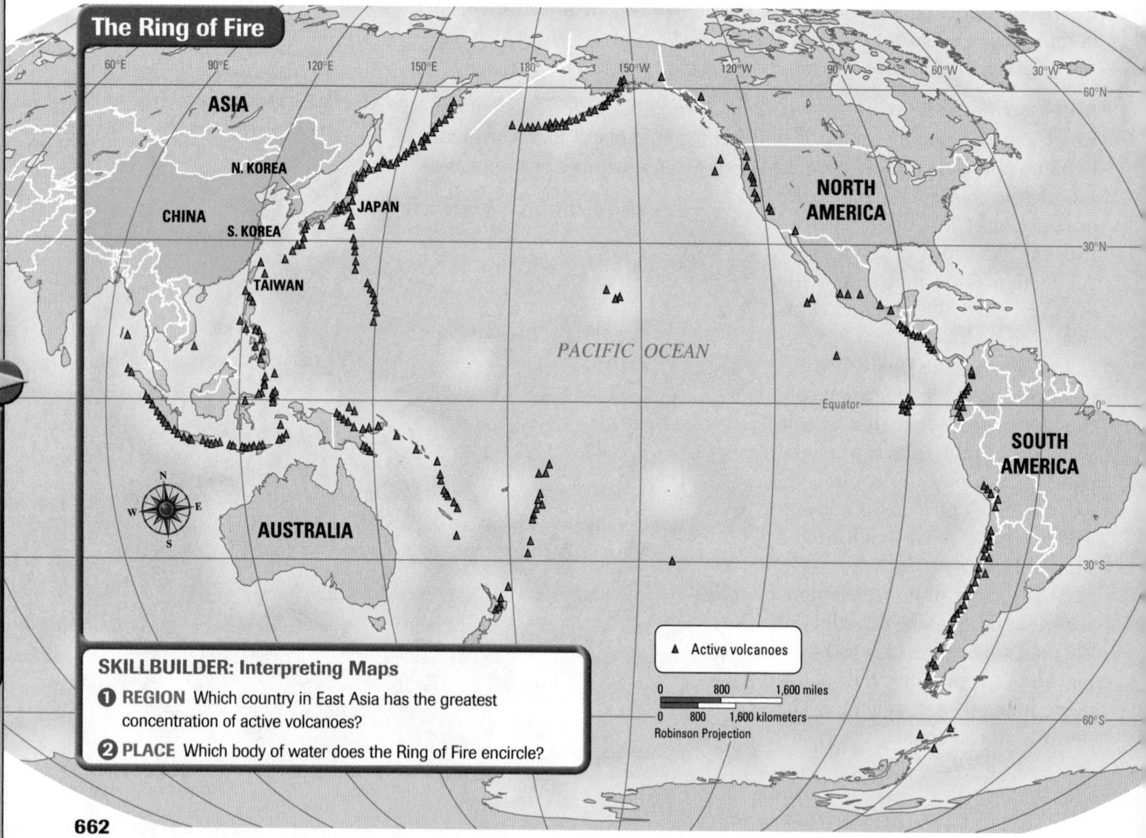

▲ Active volcanoes

0 800 1,600 miles
0 800 1,600 kilometers
Robinson Projection

SKILLBUILDER: Interpreting Maps
1. **REGION** Which country in East Asia has the greatest concentration of active volcanoes?
2. **PLACE** Which body of water does the Ring of Fire encircle?

662

DIFFERENTIATING INSTRUCTION **LESS PROFICIENT READERS**

CREATING AN EARTHQUAKE PREPARATION DIAGRAM

Objective To present geographic information in a visual format

Class Time 30 minutes

Task Create a diagram

Directions Have students create a diagram with information on how cities address earthquakes. Have them fill in information based on what they learned in this chapter section. Have students compare answers or discuss them as a group. A diagram might look like the one to the right:

CITY PLANNING FOR EARTHQUAKES		
Human life	Buildings	Utilities and Roads
warning systems	strict building codes	flexible gas & water lines, backup systems
trained hospital staff, police, rescue workers	reinforcing landfill	specially engineered roadways and bridges
	restrictions on crowding	

Preparing for Disasters

For thousands of years, people have tried to predict when natural disasters will occur. They are still trying, although modern science has provided some clues. Vulnerable nations like Japan are working to improve their defenses against the destructive power of geological forces.

PROBLEMS Many older buildings in Japan are not as likely to withstand earthquakes as newer buildings. In addition, some buildings have been constructed on ground or landfill that is not very stable. Underground gas lines are likely to rupture in the event of an earthquake, and leaking gas can catch fire. Crowded blocks and narrow streets spread the fires and hinder rescue operations.

SOLUTIONS Japan has established a strict building code. Whenever a quake rocks some area of the nation, engineers are quick to study how different types of buildings withstood the heaving ground beneath them. The results of their studies affect building codes governing construction materials and techniques. This has made newer buildings safer than older ones.

Because of the dangers, the Japanese people understand the importance of being prepared for disasters. Schoolchildren participate in yearly disaster drills with local fire-fighters. Organizations like the Japanese Red Cross Society and the Asia Pacific Disaster Management Center offer courses on disaster preparedness and management.

Japan and the other countries along the Ring of Fire cannot change the geology that shapes their land. They can, however, learn more about it and prepare to deal with disaster when it strikes next.

Geography TODAY

Earthquake Detectors

Seismographs are modern instruments for detecting ground movement. They record the intensity, direction, and duration of a movement of the ground during an earthquake.

But the ancient Chinese invented earthquake detectors almost 2,000 years ago. The model shown dates from A.D. 132 and was invented by Chang Heng.

Tremors caused a ball to drop from the mouth of a dragon into the mouth of one of eight frogs around the base of the bowl. This told the direction from which the earthquake came.

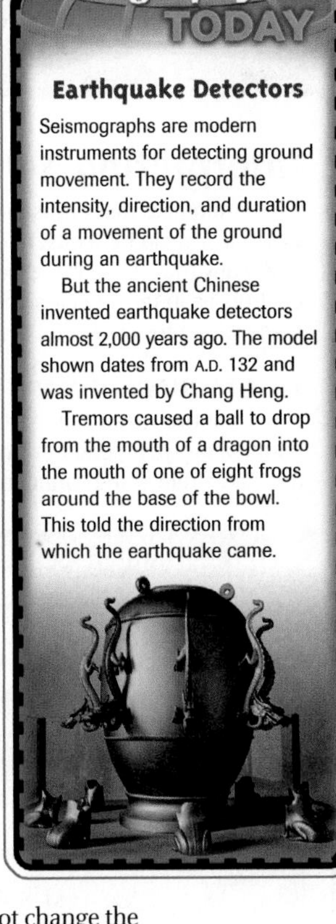

SECTION 1 Assessment

1 Places & Terms

Identify and explain the following places and terms.

- Ring of Fire
- Great Kanto earthquake
- tsunami

2 Taking Notes

HUMAN-ENVIRONMENT INTERACTION Review the notes you took for this section.

	Causes	Effects
Issue 1: Ring of Fire		

- What was the effect of subduction on Japan?
- What causes tsunamis?

3 Main Ideas

a. What are some of the natural disasters that can strike around the Ring of Fire?

b. What role do shifting plates play in earthquakes?

c. What organizations help the Japanese prepare for natural disasters?

4 Geographic Thinking

Making Inferences How will Japan respond in the future to natural disasters such as earthquakes? **Think about:**

- how it has responded so far
- its location and the frequency of earthquakes there

See Skillbuilder Handbook, page R4.

EXPLORING LOCAL GEOGRAPHY Pair with a partner and research the natural disasters that might possibly occur where you live—flood, tornado, hurricane, earthquake, and so forth. Then develop an **Emergency Procedures brochure** that lists the steps you would take to deal with such an emergency.

EAST ASIA

Instruct: Objective 3

Preparing for Disasters

- What problems does Japan face in dealing with earthquakes? *(old buildings, unstable land, crowded cities with narrow streets)*
- What are some solutions to the problems? *(strict building codes, disaster drills)*

In-Depth Resources: Unit 9
- GeoWorkshop, pp. 37–38

Geography TODAY

Earthquake Detectors

Ask students what seismographs record. *(intensity, direction, and duration of ground movement)*

Assess & Reteach

GeoFocus Have students complete the sections on causes and effects of the Ring of Fire in their GeoFocus graphic organizers.

Formal Assessment
- Section Quiz, p.452

Reteaching Activity

Divide the class into small groups. Assign one section objective to each group. Have the students in each group work together to write a brief summary of that objective. One member from each group should then share the group's summary with the class.

In-Depth Resources: Unit 9
- Reteaching Activity, p. 34

SECTION 1 ASSESSMENT ANSWERS

1. Places & Terms

Ring of Fire, p. 661
Great Kanto Earthquake, p. 662
tsunami, p. 662

2. Taking Notes

- Japanese islands were formed by subduction as the Pacific plate slid under the Eurasian plate.
- earthquakes under the ocean floor, underwater volcanic eruptions, and coastal landslides

3. Main Ideas

a. earthquakes, volcanic eruptions, tsunamis

b. Stress builds up along the edges where plates meet. Relief of stress by sudden violent movements is felt as earthquakes.

c. Japanese Red Cross Society and Asia Pacific Disaster Management Center

4. Geographic Thinking

Strict building codes; studies of earthquakes and other disasters; better building materials and techniques; disaster drills; organizations trained to deal with disaster

GeoActivity

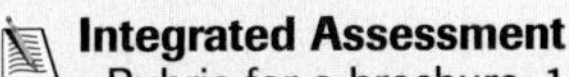

Integrated Assessment
- Rubric for a brochure, 1.13

OBJECTIVE

Interpret a proportional circle map showing Japanese earthquakes.

Instruct: Objective

Interpreting a Proportional Circle Map

- When did the earthquakes on this map occur? *(Between 1991 and 2000)*
- Where have the greatest number of earthquakes occurred according to this map? *(off the coasts of Japan, under the Pacific Ocean)*
- Which island(s) has experienced the strongest earthquakes? *(Kuril Islands)*
- Which magnitude of earthquake most commonly occurs around Japan? *(6.0-6.4)*

In-Depth Resources: Unit 9
- Map and Graph Skills, pp. 26–27

More About

The Richter Scale

Seismologists Beno Gutenberg and Charles Francis Richter introduced the Richter Scale in 1935 to measure the strength of Southern California earthquakes. They applied low numbers to the weakest local earthquakes that had been recorded up to that time. Each higher whole number represented a ten-fold increase in magnitude. Although the scale has no maximum measurement, the strongest earthquake detected thus far reached magnitude 9 on the Richter Scale. Today, newer seismographs can detect even minor earthquakes that would receive a negative number on the Richter Scale.

RAND MCNALLY **Map and Graph Skills**

Interpreting a Proportional Circle Map

The earthquake that devastated Kobe, Japan, in 1995 measured 6.8 on the Richter scale, which is a scale for measuring the magnitude of earthquakes. About 6,000 people died and many thousands more were injured. Although the Kobe quake was the most destructive in recent years, there have been many others in Japan in the 1990s. Some of these were more powerful than the Kobe quake but they did not do as much damage.

THE LANGUAGE OF MAPS A **proportional circle map** shows the relative sizes of objects or events, such as earthquakes. This map shows major earthquakes in Japan during a ten-year period beginning in 1991. The larger the circle on the map, the greater the magnitude of the earthquake as measured by the scale.

Major Earthquakes in Japan, 1991–2000

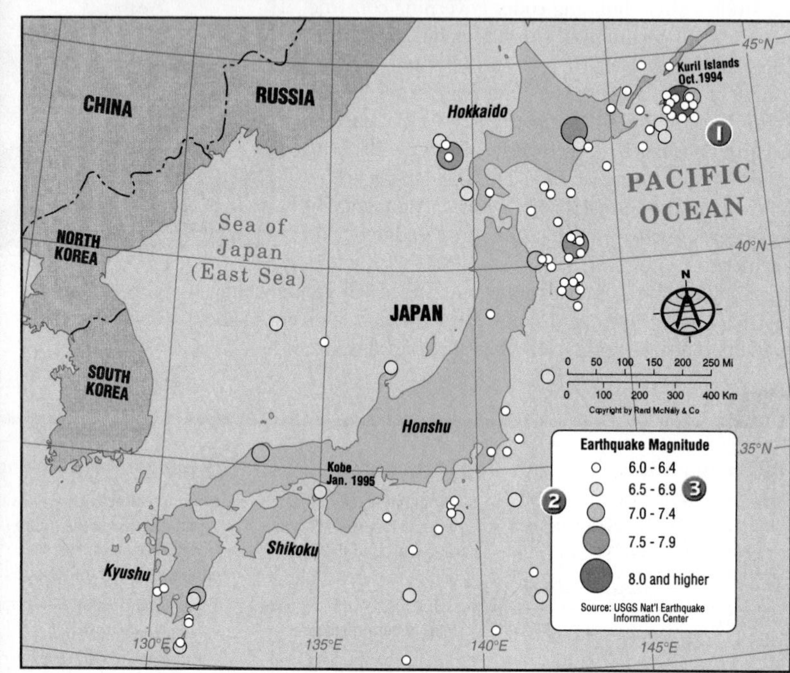

1. A cluster of circles indicates that an area is prone to frequent quakes.
2. The key explains that the bigger and darker a circle is on the map, the greater the size and intensity of the quake.
3. Values on an earthquake magnitude scale are typically between 1 and 9. This map shows earthquakes with a magnitude of 6 and higher. Each increase of .5 represents an increase in released energy. Scales for measuring earthquakes include the Richter, the moment magnitude, and others.

Map and Graph Skills Assessment

1. **Analyzing Data** What was the intensity of the earthquake that struck Kobe?
2. **Making Comparisons** On which islands did the most powerful quake occur in this period? In what range did it fall, as measured by the scale?
3. **Making Inferences** Why do you think the quake you identified in question 2 was not as destructive as the Kobe quake?

SKILLS ASSESSMENT ANSWERS

1. between 6.5 and 6.9

2. Kuril Islands; 8.0 and over

3. probably not located near big population center

Trade and Prosperity

What are some benefits of global trade?

Main Ideas

- East Asian economies became global powerhouses in the 1970s and 1980s.
- The decline of Asian economies in the 1990s created a crisis that spread around the globe.

Places & Terms

UNICEF
global economy
Jakota Triangle
recession
sweatshop

A HUMAN PERSPECTIVE At the beginning of the 1990s, the economies of East Asia were growing very rapidly. Unfortunately, there was a dark side to this prosperity. In 1995, **UNICEF (the United Nations Children's Fund)** reported that more than half a million children in East Asia were working in factories or begging on the streets. UNICEF regional director Daniel Brooks noted that, due to fast-paced economic growth, "We are seeing the erosion of family values and that includes the exploitation of children." This is one of the important issues facing the region.

Opening Doors

The process by which East Asia became an economic powerhouse took centuries. Until the 1500s, the nations of East Asia had been isolated from the rest of the world. As Western demand for Asian products grew, European traders used a variety of means—including force—to end East Asia's isolation.

Eventually, the economies of the region were to emerge as major players in the global economy. However, foreign intervention and world war lay ahead before East Asian nations achieved widespread prosperity.

OPENING TO THE WEST By the 1800s, the nations of Europe had signed treaties that gave them distinct spheres of influence in the East. These were areas where they could control trade without interference from other Western nations. In 1853, Commodore Matthew Perry set sail from the United States to Japan to persuade the Japanese to establish trade and diplomatic relations with the United States. The naval warships that accompanied Perry intimidated Japan into opening its doors to the United States and the West.

MOVEMENT Japan exports about 4½ million vehicles each year. Here, cars are about to be loaded onto a boat in the port of Narashino.

EAST ASIA

SECTION 2 OBJECTIVES

1. Examine how East Asian economies have grown by opening markets to the West.
2. Identify the key economic powers in East Asia as well as the problems they face.

Geographic Thinking

Seeing Patterns, p. 667
Making Inferences, p. 667

Focus & Motivate

How might workers be exploited? *(by working long hours for low wages in poor conditions)*

Instruct: Objective 1

Opening Doors

- What caused the end of East Asia's isolation from the West? *(European exploration, trade, and conquest)*
- When did European nations gain spheres of influence in East Asia? *(by the 1800s)*
- When did East Asia become industrialized? *(after World War II)*

In-Depth Resources: Unit 9
- Guided Reading, p. 24
- Skillbuilder Practice, p. 28
- Exploring Today's Issues, pp. 32–33

Critical Thinking Transparencies CT61
- Exports from Jakota Triangle Countries

Interpreting Photographs

Japan's Auto Exports

Have students examine the photograph. Ask them what this says about the market for Japanese cars? *(It is a big market in which the Japanese are successful in selling their products.)*

SECTION 2 PROGRAM RESOURCES

In-Depth Resources: Unit 9
- Guided Reading, p. 24
- Skillbuilder Practice, p. 28
- Building Vocabulary, p. 29
- Exploring Today's Issues, pp. 32–33
- Reteaching Activity, p. 35

Guided Reading workbook
- Section 2

Access for Students Acquiring English
- Guided Reading, p. 156
- Skillbuilder Practice, p. 158

Formal Assessment
- Section Quiz, p. 453

Integrated Assessment
- Rubric for a class report, 2.5

INTEGRATED TECHNOLOGY

Critical Thinking Transparencies CT61
- Exports from Jakota Triangle Countries

Power Presentations

TEST-TAKING RESOURCES

Strategies for Test Preparation

Test Practice Transparencies TT95

Online Test Practice

Instruct: Objective 2

- How stable is the country's economy today?
- Has the quality of life in that country changed since the 1980s?
- What changes have occurred in that country's business practices?
- Are foreigners investing heavily in that country?

When students have found information, have them write a short summary of their findings. If time permits, have them share their data with the class.

Interpreting Graphs

Exports from Jakota Triangle Countries

Have students examine the graphs. Then ask them which country has the greatest exports. *(Japan)* Which country exports seafood? *(South Korea)*

INDUSTRIALIZATION AND GLOBALIZATION After World War II, the nations of East Asia began industrializing, using cheap labor to produce goods for trade. Trade between East and West steadily increased. The labels "Made in China" and "Made in Japan" on goods became very common in the United States and Europe.

At the same time, regional economies, which had evolved from national economies, began to merge. Eventually, a **global economy** developed, in which nations became dependent on each other for goods and services. For example, Japan imported many natural resources from around the world and then transformed those resources into manufactured goods that it sold around the globe. The nations of East Asia used their supplies of cheap labor to become manufacturing powerhouses. The World Bank described this boom as an "economic miracle."

Powerful Economies of East Asia

During the 1980s and early 1990s, many Asian economies did very well. The most powerful of the Pacific Rim nations of East Asia—Japan, Taiwan, and South Korea—enjoyed record prosperity. These three countries formed a part of a zone of prosperity referred to by some as the **Jakota Triangle**—**Ja**pan, **Ko**rea (South), and **Ta**iwan. By the mid-1990s, however, these economies were experiencing problems.

Exports from Jakota Triangle Countries

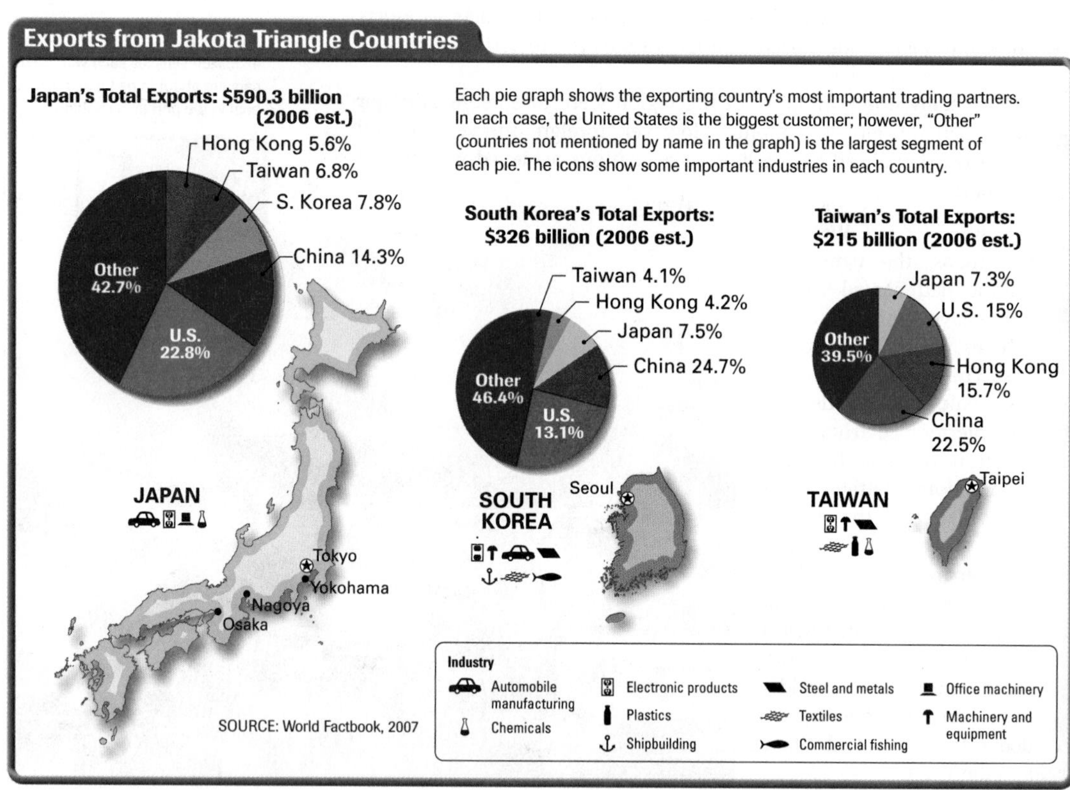

ACTIVITY OPTION **INTERNET RESEARCH**

WRITING A SUMMARY

Objective To connect geography to current economic events

Class Time One hour

Task Use the Internet to research the current status of one of the Jakota Triangle countries

Directions Have students choose one Jakota triangle country to research: Japan, South Korea, or Taiwan. Ask students to find two current pieces of economic information on that country. The following questions may serve as guides:

- Has the country recently experienced any natural disasters or harsh weather conditions that have affected its economy?
- Have economic conditions in the United States or European countries affected the subject country's economy? If so, was the effect positive or negative?
- How have the prices of key raw materials affected the subject country's manufacturing output?
- What impact have political events had on the country's economy?

ECONOMIC PROBLEMS ARISE Although some East Asian economies appeared healthy, they were burdened by debt and mismanagement. The Asian economic miracle had been based in part on efficiency and innovation. It also had been built partly on the sacrifices of very poor and very young workers, who were paid low wages.

In the mid-1990s, a series of banks and other companies went bankrupt (could not pay their debts). This sparked panic among foreign investors, who began selling their Asian stocks and currency. In some countries, riots broke out. In Japan and South Korea, ruling politicians had to resign. Japan's economy entered a **recession**—an extended decline in general business activity. The Asian economic miracle had come to an end. South Korea and Taiwan also experienced recessions. A

Geographic Thinking

Seeing Patterns
A What were some of the factors that led to recession in the region?
A Answer debt, mismanagement, business bankruptcies, stock-market decline

A GLOBAL RIPPLE EFFECT Because the economies of many nations are interconnected, the crisis in Asia spread throughout the world. Uncertainty led to concern at the New York Stock Exchange and other national exchanges. To prevent a global economic downturn, the World Bank and the International Monetary Fund stepped in, lending money to East Asian countries that promised reform. This began to reverse the downslide, but the world had learned an important lesson—a global economy could threaten prosperity as well as improve it.

THE PROMISE OF REFORM The economic crisis led to an awareness in East Asia that serious reform was necessary. Reform would have to include increased wages for adult workers, as well as a ban on child-labor and forced-labor practices. It would also mean an end to **sweatshops**. These are workplaces where people work long hours for pennies under poor conditions. By the 2000s, reforms had begun, and Asian economies were showing new signs of life.

In the next section, you will read about the expanding population of East Asia. The growth in population has had an impact on the quality of life in the region.

Assess & Reteach

GeoFocus Have students complete the sections on causes and effects of trade in their GeoFocus graphic organizer.

Formal Assessment
- Section Quiz, p. 453

Reteaching Activity
Divide students into pairs. Ask them to quiz one another about information from this section of the chapter. Have students use the section objectives and headings as guides.

In-Depth Resources: Unit 9
- Reteaching Activity, p. 35

Section 2 Assessment

1 Places & Terms
Identify and explain the following places and terms.
- UNICEF
- global economy
- Jakota Triangle
- recession
- sweatshop

2 Taking Notes
HUMAN-ENVIRONMENT INTERACTION Review the notes you took for this section.

	Causes	Effects
Issue 2: Trade		

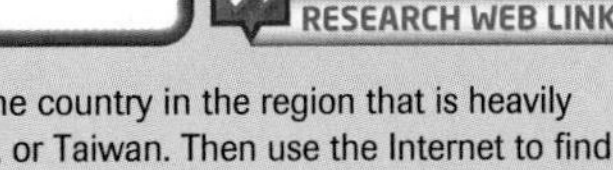

- Why is trade important to the economies of the region?
- How did the people of East Asia make possible the "economic miracle"?

3 Main Ideas
a. How was the prosperity of East Asia linked to the wider world?
b. What were some of the consequences of economic development in the region?
c. What were some of the causes of economic decline in the region?

4 Geographic Thinking
Making Inferences Why might changes in the global economy have a greater effect on South Korea and Taiwan than on China and Mongolia? **Think about:**
- the global economy
- agriculture and industry

hmhsocialstudies.com
RESEARCH WEB LINKS

EAST ASIA

GeoActivity

SEEING PATTERNS Pair with a partner and choose one country in the region that is heavily dependent on trade—for example, Japan, South Korea, or Taiwan. Then use the Internet to find out how that country's economy did in the year 2000. Give a **class report** on whether the economy is improving. 21st CENTURY

SECTION 2 ASSESSMENT ANSWERS

1. Places & Terms
UNICEF, p. 665
global economy, p. 666
Jakota Triangle, p. 666
recession, p. 667
sweatshop, p. 667

2. Taking Notes
- Their prosperity is based on trade with rest of world.
- They provided cheap labor.

3. Main Ideas
a. because it was based on trade
b. sweatshops; exploitation of children
c. debt, mismanagement, bankruptcies, exploitation of workers

4. Geographic Thinking
South Korea and Taiwan depend more upon trade for their prosperity. Mongolia and China are less dependent on trade, with agriculture playing a big role in their economies.

GeoActivity

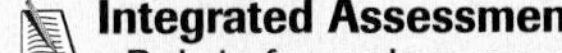
Integrated Assessment
- Rubric for a class report, 2.5

CASE STUDY OBJECTIVES

1. Examine the patterns, problems, and solutions of population growth in East Asia.
2. Describe the quality of life in East Asia.
3. Complete the Case Study Project by making a presentation on quality of life in an East Asian city.
4. Analyze primary sources for different views on population and quality of life.

SKILLBUILDER: Interpreting Charts, p. 669

Focus & Motivate

How might countries deal with overpopulation issues? *(family planning policies, change in economic and social conditions, education)*

Instruct: Objective 

Patterns of Population/Addressing Population Problems

- What was the state of most East Asian countries in the mid-20th century? *(impoverished, low quality of life, overpopulated)*
- Name two environmental stresses in East Asia during the mid-20th century. *(lack of water, lack of food)*
- What social issue did East Asian policy makers focus on to improve the quality of life? *(population control)*
- How did population policies affect East Asian women between 1950 and 2000? *(most married later and had fewer children)*

 **In-Depth Resources: Unit 9**
- Guided Reading, p. 25

CASESTUDY

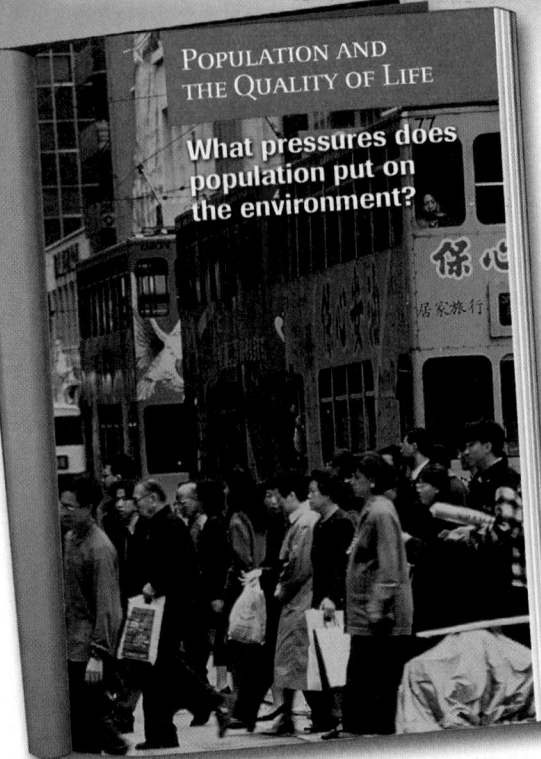

POPULATION AND THE QUALITY OF LIFE

What pressures does population put on the environment?

Trams, buses, and people crowd the streets of Hong Kong.

Because East Asia has changed so much, it's hard to imagine how different the region looked 50 years ago. Today, some of the countries and cities of the region are among the most prosperous in the world. In Japan, South Korea, and Taiwan, the statistics on per capita income, length of life, and literacy are all high. Despite recent problems, the economies are generally prosperous, as can be seen in the glittering shopping districts and luxurious residential neighborhoods of Tokyo, Seoul, and Taipei. But it wasn't always that way. If the big problem of the past was industrializing, today it is managing population.

Patterns of Population

Many of the countries of East Asia have been so successful in dealing with the basic problems of feeding their people and industrializing that they now face other problems. Several of these problems are caused by the expanding populations in the region.

THE SITUATION AT MID-CENTURY At the middle of the 20th century, the nations of East Asia ranked among the least developed in the world. In fact, statistics on health, literacy, fertility, and economics in East Asia mirrored those of the poorest region of the world—sub-Saharan Africa. Widespread poverty was the norm. Life expectancy was short. Fertility rates were high, as were infant and maternal death rates. In 1950, East Asian women often married young and gave birth to six children on average during their lifetimes. Most economies remained rural.

Addressing Population Problems

Policy makers in the region understood that population control was key to solving a wide range of social and economic woes. Among the successful programs were those that stressed education and family planning.

ENVIRONMENTAL STRESS Unrestricted population growth put tremendous strain on the quality of life in the region and on the environment. Food production on existing farmland was barely adequate. The absence of basic sanitation fouled the region's water supplies. In some countries, such as China, the water tables were drained to dangerously low levels. Fortunately, the governments of East Asia recognized this catastrophe-in-the-making. They moved quickly to reverse course.

CASE STUDY PROGRAM RESOURCES

 **In-Depth Resources: Unit 9**
- Guided Reading, p. 25
- Building Vocabulary, p. 29
- Reteaching Activity, p. 36

 **Guided Reading Workbook**
- Case Study

Access for Students Acquiring English/ESL
- Guided Reading, p. 157

 **Formal Assessment**
- Case Study Quiz, p. 454

 **Integrated Assessment**
- Rubric for a bar graph, 2.3

INTEGRATED TECHNOLOGY

 **Test Generator**
- Section Quiz

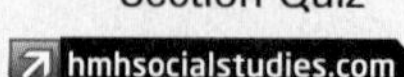

TEST-TAKING RESOURCES

 **Strategies for Test Preparation**

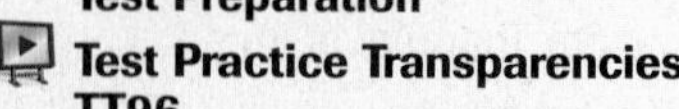 **Test Practice Transparencies TT96**

 **Online Test Practice**

PROBLEMS AND POLICIES Aggressive family planning programs were begun in the region. Birth rates began leveling off and then dropping. By the year 2000, women were marrying much later and giving birth to an average of 2.5 children. In China alone, the birth rate dropped from 6.22 children per woman in 1950–1955 to just 1.79 in the year 2009.

IMPRESSIVE RESULTS This drop in birth rates, combined with industrialization, led to fast economic growth. By the 1990s, the economies of East Asia were booming, transforming social and economic conditions. In just over a generation, the region's quality of life has improved to the point where life expectancy and literacy rates are among the highest in the world.

Population

Some Major Cities of East Asia (Metropolitan area may be much larger.)

City	Population (in millions)
Shanghai, China	14.23
Beijing, China	10.3
Seoul, South Korea	9.82
Tianjin, China	6.84
Tokyo, Japan	8.49
Hong Kong, China	6.7
Shenyang, China	4.6
Guangzhou, China	7.55
Wuhan, China	6.79
Pusan, South Korea	3.52
Chongqing, China	5.09
Xian, China	3.87
Nanjing, China	3.78
Taipei, Taiwan	2.69
Osaka, Japan	2.63

SOURCE: Statesman's Yearbook, 2009

SKILLBUILDER: Interpreting Charts

1. **HUMAN-ENVIRONMENT INTERACTION** What are the two largest cities in South Korea?
2. **REGION** Which country on the chart has most of the largest cities?

The Quality of Life

Although these changes in East Asia have been dramatic, they have not solved all of the region's problems. Some countries in the region, such as China and Japan, are among the most populous in the world. Furthermore, life expectancy in East Asia has increased from 41 years in the period 1950–1955 to 69 years in the year 2000.

SOME ONGOING PROBLEMS The huge populations of the region continue to put pressure on the environment. Even if China were to maintain a modest growth rate of one percent a year, it would still add 13 million people to its population annually.

SEE PRIMARY SOURCE A

The growing populations are concentrated in the cities of the region, where they must be provided with housing, sanitation, and transportation. Pollution, overcrowding, and flooding are all problems that are made worse by an expanding population.

However, not all family planning programs were well received. Some citizens criticized China's one-child-per-family policy as harsh and an assault on their rights. In the face of such criticism, the region's family planning efforts were expanded.

Despite these difficulties, East Asia has shown the world that rapid social and economic progress are possible. This requires that people and their leaders join hands with the world community to make difficult decisions and put in place sound policies.

SEE PRIMARY SOURCE D

A case study project on population follows on the next two pages.

EAST ASIA

Interpreting Charts

Some Major Cities of East Asia

Have students examine the chart. Ask them which city in East Asia had the largest population in the 2000s. Then ask them which Chinese city had the smallest population. *(Shanghai, China; Nanjing, China)*

SKILLBUILDER ANSWERS 1. Seoul and Pusan **2.** China

Instruct: Objective 2

The Quality of Life

- Why is population size still a problem in China despite the one-child-per-family limit? *(Life expectancy has increased.)*
- Which environmental problems are made worse because of expanding populations in East Asia? *(flooding, pollution, overcrowding)*
- What effects do expanding populations have on individuals in East Asia? *(problems finding housing, dealing with overcrowding and slow transportation, and so forth)*

DIFFERENTIATING INSTRUCTION — GIFTED AND TALENTED STUDENTS

PREPARING A PROGRESS REPORT

Objective To develop research skills and strengthen understanding of social issues in relation to geographic information

Research Time One week **Class Time** One class period

Task Prepare a progress report on efforts to curb child-labor abuses in East Asia

Directions Have students do research and prepare a report on recent progress on child-labor issues in one country of East Asia. Reports should identify past abuses, explain how they have been addressed, and describe the current situation. Reports should focus on progress in correcting child labor abuses. Encourage students to include multimedia sources (tapes of television or radio reports, photographs, and so forth) in their reports where possible.

Instruct: Objective 3

Case Study Project: Visual Presentation

- What is the main goal of this presentation? *(to present visual information on an East Asian country's population and quality of life)*
- What kinds of visuals should be included? *(maps, graphs, charts)*
- How should color be used in the presentation? *(to make information easier to understand)*
- How will people understand the visuals you select? *(oral explanation)*

Instruct: Objective 4

Using Primary Sources

- Ⓐ ***Bar Graph*** What is the source of this bar graph? *(U.S. Bureau of the Census)*
- Where is population expected to grow most? *(Asia)*
- Ⓑ ***Policy Statement*** What did President Clinton claim was China's main environmental health problem? *(pollution)*
- What effects does this problem have on the Chinese people? *(respiratory problems, health issues)*

CASESTUDY

PROJECT

A Visual Presentation

Primary sources A, B, C, D, and E offer assessments of East Asia's population challenges. Use these resources along with your own research to prepare maps, graphs, and charts that tell a story about population and quality of life in one nation of East Asia.

Suggested Steps

1. Choose one East Asian nation to study. Search for information that can be presented visually in charts and graphs. The visuals you create should explain some aspect of the nation's population and quality of life.
2. Use online and print resources to research your topic.
3. Look for information that shows relationships between population and quality of life. For example, one chart might illustrate declining birth rates while another shows rising literacy rates.
4. Include several different types of visuals: pie graphs, line and bar graphs, pictograms, population distribution maps, and so on.
5. Try to make your visuals as colorful as possible. Use color to make the information easier to understand.
6. Prepare a brief oral explanation of your visuals and the story they tell.

Materials and Supplies

- posterboard
- color markers
- computer with Internet access
- books, newspapers, and magazines
- printer

PRIMARY SOURCE Ⓐ

Bar Graph *This bar graph, prepared from U.S. Census Bureau statistics, shows where and by how much population is expected to grow from 2000 to 2050.*

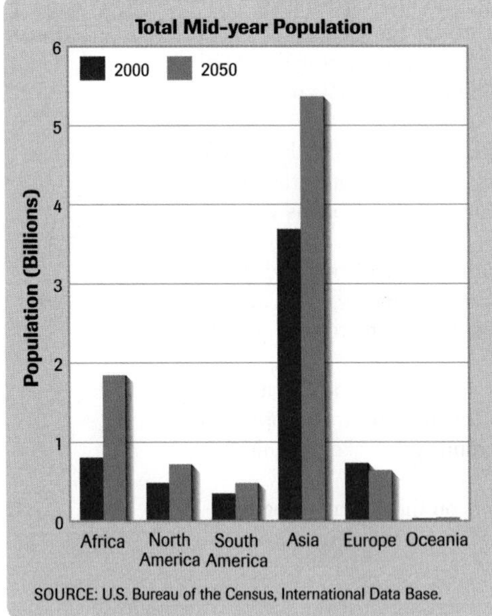

PRIMARY SOURCE Ⓑ

Policy Statement *On a trip to Hong Kong in 1998, U.S. President Bill Clinton discussed the issue of pollution in China. He noted that overcrowding and industrialization had led to serious environmental problems that would only get worse if not addressed. The following CNN news story quotes some of Clinton's remarks.*

Clinton addressed a contentious [controversial] issue separating the two countries—global warming. He also announced a series of clean air and water measures to help China, which has five of the most polluted cities in the world, according to environmentalists. . . .

"You know better than I that polluted air and water are threatening your remarkable progress," Clinton said. "Smog has caused entire Chinese cities to disappear from satellite photographs, and respiratory illness is China's number one health problem."

ACTIVITY OPTION **SKILLBUILDER LESSON**

DISTINGUISHING FACT FROM OPINION

Explaining the Skill Tell students that it is important to distinguish fact from opinion when reading. Remind them that *facts* are events, dates, statistics, or statements that can be proved to be true. *Opinions* are the judgments, beliefs, and feelings of a writer or speaker. Point out that facts are often used to support opinions and that primary sources can contain both facts and opinions.

For additional Skillbuilder practice, see p. 666 in Section 2.

Applying the Skill Have students look at primary source C on page 671. Then ask whether the following quotations from the source are more likely facts or opinions, and why.

- "Birth rates are slowing" *(fact: verifiable)*
- "Half the planet's population growth will come from Asia in the next 50 years" *(fact: verifiable)*
- "The most important resource at risk is clean water" *(opinion: not verifiable and other options might exist)*
- "Conservation is the only way to prevent catastrophe" *(opinion: not verifiable and other options could work)*

PRIMARY SOURCE C

News Analysis *In this article from Asiaweek.com, the author addresses an interesting problem posed by population growth in Asia.*

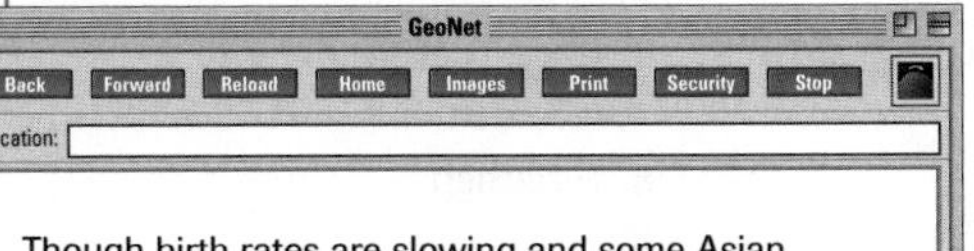

Though birth rates are slowing and some Asian countries are even worrying about a decline, overall expansion is still too high. Half the planet's population growth in the next 50 years will come from Asia—18 percent from India alone.

If consumption patterns continue, the extra bodies will put a profound stress on limited land, food, and energy supplies—particularly in developing countries. The most important resource at risk, though, is clean water, not only for drinking, but also for food production and control of hygiene-related disease. Already supplies are strained in some areas, as a result of pollution degradation or overuse in wasteful farming and industrial practices. . . . Water tables are falling in China too, particularly in the northern plain, the country's main agricultural area. Conservation is the only realistic way to prevent catastrophe.

PRIMARY SOURCE D

Fact Sheet *In 1997, Population Action International produced a fact sheet that helped explain the relationship between population control and development in East Asia.*

- **A shift to smaller families produced three important demographic changes: slower growth in the number of school-age children, a lower ratio of dependents to working-age adults, and a reduced rate of labor-force growth.** These alone were not enough to create the educated work force, high wages and savings rates, and the capital-intensive industries that now characterize the [region]. But linked to an enterprising business sector, wise public investment, and an equitable education system, demographic change soon became economic opportunity. . . .
- **With fewer children, households placed more of their earnings in savings, and governments reduced public expenditures.** In 1960, there were only 1.3 working-age adults for each child in . . . South Korea, Taiwan, Singapore, and Hong Kong. Because families chose to have fewer children, by 1995 there were 3.1 working-age adults for each child, dramatically reducing the dependency burden and allowing families to save more of their incomes.

PRIMARY SOURCE E

Political Cartoon *This cartoon was created by Steve Greenberg in 1996. It shows one cartoonist's viewpoint of the effect of a rapidly expanding population on the natural environment.*

PROJECT CheckList

Have I . . .

- ✓ fully researched my topic?
- ✓ created informative, colorful visuals that make my report clear and interesting?
- ✓ used charts and graphs to tell a story about population issues in East Asia?
- ✓ practiced explaining my report?
- ✓ anticipated questions others might ask and prepared answers?

Instruct: Objective 4

Using Primary Sources

- Ⓒ ***News Analysis*** What does the author of this article focus on? *(lack of clean water)*
- Ⓓ ***Fact Sheet*** What does the fact sheet cite as the reason why families can save more? *(having fewer children)*
- What factors, according to this fact sheet, helped further economic opportunity? *(wise public investment, enterprising businesses, an equitable education system)*
- Ⓔ ***Political Cartoon*** What is the bulldozer doing? *(destroying the homes of the animals)*
- Why is the bulldozer knocking down the tree? *(to clear space for the expanding human population)*

Assess & Reteach

GeoFocus Have students complete the cause-and-effect chart they began at the start of the chapter.

Formal Assessment
- Case Study Quiz, p. 454

Reteaching Activity
Have students take notes on the chapter, writing down key issues and ideas about population in East Asia. Then, divide the class into small groups and have each group use their notes to discuss the problems and solutions created by East Asia's growing population.

In-Depth Resources: Unit 9
- Reteaching Activity, p. 36

RUBRIC CASE STUDY PROJECT

VISUAL PRESENTATION

For the Case Study Project, students should do the following:

- Research solutions or initiatives to deal with population and the quality of life in East Asia.
- Use a variety of resources in their research.
- Prepare a brief speech to introduce the topic.
- Give a visual presentation containing a variety of data.

Grading Rubric Evaluate student performance as Exceptional, Acceptable, or Poor in each of the following categories:

	Exceptional	Acceptable	Poor
Communicates ideas and positions clearly			
Finds a variety of resources			
Presents a concise speech on the topic			
Presents a variety of data			

Reviewing Places & Terms

A. **1.** Ring of Fire, p. 661
2. Great Kanto Earthquake, p. 662
3. tsunami, p. 662
4. UNICEF, p. 665
5. global economy, p. 666
6. Jakota Triangle, p. 666
7. recession, p. 667
8. sweatshop, p. 667

B. Possible Reponses

9. 140,000 lives lost and 700,000 homes destroyed
10. the movement of shifting plates
11. exporting for trade their manufactured products
12. People work long hours for low wages, making profits for owners.
13. earthquakes, volcanic eruptions, tsunamis
14. It imports resources that it makes into products to sell around the world.
15. Reform might put an end to sweatshops.
16. fires
17. underwater volcanic eruptions and earthquakes, as well as coastal landslides
18. Japan, South Korea, Taiwan
19. prosperous economies based on manufacturing and trade
20. primarily children's issues

Chapter 29 Assessment

VISUAL SUMMARY
TODAY'S ISSUES IN EAST ASIA

Environment

The Ring of Fire
- Parts of East Asia are located along the northwestern edge of the Pacific Ocean's Ring of Fire.
- The heavily populated areas of East Asia (especially Japan) are endangered by the earthquakes, volcanic eruptions, and tsunamis along the Ring of Fire.

Economics

Trade and Prosperity
- Most of the nations of East Asia have prospered from trade with each other and with other parts of the world.
- In the second half of the 20th century, many countries in East Asia developed powerful economies.
- In the 1990s, there was a decline in the economies of the region but they have begun to recover.

Population

Case Study: Population and the Quality of Life
- East Asia has a huge population.
- Despite a reduced birth rate, the population in the region will continue to grow well into the 21st century.
- A growing population affects the quality of life in a nation.

Reviewing Places & Terms

A. Briefly explain the importance of each of the following.

1. Ring of Fire	**5.** global economy
2. Great Kanto earthquake	**6.** Jakota Triangle
3. tsunami	**7.** recession
4. UNICEF	**8.** sweatshop

B. Answer the questions about vocabulary in complete sentences.

9. How many people were killed and how many homes destroyed in the Great Kanto earthquake?
10. What is the basic cause of the physical events that characterize the Ring of Fire?
11. Upon what is the prosperity of the Jakota Triangle primarily based?
12. Why are sweatshops profitable?
13. What sorts of natural disasters occur around the Ring of Fire?
14. How does Japan participate in the global economy?
15. How might economic reform in East Asia affect sweatshops?
16. What besides earthquake damage made the Great Kanto earthquake so destructive?
17. What are three causes of tsunamis?
18. Which countries in the region experienced a recession?
19. What sorts of economies make up the Jakota Triangle?
20. With what issues does UNICEF concern itself?

Main Ideas

The Ring of Fire (pp. 661–664)

1. What causes an earthquake?
2. Why are the Japanese islands so unstable?
3. What are some Japanese organizations that help prepare for disasters?

Trade and Prosperity (pp. 665–667)

4. What effect did Western nations have on economic development in East Asia?
5. What is the connection between industrialization and globalization?
6. What are some of the things that went wrong in the economies of the region?

Case Study: Population and the Quality of Life (pp. 668–671)

7. What are some examples of the stress that population growth puts on the environment?
8. What are some effective ways to manage population growth?
9. How developed was East Asia in the middle of the 20th century?
10. How had East Asia changed by the beginning of the 21st century?

Main Ideas

1. The collision of plates creates tremendous stress. When the plates move suddenly, the result is an earthquake.
2. Japan was formed by subduction—the oceanic plate sliding under the continental plate—resulting in volcanoes that built up the islands, and earthquakes.
3. Japanese Red Cross Society and Asia Pacific Disaster Management Center
4. The opening to the West exposed the region to industrialization and helped many nations emerge as economic tigers.
5. When countries industrialize, they turn natural resources into marketable goods, and then export these around the world.
6. debt, mismanagement, social inequality, bankruptcies, decline in the stock market, and a decline in general business activity
7. inadequate food supply, lack of sanitation, foul water, low water table levels, air pollution, overcrowding
8. family planning programs; education; government limits on the number of children per family; later marriages
9. Its numbers on health, literacy, birth rates, and economics ranked it among the poorest regions of the world.
10. drop in birth rates along with industrialization led to fast economic growth

Critical Thinking

1. Using Your Notes

Use your completed chart to answer these questions.

	Causes	Effects
Issue 1: Ring of Fire		
Issue 2: Trade		

a. What are some of the effects of the Ring of Fire?

b. What role did labor play in the booming economies of East Asia after World War II?

2. Geographic Themes

a. **REGION** What are some of the ways that people respond to the dangers of living in the Ring of Fire?

b. **HUMAN-ENVIRONMENT INTERACTION** How does a rising population put a strain on the environment?

3. Identifying Themes

What might be some of the advantages of reducing population growth in the region? Which of the five themes apply to this situation?

4. Determining Cause and Effect

What might be the connection between population and trade in some of the economies of the region?

5. Making Inferences

Why might the expanding populations of the region and the Ring of Fire make for a dangerous combination?

For Additional Test Practice

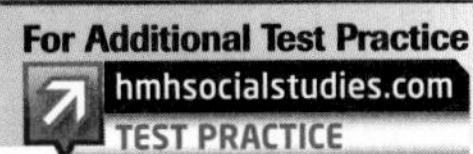

Geographic Skills: Interpreting Graphs

World Population and Growth

Use the graph to answer the questions.

1. **ANALYZING DATA** What was the population of the world in the year 1?
2. **MAKING COMPARISONS** How long did it take for the world's population to double from the year 1?
3. **MAKING COMPARISONS** How many years might it take for the world's population to double after 1974? What is the total expected to be in 2028?

Estimated population in billions: 0, 1, 2, 3, 4, 5, 6, 7, 8

Doubling Time: 54 years, 47 years, 123 years, 154 years, 1650 years

Year: 1, 1650, 1804, 1927, 1974, 2028*

SOURCE: United Nations Population Division, The World at Six Billion (1999)

*projected estimate

GeoActivity

Do research to create a bar graph showing population growth and doubling time in one country in the region. Compare it with a bar graph showing the same information for the United States. Display the two bar graphs side by side.

hmhsocialstudies.com

MULTIMEDIA ACTIVITY

Use the links at **hmhsocialstudies.com** to do research about the Ring of Fire. Focus on major eruptions, earthquakes, and tsunamis in the region.

Creating Multimedia Presentations Combine charts, maps, or other visual images in a presentation showing strategies to prepare for natural disasters along the Ring of Fire.

EAST ASIA

Critical Thinking

1. **a.** unstable physical environment caused by shifting tectonic plates, earthquakes, volcanic eruptions, tsunamis; destruction to life and property; disaster preparations
   b. Cheap labor enabled economies of East Asia to produce goods to sell around the world.
2. **a.** strict building codes; disaster drills; courses on disaster preparedness
   b. food supply; water; sanitation; overcrowding
3. Reducing population growth might lessen damage to the environment, make economic prosperity more achievable, and improve the general quality of life. Region and human-environment interaction both apply.
4. The large and well-trained work force in such countries as Japan, Taiwan, and South Korea has been a source of cheap labor to make goods to trade with the rest of the world.
5. More people will be vulnerable to the destruction caused by volcanic eruptions, earthquakes, and tsunamis.

GeoActivity

Integrated Assessment
- Rubric for a bar graph, 2.3

Formal Assessment
- Chapter Test, Forms A, B, and C, pp. 455–466

Geographic Skills

1. 250 million
2. 1650 years
3. 54 years; 8 billion

MULTIMEDIA ACTIVITY

For a multimedia presentation on the Ring of Fire, students should do the following:

- Present a concise, well-organized presentation on strategies to prepare for natural disasters.
- Summarize the impact of eruptions, earthquakes, and tsunamis.
- Produce clear, imaginative visuals for the presentation.
- Include references to the Web sites used as sources.

Grading Rubric Evaluate student performance as Exceptional, Acceptable, or Poor in each of the following categories:

	Exceptional	Acceptable	Poor
Writing and visuals are clear, focused, and logical			
Presentation clearly states topic and purpose			
Provides necessary facts and examples			
Shows strategies for preparing for disasters			

UNIT 10 ATLAS AND CHAPTER 30 PLANNING GUIDE

Physical Geography of Southeast Asia, Oceania, and Antarctica

OVERVIEW	INSTRUCTIONAL RESOURCES	
CHAPTER 30 ESSENTIAL QUESTION How does physical geography vary throughout this vast region? **Focus on the Essential Question Podcast**	**In-Depth Resources: Unit 10** • Unit Atlas Activities, p. 1 • Building Vocabulary, p. 9 • Exploring Today's Issues, pp. 28–31 **Outline Maps with Activities** • S.E. Asia, Oceania, and Antarctica: Physical, pp. 99–100 • S.E. Asia, Oceania, and Antarctica: Political, pp. 101–102 **Block Schedule Strategies** **Chapter Summaries** (English/Spanish)	**Interactive Online Edition** TOS **ExamView® Assessment Suite** (English/Spanish) TOS **CalendarPlanner** **Power Presentations with Media Gallery** **Critical Thinking Transparencies** • CT30 hmhsocialstudies.com INTERACTIVE
SECTION 1 **LANDFORMS AND RESOURCES** **MAIN IDEAS** • The region is composed of continents, peninsulas, and an abundance of islands. • The region's landforms also include volcanoes and coral reefs. • Diverse resources and numerous coastlines have shaped the economies in Southeast Asia and Oceania.	**In-Depth Resources: Unit 10** • Guided Reading, p. 3 • Building Vocabulary, p. 9 • Reteaching Activities, p. 10 • Map and Graph Skill, pp. 6–7 **Guided Reading Workbook,** Section 1	**Critical Thinking Transparencies** • CT62 Comparing Australia and New Zealand
SECTION 2 **CLIMATE AND VEGETATION** **MAIN IDEAS** • Tropical and subtropical climates are widespread in Southeast Asia and parts of Oceania. • Bands of moderate climate are found in Australia and New Zealand. • Naturally occurring diverse vegetation includes tropical forests and plants, evergreen trees, and polar lichens and mosses.	**In-Depth Resources: Unit 10** • Guided Reading, p. 4 • Building Vocabulary, p. 9 • Reteaching Activities, p. 11 **Guided Reading Workbook,** Section 2	**Map Transparencies** • MT53 Vegetation of Australia and New Zealand
SECTION 3 **HUMAN-ENVIRONMENT INTERACTION** **MAIN IDEAS** • In the Pacific, people adapted to voyaging great distances by sea. • In Australia, people are challenged by the destructive European rabbit. • Nuclear testing on Bikini Atoll has left dangerous radiation.	**In-Depth Resources: Unit 10** • Guided Reading, p. 5 • Skillbuilder Practice, p. 8 • Building Vocabulary, p. 9 • Reteaching Activities, p. 12 **Guided Reading Workbook,** Section 3	

ASSESSMENT

SE **Chapter Assessment,** pp. 702–703

Formal Assessment
- Chapter Tests, Forms A, B, and C, pp. 470–481

TOS **ExamView® Assessment Suite**

Strategies for Test Preparation

hmhsocialstudies.com TEST PRACTICE

SE **Section Assessment,** p. 692

Formal Assessment
- Section Quiz, p. 467

Integrated Assessment
- Rubric for a public service announcement, 5.2

Test Practice Transparencies TT97

SE **Section Assessment,** p. 697

Formal Assessment
- Section Quiz, p. 468

Integrated Assessment
- Rubric for a map, 2.1

Test Practice Transparencies TT98

SE **Section Assessment,** p. 701

Formal Assessment
- Section Quiz, p. 469

Integrated Assessment
- Rubric for a chart, 2.2

Test Practice Transparencies TT99

CHART KEY:

SE Student Edition	Block Scheduling	DVD/CD-ROM
TE Teacher's Edition	TOS Teacher One Stop	MP3 Audio
Printable Resource	Presentation Resource	HISTORY™

Program Resources available on TOS and @ hmhsocialstudies.com

SUPPORTING RESOURCES

- Multimedia Classroom Global History Series
- Global History Teacher's Guide

Social Studies Trade Library Collection
- World Regions Trade Collection

For more information or to purchase these resources, go to hmhsocialstudies.com

DIFFERENTIATED INSTRUCTION

English Learners	Struggling Readers	Gifted and Talented Students
Spanish/English Guided Reading Workbook **Access for Students Acquiring English/ESL** Spanish Translations, pp. 161–166 **Chapter Summaries** (English/Spanish) TE **TE Activity** Making Landform Flashcards, p. 690	**Chapter Summaries** (English/Spanish) TE **TE Activity** Identifying Climates, p. 695	TE **TE Activity** Studying Statistics, p. 685 Exploring Environmental Issues, p. 700

ENRICHMENT ACTIVITIES

The following activities are especially suitable for classes following block schedules.

SE **Student Edition,** pp. 688–703
- Interpreting a Relief Map, p. 693

hmhsocialstudies.com INTERACTIVE
- Island Formation in the Pacific, p. 690

BLOCK SCHEDULE LESSON PLAN OPTIONS: 90-MINUTE PERIOD

DAY 1

UNIT PREVIEW, pp. 674–677
Class Time 20 minutes

- **Discussion** Discuss the Unit Introduction, using the discussion prompts on TE pages 674–675.
  Class Time 10 minutes
- **Today's Issues** Introduce Today's Issues in Southeast Asia, Oceania, and Antarctica, using Exploring the Issues questions on PE pages 676–677.
  Class Time 10 minutes

UNIT ATLAS, pp. 678–687
Class Time 35 minutes

- **Groups** Divide students into groups and assign each group one section of the Atlas. Allow groups to prepare summaries of the section based on the Making Comparisons questions and any additional information. Have a student from each group present an oral summary to the class.

SECTION 1, pp. 689–693
Class Time 35 minutes

- **Discussion** As a way to prepare for the next day's review, form groups so that each includes ESL, less proficient, and gifted students. Allow time for the groups to read and discuss the section. Conclude by leading the entire class in a discussion based on the TE "Instruct: Objective" questions and the infographic on pages 690–691.

DAY 2

SECTION 1, pp. 689–693
Class Time 25 minutes

- **Section Review** Have students summarize the section based on Reviewing Places & Terms part A, items 1–5, page 702.

SECTION 2, pp. 694–697
Class Time 45 minutes

- **Outlines** Divide students into three groups and assign one to Southeast Asia, one to Australia, and one to New Zealand. Have groups discuss and prepare outlines of the text for their assigned regions.
  Class Time 20 minutes
- **Panel** To review the section, form a panel of students from each group to serve as consultants on climate and vegetation. Have other class members ask questions from the viewpoint of tourists gathering information about the next place to visit. Conclude by having each student write a brief statement indicating a place chosen and reasons for it.
  Class Time 25 minutes

SECTION 3, pp. 698–701
Class Time 20 minutes

- **Pairs** Have students read and discuss the section in pairs as preparation for the next day's review. Create pairs so that ESL or less proficient readers are linked with proficient or gifted students.

DAY 3

SECTION 3, pp. 698–701
Class Time 35 minutes

- **Identifying and Solving Problems** To help students review the section, have them create a problems-and-solutions chart. Select a student to create two columns on the chalkboard. Columns should be headed "problems" and "solutions." Have students identify problems indicated by the text for each of the section's three major headings. Have students note the solution tried and degree of success. More than one problem or solution may be noted for each heading.

CHAPTER 30 REVIEW AND ASSESSMENT, pp. 702–703
Class Time 55 minutes

- **Review** Have students summarize the chapter by answering three questions from each section listed in Main Ideas.
  Class Time 20 minutes
- **Assessment** Have students complete the Chapter 30 Assessment.
  Class Time 35 minutes

TEACHER-TESTED ACTIVITY *Nation Identification Race*

Class Time One class period

Task Students will compete to see who can identify the largest number of the region's nations and capital cities

Supplies
- Large outline maps of the region
- Construction paper
- Colored pens and/or pencils

Purpose Most students will be unfamiliar with the political geography of Southeast Asia and Oceania. Preparing for a competition may inspire students to learn the names and locations of the region's nations and capital cities.

Activity Work with students to create materials for the game, which include large maps on which the region's political divisions are outlined, and at least two sets of country-cards. (A set should include 24 cards, each bearing the name of one of the countries listed in the Regional Data File, pp. 684–687.) After gathering materials for the game, hang each outline map in a location that will be visible only to the team using it. Divide the class into at least two teams and have them line up behind a station with a set of country-cards. After signaling the start of the game, the student at the head of the line should pick up the top card, go to the map, and write the country name in the appropriate area. If the student knows the name of the country's capital, he or she should write it beneath the country name. The student should then return to the end of the line before the next team member takes a turn. At the end of the game, the teacher will determine a winner by awarding points for speed, correct placement of countries, inclusion of capital cities, spelling, etc.

Linda Tillis
Geography Teacher, South Oak Cliff High School, Dallas, Texas

TECHNOLOGY IN THE CLASSROOM

A WebQuest is a structured, "inquiry-oriented" activity that asks students to solve problems by using Web resources. Students are given a task and are asked to use the Web to help them complete the task, which usually involves drawing a conclusion or solving a problem for which there is no one correct answer. WebQuests can be very simple or highly complex. Below is a simple WebQuest to complement the material in chapter 30. To learn more about WebQuests and how to design an "official" WebQuest, go to the WebQuest link at **hmhsocialstudies.com.**

Objective Students will visit Web sites to determine the pros and cons of living on a tropical island in Oceania or Southeast Asia.

Task Have students use the specified Web sites and Chapter 30 to find out about the climate, geology, and natural resources on the islands of Oceania and Southeast Asia. Have them write letters explaining whether they would like to live on such an island.

Class Time Two class periods

1. Ask students to describe their impressions of South Pacific islands. What comes to their mind when they think of a tropical island? What have they learned from chapter 30 about the physical geography of tropical islands? Did this information match or contradict their initial ideas about Oceania and Southeast Asian islands?
2. Ask students to imagine that a friend has just made the comment "I wish I could live on a tropical island in the South Pacific–wouldn't that be great?!" How would students respond?
3. Have students use the Web sites listed at **hmhsocialstudies.com,** as well as the text in Chapter 30, to gather information to share with their friends. If there is time, you can also have them search for additional sites. They should take notes on the following aspects of the islands of Oceania and Southeast Asia: climate and weather patterns; geology and volcanic activity; and natural resources.
4. Take a class vote to see how many people would like to live on an island in Oceania or Southeast Asia. Ask students to explain their answers. What would be the most desirable things about living on an island in this region? What would be the least desirable things?
5. Ask students to use word processors to write letters to their friends describing the things they have learned about the physical geography of islands in Oceania and Southeast Asia. They may insert pictures to illustrate their points. Ask them to conclude with a statement of whether they think they would like to live on an island in this region, including a discussion of the good and not-so-good things they might encounter.

Previewing the Unit

The first pages of this unit provide an overview of Southeast Asia, Oceania, and Antarctica. The region is vast and diverse in landforms, resources, peoples, and cultures. It presents a wide range of issues.

Discussion Prompts

Exploring Prior Knowledge Ask students the following questions about Southeast Asia, Oceania, and Antarctica to determine prior knowledge:

- What country or countries do you know about in Southeast Asia? *(Answers will vary, but the most likely is Vietnam.)*
- What extreme point of the earth's axis lies in Antarctica? *(South Pole)*

Interpreting Maps Ask students to refer to the satellite image of Southeast Asia, Oceania, and Antarctica to answer the following questions:

- What continents do you recognize, from left to right? *(Africa, Asia, Australia)*
- What is the name for the narrow landform at the southern end of the Southeast Asian mainland? *(peninsula)*
- What other landform type is prominent on this map? *(island)*

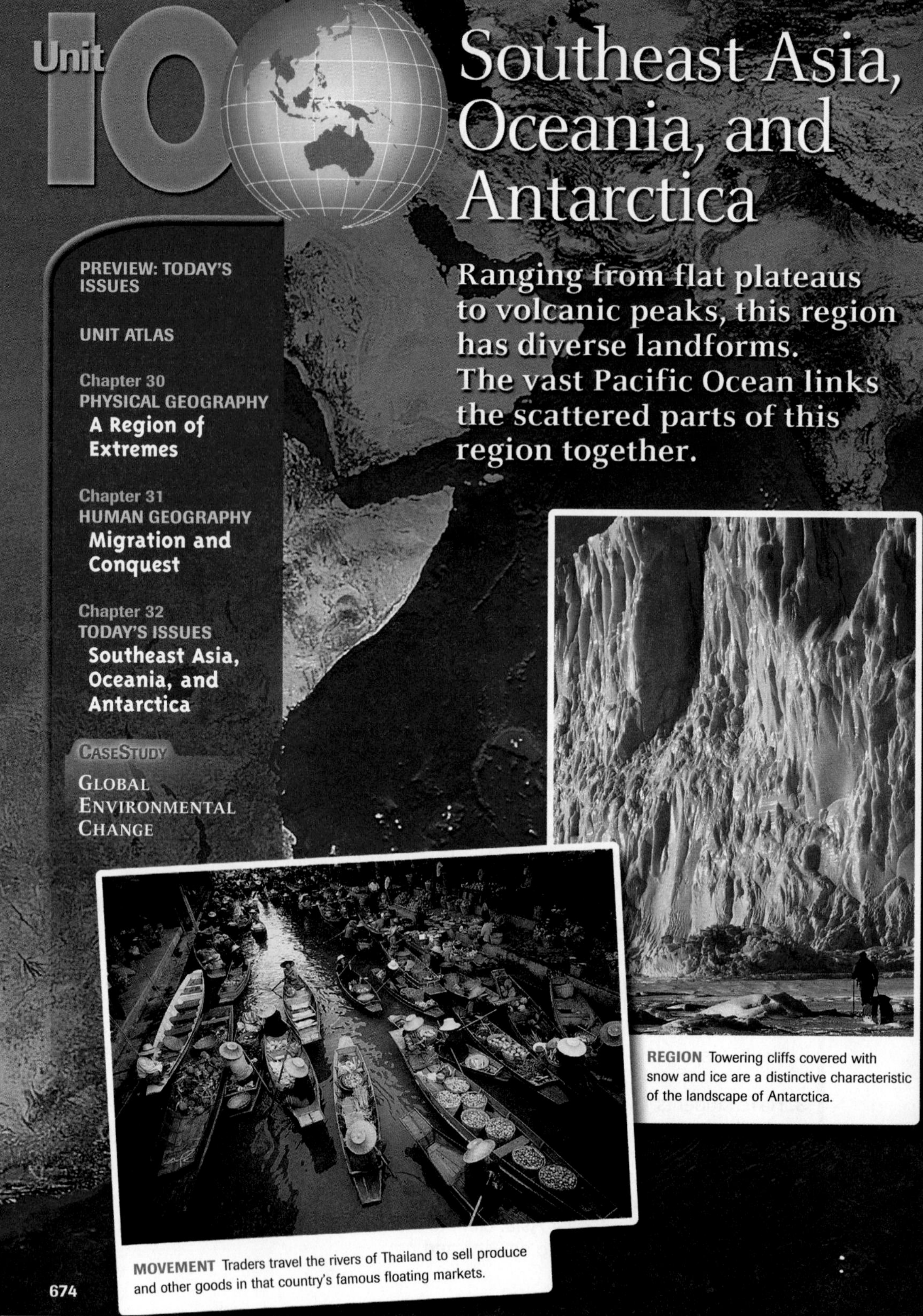

Unit 10
Southeast Asia, Oceania, and Antarctica
Ranging from flat plateaus to volcanic peaks, this region has diverse landforms. The vast Pacific Ocean links the scattered parts of this region together.
PREVIEW: TODAY'S ISSUES
UNIT ATLAS
Chapter 30 PHYSICAL GEOGRAPHY A Region of Extremes
Chapter 31 HUMAN GEOGRAPHY Migration and Conquest
Chapter 32 TODAY'S ISSUES Southeast Asia, Oceania, and Antarctica
CASESTUDY GLOBAL ENVIRONMENTAL CHANGE
674

REGION Towering cliffs covered with snow and ice are a distinctive characteristic of the landscape of Antarctica.

MOVEMENT Traders travel the rivers of Thailand to sell produce and other goods in that country's famous floating markets.

UNIT 10 ADDITIONAL RESOURCES

BOOKS FOR THE TEACHER

SarDesai, D. R. ***Southeast Asia: Past and Present.*** Westview Press, 2009. Sixth edition includes many updates, such as the 2004 tsunami and recent political unrest in Myanmar.

Robson, John. ***Captain Cook's World.*** Auckland: Random House New Zealand, 2000. The explorer's story told through maps and text.

BOOKS FOR THE STUDENT

McEvedy, Colin. ***The Penguin Historical Atlas of the Pacific.*** NY: Penguin, 1998. Valuable resource on the Pacific region.

Summers, Harry G., Jr. ***Historical Atlas of the Vietnam War.*** Boston: Houghton Mifflin, 1995. Comprehensive information about Vietnamese culture and geography.

VIDEOS

Antarctica. Hacienda Productions. Altschul Group, 1997. Introduces Antarctic research through the eyes of a student selected by the National Science Foundation.

Bali, Masterpiece of the Gods. Natl. Geographic, 1990. Shows how religion influences Balinese cultural expressions and daily life.

INTERNET

For more on the geography of Southeast Asia, Oceania, and Antarctica, visit . . .

hmhsocialstudies.com

GeoData

REGION Oceania includes the Pacific Islands not considered to be part of Southeast Asia. Some people include New Zealand and Australia, even though Australia is a continent, not an island.

LOCATION Australia is known as the "Land Down Under." It is the only inhabited continent to lie completely in the Southern Hemisphere.

HUMAN–ENVIRONMENT INTERACTION Farmers have adapted to the region's varied environments. They use terraced fields on steep Southeast Asian slopes and irrigate arid parts of Australia.

For more information on Southeast Asia, Oceania, and Antarctica . . .

hmhsocialstudies.com
RESEARCH WEB LINKS

Southeast Asia, Oceania, and Antarctica **675**

Interpreting Photographs

Thailand Floating Markets

Ask students what can be inferred from the floating markets. *(Thailand's waterways are useful for moving about and doing business.)*

Cliffs of Antarctica

Tell students that Antarctica is often referred to as a white desert. Ask what can be inferred from this term. *(Antarctica has little precipitation.)*

ACTIVITY OPTION COOPERATIVE LEARNING

CREATING A PERSUASIVE PAMPHLET

Objective To allow students to explore different aspects of the region

Class Time 30 minutes

Task Create a pamphlet that demonstrates the global importance of a subregion

Directions Divide students into groups and assign each a subregion. Have each student search for information about their subregion in newspapers and magazines. Have them use this information to compose a neatly written paragraph for a pamphlet to be constructed by the group. Display the results and ask the class to judge the pamphlet's coverage of each subregion.

Previewing Today's Issues

These pages preview the issues that affect Southeast Asia, Oceania, or Antarctica. These issues will be fully explored in Chapter 32 (pages 726–739). Use the discussion prompts that follow to determine students' prior knowledge and allow them to make comparisons to local issues.

In-Depth Resources: Unit 10
- Exploring Today's Issues, pp. 28–31

LAND CLAIMS

Several centuries ago Europeans settled in Australia despite the land claims of native people. Aboriginal petitioners today are regaining some land rights.

Discussion Prompts

- What nearby country may share this problem? *(New Zealand)*
- Do you know of other countries with a similar history? *(the United States; countries in Latin America)*

Today's Issues in Southeast Asia, Oceania, and Antarctica

Today, Southeast Asia, Oceania, and Antarctica face the issues previewed here. As you read Chapters 30 and 31, you will learn helpful background information. You will study the issues themselves in Chapter 32.

In a small group, answer the questions below. Then participate in a class discussion of your answers.

Exploring the Issues

1. LAND CLAIMS Search the Internet for information about Aboriginal land claims in Australia. What are the different sides in the conflict?
2. INDUSTRIALISM Make a list of the possible results of industrial growth, both positive and negative. How might a country reduce the negative effects?
3. ENVIRONMENTAL CHANGE Consider news stories that you've heard about global warming and the ozone hole. What are some of the predicted effects? Make a list of all the effects you can remember.

For more on these issues in Southeast Asia, Oceania, and Antarctica . . .

LAND CLAIMS

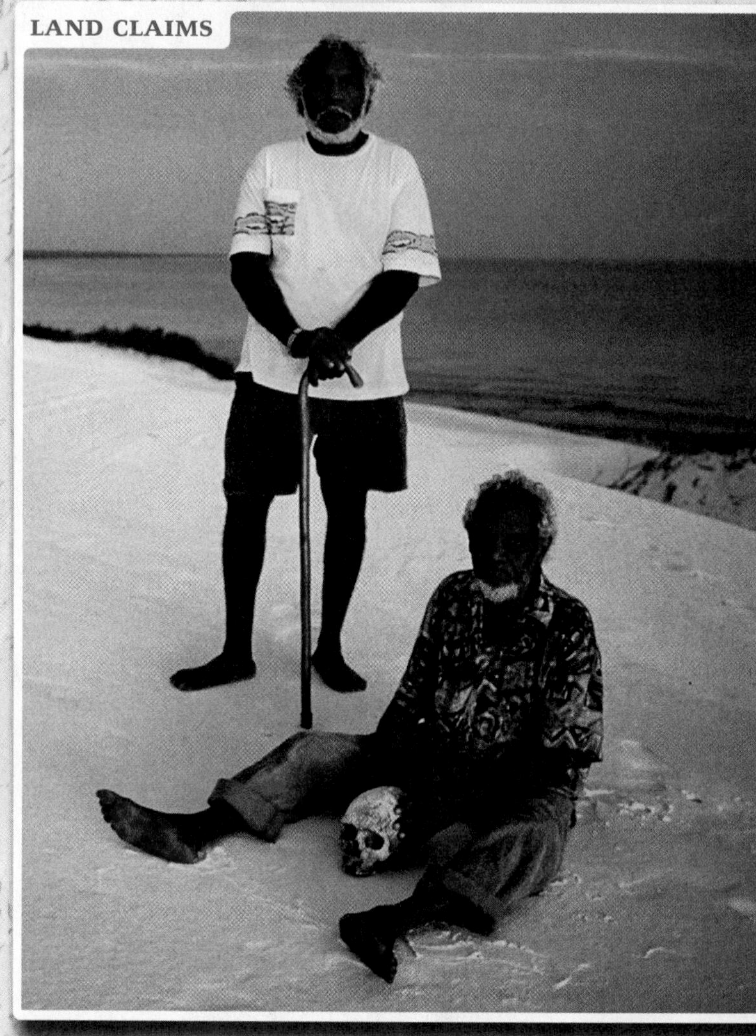

Should native people be given back their ancestors' land?

These two Aboriginal men are elders of the Wuthathi people. They have come to bury the skull of an ancestor in their homeland. Aboriginal people feel a strong spiritual connection to their land and do not want to be separated from it even in death.

EXPLORING THE ISSUES ANSWERS

1. Answers will vary, but encourage students to consider how different peoples can have very different ideas about what it means to "own" land.
2. Industrial growth might be positive if increased productivity helps to raise people's living standards. Negative effects might include environmental damage.
3. Students may have read about global warming's effect on sea levels and precipitation patterns. They might also have heard that the reduction of ozone has resulted in higher levels of UV light and increases in the incidence of skin cancer.

INDUSTRIALISM

How does industrialization affect cities?

This slum in Jakarta, Indonesia, shows how difficult it is to provide adequate housing for the thousands of people who move to cities seeking factory jobs.

CASESTUDY

ENVIRONMENTAL CHANGE

How have people changed the atmosphere?

The green and blue areas in these satellite images show where the ozone layer over Antarctica is thinnest. Ozone in the stratosphere, a layer of the atmosphere, protects the living things of earth from harmful ultraviolet radiation.

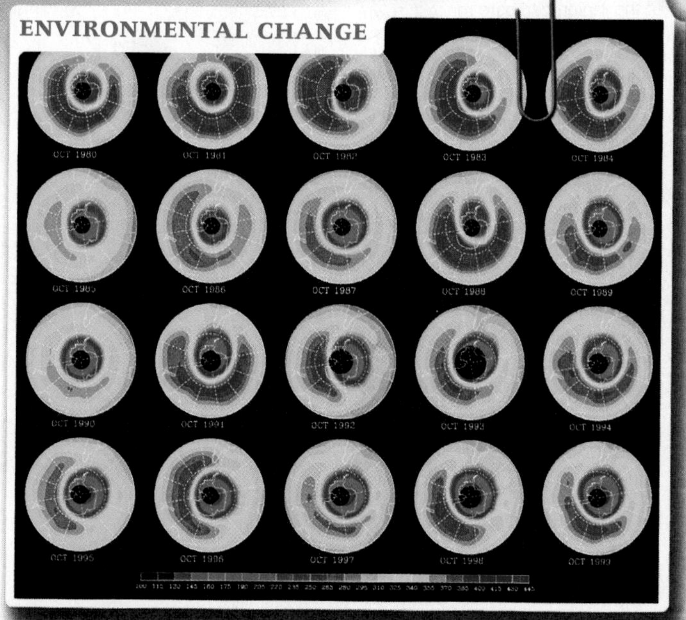

SE ASIA & OCEANIA

INDUSTRIALISM

Southeast Asia is experiencing the urban growth that typically accompanies industrialization. Like people in many parts of the world, Southeast Asians are migrating to cities to find jobs.

Discussion Prompts

- What other problems might be faced by urban Southeast Asians? *(Students might mention traffic and pollution.)*
- How are urban problems addressed locally? *(Answers will vary, but may include through city councils and civic organizations.)*

CASESTUDY

ENVIRONMENTAL CHANGE

To give students an opportunity to explore the issues surrounding environmental change, direct them to the Case Study. It begins on page 734 and concludes with a Case Study Project on pages 736–737.

Discussion Prompts

- What have you read or heard about environmental change? *(Answers will vary.)*
- What can be done about it? *(Students may discuss the importance of international cooperation.)*

ACTIVITY OPTION **INTERNET RESEARCH**

BLOCK SCHEDULING

WRITING AN OP-ED PIECE

Objective To develop basic research skills

Class Time 35 minutes

Task Identify two sources about an issue previewed on these pages and write a brief op-ed piece based on the findings

Directions Direct students to **hmhsocialstudies.com**, and follow the links to sources of information on these issues. Use examples from the newspapers or magazines as models for the students to follow.

OPTIONAL ACTIVITY If Internet access is limited or unavailable, have students use printed sources in the library.

ATLAS OBJECTIVES

1. Examine key physical features of Southeast Asia, Oceania, and Antarctica.
2. Compare data on the physical geography of Southeast Asia and Oceania.
3. Identify current political features of the region and compare to Southeast Asia in 1200.
4. Examine population figures for ethnic Chinese in Southeast Asia.
5. Learn about active volcanoes and climates in the region.
6. Identify major religions of the region.

Focus & Motivate

Ask students what they already know about landforms and climates of Southeast Asia and Oceania. Ask what human activity they have read or heard about in Antarctica. *(Answers will vary but may include islands, tropics; scientific activity in Antarctica.)*

Instruct: Objective 

Southeast Asia, Oceania, and Antarctica: Physical

- What physical feature borders the coastline of northeast Australia? *(Great Barrier Reef)*
- What oceans encircle Antarctica? *(Pacific, Atlantic, Indian)*

 **In-Depth Resources, Unit 10**
- Unit Atlas Activities, p. 1

 **Outline Maps with Activities**
- S.E. Asia, Oceania, and Antarctica: Physical, pp. 99–100

 **Map Transparencies MT51**
- S.E. Asia, Oceania, and Antarctica: Physical

Unit ATLAS

Patterns of Physical Geography

Use the Unit Atlas to add to your knowledge of Southeast Asia, Oceania, and Antarctica. As you look at the maps and charts, notice geographic patterns and specific details about the region. For example, the chart gives details about large islands in the region.

After studying the pictures, graphs, and physical map on these two pages, jot down in your notebook answers to the questions below.

Making Comparisons

1. How does the population of the region compare to that of the United States?
2. What is the world's largest island? How does its area compare to the combined area of New Guinea, Borneo, and Sumatra?
3. Which countries of this region would you consider flat? Which would you consider mountainous?

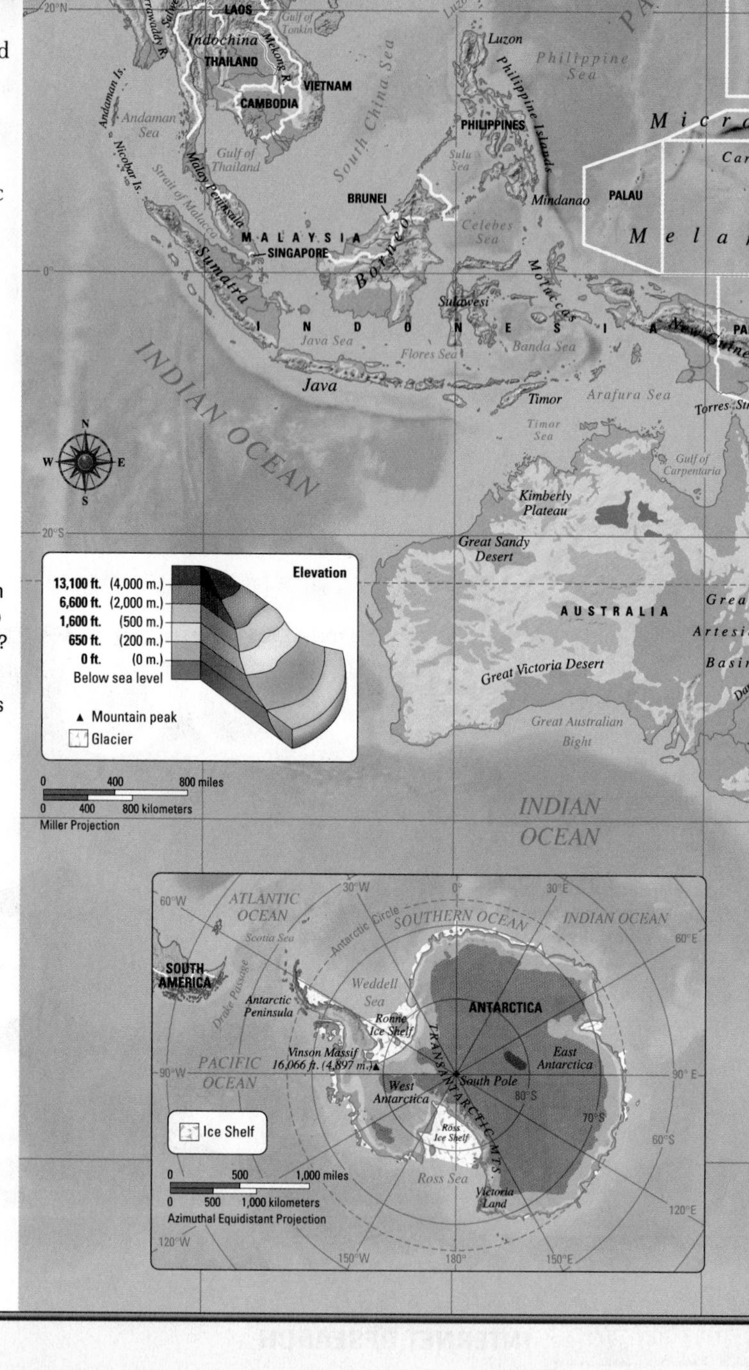

MAKING COMPARISONS ANSWERS

1. It is about 2 times greater.
2. Greenland; it is about 25,000 square miles greater than the other three combined.
3. Australia is flat; virtually all of the other countries are mountainous to some extent.

Southeast Asia, Oceania, and Antarctica: Physical

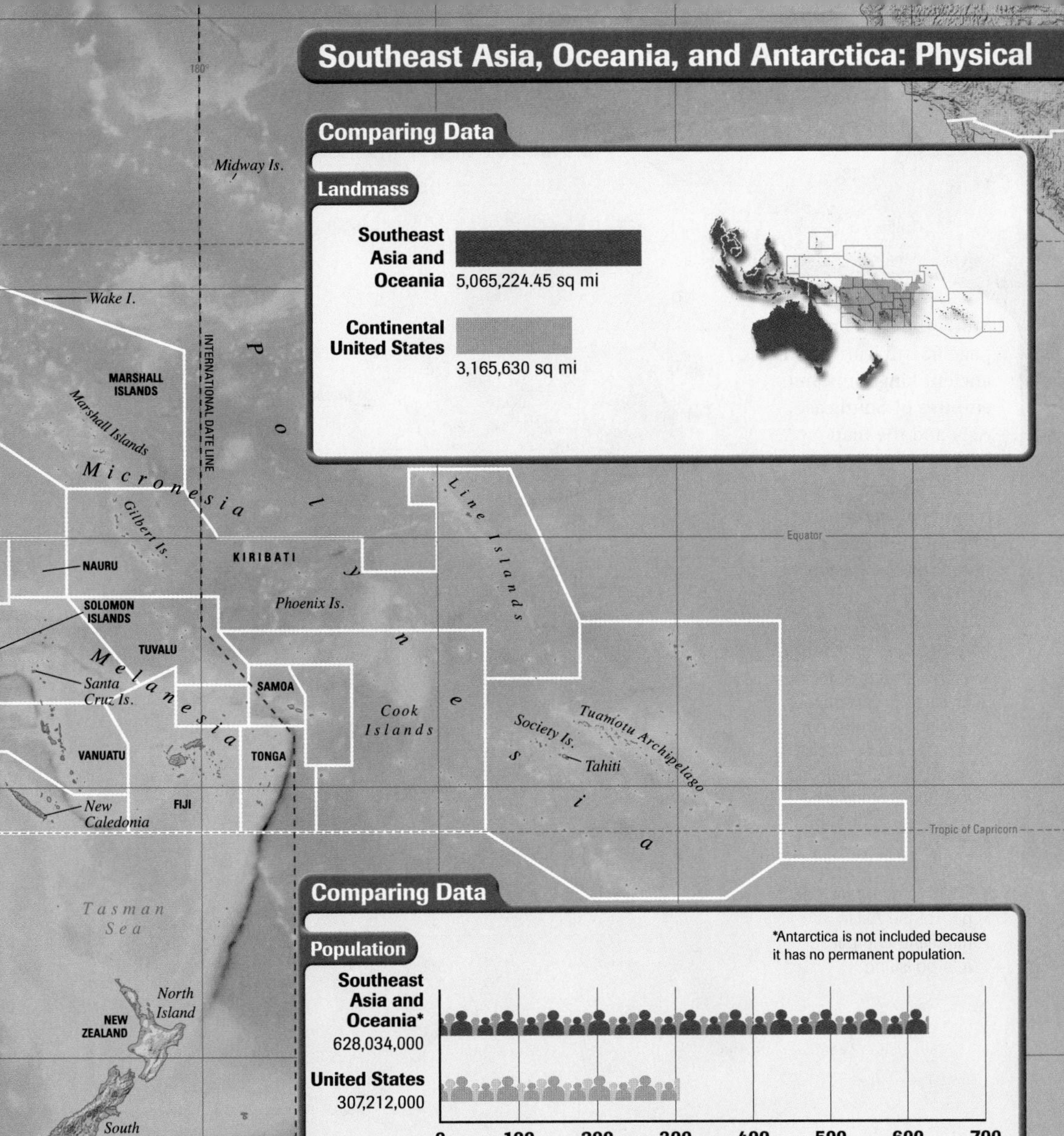

Comparing Data

Population

*Antarctica is not included because it has no permanent population.

Region	Population
Southeast Asia and Oceania*	628,034,000
United States	307,212,000

Population (in millions): 0, 100, 200, 300, 400, 500, 600, 700

Islands

World's Largest	Greenland	839,999 sq mi
U.S. Largest	Hawaii	4,021 sq mi
	New Guinea	341,631 sq mi
	Borneo	290,320 sq mi
	Sumatra	182,542 sq mi

SE ASIA & OCEANIA

679

Instruct: Objective 2

Comparing Data

- **Landmass** How does the United States compare in size to Southeast Asia and Oceania? *(it is about three-fifths the size)*
- **Population** How does the population of the United States compare to the region? *(it has about one half the population)*
- **Islands** How many islands the size of Hawaii could fit into Greenland? *(approximately 209)*

More About

The Mariana Trench

The Mariana Trench in the western Pacific Ocean is Earth's deepest known depression. It is about seven miles deep and extends for more than 1,500 miles east of the Mariana Islands. Most major oceanic trenches are found in the Pacific. The Java Trench south of Indonesia is the major depression in the Indian Ocean.

ACTIVITY OPTION — CRITICAL THINKING

ANALYZING DATA

Tell students that charts can sometimes contain data that is too general for persons seeking details. Point out that the physical geography map covers a vast region including all of Southeast Asia and Oceania. Landmasses vary widely, especially in Oceania.

Applying the Skill Have students refer to the map and consider the categories shown in the charts for comparing data. Ask the following questions:

- What categories were selected for comparison? *(Southeast Asia and Oceania, Continental United States)*
- What can be determined about Southeast Asia compared to Oceania? *(nothing)*
- How might the categories be changed to allow for more detailed comparisons? *(Southeast Asia and Oceania might be made separate categories; the large landmass of Australia might be separated from the rest of Oceania.)*

Instruct: Objective 3

Southeast Asia, Oceania, and Antarctica: Political

- Which Southeast Asian country lies west of Papua New Guinea? *(Indonesia)*
- Which countries border mainland Southeast Asia? *(China, India)*
- Which countries border the island part of Malaysia? *(Indonesia, Brunei)*

Outline Maps with Activities
- S.E. Asia and Oceania: Political, pp. 101–102

Map Transparencies MT52
- S.E. Asia and Oceania: Political

More About

The Power of Singapore Island

The history of Singapore shows the emergence of a powerful city-state. Dominated by Great Britain since 1824 and part of its Malaysian Federation, the important port city and island of Singapore formed an independent republic in 1965. This furthered its trading ties with Indonesia, which opposed Malaysia as a British colonial creation. Singapore today is a major Southeast Asian center of finance and technical expertise.

Unit ATLAS

Patterns of Human Geography

Study the map on page 681 to learn about ancient kingdoms and empires of Southeast Asia and the map on both pages to learn about the present-day nations of the region. Then write in your notebook the answers to these questions.

Making Comparisons

1. Which ancient kingdoms or empires have names similar to present-day countries in Southeast Asia? How do their locations compare?
2. Which are the largest countries in the region?
3. Which country includes part of the Asian mainland and part of a large island?

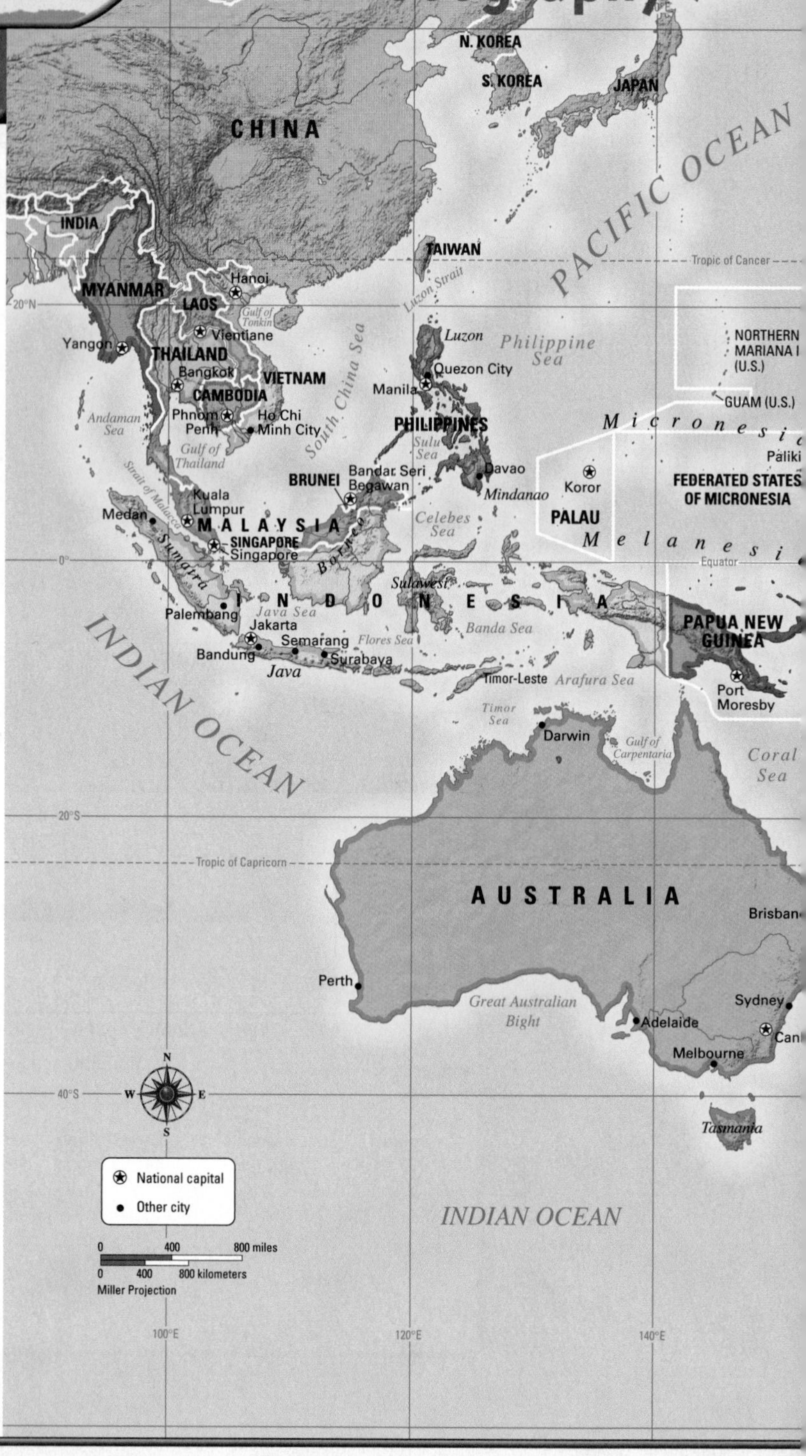

MAKING COMPARISONS ANSWERS

1. Dai Viet is similar to Vietnam and was located where northern Vietnam is today.
2. Australia, Indonesia, Myanmar, Thailand
3. Malaysia

Southeast Asia, Oceania, and Antarctica: Political

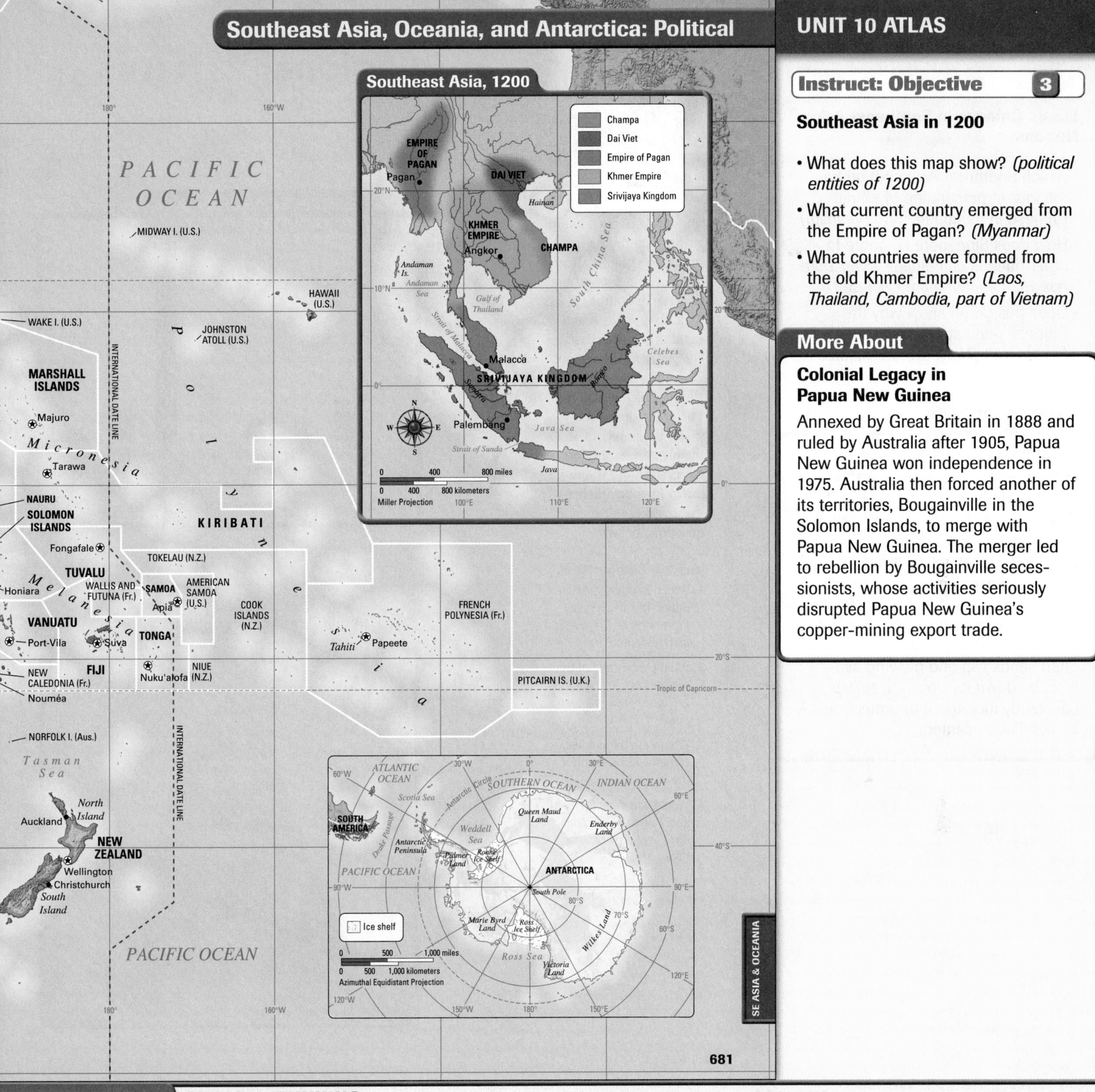

Instruct: Objective 3

Southeast Asia in 1200

- What does this map show? *(political entities of 1200)*
- What current country emerged from the Empire of Pagan? *(Myanmar)*
- What countries were formed from the old Khmer Empire? *(Laos, Thailand, Cambodia, part of Vietnam)*

More About

Colonial Legacy in Papua New Guinea

Annexed by Great Britain in 1888 and ruled by Australia after 1905, Papua New Guinea won independence in 1975. Australia then forced another of its territories, Bougainville in the Solomon Islands, to merge with Papua New Guinea. The merger led to rebellion by Bougainville secessionists, whose activities seriously disrupted Papua New Guinea's copper-mining export trade.

ACTIVITY OPTION CRITICAL THINKING

MAKING INFERENCES

Explaining the Skill Explain that geographers must often make inferences, or "read between the lines," to understand their subject.

Applying the Skill Ask students the following questions:

- What does this map show about the peoples of Southeast Asia? *(they organized politically as early as A.D. 1200)*
- What part of Southeast Asia remained generally stable? *(the part now known as Myanmar)*
- What part underwent the most upheaval? *(the old Khmer Empire, which split into several nations)*

Instruct: Objective 4

Ethnic Chinese in Southeast Asian Nations

- Which Southeast Asian nation has the lowest percentage of ethnic Chinese in its population? *(Vietnam)*
- How does Singapore compare to all other nations combined? *(Singapore has 15.5 percent more Chinese.)*
- Does this graph show why the Chinese population is large in Singapore? *(No, it provides limited information.)*

More About

Southeast Asian Volcanoes

Indonesia has approximately 130 active volcanoes, more than any other place in Southeast Asia or the world. Merapi Volcano in Java is among the most active. It has erupted at least a dozen times in recorded history and caused numerous fatalities, including about 1,300 people in 1930. Merapi's exposed lava dome often sends ash and glowing avalanches down its slope. Its activity is constantly monitored to protect nearby population centers.

Unit ATLAS

Regional Patterns

These two pages contain graphs and thematic maps. The graphs show the percentage of ethnic Chinese in Southeast Asian populations and the number of active volcanoes in the region. One map shows the climates of the region. The other shows the major religions of the region. After studying the graphs and maps, jot down in your notebook the answers to the questions below.

Making Comparisons

1. Which Southeast Asian nation has the highest proportion of Chinese in its population?
2. What percentage of the region's active volcanoes are found in Southeast Asia?
3. Where are the coldest climates to be found in the region?
4. Would you describe this as a region of religious diversity? Why or why not?

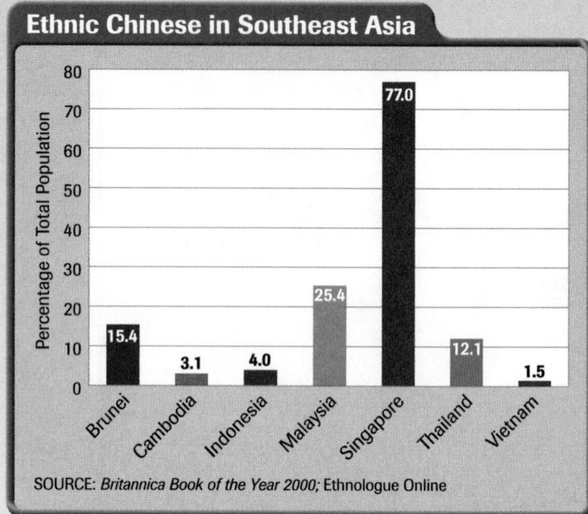

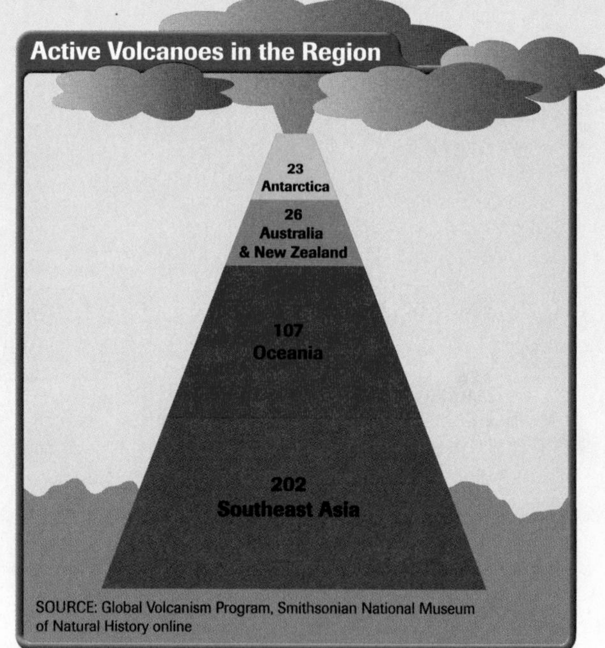

MAKING COMPARISONS ANSWERS

1. Singapore
2. 56 percent
3. Antarctica
4. Yes, it includes Islam, two branches of Christianity, two Eastern religions, and traditional religions.

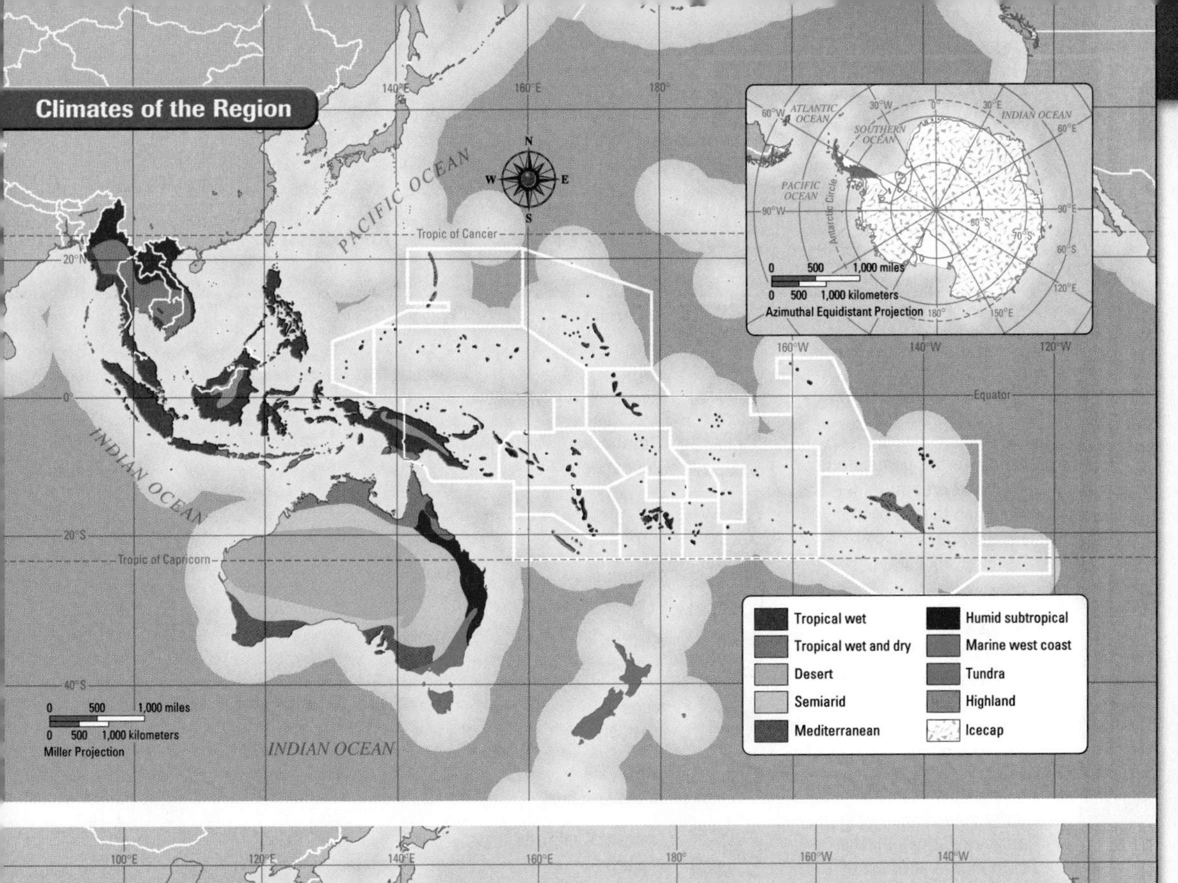

Major Religions of the Region

PACIFIC OCEAN

INDIAN OCEAN

PACIFIC OCEAN

Tropic of Cancer

Tropic of Capricorn

Equator

Confucianism
Protestant
Roman Catholic
Buddhism
Sunni Muslim
Traditional

0 500 1,000 miles
0 500 1,000 kilometers
Miller Projection

SE ASIA & OCEANIA

683

Instruct: Objective 

Active Volcanoes in the Region/Climates of the Region

- What percentage of the region's active volcanoes are found in Oceania, Australia, and New Zealand? *(about 37 percent)*
- What climates are common to mainland Southeast Asia and Australia? *(tropical wet, tropical wet and dry, humid subtropical)*
- Would you say that this is a region of climatic extremes? *(yes—climates range from icecap to tropical)*

Instruct: Objective 6

Major Religions of the Region

- What branch of Christianity is most widespread in the region? *(Protestant)*
- What are the religions of mainland Southeast Asia? *(traditional, Buddhism, Confucianism)*
- Can you identify the Southeast Asian country that is primarily Roman Catholic? *(the Philippines)*

More About

Colonialism in the Philippines

The Roman Catholic influence in the Philippines dates from the Spanish invasion in the sixteenth century. Numerous revolts occurred against Spanish colonial rule. Severe uprisings occurred shortly before Spain ceded the Philippines to the United States by treaty in 1898. In cooperation with the United States a Commonwealth of the Philippines was established in 1935. The Philippines became independent in 1946.

ACTIVITY OPTION FIVE THEMES OF GEOGRAPHY

MOVEMENT

Exploring the Theme Remind students that movement in geography can be seen in the spread of populations and religions. Point out that Confucianism originated with an ancient Chinese philosopher. In this context, have students examine the graphs and thematic maps on pages 682–683.

Understanding the Theme Ask the following questions. Which chart and thematic map reflect the theme of movement? *(Chinese in SE Asian Nations, Major Religions)* Which parts of Southeast Asia strongly display interaction with the Chinese? *(Singapore, and the part of mainland Southeast Asia that is marked for Confucianism)* What can you infer about the areas marked as Christian? *(European explorers and settlers brought Christianity to the region.)*

DATA FILE OBJECTIVE

Examine and compare data on the countries of Southeast Asia and Oceania.

CHART OBJECTIVE

Identify territories and possessions in Oceania and learn about inland explorations of Antarctica.

Focus & Motivate

Ask students if they think any Southeast Asian or Oceanic country exceeds the United States in population. *(Indonesia is closest; it has about 69 million fewer people than the United States.)*

Instruct: Objective 

Regional Data File

- Which two countries are smallest in size? *(Nauru, Tuvalu)* Have they the smallest populations? *(yes)*
- Which Southeast Asian or Oceanic country has the highest life expectancy? *(Singapore)* How does the United States compare? *(The U.S. figure is lower.)*
- Which country has the highest birthrate? *(Laos)* Which has the highest infant mortality rate? *(Laos)*

In-Depth Resources: Unit 10
• Regional Data File Activities, p. 2

Regional Data File

Study the charts on the countries of this region.

Making Comparisons

1. Compare the population and total area of Australia to that of the United States. What conclusions can you draw?
2. Make a list of the top three countries in population. What is the difference in population between the top two countries?
3. Make a list of the top three countries in total area. How does this list compare to your list of the most populous countries?

(continued on page 686)

Country Flag	Country/ Capital	Population	Life Expectancy (years)	Birthrate (per 1,000 pop.)	Infant Mortalit (per 1,000 live birth
	Australia Canberra	21,263,000	81.6	12.5	4.8
	Brunei Bandar Seri Begawan	388,000	75.7	18.2	12.3
	Cambodia Phnom Penh	14,494,000	62.1	25.7	54.8
	Fiji Suva	945,000	70.7	21.9	11.6
	Indonesia Jakarta	240,272,000	70.8	18.8	30.0
	Kiribati Tarawa	113,000	63.2	23.6	43.5
	Laos Vientiane	6,834,000	56.6	34.0	77.8
	Malaysia Kuala Lumpur	25,716,000	73.3	22.2	15.9
	Marshall Islands Majuro	65,000	71.2	30.7	25.5
	Micronesia, Fed. States of Palikir	107,000	70.9	23.1	26.1
	Myanmar Yangon	48,138,000	63.4	17.0	47.6
	Nauru (no capital)	14,000	64.2	23.9	9.3
	New Zealand Wellington	4,213,000	80.4	13.9	4.9
	Palau Melekeok	21,000	71.2	11.2	13.1
	Papua New Guinea Port Moresby	5,941,000	65.8	27.6	45.9
	Philippines Manila	97,977,000	71.1	26.0	20.6
	Samoa Apia	220,000	71.9	22.9	24.2
	Singapore Singapore	4,658,000	82.0	8.8	2.3
	Solomon Islands Honiara	596,000	73.7	27.7	19.0

For updated statistics on Southeast Asia, Oceania, and Antarctica . . .

MAKING COMPARISONS ANSWERS

1. Australia's population is roughly 7 percent of that of the United States. Its total area is roughly 78 percent of that of the United States. Compared with the United States, Australia has a low population density.
2. Indonesia, Philippines, Vietnam; 142,295,000.
3. Australia, Indonesia, Myanmar; Indonesia is the only country that appears on both lists; it is first in population and second in area.

684 UNIT 10

Doctors (per 100,000 pop.) (2000–2004)	GDP[a] (billions $US)	Import/Export (billions $US)	Literacy Rate (percentage)	Televisions (per 1,000 pop.)	Passenger Cars (per 1,000 pop.)	Total Area[b] (square miles)
247	819	160.9/161.5	99	716	513	2,988,902
101	19.4	2.61/10.67	93	637	619	2,228
16	27.9	5.37/3.58	74	9	1	69,900
34	3.6	3.12/1.20	94	110	92	7,054
13	968.5	86.6/115.6	90	143	23	741,100
N/A	0.6	0.06/0.02	N/A	23	N/A	313
N/A	15.1	2.03/1.27	69	10	N/A	91,429
70	378.9	119.5/156.4	89	174	19	127,317
N/A	0.1	0.08/0.02	94	N/A	N/A	70
N/A	0.2	0.13/0.01	89	20	N/A	271
36	56.5	3.56/6.50	90	7	4	261,970
N/A	0.6	0.02/0.00006	N/A	1	N/A	8
237	116.5	24.29/26.25	99	516	522	103,738
N/A	0.2	0.11/0.006	92	98	N/A	177
5	13.4	2.69/4.06	57	13	4	178,704
58	324.9	45.8/37.2	93	110	27	115,831
70	1.0	0.32/0.13	99	56	44	1,137
140	235.7	245/268.9	93	341	99	267
13	1.6	0.26/0.24	N/A	16	N/A	10,985

More About

British Captain James Cook

No other explorer did as much as Captain James Cook to open up the vast Pacific Ocean for Europeans. He joined the British navy in 1755 and spent more than twenty years commanding ships of discovery. He explored coastal New Zealand and mapped it for the first time. He sailed to Australia and many Pacific islands, among them the Sandwich Islands—now re-named Hawaii. He also engaged in Antarctic exploration.

More About

Tupaia

Captain James Cook was greatly indebted to the learned Polynesian Tupaia for guiding him during his Pacific explorations. They met when the Cook expedition stopped in Tahiti and learned the language. In 1768, Tupaia sailed with the expedition and contributed map-making and navigational skills. Unlike other Europeans, Captain Cook did not denigrate the ability of Polynesians to find distant islands by deliberate means.

DIFFERENTIATING INSTRUCTION GIFTED AND TALENTED STUDENTS

STUDYING STATISTICS

Objective To learn more about interpreting statistics and conducting independent study

Class Time 30 minutes

Task Write a brief justification for moving to a country listed in the Regional Data File

Directions Have students study the statistics for countries in the Regional Data File and select one with a view to moving. They should then write a brief argument to support their selection. Students may supplement the statistics with research on the Internet or from printed sources.

Instruct: Objective 2

Territories and Possessions in Oceania

- What are the U.S. possessions in Oceania? How are they administered? *(Midway Islands, Wake Island; they are administered by the Navy)*
- What other countries have interests in Oceania? *(New Zealand, France, Indonesia, Australia, Great Britain)*
- How is the U.S. territory of Guam governed? *(by a governor and a legislature)*

More About

Independence for Brunei

After discovery by the Portuguese in 1521, Brunei fell into decline and eventually came under British rule. In 1984 it became an independent Islamic sultanate linked to the British Commonwealth. Officially known as the State of Brunei Darussalam, it is about half the size of Connecticut. Brunei prospers from its oil and natural gas reserves and has one of the highest standards of living in Southeast Asia.

Unit Atlas: Regional Data File

Country Flag	Country/ Capital	Population	Life Expectancy (years)	Birthrate (per 1,000 pop.)	Infant Mortality (per 1,000 live births)
	Thailand Bangkok	65,998,000	73.1	13.4	17.5
	Timor-Leste Dili	1,132,000	67.3	26.3	40.7
	Tonga Nuku'alofa	121,000	70.7	19.8	11.6
	Tuvalu Funafuti	12,000	64.4	23.1	35.5
	Vanuatu Port-Vila	219,000	64.0	21.5	49.5
	Vietnam Hanoi	88,577,000	71.7	17.7	22.3
	United States Washington, D.C.	307,212,000	78.1	13.8	6.2

Making Comparisons *(continued)*

4. Which countries have a literacy rate below 60 percent?
5. For the countries you identified in question 4, look at their ratio of doctors to population. Is it high or low compared to other countries? What might be the relationship between literacy rate and number of doctors?

Sources:
Central Intelligence Agency, *The World Factbook*, 2010
The World Almanac and Book of Facts, 2010
World Health Organization (WHO), 2007

Notes:
[a] GDP (purchasing power parity) is defined as the sum value of all goods and services produced in the country valued at prices prevailing in the United States.
[b] Includes land and water, when figures are available

Territories and Possessions in Oceania

Name	Status
American Samoa	U.S. territory*
Cook Islands	Self-governing area in free association with New Zealand
French Polynesia	French overseas territory
Guam	U.S. territory*
Irian Jaya	Indonesian province
Midway Islands	U.S. possession*
New Caledonia	French overseas territory
Niue	Self-governing area in free association with New Zealand
Norfolk Island	Australian territory
Northern Mariana Islands	U.S. commonwealth*
Pitcairn Islands	British overseas territory
Tokelau	New Zealand territory
Wake Island	U.S. possession*
Wallis and Futuna	French overseas territory

* A commonwealth is a self-governing political unit in voluntary association with the United States; a U.S. territory is not a state but has a governor and a legislature; the U.S. possessions in the Pacific are administered by the Navy.

SOURCE: *World Book Encyclopedia 2000*

686 UNIT 10

MAKING COMPARISONS ANSWERS

4. Papua New Guinea, Timor-Leste
5. Each has a low doctor-to-population ratio. Literacy is an indicator of education, and advanced education is necessary to become a doctor.

Doctors (per 100,000 pop.) (2000–2004)	GDP[a] (billions $US)	Import/Export (billions $US)	Literacy Rate (percentage)	Televisions (per 1,000 pop.)	Passenger Cars (per 1,000 pop.)	Total Area[b] (square miles)
37	539.7	131.5/150.9	93	274	59	198,457
10	2.7	0.20/0.01	59	N/A	N/A	5,794
34	0.6	0.14/0.02	99	61	58	289
N/A	0.01	0.01/0.001	N/A	9	N/A	10
11	1.0	0.16/0.04	74	12	27	4,710
53	258.2	68.8/56.55	90	184	N/A	127,244
256	14,260.0	1,445/994.7	99	844	725	3,794,083

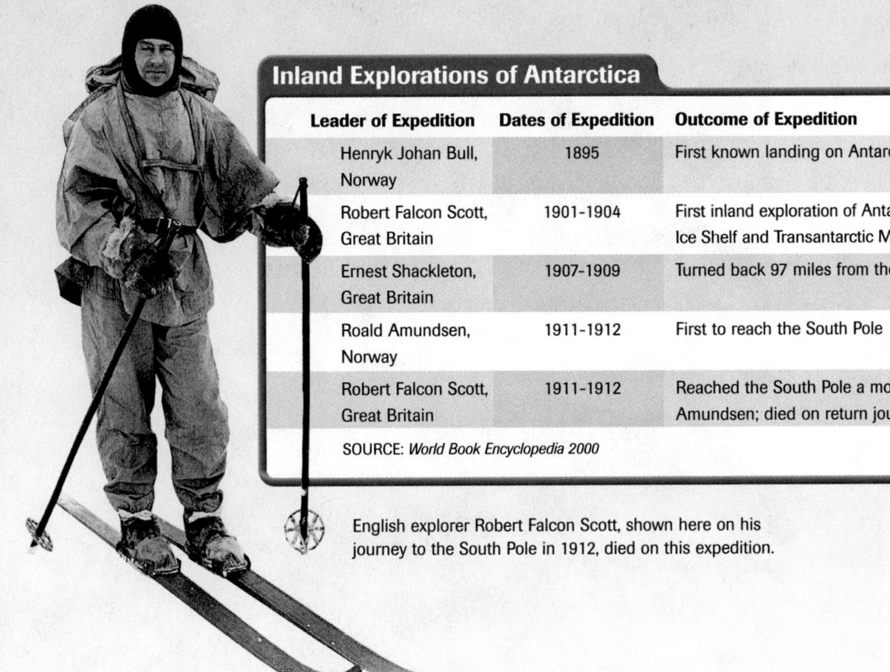

Inland Explorations of Antarctica

Leader of Expedition	Dates of Expedition	Outcome of Expedition
Henryk Johan Bull, Norway	1895	First known landing on Antarctic mainland
Robert Falcon Scott, Great Britain	1901-1904	First inland exploration of Antarctica, of Ross Ice Shelf and Transantarctic Mountains
Ernest Shackleton, Great Britain	1907-1909	Turned back 97 miles from the South Pole
Roald Amundsen, Norway	1911-1912	First to reach the South Pole
Robert Falcon Scott, Great Britain	1911-1912	Reached the South Pole a month after Amundsen; died on return journey

SOURCE: *World Book Encyclopedia 2000*

English explorer Robert Falcon Scott, shown here on his journey to the South Pole in 1912, died on this expedition.

Instruct: Objective 3

Inland Explorations of Antarctica

- When did the first European explorer reach Antarctica? *(1895)*
- What countries were expedition leaders from? *(Norway, Great Britain)*
- Who reached the South Pole in 1911-1912? *(Roald Amundsen, Robert Falcon Scott)*

More About

Norwegian Explorer Roald Amundsen

Roald Amundsen was fascinated by north and south polar exploration. He sailed for the first time in 1897 as first mate on an expedition bound for the Antarctic. After learning of American Robert E. Peary's 1909 North Pole success, he commanded the ship *Fram* on a voyage in 1910 to the South Pole. He and several companions reached it by dog team and skis in December 1911, just a month before British explorer Robert F. Scott.

ACTIVITY OPTION LINK TO HISTORY

BLOCK SCHEDULING

MAKING A POLAR EXPEDITION TIME LINE

Objective To gather key historical information and summarize it in a new format

Class Time 30 minutes

Task Make a time line showing key events in polar exploration

Supplies Needed

- large sheets of chart or drawing paper
- pens or coloring pencils

Directions Have students construct a time line that incorporates the key events of Antarctic exploration as shown in the chart on page 687. Have students conduct additional research to provide details of the explorations, such as ship names, provisions taken, size of crews, etc. Students may choose to clip photographs from newspapers or magazines to illustrate the events.

CHAPTER 30 OBJECTIVE

Identify key features of physical geography, climate and vegetation, and human-environment interaction in Southeast Asia, Oceania, and Antarctica.

Chapter 30 PHYSICAL GEOGRAPHY OF SOUTHEAST ASIA, OCEANIA, AND ANTARCTICA

A Region Of Extremes

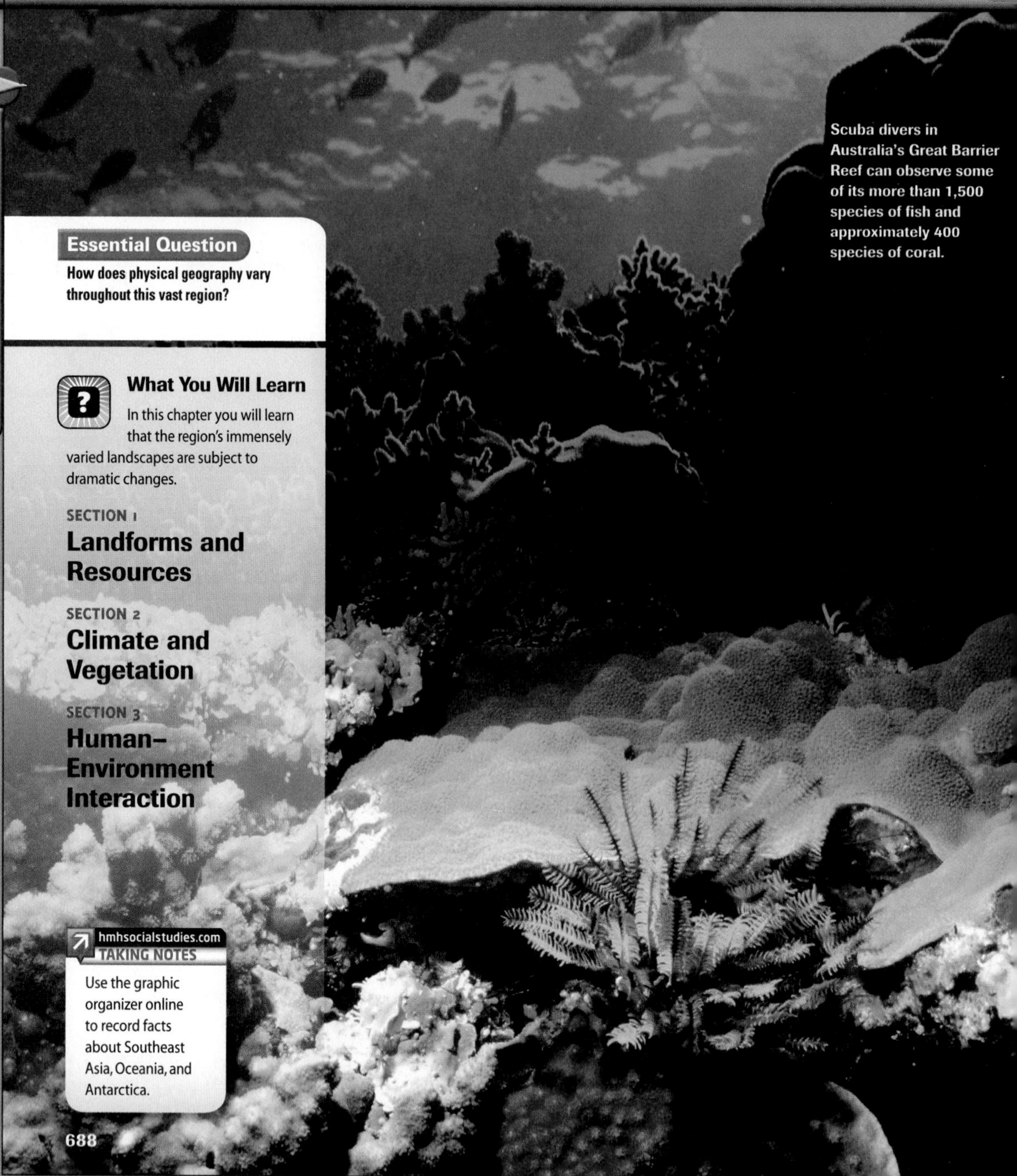

Interpreting Photographs

Australia's Great Barrier Reef

Explain that the Great Barrier Reef is a complex of coral reefs and small islands off the coast of Australia. This natural wonder extends for more than 1,250 miles and lies from 10 to 100 miles offshore.

Extension Lead a discussion about what human activities could threaten the Great Barrier Reef.

Introducing the Essential Question

- Describe the idyllic islands that have lured travellers to the South Pacific for centuries. Contrast the islands to areas in the region that have much harsher environments.
- Point out that the region contains two huge deserts—in central Australia and in Antarctica. The two deserts are quite different, of course. Australia's is very hot, and Antarctica's is very cold. What they have in common is their low precipitation rates.

hmhsocialstudies.com TAKING NOTES

Have students fill out graphic organizers in their notebooks using material from all sections in this chapter.

Critical Thinking Transparencies CT30
- GeoFocus

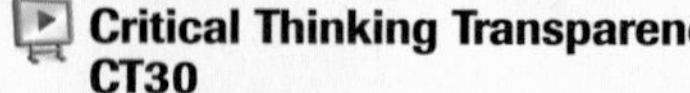
In-Depth Resources: Unit 10
- Building Vocabulary, p. 9

Scuba divers in Australia's Great Barrier Reef can observe some of its more than 1,500 species of fish and approximately 400 species of coral.

Essential Question

How does physical geography vary throughout this vast region?

What You Will Learn

In this chapter you will learn that the region's immensely varied landscapes are subject to dramatic changes.

SECTION 1
Landforms and Resources

SECTION 2
Climate and Vegetation

SECTION 3
Human–Environment Interaction

hmhsocialstudies.com TAKING NOTES

Use the graphic organizer online to record facts about Southeast Asia, Oceania, and Antarctica.

CHAPTER 30 ADDITIONAL RESOURCES

BOOKS FOR THE TEACHER

Kirkpatrick, Jamie. ***A Continent Transformed: Human Impact on the Natural Vegetation of Australia.*** Oxford University Press, USA, 2004. Includes information on the recovery of threatened species.

BOOKS FOR THE STUDENT

Heacox, Kim. ***Shackleton: The Antarctic Challenge.*** Wash., D.C.: Natl. Geographic Soc., 1999. The disastrous 1914 attempt to reach the South Pole.

Nile, Richard, and Christian Clerk. ***Cultural Atlas of Australia, New Zealand, and the South Pacific.*** NY: Facts on File, 1996. Useful geographic and historical information.

VIDEOS

Nova: Treasures of the Great Barrier Reef. PBS, 2000. Extraordinary look at the life of the world's largest reef and coral spawning.

Wayfinders: A Pacific Odyssey. Dir. and Distr. Gail Evenari, 1998. Film study of Pacific Islanders building canoes and sailing by ancient navigational methods.

INTERNET

For more on the physical geography of Southeast Asia, Oceania, and Antarctica, visit . . .

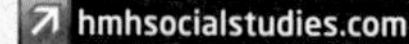
hmhsocialstudies.com

Landforms and Resources

Main Ideas

- This region includes two peninsulas of Asia, two continents, and more than 20,000 islands.
- Its landforms include mountains, plateaus, and major river systems.

Places & Terms

archipelago **low island**
Oceania **Great Barrier Reef**
high island

CONNECT TO THE ISSUES
INDUSTRIALIZATION Some countries of this region have used their resources to develop industry, with mixed results.

A HUMAN PERSPECTIVE The Aeta (EE•duh) people of the Philippines lived on the volcano Mount Pinatubo for generations. They knew this volcano so well that they timed the planting and harvesting of their crops by the amount of steam rising from a vent on its slope. In 1991, the Aeta noticed changes in the mountain and concluded that it was about to erupt. Tens of thousands of Aeta fled their homes as did countless other Filipinos. Pinatubo did erupt for the first time in 600 years, spewing ash for miles. Since then, many of the Aeta have formed new communities, but they still miss their homeland. As their story shows, the geologic processes that destroy landforms also disrupt human lives.

Southeast Asia: Mainland and Islands

Southeast Asia has two distinct subregions: the southeastern corner of the Asian mainland and a great number of islands. Both the mainland and the islands have many high mountains.

PENINSULAS AND ISLANDS The most noticeable feature of mainland Southeast Asia is that it lies on two peninsulas. The Indochinese Peninsula, located south of China, has a rectangular shape. In contrast, the Malay Peninsula is a narrow strip of land about 700 miles long, stretching south from the mainland and then curving southeast. It serves as a bridge between the mainland and islands.

Most of the islands of Southeast Asia are found in archipelagoes. An **archipelago** is a set of closely grouped islands, which sometimes form a curved arc. The Philippines and the islands of Indonesia are part of the Malay Archipelago. (See the map on page 680.) A few Southeast Asian islands, such as Borneo, are actually the high points of a submerged section of the Eurasian plate.

MOUNTAINS AND VOLCANOES On the map at right, you can see that the mainland has several mountain ranges, such as the Annamese Cordillera, running roughly north and south. These ranges fan out from a mountainous area to the north.

Southeast Asian Mountains and Rivers

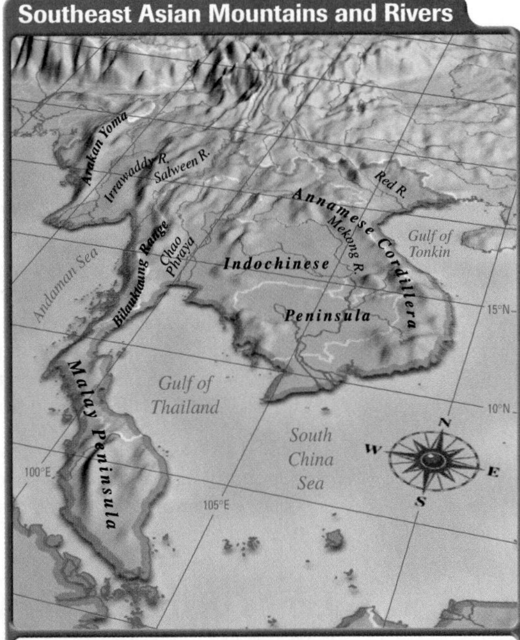

SKILLBUILDER: Interpreting Maps

1. **PLACE** Which mountain chain lies east of the Mekong River?
2. **LOCATION** How would you describe the relative location of the Chao Phraya?

SE ASIA & OCEANIA

SECTION 1 OBJECTIVES

1. Describe key landforms and resources of Southeast Asia.
2. Identify key landforms and resources of the Pacific islands, New Zealand, Australia, and Antarctica.

SKILLBUILDER: Interpreting Maps p. 689

**GeographicThinking**
Seeing Patterns, pp. 691, 692
Making Comparisons, p. 692

Focus & Motivate

Ask students how the numerous islands and coastlines found in this region might have affected its development. *(Seagoing travel and trade were important.)*

Instruct: Objective 1 appears on p. 690

Interpreting Maps

Southeast Asian Mountains and Rivers

Have students examine the map on page 689 and ask them to describe the location of the Gulf of Tonkin. *(It is to the east of the Annamese Cordillera.)*

SKILLBUILDER ANSWERS **1.** the Annamese Cordillera **2.** It's west of the Mekong, east of the Bilauktaung Range, and north of the Gulf of Thailand, into which it flows.

SECTION 1 PROGRAM RESOURCES

 **In-Depth Resources: Unit 10**
- Guided Reading, p. 3
- Building Vocabulary, p. 9
- Reteaching Activity, p. 10
- Map and Graph Skills, pp. 6–7

 **Guided Reading Workbook**
- Section 1

Access for Students Acquiring English/ESL
- Guided Reading, p. 161
- Map and Graph Skills, pp. 165–166

 **Formal Assessment**
- Section Quiz, p. 467

 **Integrated Assessment**
- Rubric for a public service announcement, 5.2

INTEGRATED TECHNOLOGY

 **Critical Thinking Transparencies CT62**
- Comparing Australia and New Zealand

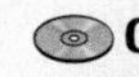 **Chapter Summaries**

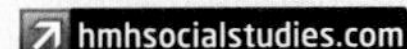

TEST-TAKING RESOURCES

 **Strategies for Test Preparation**

 **Test Practice Transparencies TT97**

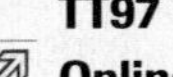 **Online Test Practice**

Instruct: Objective 

Southeast Asia: Mainland and Islands

- What is most noticeable about the arrangement of Southeast Asian islands? *(They are found in archipelagoes.)*
- How did most mountains on the islands originate? *(from volcanoes)*
- How is Southeast Asian farming connected to physical features? *(Volcanic activity and flooding rivers add nutrients to the soil, making it fertile; rivers spread into fertile deltas.)*

 **In-Depth Resources: Unit 10**
- Guided Reading, p. 3

Instruct: Objective 

Lands of the Pacific and Antarctica

- How do high islands differ from low islands? *(High islands are created by volcanoes, low islands by coral reefs.)*
- How do New Zealand and Australia compare in landforms and resources? *(New Zealand is mountainous or hilly, with rivers, fertile farmland, and forest for lumber; Australia is flat and rich in minerals.)*
- Why is icy Antarctica the object of international interest? *(mineral resources may lie beneath the ice)*

Critical Thinking Transparencies CT62
- Comparing Australia and New Zealand

Island Formation in the Pacific hmhsocialstudies.com INTERACTIVE

High (volcanic) Islands

1. Magma sometimes erupts through cracks in the ocean floor.
2. Over time, layers of lava can build up to form a volcanic cone.
3. Some volcanic cones rise above sea level and become islands.

Low (coral) Islands

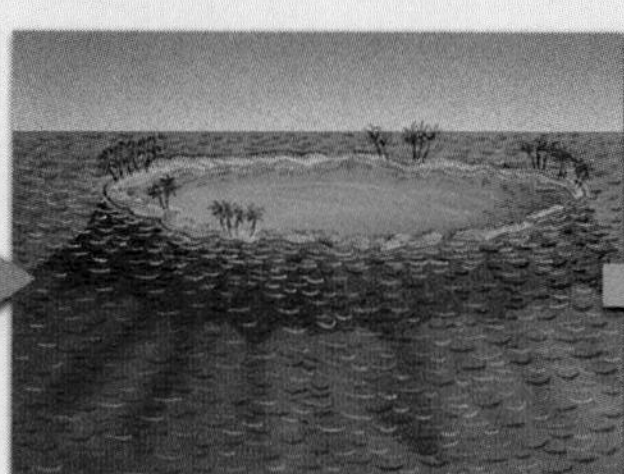

1. Some corals form reefs on the sides of volcanic islands.
2. As the island erodes, the reef continues to grow upward.
3. In time, only the low islands of the reef remain.

On the islands, most of the mountains are of volcanic origin. Southeast Asia is part of the Pacific Ring of Fire. Volcanoes and earthquakes often affect the region. In 2004, a massive earthquake struck off the coast of Sumatra, Indonesia. The resulting tsunamis killed almost 230,000 people, including at least 200,000 Indonesians.

RIVERS AND COASTLINES The mainland has several large rivers that run from the north through the valleys between the mountain ranges. Near the coast these rivers spread out into fertile deltas. For example, the Mekong (MAY-KAWNG) River begins in China and crosses several Southeast Asian nations before becoming a wide delta on Vietnam's coast. Millions of people rely on the Mekong for farming and fishing.

BACKGROUND The Mekong River forms part of the boundary between Myanmar and Laos and between Laos and Thailand.

The region's peninsulas and islands give it a long, irregular coastline with many ports. As you can imagine, these conditions have encouraged a great deal of seagoing travel and trade.

RESOURCES Fertile soil is a valuable resource. Volcanic activity and flooding rivers add nutrients to the soil. Southeast Asians also have access to plentiful fish in the rivers and nearby seas. Parts of the region have mineral resources, such as petroleum, tin, and gems.

Lands of the Pacific and Antarctica

No one knows how many islands exist in the Pacific Ocean, but some geographers estimate that there are more than 20,000. As a group, the Pacific Islands are called **Oceania.** (The Philippines, Indonesia, and other islands near the mainland are not considered part of Oceania because their people have cultural ties to Asia.) In the southwestern

BACKGROUND Oceania's islands are also called the South Sea Islands.

DIFFERENTIATING INSTRUCTION **STUDENTS ACQUIRING ENGLISH/ESL**

MAKING LANDFORM FLASHCARDS

Objective To pronounce correctly and understand names of landforms and places

Class Time 25 minutes

Task Make flashcards showing names of landforms and places that are significant in the section

Directions To help students who lack familiarity with English, pair them with proficient readers. Have pairs make a set of flashcards from index cards or note paper and take turns quizzing each other. Flashcards should show as many as ten names of landforms and places, like the Mekong River, the delta, and the Great Barrier Reef.

The high island in the background is Bora Bora, a volcanic island in French Polynesia. (See the map on page 681.) Many small coral islands surround it.

Pacific lie New Zealand and Australia, which are often considered part of Oceania, even though Australia is a continent, not an island.

OCEANIA'S MANY ISLANDS One reason geographers don't know the number of islands in Oceania is that it changes. Erosion causes some islands to vanish, while other forces create new islands. Most Pacific islands fall into two categories: **high islands** are created by volcanoes, and **low islands** are made of coral reefs. Although a few of Oceania's islands are large, most are small. If you added the land area of all the islands together, the total would be smaller than the area of Alaska.

Oceania is not rich in resources. The low islands have poor soil, and most of the islands lack minerals. But New Caledonia has nickel, chromium, and iron; New Guinea has copper, gold, and oil; Nauru has phosphate; and both Fiji and the Solomon Islands have gold. The general scarcity of resources has made it difficult to develop industry.

MAJESTIC NEW ZEALAND New Zealand has two main islands, North Island and South Island. Running down the center of South Island is a 300-mile-long mountain range, the Southern Alps. This range has 16 peaks over 10,000 feet high and more than 360 glaciers. Several rivers flow down the eastern slopes to the ocean.

North Island has hilly ranges and a volcanic plateau, but it is much less mountainous than South Island. North Island has fertile farmland and forest that support the lumber industry. In addition, its coastline has natural harbors that are used for seaports. Like South Island, North Island has many rivers running from the mountains to the sea. (A)

New Zealand has few mineral resources. However, its swift-flowing rivers have allowed its people to build dams that generate electricity.

A. Answer farm products, lumber

Seeing Patterns
(A) Judging from the information in this paragraph, what products do you think New Zealand exports?

SE ASIA & OCEANIA

Interpreting Infographics

Island Formation in the Pacific

Have students examine the infographic. Call their attention to the image of Bora Bora. Point out that Bora Bora is about fifteen square miles in size. Its harbor is a lagoon surrounded by coral islands. Ask students how the surrounding coral islands might have been formed, based on the infographic. *(They might have formed around an older, larger Bora Bora, and seawater has filled in where the volcanic island has receded.)*

More About

A Pacific Island Born in 2000

In May 2000, an international team of scientists monitored the birth of an island from underwater eruptions of the Kavachi volcano. The new island is located between Papua New Guinea and the Solomon Islands. It is estimated that island "births" occur only three or four times a century.

More About

Coral

Coral is built in layers by tiny sea animals called polyps, which build skeletal casings or shells around themselves for protection. Only the top layer of coral is alive with the latest generation of polyps, which builds its shells upon those of predecessors.

ACTIVITY OPTION | CRITICAL THINKING

MAKING INFERENCES

Explaining the Skill Tell students that they can make inferences about one place by applying knowledge they have acquired from learning about another place.

Applying the Skill Have students reread the paragraphs headed "Resources" and "Oceania's Many Islands" on pages 690–691. Ask the following questions:

- What enriches the soil in Southeast Asia? *(volcanic activity and flooding rivers)*
- How are Oceania's high islands created? Its low islands? *(by volcanoes; by coral reefs)*
- What can be inferred about the poor soil on low islands? *(Low islands are not created by volcanoes and coral does not adequately enrich low island soil.)*

More About

The Great Barrier Reef

Concerned scientists are monitoring coral reefs worldwide in an effort to prevent their decline due to human activities. The Great Barrier Reef is threatened by modern land-clearing and livestock-grazing methods that cause tons of sediment to wash into the sea, and by toxic runoff from farmlands treated with pesticides and fertilizers.

Assess & Reteach

GeoFocus Have students complete the sections on landforms and resources in their graphic organizers.

 **Formal Assessment**
- Section Quiz, p. 467

Reteaching Activity
Have students list the names of landforms introduced in this section and identify the location of each.

 **In-Depth Resources: Unit 10**
- Reteaching Activity, p. 10

Also, North Island has a volcanic area with underground steam. Engineers have found ways to use this steam to power generators.

FLAT AUSTRALIA The land mass known as Australia is the smallest continent on earth. It is also the flattest. Near the eastern coast, running roughly parallel to it, is a chain of highlands called the Great Dividing Range. Unlike New Zealand's mountains, few of these peaks rise higher than 5,000 feet. To the west of this range stretches a vast expanse of plains and plateaus, broken by only a few mountains.

Many other differences exist between Australia and New Zealand. For example, Australia has very few rivers. The largest is the Murray River, which flows into the Southern Ocean. Forestry is not a major industry in Australia, but the country is rich in minerals. It is the world's leading supplier of bauxite, diamonds, opals, lead, and coal.

Along Australia's northeast coast lies one of the wonders of nature. The **Great Barrier Reef** is often called the world's largest coral reef, although it is really a 1,250-mile chain of more than 2,500 reefs and islands. Some 400 species of coral are found there.

ICY ANTARCTICA Antarctica is the fifth largest continent. Generally circular in shape, it is centered on the South Pole. Its topography is hidden by a thick ice sheet, but under the ice lies a varied landscape. The Transantarctic Mountains divide the continent in two. East Antarctica is a plateau surrounded by mountains and valleys. West Antarctica is a group of separate islands linked only by the ice that covers them. B

Antarctica's ice sheet is the largest supply of fresh water in the world. Geologists believe that resources such as coal, minerals, and perhaps even petroleum may lie beneath the ice. But in 1991, 26 nations agreed not to mine Antarctica for 50 years. In the next section, you will read about Antarctica's harsh climate as well as the climates of Southeast Asia, Oceania, Australia, and New Zealand.

B. Answer Similarities—They are the two smallest continents; both are roughly circular. Differences—Australia is very flat, while Antarctica has a varied landscape; Antarctica is covered by ice.

BACKGROUND People in Australia and New Zealand call the waters around Antarctica the Southern Ocean.

Making Comparisons B What are similarities and differences between the physical geographies of Australia and Antarctica?

Section 1 Assessment

1 Places & Terms
Identify these terms and explain their importance in the region's physical geography.
- archipelago
- Oceania
- high island
- low island
- Great Barrier Reef

2 Taking Notes
PLACE Review the notes you took for this section.

Landforms	
Resources	

- What river begins in China and flows to the Vietnamese coast?
- What are the two main islands of New Zealand?

3 Main Ideas
a. What are the main resources of Southeast Asia?
b. What different resources do Australia and New Zealand have?
c. What landform divides the continent of Antarctica?

4 Geographic Thinking
Seeing Patterns By what processes do low islands replace high islands? **Think about:**
- the process that causes some islands to disappear
- the diagrams on page 690

SEEING PATTERNS Do research to learn about the ways that humans have damaged the Great Barrier Reef. Write the script for a **public service announcement,** telling visitors to Australia what behaviors to avoid. You might also include visuals of the Great Barrier Reef. Use standard grammar, spelling, punctuation, and sentence structure in your script.

SECTION 1 ASSESSMENT ANSWERS

1. Places & Terms
archipelago, p. 689
Oceania, p. 690
high island, p. 691
low island, p. 691
Great Barrier Reef, p. 692

2. Taking Notes
- Mekong River
- North Island and South Island

3. Main Ideas
a. fertile soil, fish, mineral resources such as petroleum, tin, and gems
b. Australia—minerals such as bauxite, diamonds, opals, lead, coal; New Zealand—fertile farmland, forests, swift-flowing rivers and volcanic areas that produce steam used to generate electricity
c. Transantarctic Mountains

4. Geographic Thinking
Coral reefs often start to build on the underwater slopes of volcanic islands. Over time, erosion wears away volcanic islands. As the original volcanic island sinks below sea level and the coral reefs rise above sea level, the high island is replaced by a low island (or islands).

GeoActivity

 **Integrated Assessment**
- Rubric for a public service announcement, 5.2

Map and Graph Skills

Interpreting a Relief Map

Two activities that are popular in New Zealand are mountain climbing and skiing. The relief map below shows mountainous areas, which are suitable to those activities. The mountains also provide some regions of New Zealand with spectacular scenery—especially in the Southern Alps of South Island.

THE LANGUAGE OF MAPS A **relief map** illustrates the differences in elevation that are found in a region. It does this with a combination of colors and shading. The lowest elevations are shown in green, and various shades of brown represent progressively higher elevations. The gray shading shows the locations of mountainous landforms.

New Zealand: Physical

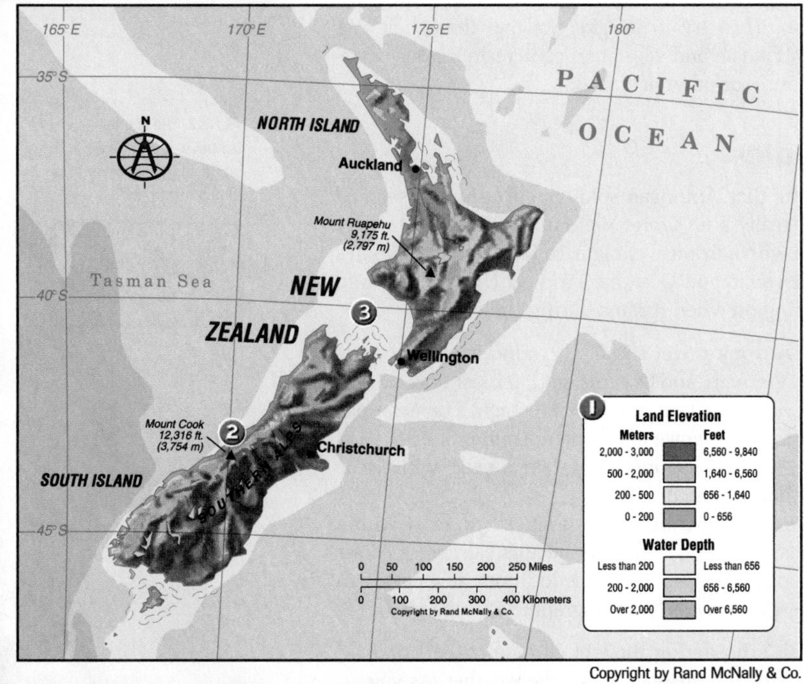

1. The key illustrates the colors used on the map and the range of elevation that each color represents.
2. The symbol for peak is ▲. The map also shows the peaks' names and elevations.
3. This map clearly shows the difference between the physical geographies of North Island and South Island.

Map and Graph Skills Assessment

1. **Seeing Patterns** Which of New Zealand's two large islands is more mountainous?
2. **Drawing Conclusions** How high is Mount Cook?
3. **Making Inferences** Which island is better suited to farming? Why?

OBJECTIVE

Understand and interpret relief maps.

Instruct: Objective

Interpreting a Relief Map

- What is represented on a relief map? *(the differences in a region's elevation)*
- How does a cartographer show relief on a map? *(with the use of colors, shading, symbols, and a key)*
- What does the key on a relief map show? *(the elevations associated with the different colors, shades, and symbols used on the map)*

 **In-Depth Resources: Unit 10**
- Map and Graph Skills, pp. 6–7

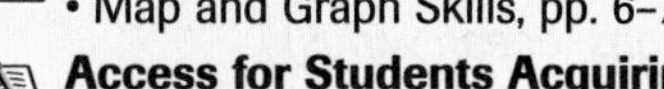
Access for Students Acquiring English/ESL
- Map and Graph Skills, pp. 165–166

More About

Mount Cook

The directors of the movie *Vertical Limit,* released in December 2000, used New Zealand's Mount Cook to simulate the fearsome heights of Mount Goodwin Austen (also known as K2), a peak in the Karakoram Range located between northern Pakistan and India and southwest China.

SKILLS ASSESSMENT ANSWERS

1. South Island

2. 12,316 feet

3. North Island; it has lower elevations, which are better suited to farming.

SECTION 2 OBJECTIVES

1. Describe the tropical climates and plants of Southeast Asia and the islands of Oceania.
2. Examine the moderate climates of Australia and New Zealand.
3. Explain the deserts of Australia and Antarctica.

GeographicThinking

Using the Atlas, p. 695
Seeing Patterns, p. 697
Making Inferences, p. 697

Focus & Motivate

Ask students what factors might affect temperatures in this region. *(elevations, ocean winds)*

Instruct: Objective 1

Widespread Tropics

- What climate is typical of the islands and coastal parts of Southeast Asia? *(tropical wet)*
- How might the formation of high islands in Oceania be linked to the abundant vegetation found on some of them? *(High islands are formed from volcanic mountains and many have rich soil.)*

In-Depth Resources: Unit 10
- Guided Reading, p. 4

Interpreting Photographs

The Rafflesia of Indonesia

Tell students that the rafflesia is known locally as the "corpse flower" because it gives off a smell of rotting meat, and that it lasts only about a week before it dies.

2 Climate and Vegetation

Main Ideas

- This region's climates range from tropical to desert to polar icecap.
- There is a great diversity of plant and animal life, including some species found nowhere else in the world.

Places & Terms

outback

CONNECT TO THE ISSUES
ENVIRONMENTAL CHANGE The hole in the ozone layer, located over Antarctica, has affected the climate of this region.

A HUMAN PERSPECTIVE During the Vietnam War, American troops were sent to fight in unfamiliar Southeast Asia. Among the hardships they endured was the tropical climate. Few had ever lived in a place that had a monsoon season with constant rain. One soldier wrote to his wife, "We live in mud and rain. I'm so sick of rain that it is sometimes unbearable. At night the mosquitoes plague me. . . . The rain drips on me until I go to sleep from exhaustion."

Another soldier wrote to a friend about the vegetation: "Try to imagine grass 8 to 15 feet high so thick as to cut visibility to one yard, possessing razor-sharp edges. Then try to imagine walking through it." As these letters make clear, climate and vegetation can create serious obstacles to military operations—or other activities.

Widespread Tropics

Although the conditions that American soldiers encountered seemed unusual to them, they really aren't rare. Vietnam is just one of many countries in this region with a tropical climate. In fact, tropical climates cover most of Southeast Asia and Oceania. Tropical climates fall into two categories, depending on when it rains during the year.

YEAR-ROUND RAINS A tropical wet climate is found in coastal parts of Myanmar, Thailand, Vietnam, and Oceania, and in most of Malaysia, Indonesia, and the Philippines. Temperatures are high. For example, most of Southeast Asia has an average annual temperature of 80°F. Parts of Southeast Asia receive over 100 inches of rain a year, with some places receiving more than 200 inches.

Although the climate is fairly consistent, variations do exist within the region. Elevation, ocean breezes, and other factors can create cooler temperatures. For example, Indonesia has some locations at such a high elevation that they have glaciers. (See the infographic on page 56.)

WET AND DRY SEASONS Bordering the wet climate is the tropical wet and dry climate, in which monsoons shape the weather. As you read in Unit 8, monsoons are winds that cause wet and dry seasons. This climate is found in parts of Myanmar, Thailand, Laos, Cambodia, and Vietnam—generally to the north or inland of the wet climate. Parts of Oceania and northern Australia also have this climate.

Although temperatures are consistently hot, rainfall varies greatly within the climate zone. Local conditions and

PLACE The Rafflesia, which is native to Indonesia, is the world's largest flower. It is almost three feet across.

SECTION 2 PROGRAM RESOURCES

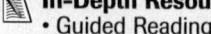

In-Depth Resources: Unit 10
- Guided Reading, p. 4
- Building Vocabulary, p. 9
- Reteaching Activity, p. 11

Guided Reading Workbook
- Section 2

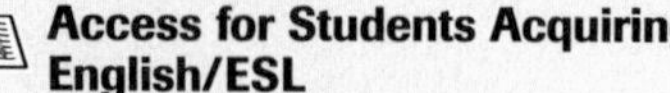

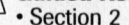

Access for Students Acquiring English/ESL
- Guided Reading, p. 162

Formal Assessment
- Section Quiz, p. 468

Integrated Assessment
- Rubric for a map, 2.1

INTEGRATED TECHNOLOGY

Map Transparencies MT53
- Vegetation of Australia and New Zealand

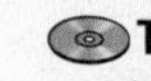

Power Presentations

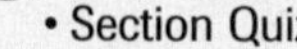

Test Generator
- Section Quiz

hmhsocialstudies.com

TEST-TAKING RESOURCES

Strategies for Test Preparation

Test Practice Transparencies TT98

Online Test Practice

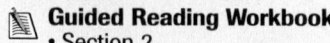

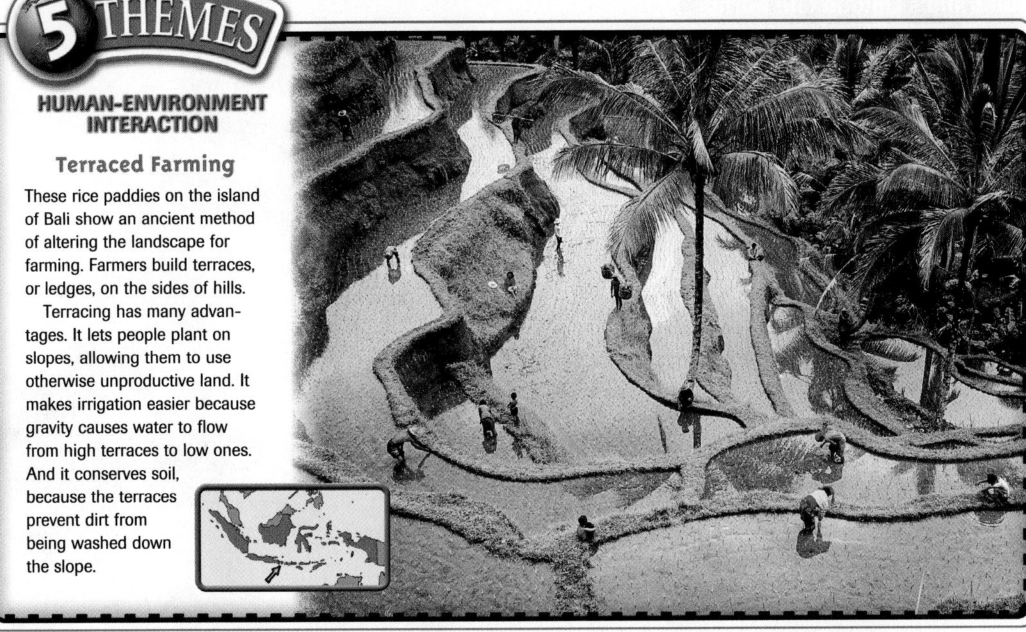

5 THEMES

HUMAN-ENVIRONMENT INTERACTION

Terraced Farming

These rice paddies on the island of Bali show an ancient method of altering the landscape for farming. Farmers build terraces, or ledges, on the sides of hills.

Terracing has many advantages. It lets people plant on slopes, allowing them to use otherwise unproductive land. It makes irrigation easier because gravity causes water to flow from high terraces to low ones. And it conserves soil, because the terraces prevent dirt from being washed down the slope.

landforms can affect precipitation amounts. For example, mountains create rain shadows.

Areas with monsoons often experience disastrous weather. During the wet season, typhoons can occur in Southeast Asia and Oceania.

TROPICAL PLANTS Southeast Asia has one of the greatest diversities of vegetation of any region. For example, it has a remarkable number of tree species. Near the equator are tropical evergreen forests, while deciduous forests are more common in the wet and dry climate zone. Teak, a valuable tree that Asians harvest commercially, comes from these deciduous forests. Southeast Asia also has many types of plants.

In general, Oceania does not have diverse vegetation. The low islands have poor soil and small amounts of rain, so plants don't grow well. Some high islands have rich, volcanic soil and plentiful rain. These islands have abundant flowers and trees, such as the coconut palm.

BACKGROUND
The tropical rain forests of the Philippines alone have more than 3,000 species of trees and 8,000 species of wild plants.

Bands of Moderate Climate

Australia is the only inhabited continent that lies completely in the Southern Hemisphere. New Zealand is even farther south. Australia and New Zealand have generally moderate climates.

HOT SUMMERS, MILD WINTERS As Section 1 explained, a mountain chain runs parallel to the east coast of Australia. The strip between the mountains and ocean is divided mostly into two climate zones. The northern part of this strip has a humid subtropical climate, with hot summers, mild winters, and heavy rainfall. It is one of Australia's wettest regions, receiving an average of 126 inches of rain a year. This climate also exists in northern Vietnam, Laos, Thailand, and Myanmar. 

A. Answer the Great Dividing Range

Geographic Thinking

Using the Atlas A Find this mountain range on the map on page 678. What is it called?

SE ASIA & OCEANIA

5 THEMES

Human-Environment Interaction: Terraced Farming

Have students examine the photograph. Tell them that rice farming in Bali and nearby places has succeeded for centuries as a way of life and worship. Plantings are timed to sustain natural methods of fertilization and pest elimination. Because yields are low, some scientists are urging a change to hybrid rice and pesticides.

- Ask students how change might affect Bali farmers. *(It may alter their way of life.)*

Instruct: Objective 2

Bands of Moderate Climate

- What climate zone occurs on the northern half of Australia's east coast? *(humid subtropical)*
- How do ocean breezes affect the climates of New Zealand and southeastern Australia? *(The breezes moderate temperatures.)*
- How has rainfall affected human settlement in Australia? *(People settled heavily along the moist east coast, leaving the dry inland relatively unpopulated.)*

Map Transparencies MT53
- Vegetation of Australia and New Zealand

DIFFERENTIATING INSTRUCTION | **LESS PROFICIENT READERS**

IDENTIFYING CLIMATES

Objective To help students learn about the climates of the region

Class Time 20 minutes

Task Respond orally to questions about climates and their locations

Directions Ask students to volunteer prior knowledge about monsoons, tropics, and deserts. Follow with questions about the section. Students should respond with information that links a kind of climate or vegetation to its place in the region.

Interpreting Photographs

Australia's Unique Life Forms

Have students examine the various images. Tell them that scientists explain the uniqueness by an evolution of these life forms in isolation. A shift of continental plates millions of years ago separated Australia from the supercontinent Gondwana which also included South America, Africa, Antarctica, and India.

CAPTION ANSWER Student answers will vary but may include koalas and poisonous snakes.

More About

Koalas

Efforts are under way in Australia to protect the koalas—popular marsupials that look like teddy bears. Koalas reside in forests of eucalyptus trees where they thrive by eating the oily shoots and leaves. Today, like wildlife in many parts of the world, koalas are threatened by human encroachment upon their habitat.

Australia's Unique Life Forms

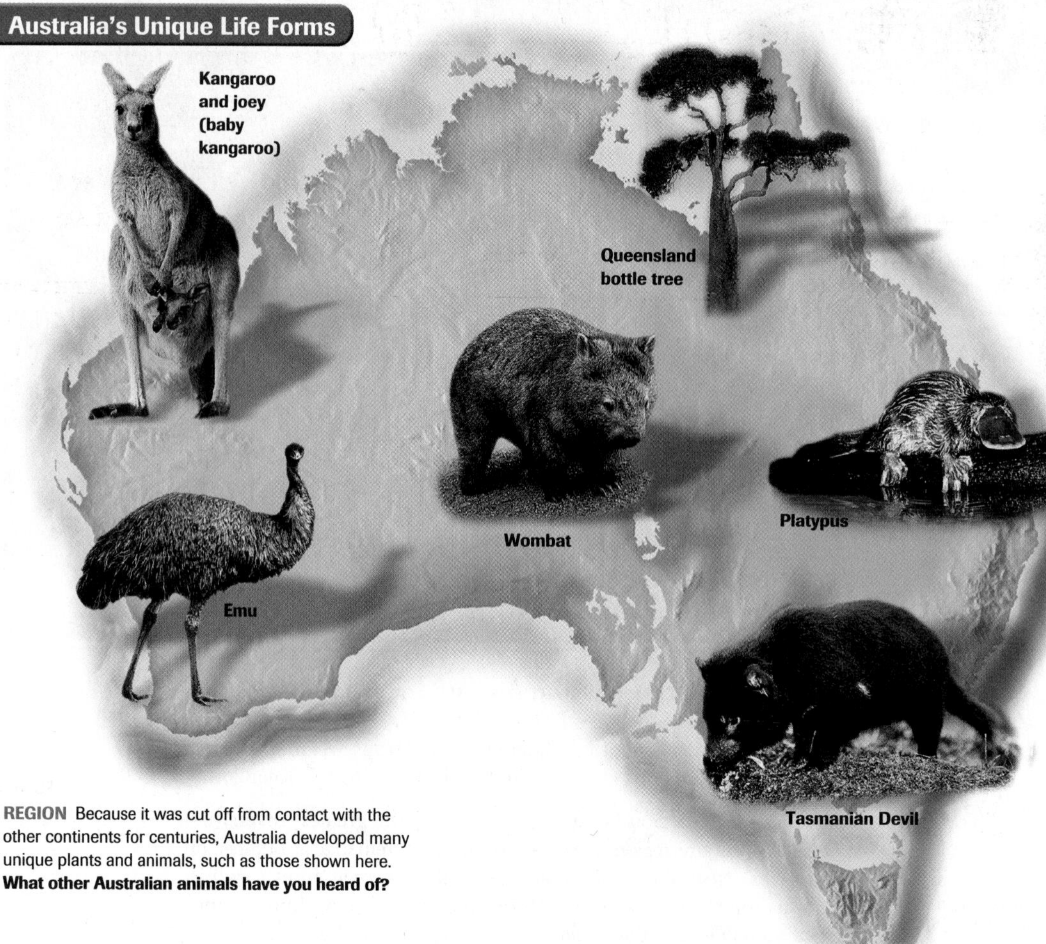

REGION Because it was cut off from contact with the other continents for centuries, Australia developed many unique plants and animals, such as those shown here. **What other Australian animals have you heard of?**

MILD SUMMERS, COOL WINTERS New Zealand and the southern part of Australia's east coast share a marine west coast climate. The seasons have mild temperatures because ocean breezes warm the land in the winter and cool it in the summer. New Zealand's forests consist primarily of evergreens and tree ferns, which thrive in such a climate.

New Zealand receives rainfall year-round, although the amount varies dramatically from one part of the country to another. For example, the mountains of South Island cause rain to fall on their western slopes, so the eastern part of the island is dryer. Mountains change the climate in another way. The mountainous inland areas of New Zealand are cooler than the coastal areas. Temperatures drop about three-and-a-half degrees for every 1,000-foot rise in elevation.

BACKGROUND This rate of temperature reduction is true in almost all mountain ranges.

Mountains influence Australia's climates, too. The Great Dividing Range forces moisture-bearing winds to rise and shed their rain before moving inland. For that reason, the marine west coast and humid subtropical climates exist only on the east coast. That coast is Australia's most heavily populated region. The moist coasts are also the only parts of Australia with enough rain for trees that grow taller than 300 feet.

ACTIVITY OPTION INTERNET RESEARCH

MAKING A WILDLIFE CONSERVATION REPORT

Objective To develop research skills and understand conservation issues

Class Time 40 minutes

Task Write a brief report based on research into the current status of an animal native to Australia

Directions Have students assume the role of wildlife conservationists. Have each of them select an animal native to Australia and find information on the Internet about its habitat and welfare. They should provide a written report about the animal's prospects. Updated links are available at **hmhsocialstudies.com.**

OPTIONAL ACTIVITY If Internet access is limited or unavailable, have students use printed sources in the library.

Hot and Cold Deserts

As you learned earlier in this book, there are many types of desert. For example, two very different deserts exist in Australia and Antarctica.

ARID AUSTRALIA One-third of Australia is desert, lying in an oval in the center of the continent. This region receives less than 10 inches of rain a year and is too dry for agriculture or for grazing. Encircling the desert is a band of semiarid climate that receives no more than 20 inches of rain a year. Crops can only be grown there by using irrigation. Several factors cause Australia's dryness. Because it lies in the tropics and subtropics, Australia is very hot, so rain evaporates easily. And as you read earlier, mountains and uplands force the winds from the ocean to rise and shed their rain on the coasts instead of the interior.

Very few people live in the dry interior. Australians call the unpopulated inland region the **outback.** The few people who live in the outback receive medical care from the Royal Flying Doctor Service. B

Geographic Thinking

Seeing Patterns

B How is the Australian outback similar to far northern Canada, which you studied in Unit 2?

B. Answer Both are isolated and sparsely inhabited, and airplanes are used as transportation.

THE WHITE DESERT With its lands located around the South Pole, Antarctica is earth's coldest, driest continent. It has an icecap climate. In the winter, inland temperatures can fall to 70°F below zero or colder. Cold air doesn't hold moisture well, so Antarctica's air has only one-tenth the water vapor found in the atmosphere of temperate regions. As a result, Antarctica receives little precipitation and is often called a polar desert. But it has heavy snow and ice cover because the snow that does fall rarely melts.

Antarctica's only plants are those, such as lichens and mosses, that can survive severe cold and long periods of darkness. Its animals are mostly sea life and birds, including several types of penguins.

In Section 3, you will learn about examples of human-environment interaction in this region.

Section 2 Assessment

1 Places & Terms

Identify this term and explain its importance in the region's physical geography.

- outback

2 Taking Notes

PLACE Review the notes you took for this section.

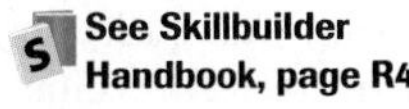

Climate	
Vegetation	

- What types of climates cover most of Southeast Asia and Oceania?
- Where are deserts found?

3 Main Ideas

a. What region has one of the greatest diversities of vegetation of any world region?

b. Why don't low islands generally have diverse vegetation?

c. What effect does elevation have on temperature in the mountains of New Zealand?

4 Geographic Thinking

Making Inferences What aspects of life in the Australian outback might be difficult? **Think about:**

- the need to fly in medical care
- activities that require water

See Skillbuilder Handbook, page R4.

EXPLORING LOCAL GEOGRAPHY Learn about the plants and animals that are native to your state. Create an **illustrated map,** like the one on page 696, showing five or six of your state's native life forms. (The examples do not have to be unique to your state, only natives of it.)

SE ASIA & OCEANIA

Instruct: Objective 3

Hot and Cold Deserts

- How much of Australia is desert and what do Australians call it? *(one-third; the outback)*
- How can Australia's desert be explained? *(Rain evaporates fast in the tropical-subtropical climate; the Great Dividing Range forces ocean winds upward to shed rain along the coast.)*
- Why is Antarctica called a desert? *(It has scant precipitation and dry air; icy temperatures of the air do not allow it to hold moisture.)*

Assess & Reteach

GeoFocus Have students complete the sections on climate and vegetation in their graphic organizers.

Formal Assessment

- Section Quiz, p. 468

Reteaching Activity

Have students write a page comparing and explaining climates discussed in the section. Ask them to incorporate an opinion about the diversity or similarity in the region.

In-Depth Resources: Unit 10

- Reteaching Activity, p. 11

SECTION 2 ASSESSMENT ANSWERS

1. **Places & Terms**
   outback, p. 697
2. **Taking Notes**
   - tropical climates
   - Australia and Antarctica
3. **Main Ideas**
   a. Southeast Asia
   b. They have poor soil and small amounts of rain.
   c. Temperature drops about three-and-a-half degrees for every 1,000-foot rise in elevation.
4. **Geographic Thinking**
   Students may say that activities such as education, gardening, and certain sports requiring water would be difficult.

GeoActivity

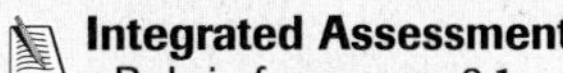

Integrated Assessment

- Rubric for a map, 2.1

SECTION 3 OBJECTIVES

1. Explain how ancient islanders traveled the Pacific.
2. Examine the invasion of rabbits in Australia and methods of control.
3. Learn about nuclear testing and its effects in the Pacific.

Making Comparisons, pp. 699, 700
Using the Atlas, p. 700
Determining Cause and Effect, p. 701

Focus & Motivate

What methods might have helped ancient peoples reach distant islands? *(developing seaworthy vessels and navigating by prevailing winds or sun, moon, stars)*

Instruct: Objective 

Traveling the Pacific

- How did Pacific Islanders navigate? *(by charts of sticks and shells, double-hulled voyaging canoes)*
- Which type of canoe shows how settlers can adapt to a new environment? *(the outrigger, used on island lagoons)*

 **In-Depth Resources: Unit 10**
- Guided Reading, p. 5

CAPTION ANSWER by showing the location of islands and indicating currents

3 Human–Environment Interaction

Main Ideas

- Pacific Islanders developed technology that enabled them to travel the Pacific Ocean.
- This region has been damaged by nuclear testing and the introduction of European animals.

Places & Terms

voyaging canoe
outrigger canoe
atoll
Bikini Atoll

CONNECT TO THE ISSUES
LAND CLAIMS The Bikini Islanders lost their homeland when the United States used it for atomic tests.

A HUMAN PERSPECTIVE In May 2000, the Smithsonian Institution honored Mau Piailug for preserving traditional navigation skills. Mau was born in Micronesia. When he was four years old, he began to sail with his grandfather, who taught the boy how to navigate without using instruments. Those methods of navigation were similar to those used by ancient Polynesians. In 1976, Mau was the navigator during an experimental voyage in which a group used a Polynesian-style canoe to travel from Hawaii to Tahiti and back. Since then, Mau has taught many people in the Pacific Islands how to navigate using traditional skills. In doing so, he passed on important knowledge of how ancient people adapted to their environment.

Traveling the Pacific

In ancient times, people around the world found ways to travel great distances in spite of geographic challenges. For example, the people of Arabia discovered that the camel was the perfect pack animal to take across the desert. Similarly, the people who settled the islands of the Pacific developed ways to travel that vast and dangerous ocean.

NAVIGATION CHARTS Most scholars believe that the people who settled the Pacific Islands came from Southeast Asia. They first used land bridges and small rafts and canoes to reach the islands closest to the mainland. In time, they ventured farther out into the Pacific, which required more sophisticated navigation methods.

Pacific Islanders not only relied on stars for navigation, but they also used charts made of sticks and shells. The sticks showed the patterns of waves commonly found in a region. The shells gave the positions of islands. Pacific Islanders closely guarded the secret of how to use these charts until the late 1800s. About that time, they began to use European methods of navigation.

HUMAN-ENVIRONMENT INTERACTION Pacific Islanders used charts like this to record patterns of waves and ocean swells. The shells mark islands. **How might these charts help sailors plan a journey?**

SECTION 3 PROGRAM RESOURCES

 **In-Depth Resources: Unit 10**
- Guided Reading, p. 5
- Skillbuilder Practice, p. 8
- Building Vocabulary, p. 9
- Reteaching Activity, p. 12

Guided Reading Workbook
- Section 3

 **Access for Students Acquiring English/ESL**
- Guided Reading, p. 163
- Skillbuillder Practice, p. 164

 **Formal Assessment**
- Section Quiz, p. 469

Integrated Assessment
- Rubric for a chart, 2.2

INTEGRATED TECHNOLOGY

 **Power Presentations**

 **Test Generator**
- Section Quiz

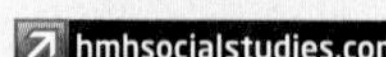

TEST-TAKING RESOURCES

 **Strategies for Test Preparation**

 **Test Practice Transparencies TT99**

 **Online Test Practice**

Polynesian Voyaging Canoe

forward sail
aft (rear) sail
navigator's seat
deck
splashguard
starboard (right) hull
steering paddle
port (left) hull
crossbeams joining the two hulls

SPECIAL CANOES To sail the vast ocean, Pacific Islanders developed huge **voyaging canoes** with double hulls, shown above. Having two hulls made the craft stable and gave it the ability to carry lots of weight. The canoes also had sails to take advantage of the winds. Cabins were sometimes built on the platform atop the hulls to shelter the voyagers and their supplies. Those supplies usually included plants that the travelers hoped to grow in their new homeland.

The large voyaging canoes were awkward to use in the lagoons of the islands where Pacific Islanders settled. In those places, they used the **outrigger canoe.** An outrigger canoe has a frame, with an attached float, extending from one side. The float helps balance the canoe. A

Geographic Thinking

Making Comparisons

A How was balance achieved in the voyaging canoes and the outrigger canoes?

A. Answer voyaging canoes– double hulls; outrigger canoes– attached floats

Invasion of the Rabbits

Just as the people who settled the Pacific Islands carried familiar plants with them, so did the Europeans who colonized Australia. They also brought European animals, such as the rabbit. The impact was disastrous. Although the rabbit is a small, timid animal, it proved to be a force strong enough to nearly ruin the Australian landscape.

THE RABBIT PROBLEM In Europe, many people raise or hunt rabbits for food. In 1859, Thomas Austin released 24 rabbits into Australia so he could hunt them. It was like infecting the continent with a cancer; the rabbit population grew faster than anyone could control it. A single pair of rabbits can have up to 184 descendants in 18 months. Plus, rabbits have few natural enemies—such as foxes—among Australia's wildlife. By 1900, Australia had more than a billion rabbits.

Interpreting Graphics

Polynesian Voyaging Canoe

Have students examine the image on page 699. Ask students where the individual responsible for steering the craft is stationed. *(to the rear of the boat, or aft)*

Instruct: Objective

Invasion of the Rabbits

- What have rabbits done to destroy vegetation in Australia? *(grazed on sparse native vegetation and crops)*
- How are rabbits responsible for erosion? *(Lands stripped of vegetation are susceptible to erosion.)*
- How is the rabbit problem linked to European colonialism? *(Rabbits were introduced by a colonist who imported them from England for the sport of hunting.)*

ACTIVITY OPTION **SKILLBUILDER LESSON**

IDENTIFYING AND SOLVING PROBLEMS

Explaining the Skill Tell students that it is possible to solve a real-life problem by gaining a deeper understanding of its cause.

Applying the Skill Ask the following questions: How could rabbits multiply so fast in Australia? *(They were not native to Australia and had no natural enemies there.)* What habits do rabbits display? *(They graze on native vegetation and crops, and live in burrows.)* How can this information be used against them? *(if a natural enemy of rabbits were introduced into the region, the rabbit population might be reduced.)*

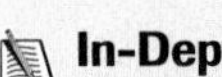

In-Depth Resources: Unit 10
- Skillbuilder Practice, p. 8

Interpreting Photographs

Australia's Rabbit Population

Point out that the rabbits had ready-made burrows to occupy when they arrived in Australia—those of the native burrowing bettong and bilby populations.

CAPTION ANSWER It would hurt it because the rabbits will eat growing crops.

Instruct: Objective 3

Nuclear Testing

- Why did the United States begin nuclear weapons testing? *(because of an arms race with the former Soviet Union)*
- Why did the United States choose Bikini Atoll? *(to avoid endangering U.S. citizens)*
- What did the Bikini Atoll testing show about the use of nuclear weapons? *(They make the environment unfit for human occupants for an unknown length of time.)*

Australia's arid climate produces sparse vegetation. Rabbits graze close to the ground, so they kill or weaken the plants that do grow. Rabbits wiped out native plants and destroyed crops. They ruined pastures, reducing the land's ability to feed herds of sheep. Areas stripped of vegetation suffered erosion. And some of Australia's native animals became endangered because of competition for food. B

Geographic Thinking

Making Comparisons

B Why are rabbits better suited to Europe than Australia?

B. Answer Europe has denser vegetation for them to eat, plus predators such as foxes, which control the rabbit population.

REGION When Australia's rabbit population gets out of control, they swarm over the landscape. **How would this affect the region's ability to grow crops?**

CONTROL MEASURES Australians have made efforts to control the number of rabbits. They imported foxes to prey on rabbits, but the growing fox population endangered Australian wildlife just as rabbits had. In the early 1900s, the government built a 2,000-mile fence to keep rabbits from spreading to the southwest. This fence succeeded only temporarily before rabbits broke through to the new region.

In the 1950s, the government infected wild rabbits with a disease called myxomatosis. More than 90 percent of the total rabbit population died. As rabbit numbers decreased, Australian ranches could support nearly twice as many sheep. But rabbits became immune to the disease, and their numbers boomed again—to 300 million by the 1990s.

Now Australians are trying a combination of methods to reduce rabbit numbers: using poison, introducing new diseases, erecting fences, and destroying the warrens and burrows where rabbits live. No one knows if this new program will provide a permanent solution.

Nuclear Testing

Australia is not the only land in this region to be scarred by the consequences of human action. Beginning in the 1940s, the United States and the Soviet Union waged an arms race in which they competed to develop more powerful nuclear weapons. As part of its weapons development program, the United States wanted to test nuclear bombs without endangering American citizens. In the 1940s and 1950s, the United States conducted 66 tests in the Pacific.

TESTS IN BIKINI ATOLL In the Marshall Islands of the central Pacific lies Bikini Atoll. An **atoll** is a ringlike coral island or string of small islands surrounding a lagoon. **Bikini Atoll** was the site of U.S. atomic-weapons tests. (Similar tests were also held on Enewetak Atoll.) C

Geographic Thinking

Using the Atlas

C Locate the Marshall Islands on the map on page 681. What are the nearest nations to them?

C. Answer Kiribati, Federated States of Micronesia

The U.S. government chose Bikini for testing because it lay far away from regular shipping and air travel routes. In 1946, the government moved the 167 Bikini Islanders to another atoll and conducted two atomic-weapons tests.

From 1951 to 1958, the U.S. government held about 60 more tests there. The most dramatic of these was the explosion of a hydrogen bomb that was code-named Bravo. That blast vaporized several islands

DIFFERENTIATING INSTRUCTION GIFTED AND TALENTED STUDENTS

EXPLORING ENVIRONMENTAL ISSUES

Objective To develop independent research and study skills concerning the environment

Class Time 40 minutes

Task Write a report about the effects of weapons testing

Directions Based on the text on pages 700–701, have students investigate the issues that surround weapons testing and prepare reports to share with the class. The reports should incorporate lines of argument and opinions about the issues.

MOVEMENT U.S. sailors and Bikini Islanders load supplies before the evacuation of Bikini Atoll in 1946. **Why do you think they used U.S. Navy landing craft instead of privately owned boats?**

BACKGROUND
The two-piece bikini bathing suit was named after the Bikini test because designers claimed the suit was "explosive."

of the Bikini Atoll and contaminated the entire area with high levels of radiation. Many islanders were injured or became ill.

LONG-TERM EFFECTS In the meantime, the Bikini Islanders remained exiled from their homeland. The first atoll to which they were moved proved to be unable to support inhabitants, so in 1948, they were moved to the island of Kili. But they soon grew unhappy because conditions there made it impossible to grow enough food or to engage in fishing.

In the late 1960s, the United States government declared Bikini Atoll safe for humans, and some islanders returned home. Then, in 1978, doctors discovered dangerous levels of radiation in the islanders' bodies. The affected islanders had to leave again. No one knows when Bikini Atoll will again be fit for human life. Many Bikinians insist that the island's topsoil must be replaced before Bikini is habitable again.

In Chapter 31, you will read more about the history and culture of Oceania, Southeast Asia, Australia, and New Zealand.

Section 3 Assessment

1 Places & Terms
Identify these terms and explain their importance in the region's physical geography.
- voyaging canoe
- outrigger canoe
- atoll
- Bikini Atoll

2 Taking Notes
HUMAN-ENVIRONMENT INTERACTION Review the notes you took for this section.

- What is an example of humans adapting to the environment?
- What are examples of humans altering the environment?

3 Main Ideas
a. How did Pacific Islanders navigate the ocean in ancient times?
b. How have Australians tried to control the rabbit problem?
c. Why have the Bikini Islanders been unable to return home?

4 Geographic Thinking
Determining Cause and Effect What do the atomic tests on Bikini reveal about the long-term effects of using atomic weapons? **Think about:**
- how the blasts affect people and the environment

hmhsocialstudies.com
RESEARCH WEB LINKS

GeoActivity

MAKING COMPARISONS Do research to learn about French atomic tests in the Pacific. Create a **chart** comparing the French tests to the U.S. tests. You might use such categories as location, impact on people, and current policy about the tests.

SE ASIA & OCEANIA

Interpreting Photographs

1946 Evacuation of Bikini Islanders

Tell students that France ceased its nuclear testing on Polynesia's Mururoa Atoll in the late 1990s but that the site continues to suffer from testing damage and leaking radioactive pollution.

CAPTION ANSWER because it was a government-sponsored relocation or because naval vessels were larger

Assess & Reteach

Have students complete the section on human-environment interaction in their graphic organizers.

Formal Assessment
- Section Quiz, p. 469

Reteaching Activity
Have students take brief notes for each of the main headings in this section. Have volunteers orally share their notes and opinions about European interaction with the environment compared to Polynesian.

In-Depth Resources: Unit 10
- Reteaching Activity, p. 12

SECTION 3 ASSESSMENT ANSWERS

1. Places & Terms
voyaging canoe, p. 699
outrigger canoe, p. 699
atoll, p. 700
Bikini Atoll, p. 700

2. Taking Notes
- ancient Pacific Islanders developing techniques and canoes to sail the ocean
- the devastation caused after Europeans introduced rabbits to Australia and the contamination of Bikini Atoll by atomic tests

3. Main Ideas
a. They used the stars and charts showing wave patterns to navigate.
b. introduction of diseases, building of fences, destruction of rabbit warrens and burrows
c. The islands remain contaminated by radiation.

4. Geographic Thinking
The tests cause illness and injury to humans and contaminate the environment for decades, perhaps longer.

GeoActivity

Integrated Assessment
- Rubric for a chart, 2.2

Reviewing Places & Terms

A.
1. archipelago, p. 689
2. Oceania, p. 690
3. high island, p. 691
4. low island, p. 691
5. Great Barrier Reef, p. 692
6. outback, p. 697
7. voyaging canoe, p. 699
8. outrigger canoe, p. 699
9. atoll, p. 700
10. Bikini Atoll, p. 700

B. Possible Responses

11. Great Barrier Reef, outback
12. An atoll is a ringlike coral island or string of small coral islands, so atolls are low islands.
13. Low islands; the Great Barrier Reef and low islands are both made of coral.
14. the Great Barrier Reef because it has a great diversity of fish and coral, while the outback is extremely arid and unpopulated
15. Southeast Asia and Oceania
16. Outrigger canoes are used in the lagoons of Pacific Islands.
17. They are double-hulled with a platform and sometimes a shelter built atop the hulls, and they have sails.
18. Bikini Atoll, where atomic tests took place
19. high islands because they are more likely to have rich soil, plentiful rainfall, diverse vegetation, and minerals
20. Bikini Atoll

Chapter 30 Assessment

VISUAL SUMMARY
PHYSICAL GEOGRAPHY OF SOUTHEAST ASIA, OCEANIA, AND ANTARCTICA

Landforms

Southeast Asia: Indochinese Peninsula; Malay Peninsula; Malay Archipelago; mountain ranges and rivers

Oceania: high islands; low islands; New Zealand–South Island and North Island; Australia–Great Dividing Range, Murray River

Antarctica: Transantarctic Mountains; East Antarctica and West Antarctica

Resources

- Southeast Asia has fish, fertile soil, and mineral resources.
- Oceania is generally poor in resources. Some islands have minerals.
- New Zealand has fertile farmland, forests, and rivers. Australia is rich in minerals.

Climate and Vegetation

- Southeast Asia and Oceania have tropical or subtropical climates. Southeast Asia has a great diversity of vegetation.
- Australia has moderate climates on its coasts and arid climates inland. New Zealand has a marine west coast climate.
- Antarctica is a polar desert.

Human-Environment Interaction

- The people who settled the Pacific Islands navigated using traditional methods and doubled-hulled canoes.
- Imported rabbits severely damaged the vegetation of Australia.
- U.S. atomic tests contaminated the Bikini Atoll with radiation.

Reviewing Places & Terms

A. Briefly explain the importance of each of the following.

1. archipelago
2. Oceania
3. high island
4. low island
5. Great Barrier Reef
6. outback
7. voyaging canoe
8. outrigger canoe
9. atoll
10. Bikini Atoll

B. Answer the questions about vocabulary in complete sentences.

11. Which of the terms above are related to Australia?
12. Are atolls high islands or low islands? Explain.
13. Is the Great Barrier Reef most closely related to high islands or low islands? Explain.
14. Which would a tourist be more likely to visit, the outback or the Great Barrier Reef? Why?
15. Which of the subregions contain archipelagoes?
16. Where in Oceania are outrigger canoes used?
17. What are the important features of voyaging canoes?
18. Which of the terms above is associated with human damage to the environment?
19. Are high islands or low islands more likely to have prosperous economies? Why?
20. Which term or terms name a place in Oceania?

Main Ideas

Landforms and Resources (pp. 689–693)

1. What are the two distinct subregions of Southeast Asia?
2. What is the physical pattern formed by the mountain ranges and rivers of mainland Southeast Asia?
3. For what purpose do engineers use the underground steam found in the volcanic area of New Zealand?
4. What is one of the many differences between the physical geographies of Australia and New Zealand?

Climate and Vegetation (pp. 694–697)

5. Where is the tropical wet and dry climate found?
6. How does the Great Dividing Range influence Australia's climate?
7. What are the main plants and animals of Antarctica?

Human-Environment Interaction (pp. 698–701)

8. On the navigation charts of Pacific Islanders, what did the shells represent?
9. Why did the rabbit population grow so quickly in Australia?
10. Why have the Bikini Islanders been unhappy with the places where the U.S. government resettled them?

Main Ideas

1. the mainland and the islands
2. the mountain ranges run roughly north and south, while the rivers flow through the valleys between them
3. to power generators
4. New Zealand is more mountainous; New Zealand has more rivers; New Zealand has forests and Australia generally does not; Australia has minerals and New Zealand generally does not.
5. parts of Myanmar, Thailand, Laos, Cambodia, Vietnam, Oceania, and northern Australia
6. It forces moisture-bearing winds to rise and shed their rain before moving inland, so that the coast has rain and the inland region is arid.
7. lichens, mosses, sea life, and birds such as penguins
8. islands
9. There were few natural predators in Australia to reduce the rabbit population.
10. Neither place was able to support inhabitants.

Critical Thinking

1. Using Your Notes
Use your completed chart to answer these questions.

Landforms	
Resources	

a. What subregion has a large diversity of both landforms and vegetation?
b. How did the type of vegetation found in Australia make it an unsuitable place for the introduction of rabbits?

2. Geographic Themes
a. **LOCATION** Where are the tropical climates of this region located relative to the equator?
b. **MOVEMENT** How does the physical geography of Southeast Asia encourage movement?

3. Identifying Themes
Consider the way that Pacific Islanders used shell maps (see page 698). How does the use of such maps demonstrate all five themes of geography?

4. Determining Cause and Effect
What are some of the negative and positive effects of volcanic activity in Southeast Asia?

5. Identifying and Solving Problems
In general, Oceania has few resources. What problem does this create for Pacific Islanders, and how might they solve it?

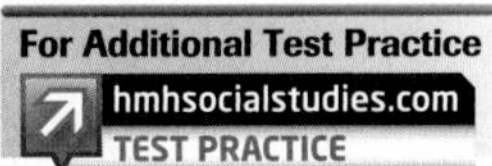

Geographic Skills: Interpreting Maps

Bikini Atoll
Use the map to answer the following questions.

1. **PLACE** Which channel leads to the lagoon inside the Bikini Atoll?
2. **LOCATION** What is the absolute location of the Bravo test site?
3. **MOVEMENT** How far did radiation travel from the Bravo test site in order to contaminate Bikini Island?

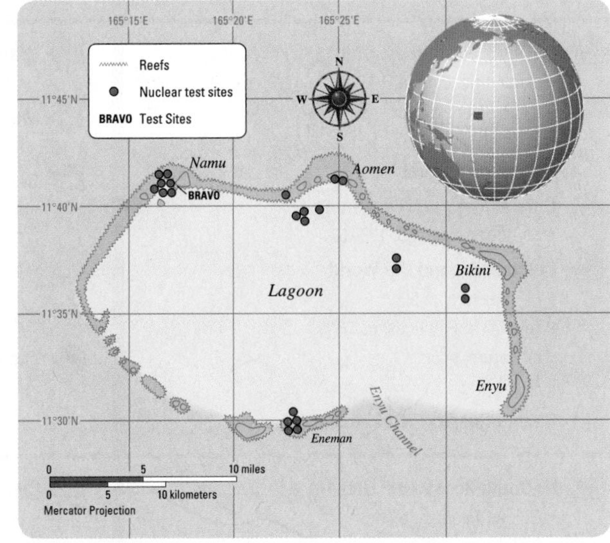

In addition to Bikini Atoll, other atolls and islands were contaminated with radiation from the U.S. atomic-weapons tests. Do research to learn the names and locations of these islands and atolls. Then create a map showing the full area of radiation contamination.

hmhsocialstudies.com
MULTIMEDIA ACTIVITY

21st CENTURY

Use the links at **hmhsocialstudies.com** to do research about active volcanoes in Southeast Asia. Look for such information as location and recent eruptions.

Writing About Geography Write a report of your findings. Include a map of the volcanoes and a chart listing recent eruptions. List the Web sites that were your sources.

CHAPTER 30 ASSESSMENT

Critical Thinking

1. a. Southeast Asia
b. Australia generally has sparse vegetation. Rabbits are heavy grazers that are better suited to regions with thick vegetation. To survive in Australia, the rabbits practically denuded the landscape.

2. a. They lie near the equator, on either side of it.
b. On the mainland, the rivers flow to the coast, where there are harbors that facilitate travel. In addition, many islands lie within easy reach by sailboat.

3. The shell maps indicate places (islands) and their approximate location in a larger region. They aid in movement, and they are an example of human-environment interaction.

4. Volcanoes have disrupted the lives of people, such as the Aeta in the Philippines. However, volcanic activity has helped to keep the soil rich and fertile, which helps agriculture to prosper.

5. Having few resources makes it difficult to develop the economy, particularly manufacturing. Pacific Islanders might pursue economic activities that don't need as many natural resources. For example, they could promote tourism.

GeoActivity

Integrated Assessment
- Rubric for a map, 2.1

Formal Assessment
- Chapter Test, Forms A, B, and C, pp. 470–481

Geographic Skills

1. Enyu Channel
2. approximately 11°42' north and 165°17' east
3. about 17 miles

SE ASIA & OCEANIA

MULTIMEDIA ACTIVITY

For the report on active volcanoes in Southeast Asia, students should:
- Create a concise, well-organized text
- Include information on both historic and recent eruptions.
- Produce a clear, imaginative visual to complement the report.
- Include references to the Web sites used as sources.

Grading Rubric Evaluate student performance as Exceptional, Acceptable, or Poor in each of the following categories:

	Exceptional	Acceptable	Poor
Writing is clear focused and logical			
Clearly states the topic and purpose			
Provides necessary facts and visual examples			
Uses correct grammar, spelling, and punctuation			

Human Geography of Southeast Asia, Oceania, and Antarctica

OVERVIEW	INSTRUCTIONAL RESOURCES	
ESSENTIAL QUESTION How have foreign powers affected Southeast Asia, Oceania, and Antarctica? **Focus on the Essential Question Podcast**	**In-Depth Resources: Unit 10** • Building Vocabulary, p. 17 **Block Schedule Strategies** **Chapter Summaries** (English/Spanish)	**Interactive Online Edition** TOS **ExamView® Assessment Suite** (English/Spanish) TOS **CalendarPlanner** **Power Presentations with Media Gallery** **Critical Thinking Transparencies** • CT31 **Video:** Dreamtime of the Aborigines hmhsocialstudies.com INTERACTIVE
SECTION 1 **SOUTHEAST ASIA** **MAIN IDEAS** • Southeast Asia has a long history of diverse cultural influences. • Nations continue to recover from the effects of European colonialism. • Some nations have highly developed economies and burgeoning cities.	**In-Depth Resources: Unit 10** • Guided Reading, p. 13 • Skillbuilder Practice, p. 16 • Building Vocabulary, p. 17 • Reteaching Activities, p. 18 **Outline Maps with Activities** • Southeast Asia, pp. 103–104 **Cultures Around the World** • Architecture, p. 55 • Traditional Practices, p. 57 • Literature, p. 58 • Music, p. 59 **Guided Reading Workbook,** Section 1	**Critical Thinking Transparencies** • CT63 History of Southeast Asia **Map Transparencies** • MT54 Cultural Regions of Oceania **Cultures Transparencies CW55, 57, 58, 59** • Angkor Wat • Celebrating Songkran • "A Plough and a Spade" by Nguyen Trai • Playing a Gong **The World's Music Audio Program**
SECTION 2 **OCEANIA** **MAIN IDEAS** • European exploration brought change and decline to traditional Pacific Island societies. • Tourism and industry exist in Island economies based on subsistence farming and fishing. • Most Islanders live in small villages, but there are a few cities.	**In-Depth Resources: Unit 10** • Guided Reading, p. 14 • Building Vocabulary, p. 17 • Reteaching Activities, p. 19 **Outline Maps with Activities** • Oceania, pp. 105–106 **Cultures Around the World** • Daily Life, p. 56 • Arts and Crafts, p. 60 **Guided Reading Workbook,** Section 2	**Cultures Transparencies CW56, 60** • Enjoying a Feast • Making Batik **The World's Music Audio Program**
SECTION 3 **AUSTRALIA, NEW ZEALAND, AND ANTARCTICA** **MAIN IDEAS** • Australia and New Zealand have a history of British colonialism that displaced native peoples. • Both nations are agricultural, but mining exists in Australia. • The nations' modern cultures show both British and distinctive influences.	**In-Depth Resources: Unit 10** • Guided Reading, p. 15 • Building Vocabulary, p. 17 • Reteaching Activities, p. 20 **Outline Maps with Activities** • Australia, New Zealand, Antarctica, pp. 107–108 **Guided Reading Workbook,** Section 3	**Map Transparencies** • MT55 Exploration and Land Claims in Antarctica **The World's Music Audio Program**

ASSESSMENT

SE **Chapter Assessment,** pp. 724–725

Formal Assessment
- Chapter Tests, Forms A, B, and C, pp. 485–496

TOS **ExamView® Assessment Suite**

Strategies for Test Preparation

hmhsocialstudies.com TEST PRACTICE

SE **Section Assessment,** p. 709

Formal Assessment
- Section Quiz, p. 482

Integrated Assessment
- Rubric for a chart, 2.2
- Rubric for a television newscast, 5.3

Test Practice Transparencies TT100

SE **Section Assessment,** p. 715

Formal Assessment
- Section Quiz, p. 483

Integrated Assessment
- Rubric for a tourist brochure, 1.13

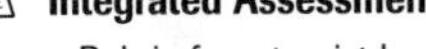

Test Practice Transparencies TT101

SE **Section Assessment,** p. 723

Formal Assessment
- Section Quiz, p. 484

Integrated Assessment
- Rubric for a Venn diagram, 2.8

Test Practice Transparencies TT102

CHART KEY:

SE Student Edition

TE Teacher's Edition

 Printable Resource

 Block Scheduling

TOS Teacher One Stop

 Presentation Resource

 DVD/CD-ROM

 MP3 Audio

 HISTORY™

Program Resources available on TOS and @ 

SUPPORTING RESOURCES

- Multimedia Classroom Global History Series
- Global History Teacher's Guide

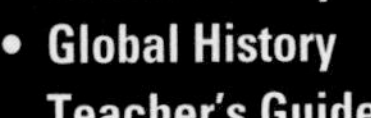

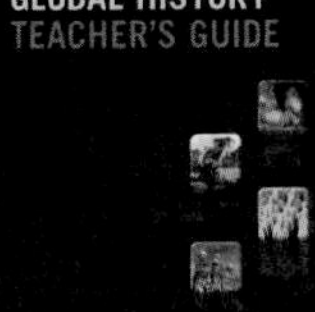

Social Studies Trade Library Collection
- World Regions Trade Collection

For more information or to purchase these resources, go to 

DIFFERENTIATED INSTRUCTION

English Learners

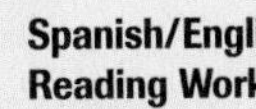
Spanish/English Guided Reading Workbook

Access for Students Acquiring English/ESL
Spanish Translations, pp. 167–170

Chapter Summaries (English/Spanish)

TE **TE Activity**
Creating a Mini-Encyclopedia, p. 721

Struggling Readers

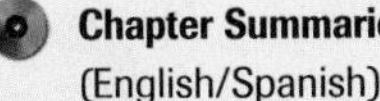
Chapter Summaries (English/Spanish)

TE **TE Activity**
Recalling the Global Picture, p. 708

Gifted and Talented Students

TE **TE Activity**
Writing a Research Proposal, p. 720

ENRICHMENT ACTIVITIES

The following activities are especially suitable for classes following block schedules.

SE **Student Edition,** pp. 704–725
- Disasters! Krakatoa, pp. 710–711
- Comparing Cultures: Regional Costumes, pp. 716–717

hmhsocialstudies.com INTERACTIVE
- Colonies in Southeast Asia, 1895, p. 706
- Cultural Regions of Oceania, p. 713
- National Claims to Antarctica, p. 720

CHAPTER 31 PACING GUIDE

BLOCK SCHEDULE LESSON PLAN OPTIONS: 90-MINUTE PERIOD

DAY 1

SECTION 1, pp. 705–709
Class Time 55 minutes

- **Panel Discussion** To help students understand Southeast Asia before and after Europeans took control, form a panel of students and moderate a discussion based on text on pages 705–707. Have students prepare for the panel discussion in class study groups or as homework.
Class Time 30 minutes
- **Summary Lists** Have students summarize the main points for the remaining headings, pages 708–709. Help students create their summary lists by leading a class discussion.
Class Time 25 minutes

DISASTERS, pp. 710–711
Class Time 20 minutes

- **Writing** After reading the Krakatoa feature, have students write a paragraph about the effects of the eruption and the formation of Anak Krakatoa.

SECTION 2, pp. 712–715
Class Time 15 minutes

- **Class Discussion** Introduce the section with a discussion based on relevant portions of "Reviewing Places & Terms" and "Main Ideas" on page 724.

DAY 2

SECTION 2, pp. 712–715
Class Time 35 minutes

- **Group Reviews/Writing** As a way to review material covered the day before, divide the class into groups. Tell groups to discuss the section from the perspective of tensions between traditional economies or lifestyles and modern changes. Have each student prepare a personal written summary as the discussions proceed.

COMPARING CULTURES, pp. 716–717
Class Time 20 minutes

- **Groups** Lead the class in a discussion of the photographs, captions, and GeoData.
Class Time 10 minutes
- **News Reports** Have students prepare news reports based on comparisons among the cultures as shown by the photographs and captions.
Class Time 10 minutes

SECTION 3, pp. 718–723
Class Time 35 minutes

- **Time Line** Have students supply supplementary information from pages 718–720 for the time line on pages 718–719. They should list the information down the page in two columns headed "Year" and "Event."

DAY 3

SECTION 3, pp. 718–723
Class Time 30 minutes

- **Charts** As a way to summarize the section, have students create charts to compare Australia and New Zealand. Help them construct the charts by selecting a student to represent each country at the chalkboard. Each student should list information supplied by class members for that country in columns headed "Land rights," "Economies," and "Cultures."

CHAPTER 31 REVIEW AND ASSESSMENT, pp. 724–725
Class Time 60 minutes

- **Review** Lead the entire class in a discussion of the chapter based on questions from the "Instruct: Objectives" on chapter pages and the "Main Ideas" from the Chapter Assessment, page 724.
Class Time 25 minutes
- **Assessment** Have students complete the Chapter 31 Assessment.
Class Time 35 minutes

TEACHER-TESTED ACTIVITY *Collage and Time Line*

Class Time Length of chapter coverage

Task Students create a class collage, individual collage time lines, and individual summary essays

Supplies
- Large sheet of white butcher paper
- Tape, glue

Purpose To help students familiarize themselves with Southeast Asia, Oceania, and Antarctica by having them collect images and stories of current events in the region

Activity The students in the class are to create a collage of current articles and pictures pertaining to Chapter 31 gathered from current newspapers, magazines, or Internet sources. The current events articles and pictures are to be taped or glued on the butcher paper. Indicate on the article or picture the date and the name of the student who posted it. At the conclusion of the unit and the final posting of articles and pictures, each student is to make a time line and then write a summary essay about the current happenings in the region.

Thomas Figurski
Geography Teacher, Thomas J. Anderson High School, Southgate Michigan

The Web lends itself well to student research because of the availability of Web sites with valuable, up-to-date information, including text and pictures. However, the Web also contains many sites that are not up-to-date or that have irrelevant, erroneous, or inappropriate information. One good way to keep students "on-task" and to ensure that they use appropriate Web sites is to have them look through a limited set of pre-selected sites. The teacher should choose sites sponsored by organizations that are generally considered reliable, such as major news sources, television networks, nonprofit organizations, or museums. If the teacher presents students with a list of acceptable sites, they can save a good deal of classroom time, and students will be less likely to end up at sites that are irrelevant or inappropriate.

Objective Students will research the geography, cultures, and politics of Indonesia and answer questions about this country.

Task Have students visit Web sites to gather information about Indonesia's geography, cultures, and politics. Have them discuss and write answers to the question "What do you think might be some challenges in governing a country made up of over 13,000 islands?"

Class Time Two class periods

1. Have students read pages 705–709, and ask them to look at the map on page 706. Have them locate the region that was controlled by the Dutch, and explain that this territory is what later became the country of Indonesia (with some contested territories struggling for autonomy and independence, such as East Timor, Aceh, and Irian Jaya/West Papua).

2. Ask students to look at the map on page 706 and figure out the approximate distance from the westernmost to the easternmost parts of the country. Have them compare that distance to the distance across the United States.

3. Explain that Indonesia is a country of over 13,000 islands. Considering its size and geographic diversity, do students think this group of islands would make a cohesive, homogeneous country that is easy to govern? Why or why not?

4. Have students go to the Web sites listed at **hmhsocialstudies.com** to find out more about Indonesia's geography, cultures, and politics. As they conduct their research, ask them to answer these questions: Approximately how many languages are spoken in Indonesia? What are the primary religions? What are some cultural customs practiced in different parts of Indonesia (provide examples from three different islands, such as Lombok, Bali, and Java)? What human rights issues affect Indonesia and its government? What is the latest news about the Indonesian government?

5. Hold a class discussion asking students to answer the question "What do you think might be some challenges in governing a country made up of over 13,000 islands?" Then have students write responses to this question.

CHAPTER 31 OBJECTIVE

Identify features of human geography in Southeast Asia, Oceania, and Antarctica.

Chapter 31 HUMAN GEOGRAPHY OF SOUTHEAST ASIA, OCEANIA, AND ANTARCTICA

Migration and Conquest

hmhsocialstudies.com VIDEO

Interpreting Maps

Three Subregions: Southeast Asia, Oceania, and Antarctica

Have students examine the map of subregions and analyze the distances between them.

Extension Ask what factors might link these disparate subregions.

Introducing the Essential Question

- Describe the conflicts involving foreign powers that have at times troubled the region. Some of those conflicts are fairly recent; for example, the war in Vietnam ended in 1975. Internal conflicts have also inflicted misery on the people. Cambodia provides an example. Its people suffered horrors during rule by the Khmer Rouge from 1975 to 1979.
- Foreign powers came to dominate some areas. Settlers from the British Isles became the largest culture groups in Australia and New Zealand.

hmhsocialstudies.com TAKING NOTES

Have students complete cluster diagrams in their notebooks using material from all sections in this chapter.

Critical Thinking Transparencies CT31
- GeoFocus

In-Depth Resources: Unit 10
- Building Vocabulary, p. 17

Three Subregions

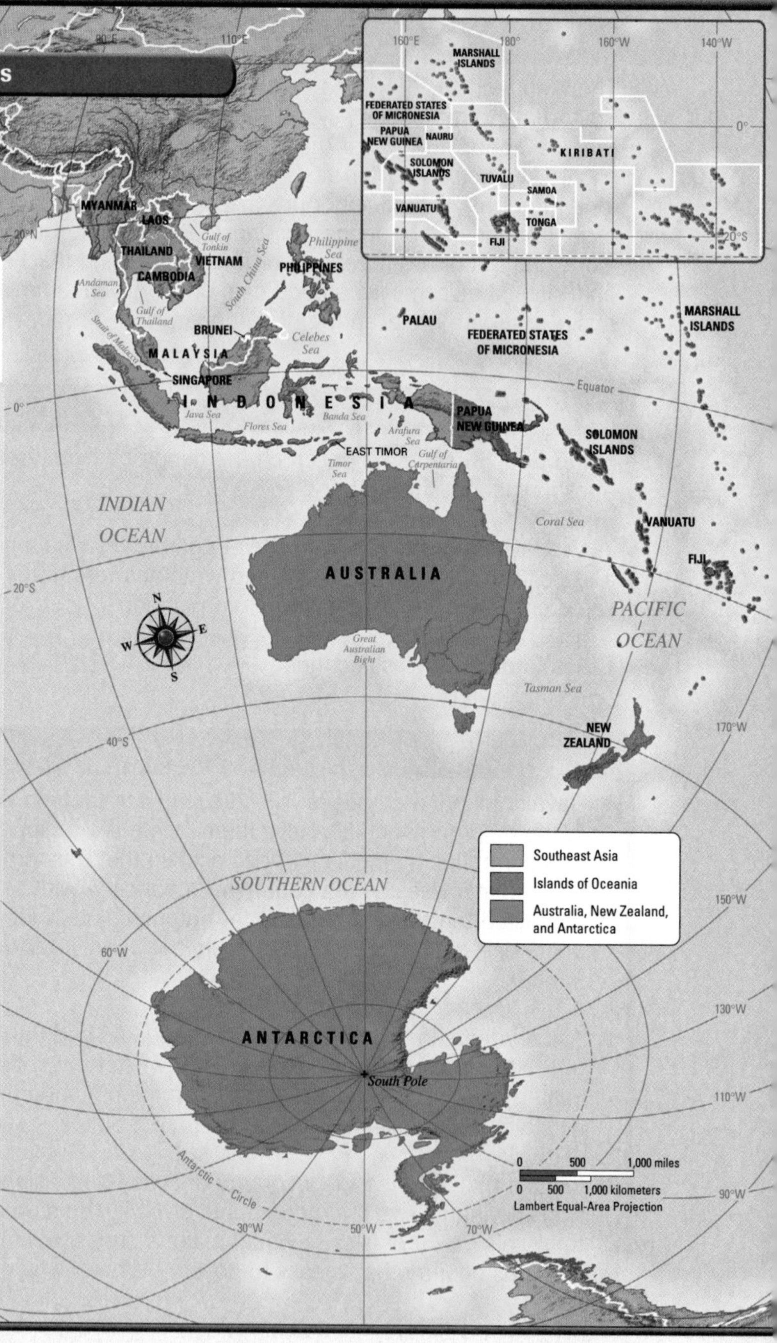

Three Subregions (map): MYANMAR, LAOS, THAILAND, VIETNAM, CAMBODIA, PHILIPPINES, BRUNEI, MALAYSIA, SINGAPORE, INDONESIA, EAST TIMOR, PAPUA NEW GUINEA, PALAU, FEDERATED STATES OF MICRONESIA, MARSHALL ISLANDS, SOLOMON ISLANDS, VANUATU, FIJI, NAURU, KIRIBATI, TUVALU, SAMOA, TONGA, AUSTRALIA, NEW ZEALAND, ANTARCTICA, South Pole, INDIAN OCEAN, PACIFIC OCEAN, SOUTHERN OCEAN, Gulf of Tonkin, South China Sea, Philippine Sea, Andaman Sea, Gulf of Thailand, Strait of Malacca, Celebes Sea, Java Sea, Flores Sea, Banda Sea, Arafura Sea, Timor Sea, Gulf of Carpentaria, Coral Sea, Tasman Sea, Great Australian Bight, Equator, Antarctic Circle

Legend: Southeast Asia; Islands of Oceania; Australia, New Zealand, and Antarctica

0 500 1,000 miles; 0 500 1,000 kilometers; Lambert Equal-Area Projection

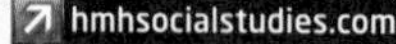

Essential Question

How have foreign powers affected Southeast Asia, Oceania, and Antarctica?

What You Will Learn

In this chapter you will learn how migration and conquest have affected the people of Southeast Asia and Oceania.

SECTION 1
Southeast Asia

SECTION 2
Oceania

SECTION 3
Australia, New Zealand, and Antarctica

hmhsocialstudies.com TAKING NOTES

Use the graphic organizer online to take notes about the history, economics, culture, and modern life of each subregion.

704

CHAPTER 31 ADDITIONAL RESOURCES

BOOKS FOR THE TEACHER

Hughes, Robert. ***The Fatal Shore.*** NY: Knopf, 1987. Best-selling, authoritative history of British colonization in Australia by a convict transportation system.

Ngor, Haing, with Roger Warner. ***A Cambodian Odyssey.*** NY: Warner, 1989. Memorable autobiographical account of torment in 1970s Cambodia.

BOOKS FOR THE STUDENT

Moorhouse, Geoffrey. ***Sydney: The Story of a City.*** NY: Harcourt, 2000. Guide to Sydney at the time of the Olympics.

Zéphir, Thierry. ***Khmer: The Lost Empire of Cambodia.*** NY: Abrams, 1998. Attractive guide to the civilization and temple complex of Angkor Wat.

SOFTWARE

Encyclopedia of the Vietnam War: A Political, Social, and Military History. CD-ROM. Santa Barbara: ABC-CLIO, 1998. Excellent source of information and commentary.

Australia Naturally! CD-ROM. Topics Entertainment, 2000. Geography and wildlife encyclopedias.

INTERNET

For more on the human geography of Southeast Asia, Oceania, and Antarctica, visit . . .

hmhsocialstudies.com

Southeast Asia

Main Ideas

- Influenced by China and India, Southeast Asia developed many vibrant, complex cultures.
- European colonialism left a legacy that continues to affect the region's politics and economics.

Places & Terms

mandala
Khmer Empire
Indochina
Vietnam War
ASEAN

CONNECT TO THE ISSUES
INDUSTRIALIZATION
Since 1960, many Southeast Asian nations industrialized, while others lagged behind.

SECTION 1 OBJECTIVES

1. Examine Southeast Asia's history of diversity.
2. Identify goals and effects of colonialism in Southeast Asia.
3. Analyze Southeast Asian economies.
4. Explain diverse cultures and lifestyles in Southeast Asia.

SKILLBUILDER: Interpreting Maps, p. 706

 **GeographicThinking**
Seeing Patterns, p. 706
Using the Atlas, pp. 708, 709
Drawing Conclusions, p. 709

Focus & Motivate

Ask students what cultural influences might be found in Southeast Asia. *(Chinese, Indian, European)*

A HUMAN PERSPECTIVE Much of Southeast Asia is haunted by its colonial past. One example is the divided island of Timor. The Netherlands ruled Western Timor, later part of Indonesia. Portugal ruled East Timor. In 1975, East Timor declared itself an independent state (even though some people living there wanted to join Indonesia). In response, Indonesia invaded the new nation and ruled it for 24 years.

In 1999, Indonesia let East Timor vote on the choice of limited self-rule within Indonesia or independence. When most voters chose independence, pro-Indonesia militias reacted with violence. The United Nations stepped in and helped East Timor prepare for nationhood. In May 2002, the country gained its independence.

The new nation is also one of the poorest. However, the development of a natural gas field in the Timor Sea should help solve East Timor's economic challenges. In fact, the revenue from the sale of the gas is expected to guarantee the new nation a steady income until 2020.

A Long History of Diversity

Since ancient times, many cultures have influenced Southeast Asia, yet it has retained its own character. Today the region includes the nations of Brunei, Cambodia, Indonesia, Laos, Malaysia, Myanmar, the Philippines, Singapore, Thailand, and Vietnam.

EARLY HISTORY China and India influenced ancient Southeast Asia. China ruled northern Vietnam from 111 B.C. to A.D. 939. Chinese art, technology, political ideas, and ethical beliefs shaped Vietnam's culture. Hinduism and Buddhism spread from India and influenced religion and art in much of Southeast Asia. Yet, Southeast Asia kept some of its own traditions, such as more equal roles for women.

Early Southeast Asian states didn't have set borders. Instead, they were ***mandalas,*** states organized as rings of power around a central court. Those regions of power changed in size over time. A *mandala's* region might overlap that of a neighbor, so rulers had to make alliances for a state to survive. The **Khmer Empire** was a powerful *mandala* that lasted roughly from the 9th to the 15th centuries in what is now Cambodia.

MOVEMENT The temple complex of Angkor Wat in Cambodia was built in the 1100s and dedicated to the Hindu god Vishnu.
How does this temple illustrate the movement of ideas?

Instruct: Objective 1

A Long History of Diversity

- What nations and religions influenced ancient Southeast Asian cultures? *(China, India; Hinduism, Buddhism)*
- How were states organized during the Khmer Empire? *(in mandalas, a region of power with a central court)*
- What happened from 1300 to 1800? *(Five powerful states emerged, national identities began to form, and cities grew.)*

 **In-Depth Resources: Unit 10**
- Guided Reading, p. 13

CAPTION ANSWER Hinduism originated in India and later traveled to Southeast Asia.

SECTION 1 PROGRAM RESOURCES

In-Depth Resources: Unit 10
- Guided Reading, p. 13
- Skillbuilder Practice, p. 16
- Building Vocabulary, p. 17
- Reteaching Activity, p. 18

Guided Reading Workbook
- Section 1

Access for Students Acquiring English/ESL
- Guided Reading, p. 167
- Skillbuillder Practice, p. 170

 **Outline Maps with Activities**
- Southeast Asia, pp. 103–104

 **Formal Assessment**
- Section Quiz, p. 482

 **Integrated Assessment**
- Rubric for a chart, 2.2
- Rubric for a television newscast, 5.3

 **Cultures Around the World**
- Architecture, p. 55
- Traditional Practices, p. 57
- Literature, p. 58
- Music, p. 59

INTEGRATED TECHNOLOGY

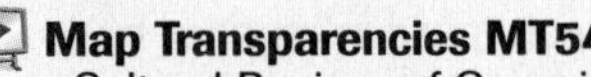

Map Transparencies MT54
- Cultural Regions of Oceania

Cultures Transparencies CW55, 57, 58, 59
- Angkor Wat; Celebrating Songkran; "A Plough and a Spade," by Nguyen Trai; Playing a Gong

Critical Thinking Transparencies CT63
- History of Southeast Asia

hmhsocialstudies.com

TEST-TAKING RESOURCES

 **Strategies for Test Preparation**

 **Test Practice Transparencies TT100**

Online Test Practice

Instruct: Objective 

Colonialism and Its Aftermath

- Why did European and Japanese powers seek control in Southeast Asia? *(to obtain the region's wealth)*
- How did colonial rule help the cause of independence? *(European rule sparked nationalism; the Japanese let Southeast Asians gain political experience.)*
- Why did the United States become involved in Vietnam? *(to prevent Communist North Vietnam from taking over South Vietnam)*

Critical Thinking Transparencies CT63
- History of Southeast Asia

Map Transparencies MT54
- Cultural Regions of Oceania

Interpreting Maps

Colonies in Southeast Asia, 1895

Have students examine the map and note how much of the area was under European control. Ask students what parts of Southeast Asia remained independent. *(Siam or Thailand)*

SKILLBUILDER ANSWERS

1. It was west of the French colony of Indochina, north of the British colony of Malaya, and east of the British colony of Burma. **2.** the Netherlands

POWERFUL STATES The years 1300 through 1800 were important to Southeast Asia's development. Five powerful states existed where Myanmar, Vietnam, Thailand, Java, and the Malay Peninsula are now. Those states were similar to *mandalas* but were larger and more complex. Trade within the region was important to their economies.

During that period, the Burmese, the Vietnamese, the Thai, and the Javanese each began to define their national identities. Urbanization, or the growth of large cities, also took place. For instance, Malacca, on the Malay Peninsula, grew to have about 100,000 people in the early 1500s.

BACKGROUND The Burmese are the people of Myanmar, which used to be called Burma; the Javanese live in Indonesia.

Colonialism and Its Aftermath

Southeast Asian states not only traded with each other but also with merchants from Arabia and India, who brought Islam to Southeast Asia. Islam attracted many followers, especially in the islands.

EUROPEAN CONTROL Large numbers of Europeans began to arrive in Southeast Asia in 1509. At that time, Europeans had little interest in setting up colonies there, except for the Spanish, who took over the Philippines. Instead, the goal of most Europeans was to obtain wealth.

Europeans used various business methods to take over much of Southeast Asia's trade. As the region's wealth flowed to Europe, local control in Southeast Asian states declined. By the 20th century, Europeans had made all of Southeast Asia except Siam (now Thailand) into colonies. A

Colonialism changed Southeast Asia. First, colonial rulers set up centralized, bureaucratic governments with set routines and regulations. Second, Europeans forced the colonies to produce commodities that would help Europe's economy. They included rubber, sugar, rice, tea, and coffee. Third, colonialism had the unintended effect of sparking nationalism. Groups that never had been allies united against European rule. And Southeast Asians who gained Western education learned about political ideas such as self-rule.

A. Answer If local rulers had less money to spend on armies, roads, and services, they would be less able to control their people.

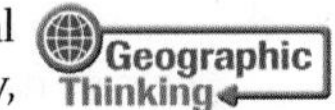

Seeing Patterns
A Why would a loss of wealth cause local control to weaken?

Colonies in Southeast Asia, 1895

hmhsocialstudies.com INTERACTIVE MAP

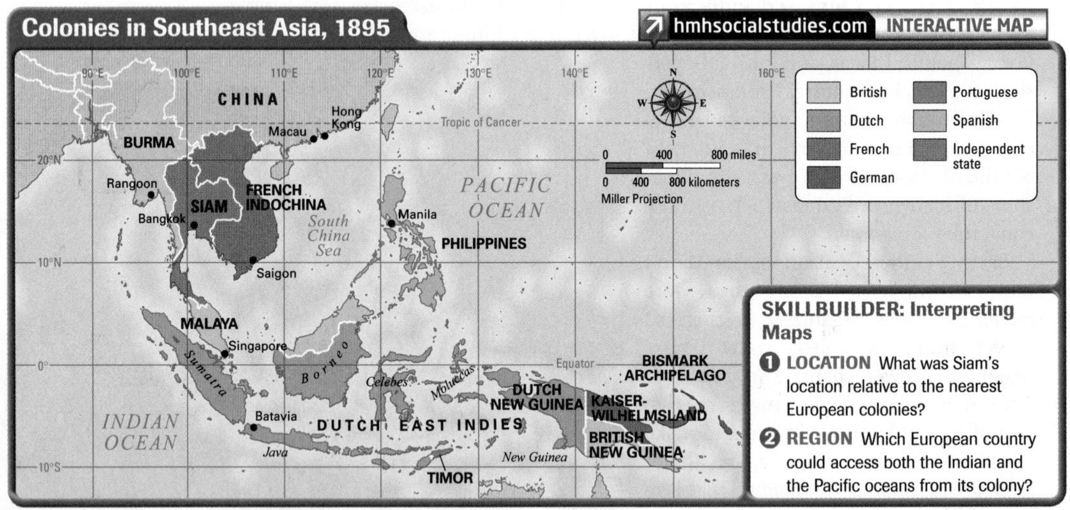

SKILLBUILDER: Interpreting Maps

1. **LOCATION** What was Siam's location relative to the nearest European colonies?
2. **REGION** Which European country could access both the Indian and the Pacific oceans from its colony?

ACTIVITY OPTION **SKILLBUILDER LESSON**

MAKING INFERENCES

Explaining the Skill Tell students that they can make inferences by "reading between the lines." Use the text on page 706 under the heading "Colonialism and Its Aftermath" to demonstrate the skill.

Applying the Skill Ask students the following questions: What characterized Southeast Asia before Europeans arrived? *(emerging states with established trading networks)* What happened during the period of European control? *(The states declined in political and economic power but later struggled for self-rule.)*

In-Depth Resources: Unit 10
- Skillbuilder Practice, p. 16

INDEPENDENCE Claiming to take back "Asia for Asians," Japan occupied Southeast Asia during World War II. Southeast Asians soon realized that Japan was exploiting the region for its own benefit just as Europe had. But unlike the Europeans, the Japanese put Southeast Asians in leadership roles, which gave them valuable experience.

After the war ended, Southeast Asian leaders sought independence. Several Southeast Asian nations gained their freedom peacefully. Indonesia had to fight from 1945 to 1949 to gain independence from the Dutch.

BACKGROUND The name *Indochina* refers to the Indian and Chinese influences on the region. The colony took up only part of the Indochinese Peninsula.

Indochina, a French colony made up of Cambodia, Laos, and Vietnam, suffered decades of turmoil. The Vietnamese defeated the French in 1954, winning independence for Cambodia, Laos, North Vietnam, and South Vietnam. The United States became involved in South Vietnam to prevent its takeover by Communist North Vietnam. The resulting conflict was the **Vietnam War** (1957-1975). In 1973, the United States withdrew. In 1975, South Vietnam surrendered, and Vietnam became one country, ruled by Communists. Also in that year, Communists took over both Cambodia and Laos.

Connect to the Issues

INDUSTRIALIZATION

Developing nations often seek foreign investors who can provide money to build industry. Most investors favor countries that show economic progress and have few political problems. This graph shows the amount of foreign investment in five Southeast Asian countries.

Foreign Direct Investment, 2002–2005

Country	Billions of U.S. Dollars
Singapore	53
Malaysia	14
Indonesia	8
Thailand	8
Philippines	4

SOURCE: United Nations Conference on Trade and Development

An Uneven Economy

Agriculture is the main source of livelihood in Southeast Asia. Several nations began to industrialize in the 1960s, but industry is unevenly distributed across the region.

TRADITIONAL ECONOMIES The people of Cambodia, Myanmar, Laos, and Vietnam depend mostly on agriculture for income. Rice is the chief food crop in those countries, as it is in almost every Southeast Asian nation. Myanmar is heavily forested and produces much of the world's teak, a yellowish-brown wood valued for its durability.

The lack of industry has many causes. The Vietnam War destroyed factories and roads. Thousands of refugees fled Vietnam, Laos, and Cambodia after the war, reducing the work force. Political turmoil, especially in Cambodia and Myanmar, has continued to block growth.

But some economic growth has occurred. For example, Vietnam has built industry and sought foreign investment and trade.

B. Answer more jobs, increased incomes, high levels of pollution, migration from the countryside to cities for jobs

INDUSTRY AND FINANCE In general, Brunei, Indonesia, Malaysia, the Philippines, Singapore, and Thailand have more highly developed economies than others in the region. Those countries have long been members of **ASEAN,** the Association of Southeast Asian Nations, an alliance that promotes economic growth and peace in the region. (The other four Southeast Asian countries did not join ASEAN until 1995 or later.)

Although these countries didn't begin to industrialize extensively until the 1960s, manufacturing has grown quickly. The processing of agricultural products is the chief industry. Other industries include the production of textiles, clothing, and electronic products. Service industries are also important. For example, Singapore is a center of finance. B

CONNECT TO THE ISSUES INDUSTRIALIZATION

B What further effects do you think industrialization will have on Southeast Asia?

SE ASIA & OCEANIA

Connect TO THE Issues

Industrialization

Southeast Asian industrialization has created issues similar to those faced by cities worldwide, such as traffic, pollution, urban sprawl.

- What does the degree of foreign investment in Singapore indicate about the country? *(It is economically and politically viable.)*
- What other information might be added to this graph? *(the types of industries attracting foreign investors)*

Instruct: Objective 

An Uneven Economy

- What is the major basis for income and industrial processing in Southeast Asia? *(agriculture)*
- Why is industry unevenly distributed in the region? *(political turmoil and effects of the Vietnam War, including the destruction of factories and disruption of the workforce)*
- How is ASEAN aiding industrial development? *(by uniting all of Southeast Asia in causes of economic growth and peace)*

ACTIVITY OPTION **INTERNET RESEARCH**

REPORTING ON THE VIETNAM WAR

Objective To develop research and reporting skills

Class Time 45 minutes

Task Investigate and report on the legacy of the Vietnam War

Directions Tell students that the Vietnam War had a lasting impact on Southeast Asia and the United States. Have students use the Internet to find information about the war's effects. You may wish to assign groups of students to different aspects of the topic, such as the war's economic legacy or its cultural legacy in the United States.

OPTIONAL ACTIVITY If Internet access is limited or unavailable, have students research the general topic of the Vietnam War and prepare reports suitable for class presentation.

Instruct: Objective 

A Rich Mosaic of Culture/Changing Lifestyles

- What influences appear in the region's sculpture and architecture? *(religious influences of Buddhism and Hinduism)*
- How are traditional ways changing in Southeast Asia? *(Many people are migrating to cities and adopting more modern lifestyles.)*
- What problems do cities face? *(shortages of housing for migrants; slums and unsafe living conditions)*

 **Cultures Around the World**
- Architecture, p. 55
- Traditional Practices, p. 57
- Literature, p. 58
- Music, p. 59

 **Cultures Transparencies CW55, 57, 58, 59**
- Angkor Wat
- Celebrating Songkran
- "A Plough and a Spade," by Nguyen Trai
- Playing a Gong

growing up in...

Thailand

Many students will be unfamiliar with *saffron,* the term used to describe the orange-yellow color of the robes of Buddhist monks. Explain to students that the spice saffron—which imparts this same orange-yellow color to foods—is made of the dried, threadlike stigmas of the saffron flower. Each flower contains only three stigmas, and the stigmas must be plucked from each flower by hand. It takes about 75,000 flowers to produce one pound of the spice, making it one of the world's most precious and expensive spices.

Energy sources and mining are significant. Brunei receives most of its wealth from petroleum and natural gas reserves. Since the 1980s, the country has restricted production in order to extend the life of its oil fields. Southeast Asia's mineral resources include tin, which is found mostly in Indonesia, Malaysia, and Thailand.

A Rich Mosaic of Culture

Although Southeast Asia has absorbed many influences from other regions, it has used them to create a culture that is distinctly its own.

RELIGIOUS DIVERSITY Southeast Asia has much religious diversity. Buddhism is widespread in the region, while the Philippines is mostly Catholic (as a result of Spanish rule), and Indonesia and Brunei are mostly Muslim. In addition, some Southeast Asians practice Hinduism, and others follow traditional local beliefs. C

Geographic Thinking

Using the Atlas
C Use the map on page 683 to learn about the major religions in Southeast Asia. What do you notice about the places where Catholicism and Islam are practiced?
C. Answer They are practiced mostly in island nations.

RICH ARTISTIC LEGACY Buddhism and Hinduism have influenced the region's sculpture and architecture. Perhaps the most famous example is the ancient temple complex of Angkor Wat in what is now Cambodia. (See page 705.) Thailand's Buddhist temples are modern examples of religious architecture.

Southeast Asia is also famous for its performing arts and literature. For example, Thailand and Indonesia have traditional forms of dance, in which richly costumed dancers act out stories. In Vietnam, poetry is highly respected. Nearly all Vietnamese know at least part of the 3,253-line poem "Kim van Kieu," which is about love and sacrifice.

About 95 percent of the people who live in Thailand are Buddhists and follow an ancient tradition of Buddhism that stresses the importance of being a monk. This has led to a unique custom. During their late teens or early twenties, many Thai men become monks for a short time.

The new monks go to live in a monastery where they meditate and study Buddhist teachings. They also shave their heads, wear saffron (orange-yellow) robes, and give up their worldly possessions. Some Thai men remain monks their whole lives, but most leave the monastery after a short period, usually a few weeks or months. After his time as a monk, a young man is considered ready for adult life.

If you grew up in Thailand, you would pass the following milestones:
- At your birth, your parents might ask a Buddhist monk to help them choose your name.
- You would have to attend school for 6 years, between ages 7 and 14. Although higher education is available, very few people can afford it.
- You could vote at age 18.
- If you were a man 18 years of age, you might be drafted to serve in the army.

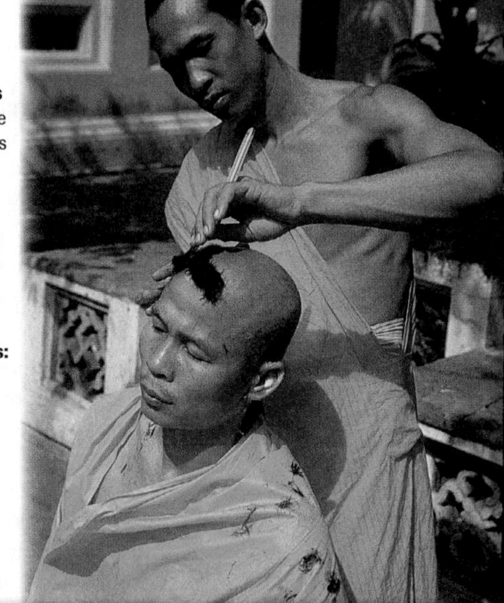

DIFFERENTIATING INSTRUCTION **LESS PROFICIENT READERS**

RECALLING THE GLOBAL PICTURE

Objective To grasp similarities among various sections of text

Class Time 20 minutes

Task Recall and relate chapters or sections of text

Directions Call primarily upon students who are less able to extract information from the printed page. Prompt them to recall and volunteer information about the movement of peoples and European colonialism based on previous text, such as the unit on Africa. Ask students to point out text in this section that provides similar information.

Changing Lifestyles

Most Southeast Asians live in rural villages and follow traditional ways. However, a growing number of people are moving to cities and leading more modern lives—a trend taking place all around the world.

THE VILLAGES In many Southeast Asian villages, people live in wood houses built on stilts for protection against floods. Roofs are usually made of thatch, although wealthy families may have a tin roof. In Laos, Myanmar, and Thailand, most villages have a Buddhist temple that serves as the center of social life. In Indonesia, most villages have a group of leaders who govern by a system that stresses cooperation.

Some Southeast Asian villagers still wear traditional clothing, such as the *longyi*—a long, tightly wrapped skirt—of Myanmar. Yet modern conveniences are slowly beginning to change village life. For instance, listening to the radio is common in Indonesia and Thailand.

PLACE People waiting at a bus stop in Kuala Lumpur, Malaysia, wear Western clothes and traditional Muslim attire.
What does this scene show about diversity in Malaysia?

THE CITIES Kuala Lumpur, Malaysia, and Singapore are examples of bustling cities with towering skyscrapers and modern business districts. In Southeast Asian cities, most people live in apartments. D

But there is a shortage of housing for the large numbers of people migrating to cities for jobs. Many of them live in makeshift shacks in slums. The dangers of doing that were shown by a disaster in Manila, Philippines. Hundreds of people had built shanties at a city dump. In July 2000, after a typhoon weakened a tower of garbage, it crashed onto those shacks and burst into flames. More than 100 people died.

Another region facing the changes caused by rural-to-urban migration is Oceania. You will read about that region in Section 2.

Geographic Thinking
Using the Atlas
D Use the map on page 680 to locate Kuala Lumpur and Singapore. How far apart are these two major cities?
D. Answer roughly 200 miles.

Interpreting Photographs

People's Attire in Malaysia
Have students examine the photograph on page 709. Ask them to point out the features of Muslim attire. *(Some students may know that many Muslims consider it a sign of modesty for women to wear a head covering. Malaysians call the head-coverings* tudungs.*)*

CAPTION ANSWER It shows either that some people are giving up traditional clothing for modern style or that there are both Muslims and non-Muslims there.

Section 1 Assessment

1 Places & Terms
Identify these terms and explain their importance in the region's history or culture.
- *mandala*
- Khmer Empire
- Indochina
- Vietnam War
- ASEAN

2 Taking Notes
PLACE Review the notes you took for this section.

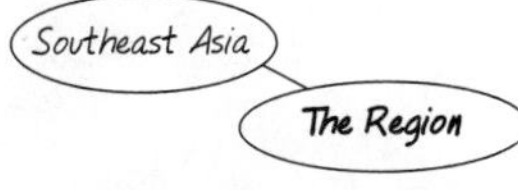

- Where did powerful states exist during the period 1300 to 1800?
- What is the only country in the region that wasn't a colony?

3 Main Ideas
a. How did China and India influence Southeast Asia?
b. How did the Vietnam War affect the economy?
c. What is village life like in Southeast Asia?

4 Geographic Thinking
Drawing Conclusions How has ASEAN helped to create a region within a region?
Think about:
- the goals of ASEAN
- differences between longtime and more recent ASEAN members

See Skillbuilder Handbook, page R5.

MAKING COMPARISONS Choose two Southeast Asian nations and research their similarities and differences. Create a **chart** comparing the two countries by using such categories as languages, religions, main economic activities, and types of government.

SE ASIA & OCEANIA

Assess & Reteach

GeoFocus Have students complete the section on Southeast Asia for the cluster diagrams.

Formal Assessment
- Section Quiz, p. 482

Reteaching Activity
Have students write a brief summary of diverse influences in Southeast Asia today and evidences of its own character and efforts toward independence.

In-Depth Resources: Unit 10
- Reteaching Activity, 18

Outline Maps with Activities
- Southeast Asia, pp. 103–104

SECTION 1 ASSESSMENT ANSWERS

1. Places & Terms
mandala, p. 705
Khmer Empire, p. 705
Indochina, p. 707
ASEAN, p. 707
Vietnam War, p. 707

2. Taking Notes
- in what is now Myanmar, Vietnam, Thailand, Java, and the Malay Peninsula
- Thailand (formerly Siam)

3. Main Ideas
a. China influenced Vietnam's art, technology, political ideas, and ethical beliefs; Hinduism and Buddhism spread from India across Southeast Asia.
b. It damaged the economy by destroying factories and roads, by causing refugees to flee, and by killing a large part of the work force.
c. Many villagers live in wood houses built on stilts with thatched or tin roofs; some villages are centered around a Buddhist temple, or are run by a group of village leaders.

4. Geographic Thinking
By promoting economic growth, ASEAN has helped its members to develop their economies, so that longtime ASEAN members make up a region of more prosperous nations within Southeast Asia as a whole.

GeoActivity

Integrated Assessment
- Rubric for a chart, 2.2

OBJECTIVES

1. Describe the 1883 eruption of the Indonesian volcano Krakatoa.
2. Learn about the consequences of eruptions by Krakatoa and four other volcanoes.
3. Research one volcanic eruption and prepare a television newscast about it.

Instruct: Objective

Krakatoa Volcanic Eruption

- What happened to Krakatoa in 1883? *(three volcanic cones on the island erupted violently)*
- Why did the Krakatoa eruption cause thousands of deaths in Java and Sumatra? *(the volcanic cones collapsed into the ocean and created deadly tsunamis)*
- What is Anak Krakatoa? *(a new volcanic island formed from lava flowing in the ocean floor beneath old Krakatoa)*

Interpreting Infographics

Krakatoa

What were the effects of the eruption according to the map and illustrations? *(People elsewhere heard explosions, volcanic ash covered a wide area, Krakatoa disappeared into the sea, tsunamis rolled toward distant coasts.)*

Disasters!

Krakatoa

Imagine an explosion so destructive that it sends volcanic ash 50 miles into the air and so loud that people hear it about 3,000 miles away. In 1883, the Indonesian volcano Krakatoa (also spelled *Krakatau*) erupted in an explosion that created those effects. But the blast was only the beginning of the disaster. The eruption caused the volcano to collapse into the sea and triggered a series of deadly tsunamis, or giant waves. The greatest of those towered 120 feet high. The tsunami swept the coasts of Java and Sumatra, killing more than 36,000 people.

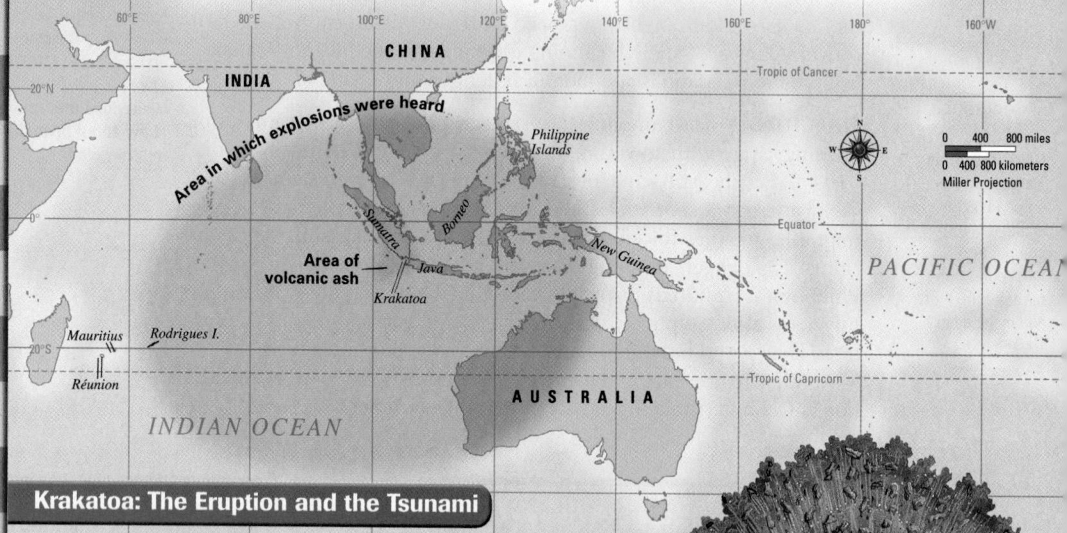

Krakatoa: The Eruption and the Tsunami

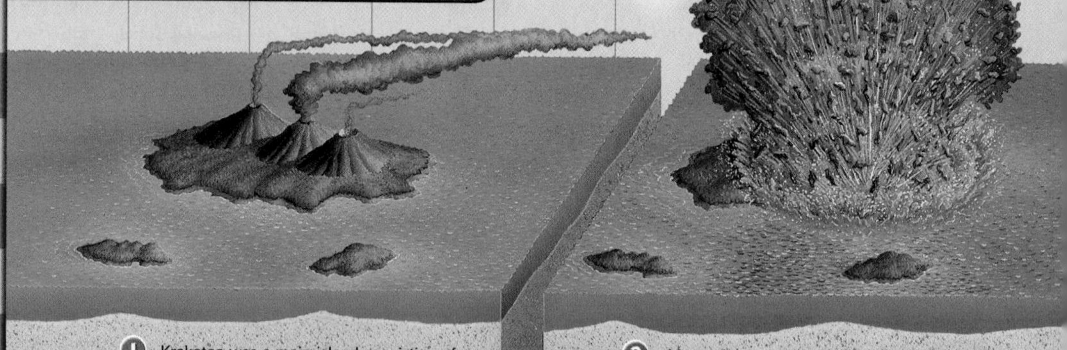

1. Krakatoa was a main island consisting of three overlapping volcano cones, plus two small islands.
2. After a few months of minor volcanic activity, Krakatoa blew up violently on August 27, 1883.

DISASTERS ADDITIONAL RESOURCES

BOOKS FOR THE TEACHER

Decker, Robert, and Barbara Decker. ***Volcanoes.*** 3rd ed. NY: W.H. Freeman, 1998. Readable text on volcanic eruptions.

Sigurdsson, Haraldur, et al., eds. ***Encyclopedia of Volcanoes.*** San Diego: Academic P, 2000. Expert articles on economic and cultural aspects of volcanoes.

BOOKS FOR THE STUDENT

Nardo, Don. ***Krakatoa.*** San Diego: Lucent, 1990. Illustrated account of the eruption and its impact on people and the environment.

Ritchie, David, and Alexander E. Gates. ***The Encyclopedia of Earthquakes and Volcanoes.*** NY: Facts on File, 2001. Excellent resource in an A-to-Z format.

VIDEOS

The Eruption of Mount St. Helens. Dir. George Casey. Graphic Films, 2000. IMAX documentary accompanied by featurette "Images of a Volcano" on videodisc edition.

Nova: In the Path of a Killer Volcano. PBS, 1993. Exciting, informative footage of Mount Pinatubo in the Philippines and the scientists who were there.

INTERNET

For more on volcanic eruptions and tsunamis, vist . . .

hmhsocialstudies.com INTERACTIVE

In the Sunda Strait, in 1927, lava began to flow through a crack in the sea floor beneath the site of the old island. By 1928, a new island was born and named Anak Krakatoa, which means "child of Krakatoa." The island is still volcanically active, but it is not considered dangerous.

3 All three cones disappeared, leaving only a small island. Massive amounts of sea water were displaced. The disturbance of the ocean created giant tsunamis. The tsunamis destroyed about 163 villages.

GeoActivity

PREPARING A NEWSCAST 

Working with a partner, use the Internet to research one of the other volcanoes listed below. Create a **television newscast** about the disaster.

- Sketch a map showing the volcano and the region affected by lava, ash, mud slides, or tsunamis.
- Create drawings, diagrams, or graphs about the disaster.
- Write a script for the newscast.

GeoData

DUST IN THE WIND

- Krakatoa threw so much ash and dust into the air that temperatures dropped by about 0.9°F around the world.
- The dust filtered light and caused spectacular sunsets around the world for about a year.
- The dust in the atmosphere also made the moon look shades of green and blue.

FIVE SIGNIFICANT VOLCANOES SINCE 1800

1800

1815
Tambora, Indonesia: 92,000 dead

1883
Krakatoa, Indonesia: 36,000 dead

1902
Mount Pelée, Martinique : 30,000 dead

1985
Nevado del Ruiz, Colombia: 25,000 dead

2010
Eyjafjallajökull, Iceland: no deaths, but air travel disrupted across northern and western Europe

2025

GeoActivities

Integrated Assessment
- Rubric for a television newscast, 5.3

More About

Tsunamis

Giant waves are caused by submarine earthquakes or landslides as well as by volcanic eruptions. Although tsunamis may travel up to 450 miles per hour, they slow as they approach the shallower areas along coastlines. The sea floor is exposed for minutes before a tsunami arrives. In 2004, many curious people on Southeast Asia's beaches went onto a newly exposed sea floor and were drowned by the waves that followed.

ACTIVITY OPTION | COOPERATIVE LEARNING

MAKING AN INFOGRAPHIC

Objective To understand volcanic activity and display information in a visual format

Class Time 30 minutes

Task Prepare a graphic that explains the behavior of various volcanoes

Supplies Needed Large sheets of white paper, drawing and coloring pencils or markers

Directions Divide students into small groups. Have each group find information on the Internet or printed reference sources about a different volcano. Be sure that students have a variety of volcanoes and locations from which to choose, including submarine and dormant, on all continents. Assign students within each group to tasks of designing, drawing, and writing caption copy for an infographic about their volcano. If possible, captions should include local lore and legends. Have the groups display their infographics for class comments.

SECTION 2 OBJECTIVES

1. Describe events in the history of Oceania.
2. Explain the region's economy.
3. Examine island cultures and lifestyles.

SKILLBUILDER: Interpreting Maps, p. 713

Seeing Patterns, p. 714
Making Comparisons, p. 715
Determining Cause and Effect, p. 715

Focus & Motivate

Ask students how physical isolation might affect the lives of Pacific Islanders. *(reliant on subsistence living and retaining traditional ways)*

Instruct: Objective

A History of the Islands

- How was Oceania first settled? *(Southeast Asian mainlanders came by canoes or land bridges.)*
- How did European contact change island societies? *(islanders died of European diseases, local customs disappeared, and islands came under foreign control)*
- What has happened to the islands since World War II? *(some have been used for nuclear tests; 12 nations have gained self-rule)*

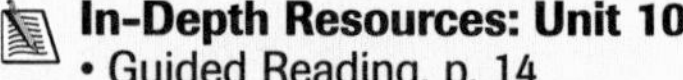

• Guided Reading, p. 14

CAPTION ANSWER Raised off of ground as protection from flooding; thatch roof allows ventilation.

Oceania

- Settled in ancient times by migrating Southeast Asians, Oceania developed three cultural regions.
- Contact with Europeans and Americans disrupted the islanders' traditional ways of life.

Places & Terms

Micronesia
Melanesia
Polynesia
subsistence activities
copra
taro

CONNECT TO THE ISSUES
ENVIRONMENTAL CHANGE A possible rise in sea level from global warming threatens some islands.

A HUMAN PERSPECTIVE Noah Idechong has fought to protect the sea life of Palau, an archipelago east of the Philippines. Palauans have always earned their living by fishing, but in the 1980s, many species of fish were in danger of extinction because they were such popular menu items in Asian restaurants. Idechong began to study the problem in 1988.

His efforts paid off. In 1994, the year Palau became independent, it banned the export of certain species, and fish populations grew again. However, in 2000, the government planned building projects that would help the economy but strain the environment. Idechong kept working to save wildlife. He said, "Palau right now needs . . . people who can say what they want Palau to look like 50 years from now." In other words, Palauans need to decide what to preserve in the face of change.

A History of the Islands

Like Palau, all the nations of Oceania except Nauru are island groups. They are Fiji, Kiribati, Marshall Islands, Federated States of Micronesia, Palau, Papua New Guinea, Samoa, Solomon Islands, Tonga, Tuvalu, and Vanuatu. (Some geographers consider Australia and New Zealand part of Oceania, but those nations are covered in Section 3.)

FIRST ISLANDERS Prehistoric people journeyed from mainland Southeast Asia to nearby Pacific islands using small rafts or canoes and land bridges that have since disappeared. In time, they developed large

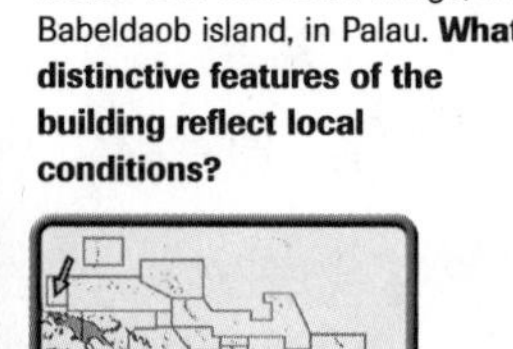

PLACE This traditional "man's house" is in Melekeok village, on Babeldaob island, in Palau. **What distinctive features of the building reflect local conditions?**

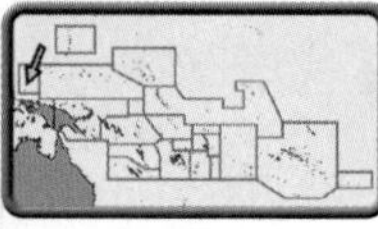

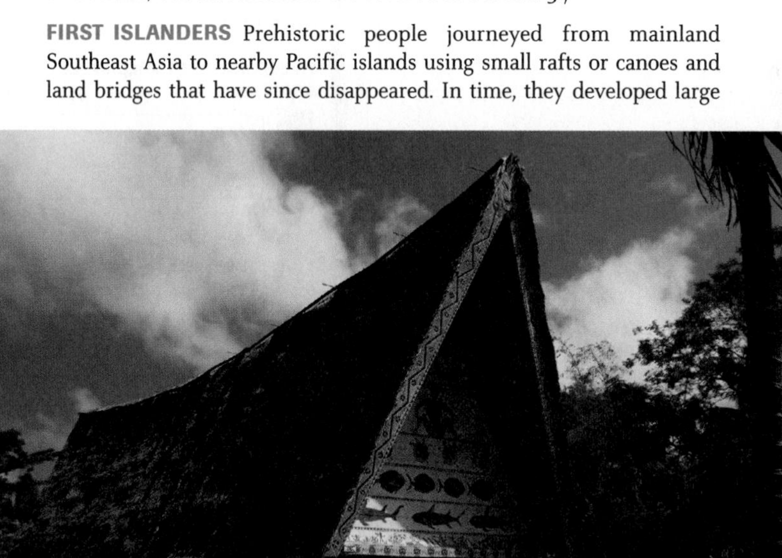

712

SECTION 2 PROGRAM RESOURCES

• Guided Reading, p. 14
• Building Vocabulary, p. 17
• Reteaching Activity, p. 19

• Section 2

Access for Students Acquiring English/ESL
• Guided Reading, p. 168

Outline Maps with Activities
• Oceania, pp. 105–106

Formal Assessment
• Section Quiz, p. 483

Integrated Assessment
• Rubric for a tourist brochure, 1.13

Cultures Around the World
• Daily Life, p. 56
• Arts and Crafts, p. 60

INTEGRATED TECHNOLOGY

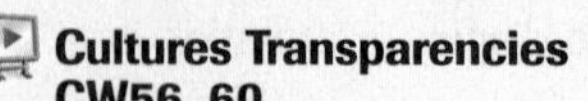

CW56, 60
• Enjoying a Feast
• Making Batik

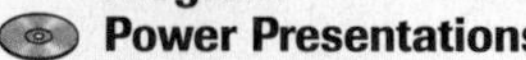

TEST-TAKING RESOURCES

Strategies for Test Preparation

TT101

Online Test Practice

Cultural Regions of Oceania

hmhsocialstudies.com INTERACTIVE MAP

SKILLBUILDER: Interpreting Maps

1. **REGION** Which of the cultural regions contains islands held by the United States?
2. **MOVEMENT** Consider what you have learned about ancient migrations of people in the Pacific Ocean. Which cultural region was the last to be settled?

voyaging canoes (see page 699) that enabled them to sail longer distances. For thousands of years, their descendants continued to migrate as far east as Hawaii, as far south as New Zealand, and as far west as Madagascar.

For centuries, the people of Oceania had little contact with the rest of the world, so they developed their own ways of life. Geographers divide Oceania into three regions, defined both by physical geography and culture. The regions are **Micronesia,** meaning "tiny islands," **Melanesia,** meaning "black islands," and **Polynesia,** meaning "many islands."

CONTACT WITH THE WEST Beginning in the 1500s, many Europeans explored the Pacific. Perhaps the most famous was the British captain James Cook, the first European to visit many of the islands.

BACKGROUND
James Cook was also one of the first Europeans to explore Australia and New Zealand. See page 718 for his portrait.

In the 1800s, European missionaries arrived and tried to convert the islanders to Christianity. Traders came for products such as coconut oil, and sailors hunted whales. Settlers started plantations on which they could grow coconuts, coffee, pineapples, or sugar.

As a result, island societies began to decline. Many islanders died of diseases brought by the Europeans. Western ways often replaced traditional customs. And Europe and the United States took control of the islands and turned them into territories and possessions.

RECENT HISTORY Oceania experienced turmoil in the 20th century. During World War II, the Allies and the Japanese fought fierce battles there to gain control of the Pacific. Afterward, some islands were used as nuclear test sites, not only by the United States (see Chapter 30) but

SE ASIA & OCEANIA

Interpreting Maps

Cultural Regions of Oceania

Have students examine the map. Ask them to locate the state of Hawaii. *(within the northern part of the largest region)*

SKILLBUILDER ANSWERS
1. Micronesia and Polynesia
2. Polynesia

More About

Pitcairn Island and H.M.S. *Bounty*

The inhabited island of the Pitcairn group is famous for its part in the mutiny of 1789 on the British merchant ship Bounty. Mutineers settled on Pitcairn Island after setting adrift their captain and eighteen of his crew in a small, poorly provisioned boat. The captain's remarkable skill safely brought the men 3,600 miles to Timor. The episode is recounted in a number of books and films.

ACTIVITY OPTION CRITICAL THINKING

DRAWING CONCLUSIONS

Explaining the Skill Tell students that drawing conclusions means analyzing what they have read and forming an opinion about its meaning. Ask them to look at the facts and then use their common sense and experience to decide what the facts mean.

Applying the Skill Allow students a few minutes to consider the "Cultural Regions of Oceania" map in relation to the text on pages 712–713. Then ask the following questions:

- What defines the three regions? *(physical geography and culture)*
- What did descendants of ancient islanders do? *(they learned to migrate long distances by canoe)*
- What can you conclude about cultural similarities among islanders separated by vast distances? *(islanders maintained contact with each other by sea travel; cultural similarities were sustained that way)*

Instruct: Objective 2

A Traditional Economy

- How do most Oceanic peoples obtain food and shelter? *(by subsistence activities)*
- What significant economic activities exist in Oceania? *(agriculture, fishing, tourism, mining)*
- How is tourism changing Oceania? *(The demand for hotels and an infrastructure to support tourism threatens island environments and traditions.)*

Interpreting Photographs

Economic Activities

Have students examine the photographs and read the captions. Ask which activity is most likely to change the lifestyle of islanders. *(tourism, as shown in the middle photograph)*

More About

Mining on Melanesia's New Caledonia

New Caledonia is rich in valuable minerals, including nickel, cobalt, copper, and chrome. Although mining is vital to the local economy, it is a mixed blessing. Mining operations have ruined mountainsides and polluted rivers. New Caledonia is working to install new technology that will be environmentally friendly.

Instruct: Objective 3 appears on page 715

Economic Activities

Many residents of Oceania make a living from traditional activities.

This resident of Fiji is husking coconuts to make copra, or the dried meat of coconuts.

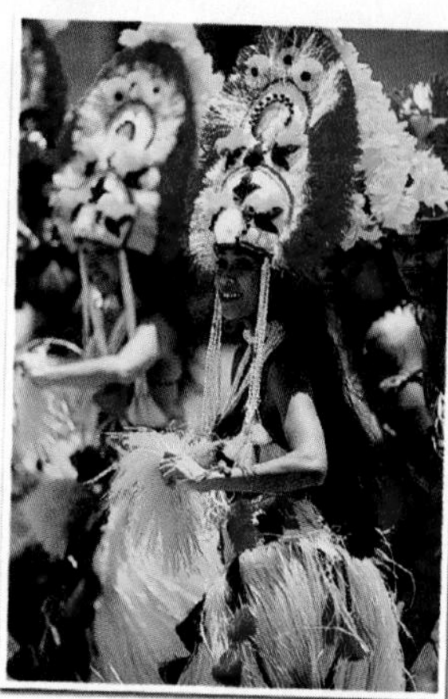

Traditional dances are often performed for tourists. These dancers are from French Polynesia.

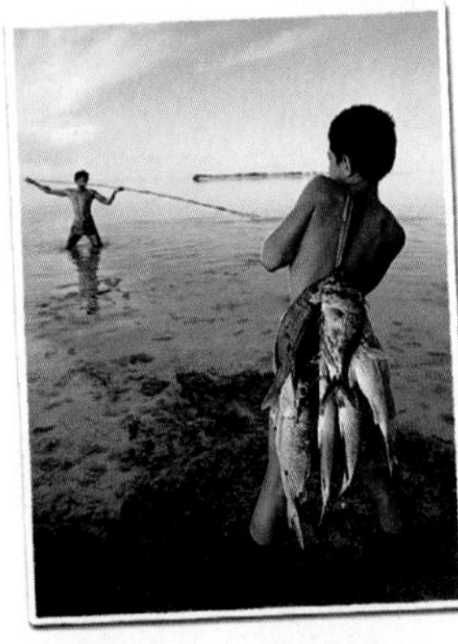

Many people of Oceania, such as these Micronesians, earn their living from fishing.

also by other countries. Gradually, inhabitants of many of the islands moved toward self-rule. Since 1962, 12 different nations have gained independence. Foreigners still rule the other islands.

A Traditional Economy

Most of Oceania has an economy in which people work not for wages but at **subsistence activities.** These are activities in which a family produces only the food, clothing, and shelter they themselves need. The tiny island of Nauru is an exception. It has a prosperous economy based on the mining of phosphates, used in fertilizer. But Nauru's phosphate deposits are expected to give out early in the 21st century.

AGRICULTURE As Chapter 30 explained, most low islands do not have plentiful or fertile soil. In spite of this, agriculture is the region's main economic activity because many high islands do have soil that supports agriculture. The chief crops are bananas, sugar, cocoa, coffee, and **copra,** which is the dried meat of coconuts. Fishing also provides a significant source of income.

OTHER ECONOMIC ACTIVITIES Since the invention of jet travel, tourism has become very important to the economy of Oceania. This has been a mixed blessing. Although tourists spend money in the islands, they also require hotels, stores, roads, and vehicles. These threaten the islands' environment and traditional ways of life.

A few islands besides Nauru have mining industries. For example, Papua New Guinea is developing a large copper mine with the help of foreign investment. Some industry also exists. Some of the larger towns have factories that produce goods such as coconut oil and soap. As in Southeast Asia, an increasing number of people in the Pacific Islands are moving to cities to find jobs. A

A. Answer its subsistence economy and the fact that many islands are not suitable for agriculture

Seeing Patterns
A Which characteristics of Oceania might account for its high levels of migration to cities?

Culture of the Islands

Oceania has a culture that blends traditional ways with the cultures of Europe and the United States.

LANGUAGE AND RELIGION Oceania is one of the most linguistically diverse regions in the world. Some 1,100 of the world's languages are spoken there. The people of Papua New Guinea alone speak 823 languages. In addition, many Pacific Islanders speak European languages. English is the most common.

Because of missionaries' work and colonialism, Christianity is the most widely spread religion. Even so, some Pacific Islanders still practice their traditional religions.

ACTIVITY OPTION **EXPLORING LOCAL GEOGRAPHY**

DEVELOPING THE LOCAL ECONOMY

Objective To gain a better understanding of global economic issues

Class Time 30 minutes

Task Plan the local economy in committee supplemented by written argument

Directions Divide students into small groups. Allow them 10 minutes to discuss the issues presented on pages 714–715 and select a delegate to attend a committee meeting. Have delegates argue the pros and cons of retaining traditional economic activities, developing tourism, and allowing (or expanding) urban growth in their community. Have delegates accept input from the remaining class "community members." Evaluate on the basis of individual contributions and a brief position statement written by each student.

THE ARTS Many Pacific Islanders produce arts and crafts, such as baskets and mats woven from the leaves of palm trees or carved wooden masks. Some islanders make a living selling such items to tourists.

Island Life

As in Southeast Asia, two distinct ways of life exist on the islands: traditional village life and more modern city life.

TRADITIONAL LIFE Ways of life varied throughout the islands. In Polynesia, most people lived in villages, ranging from small clusters of houses to large walled settlements. The houses were usually wooden with thatched roofs. Generally, a chief led each village. The villages' economies centered on fishing and farming. One major crop was **taro,** a plant with a starchy root. Taro can be eaten boiled, or it can be made into breads, puddings, or a paste called poi.

Many Polynesian societies were warlike and had frequent conflicts. In contrast, Micronesians tended to exist peacefully with their neighbors. Most Micronesians lived in extended family groups. As in Polynesia, they made a living by fishing and farming, with taro being a main crop.

In Melanesia, villages usually existed by the coast where people could fish. Inland, many people practiced shifting cultivation, moving often to let fields regain fertility. Other Melanesians were hunter-gatherers.

RECENT CHANGE Oceania has few cities, but they have been growing as many people move to them for education or jobs. Rapid urban growth has led to sprawling shantytowns and inadequate sanitation facilities. In addition, city dwellers are giving up their traditional ways of life. B

But change is also helping Oceania. Modern communications systems can unify countries consisting of scattered island groups and also can link Oceania to the rest of the world. Section 3 will describe the two most westernized nations in the region: Australia and New Zealand.

B. Answer Latin America, South Asia, Africa, and Southwest Asia

Geographic Thinking

Making Comparisons

B What other regions of the world that you have studied are experiencing these same problems in their growing cities?

Section 2 Assessment

1 Places & Terms

Identify these terms and explain their importance in the region.

- Micronesia
- Melanesia
- Polynesia
- subsistence activities
- copra
- taro

2 Taking Notes

MOVEMENT Review the notes you took for this section.

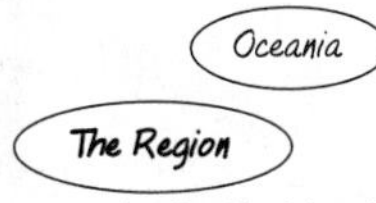

- How were the Pacific Islands first settled?
- What type of migration is happening within Oceania today?

3 Main Ideas

a. How did contact with Europeans and Americans affect the societies of the Pacific Islands?

b. What are the chief crops of Oceania?

c. What is distinctive about Oceania in terms of its languages?

4 Geographic Thinking

Determining Cause and Effect How has modern technology both helped and harmed Oceania? **Think about:**

- jet travel
- modern communications

SEEING PATTERNS Use the Internet to research several nations and territories in Oceania. Then choose the one that you think would make the best vacation spot. Create a **tourist brochure** that will persuade travelers to visit that place. Check your brochure for correct grammar, spelling, sentence structure, and punctuation.

SE ASIA & OCEANIA

Instruct: Objective 3

Culture of the Islands/Island Life

- What cultures blend in Oceania? *(traditional, European, U.S.)*
- What are Oceania's traditional economies? *(farming and fishing)*
- What Southeast Asian trend is also apparent in Oceania and causing change? *(People are moving to cities for education or jobs and abandoning traditional ways.)*

Cultures Around the World
- Daily Life, p. 56
- Arts and Crafts, p. 60

Cultures Transparencies CW56, 60
- Enjoying a Feast
- Making Batik

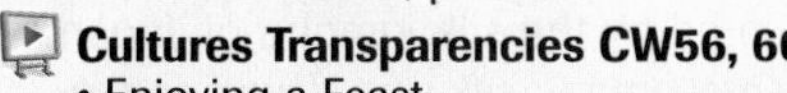
Assess & Reteach

GeoFocus Have students complete the section on Oceania in their graphic organizers.

Formal Assessment
- Section Quiz, p. 483

Reteaching Activity

Lead a class discussion about the impact in Oceania of contact with outside influences. Have students follow up with brief written summaries.

In-Depth Resources: Unit 10
- Reteaching Activity, 19

Outline Maps with Activities
- Oceania, pp. 105–106

SECTION 2 ASSESSMENT ANSWERS

1. Places & Terms

Micronesia, p. 713
Melanesia, p. 713
Polynesia, p. 713
copra, p. 714
subsistence activities, p. 714
taro, p. 715

2. Taking Notes

- In ancient times, people from Southeast Asia migrated to Pacific islands by using land bridges and small canoes or rafts.
- People are moving to the cities for jobs.

3. Main Ideas

a. Island societies declined because many islanders died of diseases, and Europeans and Americans dominated social structures.

b. bananas, sugar, cocoa, coffee, copra

c. It is one of the most linguistically diverse regions in the world, with some 1,100 languages.

4. Geographic Thinking

Jet travel has made tourism a major economic activity, but resorts have contributed to environmental damage. Modern communications can disrupt traditional values by introducing new ideas, but communications technology also helps connect people on scattered islands.

GeoActivity

Integrated Assessment
- Rubric for a tourist brochure, 1.13

OBJECTIVE

Learn about traditional costumes of different regions.

Instruct: Objective

Regional Costumes

- What features make these regional costumes unique? *(their styles and the materials from which they are made)*
- What materials were used for fabrics as early as 2700 B.C.? *(silk, cotton)*
- What theme of geography is indicated by the silk kimono of Japan? *(movement; silk was developed in China)*

More About

Saris

Saris have been worn longer than any other items of dress in history. Today, factory-made polyester saris are available, but the finest saris are made of silk woven on a handloom. India's silk industry is a huge employer of handloom weavers, dyers, and embroiderers. While saris are worn everywhere in India, blue jeans and t-shirts are popular with city dwellers.

hmhsocialstudies.com INTERACTIVE

Comparing Cultures

Regional Costumes

Blue jeans have spread around the globe and become a popular item of clothing symbolizing U.S. culture. But traditional items of clothing remain important in many regions of the world. Regional costumes are unique not only because of their styles but also because of the materials from which they are made.

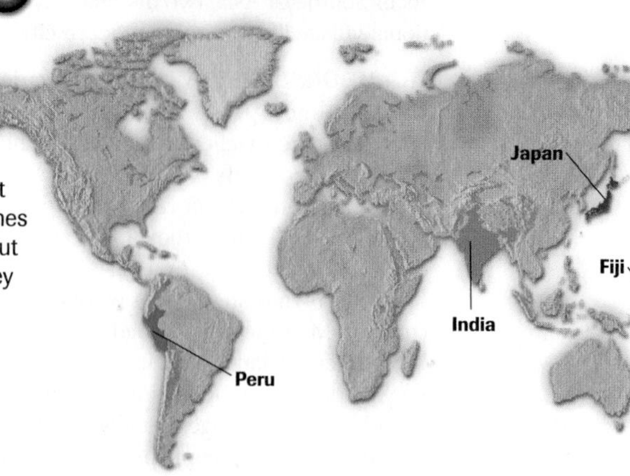

In India, the traditional garment of women for centuries has been the sari–five to seven yards of unstitched cloth wrapped around the body. The most valuable saris are made of silk, but saris of cotton and synthetic fabrics are also common.

In Fiji, traditional outfits are made from tapa cloth, a nonwoven fabric made from the inner bark of trees. This woman is wearing a skirt of tapa cloth. Fijians often decorate the cloth with geometric designs painted in brown, black, or reddish bark dyes.

SUPPORTING RESOURCES

BOOKS FOR THE TEACHER

Cosgrave, Bronwyn. ***The Complete History of Costume & Fashion: From Ancient Egypt to the Present Day.*** NY: Checkmark, 2001. Historical survey.

Neich, Roger, et al. ***Traditional Tapa Textiles of the Pacific.*** NY: Thames & Hudson, 1998. Valuable resource for the art, history, and cultural uses of tapa.

BOOKS FOR THE STUDENT

Gillow, John, and Bryan Sentance. ***World Textiles: A Visual Guide to Traditional Techniques.*** Boston: Little, Brown, 1999. Richly illustrated, encyclopedic introduction to handmade textiles from around the world.

Paterek, Josephine. ***Encyclopedia of American Indian Costume.*** Denver: ABC-CLIO, 1994. Authoritative source for Native American styles of dress and ornamentation, arranged by cultural region.

PERIODICALS

Paul, Smita Madan, and Kiran Desai. **"Sari."** *Civilization.* Oct.–Nov. 1999: 56–62. Discusses saris and silk weaving in India.

INTERNET

To learn more about regional costumes, visit . . .

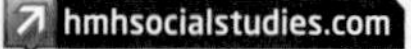

Although colorful silk kimonos symbolize Japan, neither the fabric nor the robe itself originated there. Silk was first developed in China, and kimonos are patterned after a wide-sleeved Chinese robe, the *p'ao.*

These Indians of Peru wear traditional wool clothing woven from llama hair; llamas are native to South America. Each village has it own set of traditional patterns that are woven into its cloth. Some of the designs indicate local landscapes; others depict animals or historical events.

GeoActivity

CREATING A DISPLAY 21st CENTURY

Working with a partner, use the Internet to research the linen clothing of ancient Egypt or the feather cloaks of Hawaiian chiefs. Create a **display** about this clothing.

- Draw or photocopy an illustration of the clothing. Write a caption giving interesting details about how it was made.
- Create a map showing the country where the clothing originated.

GeoData

Tapa Cloth

- Tapa cloth is also made in other Melanesian islands, New Guinea, and northern Australia.
- The most popular material for tapa is the inner bark of the mulberry.

Silk

- The Chinese began to produce silk in about 2700 B.C. and kept their methods a secret until about 140 B.C.
- The wide silk or satin sash worn with a kimono is called an obi. It is about 12 feet long.

Cotton

- South Asia was one of the first regions of the world where cotton was cultivated—starting in about 3000 B.C.
- Indian men also wear a type of wrapped garment called a dhoti. Mohandas Gandhi wore a dhoti to show his allegiance to the common Indian man.

Wool

- Wool is the fiber forming the coats of such hairy mammals as sheep, goats, camels, and llamas.
- Intricate textiles have been produced in Peru since about 1000 B.C.

GeoActivities

Creating a Display

Integrated Assessment
- Rubric for a display, 1.11

More About

Japanese Kimonos

The word "kimono" once meant "clothing" in Japanese. The kimono style evolved for centuries before it took its present form. At one time, kimonos were worn in layers and color combinations were linked to the season or the wearer's political status. In the late 1800s, Japanese officials influenced by other cultures called upon people to wear Western fashions. Japanese people today tend to don kimonos mainly to mark special occasions.

ACTIVITY OPTION | COOPERATIVE LEARNING

PLANNING A CULTURAL FASHION SHOW

Objective To understand cultural and geographic regions through styles of dress

Class Time 30 minutes

Task Produce a script for a fashion show model

Directions Divide students into groups and assign regions. Have groups produce the script for a model from their region who is entering an international fashion show. Besides describing the costume, the script should address topics of location, climate, and economy that will help models explain their region to audience members not familiar with it. Within each group, students may perform separate tasks of researcher for one or more topics, information organizer, scriptwriter, and announcer. Have the announcer read the completed script aloud for class comments.

SECTION 3 OBJECTIVES

1. Explain how Australia and New Zealand became European outposts.
2. Identify important national issues in modern Australia and New Zealand.
3. Analyze the economies of Australia and New Zealand.
4. Describe and compare cultures and lifestyles in Australia and New Zealand.

SKILLBUILDER: Interpreting Maps, p. 720

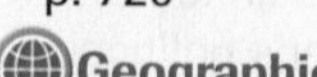

GeographicThinking
Seeing Patterns, p. 721
Making Comparisons, p. 722
Identifying and Solving Problems, p. 723

Focus & Motivate

What might Australia, New Zealand, and Antarctica have in common? *(histories of discovery and exploration by Europeans)*

Instruct: Objective 1

History: Distant European Outposts

- How were the lands conquered? *(British colonists fought Australia's native Aboriginal people and New Zealand's Maori)*
- What is the significance of the 1840 Treaty of Waitangi? *(The British took over New Zealand without understanding the Maori intent of "governorship," and this caused years of war.)*

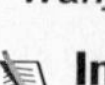

In-Depth Resources: Unit 10
- Guided Reading, p. 15

Australia, New Zealand, and Antarctica

Main Ideas
- Both Australia and New Zealand were colonized by Europeans and still have a strong European heritage.
- Because of its harsh climate, Antarctica has no permanent settlements.

Places & Terms
penal colony
Aboriginal people
Maori
Treaty of Waitangi
pakeha

CONNECT TO THE ISSUES
LAND CLAIMS The Aboriginal people of Australia are trying to reclaim ancestral lands.

A HUMAN PERSPECTIVE In 1788, Great Britain founded Sydney, Australia, as a **penal colony**—that is, a place to send prisoners. By the end of the 20th century, Sydney had overcome its origins and earned a reputation as a fun and fascinating international city. That has been due, in part, to a unique combination of physical and cultural geographic assets.

Sydney is located on a deep, beautiful harbor that not only allows the city to function as a port but also provides an arena for sailing and swimming. The mild climate there encourages such outdoor activities. In addition, Sydney has an increasingly diverse population. People who visit the city can view art and dine on food from many cultures.

In 2000, Sydney hosted the Olympic Games. With a physical environment that favors sports and a culture shaped by immigrants, the city seemed a perfect site for an international athletic event.

History: Distant European Outposts

Australia, New Zealand, and Antarctica made up the last region to be explored by Europeans. Australia and New Zealand became British colonies, even though they were already inhabited by people with ancient cultures of their own.

THE ORIGINAL INHABITANTS The **Aboriginal people** migrated to Australia from Asia at least 40,000 years ago. When Europeans arrived in Australia, there were an estimated 500 Aboriginal groups, speaking perhaps 200 different languages. The Aboriginal people had complex

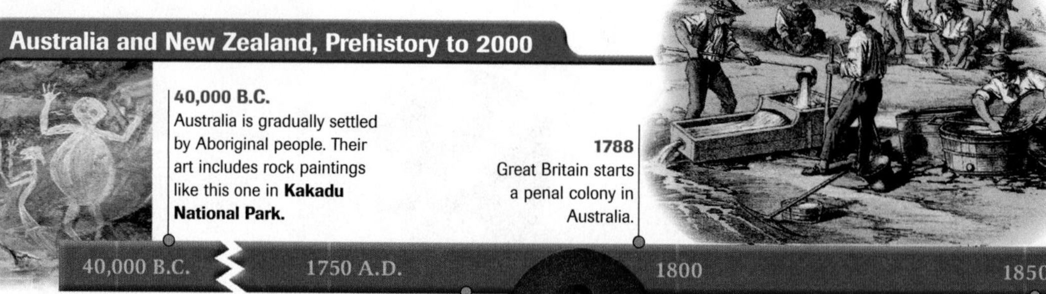

40,000 B.C. Australia is gradually settled by Aboriginal people. Their art includes rock paintings like this one in **Kakadu National Park.**

1788 Great Britain starts a penal colony in Australia.

1769–1770 **Captain James Cook** *(right)* explores New Zealand and Australia.

1851 Gold is discovered in **New South Wales,** Australia.

SECTION 3 PROGRAM RESOURCES

In-Depth Resources: Unit 10
- Guided Reading, p. 15
- Building Vocabulary, p. 17
- Reteaching Activity, p. 20

Guided Reading Workbook
- Section 3

Access for Students Acquiring English/ESL
- Guided Reading, p. 169

Outline Maps with Activities
- Australia, New Zealand, Antarctica, pp. 107–108

Formal Assessment
- Section Quiz, p. 484

Integrated Assessment
- Rubric for a Venn diagram, 2.8
- Rubric for a map, 2.1

INTEGRATED TECHNOLOGY

Map Transparencies MT55
- Exploration and Land Claims in Antarctica

The World's Music Audio Program

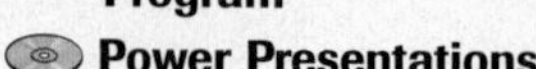

Power Presentations

Test Generator
- Section Quiz

TEST-TAKING RESOURCES

Strategies for Test Preparation

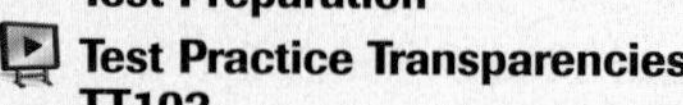

Test Practice Transparencies TT102

Online Test Practice

religious beliefs and social structures but a simple economy; they lived by hunting and gathering.

New Zealand was settled first by the **Maori,** who had migrated there from Polynesia more than 1,000 years ago. The Maori lived by fishing, hunting, and farming.

EARLY EXPLORERS During the 1600s and 1700s, several European explorers sailed in the coastal waters of New Zealand and Australia. Captain James Cook of Britain was the first to explore those two lands—New Zealand in 1769 and Australia's east coast in 1770. Antarctica was first discovered in 1820.

BACKGROUND
The name *Australia* comes from the Latin phrase *Terra Australis Incognita,* which means unknown southern land.

EUROPEAN SETTLEMENT In 1788 Britain began to colonize Australia (called New South Wales until 1820) as a place to send prisoners. Having a colony in Australia also gave Britain more Pacific naval bases. New Zealand was colonized by hunters and whalers from Europe, America, and Australia. No permanent settlements were established in Antarctica because of its cold climate.

In Australia, the British colonists had violent conflicts with the Aboriginal people, many of whom were killed. Even greater numbers of native people died from diseases brought by Europeans.

In New Zealand in 1840, the British and several Maori tribes signed the **Treaty of Waitangi,** giving Britain control over New Zealand. But the English and the Maori translations of the treaty differed. The English version gave Great Britain complete control; the Maori version gave Britain "governorship." Disagreement over who owned the land helped cause the Land Wars that lasted from 1845 to 1847 and from 1860 to 1872. In addition, tens of thousands of Maoris died from diseases.

Gold was discovered in Australia in 1851 and in New Zealand in 1861. Hundreds of thousands of people who dreamed of wealth flocked to the two countries, but few miners grew rich. Most, however, stayed there.

Connect TO THE Issues

MAORI LAND CLAIMS

Like many other cultures, the Maori believed that land could not be sold without tribal consent because the tribe, not individuals, owned it. When the English seized land or tried to buy it without tribal consent, conflicts broke out. Differing views of the Treaty of Waitangi also fueled conflicts.

The Land Wars in New Zealand lasted from 1845 to 1847 and from 1860 to 1872. A law passed in 1862 let people buy native lands, and the Maori lost most of their territory. In recent years, the Maori made land claims, and in the 1990s, they won some awards of cash and land.

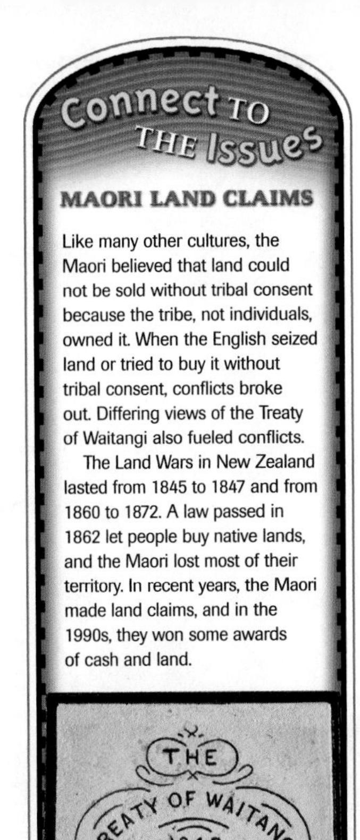

Connect TO THE Issues

Maori Land Claims

Relate to students that Native Americans also held land as community property. Explain that Shawnee Chief Tecumseh claimed that no tribe had the right to sell land any more than it had the right to sell air or the sea. Ask students what compromise might work to settle land claims by native peoples? *(Answers will vary.)*

2000
The Olympic games are held in **Sydney.**
1893
New Zealand gives women the vote.
1939–1945
Australia and New Zealand fight in World War II with the Allies.
1900
1950
2000
1861
Gold is discovered in New Zealand.
1901
Australia becomes a Commonwealth nation.

Interpreting Time Lines

Australia and New Zealand

Have students examine the time line and ask them to compare 19th-century events to similar events they might be familiar with from U.S. history. *(Students might mention the discovery of gold in California in the late 1840s. Or they might bring up the 19th Amendment to the U.S. Constitution, which gave women the right to vote in 1920.)*

ACTIVITY OPTION | CRITICAL THINKING

MAKING GENERALIZATIONS

Explaining the Skill Explain to students that making generalizations involves making broad judgments based on information. Note that similarities in geographic information can help them in making generalizations. As a preliminary to applying the skill, remind them that violent conflicts between European settlers and native peoples often occurred in U.S. history.

Applying the Skill Refer students to page 719 in the text and ask the following questions:

- What happened when Europeans began to settle in Australia? *(Violent conflicts occurred with the Aboriginal people.)*
- What occurred after the British and Maori signed the Treaty of Waitangi? *(wars based on misunderstandings about the rights of governorship)*
- What generalization can you make about colonial settlement in relation to native peoples? *(Colonial exploitation of native peoples often leads to violent conflict.)*

Interpreting Maps

National Claims to Antarctica

Have students examine the map and ask them what the nations with claims to Antarctica have in common. *(Many of the countries are relatively close to Antarctica.)*

SKILLBUILDER ANSWERS

1. Australia **2.** because every line radiating outward from the South Pole leads north

More About

Science Stations in Antarctica

The National Science Foundation manages the U.S. Antarctic program. In 1999 and 2001, daring rescue missions succeeded in retrieving ailing doctors from polar stations despite unsafe flying conditions. Temperatures below -58°F can prevent planes from gaining enough speed for takeoff, and make fuel too thick to flow.

Instruct: Objective 2

Modern Nations

- How has New Zealand implemented democratic traditions? *(self-governing in 1907, and one of the first to grant women's suffrage and establish old-age pensions)*
- How does the welfare of native people compare to that of other citizens? *(Native people are generally poorer and less educated.)*

Map Transparencies MT55
- Exploration and Land Claims in Antarctica

National Claims to Antarctica

hmhsocialstudies.com INTERACTIVE MAP

Some nations, such as Chile, claim territory close to their borders. Others, such as the United Kingdom, claim territory close to other possessions. Norway's claim is based on past explorations.

SKILLBUILDER: Interpreting Maps

1 REGION Which country has claimed the largest territory in Antarctica?

2 LOCATION Why doesn't this map have a compass rose?

REGION Twenty nations have scientific research stations in Antarctica. This one is run by U.S. scientists.

Modern Nations

Originally, several colonies existed in Australia, but in 1901, they joined into a single, independent nation. New Zealand became self-governing in 1907. Both Australia and New Zealand remained in the British Commonwealth, which is a free association of Great Britain and several of its former colonies.

RIGHTS AND LAND CLAIMS New Zealanders have a long tradition of concern for equal rights and the welfare of its citizens. In 1893, New Zealand became the first country to grant women the vote. It was also one of the first nations to provide pensions for its senior citizens.

In both Australia and New Zealand, native people generally have less education and higher rates of poverty than other citizens. Attempting to improve their lives, the Aboriginal people and the Maori have made claims for the return of their former lands. (See Chapter 32.) A

ISSUES A recent issue in Australia was a movement to withdraw from the Commonwealth. In 1999, Australia held a referendum on becoming an independent republic, but voters defeated the proposal, because Australians could not agree on how to choose a head of state.

Antarctica remains unsettled. In 1959, 12 countries drafted a treaty preserving the continent for research. By 2000, 18 countries had scientific research stations there. Seven countries have claimed territory in Antarctica, but many other countries do not recognize those claims.

A. Answer It would give them a place to live and practice their traditional ways without interference; they also might be able to earn money off the land.

CONNECT TO THE ISSUES
LAND CLAIMS
A How might land ownership improve Aboriginal and Maori lives?

DIFFERENTIATING INSTRUCTION GIFTED AND TALENTED STUDENTS

WRITING A RESEARCH PROPOSAL

Objective To develop research and persuasive writing skills
Class Time 45 minutes
Task Write a proposal to obtain funding for Antarctic research

Directions Have students assume the role of a scientist interested in research at Antarctica. Allow them to search the Internet and printed sources to become informed about scientific activities there. Have them write a proposal to a funding agency outlining the nature of their research and its importance.

Economy: Meat, Wool, and Butter

As Commonwealth members, Australia and New Zealand prospered by exporting food products and wool to the United Kingdom. So neither country developed much industry. But, since 1950, their exports to the United Kingdom have declined. To continue to prosper, Australia and New Zealand must either develop industry or find other trading partners, such as the nations of nearby Asia.

AGRICULTURE Australia and New Zealand are major exporters of farm products. New Zealand earns much of its income by selling butter, cheese, meat, and wool to other countries. Ranching is so widespread in New Zealand that in 1998 the number of farm animals (including 47.6 million sheep and 8.8 million cattle) was 15 times greater than the number of people! Crops include vegetables and fruits. For example, New Zealand is the world's largest producer of kiwi fruit.

Sheep ranching is also important in Australia, which is the largest exporter of wool in the world. Because so much of Australia is arid, less than ten percent of the land is used to grow crops.

MINING Australia earns a large part of its income from mining. It is the world's top producer of diamonds, lead, zinc, and opals. In addition, it is a major producer of bauxite, coal, copper, gold, and iron ore.

The mining industry faces one difficulty. Many deposits lie in the outback, far from cities. As a result, it is expensive to build the roads and buildings necessary for the mines to operate. Because of the high costs of mining and because Australia has historically lacked capital (money or property invested in business), Australian companies have had to rely on foreign investment. Foreign investors control about half the mining industry, so not all the profits stay within Australia. B

B. Answer Foreign investment provides the capital needed to develop industry, which can help create jobs, but the profits from the investment then leave the country.

Geographic Thinking

Seeing Patterns

B What are the pros and cons of foreign investment in industry?

MANUFACTURING AND SERVICE Unlike most developed countries, Australia does not rely heavily on manufacturing. One of the major industries in both Australia and New Zealand is the processing of food products. Because of its forests, New Zealand also produces wood and paper products.

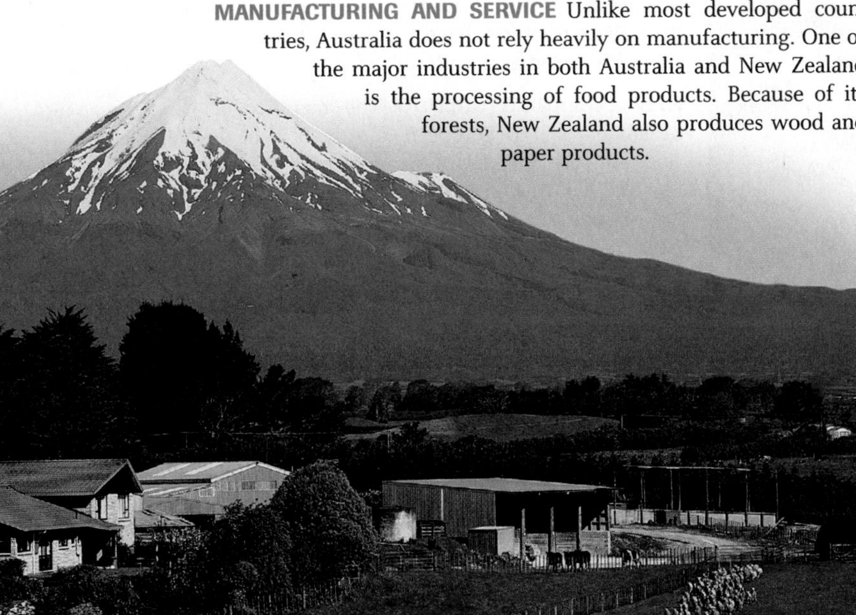

PLACE Sheep ranches dot the New Zealand landscape—here by Mount Egmont. **Why are more ranches than farms found in mountainous areas?**

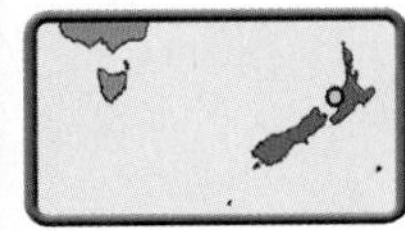

721

Instruct: Objective 3

Economy: Meat, Wool, and Butter

- How do Australia and New Zealand compare in sources of income? *(Both export farm products; Australia is the world's major exporter of wool and has income from mining; New Zealand is the world's largest producer of kiwi fruit.)*
- Why are mining operations difficult to develop in Australia? *(Capital is lacking because half the mining income goes to foreign investors.)*
- What economic challenges are faced today by both Australia and New Zealand? *(They must find new trading partners and diversify economically; manufacturing costs are high when compared to low labor costs in Asia.)*

Interpreting Photographs

New Zealand Sheep Ranches

Have students examine the photograph on page 721. Ask students why the land around the Mount Egmont might be suitable for grazing. *(streams flowing from snow at the top may help to enrich the grazing land below)*

CAPTION ANSWER Animals often can graze where the land is too steep for plowing or too dry for crops.

DIFFERENTIATING INSTRUCTION **STUDENTS ACQUIRING ENGLISH/ESL**

CREATING A MINI-ENCYCLOPEDIA

Objective To identify and understand the significance of words, terms, and names

Class Time 20 minutes

Task Construct a mini-encyclopedia of key terms and names with explanatory comments

Directions Form small groups joining ESL students with proficient speakers of English. Have each group review the chapter, selecting key words, terms, and names of individuals, such as "Maori," "Aboriginal people," "Treaty of Waitangi," "Kiri Te Kenawa." Based on group discussion, have students construct a mini-encyclopedia. An explanatory phrase or sentence should accompany each listing.

Instruct: Objective 

Distinctive Cultures/Modern Life

- What is common to the cultures of Australia and New Zealand? *(European and Christian influences are strong since most people are of British descent.)*
- How do the countries differ culturally? *(In New Zealand, 15 percent of the people are of native descent, so there is a greater blend of British and Maori cultures.)*
- How do lifestyles compare in the two countries? *(They are similar. Most people live in cities, although Australians have more pollution and traffic.)*

Interpreting Photographs

Maori *Moko*

Tell students that the traditional art of *moko*, or Maori tattooing, is undergoing a revival. It is popular among Maori young people. Moko is carved into the face by a specialist, who considers bone structure and other features. Ask students if similar customs exist in the United States. *(Students may note the recent popularity of tattooing among young people in the United States.)*

More About

Ngaio Marsh

New Zealand writer Edith Ngaio Marsh wrote mystery novels and plays. She was born in 1895 in Christchurch, and tried acting and home decorating in London before writing her first novel. *A Man Lay Dead,* published in 1934, features Inspector Roderick Alleyn.

As in all developed countries, service industries have been growing. For example, nearly 65 percent of Australia's jobs are in service industries such as government, communications, and tourism.

THE ECONOMIC FUTURE Both Australia and New Zealand want to develop a more diversified economy that is not so dependent on agriculture. But it will be difficult to develop manufacturing plants that can compete with those in nearby Asia, where the cost of labor is generally lower. Finding a way to maintain prosperity in the face of global economic change is a major issue for these two nations.

Distinctive Cultures

The British colonial past has shaped the cultures of Australia and New Zealand, but they also have developed in distinctive ways.

AUSTRALIA'S CULTURE Most Australians are of British descent, but that proportion is changing because of high rates of immigration from places like Greece, Italy, and Southeast Asia. More than 20 percent of Australians are foreign born. Only about one percent are of Aboriginal descent.

Like the British, Australians drive on the left side of the road, and many enjoy drinking tea. Christianity is the major religion. Australians speak English but also have many colorful terms that are all their own. For example, they call ranches "stations" and wild horses "brumbies."

REGION The traditional facial markings of the Maori, shown here, are called *moko.*

Australia's environment and history have influenced the arts, too. The Aboriginal people have an ancient tradition of painting human and animal figures. Some of those works can be seen on rock walls around the country. Many Australian painters of European descent have portrayed the landscape. For example, Russell Drysdale is known for his pictures of the outback. Several Australian novelists have written adventure stories about life in the bush country.

NEW ZEALAND'S CULTURE The majority of New Zealanders are of European, mostly British, descent. They are called **pakehas,** a Maori term for white people. The Maori of New Zealand fared somewhat better than the Aboriginal people of Australia; about 8 percent of New Zealand's people are descended from the Maori.

New Zealand's culture blends British and Maori ways. For example, both English and Maori are official languages. Christianity is the main religion, but some churches combine biblical and Maori teachings. C

Both cultures have shaped New Zealand's art. Maori art, including intricate woodcarvings and poetic legends, still survives. Western art also thrives. Well-known New Zealand authors have included the novelist Janet Frame and the mystery writer Ngaio Marsh. New Zealand filmmakers Jane Campion and Peter Jackson have made movies that were popular in many countries. And the opera singer Kiri Te Kanawa is admired internationally.

C. Answer Both lost lands and both lost great numbers of people to disease and conflict; however, the Maori have had a greater influence on New Zealand's culture than the Aboriginal people have had on Australia's culture.

Making Comparisons

C How are the experiences of the Aboriginal people and the Maori similar and different?

ACTIVITY OPTION **LINK TO HUMANITIES**

SURVEYING THE ARTS

Objective To learn about the arts of Australia and New Zealand

Class Time 30 minutes

Task Report about the arts in Australia and New Zealand

Directions Have students find information on the Internet or in printed sources on the arts in the two countries. Students should focus on information about the art forms of native peoples and about artists influenced by native works and by the landscapes. Have students report their findings in a class discussion, supplemented with visual aids when possible.

Modern Life

Australians and New Zealanders have similar lifestyles. For example, about 70 percent of Australians and 70 percent of New Zealanders own their own homes—usually single-family homes with enough land to grow a small garden.

CITY AND COUNTRY Australia and New Zealand are two of the most urbanized countries in the world; 89 percent of Australians and 87 percent of New Zealanders live in urban areas. Australia's big cities have the usual problems of pollution and traffic jams. In contrast, New Zealand's cities are relatively quiet, uncrowded, and pollution-free because of its small population and lack of industry.

In both Australia and New Zealand, many ranchers live far away from settlements. New Zealand has a good system of roads, even in rural areas, which aids travel. In Australia, many wealthy ranchers own private airplanes to help them cross the vast distances in the country. Some of the largest ranches in Australia can have a total land area of thousands of square miles.

RECREATION Both countries have climates that allow people to spend a great deal of time outdoors. As a result, aquatic sports, tennis, and team sports, such as rugby, cricket, and soccer, are very popular. Australia has developed its own form of football, called Australian rules football. Because New Zealand is mountainous, skiing and mountain climbing are common there.

In Chapter 32, you will read about Aboriginal land claims in Australia, industrialization in Southeast Asia, and global environmental change.

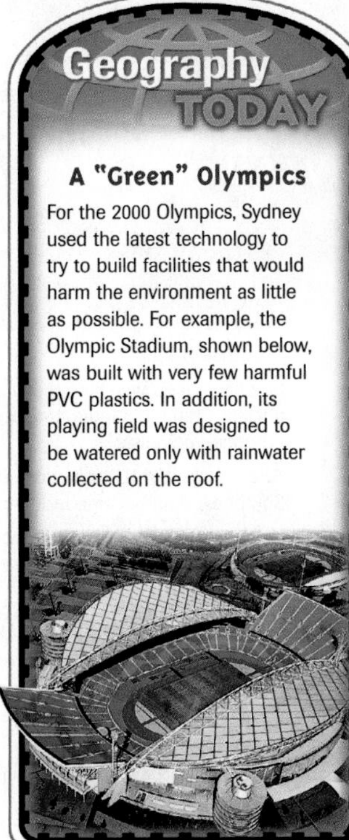

A "Green" Olympics

For the 2000 Olympics, Sydney used the latest technology to try to build facilities that would harm the environment as little as possible. For example, the Olympic Stadium, shown below, was built with very few harmful PVC plastics. In addition, its playing field was designed to be watered only with rainwater collected on the roof.

Assessment

1 Places & Terms

Identify these terms and explain their importance in the region's history or culture.

- penal colony
- Aboriginal people
- Maori
- Treaty of Waitangi
- pakeha

2 Taking Notes

MOVEMENT Review the notes you took for this section.

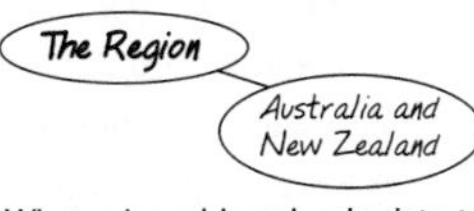

- What mineral lured colonists to Australia and New Zealand?
- To which country did Australia and New Zealand export wool?

3 Main Ideas

a. How did the Treaty of Waitangi cause a misunderstanding over land ownership in New Zealand?

b. Who owns Antarctica?

c. What are some of the British cultural influences in Australia?

4 Geographic Thinking

Identifying and Solving Problems How do you think Australia and New Zealand can solve their economic problems? **Think about:**

- their need for new markets
- Asia's large population and its relative closeness
- the Asian nations that have thriving industries

EXPLORING LOCAL GEOGRAPHY Do research to learn which farm animals and minerals (if any) are major products of your state. Create a **Venn Diagram** showing those farm animals and minerals that your state has in common with Australia and those that are unique to each.

Geography TODAY

A "Green" Olympics

"Greenfreeze" technology, or hydrocarbon (HC) refrigerant, was Sydney's choice for machines that sell soft drinks. Unlike hydrofluorocarbon refrigerant, HC does not deplete ozone or contribute to global warming. Ask students how other cities might benefit from "green" technology? *(Answers will vary.)*

Assess & Reteach

GeoFocus Have students complete the section on Australia and New Zealand in their cluster diagrams.

Formal Assessment
- Section Quiz, p. 484

Reteaching Activity
Divide students into groups. Allow them ten minutes to discuss how physical geography and history shaped the politics, economies, and cultures of modern Australia and New Zealand. Have a student from each group summarize conclusions for the class.

In-Depth Resources: Unit 10
- Reteaching Activity, p. 20

Outline Maps with Activities
- Australia, New Zealand, Antarctica, pp. 107–108

SECTION 3 ASSESSMENT ANSWERS

1. Places & Terms
penal colony, p. 718
Aboriginal people, p. 718
Maori, p. 719
Treaty of Waitangi, p. 719
pakeha, p. 722

2. Taking Notes
- gold
- United Kingdom

3. Main Ideas
a. It was issued in two versions; the English version gave the British "complete control" of the land while the Maori version gave the British "governorship." The ensuing misunderstandings helped cause wars.
b. No one; seven countries claim territory, but many other countries do not recognize those claims.
c. Australians drive on the left side of the road, drink tea, speak English, and play cricket and rugby.

4. Geographic Thinking
Australia and New Zealand might export goods to less developed Asian countries like Laos and Cambodia, or they might export food, wool, and minerals to the industrialized nations of Asia.

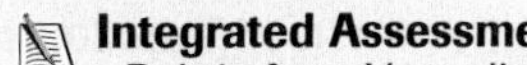

Integrated Assessment
- Rubric for a Venn diagram, p. 2.8

Reviewing Places & Terms

A. **1.** Indochina, p. 707
2. Vietnam War, p. 707
3. ASEAN, p. 707
4. Micronesia, p. 713
5. Melanesia, p. 713
6. Polynesia, p. 713
7. subsistence activities, p. 714
8. penal colony, p. 718
9. Aboriginal people, p. 718
10. Maori, p. 719

B. Possible Responses

11. Indochina was a French colony in Southeast Asia.
12. ASEAN works to promote peace and economic growth.
13. The United States tried to protect South Vietnam from Communist North Vietnam.
14. Melanesia, Micronesia, and Polynesia are the three cultural regions of Oceania.
15. Great Britain used Australia as a penal colony.
16. The Maori migrated from Polynesia.
17. They migrated to New Zealand.
18. You are likely to find subsistence activities in Melanesia, Micronesia, and Polynesia.
19. These activities may include farming and fishing.
20. Aboriginal people have been living in Australia for at least 40,000 years.

Chapter 31 Assessment

VISUAL SUMMARY
HUMAN GEOGRAPHY OF SOUTHEAST ASIA, OCEANIA, AND ANTARCTICA

Subregions of Southeast Asia

Southeast Asia
- Southeast Asia was influenced by ancient China and India and later by European colonists.
- After World War II, the nations of Southeast Asia became independent.
- Industrialization and urbanization are taking place in many countries.

Oceania
- After being isolated for centuries, the islands of Oceania came under the control of European countries and the United States.
- Since 1962, 12 nations have gained independence.
- Their economies are generally based on agriculture, tourism, and a small amount of industry.

Australia, New Zealand, and Antarctica
- The Aboriginal people of Australia and the Maori of New Zealand lost land when European colonists arrived.
- Both Australia and New Zealand are former British colonies that are now Commonwealth nations.
- They both want to diversify their economies.

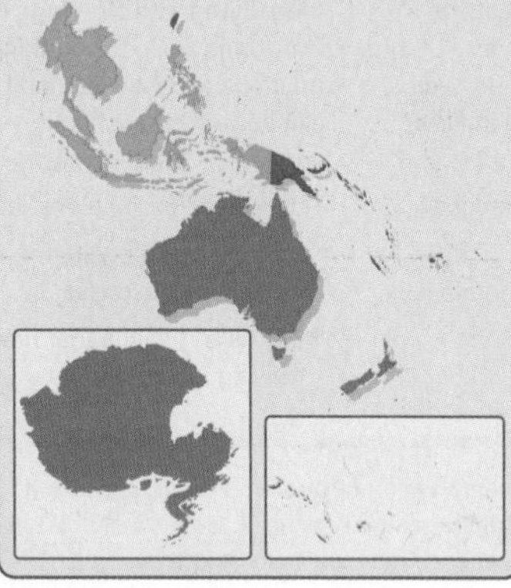

Reviewing Places & Terms

A. Briefly explain the importance of each of the following.

1. Indochina
2. Vietnam War
3. ASEAN
4. Micronesia
5. Melanesia
6. Polynesia
7. subsistence activities
8. penal colony
9. Aboriginal people
10. Maori

B. Answer the questions about vocabulary in complete sentences.

11. Which of the above terms was a French colony in Southeast Asia?
12. What are the goals of ASEAN?
13. During the Vietnam War, the United States tried to protect South Vietnam from takeover by what group?
14. What are the three cultural regions of Oceania?
15. Which European nation used Australia as a penal colony?
16. Which of the above terms is the region from which the Maori migrated?
17. What is the name of the place to which the Maori migrated?
18. Which of the above terms name regions where you are likely to find subsistence activities?
19. What are some of the subsistence activities found there?
20. How long have Aboriginal people been living in Australia?

Main Ideas

Southeast Asia (pp. 705–711)

1. What were the distinctive characteristics of the states known as *mandalas*?
2. What effect did colonialism have on Southeast Asia?
3. What are some of the major changes that Southeast Asia has undergone since 1960?
4. What are some of the arts for which Southeast Asia is known?

Oceania (pp. 712–717)

5. How far east, south, and west did Pacific Islanders migrate?
6. What caused many island societies to decline starting in the 1800s?
7. What are the major economic activities in Oceania?

Australia, New Zealand, and Antarctica (pp. 718–723)

8. What prevents Australia from benefiting completely from its mining industry?
9. What historic actions demonstrated New Zealanders' concern for equal rights and social welfare?
10. What is the major activity conducted in Antarctica?

Main Ideas

1. They did not have set borders but instead were organized as rings of power around a central court; over time, the region of power sometimes overlapped the region of a neighboring mandala.
2. Colonial powers set up bureaucratic governments, forced the colonies to produce commodities for European industries, and unintentionally sparked nationalism.
3. It is becoming more industrialized and urbanized; modern lifestyles are replacing traditional ways.
4. religious architecture and sculpture, traditional dances that act out stories, poetry
5. as far east as Hawaii, as far south as New Zealand, and as far west as Madagascar
6. Islanders died of diseases introduced by Europeans, Western ways often replaced traditional customs, and Europe and the United States took control of the islands.
7. agriculture, fishing, tourism, and some mining
8. Mining in the outback is very expensive, and historically, Australia has lacked capital; therefore, foreign investors control about half of Australia's mines, so that some of the profits leave the country.
9. It was the first country to grant women the vote and one of the first to provide pensions for its senior citizens.
10. scientific research

724 CHAPTER 31

CHAPTER 31 ASSESSMENT

Critical Thinking

1. Using Your Notes

Use your completed chart to answer these questions.

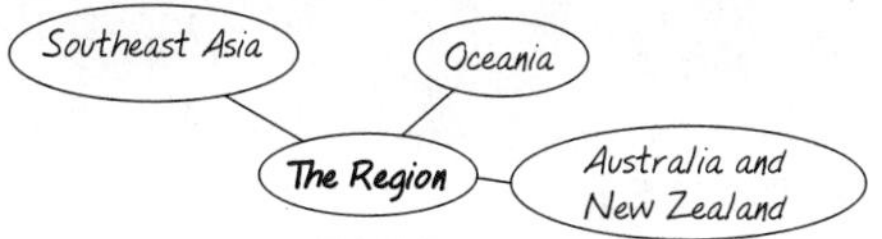

a. How does agriculture differ in the three subregions?

b. When and how did various nations of the region gain independence from European control?

2. Geographic Themes

a. **HUMAN-ENVIRONMENT INTERACTION** In what ways has the Pacific Ocean helped to shape the various cultures in this region?

b. **MOVEMENT** What role did migration play in the settling of this region?

3. Identifying Themes

Drawing on what you know about this region, what are general differences between village life and city life? What geographic themes are included in your answer?

4. Seeing Patterns

How did the arrival of Europeans affect Southeast Asia, Oceania, Australia, and New Zealand?

5. Analyzing Data

Use the Regional Data File (pages 684-687) to calculate per capita GDP (total GDP divided by population) for Indonesia, Malaysia, Philippines, Singapore, and Thailand. Rank the countries from highest to lowest. Compare your list to the graph on page 707. What pattern do you notice?

For Additional Test Practice

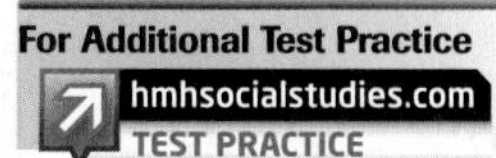

Geographic Skills: Interpreting Maps

Population Distribution of Australia

Use the map at the right to answer the following questions.

1. **REGION** How would you describe the population distribution of Australia?
2. **PLACE** Identify the two most heavily populated cities of Australia. What do you notice about their surrounding regions?
3. **PLACE** Judging from this map, would you characterize Australia as a heavily populated or lightly populated country? Explain.

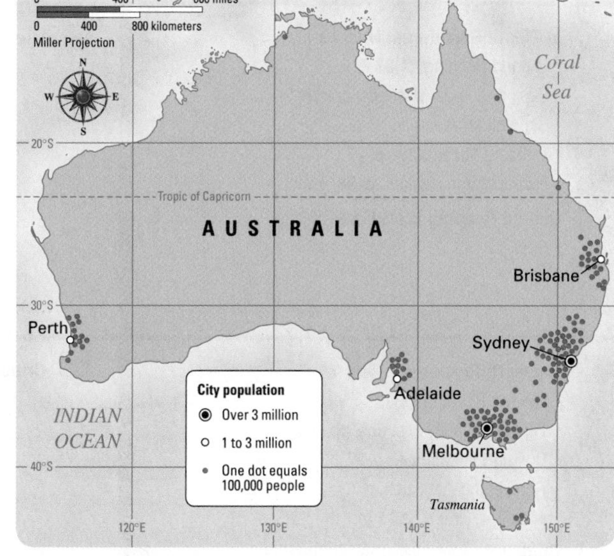

Copy this map on your own paper. Use the map on page 683 to make a climate map of Australia. Display the maps side by side with a caption explaining the link between climate and population distribution.

hmhsocialstudies.com

MULTIMEDIA ACTIVITY

Use the links at **hmhsocialstudies.com** to do research about two countries from different subregions in this unit. Look for information about government, economic activities, culture, and modern life.

Writing About Geography Write a report comparing the two countries. Include maps, charts, and graphs to help present the information. List the Web sites that were your sources.

SE ASIA & OCEANIA

Critical Thinking

1. a. main crop(s) in: Southeast Asia: rice; Oceania: bananas, coffee, sugar, cocoa, copra; Australia and New Zealand: meat, wool, dairy
b. Thailand was always independent; other Southeast Asian nations: after World War II; Australia and New Zealand: early 1900s; since 1962, 12 nations in Oceania have gained independence

2. a. Southeast Asia: trade and cultural diffusion; Oceania and New Zealand: fishing and sailing; Australia was isolated by it
b. Ancient peoples migrated to the Southeast Asian islands then to Oceania. The Aboriginal people of Australia also migrated from Asia. Later migrations brought Europeans to the region.

3. Village life is more agricultural, while city life is more industrial; region, place, human-environment interaction

4. European colonial economies and governments benefited themselves, not native peoples.

5. Singapore, $24,494; Malaysia, $9,852; Thailand, $6,265; Philippines, $3,512; Indonesia, $2,875. Greater foreign investment correlates with higher per capita GDP. The exception is Indonesia, which is third in foreign investment but fifth in per capita GDP.

GeoActivity

Integrated Assessment
- Rubric for a map, 2.1

Formal Assessment
- Chapter Test, Forms A, B, and C, pp. 485–496

Geographic Skills

1. coastal; mostly in the southeast
2. Sydney and Melbourne; surrounding regions are heavily populated
3. lightly populated because there are vast areas with no dots

MULTIMEDIA ACTIVITY

For the report comparing two countries in the region, students should:

- Present information in a well-organized and consice manner.
- Produce and clear, imaginative visual complement to the report.
- Include references to the Web sites used as sources.

Grading Rubric Evaluate student performance as Exceptional, Acceptable, or Poor in each of the following categories:

	Exceptional	Acceptable	Poor
Writing is clear focused and logical			
Clearly states the topic and purpose			
Provides necessary facts and examples			
Uses correct grammar, spelling, and punctuation			

Today's Issues: Southeast Asia, Oceania, and Antarctica

OVERVIEW	INSTRUCTIONAL RESOURCES	
ESSENTIAL QUESTION What are the relationships between the people and the land in the region? **Focus on the Essential Question Podcast**	**In-Depth Resources: Unit 10** • Building Vocabulary, p. 27 **Block Schedule Strategies** **Chapter Summaries** (English/Spanish)	**Interactive Online Edition** TOS **ExamView® Assessment Suite** (English/Spanish) TOS **CalendarPlanner** **Power Presentations with Media Gallery** **Critical Thinking Transparencies** • CT32 hmhsocialstudies.com INTERACTIVE
SECTION 1 **ABORIGINAL LAND CLAIMS** **MAIN IDEAS** • Aboriginal people lost land rights based on the British colonial doctrine of *Terra Nullius*. • British assimilation policy took away their mixed-race children. • Eddie Mabo and Wik court cases are helping Aboriginal people regain land rights.	**In-Depth Resources: Unit 10** • Guided Reading, p. 21 • Exploring Today's Issues, pp. 28–29 • Skillbuilder Practice, p. 26 • Building Vocabulary, p. 27 • Reteaching Activities, p. 32 **Guided Reading Workbook,** Section 1	**The World's Music Audio Program**
SECTION 2 **INDUSTRIALIZATION SPARKS CHANGE** **MAIN IDEAS** • Southeast Asians are leaving rural areas to find city jobs. • Growing cities in Southeast Asia are facing housing and pollution problems. • Rapid industrial growth is creating environmental problems.	**In-Depth Resources: Unit 10** • Guided Reading, p. 22 • Exploring Today's Issues, pp. 30–31 • Building Vocabulary, p. 27 • Reteaching Activities, p. 33 • Map and Graph Skills, pp. 24–25 **Guided Reading Workbook,** Section 2	**Critical Thinking Transparencies** • CT64 Push-Pull Factors in Urbanization
CASE STUDY **THE IMPACT OF ENVIRONMENTAL CHANGE** **MAIN IDEAS** • Human activities are damaging the environment. • Global warming and an ozone hole threaten global economies and people's health. • The case study project explores the issue of global environmental change.	**In-Depth Resources: Unit 10** • Guided Reading, p. 23 • GeoWorkshop, pp. 35–36 • Building Vocabulary, p. 27 • Reteaching Activities, p. 34 **Guided Reading Workbook,** Case Study	hmhsocialstudies.com INTERACTIVE • Predicted Impact of Global Warming, p. 735

ASSESSMENT

SE **Chapter Assessment,** pp. 738-739

Formal Assessment
- Chapter Tests, Forms A, B, and C, pp. 500-511

TOS **ExamView® Assessment Suite**

Strategies for Test Preparation

hmhsocialstudies.com TEST PRACTICE

SE **Section Assessment,** p. 729

Formal Assessment
- Section Quiz, p. 497

Integrated Assessment
- Rubric for a proposal, 4.11

Test Practice Transparencies TT103

SE **Section Assessment,** p. 732

Formal Assessment
- Section Quiz, p. 498

Integrated Assessment
- Rubric for a report, 2.5

Test Practice Transparencies TT104

SE **Case Study Project,** pp. 736–737

Formal Assessment
- Case Study Quiz, p. 499

Test Practice Transparencies TT105

CHART KEY:

SE Student Edition	Block Scheduling	DVD/CD-ROM
TE Teacher's Edition	TOS Teacher One Stop	MP3 Audio
Printable Resource	Presentation Resource	HISTORY™

Program Resources available on TOS and @ hmhsocialstudies.com

SUPPORTING RESOURCES

HISTORY
- **Multimedia Classroom Global History Series**
- **Global History Teacher's Guide**

Social Studies Trade Library Collection
- World Regions Trade Collection

For more information or to purchase these resources, go to hmhsocialstudies.com

DIFFERENTIATED INSTRUCTION

English Learners	Struggling Readers	Gifted and Talented Students
Spanish/English Guided Reading Workbook **Access for Students Acquiring English/ESL** Spanish Translations, pp. 171–176 **Chapter Summaries** (English/Spanish) TE **TE Activity** Discussing Environmental Issues, p. 735	 **Chapter Summaries** (English/Spanish) TE **TE Activity** Creating an Analytical Chart, p. 731	TE **TE Activity** Analyzing Data, p. 736

ENRICHMENT ACTIVITIES

The following activities are especially suitable for classes following block schedules.

SE **Student Edition,** pp. 726–739
- Interpreting a Cartogram, p. 733

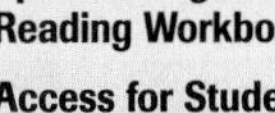

hmhsocialstudies.com INTERACTIVE
- Predicted Impact of Global Warming, p. 735

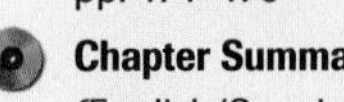

BLOCK SCHEDULE LESSON PLAN OPTIONS: 90-MINUTE PERIOD

DAY 1

SECTION 1, pp. 727-729
Class Time 60 minutes

- **Discussion** Lead the entire class in a discussion of the section, taking care to cover unfamiliar terms and legal issues.
  Class Time 25 minutes
- **Glossary** As a way to review the section, have students work in pairs to create personal glossaries of key places, terms, and ideas. The glossary should include items on the list headed Places & Terms in the Section Assessment, page 729, and the following from Main Ideas in that Assessment: *Terra Nullius, reserves, Wik decision amendment.*
  Class Time 35 minutes

SECTION 2, pp. 730-732
Class Time 30 minutes

- **Group Reports** To prepare students for the next day's review, divide students into small groups to discuss the section. Assign a reporter within each group to write a summary and post it for all class members to view.

DAY 2

SECTION 2, pp. 730-732
Class Time 25 minutes

- **Panel of Inquiry** Form a panel of students to serve as officials seeking information in order to solve citizens' problems. Have other class members assume roles of Southeast Asian rural or urban dwellers. Have the panelists pose questions for class members to answer based on problems outlined in the section.

CASE STUDY, Introduction pp. 734–735
Class Time 30 minutes

- **Discussing and Taking Notes** As a way to introduce the Case Study Project, lead the entire class in a discussion. Have students take notes of important information for each heading and subheading.

CASE STUDY PROJECT, pp. 736–737
Class Time 35 minutes

- **Discussion** Lead the entire class in a discussion of the Case Study Project and Primary Sources A through E.
  Class Time 15 minutes
- **Cooperative Learning Groups** Divide the class into groups to discuss and select an opinion on which to base a political cartoon. Have them begin construction of the cartoon and caption. Students may continue with aspects of the project as homework.
  Class Time 20 minutes

DAY 3

CASE STUDY PROJECT, pp. 736–737
Class Time 30 minutes

- **Cooperative Learning** Have groups complete the cartoon they began the day before and post them in class.

CHAPTER 32 REVIEW AND ASSESSMENT, pp. 738–739
Class Time 60 minutes

- **Review** As a way to review the issues present in the chapter, have students answer questions under the "B" heading in the "Reviewing Places & Terms" section.
  Class Time 25 minutes
- **Assessment** Have students complete the Chapter 32 Assessment.
  Class Time 35 minutes

TEACHER-TESTED ACTIVITY Product Scavenger Hunt

Class Time One week

Task Find at least fifteen products that are imported from the countries covered by Chapter 32. Create symbols for those products and mark them on a map of the region.

Supplies
- Outline map of the region provided by the teacher
- Colored pencils or markers

Purpose To demonstrate the interdependence of the United States and the countries of the region, and to reinforce the location of those countries

Activity Students will search at home or in stores for products that are manufactured in countries in the region. Students should record the name of the product and the country where it was made. If possible, students should also record the name of the store where the product was purchased and the price of the product. All countries on the map should be colored and labeled. A legend will be created to identify the symbols for the products and to show the countries involved. All countries from which products were found should be marked, using vertical lines if necessary for the smallest island nations.

Debbie Althouse
Geography Teacher, Thomas J. Anderson High School, Southgate Michigan

TECHNOLOGY IN THE CLASSROOM

The Web lends itself well to student research because of the availability of Web sites with valuable, up-to-date information, including text and pictures. However, the Web also contains many sites that are not up-to-date or that have irrelevant, erroneous, or inappropriate information. One good way to keep students "on-task" and to ensure that they use appropriate Web sites is to have them look through a limited set of pre-selected sites. The teacher should choose sites sponsored by organizations that are generally considered reliable, such as major news sources, television networks, nonprofit organizations, or museums. If the teacher presents students with a list of appropriate sites, they can save a good deal of classroom time, and students will be less likely to end up at sites that are irrelevant or inappropriate.

Objective Students will use the Internet to learn about the relationship between global warming and Antarctica.

Task Have students visit the specified Web sites to answer questions about Antarctica and global warming. Have them use computer drawing programs to illustrate the potential impacts of global warming on Antarctica

Class Time 1–2 class periods

1. Have students read pages 734–737. Ask them to describe the process of global warming and its potential long-term effects.
2. Have students visit the Web sites listed at **hmhsocial studies.com** to learn about the relationship between global warming and Antarctica. Ask them to write answers to these questions as they conduct their research: What can we learn from studying the impacts of global warming in Antarctica, and how can we get this information? Why is Antarctica particularly sensitive to the effects of global warming? What evidence has been found in Antarctica to support the global warming theory? How might other parts of the world be affected by changes in Antarctica due to global warming?
3. Have students use computer drawing programs to draw their own illustrations of the potential impacts of global warming on Antarctica and on how global warming in Antarctica might affect other parts of the Earth.

CHAPTER 32 OBJECTIVE

Examine regional issues of land claims, industrialization, and global warming, and the implications for the world community.

Chapter 32 TODAY'S ISSUES Southeast Asia, Oceania, and Antarctica

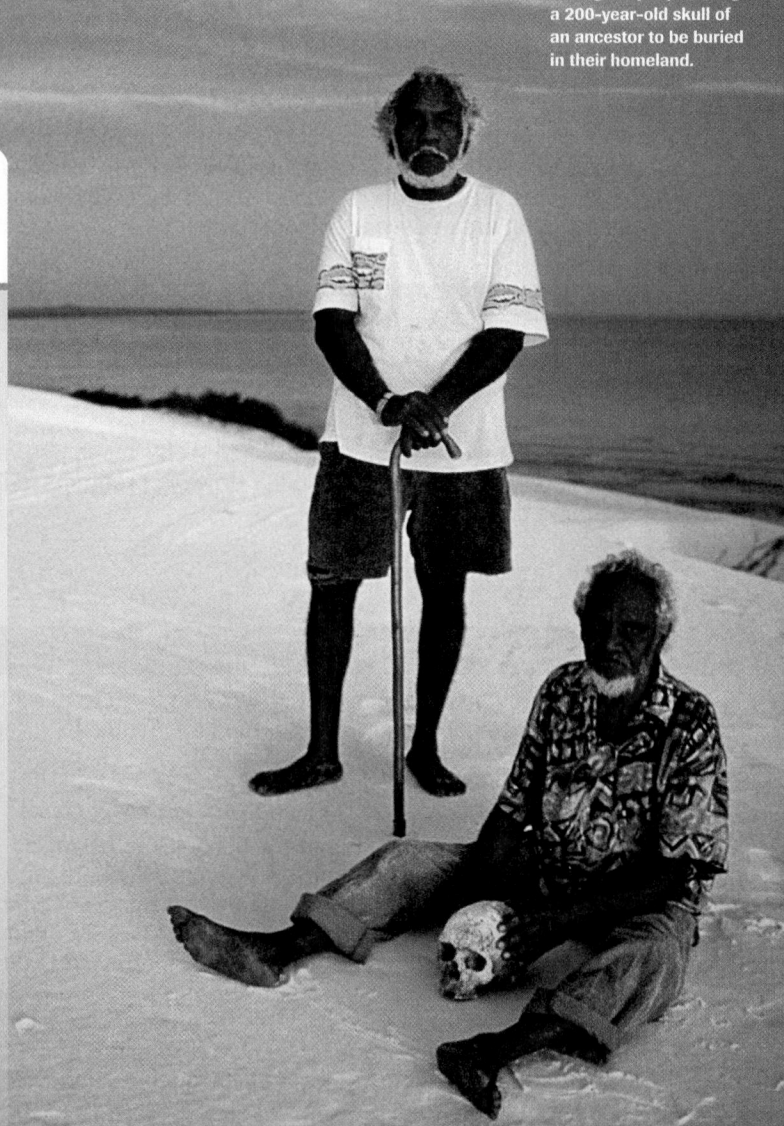

Gordon and Alick Pablo, elders of the Wuthathi Aboriginal people, bring a 200-year-old skull of an ancestor to be buried in their homeland.

Interpreting Photographs

The Wuthathi People

Have students study the photograph and caption on page 726.

Extension

Ask students to speculate about the significance of the skull.

Essential Question

What are the relationships between the people and the land in the region?

What You Will Learn

In this chapter you will see how modern life is putting stress on the region's ancient cultures and how industrialization is affecting the environment there.

SECTION 1
Aboriginal Land Claims

SECTION 2
Industrialization Sparks Change

CASE STUDY
Global Environmental Change

For more on these issues in Southeast Asia, Oceania, and Antarctica . . .

hmhsocialstudies.com CURRENT EVENTS

hmhsocialstudies.com TAKING NOTES

Use the graphic organizer online to take notes on the causes and effects of the region's issues.

726

Introducing the Essential Question

- Remind students that they have studied regions where disagreements over land have simmered for a long time. Examples include the Caucasus region and Israel. In this chapter, they will examine a conflict that began in the 1700s.
- Review possible positive and negative effects of industrialization. Point out that Southeast Asia is experiencing many of these effects.

hmhsocialstudies.com TAKING NOTES

Ask students to fill in the cause-and-effect chart as they read about the issues facing Southeast Asia, Oceania, and Antarctica today.

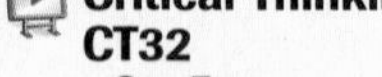

Critical Thinking Transparencies CT32
- GeoFocus

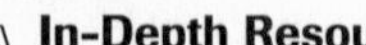

In-Depth Resources: Unit 10
- Building Vocabulary, p. 27

CHAPTER 32 ADDITIONAL RESOURCES

BOOKS FOR THE TEACHER

Dayley, Robert A. and Clark Neher. ***Southeast Asia in the New International Era.*** Westview Press, 2009. Political developments in Southeast Asia, along with the historical and cultural background of those events.

BOOKS FOR THE STUDENT

Houghton, John T. ***Global Warming: The Complete Briefing.*** Cambridge: Cambridge UP, 1997. Comprehensive discussion of the science and politics of global warming for more proficient readers.

Pringle, Laurence. ***Global Warming: The Threat of Earth's Changing Climate.*** NY: SeaStar Books, 2001. Clear, illustrated introduction to global warming issues.

PERIODICALS

Chesterman, John. **"Defending Australia's Reputation."** *Australian Historical Studies.* 32 (2001): 20–40. How the Aboriginal people obtained their civil rights.

Neutze, Max. **"Housing for Indigenous Australians."** *Housing Studies.* 15 (2000): 485–505. Study of the housing problems of Aboriginal people.

INTERNET

For more on today's issues in Southeast Asia, Oceania, and Antarctica, visit . . .

hmhsocialstudies.com

Aboriginal Land Claims

Should native people be given back their ancestors' land?

Main Ideas
- The Aboriginal people of Australia lost their ancestral lands to European colonists.
- Recently they have regained some of that land through court cases.

Places & Terms
assimilation
Stolen Generation
Land Rights Act of 1976
***Mabo* Case**
pastoral leases
***Wik* Case**

A HUMAN PERSPECTIVE In 1972, the Australian government denied the claims of some Aboriginal people trying to regain ancestral lands. In response, Aboriginal protesters erected a tent on the lawn of Old Parliament House in Canberra and named it the Aboriginal Tent Embassy. They called it an embassy to symbolize their treatment as foreigners in their own country. They chose a temporary shelter instead of a building to symbolize that they had no permanent title to land.

Over the years, the Australian government tried to get rid of the tent embassy by force, by legal action, and by ignoring it in the hope that it would disappear. But in the year 2000, the embassy still stood. Protesters also set up a second tent embassy in Sydney during the Olympics to inform the world of their ongoing struggle to regain land.

Aboriginal People Lose Land

Traditionally, the Aboriginal people had a complex relationship with land. They didn't farm or herd animals but lived by hunting and gathering whatever was available for food. Because of this, they depended completely on nature and saw many places as sacred.

BRITISH POLICY Because Aboriginal people did not use the land in the way that Westerners did—by farming it, mining it, and building on it—British colonists believed that they had no ties to the land. British authorities declared Australia to be *Terra Nullius,* a Latin term that means empty land. Therefore, the British government decided it had the right to take land without making treaties with Aboriginal leaders.

STOLEN LAND When Europeans began to settle Australia in 1788, they chose the most fertile regions. Aboriginal people tried to fight what

Aboriginal Fight for Land, 1960-Present

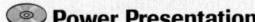

1967 Aboriginal people become Australian citizens.

1972 Protesters erect the Aboriginal Tent Embassy.

1976 Land Rights Act allows Aboriginal people to claim land in Northern Territory.

1992 The ruling in the lawsuit brought by Eddie Mabo overturns doctrine of *Terra Nullius.*

1996 The *Wik* case allows Aboriginal people to claim land leased by farmers and ranchers.

1960 — 1980 — 2000

SE ASIA & OCEANIA

SECTION 1 OBJECTIVES

1. Explain how Aboriginal people lost their land and suffered from forced assimilation.
2. Examine land claims and identify Aboriginal achievements in regaining rights.

SKILLBUILDER: Interpreting Maps, p. 728

GeographicThinking
Seeing Patterns, p. 728
Making Comparisons, p. 728
Distinguishing Fact from Opinion, p. 729

Focus & Motivate

Ask students to name other places where land issues arose from contact between Europeans and native peoples. *(Students may discuss Africa or the United States.)*

Instruct: Objective 

Aboriginal People Lose Land

- How did Aboriginal people use land? *(They used land for hunting and gathering.)*
- What was the significance of the British doctrine of Terra Nullius? *(Colonists claimed property rights on the basis that Aboriginal people did not farm, mine, or build on the land.)*
- How are Aboriginal land claims tied to grief over the "Stolen Generation"? *(Aboriginal people seek land rights to preserve their way of life and pass the culture to their descendants.)*

In-Depth Resources: Unit 10
- Guided Reading, p. 21
- Exploring Today's Issues, pp. 28–29

SECTION 1 PROGRAM RESOURCES

In-Depth Resources: Unit 10
- Guided Reading, p. 21
- Exploring Today's Issues, pp. 28–29
- Skillbuilder Practice, p. 26
- Building Vocabulary, p. 27
- Reteaching Activity, p. 32

Guided Reading Workbook
- Section 1

Access for Students Acquiring English/ESL
- Guided Reading, p. 171
- Skillbuillder Practice, p. 174

Formal Assessment
- Section Quiz, p. 497

Integrated Assessment
- Rubric for a proposal, 4.11

INTEGRATED TECHNOLOGY

Chapter Summaries
Power Presentations
Test Generator
- Section Quiz

hmhsocialstudies.com

TEST-TAKING RESOURCES

Strategies for Test Preparation

Test Practice Transparencies TT103

Online Test Practice

Instruct: Objective 2

Land Claims

- What did the Land Rights Act of 1976 mean for Aboriginal people? *(They could own their reserves and some land in the Northern Territory.)*
- What case most helped Aboriginal land claims? *(the 1992 Mabo case that overturned the doctrine of* Terra Nullius*)*
- What happened in the 1996 *Wik* case? *(Aboriginal people were granted the right to claim government-owned land taken in pastoral lease, but the law was amended under pressure from white Australians who leased and used the land.)*

Interpreting Maps

Aboriginal Land Claims

Have students examine the map and the shapes of the disputed parcels of land. Ask students what inferences they can make about the parcels. *(The parcels may incorporate reserve lands. They have been surveyed and mapped out according to latitude and longitude lines, rather than by physical boundaries.)*

SKILLBUILDER ANSWERS 1. It lies off the northeast coast of Australia, between Australia and New Guinea. **2.** about three-quarters

they saw as an invasion of their land, but they were defeated because the Europeans had superior weapons. Some Aboriginal people were forced to live on reserves, that is, tracts of less productive land set aside for them. Others lived on the edges of settlements and adopted some European ways, such as working on ranches.

STOLEN CHILDREN The Aboriginal people lost something even more precious than land. Between 1909 and 1969, the Australian government took about 100,000 mixed-race children and gave them to white families to promote assimilation. **Assimilation** occurs when a minority group gives up its culture and adopts the majority group's culture. A

Today, Aboriginal people call those children the **Stolen Generation** and feel great anger over their loss. Many Aboriginal people are fighting assimilation by passing their culture on to their children. And one reason they are seeking to regain land is to preserve their way of life.

Geographic Thinking

Seeing Patterns

A If a group assimilates, is it more or less likely to seek the return of traditional lands? Explain.

A. Answer It would probably be less likely to do so because it would no longer be living its traditional lifestyle.

Land Claims

In recent decades, the Aboriginal people have made some progress in winning their rights and regaining ownership of some of their land.

HARD-WON VICTORIES The Aboriginal people were not recognized as full citizens of Australia until 1967. In that year, 91 percent of the Australian people voted to allow the federal government to pass special laws about Aboriginal rights.

The **Land Rights Act of 1976** gave Aboriginal people the right to claim land in the Northern Territory. As a result, Aboriginal people gained ownership of the reserves where they were living and some unoccupied land that the government had owned.

THE *MABO* CASE In 1992, the High Court of Australia handed down a decision that had a tremendous effect on land claims. The case involved Eddie Mabo, a Torres Strait Islander. Mabo had been shocked to learn that under Australian law, his family did not own their traditional lands in the Murray Islands. But because the Mabos had worked the land for generations, the High Court upheld Eddie Mabo's claim. By reaching that decision in the ***Mabo* Case,** the Court recognized that Aboriginal people had owned land before the British arrived. So the *Mabo* case overturned the doctrine of *Terra Nullius,* by which Britain originally took the land. B

B. Answer The British believed that Aboriginal people had no relationship with the land; the Mabo decision acknowledges that they had a longstanding relationship with the land.

Geographic Thinking

Making Comparisons

B How does the *Mabo* decision compare with Britain's original view of Aboriginal land ownership?

Aboriginal Land Claims

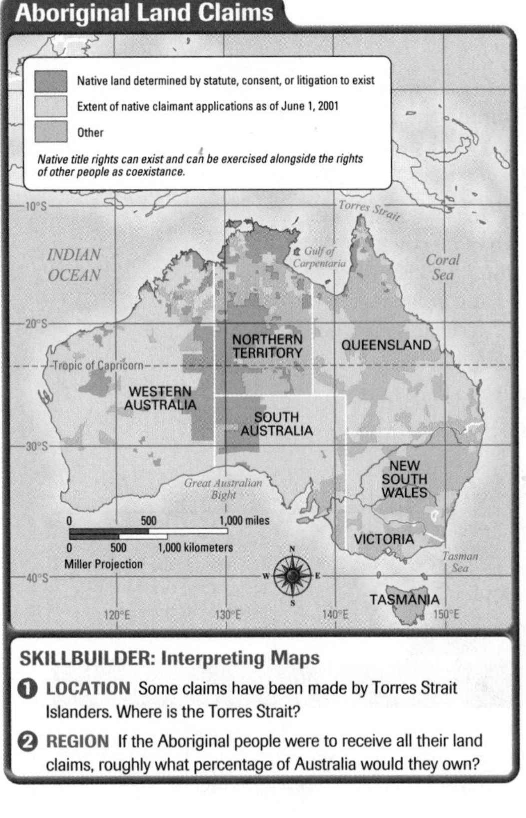

SKILLBUILDER: Interpreting Maps

1. **LOCATION** Some claims have been made by Torres Strait Islanders. Where is the Torres Strait?
2. **REGION** If the Aboriginal people were to receive all their land claims, roughly what percentage of Australia would they own?

ACTIVITY OPTION | SKILLBUILDER LESSON

DRAWING CONCLUSIONS

Explaining the Skill Tell students that drawing conclusions means analyzing what you have read and forming an opinon about its meaning. Tell students that they should use their own common sense and experience to decide what the facts mean.

Applying the Skill Refer students to the text on page 728 about British assimilation and land policies. Allow them a few minutes to think about the underlying assumption in both policies. Ask the following questions:

- How did the policies treat Aboriginal people? *(as though they were not entitled to their own children or lands)*
- How did Aboriginal people react? *(with great anger and efforts to get back their lands)*
- What conclusion can you draw about the prospects for assimilation into British culture? *(Aboriginal people will seek to keep and gain respect for their own cultural identity.)*

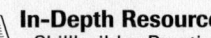

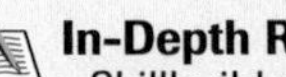
In-Depth Resources: Unit 10
- Skillbuilder Practice, p. 26

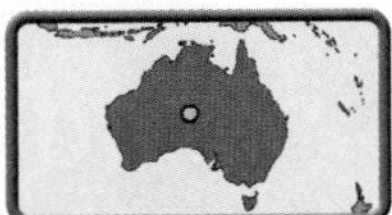

PLACE This giant outcropping, named Ayers Rock by whites, is called Uluru by the Anangu people. They consider it sacred. In 1985, the Anangu regained ownership of Uluru, but they let it be part of a national park. **How does the current arrangement address the needs of all Australians?**

THE *WIK* CASE In 1996, the High Court decided another important case. The Wik people, an Aboriginal group, claimed land that some ranchers and mining companies were using. The case involved two issues that are unique to landholding in Australia.

BACKGROUND
About 42 percent of Australia is subject to pastoral leases.

- The government still owns huge chunks of Australia. Ranchers take out **pastoral leases,** in effect renting the land from the government.
- In earlier cases, Aboriginal people had to prove their traditional relationship to a piece of land in order to claim it.

Aboriginal people could not use land that was taken up by farming or ranching, so it was hard to prove they had a tie to such land. And before 1996, white Australians assumed that pastoral leases wiped out any native land claims. But in the ***Wik* Case,** the court ruled that Aboriginal people could claim land held under a pastoral lease.

As a result, many white Australians feared having to pay Aboriginal people for land use or even losing access to some land altogether. So the national government amended the *Wik* decision to wipe out many Aboriginal land claims. In response, Aboriginal groups threatened lawsuits. No one knows how the issue will be resolved. In Section 2, you will read about industrialization, another issue related to land use.

Interpreting Photographs

Ayers Rock/Uluru

Draw a comparison for students between the events described on page 729 and similar events in the United States. In 1995, the U.S. National Park Service asked rock climbers to avoid Wyoming's Devil's Tower during the month of June. During that month, more than 20 Native American tribes hold sacred ceremonies at the Tower. Ask students what they think about such arrangements. *(Answers will vary, but students should recognize the complexities of property rights.)*

CAPTION ANSWER The Anangu people retain ownership of their sacred place but allow all Australians to visit it.

Assess & Reteach

Have students complete the section on Aboriginal land claims in their cause-and-effect charts.

Formal Assessment
- Section Quiz, p. 497

Reteaching Activity
Have students list major events and court cases in Aboriginal history, supplying a brief statement of the significance of each.

In-Depth Resources: Unit 10
- Reteaching Activity, p. 32

SECTION 1 Assessment

1 Places & Terms
Identify these terms and explain their relationship to the issue of land claims.
- assimilation
- Stolen Generation
- Land Rights Act of 1976
- *Mabo* Case
- pastoral leases
- *Wik* Case

2 Taking Notes
HUMAN-ENVIRONMENT INTERACTION Review the notes you took for this section.

	Causes	Effects
Issue 1: Land Claims		

- Why did the British believe they could take Aboriginal land?
- How did Eddie Mabo prove his family's land ownership?

3 Main Ideas
a. What was the doctrine of *Terra Nullius* and how did it affect land ownership?
b. What were reserves?
c. Why did the national government amend the *Wik* decision?

4 Geographic Thinking
Distinguishing Fact from Opinion When Britain declared Australia to be *Terra Nullius,* was that a fact or an opinion? **Think about:**
- the meaning of that term
- the Aboriginal relationship to land

See Skillbuilder Handbook, page R11.

MAKING COMPARISONS Research the Nunavut territory in Canada. Write a **proposal** for a documentary that would compare the issue of Aboriginal land claims in Australia with Inuit land claims in Canada. In the proposal, indicate the point of view the documentary would express and the type of photographs and film footage it would use.

SE ASIA & OCEANIA

SECTION 1 ASSESSMENT ANSWERS

1. Places & Terms
assimilation, p. 728
Stolen Generation, p. 728
Land Rights Act of 1976, p. 728
Mabo Case, p. 728
pastoral leases, p. 729
Wik Case, p. 729

2. Taking Notes
- Because the Aboriginal people did not farm it, mine it, or build on it, the British thought they had no ties to the land.
- He showed that his family had worked the land for generations

3. Main Ideas
a. It declared the land empty, and the British government took land without making treaties.
b. sections of less productive land set aside for Aboriginal people
c. in order to wipe out many Aboriginal land claims

4. Geographic Thinking
It was an opinion, not based on facts; because the British did not understand the Aboriginal relationship with the land, they formed the opinion that the land was empty.

GeoActivity

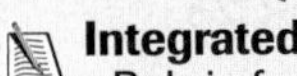

Integrated Assessment
- Rubric for a proposal, 4.11

SECTION 2 OBJECTIVES

1. Identify reasons for Southeast Asian urban growth and examine its impact.
2. Analyze other results of industrialization.

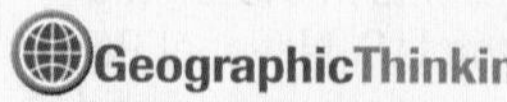

Geographic Thinking

Making Comparisons, p. 732
Drawing Conclusions, p. 732

Focus & Motivate

Ask students what problems urban dwellers in Southeast Asia might share with their counterparts in other regions of the world. *(Students may discuss overcrowding, urban sprawl, traffic jams, or air pollution.)*

Instruct: Objective 1

Moving to Find Jobs

- What "push factors" are causing urban growth in Southeast Asia? *(lost resources in rural areas; scarcity of farm plots big enough to provide a living)*
- What is the biggest "pull factor" in urban growth? *(job opportunities in factories)*

Critical Thinking Transparencies CT64
- Push-Pull Factors in Urbanization

In-Depth Resources: Unit 10
- Guided Reading, p. 22
- Exploring Today's Issues, pp. 30–31

CAPTION ANSWER The women might have more experience with sewing machines than men do, or they might work for lower wages than men.

Industrialization Sparks Change

How does industrialization affect cities?

Main Ideas
- The growth of industry in Southeast Asia has produced positive results such as new jobs and higher wages.
- The growth of industry also produced negative results such as overcrowded cities and pollution.

Places & Terms
industrialization
push-pull factors

A HUMAN PERSPECTIVE Some of the largest employers in Southeast Asia are makers of athletic shoes. They provide much-needed jobs for Southeast Asians, but many observers have accused the companies of abusing workers. For example, in 1995, Lap Nguyen began working at a shoe factory in Vietnam. In February 1996, she was promoted to team leader. A month later, she claimed that a manager who was upset about production hit her. Nguyen told a U.S. reporter about the incident.

In 1998, Nguyen talked to the press again, this time about low wages. Her managers were upset about the interview, and she eventually lost her job. The company said that she was a bad worker, but labor groups believe Nguyen lost her job for talking to reporters. As her story shows, growing industries create jobs but sometimes under harsh conditions.

Moving to Find Jobs

For many people struggling to escape poverty, any job—even one with long hours, low pay, and abusive managers—is better than none. For example, Deth Chrib of Cambodia works in a garment factory 16 hours a day, 7 days a week. She is glad she can support her family without resorting to illegal activities. Although her day is long, Deth Chrib says the job is "pretty easy, compared to working on a farm." Across Southeast Asia, people are moving from farms to cities to find work.

Because of this, **industrialization,** or the growth of industry, and the growth of cities are closely linked. It is impossible to study industrialization without studying urban growth. People move to cities because of **push-pull factors.** Push factors are forces that push people out of their homelands, while pull factors pull them to a new place.

PLACE These Cambodian women work in a factory that makes blue jeans for export to the United States and Europe.
Why do you suppose this industry hires so many women?

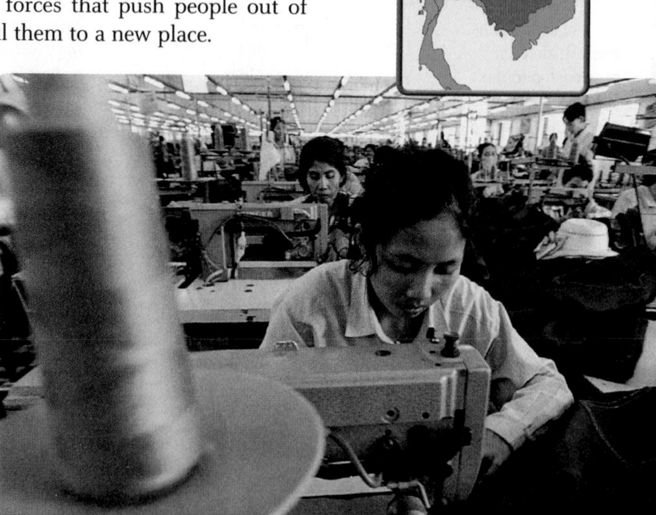

PUSH FACTORS Many forces drive rural people off their land. Push factors in Southeast Asia include the following:

- **Lost Resources** Rural areas are suffering soil erosion, deforestation, and water overuse. For example, Thailand has a water shortage in farming areas because of overpumping. Scarce resources make it hard to earn a living.

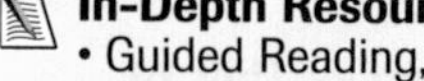

SECTION 2 PROGRAM RESOURCES

In-Depth Resources: Unit 10
- Guided Reading, p. 22
- Exploring Today's Issues, pp. 30–31
- Building Vocabulary, p. 27
- Reteaching Activity, p. 33
- Map and Graph Skills, pp. 24–25

Guided Reading Workbook
- Section 2

Access for Students Acquiring English/ESL
- Guided Reading, p. 172
- Map and Graph Skills, pp. 175–176

Formal Assessment
- Section Quiz, p. 498

Integrated Assessment
- Rubric for a report, 2.5

INTEGRATED TECHNOLOGY

Critical Thinking Transparencies CT64
- Push-Pull Factors in Urbanization

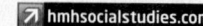

hmhsocialstudies.com

TEST-TAKING RESOURCES

Strategies for Test Preparation

Test Practice Transparencies TT104

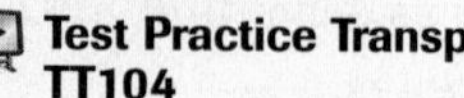

Online Test Practice

MOVEMENT Many rapidly growing Southeast Asian cities are overcrowded. That is one of several factors creating slums, such as this one in Jakarta, Indonesia. **Why would high rates of migration to cities cause overcrowding?**

- **Scarcity of Land** In the Philippines, for example, 3 percent of the country's landowners hold 25 percent of the land. Sixty percent of rural families don't have enough land to earn a living by farming.
- **Population Growth** As populations grow, land shortages become worse. Farmers who do own land often divide it among many heirs. As a result, the plots become too small to support a family.

PULL FACTORS Equally powerful forces attract people to cities. In Southeast Asia, pull factors include the following:

- **Industry** The opportunity to find a factory job is the biggest pull factor. Many people move to the city temporarily to earn money to send to relatives in rural areas. In 1993, workers in the Philippines sent $2.2 billion home, while Thai workers sent $983 million home.
- **Other Benefits** People move to cities seeking other benefits besides jobs, such as education and government services. However, the desire for education is usually related to a desire for jobs.

IMPACT ON CITIES As is true of cities all over the world, the cities of Southeast Asia are having difficulty dealing with such large numbers of immigrants. The availability of housing has not kept pace with the growing city population. As a result, many new arrivals live in slums.

A larger population generates more pollution. Traffic has increased because greater numbers of workers drive to jobs and greater numbers of trucks transport goods. This causes more air pollution; high levels of particulates are the most serious concern. In Bangkok, Thailand, an estimated 5,000 people a year die from breathing polluted air.

Another problem is the disposal of human waste. Most Southeast Asian cities do not have facilities to treat all their sewage. Untreated sewage, in turn, contaminates water supplies.

BACKGROUND
As you learned in Chapter 14, particulates are very small particles of liquids or solids.

Other Results of Industrialization

The growth of industry in Southeast Asia has done more than create rapidly growing cities. It has also affected the economy and the environment.

Interpreting Photographs

Slum in Jakarta, Indonesia

Have students examine the photograph on page 731 and ask if there is any evidence of modern amenities in the photo. *(The electrical lines and antennas suggest that some of the homes in the photo have electricity and televisions.)*

CAPTION ANSWER because the cities cannot build affordable housing fast enough to keep up with their swelling populations

Instruct: Objective 2

Other Results of Industrialization

- What economic benefits has industrial growth brought to Southeast Asia? *(increase in trade and exports, higher incomes for some people)*
- How has industry affected the environment? *(It has polluted the air, water, and soil and used up important resources.)*
- What may happen if Southeast Asians do not preserve their environment? *(Industries may leave for lack of resources and take away job opportunities.)*

DIFFERENTIATING INSTRUCTION: LESS PROFICIENT READERS

CREATING AN ANALYTICAL CHART

Objective To help students develop reading and analytical skills

Class Time 25 minutes

Task Create a chart of factors related to urban and industrial growth

Directions Help students analyze the textual information by creating a chart for this section on the board. Prompt students with questions and list responses under these categories: "push factors," "pull factors," "positive results," and "negative results." Conclude by having students write a paragraph indicating how Southeast Asians might offset the negative results of industrialization.

More About

Jakarta's Water

It is not only factories that are responsible for water pollution in Jakarta. An estimated 90 percent of the city's shallow wells have been polluted by domestic waste. In northern part of the city, nearly half the population has no access to drinking-water services—they must buy their water from traders.

Assess & Reteach

GeoFocus Have students complete the cause-and-effect chart they began at the start of this chapter.

Formal Assessment
- Section Quiz, p. 498

Reteaching Activity
Have students imagine themselves to be newcomers to a Southeast Asian city. Ask them to write a brief letter to a rural friend back home summarizing their reasons for leaving and describing their new way of life.

In-Depth Resources: Unit 10
- Reteaching Activity, p. 33

ECONOMIC EFFECTS Several Southeast Asian countries have had rapid industrial growth since the 1960s. (See Chapter 31.) One result of this has been an increase in trade and exports.

As industry has grown, the region has seen higher incomes for some citizens. In many Southeast Asian countries, the middle class is expanding. But the income gap between rich and poor remains high. This has the potential to cause social unrest because crime rates often rise in societies in which a few people have wealth while high numbers of people live in poverty. You learned about income gaps in Unit 3.

ENVIRONMENTAL EFFECTS Population growth is not the only cause of increased air and water pollution. Industry can also damage the environment. Factories can pollute the air by burning fossil fuels, and the water and soil by carelessly disposing of toxic materials.

The nature of industry in Southeast Asia makes it hard to control such pollution. A single city may contain thousands of factories and shops. Many of these industries are very small, but together they create a great deal of waste. For example, 30,000 factories in Jakarta, Indonesia, discharge pollutants into the waterways. A

Industry has also harmed the environment by using up valuable resources such as water and trees. For instance, textile companies in Bandung, Indonesia, have built illegal wells that deplete water supplies. As a result, some neighborhoods in that city have no water.

In the future, Southeast Asia must reduce the negative effects of industrialization while promoting the positive effects. Cities need to find ways to provide housing and services for all residents. Southeast Asian nations must continue to grow economically, so their citizens will have increased opportunities. The region as a whole must preserve its environment, or industries may abandon the region once its resources are gone. In the Case Study that follows, you will read about environmental changes such as global warming and the hole in the ozone layer.

A. Answer It is harder to monitor many small factories because it requires so many more visits by officials and because very small factories might be able to operate without government knowledge of their existence.

Making Comparisons
A Would it be harder to monitor the pollution created by a few large factories or many small factories? Why?

Section 2 Assessment

1 Places & Terms
Identify these terms and explain their relationship to recent events in Southeast Asia.
- industrialization
- push-pull factors

2 Taking Notes
MOVEMENT Review the notes you took for this section.

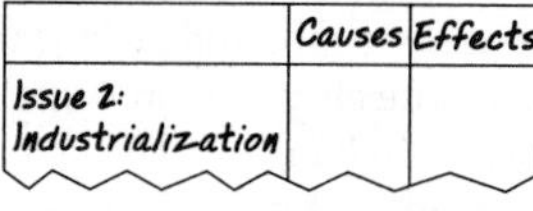

	Causes	Effects
Issue 2: Industrialization		

- Why does industrialization often lead to urbanization?
- What factors push people out of rural areas?

3 Main Ideas
a. What are good and bad aspects of factory work?
b. What are the environmental effects of industrialization?
c. What are the economic effects of industrialization?

4 Geographic Thinking
Drawing Conclusions If industries in Southeast Asia continue to use up the region's resources, how might that affect urban growth? **Think about:**
- the push factors that drive people out of rural areas

hmhsocialstudies.com
RESEARCH WEB LINKS

ASKING GEOGRAPHIC QUESTIONS Study the cartogram of industrial output on page 733. Write three geographic questions about it, such as "What geographic factors enable Thailand to have more industrial output than its neighbors?" Choose one of your questions, do research to find the answer, and write a **report** about what you learn.

SECTION 2 ASSESSMENT ANSWERS

1. Places & Terms
industrialization, p. 730 push-pull factors, p. 730

2. Taking Notes
- because people move to cities looking for jobs
- lost resources, scarcity of land, population growth

3. Main Ideas
a. Factories offer wages for legitimate work that is often easier than farm work; however, the hours are long and management can sometimes be abusive.
b. increased air and water pollution; depletion of resources
c. higher incomes for workers, expanding middle class, possibly growing income gap between rich and poor with increased conflict as a result

4. Geographic Thinking
Since lost resources often drive people from rural areas, an increase in migration to cities might be one result if industries continue to use up the region's resources, especially those in rural areas.

GeoActivity
Integrated Assessment
- Rubric for a report, 2.5

Map and Graph Skills

Interpreting a Cartogram

Even though Southeast Asia has been experiencing industrial growth as a region, not all Southeast Asian nations have prospered equally. A table listing the value of industrial output for the ten countries would give this information in numerical form. A cartogram shows the information visually.

THE LANGUAGE OF MAPS A **cartogram** is a special type of map that conveys a set of data, such as population or GDP. The sizes of the nations on the map are adjusted to reflect the amounts of data each one has. The cartogram below shows the value of industrial output for the nations of Southeast Asia.

Industrial Output of Southeast Asia

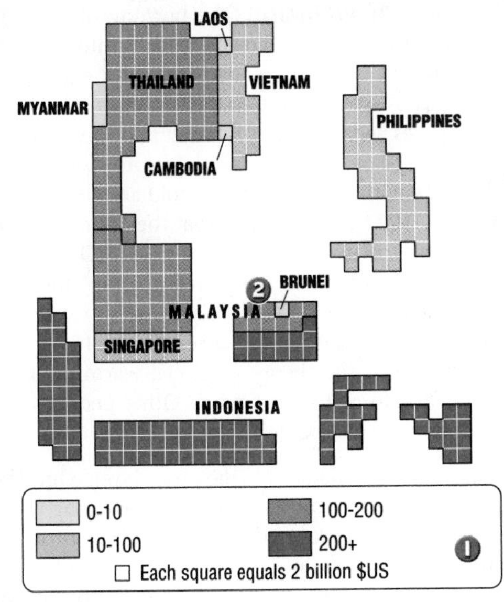

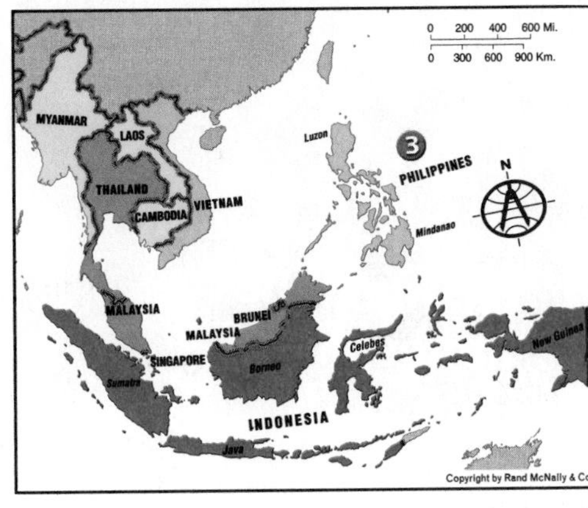

1. The key of this cartogram helps you to intrepret the value of industrial output in two ways. It tells you that each small square equals 2 billion U.S. dollars. It also identifies the colors that the cartogram uses to identify ranges of output.

2. Cartograms adjust the sizes of countries to convey relative quantities. The countries' shapes are altered because a cartogram uses squares or straight lines.

3. Comparing a cartogram to a conventional map can show which countries have more or less of the data under study than you would expect from looking at their size alone.

Map and Graph Skills Assessment

1. **Analyzing Data** According to the cartogram, how much industrial output does Thailand have?

2. **Drawing Conclusions** Which country or countries seem to have a small industrial output compared to their actual size?

3. **Drawing Conclusions** Which country or countries seem to have a large industrial output compared to their actual size?

OBJECTIVE

Understand and interpret cartograms.

Instruct: Objective

Interpreting a Cartogram

- What is a cartogram? *(A special map that represents regions, such as nations, as smaller or larger according to some measurement other than landmass—for example, population or GDP.)*
- How do cartograms represent quantity? *(Each region is represented by a cluster of squares, with each square representing a specific unit of the data being measured.)*
- Why might cartograms be a useful ancillary to conventional maps? *(because they enable you to see which regions have more or less of the data under study than you would expect from looking at their physical size alone)*

In-Depth Resources: Unit 10
- Map and Graph Skills, pp. 24–25

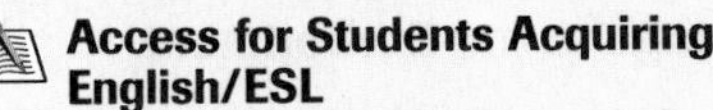

Access for Students Acquiring English/ESL
- Map and Graph Skills, pp. 175–176

Interpreting Maps

Industrial Output of Southeast Asia

Have students examine the map on page 733 and ask them to determine the industrial output of Sumatra and Borneo. *(Sumatra's output is approximately $56 billion. Borneo's output is about $26 billion.)*

SKILLS ASSESSMENT ANSWERS

1. $152 billion, or the range of $100 to 200 billion **2.** Myanmar, Laos, Cambodia **3.** Singapore

CASE STUDY OBJECTIVES

1. Identify issues of global environmental damage.
2. Identify future effects of environmental change and examine international efforts to take action.
3. Complete the Case Study Project by creating a political cartoon expressing your opinion about global environmental change.
4. Analyze primary sources for different views and data about environmental change.

SKILLBUILDER: Interpreting Maps, p. 735

Focus & Motivate

Ask students why it might be difficult to stop environmental damage. *(lack of cooperation among nations, differing opinions about the need to act and what to do)*

Instruct: Objective 1

Damage to the Environment

- What changes concern scientists? *(global warming, hole in the ozone layer)*
- Why are carbon dioxide emissions from burning fossil fuels an issue? *(carbon dioxide is a greenhouse gas that traps the sun's heat; emissions have doubled in recent decades)*
- Why are chemicals like CFCs harmful to use? *(they destroy the ozone layer that blocks ultraviolet rays from the sun)*

 **In-Depth Resources: Unit 10**
• Guided Reading, p. 23

CASESTUDY

GLOBAL ENVIRONMENTAL CHANGE

How have people changed the atmosphere?

Some people fear that global warming might cause an increase in violent weather.

As you have read in other units, many human activities harm the environment. Among these are the burning of fossil fuels and the use of chemicals such as chlorofluorocarbons (CFCs) in aerosol cans. Many scientists fear these activities are changing the environment in ways that affect the whole world.

Damage to the Environment

Scientists believe that the use of fossil fuels has begun to heat the climate, and the use of chemicals has damaged the ozone layer.

GLOBAL WARMING The burning of fossil fuels releases carbon dioxide (CO_2) into the atmosphere. Carbon dioxide is one of the greenhouse gases—gases that trap the sun's heat. Greenhouse gases serve the useful function of preventing the escape of all the sun's energy into space. Without them, the earth would be cold and lifeless.

Most scientists fear that the atmosphere now has too many greenhouse gases. CO_2 emissions have increased 50 percent since the 1970s. Scientists believe that the increase in CO_2 levels causes the atmosphere to trap too much heat, so temperatures have been gradually rising.

Some people disagree with the theory of global warming and say the temperature rise is due to natural processes. Other people say that temperatures fall within a normal range.

OZONE HOLE Another change is damage to the ozone layer, which exists high in the atmosphere. It absorbs most of the sun's damaging ultraviolet rays. In the 1970s, scientists discovered a thinning of the ozone layer over Antarctica, often called a hole in the ozone layer. Chemicals such as the chlorine found in CFCs react with ozone and destroy it. Many governments have restricted the use of such chemicals, but others have delayed passing such laws because they are costly for industry.

Looking Toward the Future

Scientists fear that many problems may result from these changes to the environment. Because of that, many people and nations around the world are trying to halt the damage before it is too late.

LONG-TERM EFFECTS One fear about global warming is that even small temperature increases could melt the world's ice caps. This would cause a rise in sea levels that might swamp coastal cities and islands. For example, the low islands of Oceania might disappear.

CASE STUDY PROGRAM RESOURCES

 **In-Depth Resources: Unit 10**
• Guided Reading, p. 23
• GeoWorkshop, pp. 35–36
• Building Vocabulary, p. 27
• Reteaching Activity, p. 34

 **Guided Reading Workbook**
• Case Study

 **Access for Students Acquiring English/ESL**
• Guided Reading, p. 173

Formal Assessment
• Case Study Quiz, p. 499

INTEGRATED TECHNOLOGY

 **Power Presentations**

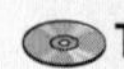 **Test Generator**
• Case Study Quiz

TEST-TAKING RESOURCES

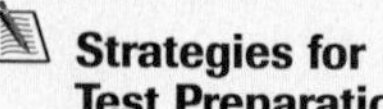
Strategies for Test Preparation

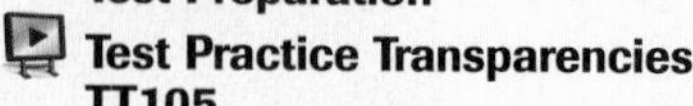
Test Practice Transparencies TT105

 **Online Test Practice**

Some people predict that global warming might change patterns of evaporation and precipitation. This could make violent storms such as typhoons and droughts more common. The location of climate zones and agricultural regions might shift, upsetting the world's economy.

SEE PRIMARY SOURCE D

People worry about the ozone layer hole because more ultraviolet rays will reach earth. Ultraviolet rays are linked to such problems as skin cancer, eye damage, and crop damage. Because it lies close to Antarctica, New Zealand may be at higher risk than other regions.

TAKING ACTION In 1992, the UN held the Earth Summit, a conference to discuss ways to pursue economic development while protecting the environment. Representatives of 178 nations attended.

SEE PRIMARY SOURCE A

In 1997, the UN held a convention in Kyoto, Japan, to discuss climate change. The conference wrote the Kyoto Protocol, guidelines for developed countries to reduce greenhouse gas emissions. In time, 165 nations signed the treaty. The United States signed the treaty, but the Senate didn't ratify it—fearing that the guidelines might harm U.S. businesses.

On the next two pages are primary sources expressing different views about environmental problems. Use them to form your own opinion.

Predicted Impact of Global Warming

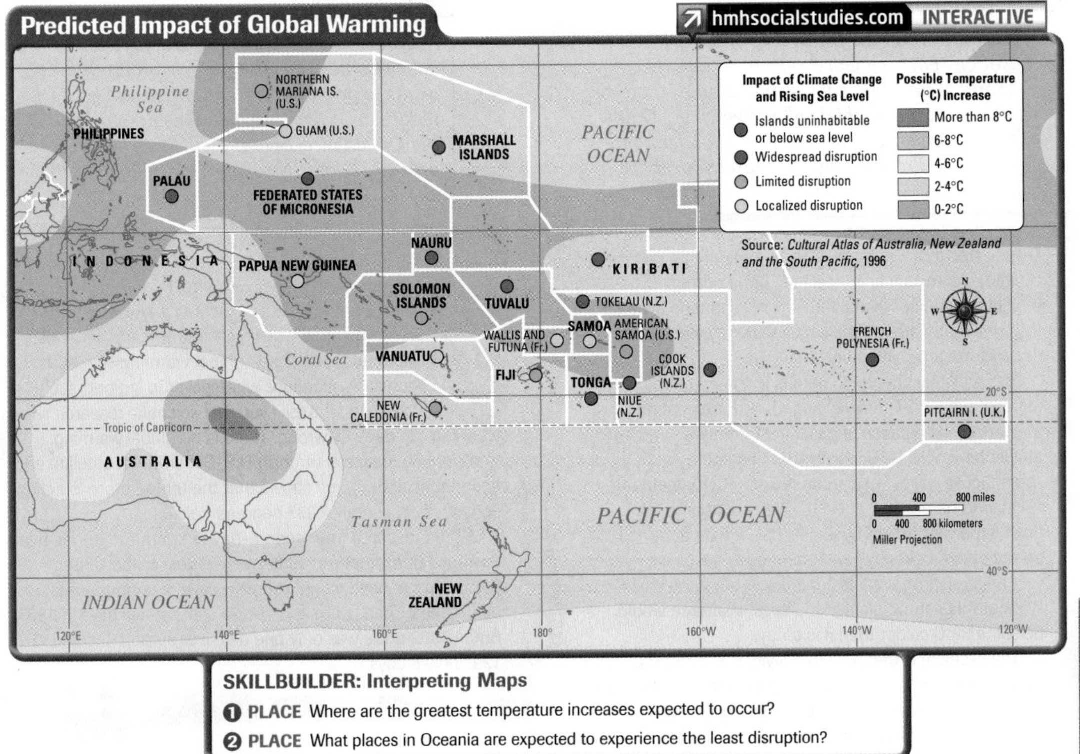

SKILLBUILDER: Interpreting Maps

1. **PLACE** Where are the greatest temperature increases expected to occur?
2. **PLACE** What places in Oceania are expected to experience the least disruption?

Instruct: Objective 2

Looking Toward the Future

- How might global warming affect coastal cities and islands? *(Global warming will melt ice caps and raise sea levels, potentially swamping coastal cities and islands.)*
- How might economies be affected by environmental change? *(Climate zones and agricultural regions might shift; ultraviolet rays might damage crops.)*
- What is the Kyoto Protocol? *(UN guidelines calling for the reduction of greenhouse emissions by developed nations.)*

In-Depth Resources: Unit 10
- GeoWorkshop, pp. 35–36

SE ASIA & OCEANIA

Interpreting Maps

Predicted Impact of Global Warming

Besides the independent nations shown here, which nations might be most interested in keeping global warming from getting worse? *(France, the United Kingdom, and the United States—because they would not want to lose overseas territories.)*

SKILLBUILDER ANSWERS

1. Australia **2.** Guam, Papua New Guinea, Vanuatu, Wallis and Futuna, Samoa

DIFFERENTIATING INSTRUCTION | STUDENTS ACQUIRING ENGLISH/ESL

DISCUSSING ENVIRONMENTAL ISSUES

Objective To develop proficiency in understanding and speaking about concepts of environmental science

Class Time 30 minutes

Task Prepare for and hold a panel discussion about issues of global environmental change

Directions Divide students into small groups so that each includes a mixture of proficient speakers of English and students learning the language. Have groups discuss the issues presented on pages 734–735. Allow time for a member from each group to participate in a panel discussion informing the class about causes of environmental damage and the reasons to take action.

Instruct: Objective 3

Case Study Project: Political Cartoon

- What is your research goal for the project? *(to form an opinion about global environmental change)*
- What questions should you consider in the process? *(theories about global environmental change; reasons people are concerned; what, if anything, should be done)*
- What should you produce for the project? *(a political cartoon that expresses your opinion about global environmental change)*

Instruct: Objective 

Using Primary Sources

- Ⓐ **Educational Pamphlet** Why was this pamphlet written? *(to help people understand the Kyoto Protocol and reasons for it)*
- What environmental problem does the pamphlet describe? *(global warming)*
- What major cause is cited for changes in the global climate? *(human activity)*
- Ⓑ **Political Commentary** What is this group's opinion of global warming? *(that there is no global warming)*
- What evidence is cited for this opinion? *(U.S. government balloon and satellite data that shows a very slight cooling; a decrease in numbers of consecutive days over 90 degrees based on figures for 1992 compared to 1936 and 1955)*

CASE STUDY

PROJECT Political Cartoon

21ST CENTURY

Primary sources A to E on these two pages present differing opinions on global environmental change. Use these sources and your own research to create a political cartoon expressing your opinion. You might use the Internet and the library for research.

hmhsocialstudies.com RESEARCH WEB LINKS

Suggested Steps

1. Use the sources here and your own research to decide if you believe that global warming and the ozone hole are problems.
2. Draw a pencil sketch of a cartoon expressing your opinion about global environmental change. As you decide what to draw, consider the following questions.
   - Do you think that the theories about environmental change are wrong? If so, why are people so concerned about the issue?
   - Do you think environmental change poses a threat to the world's climate? If so, what should be done?
3. Show the sketch to a friend to see if you have conveyed your point. Use your friend's feedback to make your cartoon more effective.
4. Create your final cartoon. You may wish to draw it lightly in pencil and then ink over the pencil marks. Post the cartoon in class.

Materials and Supplies

- Samples of political cartoons
- Drawing paper
- Pencils and erasers
- Felt-tip markers
- Computer
- Internet access

PRIMARY SOURCE A

Educational Pamphlet *In 1994, the United Nations Environment Programme and the World Meteorological Organization published a pamphlet called* Beginners Guide to the Convention *to help people understand the Kyoto Protocol and the reasons for it.*

Human beings seem to be changing the global climate. The results are uncertain, but if current predictions prove correct, the climatic changes over the coming century will be larger than any since the dawn of human civilization.

The principal change to date is in the earth's atmosphere. . . . We have changed, and are continuing to change, the balance of gases that form the atmosphere. This is especially true of such key "greenhouse gases" as carbon dioxide (CO_2), methane (CH_4), and nitrous oxide (N_2O). (Water vapour is the most important greenhouse gas, but human activities do not affect it directly.) . . . Greenhouse gases are vital because they act like a blanket around the earth. Without this natural blanket the earth's surface would be some 30°C colder than it is today.

The problem is that human activity is making the blanket "thicker." . . . The most direct result, says the scientific consensus, is likely to be a "global warming" of 1.5 to 4.5°C over the next 100 years.

PRIMARY SOURCE B

Political Commentary *The American Policy Center is a conservative group that wants to promote free enterprise and reduce government regulations. It opposed the Kyoto Protocol and published the article "There is No Global Warming."*

There is no global warming. Period.

You can't find a real scientist anywhere in the world who can look you in the eye and, without hesitation, . . . say "yes, global warming is with us."

There is no evidence whatsoever to support such claims. Anyone who tells you that scientific research shows warming trends . . . is wrong. There is no global warming.

Scientific research through U.S. Government satellite and balloon measurements shows that the temperature is actually cooling—very slightly—.037 degrees Celsius.

A little research into modern-day temperature trends bears this out. For example, in 1936 the Midwest of the United States experienced 49 consecutive days of temperatures over 90 degrees. There were another 49 consecutive days in 1955. But in 1992 there was only one day over 90 degrees and in 1997 only 5 days.

ACTIVITY OPTION CRITICAL THINKING

ANALYZING DATA

Explaining the Skill Tell students that additional information may be helpful in gaining a perspective on data. They may wish to recall information in related sources. For example, primary source D provides no explanation for showing October satellite images.

Applying the Skill After students have examined primary sources D and E and answered the relevant Objective questions, ask the following:

- What month is shown for the satellite images of ozone over Antarctica? *(October)*
- When was the news article published? *(October 10, 2000)*
- What information does the article contain that can help to explain the month chosen for the satellite data? *(the hole opens in the ozone layer each Southern Hemisphere spring, which occurs in October)*

PRIMARY SOURCE C

Data *The National Climatic Data Center collects data on temperature and precipitation. In the graph below, the line at zero represents the average annual world temperature for the period 1880 to 2000. The bars show how much the average temperatures for individual years were higher or lower than the average. Scientists use this graph to spot climate trends.*

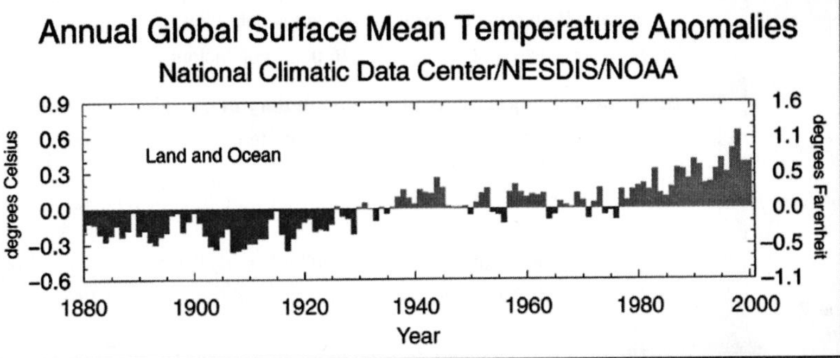

PRIMARY SOURCE D

News Article *On October 10, 2000, the* New York Times *published the article "Record Ozone Hole Refuels Debate on Climate" by Andrew C. Revkin. The article appeared in the science section of the paper.*

The hole that opens in the ozone layer over Antarctica each southern spring formed earlier and grew bigger this year than at any time since satellites have been monitoring the polar atmosphere, scientists have reported.

The finding renewed suspicions among atmospheric scientists that global warming could be indirectly abetting the chemical reactions that destroy ozone, but many still say the growth of the hole could also be the result of natural . . . variations in Antarctic weather and other conditions. . . .

The hole is closely watched because the stratosphere's . . . layer of ozone . . . absorbs ultraviolet rays, which could contribute to skin cancers and cataracts and threaten agriculture and ecosystems if they reached the surface.

PRIMARY SOURCE E

Satellite Images *Satellites took these images of ozone over Antarctica. The color blue represents areas with an extremely low concentration of ozone, while red shows a high concentration.*

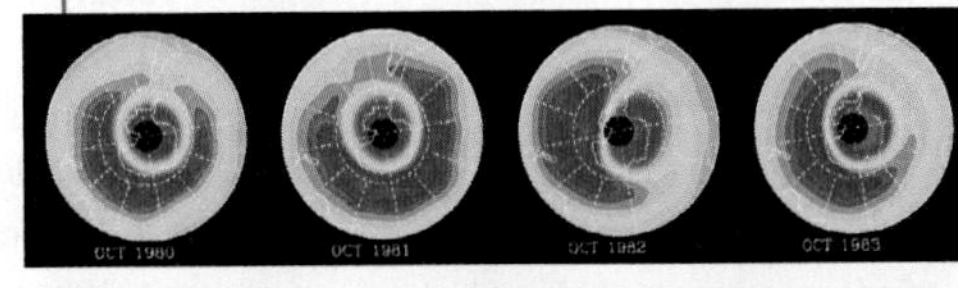
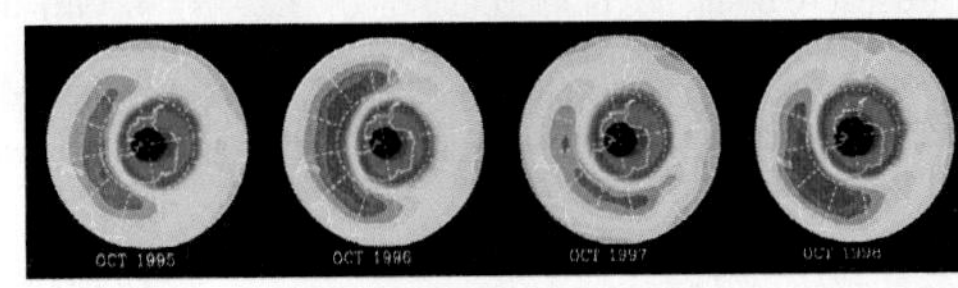

PROJECT CheckList

Have I . . .

- ✓ researched opinions on global environmental change?
- ✓ formed my own opinion based on evidence about the issue?
- ✓ created an interesting cartoon that clearly expresses that opinion?
- ✓ created a cartoon that is neat enough to print in a newspaper?

Instruct: Objective 

Using Primary Sources

- Ⓒ**Data** What is the purpose of this graph? *(to spot climate trends)*
- What can you conclude from this graph? *(temperatures have been on the rise since about 1940, dramatically since 1980)*
- Ⓓ**News Article** What event does the article publicize? *(a record ozone hole in October 2000)*
- What does the article indicate about global warming? *(that it might indirectly abet chemical reactions that destroy ozone)*
- Ⓔ**Satellite Images** What do areas of red represent? *(high concentrations of ozone)*
- What do areas of blue represent? *(areas of very low concentrations of ozone)*

Assess & Reteach

GeoFocus Have students complete the cause-and-effect chart they began at the beginning of this chapter.

Formal Assessment
- Case Study Quiz, p. 499

Reteaching Activity
Have students write a brief paragraph comparing the sources, indicating which seem most compelling and why.

In-Depth Resources: Unit 10
- Reteaching Activity, p. 34

RUBRIC CASE STUDY PROJECT

POLITICAL CARTOON

For the Case Study Project, students should:

- Develop an opinion about global environmental change, based on research
- Make a pencil sketch of a cartoon to convey the opinion, and seek feedback from a friend
- Finalize the drawing of a clear, provocative cartoon
- Create and add a caption that clearly supports the visual and post the cartoon in class

Grading Rubric Evaluate student performance as Exceptional, Acceptable, or Poor in each of the following categories.

	Exceptional	Acceptable	Poor
Drawing uses easily recognizable figures or situations			
Presents a clearly stated point of view			
Caption uses correct grammar, spelling, and punctuation			

Reviewing Places & Terms

A. **1.** assimilation, p. 728
2. Stolen Generation, p. 728
3. Land Rights Act of 1976, p. 728
4. *Mabo* Case, p. 728
5. pastoral leases, p. 729
6. *Wik* Case, p. 729
7. industrialization, p. 730
8. push-pull factors, p. 730

B. Possible Responses

9. The Stolen Generation were mixed-race children who were taken from their parents and given to white families to promote assimilation.
10. The Australian government owned the lands that were held by pastoral leases.
11. Industrialization is a pull factor that may lead to urban growth.
12. The Land Rights Act of 1976 applied to the Northern Territory.
13. The main decision in the *Mabo* Case was that Aboriginal people had owned land before the British came, thus overturning the doctrine of Terra Nullius.
14. The main decision in the *Wik* Case was that Aboriginal people could claim land held under a pastoral lease.
15. The arrival of Europeans who wanted the best lands for themselves was a push factor driving Aboriginal people from their homelands.

Chapter 32 Assessment

VISUAL SUMMARY
TODAY'S ISSUES IN SOUTHEAST ASIA, OCEANIA, AND ANTARCTICA

Government

Aboriginal Land Claims
- When the British first arrived in Australia, British authorities declared the continent to be empty. They decided they had the right to take the land without making treaties.
- Aboriginal people lost much of their land and had to live on reserves.
- Recent court cases have provided the grounds for Aboriginal people to make land claims. However, the Australian government took steps to limit those land claims.

Economics

Industrialization Sparks Change
- The growth of industry often leads to rapid urban growth. People move to cities because of push-pull factors.
- Industrialization creates higher incomes for many, but in Southeast Asia the income gap remains high. This has the potential to cause social unrest.
- Because of the use of fossil fuels and careless waste disposal, industrialization often causes pollution.

Environment

Global Environmental Change
- Many scientists believe that increases in carbon dioxide emission have caused global temperatures to rise; it is feared that global warming might lead to flooding and an increase in droughts and violent weather.
- The use of chemicals such as CFCs has been linked to a thinning of the protective ozone layer. The hole in the ozone layer may let more ultraviolet rays reach the earth and cause cancer, eye damage, and crop damage.

Reviewing Places & Terms

A. Briefly explain the importance of each of the following.

1. assimilation
2. Stolen Generation
3. Land Rights Act of 1976
4. *Mabo* Case
5. pastoral leases
6. *Wik* Case
7. industrialization
8. push-pull factors

B. Answer the questions about vocabulary in complete sentences.

9. What is the relationship between the terms *assimilation* and *Stolen Generation*?
10. Who owned the Australian lands that were held by pastoral leases?
11. Which of the above terms is a pull factor leading to urban growth?
12. To which Australian territory did the Land Rights Act of 1976 apply?
13. What was the main decision in the *Mabo* Case?
14. What was the main decision in the *Wik* Case?
15. How would you apply the term *push factors* to the experience of the Aboriginal people in Australia?

Main Ideas

Aboriginal Land Claims (pp. 727–729)

1. What does the Aboriginal Tent Embassy symbolize?
2. When the Aboriginal people fought European settlement, what enabled the Europeans to win?
3. How did Eddie Mabo prove his family's land ownership?
4. Why did white Australians fear the *Wik* decision?

Industrialization Sparks Change (pp. 730–733)

5. Why do many people in Southeast Asia move temporarily to cities?
6. How has industrialization affected cities?
7. What effect has industrial growth had on trade and exports?

Global Environmental Change (pp. 734–737)

8. What are greenhouse gases?
9. What are the arguments against the theory of global warming?
10. What health problems may increase because of the hole in the ozone layer?

Main Ideas

1. that Aboriginal people are treated as foreigners in their own country and that they have no permanent title to land
2. superior weapons
3. by showing that his family had worked the land for generations
4. They feared having to pay compensation for land use or losing access to some lands altogether.
5. to get jobs so they could earn money to send back home
6. It has sparked rapid growth, leading to problems such as slums, increased traffic, and more pollution.
7. They have increased.
8. gases, such as carbon dioxide, that trap the sun's heat
9. that the temperature increases might be due to natural processes or that higher temperatures still fall within the normal range
10. skin cancer and eye damage

Critical Thinking

1. Using Your Notes
Use your completed chart to answer these questions.

	Causes	Effects
Issue 1: Land Claims		
Issue 2: Industrialization		

a. What caused the hole in the ozone layer?
b. In what way are some of these issues linked? Explain.

2. Geographic Themes
a. **HUMAN-ENVIRONMENT INTERACTION** How has industrialization affected Southeast Asia's water supplies?
b. **MOVEMENT** What impact might global warming have upon the movement of people?

3. Identifying Themes
Consider what you have learned about Aboriginal land claims, industrialization, and global environmental change. Which of the five geographic themes relate to all three issues? Explain.

4. Determining Cause and Effect
How did the Australian government's policy of taking mixed-race children from their families affect the desire of the Aboriginal people to reclaim lands? Explain.

5. Drawing Conclusions
Overall, do you think industrialization is a positive or negative development for Southeast Asia? Explain.

For Additional Test Practice

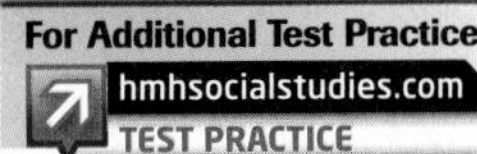

Geographic Skills: Interpreting Graphs

Annual Industrial Production Growth Rate
Use the graph to answer the following questions.

1. **PLACE** For which country were statistics for the year 2000 not available?
2. **PLACE** How would you describe the pattern of industrial growth in Thailand?
3. **REGION** In which year did Southeast Asia as a whole experience economic problems? How can you tell?

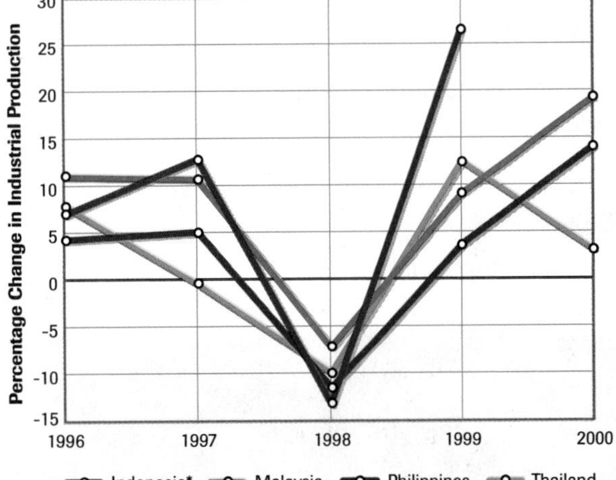

*2000 data for Indonesia were unavailable.
SOURCE: Asia Recovery Information Center online, 2001

Research the industrial production growth rate for another Southeast Asian country. Copy this graph on your own paper and add the information for the country you researched.

hmhsocialstudies.com
MULTIMEDIA ACTIVITY

Use the links at **hmhsocialstudies.com** to do research about global warming. Look for additional evidence that either supports or refutes the theory.

Creating a Database Compile statistics that either support or refute the theory of global warming. Present these statistics in tables, charts, or graphs.

SE ASIA & OCEANIA

CHAPTER 32 ASSESSMENT

Critical Thinking

1. a. the use of chemicals such as CFCs
b. Industrial uses of fossil fuels and chemicals may contribute to global warming.
2. a. Factories are depleting them; human and industrial wastes are polluting them.
b. Global warming might lead to shifts in farming regions and the submersion of some areas, causing extensive migrations.
3. Human-environment interaction is related to all three issues: The British and the Aboriginal people interacted differently with their environments, causing misunderstandings. Industrialization sometimes leads to resource depletion and pollution. Global environmental change is the result of human actions.
4. The policy increased that desire because they wanted a place where they could preserve their way of life and pass it down to future generations.
5. Positive—because it created jobs and economic opportunity; negative—because of the problems caused by rapid urban growth and because of pollution

GeoActivity

Integrated Assessment
- Rubric for a graph, 2.3

Formal Assessment
- Chapter Test, Forms A, B, and C, pp. 500–511

Geographic Skills

1. Indonesia
2. It has been up and down; it is inconsistent.
3. 1998; all four countries experienced negative growth rates.

MULTIMEDIA ACTIVITY

For their project on global warming, students should:
- Present information in a well-organized and concise manner.
- Produce clear, imaginative graphics.
- Include references to Web sites used as sources.

Grading Rubric Evaluate student performance as Exceptional, Acceptable, or Poor in each of the following categories:

	Exceptional	Acceptable	Poor
Presents information accurately			
Charts and tables present information in a manner that will aid the viewer in understanding the information			
Uses bar, line, or pie graph styles			
Presents information neatly			

World Geography

Reference Section

SKILLBUILDER HANDBOOK

Skills for reading, thinking, and researching **R1**

GLOSSARY AND SPANISH GLOSSARY

Important terms and definitions **R16**
Important terms and definitions translated into Spanish **R26**

INDEX

Index of all topics in textbook **R36**

Contents

CRITICAL THINKING AND GEOGRAPHY SKILLS

1.1 Analyzing Data R2
1.2 Making Comparisons R3
1.3 Making Inferences R4
1.4 Drawing Conclusions R5
1.5 Making Generalizations R6
1.6 Making Decisions R7
1.7 Seeing Patterns R8
1.8 Determining Cause and Effect R9
1.9 Identifying and Solving Problems R10
1.10 Distinguishing Fact from Opinion R11
1.11 Creating a Sketch Map R12
1.12 Creating Graphs and Charts R13

USING TECHNOLOGY SOURCES

2.1 Creating a Multimedia Presentation R14
2.2 Creating and Using a Database R15

R1

1.1 Analyzing Data

Defining the Skill

Analyzing data means studying quantitative information—numbers, proportions, and similar statistics. Data are often presented graphically, in graphs, charts, and maps. When you analyze data, you find patterns, make generalizations and comparisons, and locate facts.

Applying the Skill

The following line graph is titled "World Population Growth." Use the listed strategies to analyze the data presented.

How to Analyze Data

Strategy 1 Rephrase the title given for the graphic as a question that can lead you to its main idea. For example: "How has world population growth changed over time?"

Strategy 2 To understand how data are displayed, choose one point on the graph. Identify what piece of data is shown at that point. For example, in the line graph, the point on the line that is right above the horizontal number 1000 represents how many billions of people lived in the world in the year 1000—just under one-half billion.

Strategy 3 Make a comparison between two points or other parts on the graph. For example, compare the rate of world population growth between 1000 and 1500 with the rate over the following 500 years. You can see that the population barely grew at all between 1000 and 1500, but increased significantly between 1500 and 2000.

Strategy 4 Answer the question you posed in Strategy 1 in order to summarize data and note a general pattern.

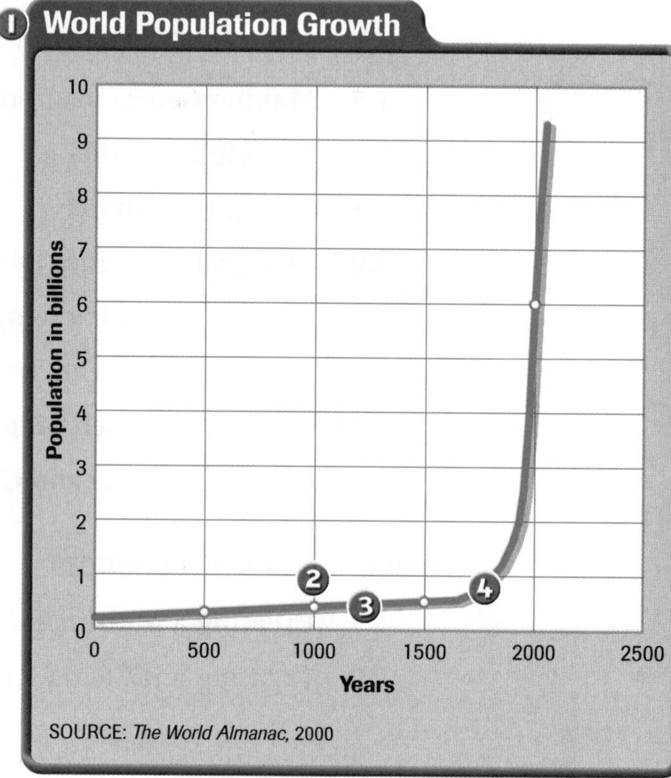

SOURCE: *The World Almanac*, 2000

Write a Summary

Summarize the most important idea in your analysis of the data shown. This summary statement might, for example, answer the question suggested by the graph title.

4 *The world's population did not even reach the 1-billion mark until the 1800s, but skyrocketed after that and is on its way to 10 billion.*

Practicing the Skill

Turn to Chapter 31, Section 1, "Southeast Asia." Find the feature on page 707 titled "Industrialization." Analyze the data in the bar graph shown. Write a summary of your analysis.

1.2 Making Comparisons

Defining the Skill

Making comparisons means thinking about similarities and differences. Two or more concepts are grouped together because of shared features, but they are distinguished from one another by other features.

Applying the Skill

The following passage tells about economic development. Use the listed strategies to compare two categories of nations.

How to Make Comparisons

Strategy 1 Note the concepts being compared. In this passage, categories of economic development are described.

Strategy 2 Look for words that signal similarities such as *both, same, similar,* and *like.* Look for words that signal differences or contrasts such as *different, in contrast, however,* and *on the other hand.*

Strategy 3 Sum up what you have learned by telling yourself (a) what concepts are being compared; (b) why they are grouped together; and (c) what their main differences are.

LEVELS OF ECONOMIC DEVELOPMENT

1 Countries of the world have two different levels of economic development. Developing nations have a low GDP per capita. (GDP is Gross Domestic Product, the value of goods and services produced within a country over a year or other period of time.) Developing nations also have limited development on all levels of economic activities. These countries lack an industrial base and struggle to provide for their citizens' basic needs. Many young countries and former colonies are found in this category.

Developed nations, 2 on the other hand, are countries with a high per capita income and varied economy. Western European nations, Canada, and the United States are highly developed economies.

Make a Chart

One way to sum up the main points of comparison is with a chart that lists features. The chart below is based on the example passage.

3

	Developing nations	*Developed nations*
GDP per capita	*low*	*high*
Variety of economic activities	*limited development; lack of industrial base*	*varied economy*
Examples	*young countries, former colonies*	*Western European nations, Canada, U.S.*

Practicing the Skill

Turn to Chapter 5, Section 3, "Human-Environment Interaction." Read "Building Cities" on page 128. Identify the main similarities and differences described, and show them in a chart.

1.3 Making Inferences

Defining the Skill

Making inferences involves using information that is directly stated in the text in order to think of, or infer, ideas that are not directly stated. You use logic and your own experience and knowledge to make inferences.

Applying the Skill

The passage below tells about a feature of the climate of South Asia. Use the listed strategies to make inferences about monsoons.

How to Make Inferences

Strategy 1 Find statements of fact and other stated ideas, such as opinions and generalizations.

Strategy 2 Ask yourself questions about the stated facts and ideas. Think of likely answers that are not directly stated. For example, the passage states that dry winds blow between October and May, and moist winds blow between June and September. Ask, "What else can I understand from that information?"

Strategy 3 Make inferences from the facts and ideas. For example, you might infer that the region has two main seasons—a long dry one and a shorter wet one.

MONSOONS

1 Although climate varies throughout South Asia, the region as a whole is greatly affected by monsoons, or seasonal winds. 2 Between October and May, dry winds blow across South Asia from the northeast. 2 Between June and September, the winds reverse and blow in from the southwest, bringing moist air from the ocean. 1 Heavy rains fall, especially in the southern and eastern portions of South Asia.

1 Rainfall is crucial to life on the subcontinent. Yet the monsoons can cause severe hardship for millions of South Asians, especially those living in the lowlands of India and Bangladesh. The monsoons are also highly unpredictable. Some areas may get too little rain, while others get too much. The monsoons are an essential but difficult feature of life in South Asia.

Make a Chart

A chart can show the inferences made from stated facts and ideas. The chart below is based on the passage you just read.

1 *Stated Facts and Ideas*	2 *Questions*	3 *Inferences*
The direction of the winds shifts seasonally, from the northeast to the southwest.	*What causes the wind patterns to change?*	*Wind patterns change as Earth changes its position relative to the sun.*
Heavy rains follow from winds coming from the ocean.	*How do ocean winds carry water?*	*Water evaporates from the ocean, is carried by the air, and condenses over land.*
The monsoons can cause severe hardship, especially in the lowlands.	*What problems do the monsoons cause in the lowlands?*	*Damaging floods can result from monsoon rains.*

Practicing the Skill

Turn to Chapter 25, Section 2, "India's Neighbors: Pakistan and Bangladesh." Read the subsection "New Countries, Ancient Lands," on pages 573–574. Use the facts and ideas to infer other ideas. Show your inferences in a chart.

1.4 Drawing Conclusions

Defining the Skill

Drawing conclusions means combining factual information with your own reasoning to formulate a statement that is likely to be true. To draw conclusions, look at the facts and think about what they mean.

Applying the Skill

The following passage offers facts about two of the world's largest lakes. Use the listed strategies to draw conclusions about the information.

How to Draw Conclusions

Strategy 1 Read carefully to identify and understand the statements of fact, the items of information that can be proved true.

Strategy 2 Think about which facts fit together and how they fit. List the facts in a diagram and use your own experiences to understand how the facts relate to each other.

Strategy 3 Come up with a statement, different from one given in the text, that draws a conclusion about the factual information.

TWO LARGE LAKES OF CENTRAL ASIA

1 The Caspian Sea, which is actually a saltwater lake, stretches for nearly 750 miles from north to south, making it the largest inland sea in the world. 1 Recently, the Caspian's water levels have been rising, and have flooded many surrounding villages and towns. 1 The sea now stands over two yards higher than it did in 1978. Nobody is certain what is causing the change. But scientists say possible causes might include climate change or more water flowing off deforested land.

1 The Aral Sea, another of the world's largest lakes, lies east of the Caspian. 1 Unlike the Caspian, the Aral Sea is shrinking. 1 Extensive irrigation projects have diverted water away from the lake. 1 Since 1960, the Aral has lost about 80 percent of its water volume.

Make a Diagram

A diagram can highlight the facts that fit together to point to a conclusion. The diagram below shows a conclusion that can be drawn from the passage above.

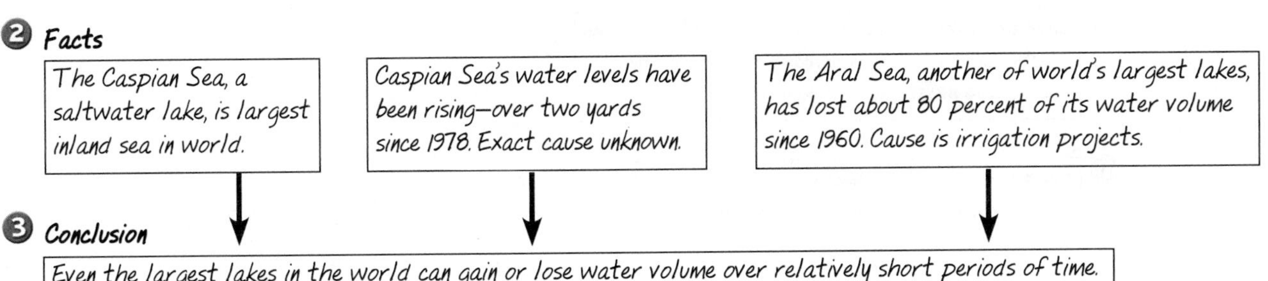

2 Facts
The Caspian Sea, a saltwater lake, is largest inland sea in world.
Caspian Sea's water levels have been rising—over two yards since 1978. Exact cause unknown.
The Aral Sea, another of world's largest lakes, has lost about 80 percent of its water volume since 1960. Cause is irrigation projects.
3 Conclusion
Even the largest lakes in the world can gain or lose water volume over relatively short periods of time.

Practicing the Skill

Turn to Chapter 10, Section 1. Read the subsection "Native Americans and the Spanish Conquest" on page 216. Make a diagram to show selected facts and the conclusion you drew from them.

1.5 Making Generalizations

Defining the Skill

Making a generalization means making a broad statement that applies to a number of examples. Generalizations can be made from examples given in one passage, in several sources, or from graphic aids.

Applying the Skill

The following two passages present examples on the same topic. Use the listed strategies to make a generalization based on the examples.

How to Make Generalizations

Strategy 1 Note the examples given on the same topic.

Strategy 2 Use a term such as *generally* or *usually* as you decide what the examples have in common.

Strategy 3 Formulate a logical, general statement that applies to all examples.

OCEANS AND MOUNTAINS

1 The Canadian coastal ranges prevent the warming of Canada's interior by blocking warm Pacific air. 1 In the United States, the western mountains trap Pacific moisture. This makes the climate in the lands to the west of the mountains rainy and those to the east very dry.

The North Atlantic Drift, a current of warm water from the tropics, flows near Europe's west coast. The prevailing westerlies, which blow west to east, pick up warmth from this current and carry it over Europe. 1 No large mountain ranges block the winds, so the influence of the westerlies extends far inland.

Make a Diagram

A diagram can show how examples add up to a generalization. The diagram below is based on the passages you just read.

1 *Example: Canadian coastal ranges block warm Pacific air from reaching Canada's interior.*

\+

1 *Example: Western mountains of the United States trap Pacific moisture, making the lands on the Pacific side moist and the eastern side dry.*

\+

1 *Example: Atlantic Ocean warmth is carried over Europe because no large mountain ranges block the winds.*

=

2 3 *Generalization: Mountains generally prevent ocean air from traveling farther inland.*

Practicing the Skill

Find passages about the humid continental climate of the United States and Canada (page 124), of Europe (page 279), and of East Asia (page 626). Make a diagram to show examples and a generalization.

1.6 Making Decisions

Defining the Skill

Making decisions means choosing between two or more courses of action. When you analyze the decisions people have made, you think about the needs they were trying to meet and the consequences of each choice.

Applying the Skill

The following passage describes the problem of rapid population growth facing the Chinese government. Use the listed strategies to analyze the decisions made.

How to Make Decisions

Strategy 1 Look for a statement of the difficulty. Think about the choices facing the group.

Strategy 2 Consider possible consequences of each choice.

Strategy 3 Identify the decisions that were made.

Strategy 4 Identify actual consequences.

CONTROLLING CHINA'S POPULATION

One out of every five people in the world lives in China. China's estimated population in the year 2000 was about 1.3 billion. 1 Because of concerns about a rapidly expanding population, 3 China in 1979 adopted a policy of one child per family. In addition, the country has age restrictions for marriage—a man must be 22 and a woman 20 before they can marry. 4 These policies have reduced China's birthrate dramatically.

4 However, the government policy of one child per family has run into opposition. Rural families, in particular, feel the need for more than one child to help work on their farms. 4 As a result, the government has relaxed the one-child policy.

Make a Flow Chart

The process of decision-making can be shown in a flow chart. The flow chart below summarizes the decisions described in the passage you just read.

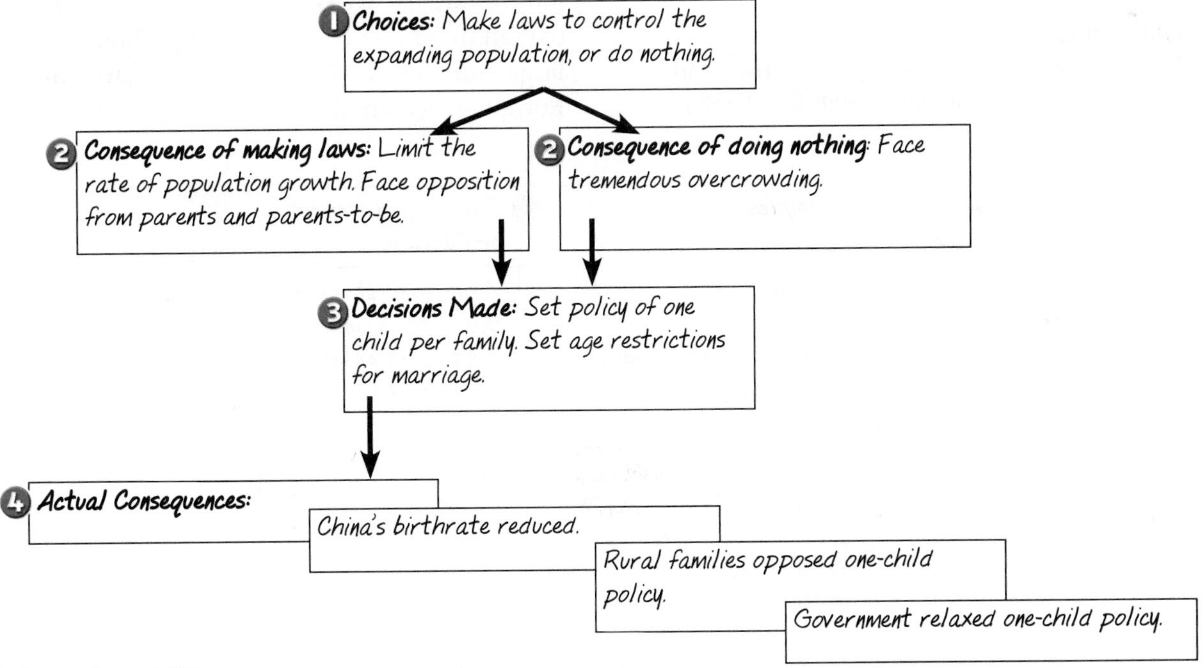

1 Choices: Make laws to control the expanding population, or do nothing.
2 Consequence of making laws: Limit the rate of population growth. Face opposition from parents and parents-to-be.
2 Consequence of doing nothing: Face tremendous overcrowding.
3 Decisions Made: Set policy of one child per family. Set age restrictions for marriage.
4 Actual Consequences:
China's birthrate reduced.
Rural families opposed one-child policy.
Government relaxed one-child policy.

Practicing the Skill

Turn to Chapter 23, Section 1. Read "New Industry Requires More Workers," on pages 525–526. Make a flow chart to show the choices faced by the nations' governments and the consequences of the decisions made.

1.7 Seeing Patterns

Defining the Skill

Seeing patterns involves seeing the overall shape, organization, or trend of geographic characteristics. It often means noting variations or contrasts, and thinking about the "rules" that describe them and could apply to similar situations. Seasonal weather cycles are one example of a pattern; economic changes are another. Graphs, maps, charts, and text passages are all sources of information that help you see patterns.

Applying the Skill

The passage below tells about the economics of oil in North Africa. Use the listed strategies to think about the pattern described.

How to See Patterns

Strategy 1 Note any directly stated main ideas about details of geographic characteristics, or changes and contrasts. (If none is directly stated, try to make your own statement of comparison, based on the details in the passage.)

Strategy 2 Notice examples that support the ideas.

Strategy 3 Use the word *pattern* in a question about the information. For this passage, you could ask, "What economic pattern is seen in the oil-producing nations of North Africa?" Your answer will sum up the pattern you see. (The chart below has a possible answer.)

AN OIL-BASED ECONOMY

1 Oil has transformed the economies of some North African countries, including Libya, Algeria, and Tunisia. 2 In Algeria, oil has surpassed farm products as the major export and source of revenue. Furthermore, oil makes up about 99 percent of Libya's exports.

1 Although oil has helped the economies of these countries, it has also caused some problems. 2 Libya, Algeria, and Tunisia face shortages of skilled labor to carry out this work. For example, Libya's labor force cannot meet the demands of the oil industry because of a lack of training and education. Oil companies are forced to give many high-paying jobs to foreign workers. Even within the oil industry, overall unemployment is still a problem. As a result, large numbers of North Africans have migrated to Europe in search of jobs.

Make a Chart

Make a chart to sum up the pattern. The chart below organizes information from the passage you have just read.

1 Main Ideas About Contrasts and Changes	2 Examples	3 Summary Statement of Pattern
The oil industry has transformed the economies of some North African countries.	Algeria—oil major export and revenue source. Libya—oil about 99 percent of exports.	A single industry can power the economy of a nation, but an unskilled labor force may not benefit.
Oil helps the economy but also causes problems.	Libya, Algeria, Tunisia face shortages of skilled workers. Libya—labor force lacks training and education. Foreign skilled workers get high-paying jobs. Unemployment, emigration.	

Practicing the Skill

Turn to Chapter 19, Section 5, "Southern Africa." Read the subsection "Success at a Cost" on pages 455–456. Use the information in it to sum up the pattern you see. Use standard grammar, sentence structure, and punctuation in your summary.

1.8 Determining Cause and Effect

Defining the Skill

A **cause** is why something happens. An **effect** is what happens. A single cause can lead to one effect or multiple effects. One effect can have multiple causes. Cause-effect chains are also common, in which a cause leads to an effect that becomes the cause of another effect, and so on.

Applying the Skill

The following paragraphs sum up major events in the recent European past. Use the listed strategies to analyze the cause-effect relationships.

How to Determine Cause and Effect

Strategy 1 Use the word *why* to formulate questions about the topic of the passage. Example: *Why was there conflict in Europe?* The answers you find will be the causes.

Strategy 2 Look for words such as *because, cause, in order to,* and *reason,* which signal causes. Look for words such as *so, consequence,* and *result,* which signal effects.

Strategy 3 Restate the cause-effect connections in your own words or in a diagram.

1 CONFLICT IN EUROPE

Western Europe experienced industrial growth in the 1800s. **2** Industrialism caused European nations to set up colonies in other lands in order to gain raw materials and markets. Many European nations saw each other as rivals in the race to gain colonies. **2** The nationalistic rivalry and competition for colonies among European nations helped cause World War I. The Allied Powers (including France) fought the Central Powers (Germany, Austria-Hungary, and their allies). The Allies won and imposed harsh terms on Germany. **2** German resentment over those terms helped cause World War II, in which Germany, led by Adolf Hitler and the Nazis, tried to conquer Europe.

Make a Diagram

A diagram can show how causes and effects are connected. Because the example passage tells how one event led to another, a cause-effect chain is a useful way to diagram its major ideas.

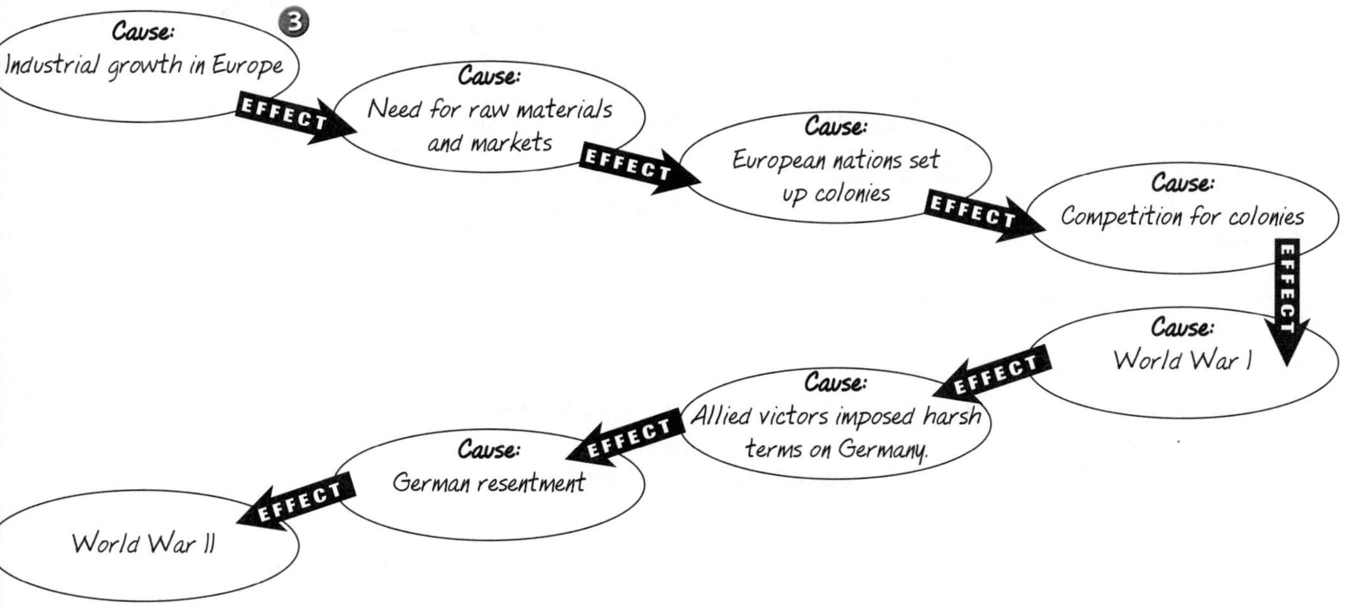

Practicing the Skill

Turn to Chapter 10, Section 4. Read the subsection "Native Peoples and Portuguese Conquest" on page 236. Make a diagram to show major cause-effect connections.

R9

1.9 Identifying and Solving Problems

Defining the Skill

Identifying and solving problems means analyzing the difficulties that are faced by individuals and groups. You determine why the difficulties exist, how people try to overcome them, and what solutions, if any, are achieved.

Applying the Skill

The following paragraph describes a general problem related to the issue of national boundaries, and offers a particular African nation as an example. Use the listed strategies to understand the problem-solution connection.

How to Identify Problems and Solutions

Strategy 1 Look for a statement of the problem. Note words such as *problem, conflict, difficulty,* or *controversy.* Use the details to ask yourself why the problem exists, and why people wish to overcome it.

Strategy 2 Identify attempts to solve the problem.

Strategy 3 Think about the outcome. Ask yourself whether the problem is solved, or whether the outcome is likely to lead to more difficulties.

ARTIFICIAL NATIONAL BOUNDARIES

Africa is a good example of how 1 boundary lines can divide groups of people or put groups that have long been enemies together in one state. When parts of Africa were divided by European colonial powers, 1 the boundary lines for Nigeria enclosed the traditional lands of the Hausa-Fulani people, the Yoruba people, and the Ibo people. Under British control, the three groups were forced to follow British rules. When Britain left, there was controversy over the control of the lands. 2 One group, the Ibo, attempted to withdraw from Nigeria and form its own nation-state, Biafra. 3 A civil war resulted, and the attempt to split away failed.

Make a Chart

A chart can help you take notes and sum up important ideas about problems and solutions. The chart below shows problems and solutions in the passage you just read.

1 Problem	Solution Attempts 2	Outcome 3
Nigerian boundary lines artificially enclose the traditional lands of three groups of people.	One group, the Ibo, attempted to form a separate nation-state.	Civil war. Attempt to split away failed.

Practicing the Skill

Turn to Chapter 8, Section 2, "Urban Sprawl." Read "Urban Sprawl's Negative Impact" and "Solutions to Sprawl." Make a chart to sum up the problem and possible solutions. Write a summary of the information presented in your chart using standard grammar, sentence structure, and punctuation.

1.10 Distinguishing Fact from Opinion

Defining the Skill

Facts are dates, numbers, names, and statements that can be proved true. **Opinions** are statements that express beliefs, values, and feelings. Although opinions cannot be proved true or false, they can be supported with facts and logical reasons. In order to decide whether to agree with stated opinions, readers must first separate opinion from fact.

Applying the Skill

The following paragraph tells how human-environment interaction affects climate and vegetation. Use the strategies listed below to distinguish fact from opinion.

How to Distinguish Fact from Opinion

Strategy 1 Notice words that reveal the author's beliefs or feelings. In the sample paragraph, *unfortunately* and *careless* show that opinions are being expressed.

Strategy 2 Look for statements about future events. These statements are opinions because they cannot be proved.

Strategy 3 Look for facts that are given as supporting reasons for the statements of opinion.

Strategy 4 Identify ways in which you can check the facts.

HUMAN IMPACT ON THE ENVIRONMENT

1 Unfortunately, the damage that humans cause to soil and vegetation is a by-product of human-environment interaction. 3 Fragile biomes such as the tundra are easily damaged. Oil pipelines crisscross tundra regions and 2 bring the threat of leakage and spills. . . .

In the United States, millions of people choose to live in the desert southwest, part of a region known as the Sunbelt. 3 The desert land is easily eroded, and housing sub-divisions destroy vegetation. In other regions of the world, 1 careless use of the land often leaves it in a condition that 2 will not support life, even with sophisticated technological intervention.

Make a Chart

The chart below analyzes the facts and opinions from the passage above.

Opinion 1 2	*Supporting Facts* 3	4 *How to Check Facts*
Human-environment interaction results in unfortunate damage to soil and vegetation.	*Fragile biomes such as the tundra are easily damaged.* *The desert land of the Sunbelt is easily eroded.* *Housing sub-divisions destroy vegetation.*	*Research current articles about human-caused damage to tundra.* *Research current articles about desert erosion in Sunbelt region.* *Research current articles about effects of development on vegetation in desert southwest.*
The tundra is threatened with oil leakage and spills.	*Oil pipelines crisscross tundra regions.*	*Research oil-industry and news sources.*
Careless use of the land often leaves it in a condition that will not support life, even with sophisticated technological intervention.	*None given*	

Practicing the Skill

Turn to Chapter 3, Section 2, and read the passage "Global Warming." Show opinions and supporting facts in a chart.

R11

I.II Creating a Sketch Map

Defining the Skill

When you are reading about routes, regions, landforms, political boundaries, or any other geographical information, try to visualize what is described. One way to clarify the information is by **creating a sketch map.** To sketch your own map, use one or more published maps as guides.

Applying the Skill

After reading the passage below, a student sketched the map shown. Read the listed strategies to see how the map was created.

WESTWARD MOVEMENT

From departure points such as Independence, Missouri, hundreds of thousands of pioneers left in covered wagons bound for the West. They blazed trails that crossed prairie, plains, desert, and mountains, moving toward the Pacific. A wagon train on the Oregon Trail might take up to six months to reach its destination 2,000 miles away.

How to Create a Sketch Map

Strategy 1 Choose a title that sums up what you will show in the map.

Strategy 2 Consider the purpose of the map as you decide which standard features need to be included. Because the main purpose of this sketch map is to show journeys, it includes a scale of distance. Other maps may require lines of latitude and longitude, for example, and a compass rose.

Strategy 3 Find one or more maps that you can use to guide the placement of elements and labels. For this sketch, the student consulted a historical map and a physical map.

Strategy 4 Create a legend to explain any symbols or colors used.

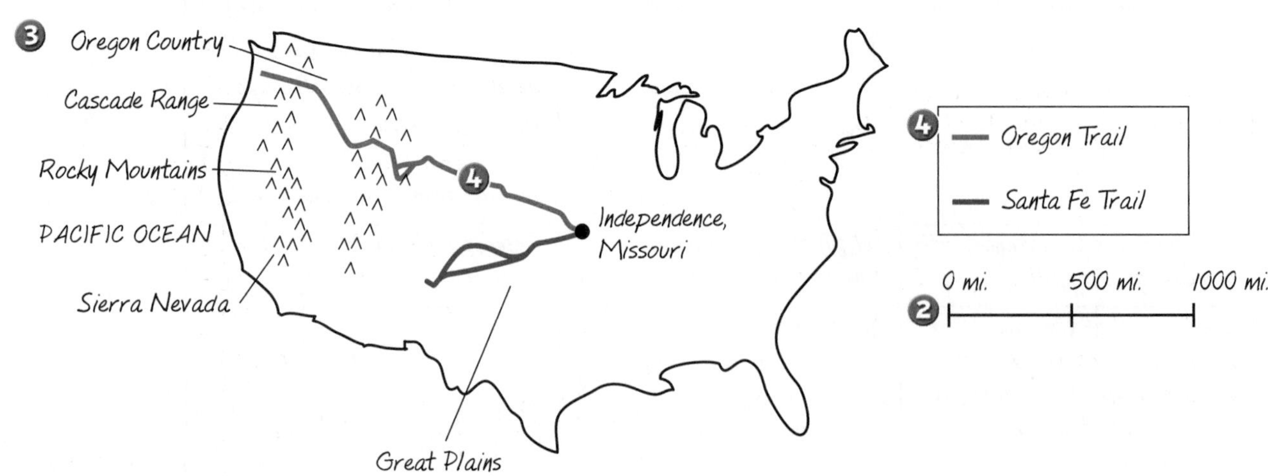

Practicing the Skill

Turn to Chapter 12, Section 1. Read the introductory paragraph "A Human Perspective" on page 273. Create a sketch map of the route of Hannibal's troops. Include the map elements needed to show why Hannibal's achievement was so remarkable.

1.12 Creating Graphs and Charts

Defining the Skill

Whenever your research provides you with information involving numbers and quantities, you can **create graphs and charts** to show patterns in your data. Software programs tend to use the terms *graphs* and *charts* interchangeably. Kinds of graphs and charts include bar graphs, line graphs, pictographs, and pie graphs, which are also called pie charts. The kind you choose depends on your data.

Applying the Skill

The three visuals below are a pie chart, a bar graph, and a line graph. Use the listed strategies to think about their purposes and parts.

How to Create Graphs and Charts

Strategy 1 Organize your numerical data. Make a table with rows and columns, or use the grid layout of a spreadsheet. The headings in your table or spreadsheet will correspond to labels in your graph.

Strategy 2 Choose the type of graph to create. Are you showing changes over time? A line graph might be best. Are you making a series of comparisons? Consider a bar graph. Do you want to show how parts make the whole? A pie chart shows percentages.

Strategy 3 In line and bar graphs, plot the data along the axes. The X-axis is horizontal; the Y-axis is vertical. Make sure that both axes are labeled with words or numbers.

Strategy 4 Include a legend to indicate what each bar, line, or section represents.

Strategy 5 Add a title.

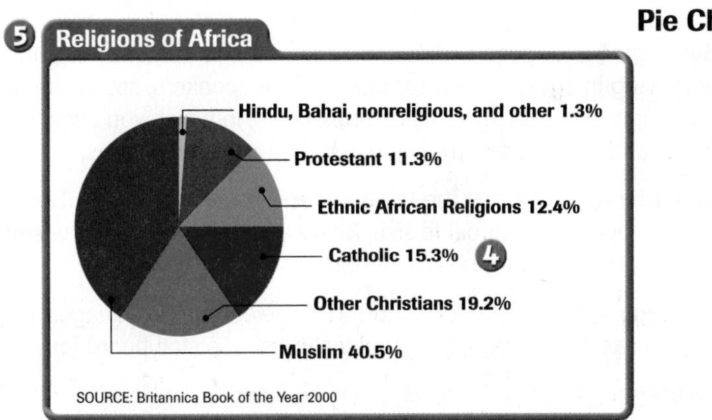

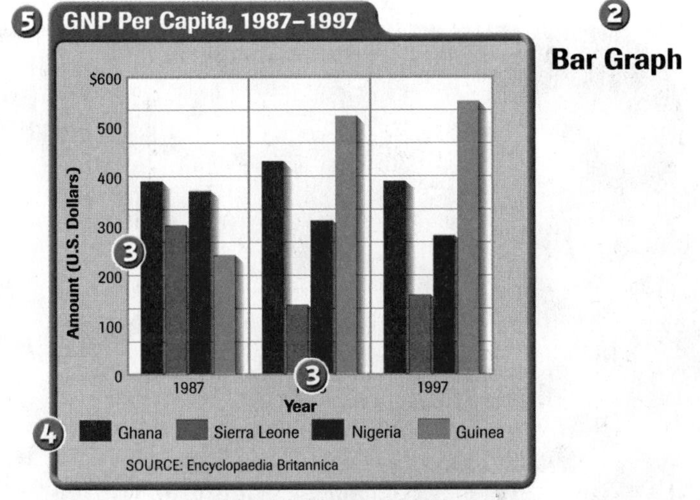

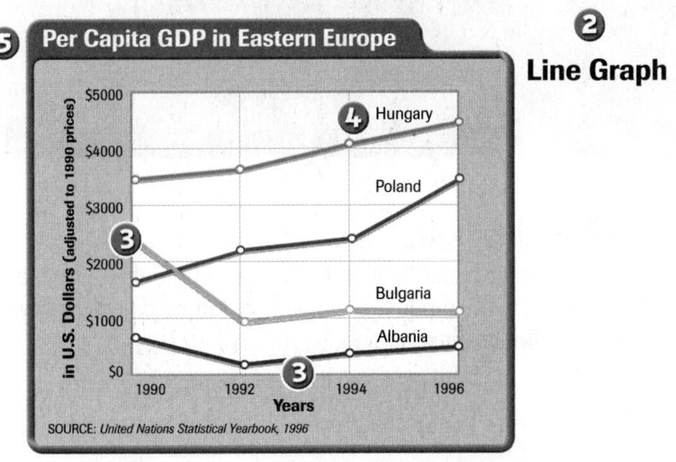

Practicing the Skill

Turn to Chapter 6, Section 3. Look at the data listed on page 147, accompanying the subsection "The Midwest." Show the data in two clearly labeled pie charts. Use graphing software if possible. Write a generalization about the information in each chart using standard grammar, sentence structure, and punctuation.

2.1 Creating a Multimedia Presentation

Defining the Skill

Print is a medium of communication. Video and audio recordings, Web pages, and photographic slides are other examples of media. To **create a multimedia presentation,** you collect and display information so that your audience watches, listens, and learns.

Applying the Skill

A multimedia presentation can incorporate high-tech electronics, but it does not have to. A photo essay with audio background, for example, is also an effective multimedia presentation. Use the listed strategies to create your own multimedia presentation.

How to Create a Multimedia Presentation

Strategy 1 Choose a topic that lends itself to multimedia. Consider using still or moving images, a script for one or more speakers, sound effects, and music. You might create a travelogue, for example, in which you show your audience a place, and develop a narrative to go with the visual images.

Strategy 2 Research the topic to get a general overview. Then narrow the topic to one of manageable size. Make an outline to show the steps you will take to develop your presentation.

Strategy 3 Collect information. Then select the text, images, and audio you plan to use. Show your plan graphically, using a storyboard format, for example.

Strategy 4 Put your presentation together.

Practicing the Skill

Turn to Chapter 4 and read Section 4, "Urban Geography." Choose a topic that you think will work well for a multimedia presentation. Do research, narrow the topic, and make an outline for a future presentation.

2.2 Creating and Using a Database

Defining the Skill

A **database** is any listing system in which related information is organized so that particular items can be retrieved. An electronic library catalog is an example of a database; new information can be added based on the categories, and users input search terms in order to pull out specific listings. Specialized software programs are used to create large, complex databases. Spreadsheet programs are frequently used to create less complex databases.

Applying the Skill

The table below is part of a database for statistics about the countries of Latin America. Use the listed strategies to understand the organization of a database.

How to Create or Use a Database

Strategy 1 Identify or name the topic of the database table.

Strategy 2 Define or identify the categories of data. In a computer database, these categories are called fields, and correspond to column headings. A field can specify names, dates or other numbers, or text.

Strategy 3 The data in each row of a database table form a record. The records are sorted by a particular field—usually alphabetically, or numerically in ascending or descending order. In the table shown, the records are sorted alphabetically by country name.

Strategy 4 To find a particular piece of data in an existing database, choose a search criterion. The table shown could lead to a list of all countries in which life expectancy is 70 or lower, for example.

1 **Regional Statistics: Latin America** (year 2000 estimates)				
Country/Capital 2	**Population** 2	2 **Life Expectancy in years** (1995–2000)	2 **Birthrate per 1,000 pop.**	**Infant Mortality per 1,000 live births** 2
3 Antigua and Barbuda/St. John's	68,000	71	22	17.1
3 Argentina/Buenos Aires	37,048,000	73	19	19.2
3 Bahamas/Nassau	310,000	74	21	18.4
Barbados/Bridgetown	259,000	76	14	14.2
Belize/Belmopan	254,000	75	32	33.9
Bolivia/La Paz, Sucre	8,281,000	4 61	30	67.0
Brazil/Brasilia	170,115,000	4 67	21	40.0
Chile/Santiago	15,211,000	75	18	10.5
Colombia/Bogota	40,037,000	4 70	26	28.0
Costa Rica/San José	3,589,000	76	22	12.6

Practicing the Skill

Use spreadsheet or database software to input the following fields from the "Regional Data File" for the 50 U.S. states, shown on pages 110–112: Name of State, Population, Population Density, Total Area (square miles). Sort the data (a) alphabetically by name of state and (b) by population, in descending order.

A

Aboriginal people *n.* people who migrated to Australia from Asia at least 40,000 years ago; the original settlers of the land. (p. 718)

absolute location *n.* the exact place on earth where a geographic feature is found. (p. 6)

acculturation *n.* the cultural change that occurs when individuals in a society accept or adopt an innovation. (p. 72)

acquired immune deficiency syndrome (AIDS) *n.* a disease caused by the human immunodeficiency virus, or HIV. (p. 465)

Aksum *n.* an important trading capital from the first to the eighth centuries A.D. in what is now Ethiopia; it flourished due to its location near the Red Sea and the Indian Ocean. (p. 431)

alluvial plain *n.* land that is rich farmland, composed of clay, silt, sand, or gravel deposited by running water. (p. 553)

Amazon River *n.* the second longest river in the world, and one of South America's three major river systems, running about 4,000 miles from west to east, and emptying into the Atlantic Ocean. (p. 203)

Andes Mountains *n.* a large system of mountain ranges located along the Pacific coast of Central and South America. (p. 201)

anti-Semitism *n.* discrimination against Jewish people. (p. 315)

apartheid (uh•PAHRT•HYT) *n.* a policy of complete separation of the races, instituted by the white minority government of South Africa in 1948. (p. 454)

Appalachian Mountains *n.* one of two major mountain chains in the eastern United States and Canada, extending 1,600 miles from Newfoundland south to Alabama. (p. 119)

aqueduct *n.* a structure that carries water over long distances. (p. 292)

aquifer *n.* an underground layer of rock that stores water. (p. 421)

archipelago *n.* a set of closely grouped islands. (pp. 553, 689)

ASEAN *n.* the Association of Southeast Asian Nations, an alliance that promotes economic growth and peace in the region. (p. 707)

Ashanti *n.* a people who live in what is now Ghana, in West Africa, and who are known for their artful weaving of colorful *asasia,* or *kente* cloth. (p. 444)

assimilation *n.* a process whereby a minority group gradually gives up its own culture and adopts the culture of a majority group. (p. 728)

Aswan High Dam *n.* a dam on the Nile River in Egypt, completed in 1970, which increased Egypt's farmable land by 50 percent and protected it from droughts and floods. (p. 426)

Atlantic Provinces *n.* the provinces in Eastern Canada—Prince Edward Island, New Brunswick, Nova Scotia, and Newfoundland. (p. 166)

atmosphere *n.* the layers of gases immediately surrounding the earth. (p. 28)

atoll *n.* a ringlike coral island or string of small islands surrounding a lagoon. (pp. 553, 700)

B

balkanization *n.* the process of breaking up a region into small, mutually hostile units. (p. 311)

Baltic Republics *n.* the countries of Latvia, Lithuania, and Estonia, located on the eastern coast of the Baltic Sea. (p. 361)

Bantu migration *n.* the movement of the Bantu peoples southward throughout Africa, spreading their language and culture, from around 500 B.C. to around A.D. 1000. (p. 448)

basic necessity *n.* food, clothing, and shelter. (p. 593)

Benelux *n.* the economic union of Belgium, the Netherlands, and Luxembourg. (p. 296)

Beringia *n.* a land bridge thought to have connected what are now Siberia and Alaska. (p. 127)

Berlin Conference *n.* a conference of 14 European nations held in 1884–1885 in Berlin, Germany, to establish rules for political control of Africa. (p. 432)

Berlin Wall *n.* a wall erected by East Germany in 1961 to cut the capital of Berlin in two, and later dismantled in 1989. (p. 298)

Bikini Atoll *n.* the isolated reef, located in the Marshall Islands of the central Pacific, that was the site of U.S. nuclear bomb tests, consequently contaminating the atoll with high levels of radiation and driving its inhabitants away. (p. 700)

biodiversity *n.* the variety of organisms within an ecosystem. (p. 245)

biological weapon *n.* a bacterium or virus that can be used to harm or kill people, animals, or plants. (p. 175)

biome *n.* a regional ecosystem. (p. 65)

biosphere *n.* all the parts of the earth where plants and animals live, including the atmosphere, the lithosphere, and the hydrosphere. (p. 28)

birthrate *n.* the number of live births per total population, often expressed per thousand population. (p. 78)

blizzard *n.* a heavy snowstorm with winds of more than 35 miles per hour and reduced visibility of less than one-quarter mile. (p. 52)

Boxer Rebellion *n.* an uprising in China in 1900, spurred by angry Chinese militants, or Boxers, over foreign control; several hundred Europeans, Christians, and Chinese died. (p. 636)

British Columbia *n.* Canada's westernmost province, located within the Rocky Mountain range. (p. 169)

Buddhism *n.* a religion that originated in India about 500 B.C. and spread to China, where it grew into a major religion by A.D. 400. (p. 638)

C

calypso *n.* a style of music that began in Trinidad and combines musical elements from Africa, Spain, and the Caribbean. (p. 227)

Canadian Shield *n.* a northern part of the interior lowlands that is a rocky, flat region covering nearly two million square miles and encircling Hudson Bay. (p. 119)

canopy *n.* the area encompassing the tops of the trees in a rain forest, about 150 feet above ground. (p. 422)

capoeira *n.* a martial art and dance that developed in Brazil from Angolans who were taken there by the Portuguese from Africa. (p. 239)

Carnival *n.* the most colorful feast day in Brazil. (p. 239)

carrying capacity *n.* the number of organisms a piece of land can support without negative effects. (p. 82)

Carthage *n.* one of the great empires of ancient Africa, situated on a triangular peninsula on the Gulf of Tunis on the coast of the Mediterranean Sea. (p. 438)

cartographer *n.* a mapmaker. (p. 10)

cash crop *n.* a crop grown for direct sale, and not for use in a region, such as coffee, tea, and sugar in Africa. (p. 433)

caste system *n.* the Aryan system of social classes in India and one of the cornerstones of Hinduism in which each person is born into a caste and can only move into a different caste through reincarnation. (p. 571)

Caucasus *n.* a region that straddles the Caucasus Mountains and stretches between the Black and Caspian seas. (p. 385)

caudillo (kow•DEE•yoh) *n.* a military dictator or political boss. (p. 249)

Central Asia *n.* a region that includes the republics of Kazakhstan, Kyrgyzstan, Tajikistan, Turkmenistan, and Uzbekistan. (p. 346)

central business district (CBD) *n.* the core of a city, which is almost always based on commercial activity. (p. 89)

cerrado (seh•RAH•doh) *n.* a savanna that has flat terrain and moderate rainfall, which make it suitable for farming. (p. 202)

Chang Jiang *n.* (or Yangtze River) the longest river in Asia, flowing about 3,900 miles from Xizang (Tibet) to the East China Sea. (p. 621)

chaparral *n.* the term, in some locations, for a biome of drought-resistant trees. (p. 66)

Chechnya *n.* one of the republics that remains a part of Russia after the collapse of the Soviet Union despite independence movements and violent upheaval. (p. 386)

chemical weathering *n.* a process that changes rock into a new substance through interactions among elements in the air or water and the minerals in the rock. (p. 43)

chernozem *n.* black topsoil, one of the world's most fertile soils. (p. 345)

cholera *n.* a treatable infectious disease that can be fatal and is caused by a lack of adequate sanitation and a clean water supply. (p. 465)

city *n.* an area that is the center of business and culture and has a large population. (p. 87)

city-state *n.* an autonomous political unit made up of a city and its surrounding lands. (p. 289)

climate *n.* the typical weather conditions at a particular location as observed over time. (p. 50)

coalition *n.* an alliance. (p. 174)

Cold War *n.* the conflict between the United States and the Soviet Union after World War II, called "cold" because it never escalated into open warfare. (p. 363)

collective farm *n.* an enormous farm in the Soviet Union on which a large team of laborers were gathered to work together during Joseph Stalin's reign. (p. 364)

Columbian Exchange *n.* the movement of plants, animals, and diseases between the Eastern and Western hemispheres during the age of exploration. (p. 136)

command economy *n.* a type of economic system in which production of goods and services is determined by a central government, which usually owns the means of production. Also called a planned economy. (pp. 91, 364)

commodity *n.* an agricultural or mining product that can be sold. (p. 462)

communism *n.* a system in which the government holds nearly all political power and the means of production. (p. 83)

confederation *n.* a political union. (p. 156)

Confucianism *n.* a movement based on the teachings of Confucius, a Chinese philosopher who lived about 500 B.C.; Confucius stressed the importance of education in an ordered society in which one respects one's elders and obeys the government. (p. 638)

coniferous *adj.* another word for needleleaf trees. (p. 66)

constitutional monarchy *n.* a government in which the ruler's powers are limited by a constitution and the laws of a nation. (p. 580)

continent *n.* a landmass above water on the earth. (p. 27)

Continental Divide *n.* the line of the highest points in North America that marks the separation between rivers flowing eastward and westward. (p. 120)

continental drift *n.* the hypothesis that all continents were once joined into a supercontinent that split apart over millions of years. (p. 29)

continentality *n.* a region's distance from the moderating influence of the sea. (p. 350)

continental shelf *n.* the earth's surface from the edge of a continent to the deep part of the ocean. (p. 36)

convection *n.* the transfer of heat in the atmosphere by upward motion of the air. (p. 54)

copra *n.* the dried meat of coconuts. (p. 714)

core *n.* the earth's center, made up of iron and nickel; the inner core is solid, and the outer core is liquid. (p. 28)

crude oil *n.* petroleum that has not been processed. (p. 497)

Crusades *n.* a series of wars launched by European Christians in 1096 to capture the Holy Land (Palestine) from Muslims. (p. 291)

crust *n.* the thin rock layer making up the earth's surface. (p. 28)

cultural crossroad *n.* a place where various cultures cross paths. (p. 310)

cultural hearth *n.* the heartland or place of origin of a major culture; a site of innovation from which basic ideas, materials, and technology diffuse to other cultures. (pp. 72, 222)

culture *n.* the total of knowledge, attitudes, and behaviors shared by and passed on by members of a group. (p. 71)

cyclone *n.* a violent storm with fierce winds and heavy rain; the most extreme weather pattern of South Asia. (p. 558)

czar *n.* the emperor of Russia prior to the Russian Revolution of 1917 and the subsequent creation of the Soviet Union in 1922. (p. 362)

D

Dead Sea *n.* a landlocked salt lake between Israel and Jordan that is so salty that almost nothing can live in its waters; it is 1,349 feet below sea level, making it the lowest place on the exposed crust of the earth. (p. 489)

debt-for-nature swap *n.* a debt-reducing deal wherein an organization agrees to pay off a certain amount of government debt in return for government protection of a certain portion of rain forest. (p. 247)

deciduous *adj.* a named characteristic of broadleaf trees, such as maple, oak, birch, and cottonwood. (p. 66)

deforestation *n.* the cutting down and clearing away of trees and forests. (p. 246)

delta *n.* a fan-like landform made of deposited sediment, left by a river that slows as it enters the ocean. (p. 43)

democracy *n.* a type of government in which citizens hold political power either directly or through elected representatives. (p. 83)

desalinization *n.* the removal of salt from ocean water. (p. 496)

desertification *n.* an expansion of dry conditions to moist areas that are next to deserts. (p. 424)

dialect *n.* a version of a language that reflects changes in speech patterns due to class, region, or cultural changes. (p. 73)

dictatorship *n.* a type of government in which an individual or a group holds complete political power. (p. 83)

diffusion *n.* the spread of ideas, inventions, or patterns of behavior to different societies. (p. 72)

dike *n.* an earthen bank used to direct or prevent the passage of water. (p. 282)

distance decay *n.* a term referring to the concept that increasing distances between places tend to reduce interactions among them. (p. 389)

diversify *v.* to increase the variety of products in a country's economy; to promote manufacturing and other industries in order to achieve growth and stability. (p. 462)

Dome of the Rock *n.* a shrine in Jerusalem, located on the Temple Mount, which houses the spot where Muslims believe Muhammad rose into heaven and where Jews believe Abraham prepared to sacrifice his son Isaac to God. (p. 511)

Dominion of Canada *n.* the loose confederation of Ontario (Upper Canada), Quebec (Lower Canada), Nova Scotia, and New Brunswick, created by the British North America Act in 1867. (p. 156)

drainage basin *n.* an area drained by a major river and its tributaries. (p. 33)

drip irrigation *n.* the practice of using small pipes that slowly drip water just above ground to conserve water to use for crops. (p. 496)

drought *n.* a long period without rain or with very minimal rainfall. (p. 53)

dynasty *n.* a series of rulers from the same family. (p. 635)

E

earthquake *n.* a sometimes violent movement of the earth, produced when tectonic plates grind or slip past each other at a fault. (p. 39)

economic system *n.* the way people produce and exchange goods. (p. 91)

economic tiger *n.* a country with rapid economic growth due to cheap labor, high technology, and aggressive exports. (p. 645)

economy *n.* the production and exchange of goods and services among a group of people. (p. 91)

ecosystem *n.* an interdependent community of plants and animals. (p. 65)

El Niño (el NEEN•YOH) *n.* a weather pattern created by the warming of the waters off the west coast of South America, which pushes warm water and heavy rains toward the Americas and produces drought conditions in Australia and Asia. (p. 57)

entrepreneur *n.* a person who starts and builds a business. (p. 575)

epicenter *n.* the point on the earth's surface that corresponds to the location in the earth where an earthquake begins. (p. 39)

equator *n.* the imaginary line that encircles the globe, dividing the earth into northern and southern halves. (p. 6)

equinox *n.* each of the two days in a year on which day and night are equal in length; marks the beginning of spring and autumn. (p. 49)

erosion *n.* the result of weathering on matter, created by the action of wind, water, ice, or gravity. (p. 43)

escarpment *n.* a steep slope with a nearly flat plateau on top. (p. 417)

estuary *n.* a broadened seaward end of a river, where the river's currents meet the ocean's tides. (p. 563)

ethnic cleansing *n.* the policy of trying to eliminate an ethnic group. (p. 320)

ethnic group *n.* a group of people who share language, customs, and a common heritage. (p. 71)

Euphrates River *n.* a river of Southwest Asia, which supported several ancient civilizations and flows through parts of Turkey, Syria, and Iraq and empties into the Persian Gulf. (p. 489)

Eurasia *n.* the combined continent of Europe and Asia. (p. 346)

euro *n.* a common currency proposed by the European Union for its member nations. (p. 305)

European Environmental Agency *n.* an agency that provides the European Union with reliable information about the environment. (p. 324)

Everglades *n.* a large subtropical swampland in Florida of about 4,000 square miles. (p. 126)

export *n.* a product or good that is sold from one economy to another. (p. 140)

F

Fang sculpture *n.* carved boxes containing the skulls and bones of deceased ancestors, created by the Fang, who live in Gabon, southern Cameroon, and Equatorial Guinea. (p. 451)

fault *n.* a fracture in the earth's crust. (p. 39)

federal republic *n.* a nation whose powers are divided among the federal, or national, government and various state and local governments. (p. 139)

feudalism *n.* a political system prevailing in Europe from about the 9th to about the 15th centuries in which a king allowed nobles the use of his land in exchange for their military service and their protection of the land. (p. 297)

fertility rate *n.* the average number of children a woman of childbearing years would have in her lifetime, if she had children at the current rate for her country. (p. 78)

First Nations *n.* a group of Canada's Native American people. (p. 159)

fjord (fyawrd) *n.* a long, narrow, deep inlet of the sea between steep slopes. (p. 273)

folk art *n.* handmade items, such as pottery, woodcarving, and traditional costumes, produced by rural people with traditional lifestyles, instead of by professional artists. (p. 314)

fossil water *n.* water pumped from underground aquifers. (p. 496)

free enterprise *n.* an economic system in which private individuals own most of the resources, technology, and businesses, and can operate them for profit with little control from the government. (p. 140)

frontier *n.* the free, open land in the American West that was available for settlement. (p. 137)

G

Ganges River *n.* river in South Asia; an important water resource flowing more than 1,500 miles from its source in a Himalayan glacier to the Bay of Bengal. (p. 560)

Gaza Strip *n.* a territory along the Mediterranean Sea just northeast of the Sinai Peninsula; part of the land set aside for Palestinians, which was occupied by Israel in 1967. (p. 527)

Geographic Information System (GIS) *n.* technology that uses digital map information to create a databank; different "data layers" can be combined to produce specialized maps. GIS allows geographers to analyze different aspects of a specific place to solve problems. (p. 13)

geography *n.* the study of the distribution and interaction of physical and human features on the earth. (p. 5)

glaciation *n.* the changing of landforms by slowly moving glaciers. (p. 44)

glacier *n.* a large, long-lasting mass of ice that moves because of gravity. (p. 44)

global economy *n.* the merging of regional economies in which nations become dependent on each other for goods and services. (p. 666)

global network *n.* a worldwide interconnected group. (p. 173)

global warming *n.* the buildup of carbon dioxide in the atmosphere, preventing heat from escaping into space and causing rising temperatures and shifting weather patterns. (p. 246)

globe *n.* a three-dimensional representation of the earth. (p. 10)

Gobi Desert *n.* a desert located in northern China and southeast Mongolia, and a prime area for finding dinosaur fossils. (p. 627)

Golan Heights *n.* a hilly plateau overlooking the Jordan River and the Sea of Galilee; a strategic location that has been the site of conflict in Southwest Asia for decades. (p. 487)

Gorée Island *n.* an island off the coast of Senegal that served as a major departure point for slaves during the slave trade. (p. 442)

Great Barrier Reef *n.* a 1,250-mile chain of more than 2,500 reefs and islands along Australia's northeast coast, containing some 400 species of coral. (p. 692)

Great Game *n.* a struggle between the British Empire and the Russian Empire for control of Central Asia in the 19th century. (p. 376)

Great Kanto Earthquake *n.* an earthquake in 1923 in Japan that killed an estimated 140,000 people and left the city of Tokyo in ruins. (p. 662)

Great Lakes *n.* a group of five freshwater lakes of central North America between the United States and Canada; the lakes are Huron, Ontario, Michigan, Erie, and Superior. (p. 121)

Great Plains *n.* a vast grassland of central North America that is largely treeless and ascends to 4,000 feet above sea level. (p. 119)

Great Zimbabwe *n.* a city established in what is now Zimbabwe by the Shona around 1000; it became the capital of a thriving gold-trading area. (p. 453)

greenhouse effect *n.* the layer of gases released by the burning of coal and petroleum that traps solar energy, causing global temperature to increase. (p. 58)

Green Revolution *n.* an agricultural program launched by scientists in the 1960s to develop higher-yielding grain varieties and improve food production by incorporating new farming techniques. (p. 569)

Gross Domestic Product (GDP) *n.* the value of only goods and services produced within a country in a period of time. (p. 95)

Gross National Product (GNP) *n.* the total value of all goods and services produced by a country in a period of time. (p. 94)

ground water *n.* the water held under the earth's surface, often in and around the pores of rock. (p. 33)

guest worker *n.* a largely unskilled laborer, often an immigrant from South and East Asia, brought in to the oil-booming countries to fill job openings that the region's native peoples find culturally or economically unacceptable. (p. 525)

H

hemisphere *n.* each half of the globe. (p. 6)

high islands *n.* Pacific islands created by volcanoes. (p. 691)

Himalaya Mountains *n.* a mountain range in South Asia that includes Mount Everest, the world's tallest mountain peak. (p. 551)

Hinduism *n.* the dominant religion of India. (p. 560)

Holocaust *n.* the Nazi program of mass murder of European Jews during World War II. (p. 298)

Huang He (hwahng huh) *n.* a river in northern China, also called the Yellow River, that starts in the Kunlun Mountains and winds east for about 3,000 miles, emptying into the Yellow Sea. (p. 621)

human resources *n.* the skills and talents of employed people. (p. 531)

humus *n.* organic material in soil. (p. 45)

hurricane *n.* a storm that forms over warm, tropical ocean waters. (p. 51)

hydrologic cycle *n.* the continuous circulation of water among the atmosphere, the oceans, and the earth. (p. 32)

hydrosphere *n.* the waters comprising the earth's surface, including oceans, seas, rivers, lakes, and vapor in the atmosphere. (p. 28)

I

Ijsselmeer (EYE•suhl•MAIR) *n.* a freshwater lake separated from the North Sea by a dike and bordered by polders. (p. 283)

illiteracy *n.* the inability to read or write. (p. 593)

Inca *n.* a member of the Quechen peoples of South America who built a civilization in the Andes Mountains in the 15th and 16th centuries. (p. 230)

Indochina *n.* a French colony comprised of Cambodia, Laos, and Vietnam; it won independence from France in 1954. (p. 707)

industrialization *n.* the growth of industry in a country or a society. (p. 730)

R19

Indus Valley civilization *n.* the largest of the world's first civilizations in what is now Pakistan; this was a highly developed urban civilization, lasting from 2500 B.C. to about 1500 B.C. (p. 573)

infant mortality rate *n.* the number of deaths among infants under age one as measured per thousand live births. (p. 79)

infrastructure *n.* the basic support systems needed to keep an economy going, including power, communications, transportation, water, sanitation, and education systems. (pp. 94, 177, 212)

innovation *n.* taking existing elements of society and creating something new to meet a need. (p. 72)

Institutional Revolutionary Party (PRI) *n.* the political party introduced in 1929 in Mexico that helped to introduce democracy and maintain political stability for much of the 20th century. (p. 218)

Islam *n.* a monotheistic religion based on the teachings of the prophet Muhammad, and the biggest cultural and religious influence in North Africa. (pp. 439, 503)

J

Jakota Triangle *n.* a zone of prosperity during the 1980s and early 1990s—Japan, South Korea, and Taiwan. (p. 666)

Jordan River *n.* a river that serves as a natural boundary between Israel and Jordan, flowing from the mountains of Lebanon with no outlet to the Mediterranean Sea. (p. 489)

junta (HOON•tah) *n.* a government run by generals after a military takeover. (p. 249)

K

Kashmir *n.* a region of northern India and Pakistan over which several destructive wars have been fought. (p. 574)

Khmer Empire *n.* a powerful empire that lasted roughly from the 9th to the 15th centuries in what is now Cambodia. (p. 706)

King Leopold II *n.* the Belgian king who opened up the African interior to European trade along the Congo River and by 1884 controlled the area known as the Congo Free State. (p. 449)

KLA (Kosovo Liberation Army) *n.* a group that fought against Serbian attempts to control the region of Kosovo in the 1990s. (p. 321)

Kunlun Mountains *n.* mountains located in the west of China that are the source of two of China's great rivers, the Huang He (Yellow) and the Chang Jiang (Yangtze). (p. 619)

Kurds *n.* an ethnic group in Southwestern Asia that has occupied Kurdistan, located in Turkey, Iraq, and Iran, for about a thousand years, and who have been involved in clashes with these three countries over land claims for most of the 20th century. (p. 516)

L

landfill *n.* a method of solid waste disposal in which refuse is buried between layers of dirt in order to fill in or reclaim low-lying ground. (p. 631)

landform *n.* a naturally formed feature on the surface of the earth. (p. 33)

landlocked *adj.* having no outlet to the sea. (p. 84)

land reform *n.* the process of breaking up large landholdings to attain a more balanced land distribution among farmers. (pp. 250, 569)

Land Rights Act of 1976 *n.* a special law passed for Aboriginal rights in Australia giving Aboriginal people the right to claim land in the Northern Territory. (p. 728)

Landsat *n.* a series of satellites that orbit more than 100 miles above the earth. Each satellite picks up data in an area 115 miles wide. (p. 12)

latitude (lines) *n.* a set of imaginary lines that run parallel to the equator, and that are used in locating places north or south. The equator is labeled the zero-degree line for latitude. (p. 6)

lava *n.* magma that has reached the earth's surface. (p. 40)

lithosphere *n.* the solid rock portion of the earth's surface. (p. 28)

llanos (LAH•nohs) *n.* a large, grassy, treeless area in South America, used for grazing and farming. (p. 202)

lock *n.* a section of a waterway with closed gates where water levels are raised or lowered, through which ships pass. (p. 129)

loess (LOH•uhs) *n.* wind-blown silt and clay sediment that produces very fertile soil. (p. 44)

longitude (lines) *n.* a set of imaginary lines that go around the earth over the poles, dividing it east and west. The prime meridian is labeled the zero-degree line for longitude. (p. 6)

Louisiana Purchase *n.* the territory, including the region between the Mississippi River and the Rocky Mountains, that the United States purchased from France in 1803. (p. 136)

low islands *n.* Pacific islands made of coral reefs. (p. 691)

M

Mabo Case *n.* in Australia, the law case that upheld Aboriginal Eddie Mabo's land claim by which the Court recognized that Aboriginal people had owned land before the British arrived. (p. 728)

Mackenzie River *n.* Canada's longest river, which is part of a river system that flows across the Northwest Territories to the Arctic Ocean. (p. 121)

magma *n.* the molten rock material formed when solid rock in the earth's mantle or crust melts. (p. 28)

malaria *n.* an infectious disease of the red blood cells, carried by mosquitoes, that is characterized by chills, fever, and sweating. (p. 466)

mandala *n.* in Tibetan Buddhism, a geometric design that symbolizes the universe and aids in meditation. (p. 583)

mandala *n.* a state organized as a ring of power around a central court, which often changed in size over time, and which was used instead of borders in early Southeast Asian states. (p. 705)

mantle *n.* a rock layer about 1,800 miles thick that is between the earth's crust and the earth's core. (p. 28)

Maori *n.* the first settlers of New Zealand, who had migrated from Polynesia more than 1,000 years ago. (p. 719)

Mao Zedong *n.* the leader of the Communists in China who defeated the Nationalists in 1949; he died in 1976. (p. 636)

map projection *n.* a way of mapping the earth's surface that reduces distortion caused by converting three dimensions into two dimensions. (p. 10)

map *n.* a two-dimensional graphic representation of selected parts of the earth's surface. (p. 10)

maquiladora *n.* a factory in Mexico that assembles imported materials into finished goods for export. (p. 220)

market economy *n.* a type of economic system in which production of goods and services is determined by the demand from consumers. Also called a demand economy or capitalism. (pp. 91, 313)

Massif Central (ma•SEEF sahn•TRAHL) *n.* the uplands of France, which account for about one-sixth of French lands. (p. 275)

Mecca *n.* the holiest city of Islam, located in Saudi Arabia, where people make pilgrimages to fulfill Islamic religious duty. (p. 503)

mechanical weathering *n.* natural processes that break rock into smaller pieces. (p. 42)

megalopolis *n.* a region in which several large cities and surrounding areas grow together. (p. 146)

Melanesia *n.* a region in Oceania meaning "black islands." (p. 713)

Meseta (meh•SEH•tah) *n.* the central plateau of Spain. (p. 275)

Mesopotamia *n.* a region in Southwest Asia between the Tigris and the Euphrates rivers, which was the location of some of the earliest civilizations in the world; part of the cultural hearth known as the Fertile Crescent. (p. 516)

métis (may•TEES) *n.* a person of mixed French-Canadian and Native American ancestry. (p. 161)

metropolitan area *n.* a functional area including a city and its surrounding suburbs and exurbs, linked economically. (pp. 87, 148)

microcredit *n.* a small loan available to poor entrepreneurs, to help small businesses grow and raise living standards. (p. 575)

Micronesia *n.* one of three regions in Oceania, meaning "tiny islands." (p. 713)

Midwest *n.* the region that contains the 12 states of the north-central United States. (p. 147)

migration *n.* the movement of peoples within a country or region. (p. 135)

Mississippi River *n.* a major river that runs north-south almost the length of the United States, from Minnesota to the Gulf of Mexico, and is part of the longest river system on the continent. (p. 121)

mistral (MIHS•truhl) *n.* a cold, dry wind from the north. (p. 279)

Mobutu Sese Seko *n.* the leader of Zaire, which is now the Democratic Republic of the Congo, from its independence in the 1960s until 1997. He brought the country's businesses under national control, profited from the reorganization, and used the army to hold power. (p. 450)

monarchy *n.* a type of government in which a ruling family headed by a king or queen holds political power and may or may not share the power with citizen bodies. (p. 83)

monsoon *n.* a seasonal wind, especially in South Asia. (p. 558)

moraine *n.* a ridge or hill of rock carried and finally deposited by a glacier. (p. 44)

mortality rate *n.* the number of deaths per thousand. (p. 79)

mosque *n.* an Islamic place of worship, where Muslims pray facing toward the holy city of Mecca. (p. 504)

Mount Kilimanjaro *n.* a volcano in Tanzania in Africa, also Africa's highest peak. (p. 417)

Mughal Empire *n.* the Muslim empire established by the early 1500s over much of India, which brought with it new customs that sometimes conflicted with those of native Hindus. (p. 568)

Muhammad *n.* the founder and a prophet of Islam, who lived part of his life in the city of Mecca. (p. 503)

multinational *n.* a corporation that engages in business worldwide. (p. 142)

Mutapa Empire *n.* a state founded in the 15th century by a man named Mutota and that extended throughout all of present-day Zimbabwe except the eastern part. (p. 453)

N

Nagorno-Karabakh *n.* the mountainous area of Azerbaijan, fought over by Armenia and Azerbaijan. (p. 386)

nation *n.* a group of people with a common culture living in a territory and having a strong sense of unity. (p. 83)

nationalism *n.* the belief that people should be loyal to their nation, the people with whom they share land, culture, and history. (p. 297)

nation-state *n.* the name of a territory when a nation and a state occupy the same territory. (p. 83)

natural resource *n.* a material on or in the earth, such as a tree, fish, or coal, that has economic value. (p. 93)

needleleaf *adj.* characteristic of trees like pine, fir, and cedar, found in northern regions of North America. (p. 66)

Nelson Mandela *n.* one of the leaders of the African National Congress who led a struggle to end apartheid and was elected president in 1994 in the first all-race election in South Africa. (p. 454)

New England *n.* the six northern states in the Northeast United States—Maine, Vermont, New Hampshire, Massachusetts, Rhode Island, and Connecticut. (p. 145)

Niger delta *n.* delta of the Niger River and an area of Nigeria with rich oil deposits. (p. 424)

Nile River *n.* the world's longest river, flowing over 4,000 miles through the Sudan Basin into Uganda, Sudan, and Egypt. (p. 416)

nomad *n.* a person with no permanent home who moves according to the seasons from place to place in search of food, water, and grazing land. (pp. 127, 378)

nonviolent resistance *n.* a movement that uses all means of protest except violence. (p. 568)

Nordic countries *n.* countries of northern Europe, including Denmark, Finland, Iceland, Norway, and Sweden. (p. 302)

NAFTA (North American Free Trade Agreement) *n.* an important trade agreement creating a huge zone of cooperation on trade and economic issues in North America. (p. 220)

North Atlantic Drift *n.* a current of warm water from the Tropics. (p. 278)

Nunavut *n.* one of Canada's territories and home to many of Canada's Inuit; it was carved out of the eastern half of the Northwest Territories in 1999. (p. 169)

O

oasis *n.* a place where water from an aquifer has reached the surface; it supports vegetation and wildlife. (pp. 421, 492)

Oceania *n.* the group of islands in the Pacific, including Melanesia, Micronesia, and Polynesia. (p. 690)

Olduvai Gorge *n.* a site of fossil beds in northern Tanzania, containing the most continuous known record of humanity over the past 2 million years, including fossils from 65 hominids. (p. 431)

oligarchy (AHL•ih•GAHR•kee) *n.* a government run by a few persons or a small group. (p. 249)

GLOSSARY

"one-commodity" country *n.* a country that relies on one principal export for much of its earnings. (p. 462)

Ontario *n.* one of Canada's Core Provinces. (p. 167)

OPEC *n.* the Organization of Petroleum Exporting Countries, a group established in 1960 by some oil-producing nations to coordinate policies on selling petroleum products. (p. 505)

Orinoco River *n.* a river mainly in Venezuela and part of South America's northernmost river system. (p. 202)

outback *n.* the dry, unpopulated inland region of Australia. (p. 697)

outrigger canoe *n.* a small ship used in the lagoons of islands where Pacific Islanders settled. (p. 699)

ozone *n.* a chemical created when burning fossil fuels react with sunlight; a form of oxygen. (p. 325)

P

Pacific Rim *n.* an economic and social region including the countries surrounding the Pacific Ocean, extending clockwise from New Zealand in the western Pacific to Chile in the eastern Pacific and including the west coast of the United States. (p. 645)

pakehas *n.* a Maori term for white people, for the New Zealanders of European descent. (p. 722)

Palestine Liberation Organization (PLO) *n.* a group formed in the 1960s to regain the Arab land in Israel for Palestinian Arabs. (p. 513)

Palestinians *n.* a displaced group of Arabs who lived or still live in the area formerly called Palestine and now called Israel. (p. 527)

pampas (PAHM•puhs) *n.* a vast area of grassland and rich soil in south-central South America. (p. 202)

Panama Canal *n.* a ship canal cut through Panama connecting the Caribbean Sea with the Pacific Ocean. (p. 226)

pandemic *n.* a disease affecting a large population over a wide geographic area. (p. 435)

Paraná River *n.* a river in central South America and one of its three major river systems, originating in the highlands of southern Brazil, travelling about 3,000 miles south and west. (p. 203)

parliament *n.* a representative lawmaking body whose members are elected or appointed and in which legislative and executive functions are combined. (pp. 158, 303)

parliamentary government *n.* a system where legislative and executive functions are combined in a legislature called a parliament. (p. 158)

particulate *n.* a very small particle of liquid or solid matter. (p. 324)

partition *n.* separation; division into two or more territorial units having separate political status. (p. 574)

pastoral lease *n.* in Australia, a huge chunk of land still owned by the government; ranchers take out leases, renting the land from the government. (p. 729)

PCB *n.* an industrial compound that accumulates in animal tissue and can cause harmful effects and birth defects; PCBs were banned in the United States in 1977. (p. 631)

peat *n.* partially decayed plant matter found in bogs. (p. 277)

penal colony *n.* a place to send prisoners. (p. 718)

per capita income *n.* the average amount of money earned by each person in a political unit. (p. 94)

permafrost *n.* permanently frozen ground. (pp. 63, 123)

polder *n.* land that is reclaimed from the sea or other body of water by diking and drainage. (p. 282)

Polynesia *n.* one of three regions in Oceania, meaning "many islands." (p. 713)

population density *n.* the average number of people who live in a measurable area, reached by dividing the number of inhabitants in an area by the amount of land they occupy. (p. 81)

population pyramid *n.* a graphic device that shows gender and age distribution of a population. (p. 79)

postindustrial economy *n.* an economic phase in which manufacturing no longer plays a dominant role. (p. 142)

Prairie Provinces *n.* in Canada, the provinces west of Ontario and Quebec—Manitoba, Saskatchewan, and Alberta. (p. 168)

precipitation *n.* falling water droplets in the form of rain, sleet, snow, or hail. (p. 50)

prevailing westerlies *n.* winds that blow from west to east. (p. 124)

prime meridian *n.* the imaginary line at zero meridian used to measure longitude east to west, and dividing the earth's east and west halves; also called the Greenwich Meridian because it passes through Greenwich, England. (p. 6)

prime minister *n.* the head of a government; the majority party's leader in parliament. (p. 158)

privatization *n.* the selling of government-owned business to private citizens. (p. 388)

province *n.* a political unit. (p. 156)

pull factor *n.* a factor that draws or attracts people to another location. (pp. 81, 211)

push factor *n.* a factor that causes people to leave their homelands and migrate to another region. (pp. 81, 211, 730)

Pyongyang *n.* the largest city in North Korea, with more than 2.5 million people. (p. 650)

Q

Qin Ling Mountains *n.* mountains in southeastern and east-central China; they divide the northern part of China from the southern part. (p. 619)

Quebec *n.* one of Canada's Core Provinces. (p. 167)

Quechua (KEHCH•wuh) *n.* the language of the Inca Empire, now spoken in the Andes highlands. (p. 231)

R

rai *n.* a kind of popular Algerian music developed in the 1920s by poor urban children that is fast-paced with danceable rhythms; was sometimes used as a form of rebellion to expose political unhappiness. (p. 440)

rain forest *n.* a forest region located in the Tropical Zone with a heavy concentration of different species of broadleaf trees. (pp. 66, 207)

rain shadow *n.* the land on the leeward side of hills or mountains that gets little rain from the descending dry air. (p. 51)

raj *n.* the period of British rule in India, which lasted for nearly 200 years, from 1857 to 1947. (p. 568)

Ramadan *n.* an Islamic practice of month-long fasting from sunup to sundown. (p. 576)

rate of natural increase *n.* also called population growth rate—the rate at which population is growing, found by subtracting the mortality rate from the birthrate. (p. 79)

recession *n.* an extended period of decline in general business activity. (p. 667)

Red Army *n.* the name of the Soviet Union's military. (p. 371)

refinery *n.* a place where crude oil is converted into useful products. (p. 497)

Reformation *n.* a movement in Western Europe beginning in 1517, when many Christians broke away from the Catholic Church and started Protestant churches; this led to mutual hostility and religious wars that tore apart Europe. (p. 297)

reggae *n.* a style of music that developed in Jamaica in the 1960s and is rooted in African, Caribbean, and American music, often dealing with social problems and religion. (p. 227)

relative location *n.* describes a place in relation to other places around it. (p. 6)

relief *n.* the difference in elevation of a landform from the lowest point to the highest point. (p. 36)

religion *n.* the belief in a supernatural power or powers that are regarded as the creators and maintainers of the universe, as well as the system of beliefs itself. (p. 75)

Renaissance *n.* a time of renewed interest in learning and the arts that lasted from the 14th through 16th centuries; it began in the Italian city-states and spread north to all of Europe. (p. 291)

representative democracy *n.* a government in which the people rule through elected representatives. (p. 139)

republic *n.* a government in which citizens elect representatives to rule on their behalf. (p. 290)

reserve *n.* public land set aside for native peoples by the government. (p. 162)

Richter scale *n.* a way to measure information collected by seismographs to determine the relative strength of an earthquake. (p. 40)

rift valley *n.* a long, thin valley created by the moving apart of the continental plates, present in East Africa, stretching over 4,000 miles from Jordan in Southwest Asia to Mozambique in Southern Africa. (p. 416)

Ring of Fire *n.* the chain of volcanoes that lines the Pacific Rim. (pp. 41, 661)

Rocky Mountains *n.* a major mountain system of the United States and Canada, extending 3,000 miles from Alaska south to New Mexico. (p. 119)

Rub al Khali *n.* also known as the Empty Quarter; one of the largest sandy deserts in the world, covering about 250,000 square miles; located on the Arabian Peninsula. (p. 491)

Russian Revolution *n.* the revolt of 1917, in which the Russian Communist Party, led by V. I. Lenin, took control of the government from the czars. (p. 363)

runoff *n.* rainfall not absorbed by soil, which can carry pesticides and fertilizers from fields into rivers, endangering the food chain. (p. 353)

S

Sahara *n.* the largest desert in the world, stretching 3,000 miles across the African continent, from the Atlantic Ocean to the Red Sea, and measuring 1,200 miles from north to south. (p. 420)

Sahel *n.* a narrow band of dry grassland, running east to west on the southern edge of the Sahara, that is used for farming and herding. (p. 424)

St. Lawrence Seaway *n.* North America's most important deepwater ship route, connecting the Great Lakes to the Atlantic Ocean by way of the St. Lawrence River. (p. 129)

St. Petersburg *n.* the old capital of Russia, established by Peter the Great, who moved it there from Moscow because St. Petersburg provided direct access by sea to Western Europe. (p. 362)

salt flat *n.* flat land made of chemical salts that remain after winds evaporate the moisture in the soil. (p. 492)

samba *n.* a Brazilian dance with African influences. (p. 239)

samurai *n.* a professional soldier in Japan who served the interests of landowners and clan chiefs. (p. 651)

satellite nation *n.* a nation dominated by another country. (p. 312)

savanna *n.* the term for the flat, grassy, mostly treeless plains in the tropical grassland region. (p. 66)

seawork *n.* a structure used to control the sea's destructive impact on human life. (p. 283)

sectionalism *n.* when people place their loyalty to their region, or section, above loyalty to the nation. (p. 136)

sediment *n.* small pieces of rock produced by weathering processes. (p. 42)

seismograph (SYZ•muh•GRAF) *n.* a device that measures the size of the waves created by an earthquake. (p. 39)

Seoul *n.* the largest city in South Korea, with a population of more than ten million people. (p. 650)

Serengeti *n.* an area of East Africa, containing some of the best grasslands in the world and many grazing animals. (p. 422)

service industry *n.* any kind of economic activity that produces a service rather than a product. (p. 142)

Sherpa *n.* a person of Tibetan ancestry in Nepal, who serves as the traditional mountain guide of the Mount Everest region. (p. 582)

Shi'ite *n.* one of the two main branches of Islam including most Iranians and some populations of Iraq and Afghanistan. (p. 517)

shogun *n.* the general of the emperor's army with the powers of a military dictator, a position created by the Japanese emperor in 1192 after a struggle between two powerful clans. (p. 651)

Siberia *n.* a region of central and eastern Russia, stretching from the Ural Mountains to the Pacific Ocean, known for its mineral resources and for being a place of political exile. (p. 349)

Siddhartha Gautama *n.* the founder of Buddhism and known as the Buddha, born in southern Nepal in the sixth century B.C. (p. 582)

Silicon Glen *n.* the section of Scotland between Glasgow and Edinburgh, named for its high concentration of high-tech companies. (p. 305)

Silk Road *n.* the 4,000-mile route between China and the Mediterranean Sea, named for the costly silk acquired in China. (p. 375)

silt *n.* loose sedimentary material containing very small rock particles, formed by river deposits and very fertile. (p. 426)

Sinhalese *n.* an Indo-Aryan people who crossed the strait separating India and Sri Lanka in the sixth century B.C. and who created an advanced civilization there, adopting Buddhism. (p. 584)

sirocco (suh•RAHK•oh) *n.* a hot, steady south wind that blows from North Africa across the Mediterranean Sea into southern Europe, mostly in spring. (p. 279)

slash-and-burn *adj.* a way of clearing fields for planting by cutting trees, brush, and grasses and burning them. (p. 210)

smart growth *n.* the efficient use and conservation of land and other resources. (p. 178)

smog *n.* a brown haze that occurs when gases released by burning fossil fuels react with sunlight. (p. 324)

society *n.* a group that shares a geographic region, a common language, and a sense of identity and culture. (p. 71)

soil *n.* the loose mixture of weathered rock, organic matter, air, and water that supports plant growth. (p. 45)

solar system *n.* consists of the sun and nine known planets, as well as other celestial bodies that orbit the sun. (p. 27)

solstice *n.* either of two times of year when the sun's rays shine directly overhead at noon at the furthest points north or south, and that mark the beginning of summer and winter; in the Northern Hemisphere, the summer solstice is the longest day and the winter solstice the shortest. (p. 49)

South, the *n.* a region that covers about one-fourth of the land area of the United States and contains more than one-third of its population. (p. 148)

South Slav *n.* a person who migrated from Poland or Russia and settled in the Balkan Peninsula around 500. (p. 319)

Spanish conquest *n.* the conquering of the Native Americans by the Spanish. (p. 217)

sphere of influence *n.* a method of dividing foreign control in China, after the country was forced to sign a series of treaties granting special privileges to the Europeans. China was partitioned for control by Britain, France, Germany, and Russia, among others. (p. 636)

state *n.* a political term describing an independent unit that occupies a specific territory and has full control of its internal and external affairs. (p. 83)

stateless nation *n.* a nation of people that does not have a territory to legally occupy, like the Palestinians, Kurds, and Basques. (p. 526)

stateless society *n.* one in which people use lineages, or families whose members are descended from a common ancestor, to govern themselves. (p. 443)

steppe *n.* the term used for the temperate grassland region in the Northern Hemisphere. (p. 66)

Stolen Generation *n.* in Australia, what Aboriginal people today call the 100,000 mixed-raced children who were taken by the government and given to white families to promote assimilation. (p. 728)

storm surge *n.* high water level brought by a cyclone that swamps low-lying areas. (p. 562)

strategic commodity *n.* a resource so important that nations will go to war to ensure its steady supply. (p. 529)

subcontinent *n.* a landmass that is like a continent, only smaller, such as South Asia, which is called the Indian subcontinent. (p. 551)

subsistence activity *n.* an activity in which a family produces only the food, clothing, and shelter they themselves need. (p. 714)

suburb *n.* a political unit or community touching the borders of the central city or touching other suburbs that touch the city. (pp. 87, 138)

sultan *n.* a ruler of a Muslim country. (p. 585)

summer monsoon *n.* the season when winds blow from the southwest across the Indian Ocean toward South Asia, from June through September, with winds stirring up powerful storms and causing severe flooding. (p. 597)

Sunni *n.* one of the two main branches of Islam, comprising about 83 percent of all Muslims, including those in Turkey, Iraq, and Afghanistan. (p. 517)

supra *n.* Georgian (Russian) term for dinner party, with many dishes and courses, toasts, and short speeches. (p. 374)

sustainable community *n.* a community where residents can live and work in harmony with the environment. (p. 178)

sweatshop *n.* a workplace where people work long hours for low pay under poor conditions to enrich manufacturers. (p. 667)

T

taiga *n.* a nearly continuous belt of evergreen coniferous forests across the Northern Hemisphere, in North America and Eurasia. (p. 351)

Taklimakan Desert *n.* a desert located in western China between the Tian Shan and Kunlun mountains. (p. 627)

Taliban *n.* a strict Muslim group in Afghanistan that has imposed rigid rules on society, including prescribed clothing styles for both men and women, restrictions on the appearance of women in public places, and regulations on television, music, and videos. (p. 519)

Tamil *n.* a Dravidian Hindu, who arrived in Sri Lanka in the fourth century, settling in the north while the Sinhalese moved further south. (p. 584)

Taoism *n.* a philosophy based on the book *Tao Te Ching* and the teachings of Lao-Tzu, who lived in China in the sixth century B.C. and believed in preserving and restoring harmony in the individual, with nature, and in the universe, with little interference from the government. (p. 638)

taro *n.* a tropical Asian plant with a starchy root, which can be eaten as a boiled vegetable or made into breads, puddings, or a paste called poi. (p. 715)

tectonic plate *n.* an enormous moving shelf that forms the earth's crust. (p. 37)

Tenochtitlan (teh•NOH•tee•TLAHN) *n.* the ancient Aztec capital, site of Mexico City today. (p. 217)

terpen *n.* high earthen platforms used in seaworks. (p. 283)

terraced farming *n.* an ancient technique for growing crops on hillsides or mountain slopes, using step-like horizontal fields cut into the slopes. (p. 211)

terrorism *n.* the use of, or threatened use of, force or violence against individuals or property for the purpose of intimidating or causing fear for political or social ends. (p. 173)

theocratic *adj.* a form of government in which religious leaders control the government, relying on religious law and consultation with religious scholars. (p. 504)

Three Gorges Dam *n.* a dam begun in the late 20th century on the Chang Jiang in China, to help control flooding, generate power, and allow ships to sail farther into China. (p. 628)

Three Kingdoms *n.* the kingdoms formed in the peninsula of Korea by A.D. 300—Koguryo in the northeast, Paekche in the southwest, and Silla in the southeast. (p. 647)

Tigris River *n.* one of the most important rivers of Southwest Asia; it supported several ancient river valley civilizations, and flows through parts of Turkey, Syria, and Iraq. (p. 489)

R24

tornado *n.* a powerful funnel-shaped column of spiraling air. (p. 51)

topographic map *n.* a general reference map; a representation of natural and man-made features on the earth. (p. 11)

topography *n.* the combined characteristics of landforms and their distribution in a region. (p. 36)

Transcaucasia *n.* a region that consists of the republics of Armenia, Azerbaijan, and Georgia; located between the Caucasus Mountains and the borders of Turkey and Iran. (p. 346)

Trans-Siberian Railroad *n.* a railroad that would eventually link Moscow to the Pacific port of Vladivostok; built between 1891 and 1903. (p. 355)

Treaty of Tordesillas *n.* a treaty between Spain and Portugal in 1494 that gave Portugal control over the land that is present-day Brazil. (p. 236)

Treaty of Waitangi *n.* the treaty signed by the British and Maori in 1840 giving Britain control over New Zealand. (p. 719)

tsunami (TSU•NAH•mee) *n.* a giant ocean wave, caused by an underwater earthquake or volcanic eruption, with great destructive power. (pp. 40, 662)

tuberculosis *n.* a respiratory infection spread by human contact, which often accompanies AIDS. (p. 466)

tundra *n.* the flat treeless lands forming a ring around the Arctic Ocean; the climate region of the Arctic Ocean. (p. 63)

typhoon *n.* a tropical storm, like a hurricane, that occurs in the western Pacific. (pp. 51, 625)

U

USSR *n.* the Union of Soviet Socialist Republics, or Soviet Union, formed in 1922 by the Communists and officially dissolved in 1991. (p. 363)

UNICEF (United Nations Children's Fund) *n.* an international watchdog and relief organization for children. (p. 665)

United Provinces of Central America *n.* the name of Central America after the region declared independence from Mexico in 1823. (p. 223)

upland *n.* a hill or very low mountain that may also contain mesas and high plateaus. (p. 275)

Ural Mountains *n.* the mountain ranges that separate the Northern European and West Siberian plains and used as the dividing line between Europe and Asia. (p. 346)

urban geography *n.* the study of how people use space in cities. (p. 87)

urbanization *n.* the dramatic rise in the number of cities and the changes in lifestyle that result. (p. 88)

urban sprawl *n.* poorly planned development that spreads a city's population over a wider and wider geographic area. (p. 176)

V

Vietnam War *n.* (1954–1975) the military conflict resulting from American involvement in South Vietnam to prevent its takeover by Communist North Vietnam. (p. 707)

volcano *n.* a natural event, formed when magma, gases, and water from the lower part of the crust or mantle collect in underground chambers and eventually erupt and pour out of cracks in the earth's surface. (p. 40)

voyaging canoe *n.* a large ship developed by Pacific Islanders to sail the ocean. (p. 699)

W

wadi *n.* a riverbed that remains dry except during the rainy seasons. (p. 488)

water table *n.* the level at which rock is saturated. (p. 33)

weather *n.* the condition of the atmosphere at a particular location and time. (p. 50)

weathering *n.* physical and chemical processes that change the characteristics of rock on or near the earth's surface, occurring slowly over many years. (p. 42)

West *n.* North American region, consisting of 13 states, that stretches from the Great Plains to the Pacific Ocean and includes Alaska to the north and Hawaii in the Pacific. (p. 148)

West Bank *n.* in Israel, a strip of land on the west side of the Jordan River, originally controlled by Jordan, which is part of the land set aside for Arab Palestinians. (p. 527)

Western Wall *n.* for Jews, the holiest site in Jerusalem; the only remaining portion of the Second Temple, built in 538 B.C. and destroyed in A.D. 70 by the Romans. (p. 510)

Wik Case *n.* in Australia, the court ruled in this case that Aboriginal people could claim land held under a pastoral lease. (p. 729)

winter monsoon *n.* the season when dry winds blow from the northeast across the Himalaya Mountains toward the sea from October through February, sometimes causing drought. (p. 597)

X

Xi Jiang (shee JYAHNG) *n.* also called the West River; the river that flows eastward through southeast China and joins the Pearl River (Zhu Jiang) to flow into the South China Sea, forming an estuary between Hong Kong and Macao. (p. 621)

Y

yurt *n.* a tent of Central Asia's nomads. (p. 379)

Z

Zionism *n.* a movement that began in the 19th century to reestablish a Jewish state in the Jewish homeland. (p. 511)

Zuider Zee (ZEYE•duhr ZAY) *n.* former inlet of the North Sea in the Netherlands. (p. 283)

R25

A

Aboriginal people [Aborígenes] *s.* gente que emigró a Australia desde Asia, hace al menos 40.000 años; los pobladores originales de la tierra. (p. 718)

absolute location [ubicación absoluta] *s.* el lugar exacto en la Tierra donde se encuentra un accidente geográfico. (p. 6)

acculturation [aculturación] *s.* el cambio cultural que ocurre cuando las personas en una sociedad aceptan o adoptan una innovación. (p. 72)

acquired immune deficiency syndrome (AIDS) [síndrome de inmunodeficiencia adquirida (SIDA)] *s.* enfermedad producida por el virus de la inmunodeficiencia humana o VIH. (p. 465)

Aksum [Aksum] *s.* una importante capital comercial desde el s. I al s. VIII de nuestra era, situada en lo que hoy es Etiopía; floreció debido a su ubicación junto al Mar Rojo y el Océano Índico. (p. 431)

alluvial plain [llanura aluvial] *s.* tierra fértil para la labranza, formada por depósitos de arcilla, limo, arena o grava producidos por las aguas corrientes. (p. 553)

Amazon River [Río Amazonas] *s.* el segundo río más largo del mundo y uno de los tres principales sistemas fluviales de América del Sur. Se extiende unas 4.000 millas (6.436 km) de oeste a este y desemboca en el Océano Atlántico. (p. 203)

Andes Mountains [Cordillera de los Andes] *s.* una larga cordillera que se extiende a lo largo de la costa del Pacífico de Centroamérica y América del Sur. (p. 201)

anti-Semitism [antisemitismo] *s.* discriminación contra los judíos. (p. 315)

apartheid [apartheid] (a-par-zeid) *s.* política de separación completa de las razas, implementada por el gobierno de la minoría blanca de Sudáfrica en 1948. (p. 454)

Appalachian Mountains [Montes Apalaches] *s.* una de las dos cordilleras más importantes en la región Este de los Estados Unidos y Canadá, que se extiende 1.600 millas (2.575 km) desde Terranova (Newfoundland) hacia el sur hasta Alabama. (p. 119)

aqueduct [acueducto] *s.* estructura para transportar agua por largas distancias. (p. 292)

aquifer [acuífero] *s.* capa subterránea de roca donde se almacena agua. (p. 421)

archipelago [archipiélago] *s.* grupo de islas cercanas. (pp. 553, 689)

ASEAN [ANSA] *s.* Asociación de Naciones del Sudeste Asiático, una alianza que promueve el desarrollo económico y la paz en la región. (p. 707)

Ashanti [Ashanti] *s.* gente que vive en lo que es ahora Ghana, en África Occidental, renombrada por sus diseños artísticos de ropa asasia o kente que usa la realeza. (p. 444)

assimilation [asimilación] *s.* proceso por el cual un grupo minoritario gradualmente se desprende de su propia cultura y adopta la cultura del grupo mayoritario. (p. 728)

Aswan High Dam [La gran presa de Asuán] *s.* presa en el río Nilo de Egipto, construida en 1970, la cual aumentó las tierras arables de Egipto en un 50 por ciento y las protegió contra las sequías y las inundaciones. (p. 426)

Atlantic Provinces [Las provincias atlánticas] *s.* las provincias en la región este del Canadá: Isla Príncipe Eduardo, Nueva Brunswick, Nueva Escocia y Terranova o Newfoundland. (p. 166)

atmosphere [atmósfera] *s.* las capas gaseosas que envuelven inmediatamente la Tierra. (p. 28)

atoll [atolón] *s.* isla coralina en forma anular o un conjunto de pequeñas islas que rodean una laguna central. (pp. 553, 700)

B

balkanization [balcanización] *s.* proceso por el cual una región se fragmenta en unidades pequeñas, mutuamente hostiles. (p. 311)

Baltic Republics [Países Bálticos] *s.* los países de Latvia, Lituania y Estonia, ubicados en la costa este del mar Báltico. (p. 361)

Bantu migration [migración bantú] *s.* desplazamiento de los pueblos bantú hacia el sur a través de África, que propagaron su lengua y su cultura desde alrededor del año 500 antes de nuestra era hasta alrededor del año 1000 de nuestra era. (p. 448)

basic necessity [necesidades básicas] *s.* alimentos, ropa y vivienda. (p. 593)

Benelux [Benelux] *s.* la unión económica de Bélgica, Países Bajos (Nederland) y Luxemburgo. (p. 296)

Beringia [Behring] *s.* puente de tierra que se cree conectaba lo que son ahora Siberia y Alaska. (p. 127)

Berlin Conference [Conferencia de Berlín] *s.* una conferencia de 14 países europeos realizada en 1884-1885 en Berlín, Alemania, para establecer normas de control político de África. (p. 432)

Berlin Wall [Muro de Berlín] *s.* muro construido por Alemania Oriental en 1961 para dividir la capital de Berlín en dos, derruido en 1989. (p. 298)

Bikini Atoll [Atolón Bikini] *s.* arrecife aislado en las Islas Marshall del Pacífico central, donde se efectuaron experimentos de bombas nucleares estadounidenses, lo que contaminó el atolón con altos niveles de radiación, y ahuyentó a sus habitantes. (p. 700)

biodiversity [biodiversidad] *s.* la variedad de organismos en un ecosistema. (p. 245)

biological weapon (arma biolûgica) *s.* bacteria o virus que se puede utilizar para daòar o matar personas, animales o plantas. (p. 175)

biome [bioma] *s.* un ecosistema regional. (p. 65)

biosphere [biósfera] *s.* todas las partes de la Tierra donde viven plantas y animales, incluyendo la atmósfera, la litosfera y la hidrosfera. (p. 28)

birthrate [índice de natalidad] *s.* el número de nacimientos vivos por total de la población, con frecuencia expresado por miles de habitantes. (p. 78)

blizzard [ventisca] *s.* tormenta de nieve fuerte con vientos de más de 35 millas (55 km) por hora y visibilidad reducida de menos de un cuarto de milla (0.40 km). (p. 52)

Boxer Rebellion [Guerra de los bóxers] *s.* rebelión en China en 1900, producida por militantes chinos enfurecidos, o bóxers, por el control extranjero; cientos de europeos, cristianos y chinos murieron. (p. 636)

British Columbia [Columbia Británica] *s.* la provincia más occidental de Canadá en las Montañas Rocosas. (p. 169)

Buddhism [Budismo] *s.* religión originda en la India por el año 500 antes de nuestra era, que se extendió hacia China, donde se convirtió en una religión importante alrededor del año 400 de nuestra era. (p. 638)

C

calypso [calypso] *s.* estilo de música que comenzó en Trinidad y combina elementos musicales de África, España y el Caribe. (p. 227)

Canadian Shield [escudo canadiense] *s.* parte norteña de las tierras bajas interiores que es una región rocosa y plana que cubre casi dos millones de millas cuadradas (cinco millones doscientos mil kilómetros cuadrados) y encierra la Bahía de Hudson. (p. 119)

canopy [bóveda] *s.* área que comprende la parte superior de los árboles en una selva tropical, a unos 150 pies (45 metros) sobre el suelo. (p. 422)

capoeira [capoeira] *s.* arte marcial y danza que desarrollaron en Brasil los angolanos que fueron llevados allí desde el África por los portugueses. (p. 239)

Carnival [Carnaval] *s.* el día de fiesta más llamativo de Brasil. (p. 239)

carrying capacity [capacidad de soporte] *s.* número de organismos que un pedazo de terreno puede soportar sin efectos negativos. (p. 82)

Carthage [Cartago] *s.* uno de los grandes imperios de África en la antigüedad, situado en una península triangular en el Golfo de Túnez en la costa del Mar Mediterráneo. (p. 438)

cartographer [cartógrafo] *s.* persona que levanta mapas. (p. 10)

cash crop [cultivo industrial o comercial] *s.* producto cultivado para la venta directa y no para uso en una región, como café, té y azúcar en África. (p. 433)

caste system [sistema de castas] *s.* el sistema ario de clases sociales en la India y uno de los pilares del hinduismo en el cual cada persona nace dentro de una casta y sólo puede pasar a otra casta mediante la reencarnación. (p. 571)

Caucasus [Cáucaso] *s.* región que comprende el sistema montañoso del mismo nombre y se extiende entre el mar Negro y el Caspio. (p. 385)

caudillo [caudillo] *s.* dictador militar o líder político. (p. 249)

Central Asia [Asia Central] *s.* región que incluye las repúblicas de Kazajstán, Kirguistán, Tayikistán, Turkmenistán y Uzbekistán. (p. 346)

central business district (CBD) [distrito comercial central (DCC)] *s.* el centro de una ciudad, en el cual casi siempre se desarrollan actividades comerciales. (p. 89)

cerrado [cerrado] *s.* una sabana que tiene terreno plano y lluvias moderadas, lo que la hace apta para la agricultura. (p. 202)

Chang Jiang [Chang Jiang] *s.* (o Río Yang-tsé) el río más largo del Asia, que fluye unas 3.900 millas (6.275 km) desde Xizang (Tibet) hasta el mar de la China oriental. (p. 621)

Chaparral [chaparral] *s.* término, en algunos lugares, para una bioma de árboles resistentes a la sequía. (p. 66)

Chechnya [Chechenia] *s.* una de las repúblicas que continúa siendo parte de Rusia después del colapso de la Unión Soviética a pesar de los movimientos independentistas y levantamientos violentos. (p. 386)

chemical weathering [meteorización química] *s.* proceso por el cual una roca se convierte en una nueva substancia a través de la interacción entre los elementos en el aire o el agua y los minerales en la roca. (p. 43)

chemozem [quimiozen] *s.* capa superior negra del suelo, una de las tierras más fértiles del mundo. (p. 345)

cholera [cólera] *s.* enfermedad infecciosa tratable que puede ser mortal y es producida por la falta de medidas higiénicas adecuadas y de suministro de agua limpia. (p. 465)

city [ciudad] *s.* zona que es el centro de los negocios y la cultura y tiene una población numerosa. (p. 87)

city-state [ciudad-estado] *s.* una unidad política autónoma compuesta por una ciudad y los terrenos circundantes. (p. 289)

climate [clima] *s.* las condiciones atmosféricas típicas de un lugar específico que se observan con el tiempo. (p. 50)

coalition (coaliciûn) *s.* alianza. (p. 174)

Cold War [Guerra Fría] *s.* el conflicto entre los Estados Unidos y la Unión Soviética después de la II Guerra Mundial, llamada "fría" porque nunca se intensificó hasta el grado de convertirse en una guerra abierta. (p. 363)

collective farm [granja colectiva] *s.* un gran equipo de peones reunidos para trabajar juntos en enormes granjas en la Unión Soviética, durante el gobierno de Jósiv Stalin. (p. 364)

Columbian Exchange [Intercambio Colombino] *s.* el intercambio de plantas, animales y enfermedades entre el hemisferio oriental y el hemisferio occidental durante la era de las exploraciones. (p. 136)

command economy [economía dirigida] *s.* tipo de sistema económico en el cual la producción de bienes y servicios es determinada por un gobierno central, el cual usualmente es dueño de los medios de producción. Llamado también "economía planificada". (pp. 91, 364)

commodity [bien de consumo] *s.* un producto agrícola o de minería que se puede vender. (p. 462)

communism [comunismo] *s.* sistema en el cual el gobierno retiene casi todo el poder político y los medios de producción. (p. 83)

confederation [confederación] *s.* una unión política. (p. 156)

Confucianism [Confucianismo] *s.* movimiento basado en las enseñanzas de Confucio, filósofo chino que vivió alrededor del año 500 antes de nuestra era; Confucio enfatizaba la importancia de la educación en una sociedad ordenada en la cual las personas respetan a sus mayores y obedecen al gobierno. (p. 638)

coniferous [conífero] adj. otro término para los árboles de hojas perennes y aciculares. (p. 66)

constitutional monarchy [monarquía constitucional] *s.* sistema de gobierno en el cual los poderes del gobernante están limitados por una constitución y las leyes de la nación. (p. 580)

continent [continente] *s.* una masa de tierra firme sobre el agua en la Tierra. (p. 27)

Continental Divide [La Divisoria Continental] *s.* la línea de los picos más altos en América del Norte que marca la separación entre los ríos que fluyen hacia el este y hacia el oeste. (p. 120)

continental drift [deriva de los continentes] *s.* la hipótesis de que los continentes fueron una vez un supercontinente que se dividió lentamente a través de millones de años. (p. 29)

continentality [continentalidad] *s.* la distancia de una región de la influencia moderadora del mar. (p. 350)

continental shelf [plataforma continental] *s.* la superficie de la Tierra desde el borde de un continente hasta la parte profunda del océano. (p. 36)

convection [convección] *s.* la transferencia de calor en la atmósfera por el movimiento ascendente del aire. (p. 54)

copra [copra] *s.* la pulpa seca del coco. (p. 714)

core [centro] *s.* el núcleo de la Tierra, compuesto de hierro y niquel; el centro interior es sólido, el centro exterior es líquido. (p. 28)

crude oil [petróleo crudo] *s.* petróleo que no ha sido procesado. (p. 497)

Crusades [Cruzadas] *s.* una serie de guerras impulsadas por los cristianos europeos en 1096 para recuperar la Tierra Santa (Palestina) de los musulmanes. (p. 291)

crust [corteza] *s.* la capa delgada de rocas que compone la superficie de la Tierra. (p. 28)

cultural crossroad [cruce cultural] *s.* un lugar donde convergen varias culturas. (p. 310)

cultural hearth [centro cultural] *s.* el centro o lugar de origen de una cultura importante; un lugar de innovaciones desde el cual se difunden ideas, materiales y tecnologías fundamentales a otras culturas. (pp. 72, 222)

culture [cultura] *s.* el total de conocimientos, actitudes y comportamientos compartidos y transmitidos por los miembros de un grupo. (p. 71)

cyclone [ciclón] *s.* una tormenta violenta con vientos fuertes y mucha lluvia; el patrón climatológico más extremo del Asia Meridional. (p. 558)

czar [zar] *s.* el emperador de Rusia antes de la Revolución de 1917 y de la subsiguiente creación de la Unión Soviética en 1922. (p. 362)

D

Dead Sea [Mar Muerto] *s.* lago salado, sin salida al mar, entre Israel y Jordania, con un nivel de salinidad tan alto que casi nada puede vivir en sus aguas; se encuentra a 1.349 pies (411 m) por debajo del nivel del mar, lo que lo convierte en el lugar más bajo en la corteza expuesta de la Tierra. (p. 489)

debt-for-nature swap [Intercambio de deuda por naturaleza] *s.* acuerdo para reducir una deuda por el cual una organización acepta pagar cierta cantidad de una deuda gubernamental a cambio de protección gubernamental de cierta parte de una selva tropical. (p. 247)

deciduous [caducifolio] adj. característica de los árboles de hojas anchas, como el arce, el roble, el abedul y el Alamo de Virginia. (p. 66)

deforestation [deforestación] *s.* el corte y la eliminación de árboles y bosques. (p. 246)

delta [delta] *s.* zona de forma de abanico formada por sedimentos depositados dejados por un río que disminuye su velocidad al desembocar en el océano. (p. 43)

democracy [democracia] *s.* tipo de gobierno en el cual los ciudadanos ejercen el poder político sea directamente o mediante representantes elegidos. (p. 83)

desalinization [desalinización] *s.* la eliminación de sal del agua del océano. (p. 496)

desertification [desertización] *s.* ampliación de condiciones secas a zonas húmedas que se encuentran próximas a desiertos. (p. 424)

dialect [dialecto] *s.* una versión de un idioma que refleja cambios en patrones de habla por factores relacionados con cambios de clase, regionales o culturales. (p. 73)

dictatorship [dictadura] *s.* tipo de gobierno en el cual un individuo o grupo de individuos tienen el poder político completo. (p. 83)

diffusion [difusión] *s.* la diseminación de ideas, invenciones o patrones de comportamiento hacia otras sociedades. (p. 72)

dike [dique] *s.* muro de tierra usado para contener o desviar el curso de las aguas. (p. 282)

distance decay [deterioro de la distancia] *s.* término que se refiere al concepto de que a mayor distancia entre dos puntos, menor interacción entre los mismos. (p. 389)

diversify [diversificar] *v.* aumentar la variedad de productos en la economía de un país; promover la industria fabril y otras industrias con el propósito de lograr el desarrollo y la estabilidad. (p. 462)

Dome of the Rock [Cúpula de la Roca] *s.* un santuario en Jerusalén, ubicado en el monte del Templo, que contiene el lugar donde los musulmanes creen que Mahoma se elevó a los cielos y donde los judíos creen que Abraham preparó el sacrificio de su hijo Isaac a Dios. (p. 511)

Dominion of Canada [Dominio de Canadá] *s.* la amplia confederación de Ontario (Alto Canadá), Quebec (Bajo Canadá), Nueva Escocia y Nuevo Brunswick, creada por el Acta de la América del Norte Británica en 1867. (p. 156)

drainage basin [cuenca de drenaje] *s.* una zona drenada por un río importante y sus afluentes. (p. 33)

drip irrigation [irrigación por goteo] *s.* la práctica de usar tubos pequeños que lentamente gotean agua justo sobre el suelo para conservar agua para usarse en los cultivos. (p. 496)

drought [sequía] *s.* un largo período sin lluvia o con precipitación mínima. (p. 53)

dynasty [dinastía] *s.* una serie de gobernantes de la misma familia. (p. 635)

E

earthquake [terremoto] *s.* un movimiento a veces violento de la tierra, producido cuando placas tectónicas se tocan o deslizan una sobre otra en una falla. (p. 39)

economic system [sistema económico] *s.* la forma como la gente produce e intercambia bienes. (p. 91)

economic tiger [tigre económico] *s.* un país con rápido crecimiento económico debido al bajo coste de la mano de obra, la alta tecnología y las exportaciones agresivas. (p. 645)

economy [economía] *s.* la producción y el intercambio de bienes y servicios entre un grupo de personas. (p. 91)

ecosystem [ecosistema] *s.* una comunidad interdependiente de plantas y animales. (p. 65)

El Niño [El Niño] *s.* un patrón meteorológico creado por el calentamiento de las aguas de las costas occidentales de América del Sur, que empuja aguas cálidas y fuertes lluvias hacia el continente americano y produce condiciones de sequía en Australia y Asia. (p. 57)

entrepreneur [empresario] *s.* persona que inicia y desarrolla un negocio. (p. 575)

epicenter [epicentro] *s.* el punto en la superficie terrestre que corresponde a la ubicación en la Tierra donde comienza un terremoto. (p. 39)

equator [ecuador] *s.* la línea imaginaria que rodea la esfera terrestre, dividiendo la Tierra en las mitades norte y sur. (p. 6)

equinox [equinoccio] *s.* cada uno de los dos días del año en los cuales el día y la noche tienen la misma duración; marca el comienzo de la primavera y el otoño. (p. 49)

erosion [erosión] *s.* el resultado del desgaste de la materia producido por la acción del viento, el agua, el hielo o la gravedad. (p. 43)

escarpment [escarpa] *s.* declive empinado de un terreno con una meseta casi plana en la cima. (p. 417)

estuary [estuario] *s.* desembocadura de un río con una amplia apertura por donde las corrientes del río chocan con las mareas del océano. (p. 563)

ethnic cleansing [limpieza étnica] *s.* la política de tratar de eliminar a un grupo étnico. (p. 320)

ethnic group [grupo étnico] *s.* un grupo de personas que comparten un idioma, costumbres y una herencia común. (p. 71)

Euphrates River [Río Éufrates] *s.* un río en el Sudoeste asiático que sirvió de apoyo a varias civilizaciones antiguas, fluye a través de regiones de Turquía, Siria e Irak y desemboca en el Golfo Pérsico. (p. 489)

Eurasia [Eurasia] *s.* los continentes combinados de Europa y Asia. (p. 346)

euro [euro] *s.* moneda común propuesta por la Unión Europea para sus naciones miembros. (p. 305)

European Environmental Agency [Agencia Europea del Medio Ambiente] *s.* esta agencia proporciona a la Unión Europea información confiable sobre el medio ambiente. (p. 324)

Everglades [Everglades] *s.* una amplia zona de terrenos pantanosos subtropicales en la Florida, de cerca de 4.000 millas cuadradas (10.400 kilómetros cuadrados). (p. 126)

export [exportación] *s.* un producto o bien que se vende desde una economía a otra. (p. 140)

F

Fang sculpture [esculturas de los fangs] *s.* cajas talladas que contienen las calaveras y los huesos de los antepasados muertos, creadas por los fangs, que vivieron en Gabón, la región sur de Camerún y Guinea Ecuatorial. (p. 451)

fault [falla] *s.* una fractura en la corteza terrestre. (p. 39)

folk art [arte folclórico] *s.* artículos hechos a mano, como cerámica, objetos tallados en madera y trajes tradicionales, elaborados por habitantes de zonas rurales que llevan estilos de vida tradicionales, no por artistas profesionales. (p. 314)

federal republic [república federal] *s.* una nación cuyos poderes están divididos entre el gobierno federal o nacional y varios gobiernos estatales o locales. (p. 139)

feudalism [feudalismo] *s.* un sistema político imperante en Europa entre el *s.* IX y el *s.* XV, en el cual el rey permitía a los nobles el uso de sus tierras a cambio de servicios militares y la protección de la tierra. (p. 297)

fertility rate [índice de fertilidad] *s.* el número promedio de hijos que una mujer en edad fértil tendría durante su vida si tuviese hijos de acuerdo con el índice vigente para su país. (p. 78)

First Nations [Primeras Naciones] *s.* un grupo de indígenas del Canadá. (p. 159)

fjord [fiordo] *s.* una entrada larga, estrecha y profunda del mar en la tierra entre pendientes empinadas. (p. 273)

fossil water [agua fósil] *s.* agua bombeada desde acuíferos subterráneos. (p. 496)

free enterprise [libre empresa] *s.* sistema económico en el cual individuos privados son dueños de la mayor parte de los recursos, la tecnología y las empresas, y pueden explotarlos para obtener ganancias con poco control del gobierno. (p. 140)

frontier [frontera] *s.* la tierra libre y abierta en el Oeste Norteamericano que estaba disponible para colonización. (p. 137)

G

Ganges River [Río Ganges] *s.* río en el Sur de Asia, un importante recurso acuático que fluye más de 1.500 millas (2.415 km) desde su fuente en un glaciar del Himalaya hasta la Bahía de Bengala. (p. 560)

Gaza Strip [Franja de Gaza] *s.* territorio a lo largo del Mar Mediterráneo, justo al noreste de la Península del Sinaí; parte del territorio asignado a los palestinos y que fue ocupado por Israel en 1967. (p. 527)

Geographic Information System (GIS) [Sistema de Información Geográfica (GIS por sus siglas en inglés)] *s.* tecnología que usa información de mapas digitalizados para crear un banco de datos; diferentes "capas de datos" pueden combinarse para producir mapas especializados. El GIS permite a los geógrafos analizar diferentes aspectos de un lugar específico para resolver problemas. (p. 13)

geography [geografía] *s.* estudio de la distribución y la interacción de las características físicas y humanas de la Tierra. (p. 5)

glaciation [glaciación] *s.* cambios en los accidentes geográficos debidos al lento movimiento de los glaciares. (p. 44)

glacier [glaciar] *s.* una masa de hielo grande y duradera que se mueve debido al efecto de la gravedad. (p. 44)

global economy [economía global] *s.* la fusión de economías regionales por la cual las naciones se vuelven dependientes unas de otras para la producción de bienes y servicios. (p. 666)

global network (red mundial) *s.* grupo que se mantiene conectado alrededor del mundo. (p. 173)

global warming [calentamiento global] *s.* la acumulación de dióxido de carbono (anhídrido carbónico) en la atmósfera, lo que evita que el calor escape al espacio, aumentando las temperaturas y ocasionando cambios en las condiciones meteorológicas. (p. 246)

globe [globo] *s.* una representación tridimensional de la Tierra. (p. 10)

Gobi Desert [Desierto de Gobi] *s.* desierto ubicado en el norte de China y en el sudeste de Mongolia, zona importante para la localización de fósiles de dinosaurios. (p. 627)

Golan Heights [Altos del Golán] *s.* meseta montañosa que se eleva sobre el Río Jordán y el Mar de Galilea; un punto estratégico que ha sido sitio de conflictos en el Sudoeste asiático durante décadas. (p. 487)

Gorée Island [Isla de Gorée] *s.* isla en las costas de Senegal que sirvió como importante punto de partida de esclavos durante el tráfico de esclavos. (p. 442)

Great Barrier Reef [La Gran Barrera de Coral] *s.* una cadena de 1.250 millas (2.000 km) de más de 2.500 arrecifes e islas a lo largo de la costa noreste de Australia, que contiene unas 400 especies de coral. (p. 692)

Great Game [El Gran Juego] *s.* un conflicto entre el Imperio Británico y el Imperio Ruso por el control del Asia Central en el *s.* XIX. (p. 376)

Great Kanto Earthquake [El Gran Terremoto de Kanto] *s.* terremoto ocurrido en 1923 en Japón que causó la muerte de aproximadamente 140.000 personas y dejó la ciudad de Tokio en ruinas. (p. 662)

Great Lakes [Grandes Lagos] *s.* grupo de cinco lagos de agua dulce en la región central de América del Norte entre los Estados Unidos y Canadá; los lagos son el Hurón, el Ontario, el Michigan, el Erie y el Superior. (p. 121)

Great Plains [Grandes Llanuras] *s.* una amplia zona de praderas en la región central de América del Norte, carente de árboles en su mayor parte, que se eleva hasta 4.000 pies (1.200 metros) sobre el nivel del mar. (p. 119)

Great Zimbabwe [El Gran Zimbabwe] *s.* un emplazamiento urbano en lo que es hoy Zimbabwe fundado por los shonas alrededor del año 1000; se convirtió en la capital de una próspera zona de comercio de oro. (p. 453)

greenhouse effect [efecto invernadero] *s.* la capa de gases emitidos por la quema de carbón y petróleo que atrapa la energía solar, elevando la temperatura de la Tierra. (p. 58)

Green Revolution [La Revolución Verde] *s.* programa agrícola lanzado por científicos en la década de 1960 para producir variedades de granos de mayor rendimiento y mejorar la producción de alimentos incorporando nuevas técnicas de labranza. (p. 569)

Gross Domestic Product (GDP) [Producto Interior Bruto (PIB)] *s.* el valor de sólo bienes y servicios producidos en un país durante un período determinado. (p. 95)

Gross National Product (GNP) [Producto Nacional Bruto (PNB)] *s.* el valor total de todos los bienes y servicios producidos por un país durante un período determinado. (p. 94)

ground water [agua subterránea] *s.* agua retenida debajo de la superficie terrestre, con frecuencia en y alrededor de los poros de las rocas. (p. 33)

guest worker [trabajador invitado] *s.* trabajadores poco calificados, a menudo inmigrantes del Sur y el Este de Asia, trasladados a los países productores de petróleo para ocupar puestos de trabajo que las personas nacidas en la región consideran cultural y económicamente inaceptables. (p. 525)

H

hemisphere [hemisferio] *s.* cada una de las dos mitades de la esfera terrestre. (p. 6)

high islands [Islas altas] *s.* islas del Pacífico creadas por volcanes. (p. 691)

Himalaya Mountains [Himalaya] *s.* cordillera del Sur de Asia que incluye el Monte Everest, el pico más alto del mundo. (p. 551)

Hinduism [Hinduismo] *s.* la religión dominante en la India. (p. 560)

Holocaust [Holocausto] *s.* programa de los nazis de asesinatos masivos de judíos europeos durante la II Guerra Mundial. (p. 298)

Huang He [Huang He] *s.* río del Norte de China, llamado también Río Amarillo, que nace en las Montañas Kunlun y se extiende unas 3.000 millas (4,800 km) hacia el Este, desembocando en el mar Amarillo. (p. 621)

human resources [recursos humanos] *s.* las aptitudes y los talentos de la gente que trabaja. (p. 531)

humus [humus] *s.* material orgánico en el suelo. (p. 45)

hurricane [huracán] *s.* una tormenta que se forma sobre las aguas cálidas de los océanos tropicales. (p. 51)

hydrologic cycle [ciclo hidrológico] *s.* la continua circulación de agua entre la atmósfera, los océanos y la Tierra. (p. 32)

hydrosphere [hidrosfera] *s.* las aguas que comprenden la superficie de la Tierra, incluyendo océanos, mares, ríos, lagos y el vapor en la atmósfera. (p. 28)

I

Ijsselmeer [Ijsselmeer] *s.* lago de agua dulce separado del Mar del Norte por un dique y bordeado por pólders. (p. 283)

illiteracy [analfabetismo] *s.* la incapacidad de leer o escribir. (p. 593)

Inca [Inca] *s.* miembro del pueblo quechua en América del Sur, que desarrolló una civilización en los Andes en los siglos XV y XVI. (p. 230)

Indochina [Indochina] *s.* colonia francesa compuesta por Camboya, Laos y Vietnam; obtuvo la independencia de Francia en 1954. (p. 707)

R29

industrialization [industrialización] *s.* el desarrollo de la industria en un país o en una sociedad. (p. 730)

Indus Valley civilization [Civilización del Valle del Indo] *s.* la más grande de las primeras civilizaciones del mundo en lo que hoy es Pakistán; fue una civilización urbana altamente desarrollada, que duró desde el 2500 hasta cerca del 1500 antes de nuestra era. (p. 573)

infant mortality rate [índice de mortalidad infantil] *s.* el número de muertes de niños menores de un año, calculado por cada mil nacimientos vivos. (p. 79)

infrastructure [infraestructura] *s.* los sistemas básicos de apoyo necesarios para mantener una economía en desarrollo, que incluyen sistemas de suministro de energía, comunicaciones, transporte, aguas, servicios sanitarios y educación. (pp. 94, 177, 212)

innovation [innovación] *s.* tomar los elementos existentes en una sociedad para crear algo nuevo con el propósito de satisfacer una necesidad. (p. 72)

Institutional Revolutionary Party (PRI) [Partido Revolucionario Institucional (PRI)] *s.* partido político creado en México, en 1929, que ayudó a introducir la democracia y mantener la estabilidad política durante la mayor parte del siglo XX. (p. 218)

Islam [Islam] *s.* religión monoteísta basada en las enseñanzas del profeta Mahoma y la mayor influencia cultural y religiosa en el Norte de África. (pp. 439, 503)

J

Jakota Triangle [Triángulo de Jakota] *s.* zona de prosperidad en la década de 1980 y comienzos de la década de 1990, que comprende Japón, Corea del Sur y Taiwán. (p. 666)

Jordan River [Río Jordán] *s.* río que sirve como frontera natural entre Israel y Jordania, y fluye desde los montes de Líbano sin desembocar en el Mar Mediterráneo. (p. 489)

junta [junta] *s.* gobierno dirigido por generales después de un golpe militar. (p. 249)

K

Kashmir [Cachemira (Kashmir)] *s.* región del Norte de la India y Pakistán sobre la que se han librado varias guerras destructivas. (p. 574)

Khmer Empire [Imperio Khmer] *s.* poderoso imperio que duró aproximadamente del siglo IX al siglo XV, en lo que hoy es Camboya. (p. 706)

King Leopold II [Rey Leopoldo II] *s.* rey de Bélgica que abrió el interior del África al comercio europeo a lo largo del río Congo y para 1884 controlaba la zona conocida como el Estado Libre del Congo. (p. 449)

KLA (Kosovo Liberation Army) [ELK (Ejército de Liberación de Kosovo)] *s.* grupo que combatió contra los intentos de los serbios de controlar la región de Kosovo en la década de 1990. (p. 321)

Kunlun Mountains [Cordillera Kunlun] *s.* cordillera ubicada en el Oeste de China que es la fuente de dos de los principales ríos de China, el Huang He (río Amarillo) y el Chang Jiang (Yangtzé) (p. 619)

Kurds [Kurdos] *s.* grupo étnico en el sudoeste de Asia, que ha ocupado la región de Kurdistán, ubicada en Turquía, Irac e Irán, por cerca de mil años, y que ha estado involucrado en enfrentamientos con estos tres países por recobrar tierras durante la mayor parte del siglo XX. (p. 516)

L

landfill [vertedero] *s.* método de eliminación de residuos sólidos por el cual los residuos son enterrados entre capas de tierra con el propósito de rellenar o recuperar terrenos bajos. (p. 631)

landform [accidente geográfico] *s.* una característica de la superficie terrestre formada naturalmente. (p. 33)

landlocked [sin litoral] adj. que no tiene salida al mar. (p. 84)

land reform [reforma agraria] *s.* proceso por el cual se dividen grandes latifundios con el propósito de lograr una distribución más equitativa de la tierra entre los agricultores. (pp. 250, 569)

Land Rights Act of 1976 [Ley de Derechos de Tierra de 1976] *s.* una ley especial promulgada en beneficio de los derechos de los aborígenes en Australia, dándoles el derecho de reclamar tierras en el Territorio Norte. (p. 728)

Landsat [Landsat] *s.* una serie de satélites que orbitan a más de 100 millas (160 km) sobre la Tierra. Cada satélite recoge información en una zona de 115 millas (185 km) de ancho. (p. 12)

latitude (lines) [latitudes (líneas)] *s.* un conjunto de líneas imaginarias que corren paralelas al ecuador, las cuales son usadas para localizar lugares al Norte y al Sur. El ecuador es denominado la línea de cero grados de latitud. (p. 6)

lava [lava] *s.* magma que ha llegado hasta la superficie terrestre. (p. 40)

lithosphere [litosfera] *s.* la capa de roca sólida de la superficie terrestre. (p. 28)

llanos [llanos] *s.* una extensa zona de praderas sin árboles de América del Sur, utilizada para pastoreo y labranza. (p. 202)

lock [esclusa] *s.* una sección de una vía acuática con puertas de entrada y salida donde se llenan o vacían de agua los espacios entre las mismas, a través de las cuales pasan los barcos. (p. 129)

loess [loess] *s.* sedimentos de limo o arcilla depositados por el viento que producen tierras muy fértiles. (p. 44)

longitude (lines) [longitud (líneas)] *s.* un conjunto de líneas imaginarias que circundan la Tierra por los polos, dividiéndola en las zonas Este y Oeste. El primer meridiano (meridiano de Greenwich) ha sido designado como la línea de cero grados para longitud. (p. 6)

Louisiana Purchase [La Compra de Louisiana] *s.* el territorio, incluyendo la región entre el río Mississippi y las Montañas Rocosas, que los Estados Unidos compró a Francia en 1803. (p. 136)

low islands [Islas bajas] *s.* islas del Pacífico formadas por arrecifes de coral. (p. 691)

M

***Mabo* Case** [el caso *Mabo*] *s.* en Australia, el proceso jurídico por el cual se declaró con lugar la reclamación de tierra del aborigen Eddie Mabo, por medio del cual el tribunal reconoció que los aborígenes eran dueños de tierras antes de la llegada de los británicos. (p. 728)

Mackenzie River [Río Mackenzie] *s.* el río más largo del Canadá, el cual es parte de un sistema fluvial que fluye a lo largo de los Territorios del Noroeste hasta el Océano Ártico. (p. 121)

magma [magma] *s.* material de roca fundida creada cuando roca sólida en el manto o corteza funde. (p. 28)

malaria [malaria] *s.* enfermedad infecciosa de los glóbulos rojos propagada por mosquitos, que se caracteriza por escalofríos, fiebre y sudor. (p. 466)

mandala [mandala] *s.* diseño geométrico usado en el budismo tibetano como símbolo del universo y que ayuda en la meditación. (p. 583)

mandala [mandala] *s.* un estado organizado como un anillo de poder alrededor de una corte central, que con frecuencia cambiaba de tamaño con el tiempo y que era usado en lugar de fronteras en los antiguos estados del sudeste asiático. (p. 705)

mantle [manto] *s.* una capa de roca de unas 1.800 millas (2.896 km) que está entre la corteza y el centro de la Tierra. (p. 28)

Maori [Maori] *s.* los primeros pobladores de Nueva Zelanda, que emigraron de Polinesia hace más de 1.000 años. (p. 719)

Mao Zedong [Mao Zedong] *s.* líder de China comunista que derrotó a los Nacionalistas en 1949; falleció en 1976. (p. 636)

map projection [proyección cartográfica] *s.* una forma de trazar el mapa de la superficie de la Tierra que reduce la distorsión causada convirtiendo tres dimensiones en dos dimensiones. (p. 10)

map [mapa] *s.* representación gráfica bidimensional de partes selectas de la superficie de la Tierra. (p. 10)

maquiladora [maquiladora] *s.* fábrica en México que ensambla materiales importados para convertirlos en productos acabados de exportación. (p. 220)

market economy [economía de mercado] *s.* tipo de sistema económico en el cual la producción de bienes y servicios se determina por la demanda de los consumidores. Llamado también economía de demanda o capitalismo. (pp. 91, 313)

Massif Central [Massif Central] *s.* las tierras altas de Francia, que abarcan un sexto del territorio francés. (p. 275)

Mecca [Meca] *s.* la ciudad más sagrada del Islam, situada en Arabia Saudita, a la que la gente hace peregrinaciones para cumplir con deberes religiosos islámicos. (p. 503)

mechanical weathering [meteorización mecánica] *s.* proceso natural por el cual las rocas se descomponen en pedazos más pequeños. (p. 42)

megalopolis [megalópolis] *s.* una región en la cual varias ciudades grandes y las áreas circundantes se unen. (p. 146)

Melanesia [Melanesia] *s.* región en Oceanía que significa "islas negras." (p. 713)

Meseta [Meseta] *s.* la planicie central de España. (p. 275)

Mesopotamia [Mesopotamia] *s.* una región en el sudoeste asiático entre los ríos Tigris y Eufrates, donde se desarrollaron algunas de las civilizaciones más antiguas del mundo; parte del corazón cultural denominado la Media Luna de las tierras fértiles. (p. 516)

métis [métis] *s.* una persona con antepasados franco-canadienses e indígenas americanos. (p. 161)

metropolitan area [área metropolitana] *s.* área funcional que incluye una ciudad y los suburbios y exurbios que la rodean, económicamente ligados entre sí. (pp. 87, 148)

microcredit [microcrédito] *s.* un pequeño préstamo disponible a los empresarios de escasos recursos para ayudar a las empresas pequeñas a desarrollarse y elevar los niveles de vida. (p. 575)

Micronesia [Micronesia] *s.* una de las tres regiones de Oceanía, el nombre significa "islas pequeñas". (p. 713)

Midwest [El Medio-Oeste] *s.* la región que contiene los 12 estados de la zona Norte-Central de los Estados Unidos. (p. 147)

migration [migración] *s.* el desplazamiento de gente dentro de un mismo país o región. (p. 135)

Mississippi River [Río Mississippi] *s.* un importante río que fluye de norte a sur por casi todo el largo de los Estados Unidos, desde Minnesota hasta el Golfo de México y forma parte del sistema fluvial más largo del continente. (p. 121)

mistral [mistral] *s.* viento frío y seco del norte. (p. 279)

Mobutu Sese Seko [Mobutu Sese Seko] *s.* líder de Zaire, la actual República Democrática del Congo, desde su independencia en la década de 1960 hasta 1997. Puso los negocios del país bajo el control nacional, se benefició de la reorganización y utilizó el ejército para conservar el poder. (p. 450)

monarchy [monarquía] *s.* tipo de gobierno en el cual una familia gobernante dirigida por un rey o una reina, tiene el poder y puede o no compartirlo con organismos ciudadanos. (p. 83)

monsoon [monzón] *s.* viento estacional, especialmente en el Asia meridional. (p. 558)

moraine [morrena] *s.* una cadena o colina de rocas transportada y finalmente depositada por un glaciar. (p. 44)

mortality rate [índice de mortalidad] *s.* el número de muertes por cada mil. (p. 79)

mosque [mezquita] *s.* un lugar de culto islámico, donde los mahometanos rezan con el rostro orientado hacia la ciudad sagrada de la Meca. (p. 504)

Mount Kilimanjaro [Monte Kilimanjaro] *s.* un volcán en Tanzania en el Africa, es el pico más alto del Africa. (p. 417)

Mughal Empire [Imperio Mughal] *s.* el imperio musulmán establecido a comienzos del siglo XVI y que se extendió por gran parte de la India, importando nuevas costumbres que algunas veces entraban en conflicto con las de los hindúes nativos. (p. 568)

Muhammad [Mahoma] *s.* fundador y profeta del Islam, que vivió parte de su vida en la ciudad de la Meca. (p. 503)

multinational [multinacional] *s.* una compañía que realiza operaciones comerciales en todo el mundo. (p. 142)

Mutapa Empire [Imperio de Monomotapa] *s.* un estado fundado en el siglo XV por un hombre llamado Mutota y que se extendió por todo lo que hoy es Zimbabwe excepto su parte oriental. (p. 453)

N

Nagomo-Karabakh [Nagorno-Karabakh] *s.* la zona montañosa de Azerbaiján, por la cual combatieron Armenia y Azerbaiján. (p. 386)

nation [nación] *s.* un grupo de personas con una cultura común que viven en un territorio y tienen un fuerte sentimiento de unidad. (p. 83)

nationalism [nacionalismo] *s.* la creencia de que la gente tiene que ser leal con su nación y con las demás personas con la que comparte la tierra, la cultura y la historia. (p. 297)

nation-state [nación-estado] *s.* nombre de un territorio cuando una nación y un estado ocupan el mismo territorio. (p. 83)

natural resource [recurso natural] *s.* un material sobre o dentro de la Tierra, como un árbol, un pez o el carbón, que tiene valor económico. (p. 93)

needleleaf [acicular] adj. característica de las hojas de ciertos árboles como el pino, el abeto y el cedro, que se encuentran en las regiones del norte de América del Norte. (p. 66)

Nelson Mandela [Nelson Mandela] *s.* uno de los líderes del Congreso Nacional Africano que dirigió la lucha contra el apartheid y fue elegido presidente en 1994, en las primeras elecciones multirraciales de Sudáfrica. (p. 454)

New England [Nueva Inglaterra] *s.* los seis estados del norte en la región noreste de los Estados Unidos: Maine, Vermont, New Hampshire, Massachusetts, Rhode Island y Connecticut. (p. 145)

Niger delta [Delta del Níger] *s.* delta del río Níger y zona de Nigeria rica en depósitos de petróleo. (p. 424)

Nile River [Río Nilo] *s.* el río más largo del mundo, que recorre más de 4.000 millas (6.436 km) a través de la cuenca del Sudán, hasta Uganda, el Sudán y Egipto. (p. 416)

nomad [nómada] *s.* persona que no tiene residencia permanente y se traslada según las estaciones de un lugar a otro en busca de alimentos, agua y tierra para pastoreo. (p. 127, 378)

nonviolent resistance [resistencia pacífica] *s.* un movimiento que usa todos los medios de protesta excepto la violencia. (p. 568)

Nordic countries [países nórdicos] *s.* países del norte de Europa, entre ellos Dinamarca, Finlandia, Islandia, Noruega y Suecia. (p. 302)

NAFTA (North American Free Trade Agreement) [NAFTA (Tratado de Libre Comercio de América del Norte)] *s.* un acuerdo comercial importante que creó una amplia zona de cooperación sobre asuntos comerciales y económicos en América del Norte. (p. 220)

North Atlantic Drift [Corriente del Atlántico Norte] *s.* una corriente de agua cálida proveniente de los Trópicos. (p. 278)

Nunavut [Nunavut] *s.* uno de los territories del Canadá, donde viven muchos de los esquimales del Canadá; fue forjado de la mitad este de los Territorios Noroestes en 1999. (p. 169)

O

oasis [oasis] *s.* un lugar donde agua de un acuífero ha llegado hasta la superficie; permite el desarrollo de vegetación y fauna. (pp. 421, 492)

Oceania [Oceanía] *s.* grupo de islas del Pacífico, que incluye Melanesia, Micronesia y Polinesia. (p. 690)

Olduvai Gorge [Garganta Olduvai] *s.* un lugar de capas fosilíferas en el norte de Tanzania, que contiene el historial más continuo que se conoce de vida humana en los últimos 2 millones de años, incluyendo fósiles de 65 homínidos. (p. 431)

oligarchy [oligarquía] *s.* un gobierno dirigido por unas cuantas personas o un pequeño grupo. (p. 249)

"one-commodity" country [país de "un solo producto"] *s.* país que depende de un producto de exportación principal para muchos de sus ingresos. (p. 462)

Ontario [Ontario] *s.* una de las Provincias más importantes del Canadá. (p. 167)

OPEC [OPEP] *s.* Organización de Países Exportadores de Petróleo, grupo establecido en 1960 por algunos países productores de petróleo para coordinar políticas sobre venta de productos de petróleo. (p. 505)

Orinoco River [Río Orinoco] *s.* río que corre principalmente por Venezuela y forma parte del sistema fluvial más hacia el norte de América del Sur. (p. 202)

outback ["outback"] *s.* zona seca y despoblada en el interior de Australia. (p. 697)

outrigger canoe [canoa con balancines] *s.* una embarcación pequeña usada en las lagunas de islas en las que se establecieron isleños del Pacífico. (p. 699)

ozone [ozono] *s.* una substancia química que se produce cuando combustibles fósiles en combustión reaccionan con la luz del sol; una forma de oxígeno. (p. 325)

P

Pacific Rim [Cuenca del Pacífico] *s.* una región económica y social que incluye los países que rodean el Océano Pacífico, la cual se extiende en el sentido de las manecillas del reloj desde Nueva Zelanda en la región occidental del Pacífico hasta Chile en la región oriental del Pacífico e incluye la costa oeste de los Estados Unidos. (p. 645)

pakehas [pakehas] *s.* término maorí para designar a las personas blancas, a los neozelandeses de ascendencia europea. (p. 722)

Palestine Liberation Organization (PLO) [Organización para la Liberación de Palestina (OLP)] *s.* grupo formado en la década de 1960 para recuperar las tierras árabes en Israel para los árabes palestinos. (p. 513)

Palestinians [Palestinos] *s.* grupo de árabes desplazados que vivían o viven todavía en la zona llamada anteriormente Palestina y ahora denominada Israel. (p. 527)

pampas [pampas] *s.* amplia zona de praderas y tierras fértiles en la región sur-central de América del Sur. (p. 202)

Panama Canal [Canal de Panamá] *s.* canal para embarcaciones a través de Panamá que conecta el Mar Caribe con el océano Pacífico. (p. 226)

pandemic [pandemia] *s.* una enfermedad que afecta a un gran número de habitantes de una amplia zona geográfica. (p. 435)

Paraná River [Río Paraná] *s.* río en la región central de América del Sur y uno de sus tres sistemas fluviales más importantes, que nace en las tierras altas del Sur del Brasil y fluye unas 3.000 millas (4.827 km) hacia el sur y el oeste. (p. 203)

parliament [parlamento] *s.* cuerpo legislativo representativo cuyos miembros son elegidos o designados y cuyas funciones legislativas y ejecutivas están combinadas. (pp. 158, 303)

parliamentary government [gobierno parlamentario] *s.* sistema en el cual las funciones legislativas y ejecutivas están combinadas en una legislatura llamada parlamento. (p. 158)

particulate [macropartícula] *s.* partícula muy pequeña de materia líquida o sólida. (p. 324)

partition [partición] *s.* separación; división en dos o más unidades territoriales con estatus político separado. (p. 574)

pastoral lease [arrendamiento pastoral] *s.* en Australia, gran extensión de terreno que todavía es propiedad del gobierno; los rancheros arriendan la tierra del gobierno. (p. 729)

PCB [PCB (policlorobifenilo)] *s.* un compuesto industrial que se acumula en el tejido animal y puede ocasionar efectos perjudiciales y defectos congénitos; el PCB fue prohibido en los Estados Unidos en 1977. (p. 631)

peat [turba] *s.* materia vegetal parcialmente descompuesta que se encuentra en las turberas. (p. 277)

penal colony [colonia penal] *s.* lugar donde son enviados los prisioneros. (p. 718)

per capita income [ingreso per cápita] *s.* la cantidad de dinero promedio que gana una persona en una unidad política. (p. 94)

permafrost [permafrost (pergelisol)] *s.* terreno permanentemente congelado. (pp. 63, 123)

polder [pólder] *s.* terreno protegido contra el mar u otra masa de agua mediante diques o drenaje. (p. 282)

Polynesia [Polinesia] *s.* una de las tres regiones de Oceanía, cuyo nombre significa, "muchas islas". (p. 713)

population density [densidad poblacional] *s.* el número promedio de habitantes de una zona mensurable, el cual se obtiene dividiendo el número de habitantes en la zona por la cantidad de tierra que ocupan. (p. 81)

population pyramid [pirámide poblacional] *s.* un dispositivo gráfico que muestra la distribución de una población por sexo y edad. (p. 79)

postindustrial economy [economía postindustrial] *s.* fase económica en la cual la manufactura no desempeña un papel dominante. (p. 142)

Prairie Provinces [Las Provincias de las Praderas] *s.* en Canadá, las provincias que se encuentran al oeste de Ontario y Quebec: Manitoba, Saskatchewan y Alberta. (p. 168)

precipitation [precipitación] *s.* gotas de agua que caen en forma de lluvia, aguanieve, nieve o granizo. (p. 50)

prevailing westerlies [vientos del oeste predominantes] *s.* vientos que soplan de oeste a este. (p. 124)

prime meridian [primer meridiano] *s.* la línea imaginaria a cero meridiano usada para medir longitud de este a oeste, y que divide la Tierra en dos mitades, este y oeste; llamado meridiano de Greenwich porque pasa por Greenwich, Inglaterra. (p. 6)

prime minister [primer ministro] *s.* la cabeza del gobierno; el líder del partido de la mayoría en el parlamento. (p. 158)

privatization [privatización] *s.* la venta de empresas propiedad del Estado a ciudadanos privados. (p. 388)

province [provincia] *s.* una unidad política. (p. 156)

pull factor [factor de atracción] *s.* un factor que atrae o arrastra a personas a otro lugar. (pp. 81, 211)

push factor [factor de empuje] *s.* un factor que hace que la gente abandone sus hogares y emigre a otra región. (pp. 81, 211, 730)

Pyongyang [Pyongyang] *s.* la ciudad más grande de Corea del Norte, con más de 2.500 millones de habitantes. (p. 650)

Q

Qin Ling Mountains [Montañas de Qin Ling] *s.* montañas de la región sudeste y este central de China; dividen la parte norte de China de la parte sur. (p. 619)

Quebec [Quebec] *s.* una de las provincias más importantes del Canadá. (p. 167)

Quechua [Quechua] *s.* idioma del Imperio Inca, hablado actualmente en las tierras de la zona andina. (p. 231)

R

rai [rai] *s.* tipo de música popular argelina compuesta en la década de 1920 por niños pobres de las zonas urbanas, con ritmos rápidos bailables; algunas veces se usó como forma de rebeldía para expresar el descontento político. (p. 440)

rain forest [selva tropical] *s.* una región selvática ubicada en la Zona Tropical con una gran concentración de diferentes especies de árboles de hojas anchas. (pp. 66, 207)

rain shadow [sombra de lluvia] *s.* la tierra del lado de sotavento de colinas o montañas que recibe muy poca lluvia del aire seco descendiente. (p. 51)

raj [raj] *s.* el período de gobierno británico en la India que duró cerca de 200 años, de 1857 a 1947. (p. 568)

Ramadan [Ramadán] *s.* práctica islámica de ayunar un mes desde que sale el sol hasta que se pone. (p. 576)

rate of natural increase [tasa de aumento natural] *s.* llamada también tasa de crecimiento demográfico; la tasa de crecimiento poblacional, que se encuentra restando la tasa de mortalidad de la tasa de natalidad. (p. 79)

recession [recesión] *s.* un período prolongado de descenso en la actividad comercial general. (p. 667)

Red Army [Ejército Rojo] *s.* nombre del ejército de la Unión Soviética. (p. 371)

refinery [refinería] *s.* lugar donde el petróleo crudo es convertido en productos útiles. (p. 497)

Reformation [Reforma] *s.* movimiento en Europa Occidental iniciado en 1517, cuando muchos cristianos se desligaron de la Iglesia Católica para fundar iglesias protestantes; esto produjo hostilidades mutuas y guerras religiosas que desgarraron a Europa. (p. 297)

reggae [reggae] *s.* un estilo de música creado en Jamaica en la década de 1960, que tiene sus raíces en la música africana, caribeña y americana, con frecuencia trata sobre problemas sociales y religión. (p. 227)

relative location [ubicación relativa] *s.* describe un lugar en relación con otros lugares que lo rodean. (p. 6)

relief [relieve] *s.* la diferencia en elevación de una forma fisiográfica, desde el punto más bajo hasta el punto más alto. (p. 36)

religion [religión] *s.* la creencia en un poder o poderes sobrenaturales que se consideran como los creadores y conservadores del universo, así como el propio sistema de creencias. (p. 75)

Renaissance [Renacimiento] *s.* época de renovado interés por la educación y las artes que duró del *s.* XIV al *s.* XVI; comenzó en los estados-ciudades italianos y se extendió hacia el norte por toda Europa. (p. 291)

representative democracy [democracia representativa] *s.* un gobierno en el cual el pueblo gobierna mediante sus representantes elegidos. (p. 139)

republic [república] *s.* gobierno en el cual los ciudadanos eligen a sus representantes para que gobiernen en su nombre. (p. 290)

reserve [reserva] *s.* terrenos públicos destinados por el gobierno para los pueblos indígenas. (p. 162)

Richter scale [escala de Richter] *s.* una forma de medir información registrada por los sismógrafos para determinar la fuerza relativa de un terremoto. (p. 40)

rift valley [Valle del Rift] *s.* un valle largo y delgado creado por la separación de las placas continentales, presente en África Oriental, el cual se prolonga por 4.000 millas (6.436 km) desde Jordania en el Sudoeste asiático hasta Mozambique en el Sur de África. (p. 416)

Ring of Fire [El Anillo de Fuego] *s.* la cadena de volcanes que bordea la cuenca del Pacífico. (pp. 41, 661)

Rocky Mountains [Las Montañas Rocosas] *s.* un importante sistema montañoso de los Estados Unidos y el Canadá que se extiende por 3.000 millas (4.827 km) desde Alaska hacia el Sur hasta Nuevo México. (p. 119)

Rub al Khali [Rub' Al Jali] *s.* conocido también como el Cuarto Vacío, uno de los desiertos arenosos más grandes del mundo, abarca cerca de 250.000 millas cuadradas (650 mil kilómetros cuadrados); ubicado en la Península Arábiga. (p. 491)

Russian Revolution [Revolución Rusa] *s.* la revuelta de 1917 por la cual el Partido Comunista Ruso dirigido por V. I. Lenin, tomó el control del gobierno de los zares. (p. 363)

runoff [escorrentía] *s.* agua de lluvia no absorbida por el suelo y que puede transportar pesticidas y fertilizantes de los campos a los ríos, poniendo en peligro la cadena alimentaria. (p. 353)

S

Sahara [Sahara] *s.* el desierto más grande del mundo, que se extiende 3.000 millas (4.827 km) por el continente africano, desde el Océano Atlántico hasta el Mar Rojo, y mide 1.200 millas (1.930 km) de norte a sur. (p. 420)

Sahel [Sahel] *s.* una banda estrecha de pradera seca, que se extiende de este a oeste en el borde sur del Sahara, usada para agricultura y pastoreo. (p. 424)

St. Lawrence Seaway [La Ruta Marítima del San Lorenzo] *s.* la ruta de barcos de aguas profundas más importante de América del Norte, la cual conecta los Grandes Lagos con el Océano Atlántico a través del Río San Lorenzo. (p. 129)

St. Petersburg [San Petersburgo] *s.* la vieja capital de Rusia, fundada por Pedro el Grande, que trasladó la capital allí desde Moscú, debido a que San Petersburgo tenía acceso directo por mar hacia Europa Occidental. (p. 362)

salt flat [salinas] *s.* terrenos planos formados por sales químicas que permanecen después de que los vientos evaporan la humedad del suelo. (p. 492)

samba [samba] *s.* danza brasileña con influencia africana. (p. 239)

samurai [samurai] *s.* soldado profesional japonés al servicio de los intereses de terratenientes y jefes de clanes. (p. 651)

satellite nation [país satélite] *s.* un país dominado por otro. (p. 312)

savanna [sabana] *s.* término para describir las llanuras herbáceas que carecen de árboles en su mayor parte, en la región de las praderas tropicales. (p. 66)

seawork [espigón] *s.* una estructura utilizada para controlar el impacto destructivo del mar en la vida humana. (p. 283)

sectionalism [faccionalismo] *s.* cuando la gente pone su lealtad a su región o sección por encima de la lealtad al país. (p. 136)

sediment [sedimento] *s.* pequeños trozos de roca producidos por la acción de los elementos. (p. 42)

seismograph [sismógrafo] *s.* un dispositivo para medir el tamaño de las ondas creadas por un terremoto. (p. 39)

Seoul [Seúl] *s.* la ciudad más grande de Corea del Sur, con una población de más de diez millones de habitantes. (p. 650)

Serengeti [Serengeti] *s.* zona de África Oriental, que tiene muchas de las mejores praderas del mundo y muchos animales de pastoreo. (p. 422)

service industry [industria de servicios] *s.* cualquier tipo de actividad económica que produce servicios en vez de productos. (p. 142)

Sherpa [Sherpa] *s.* una persona de ascendencia tibetiana en Nepal, que trabaja como guía tradicional en la región del Monte Everest. (p. 582)

Shi'ite [Shiita] *s.* una de las dos principales ramas del Islam, que incluye a la mayoría de los iraníes y parte de las poblaciones de Irak y Afganistán. (p. 517)

shogun [Shogun] *s.* el general del ejército del emperador con poderes de dictador militar, una posición creada por el emperador del Japón en 1192 después de una lucha entre dos clanes poderosos. (p. 651)

Siberia [Siberia] *s.* región del centro y la zona este de Rusia que se extiende desde los Montes Urales hasta el Océano Pacífico, conocida por sus recursos minerales y por ser un lugar de exilio político. (p. 349)

Siddhartha Gautama [Siddhartha Gautama] *s.* fundador del budismo y conocido como Buda, nacido en el Sur de Nepal en el siglo sexto antes de nuestra era. (p. 582)

Silicon Glen [Silicon Glen] *s.* sección de Escocia entre Glasgow y Edimburgo, así denominada por su alta concentración de compañías de alta tecnología. (p. 305)

GLOSSARY

Silk Road [La Ruta de la Seda] *s.* la ruta de 4.000 millas (6.436 km) entre China y el Mar Mediterráneo, así llamada por la costosa seda adquirida en China. (p. 375)

silt [limo] *s.* material sedimentario suelto que contiene partículas de roca muy pequeñas, formado por depósitos de ríos y muy fértil. (p. 426)

Sinhalese [cingalés] *s.* pueblo indo-ario que cruzó el estrecho que separa la India y Sri Lanka en el siglo sexto antes de nuestra era y creó una civilización avanzada, adoptando el budismo. (p. 584)

sirocco [siroco] *s.* viento cálido y constante del Sur que sopla desde África del Norte a través del Mar Mediterráneo hasta el Sur de Europa, usualmente en la primavera. (p. 279)

slash-and-burn [cortar y quemar] *s.* método para despejar los campos para plantar, que consiste en cortar y quemar árboles, arbustos y hierbas. (p. 210)

smart growth [crecimiento inteligente] *s.* el uso eficiente y la conservación de la tierra y otros recursos. (p. 178)

smog [smog] *s.* una niebla marrón que se produce cuando los gases liberados por combustibles fósiles en combustión reaccionan con la luz solar. (p. 324)

society [sociedad] *s.* un grupo que comparte una región geográfica, un idioma común y un sentido de identidad y cultura. (p. 71)

soil [suelo] *s.* la mezcla suelta de roca meteorizada, material orgánico, aire y agua que permiten el crecimiento de las plantas. (p. 45)

solar system [sistema solar] *s.* se compone del sol y nueve planetas conocidos, así como otros cuerpos celestes que gravitan alrededor del sol. (p. 27)

solstice [solsticio] *s.* cualquiera de dos épocas en el año cuando los rayos solares brillan directamente arriba al mediodía en los puntos más alejados al norte o al sur, y que marcan el comienzo del verano o el invierno; en el Hemisferio Norte, el solsticio de verano es el día más largo y el solsticio de invierno, el más corto. (p. 49)

South, the [sur, el] *s.* una región que cubre aproximadamente un cuarto de la superficie terrestre de los Estado Unidos y contiene más de un tercio de su población. (p. 148)

South Slav [eslavo del sur] *s.* una persona que emigró de Polonia y Rusia y se estableció en la Península Balcánica alrededor del año 500. (p. 319)

Spanish conquest [conquista española] *s.* la conquista de los pueblos indígenas americanos por los españoles. (p. 217)

sphere of influence [esfera de influencia] *s.* un método de dividir el control extranjero en China, después de que el país fuera obligado a firmar una serie de tratados otorgando privilegios especiales a los europeos. China fue dividida para el control por Gran Bretaña, Francia, Alemania y Rusia, entre otras potencias. (p. 636)

state [estado] *s.* término político para describir una unidad independiente que ocupa un territorio específico y tiene pleno control de sus asuntos internos y externos. (p. 83)

stateless nation [nación sin estado] *s.* un pueblo que no tiene un territorio que pueda ocupar legalmente, como los palestinos, los kurdos y los vascos. (p. 526)

stateless society [sociedad sin estado] *s.* una sociedad en la cual la gente usa linajes o familias cuyos miembros descienden de un antepasado común para gobernarse. (p. 443)

steppe [estepa] *s.* término usado para la región de praderas templadas en el Hemisferio Norte. (p. 66)

Stolen Generation [La Generación Robada] *s.* en Australia, término que utilizan los aborígenes actualmente para denominar a los 100.000 niños de raza mixta que fueron tomados por el gobierno y entregados a familias blancas para promover la asimilación. (p. 728)

storm surge [olas ciclónicas] *s.* altos niveles de agua producidos por un ciclón que inunda zonas de bajo nivel. (p. 562)

strategic commodity [recurso estratégico] *s.* un recurso tan importante que las naciones están dispuestas a ir a la guerra para asegurar el suministro continuo del mismo. (p. 529)

subcontinent [subcontinente] *s.* una masa de tierra similar a un continente, aunque de menor extensión, como Asia del Sur, denominada el subcontinente Indio. (p. 551)

subsistence activity [actividad de subsistencia] *s.* una actividad en la cual una familia produce únicamente los alimentos, la ropa y la vivienda que necesita. (p. 714)

suburb [suburbio] *s.* una unidad o comunidad política que linda con la ciudad central o con otros suburbios que lindan con la ciudad. (pp. 87, 138)

sultan [sultán] *s.* el gobernante de un país musulmán. (p. 585)

summer monsoon [monzón húmedo (verano)] *s.* la estación cuando los vientos soplan desde el sudoeste a través del Océano Índico hacia Asia del Sur, desde junio hasta septiembre, cuando los vientos producen fuertes tormentas y graves inundaciones. (p. 597)

Sunni [Suni] *s.* una de las dos principales ramas del Islam, la cual abarca cerca del 83 por ciento de todos los musulmanes, incluyendo los que viven en Turquía, Irak y Afganistán. (p. 517)

supra [supra] *s.* término georgiano (ruso) para designar una cena con muchos platos, brindis y discursos cortos. (p. 374)

sustainable community [comunidad sostenible] *s.* una comunidad cuyos residentes pueden vivir y trabajar en armonía con el medio ambiente. (p. 178)

sweatshop [fábrica explotadora] *s.* un lugar de trabajo donde se trabajan largas horas por salario bajo y en malas condiciones para enriquecer a los fabricantes. (p. 667)

T

taiga [taiga] *s.* una faja casi continua de bosques coníferos de hojas perennes, a través del Hemisferio Norte en América del Norte y Eurasia. (p. 351)

Taklimakan Desert [Takla-Makan] *s.* desierto ubicado en la región occidental de China entre las montañas de Tian Shan y Kunlún. (p. 627)

Taliban [Talibán] *s.* un grupo musulmán estricto en Afganistán que ha impuesto reglas muy rígidas en la sociedad, incluyendo estilos de vestuario para hombres y mujeres, restricciones en la apariencia de las mujeres en lugares públicos y reglamentos para la televisión, la música y los videos. (p. 519)

Tamil [Tamil] *s.* hindú dravídico que llegó a Sri Lanka en el *s.* IV y se estableció en el norte, mientras los sinhaleses se trasladaron más al sur. (p. 584)

Taoism [Taoísmo] *s.* filosofía basada en el libro Tao Te Ching y las enseñanzas de Lao-Tsé, que vivió en China en el siglo VI antes de nuestra era, quien creía en conservar y restaurar la armonía dentro del individuo, con la naturaleza y con el universo, con poca intervención del gobierno. (p. 638)

taro [taro] *s.* planta tropical de Asia con raíz a base de féculas, la cual se puede comer como un vegetal hervido o preparada como pan, budín o una pasta llamada "poi". (p. 715)

tectonic plate [placa tectónica] *s.* una enorme plataforma móvil que forma la corteza de la Tierra. (p. 37)

Tenochtitlan [Tenochtitlán] *s.* la antigua capital de los aztecas, donde se encuentra la Ciudad de México en la actualidad. (p. 217)

terpen [terpén] *s.* plataformas altas de tierra de barro usadas en trabajos de mar. (p. 283)

terraced farming [cultivo en andenes] *s.* una técnica antigua para cultivar la tierra en laderas o pendientes de montañas, utilizando campos horizontales a manera de peldaños, cortados en las pendientes. (p. 211)

terrorism (terrorismo) *s.* uso ilegal o amenazante de la fuerza, o violencia, contra individuos o propiedades, con el propÚsito de intimidar o causar temor con fines polÌticos o sociales. (p. 173)

theocratic [teocrático] adj. una forma de gobierno en la cual líderes religiosos controlan el gobierno con leyes religiosas y consultando con eruditos religiosos. (p. 504)

Three Gorges Dam [Presa de las Tres Gargantas] *s.* una presa que se comenzó a construir a finales del siglo. XX en Chang Jiang, China, para ayudar a controlar las inundaciones, generar energía y permitir que los barcos naveguen más hacia el interior de China. (p. 628)

Three Kingdoms [Los Tres Reinos] *s.* los reinos formados en la península de Corea por el año 300 de nuestra era: Koguryo en el norte, Paikche en el sudoeste y Silia en el sudeste. (p. 647)

Tigris River [Río Tigris] *s.* uno de los ríos más importantes del Sudoeste Asiático; sirvió de base a varias civilizaciones antiguas en el valle del río y fluye por partes de Turquía, Siria e Irak. (p. 489)

tornado [tornado] *s.* una poderosa columna de aire en espiral en forma de túnel. (p. 51)

topographic map [mapa topográfico] *s.* un mapa para referencia general; representación de características terrestres, naturales y hechas por el hombre. (p. 11)

topography [topografía] *s.* las características combinadas de formas fisiográficas y su distribución en una región. (p. 36)

Transcaucasia [Transcaucasia] *s.* una región compuesta por las repúblicas de Armenia, Azerbaiján y Georgia; situada entre el Cáucaso y las fronteras de Turquía e Irán. (p. 346)

Trans-Siberian Railroad [Ferrocarril Transiberiano] *s.* un ferrocarril que uniría Moscú con el Puerto de Vladivostok en el Pacífico; construido entre 1891 y 1903. (p. 355)

Treaty of Tordesillas [Tratado de Tordesillas] *s.* un tratado entre España y Portugal firmado en 1494, por el cual Portugal obtuvo el control de la tierra que hoy constituye el Brasil. (p. 236)

Treaty of Waitangi [Tratado de Waitangi] *s.* tratado firmado por los británicos y los maorís en 1840, por el cual Gran Bretaña obtuvo el control de Nueva Zelanda. (p. 719)

tsunami [tsunami] *s.* una ola oceánica gigantesca, producida por un terremoto o erupción volcánica subacuático, con gran poder de destrucción. (pp. 40, 662)

tuberculosis [tuberculosis] *s.* una infección respiratoria propagada a través del contacto humano, que con frecuencia acompaña al SIDA. (p. 466)

tundra [tundra] *s.* las tierras planas sin árboles que forman un aro alrededor del Océano Ártico; la región climática del Océano Ártico. (p. 63)

typhoon [tifón] *s.* una tormenta tropical, como un huracán, que se da en la región occidental del Pacífico. (pp. 51, 625)

U

USSR [URSS] *s.* la Unión de Repúblicas Socialistas Soviéticas o Unión Soviética, formada en 1922 por los comunistas y disuelta oficialmente en 1991. (p. 363)

UNICEF (United Nations Children's Fund) [UNICEF (Fondo de las Naciones Unidas para la Infancia)] *s.* organización internacional de vigilancia y ayuda para los niños. (p. 665)

United Provinces of Central America [Provincias Unidas de Centroamérica] *s.* nombre de Centroamérica después de que la región declaró su independencia de México en 1823. (p. 223)

upland [tierras altas] *s.* una colina o una montaña muy baja que también puede contener mesas y planicies altas. (p. 275)

Ural Mountains [Montes Urales] *s.* la cordillera que separa las planicies del norte de Europa y Siberia Occidental y utilizada como la línea divisoria entre Europa y Asia. (p. 346)

urban geography [geografía urbana] *s.* el estudio de cómo las personas utilizan el espacio en las ciudades. (p. 87)

urbanization [urbanización] *s.* el dramático aumento en el número de ciudades y los cambios en estilos de vida que resultan del mismo. (p. 88)

urban sprawl [expansión urbana descontrolada] *s.* desarrollo mal planificado que extiende la población de una ciudad por una zona geográfica cada vez más amplia. (p. 176)

V

Vietnam War [Guerra de Vietnam] *s.* (1954-1975) el conflicto militar producido por la intervención de Estados Unidos en Vietnam del Sur para evitar su apoderamiento por los comunistas de Vietnam del Norte. (p. 707)

volcano [volcán] *s.* un evento natural, formado cuando magma, gases y agua de la parte inferior de la corteza o capa se acumulan en cámaras subterráneas y posteriormente hacen erupción y surgen por grietas en la superficie terrestre. (p. 40)

voyaging canoe [canoas viajeras] *s.* una embarcación grande construida por habitantes de las islas del Pacífico para navegar por el océano. (p. 699)

W

wadi [wadi] *s.* lecho de un río que permanece seco excepto durante la estación lluviosa. (p. 488)

water table [nivel hidrostático] *s.* el nivel en el cual las rocas se saturan. (p. 33)

weather [clima] *s.* las condiciones atmosféricas en un lugar y tiempo específicos. (p. 50)

weathering [meteorización] *s.* proceso químico y físico que cambia las características de las rocas en o cerca de la superficie terrestre, lo cual ocurre lentamente durante el lapso de muchos años. (p. 42)

West [Oeste] *s.* región de América del Norte compuesta por 13 estados, que se extiende desde las Grandes Llanuras hasta el Océano Pacífico e incluye Alaska por el norte y Hawaii en el Pacífico. (p. 148)

West Bank [Cisjordania] *s.* en Israel, una franja de tierra en el lado oeste del Río Jordán, originalmente controlada por Jordania, que forma parte de la tierra destinada para los árabes palestinos. (p. 527)

Western Wall [El Muro de los Lamentos] *s.* para los judíos, el sitio más sagrado de Jerusalén; lo único que queda del Segundo Templo, construido en 538 antes de nuestra era y destruido en el 70 de nuestra era por los romanos. (p. 510)

***Wik* Case** [el caso *Wik*] *s.* en Australia, los tribunales dispusieron en este caso que los aborígenes pueden reclamar tierras retenidas bajo arrendamiento pastoral. (p. 729)

winter monsoon [monzón seco (invierno)] *s.* la estación cuando los vientos secos soplan desde el noreste a través de los montes Himalaya hacia el mar desde octubre hasta febrero, algunas veces causando sequías. (p. 597)

X

Xi Jiang [Xi Jiang] *s.* llamado también el Río del Oeste; río que fluye hacia el este a través del sudeste de China y se une con el Río Perla (Zhu Jiang) para desembocar en el Mar del Sur de la China, formando un estuario entre Hong Kong y Macao. (p. 621)

Y

yurt [yurt] *s.* una tienda de nómadas del Asia Central. (p. 379)

Z

Zionism [sionismo] *s.* movimiento iniciado en el siglo XIX para volver a establecer una patria judía en la tierra natal de los judíos. (p. 51)

Zuider Zee [Zuiderzee] *s.* antiguo lago interior de los Países Bajos en el Mar del Norte. (p. 283)

A

An *i* preceding a page reference in italics indicates that there is an illustration, and usually text information as well, on that page. An *m* or a *c* preceding an italic page reference indicates a map or a chart, as well as text information on that page.

Abbas, Mahmoud. *See* Mazen, Abu.
Abdul al-Aziz, 505
Abkhazia, *i372,* 386
Aboriginal people, *i676,* 718, 719, 722, *i726*, 727–729
Acadians, *m167*
acculturation
  defined, 72
acid rain, 43, *i285,* 325
aerial photography, 11, *i14*
Afghanistan, 174, *c484–485,* 488, 490, 516, 517, 518, 519, 552
Africa, 398, *i588*
  area by country, *c409, c411, c413*
  birthrate by country, *c408, c410, c412*
  blended languages in, 73
  capitals and countries of, *c408, c410, c412*
  cars per country, *c409, c411, c413*
  climate regions in, 420, *m421,* 422, 423
  colonialism in, *m404,* 432–433, 468–469
  Columbian Exchange, *c136*
  deserts in, *c402,* 420–421
  disease in, *c465, m466, i467*
  doctors by country, *c409, c411, c413*
  economic activities in, 461–463
  education in, 463
  ethnic boundaries in, *m469*
  flags of, *c408, c410, c412*
  gross domestic product by country, *c409, c411, c413*
  health care, 465–467
  imports and exports by country, *c409, c411, c413*
  independence of countries, *m473*
  infant mortality rate by country, *c408, c410, c412*
  landforms in, 415–417, *m415, i427*
  landmass of, *c402*
  languages in, *m407*
  life expectancy by country, *c408, c410, c412*
  literacy rate by country, *c409, c411, c413*
  mountains in, 417
  natural resources in, *m93,* 417–418
  one-commodity countries, *m462*
  physical geography of, *m403*
  political geography of, *m405*
  population of, *c82, c402, m406, c408, c410, c412*
  religions in, *c406*
  rivers in, *c402,* 415–416
  subregions of, *m430*
  televisions per country, *c409, c411, c413*
  vegetation in, 422–423
African Americans, *m142*
African Development Fund, 466
African National Congress (ANC), 454
AIDS (acquired immune deficiency syndrome)
  in East Africa, 435
  in Southern Africa, 456
  throughout Africa, *i401, c465, m466,* 467
airline industry. *See* industry, airline.
airplanes
  hijacking of, 173
  as terrorist weapons, 173
Alaska, *i44,* 81–82, 123, *i309*
Albania, *c268–269,* 310, 311, 313
Albanians, 319, 321, *m322*
Alberta, *c114–115, m157,* 168
Aleutian Islands, 121
Algeria, *i164, c408–409,* 417, 438, 439, 440–441, 463
Al-Ghawar, *i474, i477,* 497
Allende, Salvador, *i232*
alluvial plains, 553
Alps, *c190,* 274–275, *i274*
al-Qaeda, 173–174, 517
Amazon River, *i186, c190,* 202–203, 208, 210, *m215*
Amu Darya, 347, 353
Anak Krakatoa, *i711*
analyzing data, R2
Anatolian Peninsula, 487, 488
ANC. *See* African National Congress.
Andes Mountains, 63, *c190, i201,* 210
Andorra, *c268–269*
Angel Falls, *i200*
Angkor Wat, Cambodia, *i705,* 708
Anglo America, 117
Angola, *c408–409,* 415, 417, 451, 453, 463, *i656*
An-Nafud Desert, *c478, i486,* 492
Antarctica, *i674, m678,* 692, 697, 718–720
  climate regions in, *m683*
  inland exploration, *c687*
  national claims in, *i720, m720*
  political geography of, *m681*
  subregions of, *m704*
Antigua and Barbuda, *c196–197*
anthrax, 175
antiterrorism coalition, 174
apartheid, 454–455, 457
Apennine Mountains, 274
Appalachian Mountains, 119
Appalachian Trail, 119
aqueducts, 292
aquifers, 33, 421, 496
Arabian Desert, 62
Arabian Peninsula, *i486,* 487, 488, 492
  cultures in, 503–504
  government of, 504–505
  history of, *c504*
  modern life in, 505–506
  religious practices, 503–504, 506–507
  religious worship sites, *i508–509*
Arabian Sea, 552
Arabs, 512, 514, 515, 516, 532
Aral Sea, 348, 353–354, *i353, i354*
  runoff, 353
Ararat, Mt., *c478*
archipelago, 553
Arctic Circle, 280
Arctic Ocean, 32, 121
Argentina, 44, *c196–197,* 203, 209, 211, 232, 249, 250
Armenia, *c342–343,* 346, 370, 371, 373, 385, 386–387
art
  of Aboriginal people, 722
  culture expressed through, 77
  Italian Renaissance, *i291,* 292
  in Japan, 654
  mask making, *i656, i657*
  painting in Mexico, *i219*
  in South America, 232, *i233*
  in Southeast Asia, 708
  in United States, 143
  in West Africa, 444–445
  in Western Europe, 300
ASEAN. *See* Association of Southeast Asian Nations.
Ashanti, 444
Asian Americans, *m142*
assimilation, 728
Association of Southeast Asian Nations (ASEAN), 707
Aswan High Dam, 426–427, *m426*
Atacama Desert, 55, 209
Atlantic Coastal Plain, 119
Atlantic Ocean, 32, 121

Atlantic Provinces, *m154,* 166–167
Atlas Mountains, *c190*
atmosphere, 28
atoll, 553, 700
Australia, *i589, c684–685, i688,* 692, 695, 696, 697. *See also* Aboriginal people.
  cultures of, 722
  economic activities in, 721–722
  history of, 718–720
  Mediterranean climate region in, 62
  modern life in, 723
  natural resources in, *m93*
  physical geography of, *m678*
  plant and animal species, *i696*
  population of, *c82, m725*
Austria, *c268–269,* 296, 300, 301, 327
Austria-Hungary, 311
automobiles, 130, 143, 177
Ayers Rock (Uluru), *i729*
Azerbaijan, *c342–343,* 346, 370, 371, 373, 385, 386–387
azimuthal projection, *i18*
Aztec, 217, 218, 219

B

baby boom, *c79*
baguios, 51
Bahamas, *c196–197,* 203
Bahrain, *c484–485,* 503, *c526, c537*
Baikal, Lake, 33, *m336, i344,* 348, *i350*
Bali, 695
balkanization, 311
Balkan Mountains, 274
Balkan Peninsula, 289–290, 319
Baltic Republics, 361
Bangalore, India, 570
Bangladesh, 51, 53, *c548–549,* 551, 555, 557, 558, 560, 562, 568, 573, 574, *c575,* 576, 577, 593
Bantu, *m448*
banyas, *i367*
Barbados, *c196–197*
Basques, 293
Bedouins, *i491,* 503, 504, 515
Beijing, China, 606
Belarus, *c342–343,* 361
Belgium, *c268–269,* 296, *m404,* 449, 469
Belize, *c196–197*
Benelux countries, 296
Bengal, Bay of, 552
Bengalis, 576
Benin, *c408–409,* 444–445
benji, 456
Beringia, 127
Berlin Conference, 432, 449, 468
Berlin Wall, 298
Bhutan, *c548–549,* 551, 552, 554, 556, 558, 580–582
Biafra, 86
Bikini Atoll, 700, *i701, m701*
bin Laden, Osama, 173–174, 517
biodiversity, *m245,* 246
biological weapons, 175, 518
biome, 65
biosphere, 28
Birecik Dam, *i497*
birthrate
  defined, 8
Black Forest, 285
Blanc, Mont, *c262*
blizzards, 126
  defined, 52
bodu beru, 586
Bolívar, Simón, 231–232
Bolivia, *c196–197,* 209, 232, 247
Bora Bora, *i691*
Borneo, *c679*
Bosnia and Herzegovina, *i260, c268–269,* 310, 320, *i321*
Bospurus Strait, 488
BosWash, *m145,* 146
Botswana, *c408–409,* 415, 453, 455–456
boundaries, national
  artificial, 85
  natural, 85
Brahmaputra River, *c549,* 553, 560
brain drain, 463
Brasília, Brazil, 88, *i237,* 239
Brazil, *c196–197,* 205, 209, 210, 211, 213, *m216,* 253, 467
  cultural life in, 239
  economic activities in, 238
  history of, 236–237
  income gap in, 252
  language of, 237
  migration, 238
  natural resources in, 238
  population of, 237
  religion in, 237
British Columbia, *c114–115, m157,* 168–169
British East India Company, 568
British Empire, 303, *m304*
Brunei, *c684–685,* 705
bubonic plague, 291, *m294, i295*
Buddhism, 76–77, *i508,* 572, 582, 584, *i585,* 638, 648, *i708,* 709
Buenos Aires, Argentina, 211, *c212, i212*
Bulgaria, *c268–269,* 310, 311
bullet trains, *i655*
Burkina Faso, *c408–409*
Burundi, *c408–409,* 431
Bush, George W., 174
  war against terrorism and, 517–518, 519
buttes, *i34*
Byzantine Empire, 291, 311

C

Cajuns, *m167*
California, 124, 148–149
Cambodia, *c684–685,* 694, *i705,* 707, 708
Cameroon, *c408–409,* 417, *m417,* 448, 452
Canada, 98, *m99, i332*
  agriculture in, *m160*
  area by province/territory, *c115*
  area rank, *c115*
  arts in, 163
  Atlantic Provinces, 166–167
  capitals and provinces of, *c114*
  climate in, 62, 123, 124, *m125,* 126
  connections with United States, *m106*
  Core Provinces, 167–168
  cultural clash, *i161*
  doctors by province/territory, *c115*
  dwellings, *i380*
  economy of, 95, *m106,* 159–160, *c159, m160*
  flags of, *c114*
  government in, 158
  high school graduates by province/territory, *c115*
  history of, 155, *c156,* 157
  industry in, 159, *m160*
  infant mortality rate by province/territory, *c114*
  landforms of, 85, c102, 117–121
  languages in, 161, *m171*
  multiculturalism in, 180–181, 183
  native peoples of, *c. 1600, m104*
  natural hazards of, *m107*
  natural resources in, *m120,* 122
  Pacific Province and the Territories, 168–169
  per capita income by province/territory, *c115*
  physical geography of, *m103*
  political geography of, *m105*
  population density by province/territory, *c115*
  population of, *c82, c102, m107, c114,* 161
  population rank, *c115*

Prairie Provinces, 168
regions of, *m118*
religion in, 161
sports in, 162–163
subregions of, *m154, c166,* 167–169
territorial growth in, *m157*
territories of, *i169*
terrorism and, 174, 175
trails and waterways of, 129
transportation in, 130, *i165*
urban/rural population by province/ territory, *c115*
urban sprawl, 176–178
vegetation regions in, *m125*
weather extremes, 126
Canadian Multiculturalism Act, 180, 183
Canadian Shield, 119, 122
canals, 283–284, *m284*
canopy, 422–423
canyons, *i35*
Cape Hatteras, *i43*
Cape Verde, *c408–409*
capitalism, 388
capoeria, *i239*
Caribbean islands, 201, 203, 212, 213, *m216,* 224–225
colonies of, *c224*
economics of, 225–226
history of, 222–224
population in, 226
tourism in, 227
Carnival, 239, *i240*
carrying capacity
defined, 82
Carthage, 438
cartograms, *m22*
cartographer
defined, 10
Cascade Range, 120
Caspian Sea, 33, *m336,* 348, *m373*
caste system, 572
Caucasus, 385–387, *m385, i386*
Caucasus Mountains, *i333,* 346, *i347,* 385–386
caudillo, 249
CAUSE. *See* Citizens Against Urban Sprawl Everywhere.
CBD. *See* central business district.
Central Africa
art in, *i451*
colonialism, 449–450
economic activities in, 450
education in, 451–452
history of, 448–449
Central African Republic, *c408–409, m417,* 448, 452
Central America, 201, *m216*
culture of, 224–225
economic activities in, 225–226
history of, 222–223
Panama Canal, 226
population of, 226
tourism, 227
Central Asia, 346, 353, *m360*
ethnic groups in, 377–378, *c377*
history of, 375–376
languages in, 378
Russian winter in, 354–355
central business district (CBD), *i89, m90*
Central Siberian Plateau, 346
cerrado, 202
Ceylon, 584
CFCs. *See* chlorofluorocarbons.
Chad, *c408–409, m417,* 451
Chad, Lake, 425
Chakachamna, *i44*
Champlain, Samuel de, *i156*
Chang Jiang, *c610,* 619, 621, 628, 629, *i640–641*
Chechnya, *i334, i384,* 385, *i386,* 387
chemical weapons. *See* weapons of mass destruction.
Chernobyl, *i368, i369,* 392, 393, 395
chernozem, 345
Chicago, Illinois, 88, *m90, i98, i144,* 147, 176
Chile, *i189, c196–197,* 209, 211, *i232,* 234, 235
China, 44, 62, 174, *i508,* 552, 606, *m612, c616–617,* 623, 625, 626, 627, 637, 638, 639, 643, 644, 648, 668, 669, 690
Chinese, *c682*
chlorofluorocarbons (CFCs), 734
Chosen, 647
Christianity, 75, 370–371, 510, 532, 572, 585
chromium, 417, 531
Circassians, 515
cities, 639
in Africa, 433
defined, 87
in Eastern Europe, 314
growth in Latin America, 211, *c212*
in Japan, 630
in Oceania, 723
population in East Asia, *c669*
in Southeast Asia, *i677,* 709, 731
in Southwest Asia, 506
in United States and Canada, 128, 143, *m153, c176*
urban geography, 88–90, *m88, c89, i90*
in Western Europe, 301
in world, *m97*
Citizens Against Urban Sprawl Everywhere (CAUSE), 178
city-state, 289
cliffs, *i35, i309*
climate
changes in, 56–58, 737
factors affecting, 54–55
and population distribution, 80
response by people, 8
soil factors, 45
in United States and Canada, 123–126, 158
and weather, 50–51
climate regions, 556, *m557,* 558
in Africa, 420, *m421,* 422, 423
definition of, 59
in East Asia, 625, *m626,* 627
in Europe, *m266,* 278–280
in Latin America, *i208*
in Russia and the Republics, 350–351
in Southeast Asia, Oceania, and Antarctica, *m683*
in Southwest Asia, 491–492, *m492*
types of, 60–63, *m60–61*
coal, 122, *m204,* 277, 490, 555
cobalt, 417
cocoa, 418
coffee, 418
Cold War, 138, 363, 700
collective farms, 364, 372
Colombia, *c196–197,* 202, 211, 232
colonialism
in Africa, *i401, m404,* 449, 450, 451
in Arabian Peninsula, 505
in the Caribbean and Central America, 223–224
in Eastern Mediterranean, 511
language diffusion, 73
modern conflicts rooted in, 304
in Southeast Asia, 706–707
in United States and Canada, 135, 136, 155, 156
Colorado River, *i67, m149*
Columbian Exchange, *c136*
command economy, *i335,* 364
defined, 91
commodity, 462
Common Market. *See* European Economic Community.
communism, 138, *m312,* 320, 363, 364, *i366,* 636, 643, 644, 649
defined, 83
Comoros, *c408–409,* 453
composite maps, *i12,* 13

confederation, 156–157
Confucianism, 77, *i636,* 638, 648
Congo, Democratic Republic of, *i401, c408–409,* 417, 448, 449, 450, *i452,* 461, 469
Congo, Republic of, *c408–409,* 448, 449
Congo River, *c402,* 448
constitutional monarchies, 580, 581
Continental Divide, 120
continental drift, *i29*
continentality, 350
continental plates, 29, 661
continental shelf, 36, 620
continents, 27, *i29,* 117
convection, *i50,* 51, 54,
copper, *m93, m204,* 235
coral reefs, 691
core, of the earth, *i28*
Core Provinces, *m154,* 167–168
Coriolis effect, 54
Costa Rica, *c196–197*
costumes, *i716–717*
Cote d'Ivoire, *c408–409,* 418
creating a multimedia presentation, R14
creating and using a database, R15
creating a sketch map, R12
creating graphs and charts, R13
Croatia, *c268–269,* 310, 320
Croats, 314, 320, *m322*
Crusades, the, 291
crust, of the earth, *i28*
Cuba, *c94, c196–197,* 203, *i225*
cultural crossroads, 310
cultural hearth, 222
  defined, 72
culture, 72, 73, 75
  defined, 71
Cuzco, Peru, 210, 231
cyclones, 51, 557, 563, *i578, i579*
Cyprus, *c484–485,* 513
Czechoslovakia, 311, 312, 313
Czech Republic, *c268–269,* 310, 313, 314

D

dachas, 367
Dagestan, 385
Damavand, *c478*
dams, 426–427, *i562,* 563, 628, 630
dance, 456, 577, 586, *i714*
Danube River, *c262,* 275
Dardenelles Strait, 488
Dasht-e Kavir, 492
Dasht-e Lut, 492
Dead Sea, *i489*
death rate, 78
Death Valley, *i119*
debt-for-nature swap, 247
Deccan Plateau, 552, 556, 558
deforestation, 554, *i555,* 558, 587
  in Brazil, *i188*
  in Europe, 284–285
  in Latin America, *i244,* 245–246
  in Washington, *i100*
deltas, *i34,* 43
democracy, *i139,* 249–251, *i249, c250, i251,* 253, 289, *c303,* 469, 568, 569
  defined, 83
Denmark, *c224, c268–269,* 273, 302
Department of Homeland Security, 175
desalinization, 496
desert, 66, *i475, i491,* 558, 626, 627, 697
  in Africa, *c402,* 420–421
  human settlement of, *i70*
  in Latin America, *m194,* 209
  in Russia and the Republics, *m340,* 352
  in Southwest Asia, *c478,* 491–492
  in United States and Canada, 124, *m125*
desert climate region, *i60*
  defined, 62
desertification, *m107, i424–425*
determining cause and effect, R9
developed nations, 95
developing nations, 95
dialect, 73
diamonds, 415, 444, 456, 555
Díaz, Porfirio, 218
dictatorship
  defined, 83
didgeridoo, *i589*
disasters, *i578, i579, i640–641, i660,* 663, *i710, i711*
distinguishing fact from opinion, R11
distortion, 10
Djenné, Mali, *i398*
Djibouti, *c408–409,* 431
Dom, *c262*
Dome of the Rock, *i474, i511*
Dominica, *c196–197*
Dominican Republic, *c196–197,* 203
Dominion of Canada, 156–157
drawing conclusions, R5
drip irrigation, 496
drought, *i150, i151, m436, i437*
  defined, 53
Druze, 515
Dubai, 530
Dust Bowl, the, *m150, i151*
dust storms, 44, 53, *m150, i151*
dwellings, *i380–381*

E

earth, the, *i26, i28, i49*
earthquakes, 39–40, *i39, i40, i608, i660, m664*
  defined, 39
  detectors, *i663*
  in Haiti and Chile, 228–229
  in Ring of Fire, 41, 662
  in Turkey, *m520, i521*
  in United States and Canada, *m107*
Earth Summit, 735
East Africa, 431–435, *m431*
East Asia, 606
  area by country, *c617*
  birthrate by country, *c616*
  capitals and countries of, *c616*
  cars per country, *c617*
  climate regions, 625, *m626,* 627
  doctors by country, *c617*
  economic activities in, 665–667
  expansion of Chinese empire, *m612*
  flags of, *c616*
  gross domestic product by country, *c617*
  history of, 665–666
  imports and exports by country, *c617*
  infant mortality rate by country, *c616*
  landforms in, *c611, c617,* 619, *m620,* 621–622
  landmass of, *c610*
  languages in, *m615*
  life expectancy by country, *c616*
  literacy rate by country, *c617*
  mountains in, *c611,* 619, *m620*
  natural resources in, *m622,* 623
  physical geography of, *c611*
  political geography of, *m612–613*
  population in, *c82, c610, m615, c616, c669,* 671
  precipitation in, *m633*
  religions of, *c614*
  rivers in, *c610, m620,* 621–622
  subregions of, *m634*
  televisions per country, *c617*
  total area of countries, *c617*
  vegetation of, *m614,* 625–627
Eastern Europe
  art in, 314
  Balkan conflict in, 319, *c320,* 321
  balkanization, 311
  communism in, 363
  culture in, 314
  economic activities in, 313
  ethnic and religious animosities, 314–315, 320–321
  ethnic cleansing, 320

INDEX

ethnic groups in former Yugoslavia, 1993, *m322*
fall of communism, *m312*
gross domestic product, *c313*
history of, 310–312
modern life in, 314–315
per capita GDP, *c313*
Eastern Hemisphere, *i6*
Eastern Mediterranean
economic activities in, 513
history of, 511–513
modern life in, 514–515
religion in, 510–511
Eastern Orthodoxy, 75, 291, 515
East Germany, 298, *m317*, 325
East Timor, 705
Ebola virus, *i452*
EC. *See* European Community.
economic activities, 92
Economic Community of West African States (ECOWAS), 462
economic development, measurement of, 94
economic systems, 91
economy, 91, 92, *m93*
ecosystem, 65
ECOWAS. *See* Economic Community of West African States.
ECSC. *See* European Coal and Steel Community.
Ecuador, *c196–197*, 232, 253
EEC. *See* European Economic Community.
Egypt, 38, 42, *i398, c408–409*, 416, 426, *i426*, 438–439, *m438*
Elbe River, *c262*
Elburz Mountains, 487, 488
elevation, 11, 36, 50, *i56*
Ellesmere Island, 121
El Niño, 54, *i57*
El Salvador, *c196–197*
endangered species, 700
epicenter, 39
epidemics, *m294, c295, i295*
equator
defined, 6
Equatorial Guinea, *c408–409*, 448
Erie, Lake, 52
Eritrea, *c408–409*, 431
erosion, 43–44, *i151*, 563
defined, 43
escarpment, 417
eskers, 44
Estonia, *c342–343*, 361
estuary, 563
Ethiopia, *c410–411*, 431, 432, 433–434, *m433, m436*
ethnic cleansing, *i260*, 320
EU. *See* European Union.
Euphrates River, *i497*
Eurasia, 346
euro, 305, 327, 328
Europe, 258, 259, 298, 706, 719, 727
agriculture, 275, 277
area by country, *c269, c271*
birthrate by country, *c268, c270*
bubonic plague in, *m294, i295*
capitals and countries of, *c268, c270*
cars per country, *c269, c271*
climate of, 55, *m266*, 278–280
colonies in United States, 449
colonization of Africa, 432–433, 454, 468
Columbian Exchange, *c136*
contact with China, 636
deforestation in, 284–285
development of economies, 95
doctors by country, *c269, c271*
economic activities in, *c292*
flags of, *c268, c270*
gross domestic product by country, *c269, c271*
imports and exports by country, *c269, c271*
infant mortality rate by country, *c268, c270*
landforms in, *m273–275, m287*
landmass in, *c262*
languages in, *m267, c297*
life expectancy by country, *c268, c270*
literacy rate by country, *c269, c271*
mountains in, *c262*, 274–275
nations of, 1914, *m264*
natural resources in, *m93, m276*, 277
peninsulas, major, 273
physical geography of, *c262, m263*
political geography of, *m265*
pollution in, *i323–325*
population of, *c262, m267, c268, c270*
precipitation in, *c281*
pre-World War I, *m264*
religions of, *c266*
rivers in, *c262*, 275
social welfare in, 306
sports in, 307, *i308*
subregions of, *m288*, 289–293, 296–301, 302–307, 310–317
televisions per country, *c269, c271*
total area of countries, *c269, c271*
transportation, *c269, c271*
European Coal and Steel Community (ECSC), 325
European Community (EC), *i326*
European Economic Community (EEC), 326
European Environmental Agency, 324
European Union (EU), 86, 292, 298, 305, 325, 326, *m327*, 328, 329, *c329*
Everest, Mt., *c102, m125, c478, i539, c542, c549*, 552, 580
Everglades, the, *m36*, 126
exclave, *m387*

F

family planning, 668, 669
famines, 364, 372, *m436, i437*, 569
farming, 418, 495, 530, 575, 581–582, 637, *i695*, 721
in Africa, 423, 425, 427, 433–434, 438–439
in Canada, 159, *m160*
carrying capacity, 82
in Europe, 279
in Oceania, 714
in Soviet Union, 364, 372
in United States, 127, 140, *m141*, 147
fault, 39
favelas, 239
federal government
aviation security and, US15
Feni River, *i562*
Fertile Crescent, 516
fertility rate
defined, 78
festivals, 240–241, *i539*, 583, 586, 644
field survey, 11
Fiji, *c684–685*, 691, 712, *i714, i716*
Finland, *c268–269*, 302
First Nations, 159, 163
fishing, 159, 167, *i623*
five themes of geography
human-environment interaction, 8
location, 6
movement, 9
place, 7
region, 7–8
fjords, 273
flooding, 562, 563, *i579*, 628, 629, *m640, i641*
in Bangladesh, *i541*
defined, 53
in Netherlands, 282
in United States and Canada, *m107*, 126
floodplain, *i34*, 53
Florence, Italy, 291, 293
Florida, *m36, i118*, 124, 148
flow-line maps, *m23*

Foraker, Mt, *c102*
forestlands, 66, 351
fossil fuels, 122, 324, *c348,* 490, 497, 734
Fox, Vicente, *i218*
France, 135, 155–157, *c224, c268–269,* 296, 297–298, *m299,* 300, 325, *m404,* 505, 511, 636, 707
free enterprise system, 140
front, *i50,* 51
frontier, 137
Fuji, Mt., *i607, c611,* 662

G

Gabon, *c410–411,* 417, 448, 449, 452, 466
Gambia, *c410–411*
Gandhi, Mohandas, 568
Ganges Plain, 567
Ganges River, *i552,* 553, 557, 560, *c561*
Gaza Strip, 513, 527
GDP. *See* gross domestic product.
general reference maps. *See* topographic maps.
geographic grid, *i17*
Geographic Information System (GIS), *i12,* 13
geography. *See also* maps.
  defined, 5
  five themes of, 5–9
  study methods, 5
Georgia (Republic of), 124, *c342–343,* 346, 370, 371, *i372,* 373, 374, 385, 386
Geostationary Operational Environment Satellite (GOES), 12
Germany, *i259, c268–269,* 273, 296, 298, *m299,* 300, 301, *m317,* 320, *m404,* 469, 636
geysers, 41
Ghana, *c410–411, m442, c443,* 444, *i447,* 469, 471
GIS. *See* Geographic Information System.
glaciers, *i35,* 44
global economy, 666
Global Fund for Children's Vaccines, 466
Global Positioning System (GPS), 13, *i14*
global warming, 58, 246, 587, 734, *m735,* 736, 737
globe
  defined, 10
GMT. *See* Greenwich Mean Time.
GNP. *See* gross national product.
Gobi Desert, 620, 627
GOES. *See* Geostationary Operational Environment Satellite.
Golan Heights, *i487*
gold, *m204,* 417, 443, 453, 454, 719
Gorbachev, Mikhail, 312, 363
government, *i86, i139,* 504, 580–581, 637
  levels of, *c86*
  types of, 83
GPS. *See* Global Positioning System.
Grand Canal, 283
Grand Canyon, 42
grasslands, 66, 422
Great Barrier Reef, *i688,* 692
Great Britain, 174, *c303,* 376, 505, 511, 568, 574, 584, 636, 718, 719, 722
  antiterrorism coalition and, 518
  colonies in Africa, *m404,* 435
  colonies in Caribbean, *c224*
  colonies in United States, 135
  customs in, *i307*
  settlement of Canada, 155–157
  sports in, 307
Great Dividing Range, 692, 696
Greater Antilles, 203
Great Escarpment, 417
Great Indian Desert. *See* Thar Desert.
Great Kanto Earthquake, 662
Great Lakes, the, 33, 52, 88, 121
Great Mississippi Flood of 1993, *i8*
Great Plains, 53, 119, 122, 124, 126, *m150,* 168
Great Regina Plain, *i118*
Great Rift Valley, 416
Great Salt Lake, 33
Great Smoky Mountains, 119
Great Wall of China, *i85, i618,* 619, 635
Greece, *c268–269,* 278, 289–290, 291, *c292,* 311
greenhouse effect, *i31, c69*
  defined, 58
Greenland, *i380*
Greenwich Mean Time (GMT), 357
Greenwich meridian. *See* prime meridian.
Grenada, *c196–197*
gross domestic product (GDP), *c505*
  defined, 95
gross national product (GNP)
  defined, 94
Guatemala, *c196–197*
guest worker, 525, *c526*
Guiana Highlands, 202
Guinea, *c410–411, c443*
Guinea-Bissau, *c410–411*
Gulf Coastal Plain, 119
Gulf Stream, 55
Guyana, *c198–199*

H

Haider, Jorg, 301, 327
Hainan, 621
Haiti, *c198–199,* 224
hajj, 503
Halifax, Nova Scotia, 167
Han, 635
Hawaiian Islands, 121, 124, *i137*
Hejaz Mountains, 488
hemisphere
  defined, 6
Hermon, Mt., *c478*
Hidalgo, Miguel, *i219*
high islands, 691
highlands, *m125, m194,* 202, 209, *m340,* 625
  defined, 63
hijacking. *See* airplanes, hijacking of.
Himalaya Mountains, 38, *c190, i539, c549,* 551–552, *i551,* 580
Hinduism, 76, 560, 568, 569, 571, *i572,* 574, 583, 585, 708
Hindu Kush, 552
Hispanic Americans, *m142*
Hispaniola, 203
HISTORY Partnership, vi–vii, 153 MC1–153 MC2, 243 MC1–243 MC2, 317 MC1–317 MC2, 659 MC1–659 MC2
Hokkaido, *m624*
Holocaust, 298, 314, 512
homelessness, 254
homolosine projection, *i19*
Homowo, *i447*
Honduras, 94, *c198–199*
Hong Kong, *i241, i446, i609,* 621, 654
Hormuz, Straits of, 488
Horn of Africa, *m436*
hot springs, 41
Huang He, *c610,* 619, *i621,* 628
Hu Jintao, 637
human-environment interaction
  building dams, *i67,* 562–563
  crowding in urban Japan, 630–631
  defined, 8
  desertification, *i424–425*
  farming, 210–211
  impact on land, 282–283
  irrigation, 495
  nuclear testing, 700–701
  pollution, 560–561
  shrinking of Aral Sea, *m353*
  themes of geography, 8
  tourism, 212–213
  traveling the Pacific, 698–699, *i698, i699*

INDEX

urbanization, 211–212
humid continental climate region, *i61,* 124, *m125,* 279, *m340,* 351
defined, 62
humid subtropical climate region, *m125, m194,* 209, *m340,* 626, 695
defined, 62
Hungary, *c268–269,* 310, 311, 312, *m322,* 323
hurricanes, 49, 126
defined, 51
Hussein, Saddam, 174, 518
hydroelectric power, *m204,* 349, 490, 495, *c629*
hydrologic cycle, 32–33, *i33*
hydrosphere, 28

I

Iberian Peninsula, 274, 291
Ibo, 85–86
ice ages, *i58*
icebergs, 493
ice cap climate region, *m125*
defined, 63
ice caps, 44
Iceland, 41, *c268–269,* 302, 304, 305
ice sheets, 44, 692
identifying and solving problems, R10
Igbo, 443
Iguacu Falls, *i32*
immigration, 137, 142–143, 180–181, 182, 183, 221, 301, 525, 722
Inca, 210, 230–231
income gap, 252, *c254,* 255, 732
India, *i541, c548–549,* 551, 554, 555, 556, 557, *i558,* 638, *i716*
ancient empires of, *m567*
caste system, 572
continental drift, *i29*
economic activities in, 569–570
festivals in, *i241, i446*
Green Revolution, the, 569–570
history of, 567–568
language in, 571
modern life in, 570–571
plate movement in, 38
population, 593, *m594*
religion in, 571–572
subcontinent of, 1947 and 1972, *m574*
Indian Ocean, 32
Indochina, 707
Indo-European languages, *c74*
Indo-Gangetic Plain, 553, 556
Indonesia, *i656, i677, c684–685,* 690, 694, 705, 708, 709, *c739*
Indus River, *c548,* 553
industrialization, 136–138, 304, 362, 364, 497, 666, *i677,* 707, 730–732, *c739*
Indus Valley, *m544,* 556, 567, 573
infant mortality rate, 594
defined, 79
infrastructure, 94, 177, 212, 418, *m450, i461,* 462, 513, 530
Institutional Revolutionary Party (PRI), 218, 250
International Date Line, 357
International Organization for Migration, 463
Inuit, 155–156, 162, *i163,* 169
Iran, *c484–485,* 488, 490, 492, 497, 516, 517, *i518,* 519
Iraq, 173, 174, *c348, c484–485,* 488, 489, 516, 517, 518, 519
Ireland, 277, 302, 305
irrigation, 492, 493, *i530*
in Africa, 426–427, *i438*
Aral Sea, 348, 353
in Eastern Mediterranean, 513
in Southwest Asia, 495–496, *i496*
in the Soviet Union, 377
in western United States, *i127,* 149
Islam, 75–76, 291, *i333,* 370–371, *m439,* 503–504, 507, *i508,* 510, 517, 519, 576, 585, 586. *See also* Muslims.
islands, *i34,* 36, 121, 203, *i553,* 584–587, 620, 621, 630, 662, *c679,* 689, *i690, i691, i711,* 712
Israel, *i474, m480, c484–485,* 489, 495, 511, *m512, i514,* 515, *m533, c537*
relations with Palestine, 513, 532–535
Issyk-Kul, Lake, *m336*
Italian Peninsula, 290, 291
Italy, *i62, i259, c268–269, c292,* 293, 320, *m404*
Iturbe, Agustín de, 217

J

Jainism, 572
Jakarta, Indonesia, *i677, i731,* 732
Jakota Triangle, *c666*
Jamaica, *c198–199,* 203, 205, 213
Japan, *c95, i607, i608, i609, c616–617,* 619, 621, 623, 630–631, 636, 643, *i657,* 666, 667, 668, 669, *i717*
culture of, 654
earthquakes in, 661, *m662,* 663, *m664*
economic activities in, 652–654
empire, 1942, *m653*
history of, 651–652
modern life in, 655
volcanoes in, 661, *m662,* 663
Jerusalem, Israel, *i474, i477, i510, i513,* 532, *m533,* 534, 535
Johannesburg, South Africa, 457
Jordan, *c484–485,* 489, 511, 513, *c537*
Jordan River, 489
Juárez, Benito, 218, 251
Judaism, 75, 315, 365, 510, 532
Jutland Peninsula, 273

K

K2, *c542*
Kalahari Desert, 71, *c402,* 420, *i463*
Kamchatka Peninsula, 346
Kanchenjunga, *c542*
Kara Kum, *i347,* 352, 353
Karzai, Hamid, 517, 519
Kashmir, 574
Kauai island, 126
Kavachi, 41
Kazakhstan, *c342–343,* 346, 375, 377
Kenya, *i401, c410–411, i418,* 431, 434–435, *i434*
Kermadec Islands, 40
kettles, 44
khamsin, 42
Khan, Genghis, 642
Khan, Kublai, 625, 643
Khyber Pass, 552
Kikuyu, 435
Kili, 701
Kilimanjaro, Mt., 56, *i399,* 417
Kindu Kush Mountains, 488
Kiribati, *c684–685,* 712
Kobe, Japan, 40, *i608, i660, i661*
Koguryo, 647
Kongur, Mt., *c611*
kora, 445
Korea, *m84,* 647–650
Korean Peninsula, *m84,* 620
Korean War, 648
Kosovo, 319, 321
Kostunica, Vojislav, 321
Krakatoa, *i710, i711*
Kunlun Mountains, 619, 627
Kurdistan, 516
Kurds, *i476,* 516, 517, *i524,* 526
Kuril Islands, 346
Kuwait, 173, *c484–485,* 488, 499, 503, 505, 518, 531, *c537*
Kyoto, Japan, 654
Kyoto Protocol, 735, 736
Kyrgyzstan, *c342–343,* 347, 375, 377, *i378, i379*
Kyzyl Kum, 347, 352

L

lakes, 33, *m336*
landfill, 631
landforms
  defined, 33, *i34–35,* 36
landlocked country, 84–85
land reform, 250, 251, 569, 719, *m728*
Landsat, 12
landslides, 40
language
  in Africa, *m407,* 452
  cultural clash in Canada, 161
  as cultural expression, 73
  diffusion of, 73
  in East Asia, *m615*
  in Europe, *m267*
  in India, 571–572
  in Latin America, *m195,* 238
  in Nigeria, *c459*
  in Oceania, 714
  in South Asia, *m591*
  in Transcaucasia, *m370*
  in United States, 181
language families, 73, *m74*
La Niña, *i57*
Laos, *c684–685,* 694, 695, 705, 707, 709
Latin America, 117, 186
  area by country, *c197, c199*
  birthrate by country, *c196, c198*
  capitals and countries of, *c196, c198*
  cars per country, *c197, c199*
  climate zones in, *m194,* 207, *i208,* 209
  democracy in, 249–251, *i249, c250, i251*
  doctors by country, *c197, c199*
  energy resources of, 205
  environmental concerns in, 245–247
  farming in, 210–211
  flags of, *c196, c198*
  gross domestic product by country, *c197, c199*
  highlands in, 202
  historical political units, 1800, *m192*
  history of, 249
  imports and exports by country, *c197, c199*
  income gap in, 252–253, *c254*
  infant mortality rate by country, *c196, c198*
  landforms in, *c190,* 201–202, *m203*
  landmass in, *c190*
  land reform, 250–251
  languages in, *m195*
  life expectancy by country, *c196, c198*
  literacy rate by country, *c197, c199*
  mountains in, *c190,* 201–202
  natural resources in, *m204,* 204–205
  physical geography of, *m191*
  political geography of, *m193*
  population of, *c82, c190, c196, c198,* 211
  poverty in, *c257*
  rain forests, 245–247
  religions of, *c194*
  rivers in, *c190,* 202–203
  slash-and-burn farming, *i210,* 211, 246
  subregions of, *m216*
  televisions per country, *c197, c199*
  terraced farming, 211
  total area by country, *c197, c199*
  tourism in, 212–213
  transportation in, *c197, c199*
  urbanization of, *m195,* 211–212
  vegetation regions of, *m207*
Latinobarometro, *i251*
latitude, *i6, m15, i17, m25,* 55, *i56,* 59
  defined, 6
Latvia, *c342–343,* 361
Lebanon, *c484–485,* 490, 511, 513, 515
Leeward Islands, 203
Leizhou Peninsula, 620
Lena River, 347–348
Lesotho, *c410–411,* 453
Lesser Antilles, 203
Liberia, *c410–411,* 432
Libya, *c410–411,* 417, 438, 439–440
lichens, 66
Liechtenstein, *c268–269,* 296
Lima, Peru, 211, *c212*
linear distance, 9
lithosphere, 28
Lithuania, *c342–343,* 361
Little Ice Age, 58
Ijsselmeer, 283
llanos
  in Colombia and Venezuela, 202
location, 6, *i14, i17*
  absolute vs. relative, 6
  theme of geography, 6
locks, *i129,* 629
loess, 44
Logan, Mt., *c102*
logging, 167, 418
longitude, *i6, m15, i17, m25*
  defined, 6
Louisiana, 73, 148, *m167*
Louisiana Creole, 73
Louisiana Purchase, 136
Lower Canada, 156
low islands, 691
Luxembourg, *c268–269,* 296

M

Maastricht Treaty, 327
Mabo Case, 728
Macao Peninsula, 620
Macedonia, *c270–271,* 310, *m322*
Mackenzie River, *c102,* 121
Madagascar, *c410–411,* 423, 453
Makalu, *c542*
making comparisons, R3
making decisions, R7
making generalizations, R6
making inferences, R4
malaria, 427, *c465,* 466
Malawi, *c410–411,* 453
Malaysia, *c684–685,* 694, 705, *c739*
Maldives, *c548–549,* 551, *i553,* 584–587
Mali, *c94, i398, c410–411, m442,* 443
Malta, *c270–271*
Manchurian Plain, 620
Manchus, 635, 636, 643
mandalas, 583, 705
Mandela, Nelson, 454–455
Manitoba, 62, *c114–115, m157,* 168
mantle, of the earth, *i28*
Maori, 719, *i722*
Mao Zedong, 636, *i637*
mapmaking, science of, 11
  Geographic Information Systems (GIS), *i12,* 13
  Global Positioning System (GPS), 13, *i14*
  satellites, *i11,* 12
  surveying, 11
maps, 64, 206, 322, 494
  defined, 10
  geographic grid in, *i17*
  interpreting a population density map, *m528*
  interpreting a proportional circle map, *m664*
  projections in, 10, *i18, i19*
  reading a map, 15
  reading a population pyramid, *m596*
  reading vegetation maps, *m494*
  reading weather, *m559*
  scale in, *i16*
  science of making, 11–13
  time zones, *m357*
  topographic, 11
  types of, *i4,* 11, 20–23
Maquiladoras, 220
marine west coast climate region, 124, *m125, m194,* 209, 278–279, 696
  defined, 62
market economy, 313, *i335,* 388, 645
  defined, 91

INDEX

Marshall Islands, *c684–685,* 700, 712
Masai, 434
Massif Central, 275
Mau Mau, 435
Mauritania, *c410–411*
Mauritius, *c410–411,* 453, 463
Mauryan Empire, 567
Maya, *m222,* 223
Mazen, Abu, 513
McKinley, Mt., *c102,* 120, *c262, c478, c542*
Mecca, 503
mechanical weathering, 42
medina, 440
Mediterranean climate region, *i62,* 493
in California, 124
defined, 62
in Europe, 279–280
in Latin America, *m194,* 209
in Russia and the Republics, *m340*
in United States and Canada, *m125*
Mediterranean region
art in, 291–292
economic activities in, 292
history of, 289–291
modern life in, 292–293
Mediterranean Sea, 438, 487
megacities, 80
megalopolis, 88
defined, 146
Mekong River, 690
Melanesia, 713, 715
Mercator projection, *i19*
Mercosur, *m234*
meridian. *See* longitude.
Mesa Verde National Park, *i135*
meseta, 275
Mesopotamia, 516
mestizo, 219
métis, 161
metropolitan areas, 148. *See also* cities; suburbs; urban geography.
defined, 87
Mexico, 117, *c198–199,* 205, 208, 209, 212, *m216,* 217–221, 251, *i309, i509*
art in, 219
conquest of, 217–219
cultural mix, 218
economic activities in, 219–220
Fox, Vicente, 218
government in, 250
Institutional Revolutionary Party (PRI), 218
National Action Party, 218
natural boundaries, 85
population distribution in, *m220*
trade with United States and Canada, 160
Mexico City, Mexico, 211, *c212, i217*
Michigan, Lake, *i144,* 147
microcredit, 575
Micronesia, Federated States of, *c684–685,* 698, 712, 713, 715
Mid-Atlantic Ridge, 36
Middle Atlantic states, 145, 146
Middle East, Israeli-Palestinian conflict in, 513, 532–535
Midwest, the (United States), *m134,* 147
migrant labor, 150
migration, 73, 81, 135, 370, 371
Milosevic, Slobodan, 319, 320
minerals, 349, 417, 456, 623
in Africa, *i400, i460*
in Canada, 159
in Latin America, *m204*
in Russia and the Republics, *m359*
in South Asia, 555
in United States and Canada, 122, 146
Mississippi River
diffusion of the blues, 143
discharge rate of, *c190*
flooding along, 53, 126
length of, *c102*
meeting with Gulf of Mexico, 119
waterways in United States, *i121*
Missouri River, 53, *c102*
mistral, 279
mixed economy
defined, 91
Mobutu Sese Seku, 450, 451, 469
Mohenjo-Daro, 573–574
Mojave Desert, 124, *c402, c478*
Moldova, *c342–343,* 361
Monaco, *c270–271,* 296
monarchy, 303
defined, 83
Mongolia, *c616–617,* 619, 625, 627, 635, 644
economic activities in, 644–645
history of, 642–643
modern life in, 645–646
Mongolian Plateau, 620, 627
Mongols, 361, 625, *i642, m643,* 652
Monrovia, Liberia, 421
monsoons, *i541,* 557, 694
Montenegro, 311, 321, *m322*
Montezuma, 217, *i218*
Montreal, Canada, 128, 156, 168
moraine, 44
Morocco, *c410–411,* 438, 440, *i440,* 443
mortality rate
defined, 79
Moscow, Russia, *i332,* 361, 366, *m383*
mosque, 504, 507, *i508*
mountains, *i35,* 36, 580, *c611,* 619
altitudes of United States ranges, *c133*
in Canada, *c102*
elevation and climate, 56
in Europe, *c262,* 274–275
in Latin America, *c190*
orographic precipitation, *i50*
in Russia and the Republics, 346, *m347,* 351
in South Asia, *c542,* 551–552
in Southeast Asia, *m689*
in Southwest Asia, *c478,* 488
in United States and Canada, *c102,* 123
movement, 9, *m23,* 73
linear vs. time, 9
psychological distance, 9
theme of geography, 9
Mozambique, *c410–411,* 415, 453
Mughal Empire, 568, 576
Muhajirs, 576
Muhammad, 439, 503
multiculturalism, *i101,* 142–143, *m142,* 180–181, *c181*
Mumbai, India, 570, *i593*
Murray River, 692
mushairas, 577
music
in Caribbean, 227
culture expressed through, 77
in North Africa, 440–441
in Pakistan and Bangladesh, 577
in South America, 232
in United States, 143
in Western Europe, 300
world instruments, *i588, i589*
Muslims, *m322,* 507, 510, 515, 517, 519, 531, 532, 567, 568, 569, 574, 576, 584
Myanmar, *c684–685,* 694, 695, 705, 707, 709

N

NAFTA. *See* North American Free Trade Agreement.
Nagorno-Karabakh, 371, *m387*
Namib Desert, 55, *c402,* 420
Namibia, *c410–411,* 451, 453
Nanjing, China, *m640*
Nasser, Lake, 426, 427
national parks, 9, 41, 42, *i116,* 135, *i422, i729*
National Water Carrier, 495

Native Americans, m104, 127, 137, *m142*, 143, 159, *m171*, *i657*
NATO. *See* North Atlantic Treaty Organization.
natural gas, *m204*, *c348*, 349, 497, *i498*, 518
natural resources
in Africa, 450, 468
defined, 93
in East Asia, *m622*, 623
in Europe, *m276*
in Latin America, *m204*
in Russia and the Republics, 348–349, 356
in South Asia, 554–555, *m554*
in Southwest Asia, 489–490
in United States and Canada, 121–122
Nauru, *c684–685*, 714
Negev Desert, *c478*, 495, *i496*
Nepal, *c548–549*, 552, 554, *i555*, 556, 558, 580–581
Netherlands, the, *c224*, *c270–271*, 282–283, 296, *i300*
New Brunswick, *c114–115*, *i118*, 156–157, 162, 166, 167
New Caledonia, 691
New England, 145–147
Newfoundland, *c114–115*, 155, *m157*, 166
New Guinea, *c679*, 691
New Jersey, 81–82
New York City, 146, 180. *See also* September 11 terrorist attack.
New Zealand, *c684–685*, 691–692, 695, 696, 718–720, *i721*, 722, 723
Niagara Falls, *i99*
Nicaragua, *c198–199*
Niger, *c412–413*
Nigeria, 85–86, *c412–413*, 416, 417, 418, 424, 425, *c443*, 445, 448, *c459*
Niger River, *c402*, 416, 424
Nile River, *c190*, *c402*, 416, 426–427, *i438*
9-11 terrorist attack. *See* September 11 terrorist attack.
nomads, 127, 378, 379, *i476*, 642, 645
nonviolent resistance, 568
Noor, Queen, 529
Nordic countries, 302
noria, *i496*
Normandy, 302
North Africa
culture of, 440–441
history of, 438–439
oil, economics of, 439–440
religions in, 439
women's roles, changing, 441
North America
landforms of, 117–121
native peoples of, c. 1600, *m104*
natural resources in, *m93*
transform boundary in, 38
United States as part of, 135
North American Free Trade Agreement (NAFTA), 160, 220
North Atlantic Drift, 55, 278
North Atlantic Treaty Organization (NATO), 321
North China Plain, 620
Northeast, the (Southwest Asia), *m516*, 517, 518–519
Northeast, the (United States), *m134*, *m145*, 146–147
Northern Europe, 302–305, 306–307
British empire, 1900, *m304*
representative government, *i303*
Northern European Plain, 345
Northern Hemisphere, *i6*, 49, *i54*, 55
Northern Ireland, 305
North Island, 691
North Korea, *c616–617*, 619, 623, 626, 648, 649, 650
North Ossetia, 385
North Sea, 276, 283
North Vietnam, 707
Northwest Territories, *c114–115*, *i123*, 168–169
Norway, *c270–271*, *i272*, 302, *m305*
Nostratic language, 73
Nova Scotia, *c114–115*, 156–157, 162, 166, *m167*
nuclear energy. *See* Chernobyl.
nuclear submarines, 393
nuclear testing, 377
nuclear waste, 393, 395
nuclear weapons, 377, 392–393, *i394*, 395, *i541*, 700–701, 713, 714
Nunavut, *c114–115*, 168, *i169*
Nyasa, Lake, 38

O

oasis, *i34*, 421, *i475*, 492, *i495*
Obama, Barack, 174
Ob River, 347–348
ocean currents, 55
Oceania, *m674*, *m675*, 694
area by country, *c685*, *c687*
birthrate by country, *c684*, *c686*
capitals and countries of, *c684*, *c686*
cars per country, *c685*, *c687*
climate regions in, *m683*
cultural regions of, *m713*
doctors by country, *c685*, *c687*
economic activities in, 714
flags of, *c684*, *c686*
gross domestic product by country, *c685*, *c687*
history of, 712–714
human geography of, *m680*
imports and exports by country, *c685*, *c687*
infant mortality rate by country, *c684*, *c686*
landmass of, *c679*
language in, 714
life expectancy by country, *c684*, *c686*
literacy rate by country, *c685*, *c687*
modern life in, 715
physical geography of, *m678*
political geography of, *m681*
population of, *c82*, *c679*, *c684*, *c686*
religion in, *m683*, 714
subregions of, *m704*
televisions per country, *c685*, *c687*
territories and possessions, *c686*
total area of countries, *c685*, *c687*
traveling around, 698–699, *i698*, *i699*
oceans, 32–33, *m55*, 57, 121, 698
Ogadai, 643
Ogallala Aquifer, 33
oil, *m22*, 91, *m93*, *m204*, 205, 220, 324, *c348*, 349, 373, 377, 417–418, *m417*, 424, 425, 439, 440, *i474*, *i477*, *i490*, 497, *i498*, *m498*, *m501*, *c505*, 506, 517, 518, 525, *c529*, 555
Old Faithful, 41
Olduvai Gorge, 431
oligarchy, 249
Oman, *c484–485*, *i495*, *i496*, 503, *c526*, 531
one-child policy, 639
one-commodity countries, 462
Ontario, Canada, *c114–115*, 167
Ontario, Lake, 52
OPEC. *See* Organization of Petroleum Exporting Countries.
Operation Enduring Freedom, 174, 517
Operation Iraqi Freedom, 518
Oregon Trail, 129, 137
Organization of Petroleum Exporting Countries (OPEC), 505
Orinoco River, 202–203
orographic precipitation, *i50*, 51
Osama bin Laden. *See* bin Laden, Osama.
Ossetian people, 386
Ottawa, Canada, 157, *i158*, 167
Ottoman Empire, 311, 319, 505, 511, *m523*

INDEX

outback, 697
outrigger canoe, 699
ozone layer, 325, *i677,* 734–737

P

Pacific Islands, 698–701
Pacific Ocean, 32, 41, 121
Pacific Provinces and Territories, *m154,* 168–169
Pacific Rim, 645
Padma River, 560
Paektu, Mt., *c611*
pakehas, 722
Pakistan, 174, *i541, c548–549, i550,* 551, 552, 554, 555, 556, 568, 573–574, *c575,* 576–577
Palau, *c684–685,* 712
Palestine, 511, 512, 527, 534
Palestine Liberation Organization (PLO), 513
Palestinians, 175, *i513, i527, m533,* 535
pampas, 66
 of Argentina and Uruguay, 202
Panama, *c198–199,* 222
pandemic, 435
Pangaea, i29, 415
Papua New Guinea, *c684–685,* 712, 714
Paraguay, *c198–199,* 203, 207, 209, 253
Paraná River, *c190,* 203
parliamentary government, 158
particulates, 324
Patagonia, *i59,* 209
PCBs, 631
Pearl Harbor, 652
Pearl River. *See* Zhu Jiang.
peninsulas, 273–274, 620, 689
Pennsylvania, 146
Pentagon, 173
Perahera, 586
per capita income
 defined, 94
permafrost, 63, 123, 280, 350, 355
Persian Gulf, 487, 489, 490, 517
Persian Gulf War, 174, 499, 517, 518
Peru, 54, *i165, c198–199,* 210, 211, *i717*
Philippines, *c684–685,* 689, 690, 694, 705, 709, 731, *c739*
physical maps, *i20*
Pinatuba, Mt., 689
Pinochet, Augusto, *i189, i232*
pipelines, 373, *m417,* 426, 497, 499
Pittsburgh, Pennsylvania, 88, 117
place
 theme of geography, 7
plains, 36, 275
 of Amazon River Basin, 202
planar projection. *See* azimuthal projection.
Plateau of Tibet, 619
plateaus, *i35,* 36, 551–552
plate tectonics, 37–39
PLO. *See* Palestine Liberation Organization.
Poland, *c270–271,* 310, 311, 312
polar zones, 56, 697
polders, 282
pollution, 324, 354, 670
 in Europe, *i260,* 285, 323–325
 along the Ganges River, 560, 561
 in Japan, 630
 in Russia and the Republics, 349, *m359*
 in Southeast Asia, 731, 732
 in Southwest Asia, 499
 in United States and Canada, 177
Polynesia, 713
Polynesians, 698, *i699,* 715
population
 in Africa, *c402,* 425
 in China, *i639*
 distribution, 80–81, *m406*
 of East Asia cities, 668–669, *c669*
 of Europe, *c262*
 of Latin America, *c190,* 238
 relocation of, 525–527, 630
 in South Asia, *c542, i592*
 in Southwest Asia, *c478*
population density, *m80,* 81–82, *m528*
 in Bangladesh, *i577*
 of Canada, *m107*
 in East Asia, *m615*
 of Europe, *m267*
 in India, *m594*
 along the Nile River, 416
 of South Asia, *m547*
 of United States, *m107*
 of world regions, *c82*
population growth rate, *i3,* 78–79, *c78, c79, i540,* 670, 671, *c673*
population pyramid, *c79, m596*
 defined, 79
Portugal, 236, *c270–271,* 274, 291, *c292, m404,* 449, 468
poverty, 144, *i189,* 252–253, 254, 255, *c257,* 455, 595
Powell, Lake, *i67*
Prague, Czech Republic, 314, *i315*
prairie, *i35,* 65
Prairie Provinces, *m154, i168*
precipitation, 735
 in Africa, 421–422
 and climate regions, 59
 in East Asia, *m633*
 in Europe, *c281*
 ocean currents and, 55
 in South Asia, 557, *m565*
 in Southwest Asia, 491–492
 types of, 50–52, *i50*
 in United States coastal mountain ranges, 124
prevailing westerlies, 124
PRI. *See* Institutional Revolutionary Party.
prime meridian, *i6, m357*
 defined, 6
prime minister, 158
Prince Edward Island, *c114–115, m157,* 166
privatization, 388
proportional circle maps, *m664*
Pueblo, 127
Puerto Rico, 203
purdah, 576
Pushkin, Aleksandr, 366
push-pull factors, 211, 730
 defined, 81
 in Latin America, 211
Putin, Vladimir, *i363,* 389
Pyongyang, North Korea, 650
pyramids, 219, *i223, i398, i509*
Pyrenees Mountains, 274

Q

qanat, *i496*
Qatar, *c484–485,* 503, 506, *c526, c537*
Qawwali, 577
Qinling Shandi Mountains, 619
qualitative maps, *m22*
Quebec, *c114–115,* 162, 167, 180
Quechua, 231

R

radiation, *i368, m368,* 377
rai, 440
rain forest, 422–423, 425, 558
 in Africa, 421
 deforestation in Brazil, *i188*
 in Latin America, 207–208, *m245,* 246, 247
 medicine from, *i205*
 vegetation in, 66
rain shadow, 51, 492
Ramadan, 504, 507, 576
ranching, *i721*
rate of natural increase
 defined, 79
ratio scale, *i16*
recession, 138, 667

recycling, *c185*
Red Sea, 38, 487
refugees, *i513,* 517, 526, 527
region
formal, 7
functional, 8
perceptual, 8
theme of geography, 7–8
relief, 36
religion
in Africa, *c406*
animism, 75
in Arabian Peninsula, 506–507
architecture, *i508, i509*
in Brazil, 238
in Canada, 161
in China, 638
climates of, *m340*
as cultural expression, 75
in East Asia, *m614*
in Europe, *c266*
freedom in United States, 143
in India, 571–572
major belief systems, 75–77
in Nepal and Bhutan, 582–583
in Oceania, 714
polytheism, 75
of Russia and the Republics, *c340*
in Southeast Asia and Oceania, *m683,* 708
worldwide distribution, *c76, m76*
Renaissance, the, 291
representative democracy, *i139, c303*
Rhine River, *c262,* 275, 324
Richter Scale, 40
ridges, 36
Ridge, Tom, 175
rift valleys, *i416*
Ring of Fire, 41, 661, *m662,* 663, 690
Rio de Janeiro, Brazil, *i7, i187,* 211, *c212,* 213, 239, *i240*
Rio de la Plata, 203
Rio Grande, 85, *c102*
rivers, 33, *i34*
in Africa, *c402,* 415–416
in Canada, *c102*
in East Asia, *c610,* 621–622
erosion, 43
in Europe, *c262,* 275
flooding from, 53
in Latin America, *c190*
in South Asia, 552–553, *i552*
in Southeast Asia, *m689*
in United States, *c102*
road map (Middle East peace plan), 513
Robinson projection, *i19*
Rocky Mountains, 119–120
Roman Catholicism, 75, 291, 297
Roman Empire, *m22,* 290–292, *m290,* 296, 311
Romania, *c270–271,* 310, 311, 312, 313, 323
Rome, Italy, 293
Rosa, Monte, *c262*
Rub al-Khali, *c478, i490,* 491
rubber, *m93,* 469
Rupert's Land, 156
Russia and the Republics, 332, *c342–343, i509,* 636
area by country, *c343*
art in, 365–366
birthrate by country, *c342*
capitals and countries of, *c342*
cars per country, *c343*
climate regions of, 62, *m340,* 350–351
doctors by country, *c343*
economic system in, *i91,* 364, 388–390
ethnic groups in, *m341,* 365, *c377*
expansion of land, *m362*
extreme weather in, 354–355
federal districts of, *m389*
fighting in Chechnya, 386
flags of, *c342*
gross domestic product by country, *c343*
history of, 361–363
imports and exports by country, *c343*
income distribution in, *c391*
infant mortality rate by country, *c342*
lakes in, *c336*
landforms in, 345–348
landmass of, *c337*
life expectancy by country, *c342*
life expectancy in, *c397*
literacy rate by country, *c343*
mining in, *m359*
modern life in, 366–367
mountains in, 346–347
natural resources in, 348–349, 356
nomadic life, 378–379, *i380–381*
nuclear weapons in, 392–393
organized crime in, 390
physical geography of, *m336, m337*
political geography of, *m338–339*
population of, *c82, c337, m341, c342*
religion in, *c340,* 365
rivers and lakes in, *c336,* 347–348
subregions of, *m360*
televisions per country, *c343*
terrorism and, 174
transportation in, *m355*
unemployment in, *c391*
vegetation regions, 351–352, *m351*
Russian Revolution, 363
rust belt, 146
Rwanda, 81, *c412–413,* 431, 451

S

Sacramento, California, 88
SADC. *See* Southern African Development Community.
Sahara, 62, 420, *i420,* 443, *c478*
Sahel, 425
Sakhalin Islands, 346
salt, 443, 490
saltwater lakes, 33
Sami, 302
Samoa, *c684–685,* 712
San Andreas Fault, 38
sand dunes, 44
sandstorms, 42
San Marco, 283
San Marino, *c270–271*
Santa Fe Trail, 129
Santiago, Chile, 211, *c212*
São Paulo, Brazil, 211, *c212,* 239
São Tomé and Princípe, *c412–413,* 448
Saskatchewan, *c114–115, i118, m157,* 168
satellite nations, 312
Saudi Arabia, 38, 173, *c348, i474, i477, c484–485,* 488, 497, 503, 505, 506, *c526,* 530, *c537*
savanna, 66, 208
Scandinavia, 280, 285, 361
Scotland, 275, *i588*
sea level, *i34,* 734
seas, 29, 32–33, 36
seasons, *i49*
Seattle, Washington, 141
sediment, 42, 43, 44
seeing patterns, R8
seismograph, 39, *i663*
semiarid climate region, *i61,* 124, *m125, m194,* 208, *m340,* 493, 627
defined, 61
Senegal, *c412–413,* 467
Seoul, South Korea, *i607,* 650
September 11 terrorist attack, 173–175, 517
anthrax and, 175
Serbia, 311, 319, 321
Serbia and Montenegro, 321
Serbs, 314, 321, *m322*
Serengeti Plain, 422
Seychelles, *c412–413,* 431
Shandi Mountains, 619

INDEX

Shandong Peninsula, 620
Shanghai, China, *i81,* 637
Shatt al Arab, 489
Sherpas, *i582*
Shevardnadze, Edvard, 387
Shi Huangdi, 635
Shi'ite, 515, 516
Shintoism, 77
shogun, 651
Siberia, 129, 349, 350, *i352,* 354–355, 356
Sierra Leone, *c412–413, c443,* 444
Sierra Nevada, 120
Sikhism, 569, 572
Silicon Valley, 141
Silk Road, the, *m375,* 376
silt, 427
Singapore, 82, *c684–685,* 705, 709
Sinhalese, 584, 585
sirocco, 279
SkillBuilder Handbook
  analyzing data, R2
  creating and using a database, R15
  creating graphs and charts, R13
  creating a multimedia presentation, R14
  creating a sketch map, R12
  determining cause and effect, R9
  distinguishing fact from opinion, R11
  drawing conclusions, R5
  identifying and solving problems, R10
  making comparisons, R3
  making decisions, R7
  making generalizations, R6
  making inferences, R4
  seeing patterns, R8
slash-and-burn farming, *i210,* 211, 246, 423
slavery, 136, 223, 234, 236, 445, 449
sleeping sickness, *c465*
Slovakia, *c270–271,* 310, 313
Slovenes, *m322*
Slovenia, *c270–271,* 310, 320
smallpox, *c465*
smog, 62, 325
snowbelt, 52
snowstorms, 126
socialist realism, 366
soil, 45, *c65*
Solomon Islands, 41, *c684–685,* 691, 712
Somalia, *c412–413,* 415, 421, 431, *m436, i437,* 463
Songhai, *m442,* 443
Sonika, 443
Sonoran Desert, 124
souks, i440
South, the (United States), *m134,* 148
South Africa, *c412–413,* 415, 417, 453, 454–455, *i456,* 457, 466, 467, 469
South America, *m187,* 201, *m216*
  arts in, 232–233
  economic activities in, 233–234
  education in, 234–235
  government in, 232
  history of, 230–232
  natural resources in, *m93*
South Asia, 538
  area by country, *c549*
  birthrate by country, *c548*
  capitals and countries of, *c548*
  cars per country, *c549*
  climate regions of, 556, *m557,* 558
  doctors by country, *c549*
  economic activities in, *m547, c549*
  flags of, *c548*
  gross domestic product by country, *c549*
  imports and exports by country, *c549*
  Indus Valley civilization, *m544*
  infant mortality rate by country, *c548*
  landforms in, 38, 551, *i552,* 553
  landmass of, *c542*
  language in, *m591*
  life expectancy by country, *c548*
  literacy rate by country, *c549*
  mountains in, *c542,* 551–552
  natural resources in, 554–555, *m554*
  physical geography of, *m543*
  political geography of, *m545*
  population of, *c82, c542, m547, c548,* 593–595
  precipitation in, *m565*
  religion in, 75, *c546, m546*
  rivers in, *c542,* 552–553
  subregions of, *m566*
  televisions per country, *c549*
  total area of countries, *c549*
  using physical maps, *m20*
  using political maps, *m21*
  vegetation regions, *m557,* 558
Southeast Asia, *m674, m675*
  area by country, *c685, c687*
  area by island, *c679*
  art in, 708
  birthrate by country, *c684, c686*
  capitals and countries of, *c684, c686*
  cars per country, *c685, c687*
  climate regions in, *m683,* 694–697
  colonies in, 1895, *m706*
  doctors by country, *c685, c687*
  economic activities in, 707–708
  empires and kingdoms, 1200, *m681*
  environmental issues, 734–735
  ethnic Chinese in, *c682*
  ethnic groups in, 705
  flags of, *c684, c686*
  gross domestic product by country, *c685, c687*
  history of, 705–707
  human geography of, *m680, c682*
  imports and exports by country, *c685, c687*
  industrialization, 730–732, *c739*
  infant mortality rate by country, *c684, c686*
  landforms in, *m678, c679,* 689–690, *m689, i690*
  landmass of, *c679*
  life expectancy by country, *c684, c686*
  literacy rate by country, *c685, c687*
  modern life in, 709
  political geography of, *m680–681*
  pollution in, 732
  population of, *c82, c679, c684, c686*
  poverty in, 709
  religions in, *m683,* 708
  subregions of, *m704*
  televisions per country, *c685, c687*
  total area of countries, *c685, c687*
  urbanization, 730–731
  vegetation, 694–697
  volcanoes in, *c682*
Southern Africa
  apartheid, 454–455, 457
  cultures in, 456–457
  economic activities in, 455–456
  ethnic groups in, *m454*
  history of, 453–454
  lifestyles, modern and traditional, 457
Southern African Development Community (SADC), 462
Southern Alps, 691
Southern Hemisphere, *i6, i54,* 55
Southern Ocean, 32
South Island, 691, 696
South Korea, *i607, c616–617,* 619, 626, 648, *i649,* 650, 654, *c659,* 666, 667, 668
South Pole, 692, 697
South Vietnam, 707
Southwest Asia, 474
  area by country, *c485*
  birthrate by country, *c484*
  capitals and countries of, *c484*
  cars per country, *c485*
  climate regions of, *c478,* 491–493, *m492*
  deserts in, *c478,* 491–492
  doctors by country, *c485*

economic activities in, *m15, m483*
ethnic groups in, *c482*
ethnic regions, *m482*
flags of, *c484*
gross domestic product by country, *c485*
imports and exports by country, *c485*
infant mortality rate by country, *c484*
landforms in, 487–489
landmass of, *c478*
life expectancy by country, *c484*
literacy rate by country, *c485*
mountains in, *c478,* 488
natural resources in, 489–490, 529–530
oil, 490, 497, *i498, m498,* 499, 529–531
physical geography of, *m479*
political geography of, *m481*
population of, *c82, c478, c484,* 525–527
refugee problem, 526–527
religion in, 75, *m483*
rivers in, *m488,* 489
subregions of, *m502*
televisions per country, *c485*
total area of countries, *c485*
water resources in, 495–496, *c537*
women's roles, 531
workforce, 525–526
Soviet Union, 310, 312, 313, *m339,* 363, 364, 366, 371, 376, 385, 386, 388, *m392. See also* Russia and the Republics.
Spain, *c270–271,* 274, 291, 292, 293, 706
colonies in Latin America, *c224,* 249–251
colonies in United States, 135
conquest of Mexico, 217–219, 223–224
conquest of South America, *c230, c231,* 232
dwellings, *i381*
Spanglish, 73
spheres of influence, 636
Sri Lanka, *i539, c548–549,* 551, 553, 555, 557, 584–587
St. Elias, Mt., *c102*
St. Kitts and Nevis, *c198–199*
St. Lawrence Seaway, *i129*
St. Lucia, *c198–199*
St. Petersburg, Russia, 362, 366
St. Vincent and the Grenadines, *c198–199*
stateless nation, 526
stateless society, 443, 449
steppes, *i35,* 66, 352, 626, 627
Stolen Generation, 728
storm surges, 562
straits, *i34*
strategic commodity, 529
streams, 33, 43
subarctic climate region, *i63,* 123, *m125, m340,* 351, 625
defined, 62
subduction, 661
subtropical climate region, 124
suburbs, 138, 143, 177
defined, 87
Sudan, *c412–413,* 416, 426, 438
Suez Canal, 487, 505
sugar, 224, 225, 236
Sumatra, *c679*
sunbelt, 148
Sunni, 515, 516
supra, i374
Suriname, *c198–199*
surveying, 11, *i14*
sustainable communities, 178
Swahili, 73
swamps, *i34*
Swaziland, *c412–413,* 453, 466
Sweden, *c270–271,* 302, 303, 305
Switzerland, *c270–271,* 299
Sydney, Australia, 718, *i719, i723*
Syr Darya, 347, 353
Syria, *c484–485,* 487, 489, 511, 526
Syrian Desert, 492

T

Tagore, Rabindranath, 577
taiga, 62, 352, *i352*
Taino, 223
Tain Shan, 627
Taiwan, *c616–617,* 619, 621, 623, 626, 627, 642–643, 644–646, 654, 666, 667, 668
Tajikistan, *c342–343,* 347, 375, 377
Taklimakan Desert, 619, 627
Taliban, 174, 517, 519
Tamils, 569, 584
Tanganyika, Lake, 38, 417
Tanzania, 55, *c412–413,* 431, 432, 434
Taoism, 77, 638
Tarim Pendi Basin, 619
Taurus Mountains, 487, 488
tea, *c586*
technology, 82, 94, *i138, m141,* 530
tectonic plates, *i37,* 40, 661
Temple Mount, 510, 532, *m533*
Tennessee Valley Authority (TVA), 86
Tenochtitlán, *i186,* 217, 218, 219, *m243*
Teotihuacán, 219
terraced farming, 211, *i695*
terrorism, 173–175
coalition against. *See* antiterrorism coalition.
definition of, 173
terrorist attacks. *See* September 11 terrorist attack.
TGV, 299
Thailand, 95, *i674, c686–687,* 694, 695, 705, *i708,* 709, *c739*
Thar Desert, 553, *i556,* 557, 558
Three Gorges Dam, 623, 628–630, *m628, i629, m640*
Three Kingdoms, 647
Tibesti Mountains, 417, 420
Tien Shan, 346
Tigris-Euphrates River, *m488,* 489, 493, 495, 516
Tikal, 223
timber, *m204,* 418, 554, *i555*
time zones, world, *m357*
Timor, 705
Tisza River, *i323*
Titicaca, Lake, *i165*
Togo, *c412–413*
Tokyo, Japan, 80, *i609,* 630, 631
Toltec, 217
Tonga, *c686–687,* 712
topographic maps
defined, 11, 36
topography
defined, 36
Tordesillas, Treaty of, *m236*
Tornado Alley, *m52,* 126
tornadoes, *i48,* 51–52, *m107,* 126
defined, 51
Toronto, Canada, 156, 168
tourism, 148, 160, 212–213, 227, 434, 581–582, 714
trade routes, *m375, m442,* 443
traditional economy
defined, 91
Transantarctic Mountains, 692
Trans-Canada highway, 130
Transcaucasia, 35, 346, 351, *m360,* 370–374
transcontinental railroads, 130, *i137,* 157, *m355*
Transjordan, 512
transportation
bullet trains, *i655*
comparing cultures, *i64–65*
functions of cities, 90
highways, 130, *m131,* 177
as infrastructure, 94
Trans-Siberian Railroad, 355–356, *m355, i356*

INDEX

tributaries, 33
Trinidad and Tobago, *c198–199,* 205
tropical storms, 51, *m107*
tropical wet and dry climate region, *m125, m194,* 208, 694
defined, 61
tropical wet climate region, *i60, m194,* 207, 627, 694
defined, 60
tropical zones, 55, 124–126, 207–208, 421, 694
Tropic of Cancer, 49
Tropic of Capricorn, 49
tsunami, 40, 662, *i710*
Tuamotu Archipelago, 5
Tumbuka, 456
tundra, *m66,* 123–124, *m125,* 280, *m340, m351,* 625
defined, 63
Tunguska Event, 31
Tunisia, *c412–413,* 438, 439, 441
Turan Plain, 347
Turkey, 73, *c484–485,* 487, 488, 489, 490, *i493,* 495, *i497, i508,* 511, 516, 517, 518, 519, *m520, i521, m521, i524,* 526
Turkmenistan, *c342–343,* 347, 352, 375, 377, 378
Tuvalu, *c686–687,* 712
TVA. *See* Tennessee Valley Authority.
typhoons, *i51,* 625, *i627*
defined, 51

U

Uganda, *c412–413,* 416, 431, 434, 451, *i452, 467*
Ukraine, *c342–343, i345,* 361, 393
Uluru. *See* Ayers Rock.
UNAIDS, 466, 467
UNICEF. *See* United Nations Children's Funds.
United Arab Emirates, *c484–485,* 503, *c526,* 530, *c537*
United Kingdom, *c270–271,* 302. *See also* Great Britain.
United Nations, *i83,* 86
United Nations Children's Funds (UNICEF), 665
United Provinces of Central America, 223–224
United States, 98, *m99,* 119, 652, 707
agriculture in, *m141, c147*
area by state, *c109, c111, c113*
area rank, *c109, c111, c113*
assimilation, 181
capitals and states of, *c108, c110, c112*
climate in, 62, 123, 124, *m125,* 126
Cold War with Soviet Union, 363
connections with Canada, *m106,* 160
development of the West, *c137*
doctors by state, *c109, c111, c113*
drought in, 53
economic activities in, 95, *m106, c140*
ethnic minority distribution, *m142*
flags of, *c108, c110, c112*
government of, *i139*
high school graduates by state, *c109, c111, c113*
industry in, 137–138, 141, *m141*
infant mortality rate by state, *c108, c110, c112*
landforms of, *c102,* 117–121
landmass of, *c102*
languages in, 143
major sectors of economy, *c140*
megalopolis in, 88
Midwest, the, 147
mountains in, *c102,* 119–121
multiculturalism in, 180, *c181,* 221
native peoples of, c. 1600, *m104*
natural boundaries, 85
natural hazards of, *m107*
natural resources in, *m120,* 121–122
Northeast, the, 145–147
nuclear weapons in former Soviet Union, 393
peace talks between Armenia and Azerbaijan, 387
per capita income by state, *c109, c111, c113*
physical geography of, *m103*
political geography of, *m105*
population density by state, *c109, c111, c113*
population of, *c79,* 81–82, *c82, c102, m107, c108, c110, c112, m146, m153*
population rank, *c109, c111, c113*
postindustrial economy, 141–142
poverty in, 144
recycling in, *c185*
regions of, *m118*
religion in, 143
rivers in, *c102*
settlement of, 135–136
South, the, 148
sports in, 144
subregions of, *m134,* 145–149, 147
technology growth in, *i138*
terrorist attacks on, 173–175
tornado activity, *m52*
trade with Mexico, 220
transportation in, 121, 129, 130
urban/rural population by state, *c109, c111, c113*
urban sprawl, 176–178, *m179*
vegetation regions in, *m125*
weather extremes, 126
West, the, 148–149
Upper Canada, 156
Ural Mountains, 346
urban geography, 87–90, *m97*
urbanization, 506, 525
in Brazil, 238
in Canada, 162
defined, 88
land use patterns, 89
in Latin America, *m195,* 220
in Mediterranean climate region, 293
movement of population, 80
of northeastern United States, *m145*
in Oceania, 723
in Southeast Asia, 730–732
in United States, 128, 137, *c176*
urban sprawl, *i101,* 148
in United States and Canada, 176–178, *m179*
Uruguay, *c198–199,* 209, 211, 253
U.S.S.R. *See* Soviet Union; Russia and the Republics.
Uzbekistan, *c342–343,* 347, 352, 375, 377

V

valleys, *i35,* 43
Vancouver, Canada, 169, 178
Vanuatu, *c686–687, i712*
Vatican City, *c270–271*
vegetation, 80, *m494*
vegetation regions, 65–66
Venezuela, *c198–199,* 202, 205, 232
Venice, Italy, *i281,* 283–284, 291
Verkhoyansk, Siberia, 354
Victoria Falls, *i414*
Victoria, Lake, 417
Vietnam, *i164, c686–687,* 690, 694, 695, 705, 707
Vikings, 155, 302, 361
Vindhya Range, 552
Virginia, *i122,* 148
Virgin Islands, *i213*
volcanoes, *i2, i34,* 40–41, *m107, i228–229,* 662, *c682,* 689–690, *i710–711*
defined, 40
Volga River, 348
Vostok, Antarctica, 63

W

wadis, 488
Waialeale, Mount, 126
Waitangi, Treaty of, *i719*
war against terrorism
  in Afghanistan, 174, 517, *i517*, 518, 519
  Bush administration and, 174, 517
Washington, D.C., *m16*, *m179*
water, 33, 149, 490, 495–496, *c537*
waterfalls, *i32*, *i414*, 416
weapons of mass destruction, 518
weather, 12, 50–53, 126, 350, 354
weather extremes
  blizzards, 52
  droughts, 53
  floods, 53
  hurricanes, 51
  tornadoes, 51
  typhoons, 51
  in United States and Canada, 126
weathering, 42–43
  defined, 42
Wen Jiabao, 637
West, the (United States), *m134*, *i137*, 148–149
West Africa, 416
  art in, 444–445
  economic activities in, 443–444
  empires of, *m442*, 443
  gross national product, 1987–1997, *c443*
  history of, 442–443
  music in, 445
West Bank, 513, 527, 532
Western Europe
  art in, 300
  economic activities in, 298–300
  history of, 296–298
  modern life in, 301
  Reformation, the, 297
Western Ghats, 552
Western Hemisphere, *i6*
Western Wall, 510
West Germany, 298, *m317*
West Indies, 203
West Siberian Plain, 346
Wik Case, 729
winds
  climate effects, *i54*, *i57*
  erosion, 44
  global wind currents, *i54*
  khamsin, 42
  mistral, 279
  sirocco, 279
  tornadoes, 51–52
  over tropical ocean waters, 51
  westerlies in Europe, 278
  willy-willies, 51
Windward Islands, 203
women's roles, 595, 720
  in Arabian Peninsula, 506, *i507*
  farming in United States, 135
  in North Africa, *i441*
  in Southwest Asia, *i519*, 529, 531
wool, 721
World Trade and Development Act, 471
World Trade Center, 173. *See also* September 11 terrorist attack.
World War I, 298, *c311*
World War II, *c311*, 312, 652, 713

X

Xi Jiang, *c610*, 621, 622
Xizang Plateau, 619

Y

Yalu Jiang, *m84*, 622
Yangtze River. *See* Chang Jiang.
Yellow River. *See* Huang He.
Yemen, *c484–485*, 503, 505, *c537*
Yenisey River, 347–348
Yugoslavia, *c270–271*, 310, 311, 313, 319, *i321*, *m322*
Yukon Territory, *c114–115*, 123, *m157*, 168–169
yurts, *i72*, *i379*, *i380*, 645

Z

Zagros Mountains, 487, 488
Zaire, 471
Zambezi River, *i414*
Zambia, *c412–413*, 417, 453
Zeugma, *i497*
Zhu Jiang, 622
Zimbabwe, *c412–413*, 451, 453
Zuider Zee, 283
Zulu, 454, *i455*, 457

Acknowledgments

Unless otherwise indicated below, all video reference screens are © 2010 A&E Television Networks, LLC. All rights reserved.

TEXT ACKNOWLEDGMENTS

Unit 1, Adapted "Figure 9.51," from *Physical Geography, Second Edition.* Copyright © 1989, 1992 by West Publishing Company. Reprinted by permission of Thomson Learning.

Excerpt from "Flight of a Lifetime" by James Irwin, from *The Greatest Adventure.* Copyright © 1994 by the Association of Space Explorers.

Excerpt from "To Really See It, Leave It" by Sally Ride, from *The Greatest Adventure.* Copyright © 1994 by the Association of Space Explorers.

Unit 3, Excerpt from "Brazilian police go on trial for murder of street children" by Marina Mirabella, from CNN World News, April 26, 1996. Copyright © 1996 by Cable News Network, Inc. Reprinted by permission of Cable News Network, Inc.

Excerpt from "Hope for the no-hopers," from the *Economist,* December 23, 2000. Copyright © 2000 by the *Economist.* Reprinted by permission of the *Economist.*

Excerpt from "Rich-poor gap as wide as ever in Latin America" by Steve Gutkin, from *The Times of India Online,* September 5, 2000. Copyright © 2000 by Times Internet Limited. Reprinted by permission of Times Internet Limited. All rights reserved.

Unit 4, Excerpt from "Poland Opens Door to West, and Chills Blow Both Ways" by Edmund L. Andrews, from the *New York Times,* June 21, 1999. Copyright © 1999 by the *New York Times.* Reprinted by permission of the *New York Times.*

Excerpt from "Britain and the Single Currency," from Global Britain Briefing Note, No. 1, January 25, 1999. Copyright © 1999 by Global Britain. Reprinted by permission of Global Britain.

Unit 5, Excerpt from "Workers Bid Ill-Fated Chernobyl a Bitter Farewell" by Michael Wines, from the *New York Times,* December 15, 2000. Copyright © 2000 by the *New York Times.* Reprinted by permission of the *New York Times.*

Excerpt from "Reducing Russian Dangers," from the *New York Times,* January 21, 1999. Copyright © 1999 by the *New York Times.* Reprinted by permission of the *New York Times.*

Unit 6, Excerpt from "Cash Strapped African Leaders Beg To Be Re-Colonized" by Ron Daniels, from the *Black World Today,* August 1, 1999. Copyright © 1999 by the *Black World Today.* Reprinted by permission of the *Black World Today.*

Excerpt from "An African Success Story," from the *New York Times,* January 8, 2001. Copyright © 2001 by the *New York Times.* Reprinted by permission of the *New York Times.*

Unit 7, Excerpt from "All Sides Resist Plan by Clinton For the Mideast" by John Kifner, from the *New York Times,* December 31, 2000. Copyright © 2000 by the *New York Times.* Reprinted by permission of the *New York Times.*

Excerpt from "The Price of Peace Will Be Paid in Dreams" by John F. Kifner, from the *New York Times,* December 31, 2000. Copyright © 2000 by the *New York Times.* Reprinted by permission of the *New York Times.*

Excerpt from "A City That Echoes Eternity" by Kenneth L. Woodward, from *Newsweek,* July 24, 2000. Copyright © 2000 by Newsweek, Inc. Reprinted by permission of Newsweek, Inc. All rights reserved.

Excerpts from "City of Jerusalem," from *United Nations: General Assembly Resolution 181,* November 29, 1947. Copyright © 1947 by the United Nations. Reprinted by permission of the United Nations.

Unit 8, Excerpt from President K. R. Narayanan's state dinner toast, March 21, 2000. Copyright © 2001 by the Embassy of India, Press and Information. Reprinted by permission of the Embassy of India.

Unit 9, Excerpt from "Clinton in Hong Kong, prods China on environment," from CNN.com, July 2, 1998. Copyright © 1998 by Cable News Network, Inc. Reprinted by permission of Cable News Network, Inc.

Excerpt from "Six Billion People," from *Asiaweek.com,* October 29, 1999, Vol. 25, No. 43. Copyright © 1999 by Asiaweek. Reprinted by permission of Asiaweek.

Unit 10, Excerpt from "Record Ozone Hole Refuels Debate on Climate" by Andrew C. Revkin, from the *New York Times,* October 10, 2000. Copyright © 2000 by the *New York Times.* Reprinted by permission of the *New York Times.*

Excerpts from *Dear America, Letters Home from Vietnam* edited by Bernard Edelman. Copyright © 1985 by The New York Vietnam Veterans Memorial Commission. Reprinted by permission of Simon & Schuster.

Excerpt from "Heroes for the Planet" by Terry McCarthy, from *Time,* Apr-May 2000. Copyright © 2000 by Time, Inc. Reprinted by permission of Time, Inc.

Excerpt from "There is No Global Warming," from the American Policy Center. Copyright © 2001 by the American Policy Center. Reprinted by permission of the American Policy Center.

The editors have made every effort to trace the ownership of all copyrighted material found in this book and to make full acknowledgment for its use. Omissions brought to our attention will be corrected in a subsequent edition.

ART CREDITS

Cover *background* Provided by the SeaWiFS Project/Goddard Space Flight Center/NASA and GeoEye; *top to bottom* © Hugh Sitton/Stone/Getty Images; © George Hunter/Robertstock; © James Martin/Stone/Getty Images; © Max Dannenbaum/Riser/Getty Images.

Front Matter ii–iii Provided by the SeaWiFS Project/Goddard Space Flight Center/NASA and GeoEye; **ii** *top left* © Hugh Sitton/Stone/Getty Images; *top center* © George Hunter/Robertstock; *top right* © James Martin/Stone/Getty Images; **iii** © Max Dannenbaum/Riser/Getty Images; **v, vi–vii** Provided by the SeaWiFS Project/Goddard Space Flight Center/NASA and GeoEye; **viii** *top* © Schafer & Hill/Stone/Getty Images; *bottom* © Bob Krist/Corbis; **ix** *top* © Gala/SuperStock; *bottom* © Kevin Miller/Stone/Getty Images; **x** *bottom* © Ary Diesendruck/Stone/Getty Images; *top* © Loren McIntyre/www.lorenmcintyre.com; **xi** *bottom* © Ric Ergenbright Photography; *top* © Tony Brown/Eye Ubiquitous/Corbis; **xii** *bottom* © David Sutherland/Stone/Getty Images; *top* © TASS/Sovfoto; **xiii** *center* © Mitch Reardon; *top* © Daryl Balfour/Stone/Getty Images; *bottom* © Art Kowalsky/Alamy Ltd.; **xiv** *bottom* © John Egan/Eye Ubiquitous/Hutchison; *top* © Ali Kazuyoshi Nomachi/Pacific Press Service; **xv** *bottom* © Martin Puddy/Stone/Getty Images; *top* © Paul Harris/Stone/Getty Images; **xvi** *bottom* © John Lamb/Stone/Getty Images; *center* © Jerry Alexander; *top* © David Ball/Stone/Getty Images; **xvii** *bottom* © Robin Smith/Stone/Getty Images; *top* © Roger Mear/Stone/Getty Images; **xviii** *bottom* Illustration by Roberta Polfus; *top* © Duomo Archive/PCN; **xix** *bottom* © HO Old/Reuters; © Christopher Pillitz/Alamy Ltd.; **xxiv** kangaroo © Tim Flach/Stone/Getty Images; emu © Norman Owen Tomalin/www.bciusa.com; Tasmanian devil © John Cancalosi/Peter Arnold, Inc.; platypus © John Carnemolla/Emerald City Images; Queensland bottle tree © Patti Murray/Animals Animals, Earth Scenes. All rights reserved; wombat © Dani/Jeske/Animals Animals, Earth Scenes. All rights reserved; **xxv** *bottom left* © 1990 J.B. Handelsman/The New Yorker Collection/www.cartoonbank.com. All Rights Reserved; *bottom* Smite the Lazy Worker. Soviet poster RU/SU1748. Poster collection, Hoover Institution Archives; **A0–A1** NASA.

Maps pp. A1–A37, © Rand McNally & Company. All rights reserved.

All other maps, locators, and globe locators by GeoNova LLC.

Units Unit 1, 2 © Schafer & Hill/Stone/Getty Images; **2–3** © Earth Imaging/Stone/Getty Images; **3** © Damir Sagolj/Reuters; **4** *background* GeoNova LLC.com; **7** © Eduardo Garcia/Taxi/Getty Images; **8** © Alan S. Weiner; **10** Terrestrial Globe showing the Indian Ocean (1492), Martin Behaim. Made in Nuremberg, Germany. Bibliotheque Nationale, Paris, France. Photo © Lauros/Giraudon/Bridgeman Art Library; **11** *background* © Paul Morrell/Stone/Getty Images; *top left* National Oceanic and Atmospheric Administration/Department of Commerce; **12** *top center* © PhotoDisc/Getty Images; *top left* © Bob Krist/eStock Photo; **13** © Erwin and Peggy Bauer/www.bciusa.com; **14** background National Oceanic and Atmospheric Administration/Department of Commerce; *bottom left* © Science Museum/Science & Society Picture Library; *bottom right* © Owen Franken/Stock Boston; **top** AP/Wide World Photos; **26** © Paul Morrell/Stone/Getty Images; **30–31** Illustration by Roberta Polfus; **31** *inset bottom* Illustration by Roberta Polfus; *inset center* Illustration by Roberta Polfus; *inset top* Illustration by Roberta Polfus; **32** © Kari Kummels/SuperStock; **33** Illustration by Stephen R. Wagner; **34–35** Illustration by Ken Goldammer; **36** © Earth Satellite Corporation/Science Photo Library/Photo Researchers Inc.; **38–39** Illustration by Roberta Polfus; **40** © Chip Hires/ Gamma/Eyedea Presse; **41** © HO Old/Reuters; **42** © Image Source Pink/Getty Images; **43** AP/Wide World Photos; **44** © Jerryl Hout/www.bciusa.com; **48** © SuperStock; **50** Illustration by Stephen R. Wagner; **51** National Oceanic and Atmospheric Administration/Department of Commerce; **52** *inset* © Chris Johns/National Geographic Image Collection; **53** © Joe Raedle/Getty Images News/Getty Images; **59** © Vladpans/eStock Photo; **60** *bottom* © Michael Fogden/www.bciusa.com; *top* © Edmond Van Hoorick/SuperStock; **61** *bottom* © Daniel J. Cox/Natural Exposures; *top* © Picture Finders Ltd./eStock Photo; **62** © Charlie Waite/Stone/Getty Images; **63** © Richard Olsenius/Black Star; **67** *inset left* Used by permission of Utah State Historical Society. All rights reserved; *inset right* © Tom Till Photography; **70** © Charles O'Rear/Corbis; **72** © Adrian Arbib/Corbis; **73** From Abrams: Medical Spanglish, Medmaster; **77** © Werner Forman/Corbis; **81** © Bob Krist/Corbis; **83** © Sergio Larrain/Magnum Photos; **85** © D.E. Cox/Stone/Getty Images; **87** © Pixtal/SuperStock; **88** © Earth Imaging/Stone/Getty Images; **91** © SuperStock; **92** Photo by Sharon Hoogstraten; **94** *center right* © Lawrence Manning/Corbis; **95** *bottom center* © PhotoDisc/Getty Images.

Unit 2, 98 *bottom* © SuperStock, Inc; *top* © Superstock; **98–99** © Jim Knighton/WorldSat International/Photo Researchers Inc; **99** © Joseph Sohm/Visions of America/Corbis; **100** © Thomas E. Franklin/The Bergen Record/Getty Images News/Getty Images; **101** *bottom* © Gilles Mingasson; **101** *top* © Brian Lawrence/Imagestate; **116** © James A. Martin/SuperStock; **117** © Mark Gibson; **118** *bottom left* © Jake Rajs/Stone/Getty Images; *bottom right* © Eric Carle/Stock Boston; *top right* © Jim Schwabel/Jupiter Images; **119** © SuperStock; **122** © Jim Pickerell/Jupiter Images; **123** © Bryan and Cherry Alexander Photography/www.arcticphoto.co.uk; **126** AP/Wide World Photos;

127 © Mark Wagner/aviation-images.com; **128** © Corbis; **135** © Gala/SuperStock; **137** *bottom* The Last Spike (1869). William T. Garrett Foundry, San Francisco, after a description by David Hewes (1822-1915). 17 6/10 carat gold, alloyed with copper. Stanford Family Collection, Iris & B. Gerald Cantor Center for Visual Arts at Stanford University; *center* © Ewing Galloway/Index Stock Imagery; *top* Lewis and Clark at Three Forks, E.S. Paxson. Mural. Montana State Capitol. Courtesy of the Montana Historical Society, Helena. Photograph by John Reddy. Montana Historical Society #952-803; **138** *bottom* © Jason Reed/Photodisc/Getty Images; center © 1994 Dan McCoy/Rainbow; top AP/Wide World Photos; **143** © Terry Cryer/Corbis; **144** © Mark E. Gibson/Corbis; **147** © Mike Magnuson/ The Stock Connection; **148** AP/Wide World Photos; **150–151** AP/Wide World Photos; **151** *top and bottom* Library of Congress, Prints and Photographs Division; **153 MC1-MC2** © Ted Spiegel/Corbis; **155** © SuperStock; **156** *left* © James P. Blair/Corbis; **156** *right* The Granger Collection, New York; 158 © Kevin Miller/Stone/Getty Images; **161** © Allen McInnis; *inset* © Perry Mastrovito/Corbis; **162** © Vern McGrath/Valan Photos; **163** © Bryan & Cherry Alexander Photography/Alamy Ltd.; **164–165** bottom right © Brian Sytnyk/ Masterfile; **164** bottom *left* © Hoang Dinh Nam/AFP/Getty Images; **164** *left* © SuperStock; **165** bottom right © John Madere/Corbis; 168 © SuperStock; **169** AP/Wide World Photos; **172** © Thomas E. Franklin/The Bergen Record/ Getty Images News/Getty Images; **177** *left* AP/Wide World Photos; right © Brian Lawrence/Imagestate; **180** © Gilles Mingasson.

Unit 3, 186–187 GeoNova LLC.com; **186** *bottom right* © Loren McIntyre/www.lorenmcintyre.com; *left* The Granger Collection, New York; **187** © Ary Diesendruck/Stone/Getty Images; **188** © Luiz C. Marigo/Peter Arnold, Inc.; **189** © G. Boutin/Explorer/Photo Researchers, Inc.; *top* AP/Wide World Photos; **200** © Robert Madden/National Geographic Image Collection; **201** © Jerry Alexander/Riser/Getty Images; **202** © Christopher Pillitz/Alamy Ltd.; **205** © Robert Caputo/Aurora Photos; **210** © E.C.M. Fernandes; **211** © E.C.M. Fernandes; **212** *top* © Peter Chigmaroff/Alamy Ltd.; **213** © Don Hebert/Taxi/Getty Images; **217** © Nigel Atherton/Stone/Getty Images; **218** *bottom* © Wesley Boxce/Getty Images News/Getty Images; **center** The Granger Collection, New York; *top* The Granger Collection, New York; **219** The Cry of Dolores, Juan O'Gorman. The Granger Collection, New York; **221** © Joel Sartore/National Geographic Image Collection; **222** Wooden carved effigy in the shape of a snake. Maracayo, Puerto Rico. Courtesy, National Museum of the American Indian, Smithsonian Institution 1451100.000. Photo by NMAI Photo Service Staff; **223** © Gordon Gahan/National Geographic Image Collection; **225** © Glyn Genin; **226** © IFA /eStock Photo; **227** © Hulton Archive/Getty Images; **228–229** *background* U.S. Air Force photo/Tech. Sgt. James L. Harper Jr.; **229** *top* © Marcelo Hernandez/dpa/Corbis; **230** *bottom left* The Granger Collection, New York; *bottom right* Wooden Inka colonial period q'ero (ceremonial drinking cup) representing a puma's head. Interior of Peru. Courtesy, National Museum of the American Indian, Smithsonian Institution 105860.000 Photo by David Heald; **231** *bottom left* The Granger Collection, New York; *bottom right* AP/Wide World Photos; **232** © Reuters/Corbis; **233** *center* © Lineair/R. Giling/Peter Arnold, Inc.; *right* © Jeff Greenberg/Peter Arnold, Inc.; *left* © LMR Group/Alamy Ltd.; **235** © Gustau Nacarino/Reuters; **237** © Martin Wendler/Peter Arnold, inc.; **239** © Mireille Vautier/Alamy Ltd.; **240** *left* © Tim Holt/Photo Researchers, Inc.; *right* © Superstock; **241** © Steve Vidler/eStock Photo; top © Dinodia/Art Directors and Trip; **243** Map of Tenochtitlan and the Gulf of Mexico (1524), from Praeclara Ferdinadi Cortesii de Nova maris Oceani Hyspania Narratio by Hernando Cortes (1485-1547). Color lithograph. Newberry Library, Chicago, IL, USA. Photograph © Bridgeman Art Library; **243 MC1-MC2** © PCL/Alamy; **244** © Luiz C. Marigo/Peter Arnold, Inc.; **246** © Steve Winter/National Geographic Image Collection; **249** © 1990 J.B. Handelsman/The New Yorker Collection /www.cartoonbank.com. All Rights Reserved; **250** AP/Wide World Photos; **251** *top* © Ary Diesendruck/Stone/Getty Images; *inset* AP/Wide World Photos; **252** © Robert Frerck/Stone/Getty Images; **253** © G. Boutin/Explorer/Photo Researchers, Inc.

Unit 4, 258 © Ric Ergenbright Photography; **258–259** *background* © ESA/K. Horgan/Stone/Getty Images; **259** *top left* © Tony Brown/Eye Ubiquitous/Corbis; *top right* © C. Liewig/ABACA US; **260** © Reuters Newmedia/Corbis; **261** © Frederick Deligne and PoliticalCartoons.com; **272** © Pal Hermansen/Stone/Getty Images; **274** © Ric Ergenbright Photography; **277** © Peter Vandermark/Stock Boston; **279** © Michael Busselle/Corbis; **280** © Chad Ehlers/Stone/Getty Images; **282** Illustration by Stephen R. Wagner; *bottom left* © Paul Almasy/Corbis; **284** © Guido Alberto Rossi/Tip Images; **285** © C.T.K/Gamma/Eyedea Presse; **289** © Steve Vidler/SuperStock; **291** *top, The Virgin and Child Surrounded by Five Angels,* Sandro Botticelli. Tempera on wood panel. Musee du Louvre, Paris. Photo © SuperStock, Inc.; *bottom* © Ruggero Vanni/Corbis; **293** AP/Wide World Photos; **295** Illustration by Stephen R. Wagner; **296** *left, Portrait of Charlemagne,* Albrecht Dürer. Oil on wood panel. Germanisches Nationalmuseum, Nuremberg, Germany. Photo © SuperStock, Inc.; *center,* Self portrait, Leonardo da Vinci. Red chalk drawing. Biblioteca Reale, Turin, Italy. Photo © Scala/Art Resource, New York; right, *Portrait of Martin Luther* (1529), Lucas Cranach the Elder. Museo Poldi Pezzoli, Milan, Italy. © Bridgeman Art Library; **297** *left* The Granger Collection, New York; center, *Napoleon I on His Imperial Throne, or His Majesty, the Emperor of the French, on His Throne* (1806), Jean Auguste Dominique Ingres. Oil on canvas, 259 x 162 cm. Inv. 4; Ea 89.1; INV 5420. Musee de l'Armee, Paris. Photo © Pascal Segrette/Musée de l'Armée/Dist. Réunion des Musées Nationaux/Art Resource, New York; *right* © Margaret Bourke-White/Time & Life Pictures/Getty Images; **298** © SuperStock; **300** © Jochem Wijnands/Picture Contact/Alamy Ltd.; **302** The Granger Collection, New York; **306** © SuperStock; **307** © Culver Pictures; **308** © Christian Delangue/Gamma/Eyedea Presse; **308–309** © Duomo Archive/PCN; **309** *top* © Ron Levy Worldwide Photography; *bottom* © Bill Roth/Anchorage Daily News; **310** *center* © The Gallery Collection/Corbis; *right* © The Art Archive/Corbis; **311** *left* The Granger Collection, New York; *right* © Reuters NewMedia/Corbis; **312** AP/Wide World Photos; **314** Photo by Sharon Hoogstraten; **315** © Grant Faint/The Image Bank/Getty Images.; **317 MC1-MC2** © Goodshoot/Jupiterimages/Getty Images; **318** © Reuters Newmedia/Corbis; **319** © Ermal Meta/AFP/Getty Images; **320** AP/Wide World Photos; **321** © AFP/Getty Images; **323** © Ferenczy Europress Budapest/Gamma/Eyedea Presse; **324** © Sovfoto; **326** *top* © Reuters Newmedia/Corbis; bottom © Edmund Nägele; **329** © Oliphant/Universal Press Syndicate. Reprinted with permission. All rights reserved; **332** © Chris Hammond/Alamy Ltd.

Unit 5, 332-333 © Geosphere/Planetary Visions/Photo Researchers, Inc.; **333** *left* © Kim Karpeles/Alamy Ltd.; *right* © Choups/Alamy Ltd.; **334** © Laurent van der Stockt/Gamma/Eyedea Presse; **335** *top* © Harley Schwadron/cartoonstock.com; *bottom* © Gerd Ludwig/National Geographic Image Collection; **344** © Sarah Leen/National Geographic Image Collection; **345** © Dean Conger/National Geographic Image Collection; **346** © James Strachan/Stone/Getty Images; **347, 348** © Dean Conger/National Geographic Image Collection; **349** © Steve Ravmar/National Geographic Image Collection; **350** © TASS/Sovfoto; **352** © Dean Conger/National Geographic Image Collection; **353** Copyright © WorldSat International Inc. www.worldsat.ca All Rights Reserved.; **354, 356** © Gerd Ludwig/National Geographic Image Collection; **361** © Nikolai Semenovich Shustov/Visual Arts Library, London/Alamy Ltd.; **362** *left* © David Sutherland/Stone/Getty Images; *right* The Granger Collection, New York; *background right* © K. Scholz/Robertstock; **363** *left, Napoleon's retreat from Moscow* (Nineteenth century) Adolf Northen. Ref. No. JL0312. Sotheby's Picture Library, London; *center* © Sovfoto; *right* AP/Wide World Photos; **364** © Henri Cartier-Bresson/Magnum Photos; **365** © Dean Conger/National Geographic Image Collection; **366** *top* The Granger Collection; *bottom,* Smite the Lazy Worker. Soviet poster RU/SU1748. Poster Collection, Hoover Institution Archives; **367** © Dean Conger/National Geographic Image Collection; **368** © Igor Kostin/Sovfoto; **369** *top* © Gerd Ludwig/National Geographic Image Collection; *bottom* © Reuters/Corbis; *background* © Reuters; **371** Church of Kamravor. Ashtarak, Armenia. Photo © Borromeo/Art Resource, New York; **372** © TASS/Sovfoto; **374** © Dean Conger/National Geographic Image Collection; **376** *clockwise from top left* © David M. Schleser/Nature's Images/Photo Researchers, Inc.; © Joyce Photographics/Photo Researchers, Inc.; © O.S.F./Animals Animals, Earth Scenes; © H. Huntly Hersch/Sovfoto; © H. Huntly Hersch/Sovfoto; © Catherine Karnow/Corbis; **378** © Ergun Cagatay/Tetragon; **379** © Stefano Torrione/Hemis/Alamy Ltd. **380** © David Rosenberg/Stone/Getty Images; **380-381** © James Strachan/Stone/Getty Images **381** *top* © George Steinmetz; bottom © Johnny Stockshooter/Roberstock; **383** Map by Alex Verbitsky **384** © Laurent van der Stockt/Gamma/Eyedea Presse; **386** © R.P.G./Corbis Sygma; **388** © Steven Weinberg; **390** © Mark H. Milstein/Getty Images News/Getty Images; **392** © Itar-TASS/Corbis; **393** AP/Wide World Photos; **394** *left* AP/Wide World Photos; *right* © Gerd Ludwig/National Geographic Image Collection.

Unit 6, 398 *top* © Hugh Sitton/Stone/Getty Images; *bottom* © R. V. Webdel de Joode; **398–399** © European Space Agency/Science Photo Library/Photo Researchers, Inc.; **399** © Daryl Balfour/Stone/Getty Images; 400 © Rene Burri/Magnum Photos; **401** *top* © Wendy Stone/Odyssey Productions; bottom © Alan King; **402** © PhotoDisc/Getty Images; **414** © SuperStock; **416** © Christophe Ratier/Photo Researchers, Inc.; **418** © 1988 Christopher Pillitz; **420** © Art Kowalsky/Alamy Ltd; **422** © Wendy Stone/Odyssey Productions; **423** © Bruce Davidson; **424** © PhotoDisc/Getty Images; **424–425** *foreground* Illustration by Stephen R. Wagner; *background* © PhotoDisc/Getty Images; **426** © Lloyd Cluff/Corbis; **432** The tallest of the still erect stelae at Axum (fourth-fifth century), Axum, Ethiopia. Photo © Werner Forman/Art Resource, New York; **433** *left* The Granger Collection, New York; *right* © John Moss/Black Star; **434** © Mitch Reardon; **437** AP/Wide World Photos; **438** © Guido Alberto Rossi/Tip Images **440** © Rohan/Stone/Getty Images; **441** © Yadid Levy/Alamy; **444** © 2007 Robert Frerck/Odyssey Productions; **445** © Deborah Feingold; **446** *clockwise from top right* © Dinodia/Art Directors & Trip; © P. Treanor/Art Directors & Trip; © H. Rogers/Art Directors & Trip; **447** *top* © SuperStock; *bottom* © Robert Frerck/Odyssey Productions; **449** © Mary Evans Picture Library/The Image Works; **451** top African mask. Wood with white, ochre-yellow and greenish painting. Barbier Mueller Collection. Photo © akg-images; *bottom, Bust of a Man* (1907), Pablo Picasso. Musee Picasso, Paris. © 2008 Estate of Pablo Picasso/Artists Rights Society (ARS), New York. Reproduction, including downloading of Picasso works is prohibited by copyright laws and international conventions without the express written permission of Artists Rights Society (ARS), New York. Photo © Peter Willi/SuperStock; **452** © Malcolm Linton/Getty Images News/Getty Images; **453** View of the acropolis enclosure of Great Zimbabwe (about 1500 A.D.). Great Zimbabwe, Zimbabwe. Photo © Robert Aberman/Art Resource, New York; **455** *top left* The Granger Collection, New York; *top right* © Hulton Archive/Getty Images; *center* The Royal Collection. © 2001 Her Majesty Queen Elizabeth II; *bottom* © Mark Peters/Sipa Press; **456** © Robert Frerck/Odyssey Productions; **460–461** © Rene Burri/Magnum Photos; **461** © Gary Cook/Alamy Ltd.; **463** AP/Wide World Photos; **465** © Malcolm Linton;

467 © Wendy Stone/Odyssey Productions; **468** © Graemer Williams/Corbis; **469** AP/Wide World Photos; **471** © 1996 Alan King.

Unit 7, 474 *left* © Sylvain Grandadam/Riser/Getty Images; *right* © Bernard Gerard/Eye Ubiquitous/Hutchison; **474–475** © Jim Knighton/WorldSat International/Photo Researchers, Inc.; **475** © Ali Kazuyoshi Nomachi/Pacific Press Service; **476** © John Egan/Eye Ubiquitous/Hutchison; **477** *top* © Paul Assaker/Corbis; bottom © Mark Fiore, San Francisco/www.markfiore.com; **486** © Peter Sanders Photography; **487** © Richard T. Nowitz/Corbis; **489** © Roger Antrobus/Corbis; **490** AP/Wide World Photos; **491** © Alistair Duncan/Dorling Kindersley/DK Images; **493** © Nik Wheeler/Corbis; **495** © Alan Puzey/Stone/Getty Images; **496** background © PhotoDisc/Getty Images; *top left* © Richard Nowitz/National Geographic Image Collection; top right © H. Rogers/Art Directors & Trip; *bottom left* © Chris Rennie/Robert Harding; *bottom right* © John Lawrence Photography/Alamy Ltd; **497** © Images & Stories/Alamy Ltd.; **503** © Nabeel Turner/Stone/Getty Images; **504** Dome and minarets. Kadiomin mosque, Baghdad, Iraq. Photo © Scala/Art Resource, New York; **506** © John Henshall/Alamy Ltd.; **507** © Stern Magazine/Black Star; **508** Exterior view of Temple of Confucius in Taipei, Taiwan. Photo © SEF/Art Resource, New York; **508–509** © Hugh Sitton/Stone/Getty Images; **509** top © SuperStock; bottom © DEA/Gianni Dagli Orti/De Agostini Picture Library/Getty Images; **510** AP/Wide World Photos; **511** © Ilene Perlman/Stock Boston; **514** AP/Wide World Photos; **515** © H. Rogers/Art Directors & Trip; **517** © Getty Images/Getty Images News; 518 © EmmePi Travel/Alamy Ltd.; **519** © Richard Ashworth/Robert Harding Picture Library; **521** top © ABC Basin Ajansi/Gamma/Eyedea Presse; bottom AP/Wide World Photos; **524** © John Egan/Eye Ubiquitous/Hutchison; **525** © Thomas Hartwell/Time & Life Pictures/Getty Images; **527** © Will Yurman; **530** *top* © Ali Kazuyoshi Nomachi/Pacific Press Service; *bottom* © Baron Wolman; **531** © David Turnley/Corbis; **532** *top* AP/Wide World Photos; *bottom left* © Bettmann/Corbis; *bottom right* © Dirck Halstead/Getty Images; **535** © Mark Fiore, San Francisco/www.markfiore.com; **538** © Paul Harris/Stone/Getty Images.

Unit 8, 538–539 © Earth Imaging/Stone/Getty Images; **539** *left* © Dan Rafia/Aurora/Getty Images; right © Dominic Sansoni/Three Blind Men; **540** © Upperhall/Robert Harding Picture Library; **541** *top* © Chip Hires/Gamma/Eyedea Presse; bottom © 1998 Carlson/Milwaukee Journal Sentinel; **550** © Jon Sparks/Corbis; **551** Illustration by Stephen R. Wagner; **552** © Corbis; **553** © E. Valentin/Photo Researchers, Inc.; **554** © Dominic Sansoni/Three Blind Men; **555** © Takeshi Takahara/Photo Researchers, Inc.; **556** © Brian A. Vikander/Corbis; **558** © E. Hanumantha Rao/Photo Researchers, Inc.; **560–561** © David Sutherland/Stone/Getty Images; **562** © Pablo Bartholomew/Netphotograph.com; **563** © Stuart Franklin/Magnum Photos; **568** *top* © Bettmann/Corbis; *bottom left* The Granger Collection, New York; *bottom right* © Roderick Johnson/Linkindia; **570** © 1978 Dilip Mehta/Contact Press Images; **571** © Anthony Cassidy/Stone/Getty Images; **572** Five headed Shiva from Mandi Indian Painting, (about 1730). Photo © Eileen Tweedy/Victoria and Albert Museum London/The Art Archive; **573** © Luca I. Tettoni/Luca Tettoni Photography; **575** *left* © Neil McAllister/Alamy Ltd.; *right* © Boran Brecelj/IPAK Images; **576** © Robert Nickelsberg/Time & Life Pictures/Getty Images; **577** © Beatrice Kiener/Gamma/Eyedea Presse; **578** Illustration by Stephen R. Wagner; **578–579** National Oceanic and Atmospheric Administration/Department of Commerce; **579** *top* AP/Wide World Photos; *bottom* © Jim Holmes/Eye Ubiquitious/Hutchison; **580** Thrikheb or throne cover, Bhutan. Wool, silk, cotton, 152 x 70 cm. Private Collection, Oltromare, Geneva Switzerland. Photo © Erich Lessing/Art Resource; **581** © John Callahan/Stone/Getty Images; **582** *top* © Alison Wright/Stock Boston; *bottom* Illustration by Stephen R. Wagner **583** © Marco Brivio/Alamy Ltd.; **584** © Robert Nickelsberg/Time & Life Pictures/Getty Images; **585** © Hugh Sitton/Stone/Getty Images; **586** © Martin Puddy/Stone/Getty Images; **587** © Pete Seaward/Stone/Getty Images **588** *left* © Greig Cranna/Stock Boston; *right* © JTB Photo Communications, Inc./Alamy; **589** *top* © Neale Haynes/Buzz Pictures; bottom AP/ Wide World Photos; **592** © Upperhall/Robert Harding; **593** © Bruno Barbey/Magnum Photos; **595** © Jeroen Snijders/Linkindia; **598** Illustration by Stephen R. Wagner; **599** *top* © Dinodia Photo Library; *bottom* © H. Rogers/Art Directors & Trip; **600** *top* © Ric Ergenbright/Corbis;bottom left © Bettmann/Corbis; *bottom right* © Reuters; **603** © 1998 Carlson/Milwaukee Journal Sentinel.

Unit 9, 606 © SuperStock; **606–607** © Geosphere Project/Planetary Visions/Photo Researchers, Inc.; **607** *left* © David Ball/Stone/Getty Images; **right** © SuperStock; **608** © John Pryke/Reuters/Corbis; **609** *top* © Hugh Sitton/Stone/Getty Images; *bottom* © SuperStock; **618** © SuperStock; **619** © Jerry Alexander; **621** © Keren Su/Corbis **623** © Michael S. Yamashita/Corbis; **625** © Dr. Cynthia M. Beall & Dr. Melvyn C. Goldstein/National Geographic Image Collection; **627** © Corbis; **628** © Zou Qing/AFP/Getty Images; **629** © Imaginechina; *630* **top** © Luo Wenfa/ChinaStock; *center* © Wang Xinlin/ChinaStock; *bottom* © ChinaStock; **631** © Barry Lewis/Alamy Ltd.; **635** © Julian Calder/Stone/Getty Images; **636** *left,* Confucius (17th century), Chinese. Bibliotheque Nationale, Paris. Photo © Bridgeman Art Library, London/SuperStock; *center,* Qin Shi Huang, first emperor of China (c. 1900). From a 19th century Korean album. Or 11515. Folio No: 11v. British Library, London, Great Britain. Photograph © HIP/Art Resource, New York; *right* The Granger Collection, New York; **637** *left* © ChinaStock; right, bottom The Granger Collection, New York **638** *top left* © Christopher Liu/ChinaStock; *top right* Pendant in the Shape of a Knotted Dragon (5th-3rd century B.C.), Eastern Zhou dynasty, Warring States Period, China. Jade (nephrite), 3 1/8" x 2 1/16". The Metropolitan Museum of Art, New York. Gift of Ernest Erickson Foundation, 1985 (1985.214.99). Image copyright © The Metropolitan Museum of Art/Art Resource, New York; *center* By Permission of the British Library; *bottom* The Granger Collection, New York; **639** © Alain le Caromeu/Panos Pictures; **640** © UPI/Bettmann/Corbis; **641** *top* © UPI/Bettmann/Corbis; *bottom* © Tom Nebbia/Corbis; **642** Illustration by Patrick Whalen; **644** © Dr. Cynthia M. Beall & Dr. Melvyn C. Goldstein/National Geographic Image Collection; **646** AP/Wide World Photos; **647** © Bob Thomas/Stone/Getty Images; **649** © Jean-Léo Dugast/Panos Pictures; **651** The Granger Collection, New York; **652** *left* The Granger Collection, New York; *right, Portrait of Kisegawa of Matsubaya* (about 1796), Kitagawa Utamaro. Japanese. Fitzwilliam Museum, University of Campbridge, United Kingdom. Photo © Bridgeman Art Library; **653** *left* The Granger Collection, New York; *right* © Bettmann/Corbis; **654** © 1976 Kenneth Love; **655** © SuperStock; **656** *left,* Mask representing a female ancestor, with elaborate headdress (20th century) Chokwe Culture, Angola. Wood, fibers. Private Collection. Photo © Manu Sassoonian/Art Resource, New York; *right* © Holton Collection/SuperStock; **657** *top* Mask used as a powerful element in the ceremonies of the False Face medicine society to help appease spirits, Iroquois. Private collection. New York. Photo © Werner Forman/Art Resource, New York; *bottom* © Steve Vidler/SuperStock; **659 MC1–MC2** © Ilya Terentyev/Getty Images; **660** © John Pryke/Reuters/Corbis; **661** AP/Wide World Photos; 663 © Bzad/ChinaStock; **665** © Toshifumi Kitamura/AFP/Getty Images; **668** © John Lamb/Stone/Getty Images; **671** © 1996 Steve Greenberg/Seattle Post-Intelligencer.

Unit 10, 674 *left* © Ron Dahlquist/Stone/Getty Images; *right* © Roger Mear/Stone/Getty Images; **674–675** © Earth Imaging/Stone/Getty Images; 676 © Sam Abell/National Geographic Image Collection; **677** *top* © Sergio Dorantes/Sygma/Corbis;bottom National Oceanic and Atmospheric Administration/Department of Commerce; **687** The Granger Collection, New York; **688** © Trevor Smithers APRS/Alamy; **690** Illustration by Stephen R. Wagner; **691** © David Moore; **694** © Dani/Jeske/Animals Animals, Earth Scenes. All rights reserved; **695** © Denis Waugh/Stone/Getty Images; **696** *top left* © Tim Flach/Stone/Getty Images; *top right* © Patti Murray/Animals Animals, Earth Scenes. All rights reserved; *center* © Dani/Jeske/Animals Animals, Earth Scenes. All rights reserved; *center right* © John Carnemolla/Emerald City Images; *bottom left* © Norman Owen Tomalin/www.bciusa.com; *bottom right* © John Cancalosi/Peter Arnold, Inc.; **698** © Walter Meayers Edwards/National Geographic Image Collection; **699** Illustration by Greg Taylor/Honolulu Advertiser; **700** © John Carnemolla/Corbis; **701** © U. S. Govt. Defense Nuclear Agency/National Geographic Image Collection; **705** © Glen Allison/Stone/Getty Images; **708** © W. Robert Moore/National Geographic Image Collection; **709** © Jonathan Kim; **710–711** Illustration by Stephen R. Wagner; **711** © Georg Gerster/Photo Researchers, Inc.; **712** © Bob Krist/Corbis; **714** *top* © Peter Stone/Pacific Stock; *center* © Joe Carini/Pacific Stock; *bottom* © Amos Nachoum/Corbis; **716** *left* © Robert Frerck/Odyssey Productions; *right* © 1991 Buddy Mays; **717** *top* © 1997 Orion Press/Pacific Stock; *bottom* © Tim Graham/Alamy Ltd.; **718** *left* © D. Johanson/Institute of Human Origins; *center* The Granger Collection, New York; *right* © Mary Evans Picture Library/The Image Works; **719** *top* © Ian Paterson/Alamy Ltd.; *bottom* © Christopher Arnesen/Stone/Getty Images; **720** © George F. Mobley/National Geographic Image Collection; **721** © Steve Vidler/SuperStock; **722** © Niels Schipper; **723** AP/Wide World Photos; **726** © Sam Abell/National Geographic Image Collection; **727** © Penny Tweedie/Corbis; **729** © Robin Smith/Stone/Getty Images; **730** © Darren Whiteside/Reuters; **731** © Sergio Dorantes/Sygma/Corbis; **734** © Danita Delimont/Alamy; **736** © Scott Peterson/Getty Images News/Getty Images; **737** National Oceanic and Atmospheric Administration/Department of Commerce; **740** Provided by the SeaWiFS Project/Goddard Space Flight Center/NASA and GeoEye.

Skillbuilder Handbook, R14 AP/Wide World Photos.

The editors have made every effort to trace the ownership of all copyrighted material found in this book and to make full acknowledgment for its use. Omissions brought to our attention will be corrected in a subsequent edition.